DEVELOPMENTAL PSYCHOPATHOLOGY

DEVELOPMENTAL PSYCHOPATHOLOGY

SECOND EDITION

Volume Two: Developmental Neuroscience

Editors

DANTE CICCHETTI

and

DONALD J. COHEN

WILEY

John Wiley & Sons, Inc.

Library of Congress Cataloging-in-Publication Data:

Developmental psychopathology / editors, Dante Cicchetti & Donald Cohen.—
2nd ed.
  p.   cm.
ISBN-13: 978-0-471-23736-5, ISBN-10: 0-471-23736-1 (v. 1 : cloth)
ISBN-13: 978-0-471-23737-2, ISBN-10: 0-471-23737-X (v. 2 : cloth)
ISBN-13: 978-0-471-23738-9, ISBN-10: 0-471-23738-8 (v. 3 : cloth)
ISBN-13: 978-0-471-23735-8, ISBN-10: 0-471-23735-3 (set)
[etc.]
  1. Mental illness—Etiology. 2. Developmental psychology. 3. Mental illness—Risk factors. 4. Adjustment (Psychology). I. Cicchetti, Dante. II. Cohen, Donald J.
  RC454.4.D483 2006
  616.89—dc22

Printed in the United States of America.

10 9 8 7 6 5 4 3 2 1

These volumes are dedicated to
Marianne Gerschel.

Contents

Preface to Developmental Psychopathology, *Second Edition*

It has been over a decade since the first two volumes of *Developmental Psychopathology* were published. These volumes were extremely well received: They have been highly cited in the literature and they have served as a valuable resource for researchers and practitioners alike. The expansion of the second edition of *Developmental Psychopathology* from two to three volumes speaks to the continued growth of the field, as well as to the ascendance of theory and research in the area of neuroscience informed by a developmental perspective.

There can be no doubt that the discipline of developmental psychopathology has grown significantly in a relatively short period of time. The more than 30 years that have elapsed since the initiation of the Schizophrenia high-risk projects (Garmezy & Streitman, 1974) have been marked by significant contributions to the field. Noteworthy among these are the publication of Achenbach's (1974) first text, Rutter and Garmezy's (1983) chapter in the *Handbook of Child Psychology,* and the continued growth of the journal *Development and Psychopathology,* including the Millennium Special Issue entitled *Reflecting on the Past and Planning for the Future of Developmental Psychopathology* (Cicchetti & Sroufe, 2000). A not insignificant contributor to this rapid growth can be found in the very definitional parameters of the discipline. Theorists and researchers in the field of developmental psychopathology use a lifespan framework to elucidate the many factors that can contribute to the development of mental disorders in individuals at high risk, as well as those operative in individuals who have already manifested psychological disturbances or who have averted such disorders despite their high risk status. In essence, a developmental psychopathology perspective provides a broad, integrative framework within which the contributions of diverse disciplines can be incorporated and enhanced (Cicchetti & Sroufe, 2000). Thus, rather than having to develop new theories and methods, those working within a developmental psychopathology framework can build on and extend previously established traditions. The ability to incorporate knowledge from diverse disciplines and to encourage interdisciplinary research will expedite growth within the field of developmental psychopathology.

As with the previous edition, the current volumes were not organized exclusively around thematic psychiatric disorders. Rather, authors were encouraged to explore developmentally relevant theories, methods of assessment, and domains of functioning. Although many chapters do address specific psychiatric disorders, it is the processes that contribute to the emergence of psychopathology that are emphasized rather than the psychiatric disorders per se.

Volume I, *Theory and Method* presents various approaches to understanding developmental influences on risk and maladaptation. As previously, the volume begins with an explication of the discipline of developmental psychopathology. Within this chapter, a number of significant advances within the field are noted, including the increased attention to processes and mechanisms, the use of multiple levels of analysis, the rise of developmental neuroscience, and the evolution of translational research paradigms. Chapters address a range of topics, including approaches to diagnoses of disorders, developmental epidemiology, diverse theoretical perspectives, various contextual issues, and new frontiers in statistical techniques for developmental phenomena. The volume concludes with a chapter on prevention and intervention.

Volume II, *Developmental Neuroscience,* was added to acknowledge the significant growth in this area since the publication of the first edition of this *Handbook.* Given the seminal historical role that neuroscience played in the emergence of developmental psychopathology (Cicchetti, 1990; Cicchetti & Posner, 2005), it is only fitting that developmental neuroscience has both informed and been informed by developmental psychopathology theorizing.

Neural plasticity, brain imaging, behavioral and molecular genetics, stress and neurobiology, immunology, and environmental influences on brain development are covered in this volume.

Volume III, *Risk, Disorder, and Adaptation* presents various perspectives on contributors to disorder. For example, chapters address the role of social support, family processes, and early experience on adaptation and maladaptation. Other chapters address specific disorders, including mental retardation, language disorders, Autism, disorders of attention, obsessive-compulsive disorders, Tourette's syndrome, social anxiety, Schizophrenia, antisocial disorders, substance abuse, and dissociative disorders. A number of chapters on resilience despite adversity also are included. The volume concludes with a chapter on stigma and mental illness.

All authors were asked to conclude their chapters with discussions of future research directions and needs. Thus, these volumes serve not only to highlight current knowledge in the field of developmental psychopathology, but also to suggest avenues to pursue for progress to continue. In particular, it is increasingly important to incorporate multiple-levels-of-analysis approaches when investigating maladaptation, psychopathology, and resilience (Cicchetti & Blender, 2004; Cicchetti & Dawson, 2002). The examination of multiple systems, domains, and ecological levels in the same individuals over developmental time will yield a more complete depiction of individual patterns of adaptation and maladapation. Moreover, such methods are likely to be extremely valuable in elucidating how interventions may affect brain-behavior relations (see, e.g., Caspi et al., 2002, 2003; Cicchetti & Posner, 2005; Fishbein, 2000; Goldapple et al., 2004; Kandel, 1979, 1998, 1999). Such endeavors could result in significant progress toward understanding psychopathology, highlighting efficacious interventions, and ultimately decreasing the burden of mental illness (Cicchetti & Toth, in press).

I now turn to more personal considerations. Although Donald Cohen is no longer with us, he worked closely with me as we developed our plans for the second edition of *Developmental Psychopathology*. Given our collaboration on the first edition of the volumes and our discussions leading up to the publication of these volumes, I thought it only fitting that he be listed as my coauthor. I believe in my heart that Donald would be pleased to have his name affiliated with these volumes and when I shared this plan with his wife, Phyllis, she gave her enthusiastic endorsement. However, I hasten to add that, unfortunately, Donald's illness and untimely death precluded his active involvement in editing the chapters in these volumes. Thus, despite our many

conversations as the plan for these volumes unfolded, I alone am responsible for the final editing of all chapters.

In closing, I want to dedicate these volumes to my dear friend, Marianne Gerschel. Marianne is a true visionary and she has contributed significantly to my work in the area of developmental psychopathology. Without her belief in the value of this field, my efforts and accomplishments would have been greatly compromised.

Finally, as I write this preface, I am ending a significant era in my life. After more than two decades as the director of Mt. Hope Family Center, I am leaving Rochester to accept a position at the Institute of Child Development, University of Minnesota. There I will be the director of an interdisciplinary center that will emphasize a multiple-levels-of-analysis approach to research and intervention in developmental psychopathology.

This transition is difficult, as Mt. Hope Family Center and my colleagues there have contributed greatly to the growth and development of the field of developmental psychopathology. It is reassuring to know that Mt. Hope Family Center will continue to build upon a solid foundation under the capable directorship of my long-time collaborator and friend, Sheree L. Toth. Although I welcome the new opportunities and challenges that await me, I cannot help being a bit sad to leave. My spirits are buoyed by the knowledge that my work at Mt. Hope Family Center will continue and by my excitement at returning to my roots at the Institute of Child Development where I will have both University and community support to use the field of developmental psychopathology to extend my vision for helping disenfranchised individuals and families throughout the nation and the world.

DANTE CICCHETTI, PHD

Rochester, NY
July 2005

REFERENCES

Achenbach, T. M. (1974). *Developmental psychopathology.* New York: Ronald Press.

Caspi, A., McClay, J., Moffitt, T., Mill, J., Martin, J., Craig, I. W., et al. (2002). Role of genotype in the cycle of violence in maltreated children. *Science, 297,* 851–854.

Caspi, A., Sugden, K., Moffitt, T. E., Taylor, A., Craig, I. W., Harrington, H. L., et al. (2003). Influence of life stress on depression: Moderation by a polymorphism in the 5-HTT gene. *Science, 301,* 386–389.

Cicchetti, D. (1990). A historical perspective on the discipline of developmental psychopathology. In J. Rolf, A. Masten, D. Cicchetti, K. Nuechterlein, & S. Weintraub (Eds.), *Risk and protective factors in the development of psychopathology* (pp. 2–28). New York: Cambridge University Press.

Cicchetti, D., & Blender, J. A. (2004). A multiple-levels-of-analysis approach to the study of developmental processes in maltreated children. *Proceedings of the National Academy of Sciences, 101*(50), 17325–17326.

Cicchetti, D., & Dawson, G. (Eds.). (2002). Multiple levels of analysis. *Development and Psychopathology, 14*(3), 417–666.

Cicchetti, D., & Posner, M. I. (Eds.). (2005). Integrating cognitive and affective neuroscience and developmental psychopathology. *Development and Psychopathology, 17*(3).

Cicchetti, D., & Sroufe, L. A. (Eds.). (2000). Reflecting on the past and planning for the future of developmental psychopathology. *Development and Psychopathology, 12*(3), 255–550.

Cicchetti, D., & Toth, S. L. (in press). A developmental psychopathology perspective on preventive interventions with high-risk children and families. In A. Renninger & I. Sigel (Eds.), *Handbook of child psychology (6th ed.)*. Hoboken, NJ: Wiley.

Fishbein, D. (2000). The importance of neurobiological research to the prevention of psychopathology. *Prevention Science, 1*, 89–106.

Garmezy, N., & Streitman, S. (1974). Children at risk: Conceptual models and research methods. *Schizophrenia Bulletin, 9*, 55–125.

Goldapple, K., Segal, Z., Garson, C., Lau, M., Bieling, P., Kennedy, S., et al. (2004). Modulation of cortical-limbic pathways in major depression. *Archives of General Psychiatry, 61*(1), 34–41.

Kandel, E. R. (1979). Psychotherapy and the single synapse. *New England Journal of Medicine, 301*, 1028–1037.

Kandel, E. R. (1998). A new intellectual framework for psychiatry. *American Journal of Psychiatry, 155*, 475–469.

Kandel, E. R. (1999). Biology and the future of psychoanalysis: A new intellectual framework for psychiatry revisited. *American Journal of Psychiatry, 156*, 505–524.

Rutter, M., & Garmezy, N. (1983). Developmental psychopathology. In E. M. Hetherington (Ed.), *Handbook of child psychology* (4th ed., Vol. 4, pp. 774–911). New York: Wiley.

Contributors

Kenneth J. Aitken, MN, PhD
University of Edinburgh
Scotland, England

Francine M. Benes, MD, PhD
McLean Hospital
Belmont, Massachusetts

W. Thomas Boyce, MD
University of California
Berkeley, California

J. Douglas Bremner, MD
Emory University Hospital
Atlanta, Georgia

Claudia Buss, MSc
Trier University
Trier, Germany

Dante Cicchetti, PhD
Mt. Hope Family Center
University of Rochester
Rochester, New York
and
Institute of Child Development
University of Minnestota
Minneapolis, Minnesota

W. John Curtis, PhD
Mt. Hope Family Center
University of Rochester
Rochester, New York

Ronald Dahl, MD
University of Pittsburgh
Pittsburgh, Pennsylvania

Michelle de Haan, PhD
University of London
London, England

Jonathan Delafield-Butt, PhD
University of Edinburgh
Scotland, England

Richard A. Depue, PhD
Cornell University
Ithaca, New York

Douglas Derryberry, PhD
Oregon State University
Corvallis, Oregon

Vaibhav A. Diwadkar, PhD
Department of Psychiatry
University of Pittsburgh
Pittsburgh, Pennsylvania

Nathan A. Fox, PhD
Department of Human Development
University of Maryland
College Park, Maryland

Michael K. Georgieff, MD
School of Medicine
University of Minnesota
Minneapolis, Minnesota

Jay N. Giedd, MD
Child Psychiatry Branch
National Institute of Mental Health
Bethesda, Maryland

Nitin Gogtay, MD
Child Psychiatry Branch
National Institute of Mental Health
Bethesda, Maryland

Douglas A. Granger, PhD
Department of Biobehavioral Health
Pennsylvania State University
University Park, Pennsylvania

Gale A. Granger, PhD
Department of Molecular Biology and Biochemistry
University of California
Irvine, California

Steve W. Granger, PhD
La Jolla Allergy and Immunology Institute
Torre Pines, California

Megan R. Gunnar, PhD
Institute of Child Development
University of Minnesota
Minneapolis, Minnesota

Amie Ashley Hane, PhD
Child Development Laboratory
University of Maryland
College Park, Maryland

Mark L. Howe, PhD
Department of Psychology
Lancaster University
Lancaster, England

Almut Hupbach, PhD
McGill University
Montreal, Quebec
Canada

Mark H. Johnson, PhD
Birkbeck College
University of London
London, England

Daniel Keating, PhD
University of Michigan
Ann Arbor, Michigan

Matcheri S. Keshavan, MD
Department of Psychiatry and Behavioral Neurosciences
Wayne State University
Detroit, Michigan

David J. Kupfer, MD
University of Pittsburgh
Pittsburgh, Pennsylvania

Rhoshel K. Lenroot, MD
Child Psychiatry Branch
National Institute of Mental Health
Bethesda, Maryland

Mark F. Lenzenweger, PhD
State University of New York at Binghamton
Binghamton, New York

Monica Luciana, PhD
University of Minnesota
Minneapolis, Minnesota

Sonia J. Lupien, PhD
McGill University
Montreal, Quebec
Canada

Ann S. Masten, PhD
Institute of Child Development
University of Minnesota
Minneapolis, Minnesota

Bruce S. McEwen, PhD
Rockefeller University
New York, New York

Emese Nagy, PhD
University of Dundee
Scotland, England

Isabelle Ouellet-Morin, MPs
Laval University
Quebec, Canada

Sally Ozonoff, PhD
MIND Institute
Department of Psychiatry
U.C. Davis Medical Center
Sacramento, California

Bruce F. Pennington, PhD
University of Denver
Denver, Colorado

Koraly Pérez-Edgar, PhD
Child Development Laboratory
University of Maryland
College Park, Maryland

Daniel S. Pine, MD
Mood and Anxiety Disorders Program
National Institute of Mental Health
Bethesda, Maryland

Michael I. Posner, PhD
University of Oregon
Eugene, Oregon

Jens Pruessner, PhD
McGill University
Montreal, Quebec
Canada

Richard Rende, PhD
Brown Medical School
Providence, Rhode Island

Mary K. Rothbart, PhD
University of Oregon
Eugene, Oregon

Adam T. Schmidt, BA
University of Minnesota
Minneapolis, Minnesota

Philip Shaw, MD
Child Psychiatry Branch
National Institute of Mental Health
Bethesda, Maryland

Marjorie Solomon, PhD
University of California—Davis
Sacramento, California

Laurence Steinberg, PhD
Temple University
Philadelphia, Pennsylvania

Sheree L. Toth, PhD
Mt. Hope Family Center
University of Rochester
Rochester, New York

Colwyn Trevarthen, MSc, PhD
Department of Psychiatry
University of Edinburgh
Scotland, England

Mai T. Tu, MSc
McGill University
Montreal, Quebec
Canada

Don M. Tucker, PhD
University of Oregon
Eugene, Oregon

Marie Vandekerckhove, PhD
University of Bielefeld
Bielefeld, Germany

Delia Vazquez, MD
University of Michigan
Ann Arbor, Michigan

Irwin Waldman, PhD
Emory University
Atlanta, Georgia

Dominique Walker, PhD
McGill University
Montreal, Quebec
Canada

Greg Wallace, MA
Child Psychiatry Branch
National Institute of Mental Health
Bethesda, Maryland

CHAPTER 1

The Developing Brain and Neural Plasticity: Implications for Normality, Psychopathology, and Resilience

DANTE CICCHETTI and W. JOHN CURTIS

In recent years, the criticality of undertaking collaborations between scientists from diverse disciplines has increasingly been noted in the literature (Cicchetti & Blender, 2004; Cicchetti & Dawson, 2002; Pellmar & Eisenberg, 2000; Rodier, 2002). Two fields of inquiry that epitomize the movement toward interdisciplinary approaches to the investigation of brain-behavior relations in normality and psychopathology are neuroscience and developmental psychopathology (Cacioppo, Berntson, Sheridan, & McClintock, 2000; Cicchetti & Cannon, 1999a, 1999b; Cicchetti & Posner, 2005; Cicchetti & Tucker, 1994b; Cicchetti & Walker, 2001, 2003; Cowan & Kandel, 2001).

Several authors (Albright, Jessell, Kandel, & Posner, 2000; Cowan, Harter, & Kandel, 2000; Kandel & Squire, 2000) have described the unprecedented growth and achievements in the fields of neuroanatomy, neurochemistry, and neurophysiology that have taken place over the past half century. Despite the successes of research in these discrete areas, the present-day excitement engendered by neurobiological research emanates from the integration of several previously independent disciplines into one interdisciplinary intellectual framework known as neuroscience (Albright et al., 2000; Cowan et al., 2000; Kandel & Squire, 2000).

Cowan and colleagues (2000) reviewed the historical roots, as well as the twentieth-century phases of growth, of neuroscience. In the latter part of the nineteenth and the early decades of the twentieth centuries, a number of landmark discoveries occurred, each of which made a significant contribution to one or another of the long-established disciplines of neuroanatomy or neurophysiology. However, Cowan et al. (2000) note that none of these discoveries transcended traditional disciplinary boundaries, the defining feature of the contemporary field of neuroscience.

Kandel and Squire (2000) concluded that the modern cellular science of the nervous system was based on two fundamental discoveries: the neuron doctrine and the ionic hypothesis. Wilhelm His's description of the axon as an outgrowth from the immature nerve cell was an important step toward the formulation of the neuron doctrine. Evidence revealing that there was a discontinuity from neuron to neuron emanated from four scientific areas—embryology, histology, physiology, and pathological anatomy. The demonstration by Spanish neuroscientist Ramon y Cajal (1959) that nerve fibers have terminal structures that contact with other nerve cells but do not fuse with them—that they are contiguous rather than continuous—provided critical support for neuronal development. Ramon y Cajal established the neuron doctrine after demonstrating that the brain was composed of discrete cells called neurons that were thought to serve as elementary signaling units. In Ramon y Cajal's time, investigations of neurogenesis were conducted in the field of histology. In contemporary neuroscience, the focus has been on the molecular and cellular mechanisms involved in neuronal development. The ionic hypothesis, proffered by Alan Hodgkin, Andrew Huxley, and Bernard Katz in the late 1940s, explained the resting and action potentials of nerve cells in terms of the movement of specific ions, thereby enabling the nervous system to be comprehended in terms of physiochemical principles common to all of cell biology (Kandel & Squire, 2000).

The 1950s and 1960s witnessed the integration of neuroanatomy, neuropharmacology, neurochemistry, and behavioral science into neuroscience (Cowan et al., 2000). In early 1978, the inaugural issue of the *Annual Review of Neuroscience* was published, heralding the next phase of a multidisciplinary approach to the nervous system: the emergence of molecular neuroscience, the application of recombinant DNA technology and molecular genetics to neurobiological problems, and the unification, within a common intellectual framework, of neuroscience with the rest of the biological sciences (Ciaranello et al., 1995; Lander & Weinberg, 2000).

The emergence of molecular neuroscience enabled the field of neuroscience to surmount the intellectual barricades that had separated the study of brain processes, couched firmly in neuroanatomy and electrophysiology, from the remainder of the biological sciences, based more in biochemistry and cellular and molecular biology (Alberts et al., 1994; Cowan et al., 2000; Kandel & Squire, 2000). Kandel and Squire (2000) concluded that the modern molecular era of developmental neuroscience began in 1956 when Levi-Montalceni and Cohen isolated nerve growth factor (NGF), the first peptide growth factor to be discovered in the nervous system. The third phase in the evolution of neuroscience as a discipline, cognitive neuroscience, occurred during the 1980s and was marked by its incorporation of the methods of cognitive psychology, thereby bringing together the investigation of mental activity with the biology of the brain (see Gazzaniga, 2004; Kandel & Squire, 2000; Nelson & Bloom, 1997; Posner & DiGirolamo, 2000).

Similar to the historical growth witnessed in neuroscience, Cicchetti (1990) described developmental psychopathology as a new discipline that is the product of an integration of various disciplines, including genetics, embryology, neuroscience, epidemiology, psychoanalysis, psychiatry, and psychology, the efforts of which had previously been separate and distinct. Multiple theoretical perspectives and diverse research strategies and findings have contributed to developmental psychopathology. In fact, contributions to this field have come from virtually every corner of the biological and social sciences (Cicchetti & Sroufe, 2000).

GOALS OF THIS CHAPTER

Because developmental psychopathology and neuroscience share fundamental principles, the connection between neuroscience and developmental psychopathology can provide a compelling framework to support the study of normal and abnormal neurobiological development. In this chapter, we examine neurobiological development in normal and illustrative high-risk conditions and mental disorders. Moreover, we review relevant findings on neural plasticity and their potential contributions to the understanding of psychopathology and adaptive functioning. Additionally, we discuss the neurobiological correlates of, and contributors to, resilient adaptation. Finally, we conclude with a discussion of future work that can advance knowledge and inform prevention and intervention efforts in this area.

PRINCIPLES OF DEVELOPMENTAL NEUROSCIENCE AND DEVELOPMENTAL PSYCHOPATHOLOGY

One of the central tenets of the discipline of developmental psychopathology—that the study of normality and pathology are mutually informative—also is embraced by developmental neuroscientists (see, e.g., Cicchetti, 1990; Goldman-Rakic, 1987; Johnson, 1998). Developmental psychopathologists and developmental neuroscientists both emphasize the importance of understanding normal developmental patterns so that we can begin to investigate the ways in which deviant development may eventuate (Cicchetti & Posner, 2005). In addition, a firm knowledge base of normative biological and psychological developmental processes is essential to establish operational criteria for resilient functioning in individuals who have experienced significant adversity (Luthar, Cicchetti, & Becker, 2000).

Moreover, scientists in these two fields have long argued that one can gain valuable information about an organism's normal functioning by studying its abnormal condition (Cicchetti, 1984, 1990; Luria, 1980; Sroufe, 1990). Furthermore, developmental psycholopathologists and neuroscientists both contend that the investigation of "experiments of nature" can affirm, challenge, and augment existing etiological theories of normal and abnormal developmental processes (Cicchetti, 2003; O'Connor, 2003).

Nearly half a century ago, the embryologist Paul Weiss enunciated a view that foreshadows present-day thinking on the importance of examining the interrelation between normal and abnormal development: "Pathology and developmental biology must be reintegrated so that our understanding of the 'abnormal' will become but an extension of our insight into the 'normal,' while . . . the study of the 'abnormal' will contribute to the deepening of that very insight. Their common problems should provide foci for common orientation, so that, as they advance in joint directions, their efforts may supplement and reinforce each other to mutual benefit" (Weiss, 1961, p. 50).

Scientists within the field of neuroscience have a long history of investigating pathological phenomena to elucidate the nature of normal developmental processes (see Cicchetti, 1990, for an illustrative review). Some contemporary exemplars from neuroscience regarding how the study of atypical conditions can enhance our understanding of basic normal developmental processes include: the investigation of human microcephaly to gain insight into normal neurogenesis (Woods, 2004); the conduct of molecular genetic studies of human brain malformations in order to aid in the discovery of molecules that regulate central nervous system neuronal migration (Ross & Walsh, 2001); and neuropsychological investigations that demonstrate distinctive developmental differences following early damage to diverse areas of the prefrontal cortex and that support the critical role that the prefrontal cortex plays in the ongoing maturation of socioemotional, cognitive, and moral development (Diamond, Prevor, Callender, & Druin, 1997; Eslinger, Flaherty-Craig, & Benton, 2004).

THE BRAIN AS A DYNAMIC, SELF-ORGANIZING DEVELOPMENTAL SYSTEM

In present-day neuroscience, information in the brain is viewed as being represented and processed by distributed groups of neurons that maintain a functional interconnection based on experiential demands rather than by a strictly predetermined scheme (Black & Greenough, 1992; Courchesne, Chisum, & Townsend, 1994; Johnson, 1998). Because levels of organization and processes are reciprocally interactive, it is difficult, if not impossible, to impute ultimate causation to one level of organization over another (Cicchetti & Cannon, 1999a; Thelen & Smith, 1998).

It has become increasingly clear that the investigation of developmental processes, typical and atypical, often necessitates the simultaneous examination of individuals utilizing a multiple-levels-of-analysis approach (Cicchetti & Blender, 2004; Cicchetti & Dawson, 2002; Cicchetti & Toth, 1991; Gottlieb, Wahlsten, & Lickliter, 1998; Pellmar & Eisenberg, 2000; Thelen & Smith, 1998). In keeping with the historical tradition of prior systematizers in the field (Engel, 1977; McHugh & Slavney, 1986), *explanatory pluralism* and *methodological pluralism* have been considered to be the most suitable approaches to comprehend the nature of mental disorder (Cacioppo et al., 2000; Cicchetti & Dawson, 2002; Ghaemi, 2003; Kendler, 2005; Richters, 1997). Neuroscientists increasingly have shifted their emphasis from investigating molecules, membranes, and single neurons and tracts to examining complex neural systems (Edelman, 1987; Kandel, 1998; Thelen & Smith, 1998). In these more contemporary theoretical conceptualizations of brain-behavior relations, the brain is viewed as operating in a plastic and dynamic, self-organizing fashion, and as being less constrained by predetermined "localized" boundaries than previously thought (Cicchetti & Tucker, 1994a; Finger, 1994).

The viewpoint that the nervous system is dynamic is not exclusively a product of modern neuroscientific principles.

For example, in *The Brain of the Tiger Salamander,* C. J. Herrick (1948) restated the point that he had made in several prior publications spanning from 1908 through 1933—namely, that in all phylogenetic investigations of morphogenesis, it is important to keep in mind the conservative factor of stable genetic organization and the more labile influence of the functional requirements. Herrick (1948) contended that any morphology that overlooked the dynamic factors of tissue differentiation in terms of physiological adaptiveness lacks something and is sterile.

Systems theory approaches have historical roots in the investigations of a number of eminent developmental psychobiologists whose work occurred in the 1930s through the 1960s (see, e.g., Kuo, 1967; Lehrman, 1953; Schneirla, 1957). In contemporary developmental psychobiology, the system viewpoint is represented most elegantly in the writings of Gilbert Gottlieb (1983, 1992; Gottlieb et al., 1998).

SELF-ORGANIZATION

One of the main principles of systems theory (von Bertalanffy, 1968) is that organisms exist in a state of disequilibrium (i.e., dynamic stability) and participate in and seek out stimulation, thereby playing an active role in the construction of their own development. Thus, organisms are capable of *self-organization*—a reorganization that alters a system in an adaptive fashion when it is subjected to new constraints.

Similarly, several historically prominent developmental theorists maintain that disequilibrium enables individuals to exhibit change and flexibility throughout ontogenesis (Piaget, 1971; Werner, 1957). Such nonequilibrated systems assume a number of special properties including the ability to self-organize into patterns and nonlinearity or sensitivity to initial conditions (Prigogine, 1978). Cicchetti and Tucker (1994a) suggested that the concept of self-organization might serve as one of the mechanisms whereby individuals function in a resilient fashion despite experiencing great adversity. Furthermore, Cicchetti and Tucker (1994a) conjectured that self-organization might be a mediator of neural plasticity throughout the life course.

In self-organizing brain development, some regions of the brain serve to stabilize and organize information for other areas, whereas other regions utilize experience to fine-tune their anatomy for optimal function (Singer, 1995). In this manner, individuals can use the interaction of genetic constraints and environmental information to self-organize their highly complex neural systems. Accordingly, each individual may follow a potentially unique and partly self-determined developmental pathway of brain building.

Fundamental mechanisms of self-regulation are provided by brainstem neuromodulatory projection systems (Cicchetti & Tucker, 1994a). With widespread projections to cortical and subcortical targets, the neuromodulator systems serve as focal control points for regulating neural activity. By directing neural activity, it is expected that the neuromodular systems of the developing brain direct the activity-dependent pruning of the synaptic architecture. Each neuromodular system appears to tune neural and behavioral activity in a specific way and this specificity of effect may have direct implications for the control of neural plasticity.

THE DEVELOPING BRAIN

Wilhelm His was perhaps the preeminent contributor to research on the histogenesis of the central and peripheral nervous systems in the nineteenth century. His's discoveries included finding that changes in the shape of cells were involved in the folding of tissues, such as the neural plate. His also discovered the neural crest and the origin of the peripheral nervous system, and demonstrated that cranial and spinal ganglia are formed by cells that migrate from the neural crest (Jacobson, 1991). Moreover, His found that nerve cells originate by mitosis of stem cells near the ventricle of the neural tube rather than in the cerebral cortex itself (Jacobson, 1991). Furthermore, the concept of cell migration in the vertebrate central and peripheral nervous systems was discovered by His, initially through his observations on the origins of the peripheral nervous system from the neural crest and subsequently by his discovery that neuroblasts migrate individually from the ventricular germinal zone to the overlying mantle layer of the neural tube (Jacobson, 1991).

In 1904, His published a monograph in which he summarized more than 3 decades of his experimental work on the development of the embryonic nervous system of humans. In this monograph, he delineated the basic principles of neurogenesis for vertebrates in general. His's ideas provide the framework for the vast majority of subsequent studies of the nervous system (Sidman & Rakic, 1982). The virtual identity of the neural plate and the neural tube in all vertebrates provided suggestive evidence for the operation of very similar mechanisms in central nervous system development throughout phylogenesis.

In subsequent years, important contributions have been made by a number of investigative teams that elucidated the extraordinary diversity, organizational complexity, and precision of connections between cells in the nervous system of both vertebrates and invertebrates. Among these most prominent historical contributions to the early under-standing of neural development were those of Ramon y Cajal in Madrid, Hochstetter in Vienna, and scientists at the Moscow Brain Institute (1935–1965) and the Carnegie Institute in Baltimore (1942–1962; see review in Sidman & Rakic, 1982).

Cowan (1979) concluded that in the development of any part of the brain, eight major stages can be identified: (1) the induction of the neural plate; (2) the localized prolifer-ation of cells in different regions; (3) the migration of cells from the region in which they are generated to the places where they ultimately reside; (4) the aggregation of cells to form identifiable parts of the brain; (5) the differentiation (expression) of the immature neurons; (6) the formation of axonal pathways and synaptic connections with other neu-rons and the onset of physiological function; (7) the selec-tive death of certain cells; and (8) the elimination of some of the connections that were initially formed and the stabi-lization of others. As Steingard and Coyle (1998) noted, these stages proceed in a stepwise fashion following a genetically encoded plan that is influenced by environmen-tal events. Specifically, within each of these phases there are parallel processes of metabolic differentiation and mat-uration. Genes that take their regulatory cues from the im-mediate neurochemical (and experiential) environment regulate the onset and offset of each stage.

Moreover, each stage of brain development is dependent on the successful completion of the preceding stages. Al-terations in these processes can eventuate in aberrant neu-ral development, connectivity, or function (Rakic, 1996; Steingard & Coyle, 1998). In general, early disruption in the neurodevelopmental process is associated with a greater and more diffuse pathology (Nelson, 2000a; Volpe, 1995), while later disruptions in this process are associated with less severe pathology and more discrete neurological lesions (Steingard & Coyle, 1998). For example, if neuronal migration is disrupted, then abnormalities in cell position result. When this occurs, the neurons are said to be ectopic or heterotopic (Nowakowski, 1987). Likewise, delaying, extending, shortening, or blocking either the *progressive* (e.g., synaptogenesis and neuronal maturation) or *regres-sive* (e.g., cell death and synaptic pruning) events in the neurodevelopmental process exerts varying effects on structure-function relations, genetic regulatory processes, and on the emergence of later neurodevelopmental events that are dependent on earlier events (Keshavan & Hogarty, 1999; Nowakowski, 1987; Nowakowski & Hayes, 1999; Steingard & Coyle, 1998).

In 1939, Conel suggested that most cortical neurons in the human cerebrum were generated prenatally. More so-phisticated marking of cells has enabled neuroscientists to permanently date DNA cell replication and thereby provide direct evidence and precise time of neuron data on the ori-gin and termination of corticogenesis in primates (Johnson, 1997; Rakic, 1996, 2002a, 2002b). By utilizing the same marking of DNA replication technique in humans, we now know that humans develop their full complement of neu-rons mainly during the 4th, 5th, and 6th prenatal months (Rakic, 1981). The onset of corticogenesis in humans is ap-proximately at 6 prenatal weeks (Rakic, 1996). Through a more sophisticated autoradiographic analysis, Sidman and Rakic (1982) confirmed His's earlier discovery that all neurons destined for the neocortex were produced in the proliferative zone near the cerebral ventricle.

In the proliferative zone, precursor cells divide asyn-chronously; their nuclei move from the ventricular surface to synthesize DNA and then return to the surface to un-dergo another mitotic cycle (Rakic, 1996). There are two proliferative sites: (1) the ventricular zone, which con-tributes to cell proliferation and division in phylogeneti-cally older brain structures and (2) the subventricular zone, which contributes to cell proliferation and division in more recently evolved brain structures, such as the neocortex. These two proliferative zones generate separate glial and neuron cell lines and give rise to different forms of migra-tion, the process whereby neuronal cell bodies are dis-placed from their last cell division in the proliferative zone to their final destination in the mature brain (Johnson, 1997; Rakic, 1988a, 1988b).

In 1874, His inferred the phenomenon of neuronal cell migration by analyzing the fixed brains of human em-bryos; however, more sophisticated autoradiographic techniques have led to the discovery of the underlying cel-lular and molecular mechanisms of migration (Hatten, 1999; Price & Willshaw, 2000; Sidman & Rakic, 1982). There are two types of cell migration: tangential and ra-dial. In *tangential migration*, once cells are generated they are passively displaced and pushed further away from the proliferative zone by more recently born cells in a so-called "outside-in" gradient. This tangential form of mi-gration occurs at later developmental stages of the prenatal brain and gives rise to brain structures, such as the thalamus, dentate gyrus of the hippocampus, and many regions of the brain stem. In contrast, in *radial mi-gration*, the most recently born cell actively moves be-yond previously generated cells to create an "inside-out" gradient. This radial form of migration is visible during early stages of prenatal brain development and is found in the cerebral cortex and in some subcortical areas that have a laminar (layered) structure.

The area-specific features in the human adult neocortex are not evident in the immature cortical plate; rather, they emerge gradually over ontogenesis (Rakic, 1988b). The cells of the neocortex are not committed to differentiate the area-specific architectural and connectional features that distinguish neocortical areas in the adult at the time the neocortical plate is assembled during embryogenesis (Nowakowski, 1987; Sidman & Rakic, 1982; Steingard & Coyle, 1998). There are two primary models of cortical area differentiation that have been put forward in the literature (Johnson, 1997). Rakic (1988a, 1988b) has proposed the *protomap* hypothesis, a model whereby future cytoarchitectonic areas are thought to be genetically specified in the neuroepithelium and recapitulated in the developing cortical plate by a point-to-point migration along a radial glial scaffolding. In this "radial unit hypothesis," Rakic (1988a, 1988b) contends that the neuroepithelium is genetically programmed to generate area-specific cohorts of cortical plate neurons and that the relative positions and sizes of areas of the cerebral cortex are prespecified. Rakic's protomap hypothesis applies the same mechanisms of development to areas throughout the cerebral cortex (Johnson, 1997; O'Leary, 1989). Although the programmed emergence of discrete, cytoarchitectonic areas requires an interaction with thalamocortical afferents, the capacity of developing cortical plate neurons to differentiate features normally associated with other areas is conceived as being restricted by their commitment to specific area plates.

A contrasting viewpoint of cortical area differentiation, the *protocortex* model, has been proposed by O'Leary (1989; see also Johnson, 1997, 1998). The protocortex model emphasizes the role of epigenetic influences and applies only to the development of neocortical areas. According to the protocortex model, the neocortical epithelium is not genetically programmed to generate cortical plate cells that are committed to a particular areal fate. Rather, it is hypothesized that the neurons of the neocortical plate have the potential to develop the range of features associated with diverse neocortical areas. The differentiation of the neurons into area-specific connections and architecture requires inputs from thalamic (experiential) afferents to each region (Johnson, 1997; O'Leary, 1989).

In sum, despite their differing emphases, both the protomap and protocortex models recognize contributions from genetic and epigenetic mechanisms in the differentiation of neocortical areas as well as a vital role for thalamocortical afferents in this process. Original to the protocortex model (O'Leary, 1989) is the fact that molecular differences are thought to exist throughout the neocortex and contribute to the process of areal differentiation. Numerous investigations suggest that afferent inputs, especially thalamocortical afferents, have a fundamental role in regulating the differentiation of area-specific features (see Johnson, 1997). Thus, from the viewpoint of the protocortex model, normal cortical development is believed to enable a considerable amount of cortical plasticity. Cortical regions are capable of supporting a number of different types of representations depending on the nature of their input (Johnson, 1999).

Rakic (1996) discussed that, in the neocortex of the rhesus monkey, synaptogenesis and synapse elimination occur simultaneously and at an equal rate in all cortical regions (see also Goldman-Rakic, Bourgeois, & Rakic, 1997). Conversely, because there are known regional differences in neurobiological development, including timing of maximum brain growth, dendritic arborizations, and myelination of cortical afferents and efferents (Huttenlocher & Dabholkar, 1997; Thompson & Nelson, 2001), it is not surprising that concurrent synaptogenesis does not occur in humans. The prefrontal cortex is the last region to develop (Huttenlocher, 1994, 2002). Thus, competition between and correlated activity within neural networks drives the selective stabilization of some neural connections at the expense of others and leads to the normal parcellation of neural systems into specific structural and functional units (Courchesne et al., 1994).

The normal brain develops from a network of few elements, infrequent interactions among elements, less stability, and less structural and functional differentiation, to one of additional elements, more intricate interactions among elements, greater stability, and increased structural and functional parcellation and specialization (see, e.g., J. W. Brown, 1994; Cicchetti & Tucker, 1994a; Courchesne et al., 1994). In Chapter 3, this *Handbook,* this volume, magnetic resonance imaging studies are reviewed to present a picture of normal and abnormal brain structural development over time.

EXPERIENCE AND BRAIN DEVELOPMENT

One outgrowth of systems theorizing has been a growing acceptance of the viewpoint that neurobiological development and experience are mutually influencing (Cicchetti & Tucker, 1994a; Eisenberg, 1995; Kandel, 1998; Nelson & Bloom, 1997). For example, it has been demonstrated that, just as gene expression alters social behavior (Young, Nilson, Waymore, MacGregor, & Insel, 1999), so, too, do social experiences exert actions on the brain by feeding back on it to modify gene expression and brain structure, function, and organization (Francis, Diorio, Liu, & Meaney,

1999; Kandel, 1998). Relatedly, changes in the brain may directly exert effects on mental functioning. Conversely, alterations in mental processing can causally affect brain functioning (Bolton & Hill, 1996; Edelman, 2004).

The concept that experience can modify brain structure can be traced back at least to the writings of Cajal (see Cajal, 1913/1959), who, despite his belief that the connections that occurred between neurons unfolded according to a definite plan (i.e., the principle of connection specificity), asserted that the strength and effectiveness of these neuronal connections were not predetermined and that they could be altered by experience (Kandel & Squire, 2000). Likewise, D. O. Hebb (1949) believed that experience could alter brain structure and function and made this viewpoint a central feature of his neuropsychological theory (see Posner & Rothbart, 2004).

In current perspectives, experience is broadly construed to include not only external social and psychological events but also, for example, internal events, such as the effects of psychopathology, trauma, abuse, or injury; the actions of hormones; and the consequences of development and aging (Boyce et al., 1998; Cicchetti & Walker, 2003). For example, an investigation revealed that early life experiences could affect neurogenesis in adulthood. Mirescu, Peters, and Gould (2004) demonstrated that early adversity affects the regulation of adult neurogenesis in the hippocampus. Specifically, rats who experienced maternal deprivation when they were pups did not display the normal decrease in cell proliferatin and immature neuron production in the dentate gyrus. This finding was observed despite the fact that these rats had normal hypothalamic-pituitary-adrenal (HPA) axis activation. These results provide suggestive evidence that early adverse experience inhibits structural plasticity via a hypersensitivity to glucocorticoids and impairs the ability of the hippocampus to respond adaptively to stress that occurs in adulthood. Research with humans has similarly demonstrated that adverse early experiences may lead to the development of abnormal brain structures and functioning and sensitize developing neural networks to stressful experiences (Gunnar, 2000). Work with Romanian orphans and with children who have been abused or neglected early in life also has revealed anomalies in their brain structure and functioning (Cicchetti & Curtis, in press; Cicchetti & Rogosch, 2001a, 2001b; DeBellis, 2001; Gunnar, Morison, Chisholm, & Schuder, 2001; S. W. Parker & Nelson, 2005b; Pollak, Cicchetti, Klorman, & Brumaghim, 1997). Furthermore, it has been shown that alterations in gene expression induced by learning and by social and psychological experiences produce changes in patterns of neuronal and synaptic connections and, thus, in the func-

tion of nerve cells (Kandel, 1998, 1999; Post, Weiss, & Leverich, 1994). Such neuronal and synaptic modifications not only exert a prominent role in initiating and maintaining the behavioral changes that are provoked by experience but also contribute to the biological bases of individuality, as well as to individuals being differentially affected by similar experiences, regardless of their positive or negative/adverse valence (Cicchetti & Rogosch, 1996; Depue & Collins, 1999; Kandel, 1998).

Mechanisms of Neural Plasticity

Although brain development is guided and controlled to some extent by genetic information (Rakic, 1988a, 1998), a not insignificant portion of brain structuration and neural patterning is thought to occur through interaction of the child with the environment (Greenough, Black, & Wallace, 1987; Nelson, 1999; O'Leary, 1989). As eloquently expressed by Torsten Weisel (1994): "genes controlling embryonic development shape the structure of the infant brain; the infant's experience in the world fine tunes the pattern of neuronal connections underlying the brain's function. Such fine-tuning . . . must surely continue through adulthood" (p. 1647). Relatedly, Nelson (1999) asserted that the fine-tuning of the biological and behavioral systems that occurs beyond the early years of life is more subtle and protracted than that which is manifested in infancy. Moreover, Nelson (1999) stated that the "dramatic changes that occur in the brain long after the child's second or third birthday are in large measure brought about by the experiences the child has with his or her environment" (p. 237).

Recognizing that mechanisms of plasticity are integral to the very anatomical structure of cortical tissue, and that they cause the formation of the brain to be an extended malleable process, neuroscientists and developmental psychopathologists are presented with new avenues for understanding the vulnerability and protective aspects of the brain as contributors to the genesis and epigenesis of psychopathology and resilience (Cicchetti & Tucker, 1994a). Because the mechanisms of neural plasticity cause the brain's anatomical differentiation to be dependent on stimulation from the environment, it is now clear that the cytoarchitecture of the cerebral cortex also is shaped by input from the social environment. Since the human cerebral cortex is only diffusely structured by a genetic plan, and since the eventual differentiation of the cortex is highly reactive to the individual's active coping and "meaning making" in a particular environment, it is very likely that both abnormal and resilient outcomes following the experience of significant adversity would encompass a diverse range of neural, synaptic, and associative networks that are the physiological underpinnings of many possible individual psychological organizations (cf. Cicchetti & Tucker, 1994a; Curtis & Cicchetti, 2003). As Luu and Tucker (1996) have articulated: "To understand neuropsychological development is to confront the fact that the brain is mutable, such that its structural organization reflects the history of the organism. Moreover, this structure reflects both what is most important to the organism and what the organism is capable of at that particular time" (p. 297). Cortical development and organization should no longer be viewed as passive processes that solely depend upon genetics and environmental input. Rather, corticogenesis and organization should be conceived as processes of self-organization guided by self-regulatory mechanisms (Cicchetti & Tucker, 1994a).

Black, Jones, Nelson, and Greenough (1998) have described brain development as a complex scaffolding of three types of neural processes: gene driven, experience expectant, and experience dependent. Black et al. (1998) conceptualized *gene-driven processes* as being largely insensitive to experience. Gene-driven processes serve to guide the migration of neurons, to target many of their synaptic connections, and to determine their differentiated functions. To protect the development of the brain, much of the basic organization of most nervous systems is thought to be relatively impervious to experience. The recalcitrance to environmental influences during embryonic development was termed *canalization* by Waddington (1966). Black and colleagues (1998) note that this canalization process can be either helpful (e.g., the minimization of experiential effects on embryogenesis can aid survival) or harmful (e.g., in cases of genetic diseases, prenatal brain development proceeds along a maladaptive pathway that is largely resistant to any therapeutic interventions).

Experience-expectant processes correspond roughly to critical or "sensitive" periods and take place in early age-locked sensory system development (Greenough & Black, 1992; Greenough et al., 1987). During experience-expectant periods, the brain is primed to receive particular classes of information from the environment. The brain builds an overabundance of synapses that are then pruned back by experience to a selectively retained subset (Huttenlocher, 1990; Huttenlocher & Dabholkar, 1997). The pruning of synapses appears to be initiated by competitive interactions between neuronal connections such that inactive neural connections are eliminated and synapses that are most actively mediated by experience are selectively maintained (Greenough et al., 1987). In human embryol-

ogy, the pruning process applies to neurons, whereas postnatally it applies predominantly to synapses (Edelman, 1987). In the absence of behavioral and neural activity, cells do not die and circuits do not become pruned in an adaptive way that aids the organism in adapting to the demands of its environment.

Experience-expectant neural plasticity is usually embedded in a developmental program and requires appropriate timing and quality of the information stored for brain development to be normal. Abnormal experience or deprivation during experience-expectant development may exert enduring deleterious effects on brain and behavioral epigenesis (Black et al., 1998). Experience-expectant neural plasticity varies widely across brain systems, eventuating in highly specialized alterations that occur as a function of the timing and nature of the modified experience and the brain systems involved (Bavelier & Neville, 2002). Variations in experience-expectant neural plasticity take place as a function of a number of existing factors, including: (1) differences in the temporal expression of receptors that are necessary for synaptic plasticity; (2) differences in the molecular factors that control the development of various neural pathways; and (3) differences in the degrees of exuberant or redundant early connectivity (Bavelier & Neville, 2002).

In later development, synaptogenesis seems to be generated in response to events that provide information to be encoded in the nervous system. This *experience-dependent* synapse formation involves the brain's adaptation to information that is unique to the individual (Greenough & Black, 1992; Greenough et al., 1987). Because all individuals encounter distinctive environments, each brain is modified in a singular fashion. Experience-dependent synaptogenesis is localized to the brain regions involved in processing information arising from the event experienced by the individual. Unlike the case with experience-expectant processes, experience-dependent processes do not take place within a stringent temporal interval because the timing or nature of experience that the individual engages or chooses cannot be entirely and dependably envisioned. An important central mechanism for experience-dependent development is the formation of new neural connections in contrast to the overproduction and pruning back of synapses often associated with experience-expectant processes (Greenough et al., 1987). Because experience-dependent processes can occur throughout the life span, social interactions, psychotherapy, and pharmacotherapy have the capacity to exert a palliative influence on brains that are afflicted with disorders (Black et al., 1998; Cicchetti, 1996; Cicchetti &

Posner, 2005; Cicchetti & Sroufe, 2000; Cicchetti & Walker, 2001; Goldapple et al., 2004; Mayberg, 2003).

Neural Plasticity: Historical Aspect

In the denouement to his treatise entitled *Degeneration and Regeneration of the Nervous System,* Cajal declared: "Once development is completed, the sources of growth and regeneration are irrevocably lost. In the adult brain, nervous pathways are fixed and immutable; everything may die, nothing may be regenerated" (Cajal 1913/1959, p. 750).

After over a decade of innovative and meticulous research in which he investigated whether the brain was capable of regeneration in animals with injuries to the spinal cord, the cerebellum, or the cerebral cortex, Cajal proclaimed that "the vast majority of regenerative processes described in man are ephemeral, abortive, and incapable of completely and definitely repairing the damaged pathways" (Cajal, 1913/1959, p. 750). Since Cajal's early work, it has been known that there is some axonal regeneration subsequent to spinal cord injury; however, in the experimental conditions that Cajal designed, regeneration was limited and, therefore, not believed to have any functional significance (Stein & Dawson, 1980). Cajal's assertions served as the prevailing dogma for a large portion of the twentieth century. The widespread belief put forward by neuroscientists was that because no new neuron generation was deemed possible, rewiring of existing connections, dendritic branching, and elimination of synaptic connections were the only ways whereby neural plasticity could occur.

It was not until the 1970s that regenerative capacity was demonstrated in the adult mammalian brain. Two types of growth were found to occur in response to nerve injury (Stein & Dawson, 1980). The first is *regenerative sprouting,* a process whereby when the axons of cells are cut and the distal portion begins to degenerate, the remaining stump, including the cell body, begins to form growth cones and regenerate new terminals. In the second, known as *collateral symmetry,* a number of cells innervating a given structure are destroyed and their terminals degenerate. However, the remaining intact cells begin to grow additional new terminals (sprouting) that innervate the target area evacuated by the damaged neurons. As such, the degenerated inputs are replaced by terminals arriving from intact neurons.

In 1975, the eminent neuropsychologist Hans-Lucas Teuber declared that if one is going to have brain damage, then it would be preferable to have it early rather than late in life. Teuber based his conclusion on the findings of Margaret Kennard's experiments on the long-term effects of brain damage in monkeys of different ages. Kennard (1938) discovered that damage to the adult nervous system resulted in more deleterious and less reversible effects than similar brain damage inflicted during early development. The field's acceptance of the so-called "Kennard principle" led to the belief that little reorganization of function could occur after injury to the mature mammalian nervous system and that most structure-function relations were permanently established during the early years of life. In fact, Teuber's (1975) own studies with humans revealed that improvement in traumatic head injury cases was substantially greater when the brain damage had taken place in an early developmental period. However, scientists in the field had differing interpretations of Teuber's belief that brain damage that occurred later in development would exert more disruptive effects than damage originated earlier in life. Critics noted that the results of the experimental data of Teuber and his contemporaries in the field could be interpreted to indicate that the maturational status of the nervous system at the time of injury must be considered in any explanation of recovery or sparing of function after early brain damage (Stein & Dawson, 1980). Commentators on the aforementioned body of work reasoned that if subjects were tested at a time when the substrate for a particular function had not yet developed, then the function would appear to have been compensated when, in fact, it had never been lost (Isaacson, 1975). Depending on the location of the lesion and the precise timing of the injury, the developing brain can suffer from far more neuronal degeneration than that evidenced in the mature brain. For example, excessive amounts of excitatory amino acids, such as glutamate, produce much more severe lesions in the immature brain than in the adult brain. Thus, there are a number of instances in which early brain damage can be viewed as more disastrous than later brain damage because early lesions often result in the formation of anomalous circuitry and neural pathways as well as reduction in brain size (Black et al., 1998; Isaacson, 1975; Steingard & Coyle, 1998).

Kolb, Forgie, Gibb, Gorny, and Rowntree (1998), in their programmatic enrichment studies on brain plasticity and behavior in rats after brain injury, found that enriched experience could have varying effects upon the brain at different ages. They reported discovering compensatory changes in brain plasticity following brain injury that are similar in kind to those observed when animals learn from experience. Kolb and colleagues (1998) found that experience alters the synaptic organization of the cortex and that these changes in synaptic organization are associated with behavioral changes. The similarity between plastic changes in the brain in response either to injury or to experience suggests that it is conceivable that there may be basic mechanisms of synaptic change in the mammalian cortex that are used in many forms of neural plasticity (see also Kolb, 1995).

Accordingly, it appears that there are not any simple rules that govern whether neural plasticity occurs following lesions in early life. Most of the early neuropsychological models of the effects of brain lesions were based on work with patients, were predominantly focused on brain localization, and were couched within unidirectional models of causality (i.e., brain lesions were believed to affect behavior, but not vice versa). These early models did not take into account the dynamic interplay that occurs among brain regions and the bidirectional impact that brain and behavior exert upon each other. Modern-day research, conducted predominantly, but not exclusively, with animals, provides suggestive evidence that the mammalian central nervous system possesses much greater potential for producing new neurons and repairing damaged areas than has heretofore been thought (Cicchetti & Tucker, 1994a, 1994b; Curtis & Cicchetti, 2003).

In the developing organism, studies conducted with a variety of species also have revealed that positive or negative early life experiences can modify both brain structure and function. For example, Sur and colleagues (Sur, Garraghty, & Roe, 1988; Sur, Pallas, & Roe, 1990) trained adult ferrets, who had one hemisphere rewired at birth, to discriminate between auditory and visual stimuli that were presented to the normal hemisphere. The results of these experiments provide support for the functional equipotentiality of cortical mapping. Specifically, the findings in the Sur, Garraghty, et al. (1988) and Sur, Pallas, et al. (1990) investigations demonstrate that it is possible to rewire sensory inputs to the thalamus such that processing of auditory stimuli takes place in the primary visual cortex and vice-versa; that is, the cortical field that usually mediates vision could attain a functional organization capable of processing sound, and the cortical field that usually mediates audition could attain a functional organization capable of processing sight.

Sur and colleagues (Sharma, Angelucci, & Sur, 2000) also have demonstrated that, in ferrets whose retinal projections were routed into their auditory pathway, visually responsive neurons in the "rewired" auditory cortex, just as is the case with neurons in the primary visual cortex, were characterized by orientation modules—groups of cells that share a preferred stimulus orientation. Although the orientation tuning of neurons within the "rewired" auditory cortex was comparable to the tuning of cells in the primary visual cortex, the orientation map was less orderly. Thus, the findings of this investigation reveal that sensory afferent activity profoundly influences diverse components of cortical circuitry.

Finally, the long-held assumption that neural reorganization following injury was restricted to the period of infancy, with only modest neural reorganization possible in the child and adult, has been challenged through research with humans. Results from a number of investigations suggest that reorganization of cortical pathways can occur in the brains of older children and adults (see, e.g., Merzenich, 1998; Merzenich et al., 1996; Tallal et al., 1996). Although the majority of these neural changes to date have been demonstrated in work on sensory or motor pathways (see, e.g., Agliotti, Bonazzi, & Cortese's, 1994, work on phantom lower limb as a perceptual marker of neural plasticity), existing research provides suggestive evidence that cognitive systems (i.e., language) can reorganize beyond infancy (see, e.g., Merzenich et al., 1996; Tallal et al., 1996; also see discussions in Johnson, 1999). Thus, it is becoming quite clear that under certain conditions at least some regions of the brain can incorporate the signature of experience into the structure, function, and organization of the brain.

The process of neural plasticity is influenced by a number of neurotransmitters and growth factors. These growth factors, including nerve growth factor and brain-derived neurotrophic factor, stimulate a variety of cellular effects at the structural and functional levels that eventuate in the promotion of survival and differentiation of responsive neurons. Adaptive alterations in neuroarchitecture may occur throughout life as new synapses form, old ones disintegrate, and new neurite outgrowth occurs. The discovery of brain behavioral plasticity can make important contributions to the understanding of development through demonstrating that neural representations are dynamic processes. Moreover, experimental results that provide evidence of plasticity can give critical insights into the actual processes through which neurobiological development occurs.

Recovery of function following brain injury can be characterized as a maturational process in which the brain is thought to cause the formation of new structures via specialized mechanisms that were triggered by the injury (i.e., *causal epigenesis;* see Johnson, 1999). This viewpoint involves the restriction of fate—that is, biological tissue that initially had many possibilities for subsequent specialization throughout development is reduced to a subset of these possibilities by the injury. In contrast, according to Gottlieb's (1992) *probabilistic epigenesis* framework, brain plasticity may be conceived as a fundamental and inherent property of the developing brain. From this viewpoint, plasticity is conceptualized as allowing the neural system to retain a number of options for specialization even after brain injury. This process is influenced by neural activity rather than by molecular markers. In humans, neurobiological development is a more prolonged process than in animals, extending well into postnatal life (Nelson & Bosquet, 2000; Spear, 2000; Thompson & Nelson, 2001). Critical aspects of neurobiological development occur after middle childhood (Dahl, 2004; Giedd, 2004; Spear, 2000). Therefore, some degree of functional specialization in the cerebral cortex is likely to be influenced by the child's interaction with the postnatal environment (Johnson, 1999; Johnson et al., 2005). The extremely long juvenile period (neotony) in humans may have evolved, in part, for the primary purpose of shifting cortical specification from genetic to epigenetic control (Cicchetti & Tucker, 1994a).

During the past several decades, scientific research has begun to reveal that, within certain limits, forms of neural plasticity may take place throughout epigenesis and are not limited to early development (Cicchetti & Tucker, 1994b; Hann, Huffman, Lederhendler, & Meinecke, 1998; Kandel & Squire, 2000). The cortex, in fact, appears to be capable of organizational changes throughout the life course of the organism (Cicchetti & Tucker, 1994a; Jacobs, van Praag, & Gage, 2000). For example, Thatcher's (1992, 1994, 1997) work on the development of electroencephalogram (EEG) coherence in humans suggests that cortical organization proceeds in stages that are repeated cyclically over development. Each stage of cortical organization reflects the ongoing and dynamic shaping of cortical circuitry throughout an individual's life span. These periods of EEG coherence are thought to represent rapid synaptic growth within functionally differentiated neural systems. Neural plasticity involves the genetically driven overproduction of synapses and the environmentally driven maintenance and pruning of synaptic connections.

Neuroscientists conceive plasticity as being reflective of anatomic, chemical, or metabolic changes in the brain. Nelson (2000b) stated that neuroanatomic changes illustrate the ability of existing synapses to alter their activity through sprouting new axons, regenerating old ones, or by elaborating their dendritic surfaces. Thus, for example, loss of fibers in an area of the cortex (e.g., the corpus callosum) may eventuate in a reduction of synapses in the affected area that is subsequently compensated for by an influx of thalamic synapses into the vacated space that reestablishes communication between the hemispheres. Nelson (2000b) also defined neurochemical plasticity as the ability of synapses to alter their activity through aug-

menting the synthesis of neurotransmitters or enhancing the response of the postsynaptic receptor to the neurotransmitter. Additionally, Nelson (2000b) delineated fluctuations in cortical and subcortical metabolic activity, for example, at the site of an injury, as another possible sign of neural plasticity.

In most mammalian brain regions, neuronal birth and migration take place during a discrete period of prenatal development, followed several days later by cell death (Rakic, 1988a, 1996, 1998). In contrast, the granule cells of the dentate gyrus in the hippocampus, olfactory bulb, and cerebellum are generated predominantly during the postnatal period (Gould & Cameron, 1996). In addition, stem cells that reside in specialized niches in the brain of adult mammals continuously generate new neurons. The neurons in mammalian brains are born in two germinal regions: the subventricular zone (SVZ) and the subgranular zone (SGZ). The SVZ generates olfactory bulb neurons and the SGZ of the hippocampal formation gives rise to granule neurons of the dentate gyrus (Doetsch & Hen, 2005).

In the early adult, approximately 1% of the total olfactory bulb interneurons are added each day. Approximately 50% of these adult-generated olfactory bulb interneurons die within 15 to 45 days after their birth, after they have developed elaborate dendritic morphology and spines. In contrast to their neurogenesis, the early cell death that characterizes the adult-generated olfactory system is activity dependent. Because olfactory cues are critical for survival, the function of the newly born olfactory neurons may be to help enhance olfactory discrimination (Petreanu & Alvarez-Buylla, 2002). Interestingly, environments that are olfactory enriched enhance the length of time that adult-generated olfactory neurons survive. The increased life span of these neurons also is accompanied by improved performance on olfactory memory tasks; however, it is not known whether the improved performance was due to the newly generated neurons or to existing cells exhibiting enhanced activity (Rochefort, Gheusi, Vincent, & Lledo, 2002). Moreover, these adult-born immature neurons have electrophysiological properties that differ from those of old neurons. The unique excitability and connectivity properties may exert distinct functional consequences on the processing of olfactory information (Doetsch & Hen, 2005).

Approximately 85% of dentate gyrus neurons are generated postnatally; however, their production begins during the embryonic period (Gould & Cameron, 1996). A large population of cells reaches the dentate gyrus without undergoing final division; these precursor cells remain in the dentate gyrus and become the source of granule neurons born in the postnatal period. Granule cells are excitatory neurons that utilize glutamate as their primary neurotransmitter. A growing body of investigations indicates that excitatory input plays a prominent role in the formation of many neuronal populations.

In fact, in the mature central nervous system pools of progenitor cells appear to proliferate and migrate well into adulthood. For example, Kempermann, Kuhn, and Gage (1998) discovered that neurogenesis continues to occur in the dentate gyrus of senescent mice and can be stimulated when the mice are placed in an enriched environment. Kempermann et al. (1998) found that neurogenesis declined with increasing age; however, stimulation of adult and aged mice by changing from regular housing to an enriched environment that provided opportunities for social interaction, physical activity, and exploration brought about an increased number of survival cells. Furthermore, animals residing in enriched environments had more of their cells differentiate into neurons than did mice housed in standard conditions. These findings suggest that the new neurons were generated in the hippocampal area and that neural plasticity can take place in the aging brain in mice.

Likewise, Gould, Tanapat, McEwen, Flugge, and Fuchs (1998) discovered that new neurons are produced in the dentate gyrus of adult monkeys. Moreover, these investigators found that a single exposure to a socially stressful condition (i.e., a resident intruder unfamiliar adult male conspecific) inhibits the proliferation of granule cell precursors. Cortisol and glucocorticoids control the rate of the development of these new neurons, and it is clear that the existing neurons are not merely reorganizing their connections. Furthermore, the mature central nervous system continues to express an array of molecules that are required for the formation of neuronal networks during embryonic development (e.g., neurotrophic growth factors, embryonic forms of cell adhesion molecules, axon-guidance molecules). The presence of these molecules suggests that the degree of potential network remodeling in the mature central nervous system may be more extensive than generally thought (Lowenstein & Parent, 1999). Thus, although there is currently no unequivocal evidence that the fully developed central nervous system continues to generate new neurons and glial cells everywhere, progenitor cells with the potential to produce new cells are prevalent throughout the mature mammalian central nervous system (Gage, 2000; Lowenstein & Parent, 1999).

Two factors, adrenal steroids and excitatory input, have been identified that regulate the proliferation, migration, and survival of granule neurons during the postnatal period through adulthood. In general, increases in adrenal steroid levels or NMDA receptor activation diminish the rate of

cell proliferation, whereas decreases in adrenal steroid levels or NMDA receptor activation increase the rate of cell production. These results also suggest that decreased neurogenesis associated with increased corticosteroid levels may contribute to age-related memory deficits. Moreover, the finding that the neuronal precursor population in the dentate gyrus remains stable into old age, but that neurogenesis is slowed by high levels of adrenal steroids, suggests that these memory deficits may be reversible (Cameron & McKay, 1999). Gould (1999) also reported that activation of serotonergic receptors enhanced neurogenesis in the adult mammalian dentate gyrus. Because adult-generated hippocampal neurons are affected by, and conceivably involved in, learning and memory (Gould, Beylin, Tanapat, Reeves, & Shors, 1999), serotonergic agonists that stimulate granule cell production may prevent memory deficits.

Cells that divide in adulthood do not die soon thereafter. Thus, the cell death that occurs in adulthood does not simply remove cells that were generated incorrectly in adulthood. In fact, because granule neurons that generate in adults survive for at least 1 month and form connections, it is likely that their addition to the granule cell layer has significant functional consequences. In a study that has generated a great deal of controversy in the literature, Gould et al. (1999) discovered that stress does not alter the survival of recently produced neurons in the dentate gyrus. Accordingly, young (immature) adult-generated hippocampal cells may make them uniquely qualified to form synaptic connections rapidly and to participate in the transient storage of information. Furthermore, Gould, Beylin, et al. (1999) found that in order for learning to further enhance the number of new hippocampal neurons, the animal must be engaged in a task for which this brain region is essential. In addition, Gould, Reeves, Graziano, and Gross (1999) discovered that in adult macaque monkeys new neurons are added to the prefrontal, posterior parietal, and inferior temporal cortex. These investigators stated that these new neurons most likely originated in the subventricular zone and then migrated through white matter tracts to the neocortex, where they extended axons. Gould and colleagues hypothesized that the new neurons added to these regions of association cortex might play a role in such functions. Moreover, Gould, Reeves, et al. (1999) conjectured that these immature neurons, which continue to be added on adulthood, are capable of undergoing rapid structural changes and thereby serve as a substrate for learning and memory.

In a subsequent investigation, Gould, Vail, Wagers, and Gross (2001) compared the production and survival of adult-generated neurons and glia in the dentate gyrus, prefrontal cortex, and inferior temporal cortex. These investigators found that there were many more cells produced in the dentate gyrus than in either of the two neocortical association areas. Furthermore, a greater percentage of cells in the dentate gyrus expressed a neuronal marker than was the case for cells in either of the neocortical areas. Additionally, Gould and colleagues (2001) discovered that there was a decline in the number of cells approximately 9 weeks after they had been labeled, suggesting that some percentage of the adult-generated new cells may have a transient existence. It is believed that the short-lived nature of these newly generated neurons may make them particularly suited to play a role in learning and memory processes (cf. Gould, Tanapat, Hastings, & Shors, 1999).

The finding of neurogenesis in the neocortex of the adult primate by Gould and her colleagues (1999; Gould, Vail, et al., 2001) astonished the scientific world because, since the writings of His and Cajal, the brain has been considered to be a nonrenewable organ comprised of fully differentiated neurons (Jacobson, 1991; Rakic, 2002b). As previously noted, numerous investigations have found that adult neurogenesis in mammals only occurs unambiguously in the granule cells of the dentate gyrus and the olfactory bulb (Carleton, Petreanu, Lansford, Alvarez-Buylla, & Lledo, 2003; Gage, 2000; Kornack & Rakic, 2001b; Rakic, 1998). Not surprisingly, a number of methodological critiques of the findings of Gould, Reeves, et al. have appeared in the literature (Kornack & Rakic, 2001a; Korr & Schmitz, 1999; Nowakowski & Hayes, 2000; Rakic, 2002a, 2002b). Consequently, the conclusion put forth by some of the great systematizers in the history of developmental neurobiology, that nerve cells that subserve the highest cortical functions are irreplaceable under typical conditions, appears to continue to garner strong support from contemporary neurobiologists.

Neurobiological Pathways to Psychopathology

Just as we described with respect to normal brain development, abnormal neurobiological development also is a dynamic, self-organizing process. However, unlike the case for normal neurobiological development, the final product of abnormal brain development includes a substantial measure of misorganization (Courchesne et al., 1994). Perturbations that occur during brain development can potentiate a cascade of maturational and structural changes that eventuate in the neural system proceeding along a trajectory that deviates from that generally taken during normal neurobiological development (Cicchetti & Tucker, 1994a; Courchesne et al., 1994; Nowakowski & Hayes, 1999). Early stressors, either physiological or emotional, may alter the neurodevelopmental processes of networks, in turn generating a cascade of effects through subsequent developmental periods, conceivably constraining the child's flexibility to adapt to new challenging situations with new strategies rather than with old conceptual and behavioral prototypes (Cicchetti & Tucker, 1994a; Gunnar, 2000; Sanchez, Ladd, & Plotsky, 2001). Accordingly, early psychological trauma may eventuate not only in emotional sensitization (Maughan & Cicchetti, 2002; Rieder & Cicchetti, 1989) but also in pathological sensitization of neurophysiological reactivity (Pollak, Cicchetti, & Klorman, 1998).

Accordingly, abnormal perturbations at one stage of brain development hinder the creation of some new structures and functions, distort the form of later-emerging ones, make possible the construction of ones that normally never become manifest, and/or limit the elaboration and usage of structures and functions that had appeared earlier (Courchesne et al., 1994; Steingard & Coyle, 1998). Eventually, successively more complex, specialized, and stable abnormal neural network configurations and operations develop that differ greatly from antecedent ones (Courchesne et al., 1994). Abnormal competition between, and abnormal correlated activity within, undamaged, as well as damaged, neural networks can drive the abnormal elimination of some connections and neural elements (e.g., remote loss) and the abnormal selective stabilization of others (e.g., aberrant connections are retained or created; Courchesne et al., 1994). Such early developmental abnormalities may lead to the development of aberrant neural circuitry and often compound themselves into relatively enduring forms of psychopathology (Arnold, 1999; Cicchetti & Cannon, 1999b; Nowakowski & Hayes, 1999).

Children whose gene-driven processes construct a disordered brain are likely to experience the world in a vastly different fashion than children who do not have such a strong genetic predisposition (Black et al., 1998). Genes often exert different functional roles in divergent cell types at varying developmental periods (Alberts et al., 1994; Lewin, 2004). Consequently, defects in such genes may trigger a cascade of change that is not confined to a particular neural structure, functional system, or behavioral domain. Even if the subsequent experience-expectant and experience-dependent processes are unimpaired, the experience distorted by the neuropathology is not likely to be appropriately utilized (Black et al., 1998). Thus, children with genetically constructed abnormal brains must have their environments tailored to their specific deficits. If such environmental modifications are not introduced, then these children's subsequent experience-expectant and experience-dependent processes manifest additional aberrations and development proceeds on an even more maladaptive pathway. Pathological experience may become part of a vicious cycle, as the pathology induced in the brain structure may distort the child's experience, with subsequent alterations in cognition or social interactions causing additional pathological experience and added brain pathology (Cicchetti & Tucker, 1994a). Because experience-expectant and experience-dependent processes may continue to operate during psychopathological states, children who incorporate pathological experience during these processes may add neuropathological connections into their developing brains instead of functional neuronal connections (Black et al., 1998).

Social Experience and Brain Development and Functioning

Empirical evidence gleaned from research with rodents and nonhuman primates has demonstrated that the experience of traumatic events early in life can alter behavioral and neuroendocrine responsiveness, the morphological characteristics of the brain, and the activation of genes associated with negative behavioral and neurobiological outcomes (Sanchez et al., 2001). Moreover, the results of animal studies reveal that early traumatic experiences may exert a harmful impact on the normative developmental processes, which have been shown to be associated with long-term alterations in coping, emotional, and behavioral dysregulation; responsiveness of the neuroendocrine system to stressful experiences; brain structure; neurochemistry; and gene expression (Cicchetti & Walker, 2001; Gunnar et al., 2001). Additionally, research has discovered that depriving rodent infants of adequate social and physical stimulation from their mothers' influences the responsivity of the hypothalamic pituitary-adrenal axis to stressors in later life (Levine, 1994; Meaney et al., 1996). Furthermore, research with rodents has revealed that naturally occurring variations in maternal care alter the expression of genes whose function is to regulate behavioral and endocrine responses to stress, as well as to modify synaptic development in the hippocampus (Meaney, 2001). In particular, stressors that are imposed on mothers have been shown to increase stress reactivity in their rodent offspring. Thus, quality of parental care is a mediator of the impact that adverse environmental conditions have on neural development in rodents.

Children who are endowed with normal brains may encounter a variety of negative experiences that exert a deleterious effect on neurobiological structure, function, and organization, and contribute to distortions in the way in which these children interpret and react to their worlds (Pollak et al., 1998). In this Handbook, Chapter 4, Volume 3 (Ci-

cchetti & Valentino, 2006), the effect of child maltreatment on the structure and function of neurobiological systems was reviewed. We do not wish to restate the details of the neurobiological studies conducted to date, which demonstrate that different components of brain structure and function, each representing fairly distinct neural systems, are negatively affected by experiencing child maltreatment. Work on acoustic startle, neuroendocrine regulation, event-related potentials (ERPs), and neuroimaging have revealed that the various stressors associated with child maltreatment exert harmful effects on numerous interconnected neurobiological systems. Moreover, the neurobiological development of maltreated children is not affected in the same way in all individuals. Finally, not all maltreated children exhibit anomalies in their brain structure or function. Accordingly, it appears that the effects of maltreatment on brain microstructure and biochemistry may be either pathological or adaptive. Finally, because research with rodents and nonhuman primates has revealed that social experiences, such as maternal care giving behaviors, maternal deprivation, and maternal separation, affect gene expression, as well as brain structure and function (Kaufman & Charney, 2001; Meaney et al., 1996; Sanchez et al., 2001), it is highly probable that child maltreatment affects the expression of genes that impact brain structure, as well as basic regulatory processes (Caspi et al., 2002; Cicchetti & Blender, 2004; Kaufman et al., 2004).

Often, the investigation of a system in its smoothly operating normal or healthy state does not afford the opportunity to comprehend the interrelations among its component systems (see, e.g., Caviness & Rakic, 1978; Chomsky, 1968). Because pathological conditions enable scientists to isolate the components of the integrated system, investigation of these nonnormative conditions sheds light on the normal structure of the system. We next discuss Autism and neurodevelopmental aspects of Schizophrenia as illustrations of how the examination of brain development in mental disorder could provide insights into normal neurobiological processes.

CONTRIBUTION OF BRAIN DEVELOPMENT IN ATYPICAL POPULATIONS TO FURTHERING INSIGHTS INTO TYPICAL NEUROLOGICAL PROCESSES

Autism

Autism is a pervasive developmental disorder characterized by impairments in social communication and interaction, a wide range of cognitive and executive functioning deficits, and behavioral stereotypes (American Psychiatric Association, 1994). Over 60 years ago, Kanner (1943), who originally devised the term Autism, suggested that Autism represented a biological dysfunction that reduced the capacity of children to form emotional contact with people. However, a short time later, Kanner revised his conceptual thinking on the etiology of Autism and, along with many others, came to view it as environmentally caused, often believed to be a result of emotionally distant, rejecting parents (Bettelheim, 1967). Fortunately, more recent formulations concerning the etiology of this disorder have emphasized its probable neurobiological and genetic basis (e.g., Courchesne, 1987; Rodier, 2002).

Many neurobiological theories concerning Autism have tended to focus on possible abnormalities of individual brain structures as underlying the observed behavioral and neuropsychological symptoms observed in Autism. A range of theories focused on dysfunction of the brain have implicated abnormalities in nearly every brain system. For example, some theories have been based on animal models of medial temporal lobe dysfunction (e.g., Bachevalier, 1996; Bachevalier & Loveland, 2003), while others have emphasized abnormalities in brain structures, such as the amygdala (e.g., Baron-Cohen et al., 2000), hippocampus (e.g., DeLong, 1992), frontal cortex (e.g., Damasio & Maurer, 1978), and cerebellum (e.g., Courchesne, 1997), as well as other cortical and subcortical regions as fundamental to the etiology of Autism. Until recently, etiological formulations of Autism have failed to take into account the impact of developmental processes and the probable interconnected nature of multiple brain systems at multiple levels of analysis.

Many of the conceptualizations of neural-structural abnormalities underlying the behavioral manifestations of Autism have been based on data obtained through neuropsychological assessment of children with Autism. Such assessments have consistently demonstrated deficits in discrete areas of cognition and executive functioning. One such commonly observed deficit is in attentional functioning, whereby speed of orienting to and processing novel stimuli is reduced in those with Autism (e.g., Akshoomoff, Courchesne, & Townsend, 1997; Townsend, Harris, & Courchesne, 1996), as well as the ability to shift attention (e.g., Wainwright-Sharp & Bryson, 1993). Generally, however, individuals with Autism have been found to have widespread executive functioning impairments that are perhaps a result of the more fundamental attentional deficits found with this disorder (Ozonoff, 2001). Detailed analyses of individual components of executive functioning in those with Autism by Ozonoff and colleagues (2001)

have revealed that individuals with Autism exhibit impairments in cognitive flexibility (Ozonoff, Strayer, McMahon, & Filoux, 1994), but do not show deficits in inhibiting responses (Ozonoff & Strayer, 1997) or in working memory functioning. In addition, Frith (2001) has proposed a somewhat controversial etiological theory of Autism linking deficits in theory of mind ("mind blindness") to abnormalities in a network of brain regions, including the medial prefrontal cortex, areas in the temporal-parietal region, and the temporal poles, all of which are active in nonautistic individuals during theory of mind tasks.

Courchesne and his colleagues have begun to formulate a developmentally based theory of Autism, built upon empirical evidence derived from an examination of the neurodevelopmental course of the whole brain, and in particular the cerebellum and its interconnections with many different brain structures. Across many studies with varying methodologies, the most consistent brain structural abnormality in individuals with Autism occurs in various sites within the cerebellum and limbic system structures (Carper, Moses, Tigue, & Courchesne, 2002). The vast majority of postmortem studies have reported cerebellar pathology, while structural magnetic resonance imaging (MRI) studies consistently find evidence of hypoplasia in the cerebellum (see Courchesne, 1997, for a comprehensive review). The most common postmortem pathology of the cerebellum is a reduction in the number and size of Purkinje neurons (e.g., Bailey et al., 1998; Fatemi et al., 2000; Kemper & Bauman, 1998). Additionally, volumetric MRI studies have consistently indicated reduced size of one or another subregion of the cerebellar vermis (Carper & Courchesne, 2000; Hashimoto et al., 1995). In sum, the strongest and most consistent neuroanatomical evidence points to structural abnormalities in the cerebellum.

However, there is not a clear consensus in the Autism literature concerning the relevance of cerebellar anomalies for a disorder primarily characterized by cognitive, social, and emotional deficits, given the prevailing view that the cerebellum is primarily involved in motor function. But evidence has pointed to cerebellar involvement in a number of cognitive and emotional functions (e.g., G. Allen, Buxton, Wong, & Courchesne, 1997; Gao et al., 1996; Paradiso, Andreasen, O'Leary, Arndt, & Robinson, 1997; Xiang et al., 2003). Thus, a more current, broad view of the role of the cerebellum in overall neurobehavioral functioning creates a more reasonable scenario for implicating abnormalities in this structure as having a central underlying role in Autism.

A functional MRI (fMRI) study of the cerebellum revealed different patterns of cerebellar activation during a simple motor task (pressing a button with the thumb) in a sample of young adults with Autism compared to a nonautistic control group (G. Allen, Muller, & Courchesne, 2004). In the group with Autism, areas of the cerebellum predicted to be involved in the task exhibited more activation than observed in the control group, and areas of the cerebellum not expected to be associated with this simple motor task were activated in the group with Autism but not in the control group. The investigators concluded that the pattern of functional activation found strongly suggested that the observed functional differences were a reflection of the anatomic abnormalities (i.e., reduced cerebellar volume) found in the persons with Autism.

These authors hypothesize that many of the motor deficits commonly seen in individuals with Autism (e.g., balance problems, abnormal gait) may be related, at least in part, to both anatomical and functional abnormalities of the cerebellum. In addition, there also is evidence that cerebellar pathology can bring about a wide range of cognitive and affective deficits (G. Allen & Courchesne, 1998). In fact, one published case study reported on a child who, after surgical resection of a cerebellar tumor, exhibited behaviors after the surgery that were highly characteristic of classic symptoms of Autism, such as gaze aversion, social withdrawal, and stereotyped movements (Riva & Giorgi, 2000).

Although the neuroanatomical and neurofunctional evidence point to a clear association between cerebellar abnormalities and the behavioral manifestation of Autism, the mechanism involved remains unknown. One primary reason is that the general functional properties of the cerebellum in normal brains remain unknown to a large extent. Some preliminary evidence points to anticipatory motor deficits, given increasing evidence that the cerebellum appears to have a role in preparing many neural systems to which it maintains connections (e.g., attention, motor, affect, language) for shifts or alterations in neural responsiveness (G. Allen et al., 2004). G. Allen et al. hypothesize that the cerebellum may accomplish this task by making predictions about what might happen next based on prior learning and may alter responsiveness in the particular neural system(s) needed in upcoming moments. Thus, function in these diverse cognitive realms is not abolished in those with Autism, but lacks in coordination due to a preparatory deficit.

Another strong neuroanatomical finding in individuals with Autism is abnormal developmental changes in overall brain volume. Courchesne and colleagues have shown that brain volume of those children later diagnosed with Autism appeared to be normal at birth (according to neonatal head circumference records), but by age 2 to 4 years, volumetric

MRI data indicated that 90% of the children with Autism had a larger than average brain volume compared to nonautistic children (Courchesne et al., 2001). The observed excessive brain size was due primarily to increased white matter volume in the cerebellum and cerebrum (Courchesne et al., 2001).

Further, a study by Courchesne, Carper, and Akshoomoff (2003) has yielded evidence that there is an increased rate of growth of the brain in infants who later were diagnosed with Autism compared to those who were not, as reflected by measurements of head circumference (HC). Although HC was similar in all infants enrolled in the study during the first few months of life, those who later developed Autism exhibited a marked accelerated rate of increase in HC beginning several months after birth. On average, between birth and 6 to 14 months of age, HC increased from the 25th percentile to the 84th percentile (Courchesne et al., 2003). This increase in HC was associated with greater cerebral and cerebellar volume in these children by 2 to 5 years of age. It is striking that brain size in young children with Autism reaches its maximum by ages 4 to 5 years (Courchesne et al., 2001). Average overall maximum brain size in children with Autism is statistically equivalent to that achieved by healthy children (approximately 1350 mL), but is achieved, on average, 8 years sooner than in normally developing, healthy children (Courchesne et al., 2001). However, in adolescence and adulthood, brain size of those with Autism does not differ from that of nonautisitc individuals (Aylward, Minshew, Field, Sparks, & Singh, 2002).

Although the increases in brain volume are marked, the specific underlying cellular components of increased brain volumes are unknown to date. The increased volume found in children with Autism may potentially reflect abnormalities in any number of microstructural features, including excessive numbers of neurons and/or glial cells, excessive dendridtic arborization, and/or atypically large numbers of axonal connections (Courchesne et al., 2003). In addition, the cause of the increase in brain volume is not completely understood, but clearly reflects some type of dysregulation in one or more stages of brain developmental processes; however, it appears that the early transient period of brain overgrowth is an important underlying factor in the emergence of many of the behavioral symptoms seen in Autism. The observed overgrowth occurs during an important period of brain development when normative experience-dependent processes of neural plasticity are potentially at a maximum. This extended period of gradual axonal and dendritic growth and synapse refinement and elimination appears to occur well into the 1st decade of postnatal life. In children with Autism, however, it appears that the physical growth of the brain is compressed into a relatively short period of time, that may in turn result in aberrantly rapid and disordered growth (Courchesne et al., 2003). Such a rapid pace of growth would not allow the normal process of experience-dependent neural plasticity to take place.

Observations of disturbances in normal neurodevelopmental processes in Autism have helped to refine theory and guide research concerning the underlying biological mechanisms of this pervasive developmental disorder. The accumulated (and still growing) knowledge on normal brain development has enabled investigators in Autism to differentiate the abnormal neurodevelopmental processes that appear to underlie this disorder.

Ultimately, it appears that the key etiological feature of Autism is abnormality of the neurodevelopmental process across a wide spectrum of brain regions and networks. The emerging evidence increasingly points to abnormal regulation of brain growth in Autism, with pathological deviation from normative mechanisms underlying the typical progression through neurogenesis and synaptogenesis, followed by axon pruning and synapse elimination.

Despite the wide range of theoretical formulations and the relative paucity of consistent data pointing to a common underlying neurobiological "cause" of Autism, the study of this disorder provides an excellent example of the increasingly important role played by neuroscience in examining the potential biological contributors to a developmental disorder. Examining the evolution of theory and research in Autism also provides very useful information concerning the developmental trajectory of this disorder, and perhaps could provide insight into how the study of the development of the neural substrate underlying this disorder could inform the study of other disorders, as well as normal development. As we noted earlier, one of the fundamental tenets of developmental psychopathology is that the study of the development of disordered outcomes can be informed by an understanding of normal development (Cicchetti, 1984, 1990, 1993, 2003). Ideally, the study of normal and abnormal developmental sequelae can work in tandem to inform each other (Cicchetti, 1984, 1993; Sroufe, 1990). Autism is an excellent example of this principle at work. Also, the advances in our understanding of Autism have come as a result of close collaborations between behavioral and biological scientists working across multiple levels of analysis (Akshoomoff, Pierce, & Courchesne, 2002; Rodier, 2002). The success of such collabora-

tive, cross-disciplinary efforts in the study of Autism, and the wealth of new knowledge that has emerged as a result, serve as an excellent example of the importance of a multidisciplinary, multiple levels of analysis approach to the study of neurodevelopmental disorders.

A View from Schizophrenia

Congruent with the theoretical principles of a developmental systems approach on brain development, it is expected that a dedifferentiation and disintegration would characterize the neurobiological and psychological development and functioning of individuals with mental disorders. Much of the contemporary research in the area of neurodevelopment and Schizophrenia owes a significant portion of its historical roots to the formulations of Emil Kraepelin (1919), who conceived of Schizophrenia as a deteriorating brain disease in its natural history, albeit with an onset in early adult life. Since the 1980s, when a resurgence of interest in initiating neurobiological studies in Schizophrenia took place, Kraepelin's viewpoint has been challenged and radically altered by advances from several levels of inquiry that point to a prenatal-perinatal origin of at least some of the brain abnormalities found in individuals with Schizophrenia (Cannon, 1998; Keshavan & Hogarty, 1999; Mednick, Cannon, Barr, & Lyon, 1991; Walker & DiForio, 1997; Weinberger, 1987). During the early 1980s, a number of investigations converged and all found evidence for increased ventricle size in persons with schizophrenic illness (Shenton et al., 2001). These enlarged ventricles were present at the onset of the illness and did not protract in size as the illness proceeded over time, even in prospective longitudinal studies. This finding suggested that a neurodegenerative process was not responsible for causing the illness.

The retrospective observations of Laura Bender (1947) and Barbara Fish (1957), as well as the follow-back study by Norman Watt (1972), in which a pattern of abnormalities in neurological and behavioral parameters dating back to childhood were found in adults with Schizophrenia, laid the seeds of the neurodevelopmental hypothesis of Schizophrenia (Marenco & Weinberger, 2000). Moreover, a number of longitudinal studies demonstrated that some degree of recovery was possible in some cases of Schizophrenia (Garmezy, 1970; Tsuang, Wollson, & Fleming, 1979; Zigler & Glick, 1986), thereby casting further doubt on the Kraepelinian viewpoint that Schizophrenia is a degenerative disease of early adulthood ("dementia praecox").

Similarly, prospective longitudinal high-risk offspring studies have revealed that behavioral antecedents of

Schizophrenia occurred before the disease. Fish (1977) demonstrated that a neurobiologic disorder exists in infants and children prior to the onset of more chronic forms of Schizophrenia. Fish's (1977) discovery of pandevelopmental retardation was considered an early marker of the inherited neurointegrative defect (i.e., schizotaxia) postulated to exist in Schizophrenia by Paul Meehl (1962). Importantly, Fish noted that the phenotypic manifestations of the neurointegrative defect change over epigenesis and that the signs of dysregulation of maturation are found in many developing systems. Specifically, Fish reported that the neurointegrative disorder present from infancy disrupted the normal timing, sequence, and overall organization of development. Moreover, in a landmark prospective longitudinal investigation, Fish, Marcus, Hans, Auerbach, and Perdue (1992) discovered that the infant offspring of schizophrenic mothers displayed greater lags in their motor development during infancy and that a number of these infants themselves went on to develop Schizophrenia or schizotypal personality disorders (see also the seminal work of Walker, Davis, & Gottlieb, 1991, in this regard).

Relatedly, Cannon, Rosso, Bearden, Sanchez, and Hadley (1999), in their epidemiological investigation of the Philadelphia cohort of the National Collaborative Perinatal Project, provide compelling evidence that adverse experiences during gestation and birth, as well as deviant cognitive, motor, and behavioral functioning during early childhood, are associated with an increased risk for Schizophrenia. In particular, these investigators demonstrated that the risk for Schizophrenia increases linearly with the severity of fetal oxygen deprivation. In prior neuroimaging studies of high-risk samples (Cannon, Mednick, Parnas, & Schulsinger, 1993; Cannon et al., 2002), a history of perinatal hypoxia was found to be associated with increased severity of a neuropathological indicator of Schizophrenia (i.e., ventricular enlargement) among individuals with an elevated genetic risk for the disorder, but not among controls at low genetic risk. Together, this evidence suggests that a genetic factor in Schizophrenia may render the fetal brain particularly susceptible to the effects of oxygen deprivation and encourages search for molecular mechanisms underlying this heightened neural vulnerability.

Cannon et al. (1999) also discovered that preschizophrenic individuals show evidence of cognitive, motor, and behavioral dysfunction during the first 7 years of life (cf. Walker, Davis, et al., 1991). Because there was not evidence of significant intraindividual decline during this period within any domain of functioning, the results argue against the view that a deteriorative neural process underlies these early phenotypic expressions of liability to Schizophrenia. Rather, the findings suggest that an increasing number of diverse phenotypic signs emerge with age as the various brain systems required for their expression reach fundamental maturity. Finally, because similar functional disturbances were observed in the unaffected siblings of the preschizophrenic cases, it would appear that these cognitive, motor, and behavioral disturbances are indicators of an inherited neural diathesis to Schizophrenia (cf. Walker & Diforio, 1997).

In addition to the early and more recent work with preschizophrenic infants and children that served as an impetus for modifying the Kraepelinian (1919) view of Schizophrenia, contemporary findings have contributed to the belief that the neurobiological foundations of Schizophrenia are established, at least in part, during the development of the brain. These include the following:

1. A number of prospective longitudinal investigations has discovered an association between prenatal and perinatal complications (e.g., fetal hypoxia) and an increased risk for the later development of Schizophrenia. These findings suggest that the adverse effects of obstetric complications on the developing fetal brain may play a role in the etiology of Schizophrenia.

   As Rakic (1988a, 1988b, 1996; Sidman & Rakic, 1982) and Nowakowski (1987; Nowakowski & Hayes, 1999) have concluded, during periods of rapid brain development in which neuronal migration is occurring and synaptic connections are formed the fetal brain is especially vulnerable. Exogenous teratogens, such as maternal influenza (Brown et al., 2004; Mednick, Machon, Huttunen, & Bonett, 1988) and maternal exposure to toxoplasmosis (Brown et al., 2005), along with obstetric complications, such as perinatal hypoxia (Cannon, 1998), in concert with the genetic predisposition to Schizophrenia, may exert dramatic effects on the regions of the brain experiencing the most rapid growth. Introducing birth complications and teratogens may also place the cortical connections being established and refined at increased risk for aberrant development.

2. A number of postmortem neuropathology studies has found evidence of heterotopic displacement of neurons in various regions of the brain, including the hippocampus and the frontal and temporal cortices. These findings suggest that there are disturbances of brain development in utero in many schizophrenics.

3. Disturbances in neurogenesis, neuronal migration and differentiation, synaptogenesis, neuronal and synaptic pruning (perhaps resulting in reduced synaptic connectivity; cf. McGlashan & Hoffman, 2000), and myelina-

tion, occurring at the cellular and molecular levels, suggest that Schizophrenia is a disorder that is instantiated in brain development (Arnold, 1999; Breslin & Weinberger, 1990; Weinberger, 1987).

For example, the laminar distribution of cortical neurons is displaced inward in Schizophrenia, indicating a defect in cortical organization, suggesting that the normal process of "inside-out" neuronal migration (cf. Rakic, 1988a, 1988b) during the second trimester of gestation also is likely to be anomalous, as should the neuronal connectivity and circuitry (Arnold, 1999; Weinberger, 1995). In addition, Lewis, Hashimoto, and Volk (2005) concluded that there are atypicalities in cortical inhibitory neurons (i.e., GABA neurons) in Schizophrenia and that these abnormalities play a role in the impairments of working memory function that are a core feature of clinical Schizophrenia. Moreover, alterations in dopamine and glutamate neurotransmission in the dorso lateral prefrontal cortex (DLPFC) also are involved in the working memory dysfunction in Schizophrenia. Relatedly, Meyer-Lindenberg et al. (2005) have discovered that hippocampal dysfunction may manifest in Schizophrenia because of an inappropriate bidirectional modulatory relation with the DLPFC.

4. A growing body of neuroimaging studies has identified gross structural neuroanatomical changes in young, untreated patients in their first psychotic episode. Further, and in contrast to a Kraepelinian (1919) neurodegenerative viewpoint, these investigations also have failed to discover evidence of deterioration in these neuropathological markers with increasing length of illness (Marenco & Weinberger, 2000).

5. A number of the unaffected first-degree relatives of schizophrenic patients manifest the structural and functional brain abnormalities observed in schizophrenics, implying that such abnormalities may be mediated, in part, by genetic predisposition to the disorder (Cannon et al., 1993; Cannon, Mednick, et al., 1994). Homeobox genes, which serve as transcription factors regulating gene expression, represent potential candidate genes in disorders in which a disruption of cortical neurogenesis has been implicated, such as in Schizophrenia (Ruddle et al., 1994; Steingard & Coyle, 1998).

We wish to underscore that the extant models linking neurodevelopment and Schizophrenia point to a nonlinearity of relations. Specifically, a significant amount of time elapses between the gestational events hypothesized to create a predisposition to Schizophrenia and the onset of the symptoms of the disorder later in life. Longitudinal follow-up of individuals who have experienced traumatic insults to the brain at early stages of development, such as is likely the case in many instances of Schizophrenia, enables investigators to chart and observe the changing expression of these early lesions as development modifies behavior in general.

Alternatively, for some individuals it also is conceivable that the lesion directly affects later developmental processes via cascade, propagation, and expansion (Cicchetti & Tucker, 1994a; Courchesne et al., 1994; Post et al., 1994; Steingard & Coyle, 1998). These options all provide an opportunity to discover how brain and behavior reorganize following the experience of insults at different points in the developmental course.

Because not all persons who experience the gestational disturbances noted in the literature go on to develop clinical Schizophrenia, Gottlieb's (1992) concept of probabilistic epigenesis is evoked. Furthermore, the existing research reveals that there are a number of pathways through which the early neurodevelopmental anomalies may result in Schizophrenia. The identification of these diverse pathways to Schizophrenia provides insight into how specificity and differentiation into a syndrome may result from a commonality of initiating circumstances (i.e., equifinality; see Cicchetti & Rogosch, 1996). These multiple pathways embrace a number of possible contributors that may potentiate or mediate the links between early neurodevelopmental anomalies and Schizophrenia in genetically vulnerable individuals. These include the normal developmental changes that take place during late adolescence and early adulthood, such as: (1) synaptic pruning of the prefrontal cortex (Feinberg, 1982; McGlashan & Hoffman, 2000), (2) pubertal increases in gonadal hormones during adolescence (Spear, 2000; Walker, Sabuwalla, & Huot, 2004), (3) developmental transformations in prefrontal cortex and limbic brain regions (Dahl, 2004; Keshavan & Hogarty, 1999; Marenco & Weinberger, 2000), (4) continued myelination of intracortical connections (Benes, 1989; Gibson, 1991; Yakovlev & LeCours, 1967), (5) alterations in the balance between mesocortical and mesolimbic dopamine systems (Benes, 1989, 1997; Benes, Turtle, Khan, & Farol, 1994), (6) the stress that arises during postnatal social development (Keshavan & Hogarty, 1999; Walker & Diforio, 1997), (7) the transformations that occur in cognitive and social-cognitive development (Keating, 1990; Noam, Chandler, & LaLonde, 1995; Spear, 2000), and (8) the growing importance of the peer group (J. G. Parker, Rubin, Price, & DeRosier, 1995).

Such an integrative, interdisciplinary approach is necessary to capture the full complexity of schizophrenic illness, including the multiple pathways to, and the diverse outcomes associated with, the disorder. Thus, it appears likely that the processes underlying the normal development and maturation of cortical circuitry and connectivity may have gone awry in Schizophrenia (Arnold, 1999; Benes, 1995; McGlashan & Hoffman, 2000; Weinberger, 1987). Unraveling these misorganizations in brain development should contribute greatly to understanding the genesis and epigenesis of schizophrenic disorders.

As highlighted in the previous sections, advances in neuroscience have begun to inform neurodevelopmental theories of Autism and Schizophrenia. Other lines of research have begun to examine other forms of psychopathology (e.g., Attention Deficit/Hyperactivity Disorder, Conduct Disorder, Bipolar Disorder) in a neurodevelopmental context (see Cicchetti & Cannon, 1999a; Cicchetti & Walker, 2003). In fact, it is clear that developmental psychopathology has made great strides in recent years to incorporate multiple levels of analysis in its conceptual and empirical framework, and the understanding of the development of psychopathology generally has made great advances by employing findings from basic neuroscience and normal brain development. As previously noted, one of the fundamental tenets of developmental psychopathology is that knowledge of normal development can and should inform the study of deviant developmental trajectories eventuating in psychopathology. One logical extension of this approach is the investigation of the mechanisms and developmental pathways that eventuate in positive outcomes despite the experience of significant adversity. Knowledge from neuroscience and its associated subdisciplines has only recently been brought to bear in preliminary theoretical discussions of a biology of resilience (Charney, 2004; Curtis & Cicchetti, 2003), and, to date, no published empirical studies have incorporated this level of analysis in the investigation of resilience. As part of a complete integration of multiple levels of analysis (including biological) into the developmental psychopathology framework, we believe it is critical to begin to examine the biological contributors to resilient functioning.

RESILIENCE

Positive adaptation in the face of adversity has captured the interest and imagination of humanity over the ages. However, systematic empirical study of the phenomenon that is today referred to as resilience began only a little more than 30 years ago (Cicchetti & Garmezy, 1993; Masten, Best, & Garmezy, 1990). In the early 1970s, a few researchers investigating the development of psychopathology began to discuss the importance of examining characteristics of children who did not develop psychopathology, despite being at risk (e.g., Anthony, 1974; Garmezy, 1971, 1974), marking an important shift in theoretical depictions of the causes and consequences of psychopathology. Previously, investigations conducted on high-risk and mentally disordered populations across the life span had portrayed the developmental course as deterministic, inevitably resulting in maladaptive and pathological outcomes (Luthar et al., 2000). As researchers discovered that not all high-risk children manifested the dire consequences that extant theories of psychopathology predicted, understanding the processes through which children at risk did not develop psychopathology became viewed as important for informing theories on the development of maladaptation and pathology. The advent of modern neuroscience along with its many associated subdisciplines represents an unprecedented opportunity to augment current conceptual and methodological approaches to the study of resilience (Cowan et al., 2000).

A large volume of research over the past 3 decades has examined the psychosocial correlates of individual, interpersonal, familial, and broader environmental contributors to resilience (Luthar, 2003; Luthar et al., 2000; Masten, 2001). However, the empirical study of resilience, for various historical reasons, has focused exclusively on behavioral and psychosocial correlates of, and contributors to, the phenomenon, and has not examined biological correlates or contributors (Curtis & Cicchetti, 2003; Luthar et al., 2000). Taken as a whole, the extant empirical literature on resilience has traditionally employed behavioral indices of adversity and positive adaptation.

Although this research has yielded a wealth of knowledge concerning the psychosocial correlates of, and contributors to, resilience, early theorizing and research in resilience (e.g., Anthony, 1974; Garmezy, 1974; Murphy, 1974), as well as several subsequent large-scale longitudinal studies of resilience (e.g., Garmezy, Masten, & Tellegen, 1984; Garmezy & Tellegen, 1984; Masten & Garmezy, 1985; Werner & Smith, 1982), were undertaken prior to the inception of modern techniques for examining the neural and biological correlates of human behavior and development. In addition, the scientific study of resilience had its roots in the psychodynamic and behavioral theoretical traditions, where research was largely guided by the study of risk and symptom treatment (Masten & Reed, 2002). Within these conceptual frameworks, which dominated clinical and developmental psychology through much of the twentieth century, there was little interest in discovering the biological mechanisms that could potentially contribute to a more integrated understanding of behavioral differences (Nelson et al., 2002). Undoubtedly, the relative neglect of the brain and biology as relevant to developmental theorizing on the unfolding of adaptive and maladaptive behavioral outcomes was due, in part, to the paucity of information that existed about the structural and functional organization of the brain (Johnson, 1998; Segalowitz, 1994). There simply was not enough knowledge about brain development and function to articulate its role in the genesis and epigenesis of normal and deviant mental processes. Several cogent and extensive summaries of resilience theory and research have been published that have explicated the need to examine the processes contributing to resilience from multiple levels of analysis, in particular from the level of brain and neurobiological functioning. An important discussion has begun concerning the incorporation of the biological level of analysis into the theoretical framework of resilience (see, e.g., Curtis & Cicchetti, 2003; Luthar et al., 2000; Masten, 2001; Masten & Reed, 2002; Nelson, 1999), and preliminary proposals concerning the empirical examination of the biological foundations of resilience have recently been made (Charney, 2004; Cicchetti, 2003; Curtis & Cicchetti, 2003; Davidson, 2000). At this point in the empirical investigation of resilience, the next logical step is to include a biological perspective on resilience in order to achieve a truly complete understanding of this phenomenon.

Within the scope of this section, it is not be possible to cover all of the areas of biological functioning that might potentially contribute to resilient functioning. Rather, we focus on several broad areas that directly and/or indirectly reflect the functioning of major human biological systems that have clear links to human behavior. In particular, we consider the possible contributions of genetics, neuroendocrinology, immunology, emotion, cognition, and neural plasticity to resilient functioning. There is evidence to suggest that the environment and experience may exert an impact on these areas, thus, perhaps, playing a role in resilient functioning. Within each of these areas, we evaluate the pertinent evidence supporting the association of that particular system with resilience and suggest possible research methodologies that could be brought to bear to examine general questions and hypotheses concerning the likely relation between resilience and each area reviewed.

Going forward, it is critically important to keep in mind that biological domains do not function independently, but, more often than not, the functioning of one system influences the functional properties of one or more other systems, through a cascade of bidirectionally influenced processes (Cicchetti & Cannon, 1999a; Gottlieb, 1992; Gottlieb et al., 1998; Thelen & Smith, 1998). In addition, based on the reality that biological systems function interdependently as much as possible, the goal of future research on resilience and biology should be to increasingly incorporate multiple biological measures as part of a multiple levels of analysis approach to resilience research (Cicchetti & Curtis, in press). With this as an ideal, admittedly the challenges involved in a true integration are great. To be complete, such synthesis must involve integration at the highest level across disciplines (i.e., neuroscience and psychology), but also must examine multiple biological systems within the organism (e.g., neuroendocrine and emotion) as well as investigate different levels within the same system (e.g., neuroanatomical and neurochemical). Historically, conceptual distinctions among and within systems have been created (e.g., higher and lower order cognition) in order to more conveniently study the functional details of these systems. However, given the increasing recognition of the importance of considering many levels of interdependent processes simultaneously in order to advance the understanding of a multifaceted phenomenon, such as resilience, it is incumbent upon resilience researchers to meet the challenge of simultaneously incorporating multiple levels both across and within systems.

The discussion in this section of the chapter focuses in part on the conceptual basis for the consideration of biological processes that may potentially yield contributions to expanding our knowledge about resilience. In addition, we discuss various types of neuroimaging and other technologies, such as magnetic resonance imaging (MRI), functional MRI (fMRI), electroencephalography (EEG), event-related potentials (ERPs), assay techniques for neuroendocrine and immune functioning, and methods for investigating gene expression as methodological tools that could be employed to help answer questions about the contribution of biology to resilience. However, the discussion of these tools are secondary to what we believe is the more important general discussion of biology and resilience, as well as the research questions that should be developed to further our understanding of the interface of these two areas.

Theoretical Approach

One of the formidable challenges inherent to examining resilience from a biological perspective is the need to extend current theoretical conceptualizations about resilience in order to incorporate the various new levels of analysis potentially involved in this approach. Most investigators in the area of resilience do not have formal training in neuroscience or biology, whereas those investigators who do have such training generally have not been involved with research in the area of resilience. Given the vast range of expertise that could ultimately be required to investigate the role of biology in resilience, it is imperative that a multidisciplinary approach to both theory building and empirical investigation is brought to bear on this problem. Indeed, given that self-righting, one of the basic mechanisms underlying resilience, has its historical roots embedded in the fields of embryology and genetics (Fishbein, 1976; Waddington, 1957), we think that it is especially unfortunate that behavioral scientists have thus far eschewed the inclusion of biological measures in their research armamentaria on resilience.

In setting forth a conceptual model of biology and resilience, particular attention must be paid to the relation between the dynamic process of resilience and key components of the central nervous system, neuroendocrine, and other neurobiological systems. An explanatory model of resilience and biology will build and expand upon the extant theoretical framework around resilience, in particular, one that views resilience as a dynamic process that is influenced by neural and psychological self-organization, as well as transactions between the ecological context and the developing organism (Cicchetti & Tucker, 1994a; Egeland, Carlson, & Sroufe, 1993). Specifically, the transactional, organizational perspective (Cicchetti & Schneider-Rosen, 1986; Cicchetti & Sroufe, 1978), one of the major theoretical approaches in the field of developmental psychopathology, provides an orientation that inherently takes into account multiple levels of analysis and allows for combining biological and psychological mechanisms within the same explanatory framework (Cicchetti & Tucker, 1994a), thus providing a ready-made structure for the integration of a biological perspective into resilience. In addition, a transactional, organizational perspective is useful in that it does not ascribe ascendancy to any level of analysis over another, and it attempts to break down the traditional restrictive conceptual boundaries between nature and nurture and biology and psychology (Cicchetti & Cannon, 1999a; Gottlieb, 1992).

As we described earlier in this chapter, advocates of a self-organizing systems-theory viewpoint of neurobiological and psychological development contend that individuals actively participate in the creation of meaning by structuring and restructuring experience through self-regulated mental activity (Cicchetti & Tucker, 1994a; Mascolo, Pollack, & Fischer, 1997). Early experience and prior levels of adaptation neither doom the individual to continued maladaptive functioning nor inoculate the individual from future problems in functioning. Change takes place in a

system as new needs and environmental challenges destabilize the existing organizations, necessitating the emergence of new organizations that may prove to be more adaptive than the preexisting ones in the current context. The reorganizations that occur both within and between developmental domains (e.g., emotion, cognition) provide critical opportunities for resilient adaptation (Cicchetti & Tucker, 1994a).

Furthermore, despite the important role that genetic information plays in regulating, guiding, and controlling brain development (Rakic, 1988a, 1988b, 1995), as we noted earlier, a not insignificant portion of postnatal brain development is thought to occur through interactions and transactions of the individual with the environment (Black et al., 1998; Cicchetti & Cannon, 1999a; Johnson, 1998; O'Leary, 1989). This potential for structural and functional reorganization of the brain in response to environmental demand and afferent input shapes development in the form of a nonlinear, dynamic feedback system (Elbert, Heim, & Rockstroh, 2001). Such development proceeds hand in hand with structural modifications of the brain that can occur on both a microscopic, cellular scale with, for example, alterations in synaptic efficiency, synapse formation, and changes in properties of dendrites, as well as at a macroscopic level with functional reorganization of entire neural networks (Elbert et al., 2001). Consequently, each individual may traverse a potentially unique and partly self-determined developmental pathway of brain building that we believe may have important consequences for the development of resilient adaptation (Black et al., 1998; Cicchetti & Tucker, 1994a). Much of the underlying empirical work in support of this perspective on neural development has been in the area of sensory, language, and perceptual organization and function (e.g., Cheour et al., 1998; Elbert, Pantev, Wienbruch, Rockstroh, & Taub, 1995; Hubel & Wiesel, 1979). However, it is probable that parallel processes shape the development of higher-order, widely distributed cortical functions involved in emotion and cognition that more directly underlie complex, behaviorally manifested phenomena, including resilience.

Avoiding Reductionism

In attempting to integrate a biological perspective into the study of resilience, it is critical to avoid the potential pitfall of reducing the phenomenon of resilience to one that is exclusively mediated by biology. It is possible that the discussion of the biology of resilience could lead to the mistaken conclusion that, if biological mechanisms were associated with resilient outcomes, then the forces of biology would be of primary importance in achieving positive outcomes in the context of adversity. However, nothing could be further from the truth.

In fact, reducing psychological phenomena to components of neuroanatomical, neurochemical, neurophysiological, and genetic factors dismisses the great impact that the environment has on these processes, and demotes psychology to the realm of ephemeral behavioral marker of biological processes (see Miller & Keller, 2000). This reductionism is of particular concern in the study of psychopathology, where over the past decade there has been an increasing emphasis on the neurobiology of mental disorders, often attributing (reducing) the etiology of psychopathology to purely innate characteristics of the individual, such as genes, neuroanatomy, or brain function (Charney, Nestler, & Bunney, 1999; Torrey, 1997). More broadly, the artificial distinction between biology and behavior within the human organism contradicts years of research indicating co-actions between all levels of analysis, from the environment broadly construed to the molecular (e.g., Cicchetti & Tucker, 1994a; Gottlieb & Halpern, 2002), and it also highlights the importance of avoiding the perpetuation of the outmoded dichotomy in developmental science between nature and nurture (e.g., Hinde, 1992; Johnston, 1987). Thus, in the context of the current discussion of resilience and biology, we do not wish to convey or encourage the reduction of resilience to biological process. Rather, consistent with a transactional, organizational, general systems theory framework, we believe that biology is but one part of what should be an all-encompassing systems approach to understanding resilience, which needs to take into account all levels of analysis, from molecular to cultural.

Equifinality and Multifinality

Diversity in process and outcome are hallmarks of the developmental psychopathology perspective (Cicchetti, 1990; Cicchetti & Rogosch, 1996; Sroufe, 1989). The existence of equifinality, the recognition that a diversity of paths may eventuate in the same outcome, and multifinality, the acknowledgment that different outcomes are likely to evolve from any original starting point, challenges theorists and researchers to entertain more complex and varied approaches to how they conceptualize and investigate normal development, psychopathology, and resilience (Richters, 1997).

The application of equifinality to a biology of resilience requires that researchers be aware that a variety of developmental progressions may eventuate in disorder or resilience (Luthar et al., 2000). Clearly, biological and psychological factors both can play a role in the pathways to these diverse outcomes. Furthermore, the relative contributions of biological and psychological contributors to disorder and resilience will vary among individuals.

Likewise, the concept of multifinality alerts resilience researchers to the fact that individuals may begin on the same major developmental trajectory and, as a function of their subsequent "choices," exhibit very different patterns of maladaptation or adaptation (Sroufe, 1989; Sroufe, Egeland, & Kreutzer, 1990). The pathway to either psychopathology or resilience is influenced, in part, by a complex matrix of the individual's level of biological and psychological organization, experience, social context, timing of the adverse event(s) and experiences, and the developmental history of the individual.

Technology, Methodology, and Resilience

There is a vast array of rapidly evolving technologies in the biological sciences that can be applied to the study of development and psychopathology, many of which can now potentially play an important role in the study of the interface between biology and resilience. However, an important caveat with respect to these new tools is that the utilization of technology, without an underlying model or theoretical framework, does not serve the advancement of science (see also Peterson, 2003). In the absence of any specific, empirically based knowledge concerning the relation between biological systems and a particular behaviorally manifested psychological phenomenon (e.g., resilience), the initial challenge during the early stages of such research is to, at the very least, generate a priori, testable hypotheses that have a reasonable degree of fidelity with a clearly specified conceptual model. Although the construction of an elaborate, formal theory that specifically describes the relation between biology and resilience is overly ambitious at this juncture, it is nonetheless critical to ground empirical endeavors in some framework that is based either on a viable model or some type of functional theory.

In addition, with the continuing advances in and increasing utilization of new technologies in neuroscience and psychology, particularly neuroimaging, it is of paramount importance to avoid having the construction of theory and subsequent generation of hypotheses driven or constrained by the nature of the data that is attainable by a particular measurement technology. Thus, it is important not to exclusively conceptualize a psychological phenomenon, such as resilience, through the lens of a particular methodology. For example, fMRI is an excellent tool for localizing the functional aspects of brain regions and networks. Thus, application of this method would be ideal for answering questions about where in the brain a particular cognitive or emotional operation is taking place. However, the types of tasks that can be administered to individuals during the fMRI scanning procedure are, by necessity, often limited to those that can be physically adapted to the MRI scanner environment. Thus, the questions that can be answered by functional imaging are to a great degree dependent upon the nature and demands of the task administered, which may often be quite narrow in scope.

Furthermore, although fMRI affords excellent spatial resolution (on the order of a few millimeters), it does not provide good temporal resolution of neural activity (continuing advances in technology have somewhat improved this aspect of the technology, however). Alternatively, ERPs are an example of an ideal brain-imaging technology for detecting the temporal sequence of brain processing (resolution on the order of milliseconds), but unfortunately, the spatial resolution of ERPs is relatively poor (again, this aspect of ERP technology is also improving due to high density electrode arrays and improved source localization algorithms). Thus, the particular characteristics of these two measurement techniques in large part determine what type of data can be derived and, more fundamentally, what types of questions can be asked in research utilizing them. Of course, combining these two methods is an ideal solution for overcoming their individual limitations (e.g., de Haan & Thomas, 2002).

Moreover, as technology in biologically based areas of inquiry becomes increasingly complex and more specialized skills are required to carry out research employing these tools, researchers will naturally become more knowledgeable in the use of one particular methodology and measurement technique (e.g., fMRI). This increasing specialization may have the unintended consequence of narrowing the focus of model building and hypothesis generation. Clearly, no one individual can master all available techniques, thus pointing to the importance of collaboration across disciplines in research examining multiple levels of analysis. Ideally, a comprehensive research program would employ several measures at various levels of analysis, such as molecular genetic, neuroendocrine, functional brain imaging, neuropsychological assessment, and observational ratings of behavior.

EXPERIENCE AND THE BRAIN: A BRIEF HISTORY

From the perspective of modern neuroscience and associated disciplines, it is a given that certain types of experi-

ence result in enduring physiological changes in the brain, by way of a process referred to as neural plasticity. These changes can occur and are observed on one or more levels of analysis, including molecular, cellular, neurochemical, and anatomical brain systems, and are manifested at the highest order by changes in behavior. However, in fairly recent scientific history the fundamental question of whether experience resulted in changes in the physiological characteristics of the brain did not have a clear answer, and was a subject of active empirical inquiry.

In a comprehensive historical review of research on the relationship between experience and the brain, Rosenzweig, Bennett, and Diamond (1972) reported that the earliest recorded scientific account of physical changes in the brain as a result of experience was written in the 1780s by Michele Gaetano Malacarne, an Italian anatomist. He experimented with two dogs from the same litter, as well as pairs of parrots, goldfinches, and blackbirds, each pair from the same clutch of eggs. He trained one member of each pair to perform various tasks (in the case of the dogs) and to make specific vocalizations (the birds). He did not train the other member of the pair. After the experiment ended, he examined the animals' brains, and found that there were more folds in the cerebellum of the animals that had gone through the training procedure. Given that the cerebellum is involved in motor functioning, finding increased complexity in this part of the brain was consistent with the intensive training.

In 1791, the physiologist Samuel Thomas von Soemmering wrote that anatomical measurements might demonstrate the effects of experience on the brain, most likely in reference to the work by Malacarne (Renner & Rosenzweig, 1987). Beyond this single reference to Malacarne's work, there is no indication that any other scientists during this era attempted to follow up on this line of research (Rosenzweig et al., 1972).

In the late nineteenth century, scientists became interested in the relation between intellectual ability and training and brain anatomy in humans. Darwin (1874) wrote:

> I have shown that the brains of domestic rabbits are considerably reduced in bulk, in comparison with those of the wild rabbit or hare; and this may be attributed to their having been closely confined during many generations, so that they have exerted their intellect, instincts, senses and voluntary movements but little. (p. 53)

In this passage, Darwin is pointing out not only the hereditary nature of brain size, but also attributes it to the relative experiential deprivation of domestic rabbits compared to wild rabbits.

In the early part of the twentieth century, a scientist and inventor named Elmer Gates claimed that the results of research he conducted, similar to that of Malacarne, demonstrated support for his hypothesis of "brain building" (Renner & Rosenzweig, 1987). Gates theorized "that every conscious mental operation or experience creates in some part of the brain or nervous system new structural changes of cell and fiber . . . producing the embodiment of more mind" (1909, as cited in Renner & Rosenzweig, 1987). Gates apparently did not publish his research findings in any scientific journals; however, some of his work appeared as a series of articles in a publication called *The Metaphysical Magazine* (Renner & Rosenzweig, 1987).

In addition, Gates did not hesitate to extrapolate his work to humans. He is further quoted as saying: "The applications of these principals to human education is obvious. . . . Under usual circumstances and education, children develop less than ten percent of the cells in their brain areas. By processes of brain building, however, more cells can be put in these otherwise fallow areas, the child thus acquiring a better brain and more power of mind. . . ." (pp. 9–10, as cited in Renner & Rosenzweig, 1987). Although Gates did not quite have the details of the impact of experience on brain development correct, his bold (at the time) statements may yet prove prophetic.

In more mainstream scientific and academic circles, researchers in the last quarter of the nineteenth century failed to show that training resulted in changes in the gross anatomy of the brain. In 1895, Cajal speculated, based on the assumption that the brain does not produce new neurons, that cerebral exercise might lead to the establishment of "new and more extended intercortical connections." This notion was not to be confirmed until many years later. However, at the end of the nineteenth century, the hypothesis of an intrinsic relationship between brain size and use of the brain or intellectual ability was generally abandoned. In addition, a consensus in the scientific community developed that such anatomical changes could not be detected (if indeed there were any). Hence, scientists of this era generally gave up looking for experientially induced changes in brain anatomy.

In 1949, Donald Hebb published his seminal book, *The Organization of Behavior,* in which he outlined a comprehensive theory of behavior that attempted to integrate the physiology of the nervous system and behavioral psychology (Hebb, 1949). A central tenet of his theory was that experience modifies the brain. A few years before this book was published, Hebb (1947) reported on the first experiment that systematically compared the problem-solving ability of rats reared in different conditions. He reared two litters of rats in his home as pets. They were frequently out of their cages and had free run of Hebb's house (Hebb, 1949). At maturity, these home-raised rats scored better than laboratory-reared rats on the Hebb-Williams maze (Hebb & Williams, 1946). Hebb concluded that "*the richer experience of the pet group during development made them better able to profit by new experiences at maturity*—one of the characteristics of the 'intelligent' human being" (Hebb, 1949, p. 299, italics in the original). Subsequent replications of Hebb's research under more controlled experimental conditions resulted in similar findings (e.g., Hymovitch, 1952).

However, none of the investigators in this subsequent set of experiments discussed any role that differential brain development may have played in the behavioral results obtained. However, the thinking of these scientists was no doubt influenced by the prevailing dogma of the first half of the twentieth century concerning brain development, which held that the anatomy and physiology of the brain was fixed by a genetic blueprint. It was believed that development proceeded according to this fixed plan until adulthood, after which change in the brain was not possible, except in the case of injury and/or decay from the aging process (Renner & Rosenzweig, 1987). However, during the 1950s, some neuroscientists began to speculate that subtle aspects of the brain may be impacted by experience, such as connections between neurons and neurochemistry (Bennett, Diamond, Krech, & Rosenzweig, 1964). Unfortunately, at this time, scientific methods did not exist that would reliably allow detection of these types of brain processes, and the question reverted to a more speculative realm.

During the early 1960s, a group of scientists at the University of California, Berkeley, began to examine the relation between neurochemical changes in the brain and learning in rats. The results of a series of their early experiments confirmed their specific hypothesis of a linkage between increased cortical activity of the neurotransmitter acetylcholine (ACh), greater efficiency of synaptic transmission, and successful problem solving in rats (e.g., Krech, Rosenzweig, & Bennett, 1960). Indeed, rats who were good at learning mazes had higher ACh activity than those who were not, and it was later found that stimulation and training did, in fact, increase levels of ACh (e.g., Bennett et al., 1964). This early work lead to a now classic line of research comparing the brains of rats reared in complex environments to those reared in standard laboratory conditions.

NEURAL PLASTICITY

A recent search of literature databases in medicine and psychology by the authors yielded nearly 10,000 citations that used the term "neural plasticity" as a key word or phrase, with a seemingly exponential increase in the number of publications over the past 5 to 10 years. It would be a daunting task to synthesize the knowledge that has accumulated about neural plasticity generally, and in particular to attempt to apply this knowledge systematically in order to gain a clearer understanding of a behavioral phenomenon, such as resilience. Nearly all of the work on neural plasticity is highly technical, conveyed within specialized reports concerning the mechanisms of neural plasticity at nearly all levels of analysis, including neurochemical, molecular, genetic, and neuroanatomical, intended for a highly trained audience of neuroscientists and biologists (among others). Being able to glean something about the relevance of neural plasticity for resilience (or for that matter, any behavioral phenomenon) from such a highly technical literature is a formidable undertaking.

The study of neural plasticity in modern neuroscience and associated disciplines has brought to bear a wide range of empirical methodologies to describe all aspects of the observed dynamic processes at the synaptic and cellular levels that appear to underly neural plasticity. Neural plasticity is increasingly viewed as a dynamic nervous system process that orchestrates nearly constant neurochemical, functional, and structural CNS alterations in response to experience. It is possible that advances in the study of neural plasticity could be fruitfully employed as a model to begin to hypothesize about the biological underpinnings of resilience. Several authors recently have alluded to the possible relation between the principles of neural plasticity and resilience (e.g., Cicchetti, 2003; Curtis & Cicchetti, 2003; Davidson, 2000; Masten, 2001; Nelson, 1999), and at the conceptual level, there are several intriguing parallels between processes involved with neural plasticity and resilience. Thus, it is important to examine resilience in the context of this vast body of knowledge on neural plasticity, and to evaluate whether neural plasticity may have relevance for the study of a biology of resilience. The following sections attempt to provide a broad conceptual overview of neural plasticity, and briefly examine some of the fundamental mechanisms underlying this inherent characteristic of the brain and how it may potentially inform the study of resilience.

Plasticity: General Definition

Webster's dictionary (1979) defines plasticity as "the capacity for being molded or altered." The term plasticity is employed in a variety of fields in modern science, and until fairly recently has primarily been applied in engineering and physics to index the ability of material to change characteristics depending on environmental and thermodynamic conditions. In its purest semantic sense, plasticity simply connotes the capacity of something (e.g., a material, an organism) to change, and does not take into account the context (i.e., precipitating event[s]) in which this change may come about. In practical usage, however, it is assumed that such change takes place as a result or consequence of an event or context in the environment (e.g., expansion of a material due to increased temperature).

Plasticity can also be used to describe change in the sense of "recovery," in that the degree to which a material or system is plastic modulates the degree to which that material or system can return to its "original" condition prior to some event that leads to its modification (e.g., brain injury). However, the processes described by plasticity would imply that, regardless of the degree of recovery back to an original structural or functional state, no material (or organism) can ever return to an exact copy or duplicate of a previous condition once that initial condition has been altered. For example, a steel beam expands and contracts without structural disruption within a specified range of temperature. However, if the temperature goes beyond this range (e.g., if it becomes too hot) then the beam changes (melts), but is not able to return to its original shape after the temperature returns to normal. Analogously, the human brain is able to recover from some injuries through self-repairing mechanisms in the central nervous system. However, if the structural integrity of the physical substrate is disrupted to a great degree (e.g., a significant part of the frontal cortex is destroyed via head injury), then the organism may survive but is permanently changed, as the brain's restorative mechanisms are not able to cope with the degree of change. However, unlike the steel beam whose molecular structure may remain unchanged in the context of the expected range of expansion and contraction due to thermal changes in the environment, an organism may exhibit some degree of functional and/or behavioral recovery from brain injury, but there inevitably are differences in underlying cellular and neuroanatomical structure.

Neural Plasticity: Fundamental Concepts from Neuroscience

Plasticity is of particular interest in the field of neuroscience, and is considered to be one of the fundamental functional mechanisms of the central nervous system. In modern neuroscience, the term neural plasticity generally refers to modification of the component neural substrate of the brain and other central nervous system structures as a result of some change in conditions (generically referred to as experience), with the assumption that such modification is adaptive for the continued survival and optimal functioning of the organism. Several decades of empirical investigation have revealed that plasticity is an inherent property of the central nervous system, and that the manifestation of plasticity is part of a normative process in the mammalian central nervous system (e.g., Kempermann, van Praag, & Gage, 2000). Indeed, it has been suggested that the plasticity of the human brain, which is broadly reflected behaviorally by learning and adaptation, is one of the central defining mechanisms of the evolutionary success of the human species (Hyman & Nestler, 1993).

There is evidence that all levels of the central nervous system exhibit some form of plasticity, typically in a "bottom-up" fashion, with changes at lower levels supporting (and precipitating) changes at higher levels of the central nervous system. Many, if not all, of the lower-level changes in neural functioning are believed to underlie changes in higher-level neural processes as well as neuroanatomical structure that, in turn, are reflected in changes at higher levels of analysis (e.g., neural networks, learning, memory), producing both short-term and long-term changes. The manifestation of such changes in the neural substrate takes place at varying timescales, from milliseconds to years (Destexhe & Marder, 2004). Within neuroscience, it is clear that the term neural plasticity is used to refer to a multiplicity of processes occurring at many levels of analysis. In addition, the study of neural plasticity must include identifying not only what changes are to be classified as neural plasticity (i.e., what constitutes neural plasticity), but also the mechanisms by which these changes take place (i.e., how does neural plasticity occur), as well as the adaptive, functional, and behavioral outcomes of these changes (what are the consequences of neural plasticity) across multiple levels of analysis. Of course, in many instances the changes that constitute plasticity and the mechanisms by which these changes take place must be described in tandem in order to characterize the broad process referred to as neural plasticity.

It also is important to consider neural plasticity broadly in terms of a nonlinear dynamic feedback system, one that constantly reshapes and reorganizes the organism. Previous neuroplastic changes inevitably influence the form of, and processes underlying, changes that might take place in the future (e.g., Elbert et al., 2001; Johnson, 1999). Neural plasticity takes place as a result of some event (or experience) impinging upon the organism that precipitates a change in the central nervous system. After the change in the system has taken place, the organism is essentially "different," and the manifestations of this change are represented at multiple levels (although at varying time scales), including behavior (e.g., memory or learning). Finally, such changes can potentially bring about further instances of neural plasticity.

Neural plasticity is not only a property of the developing brain but of the adult brain as well, although the central nervous system is more likely to undergo changes during early development and within certain sensitive periods of development. Moreover, neural plasticity must be thought of in the context of the overall developmental time course of an organism, with neural plasticity being more or less likely to occur at different time points along an organism's developmental trajectory (e.g., during sensitive periods— see Cicchetti & Tucker, 1994a, 1994b).

In sum, neural plasticity is a multidimensional, highly dynamic process that is strongly consistent with the principles of self-organization of the brain. The primary dimensions of neural plasticity that need to be considered are temporal (i.e., potential developmental constraints as well as time course of neural change), level of action (i.e., cellular, genetic, neural network), precursors (i.e., precipitating event, such as enriched experience, injury), and finally, the resultant change in terms of modified neural structure function and/or observable behavior (see Figure 1.1).

Such a broad systems approach to the understanding of neural plasticity points to the necessity of a multidisciplinary approach to the potential translation of a vast body of information concerning the biochemistry of neural plasticity to the level of observable behavior. The following sections provide a brief overview of some of the types of neural plasticity, and some of the mechanisms underlying them, and begin to identify potential candidate processes that might inform the study of a biology of resilience.

Forms of Neural Plasticity: What Changes

Generally, neural plasticity has predominantly been thought of as reorganization within systems or subsystems of the central nervous system, evidenced by changes in anatomy, neurochemistry, or metabolism, and is most typically studied in the context of several types of events impinging on the central nervous system. Such measures may include physical damage to neural structures, sensory deprivation, normal development of the organism, and a variety of environmental inputs generally referred to as experience (Bavelier & Neville, 2002; Nelson, 2000b). The neuroplastic changes that take place are often dramatic, and can include observable changes in the neural substrate that are translated into changes observable at the behavioral level. Such changes that are the hallmarks of

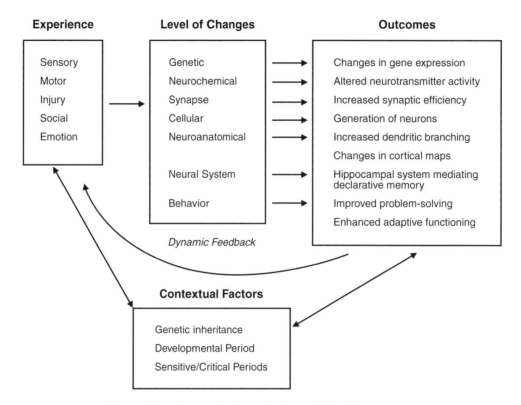

Figure 1.1   A general schematic of neural plasticity.

plasticity can occur on one or more levels of analysis, including molecular, cellular, neurochemical, neuroanatomical, and at the level of brain systems (Nelson, 1999).

Neuroplastic changes can be manifested in a number of ways, including: the characteristic behavior of single ion channels; the generation of new neural circuitry; dendritic outgrowth and the formation of synapses; the strengthening and weakening of some neural circuits through the processes of synaptogenesis and synaptic removal, respectively; and the sprouting of new axons, or elaborating their dendritic surfaces (Kolb & Gibb, 2001). Advances in the development of sophisticated molecular technologies and sensitive brain-imaging methods have enabled scientists to enhance their comprehension of the functional importance of dendritic spine heterogeneity (Segal, 2005). Empirical evidence suggests that dendritic spines may undergo complex alterations in both shape and number over time following exposure to novel experiences (Segal, 2005), thereby relating these spines to neuronal plasticity and long-term memory formation. Finally, these changes often are exhibited through observable behavioral changes. The following sections briefly summarize a sampling of different types of neural plasticity across several levels of analysis.

Short-term synaptic plasticity involves changes in synaptic activity that occur depending upon the frequency of stimulation and the history of prior activity (Schwarz, 2003). This type of plasticity allows synaptic strength to be modulated as a function of previous activity and can result in large changes in responses during physiologically relevant patterns of stimulation. Hebb (1949) originally suggested that synaptic contacts are modified as a consequence of simultaneous activation of the pre- and post-synaptic neuron (hence, the oft-cited phrase from Hebb, "cells that fire together wire together"). Long-term potentiation (LTP) and long-term depression (LTD) are forms of use-dependent plasticity at the synaptic level that have been the focus of a great deal of inquiry because of their likely correlation with some forms of learning and memory.

Synapses may show declines in transmission or increases in synaptic efficiency over time courses ranging from seconds to minutes to hours (in the case of LTP). These short- and long-term modulatory effects that neurotransmitters exert on their target neurons by way of changes in synaptic activity can be viewed as the fundamental basis of neural plasticity (Nestler & Duman, 2002), and serve as the foundation of higher levels of change within the central nervous system. For example, it is currently believed that LTP may be a key metabolic mechanism for memory formation (e.g., Chen & Tonegawa, 1997; Malenka & Nicoll, 1999), and it has been further suggested that LTP and LTD are fundamental in the process of behavior change based on experience (Post & Weiss, 1997). Other forms of synaptic plasticity also have been examined as well. For example, synaptic scaling has been examined as a general form of use-dependent regulation of synaptic transmission (e.g., Turrigiano, Leslie, Desai, Rutherford, & Nelson, 1998).

Further elaboration on neural plasticity at the cellular level is beyond the scope of this chapter. Although far removed from behavior, it is important to recognize that these molecular and cellular processes are the very building blocks that form the scaffold for neural plasticity that eventuates in changes in neuroanatomy and neural networks that are then manifested at the level of observable behavior.

Recent work has demonstrated neural plasticity in a wide range of neuroanatomical structures in the cortex. One example of this is reorganization that occurs in the motor cortex, with changes in the motor homunculus (the nonlinear map of the body across the motor cortex) observed as a consequence of the acquisition of motor skills (Steven & Blakemore, 2004). In addition, extensive training of specific limb movements in mammals leads to observable reorganization of the neural substrate of the motor cortex (e.g., Karni et al., 1995; Pascual-Leone et al., 1995).

The somatosensory cortex also has shown evidence of reorganization of representational zones as a result of somatic stimulation. In a well-established line of inquiry with musicians, Elbert and colleagues (e.g., Elbert et al., 1995; Pantev, Engelien, Candia, & Elbert, 2001) have shown enlargement in those areas of the somatosensory cortex of musicians devoted to the particular fingers used to play their instrument. Similarly, the cortical representation of the reading finger in blind Braille readers is increased compared to that of their nonreading fingers and compared to the fingers of sighted and blind non-Braille readers (Pascual-Leone & Torres, 1993). Also, there is evidence that extensive perceptual learning (experience) contributed to the correction of vision deficits in children who previously experienced visual deprivation (Grigorieva, 1996).

Other research has demonstrated neural plasticity in the form of local remapping in the primary visual cortex (V1) in animals in response to discrete retinal lesions. Most knowledge concerning alterations of the visual cortex in humans as a result of experience comes from studies of individuals deprived of sight. There is a large body of evidence indicating that the visual cortex in persons without sight is responsive to tactile and perhaps auditory stimula-

tion (e.g., Sadato et al., 1996). Neuroimaging studies have enabled the direct observation of neural plasticity in humans, and new findings continue to be published at an increasing rate demonstrating structural and functional neural plasticity of many areas of the human brain. For example, a recent structural MRI study showed that learning a second language increased the density of grey matter in the left inferior parietal cortex, with the degree of increase modulated by not only the degree of proficiency attained in the language, but also the age of acquisition (Mechelli et al., 2004).

Neural Plasticity Associated with Environmental Enrichment

Nearly all of the classic and ongoing studies of neural plasticity in animals and humans involve neuroplastic changes that impact the structure and function of primary sensory processes. Much less is known about the influence of experience on cognitive abilities, intellectual functioning, or affective and social development. A vast body of studies from the animal literature point to the direct impact of enriched rearing (relative to standard laboratory cages) on the brain and behavior of several animal species, most typically in rats. The enriched conditions (EC) for rats typically involve being housed in larger-than-standard cages, with a small maze and an assortment of toys inside, whereas control rats are reared in cages by themselves and do not have any contact with other rats. This extensive literature has indicated that being reared in enriched conditions is associated with changes in laboratory animals in neurochemical, physiological, neuroanatomical, and behavioral systems, and has revealed not only changes in the neural substrate of rats but also in their behavior.

Early studies examined changes in neurotransmitter systems in rats in response to rearing in enriched conditions, and these studies consistently demonstrated that the total activity of ACh and ChE was significantly greater in the cortex of the EC raised rats than in control rats reared in isolation, with the greatest increase in the visual cortex (e.g., Bennett et al., 1964; Krech, Rosenzweig, & Bennett, 1962). In addition, rats reared in enriched conditions were shown to have a 6% greater RNA to DNA ratio, suggesting an overall higher metabolic activity in the brains of rats reared in enriched conditions (Bennett, 1976), and there is evidence to suggest that rearing in complex environments enhances the efficiency of molecular transport through axons (Grouse, Schrier, Bennett, Rosenzweig, & Nelson, 1978). In addition, electrophysiological studies have demonstrated that rats reared in enriched conditions modify their behavior more quickly in response to environmental feedback (e.g., Leah, Allardyce, & Cummins, 1985), and other evidence points to decreased nervous system excitability in EC rats (Juraska, Greenough, & Conlee, 1983).

Numerous studies have demonstrated that the most obvious gross anatomical difference between EC reared rats and those raised in isolation is in total weight of the cortex. Replicated over 16 successive experiments, Rosenzweig et al. (1972) reported that the total cortical weight of EC rats was on average 5% greater than that of control rats, with an average 7.6% increase in the occipital (visual) cortex, 4% in the ventral cortex (which includes the hippocampus), and a 3% increase in the somatosensory cortex. These changes also were found in rats blinded before being placed in the enriched condition, or even when the differential rearing took place in total darkness (Rosenzweig et al., 1969). It thus appears that the brain effects seen in enriched rats are due to multisensory stimulation from the enriched environment, and is not restricted to the visual modality. The observed increase in cortical weight has generally been attributed to, among other factors, a 20% to 30% increase in the number of glial cells in the brains of EC rats (Diamond et al., 1966). EC rats also exhibit thicker cortical regions, with an average increase in thickness of 5% overall (Diamond, Krech, & Rosenzweig, 1964), as well as consistently larger neuronal cell bodies and nuclei than control rats (Diamond, Linder, & Raymond, 1967).

Although a 5% increase in the weight of the cortex may not seem particularly large in an absolute sense, changes of this magnitude in such a central component of the central nervous system can, and do, result in large behavioral changes. For example, destruction of less than 5% of the tissue in the rat occipital cortex can result in a functionally blind animal (Renner & Rosenzweig, 1987), and small lesions in the cortex caused by stroke or injury in humans can result in behavioral changes of great magnitude, such as aphasia or other disorders.

Over the past 30 years, Greenough and his colleagues have addressed how environmental complexity exerts an impact on the actual organization of the brain. Initial work from this laboratory demonstrated that rats reared in complex environments consistently had more high order dendritic branches and more dendritic synapses per neuron in several occipital cortical cell types and the temporal cortex, but not in the frontal cortex (e.g., Greenough, Volkmar, & Juraska, 1973). Environmental enrichment also appears to actively induce synapse formation (Greenough, Hwang, & Gorman, 1985). In addition, rats reared in enriched environments have increased relative density of dendritic spines, more synapses per neuron, and more multiple synap-

tic boutons (Jones, Klintsova, Kilman, Sirevaag, & Greenough, 1997; Turner & Greenough, 1985). Other features indicative of greater synaptic efficiency, such as larger synaptic contacts, also have been found in EC rats (e.g., Turner & Greenough, 1985).

Neuroanatomical changes as a result of enriched rearing conditions also have been found in brain regions outside the cortex. For example, Floeter and Greenough (1979) have demonstrated structural plasticity of Purkinje cell bodies, critical in coordination of movement, in the cerebellum of the Japanese macaque as a function of rearing in differential environments. Somewhat more recently, EC rats have been shown to undergo broad structural modifications of the cerebellar cortex as a result of complex motor skill learning (e.g., Kleim et al., 1998).

Given the importance of the role the hippocampus plays in memory, the influence of differential rearing experiences on this brain structure would be of particular interest. Rats reared in enriched environments have been reported to have more granule cells in the dentate gyrus, a structure adjacent to the hippocampus and a key component of the hippocampal memory circuit, as well as increases in dendritic branching and overall size of the dendritic field (e.g., Susser & Wallace, 1982). Mice reared in enriched conditions showed an overall 15% increase in the depth and number of neurons in the hippocampus (Kempermann, Kuhn, & Gage, 1997).

Behavioral Effects of Enrichment

The most consistent finding across studies is that of superior performance of EC animals in complex problem solving. For example, rats reared in enriched environments show advantages on tasks involving reversal of previously learned visual discrimination (Krech et al., 1962) and other tasks requiring response flexibility (M. J. Morgan, 1973), and are superior at response inhibition in a bar pressing task (Ough, Beatty, & Khalili, 1972) and passive avoidance tasks (e.g., Lore, 1969).

Many studies of learning in rats reared in differential environments have involved spatial problem-solving tasks with various types of mazes, demonstrating improved learning in EC rats (e.g., Brown, 1968) and mice (Kempermann et al., 1997). This superior maze performance appears to be long lasting, even with a 300 day delay period between being taken out of the complex environment and the beginning of the testing period (Denenberg, Woodcock, & Rosenberg, 1968). Others have demonstrated that pregnant rats housed in enriched conditions had offspring who performed better on a Hebb-Williams maze than offspring of mothers housed in isolated and control environments while pregnant (Kiyono, Seo, Shibagaki, & Inouye, 1985). EC rats also demonstrate more organized and complex bouts of interactions with objects than control rats, perhaps reflecting a higher level of exploratory behavior (Smith, 1972). In addition, mice reared in enriched conditions were less fearful, and exhibited lower levels of both state and trait anxiety (Chapillon, Manneche, Belzung, & Caston, 1999).

Although there are no direct human analogs to animal studies of rearing in enriched versus impoverished conditions (of course, such studies would be unethical), some nearly analogous nonexperimental paradigms involving human enrichment do exist. Programs, such as Head Start, and more recently the Abecedarian Project, have attempted to improve cognitive development and social competence in high-risk young children (e.g., Ramey & Ramey, 1998; Zigler & Valentine, 1979). The Abecedarian Project was designed as a research and intervention study, in order to test whether mental retardation correlated with inadequate environments could be prevented by providing intensive, high-quality preschool programs beginning shortly after birth and continuing at least until children entered kindergarten (Ramey & Ramey, 1992).

Generally, outcome studies of Head Start and other similar programs have shown initial IQ gains followed by subsequent declines, but with positive impact on general school and social competence (Lazar, Darlington, Murray, Royce, & Snipper, 1982). Those who participated in the Abecedarian Project, aside from a small overall advantage in IQ (approximately 5 points overall compared to children not enrolled in the Abecedarian Project), at age 12 and at age 15 also scored significantly higher on a variety of achievement tests, with the intervention group exhibiting a 50% reduction in the rate of failing a grade during elementary school (Campbell & Ramey, 1995). This project in particular has provided evidence that those children who began the program with greater risk benefited the most (Martin, Ramey, & Ramey, 1990). For example, children whose mothers had IQs less than 70 had IQs, on average, 21 points higher than the control children at 4½ years of age. This is in contrast to the mean gain of approximately 8 IQ points for the intervention sample as a whole.

In addition to the measured behavioral and intellectual advantages found in those children who participate in early enrichment interventions, one study has reported the impact of an early human enrichment program on the island of Mauritius on psychophysiological measure of arousal and orienting (Raine et al., 2001). At age 11 years, children who were randomly assigned to an enriched nursery school

intervention at ages 3 to 5 years showed greater skin conductance amplitude, faster rise times and recovery, both at rest and during a continuous performance task, compared to children who received a normal preschool educational experience. In addition, children who had experienced the enriched preschool program showed less slow-wave EEG activity both at rest and during a continuous performance task. These findings suggest both better information processing as well as a greater degree of cortical maturation in the children who participated in the early enrichment intervention (Raine et al., 2001). The results of this study are striking in that they demonstrate a strong association between early enriched preschool experience in humans and later direct measures of brain and psychophysiological functioning.

In a longitudinal follow-up of this sample, the children who participated in the environmental enrichment program at ages 3 to 5 years had lower scores on self-report measures of schizotypal personality and antisocial behavior at age 17 years, as well as showed lower rates of self-reported criminal offenses at age 23 years, compared to those who did not participate in the enrichment program (Raine, Mellingen, Liu, Venables, & Mednick, 2003). These effects were most pronounced in those children who showed signs of malnutrition at age 3 years.

Mechanisms of Neural Plasticity: How Does This Change Take Place?

The mechanism of experience-based neural plasticity begins with the organism interfacing with its environment. Experience "enters" the brain by way of afferent inputs through the sensory modalities. These signals are then relayed via established neural networks to higher cortical areas where a myriad of processes ensure proper disposition of these inputs. There are many hypothesized mechanisms to account for neural plasticity at all levels of analysis, with discrete regulatory mechanisms that occur at each level of neuroplastic change. It also appears that mechanisms governing higher levels of neural plasticity (e.g., changes in representational maps in somatosensory cortex) build upon fundamental processes at the cellular and molecular levels.

The fundamental processes underlying neural plasticity at all levels are believed to be two mechanisms underlying the modulatory effects of neurotransmitters. One of these is protein phosphorylation and the other is the regulation of gene expression (Hyman & Nestler, 1993). It would appear that protein phosphorylation is the major molecular mechanism of neural plasticity, and is generally the mechanism by which the modulation of neuronal function is achieved, through alterations in the functional state of many different types of neuronal proteins, such as ion channels, neurotransmitter receptors, and processes by which neurotransmitter storage and release is regulated (Hyman & Nestler, 1993). Protein phosphorylation regulates both presynaptic and postsynaptic neurotransmitter receptors, with corroborative evidence suggesting that phosphorylation alters the functional activity of receptors (Hyman & Nestler, 1993). In addition, protein phosphorylation plays a central role in cell growth, differentiation, and movement.

The second primary mechanism by which neurotransmitters can effect long-term changes on the function of target neurons is by regulating gene expression within those neurons. Such changes in gene expression appear to produce quantitative as well as qualitative changes in the protein components of neurons, including, for example, alterations in the numbers and types of ion channels and receptors present on the cell membrane as well as levels of proteins that regulate the morphology of neurons and the numbers of synaptic connections they form (Hyman & Nestler, 1993). Further, neurotransmitters continually regulate neuronal gene expression as a way to fine-tune the functional state of neurons in response to many varied synaptic inputs (Hyman & Nestler, 1993). Regulation of neural gene expression by neurotransmitters can, in some cases, produce quite long-lasting changes in virtually all aspects of neuronal functioning.

Within the brain, gene expression can be activated by both normative and nonnormative (i.e., drugs) physiological processes and experience. Such endogenous or exogenous processes initiate a cascade of events, beginning with incoming afferent sensory information, activate increasingly higher-level neural networks in the brain, eventually resulting in activation of neurons and networks involved with higher-order processing (e.g., language, cognition). In turn, within each of the cells involved in this process, the generation of action potentials as well as the activation of second messenger systems alters the rate of expression of specific genes and, as a result, the expression of multiple types of neuronal proteins (Hyman & Nestler, 1993). The altered levels of these proteins produce changes in processing of subsequent synaptic information by these neurons, thus leading to further changes in the processing of sensory input. It is believed that such mechanisms account for many of the longer-term consequences of experience on brain functioning. Such a regulatory process, whereby activity in one neuron regulates gene expression in another neuron, is referred to as transsynaptic regulation of gene expression, and a class of proteins termed transcription factors (e.g., c-Fos, Zif268) plays a central role in the regulation of neural gene expression (Hyman & Nestler, 1993).

Generally, changes to the central nervous system mediated by protein phosphorylation do not involve changes in protein synthesis and, therefore, are likely to have a rapid onset, be more readily reversible, and have a shorter duration compared to neural plasticity mediated by gene expression. However, both of these processes serve to mediate the long-term effects of experience on the brain. The biochemical and molecular changes brought about through these two processes, through a cascade of intermediate neural processes, lead to changes in the function and efficacy of synapses, changes in the processing of information by individual neurons, and ultimately to changes in the way multicellular neural networks within the brain communicate with each other (Hyman & Nestler, 1993). Protein phosphorylation and gene expression are in some ways considered to represent a form of molecular memory within individual neurons. Likewise, learning and memory at the level of the whole brain are mediated by accumulations of complex combinations of the fundamental types of changes in the function and efficacy of synapses brought about by these two basic processes.

The challenge of future research attempting to relate neural plasticity to particular behavioral phenomenona is to find associations between specific alterations in neural processes, brought about by phosphorylation and gene expression and behavior. This challenge is great, given the probable high degree of complexity of linkages between such distal processes, separated by multiple levels of analysis. Greenough, Black, Klintsova, Bates, and Weiler (1999) have proposed an integrative perspective on neural plasticity that may be a starting point for building a framework that enables the large gap between molecular and genetic processes involved with neural plasticity and the expression of behavior to be bridged. They advocate moving beyond a focus on synapses to a consideration of the process of neural plasticity occurring in surrounding tissue elements, cooperative regional neural networks, and diffuse endocrine modulatory effects. As increased understanding of the cellular mechanisms of neural plasticity accumulates, this new knowledge may prove to be fruitful for comprehending some of the molecular processes contributing to resilient functioning. To fully reap these potential benefits of such understanding, it is important that multidisciplinary collaborations take place between neuroscientists and developmental psychopathologists.

Connecting Neural Plasticity and Behavior

Greenough et al. (1993) have stressed that a necessary condition for the behavioral and brain effects of enrichment to be manifested in rats is direct physical interaction with the environment. Animals reared inside an enriched environment but kept in cages to prevent them from physically interacting with the environment do not show the brain or behavioral effects of their littermates who are allowed to physically interact with the enriched environment (Ferchmin, Bennett, & Rosenzweig, 1975). There is also evidence that direct physical interaction with the environment may be important for human development, as exemplified by the work of Bertenthal, Campos, and Barrett (1984), suggesting that interaction with the environment produced by self-locomotion may be an important component of cognitive and emotional development in early childhood.

Together, these motor and sensory processes facilitate learning. How learning-related neuronal activity becomes translated into changes in the structure of neurons, and the mechanisms by which environmental experience becomes translated into structural modifications of neuronal connections, is not yet completely understood (Torasdotter, Metsis, Henriksson, Winblad, & Mohammed, 1998). It appears that the general mechanism responsible for this phenomenon is gene expression, which is one of the fundamental ways that cells adjust to changes and demands placed upon them (Greenough et al., 1993). This process involves the activation of genes in the nucleus of the cell, whereby messenger RNA (mRNA) is transcribed from the genes and codes for the proteins necessary for the formation of new synapses and dendrites. Several studies have begun to show a direct link between gene expression processes and the structural changes resulting from learning (e.g., Alcantra, Saks, & Greenough, 1991).

The second stage in the process of the impact of experience on the brain is in the output, or how these neuronal changes are translated into observed changes in behavior. If neurons have more synapses, then there is more opportunity for these synapses to form or participate in networks, leading to quicker and more efficient processing. This would in turn manifest itself in observable behavior. For example, the behavioral attributes that would correlate with greater levels of neuronal connectivity are most likely the hallmark characteristics of increased flexibility in problem solving seen in rats exposed to complex environments. Finally, it is important to note that the cycle of modification of an organism in an enriched environment builds upon itself in the form of a feedback loop from the second phase to the first, with subsequent change building upon change resulting from previous experiences with the environment.

Applications of Neural Plasticity to Resilience

Although the processes and mechanisms underlying neural plasticity are beginning to be fairly well understood, the difficult challenge faced by theorists and researchers in re-

silience is to devise a model whereby mechanisms of plasticity at the neural level could be linked to the behavioral manifestation of resilience in humans. However, it is important to explicitly examine whether the principles or processes of neural plasticity can contribute to our understanding of resilience. Although understanding the process and manifestation of neural plasticity may serve as a useful heuristic in the investigation of the biological correlates of, and contributors to, resilience, neural plasticity, per se, may not serve as the ultimate explanatory biological mechanism underlying resilience. Therefore, the primary question to be addressed in the following sections is how principles of neural plasticity might inform theory and research on resilience.

Neural Plasticity and Resilience: Some Potential Linkages

A multitude of studies have consistently demonstrated the brain's ability to recover varying degrees of functioning after lesions and other injuries to its physical structure (for review, see Kolb & Gibb, 2001). Kolb and Gibb outline three ways in which the brain could manifest neuroplastic changes in response to injury. In one scenario, there could be reorganization of the remaining, intact neural substrate, most likely involving the generation of new synapses in pre-existing neural pathways. Alternatively, there could be development of entirely new neural circuitry. Finally, new neurons and supporting glia might be generated to replace some of these structures lost in the injury. It is important to consider that all of these regenerative processes most likely occur in tandem with one another, although the exact combination of processes utilized by the brain may vary depending on the developmental age of the organism at the time of injury (Kolb & Gibb, 2001). Finally, each of these neuroplastic processes may also be influenced by other factors, such as experience (i.e., training), neuromodulators, and hormones (Kolb & Gibb, 2001).

Analogous to neural plasticity that takes place in response to brain injury, resilience can be viewed as the ability of an individual to recover after exposure to trauma or adversity (Cicchetti & Rogosch, 1997; Masten et al., 1990). In this view, adversity is thought to exert a damaging effect on one or more neural substrates, and mechanisms of neural plasticity bring about recovery in an individual. This might lead to the conclusion that certain individuals, classified as resilient, may have some increased innate capacity (plasticity), above and beyond normative levels, to recover from environmental insults that impact the brain. This view of resilience conceives of adversity in the environment as "bad" for the brain, with recovery as an innate property of the brain itself. This perspective, however, does not consider the impact of a positive environment, or of the individual's active attempts at coping, on such recovery (Cicchetti, 2002; Cicchetti & Rogosch, 1997).

Another conceptualization of resilience would be one of greater than normative resistance to the impact of environmental adversity on the brain, such that resilient individuals may not succumb to the potentially damaging effects that adversity may have on the brain and other biological systems. This view of brain-adversity interaction would not strictly be classified as involving neural plasticity. Thus, for these individuals, the term recovery of function may not apply, in that they did not "lose" function at all. Despite the fact that this distinction may seem trivial, it may lead to important theoretical implications when considering the contribution of biology, and, in particular, processes described as neural plasticity, to resilience. Although quite general, the distinction between these two formulations of resilience also can generate important research questions concerning the relation of neural plasticity to resilience. Such questions underscore the importance of utilizing longitudinal research designs that can begin to examine the bidirectional relation between the brain's capacity to either resist damage from adversity versus its restorative capabilities.

Investigating Neural Plasticity and Resilience

The rapid growth in sophisticated techniques that permit imaging of the brain directly has resulted in the availability of a variety of methodologies to developmental psychopathology researchers, many of which could be utilized to examine neural plasticity, as well as brain structure and function, in detail. These new tools make it possible to now undertake empirical investigations of the relation between neural plasticity and resilience, perhaps enabling an examination of the direct linkage of these two processes. Questions about how neural plasticity may play a role in the development and maintenance of resilient functioning could be addressed, as well as whether the mechanisms of neural plasticity may operate differently in individuals classified as resilient.

Included among these new tools are: ERPs, magnetoencephalography (MEG), MRI, fMRI, positron emission tomography (PET), single-photon emission-computed tomography (SPECT), and magnetic resonance spectroscopy (MRS). Diverse information about the brain that is correlated with neural structure and functioning can be obtained by these various imaging techniques, including: (1) brain metabolic processes, such as cerebral blood flow and blood volume, and glucose metabolic rate; (2) bio-

chemical changes within brain cells, such as changes in neurotransmitter receptors; and (3) a sharp temporal resolution of brain functioning.

Among the compelling questions about resilient adaptation that could potentially be addressed utilizing brain imaging methodologies are: (1) Is brain structure and function different in resilient and nonresilient children matched on experiences of adversity? (2) Is the brain structure and function of resilient individuals who have experienced adversity different from normal children reared in nonadverse environments? (3) Are particular areas of the brain more likely to be activated in resilient than in nonresilient functioning during challenging or stressful tasks? (4) What aspects of brain structure and function differentiate individuals who function resiliently, despite experiencing early adversity, from those who function in a nonresilient fashion and who encounter adversity early in life (i.e., what is the role of early experience?) (5) Are there sensitive periods beyond which the achievement of resilience is improbable or is resilience possible to achieve across the life span? and (6) Are there changes over time in brain structure and/or functioning in individuals classified as resilient that may reflect processes of neural plasticity? The inclusion of neuroimaging techniques to the existing predominantly psychological approaches to charting the pathways to resilience, along with the biological and molecular genetic methods discussed next, results in many exciting discoveries about the complex processes that eventuate in competent outcomes despite the experience of significant adversity.

Aside from investigating the proximal relation between resilience and neural plasticity, there are several neurobiologically mediated processes (e.g., cognition, neuroendocrine functioning) that may have a direct relation to resilient outcome, some of which is described in the following sections. Although such processes may have a clear impact on resilient functioning, neural plasticity may, to some degree, be the common, underlying mechanism that mediates the relation between such processes and resilience. The behavioral manifestations of two of these realms, emotion and cognition, have been extensively investigated and their relation to resilience documented. In the sections that follow, possible links between the biological aspects of these phenomena and resilience is described.

Emotion and Resilience

Emotion encompasses a wide range of behavioral expressions and associated biological processes that play a vital role in many aspects of human development and adaptation. There are at least three primary, interrelated functional realms of emotion in humans, including perception, expression, and regulation of emotion. The first part of this section focuses on emotion regulation as a key factor in resilient outcome, while the second part reviews and examines the relation between cortical EEG asymmetry, emotion, and resilient functioning.

One important contributor to resilience at the level of individual characteristics, and often cited as a potential protective factor against adversity in studies of resilience, is the ability to regulate emotion. Emotion regulation is conceived as the intra- and extra-organismic processes by which emotional arousal is redirected, controlled, modulated, and modified to enable an individual to function adaptively in emotionally arousing situations (Cicchetti, Ackerman, & Izard, 1995; Cicchetti, Ganiban, & Barnett, 1991; Gross, 1998; Thompson, 1990). Factors, such as organizational changes in central nervous system functioning, the ontogenesis of neurological inhibition systems in the prefrontal cortex, cerebral hemisphere lateralization, the development of neurotransmitter systems, children's growing cognitive and representational skills, and the development of a coherent sense of self, are some of the important intrinsic factors that shape the development of emotion regulatory abilities (Cicchetti et al., 1991; Cole, Martin, & Dennis, 2004; Eisenberg, 2002; Fox, 1994; Fox & Davidson, 1984; Gross, 1998; Kelley & Stinus, 1984; Schore, 1994; Tucker, 1981). Extraorganismic factors that exert an influence on the ability to regulate emotion include increased parental response and tolerance of affect and the parents' socialization of affective displays during interactions (Cicchetti et al., 1991). A number of characteristics are often referred to in the context of emotion regulation, including emotional reactivity, stress reactivity, temperament, or positive and negative emotionality (e.g., Davidson, 2000; Masten et al., 1999; Masten, 2001; Watson & Clark, 1984). Generally, these constructs represent the function of a diverse set of associated brain and neuroendocrine systems, which act in concert to produce and modulate the behavioral manifestations of an individual's response to emotional challenges and stressors.

There is an unfortunate paucity of empirical studies or conceptual work directly addressing if and how emotion and the regulation of emotion may serve as a protective factor in resilience. One of the primary questions involves whether individuals classified as resilient are to a large degree impervious to the typically insidious effects of stress, a view of resilient individuals as "invulnerable" (cf. Luthar et al., 2000); alternatively, it may be more accurate to characterize resilience in this context as the unique ability to react to stress in an adaptive way. Also important is the question of how resilient individuals manifest adaptation in the face of stress and adversity at the level of biology.

Resilience, Emotional Reactivity, and Startle

Davidson (2000) has suggested that the capacity for rapid recovery from negative affective events, one specific aspect of emotion regulation, may constitute a critical component of resilient functioning. Davidson (1998a) outlines what he terms an affective chronometry, which is used to describe the time course of affective responding during experimental paradigms investigating emotion-modulated startle. In particular, Davidson (2000) has hypothesized that for resilient individuals, who tend to maintain high levels of positive affect and well-being in the context of adversity, negative affect does not persist. Thus, in this view, resilience does not entail never experiencing negative affect, but rather involves the ability to recover more quickly and to more easily return to a positive affective state, and also a heightened ability to learn from the experience of negative affect (Davidson, 2000). The specific biological underpinnings of the ability to recover quickly from negative affect are more than likely mediated by a fairly complex neural network, which has been shown to include (but is not limited to) the amygdala, several regions of the prefrontal cortex, brain stem structures, the hippocampus, and aspects of the cingulate cortex (Davidson, 2000; LeDoux, 1996, 2002).

The startle reflex is a methodological tool that has historically been utilized to examine individual differences in reaction to emotional stimuli, and is widely held to be a measure sensitive to individual differences in emotional reactivity. Generally, startle is an involuntary response to a sudden and intense tactile, visual, or acoustic stimulus that occurs across many species (Koch, 1999; Landis & Hunt, 1939). The response pattern consists of a fast twitch of facial and body muscles, which includes eye lid closure along with contraction of facial, neck, and other muscles. It is generally believed that this pattern of responding is a primitive reflex intended as a defensive response to protect against injury and as a preparation of a fight/flight response (Koch, 1999). The startle response can be easily measured in humans by recording the timing and intensity of the eye blink, which is the typical manifestation of the startle reflex.

The neuronal circuitry underlying the acoustic startle reflex is well understood in rodents and is relatively straightforward. It consists of an afferent pathway from the cochlear root neurons in the inner ear to the neurons in the nucleus reticularis pontis caudalis, and then to the motoneurons in the facial motor nucleus or the spinal cord (in the case of the whole body startle; Davis, Walker, & Lee, 1999). However, other investigators have attributed the startle reflex to a slightly more complex pathway, which may include other brain stem structures, such as the dorsal and ventral cohlear nucleus, the lateral superior olive, and the ventrolateral tegmental nucleus (see Koch, 1999, for a review). Although the neural pathway mediating the startle reflex in humans may be somewhat more complex, it is nonetheless analogous in function to the rodent model.

A vast body of research has consistently and reliably demonstrated that the startle reflex can be modulated with presentation of emotional stimuli in conjunction with the startle stimulus (e.g., Bradley, Cuthbert, & Lang, 1993; Cuthbert, Bradley, & Lang, 1996; Lang, 1995; Vanman, Boehmelt, Dawson, & Schell, 1996). Consistent findings in both animal and human research have shown that the startle reflex is amplified when accompanied by negative emotional stimuli and, conversely, the magnitude of the startle reflex is attenuated when the startle-inducing stimuli are accompanied by positive emotional stimuli.

Modulation of the startle reflex due to emotional context implies that a secondary circuit modulates the primary reflex pathway described. It appears that the central nucleus of the amygdala is critically involved in some forms of fear-potentiated startle, via a descending pathway from this structure to the nucleus pontine reticularis in the brain stem (Davis, 1992). Lesions of the central nucleus of the amygdala have been shown to block the fear-potentiated portion of the startle response, but not the baseline (e.g., Campeau & Davis, 1995; Vrana, Spence, & Lang, 1988). In addition, based on anatomical and lesion data, other structures have been implicated in the potentiation of the startle response, including the central gray and the bed nucleus of the stria terminalis, depending on the type of startle-enhancing stimuli employed (Davis et al., 1999). There has been less work directly examining the mechanism for the attenuated startle response seen with presentation of positive emotional stimuli, but it would appear likely that the amygdala also plays a central role in this phenomenon.

Investigators have examined individual differences in the human startle reflex in a variety of populations suffering from the sequelae of trauma or who are at risk for anxiety, including individuals with posttraumatic stress disorder (PTSD; e.g., Grillon, Morgan, Southwick, Davis, & Charney, 1996; C. A. Morgan, Grillon, Southwick, Davis, & Charney, 1996). In the context of threat, male combat veterans diagnosed with PTSD exhibited an exaggerated startle response. However, there are conflicting results in studies of baseline startle response (i.e., startle reflex, induced without a threat of aversive stimulus) in

those with PTSD, with some investigations showing exaggerated baseline startle (e.g., Orr, Lasko, Shalev, & Pitman, 1995), and others revealing normal baseline startle (e.g., Orr, Solomon, Peri, Pitman, & Shalev, 1997). Women with PTSD resulting from sexual assault were found to have an exaggerated baseline startle response (C. A. Morgan, Grillon, Lubin, & Southwick, 1997). However, women with PTSD associated with childhood sexual abuse had a normal startle response (Metzger et al., 1999). These conflicting results have been attributed to differences in the aversive, threatening, or stressful context of the experiment (Grillon, Morgan, Davis, & Southwick, 1998).

In addition to the fairly extensive literature on startle and adults with PTSD, a few studies have examined the startle response in children with this disorder. One such investigation examined the startle response in a small sample of children with PTSD, aged 8 to 13 years (Ornitz & Pynoos, 1989). These investigators found a reduced baseline startle amplitude in both boys and girls compared to a group of control children. These findings, which are not consistent with findings of exaggerated startle in adults with PTSD, suggest that the age at which the PTSD-inducing trauma is experienced may have an impact on the type of effect seen in subsequent baseline and modification of startle responsiveness. In a startle study of adolescents, male offspring of parents with anxiety disorders were shown to have an increased fear-potentiated startle response (in a contextual threat condition) compared to low-risk control subjects (Grillon, Dierker, & Merikangas, 1998). The baseline startle magnitude was not different for the high-risk males. However, in this study, a sex difference emerged where female offspring of parents with anxiety disorders did not show elevated startle magnitude in the threat condition but exhibited elevated baseline startle magnitude. This is in contrast to an earlier study by Grillon, Dierker, and Merikangas (1997) where both male and female offspring of parents with anxiety disorders showed exaggerated baseline startle magnitude compared to a group of low-risk control children. However, the subjects in the latter study were several years younger than those in the Grillon, Dierker, et al. (1998) study. These authors suggest that the sex difference either may be a result of differences in brain structures that underlie affective responses to threat, or that development of those vulnerable to anxiety may proceed differently for males and females. Despite the discrepant findings obtained in these studies, which may be attributable to methodological differences, in general, the results of investigations with individuals diagnosed with PTSD or at risk for anxiety disorders have implied that startle reactivity may reflect the impact of environmental stressors on the brain systems mediating startle, and may in fact serve as a vulnerability marker for the development of anxiety disorders (Grillon et al., 1996).

In a recent investigation, the first of its kind, Klorman, Cicchetti, Thatcher, and Ison (2003) examined the baseline startle response in a large sample of children maltreated by their caregivers and a group of nonmaltreated comparison children. In this study, physically abused boys demonstrated a smaller startle-reflex amplitude and slower onset latency than did demographically matched nonmaltreated comparison children, consistent with findings in Ornitz and Pynoos (1989). In contrast, the younger maltreated girls in this sample demonstrated smaller startle amplitudes than younger comparison girls, whereas the older maltreated girls showed larger startle response magnitudes than did the nonmaltreated comparison girls of similar ages. The findings for the boys in this study are suggestive of a generalized defensive reaction that may lead to reduced responsiveness to noxious stimulation and subsequent down-regulation of the startle response that may be linked to reduced cortisol levels (Klorman et al., 2003). However, the findings for the girls in this sample are more difficult to interpret, given the relative dearth of studies investigating startle in traumatized women with PTSD, as well as the differences in the trauma experienced by men (e.g., combat) and women (e.g., sexual abuse/assault) with PTSD enrolled in most studies of startle.

Although there are some inconsistencies in the literature concerning the impact of adversity on the startle reflex, there is evidence to indicate that exogenous environmental influences do reliably effect this reflex and the underlying brain stem network that modulates this response. In particular, investigation of emotion-modulated startle is yet another tool that could be employed to further our understanding of the role of emotional regulation and reactivity in the promotion of resilience. Basic investigations of emotion-modulated acoustic startle could examine individual differences in the modulation of startle reactivity in the context of positive and negative foreground stimuli, such as emotionally toned pictures from the International Affective Picture System (IAPS; Lang, Bradley, & Cuthbert, 1995). Given that there is some Q-sort personality data indicating that individuals classified as resilient are more successful with emotion regulation (e.g., Cicchetti & Rogosch, 1997; Cicchetti, Rogosch, Lynch, & Holt, 1993; Flores, Cicchetti, & Rogosch, 2005), one prediction that could be tested would be that individuals manifesting resilient functioning would display less overall increase in magnitude of the blink response when presented with unpleasant pictures than would individuals not classified as resilient but with equivalent levels of exposure to adversity.

Davidson (2000) has employed emotion-modulated startle to examine the role of the time course in affective responding and has indicated that this detailed analysis may contribute to our understanding of resilience. Davidson (2000) has suggested that by placing the acoustic-startle probes at various points before, during, and after the presentation of the emotional stimulus, then, in addition to the measurement of the response itself, the anticipatory and the recovery phases can be measured. Davidson (2000) has hypothesized that a rapid recovery phase after negative emotional stimuli is important in the development of resilience. Such a scenario suggests that negative affect, although experienced by resilient individuals, does not persist, and may be part of a ubiquitous predisposition for rapid recovery in multiple biological systems after exposure to negative and/or stressful experiences (Davidson, 2000).

Hemispheric EEG Asymmetry

Another area of emotion research directly involving the brain that may hold promise for the study of resilience is examining hemispheric asymmetries in cortical EEG activity, where a growing body of evidence has indicated differential roles for the left and right prefrontal cortex in emotion (Hugdahl & Davidson, 2003). In general, it appears that the left hemisphere participates more heavily in positive affect, whereas the right hemisphere mediates negative emotion (see reviews by Davidson, Ekman, Saron, Senulis, & Friesen, 1990; and Fox, 1991). Several investigators have found that induced positive and negative affective states can reliably shift hemispheric asymmetry (e.g., Ahern & Schwartz, 1985; Davidson et al., 1990; Jones & Fox, 1992). Negative affect induced by showing negatively toned stimuli (often in the form of film clips) increases relative right prefrontal activation as measured by EEG, while positive affect resulting from viewing positive stimuli is associated with increased activation in left prefrontal. This effect also has been demonstrated using PET to measure regional glucose metabolism, a by-product of increased neuronal activity (Sutton, Davidson, Donzella, Irwin, & Dottl, 1997; see also Pizzagalli, Shackman, & Davidson, 2003, for a selective review of PET and fMRI investigations on human emotion that have discovered lateralized activations).

In addition, many investigations have found an association between dispositional affective style and baseline levels of asymmetric activation in the prefrontal cortex (e.g., Sutton & Davidson, 1997; Tomarken, Davidson, Wheeler, & Doss, 1992). Generally, individuals with greater left frontal activation report more positive affect than those with greater right frontal activation. Other work has shown that individuals who vary in resting prefrontal EEG activation asymmetry respond differently to positive and negative emotional stimuli (e.g., Tomarken, Davidson, & Henriques, 1990; Wheeler, Davidson, & Tomarken, 1993). Specifically, Wheeler et al. (1993) found that subjects with greater relative left hemisphere activation reported more positive affect when viewing positively toned film clips and less negative affect after viewing negatively toned film clips. Thus, fairly strong experimental evidence has suggested that not only do negative and positive emotion exert an impact on relative left-right activation of prefrontal regions, but also that baseline anterior activation asymmetry is associated with differences in emotional response.

Similar results concerning frontal EEG asymmetry have been demonstrated in infants and children. For example, studies of infants have generally reported increased right frontal EEG activity during the expression of negative emotions, such as crying and sadness, and increased left frontal activation during the expression of what are termed approach emotions, such as happiness (e.g., Bell & Fox, 1994; Dawson, Panagiotides, Klinger, & Hill, 1992). Hemispheric asymmetry in EEG activity also has been observed in children of depressed mothers, with infants and toddlers of mothers experiencing depressive symptomatology showing reduced left frontal EEG activation during baseline (e.g., Dawson, Grofer Klinger, Panagiotides, Hill, & Spieker, 1992; Dawson, Frey, Panagiotides, Osterling, & Hessl, 1997; Dawson et al., 1999; Field, Fox, Pickens, & Nawrocki, 1995; Jones, Field, Fox, Lundy, & Davalos, 1997). These findings appear to be analogous with Davidson's evidence of frontal EEG asymmetry in normal adults suggesting that the left hemisphere is generally involved with positive affect. It is conceivable that the inability of mothers with depressive disorder to provide their children with adequate positive emotion and to facilitate their children's self-regulation of emotion not only affects their children's behavioral regulation capacities but also exerts an impact on the neurobiological systems that underlie these abilities (Cicchetti et al., 1991; Cicchetti & Toth, 1998; Dawson, 1994).

Finally, hemispheric EEG asymmetry has been observed in adults with depression (e.g., Allen, Iacono, Depue, & Arbisi, 1993; Henriques & Davidson, 1991). Generally, individuals diagnosed with depression have been shown to exhibit decreased left prefrontal EEG activation, although some studies have failed to replicate this finding (e.g., Reid, Duke, & Allen, 1998). However, utilizing PET to assess regional glucose metabolism, Baxter et al. (1989) reported that individuals diagnosed with depression demonstrated re-

duced left frontal activity; similar findings have been reported by Drevets et al. (1997).

Resilience and Hemispheric Asymmetry

Davidson and colleagues view individual differences in hemispheric asymmetry in prefrontal activation as a contributing factor to the development of affective style (Davidson, 1998a, 1998b). Further, Davidson (1998a, 1998b) characterizes such individual differences in hemispheric asymmetry in the context of depression as diatheses that might bias the affective style of an individual. In turn, this affective style bias may act as a risk factor for, or exacerbate a person's vulnerability to, depression.

Analogously, an important consideration is that any relation between hemispheric asymmetry and resilience is more than likely a distal one, with many intervening processes between asymmetry and the process of resilience. In addition, discussing a phenomenon, such as hemispheric asymmetry in the context of resilience, provides an opportunity to state that there is certainly no one single biological characteristic or phenomenon that is ascendant in the process of resilience over the course of development. Across time, the relative importance of various biological systems for promoting resilience may vary within an individual.

Given these caveats, one immediately obvious application of findings concerning emotion and hemispheric asymmetry for the study of resilience would be to examine individual differences in prefrontal hemispheric EEG activation in individuals who have experienced significant adversity to discern whether or not those classified as resilient based on their psychological profiles demonstrated a different pattern of EEG asymmetry than those not characterized as resilient. An often-cited group of individual characteristics predictive of good adaptation in the context of risk includes positive self-perception, a positive outlook on life, and a good sense of humor (Masten & Reed, 2002). Given the importance of these individual characteristics as protective factors, it would be reasonable to hypothesize that resilient individuals might show greater left frontal baseline EEG activity. Moreover, evidence of good emotion regulation skills and lower emotional reactivity in individuals classified as resilient could lead to the hypothesis that individuals labeled as resilient may display less reactivity to emotionally toned stimuli, as measured by changes in frontal EEG asymmetry.

Neuroendocrinology, Immunology, and Resilience

A significant amount of research with a variety of species, including rodents, nonhuman primates, and humans, has been devoted to examining the effects that stress and adversity exert on the brain and neuroendocrine and immunological systems (for reviews, see Granger, Dreschel, & Shirtcliff, 2003; Gunnar, 1998; Kaufman, Plotsky, Nemeroff, & Charney, 2000; Kiecolt-Glaser, McGuire, Robles, & Glaser, 2002; Ladd et al., 2000; McEwen, 2000; Meaney et al., 1996; Sanchez et al., 2001; Sapolsky, 1992, 1996), as well as on cognitive performance (Heffelfinger & Newcomer, 2001). However, and more relevant to resilience, the important task that lies ahead is discerning the protective processes that serve to moderate the impact of adversity on neurobiological systems, and discovering the mechanisms by which these palliative forces come into play (e.g., Charney, 2004).

To date, research that has been conducted with rodents and nonhuman primates has demonstrated that traumatic events experienced early in life can modify typical behavioral, neuroendocrine, and immunological responsiveness; brain morphology' gene expression; and neurochemistry (Meaney, 2001; Meaney et al., 1996; Sanchez et al., 2001). Work conducted with humans experiencing adversity, including children reared in orphanages, children who reside in lower-socioeconomic environments, and children who have been abused or neglected, reveals similar negative consequences on stress and brain systems, as well as gene expression (Caspi et al., 2002; Cicchetti & Rogosch, 2001a, 2001b; Cicchetti & Walker, 2001; DeBellis, 2001; DeBellis, Baum, et al., 1999a; DeBellis, Keshavan, et al., 1999b; Foley et al., 2004; Gallo & Matthews, 2003; Gunnar et al., 2001; Lupien, King, Meaney, & McEwen, 2001).

The activation of the HPA axis in response to physical and psychological perturbations is adaptive and critical for the survival of challenges to the organism's homeostasis. In this sense, the stress response can be said to serve a protective function (McEwen, 1998). However, the chronic mobilization of the stress response (i.e., hypercortisolism) also can exert damaging, even pathogenic, effects on neurons (e.g., neuronal atrophy, neurotoxicity, and neuroendangerment; Bremner, 1999; McEwen & Sapolsky, 1995; Sapolsky, 1996, 2000a, 2000b). Moreover, the elimination of glucocorticoids (i.e., hypocortisolism) also can cause damage to neurons (Gunnar & Vazquez, 2001; Heim, Ehlert, & Hellhammer, 2000).

One primary means through which hormones affect behavior is via their impact on gene expression (McEwen, 1994; Watson & Gametchu, 1999). Stress hormones have been shown to exert direct effects on the genes that control brain structure and function, including neuronal growth, neurotransmitter synthesis, receptor density and sensitivity, and neurotransmitter reuptake (McEwen, 1994; Watson & Gametchu, 1999). The glucocorticoid receptors that reside in a cell's nucleus are responsible for the influence that stress hormones exert on the expression of genes that govern brain function (Watson & Gametchu, 1999). As noted earlier in this chapter, it has been demonstrated that chronic stress eventuates in a persistent inhibition of granule cell production and changes in the structure of the dentate gyrus, suggesting a mechanism whereby stress may alter hippocampal function (Gould & Tanapat, 1999).

Moreover, close, interpersonal relationships that are discordant also can be associated with the dysregulation of the immune system (Kiecolt-Glaser et al., 2002). Social stressors can cause neurotransmitters (e.g., the catecholamines) and stress hormones to elevate substantially; furthermore, these hormones and neuromodulators exert multiple immunomodulatory effects on the functioning of the immune system (Granger et al., 2003; Segerstrom, 2000). In addition, the experience of negative emotions, such as anxiety and depression, can exert a direct impact on the cells of the immune system by either up or down regulating the secretion of proinflammatory cytokines (Granger et al., 2003; Kiecolt-Glaser et al., 2002).

Importantly, research conducted with rodents demonstrates that early social experiences do not exert immutable negative consequences for the developing nervous system. For example, the results of investigations carried out by Francis et al. (1996; see also Meaney, 2001) have revealed that interventions, such as providing opportunities for maternal handling, licking, and grooming to rat pups who had experienced prolonged periods of maternal separation early in life, alter the central circuitry of emotion that results in these rat pups having a decreased responsivity to stress in later life (Meaney, 2001). Thus, these early interventions underscore the plasticity of emotion circuitry in rat pups. It remains to be discovered whether this circuitry is capable of being modified if interventions with rat pups who have experienced pronounced periods of early maternal separation are not provided until childhood or in adulthood.

In research with humans, Nachmias, Gunnar, Mangelsdorf, Parritz, and Buss (1996) found that a secure mother-child attachment relationship buffered the functioning of the HPA axis. Specifically, securely attached toddlers who were behaviorally inhibited did not exhibit significant elevations in cortisol, whereas insecurely attached toddlers who were behaviorally inhibited displayed significant elevations in cortisol. In addition, Gunnar, Brodersen, Nachmias, Buss, and Rigatuso (1996) discovered that attachment security moderated the cortisol response to the distress of inoculation. In particular, Gunnar et al. (1996) found that the combination of behavioral inhibition and insecure attachment resulted in these toddlers exhibiting elevated cortisol levels post inoculation. Taken together, these findings suggest that the sensitive caretaking that is characteristic of the mothers of securely attached youngsters may play an important role in the modulation of the HPA axis, especially if the child possesses a behaviorally inhibited temperament.

Gunnar and colleagues (2001) found that six and a half years postadoption, children who had been reared in Romanian orphanages for greater than 8 months in their 1st year of life had higher morning (AM) basal cortisol levels than did Romanian orphans who were adopted within the first 4 months of their lives. Moreover, the longer that the Romanian orphan children were institutionalized beyond 8 months, the higher were their AM basal cortisol levels. Intervention studies would help to ascertain whether the cortisol levels of the orphans who had been institutionalized greater than 8 months were modifiable, or whether such prolonged institutionalization exerted indelible effects on the HPA axis. Likewise, longitudinal follow-up of these children who were reared in Romanian orphanages could reveal whether the functioning of the HPA axis is stable and whether those children adopted before 4 months exhibit resilient functioning, whereas those who were adopted after 8 months of institutionalization display nonresilient functioning in middle childhood. Furthermore, assessments of the quality of the parent-child relationship and of family stress could enable the detection of some of the mediators linking early experience and later outcome.

Despite the fact that the experience of persistent stress is usually associated with deleterious biological and psychological outcomes, not all organisms are affected in the same fashion (Sapolsky, 1994). It is important to note, in keeping with the general systems theory concept of multifinality, that similar stressful experiences may not exert the same impact on biological and psychological functioning in different organisms. Furthermore, the same outcomes, be they positive or negative, that were the result of stressful experiences may have eventuated from different developmental pathways (i.e., equifinality).

The confluence of a number of factors, including physical status, genetic makeup, prior experience, and developmental history, determine the differential ways in which organisms may react to a stressful event (McEwen, 1994; Sapolsky, 1994). In particular, the combination of genetic makeup, previous experience, and developmental history could either sensitize or protect the organism from subsequent stressful challenges. Additionally, more long-term stress responsiveness is characterized by interindividual variability and is related, in part, to experiential influences

on gene expression (Meaney, 2001; Meaney et al., 1996). Thus, there are multiple converging pathways—including not only the neural networks that are activated by physical, psychological, and immunological stressors, but also the influence of genetics, early experience, and ongoing life events that determine the neural response to different stressors (McEwen, 1994; Sapolsky, 1994).

The ability to measure the functioning of the HPA axis through a variety of techniques enables researchers to more precisely quantify the "stress" component of diathesis-stress models of psychopathology and to examine the relation between stress and mental disorder. Moreover, the utilization of salivary biomarkers as relatively noninvasive measures of neuroendocrine and immune functioning makes it feasible for a larger number of researchers, including those investigating the pathways to, and correlates of, resilience, to implement neuroendocrinological and immunological assays into their work.

Among the most widely employed existing measures of neuroendocrine regulation are stress-reactivity paradigms that may increase HPA axis activity. There are several such procedures that are commonly utilized in the literature on HPA axis regulation. These include the Cold Pressor Test (CPT; Bullinger et al., 1984; Edelson & Robertson, 1986), the Trier Social Stress Test (TSST; Kirschbaum, Pirke, & Hellhammer, 1993), and maternal separation paradigms (Nachmias et al., 1996). For such paradigms, saliva for subsequent cortisol assaying is typically collected three times—once at baseline, 25 to 30 minutes poststressor, and once more 25 to 30 minutes after the second collection. A number of procedures also are used to index other aspects of HPA functioning, including assessments of the diurnal regulation of cortisol, 24-hour circadian rhythm collections, and biochemical challenge tests (Vazquez, 1998). Recently, salivary alpha-amylase, a surrogate marker of the sympathetic nervous system component of the stress response, has been employed to test biosocial models of stress vulnerability (Granger et al., in press). It has been discovered that patterns of salivary alpha-amylase stress reactivity differ from those obtained utilizing salivary cortisol measurements. These findings suggest that it is important to integrate measurement of the adrenergic component of the sympathetic nervous system, as indexed by alpha amylase, into investigations of normal development and psychopathology (Granger et al., in press). Furthermore, scientists have begun to examine multiple salivary biomarkers of neuroendocrine (e.g., cortisol and dehydroepiandrosterone [DHEA]) and immune functioning (e.g., IgA, Neopterin, and possibly cytokines), as well as neuroendocrine-immune system interactions (e.g., Granger et al., 2003; Granger, Hood, Dreschel, Sergeant, & Likos, 2001; Schwartz, Granger, Susman, Gunnar, & Laird, 1998).

The incorporation of these readily obtainable salivary biomarkers in prospective longitudinal studies that also collect psychological indicators of resilient functioning may serve to enhance the understanding of the pathways to competent adaptation in the face of adverse circumstance. For example, are individuals who function resiliently more likely to return to baseline levels of neuroendocrine functioning more quickly in stress-reactivity paradigms than are individuals who are not functioning in a resilient manner? Are individuals who function in a resilient fashion less likely to develop negative neurobiological sequelae despite experiencing extreme stress? When individuals who function resiliently do evidence harmful biological sequelae, do these individuals recover their function more readily than do nonresilient individuals (i.e., do individuals who function in a resilient manner manifest greater neural plasticity)? Finally, are individuals who function resiliently better able to regulate their allostatic load—the cumulative long-term effects of physiological responses to stress (McEwen, 1998; McEwen & Stellar, 1993)?

Because they play critical roles in numerous adaptive and harmful physiological outcomes, the neuroendocrine system and the sympathetic nervous system are considered among the major mediators of allostatic processes. Repetitive social challenges in a child's environment, such as being reared in an institution and being abused or neglected, can cause disruptions in basic homeostatic and regulatory processes that are central to the maintenance of optimal physical and mental health (Repetti, Taylor, & Seeman, 2002). It is conceivable (and indeed there is some evidence at the psychological level; see Cicchetti & Rogosch, 1997) that individuals who function resiliently are more adroit at coping with stress. Relatedly, might the ability of resilient individuals to cope successfully with stress be associated with healthy, well-regulated immune functioning? For example, can the activation of the cytokines, effector molecules that are hypothesized to mediate our classic sensory functions, affect developmental plasticity via their effect on emotional, cognitive, and behavioral processes (Granger et al., 2003)? Measures of neuroendocrine regulation and reactivity and of immune function must increasingly become a part of the measurement batteries used in studies on resilient adaptation.

Cognitive Processing and Resilience

A consistent finding across several studies of resilience is that better intellectual skills are associated with more pos-

itive outcomes in individuals reared in adverse environments (e.g., Cicchetti & Rogosch, 1997; Garmezy et al., 1984; Luthar & Zigler, 1992; Masten et al., 1999; White, Moffitt, & Silva, 1989). In these studies of resilience, intellectual functioning is primarily measured with traditional measures of intellectual ability (e.g., the Peabody Picture Vocabulary Test-Revised [PPVT-R]; Dunn & Dunn, 1981), that are assumed to reflect a heterogeneous set of underlying cognitive processes that are manifested behaviorally as intelligence and adaptive functioning. These processes may include, but are not limited to, memory, attention, reasoning, and behavioral inhibition. Unfortunately, the global nature of most of these indices has, for the most part, prohibited a direct examination of which (or if) individual components of cognition may be associated with resilience.

However, some preliminary work has examined the contribution of specific facets of cognitive functioning to resilient outcomes (Curtis, 2000). This investigation was, in part, based on previous findings indicating an association between cognitive functioning and academic and social competence (Pellegrini, Masten, Garmezy, & Ferrarese, 1987). Curtis (2000) examined the relation between resilience and a set of empirically derived components of cognition, including some aspects of attention, problem solving, inhibition, creative thinking, and humor in the Project Competence cohort, a longitudinal investigation of the correlates and pathways of adaptive functioning in the face of adversity (e.g., Masten et al., 1999). These components were drawn from several measures of cognitive functioning that were administered to a subset of 90 participants in the initial assessment of this cohort in the early 1980s, when they were approximately 8 years of age.

Three composite scales of cognitive functioning were derived from these measures through a process of correlation, factor analysis, and reliability analyses: verbal ability, problem solving, and attentional functioning. Performance on these composite scales was compared across individuals classified during adolescence into one of three groups based on their level of competence across salient developmental domains and adversity. This work demonstrated that individuals classified as resilient (high adversity, high competence) during adolescence had better problem-solving ability in middle childhood, and also performed better on some aspects of attentional functioning than individuals in the same cohort classified as maladaptive (high adversity, low competence). Superior performance on the measures making up this composite may reflect good executive functioning, which would include planning ability, logic, and general problem-solving skills in the context of interpersonal relationships.

These findings suggest that good functioning on certain cognitive processes is associated with resilience in this cohort, and also begin to provide a more detailed picture of what aspects of intelligence and superior intellectual functioning serve to promote resilience. However, considering the extreme complexity of the specific operations referred to as cognition, the problem-solving composite scale from this study is very nonspecific. A variety of interdependent cognitive skills involving the coordinated action of multiple neural networks are required to solve the problems associated with this scale and other traditional assessments of higher-order cognitive processes. In general, it is difficult to extrapolate from findings from paper and pencil measures of intellectual functioning to particular cognitive processes and brain structures that may be involved in such functioning; moreover, traditional tests of intellectual and cognitive functioning have not been tied to specific functional brain regions (other than the obvious linkage between the frontal cortex and higher-cognitive functioning). Neurocognitive measures that are able to differentiate performance on specific, circumscribed cognitive processes need to be employed in order to determine in more detail the cognitive abilities that may be associated with resilience, or that might serve as protective factors for good functioning in the context of adversity. In addition, without the application of brain-imaging techniques to determine the structural and functional attributes of specific neural substrates of cognitive abilities that may be associated with resilience, or at the very least data from neuropsychological measures that include tasks that have been tied to particular brain regions, it is impossible to determine with any degree of certainty which specific cognitive abilities might be associated with resilient functioning.

Assessment of Links between Cognition and Resilience

One assessment instrument in particular, the Cambridge Neuropsychological Testing Automated Battery (CANTAB), a computer-based neuropsychological test of nonverbal memory and executive functioning, would be well suited to examining the relation between cognitive functioning and resilience (Fray, Robbins, & Sahakian, 1996). Linkages between specific CANTAB tasks and neuroanatomical systems have been established in neuroimaging studies of adults (Owen, Evans, & Petrides, 1996). This assessment was originally developed to measure cognitive functioning in geriatric populations, although normative data on children's performance on the CANTAB has recently been published (Luciana & Nelson, 2002). This assessment instrument, while providing only an indirect assessment of brain functioning, would nonetheless be a relatively inexpensive and highly accessible option for examining linkages between specific aspects of cognition and resilience. Not only is CANTAB a highly sensitive and well-validated measure of a wide range of cognitive processes, but also it potentially would allow for the investigation of the differential contribution of a number of different types of cognitive processes to resilient functioning. For example, the CANTAB could be employed to examine whether superior ability in a particular type of memory process (e.g., spatial memory span, spatial working memory, recognition memory) contributed to resilient functioning, or, alternatively, whether those who exhibit resilient functioning may exhibit high functioning in multiple realms of memory. Also, one could examine the possible differential contribution of various types of executive functioning (e.g., inhibition, logical planning, and memory) to resilient functioning.

Brain Imaging, Cognition, and Resilience

Given the consistent association between greater intelligence and resilient functioning (e.g., Cicchetti & Rogosch, 1997; Garmezy et al., 1984; Luthar & Zigler, 1992; Masten et al., 1999), previous studies examining brain functioning in those of superior intellectual ability may have some relevance for the study of resilience. A fairly well-established body of research has directly examined brain functioning in individuals with superior intellectual ability, and to date most investigations directly examining brain activity and intelligence have suggested that the brains of individuals with superior intellectual abilities are less active during problem solving than those of individuals with average intellectual abilities (e.g., Haier, Siegel, Tang, Abel, & Buschbaum, 1992; Jausovec, 2000; Jausovec & Jausovec, 2001; O'Boyle, Benbow, & Alexander, 1995). In particular, PET studies have shown that brain metabolic activity is lower during problem-solving tasks for individuals of higher intelligence (e.g., Haier et al., 1988), whereas studies of EEG activity have shown that individuals with greater intellectual ability have less complex and more coherent EEG waveforms (Anokhin, Lutzenberger, & Birbaumer, 1999; Jausovec, 2000). In addition, more intelligent individuals show a decrease in the volume of activated gray matter during an oddball task (a simple discrimination task where the participant is instructed to respond to a low frequency event, such as the infrequent presentation, e.g., 20% probability, of the letter x in the context of the frequent presentation, e.g., 80% probability, of another letter), as shown using a method of low-resolution brain electromagnetic tomography (LORETA; Jausovec & Jausovec, 2001; Pascual-Marqui, Michel, & Lehmann, 1994).

These findings are generally interpreted as reflecting greater brain efficiency in those of superior intellectual ability, whereby brain areas not needed for good performance on a particular task are not utilized, while those areas specifically relevant to the task are used in a more concentrated fashion (Haier et al., 1992; Jausovec & Jausovec, 2000, 2001). In effect, fewer and more specific brain networks are activated during problem-solving tasks.

Other investigations have recently examined the location of the neural substrate mediating intellectual functioning. In a PET study by Duncan et al. (2000), these investigators found that a diverse set of tasks designed to tap general intelligence (Spearman's g), compared to a set of control tasks, were associated with selective neural activation in the lateral frontal cortex. This result suggests that general intelligence, rather than requiring the use of multiple brain areas, may derive from a specific neural system located in the frontal cortex that mediates many different types of cognitive demands. Gray, Chabris, and Braver (2003) employed an event-related fMRI design to examine the hypothesis that general fluid intelligence is mediated by brain regions that support attentional functioning. Utilizing a relatively large number of subjects ($n = 48$) for an fMRI study, Gray et al. (2003) were able to apply a multiple regression analysis to localize brain functioning to primarily the lateral prefrontal cortex during a demanding working memory task designed to be a test of general fluid intelligence. However, contradictory to many studies showing less brain activity in those with superior intellectual ability during problem solving, Gray et al. (2003) found that higher fluid intelligence, indexed by performance on Raven's Advanced Progressive Matrices (APM; Raven, Raven, & Court, 1998), was associated with greater activity in the lateral prefrontal cortex during a fairly difficult working memory task. It is possible that this finding is a result of the relatively highly challenging nature of the task administered, in comparison to more simple tasks employed in other studies of brain function and superior intelligence.

The ERP is an index of central nervous system functioning thought to reflect the underlying neurological processing of discrete stimuli (Hillyard & Picton, 1987). ERPs represent scalp-derived changes in brain electrical activity, believed to be generated by changes in membrane poten-

tials of nerve cells, thus reflecting activity associated with neuronal connections (Hugdahl, 1995; Nelson & Bloom, 1997). ERP data is collected across a discrete temporal window (typically a few seconds), obtained by averaging time-locked segments of the EEG that follow or precede the presentation of a stimulus. In this manner, ERPs allow for monitoring of neural activity associated with cognitive processing in real time (Donchin, Karis, Bashore, Coles, & Gratton, 1986). Their particular strength lies in the high temporal resolution they provide, allowing for a finely detailed examination of the timing of cognitive operations in the brain at the level of milliseconds.

Studies utilizing ERPs to examine brain electrophysiology and intelligence have consistently demonstrated that the amount of time for ERP wave forms to reach their peak amplitude is negatively correlated with IQ, indicating that cognitive operations may be occurring more rapidly in the brains of individuals with greater intellectual ability (e.g., Barrett & Eysenck, 1994; Bazana & Stelmack, 2002; Burns, Nettelbeck, & Cooper, 2000; Jausovec & Jausovec, 2001). In particular, it appears that this difference occurs in the P300 ERP component, and not in earlier occurring components associated with lower-level sensory processes (Jausovec & Jausovec, 2001). The P300 is generally viewed as reflecting cognitive processing related to learning as well as the transfer of sensory information about a stimulus into working memory, referred to as context updating (Donchin & Coles, 1988). Latency of the P300 is associated with the amount of time it takes for an individual to evaluate the novelty or significance of a stimulus, and is typically prolonged in individuals with neurodegenerative disorders (Donchin & Coles, 1988; Hugdahl, 1995).

Other investigations have measured the relation between resting brain activity and intellectual ability. Findings from these studies have been less conclusive, but, generally, greater EEG coherence has been shown to be associated with increased intellectual ability. It is assumed that increased coherence again reflects more efficient utilization of neural networks.

Unfortunately, most studies examining the relation between intelligence and brain functioning have not been designed to delineate the relation between brain functioning and particular aspects of intelligence. Hence, the tasks employed during these studies have not been specific to any particular cognitive process, but rather have been chosen to reflect intellectual ability in general. In addition, creativity has been controlled for in many of these studies, given that persons high on measures of creativity differ from those high only on intelligence with respect to brain activity during problem-solving tasks (e.g., Carlsson, Wendt, & Risberg, 2000; Jausovec, 2000).

A major difficulty in examining the role of intelligence in promoting resilience is the vastly complex constellation of cognitive and executive functioning skills possibly associated with performance on psychometric measures of intelligence. The association between performance on some executive function tasks and IQ is moderate at best; whereas some aspects of executive functioning appear not to have a relation with IQ (e.g., Luciana & Nelson, 2002), other studies have suggested that executive functioning, subserved by the frontal cortex, is one of the underlying essential functions of creativity (Carlsson et al., 2000). Finally, many basic cognitive processes, such as attention and memory, are clearly associated with psychometric indices of intellectual functioning, but exactly how is unclear.

Thus, the first step in examining the nature of the strong association of intellectual ability with resilience would be to determine which aspects of intellectual functioning were more or less important in their contribution to resilient functioning. For example, in the Curtis (2000) study, the verbal and performance scales of an intelligence assessment loaded on two different composites of cognitive functioning, with the performance scale differentiating resilient and nonresilient groups, whereas the verbal scale did not. More comprehensive neuropsychological assessment of resilient and nonresilient individuals, such as administration of entire IQ batteries rather than abbreviated versions, would be useful in determining which aspects of traditional psychometric intelligence were important in promoting resilience. Also, it is essential that many different components of cognition and executive functioning be assessed in order to determine what particular grouping of skills may be associated with resilience. It seems unlikely that any one aspect of cognition and executive functioning alone is the critical defining feature of resilience. Rather, it seems reasonable to hypothesize that strengths on a variety of cognitive and executive functions, such as memory, attention, flexible problem solving, and inhibition, contribute to resilient functioning. However, it is of critical importance to ascertain which of these processes does or does not contribute to resilience in order to inform prevention and intervention. Utilizing instruments, such as CANTAB, a measure of more subtle and specific aspects of neuropsychological functioning, is essential in the study of cognition, executive functioning, and resilience.

Going beyond traditional neuropsychological assessment, brain-imaging studies are an important methodology to apply to investigating the role of cognition and executive functioning in resilience. Although neuropsychological as-

sessments measure aspects of cognitive functioning and allow inferences to be drawn about the neural substrate(s) involved, it is essential to employ brain imaging in order to directly determine the temporal, structural, and functional aspects of cognition and the brain (Toga & Thompson, 2003). Brain imaging allows for the direct examination of the neural substrate involved with cognition and executive functioning in individuals classified as exhibiting resilient functioning. Neuroimaging methods, such as fMRI, also can be utilized to determine if aspects of brain functioning in such individuals are unique in some way compared to competent individuals not exposed to adversity.

In addition, ERPs also can be utilized to elucidate the possible relation between cognitive efficiency and resilience. In particular, two questions can be addressed. First, it would be useful to determine whether or not individuals classified as resilient demonstrate greater cognitive efficiency in general compared to individuals not demonstrating resilience. This could be accomplished by comparing peak latencies of the P300 during cognitive tasks, such as the oddball paradigm or a recognition memory task.

Secondly, it would be informative to compare cognitive efficiency on a variety of tasks to ascertain whether there is a specific type of cognitive function that resilient individuals are able to accomplish more efficiently, or if the efficiency is an overall strength, independent of the type of cognitive operation. In this regard, it also would be informative to compare resilient individuals with those exhibiting competent functioning but not exposed to adversity. It is possible that competent functioning, despite exposure to significant adversity, may be associated with cognitive efficiency in a different way than it is for individuals not exposed to adversity. This approach can help to elucidate, at the level of brain functioning, whether speed of processing is an underlying factor in resilience, and, if so, for which type of cognitive processes is this increased efficiency important in the context of resilient functioning.

Although ERPs are particularly advantageous in determining the chronology of neural processes, this methodology does not lend itself to the precise localization of these processes. FMRI, however, does enable the localization of brain functioning with relatively great precision (see Casey, Davidson, & Rosen, 2002 and de Haan & Thomas, 2002 for relevant reviews of this methodology). FMRI is a rapidly evolving technology that has exciting, but as of yet unexplored, potential in the study of resilience. In particular, application of this methodology would be extremely useful in examining questions about the role of cognition and executive functioning in promoting resilience. For example, it would enable the examination of whether cognitive operations of those classified as resilient took place in the same or perhaps different brain systems than those experiencing adversity but not classified as resilient.

Additionally, fMRI would allow direct examination of the impact of adversity on brain structures, such as the hippocampus, which has been shown to have decreased volume in patients diagnosed with PTSD related to war combat exposure or childhood sexual and/or physical abuse (e.g., Bremner et al., 1995, 1997; Gurvits et al., 1996; Stein, Koverola, Hanna, Torchia, & McClarty, 1997; Villarreal et al., 2002). Although the cause of this volumetric reduction has not been definitively established (in fact, it is possible that reduced hippocampal volume precedes, and is a risk factor for, PTSD), the predominant view, proposed by Bremner (1999), is that reduced hippocampal volume is a result of neurotoxic effects linked to traumatic events. This neurotoxic process appears to be due to an interaction between elevated levels of glucocorticioids and excitatory neurotransmitters (e.g., glutamate), with the specific, targeted effect on the hippocampus due to its high concentration of glucocorticoid receptors (for review of this process, see McEwen & Magarinos, 1997).

In the case of individuals classified as resilient who, by definition, have been exposed to significant adversity or trauma, it would be reasonable to formulate two hypotheses: (1) As a result of this exposure to adversity over time, such individuals may have reduced hippocampal volume compared to controls but do not show expected behavioral deficits in memory. Memory functioning in these individuals may be mediated by other neuroanatomical structures and networks, thus compensating for possible diminished functional capacity of the hippocampus, or (2) Resilient individuals, despite exposure to adversity or trauma, do not have reduced hippocampal volume. In either case, volumetric MRI studies to ascertain the degree to which, if any, the hippocampus has reduced volume could be employed. In addition, functional brain imaging studies utilizing fMRI would be useful to ascertain what compensatory mechanisms are being employed (if reduced hippocampal volume were confirmed).

MRI diffusion tensor imaging (DTI), a relatively new technique that allows imaging of white matter tracts that connect neural tissue across brain areas, also holds great promise in studying cognition and resilience. DTI has provided evidence of differences in intercortical connectivity in individuals with neuropsychiatric disorders (e.g., Kubicki et al., 2002; Lim et al., 1999). Application of this technique to the study of resilience could potentially demonstrate differences between resilient individuals, non-resilient individuals exposed to adversity, and competent in-dividuals not exposed to adversity in connectivity between regions of the cerebral cortex, possibly offering evidence of neural plasticity as one of the underlying mechanisms of resilient outcome.

Genetics and Resilience

From a genetic perspective, resilience can be conceptualized as the extent to which individuals at genetic risk for maladaptation and psychopathology are not affected (Garmezy & Streitman, 1974; Luthar et al., 2000; Rende & Plomin, 1993). Additionally, there may be genetic contributors to resilient adaptation that protect some individuals in families where there is a high genetic loading for developing maladaptation and mental disorder from succumbing to these deleterious outcomes. Moreover, genes are equally likely to serve a protective function against environmental insults for some individuals. Thus, it is apparent that genetic influences on maladaptation and psychopathology operate in a probabilistic and not a deterministic manner.

To date, there has been a paucity of investigations that have examined genetic contributors to resilient functioning. Rende and Plomin (1993) have explicated the ways in which the designs and methods of quantitative behavior genetics may be utilized to uncover the genetic and environmental contributions to resilience. Herein, we provide several examples of how molecular genetic techniques may be utilized to proffer insights into the pathways to resilient adaptation.

Buccal swab sampling procedures provide a relatively easy and painless method for collecting DNA from research participants (Freeman et al., 1997; Plomin & Rutter, 1998). The buccal swabs can be easily stored in the laboratory; subsequently, the DNA is purified, ideally as soon as possible, utilizing a DNA Extraction Kit. In the particular kit used in our laboratory, the extraction solution is alloquated in 0.5 ml amounts into sterilized DNAse and RNAse free 1.5 ml microcentrifuge tubes, which are labeled and stored in a freezer at—80°C until usage. The equipment needed to extract and purify DNA is relatively inexpensive, and the methodology is not difficult to learn. Hence, it is quite feasible for researchers without expertise in molecular genetics to carry out DNA extraction in their own laboratory. Alternatively, collaborations with geneticists in universities or medical school settings could facilitate the application of these techniques.

Polymerase Chain Reaction (PCR) is a quick, fairly cost-efficient technique for producing an unlimited number of copies of any gene. The powerful duplication ability of PCR enables researchers to utilize tiny amounts of cells or tissues (such as those obtained with the buccal swabbing technique) to amplify or copy DNA and to subsequently undertake molecular genetic analysis. Although PCR itself is not very expensive, the equipment necessary to conduct subsequent molecular genetic analyses, such as a gene sequencer, is substantially more costly. The relative ease with which DNA can be collected enables even developmental psychopathologists who are not well versed in molecular genetics to obtain DNA from participants and to examine the relation of this genetic material to normal, maladaptive, and resilient behavioral outcomes.

Recently, great progress has been made in the mechanisms involved in the study of gene expression. These advances provide exciting new opportunities for enhancing knowledge not only on the genesis and epigenesis of maladaptive development and mental disorders, but also of resilience. Molecular genetic methods now exist that enable researchers to investigate the expression of particular genes or of large numbers of genes simultaneously (so called "gene profiles"). Through the utilization of complementary DNA (or cDNA) microarrays, researchers can discover the type and quantity of messenger RNA (mRNA) being produced by a given cell, thereby indicating which genes are "turned on" (i.e., activated; Hacia & Collins, 1999; Mirnics, Middleton, Lewis, & Levitt, 2001; Raychaudhuri, Sutphin, Chang, & Altman, 2001). DNA microarrays can be utilized to index changes in the expression of genes that are essential for brain function (Greenberg, 2001; Walker & Walder, 2003). By examining the concurrent and longitudinal relations among environmental, gene expression, neurobiological, hormonal, and psychological processes in individuals who have experienced significant adversity, researchers may be in a stronger position to elucidate the development of resilient adaptation. Such multiple level of analysis investigations may reveal the mechanisms responsible for activating and inhibiting the expression of genes that are probabilistically associated with maladaptive developmental outcomes and psychopathology. Likewise, these multidisciplinary approaches may proffer insights into the mechanisms that "turn on" genes that may serve a protective function for individuals experiencing significant adversity.

Utilizing animal models of learning and gene expression, several studies have begun to show a direct link between the gene expression process and structural changes in the brain that result from learning. For example, Post et al. (1998) found higher levels of mRNA and nerve growth factor (NGF) in the visual cortex and hippocampus of rats exposed to an enriched environment for 30 days, evidence that a gene transcription process was occurring. Training on a passive avoidance task resulted in significant elevation of c-*fos* mRNA levels in the chick forebrain. A gene expression transcription factor (Anokhin, Mileusnic, Shamakina, & Rose, 1991) and C-*fos* induction also has been found in the rat brain after shuttle-box training (Maleeva, Ivolgina, Anokhin, & Limborskaya, 1989), as well as in Purkinje cells in the cerebellar paramedian lobule following training of rats in a reaching task (Alcantra et al., 1991). Also, the transcription factor zif-268 has been found in the visual cortex of rats only 4 days after being placed in an enriched environment (Wallace, Withers, Weiler, & Greenough, 1991).

Thus, at the level of learning and cognition, gene expression and the subsequent cascade of processes that eventuate in structural changes in neural substrate may be one process that could be examined as a correlate of resilience. Gene expression in learning, which comes about as a result of transactions with the environment, is perhaps the foundation upon which positive adaptation to adversity is built. In addition, this multilevel perspective, showing linkages among gene expression, neurochemistry, neuroanatomy, and experiences in the environment, again points to the importance of a multiple-levels-of-analysis approach to the study of resilience.

Other work in the area of gene expression has demonstrated the relation of this process to the development of psychopathology in humans. For example, changes in gene expression due to environmental adversities have been implicated in the development of affective disorders (e.g., Post et al., 1994; Post et al., 2003). Similar to the evocation of gene expression through interaction with the environment in animal models of learning, Post et al. (1994) hypothesized that acute events in the environment can have a permanent impact on gene expression, thus accounting for long-lasting changes in subsequent behavioral responses to stressors in the environment. Thus, the interplay of early experience and gene expression processes can potentially lead to vulnerability, depression, posttraumatic stress disorder, and other disorders possibly rooted in changes in gene expression (e.g., Schizophrenia; Post et al., 1994). This formulation, a model based on electrophysiological kindling and behavioral sensitization to psychomotor stimulants and stress, emphasizes an active and dynamic process of transactions between genetic vulnerabilities and experientially mediated effects on gene expression over the entire life span. Also, Post et al. (2003) have theorized that, in addition to pathological changes in gene expression that eventuate in affective disorders, there may in fact be changes in gene expression that are adaptive and possibly serve as endogenous antidepressant mechanisms. Post et al. (2003) suggest that the proportion of pathological and adaptive changes in gene expression may be a key determining factor in an individual's propensity to have recurring episodes of affective disorder. Likewise, individuals classified as resilient may be found to have a higher proportion of adaptive gene expression processes, allowing them to maintain positive behavioral adaptation in spite of adversity (see also Cicchetti, 2003).

Very recently, molecular genetic methods have been utilized to examine the role that genetic factors, in interaction with social experience, might play in the epigenesis of maladaptive behavior. In a large, longitudinal birth cohort of male children who were studied from birth to adulthood, the investigators sought to determine why some maltreated children grow up to develop antisocial behavior where other maltreated children do not (Caspi et al., 2002). It was discovered that a functional polymorphism in the gene-encoding the neurotransmitter-metabolizing enzyme monoamine oxidase A (MAOA) moderated the effect of maltreatment. Polymorphisms are common variations that occur in the sequence of DNA among individuals. Specifically, a polymorphism is a gene that exists in more than one version (or allele), and where the rare form of the allele occurs in greater than 2% of the population. Caspi and colleagues (2002) found that the effect of child maltreatment on antisocial behavior was far less among males with high MAOA activity than among those with low MAOA activity. The investigators interpreted their findings as providing evidence that a functional polymorphism in the MAOA gene moderates the impact of early child abuse and neglect on the development of male antisocial behavior (Caspi et al., 2002).

Of relevance to research on resilience, it is conceivable that the gene for high MAOA activity may serve a protective function against the development of antisocial behavior in maltreated children (Cicchetti & Blender, 2004). Maltreated children grow up in highly stressful environments. The results of the Caspi et al. (2002) investigation suggest that some maltreated children, but not others, develop antisocial behavior via the effect that neurotransmitter system development exerts on stressful experiences. Specifically, the probability that child maltreatment will eventuate in adult violence is greatly increased among children whose MAOA is not sufficient to render maltreatment-induced changes in neurotransmitter systems inactive (Caspi et al., 2002). Thus, a gene x environment interaction appears to determine which maltreated children will, and will not, de-

velop antisocial behavior. These findings are compelling and this investigation is one of the first studies to document a genetic contribution to resilience in humans. We urge researchers to conduct additional molecular genetic studies with other samples of humans who experience similar and different types of significant adversity in order to ascertain the mechanisms underlying resilient adaptation.

CONCLUSION AND FUTURE DIRECTIONS

Although many questions remain unanswered, a great deal of progress has been made in our understanding of the construct of resilience (Luthar, 2003; Luthar et al., 2000; Masten, 2001). Much of the research focused on elucidating the correlates of, and contributors to, resilient functioning has utilized child, family, and contextual assessments (Luthar, 2003; Luthar et al., 2000). We have emphasized that the time has come to incorporate biological measures into research programs examining the determinants of resilient adaptation. We also assert that the inclusion of biological measures into the psychological research armamentaria currently employed in resilience research, as well as in resilience-promoting interventions, results in a more precise understanding of the mediators and moderators underlying resilience.

Now that the theories and neuroscience techniques are available, and since our understanding of brain development and functioning in both normality and psychopathology has grown, it seems necessary to inquire as to why there has been no research to date conducted on the biological correlates of, and contributors to, resilient adaptation. One impediment to the incorporation of biology into the field of resilience research is that most investigators who examine pathways to resilient functioning have not been trained in the various neuroscience approaches (e.g., molecular genetics, neuroimaging, psychophysiology, neuroendocrinology, immunology). Regardless, this state of affairs can be modified through a number of avenues, including: (1) changing existing training programs and philosophies for graduate and medical students; (2) fostering interdisciplinary and multidisciplinary collaborations; and (3) providing incentives and opportunities for faculty to acquire knowledge and expertise in one or more new scientific areas.

Perhaps an even larger reason for the absence of biological variables in research on resilient functioning is that evidence for the role of biology in resilience could be interpreted as representing a personal attribute of the individual and that if only the individual had this biological characteristic, then he or she could have withstood the adversities to which the individual was exposed. In essence, the individual could be blamed for not possessing the needed characteristics to function resiliently.

However, as the theoretical underpinnings of research in developmental psychopathology, dynamic developmental systems theory, and developmental neuroscience illustrate, the belief that the identification of a biological factor would inevitably result in resilience (or maladaptation for that matter) is fallacious. Our viewpoint does not reduce resilience to biology, let alone to a unitary biological variable. A multiple-levels-of-analysis perspective to resilience should not be misinterpreted as equating resilience with biology. Moreover, the inclusion of a biological perspective in resilience research should not hearken scientists back to the time when some espoused the view that there were "invulnerable" children.

To the contrary, existing theories in developmental neuroscience are very compatible with organizational and systems theories in the fields of developmental psychology and psychopathology (see Cicchetti & Cannon, 1999a, 1999b; Cicchetti & Walker, 2001, 2003). The incorporation of a biological perspective into research on resilience still requires adherence to a dynamic, transactional view that respects the importance of context. Omitting biology from the resilience equation is tantamount to omitting psychology. Biological and psychological domains are both essential to include in basic research on resilience and in resilience-promoting interventions. If we are to grasp the true complexity of the concept of resilience, then we must investigate it with a commensurate level of complexity.

Regardless of whether it may be a normal or abnormal neural system, building a brain is a dynamic, self-organizing, genetic and epigenetic, multilevel process that unfolds from the prenatal period throughout adulthood. We think that it has become essential for investigators in the disciplines of developmental neuroscience and developmental psychopathology to carry out prospective longitudinal studies that examine the same individuals over developmental time utilizing a multiple-levels-of-analysis perspective. Research also must be conducted to elucidate the similarities and differences in the fundamental neural mechanisms involved in the development of various mental disorders. Furthermore, additional molecular biological investigations on the structure and function of genes and protein involved in neural proliferation, migration, and differentiations must be implemented (Nowakowski & Hayes, 1999).

Moreover, it is important that investigations with human participants be undertaken to ascertain whether, and if so, how, specific environmental occurrences, such as the presence of serious psychopathology in caregivers, child maltreatment, repeated fostercare placement, residing in an orphanage, and/or having a mental disorder, selectively exert a deleterious impact on the development of children's various neurobiological systems as a function of the timing and duration of exposure to these adverse experiences (Cicchetti, 2002; Dawson, Ashman, & Carver, 2000; Gunnar et al., 2001; Parker & Nelson, 2005a). In a related vein, investigations must be conducted to discover what, if any, particular aspects of parenting foster optimal brain development and function in children (Bruer, 1999; Nelson, 2000b).

Now that it is evident that experience can impact the microstructure and biochemistry of the brain, a vital role for very early and continuing neural plasticity throughout epigenesis in contributing to the development of, and recovery from, various forms of maladaption and psychopathology is suggested. Research has revealed that some early lesions may not be easily reversible, despite the historically prevalent belief that brain insults occurring near the beginning of development were most amenable to reorganization and repair. Conversely, contemporary neurobiological research suggests that in some domains (e.g., sensory, motor, cognitive, memory, and linguistic) and in some areas of the brain, plasticity is possible, including new neuron generation, well into adulthood (Cicchetti & Tucker, 1994a, 1994b; Nelson, 2000a). Moreover, future research must be conducted to examine the limits of plasticity in the social and emotional domains (see Davidson, 2000; Davidson, Jackson, & Kalin, 2000, for evidence of neural plasticity in the central circuitry of emotion). It also is essential to discover the mechanisms whereby latent progenitor cells are controlled and glial cell activation is modulated, in order to elucidate the bases of the brain's self-repair processes across various neurobiological systems (Lowenstein & Parent, 1999). If scientists can discover the mechanisms underlying the neural plasticity of the circuits of specific domains in individuals with various high-risk conditions and mental disorders, then such information should provide crucial insights for prevention and intervention efforts.

In this regard, prevention research can be conceptualized as true experiments in altering the course of development, thereby providing insight into the etiology and pathogenesis of disordered outcomes (Cicchetti & Hinshaw, 2002). Relatedly, the time has come increasingly to conduct interventions that not only assess behavioral changes, but also ascertain whether abnormal neurobiological structures, functions, and organizations are modifiable or are refractory to intervention (Cicchetti, 1996). There is growing evidence that successful intervention modifies not only maladaptive behavior but also the cellular and physiological correlates of behavior (Kandel, 1979, 1998, 1999).

Unlike the belief espoused by Huttenlocher (1984) that "intervention programs, to be effective, would have to be implemented during [the] early prenatal period, and certainly prior to school age, by which time synaptic and neuronal plasticity appears to be greatly diminished, if not totally lost" (p. 495), recent demonstrations of plasticity across an array of developmental systems suggest that interventions have promise to exert ameliorative effects long beyond the early years of life (Bruer, 1999; Nelson, 2000b). A major implication of a dynamic developmental systems approach is that the implementation of intervention closely following the experience of trauma or an episode of mental illness should ameliorate the intensity and severity of the response to the illness, as well as the illness course (Toth & Cicchetti, 1999). Such interventions that are closely timed to trauma and disorder onset also should decrease the probability of developing, in a use-dependent fashion, sensitized neural systems that may cascade across development (Post et al., 1998).

As Nelson (2000b) has articulated, "the efficacy of any given intervention will depend on the capacity of the nervous system (at the cellular, metabolic, or anatomic levels) to be modified by experience" (p. 204). Likewise, Nowakowski (1987) asserted that "in order to understand how a modification in a developmental process exerts its influences, it is essential to know where the developmental process is being modified, how the structure of the mature brain will be changed, and how the structural changes that are produced will change the ability of the brain to process the information it confronts during a complex behavioral task" (pp. 568–569). Successful psychotherapy, behavioral therapy, or pharmacotherapy should change behavior and physiology by producing alterations in gene expression (transcription) that produce new structural changes in the brain (Kandel, 1979, 1999). For example, as discussed earlier, stress has been demonstrated to suppress the birth of new neurons in adulthood (see also Sapolsky, 2000a, 2000b), and serotonin has been shown to enhance the rate of neurogenesis in the dentate gyrus. Extrapolating from these findings, Jacobs and colleagues (2000) hypothesized that stress-induced decreases in dentate gyrus neurogenesis play an important causal role in precipitating episodes of major depressive disorder. Reciprocally, pharmacotherapeutic interventions for depression that increase the neurotransmission of serotonin work at least partly through their role in augmenting the birth of new neurons in the dentate gyrus, thereby contributing to the recovery from episodes of clinical depression.

A number of antidepressants have been shown to increase adult neurogenesis in the hippocampus. Santarelli and colleagues (2003) conducted a study to ascertain the functional significance of this phenomenon. These investigators demonstrated that the disruption of antidepressant-induced neurogenesis in serotonin 1A receptor null mice also blocked their behavioral responses to fluoxetine, a selective serotonin reuptake inhibitor. The results of the Santarelli et al. (2003) investigation provide suggestive evidence that the behavioral effects of antidepressant drugs may be mediated by the stimulation of neurogenesis in the hippocampus.

A substantial amount of research literature suggests that not all individuals who have similar vulnerabilities and who have been exposed to similar adverse experiences develop in a similar fashion (Luthar, 2003; Luthar et al., 2000; Masten, 2001). For example, although child maltreatment can exert a negative impact on the structure, functioning, and organization of the developing brain, it does not appear that the brains of all maltreated children are affected in the same manner. Moreover, because some maltreated children function resiliently despite having been exposed to significant adversity (Cicchetti & Rogosch, 1997; Cicchetti et al., 1993), it is likely that the experience of child abuse and neglect may exert different effects on the neurobiological structure, function, and organization in well-functioning maltreated children than it does in the typical maltreated child. Accordingly, there may be an enhanced neural plasticity in resilient individuals.

Thus, it appears that the impact of life experiences, such as child maltreatment and mental disorder, on brain microstructure and biochemistry may be either pathological or adaptive. In the future, neuroimaging investigations should be conducted in order to discern whether the brain structure, functioning, and organization of individuals who are functioning extremely well despite being exposed to significant adversity and/or having vulnerabilities to mental disorder differ from those individuals with similar experience and/or vulnerabilities who are functioning less adaptively.

Presently, we do not know if the neurobiological difficulties displayed by some persons with mental disorders or individuals who have experienced significant life adversity are irreversible or whether there are particular sensitive periods when it is more likely that neural plasticity will occur.

Moreover, it is not known whether some neural systems may be more plastic than other neural systems or whether there are particular sensitive periods when it is more likely that neural plasticity will occur. Furthermore, it is not known whether particular neural systems may be more refractory to change or have a more time-limited window when neural plasticity can occur. Consequently, it is critical that research investigations on the correlates and determinants of resilient adaptation begin to incorporate neurobiological and molecular genetic methods into their predominantly psychological measurement armamentaria (Curtis & Cicchetti, 2003).

Luthar and Cicchetti (2000) concluded that research on resilience "should target protective and vulnerability forces at multiple levels of influence" (p. 878). The incorporation of a neurobiological framework and the utilization of genetically sensitive designs into interventions seeking to promote resilient functioning or to repair positive adaptation gone awry may contribute to the ability to design individualized interventions that are based on knowledge gleaned from multiple biological and psychological levels of analysis. For example, if an individual has the polymorphism for a gene that is probabilistically associated with a particular negative behavioral outcome and if it is known how this polymorphism affects a specific neurotransmitter system, then psychopharmacological treatment can be initiated (Cicchetti & Blender, 2004). Similarly, because stressful experiences can harm the brain (e.g., Bremner, 1999; McEwen & Magarinos, 1997), biological and psychological intervention techniques can be provided to help an individual to better understand and cope with stressful situations. The identification of stress-sensitive neural processes may ultimately provide a basis for the formation of pharmacological and behavioral interventions to ameliorate the deleterious effects of early traumatic experiences (Kaufman et al., 2000; see also Post et al., 2003). Moreover, the inclusion of neurobiological assessments in evaluations of interventions designed to foster resilience enables scientists to discover whether the various components of multifaceted interventions each exert a differential impact on separate brain systems. We think that is it possible to conceptualize successful resilience-promoting interventions as examples of experience-dependent neural plasticity. If assessments of biological systems are routinely incorporated into the measurement batteries employed in resilience-facilitating interventions, then we will be in a position to discover whether the nervous systems have been modified by experience.

Despite the fact that we separately described the biological assessments that we believed would augment our knowledge base in resilience, we advocate that researchers investigating basic processes contributing to resilience and those conducting and evaluating interventions that strive to promote resilience and return function to positive levels of adaptation incorporate a multiple-levels-of-analysis approach (see Cicchetti & Dawson, 2002). Adopting such an approach is essential because, in actuality, biological and psychological systems interact and transact with one another throughout the course of development (Cicchetti & Tucker, 1994a; Gottlieb, 1992).

Furthermore, many of the biological processes that have been discussed in this chapter as possibly being related to resilience are in fact normative processes. For example, neural plasticity is one such process that has clearly been shown to be an inherent property of the central nervous system. This highlights an interesting parallel to a suggestion put forth by Masten (2001), who discusses resilience as an ordinary phenomenon that may mostly come about through the operation of "basic human adaptational systems." This perspective stresses that, although resilience is a valid, identifiable phenomenon, extraordinary individual qualities may not be necessary in order to overcome adversity. Likewise, at the biological level of analysis, normative processes may mediate resilient outcomes, as long as these systems are functioning within normal parameters. This viewpoint serves to underscore the importance of the interaction of normative systems at all levels of analysis in the promotion of resilience.

Several scholars have contended that the construct of resilience adds nothing to the more general term "positive adjustment" (see review in Luthar, Cicchetti, & Becher, 2000). Because empirical evidence has demonstrated that there are different patterns of positive adjustment that occur with and without adversity and given that there are several studies indicating that the pathways to resilience and positive adaptation may differ, it is indeed likely that positive adaptation and resilience reflect distinct constructs (Luthar et al., 2000). Moreover, the incorporation of biological and genetic measures and methods into research that strives to differentiate between individuals who function well in adversity and those who function well without (or with minimal) adversity may reveal differential neurobiological and genetic correlates of, and contributors to, resilience and positive adaptation, respectively. If distinctions between those two constructs can be made at the neurobiological, molecular genetic, and behavioral levels, then there would be strong evidence for the distinctiveness of positive adaptation and resilience.

In the beginning of the twenty-first century, it is imperative that the field of developmental psychopathology adopts a multiple-levels-of-analysis approach to the study of both deviant and adaptive functioning. New programs of research must take into account both normal and abnormal developmental processes in examining psychopathology, and intervention studies must be undertaken in order to more fully establish the characteristics of and processes underlying brain-behaviors relations. Most importantly, beyond the calls for research programs incorporating multiple levels of analysis seen in recent overviews of the field (e.g., Cicchetti & Blender, 2004; Cicchetti & Dawson, 2002), such research must actually be supported by funding agencies, many of which still view multiple-levels-of-analysis approaches to research questions as too broad and risky to merit financial support. In addition, journal editors also need to encourage such research by increasing their willingness to publish papers that investigate a phenomenon across multiple levels of analysis, some of which might fall somewhat outside the purview of the particular journal. Furthermore, research in developmental psychopathology that is driven by broadly based theory incorporating multiple levels of analysis must be increasingly encouraged by faculty in the context of graduate training.

In order to ensure that future generations of scholars in developmental psychopathology are exposed to a broad, dynamic, systems-based, multiple-levels-of-analysis perspective, graduate and undergraduate programs in clinical and developmental psychology should encourage students to take courses in a broad spectrum of areas (Cicchetti & Toth, 1991; Pellmar & Eisenberg, 2000). These might include courses on basic neurobiology, neuroendocrinology, and developmental processes, as well as courses that incorporate information on brain-imaging technology, molecular genetic methods, neuroendocrine assay techniques, and other tools involved in assessing neurobiological and genetic processes. Likewise, students in basic science areas, such as neuroscience or molecular genetics, should be encouraged to gain exposure to the fundamentals of basic normative and atypical developmental processes. Further, specific interdisciplinary programs, for both students and faculty, spanning interest areas from clinical intervention to basic neuroscience, would help to foster communication and collaborative research endeavors between the fields of developmental neuroscience and development psychopathology (see, e.g., Cicchetti & Posner, 2005).

ACKNOWLEDGMENTS

We gratefully acknowledge the support of the Spunk Fund, Inc. in the writing of this chapter.

REFERENCES

Aglioti, S., Bonazzi, A., & Cortese, F. (1994). Phantom lower limb as a perceptual marker of neural plasticity in the mature human brain. *Proceedings of the Royal Society of London Bulletin, 225,* 273–278.

Ahern, G. L., & Schwartz, G. E. (1985). Differential lateralization for positive and negative emotion in the human brain: EEG spectral analysis. *Neuropsychologia, 23,* 745–755.

Akshoomoff, N., Courchesne, E., & Townsend, J. (1997). Attention coordination and anticipatory control. In J. D. Schmahmann (Ed.), *The cerebellum and cognition* (pp. 575–598). San Diego, CA: Academic Press.

Akshoomoff, N., Pierce, K., & Courchesne, E. (2002). The neurobiological basis of Autism from a developmental perspective. *Development and Psychopathology, 14,* 613–634.

Alberts, B., Bray, D., Lewis, J., Raff, M., Roberts, K., & Watson, J. D. (1994). *Molecular biology of the cell* (3rd ed.). New York: Guilford Press.

Albright, T. D., Jessell, T. M., Kandel, E. R., & Posner, M. I. (2000). Neural science: A century of progress and the mysteries that remain. *Cell, 100,* S1–S55.

Alcantra, A. A., Saks, N. D., & Greenough, W. T. (1991). Fos is expressed in the rat during forelimb reaching task. *Society for Neuroscience Abstracts, 17,* 141.

Allen, G., Buxton, R. B., Wong, E. C., & Courchesne, E. (1997). Attentional activation of the cerebellum independent of motor involvement. *Science, 275,* 1940–1943.

Allen, G., & Courchesne, E. (1998). The cerebellum and non-motor function: Clinical implications. *Molecular Psychiatry, 3,* 207–210.

Allen, G., Muller, R.-A., & Courchesne, E. (2004). Cerebellar function in Autism: Functional magnetic resonance image activation during a simple motor task. *Biological Psychiatry, 56,* 269–278.

Allen, J. J., Iacono, W. G., Depue, R. A., & Arbisi, P. (1993). Regional electroencephalographic asymmetries in bipolar seasonal affective disorder before and after exposure to bright light. *Biological Psychiatry, 33,* 642–646.

American Psychiatric Association. (1994). *Diagnostic and statistical manual of mental disorders* (4th ed.). Washington, DC: Author.

Anokhin, A. P., Lutzenberger, W., & Birbaumer, N. (1999). Spatiotemporal organization of brain dynamics and intelligence: An EEG study in adolescents. *International Journal of Psychophysiology, 33,* 259–273.

Anokhin, K. V., Mileusnic, R., Shamakina, I. Y., & Roase, S. P. R. (1991). Effects of early experience of c-fos gene expression in the chick forebrain. *Brain Research, 544,* 101–107.

Anthony, E. J. (1974). Introduction: The syndrome of the psychologically invulnerable child. In E. J. Anthony & C. Koupernik (Eds.), *The child in his family: Children at psychiatric risk* (Vol. 3, pp. 3–10). New York: Wiley.

Arnold, S. E. (1999). Neurodevelopment abnormalities in Schizophrenia: Insights from neuropathology. *Development and Psychopathology, 11,* 439–456.

Aylward, E. H., Minshew, N. J., Field, K., Sparks, B. F., & Singh, N. (2002). Effects of age on brain volume and head circumference in Autism. *Neurology, 59,* 175–183.

Bachevalier, J. (1996). Brief report: Medial temporal lobe and Autism: A putative animal model in primates. *Journal of Autism and Developmental Disorders, 26,* 217–220.

Bachevalier, J., & Loveland, K. A. (2003). Early orbitofrontal-limbic dysfunction and Autism. In D. Cicchetti & E. Walker (Eds.), *Neurodevelopmental mechanisms in psychopathology* (pp. 215–236). New York: Cambridge University Press.

Bailey, A., Luthert, P., Dean, A., Harding, B., Janota, I., Montgomery, M., et al. (1998). A clinicopathological study of Autism. *Brain, 121,* 889–905.

Baron-Cohen, S., Ring, H. A., Bullmore, E. T., Wheelwright, S., Ashwin, C., & Williams, S. C. (2000). The amygdala theory of Autism. *Neuroscience and Biobehavioral Reviews, 24,* 335–364.

Barrett, P. T., & Eysenck, H. J. (1994). The relationship between evoked potential component amplitude, latency, contour length, variability, zero-crossings, and psychometric intelligence. *Personality and Individual Differences, 16,* 3–32.

Bavelier, D., & Neville, H. J. (2002). Cross-modal plasticity: Where and how? *Nature Reviews in Neuroscience, 3,* 443–452.

Baxter, L. R., Schwartz, J. M., Phelps, M. E., Mazziotta, J. C., Guze, B. H., Selin, C. E., et al. (1989). Reduction in prefrontal cortex glucose metabolism common to three types of depression. *Archives of General Psychiatry, 46,* 243–250.

Bazana, P. G., & Stelmack, R. M. (2002). Intelligence and information processing during an auditory discrimination task with backward masking: An event-related potential analysis. *Journal of Personality and Social Psychology, 83,* 998–1008.

Bell, M. A., & Fox, N. A. (1994). Brain development over the first year of life: Relations between EEG frequency and coherence and cognitive and affective behaviors. In G. Dawson & K. Fischer (Eds.), *Human behavior and the developing brain* (pp. 314–345). New York: Guilford Press.

Bender, L. (1947). Childhood Schizophrenia: Clinical study of 100 schizophrenic children. *American Journal of Orthopsychiatry, 17,* 40–56.

Benes, F. M. (1989). Myelination of cortical-hippocampal relays during late adolescence: Anatomical correlates to the onset of Schizophrenia. *Schizophrenia Bulletin, 15,* 585–594.

Benes, F. M. (1995). A neurodevelopmental approach to the understanding of Schizophrenia and other mental disorders. In D. Cicchetti & D. J. Cohen (Eds.), *Developmental psychopathology: Vol. 1. Theory and methods* (pp. 227–253). New York: Wiley.

Benes, F. M. (1997). Corticolimbic circuitry and the development of psychopathology during childhood and adolescence. In N. A. Krasnegor & G. R. Lyons (Eds.), *Development of the prefrontal cortex: Evolution, neurobiology, and behavior* (pp. 211–239). Baltimore: Paul H. Brookes.

Benes, F. M., Turtle, M., Khan, Y., & Farol, P. (1994). Myelination of a key relay zone in the hippocampal formation occurs in the human brain during childhood, adolescence, and adulthood. *Archives of General Psychiatry, 51,* 477–484.

Bennett, E. L. (1976). Cerebral effects of differential experiences and training. In M. R. Rosenzweig & E. L. Bennett (Eds.), *Neural mechanisms of learning and memory* (pp. 279–289). Cambridge, MA: MIT Press.

Bennett, E. L., Diamond, M. C., Krech, D., & Rosenzweig, M. R. (1964). Chemical and anatomical plasticity of the brain. *Science, 46,* 610–619.

Bertenthal, B., Campos, J., & Barrett, K. (1984). Self-produced locomotion: An organizer of emotional, cognitive, and social development in infancy. In R. Emde & R. Harmon (Eds.), *Continuities and discontinuities in development* (pp. 175–210). New York: Plenum Press.

Bettelheim, B. (1967). *The empty fortress.* New York: Free Press.

Black, J. E., & Greenough, W. T. (1992). Induction of pattern in neural structure by experience: Implications for cognitive development. In M. Lamb, A. Brown, & B. Rogoff (Eds.), *Advances in developmental psychology* (Vol. 4, pp. 1–50). Hillsdale, NJ: Erlbaum.

Black, J. E., Jones, T. A., Nelson, C. A., & Greenough, W. T. (1998). Neuronal plasticity and the developing brain. In N. E. Alessi, J. T. Coyle, S. I. Harrison, & S. Eth (Eds.), *Handbook of child and adolescent psychiatry* (pp. 31–53). New York: Wiley.

Bolton, D., & Hill, J. (1996). *Mind, meaning, and mental disorder: The nature of causal explanation in psychology and psychiatry.* Oxford, England Oxford University Press.

Boyce, W. T., Frank, E., Jensen, P. S., Kessler, R. C., Nelson, C. A., Steinberg, L., et al. (1998). Social context in developmental psychopathology: Recommendations for future research from the MacArthur Network on Psychopathology and Development. *Development and Psychopathology, 10,* 143–164.

Bradley, M. M., Cuthbert, B. N., & Lang, P. J. (1993). Pictures as prepulse: Attention and emotion in startle modification. *Psychophysiology, 30,* 541–545.

Bremner, J. D. (1999). Does stress damage the brain? *Biological Psychiatry, 45,* 797–805.

Bremner, J. D., Randall, P., Scott, M., Bronen, R., Seibyl, J., Southwick, S. M., et al. (1995). MRI-based measurement of hippocampal volume in patients with combat-related posttraumatic stress disorder. *American Journal of Psychiatry, 152,* 973–981.

Bremner, J. D., Randall, P., Vermetten, E., Staib, L., Bronen, R. A., Mazure, C. J., et al. (1997). Magnetic resonance imaging-based measurement of hippocampal volume in posttraumatic stress disorder related to childhood physical and sexual abuse-a preliminary report. *Biological Psychiatry, 41,* 23–32.

Breslin, N. A., & Weinberger, D. R. (1990). Schizophrenia and the normal functional development of the prefrontal cortex. *Development and Psychopathology, 2,* 409–424.

Brown, A. S., Begg, M. D., Gravenstein, S., Schaefer, C. A., Wyatt, R. J., Bresnahan, M. A., et al. (2004). Serologic evidence for prenatal influenza in the etiology of Schizophrenia. *Archives of General Psychiatry, 61,* 774–780.

Brown, A. S., Schaefer, C. A., Quesenberry, C. P., Liu, L., Babulas, V. P., & Susser, E. S. (2005). Maternal exposure to toxoplasmosis and risk of Schizophrenia in adult offspring. *American Journal of Psychiatry, 162*(4), 767–773.

Brown, J. W. (1994). Morphogenesis and mental process. *Development and Psychopathology, 6,* 551–563.

Brown, R. T. (1968). Early experience and problem-solving ability. *Journal of Comparative and Physiological Psychology, 65,* 433–440.

Bruer, J. (1999). *The myth of the first three years: A new understanding of early brain development and lifelong learning.* New York: Free Press.

Bullinger, M., Naber, D., Pickary, D., Cohen, R. M., Kalin, N. H., & Pert, A. (1984). Endocrine effects of the cold pressor test: Relationships to subjective pain appraisal and coping. *Psychiatry Research, 12,* 227–233.

Burns, N. R., Nettelbeck, T., & Cooper, C. J. (2000). Event-related potential correlates of some human cognitive ability constructs. *Personality and Individual Differences, 29,* 157–168.

Cacioppo, J. T., Berntson, G. G., Sheridan, J. F., & McClintock, M. K. (2000). Multilevel integrative analysis of human behavior: Social neuroscience and the complementing nature of social and biological approaches. *Psychological Bulletin, 126,* 829–843.

Cajal, R. Y. (1959). *Degeneration and regeneration of the nervous system.* New York: Hafner. (Original work published 1913)

Cameron, H. A., & McKay, R. (1999). Restoring production of hippocampal neurons in old age. *Nature Neuroscience, 2,* 894–897.

Campbell, F. A., & Ramey, C. T. (1995). Cognitive and school outcomes for high-risk African American students at middle adolescence: Positive effects of early intervention. *American Educational Research Journal, 32,* 743–772.

Campeau, S., & Davis, M. (1995). Involvement of subcorticol and corticol afferents to the lateral nucleus of the amygdala in fear conditioning measured with fear-potentiated startle in rats trained concurrently with auditory and visual conditioned stimuli. *Journal of Neuroscience, 15,* 2312–2327.

Cannon, T. D. (1998). Genetic and perinatal influences in the etiology of Schizophrenia: A neruodevelopmental model. In M. F. Lenzenweger & R. H. Dworkin (Eds.), *Originals and development of Schizophrenia* (pp. 67–92). Washington, DC: American Psychological Association.

Cannon, T. D., Mednick, S. A., Parnas, J., & Schulsinger, F. (1993). Developmental brain abnormalities in the offspring of schizophrenic mothers: I. Contributions of genetic and perinatal factors. *Archives of General Psychiatry, 50,* 551–564.

Cannon, T. D., Mednick, S. A., Schulsinger, F., Parnas, J., Praestholm, J., & Vestergaard, A. (1994). Developmental brain abnormalities in the offspring of schizophrenic mothers: II. Structural brain characteristics of Schizophrenia and schizoptypal personality disorder. *Archives of General Psychiatry, 51,* 955–962.

Cannon, T. D., Rosso, I. M., Bearden, C. E., Sanchez, L. E., & Hadley, T. (1999). A prospective cohort study of neurodevelopmental processes in the genesis and epigenesis of Schizophrenia. *Development and Psychopathology, 11,* 467–485.

Cannon, T. D., van Erp, T. G. M., Huttenen, M., Lonnqvist, J., Salonen, O., Valanne, L., et al. (2002). Perinatal hypoxia and regional brain morphology in schizophrenic patients, their siblings, and controls. *Archives of General Psychiatry, 59*(1), 17–22.

Carleton, A., Petreanu, L., Lansford, R., Alvarez-Buylla, A., & Lledo, P.-M. (2003). Becoming a new neuron in the adult olfactory bulb. *Nature Neuroscience, 6,* 507–518.

Carlsson, I., Wendt, P. E., & Risberg, J. (2000). On the neurobiology of creativity. Differences in frontal activity between high and low creative subjects. *Neuropsychologia, 38,* 873–885.

Carper, R. A., & Courchesne, E. (2000). Inverse correlation between frontal lobe and cerebellum sizes in children with Autism. *Brain, 123,* 836–844.

Carper, R. A., Moses, P., Tigue, Z. D., & Courchesne, E. (2002). Cerebral lobes in Autism: Early hyperplasia and abnormal age effects. *NeuroImage, 16,* 1038–1051.

Casey, B. J., Davidson, M., & Rosen, B. (2002). Functional magnetic resonance imaging: Basic principles of and application to developmental science. *Developmental Science, 5,* 301–309.

Caspi, A., McClay, J., Moffitt, T., Mill, J., Martin, J., Craig, I. W., et al. (2002). Role of genotype in the cycle of violence in maltreated children. *Science, 297,* 851–854.

Caviness, V. S., & Rakic, P. (1978). Mechanisms of cortical development: A review from mutations of mice. *Annual Review of Neuroscience, 1,* 297–326.

Chapillon, P., Manneche, C., Belzung, C., & Caston, J. (1999). Rearing environmental enrichment in two inbred strains of mice: 1. Effects on emotional reactivity. *Behavior Genetics, 29,* 41–46.

Charney, D. (2004). Psychobiological mechanisms of resilience and vulnerability: Implications for successful adaptation to extreme stress. *American Journal of Psychiatry, 161,* 195–216.

Charney, D., Nestler, E., & Bunney, B. (Eds.). (1999). *Neurobiology of mental illness.* New York: Oxford University Press.

Chen, C., & Tonegawa, S. (1997). Molecular genetic analysis of synaptic plasticity, activity-dependent neural development, learning, and memory in the mammalian brain. *Annual Review of Neuroscience, 20,* 157–184.

Cheour, M., Ceponiene, R., Lehtokoski, A., Luuk, A., Allik, J., Alho, K., et al. (1998). Development of language-specific phoneme representations in the infant brain. *Nature Neuroscience, 1,* 351–353.

Chomsky, N. (1968). *Language and mind.* New York: Harcourt Brace Jovanovich.

Ciaranello, R., Aimi, J., Dean, R. S., Morilak, D., Porteus, M. H., & Cicchetti, D. (1995). Fundamentals of molecular neurobiology. In D. Cicchetti & D. J. Cohen (Eds.), *Developmental psychopathology: Theory and method* (Vol. 1, pp. 109–160). New York: Wiley.

Cicchetti, D. (1984). The emergence of developmental psychopathology. *Child Development, 55,* 1–7.

Cicchetti, D. (1990). A historical perspective on the discipline of developmental psychopathology. In J. Rolf, A. Masten, D. Cicchetti, K. Nuechterlein, & S. Weintraub (Eds.), *Risk and protective factors in the development of psychopathology* (pp. 2–28). New York: Cambridge University Press.

Cicchetti, D. (1993). Developmental psychopathology: Reactions, reflections, projections. *Developmental Review, 13,* 471–502.

Cicchetti, D. (1996). Child maltreatment: Implications for developmental theory. *Human Development, 39,* 18–39.

Cicchetti, D. (2002). The impact of social experience on neurobiological systems: Illustration from a constructivist view of child maltreatment. *Cognitive Development, 17,* 1407–1428.

Cicchetti, D. (Ed.). (2003). Experiments of nature: Contributions to developmental theory. *Development and Psychopathology, 15*(4), 833–1106.

Cicchetti, D., Ackerman, B., & Izard, C. (1995). Emotions and emotion regulation in developmental psychopathology. *Development and Psychopathology, 7,* 1–10.

Cicchetti, D., & Blender, J. A. (2004). A multiple-levels-of-analysis approach to the study of developmental processes in maltreated children. *Proceedings of the National Academy of Sciences, 101*(50), 17325–17326.

Cicchetti, D., & Cannon, T. D. (1999a). Neurodevelopmental processes in the ontogenesis and epigenesis of psychopathology. *Development and Psychopathology, 11,* 375–393.

Cicchetti, D., & Cannon, T. D. (Eds.). (1999b). Neurodevelopment and psychopathology. *Development and Psychopathology, 11*(3), 375–654.

Cicchetti, D., & Curtis, W. J. (Eds.). (in press). A Multi-Level Approach to Resilience. *Development and Psychopathology, 19*(4).

Cicchetti, D., & Dawson, G. (Eds.). (2002). Multiple levels of analysis. *Development and Psychopathology, 14*(3), 417–666.

Cicchetti, D., Ganiban, J., & Barnett, D. (1991). Contributions from the study of high risk populations to understanding the development of emotion regulation. In J. Garber & K. A. Dodge (Eds.), *The development of emotion regulation and dysregulation* (pp. 15–48). New York: Cambridge University Press.

Cicchetti, D., & Garmezy, N. (1993). Prospects and promises in the study of resilience. *Development and Psychopathology, 5,* 497–502.

Cicchetti, D., & Hinshaw, S. P. (Eds.). (2002). Prevention and intervention science: Contributions for developmental theory [Editorial]. *Development and Psychopathology, 14*(4), 667–981.

Cicchetti, D., & Posner, M. I. (2005). Cognitive and Affective Neuroscience and Developmental Psychopathology [Editorial]. *Development and Psychopathology, 17*(3).

Cicchetti, D., & Rogosch, F. A. (1996). Equifinality and multifinality in developmental psychopathology. *Development and Psychopathology, 8,* 597–600.

Cicchetti, D., & Rogosch, F. A. (1997). The role of self-organization in the promotion of resilience in maltreated children. *Development and Psychopathology, 9,* 799–817.

Cicchetti, D., & Rogosch, F. A. (2001a). Diverse patterns of neuroendocrine activity in maltreated children. *Development and Psychopathology, 13,* 677–694.

Cicchetti, D., & Rogosch, F. A. (2001b). The impact of child maltreatment and psychopathology upon neuroendocrine functioning. *Development and Psychopathology, 13,* 783–804.

Cicchetti, D., Rogosch, F. A., Lynch, M., & Holt, K. (1993). Resilience in maltreated children: Processes leading to adaptive outcome. *Development and Psychopathology, 5,* 629–647.

Cicchetti, D., & Schneider-Rosen, K. (1986). An organizational approach to childhood depression. In M. Rutter, C. Izard, & P. Read (Eds.), *Depression in young people, clinical and developmental perspectives* (pp. 71–134). New York: Guilford Press.

Cicchetti, D., & Sroufe, L. A. (1978). An organizational view of affect: Illustration from the study of Down's syndrome infants. In M. Lewis & L. Rosenblum (Eds.), *The development of affect* (pp. 309–350). New York: Plenum Press.

Cicchetti, D., & Sroufe, L. A. (2000). Editorial: The past as prologue to the future: The times they've been a changin'. *Development and Psychopathology, 12,* 255–264.

Cicchetti, D., & Toth, S. L. (1991). The making of a developmental psychopathologist. In J. Cantor, C. Spiker, & L. Lipsitt (Eds.), *Child behavior and development: Training for diversity* (pp. 34–72). Norwood, NJ: Ablex.

Cicchetti, D., & Toth, S. L. (1998). The development of depression in children and adolescents. *American Psychologist, 53,* 221–241.

Cicchetti, D., & Tucker, D. (1994a). Development and self-regulatory structures of the mind. *Development and Psychopathology, 6,* 533–549.

Cicchetti, D., & Tucker, D. (Eds.). (1994b). Neural plasticity, sensitive periods, and psychopathology. *Development and Psychopathology, 6*(4), 531–814.

Cicchetti, D., & Valentino, K. (2006). An ecological transactional perspective on child maltreatment: Failure of the average expectable environment and its influence upon child development. In D. Cicchetti & D. J. Cohen (Eds.), *Developmental psychopathology: Risk, disorder, and adaptation* (2nd ed., Vol. 3). New York: Wiley.

Cicchetti, D., & Walker, E. F. (Eds.). (2001). Stress and development: Biological and psychological consequences. *Development and Psychopathology, 13*(3), 413–753.

Cicchetti, D., & Walker, E. F. (Eds.). (2003). *Neurodevelopmental mechanisms in psychopathology.* New York: Cambridge University Press.

Cole, P. M., Martin, S. E., & Dennis, T. A. (2004). Emotion regulation as a scientific construct: Methodological challenges and directions for child development research. *Child Development, 72*(2), 317–333.

Conel, J. L. (1939–1967). *The postnatal development of the human cerebral cortex* (Vol. 6). Cambridge: Harvard University Press.

Courchesne, E. (1987). A neurophysiological view of Autism. In E. Schopler & G. B. Mesibov (Eds.), *Neurobiological issues in Autism* (pp. 285–324). New York: Plenum Press.

Courchesne, E. (1997). Brainstem, cerebellar, and limbic neuroanatomical abnormalities in Autism. *Current Opinion in Neurobiology, 7,* 269–278.

Courchesne, E., Carper, R., & Akshoomoff, N. (2003). Evidence of brain overgrowth in the first year of life in Autism. *Journal of the American Medical Association, 290,* 337–344.

Courchesne, E., Chisum, H., & Townsend, J. (1994). Neural activity-dependent brain changes in development: Implications for psychopathology. *Development and Psychopathology, 6,* 697–722.

Courchesne, E., Karns, C., Davis, H. R., Ziccardi, R., Carper, R., Tigue, Z., et al. (2001). Unusual brain growth patterns in early life in patients with autistic disorder: An MRI study. *Neurology, 57,* 245–254.

Cowan, W. M. (1979). The development of the brain. *Scientific American, 241*(3), 113–133.

Cowan, W. M., Harter, D. H., & Kandel, E. R. (2000). The emergence of modern neuroscience: Some implications for neurology and psychiatry. *Annual Review of Neuroscience, 23,* 343–391.

Cowan, W. M., & Kandel, E. R. (2001). Prospects for neurology and psychiatry. *Journal of the American Medical Association, 285,* 594–600.

Curtis, W. J. (2000, April). *Cognitive functioning as a risk and protective factor in the development of competence.* Paper presented at the Poster presented at the biennial meeting of the Society for Research in Adolescence, Chicago.

Curtis, W. J., & Cicchetti, D. (2003). Moving research on resilience into the 21st century: Theoretical and methodological considerations in examining the biological contributors to resilience. *Development and Psychopathology, 15,* 773–810.

Cuthbert, B. N., Bradley, M. M., & Lang, P. J. (1996). Probing picture perception: Activation and emotion. *Psychophysiology, 33,* 103–111.

Dahl, R. (2004). Adolescent brain development: A period of vulnerabilities and opportunities [Keynote address]. *Annals New York Academy of Science, 1021,* 1–22.

Damasio, A. R., & Maurer, R. G. (1978). A neurological model for childhood Autism. *Archives of Neurology, 35,* 777–786.

Darwin, C. (1874). *The descent of man.* Chicago: Rand McNally.

Davidson, R. J. (1998a). Affective style and affective disorders: Perspectives from affective neuroscience. *Cognition and Emotion, 12,* 307–320.

Davidson, R. J. (1998b). Anterior electrophysiological asymmetries, emotion, and depression: Conceptual and methodological conundrums. *Psychophysiology, 35,* 607–614.

Davidson, R. J. (2000). Affective style, psychopathology, and resilience: Brain mechanisms and plasticity. *American Psychologist, 55,* 1196–1214.

Davidson, R. J., Ekman, P., Saron, C., Senulis, J. A., & Friesen, W. V. (1990). Approach-withdrawal and cerebral asymmetry: Emotional expression and brain physiology I. *Journal of Personality and Social Psychology, 58,* 330–341.

Davidson, R. J., Jackson, D. C., & Kalin, N. H. (2000). Emotion, plasticity, context, and regulation: Perspectives from affective neuroscience. *Psychological Bulletin, 126,* 890–909.

Davis, M. (1992). The role of the amygdala in conditioned fear. In J. Aggleton (Ed.), *The amygdala: Neurobiological aspects of emotion, memory, and mental dysfunction* (pp. 255–305). New York: Wiley.

Davis, M., Walker, D. L., & Lee, Y. (1999). Neurophysiology and neuropharmacology of startle and its affective modulation. In M. E. Dawson, A. M. Schell, & A. H. Bohmelt (Eds.), *Startle modification* (pp. 95–113). New York: Cambridge University Press.

Dawson, G. (1994). Frontal electroencephalographic correlated of individual differences in emotion expression in infants: A brain systems perspective on emotion. *Monographs of the society for research in child development, 59*(2 & 3, Serial No. 240), 135–151.

Dawson, G., Ashman, S. B., & Carver, L. J. (2000). The role of early experience in shaping behavioral and brain development and its implications for social policy. *Development and Psychopathology, 12*(4), 695–712.

Dawson, G., Frey, K., Panagiotides, H., Osterling, J., & Hessl, D. (1997). Infants of depressed mothers exhibit atypical frontal brain activity: A replication and extension of previous findings. *Journal of Child Psychology and Psychiatry and Allied Disciplines, 38,* 179–186.

Dawson, G., Frey, K., Panagiotides, H., Yamada, E., Hessl, D., & Osterling, J. (1999). Infants of depressed mothers exhibit atypical frontal electrical brain activity during interactions with mother and with a familiar, nondepressed adult. *Child Development, 70,* 1058–1066.

Dawson, G., Grofer Klinger, L., Panagiotides, H., Hill, D., & Spieker, S. (1992). Frontal lobe activity and affective behavior of infants of mothers with depressive symptoms. *Child Development, 63,* 725–737.

Dawson, G., Panagiotides, H., Klinger, L. G., & Hill, D. (1992). The role of frontal lobe functioning in the development of self-regulatory behavior in infancy. *Brain and Cognition, 20,* 152–175.

DeBellis, M. D. (2001). Developmental traumatology: The psychobiological development of maltreated children and its implications for research, treatment, and policy. *Development and Psychopathology, 13,* 539–564.

DeBellis, M. D., Baum, A. S., Birmaher, B., Keshavan, M. S., Eccard, C. H., Boring, A. M., et al. (1999a). Developmental traumatology: Pt. I. Biological stress systems. *Biological Psychiatry, 45,* 1259–1270.

DeBellis, M. D., Keshavan, M. S., Casey, B. J., Clark, D. B., Giedd, J., Boring, A. M., et al. (1999b). Developmental traumatology: Biological stress systems and brain development in maltreated children with PTSD: Pt. II. The relationship between characteristics of trauma and psychiatric symptoms and adverse brain development in maltreated children and adolescents with PTSD. *Biological Psychiatry, 45,* 1271–1284.

de Haan, M., & Thomas, K. M. (2002). Applications of ERP and fMRI techniques to developmental science. *Developmental Science, 5,* 335–343.

DeLong, G. R. (1992). Autism, amnesia, hippocampus, and learning. *Neuroscience and Biobehavioral Reviews, 16,* 63–70.

Denenberg, V. H., Woodcock, J. M., & Rosenberg, K. M. (1968). Long-term effects of preweaning and postweaning free-environment experience on rat problem-solving behavior. *Journal of Comparative and Physiological Psychology, 66,* 533–535.

Depue, R. A., & Collins, P. F. (1999). Neurobiology of the structure of personality: Dopamine, facilitation of incentive motivation, and extraversion. *Behavioral and Brain Sciences, 22,* 491–569.

Destexhe, A., & Marder, E. (2004). Plasticity in single neuron and circuit computations. *Nature, 431,* 789–803.

Diamond, A., Prevor, M. B., Callender, G., & Druin, D. P. (1997). Prefrontal cortex cognitive deficits in children treated early and continously for PKU. *Monographs of the society for research in child development, 62*(Serial No. 4).

Diamond, M. C., Krech, D., & Rosenzweig, M. R. (1964). The effects of an enriched environment on the histology of the rat cerebral cortex. *Journal of Comparative Neurology, 123,* 111–120.

Diamond, M. C., Law, F., Rhodes, H., Lindner, B., Rosenzweig, M. R., Krech, D., et al. (1966). Increases in cortical depth and glia numbers in rats subjected to enriched environments. *Journal of Comparative Neurology, 128,* 117–126.

Diamond, M. C., Linder, B., & Raymond, A. (1967). Extensive cortical depth measurements and neuron size increases in the cortex of environmentally enriched rats. *Journal of Comparative Neurology, 131,* 357–364.

Doetsch, F., & Hen, R. (2005). Young and excitable: The function of new neurons in the adult mammalian brain. *Current Opinion in Neurobiology, 15,* 121–128.

Donchin, E., & Coles, M. G. H. (1988). Is the P300 component a manifestation of context updating? *Behavioral and Brain Sciences, 11,* 355–372.

Donchin, E., Karis, D., Bashore, T. R., Coles, M. G. H., & Gratton, G. (1986). Cognitive psychophysiology and human information processing. In M. G. H. Coles, E. Donchin, & S. W. Porges (Eds.), *Psychophysiology* (pp. 244–267). New York: Guilford Press.

Drevets, W. C., Price, J. L., Simpson, J. R., Todd, R. D., Reich, T., Vannier, M., et al. (1997). Subgenual prefrontal cortex abnormalities in mood disorders. *Nature, 386,* 824–827.

Duncan, J., Seitz, R. J., Kolodny, J., Bor, D., Herzog, H., Ahmed, A., et al. (2000). A neural basis for general intelligence. *Science, 289,* 457–460.

Dunn, L. M., & Dunn, L. M. (1981). *Peabody picture vocabulary test-revised.* Circle Pines, MN: American Guidance Service.

Edelman, G. M. (1987). *Neural Darwinism: The theory of neuronal group selection.* New York: Basic Books.

Edelman, G. M. (2004). *The phenomenal gift of consciousness.* New Haven, CT: Yale University Press.

Edelson, J. T., & Robertson, G. L. (1986). The effect of the cold pressor test on vasopressin secretion in man. *Psychoneuroendocrinology, 11,* 307–316.

Egeland, B., Carlson, E. A., & Sroufe, L. A. (1993). Resilience as process. *Development and Psychopathology, 5,* 517–528.

Eisenberg, L. (1995). The social construction of the human brain. *American Journal of Psychiatry, 152,* 1563–1575.

Eisenberg, N. (2002). Emotion-related regulation and its relation to quality of social functioning. In W. Hartup & R. A. Weinberg (Eds.), *Child psychology in retrospect and prospect—In celebration of the 75th anniversary of the Institute of Child Development: The Minnesota Symposia on Child Psychology* (Vol, 32, pp. 133–171). Mahwah, NJ: Erlbaum.

Elbert, T., Heim, S., & Rockstroh, B. (2001). Neural plasticity and development. In C. A. Nelson & M. Luciana (Eds.), *Handbook of developmental cognitive neuroscience* (pp. 191–202). Cambridge, MA: MIT Press.

Elbert, T., Pantev, C., Wienbruch, C., Rockstroh, B., & Taub, E. (1995). Increased use of the left hand in string players associated with increased corticol representations of the fingers. *Science, 220,* 21–23.

Engel, G. L. (1977). The need for a new medical model: A challenge for biomedicine. *Science, 196,* 129–135.

Eslinger, P. J., Flaherty-Craig, C. V., & Benton, A. L. (2004). Developmental outcomes after early prefrontal cortex damage [Special issue]. *Brain and Cognition, 55*(1), 84–403.

Fatemi, S. H., Halt, A. R., Earle, J., Kist, D. A., Realmuto, G., Thuras, P. D., et al. (2000). Reduced Purkinje cell size in autistic cerebellum. *Biological Psychiatry, 47,* 128S.

Feinberg, I. (1982). Schizophrenia: Caused by a fault in programmed synaptic elimination during adolescence? *Journal of Psychiatry Research, 17,* 319–330.

Ferchmin, P. A., Bennett, E. L., & Rosenzweig, M. R. (1975). Direct contact with enriched environment is required to alter cerebral weights in rats. *Journal of Comparative and Physiological Psychology, 88,* 360–367.

Field, T. M., Fox, N., Pickens, J., & Nawrocki, T. (1995). Relative right frontal EEG activation in 3- to 6-month old infants of "depressed" mothers. *Developmental Psychology, 31,* 358–363.

Finger, S. (1994). *Origins of neuroscience.* New York: Oxford University Press.

Fish, B. (1957). The detection of Schizophrenia in infancy. *Journal of Nervous and Mental Disorders, 125,* 1–24.

Fish, B. (1977). Neurologic antecedents of Schizophrenia in children: Evidence for an inherited, congential neurointegrative deficit. *Archives of General Psychiatry, 34,* 1297–1313.

Fish, B., Marcus, J., Hans, S., Auerbach, J., & Perdue, S. (1992). Infants at risk for Schizophrenia: Sequelae of genetic neurointegrative defect. *Archives of general Psychiatry, 49,* 221–235.

Fishbein, H. (1976). *Evolution, development, and children's learning.* Pacific Palisades, CA: Goodyear Publishing Company.

Floeter, M. K., & Greenough, W. T. (1979). Cerebellar plasticity: Modification of purkinje cell structure by differential rearing in monkeys. *Science, 206,* 227–229.

Flores, E., Cicchetti, D., & Rogosch, F. A. (2005). Predictors of resilience in maltreated and nonmaltreated Latino children. *Developmental Psychology, 41*(2), 338–351.

Foley, D. L., Eaves, L. J., Wormley, B., Silberg, J. L., Maes, H. H., Kuhn, J., et al. (2004). Childhood adversity, monoamine oxidase: A genotype, and risk for conduct disorder. *Archives of General Psychiatry, 61*(7), 738–744.

Fox, N. A. (1991). If it's not left, it's right: Electroencephalograph asymmetry and the development of emotion. *American Psychologist, 46,* 863–872.

Fox, N. A. (1994). The development of emotion regulation: Biological and behavioral considerations. *Monographs of the Society for Research in Child Development, 59,* 2–3.

Fox, N. A., & Davidson, R. J. (1984). Hemispheric substrates of affect. In N. A. Fox & R. J. Davidson (Eds.), *The psychobiology of affective development* (pp. 353–381). Hillsdale, NJ: Erlbaum.

Francis, D., Diorio, J., LaPlante, P., Weaver, S., Seckl, J. R., & Meaney, M. J. (1996). The role of early environmental events in regulating neuroendocrine development: Moms, pups, stress, and glucocorticoid receptors. In C. F. Ferris & T. Grisso (Eds.), *Annals of the New York Academy of Sciences: Understanding aggressive behavior in children* (Vol. 794, pp. 136–152). New York: New York Academy of Sciences.

Francis, D., Diorio, J., Liu, D., & Meaney, M. J. (1999). Nongenomic transmission across generations of maternal behavior and stress responses in the rat. *Science, 286,* 1155–1158.

Fray, P. J., Robbins, T. W., & Sahakian, B. J. (1996). Neuropsychiatric applications of CANTAB. *International Journal of Geriatric Psychiatry, 11,* 329–336.

Freeman, B., Powell, J., Ball, D. M., Hill, L., Craig, I. W., & Plomin, R. (1997). DNA by mail: An inexpensive and noninvasive method for collecting DNA samples from widely dispersed populations. *Behavior Genetics, 27,* 251–257.

Frith, U. (2001). Mind blindness and the brain in Autism. *Neuron, 32,* 969–979.

Gage, F. H. (2000). Mammalian neural stem cells. *Science, 287,* 1433–1438.

Gallo, L. C., & Matthews, K. A. (2003). Understanding the association between socioeconomic status and physical health: Do negative emotions play a role? *Psychological Bulletin, 129,* 10–51.

Gao, J.-H., Parsons, L. M., Bower, J. M., Xiong, J., Li, J., & Fox, P. T. (1996). Cerebellum implicated in sensory acquisition and discrimination rather than motor control. *Science, 272,* 545–547.

Garmezy, N. (1970). Process and relative schizophrenida: Some conceptions and issues. *Schizophrenia Bulletin, 2,* 30–74.

Garmezy, N. (1971). Vulnerability research and the issue of primary prevention. *American Journal of Orthopsychiatry, 41,* 101–116.

Garmezy, N. (1974). Children at risk: Conceptual models and research methods. *Schizophrenia Bulletin, 9,* 55–125.

Garmezy, N., Masten, A. S., & Tellegen, A. (1984). The study of stress and competence in children: A building block for developmental psychopathology. *Child Development, 55,* 97–111.

Garmezy, N., & Streitman, S. (1974). Children at risk: Conceptual models and research methods. *Schizophrenia Bulletin, 9,* 55–125.

Garmezy, N., & Tellegen, A. (1984). Studies of stress resistant children: Methods, variables, and preliminary findings. In F. Morrison, C. Lord, & D. Keating (Eds.), *Advances in applied developmental psychology* (Vol. 1, pp. 231–287). New York: Academic Press.

Gazzaniga, M. S. (Ed.). (2004). *The cognitive neurosciences* (3rd ed.). Cambridge, MA: MIT Press.

Ghaemi, N. (2003). *The concepts of psychiatry: A pluralistic approach to the mind and mental illness.* Baltimore: Johns Hopkins University Press.

Gibson, K. R. (1991). Myelination and behavioral development: A comparative perspective on questions of neoteny, altriciality, and intelligence. In K. R. Gibson & A. C. Petersen (Eds.), *Brain maturation and cognitive development* (pp. 29–63). New York: Aldine de Gruyter.

Giedd, J. N. (2004). Structural magnetic resonance imaging of the adolescent brain. *Annals New York Academy of Science, 1021,* 77–85.

Goldapple, K., Segal, Z., Garson, C., Lau, M., Bieling, P., Kennedy, S., et al. (2004). Modulation of cortical-limbic pathways in major depression. *Archives of General Psychiatry, 61*(1), 34–41.

Goldman-Rakic, P. S. (1987). Development of cortical circuitry and cognitive function. *Child Development, 58,* 601–622.

Goldman-Rakic, P. S., Bourgeois, J.-P., & Rakic, P. (1997). Synaptic substrate of cognitive development: Life-span analysis of synaptogenesis in the prefrontal cortex of the nonhuman primate. In N. Krasnegor, G. R. Lyon, & P. S. Goldman-Rakic (Eds.), *Development of the prefrontal cortex* (pp. 9–26). Baltimore: Paul H. Brookes.

Gottlieb, G. (1983). The psychobiological approach to developmental issues. In P. Mussen (Ed.), *Handbook of child psychology* (pp. 1–26). New York: Wiley.

Gottlieb, G. (1992). *Individual development and evolution: The genesis of novel behavior.* New York: Oxford University Press.

Gottlieb, G., & Halpern, C. T. (2002). A relational view of causality in normal and abnormal development. *Development and Psychopathology, 14*(3), 421–436.

Gottlieb, G., Wahlsten, D., & Lickliter, R. (1998). The significance of biology for human development: A developmental psychobiological systems view. In R. Lerner (Ed.), *Handbook of child psychology: Vol. 1. Theoretical models of human development* (pp. 233–273). New York: Wiley.

Gould, E. (1999). Serotonin and hippocampal neurogenesis. *Neuropsychopharmacology, 21,* S46–S51.

Gould, E., Beylin, A., Tanapat, P., Reeves, A., & Shors, T. (1999). Learning enhances adult neurogenesis in the hippocampal formation. *Nature Neuroscience, 2,* 260–265.

Gould, E., & Cameron, H. A. (1996). Regulation of neuronal birth, migration and death in the rat dentate gyrus. *Developmental Neuroscience, 18,* 22–35.

Gould, E., Reeves, A., Graziano, M., & Gross, C. (1999). Neurogenesis in the neocortex of adult primates. *Science, 286,* 548–552.

Gould, E., & Tanapat, P. (1999). Stress and hippocampal neurogenesis. *Biological Psychiatry, 46,* 1472–1479.

Gould, E., Tanapat, P., Hastings, N. B., & Shors, T. J. (1999). Neurogenesis in adulthood: A possible role in learning. *Trends in Cognitive Sciences, 3*(5), 186–192.

Gould, E., Tanapat, P., McEwen, B. S., Flugge, G., & Fuchs, E. (1998). Proliferation of granule cell precursors in the dentale gyrus of adult monkeys is diminished by stress. *Proceedings of the National Academy of Sciences, 95,* 3168–3171.

Gould, E., Vail, N., Wagers, M., & Gross, C. G. (2001). Adult-generated hippocampal and neocortical neurons in macaques have a transient existence. *Proceedings of the National Academy of Sciences, 98*(19), 10910–10917.

Granger, D. A., Dreschel, N. A., & Shirtcliff, E. A. (2003). Developmental psychoneuroimmunology. In D. Cicchetti & E. F. Walker (Eds.), *Neurodevelopmental mechanisms in psychopathology* (pp. 293–322). New York: Cambridge University Press.

Granger, D. A., Hood, K. E., Dreschel, N. A., Sergeant, E., & Likos, A. (2001). Developmental effects of early immune stress on aggressive, socially reactive, and inhibited behaviors. *Development and Psychopathology, 13,* 599–610.

Granger, D. A., Kivilghan, K. T., Blair, C., El-Sheikh, M., Mize, J., Lisonbee, J. A., et al. (in press). Integrating the measurement of salivary a-amylase into studies of child health, development, and social relationships. *Journal of Personal and Social Relationships.*

Gray, J. R., Chabris, C. F., & Braver, T. S. (2003). Neural mechanisms of general fluid intelligence. *Nature Neuroscience, 6,* 316–322.

Greenberg, S. A. (2001). DNA microarray gene expression analysis technology and its application to neurological disorders. *Neurology, 57,* 755–761.

Greenough, W. T., & Black, J. (1992). Induction of brain structure by experience: Substrates for cognitive development. In M. Gunnar & C. A. Nelson (Eds.), *Developmental behavioral neuroscience: The Minnesota Symposia on Child Psychology* (Vol. 24, pp. 155–200). Hillsdale, NJ: Erlbaum.

Greenough, W. T., Black, J. E., Klintsova, A., Bates, K. E., & Weiler, I. J. (1999). Experience and plasticity in brain structure: Possible implications of basic research findings for developmental disorders. In S. H. Broman & J. M. Fletcher (Eds.), *The changing neurons system: Neurobehavioral consequences of early brain disorders* (pp. 51–70). New York: Oxford University Press.

Greenough, W. T., Black, J., & Wallace, C. (1987). Experience and brain development. *Child Development, 58,* 539–559.

Greenough, W. T., Hwang, H. M. F., & Gorman, C. (1985). Evidence for active synapse formation, or altered post-synaptic metabolism, in visual cortex of rats reared in complex environments. *Proceedings of the National Academy of Sciences, 82,* 4549–4552.

Greenough, W. T., Volkmar, F. R., & Juraska, J. M. (1973). Effects of rearing complexity on dendritic branching in frontolateral and temporal cortex of the rat. *Experimental Neurology, 41,* 371–378.

Greenough, W. T., Wallace, C. S., Alcantra, A. A., Anderson, B. J., Hawrylak, N., Sirevaag, A. M., et al. (1993). Development of the brain: Experience affects the structure of neurons, glia, and blood vessels. In N. J. Anastasiow & S. Harel (Eds.), *At-risk infants: Interventions, families, and research* (pp. 173–185). Baltimore, Maryland: Paul H. Brookes.

Grigorieva, L. P. (1996). Perceptual learning in overcoming the impacts of visual deprivation in children with low vision. *Human Physiology, 22,* 591–596.

Grillon, C., Dierker, L., & Merikangas, K. R. (1997). Startle modulation in children at risk for anxiety disorders and/or alcoholism. *Journal of the American Academy of Child and Adolescent Psychiatry, 36,* 925–932.

Grillon, C., Dierker, L., & Merikangas, K. R. (1998). Fear-potentiated startle in adolescent offspring of parents with anxiety disorder. *Biological Psychiatry, 44,* 990–997.

Grillon, C., Morgan, C. A., Davis, M., & Southwick, S. M. (1998). Effects of experimental context and explicit threat cues on acoustic startle in Vietnam veterans with post-traumatic stress disorder. *Biological Psychiatry, 10,* 1027–1036.

Gross, J. J. (1998). The emerging field of emotion regulation: An integrative review. *Review of General Psychology, 2,* 271–299.

Grouse, L. D., Schrier, B. K., Bennett, E. L., Rosenzweig, M. R., & Nelson, P. G. (1978). Sequence diversity studies of rat brain RNA: Effects of environmental complexity on rat brain RNA diversity. *Journal of Neurochemistry, 30,* 191–203.

Gunnar, M. R. (1998). Quality of early care and buffering of neuroendocrine stress reactions: Potential effects on the developing human brain. *Preventive Medicine, 27,* 208–211.

Gunnar, M. R. (2000). Early adversity and the development of stress reactivity and regulation. In C. A. Nelson (Ed.), *The Minnesota Symposia on Child Psychology: Vol. 31. The effects of early adversity on neurobehavioral development* (pp. 163–200). Mahwah, NJ: Erlbaum.

Gunnar, M. R., Broderson, L., Nachmias, M., Buss, K., & Rigatuso, J. (1996). Stress reactivity and attachment security. *Developmental Psychobiology, 29,* 191–204.

Gunnar, M. R., Morison, S. J., Chisholm, K., & Schuder, M. (2001). Salivary cortisol levels in children adapted from Romanian orphanages. *Development and Psychopathology, 13,* 611–628.

Gunnar, M. R., & Vazquez, D. M. (2001). Low coritsol and a flattenting of expected daytime rhythm: Potential indices of risk in human development. *Development and Psychopathology, 13,* 515–538.

Gurvits, T. V., Shenton, M. E., Hokama, H., Ohta, H., Lasko, N. B., Gilbertson, M. W., et al. (1996). Magnetic resonance imaging study of hippocampal volume in chronic, combat-related posttraumatic stress disorder. *Biological Psychiatry, 40,* 1091–1099.

Hacia, J. G., & Collins, F. S. (1999). Mutational analysis using oligonucleotide microarrays. *Journal of Medical Genetics, 36,* 730–736.

Haier, R. J., Nuechterlein, K. H., Hazlett, E., Wu, J. C., Paek, J., Browning, H. L., et al. (1988). Cortical glucose metabolic rate correlates of abstract reasoning and attention studied with positron emission tomography. *Intelligence, 12,* 199–217.

Haier, R. J., Siegel, B. V., Tang, C., Abel, L., & Buschbaum, M. S. (1992). Intelligence and changes in regional glucose metabolic rate following learning. *Intelligence, 16,* 415–426.

Hann, D., Huffman, L., Lederhendler, I., & Meinecke, D. (Eds.). (1998). *Advancing research on development plasticity: Integrating the behavioral science and neuroscience of mental health.* Bethesda, MD: National Institute of Mental Health.

Hashimoto, T., Tayama, M., Murakawa, K., Yoshimoto, T., Miyazaki, M., Harada, M., et al. (1995). Development of the brainstem and cerebellum in autistic patients. *Journal of Autism and Developmental Disorders, 25,* 1–18.

Hatten, M. (1999). Central nervous system neuronal migration. *Annual Review of Neuroscience, 22,* 511–539.

Hebb, D. O. (1947). The effects of early experience on problem-solving at maturity. *American Psychologist, 2,* 306–307.

Hebb, D. O. (1949). *Organization of behavior: A neuropsychological theory.* New York: Wiley.

Hebb, D. O., & Williams, K. (1946). A method of rating animal intelligence. *Journal of General Psychology, 34,* 56–65.

Heffelfinger, A. K., & Newcomer, J. W. (2001). Glucocorticoid effects on memory function over the human life span. *Development and Psychopathology, 13,* 491–513.

Heim, C., Ehlert, U., & Hellhammer, D. (2000). The potential role of hypocortisolism in the pathophysiology of stress-related bodily disorders. *Psychoneuroendocrinology, 25,* 1–35.

Henriques, J. B., & Davidson, R. J. (1991). Left frontal hypoactivation in depression. *Journal of Abnormal Psychology, 100,* 535–545.

Herrick, C. J. (1948). *The brain of the tiger salamander.* Chicago: University of Chicago Press.

Hillyard, S. A., & Picton, T. W. (1987). Electrophysiology of cognition. In V. Mountcastle (Ed.), *Handbook of physiology: Higher functions of the brain* (Vol. 5, pp. 519–583). Bethesda, MD: American Physiological Society.

Hinde, R. A. (1992). Developmental psychology in the context of other behavioral sciences. *Developmental Psychology, 28,* 1018–1029.

His, W. (1904). *Die Entwicklung de menschlichen Gehirns wahrend der ersten Monate.* Leipzig, Germany: Hirzel.

Hubel, D. H., & Wiesel, T. N. (1979). Brain mechanisms of vision. *Scientific American, 241,* 150–162.

Hugdahl, K. (1995). *Psychophysiology: The mind-body perspective.* Cambridge, MA: Harvard University Press.

Hugdahl, K., & Davidson, R. J. (Eds.). (2003). *At asymmetrical brain.* Cambridge, MA: MIT Press.

Huttenlocher, P. R. (1984). Synapse elimination and plasticity in developing human cerebral cortex. *American Journal of Mental Deficiency, 88*(5), 488–496.

Huttenlocher, P. R. (1990). Morphometric study of human cerebral cortex development. *Neuropsychologia, 28,* 517–527.

Huttenlocher, P. R. (1994). Synaptogenesis, synapse elimination, and neural plasticity in human cerebral cortex. In C. A. Nelson (Ed.), *Threats to optimal development: Integrating biological, psychological, and social risk factors: The Minnesota Symposia on Child Psychology* (Vol. 27, pp. 35–54). Hillsdale, NJ: Erlbaum.

Huttenlocher, P. R. (2002). *Neural plasticity: The effects of environment on the development of the cerebral cortex.* Cambridge, MA: Harvard University Press.

Huttenlocher, P. R., & Dabholkar, A. S. (1997). Developmental anatomy of prefrontal cortex. In N. Krasner, G. R. Lyton, & P. S. Goldman-Kakic (Eds.), *Development of the prefrontal cortex* (pp. 69–84). Baltimore: Paul H. Brookes.

Hyman, S. E., & Nestler, E. J. (1993). *The molecular foundations of psychiatry.* Washington, DC: American Psychiatric Press.

Hymovitch, B. (1952). The effects of experimental variations on problem solving in the rat. *Journal of Comparative and Physiological Psychology, 45,* 313–321.

Isaacson, R. L. (1975). The myth of recovery from early brain damage. In N. R. Ellis (Ed.), *Aberrant development in infancy* (pp. 1–25). Potomac, MD: Erlbaum.

Jacobs, B. L., van Praag, H., & Gage, F. H. (2000). Adult brain neurogenesis and psychiatry: A novel theory of depression. *Molecular Psychiatry, 5,* 262–269.

Jacobson, M. (1991). *Developmental neurobiology.* New York: Plenum Press.

Jausovec, N. (2000). Differences in cognitive processes between gifted, intelligent, creative and average individuals while solving complex problems: An EEG study. *Intelligence, 28,* 213–237.

Jausovec, N., & Jausovec, K. (2000). Correlations between ERP parameters and intelligence: A reconsideration. *Biological Psychology, 50,* 137–154.

Jausovec, N., & Jausovec, K. (2001). Differences in EEG current density related to intelligence. *Cognitive Brain Research, 12,* 55–60.

Johnson, M. H. (1997). *Developmental cognitive neuroscience.* Oxford, England: Blackwell Publishers.

Johnson, M. H. (1998). The neural basis of cognitive development. In D. Kuhn & R. Siegler (Eds.), *Handbook of child psychology: Cognition, perception, and language* (Vol. 2, pp. 1–49). New York: Wiley.

Johnson, M. H. (1999). Cortical plasticity in normal and abnormal cognitive development: Evidence and working hypotheses. *Development and Psychopathology, 11,* 419–438.

Johnson, M. H., Griffin, R., Csibra, G., Halit, H., Farroni, T., de Haan, M., et al. (2005). The emergence of the social brain network: Evidence from typical and atypical development. *Development and Psychopathology, 17*(3).

Johnston, T. D. (1987). The persistence of dichotomies in the study of behavioral development. *Developmental Review, 7,* 149–182.

Jones, N. A., Field, T., Fox, N. A., Lundy, B., & Davalos, M. (1997). EEG activation in 1-month-old infants of depressed mothers. *Development and Psychopathology, 9,* 491–505.

Jones, N. A., & Fox, N. A. (1992). Electroencephalogram asymmetry during emotionally evocative films and its relation to positive and negative affectivity. *Brain and Cognition, 20,* 280–299.

Jones, T. A., Klintsova, A. Y., Kilman, V. L., Sirevaag, A. M., & Greenough, W. T. (1997). Induction of multiple synapses by experience in the visual cortex of adult rats. *Neurobiology of Learning and Memory, 68,* 13–20.

Juraska, J. M., Greenough, W. T., & Conlee, J. W. (1983). Differential rearing effects responsiveness of rats to depressant and convulsant drugs. *Physiology and Behavior, 31,* 711–715.

Kandel, E. R. (1979). Psychotherapy and the single synapse. *New England Journal of Medicine, 301,* 1028–1037.

Kandel, E. R. (1998). A new intellectual framework for psychiatry. *American Journal of Psychiatry, 155,* 475–469.

Kandel, E. R. (1999). Biology and the future of psychoanalysis: A new intellectual framework for psychiatry revisited. *American Journal of Psychiatry, 156,* 505–524.

Kandel, E. R., & Squire, L. (2000). Neuroscience: Breaking down scientific barriers to the study of brain and mind. *Science, 290,* 1113–1120.

Kanner, L. (1943). Autistic disturbances of affective content. *Nervous Child, 2,* 217–250.

Karni, A., Meyer, G., Jazzard, P., Adams, M. M., Turner, R., & Ungerleider, L. G. (1995). Functional MRI evidence for adult motor plasticity during motor skill learning. *Nature, 377,* 155–158.

Kaufman, J., & Charney, D. (2001). Effects of early stress on brain structure and function: Implications for understanding the relationship between child maltreatment and depression. *Development and Psychopathology, 13,* 451–471.

Kaufman, J., Plotsky, P. M., Nemeroff, C. B., & Charney, D. S. (2000). Effects of early adverse experiences on brain structure and function: Clinical implications. *Biological Psychiatry, 48,* 778–790.

Kaufman, J., Yang, B., Douglas-Palumberi, H., Houshyar, S., Lipschitz, D., Krystal, J., et al. (2004). Social supports and serotonin transporter gene moderate depression in maltreated children. *Preceedings of the National Academy of Sciences of the United States of America, 101*(49), 17316–17321.

Keating, D. P. (1990). Adolescent thinking. In S. S. Feldman & G. R. Elliot (Eds.), *At the threshold: The developing adolescent* (pp. 54–89). Cambridge, MA: Harvard University Press.

Kelley, A. E., & Stinus, L. (1984). Neuroanatomical and neurochemical substrates of affective behavior. In N. A. Fox & R. J. Davidson (Eds.), *The psychobiology of affective development.* HIllsdale, NJ: Erlbaum.

Kemper, T., & Bauman, M. (1998). Neuropathology of infantile Autism. *Journal of Neuropathology and Experimental Neurology, 57,* 645–652.

Kempermann, G., Kuhn, H. G., & Gage, F. H. (1997). More hippocampal neurons in adult mice living in an enriched environment. *Nature, 386,* 493–495.

Kempermann, G., Kuhn, H. G., & Gage, F. H. (1998). Experience-induced neurogenesis in the senescent dentate gyrus. *Society for Neuroscience, 18,* 3206–3212.

Kempermann, G., van Pragg, H., & Gage, F. H. (2000). Activity-dependent regulation of neuronal plasticity and self-repair. *Progress in Brain Research, 127,* 35–48.

Kendler, K. S. (2005). Toward a philosophical structure for psychiatry. *American Journal of Psychiatry, 162*(3), 433–440.

Kennard, M. (1938). Reorganization of motor function in the cerebral cortex of monkeys deprived of motor and premotor areas in infancy. *Journal of Neurophysiology, 1,* 477–496.

Keshavan, M. S., & Hogarty, G. E. (1999). Brain maturational processes and delayed onset in Schizophrenia. *Development and Psychopathology, 11,* 525–544.

Kiecolt-Glaser, J. K., McGuire, L., Robles, T. F., & Glaser, R. (2002). Psychoneuroimmunology: Psychological influences on immune function and health. *Journal of Consulting and Clinical Psychology, 70,* 537–547.

Kirschbaum, C., Pirke, K. M., & Hellhammer, D. H. (1993). The "Trier Social Stress Test"-a tool for investigating psychobiological stress responses in a laboratory setting. *Neuropsychobiology, 28,* 76–81.

Kiyono, S., Seo, M. L., Shibagaki, M., & Inouye, M. (1985). Facilitative effects of maternal environmental enrichment on maze learning in rat offspring. *Physiology and Behavior, 34,* 431–435.

Kleim, J. A., Swain, R. A., Armstrong, K. A., Napper, R. M. A., Jones, T. A., & Greenough, W. T. (1998). Selective synaptic plasticity within the cerebellar cortex following complex motor skill learning. *Neurobiology of Learning and Memory, 69,* 274–289.

Klorman, R., Cicchetti, D., Thatcher, J. E., & Ison, J. R. (2003). Acoustic startle in maltreated children. *Journal of Abnormal Child Psychology, 31,* 359–370.

Koch, M. (1999). The neurobiology of startle. *Progress in Neurobiology, 59,* 107–128.

Kolb, B. (1995). *Brain plasticity and behavior.* Mahwah, NJ: Erlbaum.

Kolb, B., Forgie, M., Gibb, R., Gorny, G., & Rowntree, S. (1998). Age, experience, and the changing brain. *Neuroscience and Biobehavioral Reviews, 22,* 143–159.

Kolb, B., & Gibb, R. (2001). Early brain injury, plasticity, and behavior. In C. A. Nelson & M. Luciana (Eds.), *Handbook of developmental cognitive neuroscience* (pp. 175–190). Cambridge, MA: MIT Press.

Kornack, D. R., & Rakic, P. (2001a). Cell proliferation without neurogenesis in adult primate neocortex. *Science, 294,* 2127–2130.

Kornack, D. R., & Rakic, P. (2001b). Generation and migration of new olfactory neurons in adult primates. *Proceedings of the National Academy of Sciences, 96,* 4752–4757.

Korr, H., & Schmitz, C. (1999). Facts and fictions regarding postnatal neurogenesis in the developing human cerebral cortex. *Journal of Theoretical Biology, 200,* 291–297.

Kraepelin, E. (1919). *Dementia praecox and paraphrenia.* Edinburgh, Scotland: Livingston.

Krech, D., Rosenzweig, M. R., & Bennett, E. L. (1960). Effects of environmental complexity and training on brain chemistry. *Journal of Comparative and Physiological Psychology, 53,* 509–519.

Krech, D., Rosenzweig, M. R., & Bennett, E. L. (1962). Relations between brain chemistry and problem-solving among rats raised in enriched and impoverished environments. *Journal of Comparative and Physiological Psychology, 55,* 801–807.

Kubicki, M., Westin, C. F., Maier, S. E., Mamata, H., Frumin, M., Ersner-Herschfield, H., et al. (2002). Diffusion tensor imaging and its application to neuropsychiatric disorders. *Harvard Review of Psychiatry, 10,* 324–336.

Kuo, Z.-Y. (1967). *The dynamics of behavior development.* New York: Random House.

Ladd, C. O., Huot, R. L., Thrivikraman, K. V., Nemeroff, C. B., Meaney, M. J., & Plotsky, P. M. (2000). Long-term behavioral and neuroendocrine adaptation to adverse early experience. *Progress in Brain Research, 122,* 81–103.

Lander, E. S., & Weinberg, R. A. (2000). Genomics: Journey to the center of biology. *Science, 287,* 1777–1782.

Landis, C., & Hunt, W. A. (1939). *The startle pattern.* New York: Farrar Rinehart.

Lang, P. J. (1995). The emotion probe: Studies of motivation and attention. *American Psychologist, 50,* 372–385.

Lang, P. J., Bradley, M. M., & Cuthbert, B. N. (1995). *International affective picture system (IAPS): Technical manual and affective ratings.* Gainesville: The Center for Research in Psychophysiology, University of Florida.

Lazar, I., Darlington, R., Murray, H., Royce, J., & Snipper, A. (1982). Lasting effects of early education: A report from the Consortium for Longitudinal Studies. *Monographs of the Society for Research in Child Development, 47*(Serial No. 195).

Leah, J., Allardyce, H., & Cummins, R. (1985). Evoked cortical potential correlates of rearing environment in rats. *Biological Psychology, 20,* 21–29.

LeDoux, J. E. (1996). *The emotional brain: The mysterious underpinnings of emotional lift.* New York: Simon & Schuster.

LeDoux, J. E. (2002). *Synaptic self: How are brains become who we are.* New York: Penguin Press.

Lehrman, D. S. (1953). A critique of Konnad Lorez's theory of instinctive behavior. *Quarterly Review of Biology, 28,* 337–363.

Levine, S. (1994). The ontogeny of the hypothalamic-pituitary-adrenal axis: The influence of maternal factors. *Annuals of the New York Academy of Sciences, 746,* 275–288.

Lewin, B. (2004). *Genes VIII.* Upper Saddle River, NJ: Pearson Education, Pearson Prentice-Hall.

Lewis, D. A., Hashimoto, T., & Volk, D. W. (2005). Cortical inhibitory neurons and Schizophrenia. *Nature, 6,* 312–324.

Lim, K. O., Hedehus, M., Moseley, M., de Crespigny, A., Sullivan, E. V., & Pfefferbaum, A. (1999). Compromised white matter tract integrity in Schizophrenia inferred from diffusion tensor imaging. *Archives of General Psychiatry, 56,* 367–374.

Lore, R. K. (1969). Pain avoidance behavior of rats reared in restricted and enriched environments. *Developmental Psychology, 1,* 482–484.

Lowenstein, D. H., & Parent, J. M. (1999). Brain, heal thyself. *Science, 283,* 1126–1127.

Luciana, M., & Nelson, C. A. (2002). Assessment of neuropsychological function through use of the Cambridge Neuropsychological Testing Automated Battery: Performance in 4- to 12-year-old children. *Developmental Neuropsychology, 22,* 595–624.

Lupien, S. J., King, S., Meaney, M. J., & McEwen, B. S. (2001). Can poverty get under your skin? Basal cortisol levels and cognitive function in children from low and high socioeconomic status. *Development and Psychopathology, 13,* 653–666.

Luria, A. R. (1980). *Higher cortical functions in man.* New York: Basic Books.

Luthar, S. S. (Ed.). (2003). *Resilience and vulnerability: Adaptation in the context of childhood adversities.* New York: Cambridge University Press.

Luthar, S. S., & Cicchetti, D. (2000). The construct of resilience: Implications for intervention and social policy. *Development and Psychopathology, 12,* 857–885.

Luthar, S. S., Cicchetti, D., & Becker, B. (2000). The construct of resilience: A critical evaluation and guidelines for future work. *Child Development, 71,* 543–562.

Luthar, S. S., & Zigler, E. (1992). Intelligence and social competence among high-risk adolescents. *Development and Psychopathology, 4,* 287–299.

Luu, P., & Tucker, D. (1996). Self-regulation and cortical development: Implications for functional studies of the brain. In R. W. Thatcher, G. R. Lyon, J. Rumsey, & N. A. Krasnegor (Eds.), *Developmental neuroimaging; Mapping the development of brain behavior* (pp. 298–305). San Diego, CA: Academic Press.

Maleeva, N. E., Ivolgina, G. L., Anokhin, K. V., & Limborskaya, S. A. (1989). Patterns of c-fos expression in rat brain in the process of learning. *Genetica, 25,* 1119–1121.

Malenka, R. C., & Nicoll, R. A. (1999). Long-term potentiation: A decade of progress? *Science, 285*(5435), 1870–1874.

Marenco, S., & Weinberger, D. R. (2000). The neurodevelopemental hypothesis of Schizophrenia: Following a trail of evidence from cradle to grave. *Development and Psychopathology, 12,* 501–528.

Martin, S. L., Ramey, C. T., & Ramey, S. L. (1990). The prevention of intellectual impairment in children of impoverished families: Findings of a randomized trial of educational daycare. *American Journal of Public Health, 80,* 844–847.

Mascolo, M. F., Pollack, R. D., & Fischer, K. W. (1997). Keeping the construction in development: An epigenetic systems approach. *Journal of Constructivist Psychology, 10,* 25–49.

Masten, A. S. (2001). Ordinary magic: Resilience processes in development. *American Psychologist, 56*(3), 227–238.

Masten, A. S., Best, K., & Garmezy, N. (1990). Resilience and development: Contributions from the study of children who overcome adversity. *Development and Psychopathology, 2,* 425–444.

Masten, A. S., & Garmezy, N. (1985). Risk, vulnerability, and protective factors in developmental psychopathology. In B. Lahey & A. Kazdin (Eds.), *Advances in clinical child psychology* (Vol. 8, pp. 1–52). New York: Plenum Press.

Masten, A. S., Hubbard, J. J., Gest, S. D., Tellegen, A., Garmezy, N., & Ramirez, M. (1999). Competence in the context of adversity: Pathways to resilience and maladaptation from childhood to late adolescence. *Development and Psychopathology, 11,* 143–169.

Masten, A. S., & Reed, M. G. (2002). Resilience in development. In S. R. Snyder & S. J. Lopez (Eds.), *The handbook of positive psychology* (pp. 74–88). Oxford, England: Oxford University Press.

Maughan, A., & Cicchetti, D. (2002). The impact of child maltreatment and interadult violence on children's emotion regulation abilities. *Child Development, 73,* 1525–1542.

Mayberg, H. S. (2003). Modulating dysfunctional limbic-cortical circuits in depression: Towards development of brain-based algorithms for diagnosis and optimized treatment. *British Medical Bulletin, 65,* 193–207.

McEwen, B. S. (1994). Steroid hormone actions on the brain: When is the genome involved? *Hormones and Behavior, 28,* 396–405.

McEwen, B. S. (1998). Protective and damaging effects of stress mediators. *Seminars in Medicine of Beth Israel Deaconess Medical Center, 338,* 171–179.

McEwen, B. S. (2000). Effects of adverse experiences for brain structure and function. *Biological Psychiatry, 48,* 721–731.

McEwen, B. S., & Magarinos, A. M. (1997). Stress effects on morphology and function of the hippocampus. *Annals of the New York Academy of Sciences, 821,* 271–284.

McEwen, B. S., & Sapolsky, R. M. (1995). Stress and cognitive function. *Current Opinion in Neurobiology, 5,* 205–216.

McEwen, B. S., & Stellar, E. (1993). Stress and the individual mechanisms leading to disease. *Archives of Internal Medicine, 153,* 2093–2101.

McGlashan, T. H., & Hoffman, R. E. (2000). Schizophrenia as a disorder of developmentally reduced synaptic connectivity. *Archives of General Psychiatry, 57,* 637–648.

McHugh, P. R., & Slavney, P. R. (1986). *The perspectives of psychiatry.* Baltimore: Johns Hopkins University Press.

Meaney, M. J. (2001). Maternal care, gene expression, and the transmission of individual differences in stress reactivity across generations. *Annual Review of Neuroscience, 24,* 1161–1192.

Meaney, M. J., Diorio, J., Francis, D., Widdowson, J., LaBlante, P., Caldji, C., et al. (1996). Early environmental regulation of forebrain, glucocorticoid receptor gene expression: Implications for adrenocortical response to stress. *Developmental Neuroscience, 18,* 49–72.

Mechelli, A., Crinion, J. T., Noppeney, U., O'Doherty, J., Ashburner, J., Frackowiak, R. S., et al. (2004). Neurolinguistics: Structural plasticity in the bilingual brain. *Nature, 431,* 757.

Mednick, S. A., Cannon, T., Barr, C., & Lyon, M. (Eds.). (1991). *Fetal neural development and adult Schizophrenia.* New York: Cambridge University Press.

Mednick, S. A., Machon, R. A., Huttunen, M. O., & Bonett, D. (1988). Adult Schizophrenia following prenatal exposure to an influenza epidemic. *Archives of General Psychiatry, 45*(2), 189–192.

Meehl, P. E. (1962). Schizotaxia, schizotypy, Schizophrenia. *American Psychologist, 17,* 827–838.

Merzenich, M. M. (1998). Long-term change of mind. *Science, 282,* 1062–1063.

Merzenich, M. M., Jenkins, W. L., Johnston, P., Schreiner, C., Miller, S., & Tallal, P. (1996). Temporal processing deficits of language-learning impaired children ameliorated by training. *Science, 271,* 77–81.

Metzger, L. J., Orr, S. P., Berry, N. J., Ashern, C. E., Lasso, N. B., & Pitman, R. K. (1999). Physiologic reactivity to startling tones in women with posttraumatic stress disorder. *Journal of Abnormal Psychology, 108,* 347–352.

Meyer-Lindenberg, A. S., Olsen, R. K., Kohn, P. D., Brown, T., Egan, M. F., Weinberger, D. R., et al. (2005). Regionally specific disturbance of dorsolateral prefrontal-hipposcampal functional connectivity in Schizophrenia. *Archives of General Psychiatry, 62,* 379–386.

Miller, G. A., & Keller, J. (2000). Psychology and neuroscience: Making peace. *Current Directions in Psychological Science, 9,* 212–215.

Mirescu, C., Peters, J. D., & Gould, E. (2004). Early life experience alters response of adult neurogenesis to stress. *Nature Neuroscience, 7*(8), 841–846.

Mirnics, K., Middleton, F. A., Lewis, D. A., & Levitt, P. (2001). Analysis of complex brain disorders with gene expression microarrays: Schizophrenia as a disease of the synapse. *Trends in Neurosciences, 24,* 479–486.

Morgan, C. A., Grillon, C., Lubin, H., & Southwick, S. M. (1997). Startle abnormalities in women with sexual assault related PTSD. *American Journal of Psychiatry, 154,* 1076–1080.

Morgan, C. A., Grillon, C., Southwick, S. M., Davis, M., & Charney, D. S. (1996). Exaggerated acoustic startle reflex in Gulf War veterans with posttraumatic stress disorder. *American Journal of Psychiatry, 153,* 64–68.

Morgan, M. J. (1973). Effects of postweaning environment of learning in the rat. *Animal Behaviour, 21,* 429–442.

Murphy, L. B. (1974). Coping, vulnerability, and resilience in childhood. In G. V. Coelho, D. A. Hamburg, & J. E. Adams (Eds.), *Coping and adaptation* (pp. 69–100). New York: Basic Books.

Nachmias, M., Gunnar, M. R., Mangelsdorf, S., Parritz, R. H., & Buss, K. (1996). Behavioral inhibition and stress reactivity: The moderating role of attachment security. *Child Development, 67,* 508–522.

Nelson, C. A. (1999). Neural plasticity and human development. *Current Directions in Psychological Science, 8,* 42–45.

Nelson, C. A. (Ed.). (2000a). *The effects of early adversity on neurobehavioral development: Minnesota Symposium on Child Psychology* (Vol. 31). Mahwah, NJ: Erlbaum.

Nelson, C. A. (2000b). The neurobiological bases of early intervention. In J. Shonkoff & S. Meisels (Eds.), *Handbook of early childhood intervention* (2nd ed., pp. 204–227). New York: Cambridge University Press.

Nelson, C. A., & Bloom, F. E. (1997). Child development and neuroscience. *Child Development, 68,* 970–987.

Nelson, C. A., Bloom, F. E., Cameron, J. L., Amaral, D., Dahl, R. E., & Pine, D. (2002). An integrative, multidisciplinary approach to the study of brain-behavior relations in the context of typical and atypical development. *Development and Psychopathology, 14,* 499–520.

Nelson, C. A., & Bosquet, M. (2000). Neurobiology of fetal and infant development: Implications for infant mental health. In C. H. Zeanah (Ed.), *Handbook of infant mental health* (2nd ed., pp. 37–59). New York: Guilford Press.

Nestler, E. J., & Duman, R. S. (2002). Intracellular messenger pathways as mediators of neural plasticity. In F. E. Bloom & D. J. Kupfer (Eds.), *Psychopharmacology: The fourth generation of progress* (4th ed., pp. 234–267). Philadelphia: Lippincott, Williams, & Wilkins.

Noam, G., Chandler, M., & Lalonde, C. E. (1995). Clinical-developmental psychology: Constructivism and social cognition in the study of psychological dysfunctions. In D. Cicchetti & D. Cohen (Eds.), *Developmental psychopathology: Theory and method* (Vol. 1, pp. 424–464). New York: Wiley.

Nowakowski, R. S. (1987). Basic concepts of CNS development. *Child Development, 58,* 568–595.

Nowakowski, R. S., & Hayes, N. L. (1999). CNS development: An overview. *Development and Psychopathology, 11,* 395–418.

Nowakowski, R. S., & Hayes, N. L. (2000). New neurons: Extraordinary evidence or extraordinary conclusion? *Science, 288,* 771a.

O'Boyle, M. W., Benbow, C. P., & Alexander, J. E. (1995). Sex differences, hemispheric laterality, and associated brain activity in the intellectually gifted. *Developmental Neuropsychology, 4,* 415–443.

O'Connor, T. G. (2003). Natural experiments to study the effects of early experience: Progress and limitations. *Development and Psychopathology, 15*(4), 837–852.

O'Leary, D. (1989). Do cortical areas emerge from a protocortex? *Trends in Neurosciences, 12,* 400–406.

Ornitz, E. M., & Pynoos, R. S. (1989). Startle modulation in children with posttraumatic stress disorder. *American Journal of Psychiatry, 146,* 866–870.

Orr, S. P., Lasko, N. B., Shalev, A. Y., & Pitman, R. K. (1995). Physiologic responses to loud tones in Vietnam veterans with posttraumatic stress disorder. *Journal of Abnormal Psychology, 104,* 75–82.

Orr, S. P., Solomon, Z., Peri, T., Pitman, R. K., & Shalev, A. Y. (1997). Physiologic responses to loud tones in Israeli veterans of the 1973 Yom Kippur war. *Biological Psychiatry, 41,* 319–326.

Ough, B. R., Beatty, W. W., & Khalili, J. (1972). Effects of isolated and enriched rearing on response inhibition. *Psychonomic Science, 27,* 293–294.

Owen, A. M., Evans, A. C., & Petrides, M. (1996). Planning and spatial working memory: A positron emission topography study in humans. *European Journal of Neuroscience, 8,* 353–364.

Ozonoff, S. (2001). Advances in the cognitive neuroscience of Autism. In C. A. Nelson & M. Luciana (Eds.), *Handbook of developmental cognitive neuroscience* (pp. 537–548). Cambridge, MA: MIT Press.

Ozonoff, S., & Strayer, D. L. (1997). Inhibitory function in nonretarded children with Autism. *Journal of Autism and Developmental Disorders, 27,* 59–77.

Ozonoff, S., Strayer, D. L., McMahon, W. M., & Filoux, F. (1994). Executive function abilities in Autism and Tourette syndrome: An information processing approach. *Journal of Child Psychology and Psychiatry, 35,* 1015–1032.

Pantev, C., Engelien, A., Candia, V., & Elbert, T. (2001). Representational cortex in musicians: Plastic alterations in response to musical practice. *Annals of the New York Academy of Sciences, 930,* 300–314.

Paradiso, S., Andreasen, N. C., O'Leary, D. S., Arndt, S., & Robinson, R. G. (1997). Cerebellar size and cognition: Correlations with IQ, verbal memory and motor dexterity. *Neuropsychiatry, Neuropsychology, and Behavioral Neurology, 10,* 1–8.

Parker, J. G., Rubin, K. H., Price, J. M., & DeRosier, M. E. (1995). Peer relationships, child development, and adjustment: A developmental psychopathology perspective. In D. Cicchetti & D. J. Cohen (Eds.), *Developmental psychopathology: Risk, disorder, and adaptation* (Vol. 2, pp. 96–161). New York: Wiley.

Parker, S. W., & Nelson, C. A. (2005a). An event-related potential study of the impact of institutional rearing on face recognition. *Development and Psychopathology, 17*(3).

Parker, S. W., & Nelson, C. A. (2005b). The impact of early institutional rearing on the ability to discriminate facial expressions of emotion: An event-related potential study. *Child Development, 76*(1), 54.

Pascual-Leone, A., Nguyet, D., Cohen, L. G., Brasil-Neto, J. P., Cammarota, A., & Hallett, M. (1995). Modulation of muscle responses evoked by transcranial magnetic stimulation during the acquisition of new fine motor skills. *Journal of Neurophysiology, 74,* 1037–1045.

Pascual-Leone, A., & Torres, F. (1993). Plasticity of the sensorimotor cortex representation of the reading finger in Braille readers. *Brain, 116,* 39–52.

Pascual-Marqui, R. D., Michel, C. M., & Lehmann, D. (1994). Low resolution electromagnetic tomography: A new method for localizing electrical activity in the brain. *International Journal of Psychophysiology, 18,* 49–65.

Pellegrini, D., Masten, A., Garmezy, N., & Ferrarese, M. (1987). Correlates of social and academic competence in middle childhood. *Journal of Child Psychology and Psychiatry, 28,* 699–714.

Pellmar, T. C., & Eisenberg, L. (Eds.). (2000). *Bridging disciplines in the brain, behavioral, and clinical sciences.* Washington, DC: National Academy Press.

Peterson, B. S. (2003). Conceptual, methodological, and statistical challenges in brain imaging studies of developmentally based psychopathologies. *Development and Psychopathology, 15,* 811–832.

Petreanu, L., & Alvarez-Buylla, A. (2002). Maturation and death of adult-born olfactory bulb granule neurons: Role of olfaction. *Journal of Neuroscience, 22,* 6106–6113.

Piaget, J. (1971). *Biology and knowledge.* Chicago: University of Chicago Press.

Pizzagalli, D., Shackman, A. J., & Davidson, R. J. (2003). The functional neuroimaging of human emotion: Asymetric contributions of cortical and subcortical circuitry. In K. Hugdahl & R. J. Davidson (Eds.), *The asymmetrical brain* (pp. 511–532). Cambridge, MA: MIT Press.

Plomin, R., & Rutter, M. (1998). Child development, molecular genetics, and what to do with genes once they are found. *Child Development, 69,* 1223–1242.

Pollak, S. D., Cicchetti, D., & Klorman, R. (1998). Stress, memory, and emotion: Developmental considerations from the study of child maltreatment. *Development and Psychopathology, 10,* 811–828.

Pollak, S. D., Cicchetti, D., Klorman, R., & Brumaghim, J. (1997). Cognitive brain event-related potentials and emotion processing in maltreated children. *Child Development, 68,* 773–787.

Posner, M. I., & DiGirolamo, G. I. (2000). Cognitive neuroscience: Origins and promise. *Psychological Bullentin, 126,* 873–889.

Posner, M. I., & Rothbart, M. K. (2004). Hebb's neural networks support the integration of psychological science. *Canadian Psychologist, 45,* 265–278.

Post, R. M., Leverich, G. S., Weiss, S. R. B., Zhang, L., Xing, G., Li, H., et al. (2003). Psychosocial stressors as predisposing factors to affective illness and PTSD: Potential neurobiological mechanisms and theoretical implications. In D. Cicchetti & E. F. Walker (Eds.), *Neurodevelopmental mechanisms in psychopathology* (pp. 491–525). New York: Cambridge University Press.

Post, R. M., & Weiss, S. R. B. (1997). Emergent properties of neural systems: How focal molecular neurobiological alterations can affect behavior. *Development and Psychopathology, 9,* 907–929.

Post, R. M., Weiss, S. R. B., & Leverich, G. S. (1994). Recurrent affective disorder: Roots in developmental neurobiology and illness progression based on changes in gene expression. *Development and Psychopathology, 6,* 781–814.

Post, R. M., Weiss, S. R. B., Li, H., Smith, M. A., Zhang, L. X., Xing, G., et al. (1998). Neural plasticity and emotional memory. *Development and Psychopathology, 10*(4), 829–855.

Price, J. D., & Willshaw, D. J. (2000). *Mechanisms of cortical development.* New York: Oxford University Press.

Prigogine, I. (1978). Time, structure, and fluctuations. *Science, 201,* 777–785.

Raine, A., Mellingen, K., Liu, J., Venables, P., & Mednick, S. A. (2003). Effects of environmental enrichment at ages 3–5 years on schizotypal personality and antisocial behavior at ages 17 and 23 years. *American Journal of Psychiatry, 160,* 1627–1635.

Raine, A., Venables, P. H., Dalais, C., Mellingen, K., Reynolds, C., & Mednick, S. A. (2001). Early educational and health enrichment at age 3–5 years is associated with increased autonomic and central nervous system arousal and orienting at age 11 years: Evidence from the Mauritius Child Health Project. *Psychophysiology, 38,* 254–266.

Rakic, P. (1981). Developmental events leading to laminar and areal organization of the neocortex. In F. O. Schmitt, F. G. Worden, G. Adelman, & S. G. Dennis (Eds.), *The organization of the cerebral cortex* (pp. 7–28). Cambridge, MA: MIT Press.

Rakic, P. (1988a). Intrinsic and extrinsic determinants of neocortical parcellation: A radial unit model. In P. Rakic & W. Singer (Eds.), *Neurobiology of neocortex* (pp. 5–27). New York: Wiley.

Rakic, P. (1988b). Specification of cerebral cortex areas. *Science, 241,* 170–176.

Rakic, P. (1995). Corticogenesis in human and nonhuman primates. In M. Gazzaniga (Ed.), *The cognitive neurosciences* (pp. 127–145). Cambridge, MA: MIT Press.

Rakic, P. (1996). Development of the cerebral cortex in human and nonhuman primates. In M. Lewis (Ed.), *Child and adolescent psychiatry: A comprehensive textbook* (pp. 9–30). Baltimore: Williams & Wilkins.

Rakic, P. (1998). Young neurons for old brains? *Nature Neuroscience, 1,* 643–645.

Rakic, P. (2002a). Adult neurogenesis in mammals: An identity crisis. *Journal of Neuroscience, 22,* 614–618.

Rakic, P. (2002b). Neurogenesis in adult primate neocortex: An evaluation of the evidence. *Nature Reviews in Neuroscience, 3,* 65–71.

Ramey, C. T., & Ramey, S. L. (1992). Effective early intervention. *Mental Retardation, 30,* 337–345.

Ramey, C. T., & Ramey, S. L. (1998). Revention of intellectual disabilities: Early interventions to improve cognitive development. *Preventive Medicine, 27,* 224–232.

Raven, J., Raven, J. C., & Court, J. H. (1998). *Manual for Raven's progressive matrices and vocabulary scales.* Oxford, England: Oxford Psychologists Press.

Raychaudhuri, S., Sutphin, P. D., Chang, J. T., & Altman, R. B. (2001). Basic microarray analysis: Grouping and feature reduction. *Trends in Biotechnology, 19,* 189–193.

Reid, S. A., Duke, L. M., & Allen, J. J. B. (1998). Resting frontal electroencephalographic asymmetry in depression: Inconsistencies suggest the need to identify mediating factors. *Psychophysiology, 35,* 389–404.

Rende, R., & Plomin, R. (1993). Families at risk for psychopathology: Who becomes affected and why? *Development and Psychopathology, 5,* 529–540.

Renner, M. J., & Rosenzweig, M. R. (1987). *Enriched and impoverished environments: Effects on brain and behavior.* New York: Springer-Verlag.

Repetti, R., Taylor, S., & Seeman, T. (2002). Risky families: Family social environments and the mental and physical health of offspring. *Psychological Bulletin, 128,* 330–366.

Richters, J. E. (1997). The Hubble hypothesis and the developmentalist's dilemma. *Development and Psychopathology, 9,* 193–229.

Rieder, C., & Cicchetti, D. (1989). Organizational perspective on cognitive control functioning and cognitive-affective balance in maltreated children. *Developmental Psychology, 25,* 382–393.

Riva, D., & Giorgi, D. (2000). The cerebellum contributes to higher functions during development: Evidence from a series of children surgically treated for posterior fossa tumours. *Brain, 123,* 1051–1061.

Rochefort, C., Gheusi, G., Vincent, J.-D., & Lledo, P.-M. (2002). Enriched odor exposure increases the number of newborn neurons in the adult olfactory bulb and improves odor memory. *Journal of Neuroscience, 22,* 2679–2689.

Rodier, P. M. (2002). Converging evidence from brain stem injury in Autism. *Development and Psychopathology, 14*(3), 537–557.

Rosenzweig, M. R., Bennett, E. L., & Diamond, M. C. (1972). Brain changes in response to experience. *Scientific American, 226,* 22–29.

Rosenzweig, M. R., Bennett, E. L., Diamond, M. C., Wu, S. Y., Slagle, R., & Saffran, E. (1969). Influence of environmental complexity and visual stimulation on development of occipital cortex in the rat. *Brain Research, 14,* 427–445.

Ross, M. E., & Walsh, C. A. (2001). Human brain malformations and their lessions for neuronal migration. *Annual Review of Neuroscience, 24,* 1041–1070.

Ruddle, F. H., Bartels, J., Bentley, K., Kappen, C., Murtha, M., & Pendleton, J. (1994). Evolution of hox genes. *Annual Review of Genetics, 28,* 423–442.

Sadato, N., Pascual-Leone, A., Grafman, J., Ibanez, V., Deiber, M. P., Dold, G., et al. (1996). Activation of the primary visual cortex by Braille reading in blind subjects. *Nature, 380,* 526–528.

Sanchez, M. M., Ladd, C. O., & Plotsky, P. M. (2001). Early adverse experience as a developmental risk factor for later psychopathology: Evidence from rodent and primate models. *Development and Psychopathology, 13,* 419–450.

Santarelli, L., Saxe, M., Gross, C., Surget, A., Battaglia, F., Dulawa, S., et al. (2003). Requirement of hippocampal neurogenesis for the behavioral effects of antidepressants. *Science, 301,* 805–809.

Sapolsky, R. M. (1992). *Stress, the aging brain, and the mechanisms of neuron death.* Cambridge, MA: MIT Press.

Sapolsky, R. M. (1994). Individual differences and the stress response. *Seminars in the Neurosciences, 6,* 261–269.

Sapolsky, R. M. (1996). Stress, glucocorticoids, and damage to the NS: The current state of confusion. *Stress, 1,* 1–19.

Sapolsky, R. M. (2000a). Glucocorticoids and hippocampal atrophy in neuropsychiatric disorders. *Archives of General Psychiatry, 57,* 925–935.

Sapolsky, R. M. (2000b). The possibility of neurotoxicity in the hippocampus in major depression: A primer on neuron death. *Biological Psychiatry, 48,* 755–765.

Schneirla, T. C. (1957). The concept of development in comparative psychology. In D. B. Harris (Ed.), *An issue in the study of human behavior* (pp. 78–108). Minneapolis, MN: University of Minneapolis Press.

Schore, A. N. (1994). *Affect regulation and the origin of the self: The neurobiology of emotional development.* Hillsdale, NJ: Erlbaum.

Schwartz, E. B., Granger, D. A., Susman, E. J., Gunnar, M. R., & Laird, B. (1998). Assessing salivary cortisol in studies of child development. *Child Development, 69,* 1503–1513.

Segal, M. (2005). Dendritic spines and long-term plasticity. *Nature, 6,* 277–284.

Segalowitz, S. J. (1994). Developmental psychology and brain development: A historical perspective. In G. Dawson & K. W. Fischer (Eds.), *Human behavior and the developing brain* (pp. 67–92). New York: Guilford Press.

Segerstrom, S. C. (2000). Personality and the immune system: Models, methods, and mechanisms. *Annals of Behavioral Medicine, 22,* 180–190.

Sharma, J., Angelucci, A., & Sur, M. (2000). Induction of visual orientation modules in auditory cortex. *Nature, 404,* 841–847.

Shenton, M. E., Frumin, M., McCarley, R. W., Maier, S. E., Westin, C.-F., Fischer, I. A., et al. (2001). Morphometric magnetic resonance imaging studies: Findings in Schizophrenia. In D. D. Dougherty & S. L. Rauch (Eds.), *Psychiatric neuroimaging research: Contemporary strategies* (pp. 1–60). Washington, DC: American Psychiatric Publishing.

Sidman, R. L., & Rakic, P. (1982). Development of the human central nervous system. In W. Haymaker & R. D. Adams (Eds.), *Histology and histopathology of the nervous system* (pp. 3–145). Springfield, IL: Thomas.

Singer, W. (1995). Development and plasticity of cortical processing architectures. *Science, 270,* 758–764.

Smith, H. V. (1972). Effects of environmental enrichment on open-field activity and Hebb-Williams problem solving in rats. *Journal of Comparative and Physiological Psychology, 80,* 163–168.

Spear, L. P. (2000). The adolescent brain and age-related behavioral manifestations. *Neuroscience and Behavioral Reviews, 24,* 417–463.

Sroufe, L. A. (1989). Pathways to adaptation and maladaptation: Psychopathology as developmental deviation. In D. Cicchetti (Ed.), *Rochester Symposium on Developmental Psychopathology: The emergence of a discipline* (Vol. 1, pp. 13–40). Hillsdale, NJ: Erlbaum.

Sroufe, L. A. (1990). Considering normal and abnormal together: The essence of developmental psychopathology. *Development and Psychopathology, 2,* 335–347.

Sroufe, L. A., Egeland, B., & Kreutzer, T. (1990). The fate of early experience following developmental change: Longitudinal approaches to individual adaptation in childhood. *Child Development, 61,* 1363–1373.

Stein, D. G., & Dawson, R. G. (1980). The dynamics of growth, organization, and adaptability in the central neurons system. In J. Kagan & B. Brim (Eds.), *Constancy and change in human development* (pp. 163–228). Cambridge, MA: Harvard University Press.

Stein, M. B., Koverola, C., Torchia, M. G., & McClarty, B. (1997). Hippocampal volume in women victimized by childhood sexual abuse. *Psychological Medicine, 27,* 951–959.

Steingard, R. J., & Coyle, J. T. (1998). Brain development. In N. E. Alessi, J. T. Coyle, S. I. Harrison & S. Eth (Eds.), *Handbook of child and adolescent psychiatry* (pp. 97–107). New York: Wiley.

Steven, M. S., & Blakemore, C. (2004). Cortical plasticity in the adult human brain. In M. S. Gazzaniga (Ed.), *The cognitive neurosciences* (pp. 1243–1254). Cambridge, MA: MIT Press.

Sur, M., Garraghty, P. E., & Roe, A. W. (1988). Experimentally induced visual projections into auditory thalamus and cortex. *Science, 242,* 1437–1441.

Sur, M., Pallas, S. L., & Roe, A. W. (1990). Cross-modal plasticity in cortical development: Differentiation and specification of sensory neocortex. *Trends in Neuroscience, 13,* 227–233.

Susser, E. R., & Wallace, R. B. (1982). The effects of environmental complexity on the hippocampal formation of the adult rat. *Acta Neurobiologica Experimentalis, 42,* 203–207.

Sutton, S. K., & Davidson, R. J. (1997). Prefrontal brain asymmetry: A biological substrate of the behavioral approach and inhibition systems. *Psychological Science, 8,* 204–210.

Sutton, S. K., Davidson, R. J., Donzella, B., Irwin, W., & Dottl, D. A. (1997). Manipulating affective state using extended picture presentation. *Psychophysiology, 34,* 217–226.

Tallal, P., Miller, S. L., Bedi, G., Byma, G., Wang, X., Nagarajan, S. S., et al. (1996). Language comprehension in language-learning impaired children improved with acoustically modified speech. *Science, 271,* 81–84.

Teuber, H.-L. (1975). Recovery of function after brain injury. In *Outcome of severe damage to the central nervous system* (pp. 159–186). Amsterdam: Elsevier.

Thatcher, R. W. (1992). Cyclic cortical reorganization during early childhood. *Brain and Cognition, 20,* 24–50.

Thatcher, R. W. (1994). Psychopathology of early frontal lobe damage: Dependence on cycles of development. *Development and Psychopathology, 6,* 565–596.

Thatcher, R. W. (1997). Human frontal lobe development: A theory of cyclical cortical reorganization. In N. Krasnegor, G. R. Lyon & P. S. G. Rakic (Eds.), *Development of the prefrontal cortex: Evolution, neurobiology, and behavior* (pp. 85–113). Baltimore: Paul H. Brookes.

Thelen, E., & Smith, L. B. (1998). Dynamic systems theories. In W. Damon & R. Lerner (Eds.), *Handbook of child psychology: Vol. 1. Theoretical, models of human development* (pp. 563–634). New York: Wiley.

Thompson, R. A. (1990). Emotions and self-regulation. In R. Thompson (Ed.), *Nebraska Symposium on Motivation: Socioemotional development* (Vol. 36, pp. 367–467). Lincoln: University of Nebraska Press.

Thompson, R. A., & Nelson, C. A. (2001). Developmental science and the media: Early brain development. *American Psychologist, 56*(1), 5–15.

Toga, A. W., & Thompson, P. M. (2003). Mapping brain asymmetry. *Nature Reviews: Neuroscience, 4,* 37–48.

Tomarken, A. J., Davidson, R. J., & Henriques, J. B. (1990). Resting frontal activation asymmetry predicts emotional reactivity to film clips. *Journal of Personality and Social Psychology, 59,* 791–801.

Tomarken, A. J., Davidson, R. J., Wheeler, R. E., & Doss, R. C. (1992). Individual differences in anterior brain asymmetry and fundamental dimensions of emotion. *Journal of Personality and Social Psychology, 62,* 676–687.

Torasdotter, M., Metsis, M., Henriksson, B. G., Winblad, B., & Mohammed, A. H. (1998). Environmental enrichment results in higher levels of nerve growth factor mRNA in the rat visual cortex and hippocampus. *Behavioral Brain Research, 93,* 83–90.

Torrey, E. F. (1997). *Out of the shadows: Confronting America's mental illness crises.* New York: Wiley.

Toth, S. L., & Cicchetti, D. (1999). Developmental psychopathology and child psychotherapy. In S. Russ & T. Ollendick (Eds.), *Handbook of psychotherapies with children and families* (pp. 15–44). New York: Plenum Press.

Townsend, J., Harris, N. S., & Courchesne, E. (1996). Visual attention abnormalities in Autism: Delayed orienting to location. *Journal of the International Neuropsychological Society, 2,* 541–550.

Tsuang, M., Wollson, R. F., & Fleming, J. A. (1979). Long-term outcome of major psychoses: I. Schizophrenia and affective disorders compared with psychiatrically symptom-free surgical conditions. *Archives of General Psychiatry, 36,* 1295–1301.

Tucker, D. (1981). Lateral brain function, emotion, and conceptualization. *Psychological Bulletin, 89,* 19–46.

Turner, A. M., & Greenough, W. T. (1985). Differential rearing effects on rat visual cortex synapses: I. Synaptic and neuronal density and synapses per neuron. *Brain Research, 329,* 195–203.

Turrigiano, G. G., Leslie, K. R., Desai, N. S., Rutherford, L. C., & Nelson, S. B. (1998). Activity-dependent scaling of quantal amplitude in neocortical neurons. *Nature, 391,* 892–896.

Vanman, E. J., Boehmelt, A. H., Dawson, M. E., & Schell, A. M. (1996). The varying time courses of attentional and affective modulation of the startle eyeblink reflex. *Psychophysiology, 33,* 691–697.

Vazquez, D. M. (1998). Stress and the developing limbic-hypothalamic-pituitary-adrenal axis. *Psychoneuroendocrinology, 23,* 663–700.

Villarreal, G., Hamilton, D. A., Petropoules, H., Driscoll, I., Rowland, L. M., Griego, J. A., et al. (2002). Reduced hippocampal volume and total white matter volume in posttraumatic stress disorder. *Biological Psychiatry, 52,* 119–125.

Volpe, J. J. (1995). *Neurology of the newborn* (3rd ed.). Philadelphia: Saunders.

von Bertalanffy, L. (1968). *General system theory.* New York: Braziller.

Vrana, S. R., Spence, E. L., & Lang, P. J. (1988). The startle probe response: A new measure of emotion? *Journal of Abnormal Psychology, 97,* 487–491.

Waddington, C. H. (1957). *The strategy of genes.* London: Allen & Unwin.

Waddington, C. H. (1966). *Principles of development and differentation.* New York: Macmillan.

Wainwright-Sharp, J. A., & Bryson, S. E. (1993). Visual orienting deficits in high-functioning people with Autism. *Journal of Autism and Developmental Disorders, 23,* 1–13.

Walker, E. F., Davis, D. M., & Gottlieb, L. A. (1991). Charting the developmental trajectories to Schizophrenia. In D. Cicchetti & S. L. Toth (Eds.), *Rochester Symposium on Developmental Psychopathology: Vol. 3. Models and integrations* (pp. 185–205). Rochester, NY: University of Rochester Press.

Walker, E. F., & DiForio, D. (1997). Schizophrenia: A neural diathesis-stress model. *Psychological Review, 104,* 1–19.

Walker, E. F., Sabuwalla, Z., & Huot, R. (2004). Pubertal neuromaturation, stress sensitivity, and psychopathology. *Development and Psychopathology, 16*(4), 807–824.

Walker, E. F., & Walder, D. (2003). Neurohormonal aspects of the development of psychotic disorders. In D. Cicchetti & E. F. Walker (Eds.), *Neurodevelopmental mechanisms in psychopathology* (pp. 526–544). New York: Cambridge University Press.

Wallace, C. S., Withers, G. S., Weiler, I. J., & Greenough, W. T. (1991). Expression of the immediate early gene zif-268 influenced by brief exposure to environmental complexity in the occipital cortex of weanling rats. *Third IBRO World Congress of Neuroscience Abstracts, 3,* 25–48.

Watson, C., & Gametchu, B. (1999). Membrane-initiated steroid actions and the proteins that mediate them. *Proceedings of the Society for Experimental Biology and Medicine, 220,* 9–19.

Watson, D., & Clark, L. (1984). Negative affectivity: The disposition to experience aversive emotional states. *Psychological Bulletin, 96,* 465–490.

Watt, N. F. (1972). Longitudinal changes in the social behavior of children hospitalized for Schizophrenia as adults. *Journal of Nervous and Mental Disorders, 155,* 42–54.

Webster's new collegiate dictionary (5th ed.). (1979). Springfield, MA: Merriam-Webster.

Weinberger, D. R. (1987). Implications of normal brain development for the pathogenesis of Schizophrenia. *Archives of General Psychiatry, 44,* 660–669.

Weinberger, D. R. (1995). From neuropathology to neurodevelopment. *Lancet, 346,* 552–557.

Weisel, T. (1994). Genetics and behavior. *Science, 264,* 1647.

Weiss, P. A. (1961). Deformities as cues to understanding development of form. *Perspectives in Biology and Medicine, 4,* 133–151.

Werner, H. (1957). The concept of development from a comparative and organismic point of view. In D. B. Harris (Ed.), *The concept of development* (pp. 125–148). Minneapolis, MN: University of Minnesota Press.

Werner, E., & Smith, R. (1982). *Vulnerable but invincible: A study of resilient children.* New York: McGraw-Hill.

Wheeler, R. E., Davidson, R. J., & Tomarken, A. J. (1993). Frontal brain asymmetry and emotional reactivity: A biological substrate of affective style. *Psychophysiology, 30,* 82–89.

White, J. L., Moffitt, T. E., & Silva, P. A. (1989). A prospective replication of the protective effects of IQ in subjects at high risk for juvenile delinquency. *Journal of Consulting and Clinical Psychology, 57,* 719–724.

Woods, C. G. (2004). Human microcephaly. *Current Opinion in Neurobiology, 14,* 112–117.

Xiang, H., Lin, C., Ma, X., Zhang, Z., Bower, J. M., Weng, X., et al. (2003). Involvement of the cerebellum in semantic discrimination: An fMRI study. *Human Brain Mapping, 18,* 208–214.

Yakovlev, P. I., & LeCours, A. R. (1967). The myelogentic cycles of regional maturation of the brain. In A. Minkowski (Ed.), *Regional development of the brain in early life* (pp. 3–64). New York: Oxford.

Young, L. J., Nilson, R., Waymore, K. G., MacGregor, G. R., & Insel, T. R. (1999). Increased affiliation response to vasopressin in mice expressing the V1a receptor from a monogamous mole. *Nature, 400,* 766–768.

Zigler, E., & Glick, M. (1986). *A developmental approach to adult psychopathology.* New York: Wiley.

Zigler, E., & Valentine, J. (1979). *Project head start: A legacy of the war on poverty.* New York: Free Press.

CHAPTER 2

Collaborative Regulations of Vitality in Early Childhood: Stress in Intimate Relationships and Postnatal Psychopathology

COLWYN TREVARTHEN, KENNETH J. AITKEN, MARIE VANDEKERCKHOVE, JONATHAN DELAFIELD-BUTT, and EMESE NAGY

Survival depends upon two contrasting phenomena or processes, two ways of achieving adaptive action. Evolution must always, Janus-like, face in two directions: inward toward the developmental regularities and physiology of the living creature and outward toward the vagaries and demands of the environment. These two necessary components of life contrast in interesting ways: the inner development—the embryology or "epigenesis"—is conservative and demands that every new thing shall conform or be compatible with the regularities of the status quo ante. If we think of a natural selection of new features of anatomy or physiology—then it is clear that one side of this selection process will favour those new items which do not upset the old applecart. This is minimal necessary conservatism.

In contrast, the outside world is perpetually changing and becoming ready to receive creatures which have undergone change, almost insisting upon change. No animal or plant can ever be "ready made." The internal recipe insists upon compatibility but is never sufficient for the development and life of the organism. Always the creature itself must achieve change of its own body. It must acquire certain somatic characteristics by use, by disuse, by habit, by hardship, and by nurture. These "acquired characteristics" must, however, never be passed on to the offspring. They must not be directly incorporated into the DNA. . . . The individual body undergoes adaptive change under external pressure, but natural selection acts upon the gene pool of the population. . . . The acquired characteristics do not become unimportant by not being carried in and passed on by DNA. It is still habits which set the conditions for natural selection. And note this converse principle, that the acquisition of bad habits, at a social level, surely sets the context for selection of ultimately lethal genetic propensities. (G. Bateson, 1979, pp. 234–235)

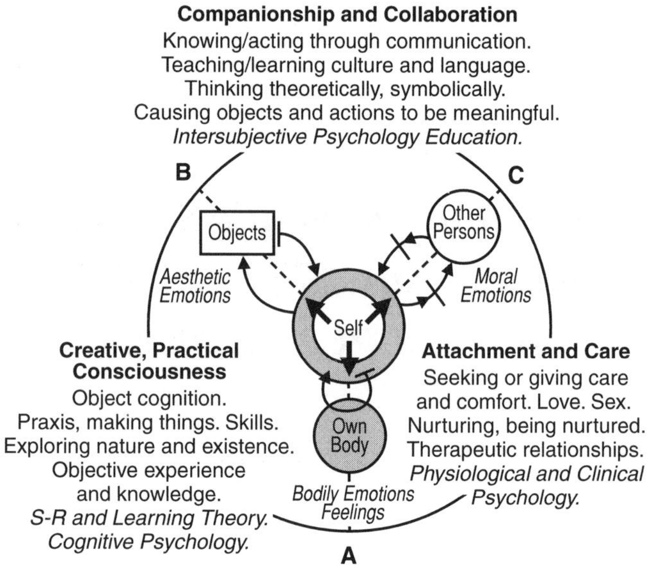

Figure 2.1 Three facets of the active self, for the body (A), for non-living objects (B), and for other subjects or persons (C); and how they are combined in behaviors: of self-protection by attachment to a carer, in private exploration of objects, and when sharing experiences in companionship. *Sources:* From "Intrinsic Motives for Companionship in Understanding: Their Origin, Development and Significance for Infant Mental Health," by C. Trevarthen, 2001a, *International Journal of Infant Mental Health, 22*(1–2), pp. 95–131; and "Stepping Away from the Mirror: Pride and Shame in Adventures of Companionship: Reflections on the Nature and Emotional Needs of Infant Intersubjectivity," by C. Trevarthen, in *Attachment and Bonding: A New Synthesis* (Dahlem Workshop Report 92), C. S. Carter, L. Ahnert, K. E. Grossman, S. B. Hrdy, M. E. Lamb, S. W. Porges, et al. (Eds.), 2005c, Cambridge, MA: MIT Press.

EPIGENISIS OF BODY AND BRAIN FOR HEALTH IN SOCIABILITY AND LEARNING

In previous publications, we have considered the implications of research on infants' capacities for communication and their developmental changes for an approach to infant mental health (Trevarthen, 2001a; Trevarthen & Aitken, 1994). The powerful innate volitions and emotions of an infant's Self for engagement with the feelings, interests, and intentions of an Other are adapted to establish affectionate *attachments.* They motivate and regulate collaborative play and learning in relations of *companionship* (Aitken & Trevarthen, 1997; Trevarthen, 2005c; Figure 2.1). This interpersonal system requires efficient initiatives from the child to attract and engage with parental responses, and it reacts to the sensitivity and quality of those responses. If the behaviors and expressions of the Other are inattentive, de-

pressed, or intrusive, or if, in experimental studies, they are briefly made noncontingent on what the infant is doing, this causes the infant to become avoidant, withdrawn, angry, and generally "dysregulated" (Murray & Trevarthen, 1985; Trevarthen, 1993a, 1993b, 2005a; Tronick, Als, Adamson, Wise, & Brazelton, 1978).

We believe the evidence shows that a young human person should be understood to require more than external regulation for emotional and autonomic equilibrium or homeostasis, and that already in the first minutes after birth, a baby can demonstrate interest for and awareness of the focused attention of a nearby person and how that person responds to the infant's expressions of conscious volitions and emotions (Trevarthen, 2005c). The rhythms of engagement obey rules that prove the movements of infant and adult are generated with matching time (Beebe, Jaffe, Feldstein, Mays, & Alson, 1985; Stern, 1974; Stern, Speiker, & Mackain, 1982; Trevarthen, 1974, 1986, 1999a). Within a few weeks, in the "primary intersubjectivity" stage (Trevarthen, 1979, 1999b; Trevarthen & Aitken, 2001), this sharing of time sense shows up in imitative mirroring of the forms of expressive movements. It exhibits *attunement* to the affective qualities in expressive movements (Stern, Hofer, Haft, & Dore, 1985), in *felt immediacy* (Bråten, 1988, 1998). It forms turn-taking "protoconversations" (M. C. Bateson, 1975, 1979) that give pleasure to both child and adult over joint coregulated performances lasting tens of seconds (Malloch, 1999; Reddy & Trevarthen, 2004; Trevarthen, 1993a, 1999a, 2005a; Trevarthen & Schögler, 2005).

As their engagements in play develop in early weeks, the mutual regulation between a mother and her infant has measurable properties of what we have described as *communicative musicality* (Malloch, 1999; Trevarthen & Malloch, 2002). Thereafter, more elaborate games, eventually incorporating orientation to and use of shared things in the nearby world, strengthens the joint awareness, co-consciousness, or what Tronick (2005) calls "dyadic states of consciousness," and establishes remembered routines of gesture and action and favorite objects and tasks. Mother and baby fabricate expressive "narrations" or "stories of meaning" (Trevarthen & Schögler, 2005) and build expectations for passing back and forth marked tricks of expression in humorous ways (Reddy, 2003, 2005; Reddy & Morris, 2004). At the end of the 1st year,

the cocreated acts, made meaningful by sharing (Trevarthen & Hubley, 1978), lead the baby to explore vocal utterances that imitate the words others use to name these "acts of meaning" and their objects (Halliday, 1975; Figure 2.2).

We propose that the infant's motives and emotions for such a rich evolving experience in approving friendships are capable, if developing abnormally in the child or if not given appropriate support from the human environment, of generating chronic stress and psychopathology that blocks the path to pleasure in human company and the path to meaning (Aitken & Trevarthen, 1997; Trevarthen, 2001a; Trevarthen & Aitken, 2001). The infant's evident psychic powers are fitted to be regulated in intimate and lively relationships, and they can suffer disorder or trauma from destructive events in these relationships. They are, however, not weak adaptations and are capable of impressive self-corrective reactions to distress. They also respond readily to sensitive forms of therapeutic communication, especially to any improvements in contact and emotionally and practically satisfying engagement with the caregiver (Trevarthen & Aitken, 2001; Trevarthen & Malloch, 2000).

Our aim in this chapter is to consider how the vitality and vulnerability of a young human person is adapted to become balanced in relationships—how the stresses and

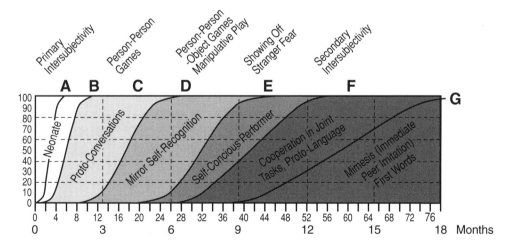

Figure 2.2 In the first 18 months of life there are marked changes in the infant's consciousness of other persons and in their motives for communication, before language. Several major transitions can be observed in self-and-other awareness at particular ages. These lead the child toward cooperative interest in actions and objects, and cultural learning. *Sources:* From "The Neurobiology of Early Communication: Intersubjective Regulations in Human Brain Development" (pp. 841–882), by C. Trevarthen, in *Handbook on Brain and Behavior in Human Development,* A. F. Kalverboer and A. Gramsbergen (Eds.), 2001b, Dordrecht, The Netherlands: Kluwer Academic; "Infant Intersubjectivity: Research, Theory, and Clinical Applications—Annual Research Review," by C. Trevarthen and K. J. Aitken, 2001, *Journal of Child Psychology, Psychiatry and Allied Disciplines, 42,* pp. 13–48; and "Regulation of Brain Development and Age-Related Changes in Infants' Motives: The Developmental Function of Regressive Periods" (pp. 107–184), by C. Trevarthen and K. J. Aitken, in *Regression Periods in Human Infancy,* M. Heimann (Ed.), 2003, Mahwah, NJ: Erlbaum.

energy costs as well as the gains and opportunities of life are regulated in the first particularly active period of development. From the beginning of an individual human life, the power of action and range of understanding are repeatedly transformed from within the child's brain and body and through engagement with a responsive human environment (Trevarthen & Aitken, 2003). Each change brings new needs for the energy of adventurous action to be balanced against nurturant care. Failure in these regulations at any stage can bring stressful and unhappy consequences (Cicchetti, 1993; Cicchetti & Cannon, 1999; Korte, Koolhaas, Wingfield, & McEwen, 2005).

We start at the beginning, with conception. A human life begins as one cell resulting from intensely emotional behavior of a man and a woman, who bring the feelings and regulations of their bodies together. This act, which involves collaborative actions of a male and a female body, and of a sperm, the woman's body, and an egg, can create a new and lasting commitment between those adults as affectionate parents of the child, two different persons who are motivated to share the future life of that child and its joys and problems. To understand this emotional commitment, and the child's active responses to it, we must explore the processes of human sympathy that build functional bridges between the processes and motives in different bodies at many levels of organization, from the cellular and anatomical to the intuitively psychological and the consciously contrived (Cicchetti & Dawson, 2002).

We summarize developmental changes in the embryo, observing the cooperative interdependency of cells during pattern formation of tissues and morphogenesis of organs in the body and brain. We follow the growing activity and awareness of the fetus in intimate vital contact with the mother's body, communicating with her in adaptive ways. Then we observe the changing motives in attachments and companionship of infancy in the family, to the beginning of language.

The inquisitive sociability of the child also brings engagements with an increasing range of persons beyond the family. Soon it is prompting the infant and toddler to learn the historical social system of meanings that governs life in community. The child is becoming more involved, by its own activity, in soliciting both biological and physiological partnerships and in discovering behavioral or psychological two-way friendships—frontiers of communication and learning in which purposes, experiences, and feelings are shared or emotional constraints on intimacy are set up. At every stage there are new opportunities and risks, new openings and new barriers (Figure 2.3).

We discover a history of mutual regulations within and between bodies and a kind of engagement of motives and emotions, of neurochemical, hormonal, and behavioral adjustments, that has evident human features from midconception, all of which may be viewed as adaptations for cooperative cultural life. An infant is an animal being evolved to become part of a universe that has been shaped by the thoughts, actions, beliefs, and moral attitudes of past generations of human adults and children, and his or her fate depends on the ways the society of adults manages life and work in the whole community, with its language, technology, and many conventions of belief and social conduct (McEwen, 2001). The causes of child psychopathology, and their potential for creating suffering in adult life, cannot be understood without relating them, not just to the regulations or disorders of the child as an individual organism, but also to his or her impulses as a person who wishes to share the emotions and practicalities of life intimately with other persons (Cicchetti, 2002; Trevarthen, 2004b).

THE IMPORTANCE OF THE CHILD'S VOLITION IN HUMAN COMPANY

In contrast to the customary emphasis in current behavioral science on the uptake, processing, and retention of forms of information for intelligence of the individual—in cognitive psychology, cognitive neuropsychology, and developmental cognitive neuroscience—we place emphasis on the anticipatory and adaptive *volitional agency* of the child (von Hofsten, 2004), the autopoietic (self-making) vital activities of the human body and especially the *motives and emotions* of the young brain that *cause and evaluate* actions and impel conscious experience and that seek human company (Cicchetti & Rogosch, 1997; Cicchetti & Tucker, 1994; Trevarthen, 1993a, 1993b, 1997). We give a fundamental causal role to *the emotional qualities in movements* that become socially necessary expressions of how motive impulses change in relation to experience and how they regulate how the child moves in contractual engagements with other persons and their motives (Trevarthen, 1998b, 2005a). We take the *prospective control of brain-generated movement* (Jeannerod, 1999; Lee, 2004), along with subtle manifestations of physiological regulations that are made apparent to the senses of other persons, to be the source of awareness and of learning about the human world. This leads to a conception of the development of the infant's awareness that differs from the constructivist theory of Piaget (1954), who, though he sought to emphasize the role of the child's actions in con-

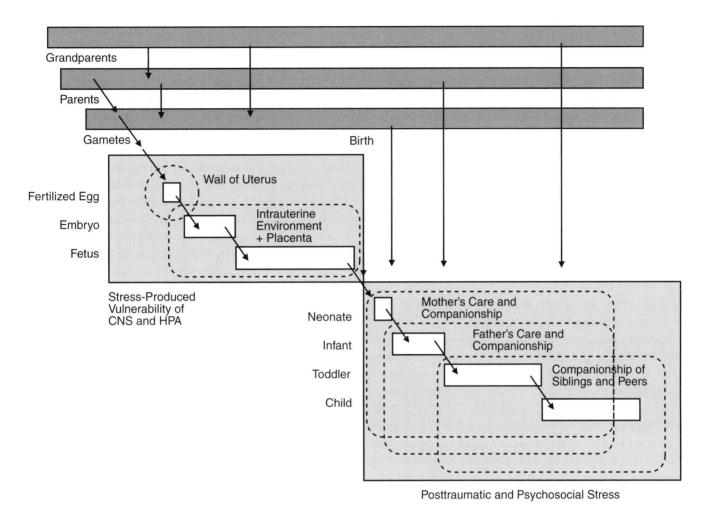

Figure 2.3   As a fertilized human egg develops into a child, it passes through different environments to which it must be adapted, first within the mother's body, then in parental care, and eventually in an increasingly wide companionship of parents, siblings, other family, and the wider society. In each environment the vitality of the child is dependent on regulations across a succession of "frontiers" with the human world, first physiological or *amphoteronomic,* then by the special direct psychological communications which we define as *synrhythmic,* and finally by sharing symbolic awareness of culture and language.

structing experience, described the infant's sensorimotor initiatives leading to imitative tracking or "accommodation" in response to unexpected present events, and to playful "assimilation" of previously mastered phenomena onto cognitive "schemas" or conceptual models of them as objects of particular future actions. This epistemological approach, to explain the genesis of knowledge, sees emotions as "mere energetics" and does not recognize the potentiality of the emotional qualities in rhythmic expressions of volition for *intersubjective sympathy of purposes.*

We propose that the development of prospective control of moving is the generator of imagination, thinking, and event-mastering "personal narrative" in music and language (Trevarthen & Schögler, 2005) and that a regeneration of motor impulses or "images of acting" prompts retrospec-

tive, imaginative awareness and the formation of memories. And all generative motor processes are coupled with and regulated by emotions that express and assess the potential risks and benefits of the actions to be executed. Motor impulses and emotions are, from the start, shared between the child and other persons (Trevarthen, 1986). They share one another's experience of action. It follows that, if there has been dysregulation by stress or trauma, all recovery of well-being in the face of acquired psychopathology involves recruitment or reactivation of these motive processes and their emotional regulations in communication. It must start with sensitivity by others for the child's volitions.

We see the growing brain as mediating *intentionally* between the vital self-sustaining needs of the child's active body and the material objects and events of the world, and therefore that the emotional systems of the central nervous system (CNS) are not only responsible for the development of *attachments* to persons who minister to the bodily needs of the infant, but also for the intense intersubjective engagements of *companionship* that make human collaborative life and the transmission of meanings possible (Trevarthen, 2001b, 2004a; Figure 2.1).

In the embryo, homeotic gene complexes, which help link genetic science to the older science of embryology (E. B. Lewis, 1994) and which are challenging theories of evolutionary change (Robert, 2001), pattern cell differentiation and tissue formation in the emerging central nervous system and impress them with the same map of morphological bisymmetry, polarity, and segmentation as for the rest of the body, anticipating the ways the body will move (Chisaka, Musci, & Capecchi, 1992; Trevarthen, 1985; Trevarthen & Aitken, 1994). These gene complexes also appear to determine the way new tissues are added to the cerebral cortex in mammalian evolution (Rakic, 1991). A division between sensory and motor parts is established, and a visceral nervous systems is defined that is adapted to ensure metabolic health of the "internal environment" of the body. The brain develops integrative cell networks that are adapted to become regulators of the behavioral activities of the whole individual self, and it couples with circulatory, digestive, and hormonal systems that mediate in the balance between energy-expending action, conservative and self-nurturing processes, and stress control.

As has been indicated, we are particularly concerned not to regard the interpersonal competence of the child, which is so important in preserving his or her well-being and in supporting vitality of action, experience and learning, as just the product of an acquired intelligent "social cognition" or as a consequence of the impressing of rational rules for life and control of emotions from the adult to the child. Viewing human cooperative life from the adult position, one can be led to assume that rational and linguistically mediated thought and communication must "construct" the child's capacities to understand or theorize about what others know and do. Research with infants has proved the inadequacy of this position (Reddy & Morris, 2004). There is a primary adaptive process of sympathetic mirroring that engages motives between the brains of any species of animal that lives in societies, and this sympathetic sociability defies reduction to a cognitive information-processing system with plastic learning capacities. Human intersubjective awareness and understanding are founded on detection of an exceptional fluency of temporospatial features of body movement between individu-als, and infants are born with the required sensory, motor, and integrative functions to participate in this (Trevarthen, 1986, 2001b).

Understanding human *sympathy of motives* requires recognition of the importance of the innate parameters of central neural action that regulate the periodicity and intensity of integrated body movements (Trevarthen, 1999a) and that generate the prospective function of the whole "self as agent" who, with specialized sensory capacities, picks up information as perceptual "affordances" to guide, check, and correct movements of the body and its parts so they will, as one integrated system, attain their intended goals effectively and efficiently. We import a new term from Greek, *synrhythmisis,* to signify the process, and we describe the motoric engagement between subjects as *synrhythmia.* Sympathy in motives and emotions is made possible by the coalescence of their regularities or rhythms, implied by this term, which means "mutual regulation." Tronick (2005) describes the awareness part of this mutual regulation as "dyadic states of consciousness."

With regard to the regulation of the vital economy of the child's body, to withstand or benefit from moderate stress or exercise and to resist the damage of excessive stress or trauma, we also need a new term in addition to the traditional *autonomics* that defines regulation of the physiological state *of the individual by the individual,* to distinguish not self-regulation, but the *mutual regulation between individuals,* to define the intimate engagement with motives and emotional signals between the child and another who is acting in ways that may affect the child's life processes in beneficial or damaging ways. The term we introduce is *amphoteronomics,* to signify "ruling together" *in a two-way relationship* or "containment." This is the process of physiological coupling, or "dyadic regulation of psychobiological states" (Tronick, 2005), that causes the goals and processes of regulation and stress to be shared and, in the beneficial case, leads to a more effective autonomic state or "allostatic balance" (McEwen, 1999) in the child, with likely benefits to the emotional health of the caregiver as well. *Allostasis* describes the dynamic adaptive changes in behavior and autonomic state that reset the goals for stress management (McEwen & Stellar, 1993). Innate adaptation to seek amphoteronomic care, we must not forget, leaves the child open to damage by neglect or abuse if the adult is incompetent to respond helpfully.

There is growing evidence that early life experiences in stressful parental care, of neglect, intrusiveness, and physical abuse, can have a lasting influence, increasing "allostatic load" throughout life and predisposing affected adults to a variety of emotional disorders, such as depression, anxiety, hostility, suicidal feelings, and substance abuse (McEwen, 2001, 2003). It is not just the pain of abuse or severe punishment that causes ill effects, but the learned anticipations of stress, which activate autonomic defenses, precipitating effects that may leave functional disorder in many regulatory systems of the brain, changing motives and awareness.

In our consideration of the situations and factors that predispose a child to psychopathology, we seek to understand what every child needs, what the universal requirements are for well-being in childhood relationships, but we must also allow for the changing needs of different ages and of different individuals whose epigenesis or constitutional adaptations may predispose them to different ways of acting, communicating, and learning. Individual differences of morphology and character are exceptionally large between human beings, as compared to other species, evidently in adaptation to the many different roles and responsibilities to be taken up by individuals in the elaborately cooperative communities we have to live in. These differences, especially those of personality or character, are not only due to the species-specific differences in genetic constitution of human beings, as study of the intrauterine development and postnatal psychology of homozygotic twins makes clear (Piontelli, 2002). Prenatal experience can leave lasting effects on individuals' emotional life and their dispositions to act, communicate, and learn.

Care and therapy, too, can be interpreted usefully only from an understanding of the nature of intrinsic regulations that assist development of a child at a given stage toward new awareness and skills, and to a different state of vital well-being, in the care and companionship of family and friends. In this intricate process of change in biological organization, genes are just one kind of player.

As Gregory Bateson (1979, see chapter epigraph) explains, survival depends on a two-way epigenetic negotiation with the environment, but it is "the developmental regularities and physiology of the living creature" that set the project. "Always the creature itself must achieve change of its own body. It must acquire certain somatic characteristics by use, by disuse, by habit, by hardship, and by nurture" (G. Bateson, 1979, p. 235).

REGULATION: BALANCING THE ENERGY BUDGET OF THE BODY IN ACTION

Life is work. A moving animal expends energy and must recuperate and hoard it (Schrödinger, 1944). As animals have evolved large multicellular bodies they have developed adaptations for survival in ecological communities of many species, and in societies where they collaborate and compete with members of their own species. The regulation of their life becomes more dependent on psychological appraisal of their own activities, on learned understanding of how to use the resources of the environment to benefit their well-being, and how this intelligence may be communicated.

Life on Different Scales, from the Single Cell to Society and the Global Culture

Even *a single-celled organism* requires adaptive processes that select resources, that are "environment-expectant" on the molecular level, and that place the cell advantageously within the motions and changes of composition or physical state of the media in which the cell lives. The cell has a surface with complex macromolecular structure that functions as a barrier and selective transport system. Its internal substance or cytoplasm contains other macromolecular structures, such as energy-producing mitochondria and protein-synthesizing Golgi bodies, each with a surface across which internal energy and material transactions are controlled. The nucleus is just one vital compartment with a surface membrane that mediates exchanges to and from the cytoplasm. This cell system is the minimal dynamic unit of any life form.

The cell as a living unit maintained by macromolecular processes has limited size, typically about 10 to 20 mm, which restricts the power of its action and its mobility. These limits are overcome by cells coalescing in *multicell organisms,* in which life functions are distributed in specialized cell groups or organs that collaborate and sum their actions. Multicellular organisms, built by a complex pattern of division, differentiation, and migratory arrangement of cells that start with the same complement of genes, exhibit distribution of work between cells and have a body form adapted to house that cooperation. In the process of cell multiplication, the actions of genes are changed by transforming their structure and especially by regulating their transcription through engagement with activating and repressing factors.

Cells reproduce by division. The linear sequence of chromosomal DNA molecules in the nucleus is replicated and, in principle, the genetic structure is allocated in equal measure to the single nuclei in each new cell. Genes confer one key source of continuity of vital adaptive structures and processes from each cell generation to the next, and from parent to offspring, but they are not the only one. There is also, from the beginning, transmission of adaptive elements through the cytoplasm and cell membrane, which is also reproduced as cells divide.

Asymmetric division, generating cell differences, is apparent in the first cell division of the fertilized zygote (Schneider & Bowerman, 2003). In the cell division cycle of a vertebrate brain, there are reciprocal interactions among genes, gene products, and molecules that regulate the expression or suppression of future gene transcription (Cayouteet & Raff, 2002; Roegiers & Jan, 2004). There are also mechanisms for the transformation of gene action in reaction to stimuli from the environment of the cell, such as in the case of dorsoventral positional information in the developing neural tube provided by graded Sonic hedgehog (SHH) molecules and then interpreted by transcription factors (Kobernick & Pierler, 2002). Sexual reproduction ensures that genetic material from different cells is combined to create new variants of cell activity that may have adaptive advantage in relation to a varying environment.

The cells, as they segregate and adhere in selective assemblies, develop different roles in collective action, generating morphogenesis of the body and its organs (Edelman, 1988), transforming the power of the organism to use the environment with benefit. There are cells, tissues, and organs that mediate in relations of the whole organism and the environment (nervous system), others that regulate the balance of functions between vital metabolic processes and action of the whole (endocrine system), and still others that retain a capacity for reproduction of that life form by production of gamete cells (sexual system).

Mobile animals have a body form adapted to move in service of a set of vital functions: They exhibit *locomotion* to search out conditions for well-being in a supportive environment and to move from potentially harmful places; they make movements of *orientation,* focusing receptors to select sensory information to guide their actions; they carry out acts of *consummation* to discover and assimilate resources for respiration and digestion, movements to eliminate waste products; and they transfer sex cells for *reproduction.* They have nervous systems that integrate action of different muscles, both visceral and somatic, to serve all these purposes.

Social animals sense one another's internal states through external changes in appearance of the body and from the quality or expression of movements made to regulate vital activities. They form communities in which individuals assume complementary roles that are adapted to benefit the group; they move together in migrations and systematic relationship to the geography of their habitat, learning and passing on habits that regulate the time and extent of movements; and they collaborate in foraging, in mating and sexual activity, and in the care of offspring.

The whole range of these behaviors, from cells to societies, participates in regulatory processes to protect, sustain, and vary the life activities of an animal species. The integration of processes in each body is mediated by circulatory and neural systems that are adapted to transport or transmit hormones, growth substances, and neurotransmitters that raise or lower the activities of receptive tissues and organs. Internal regulation between cells, between tissues, and between physiological systems shares functions with the interpersonal regulation we experience in our growth and development and in everyday life.

Autonomic, Neurohumoral, and Immunological Protection of Vital State

Regulation of living concerns the whole moving animal, integrating muscular action patterns of all body parts in concert. These patterns are initiated by "motor images" synthesized in widespread neuronal assemblies, with prospective reception of sensory information about environmental resources and affordances (Bernstein, 1967; Jeannerod, 1994). The CNS is organized to couple visceral and somatic processes and is transformed during development to increase the efficiency of the process.

The *autonomic nervous system* (ANS; Langley, 1921) consists of peripheral nerves and ganglia connected to regulatory systems of the brain stem and spinal cord that control smooth muscles and glands of the viscera. It originates in the embryo from neural crest cells that migrate from the margin of the neurectoderm to form a variety of cell types (including sense organ primordia, bipolar neurons of the dorsal sensory ganglia, sympathetic neurons, and the precursor of the adrenal gland) that become important in mediating between the environment and internal vital functions.

The ANS is responsible for automatically maintaining the internal environment by regulating blood chemistry, circulation, respiration, digestion, and the immune system responses (Bernard, 1878; Cannon, 1939). Its visceral motor outflow, divided into the *sympathetic nervous system* (SNS) and the *parasympathetic nervous system* (PNS), both of which innervate smooth muscles throughout the interior of the body and the skeletal muscles of the respiratory system in the diaphragm and chest. Their function is dynamic and adaptable, because the demands of life for a free-moving animal are constantly changing, and the system must be sensitive to plans for motor initiative and perceptuocognitive appraisal of environmental opportunities or threats. CNS structures, including forebrain limbic and neocortical tissues, are in reciprocal relation with the brain stem and diencephalic nuclei and interneuronal systems that receive input from and send output to the ANS.

The PNS has its central efferent neurons in the intermediolateral (visceral) column at the anterior and posterior ends of the spinal cord. Its function is primarily *trophotropic,* promoting energy uptake (in feeding and respiration), reducing energy expenditure (by vasoconstriction), and preserving energy resources. The principal brain stem nucleus of the *cranial PNS* is the *dorsal motor nucleus of the vagus* (DMX). The second PNS nucleus, the *nucleus ambiguous* (NA), innervates the heart and trachea, as well as skeletal muscles of the upper esophagus and pharynx via the vagus (X) and glossopharyngeal (IX) nerves. The ganglia of the parasympathetic system are in close relation to the peripheral target organs. Its preganglionic and postganglionic axons employ acetylcholine (ACh) via nicotinic receptors for the former and muscarinic receptors for the latter. Peripheral ANS action has complex variants of neurotransmitter, neuromodulation, and neurohumoral interactions.

The genital and urinary viscera are controlled by the *sacral PNS,* which originates in cell bodies in the posterior spinal cord and are located in the intermediolateral cell column of second, third, and fourth sacral segments. These neurons send preganglionic nerve fibers via the pelvic nerve to ganglia located close to or within the pelvic viscera. Postganglionic fibers are relatively short and supply cholinergic terminals to structures involved in excretory (bladder and bowel) and reproductive (fallopian tubes and uterus, prostate, seminal vesicles, vas deferens, and erectile tissue) functions.

The output to the SNS originates from the intermediolateral (visceral) thoracic and lumbar spinal cord, which connects by ACh synapses to sympathetic chain ganglia and thence to visceral organs in which the synapses are noradrenergic. Its function is *ergotropic*—to mobilize motor activity and its supporting metabolism to meet challenging circumstances—and it depends on expending energy reserves. A major sympathetic output is to the *medulla of the adrenal gland,* exciting its cells to release catecholamines *noradrenaline* (norepinephrine) and *adrenaline* (epinephrine) into the circulatory system and thus to the brain and many other organs. "Autonomic neuroendocrine activation in response to stresses serves to mobilise visceral resources in support of the requirements of 'fight and flight,' and of the attentional and cognitive demands of adaptive challenges" (Berntson, Sarter, & Cacioppo, 2003a, p. 306).

The ANS also acts as a sensory system (Dworkin, 2000). Thus, 75% of the nerve fibers in the vagus nerve are afferent, carrying information from dorsal roots of the spinal cord on the internal state of the body, from baroceptors responding to changes in blood pressure, from chemoceptors, and from other interoceptors in various tissues of the body, and these sensory inputs can influence other systems. These sensory afferents terminate in *the nucleus of the tractus solitarius* (NTS) in the brain stem, which is a major relay from visceral nuclei sending input to modulate rostral neural systems that, in turn, project to autonomic nuclei in the brain stem.

Through its connections with the *locus coeruleus* and *raphe nucleus,* the NTS exerts widespread effects in most of the brain by serotonergic, adrenergic, and noradrenergic projections. Baroceptor input reduces cortical arousal, suppresses spinal reflexes, and attenuates pain (Dworkin, 2000). Vagal projections to the medial reticular formation could be responsible for the effect of vagal nerve stimulation (VNS) on sleep and alertness.

The adrenal gland is the major link between the autonomic and endocrine systems and further expands the response repertoire of both arms of the ANS. The adrenal cortex, which is largely regulated by the *hypothalamic-pituitary-adrenocortical axis* (HPA), and the adrenal medulla, which is primarily under neural control from the SNS, have shared responsibilities in responding to stress and metabolic aberrations. The coordinated response during stress of elevated plasma *cortisol* (from the adrenal cortex) and the catecholamines *norepinephrine* and *epinephrine* (from the adrenal medullary cells) indicate that central limbic and hypothalamic centers exert combined influences to ensure the needed neurohumoral adaptations.

The ultimate integration of autonomic functions and behavior, including learned activities, is coordinated through the hypothalamus and limbic system. The whole motivating mechanism of the brain is implicated. The ANS functions

> at the interface of the vegetative and voluntary human life, maintaining and controlling *homeostasis* (stability of the internal environment) and such life and species-sustaining functions as circulation, digestion, excretion and reproduction as well as normal metabolic and endocrine physiology, and the adaptive responses to stress (flight or fight response). . . . In the broadest sense the "central and peripheral" ANS underlies the most complicated of human behavior—energy and excitement, joy and sadness, pleasure and pain; ANS activation, or lack thereof, identifies the significance and quality of behavior. These most human expressions underlie the conduct of human behavior and thus society itself. (Hamil, 2004)

Neurotransmitters in Regulation of Action and Awareness

The central nervous system carries out its integrative and regulatory functions by means of intercellular transmission, at cell junctions or synapses, of impulses that eventually excite motor activity. The patterning of behavior and its adaptation to what the environment is offering depends on how sensory information is sought for and assimilated for directing movements. Processes of behavioral coordination and attention to the environment are mediated at very different rates, even within the few seconds of immediate conscious engagement with the world—the psychological present. Changes in synaptic function lead to learning and retention of memories and the creation of different motives and emotional evaluations for dealing with experiences.

An important distinction must be made between slower changes of emotional states or interest and level of activity and the extremely rapid whole-brain assimilation of sensory information and the fine coordination of muscular excitations throughout the body in immediate adaptation to the environment (Bradford, 2004; McGeer, Eccles, & McGeer, 1978).

Neurotransmitters are chemicals released in small amounts from a nerve cell when action potentials (nerve impulses) reach a synapse attached to another nerve cell or to a muscle or gland cell (Bradford, 2004; Iversen, 2004; Thompson, 2000). They excite changes in the receptor cell that stimulate action potentials, thus propagating nerve activity, or their effect may be to inhibit cell activation. The excitatory or inhibiting effects of transmitters depend on other factors in the synaptic gap and on the surface state of the receptor cell. Neurons are specialized in their capacities to synthesize, activate, and inactivate transmitters, which are of many types with different functions in the chemical coding of intercellular messages. The efficiency of a transmitter depends on its affinity for a wide range of receptor types on the surface of the receiving cell, which vary in their molecular structure and response to the transmitter.

Until the 1970s, only six types of neurotransmitters were known in the brain: *noradrenaline (NA), dopamine (DA), serotonin or 5-hydroxytryptamine (5HT), gamma-aminobutyric acid (GABA), acetylcholine (ACh),* and *glutamate (GLU).* Since then, not only have other types of neurotransmitters been identified, including gases such as *nitrous oxide (NO),* but also the so-called *neuromodulators,* which modulate the effect of the neurotransmitters.

The main types of neurotransmitters are now classified as follows:

Monoamines (ACh, adenosine, DA, histamine, NA, 5HT). ACh released from motor nerves excites muscle contraction, and it is also released from autonomic nerves to smooth muscle activity and gland secretions. NA mediates in the excitation of smooth muscle, heart muscle, and

glands, often in opposition to ACh. Monoamines are diffuse in their effects and act to modulate the activities of the more precise functions of sensory response and motor activation; that is, they are essential in the motivational and emotional regulation of psychological functions.

Amino acids (aspartate, GABA, glycine, glutamate) performing fast, high-precision chemical signaling in the CNS in volitional and perceptual control of behavior. GABA is inhibitory and serves in focusing neural communication, increasing its differentiation and precision. Glycine is the inhibitor of the spinal cord, regulating reciprocal reflex functions. Glutamate is the main excitatory agent in the CNS, its functions being patterned by a range of transporter factors and many receptor types.

Neuropeptides (mRNA, ß-endorphin, cholecystochinin, dymorphin, enkephalins, oxytocin, somatostatin, substance P, neuropeptide Y, vasopressin, and many others). They appear to be modulators concerned more with trophotropic self-regulatory functions of the body, including states of pain and pleasure (Panksepp, 1993).

Neurotransmitters and neuromodulators act on two different kinds of receptors on the surface of postsynaptic cells: ionotropic and metabotropic (Bradford, 2004; Herlenius & Lagercrantz, 2004). The *metabotropic receptors* are G and N proteins in the bilipid layer of the cell membrane, and their effect is slow, lasting tens of milliseconds. They are essential in the preparatory modulation of integrative systems so they can efficiently and selectively respond to the environment with appropriate levels of action. Adrenergic, muscarine, and peptidergic receptors are often metabotropic and play a more modulatory role in the mature CNS.

In contrast, *ionotropic receptors* are part of ion transport gates and act very fast, in less than a millisecond. Acetylcholine, GABA, glycine and serotonin act on ionotropic receptors, and they carry out the instantaneous transactions of sensory motor coordination in the active and prospective control of behavior.

Volitions and Their Effects Mapped in the Brain

All active organisms, growing plants or moving animals, have adaptive processes that formulate viable prospects for their actions. Animals move with short- and long-term *prospective control in space and through time* (Bernstein, 1967; Lee, 1998). Each motor step in space taking a certain time must estimate effects that should follow an event of that duration and in that space, and regulate its expression accordingly. Elaborated sequences of movement must have ways of dealing with eventual risks and benefits at each and every step along the way, and this regulation requires setting desirable states or goals in advance (Jeannerod, 1999).

Some consequences of acting can be dealt with online by sensory stimulation of immediate adaptive approach or avoidance movements, but in general, the processes of life on the move require an imaginative system that maps out behavior in the future, prospecting ahead in space and time, and that, moreover, is capable of retaining information, in memory, about the consequences of acts made in the past.

A large animal's movements are guided from within a central brain. Even the most elementary neural net of a worm-like creature must represent the relationship between the form changes its output excites in the body by regimented muscular contractions, as well as the effects of stimuli that are detected by the sensory receiving organs, at the interface of the net with the world, or in the body. This relationship is constituted as "experience," which means "from acting": It has a rudimentary self-experience (Merker, 2005; Sperry, 1950; von Holst & Mittelstaedt, 1950).

For larger, more complex and forcefully active animal bodies that challenge the media in which they move in more powerful and risky ways, the anteroposterior polarity, bilateral symmetry, and dorsoventral differentiation of the body form adapted to forward progression must be represented in many systems of the brain, all of which map both the output and the sensory information the moving body will receive, looking ahead to how movements must be coordinated and regulated in consciousness (Bernstein, 1967; Paillard, 1960; Sherrington, 1906). Activation of the interlinked *somatotopic* (body-charting) or *telotopic* (direction-charting) maps of the body in the brain creates a *unified behavior field,* defined by the polarized, bisymmetric, and dorsoventrally differentiated form of the body and how that form may move and turn (Trevarthen, 1968a, 1968b, 1985; Figure 2.4). All the risks and benefits of acting in and against the outside environmental media or of ingesting components of it must also be regulated by the brain in *motives* that control the

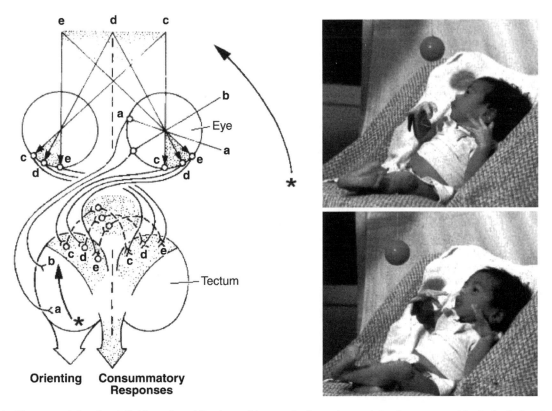

Figure 2.4   Left: The map of the visual field on the midbrain roof (tectum) of vertebrates 'plots' events outside the body in relation to the form of the body and its movements. Objects that attract interest are oriented to, which brings them into the central field, in front of the head, that is into the midline structures of the brain. These are connected to brain structures that evaluate the object, for example identifying it as food. Then "consummatory" behaviours (such as eating), make appropriate use of the object. *Sources:* From "Two Mechanisms of Vision in Primates," by C. Trevarthen, 1968a, *Psychologische Forschung, 31,* pp. 299–337; and "Vision in Fish: The Origins of the Visual Frame for Action in Vertebrates" (pp. 61–94), by C. Trevarthen, in *The Central Nervous System and Fish Behaviour,* D. Ingle (Ed.), 1968b, Chicago: University of Chicago Press. Right: A newborn infant, less than 30 minutes old, shows awareness of the changing place of a red ball being moved by a nurse, and the baby orients all arts of the body to the object. This behavior depends upon the precise mapping of the visual "image" in the brain onto the neural maps of motor coordination. Photo by Kevan Bundell.

whole interface between body and environment (Jeannerod, 1994; Trevarthen, 1998b). Consciousness is the function that regulates this motor unity of motivated purpose in a multisensory space (Merker, 2005).

Cerebral Mechanisms of Human Imagination and Memory

In the human case, these preconditions for intelligent nervous control of an active life are set up in the anatomy of an exceptionally large and complex brain by processes of cell multiplication and interneuronal tissue formation that is well advanced in the embryo stage, before there is any nervous excitation of body movement and before any of the sensory systems can transmit their excitation into the brain (Trevarthen, 1985, 2004a).

Long-term behavioral initiatives require the human agent to anticipate dangers to the substance and organization of life that might occur after many intermediate actions have been performed and to plan exploitation

of beneficial encounters with objects and events. This record and program for action requires an exceptionally large cerebral neocortex, which records a "personal narrative history" of the single conscious agent or self, the mobility and sentience of which is unified in subcortical regions (Merker, 2004, 2005; Panksepp, 1998b, 2000; Figure 2.5).

Most of all, human actions are *social*. They require that an individual's actions engage with, and discover ways of cooperating with, what other individuals do (Decety & Chaminade, 2003; Hari & Nishitani, 2004). For this to succeed, the internal motives that precipitate initiatives in action, and their autonomic regulations, of one have to be detectable to and motivating for the other. This is what is meant by "intersubjective" or "interagentive" engagement: between volitional selves and others (Aitken & Trevarthen, 1997; Trevarthen, 1998a, 1999b; Trevarthen & Aitken, 2001). The regulation of this requires what amounts to a duplication of the self in each individual; this is what Bråten (1998) calls a "virtual other."

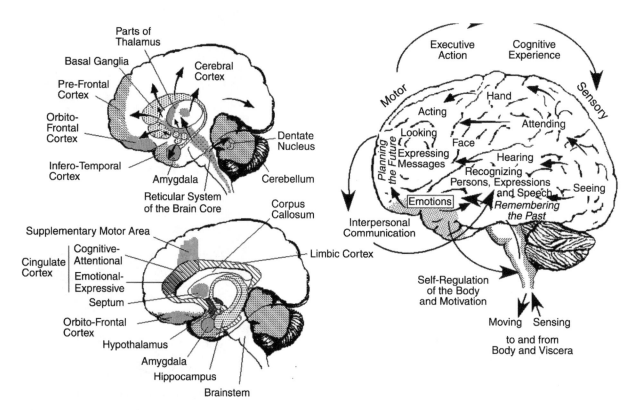

Figure 2.5 Left: Brain structures implicated in emotions and communication in the adult human. Right: Map indicating the flow of functions between brainstem and the hemispheres and between different regions of the cerebral cortex. *Sources:* From "The Neurobiology of Early Communication: Intersubjective Regulations in Human Brain Development" (pp. 841–882), by C. Trevarthen, in *Handbook on Brain and Behavior in Human Development,* A. F. Kalverboer and A. Gramsbergen (Eds.), 2001b, Dordrecht, The Netherlands: Kluwer Academic; and "Brain Development" (pp. 116–127), by C. Trevarthen, in *Oxford Companion to the Mind,* second edition, R. L. Gregory (Ed.), 2004a, Oxford, NY: Oxford University Press.

Emotion Expression and Communication of Motives and Thought: The Special Visceral Efferent System of the Parasympathetic Nervous System

The parasympathetic nerves of humans include the *special visceral efferents of the head,* which not only exert immediate dynamic regulation of vital functions of blood circulation, respiration, digestion, and excretion, but also, as an elaboration of a trend seen in other social species, express emotional states in control of intersubjective contacts and relations, that is, in communication with other subjects (Porges, 1997; Table 2.1). All the muscles of human communication, of the *eyes, face and mouth, vocal system, head and neck,* which are constantly active in natural human conversation, and which have disproportionate representation in the sensory and motor maps of the neocortex (Penfield, 1958; Figure 2.6), receive their efferents from the cranial nerves (Aitken & Trevarthen, 1997; Trevarthen, 2001b). In less sociable, primitive animals, these efferents are almost exclusively concerned with visceral, self-regulatory functions (Table 2.1).

It is of special interest that human *hands,* in addition to their extraordinary dexterity in manipulation, have become associated with the organs of communication as supremely efficient and adaptable organs of communication, capable of conveying sensitive interpersonal feelings by touch and rhythmic caresses as well as of acquiring a language ability equal to that of speech.

We note that infants are born with a capacity to imitate not only the dynamics and expressive forms of vocalizations and facial movements (such as tongue protrusion), but also isolated and apparently arbitrary gestures of the hands (such as index finger extension; Heimann, 1998; Kugiumutzakis, 1998). Neonatal hand movements are investigative, self-stimulatory, and regulative for the infant, as well as communicative, and "neoplay" with touch by the hands appears to build a self-awareness from which an awareness of objects remote from the body may be

TABLE 2.1   Cranial Nerve Nuclei, Special Visceral Sensory and Motor Functions, and Systems for Expression and Receptions of Emotion

Communication Movements	Visceral and Somatic Movements	Cranial Nerves	Visceral and Somatic Senses	Communication Senses
		1 Olfactory	Odor, taste	Smelling/tasting other
		2 Optic	Light sense, vision	Seeing other
Looking at other, directing gaze, pupil changes	Eye rotation, lens and pupil movements	3 Oculomotor	Eye-muscle sense	
Looking at other, directing gaze	Eye rotation	4 Trochlear	Eye-muscle sense	
Face expressions; vocalizing, sucking, kissing	Mastication	5 Trigeminal	Facial feelings	Feeling other's touch, feeling own face
Looking at other, eye expressions, crying	Eye rotation, lifting eyelids, tears	6 Abducent	Eye-muscle sense	
Face expressions, speech; listening to speech	Eating, control of middle ear muscles	7 Facial	Taste; tongue, mouth	Tasting/feeling other
		8 Auditory	hearing, balance	Hearing other, hearing self
Vocalizing, laughing; expression in voice; coughing	Coughing, biting, salivating, swallowing	9 Glossopharyngeal	taste	Tasting/feeling other
Vocal expression; circulatory signs; panting, gasping	Heart and gut activity, vomiting, fainting, breathing	10 Vagus	Taste; heart, lungs, gut	Feeling own emotion
Head expressions; vocalizing; laughing, coughing	Head and shoulder movements, swallowing	11 Accessory		
Vocalizing, speaking; licking, sucking	Tongue movements	12 Hypoglossal		

Sources: From "Emotion: An Evolutionary By-Product of the Neural Regulation of the Autonomic Nervous System," by S. W. Porges, 1997, *Annals of the New York Academy of Sciences, 807,* pp. 62–78; and "The Neurobiology of Early Communication: Intersubjective Regulations in Human Brain Development" (pp. 841–882), by C. Trevarthen, in *Handbook on Brain and Behavior in Human Development,* A. F. Kalverboer and A. Gramsbergen (Eds.), 2001b, Dordrecht, The Netherlands: Kluwer Academic.

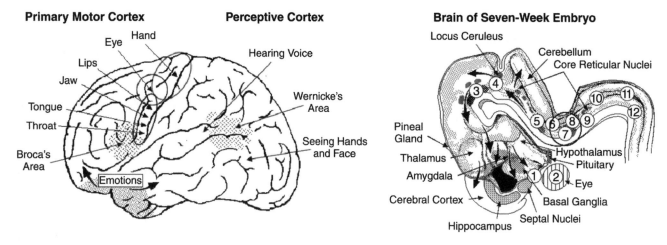

Figure 2.6 Left: Motor and perceptual systems of the cerebral cortex adapted for communication by facial expression, gesture and speech. *Sources:* From "Brain and Language," by A. R. Damasio and H. Damasio, 1992, *Scientific American, 267,* pp. 63–71; *The Excitable Cortex in Conscious Man,* by W. Penfield, 1958, Liverpool: Liverpool Press; and "Language Development: Mechanisms in the Brain," by C. Trevarthen, in *Encyclopedia of Neuroscience,* second edition, with CD-ROM, G. Adelman and B. H. Smith (Eds.), 2004d, Amsterdam: Elsevier Science. Right: Brain of a 7-week human embryo showing the locations of visceral sensory and motor nuclei involved in the sensory or motor processes of communication. These nuclei have added expressive and receptive communicative functions to their more primitive adaptations for regulation of visceral functions, such as blood circulation, heart activity, breathing, eating and digestion. *Sources:* "Emotion: An Evolutionary By-Product of the Neural Regulation of the Autonomic Nervous System" (pp. 62–78), by S. W. Porges, in *The Integrative Neurobiology of Affiliation: Vol. 807. Annals of the New York Academy of Sciences,* C. S. Carter, I. I. Lederhendler, and B. Kirkpatrick (Eds.), 1997, New York: New York Academy of Sciences; and "The Neurobiology of Early Communication: Intersubjective Regulations in Human Brain Development" (pp. 841–882), by C. Trevarthen, in *Handbook on Brain and Behavior in Human Development,* A. F. Kalverboer and A. Gramsbergen (Eds.), 2001b, Dordrecht, The Netherlands: Kluwer Academic.

conceived and their affordances explored (Adamson-Macedo, 1998, 2004). All of the expressive movements of the infant's voice, face, and hands appear to be adapted for interpersonal transmission of the impulse to know and do in dialogue (Trevarthen, 1986, 2001b, 2004d, 2005c), and all are potent vehicles for transmission of emotions and states of sympathetic motivation.

Homeostasis and Allostasis in the Integration of Autonomic and Emotional Regulations in Engagements with the World and with Society

> The ultimate integration of autonomic functions and behavior, including learned activities, is coordinated by the hypothalamus and limbic system. In the broadest sense one can view the limbic system as the cortex of the autonomic nervous system. (Kalia, 2004)

The classical reflex homeostatic model of the ANS is too restrictive and does not reflect the flexible adaptability of autonomic regulation (Berntson, Sarter, & Cacioppo, 2003b). Homeostasis requires anticipatory ANS responses, which can arise by learning, as in the salivary response of dogs trained by Pavlov, in the insulin release of a person an-

ticipating a meal (Dworkin, 2000), in conditioned fear reactions (Ohman, Flykt, & Lundqvist, 2000), and in anxiety states that are characterized by hyperattention to threat-related stimuli (Berntson, Sarter, & Cacioppo, 1998). Stimuli that are both interoceptive (sensed inside the body) and exteroceptive (sensed from the outside world) can control the ANS with anticipation, and this anticipation is changed by learning. The ANS, being in intense reciprocal relationship with many other regions of the brain and in accord with its role as regulator for the whole organism, is coordinated not only with the humoral mechanisms that control visceral functions through its connections with the hypothalamus, but also by way of the forebrain systems that mediate volitional behavior and learning.

Mental (cognitive) imagery can trigger autonomic responses, and human imaginative expectancy is fluent, dynamic, reliant on memory, and, as in dreaming, rich in prospects of dramatic, artistic, and musical experiences or activities and in language, all of which may be coupled with prospective changes in ANS activity. Conversely, somatovisceral feedback may affect cognitive and emotional processes (Berntson et al., 1998). Vagal afferents to the NTS enhance emotional memory in animals (McGaugh,

Roozendall, & Cahill, 2000), and stress hormones affect memory.

The *locus coeruleus* and the *nucleus paragigantocellularis* carry ascending visceral afferents to the basal forebrain cortical cholinergic system and cortex. Autonomic feedback can trigger panic attacks (see Bechara, Damasio, & Damasio, 2000). ACh enhances cortical processing (Sarter & Bruno, 2000) and may produce confused cognitive activity, as in the irrationality and hyperattention of anxiety states.

In the opposite sense, from processes of intentional action and engagement with experience to autonomic state, the medial frontal cortex, especially of the right hemisphere and most conspicuously in early childhood, plays a major role in affect and autonomic control, regulating both positive attachment relations and anxiety reactions (Schore, 2001a, 2003a). Research with animals has clarified this function. When the inhibitory influence of the ventromedial prefrontal cortex is absent, the instinctive fear response of the amygdala remains unchecked and triggers overwhelming aversive responses. Without prefrontal feedback regarding the level of threat, a rat remains in a maladaptive state of defensive arousal (Morgan & LeDoux, 1995). This may be compared with the speechless fear of Posttraumatic Stress Disorder (PTSD; van der Kolk, 2003).

The adaptive process that actively maintains functional stability through change is defined as *allostasis:* change of internal state set points to meet anticipated adaptive demands, for example, when one has the intention to exercise vigorously or when a threat to survival is expected (McEwen, & Stellar, 1993; McEwen, & Wingfield, 2003). Plans for active behavior include regulation over autonomic states to achieve this flexibility (Berntson & Cacioppo, 2000; McEwen, 1999). Allostasis restores homeostasis or well-being *by adaptive change of motives and regulations for behavior.* It functions to control the balance of effort or energy expenditure against energy and regulatory gains from rest and recuperation. It can incur a cost to the strength and health if regulations demand too much change.

Literally, allostasis means "achieving stability, or homeostasis, through change" (Sterling & Eyer, 1988), and a damaging or weakening response is referred to as allostatic load. Maladaptation to modern urban life, where people have to suppress the flight-fight responses of somatovisceral activation evolved for transient challenges (Dworkin, 2000) while they are subjected to prolonged somatovisceral activation with chronic psychological stresses, may have long-term health costs (McEwen, 1999, 2001).

The Function of Emotions as the Currency of Social Regulation

To understand how the integrated intelligent and passionately felt behavior of the animal can control its engagements with the external world, how it can direct movements to have desired effects, and how it can anticipate or respond to beneficial or stressful outcomes, it is helpful to divide the aims or adaptive functions of behavior into two kinds by adopting and extending the terminology of Hess (1954; Figure 2.7 and Table 2.1), who pioneered intracerebral stimulation studies of innate emotional motor systems in the diencephalon of mammals:

1. Active *ergotropic* or *energy-expending efforts* of the animal engage with the environment and change how the animal's body contacts, receives stimulation from, takes in, and changes external matter, how the matter is used to support the body and allow the animal to move about and steer its progress, and how potentially harmful events or situations are avoided.

2. *Trophotropic* or *energy-obtaining or -conserving states* increase the potential for action, either by storing energy sources from food and oxygen or absorbed heat, by taking in necessary water and nutrients, or by allowing restorative processes such as sleep. This type of restoration can be taken to include learning processes that increase the efficiency and versatility of movements.

Animal action is guided by prospective "plans" that specify environmental benefits or risks and that are selected with reference to expected outcomes of changes in the direction and goals of movement. If these aims and expectations accurately detect and anticipate the changes in contact and relationship to external objects and events consequent on moving, then the movements achieve their purpose. If the anticipations are inaccurate, then behavior may have unwanted consequences.

In the evolution of the vertebrates, a set of structures have evolved in the forebrain that amplify and extend the capacities of the regulatory mechanisms for controlling and expressing internal regulatory processes in movement. These include the *limbic structures* (Swanson, 2004), identified by Broca (1878), Papez (1937), and MacLean (1952, 2004), and extensive structures of the *emotional motor system* throughout the CNS (Holstege, Bandler, & Saper, 1996). Key limbic structures of the cerebral hemispheres identified in modern accounts of the brain mechanisms of emotional regulations

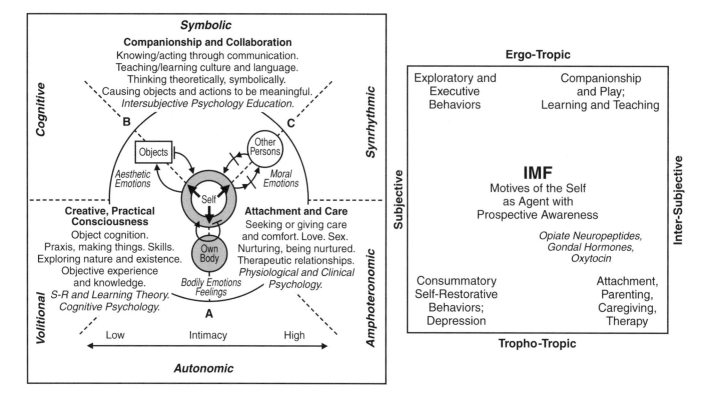

Figure 2.7 Left: Map of the three types of motive function in behavior, as illustrated in Figure One. These are regulated by different processes that either perform regulation of the individual body by voluntary actions and cognitive appraisals in relation to the physical world, or through engagement with the bodily activities and psychological processes of other persons. Human intersibjective regulations, initially by direct communication of intentions, attentions and feelings in *synrhythmisis,* leads to learned cultural communication and regulation of meanings by means of symbols. Right: A map of the regulatory "field of emotions" and the major neurochemical mediations of emotional states (see Table 2.1). Showing relations between motive principles, neuro-chemical systems of physiological and psychological self-regulation, and engagements between the subject and different objectives and partners in behaviour. *Source:* From "Action and Emotion in Development of the Human Self, Its Sociability and Cultural Intelligence: Why Infants Have Feelings like Ours" (pp. 61–91), by C. Trevarthen, in *Emotional Development,* J. Nadel & D. Muir (Eds.), 2005a, Oxford: Oxford University Press.

and their pathologies are the *amygdala,* the *hippocampus,* and the *anterior cingulate gyrus* (see later discussion).

Planned allostatic regulations drawing on experience are acquired, accessed, and modified by *emotions.* Panksepp (1998a) has classified emotions and *affective neural systems* according to their regulatory functions (Table 2.2). Unplanned stress is met by mobilization of active defensive behaviors (fight with the emotion of RAGE), or by action-reducing withdrawal (flight with the emotion of FEAR). Energetic exploration and exploitation of environmental resources is served by the inquisitive emotional behavior of SEEKING. Self-energizing and rewarding emotions of JOY/PLAY/SOCIAL AFFECTION in well-being are shared with affiliative emotions of SEXUALITY, NURTURANCE/MATERNAL CARE, and SEPARATION DISTRESS/SOCIAL BONDING.

Understanding the emotional life of children requires interpretation of the intricate forms of expressions of emotion by which even newborn infants are capable of communicating their states of purpose and their concerns for comfort and security to other human beings (Darwin, 1872/1998). Vocal expressions, which change during development in their range and power, give subtle expression to muscle actions and tensions within the body (Scherer, 1986; Zei Pollermann, 2002). Eye movements signal the direction of interest and its changes with exceptional clarity in humans, because we have a white sclera (Kobayashi & Kohshima, 2001), and movements of the lower face express feelings of joy and sadness, of wonder and anger, and of liking or loathing (Darwin, 1872/1998). There is still uncertainty about how to classify facial movements and what psychological functions to attribute to them, de-

TABLE 2.2   Emotion Systems

Affective Behavior	Distributed Neural Networks	Neuromodulators
Ergotropic		
Seeking Exploratory behavior	Ventral tegmental area (VTA) to dorsolateral hypothalamus to periaqueductal gray (PAG), with diffuse mesolimbic and mesocortical "extensions." Nucleus accumbens as basal ganglia processor for emotional "habit" systems.	DA (+), glutamate (+), many neuropeptides including opioids, neurotensin, CCK.
Play, joy, social affection	Parafascicular/centromedian thalamus, dorsomedial thalamus, posterior thalamus, projecting to more dorsal PAG (the septum is inhibitory for play; the role of other basal forebrain and hypothalamic systems is not clear).	Glutamate (+), opioids (+ in modest amounts, − in large amounts), ACh (muscarinic +), ACh (nicotinic −) DA, NE and 5HT all appear to be (−).
Rage Affective Attack	Medial amygdala to bed nucleus of stria terminalis (BNST) to anterior and ventromedial and perifornical hypothalamic to more dorsal PAG.	Substance P (+) (ACh, glutamate + may act as nonspecific modulators).
Fear	Central and lateral amygdala to anterior and medial hypothalamic to more dorsal PAG to nucleus reticularis pontine caudalis.	Glutamate (+), ACTH, and neuropeptides (DBI, CRF, CCK, alpha MSH, NPY).
Trophotropic		
Sexuality	BNST and corticomedial amygdala to preoptic and ventromedial hypothalamus to lateral and more ventral PAG.	Steroids (+), vasopressin and oxytocin. LH-RH, CCK.
Nurturance, maternal care	Anterior cingulate to BNST to preoptic hypothalamic to VTA to more ventral PAG.	Oxytocin (+), prolactin (+), DA, opioids (both + in modest amounts).
Separation distress, social bonding	Anterior cingulate/anterior thalamus to BNST/ventral septum to midline and dorsomedial thalamus to dorsal preoptic hypothalamic to more dorsal PAG (close to circuits for physical pain).	Opioids (±) oxytocin (±), prolactin (±) CRF (+) for separation distress, ACh (−).

Source: Adapted from Panksepp (1998).

Notes: + = Excitatory; − = Inhibitory.

spite the fact that they are so rich in variety with such immediate emotive effects on other persons (Oster, 2005).

STRESS: NATURE, PSYCHOLOGICAL FUNCTIONS, AND STRESS DISORDERS

The term "stress" is used to describe a host of events affecting an organism's relationship with the external or internal environment. Because stress in ordinary language is often thought of as an effect or force, as in physics or engineering, rather than a cause or an adaptive process, as implied in the original use in medical science by Hans Selye (1956), there may be confusion about the definition and meaning of the word (Dunn, Swiergeil, & Palamarchouk, 2004; Pacak & Palkovits, 2001). Nevertheless, the concept of a stress process has proved indispensable for guidance of clinical practices that seek to protect or repair individual well-being.

Stress as an Adaptive Response

All organisms, from bacteria to mammals, have evolved self-protective mechanisms of response to taxing or threatening life events. Such events are often unpredictable in

their occurrence and may have effects that are uncontrollable, traumatic, or life-threatening. Stress triggers a wide range of adaptation processes, implicating a complex of physiological, cognitive, and emotional responses (Huether, 1996), eventually leading to the general adaptation syndrome, through the phases of *alarm, resistance,* and *exhaustion* (Rozman & Doull, 2003).

When we experience a situation as stressful, physiologic and behavioral responses are initiated, leading to *allostasis and adaptation* (McEwen, 1999). Anticipated and well-controlled stress can exercise and reinforce adaptive life activities, leading to improvements in efficiency and effectiveness of vital functions and behavior. Development is stimulated and strengthened by adaptive response to stress. However, damaging stress or trauma and pain reduces life effectiveness and requires recuperation and repair. Immediately effective defenses against fatigue, illness, and pain may incur long-term costs to the organism's physiological and psychological resources and thus lead to a need for rest and processes of recovery, or, in the most socially advanced species, for protective and therapeutic care from other individuals (de Waal, 1996; Preston & de Waal, 2002).

Responses to stress may result in important changes to the body; they may replenish energy by promoting fat deposition, which can result in heart disease when the body does not burn off the energy it obtains from food. They stimulate immune cells to move to sites in the body where they are needed to fight an infection (McEwen, 2003). Stress responses can be powerful and their effects lasting. In animal studies, it has been found that even an hour-long stress can result in detectable structural changes in the brain, with a recovery period lasting for many months. Clearly, the stress response can have long-term impact on the behavior and the health of the organism and on the adaptive responses to subsequent stress events. This is relevant to the effects of child maltreatment on subsequent physical and emotional development, an area of investigation that has been termed developmental traumatology (DeBellis, 2001; DeBellis et al., 1999a, 1999b).

Basic stress reactions include automatic physiological adjustments; these are manifested in signs such as a greater release of *stress hormones (glucocorticoids),* a rise in pulse, respiration, and blood pressure, and contraction of the pupils. These reactions are in general beneficial changes that help to control or eliminate dangers to the body or the mind, to improve an organism's level of performance, and to regulate the inevitable cost of defensive responses to protect the vital resources of the organism. If not too intense, stressful situations may stimulate neuronal differentiation in slow-maturing parts of the brain with benefit to future learning processes, such as those that help a person discover ways to cope with stress or how to avoid its causes (Greenough & Black, 1992).

Corticosteroids, at high circulating levels, enhance acquisition, conditioning, and consolidation of an inescapable stressful experience. After fight-or-flight responses, corticosteroids reestablish homeostasis via feedback mechanisms (Korte, 2001). The organism needs to consolidate its memories of the predator's appearance, location, smell, and sound. This information may predict the occurrence and nature of the next encounter and thereby maximize the likelihood of survival.

Uncontrollable chronic, high-intensity stress, however, destabilizes established neural pathways and biochemical homeostasis, or compromises allostasis, the active autonomic control that adjusts psychological motives to anticipated adaptive demands (McEwen, 1999), with consequences that might endanger the integrity of a young individual directly and have indirect effects later in life, even to adulthood.

The term *hormesis* (meaning an "urging on" or "activation") is employed to designate the potential beneficial or "encouraging" effects of mild stress when it enhances the organism's future reactions to similar stress—by increas-

ing catabolic energy-mobilizing processes, enhancement of immune reactions, faster and more effective motor responses, reinforcement or reward from a subjective feeling of increased well-being, all of which help the organism to survive and adapt or learn. Hormesis in various forms is widespread among living organisms, from the *Drosophila* to humans. Studies of stress induced by radiation, heat, or chemical stimuli demonstrate that exposure to mild stress early in life frequently results in increased stress resistance later in life, increased longevity, and even retarded aging (Kristensen, Sorensen, & Loeschcke, 2003). The effect of a mild stress is likely to be mediated by alterations in gene regulation and/or gene expression and by subsequent, permanent metabolic changes. Mild stress may also increase the rate of gene mutation, permitting the population of the organism to successfully adapt to a changed environment (Goho & Bell, 2000).

The social facilitation effect of mild stress on human behavior has been investigated by social psychologists since the nineteenth century, and the facilitative effect of cognitive, somatic, and emotional anxiety on the achievement of athletes has also been widely investigated and confirmed (Hardy, 1996; Jones, Hartmann, Blaschitz, & Desoye, 1993).

In summary, early stress can lead to a cascade of responses, either adaptive, in the form of hormesis, or maladaptive, and the latter can pave the way to different paths of development and different capacities for stress resistance in prenatal and early postnatal life. Traumatic experiences early in life impress confused paths of experience and expectation, with sidetracks that are felt to lead nowhere (Siegel, 1999).

The Hypothalamus-Pituitary-Adrenal System

The stress response involves activation of the two major regulatory systems: the sympathetic nervous system and adrenal medulla (SAM) and the hypothalamo-anterior pituitary-adrenal cortical system (HPA).

The SAM, the effort or fight-flight and system, is most strongly engaged in connection with such strong and active emotional states of fear and anger as are manifested in traumatic anxiety. Its activity results in an increase of the level of the glucocorticoids *adrenaline* (epinephrine) and *noradrenaline* (norepinephrine), with effects both in the periphery and in the brain.

The HPA is the distress or conservation-withdrawal system. Corticotropin-releasing hormone (CRH) released from the paraventricular nucleus of the hypothalamus stimulates the pituitary gland to produce adrenocorticotropin hormone (ACTH). These two hormones stimulate the adrenal gland to release cortisol, the principal glucocorticoid hormone. When the stressor is terminated, glucocorticoids inhibit subsequent ACTH release from the adrenal cortex.

There are several studies supporting the hypothesis that hypersecretion of CRH is a crucial factor in depression and anxiety disorders (Nemeroff et al., 1984). It has been shown that when CRH was injected into the brains of rats, it produced many of the signs and symptoms seen in patients with depression and/or anxiety orders (Arborelius, Owens, Plotsky, & Nemeroff, 1999; Dunn & Berridge, 1990; Korte, 2001).

Limbic Mechanisms and Varieties of Stress Response

Activation of the amygdala, the anterior cingulate cortex, the hippocampus, the bed nucleus of the stria terminalis, and several brain stem regions responsible for regulating basic homeostatic functions of the individual and communication in social engagements can directly or indirectly affect the HPA circuit. The hippocampus and the anterior cingulate cortex are in a negative feedback relationship with the HPA axis, and the activation of the amygdala enhances fearful states and the stress response (Price, 2004). Research with animals, particularly rats and monkeys, has shown how these parts of the forebrain are essential for the emotional regulation of activity and experience and for active social relationships, and this knowledge has found important applications in child psychopathology (Allman, Hakeem, Erwin, Nimchinsky, & Hof, 2001; Amaral, 2003; Isaacson, 2004).

The Amygdala and the Cingulate Gyrus

Two components of the limbic system, the amygdala and the cingulate gyrus, are especially responsive to stress hormones. The *amygdala* is central in what are believed to be predominantly negative *emotionally arousing processes affecting learning* (Cahill, McGaugh, & Weinberger, 2001; Markowitsch, 1998; Price, 2004; Siebert, Markowitsch, & Bartel, 2003). In confrontation with information of a dangerous situation or a threatening social partner, the amygdala becomes active, and this is associated with manifestations of fear and anxiety, which lead the organism into a state of alertness, getting ready for flight or fight in the service of self-preservation (Adolphs, Tranel, Damasio, & Damasio, 1995; Aggleton, 1993; LeDoux, 2000). The high concentration of receptors for corticotropin-releasing factor in the amygdala, which are responsible for the release of corticosterone and ACTH, makes the amygdala especially sensitive to the influences of stress hormones (Gabrieli et al., 1995). Atro-

phy and vulnerability of neurons in this area may have severe consequences for the adaptive processing of life-threatening experience, emotional self-regulation, and the social consequences of a defensive attitude. In human adolescence, especially, attachment and the regulation of emotions of sympathy depend to a large degree on proper functioning of this part of the limbic system. Individuals with disorders of this system that cause them to display avoidance, fear, and aggression become more emotionally and also socially "blind," unable to perceive, process, or respond in a normal fashion to social and emotional stimulation (Cicchetti, 1989; Joseph, 1999).

The *cingulate cortex* has many cortisol receptors. Together with parts of the prefrontal cortex, it mediates in executive or coordinated *goal-directed motor activity* (C. S. Carter et al., 1998; Stuss et al., 2002), which requires effortful behavior, highly efficient attention, and control of inhibitory acts (Fletcher, Frith, Frackowiak, & Dolan, 1996; Markowitsch, Vandekerckhove, Lanfermann, & Russ, 2003; Nieuwenhuis, Yeung, van den Wildenberg, & Ridderinkhof, 2003; Vandekerckhove, Markowitsch, Woermann, & Mertens, in press), as well as arousal of conscious action, excitation of visual imagery, reexperiencing, and emotional processing of experiences (Cabeza & Nyberg, 1997; Fletcher et al., 1996; Markowitsch, Thiel, et al., 2000; Markowitsch et al., 2003).

In a study of preschool-age children who have high levels of cortisol, Gunnar, Tout, de Haan, Pierce, and Stansbury (1997) found that glucocorticoids affect self-control and self-regulation, requiring strenuous effort. This is possibly due to the stress hormones acting on the cingulate cortex. Brain mapping studies confirm that there is a diminished response of the anterior cingulate cortex in the presence of emotionally relevant stimuli in PTSD (Bremner et al., 2004; Shin et al., 2001). Dysfunctional recruitment of this region in PTSD may, in part, mediate symptoms such as distress and arousal on exposure to reminders of trauma.

The Hippocampus

The *hippocampal formation* also has an important role in recording the circumstances of stress (Bremner et al., 2000; Bremner & Vermetten, 2004), as well as in the functions of spatial learning and memory that may be affected by stress (Piefke, Weiss, Zilles, Markowitsch, & Fink, 2003; Tulving & Markowitsch, 1998; Vandekerckhove, in press; Vargha-Khadem et al., 1997), that is, in mapping a story of places, events, and persons that have brought fear or pain. With the temporoparietal neocortex, the hippocampus functions in the acquisition of an awareness of the environment as a place in which to live. Stress experienced before birth and extending through the postnatal period influences the slow increase in volume and the maturation of the hippocampus. The dentate gyrus of the hippocampus continues to develop after birth by neurogenesis (Malberg, 2004; McEwen, 2002; Van Praag et al., 2002).

Animal studies show that a chronic influence of glucocorticoids on the hippocampus leads to the loss of pyramidal neurons and decreased dendritic branching, and a massive acute production of glucocorticoids changes and reorganizes synaptic connectivity. Stress to the mother decreases the number of stress hormone receptors in rat pups, reducing the inhibition of the release of stress hormones, finally leading to hippocampal cell death. Prenatal exposure to stressful restraint or unavoidable electric shocks in rats led to elevated plasma ACTH and corticosterone levels and lower mineralocorticoid and glucocorticoid densities in the hippocampus (C. Henry, Kabbaj, Simon, Le Moal, & Maccari, 1994). Loss of function of mineralocorticoid (type I) receptors affects the capacity for selective attention and integration of sensory stimuli, whereas the impairment of glucocorticoid receptors (type II) affects consolidation and retrieval of information.

Prenatally stressed rats also showed more anxiety-like behavior in the elevated plus-maze test as adults than their nonstressed controls, and this behavior was positively correlated with stress-induced corticosterone responses (Korte, Buwalda, Meijer, de Kloet, & Bohus, 1995). If rats are separated from the mother after birth, they can develop extreme distress reactions (de Kloet, Korte, Rots, & Kruk, 1996). Longer periods (24 hours) of separation cause a rise in corticosterone. Rats deprived of their mother's attentions at the postnatal age of 3 days demonstrated hypercorticism (Rots et al., 1996). Stimulation from the mother protects against all these stress effects. High levels of maternal care (licking, grooming, arched-back nursing) decreased corticotropin receptor density and reduced fear of novelty in the offspring when they reached adulthood (Caldji et al., 1998).

Strong correlations have been found in humans between hippocampal volume and numbers of years of abuse or maltreatment (Bremner, 2002; Bremner & Vermetten, 2004). Severe stress causes a greater reduction in cell proliferation from adolescence to senescence, and early stress exposure accelerates a developmental reduction in hippocampal plasticity. In women, a significant correlation between total lifetime duration of depression and smaller hippocampal volumes has been found (Sheline, Sanghavi, Mintun, & Gado, 1999).

DEVELOPMENT: MUTUAL REGULATIONS IN MORPHOGENESIS OF A HUMAN MIND

> In dealing with such a complex system as the developing embryo, it is futile to inquire whether a certain organ rudiment is "determined" and whether some feature of its surroundings, to the exclusion of others, "determines" it. A score of different factors may be involved and their effects most intricately interwoven. (Harrison, 1933)

Clinical evidence and information from research with animals confirms that stress responses can occur early in interuterine development. In some cases, fetal stress changes the course of postnatal development and has lasting effects. To interpret these better we need to relate them to the unique timetable and sequence of intrauterine human development, to the special environment in which developments occur, and, above all, to the maturation of adaptive structures and processes between the embryo and fetus and the mother's body. Communication between them, and regulation of states of activity and of stress, is two-way from the start and acquires psychological attributes months before birth.

The human organism and its constituent systems and processes—at all levels, from the single cell to a culture sustained by its customs and history of beliefs—have evolved with adaptations to live and change in communities of like systems and processes (Figure 2.3). The fertilized ovum arises from a cluster of maternal cells and divides after fertilization to form a differently organized group. This fuses with the tissues of the wall of the mother's uterus to create a closely integrated living assembly, a tissue with elements from the two bodies. Vital functions of a child's body and the developing brain and behavior require interaction with a mother's body in prenatal stages and with intimate parenting through infancy and early childhood. Essential features of this development are shared with other mammals, but human childhood is long and has additional needs for sharing activity and experience.

Fetus and mother, both in adaptive states of calm inwardness, interact by way of muscular activity—of the fetal body and of the mother's uterine contractions, heartbeat, breathing, and her whole-body movements—and by various senses. In the last trimester, they respond to one another and learn.

The human infant at birth is more helpless than a newborn monkey or chimpanzee and much more developed than a newborn rat or kitten. Above all, the human infant is born with unique powers of expression and intersubjective communication of thinking (Hobson, 2002). A young baby tries to communicate self-generated purposes and interests, with emotional evaluations of experiences, including remembered or imagined ones. This condition is the adaptation of a species that employs psychological abilities of a highly evolved consciousness (Donald, 2001). This consciousness grows in a long period of dependence not only on maternal nurturance and paternal protection, but also on communication of interests and meanings in affectionate relationships with other family members and on learning with companions of all ages in play.

Both body and brain of a newborn baby have anatomical and functional adaptations for social support that lead to cultural learning. This requires, besides the linking in of systems that regulate the metabolism and energetics of behavior, affective coordination of motive processes for the acquisition of new intelligence and skills. These processes can be understood only if the *proactive, motor aspects* of engagement of the human organism with the environment and their *motivating initiatives and emotions in prospective processes of intending and imagining* are recognized, not just the sensory and perceptual processes that take in forms of information for experiences and categorizes them.

The cerebral circuits of innate human sociability adapted for this communion are founded on systems of the brain stem that were set out in the embryo (Trevarthen & Aitken, 1994). The exceptionally long human fetal period augments these structures with great cerebral and cerebellar extensions that will make it possible for a child to assimilate the skills and knowledge of the parental culture. Far from being a blank slate, the newborn infant's brain is a waiting apprentice, primed to gain competence through intent participation in the purposes, experiences, and emotional concerns of other people (Rogoff, 2003), but ready to be resistant or challenging, too.

A child has to make efforts to find and make use of the experience of intimate care and affection. Problems with development arise when the child does not seek care in a normal way, as well as when the human environment is unresponsive or in some measure abusive, rejecting, or failing to perceive the child's motivation.

Body, Brain, and Mind: Prenatal Stages and Infancy

The life of any organism has come about through the slow process of evolution, a process of transformation of whole life histories (de Beer, 1945), and an evolution of social impulses and sensibilities that find their adaptations in whole communities. The inherent features are adaptive in each case to the extent that their functions and development enable the living individual and the group to sustain well-being and gain advantage from acting in an "expected" environment.

We have set ourselves the task to examine how the developing human body and brain change through embryo, fetal, and infant stages, attempting to identify age-related periods of change and potential vulnerability and their effects in later life of that individual. This is, of course, not a new endeavor, but we believe that there is need for a fresh look to find more integrative concepts that might guide more effective diagnosis and treatment of neurodevelopmental disorders.

In human brain development, there is a long phase of prenatal growth of adaptive systems within the mother's body. This is succeeded by 2 years of infancy when the child is totally dependent on maternal care, or its equivalent provided by a mother substitute. Within the mother's body, there are few ways that the embryo or fetus can act to seek changes. Nevertheless, research on twins in utero with ultrasound shows that fetuses past midterm can act and react through contacts with one another, as well as with the mother's body (Piontelli, 2002). In the last trimester, the fetus learns the sound of the mother's voice and can move in response to the movements and tonus of her body, as well as react actively to chemical elements in the media shared with her (Lecanuet, Fifer, Krasnegor, & Smotherman, 1995).

After birth, there is a greatly expanded scope for action, for moving, and for sensing the effects. Infancy is a period in which most of the intelligent strategies for living and learning in a human world become effective, including the all-important maturation of activities of communication that engage the child's consciousness with the awareness, purposes, and emotions of other persons. After no more than 2 years, a normal child is well on the way to being a cooperative member of the community, starting to master language and a host of other cultural skills that depend on understanding and engaging with the minds of others (Trevarthen, 2004b).

The Limits of Gene Theory for Explaining Psychopathology

Just as King John was deluded to imagine a baby could produce language with no human company, so a modern behavioral scientist is misguided if he believes a gene can determine either a normal psychological function or a specific and consistent disorder. Metabolic, hormonal, neural, and other factors of the organism condition gene expression. In the end, a person's genetic constitution is just one factor in how he or she will appear, how he or she will act, know, and think, and how well his or her health will be.

The genetic constitution of a human being has its effects in critical developmental phases that are associated with specific processes that require input from the environment. *Experience-expectant* processes occur during periods when the brain is primed by its motivating or seeking activities and selective attentions to receive specific information from the environment (Cicchetti, 2002; Greenough & Black, 1992). In such periods, the brain is also producing an overabundance or "exuberance" of nerve tracts and synapses, which initiates a pruning or selective retention of elements by competitive interactions between neuronal connections for supportive or trophic factors (Edelman, 1987).

However, during sensitive learning periods, the brain is actively regulating the effects of input, and the most significant epigenetic constraint that determines what a human child's genes can accomplish after birth is that child's communicative and collaborative relationship with other persons. At the heart of this regulation of a human life course are the *emotions,* systems of neural and neurohumoral activity that keep the exploratory and executive functions of human agency on track and that regulate the moral quality of social commitments, thereby influencing every adaptive change in memory that the plasticity of the vastly retentive forebrain cortex permits.

Abnormal experience of parenting or social deprivation during experience-expectant phases of development may have enduring deleterious effects on neurobiological and behavioral epigenesis (Black, Jones, Nelson, & Greenough, 1998; Cicchetti, 2002). In the science of developmental psychopathology, a crucial principle is that the developing individual takes an active autopoietic role in the construction of a life course and in comprehending the meaning of life events (Cicchetti, 2002; Cicchetti & Tucker, 1994). The principle of *experience-dependent* synapse formation, and the neural plasticity or adaptive self-organization that mediates between nature and nurture throughout the life span, imply that each child's adaptation will be unique to that individual (Cicchetti & Tucker, 1994).

To appreciate the adaptive power of the epigenetic process described by Gregory Bateson (1979), we must survey how the structures that guide the assimilation of experience grow and become integrated in more and more elaborate self-regulatory systems of an organism, and how the regulations of different individuals who are adapted to act together may collaborate at different stages to benefit this elaboration.

Prenatal Stages and Adaptations for Interdependency with the Mother

In the early development of a child, the cell mass generated by division of the fertilized egg is dependent for its life on intimate fusion with tissues of the mother. The immobile embryo stage, with its integrated body form, differentiated physiological organs and humoral and central nervous systems, begins to regulate its own vitality while attached to the mother's circulatory system by the placenta. Birth will be a sudden transition to a far more independent life, and in the final weeks of gestation there are preparations for this event, and for the new communications with other persons that will be needed. At every stage there is both a dependency on the living environment, and a new life process advancing its autonomy with the support of that same environment.

From the Beginning, There Is Collaboration between Organisms at Many Levels

Individuation, the making of a human being, begins with sex. Two unique gene arrays are brought together through engagement of two adults with their complementary reproductive systems. The process of mating and copulation between a man and a woman requires a delicate social interplay on many levels of communication. The same is true for the couple's sexual cells. Gamete cells work together with the physiology of the sexual organs to meet and combine.

Sperm motility is probably a minor factor in the fertilization process. Sperm are found in the oviduct within 30 minutes of deposition, a time "too short to have been attained by even the most Olympian sperm relying on their own flagellar power" (Storey, 1995). Rather, the sperm appear to be carried to the oviduct by the woman's uterine muscular activity. The activity of the female genital system working together with the male ejaculate sets the stage for fertilization.

A similar reciprocity of action is found near the ampullary region of the oviduct, where fertilization takes place. Fewer than 1 in 10,000 sperm get close to the egg region (Ralt et al., 1991). Those that do must pass through a process of capacitation, where the sperm cell membrane is altered by loss of cholesterol (Cross, 1998) and carbohydrates (Wilson & Oliphant, 1987), and its membrane potential becomes more negative through loss of potassium ions. These and other negotiations of the sperm with the female genital tract are required before fertilization can take place (Töpfer-Peterson et al., 2002).

The egg is a remarkable storehouse of life-sustaining cytoplasmic molecules accumulated through oogenic maturation. The molecular supplies of energy and amino acids it holds support the early development of the embryo until it implants and fixes itself into the uterine lining. Ribosomes, RNAs, and morphogenetic factors are in place inside the egg to organize the many complex reactions of protein and nucleotide synthesis for the early cell divisions.

The sperm, in contrast, arrives with little more than its half of the genetic material and the necessary enzymes to digest the outer coverings of the egg for fusion and delivery of the genetic material. Its primary features are the motor organelle, or *flagellum,* the cell nucleus containing the haploid chromosomes, and an acrosomal cap that houses the digestive enzymes needed to lyse the egg's membrane for fusion. On reaching the egg, a sperm lines up parallel to its surface, the *zona pellucida,* and is actively tethered there (Baltz, Katz, & Cone, 1988). Egg sperm-binding proteins crosslink with receptors on the sperm surface, which appear to be responsible for the release of the acrosomal enzymes that dissolve the zona pellucida, causing the sperm cell membrane to fuse with the membrane of the egg (Leyton, Leguen, Bunch, & Saling, 1992). The process of sperm and egg fusion and subsequent gene delivery is an interactive process contributed to by both parties.

The Autopoiesis of an Individual Animal Agent

The fertilized cell, or zygote, with its new genetic potential and its new arrangement of cytoplasm, now produces a multicellular animal. Cleavage of the fertilized egg gives rise to 2, 4, 8, and 16 cells in the first few days after fertilization. Each cell has the capacity to become any cell type in the mature body; they are totipotent and can be extracted to form embryonic stem cells. From the 16-cell *morula* stage forward, however, they take courses of specialization that will eventually give rise to every diverse cell type in the human body.

At the 16-cell morula stage, cells on the inside develop into the *embryo,* but those on the outside become *trophectoderm* and give rise to the embryonic portion of the placenta, the *chorion,* which produces regulators of immune response so the mother does not reject the embryo. Chorion cells also cause the mother's uterus to retain the fetus and develop into a mingling of circulatory systems in the *placenta* that enables the fetus to get oxygen and nourishment from the mother (Figure 2.8). At the 32-cell stage, the trophectoderm has become distinct from the embryo proper.

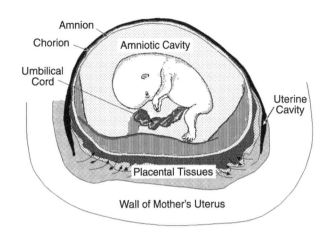

Figure 2.8 Early fetus to show the attachment between the mother's tissues and those of the fetus by the placenta. The placenta constitutes an elaborate frontier for *amphoteronomic* regulation of the vital state of both fetus and mother. *Sources:* From *Human Embryology: Prenatal Development of Form and Function,* third edition, by W. J. Hamilton, J. D. Boyd, and H. W. Mossman, 1962, Cambridge: Heffer.

Interestingly, the cells of the embryo actively support this structure, secreting proteins that cause the trophoblast cells to divide (Tanaka, Kunath, Hadjantonakis, Nagy, & Rossant, 1998).

The cells of the embryo become organized into three lines with different potential functions: (1) The *ectoderm* will give rise to the outer layer of the embryo and its brain and central nervous system; (2) the *endoderm* becomes the innermost layer and produces the digestive tube and its associated organs; and (3) the *mesoderm* will form the muscles, bones, blood, connective tissue, and the rest of the somatic organs. It was recognized by the early anatomists that the germ layers do not develop on their own. As the embryologist Pander said, ". . . each layer is not yet self-sufficient enough to create what it is destined to be; it needs the help of its companions, and therefore, although destined for different roles, all three of them collaborate . . ." (Pander, 1817, p. 12, original translation).

Reciprocity of relations between cells and between tissues drives embryological processes of body shaping. For example, the marking out of the anteroposterior embryonic axis depends on the inductive properties of two signaling centers: the *node* and the *anterior visceral endoderm* (AVE), which together determine the front end of the embryo (Bachiller et al., 2000); this will become the *head,* the lead center of the behaving individual with special receptive and signaling powers (Gans & Northcutt, 1983). The positions of the node and AVE themselves appear to be initiated by signals from the extraembryonic ectoderm, which

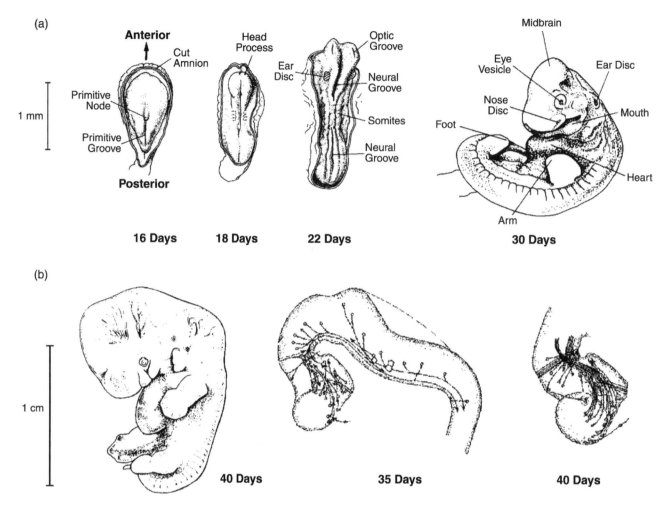

Figure 2.9   (a) Early embryos showing formation of the body and CNS. (b) Late embryo. On right, growth of the integrative tracts of the brainstem. *Source:* From "Brain Development" (pp. 116–127), by C. Trevarthen, in *Oxford Companion to the Mind,* second edition, R. L. Gregory (Ed.), 2004a, Oxford, NY: Oxford University Press.

also induce the patterning of the visceral endoderm (Brennan et al., 2001), and by trophoblast Arkadia protein (Episkopou et al., 2001). Thus, cells from the extraembryonic trophoectoderm and embryonic mesoderm and ectoderm work together in shaping the initial body pattern of the early embryo in anticipation of an active life.

Embryos develop three axial gradients of molecular constitution as foundations of the body plan: the *anteroposterior* axis extending from head to tail, the *dorsoventral* axis from the back to the belly, and the *right-left or mediolateral* axis (Figure 2.9). An important group of genes in the developmental network are the *homeotic genes* that contribute to the control of specification and cell fate (W. Bateson, 1894; E. B. Lewis, 1994; Robert, 2001). Homeotic genes guide the formation of the integrative systems of the body and brain (Boncinelli et al., 1988; E. B. Lewis, 1998). Signaling elements map the body and its segments. Hedgehog genes produce morphogens in very early stages of the em-

bryo that appear to be crucial to the regulation of whole CNS polarity, with effects on nerve cell multiplication and axon growth at subsequent stages (Echelard et al., 1993).

One of the most well-researched signaling molecules is the small protein *Sonic hedgehog* (SHH). Patterning by SHH from the notochord specifies dorsoventral polarity in the neural tube; SHH signaling in the brain rhombencephalon, mesencephalon, and telencephalon is thought to perform similar functions leading to somatotopic mapping in brain nuclei and the molecular fields of cell surface and diffusible proteins that guide patterning of nerve tracts (Marti & Bovolenta, 2002). SHH in developing limb buds specifies anteroposterior arrangement of digits, and SHH shapes the external genitalia. Of particular importance, the SHH signaling centers work in feedback relationships with gene products from neighboring induced tissue and are themselves induced, forming dynamic developmental systems (e.g., see Scherz, Harfe, McMahon, & Tabin, 2004). They induce and interact with other signaling centers, forming complex overlapping spatiotemporal developmental fields.

Morphogenesis of functional adaptive systems in the embryo is driven by cyclic processes of cell multiplication, migration, adhesion, selective cell survival or death, and epigenetic differentiation of cell functions into organs specialized for different regulatory roles, all dependent on reciprocal interactions between molecular cell surface events (determined by cell- or substrate-adhesion molecules) and activation or repression of gene activity (Edelman, 1988). Gene-regulating processes organize both the polarized and segmented body form and differentiation and integration of a coherent system of organs specialized for different vital roles. They define the ectodermal and endodermal surfaces of the body and the intermediary mesodermal sources of the skeletomuscular mechanisms of body action as well as the visceral, glandular, and circulatory systems and the fluid tissue of the blood.

A subdivision of the ectoderm, the *neurectoderm,* forms the CNS adapted to integrate volitional behavior of the whole body, its perceptuocognitive guidance, and its core regulatory emotional states that mediate between vital maintenance and adventurous engagement with the world. *Neural crest* cells, which proliferate at the margin of the neurectoderm, give rise to the autonomic nervous system. These neural control systems develop and connect with each other in interdependent concert with the somatic organs, musculature, and skeletal systems that develop from meso- and endodermal tissues. The hypothalamus and pituitary, which arise near the tip of the notochord in the location of the organizer region of the body (the *node*), are important centers responsible for production of hormones that will regulate processes of feeding, reproduction, and social affiliation in the developed individual.

We give here a brief account of how the tissues of the embryo are formed into a whole and coherent organism adapted not only for a future active life as an individual, but also for communication in the society of other human beings (Table 2.3). For more detail on the following summary of the formation of mechanisms for movement and perception in prenatal stages, see Trevarthen (1985), and for an outline of human brain development, see Trevarthen (2004a). Fetal activity, awareness, and learning are reviewed in Lecanuet et al. (1995).

Embryo: Vital Integration with the Mother's Body and Development of Human Form

An embryo human resembles the embryo of a lower vertebrate, such as a fish or a salamander. It has a central nervous system that mediates between the internal visceral systems and the soma. The latter will become the active agent for a life of free mobility, with special sensory systems for perception of the outside world. After 2 months, when the body has a distinctively human form, the cerebral hemispheres are just starting to develop.

Early Embryo (0 to 30 days)

In the first 10 days, the fertilized egg develops a protective *amniotic cavity* and a nutritive *yolk sac* and joins with the mother's life support system by means of an elaborate *chorionic sac* with many selective functions (Figure 2.9; Table 2.3). The *body axis* of the embryo is determined, the notochord appears, and mesoderm cells migrate between the ectoderm epithelium facing the amnion chamber and the endoderm epithelium facing the yolk sac. The embryo may divide in two to create homozygous twins, which, in spite of their genetic likeness, rarely develop into twins that are identical in character (Piontelli, 2002). The time of division, between 3 days and 2 weeks, determines whether the two embryos will have separate placentas and amniotic and chorionic membranes (as in all dizygotic twins), or if some or all of these structures will be shared. Division after 14 days leads to fused, or Siamese, embryos.

By 20 days, the body is polarized with left-right symmetry, the neural plate is defined, and the head process forms. A simple *circulatory system* appears between the embryo, the yolk sac, the connecting stalk, and the chorion and brings a rich food supply from the mother's blood. As the chorion develops, the yolk sac shrinks. Distances in the embryo are now too large for nutrition by diffusion; blood must circulate between the embryo and chorion, which develops rapidly from the 9th to the 20th day, when the *placenta* is established. It will enlarge with growth of the fetus. The placenta is an important endocrine regulator for the fetus, functioning as a barrier to maternal catecholamines and other substances, filtering out stressors, including cortisol (Jones, 1993). Melathonin does pass over the placenta and seems to be the agent that informs the fetus about the mother's day-night cycle, thus preparing for them to have synchronized circadian rhythms (Yellon & Longo, 1988).

In the next 10 days, the *neural tube* closes, *body segments* form with *muscle somites,* and rudiments of *special sense organs* of the head and at the tips of the digits appear. The neurectoderm develops either brain or cord tissue dependent on induction from the ectoderm/mesoderm ratio in the cell masses. The *hypothalamus* develops in the organizer region at the end of the notochord, the first motor nerve axons grow from the spinal cord, and dorsal sensory ganglia form. At this stage, *somatic and visceral columns* are defined in the CNS. The *locus coeruleus* differentiates.

TABLE 2.3   Developments in Embryo and Fetus

	Early Embryo	Late Embryo	Early Fetus	Midfetus	Last Trimester
Days from conception	0–30	30–60	60–100	100–200	200–280
Body length, mm	0.03–5	5–30	30–100	100–270	270–340
Body form and CNS development	Embryo linked to mother's body by placenta. Germ layers and body form defined. Neural tube forms and body segments appear. Hypothalamus, somatic and visceral columns in CNS, and locus coeruleus differentiate. Seratonin is present.	Main brain centers, special sense organs, and brain stem tracts and nuclei. First noradrenergic, then dopaminergic systems appear. Seratonergic neurons appear in the forebrain. Amygdala and hippocampus differentiate, with the basal ganglia.	Neocortex develops afferent and efferent tracts. Seratonin assists cortical cell differentiation and network formation. Neuroblasts develop first in hippocampus and pyriform cortex. Sexual differentiation is initiated and HPA system matures.	Right hemisphere more advanced than left. Autonomic system sufficient to allow viability in incubator from 170 d. Cholinergic activation of cortex from 140 d. Axons and dendrites of necortex cells start growth from 180 d. Brain waves start 170 d. Habituation to vibratory stimuli develops from 160 to 210 d.	Neocortical cell dendritic fields grow. Axons extend to brain stem and commissures grow between hemispheres. Visual cortex cells functional from 250 d. EEG develops rapidly, but is unreactive to stimuli. Sleep-wake cycle starts 260 d. Dopamine turnover high, GABA and glycine switch from excitatory to inhibitory function. Glutamate and aspartate increase with noradrenaline and neuromodulator galanin.
Movements		Axial twisting movements start at 50 d.	Head and arm movements, respiratory, jaw, and swallowing movements appear after 80 d.	Arm and hand movements increase and are guided by touch to explore body of fetus and surrounding objects. Postural and gestural movements show asymmetries. Heart rate changes coupled to movements from 170 d.	Respiratory movements increase. Body movements decrease. Face, tongue movements smiling, eye movements and hand gestures increase. Fetus sleeps, but wakes easily from 230 d. At term, spontaneous, automatic movements respond to perceptual guidance. Eyes open and active from 230 d.
Sensory systems and perception		Touch responses appear at 50 d.	Responses to the mother's body movements, or movements of a twin, are possible.	Vestibular responses by 100 d., auditory from 150 d., and visual from 180 d.	All sensory-perceptual systems are active before term, excepting the cortical visual system, which undergoes rapid development postterm. Fetus interacts with maternal movements and uterine contractures and learn mother's voice.

Sources: From *Human Embryology: Prenatal Development of Form and Function,* third edition, by W. J. Hamilton, J. D. Boyd, and H. W. Mossman, 1962, Cambridge, England: Heffer; "Development of Neurotransmitter Systems during Critical Periods," by E. Herlenius and H. Lagercrantz, 2004, *Experimental Neurology, 190*(Suppl. 1), pp. S8–S21; "Neuroembryology and the Development of Perceptual Mechanisms" (pp. 301–383), by C. Trevarthen, in *Human Growth,* second edition, F. Falkner and J. M. Tanner (Eds.), 1985, New York: Plenum Press; and "How Infants Learn How to Mean" (pp. 37–69), by C. Trevarthen, 2004b, in *A Learning Zone of One's Own* (SONY Future of Learning Series), M. Tokoro and L. Steels (Eds.), Amsterdam: IOS Press.

At 30 days, the cerebral hemispheres are small, thin-walled sacs with undifferentiated neuroblasts.

Late Embryo (30 to 60 days)

In the second half of the embryo period, the main components of the brain have been formed, and *eyes, vestibular canals,* and *cochlear, nose* and *mouth,* and the *hands* are rap-

idly differentiating their distinctive forms, each dedicated to the picking up of a particular kind of physical information from the environment in selective ways (Figure 2.9; Table 2.3). For most of this period, the nervous system has no electrical activity and generates no movements, and the cerebral hemispheres and cerebellum are rudimentary. In comparison, the *brain stem cell groups and tracts* are well formed (O'Rahilly & Müller, 1994). They will function as the intrinsic motive formation (Trevarthen & Aitken, 1994), activating the behavior of the whole organism.

The pathways that will supply input from the environment and excite movements now develop. First, descending efferent, then ascending pathways grow from the brain stem to the spinal cord, and the first monoamine pathways grow from the brain stem into the primordial cerebral hemisphere. Retinal fibers grow to the midbrain optic tectum, and other sensorimotor circuits of brain stem and spinal cord are formed. *Noradrenergic* neurons, later to be involved in arousal and attention, fear and anxiety, and learning and memory, appear in the CNS around 35 to 40 days. *Dopaminergic* neurons appear a little later, at a gestational age of 40 to 55 days. They will become important after birth in motor and cognitive or executive programs (Herlenius & Lagercrantz, 2004).

Throughout the development of the central nervous system, synaptic activity, with interneuronal transmitter activity, is required for the survival of the synapses. Inactive neurons suffer selective loss, or apoptosis. Very early synapses are special, however, because they require neither generation of action potentials nor the calcium ion transportation and vesicle fusions for their maintenance.

Neurotransmitters appear as the integrative systems of the CNS are forming. Enzymes to synthesize the *catecholamines,* noradrenaline (norepinephrine) and dopamine, appear in the first 2 days in the chicken embryo. In primates, catecholaminergic neurons appear in the midembryo period, at the time when the telencephalic vesicle is forming.

Neurons producing *noradrenaline* appear at 35 to 40 days in the human embryo (Sundstrom et al., 1993). They influence the generation, migration, and maturation of the cortical neurons. The birth of the first cortical neurons, the Cajal-Retzius cells, is regulated by the noradrenergic system (Naqui, Harris, Thomaidou, & Parnavelas, 1999).

Dopamine appears at around 40 to 60 gestational days in humans and is produced in the fetus at a very high level compared to adults (Sundstrom et al., 1993). Dopamine acting on the D1 receptors, which are abundant prenatally (Boyson & Adams, 1997), can directly affect gene transcription. Experimental research shows that even subtle changes in the neurotransmitter systems can directly influence early brain development. Dopamine antagonists during the prenatal period can prevent apoptosis, and lesioning noradrenergic projections prevents glia cell proliferation and in the perinatal period leads to abnormal cortical differentiation (Berger-Sweeney & Hohmann, 1997; Herlenius & Lagercrantz, 2004).

Serotonin (5-HT) can be detected in the fertilized egg and already affects the development of various organs and structures. Serotonin in the early prenatal period is also transported through the placenta from the mother. Serotonergic neurons of the forebrain appear at about 35 to 80 days in humans. The population of serotonergic receptors peaks in midgestation, precisely at the time of a very active neurogenesis, including maturation of the hippocampus. By birth, these receptors are present throughout the cortex, then are reduced rapidly at around 3 weeks after birth. Decreased serotonin levels during the early fetal period may lead to later neurodevelopmental disorders, such as Autism (D. C. Chugani, 2002). The postnatal peak followed by a subsequent decline in the level of serotonin typical of children without Autism is not seen in the brains of children with Autism.

The *amygdala* and *hippocampus* begin rapid differentiation around 50 days, with fiber connections through the lateral forebrain bundle, and the septum develops cholinergic nuclei. The *corpus striatum,* a central coordinating mechanism for adaptive movement routines, is a conspicuous swelling at 40 days. The *neostriatum, caudate, substantia nigra,* and *globus pallidus* establish mechanisms of basic instinctive motor functions.

The *oculomotor nucleus* differentiates and the *cerebellum* and *cochlear nucleus* receive cells from the proliferative zone in the hindbrain roof (rhombic lip) as the hindbrain *visceral sensory nuclei* develop. Brain development is linked with differentiation of the *gonads* and *sex organs.* The special sense organs (*eyes, nose,* and *mouth, vestibular canals,* and *cochlear, fingers,* and *toes*) are now miniatures of their final form (Figure 2.10). The fetus is hunched, hands up in front of mouth and eyes, the right hand higher than the left in most.

The wall of the *cerebral hemisphere (neocortex)* begins differentiation at about 60 days. Cortical neuron cell types (stellate cell, pyramidal cell, etc.) are determined before cells reach their place in the cortex, grow dendrites, and receive afferents. Brain stem afferents to the cortex are guided by position-specific molecules and influence cortical cell development. Efferent fibers do not grow from cortical cells until about 60 days.

Fetus: Preparing the Body and Brain for Intelligent Activities and a Sociable Life

The mammalian brain, with its large neocortex, gains its distinctive form in the fetus. Activated and directed by the core motivating processes of the brain stem, the cortex will assimilate a complex consciousness by engaging with

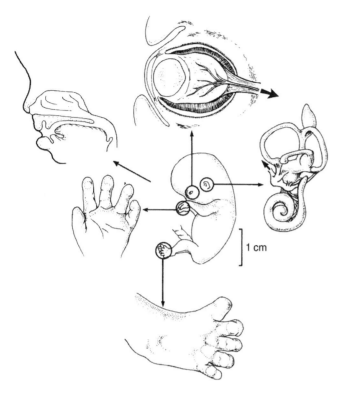

Figure 2.10   Early fetus, 60 days, with well differentiated special sense organs—eyes, nasal passages and mouth, hands, feet, semicircular canals of the vestibular system, and cochlear—at a stage when movements are just beginning and sensory terminals in the CNS have not formed. *Source:* From "Brain Development" (pp. 116–127), by C. Trevarthen, in *Oxford Companion to the Mind,* second edition, R. L. Gregory (Ed.), 2004a, Oxford, NY: Oxford University Press.

physical and social worlds. In the final weeks of fetal life the expressive organs and receptors that will couple the emotions of the child to those of parents as teachers are readied for action, and the unborn infant starts to learn an attachment to the mother's person.

Early Fetus (60 to 100 days)

Throughout its development, the *neocortex* is intimately and reciprocally connected with the earlier formed nerve systems of the brain stem and cerebellum that will control actions of the body and generate autonomic self-regulations and the emotions of social signaling (Holstege et al., 1996; Panksepp, 1998a; Figure 2.10; Table 2.3). Neurogenesis of the cerebral cortex begins.

Serotonergic (5HT) cells appear at about 35 to 84 days in the human (Herlenius & Lagercrantz, 2004). These cells send axons to the forebrain and may be of importance in the differentiation of neuronal progenitors (Gaspar, Cases, & Maroteaux, 2003). Miswiring problems due to excess or inadequate activation of specific 5HT receptors during development may be involved in the genesis of psychiatric problems, such as anxiety disorders, drug addiction, and Autism (for review, see Gaspar et al., 2003).

Neocortical neuroblasts begin to accumulate in the primordial *hippocampus* and *pyriform cortex (paleopallium)*. The latter receives olfactory axons and is a vestige of the main object-identifying and social response system of primitive vertebrates (MacLean, 1990). The neocortex is committed to receive ordered input of sensory information from the body surface and special distance receptors.

The special sense organs that formed in the late embryo become effective in exciting responses in a fixed sequence: touch to some parts at 50 days, vestibular sense at 100 days, auditory response at 150 days, and vision at 180 days (Ronca & Alberts, 1995). But the receptor surfaces are protected from stimulation before this, while the forebrain cortex cells are rapidly proliferating and thalamocortical projections are forming. The eyelids fuse at 50 days and reopen at about 170 days. Transmission of sound by the ear is blocked during the same period, the mouth is closed, and there are skin pads over the tips of the fingers.

Efferent fibers now grow from neocortical cells to thalamus, midbrain, and cerebellum. Subthalamic visual and auditory centers (superior and inferior colliculi) develop their circuits. Long corticocortical axons grow within and between the hemispheres, molding cortical folds that multiply throughout the fetal stage.

Control of *sexual differentiation* by *steroid hormones* is related to regulation of gene expression in the CNS. At 60 to 80 days, the *hypothalamus* with the medioventral reticular formation and the endocrine system of gonads and adrenals regulates development of the body and its secondary sexual features.

Now the fetus begins to move. Simple *axial twisting movements* of the body can be detected from around 60 days. Movements increase as axodendritic and axosomatic synapses form in the cortex from this time, and the number of *arm movements* increases from about 70 days. Movements influence development of tactile and vestibular systems and the face; respiratory movements affect lungs; swallowing affects formation of the mouth; and joint development benefits from limb movements (Ronca & Alberts, 1995). Fetal movements also begin to communicate with the mother through stimulating her body.

Many *hand* and *head movements* are made by 90 days, when there is a second phase of synaptogenesis, and general, cyclic movements remain throughout gestation, resembling movements of the neonate.

Nerve cells form in the cortex from 60 to 120 days, and *cortical cell death (apoptosis)* starts. Cell numbers are essentially stable from 140 days, but there is cell loss later in development. Rapid growth in the fetal cerebral wall and folding of the cortical mantle is due to neuron enlargement and *dendrite* growth.

Midfetus (100 to 200 days)

Postural and gestural movements of the fetus show *asymmetries,* and a preference observed in self-stimulatory thumb-sucking in individual fetuses of 15 weeks gestational age correlates with hand preferences seen in the 2nd year after birth (Hepper, 1995; Table 2.3). The *right hemisphere* is more advanced than the left from about 170 days to the 2nd postnatal year, apparently due to asymmetric input from subcortical systems. It is more involved in trophotropic regulations than the left hemisphere, which is richer in dopaminergic systems (Trevarthen, 1996; Tucker, 2001) and will take the lead in regulation of early communicative responses to maternal care (Schore, 1994).

At 140 days, fetuses are active approximately 25% of the time, moving about once per minute, and can actively regulate their nutrition and protein metabolism by *swallowing* amniotic fluid. From this stage until term, fetal heart rate slows appreciably and becomes more variable due to increasing parasympathetic maturation. At 170 days, the neurological and metabolic machinery for *self-maintenance* without placental support is sufficiently advanced for an infant to be viable in an incubator. The change is a sudden one, the 6-month-old fetus having achieved a characteristic state of relative functional readiness or autonomous regulation (Als, 1995).

The motor activity of the fetus is due to the maturation of neuroneuronal and neuromuscular transmission systems. The *cholinergic* activation in the human brain starts at around the 20th week of gestation (Herlenius & Lagercrantz, 2004).

Last Trimester (200 to 280 days): Preparation for Birth

Axons and *dendrites* grow from cortical cells between 180 and 260 days, following the order of the formation and migration of the cells into the cortex: first those that project to subhemispheric sites, then those that project within the hemispheres or across the *commissures* between them (Table 2.3). Visual cortex cells show changes anticipating thalamic input from the retina from about 250 days. Around 200 days, *inspiratory movements* of the chest and

responsiveness to vibroacoustic stimuli increase, related to cortical regulation of autonomic processes. Body movements decrease, and simple movements of the mouth and the tongue increase and rhythmic *mouthing movements* are present from 240 days in healthy fetuses. *Facial expressions, tongue movements, scowling, eye* and *mouth opening, blinking, yawning, smiling* are present in third trimester fetuses, as in neonates. Fetuses learn and are able to *habituate* to vibratory stimuli and "remember" them even 24 hours later.

At 230 days, the fetus is more alert and better coordinated, *waking* easily to stimulation, and showing the first *spontaneous eye movements* with lids wide open. The infant may raise *hands* to face, place them in the mouth, and suck them actively and rhythmically. Exploratory grasping occurs. For most of the last trimester the fetus is in a sleepy state, however.

The brain stem reticular formation, which will regulate sleep, spontaneous orienting, and consciousness after birth, exhibits patterned *electrical activity* first in the *pons,* at 70 days. The activity then advances through the *midbrain reticular formation* and basal ganglia, spontaneous *rhythmic brain waves* appearing in scalp electrodes at 170 days. At the time the fetus becomes viable, the *electroencephalogram* (EEG) becomes more regular, with bursts of theta waves (4 to 6 cps) synchronized within each hemisphere. Within a week or 2, this isosynchronism diminishes. At 210 days, higher-frequency bursts become more common (10 to 14 cps), this being the period of most rapid development of the EEG (170 to 250 days). There are still no electroencephalic reactions to stimuli and no sleep-wake differences. Activities at this time are probably of subcortical origin.

A distinction between *sleep* and *waking* tracings appears at 260 days. The waking EEG is similar to that of the full-term infant, but the sleep record differs, characteristics of the much younger (210 days) EEG reappearing in light sleep. Habituation to a vibratory stimulus has been studied to test responsiveness and regulation in fetuses. It is observed from about 160 days and finishes development at about 210 days, females being approximately 3 weeks earlier than males (Hepper, 1995).

The *dopamine* turnover is relatively high during the perinatal period, compared to adults. Extremely high levels of D1 receptors have been reported in the pallidum during the perinatal period (Boyson & Adams, 1997). D1 receptor stimulation regulates transcription of other genes, and it is possible that abnormal perinatal stimulation can result in long-term consequences (Herlenius & Lagercrantz, 2004).

Twenty-five to 40% of neurons contain *gamma-aminobutyric acid* (GABA), which switches from a prenatal excitatory function to an inhibitory function after birth with the appearance of the K+/Cl-KCC2 cotransporter at around 1 week of age (Miles, 1999). *Glycine,* another inhibitory amino acid neurotransmitter, similarly switches from excitatory to inhibitory function in the spinal cord and the brain stem. The disappearance of the automatic regulatory neonatal reflexes is related in part to the switch to inhibitory functions of these neurotransmitters (Fitzgerald, 1991).

Almost half of the synapses in the brain contain *glutamate* or *aspartate,* the main excitatory neurotransmitters that are most abundant around 1 to 2 years after birth in the human brain (Benitez-Diaz, Miranda-Contreras, Mendoza-Briceno, Pena-Contreras, & Palacios-Pru, 2003). Various other amino acids also show peaks and pre- or perinatal surges. They are abundant in the brain with slow transportation and slow effect and are often cosynthesized and stored with various other neurotransmitters. Many have a neuromodulatory function; that is, they assist in regulation of the synthesis and expression of the principal neurotransmitter molecules. For example, approximately 80% of the noradrenergic neurons contain *galanin,* a neuromodulator, which may control the rapid increase of noradrenergic release at birth (Herlenius & Lagercrantz, 2004).

Production of several neurotransmitters is activated around birth. The surge in the production of *noradrenaline* may contribute to the development of affectionate bonding between the mother and infant by increasing somatosensory attention (awareness of touch and temperature stimulation) and the interpersonal communication of motives of the newborn child (Sullivan, Wilson, Lemon, & Gerhardt, 1994). On the other hand, neonatal stress, including pre- and perinatal hypoxia, affects the expression and level of neurotransmitters and their receptors, and such changes could be a factor in the future mental health of the child.

Research on the behavior, psychology, and physiology of the fetus indicates that in the last trimester, functions are established in anticipation of an active postnatal life, and especially for assimilating and collaborating with maternal care (Lecanuet et al., 1995). Motor coordinations exist that are obviously adapted for visual exploration, reaching and grasping, walking, and expressive communication by facial expression and gesture (de Vries, Visser, & Prechtl, 1984, 1988; Prechtl, 1984). *Respiratory movements* and amniotic breathing appear several weeks before birth, and *heart rate* changes have been coordinated with phases of motor activity from 24 weeks (James, Pillai, &

Smoleniec, 1995). This is indicative of the formation of a prospective control of autonomic state coupled to readiness for muscular activity on the environment, a feature of brain function, which Jeannerod (1994) has cited as evidence for the formation of cerebral "motor images" underlying conscious awareness and purposeful movement. Both heart function and respiratory movements are stimulated by maternal hormones and contractures of the uterus that are both spontaneous and stimulated by oxytocin (Nathanielsz, 1995). Contractures can alter the oxygen level of the fetus by affecting placental circulation and secretion of cortisol and other hormones that might be both cause and effect of brain developments. Unlike a mature brain, which reacts to deoxygenation by a panic response, a fetal brain reacts to a drop in oxygen by protective withdrawal into inactivity.

Birth and Infancy: Regulations with a Growing Body and Brain and Development of Shared Experience

A normal birth is a highly collaborative process, the mother's body being influenced by her own hormonal system and by stimuli from the infant. In turn, the infant receives stimulation and mechanical effects from delivery that assist the onset of breathing, the transition from umbilical to pulmonary respiration. "Fetal brain expectation," readying for postnatal life, is evident in developments of prematurely born infants (Als, 1995).

Newborns with a well-integrated regulation of activity and awareness as measured by EEG sleep patterns have more successful interactions with the mother and fewer problems in later childhood and adolescence (Parmelee et al., 1994). Quiet sleep, which is a state of restful disengagement from the environment, is related to cognitive functions from early infancy through childhood, but not so consistently to attention measures. Active sleep of the neonate, which is more easily disrupted or distracted by stimuli, correlates with vigilant attention in childhood, and it correlates with regulation of norepinephrine in the frontal cortex and wakefulness. What are called indeterminate sleep patterns of the newborn indicate poor state organization and are prognostic of poorer performance on both cognitive and attention measures in childhood. Left hemisphere EEG power spectrum analysis confirms other indications that the left hemisphere is adapted for vigilance rather than recuperation, which correlates with evidence that the role of the right hemisphere, and especially the right orbitofrontal system, is complementary for establishing close regulatory affective links with the mother in infancy (Schore, 1994) and perhaps for more sustained rather than shifting vigilance (Posner & Petersen, 1990). "Poor social interactions and general socioeconomic circumstances amplify the negative effects of poor state organization, and good social interactions and socioeconomic circumstances diminish the effect confirming state organization as important for the biological environmental interface" (Parmelee et al., 1994, p. 550).

Adaptations for Mothering, on Both Sides

Newborn infants, like young of other mammalian species, are prepared for state regulation within maternal care (C. S. Carter, Lederhendler, & Kirkpatrick, 1997). They respond to the touch, movement, odor, and warmth of a mother, and sleeping with the mother may help the development of cardiac and respiratory self-regulations (McKenna & Mosko, 1994). With regard to the regulatory importance of skin contact, it is of great interest that human hair follicles can synthesize cortisol, and this is regulated by hypothalamic and pituitary hormones, including ACTH, ß-endorphin, and CRH. Thus, hair follicles assist in the coordination stress response and integrating with changing metabolic demands and neuroimmune signaling circuits (Ito, Ito, & Paus, 2005). There are positive effects of gentle massage and other forms of tactile stimulation for premature infants (Field, 2003), and these can be related to how normal mothering of the newborn involves much gentle touching of the baby (Kennell et al., 1974). Rat pups gain regulatory benefit from maternal stroking or licking, and very small preterm human neonates given tactile-kinesthetic stimulation gain more weight per day, spend more time awake and active, and show more mature habituation, orientation, motor, and range of state behaviors on the Brazelton assessment (Schanberg & Field, 1987).

Infant's arousal and expressions of distress are immediately responsive to stimulation from breast-feeding, including responses to the sugar and fat content of breast milk (Blass, 1996), and this physiological response is already linked with a sympathetic psychological or interpersonal awareness; it is facilitated if the newborn has sight of the mother's eyes (Zeifman, Delaney, & Blass, 1996). Full-term newborns show not only orienting to the nipple by so-called rooting reflexes, but an impressive control over the complex movements of suckling and swallowing for breast-feeding (Craig & Lee, 1999), and the mother has, of course, many adaptations of body, behavior, and hormonal control of milk production, stimulated by the hormones oxytocin and prolactin, that help her feed the baby.

Getting Ready to Communicate Thought and Learn Signs of Thought

The remarkable, and only recently adequately explored, abilities of newborn infants to imitate communicative expressions of adults in many forms is but part of a highly coordinated adaptation to regulate or negotiate intersubjective contact (Hobson, 2002; Trevarthen, 2005a; Figure 2.11). The attempts of the infant to imitate are accompanied by efforts to "invite" or "provoke" return imitations form the partner. Moreover, these behaviors are associated with heart rate changes that indicate *imitating* is carried out in an energetic excited phase, marked by *HR acceleration,* whereas *provocations* are accompanied by an oriented and attentive or watchful state and *HR slowing* (Nagy & Molnar, 2004).

The regulatory mechanisms of the infant brain are reactive to endocrine steroids and other hormones (McEwen, 1989, 1997a, 1997b; Suomi, 1997), but they are also ready at birth to formulate and express motivated behaviors, including coherent emotions. An intricate *mutual psychobiological dependency* is set up between a newborn infant and the care of a mother or mother substitute (DiPietro, Irizarry, Costigan, & Gurewitsch, 2004). Modern perinatal medicine finds evidence that this system of regulation cannot be fully replaced by artificial clinical mechanisms (Als, 1995), and there are concerns that the increase of elective or medically advised cesarean births may violate the principles or mutual hormonal regulation between fetus and mother in the process of natural birth (Nissen et al., 1996).

Newborns, and possibly fetuses, too, react to and gain regulation from the rhythms of maternal breathing and heart beat (McKenna & Mosko, 1994), and fetuses and infants are also supremely sensitive to maternal vocal patterns (DeCasper & Fifer, 1980; Fifer & Moon, 1995; Hepper, 1995). These emotional responses to caregivers must play a crucial role in the regulation of early brain development (Als, 1995). They are likely to guide differentiation of perceptual discrimination, cognitive processing, memory, voluntary deployment of attention to environmental objects, and executive functioning or problem solving (Schore, 1994; Tucker, 1992).

Long before the oral-vocal system is skilled in imitating speech and using it, or the hands can use symbols in a sign language or writing, the eyes, hands, face, and voice of an infant may move in coordinated exchanges of expressions of feeling with an attentive and sympathetic partner. The mechanisms for vocal expression of emotion and those for speech that develop around midgestation (de Vries et al.,

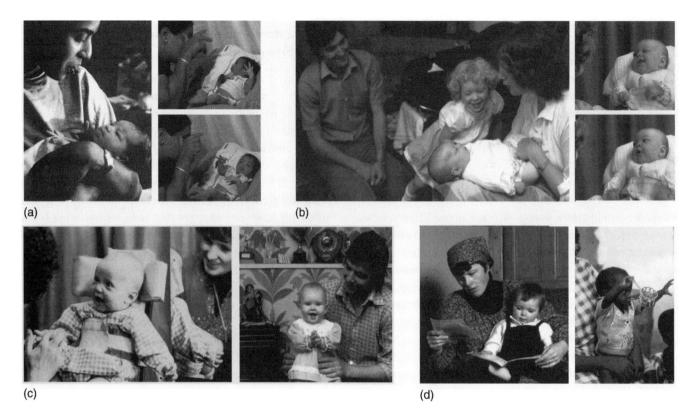

Figure 2.11   Infants communicating in the first year. a: Mutual imitations with mother or hospital nurse, less than one hour after birth (Photographs by Kevan Bundell). b: Infant in family at 3 months and in the Psychology Laboratory of Edinburgh University at 6 weeks, in protoconversation with her mother. c: Infants at 5 and 6 months enjoying practice of nursery action songs, Leanne shares "Round and round the garden" with her mother; Emma shows "Clappa clappa handies." d: One-year-olds share interests; Basilie reads with mother in Edinburgh; Adegbenro show his toy in Lagos. (Photos John and Penelope Hubley). *Source:* From "How Infants Learn How to Mean" (pp. 37–69), by C. Trevarthen, in *A Learning Zone of One's Own* (SONY Future of Learning Series), M. Tokoro and L. Steels (Eds.), 2004b, Amsterdam: IOS Press; "Action and Emotion in Development of the Human Self, Its Sociability and Cultural Intelligence: Why Infants Have Feelings like Ours" (pp. 61–91), by C. Trevarthen, in *Emotional Development,* J. Nadel & D. Muir (Eds.), 2005a, Oxford: Oxford University Press; and "Stepping Away from the Mirror: Pride and Shame in Adventures of Companionship: Reflections on the Nature and Emotional Needs of Infant Intersubjectivity," by C. Trevarthen, in *Attachment and Bonding: A New Synthesis* (Dahlem Workshop Report 92), C. S. Carter, L. Ahnert, K. E. Grossman, S. B. Hrdy, M. E. Lamb, S. W. Porges, et al. (Eds.), 2005c, Cambridge, MA: MIT Press.

1988; Piontelli, 1992; Prechtl, 1984) are organized around nuclei of the brain stem and the basal ganglia, thalamus, and limbic cortex (Ploog, 1992; Trevarthen, 2001b). These are structures that Paul MacLean (2004) identifies with the reptilian instinctive motor complex (R-complex) important in the evolutionary background of communicative behavioral routines in mammals, and which are greatly elaborated in humans.

Multimodal brain stem circuits would seem to be crucial to communication with neonates and for their first imitations, which develop into well-controlled protoconversational abilities by 6 weeks, before visual awareness has undergone rapid development in the first 6 postnatal months. Developments in the mesolimbic cortices of the temporal and frontal lobes in infants and toddlers trans-

form autonomic self-regulation, emotions in communication, and the motives for action and experience (Schore, 1994, 1998). At all stages, limbic and neocortical circuits emerge in reciprocal, dynamic, and increasing involvement with the multimodal core regulatory systems of the intrinsic motive formation (Trevarthen & Aitken, 1994) formed in utero (O'Rahilly & Müller, 1994; Panksepp, 1998a; Robbins, 1992; Tucker, Derryberry, & Luu, 2000).

Brain Events in the 1st Year

There are major transformations in brain structure and function during the 1st year of infancy: in electrical activity and EEG coherence, cortical cell anatomy and connections, myelinization, brain metabolism, neurochemistry, synaptogenesis and synaptic activity, receptor site multiplication and activation or deactivation, and gene activity (Dawson & Fischer, 1994; Nelson & Luciana, 2001). Charting of these changes with infants at accurately known ages after birth and with fine enough discrimination of different brain systems is not far advanced at present, in spite of spectacular development of noninvasive techniques.

The newborn brain is a different shape from the adult's: Frontal, parietal, and temporal lobes are relatively small. There is a conspicuous enlargement of the frontal region around the end of the 1st year. Measurements of head circumference apparently demonstrate significant age-related peaks of rate of growth at 3 to 4, 7 to 8, 10 to 11, and 15 to 18 weeks (Fischer & Rose, 1994). There are no other measurements that discriminate possible transitional events as well as these data appear to do.

Myelinization studies show that some cortical and subcortical structures undergo extensive functional development. In the first 3 months, the greatest change is observed in motor pathways, sensory roots of the spinal cord, and visual projections to the midbrain tectum, thalamus, and cortex (Barkovich, Kjos, Jackson, & Norman, 1988). Subthalamic auditory pathways are more mature than visual ones at birth, but postthalamic auditory projections develop much more slowly than the visual over the first few years. Thalamocortical tracts for touch also develop slowly.

At birth, a rapid proliferation of dendritic branches of cortical cells and synaptogenesis, which began just before term, is continuing. After 3 months, growth of major dendritic branches ceases, but synapse density continues to increase until 6 months (Bourgeois, 2001; Huttenlocher, 1990). Synaptogenesis occurs at different times in different areas of the human cortex but is largely complete by the end of the 1st year. In the visual cortex, synaptic mechanisms of layer 4 neurons undergo rapid maturation at the same time as binocular stereopsis develops (Held, 1985; Held, Birch, & Gwiazda, 1980). The first 3 months is a time when sleep regulations that were set up prenatally, and associated processes of respiration and circulatory control undergo extensive consolidation (Kohyama, 1998). These changes are linked most obviously with developments in the body's motor capacity and in visual alertness and discrimination. The infant is becoming more open to the world and more adept at social exchanges.

It is likely that a large selective elimination of interhemispheric axons of the corpus callosum takes place during the first 6 months, before the callosal axons start myelinating (Innocenti, 1983). EEG coherence studies show that different corticocortical tracts between pairs of locations in the cortex are changing in their efficiency at particular ages, and comparisons between locations in the two hemispheres indicate that cycles of development swing between left and right cortex throughout childhood (Thatcher, 1994).

PET scan evidence showing regional glucose utilization in infants' brains (H. T. Chugani, 1994, 1998) indicates that in the newborn in the primary sensory and motor cortices, thalamus, brain stem, and the vermis of the cerebellum are undergoing intense development, and the basal ganglia, hippocampus, and cingulate gyrus are also active. Parietal, temporal, and primary visual cortices, basal ganglia, and the cerebellar hemispheres are found to be developing during the first 3 months. The lateral and inferior frontal cortex shows increase of glucose consumption after 6 to 8 months, and the dorsal and medial frontal cortices show comparable increases only between 8 and 12 months. At 1 year, the infant's pattern of glucose utilization resembles that of an adult.

Foresightful Motives and Sociability: The Prefrontal Cortex

The *prefrontal cortex* (PFC) is now understood in cognitive psychology to be especially responsible for executive functioning, that is, with processes that program, control, and verify sensory information processing in the planning and organizing of behaviors (Figures 2.5 and 2.6). It is active in the selection or inhibition of specific behaviors, in initiating them and anticipating the effects. In short, from this perspective, the PFC performs complex cognitive functions integrating memory and imagination (D. A. Lewis, 1997). It is understood to have an essential role in the integration of information in future time (Fuster, 1989; Goldman-Rakic, 1987), a mastery of "time in the mind" (Pöppel & Wittmann, 1999) that accords with the close reciprocal anatomical relationship between the PFC and the cerebellum, which regulates the sensorimotor coordination of fast movements. The *dorsolateral PFC* is believed to retain transient memory traces that link the temporal discontinuities between recent events and future responses. The whole of the frontal part of the brain seems to "think ahead," and it is crucial for the integration and control of elaborate action plans and associated acts of selective attention and learning. But the *ventromedial PFC*, in association with the insula and limbic cortices, is also a regulator of *emotion* and of the motivation for efficient mental functioning in the pragmatics of social life, including the self-regulation of agency and *goal-directed activity, social self-awareness,* and *moral behavior* (Anderson, Bechara, Damasio, Tranel, & Damasio, 1999; Damasio, 1999; Damasio et al., 2000; Schore, 1994).

The frontal lobe undergoes important developments in infancy as a child becomes more active in collaborative awareness and learns to share meaningful experience with other persons (Diamond, 1991; Schore, 1994). In the last 3 months of the 1st year, when an infant is increasingly attentive to a parent's purposes (Hubley & Trevarthen, 1979; Trevarthen & Hubley, 1978) and performing expressive acts of protolanguage (Halliday, 1975), conspicuous developments in the prefrontal cortex correlate with advances in crawling and in the comprehension required for object-permanence tests of strategic attention, and for cognitive processes of executive intelligence (Bell & Fox, 1996). Evidently, brain mechanisms for action plans and locomotor maturation share common regulatory factors with motive systems that mediate in interpersonal attention and response to others' communicative expressions. Both phylogenetic and ontogenetic or developmental considerations would lead to the conclusion that this anterior part of the brain has evolved to integrate intrinsic emotional regulations with environmental information in the production of adaptive movements (Damasio, 1994; Luciana, 2001).

In the social world, the PFC appears to perform the most elaborate regulations of *expressive communication.* Complex cross-modal, or multisensory, integrations are required to match the underlying intentions and feelings in behaviors of other subjects (Diamond, 1990; Goldman-Rakic, 1987; Schore, 1994). In both monkeys and humans, parts of the PFC have a key role in the postnatal development of imitative communication skills, and in humans *Broca's area* mediates in the acquisition of all productive aspects of language, including speech (Damasio & Damasio, 1992). Research in monkeys has shown that the excitation of "mirror" neurons in frontal areas homologous with or adjacent to Broca's area "imitates" hand actions. Activation of these cells can specify either a gesture by the subject or visual perception of the same gesture in another individual (Rizzolatti & Arbib, 1998). They are part of what is now recognized as an extensive set of person-recognizing "sympathy" mechanisms distributed throughout associative and motivating regions of the cortex, including regions that mirror actions and others that are specifically involved in sympathetic reactions to visceromotor regulations and the emotional expressiveness of communication (Decety & Chaminade, 2003; Gallese, Keysers, & Rizzolatti, 2004).

Given the relative immaturity of the frontal cortex in early infancy, it is likely that unidentified subcortical motor mirror neuron components of a "sympathy system" are responsible for imitation in the 1st year, at least for the many imitations of discrete and arbitrary expressions that neonates may perform. Mirroring actions involves transmodal sensory recognitions, and there are many multimodal neural populations in the brain stem, for example, in the superior colliculus and periaqueductal gray. These are integrated with systems that formulate motor images for action and expression (Holstege et al., 1996; Panksepp, 1998a). It should be recalled that lower vertebrates that lack a neocortex are capable of communicating by emitting and perceiving stereotyped motor routines (action patterns) that are made more salient by various signs stimuli on the body of the emitter (MacLean, 1990; Tinbergen, 1951). However, it has been demonstrated that regions of the frontal and temporal cortices that become essential for face recognition and for the understanding and production of speech in adults are already active in young infants when they are presented with a picture of a person (Tzourio-Mazoyer et al., 2002).

The frontal lobes depend on receptive and regulatory functions of other cortical regions and on extensive reciprocal relations with the brain stem emotional mechanisms (Schore, 1994). Structures that have a comparativel long development in humans and that are involved in the elaboration of new functions from fetal stages to adulthood include the reticular formation, hippocampus, dorsomedial temporal lobe, and parts of the cerebellum (Gilles, Shankle, & Dooling, 1983; Yakovlev & Lecours, 1967). These all mediate in collaboration between intrinsic motivating activities and acquisition of new organization under environmental instruction.

Children with Autism show abnormalities in the anatomy and function of PFC, as well as in medial temporal and parietotemporal cortices, which correlate with their difficulties in expressive communication and awareness of other persons' feelings and intentions (Dawson et al., 2002).

Sensing Others' Feelings and States of Mind from Their Movements and Building Memories of Relationships: The Temporal Lobes

Understanding others' speech and all other forms of communicative expression involves the *superior temporal cortex* (STC), the fusiform gyrus on the ventral surface of the temporal lobe, and the left temporoparietal cortex (Wernicke's area; Damasio & Damasio, 1992; Figures 2.5 and 2.6). Emotions of interpersonal awareness, which perform the essential regulations of affective and intersubjective contact, are mediated by the entorhinal cortex, amygdala, and hippocampus of the temporal lobes.

Development of *language* is governed by principles of perception and motor expression that motivate conversational interactions between infants and their parents (Trevarthen, 1990, 2004b, 2004c, 2004d). Preverbal communication involves both limbic and neocortical mechanisms in temporal and prefrontal parts of the hemispheres, as well as many subcortical structures of forebrain, diencephalon, midbrain, and hindbrain. The *orbitofrontal cortex,* linked to the *mediolateral temporal cortex,* has a key role in regulation of the balance between psychobiological state and transactions with the environment, including affective transactions with a caregiver (Field, Fox, Pickens, & Nawrocki, 1995), and it undergoes important elaboration in infancy (Schore, 1994, 1998, 2001).

The hippocampal system (hippocampus, parahippocampus, entorhinal cortex, and perirhinal cortex) is important for forming a coherent set of memories of persons and social events and for recalling them in understanding engagements in the present (Cohen et al., 1999).

EARLY STRESS AND PSYCHOLOGICAL DEVELOPMENT: PROCESSES THAT CAUSE OR RESIST PATHOLOGY

We understand psychophysiological stress to be a product of the tension or balance between motive impulses to act on the environment and challenge it (*ergotropy*) and restorative processes that sustain vital integrity and capacity for action (*trophotropy*). The central nervous system, closely coupled to endocrine mechanisms that control essential cellular processes of organs that regulate the metabolism of the body and its internal environment, has a key role. It coordinates the balance of action and restoration and is itself both responsive to beneficial stimulation and vulnerable to excessive stress.

Developmental Neuropathology

Developmental psychopathology and developmental neuropathology have the task of explaining how the long and elaborate preparation for human intersubjective existence may go wrong at any stage of the formation of the brain's systems of motivation and prospective control of action, with the aim of improving both recognition and treatment of problems (Cicchetti, 1984, 1990; Cicchetti & Tucker, 1994).

Throughout the development of the brain, the balance of effects in a child's engagement with the outside world, and especially with other persons, determines the processes that promote further and more elaborate action and re-

sponse. Developments in the brain and body and in their genetic and epigenetic regulations undergo intrinsically regulated, age-related changes and respond to environmental stimuli and demands. Links between persons and their brains, mediated by transmitted effects of vital activities and movements of their different bodies, have importance at every stage.

Developing Autonomy in the Regulatory System of the Fetus and Coregulation before Birth

The ability of the embryo and fetus to respond adaptively to stress develops early in gestation. The most important parts of the future stress circuit, the hypothalamic region and the primordium of the hippocampus, are present in the human embryo at approximately 30 days after conception. Forebrain systems (such as the amygdala, stria terminalis) that will in future activate the HPA axis to socioemotional stressful events, are developing at the same time. The function of the HPA axis fluctuates throughout pregnancy, with a temporary suppression period in midpregnancy.

After early fetuses react to sensory stimulation around the 7th week of gestation, repeated stimulation results in an apparent hyperexcitability. This might correspond more with the development of the motor capacity of the fetus than with any experience of pain. It is also possible that the brain may react to stress earlier, when movements cannot occur. From the 16th week of gestation, increased blood flow in the fetus has been shown to follow invasive procedures (Teixeira, Glover, & Fisk, 1999), and from the 18th week, a rapid increase of the level of noradrenaline and a slower increase of the cortisol and beta-endorphin indicate the presence of a fully functioning stress response to painful invasive procedures (Gitau, Fisk, Teixeira, Cameron, & Glover, 2001). Fetuses show complex reactions to noxious stimuli long before there are thalamocortical projections to the cortex at around 26 weeks, and these reactions include stress responses that are likely to affect development (Vanhatalo & van Nieuwenhuizen, 2000).

Stress responses of the mother lead to increased glucocorticoid levels by activation of her HPA system. The fetus, however, possesses protective mechanisms to filter the effects of maternal hormones. The placenta can block the transport of glucocorticoids into the fetal circulation, partially protecting the fetus from the maternal stress response (Jones, 1993). The 11-beta-hydroxysteroid-dehydrogenase enzyme of the fetus provides another level of protection by breaking down the cortisol to inactive cortisone.

Higher circulating cortisol level leads to the HPA axis becoming suppressed to prevent the production of further cortisol, which could be damaging to the organism. However, between the 18th and 40th weeks of gestation, the negative feedback from the circulating cortisol to the HPA axis is itself reduced, which means that a high level of glucocorticoids could in fact have negative effects on fetal growth and development as the fetus opens this potential transmission of strong effects from the mother.

Although the level must be modulated, prenatal exposure to glucocorticoids in the fetus is necessary for normal growth and development. The production by the placenta of the 11-beta-hydroxysteroid-dehydrogenase enzyme, which protects the fetus from the high level of glucocorticoids, is in fact regulated by the maternal glucocorticoids. This collaborative regulation is one of the most important mechanisms to protect the fetus from too high levels of maternal glucocorticoids (van Beek, Guan, Julan, & Yang, 2004). The same enzyme is important in the development of surfactant in the fetal lung, the compound that makes the lung surface able to absorb oxygen and thereby makes the fetus independently viable (Hundertmark et al., 2002).

Measurement of fetal heart rate (FHR) acceleration to vibroacoustic stimulation (VAS) can be used from week 28 to detect the capacity of the fetus to respond and to self-regulate (habituate; Groome, Bentz, & Singh, 1995; Hepper, 1995). VAS by a vibrator applied to the mother's belly, though artificial, might be considered to act like a mother's voice to attract the readiness of the fetus to engage with her. There appears to be a change after 32 weeks, when VAS causes FHR deceleration, possibly indicative of a new alerting response (Jensen, 1984). The subthalamic brain stem auditory system is well-developed from the second trimester. Maternal emotional state can have effects on the fetal response. Fetuses of depressed mothers, but not those with anxiety disorders, have a higher baseline FHR, show a greater response to VAS, and return to their baseline levels more slowly (Allister, Lester, Carr, & Liu, 2001; Monk et al., 2004).

Winnicott (1960) identified a "primary maternal preoccupation" of expectant and new mothers. Pregnancy is associated with a dampening of the mother's physiological reaction to stressors or exercise and a temporary reduction of cognitive capacities (Barron, Mujais, Zinaman, Bravo, & Lindheimer, 1986; Buckwalter, Stolley, & Farran, 1999; deGroot, Adam, & Hornstra, 2003; Kammerer, Adams, von Castleberg, & Glover, 2002; Matthews & Rodin, 1992). All these changes reflect sympathetic activation of the mother by the fetus.

The fetus is an active agent (Smotherman & Robinson, 1987) and can stimulate labor (Challis et al., 2001). DiPietro et al. (2004, p. 518) offer evidence that the relationship between the fetus and mother is bidirectional from the start, and they propose that the capacity of the fetus to influence the mother's psychophysiological state from midgestation has been underestimated: "The observed phenomenon of maternal sympathetic activation by the fetus may serve a signal function to the pregnant woman in preparation for the consuming early demands of child rearing and redirecting maternal resources directed at competing but less relevant environmental demands." Moreover, the same research group (DiPietro, Hodgson, Costigan, Hilton, & Johnson, 1996) found that a stable synchrony of regulation is characteristic of individual maternal-fetal pairs. A mutually adapted pair of individuals forms a *single integrated system* with its own synchrony.

The Relationship after Birth

Clearly, the mother-child mutual regulation is active and functioning to assist development before birth, but all systems that have been linking a developing embryo and fetus with regulatory systems of the mother's body are transformed after birth by maturation of *attachment systems* that sustain parental care and that lead to the development of regulations of emotional companionships and shared activity that will foster the learning of knowledge and skills throughout life. The "evolutionary based dyad" of the mother and the infant (Dugdale, 1986) provides a level of protection against the negative effects of the glucocorticoids on the developing brain, just as close contact between the mother and the rat pup lowers the reactivity of the HPA axis of the pup to stressful events (Suchecki, Rosenfeld, & Levine, 1993), and offspring of more experienced rhesus monkey mothers show significantly reduced stress response and cortisol level (Kalin, Larson, Shelton, & Davidson, 1998). Evidently, rhesus mothers learn from their offspring to be better regulators of future juveniles.

The human mother's role in buffering physiological stress responses is demonstrated by a study of 18-month-old infants' cortisol levels when they were approached by a stranger in the presence of their mother; infants with secure attachment did not show a rise, but others who were insecurely attached did show a significant cortisol elevation (Gunnar, 1998). Salivary cortisol levels of human infants awaiting inoculation did not rise if the child was left with a friendly and sensitive babysitter compared to an unfriendly and insensitive one (Gunnar, Larson, Hertsgaard, Harris, & Brodersen, 1992). Evidently, the relationship with the caregiver can provide a powerful "sociobiological buffer" or psychobiological coregulation for an infant. Reduction in the level of cortisol indicates a more effective down-regulation of the stress process by the hippocampus and the prefrontal cortex (Schore, 1996, 2003a, 2003b).

Stress and Early Psychopathology

Although abnormalities in the motivating and emotional systems in the embryo brain are mainly of genetic origin (Lyon & Gadisseux, 1991) or caused by severe pathogens interfering with the action of genetic mechanisms, there is little evidence for simple, consistent effects of mutations in single genes. None of the developmental psychopathologies of socioemotional life that are recognized in diagnostic systems, including dyslexia, specific language impairment, Autistic Spectrum Disorders, and Attention-Deficit/Hyperactivity Disorder (ADHD), appears to be a direct effect of an inherited genetic fault (Dawson et al., 2002; Tager-Flusberg, 1999; Trevarthen, 2001b). All reflect the cumulative effect of stresses and traumas that interfere with the expression and development of inherent capacities to form relationships that benefit self-motivations and their development (Cicchetti & Dawson, 2002; Cicchetti & Rogosch, 1996). It follows that any psychopathological conditions, and perhaps all, may be susceptible to amelioration by adjustment of the demands of the environment, especially, in many cases, by transforming the quality and availability of human care and support—that is, by forms of treatment that act through the intersubjective route rather than, or in addition to, direct interventions with intraorganismic functions by chemical means. Communicative interactions may rebuild vital functions and self-regulatory states, mitigating the effects of early stress and posttraumatic disorders later in life.

Damage to the brain in early stages of development, especially in sensitive periods, may be linked many years later to unusual sensitivity to trauma and may be a cause of psychopathology of understanding and behavior that appears as a new problem in a child or adult. There are clinical studies indicating that prenatal stress is associated with development of ADHD in children (Weinstock, 1997). Evidence from the self-regulatory and socioemotional problems of adolescence indicates that all levels of regulation, from the physiological to the social, can carry problems from infancy that emerge in this critical period of life when the brain is undergoing a second period of accelerated growth and differentiation in adaptation to changing interpersonal and social circumstances (Cicchetti & Rogosch, 2002).

Schizophrenia is associated with pregnancy and birth complications (Stefan & Murray, 1997), and mothers of schizophrenic patients suffered more often from severe infections during pregnancy, possibly affecting cytokines and indirectly the development of monoaminergic circuits in the fetal brain (Jarskog, Xiao, Wilkie, Lauder, & Gilmore, 1997).

Increased Reactivity of the Brain Following Stress to the Fetus

Stress during critical periods of intrauterine development of mammals alters the brain's biochemistry as a result of activation of the ANS (Davis, Suris, Lambert, Heimberg, & Petty, 1997; de Kloet et al., 1996; J. P. Henry & Stephens, 1977). Biochemical changes following release of stress hormones are manifested by structural and metabolic alterations in specific areas of the brain (Bremner, 2002; Sapolsky, 1996). Cortical thickness may be reduced in regions important for functions of emotion and memory. Stress is also associated with reduced neuroplasticity, and this later facilitates the development of psychopathological conditions and functional disturbances that are difficult to characterize within standard medical and psychological criteria or diagnostic classification systems for psychological disorders. Fetal brain development is changed and may be retarded by high levels of maternal stress hormones (Glynn, Wadhwa, & Sandman, 2000). This can be reflected in premature delivery or low birthweight for gestational age and smaller head circumference (Hedegaard, 1999; Huizinck, Mulder, & Buitelaar, 2004).

The concept of "fetal and neonatal programming" (Sayer, Cooper, & Barker, 1997) also applies to the ontogeny of the neurochemical system (Herlenius & Lagercrantz, 2004). Prenatal or perinatal stress can disturb the timetable of the expression of neurotransmitters and neuromodulators and their receptors (Johnston, 1995).

> Disruption of the normal timing or intensity of neurotransmitter signaling can lead to permanent changes in proliferation differentiation and growth of their target cells during critical phases of development of the nervous system, thereby possibly providing the underlying mechanisms for neurobehavioral or neurophysiological abnormalities associated with developmental exposure to neuroactive drugs and environmental toxins. (Herlenius & Lagercrantz, 2004, p. S18)

Research on animals has shown that brain areas dense in glucocorticoid receptors, such as the hippocampus, prefrontal cortex, and septum pellucidum, respond with structural changes even to a very brief exposure to a stressor. Dendrites of the pyramidal neurons in the CA3 region of the hippocampus become shorter, with fewer branches, and the production of the granular cells will be reduced (McEwen,

1999, 2001) as a response to the increased level of glucocorticoids. High levels of prenatally administered dexamethasone (a cortisol derivative) in monkeys cause cell death (apoptosis), with an approximately 30% reduction of the volume of the hippocampus; this structural change is detectable even at 20 months after birth (Uno et al., 1994). Corticosteroids have deleterious effects on the brain and behavior of developing primates, causing inhibition of neural stem cells, neurogenesis, and migration and leading to irreversible decrease in brain weight (Edwards & Burnham, 2001; Matthews, 2001).

Prenatal stress can also cause changes in the structure of the corpus callosum, and the hemispheric laterality can be modified. Handedness in rhesus monkeys can be associated with the level of stress reactivity (Westergaard, Byrne, & Suomi, 2000). Atypical asymmetry of the dopaminergic pathways in the prefrontal cortex as a response to prenatal stress can lead to behavioral inhibition, disturbances of working memory, or inattention, and children with ADHD have been reported to exhibit an increased left prefrontal activity dominance instead of the right dominance typical of children without ADHD, that is, a deficit of right hemisphere attention and motor control (Castellanos et al., 1996).

The effects of stress hormones on affective and cognitive functioning vary, and not all are damaging (de Kloet, Oitzl, & Joels, 1999; McEwen, 1997b, 2003; Roozendaal, de Quervain, Ferry, Setlow, & McGaugh, 2001; Vandekerckhove, in press). Depending on the intensity and duration of stress, the effects may be beneficial or destructive to the adaptive functions of the developing brain and in behavior: *Brief* periods of stress can potentiate psychological functions, such as memory formation, whereas *chronic* or sustained *high-intensity* stress may disturb the brain to the extent of a total blockade of the retention of experience by the brain ("mnestic block syndrome"; Markowitsch, Kessler, Kalbe, & Herholz, 1999; Markowitsch, Kessler, Russ, et al., 1999). On the neuronal level, *moderate* duration of stress causes reversible atrophy of apical dendrites on pyramidal neurons, but basal dendrites remain unchanged. Thus, chronic stress is more dangerous than acute stress for the young brain (Garmezy & Masten, 1994). Prolonged high concentrations of glucocorticoids may lead to suppression of the immune system, hypertension, an altered vesicle distribution pattern in the brain, and irreversible brain cell death (Maccari et al., 2003; Magarinos, Verdugo, & McEwen, 1997; Sapolsky, 1993, 1996, 2000).

In rats, unpredictable stress during gestation (such as repeated loud and unanticipated noises) increases fear responses of pups, and the effects may be expressed in adult animals as behavioral problems in conflict-rich situations (Fride & Weinstock, 1988). The affected rat pup is more easily frightened, while exhibiting less exploratory behavior and heightened tendencies of behavioral and social inhibition (Fride & Weinstock, 1988; Maccari et al., 2003; Takahashi & Kalin, 1991).

Short prenatal exposure of the sheep fetus to cortisol at the end of the 1st month of gestation (considered a critical stage of development) programmed high blood pressure in the adult female and male offspring, and there were effects on regulation of gene expression in the hippocampus (Dodic et al., 2002).

A longitudinal study examining prenatal disturbance in about 10,000 women demonstrated that anxiety in late pregnancy increased behavioral/emotional problems in the child at 4 years of age (O'Connor, Heron, Golding, Beveridge, & Glover, 2002). Similarly, mothers' prenatal and postnatal stressors are correlated with temperament of their 3-year-olds (Susman, Schmeelk, Ponirakis, & Gariepy, 2001). In a population-based study of more than 3,000 women in Copenhagen, of which 70 were identified as experiencing moderate to severe stressful life events and compared with 50 nonstressed women with an intact social network, found that stress and smoking adversely affected birthweight and head circumference. The findings support the concept of a *fetal stress syndrome* with adverse effects on fetal development, including deficient brain development (Lou et al., 1995).

The fetus and the newborn react differently to various forms of stress. In general, fetuses tend to react by immobilization, decreased heart rate, and decreased breathing, with slowed metabolism caused possibly by inhibited neurotransmission (Lagercrantz, 1996). Neuromodulators, such as adenosine, neuropeptide Y, somatostatine, and opioids, may mediate this effect. At birth, the increased somatosensory input, increased level of arterial oxygen, and mechanical stimulation of the baby results in a down-regulated inhibitory and up-regulated excitatory neurotransmitter level in the brain mediated by the increased expression of the immediate early genes (Ringstedt, Tang, Persson, Lendahl, & Lagercrantz, 1995).

Stress Effects on the Brain after Birth

Prolonged and repeated separations from a contact-aversive, nonattuning mother may cause an infant to develop a state of enhanced corticotrophic activity, sympathetic-dominant agitated hyperarousal, and general hypervigilance for critical information (Perry, Pollard, Blakley, Baker, & Vigilante, 1995). Field and coworkers (Field, 1998, 2005; Field et al., 1988) found that infants of depressed mothers vocalized less, displayed increased gaze aversion, fussiness, and helplessness, and at the same time had higher heart rates and decreased vagal tone. They also show delays in growth and development at 12 months of age (Field, 1995, 1998). Dawson and her colleagues (Hessl et al., 1998) have reported slightly higher midmorning cortisol levels at home among 3-year-old children whose mothers were clinically depressed compared to children of emotionally healthy mothers. Neurophysiological signs, such as elevated salivary cortisol and disturbed sleep, might be important early indicators of risk for the development of psychopathology for children who show no clear manifestations of distress in their behavior.

The developing intelligence, memory, and imagination of a child transforms the effects stress can have in the brain and on the mind and may bring new disorders that affect life with other human beings. The classical physiological understanding of stress focuses on the peripheral neuronal and hormonal mechanism and neglects the role of the central nervous system (Dunn et al., 2004). Many neurochemical changes occur in the brain itself during or after various forms of experimental stress, notably the activation of cerebral catecholaminergic systems. Activation of cerebral noradrenergic neurons may represent a central counterpart to the peripheral ANS activation. Dopaminergic and adrenergic systems also respond, as well as endorphin systems and CRF-containing neurons. Thus, stress-related events in the CNS appear to parallel those in the periphery. The down-regulation of adrenergic receptors that occurs in chronic stress presumably represents an adaptation of the brain to deal with excess norepinephrine (NE) release, and this could explain the behavioral adaptation.

NE is known to play a role in regulating cerebral blood flow and perhaps regulates blood-brain barrier permeability. The noradrenergic projections from the locus coeruleus to the forebrain have been shown to cause the cortical desynchronization associated with arousal, and it has been suggested that this enables selective attention to novel stimuli by decreasing signal-to-noise ratios for the responses to such stimuli. NE has been postulated to play a role in neuroplasticity and has long been implicated in higher nervous functions such as learning and memory. The CRF family of peptides appears to play a critical role in anxiety and/or stress responses.

Posttraumatic Stress Disorder is the most deeply destructive consequence of severe stress on brain function; PTSD is a "physioneurosis," a mental disorder based on the persistence of biological emergency responses (van der Kolk, 2003), affecting the limbic structures that govern the

most basic social responses (MacLean, 1990). As a traumatized child grows older in a disorganized, high-stress environment, he or she might encounter traumatic situations or trauma-related narratives. When older children are exposed to stimuli that are associated with or that remind them of the original trauma—witnessing violence, being abused, or being kidnapped—critical neural pathways related to the previous experience of the threat might become reactivated, and the children may be prone to symptoms of PTSD, including poor impulse control, self-destructive behavior, phobias, anxieties, and depressive states (Cicchetti & Toth, 2000; Cytryn, McKnew, & Bunney, 1980; Kendall-Tacket, Meyer-Williams, & Finkelhor, 1993).

Traumatic memories are characterized by retention of sensory and emotional impressions that are stable and unalterable and that are likely to return vividly throughout life if triggered by reminders. The victim cannot articulate the feelings and thoughts brought back and cannot formulate a "storyline" for experiences. Such problems seriously impair the ability of a child to engage in sustained activities without distraction or to learn a range of alternatives without being disorganized or acting too impulsively on one of them. Both compliance with complex social rules and understanding of schematic representations of reality are impaired. There is evidence of atrophy of specific brain regions, in particular the hippocampus and the amygdala, which are important in cognition, memory, and emotion, and a heightened vulnerability of the self (McEwen, 1999; O'Keefe & Nadel, 1978; Starkman et al., 1999). In response to frequent chronic or massive stress situations, both children and adults may display significant reductions in emotional and social processing, in ability to learn, and in perceptual, intellectual, and memory capacities (van der Kolk, 2003).

Attachments and Shared Experience in Infancy and How Dysregulations of Interpersonal Regulations Affect Human Learning

In the half-century since Bowlby (1958) presented his theory that the infant is born with innate behavior-releasing mechanisms adapted to engage with and attract care from a loving mother, a great body of research has confirmed his insight. He was finding an explanation for the withdrawal and despair he saw in infants and toddlers who had been orphaned by war and similar behavior of infants separated from their mother for hospital care (Bowlby, 1969). There was, however, skepticism from both medical and psychological professions at first, both doubting that human nature could be so complex at birth, and that there was a specific and exclusive need for the biological mother was "disproved."

In recent decades, Bowlby's ethological model has been extended by the findings of psychobiological research on mechanisms that cause a rat pup or nursling monkey to express distress when isolated (Hofer, 1987; Kraemer, 1992). The benefits to the physiological systems of the offspring of maternal stimulation that regulate neurohumoral stress reactions have been proved. An emphasis has been placed on the plasticity of the infant brain and on the mother as a regulator of states of motivation that affect function and growth of brain structures that are critical for future regulation of social emotions and learning. In both Bowlby's ethological attachment theory and the new psychobiological attachment theory of stress regulation, the task of the newborn mammal is to commence a process of internalizing a module: a cognitive internal working model of the mother as a support for living in the world, or an internal regulator of stress-resisting neurohumoral states.

Bowlby's theory was made empirically testable by Ainsworth's Strange Situation (Lamb, Thompson, Gardner, Charnov, & Estes, 1984). Consistent differences were found between groups of 1-year-olds who were subjected to this temporary stress in the absence of their mother and then reunited with her. The classification of different attachment types—A (avoidant), B (secure), and C (resistant; Ainsworth, Blehar, Waters, & Wall, 1978)—was extended by identification of a seriously disturbed D (disorganized) group (Main & Solomon, 1986). In correlation studies to detect relationships between these infant attachment groups and mother's behaviors in populations, highly significant consistencies and some systematic cultural differences were found between maternal characteristics and their infants' approach behaviors and emotional signals toward them in the Strange Situation. The basic assumption has been that these correlations represent effects of maternal care on the development of regulatory "representations" of emotions and investigative impulses in the infant.

Now the weight of evidence is showing that infants have more complex and more variable volitions and emotions and much richer inherent capacities to perceive the motives of companions—that they play an active "mothering-expectant" part from birth in eliciting and regulating maternal behaviors. A healthy baby is, from the start, also adapted with motives for building joyful shared experience in play, with seeking emotions that explore the world with all sense, in addition to the need for receiving regulation of autonomic and HPA states and protection against brain damage from the effects of cortisol.

Because the dispositions of an infant at birth depend on unique paths of prenatal maturation of motives for both mutual regulation of vital state and stress control and motives for gaining experience from exploratory activity, there are emerging individual differences in personality, temperament, and cognitive development between children, which are affected by many prenatal factors, from genes to the nurturant support and physiological health of the mother's body. The rich variety of responses and initiatives observed in a detailed neonatal assessment (Brazelton & Nugent, 1995) proves this variability of potential in human nature at birth. A distinction must be made at the two extremes, between psychopathologies that may afflict the life of children when they are severely mistreated by neglect or abuse, and when in addition they lack adequate present psychosocial support (Lyons-Ruth, Connell, Grunebaum, & Botein, 1990), from those differences, evident in different ways at different ages, but already detectable in neonates or even before birth (Field, 1985; Piontelli, 1992), in self-confidence, adventurousness, and sociability. These should be seen as variations in adaptive motives for sustaining collaborative relationships and forms of mutual emotional support in the full course of each life.

A model is required that grants the infant a brain organization that can anticipate and immediately recognize human company in complex dynamic ways—an intersubjectivity system that is ready for intense intimate exchanges with a wide range of caregivers' states of emotional availability and willingness to share activities (Aitken & Trevarthen, 1997). Functional imaging of activity in the brain of an infant that reflects awareness of another person, as well as a fund of evidence from developmental brain science, confirms the existence of such a mechanism (Tzourio-Mazoyer et al., 2002), one evolved from the affective neural systems that regulate social encounters and cooperative behaviors in other vertebrates (MacLean, 1990).

Evidence from psychophysiology, developmental brain science, and genetics concerning how the infant-caregiver system may work to support growth of this complex endowment for regulation of intermental life and for collaboration in conscious voluntary activities converges to support the idea that there is an adaptive mutual regulatory system for *interest and purposes* and one for *affective interpersonal emotional states* that assess and direct the subconscious relationship. Developmental studies of age-related changes in normal development of securely supported infants prove that the infants' motives and the caregivers' responses are aimed, together, toward the goal of having compatible experiences so the child can acquire both a well-received and happy social personality and culturally valued knowledge and skills (Trevarthen, 2005b, 2005c).

By enriching both the situations for observation of behaviors of parents and infants and their siblings, or of infants in peer groups and in groups of children and a range of other adults inside and outside the family, and by more sensitive analysis of forms of behavior and their functions, it has been made clear that infants are truly sociable. They seek to form friendships, to protect themselves from being misunderstood and intruded upon, and to learn in "intent participation" with others in games where meanings for actions and objects are fabricated, tested, and learned (Fiamenghi, 1997; Nadel & Tremblay-Leveau, 1999; Selby & Bradley, 2003). They can cope in communication with several members of the family at once (Fivaz-Depeursinge & Corboz-Warnery, 1999; Hay, 1985).

Maternal health is critically important for these needs for sociability, of course. Bowlby was not wrong in giving the mother a privileged place, a place prepared for by the events of her pregnancy when her stimulation of and responses to her infant were already building a relationship. But the developing child is adaptable for more than one relationship, and the place of a mother can be taken by someone who is ready to build a new relationship of intimate familiarity and responsivity, one willing to pick up on the infant's capacities for regulating both self and a companion.

If the infant is in the care of a mother who has significant *clinical postnatal depression* (PND) and no other person can replace her, this is likely to depress the infant, reducing the capacity to develop self-regulation and enjoyable play with a parent (Beebe et al., in press; Field, 1984, 1992, 2005; Field et al., 1988; Murray, 1988, 1992), and in some cases the effects persist to compromise a child's capacities to take an active part in a wider social world and to profit from education (Hay & Kumar, 1995; Murray & Cooper, 1997; Murray, Woolgar, Briers, & Hipwell, 1999). However, it is also true that infants born irritable and difficult for a mother to relate to or care for, and who exhibit differences in neonatal assessment, can predispose a mother to PND (Murray, Stanley, Hooper, King, & Fiori-Cowley, 1996). PND affects all aspects of a mother's expression of affection for and interest in her infant: her holding, her attention to her infant's interests and emotions, the emotions in her voice, her responses to calls for care or for play, in addition to her capacity to give psychobiological support (Bettes, 1988; Breznitz & Sherman, 1987; Murray, Kempton, Woolgar, & Hooper, 1993; Reissland, Shepherd, & Herrera, in press-a, in press-b; Robb, 1999; Tronick & Weinberg, 1996).

The liveliness and availability of a mother is affected by her social situation, security, and relationships with the father or other partner and the wider family. Recollections from her own childhood influence how she sees the baby (Main & Goldwyn, 1984). The cultural context for mothering has powerful effects; this is a factor that gives cause for concern in the unstable present state of human communities (Nugent, 2002). A migrant mother displaced from her extended family and, perhaps most important, separated from her own mother may also be unable to respond to her infant and participate in well-regulated playful communication with shared pleasure: The experience of *belonging* is of fundamental importance (Gratier, 2003).

PTSD is a serious threat to the mother-infant system and a cause for special attention (Schechter, 2004). A woman who has experienced trauma, including abuse when a child, may find her infant's expressions of need frightening. They may precipitate pathological anxiety and emotional instability that can lead her to be insensitive or abusive to her child. An infant in the care of a mother suffering PTSD is at risk of developing frantic attempts to find contentment and disorganized attachment (Ornitz & Pynoos, 1989; Pollak, Cicchetti, & Klorman, 1998), which predisposes the child to develop serious emotional problems later in life, with the parent or in adoption. A cycle of fear and confusion can develop that disrupts all attempts of the family to function as a mutually supportive group (Archer & Burnell, 2003).

Despite the abundant evidence that childhood psychopathology can be related to emotional illness in the mother, the recognition that there is a strong set of adaptations in an infant to solicit, relate to, and benefit from communication with other persons helps explain the evidence that even badly neglected and mistreated infants can demonstrate impressive resilience and rediscover a path in childhood, adolescent, and adult relationships that is rewarding and productive of a proud life story (Luthar, Cicchetti, & Becker, 2000; Masten, 2001; Rutter, 1987; Sander, 1964).

Methods of molecular genetics have enabled researchers to discover factors that explain infant self-regulatory and behavioral differences and communication, as well as the different ways adults regulate their relationships with infants. Male and female infants differ in their psychologies and communicative behavior, as do the parenting behaviors of mothers and fathers. The differences between infants affect their expressions of sociability and sharing of interest in object-directed activities. In toddlers, these differences appear to be significant in social experience and learning with peers. These differences cannot all be explained as consequences of cultural beliefs and practices that lead to different treatment of boys and girls. It has been mentioned that seeking genetic explanations for such differences in motivation or temperament is complicated by clear evidence that epigenetic factors usually make the personalities of homozygous twins different (Piontelli, 2002), Whatever effect genes have in determining differences between male and female infants, or between those of the same sex, they will be mediated by differences arising in the hormonal systems that regulate sexual and other differentiations of bodies and brains both before and after birth. Male infants show a greater susceptibility to disturbance of their development by interpersonal stresses, including being in the care of a mother with PND (Murray et al., 1993).

It has been emphasized that confusion in the literature concerning genetic factors certainly arises from a failure of many studies to give sufficient attention to powerful interactions between socioemotional or ecological factors and the expressions of gene-related changes in basic regulatory mechanisms. None of the neurohumoral stress-regulating systems and none of the neural systems of emotion is insulated from changes due to environmental circumstances. These have evolved both to regulate and to be regulated by the risks and benefits of the behaviors they control.

In summary, a baby with neurohumoral systems of self-regulation that are partly protected from effects of stress in the caregiver's life is born ready to be actively part of intimate human relations that are regulated by sympathetic tenderness and the vitality of play (Veldman, 1994). The development of this system of mutual regulation depends on the availability and vitality of adult care, and thus on the situation of the family in relation to the wider society. Infants need available, regular, and responsive company, and all these can be weakened by fear and deprivation in the community where the caregivers make their lives. But the infant is resourceful, and some, at least, can protect themselves when parental care is deficient in sensitivity but adequate for survival. With good fortune, a young infant becomes a catalyst to a better life for the family and not an extra burden to carry (Gomes-Pedro, Nugent, Young, & Brazelton, 2002).

Especially poignant are the life stories of children who, because their biological parents have neglected or abused them, or because their homes and families have been destroyed in violent circumstances, are taken into foster care or adoption. Adoptive parents are often couples who have had a long, difficult period of waiting for children of their own. They undertake to care for and support the development of damaged children who are confused, fearful, and angry, carrying memories they can regulate in no other way. The experience of the adults and the children, and of the social services and clinicians who support their efforts to find relief from stress and a happy future, can teach much about the fragility and resourcefulness of human motives and the regulation of feelings and new experiences in attachment relationships (Archer & Burnell, 2003; Hughes, 1997, 1998).

FUTURE DIRECTIONS FOR INFANT MENTAL HEALTH: FOSTERING MOTIVES FOR CONFIDENT REGULATION OF EXPERIENCE IN AFFECTIONATE COMPANIONSHIP

> In the case of an animal, the mental states enter into the plan of the total organism and thus modify the plans of successive subordinate organisms until the ultimate smallest organism, such as electrons, are reached. (Whitehead, 1926/1953, p. 98)
>
> There are thus two sides to the machinery involved in the development of nature. On the one side there is a given environment with organisms adapting themselves to it. . . . The other side of the evolutionary machinery, the neglected side, is expressed by the word creativeness. *The organisms can create their own environment. For this purpose the single organism is almost helpless. The adequate forces require societies of cooperating organisms.* But with such cooperation and in proportion to the effort put forward, the environment has a plasticity which alters the whole ethical aspect of evolution. (Whitehead, 1926/1953, p. 140; emphasis added)

Mutual Regulations and Change in the Mother-Child Relationship

We focus our analysis of early psychosocial development and its emotional regulations on the side of the "machinery of nature" that Whitehead calls creative. We have defined two levels of mutual regulation in the development of a human mind that function from prenatal stages, both of which undergo major developments in infancy. We propose that recognition of these is essential both for understanding and diagnosing causes of psychopathology, for developing helpful parental support, for improving social support for the families, and for corrective treatments to counter risks of future psychopathology due to stress.

The *amphoteronomic* level brings the life systems of two organisms and their individual autonomic regulations into a mutually beneficial relationship that accomplishes more than either organism can do on its own. In the case of a human fetus, the growing organism is inside the mother's body and connected to her through tissue frontiers that exercise control over the passage of substances between them (Figure 2.7).

The placenta (Figure 2.8) is the main collaborative organ at this stage (Jones, 1993). It conveys essential nutrients and oxygen to the fetus and takes out CO2 and other waste. For other substances, the placenta is highly selective and acts as a barrier to the large molecules that serve as hormones in the separate autonomic regulations of both fetus and mother (Figure 2.7). The developing autonomic system (HPA, SNS, and PNS) of the fetus, with the neurochemical transmission systems that mediate between their relations with the developing sensorimotor organs of the fetal brain, act as an increasingly competent regulation for the fetus itself, but there are essential interactions with the mother, which we have reviewed here.

The *synrhythmic* level of regulation comes into full effect after birth. It couples the volitional and experiential functions of the minds of infant and mother through sympathetic response of their brains to the anatomical forms and dynamics of movement in structures of the body activated by the special visceral efferents of the cephalic SNS (Figures 2.6 and 2.7). The frontier for this regulation is in the living socioemotional space between the expressive actions of the two human beings and their minds (Figure 2.12). The efficiency of mutual psychological engagement at birth can be seen when an alert newborn free of distress is in reciprocal imitative contact with a mother or other sensitively responsive and patient adult.

We find evidence that the beginning of synrhythmic regulation begins earlier, at least by the beginning of the last trimester of gestation. In this period, mother and infant can interact not only by hormonal amphoteronomic means, but also by tactile, auditory, and vestibular stimulation of the fetus from the mother's body displacements, uterine contractures, and vocalizations and by the mother receiving stimuli from periods when the fetus is active and making limb and body movements (Veldman, 1994). Their cycles of activity interact and may become mutually entrained. This minimal communication of activities is assisted by amphoteronomic hormonal coupling, for example, by the passage of melathonin from the mother to the fetus, which helps synchronization of their day-night cycles.

At term, the fetus is expectant of a much richer traffic across the synrhythmic frontier with the mother, traffic that will be carried by an intensely active and rapidly developing visual system, as well as by the more precociously developed systems of touch and hearing. This regulation of *emergent intermental or psychological capacities* complements new amphoteronomic regulations between mother and newborn made active in breast-feeding and other caregiving activities, which are mediated by sensations of taste, olfaction, and body contact on both sides.

Synrhythmic regulations undergo conspicuous developments after birth as all modalities and new motor capacities become active in engaging motives and emotions between the infant and caregiver (Figure 2.9). We see the development of intimate protoconversations at 2 to 3 months and more testing negotiations of play and affectionate teasing from 3 months as preparatory for the person-person-object games that emerge after 6 months. These, in turn, are predictive of competence in the infant for acquisition of knowledge and skills concerning the uses of familiar objects that frequently occupy the interest of the infant's companions and for the imitation of words to name the more significant and sharable things and actions. This introduces a sociocultural level of regulation that begins the education of the child in meanings that have become essential to the life of a large society and its artifacts. We have not contrived a word for the regulation of this level, which falls outside the period of infancy, but the word "symbolic" conveys the sense of its essentially sociocultural nature.

The core of our account is that human psychological development begins in coregulated vital and volitional relationships that make significant changes to the power of communication before language begins. We affirm that support of this coregulation is critical for infant mental well-being. The basic concept is one of an agency-generating and stress-controlling system *between* two organisms, the developing child and the mother, who, for at least half of the period we have considered, is the sole partner of the infant in mutual development.

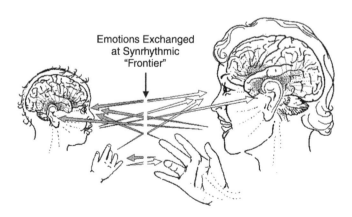

Figure 2.12 Protoconversation between mother and infant. *Synrhythmic* regulation of mutual psychological engagement by exchange of expressions of interest and emotional feelings.

Theories of Infant Mental Health and Its Needs and Risks

The past century has seen significant changes in the concept of the infant mind and *infant mental health,* concepts that can be said to have not existed at all in most of the early decades of this time (Fraiberg, 1980). It is still the case that developmental and medical scientists question the idea that a young infant has mental capacities. There have also been changes in the kinds of society that children are born into. It is likely that the threats to the well-being and sanity of young children are greater than a century ago. Certainly, a large proportion of the world's families are struggling with hunger and dangerous situations, and their children are at risk of developing socioemotional illness later in life and, in consequence, contributing to the hardships of the community—all these problems being not least in the richest countries (Brazelton, 2002). The threatened families live in communities that lack appropriate human support for their infants and for their mothers (Gomes-Pedro et al., 2002; Raphael-Leff, 2005).

It would appear urgent for medical attention to be given to more than the diagnosis and treatment of disorders of early development that have identifiable physiological, neurological, or molecular causes (or correlates), to accept remedies that are based on acceptance that the child is a source of regulatory principles that can benefit not just the body and mind of the mother, but the family and society. Children activate intrinsic forces of emotional and behavioral self-regulation in adults and their collaborative systems and organizations. But these social systems and organizations tend, by their own autopoiesis, to become endlessly extended and elaborated and overly complex in the sense that they cease to work in a creative way, like the excess of components that proliferate in the neocortex before motivated experience has pruned them. We need, perhaps, a selective apoptosis of laws, institutional management, and curricular goals to potentiate this source of social well-being. This will have to be guided by respect for the inherent motives and sympathies or "developmental principles" (Bronfenbrenner, 2002) that create human knowledge and collective understanding, not by even more quick-fix draconian measures for "national security" or "prosperity," which, driven by an excessive political anxiety, promote division and mistrust in communities and weaken families, as well as threatening the balance of relationships between human communities and the natural world (Gore, 1992).

There is abundant evidence of the damage done to the lives of infants and parents in both the richest and poorest communities of the modern world by social disadvantage, disease, deprivation, and war and how these destructive effects are motivated by greed, mistrust, and envy and by materialistic detachment, the seductive pressure of technological advances, and religious bigotry. Unfortunately, human collaborative awareness, which grows so impressively in early childhood, is capable of creating a prison of institutions, laws, and beliefs, as well as powerful methods of science that forget how they originated and what motivated their more imaginative beginnings (Whitehead, 1926/1953).

The human sciences, too, will have to learn to adopt a more coherent, multilevel view of human nature by considering the whole child in his or her family. The increasing specialization of those working on the molecular level of vital processes has led to acceptance of a reductive model of developmental causes. However, as the potential mechanisms at a genetic level of analysis are continually being revised and replaced (e.g., Pescucci, Meloni, & Renieri, 2005), we are seeing hypotheses about mechanisms coming full circle to recognize the idea that environmental factors affect the epigenetic regulation of gene expression. This will include factors "ranging from developmental progression and aging to viral infection and diet" (Jaenisch & Bird, 2003, p. 251) and inevitably, as argued here, the effects of the infants' initiatives in interactions with the human world.

Finally, we must recognize the other tendency of both psychological and scientific explanation to gravitate toward complex rational and linguistic models, which are favored by literacy and computational technology. This tendency pulls attention and explanation to the opposite pole of abstraction from the physical-reductive one. The two poles of scientific enterprise leave the middle ground of live, emotionally regulated communication in the dark.

Darwin's Legacy: Curiosity about Origins and Processes of Life Forms and an Integrative Evolutionary Biology, with Implications for Human Nature

Darwin's lasting contribution to the human sciences is a persuasive respect for origins in the prehuman past. He turned ambitious Victorian thinking about the values of human society away from elaborate artificial urgencies of imperial power and rigid adherence to scriptural explanations of human obligations, toward acceptance of forces of vitality that regulate and guide the preverbal habits and emotions of animals and infants in their evolved fitness for an ancient environment. He argued for the power of creative motives to support life and its survival. In his note-books he wrote, "Motives are the units of the universe (1998)." He knew nothing of gene molecules or neurons.

In the early part of the twentieth century, natural science, driven by a century of discovery by explorers in every habitat, was animated by a profound curiosity about and admiration for the patterns and functions of life forms and by a comparative approach that attempted to see coherent trends and homologous adaptive structures and strategies for survival across species in the "tree of life."

The first years of the twenty-first century have produced a very different science of nature. We journey in a bewildering sea of facts and correlations—about the molecular intricacies of the genome, about varieties of cell surface architecture and the chemical instabilities of cytoplasm, about the technology of stem cells and manufacturing individuals, about neuron assemblies and the capacity of the brain to process information and to change in plastic ways. Language sciences and artificial intelligence serve a brilliant technology of global electronic communication. There are changes in human industry and mobility: Employment makes mothers and fathers busy out of the home, and a global rapid transport system carries workers and their families out of their historical communities and tempts them to vacations in foreign lands away from inclement weather, where they purchase exotic objects and activities. This exuberance of production and movement can be seen as a wonderful display of human inventiveness and play, but it draws heavily on human energies, creates social divisions, and, in disadvantaged sectors, drives great numbers of children and their parents to a distracted poverty that generates forms of self-abuse and/or antagonism to society.

There are, of course, active forms of understanding in contemporary science that moderate and correct this over-rich, overconfident but narrow vision of reality and sense of mastery over nature, with recognition of regulatory homeotic processes that exercise a directive restraint on acquired diversity of genetic actions among life forms and that favor their cooperation. Among the most important of these are, first, the recognition that *emotions* of animals and humans operate on similar principles to guide social collaboration and development of the young (Panksepp, 2004), and second, a growing acceptance that the *motives* of children assist their own growth of well-being and understanding by attracting affectionate attentions from their parents and by stimulating playfulness and imaginative projects for their vitality in a growing company of peers and adult friends (Trevarthen, 1998b, 2005b, 2005c). The good health and progress of children in any world, and in

any education, depends on this display of natural enthusiasm for social life. It is the principal factor restraining the industrious compulsions of the adult world, with its intricate commercial, legal, and political fabrications. Children's needs bring human motivations back to their origins.

Here are some recent calls by respected scientists for new ideas on how science should seek a balanced view of mental life:

A neuropsychologist, introducing discoveries on the sympathetic brain, writes,

We need a theoretical vocabulary that bridges three domains: our intuitive "folk" conceptions of other people, the explanations offered by social psychology, and the explanations offered by cognitive neuroscience. And we need a method that can extract common patterns across multiple studies, to complement strict hypothesis testing of individual studies. These issues can be addressed, in part, by giving theory and experiment equal time, and by fostering an interdisciplinary approach that includes neuroscience, psychology, philosophy, anthropology and allied disciplines. (Adolphs, 2003, p. 119)

A comparative behavioral scientist who has pioneered affective neuroscience says:

Now that the cognitive revolution is gradually giving way to an emotion revolution, investigators are gradually exhibiting a new taste for the pursuit of what was once deemed scientifically unpursuable—an understanding of what affective processes really are, even in nonhuman animals. . . . Only through the integration of human and animal approaches can deep knowledge in this field be achieved. If we conflate emotions and cognitions too much in our thinking . . . we may retard a fundamental understanding of affective processes and thereby, a real understanding of how cognitive activities are modified by emotional states. (Panksepp, 2003, p. 5)

and

We should be under no illusion that as neuroscientists clarify the *parts* of the brain, they have grasped the *whole*. In general, science is better at dissecting and analyzing the parts of nature than reconstructing them into wholes. Psychology is still the best tool we possess to capture the global capacities of the neuro-mental apparatus. Without psychology we cannot make sense of the dynamic functional organization of the brain. Neuroscientists that do not respect and understand psychology and dynamic principles have little chance of understanding the functional organization of the brain. (Panksepp, 2004, p. 57)

A leader in research on the causes of emotional disorder from the molecular level up expresses his perspective thus:

Genes, early development, adult experiences, lifestyle, and stressful life experiences all contribute to the way the body adapts to a changing environment; and these factors all help to determine the cost to the body, or "allostatic load." Studies of these processes involve the disciplines of biology and psychology, but they are incomplete without the input from other fields, such as cultural anthropology, economics, epidemiology, political science, and sociology. These fields provide a description and analysis of the social and cultural institutions and economic forces that affect individual human health. (McEwen, 2001, p. 42)

These opinions clarify the limitations of both rigorously reductive theories constructed to accommodate the data from experimentation and elaborate intellectual models that are detached from spontaneous life activities. Experiments in behavioral science often appear designed primarily not just to test hypotheses, but to generate reports of novelty in professional scientific journals, which apply restrictive standards of presentation and empirical support and require statistical analysis of correlations in measurement. Modeling of cognitive processes in artificial intelligence is driven by mathematical rules to define interactions between factors in systems that have no bodies and that do not move.

In the field of child psychology, such approaches, however well-intentioned, have seemed to confirm that infants need to learn or introject a sense of emotional restraint and to acquire an articulate image or representation of another person and their states of mind to become aware of themselves and their communicative impulses, and that the mother's role is to supply a sensitively responsive patterning of movements and feelings of moving before the infant can have a self of his or her own. The mechanism of attachment of infant to the mother has been interpreted as one of instinctive appeals for a caregiver's body contact, support, calming, and nourishment. The psychobiological version of the theory, based on research to test the effects of withholding maternal stimulations on rat pups and nursling monkeys, is articulated in terms of stress reduction and the building up of a physiological system that will serve as an internal regulator and free the young animal of the need to be in such intimate dependence on maternal instincts. In attempts to find an explanation for developmental disorders of the brain that handicap communication as a child grows to adulthood, special importance has been given to verbal analysis of feelings to assist the assumed mastery of interpersonal realities.

In child psychotherapy and psychoanalysis, however, new concepts have grown, informed by infant developmental research, and by psychobiological and neuroscientific advances. These assist the interpretation of severe pathology in children, and how to deal with it (Alvarez, 1992, 1999, 2000; Edwards, 2001; Fonagy, 1998, 2001; Fonagy & Target, 2003; Maiello, 2001; Schore, 2003c). Acceptance

of the interpersonal nature of unconscious and conscious processes has always been at the heart of psychotherapeutic endeavour, now increasingly viewed from an evolutionary perspective integrating attachment theory and neurobiology (Fonagy & Target, 2003; Liotti, 1999; van der Kolk, 1994; van der Kolk, McFarlane, & Weisaeth, 1996). We find a new appraisal of intersubjective "sympathy" in psychoanalytic epistemology. Core affective states, the visceral experiencing of emotions in the therapeutic relationship, are accepted as central to the process of psychotherapeutic change.

The Role of Social Play in Development of Cooperative Awareness

Gradually, in both the human attachment literature and that concerned with maternal care of other young mammals, it has been necessary to admit that inarticulate young have powers to stimulate and guide adult affections and parenting behaviors, and that what infants require is company of a willful, aware, and emotional person who is playfully ready to gently tease, or be teased, and extend a *reaching out for fun* (Reddy, 1991, 2005). But, because the primary motivation for all work on early emotional development and social skills is to find an explanation for emotional and behavioral problems that cause concern through childhood to adolescence, and to investigate effects of insensitive or inconsistent or cruel mothering, there has been a current of theory that discourages attempts to observe healthy and happy behavior in detail. We do not understand well how joy affects the brain and what it contributes to the formation of satisfying and effective child-parent relations, how it fosters further child development, and how it motivates the kind of learning that makes the life of a young person in society full of emotional rewards and achievements and secure and realistic hopes and ambitions, though there have been clear calls for a quest (Emde, 1992; Panksepp & Burgdorf, 2003; Reddy, 2001; Stern, 1990).

We believe that the account of how human capacities for being consciously active and for becoming aware of and expressive to other persons emerge prefunctionally in formation of the bodies and brains of a human embryo and fetus, and the ways brain systems are engaged at all stages in circular regulatory relations by neurohumoral systems with the vital process of the whole body should encourage a greater faith in the powers of the infant to communicate richly. Careful observation of mutually pleasurable engagements has brought remarkable evidence of such an inborn ability. Such observations help explain the conviction of a healthy mother, who has passed through a satisfactory pregnancy and been well prepared in her neurohumoral state for love of the baby, that she is greeting a little person. The father, too, indeed all the close family and even indulgent outsiders can share this experience of engagement with a human vitality.

The developments of infancy lead to cooperation in habits and acquired understandings and emotional evaluations. The participation in shared experience is propelled forward by imitative negotiations and trickery in affectionate and carefully moderated conflicts full of enjoyment (Reddy, 2003; Reddy & Morris, 2004; Trevarthen, 2005a). Here the findings of research on animal play are of great interest (G. Bateson, 1955, 1956; Bekoff & Byers, 1998; Panksepp & Burgdorf, 2003). It seems that the joy of exuberant rivalry and immediate imitation of extravagant expressions in moving has benefit for the regulation of the positive use of near-stressful flow in activity, and above all in joint or collaborative activity. At the center of all such celebratory behaviors are rhythmic rituals of action modulated by cycles of energy expenditure and recovery (Turner, 1982). So there is a dance of life joined in every form of collaborative awareness, even one that seems to have a most serious practical purpose.

Prosocial behaviors (Bierhoff, 2002) are not merely democratic but must be guided by sympathies and "moral sentiments" (Smith, 1759/1976), such as are evident in young children. These principles are needed in assessment, therapy, and education of any person of any age who is suffering from the fear, anger, anxiety, and confusion of emotional disorder. Varieties of child emotional disorder can be related to how a child needs to develop, and is equipped by his or her nature to develop, through attachments, friendships, and a lifetime of sociability.

Understanding problems children have when the support from their mother or other caregiver is not normally responsive is, we believe, better served by research on the course of developmental change when a healthy infant is in control of actions and experiences well supported by a sympathetic and happy partner—on what can be missing. The drive to study pathology comes from a reduced or pessimistic perception that the child is a passive vessel, a receiver of developmental training.

Fitting New Brain Science to Human Needs

The final decade of the twentieth century, the "decade of the brain," brought more detailed, more accurate information about processes in living brains (Cicchetti & Cannon, 1999). New methods of anatomical investigation, of molecular neurobiology and genetics, of functional imaging, and

of standardized interrogation of mental processes by cognitive tests changed the picture. The classical theory had chains of neurons taking in sensory information and processing it into features and object schemes, then activating motor responses and inscribing categories of memory according to rewards and punishments felt in the body. That theory is gone, replaced by one that expects to find widespread patterns of activity originating in regions involved in emotional states and once thought secondary to those presumed to assemble perceptions and memories. The cortex is no longer seen as the supreme integrator of cognitive processes and language, but more like a multifaceted crystallization of impressions illuminated by arousing impulses of subcortical origins: by attentions, intentions, and above all by emotional states that evaluate the risks and benefits of the whole enterprise in subtle, adaptive ways (as emphasized by Damasio, 1994, 1999; Merker, 2005; Panksepp, 1998b, 2000; Tucker, 2001). In short, the brain has become a little more comprehensible as the organ that, with the body, moves a person, one who has a consciousness of the body and the world it is in, a consciousness that serves the skill of movements prospectively and who has emotions and memories that assist in the imagining of the potentialities and values of that future experience.

Resuscitation of interest in the neural correlates of emotional states has led to a new approach to both conscious awareness and memory, both of which had become codified in Byzantine models by one-sided adherence to experimental procedures in which subjects whose freedom of action has been severely constrained make selective responses to express judgments about questions posed by the experimenter in far too limited periods of time (Donald, 2001). The unconscious intentional preparation for rational understanding, and for its articulation in language, has returned to center stage, no longer treated as outside any possible rigorous scientific attention.

Much has been made of the discovery that brain anatomy is plastic to experience (Johnson, 1998), with classical maps of function showing disturbing instability under the influence of practice or the focus of motivation. This switch of interpretation owes much to a straw man built of exaggerations about the claims of anatomists and embryologists regarding the prefunctional mapping of systems in the neural net. But principles of somatotopy mapping between body and brain do apply and are essential to how the brain functions coherently in regulation of the time and space of behavior. Genetic mechanisms do instill adaptive programs of morphogenesis that impose crucial constraints on what the environment can do to change the rules of intelligence.

Moreover, the epigenetic process is regulated to produce age-related transformations in the enterprise of intelligence. A child's mind is not just the consequence of environmental programming and not just a history of emotive events. The abstract mathematics of dynamic systems theory makes cogent criticism of linear causal explanations of motor coordination, conscious conceptions, and memory. But no metaphor of emerging order in patterns of neural energy or their behavioral consequences can explain the initial coherence of an intention, or the emotions that evaluate its prospects. The age-related transitions depend on intrinsic transformations in constraints on brain activity that originate in motive systems that have evolved to regulate a life cycle of changes (Trevarthen & Aitken, 2003).

All these issues, no matter how much their resurgence in scientific psychology may owe to elaborate methods of brain science or molecular biology of nerve cell differentiation and communication, can be addressed and assessed by accurate investigation of the behaviors of an infant in lively engagement with the world and human society. The integrated purposefulness and awareness of newborns' movements, their emotional expressiveness and their immediate responses to the expressions of another person, and their qualities of contingent response in intimate communication prove that the human brain is designed to do the job of generating and sharing acquired mental states. Infants are born learning; they are profoundly affected in their experience and understanding by the emotions that arise between themselves in their own body and the body and mind of those who take on the responsibility of being caretakers and companions. These adaptations, with their miraculous power to absorb meanings and to create inventions of play in affectionate partnerships, carry destructive energy if the human world gives no support or imposes unsupportable stresses.

Scientific Guidelines for Care of Stressed Young Children and Their Families

Effective child psychopathology has to be multilevel and transdisciplinary (Cicchetti & Dawson, 2002; Cicchetti & Rogosch, 1996). A *whole person psychology* is needed to begin a useful science of infant mental states and to understand how stresses in relationships may predispose a child to fear and anger that will color relationships in later years. Knowing that the hippocampus or orbitofrontal cortex of the right hemisphere grows throughout life and can be stunted or deformed by emotional stresses can help focus our awareness and sympathy for the young child's plight, but it cannot replace the need for sensitive awareness of the

face, voice, and expressive gestures of the real individual child that the parents and persons offering clinical or social support have to respond to and guide. It is important that infants are born genetically different in complex ways that give them different initial strengths and fragilities, but this much should be obvious to any sensitive parent or therapist. The genes that correlate with a child's behaviors, or behaviors of family members, can give only very approximate evidence of what that child's motives are and how they will change.

Care for children at risk of pathology in consequence of neglect or abuse cannot be effective if it bypasses the intrinsic capacities of the child for sympathetic engagement with other persons' actions and feelings and for playful experimentation with the joys and risks of shared activity. Decades of experience in the recovery of happy lives from circumstances where infants have been deprived of proper human care supports the message of Bowlby's attachment theory, which has had a profound effect on medical and educational care of troubled children and on parental awareness of children's needs (Greenspan, 1981). However, Bowlby (1958) imagined the child as acquiring a cognitive internal working model of what Winnicott (1960) called a "good enough" mother. We know now, through research on the intricate signals of touch, vocalization, and eye contact in mother-infant protoconversations and games, that the infant's motives for relationships go beyond those that attract and sustain mothering (Beebe et al., 1985; Stern, 1974, 2000; Trevarthen, 1979; Tronick et al., 1978).

The lively intersubjective imagination of a child needs to participate in a generous play with meanings to make sense of the cultural world, with all its arbitrary understandings of reality. The infant is seeking to interact with intentions and interests from early weeks (Trevarthen & Aitken, 2001). The motives for this play are dynamic and rooted in the rhythmic impulses and expressive gestures of unconscious human volition. Therapy must base its effort at this level, sensitive to those rhythms and expressions (Caldwell, 2005; Nafstad & Rodbroe, 1999; Schore, 2003b).

The efficacy of improvised music therapy for achieving sympathetic communication with emotionally disturbed or mentally handicapped human beings of any age both depends on and proves this intrinsic "communicative musicality" (Bunt, 1994; Elefant, 2001; Gold, Vorachek, & Wigram, 2004; Malloch, 1999; Merker & Wallin, 2001; Nordoff & Robbins, in press; Pavlicevic, 1997; Trevarthen & Malloch, 2000, 2002; Wigram, 2004). With people whose sense of self is fragile, where meaning is lost or not easily found, music has unique powers which the resourceful music therapist can use to support integrative and self-restorative processes (Montello, 1999; Robarts, 2003, in press). We have little knowledge of how the brain mediates engagement with musicality of human expressive body movement (Panksepp & Bernatzky, 2002), but the power of this level of intersubjectivity, one that corresponds with the natural engagements of vocal and gestural play and touching with infants, is confirmed (Burford & Trevarthen, 1997).

Attachment-Based Therapy for Neglected or Abused Children and Parents Who Foster or Adopt Them

The experience of those who offer support for disturbed children and their families, and in particular those rebellious or resistant children who have been removed from their biological parents for their own protection, is that it is necessary to get into immediate responsive engagement with the child by the same kind of intuitive forms of communication as are used by affectionate and happy parents with infants and toddlers everywhere (Archer & Burnell, 2003; Hughes, 1997, 1998). In this communication, sympathy for what the child is feeling, genuine emotional response that is accepting and flexible, and good humor in play are as essential as calm attentiveness in listening to the child, and firmness in setting clear boundaries, both physical and emotional. A scientific or clinical detachment is to be avoided. For the severely abused child the recovery of joy in play requires a longer, more complex therapeutic treatment; PTSD associated with trauma distorts normal patterns of interpersonal engagement, triggering an overload of confusing sensations that frequently lead to dissociative or out of control reactions, so that the sensory and dynamic experiences of play have to be treated with clinical perception, understanding and skill (Robarts, in press; Rogers, 1995; Schore, 2001b, 2003c; Siegel, 2003; Sutton, 2002; van der Kolk et al., 1996).

Play means interaction with any impulses for adventurous and enjoyable movement and experience. It means sharing expressions of joy and surprise (Panksepp & Burgdorf, 2003). It taps a basic emotion in social sharing, one that is close to and supportive of the basic emotions for pleasure in attachment. As the ethologists have discovered by studying the instinctive movements of young animals' chasing and pretend fighting, play is affiliative (Bekoff & Byers, 1998). It strengthens and develops social bonds while sorting out social hierarchies. Play therapy draws on these psychobiological principles in a systematic way (Jernberg & Booth, 2001). For a troubled child, making happy and trusting friendships in playful and intimately affectionate responsive ways is a key to positive learning and emotional security.

Video-recorded evidence of the emotional nature and patterning of this kind of communication is beneficial not only for therapists and teachers, but also for parents attempting to guide a child to better emotional health (Beebe, 2003; Forsyth, Kennedy, & Simpson, 1995; Gutstein & Sheely, 2002; Jansen & Wels, 1998; Juffer, Bakermans-Kranenburg, & van Ijzendoorn, 2005; Schechter, 2004). This is how video feedback is employed as a detailed record of interacting behaviors and a prompt for more supportive and constructive communication.

Spontaneous and creative art therapies in dramatic acting, dance, or music all engage with the timing and expressiveness of direct intuitive communication in the present. They engage the aesthetic dynamic forms of non-verbal and verbal in expressions that are the basis of creative-constructive therapeutic change (Gilroy & Lee, 1995; Levine, Knill, & Levine, 2003; Robarts, 2003, in press). The play of communication is creative by means of an interpersonal improvisation in which partners are at the same time free to be expressive in themselves and instantly reactive to what others do, and therefore open to guidance and learning. Real intuitive engagement is necessary for the emotions between them to flourish, as with infants (Reddy & Trevarthen, 2004).

Specific memories and verbal explanations guide awareness and direct interests. In normal life, these cognitive components, built up through experiences in established relationships, strengthen the prospective control of attentions and intentions and lead to more knowledgeable and skillful action. In psychopathology, the cognitive contents of memory intrude in imagination and carry affective material that blocks effective consciousness and action. Therapy for adults requires work with these contents. At the same time, engaging with the emotions and a clear focus on the interpersonal motives that direct movements in the present can regulate disturbing or inhibiting material from memory and imagination, finding a path to more rewarding and creative purposes in relationships that are affectionate and trusting (Kerr, 2005; Kohut, 1984). A therapist aiming to help a child with developmental psychopathology by intersubjective or interpersonal means has responsibility to stay with the child through periods of resistance or rejection to find this path (Archer & Burnell, 2003).

ACKNOWLEDGMENTS

We would like to thank Dr. Jacqueline Robarts of the Nordoff Robbins Music Therapy Centre, London for her expert advice on therapy for traumatized children.

REFERENCES

Adamson-Macedo, E. N. (1998). The mind and body of the preterm neonate. *International Journal of Prenatal and Perinatal Psychology and Medicine, 10*(4).

Adamson-Macedo, E. N. (2004). Neo-haptic touch. In R. L. Gregory (Ed.), *Oxford companion to the mind* (2nd ed., pp. 637–639). Oxford, England: Oxford University Press.

Adolphs, R. (2003). Investigating the cognitive neuroscience of social behavior. *Neuropsychologia, 41,* 119–126.

Adolphs, R., Tranel, D., Damasio, H., & Damasio, A. R. (1995). Fear and the human amygdala. *Journal of Neuroscience, 15,* 5879–5892.

Aggleton, J. P. (1993). The contribution of the amygdala to normal and abnormal emotional states. *Trends in Neurosciences, 16,* 328–333.

Ainsworth, M. D. S., Blehar, M. C., Waters, E., & Wall, S. (1978). *Patterns of attachment: A psychological study of the Strange Situation.* Hillsdale, NJ: Erlbaum.

Aitken, K. J., & Trevarthen, C. (1997). Self-other organization in human psychological development. *Development and Psychopathology, 9,* 651–675.

Allister, L., Lester, B. M., Carr, S., & Liu, J. (2001). The effects of maternal depression on fetal heart rate response to vibroacoustic stimulation. *Developmental Neuropsychology, 20*(3), 639–651.

Allman, J. M., Hakeem, A., Erwin, J. M., Nimchinsky, E., & Hof, P. (2001). The anterior cingulate cortex: The evolution of an interface between emotion and cognition. In A. R. Damasio, A. Harrington, J. Kagan, B. S. McEwen, H. Moss, & R. Shaikh (Eds.), *Annals of the New York Academy of Sciences: Unity of knowledge—the convergence of natural and human science, 935,* 107–117.

Als, H. (1995). The preterm infant: A model for the study of fetal brain expectation. In J.-P. Lecanuet, W. P. Fifer, N. A. Krasnegor, & W. P. Smotherman (Eds.), *Fetal development: A psychobiological perspective* (pp. 439–471). Hillsdale, NJ: Erlbaum.

Alvarez, A. (1992). *Live company: Psychoanalytic psychotherapy with autistic, borderline, deprived and abused children.* London: Brunner-Routledge.

Alvarez, A. (1999). Addressing the deficit: Developmentally informed psychotherapy with passive, "undrawn" children. In A. Alvarez & S. Reid (Eds.), *Autism and personality* (pp. 49–61). London: Routledge.

Alvarez, A. (2000). A developmental view of "defence": The borderline psychotic child. In T. Lubbe (Ed.), *The borderline psychotic child: A selective integration.* London and Philadelphia: Routledge.

Amaral, D. G. (2003). The amygdala, social behavior, and danger detection. *Annals of the New York Academy of Sciences, 1000,* 337–347.

Anderson, S. W., Bechara, A., Damasio, H., Tranel, D., & Damasio, A. R. (1999). Impairment of social and moral behaviour related to early damage in human prefrontal cortex. *Nature Neuroscience, 2,* 1032–1037.

Arborelius, L., Owens, M. J., Plotsky, P. M., & Nemeroff, C. B. (1999). The role of corticotropin-releasing factor in depression and anxiety disorders. *Journal of Endocrinology, 160,* 1–12.

Archer, C., & Burnell, A. (2003). *Trauma, attachment and family permanence: Fear can stop you loving.* London: Jessica Kingsley.

Bachiller, D., Klingensmith, J., Kemp, C., Belo, J. A., Anderson, R. M., May, S. R., et al. (2000). The organiser factors chordin and noggin are required for mouse forebrain development. *Nature, 403,* 658–661.

Baltz, J. M., Katz, D. F., & Cone, R. A. (1988). The mechanics of sperm-egg interaction at the zona pellucida. *Biophysical Journal, 54,* 643–654.

Barkovich, A. J., Kjos, B. P. O., Jackson, D. E., Jr., & Norman, D. (1988). Normal maturation of the neonatal infant brain: MR Imaging at 1.5 T. *Radiology, 166*(1), 173–180.

Barron, W., Mujais, S., Zinaman, M., Bravo, E., & Lindheimer, M. (1986). Plasma catecholamine responses to physiologic stimuli in normal human pregnancy. *American Journal of Obstetrics and Gynecology, 154,* 80–84.

Bateson, G. (1955). A theory of play and fantasy. *Psychiatric Research Reports, 2*(Series A), 39–51.

Bateson, G. (1956). The message "This is play." In B. Schaffner (Ed.), *Group processes: Transactions of the second conference* (pp. 145–242). New York: Josiah Macy Foundation.

Bateson, G. (1979). *Mind and nature, a necessary unity.* London: Wildwood House.

Bateson, M. C. (1975). Mother-infant exchanges: The epigenesis of conversational interaction. In D. Aaronson & R. W. Rieber (Eds.), *Developmental psycholinguistics and communication disorders: Annals of the New York Academy of Sciences* (Vol. 263, pp. 101–113). New York: New York Academy of Sciences.

Bateson, M. C. (1979). The epigenesis of conversational interaction: A personal account of research development. In M. Bullowa (Ed.), *Before speech: The beginning of human communication* (pp. 63–77). Cambridge, England: Cambridge University Press.

Bateson, W. (1894). *Materials for the study of variation treated with special regard for discontinuity in the origin of species.* London: Macmillan.

Bechara, A., Damasio, H., & Damasio, A. R. (2000). Emotion, decision making and the orbitofrontal cortex. *Cerebral Cortex, 10*(3), 295–307.

Beebe, B. (2003). Brief mother-infant treatment using psychoanalytically informed video microanalysis. *Infant Mental Health Journal, 24*(1), 24–52.

Beebe, B., Jaffe, J., Buck, K., Chen, H., Cohen, P., Feldstein, S., et al. (in press). Six-week postpartum maternal depressive symptoms predict 4-month mother-infant self- and interactive regulation. *Infant Mental Health Journal.*

Beebe, B., Jaffe, J., Feldstein, S., Mays, K., & Alson, D. (1985). Interpersonal timing: The application of an adult dialogue model to mother-infant vocal and kinesic interactions. In F. M. Field & N. Fox (Eds.), *Social perception in infants* (pp. 217–248). Norwood, NJ: Ablex.

Bekoff, M., & Byers, J. A. (1998). *Animal play: Evolutionary, comparative and ecological approaches.* New York: Cambridge University Press.

Bell, M. A., & Fox, N. A. (1996). Crawling experience is related to changes in cortical organization during infancy: Evidence from EEG coherence. *Developmental Psychobiology, 29*(7), 551–561.

Benitez-Diaz, P., Miranda-Contreras, L., Mendoza-Briceno, R. V., Pena-Contreras, Z., & Palacios-Pru, E. (2003). Prenatal and postnatal contents of amino acid neurotransmitters in mouse parietal cortex. *Developmental Neurosciences, 25,* 366–374.

Berger-Sweeney, J., & Hohmann, C. F. (1997). Behavioral consequences of abnormal cortical development: Insights into developmental disabilities. *Behavioral Brain Research, 86,* 121–142.

Bernard, C. (1878). *Leçons sur les phénomènes de la vie communs aux animaux et aux végétaux* (Vol. 1). Paris: Baillière.

Bernstein, N. (1967). *Coordination and regulation of movements.* New York: Pergamon Press.

Berntson, G. G., & Cacioppo, J. T. (2000). From homeostasis to allodynamic regulation. In J. T. Cacioppo, L. G. Tassinary, & G. G. Berntson (Eds.), *Handbook of psychophysiology* (pp. 459–481). Cambridge, England: Cambridge University Press.

Berntson, G. G., Sarter, M., & Cacioppo, J. T. (1998). Anxiety and cardiovascular reactivity: The basal forebrain cholinergic link. *Behavioural and Brain Research, 94,* 225–248.

Berntson, G. G., Sarter, M., & Cacioppo, J. T. (2003a). Autonomic nervous system. In L. Nadel (Ed.), *Encyclopedia of cognitive science* (pp. 301–308). Basingstoke, England: Nature Publishing Group, Macmillan.

Berntson, G. G., Sarter, M., & Cacioppo, J. T. (2003b). Ascending visceral regulation of cortical affective information processing. *European Journal of Neuroscience, 18,* 2103–2109.

Bettes, B. (1988). Maternal depression and motherese: Temporal and intonational features. *Child Development, 59,* 1089–1096.

Bierhoff, H.-W. (2002). *Prosocial behaviour.* Hove, England: Psychology Press.

Black, J., Jones, T. A., Nelson, C. A., & Greenough, W. T. (1998). Neuronal plasticity and the developing brain. In N. E. Alessi, J. T. Coyle, S. I. Harrison, & S. Eth (Eds.), *Handbook of child and adolescent psychiatry* (pp. 31–53). New York: Wiley.

Blass, E. M. (1996). Mothers and their infants: Peptide-mediated physiological, behavioral and affective changes during suckling. *Regulatory Peptides, 66,* 109–112.

Boncinelli, E., Somma, R., Acampora, D., Pannese, M., Desposito, M., Faiella, A., et al. (1988). Organization of human homeobox genes. *Human Reproduction, 3,* 880–886.

Bourgeois, J.-P. (2001). Synaptogenesis in the neocortex of the newborn: The ultimate frontier for individuation. In C. A. Nelson & M. Luciana (Eds.), *Handbook of developmental cognitive neuroscience* (pp. 23–34). Cambridge, MA: MIT Press.

Bowlby, J. (1958). The nature of the child's tie to his mother. *International Journal of Psychoanalysis, 39,* 1–23.

Bowlby, J. (1969). *Attachment: Vol. 1. Attachment and loss.* New York: Basic Books.

Boyson, S. J., & Adams, C. E. (1997). D1 and D2 dopamine receptors in perinatal and adult basal ganglia. *Pediatric Research, 41,* 822–831.

Bradford, H. F. (2004). Neurotransmitters and neuromodulators. In R. L. Gregory (Ed.), *Oxford companion to the mind* (2nd ed., pp. 657–673). Oxford, New York: Oxford University Press.

Bråten, S. (1988). Dialogic mind: The infant and adult in protoconversation. In M. S. Cavallo (Ed.), *Nature, cognition and system* (pp. 187–205). Dordrecht, The Netherlands: Kluwer Press.

Bråten, S. (1998). Intersubjective communion and understanding: Development and perturbation. In S. Bråten (Ed.), *Intersubjective communication and emotion in early ontogeny* (pp. 372–382). Cambridge: Cambridge University Press.

Brazelton, T. B. (2002). Strengths and stresses in today's families: Looking toward the future. In J. Gomes-Pedro, J. K. Nugent, J. G. Young, & T. B. Brazelton (Eds.), *The infant and family in the twenty-first century* (pp. 23–30). New York: Brunner-Routledge.

Brazelton, T. B., & Nugent, J. K. (1995). *Neonatal Behavioural Assessment Scale* (3rd ed.). London: MacKeith Press.

Bremner, J. D. (2002). Neuroimaging studies in posttraumatic stress disorder. *Current Psychiatry Reports, 4*(4), 254–263.

Bremner, J. D., Narayan, M., Anderson, E. R., Staib, L. H., Miller, H. L., & Charney, D. S. (2000). Hippocampal volume reduction in major depression. *American Journal of Psychiatry, 157,* 115–117.

Bremner, J. D., & Vermetten, E. (2004). Neuroanatomical changes associated with pharmacotherapy in posttraumatic stress disorder. *Annals of the New York Academy of Sciences, 1032,* 154–157.

Bremner, J. D., Vermetten, E., Vythilingam, M., Afzal, N., Schmahl, C., Elzinga, B., et al. (2004). Neural correlates of the classic color and emotional Stroop in women with abuse-related posttraumatic stress disorder. *Biological Psychiatry, 15*(6), 612–620.

Brennan, J., Lu, C. C., Norris, D. P., Rodriguez, T. A., Beddington, R. S., & Robertson, E. J. (2001). Nodal signalling in the epiblast patterns the early mouse embryo. *Nature, 411,* 965–969.

Breznitz, Z., & Sherman, T. (1987). Speech patterning and natural discourse of well and depressed mothers and their young children. *Child Development, 58,* 395–400.

Broca, P. (1878). Anatomie comparée des circonvolutions cérébrales: Le grand lobe limbique et la scissure limbique dans la série des mammifères. *Revue Anthropologique, 1*(2), 385–498.

Bronfenbrenner, U. (2002). Preparing a world for the infant in the twenty-first century: The research challenge. In J. Gomes-Pedro, J. K. Nugent, J. G. Young, & T. B. Brazelton (Eds.), *The infant and family in the twenty-first century* (pp. 45–52). New York: Brunner-Routledge.

Buckwalter, K. C., Stolley, J. M., & Farran, C. J. (1999). Managing cognitive impairment in the elderly: Conceptual, intervention and methodological issues. *Online Journal of Knowledge on Synthetic Nursing, 11,* 6–10.

Bunt, L. (1994). *Music therapy: An art beyond words.* London: Routledge.

Burford, B., & Trevarthen, C. (1997). Evoking communication in Rett syndrome: Comparisons with conversations and games in mother-infant interaction. *European Child and Adolescent Psychiatry, 6,* 1–5.

Cabeza, R., & Nyberg, L. (1997). Imaging cognition: An empirical review of PET studies with normal subjects. *Journal of Cognitive Neuroscience, 9,* 1–26.

Cahill, L., McGaugh, J. L., & Weinberger, N. M. (2001). The neurobiology of learning and memory: Some reminders to remember. *Trends in Neurosciences, 24*(10), 578–581.

Caldji, C., Tannenbaum, B., Sharma, S., Francis, D., Plotsky, P. M., & Meaney, M. J. (1998). Maternal care during infancy regulates the development of neural systems mediating the expression of fearfulness in the rat. *Proceedings of the National Academy of Sciences, USA, 95,* 5335–5340.

Caldwell, P. (2005). *Creative conversations: Communicating with people with profound and multiple learning disabilities.* Brighton: Pavilion Publishing.

Cannon, W. B. (1939). *The wisdom of the body* (Rev. ed.). New York: Norton.

Carter, C. S., Lederhendler, I. I., & Kirkpatrick, B. (Eds.). (1997). *The integrative neurobiology of affiliation: Annals of the New York Academy of Sciences, 807.* New York: New York Academy of Sciences.

Carter, C. S., Perlstein, W., Ganguli, R., Brar, J., Mintun, M., & Cohen, J. D. (1998). Functional hypofrontality and working memory dysfunction in Schizophrenia. *American Journal of Psychiatry, 155*(9), 1285–1287.

Castellanos, F. X., Giedd, J. N., March, W. L., Hamburger, S. D., Vaituzis, A. C., Dickstein, D. P., et al. (1996). Quantitative brain magnetic resonance imaging in attention-deficit hyperactivity disorder. *Archives of General Psychiatry, 53,* 607–616.

Cayouteet, M., & Raff, M. (2002). Asymmetric segregation of Numb: A mechanism for neural specification from drosophila to mammals. *Nature Neuroscience, 5,* 1265–1269.

Challis, J. R., Sloboda, D., Matthews, S. G., Holloway, A., Alfaidy, N., Patel, F. A., et al. (2001). The fetal placental hypothalamic-pituitary-adrenal (HPA) axis, parturition and post natal health. *Molecular and Cellular Endocrinology, 185*(1, 2), 135–144.

Chisaka, O., Musci, T. S., & Capecchi, M. R. (1992). Developmental defects of the ear, cranial nerves and hindbrain resulting from targeted disruption of the mouse homeobox gene Hox-1.6. *Nature, 355,* 516–520.

Chugani, D. C. (2002). Role of altered brain serotonin mechanisms in Autism. *Molecular Psychiatry, 7*(Suppl. 2), S16–S17.

Chugani, H. T. (1994). Development of regional brain glucose metabolism in relation to behavior and plasticity. In G. Dawson & K. W. Fischer (Eds.), *Human behavior and the developing brain* (pp. 153–175). New York: Guilford Press.

Chugani, H. T. (1998). A critical period of brain development: Studies of cerebral glucose utilization with PET. *Preventive Medicine, 27,* 184–188.

Cicchetti, D. (1984). The emergence of developmental psychopathology. *Child Development, 55,* 1–7.

Cicchetti, D. (1989). Developmental psychopathology: Some thoughts on its evolution. *Development and Psychopathology, 1,* 1–4.

Cicchetti, D. (1990). An historical perspective on the discipline of developmental psychopathology. In J. Rolf, A. Masten, D. Cicchetti, K. Nuechterlein, & S. Weintraub (Eds.), *Risk and protective factors in the development of psychopathology* (pp. 2–28). New York: Cambridge University Press.

Cicchetti, D. (1993). Developmental psychopathology: Reactions, reflections, projections. *Developmental Review, 13,* 471–502.

Cicchetti, D. (2002). The impact of social experience on neurobiological systems: Illustration from a constructivist view of child maltreatment. *Cognitive Development, 17,* 1407–1428.

Cicchetti, D., & Cannon, T. D. (1999). Neurodevelopmental processes in the ontogenesis and epigenesis of psychopathology. *Development and Psychopathology, 11,* 375–393.

Cicchetti, D., & Dawson, G. (Eds.). (2002). Multiple levels of analysis. Special Issue. *Development and Psychopathology, 14*(3), 417–666.

Cicchetti, D., & Rogosch, F. A. (1996). Equifinality and multifinality in developmental psychopathology. *Development and Psychopathology, 8,* 597–600.

Cicchetti, D., & Rogosch, F. A. (1997). The role of self-organization in the promotion of resilience in maltreated children. *Development and Psychopathology, 9,* 797–815.

Cicchetti, D., & Rogosch, F. A. (2002). A developmental psychopathology perspective on adolescence. *Journal of Consulting and Clinical Psychology, 70,* 6–20.

Cicchetti, D., & Toth, S. L. (2000). Developmental processes in maltreated children. *Nebraska Symposium of Motivation, 46,* 85–160.

Cicchetti, D., & Tucker, D. (1994). Development and self-regulatory structures of the mind. *Development and Psychopathology, 6,* 533–549.

Cohen, H., Ryan, J., Hunt, C., Romine, L., Wszalek, T., & Nash, C. (1999). Hippocampal system and declarative (relational) memory: Summarizing the data from functional neuroimaging studies. *Hippocampus, 9,* 83–98.

Craig, C. M., & Lee, D. N. (1999). Neonatal control of nutritive sucking pressure: Evidence for an intrinsic tau-guide. *Experimental Brain Research, 124*(3), 371–382.

Cross, N. L. (1998). Role of cholesterol in sperm capacitation. *Biology of Reproduction, 59,* 7–11.

Cytryn, L., McKnew, D. H., Jr., & Bunney, W. E. (1980). Diagnosis of depression in children: A reassessment. *American Journal of Psychiatry, 137*(1), 22–25.

Damasio, A. R. (1994). *Decartes' error: Emotion, reason and the human brain.* New York: Grosset/Putnam.

Damasio, A. R. (1999). *The feeling of what happens: Body, emotion and the making of consciousness.* London: Heinemann.

Damasio, A. R., & Damasio, H. (1992). Brain and language. *Scientific American, 267,* 63–71.

Damasio, A. R., Grabowski, T. J., Bechara, A., Damasio, H., Ponto, L. L. B., Parvizi, J., et al. (2000). Subcortical and cortical brain activity during the feeling of self-generated emotions. *Nature Neuroscience, 3,* 1049–1056.

Darwin, C. (1998). *The expression of the emotions in man and animals* (3rd ed.). New York: Oxford University Press. (Original work published 1872)

Davis, L. L., Suris, A., Lambert, M. T., Heimberg, C., & Petty, F. (1997). Post-traumatic stress disorder and serotonin: New directions for research and treatment. *Journal of Psychiatry and Neuroscience, 22,* 318–326.

Dawson, G., & Fischer, K. W. (1994). *Human behavior and the developing brain.* New York: Guilford Press.

Dawson, G., Webb, S., Schellenberg, G. D., Dager, S., Friedman, S., Aylward, E., et al. (2002). Defining the broader phenotype of Autism: Genetic, brain, and behavioral perspectives. *Development and Psychopathology, 14,* 581–611.

de Beer, G. (1945). *Embryos and ancestors.* London: Oxford University Press.

DeBellis, M. D. (2001). Developmental traumatology: The psychobiological development of maltreated children and its implications for research, treatment, and policy. *Developmental Psychopathology, 13*(3), 539–564.

DeBellis, M. D., Baum, A. S., Birmaher, B., Keshavan, M. S., Eccard, C. H., Boring, A. M., et al. (1999a). A. E. Bennett Research Award—Developmental traumatology: Pt. I. Biological stress systems. *Biological Psychiatry, 15,* 1259–1270.

DeBellis, M. D., Keshavan, M. S., Clark, D. B., Casely, B. J., Giedd, J. N., Boring, A. M., et al. (1999b). A. E. Bennett Research Award—Developmental traumatology: Pt. II. Brain development. *Biological Psychiatry, 15,* 1271–1284.

DeCasper, A. J., & Fifer, W. P. (1980). Of human bonding: Newborns prefer their mother's voices. *Science, 208,* 1174–1176.

Decety, J., & Chaminade, T. (2003). Neural correlates of feeling sympathy. *Neuropsychologia, 41,* 127–138.

deGroot, R. H., Adam, J. J., & Hornstra, G. (2003). Selective attention deficits during human pregnancy. *Neuroscience Letters, 340,* 21–24.

de Kloet, E. R., Korte, S. M., Rots, W. Y., & Kruk, M. R. (1996). Stress hormones, genotype, brain organization: Implications for aggression. *Annals of the New Academy of Sciences, 94,* 179–191.

de Kloet, E. R., Oitzl, M. S., & Joels, M. (1999). Stress and cognition: Are corticosteroids good or bad guys? *Trends in Neurosciences, 22*(10), 422–426.

de Vries, J. I. P., Visser, G. H. A., & Prechtl, H. F. R. (1984). Fetal motility in the first half of pregnancy. In H. F. R. Prechtl (Ed.), *Continuity of neural functions from prenatal to postnatal life* (pp. 46–64). Oxford: Blackwell.

de Vries, J. I. P., Visser, G. H. A., & Prechtl, H. F. R. (1988). The emergence of foetal behaviour: Pt. III. Individual differences and consistencies. *Early Human Development, 16*(1), 85–103.

de Waal, F. (1996). *Good natured.* Cambridge, MA: Harvard University Press.

Diamond, A. (1990). The development and neural bases of memory functions as indexed by the A-not-B and delayed response task in human infants and infant monkeys. In A. Diamond (Ed.), *The development and neural bases of higher cognitive functions* (pp. 394–426). New York: New York Academy of Sciences.

Diamond, A. (1991). Frontal lobe involvement in cognitive changes during the first year of life. In K. R. Gibson & A. C. Petersen (Eds.), *Brain maturation and cognitive development: Comparative and cross-cultural perspectives* (pp. 127–180). New York: Aldine de Gruyter.

DiPietro, J. A., Hodgson, D. M., Costigan, K. A., Hilton, S. C., & Johnson, T. R. B. (1996). Fetal neurobehavioral development. *Child Development, 67,* 2553–2567.

DiPietro, J. A., Irizarry, R. A., Costigan, K. A., & Gurewitsch, E. D. (2004). The psychophysiology of the maternal-fetal relationship. *Psychophysiology, 41,* 510–520.

Dodic, M., Hantzis, V., Duncan, J., Rees, S., Koukoulas, I., Johnson, K., et al. (2002). Programming effects of short prenatal exposure to cortisol. *FASEB Journal, 16*(9), 1017–1026.

Donald, M. (2001). *A mind so rare: The evolution of human consciousness.* New York: Norton.

Dugdale, A. E. (1986). Evolution and infant feeding. *Lancet, 1*(8482), 670–673.

Dunn, A. J., & Berridge, C. W. (1990). Physiological and behavioral responses to corticotropin-releasing factor administration: Is CRF a mediator of anxiety or stress responses? *Brain Research Review, 15,* 71–100.

Dunn, A. J., Swiergeil, A. H., & Palamarchouk, V. (2004). Brain circuits involved in corticotropin-releasing factor: Norepinephrine interactions during stress. *Annals of the New York Academic Sciences, 1018,* 25–34.

Dworkin, B. R. (2000). Interoception. In C. T. Cacioppo, L. G. Tassinary, & G. G. Berntson (Eds.), *Handbook of psychophysiology* (pp. 482–405). Cambridge, England: Cambridge University Press.

Echelard, Y., Epstein, D. J., St-Jacques, B., Shen, L., Mohler, J., McMahon, J. A., et al. (1993). Sonic hedgehog, a member of a family of putative signalling molecules, is implicated in the regulation of CNS polarity. *Cell, 75*(7), 1417–1430.

Edelman, G. M. (1987). *Neuronal Darwinism: The theory of neuronal group selection.* New York: Basic Books.

Edelman, G. M. (1988). *Topobiology: An introduction to molecular embryology.* New York: Basic Books.

Edwards, H. E., & Burnham, W. M. (2001). The impact of corticosteroids on the developing animal. *Pediatric Research, 50,* 433–440.

Edwards, J. (Ed.). (2001). *Being alive: Building on the work of Anne Alvarez.* London & New York: Brunner-Routledge.

Elefant, C. (2001). Speechless yet communicative: Revealing the person behind the disability of Rett syndrome through clinical research on songs in music therapy. In D. Aldridge, G. Di Franco, E. Ruud, & T. Wigram (Eds.), *Music therapy in Europe.* Rome: ISMEZ.

Emde, R. N. (1992). Positive emotions for psychoanalytic theory: Surprises from infancy research and new directions. In T. Shapiro & R. N. Emde (Eds.), *Affect: Psychoanalytic perspectives* (pp. 5–54). Madison, CT: International Universities Press.

Episkopou, V., Arkell, R., Timmons, P. M., Walsh, J. J., Andrew, R. L., & Swan, D. (2001). Induction of the mammalian node requires Arkadia function in the extraembryonic lineages. *Nature, 410,* 825–830.

Fiamenghi, G. (1997). Intersubjectivity and infant-infant interaction: Imitation as a way of making contact. *Hokkaido University, Annual Report, Research and Clinical Centre for Child Development, 19,* 15–21.

Field, T. M. (1984). Early interactions between infants and their postpartum depressed mothers. *Infant Behavior and Development, 7,* 527–532.

Field, T. M. (1985). Neonatal perception of people: Maturational and individual differences. In T. M. Field & N. Fox (Eds.), *Social perception in infants* (pp. 31–52). Norwood, NJ: Ablex.

Field, T. M. (1992). Infants of depressed mothers. *Development and Psychopathology, 4,* 49–66.

Field, T. M. (1995). Infants of depressed mothers. *Infant Behaviour and Development, 18,* 1–15.

Field, T. M. (1998). Maternal depression effects on infants and early intervention. *Preventative Medicine, 27,* 200–203.

Field, T. M. (2003). Stimulation of preterm infants. *Pediatrics in Review, 24*(1), 4–11.

Field, T. M. (2005). Prenatal depression effects on fetus and neonate. In J. Nadel & D. Muir (Eds.), *Emotional development* (pp. 317–340). Oxford: Oxford University Press.

Field, T. M., Fox, N. A., Pickens, J., & Nawrocki, T. (1995). Right frontal EEG activation in 3-to-6 month old infants of depressed mothers. *Developmental Psychology, 31,* 358–363.

Field, T. M., Healy, B., Goldstein, S., Perry, S., Bendall, D., Schanberg, S., et al. (1988). Infants of depressed mothers show "depressed" behavior even with non-depressed adults. *Child Development, 59,* 1569–1579.

Fifer, W. P., & Moon, C. M. (1995). The effects of fetal experience with sound. In J.-P. Lecanuet, W. P. Fifer, N. A. Krasnegor, & W. P. Smotherman (Eds.), *Fetal development: A psychobiological perspective* (pp. 351–366). Hillsdale, NJ: Erlbaum.

Fischer, K. W., & Rose, S. P. (1994). Dynamic development of coordination of components in brain and behaviour: A framework for theory and research. In G. Dawson & K. W. Fischer (Eds.), *Human behavior and the developing brain* (pp. 3–66). New York: Guilford Press.

Fitzgerald, M. (1991). The development of descending brainstem control of spinal cord sensory processing. In M. A. Hanson (Ed.), *The fetal and neonatal brain stem: Developmental and clinical issues* (pp. 127–136). Cambridge, England: Cambridge University Press.

Fivaz-Depeursinge, E., & Corboz-Warnery, A. (1999). *The primary triangle: A developmental systems view of mothers, fathers and infants.* New York: Basic Books.

Fletcher, P., Frith, C., Frackowiak, R., & Dolan, R. (1996). Brain activity during memory retrieval: The influence of imagery and semantic cueing. *Brain, 119,* 1587–1596.

Fonagy, P. (1998). Moments of change in psychoanalytic theory: Discussion of a new theory of psychic change. *Infant Mental Health, 19,* 346–351.

Fonagy, P. (2001). Changing ideas of change: The dual components of therapeutic action. In J. Edwards (Ed.), *Being alive: Building on the work of Anne Alvarez* (pp. 14–31). London: Brunner-Routledge.

Fonagy, P., & Target, M. (2003). *Psychoanalytic theories: Perspectives from developmental psychopathology.* London and Philadelphia: Whurr.

Forsyth, P., Kennedy, H., & Simpson, R. (1995). *An evaluation of video interaction guidance in families and teaching situations* (SOED Professional Development Initiatives, 1993–1994). Edinburgh, Scotland: Scottish Office.

Fraiberg, S. (1980). *Clinical studies in infant mental health: The first year of life.* London: Tavistock.

Fride, E., & Weinstock, M. (1988). Prenatal stress increases anxiety related behavior and alters cerebral lateralization of dopamine activity. *Life Science, 42,* 1059–1065.

Fuster, J. M. (1989). *The prefrontal cortex: Anatomy, physiology and neuropsychology of the frontal lobe.* New York: Raven Press.

Gabrieli, J. D., McGlinchey-Berroth, R., Carrillo, M. C., Gluck, M. A., Cermak, L. S., & Disterhoft, J. F. (1995). Intact delay-eyeblink classical conditioning in amnesia. *Behavioural Neuroscience, 109,* 819–827.

Gallese, V., Keysers, C., & Rizzolatti, G. (2004). A unifying view of the basis of social cognition. *TRENDS in Cognitive Sciences, 8*(9), 396–403.

Gans, C., & Northcutt, R. G. (1983). Neural crest and the origin of vertebrates: A new head. *Science, 220,* 268–274.

Garmezy, N., & Masten, A. S. (1994). Chronic adversities. In M. Rutter, L. Herzov, & E. Taylor (Eds.), *Child and adolescent psychiatry* (3rd ed., pp. 191–208). Oxford: Blackwell.

Gaspar, P., Cases, O., & Maroteaux, L. (2003). The developmental role of serotonin: News from mouse molecular genetics. *Nature Reviews Neuroscience, 4,* 1002–1012.

Gilles, F. H., Shankle, W., & Dooling, E. G. (1983). Myelinated tracts: Growth patterns. In F. H. Gilles, A. Leviton, & E. G. Dooling (Eds.), *The developing brain: Growth and epidemiological neuropathology* (pp. 117–183). Boston: John Wright.

Gilroy, A., & Lee, C. (Eds.). (1995). *Art and music: Therapy and research.* London: Routledge.

Gitau, R., Fisk, N., Teixeira, J. M., Cameron, A., & Glover, V. (2001). Fetal HPA stress responses to invasive procedures are independent of maternal responses. *Journal of Clinical and Endocrinological Metabolism, 86,* 104–109.

Glynn, L. M., Wadhwa, P. D., & Sandman, C. A. (2000). The influence of corticotropin releasing hormone on human fetal development and parturition. *Journal of Prenatal and Perinatal Psychic Health, 14,* 243–256.

Goho, S., & Bell, G. (2000). The ecology and genetics of fitness in Chlamydomonas: IX. The rate of accumulation of variation in fitness under selection. *Evolution, 54,* 416–424.

Gold, C., Vorachek, M., & Wigram, T. (2004). Effects of music therapy for children and adolescents with psychopathology: A meta-analysis. *Journal of Child Psychology and Psychopathology, 45*(6), 1054–1063.

Goldman-Rakic, P. S. (1987). Development of cortical circuitry and cognitive function. *Child Development, 58,* 601–622.

Gomes-Pedro, J., Nugent, J. K., Young, J. G., & Brazelton, T. B. (Eds.). (2002). *The infant and family in the twenty-first century.* New York: Brunner-Routledge.

Gore, A. (1992). *The earth in balance: Forging a new common purpose.* London: Earth Scan Publications.

Gratier, M. (2003). Expressive timing and interactional synchrony between mothers and infants: Cultural similarities, cultural differences, and the immigration experience. *Cognitive Development, 18,* 533–554.

Greenough, W. T., & Black, J. E. (1992). Induction of brain structure by experience: Substrates for cognitive development. In M. R. Gunnar & C. A. Nelson (Eds.), *Minnesota Symposium on Child Psychology: Vol. 24. Developmental behavioral neuroscience* (pp. 155–200). Mahwah, NJ: Erlbaum.

Greenspan, S. I. (1981). *Psychopathology and adaptation in infancy and early childhood.* New York: International Universities Press.

Groome, L. J., Bentz, L. S., & Singh, K. P. (1995). Behavioral state organization in normal human term fetuses: The relationship between periods of undefined state and other characteristics of state control. *Sleep, 18,* 77–81.

Gunnar, M. R. (1998). Quality of early care and buffering of neuroendocrine stress reactions: Potential effects on the developing human brain. *Preventive Medicine, 27,* 209–210.

Gunnar, M. R., Larson, M. C., Hertsgaard, L., Harris, M. L., & Brodersen, L. (1992). The stressfulness of separation among nine-month-old infants: Effects of social context variables and infant temperament. *Child Development, 63,* 290–303.

Gunnar, M. R., Tout, K., de Haan, M., Pierce, S., & Stansbury, K. (1997). Temperament, social competence, and adrenocortical activity in preschoolers. *Developmental Psychobiologist, 31,* 65–85.

Gutstein, S. E., & Sheely, R. K. (2002). *Relationship development intervention with young children: Social and emotional development activities for Asperger syndrome, Autism, PDD, and NLD.* London: Jessica Kingsley.

Halliday, M. A. K. (1975). *Learning how to mean: Explorations in the development of language.* London: Edward Arnold.

Hamil, R. W. (2004). Autonomic nervous system: Nature and functional neuroanatomy. In G. Adelman & B. H. Smith (Eds.), *Encyclopedia of neuroscience* (3rd ed., Article 646). Amsterdam: Elsevier Science.

Hamilton, W. J., Boyd, J. D., & Mossman, H. W. (1962). *Human embryology: Prenatal development of form and function* (3rd ed.). Cambridge, England: Heffer.

Hardy, L. (1996). A test of catastrophe models of anxiety and sports performance against multidimensional anxiety theory models using the method of dynamic differences. *Anxiety, Stress and Coping: An International Journal, 9,* 69–86.

Hari, R., & Nishitani, N. (2004). From viewing of movement to imitation and understanding of other persons' acts: MEG studies of the human mirror-neuron system. In N. Kanwisher & J. Duncan (Eds.), *Functional neuroimaging of visual cognition: Attention and performance XX* (pp. 463–479). Oxford: Oxford University Press.

Harrison, R. G. (1933). Some difficulties of the determination problem. *American Naturalist, 67,* 306–321.

Hay, D. F. (1985). Learning to form relationships in infancy: Parallel attainments with parents and peers. *Developmental Review, 5,* 122–161.

Hay, D. F., & Kumar, R. (1995). Interpreting effects of mothers' postnatal depression on children's intelligence: A critique and re-analysis. *Child Psychiatry and Human Development, 253,* 165–181.

Hedegaard, M. (1999). Life style, work and stress, and pregnancy outcome. *Current Opinion in Obstetric Gynecology, 11,* 553–556.

Heimann, M. (1998). Imitation in neonates, in older infants and in children with Autism: Feedback to theory. In S. Bråten (Ed.), *Intersubjective communication and emotion in early ontogeny* (pp. 89–104). Cambridge, England: Cambridge University Press.

Held, R. (1985). Binocular vision: Behavioral and neuronal development. In J. Mehler & R. Fox (Eds.), *Neonate cognition: Beyond the blooming buzzing confusion* (pp. 37–44). Hillsdale, NJ: Erlbaum.

Held, R., Birch, E., & Gwiazda, J. (1980). Stereoacuity of human infants. *Proceedings of the National Academy of Sciences, USA, 77,* 5572–5574.

Henry, C., Kabbaj, M., Simon, H., Le Moal, M., & Maccari, S. (1994). Prenatal stress increases the hypothalamo-pituitary-adrenal axis response in young and adult rats. *Journal of Neuroendocrinology, 6,* 341–345.

Henry, J. P., & Stephens, P. M. (1977). *Stress, health and the social environment.* New York: Springer.

Hepper, P. G. (1995). The behavior of the fetus as an indicator of neural functioning. In J.-P. Lecanuet, W. P. Fifer, N. A. Krasnegor, & W. P. Smotherman (Eds.), *Fetal development: A psychobiolog
cal perspective* (pp. 405–417). Hillsdale, NJ: Erlbaum.

Herlenius, E., & Lagercrantz, H. (2004). Development of neurotransmitter systems during critical periods. *Experimental Neurology, 190* (Suppl. 1), S8–S21.

Hess, W. R. (1954). *Diencephalon: Autonomic and extrapyramidal functions.* Orlando, FL: Grune and Stratton.

Hessl, D., Dawson, G., Frey, K., Panagiotides, H., Self, H., Yamada, E., et al. (1998). A longitudinal study of children of depressed mothers: Psychobiological findings related to stress. In D. M. Hann, L. C. Huffman, K. K. Lederhendler, & D. Minecke (Eds.), *Advancing research on developmental plasticity: Integrating the behavioral sciences and the neurosciences of mental health.* Bethesda, MD: National Institutes of Mental Health.

Hobson, P. (2002). *The cradle of thought: Exploring the origins of thinking.* London: Macmillan.

Hofer, M. A. (1987). Early social relationships: A psychobiologist's view. *Child Development, 58,* 633–647.

Holstege, G., Bandler, R., & Saper, C. B. (Eds.). (1996). *The emotional motor system.* Amsterdam: Elsevier.

Hubley, P., & Trevarthen, C. (1979). Sharing a task in infancy. In I. Uzgiris (Ed.), *Social interaction during infancy: Vol. 4. New directions for child development* (pp. 57–80). San Francisco: Jossey-Bass.

Huether, G. (1996). The central adaptation syndrome: Psychosocial stress as a trigger for adaptive modifications of brain structure and brain function. *Progress in Neurobiology, 48*(6), 569–612.

Hughes, D. (1997). *Facilitating developmental attachment: The road to emotional recovery and behavioral change in foster and adopted children.* New York: Aronson.

Hughes, D. (1998). *Building the bonds of attachment: Awakening love in deeply traumatized children.* Northvale, NJ: Aronson.

Huizinck, A. C., Mulder, E. J. H., & Buitelaar, J. K. (2004). Prenatal stress and risk for psychopathology: Specific effects of induction of general susceptibility? *Psychological Bulletin, 1,* 115–142.

Hundertmark, S., Dill, A., Ebert, A., Zimmermann, B., Kotelevtsev, Y. V., Mullins, J. J., et al. (2002). Foetal lung maturation in 11beta-hydroxysteroid dehydrogenase Type 1 knockout mice. *Hormone and Metabolic Research, 34*(10), 545–549.

Huttenlocher, P. R. (1990). Morphometric study of human cerebral cortex development. *Neuropsychologia, 28,* 517–527.

Innocenti, G. M. (1983). Exuberant callosal projections between the developing hemispheres. In R. Villani, I. Papo, M. Giovanelli, S. M. Gaini, & G. Tomei (Eds.), *Advances in neurotraumatology.* Amsterdam: Excerpta Medica.

Isaacson, R. L. (2004). Hippocampus. In G. Adelman & B. H. Smith (Eds.), *Encyclopedia of neuroscience* (3rd ed., Article 58). Amsterdam: Elsevier Science.

Ito, N., Ito, T., & Paus, R. (2005). The human hair follicle has established a fully functional peripheral equivalent of the hypothamalic-pituitary-adrenal axis (HPA). *Experimental Dermatology, 14,* 158.

Iversen, L. L. (2004). Neurotransmitters. In G. Adelman & B. H. Smith (Eds.), *Encyclopedia of neuroscience* (3rd ed., Article 59). Amsterdam: Elsevier Science.

Jaenisch, R., & Bird, A. (2003). Epigenetic regulation of gene expression: How the genome integrates intrinsic and environmental signals. *Nature Genetics, 33,* 245–254.

James, D., Pillai, M., & Smoleniec, J. (1995). Neurobehavioral development in the human fetus. In J.-P. Lecanuet, W. P. Fifer, N. A. Krasnegor, & W. P. Smotherman (Eds.), *Fetal development: A psychobiological perspective* (pp. 101–128). Hillsdale, NJ: Erlbaum.

Jansen, R., & Wels, P. (1998). The effects of video home training in families with a hyperactive child. In G. Forrest (Ed.), *Psychopathology and developmental disorders* (Occasional papers, Series No. 15, pp. 63–73). London, England: Association for Child and Adolescent Mental Health.

Jarskog, L. F., Xiao, H., Wilkie, M. B., Lauder, J. M., & Gilmore, J. H. (1997). Cytokine regulation of embryonic rat dopamine and serotonin neuronal survival in vitro. *International Journal of Developmental Neurosciences, 15*(6), 711–716.

Jeannerod, M. (1994). The representing brain: Neural correlates of motor intention and imagery. *Behavioral and Brain Sciences, 17,* 187–245.

Jeannerod, M. (1999). To act or not to act: Perspectives on the representation of actions—The 25th Bartlett Lecture. *Quarterly Journal of Experimental Psychology: Section A. Human Experimental Psychology, 52*(1), 1–29.

Jensen, O. (1984). Fetal heart rate response to controlled sound stimuli during the third trimester of normal pregnancy. *Acta Obstetrics et Gynecologica Scandanavica, 63,* 193–197.

Jernberg, A. M., & Booth, P. B. (2001). *Theraplay: Helping parents and children build better relationships through attachment-based play* (2nd ed.). San Francisco: Jossey-Bass.

Johnson, M. H. (1998). Developmental cognitive neuroscience: Looking ahead. *Development and Parenting, 7,* 163–169.

Johnston, M. V. (1995). Neurotransmitters and vulnerability of the developing brain. *Brain Development, 17*(5), 301–306.

Jones, C. T. (1993). Endocrine and metabolic interaction between placenta and fetus: Pathways of maternal-fetal communication. In C. W. G. Redman, I. L. Sargent, & P. M. Starkey (Eds.), *The human placenta: A guide for clinicians and scientists* (pp. 527–557). Oxford: Blackwell Scientific.

Jones, C. T., Hartmann, M., Blaschitz, A., & Desoye, G. (1993). Ultrastructural localization of insulin receptors in human placenta. *American Journal of Reproductive Immunology, 30*(2, 3), 136–145.

Joseph, R. (1999). Environmental influences on neural plasticity, the limbic system, emotional development and attachment. *Child Psychiatry and Human Development, 29,* 187–203.

Juffer, F., Bakermans-Kranenburg, M. J., & van Ijzendoorn, M. H. (2005). The importance of parenting in the development of disorganized attachment: Evidence from a preventive intervention study in adoptive families. *Journal of Child Psychology and Psychiatry, 46*(3), 263–274.

Kalia, M. (2004). Vagus nerve and control of the autonomic nervous system. In G. Adelman & B. H. Smith (Eds.), *Encyclopedia of neuroscience* (3rd ed., Article 910). Amsterdam: Elsevier Science.

Kalin, N. H., Larson, C., Shelton, S. E., & Davidson, R. J. (1998). Asymmetric frontal brain activity, cortisol, and behavior associated with fearful temperament in rhesus monkeys. *Behavioral Neuroscience, 112,* 286–292.

Kammerer, M., Adams, D., von Castelberg, B., & Glover, V. (2002). Pregnant women become insensitive to cold stress. *BMC Pregnancy and Childbirth, 2,* 8.

Kendall-Tackett, K. A., Meyer-Williams, L., & Finkelhor, D. (1993). Impact of sexual abuse on children: A review and synthesis of recent empirical studies. *Psychological Bulletin, 113*(1), 164–180.

Kennell, J. H., Jerauld, R., Wolfe, H., Chesler, D., Kreger, N. C., McAlpine, W., et al. (1974). Maternal behavior one year after early and extended postpartum contact. *Developmental Medicine and Child Neurology, 16*(2), 172–179.

Kerr, I. (2005). Cognitive analytic therapy. *Psychiatry, 4*(5), 28–33.

Kobayashi, H., & Kohshima, S. (2001). Evolution of the human eye as a device for communication. In T. Matsuzawa (Ed.), *Primate origins of human communication and behavior* (pp. 383–401). Tokyo: Springer.

Kobernick, K., & Pierler, T. (2002). Gli-type zinc finger proteins as bipotential transducers of hedgehog signalling. *Differentiation, 70,* 69–76.

Kohut, H. (1984). *How does analysis cure?* Chicago: University of Chicago Press.

Kohyama, J. (1998). Sleep as a window on the developing brain. *Current Problems in Pediatrics, 27,* 73–92.

Korte, S. M. (2001). Corticosteroids in relation to fear, anxiety and psychopathology. *Neuroscience and Biobehavioral Reviews, 25*(2), 117–142.

Korte, S. M., Buwalda, B., Meijer, O., De Kloet, E. R., & Bohus, B. (1995). Socially defeated male rats display a blunted adrenocortical response to a low dose of 8-OH-DPAT. *European Journal of Pharmacology, 272,* 45–50.

Korte, S. M., Koolhaas, J. M., Wingfield, J. C., & McEwen, B. S. (2005). The Darwinian concept of stress: Benefits of allostasis and costs of allostatic load and the trade-offs in health and disease. *Neuroscience and Biobehavioral Reviews, 29,* 3–38.

Kraemer, G. W. (1992). A psychobiological theory of attachment. *Behavioural and Brain Sciences, 15*(3), 493–541.

Kristensen, T. N., Sorensen, J. G., & Loeschcke, V. (2003). Mild heat stress at a young age in Drosophila melanogaster leads to increased Hsp70 synthesis after stress exposure later in life. *Journal of Genetics, 82,* 89–94.

Kugiumutzakis, G. (1998). Neonatal imitation in the intersubjective companion space. In S. Bråten (Ed.), *Intersubjective communication and emotion in early ontogeny* (pp. 63–88). Cambridge, England: Cambridge University Press.

Lagercrantz, H. (1996). Stress, arousal and gene activation at birth. *News in Physiological Sciences, 11,* 214–218.

Lamb, M. E., Thompson, R. A., Gardner, W. P., Charnov, E. L., & Estes, D. (1984). Security of infantile attachment as assessed in the "Strange Situation": Its study and biological interpretation. *Behavioral and Brain Sciences, 7,* 127–171.

Langley, J. N. (1921). *The autonomic nervous system.* Cambridge, England: Heffer.

Lecanuet, J.-P., Fifer, W. P., Krasnegor, N. A., & Smotherman, W. P. (Eds.). (1995). *Fetal development: A psychobiological perspective.* Hillsdale, NJ: Erlbaum.

LeDoux, J. E. (2000). Emotion circuits in the brain. *Annual Review of Neuroscience, 23,* 155–184.

Lee, D. N. (1998). Guiding movement by coupling taus. *Ecological Psychology, 10*(3, 4), 221–250.

Lee, D. N. (2004). Tau in action in development. In J. J. Rieser, J. J. Lockman, & C. A. Nelson (Eds.), *Action, perception and cognition in learning and development* (pp. 3–49). Hillsdale, NJ: Erlbaum.

Levine, S .K., Knill, P. J., & Levine, E. G. (2003). *Principles and practice of expressive arts therapy: Towards a therapeutic aesthetic.* London: Jessica Kingsley.

Lewis, D. A. (1997). Development of the primate frontal cortex. In M. S. Keshavan & R. M. Murray (Eds.), *Neurodevelopment and adult psychopathology* (pp. 12–30). Cambridge, England: Cambridge University Press.

Lewis, E. B. (1994). Homeosis: The first 100 years. *Trends in Genetics, 10*(10), 341–343.

Lewis, E. B. (1998). The bithorax complex. *International Journal of Developmental Biology, 42,* 403–415.

Leyton, L., Leguen, P., Bunch, D., & Saling, P. M. (1992). Regulation of mouse gamete interaction by a sperm tyrosine kinase. *Proceedings of the National Academy of Sciences, USA, 89*(24), 11692–11695.

Liotti, G. (1999). Disorganization of attachment as a model for understanding dissociative psychopathology. In J. Solomon & C. George (Eds.), *Attachment disorganization* (pp. 291–317). New York: Guilford Press.

Lou, H. C., Hansen, D., Nordentoft, M., Pryds, O., Jensen, F., Nim, J., et al. (1995). Prenatal stressors of human life affect fetal brain development. *Developmental Medicine and Child Neurology, 37*(2), 185.

Luciana, M. (2001). Dopamine-opiate modulations of reward-seeking behavior: Implications for the functional assessment of prefrontal development. In C. A. Nelson & M. Luciana (Eds.), *Handbook of developmental cognitive neuroscience* (pp. 647–662). Cambridge, MA: MIT Press.

Luthar, S. S., Cicchetti, D., & Becker, B. (2000). The construct of resilience: A critical evaluation and guidelines for future work. *Child Development, 71,* 543–562.

Lyon, G., & Gadisseux, J.-F. (1991). Structural abnormalities of the brain in developmental disorders. In M. Rutter & P. Casaer (Eds.), *Biological risk factors for psychosocial disorders* (pp. 1–19). Cambridge, England: Cambridge University Press.

Lyons-Ruth, K., Connell, D. B., Grunebaum, H. U., & Botein, S. (1990). Infants at social risk: Maternal depression and family support services as mediators of infant development and security of attachment. *Child Development, 61*(1), 85–98.

Maccari, S., Darnaudery, M., Morley-Fletcher, S., Zuena, A. R., Cinque, C., & Van Reeth, O. (2003). Prenatal stress and long-term consequences: Implications of glucocorticoid hormones. *Neuroscience and Biobehavioral Reviews, 27,* 119–127.

MacLean, P. D. (1952). Some psychiatric implications of physiological studies on frontotemporal portion of limbic system (visceral brain). *Electroencephalography and Clinical Neurophysiology, 4,* 407–418.

MacLean, P. D. (1990). *The triune brain in evolution: Role in paleocerebral functions.* New York: Plenum Press.

MacLean, P. D. (2004). Triune brain. In G. Adelman & B. H. Smith (Eds.), *Encyclopedia of neuroscience* (3rd ed., Article 203). Amsterdam: Elsevier Science.

Magarinos, A. M., Verdugo, J. M. G., & McEwen, B. S. (1997). Chronic stress alters synaptic terminal structure in hippocampus. *Proceedings of the National Academy of Sciences, USA, 94,* 14002–14008.

Maiello, S. (2001). On temporal shapes: The relation between primary rhythmical experience and the quality of mental links. In J. Edwards (Ed.), *Being alive: Building on the work of Anne Alvarez* (pp. 179–194). London: Brunner-Routledge.

Main, M., & Goldwyn, R. (1984). Predicting rejection of her infant from mother's representation of her own experience: Implications for the abused-abusing intergenerational cycle. *International Journal of Child Abuse and Neglect, 8,* 203–217.

Main, M., & Solomon, J. (1986). Discovery of an insecure-disorganized/disoriented attachment pattern. In T. B. Brazelton & M. W. Yogman (Eds.), *Affective development in infancy* (pp. 95–124). Norwood, NJ: Ablex.

Malberg, J. E. (2004). Implications of adult hippocampal neurogenesis in antidepressant action. *Journal of Psychiatry and Neuroscience, 3,* 196–205.

Malloch, S. (1999). Mother and infants and communicative musicality. In I. Deliège (Ed.), *Rhythms, musical narrative, and the origins of human communication: Musicae Scientiae, 1999–2000* (pp. 29–57) [Special issue]. Liège, Belgium: European Society for the Cognitive Sciences of Music.

Markowitsch, H. J. (1998). Differential contribution of the right and left amygdala to affective information processing. *Behavioural Neurology, 11,* 233–244.

Markowitsch, H. J., Kessler, J., Kalbe, E., & Herholz, K. (1999). Functional amnesia and memory consolidation. A case of persistent anterograde amnesia with rapid forgetting following whiplash injury. *Neurocase, 5,* 189–200.

Markowitsch, H. J., Kessler, J., Russ, M. O., Frölich, L., Schneider, B., & Maurer, K. (1999). Mnestic block syndrome. *Cortex, 35,* 219–230.

Markowitsch, H. J., Thiel, A., Reinkemeier, M., Kessler, J., Koyuncu, A., & Heiss, W.-D. (2000). Right amygdalar and temporofrontal activation during autobiographic, but not during fictitious memory retrieval. *Behavioural Neurology, 12,* 181–190.

Markowitsch, H. J., Vandekerckhove, M. M. P., Lanfermann, H., & Russ, M. O. (2003). Brain circuits for the retrieval of sad and happy autobiographic episodes. *Cortex, 39,* 643–665.

Marti, E., & Bovolenta, P. (2002). Sonic hedgehog in CNS development: One signal, multiple outputs. *Trends in Neuroscience, 25*(2), 89–96.

Masten, A. S. (2001). Ordinary magic: Resilience processes in development. *American Psychologist, 56,* 227–238.

Matthews, K. A., & Rodin, J. (1992). Pregnancy alters blood pressure responses to psychological and physical challenge. *Psychophysiology, 29,* 232–240.

Matthews, S. G. (2001). Antenatal glucocorticoids and the developing brain: Mechanisms of action. *Seminars in Neonatology, 6*(4), 309–317.

McEwen, B. S. (1989). Endocrine effects on the brain and their relationship to behavior. In G. Siegel, B. Agranoff, R. W. Albers, & P. Molinoff (Eds.), *Basic neurochemistry* (4th ed., pp. 893–913). New York: Raven Press.

McEwen, B. S. (1997a). The brain is an important target of adrenal steroid actions: A comparison of synthetic and natural steroids. *Annals of the New York Academy of Sciences, 823,* 201–213.

McEwen, B. S. (1997b). Hormones as regulators of brain development: Life-long effects related to health and disease. *Acta Paediatrica Supplement, 422,* 41–44.

McEwen, B. S. (1999). Stress and hippocampal plasticity. *Annual Review of Neurosciences, 22,* 105–122.

McEwen, B. S. (2001). From molecules to mind: Stress, individual differences, and the social environment. *Annals of the New York Academy of Sciences, 93,* 42–49.

McEwen, B. S. (2002). Sex, stress and the hippocampus: Allostasis, allostatic load and the aging process. *Neurobiology of Aging, 23,* 921–939.

McEwen, B. S. (2003). Early life influences on life-long patterns of behavior and health: Mental retardation and developmental disabilities. *Research Reviews, 9,* 149–154.

McEwen, B. S., & Stellar, E. (1993). Stress and the individual: Mechanisms leading to disease. *Archives of Internal Medicine, 18,* 2093–2101.

McEwen, B. S., & Wingfield, J. C. (2003). The concept of allostasis in biology and biomedicine. *Hormonal Behaviour, 43,* 2–15.

McGaugh, J. L., Roozendall, B., & Cahill, L. (2000). Modulation of memory storage by stress hormones and the amygdala complex. In M. S. D. Gazzaniga (Ed.), *The new cognitive sciences* (2nd. ed., pp. 1081–1098). Cambridge, MA: MIT Press.

McGeer, P. L., Eccles, J. C., & McGeer, E. G. (1978). *Molecular neuroembryology of the mammalian brain.* New York: Plenum Press.

McKenna, J. J., & Mosko, S. (1994). Sleep and arousal, synchrony and independence among mothers and infants sleeping apart and together (same bed): An experiment in evolutionary medicine. *Acta Paediatrica Supplement, 397,* 94–102.

Merker, B. (2004). Cortex, countercurrent context, and dimensional integration of lifetime memory. *Cortex, 40,* 559–576.

Merker, B. (2005). The liabilities of mobility: A selection pressure for the transition to consciousness in animal evolution. *Consciousness and Cognition, 14*(1), 89–114.

Merker, B., & Wallin, N. L. (2001). Musical responsiveness in Rett disorder. In A. Kerr & I. Witt-Engerstrom (Eds.), *Rett disorder and the developing brain* (pp. 327–338). Oxford: Oxford University Press.

Miles, R. (1999). Neurobiology: A homeostatic switch. *Nature, 397,* 215–216.

Monk, C., Sloan, R. P., Myers, M. M., Ellman, L., Werner, E., Jeon, J., et al. (2004). Fetal heart rate reactivity differs by women's psychiatric status: An early marker for developmental risk? *Journal of the American Academy of Child and Adolescent Psychiatry, 43*(3), 283–290.

Montello, L. (1999). A psychoanalytic music therapy approach to treating adults traumatized as children. *Music Therapy Perspectives, 17*(2), 74–81.

Morgan, M. A., & LeDoux, J. E. (1995). Differential acquisition of dorsal and ventral medial prefrontal cortex to the acquisition and extinction of conditioned fear in rats. *Behavioural Neuroscience, 109,* 681–688.

Murray, L. (1988). Effects of postnatal depression on infant development: Direct studies of early mother-infant interactions. In R. Kumar & I. Brockington (Eds.), *Motherhood and mental illness* (Vol. 2, Causes and Consequences, pp. 159–190). London, England: John Wright.

Murray, L. (1992). The impact of postnatal depression on infant development. *Journal of Child Psychology and Psychiatry, 33*(3), 543–561.

Murray, L., & Cooper, P. J. (Eds.). (1997). *Postpartum depression and child development.* New York: Guilford Press.

Murray, L., Kempton, C., Woolgar, M., & Hooper, R. (1993). Depressed mothers' speech to their infants and its relation to infant gender and cognitive development. *Journal of Child Psychology and Psychiatry, 34*(7), 1083–1101.

Murray, L., Stanley, C., Hooper, R., King, F., & Fiori-Cowley, A. (1996). The role of infant factors in postnatal depression and mother-infant interactions. *Developmental Medicine and Child Neurology, 38*(2), 109–119.

Murray, L., & Trevarthen, C. (1985). Emotional regulation of interactions between two-month-olds and their mothers. In T. M. Field & N. Fox (Eds.), *Social perception in infants* (pp. 177–197). Norwood, NJ: Ablex.

Murray, L., Woolgar, M., Briers, S., & Hipwell, A. (1999). Children's social representations in dolls' house play and theory of mind tasks, and their relation to family adversity and child disturbance. *Social Development, 8*(2), 179–200.

Nadel, J., & Tremblay-Leveau, H. (1999). Early perception of social contingencies and interpersonal intentionality: Dyadic and triadic paradigms. In P. Rochat (Ed.), *Early social cognition: Understanding others in the first months of life* (pp. 189–212). Mahwah, NJ: Erlbaum.

Nafstad, A., & Rodbroe, I. (1999). *Co-creating communication.* Oslo, Norway: Forlaget-Nord Press.

Nagy, E., & Molnar, P. (2004). Homo imitans or Homo provocans? Human imprinting model of neonatal imitation. *Infant Behaviour and Development, 27*(1), 54–63.

Naqui, S. Z. H., Harris, B. S., Thomaidou, D., & Parnavelas, J. G. (1999). The noradrenergic system influences in fate of Cajal-Retzius cells in the developing cerebral cortex. *Developmental Brain Research, 113,* 75–82.

Nathanielsz, P. W. (1995). The effects of myometrial activity during the last third of gestation on fetal behavior. In J.-P. Lecanuet, W. P. Fifer, N. A. Krasnegor, & W. P. Smotherman (Eds.), *Fetal development: A psychobiological perspective* (pp. 369–382). Hillsdale, NJ: Erlbaum.

Nelson, C. A., & Luciana, M. (Eds.). (2001). *Handbook of developmental cognitive neuroscience.* Cambridge, MA: MIT Press.

Nemeroff, C. B., Widerlov, E., Bissette, G., Walleus, H., Karlsson, I., Eklund, K., et al. (1984). Elevated concentrations of CSF corticotropin-releasing factor-like immunoreactivity in depressed patients. *Science, 226*(4680), 1342–1344.

Nieuwenhuis, S., Yeung, N., van den Wildenberg, W., & Ridderinkhof, K. R. (2003). Electrophysiological correlates of anterior cingulate function in a go/no-go task: Effects of response conflict and trial type frequency. *Cognitive, Affective and Behavioral Neuroscience, 3,* 17–26.

Nissen, E., UvnasMoberg, K., Svensson, K., Stock, A. M., Widstrom, A. M., & Winberg, J. (1996). Different patterns of oxytocin, prolactin but not cortisol release during breastfeeding in women delivered by caesarean section or by the vaginal route. *Early Human Development, 45*(1, 2), 103–118.

Nugent, K. J. (2002). The cultural context of child development: Implications for research and practice in the twenty-first century. In J. Gomes-Pedro, J. K. Nugent, J. G. Young, & T. B. Brazelton (Eds.), *The infant and family in the twenty-first century* (pp. 87–98). New York: Brunner-Routledge.

O'Connor, T. G., Heron, J., Golding, J., Beveridge, M., & Glover, V. (2002). Maternal antenatal anxiety and children's behavioural/emotional problems at 4 years: Report from the Avon Longitudinal Study of Parents and Children. *British Journal of Psychiatry, 180,* 502–508.

Ohman, A., Flykt, A., & Lundqvist, D. (2000). Unconscious emotion, evolutionary perspective, psychophysiological data, and neuropsychological mechanisms. In R. D. Lane & L. Nadel (Eds.), *Cognitive neuroscience of emotion* (pp. 296–327). New York: Oxford University Press.

O'Keefe, J., & Nadel, L. (1978). *The hippocampus as a cognitive map.* Oxford University Press.

O'Rahilly, R., & Müller, F. (1994). *The embryonic human brain: An atlas of developmental stages.* New York: Wiley-Liss.

Ornitz, E. M., & Pynoos, R. (1989). Startle modulation in children with posttraumatic stress disorder. *American Journal of Psychiatry, 146,* 866–870.

Oster, H. (2005). The repertoire of infant facial expressions: An ontogenetic perspective. In J. Nadel & D. Muir (Eds.), *Emotional development* (pp. 261–292). Oxford: Oxford University Press.

Pacak, K., & Palkovits, M. (2001). Stressor specificity of central neuroendocrine responses: Implications for stress-related disorders. *Endocrinology Review, 22*(4), 502–548.

Paillard, J. (1960). The patterning of skilled movements. In *Handbook of physiology: Vol. III. Neurophysiology* (Sect. 1, pp. 1679–1708). Washington, DC: American Physiological Society.

Pander, C. (1817). *Beiträge zur Entwickelungseschichte des Hünchens im Eye.* Würzburg: Brönner.

Panksepp, J. (1993). Neurochemical control of moods and emotions, amino acids to neuropeptides. In M. Lewis & J. Haviland (Eds.), *The handbook of emotions* (pp. 87–107). New York: Guilford Press.

Panksepp, J. (1998a). *Affective neuroscience: The foundations of human and animal emotions.* New York: Oxford University Press.

Panksepp, J. (1998b). The periconscious substrates of consciousness: Affective states and the evolutionary origins of the SELF. *Journal of Consciousness Studies, 5,* 566–582.

Panksepp, J. (2000). Affective consciousness and the instinctual motor system: The neural sources of sadness and joy. In R. Ellis & N. Newton (Eds.), *The caldron of consciousness, motivation, affect and self-organization: Vol. 16. Advances in Consciousness Research* (pp. 27–54). Amsterdam: Benjamins.

Panksepp, J. (2003). At the interface of the affective, behavioral, and cognitive neurosciences: Decoding the emotional feelings of the brain. *Brain and Cognition, 52,* 4–14.

Panksepp, J. (2004). Affective consciousness and the origins of human mind: A critical role of brain research on animal emotions. *Impuls, 3,* 47–60.

Panksepp, J., & Bernatzky, G. (2002). Emotional sounds and the brain: The neuro-affective foundations of musical appreciation. *Behavioural Processes, 60,* 133–155.

Panksepp, J., & Burgdorf, J. (2003). "Laughing" rats and the evolutionary antecedents of human joy? *Physiology and Behavior, 79,* 533–547.

Papez, J. W. (1937). A proposed mechanism of emotion. *Archives of Neurology and Psychiatry, 38,* 725–743.

Parmelee, A. H., Sigman, M., Garbanati, J., Cohen, S., Beckwith, L., & Asarnow, R. (1994). Neonatal electroencephalographic organization and attention in early adolescence. In G. Dawson & W. Fischer (Eds.), *Human behavior and the developing brain* (pp. 537–554). New York: Guilford Press.

Pavlicevic, M. (1997). *Music therapy in context: Music, meaning and relationship.* London: Jessica Kingsley.

Penfield, W. (1958). *The excitable cortex in conscious man.* Liverpool, England: Liverpool University Press.

Perry, B. D., Pollard, R. A., Blakley, T. L., Baker, W. L., & Vigilante, D. (1995). Childhood trauma, the neurobiology of adaptation, and "use-dependent" development of the brain: How states become traits. *Infant Mental Health Journal, 16,* 271–291.

Pescucci, C., Meloni, I., & Renieri, A. (2005). Is Rett syndrome a loss-of-imprinting disorder? *Nature Genetics, 37*(1), 10–11.

Piaget, J. (1954). *The construction of reality in the child* (M. Cook, Trans.). New York: Basic Books.

Piefke, M., Weiss, P. H., Zilles, K., Markowitsch, H. J., & Fink, G. R. (2003). Differential remoteness and emotional tone modulate the neural correlates of autobiographical memory. *Brain, 126,* 850–868.

Piontelli, A. (1992). *From fetus to child.* London: Routledge.

Piontelli, A. (2002). *Twins: From fetus to child.* London: Routledge.

Ploog, D. (1992). Neuroethological perspectives on the human brain: From the expression of emotions to intentional signing and speech. In A. Harrington (Ed.), *So human a brain* (pp. 3–13). Boston, MA: Birkhäuser.

Pollak, S. D., Cicchetti, D., & Klorman, R. (1998). Stress, memory, and emotion: Developmental considerations from the study of child maltreatment. *Development and Psychopathology, 10,* 739–759.

Pöppel, E., & Wittmann, M. (1999). Time in the mind. In R. Wilson & F. Keil (Eds.), *The MIT encyclopedia of the cognitive sciences* (pp. 836–837). Cambridge, MA: MIT Press.

Porges, S. W. (1997). Emotion: An evolutionary by-product of the neural regulation of the autonomic nervous system. *Annals of the New York Academy of Sciences, 807,* 62–78.

Posner, M. I., & Petersen, S. E. (1990). The attention system of the human brain. *Annual Review of Neuroscience, 13,* 25–42.

Prechtl, H. F. R. (1984). Continuity and change in early human development. In H. F. R. Prechtl (Ed.), *Continuity of neural functions from prenatal to postnatal life* (Clinics in developmental medicine no. 94, pp. 1–13). Oxford: Blackwell.

Preston, S. D., & de Waal, F. (2002). Empathy: Its ultimate and proximate bases. *Behavioral and Brain Sciences, 25,* 1–72.

Price, J. L. (2004). Amygdala. In G. Adelman & B. H. Smith (Eds.), *Encyclopedia of neuroscience* (3rd ed., Article 442). Amsterdam: Elsevier Science.

Rakic, P. (1991). Development of the primate cerebral cortex. In M. Lewis (Ed.), *Child and adolescent psychiatry: A comprehensive textbook* (pp. 11–28). Baltimore: Williams & Wilkins.

Ralt, D., Goldenberg, M., Fetterolf, P., Thompson, D., Dor, J., Mashiach, S., et al. (1991). Sperm attraction to a follicular factor(s) correlates with human egg fertilizability. *Proceedings of the National Academy of Sciences, USA, 88,* 2840–2844.

Raphael-Leff, J. (2005). *Psychological processes of childbearing* (4th ed.). London: Anna Freud Centre.

Reddy, V. (1991). Playing with others' expectations: Teasing and mucking about in the first year. In A. Whiten (Ed.), *Natural theories of mind* (pp. 143–158). Oxford: Blackwell.

Reddy, V. (2001). Infant clowns: The interpersonal creation of humour in infancy. *Enfance, 3,* 247–256.

Reddy, V. (2003). On being the object of attention: Implications for self-other consciousness. *Trends in Cognitive Sciences, 7,* 397–402.

Reddy, V. (2005). Feeling shy and showing off: Self-conscious emotions during face-to-face interactions with live and "virtual" adults. In J. Nadel & D. Muir (Eds.), *Emotional development* (pp. 183–204). Oxford: Oxford University Press.

Reddy, V., & Morris, P. (2004). Participants don't need theories: Knowing minds in engagement. *Theory and Psychology, 14*(5), 649–667.

Reddy, V., & Trevarthen, C. (2004). What we learn about babies from engaging with their emotions. *Zero to Three, 24*(3), 9–15.

Reissland, N., Shepherd, J., & Herrera, E. (in press-a). The effect of maternal depressed mood on infant emotional reaction in a surprise-eliciting situation. *Infant Mental Health Journal.*

Reissland, N., Shepherd, J., & Herrera, E. (in press-b). Teasing play in infancy: Comparing mothers with and without self reported depressed mood during play with their babies. *European Journal of Developmental Psychology.*

Ringstedt, T., Tang, L. Q., Persson, H., Lendahl, U., & Lagercrantz, H. (1995). Expression of c-Fos, tyrozin hydroxilase, and neuropeptide mRNA in the rat brain around birth: Effects of hypoxia and hypothermia. *Pediatric Research, 37,* 15–20.

Rizzolatti, G., & Arbib, M. A. (1998). Language within our grasp. *Trends in Neurosiences, 21,* 188–194.

Robarts, J. Z. (2003). The healing function of improvised songs in music therapy with a child survivor of early trauma and sexual abuse. In S. Hadley (Ed.), *Psychodynamic music therapy: Case studies* (pp. 141–182). Gilsum, NH: Barcelona Publishers.

Robarts, J. Z. (in press). Integrative processes of affect regulation and symbol formation in music therapy with sexually abused children. *Clinical Child Psychology and Psychiatry.*

Robb, L. (1999). Emotional musicality in mother-infant vocal affect, and an acoustic study of postnatal depression. In I. Deliège (Ed.), *Rhythms, musical narrative, and the origins of human communication: Musicae Scientiae, 1999–2000,* [Special issue] (pp. 123–151). Liège, Belgium: European Society for the Cognitive Sciences of Music.

Robbins, M. (1992). Psychoanalytic and biological approaches to mental-illness: Schizophrenia. *Journal of the American Psychoanalytic Association, 40*(2), 425–454.

Robert, J. S. (2001). Interpreting the homeobox: Metaphors of gene action and activation in development and evolution. *Evolution and Development, 3*(4), 287–295.

Roegiers, F., & Jan, Y. N. (2004). Asymmetric cell division. *Current Opinion in Cell Biology, 16,* 195–205.

Rogers, P. (1995). Childhood sexual abuse: Dilemmas in therapeutic practice. *Music Therapy Perspectives, 13*(1), 24–30.

Rogoff, B. (2003). *The cultural nature of human development.* Oxford: Oxford University Press.

Ronca, A. E., & Alberts, J. R. (1995). Simulated uterine contractions facilitate fetal and newborn respiratory behavior in rats. *Physiology and Behavior, 58*(5), 1035–1041.

Roozendaal, B., de Quervain, J. F., Ferry, B., Setlow, B., & McGaugh, J. L. (2001). Basolateral amygdala-nucleus accumbens interactions in mediating glucocorticoid enhancement of memory consolidation. *Journal of Neuroscience, 21,* 2518–2525.

Rots, N. Y., De Jong, J., Workel, J. O., Levine, S., Cools, A. R., & De Kloet, E. R. (1996). Neonatal maternally deprived rats have as adults elevated basal pituitary-adrenal activity and enhanced susceptibility to apomorphine. *Journal of Neuroendocrinology, 8,* 501–506.

Rozman, K. K., & Doull, J. (2003). Scientific foundations of hormesis: Pt. 2. Maturation, strengths, limitations, and possible applications in toxicology, pharmacology, and epidemiology. *Critical Reviews in Toxicology, 33*(3, 4), 451–462.

Rutter, M. (1987). Psychosocial resilience and protective mechanisms. *American Journal of Orthopsychiatry, 57,* 316–331.

Sander, L. (1964). Adaptive relationships in early mother-child interaction. *Journal of the American Academy of Child Psychiatry, 3,* 231–264.

Sapolsky, R. M. (1993). Potential behavioral modification of glucocorticoid damage to the hippocampus. *Behavioural Brain Research, 7,* 175–182.

Sapolsky, R. M. (1996). Why stress is bad for the brain. *Science, 273,* 749–750.

Sapolsky, R. M. (2000). Glucocorticoids and hippocampal atrophy in neuropsychiatric disorders. *Archives of General Psychiatry, 57,* 925–935.

Sarter, M., & Bruno, J. P. (2000). Cortical cholinergic inputs mediating arousal, attentional processing, and dreaming: Differential afferent regulation of the basal forebrain by telencephalic and brainstem afferents. *Neuroscience, 95,* 933–952.

Sayer, A. A., Cooper, C., & Barker, D. J. (1997). Is lifespan determined in utero? *Archives of Disease in Childhood: Fetal and Neonatal Edition, 77,* F162–F164.

Schanberg, S. M., & Field, T. M. (1987). Sensory deprivation stress and supplemental stimulation in the rat pup and preterm human neonate. *Child Development, 58*(6), 1431–1447.

Schechter, D. S. (2004). How post-traumatic stress affects mothers' perceptions of their babies: A brief video feedback intervention makes a difference. *Zero to Three, 24*(3), 43–49.

Scherer, K. R. (1986). Vocal affect expression: A review and a model for future research. *Psychological Bulletin, 99,* 143–165.

Scherz, P. J., Harfe, B. D., McMahon, A. P., & Tabin, C. J. (2004). The limb bud Shh-Fgf feedback loop is terminated by expansion of former ZPA cells. *Science, 305*(5682), 396–399.

Schneider, S. Q., & Bowerman, B. (2003). Cell polarity and the cytoskeleton in the caenorhabditis elegans zygote. *Annual Review of Genetics, 37,* 221–249.

Schore, A. N. (1994). *Affect regulation and the origin of the self: The neurobiology of emotional development.* Hillsdale, NJ: Erlbaum.

Schore, A. N. (1996). The experience-dependent maturation of a regulatory system in the orbital prefrontal cortex and the origin of developmental psychopathology. *Development and Psychopathology, 8*(1), 59–87.

Schore, A. N. (1998). The experience-dependent maturation of an evaluative system in the cortex. In K. H. Pribram (Ed.), *Brain and values: Is a biological science of values possible?* (pp. 337–358). Mahwah, NJ: Erlbaum.

Schore, A. N. (2001a). The effect of a secure attachment relationship on right brain development affects regulation and infant mental health. *Infant Mental Health Journal, 22,* 7–66.

Schore, A. N. (2001b). The effects of early relational trauma on right brain development, affect regulation, and infant mental health. *Infant Mental Health, 22,* 201–269.

Schore, A. N. (2003a). *Affect dysregulation and disorders of self.* New York: Norton.

Schore, A. N. (2003b). *Affect regulation and the repair of the self.* New York: Norton.

Schore, A. N. (2003c). Early relational trauma, disorganized attachment, and the development of a predisposition to violence. In M. F. Solomon & D. J. Siegel (Eds.), *Healing trauma: Attachment, mind, body, and brain* (pp. 107–167). New York: W. W. Norton.

Schrödinger, E. (1944). *What is life? The physical aspect of the living cell.* Cambridge, England: Cambridge University Press.

Selby, J. M., & Bradley, B. S. (2003). Infants in groups: A paradigm for study of early social experience. *Human Development, 46,* 197–221.

Selye, H. (1956). *The stress of life.* New York: McGraw-Hill.

Sheline, Y. I., Sanghavi, M., Mintun, M. A., & Gado, M. H. (1999). Depression duration but not age predicts hippocampal volume loss in medically healthy women with recurrent major depression. *Journal of Neuroscience, 19,* 5034–5043.

Sherrington, C. S. (1906). *The integrative action of the nervous system.* New Haven, CT: Yale University Press.

Shin, L. M., Whalen, P. J., Pitman, R. K., Bush, G., Macklin, M. L., Lasko, N. B., et al. (2001). An fMRI study of anterior cingulate function in posttraumatic stress disorder. *Biological Psychiatry, 15,* 932–942.

Siebert, M., Markowitsch, H. J., & Bartel, P. (2003). Amygdala, affect and cognition: Evidence from 10 patients with Urbach-Wiethe disease. *Brain, 126,* 2627–2637.

Siegel, D. J. (1999). *The developing mind: Toward a neurobiology of interpersonal experience.* New York: Guilford Press.

Siegel, D. J. (2003). An interpersonal neurobiology of psychotherapy: The developing mind and the resolution of trauma. In M. F. Solomon & D. J. Siegel (Eds.), *Healing trauma: Attachment, mind, body, and brain* (pp. 1–56). New York: W. W. Norton.

Smith, A. (1976). *Theory of moral sentiments* (D. D. Raphael & A. L. Macfie, Eds.). Oxford: Clarendon Press. (Original work published 1759)

Smotherman, W. P., & Robinson, S. R. (1987). Prenatal influences on development: Behavior is not a trivial aspect of fetal life. *Development and Behavioral Pediatrics, 8,* 171–175.

Sperry, R. W. (1950). Neural basis of the spontaneous optokinetic response produced by visual inversion. *Journal of Comparative and Physiological Psychology, 43,* 483–489.

Starkman, M. N., Giordani, B., Gebarski, S. S., Berent, S., Schork, M. A., & Schteingart, D. E. (1999). Decrease in cortisol reverses human hippocampal atrophy following treatment of Cushing's disease. *Biological Psychiatry, 46,* 1595–1602.

Stefan, M. D., & Murray, R. M. (1997). Schizophrenia: Developmental disturbance of brain and mind? *Acta Paediatrica, 86,* 112–116.

Sterling, P., & Eyer, J. (1988). Allostasis: A new paradigm to explain arousal pathology. In S. Fisher & J. Reason (Eds.), *Handbook of life stress, cognition and health* (pp. 629–649). New York: Wiley.

Stern, D. N. (1974). Mother and infant at play: The dyadic interaction involving facial, vocal and gaze behaviours. In M. Lewis & L. A. Rosenblum (Eds.), *The effect of the infant on its caregiver* (pp. 187–213). New York: Wiley.

Stern, D. N. (1990). Joy and satisfaction in infancy. In R. A. Glick & S. Bone (Eds.), *Pleasure beyond the pleasure principle* (pp. 13–25). Newhaven, CT: Yale University Press.

Stern, D. N. (2000). *The interpersonal world of the infant: A view from psychoanalysis and development psychology* (2nd ed.). New York: Basic Books.

Stern, D. N., Hofer, L., Haft, W., & Dore, J. (1985). Affect attunement: The sharing of feeling states between mother and infant by means of inter-modal fluency. In T. M. Field & N. A. Fox (Eds.), *Social perception in infants* (pp. 249–268). Norwood, NJ: Ablex.

Stern, D. N., Speiker, R. K., & Mackain, K. (1982). Intonation contours as signals in maternal speech to prelinguistic infants. *Developmental Psychology, 18*(5), 727–735.

Storey, B. T. (1995). Interactions between gametes leading to fertilization: The sperm's eye view. *Reproduction, Fertility and Development, 7,* 927–942.

Stuss, D. T., Alexander, M. P., Floden, D., Binns, M. A., Levine, B., McIntosh, A. R., et al. (2002). Fractionation and localization of distinct frontal lobe processes: Evidence from focal lesions in humans. In D. T. Stuss & R. T. Knight (Eds.), *Principles of frontal lobe function* (pp. 392–407). New York: Oxford University Press.

Suchecki, D., Rosenfeld, P., & Levine, S. (1993). Maternal regulation of the hypothalamic-pituitary-adrenal axis in the infant rat: The roles of feeding and stroking. *Developmental Brain Research, 75*(2), 185–192.

Sullivan, R. M., Wilson, D. A., Lemon, C., & Gerhardt, G. A. (1994). Bilateral 6-OHDA lesions of the locus coeruleus impair associative olfactory learning in newborn rats. *Brain Research, 643,* 306–309.

Sundstrom, E., Kolare, S., Souverbie, F., Samuelsson, E. B., Pschera, H., Lunell, N. O., et al. (1993). Neurochemical differentiation of human bulbospinal monoamingergic neurons during the first trimester. *Brain Research, Developmental Brain Research, 75,* 1–12.

Suomi, S. J. (1997). Long-term effects of different early rearing experiences on social, emotional, and physiological development in nonhuman primates. In M. S. Keshavan & R. M. Murray (Eds.), *Neurodevelopment and adult psychopathology* (pp. 104–116). Cambridge: Cambridge University Press.

Susman, E. J., Schmeelk, K. H., Ponirakis, A., & Gariepy, J. L. (2001). Maternal prenatal, postpartum, and concurrent stressors and temperament in 3-year-olds: A person and variable analysis. *Development and Psychopathology 13*(3), 629–652.

Sutton, J. P. (Ed.). (2002). *Music, music therapy and trauma: International perspectives.* London: Jessica Kingsley.

Swanson, L. W. (2004). Limbic system. In G. Adelman & B. H. Smith (Eds.), *Encyclopedia of neuroscience* (3rd ed., Article 531). Amsterdam: Elsevier Science.

Tager-Flusberg, H. (1999). *Neurodevelopmental disorders.* Cambridge, MA: MIT Press.

Takahashi, L. K., & Kalin, N. H. (1991). Early developmental and temporal characteristics of stress-induced secretion of pituitary-adrenal hormones in prenatally stressed rat pups. *Brain Research, 558,* 75–78.

Tanaka, S., Kunath, T., Hadjantonakis, A.-K., Nagy, A., & Rossant, J. (1998). Promotion of trophoblast stem cell proliferation by FGF4. *Science, 282,* 2072–2075.

Teixeira, J. M., Glover, V., & Fisk, N. M. (1999). Acute cerebral redistribution in response to invasive procedures in the human fetus. *American Journal of Obstetric Gynecolgy, 181,* 1018–1025.

Thatcher, R. W. (1994). Psychopathology of early frontal lobe damage: Dependence on cycles of development. *Development and Psychopathology, 6,* 565–596.

Thompson, R. F. (2000). *The brain* (3rd ed.). New York: Worth.

Tinbergen, N. (1951). *The study of instinct.* Oxford: Clarendon Press.

Töpfer-Petersen, E., Wagner, A., Friedrich, J., Petrunkina, A., Ekhlasi-Hundrieser, M., Waberski, D., et al. (2002). Function of the mammalian oviductal sperm reservoir. *Journal of Experimental Zoology, 292,* 210–215.

Trevarthen, C. (1968a). Two mechanisms of vision in primates. *Psychologische Forschung, 31,* 299–337.

Trevarthen, C. (1968b). Vision in fish: The origins of the visual frame for action in vertebrates. In D. Ingle (Ed.), *The central nervous system and fish behaviour* (pp. 61–94). Chicago: University of Chicago Press.

Trevarthen, C. (1974). The psychobiology of speech development. In E. H. Lenneberg (Ed.), *Language and brain: Developmental aspects—Neurosciences research program bulletin* (Vol. 12, pp. 570–585). Boston: Neuroscience Research Program.

Trevarthen, C. (1979). Communication and cooperation in early infancy: A description of primary intersubjectivity. In M. Bullowa (Ed.), *Before speech: The beginning of human communication* (pp. 321–347). Cambridge, England: Cambridge University Press.

Trevarthen, C. (1985). Neuroembryology and the development of perceptual mechanisms. In F. Falkner & J. M. Tanner (Eds.), *Human growth* (2nd ed. pp. 301–383). New York: Plenum Press.

Trevarthen, C. (1986). Development of intersubjective motor control in infants. In M. G. Wade & H. T. A. Whiting (Eds.), *Motor development in children: Aspects of coordination and control* (pp. 209–261). Dordrecht, The Netherlands: Martinus Nijhoff.

Trevarthen, C. (1990). Signs before speech. In T. A. Sebeok & J. Umiker-Sebeok (Eds.), *The semiotic web* (pp. 689–755). New York: Walter de Gruyter.

Trevarthen, C. (1993a). The function of emotions in early infant communication and development. In J. Nadel & L. Camaioni (Eds.), *New perspectives in early communicative development* (pp. 48–81). London: Routledge.

Trevarthen, C. (1993b). The self born in intersubjectivity: An infant communicating. In U. Neisser (Ed.), *The perceived self: Ecological and interpersonal sources of self-knowledge* (pp. 121–173). New York: Cambridge University Press.

Trevarthen, C. (1996). Lateral asymmetries in infancy: Implications for the development of the hemispheres. *Neuroscience and Biobehavioral Reviews, 20*(4), 571–586.

Trevarthen, C. (1997). Foetal and neonatal psychology: Intrinsic motives and learning behaviour. In F. Cockburn (Ed.), *Advances in perinatal medicine* (pp. 282–291). New York: Parthenon.

Trevarthen, C. (1998a). The concept and foundations of infant intersubjectivity. In S. Bråten (Ed.), *Intersubjective communication and emotion in early ontogeny* (pp. 15–46). Cambridge, England: Cambridge University Press.

Trevarthen, C. (1998b). The nature of motives for human consciousness. *Psychology: Journal of the Hellenic Psychological Society, 4*(3), 187–221.

Trevarthen, C. (1999a). Musicality and the intrinsic motive pulse: Evidence from human psychobiology and infant communication. In I. Deliège (Ed.), *Rhythms, musical narrative, and the origins of human communication: Musicae Scientiae* (pp. 157–213). Liege, Belgium: European Society for the Cognitive Sciences of Music.

Trevarthen, C. (1999b). Intersubjectivity. In R. Wilson & F. Keil (Eds.), *The MIT encyclopedia of cognitive sciences* (pp. 413–416). Cambridge, MA: MIT Press.

Trevarthen, C. (2001a). Intrinsic motives for companionship in understanding: Their origin, development and significance for infant mental health. *International Journal of Infant Mental Health, 22*(1, 2), 95–131.

Trevarthen, C. (2001b). The neurobiology of early communication: Intersubjective regulations in human brain development. In A. F. Kalverboer & A. Gramsbergen (Eds.), *Handbook on brain and behavior in human development* (pp. 841–882). Dordrecht, The Netherlands: Kluwer Academic.

Trevarthen, C. (2004a). Brain development. In R. L. Gregory (Ed.), *Oxford companion to the mind* (2nd ed., pp. 116–127). Oxford: Oxford University Press.

Trevarthen, C. (2004b). How infants learn how to mean. In M. Tokoro & L. Steels (Eds.), *A learning zone of one's own* (SONY Future of Learning Series; pp. 37–69). Amsterdam: IOS Press.

Trevarthen, C. (2004c). Infancy, mind in. In R. L. Gregory (Ed.), *Oxford companion to the mind* (2nd ed., pp. 455–464). Oxford: Oxford University Press.

Trevarthen, C. (2004d). Language development: Mechanisms in the brain. In G. Adelman & B. H. Smith (Eds.), *Encyclopedia of neuroscience* (3rd ed., Article 397). Amsterdam: Elsevier Science.

Trevarthen, C. (2005a). Action and emotion in development of the human self, its sociability and cultural intelligence: Why infants have feelings like ours. In J. Nadel & D. Muir (Eds.), *Emotional development* (pp. 61–91). Oxford: Oxford University Press.

Trevarthen, C. (2005b). First things first: Infants make good use of the sympathetic rhythm of imitation, without reason or language. *Journal of Child Psychotherapy, 31*(1), 91–113.

Trevarthen, C. (2005c). Stepping away from the mirror: Pride and shame in adventures of companionship—Reflections on the nature and emotional needs of infant intersubjectivity. In C. S. Carter, L. Ahnert, K. E. Grossman, S. B. Hrdy, M. E. Lamb, S. W. Porges, et al. (Eds.), *Attachment and bonding: A new synthesis* (Dahlem Workshop Report 92; pp. 55–84). Cambridge, MA: MIT Press.

Trevarthen, C., & Aitken, K. J. (1994). Brain development, infant communication, and empathy disorders: Intrinsic factors in child mental health. *Development and Psychopathology, 6,* 599–635.

Trevarthen, C., & Aitken, K. J. (2001). Infant intersubjectivity: Research, theory, and clinical applications—Annual research review. *Journal of Child Psycholology, Psychiatry and Allied Disciplines, 42,* 13–48.

Trevarthen, C., & Aitken, K. J. (2003). Regulation of brain development and age-related changes in infants' motives: The developmental function of regressive periods. In M. Heimann (Ed.), *Regression periods in human infancy* (pp. 107–184). Mahwah, NJ: Erlbaum.

Trevarthen, C., & Hubley, P. (1978). Secondary intersubjectivity: Confidence, confiding and acts of meaning in the first year. In A. Lock (Ed.), *Action, gesture and symbol: The emergence of language* (pp. 183–229). New York: Academic Press.

Trevarthen, C., & Malloch, S. (2000). The dance of wellbeing: Defining the musical therapeutic effect. *Nordic Journal of Music Therapy, 9*(2), 3–17.

Trevarthen, C., & Malloch, S. (2002). Musicality and music before three: Human vitality and invention shared with pride. *Zero to Three, 23*(1), 10–18.

Trevarthen, C., & Schögler, B. (in press). Musicality and the creation of meaning: Infants' voices and jazz duets show us how, not what, music means. In C. M. Grund (Ed.), *Cross disciplinary studies in music and meaning.* Bloomington, IN: Indiana University Press.

Tronick, E. Z. (2005). Why is connection with others so critical? The formation of dyadic states of consciousness: Coherence governed selection and the co-creation of meaning out of messy meaning making. In J. Nadel & D. Muir (Eds.), *Emotional development* (pp. 293–315). Oxford: Oxford University Press.

Tronick, E. Z., Als, H., Adamson, L., Wise, S., & Brazelton, T. B. (1978). The infant's response to entrapment between contradictory messages in face-to-face interaction. *Journal of the American Academy of Child Psychiatry, 17,* 1–13.

Tronick, E. Z., & Weinberg, M. K. (1996). Depressed mothers and infants: Failure to form dyadic states of consciousness. In L. Murray & P. Cooper (Eds.), *Postpartum depression and child development* (pp. 54–81). New York: Guilford Press.

Tucker, D. M. (1992). Developing emotions and cortical networks. In M. Gunnar & C. Nelson (Eds.), *Minnesota Symposium on Child Psychology: Vol. 24. Developmental behavioral neuroscience* (pp. 75–127). Hillsdale, NJ: Erlbaum.

Tucker, D. M. (2001). Motivated anatomy: A core-and-shell model of corticolimbic architecture. In G. Gainotti (Ed.), *Handbook of neuropsychology: Vol. 5. Emotional behavior and its disorders* (2nd ed., pp. 125–160). Amsterdam: Elsevier.

Tucker, D. M., Derryberry, D., & Luu, P. (2000). Anatomy and physiology of human emotion: Vertical integration of brainstem, limbic, and cortical systems. In J. Borod (Ed.), *Handbook of the neuropsychology of emotion* (pp. 56–79). New York: Oxford University Press.

Tulving, E., & Markowitsch, H. J. (1998). Episodic and declarative memory: Role of the hippocampus. *Hippocampus, 8,* 198–204.

Turner, V. (1982). *From ritual to theatre: The human seriousness of play.* New York: Performing Arts Journals Publications.

Tzourio-Mazoyer, N., De Schonen, S., Crivello, F., Reutter, B., Aujard, Y., & Mazoyer, B. (2002). Neural correlates of woman face processing by 2-month-old infants. *NeuroImage, 15,* 454–461.

Uno, H., Eisele, D., Sakai, A., Shelton, S., Baker, E., DeJesus, O., et al. (1994). Neurotoxicity of glucocorticoids in the primate brain. *Hormones and Behavior, 28,* 336–348.

van Beek, J. P., Guan, H. Y., Julan, L., & Yang, K. P. (2004). Glucocorticoids stimulate the expression of 11 beta-hydroxysteroid dehydrogenase type 2 in cultured human placental trophoblast cells. *Journal of Clinical Endocrinology and Metabolism, 89*(11), 5614–5621.

Vandekerckhove, M. M. P. (in press). Neurovulnerability: Persistent effects of developmental stress on the brain. *Neurology, Psychiatry and Brain Research.*

Vandekerckhove, M. M. P., Markowitsch, H. J., Woermann, F. R., & Mertens, M. (in press). Bi-hemispheric activation in autobiographic memory: An fMRI study. *Behavioural Neurology.*

van der Kolk, B. A. (1994). The body keeps the score: Memory and the evolving psychobiology of posttraumatic stress. *Harvard Review of Psychiatry 1,* 253–265.

van der Kolk, B. A. (2003). Posttraumatic stress disorder and the nature of trauma. In M. F. Solomon & D. J. Siegel (Eds.), *Healing trauma: Attachment, mind, body and brain* (pp. 168–195). New York: Norton.

van der Kolk, B., McFarlane, A., & Weisaeth, L. (Eds.). (1996). *Traumatic stress: The effects of overwhelming experience on mind, body, and society.* Guilford Press.

Vanhatalo, S., & van Nieuwenhuizen, O. (2000). Fetal pain? *Brain Development, 22,* 145–150.

Van Praag, H., Schinder, A. F., Christie, B. R., Toni, N., Palmer, T. D., & Gage, F. H. (2002). Functional neurogenesis in the adult hippocampus. *Nature, 415,* 1030–1034.

Vargha-Khadem, F., Gadian, D. G., Watkins, K. E., Connelly, A., Van Paesschen, W., & Mishkin, M. (1997). Differential effects of early hippocampal pathology on episodic and semantic memory. *Science, 277,* 376–380.

Veldman, F. (1994). Confirming affectivity, the dawn of human life. *International Journal of Perinatal Psychology and Medicine, 6*(1), 11–26.

von Hofsten, C. (2004). An action perspective on motor development. *Trends in Cognitive Science, 8*(6), 266–272.

von Holst, E., & Mittelstaedt, H. (1950). Das Reafferenzprinzip. *Naturwissenschaften, 37,* 256–272.

Weinstock, M. (1997). Does prenatal stress impair coping and regulation of hypothalamic-pituitary-adrenal axis? *Neuroscience and Biobehavioural Review, 21,* 1–10.

Westergaard, G. C., Byrne, G., & Suomi, S. J. (2000). Handedness and cortisol in tufted capuchin monkey infants. *Developmental Psychobiology, 36,* 213–217.

Whitehead, A. N. (1953). *Science and the modern world* (Rev. ed.). Cambridge, England: Cambridge University Press. (Original work published 1926)

Wigram, T. (2004). *Improvisation: Methods and techniques for music therapy clinicians, educators and students.* London: Jessica Kingsley.

Wilson, W. L., & Oliphant, G. (1987). Isolation and biochemical characterization of the subunits of the rabbit sperm acrosome stabilizing factor. *Biology of Reproduction, 37,* 159–169.

Winnicott, D. W. (1960). The theory of the parent-infant relationship. *International Journal of Psychoanalysis, 41,* 585–595.

Yakovlev, P. I., & Lecours, A. R. (1967). The myelogenetic cycles of regional maturation of the brain. In A. Minkowski (Ed.), *Regional development of the brain in early life* (pp. 3–70). Oxford: Blackwell.

Yellon, S. M., & Longo, L. D. (1988). Effect of maternal pinealectomy and reverse photoperiod on the circadian melatonin rhythm in the sheep and fetus during the last trimester of pregnancy. *Biological Reproduction, 39,* 1093–1099.

Zeifman, D., Delaney, S., & Blass, E. (1996). Sweet taste, looking, and calm in 2- and 4-week-old infants: The eyes have it. *Developmental Psychology, 32,* 1090–1099.

Zei Pollermann, B. (2002). *A place for prosody in a unified model of cognition and emotion.* Proceedings of The Laboratory for Speech Prosody (Laboratoire Parole et Langage), Centre National de la Recherche Scietifique. Aix-en-Provence, France: Universitié de Provence. Available from www.lpl.univ-aix.fr/sp2002/oral.htm.

CHAPTER 3

Anatomic Brain Imaging Studies of Normal and Abnormal Brain Development in Children and Adolescents

JAY N. GIEDD, PHILIP SHAW, GREG WALLACE, NITIN GOGTAY, and RHOSHEL K. LENROOT

Neuroimaging technology has provided the means to noninvasively visualize the normal and abnormal development of the brain. This has allowed the linking of biological information such as genotypes or postmortem data with behavior through in vivo images of brain structure and function, providing a crucial bridge between developmental psychology and the broader discipline of developmental biology. The ability to correlate psychiatric illnesses with measurable brain changes has made them physically tangible in a way that has helped people to see them as biological illnesses and has been an important factor in the de-stigmatization of individuals with mental disorders and their families. On a societal level, data from neuroimaging studies of normal development in adolescence have entered social and political discourse in issues ranging from the legal age at which a teenager should drive to whether juveniles should be given the death penalty.

The excitement at being able to see this reclusive organ, so central to our personal and social selves and yet so long hidden behind its protective casing of bone, has led to a still accelerating explosion of studies using neuroimaging techniques. The purpose of this chapter is to provide a snapshot of results of those studies that provide information about the maturation of brain anatomy. As studies of normal and abnormal brain development are mutually in-

formative, we begin with discussion of studies of normal brain development and then proceed to findings associated with psychopathology.

The vast range of disorders that affect brain and behavior renders a comprehensive account beyond the scope of this chapter. Although broadly speaking the developmental trajectory of the brain extends from conception until death, we have chosen to consider as neurodevelopmental disorders those which manifest on the path toward adulthood and to somewhat arbitrarily exclude disorders normally occurring during senescence. We are also constraining our review to studies of children and adolescents. Rather than attempt an encyclopedic coverage of brain disorders, we have included reviews of literature of two general groups: those relatively common psychiatric conditions that have accrued a significant body of structural neuroimaging literature, and selected neuropsychiatric disorders with known genetic abnormalities that are illustrative of the interaction between developmental anatomy and psychopathology. Lack of attention to a particular disorder should not be interpreted as a comment about relevance of that disorder clinically.

This chapter is divided into four sections: methodological issues, typical pediatric brain development, examples of atypical brain development, and a discussion of the present and future role of structural neuroimaging in the study of neurodevelopment.

METHODOLOGY

Attention to methodological issues is crucial for interpreting results of neuroimaging studies. While the same can be said for any research tool, the ease with which neuroimaging allows one to just "look" at pictures of the brain can obscure the multitude of complex technical and statistical processes that are involved in producing imaging data. Imaging hardware and analytic techniques have been improving at a rapid rate, making comparisons between results of studies performed at different times in the development of the field a matter for caution.

Study designs have also been changing based on findings from the first generations of neuroimaging experiments. This has been particularly important in studies of neurodevelopment in children, where it was not known until the first such studies became available how much variability there is between individuals, between genders, and over the course of development.

In this section we begin with a brief history of neuroimaging techniques to provide background for a discussion of the major structural imaging modalities currently in use. We then discuss issues related to image analysis methods and study design. The goal for such a short summary of this large and dynamic field is primarily to give a sense of issues to take into consideration when evaluating neuroimaging studies.

Evolution of Neuroimaging Techniques

Imaging of the central nervous system (CNS) began with radiographs in the early 1900s, shortly after the discovery of X-rays by Roentgen in 1895 (Leeds & Kieffer, 2000). The first techniques to improve visualization of CNS structures were ventriculography, devised in 1918, which consisted of the injection of air into the ventricles; and pneumoencephalography, a variant in which air was instead injected into the spinal canal through a lumbar puncture. Both of these techniques used the low electron density of air as a type of contrast (Lewis, 1996). The presence of air made the shapes of the ventricles visible, and thus indirectly could provide information about associated CNS structures, for example, if the ventricular shape had been distorted by some CNS abnormality. Cerebral angiography provided a similar type of indirect information but in this case through visualization of the vascular system. It was

introduced by Egas Moniz in 1927, when he opacified the carotid artery through introduction of a sodium iodide solution. Substantial refinements in cerebral angiography through the 1960s eventually decreased the need for ventriculography and pneumoencephalography, but like them, it was an invasive technique only undertaken in the presence of clear clinical need.

The clinical introduction in 1971 of computed tomography (CT), originally called computerized axial tomography or CAT scanning, revolutionized the study of the CNS by allowing direct and noninvasive visualization of brain structures. It was also a radiographic technique based upon the interaction of different tissue types with X-rays, but combined multiple views using a mobile X-ray source and newly developed fast computers to create images of soft tissues like the brain. The success of CT led to intense interest during the 1970s in combining computational techniques with a variety of different physical properties for diagnostic and imaging purposes. Many of the techniques in use today originated then, including magnetic resonance imaging (MRI), magnetoencephalography (MEG), optical imaging, positron emission tomography (PET), and ultrasound.

Nuclear magnetic resonance, the basic physical principle underlying MRI, was first described during the 1940s. Felix Bloch and Edward Purcell were awarded the Nobel Prize for this achievement in 1952. They independently discovered that if a sample material is placed in a strong magnetic field and exposed to radiofrequency (RF) energy of a certain frequency, a detectable signal (or "magnetic resonance") is generated based on the interaction of the sample and the field. The potential for medical applications became apparent in the 1970s, with Raymond Damadian's discovery in 1971 that different tissues could have different magnetic resonance properties (Damadian, 1971), and Paul Lauterbur's demonstration in 1973 of a technique using magnetic field gradients to localize the source of magnetic resonance signals (Lauterbur, 1973).

The combination of these advances allowed the creation of images of tissue structure through a process in which the signal associated with a specific volume of tissue, called a *voxel,* is represented with a digital image pixel. The pixel intensity varies according to the magnetic resonance properties of the tissue, so that when the pixels are placed in their proper anatomic location an image is formed reflecting the magnetic resonance properties of the sample tissues. This is particularly useful in the brain because of the differing magnetic resonance properties of major brain components such as neurons, myelin, and cerebrospinal fluid (CSF). The ability to create highly detailed anatomical maps of brain structures resulted in MRI becoming a major imaging modality for study of the central nervous system by the 1990s.

The capabilities of MR technology have continued to rapidly improve. Image resolution is now routinely in the 1 mm to 2 mm range, within the range necessary for description of the often subtle changes associated with neurodevelopmental disorders. Some research applications are able to visualize structures down to the level of individual cortical layers, allowing the linking of data from imaging and histological studies. In addition, MRI has been particularly important in the study of neurodevelopment because it does not involve exposure to ionizing radiation. Therefore, it has become accepted as safe for use in children, including healthy children, and for multiple scans during longitudinal studies.

Parameters to Consider in Structural Pediatric Neuroimaging Studies

In the pediatric anatomic neuroimaging literature, inconsistent or contradictory findings seem to be more the rule than the exception. Differences in (1) image acquisition, (2) image analysis, (3) patient and control populations, and (4) cross-sectional versus longitudinal study design may all contribute to these discrepant findings. Parameters to consider in each of these domains are discussed next.

Image Acquisition

Major technical objectives in imaging studies of brain structure include establishing contrast between different tissue types, obtaining a sufficient degree of resolution for visualization of structure details, and minimizing exam length. MR exams are based on the principle that some types of molecules in the human body have a very slight natural magnetization. The one most frequently examined in MRI is the water molecule because it is present in the body in such high concentrations. Protons in the weakly magnetic water molecules tend to line up with the strong magnetic field of the MR scanner. A brief RF pulse temporarily disturbs this alignment, followed by a gradual return to the baseline state, a phenomenon called "relaxation." There are two different types of relaxation based on different physical properties of the tissue: spin-lattice or T1 relaxation and spin-spin or T2 relaxation. Proton density (PD) is a description of how many hydrogen atoms are in the sample. Each of these properties affects the way a tissue will look on an MR image. In an MRI session, the sequences of energy pulses (the aforementioned RF pulses and the changing magnetic gradients used for localization) are precisely timed to highlight specific features of a tissue based on T1, T2, and PD properties.

For studies of brain structure, the MRI sequence is typically designed to maximize the amount of contrast between gray matter, white matter, and CSF, as such contrasts define the boundaries of most brain structures. Images that emphasize the T1-related differences between tissues ("T1-weighted") are good at highlighting contrast between gray and white matter, while PD weighted images are better at separating gray matter and CSF, and T2 weighted images are best for seeing most types of pathology. The most common single modality used in for studies of brain neurodevelopment is the T1 weighted. However, many studies obtain a combination of T1, T2, and/or PD weighted sequences in the same session and then average them together. The advantage of this type of acquisition is that by combining information from the image sets, automated computer programs can better discriminate gray matter, white matter, and CSF (Rajapakse et al., 1996); the disadvantage is the added length of the MRI exam.

Image resolution is determined by the size of the voxels provided by a particular imaging sequence. Voxels are usually grouped into two-dimensional slices, which then are stacked to contain the data from the whole brain. The size of the voxels and thickness of the slices is especially critical for small but clinically pertinent subcortical structures. *Partial voluming* is a term for a voxel that contains two different tissue types, and so cannot be accurately assigned to either, blurring the border of small structures. Generally, resolution is purchased with the currency of time: improvements in image quality must be weighed against patient discomfort from prolonged time in the scanner.

Most of the studies reviewed in this chapter concern data obtained from T1- or T2-weighted images, which are what people are usually referring to when they say "MRI." However, MR parameters can be altered to examine other tissue characteristics. MR techniques with significant applications to complement studies of the development of brain structure include T1 and T2 relaxometry, magnetization transfer imaging (MTI), and diffusion tensor imaging (DTI).

T1 and T2 Relaxometry and Magnetization Transfer Imaging

While T1 and T2 properties of tissues can be used to generate contrast for anatomical studies, it is also possible to directly quantify how the relaxation properties of a tissue may vary by tissue type, region, developmental stage, or in the presence of pathology. Magnetization transfer imaging

(MTI) is a relative of relaxometry that has been gaining increased attention in recent years due to its ability to measure changes in WM primarily related to the status of myelination. MTI measures the impact of protons bound to macromolecules on MR-visible free water protons (Wolff & Balaban, 1989). In WM, the macromolecular pool is located primarily in myelin. As myelination occurs, it increases the concentration of tightly bound protons in tissue, which can affect signal intensity in the less tightly bound protons visualized by MR (Barkovich, 2000). The extent of this effect can be calculated on a voxel-by-voxel basis, most frequently expressed as the ratio of signal intensity obtained from standard sequences and sequences designed to saturate the bound proton pool, the magnetization transfer ratio (MTR; Wolff & Balaban, 1994).

Diffusion Tensor Imaging

DTI is a technique based on the principle of anisotropic diffusion, the tendency of water to diffuse in a particular direction based upon local structural constraints (Taylor, Hsu, Krishnan, & MacFall, 2004). Anisotropy measures are typically higher (i.e., show more directionality) in white matter than in gray matter because of directed motion of water molecules along white matter fiber tracts; anisotropy values also tend to increase in tissues as myelin increases, as during maturation (Neil, Miller, Mukherjee, & Huppi, 2002). DTI tractography provides a method for describing coherent structures, such as WM tracts, that may be informative regarding changes in connected structures (Taylor, Hsu, et al., 2004). For example, with DTI, it may be possible to determine whether a given area of cortical thinning is a local finding, is associated with a disruption in the thalamocortical tract projecting to it, or with an abnormality in the pertinent thalamic nuclei (Behrens et al., 2003).

Image Analysis

Validation of MR image analysis techniques is hindered by lack of an absolute gold standard. Postmortem data are less than ideal on several counts. When removed from the intracranial cavity and the CSF in which it is immersed, the brain collapses on its own weight, distorting in vivo morphology. Fixation and drying processes affect different brain structures to different degrees, with gray matter and white matter shrinking at separate rates. Age itself is a confound, as younger brains have higher water content and are differentially affected by fixation processes.

Studies using artificial brain models that mimic the shape and tissue characteristics of the human brain can be useful, but valid models are difficult to construct. The standard for validation of automated measures for the quantification of many structures remains a comparison to results obtained from manual tracing by expert human raters.

MR image data pixels may have only one intensity value. At the time of image acquisition, these values may range from 1 to 65,536 (2^{16}). However, to reduce the memory requirements for computation, most image analysis systems restrict this intensity value range to 256 (2^8). A general goal of structural image analysis is to classify each voxel in the image data set according to tissue characteristic (e.g., gray matter, white matter, CSF, vasculature), as well as to assign it to the structure or region in which it belongs.

Classification of tissue into different types is usually accomplished by computer algorithms that create an intensity histogram of all of the voxels in the image and then fit Gaussian functions to the distribution to infer the probabilities of a given intensity corresponding to a given type of tissue. This information is sometimes supplemented with probabilistic atlases to help determine whether a given voxel is gray matter, white matter, or CSF based on its location in the brain (Collins, Holmes, Peters, & Evans, 1995).

Once the voxels have been classified, the number of voxels in a given region may be counted to provide volume estimates of gray matter, white matter, and CSF. Lobar volumes are most commonly reported, but as greater anatomical specification is achieved smaller and smaller subregions can be accurately quantified (see Figure 3.1).

Another approach to comparing brain anatomy from MR images is to create "average" brains for each group that lend themselves to statistical analysis. The challenge to this approach is to register or align the different brains in a standardized way so that a voxel from one brain image will correspond meaningfully to a voxel from another brain image. High individual variation in cortical sulcal and gyral folding patterns makes this one-to-one correspondence difficult, although techniques to anchor the average shapes by aligning certain less variant sulci have greatly advanced the utility of this approach (see Figure 3.2; Thompson et al., 2004).

Selection of Patient Populations

A challenge shared by both genetic and imaging studies is that current psychiatric diagnostic criteria are largely descriptive. This reflects the current gaps in our knowledge about the biological mechanisms associated with observed clinical phenomena and the thus modest applicability of such knowledge to guiding treatment decisions. As greater understanding of mechanisms emerges, it is likely that di-

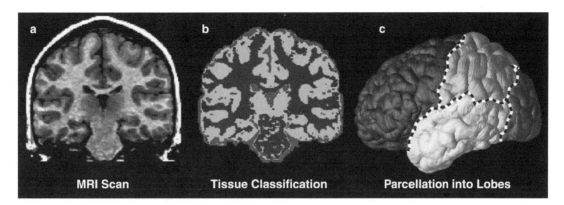

Figure 3.1 The typical sequence of processing MRI data: (a) obtain T1- and T2-weighted images, (b) segmentation procedure, and (c) parcellation of brain into subdivisions for regional quantification of tissue volumes.

agnostic schemata will change; but for now *Diagnostic and Statistical Manual of Mental Disorders IV (DSM-IV)* criteria are poorly suited to categorize homogeneous genetic or neuroanatomical subtypes.

Even when using a standard diagnostic system like the *DSM,* studies vary considerably on inclusion and exclusion criteria, most notably as to how to address the issue of co-morbidity. Some studies will attempt to exclude subjects with any comorbidity, other will include these subjects with descriptions of existing comorbidities, and some ignore the issue altogether. The effects of these decisions on imaging study outcomes are difficult to predict. Other parameters thought to affect brain morphometry that often differ between studies are handedness (Geschwind, 1978; Kertesz, Polk, Black, & Howell, 1992; Witelson, 1989) and intelligence (Andreasen et al., 1993; Reiss, Abrams, Singer, Ross, & Denckla, 1996; Willerman, Schultz, Rutledge, & Bigler, 1991). Education and socioeconomic status have been reported to influence brain size as well, although the interdependence with factors such as nutrition, prenatal care, and IQ is not clear.

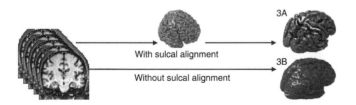

Figure 3. 2 Sulcal alignment: After careful separation of brain from nonbrain voxels, 38 sulcal curves on each subject's cortical surface are manually defined. The sulcal demarcations are used as anchors to create a deformation map, which warps the anatomy of one image onto another while matching sulcal demarcations.

Selection of Control Populations

The first neuroimaging studies performed in children typically drew their normative data from children referred for clinical reasons whose scans were subsequently read as normal. This approach is problematic on multiple counts. It has become increasingly appreciated that the type of findings typical of neurodevelopmental disorders may not be visible to even a trained radiologist, but nevertheless still have the potential to impact quantitative research measures such as cortical thickness. Some clinical diagnoses such as Attention-Deficit/Hyperactivity Disorder (ADHD) may be overrepresented in children referred for clinical scans. In addition, a small but perhaps meaningful number of healthy children may have scans read as abnormal, such that excluding these subjects confounds comparisons to clinical groups. Recruitment of healthy subjects directly from the community provides a more appropriate sampling technique for assessing normal development, although this in turn demands consideration of questions about whether a given study design is better deserved by a control population that matches population norms versus one that is as homogeneous as possible.

Cross-Sectional versus Longitudinal Study Design

The enormous normal variability in size of brain structures calls for large samples and longitudinal study designs to characterize the heterochronous developmental changes of the pediatric population. Conclusions about developmental trajectories drawn from cross-sectional data can easily be in error due to inherent statistical issues. However, multiple challenges exist in carrying out longitudinal imaging studies. Retaining subjects over the course of a study that may last decades is a task difficult to accomplish without a highly trained and stable research team. On a technical side, MRI images can be highly sensitive to differences in MR scanner hardware, and the potential for changes in hardware during the course of a lengthy longitudinal study thus can potentially affect results. Assessing the ability to maintain consistency in measurement is an essential portion of longitudinal studies. For example, in a study conducted at the NIMH, the feasibility of longitudinal studies was supported by the relative consistency of morphologic measures from scans acquired at 2- to 4-week intervals (Giedd et al., 1995). This indicated that, given a stable MRI scanning platform, quantitative differences in longitudinal scans would be reflections of genuine changes in brain structure and not from variability related to the scan acquisition itself.

TYPICAL DEVELOPMENT

Surprisingly little has been known until recently about the development of the brain in healthy children and adolescents. Postmortem data are rare and prone to sample bias due to the low mortality rate and small number of autopsies done in this age range. For example, the Yakovlev collection of roughly 500 normal brains contains only about a dozen between the ages of 4 and 18 (Haleem, 1990). This section begins with a brief review of the major steps of brain development, followed by a summary of findings from neuroimaging studies.

Key Steps in Early Brain Development

Information from postmortem studies has shown the progression of brain development through a series of critical steps (see Figure 3.3). *Primary neurulation* refers to the development of the neural tube, which is the source of future CNS development and is usually complete by 3 to 4 weeks of gestation. Abnormalities in neural tube formation result in birth defects such as spina bifida and meningomyelocele (Victor, Ropper, & Adams, 2001). Development of key forebrain and facial structures, called *prosencephalic development,* occurs during the remainder of the first trimester. The next stage is *proliferation,* which occurs for neurons primarily in the 3rd and 4th months of gestation, and for glia extends through the 1st year of life (Rakic, 1988). *Migration* occurs during the 3rd to 5th months, in which proliferating neurons migrate from their origins near the ventricles to destinations in the cortex, moving along a scaffolding of glial cells (Rakic, 1990).

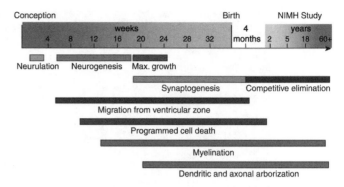

Figure 3.3   Sequence of events in brain maturation.

After migration, a period of rapid cell death called *apoptosis* occurs, resulting in the removal of approximately 50% of neurons between 6 months gestation to 1 month after birth (see Figure 3.3).

The remaining processes of brain development include proliferation and organization of synapses and the myelination of axons. Both of these begin before birth and extend well into postnatal life. The brain continues to grow rapidly in the first 2 years of life, by which time it has achieved 80% of its adult weight. Increases in size continue more slowly thereafter, with 90% of brain weight achieved by age 5 (Dekaban & Sadowsky, 1978) and a largely adult appearance of the brain by age 10 (Jernigan, Trauner, Hesselink, & Tallal, 1991). Huttenlocher (1979) found that the density of synaptic connections increases rapidly after birth, by 2 years of age reaching a level approximately 50% greater than that typically seen in adults. This is followed by a period of loss of synaptic connections called pruning. This pattern appears to occur in a similar fashion but at different rates in different brain regions. For example, the period of maximum synaptic density occurs in the visual cortex by approximately 6 months postnatally and decreases by about 50% between ages 1 and 5 years; while in the prefrontal cortex, it does not reach maximum synaptic density until approximately 24 to 36 months and does not begin to decrease until age 7 (Huttenlocher & Dabholkar, 1997).

Myelination also occurs regionally in an orderly process that begins in the brain stem at 29 weeks (Inder & Huppi, 2000). In general, myelination appears to proceed from inferior to superior and posterior to anterior. Volpe (2000) has summarized more specific principles regarding which pathways tend to be myelinated first: proximal pathways before distal, sensory pathways before motor pathways, projection before association pathways, and from the central loci toward the frontal and occipital poles, with the occipital poles maturing first. The period of time between the first appearance of myelin in a region and its reaching its mature form varies, ranging from 6 weeks in the posterior limb of the interior capsule to 69 weeks in portions of the frontal lobe (Kinney, Brody, Kloman, & Gilles, 1988). Benes (1989) compared myelination in a region along the surface of the hippocampus between children 0 to 9 years old and 10 to 19 and found a 92% increase after correction for increases in total brain volume. Although the most prolific period of myelination occurs in the 1st year of postnatal life, maturation continues for a prolonged period. Postmortem data has found changes in myelin to continue at least into the 2nd decade of life (Benes, 1989; Yakovlev & Lecours, 1967), and as discussed in the neuroimaging section below white matter volumes increase until the 4th decade (Bartzokis, 2004).

Neuroimaging Studies of Normal Brain Development

The emergence of noninvasive neuroimaging techniques, particularly MRI, revolutionized the ability to study brain development. For the first time structural changes could be mapped in healthy children and related to other aspects of development such as cognitive and emotional function. Neuroimaging has also made possible studies of large enough samples of healthy children to appreciate the enormous degree of variability present within a typically developing population. One of the more unexpected findings was the complexity and duration of postnatal brain development, with regionally specific patterns of increase and decrease occurring well into late adolescence and adulthood (Bartzokis et al., 2001; Giedd, Blumenthal, et al., 1999). Another important contribution of neuroimaging has been to make feasible longitudinal studies of brain maturation and thus begin to discern the trajectories associated with normal and abnormal development. In this section we review some of the major findings that have arisen from neuroimaging studies, with an emphasis on data obtained from our group's ongoing large-scale longitudinal studies at the National Institutes of Mental Health.

Fetal and Perinatal Brain Development

The earliest neuroimaging studies of brain development using CT in the 1970s and MRI in the 1980s focused on qualitative descriptions of gray and white matter during the first 2 years of life (Barkovich, Kjos, Jackson, & Norman, 1988; Holland, Haas, Norman, Brant-Zawadzki, & Newton, 1986; M. A. Johnson & Bydder, 1983; Levene

et al., 1982; McArdle et al., 1987). A stable developmental sequence of brain images in T1 and T2 weighted MR studies has been described. The infantile stage (less than 6 months) is characterized by a contrast pattern opposite to what is seen in adults; in T1 images of infants the cortex is lighter than the underlying axonal regions, whereas in adults the cortex is darker. The adult pattern emerges around 12 months of age, after an intervening crossover period during which gray and white matter are not well differentiated. Similar maturational-related changes in contrast are seen on T2-weighted images but slightly later. MR studies quantifying T1 and T2 relaxation times found that both significantly shortened during over the first 2 years, consistent with a substantial loss of water content in both gray and white matter in addition to arrival of macromolecular precursors to myelination and finally myelination itself (Inder & Huppi, 2000; Paus et al., 2001). As may be expected, the crossover occurs at different times in different regions of the brain, as different regions myelinate at different rates.

MRI studies performed prior to birth or of infants born prematurely have made possible the in vivo description of brain structural development from early in pregnancy (Girard, Raybaud, & Poncet, 1995; Rivkin et al., 2000). Although concerns about potential risks to the developing infant limit fetal MRI use, especially during the first trimester, no significant evidence of adverse effects has been found, increasing the likelihood that this will become a more common procedure. In addition, current interest in mapping developmental abnormalities as early in their trajectory as possible, and in delineating the role of adverse birth events in later outcome, is increasing attention to the value of obtaining prenatal brain measurements.

Huppi et al. (Huppi, Warfield, et al., 1998) applied automated methods to the quantification of gray matter, unmyelinated white matter, myelinated white matter, and CSF in preterm and full-term infants from 29 to 41 weeks gestational age. They found an increase in brain tissue volume of 22 ml/week and a fourfold linear increase of primarily cortical gray matter. The volume of myelinated white matter increased markedly between 35 weeks and term, and CSF did not show significant changes.

Myelination and gyrification are both aspects of brain development that are not easily ascertainable with ultrasonography. Interest in gyrification in particular has arisen from its applicability as an index of gestational maturation. Fetal MRI studies have described fetal brain maturation from as early as 13 weeks of gestation, including formation of the primary sulci and insula by 15 weeks. The major sulci, except for the occipital lobe, are in place by 28 weeks of gestation, after which secondary and tertiary sulci are elaborated, with nearly all gyri present by birth. The patterns of the sulci and gyri continue to increase in complexity after birth, likely related to changes in cell-packing density and maturation of subcortical tracts (Garel, Chantrel, Elmaleh, Brisse, & Sebag, 2003).

Imaging Studies in Older Children and Adolescents

Detailed structural neuroimaging studies of older children began to be reported in the 1990s. The first studies of healthy development were cross-sectional and often consisted of MRI scans collected in children being scanned as part of evaluation for a clinical complaint and whose scans were subsequently read as normal. Nonetheless, it became apparent that although overall brain volume was not changing significantly, significant remodeling appeared to be occurring, as reflected in changes in relative volumes of gray matter, white matter, and CSF (see Figure 3.4; Jernigan & Tallal, 1990; Reiss et al., 1996; Schaefer et al., 1990).

In 1989, the Child Psychiatry Branch at the National Institute of Mental Health (NIMH) initiated a large longitudinal study of normal and abnormal brain development, which is still ongoing. The study was designed to assess the hypotheses that many of the most severe neuropsychiatric disorders of childhood-onset are associated with deviations from normal brain development and that the anatomical substrates of this may be detectable by MRI. The study includes twin and nontwin healthy controls and subjects from a variety of diagnostic groups. Participants are scanned at approximate 2-year intervals, and many have been scanned three or more times, allowing the as-

- • **1440   Initial contacts - telephone screening**
- • **922   Sent parent/teacher questionnaires**
- • **490   Brought in for face-to-face exam**
- • **325   Accepted for study**
- • **272   Measurable scans acquired**

- • **Total and Regional Brain Volumes are measured and mapped**

- • **Attempt is made to bring subjects back every 2 years for studying long term brain development**

Figure 3.5   NIMH normal development study recruitment.

sessment of individual trajectories without the limitations of attempting to use cross-sectional data to address longitudinal questions (Kraemer, Yesavage, Taylor, & Kupfer, 2000). As of August 2005 the data set included approximately 3,800 scans from 1,850 subjects, about half classified as having normal development and half from various diagnostic groups, such as ADHD and childhood-onset schizophrenia (COS).

Concerns regarding potential confounds from using controls that had been referred for clinical purposes led to the adoption of a stringent screening process. The healthy control subjects are recruited from the community and undergo physical and neurological examinations, clinical interviews, family history assessment, and an extensive neuropsychological battery (see Figure 3.5).

Each child undergoes an MRI exam including a T1 weighted sequence for anatomical analysis. Once the images are acquired, they are analyzed by a variety of automated and manual techniques through collaboration with several imaging centers throughout the world. Further details of the testing and screening of this sample and the methods of image analysis are published elsewhere (Chung et al., 2001; Giedd, Blumenthal, et al., 1999; Giedd, Snell, et al., 1996; Zijdenbos, Dawant, & Margolin, 1994). In the remainder of this section, we focus on results obtained from this study.

Total Cerebral Volume

Total cerebral volume was found to increase and then decrease between ages 4 and 20 years (see Figure 3.2;

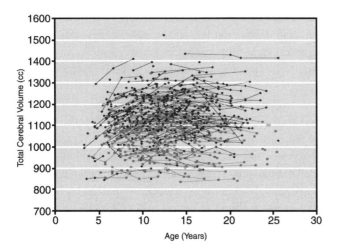

Figure 3.4   Total cerebral volume (TCV) by age for 224 females (375 scans) and 287 males (532 scans).

Giedd, Blumenthal, et al., 1999), a phenomenon not previously seen with postmortem data (Dekaban, 1977; Dekaban & Sadowsky, 1978) or previous cross-sectional imaging studies (Giedd, Snell, et al., 1996; Jernigan & Tallal, 1990). Although head circumference increases from age 4 to 18 years (approximately, 2.0 inches in boys and 1.9 inches in girls; Nellhaus, 1968), this is accounted for by an increase in thickness of the skull and soft tissues (Shapiro & Janzen, 1960) and, to a lesser degree, by an increase in ventricular volume (Jernigan & Tallal, 1990). Male brains were found to be approximately 9% larger on average than those of females. This difference was statistically significant even when controlling for height and weight. A similar finding of brains being 10% larger in boys was reported by a different group in a cross-sectional study of 85 normal children (Reiss et al., 1996).

Ventricles

In this sample, lateral ventricular volume increased robustly with age, a fact not widely appreciated for children and adolescents. Enlarged lateral ventricles in adults compared with children was also reported by Jernigan and Tallal (1990). This pattern is noteworthy in light of the fact that increased ventricular volumes, or ventricular-to-brain ratios, are associated in a nonspecific fashion with a broad range of neuropsychiatric conditions. That this phenomenon is a normally occurring event in healthy adolescents adds to the complexity of interpreting changes in ventricular volume in patient populations.

Cortical Gray Matter

Cortical gray matter volume tends to follow an inverted U developmental course, with volumes peaking at different times in different lobes (see Figure 3.6). Volume also appears to differ by sex. For example, frontal lobe gray matter reaches its maximal thickness at 11.0 years in girls and 12.1 years in boys. Temporal lobe cortical gray matter peaks at 16.7 years in girls and 16.2 years in boys. Parietal lobe cortical gray matter peaks at 10.2 years in girls and 11.8 years in boys (Giedd, Blumenthal, et al., 1999). As gray matter volume reaches its maximum at about the time of puberty, a reduction in cortical gray matter volume is interpreted as maturation, in the sense that it is becoming closer to the adult state.

To examine cortical gray matter development with greater regional specificity, we examined the change in gray matter density on a voxel-by-voxel basis in a group of 13 subjects who had each been scanned four times at approximately 2-year intervals (Gogtay, Giedd, et al., 2004).

Cortical landmarks were manually selected and used as anchors to ensure accurate matching of regions between individuals. An online animation of these changes is available as supporting material on the Proceedings of the National Academy of Sciences web site (http://www.pnas.org/cgi/content/full/0402680101).

The voxel-based measures confirmed the nonlinear and heterochronic nature of gray matter maturation seen in the earlier report based on lobar measures. Prepubertal gray matter increase is followed by loss beginning at different ages in different regions. Cortical gray matter loss occurs earliest in the primary sensorimotor areas and latest in the dorsolateral prefrontal cortex and superior temporal gyrus. The general pattern is for those regions subserving primary functions, such as motor and sensory systems, to mature earliest, and the higher-order association areas that integrate those primary functions to mature later. For instance, in the temporal lobes, the latest part to mature is the superior temporal gyrus and sulcus, which serves as a heteromodal association site integrating memory, audiovisual input, and object recognition functions, along with prefrontal and inferior parietal cortices (Calvert, 2001; Martin & Chao, 2001; Mesulam, 1998).

The cellular events underlying the observed changes in cortical thickness are not well understood. The change in gray matter density may be related to synaptic proliferation and pruning, suggested to be occurring during this age range by postmortem studies (Huttenlocher, 1994). Myelination is also occurring during this period and may result in voxel classification being changed from gray matter to white, producing an apparent loss of gray matter. Indirect evidence in support of this has been reported in cross-sectional studies of normal brain development by Sowell and colleagues (Sowell, Thompson, Tessner, & Toga, 2001) in an independent sample of healthy children and adolescents using similar voxel-based techniques. In this study of 14 children, 11 adolescents, and 10 young adults, gray matter density decrease and volume increase were spatially contemporaneous, potentially supporting the interpretation of changes in cortical thickness as being due to myelination.

Subcortical Gray Matter

In addition to the cortex, there are several gray matter structures in the center of the brain that are grouped under the term "subcortical gray matter." These include the basal ganglia, amygdala, and hippocampus. These structures are crucial components of networks combining different parts of the cortex and the peripheral system for functions such as motor control and emotional responses, many of which

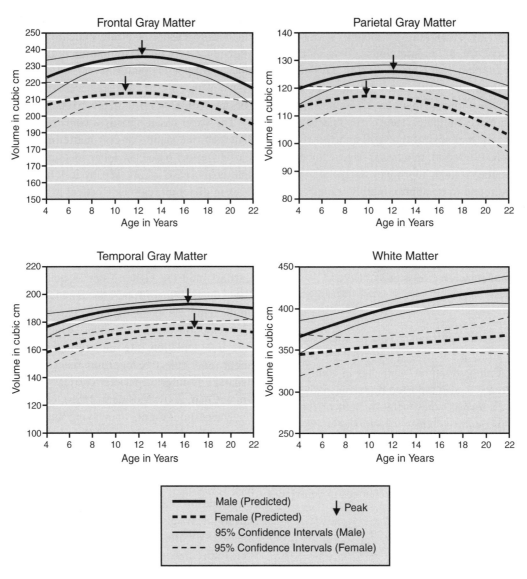

Figure 3.6 Frontal GM, parietal GM, temporal GM, and total WM trajectories: 243 scans from 145 subjects (scans acquired at approximately 2-year intervals). The arrows indicate peak volume.

show significant developmental changes over childhood and adolescence. Because of their often small size and sometimes unclear borders with neighbouring structures, most of them are difficult to quantify using automatic methods and rely on manual tracing techniques.

The basal ganglia consist of the caudate, putamen, globus pallidus, subthalamic nucleus, and substantia nigra. In addition to their central role in control of movement and muscle tone, basal ganglia structures are involved in circuits mediating higher cognitive functions, attention, and affective states. Because of the size and fuzzy border issues mentioned about, only the first three are readily quantifiable by MRI, and at present reliable automated techniques have only been established for the

caudate. Our study found that caudate volume decreases significantly from age 4 to 20 years.

The temporal lobes, amygdala, and hippocampus are integral players in the arenas of emotion, language, and memory (Nolte, 1993). Human capacity for these functions changes markedly between the ages of 4 and 18 years (Diener, Sandvik, & Larsen, 1985; Jerslid, 1963; Wechsler, 1974), although the relationship between the development of these capacities and morphological changes in the structures subserving these functions is poorly understood.

The amygdala and hippocampus have not been quantified for the longitudinal sample. In a previous report from a cross-sectional sample subset of the NIMH sample, amygdala volume increased significantly only in males, and hippocampal volume increased significantly with age only in females (Giedd, 1996). This pattern of sex-specific maturational volumetric changes is consistent with nonhuman primate studies indicating that the amygdala contains high numbers of androgen receptors (Clark, MacLusky, & Goldman-Rakic, 1988) and a smaller number of estrogen receptors (Sholl & Kim, 1989), whereas the hippocampus contains higher amounts of estrogen receptors (Morse, Scheff, & DeKosky, 1986).

Influence of estrogen on the hippocampus is further supported by both rodent and human studies. Gonadectomized female rats have lower density of dendritic spines and decreased fiber outgrowth in the hippocampus, which can be alleviated with hormone replacement (E. Gould, Woolley, Frankfurt, & McEwen, 1990; Morse et al., 1986). In humans, women with gonadal hypoplasia have smaller hippocampi (Murphy et al., 1993). A recent MRI study of 20 young adults also showed proportionately larger hippocampal volumes in females (Filipek, Richelme, Kennedy, & Caviness, 1994).

White Matter

Neurons, glial cells, and myelin are bound by lifelong reciprocal relationships in neural circuits (Fields & Stevens-Graham, 2002). Neurons influence myelin production and the proliferation and survival of oligodendrocytes (Barres & Barde, 2000) in an activity-dependent fashion (Fields, Eshete, Dudek, Ozsarac, & Stevens, 2001); oligodendrocytes secrete neuronal growth factors and influence axonal growth and clustering of ion channels at nodes (Du & Dreyfus, 2002). Oligodendrocytes also support axonal function by means of specific proteins such as CNP and PLP/DM20. Studies of knockout mice deficient in these proteins show aberrant axonal transport and axonal damage in the presence of otherwise normal myelination (Edgar & Garbern, 2004). Later-maturing myelin sheaths, such as those in association tracts and intracortical regions, tend to be thinner with greater axonal load per oligodendrocyte (Kinney, Karthigasan, Borenshteyn, Flax, & Kirschner, 1994; Yakovlev & Lecours, 1967). These characteristics may render later-myelinating areas more vulnerable to environmental or aging-related factors (Bartzokis, 2004).

Regional Volumes of White Matter. Despite their interdependence, developmental curves for WM show significant contrast to the inverted U shaped curve of gray matter (GM). The amount of WM in the brain generally increases throughout childhood and adolescence (see Figure 3.6). Although the rate of increase is age-dependent,

there do not appear to be periods of overall WM reduction for any region within the age range we have examined (Giedd, Blumenthal, et al., 1999). GM volume peaks and then begins to decrease during the 2nd decade, whereas WM volume does not begin to decrease until the 4th decade (Bartzokis et al., 2001). Unlike the regional heterogeneity seen in maturing GM, the slope of increase is approximately the same in the frontal, temporal, and parietal lobes.

Corpus Callosum. The most prominent white matter structure is the corpus callosum, consisting of approximately 200 million myelinated fibers, most of which connect homologous areas of the left and right cortex. The organization of the corpus callosum is roughly topographic, with anterior, middle, and posterior segments containing fibers from their corresponding cortical regions. The functions of the corpus callosum can generally be thought of as integrating the activities of the left and right cerebral hemispheres, including functions related to the unification of sensory fields (Berlucchi, 1981; Shanks, Rockel, & Powel, 1975), memory storage and retrieval (Zaidel & Sperry, 1974), attention and arousal (Levy, 1985), and enhancement of language and auditory functions (Cook, 1986). The relationship between improved capacities for these functions during childhood and adolescence and the noted morphologic changes is intriguing. Several studies have indicated that corpus callosum development continues to progress throughout adolescence (Allen, Richey, Chai, & Gorski, 1991; Cowell, Allen, Zalatimo, & Denenberg, 1992; Pujol, Vendrell, Junque, Marti-Vilalta, & Capdevila, 1993; Rauch & Jinkins, 1994; Thompson et al., 2000), raising the question of whether this may be related to the improvement in these cognitive capacities seen during childhood and adolescence. In the NIMH sample, total midsagittal corpus callosum area increased robustly from ages 4 to 18 years.

Diffusion Tensor Imaging, Magnetization Transfer and Relaxometry. The relatively homogeneous appearance of white matter on typical T1 and T2 images after approximately the 2nd year of life does not reflect its highly complex structure and extensive postnatal development. MRI techniques such as relaxometry, MTI, and DTI may be of particular utility to characterize nonvolumetric features of white matter. Changes in T1 and T2 relaxation rates associated with maturation were some of the first findings to be reported using MRI in the 1970s, but then received relatively little attention while investigators focused on describing anatomy based on gray/white contrast.

The growing interest in being able to use neuroimaging techniques to obtain quantitative measures of myelination as an index of brain maturation and in neural circuits as basic anatomic and functional units has led to a surge of studies using newer MR techniques to describe the maturation of myelin and white matter structures.

Neuroimaging studies assessing the maturation of myelination and white matter structures have found results consistent with the available postmortem data. A natural extension of the observation that changes in T1 and T2 contrast during the first 2 years of life could be seen with visual inspection was to derive methods to quantitatively map these relaxation-based developmental changes. Hassink and colleagues (Hassink, Hiltbrunner, Muller, & Lutschg, 1992) compared T2 relaxation values in 9 children and 8 adults and found that T2 values in the frontal lobe decreased with age. The largest decreases were found in the lateral frontal cortex, with smaller decreases in the dorsal frontal cortex, corpus callosum, and head of the caudate. Steen, Ogg, Reddick, and Kingsley (1997) created T1 relaxation maps for 19 children, 31 adolescents, and 20 adults and calculated T1 relaxation in 9 regions of interest in gray and white matter. They found that T1 values changed at different rates in gray and white matter. T1 in white matter reached the mean level for adults by 8 years old in all regions except frontal, which did not reach the mean adult level until 25 years old. The T1 relaxation value did not reach its adult level in cortical gray matter until 20 years old. The difference in T1 relaxation between children and adults was nearly twice as large in gray matter as in white. Both of these papers proposed potential contributors to the changes in relaxation values as including decreased water content, increased myelin, or structural changes.

Several studies of effects of normal development on MT measures have shown MT values increasing with maturation. Engelbrecht and colleagues (Engelbrecht, Rassek, Preiss, Wald, & Modder, 1998) found a threefold increase in myelinating white matter; gray matter during the same period also rose, but only approximately 25%, thought due to myelination within the grey matter. The more marked changes in MT than had been seen in T2 relaxation studies was thought to reflect a contribution from changes in T1 as well. Rademacher and colleagues (1999) assessed MT measures in particular fiber tracts. They obtained MT measures in children age 1, 3, 6, and 30 months in several regions of interest based on fiber tracts determined with a combination of an atlas and postmortem data from 10 adults. They were able to show that MT increased in all regions as a function of age, but that it was higher in projection and commissural fiber tracts than association tracts. This was consistent with data from the postmortem studies of Yaklovev and Lecours (1967) and others, who found the myelination process continuing longest in association tracts. Van Buchem et al. (2001) took a slightly different approach, creating a histogram of MTR in each brain tissue voxel to obtain a peak reflective of the MTR values in the brain as a whole. They found that the peak of the histogram both decreased and widened with age, likely reflecting the increasing heterogeneity of the state of myelination in different parts of the brain with maturation, compared to the relatively uniform state at birth.

Studies using DTI have also found regions of the brain to be maturing at different rates. The most marked effects were found in studies of infants, as might be expected from the rapid rates of brain changes seen with other imaging modalities and in postmortem exams during this period. Huppi, Maier, et al. (1998) obtained DTI measures in infants born from 26 to 40 weeks of gestation. They found that central white matter regions showed a significant decrease in the average diffusion constant (ADC), and relative anisotropy (RA) increased in the premature infants toward term. McGraw and colleagues (McGraw, Liang, & Provenzale, 2002) measured mean anisotropy in 66 children with an average age of 16 months to compare maturation in "compact" with "noncompact" areas of white matter. Compact white matter areas were defined as the corpus callosum, internal capsule, and cerebral peduncle, and noncompact areas were defined as frontal-parietal white matter and the corona radiate. They found that mean anisotropy was higher in the compact regions at all ages, although anisotropy values increased more rapidly after birth in the noncompact regions.

Studies of diffusion characteristics early in life have shown how anisotropy can be affected by other characteristics than increased quantities of myelin. McKinstry et al. (2002) found a transient period of increased anisotropy in cortical gray matter between 26 and 31 weeks gestational age, which then disappeared permanently, thought to correspond to a period in which radial glial processes were prominent in the cortex, before dendritic arborization obscured the directional tendency. Another group looked at children age 1 day to 17 years (Morriss, Zimmerman, Bilaniuk, Hunter, & Haselgrove, 1999). They found ADC decreased and RA increased rapidly over the first few months. However, these changes occurred prior to the stage at which myelination was known to occur from postmortem studies and before myelin-associated signal was seen on T1- or T2-weighted images. Huppi and colleagues (Huppi,

Warfield, et al., 1998) had also observed that anisotropy increased before onset of myelination. It is currently thought most likely that these changes are due to "premyelination," the stage in which oligodendroglia are beginning to wrap processes around axons and macromolecule concentrations are increasing in preparation for production of myelin (Prayer & Prayer, 2003; Wimberger et al., 1995).

DTI studies in older children show more subtle findings but also support the presence of continued maturation of white matter structures and myelination. Lovblad et al. (2003) found prolonged changes in ADC in frontal and temporal white matter. Schneider Il'yasov, Hennig, and Martin (2004) studied individuals from birth into their twenties. Although FA levels reached adult levels by 2 years in most regions of the brain, FA was still changing in deep white matter structures in the oldest individuals in their study (Schneider et al., 2004). Olesen and colleagues (Olesen, Nagy, Westerberg, & Klingberg, 2003) combined DTI with functional MRI to determine whether maturing myelination in a given tract would correlate with increased neuronal response in the pertinent cortical regions, and found that FA in the frontoparietal region correlated with the neuronal activity in the superior frontal sulcus and intraparietal lobe.

Summary

Although the total size of the human brain is already maximum size by age 6 (Giedd, Snell, et al., 1996; Sowell et al., 1999; Sowell, Thompson, Holmes, Jernigan, & Toga, 1999), the subcomponents of the brain continue to undergo dynamic changes throughout childhood and adolescence. White matter volume increases linearly, reflecting increasing myelination (Paus et al., 1999) as also supported by findings from modalities such as relaxometry, MTI, and DTI. Cortical and subcortical gray matter volume increases until early to midadolescence before beginning to trend down, presumably from synaptic pruning (Huttenlocher, 1979; Huttenlocher & Dabholkar, 1997), although increasing myelination at the cortical border may also contribute to observed cortical thinning.

The complex relationship between gross structural measures and functionally relevant factors such as neuronal connectivity and receptor density is highlighted by the remarkable degree of variability seen in overall volumes and shapes of individual trajectories in this carefully selected group of healthy children. Healthy, normally functioning children at the same age could have 80% differences in brain volume (Lange, Giedd, Castellanos, Vaituzis, & Rapoport, 1997; see Figure 3.4).

STUDIES OF ATYPICAL DEVELOPMENT

Information about normal and atypical development is mutually informative. Normal data is necessary to interpret findings from clinical populations, but the opportunity provided by illness to see how structure and function change together under the influence of pathology provides an invaluable window into their relation in healthy individuals as well. Studying pediatric populations adds the dimension of developmentally related changes in structure and function as both another complexity to account for and a target for understanding.

An enormous amount of work has been done in using neuroimaging to explore the changes in brain structure associated with neuropsychiatric disorders, although the amount of attention paid to any particular disorder varies widely. The extent of neuroimaging studies being performed in pediatric populations has lagged behind the equivalent studies in adults. This is in large part because of added complications of doing imaging studies in children, ranging from the ethical issues of performing research with children, to the lower tolerance of children for scanning procedures, to the technical issues peculiar to pediatric populations, such as smaller head sizes and age-related differences in tissue MR properties. Even so, the accelerating number of studies being performed in younger populations has made a completely comprehensive review not feasible within the scope of a single chapter; and we have, therefore, chosen to cover a subset of illustrative or common neuropsychiatric disorders affecting children and adolescents.

We have grouped the disorders in this section into three broad categories. The first consists of disorders with identified specific genetic or environmental etiologies. While there is an enormous potential catalogue of such disorders, relatively few actually have been the subject of significant neuroimaging studies in pediatric populations. For this group we have selected Fragile X, Rett Disorder, Fetal Alcohol Spectrum Disorders (FASD), and Posttraumatic Stress Disorder (PTSD), as relatively common disorders which demonstrate some of the complexity of the observed effects of even known genetic or environmental perturbations on trajectories of brain development. The second and third groups cover the most common neuropsychiatric disorders affecting children and adolescents, divided by typical age of onset: Autism, dyslexia, ADHD, and obsessive compulsive disorder (OCD) as disorders usually first seen in childhood, and Schizophrenia and mood disorders as disorders whose incidence begins to markedly increase during puberty and adolescence. Tables are provided with details about studies for those disorders with a relatively sizeable literature.

Disorders Associated with Known Genetic or Environmental Factors

A standard experimental method in developmental biology is to introduce a mutation or pathogen during the developmental process and observe how the course of development is altered (S. F. Gilbert, 2003). Neurodevelopmental disorders with known genetic or environmental etiologies provide an analogous opportunity in humans. Progress in genetic analysis methods is providing an increasingly large list of such disorders, allowing the opportunity to see how a specific perturbation impacts growth on multiple levels in a human subject.

Although studies in humans are still complicated by the often late identification of the illness and multiple other confounding factors, the identification of known etiological factors makes it feasible to develop animal models of the corresponding environmental or genetic abnormality and prospectively map their effect on the

course of brain development from much earlier stages and in a more controlled fashion. In addition, methods such as biopsy and postmortem study can be incorporated into animal studies and then correlated with less invasive measures, such as imaging data, providing important opportunities to understand how given abnormal tissue features may appear using the less invasive methods feasible for use in human studies.

If the brain is conceptualized as containing different levels of organization, abnormalities arising from known genetic abnormalities can be thought of as illnesses in which one starts at the bottom and strives to work one's way forward through the chain of causality to understand how the observed abnormalities of function are produced, in contrast to clinical disorders where one is attempting the much more difficult inverse solution (Courchesne, Townsend, & Chase, 1995). Therefore, despite the relative rarity of these disorders compared to clinical syndromes such as depression and psychosis, their potential to help unravel the relationship of genetic or environmental abnormalities to the clinical syndromes that impact functioning of individuals and society is invaluable (see Figure 3.7).

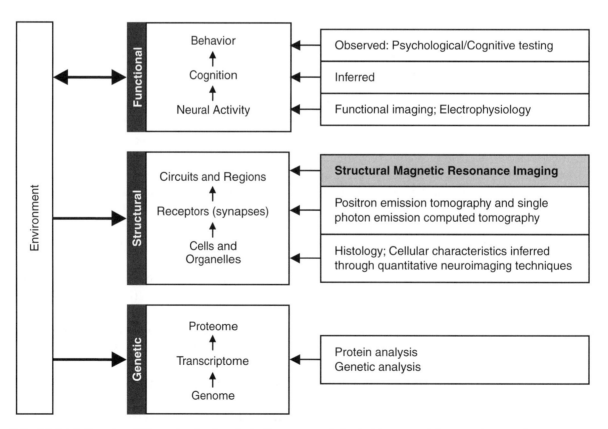

Figure 3.7   Model delineating different levels of analysis (from gene to behavior) in a causal framework. Use of this model highlights the contribution of structural neuroimaging to better understanding both typical and atypical development.

Fragile X Syndrome

Fragile X syndrome is the most common heritable cause of a developmental neuropsychiatric disorder with known genetic etiology, and second only to trisomy 21 (Down syndrome) as a genetic cause of mental retardation (Crawford et al., 1999; Freund, Reiss, & Abrams, 1993). The characteristic physical features associated with Fragile X syndrome include a long narrow face, large ears, prominent jaw, and macro-orchidism. These may become apparent only after puberty. Males, having only one X chromosome, tend to suffer more severe impairments than females, who are heterozygous for the affected X chromosome. Most males are affected with a moderate to severe degree of mental retardation; cognitive deficits in females include mild mental retardation and learning disabilities. Both sexes have a similar pattern of cognitive deficits, including impairment in short-term and working memory, visuospatial abilities, language, and executive function. The behavioral features can overlap significantly with Autistic Disorder, including poor socialization, gaze avoidance, stereotypic behavior, and unusual responses to sensory stimulation. Attention deficits and pronounced anxiety are also frequently present (Hessl, Rivera, & Reiss, 2004).

The genetic abnormality responsible is an expanded trinucleotide repeat on the X chromosome, within a gene called the Fragile X mental retardation I gene FMR1. The name Fragile X arose from initial observations of an abnormally thin region of the affected chromosome. The promoter region for this gene normally contains a CGG triplet repeat region up to 55 repeats long (Hessl et al., 2004). When the number of repeats increases to over 200, the promoter region is hypermethylated and transcription of the gene's product is repressed, resulting in the classic "full mutation" form of Fragile X. The phenotype can vary widely depending on factors such as the degree of hypermethylation, the degree of skewing of the X chromosome in females, and the presence of cellular mosaicism in degrees of triplet expansion.

Individuals with between 55 and 200 repeats have what is called the "premutation" form, which is associated with an increased risk of the full mutation appearing in the next generation. The premutation form appears to also have other functional and pathological impacts (C. J. Moore, Daly, Schmitz, et al., 2004; C. J. Moore, Daly, Tassone, et al., 2004). Approximately 25% of individuals with the premutation have an attenuated form of the typical Fragile X syndrome. In addition, a subgroup of previously normally functioning individuals has been identified who develop a clinically heterogeneous movement disorder later in life called Fragile X associated tremor/ataxia syndrome (FXTAS; Jacquemont et al., 2004), and women with the premutation have a 15% to 34% chance (Welt, Smith, & Taylor, 2004) of premature ovarian failure. Neither of these conditions is seen in individuals with the full mutation. The reasons for this are not clear, but it has been found that the repeats in the permutation form are not hypermethylated, but instead may be associated with an overexpression of FMR1 mRNA. The recognition of the potential clinical relevance of the premutation form has population implications, as it is much more prevalent than the full mutation (Moore, Daly, Schmitz, et al., 2004).

There have been several neuroimaging studies of Fragile X syndrome, although studies available to date have been cross-sectional in nature and often limited by small sample size (see Table 3.1). The initial studies by Reiss and colleagues (Reiss, Aylward, Freund, Joshi, & Bryan, 1991; Reiss, Freund, Tseng, & Joshi, 1991; Reiss, Lee, & Freund, 1994) at the Johns Hopkins Pediatric Neurodevelopmental Disorders Clinic compared males and females with the full mutation to scans from an archive of age-matched controls who were either healthy siblings of participants in the program who did not have Fragile X or subjects who had received scans for clinical reasons that were read as normal. They reported that both males and females showed decreased size of the posterior cerebellar vermis, increased fourth ventricle volume, and increased size of the hippocampus bilaterally. The finding of hippocampal enlargement was replicated in a small study by Kates, Abrams, Kaufmann, Breiter, and Reiss in 1997. They did not find any correlation of imaging findings with cognitive or behavioral measurements.

A larger follow-up study in 1995 found the caudate to be enlarged in the Fragile X group, and the amount of enlargement correlated with the degree of FMR1 methylation (Reiss, Abrams, Greenlaw, Freund, & Denckla, 1995). In addition, these authors reported that whereas caudate volume had a direct correlation with IQ in controls, it had an opposite inverse correlation in patients, suggesting that the mechanism for caudate enlargement could be different in the two groups. A relatively large caudate was also seen in a pediatric subset of this group (Eliez, Blasey, Freund, Hastie, & Reiss, 2001).

Mazzocco, Kates, Baumgardner, Freund, and Reiss (1997) compared sagittal measurement of the cerebellar vermal lobes VI and VII in 30 females with Fragile X and 32 controls. They found that the vermis was smaller in the Fragile X group; they also reported a negative correlation between the size of the vermis and the degree of autistic-like

TABLE 3.1 Structural Neuroimaging Studies of Fragile X Disorder

Study	Patients (Mean Age ± SD, or Range)	Control Subjects	Method	Findings	Comments
Reiss, Aylward, Freund, Joshi, & Bryan (1991)	14 Males (15.7, 2–43)	17 DD Males (11.1, 3–42) 18 ND males (12.5, 1–32)	T1, 5 mm sag with 1–2.5 mm gap; 3 mm axial slices no gap; manual ROI; areas measured from midsag slice, volumes from axial.	FX had dec. volume post cerebellar vermis, inc. volume 4th vent compared to controls, DD not different than controls.	DD = Developmental disability, IQ < 80. ND = Normally developing, IQ > 80, controls include normal volunteers and non-FX clinical populations.
Reiss, Freund, Tseng, & Joshi (1991)	12 Females (14.2, 6–27)	12 Females (12.9, 5–27)	T1, 5 mm sag with 1–2.5 mm gap; 3 mm axial slices no gap; manual ROI: areas measured from midsag slice, volumes from axial.	FX: areas of post cerebellar vermis VI and VII smaller, larger 4th vent volume.	Controls include normal volunteers and non-FX clinical populations.
Reiss, Lee, & Freund (1994)	6 Males 9 Females (12.9 ± 6.3)	2 Males 6 Females (10.3 ± 4.9)	T1 sagittal 3–5 mm contiguous slices, axial, T1 coronal 3 mm slice thickness, manual ROI of volumes.	Hippocampi larger in FX bilaterally, inc. with age in FX, R and L sup temp gyrus dec. with age in FX, no group x gender or gender effect.	Controls include normal volunteers and non-FX clinical populations; no correlation of volumes with cognitive measures; hippocampi volumes were not controlled for overall brain size; cross-sectional study.
Reiss, Abrams, Greenlaw, Freund, & Denckla (1995)	31 Female FX, 2 female PM (11.3 ± 4.4) 17 Male FX (10.7 ± 8.4)	70 Females (11.1 ± 3.6) 29 ND males (11.9 ± 7.5) 21 DD males (11.0 ± 9.6)	T2 axial 5 mm slices with 0–2.5 mm gap, manual ROI of areas and volumes.	Females: FX larger cerebrum, caudate, thalamus. Males: FX larger caudate, DD smaller than controls, lateral vent larger in FX, corr with IQ, caudate volume inc. with dec. gene activation.	Not all subjects had all MRI measures available due to scan quality. Study also included case study of monozygotic female twins with FX discordant for MR.
Jakala et al. (1997)	7 Male FX (29.1 ± 11.0) 9 Male PM (52.4 ± 19.7) 9 Female FX (34.2 ± 15.8) 9 Female PM (48.3 ± 15.0)	10 each, matched on age and sex (from archive)	T1, 2 mm coronal contiguous slices, manual ROI.	PM tend to smaller hippocampi than controls, FX not different than PM.	PM = Premutation form; hippocampal volumes normalized for total brain volume.
Kates, Abrams, Kaufmann, Breiter, & Reiss (1997)	6 Males 4 Females (7.1 ± 4.7)	2 Males 5 Females (8.9 ± 2.4)	MRI, manual ROI.	FX hippocampus larger.	Study compared different methods of measuring hippocampal volume.
Mazzocco, Kates, Baumgardner, Freund, & Reiss (1997)	28 Females (10.6 ± 3.2)	31 Females with LD or siblings of probands (10.3 ± 2.8)	T1, 5 mm sag with 1–2.5 mm gap, manual ROI: areas measured from midsag slice.	Some behavioral impairment corr with smaller VI+VII area and with AR.	LD = Learning disability; AR = Activation ratio; reflect number of cells with normal X chromosome; same subjects as in Reiss (1991) with additional measure of FMR1 gene expression.
Mostofsky et al. (1998)	32 Males (11.1, 1–43) 37 Females (11.4, 4–28)	28 Males with CD (9.2, 2–42) 38 Males (ND) (12.5, 1–44) 53 Females (11.3, 3–26)	T1, 1–5 mm sag with 0–1.5 mm gap, 1.5 mm coronal contiguous slices, manual ROI: areas measured from midsag slice.	Males: FX PV smaller than CD or ND. FX IC larger than CD but not ND. Females: PV smaller, not as diminished as in males. PV size corr with several cognitive measures.	CD = Cognitive disability (IQ < 80); ND = Normal development; PV = Posterior vermis; IC = Intracranial area; control subject MRIs from either documented or clinically probable non-FX subject, 11 FX; and 10 of comparison groups also met criteria for Autism; medication status not controlled. Post. vermis size not correlate with age; interpreted as most likely hypoplasia.

TABLE 3.1   Continued

Study	Patients (Mean Age ± SD, or Range)	Control Subjects	Method	Findings	Comments
Murphy et al. (1999)	8 Females with premutation (39 ± 9)	32 Females (39 ± 10)	8 FX/20 controls had scans on .5 T scanner, 7 mm contiguous axial slices; 6/11 scanned on 1.5 T for hippocampal measures, 5 mm contiguous coronal slices, manual ROI.	FX: Smaller overall brain size, caudate, and thalamus; larger hippocampi.	Volumes adjusted for intracranial volume. PET study also performed found abnormalities of metabolism in multiple areas.
Eliez, Blasey, Freund, Hastie, & Reiss (2001)	27 Females 10 Males (10.2 ± 3.8)	64 Females (10.6 ± 2.9) 21 Males (10.7 ± 2.8)	T2/PD axial 5 mm contiguous slices, segmented, manual ROI of volumes.	Caudate and ventricles larger in F, thalamus larger in FX females only.	Subjects subset of a larger study (Reiss, 1995).
Kates, Folley, Lanham, Capone, & Kaufmann (2002)	21 Full mutation FX: (4.89 ± 1.7) 12 Mosaic FX (4.96 ± 1.3) 15 DLD (5.18 ± 1.2) 12 Down syndrome (5.94 ± 1.6)	8 Males (5.79 ± 1.7)	T1, 1.5 mm contiguous slices, semiautomatic segmentation and parcellation in lobes based on Talairach grid.	All groups had smaller gm and wm temp lobe volumes, FX no difference in overall brain size, DS all volumes smaller and marked negative correlation of volume with age, DLD and DS smaller parietal wm volume.	All subjects male DLD = Developmental language delay.
Barnea-Goraly et al. (2003)	10 Females (16.7 ± 3.82)	10 Females (17.1 ± 3.82)	DTI: 6 directions, 5 mm slices/1 mm skip, not include inferior cerebellum, measure FA.	FX showed reduced FA frontal-caudate white matter on L, trend on R; dec. in sensory-motor regions bilaterally.	FA: fractional inositropy; IQ and FA measures correlated within FX; but these regions were not the same as those which differed between groups.
Kaufmann et al. (2003)	10 ideopathic Autism (7.0 ± 2.4), 27 DS (7.2 ± 2.1), 11 DS plus Autism (7.0 ± 1.8), 9 FX (5.3 ± 1.1), 13 FX plus Autism (5.7 ± 2.1)	22 Males (8.3 ± 1.9)	T1 scans, slice thickness range from 3–5 mm, gap range from 0–1.0 mm, manual ROI of midsagittal areas, report ratio of vermis areas to total intracranial area to account for DS smaller IC.	Idiopathic Autism: smaller ratio VI-VII/IC, DS: smaller IC, decreased posterior vermis, DS+Autism all vermis smaller; FX dec. posterior vermis, FX+Autism trend to higher ratio VI-VII.	All subjects were male. DS = Down syndrome; IC= Intracranial area; 4/16 DS boys also diagnosed with childhood disintegrative disorder.

features in this population, and that the vermis was relatively larger in girls who had a higher proportion of activated normal X chromosomes.

Kates, Folley, Lanham, Capone, and Kaufmann (2002) and Kaufmann et al. (2003) compared cerebellar measures in Fragile X against other neurodevelopmental disorders in addition to healthy controls; Kates, Folley, et al. included developmental language disorder and Down syndrome, and Kaufmann et al. included Down syndrome and Autism. Kates, Folley, et al. found significant age-related decreases in Down syndrome but not in Fragile X; all three disorders had smaller temporal lobes. Kaufmann et al. looked only at a midsagittal slice; they found that the vermis was smaller in Fragile X and in idiopathic

Autism, but the group with Fragile X and Autism had larger cerebellar lobes VI-VII.

One study has been reported to date looking at white matter structure in Fragile X using DTI; Barnea-Goraly and colleagues (2003) compared fractional inositropy in 10 females with the full mutation with 10 matched controls. They found significantly lower fractional inositropy in areas connecting the left frontal and caudate, and right and left sensorimotor regions; fractional inositropy in the right frontal-caudate region was lower but did not reach significance. They interpreted the abnormalities in the sensorimotor region as being consistent with findings of sensory abnormalities and stereotypic behavior, and the frontal-caudate with problems in executive function, impulsivity, and hyperactivity. FMRP is not typically found in the axons, but they hypothesized that abnormalities in the target neuron cell bodies and dendrites could impact the creation of axonal tracts during development and their maintenance afterward.

The recognition that the premutation form may also be associated with abnormalities has increased interest in exploring how the premutation form may affect brain structure. A 1999 study using manual parcellation in females with the premutation form reported decreases in overall brain size and bilateral caudate and thalamic nuclei and an increase in bilateral hippocampal size (Murphy et al., 1999). This study also performed PET imaging and reported hypometabolism in the right parietal, temporal, and occipital association areas, and bilateral hypermetabolism in the hippocampi and left cerebellum. No correlations were found between brain measures and IQ. A later study by the same group with men with the premutation form using voxel-based methods found decreases in gray matter density in the regions including the cerebellum, thalamus, and amygdala-hippocampal complex, and decreased white matter density in the cerebellum, brain stem, pons, cingulated and genu of the corpus callosum, and tracts in the temporal and frontal lobes (Moore, Daly, Tassone, et al., 2004). They again found no correlation of any brain measures with IQ.

Fragile-X associated tremor/ataxia syndrome (FXTAS) is considered to be a different disorder, arising through a different mechanism from an abnormality in the same gene which results in a gain-of-function abnormality through excess production of mRNA rather than the loss of function of the full mutation developmental disorder. The neuropathological findings in FXTAS are distinct from those in the neurodevelopmental form of Fragile X, taking the form of eosinophilic inclusions rather than abnormal dendrite morphology. Clinical MRI of men with FXTAS have shown a high number of individuals with bilateral T2 hyperintensities in the cerebellum, although this is not specific to FXTAS (Brunberg et al., 2002). FXTAS has only recently been identified in women, and neuroimaging studies are not yet available (Hagerman, Levitt, et al 2004).

FMRP1 encodes for a protein called the Fragile X mental retardation protein (FMRP; Tassone et al., 1999). FMRP is primarily found in the cell body, dendrites, and synapses. It may be particularly important in the formation of dendrites and regulation of synaptic development and in response to environmental stimulation (Darnell et al., 2001; Greenough et al., 2001; Willemsen, Oostra, Bassell, & Dictenberg, 2004). Postmortem examination in both individuals with the full mutation of Fragile X and FMRP

knockout mice has revealed the presence of morphologically immature neurons with abnormally long and thin dendritic spines and elevated spine numbers, similar to what is seen early in development and in animals with sensory deprivation (Hinton, Brown, Wisniewski, & Rudelli, 1991; Irwin, Galvez, & Greenough, 2000). Expression of FMRP has been found to increase in animal models following environmental stimulation or motor activity (Todd & Mack, 2000; Todd, Malter, & Mack, 2003). Fragile X syndrome is a neurodevelopmental disorder arising from an unstable trinucleotide repeat. It shows dosage effects associated both with the degree of expansion and its association with the X chromosome. Although the studies described here provide some important first steps toward comparing neurodevelopmental disorders directly, their methodologic limitations affect the conclusions that can be drawn. Given the nonspecific nature of cerebellar abnormalities and hippocampal abnormalities, it would be valuable to compare cerebellar differences with dosage effects, including premutation and full mutation.

Rett Syndrome

Rett syndrome is a pervasive X-linked developmental disorder first identified by Andreas Rett in 1965 (Rett, 1966). The classic presentation is almost exclusively seen in females, affecting approximately 1:10,000. It is the second most common cause of mental retardation in females after Down syndrome (Hagberg, 1995). Called by some "the paradigmatic neurodevelopmental disorder," Rett syndrome is of particular interest because of its unusual course. During the first 6 to 18 months of life, children apparently develop normally. Retrospective studies of videotapes made of children later diagnosed with Rett syndrome have shown specific patterns of abnormal motor activity during this time, suggesting that neurologic abnormalities are present, if not yet of clinical severity (Einspieler, Kerr, & Prechtl, 2005). A severe deterioration then sets in, classically moving through stages including deceleration of head growth, behavioral regression, autistic features, loss of language and hand use, onset of autonomic and motor abnormalities, and the classic hand-wringing sign. Seizures and sometimes severe mental retardation also frequently are present. However the deterioration then stops, usually by the mid-teens, and a stable state ensues that can last decades (Naidu, 1997; Neul & Zoghbi, 2004). There is a high degree of clinical heterogeneity, so far appearing to be related both to various forms of MeCP2 mutations and to different patterns of X-chromosome inactivation (Akbarian, 2003; Neul & Zoghbi, 2004).

TABLE 3.2   Structural Neuroimaging Studies of Rett Syndrome

Study	Patients (Mean Age ± SD, or Range)	Controls	Method	Findings	Comments
Casanova et al. (1991)	8 Females (5.3, 3–10)	10 Females (7, 4–10)	Area and shape for hemisphere, cc, midbrain, pons, lobes I-V and VI-VII cerebellum, head of caudate; area measured from slice.	Dec. area for cerebrum, L and R caudates.	
Murakami, Courchesne, Haas, Press, & Yeung-Courchesne (1992)	13 Females (12.0 ± 6.3)	10 Females (15.4 ± 7.5)	MRI, ROI area measured from single slices (which areas?).	Dec. volume cerebrum.	
Reiss et al. (1993)	11 Females (10.1 ± 5.2)	15 Females (11.2 ± 2.5)	MRI, ROI analysis of volumes.	Dec. volume cerebrum; more gray matter loss than white, most in frontal and caudate.	No correlation of dec. volumes and duration of illness.
Subramaniam, Naidu, & Reiss (1997)	20 Females (9.74, 3–23)	20 Females (9.03, 3–23)	MRI, ROI analysis of volumes.	Dec. volume cerebrum, caudate.	Extension of 1993 study to larger group.
Dunn et al. (2002)	9 Females (18.4, 14–26)	9 Females (23.2, 20–29)	MRI, ROI analysis of volumes.	Dec. vol. caudate.	PET scans also performed.

The earliest MRI studies of girls with Rett syndrome compared cross-sectional areas of different brain regions (see Table 3.2). Casanova et al. (Casanova et al., 1991) compared eight girls with Rett syndrome, aged 3 to 10, with 10 age- and sex-matched controls. They measured sagittal cross-sections of several structures including whole brain, corpus callosum, and cerebellum, and horizontal cross-sections of the caudate nuclei. Their findings included smaller volumes for total brain and for caudate nuclei, which trended toward being even smaller than expected when correcting for the smaller overall brain volume. Murakami examined 13 girls with Rett syndrome aged 5 to 25 and 10 controls aged 6 to 27, and found decreased volumes of total cerebrum, cerebellum, caudate nuclei, and brainstem and increased volume in the fourth ventricle. They also observed that the cerebellum and fourth ventricle appeared to be more severely affected in the older Rett syndrome girls, which they interpreted as due to increasing cerebellar atrophy with age; this effect was not seen in the supratentorial structures (Murakami, Courchesne, Haas, Press, & Yeung-Courchesne, 1992).

Reiss et al. (1993) also reported potentially age-related changes in a volumetric study of 11 Rett syndrome girls aged 5 to 15 with 15 matched controls, in that the brains of girls at the beginning of the illness course were more similar to those of controls than older girls, and that decrease in brain size did not appear to continue past a certain point. In their study the frontal region was more affected than other brain regions and gray matter more than white matter. An extension of this study in which sample sizes had been increased to 20 subjects and 20 controls found that gray matter was most reduced in the prefrontal, posterior frontal, and anterior temporal regions, while white matter was more uniformly decreased. Caudate nuclei were disproportionately smaller even after accounting for the overall smaller cerebral volume in the Rett syndrome subjects (Subramaniam, Naidu, & Reiss, 1997).

Neuropathological findings are subtle but pervasive, consistent with the imaging results. Postmortem brain volume has been found to be 14% to 34% smaller than girls of the same age and is relatively smaller even when matched for the smaller body size commonly seen in Rett's syndrome (Armstrong, 1992; Armstrong, Dunn, Antalffy, & Trivedi, 1995). Histologic studies have found reduced dendritic length and complexity in pyramidal neurons of the frontal and motor cortex, and neurons in widespread other areas of the brain are smaller and more densely packed. Multiple other abnormalities have been found in different regions of the brain in girls with Rett's syndrome. For more information, the reader is referred to the recent review by Jellinger (2003).

The low rate of familial cases of Rett syndrome delayed identification of the responsible genetic abnormality until 1999, when Amir and colleagues (1999) showed that most cases of Rett syndrome were associated with mutations in an X-linked gene called *MECP2,* which encodes for protein methyl cytosine-binding protein 2 (MeCP2). Since that time, genotyping of males in affected families has shown that the mutation is not exclusive to females, but that males tend to have a much more severe phenotype, which is often fatal early in life (Neul & Zoghbi, 2004).

The identification of MeCP2 has stimulated rapid advances in exploration of its function in Rett syndrome and in normal development, largely through animal models in which MeCP2 is impaired in different ways or at different stages of maturation. MeCP2 is a protein that suppresses gene expression through methylation of transcription factors. Using animal models, it has been possible to show that MeCP2 appears to be most active in neurons, rather than other somatic cells. In addition, elegant work by Shahbazian et al. (2002) has demonstrated that MeCP2 expression becomes detectable as neurons reach a particular stage of maturity. This delayed activity of the affected protein provides an exquisite example of how a genetic abnormality may impact the developmental course during a specific postnatal period. Early developmental milestones, such as neurogenesis and migration, appear relatively unaffected, while the later tasks of synaptogenesis and maintenance are impaired. This is consistent with the MRI findings of generalized volume deficits, most pronounced in gray matter, and the associated neuropathological findings of decreased volume and insufficient neuropil in the absence of more striking regional abnormalities. It should be noted that we have chosen not to cover the studies of neurotransmitter function in Rett Disorder as outside the scope of the chapter, but these studies support the presence of functional abnormalities on the synaptic level. Examples of more detailed recent reviews include Neul and Zoghbi (2004) and Segawa and Nomura (2005).

Fetal Alcohol Syndrome

Although concerns that parental alcohol use may have a potential adverse impact on children have been mentioned in the literature for centuries, alcohol was not identified as a teratogen associated with a specific pattern of deficits until a case series of abnormalities in 127 children born to alcoholic mothers was described by a physician in Belgium in 1968 (Lemoine, 1968; Randall, 2001). The report did not attract much notice until Jones and Smith (1973; Jones, Smith, Ulleland, & Streissguth, 1973) independently described a similar group in 1973, also coining the term Fetal Alcohol Syndrome and proposing a set of diagnostic criteria. The deficits described by both groups included growth retardation, physical malformations, a distinctive pattern of facial anomalies, decreased head size, and central nervous system damage as evidenced by low IQ and behavioral problems.

Further study of the disorder was complicated by the recognition that prenatal alcohol exposure could result in a range of presentations, not all of which exhibit the typical physical stigmata. Some variants, such as Alcohol-Related Neurodevelopmental Disorder (ARND), have no visible physical abnormalities, but cognitive and behavioral problems equally as severe as FAS. These variants are currently all included under the label Fetal Alcohol Spectrum Disorders (FASD; Hoyme et al., 2005), of which the classic FAS is the most severe. The variety of presentations has also made assessment of the prevalence of FASD difficult (Hoyme et al., 2005; Sampson et al., 1997). The need to document prenatal alcohol exposure as part of the diagnosis is often challenging, as mothers are aware of the associated stigma and may not be forthcoming. Estimates currently vary from 0.5 to 1 per 1,000 live births, with some communities showing much higher rates, often associated with disadvantaged socioeconomic status (May, Brooke, et al., 2000; May & Gossage, 2001). Sampson and colleagues performed a critical analysis of available incidence estimates for FAS and presented new estimates for both FAS and ARND. Their estimates for FAS were 2.8/1,000 in a middle-class community and 4.6/1,000 in a high-risk population, and a combined risk for FAS and ARND in the Seattle community of 9.1/1,000 (Sampson et al., 1997).

Attempts to understand the relationship of prenatal alcohol exposure to the observed disabilities has been complicated by the many other factors that may accompany maternal alcohol use and also affect prenatal development, such as access to prenatal care, maternal nutrition, and potential polysubstance use (Randall, 2001). In addition, the amount and timing of alcohol use can have a critical impact on outcome, and this information is rarely available in clinical studies (Olney et al., 2002; Streissguth, Sampson, Barr, Clarren, & Martin, 1986). Early postmortem studies showed marked structural brain abnormalities, but these may have been confounded by their primarily being performed in children with pronounced morbidity (Randall, 2001; Riley, McGee, & Sowell, 2004).

Advent of neuroimaging has allowed assessment of brain changes in less severely affected children, although difficulty controlling for dosage and timing effects is still problematic. Although severely affected children can show striking brain abnormalities, the most consistent finding is overall smaller cerebral volume in the presence of Microcephaly (see Table 3.3). Preliminary results from the neuroimaging studies have additionally found some regions to be disproportionately decreased in size, including the cerebellum and caudate (Archibald et al., 2001; Autti-Ramo et al., 2002; Sowell, Thompson, Mattson, et al., 2002; Swayze et al., 1997). The corpus callosum also appears to be impacted in a majority of cases, in keeping with generally prominent effects of alcohol exposure on development of midline structures (Autti-Ramo et al., 2002; V. P. Johnson, Swayze, Sato, & Andreasen, 1996; Sowell, Mattson, et al., 2001; Sowell, Thompson, et al., 2001; Swayze et al., 1997).

Animal models in which dosage and timing can be controlled are particularly important and have shown distinct effects on different brain regions at different periods (Olney et al., 2002). Impact of blocking NMDA receptor has been informative regarding the role of NMDA function in normal development, used in theories of other illnesses such as Schizophrenia (Olney, Newcomer, & Farber, 1999).

An important element of future neuroimaging studies of the effects of prenatal alcohol exposure will be more exploration of white matter structure, as work to date has implicated this as a particularly affected region (Bookstein, Sampson, Connor, & Streissguth, 2002; Roebuck, Mattson, & Riley, 2002; Sowell, Mattson, et al., 2001). There has also been some interesting work in animal models studying how the genetic background of the exposed fetus interacts with prenatal alcohol exposure to affect the severity of the resultant dysmorphic features (Su, Debelak, Tessmer, Cartwright, & Smith, 2001).

Posttraumatic Stress Disorder

PTSD is a specific set of symptoms associated with exposure to an extreme traumatic stressor. Research of PTSD in children began in the 1980s, when it was recognized that children report a wide range of reactions following trauma (Yule, 2001). Like adults, children can have symptoms of reexperiencing traumatic events, avoidance, numbing, and increased physiological arousal. Sleep disturbances, fear of the dark, and nightmares are common. Particularly in very young children, reaction to trauma may be more clearly exhibited through alterations in behavior, such as play centered around traumatic events or loss of previously acquired skills, social withdrawal, numbing, and antisocial behaviors. There is considerable comorbidity with depression, anxiety, and pathological grief reactions.

Little is known about the prevalence of PTSD in children, and rates from high-risk children vary widely. About 25% of children who experience road traffic accidents and 10% of children admitted to hospital after falls develop PTSD (Bryant, Mayou, Wiggs, Ehlers, & Stores, 2004; Heptinstall, 1996; Stallard, Salter, & Velleman, 2004). Biological findings in PTSD are compatible with those of a chronic stress response, with some suggestive differences; most notably, cortisol levels in PTSD are lower but show a greater dynamic range. It has thus been suggested that PTSD may be associated with hyperreactivity in the hypothalamic-pituitary-adrenal axis, leading to secondarily reduced cortisol levels through negative feedback (Yehuda, 2001).

Imaging studies of adults with PTSD have focused on combat veterans and adults with a history of sexual childhood abuse (Hull, 2002). Most (but not all) studies demonstrated a reduced volume of the hippocampus in affected subjects (Bremner et al., 1995, 1997; Gurvits et al., 1996; Myslobodsky et al., 1995; Stein, Koverola, Hanna, Torchia, & McClarty, 1997). Nonspecific white matter lesions have also been reported (Canive et al., 1997). Based on these findings, Bremner (1999) and Sapolsky (1996) postulated that stress results in long-term damage in brain structures and leads to symptoms of PTSD. According to this hypothesis, the smaller hippocampus of patients is due to the toxic effect of glucocorticoids on this particularly vulnerable brain structure. However, as noted earlier, cortisol levels are often lowered in PTSD.

In their seminal studies of children with PTSD, DeBellis et al. (1999) did not find hippocampal changes as predicted by the studies in adults. However, the affected children showed smaller intracranial and cerebral volumes than matched controls. Specific regions in the PTSD group also showed differences: The corpus callosum was smaller and the lateral ventricles proportionally larger than in controls. They also found differences in the volumes of white and gray matter of the superior temporal gyrus (De Bellis et al., 2002). To some extent, the findings differed between boys and girls: The corpus callosum effects were more marked in boys, and females had a larger cerebral volume reduction. Interestingly, a smaller corpus callosum has also been shown in children who experienced childhood neglect and, in particular, sexual abuse, a condition strongly predictive of PTSD. Because these corpus callosum changes were neither observed in healthy controls nor in children with other psychiatric disorders, this may be a relatively specific abnormality (Teicher et al., 2004). A follow-up study found that PTSD did not appear to affect the growth of the temporal lobe, amygdala, and hippocampal volumes

TABLE 3.3 Structural Neuroimaging Studies of Fetal Alcohol Spectrum Disorders

Study	Patients (Mean Age ± SD, or Range)	Control Subjects	Method	Findings	Comments
Mattson et al. (1996)	4 Males 2 Females (13.0, 8–19)	6 Males 1 Female (12.3, 8–18)	T2/PD 4 mm contiguous slices, manual ROI.	Dec. cerebral vault, basal ganglia, diencephalon; basal ganglia smaller when control for TBV.	Cerebellar vault was smaller but did not reach significance.
Sowell et al. (1996)	3 Females 6 Males (15.1, 8–22)	13 Females 11 Males (14.3, 8–24)	T1 sagittal 5 mm slice thickness, 2.5 mm gap; manual tracing of mid-sagittal section of cerebellum.	Dec. area in anterior vermis, not in posterior.	
Swayze et al. (1997)	6 Males 4 Females (15, 4–26)	101 adults, 13 adolescents, 5 children From archive	Iowa and Sioux: 1.5T, T1/T2/PD, 1.5 mm contig slices	Microcephaly in 7/10; midline abnormalities 6/10.	Patients with midline brain anomalies had the highest number of craniofacial anomalies.
Archibald et al. (2001)	8 Female FAS 6 Males FAS (11.4 ± 3.3) 4 Female PEA 8 Male PEA (12.8 ± 4.8)	20 Female 21 Male (12.8 ± 4.4)	T1: 1.2 mm contiguous; T2 4 mm contiguous slices; semi-automated segmentation, manual ROI.	FAS global volumes smaller than controls; cerebellum, parietal lobe, caudate more affected; white matter more than gm in cerebrum; hippocampus disproportionately larger; PEA findings for global volume, caudate and parietal were also smaller but not significant.	Artifact prevented obtaining temporal lobe measures on all participants.
Sowell et al. (2001)	10 Females 10 Males (FAS and PEA, 13.0 ± 4.0)	12 Females 9 Males (13.5 ± 5.2)	T1 1.2 mm contiguous slices, shape and area analysis of corpus callosum.	Corpus callosum area smaller, posterior region displaced; findings sig in FAS, less severe pattern in PEA.	CC displacement correlates with impairment in verbal learning ability.
Sowell et al. (2001)	11 Females 10 Males (13 ± 4) alcohol exposed	12 Females 9 Males (13.5 ± 5)	T1 1.2 mm contiguous slices, whole brain voxel based morphometry.	L hemisphere perisylvian cortices of temporal and parietal lobes—more gray matter, less white matter than controls.	Same population as in Sowell et al. (2001).
Autti-Ramo et al. (2002)	9 Males 8 Females (13)	17 age and gender matched	T1 sagittal 1.18 mm contiguous slices, T2 coronal 4 mm 0.8 gap, T2 and FLAIR 5 mm slices 1 mm gap.	Multiple abnormal findings in different subjects in cerebrum, cerebellum, corpus callosum; vermis hypoplasia the most consistent finding.	Mothers with known alcohol use recruited early in pregnancy; children grouped by trimester(s) during which experienced alcohol exposure; all children with wide sulci also had vermal hypoplasia.
Bookstein, Sampson, Connor, & Streissguth (2002)	60 FAS 60 FAE	30 Male 30 Female (14–37)	T1 SPGR sagittal, develop method of digitizing in set of landmarks.	FAS/FAE have widely varying collection of dysmorphies affecting cc.	Goal to describe morphometric marker for alcohol exposure in individuals without facial stigmata.
Bookstein, Streissguth, Sampson, Connor, & Barr (2002)	30 Males 15 FAS 15 FAE	15 Males subset of group above.	T1 SPGR sagittal, develop method of digitizing in set of landmarks.	Findings similar, more differentiation when incorporate behavioral measures.	Adding neuropsych to landmark measures above.

TABLE 3.3   Continued

Study	Patients (Mean Age ± SD, or Range)	Control Subjects	Method	Findings	Comments
Sowell, Thompson, Matson, et al. (2002)	14 FAS 7 PEA (12.6)	12 Female 9 Male (13.5)	T1 1.2 mm contiguous slices; T2 4 mm contiguous coronal; semi-automated volumes, surface based image analysis.	Size and shape abnormalities in inferior parietal/ perisylvian regions bilaterally, dec. brain surface in ventral aspect of frontal lobes.	
Sowell, Thompson, Peterson, et al. (2002)	14 FAS 7 PEA (11 female, 10 male, 13.9)	38 Female 45 Male (13.5)	T1 1.2 mm contiguous slices, semi-automated surface based analysis and gm density.	Sup temporal and inf parietal cortices shifted backward in left hemisphere compared to right, less asymmetry than controls in posterior inf temporal lobes (language areas).	Controls recruited from studies at two different centers.

during a period of 2 years occurring roughly during puberty (DeBellis, Hall, Boring, Frustaci, & Moritz, 2001).

Recently, pituitary volumes were investigated in 61 children with PTSD as a marker of stress-related hormonal differences. No overall differences between cases and controls were found, but a post hoc analysis suggested that the PTSD group may have had larger pituitary volumes after puberty, consistent with hypothesized increased CRH secretion (Thomas & DeBellis, 2004).

An ongoing question has been whether the smaller hippocampal volumes observed in adults were a result of PTSD or a predisposing factor. Gilbertson et al. (2002) addressed this by recruiting identical twins who were discordant for PTSD. They found smaller hippocampi in both affected and nonaffected twins, suggesting that the brain abnormality was a risk factor and not a consequence of PTSD. More recently, a first prospective study of PTSD was performed in adults to determine what abnormalities if any developed during the course of the disorder. Bonne et al. (2001) investigated 37 trauma-exposed individuals, of whom 10 later developed PTSD, obtaining imaging measures both immediately after the trauma and then after a follow-up period of 6 months. They did not find evidence of hippocampal abnormalities at either time point.

The abundance of potential confounding issues makes us question such an interpretation of brain abnormalities as markers of vulnerability or result of trauma difficult to address. The choice of controls may be important, as individuals who have been exposed to trauma but do not develop symptoms may be a better comparison group but are difficult to recruit. Another methodological problem is the high rate of psychiatric comorbidity in patients with PTSD, particularly of depression, which has also been associated

with decreased hippocampal volumes (Jelicic & Merckelbach, 2004).

In summary, the limited studies available of children with PTSD showed different findings from those reported in adults. Furthermore, due to methodological limitations, the temporal sequence between the morphological findings and the onset of symptoms is unclear, both in children and in adults with the disorder. More longitudinal studies in high-risk children are warranted to differentiate whether stress to traumatic experience can affect the developing brain or whether children with subtle brain abnormalities are particularly vulnerable to develop PTSD when exposed to traumatic experiences.

Disorders with Known Genetic or Environmental Etiology: Conclusion

The variety of brain and physical findings associated with these disorders is a graphic example of the complexity of the relationships of gene, environment, and behavior. However, one feature that is clear is that with the exception of more severe cases of FAS, the structural abnormalities associated with these disorders tend to be diffuse and subtle, albeit with some structures being more impacted than others. The availability of increasingly sophisticated voxel-based methods that are able to show differences in areas without needing to specify an a priori region of interest may be able to more effectively map relationships of these types of diffuse structural abnormalities with functional changes. MRI techniques such as DTI able to provide information about microstructural features of affected tissues may also be more informative, although the structural studies serve as an important guide regarding where to begin to look.

One of the challenges and opportunities presented by the study of disorders with known genetic or environmental causative factors is how to explain the range of resulting phenotypes. A major contribution to this is the highly complex determination of any of these behavioral features, such that the presence of other genes will affect how an insult in a specific gene is expressed. Sometimes it may be due to a genetic variation in an aspect of the associated pathway, as seen in the example of animal studies of FAS where teratogenic effects of a given dosage of alcohol were moderated by polymorphism of pertinent enzymes (Cummings, & Kavlock, 2004; Das, Cronk, Martier, Simpson, & McCarver, 2004). In PTSD, there is some evidence to suggest that a smaller hippocampus may represent a risk factor for developing the disorder. Timing of exposures is also important. Alcohol exposure can result in highly different results depending on when in pregnancy it occurs, and exposure to traumatic events may be associated with different physiological and perhaps structural effects depending on whether it occurs during childhood or after.

Another way of describing the variety of responses an individual may have to a given perturbation is in terms of resilience, an understudied area in childhood-onset neuropsychiatric disorders (Charney, 2004; Curtis & Cicchetti, 2003). A generalized attention to how specific environmental features may impact the outcome of disorders with known genetic or environmental causes has been sparse. Data from other psychiatric illnesses, for example, the increased rate of rehospitalization in patients with Schizophrenia residing in families with high levels of expressed emotion, are suggestive that such factors can significantly measure outcome (Kuipers, 1979; Miklowitz, 2004). By determining which features correlate with a better outcome in children who are faced with a particular genetic or environmental insult, it may be possible to identify areas or times of development that would be particularly important to support prospectively in affected children and their families and thus minimize the detrimental effect on the long-term developmental trajectory.

Neuropsychiatric Disorders Commonly First Diagnosed in Childhood

This section summarizes neuroimaging findings in the more common neuropsychiatric disorders typically first seen in childhood. Autistic Disorder is classified as a pervasive developmental disorder which is notable for pronounced deficits in social behavior and communication. Dyslexia is a circumscribed cognitive disorder associated with difficulties in processing written language.

Attention-Deficit/Hyperactivity Disorder is associated with difficulties in attention and impulse control, and Obsessive-Compulsive Disorder, also associated with a specific variety of difficulties in impulse control, has a significant anxiety component.

Autistic Disorder

Autism is characterized by impairments in communication and social interaction and a markedly restricted repertoire of activities and interests (Folstein & Rosen-Sheidley, 2001; Rutter, 2000). It is but one disorder that occurs along a spectrum of conditions commonly described as Autism Spectrum Disorders (ASD). ASD includes high- and low-functioning Autism, Asperger's syndrome, and a subthreshold category, termed Pervasive Developmental Disorder Not Otherwise Specified (PDD-NOS), primarily reserved for those individuals who do not meet full criteria for Autism. The onset of Autism is by definition prior to age 3 years. Recent estimates of the prevalence of Autism, strictly defined, are approximately 3 to 4 out of every 10,000 individuals (Yeargin-Allsopp et al., 2003), but this figure rises considerably when including the entire Autism spectrum (Baird et al., 2000; Chakrabarti & Fombonne, 2001). Of those diagnosed with Autism, 75% are male, approximately 70% are classified as mentally retarded, and 15% to 20% of these individuals develop seizures at some point during their lifetime.

Twin and family studies suggest a strong genetic basis for the disorder. Concordance rates for ASD and the broader phenotype (i.e., subclinical expression of the disorder) in monozygotic twins are quite high (approximately 90%), especially when contrasted with the rate among same-sex dizygotic twins (5% to 10%; Bailey et al., 1995). Such a discrepancy indicates a significant genetic loading in the transmission of autistic traits. However, no clearly defined etiology or diagnostic markers have been identified for the vast majority of cases. To date, the most prominent theories to account for the range of symptoms and characteristics present in ASD have been neuropsychological in nature. One theory regarding the basis of Autistic Disorder is that it represents an abnormality in theory of mind, a term used to describe the ability to attribute thoughts, beliefs, and desires to oneself and to others and to understand that others may have thoughts, beliefs, and desires that differ from one's own (Premack, 1978). Baron-Cohen, Leslie, and Frith (1985) first tested theory of mind abilities in individuals with ASD, finding deficits consistent with socialization difficulties observed in ASD individuals' everyday life. Ever since this seminal study, theory of mind research has had a significant and ever growing impact on the Autism field. Functional neuroimaging studies have consistently demonstrated a network of regions, including medial prefrontal cortex, posterior superior temporal sulcus, and temporal poles, as particularly important for supporting intact theory of mind ability (Frith, 2001). Theory of mind has been particularly successful in accounting for the social difficulties experienced by people with ASD, but the nonsocial aspects of the disorder generally remain unexplained.

Other researchers have described prominent abnormalities in executive functions in Autistic Disorder. Executive functions (EF) are a group of cognitive capacities that enable an individual to complete novel problem-solving tasks that require flexible thinking, future orientation, and the formulation of original strategies. EF has been linked with prefrontal functioning; however, based on functional imaging studies, it is clear that this array of cognitive capacities is subserved by various networks of brain regions, including subcortical structures and the cerebellum in addition to the previously implicated prefrontal regions (Carpenter, Just, & Reichle, 2000; Tamm, Menon, & Reiss, 2002). Potential EF deficits in Autism were investigated after noticing similarities in behavior between patients with frontal lobe injury and those with Autism (Damasio & Maurer, 1978; Rumsey, 1985) and have since been robustly demonstrated in autistic individuals and first-degree family members (Biro & Russell, 2001; Hughes, 1996; Hughes, Leboyer, & Bouvard, 1997; Hughes, Plumet, & Leboyer, 1999; Ozonoff, Strayer, McMahon, & Filloux, 1994).

In her seminal discussion of the characteristic cognitive features of Autism, Frith (1989) described the tendency of individuals with the disorder to favor local over global processing (a reverse of the typical trend) as a "weak drive for central coherence," which is the third major psychological formulation for Autism. One unusual and appealing aspect of this theoretical account is its ability to explain both strengths and weaknesses in the neuropsychological profile of individuals with ASD. A brain basis for central coherence has only begun to be investigated; Ring et al. (1999) find that when asked to complete an embedded figures task, typically developing individuals are more reliant on prefrontal regions, and ASD individuals are more reliant on primary and association visual areas. In a complementary, well-controlled functional imaging study involving only typically developing adults, there are indications that the local search component of an embedded figures task particularly activates the left superior and inferior parietal cortex (Manjaly et al., 2003).

The following sections, divided by anatomical region, aim to highlight the growing structural imaging findings for individuals with ASD (see Table 3.4). This review is not intended to be comprehensive or encyclopedic; for a detailed recent overview of structural and functional neuroimaging studies involving individuals with ASD, please see Brambilla, Hardan, et al. (2003). Similarly, for a current state of the science on neuropathological studies of ASD, please see Palmen, van Engeland, Hof, and Schmitz (2004).

Total Brain. The study of total brain size in Autism highlights many of the methodological considerations discussed in other sections of this chapter, particularly the importance of well-characterized patient and control groups (e.g., matching on or controlling for IQ), considering differences in image acquisition and analysis, and how the course of brain development (i.e., findings across different age groups and longitudinal findings) may be more informative than its end point.

In Leo Kanner's (1943) original report of Autism, he points out that 5 of the 11 subjects had notably large heads. Many subsequent studies have supported this initial observation. A postmortem study found increased brain weight in Autism (Bailey et al., 1993), and studies of head circumference (Fombonne, Roge, Claverie, Courty, & Fremolle, 1999; Lainhart et al., 1997; Miles, Hadden, Takahashi, & Hillman, 2000; Stevenson, Schroer, Skinner, Fender, & Simensen, 1997) report that approximately 1 in 5 subjects with Autism meet criteria for macrocephaly (i.e., above the 97th or 98th percentile). Taken together, these findings consistently indicate an elevated rate of macrocephaly among individuals with ASD.

Imaging studies have also been consistent in reporting enlarged brain size in Autism, although the developmental course of this enlargement has been the subject of some controversy. Piven and colleagues (Piven, Arndt, Bailey, & Andreasen, 1996) found that after controlling for IQ, brain size remained enlarged in adolescents and adults with ASD. On the contrary, Courchesne et al. (2001) and Aylward, Minshew, Field, Sparks, and Singh (2002), did not find enlargement in their adolescent and adult samples. Whether the enlargement is static or changes over time has profound implications for informing theories of the pathogenesis in Autism.

In a recent report, Courchesne, Carper, and Akshoomoff (2003) examined cross-sectional imaging and clinical data from 48 children between the ages of 2 and 5 years who were diagnosed as having ASD. Head circumference for the ASD group was smaller at birth compared to healthy controls (body length and birth weight were not statistically different) but underwent a more rapid increase between 1 to 2 months and 6 to 14 months. The accelerated rate of growth slows between ages 2 to 4 years, with the maximum size

TABLE 3.4 Structural Neuroimaging Studies of Autistic Disorder

Study	Patients (Mean Age ± SD, or Range)	Controls	Method	Findings	Comments
Courchesne, Yeung-Courchesne, Press, Hesselink, & Jernigan (1988)	16 Males 2 Females (20.9, 6–30)	9 Males 3 Females (24.8, 9–37)	Manually traced cerebellar lobules from mid-sagittal MRI scan.	Significantly smaller cerebellar vermal lobules VI and VII.	
Egaas, Courchesne, & Saitoh (1995)	45 Males 6 Females (15.5 ± 10.0)	45 Males 6 Females (15.5 ± 9.9)	Manually traced corpus callosal areas.	Smaller corpus callosum, particularly in the posterior sections.	
Piven, Arndt, Bailey, & Andreasen (1996)	26 Males 9 Females (18.4 ± 4.5)	20 Males 16 Females (20.2 ± 3.8)	T1 1.5 mm contiguous, semiautomated ROI volumes.	Total brain size enlarged in adolescents and adults with Autism, most in temporal, parietal and occipital lobes.	Findings remained after accounting for height and IQ.
Sears et al. (1999)	26 Males 9 Females (18.4 ± 4.5)	20 Males 16 Females (20.2 ± 3.8)	T1 1.5 mm contiguous slices, manual tracing of basal ganglia.	Caudate volume increased, but not putamen or globus pallidus.	Caudate enlargement related to the repetitive and restricted behaviors.
Hardan, Minshew, & Keshavan (2000)	22 Male ADI (22.4 ± 10.1)	22 Males (22.4 ± 10.0)	Area of seven subregions of the corpus callosum.	Reductions in anterior sections of the corpus callosum.	Subset reanalyzed controlling for intracranial, total brain, white matter volumes; findings persisted.
Aylward, Minshew, Field, Sparks, & Singh (2002)	58 Males 9 Females (18.8 ± 10.0)	76 Males 7 Females (18.9 ± 10.0)	T1 1.5-mm coronal contiguous slices, semiautomated measurement of whole brain volume.	Brain enlargement was observed in autistic children < 12 years and younger but not in older groups, head circumference enlarged in all ages.	Findings suggest abnormal trajectory.
Sparks et al. (2002)	45 ASD 14 DD (26 Males, 3 Females, 3.9 ± 0.4)	18 Males 8 Females (3.9 ± 0.5)	Volumes of the cerebrum, cerebellum, amygdala, and hippocampus were measured from three-dimensional coronal MR images.	ASD brain volume larger than DD and controls. Strict Autism subjects had amygdala enlargement greater than expected for cerebral volume.	ASD = Autism Spectrum Disorder; DD = Developmental delay.
Courchesne, Carper, & Akshoomoff (2003)	41 Males 7 Females (2–5)	Head circumference data were compared to two public normative samples	Head circumference, body length, and body weight measurements during the first year were obtained from medical records.	ASD reduced head circumference for the ASD group at birth; rapid increase between 1–2 months and 6–14 months and then slowing.	Abnormal trajectory as potential early marker for Autism.
Barnea-Goraly et al. (2003)	7 Males (14.6 ± 3.4)	9 Males (13.4 ± 2.8)	DTI on 3T scanner; 5 mm slices, 1.5 mm gap; 6 directions, b value =900. FA examined for whole brain using voxel based method.	Reduced fractional anisotropy in white matter areas of the ventromedial prefrontal, ant. cingulate, temporal regions; corpus callosum.	Abnormalities are consistent with regions implicated in social cognitive processes.
Boddaert et al. (2004)	16 Males 5 Females (9.3 ± 2.2)	7 Males 5 Females (10.8 ± 2.7)	T1 1.5 mm axial contiguous slices, VBM analysis.	Gray matter concentration red. in bilateral temporal lobes.	

TABLE 3.4 Continued

Study	Patients (Mean Age ± SD, or Range)	Controls	Method	Findings	Comments
De Fosse et al. (2004)	6 Males with Autism and normal language (8.3 ± 0.9) 16 Males with Autism and language impairment (9.8 ± 2.1)	11 Males with normal language (10.4 ± 2.7) 9 males with specific language impairment (SLI) (9.9 ± 2.3)	T1 1.5 mm coronal contiguous, semiautomated parcellation into 48 gyral-based divisions per hemisphere.	Reversal of asymmetry in language related regions of frontal cortex seen only in language impaired autistic and control groups.	SLI: specific language impairment.
Kates et al. (2004)	14 Male MZ twin pairs 2 Female MZ twin pairs (8.4 ± 2.6) 7 clinically concordant twin pairs, 9 discordant twin pairs	14 Males 2 Females (8.3 ± 2.4)	T1 1.5 mm coronal contiguous slices, semiautomated segmentation and parcellation into lobes.	Cerebral gm and wm similar in all twin pairs; cerebellar only similar in concordant twins. Both affected and unaffected twins showed dec. frontal, temporal, occipital wm.	
Lotspeich et al. (2004)	13 LFA males (11.6 ± 2.1) IQ: NA 18 HFA males (12.1 ± 3.4) IQ: 94 ± 17 21 Asperger's syndrome males (12.7 ± 2.6) IQ: 108 ± 20	21 Males (12.5 ± 2.8) IQ: 114 ± 10	T1 1.5–1.7 mm coronal contiguous slices, semi-automated segmentation and parcellation into lobes.	Inc. gm in LFA and HFA. Nonverbal IQ negatively related to gm in HFA; positively to wm in Asperger's syndrome.	LFA: low functioning Autism, HFA: high functioning Autism. Images acquired on 3 different scanners, one 3T and two 1.5.
Schumann et al. (2004)	19 LFA males 27 HFA males 25 Asperger's syndrome males (7.5–18.5)	27 males (7.5–18.5)	Coronal MRI images were used to trace the amygdala and the hippocampus, then outlines of these structures were also checked utilizing axial and sagittal views.	Larger amygdala found only in preadolescent autistic group (ages 7.5–12.5), LFA and HFA had bilaterally inc. hippocampal volumes.	

obtained at approximately age 5 years (8 years sooner than that of typically developing children). By adolescence there was no statistically significant difference between the groups. Severity of ASD symptoms correlated negatively with age at onset (earlier onset worse) and positively with the rate and duration of accelerated growth. The authors speculate that continued research may provide a combination of biological and behavioral markers that allow for earlier diagnosis and intervention than are currently common practice.

White and Gray Matter. Among a group of boys with Autism, Herbert et al. (2003) found a trend for cerebral white matter to be disproportionately larger than cortical gray matter and that the hippocampus-amygdaloid complex trended toward being disproportionately smaller. An extension of this study (Herbert et al., 2004), which included subjects with Developmental Language Disorder (DLD), divided white matter into an outer zone and an inner zone. Only the outer zone, composed of later myelinating axons, was larger in the Autism and DLD groups. The authors suggest that these findings are consistent with an ongoing postnatal process that affects intrahemispheric and corticocortical connections in both Autism and DLD. Other reports of white matter anomalies include a report by Courchesne et al. (2001) of an 18% increase of white matter volume in 2- to 3-year-olds with Autism but a slight decrease in this tissue type for adolescent subjects with Autism.

In examining possible brain-based differences among separate diagnoses within the Autism spectrum, Lotspeich et al. (2004) found that cerebral gray matter is enlarged in both high-functioning and low-functioning boys with Autism relative to controls, and that gray matter volume for individuals with Asperger's syndrome is intermediate between the Autism and control groups (although not statistically significantly different from either group). Gray matter may therefore covary with severity of ASD symptoms, although replication is needed to confirm these early reports.

Corpus Callosum.   The preponderance of reports suggests that corpus callosum size is slightly reduced in Autism. At least four studies indicate that the reductions occur in posterior sections (Egaas, Courchesne, & Saitoh, 1995; Manes et al., 1999; Piven, Bailey, Ranson, & Arndt, 1997; Waiter et al., 2005) of the corpus callosum; another implicates anterior sections (Hardan, Minshew, & Keshavan, 2000). Taken together with the earlier reviewed studies indicating increased brain size in ASD, these findings are consistent with the notion that larger forebrains are associated with relatively smaller corpus callosa (Jancke, Preis, & Steinmetz, 1999; Jancke, Staiger, Schlaug, Huang, & Steinmetz, 1997). Using DTI, Barnea-Goraly et al. (2004) found reduced fractional anisotropy in the genu and splenium of a small group of children and adolescents with Autism. Taken together, these findings may have implications regarding decreased lateralization and interhemispheric connectivity in ASD.

Basal Ganglia.   Findings for the basal ganglia are quite variable, including one report of an increase in caudate volume (Sears et al., 1999) in ASD and one report of volumetric differences in and around the basal ganglia in Asperger's syndrome, reflecting bilateral excess of white matter and bilateral reduction of gray matter (McAlonan et al., 2002). In contrast, two other reports (Hardan, Kilpatrick, Keshavan, & Minshew, 2003; Herbert et al., 2003) indicate that group differences in these structures are not statistically significant after controlling for total cerebral volume. Studies of brain-behavior correlates also present findings that are somewhat difficult to interpret. Consistent with the predicted brain-behavior relationship, Sears et al. found that caudate volume correlated positively with the degree of stereotyped repetitive behaviors but not with social or communication deficits in affected individuals. On the other hand, among individuals with ASD, Hardan et al. found no significant relationship between performance on motor tasks (e.g., grip strength and speed in placing grooved pegs in a board) and basal ganglia volume. These findings are not necessarily at odds with one another. The tasks utilized in Hardan et al.'s study may not capture prototypical repetitive behaviors and motor abnormalities commonly observed in ASD (as were assessed by a diagnostic interview in the Sears et al. study); thus, they may rely on a different set of neural systems.

Temporal Lobe Structures.   Postmortem studies of ASD brains consistently indicate increased cell packing density and smaller neuronal size in the limbic system (Palmen et al., 2004). Moreover, the amygdala's role in social-emotional behavior and cognition make it an obvious target for ASD imaging studies. Unfortunately, amygdala findings have been contradictory, with reports of increased volume (Abell et al., 1999; Howard et al., 2000), decreased volume (Aylward et al., 1999; Pierce, Muller, Ambrose, Allen, & Courchesne, 2001), and no statistically significant difference in volume (Haznedar et al., 2000).

Sparks et al. (2002) compared 3- to 4-year-old children with Autism, with PDD-NOS, with other developmental disorders, and typically developing children. Amygdala volumes were significantly larger in the Autism and PDD-NOS groups than in the comparison groups. Furthermore, the children with Autism had significantly larger amygdalae than the children in the less severely symptomatic PDD-NOS group.

Superficially contradictory findings may in fact be complementary after taking developmental periods into consideration. In a recently reported cross-sectional study, Schumann et al. (2004) found that the amygdala was indeed larger in preadolescent children with Autism, but among adolescents with Autism, no amygdala volume differences were observed. The pattern of findings among the typically developing controls indicates that amygdala volume continues to increase across these ages, whereas amygdala volume in children with Autism remains stable.

Turning to the hippocampus, smaller hippocampal volumes in ASD have been reported in two studies (Aylward et al., 1999; Saitoh, Karns, & Courchesne, 2001) and larger left hippocampus in one study of both preadolescent and adolescent males (Schumann et al., 2004); however, comparable hippocampal size has been reported in the majority of studies (Haznedar et al., 2000; Howard et al., 2000; Piven, Bailey, Ranson, & Arndt, 1998; Saitoh, Courchesne, Egaas, Lincoln, & Schreibman, 1995).

Consistent with Schumann et al. (2004), one study (Rojas et al., 2004) involving parents of individuals with Autism, adults with ASD, and adults with no familial history of ASD found that both parents of ASD individuals and ASD adults had larger left hippocampi than the comparison group.

Other methodologies have been utilized to examine this brain region, including voxel-based morphometry (VBM). In a VBM study of male adolescents with ASD and matched controls, Waiter et al. (2004) found that individuals with ASD had increased gray matter volume in the right fusiform gyrus, the right temporo-occipital region, the left frontal pole and medial frontal cortex relative to controls.

Similarly, Kwon, Ow, Pedatella, Lotspeich, and Reiss (2004) utilized VBM to assess potential brain-based differences among males diagnosed with high-functioning Autism, those diagnosed with Asperger's syndrome, and a control group of typically developing males. The combined ASD group had decreased gray matter density in the ventromedial regions of the temporal cortex. Also using VBM, Boddaert et al. (2004) showed decreased gray matter concentration in the superior temporal sulcus when comparing children with Autism to typically developing children. And finally, in Abell and colleagues' (1999) study utilizing VBM, individuals with ASD showed decreased gray matter volume in the right paracingulate sulcus and the left occipito-temporal cortex. The localization of these convergent findings is consistent with expectations based on previous social cognitive and functional imaging studies.

Cerebellum.   The cerebellum has been the most active area of investigation in Autism structural neuroimaging research. After indications of cerebellar abnormalities from a neuropathological investigation (Bauman & Kemper, 1985), an initial case study demonstrated incomplete development of vermal lobules VI and VII in a young man with Autism (Courchesne, Hesselink, Jernigan, & Yeung-Courchesne, 1987). This was followed by a study indicating a 19% reduction in these lobules for individuals with Autism when compared to controls (Courchesne et al., 1988). A report on a subsample of these subjects indicated more widespread involvement of the cerebellum, with a 12% reduction in cerebellar volume (Murakami, Courchesne, Press, Yeung-Courchesne, & Hesselink, 1989). In a more recent report of the sample enlarged to 50 patients and 53 controls, mean sizes of vermal lobules VI and VII were not different. However, in contrast to the Gaussian distribution of values in the control group, the values in the autistic group were bimodally distributed. Based on this distribution, two distinct subgroups were proposed, one of 86% of the patients having a mean midsagittal area of vermal lobules VI and VII 16% smaller than the control group, and the other of 12% of the patients having a 34% larger mean area.

In contrast to these studies, a number of investigators have not found differences in the midsagittal area of vermal lobules VI and VII in Autism (Hashimoto et al., 1993; Holttum, Minshew, Sanders, & Phillips, 1992; Piven, Saliba, Bailey, & Arndt, 1997). The importance of controlling for IQ in ASD neuroimaging studies was exemplified by a study of 15 high-functioning males with Autism who had smaller vermal lobules VI and VII when compared to a group of individuals matched for age and parental

socioeconomic status, but not when compared to a group matched for nonverbal IQ (Piven et al., 1992).

Although cerebellar MRI findings in Autism remain controversial, accumulating evidence of the cerebellum's role in learning and cognition (Allen, Buxton, Wong, & Courchesne, 1997) and its extensive connections to the rest of the brain make for an intriguing hypothesis in the pathogenesis of Autism. Moreover, newer studies, using refined methodologies, have noted more fine-grained differences in cerebellar volume, for example, reduced white matter volume of the cerebellum in people with ASD as compared to controls (McAlonan et al., 2005) and bilaterally increased gray matter (Abell et al., 1999).

Intriguingly, Kates and colleagues (2004) found that when they examined neuroanatomic variation among monozygotic twin pairs discordant for the narrow phenotype of Autism, cerebral structures, regardless of tissue type, exhibited high intra-class correlations, whereas the cerebellar region did not. These findings may indicate that the cerebellum, unlike cerebral structures, is vulnerable to environmental insult. The potential for relatively strong environmental influences on cerebellar development is consistent with its preferential susceptibility to insults such as alcohol, lead, and anoxia and its role in modulating responses to environmental stimuli.

Other Brain Structures/Regions.   In addition to the hippocampus and amygdala, one other subcortical structure of potential interest is the thalamus. Given its vast reciprocal connections to practically every other brain region, it likely plays an integral role in functional connectivity and networking vital to many forms and levels of information processing. Tsatsanis and colleagues (2003) showed reduced thalamic volume in ASD relative to matched controls, but only after adjusting for mean differences in total brain volume. Moreover, the relationship between thalamic volume and total brain volume was different for each of these groups; they were strongly correlated in the control group, whereas the correlation in the ASD group did not reach significance. These findings may reflect reduced connectivity between cortical and subcortical structures in ASD and may contribute to the various information-processing difficulties commonly observed in ASD.

Most studies have not found significant differences in ventricle size. One study indicates enlarged lateral ventricles in Autism (Piven et al., 1995), but two other studies find no statistical difference (Creasey et al., 1986; Hardan, Minshew, Mallikarjuhn, & Keshavan, 2001). Fourth ventricle enlargement has been reported (Gaffney, Kuperman, Tsai, Minchin, & Hassanein, 1987), but most studies that have examined it have not found differences (Garber & Ritvo, 1992; Garber et al., 1989; Kleiman, Neff, & Rosman, 1992; Piven et al., 1992).

In a qualitative MRI study of 13 high-functioning adult men with Autism five were noted to have polymicrogyria, one had macrogyria, and one had both macrogyria and schizencephaly (Piven et al., 1990). Similar cortical findings of poly- and microgyria were reported for two patients with Asperger's syndrome (Berthier, Starkstein, & Leiguarda, 1990). These anomalies most likely reflect problems in neural migration during the first 6 months of pregnancy, which may indicate a particularly vulnerable time for external factors such as infections to contribute to the pathogenesis of ASD. Other reports of cortical abnormalities include decreased parietal lobe volumes, manifest by sulcal widening, which was found in 9 of 21 autistic subjects versus none in 12 controls (Courchesne, Press, & Yeung-Courchesne, 1993); gray matter heterotopia (Gaffney & Tsai, 1987); and altered asymmetries of frontal lobe volumes (Hashimoto et al., 1989), particularly for the language association cortex (Herbert et al., 2002; De Fossé et al., 2004).

Summary. The most consistent structural abnormality in MRI studies of Autism is enlarged total brain size, although there are conflicting reports as to whether the increased size persists into adolescence/adulthood. Possibly related are findings of reduced corpus callosum size in ASD. Consistent with neuropathological studies, there is a trend toward finding abnormalities in the amygdala, hippocampus, and cerebellum. The general inconsistency in findings and lack of replicability may be due to varying methodologies, sampling procedures, and so on, and these potential confounds significantly complicate interpretation of results. Although caution is warranted, these findings are generally consistent with observed behavioral findings and the most prominent neuropsychological theories of ASD. Enlarged brains and smaller corpus callosa, for example, may be consistent with an inefficient cognitive processing style as described in the weak central coherence account. Moreover, prefrontal cortex, cerebellar, and subcortical abnormalities are consistent with the oft-reported executive dysfunction in ASD. Finally, abnormalities in the medial frontal, amygdala, and temporal regions fit with the social cognitive and emotional processing difficulties predicted by the theory of mind account. Mapping the developmental course of these brain-based abnormalities and their relationship to symptom presentation and neuropsychological impairments may help to elucidate theoretical accounts and isolate neural substrates of autistic behavior.

Dyslexia

Although there are various definitions for dyslexia, the essence of the disorder was captured nicely by this 1896 report by W. Pringle Morgan in the *British Medical Journal*: "Percy F., . . . aged 14, . . . has always been a bright and intelligent boy, quick at games, and in no way inferior to others of his age. His great difficulty has been—and is now—his inability to learn to read" (Pringle, 1896).

This straightforward concept of difficulty learning to read despite intelligence, motivation, and education belies the complexity of the many distributed systems within the central nervous system necessary to achieve a complex cognitive task such as reading. The challenge is to discern the pertinent neural circuitry subcomponents that are amenable to investigation. In this regard, studies of dyslexia are farther along than studies of most other pediatric neuropsychiatric disorders in that two distinct but interacting pathways have been well delineated and investigated. These two pathways are the orthographic, involved in the visual interpretation of symbols, and the phonologic, involved in the auditory-processing aspects.

A given person may have anomalies of none, one, or both of these pathways, and studies not accounting for different subtypes may risk "apples to oranges" comparisons, obscuring neuroanatomical differences. IQ also seems to be a parameter particularly important in dyslexia studies (Leonard et al., 2002). For instance, the literature for dyslexia subjects with high IQ tends to report large and asymmetrical brain structures, whereas the literature for dyslexia subjects with low IQ tends to report small and symmetrical brain structures.

Temporal Lobe. Most dyslexia imaging studies have focused on the planum temporale, a part of the superior temporal gryus. Interest in this region was spawned by a seminal postmortem study of 100 brains that found a left-greater-than-right asymmetry of the planum temporale (Geschwind & Levitsky, 1968). This asymmetry was thought to be related to the left hemisphere's more prominent role in language, which has been well documented from studies of people with unilateral strokes and other lesion studies. Dyslexia then was hypothesized to be related to an alteration of this normal asymmetry, and several early postmortem (Galaburda, 1995) and MRI studies (Hynd & Semrud-Clikeman, 1989; Larsen, Odegaard, Grude, & Hoien, 1989) supported this. However, subsequent larger studies have not found a link between dyslexia and loss of planum temporale asymmetry (Best & Demb, 1999; Eckert et al., 2003; Heiervang et al., 2000; Leonard et al., 1993; Leonard et al., 2001; Preis, Engelbrecht, Huang, & Steinmetz, 1998; Robichon, Levrier, Farnarier, & Habib, 2000; Rumsey et al., 1997; R. T. Schultz et al., 1994).

Relatedly, Heschl's gyrus, the primary auditory cortex, where audio input to the brain is first processed (Morosan et al., 2001), has been related to language impairment but has not been consistently demonstrated to be anomalous in dyslexia (Leonard et al., 2002).

Parietal Lobe.   Because of its functional connectivity to the temporal lobe, the parietal lobe has also been of interest in studies of dyslexia. Passive listening first activates the superior temporal gyrus and then the inferior parietal lobe (Friston, Harrison, & Penny, 2003), where the phonological inputs are mapped to orthographic symbols (Y. Chen, Fu, Iversen, Smith, & Matthews, 2002).

Here again the literature is somewhat difficult to reconcile. Three studies of high-functioning adults with dyslexia have found larger parietal areas caudal to the infra-Sylvian fissure in the dyslexia group (R. L. Green et al., 1999); exaggerated left-greater-than-right asymmetry of the planum parietale (the ascending branch of the Sylvian fissure; Leonard et al., 2001), and, in a group of dyslexic engineering students, an exaggerated left-greater-than-right asymmetry of the peri-Sylvian region that predicted nonword dictation performance (Robichon et al., 2000). However, in a study of dyslexic children with normal verbal IQ but multiple reading skill deficits, abnormal parietal asymmetries were found (Eckert et al., 2003).

Frontal Lobe.   The frontal lobe receives input from the temporal and parietal and, among other things, processes phonologic information to prepare for speech output (Gelfand & Bookheimer, 2003). Structural MRI studies of the frontal lobe in its entirety have not yielded consistent findings; however, in studies that specifically address a part of the frontal lobe, the inferior frontal gyrus, a consensus is emerging. A study of dyslexic adults found a right-greater-than-left asymmetry of the inferior frontal gyrus in the dyslexia group (Robichon et al., 2000); a voxel-based morphometry study, also of adults, found decreased left inferior frontal gyrus gray matter volume in the dyslexia group (Brown et al., 2001); and surface area measurements of the pars triangularis (the middle of the three inferior frontal gyri) were smaller in dyslexia (Eckert et al., 2003).

Cerebellum.   Functional MRI studies have implicated the cerebellum in a variety of reading and phonological

tasks (Brunswick, McCrory, Price, Frith, & Frith, 1999). The cerebellum has robust reciprocal anatomical connections to the frontal, temporal, and parietal regions previously discussed.

One structural MRI study of dyslexic adults found right-greater-than-left asymmetry of cerebellar gray matter volume in their control but not dyslexic group (Rae et al., 2002), and another found less gray matter in left and right semilunar lobule, a part of the posterior cerebellar lobe (Brown et al., 2001). A voxel-based morphometry study of dyslexic children reported less gray matter in the semilunar lobule, but only on the left (Eckert et al., 2003).

Asymmetry.   The issue of asymmetry, or more specifically, lack of typical asymmetry, is more prominently represented in the literature on dyslexia than in other disorders examined. To address interhemispheric asymmetry in a group of 16 dyslexic men age 18 to 40 years and 14 controls matched for sex, age, educational level, handedness, socioeconomic background, and general intelligence (Casanova et al., 2004), we coregistered a brain image with its left/right mirror image and examined the deformation needed to achieve alignment. From this a color-coded map of asymmetries was created, indicating a large area of asymmetry in the medial temporal lobe (a reversal of the typical left-greater-than-right in this region), but also smaller areas of asymmetry in six other regions encompassing both limbic and extrapyramidal systems. Consistent with the studies mentioned earlier, the planum temporale was not one of the areas differing in symmetry.

Summary.   For many of the pediatric-onset neuropsychiatric disorders, structural MRI anomalies have been reported for a variety of anatomically connected structures covering most general regions of the brain. This widely distributed collection of structural abnormalities suggests that studies of connectivity, such as those using DTI, may be particularly useful in dyslexia. A DTI study of dyslexic adults found white matter anomalies in the temporal-parietal region (Klingberg, Hedehus, et al., 2000). Future studies will need to continue the trend toward greater anatomical specificity and attempt to link the underlying neuroanatomic anomalies, not to dyslexia per se, but to the cognitive subcomponents of reading and language processing that come together to meet criteria for the diagnosis.

Attention-Deficit/Hyperactivity Disorder

ADHD is a clinically heterogeneous disorder with key clinical symptoms including persistent difficulty with attention, impulsivity, and hyperactivity. It is estimated to affect between 3% to 10% of children. Reports of the ratio of affected males to females have ranged from 4:1 to 9:1, with a higher male:female ratio in clinics than in community settings (American Psychiatric Association, Task Force on *DSM-IV,* 2000; Barbaresi et al., 2004; Dey & Bloom, 2005). Although many children diagnosed with the disorder show clinical improvement with maturation, approximately 30% of individuals will continue to meet criteria for the disorder in adulthood (Kessler et al., 2005).

ADHD was first described over 100 years ago (Still, 1902) as a disorder of hyperactivity mostly affecting boys. Despite its long history and high incidence its etiology and pathophysiology are not yet well understood. It has been shown to have a strong genetic component in both twin and adoption studies, with an estimated heritability of .76 obtained from multiple studies worldwide (Faraone et al., 2005). Several potential disease-susceptibility genes have been identified, including genes associated with dopamine and serotonin transmission. However, at present there is not evidence for any single gene with a strong effect.

Multiple lines of evidence from studies using structural imaging, functional imaging, and neuropsychological testing have supported the role of an abnormality in the frontostriatal regions as underlying ADHD symptoms. In this section we will review the structural neuroimaging literature, which over the past 30 years has yielded a vast amount of data on the structural anomalies associated with the disorder (see Table 3.5). We integrate some central findings in models of the pathogenesis of the disorder, focusing on recent findings. Other reviews of the literature can be found in Giedd, Blumenthal, Molloy, and Castellanos (2001) and Durston et al. (2004).

Structural Neuroimaging of ADHD.   The total brain size in ADHD is approximately 5% smaller than in age- and sex-matched controls (Castellanos et al., 1996). Generally, analyses of regional brain abnormalities should control statistically for differences among individuals in total brain volume, preferably by using analyses of covariance rather than simple ratios or proportions (Arndt et al., 1991). There are some possible exceptions, such as when entire compartments of the brain are being assessed (such as the total gray matter). In such cases, there are high correlations of total brain volume with the measures of interest, which can violate some of the assumptions underlying covariate analyses. Additionally, it can be argued that in neurodevelopmental disorders that are likely to have distributed deficits in multiple regions of the brain, covarying for total brain volume could obscure some potentially significant differences (Pfefferbaum, Lim, Rosenbloom, & Zipursky, 1990).

Most efforts to localize the brain differences between children with ADHD and children who are typically developing have focused on the frontal lobe, specifically the prefrontal cortex. This reflects some of the current hypotheses of the neurocognitive deficits that underpin the disorder. Different forms of failure of inhibition have been held to be a central deficit in ADHD, and these are linked with specific regions of the prefrontal cortex. For example, tasks such as the stop signal task (in which subjects must respond to a go signal but inhibit a response when presented with a stop signal) have been associated with activation of the right inferior frontal gyrus (Aron, Dowson, Sahakian, & Robbins, 2003; Aron, Fletcher, Bullmore, Sahakian, & Robbins, 2003). Other aspects of response inhibition, as assessed by the classic Stroop task, are supported by the anterior cingulate gyrus, and activation in subjects with ADHD is abnormal in this region (Bush et al., 1999). Others have argued for a central role of impairments in working memory in ADHD, a function typically linked with more dorsolateral regions of the prefrontal cortex (Barkley, 1997; Klingberg, Forssberg, & Westerberg, 2002).

Castellanos et al. (2002) detailed changes over time in the brain of 152 children with ADHD in the largest longitudinal study to date (see Figure 3.8 on p. 160). Children were scanned repeatedly over a 10-year period. The majority of subjects were scanned at least twice, and the trajectories of the development of the gray and white matter, the basal ganglia, and cerebellum were modeled and compared with a comparison group of age- and sex-matched typically developing children. This study examined changes at the level of entire lobes and reported overall reduction in both gray and white matter in the frontal cortex, which appeared to be fixed and nonprogressive. Notably, the reduction of volume in the frontal lobes was modest (approximately a 4% reduction compared to healthy children) and was of a similar magnitude to the reduction found in the other major lobes. In a study that compared 30 children with ADHD with their healthy siblings and healthy unrelated controls, Durston and colleagues (2004) found significant reduction in the left prefrontal gray and left prefrontal white matter in affected children and, of particular importance, a similar significant reduction in the right prefrontal gray matter in unaffected siblings relative to unrelated healthy controls. It is noteworthy that significant and near-significant volume reductions were also found in the left occipital and parietal lobes in the affected probands alone.

These findings of volume loss in several lobes might seem to run counter to the postulation of specific frontostriatal

TABLE 3.5   Structural Neuroimaging Studies of Attention Deficit and Hyperactivity Disorder

Study	Patients (Mean Age ± SD, or Range)	Control Subjects	Method	Findings	Comments
Hynd et al. (1993)	8 Males 3 Females (11.08 ± 2.52)	6 Males 5 Females (11.03 ± 2.77)	"Best" axial slice from MRI scan measured.	L caudate wider than R in normal subjects, reversed in ADHD.	High variability in measurements.
Giedd et al. (1994)	18 Males (11.9 ± 2.5)	18 Males (10.5 ± 2.3)	Midsagittal cross-sectional area of the corpus callosum, divided into seven sections, was measured from MRI scans.	Rostrum and rostral body of corpus callosum smaller in ADHD.	Rostral body correlated significantly with hyperactivity ratings.
Aylward et al. (1996)	10 Males (11.26 ± 1.62)	11 Males (10.71 ± 1.98)	Manual ROI volumes of caudate, putamen, and globus pallidus, corrected for brain volume.	Globus pallidus smaller in ADHD (significant on left).	
Castellanos et al. (1996)	57 Males (11.65 ± 2.97)	55 Males (12.03 ± 3.06)	Manual ROI volumes.	Total cerebral volume, caudate, globus pallidus smaller in ADHD.	Supports right prefrontal-striatal-cortical circuitry dysfunction in ADHD.
Filipek et al. (1997)	15 Males (12.4 ± 3.4)	15 Males (14.4 ± 3.4)	Manual ROI volumes.	R and L caudates and R anterior superior white matter smaller in ADHD, posterior white matter volumes decreased only in stimulant non-responders.	First study to quantify gray and white matter separately.
Mataro, Garcia-Sanchez, Junque, Estevez-Gonzalez, & Pujol (1997)	8 Males 3 Females (14.6 ± 0.5) IQ: 101.5 ± 8.5	16 Males 3 Females (14.8 ± 0.7) IQ: 109.4 ± 7.7	Single-slice transversal measurements of the head of the caudate nucleus.	Larger right caudate.	
Castellanos et al. (2001)	50 Females (9.7 ± 2.6)	50 Females (10.0 ± 2.5)	Manual ROI volumes.	Deceased volume in cerebellar lobules VIII to X.	
Overmeyer et al. (2001)	15 Males 3 Females ICD-10 hyperkinetic disorder (10.4 ± 1.7)	15 Males 1 Female (10.3 ± 1.2)	Voxel based morphometry.	Grey matter deficits in the R superior frontal gyrus and R posterior cingulate cortex.	Subjects also met criteria for ADHD.
Castellanos et al. (2002)	63 Females (9.4 ± 2.6) 89 Males (10.5 ± 3.1)	56 Females (10.0 ± 2.6) 83 Males (10.9 ± 3.5)	Automated ROI lobar volumes. Subjects were scanned repeatedly over a 10-year period.	Dec. volumes in cerebellum, prefrontal cortex; initially smaller caudate "normalized."	Subjects scanned repeatedly over 10-year period. The largest study of its kind. There was a correlation between all clinical measures of severity and volume loss.
Mostofsky, Cooper, Kates, Denckla, & Kaufmann (2002)	12 Males (10.1, 8.1–13.8) FSIQ: 115, 101–131	12 Males (10.2, 8.3–13.6) FSIQ: 125, 112–136	Talairach based grid to estimate lobar and sublobar volumes.	Widespread volume reduction in the prefrontal cortex.	The volume loss also affected the premotor cortex. A later study used similar methods to demonstrate volume decreases in the left deep white matter of boys with Tourette's syndrome Kates et al. (2002).
Castellanos et al. (2003)	Compared monozygotic twins, discordant for ADHD 8 Pairs of males 1 Pair of females (11.0 ± 3.2)		Automated volumetric measures of grey and white matter, basal ganglia and cerebellum.	Twin with ADHD had a significantly smaller caudate than the unaffected twin.	

(continued)

TABLE 3.5   Continued

Study	Patients (Mean Age ± SD, or Range)	Controls	Method	Findings	Comments
Hill et al. (2003)	17 Males 6 Females (9.35 ± 1.82)	16 Males 8 Females (9.36 ± 1.64)	Manual ROI volumes.	Reduction in volume of R superior prefrontal lobes. No group differences in basal ganglia. Decreased volume of cerebellar lobules 1 to V and VIII to X.	The volume reduction was associated with better performance in a test of sustained attention.
Sowell et al. (2003)	11 Females (11.6 ± 2.8) 16 Males (12.8 ± 3·2) FSIQ: 109 ± 18	17 Females (11.8 ± 3.1) 29 Males (12.2 ± 3.3) FSIQ: 114 ± 13	Surface based computational image analysis, mapping regional changes in cortical morphology and grey matter density.	Reductions in DLPFC, temporal cortex, parietal cortex; GM density increased in post. temporal and inf. parietal lobes.	
Durston et al. (2004)	30 Males (12.1 ± 2.5)	30 unaffected male siblings (11.6 ± 3.2) 30 Healthy male controls (10.7 ± 1.9)	Automated measures of grey and white matter of major lobes and cerebellum.	Smaller frontal gm, R cerebellum in ADHD.	Some volume losses also seen in unaffected siblings compared to healthy controls.

pathology in ADHD, but as the level of analysis was the entire lobe, more subregional changes affecting only a small proportion of the total lobe may have been missed. In this vein, it is interesting that more recent developments, which have allowed such regional specificity, have reported volume changes in the prefrontal cortex in areas where cortical loss would be expected on the basis of neurocognitive models. For example, using a surface-based analytic technique that

allows mapping of the entire cortex at the level of individual voxels, Sowell and colleagues (2003) reported focal abnormal cortical morphology in portions of the dorsolateral prefrontal cortex. In a group of 27 children with ADHD (compared with 47 healthy controls), they found that the brain surface extent (reflected by a decreased distance from the center of the brain) appeared to be reduced by up to 4 mm bilaterally in the inferior dorsolateral prefrontal cortex.

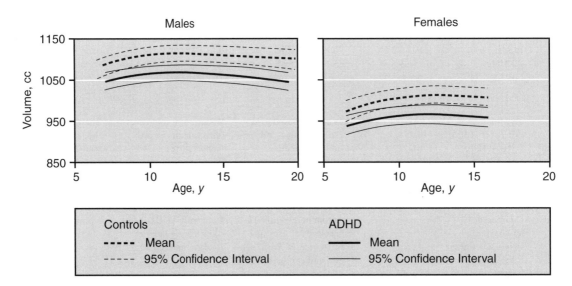

Figure 3.8 Predicted unadjusted longitudinal growth curves for total cerebral volumes for patients with ADHD and controls. *Source:* From "Developmental Trajectories of Brain Volume Abnormalities in Children and Adolescents with Attention-Deficit/ Hyperactivity Disorder," by F. X. Castellanos et al., 2002, *Journal of the American Medical Association, 288*(14), pp. 1740–1748.

By contrast, there was a trend for increase in the brain surface extent in more dorsal frontal regions. Although this study is limited by its relatively small sample size and cross-sectional nature, it is an elegant demonstration of the potential of techniques that map cortical changes at the level of individual voxels.

Overmeyer and colleagues (2001) used a different voxel-based method of estimating volume change and reported specific hits to subregions such as the right superior frontal gyrus and the posterior cingulate cortex (Overmeyer et al., 2001). Yet another approach is to use standard templates to define regions of interest, such as Talaraich-based stereotaxic grid. Mostofsky and colleagues (Mostofsky et al., 2002) adapted such as grid for pediatric brains and reported a reduction in the prefrontal and premotor gray and white matter in 12 boys with ADHD.

These automated and semiautomated techniques complement the findings of increasingly precise volumetric studies that trace regions of interest manually. Many of these earlier studies are detailed in Table 3.1 and have been discussed in Giedd et al. (2001). Recent key volumetric studies have detected smaller right-sided prefrontal brain regions measured en bloc (Castellanos et al., 1996; Filipek et al., 1997) in boys with ADHD that were correlated with neuropsychological performance on tasks that required response inhibition (Casey et al., 1997). In the first study to differentiate the gray and white matter, right anterior white matter was also reduced in ADHD boys (Filipek et al., 1997). However, this difference must be interpreted with caution as the patient group was 2 years younger on average than the controls ($p = .12$, $n = 15$ per group) and because white matter volume increases linearly with age in this age range (Paus et al., 1999; Reiss et al., 1996). The finding was replicated by another group on a larger sample of 26 children with ADHD, which found a volume loss in the right, but not left, superior prefrontal region (Hall, Dhilla, Charalambous, Gogos, & Karayiorgou, 2003). In one of the very few studies on adults with ADHD, Hesslinger and colleagues (2002) reported a significant reduction in the volume of the left orbitofrontal cortex in eight unmedicated male patients. In brief, there are consistent findings of volume reduction in the prefrontal lobe, with rapid advances in defining more precisely the exact regions which are compromised in ADHD.

The prefrontal cortex is richly interconnected with the basal ganglia in a series of parallel loops that are thought to support mechanisms of attention and motor control (Alexander, DeLong, & Strick, 1986). It has been proposed that ADHD results from dysfunction in such frontostriatal circuitry. Castellanos (2002) and others have argued that structural and neurochemical (primarily dopaminergic) anomalies may contribute to abnormal reward mechanisms in ADHD. These result in a marked intolerance to delay and preference for immediate gratification, even when this is not an optimal behavioral strategy (Sonuga-Barke, Dalen, & Remington, 2003). This theory would predict structural anomalies in the basal ganglia to parallel the changes in the frontal cortex in ADHD already discussed. A reduction or marked asymmetry in the volume of the body and/or head of the caudate nucleus has been reported by several groups (Castellanos et al., 1994, 1996, 2001, 2003; Hynd et al., 1993; Mataro, Garcia-Sanchez, Junque, Estevez-Gonzalez, & Pujol, 1997), although there is no consensus on which caudate is affected, and there are several negative findings (Bussing, Grudnik, Mason, Wasiak, & Leonard, 2002; Filipek et al., 1997; Hill et al., 2003). In the Castellanos et al. (2002) longitudinal study, the caudate emerged as the only structure showing a developmental trajectory that was not completely parallel to the healthy comparison group. Rather, over time the smaller caudate tended to normalize in size, a significant finding that will be discussed later. The inconsistencies in the many studies that measure the caudate are likely to reflect differences in methodology, such as the orientation of the slices used for definition and defining anatomical landmarks. For example, the mean coefficient of variation in the two studies that used single slice area measures of the caudate (Hynd et al., 1993; Mataro et al., 1997) was 0.22 ($SD = 0.04$), which is significantly greater than the coefficient of variation in the studies that reported volumes (Castellanos et al., 1996; Mataro et al., 1997; mean = 0.14, $SD = 0.03$, $t = 3.20$, $df = 6$, $p = .02$).

Neither of the anatomic MRI studies that reported putamen volumes detected significant diagnostic group differences (Aylward, Reiss, et al., 1996; Castellanos et al., 1996), although statistical power was insufficient in one study to rule out type II error (Aylward, Reiss, et al., 1996).

The output nuclei of the basal ganglia are the internal segment of the globus pallidus and the substantia nigra pars reticulata, but the volume of the latter cannot generally be measured with MRI, and the size of the globus pallidus can only be measured as a unit (lateral and medial segments together), and then only with difficulty. Still, this region has been found to be significantly reduced in size in ADHD (Aylward, Reiss, et al., 1996; Castellanos et al., 1996), although these two studies differed in finding the larger difference on the left and right sides, respectively.

Although total corpus callosum area has not differed from controls in any study, smaller anterior regions have generally been found in ADHD subjects (Giedd et al., 1994; Hynd et al., 1991). The largest MRI study did not confirm these differences when measurements were obtained from images that did not control for the positioning of the brain (Castellanos et al., 1996). The rostrum is the most anterior (and inferior) portion of the corpus callosum, and nearly all findings in ADHD have been anterior. The one exception was based on 15 ADHD subjects that included 5 stimulant nonresponders. The authors found that the subgroup of stimulant nonresponders had the smallest splenium area (Filipek et al., 1997). Examination of their data shows that their finding of a difference in the posterior corpus callosum would not have reached significance without the inclusion of those 5 subjects. Given the known heterogeneity and comorbidity of ADHD, we can speculate that posterior brain changes may be associated with ADHD symptoms secondary to a learning disability, which would explain the absence of benefits from stimulant treatment.

Several influential models of attention have emphasized the distributed nature of the neural systems that mediate attention. Posner and Rothbart (1998), for example, argues that the right parietal cortex plays an important role in establishing and maintaining a vigilant state and in orienting to stimuli. Volumetric deficits in both white and gray matter in the parietal lobes have been reported, complemented by a demonstration of loss of cortical density in the region (Castellanos et al., 2002; Sowell et al., 2003), although there are some negative findings (Durston et al., 2004). Automated methods that allow examination of the entire brain have also demonstrated volume losses in the cortical and occipital lobes (Castellanos et al., 2002; Durston et al., 2004). A study that defined the most severely affected regions within these lobes suggests that the changes are prominent in heteromodal cortical areas—the anterior and midtemporal cortex and inferior parietal cortex—which integrate sensorimotor percepts and allow these to guide attention (Sowell et al., 2003).

A reduction in the volume of the cerebellum is one of the most consistent findings in ADHD. Reduction in the inferior posterior, but not superior posterior, lobule is the prominent regional finding. These morphological abnormalities have been linked with two aspects of ADHD. First, poor coordination is a frequent finding in children with ADHD, and the cerebellum is important in fine motor control (Rasmussen & Gillberg, 2000). Second, many children with ADHD have deficits in time perception, being unable, for example, to estimate time intervals accurately (Barkley, Edwards, Laneri, Fletcher, & Metevia, 2001).

This may contribute to the sluggish cognitive tempo thought to characterize the high variability in performance and frequent lapses in concentration so characteristic of ADHD. Cerebrocerebellar circuits have been described which convey information from the cortex via the pons to cerebellum, which projects back to the cortex via the thalamus. Such circuits are important in determining temporal relationships and possibly in the timing of fine motor actions (Ivry, Spencer, Zelaznik, & Diedrichsen, 2002; Rubia, Noorloos, Smith, Gunning, & Sergeant, 2003).

Neuroimaging of ADHD is beginning to examine subtle structural anomalies of white matter. Several studies have reported reductions in total white matter volume in several lobes (Castellanos et al., 2002; Durston et al., 2004; Overmeyer et al., 2001). There is considerable interest in applying DTI techniques to characterize white matter changes at a more meaningful physiological level and to delineate possible white matter tract differences between children with ADHD and healthy children.

One of the most striking features of ADHD is its tendency to improve with age in a majority of cases. Little is known of the neurobiology shaping this natural history. In the only longitudinal structural study, Castellanos and colleagues (2002) reported deficits in the gray and white matter and cerebellum that did not progress over time. The only exception to the fixed, nonprogressive deficits was in the caudate nucleus, which appeared to normalize in volume in late adolescence, possibly mediating much of the clinical improvement in the syndrome. Future studies could usefully exploit the difference in outcome in children with ADHD to define structural characteristics associated with different levels of improvement.

Few studies have attempted to delineate the relative influence of genotype and environmental factors in determining the neural substrate of ADHD. One approach is to examine monozygotic (MZ) twins who are discordant for the disorder; as the twins are genetically identical, differences between them may highlight those structural differences most susceptible to environmental influences in the pathogenesis of ADHD. Castellanos and colleagues (2003) recruited nine such pairs of MZ twins discordant for ADHD and found that the only structural differences lay in a reduction in the volume of the caudate. This suggests that the caudate may be particularly susceptible to factors such as birth complications (specifically, breech presentation), which were more common in affected twins.

Most of the structural studies in ADHD have been limited by small sample size, their cross-sectional nature, and the possible confounding effects of comorbidity and mediation effects. Despite the methodological limitations, a picture begins to emerge of consistent, if complex, interconnected structural anomalies in ADHD, which fit reasonably well with some of the neurocognitive models of the disorder. At the cortical level, there is evidence for distributed subtle anomalies that may hit the regions most implicated by other modalities (such as functional imaging and lesion studies) in the mediation of attention. Particularly good evidence emerges for the involvement of the prefrontal cortices and right parietal cortex. The prefrontal cortical areas project to basal ganglia, which also demonstrate structural alterations, most convincingly found in the caudate nucleus. Thus, both components of the corticostriatal loops that mediate attention show structural change.

Obsessive-Compulsive Disorder

A similar theme of interaction between the frontal cortex and basal ganglia emerges in the pathogenesis of Obsessive-Compulsive Disorder (OCD). OCD is a common neuropsychiatric disorder characterized by repetitive, intrusive thoughts and ritualistic behaviors. It affects between 2% and 3% of the population and appears to have a bimodal incidence with one peak in childhood—perhaps as many as 80% of cases having a childhood onset—and another in adulthood (Geller et al., 2001; Swedo, Leonard, & Rapoport, 1992). There are some differences between the childhood- and adult-onset forms of the disorder: Childhood-onset OCD has a stronger familial loading, greater male preponderance, and higher incidence of tics and Tourette's syndrome (Geller et al., 1998). However, the similarities outweigh the differences, and study of the childhood form of the disorder can be particularly illuminating as confounds such as chronic symptoms and exposure to multiple medications are less prominent.

Most theorists hold that OCD is the result of imbalance in the corticostriatal-thalamic circuitry (Modell, Mountz, Curtis, & Greden, 1989; Rapoport, 1990). Specifically, the basal ganglia fail to provide sensory gating by filtering and suppressing input from frontal cortical regions. Thus, a "hyperactive" orbitofrontal cortex and anterior cingulate gyrus send outputs to the caudate and nucleus accumbens, which in turn inhibit the globus pallidus, halting its tonic discharge to the thalamus. The cessation of pallidal inhibitory activity releases the thalamus, and the thalamus feeds this excessive activity forward to frontal cortical regions, completing the cycle.

Much of the support for this model comes from functional neuroimaging studies beyond the scope of this chapter, but which have been reviewed elsewhere (Saxena, Bota, & Brody, 2001). In brief, this work has consistently demonstrated resting hypermetabolism in the orbitofrontal cortex, cingulate gyrus, and caudate in patients with OCD. In an elegant demonstration of the specificity of this hypermetabolism, several PET studies have demonstrated a partial normalization of increased orbitofrontal and caudate hypermetabolism following effective treatment (Saxena et al., 1999). During provocation of symptoms in OCD, functional imaging studies report activation of the same regions, with some recent work suggesting that different components of the frontostriatal-thalamic circuit mediate different symptom clusters (Mataix-Cols et al., 2004). Lesions studies of the effects of focal damage to the ventromedial prefrontal cortex and the basal ganglia have reported the onset of OCD as a sequela of acquired damage (Berthier, Kulisevsky, Gironell, & Heras, 1996; Giedd, Rapoport, Leonard, Richter, & Swedo, 1996; Grados, 2003; Irle, Exner, Thielen, Weniger, & Ruther, 1998; Peterson, Bronen, & Duncan, 1996; Swoboda & Jenike, 1995).

Structural Neuroimaging of OCD. The models described earlier predict trophic changes in key regions of the dysfunctional circuitry. Hyperactivity of the frontal components might lead to expansion of the anterior cingulate gryus and orbitofrontal gyrus, particularly when subjects are symptomatic. The failure of the basal ganglia to gate sensory inputs might suggest that this structure has sustained subtle damage and may thus be smaller than in healthy populations. Finally, the loss of inhibitory input to the thalamus disinhibits this structure, and a resulting hyperactivity could potentially have trophic effects.

There have indeed been reports of expansion of gray matter in the left anterior cingulate cortex in an unmedicated pediatric population (see Table 3.6; Szeszko et al., 2004). The cortical expansion was specific to the anterior cingulate and not found in other frontal regions such as the superior frontal gyrus, in keeping with the earlier theories of the pathogenesis of OCD. Rosenberg and Keshavan (1998) report a similar increase in the volume of the anterior cingulate cortex in a different population of unmedicated children and adolescents with OCD. In adult populations, there are reports of larger operculum volumes in women with OCD in a region of interest study (Jenike et al., 1996). However, this finding was not replicated by the same group using a semiautomated parcellation technique that measures 10 regions of the frontal; instead, there was reduction in the right inferior frontal and medial frontal cortex (Grachev et al., 1998). Increased cortical density specific to the orbitofrontal cortex has also been implicated in a study of adults with OCD using voxel-based morphometry (Kim et al., 2001). Again, a region of interest

TABLE 3.6   Structural Neuroimaging Studies of Obsessive-Compulsive Disorder

Study	Patients (Mean Age ± SD, or Range)	Control Subjects	Method	Findings	Comments
Luxenberg et al. (1988)	10 Males (childhood onset OCD) (20.7 ± 2.1)	10 Males (23.7 ± 2.6)	CT scans, manual trace of ROI.	Decreased volume of caudate bilaterally.	Patients were heavily comorbid with tic disorder, which may have contributed independently to the volume reduction.
Rosenberg et al. (1997)	13 Males 6 Females (12 ± 3)	13 Males 6 Females (12 ± 3)	Manual tracing of region of interest (including entire frontal lobes).	Decreased volume of caudate and putamen.	No volume difference in prefrontal lobe.
MacMaster, Rosenberg, Keshavan, & Dick (1999); Rosenberg & Keshavan (1998); Rosenberg et al. (1997)	13 Males 8 Females (7.2–17.7)	13 Males 8 Females (7.2–17.7)	Manual tracing of regions of interest, signal intensity used as measure of myelination.	Increased volume anterior cingulate and increased surface area of corpus callosum in OCD, increased signal intensity in anterior genu in OCD.	Abnormalities correlated with symptom severity.
Giedd, Rapoport, Garvey, Perlmutter, & Swedo (2000)	24 Males 10 Females (PANDAS assoc OCD and/or tics)	82 Healthy controls matched for age and gender	Semiautomated total brain volume, manual tracing of basal ganglia structures.	Enlarged caudate, putamen, globus pallidus; no diff in thalamus or TBV.	Thalamus as area from single slice.
Gilbert et al. (2000)	7 Males 14 Females (12.35 ± 2.93)	7 Males 14 Females (12.47 ± 2.64)	Manual tracing of region of interest.	Increased volume of thalamus in OCD.	Successful treatment with paroxetine in 10 of the subjects associated with partial normalization of the volume of the thalamus.
Szeszko et al. (2004)	7 Males 16 Females (12.3 ± 2.9)	12 Male 15 Female (13.6 ± 3.2)	Manual tracing of regions of interest from contiguous 1.5-mm MR images.	Decreased volume of L globus pallidus, no diff in putamen, dec. gm volume in L anterior cingulate.	Conflicts with earlier reports from this center of decreased volume in putamen (Rosenberg et al., 1997). Attributed to sample differences.

approach on the same subjects yielded discrepant results, with a finding of reduced volume of the left orbitofrontal cortex (Kang et al., 2004). Thus, the results of a region of interest approach using operator-defined regions can conflict with the results of automated measures of the same regions on the same subjects, illustrating the complexity of comparing the results of different methodologies.

The finding of enlargement or increased cortical density in the anterior cingulate and orbitofrontal cortex has not always been replicated. One of the largest studies in OCD, on 72 adults with OCD using automated voxel-based methods of determining the volume, demonstrated decrease in the gray matter of the medial orbitofrontal and anterior paracingulate gyrus (Pujol et al., 2004). Several groups, studying both children and adults, have found either a decreased or no difference in the volume of the orbitofrontal cortex (Choi et al., 2004; Szeszko et al., 1999).

The structural picture is also inconsistent in the basal ganglia, with reports in pediatric populations of an increase, decrease, or no change in the volume of the caudate,

putamen, and globus pallidus (Giedd, Rapoport, Garvey, Perlmutter, & Swedo, 2000; A. R. Gilbert et al., 2000; Rosenberg, Keshavan, Dick, et al., 1997; Szeszko et al., 2004). A similar picture emerges in adult studies, with the largest single study reporting an increase in the volume of the basal ganglia, which correlated with the reduction in the orbital and paracingulate cortices (Pujol et al., 2004), but other studies reported either no significant overall change in the basal ganglia of adults with OCD (Aylward, Harris, et al., 1996; Jenike et al., 1996) or even an increase in volume (Scarone et al., 1992).

A developmental perspective may help unravel the factors contributing to this heterogeneity. Findings of an increase in basal ganglia volume have been reported mainly in pediatric populations, in whom many of the subjects had OCD arising in association with streptococcal infection. It is possible that an inflammatory process in these pediatric subjects could account for the findings of increased volume. Differences in the protocols used to define the various components of the basal ganglia are also likely to account for some of the variance, along with measurement error inherent in manual tracings of the basal ganglia. In this regard, the findings of fully automated methods are of particular interest as they do not rely on arbitrary definitions of regions of interest. Finally, subjects with OCD in each study varied considerably in their comorbidity and history of medication. For example, in the studies of children with OCD that report smaller caudate nuclei, there are high rates of comorbid tic disorders, which may contribute independently to the volume loss (Aylward, Harris, et al., 1996; Luxenberg et al., 1988).

The thalamus serves as the final component of the circuitry held to be dysfunctional in OCD. The cessation of tonic inhibitory input from a dysfunctional striatum in OCD is thought to lead to thalamic hyperactivation, which is then fed forward to the frontal cortex. In children, a marked increase in thalamic volume has been found (A. R. Gilbert et al., 2000). An increase in the density of gray matter of the thalamus has been reported in adults (Kim et al., 2001), although a voxel-based volumetric study did not report increased thalamic volumes (Pujol et al., 2004). Volume change in the thalamus appears to reflect active symptoms as partial normalization of thalamic volume has been reported following successful treatment. One study reported a 25% reduction of the volume of the thalamus in a group of 10 children treated with paroxetine, which correlated significantly with reduction in symptoms (A. R. Gilbert et al., 2000).

White matter changes in OCD are relatively unexplored. There have been several studies examining the corpus callosum, with reports of an overall increase in the surface area of the corpus callosum in children, which correlated with symptom severity (Rosenberg, Keshavan, Dick, et al., 1997). This study used its cross-sectional data on children of different ages to delineate the possible trajectory of corpus callosum development. They reported that healthy children appeared to lag behind children with OCD in corpus callosum size, attaining equivalent posterior body and anterior and middle splenii sizes 7 to 9 years later than OCD patients. The same group further characterized the changes in the corpus callosum by studying changes in signal intensity, an index thought to reflect the degree of myelination (MacMaster, Keshavan, Dick, & Rosenberg, 1999). They found that there was a difference in children with OCD in the signal intensity in the portion of the corpus callosum that connects the ventral prefrontal cortex with the striatum. This finding is in keeping with pathophysiological models and may account for the anomalous interactions between these regions in OCD. The authors hypothesized that

the structural changes in the corpus callosum may reflect either earlier myelination of callosal fibers in children with OCD or a failure of programmed elimination of excessive callosal fibers. By adulthood, myelination is largely complete, and thus size difference in the corpus callosum between adults with OCD and healthy adults would not be predicted. In line with this prediction, Jenike et al. (1996) reported a very slight reduction in the retrocallosal region in 10 adults with OCD.

Turning to other white matter regions, Szesko and colleagues (2004) found no increase in the white matter of the anterior cingulate gyrus despite an increase in the gray matter in a pediatric population. In a large group of adults using automated voxel-based volumetric measures, Pujol and colleagues (2004) found no significant difference in white matter volumes in any brain region. Future work using DTI techniques might allow a more detailed characterization of more subtle changes in white matter in OCD.

Automated techniques such as voxel-based morphometry allow an examination of structural changes throughout the brain without any a priori region of interest. Using these techniques, several unexpected regions of the brain have been demonstrated as structurally anomalous in OCD. In adults, there has been a demonstration of volume loss in the anterior cerebellum (Pujol et al., 2004) and of increased gray matter density in similar regions (Kim et al., 2001). Although the two findings are at odds, they highlight the importance of considering the cerebellum in the pathogenesis of the disorder.

Conclusions. There are several convincing demonstrations of structural alterations in the volumes of the anterior cingulate cortex and orbitofrontal cortex, and, to a lesser extent, components of the basal ganglia and thalamus. Differences in the direction of the change—with some studies reporting increases, other decreases in these regions—are hard to reconcile. Several usual suspects are likely to be at play, including differences in comorbidity in patients with OCD, medication effects, and varying definitions of regions of interest. Developmental factors may also be important as there may be differences in the etiologies of childhood- and adult-onset cases. Many of the structural changes found in OCD may reflect symptom activity only and thus do not give an insight into the underlying structural changes that render individuals susceptible to developing the disorder. Clarifying the nature of structural changes in individuals with OCD changes is important for genetic studies, which increasingly use structural brain changes as an endophenotype.

Although the concept of parallel frontostriatal-thalamic circuits has been extremely fruitful, primate and rat studies suggest that the basic neuroanatomy of the interactions among the cortex, striatum, and thalamus is more complicated than simple parallel loops (Haber & McFarland, 2001; Mailly, Charpier, Menetrey, & Deniau, 2003). Future studies will need to address the additional complexity created by spiraling interactions within the basal ganglia. However, despite these theoretical and practical limitations, the structural findings in OCD impress by virtue of the consistency of the regions that are identified as structurally anomalous.

Disorders with Increased Onset at Adolescence

The final section considers disorders whose incidence rises during puberty and adolescence. This time can be a period of increased stress, as individuals strive to cope with physical and psychological changes amidst the new societal demands of adulthood, and the amount of difficulty with which this transition is navigated can vary widely. In addition, as described in the earlier section on normal neurodevelopment, it is now recognized that these years represent a second critical period of brain development. While the psychological and behavioral difficulties experienced by many adolescents are transitory, in some they are beginnings of what may become chronic psychiatric disorders. The relationship of the brain remodeling such as cortical synaptic pruning occurring during this time with the increasing prevalence of specific psychiatric syndromes such as Schizophrenia and mood disorders is not yet understood but is the subject of increasingly intense inquiry, as recently reviewed by Spear (2000) and Walker, Sabuwalla, & Huot (2004). The extent and complexity of the influence of hormones such as estrogen and testosterone on brain structure and function is just beginning to be appreciated. In addition, there is increasing evidence that the hypothalamic-pituitary-adrenal axis undergoes changes during puberty that may make the adolescent brain more vulnerable to long term effects of stressful experiences than either children or adults (Walker et al., 2004).

One of the challenging aspects to understanding the etiologies of these disorders is determining how genetic factors interact with maturation and with environmental influences to result in the manifestation of the clinical syndrome many years after birth. The most common conceptualization is that of a stress-diathesis model, in which genetically mediated vulnerabilities interact with environmental stresses to trigger the onset of symptoms. Maturation may affect the types of stresses that can be en-

countered, for example, typical trials of adolescence such as leaving home or increasing access to potentially neurotoxic types of substance abuse. The interaction will be different depending on the state of brain maturity. In addition, as previously described in the example of Rett syndrome, the stage of maturation can have a major effect on the expression of particular genes. It is thought that the triggering of new gene expression by changing hormone levels during puberty may be one of the factors increasing the incidence of disorders such as mood disorders and Schizophrenia.

Studying individuals as early as possible in the course of the disorder provides an approach to disentangling these factors and identifying genetic components informative regarding the pathophysiology of the syndrome. If expression of symptoms occurs in response to a combination of biologic vulnerabilities and environmental stressors, then those who become ill earlier in life may have had a more severe biological "loading" to begin with, and this may thus be easier to describe than in individuals who become ill later. In addition, attempts of an individual and/or his or her family to compensate for the presence of a disorder may introduce further relatively nonspecific alterations in the developmental trajectory that can obscure attempts to isolate contributions of the genetic component. The use of brain structural features from imaging studies as endophenotypes may help to clarify this, but interpretation of imaging studies is also challenged by difficulty of determining what findings are related to vulnerability, are evidence of disease progression, or represent compensatory reactions to a damaged system elsewhere in the brain.

In this section we review structural imaging findings in Schizophrenia, depression, and bipolar disorder, continuing to emphasize studies performed in children and adolescents with discussion of relationship of childhood and adolescent forms of the illnesses to findings in adults.

Childhood-Onset Schizophrenia

Schizophrenia is a disorder characterized by onset of psychotic symptoms and loss of function, most typically during late adolescence and young adulthood. It affects approximately 1% of individuals worldwide. Function usually begins to deteriorate during a period called the *prodrome,* a period of increasingly severe symptoms that can last weeks to years. At some point symptoms become overwhelming, often in the form of a "first break." Although most individuals recover from their first episode the risk of relapse is high, and after a period of years impairment tends to become chronic. Although Schizophrenia's frequent occurrence and high morbidity have made it one of the most thoroughly studied of the psychiatric disorders, its etiology and pathophysiology remain obscure.

It is now widely accepted that Schizophrenia is a neurodevelopmental disorder, supported by a significant genetic component, higher incidence of neurodevelopmental anomalies, and presence of nonspecific premorbid cognitive and neurologic abnormalities. It is not known what triggers the onset of psychotic symptoms in the 2nd or 3rd decade of life. Understanding the biological substrate of Schizophrenia is further complicated by factors related to having a chronic psychotic disorder such as exposure to medication or socioeconomic hardship.

COS is defined as onset of psychotic symptoms before the 13th birthday. It has been recognized since the early twentieth century (Kraepelin, Barclay, & Robertson, 1919) as a rare and severe form of the illness, which occurs one-fiftieth as frequently as adult-onset type (Beitchman, 1985; W. H. Green, Padron-Gayol, Hardesty, & Bassiri, 1992; Karno, Golding, Sorenson, & Burnam, 1988; Kramer, 1978; Volkmar, Cohen, Hoshino, Rende, & Paul, 1988). COS appears to be clinically continuous with adult-onset schizophrenia (AOS; Gordon, 1992; W. H. Green et al., 1992; Russell, Bott, & Sammons, 1989; Spencer & Campbell, 1994), and children can be diagnosed with the unmodified *DSM* criteria for Schizophrenia. COS subjects resemble poor outcome adult cases with respect to the insidious onset of symptoms and poor premorbid functioning (Alaghband-Rad et al., 1995; W. H. Green et al., 1992; Hollis, 1995). However, early developmental abnormalities in social, motor, and language domains are more striking in COS than in AOS. Some of the interest in studying this rare population arises from the hypothesis that Schizophrenia in its early-onset form may have unique or more salient pathophysiology and genetic risk factors, as demonstrated in other disorders such as diabetes (Childs & Scriver, 1986). The incidence of Schizophrenia steadily increases with age. Early-onset schizophrenia (EOS) is a term generally considered to include individuals with onset prior to adulthood.

Imaging Studies. Schizophrenia was the first psychiatric disorder to be studied using structural neuroimaging techniques (Johnstone, Crow, Frith, Husband, & Kreel, 1976), and has been the subject of an enormous and growing number of structural neuroimaging studies since (see Table 3.7). Although findings have varied between studies, likely related to some of the confounding issues stated above, some findings have been relatively consistent. Most studies have found decreased total cerebral volume and enlarged ventricles. Smaller mesial temporal lobe structures

have been the most consistently reported regional abnormality (Andreasen et al., 1986, 1990; Bilder et al., 1994; Breier et al., 1992; DeLisi et al., 1991; Jernigan, Zisook, et al., 1991; Marsh, Suddath, Higgins, & Weinberger, 1994; Shenton et al., 1992; Swayze, Andreasen, Alliger, Yuh, & Ehrhardt, 1992). Caudate volumes have been reported as enlarged in individuals who had been exposed to "typical" antipsychotics for prolonged periods, an effect which diminished when individuals were placed on the atypical antipsychotic clozaril (Chakos et al., 1994; Elkashef, Buchanan, Gellad, Munson, & Breier, 1994). Decreased thalamic volume has also been described (Andreasen et al., 1994; Flaum et al., 1995).

With the exception of the NIMH COS study described below there have been few neuroimaging studies of COS, due to the rarity of individuals with very early onset. An MRI case study of a 10-year-old boy with COS reported ventriculomegaly and a small left cerebellum (Woody, Bolyard, Eisenhauer, & Altschuler, 1987). A study of 6 children with Schizophrenia, schizophreniform disorder, or other psychosis found larger ventricular volume in three of the subjects (Hendren, Hodde-Vargas, Vargas, Orrison, & Dell, 1991). A third study likewise found enlarged ventricles in a group of 15 schizophrenic or schizophreniform disorder adolescents (mean age 16.5 years; S. C. Schultz et al., 1983).

In the largest study to date, the Child Psychiatry Branch of the NIMH has been enrolling patients in a longitudinal neuroimaging study for over a decade. Over 75 patients have participated to date, with an average age of psychosis onset of approximately 10 years and average age at study entry of approximately 14 years. Subjects undergo extensive screening and diagnostic testing to verify diagnosis. Those who participate undergo structural brain MRI scans at 2-year intervals in conjunction with clinical and neuropsychological follow-up measures and also contribute DNA for genetic analyses. The structural neuroimaging data is analyzed using a variety of automated, semi-automated and manual techniques, providing cross-sectional and longitudinal measures of total brain volume, gray and white matter, regional volumes, and cortical thickness measures (Collins, Zijdenbos, Baaré, & Evans, 1999; Thompson, Vidal, et al., 2001).

Currently available studies indicate that children with Schizophrenia show increased lateral ventricular volume, decreased total brain volume, decreased gray matter volume, and increased basal ganglia volume (probably secondary to medication effect; Frazier, Giedd, Hamburger, et al., 1996; Kumra et al., 2000; Rapoport et al., 1997, 1999; Sowell et al., 2000). There is less agreement with respect to reduced

TABLE 3.7   Structural Neuroimaging Studies of Childhood Onset Schizophrenia

Study	Patients (Mean Age ± SD, or Range)	Control Subjects	Method	Findings	Comments
Schulz et al. (1983)	15 patients with Schizophrenia or schizophreniform disorder (16.5)	18 age matched healthy controls 8 borderline patients	CAT study of ventricle volumes.	Ventricles enlarged in Schizophrenia and schizophreniform compared to other two groups.	Increased ventricular brain ratio related to poorer treatment response.
Woody, Bolyard, Eisenhauer, & Altschuler (1987)	10 year-old boy		CAT and MRI.	Enlarged ventricles and dec. left cerebellum.	Case study.
Hendren et al. (1995)	6 Males 6 Females (8–12) with early psychotic symptoms	12 subjects matched on age, gender, SES	1.5 coronal images, manual ROI.	Dec. amygdala and mesial temporal cortex volumes, decreased area of corpus callosum; decreased asymmetry measures.	MRS data obtained on subset of patients, trend to decreased NAA:Cre ratio.
Frazier et al. (1996)	COS: 13 Male 8 Females (14.6 ± 2.1)	33 controls matched for age, sex, height, weight	1.5T, 1.5 mm axial contiguous slices, semiautomated segmentation and manual tracing of ROIs.	COS smaller total cerebral volume and midsagittal thalamic area, larger ventricular volume in the COS group; COS larger basal ganglia volumes.	NIMH study. Enlarged basal ganglia possibly related to medication.
Jacobsen et al. (1997)	12 Males 12 Females with COS (14.1 ± 2.1)	28 Males 24 Females (14.3 ± 2.0)	1.5T, 1.5 mm axial contiguous slices, semiautomated segmentation and manual tracing of cerebellar ROIs.	COS had smaller volumes of vermis and volume and midsagittal areas of posterior inferior cerebellar lobe.	NIMH study. Findings present after correction for total cerebral volume.
Friedman et al. (1999)	15 Male 5 Female (14.7 ± 2.2)	Healthy controls: 9 Male 7 Female (15.6 ± 1.8) Bipolar Disorder: 8 Male 7 Female (15.3 ± 2.4)	T2/Spin density weighted axial images, 5 mm slice, 2 mm gap; manual ROIs.	Patient groups did not differ from each other. Combined patients groups show larger ventricles and smaller cerebral volume.	
Kumra et al. (2000)	COS: 25 Male 19 Female (14.4 ± 2.3) PDNOS: 22 Male 5 Female (12.3 ± 2.9)	73 Male 33 Female, age matched separately to COS and PDNOS groups	1.5T, 1.5 mm axial contiguous slices, semiautomated segmentation and manual tracing of ROIs.	COS: smaller cerebral volume, smaller midsagittal thalamic area, COS and PDNOS larger ventricles than controls.	NIMH study: Psychotic Disorder Not Otherwise Specified (PDNOS).
Sowell et al. (2000)	COS: 3 Males 6 Females (14.41.5T, 1.5 mm axial contiguous slices, semiautomated segmentation and manual tracing of ROIs)	2 Males 8 Females (12.1 ± 2.9)	1.5T T1 coronal 1.4 mm contiguous slices, semiautomated segmentation, voxel based morphometric analysis.	Larger ventricles, predominantly in the posterior horns of the lateral ventricles, and midcallosal, posterior cingulate, caudate, and thalamic abnormalities.	Average age of diagnosis 11.0 ± 2.9.

TABLE 3.7   Continued

Study	Patients (Mean Age ± SD, or Range)	Control Subjects	Method	Findings	Comments
Badura et al. (2001)	19 children with onset schizophrenia prior to age 14	Age and gender matched controls from children scanned for non-neurologic reasons	CAT study of ventricle volumes.	Increased ventricle size at onset seen only in those with onset prior to age 12, ventricle size also correlate with length of illness.	11 scans made within first year after onset of illness, rest between 2–9 years later.
Thompson, Vidal, et al. (2001)	12 COS (13.9 ± 0.8)	12 Healthy controls (13.5 ± 0.7) 10 Age-matched MDI	Longitudinal study with MRI at 3 time points, approx 2 years between scan; 1.5T, 1.5 mm axial contiguous slices, semiautomated cortical thickness measures using sulcal landmarks.	Dynamic pattern of marked gray matter loss in COS group, begin in parietal region, healthy controls show dynamic but much smaller decrease in cortical thickness; MDI group intermediate.	NIMH study: MDI = Multidimensionally impaired. MDI group provide comparison group matched for medication exposure. Decreases in cortical thickness correlate with clinical status.
James, Javaloyes, James, & Smith (2002); James, James, Smith, & Javaloyes (2004)	Early-onset schizophrenia: 9 Males 7 Females 16.6 (± 1.6)	Controls: 9 Males 7 Females	Longitudinal study with avg. 2.5 years between scans, 1.5 T1 coronal 3 mm contiguous slices, manual ROI.	Baseline smaller prefrontal cortex and thalamus, borderline larger ventricles in EOS, no evidence of progression over time during late adolescence.	Limited by small sample size.
Gogtay, Giedd, et al. (2004)	COS: 19 Males 4 Females (13.9 ± 2.5) MDI: 16 Males 3 Females (13.3 ± 3.1)	Controls: 32 Male 6 Females (13.3 ± 3.1)	Longitudinal study with average of 3 years between scans; 1.5T, 1.5 mm axial contiguous slices, automated measurement of lobar gray matter volumes.	COS group had significantly greater loss of GM than MDI or normal controls, which did not differ from each other.	NIMH study: MDI = Multidimensionally Impaired. See also Rapoport (1997, 1999), Jacobsen (1998), Giedd (1999), Keller (2003), and Sporn (2003) for other reports from this longitudinal study.

volume of medial temporal lobe structures (Jacobsen et al., 1996; Matsumoto, Simmons, Williams, Hadjulis, et al., 2001; Matsumoto, Simmons, Williams, Pipe, et al., 2001).

An updated comparison of 60 COS (mean age 14.27 + 2.41) with 110 (mean age 14.18 + 2.44) age- and sex-matched healthy volunteers extended the previous studies (Gogtay, Giedd, et al., 2004), finding that the smaller cerebral volume in COS was largely due to a robust (10%) decrease in cortical gray matter, whereas the adjusted white matter volume did not differ significantly between the COS and healthy groups. Of note is the striking reduction in parietal gray matter volume, which may be characteristic of EOS. Frontal and occipital gray matter were also reduced, albeit less extremely, only the volume of the temporal gray matter was not different between COS patients and healthy controls.

The longitudinal study design of the NIMH study has allowed the description of progressive brain volume loss in COS. It appears to be more severe than what is seen in most studies of adults. Increasing ventricular volume and

decreasing total cortical, frontal, temporal, and parietal gray matter volumes were seen across 2, 4, and 6 years after their initial scan. Here, too, regional gray/white segmentation showed the progressive loss to be for gray matter only (Giedd, Jeffries, et al., 1999; Jacobsen et al., 1998; Rapoport et al., 1997, 1999).

The rapid changes seen for COS most likely occur only during a circumscribed period, as age of onset does not appear significantly related to decreased cortical gray matter loss in adult patients (Lim et al., 1996; Marsh et al., 1997). Adolescence may provide a time-limited window in which progressive brain changes in Schizophrenia are most easily observed. This is supported by a very recent longitudinal analysis of our quantitative brain imaging data for a larger group of 36 COS patients with one or more scans, suggesting that the rate of gray matter loss slows as these COS patients reach age 20 (see Figure 3.9; Sporn et al., 2004).

This is in accordance with another follow-up study of adolescent-onset schizophrenia that documented substantially smaller prefrontal cortex and thalamus in affected

A. Total Cerebral Volume

COS curve is non-linear (cubic) ($F_{(1,159)} = 7.47$; $p < 0.0007$)

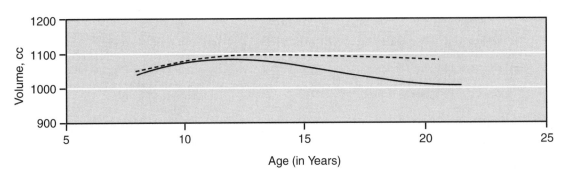

B. Total Grey Matter

COS curve is non-linear (cubic) ($F_{(1,166)} = 5.87$; $p < 0.016$)

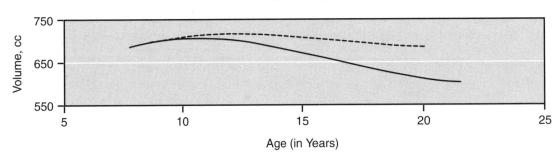

C. Lateral Ventricles

COS curve is linear ($F_{(1,129)} = 46.2$; $p < 0.001$)

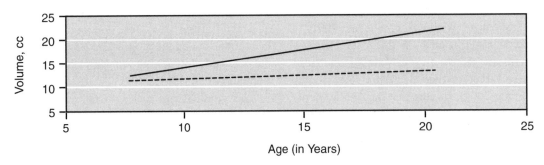

Figure 3.9 Developmental pattern for selected anatomic brain MRI measures for childhood Onset Schizophrenia ($n = 57$, 61% males, 115 scans) and healthy controls ($n = 60$, 63% males, 119 scans). Non-linear curves for total cerebral volume and total gray matter indicate decline in rate of loss that approaches zero at approximately age 21. Lateral ventricular enlargement however remained linear within the studied age period. *Source:* From "Pervasive Developmental Disorder and Childhood-Onset Schizophrenia: Comorbid Disorder or a Phenotypic Variant of a Very Early Onset Illness?" by A. L. Sporn et al., 2004, *Biological Psychiatry, 55*(10), pp. 989–994.

subjects but little evidence for progression over time between ages 18 to 20 (James, James, Smith, & Javaloyes, 2004; James, Javaloyes, James, & Smith, 2002). Recent studies of AOS, using comparable methodology, have found relatively subtle progressive loss of brain matter (DeLisi, 1999a, 1999b; Gur et al., 1998; Lieberman et al., 2001; Mathalon, Sullivan, Lim, & Pfefferbaum, 1997). An effect size comparison documents that the progressive changes are more striking during adolescence, at least for very early onset cases (Gogtay, Giedd, Janson, & Rapoport, 2001). Similarities between the follow-up imaging studies of COS and AOS include progressive ventricular expansion and cortical gray matter loss mostly in the frontal and temporal region. In addition to the frontal and temporal gray matter loss, the COS population also showed significant parietal gray matter loss.

Recently, the NIMH group and collaborators from UCLA used a computational tensor-matching strategy to compare the 3-dimensional distribution of gray matter across time on a voxel-by-voxel basis. Regionally specific cortical development across time and between subject groups was demonstrated. In the COS patients, the parietal gray matter volume loss occurs initially, with frontal and temporal gray matter changes appearing later across the adolescent years (Thompson, Vidal, et al., 2001). This is in support of the findings presented earlier, using the more automated quantitative approach and indicating that the progressive gray matter loss in COS takes place in a regular posterior-anterior wave-like fashion that was seen in all subjects in the COS study. Some support of this back-to-front wave of cortical loss as intrinsic to Schizophrenia is provided by a study of full siblings of COS patients. A recent comparison of 15 healthy siblings of COS and 32 age- and sex-matched community controls showed that the COS siblings have smaller parietal gray matter volume (Gogtay, Sporn, et al., 2004). Although limited by small sample size, these familial findings, if replicated, would suggest that a back-to-front pattern (parieto-frontal) of gray matter loss could be a trait marker in Schizophrenia.

The prospective studies have also enabled researchers to relate brain loss to medication effects. A 2-year follow-up study was done with eight patients taking typical neuroleptics at the time of the first scan and maintained on clozapine for 2 years prior to the second scan (Frazier, Giedd, Kaysen, et al., 1996) because of controversy related to the effect of neuroleptics on reported basal ganglia enlargement in Schizophrenia (Chakos et al., 1994; Elkashef et al., 1994; Keshavan et al., 1994). On follow-up, the clozapine-maintained COS group, but not eight age- and sex-matched controls also receiving a 2-year follow-up scan, demon-

strated decreased caudate and putamen volumes over time. These findings are consistent with the hypothesis that basal ganglia enlargement in COS is secondary to medication effects.

Although the MRI studies of COS have extended our knowledge of abnormal neurodevelopment, the studies discussed do not yet allow differentiation between several current alternative explanations for the precise nature of the abnormal process occurring. One version of the neurodevelopmental hypothesis of Schizophrenia proposes an early (and fixed) lesion in the prenatal or perinatal period, resulting in a disturbed late maturational response (Weinberger, 1987). This implies that specific early lesions can disrupt the later maturing regions such as the frontal-limbic circuitry and that such effects could be interaction of genetic variability (and vulnerability) and environmental factors (Lipska et al., 1995; Lipska & Weinberger, 2002). A second formulation of the neurodevelopmental hypothesis was made by Woods (1998). Based in part on the normal skull size but increased intracranial CSF space in Schizophrenia, Wood proposed that the illness be considered a progressive neurodevelopmental disorder. Neurodevelopmental genes may have multiple roles across different time periods, and etiological agents causing abnormalities in early development may have related but different effects at later stages depending on gene-environment interactions. Finally, it is possible that the progressive brain changes represent a plastic response of the brain to the illness. However, a plastic brain response to illness cannot represent the only basis for these changes, as healthy siblings of COS patients have also shown relative cortical gray matter decrease on initial scans.

Affective Disorders

Affective disorders are the most common psychiatric syndromes and among the highest causes of global burden due to disability worldwide (Costello et al., 2002). Their key features are abnormally elevated or depressed mood (or both), in conjunction with neurovegetative symptoms. Disordered thought, abnormal reality testing, and cognitive deficits may also be present during severe affective episodes (American Psychiatric Association, Task Force on *DSM-IV,* 2000). Differentiating pathological affective episodes from normal responses to life events, such as grief in response to a loss, can be quite difficult, and often represents making a division within a continuum of severity of intensity or duration.

The study of brain structural changes associated with affective disorders is much less developed than in Schizophrenia. To some extent, this may relate to the more common view that affective disorders fall more on the "functional" than "organic" end of the psychiatric spectrum (Harrison, 2002). However, it is becoming clearer that the course of illness in many individuals with bipolar or unipolar mood disorders is chronic, and at least in the case of bipolar disorder (BD), may also be associated with gradual deterioration in function. The presence of clear genetic predispositions to both depression and bipolar disorders also motivates the use of structural imaging techniques to search for brain changes that could serve as the source of vulnerability to mood symptoms.

Many of the same considerations apply to neuroimaging studies in affective disorders as already discussed in Schizophrenia. Studies in affective disorders have tended to frequently report conflicting results, possibly related to the small sample sizes of the studies, uncontrolled or unknown medication status, and heterogeneous clinical presentation (Beyer & Krishnan, 2002; Brambilla, Barale, Caverzasi, & Soares, 2002; Strakowski, Adler, & DelBello, 2002; Videbech & Ravnkilde, 2004).

A further confounding factor that has not yet received very much attention is how symptoms and physical findings in chronic affective disorders may change over the lifetime, similarly if to a less severe extent than what is seen in Schizophrenia (Kaufman, Martin, King, & Charney, 2001; Kessler, Avenevoli, & Ries Merikangas, 2001). Affective disorders, like Schizophrenia, most frequently appear during adolescence. There is evidence to suggest that there may be some differences between depression and BD in children compared with adults. For example, depression in childhood is often associated with irritability in addition to or instead of a sad mood, and tricyclic antidepressants, which are effective in adults, do not appear to show a similar benefit in children (Kaufman et al., 2001). Juvenile BD has been the object of considerable controversy, as it has been proposed that children may have BD at a rate much higher than once thought, but with a phenotype differentiated from that in adults by a high prevalence of rapid or continuous mood cycling, mixed states, and presence of ADHD symptoms ("National Institute of Mental Health Research Roundtable on Prepubertal Bipolar Disorder," 2001; Geller & Luby, 1997). There is ongoing debate in both Major Depressive Disorder and BD about whether duration criteria for episodes should be altered for younger populations (Pruett & Luby, 2004). Longitudinal studies to track how and whether a childhood affective disorder phenotype changes with maturity are currently in process. The first reports from a study in children meeting conservative criteria for BP have shown stability of symptoms during early adolescence (Geller, Tillman, Craney, & Bolhofner, 2004). More of such studies will be necessary to resolve questions about the relationship of the forms that appear during different stages of development (Pruett & Luby, 2004).

Bipolar Disorder

Bipolar Affective Disorder is characterized by the presence of manic or hypomanic episodes interspersed with periods of depression or euthymia. It was first described by Kraepelin, Barclay, and Robertson (1919) in his fundamental division of psychotic disorders as having an intermittent course as opposed the ongoing deterioration characteristic of dementia praecox, which came to be called Schizophrenia. The current *DSM* describes two variations of the disorder: BP I, which has manic or mixed episodes with or without depressed episodes, and BP II, which requires a combination of hypomanic and major depressive episodes (American Psychiatric Association, Task Force on *DSM-IV*, 2000).

Like many other psychiatric syndromes, BP appears to be a complex genetic disorder arising in response to a combination of environmental, genetic, and epigenetic influences (Craddock & Jones, 2001; Petronis, 2003). The prevalence in adolescents and adults is approximately 1% to 3% (Kashani et al., 1987; Lewinsohn, Klein, & Seeley, 1995); in first-degree family members it increases to approximately 7%, and in monozygotic twins to 60% (T. D. Gould, Quiroz, Singh, Zarate, & Manji, 2004). Unlike unipolar Major Depressive Disorder, there does not appear to be a sex differential in BP (Biederman et al., 2004). Current controversies about the proper diagnostic criteria for BP in children make prevalence difficult to estimate, but it has been traditionally accepted that onset is less frequent in children (Akiskal et al., 1985). There is some evidence from previous cross-sectional studies and current longitudinal studies that earlier-onset cases show a more severe phenotype and higher rate of affected family members, similar to what is seen in Schizophrenia and many nonpsychiatric medical disorders (Geller et al., 2004; McGlashan, 1988).

BP appears to be associated with abnormalities in the corticolimbic and corticostriatal brain circuits responsible for the regulation of emotion. Although the source of this abnormality is not known, there has been some intriguing evidence of potential abnormalities of signaling pathways active in cellular neurogenesis and resilience (T. D. Gould et al., 2004; Manji & Lenox, 2000). Structural imaging studies in adults with BP have not generally shown global differences in brain volume, supporting more regional effects than seen in an illness such as Schizophrenia (Soares, 2003). Although the literature has a relative preponderance of small studies with conflicting results, more commonly reported findings include decreased volume of the subgenual prefrontal cortex (SGPFC; a portion of the anterior cingulate) and increased volumes of subcortical structures including the amygdala, basal ganglia, and thalamus (Blumberg, Charney, & Krystal, 2002; Brambilla, Harenski, et al., 2003; Sheline, 2003). Potential abnormalities in white matter have received relatively little attention until recently, despite increased white matter hyperintensities (WMH) being the single most commonly found feature in BP (Altshuler et al., 1995). The first DTI study in BP in adults was recently published and reported significantly decreased fractional inositropy in prefrontal white matter (Adler et al., 2004).

Imaging Studies. There have been few structural imaging studies in children and adolescents with BP (see Table 3.8). Studies of temporal lobe structures have had inconsistent findings. Blumberg et al. (2003) scanned 36 individuals with BP I and 56 matched controls. She was able to compare separate groups of adolescents and adults. Similar results were found in both groups: The amygdala was significantly smaller, unlike findings in previous studies of adults, and the hippocampus was slightly smaller but did not reach significance. DelBello (DelBello, Zimmerman, Mills, Getz, & Strakowski, 2004) also found smaller amygdala volumes in her adolescent sample. B. K. Chen et al. (2004) and H. H. Chen et al. (2004) reported on a sample of adolescents with BP I, BP II, and BP-NOS and also found decreased volume of the left superior temporal gyrus (STG) and a trend toward a smaller left amygdala, STG white matter volume was smaller bilaterally. No differences were found in the hippocampus or total temporal lobe volume. Wilke and colleagues (Wilke, Kowatch, DelBello, Mills, & Holland, 2004) compared a group of 10 adolescents with BP against 26 matched archived control scans using both region of interest and voxel based methods. They found larger basal ganglia using both methods. Decreased gray matter volume in the left SGPFC and regions of the medial, temporal, and orbitofrontal lobes was seen using the voxel based method alone.

A group at the University of Cleveland compared adolescents with BP I, Schizophrenia, and controls (Dasari et al., 1999; Friedman et al., 1999). They did not find differences between the BP and schizophrenic groups in measures of total brain volume and sulcal CSF, but the two groups together had a smaller total brain volume, increased sulcal prominence, and decreased thalamic volumes compared with controls. The BP subjects had increased numbers of white matter hyperintensities (WMH) compared with the schizophrenic and control groups (Pillai et al., 2002). Two other separate research groups also identified increased

WMH in children and adolescents with BP I (Botteron, Vannier, Geller, Todd, & Lee, 1995; Lyoo, Lee, Jung, Noam, & Renshaw, 2002). Although the pathogenic significance of WMH is not clear, they have been found to be associated with increased water density in the affected area, potentially due to vascular abnormalities (Lyoo et al., 2002).

Depression

Depression is much more common and disabling in children and adolescents than once believed (Kaufman et al., 2001). The prevalence has been estimated at 2% in children (Kashani et al., 1983; Kashani & Ray, 1983) and 5% and 8% in adolescents (Lewinsohn, Clarke, Seeley, & Rohde, 1994), although the National Comorbidity Survey found a lifetime prevalence of *DSM-III-R* Major Depressive Disorder to be 14% by the end of adolescence (Kessler et al., 2001; Kessler & Walters, 1998). Early-onset depression appears to be associated with a higher risk of recurrence and more long-term morbidity (Kessler et al., 2001). It has become increasingly clear that the neurobiology of depression is different among children, adolescents, and adults on multiple measures, as addressed in a comprehensive review by Kaufman et al. (2001).

Imaging Studies. Studies of brain structure in adults with Major Depression have had highly variable results, but a few findings appear to be relatively consistent (see Table 3.9). Smaller prefrontal volume is more consistently found in adults with unipolar depression than in BD. Reduced volumes of the caudate and putamen have also been reported by several studies, although not all (Beyer & Krishnan, 2002; Lacerda et al., 2003; Pillay et al., 1998). Few studies have examined the cerebellum; two of these reported decreased cerebellar volumes (Escalona et al., 1991; Shah et al., 1992; Yates, Jacoby, & Andreasen, 1987). The relationship of the hippocampus to cognitive functions frequently impaired in depression and the observed sensitivity of the hippocampus to stress in animal models have made it the object of much more scrutiny (Campbell & MacQueen, 2004; Campbell, Marriott, Nahmias, & MacQueen, 2004). Findings have been inconsistent, although a recent meta-analysis by Videbech and Ravnkilde (2004) concluded that the evidence supported a reduction of hippocampal volume of 8% on the left side and 10% on the right side.

Depression, like BD, has been associated with a high rate of WMH, particularly in late-life depression (Coffey, Figiel, Djang, Saunders, & Weiner, 1989; Coffey et al., 1987; Lee et al., 2003; Soares & Mann, 1997; Takahashi et al., 2001; Taylor et al., 2003; Tupler et al., 2002).

TABLE 3.8 Structural Neuroimaging Studies of Bipolar Disorder

Study	Patients (Mean Age ± SD, or Range)	Control Subjects	Method	Findings	Comments
Blumberg et al. (2003)	Adult BP 22 (age 23–54) 12 Female 10 Male Adol. BP 14 (10–22) 8 Female 6 Male	Adult 33 (24–57) 17 Female 16 Male Adol. 23 (10–23) 10 Female 17 Male	1.5T T1 1.2 mm contiguous slices, manual parcellation.	Amygdala sig. smaller, hippocampus trend towards smaller size.	Findings not show age interaction.
DelBello, Zimmerman, Mills, Getz, & Strakowski (2004)	14 Male 9 Females (16.3 ± 2.4)	11 Male 9 Female (17.2 ± 1.9)	1.5T T1 1.5 mm contiguous axial slices, manual parcellation.	Smaller TCV, amygdala, larger putamen in pts.	
Friedman et al. (1999)	15 Male 5 Female (14.7 ± 2.2)	Healthy controls: 9 Male 7 Female (15.6 ± 1.8) Bipolar Disorder: 8 Male 7 Female (15.3 ± 2.4)	T2/Spin density weighted axial images, 5 mm slice, 2 mm gap; manual ROIs.	Patient groups did not differ from each other. Combined patients groups show larger ventricles and smaller cerebral volume.	
Pillai et al. (2002)	15 Male 5 Female (14.7 ± 2.2)	Healthy controls: 9 Male 7 Female (15.6 ± 1.8) Bipolar Disorder: 8 Male 7 Female (15.3 ± 2.4)	T2/Spin density weighted axial images, 5 mm slice, 2 mm gap; manual ROIs.	BP had increased white matter hyperintensities compared to other two groups.	Same study population as in Friedman (1999).
Lyoo, Lee, Jung, Noam, & Renshaw (2002)	Pt. group including mix of SCZ (42), BP (56), MDD (94), CD/ADHD (103) 30 other diagnoses as neurotic (12.4 ± 2.7)	83 control	4-point rating scale of WMH (Coffee 1990 Am J Psych).	WMH sig higher in frontal lobes of BPAD, MDD, and CD/ADHD groups.	WMH = White matter hyperintensities.
Chen et al. (2004)	8 Females 8 Males (16 ± 3; 12 BPI, 3BPII, 1 BPNOS)	9 Females 12 Males (17 ± 4, 9)	1.5 mm contiguous coronal slices; semiautomated segmentation; manual trace of hp, amyg, temp lobe, ICV.	Trend to smaller left amygdala in BPAD, in BPADI males L amygdala had positive corr with age, controls had inverse corr.	Cross-sectional study.
Chen et al. (2004)	8 Females 8 Males (16 ± 3; 12 BPI, 3BPII, 1 BPNOS)	9 Females 12 Males (17 ± 4, 9)	1.5 mm contiguous coronal slices, semiautomated segmentation, ROI tracing of STG.	Smaller STG wm volume bilaterally, smaller total STG vol on left, no other diffs.	Same subjects as above.
Wilke, Kowatch, DelBello, Mills, & Holland (2004)	5 Male 5 Female (14.47 ± 1.81)	26 Male 26 Female (14.52 ± 1.29)	3T T1 1.5 mm contiguous slices, voxel based morphometry and manual ROI.	ROI: larger basal ganglia, larger L temporal lobe; VBM: Pt larger gm volume in anterior putamen, head of caudate; decr subgenual of L ant cingulated; medial temporal, orbito-frontal.	

TABLE 3.9   Structural Neuroimaging Studies of Major Depressive Disorder

Study	Patients (Mean Age ± SD, or Range)	Control Subjects	Method	Findings	Comments
Steingard et al. (1996)	30 Males 35 Female (13.42 ± 2.32)	13 Male 5 Female Nondepressed psychiatric controls (10.78 ± 2.92)	1.5T T1 axial 5 mm slices with 1.5 mm gap, manual ROI volumes.	Depressed subjects had smaller ratio of frontal lobe volume to total volume, larger ventricular volumes.	Retrospective chart review and reanalysis of clinical MRIs, images redigitized from film.
Botteron, Raichle, Drevets, Heath, & Todd (2002)	30 Early onset females (20.2 ± 1.6) 18 Later onset 35.8 ± 8.1	8 Early age matched controls 9 Later onset age matched controls	1.5T 1 mm contiguous slices, manual parcellation.	L subgenual prefrontal cortex smaller in both groups of patients, no correlation with age.	Subjects all female.
Nolan et al. (2002)	10 Male 12 Female (9–17 yrs)	10 Male 12 Female Matched pairwise	1.5T 1.5 mm coronal contiguous slices, manual parcellation.	Larger PFC and PFC wm in non-familial MDD.	Psychotropic-naïve subjects with and without 1st deg relative with MDD.
MacMillan et al. (2003)	10 Male (13.8 ± 2.7) 13 Female (14.22 ± 1.81)	10 Male 13 Female Matched pairwise with subjects	1.5T 1.5 mm coronal contiguous slices, manual parcellation of amygdala and hippocampus.	Increased L amygdala:hippo ratio, hippocampal and amygdala volumes not differ when control for ICV and age.	Psychotropic-naïve subjects, some variation in tracing method used.
MacMaster & Kusumakar (2004)	8 Males 9 Females (14.06 ± 1.98)	8 Males 9 Females Matched pairwise	1.5T 1.5 mm coronal contiguous slices, manual parcellation.	L hippocampus smaller in patients.	9 of patients were psychotropic-naive.
Rosso et al. (2005)	3 Male 17 Female (15.35 ± .34)	8 Male 16 Female (14.08 ± .31)	1.5T 1.5 mm coronal contiguous slices, manual parcellation.	Amygdala smaller bilaterally in subjects.	

One initial study of white matter structure in late-life depression using DTI reported significantly decreased fractional inositropy in the region lateral to the anterior cingulate, which correlated with stronger family history of depressive disorders and poorer outcome (Taylor et al., 2001). Another study focused on the dorsolateral prefrontal cortex, which has been shown to have decreased metabolism associated with active depression in multiple functional studies, and found lower fractional inositropy in the right superior prefrontal cortex, even after controlling for age, sex, hypertension, and cardiovascular status (Taylor, MacFall, et al., 2004).

Structural neuroimaging studies in children are even rarer than in adults, but in similar fashion to the other neurobiological measures described, results thus far have both agreed with and contradicted findings in adults. Steingard et al. (1996) performed a retrospective chart review and reanalysis of clinical MRIs obtained from 65 children with Major Depressive Disorder, compared with 8 nondepressed psychiatric controls. Findings included a smaller ratio of the frontal lobe to total cerebral volume and a larger ratio of the ventricles to total cerebral volume, consistent with findings of decreased frontal lobe volume in adults. Botteron and colleagues (Botteron, Raichle, Drevets, Heath, & Todd, 2002) followed up the findings of significantly decreased subgenual prefrontal cortex volume in adults with mood disorders to determine whether there was an age-related effect. They compared females with early-onset depression (average age 20.2 ± 1.6 years) with later-onset depression (35.8 ± 8.1) and two groups of appropriately age-matched controls, and found that although the left subgenual prefrontal cortex was smaller in both patient groups, there did not appear to be any difference according to age of onset of symptoms.

Nolan et al. (2002) focused on psychotropic-naïve children and adolescents to minimize the potential confounding effects of medication. They compared subjects with and without a familial history of depressive disorder and found larger prefrontal cortex volumes of gray and white matter on the left side in the nonfamilial cases only. This finding was different from the smaller prefrontal volumes typically reported in adults, although the small sample size merits caution.

Three studies have reported on temporal lobe structures. MacMillan et al. (2003) studied psychotropic-naïve subjects and reported that the ratio of the volumes of the amygdala to the hippocampus was increased on the left side, although the difference in amygdala or hippocampal volumes were not statistically significant after controlling for intracranial volume and age. MacMaster and Kusumakar (2004) found decreased hippocampal volume (17%) in a group with mixed exposure to medications, again localized to the left. Findings persisted when they examined only the psychotropic-naïve subgroup. They also reported a positive correlation between hippocampal size and duration of illness and a negative correlation with age of onset. Rosso et al. (2005) examined amygdala and hippocampal volumes in a slightly larger group of primarily females. They found both the left and right amygdala to be an average of 12% smaller in patients, but did not find a difference in hippocampal volumes or total cerebral volume.

Conclusion.   Although conclusions that can be drawn from the neuroimaging literature are limited by small sample sizes and varying methodologies, there is evidence to support the presence of structural brain differences in regions known to be involved in emotional regulation, including the frontal cortex, temporal lobe structures, basal ganglia, and cerebellar vermis. All studies to date have been cross-sectional, meaning that firm conclusions cannot be drawn about the relative trajectories of brain volume changes in early- versus adult-onset depression (Kraemer et al., 2000). Nonetheless, the appearance of volumetric differences in prefrontal cortex and basal ganglia in younger populations suggests that these may be features either related to vulnerability to mood disorder or that occur early on, whereas the findings of normal hippocampal morphology in children and adolescents contrasts with the smaller volumes seen in adults.

The findings of specific rather than generalized structural differences, with clearer effects when examined in smaller regions such as the subgenual prefrontal cortex SGPFC and cerebellar vermis, indicate that approaches parcellating the brain into smaller and more functionally relevant regions may be more fruitful. In addition, the recent advances in MRI techniques such as DTI that allow more informative descriptions of white matter structure may help to elucidate the role of robust findings such as increased WMH in both children and adults with mood disorders.

A potential confounding factor that is beginning to receive more attention is the impact of medications on brain structural measures. Although it has been recognized for some time in the Schizophrenia literature that many an-

tipsychotics can affect brain structural measures (Chakos et al., 1994; Elkashef et al., 1994; Keshavan et al., 1994), there has been less attempt to account for this in the study of affective disorders, despite the frequent use of antipsychotic medications both for mood-related psychotic symptoms and as primary mood-stabilizing agents.

There is also evidence to support that the classic mood stabilizers may also affect brain structure. Findings in animal models that lithium and valproic acid may have neuroprotective effects have generated considerable interest (Manji, Moore, Rajkowska, & Chen, 2000), and three studies in humans have found brain structural correlations with lithium exposure. A study of subgenual prefrontal cortex by Drevets et al. (1997) looked at volume loss in regard to exposure to lithium and found that the subgroup that had been treated with lithium or valproic acid did not show the same cortical loss. A longitudinal study by the same group found significant increase in gray matter volume in 8 out of 10 patients with Bipolar Disorder following a 4-week trial of lithium treatment (G. J. Moore, Bebchuk, Wilds, Chen, & Manji, 2000). An independent study of anterior cingulate volume in adults with Bipolar Disorder found that treatment-naïve patients had reduced anterior cingulate volumes, whereas volumes in lithium-treated patients were not different from controls (Sassi et al., 2004).

The relationship of these findings to the pathophysiology of mood disorders and neurodevelopmental processes will benefit from the application of study designs similar to those being increasingly used in the more mature Schizophrenia literature, including exploration of state/trait differences through study of high-risk populations and longitudinal studies beginning early in the course of the disorder. Also similarly to Schizophrenia, the considerable heterogeneity of mood disorders may be more easily related to genetic vulnerabilities through the identification of particular structural or physiological characteristics which can be used as endophenotypes (Almasy & Blangero, 2001; Gottesman & Gould, 2003). Neurophysiological differences between children and adults will also be important to consider further in order to understand why children do not appear to show the same hippocampal abnormalities as seen in adults, similarly to the findings previously described in PTSD. One of the current theories regarding the pathogenesis of the hippocampal findings in depression in adults is a neurotoxic effect of hypercortisolemia (Rajkowska, 2003). As cortisol responses to stress appear to differ in children, prospective longitudinal studies extending from childhood into adulthood will be necessary to determine whether these inconsistencies in imaging findings are due to heterogeneous subtypes of the disorder or are developmental in nature.

SUMMARY AND FUTURE DIRECTIONS

In the past 25 years, neuroimaging techniques have become an essential tool in the study of normal and abnormal neurodevelopment. MRI in particular has provided the ability to include repeated direct in vivo measurements of brain structures throughout the life span, bringing into view a new level of biological organization. The newfound accessibility of brain structure measures as quantifiable phenotypes has made possible a much richer integration of human neurodevelopment and psychology within the broader field of developmental biology.

Since the first CT pictures of enlarged ventricles in individuals with Schizophrenia (Johnstone et al., 1976), neuroimaging has provided concrete evidence that psychiatric disorders are based in the brain. However, the nature of the relationship between brain structure and many brain functions is still poorly understood. For example, as of this writing, neuroimaging investigations of the childhood-onset neuropsychiatric disorders described in this chapter are not of diagnostic utility except to rule out possible central nervous system insults such as tumors, intracranial bleeds, and congenital anomalies as etiologies for the symptoms. There is no identified "lesion" common to all, or even most, children with disorders such as Autism, ADHD, Schizophrenia, dyslexia, juvenile-onset bipolar disorder, depression, PTSD, or OCD. There is enormous variation in brain structural findings even in the disorders with known genetic etiologies such as Fragile X disorder or Rett syndrome.

Attempts to link brain structure and functional capacities such as IQ are also not straightforward. As seen in the section on normal development, similar functional capacity can be found in boys of similar age but with brain volumes differing by as much as 40% (Giedd, 1996). Similarly, boys consistently have larger brain volume than girls, yet there is not a significant difference in IQ (Giedd, 1996). An individual can sustain surprisingly large amounts of damage to some parts of the brain without permanent loss of function if injury occurs sufficiently early in life (Anderson, Damasio, Tranel, & Damasio, 2000; Kennard, 1940).

Nonetheless, correlations have been identified between some aspects of brain structure and functional capacity. Several studies have shown that there are correlations of brain structural measures with IQ on both whole-brain and regional levels (Haier, Jung, Yeo, Head, & Alkire, 2004; Posthuma et al., 2002; Thompson, Cannon, et al., 2001; Toga & Thompson, 2004). Relationships between memory function and hippocampal size have also been noted in several species. Food-storing species of birds have larger hippocampi than related non-food-storing species

(Krebs, Sherry, Healy, Perry, & Vaccarino, 1989; Sherry, Vaccarino, Buckenham, & Herz, 1989), and in mammals, a similar example can be found in voles. Male voles of the polygamous species travel far and wide in search of mates; they perform better than their female counterparts on laboratory measures of spatial ability and have significantly larger hippocampi (Sherry, Jacobs, & Gaulin, 1992). Conversely, in the monogamous vole species, which do not show male-female differences in spatial ability, no sexual dimorphism of hippocampal size is seen (Jacobs, Gaulin, Sherry, & Hoffman, 1990). In humans also, correlations between memory for stories and left hippocampal volume have been noted (Goldberg, Torrey, Berman, & Weinberger, 1994; Lencz et al., 1992). A study of taxi drivers in London found that they had larger hippocampi than controls, thought to be related to their extensive amount of navigational memory required for their work (Maguire et al., 2000).

Some general impressions can be drawn from findings in neurodevelopmental disorders as well. The very early onset disorders such as Fragile X and Autism tend to have diffuse effects. In the absence of longitudinal studies, it is not known whether these are progressive. Disorders with onset during later childhood, such as OCD and ADHD, appear to show more focal structural changes. These are also relatively static compared to disorders with a marked loss of function such as Schizophrenia, which are characterized by a progressive loss of brain tissue. Rett syndrome might be expected to show a similar progressive loss of tissue during stages of the illness in which clinical deterioration is occurring, but at this time there are no longitudinal reports with which to determine if this is the case. Structural changes in mood disorders and PTSD have been less clear but have shown an intriguing relationship between developmental onset of illness and the nature of associated brain changes, in that children with depression and PTSD have not been found to have the smaller hippocampal volumes seen in adults.

The studies reviewed in this chapter, as well as the many not included here, have provided the essential first explorations of what this new tool can contribute to our understanding of typical and atypical development. It will not have escaped the reader that the findings thus far in many childhood-onset psychiatric disorders have been both inconsistent and nonspecific. As mentioned earlier, many of the inconsistencies may be attributed to methodological issues. To some extent, the lack of specificity is also not unexpected—using any phenotypic measure well, including one such as brain morphometry, involves knowing its variability and how it is impacted by factors such as age, sex, and environment (Vitzthum, 2003). The neuroimaging studies obtained to date are just starting to provide descriptions of some of these features, and the degree to which the brain shows structural differences due to these is turning out to be more significant than perhaps expected.

The realization of how much plasticity can be exhibited in even the adult brain has also begun to hint at how complex the relationship is between brain structure and development. As articulated by several investigators (Ansari & Karmiloff-Smith, 2002; Cicchetti & Cohen, 1995; Gottlieb & Halpern, 2002; M. H. Johnson, Halit, Grice, & Karmiloff-Smith, 2002; Karmiloff-Smith et al., 2004; Peterson, 2003; Rutter & Sroufe, 2000; Sameroff & Mackenzie, 2003; Thomas & Karmiloff-Smith, 2002), the structure of the brain at any time is a product of a complex interaction among genetic, epigenetic, and environmental factors ("environmental" taken broadly as including both the outside environment and the internal physiological milieu). Stresses placed on the developing individual by a mismatch between his or her capacities and demands placed by the environment will result in compensatory physiological responses and behaviors that in time may affect brain structures. Within limits this is a description of the normal learning process. However, if the mismatch is severe, this process can result in pathology, particularly if compensations result in further pathology directly or through triggering adverse environmental reactions such as increased familial stress. It is not possible to determine ex post facto from a neuroimaging study which features are related to the initial perturbation or genetic anomaly and which to downstream effects—the "inverse solution" problem, as reviewed by Courchesne et al. (1995). Longitudinal studies beginning as early as possible are the best means to try to tease apart how brain structure relates to other factors affecting the developmental trajectory (Peterson, 2003). Such studies are unfortunately difficult to perform due to logistical issues, but, as described previously, the few available to date have been fruitful in showing significant differences in trajectories that were not apparent from previous cross-sectional studies (Giedd, Blumenthal, et al., 1999; Gogtay, Giedd, et al., 2004).

Another crucial issue for neuroimaging studies of brain development is the selection of the groups to be studied. One of the basic principles from developmental biology is that of equifinality, meaning that a given phenotype can be arrived at through many paths. In the realm of neuropsychiatric disorders, the diagnostic categories are just such phenotypes. It has become increasingly clear that the diagnostic categories most frequently used in clinical practice are not necessarily the most informative for correlation with biological measures such as brain structures. The

DSM-IV states in its introduction that its diagnostic syndromes were not based strictly on biological criteria (which are not available for most psychiatric disorders), but were arrived at through balancing a variety of concerns, including historical tradition, compatibility with the *International Classification of Diseases 10,* clinical and research data, and consensus of experts in the field (American Psychiatric Association, Task Force on *DSM-IV,* 2000). In addition, the use of polythetic criteria within a categorical classification system as seen in the *DSM-IV* predisposes toward heterogeneity of individuals within a diagnostic category.

Approaches to diminish heterogeneity include identifying more homogeneous diagnostic subtypes, such as the deficit syndrome in Schizophrenia, and scoring individual symptoms on dimensional scales and clustering individuals accordingly. Both of these may be helpful in some settings, but do not necessarily have a clearer relationship to any particular biologically meaningful measure. The identification of endophenotypes is a different strategy that has been gaining attention in the study of psychiatric disorders in recent years. These are heritable traits related to the disease pathology, not due to treatment or disease-induced degeneration, and which are found in milder form in family members without the full-blown syndrome. Current examples in Schizophrenia include eye-tracking abnormalities (Calkins & Iacono, 2000; Holzman et al., 1974) and deficits in P50 suppression (Braff & Freedman, 2002; Braff, Geyer, & Swerdlow, 2001). It is theorized that these traits, being simpler than the full version of disorder, will be associated with a smaller and more easily identified set of genes (Gottesman & Gould, 2003). They also may provide a means to introduce a biologically or genetically based element into the classification of psychiatric disorders to increase the reliability and validity of psychiatric diagnoses and the likelihood of finding meaningful associations with other biological measures. Brain imaging studies organized by biologically based endophenotypes may suffer less from noise introduced by diagnostic heterogeneity. In addition, brain structural measures themselves are capturing increased attention as potential endophenotypes.

Attention to reliable and consistent diagnostic criteria gains additional importance from the current efforts to implement multicenter imaging studies; several of these are currently in process in different regions around the world. Such studies will provide an invaluable means of obtaining sufficient statistical power to address the interactions of genes and environmental factors on brain structure and function on a population level. The impact of environmental factors in particular has been understudied in neuroimaging research, an aspect that will need to be addressed if accurate representations of the relationship between genetic characteristics and outcome are to be obtained (Vineis, 2004). The additional challenges posed by attempting to match diagnostic criteria and imaging methods between different areas and even different countries will be important to consider in the design and interpretation of such studies. The development of quantitative imaging methods that are not scanner-dependent and automated image analysis methods will be particularly valuable in making it possible to combine large amounts of data between sites.

The nature of the neuroimaging measures obtained is another important methodological issue affecting specificity of findings. The measures reported for most neuroimaging studies thus far has been at the level of whole-brain and lobar volumes, which are too gross to be informative about specific functionally relevant neuroanatomic circuits. Higher field scanners and advances in acquisition techniques are making possible very high resolution that allows accurate delineation of much smaller and potentially more functionally meaningful anatomic regions.

At least equally important is the evolution of analytic techniques through concurrent progress in computational power and increasingly sophisticated statistical modeling. This is making possible the comparison of brain structural measures between groups on much finer levels, including sulcal parcellations and cluster analysis on a voxel-by-voxel basis (see Figure 3.10) (Thompson et al., 1997, 2004).

Different levels of brain organization and function are described by the many disciplines that touch on this field. To integrate these, there is a need for more studies that combine structural neuroimaging with measures from other levels of biological complexity such as genes or behavior (Toga & Mazziotta, 2002; Toga & Thompson, 2004). For example, the question regarding the relative contributions of increased myelination versus pruning to the observed loss of cortical gray matter during adolescent brain development (Sowell, Thompson, et al., 2001) will most likely benefit from using methods such as magnetization transfer that are affected by macromolecular concentrations and thus provide information about whether concentrations of myelin are increasing. Such correlations will also require increased efforts to determine the precise sources of the signals observed in structural neuroimaging studies through imaging combined with postmortem validation in animal models.

As the chief purpose of studies of brain structure is to better understand cognition and behavior, the integration of structural and functional measures is particularly important. Functional neuroimaging provides the ability to see changes in brain activity as they relate to real-time thoughts and behaviors. The plasticity of the brain in response to use implies that abnormal functional patterns may eventually be reflected in an alteration of the trajectory of brain structural

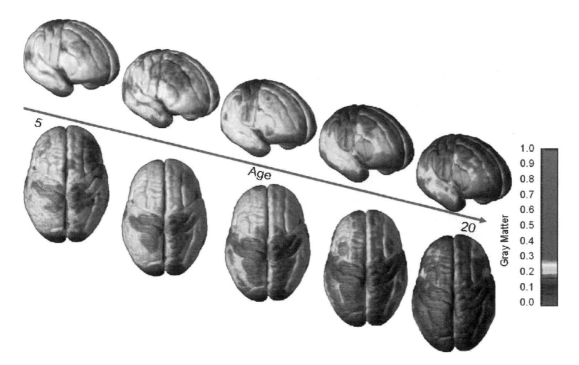

Figure 3.10 Right lateral and top views of the dynamic sequence of gray matter maturation over the cortical surface. The side bar shows a grey scale representation in units of GM volume.

development, but longitudinal studies using a combination of functional and structural modalities are necessary to determine to what extent this is actually the case (Nagy, Westerberg, & Klingberg, 2004). Along the same lines, only multimodal imaging will be able to address questions of brain function as it relates to connectivity of different brain regions. An ongoing question for fMRI studies is how the different areas of activation actually relate to each other. Being able to determine whether activated areas are parts of the same neuroanatomic circuit, and to assess the integrity of that circuit, will provide the necessary link between functional patterns, their physical foundation, and the features on the cellular, synaptic, and genetic levels that may impact them (Ramnani, Behrens, Penny, & Matthews, 2004).

Finally, to return to the statements that began this chapter, the ability to create images of the living brain has generated tremendous excitement in the scientific and lay communities. Although the initial stages of determining the capabilities of a new method like structural neuroimaging are of necessity exploratory, like any other technique neuroimaging must eventually take its place as one tool among many to address specific hypotheses arising from a clearly articulated theoretical foundation. This is particularly important for two reasons in the case of neuroimaging studies of brain development. One is the complexity of the multiple layers of potentially interacting factors and the impossibility of relating them accurately or intelligibly without a strong theoretical framework to guide interpretation. The second is the rhetorical impact of findings from neuroimaging studies. The "seeing is believing" aspect of neuroimaging studies can seem to offer the promise of concrete, objective answers to long-standing and vexatious issues, such as when adolescents have the capacity to be held responsible for their own actions. However, the relatively early stages of our ability to relate brain structural features to particular causative pathways of normal or abnormal development means that, at this point, specific findings should not be interpreted as more than indicators of potential risk factors for abnormal functioning that must be placed in the context of clinical status and as clues to the developmental processes that may be at work.

REFERENCES

Abell, F., Krams, M., Ashburner, J., Passingham, R., Friston, K., Frackowiak, R., et al. (1999). The neuroanatomy of Autism: A voxel-based whole brain analysis of structural scans. *NeuroReport, 10*(8), 1647–1651.

Adler, C. M., Holland, S. K., Schmithorst, V., Wilke, M., Weiss, K. L., Pan, H., et al. (2004). Abnormal frontal white matter tracts in bipo-

lar disorder: A diffusion tensor imaging study. *Bipolar Disorder, 6*(3), 197–203.

Akbarian, S. (2003). The neurobiology of Rett syndrome. *Neuroscientist, 9*(1), 57–63.

Akiskal, H. S., Downs, J., Jordan, P., Watson, S., Daugherty, D., & Pruitt, D. B. (1985). Affective disorders in referred children and younger siblings of manic-depressives: Mode of onset and prospective course. *Archives of General Psychiatry, 42*(10), 996–1003.

Alaghband-Rad, J., McKenna, K., Gordon, C. T., Albus, K., Hamburger, S. D., Rumsey, J. M., et al. (1995). Childhood-onset schizophrenia: The severity of premorbid course. *Journal of the American Academy of Child and Adolescent Psychiatry, 34*(10), 1273–1283.

Alexander, G., DeLong, M., & Strick, P. (1986). Parallel organization of functionally segregated circuits linking basal ganglia and cortex. *Annual Review of Neuroscience, 9,* 357–381.

Allen, G., Buxton, R. B., Wong, E. C., & Courchesne, E. (1997). Attentional activation of the cerebellum independent of motor involvement. *Science, 275*(5308), 1940–1943.

Allen, L. S., Richey, M. F., Chai, Y. M., & Gorski, R. A. (1991). Sex differences in the corpus callosum of the living human being. *Journal of Neuroscience, 11,* 933–942.

Almasy, L., & Blangero, J. (2001). Endophenotypes as quantitative risk factors for psychiatric disease: Rationale and study design. *American Journal of Medical Genetics, 105*(1), 42–44.

Altshuler, L. L., Curran, J. G., Hauser, P., Mintz, J., Denicoff, K., & Post, R. (1995). T2 hyperintensities in bipolar disorder: Magnetic resonance imaging comparison and literature meta-analysis. *American Journal of Psychiatry, 152*(8),1139–1144.

American Psychiatric Association Task Force on DSM-IV. (2000). *Diagnostic and statistical manual of mental disorders* (4th ed.). Washington, DC: Author.

Amir, R. E., Van den Veyver, I. B., Wan, M., Tran, C. Q., Francke, U., & Zoghbi, H. Y. (1999). Rett syndrome is caused by mutations in X-linked MeCP2, encoding methyl-cpg-binding protein 2. *Nature Genetics, 23*(2), 185–188.

Anderson, S. W., Damasio, H., Tranel, D., & Damasio, A. R. (2000). Long-term sequelae of prefrontal cortex damage acquired in early childhood. *Developmental Neuropsychology, 18*(3), 281–296.

Andreasen, N. C., Arndt, S., Swayze, V., II, Cizadlo, T., Flaum, M., O'Leary, D., et al. (1994). Thalamic abnormalities in Schizophrenia visualized through magnetic resonance image averaging. *Science, 266*(5183), 294–298.

Andreasen, N. C., Ehrhardt, J. C., Swayze, V. W., II, Alliger, R. J., Yuh, W. T., Cohen, G., et al. (1990). Magnetic resonance imaging of the brain in Schizophrenia: The pathophysiologic significance of structural abnormalities. *Archives of General Psychiatry, 47,* 35–44.

Andreasen, N. C., Flaum, M., Swayze, V. N., O'Leary, D. S., Alliger, R., Cohen, G., et al. (1993). Intelligence and brain structure in normal individuals. *American Journal of Psychiatry, 150*(1), 130–134.

Andreasen, N. C., Nasrallah, H. A., Dunn, V., Olson, S. C., Grove, W. M., Ehrhardt, J. C., et al. (1986). Structural abnormalities in the frontal system in Schizophrenia: A magnetic resonance imaging study. *Archives of General Psychiatry, 43,* 136–144.

Ansari, D., & Karmiloff-Smith, A. (2002). Atypical trajectories of number development: A neuroconstructivist perspective. *Trends in Cognitive Sciences, 6*(12), 511–516.

Archibald, S. L., Fennema-Notestine, C., Gamst, A., Riley, E. P., Mattson, S. N., & Jernigan, T. L. (2001). Brain dysmorphology in individuals with severe prenatal alcohol exposure. *Developmental Medicine and Child Neurology, 43*(3), 148–154.

Armstrong, D. D. (1992). The neuropathology of the Rett syndrome. *Brain Development, 14*(Suppl.), S89–S98.

Armstrong, D. D., Dunn, J. K., Antalffy, B., & Trivedi, R. (1995). Selective dendritic alterations in the cortex of Rett syndrome. *Journal of Neuropathology and Experimental Neurology, 54*(2), 195–201.

Arndt, S., Cohen, G., Alliger, R. J., Swayze, V. W., & Andreasen, N. C. (1991). Problems with ratio and proportion measures of imaged cerebral structures. *Bulletin of Clinical Neurosciences, 55,* 131–136.

Aron, A. R., Dowson, J. H., Sahakian, B. J., & Robbins, T. W. (2003). Methylphenidate improves response inhibition in adults with attention-deficit/hyperactivity disorder. *Biological Psychiatry, 54*(12), 1465–1468.

Aron, A. R., Fletcher, P. C., Bullmore, E. T., Sahakian, B. J., & Robbins, T. W. (2003). Stop-signal inhibition disrupted by damage to right inferior frontal gyrus in humans [Erratum appears in *Nature Neuroscience, 6*(12), 1329]. *Nature Neuroscience, 6*(2), 115–116.

Autti-Ramo, I., Autti, T., Korkman, M., Kettunen, S., Salonen, O., & Valanne, L. (2002). MRI findings in children with school problems who had been exposed prenatally to alcohol. *Developmental Medicine and Child Neurology, 44*(2), 98–106.

Aylward, E. H., Harris, G. J., Hoehn-Saric, R., Barta, P. E., Machlin, S. R., & Pearlson, G. D. (1996). Normal caudate nucleus in obsessive-compulsive disorder assessed by quantitative neuroimaging. *Archives of General Psychiatry, 53*(7), 577–584.

Aylward, E. H., Minshew, N. J., Field, K., Sparks, B. F., & Singh, N. (2002). Effects of age on brain volume and head circumference in Autism. *Neurology, 59*(2), 175–183.

Aylward, E. H., Minshew, N. J., Goldstein, G., Honeycutt, N. A., Augustine, A. M., Yates, K. O., et al. (1999). MRI volumes of amygdala and hippocampus in non-mentally retarded autistic adolescents and adults. *Neurology, 53*(9), 2145–2150.

Aylward, E. H., Reiss, A. L., Reader, M. J., Singer, H. S., Brown, J. E., & Denckla, M. B. (1996). Basal ganglia volumes in children with attention-deficit hyperactivity disorder. *Journal of Child Neurology, 11*(2), 112–115.

Badura, F., Trott, G. E., Mehler-Wex, C., Scheuerpflug, P., Hofmann, E., Warmuth-Metz, M., et al. (2001). A study of cranial computer tomograms in very early and early onset schizophrenia. *Journal of Neural Transmission, 108*(11), 1335–1344.

Bailey, A., Le Couteur, A., Gottesman, I., Bolton, P., Simonoff, E., Yuzda, E., et al. (1995). Autism as a strongly genetic disorder: Evidence from a British twin study. *Psychological Medicine, 25*(1), 63–77.

Bailey, A., Luthert, P., Bolton, P., Le Couteur, A., Rutter, M., & Harding, B. (1993). Autism and megalencephaly. *Lancet, 341*(8854), 1225–1226.

Baird, G., Charman, T., Baron-Cohen, S., Cox, A., Swettenham, J., Wheelwright, S., et al. (2000). A screening instrument for Autism at 18 months of age: A 6-year follow-up study. *Journal of the American Academy of Child and Adolescent Psychiatry, 39*(6), 694–702.

Barbaresi, W. J., Katusic, S. K., Colligan, R. C., Pankratz, V. S., Weaver, A. L., Weber, K. J., et al. (2002). How common is attention-deficit/hyperactivity disorder? Incidence in a population-based birth cohort in Rochester, Minn. *Archives of Pediatric and Adolescent Medicine, 156*(3), 217–224.

Barkley, R. A. (1997). Behavioral inhibition, sustained attention, and executive functions: Constructing a unifying theory of ADHD. *Psychological Bulletin, 121*(1), 65–94.

Barkley, R. A., Edwards, G., Laneri, M., Fletcher, K., & Metevia, L. (2001). Executive functioning, temporal discounting, and sense of time in adolescents with attention deficit hyperactivity disorder (ADHD) and oppositional defiant disorder (ODD). *Journal of Abnormal Child Psychology, 29*(6), 541–556.

Barkovich, A. J. (2000). Concepts of myelin and myelination in neuroradiology. *American Journal of Neuroradiology, 21*(6), 1099–1109.

Barkovich, A. J., Kjos, B. O., Jackson, D. E., Jr., & Norman, D. (1988). Normal maturation of the neonatal and infant brain: MR imaging at 1.5 T. *Radiology, 166,* 173–180.

Barnea-Goraly, N., Eliez, S., Hedeus, M., Menon, V., White, C. D., Moseley, M., et al. (2003). White matter tract alterations in fragile X syndrome: Preliminary evidence from diffusion tensor imaging. *American Journal of Medical Genetics, 118B*(1), 81–88.

Barnea-Goraly, N., Kwon, H., Menon, V., Eliez, S., Lotspeich, L., & Reiss, A. L. (2004). White matter structure in Autism: Preliminary evidence from diffusion tensor imaging. *Biological Psychiatry, 55*(3), 323–326.

Baron-Cohen, S., Leslie, A. M., & Frith, U. (1985). Does the autistic child have a "theory of mind"? *Cognition, 21*(1), 37–46.

Barres, B. A., & Barde, Y. (2000). Neuronal and glial cell biology. *Current Opinion in Neurobiology, 10*(5), 642–648.

Bartzokis, G. (2004). Age-related myelin breakdown: A developmental model of cognitive decline and Alzheimer's disease. *Neurobiology of Aging, 25*(1), 5–18; author reply 49–62.

Bartzokis, G., Beckson, M., Lu, P. H., Nuechterlein, K. H., Edwards, N., & Mintz, J. (2001). Age-related changes in frontal and temporal lobe volumes in men: A magnetic resonance imaging study. *Archives of General Psychiatry, 58*(5), 461–465.

Bauman, M., & Kemper, T. L. (1985). Histoanatomic observations of the brain in early infantile Autism. *Neurology, 35*(6), 866–874.

Behrens, T. E., Johansen-Berg, H., Woolrich, M. W., Smith, S. M., Wheeler-Kingshott, C. A., Boulby, P. A., et al. (2003). Non-invasive mapping of connections between human thalamus and cortex using diffusion imaging. *Nature Neuroscience, 6*(7), 750–757.

Beitchman, J. H. (1985). Childhood Schizophrenia: A review and comparison with adult-onset schizophrenia. *Psychiatric Clinics of North America, 8,* 793–814.

Benes, F. M. (1989). Myelination of cortical-hippocampal relays during late adolescence. *Schizophrenia Bulletin, 15*(4), 585–593.

Berlucchi, G. (1981). Interhemispheric asymmetries in visual discrimination: A neurophysiological hypothesis. *Documenta Opthalmologica Proceedings Series, 30,* 87–93.

Berthier, M. L., Kulisevsky, J., Gironell, A., & Heras, J. A. (1996). Obsessive-compulsive disorder associated with brain lesions: Clinical phenomenology, cognitive function, and anatomic correlates. *Neurology, 47*(3), 353–361.

Berthier, M. L., Starkstein, S. E., & Leiguarda, R. (1990). Developmental cortical anomalies in Asperger's syndrome: Neuroradiological findings in two patients. *Journal of Neuropsychiatry, 2,* 197–201.

Best, M., & Demb, J. B. (1999). Normal planum temporale asymmetry in dyslexics with a magnocellular pathway deficit. *NeuroReport, 10*(3), 607–612.

Beyer, J. L., & Krishnan, K. R. (2002). Volumetric brain imaging findings in mood disorders. *Bipolar Disorders, 4*(2), 89–104.

Biederman, J., Kwon, A., Wozniak, J., Mick, E., Markowitz, S., Fazio, V., et al. (2004). Absence of gender differences in pediatric bipolar disorder: Findings from a large sample of referred youth. *Journal of Affective Disorders, 83*(2/3), 207–214.

Bilder, R. M., Wu, H., Bogerts, B., Degreef, G., Ashtari, M., Alvir, J. M., et al. (1994). Absence of regional hemispheric volume asymmetries in first-episode Schizophrenia. *American Journal of Psychiatry, 151,* 1437–1447.

Biro, S., & Russell, J. (2001). The execution of arbitrary procedures by children with Autism. *Developmental Psychopathology, 13*(1), 97–110.

Blumberg, H. P., Charney, D. S., & Krystal, J. H. (2002). Frontotemporal neural systems in bipolar disorder. *Seminars in Clinical Neuropsychiatry, 7*(4), 243–254.

Blumberg, H. P., Kaufman, J., Martin, A., Whiteman, R., Zhang, J. H., Gore, J. C., et al. (2003). Amygdala and hippocampal volumes in adolescents and adults with bipolar disorder. *Archives of General Psychiatry, 60*(12), 1201–1208.

Boddaert, N., Chabane, N., Gervais, H., Good, C. D., Bourgeois, M., Plumet, M. H., et al. (2004). Superior temporal sulcus anatomical abnormalities in childhood Autism: A voxel-based morphometry MRI study. *Neuroimage, 23*(1), 364–369.

Bonne, O., Brandes, D., Gilboa, A., Gomori, J. M., Shenton, M. E., Pitman, R. K., et al. (2001). Longitudinal MRI study of hippocampal volume in trauma survivors with PTSD. *American Journal of Psychiatry, 158*(8), 1248–1251.

Bookstein, F. L., Sampson, P. D., Connor, P. D., & Streissguth, A. P. (2002). Midline corpus callosum is a neuroanatomical focus of fetal alcohol damage. *Anatomical Record, 269*(3), 162–174.

Bookstein, F. L., Streissguth, A. P., Sampson, P. D., Connor, P. D., & Barr, H. M. (2002). Corpus callosum shape and neuropsychological deficits in adult males with heavy fetal alcohol exposure. *Neuroimage, 15*(1), 233–251.

Botteron, K. N., Raichle, M. E., Drevets, W. C., Heath, A. C., & Todd, R. D. (2002). Volumetric reduction in left subgenual prefrontal cortex in early onset depression. *Biological Psychiatry, 51*(4), 342–344.

Botteron, K. N., Vannier, M. W., Geller, B., Todd, R. D., & Lee, B. C. (1995). Preliminary study of magnetic resonance imaging characteristics in 8- to 16-year-olds with mania. *Journal of the American Academy of Child and Adolescent Psychiatry, 34*(6), 742–749.

Braff, D. L., & Freedman, R. (2002). Endophenotypes in studies of the genetics of Schizophrenia. In K. L. Davis, D. S. Charney, J. T. Coyle & C. B. Nemeroff (Eds.), *Neuropsychopharmacology: The fifth generation of progress* (pp. 703–716). Philadelphia: Lippincott, Williams, & Wilkins.

Braff, D. L., Geyer, M. A., & Swerdlow, N. R. (2001). Human studies of prepulse inhibition of startle: Normal subjects, patient groups, and pharmacological studies. *Psychopharmacology (Berl), 156*(2/3), 234–258.

Brambilla, P., Barale, F., Caverzasi, E., & Soares, J. C. (2002). Anatomical MRI findings in mood and anxiety disorders. *Epidemiologiae Psichiatria Sociale, 11*(2), 88–99.

Brambilla, P., Hardan, A., di Nemi, S. U., Perez, J., Soares, J. C., & Barale, F. (2003). Brain anatomy and development in Autism: Review of structural MRI studies. *Brain Research Bulletin, 61*(6), 557–569.

Brambilla, P., Harenski, K., Nicoletti, M., Sassi, R. B., Mallinger, A. G., Frank, E., et al. (2003). MRI investigation of temporal lobe structures in bipolar patients. *Journal of Psychiatric Research, 37*(4), 287–295.

Breier, A., Buchanan, R. W., Elkashef, A., Munson, R. C., Kirkpatrick, B., & Gellad, F. (1992). Brain morphology and Schizophrenia. *Archives of General Psychiatry, 49*, 921–926.

Bremner, J. D. (1999). Does stress damage the brain? *Biological Psychiatry, 45*(7), 797–805.

Bremner, J. D., Randall, P., Scott, T. M., Bronen, R. A., Seibyl, J. P., Southwick, S. M., et al. (1995). MRI-based measurement of hippocampal volume in patients with combat-related posttraumatic stress disorder. *American Journal of Psychiatry, 152*, 973–981.

Bremner, J. D., Randall, P., Vermetten, E., Staib, L., Bronen, R. A., Mazure, C., et al. (1997). Magnetic resonance imaging-based measurement of hippocampal volume in posttraumatic stress disorder related to childhood physical and sexual abuse: A preliminary report. *Biological Psychiatry, 41*(1), 23–32.

Brown, W. E., Eliez, S., Menon, V., Rumsey, J. M., White, C. D., & Reiss, A. L. (2001). Preliminary evidence of widespread morphological variations of the brain in dyslexia. *Neurology, 56*(6), 781–783.

Brunberg, J. A., Jacquemont, S., Hagerman, R. J., Berry-Kravis, E. M., Grigsby, J., Leehey, M. A., et al. (2002). Fragile X premutation carriers: Characteristic MR imaging findings of adult male patients with progressive cerebellar and cognitive dysfunction. *American Journal of Neuroradiology, 23*(10), 1757–1766.

Brunswick, N., McCrory, E., Price, C. J., Frith, C. D., & Frith, U. (1999). Explicit and implicit processing of words and pseudowords by adult developmental dyslexics: A search for Wernicke's Wortschatz? *Brain, 122*(Pt. 10), 1901–1917.

Bryant, B., Mayou, R., Wiggs, L., Ehlers, A., & Stores, G. (2004). Psychological consequences of road traffic accidents for children and their mothers. *Psychological Medicine, 34*(2), 335–346.

Bush, G., Frazier, J. A., Rauch, S. L., Seidman, L. J., Whalen, P. J., Jenike, M. A., et al. (1999). Anterior cingulate cortex dysfunction in attention-deficit/hyperactivity disorder revealed by fMRI and the counting Stroop. *Biological Psychiatry, 45*(12), 1542–1552.

Bussing, R., Grudnik, J., Mason, D., Wasiak, M., & Leonard, C. (2002). ADHD and conduct disorder: An MRI study in a community sample. *World Journal of Biological Psychiatry, 3*(4), 216–220.

Calkins, M. E., & Iacono, W. G. (2000). Eye movement dysfunction in Schizophrenia: A heritable characteristic for enhancing phenotype definition. *American Journal of Medical Genetics, 97*(1), 72–76.

Calvert, G. A. (2001). Crossmodal processing in the human brain: Insights from functional neuroimaging studies. *Cerebral Cortex, 11*(12), 1110–1123.

Campbell, S., & MacQueen, G. (2004). The role of the hippocampus in the pathophysiology of major depression. *Journal of Psychiatry and Neuroscience, 29*(6), 417–426.

Campbell, S., Marriott, M., Nahmias, C., & MacQueen, G. M. (2004). Lower hippocampal volume in patients suffering from depression: A meta-analysis. *American Journal of Psychiatry, 161*(4), 598–607.

Canive, J. M., Lewine, J. D., Orrison, W. W., Jr., Edgar, C. J., Provencal, S. L., Davis, J. T., et al. (1997). MRI reveals gross structural abnormalities in PTSD. *Annals of the New York Academy of Science, 821*, 512–515.

Carpenter, P. A., Just, M. A., & Reichle, E. D. (2000). Working memory and executive function: Evidence from neuroimaging. *Current Opinion in Neurobiology, 10*(2), 195–199.

Casanova, M. F., Araque, J., Giedd, J., Rumsey, J. M., Casanova, M. F., Buxhoeveden, D. P., et al. (2004). Reduced brain size and gyrification in the brains of dyslexic patients: Minicolumnar pathology in dyslexia. *Journal of Child Neurology, 19*(4), 275–281.

Casanova, M. F., Naidu, S., Goldberg, T. E., Moser, H. W., Khoromi, S., Kumar, A., et al. (1991). Quantitative magnetic resonance imaging in Rett syndrome. *Journal of Neuropsychiatry and Clinical Neurosciences, 3*(1), 66–72.

Casey, B. J., Castellanos, F. X., Giedd, J. N., Marsh, W. L., Hamburger, S. D., Schubert, A. B., et al. (1997). Implication of right frontostriatal circuitry in response inhibition and attention-deficit/hyperactivity disorder. *Journal of the American Academy of Child and Adolescent Psychiatry, 36*(3), 374–383.

Castellanos, F. X. (2002). Proceed, with caution: SPECT cerebral blood flow studies of children and adolescents with attention deficit hyperactivity disorder. *Journal of Nuclear Medicine, 43*(12), 1630–1633.

Castellanos, F. X., Giedd, J. N., Berquin, P. C., Walter, J. M., Sharp, W., Tran, T., et al. (2001). Quantitative brain magnetic resonance imaging in girls with attention-deficit/hyperactivity disorder. *Archives of General Psychiatry, 58*(3), 289–295.

Castellanos, F. X., Giedd, J. N., Eckburg, P., Marsh, W. L., Vaituzis, A. C., Kaysen, D., et al. (1994). Quantitative morphology of the caudate nucleus in attention deficit hyperactivity disorder. *American Journal of Psychiatry, 151*(12), 1791–1796.

Castellanos, F. X., Giedd, J. N., Marsh, W. L., Hamburger, S. D., Vaituzis, A. C., Dickstein, D. P., et al. (1996). Quantitative brain magnetic resonance imaging in attention-deficit hyperactivity disorder. *Archives of General Psychiatry, 53*(7), 607–616.

Castellanos, F. X., Lee, P. P., Sharp, W., Jeffries, N. O., Greenstein, D. K., Clasen, L. S., et al. (2002). Developmental trajectories of brain volume abnormalities in children and adolescents with attention-deficit/hyperactivity disorder. *Journal of the American Medical Association, 288*(14), 1740–1748.

Castellanos, F. X., Sharp, W. S., Gottesman, R. F., Greenstein, D. K., Giedd, J. N., & Rapoport, J. L. (2003). Anatomic brain abnormalities in monozygotic twins discordant for attention deficit hyperactivity disorder. *American Journal of Psychiatry, 160*(9), 1693–1696.

Chakos, M. H., Lieberman, J. A., Bilder, R. M., Borenstein, M., Lerner, G., Bogerts, B., et al. (1994). Increase in caudate nuclei volumes of first-episode schizophrenic patients taking antipsychotic drugs. *American Journal of Psychiatry, 151,* 1430–1436.

Chakrabarti, S., & Fombonne, E. (2001). Pervasive developmental disorders in preschool children. *Journal of the American Medical Association, 285*(24), 3093–3099.

Charney, D. S. (2004). Psychobiological mechanisms of resilience and vulnerability: Implications for successful adaptation to extreme stress. *American Journal of Psychiatry, 161*(2), 195–216.

Chen, B. K., Sassi, R., Axelson, D., Hatch, J. P., Sanches, M., Nicoletti, M., et al. (2004). Cross-sectional study of abnormal amygdala development in adolescents and young adults with bipolar disorder. *Biological Psychiatry, 56*(6), 399–405.

Chen, H. H., Nicoletti, M. A., Hatch, J. P., Sassi, R. B., Axelson, D., Brambilla, P., et al. (2004). Abnormal left superior temporal gyrus volumes in children and adolescents with bipolar disorder: A magnetic resonance imaging study. *Neuroscience Letters, 363*(1), 65–68.

Chen, Y., Fu, S., Iversen, S. D., Smith, S. M., & Matthews, P. M. (2002). Testing for dual brain processing routes in reading: A direct contrast of Chinese character and Pinyin reading using fMRI. *Journal of Cognitive Neuroscience, 14*(7), 1088–1098.

Childs, B., & Scriver, C. R. (1986). Age at onset and causes of disease. *Perspectives in Biology and Medicine, 29,* 437–460.

Choi, J. S., Kang, D. H., Kim, J. J., Ha, T. H., Lee, J. M., Youn, T., et al. (2004). Left anterior subregion of orbitofrontal cortex volume reduction and impaired organizational strategies in obsessive-compulsive disorder. *Journal of Psychiatric Research, 38*(2), 193–199.

Chung, M. K., Worsley, K. J., Paus, T., Cherif, C., Collins, D. L., Giedd, J. N., et al. (2001). A unified statistical approach to deformation-based morphometry. *Neuroimage, 14*(3), 595–606.

Cicchetti, D., & Cohen, D. J. (1995). Perspectives on developmental psychopathology. In D. Cicchetti (Ed.), *Developmental psychopathology* (Vol. 1, pp. 3–22). New York: Wiley.

Clark, A. S., MacLusky, N. J., & Goldman-Rakic, P. S. (1988). Androgen binding and metabolism in the cerebral cortex of the developing rhesus monkey. *Endocrinology, 123,* 932–940.

Coffey, C. E., Figiel, G. S., Djang, W. T., Saunders, W. B., & Weiner, R. D. (1989). White matter hyperintensity on magnetic resonance imaging: Clinical and neuroanatomic correlates in the depressed elderly. *Journal of Neuropsychiatry and Clinical Neurosciences, 1*(2), 135–144.

Coffey, C. E., Hinkle, P. E., Weiner, R. D., Nemeroff, C. B., Krishnan, K. R., Varia, I., et al. (1987). Electroconvulsive therapy of depression in patients with white matter hyperintensity. *Biological Psychiatry, 22*(5), 629–636.

Collins, D. L., Holmes, C. J., Peters, T. M., & Evans, A. C. (1995). Automatic 3-D model-based neuroanatomical segmentation. *Human Brain Mapping, 3,* 190–208.

Collins, D. L., Zijdenbos, A. P., Baaré, W. F. C., & Evans, A. C. (1999). Animal + insect: Improved cortical structure segmentation. In *Proceedings of the annual conference on information processing in medical imaging (IPMI)* (pp. 210–223). Visegrad, Hungary: Springer.

Cook, N. D. (1986). *The brain code: Mechanisms of information transfer and the role of the corpus callosum.* London: Methuen.

Costello, E. J., Pine, D. S., Hammen, C., March, J. S., Plotsky, P. M., Weissman, M. M., et al. (2002). Development and natural history of mood disorders. *Biological Psychiatry, 52*(6), 529–542.

Courchesne, E., Carper, R., & Akshoomoff, N. (2003). Evidence of brain overgrowth in the first year of life in Autism. *Journal of the American Medical Association, 290*(3), 337–344.

Courchesne, E., Hesselink, J. R., Jernigan, T. L., & Yeung-Courchesne, R. (1987). Abnormal neuroanatomy in a nonretarded person with Autism: Unusual findings with magnetic resonance imaging. *Archives of Neurology, 44,* 335–341.

Courchesne, E., Karns, C. M., Davis, H. R., Ziccardi, R., Carper, R. A., Tigue, Z. D., et al. (2001). Unusual brain growth patterns in early life in patients with autistic disorder: An MRI study. *Neurology, 57*(2), 245–254.

Courchesne, E., Press, G. A., & Yeung-Courchesne, R. (1993). Parietal lobe abnormalities detected with MR in patients with infantile Autism. *American Journal of Roentgenology, 160,* 387–393.

Courchesne, E., Townsend, J., & Chase, C. (1995). Neurodevelopmental principles guide research on developmental psychopathologies. In D. Cicchetti (Ed.), *Developmental psychopathology* (Vol. 1, pp. 195–226). New York: Wiley.

Courchesne, E., Yeung-Courchesne, R., Press, G. A., Hesselink, J. R., & Jernigan, T. L. (1988). Hypoplasia of cerebellar vermal lobules VI and VII in Autism. *New England Journal of Medicine, 318,* 1349–1354.

Cowell, P. E., Allen, L. S., Zalatimo, N. S., & Denenberg, V. H. (1992). A developmental study of sex and age interactions in the human corpus callosum. *Developmental Brain Research, 66,* 187–192.

Craddock, N., & Jones, I. (2001). Molecular genetics of bipolar disorder. *British Journal of Psychiatry, 178*(Suppl. 41), S128–S133.

Crawford, D. C., Meadows, K. L., Newman, J. L., Taft, L. F., Pettay, D. L., Gold, L. B., et al. (1999). Prevalence and phenotype consequence of fraxa and fraxe alleles in a large, ethnically diverse, special education-needs population. *American Journal of Human Genetics, 64*(2), 495–507.

Creasey, H., Rumsey, J. M., Schwartz, M., Duara, R., Rapoport, J. L., & Rapoport, S. I. (1986). Brain morphometry in autistic men as measured by volumetric computed tomography. *Archives of Neurology, 43*(7), 669–672.

Cummings, A. M., & Kavlock, R. J. (2004). Gene-environment interactions: A review of effects on reproduction and development. *Critical Reviews in Toxicology, 34*(6), 461–485.

Curtis, W. J., & Cicchetti, D. (2003). Moving research on resilience into the 21st century: Theoretical and methodological considerations in examining the biological contributors to resilience. *Developmental Psychopathology, 15*(3), 773–810.

Damadian, R. (1971). Tumor detection by nuclear magnetic resonance. *Science, 171*(976), 1151–1153.

Damasio, A. R., & Maurer, R. G. (1978). A neurological model for childhood Autism. *Archives of Neurology, 35*(12), 777–786.

Darnell, J. C., Jensen, K. B., Jin, P., Brown, V., Warren, S. T., & Darnell, R. B. (2001). Fragile X mental retardation protein targets G quartet MRNAs important for neuronal function. *Cell, 107*(4), 489–499.

Das, U. G., Cronk, C. E., Martier, S. S., Simpson, P. M., & McCarver, D. G. (2004). Alcohol dehydrogenase 2*3 affects alterations in offspring facial morphology associated with maternal ethanol intake in pregnancy. *Alcoholism Clinical and Experimental Research, 28*(10), 1598–1606.

Dasari, M., Friedman, L., Jesberger, J., Stuve, T. A., Findling, R. L., Swales, T. P., et al. (1999). A magnetic resonance imaging study of thalamic area in adolescent patients with either Schizophrenia or bipolar disorder as compared to healthy controls. *Psychiatry Research, 91*(3), 155–162.

DeBellis, M. D., Baum, A. S., Birmaher, B., Keshavan, M. S., Eccard, C. H., Boring, A. M., et al. (1999). A. E. Bennett research award: Developmental traumatology: Pt. I. Biological stress systems. *Biological Psychiatry, 45*(10), 1259–1270.

DeBellis, M. D., Hall, J., Boring, A. M., Frustaci, K., & Moritz, G. (2001). A pilot longitudinal study of hippocampal volumes in pediatric maltreatment-related posttraumatic stress disorder. *Biological Psychiatry, 50*(4), 305–309.

DeBellis, M. D., Keshavan, M. S., Frustaci, K., Shifflett, H., Iyengar, S., Beers, S. R., et al. (2002). Superior temporal gyrus volumes in maltreated children and adolescents with PTSD. *Biological Psychiatry, 51*(7), 544–552.

De Fosse, L., Hodge, S. M., Makris, N., Kennedy, D. N., Caviness, V. S., Jr., McGrath, L., et al. (2004). Language-association cortex asymmetry in Autism and specific language impairment. *Annals of Neurology, 56*(6), 757–766.

Dekaban, A. S. (1977). Tables of cranial and orbital measurements, cranial volume, and derived indexes in males and females from 7 days to 20 years of age. *Annals of Neurology, 2,* 485–491.

Dekaban, A. S., & Sadowsky, D. (1978). Changes in brain weight during the span of human life: Relation of brain weights to body heights and body weights. *Annals of Neurology, 4,* 345–356.

DelBello, M. P., Zimmerman, M. E., Mills, N. P., Getz, G. E., & Strakowski, S. M. (2004). Magnetic resonance imaging analysis of amygdala and other subcortical brain regions in adolescents with bipolar disorder. *Bipolar Disorders, 6*(1), 43–52.

DeLisi, L. E. (1999a). Defining the course of brain structural change and plasticity in Schizophrenia. *Psychiatry Research, 92*(1), 1–9.

DeLisi, L. E. (1999b). Regional brain volume change over the lifetime course of Schizophrenia. *Journal of Psychiatric Research, 33*(6), 535–541.

DeLisi, L. E., Hoff, A. L., Schwartz, J. E., Shields, G. W., Halthore, S. N., Gupta, S. M., et al. (1991). Brain morphology in first-episode schizophrenic-like psychotic patients: A quantitative magnetic resonance imaging study. *Biological Psychiatry, 29*(5), 159–175.

Dey, A. N., & Bloom, B. (2005). Summary health statistics for U.S. children: National Health Interview Survey, 2003. *Vital Health Statistics, 10*(223), 1–78.

Diener, E., Sandvik, E., & Larsen, R. F. (1985). Age and sex effects for affect intensity. *Developmental Psychology, 21,* 542–546.

Drevets, W. C., Price, J. L., Simpson, J. R., Jr., Todd, R. D., Reich, T., Vannier, M., et al. (1997). Subgenual prefrontal cortex abnormalities in mood disorders. *Nature, 386*(6627), 824–827.

Du, Y., & Dreyfus, C. F. (2002). Oligodendrocytes as providers of growth factors. *Journal of Neuroscience Research, 68*(6), 647–654.

Dunn, H. G., Stoessl, A. J., Ho, H. H., MacLeod, P. M., Poskitt, K. J., Doudet, D. J., et al. (2002). Rett syndrome: Investigation of nine patients, including PET scan. *Canadian Journal of Neurological Sciences, 29*(4), 345–357.

Durston, S., Hulshoff Pol, H. E., Schnack, H. G., Buitelaar, J. K., Steenhuis, M. P., Minderaa, R. B., et al. (2004). Magnetic resonance imaging of boys with attention-deficit/hyperactivity disorder and their unaffected siblings. *Journal of the American Academy of Child and Adolescent Psychiatry, 43*(3), 332–340.

Eckert, M. A., Leonard, C. M., Richards, T. L., Aylward, E. H., Thomson, J., & Berninger, V. W. (2003). Anatomical correlates of dyslexia: Frontal and cerebellar findings. *Brain, 126*(Pt. 2), 482–494.

Edgar, J. M., & Garbern, J. (2004). The myelinated axon is dependent on the myelinating cell for support and maintenance: Molecules involved. *Journal of Neuroscience Research, 76*(5), 593–598.

Egaas, B., Courchesne, E., & Saitoh, O. (1995). Reduced size of corpus callosum in Autism. *Archives of Neurology, 52*(8), 794–801.

Einspieler, C., Kerr, A. M., & Prechtl, H. F. (2005). Is the early development of girls with Rett disorder really normal? *Pediatric Research, 57*(5, Pt. 1), 696–700.

Eliez, S., Blasey, C. M., Freund, L. S., Hastie, T., & Reiss, A. L. (2001). Brain anatomy, gender and IQ in children and adolescents with fragile X syndrome. *Brain, 124*(Pt. 8), 1610–1618.

Elkashef, A. M., Buchanan, R. W., Gellad, F., Munson, R. C., & Breier, A. (1994). Basal ganglia pathology in Schizophrenia and tardive dyskinesia: An MRI quantitative study. *American Journal of Psychiatry, 151*(5), 752–755.

Engelbrecht, V., Rassek, M., Preiss, S., Wald, C., & Modder, U. (1998). Age-dependent changes in magnetization transfer contrast of white matter in the pediatric brain. *American Journal of Neuroradiology, 19*(10), 1923–1929.

Escalona, P. R., McDonald, W. M., Doraiswamy, P. M., Boyko, O. B., Husain, M. M., Figiel, G. S., et al. (1991). In vivo stereological assessment of human cerebellar volume: Effects of gender and age. *American Journal of Neuroradiology, 12*(5), 927–929.

Faraone, S. V., Perlis, R. H., Doyle, A. E., Smoller, J. W., Goralnick, J. J., Holmgren, M. A., et al. (2005). Molecular genetics of attention-deficit/hyperactivity disorder. *Biological Psychiatry, 57*(11), 1313–1323.

Fields, R. D., Eshete, F., Dudek, S., Ozsarac, N., & Stevens, B. (2001). Regulation of gene expression by action potentials: Dependence on complexity in cellular information processing. *Novartis Found Symposium, 239,* 160–172.

Fields, R. D., & Stevens-Graham, B. (2002). New insights into neuron-glia communication. *Science, 298*(5593), 556–562.

Filipek, P. A., Richelme, C., Kennedy, D. N., & Caviness, V. S., Jr. (1994). The young adult human brain: An MRI-based morphometric analysis. *Cerebral Cortex, 4,* 344–360.

Filipek, P. A., Semrud-Clikeman, M., Steingard, R. J., Renshaw, P. F., Kennedy, D. N., & Biederman, J. (1997). Volumetric MRI analysis comparing subjects having attention-deficit hyperactivity disorder with normal controls. *Neurology, 48*(3), 589–601.

Flaum, M., Swayze, V. W., O'Leary, D. S., Yuh, W. T., Ehrhardt, J. C., Arndt, S. V., et al. (1995). Effects of diagnosis, laterality, and gender on brain morphology in Schizophrenia. *American Journal of Psychiatry, 152*(5), 704–714.

Folstein, S. E., & Rosen-Sheidley, B. (2001). Genetics of Autism: Complex aetiology for a heterogeneous disorder. *Nature Reviews Genetics, 2*(12), 943–955.

Fombonne, E., Roge, B., Claverie, J., Courty, S., & Fremolle, J. (1999). Microcephaly and macrocephaly in Autism. *Journal of Autism and Developmental Disorders, 29*(2), 113–119.

Frazier, J. A., Giedd, J. N., Hamburger, S. D., Albus, K. E., Kaysen, D., Vaituzis, A. C., et al. (1996). Brain anatomic magnetic resonance imaging in childhood onset schizophrenia. *Archives of General Psychiatry, 53,* 617–624.

Frazier, J. A., Giedd, J. N., Kaysen, D., Albus, K., Hamburger, S., Alaghband-Rad, J., et al. (1996). Childhood onset schizophrenia: Brain magnetic resonance imaging rescan after two years of clozapine maintenance. *American Journal of Psychiatry, 153,* 564–566.

Freund, L. S., Reiss, A. L., & Abrams, M. T. (1993). Psychiatric disorders associated with fragile X in the young female. *Pediatrics, 91*(2), 321–329.

Friedman, L., Findling, R. L., Kenny, J. T., Swales, T. P., Stuve, T. A., Jesberger, J. A., et al. (1999). An MRI study of adolescent patients with either Schizophrenia or bipolar disorder as compared to healthy control subjects. *Biological Psychiatry, 46*(1), 78–88.

Friston, K. J., Harrison, L., & Penny, W. (2003). Dynamic causal modelling. *Neuroimage, 19*(4), 1273–1302.

Frith, U. (1989). *Autism: Explaining the enigma.* Oxford: Blackwell.

Frith, U. (2001). Mind blindness and the brain in Autism. *Neuron, 32*(6), 969–979.

Gaffney, G. R., Kuperman, S., Tsai, L. Y., Minchin, S., & Hassanein, K. M. (1987). Midsagittal magnetic resonance imaging of Autism. *British Journal of Psychiatry, 151,* 831–833.

Gaffney, G. R., & Tsai, L. Y. (1987). Magnetic resonance imaging of high level Autism. *Journal of Autism and Developmental Disorders, 17*(3), 433–438.

Galaburda, A. M. (1995). Neuroanatomic basis of developmental dyslexia. *Neurologic Clinics, 11*(1), 161–173.

Garber, H. J., & Ritvo, E. R. (1992). Magnetic resonance imaging of the posterior fossa in autistic adults. *American Journal of Psychiatry, 149,* 245–247.

Garber, H. J., Ritvo, E. R., Chiu, L. C., Griswold, V. J., Kashanian, A., Freeman, B. J., et al. (1989). A magnetic resonance imaging study of Autism: Normal fourth ventricle size and absence of pathology. *American Journal of Psychiatry, 146,* 532–534.

Garel, C., Chantrel, E., Elmaleh, M., Brisse, H., & Sebag, G. (2003). Fetal MRI: Normal gestational landmarks for cerebral biometry, gyration and myelination. *Childrens Nervous Systems, 19*(7/8), 422–425.

Gelfand, J. R., & Bookheimer, S. Y. (2003). Dissociating neural mechanisms of temporal sequencing and processing phonemes. *Neuron, 38*(5), 831–842.

Geller, B., & Luby, J. (1997). Child and adolescent bipolar disorder: A review of the past 10 years. *Journal of the American Academy of Child and Adolescent Psychiatry, 36*(9), 1168–1176.

Geller, B., Tillman, R., Craney, J. L., & Bolhofner, K. (2004). Four-year prospective outcome and natural history of mania in children with a prepubertal and early adolescent bipolar disorder phenotype. *Archives of General Psychiatry, 61*(5), 459–467.

Geller, D. A., Biederman, J., Faraone, S., Agranat, A., Cradock, K., Hagermoser, L., et al. (2001). Developmental aspects of obsessive compulsive disorder: Findings in children, adolescents, and adults. *Journal of Nervous and Mental Disease, 189*(7), 471–477.

Geller, D. A., Biederman, J., Jones, J., Shapiro, S., Schwartz, S., & Park, K. S. (1998). Obsessive-compulsive disorder in children and adolescents: A review. *Harvard Review of Psychiatry, 5*(5), 260–273.

Geschwind, N. (1978). Anatomical asymmetry as the basis for cerebral dominance. *Federation Proceedings, 37*(9), 2263–2266.

Geschwind, N., & Levitsky, W. (1968). Human brain: Left-right asymmetries in temporal speech region. *Science, 161*(837), 186–187.

Giedd, J. N. (1996). Normal brain development: Ages 4–18. In K. R. R. Krishnan & M. Doraiswamy (Eds.), *Brain imaging in clinical psychiatry* (pp. 103–120). New York: Marcel Dekker.

Giedd, J. N., Blumenthal, J., Jeffries, N. O., Castellanos, F. X., Liu, H., Zijdenbos, A., et al. (1999). Brain development during childhood and adolescence: A longitudinal MRI study. *Nature Neuroscience, 2*(10), 861–863.

Giedd, J. N., Blumenthal, J., Molloy, E., & Castellanos, F. X. (2001). Brain imaging of attention deficit/hyperactivity disorder. *Annals of the New York Acadamy of Sciences, 931,* 33–49.

Giedd, J. N., Castellanos, F. X., Casey, B. J., Kozuch, P., King, A. C., Hamburger, S. D., et al. (1994). Quantitative morphology of the corpus callosum in attention deficit hyperactivity disorder. *American Journal of Psychiatry, 151*(5), 665–669.

Giedd, J. N., Jeffries, N. O., Blumenthal, J., Castellanos, F. X., Vaituzis, A. C., Fernandez, T., et al. (1999). Childhood onset schizophrenia: Progressive brain changes during adolescence. *Biological Psychiatry, 46*(7), 892–898.

Giedd, J. N., Kozuch, P., Kaysen, D., Vaituzis, A. C., Hamburger, S. D., Bartko, J. J., et al. (1995). Reliability of cerebral measures in repeated examinations with magnetic resonance imaging. *Psychiatry Research, 61,* 113–119.

Giedd, J. N., Rapoport, J. L., Garvey, M. A., Perlmutter, S., & Swedo, S. E. (2000). MRI assessment of children with obsessive-compulsive disorder or tics associated with streptococcal infection. *American Journal of Psychiatry, 157*(2), 281–283.

Giedd, J. N., Rapoport, J. L., Leonard, H. L., Richter, D., & Swedo, S. E. (1996). Acute basal ganglia enlargement and obsessive compulsive symptoms in an adolescent boy. *Journal of the American Academy of Child and Adolescent Psychiatry, 35*(7), 913–915.

Giedd, J. N., Snell, J. W., Lange, N., Rajapakse, J. C., Casey, B. J., Kozuch, P. L., et al. (1996). Quantitative magnetic resonance imaging of human brain development: Ages 4–18. *Cerebral Cortex, 6*(4), 551–560.

Gilbert, A. R., Moore, G. J., Keshavan, M. S., Paulson, L. A., Narula, V., Mac Master, F. P., et al. (2000). Decrease in thalamic volumes of pediatric patients with obsessive-compulsive disorder who are taking paroxetine. *Archives of General Psychiatry, 57*(5), 449–456.

Gilbert, S. F. (2003). *Developmental biology* (7th ed.). Sunderland, MA: Sinauer Associates.

Gilbertson, M. W., Shenton, M. E., Ciszewski, A., Kasai, K., Lasko, N. B., Orr, S. P., et al. (2002). Smaller hippocampal volume predicts pathologic vulnerability to psychological trauma. *Nature Neuroscience, 5*(11), 1242–1247.

Girard, N., Raybaud, C., & Poncet, M. (1995). In vivo MR study of brain maturation in normal fetuses. *American Journal of Neuroradiology, 16*(2), 407–413.

Gogate (sic) Gogtay, N., Giedd, J., Janson, K., & Rapoport, J. L. (2001). Brain imaging in normal and abnormal brain development: New perspectives for child psychiatry. *Clinical Neuroscience Research, 1*(4), 283–290.

Gogtay, N., Giedd, J. N., Lusk, L., Hayashi, K. M., Greenstein, D., Vaituzis, A. C., et al. (2004). Dynamic mapping of human cortical development during childhood through early adulthood. *Proceedings of the National Academy of Sciences of the United States of America, 101*(21), 8174–8179.

Gogtay, N., Sporn, A., Clasen, L. S., Nugent, T. F., III, Greenstein, D., Nicolson, R., et al. (2004). Comparison of progressive cortical gray matter loss in childhood-onset schizophrenia with that in childhood-onset atypical psychoses. *Archives of General Psychiatry, 61*(1), 17–22.

Goldberg, T. E., Torrey, E. F., Berman, K. F., & Weinberger, D. R. (1994). Relations between neuropsychological performance and brain morphological and physiological measures in monozygotic twins discordant for Schizophrenia. *Psychiatry Research, 55,* 51–61.

Gordon, C. T. (1992). Childhood-onset schizophrenia. In E. Peschel, R. Peschel, C. Howe, & J. Howe (Eds.), *Neurobiological disorders in children and adolescents.* San Francisco: Jossey-Bass.

Gottesman, I. I., & Gould, T. D. (2003). The endophenotype concept in psychiatry: Etymology and strategic intentions. *American Journal of Psychiatry, 160*(4), 636–645.

Gottlieb, G., & Halpern, C. T. (2002). A relational view of causality in normal and abnormal development. *Developmental Psychopathology, 14*(3), 421–435.

Gould, E., Woolley, C. S., Frankfurt, M., & McEwen, B. S. (1990). Gonadal steroids regulate dendritic spine density in hippocampal pyramidal cells in adulthood. *Journal of Neuroscience, 10,* 1286–1291.

Gould, T. D., Quiroz, J. A., Singh, J., Zarate, C. A., & Manji, H. K. (2004). Emerging experimental therapeutics for bipolar disorder: Insights from the molecular and cellular actions of current mood stabilizers. *Molecular Psychiatry, 9*(8), 734–755.

Grachev, I. D., Breiter, H. C., Rauch, S. L., Savage, C. R., Baer, L., Shera, D. M., et al. (1998). Structural abnormalities of frontal neocortex in obsessive-compulsive disorder [Letter, comment]. *Archives of General Psychiatry, 55*(2), 181–182.

Grados, M. A. (2003). Obsessive-compulsive disorder after traumatic brain injury. *International Review of Psychiatry, 15*(4), 350–358.

Green, R. L., Hutsler, J. J., Loftus, W. C., Tramo, M. J., Thomas, C. E., Silberfarb, A. W., et al. (1999). The caudal infrasylvian surface in dyslexia: Novel magnetic resonance imaging-based findings. *Neurology, 53*(5), 974–981.

Green, W. H., Padron-Gayol, M., Hardesty, A. S., & Bassiri, M. (1992). Schizophrenia with childhood-onset: A phenomenological study of 38 cases. *Journal of the American Academy of Child and Adolescent Psychiatry, 31,* 976–986.

Greenough, W. T., Klintsova, A. Y., Irwin, S. A., Galvez, R., Bates, K. E., & Weiler, I. J. (2001). Synaptic regulation of protein synthesis and the fragile X protein. *Proceedings of the National Academy of Sciences of the United States of America, 98*(13), 7101–7106.

Gur, R. E., Cowell, P., Turetsky, B. I., Gallacher, F., Cannon, T., Bilker, W., et al. (1998). A follow-up magnetic resonance imaging study of Schizophrenia: Relationship of neuroanatomical changes to clinical and neurobehavioral measures. *Archives of General Psychiatry, 55*(2), 145–152.

Gurvits, T. V., Shenton, M. E., Hokama, H., Ohta, H., Lasko, N. B., Gilbertson, M. W., et al. (1996). Magnetic resonance imaging study of hippocampal volume in chronic, combat-related posttraumatic stress disorder. *Biological Psychiatry, 40*(11), 1091–1099.

Haber, S., & McFarland, N. R. (2001). The place of the thalamus in frontal cortical-basal ganglia circuits. *Neuroscientist, 7*(4), 315–324.

Hagberg, B. (1995). Rett syndrome: Clinical peculiarities and biological mysteries. *Acta Paediatrica, 84*(9), 971–976.

Hagerman, R. J., Leavitt, B. R., Farzin, F., Jacquemont, S., Greco, C. M., Brunberg, J. A., et al. (2004). Fragile-X-associated tremor/ataxia syndrome (FXTAS) in females with the FMR1 premutation. *American Journal of Human Genetics, 74*(5), 1051–1056.

Haier, R. J., Jung, R. E., Yeo, R. A., Head, K., & Alkire, M. T. (2004). Structural brain variation and general intelligence. *Neuroimage, 23*(1), 425–433.

Haleem, M. (1990). *Diagnostic categories of the Yakovlev collection of normal and pathological anatomy and development of the brain.* Washington, DC: Armed Forces Institute of Pathology.

Hall, D., Dhilla, A., Charalambous, A., Gogos, J. A., & Karayiorgou, M. (2003). Sequence variants of the brain-derived neurotrophic factor (BDNF) gene are strongly associated with obsessive-compulsive disorder. *American Journal of Human Genetics, 73*(2), 370–376.

Hardan, A. Y., Kilpatrick, M., Keshavan, M. S., & Minshew, N. J. (2003). Motor performance and anatomic magnetic resonance imaging (MRI) of the basal ganglia in Autism. *Journal of Child Neurology, 18*(5), 317–324.

Hardan, A. Y., Minshew, N. J., & Keshavan, M. S. (2000). Corpus callosum size in Autism. *Neurology, 55*(7), 1033–1036.

Hardan, A. Y., Minshew, N. J., Mallikarjuhn, M., & Keshavan, M. S. (2001). Brain volume in Autism. *Journal of Child Neurology, 16*(6), 421–424.

Harrison, P. J. (2002). The neuropathology of primary mood disorder. *Brain, 125*(Pt. 7), 1428–1449.

Hashimoto, T., Tayama, M., Miyazaki, M., Murakawa, K., Shimakawa, S., Yoneda, Y., et al. (1993). Brainstem involvement in high functioning autistic children. *Acta Neuologica Scandinavica, 88,* 123–128.

Hashimoto, T., Tayama, M., Mori, K., Fujino, K., Miyazaki, M., & Kuroda, Y. (1989). Magnetic resonance imaging in Autism: Preliminary report. *Neuropediatrics, 20,* 142–146.

Hassink, R. I., Hiltbrunner, B., Muller, S., & Lutschg, J. (1992). Assessment of brain maturation by T2-weighted MRI. *Neuropediatrics, 23,* 72–74.

Haznedar, M. M., Buchsbaum, M. S., Wei, T. C., Hof, P. R., Cartwright, C., Bienstock, C. A., et al. (2000). Limbic circuitry in patients with Autism spectrum disorders studied with positron emission tomography and magnetic resonance imaging. *American Journal of Psychiatry, 157*(12), 1994–2001.

Heiervang, E., Hugdahl, K., Steinmetz, H., Inge Smievoll, A., Stevenson, J., Lund, A., et al. (2000). Planum temporale, planum parietale and dichotic listening in dyslexia. *Neuropsychologia, 38*(13), 1704–1713.

Hendren, R. L., Hodde-Vargas, J. E., Vargas, L. A., Orrison, W. W., & Dell, L. (1991). Magnetic resonance imaging of severely disturbed children: A preliminary study. *Journal of the American Academy of Child and Adolescent Psychiatry, 30*(3), 466–470.

Hendren, R. L., Hodde-Vargas, J., Yeo, R. A., Vargas, L. A., Brooks, W. M., & Ford, C. (1995). Neuropsychophysiological study of children at risk for Schizophrenia: A preliminary report. *Journal of the American Academy of Child and Adolescent Psychiatry, 34*(10), 1284–1291.

Heptinstall, E. (1996). *Healing the hidden hurt: The emotional effects of children's accidents.* London: Child Accident Prevention Trust.

Herbert, M. R., Harris, G. J., Adrien, K. T., Ziegler, D. A., Makris, N., Kennedy, D. N., et al. (2002). Abnormal asymmetry in language association cortex in Autism. *Annals of Neurology, 52*(5), 588–596.

Herbert, M. R., Ziegler, D. A., Deutsch, C. K., O'Brien, L. M., Lange, N., Bakardjiev, A., et al. (2003). Dissociations of cerebral cortex, subcortical and cerebral white matter volumes in autistic boys. *Brain, 126*(Pt. 5), 1182–1192.

Herbert, M. R., Ziegler, D. A., Makris, N., Filipek, P. A., Kemper, T. L., Normandin, J. J., et al. (2004). Localization of white matter volume increase in Autism and developmental language disorder. *Annals of Neurology, 55*(4), 530–540.

Hessl, D., Rivera, S. M., & Reiss, A. L. (2004). The neuroanatomy and neuroendocrinology of fragile X syndrome. *Mental Retardation and Developmental Disabilities Research Review, 10*(1), 17–24.

Hesslinger, B., Tebartz van Elst, L., Thiel, T., Haegele, K., Hennig, J., & Ebert, D. (2002). Frontoorbital volume reductions in adult patients with attention deficit hyperactivity disorder. *Neuroscience Letters, 328*(3), 319–321.

Hill, D. E., Yeo, R. A., Campbell, R. A., Hart, B., Vigil, J., & Brooks, W. (2003). Magnetic resonance imaging correlates of attention-deficit/hyperactivity disorder in children. *Neuropsychology, 17*(3), 496–506.

Hinton, V. J., Brown, W. T., Wisniewski, K., & Rudelli, R. D. (1991). Analysis of neocortex in three males with the fragile X syndrome. *American Journal of Medical Genetics, 41*(3), 289–294.

Holland, B. A., Haas, D. K., Norman, D., Brant-Zawadzki, M., & Newton, T. H. (1986). MRI of normal brain maturation. *American Journal of Neuroradiology, 7,* 201–208.

Hollis, C. (1995). Child and adolescent (juvenile onset) Schizophrenia. A case control study of premorbid developmental impairments. *British Journal of Psychiatry, 166*(4), 489–495.

Holttum, J. R., Minshew, N. J., Sanders, R. S., & Phillips, N. E. (1992). Magnetic resonance imaging of the posterior fossa in Autism. *Biological Psychiatry, 32,* 1091–1101.

Holzman, P. S., Proctor, L. R., Levy, D. L., Yasillo, N. J., Meltzer, H. Y., & Hurt, S. W. (1974). Eye-tracking dysfunctions in schizophrenic patients and their relatives. *Archives of General Psychiatry, 31*(2), 143–151.

Howard, M. A., Cowell, P. E., Boucher, J., Broks, P., Mayes, A., Farrant, A., et al. (2000). Convergent neuroanatomical and behavioural evidence of an amygdala hypothesis of Autism. *NeuroReport, 11*(13), 2931–2935.

Hoyme, H. E., May, P. A., Kalberg, W. O., Kodituwakku, P., Gossage, J. P., Trujillo, P. M., et al. (2005). A practical clinical approach to diagnosis of fetal alcohol spectrum disorders: Clarification of the 1996 Institute of Medicine criteria. *Pediatrics, 115*(1), 39–47.

Hughes, C. (1996). Control of action and thought: Normal development and dysfunction in Autism: A research note. *Journal of Child Psychology and Psychiatry, 37*(2), 229–236.

Hughes, C., Leboyer, M., & Bouvard, M. (1997). Executive function in parents of children with Autism. *Psychological Medicine, 27*(1), 209–220.

Hughes, C., Plumet, M. H., & Leboyer, M. (1999). Towards a cognitive phenotype for Autism: Increased prevalence of executive dysfunction and superior spatial span amongst siblings of children with Autism. *Journal of Child Psychology and Psychiatry, 40*(5), 705–718.

Hull, A. M. (2002). Neuroimaging findings in post-traumatic stress disorder: Systematic review. *British Journal of Psychiatry, 181,* 102–110.

Huppi, P. S., Maier, S. E., Peled, S., Zientara, G. P., Barnes, P. D., Jolesz, F. A., et al. (1998). Microstructural development of human newborn cerebral white matter assessed in vivo by diffusion tensor magnetic resonance imaging. *Pediatric Research, 44*(4), 584–590.

Huppi, P. S., Warfield, S., Kikinis, R., Barnes, P. D., Zientara, G. P., Jolesz, F. A., et al. (1998). Quantitative magnetic resonance imaging of brain development in premature and mature newborns. *Annals of Neurology, 43*(2), 224–235.

Huttenlocher, P. R. (1979). Synaptic density in human frontal cortex: Developmental changes and effects of aging. *Brain Research, 163,* 195–205.

Huttenlocher, P. R. (1994). Synaptogenesis in human cerebral cortex. In G. Dawson & K. Fischer (Eds.), *Human behavior and the developing brain* (pp. 137–152). New York: Guilford Press.

Huttenlocher, P. R., & Dabholkar, A. S. (1997). Regional differences in synaptogenesis in human cerebral cortex. *Journal of Comparative Neurology, 387*(2), 167–178.

Hynd, G. W., Hern, K. L., Novey, E. S., Eliopulos, D., Marshall, R., & Gonzalez, J. J. (1993). Attention deficit hyperactivity disorder (ADHD) and asymmetry of the caudate nucleus. *Journal of Child Neurology, 8*(4), 339–347.

Hynd, G. W., & Semrud-Clikeman, M. (1989). Dyslexia and neurodevelopmental pathology: Relationships to cognition, intelligence, and reading skill acquisition. *Journal of Learning Disabilities, 22,* 204–216, 220.

Hynd, G. W., Semrud-Clikeman, M., Lorys, A. R., Novey, E. S., Eliopulos, D., & Lyytinen, H. (1991). Corpus callosum morphology in attention deficit-hyperactivity disorder: Morphometric analysis of MRI. *Journal of Learning Disabilities, 24,* 141–146.

Inder, T. E., & Huppi, P. S. (2000). In vivo studies of brain development by magnetic resonance techniques. *Mental Retardation and Developmental Disabilities Research Review, 6*(1), 59–67.

Irle, E., Exner, C., Thielen, K., Weniger, G., & Ruther, E. (1998). Obsessive-compulsive disorder and ventromedial frontal lesions: Clinical and neuropsychological findings. *American Journal of Psychiatry, 155*(2), 255–263.

Irwin, S. A., Galvez, R., & Greenough, W. T. (2000). Dendritic spine structural anomalies in fragile-X mental retardation syndrome. *Cerebral Cortex, 10*(10), 1038–1044.

Ivry, R. B., Spencer, R. M., Zelaznik, H. N., & Diedrichsen, J. (2002). The cerebellum and event timing. *Annals of the New York Academy of Sciences, 978,* 302–317.

Jacobs, L. F., Gaulin, S. J., Sherry, D. F., & Hoffman, G. E. (1990). Evolution of spatial cognition: Sex-specific patterns of spatial behavior predict hippocampal size. *Proceedings of the National Academy of Sciences of the United States of America, 87,* 6349–6352.

Jacobsen, L. K., Giedd, J. N., Berquin, P. C., Krain, A. L., Hamburger, S. D., Kumra, S., et al. (1997). Quantitative morphology of the cerebellum and fourth ventricle in childhood-onset schizophrenia. *American Journal of Psychiatry, 154*(12), 1663–1669.

Jacobsen, L. K., Giedd, J. N., Castellanos, F. X., Vaituzis, A. C., Hamburger, S. D., Kumra, S., et al. (1998). Progressive reduction of temporal lobe structures in childhood-onset schizophrenia. *American Journal of Psychiatry, 155*(5), 678–685.

Jacobsen, L. K., Giedd, J. N., Vaituzis, A. C., Hamburger, S. D., Rajapakse, J. C., Frazier, J. A., et al. (1996). Temporal lobe morphology in childhood-onset schizophrenia. *American Journal of Psychiatry, 153*(3), 355–361.

Jacquemont, S., Hagerman, R. J., Leehey, M. A., Hall, D. A., Levine, R. A., Brunberg, J. A., et al. (2004). Penetrance of the fragile X-associated tremor/ataxia syndrome in a premutation carrier population. *Journal of the American Medical Association, 291*(4), 460–469.

Jakala, P., Hanninen, T., Ryynanen, M., Laakso, M., Partanen, K., Mannermaa, A., et al. (1997). Fragile-X: Neuropsychological test performance, CGG triplet repeat lengths, and hippocampal volumes. *Journal of Clinical Investment, 100*(2), 331–338.

James, A. C., James, S., Smith, D. M., & Javaloyes, A. (2004). Cerebellar, prefrontal cortex, and thalamic volumes over two time points in adolescent-onset schizophrenia. *American Journal of Psychiatry, 161*(6), 1023–1029.

James, A. C., Javaloyes, A., James, S., & Smith, D. (2002). Evidence for non-progressive changes in adolescent-onset schizophrenia. *British Journal of Psychiatry, 180,* 339–344.

Jancke, L., Preis, S., & Steinmetz, H. (1999). The relation between forebrain volume and midsagittal size of the corpus callosum in children. *NeuroReport, 10*(14), 2981–2985.

Jancke, L., Staiger, J. F., Schlaug, G., Huang, Y., & Steinmetz, H. (1997). The relationship between corpus callosum size and forebrain volume. *Cerebral Cortex, 7*(1), 48–56.

Jelicic, M., & Merckelbach, H. (2004). Traumatic stress, brain changes, and memory deficits: A critical note. *Journal of Nervous and Mental Disease, 192*(8), 548–553.

Jellinger, K. A. (2003). Rett syndrome: An update. *Journal of Neural Transmission, 110*(6), 681–701.

Jenike, M. A., Breiter, H. C., Baer, L., Kennedy, D. N., Savage, C. R., Olivares, M. J., et al. (1996). Cerebral structural abnormalities in obsessive-compulsive disorder. A quantitative morphometric magnetic resonance imaging study. *Archives of General Psychiatry, 53*(7), 625–632.

Jernigan, T. L., & Tallal, P. (1990). Late childhood changes in brain morphology observable with MRI. *Developmental Medicine and Child Neurology, 32,* 379–385.

Jernigan, T. L., Trauner, D. A., Hesselink, J. R., & Tallal, P. A. (1991). Maturation of human cerebrum observed in vivo during adolescence. *Brain, 114,* 2037–2049.

Jernigan, T. L., Zisook, S., Heaton, R. K., Moranville, J. T., Hesselink, J. R., & Braff, D. L. (1991). Magnetic resonance imaging abnormalities in lenticular nuclei and cerebral cortex in Schizophrenia. *Archives of General Psychiatry, 48,* 881–890.

Jerslid, A. T. (1963). *The psychology of adolescence* (2nd ed.). New York: Macmillan.

Johnson, M. A., & Bydder, G. M. (1983). NMR imaging of the brain in children. *Medical Bulletin, 40*(2), 175–178.

Johnson, M. H., Halit, H., Grice, S. J., & Karmiloff-Smith, A. (2002). Neuroimaging of typical and atypical development: A perspective from multiple levels of analysis. *Developmental Psychopathology, 14*(3), 521–536.

Johnson, V. P., Swayze, V. W., II, Sato, Y., & Andreasen, N. C. (1996). Fetal alcohol syndrome: Craniofacial and central nervous system manifestations. *American Journal of Medical Genetics, 61*(4), 329–339.

Johnstone, E. C., Crow, T. J., Frith, C. D., Husband, J., & Kreel, L. (1976). Cerebral ventricular size and cognitive impairment in chronic Schizophrenia. *Lancet, 2*(7992), 924–926.

Jones, K. L., & Smith, D. W. (1973). Recognition of the fetal alcohol syndrome in early infancy. *Lancet, 2*(7836), 999–1001.

Jones, K. L., Smith, D. W., Ulleland, C. N., & Streissguth, P. (1973). Pattern of malformation in offspring of chronic alcoholic mothers. *Lancet, 1,* 1267–1271.

Kang, D. H., Kim, J. J., Choi, J. S., Kim, Y. I., Kim, C. W., Youn, T., et al. (2004). Volumetric investigation of the frontal-subcortical circuitry in patients with obsessive-compulsive disorder. *Journal of Neuropsychiatry and Clinical Neuroscience, 16*(3), 342–349.

Kanner, L. (1943). Autistic disturbances of affective contact. *Nervous Child, 2,* 217–250.

Karmiloff-Smith, A., Thomas, M., Annaz, D., Humphreys, K., Ewing, S., Brace, N., et al. (2004). Exploring the Williams syndrome face-processing debate: The importance of building developmental trajectories. *Journal of Child Psychology and Psychiatry, 45*(7), 1258–1274.

Karno, M., Golding, J. M., Sorenson, S. B., & Burnam, M. A. (1988). The epidemiology of obsessive-compulsive disorder in five U.S. communities. *Archives of General Psychiatry, 45,* 1094–1099.

Kashani, J. H., Beck, N. C., Hoeper, E. W., Fallahi, C., Corcoran, C. M., McAllister, J. A., et al. (1987). Psychiatric disorders in a community sample of adolescents. *American Journal of Psychiatry, 144*(5), 584–589.

Kashani, J. H., McGee, R. O., Clarkson, S. E., Anderson, J. C., Walton, L. A., Williams, S., et al. (1983). Depression in a sample of 9-year-old children: Prevalence and associated characteristics. *Archives of General Psychiatry, 40*(11), 1217–1223.

Kashani, J. H., & Ray, J. S. (1983). Depressive related symptoms among preschool-age children. *Child Psychiatry and Human Development, 13*(4), 233–238.

Kates, W. R., Abrams, M. T., Kaufmann, W. E., Breiter, S. N., & Reiss, A. L. (1997). Reliability and validity of MRI measurement of the amygdala and hippocampus in children with fragile X syndrome. *Psychiatry Research, 75*(1), 31–48.

Kates, W. R., Burnette, C. P., Eliez, S., Strunge, L. A., Kaplan, D., Landa, R., et al. (2004). Neuroanatomic variation in monozygotic twin pairs discordant for the narrow phenotype for Autism. *American Journal of Psychiatry, 161*(3), 539–546.

Kates, W. R., Folley, B. S., Lanham, D. C., Capone, G. T., & Kaufmann, W. E. (2002). Cerebral growth in fragile X syndrome: Review and comparison with Down syndrome. *Microscopy Research and Technique, 57*(3), 159–167.

Kaufman, J., Martin, A., King, R. A., & Charney, D. (2001). Are child-, adolescent-, and adult-onset depression one and the same disorder? *Biological Psychiatry, 49*(12), 980–1001.

Kaufmann, W. E., Cooper, K. L., Mostofsky, S. H., Capone, G. T., Kates, W. R., Newschaffer, C. J., et al. (2003). Specificity of cerebellar vermian abnormalities in Autism: A quantitative magnetic resonance imaging study. *Journal of Child Neurology, 18*(7), 463–470.

Kennard, M. A. (1940). Relation of age to motor impairment in man and subhuman primates. *Archives of Neurology and Psychiatry, 44,* 377–397.

Kertesz, A., Polk, M., Black, S. E., & Howell, J. (1992). Anatomical asymmetries and functional laterality. *Brain, 115,* 589–605.

Keshavan, M. S., Bagwell, W. W., Haas, G. L., Sweeney, J. A., Schooler, N. R., & Pettegrew, J. W. (1994). Changes in caudate volume with neuroleptic treatment. *Lancet, 344,* 1434.

Kessler, R. C., Adler, L. A., Barkley, R., Biederman, J., Conners, C. K., Faraone, S. V., et al. (2005). Patterns and predictors of attention-deficit/hyperactivity disorder persistence into adulthood: Results from the national comorbidity survey replication. *Biological Psychiatry, 57*(11), 1442–1451.

Kessler, R. C., Avenevoli, S., & Ries Merikangas, K. (2001). Mood disorders in children and adolescents: An epidemiologic perspective. *Biological Psychiatry, 49*(12), 1002–1014.

Kessler, R. C., & Walters, E. E. (1998). Epidemiology of DSM-III-R major depression and minor depression among adolescents and young adults in the national comorbidity survey. *Depression and Anxiety, 7*(1), 3–14.

Kim, J. J., Lee, M. C., Kim, J., Kim, I. Y., Kim, S. I., Han, M. H., et al. (2001). Grey matter abnormalities in obsessive-compulsive disorder:

Statistical parametric mapping of segmented magnetic resonance images. *British Journal of Psychiatry, 179,* 330–334.

Kinney, H. C., Brody, B. A., Kloman, A. S., & Gilles, F. H. (1988). Sequence of central nervous system myelination in human infancy: II. Patterns of myelination in autopsied infants. *Journal of Neuropathology and Experimental Neurology, 47*(3), 217–234.

Kinney, H. C., Karthigasan, J., Borenshteyn, N. I., Flax, J. D., & Kirschner, D. A. (1994). Myelination in the developing human brain: Biochemical correlates. *Neurochemical Research, 19*(8), 983–996.

Kleiman, M. D., Neff, S., & Rosman, N. P. (1992). The brain in infantile Autism: Are posterior fossa structures abnormal? *Neurology, 42*(4), 753–760.

Klingberg, T., Forssberg, H., & Westerberg, H. (2002). Training of working memory in children with ADHD. *Journal of Clinical and Experimental Neuropsychology, 24*(6), 781–791.

Klingberg, T., Hedehus, M., Temple, E., Salz, T., Gabrieli, J. D., Moseley, M. E., et al. (2000). Microstructure of temporo-parietal white matter as a basis for reading ability: Evidence from diffusion tensor magnetic resonance imaging. *Neuron, 25*(2), 493–500.

Kraemer, H. C., Yesavage, J. A., Taylor, J. L., & Kupfer, D. (2000). How can we learn about developmental processes from cross-sectional studies, or can we? *American Journal of Psychiatry, 157*(2), 163–171.

Kraepelin, E., Barclay, R. M., & Robertson, G. M. (1919). *Dementia praecox and paraphrenia.* Edinburgh, Scotland: E. & S. Livingstone.

Kramer, M. (1978). Population changes and Schizophrenia. In L. C. Wynne, R. L. Cromwell, & S. Matthysse (Eds.), *The nature of Schizophrenia: New approaches to research and treatment* (pp. 1970–1985). New York: Wiley.

Krebs, J. R., Sherry, D. F., Healy, S. D., Perry, V. H., & Vaccarino, A. L. (1989). Hippocampal specialization of food-storing birds. *Proceedings of the National Academy of Sciences of the United States of America, 86,* 1388–1392.

Kuipers, L. (1979). Expressed emotion: A review. *British Journal of Social and Clinical Psychology, 18*(2), 237–243.

Kumra, S., Giedd, J. N., Vaituzis, A. C., Jacobsen, L. K., McKenna, K., Bedwell, J., et al. (2000). Childhood-onset psychotic disorders: Magnetic resonance imaging of volumetric differences in brain structure. *American Journal of Psychiatry, 157*(9), 1467–1474.

Kwon, H., Ow, A. W., Pedatella, K. E., Lotspeich, L. J., & Reiss, A. L. (2004). Voxel-based morphometry elucidates structural neuroanatomy of high-functioning Autism and Asperger syndrome. *Developmental Medicine and Child Neurology, 46*(11), 760–764.

Lacerda, A. L., Nicoletti, M. A., Brambilla, P., Sassi, R. B., Mallinger, A. G., Frank, E., et al. (2003). Anatomical MRI study of basal ganglia in major depressive disorder. *Psychiatry Research, 124*(3), 129–140.

Lainhart, J. E., Piven, J., Wzorek, M., Landa, R., Santangelo, S. L., Coon, H., et al. (1997). Macrocephaly in children and adults with Autism. *Journal of the American Academy of Child and Adolescent Psychiatry, 36*(2), 282–290.

Lange, N., Giedd, J. N., Castellanos, F. X., Vaituzis, A. C., & Rapoport, J. L. (1997). Variability of human brain structure size: Ages 4–20 years. *Psychiatry Research, 74*(1), 1–12.

Larsen, J. P., Odegaard, H., Grude, T. H., & Hoien, T. (1989). Magnetic resonance imaging: A method of studying the size and asymmetry of the planum temporale. *Acta Neurologica Scandinavica, 80*(5), 438–443.

Lauterbur, P. C. (1973). Image formation by induced local interactions: Examples employing nuclear magnetic resonance. *Nature, 242*(5394), 190–191.

Lee, S. H., Payne, M. E., Steffens, D. C., McQuoid, D. R., Lai, T. J., Provenzale, J. M., et al. (2003). Subcortical lesion severity and orbitofrontal cortex volume in geriatric depression. *Biological Psychiatry, 54*(5), 529–533.

Leeds, N. E., & Kieffer, S. A. (2000). Evolution of diagnostic neuroradiology from 1904 to 1999. *Radiology, 217*(2), 309–318.

Lemoine, P. (1968). Les enfants de parents alcooliques: Anomalies observées à propos de 127 cas. *Ouest Medicine, 21,* 476–482.

Lencz, T., McCarthy, G., Bronen, R. A., Scott, T. M., Inserni, J. A., Sass, K. J., et al. (1992). Quantitative magnetic resonance imaging in temporal lobe epilepsy: Relationship to neuropathology and neuropsychological function. *Annals of Neurology, 31,* 629–637.

Leonard, C. M., Eckert, M. A., Lombardino, L. J., Oakland, T., Kranzler, J., Mohr, C. M., et al. (2001). Anatomical risk factors for phonological dyslexia. *Cerebral Cortex, 11*(2), 148–157.

Leonard, C. M., Lombardino, L. J., Walsh, K., Eckert, M. A., Mockler, J. L., Rowe, L. A., et al. (2002). Anatomical risk factors that distinguish dyslexia from SLI predict reading skill in normal children. *Journal of Communication Disorders, 35*(6), 501–531.

Leonard, C. M., Voeller, K. K. S., Lombardino, L. J., Morris, M. K., Hynd, G. W., Alexander, A. W., et al. (1993). Anomalous cerebral structure in dyslexia revealed with magnetic resonance imaging. *Archives of Neurology, 50,* 461–469.

Levene, M. I., Whitelaw, A., Dubowitz, V., Bydder, G. M., Steiner, R. E., Randell, C. P., et al. (1982). Nuclear magnetic resonance imaging of the brain in children. *British Medical Journal (Clinical Research ed.), 285,* 774–776.

Levy, J. (1985). Interhemispheric collaboration: Single mindedness in the asymmetric brain. In C. T. Best (Ed.), *Hemisphere function and collaboration in the child* (pp. 11–32). New York: Academic Press.

Lewinsohn, P. M., Clarke, G. N., Seeley, J. R., & Rohde, P. (1994). Major depression in community adolescents: Age at onset, episode duration, and time to recurrence. *Journal of the American Academy of Child and Adolescent Psychiatry, 33*(6), 809–818.

Lewinsohn, P. M., Klein, D. N., & Seeley, J. R. (1995). Bipolar disorders in a community sample of older adolescents: Prevalence, phenomenology, comorbidity, and course. *Journal of the American Academy of Child and Adolescent Psychiatry, 34*(4), 454–463.

Lewis, S. (1996). Structural brain imaging in biological psychiatry. *British Medical Bulletin, 52*(3), 465–473.

Lieberman, J., Chakos, M., Wu, H., Alvir, J., Hoffman, E., Robinson, D., et al. (2001). Longitudinal study of brain morphology in first episode Schizophrenia. *Biological Psychiatry, 49*(6), 487–499.

Lim, K. O., Harris, D., Beal, M., Hoff, A. L., Minn, K., Csernansky, J. G., et al. (1996). Gray matter deficits in young onset schizophrenia are independent of age of onset. *Biological Psychiatry, 40*(1), 4–13.

Lipska, B. K., Swerdlow, N. R., Geyer, M. A., Jaskiw, G. E., Braff, D. L., & Weinberger, D. R. (1995). Neonatal excitotoxic hippocampal damage in rats causes post-pubertal changes in prepulse inhibition of startle and its disruption by apomorphine. *Psychopharmacology (Berl), 122*(1), 35–43.

Lipska, B. K., & Weinberger, D. R. (2002). A neurodevelopmental model of Schizophrenia: Neonatal disconnection of the hippocampus. *Neurotoxicity Research, 4*(5–6), 469–475.

Lotspeich, L. J., Kwon, H., Schumann, C. M., Fryer, S. L., Goodlin-Jones, B. L., Buonocore, M. H., et al. (2004). Investigation of neuroanatomical differences between Autism and Asperger syndrome. *Archives of General Psychiatry, 61*(3), 291–298.

Lovblad, K. O., Schneider, J., Ruoss, K., Steinlin, M., Fusch, C., & Schroth, G. (2003). Isotropic apparent diffusion coefficient mapping of postnatal cerebral development. *Neuroradiology, 45*(6), 400–403.

Luxenberg, J. S., Swedo, S. E., Flament, M. F., Friedland, R. P., Rapoport, J., & Rapoport, S. I. (1988). Neuroanatomical abnormalities in obsessive-compulsive disorder detected with quantitative X-ray computed tomography. *American Journal of Psychiatry, 145*(9), 1089–1093.

Lyoo, I. K., Lee, H. K., Jung, J. H., Noam, G. G., & Renshaw, P. F. (2002). White matter hyperintensities on magnetic resonance imaging of the brain in children with psychiatric disorders. *Comprehensive Psychiatry, 43*(5), 361–368.

MacMaster, F. P., Keshavan, M. S., Dick, E. L., & Rosenberg, D. R. (1999). Corpus callosal signal intensity in treatment-naive pediatric obsessive compulsive disorders. *Progress in Neuro-Psychopharmacology and Biological Psychiatry, 23*(4), 601–612.

MacMaster, F. P., & Kusumakar, V. (2004). Hippocampal volume in early onset depression. *BMC Medicine, 2*(1), 2.

MacMaster, F. P., Rosenberg, D. R., Keshavan, M. S., & Dick, E. L. (1999). Corpus callosum signal intensity in treatment-naive pediatric obsessive compulsive disorder. *Progress in Neuro-Psychopharmacology and Biological Psychiatry, 23*(4), 601–612.

MacMillan, S., Szeszko, P. R., Moore, G. J., Madden, R., Lorch, E., Ivey, J., et al. (2003). Increased amygdala: Hippocampal volume ratios associated with severity of anxiety in pediatric major depression. *Journal of Child and Adolescent Psychopharmacology, 13*(1), 65–73.

Maguire, E. A., Gadian, D. G., Johnsrude, I. S., Good, C. D., Ashburner, J., Frackowiak, R. S., et al. (2000). Navigation-related structural change in the hippocampi of taxi drivers. *Proceedings of the National Academy of Sciences of the United States of America, 97*(8), 4398–4403.

Mailly, P., Charpier, S., Menetrey, A., & Deniau, J. M. (2003). Three-dimensional organization of the recurrent axon collateral network of the substantia nigra pars reticulata neurons in the rat. *Journal of Neuroscience, 23*(12), 5247–5257.

Manes, F., Piven, J., Vrancic, D., Nanclares, V., Plebst, C., & Starkstein, S. E. (1999). An MRI study of the corpus callosum and cerebellum in mentally retarded autistic individuals. *Journal of Neuropsychiatry and Clinical Neurosciences, 11*(4), 470–474.

Manjaly, Z. M., Marshall, J. C., Stephan, K. E., Gurd, J. M., Zilles, K., & Fink, G. R. (2003). In search of the hidden: An fMRI study with implications for the study of patients with Autism and with acquired brain injury. *Neuroimage, 19*(3), 674–683.

Manji, H. K., & Lenox, R. H. (2000). Signaling: Cellular insights into the pathophysiology of bipolar disorder. *Biological Psychiatry, 48*(6), 518–530.

Manji, H. K., Moore, G. J., Rajkowska, G., & Chen, G. (2000). Neuroplasticity and cellular resilience in mood disorders. *Molecular Psychiatry, 5*(6), 578–593.

Marsh, L., Harris, D., Lim, K. O., Beal, M., Hoff, A. L., Minn, K., et al. (1997). Structural magnetic resonance imaging abnormalities in men with severe chronic Schizophrenia and an early age at clinical onset. *Archives of General Psychiatry, 54*(12), 1104–1112.

Marsh, L., Suddath, R. L., Higgins, N., & Weinberger, D. R. (1994). Medial temporal lobe structures in Schizophrenia: Relationship of size to duration of illness. *Schizophrenia Research, 11*, 225–238.

Martin, A., & Chao, L. L. (2001). Semantic memory and the brain: Structure and processes. *Current Opinion in Neurobiology, 11*(2), 194–201.

Mataix-Cols, D., Wooderson, S., Lawrence, N., Brammer, M. J., Speckens, A., & Phillips, M. L. (2004). Distinct neural correlates of washing, checking, and hoarding symptom dimensions in obsessive-compulsive disorder. *Archives of General Psychiatry, 61*(6), 564–576.

Mataro, M., Garcia-Sanchez, C., Junque, C., Estevez-Gonzalez, A., & Pujol, J. (1997). Magnetic resonance imaging measurement of the caudate nucleus in adolescents with attention-deficit hyperactivity disorder and its relationship with neuropsychological and behavioral measures. *Archives of Neurology, 54*(8), 963–968.

Mathalon, D. H., Sullivan, E. V., Lim, K. O., & Pfefferbaum, A. (1997). Longitudinal analysis of MRI brain volumes in Schizophrenia. *Schizophrenia Research, 24*(1–2), 152–152.

Matsumoto, H., Simmons, A., Williams, S., Hadjulis, M., Pipe, R., Murray, R., et al. (2001). Superior temporal gyrus abnormalities in early-onset schizophrenia: Similarities and differences with adult-onset schizophrenia. *American Journal of Psychiatry, 158*(8), 1299–1304.

Matsumoto, H., Simmons, A., Williams, S., Pipe, R., Murray, R., & Frangou, S. (2001). Structural magnetic imaging of the hippocampus in early onset schizophrenia. *Biological Psychiatry, 49*(10), 824–831.

Mattson, S. N., Riley, E. P., Sowell, E. R., Jernigan, T. L., Sobel, D. F., & Jones, K. L. (1996). A decrease in the size of the basal ganglia in children with fetal alcohol syndrome. *Alcoholism-Clinical and Experimental Research, 20*(6), 1088–1093.

May, P. A., Brooke, L., Gossage, J. P., Croxford, J., Adnams, C., Jones, K. L., et al. (2000). Epidemiology of fetal alcohol syndrome in a South African community in the Western Cape Province. *American Journal of Public Health, 90*(12), 1905–1912.

May, P. A., & Gossage, J. P. (2001). Estimating the prevalence of fetal alcohol syndrome: A summary. *Alcohol Research and Health, 25*(3), 159–167.

Mazzocco, M. M., Kates, W. R., Baumgardner, T. L., Freund, L. S., & Reiss, A. L. (1997). Autistic behaviors among girls with fragile X syndrome. *Journal of Autism and Developmental Disorders, 27*(4), 415–435.

McAlonan, G. M., Cheung, V., Cheung, C., Suckling, J., Lam, G. Y., Tai, K. S., et al. (2005). Mapping the brain in Autism: A voxel-based MRI study of volumetric differences and intercorrelations in Autism. *Brain, 128*(2), 268–276.

McAlonan, G. M., Daly, E., Kumari, V., Critchley, H. D., van Amelsvoort, T., Suckling, J., et al. (2002). Brain anatomy and sensorimotor gating in Asperger's syndrome. *Brain, 125*(7), 1594–1606.

McArdle, C. B., Richardson, C. J., Nicholas, D. A., Mirfakhraee, M., Hayden, C. K., & Amparo, E. G. (1987). Developmental features of the neonatal brain: MR imaging: I. Gray-white matter differentiation and myelination. *Radiology, 162*, 223–229.

McGlashan, T. H. (1988). Adolescent versus adult onset of mania. *American Journal of Psychiatry, 145*(2), 221–223.

McGraw, P., Liang, L., & Provenzale, J. M. (2002). Evaluation of normal age-related changes in anisotropy during infancy and childhood as shown by diffusion tensor imaging. *American Journal of Roentgenology, 179*(6), 1515–1522.

McKinstry, R. C., Mathur, A., Miller, J. H., Ozcan, A., Snyder, A. Z., Schefft, G. L., et al. (2002). Radial organization of developing preterm human cerebral cortex revealed by non-invasive water diffusion anisotropy MRI. *Cerebral Cortex, 12*(12), 1237–1243.

Mesulam, M. M. (1998). From sensation to cognition. *Brain, 121*(Pt. 6), 1013–1052.

Miklowitz, D. J. (2004). The role of family systems in severe and recurrent psychiatric disorders: A developmental psychopathology view. *Developmental Psychopathology, 16*(3), 667–688.

Miles, J. H., Hadden, L. L., Takahashi, T. N., & Hillman, R. E. (2000). Head circumference is an independent clinical finding associated with Autism. *American Journal of Medical Genetics, 95*(4), 339–350.

Modell, J. G., Mountz, J. M., Curtis, G. C., & Greden, J. F. (1989). Neurophysiologic dysfunction in basal ganglia/limbic striatal and thalamocortical circuits as a pathogenetic mechanism of obsessive-compulsive disorder. *Journal of Neuropsychiatry and Clinical Neurosciences, 1,* 27–36.

Moore, C. J., Daly, E. M., Schmitz, N., Tassone, F., Tysoe, C., Hagerman, R. J., et al. (2004). A neuropsychological investigation of male premutation carriers of fragile X syndrome. *Neuropsychologia, 42*(14), 1934–1947.

Moore, C. J., Daly, E. M., Tassone, F., Tysoe, C., Schmitz, N., Ng, V., et al. (2004). The effect of pre-mutation of X chromosome CGG trinucleotide repeats on brain anatomy. *Brain, 127*(Pt. 12), 2672–2681.

Moore, G. J., Bebchuk, J. M., Wilds, I. B., Chen, G., & Manji, H. K. (2000). Lithium-induced increase in human brain grey matter. *Lancet, 356*(9237), 1241–1242.

Morosan, P., Rademacher, J., Schleicher, A., Amunts, K., Schormann, T., & Zilles, K. (2001). Human primary auditory cortex: Cytoarchitectonic subdivisions and mapping into a spatial reference system. *Neuroimage, 13*(4), 684–701.

Morriss, M. C., Zimmerman, R. A., Bilaniuk, L. T., Hunter, J. V., & Haselgrove, J. C. (1999). Changes in brain water diffusion during childhood. *Neuroradiology, 41*(12), 929–934.

Morse, J. K., Scheff, S. W., & DeKosky, S. T. (1986). Gonadal steroids influence axonal sprouting in the hippocampal dentate gyrus: A sexually dimorphic response. *Experimental Neurology, 94,* 649–658.

Mostofsky, S. H., Cooper, K. L., Kates, W. R., Denckla, M. B., & Kaufmann, W. E. (2002). Smaller prefrontal and premotor volumes in boys with attention-deficit/hyperactivity disorder. *Biological Psychiatry, 52*(8), 785–794.

Mostofsky, S. H., Mazzocco, M. M., Aakalu, G., Warsofsky, I. S., Denckla, M. B., & Reiss, A. L. (1998). Decreased cerebellar posterior vermis size in fragile X syndrome: Correlation with neurocognitive performance. *Neurology, 50*(1), 121–130.

Murakami, J. W., Courchesne, E., Haas, R. H., Press, G. A., & Yeung-Courchesne, R. (1992). Cerebellar and cerebral abnormalities in Rett syndrome: A quantitative MR analysis. *American Journal of Roentgenology, 159,* 177–183.

Murakami, J. W., Courchesne, E., Press, G. A., Yeung-Courchesne, R., & Hesselink, J. R. (1989). Reduced cerebellar hemisphere size and its relationship to vermal hypoplasia in Autism. *Archives of Neurology, 46,* 689–694.

Murphy, D. G., DeCarli, C. D., Daly, E., Haxby, J. V., Allen, G., White, B. J., et al. (1993). X chromosome effects on female brain: A magnetic resonance imaging study of Turner's syndrome. *Lancet, 342*(8881), 1197–1200.

Murphy, D. G., Mentis, M. J., Pietrini, P., Grady, C. L., Moore, C. J., Horwitz, B., et al. (1999). Premutation female carriers of fragile X syndrome: A pilot study on brain anatomy and metabolism. *Journal of the American Academy of Child and Adolescent Psychiatry, 38*(10), 1294–1301.

Myslobodsky, M. S., Glicksohn, J., Singer, J., Stern, M., Bar-Ziv, J., Friedland, N., et al. (1995). Changes of brain anatomy in patients with posttraumatic stress disorder: A pilot magnetic resonance imaging study. *Psychiatry Research, 58*(3), 259–264.

Nagy, Z., Westerberg, H., & Klingberg, T. (2004). Maturation of white matter is associated with the development of cognitive functions during childhood. *Journal of Cognitive Neuroscience, 16*(7), 1227–1233.

Naidu, S. (1997). Rett syndrome: A disorder affecting early brain growth. *Annals of Neurology, 42*(1), 3–10.

National Institute of Mental Health research roundtable on prepubertal bipolar disorder. (2001). *Journal of the American Academy of Child and Adolescent Psychiatry, 40*(8), 871–878.

Neil, J., Miller, J., Mukherjee, P., & Huppi, P. S. (2002). Diffusion tensor imaging of normal and injured developing human brain: A technical review. *NMR Biomedicine, 15*(7–8), 543–552.

Nellhaus, G. (1968). Head circumference: Girls and boys 2–18 years. *Pediatrics, 41,* 106.

Neul, J. L., & Zoghbi, H. Y. (2004). Rett syndrome: A prototypical neurodevelopmental disorder. *Neuroscientist, 10*(2), 118–128.

Nolan, C. L., Moore, G. J., Madden, R., Farchione, T., Bartoi, M., Lorch, E., et al. (2002). Prefrontal cortical volume in childhood-onset major depression: Preliminary findings. *Archives of General Psychiatry, 59*(2), 173–179.

Nolte, J. (1993). Olfactory and limbic systems. In R. Farrell (Ed.), *The human brain: An introduction to its functional anatomy* (3rd ed., pp. 397–413). St. Louis, MO: Mosby-Year Book.

Olesen, P. J., Nagy, Z., Westerberg, H., & Klingberg, T. (2003). Combined analysis of DTI and fMRI data reveals a joint maturation of white and grey matter in a fronto-parietal network. *Brain Research. Cognitive Brain Research, 18*(1), 48–57.

Olney, J. W., Newcomer, J. W., & Farber, N. B. (1999). NMDA receptor hypofunction model of Schizophrenia. *Journal of Psychiatric Research, 33*(6), 523–533.

Olney, J. W., Wozniak, D. F., Farber, N. B., Jevtovic-Todorovic, V., Bittigau, P., & Ikonomidou, C. (2002). The enigma of fetal alcohol neurotoxicity. *Annals of Medicine, 34*(2), 109–119.

Overmeyer, S., Bullmore, E. T., Suckling, J., Simmons, A., Williams, S. C., Santosh, P. J., et al. (2001). Distributed grey and white matter deficits in hyperkinetic disorder: MRI evidence for anatomical abnormality in an attentional network. *Psychological Medicine, 31*(8), 1425–1435.

Ozonoff, S., Strayer, D. L., McMahon, W. M., & Filloux, F. (1994). Executive function abilities in Autism and Tourette syndrome: An information processing approach. *Journal of Child Psychology and Psychiatry, 35*(6), 1015–1032.

Palmen, S. J., van Engeland, H., Hof, P. R., & Schmitz, C. (2004). Neuropathological findings in Autism. *Brain, 127*(Pt. 12), 2572–2583.

Paus, T., Collins, D. L., Evans, A. C., Leonard, G., Pike, B., & Zijdenbos, A. (2001). Maturation of white matter in the human brain: A review of magnetic resonance studies. *Brain Research Bulletin, 54*(3), 255–266.

Paus, T., Zijdenbos, A., Worsley, K., Collins, D. L., Blumenthal, J., Giedd, J. N., et al. (1999). Structural maturation of neural pathways in children and adolescents: In vivo study. *Science, 283,* 1908–1911.

Peterson, B. S. (2003). Conceptual, methodological, and statistical challenges in brain imaging studies of developmentally based psychopathologies. *Developmental Psychopathology, 15*(3), 811–832.

Peterson, B. S., Bronen, R. A., & Duncan, C. C. (1996). Three cases of symptom change in Tourette's syndrome and obsessive-compulsive disorder associated with paediatric cerebral malignancies. *Journal of Neurology, Neurosurgery and Psychiatry, 61*(5), 497–505.

Petronis, A. (2003). Epigenetics and bipolar disorder: New opportunities and challenges. *American Journal of Medical Genetics C Seminars in Medical Genetics, 123*(1), 65–75.

Pfefferbaum, A., Lim, K. O., Rosenbloom, M., & Zipursky, R. B. (1990). Brain magnetic resonance imaging: Approaches for investigating Schizophrenia. *Schizophrenia Bulletin, 16,* 3, 453–476.

Pierce, K., Muller, R. A., Ambrose, J., Allen, G., & Courchesne, E. (2001). Face processing occurs outside the fusiform "face area" in Autism: Evidence from functional MRI. *Brain, 124*(Pt. 10), 2059–2073.

Pillai, J. J., Friedman, L., Stuve, T. A., Trinidad, S., Jesberger, J. A., Lewin, J. S., et al. (2002). Increased presence of white matter hyperintensities in adolescent patients with bipolar disorder. *Psychiatry Research, 114*(1), 51–56.

Pillay, S. S., Renshaw, P. F., Bonello, C. M., Lafer, B. C., Fava, M., & Yurgelun-Todd, D. (1998). A quantitative magnetic resonance imaging study of caudate and lenticular nucleus gray matter volume in primary unipolar major depression: Relationship to treatment response and clinical severity. *Psychiatry Research, 84*(2–3), 61–74.

Piven, J., Arndt, S., Bailey, J., & Andreasen, N. (1996). Regional brain enlargement in Autism: A magnetic resonance imaging study. *Journal of the American Academy of Child and Adolescent Psychiatry, 35*(4), 530–536.

Piven, J., Arndt, S., Bailey, J., Havercamp, S., Andreasen, N. C., & Palmer, P. (1995). An MRI study of brain size in Autism. *American Journal of Psychiatry, 152*(8), 1145–1149.

Piven, J., Bailey, J., Ranson, B. J., & Arndt, S. (1997). An MRI study of the corpus callosum in Autism. *American Journal of Psychiatry, 154*(8), 1051–1056.

Piven, J., Bailey, J., Ranson, B. J., & Arndt, S. (1998). No difference in hippocampus volume detected on magnetic resonance imaging in autistic individuals. *Journal of Autism and Developmental Disorders, 28*(2), 105–110.

Piven, J., Berthier, M. L., Starkstein, S. E., Nehme, E., Pearlson, G., & Folstein, S. (1990). Magnetic resonance imaging evidence for a defect of cerebral cortical development in Autism. *American Journal of Psychiatry, 147,* 734–739.

Piven, J., Nehme, E., Simon, J., Barta, P., Pearlson, G., & Folstein, S. E. (1992). Magnetic resonance imaging in Autism: Measurement of the cerebellum, pons, and fourth ventricle. *Biological Psychiatry, 31,* 491–504.

Piven, J., Saliba, K., Bailey, J., & Arndt, S. (1997). An MRI study of Autism: The cerebellum revisited. *Neurology, 49*(2), 546–551.

Posner, M. I., & Rothbart, M. K. (1998). Attention, self-regulation and consciousness. *Philosophical Transactions of the Royal Society of London. Series B, Biological Sciences, 353*(1377), 1915–1927.

Posthuma, D., De Geus, E. J., Baáre, W. F., Hulshoff Pol, H. E., Kahn, R. S., & Boomsma, D. I. (2002). The association between brain volume and intelligence is of genetic origin. *Nature Neuroscience, 5*(2), 83–84.

Prayer, D., & Prayer, L. (2003). Diffusion-weighted magnetic resonance imaging of cerebral white matter development. *European Journal of Radiology, 45*(3), 235–243.

Preis, S., Engelbrecht, V., Huang, Y., & Steinmetz, H. (1998). Focal grey matter heterotopias in monozygotic twins with developmental language disorder. *European Journal of Pediatrics, 157*(10), 849–852.

Premack, D. W. G. (1978). Does the chimpanzee have theory of mind? *Behavioral Brain Sciences, 1,* 515–526.

Pringle, W. M. (1986). A case of congenital word blindness. *British Medical Journal, 2,* 1378–1379.

Pruett, J. R., & Luby, J. L. (2004). Recent advances in prepubertal mood disorders: Phenomenology and treatment. *Current Opinion in Psychiatry, 17*(1), 31–36.

Pujol, J., Soriano-Mas, C., Alonso, P., Cardoner, N., Menchon, J. M., Deus, J., et al. (2004). Mapping structural brain alterations in obsessive-compulsive disorder. *Archives of General Psychiatry, 61*(7), 720–730.

Pujol, J., Vendrell, P., Junque, C., Marti-Vilalta, J. L., & Capdevila, A. (1993). When does human brain development end? Evidence of corpus callosum growth up to adulthood. *Annals of Neurology, 34,* 71–75.

Rademacher, J., Engelbrecht, V., Burgel, U., Freund, H., & Zilles, K. (1999). Measuring in vivo myelination of human white matter fiber tracts with magnetization transfer MR. *Neuroimage., 9*(4), 393–406.

Rae, C., Harasty, J. A., Dzendrowskyj, T. E., Talcott, J. B., Simpson, J. M., Blamire, A. M., et al. (2002). Cerebellar morphology in developmental dyslexia. *Neuropsychologia, 40*(8), 1285–1292.

Rajapakse, J. C., Giedd, J. N., DeCarli, C., Snell, J. W., McLaughlin, A., Vauss, Y. C., et al. (1996). A technique for single-channel MR brain tissue segmentation: Application to a pediatric sample. *Magnetic Resonance Imaging, 14,* 1053–1065.

Rajkowska, G. (2003). Depression: What we can learn from postmortem studies. *Neuroscientist, 9*(4), 273–284.

Rakic, P. (1988). Specification of cerebral cortical areas. *Science, 241,* 170–176.

Rakic, P. (1990). Principles of neural cell migration. *Experientia, 46,* 882–891.

Ramnani, N., Behrens, T. E., Penny, W., & Matthews, P. M. (2004). New approaches for exploring anatomical and functional connectivity in the human brain. *Biological Psychiatry, 56*(9), 613–619.

Randall, C. L. (2001). Alcohol and pregnancy: Highlights from three decades of research. *Journal of Studies on Alcohol, 62*(5), 554–561.

Rapoport, J. L. (1990). Obsessive compulsive disorder and basal ganglia dysfunction. *Psychological Medicine, 20*(3), 465–469.

Rapoport, J. L., Giedd, J. N., Blumenthal, J., Hamburger, S., Jeffries, N., Fernandez, T., et al. (1999). Progressive cortical change during adolescence in childhood-onset schizophrenia: A longitudinal magnetic resonance imaging study. *Archives of General Psychiatry, 56*(7), 649–654.

Rapoport, J. L., Giedd, J. N., Kumra, S., Jacobsen, L. K., Smith, A., Lee, P., et al. (1997). Childhood-onset schizophrenia: Progressive ventricular change during adolescence. *Archives of General Psychiatry, 54*(10), 897–903.

Rasmussen, P., & Gillberg, C. (2000). Natural outcome of ADHD with developmental coordination disorder at age 22 years: A controlled, longitudinal, community-based study. *Journal of the American Academy of Child and Adolescent Psychiatry, 39*(11), 1424–1431.

Rauch, R. A., & Jinkins, J. R. (1994). Analysis of cross-sectional area measurements of the corpus callosum adjusted for brain size in male and female subjects from childhood to adulthood. *Behavioral Brain Research, 64,* 65–78.

Reiss, A. L., Abrams, M. T., Greenlaw, R., Freund, L., & Denckla, M. B. (1995). Neurodevelopmental effects of the FMR-1 full mutation in humans. *Nature Medicine, 1*(2), 159–167.

Reiss, A. L., Abrams, M. T., Singer, H. S., Ross, J. L., & Denckla, M. B. (1996). Brain development, gender and IQ in children. A volumetric imaging study. *Brain, 119*(Pt. 5), 1763–1774.

Reiss, A. L., Aylward, E., Freund, L. S., Joshi, P. K., & Bryan, R. N. (1991). Neuroanatomy of fragile X syndrome: The posterior fossa. *Annals of Neurology, 29*(1), 26–32.

Reiss, A. L., Faruque, F., Naidu, S., Abrams, M., Beaty, T., Bryan, R. N., et al. (1993). Neuroanatomy of Rett syndrome: A volumetric imaging study. *Annals of Neurology, 34*(2), 227–234.

Reiss, A. L., Freund, L., Tseng, J. E., & Joshi, P. K. (1991). Neuroanatomy in fragile X females: The posterior fossa. *American Journal of Human Genetics, 49*(2), 279–288.

Reiss, A. L., Lee, J., & Freund, L. (1994). Neuroanatomy of fragile X syndrome: The temporal lobe. *Neurology, 44*(7), 1317–1324.

Rett, A. (1966). Uber ein eigenartiges hirnatrophisches syndrom bei hyperammonamie im kindesalter [On an unusual brain atrophy syndrome in hyperammonemia in childhood]. *Wien Med Wochenschr, 116*(37), 723–726.

Riley, E. P., McGee, C. L., & Sowell, E. R. (2004). Teratogenic effects of alcohol: A decade of brain imaging. *American Journal of Medical Genetics, 127C*(1), 35–41.

Rivkin, P., Kraut, M., Barta, P., Anthony, J., Arria, A. M., & Pearlson, G. (2000). White matter hyperintensity volume in late-onset and early-onset schizophrenia. *International Journal of Geriatric Psychiatry, 15*(12), 1085–1089.

Robichon, F., Levrier, O., Farnarier, P., & Habib, M. (2000). Developmental dyslexia: Atypical cortical asymmetries and functional significance. *European Journal of Neurology, 7*(1), 35–46.

Roebuck, T. M., Mattson, S. N., & Riley, E. P. (2002). Interhemispheric transfer in children with heavy prenatal alcohol exposure. *Alcoholism Clinical and Experimental Research, 26*(12), 1863–1871.

Rojas, D. C., Smith, J. A., Benkers, T. L., Camou, S. L., Reite, M. L., & Rogers, S. J. (2004). Hippocampus and amygdala volumes in parents of children with autistic disorder. *American Journal of Psychiatry, 161*(11), 2038–2044.

Rosenberg, D. R., & Keshavan, M. S. (1998). A. E. Bennett research award: Toward a neurodevelopmental model of obsessive compulsive disorder. *Biological Psychiatry, 43*(9), 623–640.

Rosenberg, D. R., Keshavan, M. S., Dick, E. L., Bagwell, W. W., MacMaster, F., Seymour, A. B., et al. (1997). Corpus callosal morphology in treatment-naive pediatric obsessive compulsive disorder. *Progress in Neuropsychopharmacology and Biological Psychiatry, 21*(8), 1269–1283.

Rosso, I. M., Cintron, C. M., Steingard, R. J., Renshaw, P. F., Young, A. D., & Yurgelun-Todd, D. A. (2005). Amygdala and hippocampus volumes in pediatric major depression. *Biological Psychiatry, 57*(1), 21–26.

Rubia, K., Noorloos, J., Smith, A., Gunning, B., & Sergeant, J. (2003). Motor timing deficits in community and clinical boys with hyperactive behavior: The effect of methylphenidate on motor timing. *Journal of Abnormal Child Psychology, 31*(3), 301–313.

Rumsey, J. M. (1985). Conceptual problem-solving in highly verbal, nonretarded autistic men. *Journal of Autism and Developmental Disorders, 15*(1), 23–36.

Rumsey, J. M., Donohue, B. C., Brady, D. R., Nace, K., Giedd, J. N., & Andreason, P. (1997). A magnetic resonance imaging study of planum temporale asymmetry in men with developmental dyslexia. *Archives of Neurology, 54*(12), 1481–1489.

Russell, A. T., Bott, L., & Sammons, C. (1989). The phenomenology of Schizophrenia occurring in childhood. *Journal of the American Academy of Child and Adolescent Psychiatry, 28*, 399–407.

Rutter, M. (2000). Genetic studies of Autism: From the 1970s into the millennium. *Journal of Abnormal Child Psychology, 28*(1), 3–14.

Rutter, M., & Sroufe, L. A. (2000). Developmental psychopathology: Concepts and challenges. *Developmental Psychopathology, 12*(3), 265–296.

Saitoh, O., Courchesne, E., Egaas, B., Lincoln, A. J., & Schreibman, L. (1995). Cross-sectional area of the posterior hippocampus in autistic patients with cerebellar and corpus callosum abnormalities. *Neurology, 45*, 317–324.

Saitoh, O., Karns, C. M., & Courchesne, E. (2001). Development of the hippocampal formation from 2 to 42 years: MRI evidence of smaller area dentata in Autism. *Brain, 124*(Pt. 7), 1317–1324.

Sameroff, A. J., & Mackenzie, M. J. (2003). Research strategies for capturing transactional models of development: The limits of the possible. *Developmental Psychopathology, 15*(3), 613–640.

Sampson, P. D., Streissguth, A. P., Bookstein, F. L., Little, R. E., Clarren, S. K., Dehaene, P., et al. (1997). Incidence of fetal alcohol syndrome and prevalence of alcohol-related neurodevelopmental disorder. *Teratology, 56*(5), 317–326.

Sapolsky, R. M. (1996). Why stress is bad for your brain. *Science, 273*(5276), 749–750.

Sassi, R. B., Brambilla, P., Hatch, J. P., Nicoletti, M. A., Mallinger, A. G., Frank, E., et al. (2004). Reduced left anterior cingulate volumes in untreated bipolar patients. *Biological Psychiatry, 56*(7), 467–475.

Saxena, S., Bota, R. G., & Brody, A. L. (2001). Brain-behavior relationships in obsessive-compulsive disorder. *Seminars in Clinical Neuropsychiatry, 6*(2), 82–101.

Saxena, S., Brody, A. L., Maidment, K. M., Dunkin, J. J., Colgan, M., Alborzian, S., et al. (1999). Localized orbitofrontal and subcortical metabolic changes and predictors of response to paroxetine treatment in obsessive-compulsive disorder. *Neuropsychopharmacology, 21*(6), 683–693.

Scarone, S., Colombo, C., Livian, S., Abbruzzese, M., Ronchi, P., Locatelli, M., et al. (1992). Increased right caudate nucleus size in obsessive-compulsive disorder: Detection with magnetic resonance imaging. *Psychiatry Research: Neuroimaging, 45*, 115–121.

Schaefer, G. B., Thompson, J. N., Jr., Bodensteiner, J. B., Hamza, M., Tucker, R. R., Marks, W., et al. (1990). Quantitative morphometric analysis of brain growth using magnetic resonance imaging. *Journal of Child Neurology, 5*, 127–130.

Schneider, J. F., Il'yasov, K. A., Hennig, J., & Martin, E. (2004). Fast quantitative diffusion-tensor imaging of cerebral white matter from the neonatal period to adolescence. *Neuroradiology, 46*(4), 258–266.

Schultz, R. T., Cho, N. K., Staib, L. H., Kier, L. E., Fletcher, J. M., Shaywitz, S. E., et al. (1994). Brain morphology in normal and dyslexic children: The influence of sex and age. *Annals of Neurology, 35*, 732–742.

Schultz, S. C., Koller, M. M., Kishore, R. R., Hamer, R. M., Gehl, J. J., & Friedel, R. O. (1983). Ventricular enlargement in teenage patients with Schizophrenia spectrum disorder. *American Journal of Psychiatry, 140*, 1592–1595.

Schumann, C. M., Hamstra, J., Goodlin-Jones, B. L., Lotspeich, L. J., Kwon, H., Buonocore, M. H., et al. (2004). The amygdala is enlarged in children but not adolescents with Autism; the hippocampus is enlarged at all ages. *Journal of Neuroscience, 24*(28), 6392–6401.

Sears, L. L., Vest, C., Mohamed, S., Bailey, J., Ranson, B. J., & Piven, J. (1999). An MRI study of the basal ganglia in Autism. *Progress in Neuro-Psychopharmacology and Biological Psychiatry, 23*(4), 613–624.

Segawa, M., & Nomura, Y. (2005). Rett syndrome. *Current Opinion in Neurology and Neurosurgy, 18*(2), 97–104.

Shah, S. A., Doraiswamy, P. M., Husain, M. M., Escalona, P. R., Na, C., Figiel, G. S., et al. (1992). Posterior fossa abnormalities in major depression: A controlled magnetic resonance imaging study. *Acta Psychiatrica Scandinavica, 85*, 474–479.

Shahbazian, M. D., Antalffy, B., Armstrong, D. L., & Zoghbi, H. Y. (2002). Insight into Rett syndrome: MeCP2 levels display tissue- and cell-specific differences and correlate with neuronal maturation. *Human Molecular Genetics, 11*(2), 115–124.

Shanks, M. F., Rockel, A. J., & Powel, T. P. S. (1975). The commissural fiber connections of the primary somatic sensory cortex. *Brain Research, 98*, 166–171.

Shapiro, R., & Janzen, A. H. (1960). *The normal skull.* New York: Hoeber.

Sheline, Y. I. (2003). Neuroimaging studies of mood disorder effects on the brain. *Biological Psychiatry, 54*(3), 338–352.

Shenton, M. E., Kikinis, R., Jolesz, F. A., Pollak, S. D., LeMay, M., Wible, C. G., et al. (1992). Abnormalities of the left temporal lobe and thought disorder in Schizophrenia. A quantitative magnetic resonance imaging study. *New England Journal of Medicine, 327,* 604–612.

Sherry, D. F., Jacobs, L. F., & Gaulin, S. J. (1992). Spatial memory and adaptive specialization of the hippocampus. *Trends in Neuroscience, 15,* 298–303.

Sherry, D. F., Vaccarino, A. L., Buckenham, K., & Herz, R. S. (1989). The hippocampal complex of food-storing birds. *Brain, Behavior and Evolution, 34,* 308–317.

Sholl, S. A., & Kim, K. L. (1989). Estrogen receptors in the rhesus monkey brain during fetal development. *Developmental Brain Research, 50,* 189–196.

Soares, J. C. (2003). Contributions from brain imaging to the elucidation of pathophysiology of bipolar disorder. *International Journal of Neuropsychopharmacology, 6*(2), 171–180.

Soares, J. C., & Mann, J. J. (1997). The anatomy of mood disorders: Review of structural neuroimaging studies. *Biological Psychiatry, 41*(1), 86–106.

Sonuga-Barke, E. J., Dalen, L., & Remington, B. (2003). Do executive deficits and delay aversion make independent contributions to preschool attention-deficit/hyperactivity disorder symptoms? *Journal of the American Academy of Child and Adolescent Psychiatry, 42*(11), 1335–1342.

Sowell, E. R., Jernigan, T. L., Mattson, S. N., Riley, E. P., Sobel, D. F., & Jones, K. L. (1996). Abnormal development of the cerebellar vermis in children prenatally exposed to alcohol: Size reduction in lobules I.-V. *Alcoholism-Clinical And Experimental Research, 20*(1), 31–34.

Sowell, E. R., Levitt, J., Thompson, P. M., Holmes, C. J., Blanton, R. E., Kornsand, D. S., et al. (2000). Brain abnormalities in early onset schizophrenia spectrum disorder observed with statistical parametric mapping of structural magnetic resonance images. *American Journal of Psychiatry, 157*(9), 1473–1484.

Sowell, E. R., Mattson, S. N., Thompson, P. M., Jernigan, T. L., Riley, E. P., & Toga, A. W. (2001). Mapping callosal morphology and cognitive correlates: Effects of heavy prenatal alcohol exposure. *Neurology, 57*(2), 235–244.

Sowell, E. R., Thompson, P. M., Holmes, C. J., Batth, R., Jernigan, T. L., & Toga, A. W. (1999). Localizing age-related changes in brain structure between childhood and adolescence using statistical parametric mapping. *Neuroimage, 9*(6 Pt. 1), 587–597.

Sowell, E. R., Thompson, P. M., Holmes, C. J., Jernigan, T. L., & Toga, A. W. (1999). In vivo evidence for post-adolescent brain maturation in frontal and striatal regions. *Nature Neuroscience, 2*(10), 859–861.

Sowell, E. R., Thompson, P. M., Mattson, S. N., Tessner, K. D., Jernigan, T. L., Riley, E. P., et al. (2001). Voxel-based morphometric analyses of the brain in children and adolescents prenatally exposed to alcohol. *NeuroReport, 12*(3), 515–523.

Sowell, E. R., Thompson, P. M., Mattson, S. N., Tessner, K. D., Jernigan, T. L., Riley, E. P., et al. (2002). Regional brain shape abnormalities persist into adolescence after heavy prenatal alcohol exposure. *Cerebral Cortex, 12*(8), 856–865.

Sowell, E. R., Thompson, P. M., Peterson, B. S., Mattson, S. N., Welcome, S. E., Henkenius, A. L., et al. (2002). Mapping cortical gray matter asymmetry patterns in adolescents with heavy prenatal alcohol exposure. *Neuroimage, 17*(4), 1807–1819.

Sowell, E. R., Thompson, P. M., Tessner, K. D., & Toga, A. W. (2001). Mapping continued brain growth and gray matter density reduction in

dorsal frontal cortex: Inverse relationships during postadolescent brain maturation. *Journal of Neuroscience, 21*(22), 8819–8829.

Sowell, E. R., Thompson, P., Welcome, S. E., Henkenius, A. L., Toga, A. W., & Peterson, B. S. (2003, November 22). Cortical abnormalities in children and adolescents with attention-deficit hyperactivity disorder. *Lancet, 362*(9397), 1699–1707.

Sparks, B. F., Friedman, S. D., Shaw, D. W., Aylward, E. H., Echelard, D., Artru, A. A., et al. (2002). Brain structural abnormalities in young children with Autism spectrum disorder. *Neurology, 59*(2), 184–192.

Spear, L. P. (2000). The adolescent brain and age-related behavioral manifestations. *Neuroscience and Biobehavioral Reviews, 24,* 417–463.

Spencer, E. K., & Campbell, M. (1994). Children with Schizophrenia: Diagnosis, phenomenology, and pharmacotherapy. *Schizophrenia Bulletin, 20,* 713–725.

Sporn, A. L., Addington, A. M., Gogtay, N., Ordonez, A. E., Gornick, M., Clasen, L., et al. (2004). Pervasive developmental disorder and childhood-onset schizophrenia: Comorbid disorder or a phenotypic variant of a very early onset illness? *Biological Psychiatry, 55*(10), 989–994.

Stallard, P., Salter, E., & Velleman, R. (2004). Posttraumatic stress disorder following road traffic accidents: A second prospective study. *European Child and Adolescent Psychiatry, 13*(3), 172–178.

Steen, R. G., Ogg, R. J., Reddick, W. E., & Kingsley, P. B. (1997). Age-related changes in the pediatric brain: Quantitative MR evidence of maturational changes during adolescence. *American Journal of Neuroradiolgy, 18,* 819–828.

Stein, M. B., Koverola, C., Hanna, C., Torchia, M. G., & McClarty, B. (1997). Hippocampal volume in women victimized by childhood sexual abuse. *Psychological Medicine, 27*(4), 951–959.

Steingard, R. J., Renshaw, P. F., Yurgelun-Todd, D., Appelmans, K. E., Lyoo, I. K., Shorrock, K. L., et al. (1996). Structural abnormalities in brain magnetic resonance images of depressed children. *Journal of the American Academy of Child and Adolescent Psychiatry, 35*(3), 307–311.

Stevenson, R. E., Schroer, R. J., Skinner, C., Fender, D., & Simensen, R. J. (1997). Autism and macrocephaly. *Lancet, 349*(9067), 1744–1745.

Still, G. (1902). The Coulstonian lectures on some abnormal physical conditions in children. *Lancet* (Lecture 1), 1008–1012, 1077–1082, 1163–1168.

Strakowski, S. M., Adler, C. M., & DelBello, M. P. (2002). Volumetric MRI studies of mood disorders: Do they distinguish unipolar and bipolar disorder? *Bipolar Disorders, 4*(2), 80–88.

Streissguth, A. P., Sampson, P. D., Barr, H. M., Clarren, S. K., & Martin, D. C. (1986). Studying alcohol teratogenesis from the perspective of the fetal alcohol syndrome: Methodological and statistical issues. *Annals of the New York Academy of Science, 477,* 63–86.

Su, B., Debelak, K. A., Tessmer, L. L., Cartwright, M. M., & Smith, S. M. (2001). Genetic influences on craniofacial outcome in an avian model of prenatal alcohol exposure. *Alcoholism Clinical and Experimental Research, 25*(1), 60–69.

Subramaniam, B., Naidu, S., & Reiss, A. L. (1997). Neuroanatomy in Rett syndrome: Cerebral cortex and posterior fossa. *Neurology, 48*(2), 399–407.

Swayze, V. W., II, Andreasen, N. C., Alliger, R. J., Yuh, W. T., & Ehrhardt, J. C. (1992). Subcortical and temporal structures in affective disorder and Schizophrenia: A magnetic resonance imaging study. *Biological Psychiatry, 31,* 221–240.

Swayze, V. W., II, Johnson, V. P., Hanson, J. W., Piven, J., Sato, Y., Giedd, J. N., et al. (1997). Magnetic resonance imaging of brain anomalies in fetal alcohol syndrome. *Pediatrics, 99*(2), 232–240.

Swedo, S. E., Leonard, H. L., & Rapoport, J. L. (1992). Childhood-onset obsessive compulsive disorder. *Psychiatric Clinics of North America, 15*(4), 767–775.

Swoboda, K. J., & Jenike, M. A. (1995). Frontal abnormalities in a patient with obsessive-compulsive disorder: The role of structural lesions in obsessive-compulsive behavior. *Neurology, 45*(12), 2130–2134.

Szeszko, P. R., MacMillan, S., McMeniman, M., Chen, S., Baribault, K., Lim, K. O., et al. (2004). Brain structural abnormalities in psychotropic drug-naive pediatric patients with obsessive-compulsive disorder. *American Journal of Psychiatry, 161*(6), 1049–1056.

Szeszko, P. R., Robinson, D., Alvir, J. M., Bilder, R. M., Lencz, T., Ashtari, M., et al. (1999). Orbital frontal and amygdala volume reductions in obsessive-compulsive disorder. *Archives of General Psychiatry, 56*(10), 913–919.

Takahashi, T., Murata, T., Omori, M., Kimura, H., Kado, H., Kosaka, H., et al. (2001). Quantitative evaluation of magnetic resonance imaging of deep white matter hyperintensity in geriatric patients by multifractal analysis. *Neuroscience Letters, 314*(3), 143–146.

Tamm, L., Menon, V., & Reiss, A. L. (2002). Maturation of brain function associated with response inhibition. *Journal of the American Academy of Child and Adolescent Psychiatry, 41*(10), 1231–1238.

Tassone, F., Hagerman, R. J., Ikle, D. N., Dyer, P. N., Lampe, M., Willemsen, R., et al. (1999). FMRP expression as a potential prognostic indicator in fragile X syndrome. *American Journal of Medical Genetics, 84*(3), 250–261.

Taylor, W. D., Hsu, E., Krishnan, K. R., & MacFall, J. R. (2004). Diffusion tensor imaging: Background, potential, and utility in psychiatric research. *Biological Psychiatry, 55*(3), 201–207.

Taylor, W. D., MacFall, J. R., Payne, M. E., McQuoid, D. R., Provenzale, J. M., Steffens, D. C., et al. (2004). Late-life depression and microstructural abnormalities in dorsolateral prefrontal cortex white matter. *American Journal of Psychiatry, 161*(7), 1293–1296.

Taylor, W. D., Payne, M. E., Krishnan, K. R., Wagner, H. R., Provenzale, J. M., Steffens, D. C., et al. (2001). Evidence of white matter tract disruption in MRI hyperintensities. *Biological Psychiatry, 50*(3), 179–183.

Taylor, W. D., Steffens, D. C., MacFall, J. R., McQuoid, D. R., Payne, M. E., Provenzale, J. M., et al. (2003). White matter hyperintensity progression and late-life depression outcomes. *Archives of General Psychiatry, 60*(11), 1090–1096.

Teicher, M. H., Dumont, N. L., Ito, Y., Vaituzis, C., Giedd, J. N., & Andersen, S. L. (2004). Childhood neglect is associated with reduced corpus callosum area. *Biological Psychiatry, 56*(2), 80–85.

Thomas, L. A., & DeBellis, M. D. (2004). Pituitary volumes in pediatric maltreatment-related posttraumatic stress disorder. *Biological Psychiatry, 55*(7), 752–758.

Thomas, M., & Karmiloff-Smith, A. (2002). Are developmental disorders like cases of adult brain damage? Implications from connectionist modelling. *Behavioral and Brain Sciences, 25*(6), 727–750.

Thompson, P. M., Cannon, T. D., Narr, K. L., van Erp, T., Poutanen, V. P., Huttunen, M., et al. (2001). Genetic influences on brain structure. *Nature Neuroscience, 4*(12), 1253–1258.

Thompson, P. M., Giedd, J. N., Woods, R. P., MacDonald, D., Evans, A. C., & Toga, A. W. (2000). Growth patterns in the developing brain detected by using continuum mechanical tensor maps. *Nature, 404*(6774), 190–193.

Thompson, P. M., Hayashi, K. M., Sowell, E. R., Gogtay, N., Giedd, J. N., Rapoport, J. L., et al. (2004). Mapping cortical change in Alzheimer's disease, brain development, and Schizophrenia. *NeuroImage, 23*(Suppl. 1), S2–S18.

Thompson, P. M., MacDonald, D., Mega, M. S., Holmes, C. J., Evans, A. C., & Toga, A. W. (1997). Detection and mapping of abnormal brain structure with a probabilistic atlas of cortical surfaces. *Journal of Computer Assisted Tomography, 21*(4), 567–581.

Thompson, P. M., Vidal, C., Giedd, J. N., Gochman, P., Blumenthal, J., Nicolson, R., et al. (2001). Mapping adolescent brain change reveals dynamic wave of accelerated gray matter loss in very early-onset schizophrenia. *Proceedings of the National Academy of Sciences of the United States of America, 98*(20), 11650–11655.

Todd, P. K., & Mack, K. J. (2000). Sensory stimulation increases cortical expression of the fragile X mental retardation protein in vivo. *Brain Research. Molecular Brain Research, 80*(1), 17–25.

Todd, P. K., Malter, J. S., & Mack, K. J. (2003). Whisker stimulation-dependent translation of FMRP in the barrel cortex requires activation of type I metabotropic glutamate receptors. *Brain Research. Molecular Brain Research, 110*(2), 267–278.

Toga, A. W., & Mazziotta, J. C. (2002). *Brain mapping: The methods* (2nd ed.). Amsterdam: Academic Press.

Toga, A. W., & Thompson, P. M. (2005). Genetics of brain structure and intelligence. *Annual Review of Neuroscience, 28,* 1–23.

Tsatsanis, K. D., Rourke, B. P., Klin, A., Volkmar, F. R., Cicchetti, D., & Schultz, R. T. (2003). Reduced thalamic volume in high-functioning individuals with Autism. *Biological Psychiatry, 53*(2), 121–129.

Tupler, L. A., Krishnan, K. R., McDonald, W. M., Dombeck, C. B., D'Souza, S., & Steffens, D. C. (2002). Anatomic location and laterality of MRI signal hyperintensities in late-life depression. *Journal of Psychosomatic Research, 53*(2), 665–676.

van Buchem, M. A., Steens, S. C., Vrooman, H. A., Zwinderman, A. H., McGowan, J. C., Rassek, M., et al. (2001). Global estimation of myelination in the developing brain on the basis of magnetization transfer imaging: A preliminary study. *American Journal of Neuroradiology, 22*(4), 762–766.

Victor, M., Ropper, A. H., & Adams, R. D. (2001). *Adams and Victor's principles of neurology* (7th ed.). New York: McGraw-Hill.

Videbech, P., & Ravnkilde, B. (2004). Hippocampal volume and depression: A meta-analysis of MRI studies. *American Journal of Psychiatry, 161*(11), 1957–1966.

Vineis, P. (2004). A self-fulfilling prophecy: Are we underestimating the role of the environment in gene-environment interaction research? *International Journal of Epidemiology, 33*(5), 945–946.

Vitzthum, V. J. (2003). A number no greater than the sum of its parts: The use and abuse of heritability. *Human Biology, 75*(4), 539–558.

Volkmar, F., Cohen, D., Hoshino, V., Rende, R., & Paul, R. (1988). Phenomenology and classification of the childhood psychoses. *Psychological Medicine, 18,* 191–201.

Volpe, J. J. (2000). Overview: Normal and abnormal human brain development. *Mental Retardation and Developmental Disabilities Research Review, 6*(1), 1–5.

Waiter, G. D., Williams, J. H., Murray, A. D., Gilchrist, A., Perrett, D. I., & Whiten, A. (2004). A voxel-based investigation of brain structure in male adolescents with autistic spectrum disorder. *Neuroimage, 22*(2), 619–625.

Waiter, G. D., Williams, J. H., Murray, A. D., Gilchrist, A., Perrett, D. I., & Whiten, A. (2005). Structural white matter deficits in high-functioning individuals with autistic spectrum disorder: A voxel-based investigation. *Neuroimage, 24*(2), 455–461.

Walker, E. F., Sabuwalla, Z., & Huot R. (2004). Pubertal neuromaturation, stress sensitivity, and psychopathology. *Development and Psychopathology, 16,* 807–824.

Wechsler, D. (1974). *Wechsler Intelligence Scale for Children: Revised.* New York: Psychological Corporation.

Weinberger, D. R. (1987). Implications of normal brain development for the pathogenesis of Schizophrenia. *Archives of General Psychiatry, 44,* 660–669.

Welt, C. K., Smith, P. C., & Taylor, A. E. (2004). Evidence of early ovarian aging in fragile X premutation carriers. *Journal of Clinical Endocrinology and Metabolism, 89*(9), 4569–4574.

Wilke, M., Kowatch, R. A., DelBello, M. P., Mills, N. P., & Holland, S. K. (2004). Voxel-based morphometry in adolescents with bipolar disorder: First results. *Psychiatry Research, 131*(1), 57–69.

Willemsen, R., Oostra, B. A., Bassell, G. J., & Dictenberg, J. (2004). The fragile X syndrome: From molecular genetics to neurobiology. *Mental Retardation and Developmental Disabilities Research Review, 10*(1), 60–67.

Willerman, L., Schultz, R., Rutledge, J. N., & Bigler, E. D. (1991). In vivo brain size and intelligence. *Intelligence, 15,* 223–228.

Wimberger, D. M., Roberts, T. P., Barkovich, A. J., Prayer, L. M., Moseley, M. E., & Kucharczyk, J. (1995). Identification of "premyelination" by diffusion-weighted MRI. *Journal of Computer Assisted Tomography, 19*(1), 28–33.

Witelson, S. F. (1985a). The brain connection: The corpus callosum is larger in left-handers. *Science, 229,* 665–668.

Witelson, S. F. (1985b). On hemisphere specialization and cerebral plasticity from birth. In C. T. Best (Ed.), *Hemisphere function and collaboration in the child* (pp. 33–85). Orlando, FL: Academic Press.

Witelson, S. F. (1989). Hand and sex differences in the isthmus and genu of the human corpus callosum. *Brain, 112,* 799–835.

Wolff, S. D., & Balaban, R. S. (1989). Magnetization transfer contrast (MTC) and tissue water proton relaxation in vivo. *Magnetic Resonance Medicine, 10*(1), 135–144.

Wolff, S. D., & Balaban, R. S. (1994). Magnetization transfer imaging: Practical aspects and clinical applications. *Radiology, 192*(3), 593–599.

Woods, B. T. (1998). Is Schizophrenia a progressive neurodevelopmental disorder? Toward a unitary pathogenetic mechanism. *American Journal of Psychiatry, 155*(12), 1661–1670.

Woody, R. C., Bolyard, K., Eisenhauer, G., & Altschuler, L. (1987). CT scan and MRI findings in a child with Schizophrenia. *Journal of Child Neurology, 2,* 105–110.

Yakovlev, P. I., & Lecours, A. (1967). The myelogenetic cycles of regional maturation of the brain. In A. Minkovski (Ed.), *Regional development of the brain in early life* (pp. 3–65). Oxford: Blackwell.

Yates, W. R., Jacoby, C. G., & Andreasen, N. C. (1987). Cerebellar atrophy in Schizophrenia and affective disorder. *American Journal of Psychiatry, 144*(4), 465–467.

Yeargin-Allsopp, M., Rice, C., Karapurkar, T., Doernberg, N., Boyle, C., & Murphy, C. (2003). Prevalence of Autism in a U.S. metropolitan area. *Journal of the American Medical Association, 289*(1), 49–55.

Yehuda, R. (2001). Biology of posttraumatic stress disorder. *Journal of Clinical Psychiatry, 62*(Suppl. 17), 41–46.

Yule, W. (2001). Posttraumatic stress disorder in the general population and in children. *Journal of Clinical Psychiatry, 62*(Suppl. 17), 23–28.

Zaidel, D., & Sperry, R. W. (1974). Memory impairment after commissurotomy in man. *Brain, 97,* 263–272.

Zijdenbos, A. P., Dawant, B. M., & Margolin, R. A. (1994). Automatic detection of intracranial contours in MR images. *Computerized Medical Imaging and Graphics, 18*(1), 11–23.

CHAPTER 4

Typical and Atypical Human Functional Brain Development

MARK H. JOHNSON and MICHELLE DE HAAN

Until recently, the postnatal development of human psychological functions was studied independently of their underlying neural substrates. Developmental psychologists used measures of behavior to assess theories of cognitive, perceptual, and linguistic development; developmental neuroscientists investigated detailed changes in brain structure and chemistry in humans and other species. Although occasional attempts were made to relate these two fields, only in the past decade has the hybrid field known as "developmental cognitive neuroscience" (Johnson, 2005) emerged. In assessing the progress made to date, it is interesting to note that three main approaches, each with different sets of underlying assumptions, have been taken. In this chapter, we outline these three perspectives on human functional brain development before assessing their application and different implications for understanding empirical evidence from (1) functional brain imaging, (2) the effects of early acquired brain damage, and (3) the consequences of atypical early experience.

THREE PERSPECTIVES ON THE FUNCTIONAL DEVELOPMENT OF THE HUMAN BRAIN

Relating evidence on the neuroanatomical development of the brain to the remarkable changes in motor, perceptual, and cognitive abilities during the 1st decade or so of human life presents a considerable challenge. We have identified three distinct, but not necessarily incompatible, approaches to this issue: (1) a maturational viewpoint, (2) interactive specialization, and (3) a skill-learning viewpoint. We briefly introduce these three approaches, before going on to examine their assumptions and predictions in more detail.

Maturational Viewpoint

According to the maturational viewpoint, newly emerging sensory, motor, and cognitive functions are related to the maturation of particular areas of the brain, usually regions

197

of cerebral cortex (Figure 4.1a). Much of the research to date attempting to relate brain to behavioral development in humans has taken this approach. Evidence concerning the differential neuroanatomical development of brain regions should then predict the age when a particular region is likely to become functional. Conversely, success in a new behavioral task at a given age is attributed to the maturation of a new brain region. For example, some investigators have suggested that the development into adolescence of the ability to detect error-related conflict in action-monitoring tasks is linked to maturation of the anterior cingulated cortex (Ladouceur, Dahl, & Carter, 2004). Functional brain development is in this sense depicted as the reverse of adult neuropsychological studies of patients with brain damage, with specific brain regions being added in during development instead of being "subtracted" by damage.

Despite the intuitive appeal and attractive simplicity of the maturational approach, it does not successfully explain all aspects of human functional brain development. One aspect that is difficult to account for in this view is that some of the cortical regions that are slowest to develop by neuroanatomical criteria show activity from shortly after birth and appear to mediate cognitive functions even before they would be considered anatomically fully mature. For example, the prefrontal cortex continues to mature into the teenage years according to neuroanatomical criteria, but functional imaging studies show evidence that it can be activated during the first months (see Johnson, 2005, for review). Thus, the emergence of new behaviors is not necessarily linked to a previously immature, silent neural region becoming active when it matures. In fact, where functional activity has been assessed by functional magnetic resonance imaging (fMRI) during a behavioral transition, multiple cortical and subcortical areas appear to change their response pattern (Luna et al., 2001) rather than a few specific areas becoming active. Another difficulty for the maturational viewpoint is that associations between neural and cognitive changes based on age of onset are theoretically weak due to the great variety of neuroanatomical and neurochemical measures that change at different times in different regions of the brain. Thus, it is nearly always possible to find a potential neural correlate for any behavioral change.

Interactive Specialization

In contrast to the maturational viewpoint, the interactive specialization viewpoint assumes that postnatal functional brain development, at least in the cerebral cortex, involves a process of organizing patterns of interregional interac-

a. Maturational

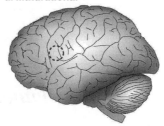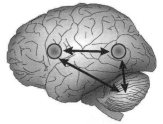

Before successful object retrieval   Successful object retrieval

b. Interactive Specialization

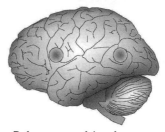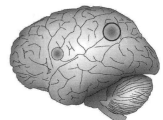

Before successful performance: poor or disorganized inter-regional interaction   Successful performance: appropriate interactions established

c. Skill Learning

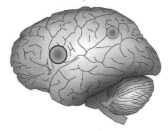

During skill acquisition: greater activation of frontal regions   After skill acquisition: greater activation of posterior regions

Figure 4.1   A hypothetical illustration of three accounts of the neural basis of an advance in behavioral abilities in infants. Panel A represents a maturational view in which maturation of one region (in this case, the dorsolateral prefrontal cortex) enables new behavioral abilities to appear. Panel B illustrates an interactive specialization view in which the onset of a new behavioral ability is due to changes in the interactions between regions that were already partially active. By this view, several regions adjust their functionality together to enable new computations. Panel C shows a third perspective, skill learning, in which certain regions become active during the acquisition of a range of new skills throughout the life span. The activation of some of these skill acquisition regions declines as expertise is developed. Thus, in some simple visuomotor tasks, infants will have more regions activated than older children and adults. These three accounts are not mutually exclusive. *Source:* From "Functional Brain Development in Humans," by M. H. Johnson, 2001, *Nature Reviews Neuroscience, 2,* pp. 475–483. Reprinted with permission. (www.nature.com)

tions (Johnson, 2000; Figure 4.1b). According to this view, the response properties of a specific brain region are partly determined by its patterns of connectivity to other regions, and their patterns of activity. During postnatal development, changes in the response properties of cortical regions occur as they interact and compete with each other to acquire their role in new computational abilities. From this perspective, some cortical regions may begin with poorly defined, general-purpose functions and consequently are partially activated in a wide range of different contexts and tasks. During development, activity-dependent interactions between regions sharpens up their functions such that their activity becomes restricted to a narrower set of circumstances (e.g., a region originally activated by a wide variety of visual objects may come to confine its response to upright human faces). The onset of new behavioral competencies during infancy will therefore be associated with changes in activity over several regions, and not just by the onset of activity in one or more additional regions.

Skill Learning

A third perspective on human functional brain development, skill learning, involves the proposal that the brain regions active in infants during the onset of new perceptual or motor abilities are similar or identical to those involved in complex skill acquisition in adults (Figure 4.1c). For example, Gauthier and colleagues (Gauthier, Tarr, Anderson, Skudlarski, & Gore, 1999) have shown that extensive training of adults to identify individual artificial objects (called "greebles") eventually results in activation of a cortical region previously preferentially activated by faces, the fusiform face area. This suggests that the region is normally activated by faces in adults, not because it is prespecified to do so, but due to our extensive expertise with that class of stimulus. Extended to ontogeny, this view would argue that development of face processing during infancy and childhood could proceed in a manner similar to acquisition of perceptual expertise for a novel visual category in adults

(see Gauthier & Nelson, 2001). Although the degree to which parallels can be drawn between adult expertise and infant development remain unclear, to the extent that the skill-learning hypothesis is correct, it presents a clear view of a continuity of mechanisms throughout the life span.

ASSUMPTIONS UNDERLYING THE THREE APPROACHES

Table 4.1 illustrates some of the assumptions that underlie the three approaches we have outlined.

Deterministic versus Probabilistic Epigenesis

Gottlieb (1992) distinguished between two approaches to the study of development: *deterministic epigenesis,* in which it is assumed that there is a unidirectional causal path from genes to structural brain changes to psychological function, and *probabilistic epigenesis,* in which interactions among genes, structural brain changes, and psychological function are viewed as bidirectional, dynamic, and emergent. In many ways, it is a defining feature of the maturational approach that it assumes deterministic epigenesis; region-specific gene expression is assumed to effect changes in intraregional connectivity that, in turn, allow new functions to emerge. A related assumption commonly made in the maturational approach is that there is a one-to-one mapping between brain and cortical regions and particular cognitive functions, such that specific computations come online following that maturation of circuitry intrinsic to the corresponding cortical region. In some respects, this view parallels mosaic development at the cellular level, in which simple organisms (such as *C. Elegans*) are constructed through cell lineages that are largely independent of each other (Elman et al., 1996). Similarly, different cortical regions are assumed to have different maturational timetables, thus enabling new cognitive functions to emerge at different ages.

TABLE 4.1   Assumptions Underlying the Three Approaches to Functional Brain Development

	Brain-Cognitive Mapping	Primary Locale of Changes	Plasticity	Cause
Maturational	One-to-one mapping. Static over development.	Intraregion connectivity matures.	A specialized mechanism invoked by stroke or injury.	Brain changes cause cognitive development.
Skill-learning	Changes during acquisition of skill.		Lifelong; no clear sensitive period.	
Interactive	Networks/neural systems. Dynamic changes during development.	Interregional connectivity changes and shapes intraregional connectivity.	An inherent property: the state of having not yet specialized. Sensitive: period determined by state of specialization.	Bidirectional relations between structure and function.

In contrast to the maturational approach, interactive specialization (IS; Johnson, 2000, 2001, 2005) has a number of different underlying assumptions. Specifically, a probabilistic epigenesis assumption is coupled with the view that cognitive functions are the emergent product of interactions between different brain regions. In this respect, IS follows views in adult functional neuroimaging. For example, Friston and Price (2001) point out that it may be an error to assume that particular functions can be localized in a certain cortical region. Rather, they suggest that the response properties of a region are determined by its patterns of connectivity to other regions as well as by their current activity states. In this view, "The cortical infrastructure supporting a single function may involve many specialized areas whose union is mediated by the functional integration among them" (pp. 276). Similarly, in discussing the design and interpretation of adult fMRI studies, Carpenter and collaborators (2001, pp. 360) have argued:

> In contrast to a localist assumption of a one-to-one mapping between cortical regions and cognitive operations, an alternative view is that cognitive task performance is subserved by large-scale cortical networks that consist of spatially separate computational components, each with its own set of relative specializations, that collaborate extensively to accomplish cognitive functions.

Extending these ideas to development, the IS approach emphasizes changes in interregional connectivity, as opposed to the maturation of intraregional connectivity. Whereas the maturational approach may be analogous to mosaic cellular development, the IS view corresponds to the regulatory development seen in higher organisms in which cell-cell interactions are critical in determining developmental fate. Mosaic development can be faster than regulatory, but the latter has several advantages; namely, regulatory development is more flexible and better able to respond to damage, and it is more efficient in terms of genetic coding. In regulatory development, genes need orchestrate only cellular-level interactions to yield more complex structures (see Elman et al., 1996).

Static versus Dynamic Mapping

As well as the mapping between structure and function at one age, we can also consider how this mapping might change during development. When discussing functional imaging of developmental disorders, Johnson, Halit, Grice, and Karmiloff-Smith (2002) point out that many investigators have assumed that the relation between brain structure

and cognitive function is unchanging during development. Specifically, in accordance with a maturational view, these researchers believe that when new structures come online, the existing (already mature) regions continue to support the same functions they did at earlier developmental stages. The "static assumption" is partly why it is acceptable to study developmental disorders in adulthood and then extrapolate back in time to early development. Contrary to this view, the IS approach as expounded by Johnson and colleagues (Johnson, 2001; Johnson et al., 2002) suggests that when a new computation or skill is acquired, there is a reorganization of interactions between different brain structures and regions. This reorganization process could even change how previously acquired cognitive functions are represented in the brain. Thus, the same behavior could be supported by different neural networks at different ages during development. For example, adult monkeys with lesions to the medial temporal lobe or inferior prefrontal convexity show marked impairments in rule learning in the delayed nonmatching-to-sample task (DNMS task; Meunier, Bachevalier, & Mishkin, 1997), indicating that both areas are key components in the neural network supporting performance on the task. By contrast, monkeys with neonatal lesions to the medial temporal lobes show similar impairments at 3 months and 2 years of age, but with inferior convexity lesions show no impairments at 3 months and only very mild ones at 2 years (Malkova, Bachevalier, Webster, & Mishkin, 2000). The authors interpret these results as showing learning of the response rule in the DNMS task depends mainly on the medial temporal lobe in young monkeys, whereas at later ages it requires functional interactions between the medial temporal lobe and inferior frontal cortex.

Stating that structure-function relations can change with development is all very well, but it lacks the specificity required to make all but the most general predictions. Fortunately, the view that there is competitive specialization of regions during development gives rise to expectations about the types of changes in structure-function relations that should be observed. Specifically, as regions become increasingly selective in their response properties during infancy, patterns of cortical activation during behavioral tasks may therefore be more extensive than those observed in adults and involve different patterns of activation. Additionally, within broad constraints, successful behavior in the same tasks can be supported by different patterns of cortical activation in infants and adults. Evidence in support of this view is discussed later in the chapter.

The basic assumption underlying the skill-learning approach is that there is a continuity of the circuitry underlying skill acquisition from birth through to adulthood (for review of the neural systems involved in perceptual and motor skill learning in adults, see Poldrack, 2002; Ungerleider, Doyon, & Karni, 2002). These circuits are likely to involve a network of structures that retains the same basic function across developmental time (a static brain-cognition mapping). However, other brain regions may respond to learning with dynamic changes in functionality similar or identical to those hypothesized in the IS framework. For example, neuroimaging studies of adults acquiring the skill of mirror reading show both increases and decreases of cortical activity over widespread regions during learning: Unskilled performance is associated with activation in bilateral occipital, parietal, and temporal lobes and the cerebellum, with acquisition of skill leading to decreases in bilateral occipital and right parietal activation and to increased inferior temporal lobe and caudate nucleus activation (Poldrack, Desmond, Clover, & Gabrieli, 1998; Poldrack & Gabrieli, 2001). According to the skill-learning view, similar dynamic changes in brain activation would occur as skills emerge during development.

Plasticity

Another way the three perspectives differ is with regard to plasticity. Plasticity in brain development is a phenomenon that has generated much controversy, with several different conceptions and definitions having been presented. According to the maturational framework, plasticity is a specialized mechanism that is activated following brain injury. According to the IS approach, plasticity is simply the state of a region's function being not yet fully specialized; that is,

there is still scope for developing more finely tuned responses. In this view, the mechanisms of plasticity remain the same throughout the life span, but the expression of plasticity is more limited in adulthood because many regions of the brain have already become specialized and there is less scope for further change. This definition corresponds well with the view of developmental biologists that development involves the increasing "restriction of fate." Finally, according to the skill-learning hypothesis view, the functional plasticity present in early development may share many characteristics with the plasticity underlying acquisition and retention of skills in adults (Karni & Bertini, 1997). The key difference from the IS approach is that in the skill-learning view, plasticity does not necessarily reduce during development (for a more detailed discussion of critical/sensitive periods for plasticity in development, see predictions for effects of brain injury and atypical experience, discussed later).

PREDICTIONS OF THE THREE APPROACHES

Some predictions of the three approaches are given in Table 4.2. Before we assess areas of empirical data in detail, we review the types of predictions that arise from the three approaches. The first set of predictions concerns the neural correlates of the onset of new abilities during development. According to a maturational view, new behavioral abilities are mediated by new components of cognition that are, in turn, allowed by the maturation of one or more brain regions. A consequence of this is a general increase in the number of structures that can be activated in tasks with

TABLE 4.2   Predictions of the Three Approaches to Functional Brain Development

	Brain Imaging 1	Brain Imaging 2	Effects of Acquired Damage	Effects of Atypical Early Experience
Maturational	New skills associated with onset of functional activity in one or more regions. An increasing number of regions active with age.	Specific regions activated by particular functions throughout development.	Need to infer specialized mechanisms of plasticity and give separate explanation for sensitive periods.	Experience accelerates or decelerates rates of maturation.
Skill learning	New skills associated with activation of skill-learning circuit. Changes in cortical activation with experience.	Skill learning of networks achieved at task onset, with other regions taking over as skill is acquired.	Damage to skill learning circuit has long-lasting and widespread effect. Otherwise, same degree of plasticity as in adults.	Effects of early deprivation are reversible because same mechanisms of skill acquisition are available in later life.
Interactive	New skills associated with changing activation of widespread network of regions. Extent of cortical activation could decrease with age.	Regions become more fine-tuned/specialized in their response properties with development.	Remaining regions can specialize in other ways to compensate for loss. When regions are specialized, plasticity terminates.	Atypical early experience may set up atypical patterns of regional specialization.

development. In contrast to these predictions, in the IS approach it is anticipated that widespread networks of brain regions will change their patterns of activation in association with the onset of new behavioral abilities. In addition, regions will become more specialized (finely tuned) in their response properties with experience. A consequence of this specialization is that, on at least some occasions, fewer brain regions are activated with development in certain tasks. Turning to the skill-learning approach, here we anticipate that the onset of new abilities will often be associated with activation of a network of skill acquisition areas. As the new behavioral ability is acquired, a different network of brain regions may become involved.

With regard to the issue of how functions are mapped onto patterns of brain activity, according to the maturational approach, if we compare two age groups in a task for which they show identical behavioral performance, we should also expect to see identical patterns of brain activation. This is not necessarily the case for the IS approach, because the exact patterns of brain activation that support a function will change according to the degree of specialization of component regions within the supporting network. Indeed, the IS approach predicts that the patterns of regional brain activation supporting a function will change during development. Although the exact nature of this change will depend on the degree of specialization achieved in different component structures, the IS view predicts a general trend for a decrease in the extent of cortical activation with increasing development/experience. The skill-learning view invokes the reactivation of one or more skill-learning circuits at the onset of a task, followed by a different pattern of activation after the skill is acquired. In this case, in many comparisons between age groups, the younger group will have acquired the skill in less depth than the older group, giving rise to different patterns of underlying brain activation. Interestingly, however, patterns of changing brain activation while adults acquire new skills should mirror the changes seen during development as infants and children acquire simpler skills.

The three perspectives yield different types of predictions about the consequences of perinatal brain damage. According to the maturational view, additional mechanisms of plasticity are activated following early damage. Specific additional explanations are then required to account for incidents of recovery of function. Also, it is not obvious why the extent of plasticity is greater earlier in life. From the IS perspective, there is a parsimonious explanation of recovery of function following perinatal damage, as the regional specialization of the remaining brain regions will be altered to compensate, particularly the corresponding regions in the other hemisphere. In cases of bi-

lateral or extensive damage, recovery is less likely. From the skill-learning perspective, plasticity is a lifelong feature of the brain. Damage to the general circuits critical for skill acquisition will have long-lasting and widespread consequences, and damage to circuits specific to acquisition of particular skills or their retention may result in more isolated impairments. Of the three approaches, IS gives the simplest account of sensitive periods for plasticity, as plasticity is reduced when specialization of corresponding regions is achieved.

With regard to the long-term effects of atypical early experience, or even variations of experience within the normal range, once again the three frameworks lead to different sets of expectations. From the skill-learning perspective, variations in early experience will determine the extent of skills acquired. Early deprivation will be potentially reversible because the same mechanisms of skill acquisition are available later in life. From the IS perspective, long-term effects of atypical early experience can result from atypical patterns of regional specialization arising early in life. Such atypical patterns of specialization may be difficult to reverse once established. Finally, under the maturational view, a primary variable influenced by the environment is the speed of maturation that may affect the level or maintenance of a skill. It is sometimes argued that early sensory deprivation may have a general slowing effect on the sequence of maturation.

BRAIN IMAGING OF TYPICAL DEVELOPMENT

In this section, we review evidence from the functional neuroimaging of normal development that pertains to the three perspectives on functional brain development. We argue that the majority of evidence currently available does not offer much support to the maturational view. Instead, behavioral change seems to be accompanied by large-scale dynamic changes in the interactions between regions, and different cortical regions become more specialized for functions as a consequence of development.

A maturational approach to human postnatal functional brain development predicts that a neural correlate of increasing behavioral abilities is an increasing number of active cortical areas. In functional imaging paradigms, therefore, infants and children should show less active regions in tasks where they show poorer behavioral performance than do adults. In contrast, if new behaviors require changes in interregional interaction, the IS view predicts a greater or equal extent of cortical activation and may find different patterns of activation early in development even in task domains where behavioral performance is similar to that of adults. Comparing activation in cases where behavioral performance is equated is critical for distinguishing the IS view from both the skill-learning view and the maturational view, as only the former predicts that the pattern of brain activation may differ with age even when performance is equated. Which of these approaches is adopted has not only theoretical implications but also practical implications for data collection. For example, if one adopts the maturational approach and is expecting a particular area to become active during development for a particular task, then brain imaging may be focused on that region rather than on the whole brain. As a consequence, any possible changes in more distant brain structures would not be detected. By contrast, if one adopts the IS approach, the importance of whole-brain imaging is clearly apparent.

A number of authors have described developmental changes in the spatial extent of cortical activation in a given situation during postnatal life. Event-related potential (ERP) experiments with infants have indicated that both for word learning (Neville, Mills, & Lawson, 1992) and face processing (de Haan, Pascalis, & Johnson, 2002) there is increasing localization of processing with age and experience of a stimulus class. That is, scalp recording leads reveal a wider area of processing for words and faces in younger infants than in older ones whose processing has become more specialized and localized. In the IS framework, such developmental changes are accounted for in terms of more pathways being partially activated in younger infants prior to experience with a class of stimuli. With increasing experience, the specialization of one or more of those pathways occurs over time. Taking the example of face processing, in early infancy both the left and the right ventral visual pathways are differentially activated by faces, but in many (although not all) adults, face processing localizes largely to the right ventral pathway (Johnson & de Haan, 2001). In the example of word recognition, ERP activity differentiating between comprehended and noncomprehended words is initially found over widespread cortical areas. This narrows to left temporal leads after children's vocabularies have reached a certain level, irrespective of maturational age (Mills, Coffey, & Neville, 1993). Changes in the extent of localization can be viewed as a direct consequence of specialization. Initially, multiple pathways are activated for most stimuli. With increasing experience, fewer pathways become activated by each specific class of stimuli. Pathways become tuned to specific functions and are therefore no longer engaged by the broad range of stimuli, as was the case earlier in development. Additionally,

there may be inhibition from pathways that are becoming increasingly specialized for that function. In this sense, there is competition between pathways to recruit functions, with the pathway best suited for the function (by virtue of its initial biases) usually winning out.

Further evidence to support the IS view comes from recent fMRI studies in children. Luna and colleagues (2001) tested participants age 8 to 30 years in an occulomotor response-suppression task. Their behavioral results showed that the adult level of ability to inhibit prepotent responses developed gradually through childhood and adolescence. The difference between prosaccade and antisaccade conditions was investigated with fMRI and revealed changing patterns of brain activation during development. Both children and adolescents had less activation than adults in a few cortical areas (superior frontal eye fields, intraparietal sulcus) and several subcortical areas, a finding broadly consistent with maturational hypotheses. However, both children and adolescents also had differential activation in regions not found to show differences in adults. Children displayed increased relative activation in the supramarginal gyrus compared to the other age groups, and the adolescents showed greater differential activity in the dorsolateral prefrontal cortex than did children or adults. These findings illustrate that the neural basis of behavior can change over developmental time, with different patterns of activation being evident at different ages, a pattern consistent with the IS and the skill-learning viewpoints.

A similar conclusion can be reached after examination of the developmental fMRI data produced by B. J. Casey and colleagues (1997; Thomas et al., 1999). These authors administered a go/no-go task to assess inhibitory control and frontal lobe function to healthy volunteers from 7 years of age to adult. The task involved participants responding to a number of letters, but withholding their response to a rarely occurring "X." More than twice the volume of prefrontal cortex activity (in the middle and superior frontal gyri) was observed in children compared to adults (for similar results, see Booth et al., 2003; Bunge, Dudukovic, Thomason, Vaidya, & Gabrieli, 2002; Durston et al., 2002; Tamm, Menon, & Reiss, 2002). One explanation of this finding is that children found the task more difficult and demanding than adults. However, children with error rates similar to those in adults showed some of the largest volumes of prefrontal activity, suggesting that task difficulty was not the important factor (Casey et al., 1997; Thomas et al., 1999). It is difficult to account for these decreases in the extent of cortical activation in terms of the progressive maturation of these areas. Some authors suggest that it reflects delayed maturation of the frontostriatal network, with the immature network requiring greater mobilization of neural processing resources to achieve the same level of performance as the mature network (Booth et al., 2003). The finding that, for children, better performance is associated with greater activation in striatal and inferior prefrontal regions is seen as consistent with this view (Durston et al., 2002). The finding that children and adults appeared to show different patterns of activation even when performance was equated is inconsistent with the skill-learning viewpoint, but not unexpected according to the IS viewpoint.

A third example of the use of fMRI to study the development of cortical activation patterns during childhood involved using the same stimulus array for two different tasks, a face-matching task and a location-matching task (Passarotti et al., 2003). For the face-matching task, younger children (10 to 12 years) showed more extensive areas of activation than did older children and adults. In general, the activation shown by the youngest group included the areas activated in adults (such as bilateral activation of the middle fusiform gyrus) but additionally extended to more lateral and anterior regions. In the location-matching condition, the children also showed more extensive activation than did adults. Whereas adults had strong right superior parietal activation, children displayed more bilateral activation of this structure, as well as additional activation in the right superior frontal gyrus. Once again, and in contrast to the maturational view, typical development appears to be associated with a reduction in the extent of activation of cortical areas and with dynamic changes in the interregional patterns of activation.

A fourth example of the use of fMRI to study the development of cortical activation patterns during childhood comes from studies of verbal fluency tasks in which participants are asked to generate words in response to a cue (e.g., to generate examples of a target category, or generate a verb that relates to a cued noun). Several studies have shown that adults (Lehericy et al., 2000) and school-age children (Gaillard et al., 2000; Hertz-Pannier et al., 1997) typically activate left hemisphere frontal cortical networks, including Broca's area, premotor, prefrontal, and supplementary motor areas, and, less consistently, temporal cortical areas, including superior temporal, middle temporal, and supramarginal gyri. In addition, some degree of activation in homologous right frontal regions is almost always found both in adults (Pujol, Deus, Losilla, & Capdevila, 1999; Springer et al., 1999) and in children (Gaillard et al., 2000; Hertz-Pannier et al., 1997). Two studies have found that both the degree to which activation is bilateral (rather than left-dominant) and the extent of this activation is greater in children than in adults (Gaillard et al., 2000; Holland et al., 2001). Thus, as in the other examples, typi-

cal development is associated with a reduction in the extent of activation of cortical areas and, as a consequence, an increased lateralization of activation to the left hemisphere with age (Holland et al., 2001).

Not all developmental imaging studies have reported decreases in extent of activation with age. For example, in the case of verbal fluency, two studies have reported that laterality and extent of activation did not differ between children and adults (Gaillard et al., 2000; Schlaggar et al., 2002), with one even showing a greater number of pixels activated in left frontal regions in adults compared to children (Gaillard et al., 2000). Another example comes from studies of the development of visuospatial working memory. These show that parts of the frontoparietal network involved in this task (superior frontal and intraparietal cortex) are more active in older children than in younger children, and that working memory capacity is significantly correlated with brain activity in the same regions (Klingberg, Forssberg, & Westerberg, 2002; Kwon, Reiss, & Menon, 2002). Diffusion tensor imaging studies suggest that these developmental increases in gray matter activation could be due to maturation of white matter connections within the frontoparietal network (Olesen, Nagy, Westerberg, & Klingberg, 2003). Interestingly, studies with adults also show increased activity in these areas with improvements in working memory following training (Olesen, Westerberg, & Klingberg, 2004).

In evaluating fMRI evidence for decreasing or increasing extent of cortical activation underlying a particular skill with age, it is important to be aware that factors other than dynamic changes in the interregional patterns of activation per se could be contributing to the observed differences. Of particular importance, technical aspects of data collection, including coil characteristics, head motion, and physiological age-related differences that could affect the fMRI BOLD signal, could contribute to apparent age-related differences in activation (see Gaillard et al., 2003). For example, a surface coil might identify more activated regions in children than adults because children have thinner skulls and scalp, and thus the coil is closer to the brain and can read the signal more clearly than in adults. By contrast, use of a head coil might lead to a finding of greater activation in adults than children, as most head coils are designed for adults, and thus children's head position in the coil would not be optimal. Thus, when interpreting the results of fMRI studies, it is important to keep in mind that technological and developmental factors may affect signal and noise detection that, in turn, may influence an interpretation of age-based differences in activation patterns (for further discussion of these issues, see Gaillard et al., 2003; Poldrack, 2002).

Studies that have examined developmental changes in prefrontal cortical activation are of particular interest in evaluating the various viewpoints, as the skill-learning and maturational views make opposing predictions about the functioning of prefrontal regions during infancy. Work on complex motor skill-learning tasks in adults shows that the prefrontal cortex is often activated during the early stages of acquisition, but this activation recedes to more posterior regions as expertise is acquired. Thus, the skill-learning view predicts greater prefrontal activation in infants than adults when performing a simple (for adults) skill. By contrast, the maturational viewpoint would predict the opposite, with lesser involvement of prefrontal areas in younger children, due to the protracted neuroanatomical development of these regions. One of the most striking features of human infants is their initial inability to perform simple motor tasks, such as reaching for an object. In addition to the examples of prefrontal involvement described earlier, activity in this region, or at least within the frontal lobe, has been reported in a number of infancy studies where action is elicited, and early damage to these structures has more severe long-term effects than damage to other cortical regions. For example, Csibra, Tucker, and Johnson (1998) examined the cortical activity associated with the planning of eye movements in 6-month-old infants. They observed eye movement related potentials over frontal sites, but not over the more posterior (parietal) sites, where they are normally observed in adults. Converging results are obtained when eye movement tasks are studied in infants with perinatal focal damage to the cortex. Infants with damage to the frontal quadrants of the brain show long-lasting deficits in visual orienting tasks, but infants with the more posterior damage that causes deficits in adults do not (Craft & Schatz, 1994; Craft, White, Park, & Figiel, 1994; Johnson, Tucker, Stiles, & Trauner, 1998). These results overall provide little support for the maturational viewpoint and are more consistent with the other two viewpoints.

In sum, the balance of evidence to date suggests that (1) new behavioral skills or developmental changes in existing skills are often accompanied by widespread changes across many regions of the cortex, (2) functional brain development involves the twin process of increasing localization and increasing specialization, and (3) frontal cortical regions, traditionally believed to be slow to mature, may be active from early in life.

BRAIN IMAGING OF ATYPICAL DEVELOPMENT

Much of the neuroimaging work on developmental disorders to date has aimed at identifying gross abnormalities in discrete brain regions, structures, or systems. Although there have been some specific claims made with regard to such deficits, recent reviews of the field tend to find instead that evidence is consistent with diffuse damage to widespread parts of the brain in developmental disorders. For example, Rumsey and Ernst (2000, p. 171) summarize their review of functional imaging of autistic disorders in this way: "Studies of brain metabolism and blood flow thus far have yet to yield consistent findings, but suggest considerable variability in regional patterns of cerebral synaptic activity." Other authors reviewing work on Autism concur with this conclusion. Deb and Thompson (1998, p. 299) state, "Various abnormalities of brain structure and function have been proposed, but no focal defect has been reliably demonstrated," and Chugani (2000, p. 183) concludes that "data from the various imaging modalities have not yet converged to provide a unifying hypothesis of brain mechanisms" with a range of cortical (frontal, medial prefrontal, temporal, anterior cingulate) and subcortical (basal ganglia, thalamus, cerebellum) structures implicated in different studies. According to Filipek (1999), a similar situation obtains with respect to Attention-Deficit/Hyperactivity Disorder (ADHD). She concludes that neuroimaging studies "have, in fact, confirmed the lack of consistent gross neuroanatomical lesions or other abnormalities in Attention Deficit" (p. 117). For ADHD, there are abnormalities in widespread cortical areas, including, at a minimum, the frontostriatal, cingulate, and parietal regions. In sum, for at least these two disorders, there is little support for the notion that discrete lesions to functional cortical areas can be observed in developmental disorders.

There may be some examples of developmental disorders that show a more focal pattern of brain abnormality. For example, the KE family shows a genetic disorder of speech and language involving a point mutation of the FOXP2 gene. Behaviorally, the affected members appear to have a deficit in sequencing articulation patterns that results in speech output that is often agrammatical and unintelligible (Vargha-Khadem et al., 1998; Watkins, Dronkers, & Vargha-Khadem, 2002). This impairment is evident from childhood and persists into adulthood. Recent reports indicate that the brains of affected family members differ from those of unaffected members and controls in several particular regions involved in speech and motor control. Among these, the evidence is most striking for the caudate nucleus, which shows reduced gray matter density and volume (Watkins et al., 2002) and shows abnormalities in activation during language tasks (Vargha-Khadem et al., 1998). This result might suggest that, at least in some genetic disorders, there may be discrete brain lesions that result in specific behavioral impairments, but it is important to note that the caudate nucleus is not the only brain area affected in this family and that imaging studies have not been conducted developmentally to determine whether the pattern of damage is already present and unchanging from early in life (as the maturational or skill-learning views might predict) or evolves with development (as the IS view would predict).

Given the assumption of the maturational approach that there is a static structure-function mapping in the brain during development, it is perhaps not surprising that the vast majority of neuroimaging studies with developmentally disordered groups involve participants from middle childhood to adulthood, and that patients are often grouped together over a wide age range (e.g., Kesler et al., 2004: Turner syndrome, 7 to 33 years; Pinter, Eliez, Schmitt, Capone, & Reiss, 2001: Down syndrome, 5 to 23 years). For the interactive specialization approach, however, age of testing is critical, and it is especially important to study infancy to understand partial causes of subsequent outcomes (Karmiloff-Smith, 1998; Paterson, Brown, Gsödl, Johnson, & Karmiloff-Smith, 1999). For this issue to be assessed, there need to be longitudinal imaging studies of clinical groups, or at least cross-sectional study at different ages. Due to the difficulties mentioned earlier, there are very few examples of studies of brain function in infants with developmental disorders. Where these have been investigated, there is evidence that abnormalities in brain structure and function may appear differently at different ages. For example, Karrer, Wojtascek, and Davis (1995, p. 146; see also Hill-Karrer, Karrer, Bloom, Chaney, & Davis, 1998) conducted an ERP study of infants with Down syndrome at 6 months using an oddball paradigm for face recognition and concluded that "infants with Down syndrome may have more subtle differences (to age matched controls) than those found in adults with Down syndrome." There are few MRI studies of developmental disorders that have compared different age groups in infancy or childhood. One recent study of Autism found evidence of hippocampal enlargement at all ages but amygdala enlargement only in children (7.5 to 12.5 years) but not adolescents (12.75 to 18 years; Schumann et al., 2004). Though few in number, these examples are consistent with the IS view that brain abnormalities in developmental disorders are not like static lesions but can change as the brain develops.

One basic question that can be addressed is whether an abnormal end state is the result of an aberrant trajectory of development or a normal developmental trajectory is merely delayed. Ideally, the question should be investigated by longitudinal studies of the developmental disorder group in question. However, in the absence of such data, the question can be asked whether the phenotypic end state of the disorder resembles any stage of the typical developmental trajectory.

If so, this could be evidence for delayed development. This approach has been taken to investigating the neurochemistry of Autism. Specifically, do individuals with Autism show a profile consistent with a delayed, but otherwise typical, developmental trajectory? Positron emission tomography (PET) studies have identified brain glucose metabolism in Autism that is higher than in age-matched controls (see Chugani, 2000, for review). However, in typical development, there is a characteristic rise and fall of glucose metabolism that parallels changes in synaptic density in the cortex. Muzik and colleagues (1999) generated a mathematical developmental function with identifiable parameters representing different stages of typical development. This allows closer comparison with developmentally disordered groups when longitudinal data are obtained. Thus, evidence for higher brain glucose metabolism (and therefore, indirectly, excess synaptic density) in Autism suggests a delayed, rather than aberrant, profile. However, a caveat to this endorsement is that in the developmental cortical network models studied by Oliver, Johnson, Karmiloff-Smith, and Pennington (2000), reduced synaptic pruning was a symptom of several *different* simulated neural networks that failed to form adequate representations of input stimuli. It is possible, therefore, that reduced synaptic pruning (and therefore elevated glucose metabolism) will be a symptom shared by several different groups with developmental disorders.

According to the maturational view, behavioral abnormalities are caused by psychological deficits that in turn are caused by functional "lesions" to the brain. In functional neuroimaging paradigms, therefore, the general expectation is that there will be fewer regions active in the disordered group than in controls, and that the regions active in controls but not in the disordered group are the neural locus of the deficit. This fits well with the subtraction methodology often employed in functional neuroimaging studies. For example, one fMRI study comparing 8-year-old children who had been born preterm or full-term found that preterm children did not activate the normal network during a semantic processing task but instead activated a network that closely resembled that used by full-term children during a phonologic processing task (Peterson et al., 2002). Furthermore, the greater the apparent reliance on the phonological pathway by preterm children, the poorer their verbal comprehension. In the maturational view, this result would be interpreted as suggesting that the brain areas involved in semantic processing were damaged in the preterm children and caused their impairments in verbal comprehension. In contrast to this view, the IS approach views developmental disorders in terms of brains that develop differently from the typical trajectory from the start. This view predicts that differences in functional activation will be seen between groups, but that this could even involve more widespread activation in developmental disorders. In other words, different patterns of regional activation may be seen for developmentally disordered groups in a given task, rather than one or more regions being functionally silent.

A further prediction of the IS view is that even if areas of behavioral competence are examined, there will still be differences in the neural processing underlying this performance (Karmiloff-Smith, 1998). This question has been examined in studies of Williams's syndrome, a syndrome portrayed by some theorists as involving islands of "sparing" (normal performance) amid clear deficits. Mills and colleagues (2000) focused on an area of behavioral competence in this disorder, face processing, and recorded ERPs during a face-matching task. Despite their "intact" behavioral performance in the task, participants with Williams's syndrome displayed different patterns of ERPs, including a lack of the normal right hemisphere asymmetry. Similar findings were obtained in another area of behavioral competence for this syndrome, where the normal left hemisphere asymmetry for words was not observed (Mills et al., 1993; Neville, Mills, & Bellugi, 1994). ERPs in response to faces have also been recorded in participants with Autism and Asperger's syndrome (McPartland & Panagiotides, 2001). However, in this case, face processing is an area of behavioral deficit. Compared with controls, the Autism group made more errors on a test of face recognition. Performance on the face recognition task was found to be related to the ERPs in several ways. In controls, a face-sensitive ERP component was larger in amplitude to faces compared with objects and was more predominant over the right hemisphere. In contrast, the autistic group showed longer latencies of this component to faces compared to objects, in the absence of any clear lateralization. These findings suggest that the poorer performance on face recognition tasks by the Autism group is reflected by slower and less lateralized (i.e., less specialized) processing of faces, as indicated by their ERPs. In addition, the different distribution of the response to faces between the autistic group and controls may reflect qualitatively different processing strategies.

EFFECTS OF EARLY ACQUIRED BRAIN DAMAGE

Both the maturational and skill-learning views would predict that early brain damage should have long-lasting detri-

mental effects, because the neural substrates through which an ability emerges or is learned and retained are destroyed. The maturational view allows for plasticity in response to such damage, but it makes no clear prediction that the extent of such plasticity should be greater for children compared to adults. The skill-learning view might predict, at least under some circumstances, more negative outcomes for early lesions to areas involved in skill acquisition, because adults would have already-learned, retained skills to fall back on, whereas children would have fewer established skills. In the IS view, however, there may be compensation for early damage. Although the damage may affect the areas that under normal circumstances would be most suitable for the task and become specialized for it, if the area is damaged early in life there is still scope for alternative neural circuitry to be recruited for the task. It is possible that this compensation could come at some price, however, as the overall amount of brain area that can take on specialized functions would be reduced (e.g., the notion of crowding; for discussion, see Vargha-Khadem & Mishkin, 1997). If the area is damaged later in life, the outcome may be less optimal, as brain areas would already have specialized for particular skills and there would be less scope for alternative neural circuitry to be recruited, as it will already be taken up by other tasks. In this section, we evaluate evidence relating to these hypotheses from studies of the effects of early lesions in three cognitive domains: face processing, memory, and language.

Face Processing

In adults, damage to the occipitotemporal cortex can result in prosopagnosia, a selective impairment in face processing. Recently, several cases of selective deficits in face processing attributed to damage sustained in infancy have been reported (developmental or congenital prosopagnosia; e.g., Bentin, Deouell, & Soroker, 1999; Farah, Rabinowitz, Quinn, & Liu, 2000; Jones & Tranel, 2001; Nunn, Postma, & Pearson, 2001). On the surface, these results are consistent with both the maturational view (early damage to the cortical face-processing system would result in a functional impairment similar to that in adults with similar damage), and the skill-learning view (early damage to the system involved in learning about faces will result in a persistent impairment in this ability). However, there are some characteristics of developmental cases of prosopagnosia that do not seem to fit either of these views. If the maturational view is correct, then it would be expected that the location of damage causing prosopagnosia would be the same in both early- and adult-onset cases (Damasio, Tranel, & Damasio,

1990). However, of the few early-onset cases where structural imaging was obtained, there was no observable structural damage (Nunn et al., 2001) or diffuse rather than focal abnormalities (Laeng & Caviness, 2001). Thus, the impairments in face processing observed do not appear to be a direct consequence of focal damage to brain areas involved in face processing in adults.

If the maturational view or the learning view were correct, then one would also expect the nature of the face-processing deficit to be similar in early- and adult-onset cases. Although some authors have concluded that the two disorders are basically similar in terms of an impairment in encoding for spatial arrangement of facial evidence (Barton, Cherkasova, Press, Intriligator, & O'Connor, 2003), there is some evidence for differences related to age of onset: Residual discrimination abilities are more limited in developmental cases (Barton, Cherkasova, & O'Connor, 2001), and covert recognition is absent in developmental cases (Barton et al., 2001; Jones & Tranel, 2001). These results are more consistent with the IS view, which would predict that the nature of the deficit would depend on the age of injury.

Other studies have taken a different approach. Instead of finding individuals with face-processing deficits that could be attributed to early lesions, these studies have found children who sustained lesions to areas known to be involved in face processing in adults and investigated the consequences for face processing. In one study of face-processing abilities in 5- to 14-year-olds who had experienced perinatal unilateral lesions, the effects were fairly mild: Fewer than half of the children showed impaired performance relative to controls on tests of face or object identity recognition (Mancini et al., 1998). Furthermore, (1) face-processing deficits were no more common than object-processing deficits following a right hemisphere lesion, (2) face-processing deficits were no more common after right-sided than left-sided damage, and (3) a face-processing deficit never occurred in the absence of an object-processing deficit. This general pattern is similar to that reported in other studies (Ballantyne & Trauner, 1999; Mancini, de Schonen, Deruelle, & Massoulier, 1994) and contrasts with the severe impairments in face and/or object recognition observed in adults with damage to similar brain regions (Farah, 2000).

Together, these results suggest that the infant face-processing system is more widely distributed and/or more plastic following damage than is the adult system. These results fail to provide convincing evidence for the maturational view or the skill-learning view. Instead, they are more consistent with the IS view that, when brain areas that typically mediate a function in adults are damaged early in life, there may be greater recovery of function than that following similar damage in adults.

Memory

Memory is among the most fundamental aspects of cognitive development, enabling individuals to amass knowledge about the world (semantic memory) and to recall everyday events (episodic memory). In adults, bilateral damage to the medial temporal lobe results in a global amnesia, reflecting this region's essential role in explicit memory. However, until recently, there were virtually no reports of memory impairments following temporal lobe damage in children. This was assumed to be either because the results of such damage were so devastating to the developing child that a global severe mental delay resulted (consistent with the skill-learning view) or because the greater plasticity of the developing brain allowed sufficient recovery to prevent clinical appearance of memory impairments (consistent with the IS view). In recent years, however, there have been reports that very early damage to a specific medial temporal lobe structure, the hippocampus, does result in amnesia (Gadian et al., 2000; Isaacs et al., 2003; Vargha-Khadem et al., 1997, 2003). On the surface, this finding appears consistent with the maturational view, in that early focal damage to a brain region believed to mediate a particular ability in adults results in a specific failure of that skill to develop. Indeed, the pattern of memory impairment observed in these children, where episodic memory is relatively impaired and semantic memory relatively spared, has been used to argue that the hippocampus is necessary for episodic memory in adults (Vargha-Khadem et al., 1997). However, the results of selective, bilateral hippocampal damage occurring in childhood appear to differ from those of similar damage occurring in adulthood (Baddeley, Vargha-Khadem, & Mishkin, 2001; Gadian et al., 2000; Vargha-Khadem et al., 1997). The deficits following early injury appear more subtle: Whereas hippocampal damage in adulthood typically results in deficits in both semantic (facts) and episodic (events) memory, damage during childhood results in clear deficits only in episodic memory, showing relatively normal development of semantic memory. For example, these children score in the low-average to average range on indices of semantic memory, such as general intellectual abilities and academic attainments, but they are severely impaired on indices of episodic memory, such as remembering a name, a message, or where a belonging was placed (Gadian et al., 2000; Vargha-Khadem et al., 1997, 2003). Also, in cases with neonatal damage, the memory deficits that these children display become apparent only about the time they first enter school or even later.

Proponents of the maturational or skill-learning view might argue that this difference in outcome can be explained by a difference in the selectivity of the medial temporal lobe between the two conditions, such that whereas the hippocampus is damaged in both, only the patients with early-onset damage show substantial sparing of the subhippocampal cortices. This possibility is in line with the suggestion that the hippocampus and the subhippocampal tissue serve different components of explicit memory, with the hippocampus mediating episodic recollection and the subhippocampal cortices mediating semantic memory and familiarity-based recognition (Baddeley et al., 2001; Mishkin, Vargha-Khadem, & Gadian, 1998). However, in the IS view, this difference in outcome can be explained by the fact that the degree of postinjury compensation and reorganization differs between the developing and the mature brain, such that only early damage allows for recovery of the functions found to be spared in early-onset amnesia. As there has currently been no published report directly comparing early-onset with adult-onset amnesia controlling for extent of damage, it is difficult to decide between these two possibilities. One piece of evidence in favor of the maturational view is a recent report indicating that, in the early-onset cases, there is no difference in the degree of long-term memory impairment for those sustaining damage before 1 year of age and those sustaining the damage between 6 and 14 years (Vargha-Khadem et al., 2003). There was evidence of a difference between the groups only on a few tests of immediate recall, where those with neonatal damage performed better than those with later damage.

Interestingly, a functional imaging study of one patient with developmental amnesia (injury neonatally, tested at 22 years of age; Maguire, Vargha-Khadem, & Mishkin, 2001) showed that, although his hippocampi are severely damaged (approximately 50% reduced in volume bilaterally), they are activated in tasks in which controls also activate the hippocampus. Specifically, during retrieval of real-world memories, the patient, Jon, activated the same brain regions as controls, including the hippocampus. Also like controls, activation in Jon's hippocampus was greater for the few autobiographical events he could recall compared to public events and general knowledge. However, in spite of these qualitative similarities, his hippocampal activation was actually greater than controls'. Specifically, he activated many homologous areas on the right that the controls did not, and he also showed a different pattern of connectivity between areas compared to controls (controls showed in-

creased connectivity of hippocampal with parahippocampal regions during retrieval of autobiographical events, whereas Jon showed increased connectivity between the hippocampus and retrosplenial cortex and the medial frontal cortex and retrosplenial cortex). These results are difficult to explain in the maturational view, but could be accounted for by the skill-learning view (Jon activates a different network because he has less memory ability) or the IS view (Jon activates a different network because his early lesions have led to reorganization and compensation).

Language

In adults, left hemisphere lesions that involve perisylvian areas result in a dramatic impairment of speech and language that is typically chronic despite rehabilitation. By contrast, damage to these regions during childhood appears to have no or only subtle effects on ultimate language abilities, and there appear to be no or only subtle effects of side of injury (in cases uncomplicated by epilepsy; e.g., see Bates & Roe, 2001; also reviewed in Vargha-Khadem, Isaacs, Watkins, & Mishkin, 2000). For example, one direct comparison of children (5 to 8 years) and adults found the classic association of left-sided damage with aphasia in adults, but found that children performed within the normal range, with no effect of lesion side (Bates et al., 2001). This result is inconsistent with the maturational view, which would predict a similar pattern of impairment in cases of childhood injury. It is also difficult to reconcile with the skill-learning view, unless the damaged areas are not involved in language learning and are only critical once the skill is fully acquired.

There is some evidence consistent with the idea that the left perisylvian areas critical for language in adults may not be key in language learning in children. This comes from data showing that even in early damage there are significant effects of lesion side and site on first stages of language development, but not involving the left perisylvian areas. For example, early delays in word comprehension and symbolic gesture are somewhat more common with perinatal right hemisphere damage, but only between 10 and 20 months of age (Vicari et al., 2000), and deficits in expressive vocabulary and expressive grammar are more common with perinatal left temporal lobe damage, but only from 10 months to 5 to 6 years (Thal et al., 1991). One interpretation is that, when children are struggling to reproduce familiar sounds from their input language for the first time, they have to extract a great deal of perceptual detail from the input. This might normally rely on the left temporal cortex, because it is known to be involved in extracting detail from perceptual inputs. This explanation is consistent with the skill-learning view and the IS view.

Overall, evidence suggests that younger children may have less consolidated and more bilateral representations of language-processing areas, which derives mostly from increased activation in the right frontal lobe (Gaillard et al., 2000; Holland et al., 2001). For example, PET studies of children who had neurosurgery to treat intractable epilepsy indicate that, especially for language perception tasks, early left hemisphere lesions are associated with enhanced activation of right hemisphere areas, whereas recruitment of regions ipsilateral to the lesions side is limited. Thus, a more diffuse, less consolidated distribution of language networks has been proposed as an explanation for recovery from dominant hemisphere brain injury in children that extends, with diminishing capacity, into adolescence (Boatman et al., 1999; Gaillard et al., 2000; Vargha-Khadem, Isaacs, van der Werf, Robb, & Wilson, 1992). It has been argued that, by adulthood, the functional role of the right hemisphere in aphasia recovery may be more limited compared with that of the perilesional structures in the left hemisphere (Karbe et al., 1998; Weiller et al., 1995).

EFFECTS OF ATYPICAL EARLY EXPERIENCE

The three perspectives on human functional brain development differ in their views as to the effects of early atypical experience. In the maturational view, differences in experience might influence the speed at which a function matures or the ultimate level of performance; in the skill-learning view, any atypical early experiences can potentially be compensated for later in development as the mechanisms for learning remain in operation in the same way; in the IS view, atypical early experiences may have long-lasting effects because they could affect the specialization and localization of function, which may not be able to be altered later in life, when there is less scope for plasticity.

There have been only a limited number of studies examining the effects of atypical early experience in humans. Several studies have examined the influence of early experience on processing of facial information. For example, Pollak and colleagues have found that perception of the facial expression of anger, but not other expressions, is altered in children who experienced the culturally atypical environment of parental abuse. Specifically, they report that, compared to nonabused children, abused children show a response bias for anger (Pollak, Cicchetti, Hornung, & Reed, 2000), identify anger based on less perceptual input (Pollak & Sinha, 2002), show altered category boundaries for anger (Pollak & Kistler, 2002), and show atypical responding to anger on tasks of selective attention (Pollak & Tolley-Schell, 2003). These results suggest that atypical frequency and content of their emotional interactions with their caregivers results in a change in the basic perception of emotional expressions in abused children. Specifically, in this case, children seem to show a hypersensitivity to anger, a finding also supported by ERP studies with this population (Pollak, Cicchetti, Klorman, & Brumaghim, 1997; Pollak, Klorman, Thatcher, & Cicchetti, 2001). However, whether these effects would disappear with sufficient exposure to a normative environment, as the skill-learning view might predict, or reflect more lasting effects, as the IS view might predict, is not clear.

Other studies have taken a different approach and investigate the perception of facial information in children who experienced deprivation of patterned visual input in the early months of life due to bilateral, congenital cataracts. These patients were tested years after their cataracts were removed and they were fitted with contact lenses (i.e., years after visual input had been restored), thus any effects of the few months of deprivation following birth would likely be absent or very minimal, according to the maturation and skill-learning views. However, investigation of these patients reveals persistent deficits in selective aspects of face processing. One study found that patients showed impairments in matching facial identity over changes in viewpoint (and tended to show an impairment in recognizing identity over changes in emotional expression), but performed normally on tests of lip reading, perception of eye gaze, and matching of emotional expressions (Geldart, Mondloch, Maurer, de Schonen, & Brent, 2002). A second study demonstrated that this difficulty in processing facial identity may be due to deficits in processing the spacing among facial features, because patients performed normally in discrimination of faces that differed only on individual features (e.g., mouth), but they were impaired in discrimination of faces that differ only in the spacing of the features (Le Grand, Mondloch, Maurer, & Brent, 2001, 2003, 2004). This was not due to a general impairment in perception of spacing of features, as they performed normally in discriminating nonface patterns whether they differed by the shape of the features or the spacing of the features. These patients also show impairments in holistic processing of faces, which actually allows them to perform better than controls on certain tasks where optimal performance relies on ignoring the whole and focusing on the features (Le Grand et al., 2004). The fact that these impairments persist even after years of visual input to compensate for the early deprivation is not consistent with the maturational or skill-learning views, but is consistent with the IS view that early atypical experience may have long-lasting consequences.

Early experience has also been studied in the context of language development. One question of interest here has been whether adults' second-language acquisition activates the same network as the primary language learned during childhood (consistent with the skill-learning and maturational views) or a different network (consistent with the IS view). Some early reports indicated that bilinguals who learned their second language late showed different activations for the two languages, whereas bilinguals who learned their second language early showed overlapping activations (e.g., Kim, Relkin, Lee, & Hirsch, 1997). However, subsequent studies have suggested that level of skill in the second language, rather than age of acquisition, is the more important variable in determining the degree of overlap of regions activated by the two languages (e.g., Chee, Tan, & Thiel, 1999; Dehaene et al., 1997; Perani et al., 1998), a result consistent with a skill-learning view.

A slightly different approach has been taken by other studies, questioning whether early exposure to a language has any long-lasting consequences. These studies have examined adults who early in life were exposed to one language for a few months or years but then were removed from that language and exposed to another one either because of adoption or emigration. One study examining Korean adults adopted between 3 and 8 years of age by French families found no evidence that the subjects could identify Korean words and no differences in brain activation to Korean versus unknown languages, but did find that the brain activation for French, though it involved the same basic network, was more widespread in the native speakers than in the adoptees (Pallier et al., 2003). Another study found that children who had heard or heard and spoken Korean during the first years of life later showed benefits from this limited early experience in learning Korean during the 1st year of college (Oh, Jun, Knightly, & Au, 2003). These lasting effects of limited periods of early exposure are difficult to explain in the maturational or skill-learning view points, but can be explained in the IS view as the effects of early experience on the specialization of the areas involved in processing speech and language.

CONCLUSIONS

The three perspectives on human functional brain development have different implications for our understanding of developmental disorders and the effects of brain damage over the first years of life. In the maturational view, genetic disorders could potentially lead to focal cortical damage and consequently to selective cognitive, motor, or perceptual disorders. Symptoms of these disorders would first become evident at the normal age of maturation of the regions concerned. However, recent reviews have concluded that there are few, if any, human developmental abnormalities of genetic origin that affect only one or two specific regions of the cortex (Johnson et al., 2002). Rather, structural and functional neuroimaging usually reveal subtle but widespread differences in the brains of groups with developmental disorders. Relatedly, claims of domain-specific cognitive deficits in syndromes such as Autism and Williams's syndrome have been challenged, replaced with hypotheses about different styles or modes of processing (e.g., Karmiloff-Smith, 1998). Finally, it is difficult to explain reports of recovery of functions following early brain damage by the maturational view, without recourse to additional special mechanisms of plasticity.

According to the interactive specialization view, developmental disorders of genetic etiology will often involve disruption of the typical biases and interactions between regions that give rise to adult patterns of cortical functional specialization. In this view, subtle symptoms should be evident from birth, but these will become compounded through the infant's abnormal interactions with its environment. Although there are currently few behavioral studies of developmental disorders during infancy, those that do exist suggest discontinuities in the patterns of behavioral and cognitive deficits through postnatal development. For example, in one such disorder, Williams's syndrome, adults present with behavioral deficits in number tasks but show surprising proficiency in some aspects of language. One study investigated whether this pattern of specific deficits is also observed in infants with Williams's syndrome, as would be expected if they have a damaged innate module for number. Standard infant paradigms for assessing number and object-naming skills were used with toddlers with Williams's syndrome (Paterson et al., 1999). The toddlers did not show the same behavioral profile as observed in adults with the syndrome, indicating that the profile of behavioral deficits in developmental disorders can change during ontogeny and that it is not appropriate to characterize such deficits in terms of damage to domain-specific modules. From the interactive specialization perspective, it may also be easier to understand recovery of function following early damage, as the same mechanisms that ensure specialization during the typical developmental trajectory could ensure a different pattern of specialization.

Both the skill-learning and IS viewpoints share the assumption of dynamic mapping, and this common assumption is overall supported by the evidence reviewed in this chapter. The main points on which these two views differ is regarding whether the brain areas involved in a task are similar or different in children versus adults who have attained a similar level of performance, and whether plasticity decreases with age. There have been relatively few studies directly assessing the former point, and studies aimed at the latter point have been more clearly consistent with the IS view in some domains (e.g., impact of brain injury on language) than others (memory, face processing).

FUTURE DIRECTIONS

Further assessment of the three perspectives on human functional brain development presented in this chapter will require more improved methods for noninvasive functional imaging and more detailed computational models that generate predictions about both neuroanatomy and behavior. With regard to new functional imaging methods, forms of optical imaging (near-infrared spectroscopy, NIRS) offer promise for studying brain function in human infants (Meek, 2002). Like fMRI, NIRS can measure changes in blood oxygenation in the brain that occur following the activation of groups of neurons within an area. Although currently lacking the spatial resolution of fMRI, the method does not involve the exposure to high magnetic fields, noise, and motion sensitivity that make using fMRI with typical infants difficult.

From the age of 6 or 7 years, MRI can be routinely used. Recent advances in MRI analysis techniques will allow the investigation of both structural and functional changes during development. The recent studies using diffusion tensor imaging (DTI) to track the development of white matter demonstrate its usefulness for understanding not only structural brain development but also the functional development of brain networks underlying emerging cognitive skills. For example, a recent study used DTI together with fMRI to study the development of the frontoparietal network involved in working memory. These authors found that DTI measures of frontoparietal white matter correlated with the fMRI response in closely located gray matter in the superior frontal sulcus and inferior parietal lobe. These results suggest that development of white matter could account for increases with age in level of activation of frontoparietal gray matter observed during working memory tasks (Olesen et al., 2004).

The basic method of EEG/ERP has been available for over 50 years, and recent advances in technology and analysis methods have opened up new possibilities for the exploration of brain function in infants and young children. In one such advance, high-density recording systems along with new algorithms for the statistical separation of sources allow better localization of the underlying brain generators of scalp-recorded voltage changes (e.g., Johnson et al., 2001). In another advance, the relation of bursts of high-frequency oscillatory activity in the brain to cognitive and perceptual tasks has begun to be studied in infants, children, and adults (e.g., Csibra, Davis, Spratling, & Johnson, 2000). In one experiment, high-frequency oscillations occurred during periods of time when previously visible objects became occluded, potentially providing a neural correlate of object permanence (Kaufman, Csibra, & Johnson, 2003).

To relate findings on brain structure and development to those on perceptual or cognitive functions, we need the explanatory bridge that can be provided by computational modeling of neural networks. There are major efforts to use connectionist models to explain aspects of typical and atypical cognitive development (Thomas & Karmiloff-Smith, 2002), but very few of these efforts currently allow interpretation of data from functional imaging or neuroanatomy. These types of investigations will provide information regarding which of the three viewpoints best describes the developmental process, and whether the answer to this question depends on the cognitive domain under study and the context in which it develops. Whatever the outcome of these investigations, a better understanding of functional brain development in human infants and children may have profound consequences for educational, clinical, and social policies.

ACKNOWLEDGMENTS

We acknowledge financial support from the United Kingdom Medical Research Council (Program Grant G9715587), Birkbeck College, and the Institute of Child Health.

REFERENCES

Baddeley, A., Vargha-Khadem, F., & Mishkin, M. (2001). Preserved recognition in a case of developmental amnesia: Implications for the acquisition of semantic memory? *Journal of Cognitive Neuroscience, 13,* 357–369.

Ballantyne, A. O., & Trauner, D. A. (1999). Facial recognition in children after perinatal stroke. *Neuropsychiatry, Neuropsychology and Behavioral Neurology, 12,* 82–87.

Barton, J. J. S., Cherkasova, M. V., & O'Connor, M. (2001). Covert recognition in acquired and developmental prosopagnosia. *Neurology, 57,* 1161–1168.

Barton, J. J. S., Cherkasova, M. V., Press, D. Z., Intriligator, J. M., & O'Connor, M. (2003). Developmental prosopagnosia: A study of three patients. *Brain and Cognition, 51,* 12–30.

Bates, E., Reilly, J., Wulfeck, B., Dronkers, N., Opie, M., Fenson, J., et al. (2001). Differential effects of unilateral lesions on language production in children and adults. *Brain and Language, 79,* 223–265.

Bates, E., & Roe, K. (2001). Language development in children with unilateral brain injury. In C. A. Nelson & M. Luciana (Eds.), *Handbook of developmental cognitive neuroscience* (pp. 281–307). Cambridge, MA: MIT Press.

Bentin, S., Deouell, L., & Soroker, N. (1999). Selective streaming of visual information in face recognition: Evidence from Congenital prosopagnosia. *NeuroReport, 10,* 823–827.

Boatman, D., Freeman, J., Vining, E., Pulsifer, M., Miglioretti, D., Minahan, R., et al. (1999). Language recovery after left hemispherectomy in children with late-onset seizures. *Annals of Neurology, 46,* 579–586.

Booth, J. R., Burman, D. D., Meyer, J. R., Zhang, L., Trommer, B. L., Davenport, N., et al. (2003). Neural development of selective attention and response inhibition. *Neuroimage, 20,* 737–751.

Bunge, S. A., Dudukovic, N. M., Thomason, M. E., Vaidya, C. J., & Gabrieli, J. D. (2002). Immature frontal lobe contributions to cognitive control in children: Evidence from fMRI. *Neuron, 33,* 301–311.

Carpenter, P. A., Just, M. A., Keller, T., Cherkassky, V., Roth, J. K., & Minshew, N. (2001). Dynamic cortical systems subserving cognition: FMRI studies with typical and atypical individuals. In J. L. McClelland & R. S. Siegler (Eds.), *Mechanisms of cognitive development* (pp. 353–386). Mahwah, NJ: Erlbaum.

Casey, B. J., Trainor, R. J., Orendi, J. L., Schubert, A. B., Nystrom, L. E., Cohen, J. D., et al. (1997). A pediatric functional MRI study of prefrontal activation during performance of a Go-No-Go task. *Journal of Cognitive Neuroscience, 9,* 835–847.

Chee, M. W., Tan, E. W., & Thiel, T. (1999). Mandarin and English single word processing studied with functional magnetic resonance imaging. *Journal of Neuroscience, 19*(8), 3050–3056.

Chugani, D. C. (2000). Autism. In M. Ernst & J. M. Rumsey (Eds.), *Functional neuroimaging in child psychiatry.* Cambridge, England: Cambridge University Press.

Craft, S., & Schatz, J. (1994). The effects of bifrontal stroke during childhood on visual attention: Evidence from children with sickle cell anemia. *Developmental Neuropsychology, 10*(3), 285–297.

Craft, S., White, D. A., Park, T. S., & Figiel, G. (1994). Visual attention in children with perinatal brain injury: Asymmetric effects of bilateral lesions. *Journal of Cognitive Neuroscience, 6*(2), 165–173.

Csibra, G., Davis, G., Spratling, M. W., & Johnson, M. H. (2000). Gamma oscillations and object processing in the infant brain. *Science, 290,* 1582–1585.

Csibra, G., Tucker, L. A., & Johnson, M. H. (1998). Neural correlates of saccade planning in infants: A high-density ERP study. *International Journal of Psychophysiology, 29,* 201–215.

Damasio, A. R., Tranel, D., & Damasio, H. (1990). Face agnosia and the neural substrates of memory. *Annual Review of Neuroscience, 13,* 89–109.

Deb, S., & Thompson, B. (1998). Neuroimaging in Autism. *Journal of Psychiatry, 173,* 299–302.

de Haan, M., Pascalis, O., & Johnson, M. H. (2002). Specialization of neural mechanisms underlying face recognition in human infants. *Journal of Cognitive Neuroscience, 14,* 199–209.

Dehaene, S., Dupoux, E., Mehler, J., Cohen, L., Paulesu, E., Perani, D., et al. (1997). Anatomical variability in the cortical representation of first and second language. *NeuroReport, 8*(17), 3809–3815.

Durston, S., Thomas, K. M., Yang, Y., Ulug, A. M., Zimmerman, R. D., & Casey, B. J. (2002). A neural basis for the development of inhibitory control. *Developmental Science, 5*(4), F9–F16.

Elman, J. L., Bates, E. A., Johnson, M. H., Karmiloff-Smith, A., Parisi, D., & Plunkett, K. (1996). *Rethinking innateness: A connectionist perspective on development.* Cambridge, MA: MIT Press.

Farah, M. J. (2000). *The cognitive neuroscience of vision.* Oxford, England: Blackwell.

Farah, M. J., Rabinowitz, C., Quinn, G. E., & Liu, G. T. (2000). Early commitment of neural substrates for face recognition. *Cognitive Neuropsychology, 17,* 117–123.

Filipek, P. A. (1999). Neuroimaging in the Developmental Disorders: The State of the Science. *Journal of Child Psychology and Psychiatry, 40*(1), 113–128.

Friston, K. J., & Price, C. J. (2001). Dynamic representation and generative models of brain function. *Brain Research Bulletin, 54*(3), 275–285.

Gadian, D. G., Aicardi, J., Watkins, K. E., Porter, D. A., Mishkin, M., & Vargha-Khadem, F. (2000). Developmental amnesia associated with early hypoxic-ischaemic injury. *Brain, 123,* 499–507.

Gaillard, W. D., Hertz-Pannier, L., Mott, S. H., Barnett, A. S., LeBihan, D., & Theodore, W. H. (2000). Functional anatomy of cognitive development: FMRI of verbal fluency in children and adults. *Neurology, 11,* 180–185.

Gaillard, W. D., Sachs, B. S., Whitnah, J. R., Ahmad, Z., Balsamo, L. M., Petrella, J. R., et al. (2003). Developmental aspects of language processing: FMRI of verbal fluency in children and adults. *Human Brain Mapping, 18,* 176–185.

Gauthier, I., & Nelson, C. A. (2001). The development of face expertise. *Current Opinion in Neurobiology, 11,* 219–224.

Gauthier, I., Tarr, M. J., Anderson, A. W., Skudlarski, P., & Gore, J. C. (1999). Activation of the middle fusiform "face area" increases with expertise in recognizing novel objects. *Nature Neuroscience, 2,* 568–573.

Geldart, S., Mondloch, C. J., Maurer, D., de Schonen, S., & Brent, H. (2002). The effects of early visual deprivation on the development of face processing. *Developmental Science, 5,* 490–501.

Gottlieb, G. (1992). *Individual development and evolution.* New York: Oxford University Press.

Hertz-Pannier, L., Gaillard, W. D., Mott, S. H., Cuenod, C. A., Bookheimer, S. Y., Weinstein, S., et al. (1997). Noninvasive assessment of language dominance in children and adolescents with functional MRI: A preliminary study. *Neurology, 48,* 1003–1012.

Hill-Karrer, J., Karrer, R., Bloom, D., Chaney, L., & Davis, R. (1998). Event-related brain potentials during an extended visual recognition memory task depict delayed development of cerebral inhibitory processes among 6-month-old infants with Down syndrome. *International Journal of Psychophysiology, 29,* 167–200.

Holland, S. K., Plante, E., Byars, A. W., Strawsburg, R. H., Schmithorst, V. J., & Ball, W. S., Jr. (2001). Normal fMRI brain activation patterns in children performing a verb generation task. *Neuroimage, 14,* 837–843.

Isaacs, E. B., Vargha-Khadem, F., Watkins, K. E., Lucas, A., Mishkin, M., & Gadian, D. G. (2003). Developmental amnesia and its relationship to degree of hippocampal atrophy. *Proceedings of the National Academy of Sciences, USA, 100,* 13060–13063.

Johnson, M. H. (2000). Functional brain development in infants: Elements of an interactive specialization framework. *Child Development, 71,* 75–81.

Johnson, M. H. (2001). Functional brain development in humans. *Nature Reviews Neuroscience, 2,* 475–483.

Johnson, M. H. (2005). *Developmental cognitive neuroscience: An introduction.* Oxford, England: Blackwell.

Johnson, M. H., & de Haan, M. (2001). Developing cortical specialization for Visual-Cognitive Function: The case of face recognition. In J. L. McClelland & R. S. Siegler (Eds.), *Mechanisms of cognitive development* (pp. 253–270). Mahwah, NJ: Erlbaum.

Johnson, M. H., de Haan, M., Oliver, A., Smith, W., Hatzakis, H., Tucker, L. A., et al. (2001). Recording and analyzing high-density event-related potentials with infants using the Geodesic Sensor Net. *Developmental Neuropsychology, 19*(3), 295–323.

Johnson, M. H., Halit, H., Grice, S., & Karmiloff-Smith, A. (2002). Neuroimaging of typical and atypical development: A perspective from multiple levels of analysis. *Development and Psychopathology, 14,* 521–536.

Johnson, M. H., Tucker, L., Stiles, J., & Trauner, D. (1998). Visual attention in infants with perinatal brain damage: Evidence of the importance of left anterior lesions. *Developmental Science, 1,* 53–58.

Jones, R. D., & Tranel, D. (2001). Severe developmental prosopagnosia in a child with superior intellect. *Journal of Clinical Experimental Neuropsychology, 23,* 265–273.

Karbe, H., Thiel, A., Weber-Luxenburger, G., Herholz, K., Kessler, J., & Heiss, W. D. (1998). Brain plasticity in poststroke aphasia: What is the contribution of the right hemisphere? *Brain and Language, 64,* 215–230.

Karmiloff-Smith, A. (1998). Development itself is the key to understanding developmental disorders. *Trends in Cognitive Sciences, 2,* 389–398.

Karni, A., & Bertini, G. (1997). Learning perceptual skills: Behavioral probes in to adult cortical plasticity. *Current Opinions in Neurobiology, 7,* 530–535.

Karrer, R., Wojtascek, Z., & Davis, M. (1995). Event-related potentials and information processing in infants with and without Down syndrome. *American Journal on Mental Retardation, 100,* 146–159.

Kaufman, J., Csibra, G., & Johnson, M. H. (2003). Representing occluded objects in the human infant brain. *Proceedings of the Royal Society of London. Series B, Biological Sciences, 270*(Suppl.), 140–143.

Kesler, S. R., Garrett, A., Bender, B., Yankowitz, J., Zeng, S. M., & Reiss, A. L. (2004). Amygdala and hippocampal volumes in Turner syndrome: A high-resolution MRI study of X-monosomy. *Neuropsychologia, 42,* 1971–1978.

Kim, K. H., Relkin, N. R., Lee, K. M., & Hirsch, J. (1997). Distinct cortical areas associated with native and second languages. *Nature, 388*(6638), 171–174.

Klingberg, T., Forssberg, H., & Westerberg, H. (2002). Increased brain activity in frontal and parietal cortex underlies the development of visuospatial working memory capacity during childhood. *Journal of Cognitive Neuroscience, 14,* 1–10.

Kwon, H., Reiss, A. L., & Menon, V. (2002). Neural basis of protracted developmental changes in visuo-spatial working memory. *Proceedings of the National Academy of Sciences, USA, 99,* 13336–13341.

Ladouceur, C. D., Dahl, R. E., & Carter, S. S. (2004). ERP correlates of action monitoring in adolescence. *Annals of the New York Academy of Sciences, 1021,* 329–336.

Laeng, B., & Caviness, V. S. (2001). Prosopagnosia as a deficit in encoding curved surface. *Journal of Cognitive Neuroscience, 13,* 556–576.

Le Grand, R., Mondloch, C. J., Maurer, D., & Brent, H. P. (2001). Early visual experience and face processing. *Nature, 410,* 890.

Le Grand, R., Mondloch, C. J., Maurer, D., & Brent, H. P. (2003). Expert face processing requires visual input to the right hemisphere during infancy. *Nature Neuroscience, 6,* 1108–1112.

Le Grand, R., Mondloch, C. J., Maurer, D., & Brent, H. P. (2004). Impairment in holistic face processing following early visual deprivation. *Psychological Science, 15,* 762–768.

Lehericy, S., Cohen, L., Bazin, B., Samson, S., Giacomini, E., Rougetet, R., et al. (2000). Functional MRI evaluation of temporal and frontal language dominance compared with the Wada test. *Neurology, 54*(8), 1625–1633.

Luna, B., Thulborn, K. R., Munoz, D. P., Merriam, E. P., Garver, K. E., Minshew, N. J., et al. (2001). Maturation of widely distributed brain function subserves cognitive development. *NeuroImage, 13*(5), 786–793.

Maguire, E. A., Vargha-Khadem, F., & Mishkin, M. (2001). The effects of bilateral hippocampal damage on fMRI regional activations and interactions during memory retrieval. *Brain, 124,* 1156–1170.

Malkova, L., Bachevalier, J., Webster, M., & Mishkin, M. (2000). Effects of neonatal inferior prefrontal and medial temporal lesions on learning the rule for delayed nonmatching-to-sample. *Developmental Neuropsychology, 18,* 399–421.

Mancini, J., Casse-Perrot, C., Giusiano, B., Girard, N., Camps, R., Deruelle, C., et al. (1998). Face processing development after a perinatal unilateral brain lesion. *Human Frontiers Science Foundation Developmental Cognitive Neuroscience Technical Report Series* (No. 98.6), 1–40.

Mancini, J., de Schonen, S., Deruelle, C., & Massoulier, A. (1994). Face recognition in children with early right or left brain damage. *Developmental Medicine and Child Neurology, 36,* 156–166.

McPartland, J., & Panagiotides, H. (2001, April). *Neural correlates of Face Perception.* Paper presented at the bi-annual conference of the Society for Research on Child Development, Minneapolis, MN.

Meek, J. (2002). Basic principles of optical imaging and application to the study of infant development. *Developmental Science, 5,* 371–380.

Meunier, M., Bachevalier, J., & Mishkin, M. (1997). Effects of orbital frontal and anterior cingulate lesions on object and spatial memory in rhesus monkeys. *Neuropsychologia, 35,* 999–1015.

Mills, D. L., Alvarez, T. D., St. George, M., Appelbaum, L. G., Bellugi, U., & Neville, H. (2000). Electrophysiological studies of face processing in Williams Syndrome. *Journal of Cognitive Neuroscience, 12,* 47–64.

Mills, D. L., Coffey, C. S. A., & Neville, H. J. (1993). Language acquisition and cerebral specialization in 20-month-old infants. *Journal of Cognitive Neuroscience, 5*(3), 317–334.

Mishkin, M., Vargha-Khadem, F., & Gadian, D. G. (1998). Amnesia and the organization of the hippocampal system. *Hippocampus 8,* 212–216.

Muzik, O., Ager, J., Janisse, J., Shen, C., Chugani, D. C., & Chugani, H. T. (1999). A mathematical model for the analysis of cross-sectional brain glucose metabolism data in children. *Progress in Neuropsychopharmacology and Biological Psychiatry, 23,* 589–600.

Neville, H. J., Mills, D. L., & Bellugi, U. (1994). Effects of altered auditory sensitivity and age of language acquisition on the development of language-relevant neural systems: Preliminary studies of Williams Syndrome. In S. H. Broman & J. Grafman (Eds.), *Atypical cognitive deficits in developmental disorders: Implications for brain function* (pp. 67–83). Hillsdale, NJ: Erlbaum.

Neville, H. J., Mills, D. L., & Lawson, D. (1992). Fractionating language: Different neural sub-systems with different sensitive periods. *Cerebral Cortex, 2,* 244–258.

Nunn, J. A., Postma, P., & Pearson, R. (2001). Developmental prosopagnosia: Should it be taken at face value? *Neurocase, 7,* 15–27.

Oh, J. S., Jun, S.-A., Knightly, L. M., & Au, T. K. (2003). Holding on to childhood language memory. *Cognition, 86,* B53–B64.

Olesen, P. J., Nagy, Z., Westerberg, H., & Klingberg, T. (2003). Combined analysis of D.T.I. & fMRI data reveals a joint maturation of white and grey matter in a fronto-parietal network. *Brain Research: Cognitive Brain Research, 18,* 48–57.

Olesen, P. J., Westerberg, H., & Klingberg, T. (2004). Increased prefrontal and parietal activity after training of working memory. *Nature Neuroscience, 7,* 75–79.

Oliver, A., Johnson, M. H., Karmiloff-Smith, A., & Pennington, B. (2000). Deviations in the emergence of representations: A neuroconstructivist framework for analysing developmental disorders. *Developmental Science, 3,* 1–23.

Pallier, C., Dehaene, S., Poline, J.-B., LeBihan, D., Argenti, A.-M., Dupoux, E., et al. (2003). Brain imaging of language plasticity in adopted adults: Can a second language replace the first? *Cerebral Cortex, 13,* 155–161.

Passarotti, A. M., Paul, B. M., Bussiere, J. R., Buxton, R. B., Wong, E. C., & Stiles, J. (2003). The development of face and location processing: An fMRI study. *Developmental Science, 6*(1), 100–117.

Paterson, S. J., Brown, J. H., Gsödl, M. K., Johnson, M. H., & Karmiloff-Smith, A. (1999). Cognitive modularity and genetic disorders. *Science, 286,* 2355–2358.

Perani, D., Paulesu, E., Galles, N. S., Dupoux, E., Dehaene, S., Bettinardi, V., et al. (1998). The bilingual brain: Proficiency and age of acquisition of the second language. *Brain, 121*(10), 1841–1852.

Peterson, B. S., Vohr, B., Kane, M. J., Whalen, D. H., Schneider, K. C., Katz, K. H., et al. (2002). A functional magnetic resonance imaging study of language processing and its cognitive correlates in prematurely born children. *Pediatrics, 110,* 1153–1162.

Pinter, J. D., Eliez, S., Schmitt, J. E., Capone, G. T., & Reiss, A. L. (2001). Neuroanatomy of Down's syndrome: A high-resolution MRI study. *American Journal of Psychiatry, 158,* 1659–1665.

Poldrack, R. A. (2002). Neural systems for perceptual skill learning. *Behavioral and Cognitive Neuroscience Reviews, 1,* 77–83.

Poldrack, R. A., Desmond, J. E., Clover, G. H., & Gabrieli, J. D. E. (1998). The neural basis of visual skill learning: An fMRI study of mirror-reading. *Cerebral Cortex, 8,* 1–10.

Poldrack, R. A., & Gabrieli, J. E. (2001). Characterizing the neural mechanisms of skill learning and repetition priming: Evidence from mirror reading. *Brain, 124,* 67–82.

Pollak, S. D., Cicchetti, D., Hornung, K., & Reed, A. (2000). Recognizing emotion in faces: Developmental effects of child abuse and neglect. *Developmental Psychology, 36,* 679–688.

Pollak, S. D., Cicchetti, D., Klorman, R., & Brumaghim, J. (1997). Cognitive brain event-related potentials and emotion processing in maltreated children. *Child Development, 68,* 773–787.

Pollak, S. D., & Kistler, D. J. (2002). Early experience is associated with the development of categorical representations of facial expressions of emotion. *Proceedings of National Academy of Sciences USA, 99,* 9072–9076.

Pollak, S. D., Klorman, R., Thatcher, J. E., & Cicchetti, D. (2001). P3b reflects maltreated children's reactions to facial display of emotion. *Psychophysiology, 38,* 267–274.

Pollak, S. D., & Sinha, P. (2002). Effects of early emotional experience on children's recognition of facial displays of emotion. *Developmental Psychology, 38,* 784–791.

Pollak, S. D., & Tolley-Schell, S. A. (2003). Selective attention to facial emotion in physically abused children. *Journal of Abnormal Psychology, 112,* 323–338.

Pujol, J., Deus, J., Losilla, J. M., & Capdevila, A. (1999). Cerebral lateralization of language in normal left-handed people studied by functional MRI. *Neurology, 52*(5), 1038–1043.

Rumsey, J. M., & Ernst, M. (2000). Functional neuroimaging of autistic disorders. *Mental Retardation and Developmental Disabilities Research Reviews, 6,* 171–179.

Schlaggar, B. L., Brown, T. T., Lugar, H. L., Visscher, K. M., Miezin, F. M., & Petersen, S. E. (2002). Functional neuroanatomical differences between adults and school-age children in the processing of single words. *Science, 296,* 1476–1479.

Schumann, C. M., Hamstra, J., Goodlin-Jones, B. L., Lotspeich, L. J., Kwon, H., Buonocore, M. H., et al. (2004). The amygdala is enlarged in children but not adolescents with Autism; the hippocampus is enlarged at all ages. *Journal of Neuroscience, 24,* 6392–6401.

Springer, J. A., Binder, J. R., Hammeke, T. A., Swanson, S. J., Frost, J. A., Bellgowan, P. S. F., et al. (1999). Language dominance in neurologically normal and epilepsy subjects: A functional MRI study. *Brain, 122*(11), 2033–2046.

Tamm, L., Menon, V., & Reiss, A. L. (2002). Maturation of brain function associated with response inhibition. *Journal of the American Academy of Child and Adolescent Psychiatry, 41,* 1231–1238.

Thal, D., Marchman, V., Stiles, J., Aram, D., Trauner, D., Nass, R., et al. (1991). Early lexical development in children with focal brain injury. *Brain and Language, 40,* 491–527.

Thomas, K. M., & Karmiloff-Smith, A. (2002). Are developmental disorders like cases of adult brain damage? Implications from connectionist modeling. *Behavioral and Brain Sciences, 25*(6), 727–788.

Thomas, K. M., King, S. W., Franzen, P. L., Welsh, T. F., Berkowitz, A. L., Noll, D. C., et al. (1999). A developmental functional MRI study of spatial working memory. *Neuroimage, 10,* 327–338.

Ungerleider, L. G., Doyon, J., & Karni, A. (2002). Imaging brain plasticity during motor skill learning. *Neurobiology of Learning and Memory, 76,* 553–564.

Vargha-Khadem, F., Gadian, D. G., Watkins, K. E., Connelly, A., Van Paesschen, W., & Mishkin, M. (1997). Differential effects of early hippocampal pathology on episodic and semantic memory. *Science, 277,* 376–380.

Vargha-Khadem, F., Isaacs, E., van der Werf, S., Robb, S., & Wilson, J. (1992). Development of intelligence and memory in children with hemiplegic cerebral palsy: The deleterious consequences of early seizures. *Brain, 115,* 315–329.

Vargha-Khadem, F., Isaacs, E., Watkins, K., & Mishkin, M. (2000). Ontogenetic specialization of hemispheric function. In J. M. Oxbury, C. E. Polkey, & M. Duchowney (Eds.), *Intractable focal epilepsy: Medical and surgical treatment* (pp. 405–418). London, England: Harcourt.

Vargha-Khadem, F., & Mishkin, M. (1997). Speech and Language outcome after hemispherectomy in childhood. In I. Tuxhorn, H. Holthausen, & H. E. Boenigk (Eds.), *Paediatric epilepsy syndromes and their surgical treatment* (pp. 774–784). London: Libbey Press.

Vargha-Khadem, F., Salmond, C. H., Watkins, K. E., Friston, K. J., Gadian, D. G., & Mishkin, M. (2003). Developmental amnesia: Effect of age at injury. *Proceedings of the National Academy of Sciences, USA, 100,* 10055–10060.

Vargha-Khadem, F., Watkins, K. E., Price, C. J., Ashburner, J., Alcock, K. J., Connelly, A., et al. (1998). Neural basis of an inherited speech and language disorder. *Proceedings of the National Academy of Sciences, USA, 95*(21), 12695–12700.

Vicari, S., Albertoni, A., Chilosi, A. M., Cipriani, P., Cioni, G., & Bates, E. (2000). Plasticity and reorganization during language development in children with early brain injury. *Cortex, 36*(1), 31–46.

Watkins, K. E., Dronkers, N. F., & Vargha-Khadem, F. (2002). Behavioral analysis of an inherited speech and language disorder: Comparison with acquired aphasia. *Brain, 125*(3), 452–464.

Weiller, C., Isensee, C., Rijntjes, M., Huber, W., Muller, S., Bier, D., et al. (1995). Recovery from Wernicke's aphasia: A positron emission tomographic study. *Annals of Neurology, 37,* 723–732.

CHAPTER 5

The Development of the Prefrontal Cortex: The Maturation of Neurotransmitter Systems and Their Interactions

FRANCINE M. BENES

For many decades, the prevailing view concerning disorders of the central nervous system was that they were either neurological or psychiatric in nature. Neurological disorders were considered to be those that altered the substance of the brain; psychiatric disorders were those that involved the emotions and were functional in nature. With the advent of pharmacological agents effective in the treatment of psychosis, depression, and anxiety, it became clear that a mental illness might entail alterations of brain circuitry and, in this respect, bear some similarity to the neurological disorders. This perspective has provided an impetus for

investigations of the pathophysiology and treatment of mental illness that have burgeoned over the past 30 years. This period has been characterized by a significant change in the approach of psychologists and neuroscientists to the study of psychopathology (Cicchetti, 1993; Cicchetti & Cannon, 1999; Cicchetti & Sroufe, 2000; Rutter & Sroufe, 2000) and how we conceptualize the etiology of mental illness during childhood, adolescence, and adulthood (Benes, 1995). Specifically, multiple levels of analysis are needed to understand how adaptation versus maladaptation contributes to normal and abnormal development, respectively

(Cicchetti & Dawson, 2002). Although Schizophrenia has been more extensively studied in recent years, affective and anxiety disorders also are addressed.

A popular hypothesis for the etiology of Schizophrenia has been that patients with this disorder might have excessive amounts of dopaminergic activity (Carlsson, 1978). With previous family studies revealing a higher incidence of Schizophrenia among the relatives of schizophrenics (Kety, Rosenthal, Wender, & Schulsinger, 1968), it was suggested that a genetic factor might be responsible for the proposed increase of dopaminergic activity (Kety & Matthysse, 1972). Viewing Schizophrenia as a genetically transmitted disorder, however, left certain clinical observations unexplained. For example, the concordance rate for Schizophrenia among monozygotic twins was found to be only 40% to 50% (Gottesman & Shields, 1972; Kety, 1983), making it virtually impossible to explain the occurrence of this disorder solely on the basis of an inherited trait. In addition, because many schizophrenics show a characteristic deterioration of functioning during the first several years of illness, at one time it seemed that a neurodegenerative process might be involved in the etiology of this disorder. It is noteworthy that several studies have indicated that schizophrenics as a group have a much higher than expected incidence of obstetrical complications (Jacobsen & Kinney, 1980; Keshavan, 2003; Parnas et al., 1982). More recently, subjects with Bipolar Disorder have also been found to have similar birthing histories (Kinney, Yurgelun-Todd, Tohen, & Tramer, 1998; Kinney et al., 1993). The most prevalent type of birth complication noted was prolonged labor. Because this is thought to be associated with hypoxemia, some believed that an early brain insult occurring in this setting might be a risk factor for Schizophrenia.

It has long been thought that Schizophrenia might represent a heterogeneous group of disorders, with some patients having a genetically transmitted disease and others a neurodegenerative one. This idea has had some appeal because these two etiologies could potentially explain some of the differences in the clinical appearance of schizophrenic patients. For example, some patients show a preponderance of so-called positive symptoms, such as hallucinations and delusions, and others show a preponderance of negative symptoms, such as poor motivation, flat affect, anhedonia, and anergia. Schizophrenics with prominent negative symptoms were found to be more likely to show volume loss in computerized axial tomography scans of their brains. This typology, however, has failed to account for the fact that most schizophrenic patients show the occurrence of both positive and negative features and cannot be easily segre-

gated into these two distinct categories. In addition, obstetrical complications alone could not explain the occurrence of neurodegeneration because birth complications are not exclusively found in the past records of schizophrenics. For example, individuals with cerebral palsy have experienced profound brain damage from severe anoxia early in life but carry no increased risk for Schizophrenia. It seemed that a two-factor model for Schizophrenia might better explain these various observations (Parnas et al., 1982), although more recently, some have come to believe that even a five-factor model may be appropriate (Serretti & Olgiati, 2004). According to the two-factor model, if a subtle brain insult occurs in the setting of susceptibility genes for Schizophrenia, then perhaps the two together could give rise to the disorder. Accordingly, a model of Schizophrenia in which both an early brain insult and a predisposing genetic trait are necessary for its occurrence (Parnas et al., 1982) seems more plausible. Such a two-factor model of Schizophrenia is consistent with Hebb's (1949) idea that both constitution and environment play central roles in the occurrence of mental illness. Interestingly, a model of this type could help explain some of the heterogeneity of Schizophrenia as a result of varying degrees of brain insult and/or genetic loading. Moreover, the precise time during early development when a brain insult occurs could further determine the specific aspects of brain circuitry that are disrupted, and this, in turn, might influence the specific behavioral manifestations that are observed clinically.

A key issue for a two-factor model of Schizophrenia is to identify the susceptibility genes for the disorder. Although evidence for a primary defect in dopamine transmission has not been forthcoming, some investigators have looked to other, more accessible phenotypic markers. For example, alterations of smooth-pursuit eye movements that have been found in both schizophrenics and their first-degree relatives could be related to a fundamental difference in the constitution of an individual who carries a gene for Schizophrenia (Holzman et al., 1988). Similarly, the schizotypal personality trait, which is more prevalent among the first-degree relatives of schizophrenics than it is among those without Schizophrenia (Kety, 1985), could also represent a predisposing constitutional trait (Parnas et al., 1982). Because schizotypes characteristically are withdrawn, are suspicious, have magical thinking, and experience some perceptual disturbances (*Diagnostic and Statistical Manual of Mental Disorders IV*, American Psychiatric Association, 1994), it is not difficult to imagine that an individual with such a personality profile, when exposed to an early brain insult, could develop the more exaggerated symptoms seen in Schizophrenia. Thus far, other types of clinical markers, such as antisaccades (Levy et al., 2004) and visual motion integration (Chen, Bidwell, & Holzman, 2005; Levy et al., 2004), have not been found to be cofamilial traits for Schizophrenia.

The discussion that follows addresses the question of how developmental neurobiology can provide a framework for investigating the nature, course, and etiology of psychiatric disorders. The chapter begins with a discussion of how we might conceptualize the interaction of constitution with environment in determining patterns of human personality and behavior. Next, the basic nature of personality is discussed in relation to several core defects in Schizophrenia that may help identify corticolimbic brain regions involved in aspects of the personality that are disturbed in Schizophrenia. This is followed by a review of the ontogenesis of corticolimbic brain areas and the major neurotransmitter systems found in them. This latter discussion lays the groundwork for a description of some recent postmortem findings in Schizophrenia research and a discussion of how neurodevelopmental disturbances theoretically could have given rise to them. Finally, the chapter concludes with a discussion of the future directions that neurobiologic studies of Schizophrenia and other psychiatric disorders, such as Bipolar Disorder, might follow so that a neurodevelopmental understanding of mental illness can eventually emerge. Overall, a basic premise of this discussion is that information in the brain is processed by distributed groups of neurons that maintain a functional interconnection based on experiential demands rather than by a strictly genetically determined scheme (Cicchetti & Dawson, 2002).

CONSTITUTION AND THE ENVIRONMENT AS DETERMINANTS OF PERSONALITY AND VULNERABILITY

Through the pioneering work of Jerome Kagan, the idea that there is a neurobiologic basis for constitutional differences among human subjects has gained widespread acceptance. This concept has grown out of the observation that a distinct subgroup of children can be identified by their fearful response to novel settings (Kagan, Reznick, Snidman, Gibbons, & Johnson, 1988). These so-called inhibited children show distinct changes in heart rate, blood pressure, and glucocorticoid release when presented with unfamiliar settings (Kagan, Resnick, & Snidman, 1988). A similar constitutional subtype in cats is also recognized. These "harm-avoidant" cats show a reduced ability to in-

teract socially with strangers and tend to hide when presented with novel stimuli (Adamec, 1991). In these fearful felines, there is an increase in the firing of neurons in the basomedial amygdala and the ventromedial hypothalamus (Adamec, 1978). It is noteworthy that the harm-avoidant temperament in cats appears very early in postnatal life, when early experience tends to bring out innate differences in temperament (Adamec, Stark-Adamec, & Livingston, 1980). For example, kittens showing more exploratory tendencies show aggressive responses to rats, whereas those with harm-avoidant tendencies become defensive when exposed to rats early in development. If a defensive cat is exposed to a dead prey, a decrease of defensive behavior is noted. Thus, postnatal experience may modify the basic temperament of cats (Adamec et al., 1980). The inhibited temperament in children also shows a tendency for postnatal modification (Kagan, Reznick, & Gibbons, 1989; Kagan, Reznick et al., 1988; Kagan & Snidman, 1991a, 1991b). For example, when inhibited children were reevaluated at age 4, their harm-avoidant patterns, in many instances, were less apparent. Experiential factors, such as parental reinforcement of nonavoidant behaviors, might serve to modify basic constitutional tendencies and become integrated as part of a child's temperament. Results from behavioral and neuroimaging studies support the view that continued development of emotional expression is related to the functional maturation of specific neural regions, such as the amygdala, throughout childhood and adolescence (Herba & Phillips, 2004).

The idea that aspects of the temperament are environmentally influenced was first suggested by the observations of Spitz (1949) of children reared either in a stimulus-enriched, nurturant environment or in an environment with both social and sensory isolation. The latter group developed an "anaclitic" depression characterized by withdrawal, lack of curiosity, and infection proneness. An animal model for environmental effects on the development of behavioral characteristics was later developed in primates to investigate whether social isolation during critical periods of early postnatal life might result in a permanent tendency toward social isolation (Harlow, 1958; Harlow, Dodsworth, & Harlow, 1965). It was found that isolative behavior can be modified by exposure of young monkeys to other, more gregarious monkeys.

Cloninger (1991) described two additional basic temperaments identifiable in humans. The "novelty-seeking" type includes features such as exploratory excitability, impulsiveness, extravagance, and disorderliness; the "reward-dependent" type shows sentimentality, persistence, attachment, and dependence. As suggested earlier, the schizotypal personality may be another constitutional variant in humans. It would be difficult to fit every individual into such categories, but aspects of several prototypes may occur in a variety of permutations and account for the diverse array present in the general population.

This discussion supports the general notion that an innate tendency toward certain behavioral responses occurs in higher mammals, particularly humans, but this can be modified by experience early in life. Each individual may carry a predisposition to certain types of basic behavioral responses, but it is likely that each also has experienced extensive modification of a constitutional framework through environmental experience. It might be operationally useful to define the individual personality as a complex function in which a dynamic equilibrium exists between basic constitution and cumulative experience (environment; Figure 5.1). According to such a model, constitution and experience would be interacting throughout the lifetime of an individual, and both would have the ability to continually modify the other. The cumulative experience of an individual and its interplay with basic constitutional tendencies would influence not only how that person responds to subsequent experience, but also how normal changes in brain maturation (see following discussion) might alter the overall response set or personality of the individual. The idea that personality is not immutable, but fluid, has come from the provocative work of Vaillant (1983), in which the "alcoholic personality," with its passive, dependent features, was found to be a state-dependent phenomenon. Individuals who have abstained from alcohol for long periods of time do not show this profile.

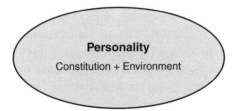

Personality
Constitution + Environment

Figure 5.1 Interaction of constitution and environment as determinants of personality. Constitution may be a genetically defined set of behavioral responses that interplay with environmental events. During the life of an individual, these two factors interact in a reciprocal fashion and give rise to what we identify as "personality." In individuals at risk for mental illness, constitution may impart selective vulnerability to individuals who have various abnormal genes related to the psychiatric disorders. In such individuals, environmental factors can influence whether and/or the degree to which the selective vulnerability is expressed.

With regard to the question of how postnatal development may play a role in the occurrence of the mental disorders, the previous remarks provide some clues. Each individual who presents with a particular mental disorder may have a preexisting set of constitutional and experiential determinants that will contribute to the nature, course, and prognosis of that illness. As noted, for a person at risk for Schizophrenia, a schizotypal constitution may provide a predisposing substrate in which an early brain injury might produce the full schizophrenic syndrome. Moreover, the severity of a brain insult could potentially determine how responsive the individual might be to conventional treatments and how debilitating the illness is. For example, schizophrenics who show evidence of volume loss in their brain also show impaired performance on neuropsychological tests and only a partial response to antipsychotic medication (Weinberger, 1987). Thus, the specific ways in which constitutional and experiential factors interact for a particular individual theoretically may result in differences in both the degree of vulnerability and the severity of the resulting illness.

THE CORTICOLIMBIC SYSTEM

There are several aspects of human behavior mediated by the corticolimbic system that are abnormal in Schizophrenia.

Personality and the Symptoms of Schizophrenia

In evolving a developmental psychopathology of the mental disorders, it is necessary to consider how the risk factors for each may alter circuitry. To do this, it is necessary to understand the mechanisms through which various types of human behavior are integrated within the central nervous system. MacLean (1990) has suggested that a careful analysis of psychiatric disorders can potentially help us to identify such mechanisms. Toward this end, an initial step is to consider what brain regions can be reasonably implicated in the generation of a particular syndrome, an approach that has been applied to the study of Schizophrenia (Benes, 1993a, 1993b).

The symptoms of Schizophrenia typically involve changes of emotion, motivation, attentional responses, sociability, and reasoning. These same general categories of behavior are also affected in Bipolar Disorder, but there are significant differences in their phenotypic expression. In a broad sense, the behaviors disturbed in Schizophrenia and Bipolar Disorder are also central features of personality, which is defined by *Dorland's Medical Dictionary* (1974, p. 1170) as "the total reaction of an individual to the surrounding environment." It has been suggested that alterations of temperament can be induced in both monkeys (Ward, 1948a, 1948b) and humans (Tow & Whitty, 1953) following surgical ablations of certain corticolimbic regions, such as the anterior cingulate cortex. In the discussion that follows, several features of personality, known to be abnormal in psychotic disorders, are considered in relation to the anterior cingulate cortex and other corticolimbic areas with which it is extensively connected.

Affectivity

A hallmark feature of Schizophrenia, particularly when it takes a chronic course, is a progressive disappearance of affect (Bleuler, 1952). Schizophrenics characteristically show a facial expression that lacks emotion, a reflection of their inability to generate appropriate affective responses to surrounding events. In some cases, an affective response is noted but is inappropriate; in others, it may be "shallow." In general, schizophrenics are unable to tolerate a high degree of emotion expressed by others around them; such an occurrence seems to predispose them to relapse (Barrelet, Ferrero, Szogethy, Giddey, & Pellizzer, 1990).

Emotional conditioning and anxiety responses are behaviors that first became apparent in mammals. They are probably mediated in part by phylogenetically primitive brain regions such as the brain stem reticular formation, hypothalamus, septal nuclei, and amygdala. This would help to account for the suggestion that fearfulness in cats appears to be modulated by these same limbic structures (Adamec, 1992). The participation of the amygdala in emotional responses was first highlighted by the work of Kluver and Bucy (1937), in which temporal lobe lesions in monkeys were associated with "psychic blindness," whereby events seem to lose their emotional implications.

Although the brain mechanisms associated with emotion continued to elude study by the neuroscience community, the past 10 years has brought a renaissance of interest in this area. For example, it is now well recognized that the amygdala plays a central role in fear conditioning (Ledoux, 2000a, 2000b). Many aspects of these responses involve the subcortical connectivity of the amygdala; however, the participation of the hippocampus is probably equally critical. Indeed, oscillatory rhythms typically associated with normal hippocampal activity have also been recorded from the amygdala (Pare & Collins, 2000). This is not surprising given the extensive connectivity that exists between these latter two regions. It is becoming increasingly clear that the learning and memory normally associated with hippocampal function may be driven, at least in part, by discharges of activity from the basolateral nuclear complex. Equally important is the connectivity between these two regions and the anterior cingulate cortex. Together they constitute the great limbic lobe delineated by Broca (1878).

Selective Attention

Bleuler (1952) was perhaps the first to emphasize that schizophrenics have great difficulty selectively focusing; this is reflected in their low scores on the continuous performance task (CPT; Kornetsky & Orzack, 1978). This loss of selective attention in Schizophrenia may be due to a defective central filtering mechanism (Detre & Jarecki, 1971) that gives rise to overinclusive thinking (Cameron, 1938; Payne & Friedlander, 1962). Typically, patients with Schizophrenia cannot distinguish relevant from irrelevant objects in their perceptual field, a defect that seems to arise early in the course of the illness and one that might involve an impairment of inhibitory mechanisms (McGhie & Chapman, 1961; see later discussion). Some believe that the cingulate and parietal cortices may cooperate in the performance of directed attention (Mesulam, 1983). In monkeys, lesions of the anterior cingulate cortex bilaterally have been associated with neglect of surrounding objects and even cage mates (Glees, Cole, Whitty, & Cairns, 1950). A similar syndrome has been observed in cats with cingulate ablations (Kennard, 1955). In humans with bilateral infarction of the cingulate gyrus, a lack of attentiveness to the surrounding environment has been observed (Laplane, Degos, Baulac, & Gray, 1981). Moreover, a recent cerebral blood flow study reported that human subjects show a marked increase of activity in the anterior cingulate region during performance of a Stroop attentional conflict paradigm (Pardo, Pardo, Janer, & Raichle, 1990). In schizophrenic subjects, a slower response to targets in the right, but not the left, visual fields, and attentional deficits similar to those following left hemispheric lesions were also noted (Posner, Early, Reisman, Pardo, & Dhawan, 1988).

It is noteworthy that abnormalities of smooth-pursuit eye movements have been found in schizophrenics and in their first-degree relatives and could reflect a latent trait for this disorder (Holzman et al., 1988). The neglect occurring with lesions of the cingulate cortex is thought to involve alterations in the relationship of the cingulate region with frontal eye field 8 (Belaydier & Maugierre, 1980), but this may be an indirect effect mediated through connections of this region with the prefrontal and inferior parietal areas. Nevertheless, the smooth-pursuit abnormalities seen in schizophrenic subjects may reflect a role of frontal eye field 8 in the attentional deficits also seen in patients with this disorder. Patients with unilateral neglect syndromes arising from lesions of the frontal or parietal regions also show some emotional disturbances, and these defects are consistent with a "parallelism in the integrity of attention and emotion" (Mesulam & Geschwind, 1978, p. 252), a concept that Bleuler first suggested to be pertinent to our understanding of Schizophrenia.

Motivation

A defect of motivation is another core feature of Schizophrenia. A model for understanding loss of motivation and interest comes from the description of massive frontal lobe lesions resulting in the apathico-akinetico-abulic syndrome (Luria, 1973). As in Schizophrenia, individuals with such lesions are passive, lack desires, and have poor hygiene (Luria, 1973). In some studies, schizophrenics who failed to activate cerebral blood flow in the dorsolateral prefrontal cortex also performed poorly on the Wisconsin Card Sort, a functional marker for this area (Weinberger, Berman, & Zec, 1986), and the differences did not appear to be related to either poor attention or global cortical dysfunction (Berman, Zec, & Weinberger, 1986). Using near-infrared imaging, studies of executive function using the Stroop interference paradigm have demonstrated significant differences between children and adults in the prefrontal area (Schroeter, Zysset, Wahl, & von Cramon, 2004). Presumably, significant changes are occurring during adolescence, when Schizophrenia typically begins. Accordingly, the timing of such developmental changes could play a critical role in determining the nature of the clinical deficits noted in patients with Schizophrenia.

Bleuler (1952) may have been the first to suspect a link between affect and motivation. He wrote, "The will, a resultant of all the various affective and associative processes, is of course disturbed in a number of ways, but above all by the breakdown of the emotions" (p. 70). The interaction of motivation and affect in humans is illustrated by a distinctive syndrome called akinetic mutism, seen in patients with bilateral destructive lesions of the anterior cingulate cortex (Barris & Schumann, 1953). Acute infarctions of this type are associated with an inability to move or speak, as well as considerable negativism. This is quite similar to the catatonic state in which muteness, lack of movement, and negativism are also observed. Patients who had akinetic mutism arising from bilateral occlusion of the anterior cerebral arteries and who later recovered have described a sudden loss of the experience of affect and a concomitant absence of the will to move (Damasio & Van Hoesen, 1983). A similar concurrence of defects in motivation and emotional experience, as seen in Schizophrenia, could arise from a disturbance in communication between the dorsolateral prefrontal area and the anterior cingulate cortex. A recent imaging study has demonstrated that there is a reduced correlation of structural parameters between the cingulate gyrus and prefrontal area (Mitelman, Shihabuddin, Brickman, Hazlett, & Buchsbaum, 2005), a change that implies that there is probably an imbalance in the functional interactions between these two regions in Schizophrenia.

Sociability

Schizophrenics have great difficulty engaging in relationships with other people, and this results in marked isolation. It is no surprise that these patients rarely marry and raise families. Female schizophrenics, in general, are unable to nurture their children. The inability of these patients to relate to others and share empathetically in their feeling states is probably central to their impaired social skills, both within family units and outside them.

The cingulate gyrus has been implicated in the mediation of interpersonal relations because ablations of this region are associated with a loss of maternal activities, such as nursing, nest building, and retrieval of the young (Slotnick, 1967; Stamm, 1955). It has been suggested that separation calls and play activities, key features associated with the appearance of social interaction, may have emerged in parallel with the development of the cingulate gyrus during the phylogenetic progression of reptiles into mammals (MacLean, 1985). MacLean has suggested that separation calls that also first appeared in mammals may be mediated by the cingulate gyrus. In support of this, vocalizations can be elicited by stimulation of the anterior cingulate region in monkeys (Smith, 1945). More extensive ablations that also include the medial prefrontal cortex and the subcallosal and preseptal cingulate cortices result in a complete loss of spontaneous isolation calls (MacLean, 1985).

If the cingulate gyrus plays a role in social interactions, it is possible that the unrelatedness and poor social skills typically observed in Schizophrenia may also be related, at least in part, to associated defects in motivation and attentiveness. It seems likely, however, that lack of interest in and neglect of one's surroundings might also contribute to diminished interactiveness.

Logical Processing

One of the most significant core defects in Schizophrenia is a formal thought disorder, in which there are illogical sequences of unrelated concepts. Attempts have been made to characterize the nature of the defective thinking found in schizophrenic patients. Toward this end, methodologies for evaluating the central processing of incoming information have been developed to study thought disorder in these patients. One such study characterized the abnormalities of central integration in schizophrenics as involving serial processing of information, but with a limited channel capacity (Callaway & Naghdi, 1982). It has also been found that, when an informational target stimulus is followed at varying intervals by a noninformational masking stimulus, a temporal delay in a two-choice forced discrimination task is observed in schizophrenics (Saccuzzo & Braff, 1986). This information-processing defect appears to be trait-dependent, rather than an epiphenomenon of the psychotic state, because individuals with the schizotypal personality profile also show it (Saccuzzo & Braff, 1986) . This latter finding implies that the thought disorder seen in Schizophrenia might be a genetically transmitted attribute, perhaps one arising from a specific alteration in neural circuitry. The left inferior parietal lobe has been implicated in the construction of logical grammatical relationships, and patients with focal left inferior parietal lesions demonstrate a marked impairment in the ability to formulate thoughts that involve the communication of relationships among ideas (Luria, 1973). It is noteworthy that neurons in monkeys' posterior parietal cortex are activated by hand-eye coordinated movements, particularly when desirable objects that can satisfy thirst or hunger are used (Mountcastle, Lynch, Georgopoulos, Sakata, & Acuna, 1975). This motivationally driven response is believed to require not only limbic connections with the parietal region but also an attentional component (Mesulam & Geschwind, 1978). Consistent with this proposal, the inferior parietal region has extensive connections with the anterior cingulate cortex and the presubiculum (E. G. Jones & Powell, 1970; Pandya & Kuypers, 1969; Petras, 1971; Seltzer & Pandya, 1978; Seltzer & Van Hoesen, 1979). Thus, interactions of this type may provide at least part of the limbic component to inferior parietal responses to desirable objects.

Luria (1973) emphasized the role of the left (dominant) inferior parietal region in the construction of logical grammatical relationships; he also described unilateral neglect syndromes in patients with right-sided posterior parietal lesions. These patients do not attend to left extracorporeal space, but they also show a peculiar inability to perceive their defects. The failure to perceive one's defects is commonly seen in schizophrenics, who are unable to notice that a listener is unable to comprehend what they are saying. The simultaneous occurrence of illogical thinking and neg-

lect in Schizophrenia is consistent with the idea that both the left and the right inferior parietal areas might be dysfunctional in this disorder. As noted earlier, neglect of the surrounding environment occurs with cingulate lesions, and the coincidence of attentional problems and disturbances of thinking could reflect the extensive connections between the anterior cingulate and inferior parietal cortices.

Corticolimbic Involvement in Disorders of Thought, Perception, Mood, and Anxiety

Based on the discussion of the symptoms of Schizophrenia and the functions of several corticolimbic regions, it has been suggested that the anterior cingulate cortex as well as the dorsolateral prefrontal region, inferior parietal lobe, and hippocampal formation with which it connects, may be of central importance to the symptomatology, and possibly even the etiology, of Schizophrenia. The functions collectively subsumed by these regions cover a broad range of behaviors, including affect, attention, motivation, social behavior, cognition, and the influence of stress on the modulation of these behaviors. It is relevant to this discussion to consider whether other psychiatric disorders may possibly involve alterations in similar cortical regions. In bipolar mood disorder, as mania alternates with depression, patients may show increases or decreases of emotional expression, motivation, attention, interpersonal relations, and thinking. On the one hand, manic individuals typically show rapid thinking and a flight of ideas from one concept to another, frequently of a grandiose nature. On the other hand, patients with depression show thinking that is slowed and often fixated on only certain ideas, usually of a self-deprecatory nature. Opposite disturbances in social behavior also occur in patients with affective disorders, with manic patients being inappropriately interactive or even intrusive, but depressed patients being very withdrawn or isolative. In considering the brain areas that might play a role in these mood disturbances, it is noteworthy that chronically depressed patients show improvement of their mood following bilateral anterior cingulotomy (Ballantine, Cassidy, Flanagan, & Marino, 1967; Tow & Whitty, 1953), a procedure that does not produce deficits in, and may even improve, overall cognitive function (Long, Pueschel, & Hunter, 1978).

Other psychiatric syndromes, such as Panic Disorder and phobias, frequently occur comorbidly with depression. Individuals with phobias have been found to have been prone to separation anxiety as children, and many were branded as school phobics during childhood (Klein, Zitrin, & Woerner, 1978). The suggestion by MacLean (1985) that the cingulate area might mediate separation behaviors (see earlier discussion) could provide a theoretical basis for understanding this syndrome, which also responds well to treatment with antidepressant medication. Another syndrome occurring comorbidly with depression is Panic Disorder, characterized by episodes of acute anxiety in which an individual experiences shortness of breath, tachycardia, profuse sweating, and pallor in response to an irrational perception of impending doom. Because the amygdala (Davis, 2000) and cingulate cortex (Anand & Dua, 1956; Kaada, Pribram, & Epstein, 1949) are involved in the regulation of autonomic visceromotor responses, it is possible that these regions, and/or areas with which they connect, could participate in the generation of panic attacks as well.

"Le Grande Lobe Limbique"

In parallel with the first appearance of mammalian features in vertebrates, Broca (1878) noted that a "limbic lobe," consisting of the septal nuclei, amygdala, hippocampus, parahippocampal (entorhinal) cortex, and cingulate gyrus, appeared along the midsagittal plane of virtually all mammalian forms (Figure 5.2). In 1947, Paul MacLean extended the concept of the limbic system by suggesting that

Comparison of Limbic Lobe and Neocortex in Mammalian Brain

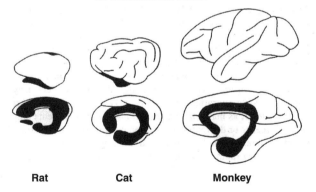

Rat   Cat   Monkey

Figure 5.2 The appearance of the brain in the rat, cat, and monkey, shown both in a lateral (above) and a midsagittal (below) view. All three brains show a contiguous loop (black) of limbic structures (including the cingulate gyrus, parahippocampal gyrus, and amygdala) that has remained remarkably similar during phylogenesis. This so-called limbic lobe is surrounded, above and laterally, by neocortex that has shown a progressive increase during phylogeny. *Source:* From "Studies on Limbic System (Visceral Brain) and Their Bearing on Psychosomatic Problems" (pp. 101–125), by P. D. MacLean, (1954). In *Recent Developments in Psychosomatic Medicine,* E. Wittkower and C. R. Kleghorn (Eds.), Philadelphia: Lippincott.

the human brain is organized into a "triune" system consisting of a reptilian brain (brain stem and other subcortical structures), an old mammalian brain (amygdala and hippocampus) that is responsible for simple feelings and emotional expression, and a new mammalian brain (neocortex) that represents a "voice of reason" in modulating emotional stimuli (MacLean, 1954, 1990).

As noted by MacLean (1985), the elaboration of this limbic lobe coincided with the appearance of audition, vocalization, maternal nurturance, and separation calls by the young, suggesting that the integration of visceral responses with cortically mediated behaviors might have facilitated the protection of young offspring. These behaviors require all three components of the so-called triune brain. Accordingly, the evolutionary trend toward developing more elaborate behaviors has involved a corresponding increase in both the amount and complexity of ties between the brain stem and old mammalian components of the limbic system. Within the spectrum of mammalian forms, there has been a striking increase in the relative proportion of neocortex to Broca's limbic lobe. Figure 5.2 shows a comparison of the limbic lobe in rat, cat, and monkey brain (MacLean, 1954). It is evident from the figure that there has been a progressive increase in the volume of the neocortex surrounding the cingulate and parahippocampal gyri. In primates and humans, this has been accompanied by the most extensive elaboration of connectivity between associative cortical regions, such as the cingulate region and the hippocampal formation, with the subcortical limbic system (Figure 5.3). The brain does not have a specific mechanism for deleting phylogenetically older circuits and instead has integrated older circuits with newly acquired ones within the corticolimbic system. As a result, there has been a progressive increase in the integration of higher cognitive processes with visceral and instinctual behaviors mediated through subcortical limbic structures. In the human brain, this additive tendency that has occurred during phylogeny has probably been adaptive because it is doubtful that the human species could have survived with cortically driven logical planning and volition without the drive that comes from limbically driven emotions.

By examining the regions that compose the corticolimbic system and their interconnections, it can be appreciated that defective integration in one or several of these areas could give rise to abnormalities in the cortical integration of emotional experience, with functions integrated primarily at the neocortical level, such as volition and logic. A psychopathological process—Schizophrenia, for example—that impacts on one or several corticolimbic regions

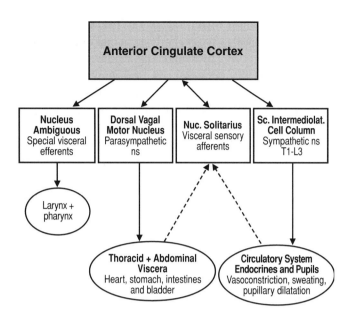

Figure 5.3   The anterior cingulate cortex and its corticobulbar and corticospinal connections, which are involved in the mediation of visceral motor and sensory responses. The anterior cingulate cortex plays a unique role in the integration of affective experience with higher cognitive function via its extensive interactions with both brain stem and spinal centers involved in autonomic processing. Corticobulbar fibers, originating in the anterior cingulate region, project to the nucleus ambiguous and the dorsal vagal motor nucleus and the preganglionic sympathetic fibers of the intermediolateral cell column to influence the outflow of activity to special visceral efferent muscles (e.g., larynx and pharynx), thoracic and abdominal viscera (e.g., the heart, esophagus, stomach, intestines, and bladder), and blood vessels and sweat glands. Extensive connections of the anterior cingulate region with the nucleus solitarius probably influence the inflow of sensory information from all viscera of the body.

could potentially give rise to a broad variety of symptoms that encompass the emotional and cognitive spheres.

The Anatomy of the Corticolimbic System

The corticolimbic system consists of the cingulate gyrus, hippocampal formation, and amygdaloid complex. All of these structures can be found on the midsagittal surface of the mammalian brain, and they interact extensively in the mediation of emotion, attention, and learning.

The Anterior Cingulate Cortex Integrates Visceral Responses with Cognition

Papez (1937) was the first to postulate that the cingulate gyrus may play a central role in the integration of emotional experience with cognition because it not only has extensive connections with the limbic system, but it also has

rich reciprocal connectivity with other associative cortical regions involved in higher cognitive functions. These patterns of connectivity lay the groundwork for the concurrence of visceral responses with thinking. As shown in Figure 5.3, autonomic responses can be altered by either stimulation or ablation of the anterior cingulate cortex. With electrical stimulation of this region in primates, visceromotor responses such as eyelid opening, pupillary dilation, respiratory movements, cardiovascular changes, and piloerection (Anand & Dua, 1956; Kaada et al., 1949; Smith, 1945) have been induced. Notably, changes in facial expression (Smith, 1945) and motor arrest (Dunsmore & Lennox, 1950; Smith, 1945) have also been observed. Extensive surgical ablation of the anterior cingulate cortex, on the other hand, has resulted in a decrease of emotional responsiveness (Ward, 1948a). Personality changes characterized by either inappropriate purring or growling without provocation have been observed in cats with cingulate lesions (Kennard, 1955); in humans, bilateral infarction of the cingulate gyrus has been associated with increased docility and indifference (Laplane et al., 1981). Interestingly, an inability to either express or experience emotion has been described in patients with bilateral cingulate gyrus infarction (Damasio & Van Hoesen, 1983). The decrease in emotional responsiveness seen in cingulotomized patients bears some resemblance to the flat affect seen in schizophrenics.

The anterior cingulate region plays a pivotal role in the integration of the more primitive portions of the limbic system with the evolving neocortex. This region has extensive reciprocal connections with several different cortical areas that include the dorsolateral prefrontal region, the hippocampal formation, and the inferior parietal lobe (E. G. Jones & Powell, 1970; Pandya & Kuypers, 1969; Petras, 1971; Seltzer & Pandya, 1978; Seltzer & Van Hoesen, 1979). Of great importance, the anterior cingulate region also has both afferent and efferent connections with nuclear groups that mediate autonomic functions (Figure 5.3), such as the periaqueductal gray (Beckstead, 1976; Domesick, 1969; Hurley, Herbert, Moga, & Saper, 1991; Wyss & Sripanidkulchai, 1984), the nucleus solitarius, the dorsal motor nucleus of the vagus (Hurley et al., 1991; Terreberry & Neafsey, 1983, 1987; Van der Kooy, McGinty, Koda, Gerfen, & Bloom, 1982), and preganglionic sympathetic neurons in the intermediolateral cell column of the thoracic spinal cord (Hurley et al., 1991). Accordingly, the anterior cingulate cortex interacts directly with centers that mediate both viscerosensory and visceromotor responses in the periphery relationships that are believed to be fundamental to its role in integrating emotional responses at the cortical level (Neafsey, Terreberry, Hurley, Ruit, & Frysztak, 1993). Either ablation (Kennard, 1955; Laplane et al., 1981; Ward, 1948a) or stimulation (Anand & Dua, 1956; Kaada, 1960; Kaada et al., 1949; Smith, 1945) of the anterior cingulate cortex results in both autonomic and affective changes. In humans with documented seizure activity arising from the cingulate cortex (Devinsky & Luciano, 1993), emotional stimulation is a frequent precipitant of ictal activity (Mazars, 1970). The majority of such patients exhibit limbically related features such as temper tantrums and fixed psychoses. In one reported case, a child with cingulate seizures was noted to run toward her mother during ictal episodes (Geier et al., 1977), a manifestation consistent with the proposed role of the cingulate cortex in mammalian separation behaviors (MacLean, 1985). Thus, the various corticolimbic connections of anterior cingulate cortex and the behavioral manifestations associated with its lesions support the idea that this region may play a particularly central role in the integration of limbic functions with higher cognitive processing (Papez, 1937).

The cingulate cortex is connected with the dorsolateral prefrontal area, frontal eye field 8, the inferior parietal lobe, and the hippocampal formation. The entorhinal region provides a key relay of information from the prefrontal area to the hippocampal formation. The prefrontal, anterior cingulate, and entorhinal cortices receive a rich supply of dopamine afferents from the midbrain ventral tegmental area (Lindvall & Bjorklund, 1984). Some of the areas are phylogenetically newer cortical regions (e.g., the dorsolateral prefrontal and inferior parietal regions) and are most extensively developed in the human brain. In contrast, the hippocampal formation is phylogenetically the oldest cortical region that first appeared in a rudimentary form in reptiles (Ulinski, 1990). The cingulate and entorhinal cortices are transitional limbic cortices that first appeared in early mammals and provide a link between the hippocampal formation and the neocortical regions (e.g., the dorsolateral prefrontal and inferior parietal regions) that are particularly well developed in humans.

The Hippocampus and Learning Mechanisms

The hippocampal formation is the oldest portion of the cortex that first appeared in reptiles. It consists of several subregions: the area dentata, sectors CA4-1, the subiculum, and the presubiculum (see Rosene & Van Hoesen, 1987). In the mammalian brain, the hippocampus has retained a characteristic three-layered organization that can be recognized using low-power optics. When examined at higher powers, there are actually five different layers distinguishable in the CA subfields. These include the stratum molec-

ulare, stratum radiatum, stratum pyramidale, stratum oriens, and alveus. The stratum pyramidale contains the majority of neuronal cell bodies; the other four laminae principally contain both efferent and afferent fiber systems. As shown in Figure 5.2, the so-called trisynaptic pathway consists of (1) perforant fibers from the entorhinal cortex that project to the outer molecular layer of the area dentata, (2) mossy fibers from the granule cells of the area dentata that project to the stratum radiatum of CA3, and (3) Schaffer collaterals of pyramidal cells in CA3 that project to the stratum radiatum of CA1.

The Amygdala and Emotionally Stimulated Learning

The amygdala is a complex corticolimbic region that lies at the temporal pole of the mammalian brain. Considered by some to be an "arbitrarily" defined set of cell groups, there are nevertheless subdivisions of this region that can be distinguished by their characteristic architecture, embryogenesis, neurotransmitter profiles, connectivity, and functional roles (Swanson & Petrovich, 1998). These include an olfactory part (central and main) that projects topographically to other regions involved in reproductive, defensive, and ingestive behavior systems in the hypothalamus, a central nucleus (CEA) that projects to autonomic centers in the brain stem, and the frontotemporal system that projects to the striatum, nucleus accumbens, hippocampus, and cortex. The latter system is distinguished from the other, more primitive components of the amygdala by its being a ventral extension of the claustrum; on this basis, it is considered to be a derivative of the frontal and temporal cortex. Whereas the central subdivisions of the amygdala have projection neurons that employ gamma-amino butyric acid (GABA) as a neurotransmitter, thus establishing their homology with the basal ganglia, the projection neurons of the basolateral complex, like those of the cortex, use glutamate as a transmitter.

The basolateral nuclear complex appears to play a complex role in associative learning and attention (Gallagher & Holland, 1994). This region regulates sensorimotor gating of the acoustic startle response (Wan & Swerdlow, 1997) and contributes to fear conditioning, possibly through a mechanism involving its GABAergic interneurons (Stutzmann & LeDoux, 1999). In this latter regard, both the central and basolateral subdivisions seem to contribute to this response. For example, lesions of the central nucleus resulted in a reduction in the suppression of behavior elicited by a conditioned fear stimulus, but the animals were able to direct their actions to avoid further presentations of this aversive stimulus (Killcross, Robbins, & Everitt, 1997). In this same study, rats with lesions of the basolatera complex were unable to avoid the conditioned aversive stimulus by their choice behavior, but exhibited normal conditioned suppression to the stimulus. Thus, it appears that discrete subdivisions of this nucleus probably contribute different components to an integrated emotional response (Killcross et al., 1997) and with recall of emotional information (Cahill & McGaugh, 1998). Although the amygdala is probably not the actual site for long-term storage of explicit or declarative memory, it appears to influence memory-storage mechanisms in other brain regions, such as the hippocampus and neocortex (Killcross et al., 1997). In one case report where there was selective bilateral damage to the amygdala, the subject was unable to acquire conditioned autonomic responses to visual or auditory stimuli, although declarative facts could be successfully paired with unconditioned stimuli (Bechara et al., 1995). The amygdala is probably involved in aversive conditioning, and the hippocampus seems to play a role in contextual associative learning (Selden, Everitt, Jarrard, & Robbins, 1991). Some authors believe the basolateral complex of the amygdala contributes to the plasticity associated with the encoding of Pavlovian fear conditioning (Fanselow & LeDoux, 1999) and may help to guide goal-directed behavior (Schoenbaum, Chiba, & Gallagher, 1998). Rats with lesions of the basolateral complex are insensitive to postconditioning changes in the value of a reinforcer, and this second-order effect is believed to reflect the presence of a positive incentive value for a conditioned stimulus (Hatfield, Han, Conley, Gallagher, & Holland, 1996).

Like the hippocampus, the cingulate cortex also works cooperatively with the basolateral complex in mediating conditioned memory. For example, rabbits with lesions of the amygdala show a decrease of discriminative avoidance learning, and this effect is believed to involve plasticity of cingulothalamic interactions (Poremba & Gabriel, 1997). Overall, the amygdala appears to be necessary for the acquisition, but not the maintenance, of associative learning that occurs when fear is used as a conditioned stimulus.

Stress appears to play a central role in modulating the activity of the basolateral nucleus of the amygdala and influences its memory-modulating systems in relation to emotionally arousing events (for a review, see Cahill & McGaugh, 1998). Both norepinephrine and dopamine show an increased release in the amygdala of stressed animals (for a review, see Stanford, 1993). For the dopamine system, acute stress is associated with a selective increase in the release of this transmitter from the medial prefrontal cortex (Thierry, Tassin, Blanc, & Glowinski, 1976); however, with more prolonged stress, the nucleus accumbens shows a similar increase (Bannon, Wolf, & Roth, 1983; Roth, Tam, Ida, Yang, & Deutch, 1988). More recent work has demon-

strated that the amygdala plays an important role in regulating the response of the medial prefrontal dopamine system to stress (Goldstein, Rasmusson, Bunney, & Roth, 1996). Whether this effect is mediated directly through the basolateral projections to the cortex or occurs indirectly via projections to the centromedian nucleus is not known. The centromedial nucleus projects to the periaqueductal gray (Hopkins & Holstege, 1978), a central relay zone for the regulation of stress-related behaviors such as freezing (LeDoux, Iwata, Cicchetti, & Reis, 1988) that involve brain stem and spinal nuclei that control the larynx, pharynx, and respiratory musculature (Holstege, Tan, Van Ham, & Bos, 1984; Jurgens & Pratt, 1979).

The connections between the amygdaloid complex and the anterior cingulate cortex may be particularly important to understanding the pathophysiology of neuropsychiatric disorders. Layer II of the anterior cingulate region, where a variety of anomalies have been detected in Schizophrenia (see earlier discussion), receives a "massive" input from the basolateral complex of the amygdala (Van Hoesen, Morecraft, & Vogt, 1993). In a series of postmortem studies, an increase of vertical fibers was found in layer II of the anterior cingulate cortex (Benes, Majocha, Bird, & Marotta, 1987; Benes, Sorensen, Vincent, Bird, & Sathi, 1992) and the entorhinal region (Longson, Deakin, & Benes, 1996), but not the prefrontal cortex. Because this latter region does not receive an appreciable input from the amygdala (Van Hoesen et al., 1993), it seemed possible that those fibers showing an increase in the anterior cingulate area might originate in a region that projects to the latter, but not the former. It is intriguing to note that intense glutamate-immunoreactivity localized to vertical axons in superficial layers of the anterior cingulate (Benes, Sorensen, et al., 1992) and entorhinal regions (Longson et al., 1996) has also been described in projection neurons of the basolateral complex (McDonald et al., 1989). Although a direct link between these two neuronal compartments cannot be established with evidence of this type, it seems likely that the basolateral nucleus and the anterior cingulate region may play a particularly important role in the pathophysiology of Schizophrenia and other neuropsychiatric disorders. The hippocampus has also been found to have abnormalities in Schizophrenia and Bipolar Disorder, particularly in sectors CA3 and CA2 (Benes, 2000).

DEVELOPMENT OF THE CORTICOLIMBIC SYSTEM

In any study of the corticolimbic system of the schizophrenic brain, the six-layered organization of the cortex is relevant to consider because alterations that occur in superficial laminae would be more likely to impact on higher cognitive processes. Also noteworthy is the fact that layer II in the anterior cingulate cortex (Van Hoesen et al., 1993) and sectors CA3 and CA2 (Benes & Berretta, 2000) receive significant projections from the basolateral amygdala. As discussed next, these same loci show a variety of abnormalities in both Schizophrenia and Bipolar Disorder. This suggests that the specific connectivity that exists in the corticolimbic system may contribute in specific ways to the pathophysiology of psychotic disorders.

Let's now consider the manner in which components of the corticolimbic system undergo ontogenetic development during pre- and postnatal life. The discussion that follows considers the ontogenesis of the hippocampal formation, followed by the neocortex. The ingrowth of afferents to the cortex and myelination of the cortex are discussed. Finally, the sequential changes that occur for both intrinsic and extrinsic transmitters of the cortex are described. The developmental of the human brain occurs at many different levels, with some that can be observed grossly and others that require sophisticated biochemical and microscopic approaches.

Gyral Development

The development of the cerebral cortex occurs at different rates that, to some extent, reflect phylogeny. There is a gradual tendency for limbic cortical areas to begin to appear during early gestation. For example, at 16 to 19 weeks of embryogenesis, the cingulate gyrus can be distinguished, but this occurs long before the parahippocampal gyrus and hippocampal formation have become discernible in the medial temporal lobe at weeks 20 to 23 (Gilles, 1983). Cortical regions undergo ontogenesis at varying rates that, to some degree, reflect phylogeny (Figure 5.4). The superior and medial frontal gyri (prefrontal regions) do not take on a clear gyral configuration until 24 to 27 weeks of gestational age, and the angular and supramarginal gyri (inferior parietal area) are not distinguished until 28 to 31 weeks (Gilles, 1983). The orbital frontal gyri, which, like the cingulate gyri, are well represented in earlier mammalian forms such as rodents, are among the last to appear.

Perturbations of ontogenesis at various stages of fetal development might be capable of inducing abnormalities in the formation of gyral patterns and corresponding disturbances in specific functional capabilities associated with these regions affected in this way. For example, in subjects with Schizophrenia, obstetrical complications have been found to include viral infections in utero during the second trimester and prolonged labor at the time of birth. It is theoretically possible that a viral infection during the second trimester, if it occurs in an individual who carries the susceptibility for Schizophrenia (Jacobsen & Kinney, 1980; Kinney et al., 2000), might result in a phenotypic form of the illness in which there are more apt to be affective or attentional problems, reflecting damage to the anterior cingulate region. On the other hand, another at-risk individual who is exposed to prolonged labor at birth might be more apt to have damage to the dorsolateral prefrontal cortex and experience disturbances in motivation. Differential disturbances associated with ontogenetic development have the potential for explaining, at least in part, the heterogeneous ways in which Schizophrenia presents clinically.

Cytoarchitectural Maturation

Both the hippocampus and cortex undergo distinct changes in their organization and appearance as ontogenes proceeds during the pre- and postnatal periods.

Hippocampus

The hippocampal formation of the human brain is a very complex structure composed of several different subsidiary regions, including the area dentata, the hippocampus proper, the subicular complex, and the entorhinal cortex (Stanfield & Cowan, 1988). The process by which it develops involves a carefully timed sequence of events, although the period during which the sequential changes occur may differ for various mammalian species. For example, in rats, the cells of the regio superior (CAI-CA2) appear during the last half of gestation (Angevine, 1965; Stanfield & Cowan, 1988); in monkeys, they appear during the first half (Rakic & Nowakowski, 1981). There is also a general tendency for neurons of the hippocampus to be generated by mitotic proliferation of precursor elements within a zone closely apposed to the ventricular surface. When a given cell has completed its mitotic proliferation, it begins to migrate upward and eventually assumes its proper position in an "inside-out" progression. This latter process occurs for the hippocampus proper, the subicular complex, and the entorhinal cortex. For the area dentata, however, the disposition of this subregion in the hippocampal formation is such that the cells migrate in an "outside-in" manner. Thus, the direction of migration occurs relative to where the proliferative epithelial zone has generated the cells. Another developmental gradient occurs along the axis lying between the entorhinal cortex and the area dentata (Stanfield & Cowan, 1988). Neurons along the ends of this so-called rhinodentate axis develop earlier; cells in the center (subicular complex and hippocampus proper) appear later.

Development of Gyral Patterns in Utero:
12–27 Weeks

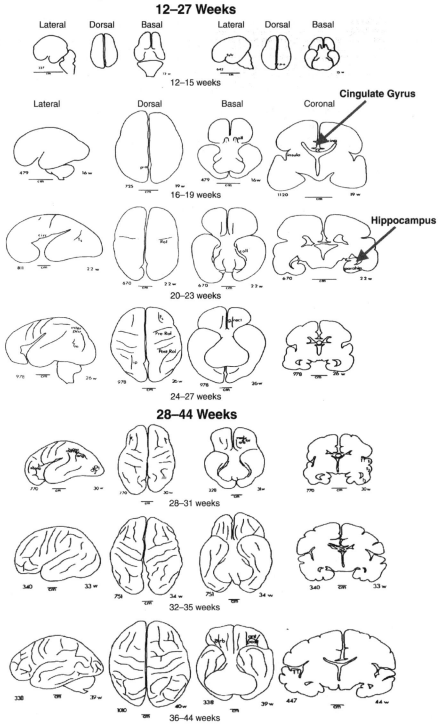

Figure 5.4 A comparison of gyral patterns in the human brain during the second and third trimesters. During the second trimester, there are very few gyri in evidence, with the exception of the cingulate gyrus that appears between 16 and 19 weeks prenatally. The hippocampal gyrus appears somewhat later, between 20 and 23 weeks prenatally. During the third trimester, the number of gyris shows a dramatic increase, especially in the prefrontal area and the superior marginal gyrus. Obstetrical complications that occur during the second trimester might tend to disrupt the normal development of limbic lobe structures, such as cingulate cortex and hippocampus, whereas during the third trimester, the prefrontal cortex might be more affected. The timing of such an insult during prenatal development could influence the types of functions that are disrupted later during the postnatal period in individuals who carry susceptibility genes for a disorder such as Schizophrenia. *Source: The Developing Human Brain: Growth and Epidemiologic Neuropathology.* Gilles, F. H., Leviton, A., and Dooling, E. C. (Eds.), John Wright. PSG Inc. Boston, 1983.

The development of the area dentata may continue well beyond birth. In rats, for example, the numbers of dentate granule cells seem to increase during both the preadult weanling and adult periods (Bayer, Yackel, & Puri, 1982), and the cells arising postnatally are thought to originate from mitotic neuroblasts (Kaplan & Bell, 1984). These newly generated granule cells of the area dentata are thought to give rise to axons that project into subfields CA3 and CA4 of the hippocampus (Stanfield & Trice, 1988). Evidence for postnatal granule cell increases has not been found in rhesus monkeys (Eckenhoff & Rakic, 1988); however, there have not, as yet, been any studies to determine whether similar postnatal changes may occur in the area dentata of the human brain. Thus, it is difficult to know whether postnatal neurogenesis might play a role in human maturation.

Parallels between the ontogenetic development of the hippocampal formation and its phylogeny in vertebrates have been described. At 8 weeks in utero, the human telencephalon is thought to be comparable to that found in mature amphibians (Hoffman, 1963). At 10 weeks, however, it is similar to that of reptiles (Crosby, 1917) and early mammalian species. In the 8-week-old fetus, rostral levels of the forebrain contain the septal nuclei situated immediately ventral to the fornix and medial frontal cortex; at more caudal levels, the fornix is contiguous with the hippocampus (Rakic & Yakovlev, 1968), also having a medial location. The appearance of limbic cortical structures in the medial forebrain of the human fetus early in prenatal development parallels that of phylogenetically earlier forms lacking neocortical structures. Thus, there are some striking similarities in the anatomical relationships of cortical and limbic forebrain structures found in reptiles, early mammals, and the human fetus. This parallelism underscores the notion that these regions are developmental precursors to transitional cortices (such as the cingulate gyrus) that predate neocortical areas such as the prefrontal and inferior parietal regions.

Cortex

The ontogenesis of all cortical regions follows a carefully timed sequence of events (Poliakov, 1965; Sidman & Rakic, 1973). All cortical neurons are generated along the ventricular surface in the so-called marginal zone and migrate toward the surface after undergoing several mitotic divisions. Poliakov (1965) described five stages of cortical development in the human brain that begin with Stage I at approximately the 7th fetal week, when postmitotic cells begin to move upward. Stage V is the longest period and occurs between the 16th fetal week and the early postnatal period. During Stage V, postmitotic neuronal cells continue migrating and reach their final destination within the cortical plate. As neurons enter the cortical plate, those destined for more superficial layers arrive later than those that occupy deeper layers and show an inside-out progression (Rakic, 1974). Studies of the motor cortex in humans have shown that by 7 months of gestation, layers V and VI have attained a more advanced degree of development than layers II and III (Marin-Padilla, 1970a; Zilles, Werners, Busching, & Schleicher, 1986). The morphological differentiation of neurons in the various layers mirrors this migratory process, such that large pyramidal neurons with a well-developed dendritic arborization and basket cells (inhibitory interneurons) can be distinguished in deeper layers sooner than in superficial layers (Marin-Padilla, 1970b). By 7.5 months in utero, pyramidal neurons in deeper portions of layer III are first beginning to show differentiation of an apical dendrite extending into layer I; in layers V and VI, these cells already have elaborate dendritic arborizations. During this same interval, incoming fibers from other regions are present in virtually all layers of the cortex. In the months immediately prior to birth, interneurons begin to appear in the deeper portions of layer III; in layers II and outer portions of III they are first beginning to form. By birth, both the second and third laminae contain pyramidal neurons; however, basket cells in layer II are largely absent (Marin-Padilla, 1970b). By 2.5 months postnatally, pyramidal neurons continue to mature, showing a dramatic increase in overall size, the amount of dendritic branching, and the numbers of dendritic spines (Michel & Garey, 1984). Interestingly, layers VI and I (the marginal zone) are the first laminae to appear and differentiate, and layers II and III are the last to form and the latest to mature (Marin-Padilla, 1970a). At birth, cortical layer II in the motor cortex of human brains is still quite immature (Marin-Padilla, 1970b). Changes in gene expression probably play an important role in regulating these events. For example, chemokines, together with gamma interferon, could play a role in promoting the migration of cells during early development and possibly also the elaboration of dendritic processes (Parlato et al., 2001). Later in development, interferons may promote dendrite retraction in the setting of injury (Kim, Beck, Lein, & Higgins, 2002).

As with the primate and human cortex, Bayer and Altman (1991) have reported that an inside-out progression is also observed in the medial prefrontal cortex of rodent brain, a homologue of the anterior cingulate region in primates and humans. Cell migration in this region occurs earlier than its does for the hippocampal formation (Bayer, Altman, & Russo, 1990). This pattern reflects

	Mitosis	Migration	Axons	Dendrites	Synapses	Myelin
1st Trimester	+++	++	+	-	-	-
2nd Trimester	-	+++	++	+	-	-
3rd Trimester	-	+	+++	+++	++	+
Postnatal Period	-	-	+	++	+++	+++

Table 5.1 The time course for mitotic division of precursor cells in the subventricular zone and their migration upward toward the cortical plate, the growth of axons and dendrites, the formation of synaptic connections, and the appearance of myelin sheaths occurs differentially during the first, second, and third trimesters. Synapse formation and myelination both occur most extensively during the postnatal period.

that described earlier for gyral development, where the cingulate gyrus differentiates weeks in advance of the parahippocampal gyrus and hippocampal formation, except that in this instance, it follows a dorsal-to-ventral course (see Table 5.1). Presumably, the analogous timing of events for the prefrontal cortex of the human brain is somewhat different, but its growth and maturation as a gyrus is likely complete by the 2nd year of life. Postnatally, the medial prefrontal cortex of rats shows a progressive expansion of its matrix as the neuropil surrounding neuronal cell bodies increases. The increase of the neuropil occurs in the preweanling period that is roughly equivalent to preadolescence in humans. The increase of the neuropil is probably related to two different events: (1) the ingrowth of fibers from other cortical and subcortical regions and (2) the collateralization of axons from neurons intrinsic to the cortex. These changes also follow an inside-out progression similar to that seen in relation to cell migration. In the medial prefrontal cortex of rat brains, the thickness is not maximal until P20, which marks the beginning of the postweanling period (Vincent, Pabreza, & Benes, 1995), an interval that is roughly equivalent to adolescence in human development.

Beyond the perinatal period, the packing density of neurons in the human cortex decreases dramatically during the 1st year of life (Blinkov & Glezer, 1968). In the dorsolateral prefrontal cortex (Brodman areas 9 and 10), neuronal density continues to decrease until 5 to 7 years of age, although in layer II of some regions, this process may continue until 12 to 15 years of age (Blinkov & Glezer, 1968).

Three- and Six-Layered Cortex

To understand how defects in the corticolimbic system can influence the processing of activity in subcortical regions,

it is useful to examine more closely the cytoarchitectural organization within the cortex of higher mammals. The cortex of reptiles has a simple three-layered organization (Ulinski, 1977); the mammalian neocortex has been expanded into six layers, which can be distinguished from one another according to the density and size of neurons, as well as their morphological appearance. For example, layer I has sparse numbers of relatively small interneurons; layers II, III, V, and VI contain large numbers of projection cells called pyramidal neurons. These cells typically send their axons out of the cortex to other, distal sites. In contrast to the pyramidal cell layers, layer IV contains abundant numbers of excitatory interneurons, called granule cells. Relative to layer IV, the deeper layers V and VI are called infragranular layers and the superficial layers I through III, supragranular layers.

Interestingly, there is a basic dichotomy between the superficial and the deep layers of the mammalian cortex. Pyramidal neurons in layers V and VI project axons primarily to subcortical structures; those in layers II and III send their axons preferentially to other cortical sites (E. G. Jones, 1984). Layer IV receives a rich supply of afferents from the thalamus (White, 1986), and layer I has a large number of incoming associative inputs from other cortical regions (Marin-Padilla, 1984). Thus, these latter two receptive layers reflect this subcortical and corticocortical relationship of the other infragranular and supragranular projection layers, respectively. In a very general sense, then, the phylogenetic development of the cortex has involved an expansion from three to six layers, and it is of more than passing interest that the three supragranular layers have a more specific role in processing associative activity and an ever-increasing role in phylogenetically more advanced species, such as primates and humans. The thickness of the supragranular layers is proportional to the amount of associative activity that a particular region mediates. For example, the primary visual cortex has a rudimentary amount of layers I through III; the tertiary visual association area 19 has a well-developed supragranular zone. Supramodal (tertiary) cortical regions such as the cingulate, prefrontal areas, and inferior parietal areas, which are associative in nature, have upper layers that are thicker than the deeper layers. Overall, the marked expansion of the associative cortex that has occurred in relation to phylogenesis of the brain has involved a dramatic increase in supragranular laminar processing.

Myelin Formation

A broadly accepted marker for the functional maturation of the central nervous system is the formation of myelin sheaths, the insulating covering that surrounds axon shafts. It has long been known that various neural pathways myelinate at different stages of pre- and postnatal development and, for humans, this process has long been thought to continue well after birth, particularly in the prefrontal cortex (Flechsig, 1920; Yakovlev & Lecours, 1967). There is a general tendency, however, for more cephalad structures to myelinate later than those found at more caudal levels of the neuraxis, and for subcortical pathways to myelinate before cortical associational paths (Yakovlev & Lecours, 1967). For example, the medial longitudinal fasciculus, a pathway that is found along the entire extent of the spinal cord and brain stem, begins myelinating as early as week 20 of the gestational period, and the medial lemniscus, a pathway confined to the brain stem, shows similar changes at gestational week 24 (Gilles, Shankle, & Dooling, 1983). In the cerebral hemispheres, the posterior limb of the internal capsule begins myelinating at gestational week 32, but the anterior limb does not show evidence of myelin formation until week 38. Interestingly, proximal portions of the cingulum bundle do not begin to myelinate until gestational weeks 38 to 39 (Gilles et al., 1983). On the other hand, some subcortical relays, such as the fornix and mammilothalamic tract, do not begin to myelinate until gestational weeks 44 and 48, respectively.

Some pathways in the corticolimbic system continue to myelinate until much later in the postnatal period (Benes, 1989; Benes, Turtle, Khan, & Farol, 1994). For example, the superior medullary lamina (Figure 5.5, upper panel), a fiber bundle found along the surface of the parahippocampal gyrus, shows an increase of myelin staining not only during the 1st and 2nd decades of life (Benes, 1989), but even as late as the 5th and 6th decades (Figure 5.5, lower panel; Benes et al., 1994). It is noteworthy that Yakovlev and Lecours (1967) had postulated that myelin formation might continue to increase in the prefrontal cortex well into the 3rd or perhaps even 4th decade of life. Although empirical evidence for this hypothesis has been lacking, the recent findings described earlier make this idea seem quite plausible.

The Formation of Synaptic Connections

Like myelination, synapse formation is a relatively late aspect of the development of the central nervous system; the preponderance of these functional connections appear during the postnatal period. There are some axons that seem primed to form synaptic connection prenatally but do not do so. For example, during embryogenesis, afferent fibers from the thalamus grow toward the cortical mantle and eventually penetrate inward toward layer IV (Wise & Jones, 1978). In rodents, however, the ingrowth of thalamo-

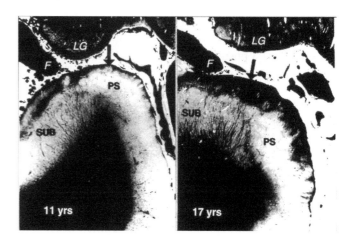

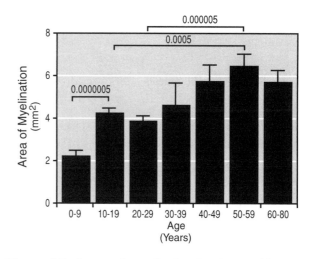

Perforant Pathway and Distal Cingulum Bundle

Figure 5.5 Increased myelination in the parahippocampal gyrus of the human brain during the postnatal period. Comparing 11- and 17-year-old subjects, an increase of myelin staining is seen in the superior medullary lamina located along the surface of the subiculum and presubiculum at the later age (upper panel). This area contains fibers of the cingulum bundle and probably some from the basolateral amygdala. When this staining was quantitated in a large cohort of 163 psychiatrically and neurologically normal individuals, a substantial increase was observed during the 2nd decade (lower panel). Although the myelin seems to plateau through the 3rd and 4th decades, it again shows a significant (50%) increase during the 5th and 6th decades. (Upper courtesy of NIMH; lower from "Myelination of a Key Relay Zone in the Hippocampal Formation Occurs in the Human Brain during Childhood, Adolescence, and Adulthood," by F. M. Benes, M. Turtle, Y. Khan, and P. Farol, 1994, *Archives of General Psychiatry, 51,* pp. 477–484.)

cortical fibers is not complete until the 3rd postnatal day, and commissural fibers begin to enter the homologous cortex in the contralateral hemisphere only by postnatal day 5 and attain a mature pattern of connectivity by postnatal day 7 (Wise & Jones, 1978). The afferent fibers seem to be present before a mature dendritic tree is in evidence, and the formation of dendritic spines may be regulated by these afferent inputs (Wise, Fleshman, & Jones, 1979). For rats, the 1st postnatal week is considered to be similar to the prenatal period of primates and, consistent with this, commissural fibers arising from the principal sulcus of the monkey brain have been reported to penetrate into the homologous cortical region of the opposite hemisphere during the late embryonic period (Goldman-Rakic, 1981).

The density of synapses first increases toward peak levels at approximately 5 to 8 years of age in the human cortex, then decreases dramatically through early adolescence (Huttenlocher, 1994; Huttenlocher & Dabholkar, 1997). The latter process is called pruning and is believed to play a role in the acquisition of mature patterns of connectivity. Presumably, weakly active synapses are eliminated as functionally reinforced ones are maintained.

Dendritic Spine Morphogenesis

An important component to the maturation of dendritic structure is the formation of spines. These structures, primarily found on the dendritic arborizations of pyramidal neurons, are associated with the appearance of enhanced functional capabilities. In the hippocampus, the process of dendritic spine morphogenesis is associated with complex changes in a variety of protein constituents, such as F-actin fibrils, debrina, and the postsynaptic density protein PSD95 (Takahashi et al., 2003). Two different isoforms of debrin are expressed during embryogenesis (Debrin E) and adulthood (Debrin A) and appear to trigger the formation of F-actin fibrils into clusters. This process is associated with the appearance of filopodia-like protuberances along the dendrites of pyramidal cells. N-methyl-D-aspartate (NMDA) receptor activity regulates F-actin clustering in mature hippocampal neurons (Halpain, Hipolito, & Saffer, 1998), but it is not yet known whether a similar mechanism is at work during embryogenesis. PSD95 is associated with the appearance of mature spine morphology with a cap and a stalk, as well as AMPA receptor trafficking (El-Hussein, Schnell, Chetkovich, Nicoll, & Bredt, 2000). It is clear that spine formation is a complex process that involves the regulation of many different classes of protein. It is well known that spines display a marked degree of plasticity, not only during prenatal development, but also even much later during the adult period. Brain-derived neurotrophic factor (BDNF) is another protein that contributes to the maintenance of dendritic spine morphology in the cortex (Gorski,

Zeiler, Tamowski, & Jones, 2003). Based on these findings, it seems likely that the appearance and resorption of spines probably involves complex changes in the regulation of transcription, translation, and post-translational modification of proteins such as debrin and PSD95.

The Development of Afferent Inputs to the Cortex

During normal brain development, the entry of various types of afferent fibers to the cortex follows a carefully timed sequence. Two principal inputs to the cortex, one arising from the thalamus and one from the contralateral cortex, show such a sequential progression. During prenatal stages in rats, fibers from the thalamus extend toward the cortical mantle and either stop immediately beneath or begin to enter layer IV (Wise & Jones, 1978). In the rat somatosensory cortex, the ingrowth of thalamocortical fibers toward specific neuronal elements, particularly those in layer IV, continues after parturition and is not complete until approximately the 3rd postnatal day (Wise et al., 1979). In contrast, commissural inputs arising from the homologous cortex of the opposite hemisphere begin entering the somatosensory cortex at 5 days postnatally and attain a mature degree of connectivity by the end of the first postnatal week.

Developmental Changes in Specific Neurotransmitter Systems

The maturation of the prefrontal cortex must involve obligatory changes in both intrinsic and extrinsic neurotransmitter systems that mediate its activity. Although there is a dearth of specific information available regarding their development in human brain, the discussion that follows considers data obtained from studies in rodents where developmental changes of cortical neurotransmitters have been extensively characterized. Although it is true that the specific timing of developmental changes can vary considerably from one species to another, there are nevertheless some general principles that can be formulated from the studies of rodent and, to a lesser extent, primate brains. In this regard, it is useful to point out that the equivalent of adolescence in rats occurs between postnatal weeks 3 and 8, and the early adult period begins at approximately postnatal day 60. Where available, studies in the developing human brain are also described.

Intrinsic Neurotransmitters

The two most broadly understood neurotransmitters that are intrinsically present in virtually all local circuits and provide excitatory and inhibitory synaptic responses are glutamate and GABA, respectively.

Glutamate.   The amino acid glutamate and the closely related compound aspartate are generally considered to be the transmitters employed by pyramidal neurons projecting to both cortical and subcortical locations (Streit, 1984). The time course for the maturation of various glutamatergic pathways is probably different. For example, the corticocortical projections originating in the visual cortex of the rat brain attain adult levels of glutamate before their corticostriatal counterparts projecting to the caudate nucleus (Johnston, 1988). Interestingly, 2 days after birth, the levels of the glutamate reuptake mechanism is 30% of the levels that are eventually seen at P15. In the visual cortex and in the lateral geniculate nucleus, the reuptake mechanism attains adult levels by P15 and P20, respectively (Kvale, Fosse, & Fonnum, 1983). High-affinity glutamate receptors also continue to change postnatally. Between P10 and P15, glutamate receptor binding activity increases by 30% and is 10 times higher than it will eventually be during adulthood (Schliebs, Kullman, & Bigl, 1986). After P15, however, the activity declines substantially through P25 (Schliebs et al., 1986). In rats monocularly deprived of visual input, the overall binding of glutamate is reduced in the lateral geniculate nucleus but not the visual cortex, and these reductions are maintained into adulthood (Schliebs et al., 1986). In the hippocampus, glutamate receptor binding increases up to P23 (Baudry, Arst, Oliver, & Lynch, 1981), possibly reflecting the persistence of long-term potentiation as an important component to both learning and memory (Johnston, 1988).

Gamma-Aminobutyric Acid.   GABA is thought to be the most important inhibitory neurotransmitter in mammalian brains, particularly in humans. Generally speaking, the activity of the GABA reuptake mechanism seems to increase before the activity of glutamate decarboxylase (GAD) shows appreciable increments (Coyle & Enna, 1976). At birth, the amount of GABA is half that seen in adults, but the adult amounts are not attained until the 2nd postnatal week. The number of GABA-immunoreactive (GABA-IR) neurons present in the medial prefrontal cortex of rat brains reaches a peak density at approximately P5, but thereafter decreases sharply between P10 and P20 as the surrounding neuropil expands (Vincent, Pabreza, et al., 1995). GABA terminals, however, increase in number between postnatal days 7 to 12 for the deeper layers of this region (Figure 5.6), but show an inside-out progression as they continue to increase in number in superficial laminae until the 3rd postna-

tal week (Vincent, Pabreza, et al., 1995). Although GAD levels are negligible at birth, they attain adult levels by the 3rd postnatal week (Johnston & Coyle, 1980).

The amount of GABA and benzodiazepine receptor activity does not begin to show appreciable increases until the 1st postnatal week, but thereafter shows a sharp rise during the 2nd week and an additional 15% increment between the 2nd and 7th postnatal weeks (Candy & Martin, 1979). In contrast, the reuptake mechanism for GABA peaks by the 2nd postnatal week, but later, in the 7th week, it decreases. In the human brain, GABA receptor binding activity shows a fivefold increase during the perinatal period (Brooksbank, Atkinson, & Balazs, 1981; Diebler, Farkas-Bargeton, & Wehrle, 1979) and an additional 100% increase for several weeks thereafter (Brooksbank et al., 1981). Functional inputs are thought to regulate the maturation of the GABA system. For example, in the cat visual cortex, dark-rearing from birth through the 6th postnatal week results in a decrease of normal GAD activity (Fosse, Heggelund, & Fonnum, 1989).

Extrinsic Neurotransmitters

Many different afferent systems project into regions of the neocortex and the hippocampal formation, but most are intrinsic to the cortex and are likely to use either glutamate or aspartate as a neurotransmitter. Afferent projections that are extrinsic to the cortex—those arising from noncortical locations—are of several different types; however, four have been particularly well investigated: (1) projections from the basal forebrain, pons, midbrain, and a diffuse region lying along the brain stem median raphe; (Lindvall, Bjorklund, & Divac, 1978) they use acetylcholine (basal nucleus; Mesulam, Mufson, Levey, & Wainer, 1984); (2) norepinephrine (locus coeruleus; P. Levitt & Moore, 1978); (3) serotonin (the raphe nuclei; Descarries, Beaudet, & Watkins, 1975); and (4) dopamine (ventral tegmental nuclei and substantia nigra; Berger, Tassin, Blanc, Moyne, & Thierry, 1974; Thierry, Blanc, Sobel, Stinus, & Glowinski, 1973). The developmental changes in each of these neurotransmitter systems are discussed separately.

Acetylcholine

Most of the acetylcholine (Ach) found in the cortex is derived from the basal forebrain (Johnston, McKinney, & Coyle, 1979), although a small amount may be synthesized by intrinsic cholinergic neurons (Bayer, 1985; Levey, Wainer, Raye, Mufson, & Mesulam, 1984). The neuronal cell bodies of the cholinergic system are generated early in gestation (Bayer, 1985), but they do not begin to accumulate appreciable amounts of choline acetyltransferase

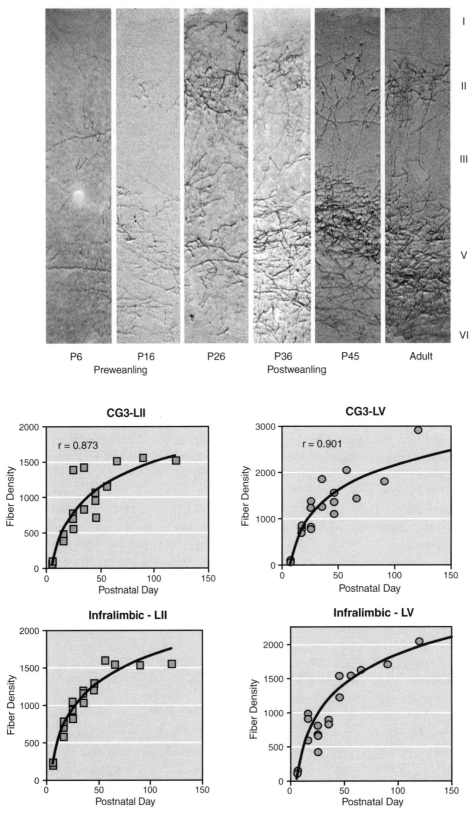

Figure 5.6 A photomontage showing an increase of fibers from the basolateral amygdala in the anterior cingulate cortex during the preweanling, postweanling, and adult periods (upper panel). Quantitative data for these fibers demonstrate a curvilinear increase between birth and the adult period (lower panel).

(ChAT) until after the 1st postnatal week, although this enzyme continues to increase at least until the 6th postnatal week (Johnston & Coyle, 1980). These changes in ChAT parallel the amount of binding activity at the receptor that mediates cholinergic effects in the cortex, the muscarinic *binding* site (Coyle & Yamamura, 1976), except that high-affinity sites for Ach are already fairly abundant at birth, and ChAT is not. The ingrowth of cholinergic fibers into the cortex occurs first in deeper layers and later in the superficial layers, a pattern that mirrors the inside-out progression seen for cortical ontogeny. In humans, cholinergic fibers have been observed to enter the cortex as early as 12 to 22 weeks of gestation (Candy et al., 1985); however, by birth, the overall levels of ChAT remain low, and adult levels are not attained until approximately age 10 (Diebler et al., 1979). In sharp contrast to rodents, muscarinic receptor activity in the human cortex is highest at birth and progressively diminishes during the 2nd through 6th decades (and possibly longer), perhaps as a result of synaptic pruning (Ravikumar & Sastary, 1985). In the human cortex, acetylcholinesterase, the enzyme that degrades Ach, is found principally in interneurons during the 1st postnatal week, but later shows a progressive increase in pyramidal cell bodies of layer III, where it reaches peak levels in young adults (Kostovic, Skavic, & Strinovic, 1988). Because upper cortical layers are predominantly involved in associative connections, these latter changes could reflect maturational changes in cognitive activity.

Norepinephrine

Noradrenergic cell bodies of the locus coeruleus undergo their last mitotic division in rat brains at gestational days 12 to 14 (Lauder & Bloom, 1974) and in monkeys at gestational days 27 to 36 (P. Levitt & Rakic, 1982). By birth, there is a rather extensive network of noradrenergic fibers in the cortex, and their density is considerably greater than that seen in adults (Coyle & Molliver, 1977). In rats, tyrosine hydroxylase (TH), the enzyme involved in the synthesis of norepinephrine and dopamine, increases steadily between the 1st and 7th postnatal weeks (Johnston & Coyle, 1980). The beta-adrenergic receptor increases sharply between the 1st and 2nd postnatal weeks, before plateauing (Harden, Wolfe, Sporn, Poulos, & Molinoff, 1977). Studies of the cat have suggested that norepinephrine may play a key role in the plasticity of synaptic connections (Kasamatsu & Pettigrew, 1976). Following monocular visualized nonvaricose fibers with a vertical orientation, it is unlikely that these fibers originated from these latter subcortical nuclei.

Serotonin

The timing of developmental changes in the serotonin (5-hydroxytryptamine or 5-HT) system is similar to that observed for the noradrenergic system (Hamon & Bourgoin, 1977; Hedner & Lundberg, 1980). Serotonin-containing neurons of the raphe nuclei in rat brains (Descarries et al., 1975) are first visualized between gestational days 13 and 17, when some of their axons have already grown toward the pyriform cortex (Wallace & Lauder, 1983). As seen with other transmitter systems in rat brains (see "Dopamine Systems"), 5-HT levels increase steadily between birth and the 4th postnatal week (Johnston, 1988). The synthesizing enzyme for 5-HT, tryptophan hydroxylase, is at 10% of adult levels by birth, but rises to adult levels by postnatal day 30 (Deguchi & Barchas, 1972). During the perinatal period, high-affinity 5-HT receptor binding activity, on the other hand, is approximately 33% of that seen in adults but does not attain adult levels until the 6th postnatal week (Uphouse & Bondy, 1981). In primates, 5-HT afferent fibers to the cortex appear to have established an adult pattern by postnatal week 6, and the levels of 5-HT continue to increase for an additional 2 to 3 weeks (Goldman-Rakic & Brown, 1982). In human brains, however, the density of $5-HT_2$ binding sites shows a linear decline between 17 and 100 years of age; in the hippocampus, a similar but less striking change in this receptor also occurs (Marcusson, Morgan, Winblad, & Finch, 1984).

It has been suggested that timing for the ingrowth of serotonergic fibers may vary according to the degree of maturity for intrinsic circuits within a given region (Lidov & Molliver, 1982). Interestingly, at birth, the serotonin projection to the sensory cortex is found preferentially within layers IV and VI, the two laminae predominantly involved in receiving thalamic afferents. Because the arrival of serotonin fibers precedes that of the thalamocortical afferents, it has been suggested that the serotonergic innervation to the cortex may provide a trophic influence on thalamic fibers and/or their target neurons (Wise & Jones, 1978).

Dopamine

Dopamine cells in the ventral tegmental area and substantia nigra of rat brains (Berger et al., 1974; Thierry et al., 1973) begin to differentiate on embryonic day 11 and continue this process through day 15 (Lauder & Bloom, 1974). Afferent dopamine fibers first arrive near the frontal cortex as early as E16 (Verney, Berger, Adrien, Vigny, & Gay, 1982); however, by birth, these axons begin to penetrate into the cortical mantle and establish an abundant innervation by postnatal week 2 for the frontal area and postnatal week 3 for the cingulate region (Berger & Verney, 1984). Dopamine afferents to the prefrontal region also follow the typical inside-out progression seen for cholinergic inputs, entering the infragranular layers first and the supragranular layers last (Kalsbeek, Voorn, Buijs, Pool, & Uylings, 1988). As shown in Figure 5.7, a full complement of dopamine fibers in the anterior cingulate cortex is not established until adulthood (Benes, Vincent, Molloy, & Khan, 1996; Kalsbeek et al., 1988; Verney et al., 1982). Dopamine concentrations also rise steadily until adulthood (Johnston, 1988). Dopamine receptors, on the other hand, are expressed in the cortex before birth and continue to increase toward adult levels through postnatal day 31 of rats (Bruinink, Lichtensteiner, & Schlumpf, 1983; Deskin, Seidler, Whitmore, & Slotkin, 1981).

Developmental Similarities among Transmitter Systems

Based on the previous discussion, there are several developmental characteristics that are similar across neurotransmitter systems, and there is no reason to believe that the situation is different for the prefrontal cortex. For example, the progenitor cells responsible for the elaboration of both intrinsic and extrinsic transmitter systems in the cortex become postmitotic long before they show appreciable differentiation of their respective neurotransmitter phenotypes. In addition, virtually all neurotransmitter systems are present in the cortex at birth but require further maturation. Finally, the postnatal development of most transmitter systems continues beyond the weaning period (similar to early adolescence in humans), during which important changes in gonadal maturity are occurring and overlap with the postweaning period (similar to late adolescence, when changes in emotional maturity are occurring). Although there is a dearth of information in this area regarding the human brain, available evidence suggests that postnatal maturation of both the cholinergic and serotonergic systems may continue throughout childhood and adolescence and, in some cases, may persist throughout the life span of the normal individual. Based on observations in rats, however, it seems likely that changes in the dopamine system are also occurring until the early adult period.

Developmental Interactions between Intrinsic and Extrinsic Cortical Projection Systems

It is evident from the previous discussion that the postnatal maturation of both intrinsic and extrinsic neurotransmitter systems is extensive. At this juncture, a reasonable question

to ask is whether these progressive postnatal changes may involve an increase in the degree to which some or all of these transmitter systems are interacting with one another.

Dopamine-GABA Interactions

A recent study has suggested that frequent appositions occur between dopaminergic afferents and both pyramidal neurons and GABAergic interneurons in the medial prefrontal cortex of adult rats (Benes, Vincent, & Molloy, 1993). As shown in Figure 5.7, the frequency of these contacts was compared for preweanling and postweanling rats, and it was found that there is a threefold increase in the number of dopamine-immunoreactive varicosities found in contact with pyramidal cells, but a fivefold increase in the number on nonpyramidal neurons in layer VI of the rat medial prefrontal cortex. In layer II of this region, there was a sevenfold increase on nonpyramidal neurons, but no change on pyramidal cells. These findings suggest that (1) postnatal increases in the interaction of one transmitter system with another probably do occur to a significant degree, (2) such changes may vary in magnitude according to cortical layer, and (3) changes of this type may occur differentially for one neuronal cell type versus another within a given cortical layer. In other words, postnatal maturational changes in the cortical neurotransmitter system may be far more complex than was heretofore suspected, and to fully understand the implications of postnatal ontogeny, a clear delineation of how changes in neurochemical markers may be reflected in alterations of specific synaptic connectivity is needed.

A variety of studies have demonstrated that both pyramidal and nonpyramidal neurons express receptors that mediate the effect of dopamine. For example, dopamine D1 receptor binding activity has been localized to nonpyramidal cells (Vincent, Khan, & Benes, 1993), but in another study it was associated with pyramidal cells (Bergson et al., 1995) in the prefrontal cortex. This apparent discrepancy can be explained by methodologic and species differences in these two studies, because messenger RNA for both the D1 and D2 subtypes has been localized in both pyramidal and nonpyramidal neurons (Huntley, Morrison, Prikhozhan, & Sealfon, 1992). Consistent with this, a large proportion of interneurons in rat medial prefrontal cortex (mPFCx) have been found to express D1 and D2 binding activities (Vincent, Khan, & Benes, 1995), and studies in which in vitro microdialysis was employed have demonstrated that agonists for both the D1 and D2 subtypes are associated with a reduction in the release of 3H-GABA (Penit-Soria, Audinat, & Crepel, 1987; Retaux, Besson, & Penit-Soria, 1991a, 1991b). Thus, as suggested by these re-

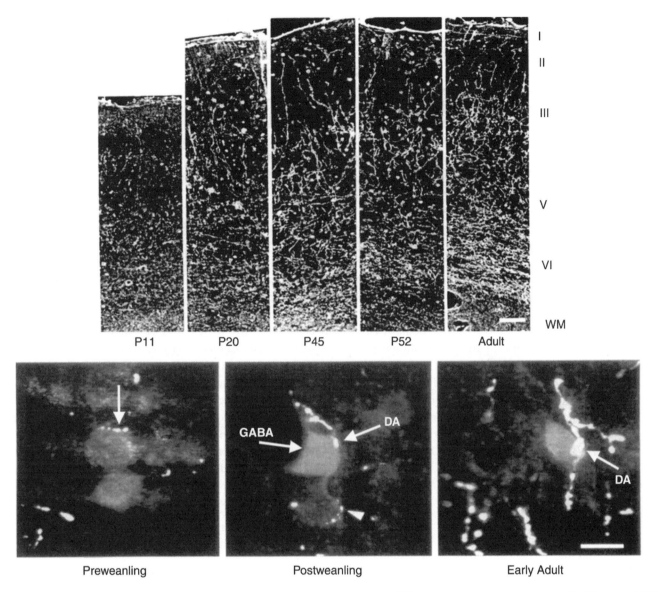

Figure 5.7   Ingrowth of dopamine fibers in the anterior cingulate cortex at different postnatal ages (upper panel). These darkfield photomicrographs show a progressive increase in the density of dopamine fibers between the preweanling (P11) period and early adulthood. Using a double localization technique, dopamine fibers also show a progressive increase in the number of contacts they form with GABAergic interneurons. *Source:*   From "Increased Interaction of Dopamine-Immunoreactive Varicosities with Gaba Neurons of Rat Medial Prefrontal Cortex Occurs during the Postweanling Period," by F. M. Benes, S. L. Vincent, R. Molloy, and Y. Khan, 1996, *Synapse, 23*(4), pp. 237–245. Reprinted with permission of Wiley-Liss a subsidiary of John Wiley & Sons, Inc.

sults, cortical dopamine projections can potentially exert a significant nonsynaptic modulatory influence on GABAergic cells in rat mPFCx.

Using a specific marker for GABAergic neurons, it has been possible to demonstrate that dopamine fibers show a progressive increase in the frequency with which they form appositions with inhibitory interneurons (Benes et al., 1996). Between the preweanling and postweanling periods, there was a 55% increase in the frequency of these interactions, and between the postweanling and early adult period

(P60) there was an additional 85% increase (see Figure 5.7). Overall, during the postnatal period, there was a 150% increase in the interaction of dopamine fibers with GABA-immunoreactive neuron somata in the medial prefrontal cortex of rat brains.

Convergence of Dopamine and Serotonin Fibers on Prefrontal Neurons

Serotonin fibers are believed to converge on the same pyramidal cells and GABA neurons that receive inputs from catecholaminergic neurons (Gellman & Aghajanian, 1993). A triple immunofluorescence study was able to confirm that this arrangement occurs in the medial prefrontal cortex of rats to an extensive degree (Taylor & Benes, 1996). It is noteworthy that pyramidal neurons also received inputs to their somata from both TH- and 5-HT-IR fibers. Because these latter cell bodies also received axosomatic inputs from GAD-IR terminals, it was concluded that the principal projection cells of this regions receive a "trivergence" of inputs from the GABA, dopamine, and serotonin systems (Benes, Taylor, & Cunningham, 2000). With regard to the serotonin system, the 5-HT2 receptor protein has been immunocytochemically localized to presumptive GABAergic interneurons in layer II of the pyriform cortex (Morilak, Garlow, & Ciaranello, 1993).

It is well-established that GABA is an inhibitory neurotransmitter that plays a pivotal role in cortical integration (E. G. Jones, 1987). There are many different subtypes of GABAergic interneurons in the cortex, but the most basic dichotomy is between basket cells that exert inhibitory effects on pyramidal neurons (E. G. Jones & Hendry, 1984) and double bouquet cells that are disinhibitory in nature (Somogyi & Cowey, 1984); the latter act by inhibiting other GABAergic cells. GABAergic interneurons play a very critical role in discriminative aspects of cortical processing, such as orientation selectivity (Sillito, 1984).

Functional Implications of Monoaminergic Convergence

Physiological studies have demonstrated that SKF38393, a D1 agonist, and RU24926, a D2 agonist, have both been found to inhibit the electrically evoked release of 3H-GABA in rat mPFC (Penit-Soria, Retaux, & Maurin, 1989; Retaux et al., 1991a, 1991b), although D2 agonists have paradoxically been found to increase the spontaneous release of GABA. This apparent paradox could potentially be explained by an initial depolarization leading to either a presynaptic inhibition or a refractor period in GABA cells. Because the D2 receptor is mainly associated with inhibitory mechanisms, the complexity of interactions between dopamine terminals and GABA cells in the prefrontal cortex might well mask a similar effect on evoked GABA release. Specifically, dopamine binding to D2 receptors on some terminals could produce an inhibition of a GABA neuron (Retaux et al., 1991b). It is plausible that dopamine fibers interact with both inhibitory and disinhibitory GABAergic elements, and this could help to explain the paradoxical effects of D2 agonists on spontaneous versus evoked release of dopamine in the prefrontal cortex. For the serotonin system, the results of an intracellular

recording study have indicated that the effect of this monoamine on GABA cells is blocked by 5-HT2 antagonists (Sheldon & Aghajanian, 1990). Overall, serotonin appears to induce hyperpolarizing postsynaptic potentials in pyramidal neurons, and these are believed to be mediated via the effect of this transmitter on GABAergic interneurons (Sheldon & Aghajanian, 1991).

Although it is clear that both dopamine and serotonin can directly influence the activity of cortical interneurons, there is very little currently known regarding any direct interactions between these two systems on individual GABAergic cells. Some investigators believe that serotonin can increase the release of dopamine in the nucleus accumbens (Broderick & Phelix, 1997), corpus striatum (Broderick & Phelix, 1997; Gudelsky & Nash, 1996; West & Galloway, 1996), and prefrontal cortex (Gudelsky & Nash, 1996). Contrariwise, others have suggested that serotonin may actually decrease the release of dopamine, because exposure to selective serotonin receptor antagonists has been associated with an increase of extracellular dopamine concentration (Howell, Czoty, & Burd, 1997; Pehek, 1996). None of these studies has attempted to assess such an interaction at the level of individual neurons. It is important to point out that functional interactions between these two monoaminergic systems may not be mediated solely at the cortical level, but could be mediated, at least in part, at midbrain levels, where the ventral tegmental area and nucleus raphe dorsalis are both located.

Postnatal Plasticity and Convergence of Dopamine-Serotonin Interactions

As noted, the serotonin systems has been found to influence the plasticity of the developing neocortex, as it exerts a trophic influence on the ingrowth of thalamocortical fibers (D'Amato et al., 1987). With respect to the current discussion, it is pertinent to ask whether serotonin might also exert a neuroplastic influence on the late ingrowth of dopamine fibers into the medial prefrontal cortex during early adulthood. To explore this issue, a series of experiments were conducted using 5,7-dihydroxytryptamine, a specific toxin to serotonergic neurons, to lesion the dorsal raphe nucleus of rat brains during the neonatal period (Taylor, Cunningham, & Benes, 1998). The distribution of TH-IR varicosities was assessed in the ventral tegmental area (VTA), where dopaminergic afferents to the cortex originate, and in the medial prefrontal area. The lesioned rats showed a marked reduction in the visualization of 5-HT-IR somata in the ventral periaqueductal gray, but the VTA showed no reduction in staining. In the medial prefrontal area, 5-HT fibers were also markedly reduced, whereas TH-IR fibers were abundantly present throughout the cortical mantle. When the numerical density of TH-IR varicosities was determined, a significant increase was noted, particularly in layer V, where the 5-HT innervation of the cortex is quite dense. These results suggest that there may be a competition between dopamine and 5-HT fiber systems within the prefrontal cortex of rat brains.

To test this hypothesis further, a second series of experiments was performed in which the dopamine projections to medial prefrontal cortex (mPFC) were lesioned using 6-OH-DOPA administration at P6. As before, the animals were allowed to mature and were sacrificed at P60. Although it was postulated that there would be a sprouting of the serotonergic fibers, a quantitative analysis revealed that the numerical density of these latter fibers was actually reduced (Cunningham, Connor, Zhang, & Benes, 2005). This finding suggests that the interaction between dopaminergic and serotonergic fibers in the cortex are much more complex than was previously believed. This paradoxical finding may be explained, at least in part, by interactions of these two monoaminergic systems at brain stem levels.

The Postnatal Ingrowth of Basolateral Amygdalar Fibers into the Cingulate Cortex

The anterior cingulate cortex (ACCx) plays a central role in the mediation of emotional, attentional, motivational, social, and cognitive behaviors (Vogt, Finch, & Olson, 1992). The amygdala, specifically its basolateral subdivision (BLA), sends a massive input to cortical layers II and V of mPFC (Amaral, Price, Pitkanen, & Carmichael, 1992; Van Hoesen et al., 1993; Vogt, Vogt, Nimchinsky, & Hof, 1997) and contributes to the recall of emotional information (McGaugh, Ferry, Vazcarjanova, & Roosendaal, 2000), aversive conditioning (Fanselow & LeDoux, 1999), decision making (Bechara, Damasio, Damasio, & Lee, 1999), and goal-directed behavior (Schoenbaum, Chiba, & Gallagher, 2000). Because these latter behaviors are all showing maturational changes during childhood and adolescence, normal postnatal changes in the distribution and synaptic connectivity of the amygdala with the anterior cingulate cortex have been characterized. Given the established role of the amygdala (LeDoux, 2000a, 2000b) and anterior cingulate cortex (Devinsky, Morrell, & Vogt, 1995) in the mediation of emotional behavior, this connectivity could play a central role in modulating the emotional component of emotionally related learning responses, particularly under conditions of stress (Gray & Bingaman, 1996).

As shown in Figure 5.6, amygdalofugal fibers become organized into a bilaminar distribution occupying cortical layers II and V by postnatal day 16 (Cunningham, Bhattacharyya, & Benes, 2002). By adulthood, this bilaminar distribution is present through the rostrocaudal extent of the anterior cingulate region, as the fiber density within these layers becomes progressively more dense. Figure 5.6 illustrates the progressive increase of basolateral amygdalar fibers between birth and the start of the adult period at postnatal day 60. During the neonatal period, there was a paucity of fibers, and those present lacked a clear laminar organization. Within 2 weeks, however, although still sparse, fibers began to organize into the characteristic bilaminar distribution seen in the adult. Subsequently, there was a striking increase in fiber density across the various postweanling time points, and this progression continued into adulthood. For each developmental time point, the density of amygdalocortical fibers shows increases in both layers II and V.

Labeled amygdalar fibers forming synapses can also be identified using an electron microscope. Contacts between labeled axons and cortical structures could be found as early as the equivalent of early adolescence (P25 in rats), but these interactions became more numerous at later time points equivalent to adulthood (P60 and P120). The most striking change was a pronounced increase of axospinous synapses that are believed to be excitatory in nature. These findings are consistent with those of Bacon, Headlam, Gabbott, & Smith (1996), which showed that dendritic spines are the principal postsynaptic target for amygdalofugal fibers in the adult.

Overall, it appears that the anterior cingulate cortex receives a progressive and dramatic ingrowth of fibers originating from the posterior aspect of the basolateral nucleus and the formation of functional synapses. Such changes are theoretically capable of providing enhanced feed-forward excitation to the anterior cingulate cortex during the equivalent of adolescence and early adulthood. Electrophysiological studies have demonstrated that stimulation of the BLA results in a preponderance of inhibitory postsynaptic potentials within the rat mPFC (Perez-Jaranay & Vives, 1991). Because amygdalocortical projection neurons are glutamatergic (McDonald et al., 1989), and are therefore likely to be excitatory in nature, the predominant target of amygdalofugal projections to the mPFC may be GABA interneurons. Presumably, stimulation of these inhibitory cells by BLA fibers results in inhibitory postsynaptic potentials in projection neurons. Indeed, amygdalofugal fibers appear to make frequent contacts with GABAergic cell bodies and processes (Benes, Bhattacharyya, & Cunningham, 2002).

These results complement a variety of other studies demonstrating late postnatal developmental changes. In addition to an estimated loss of 50% of neocortical synapses (Huttenlocher & Dabholkar, 1997), myelination continues until the 6th decade in humans (Benes, 1989; Benes et al., 1994). The amygdala itself also undergoes developmental changes during adolescence, showing increased vulnerability to kindled seizures (Terasawa & Timiras, 1968) and decreased c-Fos expression under stressful conditions (Kellogg, Awatramani, & Piekut, 1998). The postnatal increase in density of amygdalocortical fibers and their synapses described earlier parallels the emotional maturation that is associated with early and late adolescence.

As discussed in the beginning of this chapter, current theories suggest that constitutional differences in temperament may involve the amygdala and its interconnectivity with ACCx (Kagan & Snidman, 1991b). The amygdala also mediates more primitive behaviors, such as aggression, fear, and sexual activity (Armony, Servan Schreiber, Cohen, & LeDoux, 1995; Davis, 1992), all of which influence socialization. For example, cats with abnormally increased neuronal activity within the BLA show a reduced ability to interact socially and tend to hide when introduced to novel stimuli (Adamec, 1978, 1991), and animals with amygdala ablations appear to lose the fear response (Kluver & Bucy, 1937). In humans, lesions of the amygdala result in a decrease or absence of conditioned fear responses to aversive stimuli, and it is believed that the amygdala provides the affective coloration to emotionally charged stimuli (Bechara et al., 1999). Furthermore, the emotional valence provided by the amygdala is critical for appropriate processing of multimodal sensory information by the mPFC (Bechara et al., 1999; LeDoux, 1993). Patients with damage to the cingulate cortex or with therapeutic cingulotomies show a decreased ability to experience and express affect (Damasio & Van Hoesen, 1983), increased docility, and indifference (Laplane et al., 1981).

It seems evident, therefore, that cognitive and emotional development are related to amygdalocingulate connectivity. Because projections from the amygdala to ACCx have been implicated in social functioning (MacLean, 1985), the continued development of this system during adolescence may enable an individual to modulate anxiety and fear and become more socially adept. Thus, normal emotional maturation during the teenage period may involve ontogenetic changes in amygdalocingulate connectivity like those demonstrated in the present study (Cunningham et al., 2002). Contrariwise, abnormal emotional maturation could hypothetically be related to aberrant sprouting of this connectivity within the cingulate cortex during the adolescent period. Because psychosis, depression, substance abuse, violence, and suicidality all typically present during adolescence, a comprehensive understanding of postnatal changes in amygdalocingulate connections will provide a unique opportunity for increasing our understanding of both normal and abnormal behaviors that manifest during this critical stage of emotional development (Cunningham et al., 2002). By examining the boundaries between abnormal and normal development during adolescence, it may be possible to articulate more clearly the diversity in the course of development that may occur during this period (Cicchetti & Rogosch, 2002).

This discussion illustrates that it is likely that the ontogenesis of the limbic lobe spans not only the embryonic period, but also an extensive postnatal interval that includes the early adult period and possibly even beyond. During embryogenesis, the developmental processes that are operative encompass a broad range of phenomena that include the proliferation, migration, and differentiation of neurons, not only those intrinsic to the prefrontal cortex, but also ones extrinsically derived from a variety of subcortical regions that send significant projections to it. These latter fiber systems include projections from the thalamus, as well as those that originate in the dorsal raphe nucleus, ventral tegmental area, and locus coeruleus. Unlike the specific afferent systems from the thalamus, the monoaminergic systems may continue their growth and maturation for a much longer period of time that extends into adulthood. As such, these latter systems may play an important role in modulating the activity of intrinsic circuits within the prefrontal cortex and may ultimately contribute to the acquisition of mature patterns of cognitive behavior that are mediated by this region (Goldman-Rakic, 1998; Goldman-Rakic & Brown, 1982). Although their developmental time frame is different, the dopaminergic and serotonin systems converge on intrinsic prefrontal neurons and influence the nature of their activity (Lambe, Krimer, & Goldman-Rakic, 2000). This implies that these two monoaminergic systems may be particularly important to our understanding of how neuronal plasticity contributes to the sculpting of neural circuitry within the adult prefrontal cortex.

THE ROLE OF THE AMYGDALA IN THE PATHOPHYSIOLOGY OF MENTAL DISORDERS

The hypothesis that the basolateral amygdala may play a role in the pathophysiology of Schizophrenia has been suggested, in part, by the fact that this region sends a massive projection to layer II of the anterior cingulate cortex, where several microscopic anomalies have been observed in Schizophrenia (Benes & Bird, 1987; Benes et al., 1987; Benes, McSparren, Bird, SanGiovanni, & Vincent, 1991;

Benes, Sorensen, et al., 1992; Benes, Todtenkopf, & Taylor, 1997; Benes, Vincent, Alsterberg, Bird, & SanGiovanni, 1992; Woo, Walsh, & Benes, 2004). More direct evidence, however, comes from the report of a decrease of high-affinity GABA uptake in the amygdala of the postmortem schizophrenic brain (Reynolds, Czudek, & Andrews, 1990). It is relevant, therefore, to consider more closely the specific ways in which this region interacts with the hippocampal formation, particularly as both of these regions have been found to show volume reduction in brain imaging studies of Schizophrenia (for a detailed review, see Lawrie & Abukmeil, 1998).

The basolateral subdivision of the amygdala comprises a frontotemporal system that innervates several key components of the corticolimbic system, including the hippocampus formation (Swanson & Petrovich, 1998). The projections of the amygdala to the hippocampus are rather complex and include the perforant pathway terminations in the stratum moleculare of the area dentata, as well as various other fiber systems that enter the CA subfields either through the stratum oriens (i.e., to CA3) or the stratum moleculare (Pikkarainen, Ronkko, Savander, Insausti, & Pitkanen, 1999). The direct projections of the basolateral complex to the CA subfields, together with its indirect influences exerted via the entorhinal region, constitute a compelling network to consider in relation to Schizophrenia. Interestingly, blockade of the GABA$_A$ receptor results in marked changes in the regulation of emotional responses mediated by this region (Davis, Rainnie, & Cassell, 1994; Sanders & Shekhar, 1995). Because a dysfunction of the GABA system is believed to occur in the amygdala in Schizophrenia, an increased outflow of activity from this latter region to the entorhinal region and hippocampus could contribute to the disturbances in affective experience and the heightened response to stress that are observed in this disorder.

An increase of incoming amygdalar activity to the cingulate region would likely produce important shifts in the relationship of this area with the various regions to which it, in turn, projects. Recent investigations of the anterior cingulate cortex in schizophrenic patients have also suggested a model (Figure 5.8) in which there may be a loss of GABAergic neurons, particularly in layer II (Benes, McSparren, Bird, Vincent, & SanGiovanni, 1991; Benes, Vincent, et al., 1992). In this setting, excessive excitatory activity emanating from increased associative inputs could theoretically be exacerbated by diminished inhibitory activity from GABAergic basket neurons (Benes, Sorensen, et al., 1992). It has been suggested that the effects of increased excitatory inputs and decreased inhibitory activity (Benes, Sorensen, et al., 1992) could contribute to the overinclusive thinking and loss of a "central filtering" mecha-

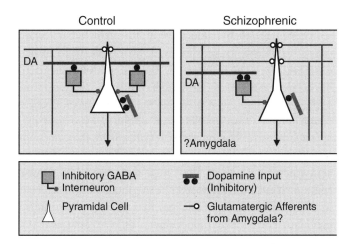

Figure 5.8 A schematic depiction of an intrinsic circuit in the anterior cingulate cortex of normal and schizophrenic individuals. In the normal circuit (left), a pyramidal neuron receives GABAergic inputs from two inhibitory interneurons. Each GABA cell receives one dopaminergic input which is inhibitory in nature. Two separate glutamatergic vertical fibers ascend to layer I, where they travel horizontally before forming excitatory connections with the distal portions of the pyramidal cell apical dendrite. In the schizophrenic circuit (right), there is only one GABAergic cell, depicting a loss and/or dysfunction of these cells. The remaining GABA cell receives an excess number of dopamine inputs, a change that has been referred to as a "miswiring." At the same time, there are four glutamatergic vertical fibers coursing toward layer I and forming excitatory connections with pyramidal cell dendrites. In the schizophrenic circuit, less inhibitory activity would be available to modulate the excessive excitatory activity arising from the vertical associative inputs. From "Amygdalo-Cortical Sprouting Continues into Early Adulthood: Implications for the Development of Normal and Abnormal Function during Adolescence," by M. G. Cunningham, S. Bhattacharyya, and F. M. Benes, 2002, *The Journal of Comparative Neurology, 453,* pp. 116–130. Reprinted with permission of Wiley-Liss a subsidiary of John Wiley & Sons, Inc.

nism, respectively, that have been described in this disorder (Detre & Jarecki, 1971). In addition, superabundant glutamatergic inputs could themselves be responsible for GABA neuron loss as a result of an excitotoxic injury (Rothman & Olney, 1986). Such an effect on inhibitory interneurons has been experimentally induced in adult rats using the excitotoxin kainic acid (Zhang et al., 1990). Because excitotoxic mechanisms have been associated with ischemic injuries to the brain (Rothman & Olney, 1986), it is possible that perinatal complication, such as prolonged labor (Jacobsen & Kinney, 1980), could result in a lower oxygen tension or high levels of glucocorticoids. Hypoxia does not appear to be a likely source of early neuronal damage in schizophrenic subjects because many different complications have been found in their obstetrical records, but most are not associated with a low oxygen tension. Rather, a nonspecific stress response, with unusually high circulating titers of glucocorticoid hormone, would be a more likely setting in which damage to the immature brain might occur (Sapolsky, 1992; Sapolsky & Meaney, 1986). Reductions in neuronal cell content (Cotterrell, Balazs, & Johnson, 1972) have been associated with high levels of corticosterone early in life, making it plausible that a variety of stressors could induce alterations of brain circuitry by triggering a nonspecific stress response. It is noteworthy that glucocorticoids seem to potentiate the excitotoxic effects of kainic acid (Stein-Behrens et al., 1992), and such a mechanism could influence the proposed role of glutamatergic afferents in the pathophysiologic changes that occur in the anterior cingulate cortex and hippocampus of schizophrenic subjects. Because the cortex develops in an inside-out fashion (Sidman & Rakic, 1973) and basket cells of layer II are particularly immature in the human brain at the time of birth (Marin-Padilla, 1970b), it is possible that GABAergic interneurons may be particularly vulnerable to the effects of perinatal complications (Benes, 1993a). In this regard, it is worth noting that, in immature rat brains, neurons with NMDA receptors may have periods in which they exhibit hypervulnerability to even moderate amounts of receptor stimulation (Ikonomidou, Mosinger, Shahid Sallett, Labruyere, & Olney, 1989). Apparently, different populations of neurons show their own periods of peak vulnerability (Olney, Sesma, & Wozniak, 1993). Because GABAergic neurons of the corpus striatum are particularly sensitive to excitotoxic degeneration in adult rats (Schwarcz & Coyle, 1977), it is possible that basket cells in various layers of the immature cortex also show selective hypersensitivity to stimulation of NMDA receptors at particular stages of development. Indeed, excessive numbers of glutamatergic inputs to superficial laminae might be a predisposing factor for a perinatal hypoxic insult to result in a failure of cortical basket neurons to mature.

Although current hypotheses regarding the etiology of Schizophrenia favor a model in which an early brain injury plays a key role in this disorder (P. B. Jones, Rantakallio, Hartikainen, Isohanni, & Sipila, 1998; Seidman et al., 2000), it is also possible that an excitotoxic injury might occur later in the life of a schizophrenic individual (Benes, 2000; Benes, Sorensen, et al., 1992). This disorder has a characteristic onset between 16 and 25 years of age (Kraepelin, 1919), a period during which the human brain shows active myelination of a key corticolimbic relay area (Benes, 1989). Because the occurrence of myelination would be associated with an increased velocity of conduction (Huxley & Stampel, 1949), this developmental change might be expected to enhance associative processing in corticolimbic areas also found to have structural alterations in schizophrenics. In the setting of excessive associative inputs to the anterior cingulate cortex, an

increased release of glutamate occurring in response to emotional stress mediated through the BLA could theoretically trigger an excitotoxic response in the anterior cingulate cortex during the 2nd or 3rd decade of life.

FUTURE DIRECTIONS

There are several directions that developmental neurobiologic studies of Schizophrenia and affective disorders can follow in the coming years. These directions are discussed here in detail.

Identification of How Circuitry Is Altered

The most essential phase of developmental neurobiologic studies of Schizophrenia and other psychiatric disorders is the precise identification of abnormalities in the intrinsic circuits of involved brain regions. Each psychiatric disorder will require appropriate neurobiologic strategies.

Schizophrenia

As shown in Figure 5.9, the vertical axons depicted in the model shown in Figure 5.8 could potentially be fibers em-

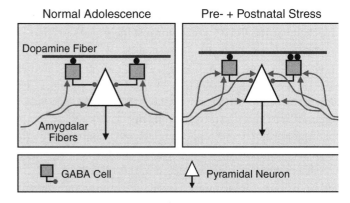

Figure 5.9 A schematic diagram similar to the one shown in Figure 5.8 showing a cortical pyramidal cell in the cingulate cortex that receives convergent inputs from dopaminergic and amygdalar fibers. Individuals exposed to both pre- and postnatal stress show a increased number of inputs from these two fiber systems. Under stressful conditions, some fibers release excess amounts of dopamine, and others release excess glutamate. At a critical stage of development, such as adolescence, these fiber systems are growing into the anterior cingulate cortex and may cause the intrinsic circuitry to decompensate in individuals exposed to severe stress during both the pre- and postnatal periods. From "Amygdalo-Cortical Sprouting Continues into Early Adulthood: Implications for the Development of Normal and Abnormal Function during Adolescence" by M. G. Cunningham, S. Bhattacharyya, and F. M. Benes, 2002, *The Journal of Comparitive Neurology, 453,* p. 124. Reprinted with permission of Wiley-Liss a subsidiary of John Wiley & Sons, Inc.

anating from the basolateral amygdala. In individuals exposed to both pre- and postnatal stress, it is hypothetically possible that this fiber system could be induced to sprout as a result of heightened activity in the basolateral nucleus of the amygdala (BLn). In this setting, a hyperinnervation of both the dopamine and amygdalar projections converging on GABAergic cells could occur and mitigate oxidative stress and potentially apoptotic cell death. If dopaminergic projections are inhibitory in nature, would their activity tend to cancel that excitatory drive coming from the amygdala? It is important to emphasize that these two fiber systems are fundamentally different in terms of their mechanisms of action. Whereas amygdala afferents to the cortex engage in synaptic connections and induce fast synaptic changes in their postsynaptic targets, dopamine fibers are modulatory in nature and induce long-lasting inhibitory changes. If the latter fibers are increased in number, especially if the release of dopamine is increased under stressful conditions, then it would be increasingly difficult for amygdalar fibers to induce depolarization in GABA cells. Inhibitory activity in the larger circuitry would be diminished. We can imagine a scenario in which the amygdalar fibers continue to release glutamate, until the inhibitory effect of dopamine is overcome. It is well-known that excitatory activity generates an influx of calcium ions that have the ability to cause an uncoupling of oxidative phosphorylation in mitochondria. This change, in turn, could potentially result in oxidative stress and the apoptosis signaling cascade being activated and underscores the importance of understanding the convergent inputs to GABAergic interneurons and the manner in which they respond to stressful conditions. This model is predicated on the idea that the circuit will decompensate under stressful conditions if the stress is occurring at a critical stage of development when dopamine and amygdalar fibers have attained a level of innervations that can produce such changes.

Affective Disorders

With regard to the affective disorders, where more postmortem work has been performed in the past 5 to 7 years, more has been learned about brain circuitry. Notably, the regions implicated in Schizophrenia also appear to be affected in Bipolar Disorder (Benes, Kwok, Vincent, & Todtenkopf, 1998; Benes, Todtenkopf, Logiotatos, & Williams, 2000; Heckers et al., 2002). This is entirely consistent with the idea that the same categories of behavior are affected in both disorders. Although the nature of the symptoms and course may vary considerably, it is not difficult to conceptualize that brain regions involved in motivation, attention, affect, stress, and learning might also show abnormalities in Schizophrenia and Bipolar Disorder. Nevertheless, it seems likely that the affective disorders will involve, either directly or indirectly, disturbances in monoaminergic integration. With regard to the corticolimbic system, it will be important to assess whether and, if so, how these monoaminergic systems are altered in individuals with depression and/or mania. Using immunocytochemical techniques, the distribution of noradrenergic and serotonergic fibers can be analyzed with respect to discrete subregions, layers, and neuronal cell types. This information can, in turn, be used to interpret the results of receptor binding activity associated with each transmitter's system. For example, depressed patients have up-regulated serotonin (Meltzer & Lowy, 1987) and noradrenergic (Siever, 1987) receptor binding activity that becomes down-regulated when they are treated with antidepressant compounds (Charney, Menkes, & Heninger, 1981).

In this latter regard, several different mechanisms could potentially result in increased receptor binding activity: (1) decreased synthesis or release of norepinephrine and 5-HT, (2) an increased rate of transmitter inactivation following release, (3) an increase in the synthesis of receptor molecules (beta, or 5-HT2), or (4) a decrease in the rate of degradation of the receptor molecule. Each of these mechanisms could, in turn, be either primarily or secondarily altered; that is, changes may arise either from an intrinsic dysregulation of the genetic mechanisms involved in their regulation or as a result of effects exerted by pre- or postsynaptic neuronal elements influencing the cell in which they are found. It will be of central importance to determine the *specific* genetic and cellular mechanisms through which the activity of the relevant transmitter system has been modified. It will also be important to assess when these changes may have appeared during the life cycle of an individual with a mood disorder. A neurodevelopmental strategy may then yield information that might eventually lead to preventive, rather than ameliorative, treatment approaches.

To understand the onset of psychopathologic states it is important to determine which corticolimbic regions show these latter changes, what types of neurons within these regions mainly account for the differences, and how the intrinsic circuits within each region have been altered as a result of such changes. In the intervening time, we have learned that subjects with Bipolar Disorder, like those with Schizophrenia, show decreases in the expression of messenger RNA for GAD65 (Guidotti et al., 2000; Heckers et al., 2002) and GAD67 (Heckers et al., 2002).

Additionally, presynaptic axon terminals containing GAD65 have been found to be significantly reduced in patients with Bipolar Disorder, but not those with Schizophrenia (Benes, Todtenkopf, et al., 2000), suggesting that neuronal cell death may be a feature of the latter, but less so in the former. In addition to cell counting studies, further evidence in support of this idea has come from a study showing an unexpected decrease of DNA damage, a marker for apoptotic injury, in Schizophrenia, but not Bipolar Disorder (Benes, Walsh, Bhattacharyya, Sheth, & Berretta, 2003). Consistent with this, a recent gene expression profiling study has demonstrated a marked up-regulation of genes associated with the apoptosis cascade in bipolar subjects, but not in schizophrenics (Benes, Burke, Matzilevich, Walsh, & Minns, 2004). The idea that Bipolar Disorder involves cell death to a greater degree than Schizophrenia is counterintuitive, given the chronic dysfunctional state that is typically found in Schizophrenia. This contrasts strikingly with the episodic nature of Bipolar Disorder and the characteristic return to normal baseline functioning following a manic or depressive episode.

Linking Risk Factor to Histopathologic Abnormalities

It will be essential to define what the risk factors for a particular illness are and whether they may be inherited or acquired. As previously discussed with respect to Schizophrenia, it is now widely believed that a genetically determined latent trait acting alone or in combination with an early brain insult may play an etiologic role in the occurrence of this disorder. Once the risk factors are specifically identified, it will be necessary to develop strategies that aim to elucidate the neurobiologic consequences for an individual who carries these risk factors—that is, how they might result in specific circuitry alterations within corticolimbic regions.

Genetic Traits

One approach that postmortem investigations can use to relate certain histopathologic abnormalities to a genetic risk factor for Schizophrenia is to carefully analyze the data observed in different subtypes of the disorder. For example, Schizophrenia both with and without superimposed mood disturbances may be variations of the same illness but with somewhat different patterns of inheritance. Bleuler (1952) was the first to suggest that Schizophrenia may be a heterogeneous group of illnesses, and the so-called Schizoaffective Disorder is probably one of its subtypes. A genetic

etiology has been suggested for Schizophrenia (Gottesman & Shields, 1972; Kendler, Gruenberg, & Tsuang, 1985; Kety & Matthysse, 1972; Kety et al., 1968), but Schizoaffective Disorder has not been extensively studied. It is possible that particularly severe affective disorder could give rise to a syndrome that, in many respects, is indistinguishable from Schizophrenia (J. J. Levitt & Tsuang, 1988). Family studies have shown different findings for the two types of Schizophrenia. For example, both affective disorder and Schizophrenia tend to occur among the family members of schizoaffective patients (Fowler, 1978; J. J. Levitt & Tsuang, 1988), and a prevalence for schizotypal personality and Schizophrenia has been found in the first-degree relatives of schizophrenics (Kendler et al., 1985). Thus, although genetic factors for the two disorders are different in some respects, they also seem to overlap. Schizoaffective patients are believed to represent a genetically heterogeneous group of patients, so it might be expected that a microscopic finding emanating from a heritable trait that is common to both disorders would be more striking in the schizophrenic patients without mood disturbances who might be considered genotypically more homogeneous. However, from the data reported for neuronal cell density in the anterior cingulate and prefrontal cortices (Benes et al., 1991), the opposite was true. In the latter study, the small neuron density was even lower in the schizoaffective group when compared to the schizophrenics without superimposed mood disturbances. This latter finding might therefore argue in favor of the lower density of interneurons not having arisen from a primary genetic defect, but rather from birth complications or some other environmental insult.

In the future, if microscopic analyses can demonstrate that an abnormality is present in schizophrenics and schizoaffectives but not in manic depressive illness, this could potentially lay the groundwork for identifying the effects of a putative genetic trait. The next step will be to assess what types of genes might be involved in generating such an abnormality and to begin the arduous task of using molecular genetic approaches to determine which products of gene expression are involved. Once the gene is identified, it will be necessary to establish what the gene normally encodes for and how this encoding process could go awry at specific developmental stages, and then produce an alteration of brain circuitry like that seen in the disorder. A general discussion of this goal is straightforward, but the specific details of how to do this are awesome in their implications.

Current approaches to the genetics of Schizophrenia deal with familial tendencies for particular characteristics and as such are at the most gross phenomic level. Because our current understanding of human genetics is at a rather rudimentary level, it is difficult to identify the phenomic equivalents for particular genes. There are genes that encode for both structural and functional protein molecules, but there are also loci that regulate the transcription of these genes by either turning them on or shutting them down. Accordingly, an alteration in the phenomic expression of a particular gene in human subjects could arise through changes in its own nucleotide sequence or the sequence for sites that regulate its expression, the so-called switches. It will also be important to determine whether a genetic variant involved in a psychiatric illness is uniformly expressed throughout the central nervous system. It is theoretically possible that there may be regional variations in the degree to which an abnormal gene is expressed, an issue that derives from the unique neurobiologic properties of the central nervous system. For example, an abnormality related to the GABA system that results in excessive GABA receptor activity could arise from a primary defect in the structure of the receptor molecule and affect its affinity properties; alternatively, it could be derived from a change in the postsynaptic regulation of gene expression for this locus as the receptor undergoes a compensatory up-regulation. There could also be primary alterations in the mechanisms through which GABA-A receptor molecules are packaged and transported to the surface of neuronal cell bodies in the anterior cingulate cortex of schizophrenics. Alternatively, there could be a primary defect in the expression of glutamate decarboxylase, the enzyme that synthesizes GABA, and this could give rise to a decrease in the amount of GABA available to interact with the receptor. The latter situation would also result in a compensatory up-regulation of GABA-A binding that secondarily, but not primarily, produces a change in the regulation of expression for the receptor gene.

The finding of increased glutamatergic afferents in superficial layers of the anterior cingulate cortex could also be attributable to a primary gene defect. In this instance, however, it will be even more complicated to define the specific mechanisms through which such a change might arise, because there is little general information regarding the genetic regulation of neuronal differentiation and the establishment of connectivity during brain ontogeny. Thus, the elucidation of such mechanisms related to specific types of neurons and specific types of fibers is not likely to be forthcoming for some time. Nevertheless, we can look forward to a time in the foreseeable future when information of this type will begin to emerge and will be available

to developmental psychopathologists for the study of mental illness.

Acquired Risk Factors

The strategies required for assessing the role of environment in the occurrence of Schizophrenia and other mental disorders will, in some respects, be different from those needed for the genetic factors. In addition to human genetic studies, it will be necessary to use animal models to assess how various types of environmental perturbations may induce alterations of brain structure and function. Animal models of behavior relevant to psychiatry have distinct limitations; nevertheless, they provide carefully controlled paradigms for evaluating the role of certain acquired factors (Henn & McKinney, 1987), and a critical use of such models can provide meaningful information.

Many different types of acquired insult have been traced to the records of schizophrenic subjects, including prolonged labor, viral infections in utero, head trauma, and emotional trauma. The heterogeneity of these factors makes it difficult to model for an early insult, unless a common denominator to all can be established. As noted, stressful conditions of any type result in an elevation of adrenal glucocorticoid levels in the blood as part of a general adaptive responsive of the body. It seems plausible that early traumatic events of any type could potentially produce a generalized insult to the brain. It does not seem likely, however, that such events would be sufficient to explain Schizophrenia or other mental illnesses, because individuals exposed to even severe anoxia resulting in cerebral palsy do not show any increased risk for psychosis. Nevertheless, studies of the effects of pre- and postnatal exposure to glucocorticoids on the development of the corticolimbic circuitry will provide important insights into the role of early stress in the etiology of Schizophrenia.

With regard to affective disorders, environmental factors are also thought to play an etiologic role, and a variety of animal models have been proposed for the study of this relationship. These have included maternal separation (Jensen & Tolman, 1962), learned helplessness (Overmeier & Seligman, 1967), behavioral despair (Porsolt, Bertin, & Jalfre, 1977), and chronic unpredictable stress (Katz, Roth, & Carroll, 1981). Studies using these and other models have attempted to establish construct validity by measuring various neurochemical markers related to monoaminergic transmitter systems to determine whether changes similar to those found in depressed patients can be elicited. For example, with the separation model, low cerebrospinal fluid (CSF) norepinephrine levels are thought to be a trait marker that predicts a greater vulnerability, and reduction of CSF hydroxyindolacetic acid (HIAA) may be a state marker reflecting the behavioral response to this experimental manipulation (Kraemer, Ebert, Lake, & McKinney, 1984). In contrast, the observation that a tricyclic antidepressant can reverse the potentiated response of such animals to subsequent separation (Kraemer & McKinney, 1979) suggests that this paradigm may also have predictive validity as a model for depression. None of these models is completely satisfactory, but they are powerful research tools for studying the role of environmental conditions in the occurrence of mental illness.

The Interactions of Genetic and Acquired Risk Factors

As suggested by Hebb (1949), the influence of environment on the occurrence of mental illness is probably dependent on the constitution of the individual on whom it is acting. In modeling developmentally for the etiology of mental disorders, it seems appropriate to postulate that an environmental factor will likely interact with constitutional factors to give rise to Schizophrenia, mood disturbances, and other psychiatric illnesses. Thus, a nonspecific insult associated with the release of neurotoxic levels of glucocorticoids could result in a diffuse loss of neurons, although the specific loci for such loss may depend on other factors that impart a *selective vulnerability*. For example, with regard to Schizophrenia, a preexisting increase of glutamatergic afferents to superficial layers of the anterior cingulate cortex could potentiate an excitotoxic injury to neurons with which they interact. In the setting of a stress response, the increased levels of circulating glucocorticoids could provide a precipitant for the increased release of glutamate at NMDA-mediated synapses (Stein-Behrens et al., 1992). Selectively bred strains of rodents will be a potent research tool to investigate the interaction of environmentally induced stress on genetically determined vulnerability for various psychiatric disorders. For example, operant responses of alcohol-preferring and alcohol-nonpreferring rats are being characterized (Murphy, Gatto, McBride, Lumeng, & Li, 1989), and differential responses of various neurotransmitters in these strains are being identified (McBride, Murphy, Lumeng, & Li, 1990). Selectively bred recombinant strains of mice are also being developed for the study of depression (Beekman, Flachskamm, & Linthorst, 2005). This general strategy will undoubtedly provide important insights into the interplay of genetic vulnerability with environmental factors.

Critical Stages for the Development of Psychopathology

It has been recognized for some time that various mental disorders frequently show a characteristic age of onset. Most schizophrenic patients will first present with symptoms at approximately 15 to 25 years of age, and this observation has led to the suggestion that normal ontogenetic changes during adolescence and early adulthood could theoretically play a role in the appearance of schizophrenic symptoms (Benes, 1988). Empiric support for such a viewpoint comes from studies of monkeys that received unilateral extirpative lesions of the dorsolateral prefrontal cortex soon after birth. There was no difference in the performance of lesioned and unlesioned monkeys on the delayed response task following recovery from the surgical procedure (Goldman-Rakic, 1981). When both sets of monkeys were again tested at approximately 2 to 3 years of age (their equivalent of pubescence), the unlesioned monkeys showed an age-appropriate performance, but the lesioned monkeys now showed a marked impairment of performance on the same task (Goldman-Rakic, 1981). These results were interpreted as indicating that late postnatal changes in the dorsolateral prefrontal region of monkeys might have provided a framework in which the previously latent effects of the lesioning could become manifest. However, the nature of these putative ontogenetic changes is not understood. Possible alterations that could play a role in the onset of Schizophrenia include a defect of synaptic elimination, which normally occurs in the cortex between 5 and 15 years of age (Feinberg, 1982), or the maturation of the cortical dopamine innervation during adolescence (Benes et al., 1996).

As discussed earlier, it is also known that changes in the myelination of a key corticolimbic relay zone occur during adolescence and again during the 5th and 6th decades of life. The fibers showing these postnatal changes probably derive from the cingulate cortex and possibly also the entorhinal cortex (Benes, 1989; Benes et al., 1994), and all of these regions have been implicated by recent postmortem investigations in the pathophysiology of Schizophrenia. An increase in the velocity of conduction would occur on these associative fibers as myelin sheaths form. An increased release of glutamate at NMDA-mediated synapses would also occur in relation to the overall increase of associative activity within this corticolimbic relay zone. In the setting of increased numbers of glutamatergic fibers into the anterior cingulate cortex, such changes elsewhere in the corticolimbic system could trigger an excitotoxic injury within this region. Thus, late postnatal changes in the maturation of the corticolimbic system could conceivably play a role in the appearance of schizophrenic symptoms during adolescence. As discussed earlier, most neurotransmitter systems, both intrinsic and extrinsic to the cortex, show appreciable postnatal changes and could create an overall environment that is permissive for the onset of Schizophrenia.

A neurodevelopmental approach to the study of mental illness will require that we obtain a clearer understanding of how various neurotransmitter systems may be undergoing normal ontogenetic changes during the critical stages identified for each illness. For example, with regard to the model of Schizophrenia described earlier, the glutamate and GABA systems both show extensive postnatal maturation up to and, in some cases, including adulthood. The dopamine system also undergoes extensive postnatal development. It will be important to know the extent to which the dopamine system interacts with the GABA (Benes et al., 1996; Verney, Alvarez, Gerrard, & Berger, 1990) and glutamate (Goldman-Rakic, Leranth, Williams, Mons, & Geffard, 1989) systems, and the degree to which such interactions could play a role in the etiology and/or treatment response of this disorder at different stages of the illness. Ultimately, abnormal interactions among these various neurotransmitter systems will be understood in relation to postnatal brain ontogeny and the complex symptomatology of the disorder.

With regard to mood disorders, maturational changes in both the noradrenergic and serotonergic systems also proceed well beyond birth and, at least in some cases, even into adulthood. If a genetic factor related to monoaminergic transmission plays a role in the etiology of the affective disorders, it will be important to define the critical developmental periods during which the expression of a relevant gene is switched on or off. Information of this type can potentially be related to periods of the life cycle when environmental factors might contribute to the actual development of a mood disorder in an individual with genetic vulnerability. The experiences of such a person could be learned through neuroplastic changes that give rise to permanently altered networks of associative connections. Because norepinephrine and serotonin have both been implicated in the establishment of cortical connectivity during ontogenesis as well as the pathophysiology of depression, an abnormal gene related to these transmitter systems could theoretically play a role in the acquisition of maladaptive responses, such as learned helplessness or sep-

aration sensitivity, in individuals with a selective vulnerability for affective disorder.

It is clear that late postnatal changes in the convergence of dopamine and serotonin fibers onto GABAergic interneurons can potentially help to lay the groundwork for the formation of both normal and abnormal wiring patterns in the corticolimbic system of the human brain. In those who carry the vulnerability for psychopathology, such changes may well contribute to the onset of mental illness during adolescence and adulthood. Our understanding of how these putative miswirings occur must rest on a solid neurobiological foundation, one in which the cellular and molecular mechanisms that control the plasticity of dopamine and serotonin fibers are better understood.

Molecular Mechanisms in Developmental Psychopathology

Future studies will consider the mechanisms that may be involved in the establishment of connections between monoaminergic fibers and intrinsic cortical neurons. Toward this end, there are several proteins that comprise a family of trophic factors, such as nerve growth factor (NGF), brain derived neurotrophic factor (BDNF), and the neurotrophins NT-3 and NT4/5, that play a role in the differentiation, survival, and maintenance of central neurons (Caleo, Menna, Chierzi, Cenni, & Maffei, 2000). The effects of BDNF and NT-3 on long-term potentiation in the hippocampus are mediated, at least in part, through specialized receptors, called Trk B and Trk C (Bramham, Southard, Sarvey, Herkenham, & Brady, 1996). This suggests that trophic changes at the molecular level contribute to the learning and memory associated with hippocampal function. During development of the cortex, GABAergic interneurons show a marked up-regulation in the expression of the genes for BDNF, NT4/5, and Trk B. It is noteworthy that these changes are believed to contribute to the intercellular signaling that occurs in nearby neurons showing evidence of apoptosis (Wang, Sheen, & Macklis, 1998). In the nigrostriatal system, the expression of messenger mRNA for BDNF, NT-3, Trk B, and Trk C influences the differentiation of neurons; BDNF and Trk B also seem to work through a dopaminergic mechanism involving the D1 receptor (Jung & Bennett, 1996). Although BDNF and NT-3 are quite active during early development, they continue to play a role in the regulation of functions, such as long-term potentiation, during the adult period (Bramham et al., 1996; Castren et al., 1993). It will be important for future studies to focus attention on these various trophic factors and their associated receptors so that we can learn more about the specific role that they may play not only in the differentiation of neurons, but also in the functional maintenance of mature synapses.

It will also be pertinent to consider what role trophic factors and/or their receptors might specifically play in the competition of 5-HT fibers with convergent dopamine (DA) inputs to GABA cells during the postnatal period. Under normal conditions, it seems reasonable to postulate that BNDF and/or its associated receptor Trk B, or possibly NT-3 and/or its receptor Trk C, might contribute to the establishment and/or maintenance of these monoaminergic connections with GABAergic interneurons. From the standpoint of normal development, it is possible that BDNF is synthesized and released by intrinsic cortical neurons, and, once in the extracellular space, this trophin could help to promote the apposition of DA and 5-HT fibers on their outer cell membrane. In other words, once released, trophic factors might be free to exert their action directly on dopaminergic fibers, particularly those that have the potential to sprout, when stimulated to do so by the appropriate molecular stimuli. In contrast, abnormal conditions may be associated with an inappropriate release of one or more trophic factors by intrinsic cortical neurons, and this could theoretically provide the setting in which aberrant connection patterns emerge. An alternative possibility is that the elaboration of trophic factors by intrinsic neurons is relatively normal in some forms of psychopathology; however, the expression of their associated receptors (e.g., Trk B or Trk C) on extrinsic fiber systems like those from the ventral tegmental dopamine neurons might be abnormal. Either way, the net result could be the formation of increased numbers of appositions on one cell type (in this case, GABA cells) if it is releasing excessive amounts of trophic factor(s) and decreased contacts with another cell type, for example, projection neurons, if these latter cells show a down-regulation of one or more trophic factor systems. If the dopamine fibers are subject to limitations in the amount of sprouting they can undergo, this may influence the number of Trk B or Trk C receptors expressed by them. A second type of intrinsic neuron, the pyramidal cell, might show the opposite effect: a proportionate decrease in the number of DA fibers forming appositions.

CONCLUSIONS

It is clear that our understanding of the development of psychopathology has benefited from the use of sophisticated molecular approaches to analyze the expression of genes.

Microscopic techniques, such as in situ hybridization and immunocytochemistry, have a high degree of spatial resolution and will complement more encompassing approaches of gene expression profiling and proteomics. Gene expression profiling makes it possible to examine the regulation of 30,000 or more individual genes and offers an extraordinary view of the dynamics of cell regulation in the corticolimbic system. Such techniques are freeing neuroscientists from the constraints of studying one gene or protein at a time and are making it possible to study the complex cascades of changes that are probably occurring within corticolimbic neurons during normal and abnormal postnatal development. Recently collected microarray data from a cohort consisting of normal controls, schizophrenics, and bipolars show dramatic changes in the regulation of signaling and metabolic pathways in the hippocampus (Konradi et al., 2004). In this study, marked reductions in the expression of genes representing the electron transport chain were observed in bipolar subjects. Rather surprisingly, schizophrenics did not show these changes, although further analysis of this databases has revealed significant changes in a broad array of genes associated with calcium channels, monoamine and peptide G-coupled protein receptors, transforming growth factor beta (TGFb) and Wnt signaling, and ribosomal regulation (Matzilevich, Burke, & Benes, 2004). Particularly noteworthy is the fact that the apoptosis pathway containing 44 different genes was significantly altered in both Schizophrenia and Bipolar Disorder, with the latter showing increased and the former decreased expression of key genes associated with cell death.

Recent studies provide support for the idea that the dopamine and serotonin systems show a significant degree of convergence and plasticity in the cingulate cortex, and the degree to which this occurs is probably similar for both pyramidal cells and GABAergic interneurons. Particularly noteworthy is the fact that the dopamine system may be capable of considerable plasticity, at least until the start of the early adult period. If the dopamine system in the human brain exhibits similar characteristics, the maturation of the limbic cortex during adolescence and early adulthood may potentially provide a window of opportunity for the induction of abnormal interactions of the monoaminergic systems with one another and with their intrinsic cortical targets. Indeed, some experimental evidence suggests that exposure to adrenal steroids during the postnatal period can result in an increase of dopamine interactions with interneurons in the medial prefronal cortex of rats also exposed to these hormones prenatally (Benes, 1997). For GABAergic interneurons, complex changes in the regulation of GAD have been observed; however, these occur whether or not there has been exposure prenatally to adrenal steroids (Stone, Walsh, & Benes, 2001). Based on these studies, an important question to ask is whether pre- and/or postnatal stress might also result in an altered distribution of serotonergic projections in the anterior cingulate cortex, one that may be reciprocal in nature to that observed for the dopamine system. If this were the case, the activity of GABAergic interneurons would be compromised by the presence of excessive dopaminergic inputs that are inhibitory in nature and diminished serotonergic inputs that are excitatory in nature. Because a combination of pre- and postnatal stress is believed to play a central role in the pathophysiology of some neuropsychiatric disorders (Benes, 1997; Walker & Diforio, 1997), it is plausible that changes in the way these two monoaminergic systems interact with one another might ultimately influence the activity of the individual cortical neurons on which they both converge.

This model appears to have predictive validity in that individuals with Schizophrenia and/or Bipolar Disorder who have a higher expected occurrence of obstetrical complications may be more likely to have an excess number of dopaminergic inputs to GABAergic interneurons. Such patients typically benefit from major tranquilizers that block dopamine receptors, as well as benzodiazepines that enhance the activity of GABA at the GABA$_A$ receptor. The model is also consistent with the fact that patients in the manic phase of Bipolar Disorder typically show an exacerbation of their symptoms with antidepressant medications. Because many of these drugs block the reuptake of serotonin, the model also predicts that the pyramidal neuron, if receiving an excessive excitatory input from this system, would show even more heightened activity.

All models have weaknesses, and the principal weakness of this model is the fact that there have not as yet been systematic studies of the effects of pre- and postnatal stress on the relative numbers of dopamine *and* serotonin fibers on pyramidal cells versus GABA cells using a colocalization technique. Monoamine G-couple protein receptors, such as the dopamine D4 and 5-HT7 subtypes, are noteworthy for their high affinity for atypical antipsychotic drugs (Lane et al., 2004; Meltzer, 1994). As described earlier, these findings fit well with those obtained for parallel postmortem studies showing changes in the both the D4 and 5-HT7 receptor subtypes. Although some aspects of the model are inferential in nature, others have been cross-validated using a combination of rat and human studies. Future studies should be directed at identifying further what effect stress might have on convergent dopaminergic and serotonergic fibers on target neurons of the cortex, how

this interaction may be influenced by exposure to pre- and postnatal stress, and how various psychotropic drugs may exert their action in relation to neuroplastic changes in these convergent monoaminergic fiber systems.

Overall, the study of abnormal conditions such as Schizophrenia and Bipolar Disorder in a neurodevelopmental context offers the potential to learn more about the structure and function of the human brain and how perturbations of its development during critical stages can result in dysfunction. Unlike Alzheimer's disease, where there is widespread degeneration of the corticolimbic system, these same regions in individuals with Schizophrenia and Bipolar Disorder show only minimal degrees of atrophy and/or neuronal cell death that is restricted to discrete loci, such as layer II in the anterior cingulate cortex and sector CA2 of the hippocampus. Similarly, these latter disorders seem to show subtle alterations in the pattern of connectivity between extrinsic and intrinsic neurons within complex circuits. By their very nature, the neuropsychiatric disorders provide a natural model system in which the wiring of the brain may be studied to understand how slight variations can result in profound disturbances of complex cognitive functions. It is in the area of gene expression that Schizophrenia and Bipolar Disorder show much more pronounced differences. In the years to come, it is reasonable to expect that our understanding of how the corticolimbic system is altered in Schizophrenia and Bipolar Disorder will continue to expand, and there will be important new insights into how the corticolimbic system is functioning under both normal and abnormal conditions (Deskin et al., 1981).

Ultimately, our understanding of the pathophysiology of psychiatric illness will have to take into account a complex interplay between the various risk factors for these illnesses and normal developmental changes in the brain. On the one hand, it is likely that a genetic factor and/or an acquired insult to the brain can alter normal brain development, perhaps focally or in a generalized way. On the other hand, once the brain of an individual who is at risk for a mental illness has been affected by environmental risk factors, then normal ontogenetic changes may trigger their expression during critical periods of postnatal development. The inherited risk factor for affective disorder is probably different from that for Schizophrenia, and the types of environmental factors that influence their expression may also be different. In applying a developmental approach to the study of Schizophrenia, mood disorders, and other forms of psychopathology that present during childhood, adolescence, and adulthood, it will be necessary to define the unique neurobiologic consequences of abnormal genes found in relation to each of these illnesses and to establish an understanding of how the expression of such genes interplays with normal ontogenetic events during a critical period of life when an individual at risk for such an illness is apt to become symptomatic.

REFERENCES

Adamec, R. E. (1978). Normal and abnormal limbic system mechanism of emotive biasing. In K. E. Livingston & O. Hornykiewicz (Eds.), *Limbic mechanisms* (pp. 405–455). New York: Plenum Press.

Adamec, R. E. (1991). Individual differences in temporal lobe sensory processing of threatening stimuli in the cat. *Physiology and Behavior, 49,* 445–464.

Adamec, R. E. (1992). Anxious personality in the cat: Its ontogeny and physiology. In B. J. Carroll & J. E. Barrett (Eds.), *Psychopathology and the brain* (pp. 153–168). New York: Raven Press.

Adamec, R. E., Stark-Adamec, C., & Livingston, K. E. (1980). The development of predatory aggression and defense in the domestic cat (Felinus Catus). I. Effects of early experience on adult patterns of aggression and defense. *Behavioral Neurology and Biology, 30,* 389–409.

Amaral, D. G., Price, J. L., Pitkanen, A., & Carmichael, S. T. (1992). Anatomical organization of the primate amygdaloid complex. In J. P. Aggleton (Ed.), *The amygdala: Neurobiological aspects of emotion, memory, and mental dysfunction* (pp. 1–66). New York: Alan R. Liss.

American Psychiatric Association. (1994). *Diagnostic and statistical manual of mental disorders* (4th ed.). Washington, DC: Author.

Anand, B. K., & Dua, S. (1956). Circulatory and respiratory changes induced by electrical stimulation of the limbic system (visceral brain). *Journal of Neurophysiology, 19,* 393–400.

Angevine, J. B. (1965). Time of neuron origin in the hippocampal region: An autoradiographic study in the mouse. *Experimental Neurology, 13,* 1–70.

Armony, J. L., Servan Schreiber, D., Cohen, J. D., & LeDoux, J. E. (1995). An anatomically constrained neural network model of fear conditioning. *Behavioral Neuroscience, 109*(2), 246–257.

Bacon, S. J., Headlam, A. J., Gabbott, P. L., & Smith, A. D. (1996). Amygdala input to medial prefrontal cortex (mPFC) in the rat: a light and electron microscope study. *Brain Research, 720*(1/2), 211–219.

Ballantine, H. T., Cassidy, W. L., Flanagan, N. W., & Marino, R. (1967). Stereotoxic anterior cingulotomy for neuropsychiatric illness and intractable pain. *Journal of Neurosurgery, 26,* 488–495.

Bannon, M. J., Wolf, M. E., & Roth, R. H. (1983). Pharmacology of dopamine neurons innervating the prefrontal, cingulate and piriform cortices. *European Journal of Pharmacology, 92,* 119–125.

Barrelet, L., Ferrero, F., Szogethy, L., Giddey, C., & Pellizzer, G. (1990). Expressed emotion and first-admission Schizophrenia nine-month follow-up in a French cultural environment. *British Journal of Psychiatry, 156,* 357–362.

Barris, R. W., & Schumann, H. R. (1953). Bilateral anterior cingulate gyrus lesions: Syndrome of the anterior cingulate gyri. *Journal of Neurology, 3,* 44–52.

Baudry, M., Arst, D., Oliver, M., & Lynch, G. (1981). Development of glutamate binding sites and their regulation by calcium in rat hippocampus. *Developmental Brain Research, 1,* 37–38.

Bayer, S. A. (1985). Neurogenesis of the magnocellular basal telencephalic nuclei in the rat. *International Journal of Developmental Neuroscience, 3,* 229–243.

Bayer, S. A., & Altman, J. (1991). *Neocortical development.* New York: Raven Press.

Bayer, S. A., Altman, J., & Russo, R. (1990). Lateral migration of cells in embryonic neocortex. *Society of Neuroscience Abstracts, 16,* 803.

Bayer, S. A., Yackel, J. W., & Puri, P. S. (1982). Neurons in the dentate gyrus granular layer substantially increase during juvenile and adult life. *Science, 216,* 890–892.

Bechara, A., Damasio, H., Damasio, A. R., & Lee, G. P. (1999). Different contributions of the human amygdala and ventromedial prefrontal cortex to decision-making. *Journal of Neuroscience, 19*(13), 5473–5481.

Bechara, A., Tranel, D., Damasio, H., Adolphs, R., Rockland, C., & Damasio, A. R. (1995). Double dissociation of conditioning and declarative knowledge relative to the amygdala and hippocampus in humans. *Science, 269*(5227), 1115–1118.

Beckstead, R. M. (1976). Convergent thalamic and mesencephalic projections to the anterior medial cortex in the rat. *Journal of Comparative Neurology, 166,* 403–416.

Beekman, M., Flachskamm, C., & Linthorst, A. C. (2005). Effects of exposure to a predator on behaviour and serotonergic neurotransmission in different brain regions of C57bl/6N mice. *European Journal of Neuroscience, 21*(10), 2825–2836.

Belaydier, C., & Maugierre, F. (1980). The duality of the cingulate gyrus in monkey: Neuroanatomical study and functional hypothesis. *Brain, 130,* 525–554.

Benes, F. M. (1988). Post-mortem structural analyses of schizophrenic brain: Study designs and the interpretation of data. *Psychiatric Developments, 6*(3), 213–226.

Benes, F. M. (1989). Myelination of cortical-hippocampal relays during late adolescence. *Schizophrenia Bulletin, 15*(4), 585–593.

Benes, F. M. (1993a). Neurobiological investigations in cingulate cortex of schizophrenic brain. *Schizophrenia Bulletin, 19*(3), 537–549.

Benes, F. M. (1993b). The relationship of cingulate cortex to Schizophrenia. In B. A. Vogt & M. Gabriel (Eds.), *Neurobiology of cingulate cortex and limbic thalamus* (pp. 581–605). Boston: Birkhäuser.

Benes, F. M. (1995). A neurodevelopmental approach to the understanding of Schizophrenia and other mental disorders. In D. Cicchetti & D. J. Cohen (Eds.), *Developmental psychopathology: Vol. 1. Theory and methods* (pp. 227–253). New York: Wiley.

Benes, F. M. (1997). The role of stress and dopamine-GABA interactions in the vulnerability for Schizophrenia. *Journal of Psychiatry Research, 31*(2), 257–275.

Benes, F. M. (2000). Emerging principles of altered neural circuitry in Schizophrenia. *Brain Research, 31*(2/3), 251–269.

Benes, F. M., & Berretta, S. (2000). Amygdalo-entorhinal inputs to the hippocampal formation in relation to Schizophrenia. *Annals of the New York Academy of Sciences, 911,* 293–304.

Benes, F. M., & Bird, E. D. (1987). An analysis of the arrangement of neurons in the cingulate cortex of schizophrenic patients. *Archives of General Psychiatry, 44*(7), 608–616.

Benes, F. M., Burke, R., Matzilevich, D., Walsh, J., & Minns, M. (2004). Differential regulation of the apoptosis pathways in hippocampus in Schizophrenia and bipolar disorder. *Society for Neuroscience Abstract.*

Benes, F. M., Bhattacharyya, S., & Cunningham, M. G. (2002). Progressive interaction of amygdalar projections with medial prefronatal GABA cells during the postnatal period. *Society for Neuroscience Abstract.*

Benes, F. M., Kwok, E. W., Vincent, S. L., & Todtenkopf, M. S. (1998). A reduction of nonpyramidal cells in sector CA2 of schizophrenics and manic depressives. *Biological Psychiatry, 44*(2), 88–97.

Benes, F. M., Majocha, R., Bird, E. D., & Marotta, C. A. (1987). Increased vertical axon numbers in cingulate cortex of schizophrenics. *Archives of General Psychiatry, 44*(11), 1017–1021.

Benes, F. M., McSparren, J., Bird, E. D., SanGiovanni, J. P., & Vincent, S. L. (1991). Deficits in small interneurons in prefrontal and cingulate cortices of schizophrenic and schizoaffective patients. *Archives of General Psychiatry, 48*(11), 996–1001.

Benes, F. M., McSparren, J., Bird, E. D., Vincent, S. L., & SanGiovanni, J. P. (1991). Deficits in small interneurons in prefrontal and anterior cingulate cortex of schizophrenic and schizoaffective patients. *Archives of General Psychiatry, 48,* 996–1001.

Benes, F. M., Sorensen, I., Vincent, S. L., Bird, E. D., & Sathi, M. (1992). Increased density of glutamate-immunoreactive vertical processes in superficial laminae in cingulate cortex of schizophrenic brain. *Cerebral Cortex, 2*(6), 503–512.

Benes, F. M., Taylor, J. B., & Cunningham, M. (2000). Convergence and plasticity of monoaminergic systems in the medial prefrontal cortex during the postnatal period: Implications for the development of psychopathology. *Cerebral Cortex, 10,* 1014–1027.

Benes, F. M., Todtenkopf, M. S., Logiotatos, P., & Williams, M. (2000). Glutamate decarboxylase(65)-immunoreactive terminals in cingulate and prefrontal cortices of schizophrenic and bipolar brain. *Journal of Chemical Neuroanatomy, 20*(3/4), 259–269.

Benes, F. M., Todtenkopf, M. S., & Taylor, J. B. (1997). Differential distribution of tyrosine hydroxylase fibers on small and large neurons in layer II of anterior cingulate cortex of schizophrenic brain. *Synapse, 25*(1), 80–92.

Benes, F. M., Turtle, M., Khan, Y., & Farol, P. (1994). Myelination of a key relay zone in the hippocampal formation occurs in the human brain during childhood, adolescence, and adulthood. *Archives of General Psychiatry, 51*(6), 477–484.

Benes, F. M., Vincent, S. L., Alsterberg, G., Bird, E. D., & SanGiovanni, J. P. (1992). Increased GABAA receptor binding in superficial layers of cingulate cortex in schizophrenics. *Journal of Neuroscience, 12*(3), 924–929.

Benes, F. M., Vincent, S. L., & Molloy, R. (1993). Dopamine-immunoreactive axon varicosities form nonrandom contacts with GABA-immunoreactive neurons of rat medial prefrontal cortex. *Synapse, 15*(4), 285–295.

Benes, F. M., Vincent, S. L., Molloy, R., & Khan, Y. (1996). Increased interaction of dopamine-immunoreactive varicosities with GABA neurons of rat medial prefrontal cortex occurs during the postweanling period. *Synapse, 23*(4), 237–245.

Benes, F. M., Walsh, J., Bhattacharyya, S., Sheth, A., & Berretta, S. (2003). DNA fragmentation decreased in Schizophrenia but not bipolar disorder. *Archives of General Psychiatry, 60*(4), 359–364.

Berger, B., Tassin, J. P., Blanc, G., Moyne, M. A., & Thierry, A. M. (1974). Histochemical confirmation for dopaminergic innervation of rat cerebral cortex after the destruction of noradrenergic ascending pathways. *Brain Research, 81,* 332–337.

Berger, B., & Verney, C. (1984). Development of the catecholamine innervation in rat neocortex: Morphological features. In L. Descarries, T. R. Reader, & H. H. Jasper (Eds.), *Monoamine innervation of cerebral cortex* (pp. 95–121). New York: Alan R. Liss.

Bergson, C., Mrzljak, L., Smiley, J. F., Pappy, M., Levenson, R., & Goldman-Rakic, P. S. (1995). Regional, cellular, and subcellular variations in the distribution of D1 and D5 dopamine receptors in primate brain. *Journal of Neuroscience, 15*(12), 7821–7836.

Berman, K. F., Zec, R. F., & Weinberger, D. R. (1986). Physiologic dysfunction of dorsolateral prefrontal cortex in Schizophrenia: II. Role of neuroleptic treatment, attention, and mental effort. *Archives of General Psychiatry, 43,* 126–135.

Bleuler, E. (1952). *Dementia praecox or the group of Schizophrenias.* New York: International Press.

Blinkov, S. M., & Glezer, I. I. (1968). *The human brain in figures and tables: A quantitative handbook.* New York: Plenum Press.

Bramham, C. R., Southard, T., Sarvey, J. M., Herkenham, M., & Brady, L. S. (1996). Unilateral LTP triggers bilateral increases in hippocampal neurothrophin and *trk* receptor mRNA expression in behaving rats: Evidence for interhemispheric communication. *Journal of Comparative Neurology, 368,* 371–382.

Broca, P. (1878). Anatomie comparée des circonvolutions cérébrales: Le grand lobe limbique et la scissure limbique dans la série des mamiferes. *Reviews in Anthropology, 1,* 385–498.

Broderick, P. A., & Phelix, C. F. (1997). I. Serotonin (5-HT) within dopamine reward circuits signals open-field behavior: II. Basis for 5-HT-DA interaction in cocaine dysfunctional behavior. *Neuroscience Biobehavioral Reviews, 21,* 227–260.

Brooksbank, B. W. L., Atkinson, D. J., & Balazs, R. (1981). Biochemical development of the human brain: II. Some parameters of the GABAergic system. *Developmental Neuroscience, 1,* 267–284.

Bruinink, A., Lichtensteiner, W., & Schlumpf, M. (1983). Pre- and postnatal ontogeny and characterization of dopaminergic D2, serotonergic S2, and spirodecanone binding sites in rat forebrain. *Journal of Neurochemistry, 40,* 1227–1237.

Cahill, L., & McGaugh, J. L. (1998). Mechanisms of emotional arousal and lasting declarative memory. *Trends in Neuroscience, 21*(7), 294–299.

Caleo, M., Menna, E., Chierzi, S., Cenni, M. C., & Maffei, L. (2000). Brain-derived neurotrophic factor is an anterograde survival factor in the rat visual system. *Current Opinion in Biology, 10*(19), 1155–1161.

Callaway, E., & Naghdi, S. (1982). An information processing model for Schizophrenia. *Archives of General Psychiatry, 39,* 339–347.

Cameron, N. (1938). Reasoning, regression and communication in schizophrenics. *Psychological Review Monographs, 50,* 1–33.

Candy, J. M., Bloxham, C. A., Thompson, J., Johnson, M., Oakley, A. E., & Edwardson, J. A. (1985). Evidence for the early prenatal development of cortical cholinergic afferents from the nucleus of meynert in the human fetus. *Neuroscience Letters, 61,* 91–95.

Candy, J. M., & Martin, I. L. (1979). The postnatal development of the benzodiazepine receptor in the cerebral cortex and cerebellum of the rat. *Journal of Neurochemistry, 32,* 655–658.

Carlsson, A. (1978). Mechanism of action of neuroleptic drugs. In M. A. Lipton, A. DiMascio, & K. F. Killam (Eds.), *Psychopharmacology: A generation of progress* (pp. 1057–1070). New York: Raven Press.

Castren, E., Pitkanen, M., Sirvio, J., Parsadanian, A., Lindholm, D., Thoenen, H., et al. (1993). The induction of LTP increases BDNF and NGF messenger RNA but decreases NT-3 messenger RNA in the dentate gyrus. *Neuroreport, 4,* 895–898.

Charney, D. S., Menkes, D. B., & Heninger, G. R. (1981). Receptor sensitivity and the mechanisms of action of antidepressant treatment. *Archives of General Psychiatry, 38,* 1160–1180.

Chen, Y., Bidwell, L. C., & Holzman, P. S. (2005). Visual motion integration in Schizophrenia patients, their first-degree relatives, and patients with bipolar disorder. *Schizophrenia Research, 74*(2/3), 271–281.

Cicchetti, D. (1993). Developmental pyschopathology: Reactions, reflections, projections. *Development and Psychopathology, 13,* 471–502.

Cicchetti, D., & Cannon, T. (1999). Neurodevelopmental processes in the ontogenesis and epigenesis of psychopathology. *Development and Psychopathology, 11,* 375–393.

Cicchetti, D., & Dawson, G. (2002). Editorial: Multiple levels of analysis. *Development and Psychopathology, 14,* 417–420.

Cicchetti, D., & Rogosch, F. A. (2002). A developmental psychopathology perspective on adolescence. *Journal of Consultation and Clinical Psychology, 70*(1), 6–20.

Cicchetti, D., & Sroufe, L. A. (2000). Editorial: The past as prologue to the future: The times, they've been a-changin. *Development and Psychopathology, 12,* 255–264.

Cloninger, C. R. (1991). Brain networks underlying personality development. In B. J. Carroll & J. E. Barrett (Eds.), *Psychopathology and the brain* (pp. 183–208). New York: Raven Press.

Cotterrell, M., Balazs, R., & Johnson, A. L. (1972). Effects of corticosteroids on the biochemical maturation of rat brain: Postnatal cell formation. *Journal of Neurochemistry, 19,* 2151–2167.

Coyle, J. T., & Enna, S. (1976). Neurochemical aspects of the ontogenesis of GABAergic neurons in the rat brain. *Brain Research, 111,* 119–133.

Coyle, J. T., & Molliver, M. (1977). Major innervation of newborn rat cortex by monoaminergic neurons. *Science, 196,* 444–447.

Coyle, J. T., & Yamamura, H. I. (1976). Neurochemical aspects of the ontogenesis of GABAergic neurons in the rat brain. *Brain Research, 118,* 429–440.

Crosby, E. C. (1917). The forebrain of alligator mississippiensis. *Journal of Comparative Neurology, 27,* 325–402.

Cunningham, M. G., Bhattacharyya, S., & Benes, F. M. (2002). Amygdalo-cortical sprouting continues into early adulthood: Implications for the development of normal and abnormal function during adolescence. *Journal of Comparative Neurology, 453*(2), 116–130.

Cunningham, M. G., Connor, C. M., Zhang, K., & Benes, F. M. (2005). Diminished serotonergic innervation of medial prefrontal cortex in the adult rat after neonatal lesions of the dopaminergic system. *Developmental Brain Research, 157,* 124–131.

Damasio, A. R., & Van Hoesen, G. W. (1983). Emotional disturbances associated with focal lesions of the limbic frontal lobe. In K. M. Heilman & P. Satz (Eds.), *Neuropsychology of human emotion* (pp. 85–110). New York: Guilford Press.

D'Amato, R. J., Blue, M. E., Largent, B. L., Lynch, D. R., Ledbetter, D. J., Molliver, M. E., et al. (1987). Ontogeny of the serotonergic projection to rat neocortex: Transient expression of a dense innervation to primary sensory areas. *Proceedings of the National Academy of Sciences, USA, 84*(12), 4322–4326.

Davis, M. (1992). The role of the amygdala in fear-potentiated startle: Implications for animal models of anxiety. *Trends in Pharmacological Science, 13*(1), 35–41.

Davis, M. (Ed.). (2000). *The role of the amygdala in conditioned and unconditioned fear and anxiety.* Oxford: Oxford University Press.

Davis, M., Rainnie, D., & Cassell, M. (1994). Neurotransmission in the rat amygdala related to fear and anxiety. *Trends in Neuroscience, 17*(5), 208–214.

Deguchi, T., & Barchas, J. (1972). Regional distribution and developmental change in tryptophan hydroxylase in rat brain. *Journal of Neurochemistry, 19,* 927–929.

Descarries, L., Beaudet, A., & Watkins, K. C. (1975). Serotonin nerve terminals in adult rat neocortex. *Brain Research, 100,* 563–588.

Deskin, R., Seidler, F. J., Whitmore, W. L., & Slotkin, T. A. (1981). Development of noradrenergic and dopaminergic receptor systems depends on maturation of their presynaptic nerve terminals in the rat brain. *Journal of Neurochemistry, 36,* 1683–1690.

Detre, T. P., & Jarecki, H. G. (1971). *Modern psychiatric treatment.* Philadelphia: Lippincott.

Devinsky, O., & Luciano, D. (1993). The contributions of cingulate cortex to human behavior. In B. A. Vogt & M. Gabriel (Eds.), *Neurobiology of cingulate cortex and limbic thalamus* (pp. 527–556). Boston: Birkhäuser.

Devinsky, O., Morrell, M. J., & Vogt, B. A. (1995). Contributions of anterior cingulate cortex to behaviour. *Brain, 118,* 279–306.

Diebler, M. F., Farkas-Bargeton, E., & Wehrle, R. (1979). Developmental changes of enzymes associated with energy metabolism and synthesis of some neurotransmitters in discrete areas of human neocortex. *Journal of Neurochemistry, 32,* 429–435.

Domesick, V. B. (1969). Projections from the cingulate cortex in the rat. *Brain Research, 12,* 296–320.

Dorland's illustrated medical dictionary (25th ed.). (1974). Philadelphia: Saunders.

Dunsmore, R. H., & Lennox, M. A. (1950). Stimulation and strychninization of supracallosal anterior cingulate gyrus. *Journal of Neurophysiology, 13,* 207–213.

Eckenhoff, M. F., & Rakic, P. (1988). Nature and fate of proliferative cells in the hippocampal dentate gyrus during the life span of the rhesus monkey. *Journal of Neuroscience, 8,* 2729–2747.

El-Hussein, A. E., Schnell, E., Chetkovich, D. M., Nicoll, R. A., & Bredt, D. S. (2000). PSD-95 involvement in maturation of excitatory synapses. *Science, 290,* 1364–1368.

Fanselow, M. S., & LeDoux, J. E. (1999). Why we think plasticity underlying Pavlovian fear conditioning occurs in the basolateral amygdala. *Neuron, 23,* 229–232.

Feinberg, I. (1982). Schizophrenia: Caused by a fault in programmed synaptic elimination during adolescence? *Journal of Psychiatry Research, 17*(4), 319–334.

Flechsig, P. (1920). *Anatomie des menschlichen Gehirns und Ruckenmarks auf myelogenetischer.* Leipzig, Germany: Gundlange.

Fosse, V. M., Heggelund, P., & Fonnum, F. (1989). Postnatal development of glutamateric, GABAergic and cholinergic neurotransmitter phenotypes in the visual cortex, lateral geniculate nucleus pulvinar and superior colliculus in cats. *Journal of Neuroscience, 9,* 426–435.

Fowler, R. C. (1978). Remitting Schizophrenia as a variant of affective disorder. *Schizophrenia Bulletin, 4,* 68–77.

Gallagher, M., & Holland, P. C. (1994). The amygdala complex: Multiple roles in associative learning and attention. *Proceedings of the National Academy of Sciences, 91,* 11771–11886.

Geier, S., Bancaud, J., Talairach, J., Bonis, A., Szikla, G., & Enjelvin, M. (1977). The seizures of frontal lobe epilepsy. A study of clinical manifestations. *Neurology, 27,* 951–958.

Gellman, R. L., & Aghajanian, G. K. (1993). Pyramidal cells in piriform cortex receive a convergence of inputs from monoamine activated GABAergic interneurons. *Brain Research, 600,* 63–73.

Gilles, F. H. (1983). Telencephalic medium and the olfacto-cerebral outpouching. In F. H. Gilles, A. Leviton, & E. C. Dooling (Eds.), *The developing human brain: Growth and epidemiologic neuropathology* (pp. 59–114). Boston: Wright-PSG.

Gilles, F. H., Shankle, W., & Dooling, E. C. (1983). Myelinated tracts: Growth patterns. In F. H. Gilles, A. Leviton, & E. C. Dooling (Eds.), *The developing human brain: Growth and epidemiologic neuropathology* (pp. 117–183). Boston: Wright-PSG.

Glees, P., Cole, J., Whitty, W. M., & Cairns, H. (1950). The effects of lesions in the cingulate gyrus and adjacent areas in monkeys. *Journal of Neurology Neurosurgery, 13,* 178–190.

Goldman-Rakic, P. S. (1981). Development and plasticity of primate frontal association cortex. In F. O. Smith (Ed.), *The organization of the cerebral cortex* (pp. 69–100). Cambridge, MA: MIT Press.

Goldman-Rakic, P. S. (1998). The cortical dopamine system: Role in memory and cognition. *Advances in Pharmacology, 42,* 707–711.

Goldman-Rakic, P. S., & Brown, R. M. (1982). Postnatal development of monoamine content and synthesis in the cerebral cortex of rhesus monkeys. *Brain Research, 256*(3), 339–349.

Goldman-Rakic, P. S., Leranth, C., Williams, S. M., Mons, N., & Geffard, M. (1989). Dopamine synaptic complex with pyramidal neurons in primate cerebral cortex. *Proceedings of the National Academy of Sciences, USA, 86*(22), 9015–9019.

Goldstein, L. E., Rasmusson, A. M., Bunney, B. S., & Roth, R. H. (1996). Role of the amygdala in the coordination of behavioral, neuroendocrine, and prefrontal cortical monoamine responses to psychological stress in the rat. *Journal of Neuroscience, 16*(15), 4787–4798.

Gorski, J. A., Zeiler, S. R., Tamowski, S., & Jones, K. R. (2003). Brain-derived neurotrophic factor is required for the maintenance of cortical dendrites. *Journal of Neuroscience, 23*(17), 6856–6865.

Gottesman, I. I., & Shields, J. (1972). *Schizophrenia and genetics: A twin study vantage point.* New York: Academic Press.

Gray, T. S., & Bingaman, E. W. (1996). The amygdala: Corticotropin-releasing factor, steroids, and stress. *Critical Reviews in Neurobiology, 10*(2), 155–168.

Gudelsky, G. A., & Nash, J. F. (1996). Carrier-mediated release of serotonin by 3,4methylenedioxymethamphetaine: Implications for serotonin-dopamine interactions. *Journal of Neurochemistry, 66,* 243–249.

Guidotti, A., Auta, J., Davis, J. M., Dwivedi, Y., Grayson, D. R., Impagnatiello, F., et al. (2000). Decrease in Reelin and glutamate acid decarboxylase$_{67}$ (GAD$_{67}$) expression in Schizophrenia and bipolar disorder. *Archives of General Psychiatry, 57,* 1061–1069.

Halpain, S., Hipolito, A., & Saffer, L. (1998). Regulation of F-actin stability in dendritic spines by glutamate receptors and calcineurin. *Journal of Neuroscience, 18*(23), 9835–9844.

Hamon, M., & Bourgoin, S. (1977). Biochemical aspects of the maturation of serotonergic neurons in the rat brain. In S. R. Berenger (Ed.), *Brain: Fetal and infant* (pp. 239–261). The Hague, Netherlands: Nijoff.

Harden, T. K., Wolfe, B. B., Sporn, J. R., Poulos, B. K., & Molinoff, P. B. (1977). Effects of 6-hydroxydopamine on the development of the *beta* adrenergic receptor/adenylate cyclase system in rat cerebral cortex. *Journal of Pharmacology and Experimental Therapeutics, 203,* 132–141.

Harlow, H. F. (1958). The nature of love. *American Psychologist, 13,* 673–685.

Harlow, H. F., Dodsworth, R. O., & Harlow, M. K. (1965). Total isolation in monkeys. *Proceedings of the National Academy of Sciences, USA, 54,* 90–97.

Hatfield, T., Han, J. S., Conley, M., Gallagher, M., & Holland, P. (1996). Neurotoxic lesions of basolateral, but not central, amygdala interfere with Pavlovian second-order conditioning and reinforcer devaluation effects. *Journal of Neuroscience, 16*(16), 5256–5265.

Hebb, D. O. (1949). *Organization of behavior.* New York: Wiley.

Heckers, S., Stone, D., Walsh, J., Shick, J., Koul, P., & Benes, F. M. (2002). Differential hippocampal expression of glutamic acid decarboxylase 65 and 67 messenger RNA in bipolar disorder and Schizophrenia. *Archives of General Psychiatry, 59*(6), 521–529.

Hedner, T., & Lundberg, P. (1980). Serotonergic development in the postnatal rat brain. *Journal of Neural Transmission, 49,* 257–279.

Henn, F. A., & McKinney, W. T. (1987). Animal models in psychiatry. In H. Y. Meltzer (Ed.), *Psychopharmacology: The third generation of progress* (pp. 687–695). New York: Raven Press.

Herba, C., & Phillips, M. (2004). Annotation: Development of facial expression recognition from childhood to adolescence: Behavioural and neurological perspectives. *Journal of Child Psychology and Psychiatry, 45*(7), 1185–1198.

Hoffman, H. H. (1963). The olfactory bulb, accessory olfactory bulb and hemisphere of some anurans. *Journal of Comparative Neurology, 120,* 317–368.

Holstege, G., Tan, J., Van Ham, J., & Bos, A. (1984). Mesencephalic projections to the facial nucleus in the cat: An autoradiographic tracing study. *Brain Research, 311,* 7–22.

Holzman, P. S., Kinglem, E., Matthysse, S., Flanagan, S., Lipton, R., Cramer, G., et al. (1988). A single dominant gene can account for eye tracking dysfunctions and Schizophrenia in offspring of discordant twins. *Archives of General Psychiatry, 45,* 641–647.

Hopkins, D. A., & Holstege, G. (1978). Amygdaloid projections to the mesencephalon, pons and medulla oblongata. *Experimental Brain Research, 32,* 529–547.

Howell, I. I., Czoty, P. W., & Burd, L. D. (1997). Pharmacological interactions between serotonin and dopamine on behavior in the squirrel monkey. *Psychopharmacology, 131,* 40–48.

Huntley, G. W., Morrison, J. H., Prikhozhan, A., & Sealfon, S. C. (1992). Localization of multiple dopamine receptor subtype mRNAs in human and monkey motor cortex and striatum. *Molecular Brain Research, 15*(3/4), 181–188.

Hurley, K. M., Herbert, H., Moga, M. M., & Saper, C. B. (1991). Efferent projections of the infralimbic cortex of the rat. *Journal of Comparative Neurology, 308,* 249–276.

Huttenlocher, P. R. (1994). Synaptogenesis in human cerebral cortex. In G. Dawson & K. W. Fischer (Eds.), *Human behavior and the developing brain* (pp. 137–152). New York: Guilford Press.

Huttenlocher, P. R., & Dabholkar, A. S. (1997). Regional differences in synaptogenesis in human cerebral cortex. *Journal of Comparative Neurology, 387*(2), 167–178.

Huxley, A. F., & Stampel, R. (1949). Evidence for saltatory conduction in peripheral myelinated nerve fibers. *Journal of Physiology, 108,* 315–339.

Ikonomidou, C., Mosinger, J. L., Shahid Salles, K., Labruyere, J., & and Olney, J. W. (1989). Sensitivity of the developing rat brain to hyperbaric/ischemic damage parallels sensitivity to N-methyl-D-aspartate neurotoxicity. *Journal of Neuroscience, 9,* 2809–2818.

Jacobsen, B., & Kinney, D. K. (1980). Perinatal complications in adopted and non-adopted schizophrenics and their controls: Preliminary results. *Acta Paediatrica Scandinavica, 238,* 103–123.

Jensen, G. D., & Tolman, C. W. (1962). Mother-Infant relationship in the monkey, Macaca Nemestrina: The effect of brief separation and mother infant specificity. *Journal of Comparative Physiology and Psychology, 55,* 131–136.

Johnston, M. V. (1988). Biochemistry of neurotransmitters in cortical development. In A. Peter & E. G. Jones (Eds.), *Cerebral cortex: Vol. 7. Development and maturation of cerebral cortex* (pp. 211–236). New York: Plenum Press.

Johnston, M. V., & Coyle, J. T. (1980). Ontogeny of neurochemical markers for noradrenergic, GABAergic and cholinergic neurons in neocortex lesioned with methylazoxymethanol acetate. *Journal of Neurochemistry, 34,* 1429–1441.

Johnston, M. V., McKinney, M., & Coyle, J. T. (1979). Evidence for a cholinergic projection to neocortex from neurons in basal forebrain. *Proceedings of the National Academy of Sciences, USA, 76,* 5392–5396.

Jones, E. G. (1984). Laminar distribution of cortical efferent cells. In A. Peters & E. G. Jones (Eds.), *Cerebral cortex: Vol. 1. Cellular components of the cerebral cortex* (pp. 521–548). New York: Plenum Press.

Jones, E. G. (1987). GABA-peptide neurons in primate cerebral cortex. *Journal of Mind and Behavior, 8,* 519–536.

Jones, E. G., & Hendry, S. H. C. (1984). Basket cells. In A. Peters & E. G. Jones (Eds.), *Cerebral cortex: Vol. 1. Cellular components of the cerebral cortex* (pp. 309–336). New York: Plenum Press.

Jones, E. G., & Powell, T. P. S. (1970). An anatomical study of converging sensory pathways within the cerebral cortex of the monkey. *Brain, 93,* 793–820.

Jones, P. B., Rantakallio, P., Hartikainen, A. L., Isohanni, M., & Sipila, P. (1998). Schizophrenia as a long-term outcome of pregnancy, delivery, and perinatal complications: A 28-year follow-up of the 1966 north Finland general population birth cohort. *American Journal of Psychiatry, 155*(3), 355–364.

Jung, A. B., & Bennett, J. P., Jr. (1996). Development of striatal dopaminergic function. III: Pre- and postnatal development of striatal and cortical mRNAs for the neurotrophin receptors trkBTK+ and trkC and their regulation by synaptic dopamine. *Developmental Brain Research, 94*(2), 133–143.

Jurgens, U., & Pratt, R. (1979). Role of the periaqueductal gray in vocal expression of emotion. *Brain Research, 167,* 367–378.

Kaada, B. R. (1960). Cingulate, posterior orbital, anterior insular and temporal pole cortex. In J. Field (Ed.), *Handbook of physiology* (Vol. 2, pp. 1345–1372). Washington, DC: American Physiological Society.

Kaada, B. R., Pribram, K. H., & Epstein, J. A. (1949). Respiratory and vascular responses in monkeys from temporal pole, insula, orbital surface and cingulate gyrus. *Journal of Neurophysiology, 12,* 347–356.

Kagan, J., Reznick, J., & Gibbons, J. (1989). Inhibited and uninhibited types of children. *Child Development, 60,* 838–845.

Kagan, J., Resnick, J. S., & Snidman, N. (1988). Biological bases of childhood shyness. *Science, 240,* 167–171.

Kagan, J., Reznick, J. S., Snidman, N., Gibbons, J., & Johnson, M. A. (1988). Childhood derivatives of inhibition and lack of inhibition to the unfamiliar. *Child Development, 59,* 1580–1589.

Kagan, J., & Snidman, N. (1991a). Infant predictors of inhibited and uninhibited profiles. *Psychological Science, 2,* 40–44.

Kagan, J., & Snidman, N. (1991b). Temperamental factors in human development. *American Psychologist, 48,* 856–862.

Kalsbeek, A., Voorn, P., Buijs, R. M., Pool, C. W., & Uylings, H. B. (1988). Development of the dopaminergic innervation in the prefrontal cortex of the rat. *Journal of Comparative Neurology, 269*(1), 58–72.

Kaplan, M. S., & Bell, D. H. (1984). Mitotic neuroblasts in the 9-day-old and 11-month-old rodent hippocampus. *Journal of Neuroscience, 4,* 1429–1441.

Kasamatsu, T., & Pettigrew, J. D. (1976). Depletion of brain catecholamines: Failure of ocular dominance shift after monocular occlusion in kittens. *Science, 194*(4261), 206–209.

Katz, R. J., Roth, K. A., & Carroll, B. J. (1981). Acute and chronic stress effects on open field activity in the rat: Implications for a model of depression. *Neuroscience and Biobehavioral Research, 5,* 247–251.

Kellogg, C. K., Awatramani, G. B., & Piekut, D. T. (1998). Adolescent development alters stressor-induced Fos immunoreactivity in rat brain. *Neuroscience, 83*(3), 681–689.

Kendler, K. S., Gruenberg, A., & Tsuang, M. T. (1985). Psychiatric illness in first-degree relatives of schizophrenic and surgical control patients. *Archives of General Psychiatry, 42,* 770–779.

Kennard, M. A. (1955). The cingulate gyrus in relation to consciousness. *Journal of Nervous and Mental Disorders, 121,* 34–39.

Keshavan, M. S. (2003). Toward unraveling the premorbid neurodevelopmental risk for Schizophrenia. In E. Walker (Ed.), *Neurodevelopmental mechanisms in psychopathology* (pp. 366–383). Cambridge, England: Cambridge University Press.

Kety, S. (1983). Mental illness in the biological and adoptive relatives of schizophrenic adoptees: Findings relevant to genetic and environmental factors in etiology. *American Journal of Psychiatry, 140*(6), 720–727.

Kety, S. (1985). Schizotypal personality disorder. An operational definition of Bleuler's latent Schizophrenia. *Schizophrenia Bulletin, 11,* 590–594.

Kety, S., & Matthysse, S. (1972). Prospects for research on Schizophrenia: An overview. *Neuroscience Research Bulletin, 10,* 456–467.

Kety, S., Rosenthal, D., Wender, P., & Schulsinger, F. (1968). The type and prevalence of mental illness in the biological and adoptive families of adopted schizophrenics. In D. Rosenthal & S. Kety (Eds.), *The transmission of Schizophrenia* (pp. 25–37). Oxford: Pergamon Press.

Killcross, S., Robbins, T. W., & Everitt, B. J. (1997). Different types of fear-conditioned behaviour mediated by separate nuclei within amygdala. *Nature, 388*(6640), 377–380.

Kim, I. J., Beck, H. N., Lein, P. J., & Higgins, D. (2002). Interferon gamma induces retrograde dendritic retraction and inhibits synapse formation. *Journal of Neuroscience, 22*(11), 4530–4539.

Kinney, D. K., Jacobsen, B., Jansson, L., Faber, B., Tramer, S. J., & Suozzo, M. (2000). Winter birth and biological family history in adopted schizophrenics. *Schizophrenia Research, 44,* 95–103.

Kinney, D. K., Yurgelun-Todd, D. A., Levy, D. L., Medoff, D., Lajonchere, C. M., & Radford-Paregol, M. (1993). Obstetrical complications in patients with bipolar disorder and their siblings. *Psychiatry Research, 48,* 47–56.

Kinney, D. K., Yurgelun-Todd, D. A., Tohen, M., & Tramer, S. (1998). Pre- and perinatal complications and risk for bipolar disorder: A retrospective study. *Journal of Affective Disorders, 50*(2/3), 117–124.

Klein, D. F., Zitrin, C. M., & Woerner, A. (1978). Antidepressant, anxiety, panic and phobia. In M. A. Lipton, A. Dimascio, & K. F. Killam (Eds.), *Psychopharmacology: A generation of progress* (pp. 1401–1410). New York: Raven Press.

Kluver, H., & Bucy, P. (1937). "Psychic blindness" and other symptoms following bilateral temporal lobectomy in rhesus monkey. *American Journal of Physiology, 119,* 352–353.

Konradi, C., Eaton, M., MacDonald, M. L., Walsh, J., Benes, F. M., & Heckers, S. (2004). Molecular evidence for mitochondrial dysfunction in bipolar disorder. *Archives of General Psychiatry, 61*(3), 300–308.

Kornetsky, C., & Orzack, M. H. (1978). Physiological and behavioral correlates of attention dysfunction in Schizophrenia patients. *Journal of Psychiatry Research, 14,* 69–79.

Kostovic, I., Skavic, J., & Strinovic, D. (1988). Acetylcholinesterase in the human frontal associative cortex during the period of cognitive development: Early laminar shifts and late innervation of pyramidal neurons. *Neuroscience Letters, 90,* 107–112.

Kraemer, G., Ebert, J. H., Lake, C. R., & McKinney, W. T. (1984). Cerebrospinal fluid measures of neurotransmitter changes associated with pharmacological alteration of the despair response to social separation in rhesus monkeys. *Psychiatry Research, 11,* 303–315.

Kraemer, G., & McKinney, W. T. (1979). Interactions of pharmacological agents which alter biogenic amino metabolism and depression: An analysis of contributing factors within a primate model of depression. *Journal of Affective Disorders, 1,* 33–54.

Kraepelin, E. (1919). *Dementia praecox and paraphrenia.* Edinburgh, Scotland: Livingston.

Kvale, I., Fosse, V. M., & Fonnum, F. (1983). Development of neurotransmitter parameters in lateral geniculate body, superior colliculus and visual cortex of the albino rat. *Developmental Brain Research, 7,* 137–145.

Lambe, E. K., Krimer, L. S., & Goldman-Rakic, P. S. (2000). Differential postnatal development of catecholamine and serotonin inputs to identified neurons in prefrontal cortex of rhesus monkey. *Journal of Neuroscience, 20*(23), 8780–8787.

Lane, H. Y., Lin, C. C., Huang, C. H., Chang, Y. C., Hsu, S. K., & Chang, W. H. (2004). Risperidone response and 5-HT6 receptor gene variance: Genetic association analysis with adjustment for nongenetic confounders. *Schizophrenia Research, 67*(1), 63–70.

Laplane, D., Degos, J. D., Baulac, M., & Gray, F. (1981). Bilateral infarction of the anterior cingulate gyri and of the fornices. *Journal of Neurological Science, 51,* 289–300.

Lauder, J. M., & Bloom, F. E. (1974). Ontogeny of monoamine neurons in the locus coeruleus, raphe nuclei and substantia nigra of the rat: I. Cell differentiation. *Journal of Comparative Neurology, 155,* 469–482.

Lawrie, S. M., & Abukmeil, S. S. (1998). Brain abnormality in Schizophrenia: A systematic and quantitative review of volumetric magnetic resonance imaging studies. *British Journal of Psychiatry, 172,* 110–120.

LeDoux, J. E. (1993). Emotional memory systems in the brain. *Behavioral Brain Research, 58,* 69–79.

LeDoux, J. E. (2000a). The amygdala and emotion. In J. P. Aggleton (Ed.), *The amygdala* (pp. 289–310). Oxford: Oxford University Press.

LeDoux, J. E. (2000b). Emotion circuits in the brain. *Annual Review of Neuroscience, 23,* 155–184.

LeDoux, J. E., Iwata, J., Cicchetti, P., & Reis, D. J. (1988). Different projections of the central amygdaloid nucleus mediate autonomic and behavioral correlates of conditioned fear. *Journal of Neuroscience, 8,* 2517–2529.

Levey, A. I., Wainer, B. H., Raye, D. B., Mufson, E. J., & Mesulam, M. M. (1984). Choline acetyltransferase immunoreactive neurons intrinsic to rodent cortex and distinction from acetylcholinesterase-positive neurons. *Neuroscience, 13,* 341–353.

Levitt, J. J., & Tsuang, M. T. (1988). The heterogeneity of schizoaffective disorder: Implications for treatment. *American Journal of Psychiatry, 145,* 926–936.

Levitt, P., & Moore, R. Y. (1978). Noradrenaline neuron innervation of the neurocortex in the rat. *Brain Research, 139,* 219–231.

Levitt, P., & Rakic, P. (1982). The time of genesis, embryonic origin and differentiation of brainstem monoamine neurons in the rhesus monkey. *Brain Research, 4,* 35–37.

Levy, D. L., O'Driscoll, G., Matthysse, S., Cook, S. R., Holzman, P. S., & Mendell, N. R. (2004). Antisaccade performance in biological relatives of Schizophrenia patients: A meta-analysis. *Schizophrenia Research, 71*(1), 113–125.

Lidov, H. G., & Molliver, M. E. (1982). The structure of cerebral cortex in the rat following prenatal administration of 6-hydroxydopamine. *Brain Research, 255*(1), 81–108.

Lindvall, O., & Bjorklund, A. (1984). General organization of cortical monoamine systems. In D. L. Descarries, T. R. Reader, & H. H. Jasper (Eds.), *Monoamine innervation of cerebral cortex* (pp. 9–40). New York: Alan R. Liss.

Lindvall, O., Bjorklund, A., & Divac, I. (1978). Organization of catecholamine neurons projecting to frontal cortex in the rat. *Brain Research, 142,* 1–24.

Long, C. J., Pueschel, K., & Hunter, S. E. (1978). Assessment of the effects of cingulate gyrus lesions by neurophysiological techniques. *Journal of Neurosurgery, 49,* 264–271.

Longson, D., Deakin, J. F., & Benes, F. M. (1996). Increased density of entorhinal glutamate-immunoreactive vertical fibers in Schizophrenia. *Journal of Neural Transmission, 103*(4), 503–507.

Luria, A. R. (1973). *The working brain.* New York: Basic Books.

MacLean, P. D. (1954). Studies on limbic system (visceral brain) and their bearing on psychosomatic problems. In E. Wittkower & C. R. Kleghorn (Eds.), *Recent developments in psychosomatic medicine* (pp. 101–125). Philadelphia: Lippincott.

MacLean, P. D. (1985). Brain evolution relating to family, play and the separation cell. *Archives of General Psychiatry, 42,* 405–417.

MacLean, P. D. (1990). *The triune brain in evolution: Role in paleocerebral functions.* New York: Plenum Press.

Marcusson, J. O., Morgan, D. G., Winblad, B., & Finch, C. E. (1984). Serotonin-2 binding sites in human frontal cortex and hippocampus: Selective loss of S-2A sites with age. *Brain Research, 311,* 51–56.

Marin-Padilla, M. (1970a). Prenatal and early postnatal ontogenesis of the human motor cortex: A Golgi study: Pt. I. The sequential development of the cortical layers. *Brain Research, 23,* 167–183.

Marin-Padilla, M. (1970b). Prenatal and early postnatal ontogenesis of the human motor cortex: A Golgi study: Pt. II. The basket-pyramidal system. *Brain Research, 23,* 185–191.

Marin-Padilla, M. (1984). Neurons of layer I: Developmental analysis. In A. Peters & E. G. Jones (Eds.), *Cerebral cortex* (Vol. 1., pp. 447–448). New York: Plenum Press.

Matzilevich, D., Burke, R. E., & Benes, F. M. (2004). Differential regulation of multiple metabolic and intracellular signaling pathways in the hippocampus of subjects with bipolar disorder (BD) and Schizophrenia (SZ). (Program no. 799.2, Abstract Viewer/Itinerary Planner). Washington, DC: Society for Neurosciences Abstracts.

Mazars, G. (1970). Criteria for identifying cingulate epilepsies. *Epilepsia, 11,* 41–47.

McBride, W. J., Murphy, J. M., Lumeng, L., & Li, T. K. (1990). Serotonin, dopamine and GABA involvement in alcohol drinking of selectively bred rats. *Alcohol, 7,* 199–205.

McDonald, A. J., Beitz, A. J., Larson, A. A., Kuriyama, R., Sellitto, C., & Madi, J. E. (1989). Co-localization of glutamate and tubulin in putative excitatory neurons of the hippocampus and amygdala: An immunohistochemical study using monoclonal antibodies. *Neuroscience, 30*(2), 405–421.

McGaugh, J. L., Ferry, B., Vazcarjanova, A., & Roosendaal, B. (2000). Amygdala: Role in modulation of memory storage. In J. P. Aggleton (Ed.), *Amygdala: A functional analysis* (2nd ed., pp. 391–404). Oxford: Oxford University Press.

McGhie, A., & Chapman, J. (1961). Disorders of attention and perception in early Schizophrenia. *British Journal of Medical Psychology, 34,* 103–116.

Meltzer, H. Y. (1994). An overview of the mechanism of action of clozapine. *Journal of Clinical Psychiatry, 55*(Suppl. B), 47–52.

Meltzer, H. Y., & Lowy, M. T. (1987). The serotonin hypothesis of depression. In H. Y. Meltzer (Ed.), *Psychopharmacology: The third generation of progress* (pp. 153–222). New York: Raven Press.

Mesulam, M.-M. (1983). The functional anatomy and hemispheric specialization of directed attention: The role of the parietal lobe and its commentary. *Trends in Neuroscience, 6,* 384–387.

Mesulam, M.-M., & Geschwind, N. (1978). On the possible role of neocortex and its limbic connections in the process of attention and Schizophrenia: Clinical cases of inattention in man and experimental anatomy in monkey. *Journal of Psychiatry Research, 14,* 249–259.

Mesulam, M.-M., Mufson, E. J., Levey, A. I., & Wainer, B. H. (1984). Atlas of cholinergic neurons in the forebrain and upper brainstem of the macaque based on monoclonal choline acetyltransferase immunohistochemistry and acetylcholinesterase histochemistry. *Neuroscience, 12,* 669–687.

Michel, A. E., & Garey, L. H. (1984). The development of dendritic spines in the human visual cortex. *Human Neurobiology, 3,* 223–227.

Mitelman, S. A., Shihabuddin, L., Brickman, A. M., Hazlett, E. A., & Buchsbaum, M. S. (2005). Volume of the cingulate and outcome in Schizophrenia. *Schizophrenia Research, 72*(2/3), 91–108.

Morilak, D. A., Garlow, S. J., & Ciaranello, R. D. (1993). Immunocytochemical localization and description of neurons expressing 5-HT-2 receptors in the rat brain. *Neuroscience, 54,* 701–717.

Mountcastle, V. B., Lynch, J. C., Georgopoulos, A., Sakata, H., & Acuna, C. (1975). Posterior parietal association cortex of the monkey: Command functions for operations within extrapersonal space. *Journal of Neurophysiology, 38,* 871–908.

Murphy, J. M., Gatto, G. J., McBride, W. J., Lumeng, L., & Li, T. K. (1989). Operant conditioning for oral ethanol in the alcohol-nonpreferring NP lines of rats. *Alcohol, 6,* 127–131.

Neafsey, E. J., Terreberry, R. R., Hurley, K. M., Ruit, K. G., & Frysztak, R. J. (1993). Anterior cingulate cortex in rodents: Connections, visceral control functions, and implications for emotions. In B. A. Vogt & M. Gabriel (Eds.), *Neurobiology of cingulate cortex and limbic thalamus: A comprehensive handbook* (pp. 206–222). Boston: Birkhäuser.

Olney, J. W., Sesma, M. A., & Wozniak, D. F. (1993). Glutamatergic, cholinergic and GABAergic systems in posterior cingulate cortex: Interactions and possible mechanisms of limbic system disease. In B. A. Vogt & M. Gabriel (Eds.), *Neurobiology of cingulate cortex and limbic thalamus* (pp. 557–580). Boston: Birkhäuser.

Overmeier, J. B., & Seligman, M. E. (1967). Effects of inescapable shock upon subsequent escape and avoidance responding. *Journal of Comparative Physiology and Psychology, 63,* 28–33.

Pandya, D. N., & Kuypers, H. G. J. M. (1969). Cortico-cortical connections in the rhesus monkey. *Brain Research, 13,* 13–36.

Papez, J. W. (1937). A proposed mechanism of emotion. *Archives of Neurology and Psychiatry, 38,* 725–743.

Pardo, J. V., Pardo, P. J., Janer, K. W., & Raichle, M. E. (1990). The anterior cingulate cortex mediated processing selection in the Stroop attentional conflict paradigm. *Proceedings of the National Academy of Sciences, USA, 87,* 256–259.

Pare, D., & Collins, D. R. (2000). Neuronal correlates of fear in the lateral amygdala: Multiple extracellular recordings in conscious cats. *Journal of Neuroscience, 20*(7), 2701–2710.

Parlato, S., Santini, S. M., Lapenta, C., Di Pucchio, T., Logozzi, M., Spada, M., et al. (2001). Expression of CCR-7, MIP-3beta, and Th-1 chemokines in type I IFN-induced monocyte-derived dendritic cells: Importance for the rapid acquisition of potent migratory and functional activities. *Blood, 98*(10), 3022–3029.

Parnas, J., Schulsinger, F., Teasdale, W., Schulsinger, H., Feldman, P. M., & Mednick, S. A. (1982). Perinatal complications and clinical outcome. *British Journal of Psychiatry, 140,* 416–420.

Payne, R. W., & Friedlander, D. (1962). Short battery of simple tests for measuring over-inclusive thinking. *Journal of Mental Science, 108,* 362–367.

Pehek, E. A. (1996). Local infusion of the serotonin antagonist ritanserin or ICS 205, 930 increases in vivo dopamine release in the rat medial prefrontal cortex. *Synapse, 24,* 12–18.

Penit-Soria, J., Audinat, E., & Crepel, F. (1987). Excitation of rat prefrontal cortical neurons by dopamine: An in vitro electrophysiological study. *Brain Research, 425,* 363–374.

Penit-Soria, J., Retaux, S., & Maurin, Y. (1989). Effets de la stimulation des récepteurs D1 et D2 dopaminergiques sur la liberation d'acide γ-[^{3}H] aminobutyrique induite electriquement dans le cortex prefrontal du rat. *Comte du Rendu de l'Academie de Sciences Paris, 309*(3), 441–446.

Perez-Jaranay, J. M., & Vives, F. (1991). Electrophysiological study of the response of medial prefrontal cortex neurons to stimulation of the basolateral nucleus of the amygdala in the rat. *Brain Research, 564*(1), 97–101.

Petras, J. M. (1971). Connections of the parietal lobe. *Journal of Psychiatry Research, 8,* 189–201.

Pikkarainen, M. S., Ronkko, S., Savander, V., Insausti, R., & Pitkanen, A. (1999). Projections from the lateral, basal, and accessory basal nuclei of the amygdalal to the hippocampal formational in rat. *Journal of Comparative Neurology, 403*(2), 229–260.

Poliakov, G. I. (1965). Development of the cerebral neocortex during the first half of intrauterine life. In S. A. Sarkisov (Ed.), *Development of the child's brain* (pp. 22–52). Leningrad, Russia: Medicina.

Poremba, A., & Gabriel, M. (1997). Amygdalar lesions block discriminative avoidance learning and cingulothalamic training-induced neuronal plasticity in rabbits. *Journal of Neuroscience, 17*(13), 5237–5244.

Porsolt, R. D., Bertin, A., & Jalfre, M. (1977). Behavioral despair in mice: A primary screening test for antidepressants. *Archives of International Pharmacodynamics, 229,* 327–336.

Posner, M. K., Early, T. S., Reisman, E., Pardo, P. J., & Dhawan, M. (1988). Asymmetries in hemispheric control of attention in Schizophrenia. *Archives of General Psychiatry, 45,* 814–821.

Rakic, P. (1974). Neurons in rhesus monkey visual cortex: Systematic relation between time of origin and eventual disposition. *Science, 183,* 425–427.

Rakic, P., & Nowakowski, R. (1981). The time of origin of neurons in the hippocampal region of the rhesus monkey. *Journal of Comparative Neurology, 196,* 99–128.

Rakic, P., & Yakovlev, P. I. (1968). Development of the corpus callosum and septum cavi in man. *Journal of Comparative Neurology, 132,* 45–72.

Ravikumar, B. V., & Sastary, P. S. (1985). Muscarinic cholinergic receptors in human fetal brain: Characterization and ontogeny of [^{3}H] quinuclidinyl benzilate bind sites in frontal cortex. *Journal of Neurochemistry, 44,* 240–246.

Retaux, S., Besson, M. J., & Penit-Soria, J. (1991a). Opposing effects of dopamine D2 receptor stimulation on the spontaneous and the electrically evoked release of [^{3}H]GABA on rat prefrontal cortex slices. *Neuroscience, 42*(1), 61–71.

Retaux, S., Besson, M. J., & Penit-Soria, J. (1991b). Synergism between D1 and D2 dopamine receptors in the inhibition of the evoked release of [^{3}H]GABA in the rat prefrontal cortex. *Neuroscience, 43*(2/3), 323–329.

Reynolds, G. P., Czudek, C., & Andrews, H. B. (1990). Deficit and hemispheric asymmetry of GABA uptake sites in the hippocampus in Schizophrenia. *Biological Psychiatry, 27,* 1038–1044.

Rosene, D. L., & Van Hoesen, G. W. (1987). The hippocampal formation of the primate brain. In A. Peters & E. G. Jones (Eds.), *Cerebral cortex: Vol. 6. Further aspects of cortical function, including hippocampus* (pp. 345–456). New York: Plenum Press.

Roth, R. H., Tam, S. Y., Ida, Y., Yang, J. X., & Deutch, A. Y. (1988). Stress and the mesocorticolimbic dopamine systems. *Annals of the New York Academy of Sciences, 537,* 138–147.

Rothman, S. M., & Olney, J. W. (1986). Glutamate and the pathophysiology of hypoxic and ischemic brain damage. *Annals of Neurology, 19,* 105–111.

Rutter, M., & Sroufe, L. A. (2000). Developmental psychopathology: Concepts and challenges. *Development and Psychopathology, 12,* 265–296.

Saccuzzo, D. P., & Braff, D. L. (1986). Information-processing abnormalities: Trait- and state-dependent component. *Schizophrenia Bulletin, 12,* 447–456.

Sanders, S. K., & Shekhar, A. (1995). Regulation of anxiety by GABAA receptors in the rat amygdala. *Pharmacological and Biochemical Behavior, 52*(4), 701–706.

Sapolsky, R. (1992). *Stress, the aging brain, and the mechanisms of neuron death.* Cambridge, MA: MIT Press.

Sapolsky, R., & Meaney, M. (1986). Maturation of the adrenocortical stress response: Neuroendocrine control mechanisms and the stress hyporesponsive period. *Brain Research Reviews, 11,* 65–76.

Schliebs, R., Kullman, E., & Bigl, V. (1986). Development of glutamate binding sites in the visual structures of the rat brain: Effect of visual pattern deprivation. *Biomedica Biophysica Acta, 45,* 4495–4506.

Schoenbaum, G., Chiba, A. A., & Gallagher, M. (1998). Orbitofrontal cortex and basolateral amygdala encode expected outcomes during learning. *Nature Neuroscience, 1*(2), 155–159.

Schoenbaum, G., Chiba, A. A., & Gallagher, M. (2000). Changes in functional connectivity in orbitofrontal cortex and basolateral amygdala during learning and reversal training. *Journal of Neuroscience, 20*(13), 5179–5189.

Schroeter, M. L., Zysset, S., Wahl, M., & von Cramon, D. Y. (2004). Prefrontal activation due to Stroop interference increases during development: An event-related fNIRS study. *Neuroimage, 23*(4), 1317–1325.

Schwarcz, R., & Coyle, J. T. (1977). Striatal lesion with kainic acid: Neurochemical characteristics. *Brain Research, 127,* 235–249.

Seidman, L. J., Buka, S. L., Goldstein, J. M., Horton, N. J., Rieder, R. O., & Tsuang, M. T. (2000). The relationship of prenatal and perinatal complications to cognitive functioning at age 7 in the New England cohorts of the National Collaborative Perinatal Project. *Schizophrenia Bulletin, 26*(2), 309–321.

Selden, N. R., Everitt, B. J., Jarrard, L. E., & Robbins, T. W. (1991). Complementary roles for the amygdala and hippocampus in aversive conditioning to explicit and contextual cues. *Neuroscience, 42*(2), 335–350.

Seltzer, B., & Pandya, D. M. (1978). Afferent cortical connections and architectonics of the superior temporal sulcus and surrounding cortex in the rhesus monkey. *Brain Research, 192,* 1–24.

Seltzer, B., & Van Hoesen, G. W. (1979). A direct inferior parietal lobule projection to the presubiculum in the rhesus monkey. *Brain Research, 179,* 157–161.

Serretti, A., & Olgiati, P. (2004). Dimensions of major psychoses: A confirmatory factor analysis of six competing models. *Psychiatry Research, 127*(1/2), 101–109.

Sheldon, P. W., & Aghajanian, G. K. (1990). Serotonin (5-HT) induces IPSPs in pyramidal layer cells of rat piriform cortex: Evidence for the involvement of a 5-HT2-activated interneuron. *Brain Research, 506,* 62–69.

Sheldon, P. W., & Aghajanian, G. K. (1991). Excitatory responses to serotonin (5-HT) in neurons of the rat piriform cortex: Evidence for mediation by 5-HT1C receptors in pyramidal cells and 5-HT2 receptors in interneurons. *Synapse, 9,* 208–218.

Sidman, R., & Rakic, P. (1973). Neuronal migration with special reference to developing human brain. *Brain Research, 62,* 1–35.

Siever, L. J. (1987). Role of noradrenergic mechanisms in the etiology of the affective disorders. In H. Y. Meltzer (Ed.), *Psychopharmacology: The third generation of progress* (pp. 493–504). New York: Raven Press.

Sillito, A. M. (1984). Functional considerations of the operation of GABAergic inhibitory processes in the visual cortex. In E. G. Jones & A. Peters (Eds.), *Cerebral cortex: Vol. 2. Functional properties of cortical cells* (pp. 91–118). New York: Plenum Press.

Slotnick, B. M. (1967). Disturbances of maternal behavior in the rat following lesions of the cingulate cortex. *Behavior, 24,* 204–236.

Smith, W. D. (1945). The functional significance of the rostral cingula cortex as revealed by its responses to electrical excitation. *Journal of Neurophysiology, 8,* 241–255.

Somogyi, P., & Cowey, A. (1984). Double bouquet cells. In A. Peter & E. G. Jones (Eds.), *Cerebral cortex: Vol. 1. Cellular components of cerebral cortex* (pp. 337–360). New York: Plenum Press.

Spitz, R. A. (1949). Hospitalism: An inquiry into the genesis of psychiatric conditions in early childhood. *Psychoanalytic Study of Children, 1,* 53–74.

Stamm, J. S. (1955). The function of the median cerebral cortex in maternal behavior of rats. *Journal of Comparative Physiology and Psychology, 48,* 347–356.

Stanfield, B. B., & Cowan, W. M. (1988). The development of hippocampal region. In A. Peters & E. G. Jones (Eds.), *Cerebral cortex: Vol. 7. Development and maturation of cerebral cortex* (pp. 91–132). New York: Plenum Press.

Stanfield, B. B., & Trice, J. E. (1988). Evidence that granule cells generated in the dentate gyrus of adult rats extend axonal projections. *Experimental Brain Research, 72,* 399–406.

Stanford, S. C. (1993). Monoamines in response and adaptation to stress. In S. C. Stanford & P. Salmon (Eds.), *Stress: From synapse to syndrome* (pp. 282–332). London: Academic Press.

Stein-Behrens, B., Elliott, E., Miller, C., Schilling, J., Newcombe, R., & Sapolsky, R. (1992). Glucocorticoids exacerbate kainic acid-induced extracellular accumulation of excitatory amino acids in the rat hippocampus. *Journal of Neurochemistry, 58,* 1730–1734.

Stone, D. J., Walsh, J. P., & Benes, F. M. (2001). Effects of pre- and postnatal stress on the rat GABA system. *Hippocampus, 11,* 492–507.

Streit, P. (1984). Glutamate and aspartate as transmitter candidates for systems of the cerebral cortex. In E. G. Jones & A. Peters (Eds.), *Cerebral cortex: Vol. 2. Functional properties of cortical cells* (pp. 119–144). New York: Plenum Press.

Stutzmann, G. E., & LeDoux, J. E. (1999). GABAergic antagonists block the inhibitory effects of serotonin in the lateral amygdala: A mechanism for modulation of sensory inputs related to fear conditioning. *Journal of Neuroscience, 19*(11), RC8.

Swanson, L. W., & Petrovich, G. D. (1998). What is the amygdala? *Trends in Neuroscience, 21*(8), 323–331.

Takahashi, H., Sekino, Y., Tanaka, S., Mizui, T., Kishi, S., & Shirao, T. (2003). Debrin-dependent actin clustering in dendritic fiopodia governs synaptic targeting of postsynaptic density-95 and dendritic spine morphogenesis. *Journal of Neuroscience, 23,* 6586–6595.

Taylor, J., & Benes, F. M. (1996). Colocalization of glutamate decarboxylase, tyrosine hydroxylase and serotonin immunoreactivity in rat medial prefrontal cortex. *Neuroscience-Net, 1,* 10001.

Taylor, J., Cunningham, M. C., & Benes, F. M. (1998). Neonatal raphe lesions increase dopamine fibers in prefrontal cortex of adult rats. *NeuroReport, 9*(8), 1811–1815.

Terasawa, E., & Timiras, P. S. (1968). Electrophysiological study of the limbic system in the rat at onset of puberty. *American Journal of Physiology, 215*(6), 1462–1467.

Terreberry, R. R., & Neafsey, E. J. (1983). Rat medial frontal cortex: A visceromotor region with a direct projection to the nucleus solitarius. *Brain Research, 278,* 245–249.

Terreberry, R. R., & Neafsey, E. J. (1987). The rat medial frontal cortex projects directly to autonomic regions of the brainstem. *Brain Research Bulletin, 19,* 639–649.

Thierry, A. M., Blanc, G., Sobel, A., Stinus, L., & Glowinski, J. (1973). Dopaminergic terminals in the rat cortex. *Science, 182,* 499–501.

Thierry, A. M., Tassin, J. P., Blanc, G., & Glowinski, J. (1976). Selective activation of the mesocortical DA system by stress. *Nature, 263,* 242–244.

Tow, P. W., & Whitty, C. W. M. (1953). Personality changes after operations on the cingulate gyrus in man. *Journal of Neurology, Neurosurgery, and Psychiatry, 16,* 186–193.

Ulinski, P. S. (1977). Intrinsic organization of snake medial cortex: An electron microscopic and Golgi study. *Journal of Morphology, 152,* 247–280.

Ulinski, P. S. (1990). The cerebral cortex of reptiles. In E. G. Jones & A. Peters (Eds.), *Cerebral cortex: Vol. 8A. Comparative structure and evolution of cerebral cortex* (Part 1, pp. 139–215). New York: Plenum Press.

Uphouse, L. L., & Bondy, S. C. (1981). The maturation of cortical serotonergic binding sites. *Developmental Brain Research, 1,* 415–417.

Vaillant, G. E. (1983). *The natural history of alcoholics.* Cambridge, MA: Harvard University Press.

Van der Kooy, D., McGinty, J. F., Koda, L. Y., Gerfen, C. R., & Bloom, F. E. (1982). Visceral cortex: Direct connections from prefrontal cortex to the solitary nucleus in the rat. *Neuroscience Letters, 33,* 123–127.

Van Hoesen, G. W., Morecraft, R. J., & Vogt, B. A. (1993). Connections of the monkey cingulate cortex. In B. A. Vogt & M. Gabriel (Eds.), *Neurobiology of cingulate cortex and limbic thalamus* (pp. 249–284). Boston: Birkhäuser.

Verney, C., Alvarez, C., Gerrard, M., & Berger, B. (1990). Ultrastructural double-labelling study of dopamine terminals and GABA-containing neurons in rat anteromedial cortex. *European Journal of Neuroscience, 2,* 960–972.

Verney, C., Berger, B., Adrien, J., Vigny, A., & Gay, M. (1982). Development of the dopaminergic innervation of the rat cerebral cortex. A light microscopic immunocytochemical study using anti-tyrosine hydroxylase antibodies. *Brain Research, 281*(1), 41–52.

Vincent, S. L., Khan, Y., & Benes, F. M. (1993). Cellular distribution of dopamine D1 and D2 receptors in rat medial prefrontal cortex. *Journal of Neuroscience, 13*(6), 2551–2564.

Vincent, S. L., Khan, Y., & Benes, F. M. (1995). Cellular colocalization of dopamine D1 and D2 receptors in rat medial prefrontal cortex. *Synapse, 19*(2), 112–120.

Vincent, S. L., Pabreza, L., & Benes, F. M. (1995). Postnatal maturation of GABA-immunoreactive neurons of rat medial prefrontal cortex. *Journal of Comparative Neurology, 355*(1), 81–92.

Vogt, B. A., Finch, D. M., & Olson, C. R. (1992). Functional heterogeneity in cingulate cortex: The anterior executive and posterior evaluative regions. *Cerebral Cortex, 2*(6), 435–443.

Vogt, B. A., Vogt, L. J., Nimchinsky, E. A., & Hof, P. R. (1997). Primate cingulate cortex chemoarchitecture and its disruption in Alzheimer's disease. In F. E. Bloom, A. Bjorklund, & T. Hokfelt (Eds.), *Handbook of Chemical Neuroanatomy* (Vol. 13, pp. 455–528). Amsterdam: Elsevier.

Walker, E., & Diforio, D. (1997). Schizophrenia: A neural diathesis-stress model. *Psychology Reviews, 104,* 667–685.

Wallace, J. A., & Lauder, J. M. (1983). Development of the serotonergic system in the rat embryo: An immunocytochemical study. *Brain Research Bulletin, 10,* 459–479.

Wan, F. J., & Swerdlow, N. R. (1997). The basolateral amygdala regulates sensorimotor gating of acoustic startle in the rat. *Neuroscience, 76*(3), 715–724.

Wang, Y., Sheen, V. L., & Macklis, J. D. (1998). Cortical interneurons upregulate neurotrophins in vivo in response to targeted apoptotic degeneration of neighboring pyramidal neurons. *Experimental Neurology, 154*(2), 389–402.

Ward, A. A. (1948a). The anterior cingulate gyrus and personality. *The frontal lobes* [Monograph]. Baltimore: Williams & Wilkins.

Ward, A. A. (1948b). The cingular gyrus: Area 24. *Journal of Neurophysiology, 11,* 13–23.

Weinberger, D. R. (1987). Implications of normal brain development for the pathogenesis of Schizophrenia. *Archives of General Psychiatry, 44,* 660–669.

Weinberger, D. R., Berman, K. F., & Zec, R. F. (1986). Physiologic dysfunction of dorsolateral prefrontal cortex in Schizophrenia: Pt. I. Regional cerebral blood flow evidence. *Archives of General Psychiatry, 43*(2), 114–124.

West, A. R., & Galloway, M. P. (1996). Regulation of serotonin-facilitated dopamine release in vivo: The role of protein kinase A activating transduction mechanisms. *Synapse, 23,* 20–27.

White. E. L. (1986). Termination of thalamic afferents in the cerebral cortes. In E G. Jones & A. Peters (Eds.), *Cerebral cortex* (Vol. 5, pp. 271–289). New York: Plenum Press.

Wise, S. P., Fleshman, J. W., Jr., & Jones, E. G. (1979). Maturation of pyramidal cell form in relation to developing afferent and efferent connections of rat somatic sensory cortex. *Neuroscience, 4*(9), 1275–1297.

Wise, S. P., & Jones, E. G. (1978). Developmental studies of thalamocortical and commissural connections in the rat somatic sensory cortex. *Journal of Comparative Neurology, 178,* 187–208.

Woo, T. W., Walsh, J. P., & Benes, F. M. (2004). Density of glutamate acid decarboxylase 67 messenger RNA-containing neurons that express the N-methyl-D-aspartate subunit NR2a is decreased in the anterior cingulate cortex in Schizophrenia and bipolar disorder. *Archives of General Psychiatry, 61,* 649–657.

Wyss, J. M., & Sripanidkulchai, K. (1984). The topography of the mesencephalic and pontine projections from the cingulate cortex of the rat. *Brain Research, 293,* 1–15.

Yakovlev, P., & Lecours, A. (1967). The myelinogenetic cycles of regional maturation of the brain. In A. Minkowski (Ed.), *Regional development of the brain early in life* (pp. 3–70). Oxford: Blackwell.

Zhang, W. Q., Rogers, B. C., Tandon, P., Hudson, P. M., Sobotka, T. J., Hong, J. S., et al. (1990). Systemic administration of kainic acid increases GABA levels in perfusate from the hippocampus of rats in vivo. *Neurotoxicology, 11,* 593–600.

Zilles, K., Werners, R., Busching, U., & Schleicher, A. (1986). Ontogenesis of the laminar structure in areas 17 and 18 of the human visual cortex: A quantitative study. *Anatomy and Embryology, 174,* 339–353.

CHAPTER 6

Early Nutritional Deficiencies in Brain Development: Implications for Psychopathology

ADAM T. SCHMIDT and MICHAEL K. GEORGIEFF

The influence of early nutrition on the developing brain has been an issue that has waxed and waned in scientific popularity over the past century (Susser & Stein, 1994). However, popular culture has recognized the importance of early nutrition in children's health for many years. The Nobel Prize-winning author Pearl S. Buck wrote about the devastating effects of starvation on young children in her 1931 classic book *The Good Earth*. In this novel, the first daughter of the main character is born at the height of a severe famine. Buck implies that the significant malnutrition the child endured early in life resulted in devastating brain damage, leaving her profoundly retarded.

Conditions such as phenylketonuria (PKU) illustrate the importance of nutritional factors in brain development. If not addressed, PKU can result in mental retardation (Huttenlocher, 2000; Sullivan & Chang, 1999). Individuals with PKU are unable to metabolize phenylalanine; the subsequent buildup of this amino acid during brain development results in a toxic reaction leading to brain damage (Huttenlocher, 2000). Reports hypothesizing a nutritional origin of some forms of mental retardation first appeared in the early 1950s, when researchers noted high amounts of phenylketones in the urine of some mentally retarded individuals (Huttenlocher, 2000). Subsequent investigations linked PKU to various neuropathologies, including diffuse white matter changes and reduced dendritic branching (Huttenlocher, 2000). Specific genetic disorders resulting in deficiencies of micronutrients (such as copper in Menkes disease), regional geographic deficiencies of trace elements (such as iodine and selenium), and low prenatal levels of maternal nutrients (such as folate and iron) have all been linked to severe neurological abnormalities and/or intellectual deficits (Hibbard & Smithells, 1965; Lozoff, 1989; Pharoah, Buttfield, & Hetzel, 1971; Prohaska, 2000; Shim & Harris, 2003; Yi-Ming, 1996).

The famines and food shortages throughout Europe during the Second World War created an interest in studying the changes in psychological and physiological functioning caused by undernutrition (Keys, 1946; Pollitt, 1988). Although much of this research pertains to adults, it is pertinent here because children likely exhibit similar psychological consequences and, by affecting the psychological state of their caregivers, parental malnutrition may exert indirect effects on children regardless of their nutritional status (Brozek, 1990).

Keys and colleagues at the University of Minnesota exposed 36 healthy males to 6 months of semistarvation followed by 3 months of controlled rehabilitation (Franklin, Schiele, Brozek, & Keys, 1948; Keys, 1946). Results indicated that during the period of semistarvation, the participants became lethargic, apathetic, less sociable, uninterested in sexual activity, less alert (except with regard to hearing), and depressed. Although the participants complained about changes in mental alertness and inability to think cogently, researchers noted no decreases on tests of memory or intellectual ability. The participants in the study exhibited unusual behaviors involving food, such as compulsive gum chewing and coffee/tea drinking (up to 40 packs of gum a day and 15 cups of coffee a day), "souping" (the practice of drinking the liquid in soup then refilling the bowl with hot salted water and repeating the process before eating the vegetables in the soup), and unusual eating habits, including novel spice concoctions, hoarding of food, and doting over every last piece of food on the plate. Many of the participants greatly increased their daily consumption of water and either began smoking or substantially increased the amount they smoked (Franklin et al., 1948). Finally, participants displayed numerous physiological reactions, such as decreased sensitivity to heat, increased sensitivity to cold, edema, skin discoloration, and reduced hair growth (Franklin et al., 1948).

During the controlled rehabilitation phase, participants were initially irritable and easily frustrated (Franklin et al., 1948). These effects were short-lived; however, weight gain and sexual interest did not immediately return to prestarvation levels. In fact, participants did not reach their prestarvation weight and level of physical fitness until almost a year after the conclusion of the semistarvation phase (Franklin et al., 1948).

These findings are important because they indicate that periods of substantial undernutrition in adults result in demonstrable (but reversible) alterations in behavior, physiology, and mood (Franklin et al., 1948; Keys, 1946). The reversibility of these symptoms suggests that, in adults, behavioral changes occur secondarily to disturbances in neurotransmitter systems. This conjecture is supported by work (with humans and animals) showing dietary manipulations resulting in rapid changes in behavior and concentration of specific neurotransmitters (Fromentin, Gietzen, & Nicolaidis, 1997; Gietzen & Magrum, 2001; Phillips, Oxtoby, Langley, Bradshaw, & Szabadi, 2000; Riedel, 2004; Pierucci-Lagha et al., 2004). In the developing brain, the effects of undernutrition may not be as amenable to rehabilitation because this condition likely impacts both neurotransmitter systems and neuroanatomic organization (Winick & Rosso, 1969).

Using a unique natural experiment, Stein, Susser, Saenger, and Marolla. (1972) investigated whether prenatal exposure to famine in the Dutch "hunger winter" of 1944 to 1945 adversely affected intellectual abilities in a sample of 19-year-old males. In September 1944, the Netherlands cooperated with Allied forces in an attempt by British paratroopers to force a bridgehead over the Rhine River (Stein et al., 1972, 1975; Susser, Brown, Klonowski, Allen, & Lindenbaum, 1998). The attempt failed, and in retaliation, the German army imposed a trade embargo on Holland. Unfortunately, even when the army lifted the embargo, previous railroad strikes and a severe winter that had frozen

the shipping channels resulted in serious food shortages in much of western Holland. At the height of the famine, daily food rations could be as low as 450 kilocalories per person, a quarter of the standard amount. The most significant period of the famine began in November 1944 and lasted until Allied armies crossed the Rhine and liberated Holland in May 1945. The severity of famine was indicated by a sharply increased death rate in the affected cities (many of these deaths were attributed to starvation), substantial (up to 25%) loss in body weight, and the occurrence of physical signs associated with severe malnourishment, such as osteomalacia and hunger edema (Stein et al., 1972, 1975).

This event was unique because it occurred at a specified time and place in a population that before and after famine had good nutrition, there was good reporting on food rations provided to the population, and excellent public health records allowed researchers to divide individuals into groups of varying exposures based on birth date and birth location. This natural experiment has generated numerous investigations on the effects of prenatal famine exposure on a multitude of psychological and medical variables.

Stein et al. (1972) grouped individuals into six birth cohorts based on their intrauterine exposure to famine: individuals born before the beginning of the famine, individuals prenatally exposed to famine in the third trimester only, individuals exposed to famine in the middle 6 months of gestation, individuals conceived during the famine and exposed in the first and second trimesters, individuals conceived during the famine and exposed during the third trimester only, and individuals conceived and born after the famine occurred. Stein and colleagues used Raven Progressive Matrices scores gathered at age 19 during military induction testing to compare these cohorts to control cohorts born during the same time frame in cities of similar size but not affected by the famine. The researchers failed to find significant declines in average IQ or increases in the rates of mild or severe mental retardation in the four groups prenatally exposed or in the one group exposed postnatally. Because many births occurred at home, the researchers could not evaluate the influence of prenatal famine exposure on the birthweight of the entire cohort; however, a subsample of births occurring in hospitals in the famine and control cities indicated no relationship of birthweight to IQ at age 19.

These findings cast doubt on the assertion that maternal malnutrition alone results in significantly lower intellectual abilities. However, the authors emphasize that their findings should not be generalized to chronically malnourished populations where the mother is likely to be malnourished before and after parturition, the child is at high risk for postnatal nutritional deficits, or deficiencies in specific trace nutrients are common. The authors suggest that their findings reveal either a high degree of protection afforded to the developing child in utero or the considerable resilience of many children in the face of prenatal insult.

Over the years, many people have speculated that nutrition affects proximal behavior (e.g., sugar increases activity levels). Although careful research has not substantiated this particular assertion, there are many clearly documented short-term effects of specific nutrients (or substances) on behavior (Beyth & Baratta, 1996; Fernstrom, 2000; Fishbein & Pease, 1994; Lieberman, 2003). However, these acute effects are not the topic of this chapter. Rather, the discussion focuses on the effects of generalized malnutrition or specific micronutrient deficiencies on the developing brain and how these insults may contribute to the later emergence of psychopathology.

Before beginning the discussion in earnest, it is important to define several terms. First, in this chapter, *early undernutrition* refers to caloric restriction occurring prenatally (sometimes even prior to conception) or in the first few years of postnatal development (prior to age 3). Second, *undernutrition* or *malnutrition* (used interchangeably throughout) refers to a general reduction in caloric intake, also known as protein energy malnutrition (PEM) or macronutrient malnutrition. Nutritional deficits can refer to either PEM or deficits in specific micronutrients such as iron (Fe), Zinc (Zn), or iodine (I). Most of the extant research concerns PEM/undernutrition, and this is the focus of the first section of this chapter; each of these three micronutrients is briefly discussed near the end of the chapter.

An unambiguous definition of what constitutes psychopathology has proven elusive (Lilienfeld & Marino, 1999; Meehl, 1979; Wakefield, 1993, 1999) but is not necessary here. We refer to major mental disorders as listed in the American Psychiatric Association's (2000) *Diagnostic and Statistical Manual of Mental Disorders,* fourth edition (*DSM-IV-TR*) as constituting a large subset of psychopathology pertinent to this discussion. Most research relevant to this review examines Schizophrenia/Schizophrenia Spectrum Disorders, internalizing disorders (such as major depression and anxiety disorders), and externalizing problems (such as Attention-Deficit/Hyperactivity Disorder [ADHD] and Antisocial Personality Disorder).

BASIC PRINCIPLES

When examining the effects of nutritional deficiencies on the developing brain and the role these may play in the genesis of psychopathology, it is important to keep in mind several core principles. First, brain development occurs in overlapping but dissociable stages, and each of these stages may be uniquely vulnerable to injury (Honig, Herrman, & Shatz, 1996; Monk, Webb, & Nelson, 2001; Morgane et al., 1993; Teicher, Andersen, Polcari, Anderson, & Navalta, 2002; Webb, Monk, & Nelson, 2001). These stages include neurulation, neurogenesis, proliferation, migration, differentiation, synaptogenesis, myelination, apoptosis, and synaptic pruning (Andersen, 2003; Monk et al., 2001; Webb et al., 2001). Disturbances in some of these processes are associated with neurobehavioral deficits—as in the nonverbal impairments and psychiatric symptoms seen in the leukodystrophies—or the hypothesis that aberrant synaptic connections play a role in the etiology of Autism and Schizophrenia (Innocenti, Ansermet, & Parnas, 2003; Keller & Persico, 2003; Percy & Rutledge, 2001; Rosebush, Garside, Levinson, & Mazurek, 1999; Van Geel, Assies, Wanders, & Barth, 1997).

Some of the initial processes of brain development (e.g., neurulation and neurogenesis) occur during a single early period, whereas other, later stages (e.g., myelination, apoptosis, and synaptic pruning) occur independently at different times in various brain regions (Monk et al., 2001; Webb et al., 2001). Thus, a brain structure/region will have its own time course through which development proceeds. Moreover, certain brain regions such as the hippocampus are more vulnerable to injury than other regions (Walsh & Emerich, 1988). Ultimately, the result of any insult to the developing brain depends on the time of onset of the insult and what developmental processes are occurring/brain structures are actively developing at that time, how innately vulnerable these processes/structures are to injury, and the magnitude of the insult (e.g., the severity and/or duration of the injury). Based on these variables, a particular deficiency can have different effects on the developing nervous system (Adams et al., 2000; Georgieff & Rao, 2001; Kretchmer, Beard, and Carlson, 1996; Morgane et al., 1993; Pollitt, 1996).

A second important principle underlying the current discussion is the concept that abnormal behavior (as in psychopathology) is the efferent expression of brain activity, and changes in neuroanatomy, neurochemistry, and neurophysiology can result in alterations in behavior (Brower & Price, 2001; Moffitt, 1993; Moffitt & Caspi, 2001; Nestor, Kimble, Berman, & Haycock, 2002; Pennington & Ozonoff, 1996; Raine, 2002). Thus, early malnutrition may lead to the expression of cognitive deficits and/or abnormal behavior stemming from alterations in fine neuroanatomy (delicate structures such as dendritic arbors and white matter tracks), neurochemistry (disturbances in neurotransmitter systems), and/or neurophysiology (the functioning of ion channels and specific receptors; Arnold, 1999; Benes & Berretta, 2001; Bowley, Drevets, Öngür, & Price, 2002; Konradi & Heckers, 2003; Molnar, Potkin, Bunney, & Jones, 2003). Although specific findings (e.g., white matter abnormalities or increased receptor density in a certain region) are sometimes difficult to replicate in new samples, disturbances in these three broad domains are consistently associated with various forms of psychopathology (Dwork, 1997; Fletcher, 1998; Jones, 1997).

The last core principle running through this discussion is the concept that genes will likely prove to be the single most important long-term determinant of behavior; however, their expression can be modified (repressed or activated) by interaction with the environment (Bunney et al., 2003; Jacobs et al., 2002; Murphy et al., 2001; Rutter, Pickles, Murray, & Eaves, 2001; Rutter & Silberg, 2002; Slutske et al., 1997). Environmental influences causing anomalous neurological development (such as chronic and severe neglect or toxicity) can have especially salient and long-term effects (Barone, Das, Lassiter, & White, 2000; Castle et al., 1999; Schettler, 2001; Weiss, 2000). Similarly, nutrition is an important environmental factor that can affect the developing brain (Georgieff & Rao, 2001; Morgane et al., 1993; Morgane, Mokler, & Galler, 2002).

This does not imply that environmental insults such as malnutrition have uniform effects on people of differing genetic characteristics. It is plausible that individual differences in the capacity to maintain homeostasis in response to challenges (thereby allowing for reasonably normal development) and in—at present—poorly explicated concepts such as neurological integrity, plasticity, and resilience are genetically or experientially determined; such factors likely modulate the effects of environmental challenges such as undernutrition (Bhutta & Anand, 2002; Engle, Castle, & Menon, 1996; Morgane et al., 1993; Nelson, 2000; Sapolsky, 2001).

Furthermore, it is rarely the case that undernutrition exists independently of other risk factors such as maternal stress, genetic predisposition, poverty, and dangerous living conditions (e.g., poor sanitation or the presence of toxins such as lead; Guesry, 1998; Pollitt, 1969; Schettler, 2001; Snodgrass, 1994; Stein & Susser; 1985; Tanner & Finn-Stevenson, 2002; Trope, Lopez-Villegas, Cecil, & Lenkinski, 2001). Pollitt reported that in developing countries, children with the greatest nutritional deficits had the poorest living conditions (i.e., lack of running water or adequate plumbing, cramped housing, and large families). Thus, malnutrition may generally exert its effects by acting

in concert (additively or synergistically) with other risk factors (Guesry, 1998; Morgane et al., 1993, 2002; Stein & Susser, 1985; Zeskind & Ramey, 1981). For example, Caspi and coworkers (2002) found that abused children with a genotype leading to higher levels of a neurotransmitter-metabolizing enzyme (monoamine oxidase) displayed lower rates of antisocial behavior. The authors interpreted these findings to be evidence of a gene-environment interaction in which the genotype influenced an individual's response to a particular environmental stimulus. It is possible that analogous mechanisms or interactions could be at work in determining the outcome of early malnutrition.

OVERVIEW

The current chapter endeavors to examine the effect of early nutritional deficits on brain development and the role this may play in the emergence of psychopathology. We begin the discussion by examining the possible link between early nutritional insults and the development of psychopathology in the context of those studies that have specifically researched this question. After this, we step back and delve into investigations that look at the affects of early malnutrition on broader issues such as cognitive development in humans and developmental neurobiology. These factors are important because they characterize a developmental path (resulting from early malnutrition) in which psychopathology may exist as part of the milieu or which may increase an individual's risk for the later development of mental illness. The chapter concludes with a brief hypothetical discussion of potential causal mechanisms that may account for the relationship between early nutritional insults and the later development of psychopathology.

STUDIES ON PSYCHOPATHOLOGY

Studies in this section are presented with regard to the spectrum of psychopathology they examine. Thus, although research in this area is sparse, studies investigating the effects of early malnutrition on Schizophrenia or Schizophrenia Spectrum Disorders, externalizing disorders (e.g., ADHD, conduct problems, and antisocial behavior), and internalizing disorders (such as depression) are discussed. In addition to other researchers, Krueger and colleagues (Krueger, 2002; Krueger, Caspi, Moffitt, & Silva, 1998; Krueger, McGue, & Iacono, 2001) have proposed the broad dimensions of externalizing and internalizing to capture more accurately the structure of common mental disorders.

These dimensions are used in the current discussion for clarity and succinctness.

Despite numerous investigations into the cognitive effects of malnutrition on children, most of the research dealing with the effects of malnutrition on the development of psychopathology concerns individuals older than 18 years. This is a significant shortcoming in our knowledge in this area because many psychiatric disorders will likely prove to have developmental origins. Thus, it is probable that these conditions have perceptible manifestations during childhood and adolescence. Similarly, early malnutrition may influence the developmental course (e.g., age of onset, severity, or progression) of psychiatric disorders. Moreover, malnutrition may be expected to exert more powerful immediate effects on the developing brain—thereby suggesting the effects of malnutrition may be more salient in individuals younger than 18. Thus, children affected by early nutritional deficits may display additional or significantly different behavioral effects than mature adults (Keys, 1946). Furthermore, it is possible that some of the cognitive manifestations of undernutrition (discussed later) may have resulted from impairments secondary to various psychiatric symptoms such as inattention or anxiety.

Much of the information regarding the relationship between early malnutrition and later psychopathology comes from data collected on cohorts prenatally exposed to famine during the Dutch hunger winter of 1944 to 1945 (A. S. Brown et al., 1996; Butler, Susser, Brown, Kaufmann, & Gorman, 1994; Hoek, Brown, & Susser, 1998; Susser, Hoek, & Brown, 1998). As discussed previously, Stein et al. (1972) found no evidence suggesting decreased intellectual abilities or increased rates of severe or mild mental retardation following prenatal famine exposure. However, years later, E. Susser (the son of the original investigators) and his collaborators revisited the famine data to examine if individuals with a history of prenatal famine exposure exhibited higher rates of psychopathology in adulthood (A. S. Brown, Cohen, Greenwald, & Susser, 2000; A. S. Brown, Susser, Lin, Neugebauer, & Gorman, 1995; Hulshoff Pol et al., 2000; Neugebauer, Hoek, & Susser, 1999; Susser & Lin, 1992; Susser et al., 1996).

Several major admonitions regarding this natural experiment should be pointed out. First, the amount of food redistribution in families is not known (Stein et al., 1972). Thus, pregnant women who occasionally received greater rations might have been supplied more calories via sacrifice of other family members (Stein et al., 1972, 1975). Second, although probably not substantially significant, it is not known how much individuals supplemented their diets with material such as tulip bulbs, which may have actually contained toxins (Stein et al., 1972, 1975). Third, these data represent a circumscribed episode of malnutrition with a previously well-nourished population who returned to this status following the famine. Therefore, these results should not be generalized to chronically malnourished populations—especially those with other substantial risk factors (Stein et al., 1972). Fourth, except for records indicating profession of father, there is no information regarding familial background. Finally, because many of the births occurred at home, it is impossible to gather information on birth or gestational complications, which, along with maternal infection and stress, may play etiological roles in the emergence of behavioral deficits and psychopathological conditions (Anand & Scalzo, 2000; A. S. Brown et al., 2000; Brown & Susser, 2002; McNeil, Cantor-Graae, & Weinberger, 2000; Teicher et al., 2002). Regardless of these essentially unavoidable imperfections, the studies discussed here provide valuable insights regarding the possible role of prenatal malnutrition in the emergence of later psychiatric disorders.

In an initial 1992 study, Susser and Lin found that women, but not men, exhibited an increased prevalence of Schizophrenia following prenatal exposure to famine in the first trimester. However, they obtained these results through a broad inclusion criterion (i.e., first trimester of gestation during periods of low food rations) and review of admission records to psychiatric hospital units from 1978 to 1989. Thus, they based exposure on a single criterion that may not have completely captured children who experienced the highest levels of exposure. Furthermore, individuals were at least 32 years old at the start of the review period. This age tends to be past the age that most males have their first psychotic episode; therefore, it is likely many men would have already made initial psychiatric contact prior to this age and were not rehospitalized during the review period (Brown et al., 1996).

In a more extensive follow-up investigation, Susser et al. (1996) used stringent inclusion criteria to define a "maximal exposure" cohort. The inclusion criteria for the other cohorts were the same as in the 1992 study. However, they defined the maximal exposure cohort to include only those individuals conceived at the height of the famine. This cohort consisted of individuals born when the general population exhibited increases in adverse health effects and new births demonstrated excess congenital malformations (which, according to Stein et al., 1975, are associated with severe prenatal starvation). These criteria ensured that the researchers dealt exclusively with the maximally exposed cohort (e.g., the cohort that underwent the most significant early insult due to the famine). These restrictions led to the identification of a cohort born between October 15, 1945, and December 31, 1945 (Hoek et al., 1996, 1998; Susser, Hoek, et al., 1998). The authors extended the period of record review back to 1970, thereby more accurately reflecting lifetime history of psychiatric admission.

Based on these data, the researchers found a significantly increased prevalence of Schizophrenia in both males and females of the maximal exposure cohort. This cohort displayed a prevalence rate for Schizophrenia nearly 2 times higher than that of the unexposed cohort. Further, the other exposed cohorts did not differ in prevalence rate from the unexposed cohort. Susser et al. (1996) demonstrated these findings using a "narrow" and a "broad" diagnostic definition of Schizophrenia. Individuals in the maximal exposure cohort had a mother malnourished during the periconceptional phase, and their prenatal famine exposure occurred early in pregnancy, generally entirely within the first trimester.

Using magnetic resonance imaging, Hulshoff Pol and colleagues (2000) found increased brain abnormalities (specifically, focal white matter hyperintensities) in a subgroup of individuals from the maximal exposure cohort. They showed that individuals from this cohort diagnosed with Schizophrenia evidenced reduced intracranial volume compared to nonexposed individuals with Schizophrenia and nondiagnosed individuals with the same level of famine exposure. The authors speculated that the decreased intracranial volumes observed only in the famine-exposed individuals with Schizophrenia resulted from an interaction between genetic risk factors and early brain stunting caused by gestational malnutrition, eventually resulting in the development of Schizophrenia. They concluded that exposure to famine early in gestation is associated with increased focal brain abnormalities, possibly secondary to specific micronutrient deficiencies. In some individuals, these aberrations may result in a higher risk for developing Schizophrenia. The researchers urge discretion when examining their findings, stressing that they obtained the results using a limited number of participants and that other confounding factors could not be completely taken into account. Nevertheless, these data provide an initial glimpse into specific structural brain changes present following severe first trimester malnutrition.

Another study by the same group expanded their inquiry to determine if males conceived at the height of the hunger winter evidenced increased prevalence of Schizophrenia spectrum personality disorders (SSPD) as defined by the *International Classification of Diseases 6* (*ICD-6;* Hoek et al., 1996). This study used methodology similar to the earlier study. Thus, the authors compared the maximal exposure cohort (see Susser et al., 1996, for a description of this cohort) to an unexposed cohort and a cohort with first trimester exposure but without maternal malnutrition at the time of conception. The authors obtained data regarding the diagnosis of SSPD from military induction records; thus, males only are represented.

The investigators found that, when compared to the other groups, the maximal exposure group demonstrated a higher prevalence of SSPDs. This increase appeared to be unique to SSPDs because the three groups did not differ from one another in the prevalence of psychoneurosis, that is, general anxiety. They noted that this relationship remains consistent when estimated socioeconomic status (SES) is taken into account. However, the authors hasten to point out that despite the increased risk in the maximal exposure group, relatively few individuals in the entire study actually met criteria for SSPD. Furthermore, they cautioned that despite the apparent care taken in making these diagnoses, no formalized diagnostic system existed at the time of these evaluations. To some extent, this caution should be applied to both of the studies previously discussed.

Using information obtained from birth and medical records in a population-based cohort born between 1924 and 1932 in Helsinki, Finland, Wahlbeck, Forsén, Osmond, Barker, and Eriksson (2001) reported on the relationship between factors indicative of prenatal undernutrition and the later development of Schizophrenia. This study found that children born to mothers with a low body mass index (BMI) prior to parturition, who were born with small placentas, and were below-average length and weight at birth, had an increased risk of developing Schizophrenia in adulthood. Furthermore, this study indicated that, independent of other predictors, children thin at 7 years of age had an increased risk for developing Schizophrenia in later life. The data also indicated that children short at birth who remained lean during childhood had a fourfold risk of developing Schizophrenia. The authors observed no differences in the risk for Schizophrenia between groups of varying SES, replicating findings from other studies.

The researchers argued that these results are consistent with the hypothesis that fetal and childhood factors (specifically undernutrition) play a role in the pathogenesis of Schizophrenia. However, given the relatively low and consistent prevalence of Schizophrenia in the population and the relatively high rate of early malnutrition, it may be more plausible to conjecture that early nutritional deficits act as predisposing or triggering circumstances. Regardless, this study suggests that malnutrition statistically increases the risk for later development of Schizophrenia.

Wahlbeck and colleagues (2001) suggest that, in their sample, nutritional status (based on maternal BMI, birth length, and slenderness in childhood) is independent of SES; however, they provide no evidence to bolster this claim. Thus, given the information available, it is impossible to discern if these measures reflect actual undernutrition or are simply corollaries of low SES or a genetic diathesis that increases risk for Schizophrenia.

Taken together, these studies suggest that the prevalence of Schizophrenia and SSPD increases in individuals who are exposed to severe malnutrition early in gestation. The findings of Wahlbeck et al. (2001) also provide evidence that Schizophrenia is (either directly or indirectly) related to suboptimal growth in utero through early childhood.

Hoek et al. (1998) speculated about potential mechanisms to explain the findings of their group. First, they noted that it was unlikely that this finding was related solely to nutritional restriction because, if such a correlation existed, one would expect to find significantly higher rates of Schizophrenia and SSPD in developing countries that commonly have serious food shortages. They indicated that it was more likely that the increased prevalence was related to a restriction in a specific micronutrient, stating that these types of deficiencies are frequently observed in both developed and developing areas. This explanation could also account for the apparent independence of SES and nutritional status described by Wahlbeck et al. (2001). This hypothesis could be investigated further by using animal models of specific micronutrient deficiencies occurring at circumscribed times during brain development that reflect a proposed pathophysiology of a disorder, for example, migration defects in Schizophrenia secondary to folate deficiency. This approach could be useful in elucidating the effects of micronutrient deficiencies on neuroanatomy, neurochemistry, and neurophysiology; however, it would fall short in illustrating possible behavioral correlates because there are currently no irrefutable animal models of mental disorders, especially Schizophrenia. Finally, Hoek and colleagues stated, their findings could have resulted from the increased level of birth complications and morbidity associated with early birth found in the most affected famine cohort. However, they noted that areas less affected by the famine experienced similar increases in obstetric complications without the concomitant rise in SSPD, making this potential confound less problematic.

Neugebauer and colleagues (1999) again used the Dutch famine data to investigate possible relationships between prenatal nutritional restriction and the subsequent development of Antisocial Personality Disorder (ASPD). The researchers used diagnostic information regarding ASPD from Dutch military induction records. According to the authors, Dutch psychiatrists considered ASPD to include a constellation of behaviors such as aggression, history of criminal activity, disregard for the truth, impulsivity, volatile temperament, unreliability, and interpersonal difficulties. Furthermore, psychiatrists categorized individuals under the subclassifications of violent or nonviolent ASPD.

Results indicated that individuals exposed to severe malnutrition in utero during the first and/or second trimesters had an increased risk for the emergence of later ASPD (specifically violent ASPD) compared to either unexposed individuals, individuals with only moderate levels of caloric restriction, and individuals severely malnourished in the third trimester alone. Malnutrition remained predictive, even after they included other proven or potential risk factors (such as low social class, low IQ, and large sibship size), for ASPD in multiple regression equations. The authors comment that the most likely explanation for this pattern of results is the lack of a particular unspecified micronutrient during this critical period of brain development. They argue that similarities in infant morbidity between cases and noncases, specificity of time and place of the findings, and the lack of third trimester effects indicate that severe malnutrition (during the first/second trimester) supersedes other environmental insults. However, they also propose a possible mechanism in which malnutrition potentiates preexisting genetic or environmental vulnerabilities.

Using a cohort of low birthweight (LBW) children, Breslau, Chilcoat, Johnson, Andreski, and Lucia (2000) examined the relationship between LBW, soft neurological signs, and subsequent intellectual/behavioral functioning at ages 6 and 11. Soft neurological signs refer to a number of various subtle neurological abnormalities in sensory, motor, and integrative skills that do not significantly impact an individual's overall functioning but may still result in suboptimal abilities in these domains (Breslau et al., 2000). Of particular importance, soft signs are not thought to reflect focal brain damage but rather a diffuse neurological pathology resulting from a variety of sources, including genetic anomalies such as microdeletions or mosaics (Breslau et al., 2000). Furthermore, studies have linked soft neurological signs to early malnutrition and deficits in IQ and behavioral functioning (Breslau et al., 2000; Galler, Ramsey, Solimano, Kucharski, & Harrison, 1984).

Breslau et al. (2000) observed a relationship between LBW and the occurrence of soft neurological signs in which LBW children are nearly twice as likely to exhibit soft signs as normal birthweight (NBW) children. The researchers found a linear relationship between LBW and the frequency of soft signs. Thus, the lower a child's weight at birth, the more likely he or she would display soft signs. Moreover, the data indicated that children evidencing soft signs consistently performed below average on tests of intellectual abilities regardless of birthweight; however, LBW children tended to score lower on the IQ test in general, thus indicating additive influences. They also found a relationship between soft signs in both LBW and NBW children and the occurrence of learning disorders (at age 11) and the occurrence of internalizing problems at age 6 and 11. In the LBW group, the investigators found a relationship between soft signs and the occurrence of externalizing behaviors, including attention problems, at age 6 but not at age 11.

Even though this study did not strictly deal with nutritional deficits, it is interesting because LBW and soft signs may be associated with undernutrition. This is particularly germane to the Breslau et al. (2000) study because many of the participants, especially those in the LBW group, lived in urban settings and came from low SES backgrounds and thus had an elevated risk for prenatal and/or postnatal malnutrition. Regardless of the nexus between LBW and soft neurological signs, the findings suggest that LBW children may be at increased risk for reductions in IQ, learning disabilities, internalizing problems, and, when younger, externalizing difficulties, including attention deficits. The reason for the apparent evaporation of differences in the externalizing domain may be increased levels of externalizing behaviors exhibited by the control groups (Moffitt, 1993) or the beneficial effects of behavioral/medical interventions.

In a follow-up to their 1986 study (to be discussed in a subsequent section of this chapter), Galler and Ramsey (1989) assessed a group of previously malnourished Barbadian children for symptoms of hyperactivity. Using parent and teacher reports, they found increased levels of hyperactivity and distractibility. These relationships remained consistent after taking into account environmental factors such as parental involvement, parental career/ knowledge of the world, stability of the home environment, number of siblings, and quality of living conditions (e.g., quantity of modern conveniences and durability of dwelling construction). Furthermore, these results concur with earlier findings (Galler, Ramsey, Solimano, & Lowell, 1983), which suggested increased attention difficulties in previously malnourished children between 5 and 11 years of age. The current study revealed an increased prevalence of speech difficulties in the formerly malnourished children as noted by teacher report. However, difficulties with socialization, emotional reactivity, and immaturity previously observed in these children (Galler, Ramsey, Soli-

mano, & Lowell, 1983) were not seen in the current investigation. According to the authors, this may have resulted from slight changes in the assessment tools (necessary to reflect the older age of the children) or interventions targeted at ameliorating some of the effects of early malnutrition. If the latter is the case, it is meaningful because it suggests that some aspects of early malnutrition (e.g., social skills) may be more amenable to educational interventions than others (e.g., attention problems; Galler & Ramsey, 1989). However, it is possible that effects such as emotional instability are more characteristic of younger children who were previously malnourished and would disappear in older children regardless of interventions (Galler & Ramsey, 1989). A shortcoming of this study is the researchers' failure to control for intellectual abilities. Thus, it is unknown if the increased attention problems observed in the experimental group are a unique aspect of undernutrition in the 1st year of life, or are a corollary of the lower intellectual skills previously reported in these children (Galler, Ramsey, & Forde, 1986).

Although not as robust as the findings for Schizophrenia, these studies imply that pre- as well as postnatal malnutrition predisposes individuals for exhibiting a variety of externalizing behaviors. It is intriguing to speculate whether the brain is susceptible to insults causing externalizing behaviors for a longer period during development, or if there are distinct etiologies of externalizing disorders, potentially linked to disruptions at various stages of brain development. Nevertheless, this handful of studies provides an impetus for future investigations on the role of malnutrition and other neurobiological risk factors in the etiology of externalizing problems.

A. S. Brown and colleagues (1995) investigated the relationship between prenatal famine exposure and the later development of affective disorders (affective psychosis and neurotic depression). The researchers defined affective psychosis and neurotic depression in accordance with *ICD-9* definitions. Thus, individuals with affective psychosis displayed disturbances in mood (either depression or mania) accompanied by mood-congruent delusions, whereas individuals with a diagnosis of neurotic depression displayed disturbances in mood (including symptoms of depression and/or anxiety) but evidenced no psychotic symptoms. They formed the groups by matching birth date and location with psychiatric admission records from 1978 to 1991.

Prenatal exposure to famine in the second trimester increased the risk of developing affective psychosis in later life; however, the authors did not find increased risk of affective psychosis resulting from first or third trimester famine exposure. These results remained significant when sex was taken into account; however, there was a significant interaction between sex and second semester famine exposure: Males but not females appeared to be at greater risk for developing affective psychosis after second semester famine exposure, whereas females had higher prevalence rates in general. The data indicated no increased risk of neurotic depression following prenatal famine exposure in any trimester or in either sex.

A possible reason for the disparity between the diagnostic categories may be that, when compared to neurotic depression, affective psychosis represents a more severe mood disorder with a greater risk of hospitalization. Furthermore, neurotic depression may be more likely triggered by life stressors, and thus differences between groups could be submerged by random variation in the population. A limitation of this study is that females usually begin exhibiting mood symptoms in adolescence. Therefore, effects of prenatal famine exposure may be observed in females if the researchers reviewed earlier hospital admission records. Additionally, A. S. Brown and his collaborators (1995) caution, their findings may not represent increased prevalence of affective psychosis, but instead may reflect increased need for hospital admission or delayed onset of symptoms in prenatally famine-exposed males. Nevertheless, these results suggest that males are at greater risk for developing serious mood disorders following significant midgestational malnutrition.

In a follow-up to their 1995 study, A. S. Brown and colleagues (2000) greatly increased their sample size by obtaining new diagnostic records. The researchers focused on unipolar and bipolar depression requiring hospitalization. Exposure to famine during the second and third trimesters related to increased hospital admissions in both males and females with unipolar and bipolar depression. The authors indicated that this effect was particularly robust if exposure occurred in the third trimester only. These results extend the findings of the 1995 study and suggest that prenatal famine exposure predisposes adults to develop serious mood disorders requiring hospitalization and characterized by either depression or mania/hypomania.

Thompson and his collaborators (Thompson, Syddall, Rodin, Osmond, & Barker, 2001) examined the relationship between LBW and the incidence of depression in old age. These investigators used data obtained from individuals born between 1920 and 1930 in the English county of Hertfordshire and who still lived in the area in the early 1990s. The authors assessed all of the participants for depressive symptoms using two measures (a self-report questionnaire and a semistructured interview) and simultaneously asked about confounding factors such as SES, recent loss, general illness, and coronary heart disease (CHD).

This study found a relationship between birthweight and depression in late life: The lower a child's birthweight, the greater the risk for developing late-life depression. The findings were more robust in males and remained significant when the researchers statistically controlled for other complicating factors such as illness, SES, and bereavement. When they specifically took into account the occurrence of CHD (another risk factor for late-life depression), the relationship grew stronger. The research indicated that males with LBW but high weight at 1 year exhibited the highest risk for late-life depression; conversely, males with above average birthweight and comparatively low weight at 1 year exhibited the lowest risk for late-life depression. Thompson et al. (2001) conjectured that this pattern indicated poor prenatal nutrition followed by compensatory growth and good prenatal nutrition followed by a regression to the mean, respectively. Because this study focused on current and not early life depression, the results should not be generalized to depression occurring outside of old age. The authors suggested that their findings provide support for aberrant fetal programming (see the conclusion of this chapter) caused by undernutrition as the major factor contributing to the future development of depression.

In summary, prenatal malnutrition appears to increase the risk for developing internalizing disorders (specifically mood disorders). It is interesting that the risk period for exposure to malnutrition in the externalizing and internalizing domains may be later than for the Schizophrenia Spectrum Disorders. The stages of brain development affected during these periods of vulnerability concur with research on the neurological sequelae of these various psychopathologies and support the timing of onset and duration of insult hypothesis. For example, the research on Schizophrenia strongly suggests that malnutrition exerts its effects in early stages of central nervous system (CNS) development, neural tube formation, and initial neuronal migration, all of which have been implicated in the etiology of Schizophrenia (Arnold, 1999; LaMantia, 1999; Rioux, Nissanov, Lauber, Bilker, & Arnold, 2003; Susser, Brown, et al., 1998). The later period of vulnerability observed in externalizing and internalizing disorders suggests that malnutrition disrupts later processes of brain development such as neurotransmitter formation, late-stage migration, and gliagenesis. Abnormalities in these processes have been implicated in the etiology of externalizing and internalizing disorders (Bowley et al., 2002; Cotter, Pariante, & Everall, 2001; Jenike et al., 1996). Further, some conditions (such as Schizophrenia) may be associated with a relatively acute injury, whereas behavioral disturbances in the externalizing and internalizing domains may be associated with insults extending over longer periods.

Despite the paucity of studies on this topic, the investigations undertaken with the Dutch famine cohort and similar samples suggest that early malnutrition increases the risk for the later development of mental disorders. Furthermore, this effect is not a general increase in vulnerability, but appears to depend on the timing and duration of the nutritional insult. Because the Dutch famine studies lack confounds such as social class, deprived environments, parental education, and extended postnatal malnutrition (which frequently accompany early malnutrition), they cannot be generalized to a chronically malnourished population. However, they provide strong support for the unique contribution of severe prenatal malnutrition in the emergence of later psychopathology.

Regrettably, few studies have addressed the role of postnatal or pre/postnatal malnutrition in the development of psychopathology. This is particularly disheartening because postnatal malnutrition is common throughout the world, and, as discussed later in the studies on cognition, it is likely that postnatal malnutrition is associated with deficits that differ from those of prenatal malnutrition.

The previous discussion suggests that early malnutrition may lead to the later development of psychopathology. Moreover, the expression of a particular psychopathology likely depends on when the insult occurred (e.g., prenatal versus postnatal or first versus second/third trimester). Another contributing factor (discussed in greater detail in the concluding remarks) is that malnutrition may exert its maximal effect if it occurs concurrently with another insult such as stress or toxicity.

Now that a plausible link has been established, it is necessary to take a step back to examine what may underlie the development of these conditions. We first examine human studies that have been designed to determine if early malnutrition results in adverse effects on cognitive/intellectual development.

PRIMER

Before beginning this section, it is necessary to note that human protein energy malnutrition or undernutrition rarely exists without concomitant micronutrient deficiencies (Gorman, 1995; Kretchmer et al., 1996).

Human Studies of Cognitive Development

One of the shortcomings of research on humans is the difficulty controlling for all potentially relevant variables, some-

times even known confounds. This limitation is particularly vexing in epidemiological research regarding the long-term consequences of early malnutrition. For example, as previously discussed, early malnutrition rarely occurs independently of other risk factors such as poverty (Engle et al., 1996; Pollitt, 1969; Stein & Susser, 1985; Tanner & Finn-Stevenson, 2002). Although there are statistical techniques that can help compensate for this comorbidity, one must still be careful when making inferences regarding experimental interventions or the interplay of particular risk factors. Secondarily, many studies using a population-based design are unable to account for other known or conjectured risk factors such as genetic predisposition, parental education, maternal stress, chaotic home environment, or other complicating physical factors such as toxin exposure, infection, or birth complications (Grantham-McGregor, 2002; Pollitt, 1969). These caveats are not indictments of these types of studies, because what such studies lack in elegant controls they often make up for in direct relevance. However, the limited control over potential third variables should be kept in mind when evaluating such studies.

There are numerous studies detailing the effects of early malnutrition on human cognitive development (Georgieff & Rao, 2001; Gorman, 1995; Pollitt, 1988). Many of these studies were conducted in developing countries, where malnutrition (or, perhaps more frequently, undernutrition) is likely chronic and may span all of development—from the periconceptional phase to adolescence and young adulthood (Grantham-McGregor, 2002). Given the growing minority and immigrant populations of developed countries such as the United States and the fact that a vast portion of children worldwide suffer from early malnutrition, a careful consideration of these studies is warranted, even for those primarily interested in industrialized populations (Pollitt, 1994). Furthermore, knowledge of successful nutritional interventions in developing countries may help to improve current U.S. government programs such as the Women, Infants and Children (WIC) program (Pollitt, 1994; Tanner & Finn-Stevenson, 2002). It is useful to review this literature to provide insight into the broad behavioral effects of early malnutrition. Further, research has linked intellectual/cognitive deficits to various types of psychopathologies (Moffitt & Caspi, 2001). Although this link may not be causal, these conditions (i.e., cognitive abilities and psychopathology) may nonetheless be connected.

Studies on neurocognitive outcomes of children who suffered early malnutrition is presented in three sections: studies concerning prenatal malnutrition and effects of LBW (where the fetus is protected from certain environmental factors such as poverty), studies on postnatal or combined pre- and postnatal malnutrition, and studies examining the effects of nutritional interventions with malnourished populations.

LBW children or children born small for gestational age (SGA) are usually the result of intrauterine growth retardation (IUGR), which is frequently associated with fetal PEM (Georgieff & Rao, 2001). Although nutritional deficits in SGA babies can result from poor maternal nutrition, they can also result from other gestational or fetal problems such as maternal hypertension, uterine infections, or genetic disorders (Georgieff & Rao, 2001).

Numerous studies have examined the neurocognitive functioning of SGA children (Georgieff, Hoffman, Pereira, Bernbaum, & Hoffman-Williamson, 1985; Low et al., 1982; Pollitt, 1996; Stein et al., 1972). Strauss and Dietz (1998), using data from the National Collaborative Perinatal Project, compared the intellectual performance and visual-motor skills of IUGR children with that of their same sex non-IUGR siblings and NBW children (without IUGR siblings). These researchers demonstrated that IUGR infants are usually born to shorter women who weigh less than the average female. Furthermore, this study revealed that NBW siblings of IUGR children were typically smaller than other NBW children, although they were not considered SGA. The authors found that, at 7 years of age, formerly IUGR infants with a head circumference significantly below normal or less than their siblings' evidenced reduced intellectual capacity and visual-motor skills compared to NBW children. However, the performance of IUGR children did not significantly differ from their non-IUGR siblings, although the data trended in this direction.

These findings suggest that reduced birthweight is a phenomenon considerably influenced by genetic factors, although it is possible that the NBW siblings were malnourished, albeit at a lesser level than their SGA siblings. Additionally, statistically correcting for genetic and environmental agents suggests that IUGR alone does not substantially contribute to the reductions in cognitive abilities noted in other studies. However, these data indicate that IUGR infants born with significantly decreased head circumference differ from the NBW population, other IUGR children without reduced head circumference, and their siblings in terms of their intellectual and visual-motor skills at 7 years of age.

In contradistinction to this study, Low and colleagues (1982) failed to find a relationship between IUGR and cognitive deficits. Their results indicated that IUGR children remained smaller than their peers at 6 years of age; however, the data revealed no significant long-term effects of IUGR on cognitive, motor, sensory, or language abilities. The IUGR group exhibited higher rates of certain difficul-

ties (such as increased language difficulties and a slightly higher fail rate in senior kindergarten), but these differences did not reach statistical significance.

The authors admitted that the small IUGR male sample may have limited statistical power to detect delays in language skills, and they rightly point out that all of the children in this study were full term, preventing generalization to preterm IUGR infants. Furthermore, this study did not assess specific neurocognitive functions (e.g., attention and recognition memory) that, because of their mediation by the hippocampus, might be more susceptible to prenatal insults such as IUGR. It is also possible that intervening environmental factors (such as a quality home environment) attenuated deficits in IUGR children. Another explanation rests on the fact that the authors meticulously matched the IUGR and control groups on factors such as obstetric complications, newborn characteristics, socioeconomic variables, and status at 1-year follow-up; thus, factors potentially contributing to the reduced cognitive performance of IUGR children in previous studies might have been eliminated in the present investigation. Moreover, although not expressly stated in this paper, it is probable that the children in both IUGR and control groups received adequate postnatal nutrition.

Other studies have expressly examined the effects of decreased head growth and caloric restriction on cognitive skills (Georgieff et al., 1985; Harvey, Prince, Bunton, Parkinson, & Campbell, 1982). Winick and Rosso (1969) demonstrated that children dying of severe malnutrition in the 1st year after birth evidence reduced brain DNA content, indicative of fewer neuronal and glial cells. Reduced head growth secondary to reduced cell numbers is an important variable to consider because microcephaly (severely reduced head size) is linked to neurodevelopmental disorders such as Fetal Alcohol Syndrome. Furthermore, some investigators have correlated small head circumference at birth with greater risk for developing psychiatric disorders such as Schizophrenia (Archibald et al., 2001; Bracha et al., 1995; Kunugi, Takei, Murray, Saito, & Nanko, 1996). Although reduced head growth is not associated with development in a specific brain region, it may be an indirect indicator of general brain maturation (Pollitt, Mueller, & Leibel, 1982).

Georgieff et al. (1985) showed that SGA infants and infants who were a size appropriate for gestational age experiencing a prolonged period of postnatal caloric deprivation (due to medical complications) exhibited reduced rates of catch-up head growth. As would be expected, SGA infants began showing this reduced growth rate after sustaining a shorter period of caloric deprivation. The reduced rates of catch-up growth in these infants resulted in smaller head circumference at 1 year, head growth curves that (although broadly within the normal range) continued to be less than optimal, and, in the most severely affected infants, below average motor development scores.

Harvey and colleagues (1982) found that children born SGA with intrauterine head growth that slowed prior to 26 weeks gestation obtained lower scores on tests of perceptual and motor skills at 5 years of age. SGA children with normal head growth performed at the same level as controls in these and other cognitive domains. The researchers combined the two SGA groups and evaluated performance strictly in terms of birthweight, ignoring rate of head growth; they determined that (taken as a single group) SGA children did not perform significantly differently from controls. Although this study did not deal with frank undernutrition, these results are an interesting corollary to the findings of Georgieff et al. (1985) because they indicate that early rate of head growth may have a long-term impact on certain cognitive abilities.

Although not entirely consistent, these studies suggest that SGA infants, especially those with decelerated rates of head growth, and children who have lower birthweight compared to siblings are at higher risk for developing subtle but detectable neurocognitive difficulties (Georgieff et al., 1985; Harvey et al., 1982). In addition, Tirosh, Gaster, Berger, Cohen, and Scher (2000) showed that birthweight and head circumference of typically developing children positively and significantly correlated with activity level and mobility in infancy. However, prenatal malnutrition in the absence of other risk factors has not been convincingly demonstrated to result in long-term decreases in cognitive abilities. It remains unclear how meaningful any deficits will be as previously malnourished children age (Guesry, 1998; Pollitt, 1996; Stein et al., 1972; Stein & Susser, 1985). Nevertheless, the relationship noted by Tirosh et al. is important because it suggests that babies born with low birthweight are less active and less able to explore their environment, thereby potentially reducing mental stimulation, which human and animal studies indicate is necessary for basic cortical organization and development (Black, 1998; Nelson, 1999). Researchers theorize that environmental stimulation is also critical for the development of other, more complex cognitive skills (Black, 1998; Nelson, 1999, 2000).

It is necessary to qualify these assertions. First, it is quite likely that the SGA infant is affected by the internal and external environments into which she or he is born, for example, by such factors as maternal substance use, stress, and genetic constitutions; postnatal nutritional factors; and

birth complications such as premature birth, hypoxia, and maternal infections. Therefore, the ultimate effects of SGA are likely graded on a continuum, depending on the combination of other vulnerabilities and assets possessed by the child (Engle et al., 1996; Stein & Susser, 1985).

Second, as stated previously, SGA infants are a heterogeneous group, and it is plausible that different etiologies of IUGR have different effects on neurological development (Black, deRegnier, Long, Georgieff, & Nelson, 2004). Finally, evidence suggests that prenatal malnutrition (especially if endured early in pregnancy) can occur without resultant low birthweight (Heasman, Clarke, Stephenson, & Symonds, 1999; Lumey, 1998). Lumey determined that prenatal malnutrition restricted to the first trimester resulted in compensatory placental growth without subsequent reductions in birthweight. For this reason, normal birthweight does not necessarily indicate the presence of adequate prenatal nutrition.

Thus, many children, despite being born the appropriate size for gestational age, may have sustained neurological insults due to prenatal malnutrition. These children, as well as SGA children, may be more vulnerable to further nutritional deprivation or other environmental insults (Berkman, Lescano, Gilman, Lopez, & Black, 2002; Galler et al., 1986; Galler & Ramsey, 1987, 1989; Ivanovic et al., 2000, 2002; Liu, Raine, Venables, Dalais, & Mednick, 2003). It is therefore difficult to dissociate the precise effects of prenatal malnutrition because the populations typically studied may not represent all prenatally malnourished individuals.

In a series of papers, Galler and colleagues (Galler & Ramsey, 1987, 1989; Galler, Ramsey, Solimano, & Lowell, 1983; Galler, Ramsey, Solimano, Lowell, & Mason, 1983; Galler et al., 1986) described the consequences of moderate to severe malnutrition sustained by Barbadian children in the 1st year of life. Galler et al. (1986) showed that, despite apparently successful nutritional rehabilitation, previously malnourished children continued to exhibit lower performance on tests of intellectual abilities up to 8 to 14 years postmalnutrition. In this study, researchers administered to participants the Wechsler Intelligence Scale for Children-Revised (WISC-R; Galler et al., 1986), and the participants' mothers completed a questionnaire assessing living circumstances, education, family relationships, and caregiver contact, among other factors. Consistent with previous evaluations (Galler, Ramsey, Solimano, Lowell, et al., 1983), results indicated that previously undernourished children had lower overall intellectual abilities and performed below controls (matched on birthweight, medical illnesses other than malnutrition, age, sex, and handedness) on the verbal and performance subscales of the

WISC-R. The researchers observed no sex differences or sex-nutrition interactions, except that (regardless of early nutritional status) females outperformed males on the Freedom from Distractibility index.

Galler et al. (1986) reported a significant correlation between scores on the WISC-R and environmental factors (e.g., poverty and maternal employment). However, early malnutrition remained significant when the authors statistically adjusted for these influences. Conversely, environmental factors remained significant when the authors statistically adjusted for early nutritional status. The significant influence of environmental factors on test performance at these older ages is interesting because this was not found in previous investigations with this cohort (Galler, Ramsey, Solimano, Lowell, et al., 1983). The authors concluded that a history of malnutrition continues to play a role in intellectual deficits at least into adolescence. However, as a child matures, the effects of an early nutritional insult may be overcome or attenuated by other environmental factors. Thus, the findings suggest that appropriate interventions may be effective in combating some of the intellectual impairments incurred in early malnutrition.

Using this same cohort, Galler and Ramsey (1987) found that previously malnourished children younger than 14 displayed deficient performance on Piaget's tests of conservation. These differences were not entirely accounted for by IQ, suggesting that these tasks assess slightly different cognitive domains. In contrast to the persisting differences on measures of IQ, previously malnourished children performed equivalent to controls by age 14. This pattern is similar to that observed in the Galler et al. (1986) study in that it suggests that effects of an early nutritional insult, initially very salient, grow less robust with time.

Another series of papers by Ivanovic and collaborators (Ivanovic et al., 2000, 2002) investigated the effects of severe early malnutrition on scholastic achievement, IQ, and brain morphology in Chilean high school graduates. Formerly undernourished and never undernourished high school graduates of low SES participated in this study. Researchers found that individuals with a history of early malnutrition obtained lower Full-Scale IQs (as assessed by the Wechsler Adult Intelligence Scale [WAIS]), lower scores on a scholastic aptitude test containing verbal and numerical items, and reduced brain volume on magnetic resonance imaging (MRI). The IQ results remained consistent across verbal and nonverbal domains in both sexes, whereas the brain volumetric difference, though significant in both sexes, emerged much more strikingly in males.

In a subsequent study with a similar population, Ivanovic et al. (2002) evaluated two groups of young adults with mean IQs of about 125 and 91, respectively. Both groups included individuals of high and low SES. They assessed participants with the same battery as in the 2000 study, now adding intellectual testing of both parents. The researchers verified the occurrence of malnutrition in the 1st year of life by reviewing hospital records. The results indicated that, regardless of SES, children with higher IQ had greater brain volume, higher maternal IQ, better prenatal nutrition as indexed by birthweight, no evidence of postnatal nutritional deficits, and higher scholastic achievement. Maternal IQ, brain volume, and postnatal nutrition significantly related to young adult IQ. Early malnutrition rarely occurred in the high SES, low IQ group; however, this group evidenced lower maternal IQ when compared to the high SES, high IQ group. Conversely, 64% of individuals with low SES and low IQ had a history of early malnutrition, and this group, in general, had maternal IQs lower than the other three groups. Additionally, the individuals in the low IQ group had similar maternal IQ, scholastic achievement, and brain volume. This led the authors to conjecture that these findings are typical correlates of low IQ.

Liu et al. (2003) conducted a very interesting study in which they assessed the effect of malnutrition at age 3 on cognitive skills at age 3 and again at age 11, while attempting to statistically control for various psychosocial risk factors (e.g., living circumstances, parental education, age of mother at time of birth, presence of mental illness in the mother, and number of children living in the home). Study participants included children living on the island of Mauritius and enrolled in the Mauritius Child Health Project, a prospective longitudinal study of children's physical and psychological health. At 3 years, children were assessed for several indicators of malnutrition: angular stomatitis, kwashiorkor, sparse fine hair, and anemia. These indicators are associated with deficiencies in vitamin A and B_2; protein, zinc, and copper; protein energy, zinc, and iron; and iron, respectively. The researchers considered a child malnourished if he or she displayed one or more of these four indicators. Assessments at age 3 included subtests from the Boehm Test of Basic Concepts-Preschool Version. Assessments at age 11 included subtests from the WISC, Trails A & B (tests of executive functions), and a test of basic reading skills.

Results indicated that children malnourished at 3 years displayed overall intellectual and verbal cognitive deficits and continued exhibiting these deficits at age 11. Moreover, at age 11 these children exhibited deficits in nonverbal abilities, scholastic skills, reading abilities, and executive functioning. They found that even though malnourished children tended to have lower parental education and higher scores on measures of social stress, the effects of malnutrition remained significant when these factors were statistically adjusted for in the analysis. Additionally, this study reported a dose-response (i.e., monotonic) relationship between indicators of malnutrition and cognitive skills, as assessed by the WISC. Thus, children with three of four indicators of malnutrition at age 3 had an IQs approximately 15 points below the mean, children with two indicators had an IQ 9 points below the mean, and children with one indicator had an IQ only 3 points below the mean.

The authors reported that anemia at age 3 years was the most significant indicator relating to lower cognitive performance at ages 3 and 11. The researchers acknowledged that they did not obtain nutritional information at age 11; hence, it is possible that these results could be explained by current or chronic malnutrition. Furthermore, the authors did not examine birth records. Therefore, factors such as birthweight and prenatal complications may have influenced the results. Nonetheless, this is a strong experimental design supporting the hypothesis that postnatal malnutrition has repercussions for later cognitive functioning. It also suggests that trace nutrients such as iron are particularly important in the manifestations of malnutrition.

The unique impact of postnatal malnutrition and its relationship with other risk factors on cognitive development remains unknown. In general, the studies presented here suggest that postnatal malnutrition is associated with discernable decreases in intellectual abilities (Berkman et al., 2002; Galler et al., 1986; Galler & Ramsey, 1987; Liu et al., 2003). Even though this assertion appears supported by the extant data, cautions similar to those detailed in the section regarding prenatal malnutrition still apply. For example, many of these studies did not directly assess potential confounding factors commonly associated with early malnutrition, such as parental IQ, biological risks (birth complications, childhood diseases, or environmental toxins), and social variables (such as a chronically neglectful or understimulating environment; Berkman et al., 2002; Guesry, 1998; Liu et al., 2003; Pollitt, 1969; Stein & Susser, 1985). Nevertheless, a majority of the studies indirectly assessed important variables and controlled for these variables in their subsequent analyses (Berkman et al., 2002; Galler et al., 1986; Galler & Ramsey, 1987; Liu et al., 2003), allowing us to be fairly confident in the assertion that postnatal malnutrition exerts deleterious effects on the developing brain.

The studies reviewed above continue to leave open the question of amelioration of the effects of early malnutri-

tion on the developing brain. Several studies addressing this point are considered next.

Generally, studies that examine amelioration of early malnutrition investigate either strictly nutritional or combined environmental/nutritional interventions (Joos, Pollitt, Mueller, & Albright, 1983; Lien, Meyer, & Winick, 1977; Pollitt, 1996; Raine, Mellingen, Liu, Venables, & Mednick, 2003; Raine et al., 2001; Winick, Meyer, & Harris, 1975; Zeskind & Ramey, 1981). The individuals in these studies are usually assumed to suffer from postnatal malnutrition, although many of the investigations did not explicitly rule out the possibility of prenatal nutritional restriction.

Pollitt and his collaborators (Pollitt, Gorman, Engle, Martorell, & Rivera, 1993) described a nutritional intervention in four rural Guatemalan villages. Beginning at various times during development (e.g., before conception, during gestation, throughout lactation, and into childhood), this project provided pregnant mothers and their children with either a high-protein, high-calorie drink known as Atole or a low-protein, low-calorie drink known as Fresco. The researchers fortified both beverages with trace minerals. Individuals in two villages received the Atole drink and individuals in the others received Fresco. Children of low SES whose mothers received Atole during gestation and until at least age 2 outperformed their peers on tests of information processing, mental ability, and academic skills, and progressed further in school than children receiving Fresco. Low SES children with shorter and later (beginning at or after age 2) periods of exposure to Atole also benefited (scoring higher on tests of numerical and reading abilities and progressing further in school than their peers), although these findings were less striking. These results are interesting because they argue for a stable, long-term improvement in intellectual, academic, and cognitive skills resulting from prenatal through postnatal nutritional supplementation in undernourished populations. Moreover, they imply that supplementation has the greatest impact/benefit on low SES individuals, perhaps because it delivers help to the children who, without it, would have fared worst. They also illustrate the differential vulnerability (or plasticity) of the brain depending on the timing of the insult and intervention.

Using data from the Mauritius health project, Raine et al. (2001) investigated the effects of an enriched educational environment on orienting and physiological arousal (measured by electroencephalography). In this study, experimenters matched children based on psychophysiological characteristics at age 3 and randomly assigned participants to an enriched preschool or a standard preschool educational experience on the island of Mauritius. The enriched preschool employed various types of enriching experiences, including well-balanced meals, education about nutrition and hygiene to parents and children, encouragement of imaginative play, interactive conversational skills, socialization, exercise, and regular field trips. Furthermore, parental involvement was highly encouraged, time-out discipline was used instead of corporal punishment, and the children's health was carefully monitored. The enriched experiences lasted for 2 years, at which time the children began grade school in typical classrooms.

Results indicated that the enriched preschool experience related to increases in orienting and physiological arousal at age 11. The authors speculated that these findings provided evidence of improved information processing or accelerated neurological maturation in children enrolled in the enriched preschool. They acknowledged that, given the multifactorial nature of the enriched experience, it was impossible to surmise which component or components explained these results, although research suggests that both nutritional and educational enrichment have unique effects on cognitive development (Grantham-McGregor, Powell, Walker, & Himes, 1991). However, these results may be explained by long-term changes in parental or child behavior caused by the early preschool experience. For example, the parental education and increased parental involvement encouraged by the preschool may have been built on and maintained after the child began grade school. Thus, the findings may represent the consequence of being raised in a more stable, lower-stress home environment and not by neurological alterations directly induced by the preschool experience. Regardless, these findings suggest that long-term alterations in physiological parameters, considered to reflect neuronal processing (Williams et al., 2000), can occur secondary to environmental enrichment and nutritional supplementation. These results are fascinating because reduced orienting and arousal responses are associated with various types of psychopathology (Banaschewski et al., 2003; Perry, Felger, & Braff, 1998; Schnur et al., 1999).

The previous studies illustrate the potential benefits of nutritional supplementation and combined nutritional/environmental enrichment in chronically undernourished populations. However, as discussed previously, undernourished children are frequently born with other genetic and environmental risks (Guesry, 1998; Pollitt, 1969; Stein & Susser, 1985). This begs the question: Can comprehensive environmental enrichment rescue a child with multiple risk factors, including malnutrition?

Winick et al. (1975) and Lien et al. (1977) addressed this question by investigating the intellectual performance of Korean children who suffered early malnutrition (prior to the age of 2) but were subsequently adopted into homes in the United States. Winick and colleagues showed that even the most severely malnourished children (below the 3rd percentile for height and weight at or before age 2) made significant advances in their physical and intellectual development after adoption. Specifically, in middle childhood, the previously malnourished children attained heights and weights above the standard for Korean children (although they continued to be smaller than American children). Furthermore, these children achieved IQ scores within the average range (mean of 102) and demonstrated academic performance comparable to their American peers. The researchers suggested that these scores were substantially greater (in excess of 40 points) than would be expected if these children remained in restricted environments. Of particular importance, this study showed a significant difference between the IQs of previously malnourished adopted children and those of adopted children with no history of malnutrition (mean IQ of the latter group was approximately 112). Winick and colleagues conjectured that these differences were partially genetic (the parents of undernourished children being more likely to have lower intellectual abilities), or a consequence of the nutritional deficits (i.e., the previously malnourished children had not been able to benefit as much from the adopted environment). Unfortunately, it is difficult to disentangle these possibilities without an assessment of parental IQ or a sibling design in which the other sibling was not malnourished.

In a study using a similar design, Lien et al. (1977) examined the roles of malnutrition on the cognitive development, growth, and academic achievement of Korean children adopted later in childhood (between 2 and 5 years of age). The researchers again found that severely, moderately, and nonmalnourished adopted children attained weight and height above standards for Korean children but below those of American children. However, they found that severely malnourished children attained IQ scores significantly lower than American children and their nonmalnourished adopted peers. Results also indicated that severely malnourished late adoptees had academic achievement scores below that of their American classmates and their late-adopted peers. The effect of nutritional deficits on academic performance remained significant when age of adoption and age of placement with the adoption agency were taken into account (this analysis was not completed on the IQ information because of the relatively small number of cases with this information provided). Interestingly, the authors found a significant effect for age of adoption on academic performance, but no evidence relating academic performance to duration of malnutrition or for an interaction between any of these factors. Secondary factors (such as behavioral or emotional concerns) may explain both later age of adoption and below-average performance on IQ and academic tests, but more would have to be known about a child's preadoptive history to completely discount this confound.

These two studies provide evidence for improved cognitive and scholastic performance following severe malnutrition in adopted children removed from pathological environments. However, the results of the second study suggest that there is a critical period in which environmental enrichment will be maximally beneficial and after which recovery is either slowed or attenuated.

We have seen that environmental enrichment (of varying degrees and types) is able to ameliorate some of the detrimental effects of malnutrition on cognitive skills; however, a subsequent question asks, Would enrichment contribute to a reduction in psychiatric correlates of malnutrition? This is especially interesting because, based on the discrepant findings of Stein et al. (1972) and Susser et al. (1996) with regard to the effect of prenatal famine exposure on cognitive deficits and Schizophrenia, it appears likely that psychopathological conditions may be more sensitive to diffuse neurological disruptions than cognitive abilities, which themselves appear more sensitive than current measures of neuropathology.

In a follow-up to their 2001 study, Raine et al. (2003) address this question. This study reported that children who experienced the enriched preschool environment exhibited significantly fewer conduct problems and schizotypal personality traits at age 17 and reduced self-reported levels of criminal offending at age 23. Court records of criminal offenses trended toward fewer offenses in the enriched group, but this did not reach conventional levels of statistical significance. Furthermore, the data showed significant interactions between environmental enrichment and early nutritional status. Thus, individuals with poorer nutritional status assessed at 3 years of age (see Liu et al., 2003), prior to the enriched preschool intervention, demonstrated significant benefits from the program. Specifically, in addition to the results presented here, the undernourished group evidenced reduced interpersonal deficits at age 23 when compared to undernourished nonenriched controls. Subsequent analyses to account for psychosocial risk factors (see Liu et al., 2003) and physiological factors at age 3 revealed no moderating effects or changes in the re-

sults. The authors argue that their findings indicate long-term behavioral benefits of enriched environmental experiences and a particularly striking long-term improvement in functioning of previously malnourished children. They acknowledge that which aspects of the enriched preschool experience contributed the most to the observed differences cannot be identified. However, they contend that the improved nutrition offered by the preschool likely played a role, especially with regard to the children who had previous nutritional deficits. This hypothesis is consistent with the findings of other research studies indicating a unique effect of nutritional supplementation on cognitive development (Grantham-McGregor et al., 1991).

The studies reviewed here (in addition to many other investigations) suggest that environmental enrichment moderates the effects of malnutrition, albeit through direct supplementation or combined nutritional and educational enrichment. Some questions remain as to how permanent and significant these effects are, but certain data indicate that, if undertaken early in development and for a sufficient duration, the beneficial effects of environmental enrichment can become stable and long-lasting (Lien et al., 1977; Pollitt, 1996; Raine et al., 2001; Winick et al., 1975). However, it would be naïve to assume that all insults, regardless of severity or genetic diathesis, can be completely alleviated by high-quality schools, nutritional supplementation, and supportive parenting (Lien et al., 1977; Pollitt, 1996). No matter the interventions employed, one cannot help but suspect that some conditions remain resistant to complete amelioration. At the same time, the inherent adaptability and plasticity of the nervous system, both in children and adults, attests to the fact that some improvement in many conditions is possible, given proper stimulation (Huntley & Jones, 2002; Nelson, 1999). For example, the studies described by Pollitt suggest that in malnourished, low SES populations, nutritional supplementation alone can have a long-term ameliorative impact on cognitive functioning. Furthermore, the reports by Lien et al., Winick et al., and Zeskind and Ramey (1981) give hope that even individuals with risk factors across multiple domains can profit from quality environmental circumstances. Essentially, plasticity exists; however, recovery from early insults such as malnutrition is likely to be incomplete.

In summary, the studies discussed in this section indicate that early malnutrition has discernable effects on cognitive skills throughout all periods of brain development (gestational and postnatal). However, research also suggests that there is potential for catch-up brain growth and improved intellectual and behavioral development if nutritional needs are restored. Additionally, other studies suggest that educational and environmental manipulations may also contribute to improved outcomes following early malnutrition. It is possible that some of the manifestations of malnutrition reported in this section (e.g., reductions in intellectual and certain cognitive abilities) may have resulted from impairments secondary to various psychiatric symptoms such as inattention or anxiety. However, with the exception of the Galler and Ramsey (1989) study, these two factors appear not to have been measured concurrently.

At this point, the discussion will again move down another level to focus on findings that shed light on the effects of early malnutrition on the structure and function of the developing and mature brain.

Neurobiology

Using a variety of dietary manipulations, many studies have linked early undernutrition to disturbances in neurotransmitter development and function and to neuroanatomic abnormalities, including fine structures (e.g., dendritic spines) and specific regions such as the hippocampus (Almeida, Tonkiss, & Galler, 1996; Hernandez-Rodriguez & Manjarrez-Gutierrez, 2001; Morgane et al., 1993, 2002; Wauben & Wainwright, 1999; Wiggins, Fuller, & Enna, 1984). These are important factors to consider because changes in brain morphology and physiology caused by malnutrition may be similar to the biological alterations observed in various psychopathologies (A. S. Brown et al., 1996).

Neurotransmitters and their receptors are important determinants of brain development before they become a critical part of the information-processing activities of neurons (Benes, Bolte-Taylor, & Cunningham, 2000; Berger-Sweeney, 1998; Bonhoeffer & Yuste, 2002; Fernandez-Ruiz, Berrendero, Hernandez, Romero, & Ramos, 1999; Franciosi, 2001; Heine, 1999; Ma et al., 2000; Nguyen et al., 2001; Retz, Kornhuber, & Riederer, 1996; van Kesteren & Spencer, 2003; Whitford, Dijkhuizen, Polleux, & Ghosh, 2002). Thus, if early malnutrition disturbs the balance of neurochemical systems, it could result in structural and/or behavioral alterations (Alvarez et al., 2002; Wauben & Wainwright, 1999; Wiggins et al., 1984).

Disruption of neurotransmitter systems due to early malnutrition can directly or indirectly affect brain development (Wauben & Wainwright, 1999). That is, a neurotransmitter may directly induce a developmental process, for example, GABA in promoting proliferation of neuronal progenitors, acetylcholine's involvement in apoptosis,

serotonin's role in synaptogenesis, and glutamate's regulation of dendritic spine formation (Nguyen et al., 2001). Therefore, if early malnutrition greatly reduces or augments neurotransmitter concentration, normal processes may not occur, or may occur in an abnormal fashion (Wauben & Wainwright, 1999). Alternatively, a neurotransmitter may be responsible for modulating other neurotransmitters, growth factors, or signaling molecules (e.g., cytosolic calcium levels, immediate early gene expression, or the mitogen-activated protein kinase cascade), which in turn regulate other developmental processes (Wauben & Wainwright, 1999). All of these downstream events can be disrupted by abnormal neurotransmitter concentrations resulting from malnutrition (Evrard, Marret, & Gressens, 1997; Wauben & Wainwright, 1999).

The amino acids tryptophan and tyrosine are precursors of the neurotransmitters serotonin and dopamine, respectively (Benes et al., 2000; Wauben & Wainwright, 1999). The blood-brain barrier contains transporters for these amino acids, which are not directly synthesized in the brain (Wauben & Wainwright, 1999). Therefore, adequate dietary intake is essential to maintain proper CNS concentrations of these compounds. Serotonin is involved in neuronal proliferation and differentiation, glia formation, and synaptogenesis (Gaspar, Cases, & Maroteaux, 2003; Morgane et al., 1993; Okado, Narita, & Narita, 2001; Wauben & Wainwright, 1999).

Hernandez-Rodriguez and Manjarrez-Gutierrez (2001) found increased tryptophan uptake across the blood-brain barrier and serotonin synthesis within the brain of gestationally malnourished rats. They observed these differences through weaning, and the increased serotonin synthesis continued after nutritional rehabilitation and normalization of tryptophan uptake. Based on these animal studies and human research suggesting analogous patterns of plasma-tryptophan ratios, these researchers postulated that similar outcomes are likely in human infants suffering from prenatal malnutrition (see Hernandez-Rodriguez & Manjarrez-Gutierrez, 2001, for review).

Manjarrez, Manuel, Mercado, and Hernandez (2003) conjectured that the increased concentration of serotonin observed in undernourished animals results in a desensitization of the serotonergic system secondary to chronic overactivation. Prenatally malnourished adult and adolescent rats also displayed decreased serotonin uptake sites, decreased serotonin fiber density, and enhanced serotonin release following hippocampal stimulation (Blatt, Chen, Rosene, Volicer, & Galler, 1994; Chen, Tonkiss, Galler, & Volicer, 1992; Mokler, Galler, & Morgane, 2003).

In addition, pre- and postnatally malnourished animals exhibit deficits in adaptation of the serotonergic system in response to chronic stress (Almeida et al., 1996; Mokler et al., 2003). Together, these results suggest that prenatal malnutrition can lead to long-lasting or even permanent alterations of the serotonergic system, potentially contributing to the later development of psychopathology (Benes et al., 2000; Fishbein & Pease, 1994; Hernandez-Rodriguez & Manjarrez-Gutierrez, 2001; Manjarrez et al., 2003).

Pre/postnatally undernourished animals also demonstrate reduced reactivity to pharmacological manipulations of the catecholaminergic system (Almeida et al., 1996; Chen, Turiak, Galler, & Volicer, 1997; Soto-Moyano et al., 1999). For example, early malnourished animals showed an attenuated response to dopamine agonists that induced stereotyped motor behaviors, reduced sensitivity to catatonic symptoms caused by dopamine antagonists, and a developmental delay in the induction of hypoactivity after administration of an adrenergic agonist (clonidine; Almeida et al., 1996; Bredberg & Paalzow, 1990; Goodlett, Valentino, Resnick, & Morgane, 1985). Other studies show decreased concentrations of dopamine and epinephrine receptors in specific brain regions of animals exposed to early undernutrition (Almeida et al., 1996; Wiggins et al., 1984).

Almeida and colleagues (1996) conjecture that these modifications are an adaptive response to initially high levels of catecholamines during brain development in undernourished animals. However, findings of increased sensitivity to the hypothermic effects of apomorphine (a dopamine agonist) but decreased sensitivity to the hypothermic effects of clonidine suggest a more complex picture in which pre/postnatal malnutrition has a differential impact on various subtypes of catecholaminergic receptors and on receptors within certain brain regions (Almeida et al., 1996; Brioni & Orsingher, 1987). For example, using a mild (8%) protein-depleted diet, Soto-Moyanoa and collaborators (1999) found increased norepinephrine release and neuronal density only in the occipital cortex of prenatally malnourished rats. Again, early malnutrition appears to cause alterations in the catecholaminergic system regardless of the precise dietary manipulation.

Prenatally malnourished animals exhibit reduced sensitivity to the effects of benzodiazepines (BZs; Almeida et al., 1996; Masur & Ribeiro, 1981; Tonkiss et al., 2000; Tonkiss, Trzcinska, Shultz, Vincitore, & Galler, 2000). This class of drugs potentiates the actions of the inhibitory neurotransmitter GABA (Almeida et al., 1996). Researchers observed long-term changes in sensitivity to BZs, similar to those found in the serotonergic system, during malnutrition and following nutritional rehabilitation (Almeida et al., 1996; Tonkiss et al., 2000).

Tonkiss and coworkers (2000) studied spatial learning in prenatally malnourished rats following administration of the GABAergic agonist chlordiazepoxide (CDP) at 30 and 90 days after birth. They found that prenatally malnourished animals responded less than control animals to a high dose of CDP at both 30 and 90 days of age, but at 90 days, the previously malnourished animals displayed greater sensitivity to a lower dose of CDP when compared to well-nourished controls. A possible reason for these differential responses may be that the drug exerts certain effects (e.g., anxiolytic versus amnesic) at high and low doses. The researchers concluded that differences between the GABAergic system of malnourished and well-nourished animals resulted in differential responses to CDP depending on age of administration and particular dosage of the drug.

Researchers have linked early malnutrition to reduced levels of GABA transmitter and increased binding of GABA and BZs to the GABA receptor complex in the CNS of rodents (Almeida et al., 1996). It is probable that the alterations in GABA binding and concentration underlie the attenuated responses to BZs and result from permanent changes in this neurotransmitter system directly caused by early malnutrition (Almeida et al., 1996; Chang, Galler, & Luebke, 2003). Again, changes in this system appear consistent across dietary manipulations, ages, and strains of animals used; therefore, they likely represent actual effects of early malnutrition and are not simply a by-product of a specific experimental design (Almeida et al., 1996). Changes in the developing GABA system are significant because GABA is a very active transmitter in early cortical development (Ben-Ari, 2002; Davies et al., 1998).

Other rodent studies reveal that early malnutrition is associated with lower sensitivity to drugs acting on the opiate system; however, studies showing specific receptor changes have not been completed (Almeida et al., 1996). Similarly, studies indicate reduced cholinergic function in the early malnourished rats (Almeida et al., 1996). Specifically, differences in muscarinic receptor density, binding, and developmental course in different brain regions are seen in previously malnourished rats. However, too few studies have been completed to draw firm conclusions regarding the effect of early malnutrition on the cholinergic system with relevance to possible behavioral effects.

Tonkiss, Almeida, and Galler (1998) used an operant procedure to show that prenatally undernourished female rats displayed sensitivity to the blockade of glutamate receptors with an N-methyl-D-aspartate (NMDA) antagonist (MK-801). The NMDA receptor is a type of glutamate receptor highly concentrated in the hippocampus and is thought to play a critical role in learning and memory (Cui et al., 2004; Nakazawa et al., 2003; Roesler et al., 2003). Tonkiss and coworkers trained rats to a stable level of performance on a differential reinforcement of low-rates (DRL) task. On this particular DRL schedule, animals did not receive a reward unless they separated their responses by at least 18 seconds. After attaining a stable performance, the researchers administered MK-801 at various doses. Results indicated that the performance of prenatally malnourished female, but not male, rats was disrupted after MK-801 administration. This experiment is interesting because it is one of the few studies to examine sex differences in generalized prenatal malnutrition. Although speculative, the increased sensitivity to NMDA blockade in prenatally malnourished females may be the result of loss or dysfunction of NMDA receptors in the hippocampus of these animals (J. A. Salinas, personal communication, April, 2000). This explanation is consistent with histological findings in other neurotransmitter systems showing decreased concentrations of various receptor types following nutritional insults (Almeida et al., 1996; Wiggins et al., 1984).

Alternatively, Fiacco and colleagues (Fiacco, Rosene, Galler, & Blatt, 2003) reported that prenatally malnourished rats displayed persistent increases in the concentration of kainate receptors (another type of glutamate receptor) in the CA3 subregion of the hippocampus, a region implicated in recognition memory (Fiacco et al., 2003; Lee & Kesner, 2003). These differences persisted through 220 days of age, but they did not emerge until 30 days after birth. Furthermore, Palmer, Printz, Butler, Dulawa, and Printz (2004) found evidence of increased NMDA receptor binding in the striatum of prenatally protein-malnourished animals, but they observed no differences in NMDA receptor binding in the hippocampus or dopamine receptor binding in the striatum. These studies suggest that changes in the glutamate system occur in rats secondary to prenatal malnutrition; however, more studies need to be completed to specify the precise nature of these changes across brain regions, age, sex, and subtypes of glutamate receptors.

This research indicates that early malnutrition appears to perturb an animal's responsiveness to pharmacological manipulation of various neurotransmitter systems (Almeida et al., 1996). Many studies show decreased receptor density for several types of neurotransmitters (dopamine, epinephrine, serotonin, acetylcholine, and GABA; Almeida et al., 1996). Researchers postulate that this represents an aspect of homeostatic functioning in early malnutrition in that down-regulation of receptors occurs in response to higher than normal levels of neurotransmitters during development (Almeida et al., 1996; Manjarrez et al., 2003). In addition, malnourished animals show decreased adaptations of the serotonergic and opioid systems in response to stress, possibly indicating permanently altered system dynamics (Almeida et al., 1996; Mokler et al., 2003). Essentially, malnutrition may exert its effects on neurochemistry not solely by affecting a single neurotransmitter system, but by perturbing the intricate balance between systems in the developing brain.

The changes in neurotransmitter systems described here appear to alter how an animal reacts and interacts with its environment. Therefore, if similar biochemical changes occur in the developing human brain, one could speculate that these perturbations will also result in modifications of behavior (Almeida et al., 1996). These behavioral changes may represent interesting correlates of certain forms of psychopathology (Almeida et al., 1996). For example, Almeida et al. (1996) reported on a study finding that, when compared to well-nourished controls, postnatally malnourished animals exhibited an anxiolytic reaction similar to that of Panic Disorder patients after chronic administration of either a tricyclic antidepressant or a monoamine oxidase inhibitor. Furthermore, numerous studies have linked dysfunction of neurotransmitter systems to the expression of various forms of psychopathology (Fishbein & Pease, 1994; Kaufman, Plotsky, Nemeroff, & Charney, 2000; Konradi & Heckers, 2003). In addition to effects on the organization of developing neurotransmitter systems, malnutrition (as noted earlier) affects structures in the brain such as the hippocampal formation. This brain region is particularly susceptible to a wide range of early insults and is implicated in various types of psychopathology (Arango, Kirkpatrick, & Koenig, 2001; DeBellis et al., 2000; Harry & Lefebvre d'Hellencourt, 2003; Heckers et al., 1998; Kimura, Reynolds, & Brien, 2000; Korte, 2001; Laakso et al., 2000, 2001; Walsh & Emerich, 1988).

Morgane et al. (2002) contend that early malnutrition results in decreased serotonergic innervation to the hippocampus due to decreased projections from the median raphe nucleus. However, as noted previously, early malnutrition results in increased serotonin release within the hippocampal formation proper. The authors propose that the disruption in input and local neurotransmitter concentration within the hippocampus leads to increased GABAergic activity in select inner neurons (Chang et al., 2003; Mokler et al., 2003; Morgane et al., 2002). Subsequently, this results in more inhibition of certain hippocampal regions, thereby potentially affecting information outflow and integration (Morgane et al., 2002).

Malnutrition results in deficits in long-term potentiation (LTP; Jordan & Clark, 1983), which is considered a candidate mechanism for learning and memory processes (Bliss & Collingridge, 1993; Kandel & Schwartz, 1982; Martin & Morris, 2002). Moreover, Morgane and colleagues (2002) stated that perturbations of hippocampal inhibitory mechanisms produce asynchronous activity of neuronal networks, potentially leading to decreased hippocampal plasticity (Morgane et al., 1993). Furthermore, Jordan and associates (Jordan, Howells, McNaughton, & Heatlie, 1982) suggested that malnutrition induces changes at the level of hippocampal synapses. In summary, early malnutrition appears to disturb hippocampal function through a variety of mechanisms (Morgane et al., 2002).

Early PEM is associated with a reduction in dendritic spine density and with abnormal spine morphology in the hippocampus, cerebral cortex, and cerebellum (Benitez-Bribiesca, De la Rosa-Alvarez, & Mansilla-Olivares, 1999; Fiala, Spacek, & Harris, 2002). A dendritic spine is a plastic structure frequently found in the cortex and is thought to play an important role in stimulus encoding and information processing (Bonhoeffer & Yuste, 2002; Coss & Perkel, 1985; Fiala et al., 2002; Segal, 2001; Whitford et al., 2002). Specifically, malnutrition may result in anomalies of spine number and shape of pyramidal cells within cortical layers III and V and the CA3 region of the hippocampus and of granule neurons within the dentate gyrus (Fiala et al., 2002). Cerebellar granule cells, Purkinje cell spines, and giant spines are reduced in early malnutrition (Fiala et al., 2002). These findings are important because research indicates that dendritic spine abnormalities exist in conditions such as mental retardation (Fiala et al., 2002).

The previous discussion supports the assertion that early malnutrition can result in distinct changes in brain neurochemistry and delicate morphology (Almeida et al., 1996; Fiala et al., 2002). However, the process of brain development is likely significantly protected (through various homeostatic and placental mechanisms) from many harmful environmental influences. This being said, the developing organism can compensate only so much before long-term changes in the chemical composition or structural organization of the developing brain result. The precise nature and extent of these changes may vary among individuals, although some general patterns (such as elevation of neurotransmitter concentrations and pathological dendritic spine formation) likely exist.

Although specific pathological mechanisms explaining behavioral changes are unclear, developmental perturbations in neurochemistry, neurophysiology, and brain morphology resulting from early malnutrition implicate candidate mechanisms that could account for behavioral

deficits. Research indicates that chronic changes in various neurotransmitter systems can affect levels of growth factors, gene expression, functioning of other transmitter systems, and the ability to acquire certain types of learning (Dudman et al., 2003; Kesslak, Chuang, & Berchtold, 2003; O'Donnell, Stemmelin, Nitta, Brouillette, & Quirion, 2003; Paule et al., 2003). Researchers have identified all of these factors as necessary components of typical CNS development (Acampora, Gulisano, & Simeone, 1999; Bar & Goffinet, 1999; Black, 1998; Cirulli, Berry, & Alleva, 2003; Cowan, 1998; Lyons et al., 1999; Nelson, 2000; Rutter & O'Connor, 2004; van Kesteren & Spencer, 2003). Therefore, significant or persistent dysfunctions in these systems (secondary to early malnutrition) may contribute to abnormal neurological development. Work by Gietzen and others (Blevins, Teh, Wang, & Gietzen, 2003; Gietzen & Magrum, 2001; Gietzen, Ross, Hao, & Sharp, 2004; Jousse et al., 2004; Truong, Magrum, & Gietzen, 2002) reveals that reductions of specific amino acids result in altered gene expression and changes in various neurotransmitter systems. These cascading effects provide a plausible mechanism for the effect of macronutrient malnutrition on neurobiology and behavior; that is, malnutrition causes decreases in important neurotransmitter systems, thus resulting in changes in growth factor concentration and in gene expression, eventually leading to modifications of behavior.

The discussion in this section focused on generalized caloric restriction/macronutrient deficiency. The reason for this emphasis is practical in that this is where many researchers have concentrated their efforts. However, as noted in the introduction, certain micronutrient deficiencies are associated with deviant brain development. Therefore, although little research exists directly linking specific micronutrient deficiencies to psychopathological outcomes, it is important to review briefly some of the extant research concerning the effect of specific micronutrient deficiencies on brain development.

PRIMER

As stated previously, it is common for deficits in micronutrients to accompany generalized protein energy malnutrition (Gorman, 1995; Kretchmer et al., 1996); conversely, it is possible to have deficits in specific micronutrients without concomitant caloric or protein restriction (Brozek, 1990; Georgieff & Rao, 2001). The latter scenario is more common in developed versus developing countries (A. S. Brown et al., 1996). As discussed earlier, A. S. Brown and colleagues postulated that deficiencies in specific micronutrients (such as folate) more fully explain the findings in the Dutch hunger winter cohort. Numerous studies have repeatedly allied early deficits of iron, zinc, and iodine with aberrant brain development and decreased cognitive skills; thus, this brief discussion focuses on these elements (Georgieff & Rao, 2001; Kretchmer et al., 1996; Yi-Ming, 1996).

Some studies have stressed the necessity of adequate levels of other micronutrients (such as vitamin B-6, selenium, manganese, copper, and choline) for proper neuronal development; however, they have been studied less extensively, especially with regard to human brain development and cognition (Castaño et al., 1997; Craciunescu, Albright, Mar, Song, & Zeisel, 2003; Fisher, Zeisel, Mar, & Sadler, 2002; Guilarte, 1989, 1993; Groziak & Kirksey, 1990; Keen et al., 1999; McCullough et al., 1990; Prohaska, 2000; Watanabe & Satoh, 1994; Yi-Ming, 1996; Zeisel, 2000). However, several studies have linked decreased periconceptional folate concentration to the development of neural tube defects in the progeny of some individuals (Czeizel & Dudas, 1992; Hibbard & Smithells, 1965). A. S. Brown et al. (1996) conjectured an association between prenatal folate deficiency and the development of Schizophrenia. Furthermore, investigators have observed lower folate levels in depressed adults, but the etiology or significance of these reductions (i.e., if they represent a symptom of or a contributor to depression) is unknown (Alpert & Fava, 1997).

Iron

Iron deficiency (ID) is one of the most common forms of undernutrition in the world (Lozoff, 1989). It is caused by chronic malnutrition or consumption of foods low in dietary iron (usually the case in developing countries), or by conditions such as maternal diabetes or IUGR (usually the cause in developed countries; Georgieff & Rao, 2001; Petry et al., 1992). A significant body of work has connected early ID to disturbances in myelination, neurotransmitter systems, metabolism, and hippocampal morphological development (Beard, 2003; de Deungria et al., 2000; Jorgenson, Wobken, & Georgieff, 2003; Kwik-Uribe, Gietzen, German, Golub, & Keen, 2000; Lozoff, 1989).

Behavioral studies with animals have shown that perinatal ID results in impaired performance of hippocampally dependent tasks, lower environmental reactivity, and decreased motor skills (Felt & Lozoff, 1996; Schmidt, Waldow, Salinas, & Georgieff, 2004). Finally, studies conducted with ID infants and children have revealed deficits in motor skills, sensory processing, recognition memory, visuospatial abilities, language skills, attention, and academic performance—some of which may persist after iron repletion (Lozoff et al., 2003; Lozoff, Jimenez, Hagen, Mollen, & Wolf, 2000; Nelson, Wewerka, Borscheid, deRegnier, & Georgieff, 2003; Roncagliolo, Garrido, Walter, Peirano, & Lozoff, 1998; Stoltzfus et al., 2001). Lozoff and colleagues (2003) contend that ID children are less socially interactive, display more inefficient information processing, and exhibit reduced activity in their physical environment. Thus, they conjecture that ID infants are less likely to receive sufficient environmental stimulation. Although some researchers have indicated that ID children display more anxious/withdrawn temperaments (Lozoff et al., 2003), no studies have expressly linked early ID to the later development of psychopathology.

Iodine

Iodine is a necessary component of various thyroid hormones. In the late 1990s, estimates indicated that approximately 1 billion people in the world were at risk for iodine deficiency (Yi-Ming, 1996). Severe maternal iodine deficiency in the preconception period (usually attributed to hypothyroidism) is associated with the development of severe mental retardation secondary to endemic cretinism (Pharoah et al., 1971). Moreover, moderately iodine-deficient children display minor (but significant) increases in reaction time and decrements on neuropsychological measures of verbal information processing, attention, and visual-motor integration (Fenzi et al., 1990; Lombardi et al., 1995). These studies suggested that the differences were time-limited and amenable to amelioration with iodine therapy. Additionally, periconceptional injection of iodized oil in at-risk populations is effective in attenuating the incidence of endemic cretinism and subsequent mental retardation (Pharoah et al., 1971). Conversely, prolonged childhood iodine deficiency may lead to lower achievement motivation and decreased learning speed, both of which become more striking with increasing age (Tiwari, Godbole, Chattopadhyay, Mandal, & Mithal, 1996). Again, no investigations have specifically examined any possible connections between early iodine deficiency and the development of mental illness (with the well-established connection between maternal iodine deficiency and mental retardation being the exception).

Zinc

Zinc is an important component of many enzyme systems and has been localized to presynaptic vesicles within limbic and cortical regions of the brain (Frederickson & Danscher, 1990; Johnson, 2001; Tuormaa, 1995). Zinc deficiency is associated with growth retardation and impaired hippocampal functioning (Sandstead et al., 1998; Tuormaa, 1995). Zinc is also critical for axonal transport and proliferation during neuronal development (Tuormaa, 1995). Animals made zinc-deficient early in gestation commonly experience fetal reabsorption or spontaneous abortion (Tuormaa, 1995). Zinc deficiency in later gestation or during lactation results in decreased forebrain and hippocampal size as well as reductions in total cell numbers (Duamah & Russell, 1984; Tuormaa, 1995).

Some researchers have linked zinc deficiency to increased hyperactivity, apathy, lethargy, sleep problems, poor appetite, aggression, and irritability (Tuormaa, 1995). Others have hypothesized that maternal zinc deficiency during gestation results in permanent alterations of neurological development, which may eventually manifest as psychiatric or neurological conditions (such as Schizophrenia, Autism, epilepsy, and Parkinson's disease; Johnson, 2001). Despite the potential seriousness of zinc deficiency, a study by Sandstead and colleagues (1998) reported that zinc-deficient children showed improved neuropsychological test performance after 10 weeks of zinc supplementation, leaving open the possibility of successful zinc rehabilitation.

FUTURE DIRECTIONS

The research reviewed in this chapter indicates that malnutrition is associated with disturbances in neurotransmitter systems necessary for normal neuronal maturation, morphological changes in delicate brain structures, and reductions in brain growth. Functional behavioral disturbances include deficits in cognitive abilities and an increased risk for psychiatric disorders, including Schizophrenia and related conditions such as externalizing behaviors and internalizing difficulties. These form and function effects persist across various models of malnutrition in animal studies and across demographic factors (country of origin and social class) in human investigations.

Isolating the specific role played by early malnutrition in the development of psychopathology in humans remains difficult because of multiple covariants. However, the problem of early malnutrition is significant for both developed and developing countries; thus, additional research is necessary to better explicate the long-term consequences of this condition. A major issue that future research should specifically address is the significance (i.e., magnitude of the effect) of malnutrition in the development of psychopathology. Specifically, does early malnutrition independently increase the risk for the development of psychopathology, or is it merely one of many important factors that, when combined, have a deleterious effect? The challenge lies in conjecturing plausible and testable mechanisms for these interactions and deriving maximally precise predictions of which factors contribute in which ways to the eventual outcomes. These are likely to be neurobiological models (concerned with cellular and molecular mechanisms) which then will inform behavioral models (tested on animals and concerned with negative correlates) based on extant relationships between form and function in the brain that are conserved across species. These studies would be complemented by statistical models that seek to explain population and subpopulation relationships among factors. Because criteria for the diagnosis of mental disorders is somewhat arbitrary and may be somewhat culturally determined, a possible way of examining this issue across settings may be to investigate more biological markers of mental disorders (such as dexamethasone suppression in depression). Although this particular test is far from perfect, this approach may provide a useful tool for examining the base rate of psychopathology in undernourished populations, where the current diagnostic system may be less effective for determining the presence or absence of a disorder.

The research reviewed supports the hypothesis that time of onset, dose, and duration of nutritional insults and interventions play critical roles in determining the nature and extent of any deficits (Morgane et al., 1993; Pollitt, 1996). What is not known is how much each of these three factors uniquely contributes to the eventual neurobehavioral outcome. Although there are no convincing animal models of psychopathology, animal studies designed to manipulate time of onset, dose, and duration of early malnutrition would help to explain the relative role of these components on neurochemistry, neuroanatomy, and some basic behavior (e.g., habit learning and recognition/spatial memory). Using neuroimaging and postmortem techniques, these findings could then be extended to human populations and, combined with evolving knowledge of the neurologic basis of psychopathology, may provide insight into the relationship between early malnutrition and the development of mental illness.

Overall, data indicate that specific micronutrient deficiencies can affect brain growth, cognitive development, and behavior. Nevertheless, adequate experiments explaining how deficits in these specific micronutrients result in the development of psychopathology (with the exception of mental retardation) have not been conducted. Examples of this approach include DNA microarray and proteomic and metabolomic assessments of targeted brain regions or processes (e.g., myelination, migration) following specific timed nutrient deficiencies. The expectation would be to identify genes and gene products that mediate neuronal form and function. For example, studies investigating the hypothesized connection between prenatal folate deficiency, potential migration defects, and the later development of Schizophrenia could be addressed using such an approach. Studies of this kind are particularly important, given the significant number of individuals (in both developed and developing countries) affected by early micronutrient deficiencies, both apart from and in combination with generalized malnutrition.

Explaining how early malnutrition exerts negative effects on the developing nervous system is also a critical direction for future investigations. Possible neuropathogenic mechanisms of early malnutrition can be broken down into direct and indirect effects. Direct effects refer to those that are the primary result of malnutrition and are considered to underlie the subsequent pathology (e.g., disrupted neurotransmitter function, brain morphology, or myelination). These primary effects could potentially work through direct nutrient contact with DNA promotor regions (as seen with zinc) or at any other posttranscriptional regulatory sites. Indirect effects refer to effects that may potentiate other pathological processes or conditions associated with a pernicious outcome, for example, where the nutrient deficiency affects pregnancy integrity, maternal stress levels, or maternal parenting style. Other indirect effects could occur through nutrient deficiency effects on metabolism that in turn influence fetal programming of brain development. It should be noted that none of these mechanisms has been irrefutably linked to the development of psychopathology. They are merely presented here as possibilities to be considered; however, investigating all of these potential mechanisms would be fruitful grounds for future scientific inquiry.

Future research will need to take the knowledge gained at the regulatory level and apply it to physiologic studies at the systems level. For example, many studies have associated disturbances in various neurotransmitter systems (e.g., monoamenergic and glutamatergic) with psychiatric disorders, including Schizophrenia, depression, and anxiety (Fishbein & Pease, 1994; Kaufman et al., 2000; Konradi & Heckers, 2003). Furthermore, evidence indicates that early malnutrition (or deficiencies in micronutrients such as iron) results in alterations in the development and eventual functioning of certain neurotransmitter systems (Hernandez-Rodriguez & Manjarrez-Gutierrez, 2001; Manjarrez et al., 2003). Although it is difficult to speculate on a specific causative mechanism, prolonged increases in neurotransmitter concentrations yielding

diminished receptor density or augmented neurotransmitter uptake may significantly alter the neurochemical milieu affecting the functioning of the entire nervous system (Almeida et al., 1996; Wauben & Wainwright, 1999). Additionally, some have postulated that neurotransmitter systems interact with each other during development (Benes et al., 2000); thus, perturbations in one system due to malnutrition may affect the developmental course of other systems (Wauben & Wainwright, 1999). For example, researchers have conjectured that changes in the glutamate, GABA, and norepinephrine systems interact with and contribute to the dysregulation of the dopamine system observed in Schizophrenia (Friedman, Temporini, & Davis, 1999; Goldman-Rakic & Selemon, 1997; Laruelle, Kegeles, & Abi-Dargham, 2003; Syvalahti, 1994). In addition, dysregulation of certain neurotransmitter systems may adversely affect dendrite formation, gene expression, and neurophysiological functioning (Gietzen et al., 2004; Jousse et al., 2004; Ma et al., 2000; van Kesteren & Spencer, 2003).

The hypothesized relationship between malnutrition and hippocampal dysfunction and between hippocampal dysfunction and psychopathology suggest that this circuit plays a role in the emergence of psychopathology following early nutritional deficits. As highlighted previously, researchers have connected early deficits of protein/protein energy, iron, or zinc to hippocampal malformation/dysfunction (de Deungria et al., 2000; Jorgenson et al., 2003; Morgane et al., 2002; Schmidt et al., 2004; Tuormaa, 1995). This specific brain structure is noteworthy because it has been implicated in various types of psychopathology, including Schizophrenia, alcohol abuse, antisocial behavior, and anxiety/depression (E. S. Brown, Rush, & McEwen, 1999; DeBellis et al., 2000; Heckers et al., 1998; Heim & Nemeroff, 1999, 2001; Korbo, 1999; Korte, 2001; Laakso et al., 2000, 2001; Rajkowska, 2000). However, it is not known whether the hippocampus plays a direct causal role, if it modulates other structures involved in the pathogenesis of the disorder (e.g., frontal lobe structures), or if disruption in this region represents more generalized brain atrophy (Graham, Heim, Goodman, Miller, & Nemeroff, 1999). It is possible that, although affected, the hippocampus itself is not the crucial contributor to a deviant behavioral outcome. Rather, it is possible that hippocampal dysfunction disrupts projections to/from other brain structures, thus deranging the functioning of a wider cortical network.

Another effect of early nutritional deficits (specifically resulting from iron deficiency and essential fatty acid deficiency) is disrupted myelination (Kwik-Uribe et al., 2000; Roncagliolo et al., 1998). This is of note because researchers have reported the occurrence of aberrant white matter structures in various psychiatric disorders (e.g., Schizophrenia and mood disorders; Cotter et al., 2001; Davis et al., 2003; Molnar, Potkin, Bunney, & Jones, 2003; Öngür, Drevets, & Price, 1998). Again, the relationship between the observed white matter abnormalities and the behavioral phenotypes of the disorder are currently unknown; however, they deserve future scrutiny because it is conceivable that the white matter changes are causally linked to psychopathology (Jones, 1997).

Maternal stress is an example of a more indirect effect that may partly explain the role of malnutrition in the emergence of mental disorders. For example, more than likely, chronic malnutrition rarely occurs in the absence of significant maternal stress (Gorman, 1995). Therefore, malnutrition could potentiate the effects of maternal stress or vice versa. The pervasiveness of maternal stress during the Second World War makes it unlikely that this factor alone can account for the pattern of deficits observed in the Dutch famine studies. Nevertheless, maternal stress cannot be ruled out as a factor contributing (either additively or synergistically) to these findings. Similarly, malnutrition of the child or infant likely occurs along with malnutrition of the mother. Thus, as suggested by the studies of Keys and colleagues (Franklin et al., 1948; Keys, 1946), significant malnutrition affects the psychological functioning of the mother and presumably her ensuing interactions with her child. Therefore, some of the consequences observed following malnutrition could partly result from disordered mother-child interactions. The magnitude of this effect—independent of other environmental/biological influences—remains unclear (Moffitt & Caspi, 2001). However, if the maternal behavior is severely abusive or pathological to the point of being unable to provide the minimal physical, perceptual, and social stimulation required for normal brain development, then a deviant outcome compounded by malnutrition is likely (Guesry, 1998; Jaffee, Caspi, Moffitt, & Taylor, 2004; Raine, Brennan, & Mednich, 1994, 1997; Stein & Susser, 1985; Tully, Arseneault, Caspi, Moffitt, & Morgan, 2004).

Some researchers have suggested that the early intrauterine environment "programs" the fetus early in gestation (Barker, 2001). This mechanism is regarded as an adaptive response helping the fetus to react during gestation to particular stressors such as malnutrition (Barker, 2001; Oliver et al., 1999; Seckl, 1998). Proponents of this theory argue that these adaptive changes become liabilities when the environmental challenge is no longer present (Barker, 2001; Oliver et al., 1999; Seckl, 1998). Barker and colleagues (Barker, Forsén, Uutela, Osmond, &

Eriksson, 2001) have invoked this fetal programming hypothesis to explain the relationship between retarded intrauterine growth and the later development of coronary heart disease. These researchers used the fetal programming hypothesis to explain their findings of a link between fetal undernutrition and the later development of depression (Thompson et al., 2001). Fetal programming in response to malnutrition could account for many of the descriptive findings regarding prenatal undernutrition; however, a precise mechanism for these alterations is still unknown (Seckl, 1998).

Another potential indirect effect connecting early malnutrition to the development of psychopathology is the decreased cognitive abilities observed in numerous studies. As discussed, research indicates that postnatal malnutrition can result in long-term reduction of intellectual abilities and cognitive skills (e.g., attention; Galler et al., 1986; Galler & Ramsey, 1987, 1989). These findings are important because intellectual ability measures obtained in middle childhood are highly stable into later life (Deary, Whalley, Lemmon, Crawford, & Starr, 2000; Deary, Whiteman, Starr, Whalley, & Fox, 2004). Other research indicates that low intelligence is an independent predictor of lifetime psychiatric contact in that lower intellectual capacity results in a significantly increased risk for developing psychiatric difficulties, including conduct problems and antisocial behavior (Moffitt, Gabrielli, Mednick, & Schulsinger, 1981; Walker, McConville, Hunter, Deary, & Whalley, 2002).

Jacobs and others (2002) found that although childhood cognitive ability and childhood psychopathology are predicted by independent genetic factors, a third genetic factor along with (unspecified) nonshared environmental factors predicts both. Thus, if postnatal malnutrition results in decreases in IQ sustained through middle childhood, these are likely permanent and may in turn lead to increased psychiatric contact. These results may be subtle and relatively small on the individual level. However, slight perturbations in the population IQ will greatly impact the number of individuals classified as mentally retarded and requiring social support services, thus increasing the financial cost to society (Tanner & Finn-Stevenson, 2002). Moreover, reductions in population IQ and specific cognitive skills (such as verbal reasoning) may increase the number of individuals requiring psychiatric support services and engaging in impulsive/delinquent behaviors (Arseneault, Moffitt, Caspi, Taylor, & Silva, 2000; Moffitt et al., 1981; Stevens, Kaplan, & Bauer, 2001; Stevens, Kaplan, & Hesselbrock, 2003).

Finally, early nutritional deficits may make an individual more vulnerable to insults (such as hypoxia) that are associated with the development of psychopathology (McNeil et al., 2000). Rao et al. (1999) provided some evidence for this hypothesis by showing that prenatally iron-deficient juvenile animals sustained more damage to the hippocampus following a hypoxic ischemic insult. Moreover, Fechner and colleagues (2001) showed that children admitted to hospital suffering from kwashiorkor exhibited decreased plasma antioxidant levels. Decreased antioxidant concentrations likely make these children more susceptible to neuronal damage/death after traumatic injuries such as anoxia or hypoxia-ischemia (Buonocore, Perrone, & Bracci, 2001; Zauner, Daugherty, Bullock, & Warner, 2002).

Similarly, compared to well-nourished children, malnourished children are more susceptible to cell damage and exhibit decreased DNA repair following an injury (Gonzalez et al., 2002). Gietzen and colleagues (1996) observed that rats with essential amino acid deficiencies displayed heightened seizure vulnerability. Research suggests that maternal zinc deficiency exacerbates the effects of prenatal alcohol exposure (Flynn et al., 1981).

These findings suggest that a nervous system already compromised by malnutrition is more vulnerable to additional insults such as toxin exposure or chronic stress. As discussed in the section on neurobiology, there is a potential for malnutrition or any early insult to alter the fundamental organization or structure of the developing brain. Although these modifications may prove beneficial in the short term (e.g., by conserving energy or reallocating resources), they may prove detrimental in the long term, possibly by decreasing behavioral and/or cellular plasticity (Barker, 2001).

Thus, malnutrition may serve as a catalyst disrupting normal development, but it may not have an enduring effect unless occurring proximally with another insult. Furthermore, the consequences of early malnutrition may not be revealed until a future stressor tries the plasticity of the system. This model is analogous to the diathesis-stress theory of mental disorders. In this model, undernutrition could be the stress (second injury), and the diathesis (initial damage) could stem from a genetic vulnerability or from other, already present environmental risk factors. Conversely, early malnutrition and its effects could be present first, so that a later infection, toxin exposure, or hypoxic/ischemic event would tip the scales toward an undesirable outcome. As discussed in the introduction, another variable to consider in this system is an individual's ability to maintain homeostasis in response to a challenge. This model may explain some of the discrepant findings in the literature. That is, it posits that each individual has his or her own threshold of how much damage via malnutrition

(or other environmental insults) he or she can endure before exhibiting an aberrant phenotype. It also hypothesizes that malnutrition exerts its maximal effect if it occurs in the context of an already compromised system. Again, this is merely a hypothesis and it should be rigorously tested (including the formulation of models that strive to describe this threshold in terms of numerical relationships and which factors are the best predictors of eventual outcome).

The question is not whether severe malnutrition (i.e., starvation) leads to adverse outcomes, because it is obvious that beyond a certain threshold of caloric restriction, conception becomes unlikely, miscarriage is inevitable, and death eventually results if adequate energy intake is not restored (Coad, Al-Rasasi, & Morgan, 2002; King, 2003; Stein et al., 1972). Rather, the question that future research should address is: Given a limited supply of energy, protein, or specific micronutrients, is an individual at an increased risk for developing psychopathology? Complicating the picture, available research suggests that generalized malnutrition rarely exists without micronutrient (iron/zinc) deficits, decreased parental intellectual abilities, deficient psychosocial stimulation, chronic childhood illness, or unsanitary living conditions (Guesry, 1998; Ivanovic et al., 2002; Pollitt, 1969; Stein & Susser, 1985). Even in the case of the Dutch hunger winter, the population was not free from significant wartime- and famine-induced stress. Therefore, it is difficult to discern if there is a unique contribution of early malnutrition to the development of psychopathology, and what, if any, is the relationship between malnutrition and other risk factors (i.e., mediational, additive, or synergistic).

Early malnutrition appears to be a topic very well suited to a multidisciplinary approach that includes basic science (neurobiology and biochemistry) as the foundation, translational research (such as using animals to model various paradigms of malnutrition), and finally comprehensive human investigations which include measures of motor, perceptual, cognitive, and intellectual abilities as well as objective measures of personality and psychopathological symptoms. These human studies should also endeavor to match participants or otherwise statistically control for potential confounds such as SES, parental education/IQ, familial history of mental illness, toxin exposure, and living circumstances. Although costly and difficult to conduct, a human study incorporating all of these components would provide valuable data that would greatly augment our understanding of the long-term effects of early malnutrition and specify how this condition interacts with other risk factors.

The potential for interactions may explain the relative effectiveness of nutritional intervention programs in developing countries compared to the often modest benefits shown by similar endeavors in countries such as the United States (Pollitt, 1996). That is, in developing countries, the population is likely to be chronically undernourished but may not exhibit elevated rates of psychopathology, and parents might provide a stable home environment. Conversely, in developed countries, individuals at risk for early malnutrition are more likely to have genetic and additional environmental risk factors, increasing their chance of expressing a deviant phenotype. This is merely a speculation and is not intended to minimize the potential impact of early malnutrition or the need to address this issue, but rather to emphasize the idea that many malnourished children (especially in developed countries) possess other substantial risk factors such as poverty, unstable home environments, deficient psychosocial stimulation, and genetic propensities, which may complicate intervention efforts. Again, designing efficient, beneficial interventions is another area that future studies should explore. Implementing successful interventions in countries such as the United States will likely entail carefully designed, targeted procedures (such as ensuring proper prenatal care and nutrition, encouraging breast feeding and parental involvement, better parental and childhood nutrition education, proper vaccinations and postnatal nutrition) that begin early and aim to treat the gestalt of the circumstances and not merely a single destructive component of the milieu (Ramey & Ramey, 1998).

REFERENCES

Acampora, D., Gulisano, M., & Simeone, A. (1999). OTX genes and the genetic control of brain morphogenesis. *Molecular and Cellular Neurosciences, 13*(1), 1–8.

Adams, J., Barone, S., Jr., LaMantia, A., Philen, R., Rice, D. C., Spear, L., et al. (2000). Workshop to identify critical windows of exposure for children's health: Neurobehavioral work group summary. *Environmental Health Perspectives, 108*, 535–544.

Almeida, S. S., Tonkiss, J., & Galler, J. R. (1996). Malnutrition and reactivity to drugs acting in the central nervous system. *Neuroscience and Biobehavioral Reviews, 20*, 389–402.

Alpert, J. E., & Fava, M. (1997). Nutrition and depression: The role of folate. *Nutrition Reviews, 55*, 145–149.

Alvarez, C., Vitalis, T., Fon, E. A., Hanoun, N., Hamon, M., Seif, I., et al. (2002). Effects of genetic depletion of monoamines on somatosensory cortical development. *Neuroscience, 115*(3), 753–764.

American Psychiatric Association. (2000). *Diagnostic and statistical manual of mental disorders* (4th ed., text rev.). Washington, DC: Author.

Anand, K. J. S., & Scalzo, F. M. (2000). Can adverse neonatal experiences alter brain development and subsequent behavior? *Biology of the Neonate, 77*, 69–82.

Andersen, S. L. (2003). Trajectories of brain development: Point of vulnerability or window of opportunity? *Neuroscience and Biobehavioral Reviews, 27*, 3–18.

Arango, C., Kirkpatrick, B., & Koenig, J. (2001). At issue: Stress, hippocampal neuronal turnover, and neuropsychiatric disorders. *Schizophrenia Bulletin, 27*, 477–480.

Archibald, S. L., Fennema-Notestine, C., Gamst, A., Riley, E. P., Mattson, S. N., & Jernigan, T. L. (2001). Brain dysmorphology in individuals with severe prenatal alcohol exposure. *Developmental Medicine and Child Neurology, 43*, 148–154.

Arnold, S. E. (1999). Neurodevelopmental abnormalities in Schizophrenia: Insights from neuropathology. *Development and Psychopathology, 11*, 439–456.

Arseneault, L., Moffitt, T. E., Caspi, A., Taylor, P. J., & Silva, P. A. (2000). Mental disorders and violence in a total birth cohort: Results from the Dunedin study. *Archives of General Psychiatry, 57*(10), 979–986.

Banaschewski, T., Brandeis, D., Heinrich, H., Albrecht, B., Brunner, E., & Rothenberger, A. (2003). Association of ADHD and conduct disorder: Brain electrical evidence for the existence of a distinct subtype. *Journal of Child Psychiatry and Allied Disciplines, 44*(3), 356–376.

Bar, I., & Goffinet, A. M. (1999). Developmental neurobiology: Decoding the Reelin signal. *Nature, 399*(6737), 645–646.

Barker, D. J. P. (2001). The malnourished baby and infant. *British Medical Bulletin, 60*, 69–88.

Barker, D. J. P., Forsén, T., Uutela, A., Osmond, C., & Eriksson, J. G. (2001). Size at birth and resilience to effects of poor living conditions in adult life: Longitudinal study. *British Medical Journal, 323*, 1–5.

Barone, S., Jr., Das, K. P., Lassiter, T. L., & White, L. D. (2000). Vulnerable processes of nervous system development: A review of markers and methods. *Neurotoxicology, 21*, 15–36.

Beard, J. (2003). Iron deficiency alters brain development and functioning. *Journal of Nutrition, 133*(5, Suppl. 1), S1468–S1472.

Ben-Ari, Y. (2002). Excitatory actions of GABA during development: The nature of the nurture. *Nature Reviews Neuroscience, 3*(9), 728–739.

Benes, F. M., & Berretta, S. (2001). GABAergic interneurons: Implications for understanding Schizophrenia and bipolar disorder. *Neuropsychopharmacology, 25*, 1–27.

Benes, F. M., Bolte-Taylor, J., & Cunningham, M. C. (2000). Convergence and plasticity of monoaminergic systems in the medial prefrontal cortex during the postnatal period: Implications for the development of psychopathology. *Cerebral Cortex, 10*, 1014–1027.

Benitez-Bribiesca, L., De la Rosa-Alvarez, I., & Mansilla-Olivares, A. (1999). Dendritic spine pathology in infants with severe protein-calorie malnutrition. *Pediatrics, 104*(2), E21.

Berger-Sweeney, J. (1998). The effects of neonatal basal forebrain lesions on cognition: Towards understanding the developmental role of the cholinergic basal forebrain. *International Journal of Developmental Neuroscience, 16*, 603–612.

Berkman, D. S., Lescano, A. G., Gilman, R. H., Lopez, S. L., & Black, M. M. (2002). Effects of stunting, diarrhoeal disease, and parasitic infection during infancy on cognition in late childhood: A follow-up study. *Lancet, 359*(9306), 564–571.

Beyth, I. J., & Baratta, A. (1996). Nutrition and behavior. *New Jersey Medicine, 93*, 45–47.

Bhutta, A. T., & Anand, K. J. S. (2002). Vulnerability of the developing brain: Neuronal mechanisms. *Clinical Perinatology, 29*, 357–372.

Black, J. E. (1998). How a child builds its brain: Some lessons from animal studies of neural plasticity. *Preventative Medicine, 27*, 168–171.

Black, L. S., deRegnier, R.-A., Long, J., Georgieff, M. K., & Nelson, C. A. (2004). *Electrographic imaging of recognition memory in 34–38 week gestation intrauterine growth restricted newborns.* Manuscript submitted for review.

Blatt, G. J., Chen, J., Rosene, D. L., Volicer, L., & Galler, J. R. (1994). Prenatal protein malnutrition effects on the serotonergic system in the hippocampal formation: An immunocytochemical, ligand binding, and neurochemical study. *Brain Research Bulletin, 34,* 507–518.

Blevins, J. E., Teh, P. S., Wang, C. X., & Gietzen, D. (2003). Effects of amino acid deficiency on monoamines in the lateral hypothalamus (LH) in rats. *Nutritional Neuroscience, 6*(5), 291–299.

Bliss, T. V. P., & Collingridge, G. L. (1993). A synaptic model of memory: Long-term potentiation in the hippocampus. *Nature, 361,* 31–39.

Bonhoeffer, T., & Yuste, R. (2002). Spine motility: Phenomenology, mechanisms, and function. *Neuron, 35,* 1019–1027.

Bowley, M. P., Drevets, W. C., Öngür, D., & Price, J. L. (2002). Low glial numbers in the amygdala in major depressive disorder. *Biological Psychiatry, 52,* 404–412.

Bracha, S., Lange, B., Gill, P. S., Gilger, J. W., Torrey, E. F., Gottesman, I. I., et al. (1995). Subclinical microcrania, subclinical macrocrania, and fifth-month fetal markers (of growth retardation or edema) in Schizophrenia: A co-twin study of discordant monozygotic twins. *Neuropsychiatry, Neuropsychology, and Behavioral Neurology, 8*(1), 44–52.

Bredberg, E., & Paalzow, L. K. (1990). Altered pharmacokinetics and dynamics of apomorphine in the malnourished rat: Modeling of the composed relationship between concentration and heart-rate response. *Pharmacology Research, 7,* 318–324.

Breslau, N., Chilcoat, H. D., Johnson, E. O., Andreski, P., & Lucia, V. C. (2000). Neurologic soft signs and low birthweight: Their association and neuropsychiatric implications. *Biological Psychiatry, 47,* 71–79.

Brioni, J. D., & Orsingher, O. A. (1987). Perinatal undernutrition alters hypothermic responses to different central agonists in recovered adult rats. *Neuropharmacology, 26,* 771–774.

Brower, M. C., & Price, B. H. (2001). Neuropsychiatry of frontal lobe dysfunction in violent and criminal behaviour: A critical review. *Journal of Neurology, Neurosurgery, and Psychiatry, 71,* 720–726.

Brown, A. S., Cohen, P., Greenwald, S., & Susser, E. (2000). Nonaffective psychosis after prenatal exposure to rubella. *American Journal of Psychiatry, 157*(3), 438–443.

Brown, A. S., & Susser, E. S. (2002). In utero infection and adult Schizophrenia. *Mental Retardation and Developmental Disabilities Research Reviews, 8*(1), 51–57.

Brown, A. S., Susser, E., Butler, P. D., Richardson Andrews, R., Kaufmann, C. A., & Gorman, J. M. (1996). Neurobiological plausibility of prenatal deprivation as a risk factor for Schizophrenia. *Journal of Nervous and Mental Diseases, 184*(2), 71–85.

Brown, A. S., Susser, E., Lin, S. P., Neugebauer, R., & Gorman, J. M. (1995). Increased risk of affective disorders in males after second trimester prenatal exposure to the Dutch hunger winter of 1944–1945. *British Journal of Psychiatry, 166,* 601–606.

Brown, E. S., Rush, A. J., & McEwen, B. S. (1999). Hippocampal remodeling and damage by corticosteroids: Implications for mood disorders. *Neuropsychopharmacology, 21,* 474–484.

Brozek, J. (1990). Effects of generalized malnutrition on personality. *Nutrition, 6,* 389–395.

Buck, P. S. (1931). *The good earth.* New York: Washington Square Press.

Bunney, W. E., Bunney, B. G., Vawter, M. P., Tomita, H., Li, J., Evans, S. J., et al. (2003). Microarray technology: A review of new strategies to discover candidate vulnerability genes in psychiatric disorders. *American Journal of Psychiatry, 160,* 657–666.

Buonocore, G., Perrone, S., & Bracci, R. (2001). Free radicals and brain damage in the newborn. *Biology of the Neonate, 79,* 180–186.

Butler, P. D., Susser, E. S., Brown, A. S., Kaufmann, C. A., & Gorman, J. M. (1994). Prenatal nutritional deprivation as a risk factor in Schizophrenia: Preclinical evidence. *Neuropsychopharmacology, 11,* 227–235.

Caspi, A., McClay, J., Moffitt, T. E., Mill, J., Martin, J., Craig, I. W., et al. (2002). Role of genotype in the cycle of violence in maltreated children. *Science, 297*(5582), 851–854.

Castaño, A., Ayala, A., Rodríguez-Gómez, J. A., Herrera, A. J., Cano, J., & Machado, A. (1997). Low selenium diet increases the dopamine turnover in prefrontal cortex of the rat. *Neurochemistry International, 30,* 549–555.

Castle, J., Groothues, C., Bredenkamp, D., Beckett, C., O'Connor, T., & Rutter, M. (1999). Effects of qualities of early institutional care on cognitive attainment. *American Journal of Orthopsychiatry, 69,* 424–437.

Chang, Y. M., Galler, J. R., & Luebke, J. I. (2003). Prenatal protein malnutrition results in increased frequency of miniature inhibitory postsynaptic currents in rat CA3 interneurons. *Nutritional Neuroscience, 6*(4), 263–267.

Chen, J. C., Tonkiss, J., Galler, J. R., & Volicer, L. (1992). Prenatal protein malnutrition in rats enhances serotonin release from hippocampus. *Journal of Nutrition, 122,* 2138–2143.

Chen, J. C., Turiak, G., Galler, J., & Volicer, L. (1997). Postnatal changes of brain monoamine levels in prenatally malnourished and control rats. *International Journal of Developmental Neuroscience, 15*(2), 257–263.

Cirulli, F., Berry, A., & Alleva, E. (2003). Early disruption of the mother-infant relationship: Effects on brain plasticity and implications for psychopathology. *Neuroscience and Biobehavioral Reviews, 27,* 73–82.

Coad, J., Al-Rasasi, B., & Morgan, J. (2002). Nutrient insult in early pregnancy. *Proceedings of the Nutrition Society, 61*(1), 51–59.

Coss, R. G., & Perkel, D. H. (1985). The function of dendritic spines: A review of theoretical issues. *Behavioral and Neural Biology, 44,* 151–185.

Cotter, D. R., Pariante, C. M., & Everall, I. P. (2001). Glial cell abnormalities in major psychiatric disorders: The evidence and implications. *Brain Research Bulletin, 55,* 585–595.

Cowan, W. M. (1998). The emergence of modern neuroanatomy and developmental neurobiology. *Neuron, 20*(3), 413–426.

Craciunescu, C. N., Albright, C. D., Mar, M. H., Song, J., & Zeisel, S. H. (2003). Choline availability during embryonic development alters progenitor cell mitosis in developing mouse hippocampus. *Journal of Nutrition, 133*(11), 3614–3618.

Cui, Z., Wang, H., Tan, Y., Zaia, K. A., Zhang, S., & Tsien, J. Z. (2004). Inducible and reversible NR1 knockout reveals crucial role of the NMDA receptor in preserving remote memories in the brain. *Neuron, 41*(5), 781–793.

Czeizel, A. E., & Dudas, I. (1992). Prevention of the first occurrence of neural tube defects by periconceptional vitamin supplementation. *New England Journal of Medicine, 327,* 1832–1835.

Davies, P., Anderton, B., Kirsch, J., Konnerth, A., Nitsch, R., & Sheetz, M. (1998). First one in, last one out: The role of GABAergic transmission in generation and degeneration. *Progress in Neurobiology, 55,* 651–658.

Davis, K. L., Stewart, D. G., Friedman, J. I., Buchsbaum, M., Harvey, P. D., Hof, P. R., et al. (2003). White matter changes in Schizophrenia: Evidence for myelin-related dysfunction. *Archives of General Psychiatry, 60,* 443–456.

Deary, I. J., Whalley, L. J., Lemmon, H., Crawford, J. R., & Starr, J. M. (2000). The stability of individual differences in mental ability from childhood to old age: Follow-up of the 1932 Scottish Mental Survey. *Intelligence, 28*(1), 49–55.

Deary, I. J., Whiteman, M. C., Starr, J. M., Whalley, L. J., & Fox, H. C. (2004). The impact of childhood intelligence on later life: Following up the Scottish Mental Surveys of 1932 and 1947. *Journal of Personality and Social Psychology, 86*(1), 130–147.

DeBellis, M. D., Clark, D. B., Beers, S. R., Soloff, P. H., Boring, A. M., Hall, J., et al. (2000). Hippocampal volume in adolescent-onset alcohol use disorders. *American Journal of Psychiatry, 157*(5), 737–744.

de Deungria, M., Rao, R., Wobken, J. D., Luciana, M., Nelson, C.A., & Georgieff, M. K. (2000). Perinatal iron deficiency decreases cytochrome c oxidase (CytOx) activity in selected regions of neonatal rat brain. *Pediatric Research, 48*(2), 169–176.

Duamah, P. K., & Russell, M. (1984). Maternal zinc status: A determination of central nervous system malformation. *British Journal of Obstetrics and Gynecology, 9*(1), 788–790.

Dudman, J. T., Eaton, M. E., Rajadhyaksha, A., Macias, W., Taher, M., Barczak, A., et al. (2003). Dopamine D1 receptors mediate CREB phosphorylation via phosphorylation of the NMDA receptor at Ser897-NR1. *Journal of Neurochemistry, 87*(4), 922–934.

Dwork, A. J. (1997). Postmortem studies of the hippocampal formation in Schizophrenia. *Schizophrenia Bulletin, 23,* 385–402.

Engle, P. L., Castle, S., & Menon, P. (1996). Child development: Vulnerability and resilience. *Social Science & Medicine, 43*(5), 621–635.

Evrard, P., Marret, S., & Gressens, P. (1997). Environmental and genetic determinants of neural migration and postmigratory survival. *Acta Paediatrica, 422*(Suppl.), 20–26.

Fechner, A., Bohme, C., Gromer, S., Funk, M., Schirmer, R., & Becker, K. (2001). Antioxidant status and nitic oxide in the malnutrition syndrome kwashiorkor. *Pediatric Research, 49*(2), 237–243.

Felt, B. T., & Lozoff, B. (1996). Brain iron and behavior of rats are not normalized by treatment of iron deficiency anemia during early development. *Journal of Nutrition, 126,* 693–701.

Fenzi, G. F., Giusti, L. F., Aghini-Lombardi, F., Bartalena, L., Marcocci, C., Santini, F., et al. (1990). Neuropsychological assessment in schoolchildren from an area of moderate iodine deficiency. *Journal of Endocrinological Investigations, 13,* 427–431.

Fernandez-Ruiz, J. J., Berrendero, F., Hernandez, M. L., Romero, J., & Ramos, J. A. (1999). Role of endocannabinoids in brain development. *Life Sciences, 65*(6/7), 725–736.

Fernstrom, J. D. (2000). Can nutrient supplements modify brain function? *American Journal of Clinical Nutrition, 71*(Suppl. 6), 1669S–1675S.

Fiacco, T. A., Rosene, D. L., Galler, J. R., & Blatt, G. J. (2003). Increased density of hippocampal kainate receptors but normal density of NMDA and AMPA receptors in a rat model of prenatal protein malnutrition. *Journal of Comparative Neurology, 456*(4), 350–360.

Fiala, J. C., Spacek, J., & Harris, K. M. (2002). Dendritic spine pathology: Cause or consequence of neurological disorders? *Brain Research Reviews, 39,* 29–54.

Fishbein, D. H., & Pease, S. E. (1994). Diet, nutrition, and aggression. *Journal of Offender Rehabilitation, 21*(3/4), 117–144.

Fisher, M. C., Zeisel, S. H., Mar, M. H., & Saldler, T. W. (2002). Perturbations in choline metabolism cause neural tube defects in mouse embryos in vitro. *Federation of American Societies for Experimental Biology (FASEB), 16*(6), 619–621.

Fletcher, P. (1998). The missing link: A failure of fronto-hippocampal integration in Schizophrenia. *Nature Neuroscience, 1,* 266–267.

Flynn, A., Miller, S. I., Martier, S. S., Golden, N. L., Sokol, R. J., & Del Villano, B. C. (1981). Zinc status of pregnant alcoholic women: A determinant of fetal outcome. *Lancet, 1,* 572–574.

Franciosi, S. (2001). AMPA receptors: Potential implications in development and disease. *Cellular and Molecular Life Sciences, 58,* 921–930.

Franklin, J. C., Schiele, B. C., Brozek, J., & Keys, A. (1948). Observations of human behavior in experimental semistarvation and rehabilitation. *Journal of Clinical Psychology, 4,* 28–45.

Frederickson, C. J., & Danscher, G. (1990). Zinc-containing neurons in hippocampus and related CNS structures. In J. Storm-Mathisen, J. Zimmer, & O. P. Ottersen (Eds.), *Progress in brain research* (pp. 71–84). Oxford: Elsevier Science, Biomedical Division.

Friedman, J. I., Temporini, H., & Davis, K. L. (1999). Pharmacologic strategies for augmenting cognitive performance in Schizophrenia. *Biological Psychiatry, 45*(1), 1–16.

Fromentin, G., Gietzen, D. W., & Nicolaidis, S. (1997). Aversion-preference patterns in amino acid or protein-deficient rats: A comparison with previously reported responses to thiamin-deficient diets. *British Journal of Nutrition, 77*(2), 299–314.

Galler, J. R., & Ramsey, F. (1987). A follow-up study of the influence of early malnutrition on development: V. Delayed development of conservation (Piaget). *American Academy of Child and Adolescent Psychiatry, 87,* 23–27.

Galler, J. R., & Ramsey, F. (1989). A follow-up study of the influence of early malnutrition on development: Behavior at home and at school. *Journal of the American Academy of Child and Adolescent Psychiatry, 89,* 254–261.

Galler, J. R., Ramsey, F., & Forde, V. (1986). A follow-up study of the influence of early malnutrition on subsequent development: 4. Intellectual performance during adolescence. *Nutrition and Behavior, 3,* 211–222.

Galler, J. R., Ramsey, F., Solimano, G., Kucharski, L. T., & Harrison, R. (1984). The influence of early malnutrition on subsequent behavioral development. IV: Soft neurologic signs. *Pediatric Research, 18*(9), 826–832.

Galler, J. R., Ramsey, F., Solimano, G., & Lowell, W. E. (1983). The influence of early malnutrition on subsequent behavioral development: II. Classroom behavior. *Journal of the American Academy of Child Psychiatry, 22*(1), 16–22.

Galler, J. R., Ramsey, F., Solimano, G., Lowell, W. E., & Mason, E. (1983). The influence of early malnutrition on subsequent behavioral development: I. Degree of impairment in intellectual performance. *Journal of the American Academy of Child Psychiatry, 22*(1), 8–15.

Gaspar, P., Cases, O., & Maroteaux, L. (2003). The developmental role of serotonin: News from mouse molecular genetics. *Nature Reviews Neuroscience, 4*(12), 1002–1012.

Georgieff, M. K., Hoffman, J. S., Pereira, G. R., Bernbaum, J. B., & Hoffman-Williamson, M. (1985). Effect of neonatal caloric deprivation on head growth and 1-year developmental status in preterm infants. *Journal of Pediatrics, 107,* 581–587.

Georgieff, M. K., & Rao, R. (2001). The role of nutrition in cognitive development. In C. A. Nelson & M. Luciana (Eds.), *Handbook of developmental cognitive neuroscience* (pp. 491–504). Cambridge, MA: MIT Press.

Gietzen, D. W., Dixon, K. D., Truong, B. G., Jones, A. C., Barrett, J. A., & Washburn, D. S. (1996). Indispensable amino acid deficiency and increased seizure susceptibility in rats. *American Journal of Physiology, 271*(1 Pt. 2), R18–R24.

Gietzen, D. W., & Magrum, L. J. (2001). Molecular mechanisms in the brain involved in the anorexia of branched-chain amino acid deficiency. *Journal of Nutrition, 131*(3), S851–S855.

Gietzen, D. W., Ross, C. M., Hao, S., & Sharp, J. W. (2004). Phosphorylation of eIF2alpha is involved in the signaling of indispensable amino acid deficiency in the anterior piriform cortex of the brain in rats. *Journal of Nutrition, 134*(4), 717–723.

Goldman-Rakic, P. S., & Selemon, L. D. (1997). Functional and anatomical aspects of prefrontal pathology in schizophrenia. *Schizophrenia Bulletin, 23*(3), 437–458.

Gonzalez, C., Najera, O., Cortes, E., Toledo, G., Lopez, L., Betancourt, M., et al. (2002). Hydrogen peroxide-induced DNA damage and DNA repair in lymphocytes from malnourished children. *Environmental and Molecular Mutagenesis, 39*(1), 33–42.

Goodlett, C. R., Valentino, M. L., Resnick, O., & Morgane, P. J. (1985). Altered development of responsiveness to clonidine in severely malnourished rats. *Pharmacology, Biochemistry and Behavior, 23,* 567–572.

Gorman, K. S. (1995). Malnutrition and cognitive development: Evidence from experimental/quasi-experimental studies among the mild-to-moderately malnourished. *Journal of Nutrition, 125*(Suppl. 8), 2239S–2244S.

Graham, Y. P., Heim, C., Goodman, S. H., Miller, A. H., & Nemeroff, C. B. (1999). The effects of neonatal stress on brain development: Implications for psychopathology. *Development and Psychopathology, 11,* 545–565.

Grantham-McGregor, S. (2002). Linear growth retardation and cognition. *Lancet, 359*(9306), 542.

Grantham-McGregor, S. M., Powell, S. P., Walker, J., & Himes, H. (1991). Nutritional supplementation, psychosocial stimulation, and mental development of stunted children: The Jamaican study. *Lancet, 338*(15), 1–5.

Groziak, S. M., & Kirksey, A. (1990). Effects of maternal restriction of vitamin B6 on neocortex development in rats: Neuron differentiation and synaptogenesis. *Journal of Nutrition, 120,* 485–492.

Guesry, P. (1998). The role of nutrition in brain development. *Preventive Medicine, 27,* 189–194.

Guilarte, T. R. (1989). Effect of vitamin B-6 nutrition on the levels of dopamine, dopamine metabolites, dopa decarboxylase activity, tyrosine, and GABA in the developing rat corpus striatum. *Neurochemical Research, 14,* 571–578.

Guilarte, T. R. (1993). Vitamin B-6 and cognitive development: Recent research findings from human and animal studies. *Nutrition Reviews, 51,* 193–198.

Harry, G. J., & Lefebvre d'Hellencourt, C. L. (2003). Dentate gyrus: Alterations that occur with hippocampal injury. *Neurotoxicology, 24,* 343–356.

Harvey, D., Prince, J., Bunton, J., Parkinson, C., & Campbell, S. (1982). Abilities of children who were small-for-gestational-age babies. *Pediatrics, 69,* 296–300.

Heasman, L., Clarke, L., Stephenson, T. J., & Symonds, M. E. (1999). The influence of maternal nutrient restriction in early to mid-pregnancy on placental and fetal development in sheep. *Proceedings of the Nutrition Society, 58,* 283–288.

Heckers, S., Rauch, S. L., Goff, D., Savage, C. R., Schacter, D. L., Fischman, A. J., et al. (1998). *Nature Neuroscience, 1*(4), 318–368.

Heim, C., & Nemeroff, C. B. (1999). The impact of early adverse experiences on brain systems involved in the pathophysiology of anxiety and affective disorders. *Biological Psychiatry, 46,* 1509–1522.

Heim, C., & Nemeroff, C. B. (2001). The role of childhood trauma in the neurobiology of mood and anxiety disorders: Preclinical and clinical studies. *Biological Psychiatry, 49,* 1023–1039.

Heine, W. E. (1999). The significance of tryptophan in infant nutrition. *Advances in Experimental Medicine & Biology, 467,* 705–710.

Hernandez-Rodriguez, J., & Manjarrez-Gutierrez, G. (2001). Macronutrients and neurotransmitter formation during brain development. *Nutrition Reviews, 59*(Suppl. 8, Pt. 2), S49–S59.

Hibbard, E. D., & Smithells, R. W. (1965). Folic acid metabolism and human embryopathy. *Lancet, 1,* 1254–1256.

Hoek, H. W., Brown, A. S., & Susser, E. (1998). The Dutch famine and Schizophrenia spectrum disorders. *Social Psychiatry and Psychiatric Epidemiology, 33,* 373–379.

Hoek, H. W., Susser, E., Buck, K. A., Lumey, L. H., Lin, S. P., & Gorman, J. M. (1996). Schizoid personality disorder after prenatal exposure to famine. *American Journal of Psychiatry, 153,* 1637–1639.

Honig, L. S., Herrmann, K., & Shatz, C. J. (1996). Developmental changes revealed by immunohistochemical markers in human cerebral cortex. *Cerebral Cortex, 6,* 794–806.

Hulshoff Pol, H. E., Hoek, H. W., Susser, E., Brown, A. S., Dingemans, A., Schnack, H. G., et al. (2000). Prenatal exposure to famine and brain morphology in Schizophrenia. *American Journal of Psychiatry, 157,* 1170–1172.

Huntley, G. W., & Jones, E. G. (2002). Introduction to a special issue on dynamical aspects of cortical structure and function. *Neuroscience, 111,* 707–708.

Huttenlocher, P. R. (2000). The neuropathology of phenylketonuria: Human and animal studies. *European Journal of Pediatrics, 159*(Suppl. 2), S102–S106.

Innocenti, G. M., Ansermet, F., & Parnas, J. (2003). Schizophrenia, neurodevelopment and corpus callosum. *Molecular Psychiatry, 8*(3), 261–274.

Ivanovic, D. M., Leiva, B. P., Pérez, H. T., Almagià, A. F., Toro, T. D., Urrutia, M. S. C., et al. (2002). Nutritional status, brain development and scholastic achievement of Chilean high-school graduates from high and low intellectual quotient and socio-economic status. *British Journal of Nutrition, 87,* 81–92.

Ivanovic, D. M., Leiva, B. P., Perez, H. T., Inzunza, N. B., Almagià, A. F., Toro, T. D., et al. (2000). Long-term effects of severe undernutrition during the first year of life on brain development and learning in Chilean high-school graduates. *Nutrition, 16,* 1056–1063.

Jacobs, N., Rijsdijk, F., Derom, C., Danckaerts, M., Thiery, E., Derom, R., et al. (2002). Child psychopathology and lower cognitive ability: A general population twin study of the causes of association. *Molecular Psychiatry, 7,* 368–374.

Jaffee, S. R., Caspi, A., Moffitt, T. E., & Taylor, A. (2004). Physical maltreatment victim to antisocial child: Evidence of an environmentally mediated process. *Journal of Abnormal Psychology, 113*(1), 44–55.

Jenike, M. A., Breiter, H. C., Baer, L., Kennedy, D. N., Savage, C. R., Olivares, M. J., et al. (1996). Cerebral structural abnormalities in obsessive-compulsive disorder: A quantitative morphometric magnetic resonance imaging study. *Archives of General Psychiatry, 53,* 625–632.

Johnson, S. (2001). Micronutrient accumulation and depletion in Schizophrenia, epilepsy, Autism and Parkinson's disease? *Medical Hypotheses, 56*(5), 641–645.

Jones, E. G. (1997). Cortical development and thalamic pathology in Schizophrenia. *Schizophrenia Bulletin, 23,* 483–501.

Joos, S. K., Pollitt, E., Mueller, W. H., & Albright, D. L. (1983). The Bacon Chow Study: Maternal nutritional supplementation and infant behavioral development. *Child Development, 54,* 669–676.

Jordan, T. C., & Clark, G. A. (1983). Early undernutrition impairs hippocampal long term potentiation in adult rats. *Behavioral Neuroscience, 97,* 319–322.

Jordan, T. C., Howells, K. F., McNaughton, N., & Heatlie, P. L. (1982). Effects of early undernutrition on hippocampal development and function. *Research in Experimental Medicine, 180,* 201–207.

Jorgenson, L. A., Wobken, J. D., & Georgieff, M. K. (2003). Perinatal iron deficiency alters apical dendritic growth in hippocampal CA1 pyramidal neurons. *Developmental Neuroscience, 25*(6), 412–420.

Jousse, C., Averous, J., Bruhat, A., Carraro, V., Mordier, S., & Fafournoux, P. (2004). Amino acids as regulators of gene expression: Molecular mechanisms. *Biochemical and Biophysical Research Communications, 313*(2), 447–452.

Kandel, E. R., & Schwartz, J. H. (1982). Molecular biology of learning modulation of transmitter release. *Science, 218*, 433–443.

Kaufman, J., Plotsky, P. M., Nemeroff, C. B., & Charney, D. S. (2000). Effects of early adverse experiences on brain structure and function: Clinical implications. *Biological Psychiatry, 48*, 778–790.

Keen, C. L., Ensunsa, J. L., Watson, M. H., Baly, D. L., Donovan, S. M., Monaco, M. H., et al. (1999). Nutritional aspects of manganese from experimental studies. *Neurotoxicology, 20*, 213–224.

Keller, F., & Persico, A. M. (2003). The neurobiological context of Autism. *Molecular Neurobiology, 28*(1), 1–22.

Kesslak, J. P., Chuang, K. R., & Berchtold, N. C. (2003). Spatial learning is delayed and brain-derived neurotrophic factor mRNA expression inhibited by administration of MK-801 in rats. *Neuroscience Letters, 353*(2), 95–98.

Keys, A. (1946). Human starvation and its consequences. *Journal of the American Dietetic Association, 22*, 582–587.

Kimura, K. A., Reynolds, J. N., & Brien, J. F. (2000). Ethanol neurobehavioral teratogenesis and the role of the hippocampal glutamate-*N*-methyl-D-aspartate receptor-nitric oxide synthase system. *Neurotoxicology and Teratology, 22*, 607–616.

King, J. C. (2003). The risk of maternal nutritional depletion and poor outcomes increases in early or closely spaced pregnancies. *Journal of Nutrition, 133*(5, Suppl. 2), S1732–S1736.

Konradi, C., & Heckers, S. (2003). Molecular aspects of glutamate dysregulation: Implications for Schizophrenia and its treatment. *Pharmacology and Therapeutics, 97*, 153–179.

Korbo, L. (1999). Glial cell loss in the hippocampus of alcoholics. *Clinical Experimental Research, 23*(1), 164–168.

Korte, S. M. (2001). Corticosteroids in relation to fear, anxiety, and psychopathology. *Neuroscience and Biobehavioral Reviews, 25*, 117–142.

Kretchmer, N., Beard, J. L., & Carlson, S. (1996). The role of nutrition in the development of normal cognition. *American Journal of Clinical Nutrition, 63*, S997–S1001.

Krueger, R. F. (2002). Personality from a realist's perspective: Personality traits, criminal behaviors, and the externalizing spectrum. *Journal of Research in Personality, 36*(6), 564–572.

Krueger, R. F., Caspi, A., Moffitt, T. E., & Silva, P. A. (1998). The structure and stability of common mental disorders (DSM-III-R): A longitudinal-epidemiological study. *Journal of Abnormal Psychology, 107*(2), 216–227.

Krueger, R. F., McGue, M., & Iacono, W. G. (2001). The higher-order structure of common DSM mental disorders: Internalization, externalization, and their connections to personality. *Personality and Individual Differences, 30*(7), 1245–1259.

Kunugi, H., Takei, N., Murray, R. M., Saito, K., & Nanko, S. (1996). Small head circumference at birth in Schizophrenia. *Schizophrenia Research, 20*(1/2), 165–170.

Kwik-Uribe, C. L., Gietzen, D., German, J. B., Golub, M. S., & Keen, C. L. (2000). Chronic marginal iron intakes during early development in mice result in persistent changes in dopamine metabolism and myelin composition. *Journal of Nutrition, 130*, 2821–2830.

Laakso, M. P., Vaurio, O., Koivisto, E., Savolainen, L., Eronen, M., Aronen, H. J., et al. (2001). Psychopathy and the posterior hippocampus. *Behavioural Brain Research, 118*, 187–193.

Laakso, M. P., Vaurio, O., Savolainen, L., Repo, E., Soininen, H., Aronen, H. J., et al. (2000). A volumetric MRI study of the hippocampus in type 1 and 2 alcoholism. *Behavioural Brain Research, 109*(2), 177–186.

LaMantia, A. (1999). Forebrain induction, retinoic acid, and vulnerability to Schizophrenia: Insights from molecular and genetic analysis in developing mice. *Biological Psychiatry, 46*(1), 19–30.

Laruelle, M., Kegeles, L. S., & Abi-Dargham, A. (2003). Glutamate, dopamine, and Schizophrenia from pathophysiology to treatment. *Annals of the New York Academy of Sciences, 1003*138–1003158.

Lee, I., & Kesner, R. P. (2003). Differential roles of dorsal hippocampal subregions in spatial working memory with short versus intermediate delay. *Behavioral Neuroscience, 117*(5), 1044–1053.

Lien, N. M., Meyer, K. K., & Winick, M. (1977). Early malnutrition and "late" adoption: A study of their effects on the development of Korean orphans adopted into American families. *American Journal of Clinical Nutrition, 30*(10), 1734–1739.

Lieberman, H. R. (2003). Nutrition, brain function and cognitive performance. *Appetite, 40*, 245–254.

Lilienfeld, S. O., & Marino, L. (1999). Essentialism revisited: Evolutionary theory and the concept of mental disorder. *Journal of Abnormal Psychology, 108*(3), 400–411.

Liu, J., Raine, A., Venables, P. H., Dalais, C., & Mednick, S. A. (2003). Malnutrition at age 3 years and lower cognitive ability at age 11 years: Independence from psychosocial adversity. *Archives of Pediatrics and Adolescent Medicine, 157*, 593–600.

Lombardi, F. A., Pinchera, A., Antonangeli, L., Rago, T., Chiovato, L., Bargagna, S., et al. (1995). Mild iodine deficiency during fetal/neonatal life and neuropsychological impairment in Tuscany. *Journal of Endocrinological Investigation, 18*, 57–62.

Low, J. A., Galbraith, R. S., Muir, D., Killen, H., Pater, B., & Karchmar, J. (1982). Intrauterine growth retardation: A study of long-term morbidity. *American Journal of Obstetrics and Gynecology, 142*, 670–677.

Lozoff, B. (1989). Iron and learning potential in childhood. *Bulletin of the New York Academy of Medicine, 65*(10), 1050–1066.

Lozoff, B., De Andraca, I., Castillo, M., Smith, J. B., Walter, T., & Pino, P. (2003). Behavioral and developmental effects of preventing iron-deficiency anemia in healthy full-term infants. *Pediatrics, 112*(4), 846–854.

Lozoff, B., Jimenez, E., Hagen, J., Mollen, E., & Wolf, A. W. (2000). Poorer behavioral and developmental outcome more than 10 years after treatment for iron deficiency in infancy. *Pediatrics, 105*(4), E51.

Lumey, L. H. (1998). Compensatory placental growth after restricted maternal nutrition in early pregnancy. *Placenta, 19*, 105–111.

Lyons, W. E., Mamounas, L. A., Ricaurte, G. A., Coppola, V., Reid, S. W., Bora, S. H., et al. (1999). Brain-derived neurotrophic factor-deficient mice develop aggressiveness and hyperphagia in conjunction with brain serotonergic abnormalities. *Proceedings of the National Academy of Sciences of the United States of America, 96*(26), 15239–15244.

Ma, W., Maric, D., Li, B. S., Hu, Q., Andreadis, J. D., Grant, G. M., et al. (2000). Acetylcholine stimulates cortical precursor cell proliferation in vitro via muscarinic receptor activation and MAP kinase phosphorylation. *European Journal of Neuroscience, 12*(4), 1227–1240.

Manjarrez, G., Manuel, A. L., Mercado, C. R., & Hernandez, R. J. (2003). Serotonergic receptors in the brain of in utero undernourished rats. *International Journal of Developmental Neuroscience, 21*, 283–289.

Martin, S. J., & Morris, R. G. M. (2002). New life in an old idea: The synaptic plasticity and memory hypothesis revisited. *Hippocampus, 12*, 609–636.

Masur, J., & Ribeiro, M. J. (1981). Chronic starvation impairs the effect of depressant drugs on CNS of rats. *Pharmacology, 23*, 64–68.

McCullough, A. L., Kirksey, A., Wachs, T. D., McCabe, G. P., Bassily, N. S., Bishry, Z., et al. (1990). Vitamin B-6 status of Egyptian mothers: Relation to infant behavior and maternal-infant interactions. *American Journal of Clinical Nutrition, 51*, 1067–1074.

McNeil, T. F., Cantor-Graae, E., & Weinberger, D. R. (2000). Relationship of obstetric complications and differences in size of brain structures in monozygotic twin pairs discordant for Schizophrenia. *American Journal of Psychiatry, 157*, 203–212.

Meehl, P. E. (1979). A funny thing happened to us on the way to the latent entities. *Journal of Personality Assessment, 43*(6), 563–581.

Moffitt, T. E. (1993). Adolescence-limited and life-course-persistent antisocial behavior: A developmental taxonomy. *Psychological Review, 100*, 674–701.

Moffitt, T. E., & Caspi, A. (2001). Childhood predictors differentiate life-course persistent and adolescence-limited antisocial pathways among males and females. *Development and Psychopathology, 13*, 355–375.

Moffitt, T. E., Gabrielli, W. F., Mednick, S. A., & Schulsinger, F. (1981). Socioeconomic status, IQ, & delinquency. *Journal of Abnormal Psychology, 90*, 152–156.

Mokler, D. J., Galler, J. R., & Morgane, P. J. (2003). Modulation of 5-HT release in the hippocampus of 30-day-old rats exposed in utero to protein malnutrition. *Brain Research, 142*(2), 203–208.

Molnar, M., Potkin, S. G., Bunney, W. E., Jr., & Jones, E. G. (2003). MRNA expression patterns and distribution of white matter neurons in dorsolateral prefrontal cortex of depressed patients differ from those in Schizophrenia patients. *Biological Psychiatry, 53*, 39–47.

Monk, C. S., Webb, S. J., & Nelson, C. A. (2001). Prenatal neurobiological development: Molecular mechanisms and anatomical change. *Developmental Neuropsychology, 19*, 211–236.

Morgane, P. J., Austin-LaFrance, R., Bronzino, J., Tonkiss, J., Díaz-Cintra, S., Cintra, L., et al. (1993). Prenatal malnutrition and development of the brain. *Neuroscience and Biobehavioral Reviews, 17*, 91–128.

Morgane, P. J., Mokler, D. J., & Galler, J. R. (2002). Effects of prenatal protein malnutrition on the hippocampal formation. *Neuroscience and Biobehavioral Reviews, 26*, 471–483.

Murphy, D. L., Li, Q., Engel, S., Wichems, C., Andrews, A., Lesch, K.-P., et al. (2001). Genetic perspectives on the serotonin transporter. *Brain Research Bulletin, 56*, 487–494.

Nakazawa, K., Sun, L. D., Quirk, M. C., Rondi-Reig, L., Wilson, M. A., & Tonegawa, S. (2003). Hippocampal CA3 NMDA receptors are crucial for memory acquisition of one-time experience. *Neuron, 38*(2), 305–315.

Nelson, C. A. (1999). Neural plasticity and human development. *Current Directions in Psychological Science, 8*, 42–45.

Nelson, C. A. (2000). *The neurobiological bases of early intervention.* Minneapolis: University of Minnesota, Institute of Child Development.

Nelson, C. A., Wewerka, S. S., Borscheid, A. J., deRegnier, R. A., & Georgieff, M. K. (2003). Electrophysiologic evidence of impaired cross-modal recognition memory in 8-month-old infants of diabetic mothers. *Journal of Pediatrics, 142*(5), 575–582.

Nestor, P. G., Kimble, M., Berman, I., & Haycock, J. (2002). Psychosis, psychopathy, and homicide: A preliminary neuropsychological inquiry. *American Journal of Psychiatry, 159*, 138–140.

Neugebauer, R., Hoek, H. W., & Susser, E. (1999). Prenatal exposure to wartime famine and development of antisocial personality disorder in early adulthood. *Journal of the American Medical Association, 281*, 455–462.

Nguyen, L., Rigo, J.-M., Rocher, V., Belachew, S., Malgrange, B., Rogister, B., et al. (2001). Neurotransmitters as early signals for central nervous system development. *Cell and Tissue Research, 305*, 187–202.

O'Donnell, J., Stemmelin, J., Nitta, A., Brouillette, J., & Quirion, R. (2003). Gene expression profiling following chronic NMDA receptor blockade-induced learning deficits in rats. *Synapse, 50*(3), 171–180.

Okado, N., Narita, M., & Narita, N. (2001). A biogenic amine-synapse mechanism for mental retardation and developmental disabilities. *Brain Development, 23*(Suppl. 1), S11–S15.

Oliver, M. H., Bloomfield, F. H., Harding, J. E., Breier, B. H., Bassett, N. S., & Gluckman, P. D. (1999). Endocrine control of perinatal programming in health and disease. *Biochemical Society Transactions, 27*, 69–73.

Öngür, D., Drevets, W. C., & Price, J. L. (1998). Glial reduction in the subgenual prefrontal cortex in mood disorders. *Proceedings of the National Academy of Sciences of the United States of America, 95*, 13290–13295.

Palmer, A. A., Printz, D. J., Butler, P. D., Dulawa, S. C., & Printz, M. P. (2004). Prenatal protein deprivation in rats induces changes in prepulse inhibition and NMDA receptor binding. *Brain Research, 996*(2), 193–201.

Paule, M. G., Fogle, C. M., Allen, R. R., Pearson, E. C., Hammond, T. G., & Popke, E. J. (2003). Chronic exposure to NMDA receptor and sodium channel blockers during development in monkeys and rats: Long-term effects on cognitive function. *Annals of the New York Academy of Sciences, 993*, 116–124.

Pennington, B. F., & Ozonoff, S. (1996). Executive functions and developmental psychopathology. *Journal of Child Psychology and Psychiatry, 37*, 51–87.

Percy, A. K., & Rutledge, S. L. (2001). Adrenoleukodystrophy and related disorders. *Mental Retardation and Developmental Disabilities Research Reviews, 7*(3), 179–189.

Perry, W., Felger, T., & Braff, D. (1998). The relationship between skin conductance hyporesponsivity and perseverations in Schizophrenia patients. *Biological Psychiatry, 44*(6), 459–465.

Petry, C. D., Eaton, M. A., Wobken, J. D., Mills, M. M., Johnson, D. E., & Georgieff, M. K. (1992). Iron deficiency of liver, heart, and brain in newborn infants of diabetic mothers. *Journal of Pediatrics, 121*(1), 109–114.

Pharoah, P. O. D., Buttfield, I. H., & Hetzel, B. S. (1971). Neurological damage to the fetus resulting from severe iodine deficiency during pregnancy. *Lancet, 1*, 308–310.

Phillips, M. A., Oxtoby, E. K., Langley, R. W., Bradshaw, C. M., & Szabadi, E. (2000). Effects of acute tryptophan depletion on prepulse inhibition of the acoustic startle (eyeblink) response and the NI/P2 auditory evoked response in man. *Journal of Psychopharmacology, 14*(3), 258–265.

Pierucci-Lagha, A., Feinn, R., Modesto-Lowe, V., Swift, R., Nellissery, M., Covault, J., et al. (2004). Effects of rapid tryptophan depletion on mood and urge to drink in patients with co-morbid major depression and alcohol dependence. *Psychopharmacology, 171*(3), 340–348.

Pollitt, E. (1969). Ecology, malnutrition, and mental development. *Psychosomatic Medicine, 31*, 193–200.

Pollitt, E. (1988). Developmental impact of nutrition on pregnancy, infancy, and childhood: Public health issues in the United States. *International Review of Research in Mental Retardation, 15*, 33–80.

Pollitt, E. (1994). Poverty and child development: Relevance of research in developing countries to the United States. *Child Development, 65*, 283–295.

Pollitt, E. (1996). Timing and vulnerability in research on malnutrition and cognition. *Nutrition Reviews, 54*(Suppl. 2, Pt. 2), S49–S55.

Pollitt, E., Gorman, K. S., Engle, P. L., Martorell, R., & Rivera, J. (1993). Early supplementary feeding and cognition: Effects over two decades. *Monographs of the Society for Research in Child Development, 58*, 1–99.

Pollitt, E., Mueller, W., & Leibel, R. L. (1982). The relation of growth to cognition in a well-nourished preschool population. *Child Development, 53*, 1157–1163.

Prohaska, J. R. (2000). Long-term functional consequences of malnutrition during brain development: Copper. *Nutrition, 16*, 502–504.

Raine, A. (2002). Annotation: The role of prefrontal deficits, low autonomic arousal, and early health factors in the development of antisocial and aggressive behavior in children. *Journal of Child Psychology and Psychiatry, 43*, 417–434.

Raine, A., Brennan, P., & Mednick, S. A. (1994). Birth complications combined with early maternal rejection at age 1 year predispose to violent crime at age 18 years. *Archives of General Psychiatry, 51*, 984–988.

Raine, A., Brennan, P., & Mednick, S. A. (1997). Interaction between birth complications and early maternal rejection in predisposing individuals to adult violence: Specificity to serious, early-onset violence. *American Journal of Psychiatry, 154*, 1265–1271.

Raine, A., Mellingen, K., Liu, J., Venables, P. H., & Mednick, S. A. (2003). Effects of environmental enrichment at ages 3–5 years on schizotypal personality and antisocial behavior at ages 17 and 23 years. *American Journal of Psychiatry, 160*(9), 1627–1635.

Raine, A., Venables, P. H., Dalais, C., Mellingen, K., Reynolds, C., & Mednick, S. A. (2001). Early educational and health enrichment at age 3–5 years is associated with increased autonomic and central nervous system arousal and orienting at age 11 years: Evidence from the Mauritius Child Health Project. *Psychophysiology, 38*, 254–266.

Rajkowska, G. (2000). Dysfunction in neural circuits involved in the pathophysiology of mood disorders: Postmortem studies in mood disorders indicate altered numbers of neurons and glial cells. *Biological Psychiatry, 48*, 766–777.

Ramey, C. T., & Ramey, S. L. (1998). Early intervention and early experience. *American Psychologist, 53*(2), 109–120.

Rao, R., de Ungria, M., Sullivan, D., Wu, P., Wobken, J. D., Nelson, C. A., et al. (1999). Perinatal brain iron deficiency increases the vulnerability of rat hippocampus to hypoxic ischemic insult. *Journal of Nutrition, 129*, 199–206.

Retz, W., Kornhuber, J., & Riederer, P. (1996). Neurotransmission and the ontogeny of human brain. *Journal of Neural Transmission, 103*, 403–419.

Riedel, W. J. (2004). Editorial: Cognitive changes after acute tryptophan depletion: What can they tell us? *Psychological Medicine, 34*(1), 3–8.

Rioux, L., Nissanov, J., Lauber, K., Bilker, W. B., & Arnold, S. E. (2003). Distribution of microtubule-associated protein MAP2-immunoreactive interstitial neurons in the parahippocampal white matter in subjects with Schizophrenia. *American Journal of Psychiatry, 160*(1), 149–155.

Roesler, R., Schroder, N., Vianna, M. R., Quevedo, J., Bromberg, E., Kapczinski, F., et al. (2003). Differential involvement of hippocampal and amygdalar NMDA receptors in contextual and aversive aspects of inhibitory avoidance memory in rats. *Brain Research, 975*(1/2), 207–213.

Roncagliolo, M., Garrido, M., Walter, T., Peirano, P., & Lozoff, B. (1998). Evidence of altered central nervous system development in infants with iron deficiency anemia at 6 mo: Delayed maturation of auditory brainstem responses. *American Journal of Clinical Nutrition, 68*, 683–690.

Rosebush, P. I., Garside, S., Levinson, A. J., & Mazurek, M. F. (1999). The neuropsychiatry of adult-onset adrenoleukodystrophy. *Journal of Neuropsychiatry and Clinical Neurosciences, 11*(3), 315–327.

Rutter, M., & O'Connor, T. (2004). Are there biological programming effects for psychological development? Findings from a study of Romanian adoptees. *Developmental Psychology, 40*(1), 81–94.

Rutter, M., Pickles, A., Murray, R., & Eaves, L. (2001). Testing hypotheses on specific environmental causal effects on behavior. *Psychological Bulletin, 127*, 291–324.

Rutter, M., & Silberg, J. (2002). Gene-environment interplay in relation to emotional and behavioral disturbance. *Annual Review of Psychology, 53*, 463–490.

Sandstead, H. H., Penland, J. G., Alcock, N. W., Dayal, H. H., Chen, X. C., Li, J. S., et al. (1998). Effects of repletion with zinc and other micronutrients on neuropsychologic performance and growth of Chinese children. *American Journal of Clinical Nutrition, 68*(Suppl. 2), S470–S475.

Sapolsky, R. M. (2001). Cellular defenses against excitotoxic insults. *Journal of Neurochemistry, 76*, 1601–1611.

Schettler, T. (2001). Toxic threats to neurologic development of children. *Environmental Health Perspectives, 109*, 813–816.

Schmidt, A. T., Waldow, K. J., Salinas, J. A., & Georgieff, M. K. (2004, May). *The long-term behavioral effects of fetal/neonatal iron deficiency in a hippocampally dependent learning task in the rat.* Paper presented at the Society for Pediatric Research, San Francisco.

Schnur, D. B., Smith, S., Smith, A., Marte, V., Horwitz, E., Sackeim, H. A., et al. (1999). The orienting response in Schizophrenia and mania. *Psychiatry Research, 88*(1), 41–54.

Seckl, J. R. (1998). Physiologic programming of the fetus. *Emerging Concepts in Perinatal Endocrinology, 25*, 939–988.

Segal, M. (2001). Rapid plasticity of dendritic spine: Hints to possible functions? *Progress in Neurobiology, 63*, 61–70.

Shim, H., & Harris, Z. L. (2003). Genetic defects in copper metabolism. *Journal of Nutrition, 133*(5, Suppl. 1), S1527–S1531.

Slutske, W., Heath, A., Dinwiddie, S., Madden, P., Bucholz, K. K., Dunne, M. P., et al. (1997). Modeling genetic and environmental influences in the etiology of conduct disorder: A study of 2,682 adult twin pairs. *Journal of Abnormal Psychology, 106*(2), 266–279.

Snodgrass, S. R. (1994). Cocaine babies: A result of multiple teratogenic influences. *Journal of Child Neurology, 9*, 227–233.

Soto-Moyano, R., Fernandez, V., Sanhuezab, M., Belmarc, J., Kusch, C., Pereza, H., et al. (1999). Effects of mild protein prenatal malnutrition and subsequent postnatal nutritional rehabilitation on noradrenaline release and neuronal density in the rat occipital cortex. *Developmental Brain Research, 116*(1), 51–58.

Stein, Z., & Susser, M. (1985). Effects of early nutrition on neurological and mental competence in human beings. *Psychological Medicine, 15*, 717–726.

Stein, Z., Susser, M., Saenger, G., & Marolla, F. (1972). Nutrition and mental performance: Prenatal exposure to the Dutch famine of 1944–1945 seems not related to mental performance at age 19. *Science, 178*, 708–713.

Stein, Z., Susser, M., Saenger, G., & Marolla, F. (1975). *Famine and human development: The Dutch hunger winter of 1944–1945.* New York: Oxford University Press.

Stevens, M., Kaplan, R., & Bauer, L. (2001). Relationship of cognitive ability to the developmental course of antisocial behavior in substance-dependent patients. *Progress in Neuro-Psychopharmacology and Biological Psychiatry, 25*(8), 1523–1536.

Stevens, M., Kaplan, R., & Hesselbrock, V. (2003). Executive cognitive functioning in the development of antisocial personality disorder. *Addictive Behaviors, 28*(2), 285–300.

Stoltzfus, R. J., Kvalsvig, J. D., Chwaya, H. M., Montresor, A., Albonico, M., Tielsch, J. M., et al. (2001). Effects of iron supplementation and anthelmintic treatment on motor and language development of pre-school children in Zanzibar: Double blind, placebo controlled study. *British Medical Journal, 323,* 1–8.

Strauss, R. S., & Dietz, W. H. (1998). Growth and development of term children born with low birth weight: Effects of genetic and environmental factors. *Journal of Pediatrics, 133,* 67–72.

Sullivan, J. E., & Chang, P. (1999). Review: Emotional and behavioral functioning in phenylketonuria. *Journal of Pediatric Psychology, 24,* 281–299.

Susser, E., Brown, A. S., Klonowski, E., Allen, R. H., & Lindenbaum, J. (1998). Schizophrenia and impaired homocysteine metabolism: A possible association. *Biological Psychiatry, 44*(2), 141–143.

Susser, E., Hoek, H. W., & Brown, A. S. (1998). Neurodevelopmental disorders after prenatal famine: The story of the Dutch famine study. *American Journal of Epidemiology, 147,* 213–216.

Susser, E., & Lin, S. P. (1992). Schizophrenia after prenatal exposure to the Dutch hunger winter of 1944–1945. *Archives of General Psychiatry, 49,* 983–988.

Susser, E., Neugebauer, R., Hoek, H. W., Brown, A. S., Lin, S., Labovitz, D., et al. (1996). Schizophrenia after prenatal famine. *Archives of General Psychiatry, 53,* 25–31.

Susser, M., & Stein, Z. (1994). Timing in pre-natal nutrition: A reprise of the Dutch famine study. *Nutritional Reviews, 52,* 84–94.

Syvalahti, E. K. (1994). Biological factors in Schizophrenia: Structural and functional aspects. *British Journal of Psychiatry* (Suppl. 23), 9–14.

Tanner, E. M., & Finn-Stevenson, M. (2002). Nutrition and brain development: Social policy implications. *American Journal of Orthopsychiatry, 72,* 182–193.

Teicher, M. H., Andersen, S. L., Polcari, A., Anderson, C. M., & Navalta, C. P. (2002). Developmental neurobiology of childhood stress and trauma. *Psychiatric Clinics of North America, 25,* 397–426.

Thompson, C., Syddall, H., Rodin, I., Osmond, C., & Barker, D. J. P. (2001). Birth weight and the risk of depressive disorder in late life. *British Journal of Psychiatry, 179,* 450–455.

Tirosh, E., Gaster, H., Berger, A., Cohen, A., & Scher, A. (2000). Neonatal neurobehavorial assessment as related to growth in infancy. *Journal of Productive and Infant Psychology, 18,* 37–41.

Tiwari, B. D., Godbole, M. M., Chattopadhyay, N., Mandal, A., & Mithal, A. (1996). Learning disabilities and poor motivation to achieve due to prolonged iodine deficiency. *American Journal of Clinical Nutrition, 63,* 782–786.

Tonkiss, J., Almeida, S. S., & Galler, J. R. (1998). Prenatally malnourished female but not male rats show increased sensitivity to MK-801 in a differential reinforcement of low rates task. *Behavioural Pharmacology, 9*(1), 49–60.

Tonkiss, J., Trzcinska, M., Shultz, P., Vincitore, M., & Galler, J. R. (2000). Prenatally protein-malnourished rats are less sensitive to the amnestic effects of medial septal infusions of chlordiazepoxide. *Behavioural Pharmacology, 11*(6), 437–446.

Trope, I., Lopez-Villegas, D., Cecil, K. M., & Lenkinski, R. E. (2001). Exposure to lead appears to selectively alter metabolism of cortical gray matter. *Pediatrics, 107*(6), 1437–1442.

Truong, B. G., Magrum, L. J., & Gietzen, D. W. (2002). GABA (A) and GABA (B) receptors in the anterior piriform cortex modulate feeding in rats. *Brain Research, 924*(1), 1–9.

Tully, L. A., Arseneault, L., Caspi, A., Moffitt, T. E., & Morgan, J. (2004). Does maternal warmth moderate the effects of birth weight on twins' attention-deficit/hyperactivity disorder (ADHD) symptoms and low IQ? *Journal of Consulting and Clinical Psychology, 72*(2), 218–226.

Tuormaa, T. E. (1995). Adverse effects of zinc deficiency: A review from the literature. *Journal of Orthomolecular Medicine, 10,* 149–164.

van Geel, B. M., Assies, J., Wanders, R. J., & Barth, P. G. (1997). X linked adrenoleukodystrophy: Clinical presentation, diagnosis, and therapy. *Journal of Neurology, Neurosurgery, and Psychiatry, 63*(1), 4–14.

van Kesteren, R. E., & Spencer, G. E. (2003). The role of neurotransmitters in neurite outgrowth and synapse formation. *Reviews in the Neurosciences, 14*(3), 217–231.

Wahlbeck, K., Forsén, T., Osmond, C., Barker, D. J. P., & Eriksson, J. G. (2001). Association of Schizophrenia with low maternal body mass index, small size at birth, and thinness during childhood. *Archives of General Psychiatry, 58,* 48–52.

Wakefield, J. C. (1993). Limits of operationalization: A critique of Spitzer and Endicott's (1978) proposed operational criteria for mental disorder. *Journal of Abnormal Psychology, 102*(1), 160–172.

Wakefield, J. C. (1999). Evolutionary versus prototype analyses of the concept of disorder. *Journal of Abnormal Psychology, 108*(3), 374–399.

Walker, N. P., McConville, P. M., Hunter, D., Deary, I. J., & Whalley, L. J. (2002). Childhood mental ability and lifetime psychiatric contact: A 66-year follow-up study of the 1932 Scottish Mental Ability Survey. *Intelligence, 30*(3), 233–245.

Walsh, T. J., & Emerich, D. F. (1988). The hippocampus as a common target of neurotoxic agents. *Toxicology, 49,* 137–140.

Watanabe, C., & Satoh, H. (1994). Brain selenium status and behavioral development in selenium-deficient preweanling mice. *Physiology and Behavior, 56,* 927–932.

Wauben, I. P. M., & Wainwright, P. E. (1999). The influence of neonatal nutrition on behavioral development: A critical appraisal. *Nutrition Reviews, 57,* 35–44.

Webb, S. J., Monk, C. S., & Nelson, C. A. (2001). Mechanisms of postnatal neurobiological development: Implications for human development. *Developmental Neuropsychology, 19,* 147–171.

Weiss, B. (2000). Vulnerability of children and the developing brain to neurotoxic hazards. *Environmental Health Perspectives, 108,* 375–381.

Whitford, K. L., Dijkhuizen, P., Polleux, F., & Ghosh, A. (2002). Molecular control of cortical dendrite development. *Annual Review of Neuroscience, 25,* 127–149.

Wiggins, R. C., Fuller, G., & Enna, S. J. (1984). Undernutrition and the development of brain neurotransmitter systems. *Life Sciences, 35,* 2085–2094.

Williams, L. M., Brammer, M. J., Skerrett, D., Lagopolous, J., Rennie, C., Kozek, K., et al. (2000). The neural correlates of orienting: An integration of fMRI and skin conductance orienting. *NeuroReport, 11*(13), 3011–3015.

Winick, M., Meyer, K. K., & Harris, R. C. (1975). Malnutrition and environmental enrichment by early adoption. *Science, 190*(4220), 1173–1175.

Winick, M., & Rosso, P. (1969). The effect of severe early malnutrition on cellular growth of human brain. *Pediatric Research, 3*(2), 181–184.

Yi-Ming, X. (1996). Trace elements in health and diseases. *Biomedical and Environmental Sciences, 9,* 130–136.

Zauner, A., Daugherty, W. P., Bullock, M. R., & Warner, D. S. (2002). Brain oxygenation and energy metabolism: Part 1. Biological function and pathophysiology. *Neurosurgery, 51,* 289–302.

Zeisel, S. H. (2000). Choline: Needed for normal development of memory. *Journal of the American College of Nutrition, 19*(Suppl. 5), S528–S531.

Zeskind, P. S., & Ramey, C. T. (1981). Preventing intellectual and interactional sequelae of fetal malnutrition: A longitudinal, transactional, and synergistic approach to development. *Child Development, 52*(1), 218–231.

CHAPTER 7

Cognitive Neuroscience and the Prefrontal Cortex: Normative Development and Vulnerability to Psychopathology

MONICA LUCIANA

Cognitive neuroscience was formalized as a scientific area of inquiry in the late 1970s, when scholars from various disciplines sought to bring together their investigations of how brain processes enabled mental functions (Gazzaniga, Ivry, & Mangun, 2002). Less formally, the field began quite a bit earlier, when Franz Joseph Gall introduced his concept of phrenology, the notion that the brain is organized around a group of cognitive tasks, each of which has a hypothesized basis in brain function. Gall proposed that when the function was frequently implemented, its corresponding brain area increased in size, causing a bump to protrude from the skull. He believed that a careful analysis of the skull's surface could reveal characteristics of an individual's personality and intellect (Gall & Spurzheim, 1810; Spurzheim, 1825). This theory

was rejected by Gall's contemporaries (Flourens, 1824), but the general goal of localizing cognitive and other behavioral functions within the brain was pursued by early experimental neuropsychologists, such as John Hughlings Jackson, in the mid-1800s (Taylor, 1958).

When Santiago Ramon y Cajal (1906/1967) used the newly developed Golgi (1906) stain to identify neurons as unitary entities that transmitted electrical impulses in a unidirectional fashion, studies of brain structure-function relations proliferated. Neuroscientific pioneers relied on lesion studies in animals and humans to craft theories of brain-behavior relations. Among these were David Hubel and Torsten Wiesel, who recorded activity from single neurons in the visual cortex of cats and demonstrated that they responded reliably to discrete forms of experiential stimulation, provoking a host of questions regarding the dynamics of experience, neurobiology, and their interactions (Hubel & Wiesel, 1962, 1965). Angelo Mosso, an Italian physiologist who studied skull defects, anticipated the development of neuroimaging when he observed an association in his patients between cerebral blood flow and increases in neuronal activity (cited in Raichle, 1998). Based on Mosso's observations in the years following World War II, scientists began to measure blood flow in the brains of laboratory animals. David Ingvar and Neils Lassen were the first to devise a method for the measurement of changes in metabolism and cerebral blood flow during cognitive performance (Raichle, 1998), a technique that gave way to positron emission tomography (PET), which was developed at Washington University in St. Louis. The successful measurement of hydrogen atoms in a magnetic field prompted the development of the first magnetic resonance imaging (MRI) scanners, and most recently, a method of tracking blood flow using MRI made functional magnetic resonance imaging (fMRI) possible (Gazzaniga et al., 2002; Raichle, 1998). Functional MRI measures and localizes activity in the behaving human brain. From a methodological standpoint, cognitive neuroscience has proliferated at an exponential rate, so that we are now able to view the dynamics of brain activity in individuals across the life span as they perform behavioral tasks.

The ability to view the living brain in action permits examination of how such activity changes or is altered in response to experiences, including illness, pharmacological treatment, and normal aging processes. In the context of the heated philosophical debates regarding nature and nurture that have motivated psychological inquiry since the field's inception, it has been natural to apply questions regarding brain-behavior relations to the study of child development. With the advent of electrophysiological recording, MRI, and fMRI, almost every conceivable cognitive function has been considered from a human developmental neuroscientific standpoint, including language development (Bates, Vicari, & Trauner, 1999; Merzenich et al., 1996), visual perception (Maurer & Lewis, 2001), face recognition (de Haan & Nelson, 1997), learning and memory (Nelson, 1995; Pascalis & Bachevalier, 1999), and attention (Johnson, 1990; Richards, 2000).

With these substantial advances in cognitive neuroscience and increased knowledge regarding postnatal brain development, there has been an escalating interest among scientists in the emergence of higher-order cognitive processes and their neural substrates. These processes include planning, foresight, and goal-directed behaviors that require integration across time and space (working memory), inhibitory control, and flexibility in selecting appropriate responses. Current theories suggest that each of these behaviors is controlled by a distributed information-processing network, orchestrated within dorsal and/or ventral regions of the prefrontal cortex (PFC). For instance, working memory and inhibitory control have been associated with dorsolateral PFC activity, and the use of these skills to pursue future goals under highly salient emotional conditions recruits the ventromedial PFC. PFC abnormalities have been noted in a number of clinical conditions such as substance abuse (associated with aberrant ventromedial PFC function) and Schizophrenia (associated with dorsolateral PFC dysfunction).

In this chapter, I consider how psychopathology can develop as a consequence of deficiencies in the PFC's ability to regulate behavior, highlighting how cognitive neuroscientific techniques have contributed to this area of inquiry. To put this discussion in context, I first briefly define what is meant by the *prefrontal cortex*. Historical perspectives on prefrontal function as derived from early studies in experimental neuropsychology are shared, followed by a discussion of behaviors that are believed to be PFC-mediated. How these behaviors develop from infancy through young adulthood is discussed next. The discussion of behavioral development emphasizes how cognitive neuroscientific techniques have been used to study the correspondences among the PFC's structural, neurophysiological, and functional developments. Once these normative principles of PFC development have been derived, their implications for psychopathology in the developmental period are considered.

THE PREFRONTAL CORTEX DEFINED

In the primate, the *frontal cortex* has been defined on anatomical and cytoarchitectural grounds. Anatomically, its posterior border is the central sulcus, a fissure that cuts across the brain's lateral surface, extending medially to separate the parietal lobe from the more anterior frontal cortex. On the inferior side, the frontal lobe is separated from the temporal lobe by the lateral fissure. Just anterior to the central sulcus is the precentral gyrus (also referred to as the primary motor cortex: Brodmann's area 4; see Figure 7.1: Pandya & Yeterian, 1990). Secondary motor areas, including the premotor cortex, frontal eye fields, supplemental motor area, and Broca's area (Brodmann's areas 6, 8, and 44) lie anterior to, and slightly beneath, the primary motor cortex. The terms *frontal cortex* and

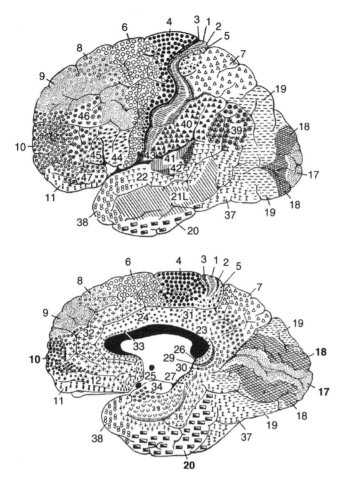

Figure 7.1 Based on cytoarchitectural characteristics, Brodmann created this anatomical map of the primate brain, including the prefrontal cortex. Each region was defined based on the presence of distinctive cellular features. *Source:* Reprinted from "Prefrontal Cortex in Relation to Other Cortical Areas in Rhesus Monkey: Architecture and Connections," by D. N. Pandya and E. H. Yeterian, 1990, *Progress in Brain Research, 85,* pp. 63–94. With permission from Elsevier.

prefrontal cortex are not synonymous. The prefrontal cortex, an expanse of tissue that constitutes about half of the human frontal cortex, describes all portions of the frontal lobe that lie anterior to these primary and secondary motor regions. Through the use of anatomical tracing techniques, the prefrontal cortex has also been defined as the projection field of the dorsomedial thalamus (Goldman-Rakic & Porrino, 1985; Rose & Woolsey, 1948; Walker, 1940). Several subdivisions of the PFC are currently recognized, including the *lateral* (lateral aspects of areas 9 to 12, 45 to 46, and the superior portion of area 47), *ventromedial* (the medial aspects of areas 9 to 12 and inferior portion of area 47), and *anterior cingulate* (areas 24, 25, and 32) cortices.

In the mature primate (including the human), the prefrontal cortex is reciprocally connected, within and between each brain hemisphere, with various cortical and subcortical structures, including the superior temporal cortex, posterior parietal cortex, posterior cingulate gyrus, thalamus, limbic system, and caudate nucleus (Cavada & Goldman-Rakic, 1989; Selemon & Goldman-Rakic, 1988). On the basis of its extensive connectivity with the rest of the brain, the PFC is in a unique position to coordinate processing among these regions so that the entire brain can function as an integrated and well-regulated unit.

HISTORICAL PERSPECTIVES ON THE PREFRONTAL CORTEX AND BEHAVIORAL REGULATION

The cognitive neuroscientific investigation of the prefrontal cortex began more than 150 years ago with a dramatic case study. In the summer of 1848, Phineas Gage was a 25-year-old construction foreman employed by the Rutland and Burlington Railroad in the state of Vermont. Known by his superiors as a highly efficient and capable man, he was assigned the difficult task of supervising a group whose mission it was to lay down new tracks for the railroad's expansion across the United States. On one fateful afternoon, Gage was preparing detonations, which required a hole to be drilled into a section of rock. The hole was then filled halfway with explosive powder, a fuse was inserted, and the powder was covered with sand. The sand had to be gently packed in with the use of an iron rod, after which the fuse was lit. Gage was momentarily distracted as he performed this sequence and reportedly began to tap the explosive powder before he had covered it with sand. A fire ignited, and the iron rod, weighing 13.5 pounds and measuring over an inch in diameter, blew upward into Gage's face (Damasio, 1994). The rod entered his left cheek, crossed the frontal region of his brain, and exited through the top of his head, landing several hundred feet away. Gage was knocked to the ground but, remarkably, was awake and communicative (Damasio, 1994; Jasper, 1995). He was cared for by John M. Harlow (1868), a local physician, who described the case in a letter written to the *New England Journal of Medicine*. Not only was it notable that Gage survived this terrible accident, living for another 15 years, but Harlow's description of Gage's change in personality was among the first scientific writings to emphasize the importance of the frontal lobe in the mediation of behavioral control.

As a consequence of the injury, Harlow commented that the "balance" between Gage's intellect and his "animal propensities" seemed to have been destroyed. Gage was described as profane, irreverent, and capricious. His friends commented that he was no longer himself. Having made a dramatic physical recovery, Gage was nonetheless eventually discharged from his leadership position due to his unpredictable behavior. He held a series of menial jobs, each of which he retained for only a short period. For a time, he became a circus attraction at Barnum's Museum in New York City. He eventually died in 1861 following a brief illness that was accompanied by grand mal seizures.

Gage's case provides an example of how a lesion to the ventromedial PFC led to behavioral *release* or disinhibition. His story remains remarkable in conveying two major points to the scientific community: first, that social behavior and individual differences in personality style can be dissociated from general intellect, and second, that aspects of an individual's personality might have a biological (brain) basis.

Around the same period of time, Paul Broca, a French neurologist, treated a stroke victim who was left with the ability to understand language, although he could not speak (Berker, Berker, & Smith, 1986). After the patient's death, it was discovered that the area of the brain that was damaged was localized to the left anterior portion of the frontal lobe, which came to be called *Broca's area*. Soon afterward, in 1876, it was demonstrated by Carl Wernicke (1908) that damage to the temporal-parietal junction, also on the left side, rendered one able to speak but unable to understand language. Together, these findings were monumental, suggesting a dissociation between discrete aspects of language and specific structures within the brain's left hemisphere.

Human case studies such as these led neuroanatomists such as Brodmann (Figure 7.1) to focus on mapping cytoarchitectural features of the cerebral cortex. These cases also inspired scientists to derive animal models of brain-behavior relations. Early animal models relied on the use of experimental focal lesions and the innovative technique of implanting electrodes into the brains of behaving animals (e.g., Hubel & Wiesel, 1962, 1965).

Carlyle Jacobsen (1935) used the lesion technique to examine the effects of bilateral frontal lobe removals on a range of cognitive functions in adult monkeys and chimpanzees. After recovery from surgery, Jacobsen's animals were physically intact, with no apparent sensory or movement difficulties. They were able to perform visual and auditory discriminations and to recall the spatial orientations of objects under immediate response conditions. However, if a delay was introduced between the presentation of a stimulus and the required response, the animals were impaired in their performance. Tasks that impose such delays are referred to as *delayed response tasks*. In the classic variant of the delayed response (DR) task (Hunter, 1913), a research subject (animal or human) is presented with two identical food wells, one of which is baited within full view with a desired object and then occluded. Following a delay interval, typically in the range of a few seconds, the subject is permitted to retrieve the object from the remembered location without the benefit of recognition memory. Although the task is very simple, it has been described over the years as a microcosm of future-directed behavior, because one must represent, through mentation, a future action that is necessary for goal attainment. That is, at the time that the desired object is hidden, one formulates a representation of that object, its motivational value, and where it can be retrieved. The nature of the action that will permit retrieval (e.g., what to do and where to do it) presumably also becomes part of the representational structure that is held in mind until that action can be executed.

Following Jacobsen's landmark finding, DR tasks became preferred means of examining the integrity of frontal lobe function in laboratory animals and, to a lesser extent, in humans with suspected frontal lobe damage. Indeed, one of the most consistently employed measures of prefrontal function has been the *spatial* DR task, where the information to be remembered concerns the desired object's location.

In addition to recent memory deficits, Jacobsen's lesioned animals demonstrated other difficulties, including loss of initiative, lethargy, and distractibility (reviewed by Jasper, 1995). In contrast to the disinhibition displayed by Phineas Gage, the disturbances experienced by these animals illustrate how PFC lesions can result in a seemingly opposite pattern of behavioral dysregulation, one that involves loss of function. Another notable finding in Jacobsen's monkeys was that individual animals' personality traits were *differentially* altered by the frontal lesions. For instance, one animal that was noted to be particularly unmanageable prior to surgery became complacent and seemingly happy afterward. The Second World Congress of Neurology in 1935 featured this work, as well as a presentation by Walter Penfield from the Montreal Neurological Institute. Penfield presented the results of a series of case studies in which patients underwent frontal lobe excisions for the treatment of brain tumors. Penfield noted that although these individuals retained a great deal of insight, introspection, and ability to follow instructions after recovery, they seemed unable to perform planned actions (Jasper, 1995; Penfield & Evans, 1935).

At one point during the meeting, according to Jasper (1995), a well-known Portuguese neurologist, Antonio Egas Moniz, asked why, if frontal lobe excisions eliminated aggressive behavior in animals, it would not be feasible to use similar surgical techniques to alleviate anxiety and frustration in humans. Upon his return to Portugal, Moniz, who coined the term *psychosurgery* (cited by Jasper, 1995), developed procedures for human frontal leucotomy (or lobotomy; both terms refer to the surgical interruption of fiber tracts that link the prefrontal cortex with other brain regions). Walter Freedman brought the practice to the United States, performing the first prefrontal leucotomy on a patient with depression in 1936. The technique was reportedly successful in regulating the behavior of difficult-to-manage cases of mental disorder and was also adopted by many well-reputed neurological institutes, including the Montreal Neurological Institute, where Penfield was approached by many patients requesting the procedure to relieve them of chronic emotional distress (Jasper, 1995). Penfield is best known for his work with intractable epilepsy (Penfield & Jasper, 1954), and the Institute's scientists became renowned for their descriptions of pre- versus postoperative behavior in humans who received lobotomies as treatments for frontal lobe epilepsy. Furthermore, Moniz won the Nobel Prize in 1949 for the use of frontal lobotomies for the treatment of mental disorders.

Prefrontal lobotomies were performed on thousands of patients in the 1930s and 1940s. When the procedure was finally subjected to increased scientific scrutiny, it was concluded that although there were a limited number of beneficial effects in extreme cases, outcomes were generally poor. The practice seems barbaric by current standards, but it must be emphasized that few treatment options were available to patients during this time period. With the advent of psychopharmacological advances in the 1960s, lobotomies became increasingly obsolete. And although the end does not necessarily justify the means, this era of prefrontal lobotomy called attention to the importance of the prefrontal cortex in the maintenance of high-level cognition and behavioral regulation. Together with findings from individual case studies, the lobotomy illustrated to the scientific community that PFC lesions could result in either behavioral excesses (disinhibition) or shortfalls (anhedonia). These paradoxical findings can be integrated by understanding that a critical function of the PFC may be to maintain behavior in a flexible but adaptive equilibrium.

It was the practice at the Montreal Neurological Institute in the 1950s and 1960s for patients undergoing frontal excisions for the treatment of epilepsy to complete comprehensive cognitive testing using standardized as well as newly developed measures. This innovative work led to reports on a number of classic neuropsychological cases and generated several influential theories regarding PFC function (Milner, 1995).

For example, Penfield's epilepsy work was notable for the case of K.M., who in 1928 at the age of 16, was struck by an overhead feeder while working in a sawmill (Milner, 1995). He sustained a penetrating injury to both frontal lobes and was comatose for more than a week. He developed severe major epileptic seizures after the injury, and like Phineas Gage, his behavior between seizures was described as irresponsible and childish. In 1938, Penfield removed an extensive area of scar tissue involving the anterior third of both of K.M.'s frontal lobes, which led to improvement in the patient's seizures as well as increased behavioral control. Brenda Milner, one of the Institute's neuropsychologists, conducted a follow-up study of K.M. in 1962, when the patient was 48 years old. She replicated earlier findings that even without a substantial portion of his prefrontal cortex, K.M. had an overall IQ in the average range, which would seem to represent a very positive outcome. However, using the newly developed Wisconsin Card Sort Task (D. A. Grant & Berg, 1948; Milner, 1963) to measure K.M.'s reasoning skills, Milner demonstrated that his performance was severely impaired. The Wisconsin Card Sort, now a classic means of assessing prefrontal function in clinical and experimental settings, presents an individual with four cards (see Figure 7.2). Each card varies on three stimulus dimensions: color, shape, and number (e.g., one card might consist of one yellow star and another might consist of four blue squares). The task is to sort additional cards on the "correct" dimension, based on feedback from an experimenter. Thus, one might start the task by sorting cards according to the color of the items on the card. After each response, the test taker is told that he or she is correct (or not). After 10 consecutively correct responses, the correct sorting criterion is changed, and the test taker must shift his or her responses, based on trial-and-error feedback, to one of the other possible dimensions. In theory, the three possible sorting dimensions have to be held simultaneously in mind to execute these behavioral shifts. Frontal lobe-lesioned patients tend to perseverate in their response sets, applying the first-learned sorting rule repeatedly, even when they are told that it is no longer correct. Milner's (1995) use of the task on a number of patients with frontal lesions, as compared to those with lesions in posterior or

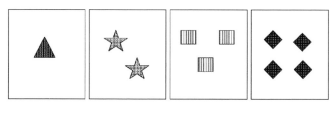

Figure 7.2 Schematic illustration of the Wisconsin Card Sort Task (Milner, 1963), one of the classic measures of prefrontal function. Individuals are presented with four display cards that vary on three dimensions: shape of the presented stimulus, stimulus color (depicted here as different patterning of stimuli), and the number of stimuli on each card. A deck of cards is also provided, and individuals must sort each card based on one of the three possible dimensions. The experimenter reinforces each sort by telling the participant that he or she is either correct or incorrect. Thus, the task requires an individual to utilize feedback to guide each response and to shift between each of the three possible sorting dimensions.

temporal regions, led her to conclude that although frontal lobe patients are appropriately responsive to environmental stimuli, they appear to have difficulty using such stimuli as cues in regulating their actions.

An alternative explanation suggested by Luria (1966) was that the dysregulated behavior of patients with frontal lobe injuries was due to an inability to verbally guide behavior. Luria's formulation was very influential, with obvious implications for understanding prefrontal development, as very young children are deficient in expressive language skills. However, his view is thought by some (i.e., Milner, 1995) to be too narrow, because frontal lobe-damaged patients exhibit difficulties on nonverbal tasks, such as stylus maze learning (Corkin, 1965; Milner, 1965), nonverbal design fluency (Jones-Gotman & Milner, 1977), spatial delayed response (Jacobsen, Wolfe, & Jackson, 1935), spatial delayed alternation (Jacobsen & Nissen, 1937), recency memory (Konorski, 1959; Milner, Corsi, & Leonard, 1991), and the temporal organization of memory (Petrides & Milner, 1982).

To summarize, although the work conducted in Montreal and elsewhere was primarily behavioral in nature, derived from a combination of animal and human clinical models that might seem primitive given today's technical advances,

it cannot be overemphasized in its importance. It represents the foundation on which the neuroscience of higher-order cognition has been built.

THE DEVELOPMENTAL COGNITIVE NEUROSCIENCE OF PREFRONTAL FUNCTION

Over the past 40 years, emphasis on single structure/single function explanations of higher-order cognition have been replaced by more contemporary views of information processing that emphasize the manner in which mentation is achieved through networks of interconnected regions (Goldman-Rakic, 1988; Mesulam, 1998). This view has provoked interest in how it is that various brain regions are able to communicate with one another and how this communication might be disrupted in psychological (as opposed to neurological) disorders. The application of cognitive neuroscientific techniques to psychopathology has also encouraged investigations of cognition-emotion interactions, how these interactions promote regulated behavior, and how they are achieved at the neural level. We know that neurochemicals form the basis of neural communication, and thus, the neurochemistry of behavioral regulation has become an area of great interest, reinforced by a desire to understand, at the cellular and network levels, the mechanisms through which psychopharmacological treatments facilitate recovery from emotional disorders. These endeavors, together with theories of psychopathology that emphasize neurodevelopmental mechanisms (Cicchetti & Walker, 2003; Weinberger, 1987), have sparked interest in how the development of the prefrontal cortex might differ from that of other brain regions and how individual differences in prefrontal development might confer vulnerability to psychopathology.

Sources of Individual Variation in Prefrontal Cortex Structure

Sources of potential variation in PFC structure and function begin at the point of conception and extend throughout the human life span. The structural development of the PFC begins prenatally. Following conception, the human embryo develops from three cellular layers: an outer ectoderm, an inner endoderm, and an intermediate mesoderm. These layers give rise to, respectively, (1) the nervous system, lenses of the eyes, outer skin, hair, and inner ear; (2) the digestive organs; and (3) the skeletal system and voluntary muscle system. Thus, the nervous system arises initially from the ectoderm layer, which comes to surround the other two layers. Its formation begins 2 to 3 weeks after conception and can be observed when the dorsal surface of the embryo begins to thicken. This thickening gives rise to the neural tube, a primitive structure that will eventually develop into the brain and spinal cord. By the 7th week of gestation, the cerebral hemispheres encompassing the brain's neocortex are visible (Spreen, Risser, & Edgell, 1995). The cellular events that lead to cortical development have not been adequately described in the human fetus due to methodological limitations, but they have been extensively examined in the nonhuman primate. It is generally assumed that a comparable sequence of events occurs in both species (Goldman-Rakic, Bourgeois, & Rakic, 1997).

Neurogenesis and Cellular Migration

Cortical development begins when mitosis promotes the generation of cells in the *ventricular zone* of the neural tube. This region develops adjacent to the ventricles of the brain. The initial *precursor* (or stem) cells, once formed, are undifferentiated. Mitosis acts on them to produce two cell lines: neuroblasts (nerve cells) and glioblasts (glial cells; Spreen et al., 1995). Using [^{3}H]thymidine, a unique autoradiographic labeling compound, it has become possible for neuroscientists to evaluate the time course of neurogenesis during the pre- and perinatal periods in nonhuman primates. This line of research, largely directed by Pasko Rakic and his colleagues at Yale University, has revealed that neurons destined for both posterior (visual) and prefrontal association cortical regions develop between embryonic day 40 (E40) and embryonic day 100 (E100) in the rhesus macaque (Rakic, 1974, 1995). After E100 (corresponding to the second trimester of human gestation), no additional formation of neurons destined for the neocortex has been observed (Rakic, 1985).

When this generative phase of neuron formation is completed, the neuroblasts move from the proliferative zone of the neural tube toward their permanent locations, a process referred to as *migration*. Proliferation and migration ensue in parallel for some time, during which an intermediate zone forms between the ventricular zone of the neural tube and the area that has been the target of developing cells (referred to as the marginal zone). By 8 to 10 weeks after conception, this intermediate zone forms the cortical plate and an underlying subplate, a secondary and transiently present locus of continued cell proliferation as well as a holding area for incoming projections from subcortical regions (Kostovic & Rakic, 1990; Rakic, 1977, 1995). In the primate, the subplate zone in the frontal cortex is as much as four times wider than what has been observed in other cortical areas, most notably the occipital cortex (Rakic, 1995). Rakic (1995) speculates that

the wider subplate is necessary to accommodate the relatively greater number of afferent fibers that form between other cortical regions and the developing frontal cortex (Kostovic & Rakic, 1990). Typically, the subplate degenerates with continued development, leaving only subtle vestiges scattered throughout the white matter of the adult cerebral hemispheres (Rakic, 1995).

As neurons continue to migrate between the 11th and 15th weeks of gestation, the cortical plate gradually forms the brain's six-layered neocortex. To achieve this laminar pattern, migration progresses in an inside-out fashion. That is, the initial layer to form within the cortical plate is the deepest (sixth) cortical layer, and the last, most superficial, layer forms when cells have migrated over relatively long distances through the five deeper layers. The cells, dependent on voltage-gated ion channels and receptors for N-methyl-D-aspartate (NMDA), are believed to use the fiber shafts of radial glial cells as scaffolds to negotiate these distances (Rakic, 1995).

This general sequence characterizes all regions of the developing cortex, including the prefrontal cortex. However, Rakic (1995) emphasizes that the migratory pathway that must be traversed by developing neurons is particularly extensive in the primate's frontal lobe. The need for cells to correctly negotiate such distances may increase the likelihood of migratory errors in the PFC. When cells root themselves in nonoptimal locations, the pattern of synaptic connectivity that results is disruptive to information processing, a process that has been hypothesized to contribute to the deficits observed in several congenital conditions, including Fetal Alcohol Syndrome (Jones & Smith, 1973, 1975), and one that has been theorized to underlie symptoms of thought disorder in Schizophrenia (Akbarian et al., 1993). Thus, accurate migration is critical for the cytoarchitectural formation of the cortex and profoundly influences its later function. Once migration is accomplished, the aggregation of cell types within each cortical layer promotes regional specialization and differentiation.

Synaptogenesis

Differentiation involves a number of processes in addition to the formation of cell bodies, including selective cell death, the growth of axons, the sprouting of dendritic processes, and the formation of functional synaptic connections (Spreen et al., 1995). The establishment of functional synaptic connections represents a significant milestone in the course of neural development, because it indicates that behavior can be guided by cortical neurons. The synaptic development of the prefrontal cortex has been studied most extensively in the nonhuman primate (Goldman-Rakic et al., 1997) and in a more limited fashion through human autopsy data (Huttenlocher, 1979).

In the rhesus macaque, the typical gestation period lasts for 165 days (~5.5 months), and the presence of the first synapses is evident 3 months prior to birth (Bourgeois, Goldman-Rakic, & Rakic, 1994). At midgestation, corticocortical and thalamocortical afferents permeate the cortical plate, and there is an overproduction of synaptic connections on the dendritic spines of pyramidal cells. (Dendrites are the postsynaptic arborizations emanating from the cell body that receive input from other cells via junctions referred to as synapses. Axons, in turn, are fibers that presynaptically propagate electrical signals to synaptic junctions. Dendrites themselves have extensions—spines—that contain synaptic contact points.) At the time of birth, the adult pattern of sulci and gyri is generally present on the surfaces of the macaque (Goldman & Galkin, 1978) and human (Spreen et al., 1995) brains. This is the time point when the maximal accumulation of synapses in the PFC occurs (Bourgeois et al., 1994) and the time point when the majority of corticocortical and thalamocortical afferents intersect the cortical plate (Schwartz & Goldman-Rakic, 1991). Spine formation continues until 30 to 60 contacts per 100 um^3 of neural tissue have formed, approximately 2 months after birth, at which time a plateau is reached. This plateau, representing synaptic density at higher-than-adult levels, is maintained throughout childhood until the onset of puberty (Bourgeois et al., 1994; Goldman-Rakic et al., 1997).

This overabundance of synapses is thought to ensure a high degree of redundancy (and hence, malleability), as multiple avenues might exist between neurons to subserve the same behavioral process. Imagine a series of highways and side roads that connect one major city to the next. To travel the distance between the two, one route might be maximally advantageous or efficient, but others are available in the event that the preferred one is impeded. These secondary routes can be used provided that they are maintained and reasonably well-traveled. Analogously, early to middle childhood would seem, on a synaptic level, to represent a time of great possibility, particularly if experience (environmental enrichment or stimulation) serves to facilitate synaptogenesis, creating multiple avenues of communication between distal brain regions. This time period might also represent a time of decreased vulnerability to injury. If the "preferred" avenue connecting distal regions

is damaged, others remain available and could be strengthened with use.

Synaptic Pruning

In the 3rd year of monkey life, corresponding to the period of adolescence/young adulthood in the human, a slow and steady decline in the number of synapses occurs. Synaptic attrition or pruning does not seem to occur in a random or haphazard way, but is a process that appears to be specific to asymmetric synaptic junctions (Goldman-Rakic et al., 1997; Rakic, 1995). Asymmetric synapses regulate excitatory transmitters, such as glutamate. The other type of junction, the symmetric synapse, regulates GABA, the major monoamines, and neuropeptides, all of which have local inhibitory functions. Symmetric synapses, once formed early in life, do not appear to change over the course of neural development or the ensuing life span (Bourgeois et al., 1994; Bourgeois & Rakic, 1993; Rakic, Bourgeois, Eckenhoff, Zecevic, & Goldman-Rakic, 1986). This change in the ratio of asymmetric to symmetric junctions alters the balance between excitatory and inhibitory neurotransmission. Pruning continues at a slight but measurable and steady rate for the remainder of the primate (macaque) life span. Huttenlocher and Dabholkar (1997) favor the view that experience has the effect of incorporating existing synapses into functional circuits and that unused synapses disappear, a process referred to as functional stabilization (Changeaux & Danchin, 1976).

Is the Prefrontal Cortex Different from Other Regions in Its Synaptic Development?

Whether or not synaptogenesis and synaptic elimination are relatively prolonged processes in the frontal cortex versus other cortical regions has been a matter of debate based on consideration of animal versus human data (Huttenlocher & Dabholkar, 1997; Rakic, 1995). It has traditionally been thought that the brain develops according to a hierarchical temporal sequence, with phylogenetically older regions maturing earlier than newer regions. Accordingly, brain development would proceed in a caudal-to-rostral sequence, with sensory areas developing prior to motor regions, and motor regions developing prior to association regions, including the prefrontal cortex. This maturational gradient would presumably be reflected equivalently in relation to all aspects of neural development, including neurogenesis, synaptogenesis, and myelination. Moreover, with respect to synaptogenesis, one expectation has been to observe concordance between a region's synaptic development and the functional maturation of behaviors subserved by that region. For instance, in the primary visual cortex, synaptogenesis rapidly increases during the first few months of human life, and this time of maximum synaptic density coincides with the development of stereoscopic vision (Huttenlocher & deCourten, 1987; Huttenlocher, deCourten, Garey, & Van Der Loos, 1982). To examine whether there is a similar concordance between synaptic density and behavioral development in the frontal cortex, Huttenlocher and Dabholkar compared the autopsied brains of fetuses, young children, and adults. Based on a quantification of synaptic density in selected brain areas, they concluded that there was a protracted course of synaptic development in the frontal lobe as compared to posterior regions, notably the primary auditory cortex in the superior temporal lobe. This finding appeared to make intuitive sense in light of the fact that the behavioral development of functions attributed to the frontal lobe also appeared to follow a sequential hierarchical course, appearing late in the 1st year of human life and reaching functional maturity many years later (as described later in the chapter).

In contrast to Huttenlocher's findings, data from nonhuman primates suggests that there is concurrent production of synapses across cortical regions (Rakic et al., 1986). Rakic and colleagues examined numerous areas of the neocortex in the brains of individual monkeys, including the prefrontal, primary visual, cingulate, motor, and somatosensory cortices, and found that the production of synapses occurs at a similar rate in all regions examined (Goldman-Rakic et al., 1997). The decline in synaptic density also appears to occur contemporaneously in these regions (Rakic et al., 1986).

These findings are difficult to reconcile. On the one hand, Rakic and colleagues have made a compelling argument in favor of their approach and general conclusions. They argue that methodological confounds may account for the apparent discrepancy between the monkey and human data (Goldman-Rakic et al., 1997; Rakic, Bourgeois, & Goldman-Rakic, 1994). On the other hand, Huttenlocher's findings are intuitively appealing and better approximate the apparent time course of the PFC's behavioral maturation in humans.

Metabolism

PET has also been used to examine brain metabolism from infancy through adolescence and into adulthood. Chugani (1998) reported changes in resting glucose metabolism from infancy to young adulthood. Newborns exhibit their highest levels of metabolism in sensory and motor regions, as well as in the hippocampus, thalamus, and brainstem. By 2 to 3 months of age, the metabolic rate

increases in primary sensory regions of the parietal and temporal cortices and in the primary motor cortex. It is also evident from monkey studies that concentrations of the major monoamine neurotransmitters, including dopamine, norepinephrine, and serotonin, rapidly increase from 2 to 5 months of postnatal life (Goldman-Rakic et al., 1997; Goldman-Rakic & Brown, 1982), as do corresponding transmitter receptor sites (Lidow & Rakic, 1992). Between 6 and 12 months of age, glucose metabolism increases in the human frontal cortex. Thus, these data seem to reinforce the notion that association areas lag behind primary sensory and motor regions in their functional development.

On a more general level and consistent with the suspected pattern of synaptogenesis in the primate brain, Chugani (1998) found that the brain's overall glucose metabolism peaks around the age of 4 years, plateaus through age 10, and begins a steady decline between 16 and 18 years, reaching adult levels late in the 2nd decade of life.

Volumetric Changes, Myelination, and White Matter Integrity

Finally, another feature of synaptic development that is being actively investigated concerns the development of white matter, which is one major constituent of brain tissue volume. Other constituents include brain gray matter (neuronal cell bodies), glial (supporting) cells, and cerebrospinal fluid. Global measures of brain volume, such as weight, potentially reflect growth in each of these structures. Brain weight increases rapidly during the first 5 years of life, reaching adult values around 10 to 12 years of age. After 5 years of age, global brain changes are relatively difficult to demonstrate, so measures that reflect structural changes must be able to detect subtle distinctions in neuronal patterning across age groups. In adults, brain anatomy and/or function can be assessed using a variety of techniques (e.g., PET, fMRI, electroencephalography, transcranial magnetic stimulation, and structural brain imaging), only some of which are appropriate for the noninvasive study of healthy children. As noted by Paus and colleagues (2001), very little is known about functional interconnectivity in the developing brain. To address this paucity of knowledge, MRI is a useful tool for investigating the anatomical features of major fiber (white matter) tracts that connect the PFC with other regions and provide information regarding functional properties of information-processing networks.

MR studies of infants have examined gray-white matter differentiation and degree of myelination (Christophe et al., 1990; B. C. Lee et al., 1986; van der Knapp & Valk, 1990). In adults, MR images indicative of white matter structure (referred to as T-1 weighted images) are more pronounced than images that are indicative of gray matter volume (T-2 weighted images). This pattern of gray-white matter differentiation is achieved over the course of postnatal development. In the healthy newborn, there is an apparent reversal of the normal adult pattern. The infant's T2-weighted (gray matter) images look like the adult's T1-weighted (white matter) images. Late in the 1st year of life, there is poor differentiation between gray and white matter, followed by acquisition of the "early adult pattern" at around 12 months of age. In a study of 145 individuals, Giedd and colleagues (1999) reported steady increases in white matter volume from ages 4 to 22 years. Each individual was scanned twice during the developmental period. Volume increases were in the range of 12% over this time period and showed a steeper progression in boys relative to girls. A number of other researchers have similarly reported increases in white matter volume from early childhood into young adulthood (Hassink, Hiltbrunner, Muller, & Lutschg, 1992; Pfefferbaum et al., 1994; Steen, Ogg, Reddick, & Kingsley, 1997).

White matter, as assessed through MR imaging, is heterogeneous and composed of a number of components, one of which is myelin, the fatty substance that insulates axons, leading to faster conduction velocities and increased synaptic efficiency. Myelination appears to follow a pronounced temporal sequence, first observed in the cerebellum and brain stem at birth, then the posterior limb of the internal capsule, optic radiations, and splenium of the corpus callosum at 6 months, followed by the frontal, parietal, and occipital lobes at 8 to 12 months (Paus et al., 2001). Progressive changes in white matter integrity have been observed throughout adolescence and are hypothesized to be due to increases in myelination (Paus et al., 2001; Pfefferbaum et al., 1994).

Genetics and Neurochemical Variation

These general mechanisms are important to characterize, but individual variations due to differences in neurotransmitter modulation of PFC function are also possible due to genetic influences. A number of neurotransmitter systems are candidates for analyses of this type, but this discussion focuses on two. Dopamine (DA) and serotonin, each of which modulates PFC-mediated behaviors, have been considered from a molecular genetic standpoint. First, by way of background, dopamine's modulation of PFC neural activity during spatial delayed response task performance

has been demonstrated in a number of classic studies (Goldman-Rakic, 1987a; Sawaguchi & Goldman-Rakic, 1991; Sawaguchi, Matsumura, & Kubota, 1988; Williams & Goldman-Rakic, 1995). Single-unit recordings have identified task-related neurons that are active during spatial delayed response performance and that differentially increase in firing rate during the initial presentation of a stimulus cue, the subsequent delay period, and as a response is being initiated (Funahashi, Bruce, & Goldman-Rakic, 1989; Kojima & Goldman-Rakic, 1982). In monkeys, neurotoxic lesions of the dorsolateral PFC produce impaired spatial delayed alternation performance that is reversed by DA agonists (Brozoski, Brown, Rosvold, & Goldman, 1979). In addition, iontophoretic applications of DA enhance task-related PFC neuronal activity (Sawaguchi, Matsumura, & Kubota, 1988, 1990a, 1990b), and pharmacological blockade of D^1 DA receptors results in reversible decrements in delayed response performance (Sawaguchi & Goldman-Rakic, 1991). In humans, pharmacological activation of D^2 DA receptors, through the use of the selective D^2 dopamine receptor agonist bromocriptine, facilitated working memory in a visuomotor spatial delayed response task (Luciana, Collins, & Depue, 1998; Luciana, Depue, Arbisi, & Leon, 1992). Haloperidol, a nonspecific DA antagonist, impaired working memory performance in the same group of subjects (Luciana & Collins, 1997). Others have reported transient Parkinsonian-like impairments in healthy people using sulpiride, a D^2 receptor antagonist (Mehta, Sahakian, McKenna, & Robbins, 1999). Agonists may reverse such deficits. For instance, bromocriptine was found to improve healthy adults' spatial memory spans (Mehta, Swainson, Ogilvie, Sahakian, & Robbins, 2001). Muller, von Cramon, and Pollmann (1998) demonstrated a facilitatory effect of a D^1 agonist in adults who completed a visuospatial delayed matching task. It is clear that dopamine's facilitation of the cellular processes that support delayed response is dose-dependent (Williams & Goldman-Rakic, 1995). Kimberg, D'Esposito, and Farah (1997) demonstrated that the optimal threshold of DA activation differs in individual human subjects. In their study, bromocriptine enhanced executive function only in individuals with low working memory capacity. Consistent with these findings, bromocriptine has been utilized to treat executive impairments in individuals with dementia (Imamura et al., 1998) and to evaluate executive function in patients with frontal lobe injuries (McDowell, Whyte, & D'Esposito, 1998). Thus, *individual differences in DA reactivity may underlie differential patterns of cognitive performance.*

Studies of DA-working memory associations in humans have focused on adults for obvious pragmatic and ethical reasons, but these associations could also be examined in developmental cohorts using noninvasive genetic (versus psychopharmacological) techniques. It has long been recognized that genes account for a substantial portion of the variability in behavior, especially in clinical conditions such as Schizophrenia (Weinberger et al., 2001).

Because these disorders are complex and likely to be mediated by interactions among candidate genes, single genes are unlikely to be specific for the disorder's presence or absence. Rather, because genes affect the biology of cells, cellular events underlie brain activity, and brain activity underlies fundamental aspects of behavior, it has been argued that genetic studies should focus on intermediate phenotypic traits, termed endophenotypes (Gottesman & Gould, 2003). These traits will not account for diagnostic classifications, but they are likely to more directly represent activity of specific genes in healthy as well as disordered people. An example is functioning of the PFC. A genetic polymorphism that impacts neurotransmission in the PFC will affect its efficiency at physiological and behavioral levels.

In theory, this hypothesis could be studied in relation to any number of candidate genes that code for various aspects of activity in major neurochemical systems. One recent focus of investigation has been the gene that encodes catechol-O-methyltransferase (COMT), a postsynaptic enzyme that methylates released dopamine to homovanillic acid (Weinberger et al., 2001). The COMT gene, located on chromosome 22q, contains a common polymorphism at position 472 (where there is a guanine-to-adenine substitution), which translates into a valine-to-methionine change in the peptide sequence (Lachman et al., 1996; Lotta et al., 1995). This change is reflected in allelic variation, whereby a given individual could possess alleles for either valine (VAL) or the methionine (MET) conversion.

At human body temperature, the MET allele has one-fourth the activity of the VAL allele, leading to decreased activity of the COMT gene and reduced catabolism of dopamine in the synapse. Furthermore, the MET and VAL alleles are codominant, so individuals with the VAL-VAL genotype have more rapid inactivation of released dopamine relative to individuals with the VAL-MET and MET-MET genotypes. Of particular importance, COMT does not appear to affect all dopamine-rich areas of the brain equivalently. It appears to be unrelated to the synaptic activity of dopamine in the striatum, due to the fact that in this region, DA activity in synapses is terminated largely by transporter reuptake into presynaptic terminals. In the PFC, DA transporter activity is less prominent and extracellular DA is more heavily regulated by catabolic processes (Weinberger et al., 2001). Hence, we would expect COMT to impact prefrontal, but not striatal, functions that are modulated by dopamine.

COMT inhibitors improve working memory functioning in rats and in humans (Gasparini, Fabrizio, Bonifati, & Meco, 1997; Liljequist, Haapalinna, Ahlander, Ying, & Mannisto, 1997), and COMT knockout mice exhibit increased extracellular DA activity in PFC but not in the striatum (Gogos et al., 1998). They also perform better than wild-type mice under stress and on working memory tasks. Recently, Egan and colleagues (2001) reported that COMT genotype predicted performance on the Wisconsin Card Sort task in a large sample of subjects that included individuals with Schizophrenia but also a majority of healthy controls. Individuals who carried the VAL allele made more perseverative errors than those who carried the MET allele. There was the predicted effect of genetic load, in that VAL-VAL individuals performed worse than VAL-MET individuals, who performed worse than MET-MET individuals. Egan and colleague's (2001) paper has rapidly become a classic in molecular genetics. His findings have been replicated by other laboratories, using other PFC measures.

A general prediction with respect to developmental populations is that individuals who carry the VAL allele will exhibit worse performance (age-corrected) than those who carry the MET allele on measures of PFC function that can be manipulated by changes in dopamine activity. Such measures might include spatial delayed response, verbal fluency, and set shifting (Dias, Robbins, & Roberts, 1996; Luciana & Collins, 1997; Vitiello et al., 1997). In contrast, psychomotor or other striatal functions would not be influenced by COMT activity. It was recently reported that children with the MET-MET genotype performed better than those with the VAL-VAL or VAL-MET genotypes on a measure of response inhibition, which has been demonstrated in other studies of children to be DA-modulated. In contrast, measures that have not been associated with prefrontal DA activity, such as self-ordered pointing, were unaffected by the COMT genotype (Diamond, Briand, Fossella, & Gehlbach, 2004).

Although these findings are intriguing, it is, of course, unlikely that PFC function can be explained by one neurochemical parameter (e.g., catabolism of DA in the synapse) or, for that matter, by a single neurotransmitter. Indeed, Egan et al. (2001) found that COMT genotype accounts for only 4% of the variation in PFC function in an adult population. Thus, it may be that interactive models might more strongly account for individual variations in PFC activity that are genetically modulated.

Another gene that expresses functional differences in dopamine receptor activity is the D4 dopamine receptor gene (DRD4), which has a variable number of tandem repeats in exon 3, a proline-rich coding region. The most common variants are 2 (DR2), 4 (DR4), and 7 (DR7) repeats. As compared with the DR2 and DR4 alleles, the DR7 repeat appears to blunt the intracellular response to dopamine (Asghari et al., 1995). D4 dopamine receptors are structurally similar to D2 receptors and are prominent in limbic brain structures. It has been suggested that D4 receptors in the shell of the nucleus accumbens modulate excitatory pathways and drug-induced sensitization (Hutchinson, LaChance, Niaura, Bryan, & Smolen, 2002; Svingos, Periasamy, & Pickel, 2000). The DRD4 genotypic variants have been examined in relation to novelty seeking, susceptibility to alcohol dependence, and reactivity to smoking cues (Hutchinson et al., 2002; Kluger, Siegfried, & Ebstein, 2002). Because of low baseline levels of DA stimulation, individuals who possess the long 7-repeat sequence may seek external activities that stimulate dopamine release and may be distracted by conditions that confer a high likelihood of encountering positive rewards.

Recently, there have been attempts to associate individual differences in dopamine receptor activity with psychopathology. For instance, a variant of the DRD4 gene has been associated with Attention-Deficit/Hyperactivity Disorder in several studies (McCracken et al., 2000; Swanson et al., 2000). This literature is complicated, and findings have not always been replicated across laboratories (Faraone, Doyle, Mick, & Biederman, 2001), which may be due in part to limitations associated with measuring single versus multiple gene effects to account for behavioral phenotypes.

Our research group has long advocated a model of behavior whereby dopamine acts as a general facilitator of information flow (leading to enhanced signal-to-noise ratios in information-processing networks), whereas serotonin (5HT) acts to regulate or constrain the tone of DA activity (Depue & Collins, 1999; Depue & Spoont, 1986; Luciana et al., 1998; Spoont, 1992). We have had a long-standing interest in dopamine-serotonin interactions with respect to limbic and cortical functions. With respect to PFC function, we have demonstrated constraint of DA-modulated spatial working memory functions by 5HT (Luciana et al., 1998), as well as 5HT modulation of affective information during working memory performance (Luciana, Burgund, Berman, & Hanson, 2001). To best understand how genetic variations in proteins that impact neurochemical transmis-

sion affect cognition, it may be more productive to examine combinations of genes (e.g., in the dopamine system) or to consider dopamine and serotonin neurotransmission from an interactive molecular genetic perspective. It is suggested here that this methodology has the potential to radically advance the developmental cognitive neuroscience of prefrontal function. In theory, there are several polymorphisms to consider in examining each transmitter system, although, as noted earlier, some have been more extensively investigated in relation to behavior than others.

For instance, a functional polymorphism in the promoter region of the 5HT transporter gene has been identified and examined in both human and primate behavioral genetic studies. Two common alleles, referred to as short (s) and long (l), in a variable repeat sequence of the gene have been differentially associated with impulsivity and negative affect in healthy people (Hariri et al., 2002). Possession of the long allele may be associated with disinhibitory behavior and may interact with dopamine genes to influence behavioral control under complex situations. Cultured cell lines that are homogeneous for the l-allele have higher concentrations of 5-HTT messenger RNA and express greater 5HT reuptake compared to cells that possess the s-allele (either heterogeneous or homogeneous variants). Humans with a similar genotype might be expected to be vulnerable to disinhibition because their higher levels of 5HT reuptake leave less serotonin available in the synapse. In contrast, humans who carry the s-allele are likely to display high levels of anxiety and fearful behavior as compared to those who are homozygous for the l-allele.

In a relatively recent study (Auerbach et al., 1999), it was reported that infants homozygous for the s-allele of the 5HT transporter gene and lacking the long repeat sequence of the DRD4 gene demonstrate maximal levels of negative emotionality and distress in daily (novel) situations. This finding could be replicated in other samples by examining DRD4 and 5HT transporter genotypes in relation to emotional characteristics, as revealed by questionnaires or behavioral tasks that require behavioral regulation. In addition, whether individuals who carry the s- versus l-alleles of the 5HT transporter vary in PFC-guided behaviors on the basis of whether they carry the MET or VAL COMT allele and/or the 7-repeat sequence of the DRD4 receptor could be investigated.

Another intriguing line of molecular genetic research concerns how genotype interacts with the environment to influence behavioral outcomes. It was recently reported that individuals who carry the s-allele of the 5HT transporter gene exhibited more objectively verified stressful life events, a higher number of depressive symptoms, and more suicidal thoughts in relation to these stressors than individuals who carry two copies of the l-allele (Caspi et al., 2003). Animal models have likewise demonstrated an interaction between the s-allele and the experience of a stressful rearing environment (peer rearing versus mother rearing) on several aspects of behavior, including alcohol preference, aggression, and hypothalamic-pituitary-adrenal activity in nonhuman primates (Barr, Schwandt, Newman, & Higley, 2004). In many cases, these associations are moderated by gender as well as age of the animal when tested.

In summary, the study of genotype-environment-behavior interactions in development, as informed by knowledge regarding the life span development of the PFC, has the potential to contribute to the nature-nurture debate by addressing how much variance in the PFC's functional development can be attributed to genetic (versus environmental) sources of influence.

Implications: Can We Identify Critical Periods in Prefrontal Cortex Development?

Overall, neurodevelopmental studies suggest the existence of two critical periods in postnatal brain and PFC development, each of which corresponds to a time of accelerated growth and synaptic refinement. One period overlaps the burst of synaptogenesis that occurs in late infancy/early childhood. It has been demonstrated that rats who are raised in impoverished learning environments have decreased synaptic density relative to those raised in more stimulating environments (Greenough & Black, 1992). In theory, the more synapses that you have and use, the less you lose later on. Hence, the other critical period corresponds to adolescence, when synaptic elimination and the progression of white matter development serve to stabilize developing information-processing networks at a functional level that will characterize most of adult life. Prior to describing the course of the PFC's apparent behavioral maturation, recent views on the functional role of the PFC are described.

THE FUNCTIONAL ROLE OF THE PREFRONTAL CORTEX

It is generally accepted that the prefrontal cortex underlies the highest level of human cognition, including planning and complex forms of goal-directed behavior. Surprisingly, PFC function has been assessed using very simple behavioral tasks, such as Jacobsen's (1935) spatial delayed response task. Numerous studies have replicated Jacobsen's

basic finding of recent memory deficits following dorsolateral prefrontal lesions (Goldman & Rosvold, 1970; Goldman-Rakic, 1987a), and many other studies have demonstrated that cells in this region are active during the delay phase of task performance (Funahashi et al., 1989; Fuster & Alexander, 1971; Niki, 1974; Sawaguchi et al., 1990a). In the monkey, lesions of the dorsolateral prefrontal cortex in the region of the principal sulcus (Brodmann's area 46) impair behavioral performance but only under delayed response conditions (Diamond & Goldman-Rakic, 1989; Goldman-Rakic, 1987a, 1987b). That is, immediate responding to reward-salient objects is not obviously affected. Spatial delayed response is also commonly referred to as *spatial working memory*. How working memory differs from other short-term forms of memory has been the subject of numerous books and articles (Baddeley, 1992; Fuster, 1997).

Working memory or "working with memory" (Moscovitch, 1992) is conceptualized as a highly active process, limited in its capacity, that requires the maintenance or manipulation of internally represented information to guide behavioral responses toward future goals (Baddeley, 1992; Fuster, 1997; Goldman-Rakic, 1987a). It involves a juxtaposition of attention, memory, and perception. For example, in the delayed response paradigm, the animal actively and effortfully works to maintain knowledge of the hidden stimulus, presumably because the stimulus object is highly desired. Given that the dorsolateral prefrontal cortex appears critical for spatial working memory performance, it was assumed for a time that all types of working memory (e.g., those that involve memory for nonspatial cues) were similarly dependent on the prefrontal cortex. Two theories are currently debated regarding whether this notion is true.

As described earlier in this chapter, the PFC can be parcellated into two general regions: the dorsal region and the ventral region. Within the dorsal and ventral areas, a further division into lateral and medial areas has been proposed. Furthermore, it has been suggested that the lateral PFC is devoted to working memory and cognitive processing (Braver & Cohen, 1999; Miller & Cohen, 2001) and that the ventromedial PFC (of which the orbitofrontal cortex is a part) controls the emotion-cognition interface (Happeney, Zelazo, & Stuss, 2004). The first theory regarding how the PFC subdivisions control behavior states that there is *domain-specific regional specialization* within the PFC (Goldman-Rakic, 1988). Accordingly, the dorsolateral prefrontal cortex in the region of the principal sulcus is critical for the representation of spatial information, and inferior regions are specialized for representing features of objects, such as their color and shape (Goldman-Rakic, 1988; Wilson, O'Scalaidhe, & Goldman-Rakic, 1993). According to this theory, the dorsal-ventral divisions of the PFC represent anterior extensions of the dorsal (spatial) and ventral (object) sensory processing pathways. This view is currently highly controversial, largely because it has not been fully supported by single unit recording and human neuroimaging studies (Miller & Cohen, 2001). Available data more strongly support a hemispheric account for how spatial versus object cues are processed in working memory. That is, the right prefrontal cortex is relatively specialized for spatial processing, and the left prefrontal cortex is specialized for nonspatial (verbal) processing (Fletcher & Henson, 2001).

A second theory, which has derived most of its support from human neuroimaging data (D'Esposito et al., 1998; Kessels, Postma, Wijnalda, & de Haan, 2000; Petrides, 1995), focuses largely on the functional specialization of the lateral PFC. It proposes regional differences in how the lateral PFC handles behaviors that demand high versus low *levels of processing*. Regardless of whether the information to be used in working memory is spatial, verbal, or object-related, the ventrolateral PFC may be recruited during low-level ("maintenance-only") tasks, whereas the dorsolateral PFC is recruited when one must not only maintain information in working memory but also manipulate it or intensively monitor performance ("maintenance-plus") tasks.

Thus, these models disagree as to whether the PFC is organized according to domain (e.g., spatial, verbal, object information) or level of processing. Both models emphasize the integral role of the lateral PFC (ventral and/or dorsal) in functions that require the cross-temporal integration of sensory cues with soon-to-be-executed responses. Other classic empirical measures that have been used to assess the integrity of similar functions in adult humans include temporal judgments (e.g., which item appeared more recently in a sequence; Milner, Corsi, & Leonard, 1991), self-ordered search tasks (Petrides & Milner, 1982), look-ahead planning tasks (Shallice, 1982), and measures of set shifting in which several different response attributes must be held simultaneously in mind and used to guide behavior in the midst of external feedback (e.g., the Wisconsin Card Sort task: Milner, 1963; Figure 7.2). When each of these tasks is dissociated into its component parts, it becomes obvious that the ability to maintain information across temporal intervals of time and link this information with appropriate responses clearly involves a number of cognitive operations, including short-term memory, attention, and the active suppression of competing information.

Given the nature of these functions, it is not surprising that another major aspect of behavior that has been associated with prefrontal functioning is behavioral inhibition, the ability to forgo immediate prepotent responding in favor of more strategic evaluative choices. As evident in the case of Phineas Gage (Harlow, 1868), damage to the anterior-most region of the PFC results in behavioral impulsivity and seeming imperviousness to socially appropriate behavior (Fuster, 1997). Experimentally, the capacity for behavioral inhibition has been assessed through variants of the go/no go task, in which the correct response to each trial is signaled by a warning stimulus that tells a research subject to either "go" (make a particular response) or "not to go" (inhibit the typical response or execute an alternative response), with the "go" response being prominent (Diamond, 2001). Other tasks that index similar functions include conflict monitoring tasks that set up a competition between prepotent responses and more effortful, but not obviously correct, ones (e.g., the Color-Word Stroop Test: Perret, 1974).

Behavioral inhibition is, in many respects, ubiquitous. It is difficult to imagine a task that does not require some level of inhibition of responses or maintenance of attention in the face of potential external or internal distractions. Adele Diamond (1990a, 1990b) has long advocated the view that the dorsolateral PFC is required when both memory and inhibitory control are simultaneously recruited by a task. Together, working memory and behavioral inhibition tasks can be said to require cognitive control over behavior. Cognitive control, as a descriptor and as a construct, is currently receiving a great deal of empirical attention in studies of PFC function.

Cognitive control is defined as the ability to flexibly shape and constrain thoughts and actions in order to accomplish goals (Bunge, Dudukovic, Thomason, Vaidya, & Gabrieli, 2002). It requires that one encode relevant environmental stimuli, select those that are appropriate based on weighing motivational signals against long-term goals, hold this important information in mind across time while ignoring extraneous distractions, select actions that are appropriate to the desired goal, and execute those actions appropriately. By definition, then, cognitive control (like working memory) is a complex construct that incorporates memory, attention, and inhibitory control. Failures of cognitive control are often associated with the presence of compelling distractors. These distractors impair one's ability to focus on long-term goals, and as a consequence, they adversely impact decision making. Because cognitive control substantially overlaps with the construct of behavioral inhibition, it tends to be assessed via the same types of conflict monitoring tasks (e.g., the Stroop Color-Word Naming Task) that require individuals to ignore irrelevant stimuli or response inhibition tasks that require the ability to inhibit prepotent response tendencies (Braver, Barch, Gray, Molfese, & Snyder, 2001; Bunge et al., 2002; Casey et al., 1998; Diamond, 1990a; Dempster, 1992; Luna et al., 2001; Ridderinkhof & van der Molen, 1997). However, the construct of cognitive control (sometimes also called "effortful control") is broader than these tasks imply, also encompassing working memory and the ability to execute decisions under highly salient emotional situations. Each of these functions relies heavily on the prefrontal cortex in conjunction with striatal, limbic, and posterior cortical regions (Casey et al., 1997; Goldman-Rakic, 1987a; Diamond, 1990a, 1990b).

As behavioral situations become more complex, the PFC must integrate activity within and across these regions. This view readily lends itself to the next major empirical and theoretical shift in the assessment of PFC function, one that posits a mechanism through which cognition and emotion interact in the service of goal-directed behavior. Cognitive control under complex conditions of high emotional salience demands a maximal level of PFC integration. This integration requires communication *within* the PFC (between its lateral and medial regions) as well as orchestration of information that is being processed within posterior cortical and subcortical regions.

The capacity of the PFC to integrate multiple sources of information and to orchestrate appropriate responses to that information is critically important from a developmental perspective. Consider, for instance, the following scenario: Imagine that you are the parent of a typical teenager. You discover that he or she attended an unchaperoned party instead of studying for the SATs. You later hear stories from other parents to suggest that there was drug and alcohol use at the party as well as sexual activity. Can you be confident in your child's ability to make safe decisions? If not, will you blame the situation? Parenting? Genes? Or are such lapses normal? One thing seems highly probable: Without adequate PFC regulation, an individual would be expected to behave based on evaluations of the immediate context. Longer-term consequences could, of course, be life-lasting, but these are not necessarily considered. Therefore, probing sources of influence over how such decisions are made during the course of development and their neural substrates has numerous public health, societal, and clinical neuroscientific implications.

From a neurobiological perspective, this situation might proceed as follows: When a child encounters positive stimuli in the form of friends and other features of a highly stimulating environment, limbic structures within the basolateral forebrain (amygdala, septum, and nucleus accumbens) are activated to encode each stimulus according to its motivational salience. While the amygdala plays a central role in tagging various stimuli according to their incentive value, the nucleus accumbens, using dopamine as its primary transmitter, translates this motivational information into behavioral actions through its connections with motor output centers in the striatum (Depue & Collins, 1999; Mogenson, Jones, & Yim, 1980). These actions might include risk-taking behaviors such as drinking alcohol and using drugs. This information is also relayed to the ventromedial prefrontal cortex, where contingencies related to positive and negative reinforcement are evaluated. That is, whether the behaviors continue will depend on evaluations of their benefits versus costs.

In parallel fashion, posterior cortical regions within the temporal and parietal lobes extract relevant stimulus cues from the environment related to stimulus features and their locations, and through interactions with the thalamus, attentional resources are directed toward these stimuli. The prefrontal cortex receives all of this information from the thalamus, sensory association regions, and the limbic-PFC interface and acts on it. If a situation is sufficiently complex, then the dorsolateral PFC (DLPFC) may be recruited to orchestrate its various inputs and to guide the appropriate selection of actions. As part of this action selection process, the DLPFC exerts inhibitory control over the nucleus accumbens-motor output interface, thereby mediating the extent to which overt behavior is swayed by motivational impulses. Thus, the DLPFC is an executive center for self-monitoring, emotional control, and action selection. It relies on the ventromedial region of the PFC for the accurate communication of data regarding environmental contingencies and whether behavioral responses must be changed in light of those contingencies.

It might be helpful at this point to interject some information regarding the ventromedial PFC (VMPFC). Depending on the species being studied, two behavioral paradigms have been commonly used to assess VMPFC activity. The first involves discrimination and reversal learning, and the second involves extinction training (Happeney et al., 2004). In reversal learning paradigms, an individual is trained through reinforcement to repeatedly select one of several stimuli, and after the individual overlearns that a given stimulus signals reward, the contingency changes such that the currently reinforced stimulus is no longer reinforced, and selection of a previously unreinforced stimulus leads to reward (Dias et al., 1996; Rolls, 1999; Rosenkilde, 1979). Extinction learning tasks are somewhat similar in that a response is reinforced until a learning criterion is met, then the reinforcement is withheld. Animals as well as humans with damage to orbitofrontal/ventromedial regions show resistance to extinction and continue to respond to the previously learned stimulus even though it is no longer being reinforced (see review by Rolls, 2004). Rolls (2004) suggests that the orbitofrontal PFC is primarily engaged when one is called on to reappraise the affective significance of stimuli and subsequently, to change behavior in the face of rapidly changing social or experiential contexts.

These findings, as well as numerous case histories similar to that of Phineas Gage's, have led researchers to focus on how the ventral and orbital regions of the PFC control motivational or affective aspects of decision making (Happeney et al., 2004). The primary challenge in this line of inquiry is to create laboratory measures that approximate the types of real-world lapses in judgment that individuals with ventral/orbital PFC lesions tend to make. One type of task, currently considered the state of the art in VMPFC assessment, presents individuals with choices that pit immediate rewards against future punishments (e.g., the Iowa Gambling Task [IGT]: Bechara, Damasio, Damasio, & Anderson, 1994). To perform successfully, one must appreciate four separate response contingencies (corresponding to four decks of cards that are simultaneously presented; see Figure 7.3), remember these contingencies over time, distinguish immediate

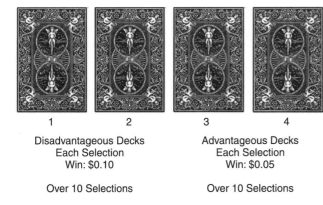

Figure 7.3 The Iowa Gambling Task requires individuals to choose from "decks" of cards to obtain monetary rewards. Two decks are advantageous in that they yield high net gains in the long run but small payoffs trial-by-trial. Two decks are disadvantageous in that they yield high net losses over time but seemingly high immediate payoffs. High-quality decision making, as assessed by the task, requires that the separate cognitive contingencies (or rules) that differentiate each deck are appreciated and that these contingencies are managed relative to the desire for high immediate rewards. It is suggested here that this task requires a high level of cognition-emotion integration that should recruit ventromedial as well as dorsolateral prefrontal regions.

from long-term outcomes, and adjust behavior accordingly. Through the use of the IGT or analogues, decision-making deficits have been identified in VMPFC patients, pathological gambling patients, and drug and alcohol abusers (Bechara, Damasio, & Damasio, 2000; Bechara, Tranel, & Damasio, 2000; Cavedini, Riboldi, Keller, D'Annucii, & Bellodi, 2002; S. Grant, Contoreggi, & London, 2000; Mazas, Finn, & Steinmetz, 2000; Rogers et al., 1999). PET scans reveal alterations in VMPFC glucose metabolism (Volkow et al., 1991).

In summary, the PFC's major function is to assist the organism in achieving behavioral control so that future goals can be attained. Available data suggest that when behavioral control is required, the DLPFC is recruited. When that control is required in the context of highly salient emotional contexts (as is typically the case in most real-life nonexperimental circumstances), the ventromedial and dorsolateral regions of the PFC must work together to regulate behavior. Because control processes are inherently integrative, requiring that multiple pieces of information are managed, our group has preferred to conceptualize them in terms of cognitive multitasking (Luciana & Nelson, 1998). What, then, is known regarding the development of these processes?

A DIMENSIONAL VIEW OF THE FUNCTIONAL DEVELOPMENT OF THE PREFRONTAL CORTEX

Available evidence suggests that cognitive control emerges dimensionally over the course of infant and child development. Recent data from our own and others' laboratories suggest that it may not asymptote until the 3rd decade of life. In the following section, several measures are referenced that have been incorporated in developmental studies. Table 7.1 includes a summary of these measures, their suggested neural correlates, and references to studies where each measure has been used. It is beyond the scope of this chapter to cover every possible test of prefrontal or executive function that has been used with developmental populations, but the following discussion highlights work that is considered classic in the field.

Infancy

Prefrontal function in the infancy period has been assessed using tasks that have rich histories in child developmental research as well as experimental neuropsychology. Surprisingly, tasks that were conceived in these seemingly disparate areas of inquiry overlap considerably in their

TABLE 7.1   Neurocognitive Measures of Prefrontal Function in Infants, Children, Adolescents, and Adults

Task Name	Applied to Age Group	What It Measures	Selected References
A-not-B Object Permanence Task	Infants	Spatial working memory	Piaget (1936); Diamond (1990a)
Object Retrieval Task	Infants	Inhibition	Diamond (1990b)
Dimensional Change Card Sort	Preschool	Set shifting	Zelazo et al. (1996)
Luria Tapping Task	Preschool	Inhibitory motor control	Luria (1966); Diamond (2001)
Day-Night Stroop Task	Preschool	Conflict monitoring; inhibition	Levin et al.,1991; Gerstadt et al. (1994)
Children's Gambling Task	Preschool	Delayed gratification	Kerr & Zelazo (2004)
Wisconsin Card Sort	Children–Adults	Set shifting; working memory	Milner (1963); Welsh et al. (1991)
Tower of Hanoi	Children–Adults	Planning; sequencing	Welsh et al. (1991)
Matching Familiar Figures Task	Children–Adults	Inhibitory control	Welsh et al. (1991)
Flanker Task	Preschool–Adult	Inhibitory control	Bunge et al. (2002); Casey et al. (1997)
Go/No Go Response Inhibition	Preschool–Adult	Inhibitiory response control	Casey et al. (1997)
Memory Span Tasks	Preschool–Adult	Memory capacity	Luciana & Nelson (1998)
Spatial Delayed Response Task	Infants–Adults	Goal-directed spatial memory	Diamond & Goldman-Rakic (1989); Luciana et al. (2005)
Intradimensional/Extradimensional Set Shifting	Preschool–Adult	Discrimination and reversal Learning; set shifting	Dias et al. (1996); Luciana & Nelson (1998); Owen et al. (1996)
Tower of London	Children–Adults	Future-directed planning	Shallice (1982); Luciana & Nelson (1998, 2002)
Spatial Self-Ordered Search	Children–Adults	Strategic searching; self-monitoring; spatial memory	Owen et al. (1990); Luciana & Nelson (1998)
Hungry Donkey Task	Children–Adults	Delayed gratificiation; reward-related decision making; contingency learning; prosocial behavior	Crone et al. (2003)
Iowa Gambling Task	Children–Adults	Delayed gratification; reward-related decision making	Bechara et al. (1994); Hooper et al. (2004); Overman et al. (2004)
Reversal Learning Tasks	Preschool–Adult	Response reappraisal and relearning of stimulus-response associations	Dias et al. (1996); Overman et al. (1996)
Resistance to Extinction	Preschool–Adult	Unlearning of previously learned associations	Happeny et al. (2004)
Spatial Delayed Recognition	Children–Adults	Recognition memory for spatial locations	Klingberg et al. (2002)
N-Back	Children–Adults	Cognitive control, inhibition, attention, working memory	Kwon et al. (2002)
Rey Auditory Verbal Learning Task	Children–Adults	Learning of a repeatedly presented word list	Sowell et al. (2001)

Note: This table is not meant to represent an all-inclusive list of tasks that have been utilized to measure frontal lobe function in individuals across the life span. However, these are measures that have been used in some of the more frequently cited studies.

demands. For instance, Adele Diamond noted a correspondence between the traditional spatial delayed response task and a measure that had been used for years in the field of child development: Piaget's (1936) A-not-B task. Piaget's AB task involves hiding an object of interest in one of two locations, in view of an infant. After a brief delay, the infant is permitted to retrieve the object. The location of hiding is varied across trials, and the infant's sense of object permanence is inferred if he or she is correct in finding the object when it is not in full view. Diamond (1990a) reported that 7- to 8-month-old infants are able to correctly retrieve objects from the first-baited location when delays are between 1 and 3 seconds in length. However, on some trials, they make the classic A-not-B error.

This error occurs over the course of two successive trials. On the first trial, the object is hidden at location A and, typically, it is successfully retrieved by the infant. On the next trial, the object is hidden at location B, again in view of the infant. The infant makes an error by searching the previously rewarded location A, despite having clearly seen that the object was hidden in a different location. This error pattern is quite robust, and the precise reason for it is one of the most thoroughly researched issues in child development. No agreement has been reached to account for the infant's behavior, which gradually improves as the infant can tolerate longer delays with increasing age. By 12 to 13 months of age, the infant can perform successfully at 10-second delays before making the A-not-B error. Because the infant performs in a manner that is similar to that of monkeys with prefrontal lesions, Diamond and Goldman-Rakic (1989; Goldman-Rakic, 1987b) suggested that infants' development of object permanence is rooted in the maturation of prefrontal regions and associated networks. If this is the case, then infants' performance patterns on A-not-B raises many puzzling issues.

For instance, one anomaly is that performance in human infants is dependent on the response mode employed (Diamond, 1990a, 1990b, 2001). When accuracy of performance is measured by direction of gaze rather than by reaching behavior, infants often appear to "know" the correct location of the hidden object even when their manual responses are incorrect. Correct performance can also be facilitated by shortening the delay interval, by allowing the infant to physically orient himself or herself toward the correct location, by using landmarks to target the correct hiding location, or by using a minimal number of hiding locations. In 9-month-olds, the number of A-trial presentations influences whether or not an error is made at the first B-trial presentation (Marcovitch, Zelazo, & Schmuckler, 2002). Indeed, what these findings seem to demonstrate is that when the task is altered in ways that decrease the demands for cognitive control, or multitasking, performance improves.

A second task in which performance accelerates at the same rate as delayed response in human infants is the *object retrieval* task (Diamond, 1990b, 2001). In this task, a desired object is placed inside a clear-sided box that has an opening only on one side. The infant's task is to retrieve the object. When the infant sees the toy directly through the open side, he or she is able to reach correctly to retrieve it. However, if the infant views the toy through a clear but occluded side, he or she exhibits a preferential tendency to try to reach through the occluded side to retrieve the toy. Hence, to perform the task correctly, the infant must inhibit this prepotent response tendency, disengage his or her

reaching behavior from his or her looking behavior, manipulate the box, and reach through its open side to retrieve the toy. This sequence requires the infant to integrate the conflicting demands of looking versus reaching behavior (Diamond, 1990b, 2001).

Individual human infants and infant rhesus macaques develop the skills necessary to perform both A-not-B and the object retrieval task at the same rate over the same developmental period of time (between 6 and 12 months in human infants and 2 to 4 months in macaques; Diamond, 1990a, 1990b; Diamond & Goldman-Rakic, 1989). Moreover, improved performance on both tasks in human infants correlates with changes in frontal EEG activity (Bell & Fox, 1992, 1997). Diamond (1990a, 1990b) suggested on the basis of these data that the dorsolateral prefrontal cortex is engaged when both inhibitory control and memory are required in the same behavior.

To summarize, Diamond's classic studies, which have relied on an integration of animal, developmental, and neuropsychological methods, suggest that the prefrontal cortex is behaviorally engaged in the monkey and human beginning in late infancy. By the time children reach preschool age, the tasks that have been informative in mapping the infant's initial expression of cognitive control processes are no longer challenging. Therefore, it has been necessary to develop slightly more complex measures to measure cognitive changes in preschool and school-age children.

Preschool and Middle Childhood

These measures have included set-shifting tasks, measures of behavioral conflict resolution, and attention tasks. When healthy adults perform set-shifting tasks such as the Wisconsin Card Sort, they are able to correctly sort cards that vary on at least three stimulus attributes (color, number, and/or shape) in response to verbal feedback. Children are unable to manage this level of complexity. On a less-demanding but analogous measure of set shifting, the *dimensional-change card sort,* it was found that 3-year-old children were able to correctly sort cards based on the first of two possible criteria that they were given. They were capable of making either conceptualization when it was presented first. However, when they were required to shift set and sort the cards using the second stimulus attribute, they persisted in sorting according to the first dimension (Kirkham & Diamond, 1999; Zelazo, Frye, & Rapus, 1996).

Thus, the ability to appreciate at least two stimulus attributes that jointly apply to objects (e.g., that the object can be referenced by either its color or its shape) is present by age 3. However, holding both attributes in mind at the same time and shifting between them is difficult. Between the ages of 3 and 6, children become progressively more adept at the task, first succeeding when they must switch between two sorting criteria at ages 4 to 5, and then becoming able to sort among three possible criteria by the age of 6. Again, children's performance on this task illustrates that the capacity for cognitive multitasking increases in a dimensional fashion in preschoolers.

The same general trend is evident for other aspects of behavioral inhibition, as exemplified by an analogue of the Stroop Color-Word Task. This task, called the Day-Night Stroop Task, was first used by Levin (Levin et al., 1991) but then modified in Adele Diamond's laboratory (Gerstadt, Hong, & Diamond, 1994). In the conventional Stroop task, individuals must read words that consist of color names (e.g., BLUE, RED, GREEN). Conflict is created by printing the words in colored fonts that are different from the word meanings (e.g., the word BLUE printed in green ink). In the Day-Night Stroop, children must respond to two cards, one of which illustrates a picture of the sun and the other that illustrates the moon. The conflict condition occurs when children are required to say "night" in response to the sun and "day" when presented with the picture of the moon. This simplified task variant eliminates the reading ability that is necessary to complete the adult version, thus reducing the child's information-processing load. The Day-Night Stroop is difficult for 3- to 4-year-olds but relatively easy for 6- to 7-year-olds. Similarly, on measures of motor inhibition (e.g., Luria's tapping task: Luria, 1966), children perform at a similar rate as on the Day-Night Stroop, improving in their speed and accuracy between the ages of 3 and 7 years (see Diamond, 2001; Diamond & Taylor, 1996; Passler, Isaac, & Hynd, 1985). Thus, through the preschool period, abilities that are apparently dependent on the PFC become increasingly well-developed, although those items and/or tasks that differentiate among children of different ages demand relatively little in the way of multitasking ability (at least as viewed from an adult perspective).

This steady developmental progression continues during middle childhood. Welsh, Pennington, and Groisser (1991) studied 110 children between the ages of 3 and 12 years using a battery of executive function measures, including visual search, verbal fluency, motor planning, the Tower of Hanoi, the Wisconsin Card Sort, and the Matching Familiar Figures test. On the more difficult tasks, including the Wisconsin Card Sort and 4-disk Tower of Hanoi tasks, an adult level of performance was reached between 10 years

(Wisconsin Card Sort) and adolescence (Tower of Hanoi, verbal fluency, and motor sequencing).

Most studies have relied on the nature of their experimental tasks to infer brain-behavior relations in children. However, Bunge et al. (2002) expanded on this general approach by examining patterns of brain activation in children, as compared to adults, who were administered measures of cognitive control. They reported inferior performance in 8- to 12-year-old children as compared to adults on no-go and incongruent trials of a flanker task.

The flanker task generally proceeded as follows. Flankers are arrows that point either to the left or to the right. On each trial, children viewed five stimuli (arrows) arranged in a row. The middle stimulus was a flanker that pointed right or left, and the general task was to look at the middle arrow to decide whether to push a response button that was on the left or the right. The other stimuli serve as distractors. On congruent trials, a right-sided button was pressed if the arrow pointed right, and a left-sided button was pressed if the arrow pointed left. On incongruent trials, the task was to respond in the direction opposite to where the arrow pointed. Finally, on no-go trials, subjects were asked to refrain from responding.

Children demonstrated a greater interference effect as indicated by slower response times across all task conditions. In adults, interference suppression activated the right ventrolateral PFC, the anterior insula, inferior parietal lobule, and putamen. In children, the left ventrolateral PFC and insula were activated along with the right inferior parietal lobule. In children, better task performers exhibited greater left PFC activation. In adults, response inhibition activated a number of PFC regions, including the bilateral ventrolateral and dorsolateral regions as well as the anterior and posterior cingulate, but these areas were not significantly activated in children as a whole. However, children who performed particularly well activated a subset of the same regions that were activated in adults.

Hence, interference suppression, strongly modulated by the anterior insular cortex, may mature to adult patterns of brain activity more quickly than response inhibition, mediated by a distributed network that includes the lateral PFC and anterior cingulate. Other studies have demonstrated robust activation of the lateral PFC in prepubescent children during response inhibition (Casey et al., 1997; Vaidya et al., 1998). However, because the study by Bunge et al. (2002) found substantial differences in 8- to 12-year-olds versus young adults, a major transition in the capacity for cognitive control may occur between the ages of 12 and 19. Similarly, Tamm, Menon, and Reiss (2002) studied go/no go performance in a small (*n* = 19) sample of 8- to 20-year-olds and found that, although age did not predict absolute accuracy of performance, it was related to performance speed or efficiency in inhibitory control. Moreover, as compared to younger subjects who activated extensive regions of the dorsolateral PFC while they performed the task, older ones showed a more focal and more restricted pattern of activation.

Interpretation across studies and across age groups is complicated by the fact that few measures of cognitive control can be (or have been) applied without alteration to children in all phases of development. Our laboratory has attempted to remedy this difficulty by using an automated task battery that not only has been investigated according to its brain-behavior correlates but includes measures that can be interpreted from a dimensional perspective.

Computerized Assessments of Frontal Lobe Function

We recently used the Cambridge Neuropsychological Testing Automated Battery (CANTAB) to study PFC functions in children ages 4 to 12 years as compared to young adults (Luciana, 2002; Luciana & Nelson, 1998, 2002). The CANTAB is a computerized neuropsychological assessment battery that was originally developed to diagnose dementia in elderly individuals (Sahakian & Owen, 1992). The most current version operates through the Windows operating system and utilizes touch screen technology. The battery consists of 13 subtests that include measures of motor skill, visual attention, memory, and working memory. All task stimuli are nonverbal, being geometric designs and simple shapes, and language proficiency is necessary only to understand the instructions prior to task initiation. The validity of the CANTAB for assessing brain-behavior relations in adults has been supported by numerous studies of patients with brain lesions, degenerative disorders, and psychiatric illness (Fowler, Saling, Conway, Semple, & Louis, 1997; Owen, Iddon, Hodges, Summers, & Robbins, 1997; Owen, Roberts, Polkey, Sahakian, & Robbins, 1991; Rahman, Robbins, & Sahakian, 1999). The impacts of psychopharmacological treatments on performance have also been examined (Coull, Middleton, Robbins, & Sahakian, 1995; Elliott et al., 1997; Lange et al., 1992). Recently, fMRI and PET have provided information regarding the neural substrates underlying adults' performance on several tasks (A. C. H. Lee, Owen, Rogers, Sahakian, & Robbins, 2000). These findings indicate that the CANTAB is sensitive to the presence of brain dysfunction in adults and that discrimination among subtypes of brain disorder is possible using profile interpretation. For

example, patients with frontal versus temporal lobe pathology differ in their performance on CANTAB's measures of working and recognition memory (Owen, Morris, Sahakian, Polkey, & Robbins, 1996; Owen, Sahakian, Semple, Polkey, & Robbins, 1995).

An even more recent development has been the use of the CANTAB to study neuropsychological function in pediatric populations (Hughes, Russell, & Robbins, 1994; Luciana, Lindeke, Georgieff, Mills, & Nelson, 1999; Luciana & Nelson, 1998, 2000, 2001; Luciana, Sullivan, & Nelson, 2001; Ozonoff, 2001). The battery has generated interest among developmental cognitive neuroscientists primarily because it emphasizes the assessment of executive functioning, including measures of planning, set shifting, spatial working memory (self-ordered search), and nonverbal memory span. We examined the feasibility of using the CANTAB to assess executive functions in a large healthy pediatric sample with the initial goal of determining the age limits of the battery's use and whether it could be administered without alteration to children. Nearly 400 typically developing children between the ages of 4 and 12 years were tested (Luciana & Nelson, 1998, 2002). Six of 13 subtests from the CANTAB were administered. In general, children found the computerized testing format motivating, and task performance was comparable in children who were native versus nonnative English speakers when English was the language used to present each task (Luciana & Nelson, 2000, 2002). A significant strength of the battery is that children can be tested on the same tests and using exactly the same item sets that are employed in adult studies. Thus, across laboratories, this battery has been successfully used, without modification, to measure cognitive functions in individuals from age 4 to over 90 years. This feature permits complex cognitive functions to be dimensionally measured from the time they are first emerging to the time when they are maximal in processing multiple pieces of information to the time when they decline due to aging. In addition, trajectories across different tasks (e.g., the life span development of planning versus the development of recognition memory) can be examined and compared within and between age groups.

Our data indicate that planning and working memory skills have not reached adult levels by the age of 12 years based on analyses of the self-ordered search and Tower of London tasks. These tasks are selected for discussion because they are relatively complex in their demands and require high levels of cognitive control for performance to be successful. Self-ordered tasks were first described by Petrides and Milner (1982) in their studies of neurological patients with frontal lobe lesions. On the CANTAB's self-ordered search task, an examinee is presented with an array of squares and told to find tokens that are hidden within the squares. The search is conducted by touching a square to "open" it. Sometimes the square is empty, and sometimes it contains a colored token. Each square is baited only once, but the examinee does not know, after any given selection, where the next token will appear. A return to an already-baited location constitutes an error. Thus, efficiency of searching is required, as is memory for locations that have been successfully searched. The task ranges in difficulty from two-item searches, generally very easy even for 4-year-olds, to eight-item searches that healthy young adults find challenging. Moreover, a strategy score is derived based on how well the examinee is able to conduct each search sequence in an organized way (Owen, Morris, Sahakian, Polkey, & Robbins, 1996). Both frontal and temporal lobe lesions are associated with mnemonic errors, but deficient strategy use has been exclusively associated with frontal lobe impairment in neurological patients (Owen, Morris, et al., 1996). When an efficient strategy is utilized, the mnemonic demands of the task are minimized. Accordingly, individuals with less than optimal functioning of the frontal lobe must depend more heavily on their memory skills in progressing through searches that involve large item sets. As expected, in healthy adults, memory span is inversely correlated with the number of forgetting errors on the task.

The Tower of London is a planning task. It requires the test taker to move colored balls, adhering to a set of rules regarding how the balls can be moved, to match a display model. At the beginning of each trial, the participant is told how many moves are minimally needed to solve that problem. The primary variable of interest is the number of problems that can be solved in the minimum possible number of moves (Shallice, 1982). The CANTAB version of the task includes problems that range in difficulty from two to five moves. In theory, one must take some time to plan the first move to solve each problem efficiently. Planning times are also calculated.

The Tower of London and self-ordered search tasks are similar in that they both require behavioral organization and/or self-monitoring to complete their most difficult items with maximal efficiency. Children's performance on both tasks has been informative as to the course of PFC maturation. First, 4- to 12-year-old children are able to complete the easiest (2- and 3-item search) trials of the self-ordered search task in a manner that is not statistically distinct from adult performance, verifying that executive skill is present by the age of 4 years. However, by adminis-

tering the task in its entirety, it is evident that several important behavioral distinctions are not evident until the most difficult (6- and 8-item search) trials are examined. By the age of 12 years, children still have not reached adult levels of task performance on these items in terms of error scores or strategy use. This finding is consistent with other reports regarding the neuropsychological development of frontal lobe functions in pubescent children (Passler et al., 1985; Welsh, Pennington, & Groisser, 1991) and with the theorized emergence of formal operational thought in early adolescence (Inhelder & Piaget, 1958). The same pattern of performance is demonstrated on the Tower of London task in terms of the ability to solve the most difficult (5-move) problems in a maximally efficient manner.

On the basis of these findings, our group suggested that future studies should focus on cohorts of adolescents in the pre- to postpubertal transition, as compared to adults, to identify when adult levels of competence are reached under conditions that demand a high level of information processing and self-organization. Arguably, these are the conditions that best approximate real-world situations that challenge an individual's capacities for cognitive control.

Adolescence to Young Adulthood

There are surprisingly few comprehensive studies that have assessed working memory and cognitive control processes in adolescents between the ages of 12 and 20 years. The frequently cited conclusion that these functions reach maturity during adolescence is largely derived from studies such as the Welsh et al. (1991) and Luciana and Nelson (2002) studies that report performance differences between prepubescent children and young adults. What is known is that a number of brain changes are occurring during the adolescent period and that because of the nature of these changes, improvements in executive control (presumed to be PFC-mediated in adults) are expected. For instance, the PFC undergoes continued structural and neurochemical refinement during adolescence (Chugani, 1998; Spear, 2000). Although gross structure and overall brain volume are relatively stable by the age of 5 years (Giedd et al., 1996; Paus et al., 2001; Reiss, Abrams, Singer, Ross, & Denckla, 1996), neuroimaging studies in humans and histological studies of animals consistently indicate that adolescence is characterized by gray matter loss in numerous areas of the cortex and that such loss is consistent with synaptic pruning (Giedd et al., 1999; Pfefferbaum et al., 1994; Sowell, Thompson, Tessner, & Toga, 2001). Sowell and colleagues (Sowell, Thompson, et al., 2001; Sowell et al., 2003) have demonstrated that gray matter loss in the PFC occurs at a more protracted rate than similar loss in the parietal cortex. At the same time, white matter development, particularly myelination, also continues throughout adolescence (Caviness, Kennedy, Richelme, Rademacher, & Filipek, 1996; Giedd et al., 1999; Pfefferbaum et al., 1994) and may be particularly pronounced in the frontal lobe (Reiss et al., 1996).

Unfortunately, there have been few attempts to directly link these structural changes with functional developments. Sowell, Delis, Stiles, and Jernigan (2001) reported that frontal gray matter decline predicted delayed verbal memory performance as well as visuospatial memory in 35 children age 7 to 16 years. In addition, recent functional neuroimaging studies have suggested that changes in PFC activity and metabolism might underlie working memory improvements. For instance, Klingberg, Forssberg, and Westerberg (2002) measured brain activity in 14 subjects age 9 to 18 years while they performed a spatial delayed recognition task under low versus high memory load conditions. They reported activation in superior and middle frontal regions, as well as regions of the parietal lobe, that increased with age and working memory capacity. Similarly, Kwon, Reiss, and Menon (2002) reported age-related increases in PFC activation associated with visuospatial 2-back performance in 23 subjects age 7 to 22 years. Despite these intriguing reports, it remains the case that few studies have comprehensively examined the normative development of executive working memory processes in larger samples of individuals spanning the age range from early adolescence to young adulthood.

One expectation is that adolescents will demonstrate a progressive ability to integrate multiple sources of information on tasks requiring memory, cross-temporal response selection, and strategic organization. To test this hypothesis, our lab is utilizing a battery of tasks, some experimental and some borrowed from clinical neuropsychology, that we have ordered based on the level of multitasking (low, moderate, and high) required for each task (Luciana, Conklin, Hooper, & Yarger, 2005). Our ordering scheme is based on the empirical literature on working memory and cognitive control, as described in the previous section. Much of the description that follows is based on Luciana et al., 2005.

At the low end of the hierarchy is a passive recognition memory task, implemented for discriminant validity purposes, that requires individuals to encode and then recognize neutrally posed human faces after a brief delay interval. Next is a spatial delayed response task (Goldman-Rakic, 1987a) that is known to be associated with PFC activation in primates. Spatial memory span,

using the Corsi Block Task (Milner, 1971), was implemented next, because its backward response condition requires the maintenance plus manipulation of multiple spatial locations in memory. Finally, a computerized self-ordered search task is used to assess strategic self-monitoring in the context of visuospatial memory (Owen, Downes, Sahakian, Polkey, & Robbins, 1990; Owen, Doyon, Petrides, & Evans, 1996; Owen, Evans, & Petrides, 1996). Because executive control processes have been recently linked with fluid aspects of global intellectual function (IQ; Gray, Chabris, & Braver, 2003), IQ is also measured.

One initial hypothesis was that adolescents would succeed at passively recognizing information before they would succeed at recall-guided action. Indeed, it was expected that recognition memory would not show pronounced development during adolescence, consistent with findings from other studies (Luciana & Nelson, 1998; Nelson, 1995). In the domain of recall, execution of an action based on the recall of a single unit of information was hypothesized to stabilize in development prior to the execution of actions based on the recall of multiple units. Recall-guided actions that occur in a fixed sequence would precede actions that must be recalled and then reordered. Finally, recall-guided reordering of information would precede the ability to strategically self-organize responses to multiple units of information in a more flexible manner.

It was expected that IQ would be unrelated to these developmental trends. Thus, consistent with our view of executive working memory as a dimensional hierarchical construct, it was expected that in the domain of nonverbal working memory, passive recognition memory would cease to show pronounced age-related change prior to adolescence, followed, in a staggered fashion, by the more active recall-guided tasks of simple delayed response, forward spatial memory span, backward spatial memory span, and strategic spatial self-organization.

This study relied on a convenience sample of families whose contact information is maintained by our Institute of Child Development in an ongoing research database. A medical and demographic history was obtained from parents through use of a structured interview questionnaire. Participants ranged in age from 9 to 17 years ($M = 12.51$, $SD = 2.93$ years), roughly balanced by gender. The sample is largely Caucasian and middle to upper middle class based on levels of parental education and family income. General intelligence, as estimated from selected subtasks of the age-appropriate version of the Wechsler Intelligence Scales (Wechsler, 1991, 1997), indicates that the sample is above average in IQ. Equal numbers of participants have not been studied in all age groups between 9 and 17, but all age groups have been sampled.

Our findings indicate that executive aspects of spatial working memory are developing well into the adolescent period in a dimensional hierarchical manner independent of general intellect. When recall must be used to strategically organize behavior (self-ordered search), development is evident up to the age of 16 years and remains stable through the age range studied. Self-ordered search errors for 6 to 8 items were converted into z-scores and are graphed in Figure 7.4 to illustrate this trend. De Luca et al. (2003) recently demonstrated that performance on the CANTAB's self-ordered search task is maximal (based on error scores) in 15- to 19- and 20- to 29-year-olds, as these groups perform better than 8- to 10-, 11- to 14-, and 50- to 64-year-olds. Their 20- to 29-year-old group also achieved the best strategy scores, which were significantly better than those produced by 8- to 10- and 50- to 64-year-olds. Similarly, De Luca et al. showed that on the Tower of London, 15- to 19- and 20- to 29-year-olds achieved significantly more perfect solutions than did 8- to 14-year-olds.

A task that required relatively simplified spatial working memory demands, the spatial delayed response task, did not index developmental changes in our study after ages 11 to 12. Recognition memory for nonverbal (face) stimuli appears to mature early, as performance did not significantly change during this broad developmental period. This pattern suggests that this ability stabilizes prior to age 9 years, consistent with what has been reported for other

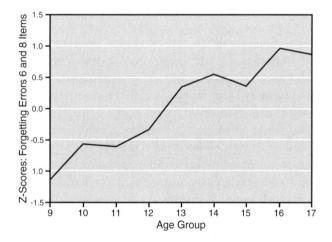

Figure 7.4 Values represent z-scores of summed forgetting errors for 6 to 8 item searches on CANTAB's spatial self-ordered search task in healthy individuals between the ages of 9 and 17 years. The ability to self-order searches of this type, perceived as relatively difficult by healthy young adults, appears to rapidly accelerate between the ages of 10 and 14 years and to plateau by age 17.

forms of nonverbal recognition memory (Luciana & Nelson, 1998, 2002). Spatial memory span showed an intermediate pattern, with development continuing up to age 13. Thus, when nonverbal working memory is deconstructed into its relevant task demands, an orderly developmental progression in skill appears evident, and this progression is paralleled by findings from the neurodevelopment literature. These findings suggest two major implications, one related to the maturation of distinct PFC regions and the other related to the organization of the prefrontal cortex by level of processing.

Maturation of Distinct Lateral Prefrontal Cortex Regions

Recognition memory has been traditionally thought to be reliant on temporal lobe memory systems regardless of the type of information that must be processed (Nelson, 1995). However, recent studies indicate that, depending on the paradigm used, recognition memory might also recruit the PFC (Petrides, 1995). Petrides found that the ventrolateral frontal cortex was activated when subjects were required to make active judgments about the familiarity of recently presented visual stimuli. The observed activation was enhanced relative to what was observed when either novel or familiar stimuli were presented and encoded in the absence of mnemonic judgments. Thus, the maintenance component of delayed-match-to-sample tasks might depend partly on the ventrolateral prefrontal cortex. However, the working memory and executive demands of the face recognition task used in our study are low (see Luciana et al., 2005). Although a delay interval was introduced, specific *responses* did not have to be held in mind over that delay. Instead, the major task was to correctly encode stimuli as they are presented, because a range of possible alternatives, including the correct one, could be reviewed prior to retrieval and response selection.

The spatial delayed response task appears to more distinctly depend on the dorsolateral prefrontal cortex in nonhuman primates (Goldman-Rakic, 1987a). A network of structures including the inferior parietal lobe, the dorsomedial thalamus, the caudate nucleus, the superior colliculus, and the hippocampus promotes successful task performance (Selemon & Goldman-Rakic, 1988). In particular, the inferior parietal lobe has the role of mapping the coordinates of spatially relevant targets in extrapersonal space, and the dorsolateral prefrontal cortex not only maintains these coordinates over time but relays this information to motor output regions so that a response can be executed at the appropriate time. Unlike recognition memory tasks, this task requires accurate encoding of the target's location in space, formulating a response based on this location, holding this recall-guided response information in mind over a delay interval, then carefully executing the response. Performance accuracy is measured with precision, at the pixel level. However, despite the animal literature, it is not possible to know whether this visuomanual task activates the PFC in humans and, if so, which subregion is critical for performance. This uncertainty is due to technical limitations imposed by neuroimaging. The task cannot be administered without a substantial modification that biases it in favor of a demand for recognition versus recall. One commonly implemented paradigm is for human subjects to view a spatial target, after which a delay interval is imposed. Then a second screen appears, consisting of the previously seen target as well as a number of distractors. One of the items on the second screen is highlighted, and the participant must indicate with a yes/no response whether the highlighted item is the same as the one he or she previously saw (Belger et al., 1998; Jonides et al., 1993). Thus, the mnemonic-motor integration that is demanded during the delay interval when the task is administered under visuomanual response conditions is absent. Whether spatial maintenance measured in this manner activates the DLPFC is currently debated. Some studies do not find PFC activation but instead report that the task relies on a network of structures in the posterior right hemisphere, including the inferior parietal lobe.

Despite the motoric demands that distinguish it from most similar tasks used in neuroimaging contexts, our spatial delayed response task is largely a maintenance-only (D'Esposito & Postle, 1999) task. One stimulus must be held in mind over a delay interval. As the delay increases, there is an increasing endogenous demand on inhibitory control mechanisms to resist distractions. The task should, as the animal literature suggests, recruit executive processing that is PFC-mediated, particularly as delay intervals become longer. However, it may be that the task is more strongly associated with ventrolateral (versus dorsolateral) PFC function in humans as opposed to animals.

PET has been used to demonstrate that forward spatial memory span activates a network of right hemisphere structures, including the ventrolateral PFC (Owen, Evans, et al., 1996). In contrast, tasks that require backward memory span, whether the stimuli are verbal or spatial, appear to activate areas of the ventrolateral but also dorsolateral PFC (Owen, 1997). We found similar age-related influences on forward and backward span in our study, which was unexpected. It may be the case that finer task-related distinctions would have been observed had we had a large enough sample to attempt to distinguish performance among each age group from 9 to 17 years.

The most demanding purely cognitive task in our battery is the spatial self-ordered search task, which requires response selection, memory, continuous updating of information, and a high degree of executive control. It also demands self-monitoring and formulation of a strategy, a task variable that has been shown to be specifically impaired in neurological patients with frontal, but not temporal, lobe lesions (Owen, Morris, et al., 1996).

The development of these skills, when demanded simultaneously, shows a protracted and extended course up to the age of 16 years. Our sample of 16- to 17-year-olds did not differ from slightly older (18- to 20-year-old) adults (Luciana et al., 2005), consistent with findings from a recent study where 15- to 19-year-olds were reported to perform similarly to 20- to 29-year-olds on this task (De Luca et al., 2003). As this type of task strongly recruits activity in the middorsolateral prefrontal cortex based on recent neuroimaging (PET; A. C. H. Lee et al., 2000; Owen, Doyon, et al., 1996; Owen, Evans, et al., 1996) and lesion (Petrides, 2000) studies, we and others have suggested that executive control is primarily mediated by this region. Overall, the pattern of findings that we observed suggests that different PFC regions reach functional maturity at different rates, with the ventrolateral region maturing prior to the dorsolateral region, which is responsible for the highest level of executive control over information processing.

Implications for Prefrontal Cortex Organization According to Processing Demand

The data presented here support behavioral development of working memory functions within the spatial domain according to level of processing demand. If the PFC is unified to promote working memory processes regardless of stimulus domain, then similar developmental trajectories should be evident for verbal and spatial tasks that have equivalent processing demands. However, if level of processing is distinctly modulated by different PFC regions, then tasks may dissociate across stimulus modalities according to their demands for executive control. These hypotheses remain to be tested in combined behavioral and neuroimaging protocols.

Cognition-Emotion Interactions and Development of the Ventromedial Prefrontal Cortex

These findings are compelling in providing evidence that the lateral PFC continues to mature well into adolescence, corresponding to the time period when myelination is progressively increasing and synaptic efficiency is improving due to the pruning back of unused connections. However, to some extent, the tasks that have just been described are somewhat "dry" and seemingly removed from the type of information processing that is demanded in daily social contexts. Such tasks have been described in terms of "cool" versus "hot" measures of cognition (Metcalfe, 2000). Hot measures of cognition include those tasks that have been described in this chapter in relation to the ventral/orbital region of the PFC.

It is only relatively recently that the functional development of the VMPFC has been investigated. Some studies (reviewed by Happeney et al., 2004) have demonstrated decreases in resistance to extinction in preschool-age children, but this phenomenon has not been thoroughly investigated. On the other hand, age-related improvements in reversal learning capacity have been described for a number of years, with an intriguing suggestion of gender differences in the rate of development of this behavior (Overman, Bachevalier, Schuhmann, & Ryan, 1996; Reavis & Overman, 2001). Infant boys (younger than 30 months) outperform girls, a finding that is consistent with evidence for developmental differences in gonadal hormones in the orbitofrontal region that might limit females' rate of learning on such tasks (Clark & Goldman-Rakic, 1989).

As mentioned earlier, the Iowa Gambling Task and similar measures are currently viewed as state of the art in VMPFC assessment because they add a strong motivational element to an otherwise complex information-processing task (see Figure 7.3). On each trial of the IGT, the test taker must select from one of four decks of cards, presented on a computer screen. After each selection, feedback is provided indicating that a certain amount of money has been won and, perhaps, also that a certain amount has been lost. Participants are instructed to attempt to win as much money as possible. Two of the decks, termed "disadvantageous decks," yield high immediate payoffs and are therefore quite compelling. However, over the course of trials, these decks will ultimately result in net loss versus gain. The other two decks, termed "advantageous decks," yield smaller immediate payoffs and can seem less compelling in the short term. However, over successive trials, choosing from these decks leads to net gains versus losses. The overall number of advantageous choices minus the number of disadvantageous choices is a measure of decision making that is directed by an appreciation of future, versus immediate, consequences. Although it has not been discussed in terms of its cognitive control or multitasking requirements, the IGT requires a lot of information to be simultaneously processed and utilized to direct future actions.

Kerr and Zelazo (2004) developed an analogue of the IGT that can be reliably administered to preschool-age children. This task utilizes two cards instead of four. Four-year-olds were found to make more advantageous decisions than 3-year-olds. Using a version of the task more similar to the original, Garon and Moore (2004) reported superior performance in 6-year-olds as compared to younger (3- to 4-year-old) children. Intriguingly, there is some suggestion in these studies of very young children that males exhibit superior performance on the task, a phenomenon that has also been reported in adults (Reavis & Overman, 2001).

IGT performance has also been compared in healthy individuals versus children and adolescents with externalizing psychopathology. Blair, Colledge, and Mitchell (2001) studied boys, ages 9 to 16 years, who had histories of behavioral difficulties and who were divided into two groups based on their scores on a measure of psychopathy. A main effect of age was reported: Older children chose more advantageously than younger children as the task progressed. Regardless of age, those with higher psychopathic tendencies chose more from disadvantageous decks, particularly later in the trial sequence. Another study (Ernst et al., 2003) examined IGT performance in 12- to 14-year-old adolescents with and without behavior disorders (ADHD or Conduct Disorder) as compared to healthy adults. No performance differences were found between healthy adolescents and healthy adults, but adolescents with and without behavioral disorders differed from one another. The IGT was administered twice to each participant, with 1 week separating the two administrations. Most of the differences between the two adolescent groups were found in the second administration. Specifically, the healthy adolescents had much higher scores in the second administration than the first, although this was not the case for the adolescents with behavior disorders.

Another recent study (Crone, Vendel, & van der Molen, 2003) examined age-related differences in performance on an analogue of the IGT (the Hungry Donkey Task) in 12- to 25-year-olds in relation to measures of cognitive and behavioral inhibition. The Hungry Donkey Task used a similar schedule of rewards and punishments as the conventional version of the IGT (Bechara et al., 1994), but rather than picking cards to win play money or to win actual money for themselves, the children were asked to open doors to find apples to feed a hungry donkey. Crone and colleagues found that Hungry Donkey Task performance was related to self-reported levels of cognitive inhibition. Protracted development of performance on the Hungry Donkey Task was also reported, in that adults (ages 18 to 25) made more advantageous choices than a group of 12- to 17-year-olds. In addition to these reports, two labs have assessed the adolescent development of IGT performance (Hooper, Luciana, Conklin, & Yarger, 2004; Overman et al., 2004).

Overman and colleagues (2004) found steady improvement on the task from sixth grade to adulthood, with differential patterns of performance evident in males versus females. Females tended to choose cards that maximized both immediate and long-term gain. Males tended to choose cards based more exclusively on their potential for long-term gain. Our group's findings were that 14- to 17-year-olds made more advantageous choices than did younger age groups on the IGT, particularly in the last two trial blocks. However, the 14- to 17-year-olds in our study performed worse than adults who have served as control subjects in other reports (Hooper et al., 2004). We also found no relation between IGT performance and performance on other measures of PFC function, such as response inhibition and working memory. Finally, although we did not find that males outperformed females on the task, we did observe gender differences in deck preferences. Specifically, females were more likely to choose from decks that yielded infrequent punishments, regardless of the magnitude of the reward associated with a given deck.

Figure 7.5 depicts adolescents' performance on the IGT relative to that of both younger children and young adults. As is evident in the figure, the skills necessary to perform the IGT with maximal efficiency appear to be developing even after the age of 17 years. Because we have not studied adults' performance as they progress into their 20s and 30s, the upper limit of this developmental progression is not known.

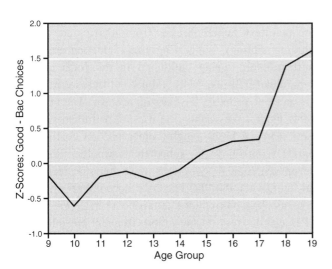

Figure 7.5 Adolescents' performance on the Iowa Gambling Task illustrates a steady developmental progression in decision-making skills that appears to accelerate after the age of 17.

Overall, these are compelling findings from the standpoint of the development of multitasking skills and the development of cognition-emotion interactions. In theory, the relatively "deficient" performance of 17-year-old adolescents on the IGT could be due to the fact that the dorsolateral PFC is challenged to mediate the cognition-emotion interface and falls somewhat short due to developmental constraints on its multitasking capacities. Whether this constraint is imposed by lack of dorsolateral PFC maturation, lack of ventromedial maturation, or the connections between them is a matter for further empirical study.

Summary

The normative development of PFC-guided behaviors has been investigated through a combination of behavioral experiments, animal lesion studies, and neuroimaging investigations. These studies converge to suggest a dimensional course of PFC development. Rudimentary levels of multitasking skill emerge late in infancy, coincident with locomotor initiation. Progressively more information can be managed and appropriately acted on during the preschool period and extending into middle childhood. Most recently, it has been suggested by neuroimaging and neurobehavioral studies that adolescence may represent a critical period in PFC maturation. This may be particularly true if the PFC must juggle both cognitive and emotional task contingencies. When multitasking is demanded in the context of high emotional salience, the PFC appears unable to respond with maximal efficiency even late in the 2nd decade of life.

INDIVIDUAL DIFFERENCES AND VULNERABILITY TO PATHOLOGY

Understanding the PFC's mediation of multitasking from a dimensional perspective holds a great deal of explanatory power. For the PFC to be taxed in its ability to orchestrate behavior, the multitasking that is demanded by a situation must exceed some critical threshold. That is, *the same situational context (or behavioral task) will not necessarily recruit the same degree of PFC activity in all people at all times.* Moreover, we know from neuroimaging studies that once a task becomes too demanding, the dorsolateral PFC more or less shuts down (Callicott et al., 1999). Thus, within an individually determined situational range, defined by an activation threshold or "on" switch at the low end and by some as yet undetermined overload indicator at the high end, the PFC effortfully works to process information that presents a challenge to the individual. Next, how neural insult or individual differences in neurochemistry might impact the PFC's processing mechanisms is considered. This discussion highlights three disorders, each of which differentially expresses (1) a developmentally mediated risk for psychopathology, (2) hypothesized dysfunction of the prefrontal cortex, and (3) neurochemical dysregulation that involves the dopamine system and its projections to the PFC, among other brain regions.

Schizophrenia: Aberrant Prefrontal Function Due to a Neurodevelopmental Lesion?

As most students of abnormal psychology are aware, Schizophrenia typically does not manifest itself until late adolescence or young adulthood (American Psychiatric Association, 1994). Its symptoms include positive indications of thought disorder, such as hallucinations or delusions, as well as deficits such as anhedonia, anergia, and an inability to form meaningful social relationships. Once symptoms begin to present themselves, behavior and the affected person's general level of function radically deteriorate. One robust finding is that individuals with Schizophrenia perform poorly on putative measures of frontal lobe function (Park & Holzmann, 1992; Perlstein, Dixit, Carter, Noll, & Cohen, 2003). The disorder is sometimes, but only rarely, seen in children. However, recent theories suggest that it is best conceptualized as a developmental disorder in which a static lesion that occurs before adulthood interacts with normal maturational events to produce later signs of the illness (see review by Lewis & Levitt, 2002). The notion that the pathological events that cause the illness are present much earlier than its presenting symptoms was suggested by Bleuler and Kraepelin over a century ago (described by Marenco & Weinberger, 2000), an idea that was elaborated on by Weinberger in the 1980s. Weinberger (1986, 1987) postulated that an early developmental lesion, perhaps occurring prenatally, was responsible for the disorder in conjunction with environmental triggers and other genetic liabilities. According to Weinberger's original model, the lesion impacted the dorsolateral prefrontal cortex and altered prefrontal dopamine transmission during adolescence, which was regarded as a critical period during which a juxtaposition of brain maturational events, environmental stress, and a demand for the PFC to assume control over behavior led to the manifestation of the disorder. Thus, in this diathesis-stress model, the PFC dysfunction that characterizes Schizophrenia is viewed as a sleeper effect, present from birth but dormant early in development and emergent only when the PFC reaches functional maturity. Other neurodevelopmental models suggest that Schizophrenia manifests itself due to later developmental events, such as failures of synaptic pruning that are specific to adolescence (reviewed by Lewis & Levitt, 2002). The neurodevelopmental hypothesis is not fully accepted but is supported by several lines of evidence, including an increased incidence of perinatal complications in people later diagnosed with Schizophrenia; the presence of soft neurological signs and other minor physical anomalies in subsets of individuals with the disease; evidence of intellectual, motor, and behavioral dysfunction prior to diagnosis; the presence of structural brain abnormalities that remain stable over time; and a course of illness that is contrary to what would be expected in a degenerative disease (Lewis & Levitt, 2002; Marenco & Weinberger, 2000). Autopsy studies of affected individuals' brains reveal evidence of migrational errors in the PFC that impact white matter development (Akbarian et al., 1993) as well as disrupted patterns of cortical connectivity (Selemon & Goldman-Rakic, 1999). In addition, minor physical anomalies, particularly deviations in craniofacial morphology (Lane, Larkin, Waddington, & O'Callaghan, 1996; Lane et al., 1997), differentiate schizophrenics from age-matched controls, suggesting that a teratogenic process that impacts development of the ectoderm layer in the developing fetus is associated with the disorder. One classic study by Walker and colleagues (Walker, Savoie, & Davis, 1994) involved the retrospective rating of home videos recorded by parents of schizophrenic children and nonaffected children, including siblings. Raters, unaware of each individual's adult diagnostic classification, viewed the videos and rated them for the presence or absence of motor idiosyncrasies and other neurological abnormalities. They were able to successfully discriminate children who would later manifest Schizophrenia from unaffected children, including siblings, suggesting that Schizophrenia might manifest itself during childhood in the form of subtle motor abnormalities. Motor abnormalities were particularly evident prior to 2 years of age. In Walker et al.'s (1994) model, these abnormalities were linked with dysfunction in the basal ganglia and a lack of cortical (prefrontal) control over subcortical (motor) processes. Neuropsychological symptoms were hypothesized to appear later, when the PFC becomes more important for cognitive, as opposed to motor, control over behavior.

Perceived stress triggers more frequent episodes of the disease and renders chronic sufferers more susceptible to impairment. As suggested by this review, individuals with the biological diathesis for Schizophrenia might have a low threshold to experience PFC overload as they are bombarded by stimuli from the environment. Thus, the individual is taxed by an information load that is significantly less in magnitude than what would challenge a healthy person, ultimately leading to PFC hypoactivation, which has been observed in PET and neuroimaging studies (Perlstein et al., 2003). The interesting aspect of the disorder, from a developmental perspective, concerns the application of normative principles of PFC development to the time course of the illness. If the model outlined in this chapter is correct regarding the normative course of PFC development, then Schizophrenia manifests itself at a point when the PFC assumes maximal control over cognition-emotion integration. If the neural processes underlying this developmental milestone can be identified in healthy adolescents, they might suggest areas of deviated function in the schizophrenic brain.

Phenylketonuria: Chronic Deviation in Prefrontal Dopamine Activity?

In contrast to Schizophrenia, another neurodevelopmental disorder that has been linked to deficits in PFC dopamine activity is phenylketonuria (PKU). Individuals with PKU suffer from a genetic lack of the enzyme phenylalanine hydroxylase (PAH); as a consequence, they are unable to metabolize phenylalanine, a naturally occurring protein that is abundantly present in the typical human's diet. When phenylalanine levels rise, they are toxic to the developing nervous system, and profound mental retardation results. Since the disorder was first recognized, neonatal screening for PKU has become the norm in most Western countries, and treatment is instituted as soon as possible after birth. Treatment involves the dietary restriction of phenylalanine. With dietary treatment, mental retardation is averted (Williamson, Koch, Azen, & Chang, 1981). However, individuals with PKU still differ cognitively from unaffected individuals, which may be due to factors related to the manner in which phenylalanine influences neurochemistry, especially in the prefrontal cortex (Diamond, Prevor, Callendar, & Druin, 1997).

Phenylalanine is involved in the synthesis of dopamine. Through the action of PAH, phenylalanine is converted in the central nervous system into tyrosine, which in turn is metabolized by tyrosine hydroxylase into dopamine (Goodwill et al., 1997; McKean & Peterson, 1970). Through several possible mechanisms, dopamine synthesis might be compromised in PKU. First, if phenylalanine is unduly restricted, as in a rigorously controlled PKU diet, then dopamine synthesis might be impaired because there is little to no phenylalanine available for conversion to tyrosine. Tyrosine is also ingested through protein-rich foods, so it

must be supplemented in PKU. However, even when phenylalanine levels are only moderately elevated, as in a restricted but not entirely efficacious diet, dopamine levels might also be decreased due to the fact that phenylalanine and tyrosine compete for transport across the blood-brain barrier (Carlson, Hyman, Bauman, & Koch, 1992; Pietz et al., 1999). If phenylalanine levels are elevated, then phenylalanine might win out in the competition for blood-to-brain transport. Once in the central nervous system, phenylalanine cannot be metabolized, and not enough tyrosine has entered the brain. Without tyrosine, dopamine is not synthesized. In theory, tyrosine depletion should impact all brain regions that use dopamine as a transmitter; however, it has been suggested that the PFC is particularly sensitive to dopamine precursor depletion (Diamond et al., 1997). If this is accurate, then individuals with treated PKU should demonstrate specific deficits in the area of executive function. Concordantly, executive function deficits have been reported in preschoolers and school-age children with PKU despite the fact that these children have IQs in the normal range. Deficits have been reported on measures of set shifting, working memory, and other aspects of higher-order problem solving (Diamond et al., 1997; Faust, Libon, & Pueschel, 1986; Pennington, van Doorninck, McCabe, & McCabe, 1985; Weglage, Pietsch, Fünders, Koch, & Ullrich, 1996; Welsh, Pennington, Ozonoff, Rouse, & McCabe, 1990; White, Nortz, Mandernach, Huntington, & Steiner, 2002). Some studies have also observed relative deficits in choice reaction times or interhemispheric transfer times (Banich, Passarotti, White, Nortz, & Steiner, 2000; Gourovitch, Craft, Dowton, Ambrose, & Sparta, 1994), suggesting that the speed of information processing is impacted in PKU. Interestingly, these deficits have been less robustly observed in adolescents and young adults with the disorder, suggesting the presence of an as yet undetermined compensatory mechanism as the PFC matures (Mazzoco et al., 1994).

When deficits are observed, they have been positively correlated with blood levels of phenylalanine (Diamond et al., 1997; Mazzoco et al., 1994; Ris, Williams, Hunt, Berry, & Leslie, 1994; Weglage et al., 1996; Welsh et al., 1990). Recently, studies have focused on the blood phenylalanine-to-tyrosine ratio as a marker of brain dopamine availability (Diamond et al., 1997). Low ratio scores have been associated with executive function deficits in several studies, one of which (Luciana, Sullivan, et al., 2001) suggests that low ratios at discrete developmental time points might confer vulnerability to later executive dysfunction.

In addition, we recently attempted a pharmacological challenge of the dopamine system in young adults with

PKU, using the dopamine antagonist haloperidol (Luciana, Hanson, & Whitley, 2003). Young adults with PKU and a group of age-matched controls completed a neurocognitive battery under the influence of haloperidol and, on a separate study day, a placebo. It was predicted that haloperidol would impair selected aspects of cognition, particularly in the realm of working memory, in both groups relative to placebo, but that the degree of impairment would be greater in the PKU sample. This prediction was only partially supported, although a composite measure of executive function impairment on haloperidol distinguished the PKU from the control group. Responses to haloperidol were variable within the PKU sample (e.g., 50% of that sample exhibited executive function impairment on haloperidol as compared to 25% of the control sample), leading us to speculate that other, individual difference factors might impact whether or not an individual with PKU suffers from chronic tyrosine depletion and whether such depletion, if present, specifically impacts the prefrontal cortex. Similar psychopharmacological investigations might be particularly illuminating if they could be conducted to compare the responses of children, adolescents, and young adults with the disorder.

Because dopamine neurotransmission is hypothesized to be specifically disrupted in PKU, another interesting avenue of research might be to investigate how PKU interacts with other genetic liabilities to determine the likelihood of cognitive dysfunction in a given individual. That is, we might predict that individuals who carry the VAL allele of the COMT gene would be at particularly high risk of prefrontal dopamine loss due to interactive effects of COMT genotype with PKU. To date, this association has not been investigated. Another association that could be investigated, particularly as cohorts of treated individuals with PKU reach middle and older adulthood, is the similarity between cognitive dysfunctions in PKU and those observed in other dopamine-related disorders such as Parkinson's disease.

In summary, because PKU is relatively well understood from a neurochemical perspective, its study has the potential to increase our understanding of other disorders that disrupt prefrontal function through neurochemical means. In addition, PKU is unique because it is diagnosed very shortly after birth and its effects can be observed in the context of a treatment that is applied throughout the life span.

In contrast, another disorder that has been associated with aberrant dopamine function (although not limited to the prefrontal cortex) is substance abuse. Substance abuse typically does not manifest itself until adolescence or adulthood, depending on an individual's environment as well as genetic predisposition.

Substance Abuse: Subcortically Generated Motivational Signals Impact Higher Levels of Information Processing

Substance abuse can be understood, only in part, as a failure of cognitive control. Current models of substance use problems emphasize that all individuals (even those who do not use drugs or alcohol) vary in their sensitivities to rewarding stimuli. Rewards can be natural unconditioned reinforcers, such as food, shelter, and warmth, that an individual will approach without prior learning. Alternatively, they can be conditioned through experience, such as likes and dislikes that pertain to specific foods and specific sources of contact comfort. Whether a stimulus is rewarding (reinforcing) or not depends on the degree to which one responds to it at a neurobiological level. Stimuli that are reinforcing activate a functional circuit in the basolateral limbic forebrain. Relevant structures include the amygdala, nucleus accumbens, dorsal striatum, and ventromedial prefrontal cortex. Using dopamine as the primary transmitter, information regarding reward salience is transmitted through this circuit (Depue & Collins, 1999). The nucleus accumbens-striatal interface ultimately allows information pertaining to positive incentives to be translated into approach behavior (Depue & Collins, 1999; Mogenson et al., 1980). If a situation or stimulus is particularly compelling, activity in this circuit would be expected to be quite robust, underlying the brain's primary reward system. Achieving control over reward-stimulated approach behavior is clearly a critical need, allowing potential sources of reward to be acquired in ways that are adaptive and appropriate to the situational context.

When the reward system is overly active, it is conjectured that an intact DLPFC must exert a greater-than-normal amount of effort to subdue hedonic impulses. Alternatively, even "typical" impulses that are generated subcortically could lead to lack of behavioral control in the absence of adequate PFC function. The impulses most relevant for drug abuse initiation are hedonic signals related to positive reinforcers and/or unconditioned natural rewards. These two mechanisms might differentially characterize drug abuse early versus later in its course as a function of (1) developmental constraints and (2) the effects of drugs on neurobehavioral systems once use is initiated. Epidemiological studies (DeWit, Adlaf, Offord, & Ogborne, 2000; B. F. Grant & Dawson, 1997, 1998; McGue, Iacono, Legrand, Malone, & Elkins, 2001) suggest that initiation of drug and alcohol use begins early, typically during adolescence. Initial use or experimentation is not necessarily aberrant, because hedonic signals may be especially compelling during adolescence, when exploratory tendencies are high. However, the course of addictive behavior (as it emerges) will vary depending on how well one can exert control over these impulses. Appropriate levels of control will be difficult, if not impossible, to achieve if the DLPFC is not functionally mature. Moreover, as noted previously, substance abusers have been shown to perform poorly on measures of VMPFC function, such as the Iowa Gambling Task. Therefore, the general trajectory of PFC maturation in adolescence, as well as sources of individual variation in this trajectory, have important ramifications for drug use initiation and maintenance.

The study of PFC development informs the study of drug abuse in two major ways. First, an understanding of the PFC's capacity for information integration and control during adolescence is important in identifying individuals who might be vulnerable to the initiation of drug use. The second area of interest concerns the impact of drug use, once initiated, on PFC-guided networks. Individuals with deficient PFC function may be most vulnerable to drug use initiation, but it may also be the case that continued use of drugs is detrimental to PFC development (e.g., Ornstein et al., 2000; Sullivan, Fama, Rosenbloom, & Pfefferbaum, 2002) due to the long-term effects of use on synaptic connections.

If our and others' laboratory data are correct regarding the maturational trajectory of PFC function, then drug use is initiated at a time when the PFC is still actively developing. Indeed, periods of pronounced functional development in a normative sample may represent periods of maximal vulnerability if drugs are used at these times.

Summary

These three disorders (Schizophrenia, phenylketonuria, and substance abuse) have several superficial features in common. Each has been associated with prefrontal dysfunction at a behavioral level and with deviations in dopamine system neurotransmission. In the case of Schizophrenia, an early lesion process critically impacts the development of cortical circuitry but is not evident until the environment becomes sufficiently stressful and that circuitry is called on to assume control over behavior. In phenylketonuria, it may be the case that affected individuals suffer from chronic tyrosine depletion, secondary to a primary deficit in phenylalanine metabolism. This depletion acutely affects neural function as the cortex is developing and may be specific to the prefrontal cortex at different points in development. Finally, although sub-stance abusers frequently exhibit deficits in behavioral control that could be attributed to deficient prefrontal function, they may be primarily characterized by an over-active approach or reward system that is difficult to restrain in the presence of reinforcing stimuli. Thus, the PFC must work in an increasingly effortful manner to keep behavior in an adaptive balance. This equilibrium can be upset by a number of processes occurring at various developmental time points.

FUTURE DIRECTIONS

The work surveyed here pertaining to the development of prefrontally guided cognitive functions in healthy children and implications of these developmental processes for psychopathology raises a number of interesting questions and ideas for future study. Some of these issues pertain to methodology; others relate more strongly to the types of questions that might guide future investigations in light of current knowledge.

On the methodological front, there has been an emphasis in the literature to date on deriving conclusions about PFC development from behavioral tasks that have been linked in adult studies to this region of the brain. However, we cannot conclude that because a task recruits PFC function in adults, it will necessarily recruit the same regions or recruit activity of the same magnitude in children and adolescents (Bunge et al., 2002; Casey, Giedd, & Thomas, 2000). Neuroimaging technology allows us to examine this issue directly in the behaving developing brain. Thus, future research should emphasize studies that combine neurobehavioral assessments with measures of functional neuroimaging.

Related to this idea, current work strongly suggests that the PFC undergoes continued structural refinement in the adolescent period (Sowell, Delis, et al., 2001; Sowell, Thompson, et al., 2001). However, only a handful of studies have attempted to address how these structural changes relate meaningfully to behavioral changes that are also prominent during this time (Klingberg et al., 2002; Kwon et al., 2002; Sowell, Delis, et al., 2001), and a need for studies of this type has been identified by others (Paus et al., 2001). In isolation, each of these reports has suggested intriguing associations between patterns of white matter development and improvement of performance on working memory or cognitive control tasks (Klingberg et al., 2002; Kwon et al., 2002) or associations between patterns of gray matter decline and mnemonic improvement on tasks that have been loosely linked to the PFC (Sowell, Delis et al., 2001). There is a sense in evaluating this literature that tasks have been selected less carefully than they might be given the vast amount of knowledge that has been gained from large-scale behavioral studies of prefrontal development (e.g., see Welsh et al., 1991). To the extent that behavioral investigations can suggest specific tasks that target processes of interest, these tasks can be brought into neuroimaging paradigms and subjected to intense scrutiny. For example, measures of response inhibition (Bunge et al., 2002) and strategic self-monitoring (De Luca et al., 2003; Luciana et al., 2005) have been found to continuously develop during adolescence, and these could be examined in relation to white matter development in dorsolateral prefrontal regions. Similarly, studies incorporating measures such as the Iowa Gambling Task (Hooper et al., 2004; Overman et al., 2004) or its cousin, the Hungry Donkey Task (Crone et al., 2003), suggest that adolescents continue to improve in their capacities for cognition-emotion integration into their 20s. These tasks could be examined in relation to synaptic integrity in the ventromedial prefrontal cortex.

Refined investigations of structure-function correlations seem destined to rely on small study samples given the current prohibitive financial and time costs of conducting neuroimaging investigations. However, one other trend that is being encouraged on a national level is for researchers to combine their resources and data sets to create large public databases (Van Horn, Grafton, Rockmore, & Gazzaniga, 2004) that can then be queried by independent investigators to consider broader issues. It might be possible to use data generated across sites to more comprehensively investigate age-related trends in the development of basic neurofunctional aspects of PFC development, particularly as investigators agree on tasks to incorporate in their assessment paradigms.

It is not sufficient, however, to rely on cross-sectional comparisons, as many investigators have done, to inform developmental theories. Prospective within-subject designs are those that have the maximal capacity to address developmental questions (see Giedd et al., 1999, for a notable example). If prospective studies can be designed that utilize multimethod approaches (e.g., combinations of behavioral, neuroimaging, and molecular genetic assessments), then growth curve models can be derived to segregate multiple sources of influence over behavior in the context of typical development. Such studies would also allow for the examination of transitions from healthy to disordered patterns of behavior within the same individuals.

Now that so much knowledge has come to the forefront regarding normative trends in PFC development, studies of

high-risk samples and children with diagnosed psychopathology are critical to truly understand how the PFC controls behavior from a multidimensional interactive perspective. One dimension of interest obviously concerns age and how and when high-level cognition emerges over time. Another dimension, though, concerns the continuum from typical to maladaptive levels of function. Clinical investigations in combination with the knowledge gained from neuroscience seem to strongly suggest that these two dimensions might interact. That is, there are vulnerable periods in the course of the normal staging of brain development when synaptic architecture is vulnerable to exogenous but also intrinsic sources of adverse influence. As described herein, these vulnerable periods include the prenatal period (when neurons are forming and migrating to targeted destinations in the cortex), early infancy (when synaptogenesis is most exuberant), and adolescence (when synaptic pruning and white matter development further refine synaptic architecture, decreasing the amount of subsequent plasticity that is possible).

Clinical descriptions also reinforce that certain forms of psychopathology are more likely to manifest themselves at some points in development rather than others. For example, according to the *Diagnostic and Statistical Manual of Mental Disorders* (American Psychiatric Association, 1994), symptoms of ADHD must manifest themselves before the age of 7 years. Schizophrenia, in contrast, is rarely seen during childhood but has a typical age of onset in adolescence or young adulthood. Affective disorders, at least in forms that are similar to what is typically seen in an adult sufferer, emerge most often postpuberty, as does substance abuse. These lines of reasoning suggest that we should focus alternatively on the toddler/preschool but also adolescent periods and the changes that are normative within these time spans to identify which processes go awry in the context of specific disorders and exactly when in relation to the expected normative developmental trajectory these processes are maximally impacted.

More refined investigations of healthy and especially high-risk children and adolescents therefore represent one critical future direction in clinical cognitive neuroscientific investigations.

The emphasis on the prefrontal cortex as a heterogeneous structure that interacts substantially with subcortical brain regions (such as the amygdala), with the anterior cingulate cortex, and with midbrain neurotransmitter regions also indicates that developmental cognitive neuroscience is at a turning point. While most investigators have focused on studying functions that are mediated by the dorsolateral prefrontal cortex (i.e., measures of cool cognition), current studies of the ventromedial prefrontal cortex and its role in decision making that is both nonsocial and also socially mediated should inspire us to target this region and so-called hot measures of executive cognition as active topics of investigation. Thus, developmental neuroscience may be at a nexus point, ready to intertwine with the emerging fields of affective and social cognitive neuroscience. For example, some paradigms that have been recently examined in social neuroscientific investigations concern how social cooperation develops between interacting partners (Rilling et al., 2002). There is an intriguing suggestion that such processes activate anterior cingulate but also ventral prefrontal regions. Because social cooperation is so critically important in the context of peer relations, studies of how it emerges and how it is mediated in adolescence would be particularly interesting.

Current interest in social cognitive neuroscience reinforces the notion that experience broadly defined interacts with more purely biological mechanisms to structure behavior. Specifically, executive control may be impacted by sociodemographic variables, by cultural factors, or by interactions between genetic liabilities and rearing conditions. Thus, future prospective studies of high-risk samples should ideally incorporate individuals with a diversity of experience to capture how these sources of influence interact with the other mechanisms described here.

CONCLUSIONS

The cognitive neuroscience of prefrontal development began in a rather unsophisticated way, with several notable case reports that were conveyed to the medical community. These reports gave way to the development of animal models of brain-behavior relations and extensions of relevant findings to human clinical and experimental neuropsychology. Our current knowledge regarding the manner in which the PFC mediates behavior is greatly enhanced by neuroimaging studies, but even these rely heavily on the foundation of experimental neuropsychology, through which behavioral tasks were creatively developed to assess working memory, inhibitory control, and set shifting.

Currently, the focus is on a reformulated theory of PFC function that is organized around cognitive control, defined by at least one researcher as the ability to flexibly modulate behavior to attain goals. The development of cognitive control was first studied by Piaget (1936), although he didn't frame his discussions of object permanence in that way. Using Piagetian tasks, it has been demonstrated that abilities dependent on the PFC later in life emerge in the infancy period. From that period onward, they continue to develop in a dimensional fashion, allowing increasingly complex pieces of information to be manipulated, monitored, and otherwise organized. This pattern of behavioral development has a parallel in brain development. Although the brain's gross structural features are present at birth, the genesis and refinement of cortical circuitry continues throughout childhood and into adolescence, culminating with the elimination of excess synapses and the continued development of white matter, including myelin. These refinements, also dimensional in their emergence, parallel what is observed in behavior (Luciana, 2002).

Typically, cognitive control has been studied using measures of working memory or behavioral inhibition. It is suggested here that control culminates with the PFC's increasing capacity to integrate and respond to cognitive as well as motivational signals that are communicated from the rest of the brain. One task that has been used in only a handful of developmental studies to date, the Iowa Gambling Task, appears to index this high demand for cognition-emotion integration. Data from our laboratory at the University of Minnesota suggest that whereas complex working memory and inhibitory control processes asymptote late in the 2nd decade of life, the processes recruited by the IGT are continuing to develop up to the age of 20 and perhaps beyond. Further investigations of how the PFC integrates emotion and cognition will be important in defining the upper limits of its development, and it is suggested that this area of inquiry is the wave of the future in developmental neuroscientific research.

Because the PFC continues to develop for the first 20-some years of the average person's life, it may be particularly vulnerable to pathological processes and events, including those that are intrinsic to the individual in terms of his or her neural development, genetics, or prenatal environment (e.g., Schizophrenia or phenylketonuria). Aberrations in other areas of the brain, such as the limbic-motor interface, as seen in substance abuse, would also be expected to have a ripple effect on PFC function. Finally, although this literature was not covered here, adverse experience, in the form of neglect, maltreatment, or socioeconomic disadvantage, has been linked to attentional dysfunction and executive impairments (Beers & DeBellis, 2002). The mechanism through which such events alter PFC function could be due to effects on developing synaptic architecture, particularly if those events occur in the time span between birth and age 5, when synaptogenesis is particularly exuberant.

It was proposed here that the PFC has a finite capacity for information integration, particularly when that integration requires control over strong motivational impulses; if that capacity is taxed through intrinsic or extrinsic stressors, executive dysfunction will result and will be observed as a failure of behavioral regulation. One challenge for developmental cognitive neuroscientists is to understand how the PFC's optimal reaction range is defined in healthy individuals between childhood and adulthood and how capacity limitations are differentially expressed in psychopathology. A multimethod approach that incorporates neuroimaging, molecular genetics, and neurobehavioral observation holds a great deal of promise in addressing this challenge in future studies.

REFERENCES

Akbarian, S., Bunney, W. E., Potkin, S. G., Wigal, S. B., Hagman, J. O., Sandman, C. A., et al. (1993). Altered distribution of nicotinamide-adenine dinucleotide phosphate-diaphorase cells in frontal lobe of schizophrenics implies disturbances of cortical development. *Archives of General Psychiatry, 50,* 227–230.

American Psychiatric Association. (1994). *Diagnostic and statistical manual of mental disorders* (4th ed.). Washington, DC: Author.

Asghari, V., Sanyal, S., Buchwaldt, S., Peterson, A., Jovanovic, V., & Van Tol, H. H. (1995). Modulation of intracellular cyclic AMP levels by different human dopamine D4 receptor variants. *Journal of Neurochemistry, 65,* 1157–1165.

Auerbach, J., Geller, V., Lezer, S., Shinwell, E., Belmaker, R. H., Levine, J., et al. (1999). Dopamine D4 receptor (DRD4) and serotonin transporter promoter (5-HTTLPR) polymorphisms in the determination of temperament in 2-month old infants. *Molecular Psychiatry, 4,* 369–373.

Baddeley, A. (1992). Working memory. *Science, 255,* 556–559.

Banich, M. T., Passarotti, A. M., White, D. A., Nortz, M. J., & Steiner, R. D. (2000). Interhemispheric interactions during childhood: II. Children with early-treated phenylketonuria. *Developmental Neuropsychology, 18*(1), 53–71.

Barr, C. S., Schwandt, M. L., Newman, T. K., & Higley, J. D. (2004). The use of adolescent nonhuman primates to model human alcohol intake: Neurobiological, genetic, and psychological variables. *Annals of the New York Academy of Sciences, 1021,* pp. 221–233.

Bates, E., Vicari, S., & Trauner, D. (1999). Neural mediation of language development: Perspectives from lesion studies of infants and children. In H. Tager-Flusberg (Ed.), *Neurodevelopmental disorders* (pp. 533–581). Cambridge, MA: MIT Press.

Bechara, A., Damasio, A. R., Damasio, H., & Anderson, S. W. (1994). Insensitivity to future consequences following damage to human prefrontal cortex. *Cognition, 50*(1/3), 7–15.

Bechara, A., Damasio, H., & Damasio, A. R. (2000). Emotion, decision making and the orbitofrontal cortex. *Cerebral Cortex, 10*(3), 295–307.

Bechara, A., Tranel, D., & Damasio, H. (2000). Characterization of the decision-making deficit of patients with ventromedial prefrontal cortex lesions. *Brain, 123*(Pt. 11), 2189–2202.

Beers, S. R., & DeBellis, M. D. (2002). Neuropsychological function in children with maltreatment-related posttraumatic stress disorder. *American Journal of Psychiatry, 159*(3), 483–486.

Belger, A., Puce, A., Krystal, J. H., Gore, J. C., Goldman-Rakic, P., & McCarthy, G. (1998). Dissociation of mnemonic and perceptual processes during spatial and nonspatial working memory using fMRI. *Human Brain Mapping, 6,* 14–32.

Bell, M. A., & Fox, N. A. (1992). The relations between frontal brain electrical activity and cognitive development during infancy. *Child Development, 63,* 1142–1163.

Bell, M. A., & Fox, N. A. (1997). Individual differences in object permanence performance at 8 months: Locomotor experience and brain electrical activity. *Developmental Psychobiology, 31,* 287–297.

Berker, E. A., Berker, A. H., & Smith, A. (1986). Translation of Broca's 1865 report: Localization of speech in the third left frontal convulation. *Archives of Neurology, 43,* 1065–1072.

Blair, R. J. R., Colledge, E., & Mitchell, D. G. V. (2001). Somatic markers and response reversal: Is there orbitofrontal cortex disfunction in boys with psychopathic tendencies? *Journal of Abnormal Child Psychology, 29*(6), 499–511.

Bourgeois, J. P., Goldman-Rakic, P. S., & Rakic, P. (1994). Synaptogenesis in the prefrontal cortex of rhesus monkeys. *Cerebral Cortex, 4,* 78–96.

Bourgeois, J. P., & Rakic, P. (1993). Changes of synaptic density in the primary visual cortex of the rhesus monkey from fetal to adult stage. *Journal of Neuroscience, 13,* 2801–2820.

Braver, T. S., Barch, D. M., Gray, J. R., Molfese, D. L., & Snyder, A. (2001). Anterior cingulate cortex and response conflict: Effects of frequency, inhibition and errors. *Cerebral Cortex, 11*(9), 825–836.

Braver, T. S., & Cohen, J. D. (1999). Dopamine, cognitive control, and Schizophrenia: The gating model. *Progress in Brain Research, 121,* 327–349.

Brozoski, T. J., Brown, R. M., Rosvold, H. E., & Goldman, P. (1979). Cognitive deficit caused by regional depletion of dopamine in prefrontal cortex of rhesus monkey. *Science, 205,* 929–931.

Bunge, S. A., Dudukovic, N. M., Thomason, M. E., Vaidya, C. J., & Gabrieli, J. D. E. (2002). Immature frontal lobe contributions to cognitive control in children: Evidence from fMRI. *Neuron, 33,* 301–311.

Cajal, S. R. (1967). The structure and connexions of neurons. In *Nobel lectures: Physiology or medicine, 1901–1921* (pp. 220–253). Amsterdam: Elsevier. (Original work published 1906)

Callicott, J. H., Mattay, V. S., Bertolino, A., Finn, K., Coppola, R., Frank, J. A., et al. (1999). Physiological characteristics of capacity constraints in working memory as revealed by functional MRI. *Cerebral Cortex, 9*(1), 20–26.

Carlson, H. E., Hyman, D. B., Bauman, C., & Koch, R. (1992). Prolactin responses to phenylalanine and tyrosine in phenylketonuria. *Metabolism: Clinical and Experimental, 41*(5), 518–521.

Casey, B. J., Cohen, J. D., O'Craven, K., Davidson, R. J., Irwin, W., Nelson, C. A., et al. (1998). Reproducibility of fMRI results across four institutions using a spatial working memory task. *NeuroImage, 8*(3), 249–261.

Casey, B. J., Giedd, J. N., & Thomas, K. M. (2000). Structural and functional brain development and its relation to cognitive development. *Biological Psychology, 54*(1/3), 241–257.

Casey, B. J., Trainor, R. J., Orendi, J. L., Schubert, A. B., Nystrom, L. E., Giedd, J. N., et al. (1997). A developmental functional MRI study of prefrontal activation during performance on a go no-go task. *Journal of Cognitive Neuroscience, 9,* 835–847.

Caspi, A., Sugden, K., Moffitt, T. E., Taylor, A., Craig, I. W., Harrington, H. L., et al. (2003). Influence of life stress on depression: Moderation by a polymorphism in the 5-HTT gene. *Science, 301,* 386–389.

Cavada, C., & Goldman-Rakic, P. S. (1989). Posterior parietal cortex in rhesus monkey: II: Evidence for segregated corticocortical networks linking sensory and limbic areas with the frontal lobe. *Journal of Comparative Neurology, 287,* 422–445.

Cavedini, P., Riboldi, G., Keller, R., D'Annucci, A., & Bellodi, L. (2002). Frontal lobe dysfunction in pathological gambling patients. *Biological Psychiatry, 51*(4), 334–341.

Caviness, V. S., Kennedy, D. N., Richelme, C., Rademacher, J., & Filipek, P. A. (1996). The human brain age 7–11 years: A volumetric analysis based on magnetic resonance images. *Cerebral Cortex, 6,* 726–736.

Changeaux, J.-P., & Danchin, A. (1976). Selective stabilization of developing synapses as a mechanism for the specification of neural networks. *Nature, 264,* 705–712.

Christophe, C., Muller, M. F., Baleriaux, D., Kahn, A., Pardou, A., Perlmutter, N., et al. (1990). Mapping of normal brain maturation in infants on phase-sensitive inversion-recovery MR images. *Neuroradiology, 32,* 173–178.

Chugani, H. T. (1998). A critical period of brain development: Studies of cerebral glucose utilization with PET. *Preventive Medicine, 27*(2), 184–188.

Cicchetti, D., & Walker, E. (Eds.). (2003). *Neurodevelopmental mechanisms in psychopathology.* Boston, MA: Cambridge University Press.

Clark, A. S., & Goldman-Rakic, P. S. (1989). Gonadal hormones influence the emergence of cortical function in nonhuman primates. *Behavioral Neuroscience, 103,* 1287–1295.

Corkin, S. (1965). Tactually-guided maze learning in man: Effects of unilateral cortical excisions and bilateral hippocampal lesions. *Neuropsychologia, 3,* 339–351.

Coull, J. T., Middleton, H. C., Robbins, T. W., & Sahakian, B. J. (1995). Contrasting effects of clonidine and diazepam on tests of working memory and planning. *Psychopharmacology, 120,* 311–321.

Crone, E. A., Vendel, I., & van der Molen, M. W. (2003). Decision-making in disinhibited adolescents and adults: Insensitivity to future consequences or driven by immediate reward? *Personality and Individual Diffferences, 34,* 1–17.

Damasio, A. R. (1994). *Descartes' error: Emotion, reason, and the human brain.* New York: G. P. Putnam's Sons.

de Haan, M., & Nelson, C. A. (1997). Recognition of the mother's face by six-month old infants: A neurobehavioral study. *Child Development, 68,* 187–210.

De Luca, C. R., Wood, S. J., Anderson, V., Buchanan, J., Proffitt, T. M., Mahoney, K., et al. (2003). Normative data from the CANTAB. I: Development of executive function over the lifespan. *Journal of Clinical and Experimental Neuropsychology, 25*(2), 242–254.

Dempster, F. N. (1992). The rise and fall of the inhibitory mechanism: Toward a unified theory of cognitive development and aging. *Developmental Review, 12,* 45–75.

Depue, R. A., & Collins, P. F. (1999). Neurobiology of the structure of personality: Dopamine, facilitation of incentive motivation, and extraversion. *Behavioral and Brain Sciences, 22*(3), 491–517.

Depue, R. A., & Spoont, M. R. (1986). Conceptualizing a serotonin trait: A behavioral dimension of constraint. *Annals of the New York Academy of Sciences, 487,* 47–62.

D'Esposito, M., Aguirre, G. K., Zarahn, E., Ballard, D., Shin, R. K., & Lease, J. (1998). Functional MRI studies of spatial and nonspatial working memory. *Cognitive Brain Research, 7*(1), 1–13.

D'Esposito, M., & Postle, B. R. (1999). The dependence of span and delayed-response performance on prefrontal cortex. *Neuropsychologia, 37*(11), 1303–1315.

DeWit, D. J., Adlaf, E. M., Offord, D. R., & Ogborne, A. C. (2000). Age at first alcohol use: A risk factor for the development of alcohol disorders. *American Journal of Psychiatry, 157*(5), 745–750.

Diamond, A. (1990a). The development and neural bases of memory functions as indexed by the A. B. & delayed response tasks in human infants and infant monkeys. In A. Diamond (Ed.), *The development and neural basis of higher cognitive functions* (Vol. 608, pp. 267–317). New York: New York Academy of Sciences Press.

Diamond, A. (1990b). Developmental time course in human infants and infant monkeys and the neural basis of inhibitory control in reaching. In A. Diamond (Ed.), *The development and neural basis of higher cognitive functions* (Vol. 608, pp. 637–676). New York: New York Academy of Sciences Press.

Diamond, A. (2001). A model system for studying the role of dopamine in prefrontal cortex during early development in humans: Early and continuously treated phenylketonuria (PKU). In C. A. Nelson & M. Luciana (Eds.), *Handbook of developmental cognitive neuroscience* (pp. 433–472). Cambridge, MA: MIT Press.

Diamond, A., Briand, L., Fossella, J., & Gehlbach, L. (2004). Genetic and neurochemical modulation of prefrontal cognitive functions in children. *American Journal of Psychiatry, 161,* 125–132.

Diamond, A., & Goldman-Rakic, P. S. (1989). Comparison of human infants and rhesus monkeys on Piaget's AB task: Evidence for dependence on dorsolateral prefrontal cortex. *Experimental Brain Research, 74,* 24–40.

Diamond, A., Prevor, M. B., Callender, G., & Druin, D. (1997). Prefrontal cortex cognitive deficits in children treated early and continuously for PKU. *Monographs of the Society for Research in Child Development, 62*(4), 1–208.

Diamond, A., & Taylor, C. (1996). Development of an aspect of executive control: Development of the abilities to remember what I said and to "do as I say, not as I do." *Developmental Psychobiology, 29,* 315–334.

Dias, R., Robbins, T. W., & Roberts, A. C. (1996). Dissociation in prefrontal cortex of affective and attentional shifts. *Nature, 380,* 69–72.

Egan, M. F., Goldberg, T. E., Kolachana, B. S., Callicott, J. H., Mazzanti, C. M., Straub, R. E., et al. (2001). Effect of COMT Val 108/158 Met genotype on frontal lobe function and risk for Schizophrenia. *Proceedings of the National Academy of Sciences, 98*(12), 6917–6922.

Elliott, R., Sahakian, B. J., Matthews, K., Bannerjea, A., Rimmer, J., & Robbins, T. W. (1997). Effects of methylphenidate on spatial working memory and planning in healthy young adults. *Psychopharmacology, 131*(2), 196–206.

Ernst, M., Grant, S. J., London, E. D., Contoreggi, C. S., Kimes, A. S., & Spurgeon, L. (2003). Decision making in adolescents with behavior disorders and adults with substance abuse. *American Journal of Psychiatry, 160*(1), 33–40.

Faraone, S. V., Doyle, A. E., Mick, E., & Biederman, J. (2001). Meta-analysis of the association between the 7-repeat allele of the dopamine D(4) receptor gene and attention deficit hyperactivity disorder. *American Journal of Psychiatry, 158*(7), 1052–1057.

Faust, D., Libon, D., & Pueschel, S. (1986). Neuropsychological function in treated phenylketonuria. *International Journal of Psychiatry in Medicine, 16,* 169–177.

Fletcher, P. C., & Henson, R. N. (2001). Frontal lobes and human memory: Insights from functional neuroimaging. *Brain, 124*(Pt. 5), 849–881.

Flourens, P. (1824). *Recherches experimentales sur les propriétés et les functions du systémique nerveux, dans les animaux vertebras.* Paris: Chez Cervot.

Fowler, K. S., Saling, M. M., Conway, E. L., Semple, J. M., & Louis, W. J. (1997). Computerized neuropsychological tests in the early detection of dementia: Prospective findings. *Journal of the International Neuropsychological Society, 3*(2), 139–146.

Funahashi, S., Bruce, C. J., & Goldman-Rakic, P. S. (1989). Mnemonic coding of visual space in the monkey's dorsolateral prefrontal cortex. *Journal of Neurophysiology, 61,* 331–349.

Fuster, J. M. (1997). *The prefrontal cortex: Anatomy, physiology, and neuropsychology of the frontal lobe* (3rd ed.). Philadelphia: Lippincott-Raven Press.

Fuster, J. M., & Alexander, G. E. (1971). Neuronal activity related to short-term memory. *Science, 173,* 652–654.

Gall, F. J., & Spurzheim, G. (1810). *Anatomie et physiologie du système nerveux en général, et du cerveau en particulier, avec des observations sur la possibilité de reconnoiter plusieurs, dispositions intellectuelles et morales de l'homme et des animaux, par la configuration de leurs têtes.* Paris: Schoell.

Garon, N., & Moore, C. (2004). Complex decision-making in early childhood. *Brain and Cognition, 55,* 158–170.

Gasparini, M., Fabrizio, E., Bonifati, E., & Meco, G. (1997). Cognitive improvement during tolcapone treatment in Parkinson's disease. *Journal of Neural Transmission, 104,* 887–894.

Gazzaniga, M. S., Ivry, R. B., & Mangun, G. R. (2002). *Cognitive neuroscience: The biology of the mind* (2nd ed.). New York: Norton.

Gerstadt, C., Hong, Y., & Diamond, A. (1994). The relationship between cognition and action: Performance of 3.5–7 year-old children on a Stroop-like day-night test. *Cognition, 53,* 129–153.

Giedd, J. N., Blumenthal, J., Jeffries, N. O., Castellanos, F. X., Liu, H., Zijdenbos, A., et al. (1999). Brain development during childhood and adolescence: A longitudinal MRI study. *Nature Neuroscience, 2*(10), 861–863.

Giedd, J. N., Snell, J. W., Lange, N., Rajapakse, J. C., Casey, B. J., Kozuch, P. I., et al. (1996). Quantitative magnetic resonance imaging of human brain development: Ages 4–18. *Cerebral Cortex, 6,* 551–560.

Gogos, J. A., Morgan, M., Luine, V., Santha, M., Ogawa, S., Pfaff, D., et al. (1998). Catechol-O-methyltransferase deficient mice exhibit sexually dimorphic changes in catecholamine levels and behavior. *Proceedings of the National Academy of Sciences, 95,* 9991–9996.

Goldman, P. S., & Galkin, T. W. (1978). Prenatal removal of frontal association cortex in the fetal rhesus monkey: Anatomical and functional consequences in postnatal life. *Brain Research, 152*(3), 451–485.

Goldman, P. S., & Rosvold, H. E. (1970). Localization of function within the dorsolateral prefrontal cortex of the rhesus monkey. *Experimental Neurology, 29,* 291–304.

Goldman-Rakic, P. S. (1987a). Circuitry of primate prefrontal cortex and regulation of behavior by representational memory. In F. Plum (Ed.), *Handbook of physiology: The nervous system* (Vol. 5, pp. 373–417). Bethesda, MD: American Physiological Society.

Goldman-Rakic, P. S. (1987b). Development of cortical circuitry and cognitive function. *Child Development, 58,* 601–622.

Goldman-Rakic, P. S. (1988). Topography of cognition: Parallel distributed networks in primate association cortex. *Annual Review of Neuroscience, 11,* 137–156.

Goldman-Rakic, P. S., Bourgeois, J.-P., & Rakic, P. (1997). Synaptic substrate of cognitive development: Lifespan analysis of synaptogenesis in the prefrontal cortex of the nonhuman primate. In N. A. Krasnegor, G. R. Lyon, & P. S. Goldman-Rakic (Eds.), *Development of the prefrontal cortex: Evolution, neurobiology, and behavior* (pp. 27–47). Baltimore: Paul H. Brookes.

Goldman-Rakic, P. S., & Brown, R. M. (1982). Postnatal development of monoamine content and synthesis in the cerebral cortex of rhesus monkeys. *Brain Research, 256*(3), 339–349.

Goldman-Rakic, P. S., & Porrino, L. J. (1985). The primate mediodorsal (MD) nucleus and its projection to the frontal lobe. *Journal of Comparative Neurology, 242,* 535–560.

Golgi, C. (1967). The neuron doctrine: Theory and facts. In *Nobel lectures: Physiology or medicine, 1901–1921* (pp. 189–217). Amsterdam: Elsevier. (Original work published 1906)

Goodwill, K. E., Sabatier, C., Marks, C., Fitzpatrick, P., Raag, R., & Stevens, R. C. (1997). Crystal structure of tyrosine hydroxylase at 2.3Å and its implications for inherited neurodegenerative diseases. *Nature Structural Biology, 4*(7), 578–585.

Gottesman, I. I., & Gould, T. D. (2003). The endophenotype concept in psychiatry: Etymology and strategic intentions. *American Journal of Psychiatry, 160,* 636–645.

Gourovitch, M. L., Craft, S., Dowton, S. B., Ambrose, P., & Sparta, S. (1994). Interhemispheric transfer in children with early-treated phenylketonuria. *Journal of Clinical and Experimental Neuropsychology, 16*(3), 393–404.

Grant, B. F., & Dawson, D. A. (1997). Age at onset of alcohol use and its association with DSM-IV alcohol abuse and dependence: Results from the National Longitudinal Alcohol Epidemiologic Survey. *Journal of Substance Abuse, 9,* 103–110.

Grant, B. F., & Dawson, D. A. (1998). Age of onset of drug use and its association with DSM-IV drug abuse and dependence: Results from the National Longitudinal Alcohol Epidemiologic Survey. *Journal of Substance Abuse, 10,* 163–173.

Grant, D. A., & Berg, E. A. (1948). A behavioral analysis of degree of reinforcement and ease of shifting to new responses in a Weigl-type card-sorting problem. *Journal of Experimental Psychology, 38,* 404–411.

Grant, S., Contoreggi, C., & London, E. D. (2000). Drug abusers show impaired performance in a laboratory test of decision making. *Neuropsychologia, 38*(8), 1180–1187.

Gray, J. R., Chabris, C. F., & Braver, T. S. (2003). Neural mechanisms of general fluid intelligence. *Nature Neuroscience, 6,* 316–322.

Greenough, W. T., & Black, J. E. (1992). Induction of brain structures by experience: Substrates for cognitive development. In M. R. Gunnar & C. A. Nelson (Eds.), *Minnesota Symposia on Child Psychology: Vol. 24. Developmental behavioral neuroscience* (pp. 155–200). Hillsdale, NJ: Erlbaum.

Happeney, K., Zelazo, P. D., & Stuss, D. T. (2004). Development of orbitofrontal function: Current themes and future directions. *Brain and Cognition, 55,* 1–10.

Hariri, A. R., Mattay, V. S., Tessitore, A., Kolachana, B., Fera, F., Goldman, D., et al. (2002). Serotonin transporter genetic variation and response of the human amygdala. *Science, 297,* 400–403.

Harlow, J. M. (1868). Recovery from the passage of an iron bar through the head. *Proceedings of the Massachusetts Medical Society, 2,* 327–346.

Hassink, R. I., Hiltbrunner, B., Muller, S., & Lutschg, J. (1992). Assessment of brain maturation by T2-weighted MRI. *Neuropediatrics, 23,* 72–74.

Hooper, C. J., Luciana, M., Conklin, H. M., & Yarger, R. S. (2004). Adolescents' performance on the Iowa Gambling Task: Implications for the development of decision-making and ventromedial prefrontal cortex. *Developmental Psychology, 40*(6), 1148–1158.

Hubel, D. H., & Wiesel, T. N. (1962). Receptive fields, binocular interaction and functional architecture in the cat's visual cortex. *Journal of Physiology, 160,* 106–154.

Hubel, D. H., & Wiesel, T. N. (1965). Binocular interaction in striate cortex of kittens reared with artificial squint. *Journal of Neurophysiology, 28,* 1041–1059.

Hughes, C., Russell, J., & Robbins, T. W. (1994). Evidence for executive dysfunction in Autism. *Neuropsychologia, 32,* 477–492.

Hunter, W. S. (1913). The delayed reaction in animals and children. *Behavior Monographs, 2,* 1–86.

Hutchinson, K. E., LaChance, H., Niaura, R., Bryan, A., & Smolen, A. (2002). The DRD4 VNTR polymorphism influences reactivity to smoking cues. *Journal of Abnormal Psychology, 111*(1), 134–143.

Huttenlocher, P. R. (1979). Synaptic density in human frontal cortex: Developmental changes and effects of aging. *Brain Research, 163,* 195–205.

Huttenlocher, P. R., & Dabholkar, A. S. (1997). Development and anatomy of prefrontal cortex. In N. A. Krasnegor, G. R. Lyon, & P. S. Goldman-Rakic (Eds.), *Development of the prefrontal cortex: Evolution, neurobiology, and behavior* (pp. 69–84). Baltimore: Paul H. Brookes.

Huttenlocher, P. R., & deCourten, C. (1987). The development of synapses in striate cortex of man. *Human Neurobiology, 6*(1), 1–9.

Huttenlocher, P. R., deCourten, C., Garey, L. J., & Van Der Loos, H. (1982). Synaptic development in human cerebral cortex. *International Journal of Neurology, 16–17,* 144–154.

Imamura, T., Takanashi, M., Hattori, N., Fujimori, M., Yamashita, H., Ishii, K., et al. (1998). Bromocriptine treatment for preservation in demented patients. *Alzheimer Disease and Associated Disorders, 12*(2), 109–113.

Inhelder, B., & Piaget, J. (1958). *The growth of logical thinking from childhood to adolescence: An essay on the construction of formal operational structures.* New York: Basic Books.

Jacobsen, C. F. (1935). Functions of the frontal association areas in primates. *Archives of Neurology and Psychiatry, 33,* 558–560.

Jacobsen, C. F., & Nissen, H. W. (1937). Studies of cerebral function in primates: IV. The effects of frontal lobe lesions on the delayed alternation habit in primates. *Journal of Comparative and Physiological Psychology, 23,* 101–112.

Jacobsen, C. F., Wolfe, J. B., & Jackson, T. A. (1935). An experimental analysis of the frontal association areas in primates. *Journal of Nervous and Mental Diseases, 82,* 1–14.

Jasper, H. H. (1995). A historical perspective: The rise and fall of prefrontal lobotomy. In H. H. Jasper, S. Riggio, & P. S. Goldman-Rakic (Eds.), *Advances in neurology: Vol. 66. Epilepsy and the functional anatomy of the frontal lobe* (pp. 97–114). New York: Raven Press.

Johnson, M. H. (1990). Cortical maturation and the development of visual attention in early infancy. *Journal of Cognitive Neuroscience, 2,* 81–95.

Jones, K. L., & Smith, D. W. (1973). Recognition of the fetal alcohol syndrome in early infancy. *Lancet, 2,* 999–1001.

Jones, K. L., & Smith, D. W. (1975). The fetal alcohol syndrome. *Teratology, 12*(1), 1–10.

Jones-Gotman, M., & Milner, B. (1977). Design fluency: The invention of nonsense drawings after focal cortical lesions. *Neuropsychologia, 15*(4/5), 653–674.

Jonides, J., Smith, E. E., Koeppe, R. A., Awh, E., Minoshima, S., & Mintun, M. A. (1993). Spatial working memory in humans as revealed by PET. *Nature, 363,* 623–625.

Kerr, A., & Zelazo, P. D. (2004). Development of "hot" executive function: The children's gambling task. *Brain and Cognition, 55,* 148–157.

Kessels, R. P., Postma, A., Wijnalda, E. M., & de Haan, E. H. (2000). Frontal-lobe involvement in spatial memory: Evidence from PET, fMRI, and lesion studies. *Neuropsychology Review, 10*(2), 101–113.

Kimberg, D. Y., D'Esposito, M. D., & Farah, M. J. (1997). Effects of bromocriptine on human subjects depend on working memory capacity. *NeuroReport, 8,* 3581–3583.

Kirkham, N. Z., & Diamond, A. (1999, April). *Integrating competing ideas in word and action.* Paper presented at the biennial meeting of the Society for Research in Child Development, Albuquerque, NM.

Klingberg, T., Forssberg, H., & Westerberg, H. (2002). Increased brain activity in frontal and parietal cortex underlies the development of visuospatial working memory capacity during childhood. *Journal of Cognitive Neuroscience, 14*(1), 1–10.

Kluger, A., Siegfried, Z., & Ebstein, R. P. (2002). A meta-analysis of the association between DRD4 polymorphism and novelty seeking. *Molecular Psychiatry, 7,* 712–717.

Kojima, S., & Goldman-Rakic, P. S. (1982). Delay-related activity of prefrontal neurons in rhesus monkeys performing delayed response. *Brain Research, 248,* 43–49.

Konorski, J. (1959). A new method of physiological investigation of recent memory in animals. *Bulletin of the Polish Academy of Sciences, 7,* 115–117.

Kostovic, I., & Rakic, P. (1990). Cytology and time of origin of interstitial neurons in the white matter in infant and adult human and monkey telencephalon. *Journal of Neurocytology, 9,* 219–242.

Kwon, H., Reiss, A. L., & Menon, V. (2002). Neural basis of protracted developmental changes in visuospatial working memory. *Proceedings of the National Academy of Sciences, 99*(20), 13336–13341.

Lachman, H. M., Papolos, D. F., Saito, T., Yu, Y. M., Szumlanski, C. I., & Weinschilboum, R. M. (1996). Human catechol-o-methyltransferase pharmacogenetics: Description of a functional polymorphism and its potential application to neuropsychiatric disorders. *Pharmacogenetics, 6,* 243–250.

Lane, A., Larkin, C., Waddington, J. L., & O'Callaghan, E. (1996). Dysmorphic features and Schizophrenia. In J. L. Waddington & P. F. Buckley (Eds.), *The neurodevelopmental basis of Schizophrenia* (pp. 79–94). Georgetown, TX: R. G. Landes.

Lane, A., Kinsella, A., Murphy, P., Byrne, M., Keenan, J., Colgan, K., et al. (1997). The anthropometric assessment of dysmorphic features in Schizophrenia as an index of its developmental origin. *Psychological Medicine, 25,* 887–894.

Lange, K. W., Robbins, T. W., Marsden, C. D., James, M., Owen, A. M., & Paul, G. M. (1992). L-dopa withdrawal in Parkinson's disease selectively impairs cognitive performance in tests of frontal lobe function. *Psychopharmacology, 107,* 394–404.

Lee, A. C. H., Owen, A. M., Rogers, R. D., Sahakian, B. J., & Robbins, T. W. (2000). Utility of CANTAB in functional neuroimaging. In M. Ernst & J. M. Ramsey (Eds.), *Functional neuroimaging in child psychiatry* (pp. 366–378). Cambridge, England: Cambridge University Press.

Lee, B. C., Lipper, E., Nass, R., Ehrlich, M. E., deCiccio-Bloom, E., & Auld, P. (1986). MRI of the central nervous system in neonates and young children. *American Journal of Neuroradiology, 7,* 605–616.

Levin, H. S., Culhane, K. A., Hartman, J., Evankovich, K., Mattson, A. J., Harward, H., et al. (1991). Developmental changes in performance on tests of purported frontal lobe functioning. *Developmental Neuropsychology, 7*(3), 377–395.

Lewis, D. A., & Levitt, P. (2002). Schizophrenia as a disorder of neurodevelopment. *Annual Review of Neuroscience, 25,* 409–432.

Lidow, M. S., & Rakic, P. (1992). Scheduling of monoaminergic neurotransmitter receptor expression in the primate neocortex during postnatal development. *Cerebral Cortex, 2,* 401–416.

Liljequist, R., Haapalinna, H., Ahlander, M., Ying, H. L., & Mannisto, P. T. (1997). Catechol-O-methyltransferase inhibitor tolcapone has minor influence on performance in experimental memory models in rats. *Behavioral Brain Research, 82,* 195–202.

Lotta, T., Vidgren, J., Tilgmann, C., Ulmanen, I., Melen, K., Julkunen, I., et al. (1995). Kinetics of human soluble and membrane-bound catechol-o-methyltransferase: A revised mechanism and description of the thermolabile variant of the enzyme. *Biochemistry, 34,* 4202–4210.

Luciana, M. (2002). The neural and functional development of human prefrontal cortex. In M. D. Haan & M. H. Johnson (Eds.), *The cognitive neuroscience of development* (pp. 157–179). Brighton, NY: Psychology Press.

Luciana, M., Burgund, E. D., Berman, M., & Hanson, K. L. (2001). Effects of tryptophan loading on working memory for spatial, verbal, and affective stimuli in healthy humans. *Journal of Psychopharmacology, 15*(4), 219–230.

Luciana, M., & Collins, P. F. (1997). Dopamine modulates working memory for spatial but not object cues in normal humans. *Journal of Cognitive Neuroscience, 9*(3), 330–347.

Luciana, M., Collins, P. F., & Depue, R. A. (1998). Opposing roles for dopamine and serotonin in the modulation of human spatial working memory functions. *Cerebral Cortex, 8,* 218–226.

Luciana, M., Conklin, H. M., Hooper, C. J., & Yarger, R. S. (2005). The development of nonverbal working memory and executive control processes in adolescents: Implications for level of processing theories of prefrontal cortex function. *Child Development, 76*(3), 697–712.

Luciana, M., Depue, R. A., Arbisi, P., & Leon, A. (1992). Facilitation of working memory in humans by a D2 dopamine receptor agonist. *Journal of Cognitive Neuroscience, 4,* 58–68.

Luciana, M., Hanson, K. L., & Whitley, C. B. (2003). Dopamine system reactivity in PKU: Acute effects of haloperidol administration on neuropsychological, physiological, and neuroendocrine functions. *Psychopharmacology, 175,* 18–25.

Luciana, M., Lindeke, L., Georgieff, M., Mills, M., & Nelson, C. A. (1999). Neurobehavioral evidence for working-memory deficits in school-aged children with histories of prematurity. *Developmental Medicine and Child Neurology, 41*(8), 521–533.

Luciana, M., & Nelson, C. A. (1998). The functional emergence of prefrontally-guided working memory systems in four-to-eight year-old children. *Neuropsychologia, 36*(3), 273–293.

Luciana, M., & Nelson, C. A. (2000). Neurodevelopmental assessment of cognitive function using the Cambridge Neuropsychological Testing Automated Battery (Cantab): Validation and future goals. In M. Ernst & J. M. Rumsey (Eds.), *Functional neuroimaging in child psychiatry* (pp. 379–397). Cambridge, England: Cambridge University Press.

Luciana, M., & Nelson, C. A. (2002). Assessment of neuropsychological function through use of the Cambridge Neuropsychological Testing Automated Battery: Performance in 4- to 12-year-old children. *Developmental Neuropsychology, 22*(3), 595–624.

Luciana, M., Sullivan, J., & Nelson, C. A. (2001). Associations between phenylalanine-to-tyrosine ratios and performance on tests of neuropsychological function in adolescents treated early and continuously for PKU. *Child Development, 72*(6), 1637–1652.

Luna, B., Thulborn, K. R., Munoz, D. P., Merriam, E. P., Garver, K. E., Minshew, N. J., et al. (2001). Maturation of widely distributed brain function subserves cognitive development. *Neuroimage, 13*(5), 786–793.

Luria, A. R. (1966). *The higher cortical functions in man.* New York: Basic Books.

Marcovitch, S., Zelazo, P. D., & Schmuckler, M. A. (2002). The effect of the number of A trials on performance on the A-not-B task. *Infancy, 3*(4), 519–529.

Marenco, S., & Weinberger, D. R. (2000). The neurodevelopmental hypothesis of Schizophrenia: Following a trail of evidence from cradle to grave. *Development and Psychopathology, 12,* 501–527.

Maurer, D., & Lewis, T. L. (2001). Visual acuity and spatial contrast sensitivity: Normal development and underlying mechanisms. In C. A. Nelson & M. Luciana (Eds.), *Handbook of developmental cognitive neuroscience* (pp. 237–251). Cambridge, MA: MIT Press.

Mazas, C. A., Finn, P. R., & Steinmetz, J. E. (2000). Decision-making biases, antisocial personality, and early-onset alcoholism. *Alcoholism: Clinical and Experimental Research, 24*(7), 1036–1040.

Mazzoco, M. M., Nord, A. M., van Doorninck, W., Greene, C. L., Kovar, C. G., & Pennington, B. F. (1994). Cognitive development among children with early-treated phenylketonuria. *Developmental Neuropsychology, 10,* 133–151.

McCracken, J. T., Smalley, S. L., McGough, J. J., Crawford, L., Del'Homme, M., Cantor, R. M., et al. (2000). Evidence for linkage of a tandem duplication polymorphism upstream of the dopamine D4 receptor gene (DRD4) with attention deficit hyperactivity disorder (ADHD). *Molecular Psychiatry, 5*(5), 531–536.

McDowell, S., Whyte, J., & D'Esposito, M. D. (1998). Differential effect of a dopaminergic agonist on prefrontal function in traumatic brain injury patients. *Brain, 121,* 1155–1164.

McGue, M., Iacono, W. G., Legrand, L. N., Malone, S., & Elkins, I. (2001). The origins and consequences of age at first drink: I. Associations with substance-use disorders, disinhibitory behavior and psychopathology, and P3 amplitude. *Alcoholism: Clinical and Experimental Research, 25,* 1156–1165.

McKean, C. M., & Petersen, N. A. (1970). Glutamine in the phenylketonuric central nervous system. *New England Journal of Medicine, 283,* 1364–1367.

Mehta, M. A., Sahakian, B. J., McKenna, P. J., & Robbins, T. W. (1999). Systemic sulpiride in young adult volunteers simulates the profile of cognitive deficits in Parkinson's disease. *Psychopharmacology, 146,* 162–174.

Mehta, M. A., Swainson, R., Ogilvie, A. D., Sahakian, B. J., & Robbins, T. W. (2001). Improved short-term spatial memory but impaired reversal learning following the dopamine D2 agonist bromocriptine in normal volunteers. *Psychopharmacology, 159,* 10–20.

Merzenich, M. M., Jenkins, W. M., Johnston, P., Schreiner, C., Miller, S. L., & Tallal, P. (1996). Temporal processing deficits of language-learning impaired children ameliorated by training. *Science, 271,* 77–81.

Mesulam, M. M. (1998). From sensation to cognition. *Brain, 121,* 1013–1052.

Metcalfe, J. (2000, April). *Hot/cool framework of cognition and emotion: Application to drug addiction.* Paper presented at the annual meeting of the Cognitive Neuroscience Society, San Francisco.

Miller, E. K., & Cohen, J. D. (2001). An integrative theory of prefrontal cortex function. *Annual Review of Neuroscience, 24,* 167–202.

Milner, B. (1963). Effects of different brain lesions on card sorting: The role of the frontal lobe. *Archives of Neurology, 9,* 90–100.

Milner, B. (1965). Visually-guided maze learning in man: Effects of bilateral hippocampal, bilateral frontal, and unilateral cerebral lesions. *Neuropsychologia, 3,* 317–338.

Milner, B. (1971). Interhemispheric differences and psychological processes. *British Medical Bulletin, 27,* 272–277.

Milner, B. (1995). Aspects of human frontal lobe function. *Advances in Neurology, 66,* 67–84.

Milner, B., Corsi, P., & Leonard, G. (1991). Frontal lobe contribution to recency judgments. *Neuropsychologia, 29,* 601–618.

Mogenson, G. J., Jones, D. L., & Yim, C. Y. (1980). From motivation to action: Functional interface between the limbic system and the motor system. *Progress in Neurobiology, 14*(2/3), 69–97.

Moscovitch, M. (1992). Memory and working-with-memory: A component process model based on modules and central systems. *Journal of Cognitive Neuroscience, 4*(3), 257–267.

Muller, U., von Cramon, D. Y., & Pollmann, S. (1998). D1 versus D2 receptor modulation of visuospatial working memory in humans. *Journal of Neuroscience, 18*(7), 2720–2728.

Nelson, C. A. (1995). The ontogeny of human memory: A cognitive neuroscience perspective. *Developmental Psychology, 31,* 723–738.

Niki, H. (1974). Differential activity of prefrontal units during right and left delayed response trials. *Brain Research, 70*(2), 346–349.

Ornstein, T. J., Iddon, J. L., Baldacchino, A. M., Sahakian, B. J., London, M., Everitt, B. J., et al. (2000). Profiles of cognitive dysfunction in chronic amphetamine and heroin users. *Neuropsychopharmacology, 23*(2), 113–126.

Overman, W. H., Bachevalier, J., Schuhmann, E., & Ryan, P. (1996). Cognitive gender differences in very young children parallel biologically based cognitive gender differences in monkeys. *Behavioral Neuroscience, 110,* 673–684.

Overman, W. H., Frassrand, K., Ansel, S., Trawalter, S., Bies, B., & Redmond, A. (2004). Performance on the Iowa card task by adolescents and adults. *Neuropsychologia, 42,* 1838–1851.

Owen, A. M. (1997). The functional organization of working memory processes within human lateral frontal cortex: The contribution of functional imaging. *European Journal of Neuroscience, 9,* 1329–1339.

Owen, A. M., Downes, J. J., Sahakian, B. J., Polkey, C. E., & Robbins, T. W. (1990). Planning and spatial working memory deficits following frontal lobe lesions in man. *Neuropsychologia, 28,* 1021–1034.

Owen, A. M., Doyon, J., Petrides, M., & Evans, A. C. (1996). Planning and spatial working memory: A positron emission tomography study in humans. *European Journal of Neuroscience, 8,* 353–364.

Owen, A. M., Evans, A. C., & Petrides, M. (1996). Evidence for a two-stage model of spatial working memory processing within the lateral frontal cortex: A positron emission tomography study. *Cerebral Cortex, 6,* 31–38.

Owen, A. M., Iddon, J. L., Hodges, J. R., Summers, B. A., & Robbins, T. W. (1997). Spatial and non-spatial working memory at different stages of Parkinson's disease. *Neuropsychologia, 35,* 519–532.

Owen, A. M., Morris, R. G., Sahakian, B. J., Polkey, C. E., & Robbins, T. W. (1996). Double dissociations of memory and executive functions in a self-ordered working memory task following frontal lobe excision, temporal lobe excision, or amygdalo-hippocampectomy in man. *Brain, 119,* 1597–1615.

Owen, A. M., Roberts, A. C., Polkey, C. E., Sahakian, B. J., & Robbins, T. W. (1991). Extradimensional versus intradimensional set-shifting performance following frontal lobe excisions, temporal lobe excisions, or amygdalo-hippocampectomy in man. *Neuropsychologia, 33,* 1–24.

Owen, A. M., Sahakian, B. J., Semple, J., Polkey, C. E., & Robbins, T. W. (1995). Visuo-spatial short-term recognition memory and learning after temporal lobe excision, frontal lobe excision, or amygdalo-hippocampectomy in man. *Neuropsychologia, 33,* 1–24.

Ozonoff, S. (2001). Advances in the cognitive neuroscience of Autism. In C. A. Nelson & M. Luciana (Eds.), *Handbook of developmental cognitive neuroscience* (pp. 537–548). Cambridge, MA: MIT Press.

Pandya, D. N., & Yeterian, E. H. (1990). Prefrontal cortex in relation to other cortical areas in rhesus monkey: Architecture and connections. *Progress in Brain Research, 85,* 63–94.

Park, S., & Holzman, P. S. (1992). Schizophrenics show spatial working memory deficits. *Archives of General Psychiatry, 49,* 975–982.

Pascalis, O., & Bachevalier, J. (1999). Neonatal aspiration lesions of the hippocampal formation impair visual recognition memory when assessed by paired-comparison task but not by delayed-nonmatching-to-sample task. *Hippocampus, 9,* 609–616.

Passler, P. A., Isaac, W., & Hynd, G. W. (1985). Neuropsychological development of behavior attributed to frontal lobe functioning in children. *Developmental Neuropsychology, 4,* 349–370.

Paus, T., Collins, D. L., Evans, A. C., Leonard, G., Pike, B., & Zjdenbos, A. (2001). Maturation of white matter in the human brain: A review of magnetic resonance studies. *Brain Research Bulletin, 54*(3), 255–266.

Penfield, W., & Evans, J. (1935). The frontal lobe in man: A clinical study of maximum removals. *Brain, 58,* 115–133.

Penfield, W., & Jasper, H. (1954). *Epilepsy and the functional anatomy of the human brain.* Boston: Little, Brown.

Pennington, B. F., van Doorninck, W. J., McCabe, L. L., & McCabe, E. R. (1985). Neuropsychological deficits in early-treated phenylketonuric children. *American Journal of Mental Deficiencies, 89*(5), 467–474.

Perlstein, W. M., Dixit, N. K., Carter, C. S., Noll, D. C., & Cohen, J. D. (2003). Prefrontal cortical dysfunction mediates deficits in working memory and prepotent responding in Schizophrenia. *Biological Psychiatry, 53*(1), 25–38.

Perret, E. (1974). The left frontal lobe of man and the suppression of habitual responses in verbal categorical behaviour. *Neuropsychologia, 12,* 527–537.

Petrides, M. (1995). Functional organization of the human frontal cortex for mnemonic processing: Evidence from neuroimaging studies. *Annals of the New York Academy of Sciences, 769,* 85–96.

Petrides, M. (2000). Dissociable roles of mid-dorsolateral prefrontal and anterior inferotemporal cortex in visual working memory. *Journal of Neuroscience, 20*(19), 7496–7503.

Petrides, M., & Milner, B. (1982). Deficits in subject-ordered tasks after frontal and temporal-lobe lesions in man. *Neuropsychologia, 20,* 249–262.

Pfefferbaum, A., Mathalon, D. H., Sullivan, E. V., Rawles, J. M., Zipursky, R. B., & Lim, K. O. (1994). A quantitative magnetic resonance imaging study of changes in brain morphology from infancy to late adulthood. *Archives of Neurology, 51*(9), 874–887.

Piaget, J. (1936). *The construction of reality in the child* (M. Cook, Trans.). New York: Basic Books.

Pietz, J., Kreis, R., Rupp, A., Mayatepek, E., Rating, D., Boesch, C., et al. (1999). Large neutral amino acids block phenylalanine transport into brain tissue in patients with phenylketonuria. *Journal of Clinical Investigation, 103*(8), 1169–1178.

Rahman, S., Robbins, T. W., & Sahakian, B. J. (1999). Comparative cognitive neuropsychological studies of frontal lobe function: Implications for therapeutic strategies in frontal variant frontotemporal dementia. *Dementing Geriatric Cognitive Disorders, 10*(Suppl. 1), 15–28.

Raichle, M. E. (1998). Behind the scenes of functional brain imaging: A historical and physiological perspective. *Proceedings of the National Academy of Sciences, USA, 95,* 765–772.

Rakic, P. (1974). Neurons in the monkey visual cortex: Systematic relation between time of origin and eventual disposition. *Science, 183,* 425–427.

Rakic, P. (1977). Prenatal development of the visual system in the rhesus monkey. *Philosophical Transactions of the Royal Society of London. Series B, Biological Sciences, 278,* 245–260.

Rakic, P. (1985). Limits of neurogenesis in primates. *Science, 227,* 154–156.

Rakic, P. (1995). The development of the frontal lobe: A view from the rear of the brain. In H. H. Jasper, S. Riggio, & P. S. Goldman-Rakic (Eds.), *Advances in neurology: Vol. 66. Epilepsy and the functional anatomy of the frontal lobe* (pp. 1–8). New York: Raven Press.

Rakic, P., Bourgeois, J. P., Eckenhoff, M. F., Zecevic, N., & Goldman-Rakic, P. S. (1986). Concurrent overproduction of synapses in diverse regions of the primate cerebral cortex. *Science, 232*(4747), 232–235.

Rakic, P., Bourgeois, J. P., & Goldman-Rakic, P. S. (1994). Synaptic development of the cerebral cortex: Implications for learning, memory, and mental illness. *Progress in Brain Research, 102,* 227–243.

Reavis, R., & Overman, W. H. (2001). Adult sex differences on a decision-making task previously shown to depend on the orbital prefrontal cortex. *Behavioral Neuroscience, 115,* 196–206.

Reiss, A. L., Abrams, M. T., Singer, H. S., Ross, J. L., & Denckla, M. B. (1996). Brain development, gender and IQ in children. A volumetric imaging study. *Brain, 119*(Pt. 5), 1763–1774.

Richards, J. E. (2000). Localizing the development of covert attention in infants using scalp event-related potentials. *Developmental Psychology, 36,* 91–108.

Ridderinkhof, K. R., & van der Molen, M. W. (1997). Mental resources, processing speed, and inhibitory control: A developmental perspective. *Biological Psychology, 45*(1/3), 241–261.

Rilling, J. K., Gutman, D. A., Zeh, T. R., Pagnoni, G., Berns, G. S., & Kilts, C. D. (2002). A neural basis for social cooperation. *Neuron, 35*(2), 395–405.

Ris, M. D., Williams, S. E., Hunt, M. M., Berry, H. K., & Leslie, N. (1994). Early-treated phenylketonuria: Adult neuropsychologic outcome. *Journal of Pediatrics, 124,* 388–392.

Rogers, R. D., Everitt, B. J., Baldacchino, A., Blackshaw, A. J., Swainson, R., Wynne, K., et al. (1999). Dissociable deficits in the decision-making cognition of chronic amphetamine abusers, opiate abusers, patients with focal damage to prefrontal cortex, and tryptophan-depleted normal volunteers: Evidence for monoaminergic mechanisms. *Neuropsychopharmacology, 20*(4), 322–339.

Rolls, E. T. (1999). *The brain and emotion.* Oxford: Oxford University Press.

Rolls, E. T. (2004). The functions of the orbitofrontal cortex. *Brain and Cognition, 55,* 11–29.

Rose, J. E., & Woolsey, C. N. (1948). The orbitofrontal cortex and its connections with the mediodorsal thalamus in rabbit, sheep, and cat. *Research Publications of the Association for Research on Nervous and Mental Disorders, 27,* 210–232.

Rosenkilde, C. E. (1979). Functional heterogeneity of the prefrontal cortex in the monkey: A review. *Behavioral and Neural Biology, 25,* 301–345.

Sahakian, B. J., & Owen, A. M. (1992). Computerised assessment in neuropsychiatry using CANTAB. *Journal of the Royal Society of Medicine, 85,* 399–402.

Sawaguchi, T., & Goldman-Rakic, P. S. (1991). D1 dopamine receptors in prefrontal cortex: Involvement in working memory. *Science, 251,* 947–950.

Sawaguchi, T., Matsumura, M., & Kubota, K. (1988). Dopamine enhances the neuronal activity of a spatial short term memory task in the primate prefrontal cortex. *Neuroscience Research, 5,* 465–473.

Sawaguchi, T., Matsumura, M., & Kubota, K. (1990a). Catecholamine effects on neuronal activity related to a delayed response task in monkey prefrontal cortex. *Journal of Neurophysiology, 63*(6), 1385–1400.

Sawaguchi, T., Matsumura, M., & Kubota, K. (1990b). Effects of dopamine antagonists on neuronal activity related to a delayed response task in monkey prefrontal cortex. *Journal of Neurophysiology, 63*(6), 1401–1412.

Schwartz, M. L., & Goldman-Rakic, P. S. (1991). Callosal and intrahemispheric connectivity of the prefrontal association cortex in rhesus monkey: Relation between intraparietal and principal sulcal cortex. *Journal of Comparative Neurology, 226,* 403–420.

Selemon, L. D., & Goldman-Rakic, P. S. (1988). Common cortical and subcortical targets of the dorsolateral prefrontal and posterior parietal cortices in the rhesus monkey: Evidence for a distributed neural network subserving spatially-guided behavior. *Journal of Neuroscience, 8,* 4049–4068.

Selemon, L. D., & Goldman-Rakic, P. S. (1999). The reduced neuropil hypothesis: A circuit-based model of Schizophrenia. *Biological Psychiatry, 45,* 17–25.

Shallice, T. (1982). Specific impairments in planning. *Philosophical Transactions of the Royal Society of London. Series B, Biological Sciences, 298,* 199–209.

Sowell, E. R., Delis, D., Stiles, J., & Jernigan, T. L. (2001). Improved memory functioning and frontal lobe maturation between childhood and adolescence: A structural MRI study. *Journal of the International Neuropsychological Society, 7,* 312–322.

Sowell, E. R., Peterson, B. S., Thompson, P. M., Welcome, S. E., Henkenius, A. L., & Toga, A. W. (2003). Mapping cortical change across the human lifespan. *Nature Neuroscience,* 1–7.

Sowell, E. R., Thompson, P. M., Tessner, K. D., & Toga, A. W. (2001). Mapping continued brain growth and gray matter density reduction in dorsal frontal cortex: Inverse relationships during postadolescent brain maturation. *Journal of Neuroscience, 21*(22), 8819–8829.

Spear, L. P. (2000). The adolescent brain and age-related behavioral manifestations. *Neuroscience and Biobehavioral Reviews, 24,* 417–463.

Spoont, M. R. (1992). The modulatory role of serotonin in neural information processing: Implications for human psychopathology. *Psychological Bulletin, 112,* 330–350.

Spreen, O., Risser, A. T., & Edgell, D. (1995). *Developmental neuropsychology.* New York: Oxford University Press.

Spurzheim, J. G. (1825). *Phrenology, or doctrine of the mind* (3rd ed.). London: Knight.

Steen, R. G., Ogg, R. J., Reddick, W. E., & Kingsley, P. B. (1997). Age-related changes in the pediatric brain: Quantitative MR evidence of maturational changes during adolescence. *American Journal of Radiology, 18,* 819–828.

Sullivan, E. V., Fama, R., Rosenbloom, M. J., & Pfefferbaum, A. (2002). A profile of neuropsychological deficits in alcoholic women. *Neuropsychology, 16*(1), 74–83.

Svingos, A. L., Periasamy, S., & Pickel, V. M. (2000). Presynaptic dopamine D(4) receptor localization in the rat nucleus accumbens shell. *Synapse, 36,* 222–232.

Swanson, J. M., Flodman, P., Kennedy, J., Spence, M. A., Moyzis, R., Schuck, S., et al. (2000). Dopamine genes and ADHD. *Neuroscience and Biobehavioral Reviews, 24*(1), 21–25.

Tamm, L., Menon, V., & Reiss, A. I. (2002). Maturation of brain function associated with response inhibition. *Journal of the American Academy of Child and Adolescent Psychiatry and Allied Disciplines, 41*(10), 1231–1238.

Taylor, J. (Ed.). (1958). *Selected writings of John Hughlings Jackson* (Vols. 1–2). London: Staples Press.

Vaidya, C. J., Austin, G., Kirkorian, G., Ridlehuber, H. W., Desmond, J. E., Glover, G. H., et al. (1998). Selective effects of methylphenidate in attention deficit hyperactivity disorder: A functional magnetic resonance study. *Proceedings of the National Academy of Sciences, USA, 95,* 14494–14499.

van der Knapp, M. S., & Valk, J. (1990). MR imaging of the various stages of normal myelination during the first year of life. *Neuroradiology, 31,* 459–470.

Van Horn, J. D., Grafton, S. T., Rockmore, D., & Gazzaniga, M. S. (2004). Sharing neuroimaging studies of human cognition. *Nature Neuroscience, 7*(5), 473–481.

Vitiello, B., Martin, A., Hill, J., Mack, C., Molchan, S., Martinez, R., et al. (1997). Cognitive and behavioral effects of cholinergic, dopaminergic, and serotonergic blockade in humans. *Neuropsychopharmacology, 16*(1), 15–24.

Volkow, N. D., Fowler, J. S., Wolf, A. P., Hitzemann, R., Dewey, S., Bendriem, B., et al. (1991). Changes in brain glucose metabolism in cocaine dependence and withdrawal. *American Journal of Psychiatry, 148*(5), 621–626.

Walker, A. E. (1940). A cytoarchitectural study of the prefrontal area of the macaque monkey. *Journal of Comparative Neurology, 73,* 59–86.

Walker, E. F., Savoie, T., & Davis, D. (1994). Neuromotor precursors of Schizophrenia. *Schizophrenia Bulletin, 20,* 441–451.

Wechsler, D. (1991). *Wechsler Intelligence Scale for Children: Third revision.* San Antonio, TX: Psychological Corporation.

Wechsler, D. (1997). *Wechsler Adult Intelligence Scale* (3rd. ed.). San Antonio, TX: Psychological Corporation.

Weglage, J., Pietsch, M., Fünders, B., Koch, H. G., & Ullrich, K. (1996). Deficits in selective and sustained attention processes in early treated children with phenylketonuria: Results of impaired frontal lobe functions? *European Journal of Pediatrics, 155,* 200–204.

Weinberger, D. R. (1986). The pathogenesis of Schizophrenia: A neurodevelopmental theory. In H. A. W. Naurallah & D. R. Weinberger (Eds.), *The neurology of Schizophrenia* (pp. 397–406). Amsterdam: Elsevier.

Weinberger, D. R. (1987). Implications of normal brain development for the pathogenesis of Schizophrenia. *Archives of General Psychiatry, 44,* 660–669.

Weinberger, D. R., Egan, M. F., Bertolino, A., Callicott, J. H., Lipska, B. K., Berman, K. F., et al. (2001). Prefrontal neurons and the genetics of Schizophrenia. *Biological Psychiatry, 50*(11), 825–844.

Welsh, M. C., Pennington, B. F., & Groisser, D. B. (1991). A normative-developmental study of executive function: A window on prefrontal function in children. *Developmental Neuropsychology, 7*(2), 131–149.

Welsh, M. C., Pennington, B. F., Ozonoff, S., Rouse, B., & McCabe, E. R. B. (1990). Neuropsychology of early-treated phenylketonuria: Specific executive function deficits. *Child Development, 61,* 1697–1713.

Wernicke, C. (1908). The symptom-complex of aphasia. In A. Church (Ed.), *Diseases of the nervous system* (pp. 265–324). New York: Appleton.

White, D. A., Nortz, M. J., Mandernach, T., Huntington, K., & Steiner, R. D. (2002). Age-related working memory impairments in children with prefrontal dysfunction associated with phenylketonuria. *Journal of the International Neuropsychological Society, 8,* 1–11.

Williams, G. V., & Goldman-Rakic, P. S. (1995). Modulation of memory fields by dopamine D1 receptors in prefrontal cortex. *Nature, 376,* 572–575.

Williamson, M. L., Koch, R., Azen, C., & Chang, C. (1981). Correlates of intelligence tests results in treated phenylketonuric children. *Pediatrics, 68,* 161–167.

Wilson, F. A. W., O'Scalaidhe, S. P., & Goldman-Rakic, P. S. (1993). Dissociation of object and spatial processing in primate prefrontal cortex. *Science, 260,* 1955–1958.

Zelazo, P. D., Frye, D., & Rapus, T. (1996). An age-related dissociation between knowing rules and using them. *Cognitive Development, 11,* 37–63.

CHAPTER 8

Neuropsychological Perspectives on Developmental Psychopathology

SALLY OZONOFF, BRUCE F. PENNINGTON, and MARJORIE SOLOMON

This chapter explores the utility of neuropsychological conceptualizations of developmental psychopathology. Simply put, the field of neuropsychology is concerned with understanding brain-behavior relations. Although this field is over 200 years old, through most of its history it has been focused on understanding brain-behavior relations in mature humans and other animals mainly by examining the effects of acquired lesions. The application of a neuropsychological approach to understanding disorders of development, especially developmental psychopathology, is a relatively recent phenomenon. With a few exceptions (Orton, 1925), most of this work has been done in the past 40 years (see Benton, 1974, for a brief review of some early work in this field).

It is important to appreciate how much has changed in those 40-odd years. In the mid-1960s, few psychopathologies were regarded as brain disorders, partly because the dominant psychoanalytic and behaviorist paradigms emphasized environmental etiologies and partly because the methods for measuring brain structure and function were

so rudimentary. A strict dualistic distinction was often drawn between "organic" and "functional" disorders, with most psychiatric disorders regarded as functional. Thus, findings that challenged these views, such as evidence for heritability of disorders like Schizophrenia (Gottesman & Shields, 1976), were surprising and controversial. Neuropsychologists were critical to overturning the dominant environmental/functional view of psychopathology. They had already developed test batteries with proven sensitivity to the presence, lateralization, and localization of acquired brain damage (e.g., Reitan & Davison, 1974). When these batteries were then used with patients with psychiatric disorders, notably Schizophrenia, it became clear that several diagnoses had correlated neuropsychological dysfunction (e.g., Heaton, Baade, & Johnson, 1978), and could be thought of as brain disorders.

Behavioral methods for evaluating neuropsychological functions in children began to be developed around the same time. One impetus was the clinical need to measure the effects of childhood neurological disorders, such as focal lesions, closed head injuries, and seizures. This work led to the emergence of the field of child clinical neuropsychology. It was soon reported that childhood brain damage was associated with psychopathology (Shaffer, 1973). Rutter (1977), using epidemiological data from the Isle of Wight studies, demonstrated that children with brain damage had a rate of emotional disturbance (34.3%) almost 6 times higher than the rate (6.6%) found in healthy controls and 3 times higher than the rate (11.5%) found in children with nonneurological physical disorders. So brain damage in childhood impaired not only cognitive development but emotional and behavioral development as well. Moreover, the association between psychopathology and brain dysfunction was found to run in the opposite direction. When neuropsychological batteries appropriate for children were applied to childhood psychiatric disorders, such as Autism and Attention-Deficit/Hyperactivity Disorder (ADHD), neuropsychological deficits were found. These batteries were also applied to childhood genetic syndromes like Turner's syndrome and early treated phenylketonuria, and particular patterns of deficits were found. The finding that somewhat distinct neuropsychological phenotypes were characteristic of *both* behaviorally and etiologically defined disorders contributed to the view that all these disorders had a neurodevelopmental origin and could be explained by the same paradigm.

Around the same time, the field of developmental neuropsychology began to emerge to address fundamental questions about the origins of the brain-behavior relations found in adults: Is there innate or progressive left hemisphere lateralization of language function (Lenneberg, 1967; Segalowitz & Gruber, 1977)? Is the young brain more plastic after brain damage than the mature brain (Goldman-Rakic, Isseroff, Schwartz, & Bugbee, 1983; Kennard, 1940)? How does localization of function emerge in development, and how plastic are these localizations (Neville, 1977)? Obviously, contributions from child clinical and developmental neuropsychology are mutually informative. The overall goal is to explain both typical and atypical behavioral development using the same paradigm. This is the goal of the relatively new field of developmental cognitive neuroscience, which has its roots in the earlier work described here, but which has recently shown dramatic growth, partly because of the advent of new technologies.

In sum, in a scant 40 years, the neuropsychological approach to understanding developmental psychopathological disorders has evolved considerably, as the work reviewed here demonstrates. The neuropsychological approach is no longer new and has been applied to explain the manifestations and potential underlying mechanisms of many different childhood disorders. It is now time to take a critical look at how this model has proven useful and, when it has failed, what we have learned from its limitations. The neuropsychological model holds great promise for improving our understanding of multiple aspects of developmental psychopathology, as well as enhancing our knowledge of typical development. It may be useful for refining diagnosis, better predicting prognosis, and matching specific treatments to specific subtypes or profiles within a more broadly defined condition. On the other hand, rapid technological and scientific advances in fields as diverse as genetics, imaging, and connectionist modeling have led to postmodularity conceptualizations of the brain that may limit the utility of certain basic tenets of the neuropsychological perspective on developmental psychopathology.

This chapter reviews the multilevel model for analyzing developmental psychopathology laid out in the first edition of these volumes (Pennington & Welsh, 1995) and further developed in Pennington (2002). Four broad levels of analysis are discussed: etiology, brain mechanisms, neuropsychology, and behavior. Next, we focus on the neuropsychological level of analysis and its promise of providing a bridge between brain and behavior, identifying mechanisms that may be closer to and more consistent with biology than are symptoms themselves. In the third section, we examine two forms of developmental psychopathology, Autism Spectrum Disorders and Posttraumatic Stress Disorder, applying a neuroscientific perspective. Exploring these very different disorders provides a rigorous test of the neuropsychological model. After this, limitations of the neuropsychological model and ways it may not live up to its promises are discussed. Implications for future research conclude the chapter.

THE NEUROSCIENTIFIC PERSPECTIVE

In our model of developmental psychopathology (Pennington, 2002), there are four levels of analysis: the *etiological* level that examines genetic and environmental influences that heighten the risk of psychopathology, the *brain mechanisms* that these etiologies act on, the *neuropsychological processes* that are in turn disrupted by alterations in brain development, and the *symptoms* or behavioral phenotypes that are the final product of the three preceding levels. A basic tenet of multilevel analytic frameworks is that psychopathology cannot be reduced to any one level (Cicchetti & Dawson, 2002; Nelson et al., 2002). When the field of developmental psychopathology was relatively new, much work was invested in understanding the symptom level, the specific behaviors or signs associated with specific conditions. Diagnostic taxonomies struggled to delineate symptoms that were reliably associated with a disorder and that distinguished it from other disorders. Although this work was absolutely necessary, it was not sufficient for the maturing field of developmental psychopathology, leaving many questions about causes, mechanisms, and, ultimately, treatments unanswered. Many interventions are developed from theories of causation, highlighting the importance of an understanding of underlying mechanisms. Furthermore, apparent developmental discontinuities or dissociations at the symptom level of analysis may be clarified at deeper levels of analysis. One of the basic principles fundamental to this chapter is that recent contributions from etiological, brain, and neuropsychological research have significantly matured the field of developmental psychopathology. This chapter is concerned primarily with the third level of analysis in this model, the neuropsychological level, but processes at different levels are interactive and reciprocal and so it is essential that we consider all levels.

Pennington's (2002) model chose four levels of analysis; this heuristic has proven quite useful, as we hope to illustrate in this chapter, but it remains to be seen whether four levels will be sufficient to capture the variability within and across developmental psychopathology. As our understanding of the brain improves with new innovations in technology, it may become clear that the neural level of analysis needs to be further subdivided into anatomical and chemical functional units, to take just one example. For now, we illuminate the four levels originally postulated by Pennington (1991, 2002) but return to the issue of this model's limits later in the chapter.

We propose that this four-level heuristic is valuable for understanding all developmental psychopathologies, not just those with robust evidence of biological etiology or brain involvement. Indeed, it is a basic premise of our model that the manifestations of all developmental psychopathologies are mediated by brain processes. As such, all require some understanding of the neuropsychological processes that bridge the brain and behavior levels of analysis. Even a condition with purely social-environmental (i.e., interpersonal) etiologies, with no genetic influence or neurological trauma associated with it, still alters brain development and function. Indeed, we believe it is fundamentally incorrect to distinguish between mind and brain, functional and organic, psychological and physiological, environmental and biological, nature and nurture. All

pathological processes act at some point on the brain, changing its organization and function and resulting in a pattern of atypical behavior. Thoughts, feelings, actions, indeed every aspect of behavior ultimately originate in neurons firing in particular patterns. All social influences affect brain development in some way, and all psychological processes are executed by brain mechanisms.

Two examples illustrate this close interplay between brain and behavior. It has long been observed that adults who were abused or neglected during childhood are at much greater risk for affective disorders. It is now becoming clear that traumatic early events and other early experiences alter brain development and, in this way, contribute to the development of psychopathology (Grossman et al., 2003). Persistent changes have been found in hypothalamic neurons and receptors in mice exposed to repeated maternal separations during infancy (Heim & Nemeroff, 1999). The second example comes from a treatment study of Obsessive-Compulsive Disorder (OCD) that scanned participants before and after treatment using positron emission tomography (PET). Some participants were treated with medication and others with psychotherapy. Regardless of the treatment strategy, both showed metabolic changes in the same neural systems at the outcome scan (Schwartz, Stoessel, Baxter, Martin, & Phelps, 1996). What surprised many about this study was that psychotherapy alters brain activity, and in the same way that effective medications for OCD do. These two examples clearly demonstrate that mind and brain are one and the same and that psychological constructs (i.e., psychotherapy, personality, social experiences, interpersonal risk factors) affect behavior because they affect brain function. Clearly, then, it is not enough to frame an explanation of a psychopathology purely in terms of mental or psychological constructs. But neither is it satisfactory to explain the condition only at the etiological or brain levels, in terms of gene mutations or receptor densities. We need to understand how genetic or brain differences lead to changes in behavior; in our model, these mechanisms can be elucidated at the neuropsychological level of analysis.

Complicating this model are bidirectional influences among the levels. The causal arrows do not run in only one direction, from the etiological or brain levels to behavior. A child's behavior constrains his or her experiences and creates certain environmental consequences, which in turn change brain development. Although experiences and environment do not change genes and DNA sequences, there is emerging evidence that they can influence gene activity. For example, early stress experiences can change the expression of the gene that produces the glucocorticoid receptor (Meaney et al., 1996). In rat pups, maternal separation causes increased corticotropin-releasing factor messenger RNA expression in several brain regions, including the amygdala (Caldji, Francis, Sharma, Plotsky, & Meaney, 2000). It should not be surprising that signals from the environment are capable of activating the DNA necessary to produce the appropriate proteins the organism needs to function in the environment, yet this direction of gene-environment interaction has rarely been appreciated (Gottlieb, 1998).

Four Levels of Analysis

With this introduction to the neuroscientific model of developmental psychopathology, we proceed to more detailed descriptions of the four levels of analysis. The symptoms of a disorder are end points of a complicated developmental process that includes multiple interacting levels and pathways. The science of developmental psychopathology has been successful at characterizing the outputs of this process, but is only beginning to understand its inputs. Therefore, we begin at the beginning, with the etiological level.

At the *etiological level,* both genetic and environmental factors work, separately or together, to cause psychopathology. As discussed earlier, there has been a tendency to view some conditions as more biological or genetic in origin and others as more social-environmental or interpersonal. It is becoming increasingly evident, however, that most developmental psychopathologies are caused by an interaction of genetic and environmental factors (Pennington, 2002) and that there is moderate genetic influence on most behavioral traits (Plomin & Rutter, 1998). Genes do not simply act very early in development and then hand the organism over to the environment. They turn off and on across the life span, and their expression can be changed by both the internal and external environments (Gottlieb, 1998). Psychopathologies likely result from specific combinations of biological and psychosocial risks (e.g., specific gene mutations, general susceptibility alleles, difficult life events, socioeconomic adversity, environmental exposures) and protective factors (good prenatal care, nutrition, protective alleles, parenting, safe physical environment, access to community resources and support). Studies at the etiological level use multiple research methods, including behavioral and molecular genetics.

Etiological factors do not "code" for behavior directly. They influence behavior through their impact on the process of brain development. Thus, the next level in our model is the *brain mechanism level.* There are many examples of specific genetic mutations that affect the development of specific brain structures. Genetic variations can alter the migration of neurons, their organization into functional units such as columns and minicolumns, and their dendritic connections to other neurons. Neurons communicate with each other and with the rest of the body through chemical messengers (neurotransmitters and neuromodulators) that are released by one cell and bind to receptors on other cells. Receptors are proteins coded for by genes, and thus variations in their structure and function are under genetic control.

It is clear that genetics alone do not determine brain development. Since the landmark experiments of Hubel and Wiesel (1970) demonstrated the essential role that experiential input played in the organization and function of the feline visual system, it has been evident that the environment plays a very important role in shaping the developing brain. With approximately 10^{11} neurons and 10^{15} connections between them, it is logically impossible for 30,000 human genes to determine all the locations and connections of all the neurons in the brain (Changeux, 1985). Instead, the developing brain overproduces neurons, dendrites, and synapses, and experience "selects" which elements to preserve. During the course of typical development, those neurons and connections that are used are strengthened and those that are not used die. In some forms of psychopathology, such as Autism, there is evidence that these production and pruning processes do not take place in the typical way, resulting in disastrous deviations in development. The distribution of head size for children with Autism as a group is shifted by up to 1 standard deviation, and a substantial minority (up to 20%) exhibit macrocephaly (head circumference greater than the 97th percentile; Lainhart et al., 1997). A recent study reported that children with Autism are born with significantly smaller than normal head circumference, but by the first birthday have, as a group, mean head circumference at the 84th percentile, suggesting rapid and excessive early brain growth and failure of the typical pruning processes (Courchesne, Carper, & Akshoomoff, 2003).

As summarized earlier, it is clear that early experiences modify brain function and in this way may contribute to the development or prevention of psychopathology (see Grossman et al., 2003, for a recent review). Later experiences can also alter brain structure by adding or subtracting dendrites or synapses and by modifying existing synapses (Greenough, Black, & Wallace, 1987) and, possibly, by creating new neurons, even in adulthood (Gould,

Reeves, Graziano, & Gross, 1999), although this latter finding is controversial and more work is needed. Thus, experience and genetics play a major role in shaping the central nervous system across the life span.

Research methods used to explore brain level include animal lesion studies, neurochemical studies, and structural and functional neuroimaging. Relatively recent and rapid technological advances in neuroimaging have greatly illuminated brain processes involved in typical and atypical development.

The next level in our analytic framework is the *neuropsychological level.* This level bridges the gap between mind and body, making it the most challenging conceptually. One of its goals is to explain how variations in neural networks lead to changes in behavior. That is, *how* specifically do changes in the brain translate into functional differences, both psychopathological and normative, among people? An equally important goal of the neuropsychological level of analysis is to provide more parsimonious explanations of behavior than does a list or description of symptoms. A major presumption of the neuropsychological level is that variations in behavior can be reduced to variations in a smaller number of neuropsychological processes. The language of neuropsychological mechanisms is presumably closer to and more consistent with brain architecture than are symptoms or psychological constructs. With the rapid advances occurring in neuroscience, the neuropsychological level is poised to undergo rapid development. One of the most exciting recent developments at the neuropsychological level has been the use of functional neuroimaging technology to observe the brain as individuals engage in the execution of simple neuropsychological tasks. The rest of this chapter discusses this level of analysis more deeply.

Finally, the *symptom level* of analysis describes in a (supposedly) atheoretical manner the clusters of behaviors that define specific disorders. The developmental psychopathology field has been largely focused at this level thus far. The fruits of this labor include current diagnostic taxonomies, such as the *Diagnostic and Statistical Manual of Mental Disorders* (*DSM*) and *International Classification of Diseases.* These systems have been refined through multiple revisions so that behavioral descriptions have become increasingly more reliable and valid. The symptom level of analysis continues to wrestle with a number of crucial issues, including (1) phenotypic variability, (2) external validity, (3) comorbidity, and (4) discontinuities across development. Many of these issues can be resolved using tools from neuropsychology, as discussed later.

Promises of the Neuropsychological Level of Analysis

Understanding the neuropsychological processes that underlie a disorder can help move the field of developmental psychopathology along in a number of ways.

Phenotypic Variability

One major concern of the symptom level of analysis is phenotypic heterogeneity. Different individuals diagnosed with the same condition do not present with the exact same symptom patterns. For most conditions, a list of potential symptoms is included in the diagnostic criteria, of which only a subset must be demonstrated for the diagnosis to be made. For some diagnoses, such as Autism, it is possible for two individuals to display completely different sets of symptoms (as only 6 symptoms from a list of 12 must be present). There are also symptoms that are common to a number of disorders, and there are a host of behaviors that are commonly associated with particular syndromes that are not included in the diagnostic criteria. One challenge for the symptom level of analysis is to explain this heterogeneity.

The neuropsychological level of analysis provides some assistance with this challenge. Symptoms can be classified into one of four categories: (1) primary or core symptoms, (2) correlated or concomitant symptoms, (3) secondary symptoms, and (4) artifactual symptoms (Pennington & Ozonoff, 1991; Rapin, 1987). Primary symptoms are close to universal in individuals with the disorder, are relatively specific to the disorder, have causal precedence in development, and persist with age. Most important, primary symptoms are the observable behaviors that are caused by the underlying neuropsychological deficit(s).

Correlated or concomitant symptoms have an etiology similar to that of core symptoms but arise from the involvement of different brain systems. For example, many children with dyslexia also demonstrate specific language impairments. These broader verbal disabilities are presumed to arise from the same genetic influences that cause dyslexia, but the brain systems disrupted are more extensive than those that lead to dyslexia. Not all children with a disorder will display correlated symptoms; symptom expression is dependent on the extent of disruption of brain development. Secondary symptoms are caused by primary or correlated symptoms. For example, the difficulties in peer relationships experienced by many children with ADHD are likely secondary to the primary symptoms of inattention, distractibility, and hyperactivity, which can make social interactions difficult. Finally, artifactual symptoms are those that appear to be associated with a disorder but are an artifact of biased ascertainment or other processes that serve to artificially increase the apparent co-occurrence of the behaviors. For example, behavioral disorders and delinquency in children with learning disabilities may be artifactual symptoms that are due to ascertainment biases.

Neuropsychological studies can be critical to determining which of many possible candidate symptoms are primary to a disorder. First, there must be a consistent pattern of results across studies demonstrating difficulties in the domain, relative to others without the disorder, matched on developmental level. Evidence of both specificity and universality can be provided by discriminant function analyses that attempt to classify individuals on the basis of their performance in the neuropsychological domain. Longitudinal and cross-sectional studies across a wide developmental range can address both persistence and precedence. Most powerful are prospective studies that identify and follow children at risk of developing a disorder, examining the onset, developmental trajectory, and predictive significance of key neuropsychological skills and deficits.

External Validity

A second way that neuropsychological analyses can be useful to developmental psychopathology is in establishing whether diagnostic classifications are meaningful and have explanatory power. Another issue raised at the symptom level of analysis is overlap among diagnostic categories. Some forms of developmental psychopathology share symptoms, raising concern that dimensional phenomena have been inappropriately parsed into categorical classifications. A powerful method of deciding whether two conditions are truly different is the process of external validation. The most essential component of this process is examining whether the conditions differ on external criteria not involved in the original definition of the syndromes (Fletcher, 1985). Typical means of establishing external validity involve comparison of the conditions' early history, developmental course, outcome, neuropsychological profiles, etiologies, and treatment response. Distinct syndromes should differ along at least one of these dimensions (Fletcher, 1985; Pennington, 1991). What is essential to external validation is that the dimensions on which the two conditions are compared fall outside the measurement domains used to initially define the syndromes.

One example of the potential power of the neuropsychological perspective in this regard comes from recent research on Autism Spectrum Disorders. Asperger's syndrome is a subtype of Autism Spectrum Disorders that shares the social disabilities and restricted, repetitive behaviors of Autism, but in which language abilities are well developed and cognitive functioning is not impaired. Ever since it was first described in the English-language literature (Wing, 1981), there have been questions about its relationship to high-functioning Autism (i.e., Autism without accompanying mental retardation). Research comparing Asperger's syndrome and high-functioning Autism provides mixed evidence of their external validity, and a consensus is beginning to emerge that the two conditions are more similar than different. Neuropsychological studies have found impairments in executive function, social cognition, and motor skills in both subtypes (summarized in Ozonoff & Griffith, 2000). The one exception is that most research finds that individuals with Asperger's syndrome perform better on language tests than those with high-functioning Autism (Klin, Volkmar, Sparrow, Cicchetti, & Rourke, 1995; Ozonoff, South, & Miller, 2000), but this finding is likely an artifact of the group definition process requiring normal language onset for the Asperger's diagnosis. Some studies have found visual-spatial deficits in Asperger's syndrome (Klin et al., 1995) rather than the strengths typical of Autism, but several other studies have failed to replicate this finding and some have actually found visual-spatial superiorities in individuals with Asperger's syndrome (Manjiviona & Prior, 1995; Ozonoff et al., 2000; Szatmari, Tuff, Finlayson, & Bartolucci, 1990). Prior (2000, p. 8), in an editorial devoted to the issue of Asperger's syndrome's external validity, concluded, "One message to emerge from the papers is that it seems currently impossible to reliably distinguish between Asperger syndrome and high-functioning Autism on any acceptable clinical or pragmatic grounds." Supportive evidence has been provided from the etiological level, suggesting that high-functioning Autism and Asperger's syndrome often co-occur in families (Bolton et al., 1994; Jamain et al., 2003) and thus appear to share similar genetic influences (Volkmar, Klin, & Pauls, 1998). But the neuropsychological studies have been the most influential in this debate.

Comorbidity

Another significant issue that arises, but is not resolved, at the symptom level of analysis is that of comorbidity. It is not at all uncommon to find that a child suffers from more than one form of developmental psychopathology. Many explanations for this phenomenon have been proposed (Caron & Rutter, 1991; Simonoff, 2000), from artifactual reasons to causal relationships. Comorbidity is more likely in a sample ascertained from a clinic, the most common source of research participants, as individuals with more symptoms are more likely to seek professional consultation. When affected individuals are recruited from the community, the apparent association between two disorders often disappears. Rater biases occur when a reporter (a parent, a teacher, or the child himself or herself) who is concerned about certain difficulties adopts a negative rating set (or "negative halo"), endorsing both symptoms that are truly present as well as additional behaviors that are not problematic. Another artifactual explanation for comorbidity is definitional overlap between diagnostic categories. For certain diagnoses, such as the externalizing behavior disorders, there is symptomatic overlap, such that the same or similar behaviors are included in multiple sets of diagnostic criteria. This can also increase the apparent rate of comorbidity.

Once these artifactual explanations have been ruled out, there are a number of explanations for the common occurrence of multiple developmental psychopathologies. Disorders may occur together because they share similar risk factors or because having one disorder places an individual at risk for the other disorder. That is, one disorder is a consequence of or secondary to the other. These hypotheses are not easily tested with neuropsychological models and are best examined through genetic analyses, including family, twin, and molecular studies. The interested reader is referred to Neale and Kendler (1995).

Developmental Discontinuities

A final set of questions that arise when examining developmental psychopathologies at the symptom level of analysis are related to discontinuities in symptom manifestation across development. It is more the rule than the exception to find that symptoms transform and change with age. A behavior that is prominent during one developmental period may be absent or of minor significance at another age. A symptom may manifest differently at different developmental periods, as in depression, in which the primary mood abnormality in adolescence and adulthood is low mood, but in earlier childhood is more often manifest as irritable mood. It is a fundamental part of our model that discontinuities at the level of observable behavior may hide continuities at deeper levels of analysis, those concerned with mechanisms (Pennington & Ozonoff, 1991). For example, hyperactive behavior is much less common in adults with ADHD than in children. If the underlying neuropsychological mechanism in ADHD is understood as a deficit in response inhibition (Barkley, 1997), then this apparent discontinuity is easily resolved. Hyperactivity is

conceptualized as only one of several manifestations of response disinhibition; others include difficulty curbing immediate reactions or thinking about consequences before doing or saying something, problems that are evident even in adults with ADHD. It must be noted that discontinuities in underlying neuropsychological deficits are also possible, but these are often more apparent than real, secondary to the necessity of using different measurement tools at different ages. If a broad sequence of developmentally appropriate measures of the neuropsychological domain are carefully chosen, then we often observe "heterotypic neuropsychological continuity" across development (Pennington & Ozonoff, 1991).

Further Promises

Neuropsychological perspectives may contribute to our understanding of developmental psychopathology in several additional ways. One possibility is that neuropsychological profiles can be used to clarify diagnosis or provide an objective diagnostic test. For some disorders, we have already begun to achieve this goal. We have a good understanding of the primary neuropsychological deficits associated with dyslexia, for example. These impairments fall in the domain of phonological processes, including phonological awareness and phonological decoding of written language (Torgesen, 1995). Specific performance profiles on neuropsychological tests (e.g., phonological processes significantly discrepant from age norms or from the child's own intellectual level) are widely used for diagnostic purposes in clinics that serve children with learning disabilities and in schools. The neuropsychology of dyslexia is a mature field, relative to other forms of developmental psychopathology, and for most disorders, including those we discuss later in this chapter, the promise of using neuropsychological functioning to clarify diagnosis is far from being achieved. In Autism, for example, there has been great debate about the nature of the underlying neuropsychological dysfunction. In the first edition of these volumes, Pennington and Welsh (1995) characterized Autism as a primary disorder of social cognition, whereas newer conceptualizations emphasize core deficits in emotional processes, and theories that focus on other cognitive abnormalities also exist. Using performance profiles on neuropsychological tests to bootstrap diagnosis of Autism Spectrum Disorders, while conceptualizations of the neuropsychological phenotype are still in flux, would be a mistake.

Another potential promise of the neuropsychological level is to better match treatments to subtypes within a disorder. This goal has again been achieved in the dyslexia field, where the treatments are explicitly geared toward improvement of the deficient phonological skills (e.g., Lindamood & Lindamood, 1998; Torgesen & Bryant, 1994). As another example, better understanding of the neuropsychology of ADHD might improve our efforts to target particular symptoms more precisely with medications and behavioral interventions that affect selective processes, such as working memory, response inhibition, and delay aversion (Castellanos & Tannock, 2002).

So far, these examples illustrate how research at the neuropsychological level might refine understanding at the behavioral or symptom level. Neuropsychological influences on other levels are also possible (e.g., neuropsychological research informing understanding of etiologic mechanisms). In fact, this is what we argue is the case in the PTSD field. Many, probably most, developmental psychopathologies are influenced by genetic factors, yet none follows classic Mendelian patterns of inheritance. In even those disorders with high heritability, such as Autism, what is inherited does not appear to be the disease itself, but a broader set of behaviors and traits that are more or less normally distributed throughout the population (Bailey, Palferman, Heavey, & LeCouteur, 1998). For this reason, using diagnostic classifications to find susceptibility genes would not be predicted to be successful, and indeed this has been the case for Autism (Piven, 2001). Neuropsychological abilities and deficits are often dimensionally distributed, both within the general population and within affected families, and thus may better index genetic liability than dichotomous diagnostic categories.

It has also been proposed that specific neuropsychological patterns may have distinct etiologic bases. One example comes from Williams' syndrome, a rare genetic disorder caused by a small deletion on chromosome 7. Individuals with Williams' syndrome have mental retardation, but their cognitive abilities are not affected similarly across the board. Visuospatial abilities, such as pattern construction, are significantly impaired, but verbal abilities are relatively spared (Bellugi, Mills, Jernigan, Hickok, & Galaburda, 1999). The microdeletion on chromosome 7 typically includes the genes for both elastin, a protein in connective tissue, and LIM-kinase, a protein co-enzyme expressed in the brain. However, the deletion can vary in size, and it has been proposed that genotype-phenotype mapping may elucidate the genes responsible for specific physical, behavioral, and neuropsychological manifestations of the syndrome. Two samples of individuals with Williams' syndrome have been described, one of which had the elastin but not the LIM-kinase gene deleted and the other of which had both genes deleted. In the first sample, the typical visuoconstructive deficit was not evident, lead-

ing to the suggestion that this cognitive ability is influenced by the LIM-kinase gene (Frangiskakis et al., 1996). A later study failed to replicate this finding, however (Tassabehji et al., 1999). It has also been suggested that distinct components of the dyslexia phenotype are associated with distinct genotypes (Grigorenko et al., 1997), but this study, too, awaits replication. Nevertheless, these syndromes provide exciting examples of the potential of the neuropsychological method to guide us toward etiological mechanisms (see also Flint, 1999; Fossella et al., 2002).

Neuropsychological Domains Relevant to Developmental Psychopathology

The neuropsychological level of analysis seeks to provide a bridge between behavior and the brain. The brain is a highly complex organ, containing billions of neurons and trillions of connections among them. Similarly, human behavior is highly complex. The task of mapping brain and behavior would be daunting, if not impossible, if there were not some model for describing the functional units of the human nervous system. Two such approaches are the traditional lesion model of neuropsychology and the functional model described by Luria (1966).

Luria's Model

Luria (1966) described three functional brain units: the arousal/motivation system, the perception/memory system, and the action selection system, each of which map onto integrated but distinct neural circuits. The perception/memory system creates and stores and/or activates existing representations of the organism's context that come from the environment through the sensory organs to the brain. The neural circuits involved in this process lie primarily in the posterior cortex and the hippocampus, but there are rich reciprocal connections to other areas of the brain that permit these representations of environmental context to affect behavior and vice versa. Disruptions of components of the perception/memory system occur in a variety of neurological diseases, such as Alzheimer's and other dementias, and focal lesions due to stroke or injury, but few forms of developmental psychopathology appear due to involvement of this system.

Representations generated by the perception/memory system serve as inputs to the motivation/arousal system. This component of Luria's organizational model accomplishes one of the key adaptive tasks for any behaving organism, which is to adjust motivational state to fit changing environmental circumstances. This system appraises the context in which the organism finds itself and generates appropriate arousal and motivational states. When the system is dysfunctional, as in the development of psychopathology, motivational states inappropriate to context may be activated. The neural components of the motivation/arousal system include the neocortex, the limbic system, and the brain stem. At the lowest level, brain stem nuclei with diffuse projections to other regions release excitatory and inhibitory neurotransmitters that modulate arousal in the rest of the brain to match current contexts and goals. Circuits in the brain stem and midbrain also mediate automatic behavioral responses to certain environmental stimuli (e.g., pain, taste). Some of these responses are reflexive, but other motivational responses can be modified at higher levels. The amygdala, for example, allows the rapid extraction of valence from environmental input and the learning of associations between stimuli. The orbitofrontal cortex is specialized for rapidly reversing the link between reinforcers and actions as the context changes, inhibiting or reversing motivated behaviors mediated by lower structures. Thus, there are some virtually innate motivational states that appear to have almost reflexive effects on behavior, but higher structures can modify these responses. The learning of new associations mediated by the amygdala is rapid, which is important for survival, but not flexible (e.g., learned associations are not quick to be unlearned), which can be disadvantageous and lead to psychopathology, such as mood and anxiety disorders.

The action selection system, modified by input from the motivation system, then plans and executes actions (and thoughts) to deal with the environmental context and, in humans, to contend with future contexts. When current and future conditions differ, this ability to select responses evoked by simulated contexts can give rise to both adaptive behaviors, such as foresight and courage, and maladaptive behaviors seen in certain psychopathologies, such as avoidance. Because the range of possible actions is infinite, it is hypothesized that the motivation system helps the organism quickly narrow the range. One important functional component of the action selection system serves to further constrain possible behavior choices by *deselecting* options that are not appropriate through inhibitory processes. Many developmental psychopathologies appear to involve difficulty both in selecting context-appropriate actions and in inhibiting context-inappropriate actions; these deficits may be manifest as hyperactivity, echolalia, tics, compulsions, stereotypies, ruminations, antisocial behavior, hallucinations, and/or delusions.

The action selection system, modified by input from the motivation system, then plans and executes actions (and

Three main brain structures interact in the action selection system: the frontal cortex, the basal ganglia, and the thalamus. The prefrontal cortex makes connections with components of the basal ganglia, which in turn makes connections to the thalamus, which sends a feedback connection to prefrontal cortex (Casey, Durston, & Fossella, 2001). Each level of the circuit performs a somewhat different function. The prefrontal cortex mediates planning. It receives and integrates input from all over the brain, providing contextual constraints on the action selection system and exerting top-down control over areas of the cortex. Different portions of the prefrontal cortex maintain different kinds of information about current context in working memory to guide action. The basal ganglia then play an important role in initiating actions (O'Reilly & Munakata, 2000); when sufficient evidence accumulates that a given action is warranted, circuits within the basal ganglia fire, leading to reduced thalamic inhibition of the given areas of the prefrontal cortex, resulting in output (action or thought).

Lesion Models

Another taxonomic approach comes from the lesion model of adult neuropsychology, in which acquired damage to specific brain structures defines particular cognitive deficits. The functional domains defined by the lesion model have traditionally included executive function, spatial reasoning, phonological processing, social cognition, and memory. In the traditional neuropsychological model, these functional systems are subserved by different cortical networks. Certainly other functional systems (e.g., motor) exist, but these appear less relevant to developmental psychopathology. Here we consider the domains most often impaired in developmental psychopathologies.

Executive functions are goal-directed, future-oriented behaviors that include such components as organization, planning, goal generation and monitoring, inhibition, and flexibility. Deficits in these behaviors are commonly found as a result of injury to the prefrontal cortex. Goldman-Rakic (1987) emphasized the role of the prefrontal cortices in holding goal-related representations online (in so-called working memory), allowing the organism to solve problems that cannot be worked out strictly on the basis of previously learned associations. Cohen and Servan-Schreiber (1992) postulated that the core function of the prefrontal cortices is to maintain an internal representation of context in working memory to guide behavior in complex or novel situations. Thus, when an organism must compute a new response, the frontal cortex is used to hold online relevant representations of context and goals, as well as partial and final products of computation, in a dynamic system. Proper functioning of this system is required for (1) strategic allocation of attention, (2) inhibition of irrelevant responses, (3) appropriate shifting of cognitive set, (4) relating information appropriately over time and space, and (5) adjusting behavior in relation to evolving contexts. Much of social behavior and social development would appear to depend on these capacities. Consequently, we would expect the domain of executive functions to be particularly important for understanding deficits in social behavior, which is the domain of much of developmental psychopathology. Indeed, executive function deficits are being found in a number of developmental psychopathologies.

Social cognition is the domain of neuropsychology that includes the information-processing mechanisms that underlie social behavior. Specific functions that fall in this domain are emotion perception, face processing, social perspective taking, pragmatic aspects of language production and comprehension, attachment, affect regulation, self-knowledge, and emotional biases on judgment (Ochsner & Lieberman, 2001). As just discussed, some aspects of social cognition appear to require executive functions and to be mediated by the prefrontal cortex, so this is not a wholly independent category. Other parts of the brain are also important for some social and emotional functions, and hence separate pathologies that involve disruptions in these neural systems are possible. For example, face perception depends on regions of the visual cortex, such as the fusiform gyrus (also sometimes known as the "fusiform face area" or FFA), as well as aspects of the temporal lobes, such as the superior temporal sulcus (STS; Haxby, Hoffman, & Gobbini, 2000; Kanwisher, McDermott, & Chun, 1997). The amygdala is thought to play a major role in identifying negative affect, particularly fear, and recognizing threat (Adolphs et al., 1999). Functional imaging studies suggest that similar areas (orbitofrontal cortex, FFA, STS) are activated when mental states are processed (Gallagher et al., 2000; Stuss, Gallup, & Alexander, 2001).

A third functional system is the *phonological processing* system, which in the majority of individuals is subserved by the perisylvian areas of the left hemisphere, including Wernicke's area in the posterior left temporal lobe and Broca's area in the premotor portion of the left frontal lobe. Phonological abilities have a protracted course of development; consistent with this and with their relatively late appearance on an evolutionary scale, phonological processes are subject to considerable individual variation, and disorders of phonological processing have a high prevalence rate (up to 10% of the population). Language processes are very important in understanding developmental psychopathology, both because primary deficits in language processes can disrupt the development of social

skills and because primary deficits in social skills can disrupt language development. Given this close reciprocal relationship, it is not surprising that many developmental psychopathologies involve associated symptoms consistent with deficient phonological processes, such as comorbid language disorders and language-based learning disabilities. Understanding the causal basis of such overlap is one of the challenges for developmental psychopathology.

The lesion model's functional organization of neuropsychological systems has a long research tradition and has often been used in research studies. Its assumption of one-to-one structure-function relationships appears to be too simplistic, however. Brain functions are rarely localizable to specific cortical regions but are products of the aggregate functioning of cortical and subcortical networks. One of the most serious weaknesses of the lesion model is that it is not a developmental model. Developing brains exhibit greater plasticity than mature ones. Consequently, when they are injured, there is not the same loss of function as in adults, with alternative neural connections potentially able to support behavior (Moses & Stiles, 2002). Luria's functional organization of the central nervous system is appealing because it appears more consistent with accumulating neuroscientific evidence of how the brain works. Both models are simplifications of highly interactive, complex systems, however, and both have limitations, which we turn to later in the chapter. Nonetheless, both afford some heuristic for translating from behavior to brain and back again and current neuropsychological research on developmental psychopathology, such as that reviewed in the next section, has relied on these models, so we use them for the time being.

THE NEUROPSYCHOLOGY OF SPECIFIC DEVELOPMENTAL PSYCHOPATHOLOGIES

In this section, we examine two developmental psychopathologies in depth: Autism and Posttraumatic Stress Disorder. The Autism Spectrum Disorders provide fertile ground for examining the utility of the four-level model of developmental psychopathology just outlined. A large amount of research has been conducted at each of the levels, but the etiologies and brain mechanisms involved and the mechanisms by which they lead to symptoms are still largely unknown. This creates many explanatory voids that the neuropsychological level can attempt to fill. Indeed, the lack of definitive etiologies has stimulated a great deal of neuropsychological research since the disorder was first described by Kanner (1943). Published work has moved from largely descriptive accounts of symptoms to sophisticated empirical delineations of information-processing profiles. Several unifying neuropsychological models that attempt to bring together all the symptoms of Autism under one roof have been proposed, stimulating more experimental research and new scientific debates. In this sense, the neuropsychology of Autism is a much broader and more active field than that of PTSD, the other psychopathological condition we discuss in this chapter, which is more focused, perhaps because its etiology appears simpler. As the Autism field has gained maturity, however, new questions have been raised and a variety of potential limitations of the neuropsychological model of developmental psychopathology have become apparent. The comparison of Autism, a disorder with high heritability, and PTSD, a condition with (by definition) major environmental contributions to etiology, provides other interesting contrasts, including the relative mind-body problems each face, how their respective explanatory models have attempted to resolve these issues, and how research at different levels of analysis has proceeded at different rates and with varying degrees of dependence/independence.

For each disorder, we begin with the fourth level of analysis, that is, definition and description of the symptoms. We then proceed from level 1, the etiological level, through level 3, the neuropsychological level. It should be noted that this ordering of the levels is practical, but not conceptually elegant. By placing symptoms and background first, this order makes it easier for the reader to follow the other levels of analysis. By placing neuropsychology last, however, this order de-emphasizes the fact that this level forms a bridge between brain and behavior. For both Autism and PTSD, we report the literature in such a way as to highlight both the promises of the neuropsychological approach outlined earlier and the apparent limitations of the approach that are emerging. This latter topic is further developed in the final section of the chapter.

AUTISM SPECTRUM DISORDERS

In this section, we review the empirical research on the group of conditions collectively called Autism Spectrum or Pervasive Developmental Disorders.

Level 4: Symptoms, Diagnostic Definitions, and Epidemiology

As specified in the *Diagnostic and Statistical Manual of Mental Disorders,* fourth edition, text revision (*DSM-IV-TR;* American Psychiatric Association [APA], 2000), there are five Pervasive Developmental Disorders (PDD): Autistic Disorder, Asperger's Disorder, Rett's Disorder, Childhood Disintegrative Disorder, and Pervasive Developmental Disorder Not Otherwise Specified. Symptoms of Autistic Disorder fall in the three areas of social relatedness, communication, and behaviors and interests. In the social domain, symptoms include impaired use of nonverbal behaviors (e.g., eye contact, facial expression, gestures) to regulate social interaction, failure to develop age-appropriate peer relationships, little seeking to share enjoyment or interests with other people, and limited social-emotional reciprocity. Communication deficits include delay in or absence of spoken language, difficulty initiating or sustaining conversation, idiosyncratic or repetitive language, and imitation and pretend play deficits. In the behaviors and interests domain, there are often encompassing, unusual interests, inflexible adherence to nonfunctional routines, stereotyped body movements, and preoccupation with parts or sensory qualities of objects (APA, 2000). To meet criteria for Autistic Disorder, an individual must demonstrate at least 6 of the 12 symptoms, with at least two coming from the social domain and one each from the communication and restricted behaviors/interests categories. At least one symptom must have been present before 36 months of age.

The onset of Autism occurs before age 3, at two peak periods. The majority of children display developmental abnormalities within the first 2 years of life. A smaller group of children with Autism display a period of normal or mostly normal development, followed by a loss of communication and social skills and onset of Autism (Kurita, 1985). The regression occurs most commonly between 12 and 24 months of age, although in rare cases can occur after age 2 but before the third birthday.

Asperger's Disorder (or Asperger's syndrome) shares the social disabilities and restricted, repetitive behaviors of Autism, but language abilities are well developed and intellectual functioning is not impaired. Its symptoms are identical to those just listed for Autistic Disorder, except that there is no requirement that the child demonstrate any difficulties in the second category, communication. Although described almost 60 years ago by Austrian pediatrician Hans Asperger (1944), the Asperger's syndrome diagnosis was not included in the *DSM* until the fourth edition. In the *DSM-IV* diagnostic system, the main point of differentiation from Autistic Disorder, especially the higher-functioning subtype, is that those with Asperger's syndrome do not exhibit significant delays in the onset or early course of language. As specified in the *DSM-IV,* nonechoed, communicative use of single words must be demonstrated by age 2 and meaningful phrase speech by age 3. Most parents of children with Asperger's syndrome are not concerned about early language development and may even report precocious language abilities, such as a large vocabulary and adult-like phrasing from an early age. Autistic Disorder must be ruled out before a diagnosis of Asperger's syndrome is justified. *DSM-IV-TR* mandates that the diagnosis of Autism always takes precedence over that of Asperger's syndrome. Thus, if a child meets criteria for Autistic Disorder, the diagnosis must be Autism even if he or she displays excellent structural language, average or better cognitive skills, and other typical features of Asperger's syndrome.

Individuals who meet criteria for Autistic Disorder and are intellectually normal are considered high functioning. Research comparing Asperger's syndrome and high-functioning Autism provides mixed evidence of their external validity. Early history differences are evident between the disorders, with children with Asperger's syndrome showing fewer and less severe symptoms and better language in the preschool years than children with high-functioning Autism, but these group differences are likely artifacts of the diagnostic definitions (Ozonoff et al., 2000). Follow-up studies demonstrate similar trajectories in outcome (Ozonoff et al., 2000; Szatmari et al., 2000). As summarized earlier, neuropsychological research suggests that the two conditions are more similar than different.

Two other conditions also appear in *DSM-IV* in the PDD category: Rett's Disorder and Childhood Disintegrative Disorder. Both involve a period of typical development, followed by a loss of skills and regression in development. The classic symptoms of Rett's Disorder, seen primarily in females, include unsteady gait, lack of language, lack of functional hand use, almost constant stereotyped hand movements, including repetitive wringing, "washing," twisting, clapping, or rubbing of the hands in the midline, very severe cognitive deficits, and lack of typical social interaction. Recently, a gene was isolated on the X chromosome MECP2, which appears responsible for most cases of Rett's Disorder (Amir et al., 1999). In Childhood Disintegrative Disorder, an abrupt and severe regression occurs after at least 2 (and up to 10) years of normal development. After the loss of skills, the child has all the characteristics of severe Autism and severe mental retardation, but unlike typical Autism, there is little developmental growth after treatment and the condition continues as a chronic, severe, developmental disability.

The fifth and final condition that falls within the PDD category is Pervasive Developmental Disorder Not Otherwise Specified (PDD-NOS). This label is used for children who experience difficulties in at least two of the three Autism-related symptom clusters (clear difficulty relating to others, as well as either communication problems or repetitive behaviors) but who do not meet criteria for any of the other PDDs. The same list of 12 symptoms is used to diagnose PDD-NOS, but only one difficulty in the "reciprocal social interaction" domain and one symptom from either the "communication deficits" or "repetitive, restricted behaviors" domains is required. Children with PDD-NOS have autistic-like behaviors and difficulties, but either have too few symptoms or a different pattern of symptoms than the other conditions in the PDD category. For example, a child might be diagnosed with PDD-NOS if he or she displayed only four of the *DSM-IV* symptoms (ruling out Autistic Disorder), displayed a delay in language onset (ruling out Asperger's syndrome), and showed no regression in development (ruling out both Rett's and Childhood Disintegrative Disorders).

Epidemiology

Early research suggested that Autism (strictly defined, meeting full criteria for the disorder) occurred at the rate of 4 to 6 affected individuals per 10,000 (Lotter, 1966; Wing & Gould, 1979). An influential study conducted in the mid-1980s broadened diagnostic criteria somewhat and found a rate of 10 per 10,000 in a total population screening of a circumscribed geographic region in Canada (Bryson, Clark, & Smith, 1988). Newer studies have utilized standardized diagnostic measures of established reliability and validity and employed active ascertainment techniques. These surveys have given prevalence estimates of 60 to 70 per 10,000 or approximately 1/150 across the spectrum of Autism and 1/500 for children with the full syndrome of Autistic Disorder (Chakrabarti & Fombonne, 2001). One obvious reason for the rise in rates is that more recent research has examined all Autism Spectrum Disorders, whereas early surveys looked at rates of only strictly defined Autism. However, in studies that have broken down the rates by specific *DSM-IV* PDD subtypes, it is clear that the prevalence of classic Autism itself is higher. This may suggest that broader criteria or better detection of mild cases alone are not enough to account for the rise in prevalence. Chakrabarti and Fombonne (2001) reported a rate of 16.8 per 10,000 for *DSM-IV* Autistic Disorder, which is 3 to 4 times higher than suggested in the 1960s and 1970s and over 1.5 times higher than thought in the 1980s and 1990s.

Several reasons for the rising prevalence rates have been proposed, from artifactual explanations to newly emerging environmental and biological risk factors. In the first category are increased awareness among clinicians and the general public, better identification and referral practices, more sensitive diagnostic tools, and broader classification systems. There is no doubt that the ability of clinicians to identify more subtle manifestations of Autism Spectrum Disorders and to discriminate Autism from mental retardation has improved; it is also clear that the current diagnostic system of *DSM-IV* is broader in the net it casts than were previous classification systems. Whether these changes in referral and practice alone can account for the large increase is uncertain, and hypotheses abound about environmental factors that may have emerged in the past few decades to put infants and young children at greater risk for developing Autism. These are covered, along with other etiologic factors, in the next section.

Level 1: Etiology—Genes, Environmental Factors, and Interactions

Kanner (1943, p. 42) suggested that autistic children were born with "an innate inability to form the usual, biologically provided affective contacts with people." Later, however, his thinking came into line with that of his contemporaries trained in the psychoanalytic tradition predominant at the time. It was mistakenly suggested that Autism was the result of inadequate nurturance by emotionally cold, rejecting parents (Bettelheim, 1967), a theory that prevailed until the late 1960s. Rimland (1964) did a tremendous service to the field when he provided powerful arguments that Autism had an organic etiology. The finding that approximately 25% of children with Autism developed seizures in adolescence also strongly suggested that Autism was a neurodevelopmental condition with underlying organic brain dysfunction (Schain & Yannet, 1960).

Genetic factors appear to play a strong role in the development of Autism (Bailey et al., 1995; International Molecular Genetic Study of Autism Consortium, 2001). The recurrence risk for Autism after the birth of one child with the disorder is 3% to 6%, a rate that far exceeds that in the general population (Bailey, Palferman, et al., 1998). The concordance rate for Autism in monozygotic (MZ) twins is greatly elevated relative to that for dizygotic (DZ) twins. The most recent twin studies, which used standardized diagnostic measures and total population screening, found concordance rates for strictly defined Autistic Disorder of 60% in MZ pairs, but only 5% in DZ pairs. MZ concordance rates of up to 90% are reported when including social and communication abnormalities broader than Autistic Disorder. Twin studies yield a heritability estimate greater than .90 (Bailey et al., 1995; LeCouteur et al.,

1996). And there is evidence of familial transmission of an extended set of cognitive and social anomalies that are milder than but qualitatively similar to Autism (the so-called broader Autism phenotype; Bailey, Palferman, et al., 1998). Family members also suffer from higher than average rates of anxiety and affective disorders and learning disabilities. Collectively, these features of the broader Autism phenotype have been found in 15% to 45% of family members of people with Autism in different samples (Bailey, Palferman, et al., 1998).

Advances in the molecular genetics of Autism have been rapid, but the results are so far inconclusive. One reason is that the inheritance pattern appears far from simple, with statistical models suggesting that several and perhaps as many as 10 genes are involved in conferring susceptibility (Pickles et al., 1995; Risch et al., 1999). Case reports have demonstrated a link between Autism and a wide variety of chromosomal anomalies, with one review (Gillberg, 1998) reporting associations with all but three chromosomes. It is not yet clear which associations are random and which may provide clues about etiology. The one cytogenetic abnormality that has been consistently replicated in a small proportion of children with Autism is a duplication of material on chromosome 15 (Rutter, 2000). Molecular genetic studies have found linkage and/or association with a number of different chromosomal regions, with the strongest support and replication across studies for sites on 2q, 7q, and perhaps 13q (Collaborative Linkage Study of Autism, 2001; International Molecular Genetics Study of Autism Consortium, 2001).

Twin studies also make it clear that Autism is not a purely genetic disorder, as concordance rates among identical twins fall short of 100%. There can be tremendous phenotypic variability even among MZ twins, with one twin displaying severe Autism and the other the broader phenotype, for example. Fifty point IQ differences within MZ pairs have been reported (Rutter, 1999). The search for other factors that influence the development and severity of Autism is intense and has received much media attention. It has been suggested that environmental factors, including vaccination, heavy metal or pesticide exposure, viral agents, and food products, may interact with genetic susceptibility to trigger Autism, cause it alone, or mediate the expression and severity of the disorder (Hornig & Lipkin, 2001). A few of the most influential theories regarding environmental factors are reviewed in this section.

Many parents report gastrointestinal (GI) disturbances in their children with Autism, such as persistent diarrhea, constipation, abdominal distention, or pain. There are multiple theories for the origin of GI pathology in Autism, including food allergies, metabolic problems, and disruption of gut flora due to antibiotic overuse. The potential environmental etiologic agent that has received the most attention is immunizations. Wakefield et al. (1998) described a case series of 12 children with GI disturbances that were reported to begin around the time that autistic behaviors became evident. He postulated that these children had a new subtype of "regressive Autism" that was induced by the measles, mumps, rubella (MMR) vaccination. The postulated mechanism was a persistent measles virus infection resulting in damage to the intestinal lining, increased permeability, and absorption of toxic peptides that cause central nervous system dysfunction and behavioral regression. Three recent studies do not support this hypothesis, however. Taylor et al. (1999, 2002) identified 498 children with Autism born since 1979 and linked clinical records to independently recorded immunization data. No evidence of a change in trend in incidence or age at diagnosis was associated with the introduction of the MMR vaccination in 1988. The most recent study followed all children born in Denmark between 1991 and 1998 and strongly supported the findings of Taylor and colleagues, again failing to find any increase in vaccinated relative to unvaccinated children and any temporal clustering of cases of Autism after immunization (Madsen et al., 2002).

Another proposed environmental risk factor for Autism is exposure to environmental toxins during the prenatal or infancy periods (Bernard, Enayati, Roger, Binstock, & Redwood, 2002; Edelson & Cantor, 1998; London & Etzel, 2000) or metabolic abnormalities that impair the natural detoxification process. It is well established that certain early exogenous exposures (e.g., mercury, lead, ethanol) can have neurotoxin effects and lead to developmental disabilities (Burbacher, Rodier, & Weiss, 1990; Needleman, Schell, Bellinger, Leviton, & Allred, 1990), although none has been specifically associated with Autism in the empirical literature. One possible source of excessive mercury exposure that has received attention is thimerosal, an ethylmercury-based preservative included in several vaccines to prevent bacterial contamination. MMR, polio, and varicella vaccines have never contained thimerosal, but it has been included in multiple-use vaccines since the 1930s. Concerns have been raised recently that the cumulative exposure to ethylmercury, via thimerosal, is now far greater than in the past due to the increased number of vaccines given to children, especially before age 2. This is a controversial theory that has provoked strong reactions on both sides, but current scientific evidence has not yet proven or disproven a link between thimerosal and neurodevelopmental disorders (Stratton, Gable, & McCormick, 2001).

To summarize this section, research at the etiologic level is accumulating rapidly, and there are many theories about causal agents. All theories postulate biological mechanisms that are thought to produce brain changes that lead in turn to the symptoms of Autism. There are no viable social-environmental hypotheses of Autism etiology, but a diathesis-stress model (with the environmental stressors biological in nature) may have utility. We turn next to the brain changes that the putative etiologic agents are thought to cause.

Level 2: Brain Mechanisms

Kanner's (1943) original description noted unusually large head size in a proportion of children with Autism, and macrocephaly (head circumference >97th percentile) has been confirmed in approximately 20% of individuals with Autism (Fombonne, Roge, Claverie, Courty, & Fremolle, 1999; Lainhart et al., 1997). The increase in head volume reflects an increase in brain volume, which is not apparent at birth but is present by the first birthday (Courchesne et al., 2003) and is hypothesized to be due to both overgrowth and the failure of normal pruning mechanisms (Piven, Arndt, Bailey, & Andreasen, 1996). Recent studies have suggested that excessive growth may be followed by a period of abnormally slow or arrested growth later in childhood (Courchesne, 2004).

Aside from macrocephaly, structural neuroimaging studies have yielded inconsistent results, possibly stemming from methodological issues such as small samples, inappropriate or no control groups, and inconsistent use of covariates, including age, gender, IQ, and total brain volume. Studies have demonstrated decreased volume of the cerebellar vermis, particularly lobules VI and VII (Courchesne, Yeung-Courchesne, Press, Hesselink, & Jernigan, 1988), but this finding has not always been replicated by other research teams (Hardan, Minshew, Harenski, & Keshavan, 2001; Piven, Bailey, Ranson, & Arndt, 1997). The body and posterior portions of the corpus callosum have been reported to be significantly smaller than normal (Piven et al., 1997). Saitoh, Karns, and Courchesne (2001) found that the area dentata (dentate gyrus and CA4) of the hippocampus was significantly smaller on the MRI of children with Autism than normal children, and Sparks et al. (2002) reported increased hippocampal and amygdala volumes in children with Autism Spectrum Disorders.

Structural MRI results are variable across studies and do not point to any signature abnormality characteristic of

Autism Spectrum Disorders, and regional volumetric changes do not directly measure brain function and thus are not the most sensitive index of the brain-level mechanisms operative in these disorders. Functional brain imaging studies have more consistently demonstrated differences in samples of children with Autism (Cody, Pelphrey, & Piven, 2002). Two recent studies found reduced cerebral blood flow bilaterally in the superior temporal gyrus and left frontal cortex (Ohnishi et al., 2000; Zilbovicius et al., 2000) in children with Autism at rest (e.g., not engaged in task performance). In activation studies that examine brain regions used to perform specific tasks, several research groups have found that individuals with Autism show reduced or different patterns of brain activity compared to controls. In one study in which participants had to identify facial expressions of emotion, those with Autism activated the fusiform gyrus (part of the temporal lobes), the left amygdala, and the left cerebellum significantly less than controls did (Critchley et al., 2000). Two other studies, discussed in more detail in the neuropsychology section, found reduced or absent activation of similar brain regions during social reasoning tasks (Baron-Cohen et al., 1999; Schultz et al., 2000). Different patterns of activation were also found in a study that examined brain function during a visual search task that is often a strength for individuals with Autism. Participants with Autism demonstrated reduced activation of prefrontal cortex but increased activation of ventral occipitotemporal networks relative to controls (Ring et al., 1999). Thus, even when performance is not deficient, the brains of people with Autism Spectrum Disorders show distinct functional differences from typical patterns.

The changes present in detailed autopsy studies of a limited number of individuals with Autism (most of whom also had significant mental retardation and seizures) consist of increased neuronal density, particularly in the hippocampus, olivary dysplasia, scattered areas of cortical and white matter dysplasia, including neuronal ectopias, and other nonspecific developmental abnormalities in the brain stem and cerebellum (Bailey, Luthert, et al., 1998; Palmen, van Engeland, Hof, & Schmitz, 2004). Bauman and Kemper (1988) reported increased cell packing, reduced cell size, and reduced dendritic connections in the limbic system. Casanova and colleagues (Casanova, Buxhoeveden, Switala, & Roy, 2002) have developed a computer program that can quantify the size and density of the parallel vertical columns that organize the human neocortex. The basic unit is the minicolumn, a chain of neurons oriented perpendicular to the cortical surface, surrounded by axons and dendrites that make lateral connections. Casanova et al. found smaller, less compact, and more numerous minicolumns in the superior and middle temporal gyrus and superior and middle frontal gyrus in those with Autism, relative to typical and dyslexic controls. As we discuss in the next section, these findings have potential implications for neuropsychological theories of Autism.

Level 3: Neuropsychology

Research at the neuropsychological level of analysis has been very active, perhaps because the behavior of individuals with Autism has always made clear that the profile of strengths and weaknesses is an interesting and unusual one. In Kanner's (1943) original paper, he highlighted both deficits and talents. He mentioned precocious reading, prodigious memory, and well-developed visual-spatial skills, alongside a fundamental inability to relate to others, a failure to use language to convey meaning, and an obsessive desire for the maintenance of sameness. Several subsequent studies have demonstrated an uneven profile of ability in Autism, with impaired performance on tasks that require language, abstract reasoning, integration, and sequencing, but spared ability on tasks that require visual-spatial processing, attention to detail, and rote memory abilities (Green, Fein, Joy, & Waterhouse, 1995). Next, we describe empirical findings in the domains defined by traditional neuropsychological conceptualizations of the brain's functions (e.g., attention, memory, social cognition, language, and executive functions), highlighting both empirical findings and theoretical models.

Attention

Many investigations have documented attentional abnormalities in individuals with Autism (for a review, see Allen & Courchesne, 2001), but the deficits are variable across different components of attention and present a different profile from other disorders. It has been noted in case studies and in the clinical literature for many years that individuals with Autism appear to have "overfocused" attention, responding to only a subset of environmental cues during learning situations (e.g., Lovaas, Koegel, & Schreibman, 1979). Deficits relative to controls have been found in the shifting of attention between sensory modalities. In one study, adults with average IQ and Autism performed as well as typical controls on a task that required no shifting of attention, but performance was over 6 standard deviations below that of controls when rapid alternation of attention between auditory and visual channels was required

(Courchesne et al., 1994). Several studies using the visuospatial orienting task of Posner (1980) have documented that people with Autism take longer to disengage and move attention than controls matched on ability (Casey, Gordon, Mannheim, & Rumsey, 1993; Townsend et al., 1999; Wainwright-Sharp & Bryson, 1993). In contrast, a number of studies have suggested that the ability to *sustain* attention is a relatively spared ability in Autism, with normal function on continuous performance tests found in several investigations (Buchsbaum et al., 1992; Casey et al., 1993; Garretson, Fein, & Waterhouse, 1990; Goldstein, Johnson, & Minshew, 2001; Noterdaeme, Amorosa, Mildenberger, Sitter, & Minow, 2001). This profile of attentional strengths and weaknesses distinguishes children with Autism from those with ADHD. Children with ADHD have little difficulty disengaging and shifting attention (Swanson et al., 1991), but they demonstrate severe impairment in sustaining attention and controlling impulses.

Memory

The memory of people with Autism has been extensively studied, stimulated by early research that likened Autism to amnesia (Boucher & Warrington, 1976). The amnesic analogy has received some support from the neuroanatomical research reviewed in the previous section (Aylward et al., 1999; Bauman & Kemper, 1988; Saitoh et al., 2001; Salmond, de Haan, Friston, Gadian, & Vargha-Khaden, 2003) and renewed interest due to the current popularity of an "amygdala theory" of Autism (Baron-Cohen et al., 2000). Proposed similarity at the neuropsychological level has been more controversial. Amnesic subjects typically demonstrate three patterns: (1) intact immediate and short-term memory but deficient long-term memory, (2) reduced primacy but normal recency effects, and (3) a flatter learning curve. Similar patterns have been hypothesized to also exist in Autism (Bachevalier, 1994; Boucher & Warrington, 1976; DeLong, 1992).

In the opening paragraphs of his seminal paper describing the syndrome of Autism, Kanner (1943) commented on the extraordinary memories of the children he was describing, particularly their ability to recite long lists of items or facts. Experimental studies have confirmed this observation. Hermelin and Frith (1971) demonstrated that children with Autism were as able as mental age controls to repeat back strings of words, and Prior and Chen (1976) demonstrated typical recall of both single items and lists in a visual memory task.

Another piece of the Autism-amnesia analogy concerns primacy and recency effects. O'Connor and Hermelin (1967) were the first to note that primacy effects in list learning tended to be weaker than recency effects in Autism; these results were replicated by Boucher (1981). This pattern is also characteristic of adults with amnesia (Baddeley & Warrington, 1970). Hermelin and Frith (1971) attempted, unsuccessfully, to attenuate strong recency effects by composing sentences in which the beginning part of the word string was made up of meaningful sentence fragments, and the latter part was composed of random verbal material. The children with Autism continued to demonstrate strong recency and weak primacy effects even under these conditions. Deficient primacy but intact recency memory has been replicated more recently by Renner, Klinger, and Klinger (2000). As recency effects rely more purely on rote auditory mechanisms, whereas recall of the first part of a list requires further processing and encoding of the material, less developed primacy effects in Autism may be secondary to organizational and encoding impairments rather than to memory deficits per se, an issue to which we return later.

In a pioneering series of experiments, Hermelin, O'Connor, and colleagues found that the advantage in remembering meaningful over random material typically seen in normally developing individuals is not apparent in Autism; that is, individuals with Autism do not appear to use the syntactic and semantic cues that aid others in recalling material. For example, two studies demonstrated that children with Autism were just as capable of recalling random verbal material (e.g., unconnected words) as they were of remembering meaningful sentences (Hermelin & O'Connor, 1967; Hermelin & Frith, 1971). Later experiments clarified that children with Autism are not incapable of using semantic cues in recall but do appear to be less efficient in doing so and less likely to use this strategy spontaneously. Fyffe and Prior (1978) failed to replicate earlier results, finding that children with Autism recalled sentences significantly better than random word lists. Relative to controls, however, recall of sentences was deficient and recall of random material was adequate. Thus, although the group with Autism did appear to make use of meaning in recall, their advantage was not as great as in the mentally handicapped or typically developing control groups. Tager-Flusberg (1991) replicated this pattern, finding that recall of related and unrelated word lists was equivalent in the group with Autism; however, their memory for meaningful material was less efficient than that of controls.

Deficits in working memory have sometimes been found in Autism. Working memory is defined as the ability to maintain information in an activated, online state to guide cognitive processing (Baddeley, 1986) and is thought to be subserved by the prefrontal cortex. An initial study found that subjects with Autism were significantly impaired relative to controls on working memory tasks but not on measures of short- and long-term recognition memory, cued recall, or new learning ability (Bennetto, Pennington, & Rogers, 1996). Later studies have been less consistent. In an investigation by Russell and colleagues (Russell, Jarrold, & Henry, 1996), a group with both Autism and mental retardation did not differ from matched controls on three measures of verbal working memory. In another study, no group differences were found in a higher-functioning sample, relative to matched comparison groups with Tourette's syndrome and typical development, on three tasks of working memory (Ozonoff & Strayer, 2001).

The evidence reviewed here suggests that Autism is not a primary disorder of long-term memory. Rather, difficulty appears to occur at the stage of encoding and organizing material. It is the overlay or additional requirement of higher-order processing that makes certain memory tasks difficult for people with Autism.

Language

In most children with Autism, impairment in language and communication is apparent early in life. Use of gesture to communicate is also notably restricted. Language does not always develop and, when it does, its onset is often delayed. For those who do speak, phonology and syntax are often consistent with mental age, but abnormalities in pragmatics, that is, language used to communicate socially (Tager-Flusberg & Anderson, 1991), are characteristic. Even mildly affected children show difficulty adapting their discourse to the listener's response or perspective and taking turns in conversation. Although high-functioning children with Autism are willing to engage in conversation, they often give no response, repeat questions and comments, and do not spontaneously elaborate; their conversational exchanges with others are marked by disjointedness, lack of reciprocity, and noncontextual utterances (Adams, Green, Gilchrist, & Cox, 2002; Capps, Kehres, & Sigman, 1998). Autism was at one time considered a disorder of language (Rutter, 1978), but more recent theories emphasize impairments in social cognition and attribute universal difficulties with pragmatic language to higher-order social information-processing deficits. We turn now to this large body of research.

Social Cognition

Problems perceiving faces and emotions have been documented in a number of studies. Using a crossmodal para-digm in which subjects had to match affective and nonaffective auditory and visual stimuli, Hobson (1986) found that the group with Autism committed significantly more errors than controls matched on nonverbal IQ when matching affective material, but performed as well as controls on nonaffective crossmodal matching. Weeks and Hobson (1987) demonstrated that children with Autism preferred to sort faces by nonemotional attributes, such as hairstyles and accessories, than by emotional expressions. When required to sort faces by emotion, performance was significantly impaired relative to controls. Other researchers using different paradigms have replicated the finding that individuals with Autism are selectively impaired on affect-matching tasks, relative both to performance of comparison subjects matched on nonverbal IQ and to their own performance on nonaffective control tasks (Bormann-Kirschkel, Vilsmeier, & Baude, 1995; MacDonald et al., 1989).

A methodological issue was raised, however, suggesting that the role of verbal ability in emotion perception was not adequately controlled in early studies (Ozonoff, Pennington, & Rogers, 1990). If some verbal mediation is required to process affective information, then failure to match on verbal ability may account for group differences, rather than a primary deficit in emotion perception being responsible. Most initial studies matched control samples on nonverbal IQ alone. Subsequent investigations showed that when individuals with Autism were matched with control subjects on the basis of verbal ability, group differences were no longer apparent on emotion sorting, matching, and naming tasks (Braverman, Fein, Lucci, & Waterhouse, 1989; Davies, Bishop, Manstead, & Tantam, 1994; Hobson, Ouston, & Lee, 1988, 1989a; Loveland et al., 1997; Ozonoff et al., 1990; Prior, Dahlstrom, & Squires, 1990). Language ability and verbal IQ account for large amounts of variance in emotion perception scores, with intercorrelations in the .60 to .70 range (Fein, Lucci, Braverman, & Waterhouse, 1992). Capps, Yirmiya, and Sigman (1992) found deficits in recognizing only complex emotions, such as pride and embarrassment. Similarly, Adolphs and colleagues (Adolphs, Sears, & Piven, 2001) found no group differences in recognition of simple emotions but impairment when making social judgments, such as trustworthiness or approachability, from faces. These results suggest that there are a number of moderating variables that account for variance in emotion perception abilities in Autism. Group differences between samples with and without Autism may be secondary to linguistic, cognitive, pragmatic, or theory of mind deficits rather than reflecting a specific emotion-processing impairment. Research has also demonstrated that emotion perception deficits are not specific to people with Autism, having also been documented in individuals with mental retardation (Hobson, Ouston, & Lee, 1989b), learning disabilities (Holder & Kirkpatrick, 1991), and Schizophrenia (Novic, Luchins, & Perline, 1984). It should be noted, however, that the emotion tasks used have all been poor approximations of naturalistic, real-world opportunities for emotion perception. Structured laboratory tests of this type are susceptible to compensation. Better tasks that measure basic, online affective processes, particularly those that develop early in life, are needed to fully test emotion-related hypotheses in Autism.

Several studies have also explored potential differences in more basic processes involved in understanding faces. As with emotion perception, results have been somewhat mixed, with some studies finding that identity matching and basic facial perception appear to be normal (Adolphs et al., 2001; Ozonoff et al., 1990; Volkmar, Sparrow, Rende, & Cohen, 1989), whereas other studies find deficits in these abilities (Boucher, Lewis, & Collis, 1998; Klin et al., 1999). New techniques that have only recently become available suggest that the mechanisms underlying face processing, regardless of accuracy, may be different in people with and without Autism. Recent eye-tracking and behavioral studies have demonstrated that individuals with Autism use an atypical and disorganized approach to viewing faces, including an unusual focus on nonfeature areas of the face, such as the mouth (Joseph & Tanaka, 2003; Klin, Jones, Schultz, Volkmar, & Cohen, 2002; Pelphrey et al., 2002), instead of the normal focus on the eyes (Emery, 2000). Dawson et al. (2002) used event-related potentials (ERP) to study response to familiar faces (i.e., their mother's) and unfamiliar faces in young children with Autism and matched controls. Only those with Autism failed to show a difference in ERP response to the familiar versus unfamiliar face, although they did show the expected response to familiar versus unfamiliar objects. Another important study, by Schultz et al. (2000), found that people with Autism and Asperger's syndrome use the inferior temporal gyrus, the part of the brain that normally makes sense of objects, when they look at faces and do not activate typical face-processing structures, such as the fusiform gyrus. These studies suggest that even when people with Autism can figure out what someone's eyes or face conveys, they do so in a different, possibly less efficient manner.

Another aspect of social cognition in Autism that has received a great deal of research attention is the theory of mind hypothesis, which became prominent in Autism research in the 1980s and 1990s and has been posited as able to explain many characteristics of the disorder. Early studies demonstrated that children with Autism have specific difficulties in understanding states of mind such as false belief, ignorance, and second-order belief (beliefs about beliefs) in other people (Baron-Cohen, 1989a; Baron-Cohen, Leslie, & Frith, 1985). Deficits in theory of mind have been proposed to cause many of the social and language impairments that are part of Autism (Frith, 1989; Frith, Happé, & Siddons, 1994; Happé, 1993). The theory of mind account of Autism has been a very influential hypothesis that has generated a great deal of empirical research.

Recent functional imaging research has examined the neural foundations of theory of mind skills. Baron-Cohen and colleagues (1999) used fMRI to examine brain function while participants looked at pictures of eyes and made judgments about what mental states the eyes conveyed. They found that typical adults relied heavily on both the amygdala and the frontal lobes to perform this task. In contrast, adults with either high-functioning Autism or Asperger's syndrome used the frontal lobes much less than the normal adults and did not activate the amygdala at all when looking at the pictures of eyes. Instead, they used the superior temporal gyrus, which is not typically active during this task in people without Autism (Baron-Cohen et al., 1999). Happé et al. (1996) found that adults with Asperger's syndrome used different regions of the prefrontal cortex than typical controls when engaged in reasoning about mental states. A recent report found significantly less activation in the medial prefrontal cortex and the superior temporal sulcus, relative to controls, in adults with Autism Spectrum Disorders. Activation in the extrastriate cortex was high (and equivalent) in both groups, but the Autism spectrum group alone showed reduced connectivity between this region and the superior temporal sulcus, suggesting an information transfer bottleneck within this mentalizing network (Castelli, Frith, Happé, & Frith, 2002).

A limitation of the theory of mind hypothesis of Autism is that theory of mind skills do not begin to emerge in typical development until after symptoms of Autism are already present. Thus, they lack the developmental precedence necessary for causal explanatory power. Recent work has focused on potential precursors of later theory of mind development. One purported precursor is joint attention behavior, which typically emerges around the first birthday and involves sharing attention to an object with another person. It is evident usually through pointing, referential looking, and shared affect. Many studies have demonstrated a paucity or absence of joint attention behaviors in young children with Autism (Baron-Cohen, 1989b; Mundy & Sigman, 1989), and some have hypothesized that this is the earliest sign of the failure to appreciate the minds of others exhibited by these children (Baron-Cohen, 1991; Mundy, Sigman, & Kasari, 1993).

Rogers and Pennington (1991) proposed that the symptoms of Autism might stem from impairment in another very early social process, that of imitation. Based on a theoretical model of early interpersonal processes developed by Stern (1985) and evidence that newborns are capable of imitating some body movements (Meltzoff & Moore, 1977), it has been proposed that infants and young children come to understand the behavior, subjective experiences, and mental states of other people through imitation, social mirroring, and affect sharing (Meltzoff & Gopnik, 1993; Rogers & Pennington, 1991). An early impairment in motor imitation could have cascading consequences that profoundly alter later social development. Many studies have documented imitation deficits in young children with Autism (e.g., Jones & Prior, 1985; Rogers, Hepburn, Stackhouse, & Wehner, 2003) and even in older, higher-functioning individuals with the disorder (Rogers, Bennetto, McEvoy, & Pennington, 1996). More work examining the developmental emergence and relationships among joint attention, imitation, other early social processes, and later theory of mind is needed.

Another limitation of the theory of mind hypothesis is that not all children with Autism lack a theory of mind. Studies have shown that higher-functioning individuals are often able to pass theory of mind tasks (Bowler, 1992; Ozonoff, Pennington, & Rogers, 1991). Nor are theory of mind deficits specific to Autism. A meta-analysis found significant theory of mind deficits in individuals with mental retardation as well as those with Autism (Yirmiya, Erel, Shaked, & Solomonica-Levi, 1998). Other linguistically handicapped children, including those who are deaf (Peterson & Siegal, 1995), may show theory of mind handicaps but not the other social and pragmatic impairments. Recent studies have failed to find deficits in the understanding of simple mental states, such as intentions, in young children with Autism (Carpenter, Pennington, & Rogers, 2001). These findings collectively have tempered early claims to have discovered the "core" psychological defect of Autism, as has the inability of this theory to account for the repetitive and stereotyped behaviors of Autism, as well as the cognitive strengths in visual-spatial processing that are often evident (Hughes, 2002). In recent years, there has been increasing debate and reevaluation of the theory, especially in terms of claims regarding its modularity or componential quality in brain development and dysfunction (Garfield, Peterson, & Perry, 2001; Tager-Flusberg, 2001). Questions about its relation to other

prominent neuropsychological deficits, such as executive function, have also been raised. We turn to this topic next.

Executive Function

Investigation of executive functions has been another active area of research in Autism. Beginning with Rumsey (1985), many studies have documented deficient performance on tests of executive function (EF). The dysfunction most often found is perseveration of behavior, that is, continuing to perform actions that are no longer appropriate or relevant given the context. An example of this is sorting by previously correct rules despite feedback that their strategies were incorrect (Prior & Hoffmann, 1990; Rumsey & Hamburger, 1988). Several research groups have found that executive deficits are apparent in Autism even relative to controls with other neurodevelopmental disorders (Ozonoff, Pennington, & Rogers, 1991; Szatmari, Tuff, Finlayson, & Bartolucci, 1990). In one study, performance on the Tower of Hanoi, a test of planning, correctly predicted diagnosis in 80% of subjects, whereas other neuropsychological variables (e.g., theory of mind, memory, emotion perception, spatial abilities) predicted group membership at no better than chance levels. Following the sample longitudinally, Ozonoff and McEvoy (1994) found that deficits on the Tower of Hanoi and Wisconsin Card Sorting Test (WCST) were stable over a 2.5-year period. Not only did EF abilities not improve during the follow-up interval, they showed a tendency to decline relative to controls over time. Shu, Lung, Tien, and Chen (2001) reported significant deficits on WCST performance in a sample of 26 Taiwanese children with Autism, relative to matched controls. Because these children were raised in a completely different culture and environment from the Western children who participate in most EF studies, the authors suggested that executive dysfunction may be a core impairment in Autism. In a review of the EF literature, Pennington and Ozonoff (1996) reported that 13 out of the 14 studies existing at the time of publication demonstrated impaired performance on at least one EF task in Autism, including 25 of the 32 executive tasks used across those empirical studies. The magnitude of group differences tended to be quite large, with an average effect size (Cohen's d) across all studies of .98, marked by especially large effect sizes for the Tower of Hanoi (d = 2.07) and the WCST (d = 1.04). Recently, significant group differences on the Intradimensional/Extradimensional Shift task of the Cambridge Neuropsychological Test Automated Battery were found in a very large sample of individuals with Autism and matched controls recruited from the Collaborative Programs of Excellence in Autism network funded by the National Institutes of Health (Ozonoff et al., 2004). This work was important in replicating the flexibility impairment of Autism across samples collected at seven independent sites in individuals ranging in age from 6 to 47 years.

Two research groups have tested age-related EF development in very young children with Autism. McEvoy, Rogers, and Pennington (1993) studied preschool-age children with Autism (mean age = 5 years) and matched developmentally delayed and typically developing control groups. Significant group differences were found on the spatial reversal task, a measure of flexibility developed for infants and nonhuman primates, but no group differences were evident on three other EF measures. It was suggested that these tasks may have been less developmentally appropriate for the sample. However, in another investigation by the same research team (Griffith, Pennington, Wehner, & Rogers, 1999) studying even younger preschool children with Autism (mean age = 4 years), there were no differences in performance on any of eight executive tasks (including the spatial reversal task), compared to a developmentally delayed group matched on chronological age and both verbal and nonverbal mental age. Likewise, in a larger study of even younger children with Autism (mean age = 3 years), Dawson et al. (2002) reported no significant differences on six EF tasks (again including spatial reversal), relative to developmentally delayed and typically developing control groups matched on mental age. This work raises the possibility that EF deficits in children with Autism emerge with age and are not present (at least relative to other samples with delayed development) early in the preschool range. Because executive functions are just beginning to develop during the early preschool period in all children, a relative lack of variance across groups may explain this apparent developmental discontinuity. Differences in the way EF is measured at different ages may also contribute to this finding. The executive tests that have been administered to very young children with Autism do not require the same use of arbitrary rules (Biro & Russell, 2001) and social feedback (Ozonoff, 1995) that those given to older individuals do. If these features are central to the EF performance deficits of Autism, then the discontinuity between earlier and later development may be due simply to measurement differences. Further work, particularly longitudinal research, is needed to examine when during development specific executive difficulties emerge and what their developmental precursors may be.

Another recent research trend has been to study the relationships between EF and other cognitive and social-cognitive processes. The explanatory power of executive dysfunction for Autism would be greatest if individual differences in EF predicted variations in other impairments or in symptoms of Autism. In fact, one of the initial appeals of the EF hypothesis of Autism was its apparent ability to account for the repetitive and stereotyped behaviors of the disorder (Turner, 1997), something that the theory of mind and other neuropsychological models of Autism had failed to explain (Hughes, 2002). Empirical support for a relationship between executive dysfunction and repetitive behaviors is mixed. Turner reported that perseveration on a set-shifting task was correlated with more primitive stereotyped behaviors, such as hand flapping, and impoverished generativity was correlated with "higher-level" repetitive behaviors such as circumscribed interests. In contrast, South, Ozonoff, and McMahon (in press) found no significant correlations between any category of repetitive behavior and any EF variable. For example, the correlations between the number of perseverations on the WCST and various forms of repetitive behavior ranged from a low of $r = -.03$ for lifetime history of circumscribed interests to a high of $r = .16$ for lifetime history of unusual obsessions with objects. This sample was significantly older (mean age = 14 years) and more intellectually capable (mean VIQ = 111) than Turner's sample, so direct comparisons are difficult and further research is clearly needed.

Other work has explored the relationship between executive function and theory of mind skills. In a study designed to examine theory of mind and strategic deception abilities (Russell, Mauthner, Sharpe, & Tidswell, 1991), children with Autism were taught to play a game in which they competed with an experimenter for a piece of candy. The candy was placed in one of two boxes with windows that revealed the contents of the box to subjects but not to the experimenter. The objective of the task was to fool the experimenter into looking for the candy in the empty box. It was explained that the strategy of pointing to the empty box would be successful in winning the candy, whereas pointing to the box that actually contained the chocolate would result in losing it. Even after many trials, the subjects with Autism were unable to point to the empty box, despite the consequences of this strategy. Russell et al. first attributed these results to a perspective-taking deficit that caused an inability to engage in deception. In a follow-up study, Hughes and Russell (1993) demonstrated that significant group differences remained even after the element of social deception was removed from the task. Subjects were simply instructed to point to the empty box to get the candy. Even with no opponent present, the subjects with Autism persisted in using the inappropriate strategy. On the basis of these results, Hughes and Russell reattributed the pattern of performance to a deficit in disengaging from the object and using internal rules to guide behavior, rather than to a social or perspective-taking dysfunction. This work led the way for several other studies that explored the hypothesis that some degree of executive control is necessary for successful performance on theory of mind tasks and, by extension, for the development of theory of mind (e.g., Russell, Saltmarsh, & Hill, 1999).

The opposite hypothesis, that some level of social awareness is necessary for executive function, has also received support. In the WCST, for example, feedback is provided by the examiner after each card is sorted; successful set shifting requires using this feedback to alter behavior. If, however, feedback supplied in a social context is less salient or more difficult to process for people with Autism, they may perform poorly on EF tasks for primarily social reasons. A few studies have contrasted performance on executive tests when they are administered in the traditional manner, by human examiners, to performance when they are administered by computer. Ozonoff (1995) reported that the WCST was significantly easier for individuals with Autism when it was given by computer, with group differences considerably smaller in the computer administration than the human administration conditions. In the group with Autism, the number of perseverations was cut in half on the computerized version of the task, but performance did not differ across conditions in the typically developing control group (Ozonoff, 1995). This finding has been replicated by two independent research groups (Griffith & Pennington, 2003; Pascualvaca, Fantie, Papageorgiou, & Mirsky, 1998). This suggests that the format of the executive task, particularly the nature of the feedback (social versus nonsocial), may have a much greater impact on performance for people with Autism than has been appreciated. Thus, it has been difficult to tease apart the relative primacy of executive function and mentalizing or other social deficits in the chain of cognitive impairments that are involved in Autism.

It has also become clear that other non-EF skills, such as language and intelligence, may contribute to EF deficits. Liss et al. (2001) gave a battery of EF tests to children with high-functioning Autism and a control group of children with language disorders. The only group difference, more perseverative errors on the WCST by the Autism group, disappeared when Verbal IQ was statistically controlled. Ozonoff (Miller & Ozonoff, 2000; Ozonoff & McEvoy, 1994; Ozonoff & Strayer, 2001) has also identified significant relations between IQ and EF performance in people with Autism. And Perner and Lang (2002) reported a pair of large studies of typically developing preschool children

in which the correlation between EF and a language task was just as high as its correlation with a false belief task.

Finally, it is apparent that EF deficits are not specific to Autism but are found in many other disorders, including ADHD (Shallice et al., 2002), Obsessive-Compulsive Disorder (Spitznagel & Suhr, 2002), and Schizophrenia (Bustini et al., 1999). Thus, the EF account of Autism has failed, like the theory of mind account, as a grand cognitive theory of Autism. EF deficits are not specific to Autism, universal in individuals with the condition, nor precedent in development.

Central Coherence

A third theory put forth as an integrative explanation for the pattern of symptoms seen in Autism is that of weak central coherence (Frith & Happé, 1994). This theory suggests that the core psychological impairment in Autism is the failure to process information in context. The information processing of typically developing individuals is motivated by a "drive" to achieve higher-level meaning and a preference for global processing. Frith (1989) first introduced the idea that it is this drive for central coherence that is missing in Autism, resulting instead in detail-focused processing. Central coherence theory predicts that people with Autism will perform poorly on tasks that require integration of constituent parts into coherent wholes, but will perform normally (or even in a superior fashion) on tasks that require a focus on detail or "local processing." They should also show preserved or enhanced performance on tasks in which the typical tendency to use contextual information actually interferes with performance, because central coherence theory predicts that people with Autism would be relatively impervious to context effects. An essential feature of central coherence theory is that the detail orientation of Autism is a consequence of a deficit in global processing.

Central coherence theory has intuitive appeal, as it appears to explain both the neuropsychological deficits and the particular cognitive strengths of people with Autism (Happé, 1999). It also has potential to account for some behavioral symptoms of the condition that other theories have failed to explain, such as repetitive and stereotyped behaviors. For example, weak central coherence could explain the focus on technicalities and trivia seen in the circumscribed interests of people with Autism Spectrum Disorders, as well as their insistence on sameness in the environment.

Several studies have supported the central coherence theory of Autism. Frith and colleagues found that children with Autism were significantly more accurate in discovering figures embedded in complex pictures than controls matched on mental and chronological age (Shah & Frith, 1983). This research team also found evidence that weak central coherence played a role in the strong performance of people with Autism on the Wechsler Block Design subtest (Shah & Frith, 1993). They found that presegmenting the designs significantly improved performance for participants without Autism (both those with typical development and those with mental retardation), presumably because of the strong tendency to process the unsegmented designs as a gestalt. The performance of people with Autism, however, was not enhanced by presegmentation, suggesting that this group had a natural tendency to see the stimuli in terms of parts rather than as a whole and did not need the parts to be explicitly highlighted. Other supportive evidence of central coherence deficits in Autism came from verbal tasks. Several studies have shown that individuals with Autism fail to use sentence context to determine the correct pronunciation of homographs, words with one spelling but two meanings (e.g., *lead;* Frith & Snowling, 1983; Happé, 1997; Jolliffe & Baron-Cohen, 2000). In global-local tasks, in which large stimuli (usually either letters or numbers) are composed of smaller similar stimuli (also letters or numbers), people with Autism show an advantage at identifying the local details that slow and make less accurate identification of global patterns (Rinehart, Bradshaw, Moss, Brereton, & Tonge, 2000).

Later studies have not fully confirmed these results, however. Several subsequent investigations have used the Embedded Figures Test, with one study finding no superiority in accuracy (Ozonoff et al., 1991), another failing to replicate the accuracy results but demonstrating significantly faster reaction time on the part of people with Autism Spectrum Disorders (Jolliffe & Baron-Cohen, 1997), and a third failing to find superiority in either accuracy or reaction time (Rodgers, 2000). A prediction of central coherence theory is that there should be little difference in performance when the context in which the shape is embedded is meaningful or nonmeaningful, as the deficit in global processing leads to little or no encoding of context. Two studies used adaptations of the Embedded Figures Test in which the meaningfulness of the context was manipulated. Both investigations found that the performance of participants with Autism was affected by the contextual information in the same manner as the controls (Brian & Bryson, 1996; Lopez & Leekam, 2003). Brian and Bryson also examined memory for the contextual information and found that it was as good as

controls, demonstrating that the context *was* being actively processed and encoded.

Mixed results have been obtained on global-local tasks as well. Later investigations have failed to replicate the superiority at identification of local targets (Rodgers, 2000) or the deficiency of processing global configurations (Mottron, Burack, Stauder, & Robaey, 1999; Ozonoff, Strayer, McMahon, & Filloux, 1994). In an elegant experimental design, Plaisted, Swettenham, and Rees (1999) demonstrated that administration procedures have large effects on performance and could account for the inconsistent pattern of results across studies. They found normal global processing in Autism using a selective attention procedure in which participants focused on only one level (either global or local) for long blocks of stimulus presentation, but a local advantage in Autism during a divided attention procedure in which participants had to shift between global and local levels from trial to trial. This suggests that difficulty switching attention (an executive or attentional deficit) may be part of poor performance and argues against a pure central coherence explanation for the deficit found on such global-local tasks.

Findings have been similarly inconsistent using other paradigms. Happé (1996) first reported that individuals with Autism were much less likely than control participants to succumb to visual illusions, which are dependent on context. However, Ropar and Mitchell (1999) failed to replicate this nonsusceptibility, using the same illusions employed in the Happé study. They also reported low and nonsignificant correlations among visual illusion nonsusceptibility and several visuospatial tasks also thought to measure weak central coherence (e.g., Block Design, Embedded Figures Test; Ropar & Mitchell, 2001), further questioning the construct and its selective association with Autism.

These nonreplications, particularly the repeated findings that individuals with Autism do appear to use context and perceive gestalts (Brian & Bryson, 1996; Lopez & Leekam, 2003; Mottron et al., 1999; Ozonoff et al., 1994; Ropar & Mitchell, 1999), have suggested a modified version of central coherence theory. It has been proposed that the cognition of people with Autism does involve some "local bias" or preference for detail-oriented processing but that this is not due to a deficit in global processing. Several recent investigations have supported this notion. Plaisted and colleagues (Plaisted, Saksida, Alcantara, & Weisblatt, 2003) found that a group of participants with Autism demonstrated enhanced ability to identify individual features of a stimulus but also were as good as controls at integrating these features to see the significance of the configuration of the features.

In a final study of interest, weak central coherence was found to be more common in a group of adolescents with high-functioning Autism than developmental norms for the tests would predict, but was far from universal, with half of those with Autism demonstrating performance across several tests indicative of *strong* central coherence (Teunisse, Cools, van Spaendonck, Aerts, & Berger, 2001). Given the mixed results of studies of weak central coherence, its status as a core neuropsychological impairment of Autism is currently uncertain (Hoy, Hatton, & Hare, 2004).

Conclusion

Although aspects of the central coherence theory describe well the cognition of Autism, it has fared similarly to the executive function and theory of mind accounts in failing as a grand theory capable of organizing the behavioral and cognitive strengths and weaknesses of Autism within one unifying theory. So, we do not have a convincing single deficit theory of Autism. Part of the puzzle of this disorder is that it involves multiple neuropsychological deficits, but at the same time there is specificity to the profile of strengths and weaknesses. There are several broad solutions to this puzzle, but we do not yet know enough to distinguish among them. One possibility is a developmental cascade model (e.g., Fein, Pennington, Markowitz, Braverman, & Waterhouse, 1986; Rogers & Pennington, 1991), in which one early deficit disrupts the enculturation through which many distinctive human cognitive capacities develop. Another is that there are neuropsychological subtypes of Autism, each with its own primary deficit. A third possibility is that the notion of a single primary neuropsychological deficit is too simple, and that what is required is two or more interacting primary deficits. A final possibility is that the seemingly disparate multiple deficits that have been observed all share some general underlying cognitive characteristic, such as complex information processing, and it is the deficit in that cognitive process that is primary.

Evaluating these possibilities in light of the empirical findings just reviewed, it remains possible that some early developing aspect of basic affective or interpersonal processing is the primary deficit in infants with Autism and that this deficit "unhooks" these infants from normal socialization, thus producing a cascade of deficits in the domains reviewed here: attention, memory, language, social cognition, executive functions, and central coherence. Unfortunately, our knowledge of affective processes in typical

infants, especially infants with Autism, is very sparse, so it is difficult to critically examine this hypothesis at the present time. None of the three other possible solutions to the puzzle of the neuropsychology of Autism—subtypes with their own primary deficits, multiple interacting deficits, or a deeper core cognitive deficit—can be clearly rejected at this point. The evidence reviewed in this section suggests it is unlikely that deficits in memory will be on the list for subtype or multiple interacting deficit causal theories of Autism. It is possible, although not probable, that difficulties in attention shifting, theory of mind, imitation, affective processes, executive functions, and central coherence may define different subtypes of Autism. It is more plausible, but equally undetermined, that some or all of these impairments are components of a set of interacting deficits that as a configuration are primary to Autism. Finally, we turn to our fourth possible solution to the puzzle, that of a deeper core cognitive deficit.

Minshew (Minshew, Goldstein, & Siegel, 1997) has proposed that the central cognitive deficit in Autism is one of complex information processing. Any neuropsychological task, be it perceptual, spatial, verbal, or motor, that requires less information processing will be spared, according to this account, and those that require higher-order information processing will be impaired. The review of the Autism literature across many neuropsychological domains appears to support this theory. We have summarized the relative sparing of simple language processes (e.g., phonology, syntax), simple executive functions (e.g., inhibition), simple attentional processes (e.g., selective and focused attention), and simple memory functions (e.g., rote and recognition), with complementary dysfunction in each of these domains at the level of more complex processes (e.g., language pragmatics, cognitive flexibility, abstraction, attention shifting, working memory). The complex information-processing theory is also compatible with recent neurological findings of enlarged brains (Courchesne et al., 2003) with increased number of cortical columns of reduced size and density (Casanova et al., 2002), which could significantly disrupt neural networks, increase noise in the computational system, and lower efficiency of information processing (Casanova et al., 2002).

There is an important conceptual challenge for this theory, however, which is the need for a more detailed and principled account of what makes a cognitive task complex or not. Does complexity just equal difficulty? Chapman and Chapman (1973) argued a long time ago that many demonstrations of apparently specific cognitive deficits in Schizophrenia did not equate the experimental and comparison tasks for difficulty. It is not too surprising that subjects with an extreme neurodevelopmental disorder like Schizophrenia would perform differentially worse on difficult cognitive tasks. A similar pattern would be expected in mental retardation syndromes and in Autism. So, for the complex information-processing theory to work, we need an explicit definition of cognitive complexity that is derived independently of the empirical results in Autism, yet explains the specific pattern of cognitive strengths and weaknesses found in Autism, which differ from those found in Schizophrenia or mental retardation.

A second challenge to the complex information-processing theory of Autism is that it does not adequately explain the very early symptoms of Autism that are often apparent before the first birthday (Osterling & Dawson, 1994). Autism is particularly interesting because impairments in very basic interpersonal processes coexist with spared abilities in certain cognitive domains, such as memory and visual-spatial processes. The complex information-processing theory cannot explain why a 2-year-old with Autism can put together puzzles at a 3-year mental age level but is not able to point, a developmentally simpler skill normally apparent by 1 year of age.

Recent genetic advances make it clear that a number of interacting genes may be needed for the development of Autism. It is implausible that all genes (and other potential environmental factors) confer susceptibility for a single specific neuropsychological deficit. Moreover, such modular hypotheses are unable to account for the variations across the spectrum of Autism in severity and pattern of symptoms and deficits. These variations make subtypes and multiple deficit theories more likely, but more work is needed to identify the relevant deficits. Although research on the neuropsychology of Autism has been very active, it is far from definitive at this point. Like the blind men describing the elephant, the theories proposed depend largely on the characteristics of the participants and the neuropsychological domains being studied. Researchers who study young children focus on early interpersonal deficits; those who study older and higher-functioning individuals focus on cognitive impairments. No model accounts for everything. A major test of any viable future model will be its ability to explain early appearing infant symptoms. Research on the very early development of infants at family risk for the disorder will help identify such deficits, as will a more careful dissection of the typical development of early social cognition. Until we have a better model of typical very early social-emotional development (prejoint attention), answers to the Autism puzzle may remain elusive.

In the next section, we apply the neuroscientific model of developmental psychopathology to a very different condition, Posttraumatic Stress Disorder, and see how the four levels of explanation, particularly the neuropsychological model, fare.

POSTTRAUMATIC STRESS DISORDER

This section of the chapter reviews the literature on Posttraumatic Stress Disorder (PTSD) as it pertains to the four levels discussed earlier. Although once considered an adult disorder, PTSD is highly relevant to the field of developmental psychopathology, as it is a relatively common consequence of child abuse, which affects at least 15 of every 1,000 children in the United States (Daro & Donnelly, 2002). PTSD was selected as the focal disorder for this section because it presents several interesting and complex challenges for the neuropsychological model of developmental psychopathology.

First, PTSD is unique among mental disorders in that, by definition, it is the result of a specific etiological-level environmental event (e.g., a trauma). In this respect, PTSD is very different from Autism, which is a highly heritable disorder for which environmental risk factors have yet to be identified. But, as is discussed later, there are also genetic influences on PTSD, which represents a relatively simple example of a diathesis-stress model of developmental psychopathology, with a defined stressor. Second, PTSD is a disorder involving stark contrasts in neuropsychological symptoms. Vivid, intrusive, and arousing memories present alongside amnesia, forgetting, and numbing. Symptoms of dissociation also may be part of the disorder. Third, other conditions, including depression and Generalized Anxiety Disorder, frequently are comorbid with PTSD, making syndrome definition challenging.

As described in more detail later, reasonable conceptual neuropsychological models of PTSD have been developed. There has been tremendous growth in empirical work to explain the neurobiology of anxiety, fear, and stress. So another reason PTSD was chosen for this section is that much of this recent neuroscience research is relevant to PTSD and offers new information about the brain mechanisms involved in the disorder. In fact, some researchers (see LeDoux, 2002, p. 294) have chosen to focus on PTSD because, at the neuropsychology level, the disorder offers the clearest available model of classical conditioning in a mental disorder (Pitman, Shalev, & Orr, 1999). Furthermore, a merger between the brain and neuropsychological levels appears to be occurring in studies of PTSD.

Pennington (2002) states that the four-level framework is not intended as a grand theory of any disorder but as an organizing structure potentially capable of incorporating and assimilating new discoveries at each level. The neuropsychological level, in particular, is likely to undergo significant changes as a consequence of advances in computational and affective neuroscience. A comprehensive review of factors involved in the etiology, neurobiology, and neuropsychology of PTSD offers an opportunity to explore these propositions. As before, we have chosen to organize this section with symptoms first because it is easier to read, although, particularly in the case of PTSD where the neuropsychology of the condition is well understood, this sequence downplays the centrality of the neuropsychological domain in bridging the mind-body gap.

Level 4: Symptoms, Diagnostic Definitions, and Epidemiology

Although military psychiatrists have long recognized that exposure to war-related atrocities can produce persistent stress symptoms in previously well-adjusted individuals, it was not until after the Vietnam War that Posttraumatic Stress Disorder was included in the *Diagnostic and Statistical Manual of Mental Disorders* (APA, 1980). Members of the *DSM-III* task force eventually agreed to the inclusion of PTSD as it became clear that a similar syndrome occurred in survivors of other traumas, including rape, abuse, natural disasters, and concentration camp confinement.

DSM-IV (APA, 1994) broadened the definition of PTSD, creating what some have called "bracket creep" in the boundaries of the syndrome (McNally, 2003). To meet the *DSM-IV* diagnostic criteria for PTSD, individuals must be exposed to a traumatic event in which they experience or witness events that involve the threat of death or serious damage to the integrity of self or other, and their response must involve intense fear, helplessness, or horror. Thus, to be diagnosed with PTSD, one need not actually be involved in the trauma: It is enough to be either vicariously involved or to be horrified about what has happened to others. *DSM-IV* stipulates that in children, this intense reaction may be expressed by disorganized or agitated behavior.

Three symptom clusters define PTSD: reexperiencing, avoiding, and increased arousal. To meet diagnostic criteria, the individual must have one symptom from the first cluster that indicates that the traumatic event is persistently reexperienced in either intrusive and distressing recollections of the event, in recurrent and distressing dreams of the

event, in acting or feeling that the event is reoccurring, in psychological distress at exposure to cues that symbolize the event, or in physiologic reactivity to these cues. *DSM-IV* notes variations in the first three of these for young children, such that reexperiencing may be acted out in repetitive play, nightmares need not have content specific to the trauma, and trauma-specific reenactments may occur.

The individual must also experience three or more symptoms related to avoidance and general numbing of responsiveness. These include efforts to avoid thoughts, feelings, or conversations associated with the trauma; efforts to avoid activities, places, or people that arouse recollections of the trauma; amnesia for important aspects of the trauma; diminished interest or participation in significant activities; feelings of detachment and estrangement; restricted range of affect; and a sense of foreshortened future. Two or more symptoms of hyperarousal must also be present to meet PTSD criteria. These include difficulty falling or staying asleep, irritability, concentration problems, hypervigilance, and/or an exaggerated startle response.

Two final criteria for the PTSD diagnosis are that the symptoms last at least 1 month and cause functional impairment. Symptoms may be defined as acute or chronic depending on whether they are present for less or more than 3 months. PTSD onset is viewed as delayed if it occurs 6 months or more after the trauma. One of the distinctive symptoms of PTSD is the repetitive experiencing of traumatic and richly detailed memories or flashbacks that intrude into consciousness and/or dreams. These memories may be highly detailed and laden with affective content. Although some degree of reexperiencing a trauma is relatively common, in PTSD these symptoms do not fade over time.

DSM-III-R (APA, 1987) first recognized that PTSD could develop in children as well as adults. Initially, diagnostic criteria for children were simply a downward extension from observations made in adults. In *DSM-IV-TR* (APA, 2000), there are now specific descriptions of how symptoms may manifest in children. A child's response to a traumatic event may be manifested as disorganized or agitated behavior rather than intense fear or horror, for example. It is also noted that children may represent the trauma through repetitive play and that frightening dreams may occur without content that is recognizably related to the trauma.

A common trauma leading to PTSD in childhood is chronic and/or severe physical, emotional, or sexual abuse. Child maltreatment represents the greatest failure of the environment to provide the expectable experiences that are vital to normal child development (Cicchetti & Lynch,

1995). As we summarize later, trauma and abuse can affect attachment, interfere with and/or bias information processing, dysregulate mood, and enhance the stress response throughout life (Maughan & Cicchetti, 2002; Teicher et al., 2003). Despite recent advances in the conceptualization of pediatric PTSD, more work to understand the nature and extent of stress reactions in children is needed (Lonigan, Phillips, & Richey, 2003; Yule, Perrin, & Smith, 2001). For example, it is not well understood why symptoms of PTSD in chronically abused children often are not as prominent as those following other traumas and may be obscured by other social, cognitive, and behavioral problems (van der Kolk, 2003).

Epidemiology

Community-based studies of PTSD show a lifetime prevalence of approximately 8% of the adult population (Kessler, Sonnega, Bromet, Hughes, & Nelson, 1995). At-risk individuals, including combat veterans, victims of crime, and victims of natural disasters, face a much higher prevalence rate, with estimates ranging from 3% to 58%. Women are twice as likely as men to develop PTSD (Kessler et al., 1994).

Traumatic events faced by men, women, and children tend to differ, as do those experienced by individuals from different ethnicities and social classes. Pynoos, Steinberg, and Wraith (1995) have developed a typology of reported traumatic exposures experienced by children and adolescents. These include small- and large-scale natural disasters, accidents, intra- and extrafamilial violence, and life-threatening illnesses and medical procedures. Terrorist attacks, including those occurring on September 11, 2001, offer a new class of traumatic events for study (North, 2004). Traumatic stress in school-age children and adolescents is a complex phenomenon involving a wide variety of emotional, cognitive, perceptual, sensory, and physiological experiences (Pynoos, Steinberg, & Piacentini, 1999).

The prevalence of PTSD in children in the community is not known. One estimate, based on a study of 386 older adolescents, is that 6.3% met the *DSM-III-R* lifetime criteria for PTSD (Reinherz, Giaconia, Lefkowitz, Pakiz, & Frost, 1993). Widely varying rates of PTSD have been found in children exposed to extreme stressors. For example, Terr (1979) reported that the incidence of psychic trauma was 100% after the Chowchilla bus kidnapping. Yule, Udwin, and Murdoch (1990) found that approximately 50% of the survivors of the sinking of the cruise ship *Jupiter,* which had more than 400 British schoolchildren on board, met the criteria for PTSD in the 1st year following the incident. Green et al. (1991) reported that of the 179 children age 2 to 15 examined after the Buffalo Creek disaster, 37% received probable PTSD diagnoses based on a retrospective review of records. A consensus is emerging that approximately one-third of children may develop PTSD following traumatic events (Breslau, Davis, Andreski, & Peterson, 1991; Resnick, Kilpatrick, Dansky, Saunders, & Best, 1993; Yule & Udwin, 1991). Factors such as type of trauma, extent of exposure, age, gender, level of premorbid functioning, social support, and coping style appear to moderate the risk of developing PTSD symptoms after exposure to a traumatic event (Lonigan et al., 2003; Pine & Cohen, 2002).

Several studies have found that persons with PTSD and PTSD symptoms are at risk for a variety of other problems later in life, including suicidality, premature death, sexual revictimization, and somatization symptoms (Lonigan et al., 2003). About 80% of adults with PTSD also have a comorbid diagnosis of alcohol abuse, depression, Generalized Anxiety Disorder, or Panic Disorder. It is unclear, however, whether these conditions are risk factors for PTSD or results of PTSD, or whether PTSD and these conditions are each related to some third factor (Pennington, 2002).

Level 1: Etiology—Genes, the Environment, and Transactions

PTSD is a disorder whose etiology appears best explained by a diathesis-stress model. The precipitant of PTSD is fairly clearly defined by the diagnostic criteria themselves, and this makes it a clean example of a disorder caused in part by an environmental stressor. To understand the diathesis part of the etiologic model, we examine genetic factors contributing to the vulnerability to develop PTSD and, in doing so, touch on etiological factors implicated in other anxiety disorders. Molecular genetics, behavioral genetics, and animal models are discussed, as well as selected environmental factors and transactions between genes and the environment. As will become evident, there is a close relationship between genes and brain development. Thus, some of the effects discussed in this section are further elaborated in later parts of the review concerning the brain level.

Genetics

Molecular and behavioral genetics methods have been applied to the study of anxiety disorders. Efforts to discover genes specific to PTSD, like those to locate putative genes responsible for Panic Disorder, phobias, and Obsessive-Compulsive Disorder, have proven unsuccessful. Molecular genetics work has been hampered, in part, by difficulty drawing boundaries between different anxiety disorder phenotypes and nonclinical anxiety that is part of typical development (Smoller, Finn, & White, 2003). There have been few published molecular genetic studies of PTSD. Comings, Muhleman, and Gysin (1996) reported a potential association between a TaqI DRD2 receptor polymorphism and PTSD, but this was not replicated in a subsequent study (Gelernter et al., 1999).

Given that PTSD requires an external trigger, it is difficult to perform family studies of the disorder. Davidson and colleagues (Davidson, Tupler, Wilson, & Connor, 1998) found that relatives of individuals with both PTSD and depression were more likely to suffer from depression. However, having PTSD alone was not associated with an increased family risk for either disorder.

Several studies based on a group of more than 4,000 twin pairs consisting of Vietnam veterans and their twins have provided strong evidence for both environmental and genetic influences on the development of PTSD (Goldberg, True, Eisen, & Henderson, 1990; True et al., 1993). In MZ twin pairs discordant for heavy combat exposure, Goldberg et al. found that individuals exposed to war trauma were 9 times more likely to have PTSD than cotwins not serving in Vietnam. After controlling for combat exposure, True and colleagues found that heritabilities for PTSD symptoms were 13% to 30% for reexperiencing symptoms, 30% to 34% for avoidance symptoms, and 28% to 32% for arousal symptoms.

Inherited personality traits also may mediate the response to trauma. Several studies have found that neuroticism and extraversion, both of which are moderately heritable, are related to who develops PTSD after a trauma and to the severity of the symptoms (see Fauerbach, Lawrence, Schmidt, Munster, & Costa, 2000). Emotionality, conceptualized as neuroticism, anxiety, electrodermal lability, and lowered habituation, appears to be an important moderator of how conditionable an individual is to fear responses (Pitman et al., 1999). Anxiety sensitivity, a psychological construct incorporating concern over anxiety-related sensations, also is highly heritable (Stein, Jang, & Livesley, 1999).

Animal studies indicate that individual differences in reactivity to stress and novelty are partly genetically mediated (Sanchez, Ladd, & Plotsky, 2001). For example, in squirrel monkeys separated from their mother, cortisol levels measured 1 day after separation show significant post-natal rearing effects, whereas by 3 to 7 days, the effects of separation are minimal and heritability is significant (Lyons, Martel, Levine, Risch, & Schatzberg, 1999). In further support of the heritability of vulnerability to anxiety disorders, an animal model using mice bred to exhibit characteristics of learned helplessness showed that animals with this genetic predisposition respond differently to trauma than mice not bred for these characteristics. Specifically, exposure to stress produced physiologic symptoms of analgesia, cognitive deficits, and hypothalamic-pituitary-adrenal (HPA) dysregulation (King, Abend, & Edwards, 2001). HPA dysregulation, which is hypothesized to be an important component in PTSD and affective and anxiety disorders, is explored in more detail in the brain mechanisms section.

Environment and Transactions

Numerous factors can be considered part of the environment. As discussed earlier, the most central environmental factor to PTSD is the trauma. Here we examine the role of other environmental factors, particularly the contribution of parenting behavior, to the child's experience of stress. Research suggests that parents and caretakers greatly influence the child's experience of trauma. In situations of imminent danger, parental reactions of extreme anxiety may exacerbate the child's fearfulness (Pynoos et al., 1999). Parents can play a role in maintaining anxious behavior in their children after traumatic stress by modeling and reinforcing anxious and/or avoidant behavior and not encouraging the development of coping behaviors (Hudson, Kendall, Coles, Robin, & Webb, 2002). In general, the presence of a caring adult mitigates the effects of childhood stress (Masten, Best, & Garmezy, 1990). In the opposite scenario, when a parent is the agent of the trauma, as in child maltreatment, there is a serious challenge to the species-typical environmental transactions that play a critical role in the emergence and timing of normal developmental processes (Cicchetti & Lynch, 1995; Cicchetti & Toth, 2000).

At the biological level, animal studies have shown that typical variations in maternal care "program" the expression of genes regulating behavioral and endocrine stress responses in offspring. Hippocampal synaptic development is affected by maternal care such that long-term potentiation, important in the processes of learning and memory, may be enhanced. Furthermore, characteristics of maternal care influence oxytocin receptor gene expression in female offspring, and this appears to form the basis of intergenerational transmission of individual differences in stress reactivity (Meaney, 2001).

To summarize, the etiology of PTSD appears to require both a stressor (by definition) and a diathesis or predisposition that may be biologically and/or environmentally mediated.

Level 2: Brain Mechanisms

Research over the past decade has produced tremendous advances in our understanding of the pathophysiology of negative emotional states, including those associated with stress and fear. This proliferation of work is due to several factors, including the development of compelling animal models and of noninvasive structural and functional neuroimaging techniques for humans.

Traumatic stress is hypothesized to affect complex and interrelated neurochemical and structural aspects of brain development and functioning, including the HPA axis, neurotransmitter systems, limbic structures (particularly the hippocampus and amygdala), and psychophysiologic responses. As highlighted next, results of animal and human brain studies require integration into the evolving literature on the neuropsychology of PTSD.

The Hypothalamic-Pituitary-Adrenal Axis

Stress early in life is related to long-term alterations in bodily systems that mediate the stress response. In mammals, the HPA axis (sometimes referred to as the limbic-hypothalamic-pituitary-adrenal or LHPA axis, given its connections with the limbic system) is the major neuroendocrine stress response system. The HPA axis is activated in stressful conditions to mount the organism's "fight or flight" response. Corticotropin-releasing factor (CRF) is released from the hypothalamus. This stimulates the release of adrenocorticotropin hormone (ACTH) from the pituitary, which, in turn, causes glucocorticoids (cortisol in humans) to be released from the adrenal glands. This process has a negative feedback effect on the pituitary, hypothalamus, and hippocampus.

Persistent changes in CRF in the central nervous system are hypothesized to mediate the association between stressful experiences and the development of mood and anxiety disorders. It has been suggested that the relationship between early life stress and later psychiatric disorders is related to persistent elevations in CRF neurotransmission and alterations in other neurotransmitter systems. Animal studies have supported the relationship between CRF and negative affect. In the laboratory, administration of CRF produces effects that mimic stress, depression, and anxiety, including increases in heart rate and

arterial pressure, disruption of sleeping, and suppression of exploratory behavior (Heim & Nemeroff, 1999). CRF also acts on the central nervous system to trigger additional neurochemical stress responses, such as those involved in the noradrenergic system and those associated with the brain stem and locus coeruleus (Bremner, 2003). Extreme trauma may produce oscillation between noradrenergic overactivity and depletion. The stress response system also may interact with the endogenous opiate system to produce effects described next.

In addition to CRF, other neuropeptides and amino acids thought to mediate the stress response include endogenous opioid peptides, neurotensin, somatostatin, cholecystokinin, neuropeptide Y, substance P, vasopressin, and oxytocin. Neuropeptides can function as both hormones (in the body) and neurotransmitters in the central nervous system. Stress is associated with endogenous opiate release, which may be related to the analgesia or numbing produced by the body in stressful situations. Cholecystokinin and neuropeptide Y have been associated with anxiolytic-like responses in several anxiety models (Heilig et al., 1993; Vermetten & Bremner, 2002). Oxytocin and vasopressin play a role in social attachment and may thereby mediate the role of early stressors in producing vulnerability to PTSD.

Glucocorticoids, through their metabolic and immune modulating effects, help the organism maintain homeostasis in the face of stress. Although necessary for survival, persistent elevations in glucocorticoids may damage the central nervous system and physical organs. High levels of cortisol have been associated with damage to the hippocampus in humans, including neuronal loss, inhibited neurogenesis, delayed myelination, and abnormalities in synaptic pruning (Sapolsky, 2000).

Findings related to cortisol in PTSD are not straightforward, however. Some studies find that traumatized children have significantly elevated cortisol levels, relative to controls (DeBellis et al., 1999); others have shown that the pattern of daily cortisol levels varies depending on other factors, including the type of maltreatment experienced by the child and its severity. For example, Cicchetti and Rogosch (2001a) found that children who experienced the most extensive maltreatment, including sexual and physical abuse as well as neglect and emotional abuse, showed significantly elevated morning cortisol levels relative to other maltreated children and to nonmaltreated children. These authors also found that clinical-level internalizing and externalizing symptoms in maltreated and other children were associated with different patterns of cortisol levels and daily fluctuation (Cicchetti & Rogosch, 2001b). Cortisol findings in adults are different, however, possibly due to the down-regulation of an overly challenged HPA axis. Studies of adults with PTSD have generally found dysregulation of the HPA axis characterized by a blunted response to ACTH and without increased cortisol secretion (DeBellis et al., 1994; Yehuda, 1997).

Neurotransmitters

Catecholamines, including dopamine, and serotonin have been hypothesized to play a role in some of the cognitive features of PTSD, depression, and other anxiety disorders. Dopamine innervation of the medial prefrontal cortex is vulnerable to even mild stress. The medial prefrontal cortex is recognized to play a role in the neuropsychological construct of working memory, with dopamine necessary for its function. This explanation is consistent with neuropsychological studies that suggest that working memory may be impaired in PTSD.

Long-term chronic stressors also result in altered serotonergic functions—an example of the cross-talk and coregulation that exist between the 5HT system and the LHPA axis, two neurobiological systems linked to stress and mood regulation (Lopez, Akil, & Watson, 1999). Animal models suggest that stress increases serotonin turnover in the medial prefrontal cortex, nucleus accumbens, amygdala, lateral hypothalamus, and locus coeruleus. Chronic shock that produces learned helplessness states is associated with reduced serotonin release in the frontal cortex, suggesting that serotonin synthesis is not able to keep pace with demand in this situation (Wu et al., 1999). Supporting this hypothesis are animal studies showing that the capability for increased serotonin metabolism during exposure to inescapable stressors prevents the development of learned helplessness (e.g., Ronan, Steciuk, Kramer, Kram, & Petty, 2000).

The Limbic System

Components of the limbic system, including the hippocampus and amygdala, and closely related structures, such as the orbitofrontal cortex and the anterior cingulate, have been proposed to play a role in the development of PTSD symptoms. The hippocampus is a highly plastic structure. Under stressful conditions, reduced levels of dendritic branching, neuronal loss, and inhibition of neuronal migration in this structure have been reported (Bremner, 2003). Conversely, animal models have demonstrated that administration of selective serotonin reuptake inhibitors (SSRIs) increases dendritic branching and neurogenesis in the hippocampus (Malberg, Eisch, Nestler, & Duman, 2000). Chronic stress also may be associated with potentiated release of norepinephrine in the hippocampus (Nisenbaum,

Zigmond, Sved, & Abercrombie, 1991). It has been suggested that early abuse and neglect affect the maturation of the hippocampus, and it has been hypothesized that this effect accounts for the tendency of abused and neglected children to misinterpret sensory information as more dangerous or threatening than it actually is (van der Kolk, 2003).

Numerous studies have shown that the amygdala is necessary for the establishment of fear conditioning (LeDoux, 1996, 2002). The amygdala rapidly appraises incoming information from the environment and determines whether it constitutes a threat. Projections from the central amygdala initiate the HPA axis response. These projections run from the amygdala to the medulla and hypothalamus and initiate sympathetic and parasympathetic nervous system responses. The amygdala also projects to the brain stem and activates a startle response and other defensive behaviors. Once amygdala circuits are activated and become "trained" through repeated or extreme exposure to fear, they are very hard to modify, and the memories and behaviors associated with them are difficult to extinguish (LeDoux, 1996). Amygdala activation in response to sensory stimuli reminiscent of a trauma then can result in misinterpretation of neutral stimuli as threats. When this occurs, responses are stereotyped and totalistic and prevent new learning from occurring.

Structural and Functional Imaging Studies

The most consistent finding in structural MRI studies of PTSD is reduced hippocampal volume. It is possible that this contributes to memory problems associated with PTSD. Neuroimaging studies of PTSD also implicate regions of the limbic system involved in learning, memory, and emotional regulation (Horner & Hamner, 2002). Several structural MRI studies of Vietnam veterans with PTSD have reported reduced hippocampal volume. Bremner, Randall, Scott, et al. (1995) found right hippocampal volumes to be reduced by 8% in 26 veterans with PTSD, compared with age- and gender-matched healthy controls. Gurvits et al. (1996) reported bilateral volume reductions of 26% in veterans with PTSD relative to healthy controls, even after controlling for age, brain volume, alcohol abuse history, and combat exposure.

Structural MRI studies of individuals who have experienced sexual abuse have produced similar results. In adult survivors of child abuse, Bremner et al. (1997) found 12% reductions in left hippocampal volume compared to matched controls. Stein, Koverola, Hanna, Torchia, and McClarty (1997) reported a 5% reduction in left hippocampal volume versus controls without a history of abuse matched on sociodemographic variables.

It is unclear whether these changes in hippocampal volume are a cause, an effect, or an incidental or nonspecific finding of PTSD. Several animal models suggest, for example, that prolonged glucocorticoid exposure produces hippocampal atrophy (Sapolsky, 2000). In contrast, Gilbertson et al. (2002) question whether hippocampal atrophy is an effect of chronic stress. In a twin study of Vietnam veterans and their twins who were not involved in combat, these researchers found concordance in hippocampal volume of the twins regardless of combat status. This result suggests that reduced hippocampal volume may be an inherited risk factor for PTSD (part of the diathesis), although it could also be a nonspecific finding.

Several functional imaging studies of patients with PTSD have found brain changes that appear to correspond to the emotional reexperiencing symptoms of PTSD (for a review, see Pine, 2003). Symptom provocation designs use visual and script-driven imagery and auditory reminders of traumatic events to trigger reexperiencing symptoms. These studies show decreased functioning in the prefrontal, parietal, and temporal cortex and the hippocampus. Increased activation in the posterior cingulate, motor cortex, amygdala (Rauch et al., 1996; Shin et al., 1999), and anterior cingulate (Liberzon, Abelson, Flagel, Raz, & Young, 1999; Shin et al., 1997) have also been reported, although one recent study using an emotional Stroop paradigm found decreased anterior cingulate blood flow during exposure to emotion words (Bremner, Vermetten, Vythilingam, et al., 2004).

Other Brain- and Nervous System-Level Findings

Physiological hypersensitivity has been found in PTSD patients, which appears to be a result of traumatic exposure and part of the pathophysiology of the disorder (i.e., sensitization of the fear response). PTSD patients show specific signs of increased peripheral physiological responding to both audiovisual and imagined stimuli similar to the traumatic event. Higher heart rate to loud startling tones is one of the most replicated combat-related PTSD findings, and a recent twin study of Vietnam combat veterans has shown this to be an acquired sign of PTSD, as opposed to a preexisting vulnerability (Orr et al., 2003). This exaggerated startle response presumably reflects a sensitization of the fear response (Orr, Lasko, Shalev, & Pitman, 1995). Using an acoustic startle paradigm, Klorman, Cicchetti, Thatcher, and Ison (2003) found that maltreated boys showed smaller increases in amplitude of eyeblink and smaller reductions in blink latency than comparison boys as the startle probe increased in loudness. Although this is not consistent with findings for adult males with PTSD, who exhibit the reverse of these findings, this was interpreted as sensitization to noxious stimuli in the maltreated group. This sensitization interpretation is consistent with studies that have shown that at 1 and 4 months posttrauma, individuals with PTSD, compared to those who do not develop the disorder, show greater heart rate responses but lower skin conductance and blunted eyeblink response to startle (Shalev et al., 2000).

Exposure to internal or external trauma cues has been found to produce strong sympathetic reactivity even years after the trauma (Buckley, Blanchard, & Neill, 2000). Results of a study of more than 1,300 Vietnam veterans combined audiovisual and script-driven imagery and found heightened physiologic reactivity to trauma-related cues in the veterans with PTSD (Keane et al., 1998). Such increased arousal is consistent with the fear conditioning model described later, although there are individual differences in psychophysiological responses (Liberzon et al., 1999).

Another possible consequence of trauma is altered brain hemispheric laterality, as shown by functional neuroimaging studies (van der Kolk, 2003). Using a symptom provocation paradigm and PET, Rauch et al. (1996) found pronounced hemispheric lateralization in adults with PTSD who were exposed to reminders of trauma. Teicher, Andersen, Polcari, Anderson, and Navalta (2002) found that patients with a history of abuse in childhood used their left hemisphere predominantly when thinking about neutral memories and their right hemisphere when recalling an early upsetting memory. Control subjects had a more integrated and bilateral response to recalling neutral and traumatic events. In this study, the right hemisphere of the abused participants was as developed as that of control subjects, but their left hemispheric development was arrested. Van der Kolk completed another study with children with trauma histories and found a similar pattern of frontal lobe asymmetry.

In summary, there are several consistent findings at the brain level of research on PTSD. The HPA axis is clearly disrupted by the experience of trauma and/or chronic stress. The size and functioning of the hippocampus and amygdala appear malleable in response to trauma, although the Gilbertson et al. (2002) twin study contradicts this. Physiological hypersensitivity is often found in individuals with PTSD, both adults and children, relative to those without a trauma history. As will be illustrated in the next section, these findings are highly consistent with those found at the neuropsychological level of analysis.

Level 3: Neuropsychology

The neuropsychology of PTSD may be inherently less complex than that of Autism because the causal mechanisms are clearer, because the epigenetic process of the disorder starts later in development and thus may have less profound consequences, and because the symptoms defining the disorder are less heterogeneous than in Autism and correspond more neatly to traditional neuropsychological domains (i.e., attention, memory, arousal). Perhaps because of this, the neuropsychological research that has been done on PTSD is more focused than that of Autism. It is more closely intertwined with research at the brain level than is Autism research, as the neural mechanisms of fear and stress responses appear to be better understood than the neural mechanisms of the cognitive processes that may mediate autistic symptoms. Over the past decade, the brain level has been where the action is in PTSD research. This creates an opportunity for more basic empirical neuropsychological research as well as studies that integrate findings between the two levels.

This section begins with a review of the extant literature on the neuropsychology of PTSD. Two relatively well-established neuropsychological theories of PTSD—the classical conditioning and the cognitive-behavioral/information-processing models—are then described, with connectionist neural network model of PTSD that is able to incorporate both theories. A discussion of each model's strengths and limitations follows. Criteria used to evaluate neuropsychological theories were set forth in the beginning of this chapter. These include the model's ability to answer questions related to phenotypic variability, external validity, comorbidity, and developmental trajectory. Similar general guidelines to evaluate specific theories of PTSD have been established by Jones and Barlow (1990). These include being able to explain the diverse symptoms of reexperiencing, avoidance, emotional numbing, and persistent arousal, as well as being able to explain individual differences in vulnerability to PTSD symptoms and variability in the severity of symptoms. Brewin, Dalgleish, and Joseph (1996) added several more recommendations, including that the theory explain comorbidities and make novel predictions.

Because several PTSD symptoms appear related to memory processes (both deficient, as in amnesia, and enhanced, as in intrusive memories), most neuropsychological studies of the disorder have focused on memory and/or attention function. More recent work has also explored executive functions, but this area requires further study.

Memory

Studies have explored general memory impairment, performance on list-learning tasks, and trauma-related amnesia. They generally find that PTSD patients of different ages exhibit deficits in these areas. Although results need to be interpreted with caution due to lack of statistical control for potential confounds, including psychiatric comorbidity, medical illness, and substance abuse, several studies have found that patients with PTSD have deficits in declarative memory for information not related to the trauma (Bremner, Vermetten, Afzal, & Vythilingam, 2004; Horner & Hamner, 2002). Vietnam veterans have been shown to display a pattern of short-term memory impairment (Bremner et al., 1993; Uddo, Vasterling, Brailey, & Sutker, 1993), as have adult survivors of child abuse (Bremner, Randall, Capelli, et al., 1995) and rape (Jenkins, Langlais, Delis, & Cohen, 1998). Autobiographical memory was reduced in inpatient adolescents who had experienced traumas, with high negative correlations between number and severity of traumatic events and the specificity of autobiographical memory (de Decker, Hermans, Raes, & Eelen, 2003). Yehuda et al. (1995) found that adult veterans with PTSD exhibited memory deficits as assessed by a list-learning task. Compared with control subjects, individuals with PTSD showed a significant reduction in retention of previously learned lists when a distracting intervening list was presented. This was interpreted as compatible with the idea that intruding thoughts or flashbacks produced declarative memory deficits. Although intrusions and amnesia appear to be opposite problems, they may be related in that intrusive memories may interfere with the capacity to process other material.

Moradi, Doost, Taghavi, Yule, and Dalgleish (1999) studied children ages 11 to 17 with PTSD using the Rivermead Behavioral Memory Test (Wilson et al., 1998), a measure of memory in everyday contexts. They found that children with PTSD were significantly impaired relative to a control group on a global measure of memory. Clark et al. (2003) explored working memory for neutral verbal information using PET technology and a task requiring detection of different colored target words. They found that individuals with PTSD showed significantly less activation in the left dorsolateral prefrontal cortex, which is typically involved in monitoring and manipulating working memory content.

Both the incidence and the mechanism of amnesia in PTSD remain controversial. One study reported that more than 30% of adults who were sexually abused as children were amnestic about the abuse for many years (Williams, 1994), but this study has been criticized on methodological grounds, and the concept of repressed memories of abuse is hotly debated (see McNally, 2003). Brewin et al. (1996) have conceptualized amnesia as the absence of verbally accessible knowledge, leaving only unconscious, situationally accessible knowledge available. In this model, amnesia is the result of a strategy to avoid trauma-related stimuli by not attending to the negative emotions associated with the trauma. However, McNally, Metzger, Lasko, Clancy, and Pitman (1998) found that in a directed forgetting task, children with PTSD exhibited recall deficits for positive and neutral words only, as opposed to trauma-related words. Factors related to depth of encoding and retrieval, including the degree of elaboration, organization, and rehearsal of memories, may also play a role in the forgetting of unpleasant trauma-related memories (Koutstaal & Schacter, 1997).

Attention and Executive Function

Neuropsychological studies of attention in PTSD have adopted several approaches. Research in this area has examined such components of attention as sustained attention, learning of new material, shifting attention, and ideational fluency, as well as issues of attention allocation and bias.

Vasterling, Brailey, Constans, and Sutker (1998) studied Gulf War veterans with PTSD and a control group without PTSD who had also participated in combat in this war. Significant sustained attention, mental manipulation, initial acquisition of information, and retroactive interference differences were observed between the groups, as were errors of commission and intrusion. Results suggested that trauma-related intrusions may reflect a more general pattern of disinhibition. This study also found that disinhibition and intrusions on cognitive tasks correlated positively with reexperiencing symptoms and negatively with avoidance and numbing symptoms. Vasterling et al. (2002) found that Vietnam veterans with PTSD scored significantly worse than Vietnam veterans without PTSD on tasks of sustained attention, working memory, and learning, but not on focused attention or shifting attention measures. These findings were independent of intellectual functioning.

Beers and DeBellis (2002) found that children with PTSD made significantly more errors on measures of freedom from distractibility, including the Stroop Color Word Test. They also made more omission errors on a test of sustained attention. Shields and Cicchetti (1998) found attention deficits in maltreated children ages 6 to 12 relative to controls.

Studies have shown that persons with PTSD exhibit attentional biases that favor the processing of trauma-related material. Several studies employing word list-learning tasks with trauma-related and neutral words have shown that Vietnam veterans with PTSD exhibit an enhancement of implicit memory for words related to the trauma versus control subjects (Amir, Kaplan, & Kotler, 1996; Zeitlin & McNally, 1991). Emotional Stroop tasks use emotionally

laden words related to the trauma (i.e., body bag), interspersed with nonemotional words. Words are printed in different colors and participants must name the ink color and suppress the prepotent tendency to read the words. Studies employing these paradigms have found that PTSD patients have an attentional bias to trauma-related words, resulting in an enhanced Stroop effect (greater interference of word reading on color naming). This has been shown for Vietnam veterans (McNally, Kaspi, Riemann, & Zeitlin, 1990), rape and sexual abuse victims (Bremner et al., 2004; Foa, Feske, Murdock, Kozak, & McCarthy, 1991), and survivors of motor vehicle accidents (Bryant & Harvey, 1997). Stroop interference for words related to trauma appears to be correlated with the severity of the PTSD symptoms as assessed by standardized measures (McNally et al., 1990) and self-reports (Cassidy, McNally, & Zeitlin, 1992). It has been suggested that reduced capacities to inhibit unwanted or situationally inappropriate information may cause individuals with PTSD to have difficulty focusing, particularly under stressful or novel conditions (Weinstein, Fucetola, & Mollica, 2001).

Koenen et al. (2001) studied 16 patients with PTSD (primarily women) and 53 neurologically intact control subjects (primarily men ages 20 to 64). Patients with PTSD were significantly more impaired on delayed alternation, object alternation, and delayed nonmatch-to-sample tasks, suggesting overlapping deficits in dorsolateral and orbital regions of the prefrontal cortex. Beers and DeBellis (2002) found that on the Wisconsin Card Sorting Task (Heaton, Chelune, Talley, Kay, & Curtiss, 1993) subjects with PTSD completed fewer categories than control subjects. These authors also showed that ideational fluency in children with PTSD, as assessed by the animal naming and FAS tasks, was compromised. Another study of children ages 11 to 17 with PTSD found significantly lower performance than controls on measures of planning and cognitive flexibility (Moradi et al., 1999).

Social Cognition

Research on social cognition in children with PTSD emanates primarily from work on child maltreatment. Several early studies demonstrated that maltreated children show atypical patterns of emotion expression and recognition relative to children who have not been maltreated (Camras et al., 1990; Gaensbauer & Hiatt, 1984). More recent studies have converged in finding that maltreated children have particular difficulty interpreting anger. Pollak, Cicchetti, Hornung, and Reed (2000) found that, compared with control children, physically abused preschoolers had a response bias toward incorrect interpretation of anger when presented with brief emotional stories and asked to match the feeling of the protagonist with a photograph of a model posing with a facial expression. They also found that physically abused and neglected children generally detected fewer differences between facial expressions than did children in the control group. Pollak, Cicchetti, Klorman, and Brumaghim (1997) conducted an event-related brain potential study and found that, compared to control children, children with maltreatment histories had larger P3b amplitudes when shown angry versus happy and neutral faces. A later study failed to find increased P3b amplitudes to fearful faces (Pollak, Klorman, Thatcher, & Cicchetti, 2001). This suggests that maltreated children may allocate greater attentional resources to angry faces than to other expressions of emotion.

In summation, existing studies of the neuropsychology of PTSD suggest that it involves general deficits in short-term memory, sustained attention, working memory, learning, inhibition, and comprehension and expression of emotions. These deficits appear to be exacerbated by exposure to emotional stimuli reminiscent of the trauma. Individuals with PTSD attend to information in atypical and distorted ways. Trauma-related materials both heighten and dampen arousal levels; some aspects of memory are impaired and others are accentuated.

Neuropsychological Models

We now turn to a discussion of the conceptual neuropsychological models that have been used to explain PTSD and explore their ability to account for these empirical findings.

Classical Conditioning Models. PTSD has been conceptualized as a case of classical conditioning (see Barlow, 1988; Pitman et al., 1999). In the classical conditioning model, the traumatic stimulus (unconditioned stimulus) has induced an intense unpleasant reaction of fear, helplessness, or horror (unconditioned response). External and internal cues present at the time of this trauma (conditioned stimuli) become paired with the traumatic experience and evoke intense emotional responses on future occasions (conditioned responses). This results in fearful reexperiencing symptoms associated with the original trauma. As mentioned earlier, this type of fear conditioning, which is hypothesized to involve the limbic system, especially the amygdala, is thought to be involved in other anxiety disorders, including Panic Disorder and phobias (LeDoux, 2002). So what began as a purely psychological construct as part of the behaviorist paradigm has now become a neuropsychological construct as the underlying brain mechanisms have been understood. As we will see, this conditioning theory of PTSD needs to be

broadened to account for individual differences in susceptibility to PTSD, the developmental trajectory of PTSD, other symptoms of PTSD, such as numbing and trauma-related amnesia, and other neuropsychological deficits associated with PTSD, such as impairments in attention and declarative memory.

Extinction and sensitization, two other processes related to fear conditioning, are important for explaining PTSD. To explain these phenomena, brain-level findings must be considered in combination with conceptual neuropsychological models. In PTSD, there is likely a sensitization process whereby repetitive exposure to stimuli elevates the sensitivity of limbic system networks, reduces extinction of the conditioned fear, and/or causes sensitization of the HPA axis. PTSD sufferers also avoid reminders of the trauma, thus robbing themselves of new learning opportunities that would extinguish fear conditioning. Thus, the fear conditioning model can explain many PTSD symptoms, including reexperiencing, avoidance, and high arousal. It does not, however, account for all *DSM* symptoms, including numbing, feelings of estrangement, and a sense of a foreshortened future. Similarly, the classical conditioning model does not offer insights as to why some people are more likely than others to develop PTSD symptoms and why symptom severity levels differ. As mentioned earlier, it is hypothesized that certain etiological factors may result in increased vulnerability to acute stress reactions, but these are not part of the fear conditioning model.

Similarly, genetic and brain-level findings need to be used in concert with neuropsychological findings in explaining PTSD comorbidities. Classical conditioning models do not account for the common co-occurrence of depression with PTSD, for example, but HPA axis dysregulation and limbic system abnormalities may explain comorbidities. Disruptions in different parts of these circuits might lead to one or a combination of disorders.

In addition, the classical conditioning model does not offer a way to think about the developmental trajectory of PTSD or developmental discontinuities in PTSD symptoms. It does not explain trauma-related amnesia. Furthermore, it does not predict the declarative memory, sustained attention, and learning deficits found in the empirical research reviewed earlier. In sum, fear conditioning may indeed lie at the heart of PTSD, but the classical conditioning model needs to be broadened to account for individual differences, developmental differences, and other features of PTSD.

Cognitive-Behavioral/Information-Processing Models. Cognitive-behavioral/information-processing models build on the concept of fear conditioning but further propose that traumatic experiences strengthen connections among distributed cognitive, behavioral, and physiological memory representations related to the trauma (see Foa & Kozak, 1986). Activation of any part of the trauma memory network can reactivate the whole structure. When an input to the system matches the emotional memory network (e.g., the noise of a gunshot), it is reactivated, and the trauma response is reexperienced in the form of arousal, vivid and intrusive memories, and fear. Traumas themselves are forms of powerful but discrepant information that is not easily assimilated into existing cognitive schemata for the way the world works (Brewin et al., 1996; Foa, Steketee, & Rothbaum, 1989). As a result of trauma exposure, PTSD patients develop serious perceptual distortions in the way they process information. Arousal also results: Traumas are believed to involve unpleasant and excessive arousal. The individual avoids trauma cues: Avoidance prevents new learning so that new and more inclusive schemata can be formed.

Brewin et al. (1996) proposed a dual representation model that differentiates conscious and unconscious processes. In this model, both conscious and unconscious information is accessed automatically when physical features or meanings in the current situation resemble those of the trauma. Attentional and memory processes favor trauma-related information over neutral information, perpetuating the experiencing of traumatic information.

Cognitive-behavioral models provide explanations for the major clusters of PTSD symptoms. Reexperiencing is seen as a result of memory network activation when there is a match between existing cognitive schemata and the environment. This is especially problematic because attention and memory are believed to favor trauma-related information. Avoidance is viewed as the strategy used by the individual to prevent confrontation with reexposure to cues. Arousal is seen as an element of the traumatic memory network and part of the experience of discrepant horrific information. Memories can be activated without conscious awareness.

One of the major advantages of cognitive-behavioral/information-processing models of PTSD is that they allow more room for considering the role of cognition in the development of symptoms than do classical conditioning paradigms. This type of memory network model also is consistent with empirical findings suggesting that trauma-related stimuli are overwhelming and affect learning and memory. Although these models do not provide an explanation for who develops symptoms, they do provide a means of explaining why some PTSD symptoms are worse than

others based on the size and interconnectivity of the cognitive, behavioral, and physiologic components of the trauma-related memory structure. Cognitive-behavioral/information-processing models also are more able to include a developmental dimension as they can incorporate information about age-graded development in cognitions that trigger symptoms (Pynoos et al., 1999). This enables one to make predictions about the course of PTSD symptoms and about the likelihood of developing trauma symptoms at different points in the life course.

Cognitive-behavioral/information-processing models have their limitations, however. They do not explain why certain disorders are comorbid with PTSD. They do not explain why depression, which may also involve a traumatic precipitant, has symptoms distinct from PTSD. Similarly, these models provide no explanation for general short-term memory problems or amnesia.

Neural Network Models. Over the past 15 years, various researchers have employed neural network models to develop insight into how the brain processes information. Rumelhart, McClelland, and the Parallel Distributed Processing Group (1986) were among the first to attempt to model the microstructure of cognition with greater fidelity to brain structures and processes. Pitman and Orr (1990) were the first to use network models to enhance the understanding of PTSD.

Network theory simultaneously considers the structure created by multiple stimulus-response pairs. There is no executive process in the network. Instead, elements of the network are dynamically interdependent: The activation of one element enhances the activation of all others with which it is positively connected and diminishes the activation of all other elements with which it is negatively connected. Relationships between the nodes in the network are frequently nonlinear. This means that a small change in one processing node can create large changes in others. The term "spreading activation" is used to describe the process whereby one portion of the network influences others. Most recent models used to describe PTSD are connectionist models, meaning that all nodes and layers of the network are connected to one another.

Network models allow one to model the complex elements of a fear structure, including emotional processes (see Tryon, 1999, for a description of a bidirectional associative memory explanation of PTSD). Fear can be understood as a structure in the memory network that contains information about external stimuli, as well as verbal and nonverbal reactions to their meanings. Connections between the parts of the network are both excitatory and inhibitory and mediate psychophysiological responses to script-driven imagery and to escape and avoidance behavior. In this kind of a network, short-term, within-session habituation is thought to evoke a change in the fear structure. The reduction of arousal in the presence of fear cues causes new memories. (This is thought to be the mechanism through which systematic desensitization occurs.) Other disorders and typical fears involve memory structures, but in PTSD the network responses are more ready, intense, large, and easily accessible.

Pitman and Orr (1990) and Tryon (1999) suggested that networks for memories are created through memory "wells" in a flat memory surface (i.e., attractors in a multidimensional space). A visual representation of such a model is a rubber sheet held taut with a ball bearing placed on it; the indentation made by the ball bearing is the memory well. These wells are attractors because another ball bearing placed on the sheet would roll to the indentation. PTSD memories are though to create similar "basins of attraction." Normal memory formation also involves the creation of wells. In PTSD, abnormally deep and attractive basins are formed, as if a heavier ball bearing were placed on the rubber sheet, thereby drawing multiple stimuli into the well. The traumatic incident warps the gradient of memory recall such that previously innocuous stimuli roll into the superbasin of the trauma memory well. The gradient becomes so warped that it incorporates stimuli relating to other memories. Network models also have a drive toward pattern completion, meaning that once activation is initiated, it spreads throughout the network.

Such theoretical neural network models offer potential explanations for many PTSD symptoms, although they have yet to be empirically tested. Reexperiencing symptoms may be explained by the warped gradient of memory retrieval that incorporates unrelated and irrelevant stimuli and memories. Emotional numbing and other avoidance-related phenomena could occur when the person tries to prevent pattern completion by avoiding the emotional states capable of triggering the memory recall. Arousal symptoms may occur because of pattern completion tendencies and because even partial cues trigger recall.

Several novel predictions can be made from this neural network model. First, quality and duration of memory recall, as well as efficiency of pattern completion, are hypothesized to correlate with the severity of PTSD symptoms because activation will spread through the network more widely, efficiently, and quickly. This can be extended to suggest that some individuals have a genetic predisposition to process information and complete patterns rapidly, and this may be disadvantageous if they are exposed to trauma. Second, state-dependent memory ef-

fects are proposed to be operating because emotions are coded with cognitions. For example, fearful memories are more likely to be recalled when the person is frightened versus happy. Emotions participate equally with cognitions in facilitating recall. Entire memories can be retrieved by purely cognitive or purely emotional cues. A third prediction of neural network models is that logical reciprocal inhibition should be operative; thus, there may be some equally strong memories capable of inhibiting trauma-related ones. Finally, persons with more severe PTSD will have fear structures with broader associative structures. The associative structures can be mapped, studied, and used therapeutically. These predictions have yet to be tested.

In conclusion, the neuropsychology of PTSD is relatively well understood, albeit not as extensive as that of Autism, where the symptom profile is broader and thus there is more to explain. However, there are still opportunities to replicate existing studies of PTSD and design new ones that deepen our understanding of memory, learning, attention, and executive functions in this disorder. Relatively little is known, for example, about traumatic amnesia and numbing. Neuropsychological studies also may provide useful information about individual differences in vulnerability to PTSD, symptom profiles, symptom severity, and developed fear structures after a traumatic event.

The neuropsychological models described here also raise interesting issues about treatment matching. In particular, the neural network model provides several novel ideas about constructs that may be useful to study and then employ in PTSD interventions. First, it may be fruitful to better understand and measure a variable assessing ease of pattern completion and spreading activation, as these constructs may be related to who develops PTSD, symptom severity, and how to "cure" the disorder. Second, studies of the existence of logical reciprocal inhibition may help shrink traumatic memory structures or wells and provide additional clues for treatments. Finally, through careful mapping of individual fear structures, it may be possible to develop individually tailored exposure or information-processing therapies that help reduce the hold of traumatic memories.

"RETROFITTING THE BRIDGE": LIMITATIONS OF AND FUTURE DIRECTIONS FOR THE NEUROSCIENTIFIC MODEL

In earlier papers, we made a plea for parsimony (Pennington & Ozonoff, 1991). We suggested that initial neuroscientific models of developmental psychopathologies, as we moved from the atheoretical descriptive stage to an understanding of the three deeper levels of analysis, should be simple. That is, we should propose complexity only as the model demonstrates the need for it. This was an appropriate starting point for an emerging developmental science, but it is now time to reevaluate the simpler models put forth in this chapter to see how far they have taken us. In the preceding discussions of Autism and PTSD, we highlighted both the strengths and the limitations of the neuropsychological models relevant to each condition. In each case, but to differing degrees, extant models have not adequately accounted for the complexities of these developmental psychopathologies. In this final section, we explore how they have broken down and how the limitations they expose may help us improve future neuropsychological models of developmental psychopathology.

Revisiting the Promise of the Neuropsychological Level

At the outset of this chapter, we suggested that the neuropsychological level provided an important bridge between biology and behavior. We maintain the point that some functional bridge that translates brain dysfunction to behavioral symptoms is necessary. We have chosen to call this bridge "neuropsychology," but it is possible that this term has itself become reified. That is, what is really required at the bridging level is some computational algorithm, some translation of inputs to output, but this bridge may or may not be best conceptualized through the traditional domains of neuropsychology. For an alternative account of this bridging level, we summarize the model of David Marr (1982), an influential visual scientist, who proposed three interdependent levels in cognitive science: (1) a computational level, (2) an algorithmic level, and (3) an implementation level. The *computational* level is Marr's highest level (that most related to observed behavior) and is concerned with characterizing the function or goal of a particular piece of information processing or input-output mapping (e.g., stereopsis, printed word recognition, face recognition). A computational theory provides a formal account of the nature of the inputs and outputs and the mapping between them in a particular cognitive computation and incorporates what we know about real-world constraints on that computation. For many of the functions relevant for understanding psychopathology (e.g., emotion perception, mood regulation), we currently lack adequate theories even at this highest computational level.

The next level in Marr's (1982) framework is the *algorithm,* which concerns how a particular mapping is actually

computed and must specify the nature of the input and output representations and the actual mathematical algorithm for computing an output from an input. A connectionist or parallel distributed processing model, which computes the mapping from input to output in a given domain, is an example of the algorithm level. The third and lowest (or most internal) level is that of *implementation* and is concerned with how these representations and algorithms are realized in the physical system of the brain.

How do the levels in the neuroscientific framework we have proposed in this chapter map onto Marr's (1982) levels? Basically, our symptom level would correspond to the behavioral phenomenon (e.g., stereopsis) that Marr's levels are intended to explain; this behavioral level is not an explicit level in Marr's model. The computational and algorithmic levels together roughly equal the neuropsychological level in our framework. In seeking the primary neuropsychological deficit(s) in a given psychopathology, we are testing theories of which particular input-output mappings are impaired, with the long-term goal of providing an algorithmic or neurocomputational account of this deficit and how it explains the symptoms that define the disorder. Marr's implementation level corresponds to our brain level. Finally, because Marr did not aspire to explain individual differences, he did not need an etiological level. But of course, this level is key in any explanation of a psychopathology, which must account for why some people are more at risk for a given disorder than others.

It is hard to imagine that we could ever dispense with a bridging level, whether Marr's (1982) computational level, our neuropsychological level, or some other, in an explanation of normal and abnormal behavior. Even if we had complete accounts of etiologies and symptoms, we would still want a functional account of how one is translated into the other. So, although it is important not to reify the neuropsychological level, it appears necessary to the mature accounts of all psychopathological disorders.

One implication of Marr's (1982) approach and ours is that these levels are logically and causally related and that progress at one level will change our understanding at another. This is an example of the network theory of scientific truth in action. Terms and concepts at each level of analysis are not in tight compartments; rather, their meaning changes as we learn more about other levels of analysis. For instance, the language of symptoms is not theory-neutral. Instead, which symptoms are highlighted in the definition of a disorder and how they are defined changes as we understand more about other levels of analysis. The same applies to the other levels of analysis. A purely psychological construct, such as classical conditioning of the fear response, takes on different meanings as we understand more about the neural implementation of fear conditioning in the amygdala and other structures. Similarly, the meaning of symptoms of anxiety disorders will also change with this increased understanding, as will which genetic or environmental risk factors are considered candidates for understanding individual differences in anxiety. So, as you read our reviews of Autism and PTSD, you may have noticed that it was sometimes hard to decide which level a particular finding belonged to. How would we classify a finding of heightened amygdala activity in response to angry faces in individuals with a particular allele of the serotonin transporter gene? Obviously, it belongs to three, if not all four levels of analysis.

A closely related point is that methods that bridge levels of analysis are particularly informative. Functional neuroimaging studies, including fMRI and ERP studies, by definition bridge at least two levels of analysis, and when applied to psychopathology, include three: symptoms, cognition, and brain function. Behavioral and molecular genetic studies of psychopathology bridge at least two levels of analysis, etiology and symptoms, and potentially three (if cognitive measures are added) or even four (if the study also includes functional neuroimaging). An integrated explanation of a given developmental psychopathology will require converging findings across levels of analysis.

The *Diagnostic and Statistical Manual of Mental Disorders* is described as an atheoretical taxonomy, based largely on the symptom level of analysis. A more pathogenesis-driven classification system would look considerably different (Pennington, 2002). For example, PTSD could be categorized as a disorder of HPA dysregulation along with other anxiety disorders (a combination etiological-level and brain-level explanation), a disorder of hippocampal pathology due to excess glucocorticoids like Cushing's disease or Schizophrenia (an alternative brain-level explanation), a disorder of unfortunate conditioning of the limbic system's fear circuits like Panic Disorder (more of a neuropsychology explanation), or a disorder of Luria's arousal motivation system along with other anxiety disorders and Bipolar Disorder (an alternative neuropsychological conception). We do not yet know which conceptualization will turn out to be most useful; neuropsychology may be part of the answer, but not the whole answer.

Modules or Networks? Single or Multiple Deficits?

Another limitation of neuropsychological models that has been readily recognized for many years is their modularity (e.g., Karmiloff-Smith, 1992). As discussed earlier in this chapter, the most familiar and traditional approach to linking behavior to brain mechanisms is the lesion model, derived from the study of (usually adult) patients with acquired brain insults. This model infers that the injured regions control the functions that are deficient postinjury and, by analogy to the normal brain, attributes specific cognitive functions to distinct brain regions. This model is a simplification that has worked in many ways, launching the fields of experimental cognitive science and neuroscience (Finger, 1994). Decades of elegant experiments have confirmed, in broad strokes, that particular brain regions are indeed involved in particular cognitive functions. For example, there is little doubt that the temporal cortex of the dominant hemisphere is specialized for producing and comprehending language (Dick et al., 2001). It is also clear, however, that multiple additional brain regions are active during language-related tasks.

Just as typical neuropsychological development involves complex, dynamic, distributed neural systems, so, too, does atypical neuropsychological development (Oliver, Johnson, Karmiloff-Smith, & Pennington, 2000). Thus, it is unlikely that any one neuropsychological deficit or damage to any one brain region could explain all manifestations of complex syndromes like Autism or PTSD. Many different theories of Autism are based on modular conceptualizations of neuropsychological function, from the executive dysfunction theory (Russell, 1997), to Leslie's (1992) theory of mind module, to the recent amygdala theory of Autism (Baron-Cohen et al., 2000). It is likely that each of these (and other) theories will turn out to be only partial models that explain some, but not all, features of Autism. There appear to be a number of interacting genes, as well as other unknown nongenetic factors, required for development of the disorder. It is unlikely that each of these etiologic risks would operate on the same functional neuropsychological (or neural) system, making a single deficit model both biologically and theoretically implausible. Indeed, it is unlikely that genes have specific effects on regions of the cortex or cognitive functions, but affect brain development in a general way (Shatz, 1992).

Similarly, dysfunction of a single neuropsychological module cannot explain the wide variation in abilities and deficits that are part of Autism, nor the continuum of severity from higher functioning to seriously disabled. During development, many paths lead to the same end (equifinality), and the same causes can have different outcomes (multifinality; Cicchetti & Rogosch, 1996). This is incompatible with single primary deficit accounts of developmental psychopathologies (Yeung-Courchesne & Courchesne, 1997). Focus on unitary mechanisms, at whatever level, is inappropriate for a complex phenotype.

Developmental Issues

It must be admitted that early (and even current) applications of a neuropsychological approach to disorders in children have often lacked a developmental perspective. For instance, more than 100 years ago, Hinshelwood (1896) explained developmental dyslexia as "congenital word blindness" and postulated abnormal development of the left angular gyrus as the cause. His theory was based on the discovery by Dejerine that a form of acquired dyslexia in adults followed damage to that brain structure. This theory ignores development on two counts. First, it assumes that the same structure serves reading in both children and adults. Second, it comes close to assuming that there is an innate brain center for a function that could not have evolved! Obviously, any reading "centers" in the brain must emerge as a result of instruction and experience. Explaining Autism as congenital mind blindness commits some of these same conceptual errors. Even though theory of mind, unlike reading, did evolve, it is very unlikely to be innate or localized.

The implicit assumption has often been that brain-behavior relations are static across development and hence similar in adults and children. Therefore, the same constructs and even measures could be used across ages. In this "static neuropsychological deficit" approach to understanding developmental disorders, it is further assumed that a mapping exists between damage to or dysfunction in a localized brain structure and a particular cognitive deficit, and that cause runs from the neural to the cognitive level (Oliver et al., 2000). As a consequence of these assumptions, such disorders have often been studied at later ages, close to their developmental end state. As discussed by Oliver et al., recent findings in developmental neuroscience have questioned these core assumptions of the static neuropsychological approach and call for a radically different approach to understanding brain-behavior interactions in both developmental disorders and the mature brain. In this alternative neuroconstructionist or connectionist approach, the specializations found in the mature brain are *products* of development rather than innate, prewired modules. Atypical development results from subtle, often widespread, differences in the initial state which lead to "alternative developmental trajectories in the emergence of representations within neural networks" (p. 1). It follows that the neuropsychological phenotype observed in a given developmental disorder will change with age and that the mapping from the initial to the final state will be complex.

Broca himself noted that lesions resulting in aphasia in adults do not usually prevent children from learning to talk (Moses & Stiles, 2002). Traditional neuropsychological models that ascribe language functions to the left temporal cortex do not explain this phenomenon, just as the neuropsychological model of Autism discussed in this chapter had very little to say about plasticity and resilience. No explanations are provided for the remarkable progress that is sometimes evident after intensive early intervention (Lovaas, 1987). Attributing Autism to a defect in the theory of mind module (Leslie, 1992), as just one example, does not help us understand why some children fare so well with early treatment and what changes in cortical organization take place during intervention. Functional brain imaging studies have pointed to different patterns of activation during task performance in individuals with Autism. Do these differences indicate dysfunction or plasticity (or perhaps both)? What are the limitations to plasticity? Such questions are impossible to answer until the field of developmental neuroscience matures and we know more about typical patterns of brain activation across development.

The Role of Emotion and Related Constructs

One conclusion of this chapter is that the traditional list of neuropsychological domains is not sufficient to account for psychopathology. We need to broaden the list; once we do, it will include many psychological constructs not traditionally considered neuropsychological (e.g., emotion) and not nearly as well understood or studied as the domains of memory and attention. There is a clear need for better neuropsychological models of motivation, emotion regulation, and social cognition. Neuropsychological models of Autism have been difficult to build without a good theory of normal social cognitive and emotional development or a clear understanding of the neural networks that subserve it. Many forms of psychopathology involve dysregulated emotional states and/or deficient social cognitive abilities, yet there are few standardized or naturalistic measures of these processes and little exploration of their role in psychopathology. Even research on affective disorders has, until recently, shed little light on precisely what is disordered about emotion in these conditions (Davidson, 1998). Some recent attempts to integrate emotion and neuropsychological performance can be seen in the PTSD field, where emotional Stroop tasks have been used to explore processing of emotionally charged versus emotionally neutral stimuli. Recent research on individuals with Bipolar Disorder has examined emotional state-dependent recall (Murphy & Sahakian, 2001). Neuroimaging studies are beginning to illuminate the types of brain changes that accompany the experience of emotional states (Damasio et al., 2000). Psychophysiological measures also hold promise for assessing arousal levels that are constituent parts of emotions, and it has been suggested that emotional arousal influences memory encoding and consolidation (Hamann, 2001). Future work should continue down these exciting paths.

Temperament is another area that is critical to consider when assessing psychopathology and neuropsychological functioning. Some recent and innovative research programs have attempted to integrate findings from the diverse fields of temperament research, neuropsychology, and neuroimaging (see Posner, 2002). For example, it has been suggested that it is necessary to study components of temperament to understand individual differences in the development of attentional networks in early childhood (Rothbart & Posner, 2001). Effortful control is one temperamental variable related to the development of executive attention. Studies have shown it to be positively associated with the development of conscience (Kochanska, Murray, & Coy, 1997) and empathy (Rothbart, Ahadi, & Hershey, 1994) and inversely correlated with negative affect. In this view, the development of attentional networks and the development of emotional self-regulation are inextricably linked and must be studied in an integrated way.

A third area of social cognition that is rarely considered in neuropsychological research on developmental psychopathology is the role of individual differences in attribution style and perception of the environment. This is critical in a disorder like PTSD, where an individual's perceptions of a traumatic stimulus can influence symptom severity and mediate outcome. Yet there is little systematic research in this area.

CONCLUSION

We have come a long way in the 40 years or so that the neuropsychological model has been applied to better understand the bases of child psychopathologies. Not long ago, most forms of psychopathology were considered social-interpersonal in origin; now, it is clear that most involve some form of brain difference, regardless of whether the etiological mechanisms are environmental or biological. Research at the neuropsychological level of analysis was important to this realization. Early studies administered traditional neuropsychological batteries to children with psychopathology and found that even those with social-environmental etiologies displayed distinct impairments. The limits of this approach have become apparent over time, and it is no longer terribly informative to document that a particular form of psychopathology is associated with a particular neuropsychological deficit or deficits. We argue that the neuropsychological perspective is nevertheless critical as a computational bridge or heuristic for explaining how genes, neurotransmitters, and specific patterns of brain activation are displayed as symptoms. Now is an exciting time to be a developmental psychopathologist, as the emerging ability to image the living brain at work and computationally model its inputs and outputs may ultimately open what was once a black box.

REFERENCES

Adams, C., Green, J., Gilchrist, A., & Cox, A. (2002). Conversational behaviour of children with Asperger syndrome and conduct disorder. *Journal of Child Psychology and Psychiatry, 43,* 679–690.

Adolphs, R., Sears, L., & Piven, J. (2001). Abnormal processing of social information from faces in Autism. *Journal of Cognitive Neuroscience, 13,* 232–240.

Adolphs, R., Tranel, D., Hamann, S., Young, A. W., Calder, A. J., Phelps, E. A., et al. (1999). Recognition of facial emotion in nine individuals with bilateral amygdala damage. *Neuropsychologia, 37,* 1111–1117.

Allen, G., & Courchesne, E. (2001). Attention function and dysfunction in Autism. *Frontiers in Bioscience, 6,* 105–119.

American Psychiatric Association. (1980). *Diagnostic and statistical manual of mental disorders* (3rd ed.). Washington, DC: American Psychiatric Press.

American Psychiatric Association. (1987). *Diagnostic and statistical manual of mental disorders* (3rd ed., rev.). Washington, DC: Author.

American Psychiatric Association. (1994). *Diagnostic and statistical manual of mental disorders* (4th ed.). Washington, DC: Author.

American Psychiatric Association. (2000). *Diagnostic and statistical manual of mental disorders* (4th ed., text rev.). Washington, DC: Author.

Amir, M., Kaplan, Z., & Kotler, M. (1996). Type of trauma, severity of posttraumatic stress disorder core symptoms, and associated features. *Journal of General Psychology, 123,* 341–351.

Amir, R. E., Van Den Veyver, I. B., Wan, M., Tran, C. Q., Franke, U., & Zoghbi, H. (1999). Rett syndrome is caused by mutations in X-linked MECP2, encoding methyl CpG binding rotein 2. *Nature Genetics, 23,* 185–188.

Asperger, H. (1944). "Autistic psychopathy" in childhood. *Archiv fur Psychiatrie und Ervenkrankheiten, 117,* 76–136.

Aylward, E. H., Minshew, M. J., Goldstein, G., Honeycutt, N. A., Augustine, A. M., Yates, K. O., et al. (1999). MRI volumes of amygdala and hippocampus in non-mentally retarded autistic adolescents and adults. *Neurology, 52,* 2145–2150.

Bachevalier, J. (1994). Medial temporal lobe structures and Autism: A review of clinical and experimental findings. *Neuropsychologia, 32,* 627–648.

Baddeley, A. D. (1986). *Working memory.* Oxford: Clarendon Press.

Baddeley, A. D., & Warrington, E. K. (1970). The distinction between long and short-term memory. *Journal of Verbal Learning and Verbal Behavior, 9,* 176–189.

Bailey, A., LeCouteur, A., Gottesman, I., Bolton, P., Simonoff, E., Yuzda, E., et al. (1995). Autism as a strongly genetic disorder: Evidence from a British twin study. *Psychological Medicine, 25,* 63–77.

Bailey, A., Luthert, P., Dean, A., Harding, B., Janota, I., Montgomery, M., et al. (1998). A clinicopathological study of Autism. *Brain, 121,* 889–905.

Bailey, A., Palferman, S., Heavey, L., & LeCouteur, A. (1998). Autism: The phenotype in relatives. *Journal of Autism and Developmental Disorders, 28,* 369–392.

Barkley, R. A. (1997). Behavioral inhibition, sustained attention, and executive functions: Constructing a unifying theory of ADHD. *Psychological Bulletin, 121,* 65–94.

Barlow, D. H. (1988). *Anxiety and its disorders: The nature and treatment of anxiety and panic.* New York: Guilford Press.

Baron-Cohen, S. (1989a). The autistic child's theory of mind: A case of specific developmental delay. *Journal of Child Psychology and Psychiatry, 30,* 285–297.

Baron-Cohen, S. (1989b). Perceptual role taking and protodeclarative pointing in Autism. *British Journal of Developmental Psychology, 7,* 113–127.

Baron-Cohen, S. (1991). Precursors to a theory of mind: Understanding attention in others. In A. Whiten (Ed.), *Natural theories of mind: The evolution, development and simulation of everyday mindreading* (pp. 233–251). Oxford: Basil Blackwell.

Baron-Cohen, S., Leslie, A. M., & Frith, U. (1985). Does the autistic child have a "theory of mind"? *Cognition, 21,* 37–46.

Baron-Cohen, S., Ring, H. A., Bullmore, E. T., Wheelwright, S., Ashwin, C., & Williams, S. C. (2000). The amygdala theory of Autism. *Neuroscience and Biobehavioral Review, 24,* 355–364.

Baron-Cohen, S., Ring, H. A., Wheelwright, S., Bullmore, E., Brammer, M., Simmons, A., et al. (1999). Social intelligence in the normal and autistic brain: An fMRI study. *European Journal of Neuroscience, 11,* 1891–1898.

Bauman, M., & Kemper, T. L. (1988). Limbic and cerebellar abnormalities: Consistent findings in infantile Autism. *Journal of Neuropathology and Experimental Neurology, 47,* 369.

Beers, S. R., & DeBellis, M. D. (2002). Neuropsychological function in children with maltreatment-related PTSD. *American Journal of Psychiatry, 159,* 483–486.

Bellugi, U., Mills, D., Jernigan, T., Hickok, G., & Galaburda, A. (1999). Linking cognition, brain structure, and brain function in Williams syndrome. In H. Tager-Flusberg (Ed.), *Neurodevelopmental disorders* (pp. 111–136). Cambridge, MA: MIT Press.

Bennetto, L., Pennington, B. F., & Rogers, S. J. (1996). Impaired and intact memory functions in Autism: A working memory model. *Child Development, 67,* 1816–1835.

Benton, A. L. (1974). Clinical neuropsychology of childhood: An overview. In R. M. Reitan & L. A. Davison (Eds.), *Clinical neuropsychology: Current status and applications* (pp. 47–53). New York: Wiley.

Bernard, S., Enayati, A., Roger, H., Binstock, T., & Redwood, L. (2002). The role of mercury in the pathogenesis of Autism. *Molecular Psychiatry, 7*(Suppl. 1), S42–S43.

Bettelheim, B. (1967). *The empty fortress.* New York: Free Press.

Biro, S., & Russell, J. (2001). The execution of arbitrary procedures by children with Autism. *Development and Psychopathology, 13,* 97–110.

Bolton, P., MacDonald, H., Pickles, A., Rios, P., Goode, S., Crowson, M., et al. (1994). A case-control family history study of Autism. *Journal of Child Psychology and Psychiatry, 35,* 877–900.

Bormann-Kischkel, C., Vilsmeier, M., & Baude, B. (1995). The development of emotional concepts in Autism. *Journal of Child Psychology and Psychiatry, 36,* 1243–1259.

Boucher, J. (1981). Immediate free recall in early childhood Autism: Another point of behavioral similarity with the amnesic syndrome. *British Journal of Psychology, 72,* 211–215.

Boucher, J., Lewis, V., & Collis, G. (1998). Familiar face and voice matching and recognition in children with Autism. *Journal of Child Psychology and Psychiatry, 39,* 171–181.

Boucher, J., & Warrington, E. K. (1976). Memory deficits in early infantile Autism: Some similarities to the amnesic syndrome. *British Journal of Psychology, 67,* 73–87.

Bowler, D. M. (1992). "Theory of mind" in Asperger's syndrome. *Journal of Child Psychology and Psychiatry, 33,* 877–893.

Braverman, M., Fein, D., Lucci, D., & Waterhouse, L. (1989). Affect comprehension in children with pervasive developmental disorders. *Journal of Autism and Developmental Disorders, 19,* 301–316.

Bremner, J. D. (2003). Long-term effects of childhood abuse on brain and neurobiology. *Child and Adolescent Psychiatric Clinics of North America, 12,* 271–292.

Bremner, J. D., Randall, P. R., Capelli, S., Scott, T., McCarthy, G., & Charney, D. S. (1995). Deficits in short-term memory in adult survivors of childhood abuse. *Psychiatry Research, 59,* 97–107.

Bremner, J. D., Randall, P. R., Scott, T. M., Bronen, R. A., Seibyl, J. P., Southwick, S. M., et al. (1995). MRI-based measurement of hippocampal volume in combat-related posttraumatic stress disorder. *American Journal of Psychiatry, 152,* 973–981.

Bremner, J. D., Randall, P. R., Vermetten, E., Staib, L., Bronen, R. A., Mazure, C., et al. (1997). Magnetic resonance imaging-based measurement of hippocampal volume in posttraumatic stress disorder related to childhood physical and sexual abuse: A preliminary report. *Biological Psychiatry, 41,* 23–32.

Bremner, J. D., Scott, T. M., Delaney, R. C., Southwick, S. M., Mason, J. W., Johnson, D. R., et al. (1993). Deficits in short-term memory in post-traumatic stress disorder. *American Journal of Psychiatry, 150,* 1015–1019.

Bremner, J. D., Vermetten, E., Afzal, N., & Vythilingam, M. (2004). Deficits in verbal declarative memory function in women with childhood sexual abuse-related posttraumatic stress disorder. *Journal of Nervous and Mental Diseases, 192,* 643–649.

Bremner, J. D., Vermetten, E., Vythilingam, M., Afzal, N., Schmahl, C., Elzinga, B., et al. (2004). Neural correlates of the classic color and emotional Stroop in women with abuse-related posttraumatic stress disorder. *Biological Psychiatry, 55,* 612–620.

Breslau, N., Davis, G. C., Andreski, P., & Peterson, E. (1991). Traumatic events and posttraumatic stress disorder in an urban population of young adults. *Archives of General Psychiatry, 48,* 216–222.

Brewin, C. R., Dalgleish, T., & Joseph, S. (1996). A dual representation theory of posttraumatic stress disorder. *Psychological Review, 103,* 670–686.

Brian, J. A., & Bryson, S. E. (1996). Disembedding performance and recognition memory in Autism/PDD. *Journal of Child Psychology and Psychiatry, 37,* 865–872.

Bryant, R. A., & Harvey, A. G. (1997). Attentional bias in post-traumatic stress disorder. *Journal of Traumatic Stress, 10,* 635–644.

Bryson, S. E., Clark, B. S., & Smith, I. M. (1988). First report of a Canadian epidemiological study of autistic syndromes. *Journal of Child Psychology and Psychiatry, 29,* 433–445.

Buchsbaum, M. S., Siegel, B. V., Wu, J. C., Hazlett, E., Sicotte, N., Haier, R., et al. (1992). Attention performance in Autism and regional brain metabolic rate assessed by positron emission tomography. *Journal of Autism and Developmental Disorders, 22,* 115–125.

Buckley, T. C., Blanchard, E. B., & Neill, W. T. (2000). Information processing and PTSD: A review of empirical literature. *Clinical Psychology Review, 20*, 1041–1065.

Burbacher, T. M., Rodier, P. M., & Weiss, B. (1990). Methylmercury developmental neurotoxicity: A comparison of effects in humans and animals. *Neurotoxicology and Teratology, 12*, 191–202.

Bustini, M., Stratta, P., Daneluzzo, E., Pollice, R., Prosperini, P., & Rossi, A. (1999). Tower of Hanoi and WCST performance in Schizophrenia: Problem-solving capacity. *Journal of Psychiatric Research, 33*, 285–290.

Caldji, C., Francis, D., Sharma, S., Plotsky, P. M., & Meaney, M. J. (2000). The effects of early rearing environment on the development of GABAA and central benzodiazepine receptor levels and novelty-induced fearfulness in the rat. *Neuropsychopharmacology, 22*, 219–229.

Camras, L. A., Ribordy, S., Hill, J., Martino, S., Sachs, V., Spaccarelli, S., et al. (1990). Maternal facial behavior and the recognition and production of emotional expression by maltreated and nonmaltreated children. *Developmental Psychology, 26*, 312.

Capps, L., Kehres, J., & Sigman, M. (1998). Conversational abilities among children with Autism and children with developmental delays. *Autism, 2*, 325–344.

Capps, L., Yirmiya, N., & Sigman, M. (1992). Understanding of simple and complex emotions in non-retarded children with Autism. *Journal of Child Psychology and Psychiatry, 33*, 1169–1182.

Caron, C., & Rutter, M. (1991). Comorbidity in child psychopathology: Concepts, issues, and research strategies. *Journal of Child Psychology and Psychiatry, 32*, 1063–1080.

Carpenter, M., Pennington, B. F., & Rogers, S. J. (2001). Understanding of others' intentions in children with Autism. *Journal of Autism and Developmental Disorders, 31*, 589–599.

Casanova, M. F., Buxhoeveden, D. P., Switala, A. E., & Roy, E. (2002). Minicolumnar pathology in Autism. *Neurology, 58*, 428–432.

Casey, B. J., Durston, S., & Fossella, J. (2001). A mechanistic model of cognitive control: Clinical, neuroimaging, and lesion studies. *Clinical Neuroscience Research, 1*, 267–282.

Casey, B. J., Gordon, C. T., Mannheim, G. B., & Rumsey, J. M. (1993). Dysfunctional attention in autistic savants. *Journal of Clinical and Experimental Neuropsychology, 15*, 933–946.

Cassidy, K. L., McNally, R. J., & Zeitlin, S. B. (1992). Cognitive processing of trauma cues in rape victims with post-traumatic stress disorder. *Cognitive Therapy Research, 16*, 283–295.

Castellanos, F. X., & Tannock, R. (2002). Neuroscience of attention-deficit/hyperactivity disorder: The search for endophenotypes. *Nature Reviews Neuroscience, 3*, 617–628.

Castelli, F., Frith, C., Happé, F., & Frith, U. (2002). Autism, Asperger syndrome and brain mechanisms for the attribution of mental states to animated shapes. *Brain, 125*, 1839–1849.

Chakrabarti, S., & Fombonne, E. (2001). Pervasive developmental disorders in preschool children. *Journal of the American Medical Association, 285*, 3093–3099.

Changeux, J. P. (1985). *Neuronal man.* New York: Oxford University Press.

Chapman, L. J., & Chapman, J. P. (1973). Problems in the measurement of cognitive deficit. *Psychological Bulletin, 79*, 380–385.

Cicchetti, D., & Dawson, G. (2002). Multiple levels of analysis. *Development and Psychopathology, 14*, 417–420.

Cicchetti, D., & Lynch, M. (1995). Failures in the expectable environment and their impact on individual development: The case of child maltreatment. In D. Cicchetti & D. Cohen (Eds.), *Developmental psychopathology: Vol. 2. Risk, disorder and adaptation* (pp. 32–71). New York: Wiley.

Cicchetti, D., & Rogosch, F. A. (1996). Equifinality and multifinality in developmental psychopathology. *Development and Psychopathology, 8*, 597–600.

Cicchetti, D., & Rogosch, F. A. (2001a). Diverse patterns of neuroendocrine activity in maltreated children. *Development and Psychopathology, 13*, 677–693.

Cicchetti, D., & Rogosch, F. A. (2001b). The impact of child maltreatment and psychopathology on neuroendocrine function. *Development and Psychopathology, 13*, 783–804.

Cicchetti, D., & Toth, S. L. (2000). Developmental processes in maltreated children. In D. Hansen (Ed.), *Nebraska Symposium on Motivation: Vol. 46. Child maltreatment* (pp. 85–160). Lincoln: University of Nebraska Press.

Clark, C. R., McFarlane, A. C., Morris, P., Weber, D. L., Sonkkilla, C., Shaw, M., et al. (2003). Cerebral function in posttraumatic stress disorder during verbal working memory updating: A positron emission tomography study. *Biological Psychiatry, 53*, 474–481.

Cody, H., Pelphrey, K., & Piven, J. (2002). Structural and functional magnetic resonance imaging of Autism. *International Journal of Developmental Neuroscience, 20*, 421–438.

Cohen, J. D., & Servan-Schreiber, D. (1992). Context, cortex, and dopamine: A connectionist approach to behavior and biology in Schizophrenia. *Psychological Review, 99*, 45–77.

Collaborative Linkage Study of Autism. (2001). An autosomal genomic screen for Autism. *American Journal of Medical Genetics, 105*, 609–615.

Comings, D. E., Muhleman, D., & Gysin, R. (1996). Dopamine D2 receptor (DRD2) gene and susceptibility to posttraumatic stress disorder: A study and replication. *Biological Psychiatry, 40*, 368–372.

Courchesne, E. (2004). Brain development in Autism: Early overgrowth followed by premature arrest of growth. *Mental Retardation and Developmental Disabilities, 10*, 106–111.

Courchesne, E., Carper, R., & Akshoomoff, N. (2003). Evidence of brain overgrowth in the first year of life in Autism. *Journal of the American Medical Association, 290*, 337–344.

Courchesne, E., Townsend, J., Akshoomoff, N. A., Saitoh, O., Yeung-Courchesne, R., Lincoln, A. J., et al. (1994). Impairment in shifting attention in autistic and cerebellar patients. *Behavioral Neuroscience, 108*, 848–865.

Courchesne, E., Yeung-Courchesne, R., Press, G. A., Hesselink, J. R., & Jernigan, T. L. (1988). Hypoplasia of cerebellar vermal lobules VI and VII in Autism. *New England Journal of Medicine, 318*, 1349–1354.

Critchley, H. D., Daly, E. M., Bullmore, E. T., Williams, S. C. R., Van Amelsvoort, T., Robertson, D. M., et al. (2000). The functional neuroanatomy of social behaviour: Changes in cerebral blood flow when people with autistic disorder process facial expressions. *Brain, 123*, 2203–2212.

Damasio, A. R., Grabowski, T. J., Bechara, A., Damasio, H., Ponto, L. L., Parvizi, J., et al. (2000). Subcortical and cortical brain activity during the feeling of self-generated emotions. *Nature Neuroscience, 3*, 1049–1056.

Daro, D., & Donnelly, A. C. (2002). Charting the waves of prevention: Two steps forward, one step back. *Child Abuse and Neglect, 26*, 731–742.

Davidson, J. R., Tupler, L. A., Wilson, W. H., & Connor, K. M. (1998). A family study of chronic posttraumatic stress disorder following rape trauma. *Journal of Psychiatric Research, 32*, 301–309.

Davidson, R. J. (1998). Introduction to the special issue on neuropsychological perspectives on affective and anxiety disorders. *Cognition and Emotion, 12*, 273–275.

Davies, S., Bishop, D., Manstead, A. S. R., & Tantam, D. (1994). Face perception in children with Autism and Asperger's syndrome. *Journal of Child Psychology and Psychiatry, 35*, 1033–1057.

Dawson, G., Munson, J., Estes, A., Osterling, J., McPartland, J., Toth, K., et al. (2002). Neurocognitive function and joint attention ability in young children with Autism spectrum disorder versus developmental delay. *Child Development, 73,* 345–358.

DeBellis, M. D., Baum, A. S., Birmaher, B., Keshavan, M. S., Eccard, C. H., Boring, A. M., et al. (1999). Developmental traumatology: Pt. I. Biological stress systems. *Biological Psychiatry, 45,* 1235–1236.

DeBellis, M. D., Chrousos, G. P., Dorn, L. D., Burke, L., Helmers, K., Kling, M. A., et al. (1994). Hypothalamic-pituitary-adrenal axis dysregulation in sexually abused girls. *Journal of Clinical Endocrinology and Metabolism, 78,* 249–255.

de Decker, A., Hermans, D., Raes, F., & Eelen, P. (2003). Autobiographical memory specificity and trauma in inpatient adolescents. *Journal of Clinical Child and Adolescent Psychology, 32,* 22–31.

DeLong, G. R. (1992). Autism, amnesia, hippocampus, and learning. *Neuroscience and Biobehavioral Reviews, 16,* 63–70.

Dick, F., Bates, E., Wulfeck, B., Utman, J., Dronkers, N., & Gernsbacher, M. A. (2001). Language deficits, localization, and grammar: Evidence for a distributive model of language breakdown in aphasic patients and neurologically intact individuals. *Psychological Review, 108,* 759–788.

Edelson, S. B., & Cantor, D. S. (1998). Autism: Xenobiotic influences. *Toxicology and Industrial Health, 14,* 553–563.

Emery, N. J. (2000). The eyes have it: The neuroethology, function and evolution of social gaze. *Neuroscience and Biobehavioral Reviews, 24,* 581–604.

Fauerbach, J. A., Lawrence, J. W., Schmidt, C. W., Munster, A. M., & Costa, P. T. (2000). Personality predictors of injury-related posttraumatic stress disorders. *Journal of Nervous and Mental Diseases, 188,* 510–517.

Fein, D., Lucci, D., Braverman, M., & Waterhouse, L. (1992). Comprehension of affect in context in children with pervasive developmental disorders. *Journal of Child Psychology, 33,* 1157–1167.

Fein, D., Pennington, B. F., Markowitz, P., Braverman, M., & Waterhouse, L. (1986). Toward a neuropsychological model of infantile Autism: Are the social deficits primary? *Journal of the American Academy of Child Psychiatry, 25,* 198–212.

Finger, S. (1994). *Origins of neuroscience: A history of explorations into brain function.* New York: Oxford University Press.

Fletcher, J. M. (1985). External validation of learning disability typologies. In B. P. Rourke (Ed.), *Neuropsychology of learning disabilities: Essentials of subtype analysis* (pp. 187–211). New York: Guilford Press.

Flint, J. (1999). The genetic basis of cognition. *Brain, 122,* 2015–2031.

Foa, E. B., Feske, U., Murdock, T. B., Kozak, M. J., & McCarthy, P. R. (1991). Processing of threat-related information in rape victims. *Journal of Abnormal Psychology, 100,* 156–162.

Foa, E. B., & Kozak, M. J. (1986). Emotional processing of fear: Exposure to corrective information. *Psychological Bulletin, 99,* 20–35.

Foa, E. B., Steketee, G., & Rothbaum, B. O. (1989). Behavioral/cognitive conceptualization of post-traumatic stress disorder. *Behavior Therapy, 20,* 155–176.

Fombonne, E., Roge, B., Claverie, J., Courty, S., & Fremolle, J. (1999). Microcephaly and macrocephaly in Autism. *Journal of Autism and Developmental Disorders, 29,* 113–119.

Fossella, J., Sommer, T., Fan, J., Yanhong, W., Swanson, J. M., Pfaff, D. W., et al. (2002). Assessing the molecular genetics of attention networks. *BMC Neuroscience, 3,* 1–14.

Frangiskakis, J. M., Ewart, A. K., Morris, C. A., Mervis, C. B., Bertrand, J., Robinson, B. F., et al. (1996). LIM-kinase1 hemizygosity implicated in impaired visuospatial constructive cognition. *Cell, 86,* 59–69.

Frith, U. (1989). *Autism: Explaining the enigma.* Oxford: Basil Blackwell.

Frith, U., & Happé, F. (1994). Autism: Beyond theory of mind. *Cognition, 50,* 115–132.

Frith, U., Happé, F., & Siddons, F. (1994). Autism and theory of mind in everyday life. *Social Development, 3,* 108–124.

Frith, U., & Snowing, M. (1983). Reading for meaning and reading for sound in autistic and dyslexic children. *British Journal of Developmental Psychology, 1,* 329–342.

Fyffe, C., & Prior, M. (1978). Evidence for language recoding in autistic, retarded and normal children: A re-examination. *British Journal of Psychology, 69,* 393–402.

Gaensbauer, T. J., & Hiatt, S. (1984). Facial communication of emotion in early infancy. In N. Fox & R. Davidson (Eds.), *The psychobiology of affective development* (pp. 207–230). Hillsdale, NJ: Erlbaum.

Gallagher, H. L., Happé, F., Brunswick, N., Fletcher, P. C., Frith, U., & Frith, C. D. (2000). Reading the mind in cartoons and stories: An fMRI study of "theory of mind" in verbal and nonverbal tasks. *Neuropsychologia, 38,* 11–21.

Garfield, J. L., Peterson, C. C., & Perry, T. (2001). Social cognition, language acquisition, and the development of the theory of mind. *Mind and Language, 16,* 494–541.

Garretson, H. B., Fein, D., & Waterhouse, L. (1990). Sustained attention in children with Autism. *Journal of Autism and Developmental Disorders, 20,* 101–114.

Gelernter, J., Southwick, S., Goodson, S., Morgan, A., Nagy, L., & Charney, D. S. (1999). No association between D2 dopamine receptor (DRD2) "A" system alleles, or DRD2 haplotypes, and posttraumatic stress disorder. *Biological Psychiatry, 45,* 620–625.

Gilbertson, M. W., Shenton, M. E., Ciszewski, A., Kasai, K., Lasko, N. B., Orr, S. P., et al. (2002). Smaller hippocampal volume predicts pathologic vulnerability to psychological trauma. *Nature Neuroscience, 5,* 1111–1113.

Gillberg, C. (1998). Chromosomal disorders and Autism. *Journal of Autism and Developmental Disorders, 28,* 415–425.

Goldberg, J., True, W. R., Eisen, S. A., & Henderson, W. G. (1990). A twin study of the Vietnam War on posttraumatic stress disorder. *Journal of the American Medical Association, 263,* 1227–1232.

Goldman-Rakic, P. S. (1987). Development of cortical circuitry and cognitive function. *Child Development, 58,* 601–622.

Goldman-Rakic, P. S., Isseroff, A., Schwartz, M. L., & Bugbee, N. M. (1983). The neurobiology of cognitive development. In P. H. Mussen (Ed.), *Handbook of child psychology: Biology and infancy development* (pp. 311–344). New York: Wiley.

Goldstein, G., Johnson, C. R., & Minshew, N. J. (2001). Attentional process in Autism. *Journal of Autism and Developmental Disorders, 31,* 433–440.

Gottesman, I. I., & Shields, J. (1976). A critical review of recent adoption, twin, and family studies of Schizophrenia: Behavioral genetics perspectives. *Schizophrenia Bulletin, 2,* 360–401.

Gottlieb, G. (1998). Normally occurring environmental and behavioral influences on gene activity: From central dogma to probabilistic epigenesis. *Psychological Review, 105,* 792–802.

Gould, E., Reeves, A. J., Graziano, M. S., & Gross, C. G. (1999). Neurogenesis in the neocortex of adult primates. *Science, 286,* 548–552.

Green, B. F., Korol, M., Grace, M. C., Vary, M. G., Leonard, A. C., Gleser, G. C., et al. (1991). Children and disaster: Age, gender, and parental effects on PTSD symptoms. *Journal of the American Academy of Child and Adolescent Psychiatry, 30,* 945–951.

Green, L., Fein, D., Joy, S., & Waterhouse, L. (1995). Cognitive functioning in Autism: An overview. In E. Schopler & G. B. Mesibov

(Eds.), *Learning and cognition in Autism* (pp. 13–31). New York: Plenum Press.

Greenough, W. T., Black, J. E., & Wallace, C. S. (1987). Experience and brain development. *Child Development, 58,* 539–559.

Griffith, E. M., & Pennington, B. F. (2003). *Manipulating feedback normalizes perseveration in individuals with Autism.* Unpublished doctoral dissertation, University of Denver.

Griffith, E. M., Pennington, B. F., Wehner, E. A., & Rogers, S. J. (1999). Executive functions in young children with Autism. *Child Development, 70,* 817–832.

Grigorenko, E. L., Wood, F. B., Meyer, M. S., Hart, L. A., Speed, W. C., Shuster, A., et al. (1997). Susceptibility loci for distinct components of developmental dyslexia of chromosomes 6 and 15. *American Journal of Human Genetics, 60,* 27–39.

Grossman, A. W., Churchill, J. D., McKinney, B. C., Kodish, I. M., Otte, S. L., & Greenough, W. T. (2003). Experience effects on brain development: Possible contributions to psychopathology. *Journal of Child Psychology and Psychiatry, 44,* 33–63.

Gurvits, T. V., Shenton, M. E., Hokama, H., Ohta, H., Lasko, N. B., Gilbertson, M. W., et al. (1996). Magnetic resonance imaging study of hippocampal volume in chronic combat-related posttraumatic stress disorder. *Biological Psychiatry, 40,* 1091–1099.

Hamann, S. (2001). Cognitive and neural mechanisms of emotional memory. *Trends in Cognitive Sciences, 5,* 394–400.

Happé, F. G. E. (1993). Communicative competence and theory of mind in Autism: A test of relevance theory. *Cognition, 48,* 101–119.

Happé, F. G. E. (1996). Studying weak central coherence at low levels: Children with Autism do not succumb to visual illusions. *Journal of Child Psychology, 37,* 873–877.

Happé, F. G. E. (1997). Central coherence and theory of mind in Autism: Reading homographs in context. *British Journal of Developmental Psychology, 15,* 1–12.

Happé, F. G. E. (1999). Autism: Cognitive deficit or cognitive style? *Trends in Cognitive Sciences, 3,* 216–222.

Happé, F. G. E., Ehlers, S., Fletcher, P., Frith, U., Johansson, M., Gillberg, C., et al. (1996). "Theory of mind" in the brain. Evidence from a PET scan study of Asperger syndrome. *NeuroReport, 8,* 197–201.

Hardan, A. Y., Minshew, N. J., Harenski, K., & Keshavan, M. S. (2001). Posterior fossa magnetic resonance imaging in Autism. *Journal of American Academy of Child and Adolescent Psychiatry, 40,* 666–672.

Haxby, J. V., Hoffman, E. A., & Gobbini, M. I. (2000). The distributed human neural system for face perception. *Trends in Cognitive Sciences, 4,* 223–233.

Heaton, R. K., Baade, L. E., & Johnson, K. L. (1978). Neuropsychological test results associated with psychiatric disorders in adults. *Psychological Bulletin, 85,* 141–162.

Heaton, R. K., Chelune, G. J., Talley, J. L., Kay, G. G., & Curtiss, G. (1993). *Wisconsin Card Sorting Test manual: Revised and expanded.* Odessa, FL: Psychological Assessment Resources.

Heilig, M., McLeod, S., Brot, M., Heinrichs, S. C., Menzaghi, F., Koob, G. F., et al. (1993). Anxiolytic-like action of neuropeptide Y: Mediation by Y1 receptors in amygdala, and dissociation from food intake effects. *Neuropsychopharmacology, 8,* 363.

Heim, C., & Nemeroff, C. B. (1999). The impact of early adverse experiences on brain systems involved in the pathophysiology of anxiety and affective disorders. *Biological Psychiatry, 46,* 1509–1522.

Hermelin, B., & Frith, U. (1971). Psychological studies of childhood Autism: Can autistic children make sense of what they see and hear? *Journal of Special Education, 5,* 107–117.

Hermelin, B., & O'Connor, N. (1967). Remembering of words by psychotic and subnormal children. *British Journal of Psychology, 58,* 213–218.

Hinshelwood, J. (1896). A case of dyslexia: A peculiar form of word blindness. *Lancet, 2,* 1451–1453.

Hobson, R. P. (1986). The autistic child's appraisal of expressions of emotion. *Journal of Child Psychology and Psychiatry, 27,* 321–342.

Hobson, R. P., Ouston, J., & Lee, A. (1988). Emotion recognition in Autism: Coordinating faces and voices. *Psychological Medicine, 18,* 911–923.

Hobson, R. P., Ouston, J., & Lee, A. (1989a). Naming emotion in faces and voices: Abilities and disabilities in Autism and mental retardation. *British Journal of Developmental Psychology, 7,* 237–250.

Hobson, R. P., Ouston, J., & Lee, A. (1989b). Recognition of emotion by mentally retarded adolescents and young adults. *American Journal of Mental Retardation, 93,* 434–443.

Holder, H. B., & Kirkpatrick, S. W. (1991). Interpretation of emotion from facial expressions in children with and without learning disabilities. *Journal of Learning Disabilities, 24,* 170–177.

Horner, M. D., & Hamner, M. B. (2002). Neurocognitive functioning in posttraumatic stress disorder. *Neuropsychology Review, 12,* 15–30.

Hornig, M., & Lipkin, W. I. (2001). Infectious and immune factors in the pathogenesis of neurodevelopmental disorders: Epidemiology, hypotheses, and animal models. *Mental Retardation and Developmental Disabilities Research Reviews, 7,* 200–210.

Hoy, J. A., Hatton, C., & Hare, D. (2004). Weak central coherence: A cross-domain phenomenon specific to Autism? *Autism, 8,* 267–281.

Hubel, D. H., & Wiesel, T. N. (1970). The period of susceptibility to the physiological effects of unilateral eye closure in kittens. *Journal of Physiology, 206,* 419–436.

Hudson, J. L., Kendall, P. C., Coles, M. E., Robin, J. A., & Webb, A. (2002). The other side of the coin: Using intervention research in child anxiety disorders to inform developmental psychopathology. *Development and Psychopathology, 14,* 819–841.

Hughes, C. (2002). Executive functions and development: Emerging themes. *Infant and Child Development, 11,* 201–209.

Hughes, C., & Russell, J. (1993). Autistic children's difficulty with mental disengagement from an object: Its implications for theories of Autism. *Developmental Psychology, 29,* 498–510.

International Molecular Genetic Study of Autism Consortium. (2001). A genomewide screen for Autism: Strong evidence for linkage to chromosomes 2q, 7q, and 16p. *American Journal of Human Genetics, 69,* 570–581.

Jamain, S., Quach, H., Betancur, C., Rastam, M., Colineaux, C., Gillberg, I. C., et al. (2003). Mutations of the X-linked genes encoding neuroligins NLGN3 and NLGN4 are associated with Autism. *Nature Genetics, 34,* 27–29.

Jenkins, M. A., Langlais, P. J., Delis, D., & Cohen, R. (1998). Learning and memory in rape victims with posttraumatic stress disorder. *American Journal of Psychiatry, 155,* 278–279.

Jolliffe, T., & Baron-Cohen, S. (1997). Are people with Autism and Asperger syndrome faster than normal on the embedded figures test? *Journal of Child Psychology and Psychiatry, 38,* 527–534.

Jolliffe, T., & Baron-Cohen, S. (2000). Linguistic processing in high-functioning adults with Autism or Asperger's syndrome: Is global coherence impaired? *Psychological Medicine, 30,* 1169–1187.

Jones, J. C., & Barlow, D. H. (1990). The etiology of post-traumatic stress disorder. *Clinical Psychology Review, 10,* 299–328.

Jones, V., & Prior, M. R. (1985). Motor imitation abilities and neurological signs in autistic children. *Journal of Autism and Developmental Disorders, 15,* 37–46.

Joseph, R. M., & Tanaka, J. (2003). Holistic and part-based faced recognition in children with Autism. *Journal of Child Psychology and Psychiatry, 44,* 529–542.

Kanner, L. (1943). Autistic disturbances of affective content. *Nervous Child, 2,* 217–250.

Kanwisher, N., McDermott, J., & Chun, M. M. (1997). The fusiform face area: A module in human extrastriate cortex specialized for face perception. *Journal of Neuroscience, 17,* 4302–4311.

Karmiloff-Smith, A. (1992). *Beyond modularity: A developmental perspective on cognitive science.* London: MIT Press.

Keane, T. M., Kolb, L. C., Kaloupek, D. G., Orr, S. P., Blanchard, E. B., Thomas, R. G., et al. (1998). Utility of psychophysiological measurement in the diagnosis of posttraumatic stress disorder: Results from a Department of Veterans Affairs Cooperative Study. *Journal of Consulting and Clinical Psychology, 66,* 914–923.

Kennard, M. (1940). Relation of age to motor impairment in man and in subhuman primates. *Archives of Neurology and Psychiatry, 44,* 377–397.

Kessler, R. C., McGonagle, K. A., Zhao, S., Nelson, C. B., Hughes, M., Eshleman, S., et al. (1994). Lifetime and 12-month prevalence of DSM-III-R psychiatric disorders in the United States. *Archives of General Psychiatry, 51,* 8–19.

Kessler, R. C., Sonnega, A., Bromet, R., Hughes, M., & Nelson, C. B. (1995). Posttraumatic stress disorder in the National Comorbidity Survey. *Archives of General Psychiatry, 52,* 1048–1060.

King, J. A., Abend, S., & Edwards, E. (2001). Genetic predisposition and the development of posttraumatic stress disorder in an animal model. *Biological Psychiatry, 50,* 231–237.

Klin, A., Jones, W., Schultz, R., Volkmar, F., & Cohen, D. (2002). Visual fixation patterns during viewing of naturalistic social situations as predictors of social competence in individuals with Autism. *Archives of General Psychiatry, 59,* 809–816.

Klin, A., Sparrow, S. S., de Bildt, A., Cicchetti, D. V., Cohen, D. J., & Volkmar, F. R. (1999). A normed study of face recognition in Autism and related disorders. *Journal of Autism and Developmental Disorders, 29,* 499–510.

Klin, A., Volkmar, F. R., Sparrow, S. S., Cicchetti, D. V., & Rourke, B. P. (1995). Validity and neuropsychological characterization of Asperger syndrome: Convergence with nonverbal learning disabilities syndrome. *Journal of Child Psychology and Psychiatry, 36,* 1127–1140.

Klorman, R., Cicchetti, D., Thatcher, J. E., & Ison, J. R. (2003). Acoustic startle in maltreated children. *Journal of Abnormal Child Psychology, 31,* 359–370.

Kochanska, G., Murray, K. T., & Coy, K. (1997). Inhibitory control as a contributor to conscience in childhood: From toddler to early school age. *Child Development, 68,* 263–267.

Koenen, K. C., Driver, K. L., Oscar-Berman, M., Wolfe, J., Folsom, S., Huang, M. T., et al. (2001). Measures of prefrontal system dysfunction in posttraumatic stress disorder. *Brain and Cognition, 45,* 64–78.

Koutstaal, W., & Schacter, D. L. (1997). Intentional forgetting and voluntary thought suppression: Two potential methods for coping with childhood trauma. In D. Spiegel (Ed.), *Repressed memories* (pp. 77–122). Washington, DC: American Psychiatric Press.

Kurita, H. (1985). Infantile Autism with speech loss before the age of thirty months. *Journal of the American Academy of Child Psychiatry, 24,* 191–196.

Lainhart, J. E., Piven, J., Wzorek, M., Landa, R., Santangelo, S. L., Coon, H., et al. (1997). Macrocephaly in children and adults with Autism. *Journal of the American Academy of Child and Adolescent Psychiatry, 36,* 282–290.

LeCouteur, A., Bailey, A. J., Goode, S., Pickles, A., Robertson, S., & Gottesman, I. (1996). A broader phenotype of Autism: The clinical spectrum in twins. *Journal of Child Psychology and Psychiatry, 37,* 785–801.

LeDoux, J. E. (1996). *The emotional brain: The mysterious underpinnings of emotional life.* New York: Touchstone.

LeDoux, J. E. (2002). *Synaptic self: How our brains become who we are.* New York: Penguin.

Lenneberg, E. (1967). *Biological foundations of language.* New York: Wiley.

Leslie, A. M. (1992). Pretense, Autism, and the theory-of-mind module. *Current Directions in Psychological Science, 1,* 18–21.

Liberzon, I., Abelson, J. L., Flagel, S. B., Raz, J., & Young, E. A. (1999). Neuroendocrine and psychophysiologic responses in PTSD: A symptom provocation study. *Neuropsychopharmacology, 21,* 40–50.

Lindamood, P., & Lindamood, P. (1998). *The Lindamood Phoneme Sequencing Program for reading, spelling, and speech (the LiPS program).* Austin, TX: ProEd.

Liss, M., Fein, D., Allen, D., Dunn, M., Feinstein, C., Morris, R., et al. (2001). Executive functioning in high-functioning children with Autism. *Journal of Child Psychology and Psychiatry, 42,* 261–270.

London, E., & Etzel, R. A. (2000). The environment as an etiologic factor in Autism: A new direction for research. *Environmental Health Perspective, 108,* 401–404.

Lonigan, C. J., Phillips, B. M., & Richey, J. A. (2003). Posttraumatic stress disorder in children: Diagnosis, assessment, and associated features. *Child and Adolescent Psychiatric Clinics of North America, 12,* 171–194.

Lopez, B., & Leekam, S. R. (2003). Do children with Autism fail to process information in context? *Journal of Child Psychology and Psychiatry, 44,* 285–300.

Lopez, J. F., Akil, H., & Watson, S. J. (1999). Neural circuits mediating stress. *Biological Psychiatry, 46,* 1461–1471.

Lotter, V. (1966). Epidemiology of autistic conditions in young children: I. Prevalence. *Social Psychiatry, 1,* 124–137.

Lovaas, O. I. (1987). Behavioral treatment and normal educational and intellectual functioning in young autistic children. *Journal of Consulting and Clinical Psychology, 55,* 3–9.

Lovaas, O. I., Koegel, R. L., & Schreibman, L. (1979). Stimulus overselectivity in Autism: A review of research. *Psychological Bulletin, 86,* 1236–1254.

Loveland, K. A., Tunali-Kotoski, B., Chen, Y. R., Ortegon, J., Pearson, D. A., Brelsford, K. A., et al. (1997). Emotion recognition in Autism: Verbal and nonverbal information. *Development and Psychopathology, 9,* 579–593.

Luria, A. R. (1966). *The higher cortical functions in man.* New York: Basic Books.

Lyons, D. M., Martel, F. L., Levine, S., Risch, N. J., & Schatzberg, A. F. (1999). Postnatal experiences and genetic effects on squirrel monkey social affinities and emotional distress. *Hormones and Behavior, 36,* 226–275.

MacDonald, H., Rutter, M., Howlin, P., Rios, P., LeCouteur, A., Evered, C., et al. (1989). Recognition and expression of emotional cues by autistic and normal adults. *Journal of Child Psychology and Psychiatry, 30,* 865–877.

Madsen, K. M., Hviid, A., Vestergaard, M., Schendel, D., Wohlfahrt, J., Thorsen, P., et al. (2002). A population-based study of measles, mumps, and rubella vaccination and Autism. *New England Journal of Medicine, 347,* 1477–1482.

Malberg, J. E., Eisch, A. J., Nestler, E. J., & Duman, R. S. (2000). Chronic antidepressant treatment increases neurogenesis in adult rat hippocampus. *Journal of Neuroscience Research, 15,* 9104–9110.

Manjiviona, J., & Prior, M. (1995). Comparison of Asperger syndrome and high-functioning autistic children on a test of motor impairment. *Journal of Autism and Developmental Disorders, 25,* 23–39.

Marr, D. (1982). *Vision.* San Francisco: Freeman.

Masten, A. S., Best, K. M., & Garmezy, N. (1990). Resilience and development: Contributions from the study of children who overcome adversity. *Development and Psychopathology, 2,* 425–444.

Maughan, A., & Cicchetti, D. (2002). Impact of child maltreatment and interadult violence on children's emotion regulation abilities and socioemotional adjustment. *Child Development, 73,* 1525–1542.

McEvoy, R. E., Rogers, S. J., & Pennington, B. F. (1993). Executive function and social communication deficits in young autistic children. *Journal of Child Psychology and Psychiatry, 34,* 563–578.

McNally, R. J. (2003). Progress and controversy in the study of posttraumatic stress disorder. *Annual Review of Psychology, 54,* 229–252.

McNally, R. J., Kaspi, S. P., Riemann, B. C., & Zeitlin, S. B. (1990). Selective processing of threat cues in posttraumatic stress disorder. *Journal of Abnormal Child Psychology, 99,* 398–402.

McNally, R. J., Metzger, L. J., Lasko, N. B., Clancy, S. A., & Pitman, R. K. (1998). Directed forgetting of trauma cues in adult survivors of childhood sexual abuse with and without posttraumatic stress disorder. *Journal of Abnormal Psychology, 107,* 596–601.

Meaney, J. J., Diorio, J., Francis, D., Widdowson, J., LaPlante, P., Caldji, C., et al. (1996). Early environmental regulation of forebrain glucocorticoid receptor gene expression: Implications for adrenocortical response to stress. *Developmental Psychobiology, 18,* 49–72.

Meaney, M. J. (2001). Maternal care, gene expression, and the transmission of individual differences in stress reactivity across generations. *Annual Review of Neuroscience, 24,* 1161–1192.

Meltzoff, A., & Gopnik, A. (1993). The role of imitation in understanding persons and developing a theory of mind. In S. Baron-Cohen, H. Tager-Flusberg, & D. J. Cohen (Eds.), *Understanding other minds: Perspectives from Autism* (pp. 335–366). New York: Oxford University Press.

Meltzoff, A., & Moore, M. K. (1977). Imitation of facial and manual gestures by human neonates. *Science, 198,* 75–78.

Miller, J. N., & Ozonoff, S. (2000). The external validity of Asperger disorder: Lack of evidence from the domain of neuropsychology. *Journal of Abnormal Psychology, 109,* 227–238.

Minshew, N. J., Goldstein, G., & Siegel, D. J. (1997). Neuropsychologic functioning in Autism: Profile of a complex information processing disorder. *Journal of the International Neuropsychological Society, 3,* 303–316.

Moradi, A. R., Doost, H. T. N., Taghavi, M. R., Yule, W., & Dalgleish, T. (1999). Everyday memory deficits in children and adolescents with PTSD: Performance on the Rivermead Behavioral Memory Test. *Journal of Child Psychology and Psychiatry, 40,* 357–361.

Moses, P., & Stiles, J. (2002). The lesion methodology: Contrasting views from adult and child studies. *Developmental Psychobiology, 40,* 266–277.

Mottron, L., Burack, J. A., Stauder, J. E. A., & Robaey, P. (1999). Perceptual processing among high-functioning persons with Autism. *Journal of Child Psychology and Psychiatry, 40,* 203–211.

Mundy, P., & Sigman, M. (1989). The theoretical implications of joint attention deficits in Autism. *Development and Psychopathology, 1,* 173–183.

Mundy, P., Sigman, M., & Kasari, C. (1993). The theory of mind and joint-attention deficits in Autism. In S. Baron-Cohen, H. Tager-Flusberg, & D. Cohen (Eds.), *Understanding other minds: Perspectives from Autism* (pp. 181–203). Oxford: Oxford University Press.

Murphy, F. C., & Sahakian, B. J. (2001). Neuropsychology of bipolar disorder. *British Journal of Psychiatry, 41,* S120–S127.

Neale, M. C., & Kendler, K. S. (1995). Models of comorbidity for multifactorial disorders. *Journal of Human Genetics, 57,* 935–953.

Needleman, H. L., Schell, A., Bellinger, D., Leviton, A., & Allred, E. N. (1990). The long-term effects of exposure to low doses of lead in childhood: An 11-year follow-up report. *New England Journal of Medicine, 322,* 83–88.

Nelson, C. A., Bloom, F. E., Cameron, J. L., Amaral, D., Dahl, R. E., & Pine, D. (2002). An integrative, multidisciplinary approach to the study of brain-behavior relations in the context of typical and atypical development. *Development and Psychopathology, 14,* 499–520.

Neville, H. (1977). Electroencephalographic testing of cerebral specialization in normal and congenitally deaf children: A preliminary report. In S. J. Segalowitz & F. A. Gruber (Eds.), *Language development and neurological theory* (pp. 121–131). New York: Academic Press.

Nisenbaum, L. K., Zigmond, M. J., Sved, A. F., & Abercrombie, E. D. (1991). Prior exposure to chronic stress results in enhanced synthesis and release of hippocampal norepinephrine in response to a novel stressor. *Journal of Neuroscience, 11,* 1478–1484.

North, C. S. (2004). Approaching disaster mental health research after the 9/11 World Trade Center terrorist attacks. *Psychiatric Clinics of North America, 27,* 589–602.

Noterdaeme, M., Amorosa, H., Mildenberger, K., Sitter, S., & Minow, F. (2001). Evaluation of attention problems in children with Autism and children with a specific language disorder. *European Child and Adolescent Psychiatry, 10,* 58–66.

Novic, J., Luchins, D. J., & Perline, R. (1984). Facial affect recognition in Schizophrenia: Is there a differential deficit? *British Journal of Psychiatry, 144,* 533–537.

Ochsner, K. N., & Lieberman, M. D. (2001). The emergence of social cognitive neuroscience. *American Psychologist, 56,* 717–734.

O'Connor, N., & Hermelin, B. (1967). Auditory and visual memory in autistic and normal children. *Journal of Mental Deficiency Research, 11,* 126–131.

Ohnishi, T., Matsuda, H., Hashimoto, T., Kunihiro, T., Nishikawa, M., Uema, T., et al. (2000). Abnormal regional blood flow in childhood Autism. *Brain, 123,* 1838–1844.

Oliver, A., Johnson, M. H., Karmiloff-Smith, A., & Pennington, B. (2000). Deviations in the emergence of representations: A neuroconstructivist framework for analysing developmental disorders. *Developmental Science, 3,* 1–40.

O'Reilly, R. C., & Munakata, Y. (2000). *Computational explorations in cognitive neuroscience: Understanding the mind by simulating the brain.* Cambridge, MA: MIT Press.

Orr, S. P., Lasko, N. B., Shalev, A. Y., & Pitman, R. K. (1995). Physiologic responses to loud tones in Vietnam veterans with posttraumatic stress disorder. *Journal of Abnormal Psychology, 104,* 75–82.

Orr, S. P., Metzger, L. J., Lasko, N. B., Macklin, M. L., Hu, F. B., Shalev, A. Y., et al. (2003). Physiologic responses to sudden, loud tones in monozygotic twins discordant for combat exposure. *Archives of General Psychiatry, 60,* 283–288.

Orton, S. T. (1925). "Word-blindness" in school children. *Archives of Neurology and Psychiatry, 14,* 582–615.

Osterling, J., & Dawson, G. (1994). Early recognition of children with Autism: A study of first birthday home video tapes. *Journal of Autism and Developmental Disorders, 24,* 247–259.

Ozonoff, S. (1995). Reliability and validity of the Wisconsin Card Sorting Test in studies of Autism. *Neuropsychology, 9,* 491–500.

Ozonoff, S., Coon, H., Dawson, G., Joseph, R., Klin, A., McMahon, W. M., et al. (2004). Performance on CANTAB subtests sensitive to frontal lobe function in people with autistic disorder: Evidence from the CPEA network. *Journal of Autism and Developmental Disorders, 34,* 139–150.

Ozonoff, S., & Griffith, E. M. (2000). Neuropsychological function and the external validity of Asperger syndrome. In A. Klin, F. Volkmar, &

S. S. Sparrow (Eds.), *Asperger syndrome* (pp. 72–96). New York: Guilford Press.

Ozonoff, S., & McEvoy, R. E. (1994). A longitudinal study of executive function and theory of mind development in Autism. *Development and Psychopathology, 6,* 415–431.

Ozonoff, S., Pennington, B. F., & Rogers, S. J. (1990). Are there emotion perception deficits in young autistic children? *Journal of Child Psychology and Psychiatry, 31,* 343–361.

Ozonoff, S., Pennington, B. F., & Rogers, S. J. (1991). Executive function deficits in high-functioning autistic individuals: Relationship to theory of mind. *Journal of Child Psychology and Psychiatry, 32,* 1081–1105.

Ozonoff, S., South, M., & Miller, J. N. (2000). DSM-IV-defined Asperger syndrome: Cognitive, behavioral, and early history differentiation from high-functioning Autism. *Autism, 4,* 29–46.

Ozonoff, S., & Strayer, D. L. (2001). Further evidence of intact working memory in Autism. *Journal of Autism and Developmental Disorders, 31,* 257–263.

Ozonoff, S., Strayer, D. L., McMahon, W. M., & Filloux, F. (1994). Executive function abilities in Autism and Tourette syndrome: An information processing approach. *Journal of Child Psychology and Psychiatry, 35,* 1015–1032.

Palmen, S. J. M. C., van Engeland, H., Hof, P. R., & Schmitz, C. (2004). Neuropathological findings in Autism. *Brain, 127,* 2572–2583.

Pascualvaca, D. M., Fantie, B. D., Papageorgiou, M., & Mirsky, A. F. (1998). Attentional capacities in children with Autism: Is there a general deficit in shifting focus? *Journal of Autism and Developmental Disorders, 28,* 467–478.

Pelphrey, K. A., Sasson, N. J., Reznick, J. S., Paul, G., Goldman, B. D., & Piven, J. (2002). Visual scanning of faces in Autism. *Journal of Autism and Developmental Disorders, 32,* 249–261.

Pennington, B. F. (1991). *Diagnosing learning disorders: A neuropsychological framework.* New York: Guilford Press.

Pennington, B. F. (2002). *The development of psychopathology: A neuroscience approach.* New York: Guilford Press.

Pennington, B. F., & Ozonoff, S. (1991). A neuroscientific perspective on continuity and discontinuity in developmental psychopathology. In D. Cicchetti & S. L. Toth (Eds.), *Rochester Symposium on Developmental Psychopathology: Vol. III. Models and integrations* (pp. 117–159). Rochester, NY: University of Rochester Press.

Pennington, B. F., & Ozonoff, S. (1996). Executive functions and developmental psychopathologies. *Journal of Child Psychology and Psychiatry, 37,* 51–87.

Pennington, B. F., & Welsh, M. C. (1995). Neuropsychology and developmental psychopathology. In D. Cicchetti & D. J. Cohen (Eds.), *Manual of developmental psychopathology* (pp. 254–290). New York: Wiley.

Perner, J., & Lang, B. (2002). What causes 3-year-olds' difficulty on the dimensional change card sorting task? *Infant and Child Development, 11,* 93–105.

Peterson, C. C., & Siegal, M. (1995). Deafness, conversation and theory of mind. *Journal of Child Psychology and Psychiatry, 36,* 459–474.

Pickles, A., Bolton, P. F., MacDonald, H., Bailey, A., LeCouteur, A., Sim, C. H., et al. (1995). Latent-class analysis of recurrence risks for complex phenotypes with selection and measurement error: A twin and family history study of Autism. *American Journal of Human Genetics, 57,* 717–726.

Pine, D. S. (2003). Developmental psychobiology and response to threats: Relevance to trauma in children and adolescents. *Society of Biological Psychiatry, 53,* 796–808.

Pine, D. S., & Cohen, J. A. (2002). Trauma in children and adolescents: Risk and treatment of psychiatric sequelae. *Biological Psychiatry, 51,* 519–531.

Pitman, R. K., & Orr, S. P. (1990). The black hold of trauma. *Biological Psychiatry, 27,* 469–471.

Pitman, R. K., Shalev, A. Y., & Orr, S. P. (1999). Posttraumatic stress disorder: Emotion, conditioning, and memory. In M. S. Gazzaniga (Ed.), *The new cognitive neurosciences* (2nd ed., p. 78). Cambridge, MA: MIT Press.

Piven, J. (2001). The broad Autism phenotype: A complementary strategy for molecular genetic studies of Autism. *American Journal of Medical Genetics, 8,* 34–35.

Piven, J., Arndt, S., Bailey, J., & Andreasen, N. (1996). Regional brain enlargement in Autism: A magnetic resonance imaging study. *Journal of the American Academy of Child and Adolescent Psychiatry, 35,* 530–536.

Piven, J., Bailey, J., Ranson, B. J., & Arndt, S. (1997). An MRI study of the corpus callosum in Autism. *American Journal of Psychiatry, 154,* 1051–1056.

Plaisted, K., Saksida, L., Alcantara, J., & Weisblatt, E. (2003). Towards an understanding of the mechanisms of weak central coherence effects: Experiments in visual configural learning and auditory perception. *Philosophical Transactions of the Royal Society of London, 358,* 375–386.

Plaisted, K., Swettenham, J., & Rees, L. (1999). Children with Autism show local precedence in a divided attention task and global precedence in a selective attention task. *Journal of Child Psychology and Psychiatry, 40,* 733–742.

Plomin, R., & Rutter, M. (1998). Child development, molecular genetics, and what to do with genes once they are found. *Child Development, 69,* 1223–1242.

Pollak, S. D., Cicchetti, D., Hornung, K., & Reed, A. (2000). Recognizing emotion in faces: Developmental effects of child abuse and neglect. *Developmental Psychology, 36,* 679–688.

Pollak, S. D., Cicchetti, D., Klorman, R., & Brumaghim, J. (1997). Cognitive brain event-related potentials and emotion processing in maltreated children. *Child Development, 68,* 773–787.

Pollak, S. D., Klorman, R., Thatcher, J. E., & Cicchetti, D. (2001). P3b reflects maltreated children's reactions to facial displays of emotion. *Psychophysiology, 38,* 267–274.

Posner, M. I. (1980). Orienting of attention. *Quarterly Journal of Experimental Psychology, 32,* 3–25.

Posner, M. I. (2002). Convergence of psychological and biological development. *Developmental Psychobiology, 40,* 339–343.

Prior, M. R. (2000). Guest editorial: Special issue on Asperger syndrome. *Autism, 4,* 5–8.

Prior, M. R., & Chen, C. S. (1976). Short-term and serial memory in autistic, retarded, and normal children. *Journal of Autism and Childhood Schizophrenia, 6,* 121–131.

Prior, M. R., Dahlstrom, B., & Squires, T. L. (1990). Autistic children's knowledge of thinking and feeling states in other people. *Journal of Child Psychology and Psychiatry, 31,* 587–601.

Prior, M. R., & Hoffmann, W. (1990). Neuropsychological testing of autistic children through an exploration with frontal lobe tests. *Journal of Autism and Developmental Disorders, 20,* 581–590.

Pynoos, R. S., Steinberg, A. M., & Piacentini, J. C. (1999). A developmental psychopathology model of childhood traumatic stress and intersection with anxiety disorders. *Biological Psychiatry, 46,* 1542–1554.

Pynoos, R. S., Steinberg, A. M., & Wraith, R. (1995). A developmental model of childhood traumatic stress. In D. Cicchetti & D. J. Cohen (Eds.), *Developmental psychopathology: Risk, disorder, and adaptation* (pp. 72–95). New York: Wiley.

Rapin, I. (1987). Searching for the cause of Autism: A neurologic perspective. In D. J. Cohen & A. M. Donnellan (Eds.), *Handbook of*

Autism and pervasive developmental disorders (pp. 710–717). New York: Wiley.

Rauch, S. L., van der Kolk, B. A., Fisler, R. E., Alpert, N. M., Orr, S. P., Savage, C. R., et al. (1996). A symptom provocation study of post-traumatic stress disorder using positron emission tomography and script-driven imagery. *Archives of General Psychiatry, 53,* 380–387.

Reinherz, H. Z., Giaconia, R. M., Lefkowitz, E. S., Pakiz, B., & Frost, A. K. (1993). Prevalence of psychiatric disorders in a community population of older adolescents. *Journal of the American Academy of Child and Adolescent Psychiatry, 32,* 369–377.

Reitan, R. M., & Davison, L. A. (1974). *Clinical neuropsychology: Current status and applications.* New York: Wiley.

Renner, P., Klinger, L. G., & Klinger, M. R. (2000). Implicit and explicit memory in Autism: Is Autism an amnesic disorder? *Journal of Autism and Developmental Disorders, 30,* 3–14.

Resnick, H. S., Kilpatrick, D. G., Dansky, B. S., Saunders, B. E., & Best, C. L. (1993). Prevalence of civilian trauma and posttraumatic stress disorder in a representative national sample of women. *Journal of Consulting and Clinical Psychology, 61,* 984–991.

Rimland, E. R. (1964). *Infantile Autism: The syndrome and its implications for a neural theory of behavior.* New York: Appleton-Century-Crofts.

Rinehart, N. J., Bradshaw, J. L., Moss, S. A., Brereton, A. V., & Tonge, B. J. (2000). Atypical interference of local detail on global processing in high-functioning Autism and Asperger's disorder. *Journal of Child Psychology and Psychiatry, 41,* 769–778.

Ring, H. A., Baron-Cohen, S., Wheelwright, S., Williams, S. C., Brammer, M., Andrew, C., et al. (1999). Cerebral correlates of preserved cognitive skills in Autism: A functional MRI study of embedded figures task performance. *Brain, 122,* 1305–1315.

Risch, N., Spiker, D., Lotspeich, L., Nouri, N., Hinds, D., Hallmayer, J., et al. (1999). A genomic screen of Autism: Evidence for a multilocus etiology. *American Journal of Human Genetics, 65,* 493–507.

Rodgers, J. (2000). Visual perception and Asperger syndrome: Central coherence deficit or hierarchization deficit? *Autism, 4,* 321–329.

Rogers, S. J., Bennetto, L., McEvoy, R., & Pennington, B. F. (1996). Imitation and pantomime in high functioning adolescents with Autism spectrum disorders. *Child Development, 67,* 2060–2073.

Rogers, S. J., Hepburn, S. L., Stackhouse, T., & Wehner, E. (2003). Imitation performance in toddlers with Autism and those with other developmental disorders. *Journal of Child Psychology and Psychiatry, 44,* 763–781.

Rogers, S. J., & Pennington, B. F. (1991). A theoretical approach to the deficits in infantile Autism. *Development and Psychopathology, 3,* 137–162.

Ronan, P. J., Steciuk, M., Kramer, G. L., Kram, M., & Petty, F. (2000). Increased septal 5-HIAA efflux in rats that do not develop learned helplessness after inescapable stress. *Journal of Neuroscience Research, 61,* 101–106.

Ropar, D., & Mitchell, P. (1999). Are individuals with Autism and Asperger's syndrome susceptible to visual illusions? *Journal of Child Psychology and Psychiatry, 40,* 1287–1293.

Ropar, D., & Mitchell, P. (2001). Susceptibility to illusions and performance on visuospatial tasks in individuals with Autism. *Journal of Child Psychology and Psychiatry, 42,* 539–549.

Rothbart, M. K., Ahadi, S. A., & Hershey, K. L. (1994). Temperament and social behavior in childhood. *Merrill-Palmer Quarterly, 40,* 21–39.

Rothbart, M. K., & Posner, M. I. (2001). Mechanism and variation in the development of attentional networks. In C. A. Nelson & M. Luciana (Eds.), *Handbook of developmental cognitive neuroscience* (pp. 353–363). Cambridge, MA: MIT Press.

Rumelhart, D. E., McClelland, J. L., & The PDP Research Group. (1986). *Parallel distributed processing: Explorations in the microstructure of cognition* (Vol. 1). Cambridge, MA: MIT Press.

Rumsey, J. M. (1985). Conceptual problem-solving in highly verbal, nonretarded autistic men. *Journal of Autism and Developmental Disorders, 15,* 23–36.

Rumsey, J. M., & Hamburger, S. D. (1988). Neuropsychological findings in high-functioning men with infantile Autism, residual state. *Journal of Clinical and Experimental Neuropsychology, 10,* 201–221.

Russell, J. (1997). *Autism as an executive disorder.* New York: Oxford University Press.

Russell, J., Jarrold, C., & Henry, L. (1996). Working memory in children with Autism and with moderate learning difficulties. *Journal of Child Psychology and Psychiatry, 37,* 673–686.

Russell, J., Mauthner, N., Sharpe, S., & Tidswell, T. (1991). The "windows task" as a measure of strategic deception in preschoolers and autistic subjects. *British Journal of Developmental Psychology, 9,* 331–349.

Russell, J., Saltmarsh, R., & Hill, E. (1999). What do executive factors contribute to the failure on false belief tasks by children with Autism? *Journal of Child Psychology and Psychiatry, 40,* 859–868.

Rutter, M. (1977). Brain damage syndromes in childhood: Concepts and findings. *Journal of Child Psychology and Psychiatry, 18,* 1–21.

Rutter, M. (1978). Language disorder and infantile Autism. In M. Rutter & E. Schopler (Eds.), *Autism: A reappraisal of concepts and treatment* (pp. 85–104). New York: Plenum Press.

Rutter, M. (1999). The Emanuel Miller memorial lecture 1998: Autism: Two-way interplay between research and clinical work. *Journal of Child Psychology and Psychiatry, 40,* 169–188.

Rutter, M. (2000). Genetic studies of Autism: From the 1970s into the millennium. *Journal of Abnormal Child Psychology, 28,* 3–14.

Saitoh, O., Karns, C. M., & Courchesne, E. (2001). Development of the hippocampal formation from 2 to 42 years: MRI evidence of smaller area dentata in Autism. *Brain, 124,* 1317–1324.

Salmond, C. H., de Haan, M., Friston, K. J., Gadian, D. G., & Vargha-Khadem, F. (2003). Investigating individual differences in brain abnormalities in Autism. *Philosophical Transactions of the Royal Society of London. Series B, Biological Sciences, 358,* 405–413.

Sanchez, M. M., Ladd, C. O., & Plotsky, P. M. (2001). Early adverse experience as a developmental risk factor for later psychopathology: Evidence from rodent and primate models. *Development and Psychopathology, 13,* 419–449.

Sapolsky, R. M. (2000). Glucocorticoids and hippocampal atrophy in neuropsychiatric disorders. *Archives of General Psychiatry, 57,* 925–935.

Schain, R., & Yannet, H. (1960). Infantile Autism: An analysis of 50 cases and a consideration of certain relevant neurophysiological concepts. *Journal of Pediatrics, 57,* 550–567.

Schultz, R. T., Gauthier, I., Klin, A., Fulbright, R. K., Anderson, A. W., Volkmar, F., et al. (2000). Abnormal ventral temporal cortical activity during face discrimination among individuals with Autism and Asperger syndrome. *Archives of General Psychiatry, 57,* 331–340.

Schwartz, J. M., Stoessel, P. W., Baxter, L. R., Jr., Martin, K. M., & Phelps, M. E. (1996). Systematic changes in cerebral glucose metabolic rate after successful behavioral modification treatment of obsessive-compulsive disorder. *Archives of General Psychiatry, 53,* 109–113.

Segalowitz, S. J., & Gruber, F. A. (1977). *Language development and neurological theory.* New York: Academic Press.

Shaffer, D. (1973). Psychiatric aspects of brain injury in childhood: A review. *Developmental Medicine and Child Neurology, 15,* 211–220.

Shah, A., & Frith, U. (1983). An islet of ability in autistic children. *Journal of Child Psychology and Psychiatry, 24,* 613–620.

Shah, A., & Frith, U. (1993). Why do autistic individuals show superior performance on the block design task? *Journal of Child Psychology and Psychiatry, 34,* 1351–1364.

Shalev, A. Y., Peri, T., Brandes, D., Freedman, S., Orr, S. P., & Pitman, R. K. (2000). Auditory startle response in trauma survivors with posttraumatic stress disorder: A prospective study. *American Journal of Psychiatry, 157,* 255–261.

Shallice, T., Marzocchi, G. M., Coser, S., Del Savio, M., Meuter, R. F., & Rumiati, R. I. (2002). Executive function profile of children with attention deficit hyperactivity disorder. *Developmental Neuropsychology, 21,* 43–71.

Shatz, C. (1992). Dividing up the neocortex. *Science, 258,* 237–238.

Shields, A., & Cicchetti, D. (1998). Reactive aggression among maltreated children: The contributions of attention and emotion dysregulation. *Journal of Clinical Child Psychology, 27,* 381–395.

Shin, L. M., McNally, R. J., Kosslyn, R. J., Thompson, W. L., Rauch, S. L., Alpert, N. M., et al. (1999). Regional bloodflow during script-driven imagery in childhood sexual abuse-related PTSD: A PET investigation. *American Journal of Psychiatry, 156,* 575–584.

Shin, L. M., McNally, R. J., Kosslyn, S. M., Thompson, W. L., Rauch, S. L., Alpert, N. M., et al. (1997). A positron emission tomographic study of symptom provocation in PTSD. *Annals of the New York Academy of Sciences, 821,* 521–523.

Shu, B.-C., Lung, F.-W., Tien, A. Y., & Chen, B.-C. (2001). Executive function deficits in non-retarded autistic children. *Autism, 5,* 165–174.

Simonoff, E. (2000). Extracting meaning from comorbidity: Genetic analyses that make sense. *Journal of Child Psychology and Psychiatry, 41,* 667–674.

Smoller, J. W., Finn, C., & White, C. (2003). The genetics of anxiety disorders: An overview. *Philosophical Transactions of the Royal Society of London. Series B, Biological Sciences, 358,* 303–314.

South, M., Ozonoff, S., & McMahon, W. M. (in press). Repetitive behavior profiles in Asperger syndrome and high-functioning Autism. *Journal of Autism and Developmental Disorders.*

Sparks, B. F., Friedman, S. D., Shaw, D. W., Aylward, E. H., Echelard, D., Artru, A. A., et al. (2002). Brain structural abnormalities in young children with Autism spectrum disorder. *Neurology, 59,* 184–192.

Spitznagel, M. B., & Suhr, J. A. (2002). Executive function deficits associated with symptoms of schizotypy and obsessive-compulsive disorder. *Psychiatry Research, 110,* 151–163.

Stein, M. B., Jang, K. L., & Livesley, W. J. (1999). Heritability of anxiety sensitivity: A twin study. *American Journal of Psychiatry, 156,* 246–251.

Stein, M. B., Koverola, C., Hanna, C., Torchia, M. G., & McClarty, B. (1997). Hippocampal volume in women victimized by childhood sexual abuse. *Psychological Medicine, 27,* 951–959.

Stern, D. N. (1985). *The interpersonal world of the infant.* New York: Basic Books.

Stratton, K., Gable, A., & McCormick, M. C. (2001). *Immunization safety review: Thimerosal-containing vaccines and neurodevelopmental disorders.* Washington, DC: National Academy Press.

Stuss, D. T., Gallup, G. G., & Alexander, M. P. (2001). The frontal lobes are necessary for "theory of mind." *Brain, 124,* 279–286.

Swanson, J. M., Posner, M., Potkin, S. G., Bonforte, S., Youpa, D., Fiore, C., et al. (1991). Activating tasks for the study of visual-spatial attention in ADHD children: A cognitive anatomic approach. *Journal of Child Neurology, 6,* S119–S127.

Szatmari, P., Bryson, S. E., Streiner, D. L., Wilson, F., Archer, L., & Ryerse, C. (2000). Two-year outcome of preschool children with Autism or Asperger's syndrome. *American Journal of Psychiatry, 157,* 1980–1987.

Szatmari, P., Tuff, L., Finlayson, A. J., & Bartolucci, G. (1990). Asperger's syndrome and Autism: Neurocognitive aspects. *Journal of the American Academy of Child and Adolescent Psychiatry, 29,* 130–136.

Tager-Flusberg, H. (1991). Semantic processing in the free recall of autistic children: Further evidence for a cognitive deficit. *British Journal of Developmental Psychology, 9,* 417–430.

Tager-Flusberg, H. (2001). A re-examination of the theory of mind hypothesis of Autism. In J. Burack, T. Charman, N. Yirmiya, & P. Zelazo (Eds.), *The development of Autism: Perspectives from theory and research* (pp. 173–193). London: Erlbaum.

Tager-Flusberg, H., & Anderson, M. (1991). The development of contingent discourse ability in autistic children. *Journal of Child Psychology and Psychiatry, 32,* 1123–1134.

Tassabehji, M., Metcalfe, K., Karmiloff-Smith, A., Carette, M. J., Grant, J., Dennis, N., et al. (1999). Williams syndrome: Use of chromosomal microdeletions as a tool to dissect cognitive and physical phenotypes. *American Journal of Human Genetics, 64,* 118–125.

Taylor, B., Miller, E., Farrington, C. P., Petropoulos, M. C., Favot-Mayaud, I., Li, J., et al. (1999). Autism and measles, mumps, and rubella vaccine: No epidemiological evidence for a causal association. *Lancet, 353,* 2026–2029.

Taylor, B., Miller, E., Lingam, R., Andrews, N., Simmons, A., & Stowe, J. (2002). Measles, mumps, and rubella vaccination and bowel problems or developmental regression in children with Autism: Population study. *British Medical Journal, 324,* 393–396.

Teicher, M. H., Andersen, S. L., Polcari, A., Anderson, C. M., & Navalta, C. P. (2002). Developmental neurobiology of childhood stress and trauma. *Psychiatric Clinics of North America, 25,* 397–426.

Teicher, M. H., Andersen, S. L., Polcari, A., Anderson, C. M., Navalta, C. P., & Kim, D. M. (2003). The neurobiological consequences of early stress and childhood maltreatment. *Neuroscience and Biobehavioral Reviews, 27,* 33–44.

Terr, L. C. (1979). The children of Chowchilla. *Psychoanalytic Study of the Child, 34,* 547–623.

Teunisse, J.-P., Cools, A. R., van Spaendonck, K. P. M., Aerts, F. H. T. M., & Berger, H. J. C. (2001). Cognitive styles in high-functioning adolescents with autistic disorder. *Journal of Autism and Developmental Disorders, 31,* 55–66.

Torgesen, J. K. (1995). *Phonological awareness: A critical factor in dyslexia.* Baltimore: Orton Dyslexia Society.

Torgesen, J. K., & Bryant, B. (1994). *Phonological awareness training program.* Austin, TX: ProEd.

Townsend, J., Courchesne, E., & Egaas, B. (1996). Slowed orienting of covert visual-spatial attention in Autism: Specific deficits associated with cerebellar and parietal abnormality. *Development and Psychopathology, 8,* 563–584.

True, W. R., Rice, J., Eisen, S. A., Heath, A. C., Goldberg, J., Lyons, M. J., et al. (1993). A twin study of genetic and environmental contributions to liability for posttraumatic stress symptoms. *Archives of General Psychiatry, 50,* 257–264.

Tryon, W. W. (1999). A bidirectional associative memory explanation of posttraumatic stress disorder. *Clinical Psychology Review, 199,* 789–818.

Turner, M. (1997). Towards an executive dysfunction account of repetitive behavior in Autism. In J. Russell (Ed.), *Autism as an executive disorder* (pp. 57–100). New York: Oxford University Press.

Uddo, M., Vasterling, J. T., Brailey, K., & Sutker, P. B. (1993). Memory and attention in posttraumatic stress disorder. *Journal of Psychopathology and Behavioral Assessment, 15,* 43–52.

van der Kolk, B. A. (2003). The neurobiology of childhood trauma and abuse. *Child and Adolescent Psychiatric Clinics of North America, 12,* 293–317.

Vasterling, J. J., Brailey, K., Constans, J. I., & Sutker, P. B. (1998). Attention and memory dysfunction in posttraumatic stress disorder. *Neuropsychology, 12,* 125–133.

Vasterling, J. J., Duke, L. M., Brailey, K., Constans, J. I., Allain, A. N., Jr., & Sutker, P. B. (2002). Attention, learning, and memory performances and intellectual resources in Vietnam veterans: PTSD and no disorder comparisons. *Neuropsychology, 16,* 5–14.

Vermetten, E., & Bremner, J. D. (2002). Circuits and systems in stress: I. Preclinical studies. *Depression and Anxiety, 15,* 126–147.

Volkmar, F. R., Klin, A., & Pauls, D. (1998). Nosological and genetic aspects of Asperger syndrome. *Journal of Autism and Developmental Disorders, 28,* 457–463.

Volkmar, F. R., Sparrow, S. S., Rende, R. D., & Cohen, D. J. (1989). Facial perception in Autism. *Journal of Child Psychology and Psychiatry, 30,* 591–598.

Wainwright-Sharp, J. A., & Bryson, S. E. (1993). Visual orienting deficits in high-functioning people with Autism. *Journal of Autism and Developmental Disorders, 23,* 1–13.

Wakefield, A. J., Murch, S. H., Anthony, A., Linnell, J., Casson, D. M., Malik, M., et al. (1998). Ileal-lymphoid-nodular hyperplasia, non-specific colitis, and pervasive developmental disorder in children. *Lancet, 351,* 637–641.

Weeks, S. J., & Hobson, R. P. (1987). The salience of facial expression for autistic children. *Journal of Child Psychology and Psychiatry, 28,* 137–151.

Weinstein, C. S., Fucetola, R., & Mollica, R. (2001). Neuropsychological issues in the assessment of refugees and victims of mass violence. *Neuropsychology Review, 11,* 131–141.

Williams, L. M. (1994). Recall of childhood trauma: A prospective study of child sexual abuse. *Journal of Consulting and Clinical Psychology, 62,* 1167–1176.

Wilson, B., Clare, L., Baddeley, A., Cockburn, J., Watson, P., & Robyn, T. (1998). *The Rivermead Behavioural Memory Test (RBMT).* St. Edmunds, England: Thames Valley Test Company.

Wing, L. (1981). Asperger's syndrome: A clinical account. *Psychological Medicine, 11,* 115–129.

Wing, L., & Gould, J. (1979). Severe impairments of social interaction and associated abnormalities in children: Epidemiology and classification. *Journal of Autism and Developmental Disorders, 9,* 11–29.

Wu, J., Kramer, G. L., Kram, M., Steciuk, M., Crawford, I. L., & Petty, F. (1999). Serotonin and learned helplessness: A regional study of 5-HT1A receptors and the serotonin transport site in rat brain. *Journal of Psychiatric Research, 33,* 17–22.

Yehuda, R. (1997). Sensitization of the hypothalamic-pituitary-adrenal axis in posttraumatic stress disorder. *Annals of the New York Academy of Sciences, 821,* 57–75.

Yehuda, R., Keefe, R. S., Harvey, P. D., Levengood, R. A., Gerber, D. K., Geni, J., et al. (1995). Learning and memory in combat veterans with posttraumatic stress disorder. *American Journal of Psychiatry, 152,* 137–139.

Yeung-Courchesne, R., & Courchesne, E. (1997). From impasse to insight in Autism research: From behavioral symptoms to biological explanations. *Development and Psychopathology, 9,* 389–419.

Yirmiya, N., Erel, O., Shaked, M., & Solomonica-Levi, D. (1998). Meta-analyses comparing theory of mind abilities of individuals with Autism, individuals with mental retardation, and normally developing individuals. *Psychological Bulletin, 124,* 283–307.

Yule, W., Perrin, S., & Smith, P. (2001). Traumatic events and posttraumatic stress disorder. In W. K. Silverman & P. D. A. Treffers (Eds.), *Anxiety disorders in children and adolescents: Research, assessment and intervention* (pp. 212–234). New York: Cambridge University Press.

Yule, W., & Udwin, O. (1991). Screening child survivors for PTSD: Experiences from the "Jupiter" sinking. *British Journal of Clinical Psychology, 30,* 131–138.

Yule, W., Udwin, O., & Murdoch, K. (1990). The "Jupiter" sinking: Effects on children's fears, depression and anxiety. *Journal of Child Psychology and Psychiatry, 31,* 1051–1061.

Zeitlin, S. B., & McNally, R. J. (1991). Implicit and explicit memory bias for threat in post-traumatic stress disorder. *Behavior Research and Therapy, 29,* 451–457.

Zilbovicius, M., Boddaert, N., Belin, P., Poline, J. B., Remy, P., Mangin, J. F., et al. (2000). Temporal lobe dysfunction in childhood Autism: A PET study. *American Journal of Psychiatry, 157,* 1988–1993.

CHAPTER 9

Psychophysiological Methods for the Study of Developmental Psychopathology

NATHAN A. FOX, AMIE ASHLEY HANE, and KORALY PÉREZ-EDGAR

Psychophysiology may be defined as that area of research examining the interaction of physiological systems and psychological states. It involves both the measurement of reactions of a physiological system to changes in psychological state and the influence of a physiological system on the initiation, presentation, and termination of psychological behavior. In this sense, psychophysiology is truly bidirectional, involving both input and output systems that guide, reflect, and accompany psychological behavior. A good example of this can be seen in work indicating that prolonged exposure to abuse and maltreatment can reshape the functioning of core regulatory systems (Cicchetti & Rogosch, 2001; Glaser, 2000; Hart, Gunnar, & Cicchetti, 1995). It appears that along with behavioral and psychological systems, central physiological mechanisms will also reorganize to maximally adapt to the demands of the environment (Campos, Campos, & Barrett, 1989), however aberrant. It is because of this bidirectional relationship that developmental psychophysiology holds great promise for the study of developmental psychopathology.

Developmental psychophysiology also holds the promise of helping the field expand its research boundaries to incorporate multiple levels of analyses. For example, Sroufe and Rutter (1984) contend that developmental psychopathology should emphasize four broad areas of study: (1) the origins and time course of early appearing psychopathology, (2) the varying manifestations of disorder with development, (3) the precursors and sequelae of these disorders, and (4) the relationship of maladaptation to nondisordered patterns of behavior. To do so, researchers must be able to examine and compare developmental processes that act and interact at the behavioral, cognitive, affective, and psychophysiological levels. In this way, researchers can build a multidimensional model of the mechanisms and manifestations of developmental psychopathology.

For example, in assessing risk, Cicchetti and Dawson (2002) note that risk factors can appear at varying levels, ranging from the molecular to the environmental. Although any single risk factor may not be sufficient for a disorder to manifest, the collective risk found in the pooling of vulnerabilities across levels of functioning may lead to the larger overarching disorders described clinically. In addition, because risk factors tend to act synergistically rather than additively and are rarely found in isolation (Cicchetti & Dawson, 2002), the use of multiple levels of analysis is also critical to outlining the bidirectional nature of the physiology-behavioral link (Kagan, Snidman, McManis, Woodward, & Hardway, 2002).

However, out of either necessity or long-standing tradition, researchers often treat psychopathology as a binary system. That is, participants in studies are often divided into two exclusive groups that are labeled disordered and nondisordered. Our schemes for categorizing and diagnosing psychopathology are dependent on documenting a compendium of behaviors, affects, and cognitions that are both highly variable and dynamic in nature. Indeed, even in the case of developmental disorders with clear genetic markers, such as Down syndrome and Fragile X, the path between genotype and phenotype is so complex that a simple karyotype tells us very little about the psychological state of the individual in question. Therefore, one of the main goals for developmental psychopathology has been to create more precise and nuanced profiles of individual developmental disorders, incorporating both observed behavior and underlying developmental mechanisms. In the past 2 decades, psychophysiological measures have become a central tool in this endeavor.

The increasing use of developmental psychophysiology in developmental psychopathology research has evolved from the unique strengths of the psychophysiological approach and the insights it allows into the processes underlying or accompanying early maladaptation. Inherent in the developmental psychopathological approach is the study of the manner in which early dispositions lead to adaptations in psychological behavior over time. Trajectories of human development are an outgrowth of the interaction between a given nervous system's readiness and reactivity and the adaptations of that nervous system across time. Behavioral change is a result of initial dispositions responding to dynamic and challenging environmental contexts. Research involving measurement of physiological systems thus holds great promise for elucidating important aspects of the bidirectional influences on individual trajectories across development.

In this chapter, we start with the basic tenets and strengths of psychophysiological research. We then systematically examine and review research exploring a variety of physiological systems, detailing issues of approach and measurement. We end this chapter with some thoughts on the future directions of this type of research for the field of developmental psychopathology.

STRENGTHS OF THE PSYCHOPHYSIOLOGICAL APPROACH

The use of physiological measures in behavioral research provides a number of advantages, permitting a window onto the bidirectional influence that physiological systems have on behavior and behavior on physiology. However, it is important to note that psychophysiology does not convey a special truth to data independent of behavior. Often, investigators will claim that physiological responses are more objective than behavioral analysis. In fact, such measures are no more essential than precise behavioral measurement. As van der Molen and Molenaar (1994, p. 466) noted, "The usefulness of psychophysiological measures depends on the demonstration of the sensitivity of the measures to task manipulations derived from developmental psychology." Psychophysiology does provide, however, a means for understanding a level of processing that may not be accessible through observation alone.

Psychophysiology illuminates the link between physiology and behavior, opening up the possibility of supplementing behavioral classifications with the structure, function, and timing of underlying physiological and neural events. Psychophysiology also allows developmental researchers to incorporate a multiple-measures approach, giving them an ability to create multidimensional profiles of the areas of interest and examine associations and disassociations between physiology and behavior. Finally, this approach is exceedingly useful for preverbal and compromised populations, which are often at the heart of developmental psychopathology.

Understanding the Physiology-Behavior Connection

A major strength of the psychophysiological approach is that one can examine the action of a targeted physiological system as it changes in response to psychological challenge. The nature of that change, the manner in which physiological change energizes, arouses, or inhibits behavior, may provide insight into psychological responses to challenge. Knowledge of the underlying physiology of that system as well as an understanding of what aspects of that system are being reflected in its measurement is critical if accurate interpretation of the change in physiology is to be made. At a very basic level, it is important to understand how the physiological system works, that is, how it activates or inhibits behavior. Similarly, it is crucial to understand which measures of a particular physiological system best reflect these processes.

For many years, for example, heart rate increases in mobile infants who were exposed to unfamiliar adults were assumed to reflect the state of fear in the infants. Infants were approached by an unfamiliar adult while researchers monitored cardiac activity. Increases in heart rate were thought to reflect the infant's fear of the stranger. Increases and decreases in heart rate, however, are multiply determined. Heart rate change could be the result of metabolic, motor, or psychological change or some combination thereof. Infants who actively moved in response to stranger approach would show heart rate increases, as would an infant who would sit still and cry during this situation. Heart rate increases could not differentiate among these different behavioral responses. The lack of specificity of the physiological response and the multidetermined nature of the response raise important caveats in interpreting heart rate changes during certain types of challenge. Often, however, researchers fall back on the presumed psychological explanation for heart rate change (e.g., arousal, fear, anxiety) without first examining other potential confounding influences.

Linking multidetermined physiological responses to diffuse and nonspecific psychological states (e.g., arousal or anxiety) leads to a lack of precision in the association between the physiological change and the psychological state. This lack of precision in identifying the physiological factors involved in the increased heart rate and the lack of precision in the definition of the underlying psychological state do not facilitate further understanding of the phenomenon of interest. Thus, the very strength of the psychophysiological approach, linking physiological and behavioral change, may sometimes be a critical weakness, particularly when the underlying physiological processes are not well understood.

On the other hand, there are examples from the psychophysiology literature in which knowledge of physiological mechanisms assists in the interpretation of behavioral change. Porges (Porges & Byrne, 1992) has shown that by using complex filtering and statistical techniques, one can identify and extract the component of heart rate, reflecting parasympathetic influence. Vagal tone is a quantification of the variability in heart rate due to respiratory influences that are primarily vagal in origin. The level of vagal tone of an individual or changes in vagal tone as a result of psychological challenge may be interpreted as reflecting the influence of parasympathetic tone or vagal activity on heart rate. The obvious benefit of such precision is that it allows one to examine the relationship of this system to both higher cortical responses and other connected peripheral responses. For example, one can map out the manner in which changes

in vagal tone affect brain stem nuclei and upstream cortical centers that may modulate attention. Similarly, one can examine the influence of cortical regions on the brain stem nuclei, which control parasympathetic tone. In addition, because vagus nerve activity affects multiple organ sites, one can begin to describe the manner in which individual differences in vagal tone affect physiological and psychological organization and preparedness for action and behavior. Finally, the precision of physiological description and links to specific psychological behaviors allows one to develop models for how certain initial dispositions may adapt to changing environmental challenges.

Assessing Function through the Timing of Physiological Change

Yet another strength of the psychophysiological approach can be found in its ability to reflect the importance of timing of physiological events underlying or accompanying behavior. Each physiological system commonly measured in psychophysiological research has its distinct time course, which affects and is affected by psychological challenge and behavioral response. For example, recording brain electrical activity (i.e., electroencephalogram, EEG) during repeated stimulus presentation allows the creation of event-related potentials (ERPs), which reflect the timing of neural processing. These ERPs may reflect the immediate processing of sensory information at the millisecond level as well as higher-order cortical processing at the level of hundreds of milliseconds. Continuing the time line, measures of the autonomic nervous system (e.g., heart rate) provide information at the level of seconds, and activity in the limbic-hypothalamic-pituitary-adrenal (LHPA) axis is at the level of minutes. The varying time course for different physiological systems directly reflects their function in the individual's response to psychological challenge, be it to evaluate the stimulus (milliseconds), divert resources such as blood and oxygen to muscle to respond (seconds), or organize a response to provide energy toward restoring homeostasis in the body (minutes). The timing of physiological responses links directly to the behaviors under study and may provide insight into the function of the behavior in response to the particular challenge.

Providing Multidimensional Biobehavioral Profiles

The use of multiple measures applied to experimental settings allows for a richer and more nuanced analysis of data, particularly when interested in performance differences across two or more groups. A central strategy in developmental psychopathology research is to contrast the performance of a clinical or high-risk group on a particular task with that of a healthy control group. The addition of multiple measures allows for the addition of analyses that focus on individual differences across two or more physiological systems, which are often both theoretically and statistically stronger avenues for discovery. Perhaps as important, researchers can now look to between-group differences in within-group response patterns. This allows for the examination of individual and group profiles, which may produce a more stable or informative picture of a given disorder than would isolated bits of data. This is in line with the call for more holistic, person-oriented research strategies (e.g., Bergman & Magnusson, 1997; von Eye & Bergman, 2003) that focus on the significance of single variables and of patterns in development, the developmental study of syndromes (typical patterns), and the detection of "white spots" in development in characterizing the individual as an "organized whole."

This is not to say that each individual measure, even if a core indicator of the disorder or maladjustment, need be deviant or abnormal. Rather, a great deal of insight can be gained in finding patterns of normality and abnormality across measures as well as in creating broad behavioral and psychophysiological profiles. That is, disorder or risk may manifest in the dysregulation of responses across systems rather than alterations within an individual system (Bauer, Quas, & Boyce, 2002). An early example can be seen in Ax's (1970) work demonstrating that Schizophrenia is marked by poor coordination across systems (in this case, heart rate and respiration) rather than dysregulation within a single system.

It is in this endeavor that developmental psychopathology can benefit from its *developmental* roots. In the case of psychophysiological measures, their use in the study of psychopathology should not come with the expectation that the measure(s) will necessarily be patently deviant. There may be cases, such as institutionalization (Carlson & Earls, 1997), in which differences are apparent, but it is just as likely that a measure falls within the normal developmental distribution. The greatest information may be found when the measure is placed in the larger context of a physiological or behavioral profile.

For example, Raine (Raine, Venables, & Williams, 1990) collected heart rate, skin conductance, and EEG measures from a group of British adolescents ages 14 to 16. Ten years later, Raine and colleagues returned to see that 17 of the original 101 children now had criminal records. When comparing these two groups, Raine and colleagues found that the adolescents who went on to have a criminal record had lower heart rates as well as dampened electrodermal and EEG arousal. Although the individual findings do not point to any gross deviance, disorder, or, to use a nineteenth-century term, degeneracy, they do point to an interconnected physiological system that may create a profile that is vulnerable to antisocial behavior.

Understanding Dissociations between Physiology and Behavior

It is of obvious interest to examine physiological change, concurrent with behavioral change, in response to a specific psychological challenge. Such associations provide another level of analysis around which one may interpret behavior, understanding the significance of the physiological change as i affects or supports a behavioral response. However, disassociations between overt behavior and physiology may also be of interest for understanding the individual's response to psychological challenge. In this instance, measurement of physiological change may provide important information that may not be readily apparent to the observer. An example of this may be found in the work of James Gross (Rottenberg, Kasch, Gross, & Gotlib, 2002) on emotion regulation. Gross and colleagues asked subjects who were watching videos designed to elicit different emotions to either freely respond or to inhibit their affective responses, measuring both overt behavior and autonomic responses. During the period in which subjects were inhibiting their affective responses, there was a noticeable decrease in observable behavior. However, these same subjects displayed a significant increase in autonomic activity (e.g., heart rate, blood pressure). This dissociation between behavior and psychophysiology was linked to more extreme concurrent depression and a decreased likelihood for satisfactory recovery. Dissociations between overt behavior and physiology may provide important information about psychological processes, in this case, inhibition of emotional behavior.

The issue of dissociation between physiology and behavior is complex, however. In the case of Gross's studies, subjects were given specific instructions and acknowledged complying with such instructions via self-report. However, in the absence of such task specificity and instruction, it is often difficult to interpret physiological change without a concurrent behavioral response. This dilemma underlies the first of two cardinal rules regarding psychophysiological research: Whenever possible, physiological responses should be anchored to behavior. Practically, this means that one should usually not interpret physiological change in the absence of concurrent behavioral change. There are, however, multiple exceptions to this rule. First, as described earlier, if subjects are asked to inhibit behavior, then their physiological response becomes of interest independent of behavioral response. Second, tasks assessing sensory processing may not require a behavioral response. For example, examining brain stem auditory evoked responses or even mismatch negativity (i.e., an early ERP component that reflects a discrepancy between a stimulus and the traces in short-term memory produced by the immediately preceding stimulus) to auditory tones does not require active response from the subject. In these instances, it is not necessary to link behavioral response to physiology. It is in cases of complex cognitive or affective challenges that the interpretation of a physiological response without a behavioral anchor is problematic. Due to the complexity of the systems involved and the multidetermined processes influencing these responses, it is often difficult in such instances to specify the source of the physiological change and its contribution to a discrete psychological state.

Providing Insight into the Behavior of Preverbal and Young Children

An additional strength of the psychophysiological approach lies in its ability to provide insight into the behavior of preverbal infants and young children who cannot self-report or participate in interviews. In such cases, the psychophysiological approach provides a window onto reactivity and processing of stimuli that, together with behavioral analysis, offer a reasonable basis for judging an infant's or young child's response to psychological challenge. This is of particular importance when examining developmental psychopathology because researchers are often faced with the task of distinguishing between overlapping and nondistinct symptomatology due to children's limited behavioral repertoires.

The utility of these methods with infant and young child populations comes with several important caveats. It should come as little surprise that accompanying physical and psychological development is the development and change in underlying physiological systems, which support both of these areas. In some instances, the maturation of the system is rapid, over the 1st year of life, whereas for other systems there is consistent change through adolescence. For example, autonomic control systems change rapidly over the 1st year, and although mean heart rate levels change with development, the physiological system of vagal and sympathetic innervations, the links to respiratory control and blood pressure exist at birth and are stably in place by the end of the 1st year of life. On the other hand, concomitant with maturation of brain regions, particularly in corti-

cal areas, there are significant changes in frequency and amplitude of the EEG through adolescence. There are also major changes in the morphology of the components that are evoked by exogenous stimuli and that form the ERP. These changes in the physiology of the system directly affect the measurement of the system.

QUESTIONS ADDRESSED BY THE PSYCHOPHYSIOLOGICAL APPROACH

There are three broad areas in which psychophysiological methods are meaningfully applied: (1) examination of basic cognitive processes, (2) measurement of variations in physiological arousal and reactivity, and (3) examination of the processes surrounding motivation and emotion. In each of these areas, psychophysiology has a long history of research with both "normal" and clinical populations. In general, certain methods are more applicable for specific areas as opposed to others. Thus, for example, when examining basic cognitive processes such as attention, sensory processing, perceptual sensitivity, or memory, most of the work has entailed the use of ERP methods. Such methods require precision in stimulus definition and the timing of stimulus presentation and provide information about the timing and intensity of neural events involved in different aspects of cognitive processing. For studies in the preparedness of the system to react or respond to psychological challenge (e.g., arousal and reactivity), measures of the autonomic nervous system have been most commonly used. Assessments of arousal have traditionally been accomplished via measurement of sympathetic and parasympathetic activity. Such studies may examine heart rate, skin conductance, or sympathetic activity during a resting or baseline state and then during subsequent challenge and recovery to baseline. The use of psychophysiological methods to study emotion and motivation covers a wide range of methods, including those examining specific neural systems (e.g., the "fear" system) and those examining broad motivational processes (e.g., approach versus withdrawal). Included as well in this area is the work on the stress response and the physiological system involved.

The wide array of methods in part reflects the history of behavioral research in emotion, where precision in both the stimulus characteristics eliciting emotion and the approach to quantifying or identifying the presence of emotion have undergone important advances in only the past 30 years. This range of approaches has led to a range of studies, only some of which specify the nature of the stimulus and context in which it is presented. As well, among studies of emotion or motivation only some anchor the physiological response to behavior, making interpretation of the physiological change ambiguous.

The following sections of this chapter are divided along these three broad domains. We first cover those methods useful for examining cognitive processes such as attention and review the empirical findings that are relevant for understanding both normative and clinical patterns of behavior in development. We then provide an overview of the methods used to examine the physiological organization of arousal and reactivity. The third section provides a review of those methods that may be useful for examining motivation, emotion, and emotion regulation in children. The literature discussed in each of the three broad domains illustrates how the application of psychophysiological methods has contributed to our current understandings of individual differences in developmental trajectories generally and developmental psychopathology in particular.

PHYSIOLOGICAL MEASURES OF COGNITIVE PROCESSING

In the psychophysiological literature there is often the implicit assumption of a dichotomy between cognition and emotion such that central nervous system measures are appropriate for the study of cognition and peripheral nervous system measures are suitable for studies of emotion (Keller, Hicks, & Miller, 2000). However, over the past 2 decades there has been a growing understanding of the interconnections between cognition and emotion in shaping both normative and disordered functioning and development. For example, recent research has suggested that individual biases to process or attend to negative threat information may play an important role in the development and maintenance of anxiety disorders in both children and adults (E. Fox, Russo, Bowles, & Dutton, 2001). In psychophysiology research, much of the work examining the relationship between cognition and emotion has relied on the ERP as a central methodological tool. This is due to the fact that these measures are very well suited to address questions of speed and efficiency of processing as well as perceptual sensitivity to variations in stimulus complexity. In addition, prepulse inhibition has been used to tap into basic cognitive processes and is therefore also explored in this section.

Event-Related Potentials

ERPs are currently the best noninvasive method for measuring the physiological manifestations of psychological processes within a small temporal window (Deldin,

Shestyuk, & Chiu, 2003; Fabiani, Gratton, & Coles, 2000). ERPs are able to supplement the broad neuropsychological and neuroanatomical correlates of psychopathology assessed through the use of EEG, positron emission tomography (PET), and magnetic resonance imaging (MRI) by providing a more direct link between physiology and discrete instances of information processing.

There are four basic questions that can be asked with ERP data (Rugg & Coles, 1995). First, do the waveforms differ across experimental groups as a function of stimuli characteristics? Second, when do these differences appear? This question can be answered by looking at the timing of the divergence point. Presumably, divergences in the waveform indicate when processing begins to differ across stimuli or conditions. Third, are the processes underlying performance evoked to a different degree? This question is answered by measuring any differences in amplitude across the waveform. Fourth, do the ERPs fit any standard pattern? Psychophysiologists look for standard components, and deviations from the standard waveform are often taken as signs of deviance, delay, or immaturity. For example, individuals normally produce a smaller P50 ERP component to the second of a pair of identical stimuli. Schizophrenic individuals do not show a reduced P50 to the second stimulus, suggesting poor sensory filtering (Light & Braff, 1998; D. A. Smith, Boutros, & Schwarzkopf, 1994). These data suggest that poor sensory gating may lead to the perceptual and attentional deficits seen in Schizophrenia by allowing irrelevant or distracting information to interfere with normal functioning (Braff & Geyer, 1990).

Aside from marking the general processing of a particular stimulus, ERPs are also sensitive to the particular meaning the stimulus holds for the individual. For example, given a presentation of positive, negative, and emotionally neutral stimuli, researchers can use the neutral stimuli as a baseline against which to compare the processing of the affectively charged stimuli. One could then see if an individual's phenotypic presentation of, for example, depression is linked to an overresponse to the presentation of negative stimuli or an underresponse when presented with positive stimuli. The temporal resolution of the ERP also makes it a useful tool in the study of psychopathology because the core phenomena of emotion and attention are brief and require fast resolution to accurately reflect timing and intensity (Davidson, 1994). It is this sensitivity that makes ERP-based research attractive to researchers interested in the psychological, as well as biological, components of psychopathology.

Methodology for Event-Related Potentials

ERPs are time-locked electrophysiological recordings timed to the presentation of a specific stimulus or class of stimuli (Coles & Rugg, 1995). The ERP for a particular condition or subset of the data is calculated by averaging over the EEG signals collected for each individual trial. The waveform produced is characterized by the size (amplitude) and timing (latency) of deflections in the wave. Increases in component amplitude and/or decreases in latency are taken as evidence that individuals are investing greater cognitive resources in processing the stimuli presented to them. Specific deflections or components are designated by their polarity (P = Positive; N = Negative) and either their order of appearance (e.g., N1, P1, N2) or their specific latency (e.g., N170, P360). For example, the P300 is a positive wave that occurs approximately 300 to 600 msec after stimulus onset and is maximal over central-parietal sites. The amplitude of the P300 is thought to vary with the task relevance and probability of a stimulus (R. Johnson, 1993) and marks the evaluation of stimulus significance. A detailed discussion of the methodology underlying ERP research can be found in Picton et al. (2000) and M. J. Taylor and Baldeweg (2002).

Although derived from a common electrocortical substrate, EEG and ERP measures appear to comment on different aspects of a particular behavior or process. For example, in their study of verbal and spatial working memory in adults, Gevins, Smith, McEvoy, and Yu (1997) found that changes in EEG were more likely tied to changes in the functional networks underlying task performance, whereas their ERP data were indexing the specific "operations being performed on internal representations" (p. 383). Along the same lines, Sobotka, Davidson, and Senulis (1992) found that EEG measures were more sensitive to incentive variations than were ERP measures.

There are a number of developmental changes that occur in the ERP through infancy and childhood (Cheour, Leppänen, & Kraus, 2000). First, the waveform becomes more complex and new components appear. For example, the Nc (negative component) generated by infants to stimuli will differentiate over time into an adult component (Richards, 2003). Second, ERP amplitudes appear to follow an inverted U shape as a function of age, perhaps reflecting greater processing demands and inefficiency during task performance (Ridderinkhof & van der Stelt, 2000). Third, ERP latencies grow progressively shorter, indicating an increase in processing speed (Thomas & Crow, 1994), perhaps due to more extensive myelination. Fourth, there are on occasion indications of a polarity shift in components over time (Novak, Ritter, Vaughan, & Wiznitzer, 1990). Finally, the localization of the component generator becomes more differentiated (M. J. Taylor & Baldeweg, 2002).

By far the most common use of the ERP has been to examine the physiological correlates of attentional processes.

This is true for both children and adults in healthy and clinical populations. Hillyard and Hansen (1986, p. 227) have suggested that the term attention "has become more of a chapter-heading word, encompassing a diverse set of processes and paradigms, than a precisely defined theoretical construct," but one cannot deny the central role attentional processes play in development. From birth, adaptive functioning is often dependent on the individual's ability to appropriately select those aspects of the environment that are of interest from among the constant and simultaneous presentation of competing stimuli. Ridderinkhof and van der Stelt (2000) argue that age-related improvements in this ability, particularly when under strong voluntary control, are one of the most profound advances in information processing that takes place in childhood. The advantage of the ERP paradigm is that it often forces the researcher to break down the larger construct of attention into its constituent parts in order to collect quantifiable data.

Traditionally, performance in attentional selection tasks is monitored via the speed and/or accuracy of an overt behavior in response to the information (e.g., stimulus identity or location) presented. For example, reaction times in response to cued and noncued visual targets have been compared as an indicator of the individual's ability to disengage and reorient attention (Posner & Cohen, 1984). As the various components in the standard ERP wave are thought to reflect different stages of processing, these data may help verify the mechanisms that shape overt behavior.

There are a number of standard paradigms in use for studying attention in both children and adults. Ridderinkhof and van der Stelt (2000) provide a very extensive review of attentional studies in developmental psychophysiology. As a result, the following discussion highlights only three types of tasks used in the field and the findings generated so far. Each discussion briefly notes the normative data in adults and children and then turns to findings with clinical and at-risk groups.

The first set of tasks is commonly labeled interference tasks. In this paradigm, participants are asked to overtly respond to information presented in one stimulus domain. Researchers look to see if performance is either hindered or facilitated by information in a second stimulus domain. The classic example of an interference or conflict task can be found in the Stroop (1935) paradigm. The traditional Stroop task presents individuals with a series of words and asks them to name the color in which the word is written, while disregarding the actual meaning of the word. Individuals are faster to respond when presented with congruent stimuli (the word RED in red ink) than when the stimuli are incongruent (the word RED in blue ink).

The earliest ERP study of the traditional Stroop task (Duncan-Johnson & Kopell, 1981) found no consistent differences across conditions. The researchers concluded that Stroop interference was related to conflicts in response selection rather than in the stimulus evaluation processes. However, more recent studies have indicated that there are detectible differences in ERPs generated by the traditional (color-word) Stroop (Ilan & Polich, 1999; Liotti, Woldroff, Pérez, & Mayberg, 2000; Schack, Chen, Mescha, & Witte, 1999; West & Alain, 1999). Early in the ERP wave, studies have found a distinct N1-P2-N2 complex (e.g., West & Alain, 2000b). These components are thought to index early sensory processing and low-level attention allocation (Hillyard, Luck, & Mangun, 1994). Traditional Stroop studies for the most part have not detected differences at this early stage across their two conditions: congruent versus noncongruent color words (however, see Atkinson, Drysdale, & Fulham, 2002). Rather, these studies have focused on more endogenous components, the P3 and N4 (e.g., Ilan & Polich, 1999). The larger amplitudes noted in the incongruent condition are thought to reflect the stimulus evaluation time and attentional requirements needed to ultimately suppress the information carried in the incongruent trials (West & Alain, 2000a). This interpretation also carries over to the positive slow wave prominently seen in traditional ERP studies (West & Alain, 2000b).

In the emotional Stroop, emotion words are substituted for the color words used in the traditional task. A number of emotional Stroop studies (Pérez-Edgar, 2001; Pérez-Edgar & Fox, 2003) have found that the general morphology of early ERP components (P1-N1-P2-N2) is roughly similar to those found in the traditional Stroop studies (e.g., West & Alain, 2000b). However, the later components (P3 and N4) were either attenuated or nonexistent. Overall, they indicate that there may be early processing differences across words of varying emotional valence, in line with data from other non-Stroop studies of emotion words (Shalev & Algom, 2000). A late slow wave also appears to distinguish between word categories. In particular, words conveying negative emotions seem to require or attract greater processing resources, as indexed by larger amplitudes and shorter component latencies (Hillyard et al., 1994; Schack et al., 1999).

The second major design, deviance detection tasks, requires participants to attend to the presence of a specific stimulus (the target) during the presentation of both target and nontarget stimuli. The most common deviance detection task is the oddball task. Prototypically, participants are asked to respond as quickly as possible to the presentation of a target that is embedded in a sequence of rare targets and frequent nontargets (Ridderinkhof & van der Stelt, 2000). One can also present a passive oddball design, during which no overt response is given. In fact, researchers often present participants with a book to read or video to watch in order to guarantee that they do not pay attention to the stimuli. This variant is used to examine the individual's bias in orienting to deviance or novelty and is quite useful to developmental researchers as no overt instructions need be given or followed.

Among adults, target detection in oddball tasks has been associated with increased P300, an enhanced N2, and a slow wave. The N2 is thought to reflect stimulus comparisons necessary for discriminating between the target and nontarget stimuli (Oades, Dittmann-Balcar, & Zerbin, 1997), and the slow wave may be associated with further elaboration of the target stimulus (Sutton & Ruchkin, 1984). Among individuals with Posttraumatic Stress Disorder (PTSD), oddball paradigms often produce attenuated P300s (Charles et al., 1995; MacFarlane, Weber, & Clark, 1993) and a delayed N200. McFarlane et al. suggested that the delayed latencies for the N200 reflect more time spent in stimulus discrimination, which allowed for fewer resources in later processing, as seen in the P300.

Subtracting the ERPs generated by the standard stimuli from the ERPs for the deviant stimuli produces a difference wave with a negative component that is maximal in frontal-central electrode sites and often peaks 200 msec poststimulus (Näätänen, 1990). This component, the mismatch negativity (MMN), is thought to reflect the mismatch between the current stimulus and the traces in short-term memory produced by the immediately preceding stimulus (Näätänen, 1992; for a review, see Cheour et al., 2000).

The developmental literature indicates that the MMN response can be seen very early, even in newborns (Kurtzberg, Vaughan, Kreuzer, & Flieger, 1995), although there is some controversy over the stability of amplitude (Kurtzberg et al., 1995; van der Stelt, Gunning, Snel, & Kok, 1997) and latency (A. H. Lang et al., 1995; van der Stelt et al., 1997) over time. One of the main reasons for the lack of consistency is due to the large inter- and intrasubject variability in young children (Kurtzberg et al., 1995). Studies focusing on the P3 (M. J. Taylor & Eals, 1996), N2 (Oades et al., 1997), and slow wave (Wijker, 1991) also indicate that the stimulus evaluation processes necessary for the task are present even in young children and that over time children make quantitative improvements in the efficiency of processing (i.e., shorter latencies and smaller amplitudes).

Reduced MMN amplitudes have been detected in individuals with depression (Ogura et al., 1993) and Schizophrenia (Catts et al., 1995; Javitt, Doneshka, Grochowski, & Ritter, 1995; Javitt, Grochowski, Shelley, & Ritter, 1998; O'Donnell et al., 1993). The degree of attenuation among schizophrenics was correlated with ratings of negative symptoms (such as social withdrawal) but not positive symptoms (e.g., hallucinations and delusions; Catts et al., 1995; Javitt, Shelley, & Ritter, 2000). In a study of social withdrawal in young children, Bar-Haim and colleagues (Bar-Haim, Marshall, Fox, Schorr, & Gordon-Salant, 2003) found that children who were withdrawn in a novel social situation had smaller MMN amplitudes and longer latencies than their more sociable counterparts. Combined with the adult clinical and personality findings, Bar-Haim et al. speculated that individuals with a tendency for social withdrawal may share a difficulty in the early stages of auditory processing, which in turn shapes their subjective perception of their environment. A similar mechanism of perceptual processing may be at play in Attention-Deficit/Hyperactivity Disorder (ADHD), which has also been linked to attenuated MMN amplitudes (Kemner et al., 1996).

In the third major set of tasks, attention is primed on a trial-by-trial basis by a cue stimulus that instructs the individual on the identity or location of the target stimulus to attend to. By varying the location or identity of the target and cue, the tasks require participants to repeatedly disengage, orient, and reengage attention. The assumption is that the presence of the cue will prime mechanisms of selective attention, ensuring that the target stimulus will receive preferential processing while the processing of alternative stimuli is suppressed (Posner & Cohen, 1984). Examples of these shifting tasks are often referred to as Posner cued-attention tasks, and they consistently produce a "validity effect" marked by faster reaction times when responding to stimuli that appear in a previously cued location (valid trials) versus stimuli that are not cued (invalid trials).

There are a growing number of studies using ERP measures to observe neural activity during the Posner cued-attention task and address the timing of attentional mechanisms triggered by the task. The data indicate that the presentation of the cue engages attention during early perceptual processing (Luck, Heinze, Mangun, & Hillyard, 1990). As such, early ERP components (e.g., P1 and N1) generated by stimuli preceded by valid cues have greater amplitudes than ERP components corresponding to stimuli that were invalidly cued. The findings are most pronounced for posterior electrode sites.

For example, Anllo-Vento (1991) presented 6- and 8-year-old children with a centrally located arrow cue. They found an enhanced negativity from 200 to 500 msec after

the presentation of the cue, which was maximal in the hemisphere contralateral to the cued visual field. This "early directing attention negativity" was thought to reflect the selective recruitment of processes associated with spatial attention orienting. The presentation of the target in the validly cued location produced enhanced N1 and P1 amplitudes, reflecting the modulation of sensory areas by attention. Similar results were found in a recent study of 7-year-old children using peripheral, and presumably more exogenous, visual cues (Pérez-Edgar & Fox, 2005). These data indicate that attentional priming mechanisms are largely in place in young children.

Event-Related Potentials in the Study of Developmental Psychopathology

As noted in the discussion of specific tasks, affective processes have increasingly been incorporated into ERP studies (e.g., Gunnar & Nelson, 1994), expanding our understanding of the neural processing of affective behavior. This in turn is shaping the way ERP studies are incorporated into studies of risk and psychopathology.

For example, recent work suggests that late components of the ERP may reflect the discrepant nature of stimuli undergoing cognitive or affective processing (Pauli et al., 1997). In particular, affective stimuli elicit larger P300s and late positive slow waves than neutral stimuli (Kostandov & Azumanov, 1977; Williamson, Harpur, & Hare, 1991). This effect is even more pronounced when the stimuli are tailored to individual subject concerns. For example, Pauli and colleagues found that panic patients showed larger P300s and positive slow waves to somatic words versus nonsomatic stimuli.

Similar effects have been found when generally content-neutral stimuli are given affective significance. For example, introverted subjects performing a lexical decision task (De Pascalis, Fiore, & Sparita, 1996), a stimulus detection task (De Pascalis, 1994), and a stimulus prediction task (Bartussek, Diedrich, Naumann, & Collet, 1993) did not differ from extraverted subjects when the task was affect-neutral. However, when the experimenter introduced competition, providing win/loss feedback after each trial or set of trials, differences emerged. More specifically, introverts showed larger peak amplitudes (particularly the N2, P3, and P6) to loss feedback and extraverts showed larger peak amplitudes to win feedback.

In the adult literature, ERPs have been used with greater frequency to explore the information-processing mechanisms thought to underlie various disorders. In the case of Major Depression, for example, ERPs have been used to study negative biases in attention and memory

(Deldin et al., 2003). Specifically, the data indicate that depressed individuals are more likely to attend to and later recall more negative information, relative to nondepressed controls (B. P. Bradley, Mogg, & Williams, 1995). This cognitive style has been implicated in both the etiology and the maintenance of depressive symptomatology (Williams, Watts, MacLeod, & Matthews, 1997). ERPs allow for an examination of the mechanisms that may fuel the observed biases. In one such study, Deveney and Deldin (2004) found that depressed individuals showed larger amplitudes in a late slow wave when presented with pictures of faces expressing negative emotions. The slow wave has been associated with either elaborative encoding or subsequent retrieval processes of memory (R. Johnson, 1995). In addition, Deveney and Deldin's findings were strongest in the left posterior region, an area associated with face processing in working memory. Taken together, the psychophysiological measure helps test and refine our understanding of previously collected behavioral data.

A representative example of recent work in the developmental psychopathology literature can be found in Pollak's work with maltreated children (Pollak, Cicchetti, Klorman, & Brumaghim, 1997; Pollak, Klorman, Thatcher, & Cicchetti, 2001). Maltreatment and abuse place children at an extremely high risk for psychopathology (Cicchetti & Toth, 1995), and one area of particular concern is emotional functioning. For example, maltreated children appear to have a bias toward negative emotions. In infancy they manifest negative emotional expressions earlier and more often than nonabused peers (Gaensbauer & Hiatt, 1984). Over time, they are primed to detect negative affect in the environment (Weiss, Dodge, Bates, & Pettit, 1992) and have difficulty interpreting and responding to potentially hostile gestures in others (Klimes-Dougan & Kistner, 1990). Maltreatment and abuse may selectively increase children's psychological sensibilities to specific emotional cues, such as an angry face (Pollak et al., 2001).

Pollak and colleagues (1997) found that the ERP responses of maltreated children when processing emotion faces were sensitive to the context and attentional demands of the task at hand. Children ages 7 to 11 were presented with photographs of a single individual posing with either a happy, angry, or neutral facial expression. In this study, maltreated children had smaller component amplitudes and slower reaction times than their nonmaltreated counterparts when responding to the emotion faces. When asked to specifically attend to the angry faces, the maltreated children showed an increase in amplitude over the happy face condition, whereas the other children showed an equivalent response. These data indicate that the emotion processing

need not be completely stimulus-driven, but may depend on the contextual importance of the stimulus and task at hand. Indeed, a follow-up study (Pollak et al., 2001) indicated that the effect was specific to angry faces, suggesting that maltreated children do not exhibit a global deficit in emotional information processing.

Future Directions in the Use of Event-Related Potentials

ERP measures have allowed researchers to examine the processing mechanisms that bridge the presentation of a stimulus with the observation of overt behavior. Indeed, the technology opens a window onto cognition even in the absence of behavior. In general, it appears that affective information can influence the topography of ERP components if the affective loading of the stimulus is high and the individual attends to stimulus meaning (Johnston & Wang, 1991; Williamson, Harpur, & Hare, 1991). The ERP has proven to be a robust, noninvasive measure amenable across a wide age range of uses, yet there are a number of considerations that should be kept in mind when collecting and interpreting such data.

First, a better understanding of the development of the ERP, independent of our interest in psychopathology, will be needed to make the best use of the methodology. One cannot presume that measures from children and adults are equivalent in structure or function. For example, many of the studies incorporating ERP measures into the study of emotion and emotional processing have used pictures of facial affect as the central stimulus (e.g., M. H. Johnson & Morton, 1991; Nelson, 1987; Pollak et al., 1997). These stimuli are relatively easy to produce, can be standardized and incorporated across a set of studies, and are in most cases appropriate for use across a wide developmental range. Indeed, ERP measures have been successfully used in studies with participants as young as 6 months (e.g., Nelson, 1994). Although the technology allows researchers to compare children and adults on identical measures generated via identical stimuli presented in the context of the same task, there are important developmental differences involving both the psychophysiological measures of interest themselves and the processing mechanisms they are thought to reflect.

The ERPs generated in children by the task at hand often do not correspond to those of adults. These age-related differences are more pronounced the younger the child. For example, as noted earlier, adults participating in an oddball paradigm display an enhanced N2 component to the presentation of the target stimulus approximately 200 msec after onset (Oades et al., 1997). Infants participating in similar procedures display a large negative component (morphologically similar to an adult slow wave) occurring approximately 400 to 800 msec after the stimulus. This component is known as the Nc because it is negative in polarity and maximal in central sites (Richards, 2003).

Even when dealing with older children, who often generate ERP waves that are morphologically comparable to those of adults, one cannot assume that visual similarity reflects an equal similarity in the psychological processes involved. This becomes evident when trying to compare the performance of children and adults across conditions of the same task. For example, Kestenbaum and Nelson (1992) presented 7-year-old children and adults with pictures of angry, happy, fearful, and surprised faces and asked them, across two conditions, to respond to either the happy or angry face. Adults in this study showed greater ERP (e.g., P300) amplitudes to the happy faces. The children, however, showed larger amplitudes for the angry faces. In addition, this finding held only when calculating the area scores for the component. When peak values were calculated there was no differentiation across valence. The method of analysis made no difference in the adult data.

Because ERPs are derived from raw EEG signals, the issues and concerns discussed in that section are also applicable here. For example, ERP component amplitude is sensitive to the overall power of the EEG signal. As a result, age-related changes in ERP amplitude to the presentation of a particular stimulus need not solely reflect developmental changes in the ability to process or derive meaning from that stimulus. Rather, it may be largely driven by maturational changes in the overall strength of the EEG signal. Group differences observed in the ERP may also similarly be rooted in variations in the underlying EEG substrate. For example, Lazzaro and colleagues (Lazzaro, Gordon, Whitmont, Meares, & Clarke, 2001) found that amplitude reductions in the P3 component of children with ADHD could be linked to prestimulus increases in theta wave activity.

As such, it is important that any age-related changes in the ERP can be traced to manipulations of the task or conditions at hand. If not, it is difficult to disentangle results from the general effects of brain maturation. For example, after reviewing a variety of deviance detection (oddball) studies focusing on the P300 and finding that age-related changes in topography were invariant across myriad stimulus and task demands, M. J. Taylor (1988) came to the somewhat controversial conclusion that the findings were due to the expression of brain maturation, not developmental changes in specific cognitive abilities.

Prepulse Inhibition

It has long been surmised that seemingly simple human reflexes do not function in isolation in the intact nervous system (Fearing, 1930). For instance, at the turn of the previous century, Bowditch and Warren (1890) documented that the human patellar (i.e., knee-jerk) reflex was substantially suppressed when subjects clinched their hands in response to a bell milliseconds before the knee was stimulated. Years later, Hilgard (1933) documented changes in the amplitude of the eyeblink (i.e., startle) reflex in response to the presentation of a loud, startle-evoking noise when a visual stimulus (i.e., flashing light) was presented prior to the auditory stimulus. Further, Hilgard found that temporal variation in the presentation of the visual stimuli served to differentially modify the acoustic startle response. These early studies mark the first evidence to suggest that reflexes, previously thought to be isolated functions of the central nervous system, are in fact modulated by psychophysiological processes (M. E. Dawson, Schell, & Böhmelt, 1999). Hence, measurement of the degree of modulation in the startle response permits exploration of psychological states on physiological responding.

Graham, Putnam, and Leavitt (1975) showed that the presentation of a nonstartling, neutral, "lead" probe (e.g., a series of tones) immediately prior to the startle probe yields an attenuation of the blink amplitude, a phenomenon referred to as prepulse inhibition, defined formally as "the normal suppression of the startle reflex when the intense startling stimulus is preceded 30 to 500 msec by a weak lead stimulus" (Swerdlow & Geyer, 1999, p. 115). The opposite pattern was documented for lead stimuli that were presented at longer (>1,400 msec) intervals, describing a phenomenon referred to as long-lead facilitation. Graham's findings regarding the inhibition or facilitation of startle relative to temporal variation in the presentation of lead stimuli has been well replicated and is a robust phenomenon in adults (Ornitz, 1999).

The neural circuitry involved in prepulse inhibition is regulated by forebrain and limbic structures that descend on the pallidum and pontine tegmentum. This top-down pathway is not direct and involves inputs to the striatum from the limbic cortex, striatal connections to the pallidum from the striatum, and inputs to the pontine tegmentum from the pallidum. Such top-down effects of higher-level processes on brain stem modulation of startle are related to early attention and sensory processing of input. The temporal variation in the presentation of the lead stimuli, relative to the experimental stimuli (i.e., affective; see discussion of affective modulation of startle later in chapter) and the startle probe, has been investigated and findings here mark an important contribution to understanding the role of attention and affect in startle modulation. In their review of this literature, M. M. Bradley, Cuthbert, and Lang (1999, pp. 167–169) have summarized these findings into six general conclusions:

> First, strong inhibitory effects are obtained when blink reflexes are elicited immediately after picture onset. Second, reflex inhibition is maximal 300 msec after picture onset, which is somewhat later than is typically found for simpler foreground stimuli. Third, at the point of maximum inhibition (300 msec), reflex inhibition is significantly larger for emotional pictures (pleasant or unpleasant), compared with neutral materials. Fourth, reflexes continued to be relatively inhibited, compared with responses elicited in the interpicture interval, for up to 3 s after picture presentation, at which time reflex magnitude appears to asymptote for all picture contents. . . . Fifth, by 500 msec after picture onset, reflexes are significantly augmented for unpleasant, compared with pleasant materials, suggesting that affective modulation has been initiated by this time. Affective modulation then continues throughout the picture-viewing interval. Sixth, no significant effects of affective valence are found for reflexes elicited after picture offset.

Bradley and her colleagues interpret such effects as the result of attentional mechanisms involved in the initial processing of the foreground stimulus. Essentially, the more interesting the prepulse stimulus is, the more resources are involved in the encoding of it. However, at the point at which encoding of the stimulus is complete (at approximately 500 msec), the affective quality of the stimulus has been perceived and the startle reflex will henceforth be modulated by the affective nature of that stimulus until the time when the stimulus is no longer presented.

According to Graham and colleagues (1975), prepulse inhibition is due to a "transient detecting reaction" that serves to suppress startle reactions temporarily to ensure that perceptual processing of the lead stimulus is complete. In this way, prepulse inhibition serves a protective function, inasmuch as attenuated startle reactions allow for increased allocation of cognitive resources to the stimulus encoding process. Thus, the individual differences in prepulse inhibition are of scientific interest in their own right, as variation in the degree to which the startle response of participants is modulated following the presentation of simple lead stimuli is thought to be an indicator of individual differences in attention and sensory processing as relevant to initial perceptual encoding of information at lower brain stem levels (Ornitz, Hanna, & Traversay, 1992).

Startle Methodology

The startle reflex is thought to be a primitive defensive response that may serve at least two purposes: (1) to avoid bodily injury, as in the function of the eyeblink; and (2) to halt ongoing activity and prepare the organism for fight or flight in the face of looming threat (P. J. Lang, 1995). Landis and Hunt (1939) were the first to provide a detailed depiction of the startle response in humans. These researchers used slow-motion video documentation to characterize the response that followed the presentation of a pistol shot. They reported that the startle response consists of a forward head thrust, descending flexor wave reaction, and the sudden closure of the eyes. It is the last of these responses that is used as the index of startle amplitude, as it has been shown to be the earliest, fastest, and most stable process involved in the startle response (P. J. Lang, Bradley, & Cuthbert, 1992). There is considerable variability in the degree of amplitude of the startle reflex related to attention and affective processes. This variability in amplitude is used as an index of an organism's underlying emotional state. Researchers interested in the affective modulation of the startle reflex tend to rely also on additional psychophysiological indices of emotional reactivity and attention, including heart rate, blood pressure, skin conductance, ERPs, and facial electromyographic responses. These are also incorporated into the protocol to confirm that the appropriate/desired level of affective arousal has been achieved by the emotional stimulus (M. M. Bradley et al., 1999).

The eyeblink startle reflex is measured with electromyogram (EMG) by placing two electrodes under one eye. The EMG waveforms are rectified and integrated (see van Boxtel, Boelhouwer, & Bos, 1998, for a full review) and scored for degree of amplitude in the EMG response. Onset of the eyeblink reflex is triggered most often with the presentation of brief, high-intensity white noise for baseline startle and during the presentation of experimental stimuli. Experimental stimuli have ranged from visual stimuli such as pleasant or unpleasant pictures or videos (M. M. Bradley & Lang, 2000; Cuthbert, Bradley, & Lang, 1996; P. J. Lang, Bradley, & Cuthbert, 1990), administration of shocks (Hamm & Stark, 1993), use of air blasts administered to the neck (Grillon & Ameli, 1998), and manipulation of levels of light and darkness (Grillon, Morgan, Davis, & Southwick, 1998; Walker & Davis, 1997). According to Grillon and Baas (2003), the method used to assess the degree of change in startle amplitude between the control and experimental conditions has major implications for the results of a study and should be based on knowledge of the particular underlying system being assessed. The startle paradigm is ideal for use with infants and young children as well as adults and the elderly. However, choice of emotional stimuli used for experimental conditions must be appropriate for the particular age group targeted in the study (Grillon & Baas, 2003).

Prepulse Inhibition and the Study of Developmental Psychopathology

The literature exploring the role of attention in the modulation of the startle reflex in infants and children provides preliminary evidence for a meaningful developmental trend in the degree to which variable lead intervals affect startle responses. In his review of this literature, Ornitz (1999) concludes that there is little evidence for the presence of prepulse inhibition prior to the age of 8 years. For instance, there is a 25% response inhibition in 2- to 6-month-olds, 23% inhibition in 3-year-olds, and 30% inhibition in 5-year-old boys (Ornitz, Guthrie, Kaplan, Lane, & Norman, 1986). After age 8, however, adult-like levels of prepulse inhibition are evident. This effect is consistent with the notion that prior to the middle of childhood, young children lack impressive degrees of inhibitory control. This notion regarding inhibitory control is further supported by data that have revealed peaks in the degree of long lead stimulus startle facilitation in 3-year-olds relative to adults and children older than 8 (Ornitz et al., 1986). Ornitz suggests that these findings provide preliminary evidence that the brain stem mechanisms that mediate startle response modulation are developing during childhood and are not fully mature until approximately age 8. Such a conclusion is indeed tentative at best, as no replication of Ornitz's developmental findings yet exists. The notion that these patterns of findings are due to the increase in the development of inhibitory control across the preoperational to concrete operational years is certainly plausible. One important contribution to this area will be the examination of attentional modulation of startle in children between ages 3 and 8, during the transition from preschool to middle childhood.

To date, there are only a few published studies that have examined the role of startle modulation in childhood psychopathology. Two are investigations of attentional modulation of startle undertaken by Ornitz and his colleagues. In the earliest of these works, Ornitz and Pynoos (1989) examined startle modulation based on variable lead intervals, on the premise that the exaggerated startle pattern manifested by individuals with PTSD would yield atypical patterns in attentional modulation of startle assessed in the laboratory. They anticipated that children with PTSD would show a reduction in prepulse inhibition and enhanced startle facilitation due to longer lead inter-

vals. Ornitz and Pynoos assessed their small sample of children with PTSD and a normative sample of nonmatched controls multiple times across 2 years (six of the children in the study had onset of PTSD following a sniper attack at their school playground and a seventh child in the study witnessed the murder of his father). The children with PTSD showed less startle inhibition with prestimulation relative to controls. Close examination of the case that witnessed murder revealed that the reduced prepulse inhibition was quite variable across the 2 years following the incident, with the most pronounced effects emerging at assessments closest temporally to the traumatic event. The authors concluded that the lack of prepulse inhibition of the PTSD group relative to normal controls might indicate a slowing in the normal development of the brain stem mediated function due to severe stress. Additionally, although marked by many limitations, including the lack of a matched control sample and a small sample size, this study provides preliminary evidence to suggest that the deviant startle pattern in children with PTSD is most pronounced at temporal points closest to the traumatic incident and may ameliorate over time.

In another study of childhood psychopathology and startle modulation, Ornitz and his group (Ornitz et al., 1992) examined differences in prepulse inhibition and long-lead facilitation of startle in boys ages 6 to 11 diagnosed with ADHD, primary nocturnal enuresis, and the comorbid condition (i.e., both ADHD and enuresis) relative to normal peers. In their clinical sample, a high degree of comorbidity between nocturnal enuresis and ADHD was found (with enuresis occurring in some 30% of boys with ADHD). Hence, Ornitz and his colleagues explored the extent to which previously documented (Anthony, 1990) startle abnormalities in children with ADHD are more closely related to the attention deficit primary to their condition or to the physiological immaturity associated with nocturnal enuresis. The findings of this study are indeed quite telling, for although no ADHD effects were noted, all enuretic boys (i.e., children with both primary and secondary nocturnal enuresis) showed immature patterns of prepulse inhibition and long-lead facilitation that were comparable to levels found in 5-year-old children. The authors interpreted these findings as providing evidence for underdeveloped mesopontine reticular mechanisms, which serve to mitigate the lower-level processing of the signals associated with urinary continence. During sleep, appropriate functioning of the inhibitory functions involved in urinary continence are dependent on the modulation of sensory input to indicate bladder fullness by the spinal reflex activity of the pontine micturition center. This pathway may be anatomically and functionally related to the pathways involved in startle modulation, inasmuch as the processing of sensory information relevant to startle is modulated by an inhibitory pathway that parallels the inhibitory pathway in the mesopontine lateral tegmental area associated with the processing of sensory signals from the bladder. Hence, "primary nocturnal enuresis can be considered a disorder of early sensory processing, that is, a dysfunction of subcortical preattentive mechanisms" (p. 447).

Such a finding marks an important contribution to current understandings of developmental psychophysiology on several grounds. First, a good deal of research has sought to understand the neurophysiological nature of nocturnal enuresis with little resolution. For instance, as Ornitz and his colleagues indicate, deviant sleep patterns, arousal mechanisms, and bladder functions have been implicated as the source of nocturnal enuresis, and each of these literatures has been met with mixed results. The findings involving startle modulation offer new and exciting directions for understanding the nature of primary nocturnal enuresis as a deficit in early sensory processing. The lack of effect for the boys with ADHD suggests that ADHD is perhaps less related to lower-level preattentive mechanisms than it is to higher-level processing, such as executive functions located in the prefrontal cortex.

Future Directions in the Use of Prepulse Inhibition

The use of the startle methodology to the field of developmental psychopathology, although still very much in its infancy, holds promise. Studies of the temporal variation of lead intervals provide windows onto the role of the most basic processes, including that of early preattentive sensory processing, on pathological development. Ornitz's work (Ornitz et al., 1992; Ornitz & Pynoos, 1989) has demonstrated that central nervous system immaturity associated with basic processing is associated with childhood-onset PTSD and primary nocturnal enuresis, and not ADHD. Indeed, issues of sensory gating are relevant to many psychopathological conditions, particularly Schizophrenia and conditions of anxiety, learning disabilities, mental retardation, and Pervasive Developmental Disorders. It is especially important to note that the prepulse inhibition paradigm is ideal for use with such compromised populations, as the laboratory paradigm places no burden on the participant to read or socially interact with an experimenter. As such, the prepulse inhibition methodology can meaningfully be applied to special populations of children, and its use should yield great strides in uncovering

the aberrant sensory processing associated with a diversity of psychopathological conditions.

MEASURES OF PHYSIOLOGICAL AROUSAL

Although variations in psychopathology differ in etiology, developmental course, disruptiveness, and amenability to treatment, they are thought to share some core characteristics. Chief among these is the notion that children diagnosed with or at risk for psychopathology have a difficult time adjusting and adapting to the shifting demands of their environment. A good deal of work in developmental psychopathology has focused on individual differences in the preparedness of the system to react or respond to psychological challenge. Related to this are differences in level of reactivity to threatening stimuli and in the subsequent regulation of fight/flight responses. Measures covered in this section include measures of autonomic arousal, including heart rate, preejection period, electrodermal activity, and vagal tone, as well as additional measures of physiological arousal, namely, cortisol and EEG power.

Walter Cannon (1915) offered the earliest account of the functional significance of the autonomic nervous system (ANS). According to Cannon, the ANS served to keep the organism in a state of homeostasis, with two separate branches of the ANS (sympathetic and parasympathetic) serving in reciprocal harmony. The ANS is of interest to psychopathological processes because it plays a central role in mitigating somatic responses that are associated with perceived environmental threat (Boyce et al., 2001).

In a classic paper on the relationship between somatic and psychological processes, Cannon (1928) reported associations between negative affect and heart rate, hypertension, the digestive system, the menstrual cycle, thyroid function, and the immune system. ANS reactivity has been found to correlate with behavioral inhibition in infants and young children (N. A. Fox, 1989), internalizing and externalizing psychopathology in middle childhood (Raine, 2002), and ADHD and Conduct Disorder in adolescents (Beauchaine, Katkin, Strassburg, & Snarr, 2001).

This portion of the chapter first discusses the measurement of sympathetic activation and includes discussion of measures of heart rate via electrocardiogram (ECG), preejection period, and electrodermal activity. Measurement of the activation of the parasympathetic branch of the ANS is discussed next, followed by a review of the findings regarding autonomic reactivity and the development of psychopathology.

Measures of Sympathetic Activity and Reactivity

The sympathetic branch of the ANS prepares the body for the release of energy and is activated during fear-eliciting situations. Activation of this branch yields an increase in blood circulation to the muscles vis-à-vis increases in heart rate and force of heartbeats (Ohman, Hamm, & Hugdahl, 2000). Sweat glands also respond during activation of the sympathetic branch, such that increases in perceived threat result in filling of eccrine sweat glands. Psychologically, sympathetic autonomic reactivity is of interest to psychophysiologists because of its relationship to the activation of the approach-withdrawal system, the motivational system implicated in individual differences in arousal (Fowles, 1980).

Heart Rate

According to Fowles (1980), heart rate is a sympathetic manifestation of Gray's (1975) behavioral activation system (BAS). In his landmark theoretical paper, Fowles points to the abundant body of early empirical evidence that found associations between heart rate acceleration and behavioral activation when level of somatic activity is controlled (e.g., Belanger & Feldman, 1962; Ehrlich & Malmo, 1967). According to Gray, the BAS also mitigates behavioral response patterns of active avoidance. Fowles cites additional work, such as that of Obrist (1976, as cited by Fowles, 1980), that found heart rate accelerations during conditions in which participants were able to actively avoid shocks based on successful task performance. In Fowles' own words, "The BAS represents a central control system which responds to incentives and whose activity is reflected in increased HR [heart rate]" (p. 92). It is important to note, however, that simple estimates of heart rate are by no means uncontaminated estimates of sympathetic functioning, as patterns of heart rate acceleration and deceleration are associated with both somatic activity (Fowles, 1980) and respiration (Porges, McCabe, & Yongue, 1982). Hence, heart rate is an index of activation of the BAS (either in the form of reward seeking or active avoidance of punishment) when degree of somatic activity and respiration are controlled.

ECG is a psychophysiological measure that involves recording the electrical potentials of the heart during each cardiac cycle (Papillo & Shapiro, 1990). Heart rate is perhaps the most salient and easily observable manifestation of sympathetic ANS arousal. The large bioelectrical signals generated by the heart are recorded from placement of electrodes on the body's surface. Although as many as 12 leads can be tactically placed on the limbs and chest to di-

agnose irregularities of the heart, psychophysiologists are typically interested in heart rate alone, which can be reliably recorded from as few as two electrode sites. Positioning of the ECG electrodes is not a critical consideration in ECG setup, as the large electrical signals can be recorded from almost any site in the general region of the heart. Although it is not within the scope of this chapter to provide a depth of knowledge about ECG indices (see Papillo & Shapiro, 1990), guidelines for those interested in psychophysiological research can be found in Jennings (1981).

There are two indices determined by ECG that warrant mention. The first is simple heart rate, which is determined by the number of beats per some prespecified unit of time, typically 1 minnte. Heart period, or the interbeat interval, is the elapsed time between two successive heart cycles and is usually determined online by a computer. The decision of which index is most appropriate depends on a number of considerations, including whether the research questions involve analysis of individual or group differences, if the participants are infants or adults, and whether raw scores or change scores are desired (Graham, 1978; Graham & Jackson, 1970; Jennings, Stringfellow, & Graham, 1974).

Systolic Time Intervals

More recent work in autonomic reactivity has relied on the use of measurement of the systolic time interval as an estimate of autonomic reactivity. Measurement of the preejection period (PEP) is one such estimate and is defined operationally as the temporal latency between the onset of isovolumetric contraction (i.e., ventricular depolarization) and the onset of left ventricular ejection (Sherwood, 1993; Uchino, Cacioppo, Malarkey, & Glaser, 1995). The PEP is obtained by collecting both ECG and an impedance signal of thoracic blood flow, such that PEP equals the temporal interval from the Q wave on ECG to the B point on the dZ/dt signal. Shorter intervals indicate greater sympathetic activation. The PEP of the cardiac cycle is a sensitive measure of sympathetic tone that is free of parasympathetic influence inasmuch as the ventricular myocardium is innervated almost exclusively by the sympathetic nervous system (Cacioppo, Uchino, & Bernston, 1994).

Electrodermal Activity

Another method for gauging activation of the sympathetic ANS involves the measurement of electrodermal activity (EDA). Before the turn of the previous century, Vigouroux (1879, as cited by M. E. Dawson, Schell, & Filion, 2000) began using degree of tonic skin resistance as a clinical diagnostic tool. Fere (1888, as cited by M. E. Dawson et al.,

2000), extending Vigouroux's work, revealed that skin resistance could be measured by passing a small electrical current between two electrodes placed on the skin. Contemporary psychophysiological researchers are still quite interested in the degree of skin resistance—often conceptualized as its opposite, skin conductance—that is elicited following the passage of an electrical current between two electrodes placed on the skin.

EDA is the result of activity of eccrine sweat glands found on the surface of the body and largely concentrated in the hands and feet. The eccrine glands are responsible for regulation of skin temperature, although the glands located on the hands and feet are also thought to play a role in grasping and are more reactive to emotional versus thermal stimuli then are eccrine glands located on other skin surfaces. The relationship between sweat gland and electrical activity is such that, as the sympathetic ANS is activated, sweat fills sweat ducts on the surface of the skin and electrical conduction is increased (M. E. Dawson et al., 2000). Eccrine sweat gland activity is controlled by cholinergic innervation from fibers that originate in the sympathetic system. Hence, unlike cardiac functioning, EDA receives no parasympathetic input (Fowles, 1980).

Functionally, EDA is thought to reflect activation of the behavioral inhibition system (BIS; Fowles, 1980; Gray, 1975). In his synthesis of the EDA literature, Fowles called on studies such as Elliott's (1969) study of autonomic arousal and Stroop performance and Haywood's (1963) work in autonomic reactivity and delay of auditory feedback to illustrate the utility of EDA as a measure of the BIS, as these studies revealed that autonomic reactivity was manifest by EDA (but not heart rate) during conditions of nonreward. Fowles cautions, however, that EDA's index of activation of the BIS is confounded by degree of cognitive activity (e.g., orienting, itself mediated by the BIS) involved in the laboratory paradigm (Szpiler & Epstein, 1976), frequency of response required by a task (with frequent responding yielding nonspecific EDA patterns; Schneider & Fowles, 1978), and degree of hydration of the skin (Bundy & Mangan, 1979). However, with careful experimental control, Fowles has suggested that EDA can be used to assess degree of emotional arousal stemming from activation of the BIS.

Measures of Parasympathetic Activity and Reactivity

The parasympathetic branch of the ANS serves a catabolic, energy-restoring function (Ohman et al., 2000). Activities supported by the parasympathetic branch include gastric and intestinal motility, secretion of digestive juices, salivation, and increased blood flow to the gastrointestinal tract. Cells of the parasympathetic branch are located in the nuclei of the cranial nerves (3, 7, 9, and 10) and in the sacral region of the spinal cord. Focus on this division of the ANS has been centered on the role of the vagus, the cranial nerve that regulates deceleratory parasympathetic activity (Beauchaine, 2001) and hence mediates patterns of cardiac reactivity during periods of orienting and fight/flight responding. Historically, interest in the parasympathetic branch of the ANS was based on the notion that it worked with the sympathetic branch in a symbiotic fashion such that each were separate, antagonistically related components of one unitary system. However, evidence offered by Porges (1995) indicates that the parasympathetic system is more complex than previously thought.

Heart Rate Variability (Vagal Tone)

Quantification of heart rate variability is used as an index of parasympathetic functioning, or vagal tone. The vagus itself contains both afferent and efferent fibers that play a role in cardiac functioning. Efferent vagal fibers from the brain stem extend to the sonoatrial (SA) node. Activation of these inhibitory fibers yields a decrease in SA firing, which yields a general attenuation in heart rate. Afferent fibers, originating in the heart, extend to the nucleus tractus solitarius and provide feedback to the brain that ultimately serves to regulate generalized cardiac functioning. Vagal tone, or RSA, is the result of vagal efference occurring during exhalation (slowing the heart) and of vagal efference during inhalation (increasing heart rate). Because the sympathetic regulation of the heart via acceleratory sympathetic projections to the SA node confound simple estimates of heart rate, neither heart rate nor heart period alone can serve as an uncontaminated index of RSA.

The simplest methods for gauging RSA rely on the range, variance, or standard deviation of the cardiac interbeat interval. The peak-to-trough method proposed by Fouad, Tarazi, Ferrario, Fighaly, and Alicandri (1984) involves the monitoring of both interbeat interval and respiration and is the mathematical difference between the longest interbeat interval corresponding to expiration and the shortest interbeat interval corresponding to inspiration. Porges (1986) recommended using spectral analysis to isolate the portion of variance within the interbeat interval that is due to RSA from that which is due to heart rate.

The functional significance of the RSA is provided by Porges's (1995) polyvagal theory. Porges argued that the vagal system is controlled by two very distinct motor systems, each of which has different evolutionary origins and locations. One system originates in the dorsal motor nucleus, is phylogenetically older, and is termed the *vegetative vagus*. This system is associated with reflexive regulation of primitive functions, including the deceleration of heart rate during states of attentiveness and primitive behavioral freezing in the face of perceived threat. The other motor system is purely mammalian, originates in the nucleus ambiguous, and is called the *smart vagus* because it is associated with attention and orienting responses. In the face of impending threat, higher-order mammals must first orient and then either become engaged or enter into a fight-or-flight behavioral pattern. Engagement is associated with vagal withdrawal, and the emotional reaction triggered by a fight/flight response system is associated with a nearly complete vagal suppression, or "vagal break," which is accompanied by sympathetic heart rate acceleration. As such, cardiac reactivity postorientation, during engagement of the fight/flight system, is mediated by the activation of the smart vagus. The vegetative vagus, in contrast, mediates heart rate deceleration during orienting behavior (Porges, 1995).

As Beauchaine cautions (2001), the functional significance of RSA is by no means clear-cut and is largely dependent on the context in which RSA data are collected. According to his review, RSA reflects generalized temperamental reactivity and emotionality when it is obtained during quiescent states, such that high-RSA infants are more likely to be extremely emotionally reactive (i.e., either affectively negative or positive in response) than infants who have lower levels of RSA (N. A. Fox, 1989; Stifter & Fox, 1990; Stifter, Fox, & Porges, 1986). In contrast, when RSA is obtained during specific environmental demands, the measure will reflect the manifestation of either attentional focus *or* emotion regulation. For example, in a sample of boys ages 5 to 9 years, Weber, van der Molen, and Molenaar (1994) found that RSA decreased significantly from baseline during an attention-demanding task. Indeed, Beauchaine argues that there is ample consistency in the infant, childhood, and adult literature to conclude that periods of cognitive engagement result in partial vagal withdrawal.

The literature exploring emotional reactivity to specific emotionally charged events is less clear. Calkins and Fox (1997) reported RSA reduction from baseline in preschoolers during the presentation of *both* affectively positive and negative events. Beauchaine (2001) suggests that although moderate degrees of vagal withdrawal are associated with adaptive responses to danger, excessive vagal withdrawal is associated with emotional lability, or dysregulation, and is therefore an important index of psychopathology, particu-

larly when parasympathetic reactivity is supplemented with measures of sympathetic reactivity such as EDA and heart rate, which can then serve to help specify whether or not activation involves Gray's (1975) BAS or BIS.

Autonomic Reactivity and Developmental Psychopathology

Most substantive work in the area of autonomic reactivity and childhood psychopathology has emphasized the rol of the BIS, BAS, and, more recently, the parasympathetic regulatory system in the childhood onset of aggression and impulsivity (Beauchaine et al., 2001; Boyce et al., 2001; Harden & Pihl, 1995; Herpertz et al., 2003; Raine, 2002). For instance, the application of both sympathetic and parasympathetic measures of reactivity to childhood externalizing disorders has yielded great strides in the disentanglement of the distinctive etiological underpinnings of ADHD and Conduct Disorder (Beauchaine et al., 2001). More general studies of childhood psychopathology have revealed distinctive patterns of autonomic reactivity associated with internalizing versus externalizing conditions.

Boyce and his colleagues (2001) conducted a cross-sectional investigation of autonomic reactivity, including measures of sympathetic and parasympathetic responding and psychopathology, in a sample of 6- and 7-year-olds. Included in their reactivity protocol were indices of heart rate, RSA, and PEP. Autonomic reactivity measures were obtained at baseline and across various challenging contexts, including a structured interview, a digit span task, placement of lemon juice on the tongue, and during the showing of two emotion videos designed to evoke fear and sadness. Children were divided into four symptom groups: children with low symptoms on both internalizing and externalizing, high internalizing children, high externalizing children, and children who scored high on both externalizing and internalizing disorders.

Results revealed that children who scored high on internalizing problems showed significantly more parasympathetic reactivity (low RSA). Children who scored high on externalizing manifested lower degrees of parasympathetic and sympathetic reactivity than children in the low symptom group. Subsequent analyses examining the discriminant validity of the autonomic profiles of the sample revealed that children with high internalizing problems could be significantly discriminated from children in the low symptoms group based on a profile of high parasympathetic reactivity during challenge tasks and recovery from those tasks. Externalizing children, in contrast, were significantly discriminated from the other three groups based on a profile that reflected a generalized (i.e., non-task-specific) pattern of low sympathetic and parasympathetic reactivity. Children in the high internalizing/externalizing group showed lower generalized sympathetic reactivity only. Child gender and patterns of autonomic reactivity were also explored in this study, and no evidence of main or moderating effects were found. Hence, results of this study are indicative of differential degrees of reactivity that are specific to each of the broadband classifications of childhood pathology. High internalizers in Boyce's study showed dysregulation in fight/flight responding during and after challenging paradigms, providing evidence that the underlying substrate of childhood anxiety and depression is related to the perception of environmental threat. In contrast are externalizers, who manifest a generalized pattern of autonomic underarousal that does not seem to be linked to any specific event. Such children manifested global dysregulation in the fight/flight system and abnormal levels of reactivity related to BAS functioning.

In a similar study, Harden and Pihl (1995) found that boys who were classified as high on internalizing and externalizing behavior problems evidenced an ANS profile of hyperreactivity when compared to children with no behavior problems or problems of only the externalizing variety. In their sample of 51 10-year-old boys, ANS reactivity was gauged with EMG, finger pulse amplitude, and interbeat interval of the cardiac cycle during a laboratory paradigm in which the children were rewarded for correct responses to a series of challenging arithmetic questions (the Arithmetic Stress Task, adapted from Carroll, Turner, & Hellawell, 1986). Results of the test of group differences across the psychophysiological indices revealed that boys who were both disruptive and anxious manifested significantly higher degrees of sympathetic reactivity than either the disruptive group or the controls, and the group of boys who had histories of disruptive behavior without anxiety manifested sympathetic underarousal as indexed by low levels of EDA during the cognitive stress task.

Indeed, there is an ample body of evidence to suggest that global ANS underarousal may constitute an early marker for subsequent antisocial behavior in adulthood. In a recent review, Raine (2002, p. 417) suggests that low resting heart rate "is the best-replicated biological correlate of antisocial and aggressive behavior in children." In his meta-analysis of 29 studies that examined resting heart rate and antisocial behavior in children and adolescents, the combined effect size was robust ($r = .56$), was equal in strength for both males and females, and was found across various types of measurement and in data collected across multiple countries (Raine, 1996). Raine (2002) also suggests that heart rate findings are particularly diagnostically signifi-

cant (when compared to other ANS measures), inasmuch as no other psychopathological condition is associated with low heart rate. ANS underarousal when assessed by heart rate also appears to be a strong biological marker for the condition, as it has been found to contribute *unique variance* to childhood violence beyond the effects of contextual factors such as family risk and *interacts* with psychosocial risk factors. For instance, Farrington (1997) showed that the joint effect of low resting heart rate and a poor parent-child relationship placed boys at the most risk for becoming violent offenders in adulthood. According to Raine (2002), the heart rate findings in children at risk for the development of antisocial behavior holds much promise for the advancement of current understandings regarding etiological contributions to the disorder as well as psychopharmacological treatment of violent behavior in childhood.

Recent work to uncover the ANS correlates of childhood externalizing behaviors has turned to the role of the parasympathetic branch (Beauchaine et al., 2001; Herpetz et al., 2003; Pine, Wasserman, & Coplan, 1996). In their study of aggressive behavior in children, Pine and his colleagues showed that childhood aggression was associated with increased parasympathetic reactivity, as manifest by reduced levels of vagal tone. Beauchaine and his colleagues have extended the literature in ANS reactivity and conditions of externalizing by examining the sympathetic and parasympathetic reactivity profiles of adolescent boys with ADHD with and without the comorbid condition of Conduct Disorder (CD) and normal controls. Differentiation between these two conditions is of particular relevance to understanding the ANS underpinnings of childhood aggression, as both groups are characterized by disinhibition, with aggression and antisocial behavior unique to only one group. Results of this study revealed that both clinical groups manifested less BIS activity (i.e., lower levels of EDA) relative to normal controls. Further, children with CD and ADHD showed reduced BAS activity (i.e., lengthened PEPs) relative to normal controls and children with only ADHD. Finally, children with comorbid ADHD/CD exhibited parasympathetic hyperreactivity, as evidenced by low vagal tone. Hence, results of this important study show that although BIS dysfunction is common among both groups of externalizers, reduced regulatory control in fight/flight responding and sympathetic underarousal is specific to the more aggressive, antisocial children with CD.

Herpertz and his colleagues (2003) conducted a similar study of externalizing disorder and ANS reactivity. Their study included children with an exclusive ADHD diagnosis, the comorbid ADHD/CD condition, and a group of children with an exclusive CD diagnosis, the inclusion of which permitted the drawing of more definitive conclusions as to whether CD by itself is associated with autonomic dysregulation. Results of this study revealed that low resting heart rate was exclusive to the two groups of CD children, confirming Raine's (2002) contention that poorly regulated BAS activity is specific to children with aggressive and/or antisocial tendencies.

Future Directions in the Use of Autonomic Nervous System Measures

As indicated by Raine (2002), examination of ANS reactivity has led to great strides in understanding the physiological nature of childhood aggression. However, the work in this area to date is far from exhaustive for externalizing or internalizing behavior problems. For instance, Beauchaine and his colleagues (2001) have indicated that although findings regarding parasympathetic dysregulation in aggressive and antisocial behavior are promising, additional work in RSA has revealed similar patterns of dysfunction in anxiety disorders, suggesting that parasympathetic reactivity is a generalized, nonspecific marker of emotion dysregulation.

It is somewhat paradoxical that although autonomic arousal is the psychophysiological measure with the longest history, it has perhaps contributed the least to current understandings of normative and aberrant psychological development. Future work would do well to emphasize the differential role of sympathetic and parasympathetic reactivity to childhood psychopathology, as dysregulation accompanied by distinctive BIS-BAS profiles seems to underscore problems of internalizing and externalizing behaviors.

Cortisol

Beginning in the 1930s (Lovallo & Thomas, 2000), researchers have focused on the LHPA system as a central regulator of the body's metabolic stress response. The LHPA system is central to normal daily functioning in that it allows the organism to respond to external events, both positive and negative, active and sedate, while still maintaining overall functioning within the relatively narrow confines of healthy adaptation. The LHPA system is most often studied via its main glucocorticoid, cortisol (Lovallo & Thomas, 2000).

Cortisol acts as an allostatic regulator (McEwen & Lasley, 2003; McEwen & Wingfield, 2003). That is, cortisol acts to maintain physiological systems in working balance (allostasis) as they react to normal changes in functioning. This is in contrast to homeostatic regulators, which strive to bring the individual to a set point of functioning (Bauer et al., 2002). Cortisol fine-tunes multiple physiological systems to meet continual changes in both the external and internal environments. Its impact is wide-ranging and is not simply tied to moments of high stress, as would normally be defined for research in psychopathology. For example, exercise will increase cortisol secretion if its duration challenges metabolic and cardiovascular expenditures (Sung, Lovallo, Pincomb, & Wilson, 1990).

As a daily regulator, cortisol is marked by a stable diurnal rhythm of secretion. The diurnal cycle is marked by peak cortisol levels in the early morning hours that then bottom out in the midafternoon. The magnitude of this cycle is quite extreme, such that there is often a 10-fold difference in cortisol levels between the peak and the trough (Goodyer, Park, Netherton, & Herbert, 2001). This pattern suggests that LHPA activity is providing the "wake-up energy" needed to transition from a sleep state to the active events of the day (Erickson, Drevets, & Schulkin, 2003).

The allostatic load of an environment is tied to the frequency, intensity, and predictability of the demands placed on the individual. Prolonged functioning under high allostatic load can lead to alterations in central regulatory mechanisms in terms of both daily functioning and in response to acute stressors (Johnston-Brooks, Lewis, Evans, & Whalen, 1998). This dysregulation, which is itself a form of allostatic load, may act as a causal mechanism for both psychological disorders and their behavioral precursors (Bauer et al., 2002). The impact of this type of disturbance may be particularly high in childhood given that early exposure to stress may produce lifelong effects on neuroendocrine function that may be behaviorally transmitted to future generations (McEwen, 1999).

Cortisol Methodology

In the literature, LHPA activity in children has been assessed through the use of serum cortisol, urinary cortisol (Kruesi, Schmidt, Donnelly, Hibbs, & Hamburger, 1989; Tennes & Kreye, 1985), adrenocorticotropin hormone (ACTH), and, most commonly, salivary cortisol (Schmidt, Fox, Sternberg, et al., 1999; Schmidt et al., 1997). Unlike more cumulative measures of LHPA functioning, salivary cortisol is sensitive to variations in cortisol levels throughout the day (Bauer et al., 2002). It is highly correlated with cortisol levels in the blood and cerebral spinal fluid, and, unlike with serum cortisol, collecting salivary cortisol is a benign, noninvasive process that can be used with relative ease across a wide age range. Most studies have asked children to either deposit saliva directly into a small container or have had children chew on a dry piece of cotton soaked in a sugary substance. The sample is then squeezed out of the cotton into a container for assaying.

Given that collection is relatively simple, researchers have the luxury of collecting multiple samples both within and across a period of time. Depending on the exact parameters of the study, researchers are then faced with a choice of how best to summarize and quantify LHPA activity. For example, a review of the literature indicates that studies have employed a variety of measures, including basal level, median level, daily range, reactivity to stress, pulse amplitude, and frequency. These measures capture different facets of the LHPA system's dual role: regulation and reactivity.

Each particular measure provides very different views into the relationships between the LHPA axis, behavior, and affect (Gunnar & Donzella, 2002; Tout, de Haan, Kipp-Campbell, & Gunnar, 1998). For example, Schmidt et al. (1997) found a significant positive correlation between temperamental withdrawal and basal cortisol levels. However, there were no group differences when comparing the same children after a series of startle probes. Findings such as these reflect the fact that different measures are linked to different patterns of neural activity. That is, although stress-induced cortisol is produced after an acute activation of the paraventricular nucleus of the hypothalamus, basal levels of cortisol are governed by neuronal projections originating in brain nuclei associated with biological clocks (Gunnar & Donzella, 2002).

The particular cortisol measure used may also greatly affect the strength of the available data. For example, Gunnar and Donzella (2002) argue that it is relatively difficult to elicit increases in cortisol among young children through the introduction of the mild stressors normally approved for laboratory use. Given that one cannot dramatically increase the potency of the stressors, Boyce et al. (2001) suggest expanding the way reactivity is defined. Currently, reactivity is most often defined as the difference between baseline arousal and stress-induced arousal. It may be more informative to try to capture the broader pattern of response. This includes the magnitude of the physiological response, the variability of the response, recovery time, and the ability to habituate to the triggering stimulus. Boyce (Boyce et al., 2001) has speculated that reactive children have difficulty regulating their initial arousal response and that this difficulty extends from their physiological responses to their behavioral coping strategies. To examine children's ability to dampen a response after an acute stressor, one needs to have multiple measures of cortisol after the introduction of the triggering stimulus (Ramsay & Lewis, 2003).

Cortisol and Developmental Psychopathology

Not all individuals with objectively high allostatic loads exhibit psychological distress. Individual differences in vulnerability have been tied to differences in resting physiological arousal as well as reactivity to an environmental stimulus. The hippocampus, a central limbic structure, is considered a primary regulator of cortisol during both normal activity and periods of high stress (Jacobson & Sapolsky, 1991). It performs through negative feedback regulation, inhibiting secretion during normal functioning (shaping the nadir seen in the diurnal cycle) and in times of acute stress. In the hippocampus, it has been suggested that one set of receptors (mineralocorticoid; MR) regulates diurnal variations in cortisol levels and another (glucocorticoid; GR) regulates stress-related secretion (Dallman et al., 1987).

This division of labor is an important factor in shaping individual responses to environmental change. The diurnal cycle regulated by MR is sensitive to negative feedback, helping to ensure regularity (Munck, Guyre, & Holbrook, 1984). However, negative control of the acute GR response is weakened by strong activation of the amygdala (Lovallo & Thomas, 2000). Hyperarousal of the amygdala, in turn, is thought to play a central role in shaping the fear response in both animals (LeDoux, 1996) and humans (Kagan, 1984). In young children, it has been linked to individual differences in temperamental shyness and social withdrawal (Garcia Coll, Kagan, & Reznick, 1984). The data indicate that the LHPA axis response is not governed solely by the nature of the stressor. Rather, individual differences in stress response often result from the individual's cognitive and emotional reactions to the stimulus (Lazarus & Folkman, 1984).

The LHPA axis is one actor among an interconnected system of regulators that help the individual respond to the environment. Individual differences in the way these systems interact and respond may help our understanding of phenotypic differences in behavior. Unlike the catecholamines of the sympathetic-adrenal-medullary (SAM) system, which act quickly to generate the fight-or-flight response (Henry, 1992), the glucocorticoids produced by the LHPA axis are slow-acting steroid hormones. Cortisol must be synthesized on demand and acts by affecting protein synthesis. Cortisol is released by the adrenal cortex only after a signal from the anterior pituitary, which must, in turn, be signaled by the release of corticotropin-releasing hormone (CRH) from the hypothalamus (Bauer et al., 2002). As a result, although cortisol is released within 10 to 30 minutes after a stressor, its effects on target tissues may not be evident for over an hour (Kirschbaum & Hellhammer, 1994).

Henry (1992) has argued that the SAM system acts to generate a "defense reaction," whereas the LHPA system activates a "defeat reaction." The SAM system is thought to mount an effortful response to a stimulus that is considered manageable or under personal control (Peters et al., 1998). For example, individuals with a Type A personality are likely to show larger SAM responses, even as early as 3 years of age (Brown & Tanner, 1988; Lundberg, 1986). In contrast, adults show a larger LHPA response to situations that are deemed uncontrollable (Peters et al., 1998) or are likely to provoke fear and frustration (Lovallo & Thomas, 2000).

For children, the response is particularly strong if it involves a situation whose outcome they view as highly important (Gunnar, Brodersen, Nachmias, Buss, & Rigatuso, 1997; Kirschbaum & Hellhammer, 1994). Lewis and Ramsay (2002) found that at age 4 children who exhibited embarrassment and shame after failure had higher levels of salivary cortisol. They argued that cortisol levels might differentially reflect stress experienced after negative evaluations. These data are also in line with the temperament literature which indicates that behaviorally inhibited children are likely to show elevated cortisol levels at baseline (Kagan, Reznick, & Snidman, 1987; Schmidt et al., 1997).

In both children and adults, the cortisol response is closely tied to individual variations in the affect-stress response. A prime example of this can be found in a growing literature indicating that the relationship between LHPA activity and behavior varies as a function of gender. To begin with, men and women appear to differ in the experiences they consider stress-inducing (A. Taylor, Fisk, & Glover, 2000). The assumption is that the stress response in women involves less sympathetic arousal, is primarily defensive, and is likely to be moderated by social context. For example, college-age women showed elevated cortisol levels after experiencing a social stressor in the form of social rejection (Stroud, Salovey, & Epel, 2002). Their male counterparts showed greater reactivity to an achievement challenge involving difficult mathematical and verbal problems. Over time, these variations in stress response may alter the relationship between basal cortisol levels and behavior.

Boys and girls also differ in how dysregulation is manifested in behavior. In general, boys are more likely to show high levels of externalizing behavior, whereas girls show more internalizing behavior (Merrell & Dobmeyer, 1996; Keiley, Bates, Dodge, & Pettit, 2000). This dichotomy suggests that the developmental role of underlying regulatory mechanisms also differs. For example, Carrion et al. (2002) found that girls with PTSD had higher basal cortisol levels than boys with equivalent levels of PTSD. Klimes-Dougan and colleagues (Klimes-Dougan, Hastings, Granger, Usher, & Zahn-Waxler, 2001) also found differing diurnal rhythms between male and female adolescents at risk for psychopathology. This is in line with data from a nonclinical sample that LHPA activity helps sustain temperamental biases from infancy to early childhood in boys, but not girls (Pérez-Edgar, Fox, Schmidt, & Schulkin, 2004).

This is not to say that the SAM response is "good" and the LHPA response is "bad." Indeed, Munck (Munck et al., 1984) argues that the LHPA response must step in to suppress the initial fight/flight response and prevent lasting damage to the individual by regulating sympathetically mediated changes in cardiovascular function, metabolism, and immune function (Sapolsky, Romero, & Munck, 2000). In addition, brief and periodic increases in cortisol may enhance focused attention on emotionally arousing stimuli and marshal cognitive forces for a response (Erickson et al., 2003). As such, it appears that the SAM and LHPA systems must work in tandem to provide the optimal level of arousal and attentional engagement that higher-order cognitive mechanisms rely on.

The growing consensus in the psychopathology literature holds that dysregulation of the LHPA system, often due to prolonged periods of high allostatic load, disrupts the individual's ability to self-regulate and adapt to shifting environmental demands. This leaves the individual vulnerable to psychological maladaptation. The data, as outlined next, indicate that this mechanism may be central to psychopathology in both children and adults, playing a role in its etiology, maintenance, and perhaps intergenerational transmission.

For example, findings from the adult literature suggest that PTSD may be linked to hippocampal attrition, as seen in reduced volume (Bremner, Krystal, Southwick, & Charney, 1995; Gurvitis, Shenton, Hokama, & Ohta, 1996), decreased blood flow (Semple et al., 1993, but not Rauch et al., 1996), and poor working memory performance (Bremner et al., 1995). Both Nadel and Jacobs (1998) and Yehuda (1997) have suggested that the damage is due to stress-related steroid exposure via dysregulation in the LHPA axis. In the glucocorticoid cascade hypothesis, the presence of cortisol in GR and MR during stress negatively impacts hippocampal neurons (Lovallo & Thomas, 2000). Damage to the hippocampus, a critical feedback site, may disrupt diurnal regulation and lead to chronically high levels of cortisol, further increasing the system's vulnerability to future stress. Along the same lines, disturbances in autobiographical memory in depressed adults have been linked to hippocampal damage due to excessive cortisol secretion (Axelson et al., 1993).

Parallel work in the developmental literature suggests that a similar mechanism may also shape behavior and psychological adjustment in children. For example, Gunnar and Nelson (1994) found a diminished late positive component in the ERPs of 12-month-olds with high levels of cortisol, reflecting the dampening effect of cortisol on hippocampal activity and perhaps also development. Some (e.g., Goodyer, Park, Netherton, et al., 2001) have speculated that this disruption of the hippocampus will directly impact memory formation, particularly memories of an autobiographical nature, thus placing the child at risk for later difficulties (Lynch & Cicchetti, 1998; Pollak, Cicchetti, & Klorman, 1998).

Under normal circumstances, the LHPA system goes through at least two major shifts in functioning and reactivity in the 1st year of life. The first 3 months sees the emergence of the cortisol diurnal rhythm and a reduction in the cortisol response to a specific stressor. In the next 9 months, the cortisol response to nonspecific general stressors decreases again (Gunnar, Brodersen, Krueger, & Rigatuso, 1996). This buffering can be seen in the fact that routine examinations by a pediatrician will trigger a cortisol response in the young infant (Gunnar, Brodersen, Nachmias, Buss, & Rigatuso, 1996) but will not do so in the 2nd year of life. This developmental progression is sensitive to environmental characteristics. Indeed, the connection between early life events and later LHPA activity is sensitive to extremely subtle environmental differences. For example, 8-week-old infants who underwent an assisted delivery (e.g., forceps) show a larger cortisol response to inoculation than do infants who had vaginal or cesarean deliveries (A. Taylor et al., 2000).

Similar mechanisms may be at play for children of highly stressed or depressed mothers, shaping behavior through both biological and environmental channels. Stress during pregnancy, as measured by morning cortisol levels, has been associated with delays in motor and mental development at 8 months of age (Huizink, Robles de Medina, Mulder, Visser, & Buitelaar, 2003). Depressed mothers often provide detached and inconsistent care to their children (Ashman, Dawson, Panagiotides, Yamada, & Wilkinson, 2002; G. Dawson & Ashman, 2000). Unpredictability in the environment has, in turn, been suggested as a possible factor in LHPA dysfunction. In fact, depressed mothers have higher salivary cortisol levels than nondepressed mothers, and these elevations are associated with more depressed behaviors in the infants (Field et al., 1988). At age 3, children of depressed mothers displayed higher baseline cortisol levels than children of nondepressed mothers (Hessl et al., 1996). Recently, Ashman et al. examined the effect of maternal depression on offspring LHPA activity as a function of the timing of depressive episodes and found

that the presence of depression in the first 2 years of life was the best predictor of cortisol production at age 7.

Given these data, it is not hard to imagine that a prolonged disruption in a child's environment could have profound effects on allostatic load and the body's ability to self-regulate. As a relatively benign example, infants with colic show a flattening of the normal daily cortisol cycle (Finsterwald, Selig, Schieche, Wurmser, & Papousek, 2000; B. P. White, Gunnar, Larson, Donzella, & Barr, 2000), which may reflect the toll of persistent crying and the disruption to normal daily events (e.g., colicky babies tend to have bouts of interrupted sleep).

In general, the literature indicates that children with severe difficulties in their caretaking environment have either chronically high cortisol levels or unusually low basal cortisol levels with occasional spikes (Flinn & England, 1995). Chaotic or unpredictable schedules also contribute to the blunting of the normal diurnal rhythm (Gunnar & Vazquez, 2001). For example, maltreatment and abuse may produce chronic disruptions of the LHPA axis and play a central role in the development of psychopathology. DeBellis et al. (1999) found that cortisol concentrations in abused children were positively correlated with the duration of trauma and the intensity of symptoms in children subsequently diagnosed with PTSD. Indeed, Cicchetti and Rogosch (2001) found that cortisol patterns also reflected the form of the abuse experienced by the child. Carrion et al. (2002) found that young children with PTSD exhibited elevated basal cortisol levels and a flattening of the diurnal cycle.

To date, most studies have assessed outcomes in two broad categories: internalizing and externalizing behavior. Studies generally look at either one form of behavior or the other. When included in a single study, internalizing and externalizing behaviors are often treated as orthogonal to each other, despite the fact that these behaviors are often highly related (e.g., Granger, Weisz, & Kauneckis, 1994).

In general, the data indicate that low LHPA activation is associated with externalizing, aggressive, or disruptive behavior in children (McBurnett et al., 1991; Tout et al., 1998). For example, Van Goozen et al. (1998) had boys ages 8 to 11 diagnosed with Oppositional Defiant Disorder (ODD) or CD participate in a competitive stressor. Compared to the control children, the boys with ODD/CD had lower baseline levels of cortisol. However, there were no differences in stress-induced cortisol across groups. Pajer and colleagues (Pajer, Gardner, Rubin, Perel, & Neal, 2001) found a similar relationship between low resting cortisol and externalizing behavior in a group of 15- to 17-year-old girls diagnosed with CD.

In contrast to externalizing behavior, internalizing problems have been linked to higher levels of adrenocortical activation in children (Ashman et al., 2002; Gunnar, Tout, de Haan, Pierce, & Stansbury, 1997; Kagan, Reznick, & Snidman, 1988; Schmidt et al., 1997). For example, Granger et al. (1994) found that among a group of clinic-referred children, those with the highest levels of cortisol reactivity displayed more internalizing behavior (social withdrawal and anxiety) than the children with low reactivity. Similarly, children with clinically significant levels of internalizing difficulties show significantly larger cortisol responses to a mild stressor in the form of a potentiated startle (Ashman et al., 2002). Granger et al. also found that a continuous measure of cortisol activity predicted over-controlled behaviors, defined as a composite of social withdrawal, anxiety, depression, and somatic complaints. This is in line with data indicating that temperamentally inhibited children also show higher cortisol levels at rest (Kagan et al., 1987).

However, there are indications that this pattern of data is not universal. For example, some studies have shown a positive correlation between cortisol levels and externalizing behavior. Tout et al. (1998) observed children at playtime in a preschool and found that increased cortisol reactivity (a measure reflecting the tendency to have frequent high morning cortisol levels) was associated with angry and aggressive behaviors. Recent findings also suggest that normally developing preschoolers showing high levels of cortisol are higher in both internalizing and externalizing difficulties 2 years later at the end of first grade (Essex, Klein, Cho, & Kalin, 2002).

In addition, Gunnar and Vazquez (2001) have argued that young children at risk for psychopathology often exhibit lower basal cortisol levels, not higher levels, as would be expected. The accompanying flattening of the diurnal cycle in these cases is due to lower cortisol levels in the morning, the normal peak in the cycle, rather than higher levels at the trough, as is often seen with depressed adults. Also evident in this pattern of "hypocortisolism" is a blunting of the cortisol stress response to an acute trigger (Heim, Ehlert, & Hellhammer, 2000). Henry (1993) suggests that hypocortisolism in response to stressors may be associated with a lack of ego involvement, repression or passive coping, and emotional indifference. Hypocortisolism may also reflect chronic allostatic adjustments (McEwen, 1998), often seen as an extended period of elevated cortisol in response to trauma or stress (Hellhammer & Wade, 1993). Granger et al. (1998), for example, found that children under chronic stress had subnormal cortisol levels in nonstressful conditions.

Indeed, the most dramatic example of hypocortisolism can be found in environments marked by maltreatment, neglect, and natural or sociopolitical disaster, including children reared in orphanages (Carlson & Earls, 1997), cloth-reared monkeys (Boyce, Champoux, Suomi, & Gunnar, 1995), and adolescent survivors of earthquake with subsequent symptoms of PTSD (Goenjian et al., 1996). Yehuda (Yehuda, Boisoneau, Mason, & Giller, 1993; Yehuda, Southwick, et al., 1993) has argued that hypocortisolism may be due to early life stresses that result in a negative regulation of the LHPA axis, which may in turn create an inability to effectively deal with subsequent stressors.

The studies reviewed so far indicate that disruptions in the child's environment may disrupt LHPA functioning and place the child at higher risk for psychopathology. Studies focused on childhood depression illustrate the consequences of LHPA dysfunction on subsequent development.

Goodyer and colleagues (Goodyer, Herbert, Tamplin, & Altham, 2000a, 2000b) have found that among healthy adolescents at high risk for depression there is a high correlation between cortisol levels and subsequent diagnoses of Major Depression. In addition, approximately one-quarter of children and adolescents with depression show elevated cortisol levels (Rao et al., 1996). For example, Goodyer and colleagues (Goodyer, Park, & Herbert, 2001) followed a group of clinically depressed 8- to 16-year-olds across a 72-week period, collecting morning and evening cortisol samples for two consecutive days at three points in the study: inception, 36 weeks, and 72 weeks. Those children whose symptoms had not diminished were classified as chronically depressed. The other children were placed in the recovery group. At each of the collection points, the children in the chronically depressed group had higher evening cortisol levels than the children in the recovered group.

In addition, Goodyer, Park, and Herbert (2001) found that adverse life events over the course of the study were associated with elevated cortisol levels at inception. They speculated that cortisol hypersecretion might affect cognitive processes that influence risk for adverse events. Indeed, there are initial indications (E. P. Davis, Bruce, & Gunnar, 2002; Vedhara, Hyde, Gilchrist, Tytherleigh, & Plummer, 2000) that LHPA activity may be related to both the development and current functioning of the prefrontal cortex, specifically the anterior cingulate cortex (ACC). Poor prefrontal functioning has, in turn, been linked to the appearance of behavioral maladjustment (Bush et al., 1999; E. P. Davis et al., 2002) and poor or risky decision making. Given that the ACC is undergoing significant maturation during childhood (Janowsky & Carper, 1996; Rothbart, Posner, & Hershey, 1995), one may speculate that this process may impact the observed relationship between cortisol and behavior. Unfortunately, the extant literature cannot at this time address basic questions concerning the direction of the effect and the potential causal bases.

Future Directions in the Use of Cortisol

For the most part, studies examining the relationship between cortisol and psychopathology have relied on two basic measures: baseline cortisol and acute cortisol after the introduction of a stressor. These measures have added to our understanding of the impact of the LHPA system on affect and behavior. However, recent work suggests that an additional quantification of LHPA functioning may greatly help. That is, an examination of variations in the diurnal cycle may allow researchers to examine the *shape* of the cortisol cycle in response to environmental challenges (Gunnar & Vazquez, 2001). An example of this research strategy can be found in the child care studies overseen by Gunnar and her colleagues.

A number of studies have now noted that children in full-time center-based child care often show an increase in cortisol levels throughout the day (Tout et al., 1998; Watamura, Sebanc, & Gunnar, 2002), rather than the expected dip in cortisol seen in children tested in the home setting (Watamura, Donzella, Alwin, & Gunnar, 2003). Watamura et al. (2003) note that cortisol increases appear to emerge in infancy, peak in the toddler years, and disappear by the early school years. The available data suggest that the increase in cortisol is linked to the increasing social demands and complexity of the child's environment as he or she moves from infancy into toddlerhood (Dettling, Gunnar, & Donzella, 1999; Tout et al., 1998; Watamura et al., 2003). The subsequent downturn in the trend is presumably due to the child's increasing ease when engaged in social interactions.

The data also suggest that the developmental trends in cortisol production are context-specific. That is, children appear to revert to the "normal" cortisol rhythm when not in the child care setting (Watamura et al., 2003). Because older children in full-day child care also show the expected dips in afternoon cortisol levels, it does not appear that mild environmental challenges, even if relatively frequent, permanently alter the diurnal cortisol pattern. This is in contrast to the abuse and maltreatment literature, which finds that prolonged adversity can flatten the diurnal cycle (Carrion et al., 2002). As such, these data point to the importance of noting individual differences in both context and developmental state when examining cortisol production throughout the day. In this way, research may be better

able to capture both the regulatory and reactive functions of the LHPA axis.

Electroencephalogram

The use of EEG to assess human behavior and development began quite early with the work of Berger (1929, 1932). Although the first reports were met with skepticism, the measure was soon widely accepted in the biomedical research community, particularly after a live demonstration at a 1935 meeting of the Physiological Society in London convinced people of its usefulness (Davidson, Jackson, & Larson, 2000). Much of the early work was hampered by the fact that reports were largely descriptive, used adult indices of behavior (e.g., alertness) even when dealing with children and infants, and were reliant on cumbersome, and perhaps inaccurate, manual analyses of the EEG data (e.g., J. R. Smith, 1938a, 1938b, 1938c).

Many of the methodological issues limiting the early research were beginning to subside by the 1960s, when Hagne and colleagues (Hagne, 1968, 1972; Hagne, Persson, Magnusson, & Petersén, 1973) began their longitudinal studies of EEG development. The introduction of quantitative EEG analysis through the use of computers and the fast Fourier transform greatly increased the scope of data available to the researcher. These include waveform amplitude (Matousek & Petersén, 1973), absolute and relative power (Clarke, Barry, McCarthy, & Selikowitz, 2001c), dominant and subordinate frequency analysis (Katada & Koike, 1990), mean frequency (Chabot & Serfontein, 1996), the wave percentage time (Matsuura et al., 1985), EEG asymmetry (Davidson, 1995), and the coherence of the EEG signal across regions (Chabot & Serfontein, 1996; Thatcher, 1992).

Taking advantage of these technological advances, Hagne was able to emphasize the importance of changes in relative power and peak frequency. For example, she found that the ratio between delta (1.5 to 3.5 Hz) and theta (3.5 to 7.5 Hz) frequency changes between 8 and 12 months of age due to an increase in theta and a decrease in delta (Hagne, 1968, 1972). These shifts in relative power were then linked to patterns of change in behavior.

In addition to examining normal functioning and development, the use of EEG measures to examine psychopathology in adults and children began fairly early. P. A. Davis and Davis (1939), for example, collected resting EEG from a large sample of psychotic adults and found that the patients demonstrated significantly less alpha activity than did control subjects. Later studies also found a similar pattern in anxious adults (Duffy, 1962). Investigations of ADHD, then known as minimal brain dysfunction syndrome, began in the 1930s (Jasper, Solomon, & Bradley, 1938).

Linked to a relatively long history of EEG experimentation, the past 3 decades have seen exponential growth in the use of EEG measures in psychological research. This section reviews the collection and interpretation of the EEG signal, our current understanding of the normal developmental progression, and its application to the study of developmental psychopathologies.

Electroencephalogram Methodology

EEG is collected via electrodes placed on the scalp either singly or by group as part of a net or cap system. Distributed in a standard placement design (Jasper, 1958), the electrodes are referred to by the cerebral lobe their scalp locations are closest to (e.g., F = Frontal, P = Parietal) and their relative location on the scalp (Odd numbers = Left hemisphere, Even numbers = Right hemisphere, z = Midline). The electrical activity recorded via the electrodes is referenced to relatively inactive electrode site(s), and the signal is then saved offline for further processing and analysis. The collected signal is thought to be derived from the summation of postsynaptic potentials. This rhythmic electrocortical activity is regulated by the thalamus (Larson, White, Cochran, Donzella, & Gunnar, 1998), particularly through the nucleus reticularis (Steriade, Deschenes, Domich, & Mulle, 1985).

Before statistical analyses begin, EEG power is normally aggregated across frequency bins to form measures of band power. Different epochs of the same condition are then averaged to provide more reliable estimates of spectral power, in much the same way as behavioral reaction time data. A more detailed discussion of the steps involved in EEG collection and processing can be found in Davidson, Jackson, et al. (2000) and Pivik et al. (1993).

EEG data are primarily characterized along the dimensions of amplitude and frequency, which are often used to describe the differences across major behavioral states (Pilgreen, 1995). In adults, deep sleep is associated with large and very slow waves in the delta frequency range (1 to 4 Hz). Drowsiness is characterized by reduced amplitude theta activity (5 to 7 Hz), although delta activity is also common. Alpha activity (8 to 13 Hz) is often linked to a state of "relaxed wakefulness," and points of high alert and attention are marked by low-amplitude fast activity (>13 Hz). Much of the literature has focused on quantifying alpha activity in response to experimental task manipulations.

EEG measures have proven particularly attractive in the laboratory because the signal derived has good temporal resolution, in the realm of milliseconds. Indeed, EEG can detect neuronal changes in activity almost instantaneously (Davidson, Jackson, et al., 2000). This is particularly important when dealing with processes that are fast-acting, irregular, and spontaneous, such as emotion. Behaviors that are fleeting (lasting only a second) can be easily detected given that EEG is often sampled 200 times per second. This compares favorably with the long lag times found with functional MRI (fMRI) and PET, compensating for the relatively poor spatial resolution seen in the EEG signal.

On this point, Davidson, Jackson, et al. (2000) argue that even when using high-density electrode arrays, which can collect data from up to 256 sites (compared to traditional 16- and 32-channel collection protocols), EEG recording will always lag behind metabolic and hemodynamic imaging. This is due in part to spatial resolution a full order of magnitude coarser than that found with fMRI, the distortion produced via transmission through the skull, and the fact that a particular distribution of scalp potentials can be produced by different combinations of neuronal generators.

In addition, there are some methodological concerns in collecting EEG that are common when dealing with children. First, the validity of EEG data is dependent on the analysis of a clean signal that is free of motor or movement artifact and was generated under the specific mental states of interest (e.g., at rest or alert attention). However, one cannot instruct infants and young children to either sit still or focus attention solely on the stimuli of interest. As such, researchers rely on both methodological creativity and analytical skill in circumventing these difficulties. For example, Fox (e.g., N. A. Fox, Henderson, Rubin, Calkins, & Schmidt, 2001; N. A. Fox et al., 1995) presents infants with a spinning bingo wheel filled with colorful balls to capture the infant's attention and minimize extraneous movement. For analysis, these data are then processed to remove any movement artifacts. Even when the difficulties with artifact and attention are minimized, however, there remain concerns over the meaningfulness of the underlying data.

N. A. Fox, Schmidt, and Henderson (2000) point out that electrode placement protocol agreed on for adults (Jasper, 1958) is not necessarily appropriate for use with young children. First, it is not clear if the ratio of distances across electrode sites is stable across development, indicating that our measures may not correspond to the actual geometry or topography of the brain. Second, morphological changes in the brain throughout development may shift the location from which electrical activity is emanating. This would greatly complicate the already thorny issue of localizing the source of the EEG signal.

In documenting the change in EEG functioning over time, a number of researchers caution against using absolute power (Benninger, Matthis, & Scheffner, 1984). In particular, changes in bone thickness, skull resistance, and impedance may distort absolute power values. Instead, relative power may have better test-retest reliability (John et al., 1980) and may be more sensitive to changes in the frequency composition of the EEG with age (Clarke, Barry, McCarthy, & Selikowitz, 2001a). Relative power is expressed as the percentage of power in a specific frequency bin at each electrode site relative to total power (in all frequency bins) at the same electrode site (Marshall, Bar-Haim, & Fox, 2002).

Despite these limitations, the ease of assembling and using the equipment necessary for EEG collection, and its noninvasiveness, has made it a common tool for psychophysiological research with individuals of all ages. This has allowed researchers to document the major developmental changes that take place between the burst-suppression non-state-dependent EEG patterns seen in premature infants (less than 28 weeks conceptual age) and the organized and coherent patterns seen in normal adults. An example can be seen in Marshall et al.'s (2002) study of changes in relative power and peak frequency in children from ages 4 months to 4 years (see Figures 9.1 and 9.2).

In the 1st year of life, activity in the lower frequencies (delta and theta) decreases, whereas alpha activity increases into early adolescence and beta continues to mature into adulthood (M. J. Taylor & Baldeweg, 2002). Indeed, the normal adult EEG pattern is usually not established until 25 to 30 years of age, a point in time that corresponds to the final state of myelination (Pilgreen, 1995). The alpha band, central to many studies, migrates from the 3 to 5 Hz band in the 1st year to 6 to 9 Hz in early childhood and later settles into the 8 to 13 Hz band in adulthood (Marshall et al., 2002). Throughout the process, the rate of maturation is at its most rapid in the posterior cites and its slowest in anterior locations (Benninger et al., 1984; Gasser, Jennen-Steinmetz, Sroka, Verleger, & Mocks, 1988).

Electroencephalogram in the Study of Developmental Psychopathology

Building on these developmental data, quantitative measures of EEG have been used to examine a number of core cognitive (Bell & Fox, 1994) and emotional (G. Dawson, Panagiotides, Grofer Klinger, & Hill, 1992) processes. In both domains, the strategy has been to create a functional link between changes in behavioral performance and the purported underlying neural mechanisms by noting changes in electrocortical signals thought to reflect activity in these same neural mechanisms.

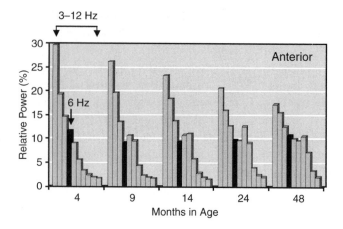

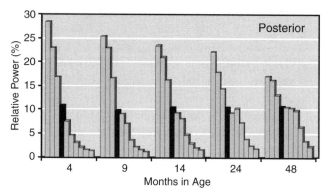

Figure 9.1   Power spectra for relative power in the 3 to 12 Hz bins for anterior (F3, F4, C3, C4) and posterior (P3, P4, O1, O2) electrode sites between 4 and 48 months of age. The 6 Hz bin is indicated in black. Adapted from "Development of the EEG from 5 Months to 4 Years of Age," by P. J. Marshall, Y. Bar-Haim, and N. A. Fox, 2002, *Clinical Neurophysiology, 113,* pp. 1199–1208.

Early on, this work was hindered by the belief that many of the brain regions of interest were not well developed in childhood. The frontal cortex is directly involved in a number of the components underlying higher-order cognition and emotion, including the facilitation of emotional expression, the organization of cognitive processes associated with emotion, and the ability to regulate emotion (G. Dawson, 1994; N. A. Fox et al., 2000). However, the general consensus had long been that there was minimal frontal lobe development until middle childhood (Bell & Fox, 1992). As a result, much of our understanding of the relationship between EEG and development was limited to posterior sites. However, a number of studies have demonstrated that changes in frontal lobe activity occur as early as the 1st year of life (Chugani & Phelps, 1986; N. A. Fox & Bell, 1990), although frontal lobe development does lag behind growth in other brain regions. These studies further emboldened researchers to incorporate these tools in their

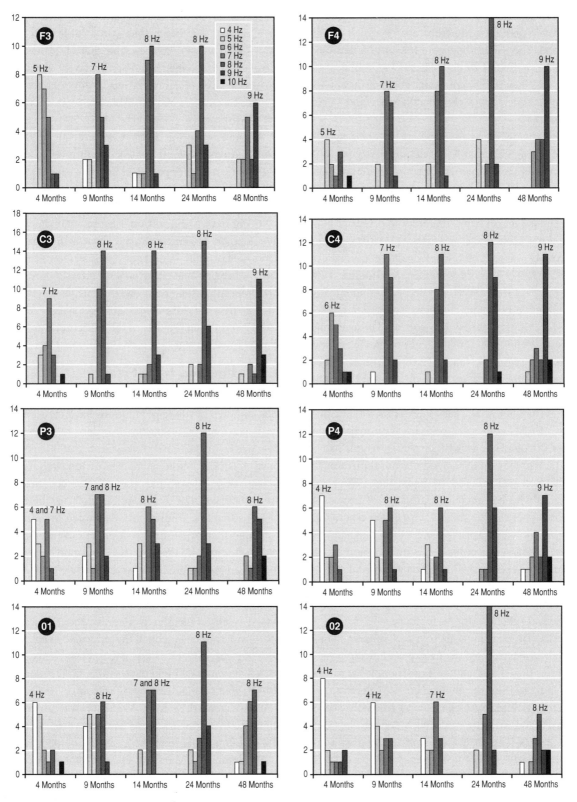

Figure 9.2 The distribution of the peak frequency of relative power within the 3 to 10 Hz range in the first 4 years of life. The bars indicate the number of participants whose peak frequency fell in each 1 Hz bin. Modal frequencies are indicated for each site and age. Adapted from "Development of the EEG from 5 Months to 4 Years of Age," by P. J. Marshall, Y. Bar-Haim, and N. A. Fox, 2002, *Clinical Neurophysiology, 113,* pp. 1199–1208.

work. For example, Bell and Fox observed infants performing the A-not-B task monthly from ages 6 to 12 months. Their data provided added support to the notion that A-not-B performance is linked to dorsolateral prefrontal cortex development by showing a significant correlation between EEG power recorded from the frontal sites and performance on the task.

In addition to power and frequency, EEG coherence has proven to be an important tool in assessing early brain development. Coherence quantifies the phase relationship between two processes at a specific frequency band. Coherence can range from 0 (there is no phase relationship) to 1 (the two signals are either completely in or out of phase with each other). Coherence measures will shift over time depending on age and the processes of interest. For example, Thatcher (1992; Thatcher, Walker, & Giudice, 1987) has found that over time there is increased communication between anatomically distant locations, coupled with an increased differentiation across the cortex. These changes may be due to either the activity level of axonal connections across two regions (Nunez, 1981) or the activity of short- and long-fiber networks or the axons (Thatcher, Krause, & Hrybyk, 1986; Thatcher et al., 1987).

Thatcher (Thatcher et al., 1987) has argued that changing patterns of EEG coherence coincide with major points of transition in cognitive growth, providing neural mechanisms by which to explain observed behavioral differences. For example, Bell and Fox (1996) found that EEG coherence in infants who had moderate amounts of experience crawling was higher than in infants with either no crawling experience or who were proficient crawlers. It appears that the increase in coherence coincided with a period of time during which a new, core skill was being consolidated, requiring the coordination of multiple systems. Once mastered, the newly efficient process no longer required as complex a neural substrate for performance.

Beyond EEG findings in normative development, a number of studies have examined the EEG correlates of psychopathology in children and adults. For example, studies in depression indicate that the thalamocortical regulation of EEG rhythm (particularly alpha power) normally seen in adults is disrupted in individuals with depression (Lindgren et al., 1999). This is evident during sleep, which is marked by elevated levels of fast-frequency EEG (>16 Hz) and a reduction of low-frequency activity (Armitage, Hudson, Trivedi, & Rush, 1995) in depressed adults. These findings are of particular interest because sleep disturbances and abnormalities are linked to increased risk for relapse (Giles, Jarrett, Biggs, Guzick, & Rush, 1989) and suicide (Fawcett et al., 1989).

In the developmental literature, the most extensive empirical work has been done with children diagnosed with ADHD. Typically, studies find that children with ADHD have decreased alpha and beta activity most apparent in posterior sites (Chabot & Serfontein, 1996; Clarke et al., 2001c; Lazzaro et al., 1998). In contrast, there is often increased frontal theta (Clarke et al., 2001c; Lazzaro et al., 1998) and posterior delta (Clarke et al., 2001c) activity. The findings are most acute in children who show signs of hyperactivity, as opposed to inattentiveness (Clarke et al., 2003). These data have been interpreted as indicating that children with ADHD are cortically hypoaroused (Lubar, 1991) or have a maturational lag in central nervous system development (Clarke, Barry, McCarthy, & Selikowitz, 1998). The latter interpretation is bolstered by coherence data indicating that children with ADHD show less cortical differentiation than their non-ADHD peers (Barry, Clarke, McCarthy, & Selikowitz, 2002; Chabot & Serfontein, 1996). A thorough review of the EEG literature with ADHD can be found in Barry, Clarke, and Johnstone (2003).

Future Directions in the Use of Electroencephalogram

EEG studies in young populations have focused on children with learning or attention disorders (Barry et al., 2003; Marshall, Fox, & BEIP Core Group, 2004). These studies have generally found increases in low-frequency spectral power (e.g., delta and theta) and decreases in high-frequency spectral bands (e.g., alpha or beta). Until recently, very few studies have examined the effects of environment or sociocultural risk on EEG functioning. Among these studies, it appears that environmental deprivation may keep theta and delta power levels elevated beyond the normal developmental period (Harmony et al., 1988; Harmony, Marosi, Diaz de Leon, Becker, & Fernandez, 1990), whereas enrichment may depress theta and delta power (Raine et al., 2001). Given the extensive behavioral data indicating the effects of adverse environments, such as maternal depression (Field et al., 1988; G. Dawson & Ashman, 2000), institutionalization (Carlson & Earls, 1997), and abuse (Cicchetti & Toth, 1995), on socioemotional development, this appears to be an important avenue of study that could benefit from the introduction of EEG measures.

For example, Marshall et al. (2004) compared resting EEG in a group of institutionalized infants in Bucharest, Romania, to age-matched children living with their families in the greater Bucharest area. They found that the children in the institution showed more relative power in the lower-frequency bands and less relative alpha power than their community-based counterparts. In light of similar data from children with ADHD (Barry et al., 2003) and Autism (G. Dawson, Klinger, Panagiotides, Lewy, & Castellow, 1995), it may be that EEG activity across power bands may serve as a marker for deviations or lags in development that are common to a variety of disorders or contexts (Marshall et al., 2004). This is in line with Keller et al.'s (2000) note that EEG power is multidetermined and driven by a number of summating and overlapping mechanisms. Comparisons across groups and contexts, such as those noted here, may allow us to better delineate the functional significance of resting EEG activity.

MEASURES OF MOTIVATION AND EMOTION

The use of psychophysiological methods to study emotion and motivation are relevant to the study of developmental psychopathology, particularly for disorders of affect and disinhibition. Measures covered in this section tap into the physiological substrates of the neural fear system and of the appetitive/aversive motivational systems and include EEG asymmetry and affective modulation of the startle reflex.

Electroencephalogram Asymmetry

Like the ERP, EEG asymmetry is derived from measures of raw EEG power, and, like the ERP, measures of the relative difference in activation across sites provide an additional perspective on the links between physiology and behavior. In particular, differences in EEG asymmetry have been used to examine individual differences in motivation systems both as a stable individual trait and in response to transient environmental characteristics. Indeed, the relative difference in activation across sites may be more important in determining behavior than the absolute amount of activation in a region (Davidson, Chapman, Chapman, & Henriques, 1990). This is borne out in part by the very extensive literature linking asymmetries in EEG activity to individual differences in affect in both healthy and clinical populations.

Electroencephalogram Asymmetry Methodology

EEG asymmetry is normally calculated by comparing power in two homologous electrodes (e.g., F3 and F4). Frontal EEG asymmetry is determined by subtracting the natural log of alpha power seen in the left electrode from the natural log of the alpha power in the right electrode (lnF4–lnF3). Because EEG power is inversely related to activation, a negative number indicates that an individual is showing more activity in the right frontal lobe relative to

the left (Davidson, Jackson, et al., 2000). It is also important to note the level of activity within each lobe as this will help to explain the pattern (e.g., hyper- or hypoactivation in a particular location across individuals or conditions) underlying a particular asymmetry finding (Schmidt, 1999).

Electroencephalogram Asymmetry and Developmental Psychopathology

Davidson (1984a, 1984b, 1995) and others have argued that resting frontal EEG activation reflects an underlying motivation bias to respond to the environment in a particular hedonic manner. Individuals with right frontal EEG asymmetry are more likely to respond to the environment with negative or withdrawal emotions and behavior. In contrast, individuals showing left frontal EEG asymmetry are more likely to exhibit positive or approach responses. For example, studies have found that adults who display a pattern of greater right frontal asymmetry at rest rate film clips more negatively (Tomarken, Davidson, & Henriques, 1990) and are less sociable in a dyadic interaction (Schmidt & Fox, 1994) than are individuals with left frontal EEG asymmetry at rest.

Schmidt (1999) found that female undergraduates who rated themselves as high in shyness were likely to show right frontal EEG asymmetry due to left frontal hypoactivation. Their sociable counterparts, on the other hand, displayed more left frontal asymmetry. Schmidt further decomposed the data to compare participants who were high in shyness but varied in their level of sociability. He found that these two groups differed in the absolute power in the left frontal lobe, suggesting that there may be different types of shyness distinguishable at the behavioral (Cheek & Buss, 1981) and psychophysiological (Schmidt & Fox, 1994) levels.

Work by Tomarken and colleagues (Tomarken, Davidson, Wheeler, & Kinney, 1992) suggests that differences in asymmetry observed across individuals are rooted in functional, not structural, differences in the brain. As such, EEG asymmetry reflects functional changes in activity as well as underlying motivational biases. For example, individuals who show a pattern of left frontal asymmetry at rest may display right frontal asymmetry when presented with aversive film clips (Jones & Fox, 1992; Tomarken et al., 1990).

Adults who exhibit a stable pattern of right frontal EEG asymmetry over the course of 3 weeks report more intense negative affect when presented with negative emotional film clips (Wheeler, Davidson, & Tomarken, 1993). Participants in the same study who displayed stable left asymmetry reported more intense positive emotion when presented with positive film clips. It appears that stable patterns of asymmetry do not simply increase general arousal, creating more intense affective responses across the board. Rather, the motivational or processing bias appears to be limited to a particular region in the affective spectrum.

EEG asymmetry may serve as a psychophysiological marker of risk for maladaptive behaviors and psychopathology. Right frontal EEG asymmetry appears to be linked to difficulty in regulating negative arousal, a bias toward negative affect, and the display of withdrawal behaviors when confronted with threat—factors that are all related to psychopathology and maladaptation.

In the adult literature, depressed individuals display less left frontal activation (Henriques & Davidson, 1991) and greater right frontal activation (Henriques & Davidson, 1990) than nondepressed individuals. Supplementing the frontal asymmetry literature, Heller (1993) has suggested that emotional functioning may also be modulated by activity in posterior brain regions. Specifically, Heller has found that depressed individuals show less EEG activity in right parietal sites. This has been replicated in a number of studies with varying experimental tasks (e.g., Bruder et al., 1995; Keller, Deldin, Gergen, & Miller, 1995) and is thought to reflect the hypoarousal often found in depression (Heller & Nitschke, 1997).

Anxiety has also been linked to greater right frontal activity, specifically in Panic Disorder (Reiman, Raichle, Butler, Herscovitch, & Robins, 1984), Generalized Anxiety Disorder (Wu et al., 1991), social phobia (Davidson, Marshall, Tomarken, & Henriques, 2000), and nonclinical individuals self-rated as high in trait anxiety (Reivich, Gur, & Alavi, 1983). Here, the direction of the effect indicates that anxiety is marked by elevated levels of negative affect and withdrawal tendencies, coupled with increased autonomic arousal. This is borne out in data indicating increased EEG activity in parietal sites (Heller, 1993).

Paralleling the adult literature, a similar pattern of frontal EEG asymmetry has been found in the 1st year of life. Davidson and Fox (1982) found that 10-month-old infants were more likely to show left frontal asymmetry when viewing a person smiling than when presented with the same individual crying. Infants of the same age also show shifts in EEG asymmetry in response to the approach of an unfamiliar adult (N. A. Fox & Davidson, 1987) and maternal separation (N. A. Fox & Davidson, 1988).

EEG measures at baseline also predict later behavior, such that infants with right frontal asymmetry will cry sooner to maternal separation than will infants with left frontal asymmetry (Davidson & Fox, 1989). In early childhood, children with right frontal asymmetry are also more likely to be behaviorally inhibited and show difficulty with social interactions (e.g., N. A. Fox et al., 1995, 2001). Infants who displayed a stable pattern of right frontal asymmetry across time also show a stable pattern of behavioral inhibition across progressively larger time windows of 2 (N. A. Fox, Calkins, & Bell, 1994), 4 (N. A. Fox et al., 2001), and 7 years.

Henderson, Fox, and Rubin (2001) found that infant temperament predicted social wariness in early childhood only for those children who displayed a pattern of right frontal EEG asymmetry in infancy. School-age children asked to prepare a potentially embarrassing speech, a task designed to elicit social stress, showed increases in right frontal EEG asymmetry that paralleled increases in anxiety (Schmidt, Fox, Schulkin, & Gold, 1999). Baving, Laucht, and Schmidt (2002) assessed EEG asymmetry in anxious children at ages 8 or 11 relative to nonanxious control groups and found that anxious girls showed more right frontal asymmetry.

In addition, parallel data indicate that children who consistently display high levels of sociability in the first 4 years of life were more likely to exhibit left frontal EEG asymmetry (N. A. Fox et al., 2001). However, increased sociability, when coupled with right frontal EEG asymmetry, may place a child at increased risk for externalizing behavior problems (N. A. Fox, Schmidt, Calkins, Rubin, & Coplan, 1996).

Future Directions in the Use of Electroencephalogram Asymmetry

EEG asymmetry has been used to examine both individual and group differences in motivational and affective biases. The measure has provided a theoretically grounded and empirically supported mechanism by which to gauge trait- and state-based variations in a core psychological construct. Future work, while continuing on this path, will also need to examine secondary measures that may moderate the relationship between EEG asymmetry and behavior. As an example of exogenous and endogenous factors that may shape individual differences in EEG asymmetry, our discussion now briefly turns to the effects of parental characteristics (exogenous) and gender (endogenous) on the relationship of interest.

Psychopathology in children arises from multiple factors, including temperament, environmental characteristics, and parenting. As a result, developmental outcomes must be placed in the context of development to be fully understood. Based on this understanding of pathogenesis, a great deal of research has focused on the impact of maternal depression on infant physiology and behavioral outcomes. Women who are depressed display less positive affect toward their infant, provide less stimulation (Field et al., 1988; Jones, Field, & Davlos, 2000), and often display unpredictable response patterns to their child's distress (G. Dawson & Ashman, 2000). Infants of depressed mothers, who are at a greater risk for future disorders (e.g., Murray & Cooper, 1997), display less positive affect and increased irritability (Cohn, Matias, Tronick, Connell, & Lyons-Ruth, 1986; Field, 1986; Field et al., 1985) and show greater frontal activation (Field, Fox, Pickens, & Nawrocki, 1995; G. Dawson, Grofer Klinger, Panagiotides, Hill, & Spieker, 1992) than do infants with nonsymptomatic mothers. In early childhood, these children are also more likely to show greater levels of behavioral maladaptation, particularly internalizing problems (Ashman, Dawson, Panagiotides, Yamada, & Wilkinson, 2002).

These data indicate that parental characteristics shape psychophysiology in the first years of life, although we do not have the research needed to determine the relative importance of environmental and heritable factors. However, it does appear that the effects of exposure to risk factors for later maladaptation are evident within the individual very early, perhaps within the first 3 months of age (Field et al., 1995). These effects have also been shown to carry on into early childhood, such that preschoolers with depressed mothers show greater right frontal EEG asymmetry and manifest less empathic responses to distress in others (Jones et al., 2000).

In terms of endogenous factors that may affect the link between EEG and behavior, there is growing evidence that the pattern of EEG asymmetry and its relationship to affect and behavior vary as a function of gender in both children (Baving, Laucht, & Schmidt, 1999, 2002; Henderson et al., 2001) and adults (e.g., Kline, Allen, & Schwartz, 1998; Kline, Blackhart, & Schwartz, 1999). These findings are joined by gender-linked differences in raw EEG patterns among depressed individuals (Armitage et al., 2000; Armitage, Hudson, Trivedi, & Rush, 1995). This underscores studies indicating that Major Depressive Disorder is twice as prevalent in adolescent and adult females as in their male counterparts (Angold, Erklani, Silberg, Eaves, & Costello, 2002; American Psychiatric Association, 1994) and suggests that measures of EEG asymmetry may reflect the differential mechanisms at play.

Taken together, the adult and developmental data indicate that EEG asymmetry may reflect stable individual differences in temperament and motivation that are early appearing and may endure into adulthood. Resting frontal EEG asymmetry may reflect the valence of the motivational or affective bias, and the absolute power of the EEG

signal may reflect the intensity of the affective experience (Schmidt & Fox, 1999).

Measures of electrocortical activity have proven to be extremely useful in developmental psychopathology. The technology is noninvasive, relatively easy to employ, and amenable to use across a wide age spectrum. As a result, researchers have available to them a set of interrelated, but distinct, measures to address questions of trait-level differences in functioning and motivation as well as changes that occur in response to change in the environment.

Affective Modulation of the Startle Reflex

The startle reflex is a defensive response, and hence, theoretically, should be enhanced when an organism is presented with an aversive or threatening stimulus. This is the basis for research that uses the startle paradigm to explore emotional reactivity. According to P. J. Lang (1995, p. 372), "Defensive reflexes, including startle, increase in amplitude when an organism is aversively motivated . . . [and] . . . defensive reflexes are reduced in amplitude when an organism is positively motivated." It is not within the scope of the current work to provide a depth of knowledge into the nature and the neural circuitry involved in such appetitive and aversive motivational systems (see P. J. Lang, 1995, for a full review). However, there is considerable evidence to support this claim, as Davis and colleagues (M. Davis, Hitchcock, & Rosen, 1987) have documented that the neural circuitry involved in conditioned fear is the same as that involved in fear-conditioned startle potentiation. Two neural circuits are believed to be responsible for fear-potentiated startle in rats. The first is the primary brain stem pathway, which transfers auditory input to the reflex effectors vis-à-vis the reticular formation. The second path mitigates transmissions in the primary circuit, as projections from the central nucleus of the amygdala to the reticular locus of the primary pathway described earlier. Davis and his colleagues have shown that the primary neural circuit attenuates or ameliorates startle responses. Additionally, lesions of the amygdala have been found to eradicate the startle response (Boulis & Davis, 1989; Hitchcock & Davis, 1986; Rosen & Davis, 1988).

According to M. M. Bradley, Cuthbert, and Lang (1999), affective modulation of the startle reflex is a robust method for measuring the activation of the underlying appetitive and aversive, or approach-withdrawal, systems, particularly because it captures the state of the organism prior to the onset of fight/flight behavior. The startle reflex itself is an index of the preparatory state of the organism prior to initiation of the flight response, which is consistent with literature that has found fear-induced freezing in rodents to be associated with startle potentiation; no such relationship exists when the animal is in an active state or responding to aversive stimuli. For instance, Grillon, Ameli, Woods, Marikangas, and Davis (1991) showed that the startle reflex is consistently potentiated in humans when the experimental condition involves a verbally instructed threat. Essentially, once the flight component of the fight/flight system is engaged, startle potentiation is no longer a useful measure of emotional reactivity, as affective startle modulation will be eradicated once the organism has become overtly reactive. In short, potentiation of the startle reflex during presentation of affectively negative stimuli is an early indicator that the organism has detected a threat; as such, it is an index of the activation of the appetitive/aversive motivational systems.

Affective Modulation of Startle Methodology

The methods of data collection for the startle paradigm were previously discussed in this chapter (see discussion of prepulse inhibition). The setup and collection of data in studies that seek to explore affective modulation are identical in terms of lead placement and outcome measure (magnitude of the blink reflex following a startling probe). However, whereas studies of prepulse inhibition involve manipulation of the timing of the lead interval of a nonstartling, benign, prepulse stimulus, the paradigm to assess affective modulation involves manipulating the affective state of the subject prior to or during presentation of the startle probe.

Lang and his colleagues have explored the affective modulation of the startle reflex for well over a decade and have provided empirical support for the notion that the amplitude of the startle reflex varies systematically based on the ongoing emotional valence of individuals. Using a sample of undergraduates, Vrana, Spence, and Lang (1988) showed that acoustic startle probes were augmented during the presentation of negatively valenced slides, which included photographic stimuli of such unpleasant images as starving children, angry human faces, violent death scenes, and an aimed gun. In contrast, when undergraduates viewed positively valenced pictures such as those depicting happy babies, attractive nudes, and chocolate, startle responses to acoustic probes were attenuated. A later study (M. M. Bradley, Cuthbert, & Lang, 1990) extended this early work by demonstrating a linear relationship between the degree of emotional arousal participants reported while viewing foreground stimuli and startle potentiation, beyond the potential effects of startle probe modality (i.e., acoustic versus visual) and participant self-

reported interest in the foreground stimuli. Another study by this research group (Cuthbert et al., 1996) showed that the affective modulation of startle potentiation is linearly related to the degree of arousal of the foreground stimuli, such that blink potentiation in the presence of negative stimuli and blink inhibition in the case of positive stimuli were most pronounced when participants reported that the corresponding stimuli elicited high degrees of arousal.

Affective Modulation of Startle and Developmental Psychopathology

The developmental literature on the role of startle modulation in both normative and abnormal processes is still in its infancy. Indeed, very few published studies have examined the role of affective modulation of startle in infants or children, and the little work that has been done has yielded mixed findings. In her study of 5-month-old infants, Balaban (1995) found early evidence for the emergence of the adult affectively modulated startle responsiveness. Specifically, infants showed startle potentiation while viewing pictures of happy faces and attenuated eyeblink magnitude while viewing photos of angry faces. In contrast are two known studies that sought to replicate this pattern in older children. McManis, Bradley, Cuthbert, and Lang (1995) examined affective startle modulation in children ages 7 to 10 and found no evidence of a generalized adult-like response pattern, although further analyses revealed that girls showed the typical affectively modulated pattern but boys did not. Similarly, Cook, Hawk, Hawk, and Hummer (1995) found no evidence of the affective modulation of startle in their school-age sample. Given only the infant evidence, it could be concluded that affective modulation of the startle reflex is salient in the early months of life. However, Cook et al. and McManis et al. show no evidence for the phenomenon in middle childhood. As pointed out by Ornitz (1999), there is much yet to be learned about the normal development of affective modulation of startle. Certainly, three studies alone do not provide sufficient resolution to this issue. For instance, one plausible explanation forwarded by Ornitz for the infant findings in light of the null findings for the same effect in older samples is that the infant pattern of responding is due to attentional focus, in that angry faces perhaps mark a more novel, and therefore interesting, set of stimuli to infants than neutral or happy faces.

Given the general scarcity of findings of affective modulation of startle in children, normal or atypical, one must turn to the adult literature to consider the contribution and relevance of the paradigm to issues related to developmental psychopathology. The degree of affective modulation in the startle response has been examined in studies of psychopaths (Patrick, Bradley, & Lang, 1993) and fearful (Cook, Hawk, Davis, & Stevenson, 1991) and clinically depressed (Allen, Trinder, & Brennen, 1999) adults and in anxiety disorders, including PTSD (Morgan, Grillon, Southwick, Davis, & Charney, 1995) and specific phobia (Hamm, Cuthbert, Globisch, & Vaitl, 1997; Vrana, Constantine, & Westman, 1992).

Perhaps the best evidence for the contribution of the startle paradigm to the study of abnormal psychological development comes from the literature investigating the affective modulation of startle response in criminals and psychopaths (Patrick, 1994; Patrick et al., 1993). By definition, psychopathic individuals show marked abnormalities in affective responsiveness. According to Cleckley's (1976) criteria, individuals with primary psychopathy manifest antisocial behaviors due to an underlying deficit in emotional processing. Lykken's (1957) landmark study revealed that, relative to normal controls, psychopathic adults showed less anxiety on measures of self-report, less galvanic skin response reactivity to a conditioned shock, and less avoidance of punishment during a test of avoidance learning. This work provided the earliest evidence that the primary deficit in psychopaths involves a lack of anxiety. The predominant theory of psychopathy still contends that the central deficit in individuals who meet the criteria for true psychopathy is a lack of behavioral inhibition in response to punishment or nonreward (Fowles, 1980; Patrick, 1994).

According to Patrick (1994), the literature offering evidence for a lack of fear in psychopathic samples is limited by the use of autonomic indices, which confound assessments of the behavioral inhibition system with more generalized sympathetic arousal and higher-level processing. Further, although autonomic measures such as electrodermal activity should, theoretically, increase with activation of the behavioral inhibition system (Fowles, 1980), empirical support for this claim in normative samples does not abound (e.g., see Fowles, Kochanska, & Murray, 2000; Keltikangas-Järvinen, Kettunen, Ravaja, & Näätänen, 1999). Hence, autonomic measures fail to provide satisfactory evidence for Lykken's (1957) and Cleckley's (1976) notions regarding the affective deficit involved in psychopathy.

Patrick and his colleagues (1993) used startle methodology and autonomic measures to examine affective processing of psychopathic and nonpsychopathic men among a population of incarcerated sex offenders. They examined the degree of startle potentiation during the presentation of emotionally pleasant, unpleasant, or neutral pictures. Results showed that there were no statistically significant differences between incarcerated, nonpsychopathic men and a control sample of college students. In other words, for these two groups, startle responses were appropriately inhibited during presentation of positive stimuli and potentiated during presentation of negative stimuli.

In stark contrast was the psychopathic group, who not only failed to show startle potentiation during the presentation of the negatively valenced photos, but instead showed an inhibition in their blink amplitude relative to neutral slides. Hence, the psychopathic group manifested startle inhibition during presentation of both positively *and* negatively valenced stimuli, providing profound evidence that the nature of emotional processing between these two groups is quite discrepant. An additional subgroup of men in the study who were classified as "mixed" fell between the cutoff for clinical diagnosis of psychopathy but scored higher than average on the index of psychopathy used in this study. When this subgroup was added to the group of psychopaths, a correlation was found between degree of emotional detachment and startle potentiation to negative stimuli, such that individuals who were the most emotionally detached showed the highest levels of startle inhibition during presentation of negative stimuli (or the reversed startle potentiation effect). No between-group differences were found for autonomic response patterns: All participants showed increases in skin conductance reactions to both positive *and* negative stimuli and all showed normal patterns of heart rate deceleration.

Future Directions in the Use of Affective Startle

The application of the startle paradigm to the study of psychopathy by Patrick and his colleagues (1993) has yielded important contributions that would not have been obtained via the use of other psychophysiological measures. We suggest that startle methodology holds great promise for the early assessment of psychological risk. Methodologically, data collection is relatively clear-cut and lends itself to work with young children and infants. The ability to tap "pure" responses directly based on the neural circuitry involved in the processing of fear and pleasure (Ornitz, 1999) makes interpretation of startle data quite clean.

One logical extension of the current work in affective startle is to attempt to replicate the findings of Patrick and his colleagues (1993) in samples of children and/or adolescents. For instance, an examination of affective startle responses in a clinical sample of conduct disordered boys is currently under way in our laboratory. This work will extend the work of Patrick and his colleagues in psychopathy by establishing the degree to which the physiologically based absence of fear manifest by adult criminal samples is evident among the group of children who are at greatest risk for subsequent development of the adult condition.

One study by Schmidt and Fox (1999) also demonstrates the benefits of using the startle methodology to assess degree of risk for deviant development. Schmidt and Fox found amplified fear-potentiated startle in a subgroup of negatively reactive 9-month-olds at risk for behavioral inhibition in childhood, which can act as a precursor to anxiety disorders in childhood. This increase in startle amplitude was specific to a laboratory stranger approach paradigm, as no differences in baseline startle were found. This work provides evidence that amplified startle responses may be used as an index of early risk for the subsequent development of anxiety-related conditions.

In short, although the developmental literature in affective modulation of startle is far from sufficient, adult studies such as those of Patrick and his colleagues (Patrick, 1994; Patrick et al., 1993) and infant work by Schmidt and Fox (1999) illustrate the potential benefits of applying the measure to young samples who are at risk for the development of conditions associated with the processing of fear, be it increased or deficient fear-related reactivity. Of particular importance, following such children who have manifested early behavioral and physiological risk across childhood and adolescence will enable researchers to explore the degree to which environmental factors alter the developmental trajectories of children marked by physiologically substantiated risk.

CONCLUSIONS AND FUTURE DIRECTIONS

Unlike many chronic diseases, psychopathology, in the form of either the diagnosable disorder or its developmental precursors, is often evident early in life (Giaconia, Reinherz, Silverman, & Pakiz, 1994; Institute of Medicine, 1989; World Health Organization, 2000). This early appearance is a vital component of attempts to both treat and prevent psychopathology in the population. This is in line with Kohlberg, LaCrosse, and Ricks's (1972, p. 217) view that the ability to predict outcome is the "single most important area of study of clinical theory and practice with children." Yet, although researchers and clinicians are skilled at describing and categorizing these early phenotypes, their larger work is hampered by the fact that the phenotypes are only moderately predictive of later psychopathology (Kagan, 1994).

In addressing these concerns, Sroufe and Rutter (1984) have made the distinction between developmental coherence and developmental stability. That is, although psychologists

have found very few traits or abilities that remain truly stable over time, the course of an individual's development is both lawful and coherent in nature. They argue that continuity lies not in the presence of a specific behavior across time, but in the lawful relationship between early and later behavior, even if the link is exceedingly complex. This is true in the case of both normative and atypical development (Cicchetti & Sroufe, 1978). This view of development as a dynamic yet lawful progression suggests that researchers must rely on multiple measures, collected over time, to describe and assess the relationships among the components within the person-biology-experience structure. These multiple measures are then used to assess multiple components of the observed outcomes. These include the factors, processes, and mechanisms involved in producing both typical and atypical development (Garmezy, 1996).

In looking for the antecedents of later psychopathology, researchers familiar with the adult presentation of a disorder may begin their study of children by trying to find phenotypically similar behaviors in the young. For example, does the 7-year-old bipolar child behave similarly to the 27-year-old bipolar adult (Biederman et al., 2003; Tillman & Geller, 2003)? The same is true for high-risk studies in which risk is linked to one proscribed outcome. Erlenmeyer-Kimling (1996) points out that many Schizophrenia studies predicted that their participants would either be "manifestly schizophrenic or clinically unremarkable." Instead, the data indicate that children at risk for a specific disorder can display their vulnerability in a wide variety of behaviors. These findings reinforce Sroufe and Rutter's (1984) suggestion that researchers may do better in deemphasizing phenotypic mirrors throughout development and instead focus on failures in adaptation, which are defined through core developmental issues.

As the preceding discussion makes clear, psychophysiological measures are ideal for this work. Varying in the systems of interest, the time course of measures, and the psychological constructs addressed, psychophysiological measures, particularly when used in combination, can provide an additional window onto the psychological mechanisms underlying both risk and resilience in early development. The flexibility found in psychophysiology allows researchers to address some of the core questions surrounding developmental psychopathology. To illustrate, we can use Keller et al.'s (2000) summary of important questions that the field of developmental psychopathology should address.

First, what are the psychological and physiological causes of the psychophysiological differences? Systematic use of psychophysiological measures that are anatomically and functionally well-defined, like the startle response, in conjunction with traditional behavioral measures, will help target the root forces underlying observed differences. Second, at what stage of processing do individuals with psychopathology begin to diverge from controls? This question can be answered at the micro level across the span of milliseconds, as seen in the ERP, or at the level of the relatively laconic LHPA system. Third, under what conditions are individuals with psychopathology able to mimic controls in their performance of mental operations? This question is analogous to studies attempting to examine the conditions under which children display adult-like performance on a task. Psychophysiological measures allow researchers to address this question across a number of domains, from cognition to motivation and emotion. Fourth, do the processing differences seen within or across diagnostic groups reflect a deficit or a compensatory tactic? This question is of particular interest when comparisons between psychophysiological and behavioral data show a dissociation in findings. If, for example, two groups of children display identical behavioral outcomes in a task but diverging psychophysiological functioning, one may then begin to explore the possibility that the groups are using different strategies or processes to achieve the presented goal.

In addition to Keller et al.'s (2000) questions, psychophysiology can also help address two interrelated issues of central importance in developmental psychopathology: differential diagnosis and comorbidity. To date, *Diagnostic and Statistical Manual of Mental Disorders* diagnostic categories are almost exclusively reliant on observed behavior coupled with self- or parent report (American Psychiatric Association, 1994). However, as our understanding of the biological substrates of behavior grows, it may be wise to incorporate psychophysiological measures into the diagnostic process. The early work in this process can be illustrated by recent research with ADHD. ADHD is a highly comorbid disorder often co-occurring with Conduct Disorder and Oppositional Defiant Disorder (Bird, Gould, & Staghezza-Jaramillo, 1994), anxiety disorders (August, Realmuto, MacDonald, & Nugent, 1996), depression (Woolston et al., 1989), and learning difficulties (August & Garfinkel, 1990). For example, 40% to 70% of children with ADHD are also diagnosed with either ODD or CD (Banaschewski et al., 2003), and these children tend to exhibit more psychosocial difficulties than their counterparts who also have ADHD but show no co-occurring psychopathology (Kuhne, Schacher, & Tannock, 1997).

Recent work has attempted to aid diagnosis and classification through the use of psychophysiological measures. For example, Mann et al. (Mann, Lubar, Zimmerman, Miller, & Muenchen, 1992) found that EEG measures incorporated into a discriminant function analysis could accurately predict group membership 80% of the time. Chabot and Serfontein (1996) found that a similar analysis using nine EEG variables had a correct classification rate of 95% and 93% for ADHD and non-ADHD children, respectively. Clarke and colleagues (Clarke, Barry, McCarthy, & Selikowitz, 2001b) used EEG-based cluster analyses to create three distinct subtypes within their sample of boys with ADHD. In a related vein, Banaschewski et al. (2003) have used ERP component differences to argue that ADHD comorbid with Conduct Disorder constitutes a "separate psychopathological entity" from ADHD in its pure form.

With the addition of new sources of information, particularly if they bring information from a different level of functioning, we may better define the boundaries and characteristics of our target population (Kagan, 1996). This allows the researcher to reduce the amount of heterogeneity within a group or even create subgroupings (Cicchetti & Rogosch, 1996; Richters, 1997). In this way, research can continue with greater precision, parsing out the multiple pathways to and manifestations of an underlying maladaptation. From a historical perspective, the addition of new technology, coupled with rigorous methodology, has moved the study of pathology in childhood from the nineteenth century's reliance on "degeneracy" as the broad-brush answer to maladaptation (S. H. White, 1996) to the current complex, and perhaps confusing, network of explanatory mechanisms.

Further complicating our understanding of deviant processes underlying pathological states is the dynamic nature of the system itself. Although the use of psychophysiological indices provides a window onto the biology underlying behavior, these measures are not impervious to contextual forces. Indeed, the transactional model set forth by Sameroff and Chandler (1975), which emphasized dynamic relationships between the child and his or her environment across time, is quite meaningfully applied to studies of psychophysiology, as physiological mechanisms reorganize in response to environmental demands (Campos et al., 1989). Our model of neuroplasticity holds that behavioral change is the result of a complex series of transactions between genetic programs that direct the formation and connectivity of brain structures and environmental modifiers of these codes (N. A. Fox, Calkins, & Bell, 1994). An emergent body of literature supports this notion, as changes in physiology based on environmental circumstances have been documented in humans (N. A. Fox et al., 2001) and nonhuman primates (Bennett et al., 2002). Curtis and Cicchetti (2003, p. 803) have indicated that "the incorporation of a biological perspective into research on resilience still requires adherence to a dynamic, transactional view that respects the importance of context."

Given such evidence, it is clear that the field of physiology will make a significant contribution to the study of psychopathology only by rising to the challenges posed by the transactional model of development. One way to do this is by studying children early—an option nicely accommodated with the use of psychophysiological measures. Groups found to be at risk behaviorally and/or physiologically should then be followed at critical junctures of development and reevaluated not only behaviorally or psychophysiologically but also in terms of the presence or absence of environmental stressors. Indeed, Sameroff and MacKenzie (2003) caution that the success of such models hinges on the outlining of a careful schedule of assessments that target the developmental periods when the environment and the child are most likely to be altered by each other (and hence most likely to change).

It is because of the bidirectional environment-physiology relationship that developmental psychophysiology holds great promise for the study of developmental psychopathology, as psychophysiological measures allow for the quantification of proximal influences at the most basic biological level. However, our greatest potential for contribution may also be our downfall, as research attempts that fail to monitor the degree of change in physiology in accordance with the presence or absence of relevant ecological influences will lead to short-sighted, overly simplistic conclusions. Research programs that adhere to transactionally oriented designs will likely be the most profitable in advancing current understanding regarding the antecedents and consequences of normative and aberrant development. Indeed, measures of psychophysiology reflect only one dimension of an intricate ensemble of systems, individual and contextual, which together alter the course of development.

REFERENCES

Allen, N. B., Trinder, J., & Brennen, C. (1999). Affective startle modulation in clinical depression: Preliminary findings. *Biological Psychiatry, 46,* 542–550.

American Psychiatric Association. (1994). *Diagnostic and statistical manual of mental disorders* (4th ed.). Washington, DC: Author.

Angold, A., Erklani, A., Silberg, J., Eaves, L., & Costello, E. J. (2002). Depression scale scores in 8–17-year-olds: Effects of age and gender. *Journal of Child Psychology and Psychiatry and Allied Disorders, 43,* 1052–1063.

Anllo-Vento, M. L. (1991). *Visual-spatial selective attention and reading ability in children: A study using event-related potentials and behavioral measures.* Unpublished doctoral dissertation, University of North Carolina at Greensboro.

Anthony, B. J. (1990). Blink modulation in attention-deficit disorder [Abstract]. *Psychophysiology, 27*(Suppl.), S6.

Armitage, R., Emslie, G. J., Hoffman, R. F., Weinberg, W. A., Kowatch, R. A., Rintelmann, J., et al. (2000). Ultradian rhythms and temporal coherence in sleep EEG in depressed children and adolescents. *Biological Psychiatry, 47,* 338–350.

Armitage, R., Hudson, A., Trivedi, M., & Rush, A. J. (1995). Sex differences in the distribution of EEG frequencies during sleep: Unipolar depressed outpatients. *Journal of Affective Disorders, 34,* 121–129.

Ashman, S. B., Dawson, G., Panagiotides, H., Yamada, E., & Wilkinson, C. W. (2002). Stress hormone levels of children of depressed mothers. *Development and Psychopathology, 14,* 333–349.

Atkinson, C. M., Drysdale, K. A., & Fulham, W. R. (2002). Event-related potentials to Stroop and reverse Stroop stimuli. *International Journal of Psychophysiology, 47,* 1–21.

August, G. J., & Garfinkel, B. D. (1990). Comorbidity of ADHD and reading disability among clinic-referred children. *Journal of Abnormal Child Psychology, 18,* 29–45.

August, G. J., Realmuto, G. M., MacDonald, A. W., III., & Nugent, S. M. (1996). Prevalence of ADHD and comorbid disorders among elementary school children screened for disruptive behavior. *Journal of Abnormal Child Psychology, 24,* 571–595.

Ax, A. F. (1970). Autonomic conditioning in chronic Schizophrenia. *Journal of Abnormal Psychology, 76,* 140–154.

Axelson, D. A., Doraiswamy, P. M., McDonald, W. M., Boyko, O. B., Tupler, L. A., Patterson, L. J., et al. (1993). Hypercortisolemia and hippocampal changes in depression. *Psychiatry Research, 47,* 163–173.

Balaban, M. T. (1995). Affective influences on startle in five-month-old infants: Reactions to facial expressions of emotion. *Child Development, 66,* 28–36.

Banaschewski, T., Brandeis, D., Heinrich, H., Albrecht, B., Brunner, E., & Rothenberger, A. (2003). Association of ADHD and conduct disorder: Brain electrical evidence for the existence of a distinct subtype. *Journal of Child Psychology and Psychiatry and Allied Disciplines, 44,* 356–376.

Bar-Haim, Y., Marshall, P. J., Fox, N. A., Schorr, E. A., & Gordon-Salant, S. (2003). Mismatch negativity in socially withdrawn children. *Biological Psychiatry, 54,* 17–24.

Barry, R. J., Clarke, A. R., & Johnstone, S. J. (2003). A review of the electrophysiology in attention-deficit/hyperactivity disorder: I. Qualitative and quantitative electroencephalography. *Clinical Neurophysiology, 114,* 171–183.

Barry, R. J., Clarke, A. R., McCarthy, R., & Selikowitz, M. (2002). EEG coherence in attention-deficit/hyperactivity disorder: A comparative study of two DSM-IV types. *Clinical Neurophysiology, 113,* 579–585.

Bartussek, D., Diedrich, O., Naumann, E., & Collet, W. (1993). Introversion-extraversion and event-related potential (ERP): A test of J. A. Gray's theory. *Personality and Individual Differences, 14,* 565–574.

Bauer, A. M., Quas, J. A., & Boyce, W. T. (2002). Associations between physiological reactivity and children's behavior: Advantages of a multisystem approach. *Journal of Developmental and Behavioral Pediatrics, 23,* 102–113.

Baving, L., Laucht, M., & Schmidt, M. H. (1999). Atypical frontal brain activation in ADHD: Preschool and elementary school boys and girls.

Journal of the American Academy of Child and Adolescent Psychiatry, 38, 1363–1371.

Baving, L., Laucht, M., & Schmidt, M. H. (2002). Frontal brain activation in anxious school children. *Journal of Child Psychology and Psychiatry and Allied Disciplines, 43*, 265–274.

Beauchaine, T. P. (2001). Vagal tone, development, and Gray's motivational theory: Toward an integrated model of autonomic nervous system functioning in psychopathology. *Development and Psychopathology, 13*, 183–214.

Beauchaine, T. P., Katkin, E. S., Strassberg, Z., & Snarr, J. (2001). Disinhibitory psychopathology in male adolescents: Discriminating conduct disorder from attention deficit/hyperactivity disorder through concurrent assessment of multiple autonomic states. *Journal of Abnormal Psychology, 110*, 610–624.

Belanger, D., & Feldman, S. M. (1962). Effects of water deprivation upon heart rate and instrumental activity in the rat. *Journal of Comparative and Physiological Psychology, 55*, 220–225.

Bell, M. A., & Fox, N. A. (1992). The relations between frontal brain electrical activity and cognitive development during infancy. *Child Development, 63*, 1142–1164.

Bell, M. A., & Fox, N. A. (1994). Brain development over the first year of life: Relations between EEG frequency and coherence and cognitive and affective behaviors. In G. Dawson & K. W. Fischer (Eds.), *Human behavior and the developing brain* (pp. 314–345). New York: Guilford Press.

Bell, M. A., & Fox, N. A. (1996). Crawling experience is related to changes in cortical organization during infancy: Evidence from EEG coherence. *Developmental Psychobiology, 29*, 551–561.

Bennett, A. J., Lesch, K. P., Heils, A., Long, J. C., Lorenz, J. G., Shoat, S. E., et al. (2002). Early experience and serotonin transporter gene variation interact to influence primate CNS function. *Molecular Psychiatry, 7*, 118–122.

Benninger, C., Matthis, P., & Scheffner, D. (1984). EEG development of healthy boys and girls: Results of a longitudinal study. *Electroencephalography and Clinical Neurophysiology, 57*, 1–12.

Berger, H. (1929). Über das Elektrenkephalogramm des Menschen: I. *Archiv für Psychiatri und Nervenkrankheiten, 87*, 527–570.

Berger, H. (1932). Über das Elektrenkephalogramm des Menschen: IV. *Archiv für Psychiatri und Nervenkrankheiten, 97*, 6–26.

Bergman, L. R., & Magnusson, D. (1997). A person-oriented approach in research on developmental psychopathology. *Development and Psychopathology, 9*, 291–319.

Biederman, J., Mick, E., Faraone, S. V., Spencer, T., Wilens, T. E., & Wozniak, J. (2003). Current concepts in the validity, diagnosis and treatment of pediatric bipolar disorder. *International Journal of Neuropsychopharmacology, 6*, 293–300.

Bird, H. R., Gould, M. S., & Staghezza-Jaramillo, B. M. (1994). The comorbidity of ADHD in a community sample of children aged 6 through 16 years. *Journal of Child and Family Studies, 3*, 365–378.

Boulis, N. M., & Davis, M. (1989). Footshock-induced sensitization of electrically elicited startle reflexes. *Behavioral Neuroscience, 103*, 504–508.

Bowditch, H. P., & Warren, J. W. (1890). The knee-jerk and its physiological modifications. *Journal of Physiology, 11*, 25–64.

Boyce, W. T., Champoux, M., Suomi, S. J., & Gunnar, M. R. (1995). Salivary cortisol in nursery-reared rhesus monkeys: Reactivity to peer interactions and altered circadian activity. *Developmental Psychobiology, 28*, 257–267.

Boyce, W. T., Quas, J., Alkon, A., Smider, N. A., Essex, M. J., Kupfer, D. J., et al. (2001). Autonomic reactivity and psychopathology in middle childhood. *British Journal of Psychiatry, 179*, 144–150.

Bradley, B. P., Mogg, K., & Williams, R. (1995). Implicit and explicit memory for emotion-congruent information in clinical depression and anxiety. *Behaviour Research and Therapy, 33*, 755–770.

Bradley, M. M., Cuthbert, B. N., & Lang, P. J. (1990). Startle reflex modification: Emotion or attention? *Psychophysiology, 27*, 513–522.

Bradley, M. M., Cuthbert, B. N., & Lang, P. J. (1999). Affect and the startle reflex. In M. E. Dawson, A. M. Schell, & A. H. Böhmelt (Eds.), *Startle modification: Implications for neuroscience, cognitive science, and clinical science* (pp. 157–185). New York: Cambridge University Press.

Bradley, M. M., & Lang, P. J. (2000). Affective reactions to acoustic stimuli. *Psychophysiology, 37*, 204–215.

Braff, D. L., & Geyer, M. A. (1990). Sensorimotor gating and Schizophrenia: Human and animal model studies. *Archives of General Psychiatry, 47*, 181–188.

Bremner, J. D., Krystal, J. H., Southwick, S. M., & Charney, D. S. (1995). Functional neuroanatomical correlates of the effects of stress on memory. *Journal of Traumatic Stress, 8*, 527–553.

Brown, M. S., & Tanner, C. (1988). Type A behavior and cardiovascular responsivity in preschoolers. *Nursing Research, 37*, 152–155.

Bruder, G. E., Tenke, C. E., Stewart, J. W., Towey, J. P., Leite, P., Voglmaier, M. M., et al. (1995). Brain event related potential to complex tones in depressed patients: Relation to perceptual asymmetry and clinical features. *Psychophysiology, 32*, 373–381.

Bundy, R. S., & Mangan, S. M. (1979). Electrodermal indices of stress and cognition: Possible hydration artifacts. *Psychophysiology, 16*, 30–33.

Bush, G., Vogt, B. A., Holmes, J., Dale, A. M., Greve, D., Jenike, M. A., et al. (1999). Dorsal anterior cingulate cortex: A role in reward-based decision making. *Proceedings of the National Academy of Sciences, 2002*, 523–528.

Cacioppo, J. T., Uchino, B. N., & Berntson, G. G. (1994). Individual differences in the autonomic origins of heart rate reactivity: The psychometrics of respiratory sinus arrhythmia and preejection period. *Psychophysiology, 31*, 412–419.

Calkins, S. D., & Fox, N. A. (1997). Cardiac vagal tone indices of temperamental reactivity and behavioral regulation in young children. *Developmental Psychobiology, 31*, 125–135.

Campos, J. J., Campos, R. G., & Barrett, K. C. (1989). Emergent themes in the study of emotional development and emotion regulation. *Developmental Psychology, 25*, 394–402.

Cannon, W. B. (1915). *Bodily changes in pain, hunger, fear and rage: An account of recent researches into the function of emotional excitement.* Oxford: Appleton.

Cannon, W. B. (1928). Neural organization for emotional expression. I C. Mirchenson & M. L. Reymert (Eds.), *Feelings and emotions: The Wittenberg Symposium* (pp. 82–103). Worcester: Clark University Press.

Carlson, M., & Earls, F. (1997). Psychological and neuroendocrinological sequelae of early social deprivation in institutionalized children in Romania. *Annals of the New York Academy of Sciences, 807*, 419–428.

Carrion, V. G., Weems, C. F., Ray, R. D., Glaser, B., Hessl, D., & Reiss, A. L. (2002). Diurnal salivary cortisol in pediatric posttraumatic stress disorder. *Biological Psychiatry, 51*, 575–582.

Carroll, D., Turner, J. R., & Hellawell, J. C. (1986). Heart rate and oxygen consumption during active psychological challenge: The effects of level of difficulty. *Psychophysiology, 23*, 174–181.

Catts, S. V., Shelley, A. M., Ward, P. B., Liebert, B., McConaghy, N., Andrews, S., et al. (1995). Brain potential evidence for an auditory sensory memory deficit in Schizophrenia. *American Journal of Psychiatry, 152*, 213–219.

Chabot, R., & Serfontein, G. (1996). Quantitative electroencephalographic profiles of children with attention deficit disorder. *Biological Psychiatry, 40,* 951–963.

Charles, G., Hansenne, M., Anssea, M., Pitchot, W., Machowski, R., Schittecatte, M., et al. (1995). P300 in posttraumatic stress disorder. *Neuropsychobiology, 32,* 72–74.

Cheek, J. M., & Buss, A. H. (1981). Shyness and sociability. *Journal of Personality and Social Psychology, 41,* 330–339.

Cheour, M., Leppänen, P. H., & Kraus, N. (2000). Mismatch negativity (MMN) as tool for investigating auditory discrimination and sensory memory in infants and children. *Clinical Neurophysiology, 111,* 4–16.

Chugani, H. T., & Phelps, M. E. (1986). Maturational changes in cerebral function in infants determined by 18FDG positron emission tomography. *Science, 231,* 840–843.

Cicchetti, D., & Dawson, G. (2002). Editorial: Multiple levels of analysis. *Development and Psychopathology, 14,* 417–420.

Cicchetti, D., & Rogosch, F. A. (1996). Equifinality and multifinality in developmental psychopathology. *Development and Psychopathology, 8,* 597–600.

Cicchetti, D., & Rogosch, F. A. (2001). Diverse patterns of neuroendocrine activity in maltreated children. *Development and Psychopathology, 13,* 677–693.

Cicchetti, D., & Sroufe, L. A. (1978). An organizational view of affect: Illustrations from the study of Down syndrome infants. In M. Lewis & L. Rosenblum (Eds.), *The development of affect* (pp. 1247–1251). New York: Plenum Press.

Cicchetti, D., & Toth, S. (1995). A developmental psychopathology perspective on child abuse and neglect. *Journal of the American Academy of Child and Adolescent Psychiatry, 34,* 541–565.

Clarke, A. R., Barry, R. J., McCarthy, R., & Selikowitz, M. (1998). EEG analysis in attention-deficit/hyperactivity disorder: A comparative study of two subtypes. *Psychiatry Research, 81,* 19–29.

Clarke, A. R., Barry, R. J., McCarthy, R., & Selikowitz, M. (2001a). Age and sex effects in the EEG: Development of the normal child. *Clinical Neurophysiology, 112,* 806–814.

Clarke, A. R., Barry, R. J., McCarthy, R., & Selikowitz, M. (2001b). EEG-defined subtypes of children with attention-deficit/hyperactivity disorder. *Clinical Neurophysiology, 112,* 2098–2105.

Clarke, A. R., Barry, R. J., McCarthy, R., & Selikowitz, M. (2001c). Excess beta activity in children with attention-deficit/hyperactivity disorder: An atypical electrophysiological group. *Psychiatry Research, 103,* 205–218.

Clarke, A. R., Barry, R. J., McCarthy, R., Selikowitz, M., Brown, C. R., & Croft, R. J. (2003). Effects of stimulant medications on the EEG of children with attention-deficit/hyperactivity disorder predominantly inattentive type. *International Journal of Psychophysiology, 47,* 129–137.

Cleckley, H. M. (1976). *The mask of sanity* (5th ed.). St Louis, MO: Mosby.

Cohn, J., Matias, R., Tronick, E., Connell, D., & Lyons-Ruth, K. (1986). Face-to-face interactions of depressed mothers and their infants. In E. Tronick & T. Field (Eds.), *Maternal depression and infant disturbance* (pp. 15–23). San Francisco: Jossey-Bass.

Coles, M. G. H., & Rugg, M. D. (1995). Event related potentials: An introduction. In M. D. Rugg & M. G. H. Coles (Eds.), *Electrophysiology of mind: Event related brain potentials and cognition* (pp. 1–26). New York: Oxford University Press.

Cook, E. W., Hawk, L. W., Davis, T. L., & Stevenson, V. E. (1991). Affective individual differences and startle reflex modulation. *Journal of Abnormal Psychology, 100,* 5–13.

Cook, E. W., Hawk. L. W., Hawk, T. M., & Hummer, K. (1995). Affective modulation of startle in children. *Psychophysiology, 32,* S25.

Curtis, W. J., & Cicchetti, D. (2003). Moving research on resilience into the 21st century: Theoretical and methodological considerations in examining the biological contributors to resilience. *Development and Psychopathology, 15,* 773–810.

Cuthbert, B. N., Bradley, M. M., & Lang, P. J. (1996). Probing picture perception: Activation and emotion. *Psychophysiology, 33,* 103–111.

Dallman, M. F., Akana, S. F., Cascio, C. S., Darlington, D. N., Jacobson, L., & Levin, N. (1987). Regulation of ACTH secretion: Variations on a theme of B. *Recent Progress in Hormonal Research, 43,* 113–173.

Davidson, R. J. (1984a). Affect, cognition, and hemispheric specialization. In C. E. Izard, J. Kagan, & R. Jajonc (Eds.), *Emotion, cognition, and behavior* (pp. 320–365). New York: Cambridge University Press.

Davidson, R. J. (1984b). Hemispheric asymmetry and emotions. In K. R. Scherer & P. Ekman (Eds.), *Approaches to emotion* (pp. 39–57). Hillsdale, NJ: Erlbaum.

Davidson, R. J. (1994). Temperament, affective style, and frontal lobe asymmetry. In G. Dawson & K. W. Fischer (Eds.), *Human behavior and the developing brain* (pp. 518–536). New York: Guilford Press.

Davidson, R. J. (1995). Cerebral asymmetry, emotion, and affective style. In R. J. Davidson & K. Hugdahl (Eds.), *Brain asymmetry* (pp. 361–387). Cambridge, MA: MIT Press.

Davidson, R. J., Chapman, J. P., Chapman, L. J., & Henriques, J. B. (1990). Asymmetrical brain electrical activity discriminates between psychometrically matched verbal and spatial cognitive tasks. *Psychophysiology, 27,* 528–543.

Davidson, R. J., & Fox, N. A. (1982). Asymmetrical brain activity discriminates between positive and negative affective stimuli in human infants. *Science, 218,* 1235–1237.

Davidson, R. J., & Fox, N. A. (1989). Frontal brain asymmetry predicts infants' response to maternal separation. *Journal of Abnormal Psychology, 98,* 127–131.

Davidson, R. J., Jackson, D. C., & Larson, C. L. (2000). Human electroencephalography. In J. T. Cacioppo, L. G. Tassinary, & G. G. Berntson (Eds.), *Handbook of psychophysiology* (2nd ed., pp. 27–52). New York: Cambridge University Press.

Davidson, R. J., Marshall, J. R., Tomarken, A. J., & Henriques, J. B. (2000). While a phobic waits: Regional brain electrical and automatic activity predict anxiety in social phobics during anticipation of public speaking. *Biological Psychiatry, 47,* 85–95.

Davis, E. P., Bruce, J., & Gunnar, M. R. (2002). The anterior attention network: Associations with temperament and neuroendocrine activity in 6-year-old children. *Developmental Psychobiology, 40,* 43–56.

Davis, M., Hitchcock, J. M., & Rosen, J. B. (1987). Anxiety and the amygdala: Pharmacological and anatomical analysis of the fear-potentiated startle paradigm. In G. H. Bower (Ed.), *The psychology of learning and motivation: Advances in research and theory* (Vol. 21, pp. 263–305). San Diego: Academic Press.

Davis, P. A., & Davis, H. (1939). The electroencephalograms of psychotic patients. *American Journal of Psychiatry, 95,* 1007–1025.

Dawson, G. (1994). Development of emotional expression and emotion regulation in infancy. In M. D. Rugg & M. G. H. Coles (Eds.), *Electrophysiology of mind: Event related brain potentials and cognition* (pp. 346–369). New York: Oxford University Press.

Dawson, G., & Ashman, S. B. (2000). On the origins of a vulnerability to depression: The influence of the early social environment on the development of psychological systems related to risk for affective disorder. In C. A. Nelson (Ed.), *Minnesota Symposia on Child Psychology:*

The effects of early adversity on neurobehavioral development (pp. 245–279). Mahwah, NJ: Erlbaum.

Dawson, G., Grofer Klinger, L., Panagiotides, H., Hill, D., & Spieker, S. (1992). Frontal lobe activity and affective behavior of infants of mothers with depressive symptoms. *Child Development, 63,* 725–737.

Dawson, G., Klinger, L. G., Panagiotides, H., Lewy, A., & Castelloe, P. (1995). Subgroups of autistic children based on social behavior display distinct patterns of brain activity. *Journal of Abnormal Child Psychology, 23,* 569–583.

Dawson, G., Panagiotides, H., Grofer Klinger, L., & Hill, D. (1992). The role of frontal lobe functioning in the development of infant self-regulatory behavior. *Brain and Cognition, 20,* 152–175.

Dawson, M. E., Schell, A. M., & Böhmelt, A. H. (1999). Startle modification: Introduction and overview. In M. E. Dawson, A. M. Schell, & A. H. Böhmelt (Eds.), *Startle modification: Implications for neuroscience, cognitive science, and clinical science* (pp. 257–275). New York: Cambridge University Press.

Dawson, M. E., Schell, A. M., & Filion, D. L. (2000). The electrodermal system. In J. T. Cacioppo, L. G. Tassinary, & G. G. Bernston (Eds.), *Handbook of psychophysiology* (2nd ed., pp. 200–223). New York: Cambridge University Press.

DeBellis, M. D., Baum, A. S., Birmaher, B., Keshavan, M. S., Eccard, C. H., Boring, A. M., et al. (1999). Developmental traumatology: I. Biological stress systems. *Biological Psychiatry, 45,* 1259–1270.

Deldin, P. J., Shestyuk, A. Y., & Chiu, P. H. (2003). Event-related brain potential indices of memory biases in major depression. In M. F. Lenzenweger & J. M. Hooley (Eds.), *Principles of experimental psychopathology: Essays in honor of Brendan A. Maher* (pp. 195–209). Washington, DC: American Psychological Association.

De Pascalis, V. (1994). Personality and temperament in the event-related potentials during stimulus recognition tasks. *Personality and Individual Differences, 16,* 877–889.

De Pascalis, V., Fiore, A. D., & Sparita, A. (1996). Personality, event-related potential (ERP), and heart rate (HR): An investigation of Gray's theory. *Personality and Individual Differences, 20,* 733–746.

Dettling, A. C., Gunnar, M. R., & Donzella, B. (1999). Cortisol levels of young children in full-day child care centers: Relations with age and temperament. *Psychoneuroendocrinology, 24,* 519–536.

Deveney, C. M., & Deldin, P. J. (2004). Memory of faces: A slow wave ERP study of major depression. *Emotion, 4,* 295–304.

Duffy, E. (1962). *Activation and behavior.* New York: Wiley.

Duncan-Johnson, C. C., & Kopell, B. S. (1981). The Stroop effect: Brain potentials localize the source of interference. *Science, 214,* 938–940.

Ehrlich, D. J., & Malmo, R. B. (1967). Electrophysiological concomitants of simple operant conditioning in the rat. *Neuropsychologia, 5,* 219–235.

Elliott, R. (1969). Tonic heart rate: Experiments on the effects of collative variables lead to a hypothesis about its motivational significance. *Journal of Personality and Social Psychology, 12,* 211–228.

Erickson, K., Drevets, W., & Schulkin, J. (2003). Glucocorticoid regulation of diverse cognitive functions in normal and pathological emotional states. *Neuroscience and Behavioral Reviews, 27,* 233–246.

Erlenmeyer-Kimling, L. (1996). A look at the evolution of developmental models of Schizophrenia. In S. Matthysse, D. L. Levy, J. Kagan, & F. M. Benes (Eds.), *Psychopathology* (pp. 229–252). Cambridge, England: Cambridge University Press.

Essex, M. J., Klein, M. H., Cho, E., & Kalin, N. H. (2002). Maternal stress beginning in infancy may sensitize children to later stress exposure: Effects on cortisol and behavior. *Biological Psychiatry, 52,* 776–784.

Fabiani, M., Gratton, G., & Coles, M. G. H. (2000). Event-related brain potentials: Methods and theory. In J. T. Cacioppo, L. G. Tassinary, &

G. G. Berntson (Eds.), *Handbook of psychophysiology* (pp. 53–84). Cambridge, England: Cambridge University Press.

Farrington, D. P. (1997). The relationship between low resting heart rate and violence. In A. Raine & P. A. Brennan (Eds.), *Biosocial bases of violence* (pp. 89–105). New York: Plenum Press.

Fawcett, J., Zajecka, J. M., Kravitz, H. M., Edwards, J., Jeffriess, H., & Scorza, E. (1989). Fluoxetine versus amitriptyline in adult outpatients with major depression. *Current Therapeutic Research, 45,* 821–832.

Fearing, F. (1930). *Reflex action: A study in the history of physiological psychology.* Oxford: Wiliams & Wilkins.

Fere, C. (1888). Note sur les modifications de la tension électrique dans le corps humain. *Comptes Rendus des Séances de la Société de Biologie, 5,* 217–219. (Reprinted in S. W. Porges & M. G. H. Coles, 1976) *Psychophysiology.* Stroudsberg, PA: Dowden, Hutchinson & Ross.

Field, T. (1986). Models for reactive and chronic depression in infancy. In E. Z. Tronick & T. Field (Eds.), *Maternal depression and infant disturbance* (pp. 47–60). San Francisco: Jossey-Bass.

Field, T., Fox, N. A., Pickens, J., & Nawrocki, T. (1995). Relative right frontal EEG activation in 3- to 6-month-old infants of depressed mothers. *Developmental Psychology, 31,* 358–363.

Field, T., Healy, B., Goldstein, S., Perry, S., Bendall, D., Schanberg, S., et al. (1988). Infants of depressed mothers show "depressed" behavior even with non-depressed adults. *Child Development, 59,* 1569–1579.

Field, T., Sandberg, D., Garcia, R., Vega-Lahr, N., Goldstein, S., & Guy, L. (1985). Prenatal problem, postpartum depression, and early mother-infant interaction. *Developmental Psychology, 12,* 1152–1156.

Finsterwald, J., Selig, M. A., Schieche, M., Wurmser, H., & Papousek, M. (2000, July). *Individual differences in self-regulation in excessively crying infants: A microanalytical approach.* Paper presented at the International Conference of Infant Studies, Brighton, England.

Flinn, M. V., & England, B. G. (1995). Childhood stress and family environment. *Current Anthropology, 36,* 854–866.

Fouad, F. M., Tarazi, R. C., Ferrario, C. M., Fighaly, S., & Alicandri, C. (1984). Assessment of parasympathetic control of heart rate by a non-invasive method. *American Journal of Physiology, 246,* H838–H842.

Fowles, D. C. (1980). The three arousal model: Implications of Gray's two-factor learning theory for heart rate, electrodermal activity and psychopathy. *Psychophysiology, 17,* 87–104.

Fowles, D. C., Kochanska, G., & Murray, K. (2000). Electrodermal activity and temperament in preschool children. *Psychophysiology, 37,* 777–787.

Fox, E., Russo, R., Bowles, R., & Dutton, K. (2001). Do threatening stimuli draw or hold visual attention in subclinical anxiety? *Journal of Experimental Psychology: General, 130,* 681–700.

Fox, N. A. (1989). Psychophysiological correlates of emotional reactivity during the first year of life. *Developmental Psychology, 25,* 364–372.

Fox, N. A., & Bell, M. A. (1990). Electrophysiological indices of frontal lobe development: Relations to cognitive and affective behavior in human infants over the first year of life. *Annals of the New York Academy of Sciences, 608,* 677–704.

Fox, N. A., Calkins, S., & Bell, M. A. (1994). Neural plasticity and development in the first two years of life: Evidence from cognitive and socioemotional domains of research. *Development and Psychopathology, 6,* 677–696.

Fox, N. A., & Davidson, R. J. (1987). Electroencephalogram asymmetry in response to the approach of a stranger and maternal separation in 10-month-old infants. *Developmental Psychology, 23,* 233–240.

Fox, N. A., & Davidson, R. J. (1988). Patterns of brain electrical activity during facial signs of emotion in 10-month-old infants. *Developmental Psychology, 24*, 230–236.

Fox, N. A., Henderson, H. A., Rubin, K. H., Calkins, S. D., & Schmidt, L. A. (2001). Continuity and discontinuity of behavioral inhibition and exuberance: Psychophysiological and behavioral influences across the first four years of life. *Child Development, 72*, 1–21.

Fox, N. A., Rubin, K. H., Calkins, S. D., Marshall, T. R., Coplan, R. J., Porges, S. W. et al. (1995). Frontal activation asymmetry and social competence at four years of age. *Child Development, 66*, 1770–1784.

Fox, N. A., Schmidt, L. A., Calkins, S. D., Rubin, K. H., & Coplan, R. J. (1996). The role of frontal activation in the regulation and dysregulation of social behavior during the preschool years. *Development and Psychopathology, 8*, 89–102.

Fox, N. A., Schmidt, L. A., & Henderson, H. A. (2000). Developmental psychophysiology: Conceptual and methodological perspectives. In J. T. Cacioppo, L. G. Tassinary, & G. G. Berntson (Eds.), *Handbook of psychophysiology* (pp. 665–686). New York: Cambridge University Press.

Gaensbauer, T. J., & Hiatt, S. (1984). Facial communication of emotion in early infancy. In N. A. Fox & R. J. Davidson (Eds.), *The psychobiology of affective development* (pp. 207–230). Hillsdale, NJ: Erlbaum.

Garcia Coll, C., Kagan, J., & Reznick, J. S. (1984). Behavioral inhibition in young children. *Child Development, 55*, 1005–1019.

Garmezy, N. (1996). A paradoxical partnership: Some historical and contemporary referents linking adult schizophreniform disorder and resilient children under stress. In S. Matthysse, D. L. Levy, J. Kagan, & F. M. Benes (Eds.), *Psychopathology* (pp. 200–228). Cambridge, England: Cambridge University Press.

Gasser, T., Jennen-Steinmetz, C., Sroka, L., Verleger, R., & Mocks, J. (1988). Development of the EEG of school-age children and adolescents: II. Topography. *Electroencephalography and Clinical Neurophysiology, 69*, 100–109.

Gevins, A., Smith, M. E., McEvoy, L., & Yu, D. (1997). High resolution EEG mapping of cortical activation related to working memory: Effects of task difficulty, type of processing, and practice. *Cerebral Cortex, 7*, 374–385.

Giaconia, R. M., Reinherz, H. Z., Silverman, A. B., & Pakiz, B. (1994). Ages of onset of psychiatric disorders in a community population of older adolescents. *Journal of the American Academy of Child and Adolescent Psychiatry, 33*, 706–717.

Giles, D. E., Jarrett, R. B., Biggs, M. M., Guzick, D. S., & Rush, A. J. (1989). Clinical predictors of recurrence in depression. *American Journal of Psychiatry, 146*, 764–767.

Glaser, D. (2000). Child abuse and neglect and the brain: A review. *Journal of Child Psychology and Psychiatry and Allied Disorders, 41*, 97–116.

Goenjian, A. K., Yehuda, R., Pynoos, R. S., Steinberg, A. M., Tashjian, M., Yang, R. K., et al. (1996). Basal cortisol, dexamethasone suppression of cortisol, and MHPG in adolescents after the 1988 earthquake in Armenia. *American Journal of Psychiatry, 153*, 929–934.

Goodyer, I. M., Herbert, J., Tamplin, A., & Altham, P. M. (2000a). First-episode major depression in adolescents: Affective, cognitive and endocrine characteristics of risk status and predictors of onset. *British Journal of Psychiatry, 176*, 142–149.

Goodyer, I. M., Herbert, J., Tamplin, A., & Altham, P. M. (2000b). Recent life events, cortisol, dehydroepiandrosterone and the onset of major depression in high-risk adolescents. *British Journal of Psychiatry, 177*, 499–504.

Goodyer, I. M., Park, R. J., & Herbert, J. (2001). Psychosocial and endocrine features of chronic first-episode major depression in 8–16 year olds. *Biological Psychiatry, 50*, 351–357.

Goodyer, I. M., Park, R. J., Netherton, C. M., & Herbert, J. (2001). Possible role of cortisol and dehydroepiandrosterone in human development and psychopathology. *British Journal of Psychiatry, 179*, 243–249.

Graham, F. (1978). Constraints of measuring heart rate and period sequentially through real and cardiac time. *Psychophysiology, 15*, 492–495.

Graham, F., & Jackson, J. C. (1970). Arousal systems and infant heart rate responses. *Advances in Child Development and Behavior, 5*, 59–117.

Graham, F., Putnam, L., & Leavitt, L. (1975). Lead-stimulation effects on human cardiac orienting and blink reflexes. *Journal of Experimental Psychology, 1*, 161–169.

Granger, D. A., Serbin, L. A., Schwartzman, A., Lehoux, P., Cooperman, J., & Ikeda, S. (1998). Children's salivary cortisol, internalizing behaviour problems, and family environment: Results for the Concordia Longitudinal Risk Project. *International Journal of Behavioral Development, 22*, 707–728.

Granger, D. A., Weisz, J. R., & Kauneskis, D. (1994). Neuroendocrine reactivity, internalizing behavior problems and control-related cognitions in clinic referred children and adolescents. *Journal of Abnormal Psychology, 103*, 267–276.

Gray, J. A. (1975). *Elements of a two-process theory of learning.* New York: Academic Press.

Grillon, C., & Ameli, R. (1998). Effects of threat and safety signals on startle during anticipation of aversive shocks, sounds, or airblasts. *Journal of Psychophysiology, 12*, 329–337.

Grillon, C., Ameli, R., Woods, S. W., Marikangas, K., & Davis, M. (1991). Fear potentiated startle in humans: Effects of anticipatory anxiety on the acoustic blink reflex. *Psychophysiology, 28*, 588–595.

Grillon, C., & Baas, J. (2003). A review of the modulation of the startle reflex by affective states and its application to psychiatry. *Clinical Neurophysiology, 114*, 1557–1579.

Grillon, C., Morgan, C. A., III, Davis, M., & Southwick, S. M. (1998). Effect of darkness on acoustic startle in Vietnam veterans with PTSD. *American Journal of Psychiatry, 155*, 812–817.

Gunnar, M. R., Brodersen, L., Krueger, K., & Rigatuso, J. (1996). Dampening of adrenocortical responses during infancy: Normative changes and individual differences. *Child Development, 67*, 877–889.

Gunnar, M. R., Brodersen, L., Nachmias, M., Buss, K., & Rigatuso, R. (1996). Stress reactivity and attachment security. *Developmental Psychobiology, 29*, 10–36.

Gunnar, M. R., & Donzella, B. (2002). Social regulation of the cortisol levels in early human development. *Psychoneuroendocrinology, 27*, 199–220.

Gunnar, M. R., & Nelson, C. A. (1994). Event-related potentials in year-old infants: Relations with emotionality and cortisol. *Child Development, 65*, 80–94.

Gunnar, M. R., Tout, K., de Haan, M., Pierce, S., & Stansbury, K. (1997). Temperament, social competence, and adrenocortical activity in preschoolers. *Developmental Psychobiology, 31*, 65–85.

Gunnar, M. R., & Vazquez, D. M. (2001). Low cortisol and a flattening of expected daytime rhythm: Potential indices of risk in human development. *Development and Psychopathology, 13*, 515–538.

Gurvitis, T. V., Shenton, M. E., Hokama, H., & Ohta, H. (1996). Magnetic resonance imaging study of hippocampal volume in chronic, combat-related posttraumatic stress disorder. *Biological Psychiatry, 40*, 1091–1099.

Hagne, I. (1968). Development of the waking EEG in normal infants during the first year of life. In P. Kellaway & I. Petersén (Eds.), *Clinical electroencephalography of children* (pp. 97–118). New York: Grune & Stratton.

Hagne, I. (1972). Development of the EEG in normal infants during the first year of life. *Acta Pediatrica Scandinavica* (Suppl. 232), 25–32.

Hagne, I., Persson, J., Magnusson, R., & Petersén, I. (1973). Spectral analysis via fast Fourier transform of waking EEG in normal infants. In P. Kellaway & I. Petersén (Eds.), *Automation of clinical EEG* (pp. 103–143). New York: Raven.

Hamm, A. O., Cuthbert, B. N., Globisch, J., & Vaitl, D. (1997). Fear and the startle reflex: Blink modulation and autonomic response patterns in animal and mutilation fearful subjects. *Psychophysiology, 34,* 97–107.

Hamm, A. O., & Stark, R. (1993). Sensitization and aversive conditioning: Effects on the startle reflex and electrodermal responding. *Integrative Physiological and Behavioral Sciences, 28,* 171–176.

Harden, P. W., & Pihl, R. O. (1995). Stress response in anxious and nonanxious disruptive boys. *Journal of Emotional and Behavioral Disorders, 3*(3), 183.

Harmony, T., Alvarez, A., Pascual, R., Ramos, A., Marosi, E., Diaz de Leon, A. E., et al. (1988). EEG maturation of children with different economic and psychosocial characteristics. *International Journal of Neuroscience, 41,* 103–113.

Harmony, T., Marosi, E., Diaz de Leon, A. E., Becker, J., & Fernandez, T. (1990). Effect of sex, psychosocial disadvantages and biological risk factors on EEG maturation. *Electroencephalography and Clinical Neurophysiology, 75,* 482–491.

Hart, J., Gunnar, M., & Cicchetti, D. (1995). Salivary cortisol in maltreated children: Evidence of relations between neuroendocrine activity and social competence. *Development and Psychopathology, 7*(1), 11–26.

Haywood, H. C. (1963). Differential effects of delayed auditory feedback on palmar sweating, heart rate, and pulse pressure. *Journal of Speech and Hearing Research, 6,* 181–186.

Heim, C., Ehlert, U., & Hellhammer, D. H. (2000). The potential role of hypocortisolism in the pathophysiology of stress-related bodily disorders. *Psychoneuroendocrinology, 25,* 1–35.

Heller, W. (1993). Gender differences in depression: Perspectives from neuropsychology. *Journal of Affective Disorders, 29,* 129–143.

Heller, W., & Nitschke, J. B. (1997). The puzzle of regional brain activity in depression and anxiety: The importance of subtypes and comorbidity. *Cognition and Emotion, 12,* 421–428.

Hellhammer, D. H., & Wade, S. (1993). Endocrine correlates of stress vulnerability. *Psychotherapy Psychosomatics, 60,* 8–17.

Henderson, H. A., Fox, N. A., & Rubin, K. H. (2001). Temperamental contributions to social behavior: The moderating roles of frontal EEG asymmetry and gender. *Journal of the American Academy of Child and Adolescent Psychiatry, 40,* 68–74.

Henriques, J. B., & Davidson, R. J. (1990). Regional brain electrical asymmetries discriminate between previously depressed subjects and healthy controls. *Journal of Abnormal Psychology, 99,* 22–31.

Henriques, J. B., & Davidson, R. J. (1991). Left frontal hypoactivation in depression. *Journal of Abnormal Psychology, 100,* 535–545.

Henry, J. P. (1992). Biological basis of the stress response. *Integrative Physiological and Behavioral Science, 27,* 66–83.

Henry, J. P. (1993). Psychological and physiological responses to stress: The right hemisphere and the hypothalamo-pituitary-adrenal system. An inquiry into problems of human bonding. *Integrative Physiological and Behavioral Science, 28,* 368–387.

Herpertz, S. C., Mueller, B., Wenning, B., Qunaibi, M., Linchterfeld, C., & Herpertz-Dahlmann, B. (2003). Autonomic responses in boys with externalizing disorders. *Journal of Neural Transmission, 110,* 1181–1195.

Hessl, D., Dawson, G., Frey, K., Panagiotides, H., Self, J., Yamada, E., et al. (1996, May). *A longitudinal study of children of depressed moth-ers: Psychobiological findings related to stress.* Poster presented at the NIMH Conference for Advancing Research on Developmental Plasticity, Chantilly, VA.

Hilgard, J. R. (1933). Reinforcement and inhibition of eyelid reflexes. *Journal of General Psychology, 8,* 85–113.

Hillyard, S. A., & Hansen, J. C. (1986). Attention: Electrophysiological approaches. In M. G. H. Coles, E. Donchin, & S. W. Porges (Eds.), *Psychophysiology: Systems, processes, and applications* (pp. 227–243). New York: Guilford Press.

Hillyard, S. A., Luck, S. J., & Mangun, G. R. (1994). The cueing of attention to visual field locations: An analysis with ERP recordings. In H. J. Heinze, T. F. Munte, & G. R. Mangun (Eds.), *Cognitive electrophysiology* (pp. 1–25). Boston: Birhäuser.

Hitchcock, J. M., & Davis, M. (1986). Lesions of the amygdala, but not of the cerebellum or red nucleus, block conditioned fear as measured with the potentiated startle paradigm. *Behavioral Neuroscience, 100,* 11–22.

Huizink, A. C., Robles de Medina, P. G., Mulder, E. J. H., Visser, G. H. A., & Buitelaar, J. K. (2003). Stress during pregnancy is associated with developmental outcome in infancy. *Journal of Child Psychology and Psychiatry and Allied Disorders, 44,* 810–819.

Ilan, A. B., & Polich, J. (1999). P300 and response time from a manual Stroop task. *Clinical Neurophysiology, 110,* 367–373.

Institute of Medicine. (1989). *Research on children and adolescents with mental, behavioral, and developmental disorders.* Washington, DC: National Academy Press.

Jacobson, L., & Sapolsky, R. (1991). The role of the hippocampus in feedback regulation of the hypothalamic-pituitary-adrenocortical axis. *Endocrinology Review, 12,* 118–134.

Janowsky, J. S., & Carper, R. (1996). Is there a neural basis for cognitive transitions in school-age children? In A. J. Sameroff & M. M. Haith (Eds.), *The five to seven year shift: The age of reason and responsibility* (pp. 33–60). Chicago: University of Chicago Press.

Jasper, H. H. (1958). The ten-twenty electrode system of the International Federation. *Electroencephalography and Clinical Neurophysiology, 10,* 371–375.

Jasper, H. H., Solomon, P., & Bradley, C. (1938). Electroencephalographic analyses of behaviour problem children. *American Journal of Psychiatry, 95,* 641–658.

Javitt, D. C., Doneshka, P., Grochowski, S., & Ritter, W. (1995). Impaired mismatch negativity generation reflects widespread dysfunction of working memory in Schizophrenia. *Archives of General Psychiatry, 52,* 550–558.

Javitt, D. C., Grochowski, S., Shelley, A. M., & Ritter, W. (1998). Impaired mismatch negativity (MMN) generation in Schizophrenia as a function of stimulus deviance, probability, and interstimulus/interdeviant interval. *Electroencephalography and Clinical Neurophysiology, 108,* 143–153.

Javitt, D. C., Shelley, A. M., & Ritter, W. (2000). Associated deficits in mismatch negativity generation and tone matching in Schizophrenia. *Clinical Neurophysiology, 111,* 1733–1737.

Jennings, J. R. (1981). Publication guidelines for heart rate studies in man. *Psychophysiology, 18,* 226–231.

Jennings, J. R., Stringfellow, J. C., & Graham, M. (1974). A comparison of the statistical distributions of beat-by-beat heart rate and heart period. *Psychophysiology, 11,* 207–210.

John, E. R., Ahn, H., Prichep, L., Trepetin, M., Brown, D., & Kaye, H. (1980). Developmental equations for the electroencephalogram. *Science, 210,* 1255–1258.

Johnson, M. H., & Morton, J. (1991). *Biology and cognitive development: The case of face recognition.* Oxford: Blackwell.

Johnson, R. (1993). On the neural generators of the P300 component of the event-related potential. *Psychophysiology, 30,* 90–97.

Johnson, R., Jr. (1995). Event-related potential insights into the neurobiology of memory systems. In F. Boller & J. Grafman (Eds.), *Handbook of neuropsychology* (Vol. 10, pp. 135–159). New York: Elsevier Science.

Johnston, V. S., & Wang, X.-T. (1991). The relationship between menstrual phase and the P3 component of ERPs. *Psychophysiology, 38,* 400–409.

Johnston-Brooks, C. H., Lewis, M. A., Evans, G. W., & Whalen, C. K. (1998). Chronic stress and illness in children: The role of allostatic load. *Psychosomatic Medicine, 60,* 597–603.

Jones, N. A., Field, T., & Davlos, M. (2000). Right frontal EEG asymmetry and lack of empathy in preschool children of depressed mothers. *Child Psychiatry and Human Development, 30,* 189–204.

Jones, N. A., & Fox, N. A. (1992). Electroencephalogram asymmetry during emotionally evocative films and its relation to positive and negative affectivity. *Brain and Cognition, 20,* 280–299.

Kagan, J. (1984). Behavioral inhibition to the unfamiliar. *Child Development, 55,* 2212–2225.

Kagan, J. (1994). *Galen's prophecy: Temperament in human nature.* New York: Basic Books.

Kagan, J. (1996). Editor's introduction: Methods in the developmental study of madness. In S. Matthysse, D. L. Levy, J. Kagan, & F. M. Benes (Eds.), *Psychopathology* (pp. 155–160). Cambridge, England: Cambridge University Press.

Kagan, J., Reznick, S., & Snidman, N. (1987). The physiology and psychology of behavioral inhibition in children. *Child Development, 58,* 1459–1473.

Kagan, J., Reznick, S., & Snidman, N. (1988). Temperamental influences on reactions to unfamiliarity and challenge. *Advances in Experimental Medicine and Biology, 245,* 319–339.

Kagan, J., Snidman, N., McManis, M., Woodward, S., & Hardway, C. (2002). One measure, one meaning: Multiple measures, clearer meaning. *Development and Psychopathology, 14,* 463–475.

Katada, A., & Koike, T. (1990). Developmental process of electroencephalogram by follow-up recording of normal and mentally retarded children's EEGs. *Japanese Psychological Research, 32,* 192–201.

Keiley, M. K., Bates, J. E., Dodge, K. A., & Pettit, G. S. (2000). A cross-domain growth analysis: Externalizing and internalizing behaviors during 8 years of childhood. *Journal of Abnormal Child Psychology, 28,* 161–179.

Keller, J., Deldin, P. J., Gergen, J. A., & Miller, G. A. (1995, October). *Evidence for a semantic processing deficit in depression.* Paper presented at the annual meeting of the Society for Psychophysiological Research, Toronto, Ontario, Canada.

Keller, J., Hicks, B. D., & Miller, G. A. (2000). Psychophysiology in the study of psychopathology. In J. T. Cacioppo, L. G. Tassinary, & G. G. Bentson (Eds.), *Handbook of psychophysiology* (pp. 719–750). New York: Cambridge University Press.

Keltikangas-Järvinen, L., Kettunen, J., Ravaja, N., & Näätänen, P. (1999). Inhibited and disinhibited temperament and autonomic stress reactivity. *International Journal of Psychophysiology, 33,* 185–196.

Kemner, C., Verbaten, M. N., Koelega, H. S., Buitelaar, J. K., van-der-Gaag, R., & van Engeland, H. (1996). Event-related brain potentials in children with attention-deficit and hyperactivity disorder: Effects of stimulus deviancy and task relevance in the visual and auditory modality. *Biological Psychiatry, 40,* 522–534.

Kestenbaum, R., & Nelson, C. A. (1992). Neural and behavioral correlates of emotion recognition in children and adults. *Journal of Experimental Child Psychology, 54,* 1–18.

Kirschbaum, C., & Hellhammer, D. H. (1994). Salivary cortisol in psychoneuroendocrine research: Recent developments and applications. *Psychoneuroendocrinology, 19,* 313–333.

Klimes-Dougan, B., Hastings, P. D., Granger, D. A., Usher, B. A., & Zahn-Waxler, C. (2001). Adrenocortical activity in at-risk and normally developing adolescents: Individual differences in salivary cortisol basal levels, diurnal variation, and responses to social challenges. *Development and Psychopathology, 13,* 695–719.

Klimes-Dougan, B., & Kistner, J. (1990). Physically abused preschoolers' responses to peers' distress. *Developmental Psychology, 26,* 599–602.

Kline, J. P., Allen, J. J. B., & Schwartz, G. E. (1998). Is left frontal brain activation in defensiveness gender specific? *Journal of Abnormal Psychology, 107,* 149–153.

Kline, J. P., Blackhart, G. C., & Schwartz, G. E. (1999). Gender specificity of resting anterior electroencephalographic asymmetry and defensiveness in the elderly. *Journal of Gender-Specific Medicine, 2,* 35–39.

Kohlberg, L., LaCrosse, J., & Ricks, D. (1972). The predictability of adult mental health from childhood behavior. In B. Wolman (Ed.), *Manual of child psychopathology* (pp. 1217–1284). New York: McGraw-Hill.

Kostandov, E., & Azumanov, Y. (1977). Averaged cortical evoked potentials to recognized and non-recognized verbal stimuli. *Acta Neurobiologiae Experimentalis, 37,* 311–324.

Kruesi, M. J. P., Schmidt, M. E., Donnelly, M., Hibbs, E. D., & Hamburger, S. D. (1989). Urinary free cortisol output and disruptive behavior in children. *Journal of the American Academy of Child and Adolescent Psychiatry, 28,* 441–443.

Kuhne, M., Schacher, R., & Tannock, R. (1997). Impact of comorbid oppositional or conduct problems on attention-deficit hyperactivity disorder. *Journal of the American Academy of Child and Adolescent Psychiatry, 36,* 1715–1725.

Kurtzberg, D., Vaughan, H. G., Kreuzer, J. A., & Flieger, K. Z. (1995). Developmental studies and clinical implications of mismatch negativity: Problems and prospects. *Ear and Hearing, 16,* 105–117.

Landis, C., & Hunt, W. (1939). *The startle pattern.* Oxford: Farrar & Rinehart.

Lang, A. H., Eerola, O., Korpilahti, P., Holopainen, I., Salo, S., & Aaltonen, O. (1995). Practical issues in the clinical application of mismatch negativity. *Ear and Hearing, 16,* 117–129.

Lang, P. J. (1995). The emotion probe: Studies of motivation and attention. *American Psychologist, 50,* 372–385.

Lang, P. J., Bradley, M. M., & Cuthbert, B. N. (1990). Emotion, attention, and the startle reflex. *Psychological Review, 97,* 377–395.

Lang, P. J., Bradley, M. M., & Cuthbert, B. (1992). A motivational analysis of emotion: Reflex-cortex connections. *Psychological Science, 3,* 44–49.

Larson, M., White, B. P., Cochran, A., Donzella, B., & Gunnar, M. R. (1998). Dampening of the cortisol response to handling at 3-months in human infants and its relation to sleep, circadian cortisol activity, and behavioral distress. *Developmental Psychobiology, 33,* 327–337.

Lazarus, R. S., & Folkman, S. (1984). *Stress, appraisal, and coping.* New York: Springer.

Lazzaro, I., Gordon, E., Whitmont, S., Meares, R., & Clarke, S. (2001). The modulation of late component event related potentials by prestimulus EEG theta activity in ADHD. *International Journal of Neuroscience, 107,* 247–264.

Lazzaro, I., Gordon, E., Whitmont, S., Plahn, M., Li, W., Clarke, S., et al. (1998). Quantitative EEG activity in adolescent attention deficit hyperactivity disorder. *Clinical Electroencephalography, 29,* 37–42.

LeDoux, J. E. (1996). *The emotional brain: The mysterious underpinnings of emotional life.* New York: Simon & Schuster.

Lewis, M., & Ramsay, D. (2002). Cortisol response to embarrassment and shame. *Child Development, 73,* 1034–1045.

Light, G. A., & Braff, D. L. (1998). The "incredible shrinking" P50 event-related potential. *Biological Psychiatry, 43,* 918–920.

Lindgren, K. A., Larson, C. L., Schaefer, S. M., Abercrombie, H. C., Ward, R. T., Oakes, T. R., et al. (1999). Thalamic metabolic rate predicts EEG alpha power in healthy controls but not in depressed patients. *Biological Psychiatry, 45,* 943–952.

Liotti, M., Woldroff, M. G., Pérez III, R., & Mayberg, H. S. (2000). An ERP study of the temporal course of the Stroop color-word interference effect. *Neuropsychologia, 38,* 701–711.

Lovallo, W. R., & Thomas, T. L. (2000). Stress hormones in psychophysiological research: Emotional, behavioral, and cognitive implications. In J. T. Cacioppo, L. G. Tassinary, & G. G. Berntson (Eds.), *Handbook of psychophysiology* (2nd ed., pp. 342–367). Cambridge, England: Cambridge University Press.

Lubar, J. F. (1991). Discourse on the development of EEG diagnostics and biofeedback for attention-deficit/hyperactivity disorders. *Biofeedback and Self Regulation, 16,* 201–225.

Luck, S. J., Heinze, H. J., Mangun, G. R., & Hillyard, S. A. (1990). Visual event-related potentials index focused attention within bilateral stimulus arrays. II. Functional dissociation of P1 and N1 components. *Electroencephalography and Clinical Neurophysiology, 75*(6), 528–542.

Lundberg, U. (1986). Stress and Type A behavior in children. *Journal of the American Academy of Child and Adolescent Psychiatry, 25,* 771–778.

Lykken, D. T. (1957). A study of anxiety in the sociopathic personality. *Journal of Abnormal and Social Psychology, 55,* 6–10.

Lynch, M., & Cicchetti, D. (1998). Trauma, mental representation, and the organization of memory for mother-referent material. *Development and Psychopathology, 10,* 739–759.

MacFarlane, A. C., Weber, D. L., & Clark, C. R. (1993). Abnormal stimulus processing in posttraumatic stress disorder. *Biological Psychiatry, 34,* 103–116.

Mann, C. A., Lubar, J. F., Zimmerman, A. W., Miller, C. A., & Muenchen, R. A. (1992). Quantitative analysis of EEG in boys with attention-deficit-hyperactivity disorder: A controlled study with clinical implications. *Pediatric Neurology, 8,* 30–36.

Marshall, P. J., Bar-Haim, Y., & Fox, N. A. (2002). Development of the EEG from 5 months to 4 years of age. *Clinical Neurophysiology, 113,* 1199–1208.

Marshall, P. J., Fox, N. A., & BEIP Core Group. (2004). A comparison of the electroencephalogram between institutionalized and community children in Romania. *Journal of Cognitive Neuroscience, 16,* 1327–1338.

Matousek, M., & Petersén, I. (1973). Automatic evaluation of EEG background activity by means of age-dependent EEG quotients. *Electroencephalography and Clinical Neurophysiology, 35,* 603–612.

Matsuura, M., Yamamoto, K., Fukuzawa, H., Okubo, Y., Uesugi, H., Moriwa, M., et al. (1985). Age development and sex differences of various EEG elements in healthy children and adults: Quantification by a computerized wave form recognition method. *Electroencephalography and Clinical Neurophysiology, 60,* 394–406.

McBurnett, K., Lahey, B. B., Frick, P. J., Risch, C., Loeber, R., Hart, E. L., et al. (1991). Anxiety, inhibition, and conduct disorder in children: II. Relation to salivary cortisol. *Journal of the American Academy of Child and Adolescent Psychiatry, 30,* 192–196.

McEwen, B. S. (1998). Protective and damaging effects of stress mediators. *New England Journal of Medicine, 338,* 171–179.

McEwen, B. S. (1999). Stress and hippocampal plasticity. *Annual Review of Neuroscience, 22,* 105–122.

McEwen, B., & Lasley, E. N. (2003). Allostatic load: When protection gives way to damage. *Advances in Mind-Body Medicine, 19,* 28–33.

McEwen, B., & Wingfield, J. C. (2003). Response to commentaries on the concept of allostasis. *Hormones and Behavior, 43,* 28–30.

McManis, M. H., Bradley, M. M., Cuthbert, B., & Lang, P. (1995). Kids have feelings too: Children's physiological response to affective pictures. *Psychophysiology, 32,* S53.

Merrell, K. W., & Dobmeyer, A. C. (1996). An evaluation of gender differences in self-reported internalizing symptoms of elementary-age children. *Journal of Psychoeducational Assessment, 14,* 196–207.

Morgan, C. A., Grillon, C., Southwick, S. M., Davis, M., & Charney, D. S. (1995). Fear-potentiated startle in posttraumatic stress disorder. *Biological Psychiatry, 36,* 378–385.

Munck, A., Guyre, P. M., & Holbrook, N. J. (1984). Physiological functions of glucocorticoids in stress and their relation to pharmacological actions. *Endocrinology Review, 5,* 25–44.

Murray, L., & Cooper, P. J. (1997). Postpartum depression and child development. *Psychological Medicine, 27,* 253–260.

Näätänen, R. (1990). The role of attention in auditory information processing as revealed by event-related potentials and other brain measures of cognitive function. *Behavioral Brain Sciences, 13,* 201–288.

Näätänen, R. (1992). *Attention and brain function.* Hillsdale, NJ: Erlbaum.

Nadel, L., & Jacobs, W. J. (1998). Traumatic memory is special. *Current Directions in Psychological Science, 7,* 154–157.

Nelson, C. A. (1987). The recognition of facial expressions in the first two years of life: Mechanisms of development. *Child Development, 58,* 889–909.

Nelson, C. A. (1994). Neural correlates of recognition memory in the first postnatal year. In G. Dawson & K. W. Fischer (Eds.), *Human behavior and the developing brain* (pp. 269–313). New York: Guilford Press.

Novak, G. P., Ritter, W., Vaughan, H. G., & Wiznitzer, M. L. (1990). Differentiation of negative event-related potentials in an auditory discrimination task. *Electroencephalography and Clinical Neurophysiology, 75,* 255–275.

Nunez, P. (1981). *Electrical fields of the brain.* New York: Oxford University Press.

Oades, R. D., Dittmann-Balcar, A., & Zerbin, D. (1997). Development and topography of auditory event-related potentials (ERPs): Mismatch and processing negativity in individuals 8–22 years of age. *Psychophysiology, 34,* 677–693.

Obrist, P. A. (1976). The cardiovascular-behavioral interaction as it appears today. *Psychophysiology, 13,* 95–107.

O'Donnell, B. F., Shenton, M. E., McCarley, R. W., Faux, S. F., Smith, R. S., Salisbury, D. F., et al. (1993). The auditory N2 component in Schizophrenia: Relationship to MRI temporal lobe gray matter and to other ERP abnormalities. *Biological Psychiatry, 33,* 26–40.

Ogura, C., Nageishi, Y., Omura, F., Fukao, K., Ohta, H., Kishimoto, A., et al. (1993). N200 component of event-related potentials in depression. *Biological Psychiatry, 33,* 720–726.

Ohman, A., Hamm, A., & Hugdahl, K. (2000). Cognition and the autonomic nervous system: Orienting, anticipation, and conditioning. In J. T. Cacioppo, L. G. Tassinary, & G. G. Berntson (Eds.), *Handbook of psychophysiology* (2nd ed., pp. 533–575). New York: Cambridge University Press.

Ornitz, E. M. (1999). Startle modification in children and developmental effects. In M. E. Dawson, A. M. Schell, & A. H. Böhmelt (Eds.), *Startle modification: Implications for neuroscience, cognitive science, and clinical science* (pp. 245–266). New York: Cambridge University Press.

Ornitz, E. M., Guthrie, D., Kaplan, A. R., Lane, S. J., & Norman, R. J. (1986). Maturation of startle modulation. *Psychophysiology, 23,* 624–634.

Ornitz, E. M., Hanna, G. L., & De Traversay, J. D. (1992). Prestimulation-induced startle modulation in attention-deficit hyperactivity disorder and nocturnal enuresis. *Psychophysiology, 29,* 437–451.

Ornitz, E. M., & Pynoos, R. S. (1989). Startle modulation in children with posttraumatic stress disorder. *American Journal of Psychiatry, 146,* 866–870.

Pajer, K., Gardner, W., Rubin, R. T., Perel, J., & Neal, S. (2001). Decreased cortisol levels in adolescent girls with conduct disorder. *Archives of General Psychiatry, 58,* 297–302.

Papillo, J. F., & Shapiro, D. (1990). The cardiovascular system. In J. T. Cacioppo & L. G. Tassinary (Eds.), *Principles of psychophysiology: Physical, social, and inferential elements* (pp. 456–512). New York: Cambridge University Press.

Patrick, C. J. (1994). Emotion and psychopathy: Startling new insights. *Psychophysiology, 31,* 319–330.

Patrick, C. J., Bradley, M. M., & Lang, P. J. (1993). Emotion in the criminal psychopath: Startle reflex modulation. *Journal of Abnormal Psychology, 102,* 82–92.

Pauli, P., Dengler, W., Wiedemann, G., Montoya, P., Flor, H., Birbaumer, N., et al. (1997). Behavioral and neurophysiological evidence for altered processing of anxiety related words in panic disorder. *Journal of Abnormal Psychology, 106,* 213–220.

Pérez-Edgar, K. (2001). *Attentional control in emotional contexts: The potential role of temperament.* Unpublished doctoral dissertation, Harvard University, Cambridge, MA.

Pérez-Edgar, K., & Fox, N. A. (2003). Individual differences in children during an emotional Stroop task: A behavioral and electrophysiological study. *Brain and Cognition, 52,* 33–51.

Pérez-Edgar, K., & Fox, N. A. (2005). A behavioral and electrophysiological study of children's selective attention under neutral and affective conditions. *Journal of Cognition and Development, 6,* 89–116.

Pérez-Edgar, K., Fox, N. A., Schmidt, L. A., & Schulkin, J. (2004). *A longitudinal analysis of individual differences across gender and temperament in the relations between cortisol and socioemotional maladjustment in early childhood.* Manuscript submitted for publication.

Peters, M. L., Godaert, G. L., Ballieux, R. E., van Vliet, M., Willemsen, J. J., Sweep, F. C., et al. (1998). Cardiovascular and endocrine responses to experimental stress: Effects of mental effort and controllability. *Psychoneuroendocrinology, 23,* 1–17.

Picton, T. W., Bentin, S., Berg, P., Donchin, E., Hillyard, S. A., Johnson, R., Jr., et al. (2000). Guidelines for using human event-related potentials to study cognition: Recording standards and publication criteria. *Psychophysiology, 37,* 127–152.

Pilgreen, K. L. (1995). Physiologic, medical, and cognitive correlates of electroencephalography. In P. L. Nunez (Ed.), *Necrotic dynamics and human EEG rhythms* (pp. 195–248). New York: Oxford University Press.

Pine, D. S., Wasserman, G., & Coplan, J. (1996). Cardiac profile and disruptive behavior in boys at risk for delinquency. *Psychosomatic Medicine, 58,* 342–353.

Pivik, R. T., Broughton, R. J., Coppola, R., Davidson, R. J., Fox, N. A., & Nuwer, M. R. (1993). Guidelines for the recording and quantitative analysis of electroencephalographic activity in research contexts. *Psychophysiology, 30,* 547–558.

Pollak, S. D., Cicchetti, D., & Klorman, R. (1998). Stress, memory, and emotion: Developmental considerations from the study of child maltreatment. *Development and Psychopathology, 10,* 511–528.

Pollak, S. D., Cicchetti, D., Klorman, R., & Brumaghim, J. (1997). Cognitive brain event-related potentials and emotion processing in maltreated children. *Child Development, 68,* 773–787.

Pollak, S. D., Klorman, R., Thatcher, J. E., & Cicchetti, D. (2001). P3b reflects maltreated children's reactions to facial displays of emotion. *Psychophysiology, 38,* 267–274.

Porges, S. W. (1986). Respiratory sinus arrhythmia: Physiological basis, quantitative methods, and clinical implications. In P. Grossman, K. Janssen, & D. Vaitl (Eds.), *Cardiorespiratory and cardiosomatic psychophysiology* (pp. 101–115). New York: Plenum Press.

Porges, S. W. (1995). Cardiac vagal tone: A physiological index of stress. *Neuroscience and Biobehavioral Reviews, 19,* 225–233.

Porges, S. W., & Byrne, E. A. (1992). Research methods for the measurement of heart rate and respiration. *Biological Psychology, 34,* 93–130.

Porges, S. W., McCabe, P. M., & Yongue, B. G. (1982). Respiratory–heart rate interactions: Psychophysiological implications for pathophysiology and behavior. In J. Cacioppo & R. Petty (Eds.), *Perspectives in cardiovascular psychophysiology* (pp. 223–264). New York: Guilford Press.

Posner, M. I., & Cohen, Y. (1984). Components of visual orienting. In H. Bouma & D. Bowhuis (Eds.), *Attention and performance X* (pp. 531–556). Hillsdale, NJ: Erlbaum.

Raine, A. (1996). Autonomic nervous system activity and violence. In D. M. Stoff & R. B. Cairns (Eds.), *Neurobiological approaches to clinical aggression research* (pp. 145–168). Mahwah, NJ: Erlbaum.

Raine, A. (2002). Annotation: The role of prefrontal deficits, low autonomic arousal, and early health factors in the development of antisocial and aggressive behavior in children. *Journal of Child Psychology and Psychiatry, 43,* 417–434.

Raine, A., Venables, P. H., Dalais, C., Mellijngen, K., Reynolds, C., & Mednick, S. A. (2001). Early educational and health enrichment at ages 3–5 years is associated with increased autonomic and central nervous system arousal and orienting at age 11 years: Evidence from the Mauritius Child Health Project. *Psychophysiology, 38,* 254–266.

Raine, A., Venables, P. H., & Williams, M. (1990). Relationships between central and autonomic measures of arousal at age 15 years and criminality at age 24 years. *Archives of General Psychiatry, 47,* 1003–1007.

Ramsay, D. S., & Lewis, M. (2003). Reactivity and regulation in cortisol and behavioral responses to stress. *Child Development, 74,* 456–464.

Rao, U., Dahl, R. E., Ryan, N. D., Birmaher, B., Williamson, D. E., Giles, D. E., et al. (1996). The relationship between longitudinal clinical course and sleep and cortisol changes in adolescent depression. *Biological Psychiatry, 40,* 474–484.

Rauch, S. L., van der Kolk, B. A., Fisler, R. E., Alpert, N. M., Orr, S. P., & Savage, C. R. (1996). A symptom provocation study of posttraumatic stress disorder using positron emission tomography and script-driven imagery. *Archives of General Psychiatry, 53,* 380–387.

Reiman, E. M., Raichle, M. E., Butler, F. K., Herscovitch, P., & Robins, E. (1984). A focal brain abnormality in panic disorder, a severe form of anxiety. *Nature, 310,* 683–685.

Reivich, M., Gur, R., & Alavi, A. (1983). Positron emission tomographic studies of sensory stimuli cognitive processes and anxiety. *Human Neurobiology, 2,* 25–33.

Richards, J. E. (2003). Attention affects the recognition of briefly presented visual stimuli in infants: An ERP study. *Developmental Science, 6,* 312–328.

Richters, J. E. (1997). The Hubble hypothesis and the developmentalist's dilemma. *Development and Psychopathology, 9,* 193–229.

Ridderinkhof, K. R., & van der Stelt, O. (2000). Attention and selection in the growing child: Views derived from developmental psychophysiology. *Biological Psychology, 54,* 55–106.

Rosen, J. B., & Davis, M. (1988). Enhancement of acoustic startle by electrical stimulation of the amygdala. *Behavioral Neuroscience, 102,* 195–202.

Rothbart, M. K., Posner, M. I., & Hershey, K. L. (1995). Temperament, attention, and developmental psychopathology. In D. Cicchetti & D.

Cohen (Eds.), *Developmental psychopathology: Vol. 1. Theory and methods* (pp. 315–340). New York: Wiley.

Rottenberg, J., Kasch, K. L., Gross, J. J., & Gotlib, I. H. (2002). Sadness and amusement reactivity differentially predict concurrent and prospective functioning in major depressive disorder. *Emotion, 2,* 135–146.

Rugg, M. D., & Coles, M. G. H. (1995). The ERP and cognitive psychology: Conceptual issues. In M. D. Rugg & M. G. H. Coles (Eds.), *Electrophysiology of mind: Event-related brain potentials and cognition* (pp. 27–39). Oxford: Oxford University Press.

Sameroff, A. J., & Chandler, M. J. (1975). Perinatal risk and the continuum of caretaking casualty. In F. Horowitz, M. Hetherington, S. Scarr-Salapatek, & G. Siegel (Eds.), *Review of child development research* (Vol. 4, pp. 187–244). Chicago: Society for Research in Child Development.

Sameroff, A. J., & MacKenzie, M. J. (2003). Research strategies for capturing transactional models of development: The limits of the possible. *Development and Psychopathology, 15,* 613–640.

Sapolsky, R. M., Romero, L. M., & Munck, A. U. (2000). How do glucocorticoids influence stress responses? Integrating permissive, suppressive, stimulatory, and preparative actions. *Endocrinology Review, 21,* 55–89.

Schack, B., Chen, A. C. N., Mescha, S., & Witte, H. (1999). Instantaneous EEG coherence analysis during the Stroop task. *Clinical Neurophysiology, 110,* 1410–1426.

Schmidt, L. A. (1999). Frontal brain electrical activity in shyness and sociability. *Psychological Science, 10,* 316–321.

Schmidt, L. A., & Fox, N. A. (1994). Patterns of cortical electrophysiology and autonomic activity in adults' shyness and sociability. *Biological Psychology, 38,* 183–198.

Schmidt, L. A., & Fox, N. A. (1999). Conceptual, biological, and behavioral distinctions among different categories of shy children. In L. A. Schmidt & J. Schulkin (Eds.), *Extreme fear, shyness, and social phobia: Origins, biological mechanisms, and clinical outcomes* (pp. 47–66). New York: Oxford University Press.

Schmidt, L. A., Fox, N. A., Rubin, K. H., Sternberg, E. M., Gold, P. W., Smith, C. C., et al. (1997). Behavioral and neuroedocrine responses in shy children. *Developmental Psychobiology, 30,* 127–140.

Schmidt, L. A., Fox, N. A., Schulkin, J., & Gold, P. W. (1999). Behavioral and psychophysiological correlates of self-presentation in temperamentally shy children. *Developmental Psychobiology, 35,* 119–135.

Schmidt, L. A., Fox, N. A., Sternberg, E. M., Gold, P. W., Smith, C. C., & Schulkin, J. (1999). Adrenocortical reactivity and social competence in seven-year-olds. *Personality and Individual Differences, 26,* 977–985.

Schneider, R. E., & Fowles, D. C. (1978). A convenient, non-hydrating electrolyte medium for the measurement of electrodermal activity. *Psychophysiology, 15,* 483–486.

Semple, W. E., Goyer, P., McCormick, R., Morris, E., Compton, B., Muswick, G., et al. (1993). Preliminary report: Brain blood flow using PET in patients with posttraumatic stress disorder and substance abuse histories. *Biological Psychiatry, 34,* 115–118.

Shalev, L., & Algom, D. (2000). Stroop and Garner effects in and out of Posner's beam: Reconciling two conceptions of selective attention. *Journal of Experimental Psychology: Human Perception and Performance, 26,* 997–1017.

Sherwood, A. (1993). Use of impedance cardiography in cardiovascular reactivity research. In J. Blascovich & E. S. Katikin (Eds.), *Cardiovascular reactivity to psychological stress and disease* (pp. 157–199). Washington, DC: American Psychological Association.

Smith, D. A., Boutros, N. N., & Schwarzkopf, S. B. (1994). Reliability of P50 auditory event-related potential indices of sensory gating. *Psychophysiology, 31,* 495–502.

Smith, J. R. (1938a). The electroencephalogram during normal infancy and childhood: I. Rhythmic activities present in the neonate and their subsequent development. *Journal of Genetic Psychology, 53,* 431–453.

Smith, J. R. (1938b). The electroencephalogram during normal infancy and childhood: II. The nature and growth of alpha waves. *Journal of Genetic Psychology, 53,* 455–469.

Smith, J. R. (1938c). The electroencephalogram during normal infancy and childhood: III. Preliminary observations on the pattern sequence during sleep. *Journal of Genetic Psychology, 53,* 471–482.

Sobotka, S. S., Davidson, R. J., & Senulis, J. A. (1992). Anterior brain electrical asymmetries in response to reward and punishment. *Electroencephalography and Clinical Neurophysiology, 83,* 236–247.

Sroufe, L. A., & Rutter, M. (1984). The domain of developmental psychopathology. *Child Development, 55,* 17–29.

Steriade, M., Deschenes, M., Domich, L., & Mulle, C. (1985). Cortically elicited spike-wave discharge in thalamic neurons. *Electroencephalography and Clinical Neurophysiology, 41,* 641–644.

Stifter, C. A., & Fox, N. A. (1990). Infant reactivity: Physiological correlates of newborn and 5-month temperament. *Developmental Psychology, 26,* 582–588.

Stifter, C. A., Fox, N. A., & Porges, S. W. (1986). Facial expressivity and vagal tone in 5- and 10-month-old infants. *Infant Behavior and Development, 12,* 127–137.

Stroop, J. R. (1935). Studies of interference in serial verbal reactions. *Journal of Experimental Psychology, 18,* 643–662.

Stroud, L. R., Salovey, P., & Epel, E. S. (2002). Sex differences in stress responses: Social rejection versus achievement stress. *Biological Psychiatry, 52,* 318–327.

Sung, B. H., Lovallo, W. R., Pincomb, G. A., & Wilson, M. F. (1990). Effects of caffeine on blood pressure response during exercise in normotensive healthy young men. *American Journal of Cardiology, 65,* 909–913.

Sutton, S., & Ruchkin, D. S. (1984). The late positive complex: Advances and new problems. *Annals of the New York Academy of Sciences, 425,* 1–23.

Swerdlow, N. R., & Geyer, M. A. (1999). Neurophysiology and neuropharmacology of short lead interval startle modification. In M. E. Dawson, A. M. Schell, & A. H. Böhmelt (Eds.), *Startle modification: Implications for neuroscience, cognitive science, and clinical science* (pp. 14–133). New York: Cambridge University Press.

Szpiler, J. A., & Epstein, S. (1976). Availability of an avoidance response as related to autonomic arousal. *Journal of Abnormal Psychology, 85,* 73–82.

Taylor, A., Fisk, N. M., & Glover, V. (2000). Mode of delivery and subsequent stress response. *Lancet, 355,* 120.

Taylor, M. J. (1988). Developmental changes in ERPs to visual language stimuli. *Biological Psychology, 26,* 321–339.

Taylor, M. J., & Baldeweg, T. (2002). Application of EEG, ERP, and intracranial recordings to the investigation of cognitive functions in children. *Developmental Science, 5,* 318–334.

Taylor, M. J., & Eals, M. (1996). An event-related potential study of development using visual semantic tasks. *Journal of Psychophysiology, 10,* 125–139.

Tennes, K., & Kreye, M. (1985). Children's adrenocortical responses to classroom activities and tests in elementary school. *Psychosomatic Medicine, 47,* 451–460.

Thatcher, R. W. (1992). Cyclic cortical reorganization during early childhood. *Brain and Cognition, 20,* 24–50.

Thatcher, R. W., Krause, P., & Hrybyk, M. (1986). Corticocortical association fibers and EEG coherence: A two compartment model. *Electroencephalography and Clinical Neurophysiology, 64,* 123–143.

Thatcher, R. W., Walker, R. A., & Giudice, S. (1987). Human cerebral hemispheres develop at different rates and ages. *Science, 236,* 1110–1112.

Thomas, D. G., & Crow, C. D. (1994). Development of evoked electrical brain activity in infancy. In G. Dawson & K. W. Fischer (Eds.), *Human behavior and the developing brain* (pp. 207–231). New York: Guilford Press.

Tillman, R., & Geller, B. (2003). Definitions of rapid, ultrarapid, and ultradian cycling and of episode duration in pediatric and adult bipolar disorders: A proposal to distinguish episodes from cycles. *Journal of Child and Adolescent Psychopharmacology, 13,* 267–271.

Tomarken, A. J., Davidson, R. J., & Henriques, J. B. (1990). Frontal brain asymmetry predicts affective responses to films. *Journal of Personality and Social Psychology, 59,* 791–801.

Tomarken, A. J., Davidson, R. J., Wheeler, R. E., & Kinney, L. (1992). Psychometric properties of resting anterior EEG asymmetry: Temporal stability and internal consistency. *Psychophysiology, 29,* 576–592.

Tout, K., de Haan, M., Kipp-Campbell, E., & Gunnar, M. R. (1998). Social behavior correlates of adrenocortical activity in daycare: Gender differences and time-of-day effects. *Child Development, 69,* 1247–1262.

Uchino, B. N., Cacioppo, J. T., Malarkey, W., & Glaser, R. (1995). Individual differences in cardiac sympathetic control predict endocrine and immune responses to acute psychological stress. *Journal of Personality and Social Psychology, 69,* 736–743.

Van Boxtel, A., Boelhouwer, A. J. W., & Bos, A. R. (1998). Optimal EMG signal bandwidth and interelectrode distance for the recording of acoustic, electrocutaneous, and photic reflexes. *Psychophysiology, 35,* 690–697.

van der Molen, M. W., & Molenaar, P. C. M. (1994). Cognitive psychophysiology: A window to cognitive development and brain maturation. In G. Dawson & K. W. Fischer (Eds.), *Human behavior and the developing brain* (pp. 456–490). New York: Guilford Press.

van der Stelt, O., Gunning, W. B., Snel, J., & Kok, A. (1997). No electrocortical evidence of automatic mismatch dysfunction in children of alcoholics. *Clinical and Experimental Research, 21,* 569–575.

van Goozen, S. H. M., Matthys, W., Cohen-Kettenis, P. T., Gispen-de Wiend, C., Wiegant, V. M., & van Engeland, H. (1998). Salivary cortisol and cardiovascular activity during stress in oppositional-defiant disorder boys and normal controls. *Biological Psychiatry, 43,* 531–539.

Vedhara, K., Hyde, J., Gilchrist, I. D., Tytherleigh, M., & Plummer, S. (2000). Acute stress, memory, attention and cortisol. *Psychoneuroendocrinology, 25,* 535–549.

Vigouroux, R. (1879). Sur le rôle de la résistance électrique des tissues dans l'électrodiagnostic. *Comptes Rendus Société de Biologie (Series 6), 31,* 336–339.

von Eye, A., & Bergman, L. R. (2003). Research strategies in developmental psychopathology: Dimensional identity and the person-oriented approach. *Development and Psychopathology, 15,* 553–580.

Vrana, S. R., Constantine, J. A., & Westman, J. S. (1992). Startle reflex modification as an outcome measure in the treatment of phobia: Two case studies. *Behavioral Assessment, 14,* 279–291.

Vrana, S. R., Spence, E. L., & Lang, P. J. (1988). The startle probe response: A new measure of emotion? *Journal of Abnormal Psychology, 97,* 487–491.

Walker, D. L., & Davis, M. (1997). Anxiogenic effects of high illumination levels assessed with the acoustic startle response in rats. *Biological Psychiatry, 42,* 461–471.

Watamura, S. E., Donzella, B., Alwin, J., & Gunnar, M. R. (2003). Morning-to-afternoon increases in cortisol concentrations for infants and toddlers at child care: Age differences and behavioral correlates. *Child Development, 74,* 1006–1020.

Watamura, S. E., Sebanc, A. M., & Gunnar, M. R. (2003). Rising cortisol at childcare: Relations with nap, rest, and temperament. *Developmental Psychobiology, 40,* 33–42.

Weber, E. J., Van der Molen, M. W., & Molenaar, P. C. (1994). Heart rate and sustained attention during childhood: Age changes in anticipatory heart rate, primary bradycardia, and respiratory sinus arrhythmia. *Psychophysiology, 31,* 164–174.

Weiss, B., Dodge, K. A., Bates, J. E., & Pettit, G. S. (1992). Some consequences of early harsh discipline: Child aggression and a maladaptive social information processing style. *Child Development, 63,* 1321–1335.

West, R., & Alain, C. (1999). Event-related neural activity associated with the Stroop task. *Cognitive Brain Research, 8,* 157–164.

West, R., & Alain, C. (2000a). Age-related decline in inhibitory control contributes to the increased Stroop effect observed in older adults. *Psychophysiology, 37,* 179–189.

West, R., & Alain, C. (2000b). Effects of task context and fluctuations of attention on neural activity supporting performance of the Stroop task. *Brain Research, 873,* 102–111.

Wheeler, R. E., Davidson, R. J., & Tomarken, A. J. (1993). Frontal brain asymmetry and emotional reactivity: A biological substrate of affective style. *Psychophysiology, 30,* 82–89.

White, B. P., Gunnar, M. R., Larson, M. C., Donzella, B., & Barr, R. G. (2000). Behavioral and physiological responsivity, and patterns of sleep and daily salivary cortisol in infants with and without colic. *Child Development, 71,* 862–877.

White, S. H. (1996). Developmental psychopathology: From attribution toward information. In S. Matthysse, D. L. Levy, J. Kagan, & F. M. Benes (Eds.), *Psychopathology* (pp. 161–197). Cambridge, MA: Cambridge University Press.

Wijker, W. (1991). *ERP ontogenesis in childhood.* Unpublished doctoral dissertation, University of Amsterdam, The Netherlands.

Williams, J. M. G., Watts, F. N., MacLeod, C., & Matthews, A. (1997). *Cognitive psychology and emotional disorders.* Oxford: Wiley.

Williamson, S., Harpur, T. J., & Hare, R. D. (1991). Abnormal processing of affective words by psychopaths. *Psychophysiology, 28,* 260–271.

Woolston, J. L., Rosenthal, S. L., Riddle, M. A., Sparrow, S. S., Cicchetti, D., & Zimmerman, L. D. (1989). Childhood comorbidity of anxiety/affective and behavior disorders. *Journal of the American Academy of Child and Adolescent Psychiatry, 28,* 707–713.

World Health Organization. (2000). International Consortium in Psychiatric Epidemiology: Cross-national comparisons of the prevalence and correlates of mental disorders. *Bulletin of the World Health Organization, 78,* 413–426.

Wu, J. C., Buschsbaum, M. S., Hershey, T. G., Hazlett, E., Sciotte, N., & Johnson, J. C. (1991). PET in generalized anxiety disorder. *Biological Psychiatry, 29,* 1181–1199.

Yehuda, R. (1997). Sensitization of the hypothalamic-pituitary-adrenal axis in posttraumatic stress disorder. *Annals of the New York Academy of Sciences, 821,* 57–75.

Yehuda, R., Boisoneau, D., Mason, J. W., & Giller, E. L. (1993). Glucocorticoid receptor number and cortisol excretion in mood, anxiety, and psychotic disorders. *Biological Psychiatry, 34,* 18–25.

Yehuda, R., Southwick, S. M., Krystal, J. H., Bremner, J. D., Charney, D. S., & Mason, J. W. (1993). Enhanced suppression of cortisol following dexamethasone administration in posttraumatic stress disorder. *American Journal of Psychiatry, 150,* 83–86.

CHAPTER 10

Behavioral and Molecular Genetics and Developmental Psychopathology

RICHARD RENDE and IRWIN WALDMAN

Although the perception of behavioral genetic research by developmentalists has undergone a number of transformations over the past few decades (ranging from resistance to widespread acceptance), the fundamental purpose of elucidating and understanding both genetic and environmental contributions to behavioral development (both adaptive and maladaptive) has not wavered in importance or effort. As indicated in the title of this chapter, the most notable advancement in the field over the past decade has been the expansion of traditional behavioral genetic research (e.g., twin, family, and adoption studies) to include state-of-the-art molecular genetic approaches. Indeed, it may be argued

that behavioral genetics, both as an empirical enterprise and as a theoretical orientation, has forcefully shaped the direction of the conceptual and methodological approaches that are currently being applied to understanding the etiological architecture of psychopathology (Rende, 2004). Of particular note is the emphasis on both genetic and nongenetic contributions to etiology, including overt attention to a number of mechanisms by which genes and environment interrelate.

This chapter examines advancements in the field that have been influenced by and/or have implications for developmental psychopathology. As discussed in detail in the first edition to these volumes (Rende & Plomin, 1995), developmental psychopathology and behavioral and molecular genetics have many avenues for fruitful overlap. For example, core issues in developmental psychopathology, such as the delineation between normative and maladaptive—the "distinction" between the normal and

This work was supported by a number of grants funded by the National Institutes of Health, including MH001559, MH062989, DA016795, CA0841719, and MH001818. We thank Dante Cicchetti for many good suggestions for improving the content of this chapter.

abnormal—are particularly rich topics for behavioral genetic methodologies as well as molecular strategies. Similarly, themes that have been prominent for decades in behavioral genetics, such as the developmental interplay between genetic and environmental influence, are quite consistent with the systemic and interdisciplinary foundation of developmental psychopathology and are beginning to take on new meaning with the inclusion of molecular genetic techniques.

With this natural and fruitful merger between developmental psychopathology and behavioral and molecular genetics in mind, this chapter is organized around four core topics: theoretical and methodological foundations of behavioral genetics, advances in behavioral genetics and developmental psychopathology, molecular genetic approaches to developmental psychopathology, and future directions. Our goal is to illuminate critical themes that have emerged over the past decade that have shaped current thinking and hold promise for yielding future insights into our understanding of the development of psychopathology. Furthermore, we emphasize that for the purposes of this chapter, we are drawing a distinction between behavioral genetics and molecular genetics. This heuristic is organizational and allows us an opportunity to discuss in turn the yield of traditional behavioral genetic approaches that utilize natural experiments (i.e., genetically informative designs) as well as the newer enterprise of examining DNA (and environments) in relation to behavioral development. In principle, these two domains represent complementary and mutually informative strategies for studying the complex mix of genes and environment in a developmentally sensitive framework aimed at elucidating mechanisms that either promote or buffer against psychopathology.

THEORETICAL AND METHODOLOGICAL FOUNDATIONS OF BEHAVIORAL GENETICS

Prior to reviewing the many advances that have occurred in behavioral and molecular genetics, it is worthwhile to highlight the theory that not only provides a foundation for behavioral genetic research but also unifies current thinking in behavioral and molecular genetics. (Table 10.1 presents definitions for key terms in this section on behavior genetics.) For many decades, behavioral genetics has relied on quantitative genetic theory, which is a framework for understanding individual differences on a trait (continuous or categorical) in a population. Quantitative genetic theory postulates that individual differences (or variation) on a phenotype may be attributed to both genetic and nongenetic

TABLE 10.1 A Glossary of Terms for Behavioral Genetics

Term	Definition
Additive genetic effects	Genetic effects on individual differences on a trait or disorder that statistically add up to produce variation in the population.
Adoption design	A class of natural experiments that utilize a disentangling of genetic relatedness and rearing environment.
Gene × Environment correlation	Genetic effects that contribute to the level of an environmental variable.
Gene × Environment interaction	Genetic effects on a trait or disorder that are dependent on the level of an environmental variable.
Genetically informative design	A class of natural experiments that provide manipulation of genetic relatedness and/or rearing environment.
Heritability	A descriptive statistic that assigns an effect size to the genetic contribution to a trait or disorder that is attributable to inheritance.
Knock-out gene studies	Studies in model organisms, such as mice, in which one or both copies of a gene are deactivated and the effects on behavior and/or cognition are examined.
Liability	A theoretical construct in quantitative genetic theory that reflects the underlying effects of genes on a multifactorial disorder.
Multifactorial	Quantitative genetic model that incorporates the net effect of multiple genetic and environmental influences on a trait.
Nonshared environment	A descriptive statistic that assigns an effect size to the portion of unexplained variance on a trait or disorder.
Polygenic	Genetic influences that reflect effects of multiple genes on a trait.
Shared environment	A descriptive statistic that assigns an effect size to nongenetic or environmental influences on a trait or disorder that promote similarity among individuals reared together.
Twin design	A natural experiment that compares the similarity of monozygotic (MZ) and dizygotic (DZ) twins.
Zygosity	An indicator of genetic relatedness based on an additive genetic model.

influences. One key feature of the theory is that genetic influences reflect the impact of a number of genes rather than one gene, and as such, the theory relies on polygenic influence. It is postulated that a combined effect of such genes contributes to the manifestation of individual differences on a trait (or variation i'n the population on that trait). The fundamental quantitative genetic model assumes that this combined effect is additive, such that variation in each gene contributes (or adds up) to shape phenotypic variation. Alternative nonadditive effects (such as dominance) are possible and can be accommodated in the model. A similar perspective applies to nongenetic (or environmental) influence in quantitative genetic theory, as it is typically assumed that a number of environmental influences may also have an additive effect in producing phenotypic variation in the population. Finally, the model assumes error or nonexplained influences on phenotypic variation. Thus, the fundamental model is multifactorial (in that it assumes an unspecified number of both genetic and nongenetic influences) and polygenic (by assuming that a number of genes impact the manifestation of the phenotype).

Quantitative genetic theory has been utilized for decades in behavioral genetics by the application of genetically informative designs, which typically are natural experiments that provide some manipulation of genetic and nongenetic factors. The most commonly used paradigm is the twin method, which was formally proposed in the 1920s (Rende, Plomin, & Vandenberg, 1990), when there was clear recognition that there are two types of twins, monozygotic (MZ) and dizygotic (DZ). MZ twins share 100% of their genes and are thus also referred to as identical twins. DZ twins are, from a genetic perspective, biological siblings who are the same age and are thus also referred to as fraternal twins. The classic twin paradigm capitalizes on this natural experiment by comparing the similarity of MZ and DZ twins; if MZ twins are more similar on a trait than DZ twins, then heritability is assumed to be important for that trait and responsible for the difference in twin similarity. This inference is dependent in part on the equal environments assumption, which states that the rearing environment of MZ and DZ twins does not differ and thus differences in twin similarity are attributable to heritable factors and not environmental influences.

A powerful design is the adoption paradigm, which refers to a variety of methods that utilize both adoptive and nonadoptive (or biological) family members. The fundamental principle underlying the information yield of adoption studies is the cleaving of biological parentage and social rearing environment. One comparison examines the similarity of biological parents and their offspring that were adopted, typically very early in life, as an index of genetic contributions to a trait. The similarity between adoptive parents and their adopted offspring provides a direct measure of environmental influence, assuming that there is no selective placement (matching of adoptive parent traits to biological parent traits). Other adoption designs include comparisons of biological and adoptive siblings. Given the clear distinction between biological parentage and social environment in the adoption design, there are also opportunities to examine the interplay of genes and environment (e.g., the genetic contribution of the biological parent[s]

crossed by the environmental influence of the adoptive parents), including gene-environment interaction and gene-environment correlation.

Research over the past decade has also capitalized on other natural experiments. The combined twin-sibling design expands the classical twin paradigm to include other sibling types of varying genetic similarity, including full biological siblings, half-siblings, and unrelated siblings. This paradigm is useful in that it combines features of both the twin and adoption paradigms and allows an integrated picture of sibling similarity as a function of a broad range of biological relatedness, or zygosity. A combination of the twin and adoption study methodology yields comparisons of twins reared apart and twins reared together, a more rare but nonetheless highly informative design. As discussed later in this chapter, there is current interest in the children of twins design, which examines the offspring of MZ and DZ twins.

All of these designs have one commonality: a naturally existing differentiation (either in level of genetic relatedness or in genetic versus social parentage) that can be modeled to yield information on both genetic and environmental contributions to individual differences on a trait. As discussed in the first edition to these volumes, a major advance in behavioral genetics was the development of biometrical model fitting, or the application of systematic analytic models that could test the fit of alternative models combining the effects of genes and environment. Biometrical models are used to quantify the statistical effect size of both genetic and environmental influence. Genetic effects are captured by the construct of *heritability,* which is a descriptive statistic that assigns an effect size to genetic influence. Environmental influences that promote similarity among family members are captured by the descriptive statistic *shared environment* (or common environment). Nonfamilial resemblance (including error of measurement) is indicated by the descriptive statistic *nonshared environment.* Most behavioral genetic studies utilize a genetically informative design and biometrical models to provide parameter estimates of these three basic descriptive statistics. It should be noted that these three descriptive statistics correspond to the basic theoretical constructs proposed by quantitative genetic theory, as described earlier. Also, as discussed later in this chapter, these descriptive statistics are often calculated for a theoretical construct of liability to psychopathology when the outcome measure of interest is a diagnosed disorder.

Before turning to the behavioral genetic literature, two considerations must be emphasized. First, as described earlier, genetically informative designs are natural experiments and must be recognized as having the limitations inherent in any nonexperimental approach to behavior. Second, given that the constructs of heritability, shared environment, and nonshared environment are descriptive statistics, they are specific to the population studied as well as the methods used to study that population. Thus, these indicators may and do change across studies, environmental contexts, age, and generation. Indeed, some of the major advances in behavioral genetics have come from explicitly modeling how these descriptive statistics change based on these considerations. We now turn to the vast yield of behavioral genetic studies with particular relevance for developmental psychopathologists.

ADVANCES IN BEHAVIORAL GENETICS AND DEVELOPMENTAL PSYCHOPATHOLOGY

Traditional behavioral genetic research has continued at a rapid pace with an extraordinary number of high-quality papers represented in journals. Much of the work over the past decade has relied on the benchmark twin paradigm, although, as discussed later, other alternative and complementary designs have also been utilized. As has been the case with behavioral genetic research over the past few decades, many studies have gone beyond the "simplistic" delineation of heritable and nonheritable influences to address themes of fundamental importance to developmental psychopathology. In this section, we highlight four such themes that have been prominent over the past decade: (1) construction of developmental models of psychopathology, (2) use of genetically informative designs to understand environmental contributions to psychopathology, (3) use of genetically informative designs to hone in on the heritable contributions to psychopathology, and (4) advancement in methods that have potential for improving the yield of information for developmental psychopathology.

Developmental Models of Psychopathology

Behavioral genetic research has often involved developmentally informative designs, including both cross-sectional and longitudinal studies. The fruit of these labors is becoming more clear as empirically supported models of the development of various forms of psychopathology are emerging. Perhaps the clearest examples of how behavioral genetic studies have yielded potentially useful developmental models have come from research on substance use,

especially research on tobacco and alcohol use. We begin this section with a focus on tobacco use and then progress through other domains that have been studied.

Since a landmark paper by Carmelli, Swan, Robinette, and Fabsitz (1992) provided evidence for the heritability of smoking using the classic twin method, there have been a number of twin studies focused on varying levels of smoking intensity, ranging from initiation to smoking persistence to dependence. As discussed in reviews by Sullivan and Kendler (1999) and Li, Cheng, Ma, and Swan (2003), both genetic and shared environmental factors (i.e., environmental factors that operate to produce similarity in family members) are implicated for all of these indicators of smoking behavior, but the relative mix appears to be different for different levels of smoking intensity. For example, using meta-analysis, Li et al. (2003) have determined that smoking initiation is influenced significantly both by genetic factors (with heritability estimates of .37 for males, and .55 for females) and by shared environmental factors (.49 for males, and .24 for females). Li et al. also provide evidence of substantial heritability of smoking persistence (.59 for males and .46 for females), with shared environmental influences being more prominent for females (.28) than for males (.08). Sullivan and Kendler (1999) reached somewhat similar conclusions, suggesting substantial heritability of smoking initiation (approximately .60) along with significant shared environmental influences (approximately .20), with genetic factors being primarily responsible (heritability of approximately .70) for the transition to nicotine dependence and less impact observed for shared environmental influences.

It is of particular note that both Li et al. (2003) and Sullivan and Kendler (1999) emphasize the importance of shared environmental factors as well as genes on smoking initiation, which typically occurs during adolescence. Although there have been fewer behavioral genetic studies of adolescent tobacco use, compared to the number of reports on adults (Maes et al., 1999; McGue, Elkins, & Iacono, 2000), the studies to date have yielded intriguing results. First, there is strong evidence for shared environmental influences on smoking (Boomsma, Koopsman, van Doornen, & Orlebeke, 1994; Han, McGue, & Iacono, 1999; Koopsman, van Doornen, & Boomsma, 1997; Koopsman, Slutske, Heath, Neale, & Boomsma, 1999; McGue et al., 2000; Rende, Slomkowski, McCaffery, Lloyd-Richardson, & Niaura, 2005; Slomkowski, Rende, Novak, Lloyd-Richardson, & Niaura 2005; Vink, Willemsen, & Boomsma, 2003; White, Hopper, Wearing, & Hill, 2003), suggesting that there are etiological factors that promote twin resemblance independent of genetic related-ness and thus are thought to represent social effects. Most typically, shared environmental effects have been most prominent for either initiation of smoking or an index of "ever smoking" (i.e., without taking into account intensity of smoking), leading to claims that environmental influ-ences on initial experiences with cigarettes are critical (McGue et al., 2000) and perhaps even more influential than genetic contributions (Stallings, Hewitt, Beresford, Heath, & Eaves, 1999; White et al., 2003).

The results of a number of studies suggest that the pro-gression from smoking initiation to higher levels of smok-ing intensity (e.g., persistence, regular use, nicotine dependence) depend in part on the activation of gene sys-tems not implicated in initial exposure to cigarettes. For example, some longitudinal studies have suggested that progression from initial use to regular use reflects in part the expression of genetic susceptibility with little contri-bution from social influences (Boomsma et al., 1994; Koopsman et al., 1997, 1999). Although there is some ev-idence of overlap between the genetic contributions to ini-tiation and either persistence or dependence, a number of studies that have utilized multivariate models have re-ported that there are genetic influences unique to these higher levels of smoking intensity. Kendler et al. (1999) have proposed unique genetic influences (i.e., separable from those that influence smoking initiation) for nicotine dependence; Madden et al. (1999; Madden, Pedersen, Kaprio, Koskenvou, & Martin, 2004) and Heath, Martin, Lynskey, Todorov, and Madden (2002) have shown that smoking persistence involves genetic contributions that are separable from those found for smoking initiation.

Taken together, a number of behavioral genetic studies, both cross-sectional and longitudinal, and representing in-formative samples taken from a variety of cultures, support the notion that shared experiences between family members (i.e., the shared environment) is a critical risk factor that in-creases risk for initiating smoking in adolescence. These same studies also support the notion that genes contribute to this risk, and that these genes influence in part progression to higher levels of smoking intensity. However, there is sup-port for the contention that a unique set of genetic factors are activated by exposure to tobacco and influence progres-sion to smoking persistence and nicotine dependence. This straightforward developmental model is not only well sup-ported empirically, but offers an intuitive appeal (social fac-tors promote risky behavior, whereas biological factors become most prominent in terms of responsivity to exposure to a substance). One fundamental implication for develop-

mental psychopathology is the potential utility to consider environmental factors (especially those that are shared by family members) as targets for prevention and intervention models aimed at reducing the likelihood of smoking initia-tion in adolescence (e.g., McGue et al., 2000). A comple-mentary implication is that attention to genetic and biological factors will be critical for understanding individ-ual differences in responsivity to tobacco exposure (Swan et al., 2003). Of note here is the possibility that such genetic sensitivity may be apparent even in adolescence as both high frequency of smoking and symptoms of dependence have a heritable component (McGue et al., 2000; Rende et al., 2005). Thus, although the typical trajectory of influences may involve social (and genetic) effects on initiation in ado-lescence and later contributions of genes to persistence and dependence in adulthood, it may be that the developmental trajectory may be much more rapid in some youth, perhaps especially those at high genetic risk.

This fundamental developmental model that emphasizes environmental contributions to exposure and genetic foun-dations for sensitivity once exposed appears to hold prom-ise for substances other than tobacco. A number of twin studies of alcohol use in adolescence report robust shared environmental effects (Buster & Rogers, 2000; Cleveland & Wiebe, 2003; McGue, Iacono, Legrand, & Elkins, 2001; Rose, Dick, Viken, & Kaprio, 2001; Viken, Kaprio, Kosken-vuo, & Rose, 1999). Of particular interest from a develop-mental perspective is the distinction between initiation of drinking and engaging in heavier levels of use. Initiation of drinking in adolescence (i.e., comparing adolescents who have never had a drink to those who have) has been reported to be highly influenced by shared environmental effects (Rose, Dick, Viken, Pulkkinen, & Kaprio, 2001; Viken et al., 1999), whereas escalation to high levels of drinking (such as drinking to intoxication) appears to be less im-pacted by shared environmental influences but more indica-tive of genetic differences (Viken et al., 1999). Furthermore, a combined sibling/twin/adoption study of substance initiation, use, and problem use in adolescence has supported this general model for a number of sub-stances, including tobacco, alcohol, and other drugs such as marijuana (Rhee et al., 2003). Expanding the findings dis-cussed earlier for tobacco use, this study provided evidence that shared environmental factors contribute to initiation for alcohol, tobacco, and any drug use, and that heritability is more pronounced for problem use in adolescence than for initiation of any drug use. It may be suggested, then, that there is compelling evidence of a clear developmental model for substance use, with roles for shared environment and genes in the etiology of exposure to and initial use of substances and potentially unique genetic factors specific to sensitivity to repeated exposure to the substances and hence progression of use. Again, although this model commences with initial exposure to substances in adolescence, the rate of progression to higher levels of use may also begin in adolescence and continue into adulthood.

Developmental models from a behavioral genetic perspective have begun to emerge for other domains of behavior. The theme of shared environmental influences exerting an impact prior to the activation of genetic effects has been prominent in research on depression. A fundamental difference from the work reviewed for substance use has been the developmental epochs of interest: Shared environment has been shown to affect depressive symptoms in childhood, with evidence that genetic effects become detectable in adolescence. For example, Rice et al. (2002), using cross-sectional analyses in a population-based sample of twins, have shown that shared environmental influences were prominent for children ages 8 to 10 years, whereas genetic factors were most influential for adolescents (ages 11 to 17). Further longitudinal analyses have confirmed this pattern detected from the cross-sectional study, with evidence for new genetic influences that emerge in adolescence (Scourfield et al., 2003). This line of work has also suggested that the activation of genetic influences in adolescence may be related to genetic correlation with experiencing negative life events (Rice, Harold, & Thapar, 2003). Silberg et al. (1999) have made a similar argument, presenting analyses derived from the Virginia Twin Study of Adolescent Behavioral Development supporting the notion that a set of genes common to both depression and life stress is activated in adolescence, particularly for girls once puberty is achieved.

From a developmental perspective, an additional intriguing idea is that there are links between anxiety in childhood and depression in adolescence. Studies of offspring of depressed parents have long supported the contention that familial risk for depression first manifests as anxiety in childhood, followed by depression in adolescence (Rende, Wickramaratne, Warner, & Weissman, 1995; Warner, Weissman, Mufson, & Wickramaratne, 1999) and adulthood (Rende, Warner, Wickramaratne, & Weissman, 1999). Behavioral genetic work posits two unique pathways underlying this association, as exemplified by work conducted by Silberg and coworkers (Silberg, Rutter, & Eaves, 2001; Silberg, Rutter, Neale, & Eaves, 2001). These authors provide evidence of genetic links between childhood anxiety (Overanxious Disorder and simple phobias) and depression in adolescence, as well as support

for (shared) environmental links between separation anxiety in childhood and depression in adolescence. Thus, these authors suggest that there may be etiologically distinct syndromes of depression, essentially one reflecting environmental effects and one more genetically driven.

From the genetic perspective, Eaves, Silberg, and Erkanli (2003) have presented a model arguing that the developmental pathway is complex and must take into account at least three streams of influence: direct genetic continuity between anxiety in childhood and depression in adolescence, gene-environment interaction (genes that contribute to early anxiety also confer sensitivity to life events that may manifest as depression), and gene-environment correlation (genes that contribute to early anxiety also increase likelihood of exposure to life events that influence depression). From the environmental perspective, the Silberg, Rutter, and Eaves (2001) and Silberg, Rutter, Neale, et al. (2001) emphasis on potential shared environmental influences on depression is consistent with research using De-Fries-Fulker analysis, an analytic technique that examines the etiology of extreme scores in a distribution (Purcell & Sham, 2003; Rende & Slomkowski, in press). A number of studies using this method have shown that high levels of depressive symptoms in adolescence (e.g., symptom scores that are in a clinically significant range) are substantially influenced by shared environment, whereas individual differences in depressive symptoms are not (Deater-Deckard, Reiss, Hetherington, & Plomin, 1997; Eley, 1997; Rende, Plomin, Reiss, & Hetherington, 1993; Rice et al., 2002).

There is thus accumulating data and theory concerning developmental pathways to depression, including an emphasis on different developmental periods (childhood versus adulthood) as well as the possibility of etiological and phenotypic heterogeneity. This body of work is especially appealing in that it is hypothesis-generating and cuts across both high-risk studies of offspring of depressed parents (e.g., Rende et al., 1999) and twin studies (Silberg, Rutter, & Eaves, 2001; Silberg, Rutter, Neale, et al., 2001). Thus, the fundamental developmental association of anxiety in childhood and depression in adolescence may in fact represent two distinct pathways. First, there is the proposition that one form of depression onsets in childhood, as manifested by separation anxiety, with heterotypic continuity accounting for the expression of depression in adolescence, as mediated by shared environmental factors. A second proposition is that a more genetic form of depression, resulting from a common set of genes, includes expression of Overanxious Disorder and phobia in childhood and depression in adolescence, again as a form of heterotypic continuity. What has not been broached from the behavioral genetic perspective is continuity into adulthood. There is little evidence of shared environmental influences on depression in adulthood, as most studies have shown only genetic effects (Sullivan et al., 2000). The one study to date of Major Depressive Disorder in adolescence has also provided evidence of genetic, but not shared environmental, influence (Glowinski, Madden, Bucholz, Lynskey, & Heath, 2003). Thus, it is clear that in the future, developmental models of depression will need to generate testable propositions concerning etiological influences that span from childhood into adulthood (e.g., Kendler, Gardner, & Prescott, 2002).

The theme of etiological heterogeneity has been prominent in developmental behavioral genetic studies of antisocial behavior. Retrospective reports gathered from adults have suggested that both genes and shared environment contribute to juvenile antisocial behavior (Jacobson, Prescott, & Kendler, 2000), with some evidence that a different set of genetic factors may operate in childhood versus adolescence and adulthood (Jacobson et al., 2000). It has been suggested that such unique genetic influence on childhood antisocial behavior reflects an increased heritability for early-onset delinquency (Taylor, Iacono, & McGue, 2000). An informative approach has been taken by Eley, Lichtenstein, and Moffitt (2003), as they incorporated two methodological features in a twin study: a longitudinal sampling frame (with measurement occurring at 8 to 9 years of age and again at 13 to 14 years of age) and a distinction between aggressive and nonaggressive antisocial behavior. These features allowed for the calculation of genetic and environmental influences at each time point for each subtype of antisocial behavior, as well as for the application of longitudinal behavioral genetic models aimed at understanding the etiology of continuity across time points. Eley et al. report that aggressive antisocial behavior was influenced primarily by genes in childhood, with genes and shared environment both contributing to adolescent antisocial behavior. Nonaggressive antisocial behavior was influenced by both genes and antisocial behavior in both childhood and adolescence. Perhaps most important, the continuity in aggressive antisocial behavior from childhood to adolescence was mediated primarily by genetic influences, suggesting that aggressive antisocial behavior is a stable heritable phenotype, in contrast to nonaggressive antisocial behavior, which was more strongly affected by the environment. Additional longitudinal studies, especially those that extend beyond adolescence and into adulthood, hold potential for shedding more light on the different developmental pathways leading

to subtypes of antisocial behavior. Of note in the Eley et al. approach is the emphasis on testing models that apply essentially not only to subtypes but to individual trajectories, an approach that has potential for understanding the etiology of complex phenotypes that undoubtedly reflect a number of heterogeneous behavioral types.

It is also worth noting that eating disorders—and related phenotypes such as eating attitudes and behaviors—have been examined using behavioral genetic approaches. A number of twin studies have demonstrated that eating disorders, especially bulimia nervosa, show evidence of substantial heritability and typically little evidence of shared environmental influence (Bulik, Sullivan, Wade, & Kendler, 2000; Bulik & Tozzi, 2004). There is also evidence that heritable influences are detectable for bulimic symptoms in adolescence (Rowe, Pickles, Simonoff, Bulik, & Silberg, 2002). Other types of eating behaviors also show evidence of significant heritability, including symptoms of binge eating (Reichborn-Kjennerud, Bulik, Tambs, & Harris, 2004) and indicators of eating behaviors such as emotional and uncontrolled eating (Tholin, Rasmussen, Tynelius, & Karlsson, 2005). To date, however, few studies have taken an explicit developmental perspective to examine if there are age-based changes in the etiology of eating behaviors. Two papers illustrate the potential utility of this approach. Klump, McGue, and Iacono (2000) reported that eating attitudes and behaviors were more heritable in adolescent (17-year-old) versus preadolescent (11-year-old) twins, whereas shared environmental factors were more salient in preadolescence. Further work with this sample traced the onset of heritability of eating attitudes and behaviors to the onset of puberty, as heritability could be detected in the subsample of 11-year-old twins who had reached puberty, but not in the prepubertal twins (Klump, McGue, & Iacono, 2003). Thus, a potentially important direction for future studies of eating disorders and behaviors will be tracking developmentally timed changes in the etiological contributions of genes and environment.

It is clear that behavioral genetic research has begun to make substantial progress in bringing a developmental framework to the study of psychopathology. We have focused on behavioral genetic study of symptom areas such as substance use, depression, and antisocial behavior, which has yielded especially interesting data and theory over the past decade. One additional point is that much less attention has been given to work spanning other developmental transitions, such as the progression to later life, although examples of the utility of a life span perspective are emerging (Gillespie et al., 2004). As developmental psychopathology is not synonymous with studying only childhood and adolescence, but rather encompasses a theoretical framework concerning development through the life span, such work is also needed to further the yield of behavioral genetic research.

Elucidating Environmental Influences on Psychopathology

The developmental studies reviewed earlier highlight a tradition in behavior genetics that is now well recognized but was not always appreciated by developmentalists: Behavior genetics attempts to study both genetic and environmental influences on psychopathology. The studies discussed thus far provided evidence of environmental influences on the development of substance use, depression, and antisocial behavior. Contrary to prior decades of behavioral genetic research (e.g., Dick & Rose, 2002; Rende, 2004), the emphasis is now on shared environmental influences, environmental factors that promote similarity among family members independent of genetic influences.

New directions for studying the environment have resulted from incorporating measurable features of the environment into genetically informative designs to tease apart "pure" environmental influence that is shown to be independent of genes (e.g., Rutter, Pickles, Murray, & Eaves, 2001). There have been a wide variety of such studies in the past decade, many of which have presented evidence in favor of specific environmental contributions to psychopathology. For example, there has been interest in the broader social context, such as the neighborhood. Rose et al. (2003) have used a "double dyad" design composed of twins and their classmates to gauge effects of the neighborhood and have shown similarity of the dyads for smoking and drinking patterns, suggesting an environmental impact of the neighborhood. Caspi, Taylor, Moffitt, and Plomin (2000) used the classic twin paradigm to show that neighborhood deprivation accounted for a significant portion of the shared environmental effect on emotional and behavioral problems in toddlers. Broadening the focus on social context, Rose, Kaprio, Winter, Koskenvuo, and Viken (1999) have shown that socioregional differences strongly affect the likelihood of adolescent abstinence from alcohol and affect the extent to which abstinence aggregates in the family. These studies point to the potential impact of the broad social context that may function independently from genetic influences.

A number of studies have used similar strategies to further our knowledge of the effects of family environment on the development of psychopathology. Meyer et al. (2000) have used an extended twin-family design to show that family discord and maladaptation operate as a "true" envi-ronmental effect, shared by family members, on antisocial behavior in childhood and adolescence. Similar support for environmental influences on antisocial behavior has come from twin studies focusing on physical maltreatment (Jaffee, Caspi, Moffitt, & Taylor, 2004) and maternal expressed emotion (Caspi et al., 2004). Jaffee et al. have shown that physical maltreatment has a direct environmental effect on antisocial behavior in childhood after controlling for the net effects of genes. They also reported that twin similarity for physical maltreatment is not due to genes but reflects the shared experiences of being in an abusive home, furthering the evidence that physical maltreatment represents an environmental influence on development. Caspi et al. utilized comparisons of MZ twins who experienced differential maternal treatment, and demonstrated that the MZ twins who received more maternal negativity and less maternal warmth had higher levels of antisocial behavior than their identical cotwins. As this design implicitly controls for genetic similarity by focusing on differences within MZ pairs, it provides direct evidence of environmental influence on antisocial behavior.

The interaction between family members has also been highlighted as a potential environmental mechanism for substance use, especially smoking. The smoking behavior of parents and siblings appears to function primarily as an environmental risk for smoking in adolescence, although some genetic effects on this relationship emerge in adulthood (Vink, Willemsen, & Boomsma, 2003). Slomkowski and coworkers (2005) have shown that this proposed sibling effect on smoking is an environmental process that is moderated by having high levels of sibling social connectedness (a composite of time spent together, mutual friendships, and warmth). Taken together, these diverse studies share the framework of using genetically informative designs to not only establish the existence of environmental effects, but to elucidate specific measurable features of the family environment that may serve as targets for intervention and prevention efforts.

A related theme to emerge from the developmental studies of psychopathology discussed earlier is the necessity to consider models that make explicit the interplay of genetic and environmental influences. Although elegant models of gene-environment interplay have been offered in behavioral genetics for over 2 decades with clear specification of the distinction between gene-environment interaction and gene-environment correlation (see Rende & Plomin, 1995), there has been an infusion of increased recognition of the importance of this topic. A number of theoretical papers devoted to gene-environment interplay have emerged in the past few years. These have included increasing recognition of the expansion of the classic twin paradigm to consider both gene-environment interaction and correlation (Kendler, 2001). Attention to the conceptual and methodological issues involved in studying gene-environment correlations and interactions particularly with respect to developmental psychopathology have also been offered (Rutter, 2002; Rutter et al., 1997; Rutter & Silberg, 2002). The importance of gene-environment interplay has been recognized for a number of domains, including Schizophrenia (Tsuang, 2000; Tsuang, Stone, & Faraone, 2001) and alcohol dependence (Heath & Nelson, 2002).

In addition to conceptual and theoretical papers, there have been a number of empirical studies that have taken on gene-environment interplay using a variety of designs. Returning to the theme of socioregional influences on alcohol use, genetic effects on adolescent drinking are more pronounced in urban versus rural settings, a form of gene-environment interaction (Dick, Rose, Viken, Kaprio, & Koskenvou, 2001; Rose, Dick, Viken, & Kaprio, 2001). Gene-environment interaction has also been implicated for the effects of parental drinking on adolescent drinking, as there is evidence that (especially for boys) exposure to parental drinking increases heritability (Cleveland & Wiebe, 2003).

The study of gene-environment interplay and depression highlights the complexity of the issue. It has been long recognized that exposure to stressful life events increases risk for depression, both in adolescence and adulthood. Behavioral genetic approaches have been well positioned to examine mechanisms underlying this association, including both gene-environment interaction (genetic factors influence the sensitivity to life events that promotes depression) and gene-environment correlation (genetic factors contribute to exposure to life events that promote depression). Behavioral genetic studies suggest that both mechanisms may be at work. Twin studies have shown that genetic factors associated with Major Depressive Disorder are also correlated with the probability of experiencing stressful life events, particularly in the interpersonal and occupational/financial domains (Kendler & Karkowski-Shuman, 1997). Kendler et al. (1999) estimate that such gene-environment correlation accounts for about one-third of the association between stressful life events and depression, with the implication being that there are causal effects between stress exposure and depression onset. With respect to adolescent depression (particularly in girls), there is also evidence that there is an environmental pathway between exposure to life events and depression (Silberg, Rutter, Neale, et al., 2001). These studies suggest that genetic factors influence susceptibility to such exposure and that there may be correlation between

genetic factors that affect depression likelihood as well as exposure to life events.

The complexity of the pathways linking genetic susceptibility to and control over effects of the environment has also come to light in studies evaluating the effects of prenatal exposure to tobacco. Historically similar to research on life events, research on maternal smoking during the prenatal period has often been considered an environmental risk factor for behavioral problems in childhood, especially conduct problems. Behavioral genetic methodology has been used to reexamine this supposed link, opening up the possibility that some of the association may not be causal but may reflect a "spurious" association due to familial transmission of a latent "antisocial" trait that similarly influences maternal smoking and childhood conduct problems. Two studies in particular have examined this topic. Silberg et al. (2003) used a combined family-twin design to explore links between maternal smoking and childhood conduct problems; they concluded that the fundamental pathway (for boys) was genetic transmission of a latent factor that influenced expression of antisocial behavior. Maughan, Taylor, Caspi, and Moffitt (2004) also used parental data collected in a twin study of childhood and also concluded that there was evidence of correlated genetic effects. These authors highlight potential environmental confounds such as maternal mating with antisocial men and living in disadvantaged circumstances.

It is clear that current behavioral genetic theory and research has taken seriously the role of environmental influences on the development of psychopathology. The fundamental advance has come from incorporating specific measures of the environment into the classic behavioral genetic models, permitting insight into environmental effects, gene-environment interaction, and gene-environment correlation. The range of environmental factors considered to date (including socioregional and neighborhood effects, family dynamics involving parents and siblings, exposure to life stress, and prenatal exposure to tobacco) is impressive and speaks to the theory-driven nature of this work. The primary conclusion that may be reached at this point is that the impact of the environment may involve a variety of mechanisms, depending in part on the area of psychopathology being studied and the developmental epoch of interest.

Genetically Informative Designs and the Heritable Component of Behavior

The advancements made in understanding environmental contributions to the development of psychopathology have resulted in large measure from including specific dimensions of the environment in behavioral genetic studies. A similar spirit drives the use of behavioral genetic designs to elucidate the behavioral expression of genetic influence. Indeed, it has been well recognized that a major barrier to progress is the lack of specified indicators of genetic influence for many domains of psychopathology. Work in this area is progressing in two complementary ways. One fundamental area for advance involves the identification of genetic markers along with indication of their functional significance in the brain. This topic is reviewed in the section on molecular genetics. A second area relies on the application of traditional paradigms used in behavioral genetics to elucidate behavioral indicators of the genetic signal. We focus here on this approach and review various strategies that have been used to date.

Before presenting exemplars of the behavioral genetic approach to uncovering indicators of genetic influence, we present some of the conceptual underpinnings that are especially important for this enterprise. For nearly 40 years, behavioral genetic research has promoted the concept of genetic liability to disorder as opposed to inheritance of the disorder per se (Rende & Plomin, 1995). It is noted here that the term "liability" traditionally refers either to a theoretical construct of genetic influence that is *inferred* but not measured, or to a statistical representation of the effect size of this theoretical parameter. As discussed earlier, this fundamental construct has essentially been accepted for nearly all domains of psychopathology, including rare conditions such as Autism, Schizophrenia, and Bipolar Disorder. In terms of charting progress in behavioral genetics, the construct of liability, and the statistical modeling of it using biometrical models, has essentially delivered its yield and now provides a foundation for attempts to isolate specific indicators of such liability.

In this regard, there is consensus that a critical step for behavioral genetics is to identify putative phenotypes that best reflect the expression of genes (Gottesman & Gould, 2003; Merikangas & Risch, 2003). Broad clinical descriptors such as psychiatric diagnoses represent the "end product" of gene-environment interplay and, as targets for genetic investigations, are not maximally informative about specific indicators that reside closer to the genetic signal (Gottesman & Gould, 2003; Merikangas & Risch, 2003). There have been multiple suggestions for improving the resolution of genetic studies, including genetic studies that incorporate measurement of the environment, via the refinement of "candidate phenotypes" that may be more informative of underlying genetic liability. This is precisely the area in which traditional behavioral genetic designs may shed new light on our understanding of psychopathology, if they are aimed at measurable indicators of genetic

liability to move the field closer to the putative genetic effect.

This approach is best exemplified by the search for *endophenotypes,* typically regarded as biological markers that may begin to flag the mechanisms representing genetic liability. Although there has been extensive interest in endophenotypes for decades, this area is taking on new momentum in the era of genomics research. Gottesman and Gould (2003) have provided a number of criteria that could be used to uncover so-called endophenotypes, which include traits or markers that may reflect more closely the expression of vulnerability genes (see our expanded discussion of endophenotypes in the section on molecular genetics). A similar construct with somewhat different implications is captured by the phrase *intermediate phenotype* (e.g., Enoch, Schuckit, Johnson, & Goldman, 2003). Although sometimes used interchangeably with endophenotype, this term is also used to refer to genetically driven dimensions or indicators of behavior that are conceptually tied to a domain of psychopathology without representing full expression of a diagnosed condition or syndrome. We propose that this term sometimes differs in spirit from endophenotype in that it refers more to *phenotypic* traits associated with a form of psychopathology that more closely reflect the genetic signals underlying a disorder or syndrome, as opposed to more distal biological markers of underlying genetic risk (which is the spirit of an endophenotype). We belabor this point primarily to indicate that the gene-brain system-behavior chain is complex, such that there may be many indicators of genetic contribution to psychopathology. These can range from biological markers that represent the expression of genetic risk for a disorder (such as regulation of a neurotransmitter, underlying brain pathology) to behavioral traits that better reflect phenotypic expression of genetic risk (such as being a personality trait that is highly heritable that conveys likelihood for developing a specific form of psychopathology) to identification of indicators of a disorder that appear to be more heritable than others (e.g., subtypes of a disorder, specific symptoms of a disorder).

An excellent illustration of the range of phenotypic markers that may be investigated is provided by Swan et al. (2003). With particular reference to genetic studies of tobacco use, these authors have provided a "class" system to make the point that candidate phenotypes may take many forms, including more precise clinical descriptors, underlying trait characteristics, and specific indicators of biological mechanisms. Specifically, they present four such classes, ranging from the least informative for genetic studies (Class I) to the most informative (Class IV):

Class I: Relatively crude, broad summary or cross-sectional measures of smoking behaviors, such as ever/never smoker, current/former/never smoker, age at initiation, and average number of cigarettes smoked per day.

Class II: Measures or indicators of tobacco dependence, such as time to first cigarette in the morning or number of quit attempts.

Class III: Classifications that emphasize the process of or progression toward the development of regular smoking or tobacco dependence, such as smoking topography, uptake slope, or trajectory.

Class IV: Nicotine pharmacokinetic parameters (the effects of the body on the drug, i.e., nicotine absorption, metabolism), and pharmacodynamic effects (the effects of the drug on the body, including physiological responses, heightened concentration, and changes in receptor function and density).

We thus present progress made in the field to date, being mindful of the multiple ways that behavior genetic designs can illuminate with specificity heritable underpinnings of psychopathology. One area of research continues a tradition of behavioral genetic work that attempts to understand the specificity and nonspecificity of heritable influences on psychopathology. This work serves an important function by establishing the broad landscape for genetic studies, approaching the classic issue of lumping versus splitting disorders from the perspective of etiology. *Lumping* refers to explaining the etiology of a number of disorders via common genetic influences, such as having a shared genetic etiology to comorbid disorders. *Splitting* refers to decomposing a heterogeneous disorder into etiologically independent subtypes.

A number of twin studies have begun to clarify both a common genetic vulnerability to substance use and drug-specific effects (Tsuang, Bar, et al., 2001), providing evidence in favor of lumping. For example, multivariate biometrical modeling of data collected on adult males as part of the Vietnam Era Twin Registry has shown that there is a common genetic influence that affects abusing a number of drugs, including marijuana, sedatives, stimulants, heroin, and psychedelics (Tsuang et al., 1998). Similarly, Kendler, Jacobson, Prescott, and Neale (2003) reported a singular genetic factor that influenced risk for illicit use and abuse/dependence of cannabis, cocaine, hallucinogens, sedatives, stimulants, and opiates in a study of adult male twins ascertained from the Virginia Twin Registry. There may also be a common genetic vulnerability that underlies risk for nicotine and alcohol dependence in men (True,

Xian, et al., 1999). The theme of common genetic risk has also arisen in studies of tobacco, alcohol, and caffeine (Hettema, Corey, & Kendler, 1999).

Common genetic vulnerability has been shown across a number of psychiatric disorders and domains of psychopathology. Biometrical modeling has provided evidence of shared genetic risk for the following: anorexia nervosa and Major Depressive Disorder (Wade, Bulik, Neale, & Kendler, 2000); Attention-Deficit/Hyperactivity Disorder and Oppositional-Defiant Disorder/Conduct Disorder (Nadder, Rutter, Silberg, Maes, & Eaves, 2002); Generalized Anxiety Disorder and Panic Disorder (Scherrer et al., 2000); Posttraumatic Stress Disorder, alcohol and drug dependence (Xian et al., 2000); alcohol dependence and marijuana dependence (True, Heath, et al., 1999); pathological gambling and Antisocial Personality Disorder (Slutske et al., 2001); and Major Depressive Disorder, alcohol dependence, marijuana dependence, and Antisocial Personality Disorder (Fu et al., 2002). Although some of these studies also reported evidence of disorder-specific genetic effects, it is clear that a fundamental conclusion is that the construct of lumping from the perspective of genetics is alive and flourishing.

A different approach has been taken when examining alternative phenotypes (i.e., those that might reflect genetic effects more closely than more traditional diagnostic measures). Indeed, it could be argued that the strong evidence for common genetic factors may reflect, in part, the imprecision of measurement offered by traditional diagnostic categories. Research on Attention-Deficit/Hyperactivity Disorder (ADHD) provides a good example of this tradition of searching for more heritable indicators characteristic of the splitting perspective. One approach has focused on latent class analysis of the symptoms of ADHD in twin samples, the intent being to identify empirically different classes of this syndrome and to determine if there is evidence of class-specific heritability. To date, the studies conducted support this contention and provide evidence of multiple independent forms of ADHD, reflecting subtype-specific genetic effects (Neuman et al., 2001; Rasmussen et al., 2004; Todd, Rasmussen, et al., 2001).

Similar research on other domains of psychopathology have focused on isolating more specific indicators of genetic influence than those offered by analyzing traditional diagnostic categories. Using an Australian sample of twins, Lessov et al. (2004) have reported that five symptoms of nicotine dependence (tolerance, withdrawal, experiencing difficulty quitting, time to first cigarette in the morning, and number of cigarettes smoked per day) represent the most heritable components of nicotine dependence. It has also been shown that failed smoking cessation and nicotine withdrawal are both heritable, with partial correlation between these indicators of genetic vulnerability (Xian et al., 2003). An interesting aspect to this study is that Xian et al. focused on a subsample of twins (drawn from the Vietnam Era Twin Registry) in which both members of the twin pair were lifetime smokers and had made at least one attempt to quit smoking. This permitted a fine-grained analysis of a number of individual nicotine withdrawal symptoms. Slutske et al. (1999) analyzed the etiological architecture of a number of alcoholism symptoms and found a wide range in the resultant heritabilities (from .03 to .53). Given the overlapping confidence intervals surrounding these heritability estimates, the authors cautioned against the likelihood of identifying "more or less heritable" symptoms of alcoholism, although they noted the potential importance of pursuing this topic. Other research on alcohol disorders has shown that individual differences in alcohol intake are due to genetic effects, with additional genes contributing to alcohol dependence (Whitfield et al., 2004). This study is unique (and arguably approaches Class II phenotypes) because it utilized multiple assessments to determine repeatability of intake as the phenotype of interest.

Although a number of twin studies have shown that Major Depressive Disorder (MDD) is heritable (Sullivan et al., 2000), the family study paradigm has been informative over a number of years by documenting specific clinical features that are associated with familial aggregation. Studies using extensions of the family design have provided further clarification. In a landmark study, Weissman et al. (2005) have shown the transmission of risk for MDD across three generations. The three-generation analysis yielded two findings that build on prior research with important implications for genetic studies: (1) Rates of depression are highest in the third-generation offspring who have both parents and grandparents with moderately to severely impairing depression; and (2) Anxiety Disorders are the first manifestation of familial risk for depression. This work is critical in that it has identified clinical characteristics of depression (impairment) linked to familial transmission, expanded familial transmission across generations, and permitted insight into the developmental trajectory o risk in childhood (Anxiety Disorders) and adolescence and adulthood (depression). Similarly, Klein, Lewinsohn, Rohde, Seeley, and Durbin (2002) have found that severity of depression (involving both recurrence of episodes and impairment) is the most salient marker of familial aggregation, as opposed to specific symptoms of depression. The work of Klein and colleagues is important developmentally as they have utilized a bottom-up (see Rende & Weissman, 1999) design focusing on relatives of adolescents with

MDD (as opposed to the more traditional top-down design focused on offspring of depressed parents). Their work (see also Klein, Lewinsohn, Seeley, & Rohde, 2001) has demonstrated that depression with onset in adolescence is a highly familial phenotype and thus converges well with the more vast literature on offspring of depressed parents. Indeed, Wickramaratne, Warner, and Weissman (2000) have shown, using data from the Weissman top-down longitudinal intergenerational study mentioned earlier, that early-onset depression is heterogeneous and not informative for genetic studies without reference to familial loading. Interestingly, the converging evidence for the importance of clinical severity/impairment as a marker of familial risk for depression has also been found in analyses of twin samples (Kendler et al., 1999).

The studies reviewed in this section represent a number of ways in which behavioral genetic work has begun to unravel the etiological architecture of psychopathology. The studies discussed thus far, however, have all been focused at the level of symptomatology, and it is clear that progress in the field will come about in part by linking symptom presentation with attempts to conceptualize and measure putative endophenotypes or intermediate phenotypes. Studies focused on Obsessive-Compulsive Disorder (OCD) illustrate well how this leap may occur. There have been efforts to examine the complex spectrum of symptoms that may manifest as part of OCD and to employ statistical methods to generate a number of specific dimensions that are partly distinct etiologically. Mataix-Cols, do Rosario-Campos, and Leckman (2005) reviewed a number of factor analytic studies and derived four symptom dimensions of OCD: symmetry/ordering, hoarding, contamination/cleaning, and obsessions/checking. Of particular relevance is that these authors speculated that these symptom dimensions may represent viable endophenotypes for genetic studies of OCD. Miguel et al. (2005) have furthered this argument by proposing that dimensional components of OCD such as these may underlie the genetic contributions to distinctive phenotypic subgroups of the disorder. These models of OCD provide both a theoretical foundation for genetic studies and measurable endophenotypes that may be evaluated as indicators of genetic influence by behavioral genetic paradigms.

To date, most domains of psychopathology of interest to developmentalists are at this formative stage in terms of conceptualizing endophenotypes, a necessary step that precedes their measurement and testing in genetically informative designs. For example, research on depression, anxiety, antisocial behavior, and substance use have lagged behind progress achieved for other areas of dysfunction such as

Schizophrenia, where there is a long history of examining endophenotypes (Gottesman & Erlenmeyer-Kimling, 2001; Tsuang, 2001) and much activity in this area using both family and twin designs (Glahn et al., 2003; Seidman et al., 2002). However, two areas of research have begun to measure and test putative endophenotypes and reflect important conceptual progress. First, endophenotypic indicators of risk for ADHD have received attention. Stins, van Baal, Polderman, Verhulst, and Boomsma (2004) have used the twin paradigm to demonstrate genetic effects on performance of the Stroop task, an indicator of frontal functioning, in a large sample of 12-year-olds. They suggest that performance on this task may serve as a potential endophenotype for genetic studies of ADHD and other disorders that reflect frontal dysfunction. Nigg, Blaskey, Stawicki, and Sachek (2004) have taken a neuropsychological approach by examining executive and regulatory measures in parents and siblings of children with ADHD and have presented a neurogenetic model for a subset of executive functions. Nonaffected siblings of ADHD probands have also been shown to have a deficient response inhibition, which has been argued to represent potential genetic vulnerability to ADHD (Slaats-Willemse, Swaab-Barneveld, de Sonneville, van der Meulen, & Buitelaar, 2003). These three studies provide prototype designs (both twin and family) with appropriate attention to specified and measurable endophenotypes. A similar spirit has guided research on reduced P300 amplitude as a potential endophenotype indexing familial (genetic) risk for alcoholism. Both family (Hesselbrock, Begleiter, Porjesz, O'Connor, & Bauer, 2001) and twin (Carlson, Iacono, & McGue, 2002, 2004) studies have supported this idea by focusing on nonaffected family members. This group of studies on alcoholism, along with the studies on ADHD, represent significant progress by explicitly testing endophenotypes using informative family and twin designs.

Method Development in Behavioral Genetics

Behavioral genetic research has always been associated with method development. For a number of years, such method development was primarily analytic, including the advent of biometrical model fitting, which became a benchmark of modern work (see Rende & Plomin, 1995). In this section, we wish to emphasize that research design represents another domain for advancement in behavior genetics. For example, historically, the twin and adoption paradigms that represented the advent of the fundamental behavioral genetic designs were expanded to include designs such as twins reared apart, sibling adoption studies, and combined twin and sibling paradigms. A newer design of particular relevance for the study of developmental psychopathology is the children of twins paradigm.

A number of papers have argued that the children of twins design (COT) offers a unique opportunity to resolve issues pertaining to genetic and environmental transmission within families, with obvious application to developmental psychopathology. Two papers (D'Onofrio et al., 2003; Silberg & Eaves, 2004) have presented both a theoretical and an analytic framework for the COT design, and both papers have suggested that a unique contribution of this approach is the ability to differentiate environmental effects from genetic effects with more precision than is offered by more traditional behavioral genetic designs. Applications of this design have shown, for example, that the familial environment (presence or absence of exposure to parental alcoholism) moderates the expression of high genetic risk for alcoholism (Jacob et al., 2003); that prenatal exposure to tobacco represents an environmental contribution to birthweight (D'Onofrio et al., 2003); and that environmental factors (including gene-environment interplay) contribute to the association between parental alcoholism and offspring suicide attempts (Glowinski et al., 2004). Of particular interest in the COT is the focus on vertical transmission (intergenerational transmission), which is typically lacking in the traditional twin paradigm (which focuses on horizontal transmission). Thus, the COT expands the utility of the top-down or high-risk design that has played a critical role in developmental psychopathology (Rende & Weissman, 1999) by adding a genetically informative component. This combination of elements from the family and twin paradigms offers unique opportunities to understand in much greater detail the genetic and environmental mechanisms underlying transmission of familial risk for psychopathology.

Summary

This section has considered the substantial progress that has been made in the behavioral genetic study of psychopathology, especially as it relates to the fundamental tenets of developmental psychopathology. Behavioral genetic designs have been especially useful in mapping out potential etiological pathways to psychopathology that span developmental epochs (e.g., childhood to adolescence, adolescence to adulthood). We have gained much insight over the past decade on the role of environmental influences on psychopathology, particularly shared environmental effects in childhood and adolescence. Similar effort has been devoted to refining our conception and measurement of the indicators of genetic influence on psychopathology. Finally, advances in behavioral genetic designs have also begun to make important contributions to our understanding of the development of psychopathology.

MOLECULAR GENETIC APPROACHES TO DEVELOPMENTAL PSYCHOPATHOLOGY

The previous section provides ample evidence of the contribution of behavioral genetics to our understanding of psychopathology. In addition, behavioral genetics has had a major impact on our conceptualization of genetic influence on psychiatric disease as well as helped shape the methodology used in molecular genetic studies (Rende, 2004). Indeed, behavioral and molecular genetic studies of psychopathology have become intricately linked, especially as behavioral genetic work lays a strong foundation for current molecular investigations.

Before turning exclusively to advances in molecular genetic approaches to psychopathology, we expand on the ways behavioral genetics has helped shape the focus and direction of genomic research. First, the vast empirical yield of behavioral genetic research demonstrating that heritability estimates do not fully explain the distribution of disorder in the population, even for severe diseases such as Schizophrenia and Bipolar Disorder, helped revamp genetic search strategies by changing the underlying genetic model. Specifically, the *empirical* evidence for genetic *and* environmental influences on nearly all forms of psychopathology gathered from behavioral genetic studies resulted in a paradigm shift in psychiatric genetics. Mendelian models of single-gene influence have been discarded in favor of multifactorial models that incorporate the effects of many probabilistic genes along with nongenetic influences, as represented in the fundamental quantitative genetic model (Rende, 2004). This shift has in fact occurred for most common diseases, of which psychiatric disorder is but one class (Conneally, 2003; Merikangas & Risch, 2003; van den Bree & Owen, 2003).

This paradigm shift is reflected in the de-emphasis (or reworking) of genetic strategies best suited for detecting single or major gene effects on disorder, in favor of alternative strategies aimed at detecting the correlation of genes of small effect size with complex disease (see Conneally, 2003; Merikangas & Risch, 2003; van den Bree & Owen, 2003). The emphasis in behavioral genetics on the complexity of the phenotype, as well as the construct of genetic liability, has also helped shape molecular studies by focusing attention on intermediate phenotypes and endophenotypes. Finally, the importance of the environment has been recognized in molecular studies that assess gene-environment interaction. The progress in the field of molecular genetics that is reviewed here is thus conceptually linked with behavioral genetics by quantitative genetic theory, the theoretical foundation that has guided behavioral genetics for decades, and also logically derives from the substantial empirical findings derived from behavioral genetic studies.

Overview

Over the past decade, molecular genetic studies of psychopathology have transitioned from the potential to the real. Whereas quantitative genetic studies have increased our knowledge of the etiology of various disorders in a general manner by characterizing abstract, anonymous genetic and environmental variance components, only molecular genetic studies can point to specific genetic risk factors and their consequent etiological mechanisms. At the time the first edition to these volumes was published over a decade ago, molecular genetic studies of psychopathology represented an unrealized dream, the discussion of which was confined to the "Future Directions" section of the chapter. Much of the actualization of the potential of such studies stems from technological rather than conceptual developments. Advances in DNA collection methods using minimally invasive procedures (i.e., buccal cells versus venipuncture; Freeman et al., 1997), advances in genotyping methods (Craig & McClay, 2002), and the proliferation of DNA markers culminating in the sequencing of the human genome and successive improvements to databases in which DNA markers such as single nucleotide polymorphisms (SNPs) are catalogued (Reich, Gabriel, & Altshuler, 2003) all have contributed to the rapid progress in molecular genetic studies of various forms of psychopathology seen since the publication of the first edition of these volumes.

In this section, we first describe some fundamental aspects of the design and analysis of molecular genetic studies, including the concepts of association and linkage, the basics of genome scans and candidate gene studies, and important considerations in the search for genes that underlie complex traits (i.e., those that are thought to have multiple genetic and environmental causes). We proceed with a consideration of some of the more important themes that are emerging in molecular genetic studies of psychopathology that are important for guiding future research in this domain. These include the *replicability and consistency* of findings of association and linkage between a gene and a disorder, the *specificity* of association and/or linkage findings to particular diagnostic subtypes or symptom dimensions, and the *heterogeneity* of association and/or linkage with a particular disorder due to characteristics of individuals such as age, sex, or age of onset or due to aspects of the environment (i.e., gene-environment interactions). The last theme involves the use of endophenotypes in molecular genetic studies of psychopathology, examining association and/or linkage with some underlying biological or psychological mechanism that is thought to more directly reflect the gene's action than does the disorder of interest. We illustrate these themes using examples from molecular genetic studies of several disorders, including ADHD, Schizophrenia, depression and Bipolar Disorder, antisocial behavior, and Autism. We focus primarily on candidate gene studies but also consider findings from genome scans where applicable. Wherever possible, we also highlight ways in which developmental psychopathology concepts can elucidate current molecular genetic findings and directions for future research. To facilitate the reading of this section, Table 10.2 presents definitions of key terms.

Association and Linkage

In contrast to behavioral genetic studies, which estimate broad, abstract components of genetic and environmental variance that contribute to the liability underlying a disorder, molecular genetic studies examine the role of specific genes or genomic regions that may contribute to the etiology of a given disorder. Molecular genetic studies of disorders test for association and/or linkage between a given disorder and particular candidate genes or genomic regions. In association studies, the frequency of high-risk and low-risk forms of a candidate gene (i.e., high- and low-risk alleles) are typically contrasted in cases and controls (i.e., individuals ascertained based on the presence of the target disorder versus a sample selected based on the absence of the disorder who are matched on a variety of background characteristics), with the expectation that cases will show higher frequencies of the high-risk allele than controls. Several variations on the classic case-control association design have been developed (e.g., a comparison of symptom levels in individuals who have 0, 1, or 2 copies of the high-risk allele of a particular gene in a nonreferred sample, or in siblings that differ in the number of high-risk alleles). One very important variation is family-based association methods, such as the haplotype-based Haplotype Relative Risk (HHRR; Falk & Rubenstein, 1987; Terwilliger & Ott, 1992), which contrast the alleles that are transmitted with those that are not transmitted by parents to their affected children. In this design, the nontransmitted alleles serve as controls for the transmitted alleles, which are expected to be high-risk alleles that are disproportionately transmitted to the affected children if there is

TABLE 10.2 A Glossary of Terms for Molecular Genetic Studies

Term	Definition
Allele	One of the alternative forms of a DNA marker.
Association	A nonrandom difference in the frequency of alternative forms of a DNA marker between individuals with and without some diagnosis or across levels of a trait.
Candidate gene study	A study that conducts a targeted test of the association of one or more DNA markers in a specific gene with a disorder or trait.
Endophenotype	Constructs posited to underlie psychiatric disorders or psychopathological traits and to be more directly influenced by the genes relevant to disorder than are the manifest symptoms.
Genome scan	An exploratory search across the whole genome for genes related to a disorder or trait.
Haplotype	A particular configuration of alleles at multiple DNA markers in close contiguity within a chromosomal region.
Knock-out gene studies	Studies in model organisms, such as mice, in which one or both copies of a gene are deactivated and the effects on behavior and/or cognition are examined.
Linkage	The correlation of a disorder and DNA markers within families, typically tested by examining the cosegregation of the presence or absence of the disorder with sharing particular allele(s) of a DNA marker.
Polymorphism	A DNA marker that varies among individuals in the population.
Population stratification	An association between a DNA marker and a disorder or trait that is not due to the causal effects of the gene, but is instead due to the mixture of subsamples (e.g., ethnic groups) that differ in both allele frequencies and symptom levels or diagnostic rates.
SNP	Single nucleotide polymorphism: a single nucleotide base that varies among individuals in the population.
Transmission Disequilibrium Test (TDT)	A within-family test of association and linkage that is robust to the potentially biasing effects of population stratification, the TDT contrasts the transmitted and nontransmitted alleles from *heterozygous* parents only (i.e., parents with two different alleles) to their children diagnosed with the target disorder.
VNTR	Variable number of tandem repeats: a DNA marker that consists of a number of base pairs that are repeated a varying number of times across individuals in the population.
UTR	An untranslated region of the gene, meaning a part of the gene that is not involved directly in the coding of proteins.

indeed an association between the disorder and the gene. Family-based association designs were developed to avoid the problem of population stratification that often can plague conventional case-control association studies, leading to false positive results. This problem occurs when case and control samples differ not only in the rates (or symptom levels) of the disorder, but in the frequency of high- and low-risk alleles for reasons other than the causal effects of the gene on the disorder. This mixture of subsamples that differ in both allele frequencies and symptom levels/diagnostic rates induces an association in the overall sample that may occur even in the absence of any true relation between the gene and the disorder in either of the \ subsamples. The most common source of population stratification is thought to be ethnic group differences, wherein ethnic groups differ both in allele frequencies and rates of disorder, although in principle stratification effects may be due to any form of population structure (e.g., socioeconomic status differences) that varies between cases and controls. Within-family association methods are thought to avoid the biasing effects of population stratification because the transmitted and nontransmitted alleles come from the same individuals within the sample of cases.

In linkage studies, typically the correlation of a disorder and anonymous DNA markers is examined within family members (e.g., sibling pairs, parents and their children). In classical linkage studies, this involves examining the cosegregation of the presence or absence of the disorder with sharing particular alleles of a DNA marker through large family pedigrees. Note that in linkage analysis, it is commonly assumed that the anonymous DNA markers are not themselves the genes contributing to the etiology of the disorder, but may be "linked" with them due to their close contiguity on the chromosome, which results in their frequent coinheritance during meiosis. In the case of strong linkage, there is a strong co-occurrence among relatives of the presence or absence of the disorder with sharing the same DNA marker allele *identical by descent* (IBD), which means that the shared allele is not merely of the same type (*identical by state* or IBS), but is indeed the identical allele transmitted by a common ancestor. Classical linkage analyses are commonly *model-based,* meaning that the researcher must specify a number of parameters a priori, including the base rate of the disorder, the allele frequencies, and the penetrances of the genotypes. (The investigator also can examine genetic heterogeneity by modeling the proportion of families in which the disorder is linked to the genomic region.) Needless to say, in most instances, the values of most, if not all, of these parameters would be unknown. This led statistical geneticists to develop *model-free* linkage analytic methods, which require the specification of few or no parameters a priori. Model-free analyses typically are both more flexible and less powerful than model-based linkage analyses, in which values of the parameters are correctly specified. A common form of model-free linkage analysis involves estimating the proportion of alleles shared IBD among affected sibling pairs for each DNA marker examined. A departure of the proportion of alleles shared IBD from the expected Mendelian proportions (namely, .25, .50, .25, for 0, 1, and 2 alleles shared IBD, respectively) suggests that the genomic region in which that DNA marker resides is linked with the disorder.

Like association analyses, linkage analyses have undergone many important refinements. First, there has been a shift in contemporary linkage studies toward the use of many smaller family pedigrees or large numbers of affected sibling pairs rather than a reliance on a few very large family pedigrees. Second, linkage analyses of specific targeted candidate genes, rather than of large numbers of anonymous DNA markers, are becoming more common. One statistical genetic tool that has become quite popular for such studies is the Transmission Disequilibrium Test (TDT; Spielman, McGinnis, & Ewens, 1993). The TDT is similar to the aforementioned HHRR, in that both statistics contrast the transmitted and nontransmitted alleles from parents to their affected children. The only methodological difference between the analytic methods is that the TDT contrasts the transmitted and nontransmitted alleles only from *heterozygous* parents (i.e., parents with one high-risk and one low-risk allele), as opposed to contrasting the alleles transmitted by all parents, as in the HHRR. Nonetheless, the TDT possesses a number of important statistical properties that distinguish it from the HHRR, including being a test of linkage as well as association, being robust to population stratification, and enabling one to include multiple affected offspring from a given family in a test of linkage. In contrast, the HHRR is a test of association only, is not completely robust to the biasing effects of population stratification, and cannot accommodate data from multiple affected offspring from the same family due to the violation of the assumption of observational independence. Given its favorable characteristics, it is little wonder that the TDT has received so much use and attention regarding its statistical properties as compared with alternative statistical genetic methods in the genetics literature. In addition, the TDT has been extended by a number of researchers (e.g., Rabinowitz, 1997; Waldman, Robinson, & Rowe, 1999) to enable the examination of linkage between a candidate gene or DNA marker and multiple continuous as well as categorical variables (e.g., symptom levels of a disorder instead of or in addition to a diagnosis).

The Genetics of Complex Traits

A number of geneticists (e.g., Chakravarti, 1999; Lander & Schork, 1994; Risch, 2000; Risch & Merikangas, 1996) have highlighted important differences between the genetics of simple Mendelian diseases and of complex traits or disorders and have focused on the special challenges posed by the search for genes that underlie the latter. These geneticists define a *complex trait* as any phenotype that does not exhibit classic Mendelian recessive or dominant inheritance attributable to a single gene locus (Lander & Schork, 1994). Complex traits and disorders have a number of features that distinguish them from Mendelian diseases. First, complex traits are thought to result from the effects of multiple genetic and environmental influences. Second, each of the multiple genes thought to underlie complex disorders likely confers only a relatively small risk for the disorder. Third, these genes are likely to have fairly low penetrance (i.e., the probability of developing the disorder given the presence of the high-risk allele or genotype) and have a relatively high allele frequency in the population. Fourth, there is likely to be genetic heterogeneity for complex traits, such that the same genotype can result in different phenotypes (i.e., multifinality or pleiotropy) and different genotypes can result in the same phenotype (i.e., equifinality or final common pathway). Fifth, there is likely to be the presence of phenocopies (i.e., disorders caused by environmental influences that have the same symptom presentation as the inherited disorder) for complex disorders. Sixth, specific environmental influences are more likely to be important risk factors for complex disorders, and there may be the presence of gene- or genotype-by-environment interaction. Suffice to say, for complex traits and disorders it is most likely that the etiology and risk to relatives is composed of a multitude of susceptibility genes, each contributing only a small magnitude of the overall risk for the disorder. Indeed, most researchers consider the underlying causes of almost all forms of psychopathology to be polygenic (i.e., influenced by many genes and environmental factors).

Genome Scans and Candidate Gene Studies

Broadly speaking, there are two general strategies for finding genes that contribute to the etiology of a disorder. The first is a genome scan, in which linkage is examined between a disorder and a large number of DNA markers scattered at approximately equal distances across the genome. Genome scans may be thought of as exploratory searches for putative genes that contribute to the etiology of a disorder. What makes genome scans exploratory is that neither the location of the relevant genes nor their function or etiological relevance is known a priori. On the other hand, the fact that major genes have been found for many medical diseases via genome scans is testament to the usefulness of this method. Unfortunately, the power of linkage analyses in genome scans is typically quite low, making it very difficult, if not impossible, to detect genes that account for less than ~15% of the variance in a disorder. Given this, the promise for genome scans of complex traits (e.g., disorders in which multiple genes and environmental influences contribute to their etiology) remains largely unknown.

In many ways, candidate gene studies are polar opposites of genome scans. In contrast to the exploratory nature of genome scans, well-conducted candidate gene studies represent a targeted test of the role of specific genes in the etiology of a disorder. In addition, the location, function, and etiological relevance of candidate genes is most often known or strongly hypothesized a priori, although the specific polymorphism chosen for study in the candidate gene may itself not be functional and the functional mutation(s) in the candidate gene may be as yet unidentified. A big advantage of well-conducted candidate gene studies in comparison with genome scans is that positive findings are easily interpretable because one already knows the gene's location, function, and etiological relevance. Some disadvantages of candidate gene studies are that one cannot find genes that one has not looked for; also, there are still not that many strong candidate genes for psychiatric disorders, and the same candidate genes tend to be examined for almost all psychiatric disorders, regardless of how disparate the disorders may be in terms of their symptomatology or conjectured pathophysiology. In well-designed studies, however, candidate genes are selected based on the known or strongly hypothesized role of their gene product in the etiology of the disorder (i.e., its pathophysiological function and etiological relevance). Thus, with respect to psychiatric disorders, most of the candidate genes heretofore examined underlie various aspects of disorder-relevant neurotransmitter pathways (e.g., dopaminergic candidate genes for ADHD and Schizophrenia, serotonergic candidate genes for depression and Anxiety Disorders). With regard to ADHD, for example, this is a result of the strongly conjectured role of the dopaminergic (and, to a lesser extent, noradrenergic) system in the etiology and pathophysiology of ADHD (e.g., Biederman & Spencer, 1999; F. Levy, 1991; Pliszka, McCracken, & Maas, 1996), as well as the observation that stimulant medications, the most common and effective treatment for ADHD, appear to act primarily by regulating dopamine levels in the brain (Seeman & Madras, 1998; Solanto, 1984). Another justification for the selection of ADHD candidate genes within the dopaminergic system involves the results of knock-out gene studies in mice, in which the behavioral effects of the deactivation of these genes is examined. Results of such studies have markedly strengthened the consideration of genes within the dopaminergic system as candidate genes for ADHD, including the dopamine transporter gene (DAT1; Giros, Jaber, Jones, Wightman, & Caron, 1996), and the dopamine receptor D3 and D4 genes (DRD3 and DRD4; Accili et al., 1996; Dulawa, Grandy, Low, Paulus, & Geyer, 1999; Rubenstein et al., 1997).

To address the four aforementioned themes in this section of the chapter, we review various studies of association and linkage between psychiatric disorders and candidate genes within neurotransmission pathways. Candidate genes for neurotransmitter systems may include (1) *precursor genes* that affect the rate at which neurotransmitters are produced from precursor amino acids (e.g., tyrosine hydroxylase for dopamine and tryptophan hydroxylase for serotonin); (2) *receptor genes* that are involved in receiving neurotransmitter signals (e.g., genes corresponding to the five dopamine receptors, DRD1, D2, D3, D4, and D5, and to the numerous serotonin receptors); (3) *transporter genes* that are involved in the reuptake of neurotransmitters back into the presynaptic terminal (e.g., the dopamine transporter gene, DAT1, and the serotonin transporter gene, 5HTT); (4) *metabolite genes* that are involved in the metabolism or degradation of these neurotransmitters (e.g., the gene for catechol-O-methyltransferase, COMT, and for monoamine oxidase A and B, MAOA and MAOB); and (5) genes that are responsible for the *conversion* of one neurotransmitter into another (e.g., dopamine beta hydroxylase, or DbH, which converts dopamine into norepinephrine).

Studies of association and linkage between psychiatric disorders and candidate genes, as well as genome scans for these disorders, are appearing in the literature at an accelerating rate; thus, this review is necessarily somewhat incomplete. Rather than attempting a comprehensive review of all candidate gene studies and genome scans for all psychiatric disorders, we selectively review such studies to illustrate the burgeoning investigation of the four overarching themes mentioned earlier, which we feel provide a meaningful structure for exploring etiology in developmental psychopathology studies.

Replicability and Consistency of Findings

Perhaps the greatest challenge of molecular genetic studies of complex traits and disorders is replication. Numerous researchers have raised concerns regarding the replication of association and linkage findings for both psychiatric disorders and medical diseases (e.g., Crowe, 1993; Kidd, 1993).

At the extreme, the editors of certain journals have decided to ban case-control association studies or association findings from a single sample unaccompanied by evidence for replication. Indeed, for almost any psychiatric disorder and any associated candidate gene or linked genomic region studied, there are both positive and negative findings published. It may be cold comfort to recognize that such mixed findings are by no means the exclusive province of psychiatric genetics, as medical genetic studies also have found failures to replicate (e.g., linkage findings for Type I diabetes; Concannon et al., 1998). To render this phenomenon of mixed findings more tangible, we provide a number of examples from studies of association and linkage for several psychiatric disorders. We begin by discussing the results of candidate gene studies of the dopamine receptor D4 gene (i.e., DRD4) and ADHD, given that this is perhaps the most frequently studied candidate gene for ADHD and that it well illustrates both the difficulties of interpreting such mixed findings and the aid that meta-analysis can provide toward that end. We then proceed to discuss the first two genome scans for ADHD and their (almost totally) nonoverlapping findings, as well as the conclusions from meta-analyses of genome scans for Schizophrenia and Bipolar Disorder.

Attention-Deficit/Hyperactivity Disorder and the Dopamine Receptor D4 Gene

Initial interest in DRD4 as a candidate gene for ADHD was sparked by association studies that linked the gene to the personality trait of novelty seeking (Benjamin et al., 1996; Ebstein et al., 1996), which has been compared to the high levels of impulsivity and excitability often seen in ADHD. Further interest in DRD4 as a candidate gene for ADHD has been generated from knock-out mouse studies. Rubinstein et al. (1997) compared the behavior of homozygous DRD4 knock-out mice and wild-type controls following administration of cocaine and methamphetamine and noted that the knock-out mice showed a heightened response to cocaine and methamphetamine injection relative to controls, as measured by increases in locomotor behavior. In addition, several studies have suggested that the 7-repeat of a 48 base pair VNTR (i.e., variable number of tandem repeats) in exon 3 of the gene differs, albeit slightly, from the 2- and 4-repeats in secondary messenger (i.e., cAMP) activity and possibly also in response to the antipsychotic medication clozapine (Ashgari et al., 1994, 1995).

Such findings suggest the potential involvement of DRD4 in the pathophysiology of ADHD; thus, LaHoste et al. (1996) conducted an association study of DRD4 with

ADHD in children in a small case-control sample (n = 39 cases and 39 ethnically matched controls). The authors reported increased prevalence of the 7-repeat allele and genotype in cases (29% and 49%, respectively) compared to controls (12% and 21%, respectively). A number of replication studies have investigated the relation between the exon 3 VNTR of DRD4 and ADHD (7 case-control and 14 within-family studies), the findings and methods of which have been described in a number of reviews (Swanson et al., 1998; Thapar, Holmes, Poulton, & Harrington, 1999). The findings of association between ADHD and DRD4 were replicated in some of these studies but not in others, and thus, it is noteworthy that there is a meta-analysis of these case-control and within-family association studies (Faraone, Doyle, Mick, & Biederman, 2001), which demonstrated a significant DRD4-ADHD association for both types of studies (case-control: $p = .00000008$; relative risk = 1.9, 95% CI: 1.4 to 2.2; within-family: $p = .02$; relative risk = 1.4, 95% CI: 1.1 to 1.6). Although the evidence was notably stronger for the case-control studies, it is possible that this is the result of biasing effects of population stratification or some other systematic difference, such as greater power for case-control than within-family designs. Since the publication of this meta-analysis, two additional studies have been published examining the relation between the exon 3 VNTR of DRD4 and ADHD. The first study reported increased prevalence of the 7-repeat allele in a clinical sample compared to a control group (Roman et al., 2001), whereas the second study reported significant preferential nontransmission of the 7-repeat allele to ADHD offspring (Manor et al., 2002). These conflicting findings further demonstrate the importance of meta-analysis for integrating such data when studying the genetic basis of complex disorders such as ADHD.

Population Samples

In addition to examining the relation of DRD4 to ADHD when defined as a discrete diagnostic category, researchers have investigated whether DRD4 might influence specific behavioral traits that are continuously distributed in the population and that, at their extreme end, are thought to represent ADHD. For example, Curran et al. (2001) tested for association between the exon 3 VNTR of DRD4 and severity of ADHD symptoms, which were assessed by questionnaire and defined along a continuum, in a large epidemiological sample. The authors selected for their sample children who scored at either the high or low extreme end of this continuum and reported that the 7-repeat allele was significantly more prevalent among high scorers than low scorers ($\chi^2 = 8.63$, $p = .003$, Odd ratio = 2.09). In a similar study, Mill et al. (2002) tested the relation between the exon 3 VNTR of DRD4 and ratings of hyperactive and impulsive behaviors in a sample of 1,037 children participating in a longitudinal study. The children were assessed at ages 7, 9, 11, 13, and 15. Rather than dichotomizing their sample, Mill et al. used the continuous symptom scores to test for association between the 7-repeat allele and each behavioral dimension. The authors reported no evidence for association between DRD4 and either behavioral trait at any of the assessment points. Thus, the two studies reviewed show conflicting results regarding the association between DRD4 and hyperactive-impulsive behavior in the general population.

Other researchers have investigated the relation between DRD4 and the normal development of attention processes. Auerbach, Benjamin, Faroy, Geller, and Ebstein (2001) assessed sustained attention abilities using an orientation task in a sample of 64 1-year-old infants. The authors reported that infants with the 7-repeat allele took significantly longer to orient to objects and showed significantly shorter periods of focused attention on these objects than infants without the 7-repeat allele ($F(1,55) = 4.65$, Effect size = .074 and $F(1,55) = 8.06$, Effect size = .120, respectively). In a sample of older children, Schmidt, Fox, Pérez-Edgar, Hu, and Hamer (2001) tested the relation between the DRD4 exon 3 VNTR and inattention as assessed by the Attention Problems subscale of the Child Behavior Checklist (Achenbach & Edelbrock, 1981). As part of a longitudinal study, the authors collected data on a population sample of 174 children at age 4 and age 7. Association analyses showed a relation between the 7-repeat allele and increased attention problems at age 4 ($F(1,159) = 4.79$, $p = .030$, Standardized mean difference = 0.35) and age 7 ($F(1,106) = 4.16$, $p = .044$, Standardized mean difference = 0.40) such that children with one or more copies of the 7-repeat allele had higher scores than children with no copies. These two studies demonstrate a relation between the DRD4 exon 3 VNTR and the development of attention processes in the normal population.

Multimarker Data

Our review of studies testing for linkage and association between DRD4 and ADHD has thus far been limited to studies that have tested this relation using only the exon 3 VNTR. A number of studies have tested for linkage and association at additional polymorphisms within DRD4, and some of these studies have created haplotypes using these markers to test for the presence of susceptibility loci for ADHD. Barr and colleagues (2000, 2001) examined the relation between DRD4 and ADHD at three loci in addition to the exon 3 VNTR. In the first published study, the authors genotyped subjects at the VNTR, a mononucleotide repeat in intron 1, and a 12-bp repeat in exon 1. In addition to the significant linkage result with the 7-repeat allele of the exon 3 VNTR (previously reported in Sunohara et al., 2000), the authors reported a trend for linkage between the 142-bp allele of the intron 1 mononucleotide repeat ($\chi^2 = 3.57$, $p = .059$, Relative risk = 0.65) but not for either allele of the exon 1 12-bp repeat ($\chi^2 = 0.43$, $p = .513$, Relative risk = 1.33; Barr et al., 2000). Of particular importance, haplotypes constructed from genotypes at these three markers showed strong evidence for linkage between DRD4 and ADHD, with a haplotype containing the exon 3 7-repeat allele and the intron 1 140-bp allele showing preferential transmission to affected children ($\chi^2 = 4.90$, $p = .027$, Relative risk = 2.08). In a subsequent study, Barr et al. (2001) tested for linkage with ADHD at three additional polymorphisms located in the 5′ UTR of DRD4. These polymorphisms included a 120-bp repeat 1.2 kb upstream of the transcription start site and two SNPs also upstream from the start site at positions −521 and −616. The authors reported a trend for linkage between the 1-repeat allele of the 120-bp repeat and ADHD ($\chi^2 = 1.66$, $p = .198$, Relative risk = 1.35) as well as the SNP at position −616 ($\chi^2 = 2.04$, $p = .154$, Relative risk = 1.37). There was no evidence of linkage between ADHD and the SNP at position −521 ($\chi^2 = 0.818$, $p = .366$, Relative risk = 1.20). Although none of the haplotypes containing alleles suggestive of linkage with ADHD in the single marker analyses showed preferential transmission to affected children, one haplotype containing the opposite alleles at the two markers that were suggestive of linkage did show a trend toward preferential nontransmission ($\chi^2 = 3.571$, $p = .059$, Relative risk = 2.11). Thus, these studies further support a relation between DRD4 and ADHD.

In addition to the studies by Barr et al. (2001), three other research groups have examined the relation between ADHD and DRD4 polymorphisms other than the exon 3 VNTR. McCracken et al. (2000) tested for linkage at the 120-bp repeat in the 5′ UTR of DRD4 described earlier (Barr et al., 2001). The authors reported significant preferential transmission of the 2-repeat allele to affected offspring ($\chi^2 = 5.40$, $p = .020$, Relative risk = 1.35), and this relation strengthened when the sample was restricted to include only children with Inattentive ADHD subtype ($\chi^2 = 8.00$, $p = .005$, Relative risk = 1.80). Nonetheless, it should be noted that it was the 1-repeat allele, and not the 2-repeat

allele, that showed a trend toward preferential transmission in the study by Barr et al. (2001). In addition to single marker analyses, McCracken et al. also conducted haplotype analyses using genotypic data from the 5′ UTR repeat and the exon 3 VNTR. These analyses revealed a trend for preferential transmission of a haplotype containing both the 7-repeat allele of the exon 3 VNTR and the 2-repeat allele of the 5′ UTR repeat ($\chi^2 = 1.92$, $p = .165$, Relative risk = 1.29), and the significant preferential nontransmission of a haplotype containing non-7-repeat alleles of the exon 3 VNTR and the 1-repeat allele of the 5′ UTR repeat ($\chi^2 = 4.17$, $p = .040$, Relative risk = 0.72).

In a similar study, Todd, Neuman, et al. (2001) tested for association at the exon 3 VNTR and the 5′ UTR repeat in a sample of twins drawn from the general population. In contrast to the previously reviewed study, Todd et al. did not find evidence suggestive of linkage at either individual marker (exon 3 7-repeat: $\chi^2 = 0.30$, $p = .58$, Relative risk = 1.11; 5′ UTR 1-repeat: $\chi^2 = 0.59$, $p = .44$, Relative risk = 1.16). They did report significant preferential transmission of a haplotype containing both the 7-repeat allele of the exon 3 VNTR and the 1-repeat allele of the 5′ UTR repeat ($\chi^2 = 4.45$, $p = .04$, Relative risk = 4.50), but this result became nonsignificant when they corrected for conducting multiple tests (adjusted $p = .25$).

The final study to test for linkage between a DRD4 polymorphism other than the exon 3 VNTR and ADHD was conducted by Payton et al. (2001). The authors genotyped subjects at the 5′ UTR SNP at position −521 described earlier (Barr et al., 2001), and similar to that study, they reported no evidence for association between this 5′ UTR DRD4 SNP and ADHD ($\chi^2 = 0.19$, $p = .75$, Relative risk = 1.10).

To summarize, the meta-analysis conducted by Faraone et al. (2001) suggests a strong relation between the 7-repeat allele of the exon 3 VNTR of DRD4. In addition, studies testing the relation in the general population between behaviors associated with ADHD such as hyperactivity and sustained attention abilities support the hypothesis that DRD4 may influence these traits in normal development and not just in children with ADHD. Finally, despite the conflicting results across some of the reviewed studies, examinations of multiple markers within DRD4 are beginning to provide additional data that may lead to a better understanding of the relation between DRD4 and ADHD.

This difficulty in making sense of the mixed findings from candidate gene studies is not limited to the association and linkage between ADHD and DRD4. For example, numerous studies have been conducted of the association between Schizophrenia and the dopamine receptor D3 gene

(DRD3) and the serotonin receptor 2A gene (HTR2A), with the predictable pattern of mixed findings. Meta-analyses of these associations were conducted (Williams, McGuffin, Nothen, & Owen, 1997; Williams et al., 1998) and detected significant associations across studies, despite the fact that the magnitude of these associations was fairly modest (i.e., Odds Ratios $\cong$ 1.3). An informal perusal of results of these studies might (incorrectly) conclude that association between these genes and Schizophrenia is absent, thus highlighting the importance of formal, statistical evaluations of the associations across studies using meta-analysis. In addition to serving as an effective mechanism for combining results and testing their significance across studies, meta-analytic procedures also provide an estimate of the magnitude of association, quantify the degree of heterogeneity in the effect sizes across studies, and can include moderator variables that may meaningfully explain any variability observed in the effect sizes across studies. Such moderators can represent either important substantive variables (e.g., representation of diagnostic subtypes, rates of comorbid disorders) or methodological features (e.g., male:female ratios, location of the study) that differ across studies.

Problems in interpreting the results of molecular genetic studies are not limited to candidate gene studies of association. For example, two genome scans for ADHD have been published (Bakker et al., 2003; Ogdie et al., 2003) that examined allele sharing in affected sibling pairs with an average marker spacing of ~10 cM. Ogdie et al. examined linkage in 270 affected sib pairs from 204 families in the United States and found linkage on the short arm of chromosome 16 (16p13), suggestive linkage on the short arm of chromosome 17 (17p11), and nominal (i.e., weaker) support for linkage in four additional chromosomal regions (i.e., on the short arm of chromosome 5 [5p13] and on the long arms of chromosomes 6, 11, and 20 [6q14, 11q25, and 20q13]). Bakker et al. examined linkage in 164 affected sib pairs in 106 Dutch families and found suggestive linkage to two regions, the long arm of chromosome 15 (15q15.1) and the short arm of chromosome 7 (7p13), and nominal support for linkage in seven additional chromosomal regions (3q13.32, 4p16.3, 5p13.1, 6q26, 9q33.3, 10cen, and 13q33.3). It is noteworthy that only one of these chromosomal regions (5p13) showed linkage in both the U.S. and Dutch samples and that evidence for linkage to the remaining 13 chromosomal regions was found in one of the samples but not the other. These linkage findings again highlight the difficulties inherent in drawing inferences regarding linkage from a few studies with relatively small samples, in which it is

likely that the genomic regions suggestive of linkage will differ appreciably across studies *for statistical reasons alone.* That is, although there may be other reasons for the discrepant findings across these two studies, such as differences in the populations sampled or in the assessment or diagnostic methods used, the stochastic fluctuations associated with few studies of small sample size are sufficient to cause such discrepancies.

In contrast to ADHD, many more genome scans have been conducted for Schizophrenia, Bipolar Disorder, and Autism. Nonetheless, a casual perusal of the scans for these disorders would lead to a similar impression as that for the scans of ADHD, namely, that there is greater *nonoverlap* than there is overlap of the genomic regions of interest across studies. Indeed, some reviewers of the numerous genome scans for Schizophrenia have stated that the available evidence from all of these studies provides about as much support for linkage at almost any location in the genome as evidence against linkage at these same genomic locations! Fortunately, methods for the meta-analysis of genome scans have been developed (e.g., Badner & Gershon, 2002b; Wise, Lanchbury, & Lewis, 1999) and applied to the genome scans for Schizophrenia, Bipolar Disorder, and Autism. In contrast to the apparently inconsistent picture of results yielded by conventional reviews of these studies, meta-analyses yield a more consistent and coherent summary of the findings. For example, one of the most exciting findings in psychiatric genetics is the linkage of Autism to the long arm of chromosome 7 (7q), as well as the observation that this linkage finding appeared to replicate across a few independent studies. Nonetheless, Hutcheson et al. (2003) simultaneously analyzed the 7q linkage data from multiple samples but were unable to find a specific narrow location that was common across studies or an associated polymorphism that explained the linkage to the 7q region. Fortunately, a meta-analysis of four genome scans (Badner & Gershon, 2002b) yielded convincing evidence for the replication of the linkage of Autism to the 7q region. Indeed, this was the only genomic region for which linkage findings replicated across the four genome scans.

For Schizophrenia, a meta-analysis of 20 genome scans found significant linkages on the short arms of chromosomes 3, 6, 8, 10, and 14 and on the long arms of chromosomes 1, 5, 6, 11, 15, 16, 17, 18, 20, and 22 (Lewis et al., 2003). For Bipolar Disorder, a meta-analysis of 18 genome scans found significant linkages on the short arms of chromosomes 9 and 18 and the long arms of chromosomes 8, 10, 14, and 18 (Segurado et al., 2003). Although the findings from these meta-analyses suggest greater consistency in the results of genome scans for these disorders, particularly

Schizophrenia, than do previous reviews, even the results of such meta-analyses are somewhat dependent on the particular meta-analytic methods employed. For example, using an alternative meta-analytic method on published genome scans, Badner and Gershon (2002a) found significant replicable results for both Schizophrenia and Bipolar Disorder only on the long arms of chromosomes 13 and 22, and for Schizophrenia also on the short arm of chromosome 8. Although the meta-analytic methods used in these studies differed substantially, it is noteworthy that only one location (22q for Schizophrenia) was identified by both methods. These results reinforce the notion that, though useful, meta-analyses are not a magic wand for detecting replicable linkage findings across studies. In addition, even in the presence of replicated linkage findings, it can be very difficult to narrow down the specific chromosomal location that harbors the particular candidate gene of interest (Roberts, MacLean, Neale, Eaves, & Kendler, 1999), the necessary step in identifying the particular genetic risk factor that contributes to the etiology of the disorder.

Specificity of Findings to Diagnostic Subtypes or Symptom Dimensions

Although replication of association and linkage findings is essential for establishing the validity of the relations between genes and disorders, they may not be particularly informative regarding the specific phenotype(s) influenced by the gene. Following the example mentioned earlier, the demonstration of replicated association between DRD4 and ADHD across studies does not inform us as to whether DRD4 is also a risk factor for the other disruptive disorders (i.e., Oppositional Defiant Disorder and Conduct Disorder) that have been shown to substantially overlap with ADHD both phenotypically and genetically (e.g., Biederman, Newcorn, & Sprich, 1991; Waldman, Rhee, Levy, & Hay, 2001), or whether the effects of DRD4 on ADHD are actually more specific, being confined to a particular diagnostic subtype or symptom dimension. Indeed, this difference in approaches corresponds to the lumping versus splitting distinction that has long characterized much research in a variety of psychopathology domains. For example, some researchers examining the genetics of such disorders in both quantitative and molecular genetic studies have argued for the lumping approach that transcends specific disorders in favor of a broad externalizing dimension (Krueger et al., 2002; S. E. Young et al., 2002), whereas other researchers have demonstrated the benefits of examining the genetics of specific diagnostic subtypes or symptom dimensions (Lowe et al.,

2004; Waldman et al., 1998). In our view, it is likely that there is merit in pursuing both approaches, given that some genes may act in a pleiotropic manner to confer risk on a number of related disorders, whereas other genes may be quite specific in their influence, by demonstrating effects only on a particular facet of a single disorder. We provide some tangible examples to help illustrate these different possibilities.

Specificity in Association and Linkage between Dopamine Genes and Attention-Deficit/Hyperactivity Disorder

Several candidate gene studies of ADHD have examined the specificity of association and/or linkage findings to particular diagnostic subtypes or symptom dimensions. The conceptual rationale underlying such studies is that it is highly unlikely that whatever genes confer risk for ADHD work at the level of the overall diagnosis, and that nature so closely resembles the current version of the *Diagnostic and Statistical Manual of Mental Disorders* (*DSM*). We think it is much more likely that whatever genes contribute to risk for ADHD do so by conferring risk for specific diagnostic subtypes or symptom dimensions. Although this area of molecular genetic research is only in its infancy, there have been a few examples of such findings in this research domain. For example, Waldman et al. (1998) found that DAT1 is associated and linked with the Combined subtype, but not the Inattentive subtype, and appears to be related more strongly to hyperactive-impulsive than inattentive symptoms of the disorder. Similarly, Eisenberg et al. (1999) reported an association between the valine/valine genotype of COMT and the Hyperactive-Impulsive and Combined, but not the Inattentive, ADHD subtypes. In contrast, Lowe et al. (2004) found that the association and linkage between DRD5 and ADHD was significant for the Combined and Inattentive subtypes, but not for the Hyperactive-Impulsive subtype. Holmes et al. (2002) found that DRD4 is related to ADHD only when it is accompanied by Conduct Disorder. Although other researchers have focused on examining genetic influences on higher-order diagnostic constructs, such as an externalizing symptom dimension (e.g., Krueger et al., 2002; S. E. Young et al., 2002), and have advocated the utility of studying the genetics of broad diagnostic constructs that span several *DSM-IV* diagnoses, we believe that these results for ADHD suggest that examining association and linkage with more specific diagnostic subtypes or symptom dimensions also will be a fruitful approach. Pursuing both of these possibilities simultaneously in a two-pronged approach is ideal, given the primitive stage of our knowledge of the association between specific genes and disorders and the likelihood that some genes will be risk factors for several related disorders, whereas others will confer risk only on narrower disorder phenotypes.

Specificity of genetic influences to diagnostic subtypes or symptom dimensions in the psychiatric genetics literature is not confined to studies of ADHD or to studies of association with candidate genes. For example, in molecular genetic studies of Schizophrenia, one of the several studies reporting linkage to the short arm of chromosome 6 analyzed quantitative Schizophrenia symptom dimensions in addition to the diagnosis of Schizophrenia (Brzustowicz et al., 1997) and found linkage with positive but not negative symptoms. Similarly, in linkage studies of reading disability (e.g., Fisher et al., 1999; Grigorenko et al., 1997), linkage findings appeared to be specific to different reading disability phenotypes on chromosome 6p (phonological awareness, phonological decoding, and irregular word reading) versus 15q (single-word reading). The linkage findings for chromosome 6p were replicated in two independent family samples (Fisher et al., 1999; Gayan et al., 1999) but failed to replicate in a third sample (Field & Kaplan, 1998). These studies suggest that dissecting the Schizophrenia and reading disability phenotypes into more specific components, as well as examining the manifest diagnosis, may help significantly in finding susceptibility loci for these (and other) disorders. In the meta-analysis of genome scans of Bipolar Disorder described earlier (Segurado et al., 2003), different genomic regions were found to be linked with somewhat different Bipolar Disorder diagnostic phenotypes. Whereas a region on the long arm of chromosome 14 was found to be linked with Bipolar Disorder I, Schizoaffective Disorder-Bipolar type, and Bipolar Disorder II, regions on the short arm of chromosome 9 and the long arm of chromosome 10 were found to be linked only with Bipolar Disorder I and Schizoaffective Disorder-Bipolar type (Segurado et al., 2003). In addition, nominally significant evidence for linkage was found for all of these diagnostic phenotypes and for recurrent Major Depression on chromosome 18 (Segurado et al., 2003). Similarly, in a multisite candidate gene study examining association and linkage between the dopamine transporter gene (DAT1) and Bipolar Disorder diagnostic phenotypes (Waldman, Robinson, & Feigon, 1997), the relation between this gene and the disorder varied by the breadth of the Bipolar Disorder diagnostic phenotype examined. Specifically, in a sample from Cardiff, Wales, DAT1 appeared to be associated and linked with a narrow Bipolar Disorder diagnostic phenotype comprising Bipolar Disorder I and II, whereas in a sample from San Diego, DAT1 appeared to be associated and linked with a broad Bipolar Disorder diagnostic phenotype comprising not only Bipolar Disorder I and II but also recurrent unipolar depression.

Focus on Alternative Pathways Underlying Psychopathological and Normal Development

It is also worth noting that the lumping versus splitting distinction bears some similarities to developmental psychopathologists' differentiation among a number of alternative pathways that individuals' development may take. In particular, developmental psychopathologists make use of the terms equifinality and multifinality, developed in general systems theory (von Bertalanffy, 1968; as cited in Cicchetti & Rogosch, 1996, 1999), to refer to two general types of developmental pathways. *Equifinality* refers to the scenario where several distinct causes or developmental processes can eventuate in the same outcome, whereas *multifinality* refers to the scenario where a particular cause or developmental process can result in a multiplicity of outcomes (Cicchetti & Rogosch, 1996, 1999). Equifinality is quite similar to the concept of "final common pathway" that is discussed in many accounts of the etiology of psychopathology. An example of this is if multiple genes within the dopaminergic neurotransmitter system conferred risk for ADHD in an interchangeable manner, such that having the high-risk alleles for any of a critical number of these genes would be more important than having high-risk alleles for a particular subset of such genes. Multifinality occurs when the same causal process or developmental event differs in its effects or outcome, depending on other causes, developmental contexts, or an individual's choices (Cicchetti & Rogosch, 1996). Many readers will note that multifinality can thus be construed as an example of moderation, in which the relation between a cause and some outcome varies depending on other factors, which can be studied and modeled in appropriate analyses. An example of multifinality mentioned earlier is the finding that DRD4 may be a risk factor for ADHD only when it is accompanied by Conduct Disorder (Holmes et al., 2002). If replicated, this would indicate that the role of DRD4 as a risk factor for ADHD differs as a function of developmental context, namely, the presence or absence of overlapping Conduct Disorder. Other examples of multifinality are better construed as cases of heterogeneity, to be discussed later. These might include gene-gene and gene-environment interactions, in which the role of a given genetic risk factor for the development of a disorder might differ as a function of the allele(s) at another gene(s) or aspects of the environment to which the individual is exposed.

Focus on Continuities and Discontinuities between Normal and Abnormal Development

Developmental psychopathologists also are quite cognizant of the fact that an individual's developmental outcome (e.g., diagnostic status for some disorder) is not static but can change over time and place (Cicchetti, 1993; Sroufe & Rutter, 1984). Consistent with this is the recognition that an individual's diagnostic status is somewhat arbitrary, based on surpassing a prespecified diagnostic threshold. Given what at times are only minor differences in the symptom levels of individuals above and below the diagnostic threshold, developmental psychopathologists are interested in the similarities and differences in adjustment between such individuals. This is only one example of developmental psychopathologists' interest in the continuities and discontinuities between normal and abnormal adjustment. Another example concerns the extent to which the causes of an abnormal developmental outcome (e.g., a disorder such as ADHD) are the same or different from those of the corresponding normal range trait (e.g., the temperamental trait of activity level). Consistent with this notion are findings of associations between several candidate genes that are related to ADHD (e.g., DRD4, 5HTT) and normal-range traits such as activity levels and attention in young children (e.g., Auerbach et al., 2001).

Heterogeneity of Findings Based on Characteristics of Participants or Environments

A third theme important for future studies of candidate genes or genomic loci and developmental psychopathological disorders and traits involves the heterogeneity of association and/or linkage due to characteristics of individuals such as age, sex, or age of onset or due to aspects of the environment (i.e., gene-environment interactions). Just as it is implausible that the *DSM* is so closely aligned with nature that associations with candidate genes will be found only or primarily with *DSM* diagnoses, as opposed to more specific diagnostic subtypes or symptom dimensions, it is equally implausible that such associations will be equal for males and females, younger and older individuals, individuals whose disorders onset at younger and at older ages, and individuals who are exposed to widely disparate environmental contexts. Although there is at present a limited literature on such moderators of the relations between candidate genes or genomic loci and psychiatric disorders or psychopathological traits, there is considerable interest in such effects, and this literature is burgeoning. In this section, we review several studies that examined differences in association and linkage between disorders and candidate genes or genomic loci as a function of sex, age, age of onset, or environmental context.

Surprisingly few molecular genetic studies of psychiatric disorders or developmental psychopathological traits have examined such sources of heterogeneity, particularly given research showing that several candidate genes show important sex or age differences in expression. In the dopamine system, for example, levels of the dopamine transporter have been shown to be higher in males than females (e.g., Mozley, Gur, Mozley, & Gur, 2001) and to decline appreciably with age (e.g., Volkow et al., 1994). Similarly, in a study of knock-out mice in which one copy of the COMT gene was deactivated, motor activity, aggression, anxiety, and dopamine levels in the prefrontal cortex differed substantially between males and females (Gogos et al., 1998). Despite these findings, none of the published studies of DAT1 and ADHD have examined sex or age differences in association. Studies of association and linkage between COMT and ADHD have yielded mixed findings. In one study (Qian et al., 2003), however, analyses were conducted separately by sex and suggested sexually dimorphic findings, with the low-activity methionine allele being associated with ADHD in boys but the high-activity valine allele being associated with ADHD in girls. Although these results are preliminary, confined to one study, and need to be replicated, they embody the type of heterogeneity analyses that we believe may be useful for elaborating the nature of the relations between candidate genes and psychiatric disorders and developmental psychopathological traits.

Other sources of heterogeneity also may be important from a genetic perspective. In the medical genetics literature, for example, several genes are risk factors for disorder or disease contingent on age of onset. The first genetic locus found to contribute to breast cancer (i.e., BRCA1) was found to be linked with the disease only once early-onset cases were clearly distinguished from late-onset cases in the linkage analysis (Hall et al., 1990). Similarly, several genes for Alzheimer's disease (i.e., APP, APOE, PSEN1, and PSEN2) were identified as risk factors only for the early-onset form of the disease (Crutz & Van Broeckhoven, 1998). Despite these findings, to our knowledge no published candidate gene study of ADHD or any other developmental disorder has examined whether findings of association vary by age of onset. Another important source of heterogeneity may be the parent who transmitted a particular risk allele. Such transmitting parent effects are interesting from a genetic perspective because they may represent cases of imprinting, in which one parental allele has been deactivated due to methylation. Few studies have examined transmitting parent effects on candidate genes for ADHD or other psychiatric disorders. Kirley et al. (2002) tested transmitting parent effects for several candidate genes in the dopaminergic system and found that association and linkage between ADHD and tyrosine hydroxylase (TH) and, to a lesser extent, the dopamine receptor D2 gene (DRD2) was stronger for paternally than maternally transmitted alleles.

Although developmental psychopathology researchers have long been excited by the prospect of gene-environment interaction, and many have contended that one cannot understand the development of psychopathology without the consideration of such processes, there are few published studies of gene-environment interactions for psychiatric disorders or developmental psychopathological traits. There have been two high-profile published examples of gene-environment interactions for psychopathology that have garnered considerable attention and interest (Caspi et al., 2002, 2003). In the first of these, risk for adolescent serious antisocial behavior and violence based on abuse during early childhood was found to depend on alleles at the monoamine oxidase A gene (MAOA; Caspi et al., 2002). In the second, risk for depression during early adulthood was a multiplicative function of both life stress and alleles at the serotonin transporter gene (5HTT; Caspi et al., 2003). Notable features of these studies were the careful measurement of both the psychopathology outcomes and the environmental risk factors, as well as the use of functional mutations in both candidate genes. In addition, it is important to recognize the symmetrical nature of such gene-environment interactions, that is, that gene-environment interaction refers both to the moderation of the effects of environmental risk factors as a function of individuals' genotypes at a particular gene and to the moderation of individuals' genetic predispositions for a certain disorder or trait as a function of the environmental facets to which they are exposed and that they experience. Although no gene-environment interactions for developmental disorders such as ADHD have been examined to date, it would be easy to test whether the effects of various of the candidate genes mentioned earlier differ as a function of environmental risk factors, such as pre- or perinatal complications, maternal smoking or drinking during pregnancy, or other relevant environmental risk factors that have been posited and/or studied in the literature.

Focus on Resilience and Risk

Developmental psychopathologists are interested in, and frequently examine the role of, risk factors in the develop-

ment of psychopathology; they are also interested in resilience. Resilience may be construed as the ability of individuals to attain adequate developmental outcomes, despite their having experienced various risk factors or adverse experiences at an earlier developmental stage. Developmental psychopathologists are thus interested in studying the pathways to adaptive outcomes of individuals at risk for psychopathology (e.g., Rolf, Masten, Cicchetti, Nuechterlein, & Weintraub, 1990) and of those who grow up in contexts that are extremely stressful or even abusive (e.g., Cicchetti, Rogosch, Lynch, & Holt, 1993; Masten & Coatsworth, 1998). Developmental psychopathologists also acknowledge that individuals may traverse developmental pathways that cycle between adaptive and maladaptive outcomes (Cicchetti & Richters, 1993), and they are interested in studying the dynamic aspects of these straight and deviant pathways (Robins & Rutter, 1990). In its most basic form, the concept of resilience can thus also be construed as a form of moderation, similar to multifinality, in which the relation between a risk factor and an outcome variable differs as a function of some protective factor. It would be fairly easy and straightforward to extend both the concept and design of gene-environment interaction studies to explicitly incorporate tests of resilience as well as risk factor models. The investigations by Caspi and colleagues (2002, 2003) cited earlier represent first steps in this direction of examining gene-environment interactions within a developmental psychopathology context.

The Use of Endophenotypes to Aid in Finding Genes for Disorders

Many studies of risk factors for psychopathology are limited to examining the association between a particular risk factor and a disorder. A developmental psychopathology approach attempts to transcend these simple associations in several ways. First, developmental psychopathologists strive to design their studies not only to establish an association between a disorder and one or more risk factors, but also to be informative regarding the specific causal mechanisms that underlie such associations. Hence, a focus on neurodevelopmental endophenotypic mechanisms underlying the development of psychopathology is well in keeping with this perspective. Second, most studies of the etiology of psychopathology can be best thought of as snapshots of development, given that they characterize individual participants' outcomes at a particular developmental point in time. Even in the absence of longitudinal data, developmental psychopathologists strive to place their etiological findings in proper developmental perspective.

The fifth and final theme involves the use of endophenotypes in molecular genetic studies of psychiatric disorders and developmental psychopathological traits. Clearly, there is a large gap between candidate genes and the manifest symptoms of disorders as typically assessed by interviews or rating scales. It is desirable from both a conceptual and an empirical perspective to find valid and meaningful mediational or intervening constructs that may help to bridge this gap. The term endophenotype is often used to describe such constructs and the variables that are used to measure them. Endophenotypes were first described with respect to psychiatric disorders by Gottesman and Shields (1972, p. 637) over 30 years ago in their application to the genetics of Schizophrenia as "internal phenotypes discoverable by a biochemical test or microscopic examination" (Gottesman & Gould, 2003). More generally, endophenotypes refer to constructs that are thought to underlie psychiatric disorders or psychopathological traits and to be more directly influenced by the genes relevant to disorder than are the manifest symptoms. As such, they are closer to the immediate products of such genes (i.e., the proteins they code for) and are thought to be more strongly influenced by the genes that underlie them than the manifest symptoms that they in turn undergird. Endophenotypes also are thought to be "genetically simpler" in their etiology than are complex traits such as manifest disorders or their symptom dimensions (Gottesman & Gould, 2003). This means that the underlying structure of genetic influences on endophenotypes is simpler than that of complex disorders and traits in that there are fewer individual genes (or sets thereof) that contribute to their etiology.

A number of researchers have outlined criteria for evaluating the validity and utility of putative endophenotypes (e.g., Castellanos & Tannock, 2002; Doyle et al., in press; Gottesman & Gould, 2003; Waldman, in press). These include the following: (1) The endophenotype is related to the disorder and its symptoms in the general population; (2) the endophenotype is heritable; (3) the endophenotype is expressed regardless of whether the disorder is present; (4) the endophenotype and disorder are associated within families (i.e., they cosegregate); and (5) in addition to the endophenotype occurring in family members with a disorder to a greater extent than in family members who are unaffected (viz., criteria 4), it also will occur in the unaffected relatives of family members with a disorder at a higher rate than in randomly selected individuals from the general population (given that the endophenotype reflects the inherited liability to a disorder).

In addition to these criteria, several other criteria are pertinent to the validity and utility of endophenotypes.

First, it is important that the genetic influences that underlie the endophenotype also underlie the disorder and that at least some (but likely not all) of the genetic influences that underlie the disorder underlie the endophenotype. Note that this last criterion is asymmetrical, in that a higher proportion of the genetic influences on the endophenotype will be shared in common with those on the disorder, rather than vice versa. This criterion follows from the notion mentioned earlier that endophenotypes are thought to be genetically simpler than are complex traits such as disorders, in the sense that fewer genes contribute a greater magnitude to their etiology (Gottesman & Gould, 2003). Second, measures of the endophenotype must show association and/or linkage with one (or more) of the candidate genes or genetic loci that underlie the disorder. Third, the endophenotype measure must *mediate* the association and/or linkage between the candidate gene or genetic locus and the disorder, meaning that the effects of a particular gene or locus on a disorder are expressed—either in full or in part—through the endophenotype. The prerequisites for this causal scenario are that the candidate gene influences both the disorder and the endophenotype and that the endophenotype influences the disorder.

Putative endophenotypes have begun to be used in genetic studies of a number of disorders and developmental psychopathological traits, and the validity and utility of such endophenotypes have begun to be investigated. For example, the use and evaluation of putative endophenotypes in studies of the genetics of ADHD is in its infancy, such that only a few studies have examined association and linkage between candidate genes and plausible measures of endophenotypes for ADHD. In one of the first candidate gene studies of ADHD endophenotypes, Swanson et al. (2000) examined association of the 7-repeat allele of the 48 base pair VNTR in exon 3 of DRD4 in a small sample of 32 ADHD children. Surprisingly, the authors found that although ADHD children with the 7-repeat allele exhibited hyperactive-impulsive behaviors typical of the disorder, their performance on reaction time tasks of attention resembled that of non-ADHD children, whereas children without the DRD4 7-repeat allele showed slower reaction time deficits. In one study (Langley et al., 2004), association between the 7-repeat allele and several neuropsychological tests of executive function endophenotypes was assessed in a sample of 133 6- to 13-year-old drug naïve ADHD children. These tests included a continuous performance test (CPT), the Matching Familiar Figures Test (MFFT), a Go/No Go task, and the Stop Task. Consistent with predictions, ADHD children with one or more copies of the 7-repeat allele committed more errors on the MFFT and showed faster reaction times on the Stop Task and when committing errors on the MFFT.

In another study, Loo et al. (2003) examined association between the DAT1 10-repeat allele of the 3′ UTR VNTR and both cognitive and psychophysiological endophenotypes in a sample of 27 children with ADHD. Children with 2 copies of the 10-repeat allele performed worse than children with 0 or 1 copy on various CPT measures, including signal detection indices of inattention and impulsivity, omission and commission errors, and reaction time variability. In addition, children with 2 copies of the 10-repeat allele differed from children with 0 or 1 copy in their psychophysiological response to stimulant medication, such that children with 2 copies showed greater increases in EEG indices of cortical activation and arousal on stimulant medication relative to baseline. Several other studies have provided suggestive evidence for association between candidate genes and endophenotype measures. In a study of ADHD and COMT, Eisenberg et al. (1999) found a trend for greater CPT false alarms in children with the val/val genotype than in children with the met/met genotype. It is noteworthy that the val/val genotype also was overrepresented in ADHD children with the Combined and Hyperactive-Impulsive subtypes. Finally, in a sample of 200 nonreferred adults, Fossella et al. (2002) reported associations between the index of executive control on the Attention Network Task and polymorphisms in DRD4 and MAOA. Polymorphisms in MAOA were also associated with the alerting component of the Attention Network Task. It would be interesting for future studies to attempt to replicate such findings in clinical samples of children with ADHD.

As stated earlier, a prerequisite for the validity and utility of putative endophenotype measures is their heritability and the overlap of their genetic influences with those on the disorder of interest. Similar to molecular genetic studies of association and linkage between candidate genes and endophenotypic measures, quantitative genetic studies of the heritability of such measures and of the etiology of their overlap with ADHD symptoms also are in their infancy. As such, these studies have tended to include very small samples of twins drawn from either nonreferred adult or child populations (e.g., Fan, Wu, Fossella, & Posner, 2001; Holmes et al., 2002) or a mixture of nondisordered and ADHD child populations (Kuntsi & Stevenson, 2001). Likely due to the conjunction of very small twin samples and the distributional shortcomings of the endophenotypic measures (e.g., significant nonnormality, the presence of dramatic outliers, ceiling effects), some of these studies have yielded anomalous findings, which include near-zero

and negative heritabilities (Fan et al., 2001; Kuntsi & Stevenson, 2001), enormous confidence intervals around the genetic and environmental parameter estimates and/or twin correlations (Fan et al., 2001; Holmes et al., 2002; Kuntsi & Stevenson, 2001), and negative MZ and DZ twin correlations (Holmes et al., 2002). Although estimation of the heritability of endophenotypic measures and of the magnitude of overlapping genetic influences with disorder are important steps in evaluating the validity and utility of putative endophenotypes, these extant studies represent merely the beginning of such research. Specifically, future studies must be conducted on much larger twin samples, using a broader range of endophenotypic measures, with greater attention paid to the distributional and psychometric properties of such measures. Similar criteria apply to future studies of association and linkage between ADHD candidate genes and putative endophenotypic measures.

Fortunately, the investigation of putative endophenotypes is much more developed for other disorders, Schizophrenia in particular. A number of psychophysiological and cognitive-neuropsychological endophenotypic constructs have been investigated for Schizophrenia, including sensorimotor gating, smooth pursuit eye-tracking, and working memory. Given that this literature has been reviewed in detail by Gottesman and Gould (2003), we provide only a brief summary here. Studies of sensorimotor gating have documented deficits in P50 suppression among both schizophrenic patients and their unaffected first-degree relatives (e.g., Siegel, Waldo, Mizner, Adler, & Freedman, 1984). This index has been shown to be heritable in twin studies (e.g., D. A. Young, Waldo, Rutledge, & Freedman, 1996) and has been used to find linkage to a region on chromosome 15 (Freedman et al., 1997) and association and linkage with the a7 nicotinic acetylcholine receptor gene that resides in this chromosomal location (Leonard et al., 2002). Deficits in smooth pursuit eye movements have been shown in both schizophrenic patients and their unaffected first-degree relatives and to be heritable in twin studies (Conklin, Curtis, Katsanis, & Iacono, 2000) and has been found to be linked with a region on the short arm of chromosome 6, for which linkage has been replicated across multiple genome scans of Schizophrenia (Arolt et al., 1996). Finally, the endophenotypic findings pertinent to Schizophrenia that have received the most attention in the literature concern the relations among the disorder, neuropsychological and brain imaging indices of working memory, and the gene for COMT, which is the major mechanism of control of dopamine levels in the prefrontal cortex. Several studies have implicated working memory deficits in both schizophrenic patients and their unaffected first-degree relatives (e.g., Conklin et al., 2000), as well as the heritability of such measures in twin studies (Cannon et al., 2000) and have demonstrated the primacy of dorsolateral prefrontal cortical regions to working memory function in general (R. Levy & Goldman-Rakic, 2000) and to schizophrenic patients' deficits therein (Egan et al., 2001; Manoach et al., 2000). The gene for COMT is located on the long arm of chromosome 22, a location that has been linked to Schizophrenia in several genome scans, and COMT itself has shown association and linkage with Schizophrenia in several studies (Karayiorgou et al., 1995, 1998). In one study (Egan et al., 2001), COMT was associated and linked with performance on the Wisconsin Card Sorting test, a commonly used measure of working memory, and functional magnetic resonance imaging indices of activity in the dorsolateral prefrontal cortex in schizophrenic patients, their unaffected first-degree relatives, and unselected controls. The bridges built among several of the criteria for the validity and utility of putative endophenotypes go a long way toward establishing sensorimotor gating, smooth pursuit eye-tracking, and working memory as useful endophenotypes. The burgeoning literatures on endophenotypes for other disorders, such as childhood ADHD, can benefit considerably by emulating the research designs and methods used in the literature on Schizophrenia endophenotypes.

Summary

In this section of the chapter, we have tried to summarize some of the most exciting developments in molecular genetic studies of developmental psychopathology and specific psychiatric disorders. Rather than merely reviewing extant findings for several disorders, we have focused on several emerging themes in these literatures that should guide future research. These themes included the *replicability and consistency* of findings of association and linkage between a gene and a disorder, the *specificity* of association and/or linkage findings to particular diagnostic subtypes or symptom dimensions, the *heterogeneity* of association and/or linkage with a particular disorder due to characteristics of individuals or to aspects of their environments (i.e., gene-environment interactions), and the use of *endophenotypes* (i.e., underlying biological or psychological mechanisms thought to more directly reflect the gene's action) in molecular genetic studies of psychopathology. We illustrated these themes using examples from molecular genetic studies of several disorders, including ADHD, Schizophrenia, Major Depression, Bipolar Disorder, antisocial behavior, and Autism. It is our hope that these themes not

only provide a glimpse of the extant molecular genetic research on psychopathology and its development, but will help to set the research agendas for future such studies.

FUTURE DIRECTIONS

The wealth of approaches and information reviewed in this chapter set the stage for a potentially critical next decade of research in behavioral and molecular genetics. Over the past decade, it has become clear that the mission of both behavioral and molecular genetics is to increase our understanding of *mechanisms* that influence the course of adaptive and maladaptive behavior throughout the life span, rather than document empirically the extent to which genetic and environmental influences impact different forms of psychopathology. These mechanisms have begun to be specified in terms of genetic loci, specific environmental influences, and examples of gene-environment interplay. In this spirit, we speculate on the critical areas for investigation that will further our understanding of developmental processes.

At the center of future research will be the continued effort to conduct genomic research on psychopathology. In predicting the next decade, a brief consideration of the past 2 decades is informative. As we entered the 1990s, excitement lay in the idea of identifying specific genes responsible for the etiology of many diseases, including psychiatric disorders. This excitement soon waned, however, as it became clear that many diseases had complex etiologies involving both multiple genetic loci and many environmental influences. Excitement was generated again, however, by embracing the quantitative genetic model to incorporate both conceptual and methodological approaches geared toward such elusive probabilistic effects. Indeed, much of this chapter has been devoted to the execution of this goal, with many fine examples from both behavioral genetic and molecular genetic paradigms. The conceptual convergence of approaches of work reviewed in this chapter supports the contention that there is general agreement that the quantitative genetic model (i.e., a multifactorial model that includes multiple genetic and environmental effects along with the possibility of gene-environment interplay) provides to date the best representation of the etiology of most forms of psychopathology.

The fundamental issue facing the field now, however, is the extent to which we can empirically make substantial inroads that will further our understanding of development and pathogenesis. For example, it is currently recognized that progress in molecular genetics has gone slower than may have been anticipated (Plomin & McGuffin, 2003) and that the study of genetic influences on complex diseases poses a number of difficulties and complexities (Conneally, 2003; van den Bree & Owen, 2003). Furthermore, the extent to which genomics research will have a major impact on our understanding of psychopathology has been questioned (Merikangas & Risch, 2003), and the rationale driving genomic search strategies has been challenged with a perspective informed by considerations of public health impact (Merikangas & Risch, 2003). It is thus fair to say that although the conceptual model driving genomic research on psychopathology is not questioned, there are many concerns about our ability as a field to make true inroads over the next decade.

It is always clear that technological and analytic advances may propel new directions of research, especially in fields such as genetics. Speculation on what these advances may be are beyond the scope of this chapter, but it is reasonable to suggest the possibility that our approach to understanding genetic influence will be altered, to some degree, by advances in genomics, including developments pertaining to the analysis of genetic effects. However, given this, it will be critical that the field of genomics seriously considers critiques such as those offered by Merikangas and Risch (2003, 2004) and that behavioral and molecular genetics devise well-defined and rational strategies to combat the complexities inherent in studying complex phenotypes such as psychopathology.

Given these considerations, we postulate that many of the advances over the next decade will not necessarily come from molecular genetics, but rather from new applications of behavioral genetics that may set the stage for future progress on the genomic front. We are still at a relatively crude stage in our understanding, conceptualization, and measurement of phenotypes that will provide solid targets for genomic investigations. We have reviewed a number of approaches that have been used to define, refine, and create phenotypes that reside closer to the putative genetic signals that family, twin, and adoption paradigms have detected for decades. There is still a surprising lack of attention to identifying and testing endophenotypes for many forms of psychopathology, and we speculate that this area of investigation will produce much greater yields over the next decade. In particular, it is hoped that the field that relies on quantitative genetic theory will focus intensive effort on elucidating the nebulous construct of "genetic liability" that has provided the foundation for most work conducted in psychopathology over the past few decades. We have already described the ways endophenotypes have begun to be targets for molecular genetic investigations; as more progress is made in the conceptualization, measurement, and

testing of endophenotypes using behavioral genetic strategies, it will surely improve the fruitful translation to genomic search strategies.

In this regard, it is imperative, and thus a target for future directions, that behavioral genetic research becomes more interdisciplinary, with more explicit links with cognitive, biological, and brain sciences. Integration of both additional perspectives and methodologies into genetically informative designs clearly hold promise for generating new models of risk mechanisms that reside between the gene and the phenotype. Some examples of such endophenotypes were presented in this chapter; these are clearly needed for essentially all forms of developmental psychopathology. Furthermore, as represented in some of the research on ADHD, alcoholism, and Obsessive-Compulsive Disorder, establishing links between different endophenotypes and varying clinical characteristics may revamp our understanding of etiology and provide newer and more rational targets for molecular studies. It is not far-fetched to speculate that molecular genetic studies may be better served by focusing on underlying endophenotypic processes that have a multitude of connections with a number of clinical conditions and symptom profiles. As the variety and complexity of measures increase in behavioral and molecular genetics, it will be imperative to also begin to consider approaches such as multiple levels of analysis to fully take advantage of the range of biological and psychological systems implicated in the development of psychopathology (Cicchetti & Blender, 2004; Cicchetti & Dawson, 2002).

Thus far, we have considered future directions that pertain to genetic influence. It is clear from the studies reviewed in this chapter that there is particular excitement concerning the use of genetically informative designs to elucidate environmental influences and, specifically, more "pure" indices of the environment. We have cited many examples coming from studies using traditional approaches such as twin and twin-sibling designs as well as evidence deriving from newer paradigms such as the children of twins design. Given that quantitative genetic theory, and behavioral genetics as a field, has always devoted as much attention to the environment as the genome, this is probably not surprising. However, it is especially interesting that such a focus not only continues but arguably expands in the genomic era (Merikangas, 2005), and it is assumed that future work will further this emphasis on the environment. Indeed, much of the progress made over the past decade has resulted from inclusion of measured environmental risks that were of clear theoretical importance to the domain of interest (again paralleling the inclusion of putative genetic risk in the form of genetic markers). Thus, behavioral genetics has not just provided evidence of the importance of the environment, but in fact has begun to fill in the black box with specific indicators of environmental effects, ranging from family dynamics to neighborhood and cultural influences. We note here that the measurement of the environment in behavioral genetic studies may also, like the measurement of the phenotype, be subject to conceptual and methodological advances. We anticipate that progress over the next decade will come about by further development of our ability to measure environmental process. For example, behavioral genetic work on the family environment has begun to incorporate a variety of methodologies (e.g., self-report, videotaped interactions); such attention to the environment will undoubtedly expand our understanding of nongenetic influences on development (Neiderhiser et al., 2004; Reiss et al., 2001; Rende, Slomkowski, Lloyd-Richardson, & Niaura, 2005).

It is also clear that methodologies are being directed at understanding gene-environment interplay both in behavioral genetic and molecular genetic designs. Such work is critical, especially as intriguing conceptual models for gene-environment interplay (e.g., gene-environment interaction, gene-environment correlation) have been available for over 2 decades. Current molecular studies emphasizing gene-environment interaction (Caspi et al., 2002, 2003) are important reminders that examining main effects of genes must be complemented by other strategies that examine how genetic risk is expressed in environmental context. In addition to further study of gene-environment interaction, we also anticipate more emphasis on gene-environment correlation, especially as this topic has received much attention over the past 2 decades as having particular relevance to behavior, development, and psychopathology.

As the field moves toward a better understanding of genetic and environmental mechanisms, it is anticipated that more satisfying developmental models will follow. We presented a number of studies that have begun to sketch out the developmental trajectory for a number of forms of psychopathology, and these set the stage well for more mechanistic studies that indicate not only the *how* but the *when* of potential risk factors and their consequences. It is clear that much of the work in behavioral genetics has reflected a developmental sensitivity, and it appears as if many investigations are contributing to the construction of etiological models that extend across different developmental epochs. For example, we noted how research on depression has focused on early manifestations of familial risk in childhood (in the form of Anxiety Disorders) and

has, through the use of longitudinal and multigenerational studies, studied trajectories of such risk through adulthood. Studies focused on substance use offer another example of how behavioral genetic research has begun to identify developmental pathways. An especially exciting area for future studies will be examining how specific environmental influences and endophenotypes come together developmentally. For example, although endophenotypes are purported to represent the genetic signal, this should not be misinterpreted to mean that such signals are necessarily present early in life, and then interact with later environmental influences (although this may be a plausible model for some forms of psychopathology). Environmental influences may operate early in the life span and in fact predate the emergence of endophenotypes, such as emerging cognitive abilities that arise in the transitions to adolescence and adulthood. Incorporating a developmental perspective will undoubtedly expand our understanding of endophenotypes, environmental influence, and mechanisms of risk for psychopathology.

One final direction concerns implications for intervention. To date, there have been limited attempts to translate behavioral genetic findings into intervention models, with, of course, even fewer attempts to do so from molecular genetic studies. However, given the assumption that the next decade will yield many more insights into the processes by which genes and environment influence risk for and protection from psychopathology, along with the potential critical periods of influence, it will become a critical concern to translate these findings into intervention programs. Many opportunities present currently, especially in the form of specifying environmental effects on psychopathology. For example, there is robust and replicable evidence from a number of behavioral genetic studies that shared environmental effects are of critical importance for the initiation of substance use in adolescence, as well as exemplars of potential mechanisms for such influence. To make this point concrete, we have reviewed a number of studies demonstrating shared environmental effects on smoking initiation in adolescence, which, as argued by McGue et al. (2002), provides a solid foundation for intervention studies. Recent research has identified sibling influences as one such mechanism that reflects the impact of shared environment after controlling for genetic effects (Slomkowski et al., 2005). Thus, prevention programs that target transmission of smoking from older to younger siblings may be able to focus on a number of mechanisms that could reduce the likelihood of younger sibling smoking (Rende, Slomkowski, Lloyd-Richardson, et al., 2005). This is just one example of how behavioral genetic research can begin to move from etiological models emphasizing classes of effects (genetic versus environmental) to work that identifies putative mechanisms that operate at potentially critical developmental periods. Although the translation of research on genetic effects to implications for intervention must await further progress, it may be argued that genetically informative designs have already provided information that could begin to filter into intervention strategies. Such an end result would clearly demonstrate the utility of behavioral and molecular genetic research on developmental psychopathology and will represent perhaps the most important direction for future research.

REFERENCES

Accili, D., Fishburn, C. S., Drago, J., Steiner, H., Lachowicz, J. E., Park, B. H., et al. (1996). A targeted mutation of the D3 dopamine receptor gene is associated with hyperactivity in mice. *Proceedings of the National Academy of Sciences, 93,* 1945–1949.

Achenbach, T. M., & Edelbrock, C. S. (1981). Behavioral problems and competencies reported by parents of normal and disturbed children aged four through sixteen. *Monographs of the Society for Research in Child Development, 46,* 1–82.

Arolt, V., Lencer, R., Nolte, A., Muller-Myhsok, B., Purman, S., & Schurmann, M. (1996). Eye tracking dysfunction is a putative phenotypic susceptibility marker of schizophrenia and maps to a locus on chromosome 6p in families with multiple occurrence of the disease. *American Journal of Medical Genetics, 67,* 564–579.

Ashgari, V., Sanyal, S., Buchwaldt, S., Paterson, A., Jovanovic, V., & Van Tol, H. M. (1995). Modulation of intracellular cyclic AMP levels by different human dopamine D4 receptor variants. *Journal of Neurochemistry, 65,* 1157–1165.

Asghari, V., Schoots, O., van Kats, S., Ohara, K., Jovanovic, V., Guan, H. C., et al. (1994). Dopamine D4 receptor repeat: Analysis of different native and mutant forms of the human and rat genes. *Molecular Pharmacology, 46,* 364–373.

Auerbach, J. G., Benjamin, J., Faroy, M., Geller, V., & Ebstein, R. (2001). DRD4 related to infant attention and information processing: A developmental link to ADHD? *Psychiatric Genetics, 11,* 31–35.

Badner, J. A., & Gershon, E. S. (2002a). Meta-analysis of whole-genome linkage scans of bipolar disorder and Schizophrenia. *Molecular Psychiatry, 7,* 405–411.

Badner, J. A., & Gershon, E. S. (2002b). Regional meta-analysis of published data supports linkage of autism with markers on chromosome 7. *Molecular Psychiatry, 7,* 56–66.

Bakker, S. C., van der Meulen, E. M., Buitelaar, J. K., Sandkuijl, L. A., Pauls, D. L., Monsuur, A. J., et al. (2003). A whole-genome scan in 164 Dutch sib pairs with attention-deficit/hyperactivity disorder: Suggestive evidence for linkage on chromosomes 7p and 15q. *American Journal of Human Genetics, 72,* 1251–1260.

Barr, C. L., Feng, Y., Wigg, K. G., Schachar, R., Tannock, R., Roberts, W., et al. (2001). 5'-untranslated region of the dopamine D4 receptor gene and attention-deficit hyperactivity disorder. *American Journal of Medical Genetics, 105,* 84–90.

Barr, C. L., Wigg, K. G., Bloom, S., Schachar, R., Tannock, R., Roberts, W., et al. (2000). Further evidence from haplotype analysis for linkage of the dopamine D4 receptor gene and attention-deficit hyperactivity disorder. *American Journal of Medical Genetics, 96,* 262–267.

Benjamin, J., Li, L., Paterson, C., Greenberg, B. D., Murphy, D. L., & Hamer, D. H. (1996). Population and familial association between the D4 dopamine receptor gene and measures of novelty seeking. *Nature Genetics, 12,* 81–84.

Biederman, J., Newcorn, J., & Sprich, S. (1991). Comorbidity of attention deficit hyperactivity disorder with conduct, depressive, anxiety, and other disorders. *American Journal of Psychiatry, 148,* 564–577.

Biederman, J., & Spencer, T. (1999). Attention-deficit/hyperactivity disorder (ADHD) as a noradrenergic disorder. *Biological Psychiatry, 46,* 1234–1242.

Boomsma, D. I., Koopsman, J. R., van Doormen, L. J., & Orlebeke, J. F. (1994). Genetic and social influences on starting to smoke: A study of Dutch adolescent twins and their parents. *Addiction, 89,* 219–226.

Brzustowicz, L. M., Honer, W. G., Chow, E. W., Hogan, J., Hodgkinson, K., & Bassett, A. S. (1997). Use of a quantitative trait to map a locus associated with severity of positive symptoms in familial Schizophrenia to chromosome 6p. *American Journal of Human Genetics, 61,* 1388–1396.

Bulik, C. M., Sullivan, P. F., Wade, T. D., & Kendler, K. S. (2000). Twin studies of eating disorders: A review. *International Journal of Eating Disorders, 27,* 1–20.

Bulik, C. M., & Tozzi, F. (2004). Genetics in eating disorders: State of the science. *CNS Spectrum, 9,* 511–515.

Buster, M. A., & Rogers, J. L. (2000). Genetic and environmental influences on alcohol use: DF analysis of NLSY kinship data. *Journal of Biosocial Sciences, 32,* 177–189.

Cannon, T. D., Huttunen, M. O., Lonnqvist, J., Tuulio-Henriksson, A., Pirkola, T., & Glahn, D. (2000). The inheritance of neuropsychological dysfunction in twins discordant for Schizophrenia. *American Journal of Human Genetics, 67,* 369–382.

Carlson, S. R., Iacono, W. G., & McGue, M. (2002). P300 amplitude in adolescent twins discordant and concordant for alcohol use disorders. *Biological Psychiatry, 61,* 203–227.

Carlson, S. R., Iacono, W. G., & McGue, M. (2004). P300 amplitude in nonalcoholic adolescent twin pairs who become discordant for alcoholism as adults. *Psychophysiology, 41,* 841–844.

Carmelli, D., Swan, G. E., Robinette, D., & Fabsitz, R. (1992). Genetic influence on smoking: A study of male twins. *New England Journal of Medicine, 327,* 829–833.

Caspi, A., McClay, J., Moffitt, T. E., Mill, J., Martin, J., Craig, I. W., et al. (2002). Role of genotype in the cycle of violence in maltreated children. *Science, 297,* 851–854.

Caspi, A., Moffitt, T. E., Rutter, M., Taylor, A., Arseneault, L., Tully, L., et al. (2004). Maternal expressed emotion predicts children's antisocial behavior problems: Using monozygotic-twin differences to identify environmental effects on behavioral development. *Developmental Psychology, 40,* 149–161.

Caspi, A., Sugden, K., Moffitt, T. E., Taylor, A., Craig, I. W., Harrington, H., et al. (2003). Influence of life stress on depression: Moderation by a polymorphism in the 5-HTT gene. *Science, 301,* 386–389.

Caspi, A., Taylor, A., Moffitt, T. E., & Plomin, R. (2000). Neighborhood deprivation affects children's mental health: Environmental risks identified in a genetic design. *Psychological Science, 11,* 338–342.

Castellanos, F. X., & Tannock, R. (2002). Neuroscience of attention-deficit/hyperactivity disorder: The search for endophenotypes. *Nature Reviews Neuroscience, 3,* 617–628.

Chakravarti, A. (1999). Population genetics: Making sense out of sequence. *Nature Genetics, 21,* 56–60.

Cicchetti, D. (1993). Developmental psychopathology: Reactions, reflections, projections. *Developmental Review, 13,* 471–502.

Cicchetti, D., & Blender, J. A. (2004). A multiple-levels-of-analysis approach to the study of developmental processes in maltreated children. *Proceedings of the National Academy of Sciences, 101,* 17325–17326.

Cicchetti, D., & Dawson, G. (2002). Multiple levels of analysis. *Development and Psychopathology, 14,* 417–420.

Cicchetti, D., & Richters, J. E. (1993). Developmental considerations in the investigation of conduct disorder. *Development and Psychopathology, 5,* 331–344.

Cicchetti, D., & Rogosch, F. A. (1996). Equifinality and multifinality in developmental psychopathology. *Development and Psychopathology, 8,* 597–600.

Cicchetti, D., & Rogosch, F. A. (1999). Conceptual and methodological issues in developmental psychopathology research. In P. C. Kendall, J. N. Butcher, & G. N. Holmbeck (Eds.), *Handbook of research methods in clinical psychology* (pp. 433–465). New York: Wiley.

Cicchetti, D., Rogosch, F. A., Lynch, M., & Holt, K. (1993). Resilience in maltreated children: Processes leading to adaptive outcome. *Development and Psychopathology, 5,* 629–647.

Cleveland, H. H., & Wiebe, R. P. (2003). The moderation of genetic and shared-environmental influences on adolescent drinking by levels of parental drinking. *Journal of Studies on Alcohol, 64,* 182–194.

Concannon, P., Gogolin-Ewens, K. J., Hinds, D. A., Wapelhorst, B., Morrison, V. A., Stirling, B., et al. (1998). A second-generation screen of the human genome for susceptibility to insulin-dependent diabetes mellitus. *Nature Genetics, 19,* 292–296.

Conklin, H. M., Curtis, C. E., Katsanis, J., & Iacono, W. G. (2000). Verbal working memory impairment in Schizophrenia patients and their first-degree relatives: Evidence from the Digit Span task. *American Journal of Psychiatry, 157,* 275–277.

Conneally, P. M. (2003). The complexity of complex diseases. *American Journal of Human Genetics, 72,* 229–232.

Craig, I. W., & McClay, J. (2002). Molecular genetics in a post-genomic world. In R. Plomin, J. C. DeFries, I. W. Craig, & P. McGuffin (Eds.), *Behavioral genetics in the post-genomic era.* Washington, DC: American Psychological Association.

Crowe, R. R. (1993). Candidate genes in psychiatry: An epidemiological perspective. *American Journal of Medical Genetics, 48,* 74–77.

Crutz, M., & Van Broeckhoven, C. (1998). Molecular genetics of Alzheimer's disease. *Annals of Medicine, 30,* 560–565.

Curran, S., Mill, J., Sham, P., Rijsdijk, F., Marusic, K., Taylor, E., et al. (2001). QTL association analysis of the DRD4 exon 3 VNTR polymorphism in a population sample of children screened with a parent rating scale for ADHD symptoms. *American Journal of Medical Genetics, 105,* 387–393.

Deater-Deckard, K., Reiss, D., Hetherington, E. M., & Plomin, R. (1997). Dimensions and disorders of adolescent adjustment: A quantitative genetic analysis of unselected samples and selected extremes. *Journal of Child Psychology and Psychiatry, 38,* 515–525.

Dick, D. M., & Rose, R. J. (2002). Behavior genetics: What's new? What's next? *Current Directions in Psychological Science, 11,* 70–74.

Dick, D. M., Rose, R., Viken, R. J., Kaprio, J., & Koskenvou, M. (2001). Exploring gene-environment interactions: Socioregional moderation of alcohol use. *Journal of Abnormal Psychology, 110,* 625–632.

D'Onofrio, B. M., Turkheimer, E. N., Eaves, L. J., Corey, L. A., Berg, K., Solaas, M. H., et al. (2003). The role of the children of twins design in elucidating causal relations between parent characteristics and child outcomes. *Journal of Child Psychology and Psychiatry, 44,* 1130–1140.

Doyle, A. E., Faraone, S. V., Seidman, L. J., Willcutt, E., Nigg, J. T., Waldman, I. D., et al. (in press). Are endophenotypes based on measures of executive functions useful for molecular genetic studies of ADHD? *Journal of Child Psychology and Psychiatry.*

Dulawa, S. C., Grandy, D. K., Low, M. J., Paulus, M. P., & Geyer, M. A. (1999). Dopamine D4 receptor-knock-out mice exhibit reduced exploration of novel stimuli. *Journal of Neuroscience, 19,* 9550–9556.

Eaves, L., Silberg, J., & Erkanli, A. (2003). Resolving multiple epigenetic pathways to adolescent depression. *Journal of Child Psychology and Psychiatry, 7,* 1006–1014.

Ebstein, R. P., Novick, O., Umansky, R., Priel, B., Osher, Y., Blaine, D., et al. (1996). Dopamine D4 receptor (DRD4) exon III polymorphism associated with the human personality trait of novelty seeking. *Nature Genetics, 12,* 78–80.

Egan, M. F., Goldberf, T. E., Kolachana, B. S., Callicolt, J. H., Mazzanti, C. M., & Straub, R. E. (2001). Effect of COMT Val108/158 Met genotype on frontal lobe function and risk for Schizophrenia. *Proceedings of the National Academy of Sciences of the United States of America, 98,* 6917–6922.

Eisenberg, J., Mei-Tal, G., Steinberg, A., Tartakovsky, E., Zohar, A., Gritsenko, I., et al. (1999). Haplotype relative risk study of catechol-O-methyltransferase (COMT) and attention deficit hyperactivity disorder (ADHD): Association of the high-enzyme activity Val allele with ADHD impulsive-hyperactive phenotype. *American Journal of Medical Genetics, 88,* 497–502.

Eley, T. C. (1997). Depressive symptoms in children and adolescents: Etiological links between normality and abnormality: A research note. *Journal of Child Psychology and Psychiatry, 38,* 861–865.

Eley, T. C., Lichtenstein, P., & Moffitt, T. E. (2003). A longitudinal behavioral genetic analysis of the etiology of aggressive and nonaggressive antisocial behavior. *Development and Psychopathology, 15,* 383–402.

Enoch, M. A., Schuckit, M. A., Johnson, B. A., & Goldman, D. (2003). Genetics of alcoholism using intermediate phenotypes. *Alcoholism: Clinical and Experimental Research, 27,* 169–176.

Falk, C. T., & Rubenstein, P. (1987). Haplotype relative risk: An easy reliable way to construct a proper control sample for risk calculations. *Annals of Human Genetics, 51,* 227–233.

Fan, J., Wu, Y., Fossella, J. A., & Posner, M. I. (2001). Assessing the heritability of attentional networks. *BMC Neuroscience, 2,* 14.

Faraone, S. V., Doyle, A. E., Mick, E., & Biederman, J. (2001). Meta-analysis of the association between the 7-repeat allele of the dopamine D(4) receptor gene and attention deficit hyperactivity disorder. *American Journal of Psychiatry, 158,* 1052–1057.

Field, L. L., & Kaplan, B. J. (1998). Absence of linkage of phonological coding dyslexia to chromosome 6p23-p21.3 in a large family dataset. *American Journal of Human Genetics, 63,* 1448–1456.

Fisher, S. E., Marlow, A. J., Lamb, J., Maestrini, E., Williams, D. F., Richardson, A. J., et al. (1999). A quantitative-trait locus on chromosome 6p influences different aspects of developmental dyslexia. *American Journal of Human Genetics, 64,* 146–156.

Fossella, J., Sommer, T., Fan, J., Wu, Y., Swanson, J. M., Pfaff, D. W., et al. (2002). Assessing the molecular genetics of attention networks. *BMC Neuroscience, 3,* 14.

Freedman, R., Coon, H., Myles-Worsley, M., Orr-Urtreger, A., Olincy, A., & Davis, A. (1997). Linkage of a neurophysiological deficit in Schizophrenia to a chromosome 15 locus. *Proceedings of the National Academy of Sciences of the United States of America, 94,* 587–592.

Freeman, B., Powell, J., Ball, D., Hill, L., Craig, I., & Plomin, R. (1997). DNA by mail: An inexpensive and noninvasive method for collecting DNA samples from widely dispersed populations. *Behavior Genetics, 27,* 251–257.

Fu, Q., Heath, A. C., Bucholz, K. K., Nelson, E., Goldberg, J., Lyons, M. J., et al. (2002). Shared genetic risk of major depression, alcohol dependence, and marijuana dependence: Contribution of antisocial personality disorder in men. *Archives of General Psychiatry, 59,* 1125–1132.

Gayan, J., Smith, S. D., Cherny, S. S., Cardon, L. R., Fulker, D. W., Brower, A. M., et al. (1999). Quantitative-trait locus for specific language and reading deficits on chromosome 6p. *American Journal of Human Genetics, 64,* 157–164.

Gillespie, N. A., Kirk, K. M., Evans, D. M., Heath, A. C., Hickie, I. B., & Martin, N. G. (2004). Do the genetic or environmental determinants of anxiety and depression change with age? A longitudinal study of Australian twins. *Twin Research, 7,* 39–53.

Giros, B., Jaber, M., Jones, S. R., Wightman, R. M., & Caron, M. G. (1996). Hyperlocomotion and indifference to cocaine and amphetamine in mice lacking the dopamine transporter. *Nature, 379,* 606–612.

Glahn, D. C., Therman, S., Manninen, M., Huttenen, M., Kaprio, J., Lonnqvist, J., et al. (2003). Spatial working memory as an endophenotype for Schizophrenia. *Biological Psychiatry, 53,* 624–626.

Glowinski, A. L., Jacob, T., Bucholz, K. K., Scherrer, J. F., True, W., & Heath, A. C. (2004). Paternal alcohol dependence and offspring suicidal behaviors in a children-of-twins study. *Drug and Alcohol Dependence, 76,* S69–S77.

Glowinski, A. L., Madden, P. A., Bucholz, K. K., Lynskey, M. T., & Heath, A. C. (2003). Genetic epidemiology of self-reported lifetime DSM-IV major depressive disorder in a population-based twin sample of female adolescents. *Journal of Child Psychology and Psychiatry, 44,* 988–996.

Gogos, J. A., Morgan, M., Luine, V., Santha, M., Ogawa, S., Pfaff, D., et al. (1998). Catechol-O-methyltransferase-deficient mice exhibit sexually dimorphic changes in catecholamine levels and behavior. *Proceedings of the National Academy of Sciences of the United States of America, 95,* 9991–9996.

Gottesman, I. I., & Erlenmeyer-Kimlimg, L. (2001). Family and twin strategies as a head start in defining prodromes and endophenotypes for hypothetical early-interventions in Schizophrenia. *Schizophrenia Research, 51,* 93–102.

Gottesman, I. I., & Gould, T. D. (2003). The endophenotype concept in psychiatry: Etymology and strategic intentions. *American Journal of Psychiatry, 160,* 636–645.

Gottesman, I. I., & Shields, J. (1972). *Schizophrenia and genetics: A twin study vantage point.* New York: Academic Press.

Grigorenko, E. L., Wood, F. B., Meyer, M. S., Hart, L. A., Speed, W. C., Shuster, A., et al. (1997). Susceptibility loci for distinct components of developmental dyslexia on chromosomes 6 and 15. *American Journal of Human Genetics, 60,* 27–39.

Hall, J. M., Lee, M. K., Newman, B., Morrow, J. E., Anderson, L. A., Huey, B., et al. (1990). Linkage of early-onset familial breast cancer to chromosome 17q21. *Science, 250,* 1684–1689.

Han, C., McGue, M. K., & Iacono, W. G. (1999). Lifetime tobacco, alcohol and other substance use in adolescent Minnesota twins: Univariate and multivariate behavioral genetic analyses. *Addiction, 94,* 981–993.

Heath, A. C., Martin, N. G., Lynskey, M. T., Todorov, A. A., & Madden, P. A. (2002). Estimating two-stage models for genetic influences on alcohol, tobacco or drug use initiation and dependence vulnerability in twin and family data. *Twin Research, 5,* 113–124.

Heath, A. C., & Nelson, E. C. (2002). Effects of the interaction between genotype and environment: Research into the genetic epidemiology of alcohol dependence. *Alcohol Research and Health, 26,* 193–201.

Hesselbrock, V., Begleiter, H., Porjesz, B., O'Connor, S., & Bauer, L. (2001). P300 event-related potential amplitude as an endophenotype of alcoholism: Evidence from the collaborative study on the genetics of alcoholism. *Journal of Biomedical Science, 8,* 77–82.

Hettema, J. M., Corey, L. A., & Kendler, K. S. (1999). The multivariate genetic analysis of the tobacco, alcohol, and caffeine in a population based sample of male and female twins. *Drug and Alcohol Dependence, 57,* 69–78.

Holmes, J., Payton, A., Barrett, J., Harrington, R., McGuffin, P., Owen, M., et al. (2002). Association of DRD4 in children with ADHD and comorbid conduct problems. *American Journal of Medical Genetics, 114,* 150–153.

Hutcheson, H. B., Bradford, Y., Folstein, S. E., Gardiner, M. B., Santangelo, S. L., Sutcliffe, R. L., et al. (2003). Defining the autism minimum candidate gene region on chromosome 7. *American Journal of Medical Genetics, 117B,* 90–96.

Jacob, T., Waterman, B., Heath, A., True, W., Bucholz, K. K., Haber, R., et al. (2003). Genetic and environmental effects on offspring alcoholism: New insights using an offspring-of-twins design. *Archives of General Psychiatry, 60,* 1265–1272.

Jacobson, K. C., Prescott, C. A., & Kendler, K. S. (2000). Genetic and environmental influences on juvenile antisocial behaviour based on two occasions. *Psychological Medicine, 30,* 1315–1325.

Jaffee, S. R., Caspi, A., Moffitt, T. E., & Taylor, A. (2004). Physical maltreatment victim to antisocial child: Evidence of an environmentally mediated process. *Journal of Abnormal Psychology, 113,* 44–55.

Karayiorgou, M., Gogos, J. A., Galke, B. L., Wolyniec, P. S., Nestadt, G., & Antonarakis, S. E. (1998). Identification of sequence variants and analysis of the role of the catechol-O-methyl-transferase gene in Schizophrenia susceptibility. *Biological Psychiatry, 43,* 425–431.

Karayiorgou, M., Morris, M. A., Morris, B., Shprintzan, R. J., Goldberg, R., Borrow, J., et al. (1995). Schizophrenia susceptibility associated with interstitial deletions of chromosome 22q11. *Proceedings of the National Academy of Sciences of the United States of America, 92,* 7612–7616.

Kendler, K. S. (2001). Twin studies of psychiatric illness: An update. *Archives of General Psychiatry, 58,* 1005–1014.

Kendler, K. S., Gardner, C. O., & Prescott, C. A. (2002). Toward a comprehensive developmental model for major depression in women. *American Journal of Psychiatry, 159,* 1133–1145.

Kendler, K. S., Jacobson, K. C., Prescott, C. A., & Neale, M. C. (2003). Specificity of genetic and environmental risk factors for use and abuse/dependence of cannabis, cocaine, hallucinogens, sedatives, stimulants, and opiates in male twins. *American Journal of Psychiatry, 160,* 687–695.

Kendler, K. S., & Karkowski-Shuman, L. (1997). Stressful life events and genetic liability to major depression: Genetic control of exposure to the environment? *Psychological Medicine, 27,* 539–547.

Kendler, K. S., Neale, M. C., Sullivan, P., Corey, L. A., Gardner, C. O., & Prescott, C. A. (1999). A population-based twin study in women of smoking initiation and nicotine dependence. *Psychological Medicine, 29,* 299–308.

Kidd, K. K. (1993). Associations of disease with genetic markers: Deja vu all over again. *American Journal of Medical Genetics, 48,* 71–73.

Kirley, A., Hawi, Z., Daly, G., McCarron, M., Mullins, C., Millar, N., et al. (2002). Dopaminergic system genes in ADHD: Toward a biological hypothesis. *Neuropsychopharmacology, 27,* 607–619.

Klein, D. N., Lewinsohn, P. M., Rohde, P., Seeley, J. R., & Durbin, C. E. (2002). Clinical features of depressive disorder in adolescents and their relatives: Impact on familial aggregation, implications for phenotype definition, and specificity of transmission. *Journal of Abnormal Psychology, 111,* 98–106.

Klein, D. N., Lewinsohn, P. M., Seeley, J. R., & Rohde, P. (2001). A family study of major depressive disorder in a community sample of adolescents. *Archives of General Psychiatry, 58,* 13–20.

Klump, K. L., McGue, M., & Iacono, W. G. (2000). Age differences in genetic and environmental influences on eating attitudes and behaviors in preadolescent female twins. *Journal of Abnormal Psychology, 109,* 239–251.

Klump, K. L., McGue, M., & Iacono, W. G. (2003). Differential heritability of eating attitudes and behaviors in prepubertal versus pubertal twins. *International Journal of Eating Disorders, 33,* 287–292.

Koopsman, J. R., Slutske, W. S., Heath, A. C., Neale, M. C., & Boomsma, D. I. (1999). The genetics of smoking initiation and quantity smoked in Dutch adolescent and young adult twins. *Behavior Genetics, 29,* 383–393.

Koopsman, J. R., van Doornen, L., & Boomsma, D. I. (1997). Associations between alcohol use and smoking in adolescent and young adult twins: A bivariate genetic analysis. *Alcoholism: Clinical and Experimental Research, 21,* 537–546.

Krueger, R. F., Hicks, B. M., Patrick, C. J., Carlson, S. R., Iacono, W. G., & McGue, M. (2002). Etiologic connections among substance dependence, antisocial behavior, and personality: Modeling the externalizing spectrum. *Journal of Abnormal Psychology, 111,* 411–424.

Kuntsi, J., & Stevenson, J. (2001). Psychological mechanisms in hyperactivity: II. The role of genetic factors. *Journal of Child Psychology and Psychiatry and Allied Disciplines, 42,* 211–219.

LaHoste, G. J., Swanson, J. M., Wigal, S. B., Glabe, C., Wigal, T., King, N., et al. (1996). Dopamine D4 receptor gene polymorphism is associated with attention deficit hyperactivity disorder. *Molecular Psychiatry, 1,* 121–124.

Lander, E. S., & Schork, N. S. (1994). Genetic dissection of complex traits. *Science, 265,* 2037–2048.

Langley, K., Marshall, L., van den Bree, M., Thomas, H., Owen, M., O'-Donovan, M., et al. (2004). Association of the dopamine D4 receptor gene 7-repeat allele with neuropsychological test performance of children with ADHD. *American Journal of Psychiatry, 161,* 133–138.

Leonard, S., Gault, J., Hopkins, J., Logel, J., Vianzon, R., Short, M., et al. (2002). Association of promoter variants in the a7 nicotinic acetylcholine receptor subunit gene with an inhibitory deficit found in Schizophrenia. *Archives of General Psychiatry, 59,* 1085–1096.

Lessov, C. N., Martin, N. G., Statham, D. J., Todorov, A. A., Slutske, W. S., Bucholz, K. K., et al. (2004). Defining nicotine dependence for genetic research: Evidence from Australian twins. *Psychological Medicine, 35,* 865–879.

Levy, F. (1991). The dopamine theory of attention deficit hyperactivity disorder (ADHD). *Australian and New Zealand Journal of Psychiatry, 25,* 277–283.

Levy, R., & Goldman-Rakic, P. S. (2000). Segregation of working memory functions within the dorsolateral prefrontal cortex. *Experimental Brain Research, 133,* 23–32.

Lewis, C. M., Lewinson, D. F., Wise, L. H., DeLisi, L. E., Straub, R. E., Horvatta, I., et al. (2003). Genome scan meta-analysis of Schizophrenia and bipolar disorder: Part II. Schizophrenia. *American Journal of Human Genetics, 73,* 34–48.

Li, M. D., Cheng, R., Ma, J. Z., & Swan, G. E. (2003). A meta-analysis of estimated genetic and environmental effects on smoking behavior in male and female adult twins. *Addiction, 98,* 23–31.

Loo, S. K., Specter, E., Smolen, A., Hopfer, C., Teale, P. D., & Reite, M. L. (2003). Functional effects of the DAT1 polymorphism on EEG

measures in ADHD. *Journal of the American Academy of Child and Adolescent Psychiatry, 42,* 986–993.

Lowe, N., Kirley, A., Hawi, Z., Sham, P., Wickham, H., Kratochvil, C. J., et al. (2004). Joint analysis of the DRD4 marker concludes association with attention-deficit/hyperactivity disorder confined to the predominantly inattentive and combined subtypes. *American Journal of Human Genetics, 74,* 348–356.

Madden, P. A., Heath, A. C., Pedersen, N. L., Kaprio, J., Koskenvuo, M. J., & Martin, N. G. (1999). The genetics of smoking persistence in men and women: A multicultural study. *Behavior Genetics, 29,* 423–431.

Madden, P. A., Pedersen, N. L., Kaprio, J., Koskenvou, M. J., & Martin, N. G. (2004). The epidemiology and genetics of smoking initiation and persistence: Crosscultural comparisons of twin study results. *Twin Research, 7,* 82–97.

Maes, H., Woodward, C., Murrelle, L., Meyer, J., Silberg, J., Hewitt, J., et al. (1999). Tobacco, alcohol and drug use in eight- to sixteen-year-old twins: The Virginia Twin Study of Adolescent Behavioral Development. *Journal of Studies on Alcohol, 60,* 293–305.

Manoach, D. S., Goolub, R. L., Benson, E. S., Searl, M. M., Goff, D. C., Halpern, E., et al. (2000). Schizophrenic subjects show aberrant fMRI activation of dorsolateral prefrontal cortex and basal ganglia during working memory performance. *Biological Psychiatry, 48,* 99–109.

Manor, I., Tyano, S., Eisenberg, J., Bachner-Melman, R., Kotler, M., & Ebstein, R. P. (2002). The short DRD4 repeats confer risk to attention deficit hyperactivity disorder in a family-based design and impair performance on a continuous performance test (TOVA). *Molecular Psychiatry, 7,* 790–794.

Masten, A., & Coatsworth, J. D. (1998). The development of competence in favorable and unfavorable environments: Lessons from research on successful children. *American Psychologist, 53,* 205–220.

Mataix-Cols, D., do Rosario-Campos, M. C., & Leckman, J. F. (2005). A multidimensional model of obsessive-compulsive disorder. *American Journal of Psychiatry, 162,* 228–238.

Maughan, B., Taylor, A., Caspi, A., & Moffitt, T. E. (2004). Prenatal smoking and early childhood conduct problems: Testing genetic and environmental explanations of the association. *Archives of General Psychiatry, 61,* 836–843.

McCracken, J. T., Smalley, S. L., McGough, J. J., Crawford, L., Del'Homme, M., Cantor, R. M., et al. (2000). Evidence for linkage of a tandem duplication polymorphism upstream of the dopamine D4 receptor gene (DRD4) with attention deficit hyperactivity disorder (ADHD). *Molecular Psychiatry, 5,* 531–536.

McGue, M., Elkins, I., & Iacono, W. G. (2000). Genetic and environmental influences on adolescent substance use and abuse. *American Journal of Medical Genetics, 96,* 671–677.

McGue, M., Iacono, W. G., Legrand, L. N., & Elkins, I. (2001). Origins and consequences of age at first drink. II. Familial risk and heritability. *Alcoholism: Clinical and Experimental Research, 25,* 1166–1173.

Merikangas, K. R. (2005). The significance of social connectedness: Comments on Slomkowski et al., 2005. *Addiction, 100,* 442–443.

Merikangas, K. R., & Risch, N. (2003). Will the genomics revolutionize psychiatry? *American Journal of Psychiatry, 160,* 625–635.

Merikangas, K. R., & Risch, N. (2004). Genomic priorities and public health. *Science, 302,* 599–601.

Meyer, J. M., Rutter, M., Silberg, J. L., Maes, H. H., Simonoff, E., Shillady, L. L., et al. (2000). Familial aggregation for conduct disorder symptomatology: The role of genes, marital discord and family adaptability. *Psychological Medicine, 30,* 759–774.

Miguel, E. C., Leckman, J. F., Rauch, S., do Rosario-Campos, M. C., Hounie, A. G., Mercadante, M. T., et al. (2005). Obsessive-compulsive disorder phenotypes: Implications for genetic studies. *Molecular Psychiatry, 10,* 258–275.

Mill, J. S., Caspi, A., McClay, J., Sugden, K., Purcell, S., Asherson, P., et al. (2002). The dopamine D4 receptor and the hyperactivity phenotype: A developmental-epidemiological study. *Molecular Psychiatry, 7,* 383–391.

Mozley, L. H., Gur, R. C., Mozley, P. D., & Gur, R. E. (2001). Striatal dopamine transporters and cognitive functioning in healthy men and women. *American Journal of Psychiatry, 158,* 1492–1499.

Nadder, T. S., Rutter, M., Silberg, J. L., Maes, H. H., & Eaves, L. J. (2002). Genetic effects on the variation and covariation of attention deficit-hyperactivity disorder (ADHD) and oppositional-defiant disorder/conduct disorder (ODD/CD) symptomatologies across informant and occasion of measurement. *Psychological Medicine, 32,* 39–53.

Neiderhiser, J. M., Reiss, D., Pedersen, N. L., Lichtenstein, P., Spotts, E. L., Hansson, K., et al. (2004). Genetic and environmental influences on mothering adolescents: A comparison of two samples. *Developmental Psychology, 40,* 335–351.

Neuman, R. J., Heath, A., Reich, W., Bucholz, K. K., Madden, P. A. F., Sun, L., et al. (2001). Latent class analysis of ADHD and comorbid symptoms in a population sample of adolescent female twins. *Journal of Child Psychology and Psychiatry, 42,* 933–942.

Nigg, J. T., Blaskey, L. G., Stawicki, J. A., & Sachek, J. (2004). Evaluating the endophenotype model of ADHD neuropsychological deficit: Results for parents and siblings of children with ADHD combined and inattentive subtypes. *Journal of Abnormal Psychology, 113,* 614–625.

Ogdie, M. N., Macphie, I. L., Minassian, S. L., Yang, M., Fisher, S. E., Francks, C., et al. (2003). A genomewide scan for attention-deficit/hyperactivity disorder in an extended sample: Suggestive linkage on 17p11. *American Journal of Human Genetics, 72,* 1268–1279.

Payton, A., Holmes, J., Barrett, J. H., Hever, T., Fitzpatrick, H., Trumper, A. L., et al. (2001). Examining for association between candidate gene polymorphisms in the dopamine pathway and attention-deficit hyperactivity disorder: A family-based study. *American Journal of Medical Genetics, 105,* 464–470.

Pliszka, S. R., McCracken, J. T., & Maas, J. W. (1996). Catecholamines in attention-deficit hyperactivity disorder: Current perspectives. *Journal of the American Academy of Child and Adolescent Psychiatry, 35,* 264–272.

Plomin, R., & McGuffin, P. (2003). Psychopathology in the postgenomic era. *Annual Review of Psychology, 54,* 205–228.

Purcell, S., & Sham, P. C. (2003). A model-fitting implementation of the DeFries-Fulker model for selected twin data. *Behavior Genetics, 33,* 271–278.

Qian, Q., Wang, Y., Zhou, R., Li, J., Wang, B., Glatt, S., et al. (2003). Family-based and case-control association studies of catechol-O-methyltransferase in attention deficit hyperactivity disorder suggest genetic sexual dimorphism. *American Journal of Medical Genetics, 118B,* 103–109.

Rabinowitz, D. (1997). A transmission/disequilibrium test for quantitative trait loci. *Human Heredity, 47,* 342–350.

Rasmussen, E. R., Neuman, R. J., Heath, A. C., Levy, F., Hay, D. A., & Todd, R. D. (2004). Familial clustering of latent class and DSM-IV defined attention-deficit/hyperactivity disorder (ADHD) subtypes. *Journal of Child Psychology and Psychiatry, 45,* 589–598.

Reich, D. E., Gabriel, S. B., & Altshuler, D. (2003). Quality and completeness of SNP databases. *Nature Genetics, 33,* 457–458.

Reichborn-Kjennerud, T., Bulik, C. M., Tambs, K., & Harris, J. R. (2004). Genetic and environmental influences on binge eating in the absence of compensatory behaviors: A population-based twin study. *International Journal of Eating Disorders, 36,* 307–314.

Reiss, D., Cederblad, M., Pedersen, N. L., Lichtenstein, P., Elthammar, O., Neiderhiser, J. M., et al. (2001). Genetic probes of three theories of maternal adjustment: II. Genetic and environmental influences. *Family Process, 40,* 261–272.

Rende, R. (2004). Beyond heritability: Biological process in social context. In C. Garcia-Coll, E. L. Bearer, & R. M. Lerner (Eds.), *Nature and nurture: The complex interplay of genetic and environmental influences on human behavior and development* (pp. 107–126). New York: Guilford Press.

Rende, R., & Plomin, R. (1995). Nature, nurture, and development of psychopathology. In D. Cicchetti & D. Cohen (Eds.), *Developmental psychopathology: Vol. 1. Theory and method* (pp. 291–314). New York: Wiley.

Rende, R., Plomin, R., Reiss, D., & Hetherington, E. M. (1993). Genetic and environmental influences on depressive symptoms in adolescence: Etiology of individual differences and extreme scores. *Journal of Child Psychology and Psychiatry, 34,* 1387–1398.

Rende, R., Plomin, R., & Vandenberg, S. (1990). Who discovered the twin method? *Behavior Genetics, 20,* 277–285.

Rende, R., & Slomkowski, C. (in press). DeFries-Fulker analysis. In B. Everitt & D. C. Howell (Eds.), *Encyclopedia of behavioral statistics.* Hoboken, NJ: Wiley.

Rende, R., Slomkowski, C., Lloyd-Richardson, E. E., & Niaura, R. (2005). Improving understanding of sibling effects on adolescent smoking: Response to the commentaries. *Addiction, 100,* 443–444.

Rende, R., Slomkowski, C., McCaffery, J., Lloyd-Richardson, E., & Niaura, R. (2005). A twin-sibling study of smoking in adolescence: Etiology of individual differences and extreme scores. *Nicotine and Tobacco Research, 7,* 413–419.

Rende, R., Warner, V., Wickramaratne, P., & Weissman, M. M. (1999). Sibling aggregation for psychiatric disorders in offspring at high and low risk: Ten-year follow-up. *Psychological Medicine, 29,* 1291–1298.

Rende, R., & Weissman, M. M. (1999). Assessment of family history of psychiatric disorders. In D. Shaffer, C. P. Lucas, & J. E. Richters (Eds.), *Diagnostic assessment in child and adolescent psychopathology* (pp. 230–255). New York: Guilford.

Rende, R., Wickramaratne, P., Warner, V., & Weissman, M. M. (1995). Sibling resemblance for psychiatric disorders in offspring at high and low risk for depression. *Journal of Child Psychology and Psychiatry, 36,* 1353–1363.

Rhee, S. H., Hewitt, J. K., Young, S. E., Corley, R. P., Crowley, T. J., & Stallings, M. C. (2003). Genetic and environmental influences on substance initiation, use, and problem use in adolescents. *Archives of General Psychiatry, 60,* 1256–1264.

Rice, F., Harold, G. T., & Thapar, A. (2002). Assessing the effects of age, sex, and shared environment on the genetic aetiology of depression in childhood and adolescence. *Journal of Child Psychology and Psychiatry, 43,* 1039–1051.

Rice, F., Harold, G. T., & Thapar, A. (2003). Negative life events as an account of age-related differences in the genetic aetiology of depression in childhood and adolescence. *Journal of Child Psychology and Psychiatry, 44,* 977–987.

Risch, N. J. (2000). Searching for genetic determinants in the new millennium. *Nature, 405,* 847–856.

Risch, N. J., & Merikangas, K. (1996). The future of genetic studies of complex human diseases. *Science, 273,* 1516–1517.

Roberts, S. B., MacLean, C. J., Neale, M. C., Eaves, L. J., & Kendler, K. S. (1999). Replication of linkage studies of complex traits: An examination of variation in location estimates. *American Journal of Human Genetics, 65,* 876–884.

Robins, L. N., & Rutter, M. (Eds.). (1990). *Straight and deviant pathways from childhood to adulthood.* New York: Cambridge University Press.

Rolf, J., Masten, A. S., Cicchetti, D., Nuechterlein, K. H., & Weintraub, S. (Eds.). (1990). *Risk and protective factors in the development of psychopathology.* New York: Cambridge University Press.

Roman, T., Schmitz, M., Polanczyk, G. B., Eizirik, M., Rohde, L. A., & Hutz, M. H. (2001). Attention-deficit hyperactivity disorder: A study of association with both the dopamine transporter gene and the dopamine D4 receptor gene. *American Journal of Medical Genetics: Part B, Neuropsychiatric Genetics, 105,* 471–478.

Rose, R. J., Dick, D. M., Viken, R. J., & Kaprio, J. (2001). Gene-environment interaction in patterns of adolescent drinking: Regional residency moderates longitudinal influences on alcohol use. *Alcoholism: Clinical and Experimental Research, 25,* 637–643.

Rose, R. J., Dick, D. M., Viken, R. J., Pulkkinen, L., & Kaprio, J. (2001). Drinking or abstaining at age 14? A genetic epidemiological study. *Alcoholism: Clinical and Experimental Research, 25,* 1594–1604.

Rose, R. J., Kaprio, J., Winter, T., Koskenvuo, M., & Viken, R. J. (1999). Familial and socioregional environmental effects on abstinence from alcohol at age sixteen. *Journal of Studies on Alcohol, 13,* 63–74.

Rose, R. J., Viken, R. J., Dick, D. M., Bates, J. E., Pulkkinen, L., & Kaprio, J. (2003). It does take a village: Nonfamilial environments and children's behavior. *Psychological Science, 14,* 273–277.

Rowe, R., Pickles, A., Simonoff, E., Bulik, C. M., & Silberg, J. L. (2002). Bulimic symptoms in the Virginia Twin Study of Adolescent Behavioral Development: Correlates, comorbidity, and genetics. *Biological Psychiatry, 51,* 172–182.

Rubinstein, M., Phillips, T. J., Bunzow, J. R., Falzone, T. L., Dziewczapolski, G., Zhang, G., et al. (1997). Mice lacking dopamine D4 receptors are supersensitive to ethanol, cocaine, and methylphenidate. *Cell, 90,* 991–1001.

Rutter, M. (2002). The interplay of nature, nurture, and developmental influences: The challenge ahead for mental health. *Archives of General Psychiatry, 59,* 996–1000.

Rutter, M., Dunn, J., Plomin, R., Simonoff, E., Pickles, A., Maughan, B., et al. (1997). Integrating nature and nurture: Implications of person-environment correlations and interactions for developmental psychopathology. *Development and Psychopathology, 9,* 335–364.

Rutter, M., Pickles, A., Murray, R., & Eaves, L. (2001). Testing hypotheses on specific environmental causal effects on behavior. *Psychological Bulletin, 127,* 291–324.

Rutter, M., & Silberg, J. (2002). Gene-environment interplay in relation to emotional and behavioral disturbance. *Annual Review of Psychology, 53,* 463–490.

Scherrer, J. F., True, W. R., Xian, H., Lyons, M. J., Eisen, S. A., Goldberg, J., et al. (2003). Evidence for genetic influences common and specific to symptoms of generalized anxiety and panic. *Journal of Affective Disorders, 57,* 25–35.

Schmidt, L. A., Fox, N. A., Pérez-Edgar, K., Hu, S., & Hamer, D. H. (2001). Association of DRD4 with attention problems in normal childhood development. *Psychiatric Genetics, 11,* 25–29.

Scourfield, J., Rice, F., Thaper, A., Harold, G. T., Martin, N., & McGuffin, P. (2003). Depressive symptoms in children and adolescents: Changing aetiological influences with development. *Journal of Child Psychology and Psychiatry, 44,* 968–976.

Seeman, P., & Madras, B. K. (1998). Anti-hyperactivity medication: Methylphenidate and amphetamine. *Molecular Psychiatry, 3,* 386–396.

Segurado, R., Detera-Wadleigh, S. D., Levinson, D. F., Lewis, C. M., Gill, M., Nurnberger, J. I., et al. (2003). Genome scan meta-analysis of Schizophrenia and bipolar disorder: Part III. Bipolar disorder. *American Journal of Human Genetics, 73,* 49–62.

Seidman, L. J., Faraone, S. V., Goldstein, J. M., Kremen, W. S., Horton, N. J., Makris, N., et al. (2002). Left hippocampal volume as a vulnerability indicator for Schizophrenia: A magnetic resonance imaging morphometric study of nonpsychotic first-degree relatives. *Archives of General Psychiatry, 59,* 839–849.

Siegel, C., Waldo, M., Mizner, G., Adler, L. E., & Freedman, R. (1984). Deficits in sensory gating in schizophrenic patients and their relatives: Evidence obtained with auditory evoked responses. *Archives of General Psychiatry, 41,* 607–612.

Silberg, J. L., & Eaves, L. J. (2004). Analysing the contributions of genes and parent-child interaction to childhood behavioural and emotional problems: A model for the children of twins. *Psychological Medicine, 34,* 347–356.

Silberg, J. L., Parr, T., Neale, M. C., Rutter, M., Angold, A., & Eaves, L. J. (2003). Maternal smoking during pregnancy and risk to boys' conduct disturbance: An examination of the causal hypothesis. *Biological Psychiatry, 53,* 130–135.

Silberg, J. L., Pickles, A., Rutter, M., Hewitt, J., Simonoff, E., Maes, H., et al. (1999). The influence of genetic factors and life stress on depression among adolescent girls. *Archives of General Psychiatry, 56,* 225–232.

Silberg, J. L., Rutter, M., & Eaves, L. (2001). Genetic and environmental influences on the temporal association between earlier anxiety and later depression in girls. *Biological Psychiatry, 49,* 1040–1049.

Silberg, J. L., Rutter, M., Neale, M., & Eaves, L. (2001). Genetic moderation of environmental risk for depression and anxiety in adolescent girls. *British Journal of Psychiatry, 179,* 116–121.

Slaats-Willemse, D., Swaab-Barneveld, H., de Sonneville, L., van der Meulen, E., & Buitelaar, J. (2003). Deficient response inhibition as a cognitive endophenotype of ADHD. *Journal of the American Academy of Child and Adolescent Psychiatry, 42,* 1242–1248.

Slomkowski, C., Rende, R., Novak, S., Lloyd-Richardson, E., & Niaura, R. (2005). Sibling effects on smoking in adolescence: Evidence for social influence from a genetically-informative design. *Addiction, 100,* 430–438.

Slutske, W. S., Eisen, S., Xian, H., True, W. R., Lyons, M. J., Goldberg, J., et al. (2001). A twin study of the association between pathological gambling and antisocial personality disorder. *Journal of Abnormal Psychology, 110,* 297–308.

Slutske, W. S., True, W. R., Scherrer, J. F., Heath, A. C., Bucholz, K. K., Eisen, S. A., et al. (1999). The heritability of alcoholism symptoms: "Indicators of genetic and environmental influence in alcohol-dependent individuals" revisited. *Alcoholism: Clinical and Experimental Research, 23,* 759–769.

Solanto, M. V. (1984). Neuropharmacological basis of stimulant drug action in attention deficit disorder with hyperactivity: A review and synthesis. *Psychological Bulletin, 95,* 387–409.

Spielman, R., McGinnis, J., & Ewens, W. (1993). Transmission test for linkage disequilibrium: The insulin gene region and insulin-dependent diabetes mellitus (IDDM). *American Journal of Human Genetics, 52,* 506–516.

Sroufe, L. A., & Rutter, M. (1984). The domain of developmental psychopathology. *Child Development, 55,* 17–29.

Stallings, M. C., Hewitt, J. K., Beresford, T., Heath, A. C., & Eaves, L. J. (1999). A twin study of drinking and smoking onset and latencies from first use to regular use. *Behavior Genetics, 29,* 409–421.

Stins, J. F., van Baal, C. G., Polderman, T. J., Verhulst, F. C., & Boomsma, D. I. (2004). Heritability of Stroop and flanker performance in 12-year old children. *BMC Neuroscience, 5,* 49.

Sullivan, P. F., & Kendler, K. S. (1999). The genetic epidemiology of smoking. *Nicotine and Tobacco Research, 1*(Suppl. 2), S51–S57.

Sullivan, P. F., Neale, M. C., & Kendler, K. S. (2000). Genetic epidemiology of major depressive disorder: Review and meta-analysis. *American Journal of Psychiatry, 157,* 1552–1562.

Sunohara, G. A., Roberts, W., Malone, M., Schachar, R. J., Tannock, R., Basile, V. S., et al. (2000). Linkage of the dopamine D4 receptor gene and attention-deficit/hyperactivity disorder. *Journal of the American Academy of Child and Adolescent Psychiatry, 39,* 1537–1542.

Swan, G. E., Hudman, K. S., Jack, L. M., Hemberger, K., Carmelli, D., Khroyan, T. V., et al. (2003). Environmental and genetic determinants of tobacco use: Methodology for a multidisciplinary, longitudinal family-based investigation. *Cancer Epidemiology Biomarkers Prevention, 12,* 994–1005.

Swanson, J. M., Oosterlaan, J., Murias, M., Schuck, S., Flodman, P., Spence, M. A., et al. (2000). Attention deficit/hyperactivity disorder children with a 7-repeat allele of the dopamine receptor D4 gene have extreme behavior but normal performance on critical neuropsychological tests of attention. *Proceedings of the National Academy of Sciences of the United States of America, 97,* 4754–4759.

Swanson, J. M., Sunohara, G. A., Kennedy, J. L., Regino, R., Fineberg, E., Wigal, T., et al. (1998). Association of the dopamine receptor D4 (DRD4) gene with a refined phenotype of attention deficit hyperactivity dosorder (ADHD): A family-based approach. *Molecular Psychiatry, 3,* 38–41.

Taylor, J., Iacono, W. G., & McGue, M. (2000). Evidence for a genetic etiology of early-onset delinquency. *Journal of Abnormal Psychology, 109,* 634–643.

Terwilliger, J. D., & Ott, J. (1992). A haplotype-based haplotype relative risk statistic. *Human Heredity, 42,* 337–346.

Thapar, A., Holmes, J., Poulton, K., & Harrington, R. (1999). Genetic basis of attention deficit and hyperactivity. *British Journal of Psychiatry, 174,* 105–111.

Tholin, S., Rasmussen, F., Tynelius, P., & Karlsson, J. (2005). Genetic and environmental influences on eating behavior: The Swedish Young Male Twins Study. *American Journal of Clinical Nutrition, 81,* 564–569.

Todd, R. D., Neuman, R. J., Lobos, E. A., Jong, Y. J., Reich, W., & Heath, A. C. (2001). Lack of association of dopamine D4 receptor gene polymorphisms with ADHD subtypes in a population sample of twins. *American Journal of Medical Genetics, 105,* 432–438.

Todd, R. D., Rasmussen, E. R., Neuman, R. J., Reich, W., Hudziak, J. J., Bucholz, K. K., et al. (2001). Familiality and heritability of subtypes of attention deficit hyperactivity disorder in a population sample of adolescent female twins. *American Journal of Psychiatry, 158,* 1891–1898.

True, W. R., Heath, A. C., Scherrer, J. F., Xian, H., Lin, N., Eisen, S. A., et al. (1999). Interrelationships of genetic and environmental influences on conduct disorder and alcohol and marijuana dependence symptoms. *American Journal of Medical Genetics, 88,* 391–397.

True, W. R., Xian, H., Scherrer, J. F., Madden, P. A., Buchholz, K. K., Heath, A. C., et al. (1999). Common genetic vulnerability for nicotine and alcohol dependence in men. *Archives of General Psychiatry, 56,* 655–661.

Tsuang, M. T. (2000). Schizophrenia: Genes and environment. *Biological Psychiatry, 47,* 210–220.

Tsuang, M. T. (2001). Defining alternative phenotypes for genetic studies: What can we learn from studies of Schizophrenia? *American Journal of Medical Genetics, 105,* 8–10.

Tsuang, M. T., Bar, J. L., Harley, R. M., & Lyons, M. J. (2001). The Harvard Twin Study of Substance Abuse: What we have learned. *Harvard Review of Psychiatry, 59,* 839–849.

Tsuang, M. T., Lyons, M. J., Meyer, J. M., Doyle, T., Eisen, S. A., Goldberg, J., et al. (1998). Co-occurrence of abuse of different drugs in men: The role of drug-specific and shared vulnerabilities. *Archives of General Psychiatry, 55,* 967–972.

Tsuang, M. T., Stone, W. S., & Faraone, S. V. (2001). Genes, environment, and Schizophrenia. *British Journal of Psychiatry, 178,* S19–S24.

van den Bree, M. B., & Owen, M. J. (2003). The future of psychiatric genetics. *Annals of Medicine, 35,* 122–134.

Viken, R. J., Kaprio, J., Koskenvuo, M., & Rose, R. J. (1999). Longitudinal analyses of the determinants of drinking and of drinking to intoxication in adolescent twins. *Behavior Genetics, 29,* 455–461.

Vink, J. M., Willemsen, G., & Boomsma, D. I. (2003). The association of current smoking behavior of parents, siblings, friends, and spouses. *Addiction, 98,* 923–931.

Volkow, N. D., Fowler, J. S., Wang, G. J., Logan, J., Schlyer, D., MacGregor, R., et al. (1994). Decreased dopamine transporters with age in healthy human subjects. *Annals of Neurology, 36,* 237–239.

Wade, T. D., Bulik, C. M., Neale, M., & Kendler, K. S. (2000). Anorexia nervosa and major depression: Shared genetic and environmental risk factors. *American Journal of Psychiatry, 157,* 469–471.

Waldman, I. D. (in press). Statistical approaches to complex phenotypes: Evaluating neuropsychological endophenotypes for ADHD. *Biological Psychiatry.*

Waldman, I. D., Rhee, S. H., Levy, F., & Hay, D. A. (2001). Genetic and environmental influences on the covariation among symptoms of attention deficit hyperactivity disorder, oppositional defiant disorder, and conduct disorder. In D. A. Hay & F. Levy (Eds.), *Attention, genes and ADHD* (pp. 115–138). Hillsdale, NJ: Erlbaum.

Waldman, I. D., Robinson, B. F., & Feigon, S. A. (1997). Linkage disequilibrium between the dopamine transporter gene (DAT1) and bipolar disorder: Extending the Transmission Disequilibrium Test (TDT) to examine genetic heterogeneity. *Genetic Epidemiology, 14,* 699–704.

Waldman, I. D., Robinson, B. F., & Rowe, D. C. (1999). A logistic regression based extension of the TDT for continuous and categorical traits. *Annals of Human Genetics, 63,* 329–340.

Waldman, I. D., Rowe, D. C., Abramowitz, A., Kozel, S. T., Mohr, J. H., Sherman, S. L., et al. (1998). Association and linkage of the dopamine transporter gene and attention-deficit hyperactivity disorder in children: heterogeneity owing to diagnostic subtype and severity. *American Journal of Human Genetics, 63,* 1767–1776.

Warner, V., Weissman, M. M., Mufson, L., & Wickramaratne, P. J. (1999). Grandparents, parents, and grandchildren at high risk for depression: a three-generation study. *Journal of the American Academy of Child and Adolescent Psychiatry, 38,* 289–296.

Weissman, M. M., Wickramaratne, P., Nomura, Y., Warner, V., Verdeli, H., Pilowsky, D. J., et al. (2005). Families at high and low risk for depression: A 3-generation study. *Archives of General Psychiatry, 62,* 29–36.

White, V. M., Hopper, J. L., Wearing, A. J., & Hill, D. J. (2003). The role of genes in tobacco smoking during adolescence and young adulthood: A multivariate behaviour genetic investigation. *Addiction, 98,* 1087–2000.

Whitfield, J. B., Zhu, G., Madden, P. A., Neale, M. C., Heath, A. C., & Martin, N. G. (2004). The genetics of alcohol intake and of alcohol dependence. *Alcoholism: Clinical and Experimental Research, 28,* 1153–1160.

Wickramaratne, P. J., Warner, V., & Weissman, M. M. (2000). Selecting early onset MDD probands for genetic studies: Results from a longitudinal high-risk study. *American Journal of Medical Genetics, 96,* 93–101.

Williams, J., McGuffin, P., Nothen, M., & Owen, M. J. (1997). Meta-analysis of association between the 5-HT2a receptor T102C polymorphism and Schizophrenia. EMASS Collaborative Group: European Multicentre Association Study of Schizophrenia. *Lancet, 349,* 1221.

Williams, J., Spurlock, G., Holmans, P., Mant, R., Murphy, K., Jones, L., et al. (1998). A meta-analysis and transmission disequilibrium study of association between the dopamine D3 receptor gene and Schizophrenia. *Molecular Psychiatry, 3,* 141–149.

Wise, L. H., Lanchbury, J. S., & Lewis, C. M. (1999). Meta-analysis of genome searches. *Annals of Human Genetics, 63,* 263–272.

Xian, H., Chantarujikapong, S. I., Scherrer, J. F., Eisen, S. A., Lyons, M. J., Goldberg, J., et al. (2000). Genetic and environmental influences on posttraumatic stress disorder, alcohol, and drug dependence in twin pairs. *Drug and Alcohol Dependence, 61,* 95–102.

Xian, H., Scherrer, J. F., Madden, P. A., Lyons, M. J., Tsuang, M., True, W. R., et al. (2003). The heritability of failed smoking cessation and nicotine withdrawal in twins who smoked and attempted to quit. *Nicotine and Tobacco Research, 5,* 141–144.

Young, D. A., Waldo, M., Rutledge, J. H., & Freedman, R. (1996). Heritability of inhibitory gating of the P50 auditory-evoked potential in monozygotic and dizygotic twins. *Neuropsychobiology, 33,* 113–117.

Young, S. E., Smolen, A., Corley, R. P., Krauter, K. S., DeFries, J. C., Crowley, T. J., et al. (2002). Dopamine transporter polymorphism associated with externalizing behavior problems in children. *American Journal of Medical Genetics, 114,* 144–149.

CHAPTER 11

Temperament, Attention, and Developmental Psychopathology

MARY K. ROTHBART and MICHAEL I. POSNER

Cicchetti and Toth (1995) have described two major goals of a developmental approach to psychopathology. The first is to study the development of individual capacities across the life span. The second is to examine the relation between outcomes and earlier adaptations in functioning, considering distal as well as proximal influences on development. A temperament approach to development and psychopathology is concerned with the constitutionally based dispositions that underlie the individual's social and emotional development. Temperament also provides a view of distal influence that is evolutionary in scope, identifying variations in affective-motivational and attentional adaptations to human life that are both inherited and shaped by experience. Along with attention, these include emotion related to threatening input that organizes motor and autonomic circuits to support avoidant behavior and perceptual path-

ways to enhance information relevant to threat and safety (Derryberry & Rothbart, 1984; Derryberry & Tucker, 1992; Gray, 1982; Ohman, 2000). They also include affect related to incentives that support approach, perceptual pathways that enhance information relevant to reward, and affect related to goal blockage and loss that supports attack and withdrawal.

Except in rare cases, we all exhibit these adaptations, and we share a number of them with nonhuman animals (Panksepp, 1998). Individuals vary in the reactivity of their affective motivational systems and in the self-regulatory capacities, such as attention, that modulate them (Rothbart & Derryberry, 1981). As the child develops, initially more reactive forms of regulation such as approach and fearful inhibition are increasingly supplemented by capacities of voluntary or effortful control

(Posner & Rothbart, 1998; Rothbart & Bates, 1998). These patterns of regulation may "promote a progressive stabilization of synapses within the brain, contributing to the structural organizations central to personality" (Derryberry & Reed, 1994, p. 633). The self-organization of social and emotional development based on temperament and experience provides a further proximal basis for thinking about psychopathology and its development (Cicchetti & Tucker, 1994).

In this chapter, we consider relations between temperament and the development of psychopathology. We define temperament as constitutionally based individual differences in reactivity and self-regulation, as observed in the domains of emotionality, motor activity, and attention (Rothbart, 1989c; Rothbart & Derryberry, 1981). By reactivity, we mean characteristics of the individual's responsivity to changes in stimulation, as reflected in somatic, autonomic, and endocrine nervous systems. By self-regulation, we mean processes modulating this reactivity, including behavioral approach, avoidance, inhibition, and attentional self-regulation. In our view, individual differences in temperament constitute the earliest expression of personality and the substrate from which later personality develops. By tracing the development of temperament and the adaptations it supports across different periods of the life span, we can illuminate our understanding of the development of risk for psychopathology.

In the previous edition of this chapter (Rothbart, Posner, & Hershey, 1995), we identified a number of ways that temperament might shape individual adaptation and vice versa. These include (1) individual differences that in the extreme may constitute the psychopathology or dispose the person toward it; (2) characteristics evoking reactions in others that can promote the risk of psychopathology or buffer it; (3) characteristics influencing the person's "niche picking," putting him or her at greater or lesser risk for psychopathology; (4) temperamental influences on the form of a disorder, its course, and the likelihood of its recurrence; (5) temperamental biases in information processing about the self and the world, increasing or decreasing the likelihood of psychopathology; (6) temperamental regulation or buffering against the effects of risk factors or stress; (7) temperamental heightened responsiveness to environmental events; and (8) interaction among temperament systems, some of them later developing. Two major temperamental control systems are fear, developing late in the 1st year, inhibiting approach and expressive tendencies, and effortful control, developing during the preschool years and beyond. In addition, (9) temperamental dispositions may shape different devel-

opmental pathways to a given outcome, and individual dispositions may allow for multiple outcomes (Cicchetti & Cohen, 1995). Finally, (10) temperament characteristics and caregiving environment may make independent contributions to outcomes or may interact in increasing or decreasing risk of disorder; and (11) disorders themselves may change aspects of temperament. We have been impressed at the number of studies during the past decade that speak to these issues, and we revisit them in the course of our discussion.

This chapter has two major sections. In the first, we describe findings on individual differences in temperament and attention and consider their links to neural networks. We then discuss theories and research relating temperament to the development of risk conditions for psychopathology. Individual differences in attentional capacities, a major aspect of temperament, are critical to our understanding of these issues.

We begin the chapter with a brief historical introduction, followed by a discussion of dimensions of temperament that have emerged from conceptual and factor-analytic studies of temperament early in life (Bates, Freeland, & Lounsbury, 1979; Hagekull & Bohlin, 1981; Rothbart, 1981; Sanson, Prior, Garino, Oberklaid, & Sewell, 1987). These dimensions include fear (distress and behavioral inhibition to novelty), anger or irritability, positive affect and approach, activity level, and attentional persistence. We note similarities between these dimensions and the "Big Five" and "Big Three" personality factors identified in research on adults (Goldberg, 1990). We then consider temperament dimensions in connection with models for developmental psychopathology and review recent research on temperament, attention, and the development of psychopathology.

HISTORICAL APPROACHES

We begin our brief history with a discussion of temperament typologies. We then consider factor analytic approaches to the study of temperament.

The Greco-Roman Typology

The ancient Western typology of temperament was developed by Greek and Greco-Roman physicians, including Theophrastus, Vindician, and Galen (S. Diamond, 1974). Like later approaches to temperament, the fourfold typology related individual differences in behavior and emotionality to variability in the human constitution as it was understood at the time. The temperamental syndrome of *melancholia* (a tendency to negative and depressed mood) and its relation to a predominance of black bile was developed in the fourth century B.C. writings of Theophrastus, and the complete fourfold typology of temperament as linked to the Hippocratic bodily humors was present by the time of Vindician in the fourth century A.D. (S. Diamond, 1974).

In addition to the melancholic type, the fourfold typology included descriptions of the *choleric* person (quick-tempered and touchy, easily aroused to anger, with a predominance of yellow bile), the *phlegmatic* (apathetic and sluggish, not easily stirred to emotion, with a predominance of phlegm), and the *sanguine* person (characterized by warmth, optimism, and lively expressiveness, with a predominance of blood). The fourfold temperament typology was endorsed throughout the Middle Ages and Renaissance (cf. Burton, 1621/1921; Culpeper, 1657) and discussed by Kant (1798/1978). More recently, Eysenck's (1970) work made use of the typology, and Merenda (1987) has argued that it constitutes a four-factor model for our current understanding of temperament and personality. Recently, Watson and Clark (1995) discussed the melancholic temperament in connection with links between negative emotionality and psychopathology.

If we look at woodcuts from the Middle Ages representing the four temperament types, the behaviors depicted often do appear pathological. The choleric man is depicted beating a woman, the phlegmatic person is asleep in bed while others are working, and the melancholic person is seen in depressed attitude or portrayed as a distraught lover (e.g., Carlson, 1984, p. 613). The sanguine type is often depicted as better adjusted than the other three, but even the sanguine individual may be shown overeating or overdrinking. These images suggest that, at the extreme, individual differences in temperament may in themselves constitute maladaptations. One of the issues immediately raised by these historical treatments of temperament and psychopathology is thus the relation between a temperamental extreme and a psychopathological condition.

The Typological Approach of Carl Jung

In this century, the type construct has been modified conceptually, resulting in dimensional and factor-analytically derived approaches to an understanding of individual differences. Even the psychological types put forward by Jung (1923) differ in important ways from the fourfold typology. To Jung, introverted and extraverted qualities were pre-

dominant human attitudes, related to thinking, feeling, sensation, and intuition. Unlike the ancients, or Kagan's (1989) view of inhibited and uninhibited types as qualitatively different classes of individuals, Jung did not view psychological types as representing qualitative differences. Instead, he described them as "Galtonesque family portraits, which sum up in a cumulative image the common and therefore typical characters, stressing these disproportionately, while the individual features are just as disproportionately effaced" (1923, p. 513).

Jung's approach to the type is similar to the idea of the prototype in cognition (Posner & Keele, 1968; Rosch, 1973); it is also related to principles of trait measurement. In deriving a score for an individual on a temperament or personality trait, the individual's item scores on a scale are aggregated to describe a single score that represents similarity of response across time and situations. This trait score can be seen as the *individual's* "common and therefore typical" characteristics, "stressing these disproportionately"; the influence of particular situations or other important factors is also "just as disproportionately effaced." The type can then be seen as a set of traits that tend to occur together in groups of individuals. Factor-analytic approaches to temperament and personality identify clusters of characteristics that tend to covary; results of this work are described in more detail later.

Jung also suggested that introverted *and* extraverted tendencies are present in all persons, but, for a given person, one attitude tends to become more elaborated and conscious, while the other is less elaborated, more primitive, and, for the most part, unconscious. Differentiation between extraversion and introversion, he wrote, can be seen early in life:

> The earliest mark of extraversion in a child is his quick adaptation to the environment, and the extraordinary attention he gives to objects, especially to his effect upon them. Shyness in regard to objects is very slight; the child moves and lives among them with trust. He makes quick perceptions, but in a haphazard way. Apparently he develops more quickly than an introverted child, since he is less cautious, and as a rule, has no fear. Apparently, too, he feels no barrier between himself and objects, and hence he can play with them freely and learn through them. He gladly pushes his undertakings to an extreme, and risks himself in the attempt. Everything unknown seems alluring. (1928/1953, p. 303)

As objects, Jung (1923) included both physical and social entities, so that the more introverted child would show a tendency to dislike new social situations, approaching strangers with caution or fear, and the introverted adult to dislike new situations or social gatherings, demonstrating hesitation and reserve. Jung suggests that the introvert would also be inclined toward pessimism about the outcome of future events. The extraverted person would show more ready approach and action toward social and physical objects (impulsivity) and greater sociability and optimism about the future.

Jung also related extraversion-introversion to psychopathology. He took over a distinction between two types of neurosis put forward by Janet and developed the idea that the extravert is predisposed to hysteria, "characterized by an exaggerated rapport with the members of his circle, and a frankly imitatory accommodation to surrounding conditions" (Jung, 1923, p. 421), combined with a tendency toward experiencing somatic disorders. The introvert was seen as prone to psychasthenia, "a malady which is characterized on the one hand by an extreme sensitiveness, on the other by a great liability to exhaustion and chronic fatigue" (p. 479).

Factor-Analytic Studies

Extraversion-introversion also emerged from factor-analytic studies of temperament in adults. Early factor-analytic studies were carried out in Great Britain by Webb and Burt. Webb (1915) analyzed items assessing emotionality, activity, qualities of the self, and intelligence, and identified two factors. One he labeled "w," defined as "consistency of action resulting from deliberate volition or will" (p. 34). This factor bears similarities to the higher-order personality factor recently labeled control, constraint, or conscientiousness (Digman & Inouye, 1986) and to temperamental effortful control. A second factor assessed negative emotionality, sometimes labeled emotional stability-instability; Eysenck would later call it neuroticism. By 1938, Burt had also identified the factor of extraversion-introversion. Later factor-analytic work has repeatedly identified three factors similar to these: extraversion (the first factor that is usually extracted from a large data set of personality descriptors), neuroticism, and conscientiousness (Costa & McCrae, 1988; Goldberg, 1990; John, 1989). These three factors, with the additional factors of agreeableness and openness to experience, as derived from factor analyses on trait descriptive words and personality items, constitute what have been called the Big Five personality factors.

In Eysenck's (1944, 1947) early factor-analytic work on male neurotic subjects, factors of extraversion-introversion and neuroticism were extracted. He also reported support for Jung's distinction between more extraverted (hysteric) symptoms and more introverted (dysthymic or psychas-

thenic) symptoms in neurosis. Eysenck (1947) also reviewed results of a factor analysis of Ackerson's (1942) data describing a large sample of children studied by the Illinois Institute for Juvenile Research. These data yielded a general neuroticism factor, along with a factor that distinguished between more introverted behavior problems "(sensitive, absent-minded, seclusive, depressed, daydreams, inefficient, queer, inferiority feelings, and nervous), and extraverted behavior problems (such as stealing, truancy from home and school, destructive, lying, swearing, disobedient, disturbing influence, violent, rude and egocentric)" (Eysenck & Eysenck, 1985, p. 53).

There has since been extensive replication of this factor structure of psychopathology in childhood, distinguishing between internalizing problems, including inhibition, shyness, and anxiety related to introversion, and externalizing problems, including aggressive and acting-out problems related to extraversion (Achenbach & Edelbrock, 1978; Cicchetti & Toth, 1991). Results of these analyses, combined with evidence for stability of extraversion-introversion across long periods (see reviews by Bronson, 1972; Kagan, 1998; and Rothbart, 1989a), suggest that individual differences on extraversion-introversion may be basic to both a description of temperament and, in their extremes, to an individual's likelihood of demonstrating particular kinds of behavior problems or psychopathology. Later, we describe some direct and indirect links between temperament, caregiving, and risk for psychopathology. First, however, we discuss the structure of temperament.

TEMPERAMENT DIMENSIONS IN DEVELOPMENT

Much of the early research and thinking in the field of temperament in childhood has relied on Thomas and Chess's pioneering work in the New York Longitudinal Study (NYLS; A. Thomas & Chess, 1977; A. Thomas, Chess, Birch, Hertzig, & Korn, 1963). Dimensions of temperament identified by the NYLS included activity level, threshold, mood, rhythmicity, approach/withdrawal, intensity, adaptability, distractibility, and attention span/persistence. Chess and Thomas (1986; A. Thomas, Chess, & Birch, 1968) also developed the important idea of "goodness of fit" to describe situations in which there is a "match" between the temperamental characteristics of the child and the expectations of others and/or demands of the situation. In their model, a good fit would predict a more favorable mental health outcome; a poor fit or incompatibility would predict impaired function and risk of development of behavior disorders.

In their case studies of children who survived an up-bringing in multiproblem families with mental illness in one or more parents, Radke-Yarrow and Sherman (1990) identified two key protective factors. The first is very similar to Chess and Thomas's (1986) goodness-of-fit idea: "One key factor is a *match* between a psychological or physical *quality* in the child and a core *need* in one or both of the parents that the child fulfills" (Radke-Yarrow & Sherman, 1990, p. 112). The second, an extension of the first, is "the child's clear conception that there is something good and special about himself or herself. The child quality is then a source of positive self-regard for the child, as well as need-satisfying to the parent" (p. 112).

Child qualities providing a match or mismatch with parental need could be gender, appearance, intellectual or physical aptitude, or temperament. In American society generally, a positive and outgoing temperament may represent a particularly auspicious match between the child and many situational requirements; in school, effortful and/or fear control may provide a better match (Lerner, Nitz, Talwar, & Lerner, 1989). In other cultures, reserve rather than extraversion may be more generally valued (Chen, Rubin, & Li, 1995: Chen, Rubin, & Sun, 1992).

"Difficulty" in the New York Longitudinal Study Typology

A. Thomas, Chess, and associates (1963, 1968) also identified groups of children they designated as "easy," "difficult," and "slow to warm up," and their construct of "difficultness" has been frequently used in studies of the development of behavior problems. This construct stemmed from results of a factor analysis of data from the original NYLS, which identified a cluster of five temperament dimensions: approach/withdrawal, mood, intensity, adaptability, and rhythmicity, labeled as "difficult" (A. Thomas et al., 1963). In algorithms for assessing difficulty, developed by Carey and McDevitt (1978), Fullard, McDevitt, and Carey (1984), and others, difficulty is derived from extreme scores on all five dimensions.

There are several problems with the use of the difficulty construct in temperament research (for a discussion of this issue, see Plomin, 1982; Rothbart, 1982). One is the wide variability of operationalizations of the construct. Because factor analyses of data collected on the NYLS dimensions have frequently failed to yield loadings for rhythmicity in the difficulty factor (Bates, 1989), these studies often delete rhythmicity measurements or use varying composites, depending on the outcome of the factor analysis or the particular measures used in the study. Those based on the

Carey and McDevitt (1978) or Fullard et al. (1984) algorithms always include it. Inconsistency in the use of difficulty as a construct then creates serious problems for knowing what is meant by difficulty in any given study, and greater precision will result only when assessments of the construct are psychometrically sound and comparable across studies.

Bates (1980, 1989) argued that the core variable of measures of difficulty is negative emotionality, and his work used measures assessing this variable. Factor-analytic work by Bates and others also identified two kinds of negative emotionality in infancy: The first is related to children's responses to novelty and the second, more general distress proneness (Bates et al., 1979). Bates's research indicated that the two varieties of negative emotionality may be differentially related to specific behavior problems that develop later, and differentiated temperamental contributions to behavioral problems and psychopathology have consistently been found in recent research, as indicated later in this chapter and in Rothbart and Bates (in press). This differentiation is lost in the more general NYLS-based difficulty construct.

Another way of looking at difficulty is to say that some children are labeled by their caregivers as problem children at an early age, and this labeling is likely influenced by the child's temperament. Use of the terms "easy" and "difficult" may be further extended as a parent has more than one child ("The first was easy, but the second was difficult"). The terms may be applied in an endearing way or used to indicate the source of problems in family relationships. Attributions about the child may in turn contribute to developmental outcomes in the child's adaptation. Nevertheless, social attributions and values take us to a different level of analysis from measurement of temperamental dispositions in the child.

Revised Dimensions of Temperament in Infancy

In the original clinical application of the NYLS work (A. Thomas et al., 1968), no attempts were made to avoid conceptual overlap across the nine dimensions, so that individual questionnaire scales based on the NYLS have sometimes been highly overlapping in meaning. Findings of relatively high intercorrelations among scale scores designed to assess the NYLS dimensions have not been too surprising, given that a behavioral item might, in some cases, belong as easily to any one of three different scales (Rothbart & Mauro, 1990). Lack of internal homogeneity within individual scales based on some of the NYLS dimensions has also been found, which, when combined with lack of independence among scales, has led researchers in Sweden and Australia to attempt item-level factor analysis of NYLS-based parent report scales (Hagekull & Bohlin, 1981; Sanson et al., 1987).

Results of item-level factor analysis in turn led to identification of a smaller number of factors that correspond well to dimensions of temperament derived from other developmentally based theoretical approaches to temperament (Buss & Plomin, 1975, 1984; Rothbart & Derryberry, 1981). These factors include distress and inhibition to novelty (including behavioral inhibition), other distress proneness or irritability, positive affect and approach, activity level, and persistence (Rothbart & Mauro, 1990).

Gartstein and Rothbart (2003) recently studied the factor structure of expanded scales measuring parent-reported infant temperament, adapted from dimensions identified in research on temperament in childhood. Factor analysis of a large data set describing 3- to 12-month-old children yielded three broad dimensions: *surgency/extraversion,* defined primarily from scales of approach, vocal reactivity, high-intensity pleasure (stimulation seeking), smiling and laughter, activity level and perceptual sensitivity; *negative affectivity,* with loadings from sadness, frustration, fear, and, loading negatively, falling reactivity; and *orienting/regulation,* with loadings from low-intensity pleasure, cuddliness, duration of orienting and soothability, and a secondary loading for smiling and laughter. As early as infancy, there is thus evidence for three broad temperament dimensions.

Dimensions of Temperament in Childhood

We have also developed a highly differentiated and comprehensive parent report instrument called the Children's Behavior Questionnaire, or CBQ (Rothbart, Ahadi, Hershey, & Fisher, 2001). Across a number of data sets using the CBQ, three temperament systems of surgency/extraversion, negative affectivity, and effortful control have emerged from research on temperament in children 3 to 7 years of age (Lonigan & Phillips, 2001; Rothbart, Ahadi, & Hershey, 1994; Rothbart et al., 2001). The surgency factor is primarily defined by scales assessing positive emotionality and approach, including positive anticipation, high-intensity pleasure (sensation seeking), activity level, impulsivity, smiling and laughter, and a negative loading from shyness. The negative affectivity factor involves positive loadings for shyness, discomfort, fear, anger/frustration, and sadness, and a negative loading from soothability-falling reactivity. The effortful control factor is defined by positive loadings from inhibitory control, attentional focusing, low-intensity pleas-

ure (non-risk-taking pleasure), and perceptual sensitivity. These broader factors suggest a hierarchical structure to temperament, with more narrow constructs related to each other at a higher level in the hierarchy. Questions regarding breadth of temperamental predictors of psychopathology are addressed later in the chapter.

The Big Five Factors of Personality and Temperament

These childhood temperament factors conceptually and empirically map fairly well on the extraversion/positive emotionality, neuroticism/negative emotionality, and conscientiousness/constraint dimensions found in Big Five studies of the adult personality (Ahadi & Rothbart, 1994; Rothbart, Ahadi, & Evans, 2000). These broad temperament constructs further suggest that temperament dimensions go beyond lists of unrelated traits and generalized characteristics of positive and negative emotionality. Particularly important are temperament-based interactions between the child's motivational impulses and his or her efforts to constrain them.

We (Ahadi & Rothbart, 1994; Rothbart, 1989d; Rothbart & Ahadi, 1994) and Martin and Presley (1991) have indicated possible relationships between temperament factors identified for childhood and personality factors identified for adults, and in our adult research program, we have found empirical links between negative affectivity and big five neuroticism, surgency/extraversion, and extraversion, and effortful control and conscientiousness (Evans & Rothbart, 2004; Rothbart, Ahadi, et al., 2000).

In the next section, we describe conceptual and neural models developed to enhance our understanding of these dimensions. The first two dimensions are positive affectivity and approach (surgency/extraversion) and fear (distress and latency to approach novel or challenging stimuli). The third dimension, anger/irritability, is seen, along with fear, discomfort, and sadness, to represent part of a general susceptibility to negative affect. These dimensions are particularly interesting because they are related to differences observed in nonhuman animals (Gosling & John, 1999; Panksepp, 1998) and to factor structures extracted from studies of personality in adults. The fourth dimension, effortful control, is further discussed in connection with a neural model for individual differences in alerting, orienting, and executive attention (Posner & Fan, in press). We begin our more specific discussion with a consideration of positive affectivity/approach and fear.

NEURAL MODELS

Cloninger (1986, 1987), Gray (1979, 1982), LeDoux (1987, 1989), Panksepp (1982, 1986a, 1998), and Zuckerman (1984) have all made contributions to the development of neural models for temperament (Rothbart, Derryberry, & Posner, 1994). LeDoux identifies emotions as broadly integrative systems ordering feeling, thought, and action. In his analysis, emotions are seen to be the output of information-processing networks assessing the meaning or affective significance of events for the individual (LeDoux, 1989). Whereas object recognition systems and spatial processing systems address the questions "What is it?" and "Where is it?," respectively, neural emotion-processing networks answer the questions "Is it good for me?" and "Is it bad for me?," in turn influencing the organism's behavioral answers to the questions "What shall I do about it?" or simply "What shall I do?"

In the neural processing of emotion, thalamic connections route information about object qualities of a stimulus through sensory pathways, while simultaneously routing information for evaluative analysis to the limbic system and the amygdala, where memories of the affective meaning of the stimulus further influence the process (LeDoux, 1989). Later stages of object processing update the emotional analysis based on early sensory information, but, in the meantime, back projections from the amygdala influence the subsequent sensory processing of the stimulus. Output of the amygdala to organized autonomic reactions via the hypothalamus and to motor activation via the corpus striatum constitutes the motivational aspect of the emotions.

In this view, emotional processing can be seen as information processing of a special sort. Attentional neural networks can then act on emotional information similarly to their action on output of other data-processing systems, including those for object recognition, language, and motor control, each of which in turn has its own underlying neural networks (Posner & Fan, in press; Posner & Petersen, 1990). Neuroimaging studies demonstrate connections between emotional processing networks and the anterior attention system, including the anterior cingulate, that allow attentional influence on the selection of emotional information for conscious processing, a consequence of which is that we may or may not be aware of our emotional evaluations (Bush, Luu, & Posner, 2000; Posner & Rothbart, 1992). However, the attentional controls on emotion may be somewhat limited and difficult to establish. Panksepp (1998, p. 319) lays out anatomical reasons why the regula-

tion of emotion may pose a difficult problem for the child as follows:

> One can ask whether the downward cognitive controls or the upward emotional controls are stronger. If one looks at the question anatomically and neurochemically, the evidence seems overwhelming. The upward controls are more abundant and electrophysiologically more insistent: hence one might expect they would prevail if push came to shove. Of course, with the increasing influence of cortical functions as humans develop, along with the pressures for social conformity, the influences of the cognitive forces increase steadily during maturation. We can eventually experience emotions without sharing them with others. We can easily put on false faces, which can make the facial analysis of emotions in real-life situations a remarkably troublesome business.

Attentional systems can act on and influence conscious aspects of emotional analyses, and emotion also influences the focusing and shifting of attention (Derryberry & Reed, 1994, 1996; Gray, 1982). An important aspect of social adaptation involves the appropriateness of the person's social interaction and related acceptance by others (Parker & Asher, 1987). Information about the state of others is an important contributor to appropriate social action, and failure of access of this information to action and consciousness can be a critical element in the development of disordered functioning (Blair, Jones, Clark, & Smith, 1997). Focusing attention on threatening stimuli or on the self also may make access to information about others less accessible. These are important examples of information-processing aspects of temperament, with implications for social development and psychopathology.

Positive Affectivity and Approach

We now briefly consider neural models developed to describe a physical substrate for approach and inhibition. Based on animal research, Gray (1979, 1982) described the behavioral activation system (BAS), involving sensitivity to rewards, and the behavioral inhibition system (BIS), involving sensitivity to punishment, nonreward, novelty, and innate fear stimuli. These two systems are seen as mutually inhibitory, with their balance determining degrees of extraversion-introversion. Gray (1971, 1975) also posited a fight/flight system moderating unconditioned punishment. According to Gray's model of the BAS, reward-related projections from the amygdala to the nucleus accumbens activate the next step in a motor program that maximally increases proximity to the desired stimulus. Converging dopaminergic projections to the accumbens enable the switch to this neuronal set, facilitating goal-oriented behavior (Gray, 1994; Gray & McNaughton, 1996).

In a broader behavioral facilitation system (BFS), Depue and Collins (1999) propose a circuit involving the nucleus accumbens, ventral pallidum, and dopaminergic neurons that codes the intensity of the rewarding stimuli, while related circuits involving the medial orbital cortex, amygdala, and hippocampus integrate the "salient incentive context." Individual differences in the functioning of this network are thought to arise from functional variation in dopaminergic projections that encode the intensity of the incentive motivation and facilitate contextual processing across multiple limbic and frontal sites. As development proceeds, dopaminergic facilitation helps to stabilize synaptic contacts in the medial orbital and limbic circuits and thus to enhance responsivity to positive incentive stimuli (Depue & Collins, 1999).

Depue and Iacono (1989) originally posited the BFS to help account for Bipolar Affective Disorders. The BFS involves the individual's initiation of locomotor activity, incentive-reward motivation, exploration of environmental novelty (if the stimulus and its context do not induce opposing fear reactions), and irritable aggression. In Depue and Iacono's model, nucleus accumbens dopamine (DA) activity "appears to modulate the flow of motivational information from the limbic system to the motor system, and thereby contributes to the process of initiating locomotor activity, incentive, and goal-directed behavior" (p. 470). Panksepp (1982, 1986a, 1998) also reviewed the literature on DA effects, concluding that "the general function of DA activity in appetitive behavior is to promote the expression of motivational excitement and anticipatory eagerness— the heightened energization of animals searching for and expecting rewards" (1986a, p. 91). Cloninger (1986, 1987) specified a novelty-seeking dimension related to DA functioning, as did Zuckerman (1984) in his dimension of sensation seeking (see review by Rothbart, 1989b).

Tellegen's (1985) factor-analytic research on personality in adults identified positive emotionality, a broad factor that includes positive affect and anticipation, and Watson and Clark (1997) have argued that there is a positive affect core to individual differences in extraversion. In research on infants (Rothbart, 1988; Rothbart, Derryberry, & Hershey, 2000), we have found expressions of positive affect (smiling and laughter) to be positively related to infants' rapid latency to approach objects and to predict anticipatory eagerness about upcoming positive events when the same children were 7 years old.

In recent functional magnetic resonance imaging (fMRI) research, Canli et al. (2001) found that the brain's activation to positive and negative pictures varied depending on the subject's temperament or personality. Persons higher in extraversion showed greater brain response to positive than to negative stimuli in widespread frontal, temporal, and limbic activation of both hemispheres. Subjects higher in neuroticism reacted more to the negative than to the positive stimuli, and showed more circumscribed activation (frontotemporal) on the left side and deactivation in a right frontal area. These findings also demonstrated a positive emotional bias for extraverts and a negative bias for those high in neuroticism.

A quite different set of brain areas proved to be active in studies of persistence, a dimension of personality conceptually related to effortful control in temperament (Gusnard et al., 2003). The effects of persistence acted strongly on midline and lateral prefrontal areas that are quite different from those found active for positive and negative affect, suggesting regulatory aspects of persistence. An increasingly popular view is that effortful control (persistence) is represented in midline frontal areas and acts to regulate brain areas like the amygdala that are more clearly related to reactive aspects of negative affect (Posner & Rothbart, 2000).

Fear and Behavioral Inhibition

Factor analyses of infant temperament questionnaires have reliably yielded two distress factors: one involving distress to novelty, and the other, irritability, including distress to limitations or frustration (Rothbart & Mauro, 1990). In our recent revision of the Infant Behavior Questionnaire, we also found a higher-order negative emotionality factor that includes fear and frustration (Gartstein & Rothbart, 2003). The distress to novelty factor is linked to an extended latency to approach new objects (Rothbart, 1988), and a combination of behavioral inhibition and distress proneness to novelty appears to correspond to the introverted pole of a broader extraversion-introversion dimension.

Fear is an emotional response activated in the presence of threat or signals of upcoming danger, and its function appears to be a defensive one. Fear activation is accompanied by inhibition of ongoing motor programs and preparation of response systems controlling coping options such as fleeing, fighting, or hiding (see review by Rothbart, Derryberry, et al., 1994). In Gray's (1991) model, the fear-related BIS is based on circuits that include the orbital frontal cortex, medial septal area, and the hippocampus. However, the amygdala has been more often identified as the critical structure in the processing of conditioned fear (LeDoux, 1989).

Emotional networks involving the amygdala also appear to respond more strongly to novel than to familiar stimuli (Nishijo, Ono, & Nishino, 1988). Lesions of the amygdala in rodents disrupt autonomic and cortisol reactions, behavioral freezing, and fear vocalizations, and similar findings have been reported in primates (Lawrence & Calder, in press). In humans, functional neuroimaging studies by Calder, Lawrence, and Young (2001) and others support involvement of the amygdala in both acquiring and expressing fear, although not in the voluntary production of facial expressions of fear (A. K. Anderson & Phelps, 2002). The amygdala also is involved in the recognition of fear in the human face (Calder et al., 2001), and there is evidence in humans with amygdalar damage of reduced fear experience (Adolphs et al., 1999; Sprengelmeyer et al., 1999).

Projections from the amygdala implement autonomic and behavioral components of fear, including startle, motor inhibition, facial expression, and cardiovascular and respiratory change (Davis, Hitchcock, & Rosen, 1987). Individual variability in the structure and functioning of any of these subsystems may be related to variations in behavioral expressions of fear, and multiple components of other affective motivational systems such as approach/positive affect and anger/irritable distress would also be expected.

The amygdala also appears to affect information processing within the cortex. For example, the basolateral nucleus of the amygdala projects to frontal and cingulate regions involved in the executive attention system (Posner & Petersen, 1990), as well as to ventral occipital and temporal pathways involved in processing object information. These connections are consistent with the finding that anxious individuals show enhanced attention to threatening sources of information (e.g., Derryberry & Reed, 1994).

A psychobiological analysis of fear suggests that there may be less disagreement about temperament variables than had been previously thought. Fear includes components of arousal, felt emotion, motor response preparation for flight and/or attack (with responses often inhibited), and attention to the fear-inducing stimulus and/or possible escape routes (Davis et al., 1987). When temperament researchers study the construct, they sometimes stress its motivational aspects (e.g., A. Thomas & Chess's, 1977, approach/withdrawal; Kagan's, 1994, behavioral inhibition), its distress proneness aspects (Buss & Plomin's, 1975, emotionality; Goldsmith & Campos's, 1982, fear), its duration and susceptibility to interventions (Rothbart's, 1981, soothability),

its relation to arousal (Strelau's, 1983, reactivity), or multiple components of response (Rothbart & Derryberry's, 1981, fear). If we take the broader view of fear as suggested by the neuroscience analysis, however, agreement is more evident. Intercorrelations among scales measuring the differently named constructs further support this contention (Goldsmith, Rieser-Danner, & Briggs, 1991).

Differences in cerebral hemispheric activation have been related to temperamental tendencies toward approach versus inhibition-withdrawal. Evidence from electrophysiological (EEG) and lesion studies has related higher anterior left hemisphere activation in response to stimulation to increased positive affect and/or decreased negative affect (see reviews by Davidson et al., 2003; Davidson & Tomarken, 1989). The reverse relationships—higher anterior right hemisphere activation related to higher negative affect and/or decreased positive affect—have also been reported. Resting EEG asymmetries have also been related to positive and negative emotional reactivity (e.g., Davidson & Fox, 1989; Tomarken, Davidson, Wheeler, & Doss, 1992). Harmon-Jones and Allen (1997), for example, reported greater left than right-frontal cortical activity in women subjects with higher scores on Carver and White's (1994) BAS questionnaire. The BIS measure was not related to asymmetry. Buss et al. (2003) found relations between extreme right EEG asymmetry and basal and reactive cortisol, replicating primate findings from Kalin and his colleagues (Kalin, Larson, Shelton, & Davidson, 1998).

N. A. Fox, Calkins, and Bell (1994) found that infants with stable right frontal EEG asymmetry between 9 and 24 months of age displayed more fearfulness and inhibition in the laboratory than other children. At 4 years, children who showed more reticence and social withdrawal were also more likely to show right frontal asymmetry. Calkins, Fox, and Marshall (1996) reported that children selected for high motor activity and negative affect to laboratory stimulation at 4 months showed greater right frontal asymmetry at 9 months, mother reports of greater fear at 9 months, and more inhibited behavior at 14 months. However, no concurrent relation was found between behavior and frontal asymmetry at 9 and 14 months, and greater activation of both right and left frontal areas was related to higher inhibition scores at 14 months. Calkins et al. suggest a need to differentiate between fearful and angry distress, as discussed in the "Revised Dimensions of Temperament in Infancy" section. They also hypothesize that infant high motor/high negative affect and high motor/high positive affect may be associated with different kinds of problems developing later. For high motor/high positive affect, the problems would be associated with difficulties in control rather than inhibition.

Anger/Irritability and Aggressive Behavior

In Gray's (1991) model, a fight/flight system is constituted by circuits connecting the amygdala, ventromedial nucleus of the hypothalamus, central gray region of the midbrain, and somatic and motor effector nuclei of the lower brain stem, processing information involving unconditioned punishment and nonreward. When there is detection of painful or frustrating input, the brain stem effectors produce aggressive or defensive behavior. Panksepp (1982) discusses similar neural circuitry in terms of a "rage" system (see review by Rothbart, Derryberry, et al., 1994).

Important distinctions have more recently been made among different varieties of aggression and anger, in relation to their underlying neural systems. Aggression as a self-defense reaction seems to be based on the functioning of the same amygdala circuits as those involved in the production of fear (Blanchard & Takahashi, 1988). Aggression linked to protection of resources, competition, and offensive aggression, on the other hand, involves a different neural system based on the monoamine dopamine (Lawrence & Calder, in press). The DA system has been linked to both the production of offensive aggression (Smeets & González, 2000) and to the recognition of anger in the human face (Lawrence, Calder, McGowan, & Grasby, 2002). In Lawrence et al.'s study, DA blockade impaired the recognition of anger, whereas recognition of other emotions and of facial identity was spared.

Depue and Iacono (1989) suggest that the dopaminergic system may facilitate irritable aggression aimed at removing a frustrating obstacle, consistent with findings that DA agonists (e.g., amphetamine) can enhance aggressive behaviors. Their view suggests links between approach and frustration/anger, and, in fact, infants' and children's activity level and anger have been consistently positively related in parent-reported temperament (Rothbart & Derryberry, 2002). Moreover, infant activity level predicts not only positive emotionality at age 7 years, but also anger/frustration and low soothability-falling reactivity (Rothbart, Derryberry, et al., 2000). Together with findings relating 7-year surgency to aggression (Rothbart, Derryberry, et al., 2000), this suggests that strong approach tendencies may be linked to negative as well as positive emotions (Derryberry & Reed, 1994; Rothbart, Derryberry, et al., 2000). Children who quickly grasped objects during infancy showed 7-year high levels of positive anticipation and impulsivity, as well as high anger/frustration and aggression, again suggesting that strong approach tendencies can contribute to later specific negative emotions as well as to positive emotionality.

Negative Emotionality or General Distress Proneness

Negative emotionality or distress proneness is often viewed as a general dimension subsuming the emotions of fear, anticipatory anxiety, sadness, frustration/anger, guilt, and discomfort. For example, the Five-Factor model of adult personality includes negative emotions as components of the neuroticism superfactor. Neuroticism/negative emotionality has been found to be orthogonal to extraversion/positive emotionality (Eysenck & Eysenck, 1985; Tellegen, 1985; Watson, & Clark, 1992). As evident in our previous discussion, however, the positive relationship between anger/frustration and strong approach tendencies suggests that a more differentiated model is needed.

There are several possibilities for neural systems supporting higher-order negative emotion reactions. One is the link between systems supporting fear and self-defensive aggression (Blanchard & Takahashi, 1988). Defensive aggression in animal models seems to be based on the same amygdalar circuits as fear, and in humans, anger in response to threat may also be linked to fear. Negative affect systems are also regulated by more general neurochemical systems, including dopaminergic and serotonergic projections arising from the midbrain, and by circulating gonadal and corticosteroid hormones (Rothbart, Derryberry, et al., 1994; Zuckerman, 1995). Neurochemical influences may thus also provide coherence of emotional states in an individual and support more general factors of temperament such as negative emotionality.

For example, serotonergic projections from the midbrain raphe nuclei appear to moderate limbic circuits related to anxiety and aggression (Spoont, 1992). Low serotonergic activity may thus increase an individual's vulnerability to both fear and frustration, contributing to a general factor of negative affectivity, including depression. Molecular genetics studies related to serotonin function are therefore of interest in identifying negative affect as a general diathesis. Lesch et al. (1996), for example, have reported relations between a polymorphism of the serotonin transporter gene and measures of anxiety, depression, and neuroticism.

Affiliativeness/Agreeableness

We share with other animals, including mammals, birds, and fish, systems of affiliation that support pair bonds and care of the young (Insel, 2003). Panksepp (1986b) indicates that affiliative and prosocial behaviors may depend in part on opiate projections from higher limbic regions (e.g., amygdala, cingulate cortex) to the ventromedial hypothalamus, with brain opiates promoting social comfort and bonding, and opiate withdrawal promoting irritability and aggressiveness. Because ventromedial hypothalamic lesions dramatically increase aggression, Panksepp also suggests that this brain region normally inhibits aggressive behaviors controlled by the midbrain's central gray area. Hypothalamic projections can allow for friendly, trusting, and helpful behaviors between members of a species by suppressing aggressive tendencies. Mechanisms underlying prosocial and aggressive behaviors would in this way be reciprocally related, in keeping with the bipolar agreeableness-hostility dimension found in Five Factor model of personality.

Panksepp (1993) has also reviewed research suggesting links between social bonding and the hypothalamic neuropeptide oxytocin (OXY), involved in maternal behavior, feelings of social acceptance and social bonding, and reduction of separation distress. OXY is also released during sexual activity by both females and males. In Cloninger's (1987) theory, *reward dependence* is a dimension ranging from being emotionally dependent, warmly sympathetic, sentimental, persistent, and sensitive to social cues to being socially detached, cool, tough-minded, and independently self-willed. He sees reward dependence as related to social motivation; it is thus similar to dimensions of affiliativeness or agreeableness.

Agreeableness, including at the high end the prosocial emotions and behaviors and affiliative tendencies, and at the low end aggression and manipulativeness, has been increasingly studied in childhood (Graziano, 1994; Graziano & Eisenberg, 1997; Graziano & Tobin, 2002). Like other originally bipolar dimensions, prosocial and antagonistic dispositions have been studied separately (Bohart & Stipek, 2001), and Graziano and Eisenberg (1997) suggest that the two dispositions may be separable, even though they are negatively related. In a related argument, Shiner and Caspi (2003) point out that antisocial and prosocial behaviors have different etiologies (Krueger, Hicks, & McGue, 2001). Any temperamental predisposition to prosocial behavior needs to be seen as an open system, interacting with social experience for its outcomes. In research linking parent-reported temperament to personality in early and middle childhood, two forms of extraversion/surgency have been identified; one is linked to prosocial behavior and the other to antisocial behavior and aggression (Rothbart & Victor, 2004), again suggesting the importance of socialization to the development of pro- or antisocial behavior.

Attentional Networks

Functional neuroimaging has allowed many cognitive tasks to be analyzed in terms of the brain areas they activate, and studies of attention have been among the most examined (Corbetta & Shulman, 2002; Driver, Eimer, & Macaluso, in press; Posner & Fan, in press). Imaging data support the presence of three networks related to different aspects of attention. These networks carry out the functions of alerting, orienting, and executive control (Posner & Fan, in press). A summary of the anatomy and transmitters involved in the three networks is shown in Table 11.1.

Alerting is defined as achieving and maintaining a state of high sensitivity to incoming stimuli; orienting is the selection of information from sensory input; executive control involves the mechanisms for monitoring and resolving conflict among thoughts, feelings, and responses.

The alerting system has been associated with frontal and parietal regions of the right hemisphere. A particularly effective way to vary alertness has been to use warning signals prior to targets. The influence of warning signals on alertness is thought to be due to modulation of neural activity by the neurotransmitter norepinephrine (Marrocco & Davidson, 1998).

Orienting involves aligning attention with a source of sensory signals. This may be overt, as in eye movements, or may occur covertly, without any movement. Orienting to visual events has been associated with posterior brain areas, including the superior parietal lobe and temporal parietal junction and the frontal eye fields (Corbetta & Shulman, 2002). Orienting can be manipulated by presenting a directional or symbolic cue indicating where in space a person should attend, thereby directing attention to the cued location (Posner, 1980). Event-related fMRI studies have suggested that the superior parietal lobe is associated with orienting following the presentation of a symbolic cue (Corbetta & Shulman, 2002). The superior parietal lobe in humans is closely related to the lateral intraparietal area in monkeys, which is known to produce eye movements (R. A. Anderson, 1989). When a target occurs at an uncued location and attention has to be disengaged and moved to a new

TABLE 11.1 Brain Areas and Neuromodulators Involved in Attention Networks

Function	Structures	Modulator
Orient	Superior parietal	
	Temporal parietal junction	
	Frontal eye fields	
	Superior colliculus	Acetylcholine
Alert	Locus coeruleus	
	Right frontal and parietal cortex	Norepinephrine
Executive attention	Anterior cingulate	
	Lateral ventral prefrontal	
	Basal ganglia	Dopamine

location, there is activity in the temporal parietal junction (Corbetta & Shulman, 2002). Lesions of the parietal lobe and superior temporal lobe have been consistently related to difficulties in orienting (Karnath, Ferber, & Himmelbach, 2001).

The second major temperamental control system over reactive approach and action (the first is reactive fear) is effortful control, supported by development of the executive attention network. Executive control of attention is often studied by tasks that involve conflict, such as various versions of the Stroop task. In the Stroop task, subjects must respond to the color of ink (e.g., red) while ignoring the color word name (e.g., blue; Bush et al., 2000). Resolving conflict in the Stroop task activates midline frontal areas (anterior cingulate) and the lateral prefrontal cortex (Botwinick, Braver, Barch, Carter, & Cohen, 2001; Fan, Flombaum, McCandliss, Thomas, & Posner, 2003). There is also evidence for the activation of this network in tasks involving conflict between a central target and surrounding flankers that may be congruent or incongruent with the target (Botwinick et al., 2001; Fan, McCandliss, Sommer, Raz, & Posner, 2002). Experimental tasks may provide a means of fractionating the functional contributions of different areas within the executive attention network (MacDonald, Cohen, Stenger, & Carter, 2000).

Regulatory Functions of Attention

The anterior cingulate gyrus, one of the main nodes of the executive attention network, has been linked to a variety of specific functions in attention (Posner & Fan, in press), working memory (Duncan et al., 2000), emotion (Bush et al., 2000), pain (Rainville, Duncan, Price, Carrier, & Bushnell, 1997), and monitoring for conflict (Botwinick et al., 2001) and for error (Holroyd & Coles, 2002). These functions have been well documented, but no single rubric seems to explain all of them. In emotion studies, the cingulate is often seen as part of a network involving orbital frontal and limbic (amygdala) structures. The frontal areas seem to have an ability to interact with the limbic system (Davidson, Putnam, & Larson, 2000), which could fit well with the idea that attention subserves self-regulation.

A specific test of a self-regulatory role for the cingulate involves exposure to erotic films, with the requirement to regulate any resulting arousal. The cingulate activity shown by fMRI was found to increase in relation to the regulatory instruction (Beauregard, Levesque, & Bourgoulin, 2001). In a different study, cognitive reappraisal of photographs producing negative affect showed a positive correlation between the extent of cingulate activity and the amount of affect to be controlled (Ochsner, Bunge, Gross, & Gabrieli, 2002). Similarly, in a study in which hypno-

tism was used to control the perception of pain, cingulate activity reflected the degree of pain as rated by the subject under hypnotism rather than the physical intensity of the heat stimulus (Rainville et al., 1997). These results show a role for the anterior cingulate in regulating limbic activity related to emotion and provide evidence for its role as a part of a network involved in regulation, cognition, and affect (Bush et al., 2000).

In experimental paradigms like the Stroop and flanker tasks, conflict is introduced by the need to respond to one aspect of the stimulus while ignoring another (Bush et al., 2000; Fan, Flombaum, et al., 2003). Cognitive activity that involves this kind of conflict activates the dorsal anterior cingulate and lateral prefrontal cortex. Large lesions of the anterior cingulate either in adults (Damasio, 1994) or children (S. W. Anderson, Damasio, Tranel, & Damasio, 2000) result in great difficulty in regulating behavior, particularly in social situations. Smaller lesions may produce only a temporary inability to deal with conflict in cognitive tasks (Turken & Swick, 1999; Ochsner et al., 2002).

A major advantage of viewing attention in relation to self-regulation is that knowledge of the development of a specific neural network can be linked to the ability of children and adults to regulate their thoughts and feelings. Over the early years of life, regulation of emotion and behavior is a major issue of development, and issues of dysregulation continue to play a role in psychopathology in adults.

TEMPERAMENT AND ADAPTATION

Developmental studies of nondisordered children are consistent with models such as Gray and McNaughton's (1996), where an anxiety-related behavioral inhibition system inhibits an approach-related behavioral activation system. Fearful inhibition is well developed by the end of the 1st year of life, and if a disposition to behavioral inhibition is strong, expressive, approach and avoidance behavior will be moderated under novel or challenging situations. In nondisordered children, measures of infants' fearfulness in the laboratory negatively predict mothers' reports of children's impulsivity, activity, and aggression at age 7. Fearfulness in infancy also positively predicted susceptibility to guilt and shame, two powerful socializing emotions (Rothbart, Ahadi, et al., 1994; Rothbart, Derryberry, et al., 2000).

Approach, Frustration, and Aggression

Together with the earlier finding relating 7-year surgency to aggression (Rothbart, Derryberry, et al., 1994), this suggests that strong approach tendencies may contribute to negative as well as positive emotionality (Derryberry & Reed, 1994; Rothbart, Derryberry, et al., 1994). Infants who showed strong approach in their short-latency grasps of objects at 6.5, 10, and 13.5 months showed high levels of positive anticipation and impulsivity, along with high anger/frustration and aggression at 7 years. This again suggests that strong approach tendencies contribute to later negative as well as positive emotionality.

Children showing rapid approach as infants also tended to be low in attentional and inhibitory control at age 7, and suggesting that strong approach tendencies may constrain the development of voluntary self-control. If approach tendencies are viewed as the "accelerator" toward action and inhibitory tendencies as the "brakes," it is not surprising that stronger accelerative tendencies may weaken the braking influence of inhibitory control (Rothbart & Derryberry, 2002).

In our laboratory study, frustration at 6 and 10 months predicted 7-year anger/frustration but not fear, as well as other components of negative affectivity, including high discomfort, high guilt/shame, and low soothability (Rothbart, Derryberry, et al., 2000). Greater infant frustration in the laboratory was also related to higher 7-year activity level, positive anticipation, impulsivity, aggression, and high-intensity pleasure. Whereas infant fear is thus related to relatively weak approach behavior and to internalizing tendencies in childhood, infant frustration is related to stronger approach and to externalizing as well as internalizing tendencies. This finding is consistent with Panksepp's (1998) suggestion that unsuccessful reward-related activities may activate the anger/frustration functions of a rage system. Strong approach tendencies may include positive expectations and frustrated reactions under conditions when those expectations are not met.

Fear, Aggression, and Over-Control

Fear appears to take on an important inhibitory role in early development, constraining approach and aggression, acting as a protective factor for the development of externalizing, and contributing to the development of conscience. In addition to Kochanska's findings on fear and the development of conscience (reviewed by Rothbart & Bates, in press), children with concurrent Attention-Deficit/Hyperactivity Disorder (ADHD) and anxiety also show reduced impulsivity relative to children with ADHD alone (Pliszka, 1989), and aggressiveness appears to decrease between kindergarten and first grade in children who show internalizing patterns of behavior (Bates, Maslin, & Frankel, 1995).

From an evolutionary point of view, fearful inhibition can serve to protect the individual from approaching potentially harmful objects or situations. Nevertheless, the fearful form of inhibitory control remains a relatively reactive process that can be easily elicited by situational cues. In the course of development, this system can lead to rigid and overcontrolled patterns of behavior that can limit the individual's positive experiences with the world (Block & Block, 1980; Kremen & Block, 1998).

Shiner and her colleagues have recently been studying the continuity of personality from the period 8 to 12 years to 20 years (Shiner, Masten, & Tellegen, 2002) and 30 years (Shiner, Masten, & Roberts, 2003). Tellegen's self-report MPQ contains three broad personality factors. Positive emotionality (PEM) includes scales for well-being, achievement, social potency, and social closeness. Negative emotionality (NEM) includes scales for stress reaction, alienation, and aggression. Constraint (CON) includes scales for control, harm avoidance, and traditionalism. PEM was moderately predicted at age 20 by childhood mastery motivation, surgent engagement, and self-assurance in middle childhood (Shiner et al., 2002). PEM was also related to concurrent social and romantic competencies at 20 years, but not to any of the childhood measures of adaptation. NEM at 20, however, was related to childhood low adaptation in all areas and to all concurrent adaptation measures except romantic competence. Even controlling for childhood personality, lower academic achievement and greater conduct problems in childhood continued to predict adult NEM. Childhood mastery motivation and surgent engagement were inversely related to NEM in adulthood. At age 20, CON was predicted by earlier lower self-assurance and higher academic competence, but when childhood personality was controlled, it was not related to childhood adaptation.

Shiner et al. (2002) suggest on the basis of longitudinal findings that positive emotionality might be more closely linked to current adaptation, whereas negative emotionality shows more continuity with earlier adaptation. Later in the chapter, we note strong links between negative emotionality and psychopathology, both in childhood and adulthood. Negative emotionality is also particularly linked to behavior problems when effortful control is low (Eisenberg, Fabes, Guthrie, & Reiser, 2000). How might this occur? First, mental processing related to distress may have involved attempts to decrease distress, possibly including calling up repeated memories of the negative event. Positive experiences are likely to have been less rehearsed. Thus, when mental processing has been tied to difficult and painful situations in the past, one may face not only current problems, but also representations in memory of adaptations to events. Well-practiced associations make links between negative affect, cognition, and action links stronger. Thus, early failure, such as poor achievement in school, may create the possibility of long-term negative affect that extends to a range of achievement situations later in life. Shiner et al. also found that adults high on negative emotionality were particularly upset by daily problems (Suls, Martin, & David, 1998).

Preschool Behavior and Adult Problems

Caspi et al. (2003) linked observations of 1,000 children at age 3 to their self-reported personality at age 26 (96% of the original sample). Undercontrolled children (10% of the sample) had been temperamentally impulsive, restless, distractible, and negativistic at age 3; confident children (28%) were friendly, eager, and somewhat impulsive; inhibited children (8%) were fearful, reticent, and easily upset; reserved children (15%) were timid but not extreme in shyness; well-adjusted children (40%) appeared to be capable of self-control, were adequately self-confident, and did not become upset during testing. At age 26, previously undercontrolled children were higher in negative emotionality, more alienated, and subject to stress reactions. They also tended to follow a traditional morality. Formerly inhibited and reserved children were high in harm avoidance, low in social potency (less vigorous, dynamic, forceful), and low in achievement. Both previously undercontrolled and confident children were low in harm avoidance. Confident children were high on social potency, whereas inhibited children were high in constraint and low in positive emotionality.

Caspi et al.'s (2003) findings provide evidence that the temperament of the child truly provides a core for the developing aspects of personality. Undercontrolled children, who combined extraversion/surgency, negative affect, and low attentional control at age 3, showed neurotic and alienated tendencies as adults. Confident extraverted children were confident and unfearful as adults. The more shy and fearful inhibited and reserved children maintained their caution and harm avoidance and were low in social potency, whereas the more extreme inhibited children were also high in constraint (a mixture of fearfulness and self-control) and low in positive emotionality and social support. The most interesting aspect of the results, however, go beyond temperament to touch on alienation, traditional values, and social support. Additional research on these topics is needed.

TEMPERAMENT, ATTENTION, AND PSYCHOPATHOLOGY

In this section, we discuss studies that have linked temperament and attention to the development of behavior problems and other forms of psychopathology. Two concerns must be taken into account, however, in reviewing this literature. First, although studies have identified links between temperament and behavior problems or psychopathology, it is difficult to determine the direction of influence. Although temperament extremes may predispose a person to problems, an alternative interpretation is that the problems associated with the disorder lead to extremes in the behavior measured as temperament. For example, punishment from peers and teachers may lead to increased negative affect in the child. Asendorpf's (1989, 1990) model for the development of shyness follows two developmental routes: one is early appearing and related directly to temperament (social fearfulness); the other is indirect and operates through peer rejection and punishment. In the latter case, the child's shyness may have been not present initially but is shaped through social experience. In Asendorpf and van Aken's (1994) longitudinal research, only the latter form of shyness was related to the development of later problems in self-evaluation.

Another important issue raised by a number of investigators (e.g., Barron & Earls, 1984; Prior, Sanson, Oberklaid, & Northam, 1987; Sanson, Prior, & Kyrios, 1990; Wertlieb, Wiegel, Springer, & Feldstein, 1987), is the possible confounding of assessments of temperament and behavior problems, especially when they are assessed by the same rater (usually the mother). For example, items used to measure temperamental dimensions such as activity, approach/withdrawal, and adaptability may be very similar to items assessing behavior problems such as hyperactivity, anxiety, and oppositional behavior. Bates (1990), on the other hand, argued that if temperament contributes to the development of behavior problems, then conceptual overlap across constructs would be theoretically expected.

Lengua, West, and Sandler (1998) addressed possible contamination of measures by eliminating overlapping items between temperament and symptom measures; associations were nevertheless found between negative emotionality and depression, and between impulsivity and conduct problems in a large sample of children of divorce. In further support of Lengua et al.'s findings, Lemery, Essex, and Smider (2002) asked experts to categorize CBQ items (Rothbart et al., 2001) and behavior problem symptoms (Preschool Behavior Questionnaire; Behar & Stringfield, 1974) as temperament and/or behavior problem constructs. Factor analysis of longitudinal multi-informant combined data was also used. With the latter method, 9% of temperament and 23% of symptom items were confounded.

Removing all confounded items did not affect the extensive relation between the two measures, including mothers' reports of temperament predicting fathers' and caregivers' reports of behavior problems. Temperament at 3 to 4 years also predicted later *Diagnostic and Statistical Manual of Mental Disorders IV* (*DSM-IV*) symptoms at age 5 (Lemery et al., 2002). Activity level, attentional focusing, and inhibitory control predicted ADHD better than internalizing or externalizing, but the general finding was that high negative emotionality and low effortful control predicted children's problems. Because the CBQ allowed further differentiation of the negative affectivity construct, anger was found to predict externalizing, whereas fear and shyness predicted internalizing problems.

Finally, Sheeber (1995; Sheeber & Johnson, 1994) used a treatment outcome study to address the overlap issue. In her research, parents were trained in a temperament-focused approach to parenting. In posttreatment assessment, differences were found for the trained parents in behavior problem ratings, but not temperament ratings. Children's behavior was reported as improved on both internalizing and externalizing measures. Although the temperament-focused content may have influenced this finding, Sheeber (1995) reviews another study with similar findings that used a behavior management program (Webster-Stratton & Eyberg, 1982).

Models and Research

Clark, Watson, and Mineka (1994) follow Tellegen (1985) in describing negative affectivity (NA) or neuroticism as a temperamental sensitivity to negative stimuli. Those high in NA

> experience a broad range of negative moods, including not only fear/anxiety and sadness/depression but also such emotions as guilt, hostility, and self-dissatisfaction (Watson & Clark, 1984). A wide range of nonmood variables are related to this affective core, including negative cognitions (Clark, Beck, & Stewart, 1990), somatic complaints (Watson & Pennebaker, 1989), negativistic appraisals of self and others (Gara et al., 1993), diverse personality characteristics such as hardiness, pessimism, and low self-esteem, and various indices of job, marital and life dissatisfaction. (Clark et al., 1994, p. 104)

Watson, Clark, and Harkness (1994) also identify an affective core to positive affectivity or extraversion, ranging from "joyful, enthusiastic, energetic, friendly, bold, assertive, proud, and confident" to "dull, flat, disinterested, and unenthusiastic" (p. 106). In their review of the adult literature, including measures of negativity predating the onset of depression, Watson et al. concluded that temperamental negative affect is generally related to the mood disorders of both depression and anxiety, whereas low positive affect appears to be more specifically related to depression. In this case, two general temperamental dispositions would be seen as predispositions to depression, one to anxiety.

As noted earlier, externalizing disorders include aggression, overactivity, delinquency, ADHD, Conduct Disorder, and Antisocial Disorder (Achenbach & Edelbrock, 1978; Cicchetti & Toth, 1991). Using factor scores derived from *DSM-IV* items to assess these problems, scores based on hyperactivity-impulsivity, Conduct Disorder, and Oppositional Defiant Disorder are highly intercorrelated, and all three are highly correlated with attentional problems (Hartman et al., 2001). Internalizing problems include extreme shyness or inhibition, sensitivity, anxiety and depression. In Hartman et al.'s study of measures of child psychopathology based on the *DSM-IV*, anxiety and depression scores were highly intercorrelated, and both were correlated with attention problems. The temperamental characteristic most often linked to internalizing problems is negative emotionality, but links have also been made between low positive emotionality and depression and between the mood disorders and attentional control. Theoretical and empirical models are increasingly using both temperamental and environmental variables in predicting outcomes.

Differentiated Negative Emotionality and Behavior Disorders

We first consider studies in which differentiated measures of affect and self-regulation (effortful control) were used to predict both internalizing and externalizing behavior problems. In the Bloomington Longitudinal Study (BLS), infant and toddler Infant Characteristics Questionnaire (ICQ) temperamental difficultness (frequent and intense negative affect and attention demanding) predicted later externalizing and internalizing problems, as seen in the mother-child relationship, from the preschool to the middle-childhood periods (Bates & Bayles, 1988; Bates, Bayles, Bennett, Ridge, & Brown, 1991; Bates et al., 1985; Lee & Bates, 1985). Early negative reactivity to novel situations (unadaptability) predicted less consistently, but when it did, it predicted internalizing problems to a greater extent than externalizing problems. Early resistance to control (perhaps akin to the manageability dimension of Hagekull, 1989, and at least partly related to the construct of effortful control) predicted externalizing problems more than internalizing problems. This was also found in predicting externalizing problems at school in both the BLS and in a separate longitudinal study, the Child Development Project (CDP; Bates, Pettit, Dodge, & Ridge, 1998).

In a structural modeling analysis of CDP data dealing with the overlap in externalizing and internalizing symptoms, Keiley, Lofthouse, Bates, Dodge, and Pettit (2003) separated mother and teacher reports of 5 to 14 year olds' behavior problems into pure externalizing, pure internalizing, and covarying scores, and then considered early childhood predictors of each of these scores. Resistant temperament (unmanageability) predicted the mother- and teacher-rated externalizing problems but not the internalizing ones. Unadaptable temperament (fear) their internalizing scores, and to a lesser degree, *negatively,* their externalizing scores. That is, fearful temperament predicted higher levels of internalizing problems and, less strongly, lower levels of externalizing problems. Finally, difficult temperament (negative emotionality and demandingness) predicted neither of the pure scores but only the covarying externalizing plus internalizing score for mothers.

These predictions are all consistent with the models described at the beginning of this chapter where temperament extremes either constitute pathology dimensions or predispose to risk for these conditions. The linkages are of modest size, but they obtain from early in life. They are also not eliminated when family and parenting characteristics are included in prediction, so they are not simply artifacts of family functioning. Also supporting the general pattern, Gilliom and Shaw (2004) found, in a sample of preschool-age boys from low-income families, that high levels of negative emotionality were associated with initial levels of both externalizing and internalizing problems, whereas high levels of fearfulness were associated with high initial levels of internalizing problems and with increases in internalizing problems over time and with decreases in externalizing problems over time.

In the Dunedin longitudinal study (Caspi & Silva, 1995), ratings based on the child's behavior during testing sessions, aggregated from ages 3 and 5 years, predicted ratings of parents and teachers over ages 9 to 11 and in early adolescence (over ages 13 and 15). A temperament dimension combining lack of control, irritability, and distractibility predicted for both genders externalizing problems more strongly than internalizing problems or positive competencies. Early approach (positive responses to strangers and new test materials) predicted, inversely, internalizing problems better than externalizing problems for boys. It did not predict either kind of problem for girls. Early sluggishness (a factor combining a lack of positive affect, passivity, and wariness/withdrawal from novelty) predicted later internalizing and externalizing problems for girls, but not boys, as well as the relative absence of positive competencies for both girls and boys. The discovery of differentiated patterns in these studies has been found despite the tendency for externalizing and internalizing adjustment scores to be correlated with each other. Caspi and Silva report somewhat similar patterns of linkage between early temperament and self-reported personality patterns on Tellegen's Multidimensional Personality Questionnaire, with undercontrolled children tending as adults to be low on harm/avoidance and high on social alienation, and inhibited children high on harm/avoidance, low on aggression, and low on social potency.

In a Swedish study, Hagekull (1994) found that parent-reported Emotionality, Activity, Sociability, Impulsivity (EASI) sociability/shyness aggregated over mothers' and fathers' questionnaires at 28 and 36 months predicted age 48-month aggregated parent ratings of internalizing problems. Early impulsivity also predicted later externalizing but not internalizing problems and lower ego strength. Early activity predicted later externalizing and, inversely, later internalizing. Negative emotionality predicted both kinds of behavior problems as well as lowered ego strength. This pattern of findings is consonant with the BLS and Dunedin studies.

Another group of studies considered relations between parent ratings on the Middle Childhood Temperament Inventory (Hegvik, McDevitt, & Carey, 1982) and adjustment. Wertlieb et al. (1987) found parent ratings of high negative mood to be correlated with both externalizing and internalizing disorders. Scales having to do with manageability (activity, nonadaptability, and intensity) and self-regulation (nonpersistence and nonpredictability), on the other hand, tended to have higher correlations with externalizing than with internalizing. Guerin, Gottfried, Oliver, and Thomas (1994) found a similar pattern of correlations between parent temperament reports and teacher adjustment reports at age 10 years, except that negative mood correlated more strongly with teacher reports of externalizing than internalizing behavior problems; similar relations were found between age 10 parent temperament ratings and age 11 teacher ratings. Teglasi and MacMahon (1990) found a similar pattern, with manageability and self-regulation temperament scales correlating more strongly with externalizing adjustment scales than with internalizing scales. In addition, their negative reaction to novelty scale was more closely associated with internalizing than externalizing scales, and mood was moderately to highly correlate with both kinds of adjustment.

McClowry et al. (1994) found parent-rated negative emotional reactivity to be related to both internalizing and externalizing problems, with low task persistence (self-regulation) correlated only with externalizing. Their approach scale did not correlate with either internalizing or externalizing. However, in research by Rothbart, Derryberry, et al. (2000), infant activity and smiling, related to extraversion, predicted 7-year aggressiveness and negativism; infant fear predicted lower levels of aggressiveness and higher levels of fear, sadness, empathy, guilt, and shame.

Examining the link between temperament and behavior problems in older children (6- and 9-year-olds), Wertlieb et al. (1987) found high activity, withdrawal, distractibility, and intensity and low adaptability, persistence, negative mood, and unpredictability to be significantly related to higher behavior problem scores. Internalizing behavior scores (reflecting anxiety, phobias, social withdrawal, etc.) and externalizing behavior scores (reflecting hyperactivity, aggression, etc.) were also found to be differentially related to temperament. Withdrawal was more associated with internalizing scores, and high activity, distractibility, and low threshold more associated with externalizing scores.

Biederman et al. (1990), in a longitudinal cohort of highly inhibited and highly uninhibited children, found that inhibited children accounted for the majority of diagnoses of Anxiety Disorder (especially phobias) in their sample, and uninhibited children, the majority of the externalizing disorders (especially Oppositional Disorder). Despite the extreme sample, some extremely inhibited children later received attention deficit diagnoses, and some extremely uninhibited children received anxiety diagnoses, such as Overanxious Disorder. These results are similar to the more general pattern based on parent report studies and dimensional adjustment scores, in which there are some, if typically smaller, cross-domain correlations.

Rothbart, Ahadi, et al. (1994) considered relations between parent reports of temperament on the CBQ and adjustment on a newly developed questionnaire on social behavior patterns in a group of 6- and 7-year-olds. A second-order factor composite index of temperamental negative affectivity predicted the full range of social traits, including aggressiveness, guilt, help seeking, and negativity. However, components of the general negative affect factor were associated with the social traits in a more differentiated way: Fear and sadness were more related to traits such as empathy; anger and discomfort were more related to aggression and help seeking.

In summary, these findings indicate that fear-related negative affect is particularly related to internalizing disorders, and anger and irritability to externalizing disorders. In addition, although self-regulation is related to both internalizing and externalizing problems, it appears to be more strongly related to externalizing disorders. Fearful negative affect also appears to predict later lower externalizing problems, in keeping with its aspects as a control system. Thus, when negative affect is decomposed, there appear to be greater possibilities for differentiating the disposition to mood and behavior problems. Effortful control is also an important negative predictor of later problems. This control may serve both emotional and behavioral regulation. In the future, the uses of more highly differentiated measures of temperament are likely to lead to a better understanding of the development of adjustment and psychopathology.

Generality of Links with Negative Affectivity: Genetics Studies

Behavior genetics studies have also examined the generality of negative affect links to mood disorders, suggesting a general negative affect predisposition to anxiety and depression. The genetic correlation between anxiety and depression symptoms in adult twins is in the vicinity of 1.00, indicating shared genetic influence on these two disorders (Kendler, Heath, Martin, & Eaves, 1987). Given this overlap, Pennington (2002) suggests that more specific syndromes may be related to environmental events, with threat related to anxiety and loss to depression (Eley & Stevenson, 2000).

Considering again the model of temperamental extremes, predisposing to psychopathology, we might expect individual differences in fear or behavioral inhibition to be related to susceptibility to anxiety and a tendency toward social withdrawal. Wolfson, Fields, and Rose (1987) found that preschool children with Anxiety Disorders were reported by their mother to be less adaptable, more negative in mood, and more "difficult" than a nonanxious control group, and internalizing problems were related to high temperamental withdrawal. Rosenbaum et al. (1988) studied 2- to 7-year-old children of parents with Agoraphobia or Panic Disorder. Compared with children of psychiatric controls, the rates of behavioral inhibition were close to 80% for the children of the Agoraphobic or Panic Disorder parents, and approximately 15% for non–Major Depression controls. In a study of adult subjects with Major Depression, the codiagnosis of Agoraphobia or Panic Disorder has been found to be positively related to risk for psychiatric disorders in their children, especially risk for Major Depression and separation anxiety (Weissman, 1989). Weissman concluded that there may be a common underlying process constituting a vulnerability (diathesis) for both Panic Disorder and Major Depression. High comorbidity of anxiety and depression further suggest that differentiating the two is difficult, even at the level of clinical diagnosis (Kovacs & Devlin, 1998).

Imaging studies may cast further light on this question. K. M. Thomas et al. (2001) carried out an fMRI study on amygdala functions, comparing a small sample of children with anxiety and Major Depression diagnoses in comparison with controls. Differential findings were reported for anxious and depressed children, with anxious children showing a stronger right amygdala response to fear faces and depressed children showed a decreased left amygdala response to all faces.

Kagan, Snidman, Zentner, and Peterson (1999) reported that highly reactive infants at 4 months were likely to be behaviorally inhibited at 4 years and to exhibit more anxious symptoms at age 7. Behavioral inhibition in toddlers also predicted general social anxiety at age 13, particularly for girls (Schwartz, Snidman, & Kagan, 1999). Recent genetics contributions to the fear/phobia literature suggest a continuum of diathesis, from fearfulness to phobias. In a twin study by Kendler, Myers, Prescott, and Neale (2001), the lifetime history of multiple phobias as well as irrational fears was assessed. For a sample of males, a common genetic factor was found for five phobia subtypes, as well as genetic factors specific to each subtype, and a common familial environmental factor. Kendler et al. also analyzed irrational fears, with findings consistent with the idea that the irrational fears were a mild manifestation of the same genetic risk factor that produced clinical phobias. A previous study of women subjects was in agreement with these findings for men (Kendler, Neal, Kessler, Heath, & Eaves, 1992).

Temperament and Environment Influences

Rubin and Burgess (2001) have reviewed research on links between temperamental behavioral inhibition, social withdrawal, and maladaptation. They distinguish, as did Rubin and Asendorpf (1993), between children who isolate themselves from the peer group (social withdrawal) and children who have been rejected by the peer group (social isolation). Their model posits that inhibited children withdraw from the peer group, thereby failing to develop social interaction skills, becoming increasingly uncomfortable among peers, and finally facing social isolation from the peer group. This experience, in turn, is expected to encourage negative self-perceptions with respect to social relationships and social competence. Rubin (1993) identified a group of 11-year-old children above the clinical cutoff on depression inventory scores. Compared with nondepressed 11-year-olds, the depressed children at age 7 had been high on social withdrawal and negative self-perception of social competence. The groups did not differ on 7-year-old aggression or popularity, suggesting that, contrary to expectation, the negative self-perception appeared to precede social isolation.

Rubin and Burgess (2001) suggest that relative right frontal EEG activation in inhibited children may be related to low left hemisphere-related affective regulation. They note Eisenberg, Shepard, Fabes, Murphy, and Guthrie's (1998) findings that early school-age children's shyness was related to distress, upset, and nervousness and negatively related to excitement and enthusiasm. Higher levels of negative emotions were also related to avoidant coping in social problem situations.

Finally, Rubin and Burgess (2001) review research indicating that mothers of anxious and avoidant children tend to direct, control, and protect their children. They note, however, that the influence could well be bidirectional, with children's apparent vulnerability leading to parental overprotection. It is worthy of note that several studies have now reported that anxious children whose mothers are more demanding and less protective show more favorable outcomes. For a more complete report of this work, see Rothbart and Bates (in press).

Bidirectionality brings up the model in which characteristics evoke reactions in others that can increase risk or buffer it. Bidirectionality can also apply to externalizing disorders such as Conduct Disorder, where parents are found to reject or punish their children. Studies where conduct-disordered boys interact with other mothers as well as their own find no differences between the two groups of mothers' commands and negative responses to the boys, influence on the adults' responses (K. E. Anderson, Lytton, & Romney, 1986). Given shared genetic endowment, both parents and children may also share biologically based temperamental dispositions. If parents also tend to be more fearful, for example, they may seek to control situations and to protect their children.

Studies have investigated the relationship of temperament to observations of naturalistic mother-child interaction in preschool-age children. Stevenson-Hinde and Simpson (1982) found that mothers reported effects of difficult-to-manage behavior on all relationships in the family, including interactions with siblings and mother-father interactions. In comparison to mothers of more manageable children, these mothers also reported higher levels of anxiety and irritability in themselves, many commenting that they "did not used to be like this." Rutter and Quinton (1984) reported that children showing negative mood, low regularity, low malleability, and fastidiousness were more likely to be the focus of depressed parents' criticism, hostility, and irritability. In Rutter's (1990, p. 191) terms, "The interactive process reflects a pattern in which the children's attributes make them a focus for the discord (thus increasing exposure to the risk variable) and increase the probability that exposure will set in motion a train of adverse interactions that will prolong the risk."

Lee and Bates (1985) observed mothers' interacting with 2-year-olds at home, where the mothers were trying to control their toddlers' "trouble" behavior. They found that more distress-prone ("difficult") children approached trouble more often, resisted their mothers' attempts to control them, and had mothers who were more likely both to use more aversive discipline and to give in to their children. Lee and Bates noted that these early interactions resembled the coercive cycle of behavior described in socially aggressive boys and their mothers (G. R. Patterson, 1977, 1980). Even at early ages, children who present their mother with more troublesome, resistant behavior may encourage their mothers to use aversive discipline tactics more frequently or to give in, and these in turn may be the antecedents of a coercive cycle of parent-child interactions related to problems with aggression (G. R. Patterson, 1980).

Activation and inhibition are both important in the development of children's conduct problems. G. R. Patterson (1980) reported that parents of nonaggressive problem children are effective in stopping their children's aversive behavior on three out of every four times they use punishment. When parents of aggressive problem children employ punishment, however, the likelihood that the child will persist in the problem behavior increases rather than decreases (G. R. Patterson, 1977, 1980; Snyder, 1977). In our laboratory, we have found (Hershey, 1992) that more aggressive (by mothers' report) 7-year-old children show less inhibitory control, that is, they respond more quickly after encountering an error message in a catch trial in an experimental task, than less aggressive 7-year-olds.

Extraversion and introversion may also be related to inhibitory control. Nichols and Newman (1966) asked subjects to view a visual pattern and match a subsequent pattern against it. Rewards and punishments were preprogrammed and noncontingent on subject response. On trials following punishment, introverts responded more slowly, but extraverts responded more *quickly*. Subjects who were more slowed by punishment performed better on the go/no go task (C. M. Patterson, Kosson, & Newman, 1987). In a study with young children, Saltz, Campbell, and Skotko (1983) found that, in support of Luria's (1961) observations, increasing the loudness of a "no go" command increased 3- to 4-year-old children's likelihood of performing a prohibited act. They also found that increasing loudness decreased the likelihood of responding for children 5 to 6 years of age, indicating developmental change in the excitatory and inhibitory control and their balance during the preschool years. Development of the executive attention system underlying effortful control may be related to these findings.

In addition to their relationship to disinhibiting psychopathologies, positive, outgoing characteristics of the young child have been identified as a general *protective* factor for the development of risk factors and psychopathology. More active and outgoing children are likely to show fewer negative effects of institutionalization, possibly because they are more likely to receive greater attention from adult caregivers (Schaffer, 1966). Werner's (1986; Werner & Smith, 1982) longitudinal studies in Hawaii indicate that more positive affective and expressive characteristics in the young child from an at-risk population are associated with fewer psychosocial problems later in life. In addition, higher positive affect appears to be a negative predictor of problems with depression (Mineka, Watson, & Clark, 1998).

Effortful Control and Psychopathology

A second inhibitory influence on impulsivity in addition to fear or behavioral inhibition is the attentionally influenced capacity to withhold prohibited responses and activate prescribed ones, that is, effortful control. It has been suggested that this function may be divided into monitoring for conflict and executing inhibitory control (Botwinick et al., 2001). Monitoring for conflict has been related to anterior cingulate function, whereas lateral prefrontal areas may be more related to executing the inhibitory operation. In our 7-year-old sample, inhibitory control was predicted by infants' longer latency to approach toys at 11 and 13 months and by their lower activity level in the laboratory at 13 months (Rothbart, Derryberry, et al., 2000). At 7 years, inhibitory control was concurrently related to attentional control and empathy, and negatively to aggression. Inhibitory control was also moderately positively related to guilt/shame, although uncorrelated with behavioral inhibition as assessed in shyness.

Several components of effortful control have been identified in the development of behavior problems. Poor delay of gratification has been identified as a risk factor for aggressive and delinquent behaviors, and high delay of gratification to adaptive behaviors (Krueger, Caspi, Moffitt, White, & Stouthamer-Loeber, 1996). In clinic-referred children, Huey and Weisz (1997) found externalizing problems to be related to underregulation of behavior, and internalizing problems to high behavioral inhibition and low regulative resiliency. Eisenberg et al. (1996) reported correlations between teacher and parent ratings of low emotional and behavioral self-regulation and acting-out behavior problems. Eisenberg, Guthrie, et al. (2000) directly predicted internalizing problems from low behavioral regulation and high negative emotionality, and found moderating effects of negative emotionality on the relation between low attentional regulation and externalizing problems in grade school children (only children high in emotionality showed the relation).

Eisenberg et al. (2001) compared the temperament of school-age children with externalizing problems to those with internalizing problems and nondisordered children. Children with externalizing problems showed higher anger and impulsivity and lower regulation. Eisenberg et al. (1998) also found, in nondisordered children, that high internalizing negative emotion at age 4 to 6 years predicted shyness at ages 6 to 8 and 8 to 10, but chiefly for children low in the ability to control attention shifting. Lack of emotional, behavioral, and attitudinal control in the preschool period, assessed via negativism, emotional lability, restlessness, and short attention span, has predicted externalizing behaviors in adolescents (Caspi, Henry, McGee, Moffitt, & Silva, 1995). In a multiple regression analysis, lack of control and low approach independently predicted boys' anxiety; lack of control and sluggishness were independent predictors for girls. Both lack of control and response to novelty (behavioral inhibition) predicted children's later problems with anxiety. Preschool lack of control has also been found to distinguish between life-course-persistent antisocial behavior and antisocial behavior limited primarily to the period of adolescence (Moffitt, Caspi, Dickson, Silva, & Stanton, 1996). There is also strong evidence of links between high levels of control and positive or adaptive outcomes (see review by Eisenberg, Fabes, Guthrie, & Reiser, 2002).

Merikangas, Swendsen, Preisig, and Chazan (1998) studied adults with psychiatric disorders and their 7- to 17-year-old children. Externalizing or substance use disorders in the offspring were associated with low attentional control and high activity across the life span. Anxiety and depression were associated with low adaptability and approach/withdrawal, and comorbidity of externalizing and internalizing disorders was associated with both clusters of temperament characteristics and with high clinical severity and impairment.

In a study of temperament, externalizing problems, and internalizing problems in older adolescents using the Attention Network Task (Fan et al., 2002), conflict performance on computerized measures of executive attention was related to mother-reported adolescents' self-regulation and negative affectivity (Ellis, 2002). Adolescents' performance was related to teacher assessment of risk for developing antisocial behaviors. Executive attention scores, mother- and self-report self-regulation, and parental monitoring all contributed unique variance to the prediction of problem behavior scores, with individual difference variables accounting for relatively more variance than parenting variables. Mother- and self-reported self-regulation, self-reported affiliativeness and approach tendencies, and gender contributed to prediction of depressive mood scores. Parenting variables did not add significant variance to predicting depressive mood.

In summary, in addition to lack of inhibitory reactions to punishment (the BIS), lack of attentional or effortful control has been related to externalizing problems. We now consider how temperament may be related to family interaction that, in turn, can shape outcomes.

Additive Effects of Temperament and Parenting

In one model temperament and the caregiving environment make independent contributions to psychopathology outcomes, and often, temperament and parenting have shown additive contributions to behavior problems. Campbell (1991) reported results from two longitudinal samples. The first included 3-year-olds referred by parents; the second, a 3-year-old group rated by their teachers as inattentive, overactive, and impulsive, and a matched control group from the same class. Data were collected in home visits, laboratory, and preschool classrooms, and children in both samples have been followed longitudinally. There was consistency of ratings of externalizing behavior problems across parents and teachers of preschool, first-grade, and fourth-grade children, and relations were found between early inattention, hyperactivity, and the development of poor impulse control, and aggression and noncompliance. In addition, higher levels of externalizing problems in preschool children were found to be related to both higher levels of stress in the family and the mother's use of more negative control strategies. In support of this model, Keenan and Shaw (1994) found in a low-income sample that a composite of temperamental difficultness and resistance to control predicted laboratory measures of aggression in 18-month-old boys, but not girls.

By combining measures of temperament in the first 3 years, mothers' positive involvement (affection, teaching), and 3-year behavior problems, Bates and Bayles (1988) were able to predict both externalizing and internalizing behavior problems at 6 years. Fisher and Fagot (1992) also found that toddler temperament and parental discipline practices were independently related to children's antisocial and coercive behavior at 5 to 7 years.

Interactive Effects

Another model involves interactive effects of temperament and parenting, and these also have been found. These are reviewed in Rothbart and Bates (in press), where recent contributions to the literature make this a particularly exciting area of research. For example, in the 1,500-subject Australian Temperament Study, infant difficult temperament had little direct relationship with 7- to 8-year-old hostile-aggressive problems, but when this temperament occurred in a setting reflecting poor mother-child relationships, the level of risk for behavior problems substantially increased (Swanson et al., 2000). Belsky, Hsieh, and Crnic (1998) also found that parenting of male infants was more predictive of externalizing behavior problems at 3 years for infants high in negativity versus those low in negativity.

Stice and Gonzales (1998) reported a moderating effect for temperament; maternal control and support were more strongly related to antisocial behavior among adolescents who were high on negative affectivity and behavioral undercontrol. Maziade et al. (1990) found that 7-year-old child difficulty in dysfunctional families with lack of parental rule clarity, consistency, and consensus predicted later oppositional and attention deficit disorders at 12 and 16 years. Few children with difficult temperament and a well-functioning family developed behavior disorders, and few of the very easy children at 7 showed problems at 12, regardless of family functioning.

Lengua, Wolchik, Sandler, and West (2000) found that both temperament (high positive emotionality, low negative emotionality, and impulsivity) and parenting (low rejection and inconsistent parenting) independently predicted successful adjustment after parental divorce. Interactive effects were found for dysfunction. Rejection was most strongly associated with behavior problems in children low in positive affect and inconsistency with problems for highly impulsive children. Belsky et al. (1998) found that parenting of male infants was more predictive of externalizing behavior problems at age 3 years for infants high in negativity. Shaw et al. (1998) regressed out main effects in predicting 24-month externalizing and found a remaining sex × temperament × parenting interaction. For boys, noncompliant temperament and mother rejection exerted independent effects on externalizing. For girls, noncompliant temperament predicted later behavior problems only when combined with mother rejection.

In a setting where negativity was not measured, Bates et al. (1998) found that 13- and 24-month-old children's resistance to control interacted with mothers' restrictive control at 6, 13 and 24 months to predict externalizing in middle childhood. For mothers who were low in control, negative correlations were found between earlier temperament and externalizing; when mothers were high in restrictive control, lower correlations were found. Bates et al. carried out a conceptual replication of this finding in a second study and suggested that resistance to control may reflect strong approach, weak fear, and/or low effortful control. Parental control may be more likely to lead to coercive cycles of interaction when the child is also highly negative, but when control is the main issue, children may actually benefit from mother's intervention.

Overall, these findings suggest that there are particular temperamental vulnerabilities that may make some children more susceptible than others to negative environments. In a recent study, Caspi et al. (2002) added an exciting molecular genetics contribution to this literature, looking specifically at the relation between child maltreatment and the child's possession of the MAOA gene, which has been related to the development of aggressivity in monkeys. Maltreatment was assessed between the ages of 3 and 11 years, and antisocial outcomes were predicted for male teenagers and adults. A significant gene-environment interaction was found, indicating that the effect of maltreatment was stronger in males with low MAOA activity.

This finding will require replication, but a link has also been reported between the same gene (MAOA) and the ability of normal subjects to regulate conflict in the Attention Network Test (Fossella, Posner, Fan, Swanson, & Pfaff, 2002). When people with two different alleles of the MAOA gene were studied in fMRI (Fan, Fossella, et al., 2003), a difference was observed in the amount of activity in the anterior cingulate, which is an important node in the executive attention network (Fan et al., 2002). MAOA is also linked to the regulation of norepinephrine, dopamine, and serotonin, 5-HT and thus appears to provide protection for antisocial outcomes given stressful early experience. The authors argue that studying other genotypes associated with stress responses may promote an understanding of "how stressful experiences are converted into antisocial behavior toward others in some, but not all, victims of maltreatment" (Caspi et al., 2002, p. 853).

In summary, evidence has increasingly been found for interactions between child temperament and caregiver treatment in psychopathology outcomes. In addition, studies continue to find additive contributions to temperament and caregiver treatment in child outcomes. The coercion model suggests that child characteristics can influence parental reactions, leading to increased risk of externalizing psychopathology.

Gender Influences

With the exception of activity level (Eaton, 1994), sex differences are rarely found in early assessments of temperament (Rothbart, 1986), but behavior problems develop disproportionately in boys. Girls are at greater risk than boys for depression (Zahn-Waxler, Cole, & Barrett, 1991), and antisocial behavior is generally found at higher rates for males than for females (Eagly & Steffen, 1986). Research results currently describe interplay among temperament, social experience, and gender in the development of depressive mood; two studies suggest that antecedents for depressive mood may be somewhat gender-specific (Block, Gjerde, & Block, 1991; G. R. Patterson & Capaldi, 1990).

Measuring depressive mood at age 18, with self-reported anxiety partialed out, Block et al. (1991) found that girls' depressive mood was predicted from intropunitive, oversocialized, and overcontrolling behavior at age 7 and from higher preschool IQ. Boys' depressive mood, on the other hand, was predicted from higher aggressive, self-aggrandizing, and undercontrolled behavior at age 7, and from lower preschool IQ. Variables assessing undercontrol for males and overcontrol for females were also found to be concurrently related to depressive mood at age 18 for this sample (Gjerde, Block, & Block, 1988). Block et al. noted that their findings were congruent with findings of a positive relationship between Conduct Disorder and depression for male but not for female clinically depressed preadolescents (Edelbrock & Achenbach, 1980; Puig-Antich, 1982).

G. R. Patterson and Capaldi (1990) provided further information on this point in research with two samples of forth-grade boys. Their research results supported a model in which peer rejection is a central mediating influence on depressed mood. In this model, for at least some boys, undercontrolled behavior is seen to lead to peer rejection, which in turn is related to development of depressive mood. For girls, on the other hand, Zahn-Waxler et al. (1991) offered a developmental model for depression, highlighting vulnerability to depression in highly socialized girls. Once again, gender may be a moderating variable in the relation between temperament and the development of depressive mood.

In a further analysis of gender and psychopathology, Maziade, Cote, Bernier, Boutin, and Thivierge (1989) suggested that boys' "difficult" temperament is more stable than girls' and that girls are prone to become less difficult over time even when there is stress in the family. In addition, Earls and Jung (1987) reported that marital discord and maternal depression are related to behavior problems in boys but not in girls. They speculated that boys may be under different socialization pressures than girls, especially when the mother is under stress, although the direction of effects might also be reversed, with boys' greater externalizing problems creating higher levels of stress for the mother and for her relationship with the father.

The reader will have noted the important links between failures of self-regulation and developmental disorders. In the final sections of our review, we consider what we have learned about attention systems in relation to the development of psychopathology.

ATTENTION AND PSYCHOPATHOLOGY

The ability of attention to regulate distress can be traced to early infancy (Harman, Rothbart, & Posner, 1997). In infants as young as 3 months, we have found that orienting to a visual stimulus provided by the experimenter produces powerful if only temporary soothing of distress. One of the major accomplishments of the first few years is for infants to develop the means to achieve this regulation on their own. These events have been reviewed in Rothbart and Rueda (2005) and Rothbart, Posner, and Kieras (in press).

A sign of the control of cognitive conflict is found late in the 1st year of life (A. Diamond, 1991). For example, in A-not-B tasks, children are trained to reach for a hidden object at location A, and then tested on their ability to search for the hidden object at a new location B. Children younger than 12 months tend to look in the previous location A, even though they see the object disappear behind location B. After the 1st year, children develop the ability to inhibit the prepotent response toward the trained location A and successfully reach for the new location B. During this period, infants develop the ability to resolve conflict between line of sight and line of reach when retrieving an object. At 9 months of age, line of sight dominates completely. If the open side of a box is not in line with the side in view, infants will withdraw their hand and reach directly along the line of sight, striking the closed side (A. Diamond, 1991). In contrast, 12-month-old infants can simultaneously look at a closed side while reaching through the open end to retrieve a toy.

The ability to use context to reduce conflict can be traced developmentally using the learning of sequences of locations. Infants as young as 4 months can learn to anticipate the location of a stimulus, provided the association in the sequence is unambiguous (Haith, Hazan, & Goodman, 1988). In unambiguous sequences, each location is invariably associated with another location (e.g., 123; Clohessy, Posner, & Rothbart, 2001). Because the location of the current target is fully determined by the preceding item, one type of information needs to be attended to, and there is therefore no conflict (e.g., location 3 always follows location 2). Adults can learn unambiguous sequences of spatial locations implicitly even when attention is distracted by a secondary task (Curran & Keele, 1993).

Ambiguous sequences (e.g., 1213) require attention to the current association in addition to the context in which the association occurs (e.g., location 1 may be followed by location 2 or by location 3). Ambiguous sequences pose conflict because for any association, there exists two strong candidates that can be disambiguated only by context. When distracted, adults are unable to learn ambiguous sequences of length six (e.g., 123213; Curran & Keele, 1993), a finding that demonstrates the need for higher-level attentional resources to resolve this conflict. In young children, even simple ambiguous associations (e.g., 1213) were not performed at above chance level until about 2 years of age (Clohessy et al., 2001).

Developmental changes in executive attention were found during the 3rd year of life using a conflict key-pressing task (spatial conflict; Gerardi-Caulton, 2000). Because children of this age do not read, location and identity, rather than word and ink color, served as the dimensions of conflict. Children sat in front of two response keys, one located to the child's left and one to the right. Each key displayed a picture, and on every trial a picture identical to one member of the pair appeared on either the left or right side of the screen. Children were rewarded for responding to the identity of the stimulus regardless of its spatial compatibility with the matching response key (Gerardi-Caulton, 2000). Reduced accuracy and slowed reaction times for spatially incompatible relative to spatially compatible trials reflect the effort required to resist the prepotent response and resolve conflict between these two competing dimensions. Performance on this task produces a clear interference effect in adults and activates the anterior cingulate (Fan, Flombaum, et al., 2003). Children 24 months of age tended to perseverate on a single response; 36-month-old children performed at high accuracy levels but, like adults, responded more slowly and with reduced accuracy to incompatible trials.

At 30 months, when toddlers were first able to successfully perform the spatial conflict task, we found that performance on this task was significantly correlated with

their ability to learn the ambiguous associations in the sequence learning task (Rothbart, Ellis, Rueda, & Posner, 2003). This finding, together with the failure of 4-month-olds to learn ambiguous sequences, holds out the promise of being able to trace the emergence of executive attention during the first months and years of life.

The importance of being able to study the emergence of executive attention is enhanced because cognitive measures of conflict resolution in these laboratory tasks have been linked to aspects of children's temperament. Signs of the development of executive attention by cognitive tasks relate to a temperament individual differences measure obtained from caregiver reports called effortful control. Children relatively less affected by spatial conflict received higher parental ratings of temperamental effortful control and higher scores on laboratory measures of inhibitory control (Gerardi-Caulton, 2000). We regard effortful control as reflecting the efficiency with which the executive attention network operates in naturalistic settings.

Assessing Individual Differences in Attentional Networks

The Attention Network Test (ANT) examines the efficiency of the three brain networks we have discussed (Fan et al., 2002). The ANT procedure uses differences in reaction times (RT) between conditions to measure the efficiency of each network. The procedure for the ANT is illustrated in Figure 11.1. Subtracting RTs obtained in the double-cue condition from RTs in the no-cue condition gives a measure of alerting due to a warning signal. Subtracting RTs to targets at the cued location (spatial cue) from trials using a central cue gives a measure of orienting. Subtracting RTs for congruent from incongruent target trials provides a measure of conflict and marks the executive attention network.

The ANT has some useful properties as a measure of attentional efficiency. It does not use language stimuli, so it can be used with children, speakers of any language, patients unable to read, or special populations. In about 20 minutes, the test provides a measure of the efficiency of the alerting, orienting, and conflict networks with reasonable reliability, in addition to overall RT and error rates. Measuring the three networks' scores in the same test also allows assessment of possible patterns of interactions between them. We do not exclude the possibility that certain psychopathologies or brain-injured patients would have a dysfunction in the way the attentional networks interact.

In a sample of 40 normal persons, network scores were reliable over two successive presentations. In addition, no

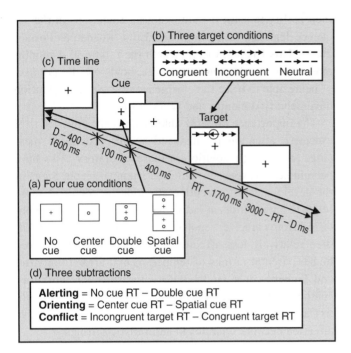

Figure 11.1 The figure illustrates the Attention Network Test (ANT). Each trial begins with one of the four cues shown in a. The three targets are shown in b. The time course of each trial is shown in c. At the bottom are the subtractions that provide the measurement of the efficiency of each network. Adapted from "Testing the Efficiency and Independence of Attentional Networks," by J. Fan, B. D. McCandliss, T. Sommer, M. Raz, and M. I. Posner (April, 2002), *Journal of Cognitive Neuroscience, 3,* pp. 340–347. © 2002 by the Massachusetts Institute of Technology.

correlation was found among the three network scores. An analysis of RTs in this task showed large main effects for cuing and for the type of target, but only two small but significant interactions (Fan et al., 2002). They both involved very small reductions in conflict when either no warning cue is provided or when the cue is at the location of the target. The latter interaction is to be expected because the effective eccentricity of flankers is increased when attention is on the central arrow. The first finding appears to arise because with no warning, the subject is generally slow and some conflict resolution may occur during the longer overall RT. This effect also appears to be responsible for a small but significant negative correlation between alerting and conflict ($r = -.18$), found in a larger sample of more than 200 people who had taken the ANT (Fossella et al., 2002).

Recently, ANT scores have been used as a phenotype to assay the heritability of each of the attentional functions with a sample of 26 pairs of monozygotic and dizygotic twins (Fan, Wu, Fossella, & Posner, 2001). In accordance with their neuroanatomical and behavioral independence, the three attentional networks showed different heritability indexes. Despite the small scale of the study, the executive network scores showed a significant correlation ($r = .73$) between monozygotic twins. This correlation was also significant, although weaker, for the alerting scores ($r = .46$), while the orienting network showed no evidence of heritability.

A child version of the ANT has been developed that is appropriate for children from about 4 years of age. In previous work, we found that children work best when there is a story and when there is clear feedback on their performance (Berger, Jones, Rothbart, & Posner, 2000). In the child version of the ANT, five colorful fish replaced the arrows that typically appear in the flanker task. Children are invited to help the experimenter feed the middle fish by pressing a button corresponding to the direction in which it is swimming. Visual feedback (the middle fish smiles and bubbles come out of its mouth) and auditory feedback (a "woohoo" sound) is provided when the response has been successful. In each trial, the flanker fish are swimming in the same (congruent) or opposite (incongruent) direction as the center fish.

Using the child ANT, the developmental course of the attentional networks has been studied (Rueda, Fan, et al., 2004; Rueda, Posner, & Rothbart, 2004). As in the adult data, the child study revealed independence among the three network scores. Despite a common decline in RT, each network also showed a different developmental course. Significant improvement in conflict resolution was found up until age 7 as compared to younger children, but a remarkable stability in both RT and accuracy conflict scores from the age of 7 to adulthood. Alerting scores showed some improvement in late childhood and continued development between 10 years old and adulthood. Finally, the orienting score at the age of 6 was similar to adult levels. The normal development of these networks may be important in understanding issues related to developmental pathologies such as those in Autism, ADHD, and anxiety and depression.

DEVELOPMENT AND ATTENTIONAL PATHOLOGIES

Attention is a very frequent symptom of many forms of psychopathology. However, without a real understanding of the neural substrates of attention, this has been a somewhat empty classification. This situation changed with the systematic application of our understanding of attentional networks to pathological issues. Viewing attention in terms of underlying neural networks provides a means of classifying disorders that differs from the usual internalizing versus externalizing classification that we applied earlier in the chapter. A number of abnormalities involving attention, including Alzheimer's dementia, anxiety, ADHD, Autism, Borderline Personality Disorder, depression, and Schizophrenia, have been studied either with the ANT (Fan et al., 2002), which measures the efficiency of all three networks (see Figure 11.1), or parts of the task that measure one or two of the networks.

Alerting

The alerting network is obtained in the ANT by subtracting RTs following a warning of when a target will occur from RTs when participants do not receive any warning signal. Alerting shows the longest period of development of any of the networks, not reaching adult levels even by age 10 (Rueda, Fan, et al., 2004). Young participants have larger alerting scores than adults because they have abnormally long RTs without a warning signal. These effects are reduced with age. One effect of a warning signal is to improve the alert state, but there may be other influences as well. For example, children may rehearse the task after the warning signal, and this may allow them to respond more quickly, and they may be caught somewhat unawares when a target occurs without warning. Because the ANT is so simple, adults don't seem to need to rehearse during the warning interval once the task has been well learned.

It is also known that patients with anterior and posterior right hemisphere damage have problems when tasks are given without warning (Posner, Inhoff, Friedrich, & Cohen, 1987; Robertson, Mattingley, Rorden, & Driver, 1998). This arises because patients, like young children, have very long RTs in the absence of warning. Robertson has argued that the inability to maintain the alert state without a warning signal is a major contributor to the reduced attention to the side of space opposite the lesion, found more strongly in patients with right than with left posterior lesions.

A study using the ANT has shown that normal elderly persons also show dramatically larger alerting effects than young adults, resembling what is found with children (Fernandez-Duque & Black, in press). The study also found that normally developing older adults and Alzheimer's patients showed the same elevated alerting scores, but only the Alzheimer's patients showed increased difficulty in resolving conflict (see also our later discussion of executive attention).

Attention-Deficit/Hyperactivity Disorder

Studies of ADHD have linked the disorder to aspects of both attention and sensation seeking, a component of extraversion/surgency (Swanson et al., 2001). Many theories of ADHD have also suggested a deficit in executive functions (Barkley, 1997). However, in early work using a spatial orienting task, the most compelling deficit appeared to be a difficulty in maintaining the alert state in the absence of a warning signal (Swanson et al., 1991). This difficulty might arise from right hemisphere damage, which has also been reported to be a feature in many studies of ADHD.

More recent studies using the ANT have replicated problems with alerting in ADHD, again mostly due to the inability to maintain the alert state when no warning signal was used (Beane & Marrocco, 2004; Booth, Carlson, & Tucker, 2001). In one of these studies (Booth et al., 2001), the ANT was used to discriminate the Inattentive subtype from normal children and the Combined subtype. The alerting network best distinguished the different forms of ADHD, with Inattentive children showing less ability to maintain the alert state in the absence of warning signals. Neuroimaging studies of ADHD children have generally shown right frontal, cingulate, and basal ganglia deficits (Casey et al., 1997). Because right frontal areas have been related both to problems with the alert state and with inhibitory control, there could be links between the ANT results and these imaging studies, but this research has not yet been done.

Casey, Durston, and Fossella (2001) used three different tasks that rely on different processes (stimulus selection, response selection, and response execution) to analyze executive functions in different types of developmental disorders (Schizophrenia, Sydenham's chorea, Tourette's syndrome, and ADHD). They suggest that each of the cognitive operations is implemented in a particular basal ganglia-thalamocortical circuit. Stimulus processing seems to be related to connections among basal ganglia, thalamus, and the dorsolateral prefrontal cortex, whereas response processing is associated with connections of subcortical structures to the lateral orbital frontal cortex. Schizophrenic patients exhibited deficits in stimulus election, Sydenham's chorea patients in response selection, Tourette's syndrome children in response execution, and ADHD children in both stimulus selection and response execution, suggesting that specific cognitive operations related to executive attention can be independently damaged.

For a number of years it has been thought that ADHD related to problems with dopamine and other catecholamine function (Wender, 1971). In molecular genetics research, the dopamine theory found support in replicated findings that one allele (the 7-repeat) of the dopamine 4 receptor gene is overrepresented in children with ADHD and also is associated with a temperament featuring high sensation seeking (see Swanson et al., 2001, for a recent summary). Sensation seeking is a lower-order construct of extraversion. This finding has been well replicated for the syndrome of ADHD, but the allele has not been associated with a cognitive deficit in executive function in a study of children with and without the 7-repeat allele (Swanson et al., 2000). The 7-repeat was associated with ADHD but not with the cognitive deficit that usually accompanies ADHD (Swanson et al., 2000). This finding led to the suggestion that there may be two routes to ADHD. One would involve a temperamental extreme of sensation seeking (or extraversion), the frequency of which might be increased by the presence of the repeat version of the dopamine 4 receptor gene. This route need not involve a cognitive deficit. A second route to ADHD would involve cognitive deficits that might be either genetic or due to early brain injury or other experiential factors.

Orienting

Orienting network efficiency is obtained from the ANT by subtracting the spatial cue RTs from the center cue RTs.

Anxiety and Depression

There is much new information on the role of attention in anxiety, depression, and mood disorders. In a series of studies, subclinical college students with high scores on trait anxiety were cued to attend to a location by a positive, negative, or neutral face. Trials on which the cue to the location was negative and invalid produced longer reaction times for the trait anxiety subjects (E. Fox, Ricardo, & Dutton, 2002; E. Fox, Russo, Bowles, & Dutton, 2001). These results replicate and extend previous studies by Derryberry and Reed (1994) and together suggest that trait anxiety influences the ability to disengage, particularly from threat stimuli. Derryberry and Reed suggest that this finding may be dependent on relatively low levels of effortful control. Subjects high in effortful control but suffering from depression did not have difficulty disengaging from negative affect.

A symptom of depression is the tendency to dwell on negative ideation (Beck, 1976). Vasey and Macleod (2001) reviewed recent studies on trait-anxious children, finding evidence of their making threatening interpretations of ambiguous stimulus material, overestimating the likelihood of future negative events, and showing a negative bias toward threatening information. Negative bias has also been noted in children's speeded detection of dot probes in the vicinity of threatening words (Bijttebier, 1998; Schippel, Vasey, Cravens-Brown, & Bretveld, 2003). In temperament research, the ability to control attention was found to be neg-

atively related to negative affect (Derryberry & Rothbart, 1988; Rothbart, Ahadi, et al., 2000), congruent with the interpretation that good attentional mechanisms may serve to protect against negative ideation.

Children with a history of abuse have also been found to be hypersensitive to the recognition of angry faces, misclassifying objectively neutral faces as angry (Pollak & Kistler, 2002). Together, these findings suggest that both temperament and experience can influence aspects of attention toward threat stimuli, perhaps by both enlarging the boundary of the classification and increasing the time to dwell on these stimuli. Because orienting to cues and targets can be studied in children from birth onward (Pollak & Kistler, 2002), it is possible to use these findings to obtain more information on the effect of anxiety on normal development and to determine the degree to which it predicts later problems given stressful experience.

Brain systems related to unipolar depression have been explored in a number of imaging studies (Drevets & Raichle, 1998; Liotti, Maybert, McGinnis, Brannan, & Jerabeck, 2003). These studies have generally shown the importance of midline frontal areas, including the anterior cingulate and orbital prefrontal cortex. In normal persons, these areas are related to the experience and control of emotion (Bush et al., 2000), behavior and cognition (Drevets, 2000), and self-image (Gusnard et al., 2003). The areas appear to function abnormally in depressed persons exposed to material producing a sad mood, whether or not they were currently depressed. The overlap between brain activities in currently depressed people with those who have suffered from depression in the past may explain the frequent occurrence of multiple depressive bouts.

Autism

Autism is a disorder that has been linked to the orienting system (Akshoomoff, Pierce, & Courchesne, 2002; Landry & Bryson, 2004; Rodier, 2002). It is well-known that autistic persons do not normally orient to faces. However, Landry and Bryson (2004) report autistic difficulty in orienting in tasks that involve nonsocial stimuli similar to those used in the ANT. Similar deficits in the ability to disengage and move attention have been reported in Autism in relation to abnormal development of the cerebellum (Akshoomoff et al., 2002). We do not know if this abnormality is due only to cerebellar deficits, as many of the patients also show parietal abnormalities as well (Allen & Courschesne, 2001). Moreover, the pattern of advantages and difficulties in orienting displayed by autistic persons (summarized in Allen & Courschesne, 2001) suggest that the core difficulty may lie in executive control of orienting rather than being a result of simply parietal or cerebellar deficit. These results may serve to related the orienting difficulties in Autism to higher-level executive deficits (Frith, 2001). Rodier has some evidence that the orienting abnormalities found in Autism might relate to a gene associated with migration of cells in early development.

Executive Function

Executive network efficiency in the ANT is obtained by subtracting the congruent trial RTs from the incongruent trial RTs.

Borderline Personality Disorder

Borderline Personality Disorder is characterized by very great lability of affect and problems in interpersonal relations. In some cases, patients are suicidal or carry out self-mutilation. Because this diagnosis has been studied largely by psychoanalysts and has a very complex definition, it might at first be thought of as a poor candidate for a specific pathophysiology involving attentional networks. However, we focused on the temperamentally based core symptoms of negative emotionality and difficulty in self-regulation (Posner et al., 2002). We found that patients were very high in negative affect and relatively low in effortful control (Rothbart, Ahadi, et al., 2000), and defined a temperamentally matched control group of normal persons without personality disorder who were equivalent in scores on these two dimensions. Our study with the ANT found a deficit specific to the executive attention network in borderline patients (Posner et al., 2002). Preliminary imaging results suggested overgeneralization of responding in the amygdala and reduced responding in the anterior cingulate and related midline frontal areas (Posner et al., 2002). Patients with higher effortful control and lower conflict scores on the ANT were also the most likely to show the effects of therapy. This methodology shows the utility of focusing on the core deficits of patients, defining appropriate control groups based on matched temperament, and using specific attentional tests to help determine how to conduct imaging studies.

Schizophrenia

A number of years ago, never-medicated schizophrenic patients were tested both by imaging and with a cued detection task similar to the orienting part of the ANT. At rest, these subjects showed a focal decrease in cerebral blood flow in the left globus pallidus (Early, Posner, Reiman, & Raichle, 1989), a part of the basal ganglia with close ties to the anterior cingulate. These subjects showed a deficit in orienting similar to what had been found for left parietal

patients (Early et al., 1989). When their visual attention was engaged, they had difficulty shifting attention to the right visual field. However, they also showed deficits in conflict tasks, particularly when they had to rely on a language cue. It was concluded that the overall pattern of their behavior was most consistent with a deficit in the anterior cingulate and basal ganglia, parts of a frontally based executive attention system.

The deficit in orienting rightward has been replicated in first-break schizophrenics, but it does not seem to be true later in the disorder (Maruff, Currie, Hay, McArthur-Jackson, & Malone, 1995), nor does the pattern appear to be part of the genetic predisposition for Schizophrenia (Pardo et al., 2000). First-break schizophrenic subjects often have been shown to have left hemisphere deficits, and there have been many reports of anterior cingulate and basal ganglia deficits in patients with Schizophrenia (Benes, 1999). The anterior cingulate may be part of a much larger network of frontal and temporal structures that operate abnormally in Schizophrenia (Benes, 1999).

A recent study using the ANT casts some light on these results (Wang et al., in press). In this case, the schizophrenic patients were chronic and were compared with a similarly aged control group. The schizophrenic patients had much greater difficulty resolving conflict than did the normal controls. The deficit in patients was also much larger than that found for borderline personality patients. There was still a great deal of overlap between the patients and normal subjects, however, indicating that the deficit is not suitable for making a differential diagnosis. The data showed a much smaller orienting deficit of the type that had been reported previously. These findings suggest that there is a strong executive deficit in chronic Schizophrenia, as would be anticipated by Benes's (1999) theory. It remains to be determined whether this deficit exists prior to the initial symptoms or develops with the disorder.

Chromosome 22q11.2 Deletion Syndrome

This is a complex syndrome that involves a number of abnormalities, including facial and heart structure but also a mental retardation to deletion of a number of genes. Children with the deletion are at high risk for developing Schizophrenia. Among the genes deleted in this syndrome is the COMT gene, which has been associated with performance in a conflict task (A. Diamond, Briand, Fossella, & Gehlbach, 2004) and with Schizophrenia (Egan et al., 2003). In light of these findings, it was to be expected that the disorder would produce a large executive deficit (Simon et al., in press; Sobin et al., 2004). Sobin has reported in another paper (Sobin, Kiley-Bradeck, & Karayiorgou, 2005) that the deficit in resolving conflict is associated with the ability to inhibit a blink following a cue that a loud noise would be presented shortly (prepulse inhibition). The authors indicate that the association of the high-level attention and prepulse inhibition deficit suggests a pathway that includes both the basal ganglia and the anterior cingulate.

Summary

Many neurological and psychiatric disorders produce difficulty in attention. Data to date suggest that disorders have specific influences on attentional networks. However, a number of disorders influence the same network (e.g., Schizophrenia, Borderline Personality Disorder, and Alzheimer's dementia affect executive attention), and the same disorder can influence more than one network (e.g., Schizophrenia may affect both the executive and orienting network, although perhaps at different stages of the disorder). These findings reduce the utility of attention as a means of classifying disorders, but they may be useful in understanding their etiology and suggesting methods of treatment, at least of the attentional symptoms.

SUMMARY AND FUTURE DIRECTIONS

In this chapter, we described recent findings on the structure and development of temperament and related temperament and attention to the development of psychopathology. We noted that temperament involves a number of interacting systems, each of which follows its own course of development. We identified two major control systems of temperament, reactive fearfulness and self-regulatory effortful control, with the latter based on the development of executive attention that serves to moderate or break the approach and incentive-related systems and allow activation of lower probability responses.

We described a hierarchical structure of temperament. General negative affectivity includes dispositions toward fear, frustration/anger, sadness, and discomfort, as well as low soothability. General surgency, or extraversion, includes impulsivity, high-intensity pleasure, activity, and sociability. Effortful control includes inhibitory control, low-intensity pleasure, attentional shifting and attentional focusing. These three higher-order general dimensions of temperament are related to three of the Big Five factors, as well as the Big Three factors in adult personality.

As suggested by Cicchetti and Cohen (1995), there are multiple routes to psychopathology, as well as to positive adaptation, and the influence of a given temperamental characteristic may vary depending on other temperamental or contextual influences. The nature of the person's experiences and the choice of settings will also be influenced by affect and regulated by attention. Although experiences may be chosen on the basis of their affective consequences, they may also be influenced by the planning processes that are part of temperamental effortful control.

Temperamental factors may predispose children and adults to psychopathological outcomes and contribute to the maintenance, reduction, or intensification of an outcome. In addition, a given temperamental characteristic may predispose to more than one psychopathology outcome. Temperament is related to both risk and protective factors in the development of psychopathology; it may influence risk of recurrence of the disorder and may bias information processing about the self, leading to further risk or protective factors for the development of psychopathology. In addition, experience, including the experience of disorder, will affect the range of stimuli activating the temperamental response and the intensity and regulation of the reaction.

Temperament involves constitutional differences in reactivity and self-regulation. In this chapter, we were able to make connections between disorders and attentional networks. These connections are possible due to the increasing use of brain imaging studies of common aspects of brain networks and of individual differences. Temperamental differences in extraversion, negative affect, and persistence tasks can provide clues for understanding the genes responsible for the relatively high heritability of temperament scales. We expect the search for brain mechanisms underlying temperament and for candidate genes involved in producing these effects to be a major topic of research in the future.

The ability of temperamental differences to predict disorders has been impressive, but it is not yet possible to determine the direction of these effects. Increased understanding of the brain networks and genetic mechanisms related to temperamental dimensions could improve this picture and allow us to understand which aspects of temperament predictions of disorders are causative. A large number of disorders have now been shown to produce different specific effects on attention networks. Although these effects might not be reliable enough to be used as differential diagnoses, they do provide clues to the anatomy impaired by the disorder and in the future may guide more specific therapeutic strategies.

When we wrote this chapter for the first edition of the *Handbook,* we speculated on possible relations between temperament and psychopathology and on brain systems related to reactivity and self-regulation. Evidence for these connections has vastly improved in the 8 intervening years. We expect by the time the *Handbook* is again rewritten, these trends will be even more developed, and we hope that they will lead to both better understanding and more certain improvements in treatment.

REFERENCES

Achenbach, T. M., & Edelbrock, C. S. (1978). The classification of child psychology: A review and analysis of empirical efforts. *Psychological Bulletin, 85,* 1275–1301.

Ackerson, L. (1942). *Children's behavior problems* (Vol. 2). Chicago: University of Chicago Press.

Adolphs, R., & Tranel, D., Hamann, S., Young, A. W., Calder, A. J., Phelps, E. A., et al. (1999). Recognition of facial emotion in nine individuals with bilateral amygdala damage. *Neuropsychologia, 37*(10), 1111–1117.

Ahadi, S. A., & Rothbart, M. K. (1994). Temperament, development and the Big Five. In C. Halverson, R. Martin, & G. Kohnstamm (Eds.), *The developing structure of temperament and personality from infancy to adulthood* (pp. 189–208). Hillsdale, NJ: Erlbaum.

Akshoomoff, N., Pierce, K., & Courchesne, E. (2002). The neurobiological basis of Autism from a developmental perspective. *Development and Psychopathology, 14,* 613–634.

Allen, G., & Courschesne, E. (2001). Attention function and dysfunction in Autism. *Frontiers in Bioscience, 6,* 105–119.

Anderson, A. K., & Phelps, E. A. (2002). Is the human amygdala critical for the subjective experience of emotion?: Evidence of intact dispositional affect in patients with amygdala lesions. *Journal of Cognitive Neuroscience, 14,* 709–720.

Anderson, K. E., Lytton, H., & Romney, D. M. (1986). Mothers' interactions with normal and conduct-disordered boys: Who affects whom? *Developmental Psychology, 22,* 604–609.

Anderson, R. A. (1989). Visual eye movement functions of the posterior parietal cortex. *Annual Review of Neuroscience, 12,* 377–403.

Anderson, S. W., Damasio, H., Tranel, D., & Damasio, A. R. (2000). Long-term sequelae of prefrontal cortex damage acquired in early childhood. *Developmental Neuropsychology, 18,* 281–296.

Asendorpf, J. B. (1989). Shyness as a final common pathway for two different kinds of inhibition. *Journal of Personality and Social Psychology, 53,* 481–492.

Asendorpf, J. B. (1990). Development of inhibition during childhood: Evidence for situational specificity and a two-factor model. *Developmental Psychology, 26,* 721–730.

Asendorpf, J. B., & van Aken, M. A. G. (1994). Traits and relationship status: Stranger versus peer group inhibition and test intelligence versus peer group competence as early predictors of later self-esteem. *Child Development, 65,* 1786–1798.

Barkley, R. A. (1997). Behavioral inhibition, sustained attention, and executive functions: Constructing a unifying theory of ADHD. *Psychological Bulletin, 121,* 65–94.

Barron, A. P., & Earls, F. (1984). The relation of temperament and social factors to behavior problems in three-year-old children. *Journal of Child Psychology and Psychiatry, 25,* 23–33.

Bates, J. E. (1980). The concept of difficult temperament. *Merrill-Palmer Quarterly, 26,* 299–319.

Bates, J. E. (1989). Applications of temperament concepts. In G. A. Kohnstamm, J. E. Bates, & M. K. Rothbart (Eds.), *Temperament in childhood* (pp. 321–355). New York: Wiley.

Bates, J. E. (1990). Conceptual and empirical linkages between temperament and behavior problems: A commentary on the Sanson, Prior, and Kyrios study. *Merrill-Palmer Quarterly, 36,* 193–199.

Bates, J. E., & Bayles, K. (1988). The role of attachment in the development of behavior problems. In J. Belsky & T. Nezworski (Eds.), *Clinical implications of attachment: Child psychology* (pp. 253–299). Hillsdale, NJ: Erlbaum.

Bates, J. E., Bayles, K., Bennett, D. S., Ridge, B., & Brown, M. M. (1991). Origins of externalizing behavior problems at eight years of age. In D. Pepler & K. Rubin (Eds.), *Development and treatment of childhood aggression* (pp. 93–120). Hillsdale, NJ: Erlbaum.

Bates, J. E., Freeland, C. A. B., & Lounsbury, M. L. (1979). Measurement of infant difficultness. *Child Development, 50,* 794–803.

Bates, J. E., Maslin, C. A., & Frankel, K. A. (1985). Attachment security, mother-child interaction, and temperament as predictors of behavior-problem ratings at age three years. In I. Bretherton & E. Waters (Eds.), *Growing points in attachment theory and research: Society for Child Development monographs* (Serial No. 209, pp. 167–193).

Bates, J. E., Pettit, G. S., Dodge, K. A., & Ridge, B. (1998). Interaction of temperamental resistance to control and restrictive parenting in the development of externalizing behavior. *Developmental Psychology, 34,* 982–995.

Beane, M., & Marrocco, R. (2004). Cholinergic and noradrenergic inputs to the posterior parietal cortex modulate the components of exogenous attention. In M. I. Posner (Ed.), *Cognitive neuroscience of attention* (pp. 313–325). New York: Guilford Press.

Beauregard, M., Levesque, J., & Bourgouin, P. (2001). Neural correlates of conscious self-regulation of emotion. *Journal of Neuroscience, 21,* 6993–7000.

Beck, A. T. (1976). *Cognitive therapy and the emotional disorders.* Madison, CT: Meridian.

Behar, L., & Stringfield, S. (1974). A behavior rating scale for the preschool child. *Developmental Psychology, 10,* 601–610.

Belsky, J., Hsieh, K.-H., & Crnic, K. (1998). Mothering, fathering, and infant negativity as antecedents of boys' externalizing problems and inhibition at age 3 years: Differential susceptibility to rearing experience? *Development and Psychopathology, 10,* 301–319.

Benes, F. M. (1999). Model generation and testing to probe neural circuitry in the cingulate cortex of postmortem schizophrenic brains. *Schizophrenia Bulletin, 24,* 219–229.

Berger, A., Jones, L., Rothbart, M. K., & Posner, M. I. (2000). Computerized games to study the development of attention in childhood. *Behavioral Research Methods and Instrumentation, 32,* 297–303.

Biederman, J., Rosenbaum, J. F., Hirshfeld, D. R., Faraone, S. V., Bolduc, E. A., Gersten, M., et al. (1990). Psychiatric correlates of behavioral inhibition in young children of parents with and without psychiatric disorders. *Archives of General Psychiatry, 47,* 21–26.

Bijttebier, P. (1998). *Monitoring and blunting coping styles in children.* Unpublished doctoral thesis, University of Leuven, Belgium.

Blair, R. J. R., Jones, L., Clark, F., & Smith, M. (1997). The psychopath: A lack of responsiveness to distress cues? *Physiology, 34,* 192–198.

Blanchard, D. C., & Takahashi, S. N. (1988). No change in intermale aggression after amygdala lesions which reduce freezing. *Physiology and Behavior, 42*(6), 613–616.

Block, J. H., & Block, J. (1980). The role of ego-control and ego-resiliency in the organization of behavior. In W. A. Collins (Ed.),

Minnesota Symposia on Child Psychology (Vol. 13, pp. 39–101). Hillsdale, NJ: Erlbaum.

Block, J. H., Gjerde, P. F., & Block, J. H. (1991). Personality antecedents of depressive tendencies in 18-year-olds: A prospective study. *Journal of Personality and Social Psychology, 60,* 726–738.

Bohart, A. C., & Stipek, D. J. (2001). What have we learned? In A. C. Bohart & D. J. Stipek (Eds.), *Constructive and destructive behavior: Implications for family, school, and society* (pp. 367–397). Washington, DC: American Psychological Association.

Booth, J., Carlson, C. L., & Tucker, D. (2001, June). *Cognitive inattention in the ADHD subtypes.* Paper presented at the 10th meeting of the International Society for Research in Child and Adolescent Psychopathology, Vancouver, Canada.

Botwinick, M. M., Braver, T. S., Barch, D. M., Carter, C. S., & Cohen, J. D. (2001). Conflict monitoring and cognitive control. *Psychological Review, 108,* 624–652.

Bronson, W. C. (1972). The role of enduring orientations to the environment in personality development. *Genetic Psychology Monographs, 86,* 3–80.

Burt, C. (1938). The analysis of temperament. *British Journal of Medical Psychology, 17,* 158–188.

Burton, R. (1921). *The anatomy of melancholy.* Oxford: Oxford University Press. (Original work published 1621)

Bush, G., Luu, P., & Posner, M. I. (2000). Cognitive and emotional influences in anterior cingulate cortex. *Trends in Cognitive Sciences, 4,* 215–222.

Buss, A. H., & Plomin, R. (1975). *A temperament theory of personality development.* New York: Wiley.

Buss, A. H., & Plomin, R. (1984). *Temperament: Early developing personality traits.* Hillsdale, NJ: Erlbaum.

Buss, K. A., Schumacher, J. R. M., Dolski, I., Kalin, N. H., Goldsmith, H. H., & Davidson, R. J. (2003). Right frontal brain activity, cortisol, and withdrawal behavior in 6-month-old infants. *Behavioral Neuroscience, 117*(1), 11–20.

Calder, A. J., Lawrence, A. D., & Young, A. W. (2001). Neuropsychology of fear and loathing. *Nature Reviews Neuroscience, 2*(5), 352–363.

Calkins, S. D., Fox, N. A., & Marshall, T. R. (1996). Behavioral and psychological antecedents of inhibition in infancy. *Child Development, 67,* 523–540.

Campbell, S. B. (1991). Longitudinal studies of active and aggressive preschoolers: Individual differences in early behavior and in outcome. In D. Cicchetti & S. L. Toth (Eds.), *Rochester Symposium on Developmental Psychopathology: Vol. 2. Internalizing and externalizing expressions of dysfunction* (pp. 57–89). Hillsdale, NJ: Erlbaum.

Canli, T., Zhao, Z., Desmond, J. E., Kang, E. J., Gross, J., & Gabrieli, J. D. E. (2001). An fMRI study of personality influences on brain reactivity to emotional stimuli. *Behavioral Neuroscience, 115,* 33–42.

Carey, W. B., & McDevitt, S. C. (1978). Revision of the infant temperament questionnaire. *Pediatrics, 61,* 735–739.

Carlson, N. R. (1984). *Psychology: The science of behavior.* Boston: Allyn & Bacon.

Carver, C. S., & White, T. L. (1994). Behavioral inhibition, behavioral activation, and affective responses to impending reward and punishment: The BIS/BAS scales. *Journal of Personality and Social Psychology, 67,* 319–333.

Casey, B. J., Durston, S., & Fossella, J. A. (2001). Evidence for a mechanistic model of cognitive control. *Clinical Neuroscience Research, 1,* 267–282.

Casey, B. J., Trainor, R. J., Orendi, J. L., Schubert, A. B., Nystrom, L. E., Giedd, J. N., et al. (1997). A developmental functional MRI study of prefrontal activation during performance of a go-no-go task. *Journal of Cognitive Neuroscience, 9,* 835–846.

Caspi, A., Harrington, H., Milne, B., Amell, J. W., Theodore, R. F., & Moffitt, T. E. (2003). Children's behavioral styles at age 3 are linked to their adult personality traits at age 26. *Journal of Personality, 71*(4), 495–513.

Caspi, A., Henry, B., McGee, R. O., Moffitt, T. E., & Silva, P. A. (1995). Temperamental origins of child and adolescent behavior problems: From age three to age fifteen. *Child Development, 66,* 55–68.

Caspi, A., McClay, J., Moffitt, T., Mill, J., Martin, J., Craig, I. W., et al. (2002). Role of genotype in the cycle of violence in maltreated children. *Science, 297,* 851–854.

Caspi, A., & Silva, P. A. (1995). Temperamental qualities at age three predict personality traits in young adulthood: Longitudinal evidence from a birth cohort. *Child Development, 66,* 486–498.

Chen, X., Rubin, K. H., & Li, B.-S. (1995). Depressed mood in Chinese children: Relations with school performance and family environment. *Journal of Consulting and Clinical Psychology, 63,* 938–947.

Chen, X., Rubin, K. H., & Sun, Y. (1992). Social reputation and peer relationships in Chinese and Canadian children: A cross-cultural study. *Child Development, 63,* 1336–1343.

Chess, S., & Thomas, A. (1986). *Temperament in clinical practice.* New York: Guilford Press.

Cicchetti, D., & Cohen, D. J. (Eds.). (1995). *Developmental psychopathology: Vol. 2. Risk, disorder, and adaptation.* New York: Wiley.

Cicchetti, D., & Toth, S. L. (Eds.). (1991). *Rochester Symposium on Developmental Psychopathology: Vol. 2. Internalizing and externalizing expressions of dysfunction.* Hillsdale, NJ: Erlbaum.

Cicchetti, D., & Toth, S. L. (1995). Developmental psychopathology and disorders of affect. In D. Cicchetti & D. J. Cohen (Eds.), *Developmental psychopathology: Vol. 2. Risk, disorder, and adaptation* (pp. 369–420). New York: Wiley.

Cicchetti, D., & Tucker, D. (1994). Development and self-regulatory structures of the mind. *Development and Psychopathology, 61,* 533–549.

Clark, D. A., Beck, A. T., & Stewart, B. (1990). Cognitive specificity and positive-negative affectivity: Complementary or contradictory view on anxiety and depression? *Journal of Abnormal Psychology, 99,* 148–155.

Clark, L. A., Watson, D., & Mineka, S. (1994). Temperament, personality, and the mood and anxiety disorders. *Journal of Abnormal Psychology, 103,* 103–116.

Clohessy, A. B., Posner, M. I., & Rothbart, M. K. (2001). Development of the functional visual field. *Acta Psychologica, 106,* 51–68.

Cloninger, C. R. (1986). A unified biosocial theory of personality and its role in the development of anxiety states. *Psychiatric Developments, 3,* 167–226.

Cloninger, C. R. (1987). A systematic method for clinical description and classification of personality variants. *Archives of General Psychiatry, 44,* 573–588.

Corbetta, M., & Shulman, G. L. (2002). Control of goal-directed and stimulus-driven attention in the brain. *Nature Reviews Neuroscience, 3,* 201–215.

Costa, P. T., Jr., & McCrae, R. R. (1988). From catalog to classification: Murray's needs and the five-factor model. *Journal of Personality and Social Psychology, 55,* 258–265.

Curran, T., & Keele, S. W. (1993). Attentional and nonattentional forms of sequence learning. *Journal of Experimental Psychology: Learning, Memory, and Cognition, 19,* 189–202.

Damasio, A. R. (1994). *Descartes' error: Emotion, reason and the brain.* New York: G. P. Putnam.

Davidson, R. J., & Fox, N. A. (1989). Frontal brain asymmetry predicts infants' response to maternal separation. *Journal of Abnormal Psychology, 98,* 127–131.

Davidson, R. J., Putnam, K. M., & Larson, C. L. (2000). Dysfunction in the neural circuitry of emotion regulation: A possible prelude to violence. *Science, 289,* 591–594.

Davidson, R. J., Scherer, K. R., Goldsmith, H. H., Pizzagalli, D., Nitschke, J. B., Kalin, N. H., et al. (2003). Part I, Neuroscience. In R. J. Davidson & K. R. Scherer (Eds.), *Handbook of affective sciences* (pp. 3–128). London: Oxford University Press.

Davidson, R. J., & Tomarken, A. J. (1989). Laterality and emotion: An electrophysiological approach. In F. Boller & J. Grafman (Eds.), *Handbook of neuropsychology* (pp. 419–441). Amsterdam, The Netherlands: Elsevier.

Davis, M., Hitchcock, J. M., & Rosen, J. B. (1987). Anxiety and the amygdala: Pharmacological and anatomical analysis of the fear-potentiated startle paradigm. In G. Bower (Ed.), *The psychology of learning and motivation: Advances in research and theory* (Vol. 21, pp. 263–305). San Diego: Academic Press.

Depue, R. A., & Collins, P. F. (1999). Neurobiology of the structure of personality: Dopamine, facilitation of incentive motivation, and extraversion. *Behavioral and Brain Sciences, 22,* 491–569.

Depue, R. A., & Iacono, W. G. (1989). Neurobehavioral aspects of affective disorders. In M. R. Rosenzweig & L. Y. Porter (Eds.), *Annual review of psychology* (Vol. 40, pp. 457–492). Palo Alto, CA: Annual Reviews.

Derryberry, D., & Reed, M. A. (1994). Temperament and the self-organization of personality. *Development and Psychopathology, 6,* 653–676.

Derryberry, D., & Reed, M. A. (1996). Regulatory processes and the development of cognitive representations. *Development and Psychopathology, 8,* 215–234.

Derryberry, D., & Rothbart, M. K. (1984). Emotion, attention, and temperament. In C. Izard, J. Kagan, & R. Zajonc (Eds.), *Emotion, cognition, and behavior* (pp. 132–166). Cambridge, England: Cambridge University Press.

Derryberry, D., & Rothbart, M. K. (1988). Arousal, affect, and attention as components of temperament. *Journal of Personality and Social Psychology, 55,* 958–966.

Derryberry, D., & Tucker, D. M. (1992). Neural mechanisms of emotion. *Journal of Consulting and Clinical Psychology, 60,* 329–338.

Diamond, A. (1991). Neuropsychological insights into the meaning of object concept development. In S. Carey & R. Gelman (Eds.), *The epigenesis of mind: Essays on biology and cognition* (pp. 67–110). Hillsdale, NJ: Erlbaum.

Diamond, A., Briand, L., Fossella, J., & Gehlbach, L. (2004). Genetic and neurochemical modulation of prefrontal cognitive functions in children. *American Journal of Psychiatry, 161,* 125–132.

Diamond, S. (1974). *The roots of psychology.* New York: Basic Books.

Digman, J. M., & Inouye, J. (1986). Further specification of the five robust factors of personality. *Journal of Personality and Social Psychology, 50,* 116–123.

Drevets, W. C. (2000). Neuroimaging studies of mood disorders. *Biological Psychiatry, 18,* 813–829.

Drevets, W. C., & Raichle, M. E. (1998). Reciprocal suppression of regional cerebral blood flow during emotional versus higher cognitive processes: Implications for interactions between emotion and cognition. *Cognition and Emotion, 12,* 353–385.

Driver, J., Eimer, M., & Macaluso, E. (2004). Neurobiology of human spatial attention: Modulation, generation, and integration. In N. Kanwisher & J. Duncan (Eds.), *Attention and performance XX: Func-*

tional brain imaging of visual cognition (pp. 267–300). Oxford: Oxford University Press.

Duncan, J., Seitz, R. J., Kolodny, J., Bor, D., Herzog, H., Ahmed, A., et al. (2000). A neural basis for general intelligence. *Science, 289,* 457–460.

Eagly, A. H., & Steffen, V. J. (1986). Gender and aggressive behavior: A meta-analytic review of the social-psychological literature. *Psychological Bulletin, 100,* 309–330.

Earls, F., & Jung, K. G. (1987). Temperament and home environment characteristics and causal factors in the early development of childhood psychopathology. *Journal of the American Academy of Child and Adolescent Psychiatry, 26,* 491–498.

Early, T. S., Posner, M. I., Reiman, E. M., & Raichle, M. E. (1989). Left striato-pallidal hyperactivity in Schizophrenia: Part I. Phenomenology and thought disorder. *Psychiatric Developments, 2,* 85–121.

Eaton, W. O. (1994). Temperament, development, and the five-factor model: Lessons from activity level. In C. F. Halverson Jr., G. A. Kohnstamm, & R. P. Martin (Eds.), *The developing structure of temperament and personality from infancy to adulthood* (pp. 173–187). Hillsdale, NJ: Erlbaum.

Edelbrock, C., & Achenbach, T. M. (1980). A typology of Child Behavior Profile patterns: Distribution and correlates in disturbed children aged 6 to 16. *Journal of Abnormal Child Psychology, 8,* 441–470.

Egan, M. F., Kojima, M., Callicott, J. H., Goldberg, T. E., Kolachana, B. S., Bertolino, A., et al. (2003). The BDNF val66met polymorphism affects activity-dependent secretion of BDNF and H. *Cell Publication, 112* 257–269.

Eisenberg, N., Cumberland, A., Spinrad, T. L., Fabes, R. A., Shepard, S. A., Reiser, M., et al. (2001). The relations of regulation and emotionality to children's externalizing and internalizing problem behavior. *Child Development, 72,* 1112–1134.

Eisenberg, N., Fabes, R. A., Guthrie, I. K., Murphy, B. C., Maszk, P., Holgren, R., et al. (1996). The relations of regulation and emotionality to problem behavior in elementary school children. *Development and Psychopathology, 8,* 141–162.

Eisenberg, N., Fabes, R. A., Guthrie, I. K., & Reiser, M. (2000). Dispositional emotionality and regulation: Their role in predicting quality of social functioning. *Journal of Personality and Social Psychology, 78*(1), 136–157.

Eisenberg, N., Fabes, R. A., Guthrie, I. K., & Reiser, M. (2002). The role of emotionality and regulation in children's social competence and adjustment. In L. Pulkinnen & A. Caspi (Eds.), *Paths to successful development: Personality in the life course* (pp. 46–70). Cambridge, England: Cambridge University Press.

Eisenberg, N., Guthrie, I. K., Fabes, R. A., Shepard, S., Losoya, S., Murphy, B. C., et al. (2000). Prediction of elementary school children's externalizing problem behaviors from attentional and behavioral regulation and negative emotionality. *Child Development, 71,* 1367–1382.

Eisenberg, N., Shepard, S. A., Fabes, R. A., Murphy, B. C., & Guthrie, I. K. (1998). Shyness and children's emotionality, regulation, and coping: Contemporaneous, longitudinal, and across-context relations. *Child Development, 69,* 767–790.

Eley, T. C., & Stevenson, J. (2000). Specific life events and chronic experiences differentially associated with depression and anxiety in young twins. *Journal of Abnormal Child Psychology, 28,* 383–394.

Ellis, L. K. (2002). *Individual differences and adolescent psychosocial development.* Unpublished doctoral dissertation, University of Oregon, Eugene.

Evans, D., & Rothbart, M. K. (2004). *A hierarchal model of temperament and the Big Five.* Manuscript submitted for publication. Available from evansde@moffitt.usf.edu.

Eysenck, H. J. (1944). Types of personality: A factorial study of 700 neurotics. *Journal of Mental Science, 90,* 851–861.

Eysenck, H. J. (1947). *Dimensions of personality.* London: Routledge & Kegan Paul.

Eysenck, H. J. (1970). *The structure of human personality* (3rd ed.). London: Methuen.

Eysenck, H. J., & Eysenck, M. W. (1985). *Personality and individual differences.* New York: Plenum Press.

Fan, J., Flombaum, J. I., McCandliss, B. D., Thomas, K. M., & Posner, M. I. (2003). Cognitive and brain mechanisms of conflict. *NeuroImage, 18,* 42–57.

Fan, J., Fossella, J., Sommer, T., Wu, Y., & Posner, M. I. (2003). Mapping the genetic variation of executive attention onto brain activity. *Proceedings of the National Academy of Sciences of the USA, 100,* 7406–7411.

Fan, J., McCandliss, B. D., Sommer, T., Raz, M., & Posner, M. I. (2002). Testing the efficiency and independence of attentional networks. *Journal of Cognitive Neuroscience, 3,* 340–347.

Fan, J., Wu, Y., Fossella, J., & Posner, M. I. (2001). Assessing the heritability of attentional networks. *BioMed Central Neuroscience, 2,* 14.

Fernandez-Duque, D., & Black, S. (in press). *Attentional networks in normal aging and Alzheimer's disease.* Manuscript submitted for publication.

Fisher, P. A., & Fagot, B. I. (1992, April). *Temperament, parental discipline, and child psychopathology: A social-interactional model.* Paper presented at the annual convention of the Western Psychological Association, Portland, OR.

Fossella, J., Posner, M. I., Fan, J., Swanson, J. M., & Pfaff, D. M. (2002). Attentional phenotypes for the analysis of higher mental function. *Scientific World Journal, 2,* 217–223.

Fox, E., Ricardo, R., & Dutton, K. (2002). Attentional bias for threat: Evidence for delayed disengagement from emotional faces. *Cognition and Emotion, 16,* 355–379.

Fox, E., Russo, R., Bowles, R. J., & Dutton, K. (2001). Do threatening stimuli draw or hold attention in subclinical anxiety? *Journal of Experimental Psychology: General, 130,* 681–700.

Fox, N. A., Calkins, S. D., & Bell, M. A. (1994). Neural plasticity and development in the first two years of life: Evidence from cognitive and socioemotional domains of research. *Development and Psychopathology, 6,* 677–696.

Frith, U. (2001). Mind blindness and the brain in Autism. *Neuron, 32*(6), 969–979.

Fullard, W., McDevitt, S. C., & Carey, W. B. (1984). Assessing temperament in one- to three-year-old children. *Journal of Pediatric Psychology, 9,* 205–217.

Galen, N. (1652). *Galen's art of physik* (N. Culpeper, Trans.). London: Peter Cole.

Gara, M. A., Woolfolk, R. L., Cohen, B. D., Goldston, R. B., Allen, L. A., & Novalany, J. (1993). Perception of self and other in major depression. *Journal of Abnormal Psychology, 102,* 93–100.

Gartstein, M. A., & Rothbart, M. K. (2003). Studying infant temperament via the revised Infant Behavior Questionnaire. *Infant Behavior and Development, 26,* 64–86.

Gerardi-Caulton, G. (2000). Sensitivity to spatial conflict and the development of self-regulation in children 24–36 months of age. *Developmental Science, 3,* 397–404.

Gilliom, M., & Shaw, D. S. (2004). Codevelopment of externalizing and internalizing problems in early childhood. *Development and Psychopathology, 16*(2), 313–333.

Gjerde, P. F., Block, J., & Block, J. H. (1988). Depressive symptoms and personality during late adolescence: Gender differences in the externalization-internalization of symptom expression. *Journal of Abnormal Psychology, 97,* 475–486.

Goldberg, L. R. (1990). An alternative "description of personality": The Big-Five factor structure. *Journal of Personality and Social Psychology, 59,* 1216–1229.

Goldsmith, H. H., & Campos, J. J. (1982). Toward a theory of infant temperament. In R. Emde & R. Harmon (Eds.), *Attachment and affiliative systems* (pp. 161–193). New York: Plenum Press.

Goldsmith, H. H., Rieser-Danner, L. A., & Briggs, S. (1991). Evaluating convergent and discriminant validity of temperament questionnaires for preschoolers, toddlers, and infants. *Developmental Psychology, 27,* 566–579.

Gosling, S. D., & John, O. P. (1999). Personality dimensions in nonhuman animals: A cross-species review. *Current Directions in Psychological Science, 8,* 69–75.

Gray, J. A. (1971). *The psychology of fear and stress.* New York: McGraw-Hill.

Gray, J. A. (1975). *Elements of a two-process theory of learning.* New York: Academic Press.

Gray, J. A. (1979). A neuropsychological theory of anxiety. In C. E. Izard (Ed.), *Emotions in personality and psychopathology* (pp. 303–335). New York: Plenum Press.

Gray, J. A. (1982). *The neuropsychology of anxiety.* New York: Oxford University Press.

Gray, J. A. (1991). The neuropsychology of temperament. In J. Strelau & A. Angleitner (Eds.), *Explorations in temperament: International perspectives on theory and measurement* (pp. 105–128). New York: Plenum Press.

Gray, J. A. (1994). Framework for a taxonomy of psychiatric disorder. In S. H. M. van Goozen, N. E. Van de Poll, & J. A. Sargeant (Eds.), *Emotions: Essays on emotion theory* (pp. 29–59). Hillsdale, NJ: Erlbaum.

Gray, J. A., & McNaughton, N. (1996). The neuropsychology of anxiety: Reprise. In D. A. Hope (Ed.), *Nebraska Symposium on Motivation: Perspectives on anxiety, panic, and fear* (Vol. 43, pp. 61–134). Lincoln: University of Nebraska Press.

Graziano, W. G. (1994). The development of agreeableness as a dimension of personality. In C. F. Halverson, G. A. Kohnstamm, & R. P. Martin (Eds.), *The developing structure of temperament and personality from infancy to adulthood* (pp. 339–354). Hillsdale, NJ: Erlbaum.

Graziano, W. G., & Eisenberg, N. (1997). Agreeableness: A dimension of personality. In R. Hogan, J. A. Johnson, & S. Briggs (Eds.), *Handbook of personality psychology* (pp. 795–824). San Diego: Academic Press.

Graziano, W. G., & Tobin, R. M. (2002). Agreeableness: Dimension of personality or social desirability artifact? *Journal of Personality, 70*(5), 695–727.

Guerin, D. W., Gottfried, A. W., Oliver, P. H., & Thomas, C. W. (1994). Temperament and school functioning during early adolescence. *Journal of Early Adolescence, 14,* 200–225.

Gusnard, D. A., Ollinger, J. M., Shulman, G. L., Cloninger, C. R., Price, J. L., Van Essen, D. C., et al. (2003). Persistence and brain circuitry. *Proceedings of the National Academy of Sciences of the United States, 100,* 3479–3484.

Hagekull, B. (1989). Longitudinal stability of temperament within a behavioral style framework. In G. A. Kohnstamm, J. E. Bates, & M. K. Rothbart (Eds.), *Temperament in childhood* (pp. 283–297). Chichester, England: Wiley.

Hagekull, B. (1994). Infant temperament and early childhood functioning: Possible relations to the five-factor model. In J. C. J. Halverson, G. A. Kohnstamm, & R. P. Martin (Eds.), *The developing structure of temperament and personality* (pp. 227–240). Hillsdale, NJ: Erlbaum.

Hagekull, B., & Bohlin, G. (1981). Individual stability in dimensions of infant behavior. *Infant Behavior and Development, 4,* 97–108.

Haist, F., Adamo, M., Westerfield, M., Courchesne, E., & Townsend, J. (2005). The functional neuroanatomy of spatial attention in Autism spectrum disorder. *Developmental Neuropsychology, 27*(3), 425–458.

Haith, M., Hazan, C., & Goodman, G. S. (1988). Expectation and anticipation of dynamic visual events by 3.5-month-old babies. *Child Development, 59,* 467–479.

Harman, C., Rothbart, M. K., & Posner, M. I. (1997). Distress and attention interactions in early infancy. *Motivation and Emotion, 21,* 27–43.

Harmon-Jones, E., & Allen, J. J. B. (1997). Behavioral activation sensitivity and resting frontal EEG asymmetry: Covariation of putative indicators related to risk for mood disorders. *Journal of Abnormal Psychology, 106,* 159–163.

Hartman, C., Hox, J., Mellenbergh, G. J., Boyle, M. H., Offord, D. R., Racine, Y., et al. (2001). DSM-IV internal construct validity: When a taxonomy meets data. *Journal of Child Psychology and Psychiatry and Allied Disciplines, 42,* 817–836.

Hegvik, R. L., McDevitt, S. C., & Carey, W. B. (1982). The Middle Childhood Temperament Questionnaire. *Developmental and Behavioral Pediatrics, 3,* 197–200.

Hershey, K. L. (1992). *Concurrent and longitudinal relationships of temperament to children's laboratory performance and behavior problems.* Unpublished doctoral dissertation, University of Oregon, Eugene.

Holroyd, C. B., & Coles, M. G. H. (2002). The neural basis of human error processing: Reinforcement learning, dopamine and the error related negativity. *Psychological Review, 109,* 679–709.

Huey, S. J., Jr., & Weisz, J. R. (1997). Ego control, ego resiliency, and the five-factor model as predictors of behavioral and emotional problems in clinic-referred children and adolescents. *Journal of Abnormal Psychology, 106,* 404–415.

Insel, T. R. (2003). Is social attachment an addictive disorder? *Physiology and Behavior, 79*(3), 351–357.

John, O. P. (1989). Towards a taxonomy of personality descriptors. In D. M. Buss & N. Cantor (Eds.), *Personality psychology: Recent trends and emerging directions* (pp. 261–271). New York: Springer-Verlag.

Jung, C. G. (1923). *Psychological types or the psychology of individuation.* New York: Harcourt.

Jung, C. G. (1953). *Contributions to analytic psychology.* In F. Fordham (Ed.), *An introduction to Jung's psychology.* New York: Plenum Press. (Original work published 1928)

Kagan, J. (1989). The concept of behavioral inhibition to the unfamiliar. In J. S. Reznick (Ed.), *Perspectives on behavioral inhibition* (pp. 1–24). Chicago: University of Chicago Press.

Kagan, J. (1994). *Galen's prophecy: Temperament in human nature.* New York: Basic Books.

Kagan, J. (1998). Biology and the child. In W. S. E. Damon & N. V. E. Eisenberg (Eds.), *Handbook of child psychology: Vol. 3. Social, emotional and personality development* (5th ed., pp. 177–235). New York: Wiley.

Kagan, J., Snidman, N., Zentner, M., & Peterson, E. (1999). Infant temperament and anxious symptoms in school age children. *Development and Psychopathology, 11,* 209–224.

Kalin, N. H., Larson, C., Shelton, S. E., & Davidson, R. J. (1998). Asymmetric frontal brain activity, cortisol, and behavior associated with fearful temperament in rhesus monkeys. *Behavioral Neuroscience, 112,* 286–292.

Kant, I. (1978). *Anthropology from a pragmatic point of view.* Carbondale: Southern Illinois University Press. (Original work published 1798)

Karnath, H.-O., Ferber, S., & Himmelbach, M. (2001). Spatial awareness is a function of the temporal not the posterior parietal lobe. *Nature, 411,* 951–953.

Keenan, K., & Shaw, D. S. (1994). The development of aggression in toddlers: A study of low-income families. *Journal of Abnormal Child Psychology, 22,* 53–77.

Keiley, M. K., Lofthouse, N., Bates, J. E., Dodge, K. A., & Pettit, G. S. (2003). Differential risks of covarying and pure components in mother and teacher reports of externalizing and internalizing behavior across ages 5 to 14. *Journal of Abnormal Child Psychology, 31,* 264–283.

Kendler, K. S., Heath, A. C., Martin, N., & Eaves, L. J. (1987). Symptoms of anxiety and depression and generalized anxiety disorder: Same genes (partly) different environments? *Archives of General Psychiatry, 44,* 451–457.

Kendler, K. S., Myers, J., Prescott, C. A., & Neale, M. C. (2001). The genetic epidemiology of irrational fears and phobias in men. *Archives of General Psychiatry, 58,* 257–265.

Kendler, K. S., Neale, M. C., Kessler, R. C., Heath, A. C., & Eaves, L. J. (1992). The genetic epidemiology of phobias in women: The inter-relationship of agoraphobia, social phobia, situational phobia, and simple phobia. *Archives of General Psychiatry, 49,* 273–281.

Kovacs, M., & Devlin, B. (1998). Internalizing disorders in childhood. *Journal of Child Psychology and Psychiatry and Allied Disciplines, 39,* 47–63.

Kremen, A. M., & Block, J. (1998). The roots of ego-control in young adulthood: Links with parenting in early childhood. *Journal of Personality and Social Psychology, 75,* 1062–1075.

Krueger, R. F., Caspi, A., Moffitt, T. E., White, J., & Stouthamer-Loeber, M. (1996). Delay of gratification, psychopathology, and personality: Is low self-control specific to externalizing problems? *Journal of Personality, 64,* 107–129.

Krueger, R. F., Hicks, B. M., & McGue, M. (2001). Altruism and antisocial behavior: Independent tendencies, unique personality correlates, distinct etiologies. *Psychological Science, 12,* 397–402.

Landry, R., & Bryson, S. E. (2004). Impaired disengagement of attention in young children with Autism. *Journal of Child Psychology and Psychiatry, 45,* 1115–1122.

Lawrence, A. D., & Calder, A. J. (in press). Homologizing human emotions. In D. Evans & P. Cruse (Eds.), *Emotion, evolution, and rationality.* Oxford: Oxford University Press.

Lawrence, A. D., Calder, A. J., McGowan, S. W., & Grasby, P. M. (2002). Selective disruption of the recognition of facial expressions of anger. *NeuroReport, 13,* 881–884.

LeDoux, J. E. (1987). Cognitive-emotional interactions in the brain. *Cognition and Emotion, 3*(4), 267–289.

LeDoux, J. E. (1989). Emotion. In F. Plum (Ed.), *Handbook of physiology: Vol. V. Higher functions of the brain* (pp. 419–460). Bethesda, MD: American Physiological Society.

Lee, C. L., & Bates, J. E. (1985). Mother-child interaction at age two years and perceived difficult temperament. *Child Development, 56,* 1314–1325.

Lemery, K. S., Essex, M. J., & Smider, N. A. (2002). Revealing the relation between temperament and behavior problem symptoms by eliminating measurement confounding: Expert ratings and factor analyses. *Child Development, 73,* 867–882.

Lengua, L. J., West, S. G., & Sandler, I. N. (1998). Temperament as a predictor of symptomatology in children: Addressing contamination of measures. *Child Development, 69,* 164–181.

Lengua, L. J., Wolchik, S. A., Sandler, I. N., & West, S. G. (2000). The additive and interactive effects of parenting and temperament in predicting problems of children of divorce. *Journal of Clinical Child Psychology, 29,* 232–244.

Lerner, J. V., Nitz, K., Talwar, R., & Lerner, R. M. (1989). On the functional significance of temperamental individuality: A developmental contextual view of the concept of goodness of fit. In G. A. Kohnstamm, J. E. Bates, & M. K. Rothbart (Eds.), *Temperament in childhood* (pp. 509–522). Chichester, England: Wiley.

Lesch, K. P., Bengel, D., Heils, A., Sabol, S. Z., Greenberg, B. D., Petri, S., et al. (1996). A gene regulatory region polymorphism alters serotonin transporter expression and is associated with anxiety-related personality traits. *Science, 274,* 1527–1531.

Liotti, M., Mayberg, H. S., McGinnis, S., Brannan, S. L., & Jerabeck, P. (2003). Unmasking disease-specific cerebral flow abnormalities: Mood challenge in patients with remitted unipolar depression. *American Journal of Psychiatry, 159,* 183–186.

Lonigan, C. J., & Phillips, B. M. (2001). Temperamental influences on the development of anxiety disorders. In M. E. Vasey & M. R. Dadds (Eds.), *The developmental psychopathology of anxiety* (pp. 60–91). New York: Oxford University Press.

Luria, A. R. (1961). *The role of speech in the regulation of normal and abnormal behavior.* New York: Liveright.

MacDonald, A. W., Cohen, J. D., Stenger, V. A., & Carter, C. S. (2000). Dissociating the role of the dorsolateral prefrontal and anterior cingulate cortex in cognitive control. *Science, 288,* 1835–1838.

Marrocco, R. T., & Davidson, M. C. (1998). Neurochemistry of attention. In R. Parasuraman (Ed.), *The attention brain* (pp. 35–50). Cambridge, MA: MIT Press.

Martin, R., & Presley, R. (1991, April). *Dimensions of temperament during the preschool years.* Paper presented at the biennial meeting of the Society for Research in Child Development, Seattle, WA.

Maruff, P., Currie, J., Hay, D., McArthur-Jackson, C., & Malone, V. (1995). Asymmetries in the covert orienting of visual spatial attention in Schizophrenia. *Neuropsychologia, 31,* 1205–1223.

Maziade, M., Caron, C., Cote, R., Merette, C., Bernier, H., Laplante, B., et al. (1990). Psychiatric status of adolescents who had extreme temperaments at age 7. *American Journal of Psychiatry, 147,* 1531–1536.

Maziade, M., Cote, R., Bernier, H., Boutin, P., & Thivierge, J. (1989). Significance of extreme temperament in infancy for clinical status in preschool years 11: Patterns of temperament and implications for the appearance of disorders. *British Journal of Psychiatry, 154,* 544–551.

McClowry, S. G., Giangrande, S. K., Tommasini, N. R., Clinton, W., Foreman, N. S., Lynch, K., et al. (1994). The effects of child temperament, maternal characteristics, and family circumstances on the maladjustment of school-age children. *Research in Nursing and Health, 17,* 25–35.

Merenda, P. F. (1987). Toward a four-factor theory of temperament and/or personality. *Journal of Personality Assessment, 51,* 367–374.

Merikangas, K. R., Swendsen, J. D., Preisig, M. A., & Chazan, R. Z. (1998). Psychopathology and temperament in parents and offspring: Results of a family study. *Journal of Affective Disorders, 51,* 63–74.

Mineka, S., Watson, D., & Clark, L. A. (1998). Comorbidity of anxiety and unipolar mood disorders. *Annual Review of Psychology, 49,* 377–412.

Moffitt, T. E., Caspi, A., Dickson, N., Silva, P. A., & Stanton, W. (1996). Childhood-onset versus adolescent-onset antisocial conduct in males: Natural history from age 3 to 18. *Development and Psychopathology, 8,* 399–424.

Nichols, S., & Newman, J. P. (1986). Effects of punishment on response latency in extraverts. *Journal of Personality and Social Psychology, 50,* 624–630.

Nishijo, H., Ono, T., & Nishino, H. (1988). Single neuron responses in amygdala of alert monkey during complex sensory stimulation with affective significance. *Journal of Neuroscience, 8,* 3570–3583.

Ochsner, K. N., Bunge, S. A., Gross, J. J., & Gabrieli, J. D. E. (2002). Rethinking feelings: An fMRI study of the cognitive regulation of emotion. *Journal of Cognitive Neuroscience, 14,* 1215–1229.

Ohman, A. (2000). Fear and anxiety: Evolutionary, cognitive, and clinical perspectives. In M. Lewis & J. M. Haviland-Jones (Eds.), *Handbook of emotions* (2nd ed., pp. 573–593). New York: Guilford Press.

Panksepp, J. (1982). Toward a general psychobiological theory of emotions. *Behavioral and Brain Sciences, 5,* 407–468.

Panksepp, J. (1986a). The neurochemistry of behavior. *Annual Review of Psychology, 37,* 77–107.

Panksepp, J. (1986b). The psychobiology of prosocial behaviors: Separation distress, play, and altruism. In C. Zahn-Waxler, E. M. Cummings, & R. Iannotti (Eds.), *Altruism and aggression: Biological and social origins* (pp. 19–57). Cambridge, MA: Cambridge University Press.

Panksepp, J. (1993). Neurochemical control of moods and emotions: Amino acids to neuropeptides. In M. Lewis & J. M. Haviland (Eds.), *Handbook of emotions* (pp. 87–107). New York: Guilford Press.

Panksepp, J. (1998). *Affective neuroscience: The foundations of human and animal emotions.* New York: Oxford University Press.

Pardo, P. J., Knesevich, M. A., Vogler, G. P., Pardo, J. V., Towne, B., Cloninger, C. R., et al. (2000). Genetic and state variables of neurocognitive dysfunction in Schizophrenia: A twin study. *Schizophrenia Bulletin, 26,* 459–477.

Parker, J. G., & Asher, S. R. (1987). Peer relations and later personal adjustment: Are low-accepted children at risk? *Psychological Bulletin, 102,* 357–389.

Patterson, C. M., Kosson, D. S., & Newman, J. P. (1987). Reaction to punishment, reflectivity, and passive avoidance learning in extraverts. *Journal of Personality and Social Psychology, 52,* 565–575.

Patterson, G. R. (1977). Accelerating stimuli for two classes of coercive behaviors. *Journal of Abnormal Child Psychology, 5,* 335–350.

Patterson, G. R. (1980). Mothers: The unacknowledged victims. *Monographs of the Society for Research in Child Development, 45*(5, Serial No. 186), 1–64.

Patterson, G. R., & Capaldi, D. M. (1990). A mediational model for boys' depressed mood. In J. Rolf, A. S. Masten, D. Cicchetti, K. H. Neuchterlin, & S. Weintraub (Eds.), *Risk and protective factors in the development of psychopathology* (pp. 141–163). New York: Cambridge University Press.

Pennington, B. F. (2002). *The development of psychopathology: Nature and nurture.* New York: Guilford Press.

Pliszka, S. R. (1989). Effect of anxiety on cognition, behavior, and stimulant response in ADHD. *Journal of the American Academy of Child and Adolescent Psychiatry, 28,* 882–887.

Plomin, R. (1982). The concept of temperament: A response to Thomas, Chess, and Korn. *Merrill-Palmer Quarterly, 28,* 25–33.

Pollak, S. D., & Kistler, D. J. (2002). Early experience is associated with the development of categorical representations for facial expressions of emotion. *Proceedings of the National Academy of Sciences of the United States, 99,* 9072–9076.

Posner, M. I. (1980). Orienting of attention: The 7th Sir F. C. Bartlett Lecture. *Quarterly Journal of Experimental Psychology, 32,* 3–25.

Posner, M. I., & Fan, J. (in press). Attention as an organ system. In J. Pomerantz (Ed.), *Neurobiology of perception and communication: From synapse to society. The Fourth De Lange Conference.* Cambridge, England: Cambridge University Press.

Posner, M. I., Inhoff, A., Friedrich, F. J., & Cohen, A. (1987). Isolating attentional systems: A cognitive-anatomical analysis. *Psychobiology, 15,* 107–121.

Posner, M. I., & Keele, S. W. (1968). On the genesis of abstract ideas. *Journal of Experimental Psychology, 77,* 353–363.

Posner, M. I., & Petersen, S. E. (1990). The attention system of the human brain. *Annual Review of Neuroscience, 13,* 25–42.

Posner, M. I., & Rothbart, M. K. (1992). Attention and conscious experience. In A. D. Milner & M. D. Rugg (Eds.), *The neuropsychology of consciousness* (pp. 91–112). London: Academic Press.

Posner, M. I., & Rothbart, M. K. (1998). Attention, self-regulation, and consciousness. *Philosophical Transactions of the Royal Society of London. Series B, Biological Sciences, 353,* 1915–1927.

Posner, M. I., & Rothbart, M. K. (2000). Developing mechanisms of self regulation. *Development and Psychopathology, 12,* 427–441.

Posner, M. I., Rothbart, M. K., Vizueta, N., Levy, K., Thomas, K. M., & Clarkin, J. (2002). Attentional mechanisms of borderline personality disorder. *Proceedings of the National Academy of Sciences, 99,* 16366–16370.

Prior, M. R., Sanson, A., Oberklaid, F., & Northam, E. (1987). Measurement of temperament in one- to three-year-old children. *International Journal of Behavioral Development, 10,* 131–132.

Puig-Antich, J. (1982). Major depression and conduct disorder in prepuberty. *Journal of the American Academy of Child Psychiatry, 21,* 118–128.

Radke-Yarrow, M., & Sherman, T. (1990). Hard growing: Children who survive. In J. E. Rolf, A. S. Masten, D. Cicchetti, K. H. Neuchterlein, & S. Weintraub (Eds.), *Risk and protective factors in the development of psychopathology* (pp. 97–119). New York: Cambridge University Press.

Rainville, P., Duncan, G. H., Price, D. D., Carrier, B., & Bushnell, M. C. (1997). Pain affect encoded in human anterior cingulate but not somatosensory cortex. *Science, 277,* 968–970.

Robertson, I. H., Mattingley, J. B., Rorden, C., & Driver, J. (1998). Phasic alerting of neglect patients overcomes their spatial deficit in visual awareness. *Nature, 395,* 169–172.

Rodier, P. M. (2002). Converging evidence for brain stem injury during Autism. *Development and Psychopathology, 14,* 537–559.

Rosch, E. (1973). On the internal structure of perceptual and semantic categories. In T. E. Moore (Ed.), *Cognitive development and the acquisition of language* (pp. 110–129). New York: Academic Press.

Rosenbaum, J. E., Biederman, J., Gersten, M., Hirshfeld, D. R., Meminger, S. R., Herman, J. B., et al. (1988). Behavioral inhibition in children of parents with panic disorder and agoraphobia: A controlled study. *Archives of General Psychiatry, 45,* 463–470.

Rothbart, M. K. (1981). Measurement of temperament in infancy. *Child Development, 52,* 569–578.

Rothbart, M. K. (1982). The concept of difficult temperament: A critical analysis of Thomas, Chess, & Korn. *Merrill-Palmer Quarterly, 28,* 35–40.

Rothbart, M. K. (1986). Longitudinal observation of infant temperament. *Developmental Psychology, 22,* 356–365.

Rothbart, M. K. (1988). Temperament and the development of inhibited approach. *Child Development, 59,* 1241–1250.

Rothbart, M. K (1989a). Behavioral approach and inhibition. In S. Reznick (Ed.), *Perspectives on behavioral inhibition* (pp. 139–157). Chicago: University of Chicago Press.

Rothbart, M. K. (1989b). Biological processes of temperament. In G. Kohnstamm, J. Bates, & M. K. Rothbart (Eds.), *Temperament in childhood* (pp. 77–110). Chichester, England: Wiley.

Rothbart, M. K (1989c). Temperament in childhood: A framework. In G. Kohnstamm, J. Bates, & M. K. Rothbart (Eds.), *Temperament in childhood* (pp. 59–73). Chichester, England: Wiley.

Rothbart, M. K. (1989d). Temperament and development. In G. Kohnstamm, J. Bates, & M. K. Rothbart (Eds.), *Temperament in childhood* (pp. 187–248). Chichester, England: Wiley.

Rothbart, M. K., & Ahadi, S. A. (1994). Temperament and the development of personality. *Journal of Abnormal Psychology, 103,* 55–66.

Rothbart, M. K., Ahadi, S. A., & Evans, D. E. (2000). Temperament and personality: Origins and outcomes. *Journal of Personality and Social Psychology, 78,* 122–135.

Rothbart, M. K., Ahadi, S. A., & Hershey, K. L. (1994). Temperament and social behavior in childhood. *Merrill-Palmer Quarterly, 40,* 21–39.

Rothbart, M. K., Ahadi, S. A., & Hershey, K. L., & Fisher, P. (2001). Investigations of temperament at three to seven years: The Children's Behavior Questionnaire. *Child Development, 72,* 1394–1408.

Rothbart, M. K., & Bates, J. E. (1998). Temperament. In W. Damon (Series Ed.) & N. Eisenberg (Vol. Ed.), *Handbook of child psychology: Vol. 3. Social, emotional and personality development* (5th ed., pp. 105–176). New York: Wiley.

Rothbart, M. K., & Bates, J. E. (in press). Temperament in children's development. In W. Damon, R. Lerner, & N. Eisenberg (Eds.), *Handbook of child psychology: Vol. 3. Social, emotional and personality development* (6th ed.). Hoboken, NJ: Wiley.

Rothbart, M. K., & Derryberry, D. (1981). Development of individual differences in temperament. In M. E. Lamb & A. L. Brown (Eds.), *Advances in developmental psychology* (Vol. 1, pp. 37–86). Hillsdale, NJ: Erlbaum.

Rothbart, M. K., & Derryberry, D. (2002). Temperament in children. In C. von Hofsten & L. Bäckman (Eds.), *Psychology at the turn of the millennium: Vol. 2. Social, developmental, and clinical perspectives* (pp. 17–35). East Sussex, England: Psychology Press.

Rothbart, M. K., Derryberry, D., & Hershey, K. (2000). Stability of temperament in childhood: Laboratory infant assessment to parent report at seven years. In V. J. Molfese & D. L. Molfese (Eds.), *Temperament and personality development across the life span* (pp. 85–119). Hillsdale, NJ: Erlbaum.

Rothbart, M. K., Derryberry, D., & Posner, M. I. (1994). A psychobiological approach to the development of temperament. In J. E. Bates & T. D. Wachs (Eds.), *Temperament: Individual differences at the interface of biology and behavior* (pp. 83–116). Washington, DC: American Psychological Association.

Rothbart, M. K., Ellis, L. K., Rueda, M. R., & Posner, M. I. (2003). Developing mechanisms of temperamental effortful control. *Journal of Personality, 71,* 1113–1143.

Rothbart, M. K., & Mauro, J. A. (1990). Questionnaire measures of infant temperament. In J. W. Fagen & J. Colombo (Eds.), *Individual differences in infancy: Reliability, stability and prediction* (pp. 411–429). Hillsdale, NJ: Erlbaum.

Rothbart, M. K., Posner, M. I., & Hershey, K. (1995). Temperament, attention, and developmental psychopathology. In D. Cicchetti & J. D. Cohen (Eds.), *Handbook of developmental psychopathology* (Vol. 1, pp. 315–340). New York: Wiley.

Rothbart, M. K., Posner, M. I., & Kieras, J. (in press). Temperament, attention, and the development of self-regulation. In K. McCartney & D. Phillips (Eds.), *The Blackwell handbook of early child development.* Oxford, England: Blackwell.

Rothbart, M. K., & Rueda, M. R. (2005). The development of effortful control. In U. Mayr, E. Aw, & S.W. Keele (Eds.), *Developing individuality in the human brain: A tribute to Michael I. Posner* (pp. 167–188). Washington, DC: American Psychological Association.

Rothbart, M. K., & Victor, J. B. (2004, October). *Temperament and personality development: The CTPQ (Children's Temperament and Personality Questionnaire).* Paper presented at the annual Occasional Temperament Conference, Athens, GA.

Rubin, K. H. (1993). The Waterloo Longitudinal Project: Correlates and consequences of social withdrawal from childhood to adolescence. In H. H. Rubin & J. Adendorph (Eds.), *Social withdrawal, inhibition, and shyness in childhood* (pp. 291–314). Hillsdale, NJ: Erlbaum.

Rubin, K. H., & Asendorpf, J. (Eds.). (1993). *Social withdrawal, inhibition, and shyness in childhood.* Hillsdale, NJ: Erlbaum.

Rubin, K. H., & Burgess, K. B. (2001). Social withdrawal and anxiety. In M. W. Vasey & M. R. Dadds (Eds.), *The developmental psychopathology of anxiety* (pp. 407–434). New York: Oxford University Press.

Rueda, M. R., Fan, J., Halparin, J., Gruber, D., Lercari, L. P., McCandliss, B. D., et al. (2004). Development of attention during childhood. *Neuropsychologia, 42,* 1029–1040.

Rueda, M. R., Posner, M. I., & Rothbart, M. K. (2004). Attentional control and self regulation. In R. F. Baumeister & K. D. Vohs (Eds.), *Handbook of self-regulation: Research, theory, and applications* (pp. 283–300). New York: Guilford Press.

Rutter, M. (1990). Psychosocial resilience and protective mechanisms. In J. Rolf, A. S. Masten, D. Cicchetti, K. H. Neuchterlein, & S. Weintraub (Eds.), *Risk and protective factors in development of psychopathology* (pp. 181–214). New York: Cambridge University Press.

Rutter, M., & Quinton, D. (1984). Long-term follow-up of women institutionalized in childhood: Factors promoting good functioning in adult life. *British Journal of Developmental Psychology, 18,* 225–234.

Saltz, E., Campbell, S., & Skotko, D. (1983). Verbal control of behavior: The effects of shouting. *Developmental Psychology, 19,* 461–464.

Sanson, A., Prior, M., Garino, E., Oberklaid, F., & Sewell, J. (1987). The structure of infant temperament: Factor analysis of the revised Infant Temperament Questionnaire. *Infant Behavior and Development, 10,* 97–104.

Sanson, A., Prior, M., & Kyrios, M. (1990). Contamination of measures in temperament research. *Merrill-Palmer Quarterly, 36,* 179–192.

Schaffer, H. R. (1966). The onset of fear of strangers and the incongruity hypothesis. *Journal of Child Psychology and Psychiatry, 7,* 95–106.

Schippel, P., Vasey, M. W., Cravens-Brown, L. M., & Bretveld, R. A. (2003). Suppressed attention to rejection, ridicule, and failure cues: A unique correlate of reactive but not proactive aggression in youth. *Journal of Clinical Child and Adolescent Psychology, 32,* 40–55.

Schwartz, C. E., Snidman, N., & Kagan, J. (1999). Adolescent social anxiety as an outcome of inhibited temperament in childhood. *Journal of the American Academy of Child and Adolescent Psychiatry, 38,* 1008–1015.

Shaw, D. S., Winslow, E. B., Owens, E. B., Vondra, J. I., Cohn, J. F., & Bell, R. Q. (1998). The development of early externalizing problems among children from low-income families: A transformational perspective. *Journal of Abnormal Child Psychology, 26,* 95–107.

Sheeber, L. B. (1995). Empirical dissociations between temperament and behavior problems: A response to the Sanson, Prior, and Kyrios study. *Merrill-Palmer Quarterly, 41*(4), 554–561.

Sheeber, L. B., & Johnson, J. H. (1994). Evaluation of a temperament-focused, parent-training program. *Journal of Clinical Child Psychology, 23,* 249–259.

Shiner, R., & Caspi, A. (2003). Personality differences in childhood and adolescence: Measurement, development, and consequences. *Journal of Child Psychology and Psychiatry and Allied Disciplines, 44*(1), 2–32.

Shiner, R. L., Masten, A. S., & Roberts, J. M. (2003). Childhood personality foreshadows adult personality and life outcomes two decades later. *Journal of Personality and Social Psychology, 71*(6), 1145–1170.

Shiner, R. L., Masten, A. S., & Tellegen, A. (2002). A developmental perspective on personality in emerging adulthood: Childhood antecedents and concurrent adaptation. *Journal of Personality and Social Psychology, 83*(5), 1165–1177.

Simon, T. J., Bish, J. P., Bearden, C. E., Ding, L., Ferrante, S., Nguyen, V., et al. (in press). A multi-level analysis of cognitive dysfunction and psychopathology associated with chromosome 22q11.2 deletion syndrome in children development and psychopathology. *Developmental Psychopathology.*

Smeets, W. J. A. J., & González, A. (2000). Catecholamine systems in the brain of vertebrates: New perspectives through a comparative approach. *Brain Research, 33,* 308–379.

Snyder, J. A. (1977). A reinforcement analysis of interaction in problem and nonproblem children. *Journal of Abnormal Psychology, 86,* 528–535.

Sobin, C., Kiley-Brabeck, K., Daniels, S., Blundell, M., Anyane-Yeboa, K., & Karayiorgou, M. (2004). Networks of attention in children with the 22q11 deletion syndrome. *Developmental Neuropsychology, 26*(2), 611–626.

Sobin, C., Kiley-Brabeck, K., & Karayiorgou, M. (2005). Association between prepulse inhibition and executive visual attention in children with 22q11 deletion syndrome. *Molecular Psychiatry, 10,* 553–562.

Spoont, M. R. (1992). Modulatory role of serotonin in neural information processing: Implications for human psychopathology. *Psychological Bulletin, 112,* 330–350.

Sprengelmeyer, R., Young, A. W., Schroeder, U., Grossenbacher, P. G., Federlein, J., Buettner, T., et al. (1999). Knowing no fear. *Proceedings of the Royal Society of London. Series B, Biological Sciences, 266*(1437), 2451–2456.

Stevenson-Hinde, J., & Simpson, A. E. (1982). Temperament and relationships. In R. Porter & G. M. Collins (Eds.), *Temperamental differences in infants and young children* (pp. 51–65). London: Pitman.

Stice, E., & Gonzales, N. (1998). Adolescent temperament moderates the relations of parenting to antisocial behavior and substance use. *Journal of Adolescent Research, 13,* 5–31.

Strelau, J. (1983). *Temperament personality activity.* New York: Academic Press.

Suls, J., Martin, R., & David, J. P. (1998). Person-environment fit and its limits: Agreeableness, neuroticism, and emotional reactivity to interpersonal conflict. *Personality and Social Psychology Bulletin, 24*(1), 88–98.

Swanson, J. M., Kraemer, H. C., Hinshaw, S. P., Arnold, L. E., Conners, C. K., Abikoff, H. B., et al. (2001). Clinical relevance of the primary findings of the MTA: Success rates based on severity of ADHD and ODD symptoms at the end of treatment. *Journal of the American Academy of Child and Adolescent Psychiatry, 40*(2), 168–179.

Swanson, J. M., Oosterlaan, J., Murias, M., Moyzis, R., Schuck, S., Mann, M., et al. (2000). ADHD children with 7-repeat allele of the DRD4 gene have extreme behavior but normal performance on critical neuropsychological tests of attention. *Proceeds of the National Academy of Sciences, 97,* 4754–4759.

Swanson, J. M., Posner, M. I., Potkin, S., Bonforte, S., Youpa, D., Cantwell, D., et al. (1991). Activating tasks for the study of visual-spatial attention in ADHD children: A cognitive anatomical approach. *Journal of Child Neurology, 6,* S119–S127.

Teglasi, H., & MacMahon, B. V. (1990). Temperament and common problem behaviors of children. *Journal of Applied Developmental Psychology, 11,* 331–349.

Tellegen, A. (1985). Structures of mood and personality and their relevance to assessing anxiety, with an emphasis on self-report. In A. H. Tuma & J. D. Maser (Eds.), *Anxiety and the anxiety disorders* (pp. 681–706). Hillsdale, NJ: Erlbaum.

Thomas, A., & Chess, S. (1977). *Temperament and development.* New York: Brunner/Mazel.

Thomas, A., Chess, S., & Birch, H. G. (1968). *Temperament and behavior disorders in children.* New York: New York University Press.

Thomas, A., Chess, S., Birch, H. G., Hertzig, M. E., & Korn, S. (1963). *Behavioral individuality in early childhood.* New York: New York University Press.

Thomas, K. M., Drevets, W. C., Dahl, R. E., Ryan, N. D., Birmaher, B., Eccard, C. H., et al. (2001). Amygdala response to fearful faces in anxious and depressed children. *Archives of General Psychiatry, 58,* 1057–1063.

Tomarken, A. J., Davidson, R. J., Wheeler, R. E., & Doss, R. C. (1992). Individual differences in anterior brain asymmetry and fundamental dimensions of emotion. *Journal of Personality and Social Psychology, 62,* 676–687.

Turken, A. U., & Swick, D. (1999). Response selection in the human anterior cingulate cortex. *Nature Neuroscience, 2,* 920–924.

Vasey, M. W., & MacLeod, C. (2001). Information-processing factors in childhood-anxiety: A review and developmental perspective. In M. E. Vasey & M. R. Dadds (Eds.), *The developmental psychopathology of anxiety* (pp. 253–277). New York: Oxford University Press.

Wang, K. J., Fan, J., Dong, Y., Wang, C., Lee, T. M. C., & Posner, M. I. (in press). Selective impairment of attentional networks of orienting and executive control in Schizophrenia. *Schizophrenia Research.*

Watson, D., & Clark, L. A. (1984). Negative affectivity: The disposition to experience aversive emotional states. *Psychological Bulletin, 96,* 465–490.

Watson, D., & Clark, L. A. (1992). Affects separable and inseparable: A hierarchical model of the negative affects. *Journal of Personality and Social Psychology, 62,* 489–505.

Watson, D., & Clark, L. A. (1995). Depression and the melancholic temperament. *European Journal of Personality, 9,* 351–366.

Watson, D., & Clark, L. A. (1997). The measurement and mismeasurement of mood: Recurrent and emergent issues. *Journal of Personality Assessment, 68,* 267–296.

Watson, D., Clark, L. A., & Harkness, A. R. (1994). Structures of personality and their relevance to psychopathology. *Journal of Abnormal Psychology, 103,* 18–31.

Watson, D., & Pennebaker, J. (1989). Health complaints, stress, and distress: Exploring the central role of negative affectivity. *Psychological Review, 96,* 235–254.

Webb, E. (1915). Character and intelligence. *British Journal of Psychology Monographs, 1*(Serial No. 3), 99.

Webster-Stratton, C., & Eyberg, S. M. (1982). Child temperament: Relationship with child behavior problems and parent-child interactions. *Journal of Clinical Child Psychology, 11,* 123–129.

Weissman, M. M. (1989). Anxiety disorders in parents and children: A genetic-epidemiological perspective. In J. S. Reznick (Ed.), *Perspectives on behavioral inhibition* (pp. 241–254). Chicago: University of Chicago Press.

Wender, P. (1971). *Minimal brain dysfunction in children.* New York: Wiley-Liss.

Werner, E. E. (1986). The concept of risk from a developmental perspective. In B. Keogh (Ed.), *Advances in special education: Developmental problems in infancy and the preschool years* (pp. 1–23), Greenwich, CT: JAI Press.

Werner, E. E., & Smith, R. S. (1982). *Vulnerable, but invincible: A longitudinal study of resilient children and youth.* New York: McGraw-Hill.

Wertlieb, D., Wiegel, C., Springer, T., & Feldstein, M. (1987). Temperament as a moderator of children's stressful experiences. *American Journal of Orthopsychiatry, 57,* 234–245.

Wolfson, J., Fields, J. H., & Rose, S. (1987). Symptoms, temperament, resiliency, and control in anxiety-disordered preschool children. *Journal of the American Academy of Child and Adolescent Psychiatry, 26,* 16–22.

Zahn-Waxler, C., Cole, P. M., & Barrett, K. C. (1991). Guilt and empathy: Sex differences and implications for the development of depression. In J. Garber & K. A. Dodge (Eds.), *The development of emotion regulation and dysregulation* (pp. 243–272). New York: Cambridge University Press.

Zuckerman, M. (1984). Sensation seeking: A comparative approach to a human trait. *Behavioral and Brain Sciences, 7,* 413–471.

Zuckerman, M. (1995). Good and bad humors: Biochemical bases of personality and its disorders. *Psychological Science, 6*(6), 325–332.

CHAPTER 12

Motivation, Self-Regulation, and Self-Organization

DOUGLAS DERRYBERRY and DON M. TUCKER

For most of its history, psychology has emphasized external forces that arise from the environment to shape human personality. This view began during the behaviorist era, when learned connections between external stimuli and responses were viewed as central. It has continued during the cognitive era, though the emphasis has, of course, shifted from the external world to representations of the environment. This general environmental paradigm in psychology has provided many useful constructs for understanding psychopathology and its development. We now have a number of models through which external environments, internal representations, and adaptive or maladaptive behaviors can be linked (Beck & Clark, 1997; M. W. Eysenck, 1997; Wells & Matthews, 1994).

Nevertheless, the recent advent of neuroscience research has provided an additional perspective for viewing human personality, one that emphasizes internal biological processes along with external events and their representations (Cicchetti & Tucker, 1994; Derryberry & Rothbart, 1997). Although in many instances, neuroscience data converge quite well with psychological constructs, in other instances, the biological perspective suggests that a much broader view is required than that provided by most psychological models. For example, we often think of an external stimulus as being processed within the cortex, as if the cortex were some highly complex electronic computer. What we find, however, is that the information within the cortex is embodied in a chemical framework where its processing is modulated by preexisting constellations of amines, peptides, steroids, and other neurochemicals (Herbert, 1994). Moreover, fluctuations in this neuromodulatory framework are in large part driven by internal processes related to biological rhythms, moods, and motivational states that are not often addressed in psychological models. Similarly, in psychological theory, we attempt to define memory processes in relation to their functional characteristics, such as long term or short term, or to their phenomenal and behavioral manifestations, such as episodic, contextual, or procedural. In contrast, the neurophysiological perspective points to specific internal circuits that integrate cortical with limbic networks and that engage brain stem motivational and arousal regulatory systems. Although analysis of these memory circuits points the way to the adaptive, motivational control of each level of the neuraxis, it also raises the issue of how to relate neurophysiological mechanisms to psychological concepts of memory, motivation, and cognitive function.

In this chapter, we discuss the contribution of neurophysiological mechanisms and their associated internal states to motivation, personality, and psychopathology. We begin by focusing on the neurophysiological evidence of separable motivational systems related to appetitive and defensive needs. A main emphasis is on the vertical integration of these systems, extending from the brain stem to the limbic systems to the cortex. We consider ways in which elementary motivational controls arising from brain stem and limbic regions shape more complex cortical processes of appraisal, concept formation, and self-regulation. As will be seen, individual differences in the appetitive and defensive systems are related to major personality dimensions such as extraversion/impulsivity and neuroticism/anxiety, respectively. In addition, we review models suggesting that individuals at the extreme of these dimensions, whose motivational systems tend to be under- or overreactive, will be most vulnerable to psychopathology. In simplest terms, excessive appetitive function can give rise to externalizing disorders, whereas extreme defensive function can underlie internalizing problems.

The chapter's second section attempts to fill in this preliminary framework by focusing on the regulatory functions carried out by the motivational systems. We suggest that *self-regulation* is a process through which motivational systems coordinate the functioning of component regulatory subsystems: The body is regulated through the endocrine, autonomic, and motor subsystems, and the brain is regulated through subsystems related to arousal and attention. An underlying theme is that the efficiency of the regulation will depend on the status of the regulatory subsystems; that is, if one of the subsystems is impaired or imbalanced, then the effective functioning of the motivational system as a whole may be compromised. Examining individual variability in these subsystems provides a broad view of children's sources of vulnerability and, at the same time, a more specific view of their actual symptoms. It also helps distinguish involuntary from voluntary forms of self-regulation and by so doing, helps underscore the difficulties inherent in children's attempts to cope with their problems.

The chapter's final section extends these regulatory functions to address self-organization. We propose that development does not proceed through a simple process of environmental "instruction," but through an internal process of selection guided by the child's developing motivational systems. By emphasizing these internal selective pressures, we explore the notion that children construct representations of the world that serve their motivational needs. In the chapter's final section, we return to an environmental perspective and consider ways that different environments may constrain the differentiation of the child's motivational systems. Depending on both the environment's input and the child's internal states, personalities can organize themselves along many different paths. Viewing development in terms of a self-organizing process provides a broader view of environmental influences and, again, a more specific view of the child's symptoms and experience.

MOTIVATIONAL SYSTEMS

Our discussion of motivational systems emphasizes two general systems, one related to appetitive needs and the other to defensive needs. We first lay out the anatomy and physiology of these systems, emphasizing their distributed nature across the nervous system. As will be seen, the brain stem pattern generation systems appear to provide complete packages of behavioral and autonomic response for simple creatures. For more complex organisms such as higher mammals, these systems become integrated with evaluative, mnemonic, and planning functions that have more extended, and less direct, influences on behavior. We then relate these systems to human personality, suggesting that individual differences in the reactivity of appetitive and defensive systems contribute to personality dimensions of positive emotionality (extraversion) and negative emotionality (neuroticism). Finally, we discuss the clinical vulnerabilities facing individuals falling at the extremes of these motivational system/personality disorders.

Defensive Systems

Instead of being localized within a small set of structures, the brain's defensive circuitry is widely distributed. This distribution reflects the brain's evolution: Defensive functions are patterned in discrete modules in the more primitive regions of the brain stem, are elaborated further with the evolution of the limbic regions, and are ultimately interwoven with memory and concept formation within the cortex. Whereas more primitive structures supported immediate responses to proximal dangers, the more recent circuits respond in a highly evaluative and planful manner to dangers that are extended in both space and time.

Beginning with the brain stem, the past 10 years has seen increased interest in a region known as the periaqueductal gray (PAG). The PAG receives sensory information from the immediate environment and organizes responses through descending projections to motor and autonomic cell groups within the medulla (see Figure 12.1). Of greatest interest is the PAG's organization in distinct columns

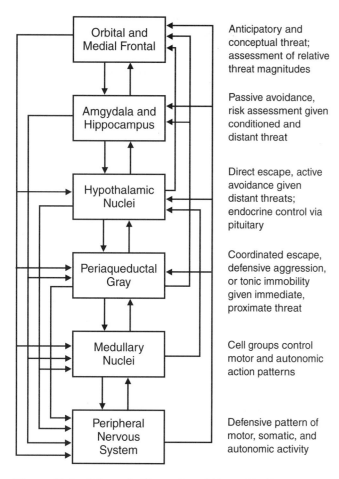

Anticipatory and conceptual threat; assessment of relative threat magnitudes

Passive avoidance, risk assessment given conditioned and distant threat

Direct escape, active avoidance given distant threats; endocrine control via pituitary

Coordinated escape, defensive aggression, or tonic immobility given immediate, proximate threat

Cell groups control motor and autonomic action patterns

Defensive pattern of motor, somatic, and autonomic activity

Figure 12.1 Schematic illustration of hierarchically organized defensive circuitry. Higher levels allow for more coordinated defensive reactions in response to threats that are more distant in temporal and spatial terms. Each level carries out increasingly sophisticated interoceptive as well as exteroceptive processing. Ascending and descending connections are extensive, allowing for a vertical integration within which diverse functional loops or activation patterns can emerge.

devoted to specific behavioral options. At least two of these PAG columns are devoted to defense. The caudal portion of the lateral column activates explosive escape behavior, as occurs when a prey animal is closely threatened by a predator but an escape route is available. In contrast, rostral regions of the lateral column elicit defensive aggression, as occurs when the threatened animal is cornered and cannot escape. Besides promoting active motor and autonomic responses, these defensive regions promote a nonopioid form of analgesia, serving to limit pain processing in defensive situations. In contrast to such active forms of coping, a ventrolateral column produces profound hyporesponsivity (i.e., tonic immobility), as occurs when an animal has been captured and copes by playing dead.

This passive action is accompanied by decreased sympathetic activation and an opioid analgesia. Thus, the PAG is capable of integrating three forms of defensive behavior (escape, defensive aggression, and tonic immobility), depending on the threat's proximity and the availability of escape routes (Bandler & Keay, 1996; Bandler & Shipley, 1994; Floyd, Price, Ferry, Keay, & Bandler, 2001).

The PAG defensive columns are reciprocally interconnected with major components of the limbic system. First, extensive connections exist between the PAG and various hypothalamic regions such as the anterior and ventromedial nuclei (Swanson, 2000). It has been suggested that the hypothalamus provides better sensory processing of more distant dangers, more time for organization of a suitable response, and thus what is referred to as *directed escape* (Gray & McNaughton, 1996). Second, the hypothalamus is reciprocally connected with the more recently evolved amygdala, which is in turn reciprocally connected with the PAG (Swanson, 2000). The amygdala allows conditioned fear reactions, where an originally neutral stimulus such as a sound predicts that a threat is present or imminent in the environment (LeDoux, 1996). In some cases, such reactions can be instantly triggered via direct inputs from the thalamus to the amygdala. The amygdala also receives extensive projections from sensory and association areas of the cortex, allowing it to modify fear responses based on complex combinations of highly processed information. Third, the hippocampus (which projects to both the amygdala and hypothalamus) may play a role in anxiety through a behavioral pattern called *risk assessment*. This occurs in conflict situations where both appetitive and defensive motives are active, as when an animal proceeds to forage in an area that was just vacated by a predator (Blanchard & Blanchard, 1988; Gray & McNaughton, 1996).

Each of these regions—the PAG, hypothalamus, amygdala, and hippocampus—are reciprocally connected with the cortex. In fact, distinct topographic circuits have been traced interconnecting the PAG, hypothalamus, amygdala, and frontal lobe (Floyd et al., 2001). Within the frontal lobe, two major emotion-related networks have recently been delineated (Carmichael & Price, 1995a, 1995b). The first is the *orbital network*, an interconnected set of roughly 13 regions located on the ventral surface of the frontal lobe. The orbital network is closely interconnected with adjacent ventral circuits within the temporal pole and insula. This complexity indicates multiple functions, but only a few have been characterized. For example, the orbital region involves a massive convergence of highly processed sensory and visceral information, suggesting that it is involved in relating affective significance to cortical inputs or representations (Carmichael & Price, 1995b; Schoenbaum, Chiba, & Gallagher, 2003). In addition, the orbital region is involved in computing the relative magnitude of incentive input, as would be required in determining which is the greater of two threats (Schultz, Tremblay, & Hollerman, 2000). Finally, the orbital region appears to play a role in controlling behavior in conflict situations, when incentive values need to be reversed and reattached (Schoenbaum, Setlow, Nugent, Saddoris, & Gallagher, 2003). Thus, the orbital cortex seems well designed for recognizing complex and perhaps abstract threats, for determining their magnitude, and for adjusting representations when motivational conditions change.

In general, it appears that the orbital frontal cortex, associated ventral limbic networks (including the temporal pole and insula), and the amygdala are integral to elaboration of more primitive defensive reactions organized in the brain stem and hypothalamic centers. Several lines of evidence suggest that these ventral limbic networks are functionally exaggerated in humans with chronically activated defensive systems, such as those experiencing chronic anxiety (Tucker & Derryberry, 1992). It has also been suggested that interactions between the ventral limbic structures and the neostriatum (caudate and putatmen) may promote highly routinized and habitual behavior. At an elementary level, engaging well-routinized action plans is critical to fight-or-flight behavior, and this modulatory influence may be adaptive at a cognitive level in humans, facilitating well-learned patterns of thought and action under stress. However, the pathological implications may be seen in behavioral compulsions and cognitive obsessions associated with exaggerated activations of the neostriatum and orbital frontal cortex in the chronic anxiety of Obsessive-Compulsive Disorder (Baxter, Phelps, Mazziotta, & Guze, 1987; Gehring, Himle, & Nisenson, 2000).

The second frontal network characterized by Carmichael and Price (1995a) is the *medial network*. Consisting of roughly 12 interconnected regions, the medial network subserves a number of functions. In general, it can be viewed as serving visceromotor functions complementing the orbital network's viscerosensory functions (Luu & Tucker, 2001). For example, specific areas within the medial network project to the same subcortical circuitry (e.g., amygdala, PAG) described earlier (Floyd et al., 2001). Presumably, the cortical input helps to fine-tune the unfolding fear response based on more elaborate input provided by the orbital network. Other medial regions, such as subfields within the anterior cingulate area, project to downstream cortical motor areas,

including the supplemental motor area and the motor cortex. The cingulate region has been described as providing the motivational drive that is articulated, in terms of axial, proximal, and distal components, in the subsequent motor areas (Goldberg, 1985). This may seem at odds with the fine-tuning function, though it is possible that the fine-tuning applies to involuntary defensive behaviors, whereas the drive function applies to more voluntary responses. Thus, the cingulate region may provide the conscious and active sense of *agency* involved in voluntary behavior.

It can be seen that defensive circuits are quite extensive and follow an evolutionary course. Whereas the more primitive regions provide adaptive mechanisms for dealing with simple, close, and immediate threats, the more recently evolved limbic and cortical networks allow for more complex evaluation of the danger based on multiple sources of information. Evaluation is able to extend into the future, enabling more flexible and planful behavioral responses. As will be become clearer in subsequent sections, these more advanced functions remain regulated by subcortical mechanisms (and vice versa), such that all levels work together as the response unfolds. This form of *vertical integration* is characteristic of many functions within the brain and provides a useful perspective for viewing their development and pathology (Tucker, Derryberry, & Luu, 2000). We return to these issues after briefly describing the appetitive systems.

Appetitive Systems

The construct of an appetitive neural system has been explored by several researchers. The underlying circuitry has been discussed in terms of an "expectancy-foraging system" (Panksepp, 1998), a "behavioral activation system" (Gray, 1994), and a "behavioral facilitation system" (Depue & Collins, 1999). Panksepp's more primitive appetitive system regulates processes activated by states of need (e.g., hunger) and functions to activate approach/exploratory behavior along with an emotional state of desire. In contrast, the circuitry emphasized by Gray and Depue is more recently evolved and designed to detect conditioned signals of reward and nonpunishment. Given such signals, the circuitry facilitates approach behavior directed toward the positive incentive, along with emotional states of hope (given expected reward) and relief (given nonpunishment).

The actual neural circuitry underlying appetitive motivation has not been well characterized. It appears to be distributed vertically throughout the brain, flowing through some of the same structures involved in defensive functions.

For example, columns within the PAG appear to be related to appetitive functions of sex (Holstege & Boers, 2001) and drinking (Sewards & Sewards, 2000). At the limbic level, specific hypothalamic regions contribute to sex, hunger, and thirst. Animal research suggests that the basolateral amygdala plays a role in conditioned rewards (Schoenbaum, Setlow, et al., 2003), and human positron emission tomography (PET) scans have shown left amygdala activation during the viewing of positive pictures (Hamann, Ely, Hoffman, & Kilts, 2002). Finally, much evidence suggests that the orbital and medial prefrontal networks also contribute to appetitive motivation (e.g., Depue & Collins, 1999). Animal research suggests that reciprocal connections between the basal lateral amygdala and orbital cortex may encode information regarding expected rewarding outcomes (Schoenbaum, Chiba, et al., 2003). PET scans have shown orbital cortex and amygdala activity to covary as a function of stimulus category (food versus nonfood) in hungry humans (Morris & Dolan, 2001). Orbital neurons also encode the magnitude of a reward, firing more strongly to a monkey's preferred reward (Schultz et al., 2000).

One region that may play a unique role in appetitive behavior is the nucleus accumbens. The accumbens is a component in a reentrant loop through which cortical information is projected to the subcortical ventral striatum and eventually returned to the cortex by means of the mediodorsal thalamus and its projections to the frontal lobe. Activity within the loop passing through the nucleus accumbens can sustain activity in the medial prefrontal network. Multiple functions are involved, but a major one in relation to the accumbens loop is that of computing motivational intensity and regulating approach behavior (Depue & Collins, 1999). The loop as a whole, along with many other limbic and frontal regions, is modulated by dopamine projections from the brain stem's ventral tegmental region. Many theorists have focused on the core notion that reward-related dopamine firing facilitates approach behavior via the nucleus accumbens and its prefrontal projections (e.g., Depue & Collins, 1999; Pickering & Gray, 2001). This is an attractive model, but it should be noted that mediofrontal dopamine increases during stress (e.g., Benes, 1994), and thus a broader view of dopaminergic function seems necessary.

Another important question for understanding the influence of appetitive systems is how they engage not only hedonic responsiveness but the exploratory behavior that leads to new appetitive goals. In humans, positive affect, such as that induced by receiving a small, unexpected gift in a psychology experiment, leads to a more holistic, expansive cognitive set (Isen, 2000). In animals, there are sugges-

tions that behavior under rewarding conditions that are consistent with expectancies leads to engagement of a broad, contextual representation of the environment, supported by the dorsal limbic pathway (the hippocampus, posterior cingulate cortex, and anterior ventral thalamic nuclei; Gabriel, Kubota, Sparenborg, Straube, & Vogt, 1991). This context-updating mode of learning is suitable when ongoing events confirm the animal's contextual expectancies. It contrasts with the engagement of the ventral limbic, anterior cingulate, amygdalar, and mediodorsal thalamic circuit under conditions of context violation, when rapid adjustments of learning contingencies must be made. Whereas the context-updating, feed-forward mode of learning seems to dominate under appetitive conditions, the context-violation, feedback mode of learning seems to dominate under defensive conditions (Luu & Tucker, 2003).

Motivational Systems and Personality

One of the most interesting aspects of the appetitive and defensive motivational systems is their relevance to personality. Relating personality to the brain is a complex project facing difficulties from both psychological and physiological perspectives. From a physiological point of view, the motivational systems are so wide-ranging that individual differences may occur at different levels (e.g., brain stem, limbic, cortical components) within the system. A related issue arises from a psychological perspective, where it is difficult to ascertain what level of trait specificity (e.g., neuroticism, anxiety, social anxiety) is best suited for linking to a motivational system. Ultimately, we need to be as specific as possible, but at this point, the required knowledge is simply lacking. Therefore, we begin by addressing personality at a relatively general level and attempt to become more specific as the chapter proceeds. As will be seen, the more general traits map fairly well onto subcortical systems, whereas the more specific traits appear to require a cortical level of analysis.

The simplest approach links individual differences in appetitive and defensive systems to the general dimensions of extraversion or impulsivity and neuroticism or anxiety, respectively (H. J. Eysenck & Eysenck, 1985; Watson & Clark, 1992). Thus, a child with strong appetitive motivation should be sensitive to reward signals in the environment and should show vigorous approach behavior directed toward the rewards. Although some would speak of a dimension of "positive emotionality," this may be somewhat strong because children with strong appetitive motivation are not immune to negative emotions. Specifically, such children may be vulnerable to frustration when their strong desires are blocked or delayed (Derryberry & Rothbart, 1997; Panksepp, 1998). Thus, terms such as "reward-oriented" and "impulsive" may be more appropriate. In any event, we would expect such children to be generally positive, with much of their positivity reflected in social affiliation, because others can be a strong source of reward. Behaviorally, they should tend to show vigorous approach behaviors, contributing to a generally high activity level. At a cognitive level, children with strong appetitive motivation should tend to focus on positive events and to be generally optimistic.

In contrast, children with a strong defensive system will be more sensitive to environmental punishment and will tend to avoid such events. Again, some theorists have used the dimension of "negative emotionality" to describe these children, but terms such as "anxious" and "fearful" seem more suitable. The reasoning here is that many anxious children will also experience much relief (or security or comfort) when their anxiety subsides. In general, anxious children will tend to show inhibited behavior (i.e., passive avoidance), though sometimes they may resort to active avoidance or even defensive aggression. Their cognition will tend to focus on impending or imagined dangers, along with a generally pessimistic view of the future.

One advantage of this type of dimensional approach is that it allows one to combine dimensions to appreciate more subtle personality differences. For example, a child's strong appetitive system may be accompanied by either a weak or a strong defensive system. The impulsive child with a weak defensive system will be not only reward-oriented, but also somewhat fearless and poor at inhibiting approach in potentially punishing situations. In contrast, the impulsive child with a strong defensive system would be sensitive to both rewards and punishments in the environment and is likely to show inhibition, despite their strong approach, when punishment is present. Such a child may be quite emotional, showing hope, fear, frustration, and relief across different situations.

Extensions to Psychopathology

A related advantage of a dimensional approach is its relevance to psychopathology. An underlying assumption is that most cases of psychopathology are extreme expressions of normal personality: A motivational system becomes overreactive or underreactive, with this extreme reactivity placing the child at risk of developing maladaptive behavior. The causes of over- or underreactivity may be partly genetic or biologically based, but problems can also arise

from learning and the environment. Whatever the cause, specific neural structures become unbalanced, leading to various types of vulnerability.

For example, children with overreactive appetitive systems may show symptoms related to impulsive disorders (e.g., Attention-Deficit/Hyperactivity Disorder [ADHD], Conduct Disorder), such as oversensitivity to reward and approach behavior that is too strong or misguided. In contrast, children with underreactive appetitive systems may be prone to depressive symptoms, such as an insensitivity to reward, feelings of hopelessness, and difficulty mobilizing approach. On the defensive side, a child with overreactive defense systems will be most vulnerable to anxiety symptoms, such as excessive worrying about future events and inappropriate avoidance behavior. In contrast, those with a week defensive system may be prone to disinhibited types of problems (e.g., undersocialized Conduct Disorder), resulting from their insensitivity to potential punishment and lack of inhibition (Derryberry & Rothbart, 1997; Fowles, 1994; Gray, 1994).

Further specification of symptoms can be made by considering the different levels within the motivational systems. Some children may show overactive defensive functions at multiple subcortical and cortical levels. This would be unfortunate, setting the child up for many forms of fear (e.g., Overanxious Disorder). For others, however, the reactivity may be focused at a single level within the system. Evidence suggests that panic attacks arise from overactivation within the PAG, in particular the columns related to explosive escape. Presumably, the circuits become disinhibited as serotonin levels drop, resulting in spontaneous attacks of extreme fear and an urge to escape (Graeff, 1991; Gray & McNaughton, 1996). Higher levels within the limbic system may play a stronger role in anticipatory forms of anxiety, such as those resulting from classical conditioning. Childhood phobias related to animals, other people, and school may have their roots in limbic structures such as the amygdala (Gray & McNaughton, 1996). Still higher levels within the cortex may underlie more subtle forms of anxiety, such as fears of failure, evaluation, and rejection, many of which are related to future uncertainties. Thus, different anxious symptoms can be predicted based on the different levels within the defensive circuitry. Nevertheless, given the integration seen across the levels of the defensive system, one would expect anxious symptoms to be related, co-occurring in different children to different degrees. For example, a child with panic problems (brain stem) may develop anticipatory anxiety (limbic) and even evaluation anxiety (cortical) regarding his or her panic attacks.

A multidimensional approach is also helpful in predicting the interactions that may increase vulnerability. For example, the children most likely to show impulsive problems should be those with a strong appetitive system accompanied by a weak defensive system. Such children will tend to vigorously approach a potential reward, without fear or inhibition given potential punishments. However, if the strong approach tendency is accompanied by moderate or strong fear, then the child will have some degree of inhibition over his or her impulsivity. Conversely, the children most vulnerable to anxiety disorders should be those with a strong defensive system and a weak appetitive system. The lack of reward sensitivity and approach tendencies makes it easier for the child to avoid certain threatening situations, especially social situations. If the anxiety is accompanied by moderate or strong appetitive tendencies, then the potential rewards from social interaction might mobilize approach and thus overcome the avoidant tendencies. Although more research is needed, recent studies provide preliminary support for such predictions (Caspi, Henry, McGee, Moffitt, & Silva, 1995; Eisenberg et al., 2001; Quay, 1993).

As can be seen from these examples, these simple dual-system approaches also provide a useful perspective for understanding comorbid disorders. For example, a good proportion of children suffering from ADHD also experience anxiety (Pliszka, 1992). This would make sense if such children possessed a strong appetitive system that promoted the hyperactive approach tendencies of ADHD, along with a strong defensive system that promoted the anxiety. Another example is comorbid anxiety and depression, which appears to be quite common in anxious adults (Mineka, Pury, & Luten, 1995). Here, one would suspect a strong defensive system along with a weak appetitive system, with the weak appetitive system contributing to the anhedonia and low approach symptoms of depression.

Interestingly, most anxious depressions begin with an anxious rather than depressed episode. One explanation is that prolonged defensive reactivity to stress may progressively suppress appetitive functioning, eventually leading to a depressive state. The reduced appetitive functioning could be due to inhibitory projections from the defensive to the appetitive system, or from the depletion of a crucial neuromodulator (e.g., dopamine) used by both systems. In other instances, a sudden drop in appetitive functioning may be brought on by environmental changes, such as the loss of a parent or good friend. The drop in appetitive functioning may disinhibit activity in the defensive system (by weakening the inhibitory connections), again resulting in depression accompanied by anxiety. It can be seen that this type of dual-system model provides multiple approaches to understanding comorbid disorders.

To summarize, we have traced the vertical structure of two complementary and interacting motivational systems. This general framework provides a useful approach to conceptualizing personality differences, suggesting that personality is grounded in relative strengths of appetitive and defensive systems. Moreover, it provides a useful starting point for considering childhood psychopathology, which can be tied to imbalances in a child's tendencies to approach rewards and/or avoid punishments. Although it is beyond the scope of this chapter, we note that future research will describe additional motivational systems, such as one related to nurturant forms of behavior (Depue & Morrone-Strupinsky, in press; MacDonald, 1992). Individual differences would most likely be related to a personality dimension of agreeableness/hostility, which would advance our understanding of the more callous and aggressive forms of psychopathology.

Hierarchical Organization

Given such extensions to personality and psychopathology, it is worth briefly returning to the construct of hierarchical organization illustrated in Figure 12.1. Theorists have long emphasized the hierarchical structure of the brain, a structure evident from phylogenetic, ontogenetic, and functional perspectives. The classic approach has been a top-down approach, viewing development as a process through which higher regions exert increasing control over more primitive regions. For example, primitive panic-like forms of fear may be inherent in the brain stem, but these are gradually brought under control by the anticipatory, evaluative, and memorial capacities of the limbic and cortical regions. With development, representations provide increasing control over emotions such as hope, fear, and anger, shaping them in terms of cultural beliefs, values, and rules.

This form of top-down model often views psychopathology as resulting from failures at the highest levels, such that the motivations or behaviors are inappropriately released from inhibition. A child may become chronically anxious, for example, because cortical representations or inhibitory mechanisms are not strong or accurate enough to construct the situation as safe and inhibit the fear. Or, from a more recent cognitive perspective, some representations may be too strong or biased (e.g., catastrophic thinking) and function to amplify more primitive fear tendencies. Rather than simply disinhibiting subcortical fears, the cortex can also directly enhance the fear to problematic levels. Much current theorizing speaks in terms of disinhibition or dysregulation, and clearly there is a lot to be gained from this perspective.

In contrast to such top-down approaches, however, other theorists have emphasized bottom-up approaches, in which lower-level processes influence higher levels. Physiological bases can be seen in the ascending projections illustrated in the defensive circuitry of Figure 12.1, which appear to be as extensive as the descending connections. Given that subcortical regions tend to precede cortical regions in development, a child born with strong subcortical fear circuitry may subsequently learn to view and think about the world in an anxious way. Thus, subcortical regions provide a motivational foundation on which cortical representations are framed. As described earlier, this type of approach suggests that some forms of psychopathology develop because overreactive or underreactive motivational systems shape cognition in a maladaptive way. In subsequent sections, we describe ascending regulatory functions, such as the dopaminergic regulation of frontal lobe functions. Imbalances in the subcortical dopamine projections appear influential in disorders such as ADHD and Schizophrenia (Benes, 1994). At even lower levels, peripheral cortisol has been found to regulate activity in the brain stem, limbic, and cortical regions, providing a hormonal pathway through which vulnerabilities may arise (Gunnar, 1994). Although this bottom-up approach has not been as influential as the top-down approach, it is likely to gain in power as we learn more about the biological nature of the nervous system, in particular, its relations to the endocrine and immune systems.

Most recently, many theorists have come to view the bottom-up and top-down frameworks as complementary. This can be done in different ways, but a useful example can be seen in the notion of vertical integration. As alluded to earlier, the idea is that the nervous system can be viewed as a set of vertically evolved modules interconnected through overlapping reciprocal connections, as depicted in Figure 12.1. Activation may arise at several levels within this system, depending on the nature of the input and the current reactivity of the individual modules. But regardless of whether it begins relatively high or low in the system, activation will spread such that all components are brought into play. When a child becomes anxious, we see changes in peripheral cortisol and autonomic activity, as well as coordinated activity within the medulla, PAG, hypothalamus, amygdala, and cortex. In some cases, the primary flow may be top-down; in others, it is bottom-up. In either case, the two flows will work to support one another, with the bottom-up flow establishing the general framework and the top-down serving to fill in the details of the motivational state. To some extent, this vertical processing can be viewed as a microgenetic process, characterized by movement from general to more specific functions (Derryberry & Tucker, 1991).

Because information and regulatory activity run in both directions, the stage is set for dynamic interactions between the various hierarchical levels. For example, fear-related excitation ascending from the amygdala might trigger inhibition from the cortex, such that a negative feedback loop is established and anxiety is suppressed. In other instances, ascending excitation may trigger descending excitation, setting up a positive feedback loop that amplifies cortical beliefs of danger and subcortical feelings of fear. Such patterns of self-amplifying activity are common in both defensive and appetitive situations and constitute serious challenges to self-regulation. We introduce additional examples of dynamic interactions in later sections of the chapter.

Although approaches emphasizing simple motivational systems are helpful, it is clear that they face several shortcomings. On the one hand, these approaches focus on motivational systems in isolation, without relating them to other brain systems that may also contribute to psychopathology. In addition, the models are fairly good at predicting reactive responses and general symptoms, but they do not shed much light on the child's active efforts to cope with these symptoms. Furthermore, such models remain rather vague regarding the specific nature of the child's symptoms. The next section begins to address these issues by focusing on the regulatory functions carried out by the motivational systems.

MOTIVATIONAL SYSTEMS AND SELF-REGULATION

Recent years have seen an increasing interest in processes referred to as emotion regulation, behavior regulation, and self-regulation. Unfortunately, these terms are often used vaguely and interchangeably, making it difficult for researchers to communicate effectively. Our approach attempts to define the regulatory processes as clearly as possible. In this view, a regulatory process is one that does not directly transmit or process information, but rather adjusts (e.g., by facilitating or inhibiting) the processing in the systems that it targets (Wise, 1987). Thus, the motivational systems described earlier are actually high-level regulatory systems; they respond to various types of rewards and punishments by adjusting the reactivity of other subsystems within the brain. These subsystems are themselves regulatory in nature, adjusting the processing in other information-processing systems. To an extent, the motivational systems can be viewed as forming the highest level in a hierarchy of regulatory systems. Thus, Panksepp (1998) suggests that the motivational systems function as "executive" regulatory systems within the brain.

Regulatory Subsystems

In the following paragraphs, we discuss six general types of regulation orchestrated by the motivational systems. As illustrated in Figure 12.2, the appetitive and defensive systems regulate three types of peripheral systems, the motor,

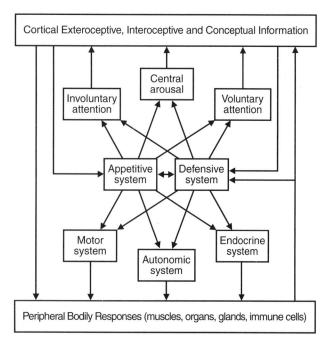

Figure 12.2 Simplified illustration of the major regulatory subsystems controlled by appetitive and defensive motivational systems. Cortical and subcortical input is monitored by motivational systems. Given a significant input, the motivational system coordinates responses via motor, autonomic, and endocrine adjustments and also coordinates perceptual and conceptual processing via adjustments of central arousal systems (dopamine, serotonin, norepinephrine, acetylcholine), involuntary attentional systems, and voluntary frontal attentional mechanisms. Lateral ascending lines represent interoceptive information from the body. Lateral descending lines represent cortical and direct thalamic information to the motivational systems. Not illustrated are direct and cortical inputs to the motor system, as well as reciprocal inputs from the six regulatory systems to the motivational systems.

autonomic, and endocrine systems, to produce complex behavior. To support this behavior, the motivational systems also recruit central regulatory systems involved in modulating perceptual and conceptual activity in the forebrain. These central systems are involved in processes of arousal, involuntary attention, and voluntary attention. By adjusting these regulatory subsystems, ongoing motives can orchestrate a state of reactivity throughout the organism that is adaptive, given ongoing needs. Thus, motivational systems function at a high level to coordinate activity in the body and brain.

A major thrust of our approach is based on evidence that individual differences arise not only in the motivational circuitry itself, but also in the regulated subsystems. Although the systems are designed to be adaptive, individual variability will cause the overall motivational state to differ in efficiency across individuals. In most cases, the states are generally efficient and adaptive, but for some, imbalances in arousal or attention may lead to states that are maladaptive; that is, the regulation is ineffective such that appetitive motivation often leads to frustration rather than reward, and/or defensive states result in fear rather than relief. We hope to show that considering the regulatory challenges within the subsystems provides a more specific view of the source and nature of the child's symptoms.

Regulation of Peripheral Arousal

Traditional approaches to motivation and emotion have long emphasized the role of the body. Consistent with these approaches, all levels within the motivational systems (i.e., PAG, hypothalamus, amygdala, cortex) project extensively to cell groups in the medulla and hypothalamus related to autonomic and endocrine activity, respectively (Holstege, Bandler, & Saper, 1996). Although older models emphasized a unitary notion of "peripheral arousal," motivational states are now known to involve specific patterns of activity across the autonomic and endocrine systems. These patterns are important in at least two ways. They provide a peripheral physiological state, involving multiple organs and glands that supports the motor response required in an appetitive or defensive situation. In addition, the peripheral adjustments feed back on the brain as interoceptive sensory information, whose processing gives rise to the emotional feelings (e.g., fear, hope, relief, frustration) that accompany the motivational state. In later sections, we argue that such emotional feelings are represented in the cortex and play a central role in guiding motivated behavior.

Individual differences in the autonomic and endocrine levels systems can have profound effects on the efficiency of the motivational state. At the endocrine level, for example, the relatively long-lasting secretion of cortisol promotes energy utilization throughout the body, an adaptive function for appetitive and especially defensive goals. However, cortisol also crosses the blood-brain barrier, where it potentiates fear-related circuitry in the amygdala (Schulkin, McEwen, & Gold, 1994). Thus, a child with an intense or prolonged cortisol response can set up a positive feedback loop that intensifies and prolongs his or her anxiety. Research by Gunnar and her colleagues (Stansbury & Gunnar, 1994) has found interesting differences in cortisol patterns between children. When faced with a new social situation, children who are more outgoing show an initially strong but rapidly recovering cortisol response as they engage other children. In contrast, more inhibited children show an initially weak cortisol response but then more intense and prolonged response when they finally approach the other children (Gunnar, 1994).

The autonomic nervous system is another important source of variability. One area of active interest has been the balance between sympathetic and parasympathetic divisions, as assessed through constructs such as vagal tone (Porges, Doussard-Roosevelt, & Maiti, 1994). In general, parasympathetic dominance, as reflected in a higher vagal tone, appears related to several positive emotional and behavioral outcomes (Beauchaine, 2001). Children with weak vagal tone may show delays in responding in motivational situations, as well as prolonged responses and a slower return to homeostasis. This peripheral imbalance may enhance negative affect and impair more central regulatory processes involving attention. It is worth noting that the peripheral autonomic nervous system is not entirely separate from the brain's central arousal systems. Links have been drawn between the peripheral sympathetic system and the central noradrenergic arousal system (see later discussion). Thus, peripheral imbalances between sympathetic and parasympathetic divisions may also be reflected in the central monoamine imbalances related to problems of depression and anxiety.

Motor Regulation

Traditional motivation models focused on motor responses as the basic target of motivational regulation. Again, this would be a primarily regulatory function; rather than directly transmitting information or activating a response, the motivational circuits potentiate a set of responses that might be adaptive given the current situation. The simplest example here would be functioning at the level of the PAG, where a defensive state potentiates three response options: escape, defensive aggression, and immobility. Converging

environmental signals, conveying the threat proximity and escape routes, can then release the most appropriate reaction. Response processing will be more complex at higher levels such as the cortex, but again, the motivational influence is primarily regulatory, potentiating one set of options and perhaps depotentiating others.

At higher levels of the motor system, an important framework has come from the recognition of dual-motor pathways within the frontal lobe (Goldberg, 1985; Passingham, 1987; Tanji & Shima, 1996). In the mediodorsal pathway (cingulate gyrus and supplementary motor area), actions appear to be organized through feed-forward control, launched toward goals set by internal urges. In the ventrolateral pathway (orbital and lateral frontal), actions appear to be organized through feedback control, in which external sensory targets are used as criteria for adjusting the action sequentially. Although these are action regulation systems, they appear to be based on motivational controls from the limbic networks at the dorsal (medial) and ventral (orbital) bases of the frontal pathways (Luu & Tucker, 2003; Tucker, 2001).

Various psychopathologies may be facilitated by imbalances between these two action regulation systems. Neurological evidence indicates that with extensive lesions of the cingulate cortex and mediodorsal pathway, subjects show akinetic mutism or pseudodepression, as if losing the projectional, visceral, internal feed-forward control over behavior generally (Blumer & Benson, 1975; Goldberg, 1985). With lesions of the orbital frontal lobe, patients show a pseudopsychopathic mode of behavior, as if losing the inhibitory feedback control over behavior provided by the viscerosensory function (Blumer & Benson, 1975; Luu & Tucker, 2003). Although we have little evidence of overreactivity in these motor systems, it is reasonable to predict that an imbalance favoring the medial or projectional system would potentiate impulsive appetitive tendencies and interfere with the constraint required in defensive states. In contrast, a strong ventrolateral pathway may allow individuals to function more effectively in defensive states, but their feedback control and checking may impair appetitive approach behavior.

Regulation of Central Arousal

Another important regulatory mechanism involves connections from the motivational systems to the reticular cell groups in the brain stem. Most relevant here are the norepinephrine projections from the locus coeruleus, the serotonergic projections from the raphe nuclei, the dopaminergic projections from the ventral tegmental area, and the cholinergic projections from the nucleus basalis. Each of these systems sends extensive ascending projections to the fore-brain, making them capable of modulating perceptual, conceptual, and response processing in the cortical and limbic regions. A motivational state arising in the amygdala may adjust firing rates in all four of these arousal systems. Because each system has distinct (though overlapping) cortical targets and distinct modulatory effects, the amygdala can thus establish a state of general cortical readiness that is appropriate to the motivational state. Although these complex modulatory states remain beyond current understanding, we can begin to see how certain components may contribute to adaptive processing. For example, some defensive states may feature strong dopaminergic activation, which tends to focus attention on the source of threat and to bias processing in favor of relatively routinized responses. In contrast, appetitive states may recruit noradrenergic projections, which serve to enhance signal: noise ratios, enable attentional shifts, and broaden the scope of processing (Derryberry & Tucker, 1991; Tucker & Derryberry, 1992; Tucker et al., 2000).

Individual differences in the central arousal system appear crucial to psychopathology. Although they contribute to many motivational states, the arousal systems tend to be strongly recruited in stressful or defensive contexts. If the stress is prolonged, the neurochemical systems can become depleted or at least imbalanced. Such imbalances in norepinephrine, serotonin, and dopamine form the foundation of biological models of depression and are the primary targets of pharmacological treatments (Davis, Charney, Coyle, & Nemeroff, 2002). For example, depletions in projections related to appetitive approach behaviors (e.g., dopamine, norepinephrine) may contribute to the anhedonia and impaired approach evident in depression. These systems have also been implicated in anxiety and impulsive disorders. For example, serotonin appears to exert a general inhibition of brain stem (PAG) and limbic circuits related to fear and aggression (Depue & Spoont, 1986; Graeff, 1991). If serotonin is too low, then normally constrained response patterns can be disinhibited, resulting in panic attacks and perhaps anger attacks (Barlow, Chorpita, & Turovsky, 1996). Furthermore, the ascending arousal systems contribute to a wide range of cognitive processes. Dopaminergic projections to the frontal lobe enable working memory, attention, and other frontal functions. Recent research suggests that an optimal level of dopaminergic facilitation is required for effective frontal control; if dopamine is too high or too low, executive functions can suffer (Arnstein, 1998). Thus, a child with low dopamine may have trouble focusing attention and show symptoms related to ADHD. In contrast, a child with high dopamine, as can occur in anxi-

ety, may become overfocused and have difficulty shifting attention. Serotonin, norepinephrine, and acetylcholine also play important roles in regulating attentional processes.

Although the central arousal systems appear crucial to a variety of disorders, it is clear that their effects are complex and that more research is needed. Each of these neuromodulators functions through multiple receptors, exerting distinct effects depending on the targeted receptor (Uphouse, 1998). In addition, activity in the cell bodies is not simply regulated by motivational systems, but is also subject to a variety of rhythmic, peptide, and hormonal (e.g., cortisol) effects (Herbert, 1994). Nevertheless, studying these systems is an area of intense activity, and progress will accelerate in the coming years.

Regulation of Attention

Limbic and brain stem motivational circuits also project on more specific regulatory systems involved in attention. The attentional systems are closely related to the arousal systems, but appear to exert more specific and flexible effects on their targets. In general, attention refers to a selective facilitation of specific information that arises apart from the automatic activation of input pathways. In other words, incoming information may be to some extent processed "automatically" without attention. When attention is aligned with an activated pathway (or in advance of its activation), that information is facilitated for extended processing. Posner (Posner & Raichle, 1994; Posner & Rothbart, 1998) has described a "posterior attentional system" responsible for the involuntary orienting of attention from one spatial location to another. The system consists of a network with separable regions contributing to attentional "disengagement" (parietal cortex), "movement" (superior colliculus), and "engagement" (thalamic pulvinar nucleus). This posterior network is labeled "involuntary attention" in Figure 12.2.

Whereas the orienting system is thought to function in a primarily reactive manner, another system, the anterior attentional system, is thought to be responsible for voluntary control (see Figure 12.2). The anterior system involves distributed circuits within the frontal lobe, with the anterior cingulate region playing a pivotal role. The anterior system regulates the posterior system so as to provide voluntary control over orienting. It also functions to inhibit dominant response tendencies, to inhibit dominant conceptual associations, and to monitor and correct erroneous responses (Posner & DiGirolamo, 1998; Posner & Raichle, 1994). A similar set of executive functions can be found in Shallice's (Shallice et al., 2002; Stuss, Shallice, Alexander, & Picton, 1995) construct of a "supervisory attentional system."

In describing these processes, we place most emphasis on the voluntary attentional mechanisms and the role they play in facilitating motivated behavior. We first describe the targets of the attentional regulations, which include exteroceptive, interoceptive, and conceptual information. We then consider individual differences in such attentional control, illustrating ways poor control may impair motivational function and thereby promote psychopathology.

Exteroceptive Input

Adaptive functioning often requires flexible attention to multiple sources of external information. In appetitive contexts, a child who can be attentive to both the rewarding goal and potentially frustrating obstacles is best able to avoid the obstacles and obtain the reward. In a defensive situation, the child who attends to both the threat and the sources of safety can best avoid the threat, approach the source of safety, and obtain relief from anxiety. In more complex situations, such as social situations, the child may need to attend to several other children simultaneously, monitoring positive and negative signals through several channels (e.g., facial expressions, tone of voice). If attention is biased or limited, then the flexibility required in such situations can easily be compromised (Derryberry & Reed, 1994b; Derryberry & Reed, 2002).

Much evidence has demonstrated attentional biases related to personality and clinical problems, though this is primarily true for defensive rather than appetitive functions. Anxious adults allocate greater attention to threatening visual information, such as a negative word or photograph or a failure-related signal in a game context (for review, see M. W. Eysenck, 1997). Similar biases have been found in children (Vasey & Daleiden, 1996). Our research with college students suggests that the underlying problem is not one of moving attention toward environmental dangers; rather, the difficulty lies in disengaging and shifting from such threats once they are engaged (Derryberry & Reed, 1994a). In addition, anxiety promotes focusing or narrowing of attention. Such narrowing may take the form of focusing on a central portion of the visual field at the expense of the peripheral field (e.g., A. Mathews & Macintosh, in press) or focusing on local details of a figure at the expense of the global form (Derryberry & Reed, 1998). These cognitive effects are reminiscent of the routinized and restricted attention engaged by strong ventral limbic and orbital frontal control in defensive responses.

Many of these biases probably arise from motivational effects on involuntary attentional mechanisms. As discussed in more detail later, some children may be able to attenuate these effects by voluntarily controlling attention. If attention becomes overfocused, the child may be able to broaden attention and regain perspective. If attention becomes too strongly engaged, he or she can intentionally disengage and attend to something else (Derryberry & Reed, 2002).

Interoceptive Input

A more subtle form of perceptual regulation involves attention to interoceptive feelings. Although feelings tend to be neglected in much of the literature, their regulation is evident even at the primitive level of the PAG. In defensive states, the PAG can recruit both opioid and nonopioid analgesic mechanisms to suppress pain information that might prove distracting and interfere with efficient coping (Bandler & Keay, 1996). Given the more complex interoceptive representations afforded by the cortex, more sophisticated attentional regulation can be implemented.

Self-report data suggest that the cortex can represent at least three types of feelings: positive affect, negative affect, and energy (e.g., Matthews, 1997). These can be combined with other somatic information in more complex representations of emotions, such as fear, relief, pleasure, and frustration. When related to other information, interoceptive feelings can be extremely useful in evaluating incoming information (stimulus-outcome evaluations) and potential responses (response-outcome evaluations). Such evaluations are consistent with findings regarding the orbital and medial prefrontal networks (e.g., Schoenbaum, Chiba, et al., 2003).

Nauta (1971) first suggested that disconnections in the frontal lobe may promote an "interoceptive agnosia," where a person can recognize an object but fail to perceive its affective significance. In normal behavior, Nauta pointed out that linked affective information can serve as "navigational markers" or "affective reference points" for guiding behavior. More recently, Damasio (1994) has used similar ideas in his model of "somatic markers": internal affective information that allows a rapid affective guidance of behavior. Again, a basic assumption is that deficits or imbalances in these markers may lead to poorly directed and organized behavior, and to psychopathic behavior in extreme cases.

In regulatory terms, individuals may vary in their ability to use attention to modulate aspects of their interoceptive state. For example, some children may be able to suppress their fear by shifting attention from anxious feelings. Similarly, some may be able to suppress their appetitive behavior by disengaging from hopeful rewarding sensations. Other forms of interoceptive regulation may focus more specifically on energetic feelings. Children may learn to initiate difficult activities or to sustain effortful behavior by amplifying the energetic feelings arising from the body. Although such processes are difficult to study, we suspect that they provide a rather basic form of self-regulation. Such control most likely depends on voluntary attentional mechanisms of the frontal lobe (Derryberry & Rothbart, 1997).

Conceptual Processing

Perhaps the most important form of regulation arising from motivated attention is that involving conceptual processing. Such regulation is a function of Posner's anterior attentional system and Shallice's supervisory attentional system. One aspect of this regulation concerns the inhibition of dominant or prepotent conceptual associations, allowing concepts to be rearranged to form new ideas and beliefs. For example, an anxious child faced with a threatening event, such as an upcoming test, may use attention to manipulate information relevant to his or her potential performance. The child may attend to the test's content and difficulty, as well as to his or her own intelligence and ability to study for the exam. If done objectively with little bias, such conceptual regulation should allow the child to come up with a rational and effective coping strategy or plan of study.

The problem for many anxious children is that the appraisal processes can become negatively biased and relatively automatic (Beck & Clark, 1997). Anxious children are likely to overestimate the degree of threat and to underestimate their coping ability, thereby increasing their anxiety. However, if attention can be used to inhibit these automatic associations, the child should be able to more accurately appraise the threat (e.g., "The test will be hard, but it's not that important and it's not immediate") and his or her ability to cope ("I'm not good at tests, but I can study harder") at the conceptual level. Such conceptual regulation will not be easy for the child (or even for adults), but it provides a direct way through which the defensive system can help attenuate fear.

Other examples can be found in the conceptual processing underlying causal attributions. Evidence suggests that anxious people tend to attribute negative events to internal causes, often blaming themselves for negative outcomes (Mineka et al., 1995). Although internal attributions are not necessarily inaccurate or maladaptive, they do tend to enhance anxious and depressive symptoms. If this automatic tendency can be inhibited, however, then a less debilitating attribution can be constructed (e.g., "I failed the test because math is difficult and not because I'm dumb"). Similarly, depressed and anxious individuals tend to make

uncontrollable attributions, feeling that there is nothing they can do to improve the situation. If this belief can be suppressed, they may be able to view a negative outcome as controllable and then formulate new options for coping in the future (e.g., "I failed the test, but I can study harder in the future").

Individual Differences in Attentional Control

It should be evident from the previous examples that attention can play a role in regulating the appraisal and attributional processes thought to be so important to emotion. Unfortunately, many of these regulations are quite difficult, because the regulated processes involve automatic activation or involuntary attentional biases. Thus, individual differences in the voluntary attentional ability to constrain more reactive processing can have crucial effects on the efficiency with which motivational states function.

Individual differences in voluntary attention have been of special interest in the developmental literature. Rothbart and her colleagues (Rothbart, Ahadi, & Hershey, 1994; Rothbart, Derryberry, & Posner, 1994) have investigated a dimension of "effortful control" thought to reflect individual variability in the anterior attentional system. Effortful control is assumed to function by allowing the child to suppress more reactive tendencies associated with appetitive and defensive processes. Consistent with this notion, effortful control and similar measures have been found related to a variety of positive outcomes. Children with good control tend to show more positive affect, less negative affect, more empathy, more social competence, enhanced conscience, and enhanced compliance (e.g., Eisenberg, Fabes, Guthrie, & Reiser, 2000; Kochanska, Murray, & Harlan, 2000; Rothbart, Ahadi, et al., 1994). Research also suggests that effortful control may serve as a protective factor, limiting the vulnerability arising from extreme appetitive or defensive reactivity. Eisenberg and her colleagues (2001) found internalizing behaviors in 4- to 8-year-olds to be predicted by low effortful control, low impulsivity, and sadness, whereas externalizing problems were related to low effortful control, anger, and impulsivity. However, another study found effortful control to predict internalizing and externalizing problems in a nonlinear way, with low and high levels of control associated with problem behaviors (Murray & Kochanska, 2002).

One of the difficulties inherent in research on effortful control is that the individual difference measures often blend together a variety of attentional and response-related processes. The capacity is most likely multidimensional, making specific predictions difficult. It is also likely to rely on several different frontal regions. In a recent fMRI study, participants were asked to view negative photos and cognitively reappraise them. This effortful reappraisal tended to decrease negative affect, but to differing degrees in different individuals. Across individuals, success in reducing negative affect was positively correlated with anterior cingulate activity, the general region of Posner's anterior attentional system. However, the reappraisal process itself was most strongly accompanied by activation of the lateral and medial prefrontal regions, along with decreased activation in orbital and amygdaloid regions (Ochsner, Bunge, Gross, & Gabrieli, 2002).

Our research with college students has tried to simplify this situation by measuring voluntary regulation that is primarily attentional. We use a 20-item self-report measure of attentional control along with reaction time tasks designed to target specific attentional processes. We have found the Attentional Control scale to predict attentional performance in perceptual, conceptual, and response-related tasks (Derryberry, 2002). One study employed a design where an initial cue drew attention to either a threatening location (i.e., where points were likely to be lost) or a safe location (i.e., where points were unlikely to be lost). All anxious participants showed delays in disengaging attention for a cued threatening location for 250 milliseconds. By 500 milliseconds after the cue, however, anxious persons with good attention were able to disengage and shift to the safer location, whereas those with poor attention still had difficulty shifting from the threatening location. This pattern suggests that anxious people with poor voluntary attention will be more vulnerable when it comes to coping with threat, because they have difficulty shifting from danger to find a source of safety (Derryberry & Reed, 2002).

More recently, we have begun collecting data relating attentional control to various forms of coping. Students with good attention tended to employ more difficult but effective strategies, such as active coping, planning, and positive reappraisal. In contrast, those with poor attention favored simpler and less effective strategies, such as denial, disengagement, and venting. Some coping strategies were predicted by motivational as well as attentional tendencies. For example, the positive reappraisal strategy was associated with good attention and a strong appetitive tendency, restraint coping was predicted by good attention and strong defensive tendencies, and venting was predicted by strong defensive tendencies and poor attention (Derryberry & Pilkenton-Taylor, 2005).

In general, we suspect that attentional skills enable children to incorporate more complex and more effective coping strategies into their defensive and appetitive moti-

vation. In terms of Figure 12.2, the functional capacity of the voluntary attentional link may prove pivotal to effective coping. Children with good attention should be better able to inhibit reflexive biases, to assess more information, and thereby to arrive at a more adaptive coping strategy. Unfortunately, children with poor attentional control may have to rely on simpler and less effective techniques such as distraction and venting. Such techniques may often fail, leaving the child with increasing anxiety or frustration and a desire to avoid the situation. If the situation is avoided, then the child loses the opportunity to learn about the threats and new ways of coping.

To summarize, we have argued that motivational systems exert wide-ranging regulatory effects. Regulation of motor, autonomic, and endocrine systems prepares the peripheral body, and regulation of central arousal and attention guides the processing of exteroceptive, interoceptive, and conceptual information. If certain regulatory subsystems are impaired, then the motivational process as a whole will suffer, leaving the child vulnerable to impulsive and anxious disorders. To understand these disorders, it is necessary to focus on the regulatory subsystems and to determine how their functioning may enhance or impair overall motivational performance. We suspect that the capacity for voluntary attentional control may prove to be the most influential of these regulatory effects.

Interactions between Motivational Systems

Our discussion so far has been simplistic in implying that only one motivational system is active at a time. In reality, most environments contain both positive and negative signals, resulting in the simultaneous activation of appetitive and defensive systems. Similarly, at a conceptual level, most of the child's thinking will consist of both positive and negative elements, as is usually the case in thinking about the self or the future. By considering contexts in which motivational systems might interact, a more informed view of self-regulation can be attained.

Reactive Interactions

The most common type of interaction involves the inhibition of appetitive motivation by defensive motivation. Positive and negative incentives are present in the environment, but the defensive system inhibits approach behavior to protect the individual. We have suggested that this type of behavioral inhibition provides the child with an initial, reactive means of self-control (Derryberry & Rothbart, 1997). The effectiveness of this regulation depends on both the strength of the approach motive and the strength of the defensive inhibition. As mentioned earlier, the regulation of approach will become increasingly effective as appetitive motivation decreases and defensive motivation increases. Thus, children with strong appetitive and weak defensive systems should be most vulnerable to impulsive, disinhibited forms of behavior.

To provide a less familiar example, anxious children often find themselves in conflict situations, where they might want to join other children in play but their fear holds them back. In some instances, the fearful child's attention may be caught by some positive signal, such as the smiles or laughter of the other children. If attention orients to these signals, their impact on the child's appetitive system is enhanced, leading to a progressive increase in the desire or tendency to approach. At some point, the appetitive motivation may surpass that of the defensive system, such that the child approaches and plays with the other children. As illustrated, this can be an entirely reactive form of regulation, driven primarily by changes in the environmental balance of positive to negative signals.

In brief, we have described two simple forms of reactive regulation arising from interactions between motivational systems. The defensive system can constrain approach behavior, and the appetitive system can attenuate fearful behavior. Viewing this regulation as a temporal process, in which a less dominant system progressively weakens the stronger system, provides a useful framework for more voluntary forms of self-control.

Voluntary Self-Control

In this view, self-control or "will" arises in a situation where two motives are in conflict, with the initially weaker motive recruiting voluntary processes to supersede the dominant motive. More specifically, the weaker motive can employ attention to suppress the exteroceptive, interoceptive, and conceptual pathways that fuel the stronger motive and to facilitate the pathways that support itself. These attentional influences are difficult and energy-demanding, resulting in feelings of effort and agency on the part of the person. These internal feelings of resistance, effort, and agency are central components of the general experience of will.

For children with strong appetitive motivation, one of their common challenges will be to bring their impulsivity under control. They may often find themselves in situations where the appetitive system is dominant and the defensive inhibitory system is active but not strong enough to rein in the approach tendencies. However, if the defensive system can access voluntary frontal capacities, it can amplify its influence and eventually overcome the approach tenden-

cies. If tempted to steal, for example, the child may shift attention away from the rewarding object and its associated positive feelings. He or she may amplify conceptual beliefs that it would be bad to steal and good to resist this temptation. The child would also be likely to attend to potential outcomes related to possible actions such as the possibility of being punished or feeling guilty afterward and of feeling proud and competent if the impulse is controlled. Although there are different attentional strategies that can be deployed, the basic idea is to redirect support (exteroceptive, interoceptive, and conceptual informational support) from the dominant to the subordinate motive.

For children with stronger defensive tendencies, the main regulatory challenge will be overcoming their fear and approaching a situation they would rather avoid. Various strategies can again be used, such as reorienting from the threatening aspects of the situation and their anxious feelings to safer aspects and feelings of relief or assurance. Also, the child can call on beliefs about what should be done ("I should be friendly"), what should not be done ("I shouldn't be a coward"), and what can be done ("I can do this"), as well as gain strength by accessing potential feelings of guilt and pride related to avoiding and approaching, respectively. Clearly, such self-control can be extremely difficult for the child, and he or she will often fail. But if adequate representations and attentional skills are available, and if the necessary effort can be sustained, quite difficult forms of coping can be accomplished. As mentioned earlier, children with good effortful control are likely to benefit from their attentional skills.

The most influential research on self-control is that done by Mischel and his colleagues. Working with a delay of gratification task, these researchers demonstrated that the ability to delay depends on various attentional strategies that serve to amplify the "cool" relative to the "hot" aspects of the situation (Metcalfe & Mischel, 1999). For example, children are better able to delay eating a marshmallow when they look away from it or think of it as a puffy white cloud. Nor do they want to think about how good it might taste. One of the most remarkable aspects of this research is the apparent stability of the underlying skills. Preschool ability to delay gratification predicts competent coping during adolescence (Shoda, Mischel, & Peake, 1990) and even competent coping with rejection in the early 30s (Ayduk et al., 2000).

Such stability is consistent with the idea that self-control depends on underlying frontal capacities such as attention. Given the importance of attention in motivational functioning and self-control, it seems clear that attention should be a key target of intervention and treatment. Such a focus is evident in pharmacological approaches, though the effect is relatively indirect; for example, various antidepressants and stimulants manipulate the central monoamine systems, which in turn influence frontal functioning. It is also central to cognitive-behavioral approaches, where a main goal is to help the patient to deploy attention in a more voluntary and effective way and thereby to overcome automatic and maladaptive patterns of thought (Wells & Matthews, 1994).

Constraints on Self-Control

Although voluntary self-control is one of our greatest strengths, it is a capacity that is limited in many ways. It depends not only on the child's frontal attentional capacity, but also on the strength of the to-be-regulated motives. In anxiety, for example, there are many reactive components that can constrain self-control. For example, anxiety often involves a strong autonomic response, resulting in intense feelings of tension. These anxious feelings can capture attention, leading to a state of self-consciousness that interferes with other processing (Hamilton & Ingram, 2001; Matthews, 1997). Regarding attention, we have noted that anxiety tends to narrow attention and to impair disengagement (Tucker & Derryberry, 1992). Working together, these reactive elements render the anxious state very difficult to moderate through voluntary attention.

In addition, self-control can be limited by physiological changes indirectly related to frontal attentional mechanisms. Research by Baumeister (e.g., Muraven, Tice, & Baumeister, 1998) has shown that self-control tends to decrease following its exertion, leading to breakdowns in control on subsequent tasks. A simple explanation for such breakdowns is that self-control requires some type of "energy" in the form of neurochemicals that facilitate frontal activity (e.g., dopamine, serotonin). If these substances are limited, then they are likely to become depleted during effortful or prolonged self-control. Alternatively, the depletion could occur within one of the higher-level motivational systems (e.g., defensive), such that the initially controlled system (e.g., appetitive) becomes disinhibited and thus rebounds (Grossberg & Gutowski, 1987). In either case, these types of dynamic fluctuations help explain why a child's symptoms may fluctuate across time, despite changes in external rewards and punishments. The child may initially be able to voluntarily control his or her behavior, but symptoms return as the child's resources are fatigued.

In summary, our discussion of self-regulation has emphasized the idea that motivational systems are complex self-regulating systems. They carry out a rapid reorganization or tuning of the brain, a coordinated and distributed regulation aimed at promoting a processing state that is adaptive given current motivational needs. The effectiveness of this state in meeting these needs will depend not only on the motivational system itself, but also on the efficiency of the regulated endocrine, autonomic, motor, arousal, and attentional systems. Moreover, because these component systems are shared by other motivational systems, it is necessary to consider interactions between the systems. Whereas some interactions may involve reactive suppression of one system by the other, in conflict situations voluntary self-control can be brought into play. Such voluntary effort provides a form of regulation that goes beyond the influence of the environment and dominant motivational system to provide more effective possessing.

When applied to personality and psychopathology, an emphasis on the regulatory nature of motivational systems provides a better understanding of the active and reactive nature of children's coping. Vulnerabilities to externalizing disorders can be seen to arise from multiple sources, such as an overactive appetitive system and underactive defensive system or a weak attentional capacity. Conversely, the problematic coping involved in internalizing behavior can result from overly strong defensive tendencies, weak appetitive motivation, or weak attention. Although voluntary attention can provide highly effective regulation, some attentional strategies are demanding and beyond the child's capabilities. In addition, the child's reactive tendencies may be too strong to constrain, or the attentional capacity itself may weaken across time. As a result, some children may be forced to rely on less efficient regulatory strategies that provide only short-term relief.

Although a regulatory emphasis is helpful in understanding the child's coping efforts, the approach remains limited in accounting for the specific types of impulses or fears that become important in children's personalities. To address such issues of content, it is helpful to step back and adopt a stronger developmental view of motivational systems across time. The development perspective shows that regulatory mechanisms such as arousal and attention are not only designed to modulate ongoing information processing, but in addition, they are designed to modulate the storage of that information in memory. As will be seen in the next section, motivational processes can be viewed as developmental facilitators by functioning to select significant information for storage in memory, information that will guide motivational function in the future. By examining this progressive selection, we can better understand the extent to which the child's personality is "self-organized" and in turn, the varying content of the child's hopes and fears.

MOTIVATION AND SELF-ORGANIZATION

The developing brain is often viewed as a highly plastic organ that receives instructions from the environment. Such a perspective has much to offer, shedding light on the importance of the environment in both adaptive and maladaptive development. However, the brain's regulatory capacity suggests that more than simple environmental instruction is involved. In this final section, we suggest that personality development can also be viewed as a selective process, through which underlying motivational processes select specific types of environmental information to be represented in the brain (Cicchetti & Tucker, 1994; Derryberry & Reed, 1994b). The motivational systems can be viewed as a generative core of the brain: They establish regulatory states designed to promote adaptive sensory-response organization based on the child's needs. Working together with environmental input, these internal selective processes lead to the construction of progressively complex representations of the self and the world. As will be seen, such an approach provides a view of the differentiation that occurs with development, as well as the integrative aspects of self-organization. In turn, examining the differentiation and integration provides a more precise view of the primary symptoms to which children may become vulnerable.

Motivation and Learning

Motivational systems can influence memory in multiple ways. To begin, motives will influence the types of environment to which the child is exposed (Scarr & McCartney, 1983). This can be done at the most general level through regulation of the child's approach tendencies. Children with strong approach motivation are more likely to expose themselves to various types of exciting, novel, and social environments. In contrast, more inhibited children are likely to avoid these environments and to selectively approach less threatening situations. Through such motivated response regulation, children can frequently select the type of environment and information that they learn.

Moreover, even when children are forced to approach a certain environment (e.g., school), motivational differences will be important in regulating what they learn. As describe earlier, a key regulation carried out by motivational systems is that of the multiple arousal systems ascending to the cortex. Much evidence suggests that the relevant neuromodulators (e.g., norepinephrine, dopamine, acetylcholine) are involved in memory, contributing in various ways to the se-

lection of synapses for stabilization in the cortex. Even peripheral arousal mechanisms, such as the hormones cortisol and epinephrine, are involved in consolidation of long-term memory (McGaugh & Cahill, 2002; Schultz, 1998; Singer, 1990). Thus, regardless of the environment, differences in children's motivational and arousal reactions are likely to lead to different memories. Reward-oriented children may show greater arousal following an academic success than failure, leading to a progressive memory structure that emphasizes their previous successes. In contrast, more anxious children should show greater arousal following failure and a corresponding negative memory.

Furthermore, much evidence suggests that attention facilitates memory. The Pearce-Hall (1980) model of classical conditioning proposes that attention must be paid to the conditioned stimulus to allow it to gain or lose associative strength (Pearce, 1987). Models of observational learning also assume that attention is fundamental to the storage of information in memory. Attention may be less important for simple forms of sequence learning, but more complex sequences that involve hierarchical associations do require attention (e.g., Curran & Keele, 1993). Based on these and additional findings that emotional stimuli tend to be preferentially attended, one would expect enhanced memory for emotional stimuli. Indeed, many studies have now shown better memory for simple emotional stimuli compared to neutral stimuli (e.g., Hamann, 2001). Memory also tends to be better for emotional episodes, which may be partly due to the attention allocated during the elaboration and rehearsal of such episodes (Ochsner & Schacter, 2000). Combined with additional findings that certain types of personalities preferentially attend to certain stimuli, one would further expect relations between personality and memory. Consistent with this hypothesis, anxious individuals tend to show preferential attention to and memory of threatening information (e.g., McCabe, 1999; McNally, Lasko, Macklin, & Pitman, 1995; Reidy & Richards, 1997). Thus, personality differences may differentially bias attention and thereby lead to distinct patterns of memory.

If children with strong defensive systems pay more attention to environmental threats, then across time, they are likely to develop strong representations of various types of dangers. These representations may be further strengthened by anticipatory attention when worrying about some danger before it occurs, as well as by elaboration and rumination after it occurs. The resulting representations may be wide-ranging in their focus, but with many tending to pivot around some threatening aspects of the self or other people. For example, some children may develop elaborate subjective representations of shortcomings in their self-concept, perhaps accompanied by objective representations of the negative ways other people might view them. These types of representations would tend to fuel evaluative fears related to social anxiety. Along related lines, some children may develop strong representations of the sources of safety that help attenuate their fears, representations that tend to emphasize their dependence and reliance on others for security. Such representations may contribute to problems involving Attachment Disorder and school phobia. Other anxious children articulate threat-related representations that are less self-oriented or social in nature. Examples here would be representations related to physical dangers in the environment, such as certain types of animals and heights (Derryberry & Reed, 1996).

Although more longitudinal research is needed, the regulation of arousal and attentional systems should allow underlying motivational systems to progressively construct representations that are relevant to the child's appetitive and defensive needs. This makes adaptive sense in that the motivational systems selectively stabilize information that can enhance their future performance. It is important to note that the developing cortical representations feed back on the subcortical motivational circuits, allowing them to function as cortical or cognitive extensions of the child's motives. In a sense, the more primitive motivational circuitry organizes itself by assimilating the representational capacities of the more advanced cortical architecture (Derryberry & Reed, 1994b; Panksepp, 1998). As discussed in subsequent sections, the representations can serve as more complex recognition mechanisms for predicting and detecting significant environmental events. In addition, the representations can serve to guide the child's behavior by providing navigational markers as he or she attempts to cope with the situation.

Self-Organized Representations

In the discussion that follows, we adopt a broad perspective of cortical representations as rooted in underlying limbic and brain stem circuitry. The representations are highly distributed across the cortex, interconnecting regions that serve exteroceptive, conceptual/episodic, interoceptive, and response processing. Exteroceptive processing is carried out by posterior sensory and association regions, whereas conceptual and episodic memories are focused in posterior and frontal association areas. Interoceptive representations are also located in frontal regions, including the orbital, medial, and insular regions.

Finally, the response-related functions are also frontal, including cingulate, premotor, and motor regions (i.e., the medial and orbital/lateral trends described earlier).

All these regions are extensively interconnected and participate, to varying degrees, in the representational process. One can, of course, focus on more specific representations localized in circumscribed regions, but for personality and psychopathology, the interactions between representational fields is equally important. This notion of distributed representations is illustrated in Figure 12.3.

As connections between exteroceptive and interoceptive regions become stabilized, the child becomes able to relate stimuli to emotional feelings. Many types of emotional representations may be stored in the frontal lobe, but particularly important will be those related to motivational outcomes, that is, whether an appetitive stimulus results in pleasure or frustration and whether a defensive stimulus results in pain or relief. Thus, the exteroceptive-interoceptive connections provide a rapid means of stimulus-outcome evaluation, allowing a direct connection between a stimulus and a specific hedonic outcome. Similarly, connections from conceptual regions to interoceptive regions afford an instantaneous evaluation of ideas, beliefs, and

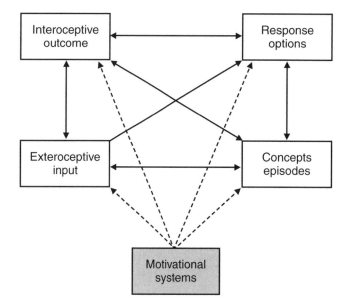

Figure 12.3 Illustration of distributed cortical representations. Information is stored in different cortical regions regarding exteroceptive, interoceptive, conceptual, and response information. In this example, interoceptive information involves hedonic outcomes such as pleasure, frustration, pain, and relief, which can be used in evaluating various sensory and response options. Ascending connections reflect the role of subcortical motivational systems in development and online modulation of representations.

conceptual aspects of the self. As they feed back into the subcortical motivational circuits, such cortical connections can enhance the detection or recognition function of the subcortical systems (Damasio, 1994; Derryberry & Reed, 1994b; Schoenbaum, Chiba, et al., 2003). Finally, connections between motor regions and interoceptive regions afford a rapid evaluation of potential response options, prior to their actual execution. Response selection under appetitive and defensive conditions may thus be biased in favor of responses related to pleasurable and relieving outcomes. These processes will help support the guidance function of the motivational system. To return to Nauta's (1971) seminal ideas, the stimulus-outcome and response-outcome links establish the navigational markers for guiding behavior.

We do not mean to imply that these distributed representations are completely stable or hardwired, for the system must remain plastic and responsive to environmental changes. In addition, the person's internal hormonal and arousal states appear capable of modulating the links among various cortical regions, in a sense reconfiguring the representational network to fit current needs. For example, ascending cholinergic projections preferentially target connections between exteroceptive and interoceptive regions, suggesting that this neuromodulator facilitates stimulus-outcome evaluations. Ascending dopamine projections preferentially target interoceptive and response areas, suggesting that they may facilitate response-outcome processing.

But in terms of personality, the important point is that as the child develops, projections to the cortex will progressively sculpt the representations to support the child's motives. The child's appetitive system will function to tune exteroceptive circuits to many types of rewards (e.g., smiles, food, excitement) that the child experiences. Conceptual and episodic pathways will similarly be molded to represent rewarding information, such as the positive traits of the self, positive aspects of other people, positive events in the past, and positive events in the future. Interoceptive circuitry will be shaped by underlying needs and desires, as well as the outcome states of pleasure and frustration. The response repertoire will accordingly be selected in favor of various approach strategies and actions. In contrast, the child's defensive system will promote cortical representations aimed at detecting danger and guiding avoidance behavior. Exteroceptive regions will be tuned to potential dangers such as sources of pain and disapproval, whereas interoceptive regions will be shaped by experiences of pain, fear, and relief. Conceptual and episodic regions will be shaped to store memories regarding negative traits and

events, and motor pathways will be stabilized that have been successful in avoiding pain and obtaining relief.

When approached in these simple terms, the developmental process and resultant cortical connectivity appear fundamentally adaptive: As their representational capacity becomes more finally tuned, children should become more and more efficient at anticipating and satisfying their needs. Unfortunately, this adaptive process can be undermined in a variety of ways. Because the child's representations are so central to understanding his or her symptoms, we consider these problems in some detail in the next section.

Problems of Representation

A general source of risk involves imbalances in the strength of the underlying motivational systems. In simplest terms, problems can arise because the motivational imbalance biases the representational process in favor of one type of information when, in reality, the world consists of both positive and negative information. Focusing on the self-concept, for example, children with a strong appetitive and weak defensive system may overrepresent their positive attributes and underrepresent their negative attributes. Such representations might be adaptive in motivating the child to approach difficult tasks, but they can also lead to frustration and disappointment when the situation is beyond the child's abilities. As discussed in more detail later, the weak defensive system may also undermine representations important for emotions such as guilt and empathy. In contrast, children with a strong defensive and weak appetitive capacity will tend to develop representations that emphasize their negative attributes and underemphasize positive attributes. Though such humility can have its advantages, these children are likely to suffer in a variety of ways and, at the same time, to blame themselves for their conceived inadequacies. In the worst cases, children may represent themselves not only as negative, but also as powerless in overcoming their shortcomings. These are, of course, highly simplified examples, intended only to establish a general framework for examining more specific representational problems.

The more specific problems can be approached in light of the regulatory functions carried out by the motivational systems. As discussed earlier, the motivational systems function by regulating subsystems controlling autonomic/endocrine activity, central arousal, response activity, and attention (Figure 12.2). Children will vary not only in the reactivity of the central motivational circuits, but also in terms of these subsystems. If one or more of these subsystems is too weak or too strong, the efficiency of the regulation will suffer, and this inefficiency may bias representational development.

For example, some children tend to have particularly strong autonomic reactions, perhaps related to low vagal tone. The autonomic activity is likely to attract attention, leading to representations with strong links between interoceptive information and exteroceptive and conceptual elements. Such an interoceptive emphasis can prove adaptive or maladaptive, depending on the nature of the representation. If an anxious child has a strong autonomic reaction when meeting a new child, attention may become self-focused and the child may lose track of important events in the social situation (Matthews, 1997). This distraction would lead to an impoverished representation of the external aspects of the interaction (e.g., characteristics of the other child), which would in turn impair his or her performance in subsequent encounters. In addition, the strong autonomic activity and self-focused attention could lead the child to make an internal rather than external attribution, blaming the self if the interaction was unpleasant. The idea here is that the focus on the body, as the physical locus of the self, helps establish a stronger link between the negative feeling and the self rather than between the negative feeling and the other child (Dienstbier, 1984).

In other instances, strong autonomic reactions may facilitate more useful representations such as those supporting conscience and moral behavior. Intense autonomic reactions following a transgression may again cause the anxious child to focus on the self, increasing the odds that he or she will make an internal attribution and internalize the relevant moral principle (Dienstbier, 1984; Kochanska, 1997). The intense autonomic reaction makes it easier for the child to link the negative feeling to activated conceptual content (i.e., a moral principle). This could be one of the pathways that contribute to the facilitated moral development and vulnerability to guilt evident in anxious children. In contrast, the absence of strong autonomic reactivity may contribute to impaired moral development evident in psychopathic individuals. This autonomic relation is consistent with evidence that adult psychopaths and children with ADHD and Conduct Disorder tend to show decreased autonomic reactivity (Beauchaine, Katkin, Strassberg, & Snarr, 2001). In some of these children, the inability to generate and experience aversive autonomic activity may contribute to the development of deficient interoceptive markers in their representations. Besides problems in guiding behavior, such representations may lead to deficiencies in moral internalization and emotions such as guilt and remorse (e.g., Damasio, 1994; Nauta, 1971). Functional MRI studies indicate that moral emotions activate orbital and medial frontal networks, along with areas of the superior temporal sulcus (Moll et al., 2002).

A more wide-ranging source of representational problems arises from imbalances in the central arousal systems. As described earlier, ascending projections releasing dopamine, serotonin, norepinephrine, and acetylcholine are recruited in varying combinations during different motivational states. These neuromodulators function to regulate ongoing cortical processing and to facilitate storage of information in memory. To build on the interoceptive example described earlier, cholinergic projections from the nucleus basalis target the entire cortex but are particularly dense in the paralimbic regions that feed into the limbic system. Deficits in acetylcholine have a variety of effects on memory, but from an anatomical perspective, they would likely diminish the interoceptive facets of representations, perhaps promoting deficits in behavioral guidance similar to those with weak autonomic reactivity. In addition, cholinergic deficits could impair connections from the cortical representations to the limbic motivational circuits. Such a disconnection would make it more difficult for the individual to detect a motivationally relevant external or conceptual event, resulting in relatively apathetic behavior (Mesulam, 1988).

Additional representational problems may arise from dopamine imbalances. If dopamine is too low, as appears to occur in ADHD, the child will have difficulty focusing attention on central details of the situation. As a result, his or her representations, in the classroom and elsewhere, may often be missing important central details. In contrast, dopamine appears to be high in certain anxiety disorders, giving rise to narrowed attention and tightly coupled information processing (Tucker & Derryberry, 1992). Such a mode of processing could promote representations that overemphasize central aspects of an episode (e.g., "I was bad"), at the expense of more peripheral but still relevant information (e.g., mitigating circumstances). This is consistent with findings that children undergoing painful medical procedures show quite accurate memory for details, though their memory decreases with the extent of distress (Chen, Zeltzer, Craske, & Katz, 2000). It is also consistent with certain paranoid forms of thought, in which a set of relatively unrelated events are woven together in a tight, inflexible belief system, often with a general neglect of the big picture (Tucker & Derryberry, 1992).

A final source of representational problems arises from deficits in frontal attentional functioning. As described earlier, frontal attentional networks appear capable of constraining more reactive attentional effects elicited by the motivations. If frontal mechanisms are weak, attention will be driven in a more reactive way by subcortical mechanisms (e.g., overfocusing from dopamine, difficulties in disengaging). In these cases, different types of information may be equally available to the child, but attentional biases would impair the balanced representation of that information in memory. Anxious children with poor attentional control may form episodic representations of social situations that emphasize only the threats (e.g., looks of anger, disapproval). If the child has better control, he or she may be able to disengage from the threats and take advantage of other information (e.g., looks of reassurance, support). The resulting representation that related safety to other people and behaviors would help in guiding their future social interactions toward relieving outcomes. Without such control, the child's representations are likely to emphasize threat, thus making it easier for the child to worry about threat and to expect threat in a social situation (i.e., to be more socially anxious). On the other hand, it is also possible that some anxious children with poor attention may come to focus very strongly on a source of safety in a threatening situation. A young child may form representations that emphasize the presence of the parent, and older children may emphasize their friends as sources of support and reassurance. If the representations are imbalanced to the extent that the child relies too heavily on others, then symptoms related to dependency and attachment problems might be supported. Because coping responses are linked to another person instead of the self, the child lacks a sense of agency and control when the source of support is not present (Derryberry & Reed, 1994b).

More generally, its worth noting that social situations involve rather subtle and fast-moving events, requiring attentional shifts from one's feelings, to what one wants to say, to what the other is saying, to what the other might be thinking, and so on. Even for a child with relatively good attention, it is fairly easy to become overloaded in social situations (Rapee & Heimberg, 1997). If attention cannot keep up with the pace of the interaction, or if it becomes inappropriately focused on the self, a good deal of information relevant to both threat and safety is likely to be missed. The consequent representation will be impoverished and of limited help in guiding future social performance. Links between attentional control and social competence have been demonstrated in the work of Eisenberg and her colleagues (2000).

Similar effects of attention can be seen in conceptual and episodic representations of the self. Many anxious children are likely to preferentially attend to the more negative components of their personality, leading to an overemphasis on negative rather than positive traits. Similarly, reward-oriented children are likely to develop self-representations that emphasize their positive attributes. Adult studies suggest that some individuals tend to interlink self-related traits into relatively separate positive and negative structures, creating a compartmentalized form of representation (Showers & Kling, 1996). Such representations are likely to become problematic for children with poor attentional control: Spreading activation within the negative compartment would lead to increasing feelings of worthlessness of the anxious child, perhaps promoting the global forms of attribution evident in some anxious and depressed individuals. The compartmentalized situation may seem better for the appetitive child, but even here, the spreading activation could lead to overconfidence, grandiosity, and poor decisions. In contrast, children with good control of attention could inhibit this spreading activation and may compensate by shifting attention from a bad trait to a good trait ("I'm bad at math but good at spelling"). This type of cognitive coping strategy would be likely to lead to an integrative self-organization (Showers & Kling, 1996). As the integrative organization develops, anxious children will be better able to attenuate their self-related fears by focusing on their positive traits, and impulsive children will be better able to constrain their grandiosity by focusing on their negative traits. Neuroimaging studies suggest that episodic and semantic information regarding the self activates circuitry in anterior, polar regions of the frontal lobe (Craik et al., 1999).

Although more research is necessary, we suspect that in the long run, representations that are relatively balanced in terms of positive and negative components will serve a protective function for many children. As described earlier, representations can become imbalanced if one motivational system tends to dominate the other, or if components within the systems, such as autonomic, arousal, and attentional activity, are overly strong or weak in the system as a whole. Even given such imbalances between and within the motivational systems, the possibility remains that children with good attention may be able to exert effort and restore more balanced and objective representations.

Environmental Influences

So far, our discussion of self-organization has focused on the development of the representational functions of motivational systems. We have suggested that representations may be related to specific symptoms, which arise from the balance between the two motivational systems and the functioning of components within the systems. The major limitation of this approach arises from its emphasis on internal at the expense of external environmental influences. It is clearly beyond the scope of this chapter to discuss the countless ways the environment influences self-organization. What we hope to provide instead is a general framework that organizes environmental influences into a set of domains that are particularly important to personality organization. These domains include environmental influences related to social inclusion, social status, achievement, morality, and intellectual development.

A second shortcoming involves our emphasis on two motivational systems and a small set of emotions (fear, hope, relief, frustration, pride, guilt). Although such a simple approach provides a useful starting point, it fails to explain a wide range of more complex human motives and emotions. It is worth emphasizing that future advances may delineate additional, distinct circuits related to more specific motives and emotions. In the mean time, however, it is worthwhile to examine the extent to which such emotions can be generated through a differentiation of our basic motivational systems. Therefore, in considering the different environmental domains through which children develop, we also examine the possibility that these domains allow a differentiation of basic appetitive and defensive motives into more specific motives related to more complex emotions.

In a sense, we are adopting an inside-out approach to the environment, attempting to organize environmental influences in terms of their relevance to internal motivational and developmental processes. As will be seen, the emotional and motivational consequences of each domain can be viewed in terms of internally generated appetitive and defensive processes. At the same time, the domains are characterized by distinct external incentives. It is assumed that the strengths of these incentives will differ across children, resulting from values of their family, their educational opportunities, and so on. As a result, children's appetitive tendencies may differentiate along various pathways, depending on the availability of these various incentives. Some children may develop extensively in areas such as social inclusion and morality, and others in areas such as social status and achievement. If development is frustrated in one of these domains, the child may select another domain that better fits his or her motivational goals and efficiency. This general process is illustrated in Figure 12.4.

Many theorists have emphasized the caregiver and early attachment relationship as fundamental to social development. Although this vast literature is beyond our scope, attachment theorists have proposed that representations of the self and the self in relation to another person can be strongly influenced by the quality of the early caregiving matrix (e.g., Bowlby, 1988). The most severe disruptions in this initial environment arise in cases where children are physically abused, sexually abused, or neglected. When studied using narrative story stems, maltreated children have been found to reflect more negative representations of the self and also the mother (Toth, Cicchetti, Macfie, & Emde, 1997). Interestingly, no differences were found in positive representations between maltreated and nonmaltreated children, a finding consistent with the notion that representations may be shaped by separable motivational systems. In addition, longitudinal work suggests that the negative representations of maltreated children tend to coalesce and consolidate as development proceeds (Toth, Cicchetti, Macfie, Maughan, & VanMeenan, 2000). Furthermore, several investigations indicate that maltreated children tend to generalize their negative representations, making them vulnerable to future relationship problems (e.g., Lynch & Cicchetti, 1991). Clearly, representations of the self and others appear to be highly sensitive to the early caregiving environment and thus constitute an important target for intervention.

A related environmental domain involves social groups. From an evolutionary perspective, crucial resources and protection can be gained or lost depending on whether one is included in or excluded from a group. Thus, it is not surprising that the hope for acceptance and the fear of rejection are two of our strongest social motives. Social environments differ in their potential for acceptance and rejection, and children are differentially sensitive to these two outcomes (Gazelle & Ladd, 2003). As a result, children develop representations of the self, of others, and of the self in relation to others that help them navigate the social world. Whether the self is represented as acceptable or unacceptable and whether others are viewed as accepting or rejecting will be central to the child's personality (Asher & Paquette, 2003; Gazelle & Ladd, 2003; Leary, Tambor, Terdal, & Downs, 1995). When accepted, children will experience positive feelings related to affection, belongingness, and support. If rejection occurs and is internally attributed, then feelings of rejection, loneliness, anxiety, and sadness are likely. For children initially prone to aggression, early rejection can exacerbate antisocial development and more resentful and hostile emotions (Dodge et al., 2003).

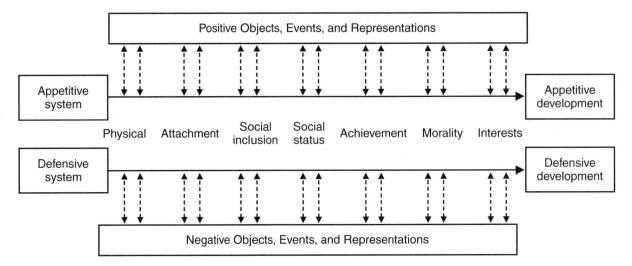

Figure 12.4 Illustration of interaction between developing motivational systems and the environment. Environment refers to objects, events, and related concepts in physical, social, achievement, and moral domains. Each domain is capable of providing various rewarding or punishing inputs to the appetitive and defensive systems, as a result of which the motivational systems facilitate and form connections with representations of domain-related objects and events. Dotted lines reflect potential branches of the motivational systems within the environmental domains.

Related to social inclusion are environmental incentives involving social status (e.g., popularity and dominance). Varying emphases on status appear in different families and peer groups, and again, children are more or less sensitive to such matters (Lease, Musgrove, & Axelrod, 2002). Whether children represent themselves and others as superior or inferior can have strong impact on their self-evaluation and treatment of others (Leary et al., 1995). On the emotional side, status representations focusing on the self can generate feelings such as pride, superiority, inferiority, and shame. When focused on others, status representations can generate feelings of respect or disrespect. Again, such representations of self and others can have potent influences on interpersonal behavior.

Another crucial domain is that of achievement, encompassing environmental events ranging from tasks around the house, to skills in games and sports, to academic performance. Motivational approaches to achievement have long emphasized the relative strengths of motives to approach success and to avoid failure (Atkinson, 1983). More recently, the child's fear of failure has been dissociated into a more active form of defensive approach along with the avoidance of achievement contexts (Elliot & Church, 1997). Although such models fit well with appetitive and defensive motivational systems, it is clear that different families, peer groups, and cultures put varying emphasis on achievement. As a simple example, parents set different standards for successful academic performance, requiring A's, B's, C's, and in some cases even less. It is natural for the child to internalize these standards and to use them in self-evaluation. Whether the child represents the self as a success or a failure will have potent motivational and emotional consequences. On the motivational side, the representations will be crucial to the child's sense of self-efficacy and perceived control (Skinner, Zimmer-Gembeck, & Connell, 1998). On the emotional side, the child may feel incompetent and ashamed given failure but competent and proud given success.

For some children, a particularly central domain will be the moral domain. Here, we simply refer to the environmental rules about what is right and wrong, as transmitted through the child's parents, peers, and belief systems. The appetitive motivation may vary from simply hoping to being a "good" person to the hope of religious salvation. The defensive component may promote a fear of being "bad" and even religious damnation. Again, there will be wide-ranging differences in the ethical standards to which children are exposed. Like the achievement-related representations, those in the ethical domain come to constitute important standards in evaluating the self and others. Whether children view themselves and others as good or bad will have a strong impact on their private and social experiences. Relevant feelings include those of righteousness, virtuousness, guilt, and shame. In regard to others' morality, emotions such as admiration, approval, condemnation, and contempt may come into play.

A final domain entails the more abstract intellectual realm that becomes important for older children and adolescents. Rather than centering on other people, achievements, and ethical standards, this is in many ways a more open domain involving the primarily appetitive pleasures that can be derived from the manipulation of ideas. The domain may begin with simple intellectual activities such as fantasy, reading, and hobbies and expand into more complex philosophical, scientific, and aesthetic interests in some children. Again, there are enormous differences in the intellectual environments to which children are exposed. To the extent to which they develop, intellectual pursuits provide perhaps the most subtle forms of emotion, such as the curiosity and sense of wonder about what is unknown, the intellectual pleasures that arise from acquired understanding, and the aesthetic pleasures that arise from art. Although we have emphasized the appetitive side of the intellectual domain, beliefs can certainly be used for defensive purposes. Typical examples are an anxious or mistreated child's retreat into a fantasy world, or adoption of a strong religious belief as a source of relief and solace.

The grouping of environments into more simple domains provides a view of how relatively simple motivational systems may differentiate along different pathways to generate more complex representations and emotions. The nature of the domain will determine the type of exteroceptive, interoceptive, conceptual, and response information that compose the child's representations. Given that these pathways differ in their availability across children, such an approach also helps highlight the different trajectories along which personality may self-organize. Thus, different children's underlying appetitive and defensive tendencies may differentiate in distinct branching patterns related to acceptance-rejection, superiority-inferiority, success-failure, and pride-guilt. To better understand the child's symptoms, more research needs to focus on these branches and, eventually, on the individual twigs along them.

In addition to clarifying the differentiation that occurs with personality development, an emphasis on environmental domains provides a view of the integrative processes at work in self-organization. On the one hand, we have already emphasized the extent to which the child's cortical representations are vertically integrated: They are fundamentally rooted in subcortical limbic and brain stem structures. However, once the cortical branching in environmental domains is considered, we can see another form of organization, within which the differentiated motives function together to support one another. In other words, these domains are highly complementary and can thus facilitate one another.

For example, a child with high status (e.g., popularity) in one group will have an easier time being accepted into a new social group. In addition, both achievement and ethical success can support inclusion and status; that is, children who are competent and ethical are most likely to be accepted and attain status in a group. Similarly, development in the intellectual domain can facilitate the child's potential in achievement and ethical domains, as well as in inclusion and status domains. Thus, not only are there many different branches along which children can develop, but many of these branches can grow together to support one another.

In addition to this supportive function, the different domains can substitute for one another in satisfying the child's needs. If development of a motivational system is suppressed in one domain, it is likely to develop in another. A child who is unsuccessful in academics may satisfy his or her hope for success in athletics. A child who is generally unsuccessful in the achievement domain may turn to ethics or status to satisfy appetitive needs. From this perspective, self-organization is similar to an evolutionary process in that a wide variety of environmental or representational niches are available for motivational development. Although children may have problems in some areas, it seems unlikely that the self-organization process will be blocked or disrupted. Rather, it will tend to develop along a different trajectory, taking advantage of the niches that are available. When viewed in this way, a clear distinction between normal and abnormal development becomes more difficult to make. As Fischer et al. (1997) point out, psychopathology can be viewed as adaptive development, albeit along distinctive pathways.

FUTURE DIRECTIONS

Although much progress has been made in understanding the general functioning of regulatory processes, it is clear that we are only beginning to appreciate their complexity. Greater understanding will require research in a number of directions. One of the most important directions will approach motivational functions in light of the broader regulatory systems within which they are embedded. Our treatment here has focused on regulatory subsystems as outputs of the motivational systems, physically adjusted in light of significant inputs. However, these regulatory systems are affected by additional biological influences, such as biological rhythms and states, causing them to vary through tonic states that are to some extent independent of the motivational influence. Moreover, the regulatory systems are widespread in their effects, feeding back to modulate the motivational and attentional systems (e.g.,

Derryberry & Tucker, 1991; Herbert, 1994). As we learn more about this modulation, models will allow more dynamic views of how motivation might be influenced by fluctuating arousal, hormonal, and health states.

A major influence on motivational and attentional systems arises from converging arousal systems employing serotonin, norepinephrine, and dopamine as neuromodulators. These systems are currently manipulated in pharmacological treatments of attentional, anxiety, and depressive disorders. Although such treatments often provide relief, it is fair to say that the underlying mechanisms are poorly understood and that the advisability of manipulating arousal systems in children is questionable. Thus, more research is needed on these systems, particularly regarding their specific functions, their development across time, and the effects of manipulating this development pharmacologically.

At a broader level, future research will explore the extent to which motivational, attentional, and arousal systems are embedded in a modulatory influence arising from the peripheral endocrine system. For example, circulating cortisol released from the adrenal gland appears to interact with central circuits related to anxiety and arousal, possibly potentiating fear reactivity across relatively long time frames (e.g., Gunnar, 1994; Schulkin, Gold, & McEwen, 1998). Similarly, circulating testosterone appears to play a role in potentiating aggressive behavior. Primate research suggests that offensive forms of aggression are related to high plasma testosterone and low cortisol, whereas defensive aggression involves high cortisol (Kalin, 1999).

At an even broader level, much evidence suggests that the peripheral immune system is also capable of adjusting central motivation and arousal (Maier & Watkins, 1998). For example, cells of the immune system release many types of cytokines, some of which (the interleukins and interferons) interact with brain stem circuitry to produce "sickness behavior." This is an organized motivational state characterized by fever, fatigue, immobility, and social withdrawal, presumably designed to complement other components of the immune response (Dantzer et al., 1998). Some researchers are pursuing relations between sickness behavior and depression, attempting to establish basic links between peripheral health and central motivational and psychiatric states (Hickie & Lloyd, 1995).

As we learn more about endocrine and immune effects on the brain, theories will come to appreciate the extent to which motivation is embodied, that is, embedded within and shaped by the body's major regulatory systems. Such theories will deepen our understanding of the difficulties involved in voluntary self-regulation and, when applicable, open up a variety of peripherally focused treatment options.

Along with this emphasis on peripheral influences, future research will continue to focus on the central motivational systems themselves. A particularly important line of research will investigate additional systems besides the general appetitive and defensive systems emphasized here. Panksepp (1998) has provided a valuable start in this direction, describing systems related to exploration, fear, anger, sadness, and affiliation. We suspect that systems related to nurturant and affiliative motivation may prove central to personality and psychopathology (Depue & Morrone-Stupinsky, in press; MacDonald, 1992). Variability in such systems contributes to the major trait dimension of agreeableness. Children with stronger nurturant tendencies are likely to show behaviors such as trust, empathy, and kindness. Such prosocial behaviors will be less common in children with weaker tendencies.

It is relatively easy to see how affiliative/nurturant tendencies might interact with other motivational tendencies. For example, deficiencies in nurturant tendencies, when combined with strong appetitive or weak defensive tendencies, may help to explain the more callous and aggressive forms of conduct problems. Perhaps more intriguing is the regulatory potential of nurturant motivation. Although speculative, it is worth noting that parental behavior, which reflects nurturance at its most extreme, often involves very strong suppression of "selfish" needs as the parents attempt to provide resources and protection for their children. The fact that such behavior is seen across the animal kingdom suggests a powerful form of self-regulation with very deep roots. Studying the development of nurturance should provide new insights regarding self-regulation and its failures.

In addition to investigating new motivational systems, future research will attempt to further differentiate the existing systems. We have tried to give several examples of how the defensive system might eventually come to be understood as a set of interacting subsystems. One approach arose from the notion of vertical integration, within which one can identify primitive brain stem fear mechanisms, anticipatory limbic-related anxiety capacities, and the more abstract conceptual fears afforded by the cortex. Although we emphasized the functional integration across these defensive systems, the hierarchically organized subsystems remain separable, suggesting that imbalances at different levels may give rise to different forms of fear and anxiety. As mentioned earlier, more primitive subsystems may contribute to certain types of panic and depressed feelings, whereas imbalances at the higher levels may move the child toward anticipatory forms of anxiety (e.g., Gray & McNaughton, 1996).

Along with such vertical differentiation, future research will provide new views of the extent to which the defensive system is laterally differentiated. Our earlier example focused on the idea that vulnerable children may develop different forms of anxiety depending on their environments. As illustrated in Figure 12.3, a general fear system may develop a variety of branches related to fears of injury, rejection, achievement, and so on. Although we described such fears as a result of selection within a general defensive system, future research may well discover that these and other fears reflect activity in distinct anxiety-related systems. In other words, there may be 10 specialized anxiety systems within the brain, which tend to covary in the individual because they are all influenced by common regulatory systems (e.g., serotonin, cortisol). To the extent that such separable systems can be isolated, we will be better able to predict children's specific vulnerabilities and alleviate them in a precise manner.

Beyond the motivational systems, future research will extend our understanding of higher-level regulatory mechanisms involved in cognition. The research described here has spoken in relatively general terms, such as attention and arousal, though we have at times alluded to other executive functions. One of the challenges of future research will be to specify the basic cognitive operations related to attention, such as the capacity to monitor action and detect errors, to inhibit dominant response tendencies, to inhibit conceptual pathways, to activate conceptual pathways, to hold and operate on information in working memory, to voluntarily retrieve information from long-term memory, to manipulate mental images, to produce internal speech, and to plan. Again, an important issue will be the extent to which these frontal operations vary independently, or whether they tend to cohere as a function of frontally projecting dopaminergic constraints.

A closely related research area will assess how motivational states may differentially bias these executive processes. Motivation has traditionally been viewed as a descending influence that serves to potentiate relevant response options, such as the freezing, fleeing, or fighting options relevant in a dangerous situation (Gallistel, 1980). However, it is also possible to view motivation as exerting an ascending cortical influence that serves to potentiate sets of cognitive operations (e.g., error detection, conceptual inhibition, short-term memory facilitation) that are adaptive given the information-processing requirements of the ongoing state. Some types of anxiety, such as social anxiety, may facilitate conceptual pathways involved in self-evaluation and error detection, such that individuals tend to "search" for aspects of their behavior that might

lead to rejection. Other types of anxiety may limit conceptual processing while facilitating anticipatory processing, thus allowing the person to better anticipate potential threats in the future (Tucker & Derryberry, 1992). It can be seen that individual differences in the capacity for anticipatory or self-referential processing may bias a child toward different forms of anxiety.

Given this type of functional understanding, future theorizing may shift from the current focus on motivational processes to models that place equal emphasis on variability in children's patterns of cognitive skills. Such models should prove valuable from a developmental perspective because they allow motivation and personality to be linked more directly to the development of specific cognitive skills. A well-known example is the progressive control over impulsive tendencies afforded by the development of internal speech. More recently, Posner and Rothbart (1998) have attempted to trace the development of attentional subsystems and their consequences for emotional development. Moreover, models emphasizing cognitive skills along with motivational tendencies should prove particularly valuable in the study of developmental psychopathology. By incorporating more individual difference variables and examining these variables in various combinations, such models will provide greater resolution in predicting a child's unique vulnerabilities. It may turn out that some cases of childhood anxiety are primarily rooted in an overreactive defensive system, whereas others arise from executive deficits such as poor short-term memory or conceptual inhibition.

Another promising aspect of such a hybrid motivational-cognitive model is that the relevant skills can be assessed longitudinally. If vulnerabilities are detected, prevention techniques can be implemented aimed at strengthening the problematic skill area. For example, various types of mental exercises, ranging from meditative to game-like techniques, can be employed to strengthen relevant systems or skills. Such techniques are already being developed to improve attention (e.g., Wells & Matthews, 1994), and we suspect that other executive processes can also be enhanced. It is worth noting that progress in computer science will lead to increasingly realistic and enjoyable simulations that might be used to exercise relevant brain regions. At the same time, developments in brain imaging will make it increasingly possible to monitor the efficacy of such interventions.

SUMMARY AND CONCLUSIONS

We have described an approach to personality and psychopathology that emphasizes internal biological processes. We began with the idea that the brain is organized around two basic motivational systems related to appetitive and defensive needs. The motivational systems can be viewed as relatively primitive coping systems, usually functioning in a reactive way but also capable of voluntary functioning. The coping function is accomplished by means of the coordination of other brain systems underlying endocrine, autonomic, motor, arousal, and attentional functions. The consequent motivational state accomplishes two adaptive goals: First, it modulates ongoing information processing to facilitate appetitive and defensive goals; second, it modulates memory storage so as to optimize its functioning in the future. Across time, the motivational states gradually shape the connectivity within the forebrain, guiding a progressive process of personality development and self-organization. This process of self-organization, through which the motivational systems unfold in terms of selected representations, are highly sensitive to the environment, such that different personalities self-organize along diverse pathways.

This view of development provides an especially rich approach to personality. It begins with a focus on individual differences in the relative strengths of the appetitive and defensive systems. This focus provides a general view of personality traits such as extraversion and neuroticism but has difficulty predicting more specific traits and behaviors. This shortcoming can be attenuated by considering individual differences in the component systems related to endocrine, autonomic, motor, arousal, and attentional regulations. In particular, we have tried to point out that it is not simply the strength of the motivational state that is important, but also the efficiency with which the components function. If one or more components are out of balance (e.g., too weak or too strong), the resulting motivational state will tend to be less efficient. Still, such a view remains relatively silent regarding the specific experiences and symptoms evident in different children. To better understand these symptoms, it is crucial to examine the environment in which the child develops. We have suggested that the child's motivational systems will branch within the cortex, establishing representational extensions that are in large part dependent on the environment.

In terms of psychopathology, an implicit assumption is that the problems faced by most children and adults fall within the normal realm of personality. In some cases, symptoms arise because the child is prone to extreme or intense motivational functioning, and in other cases because the regulatory processes are ineffective. Again, we find it useful to view these motivational systems as coping systems, shaped through evolutionary history to enable our species to cope adaptively. The modern world is complex,

however, and children differ in the coping resources (e.g., attentional skills, supportive representations, supportive environments) that are available to them. As a result, children differ dramatically in the efficiency of their coping efforts, and thus in their vulnerability to psychopathology.

An underlying theme of the chapter has been that attention, in particular the frontal systems related to voluntary control, is critical to the child's vulnerability. Indeed, much research suggests that good attention can serve to reduce the child's vulnerability to both internalizing and externalizing disorders. We should emphasize, however, that attention is still poorly understood and is by no means completely separate from other regulatory mechanisms such as arousal. In addition, other executive skills are likely to be important to motivational functioning. As we gain better understanding of how the different regulatory and executive systems work together during various motivational states, we hope techniques will be developed that provide children with greater capacity for self-control.

Although we have consistently emphasized regulatory systems, we should end by noting the importance of the child's representations and the environment. A child might have exceptional attentional control, but in the absence of the appropriate environmental stimulus or internal representation, that attentional control is not going to be that helpful. Children must learn what to attend to in different situations, and moreover, they must have the knowledge or representations that can serve as the objects and guides of attention. Fortunately, by viewing psychopathology in relation to normal personality, we have a fairly direct way of discovering which types of representations are likely to be adaptive in helping the child to cope.

Finally, we would emphasize the child's representations as being particularly important in the study of psychopathology. The child's representations provide the most direct source of his or her experience. To really understand the child's problems, it seems that in many cases, the most useful perspective is one that focuses on the child's personal experiences, that is, how different feelings emerge in relation to different external stimuli, different thoughts, and different response options. If we can better understand the ways the underlying representations are motivated, they will become all the more useful in diagnosis and treatment.

REFERENCES

Arnstein, A. F. T. (1998). Catecholamine modulation of prefrontal cognitive function. *Trends in Cognitive Science, 2,* 436–447.

Asher, S. R., & Paquette, J. A. (2003). Loneliness and peer relations in childhood. *Current Directions in Psychological Science, 12,* 75–78.

Atkinson, J. W. (1983). *Personality, motivation, and action: Selected papers*. New York: Praeger.

Ayduk, O., Mendoza-Denton, R., Mischel, W., Downey, G., Peake, P., & Rodriguez, M. (2000). Regulating the interpersonal self: Strategic self-regulation for coping with rejection sensitivity. *Journal of Personality and Social Psychology, 79*, 776–792.

Bandler, R., & Keay, K. A. (1996). Columnar organization in the midbrain periaqueductal gray and the integration of emotional expression. In G. Holstege, R. Bandler, & C. B. Saper (Eds.), *Progress in brain research: Vol. 107. The emotional motor system* (pp. 285–300). Amsterdam: Elsevier.

Bandler, R., & Shipley, M. T. (1994). Columnar organization in the midbrain periaqueductal gray: Modules for emotional expression? *Trends in Neurosciences, 17*, 379–389.

Barlow, D. H., Chorpita, B. F., & Turovsky, J. (1996). Fear, panic, anxiety, and disorders of emotion. In D. A. Hope (Ed.), *Nebraska Symposium on Motivation: Vol. 43. Perspectives on anxiety, panic, and fear* (pp. 251–328). Lincoln: University of Nebraska Press.

Baxter, L. R., Phelps, M. E., Mazziotta, M. E., & Guze, J. C. (1987). Local cerebral glucose metabolic rates in obsessive-compulsive disorder: A comparison with rates in unipolar depression and in normal controls. *Archives of General Psychiatry, 44*, 211–218.

Beauchaine, T. P. (2001). Vagal tone, development, and Gray's motivational theory: Toward an integrated model of autonomic nervous system functioning in psychopathology. *Development and Psychopathology, 13*, 183–214.

Beauchaine, T. P., Katkin, E. S., Strassberg, Z., & Snarr, J. (2001). Disinhibitory psychopathology in male adolescents: Discriminating conduct disorder from attention-deficit/hyperactivity disorder through concurrent assessment of multiple autonomic states. *Journal of Abnormal Psychology, 110*, 610–624.

Beck, A. T., & Clark, D. A. (1997). An information processing model of anxiety: Automatic and strategic processes. *Behavioural Research and Therapy, 35*, 49–58.

Benes, F. M. (1994). Developmental changes in stress adaptation in relation to psychopathology. *Development and Psychopathology, 6*, 723–739.

Blanchard, D. C., & Blanchard, R. J. (1988). Ethoexperimental approaches to the biology of emotion. *Annual Review of Psychology, 39*, 43–68.

Blumer, D., & Benson, D. F. (1975). Personality changes with frontal and temporal lobe lesions. In D. F. Benson & D. Blumer (Eds.), *Psychiatric aspects of neurologic disease* (pp. 151–170). New York: Grune & Stratton.

Bowlby, J. (1988). *A secure base*. New York: Basic Books.

Carmichael, S. T., & Price, J. L. (1995a). Limbic connections of the orbital and medial prefrontal cortex in macaque monkeys. *Journal of Comparative Neurology, 363*, 615–641.

Carmichael, S. T., & Price, J. L. (1995b). Sensory and premotor connections of the orbital and medial prefrontal cortex of macaque monkeys. *Journal of Comparative Neurology, 363*, 642–664.

Caspi, A., Henry, B., McGee, R. O., Moffitt, T. E., & Silva, P. A. (1995). Temperamental origins of child and adolescent behavior problems: From age three to age fifteen. *Child Development, 66*, 55–68.

Chen, E., Zeltzer, L., Craske, M., & Katz, E. (2000). Children's memory for painful cancer treatment procedures: Implications for distress. *Child Development, 71*, 933–947.

Cicchetti, D., & Tucker, D. (1994). Development and self-regulatory structures of the mind. *Development and Psychopathology, 6*, 533–549.

Craik, F. I. M., Moroz, T. M., Moscovitch, M., Stuss, D. T., Winocur, G., Tulving, E., et al. (1999). In search of the self: A positron emission tomography study. *Psychological Science, 10*, 26–34.

Curran, T., & Keele, S. W. (1993). Attentional and nonattentional forms of sequence learning. *Journal of Experimental Psychology: Learning, Memory, and Cognition, 19*, 189–202.

Damasio, A. R. (1994). *Descartes' error: Emotion, reason, and the human brain*. New York: G. P. Putnam's Sons.

Dantzer, R., Bluthe, R., Gheus, G., Cremona, S., Laye, S., Parnet, P., et al. (1998). Molecular basis of sickness behavior. *New York Academy of Sciences, 856*, 132–138.

Davis, K. L., Charney, D., Coyle, J. T., & Nemeroff, C. (Eds.). (2002). *Neuropsychopharmacology: The fifth generation of progress. An official publication of the American College of Neuropsychopharmacology*. New York: Lippincott, Williams, & Wilkins.

Depue, R. A., & Collins, P. F. (1999). Neurobiology of the structure of personality: Dopamine, facilitation of incentive motivation, and extraversion. *Behavioral and Brain Sciences, 22*, 521–555.

Depue, R. A., & Morrone-Strupinsky, J. V. (in press). A neurobehavioral model of affiliative bonding: Implications for conceptualizing a human trait of affiliation. *Behavioral and Brain Sciences*.

Depue, R. A., & Spoont, M. R. (1986). Conceptualizing a serotonin trait: A behavioral dimension of constraint. *Annals of the New York Academy of Science, 487*, 47–62.

Derryberry, D. (2002). Attention and voluntary control. *Self and Identity, 1*, 105–111.

Derryberry, D., & Pilkenton-Taylor, C. (2005). *Individual differences in attention predict coping styles*. Manuscript in preparation.

Derryberry, D., & Reed, M. A. (1994a). Temperament and attention: Orienting toward and away from positive and negative signals. *Journal of Personality and Social Psychology, 66*, 1128–1139.

Derryberry, D., & Reed, M. A. (1994b). Temperament and the self-organization of personality. *Development and Psychopathology, 6*, 653–676.

Derryberry, D., & Reed, M. A. (1996). Regulatory processes and the development of cognitive representations. *Development and Psychopathology, 8*, 215–234.

Derryberry, D., & Reed, M. A. (1998). Anxiety and attentional focusing: Trait, state and hemispheric influences. *Personality and Individual Differences, 25*, 745–761.

Derryberry, D., & Reed, M. A. (2002). Anxiety-related attentional biases and their regulation by attentional control. *Journal of Abnormal Psychology, 111*, 225–236.

Derryberry, D., & Rothbart, M. K. (1997). Reactive and effortful processes in the organization of temperament. *Development and Psychopathology, 9*, 633–652.

Derryberry, D., & Tucker, D. M. (1991). The adaptive base of the neural hierarchy: Elementary motivational controls on network function. In R. Dienstbier (Ed.), *Nebraska Symposium on Motivation: Vol. 38. Perspectives on motivation* (pp. 289–342). Lincoln: University of Nebraska Press.

Dienstbier, R. A. (1984). The role of emotion in moral socialization. In C. E. Izard, J. Kagan, & R. B. Zajonc (Eds.), *Emotions, cognition, and behavior* (pp. 484–514). Cambridge, England: Cambridge University Press.

Dodge, K. A., Lansford, J. E., Burks, V. S., Bates, J. E., Pettit, G. S., Fontaine, R., et al. (2003). Peer rejection and social information-processing factors in the development of aggressive behavior problems in children. *Child Development, 74*, 374–393.

Eisenberg, N., Cumberland, A., Spinrad, T., Fabes, R., Shepard, S., Reiser, M., et al. (2001). The relations of regulation and emotionality to children's externalizing and internalizing problem behavior. *Child Development, 74,* 1112–1134.

Eisenberg, N., Fabes, R. A., Guthrie, I. K., & Reiser, M. (2000). Dispositional emotionality and regulation: Their role in predicting quality of social functioning. *Journal of Personality and Social Psychology, 78,* 136–157.

Elliot, A. J., & Church, M. A. (1997). A hierarchical model of approach and avoidance achievement motivation. *Journal of Personality and Social Psychology, 72,* 218–232.

Eysenck, H. J., & Eysenck, M. W. (1985). *Personality and individual differences: A natural science approach.* New York: Plenum Press.

Eysenck, M. W. (1997). *Anxiety and cognition: A unified theory.* Hove, England: Psychology Press.

Fischer, K. W., Ayoub, C., Singh, I., Noam, G., Maraganore, A., & Raya, P. (1997). Psychopathology as adaptive development along distinctive pathways. *Development and Psychopathology, 9,* 749–779.

Floyd, N. S., Price, J. L., Ferry, A. T., Keay, K. A., & Bandler, R. (2001). Orbitomedial prefrontal cortical projections to hypothalamus in the rat. *Journal of Comparative Neurology, 432,* 307–328.

Fowles, D. C. (1994). A motivational theory of psychopathology. In W. G. Spaulding (Ed.), *Nebraska Symposium on Motivation: Vol. 41. Integrative views of motivation, cognition, and emotion* (pp. 181–238). Lincoln: University of Nebraska Press.

Gabriel, M., Kubota, Y., Sparenborg, S., Straube, K., & Vogt, B. A. (1991). Effects of cingulate cortical lesions on avoidance learning and training-induced unit activity in rabbits. *Experimental Brain Research, 86*(3), 585–600.

Gallistel, C. R. (1980). *The organization of action: A new synthesis.* Hillsdale, NJ: Erlbaum.

Gazelle, H., & Ladd, G. W. (2003). Anxious solitude and peer exclusion: A diathesis-stress model of internalizing trajectories in childhood. *Child Development, 74,* 257–278.

Gehring, W. J., Himle, J., & Nisenson, L. G. (2000). Action-monitoring dysfunction in obsessive-compulsive disorder. *Psychological Science, 11,* 1–6.

Goldberg, G. (1985). Supplementary motor area structure and function: Review and hypotheses. *Behavioral and Brain Science, 8,* 567–616.

Graeff, F. G. (1991). Neurotransmitters in the dorsal periaqueductal gray and animal models of panic anxiety. In M. Briley & S. E. File (Eds.), *New concepts in anxiety* (pp. 288–312). London: Macmillan.

Gray, J. A. (1994). Framework for a taxonomy of psychiatric disorder. In S. H. M. van Goozen, N. E. Van de Poll & J. A. Sergeant (Eds.), *Emotions: Essays on emotion theory* (pp. 29–60). Hillsdale, NJ: Erlbaum.

Gray, J. A., & McNaughton, N. (1996). The neuropsychology of anxiety: Reprise. In D. A. Hope (Ed.), *Nebraska Symposium on Motivation: Vol. 43. Perspectives on anxiety, panic, and fear* (pp. 61–134). Lincoln: University of Nebraska Press.

Grossberg, S., & Gutowski, W. E. (1987). Neural dynamics of decision making under risk: Affective balance and cognitive-emotional interactions. *Psychological Review, 94,* 300–318.

Gunnar, M. R. (1994). Psychoendocrine studies of temperament and stress in early childhood: Expanding current models. In J. E. Bates & T. D. Wachs (Eds.), *Temperament: Individual differences at the interface of biology and behavior* (pp. 175–198). Washington, DC: American Psychological Association.

Hamann, S. B. (2001). Cognitive and neural mechanisms of emotional memory. *Trends in Cognitive Sciences, 5,* 394–400.

Hamann, S. B., Ely, T. D., Hoffman, J. M., & Kilts, C. D. (2002). Ecstasy and agony: Activation of the human amygdala in positive and negative emotion. *Psychological Science, 13,* 135–141.

Hamilton, N. A., & Ingram, R. E. (2001). Self-focused attention and coping: Attending to the right things. In C. R. Snyder (Ed.), *Coping with stress: Effective people and processes* (pp. 178–195). New York: Oxford University Press.

Herbert, J. (1994). Peptides in the limbic system: Neurochemical codes for co-ordinated adaptive responses to behavioural and physiological demand. *Progress in Neurobiology, 41,* 723–791.

Hickie, I., & Lloyd A. (1995). Are cytokines associated with neuropsychiatric syndromes in humans? *International Journal of Immunopharmacology, 17,* 677–683.

Holstege, G., Bandler, R., & Saper, C. B. (Eds.). (1996). *Progress in brain research: Vol. 107. The emotional motor system.* Amsterdam: Elsevier.

Holstege, G., & Boers, J. (2001). The neuronal systems of mating. In W. Everaerd & E. Laan (Eds.), *Sexual appetite, desire and motivation: Energetics of the sexual system* (pp. 1–11). Amsterdam, The Netherlands: Koninklijke Nederlandse Akademie van Wetenschappen.

Isen, A. M. (2000). Positive affect and decision making. In M. Lewis & J. M. Haviland-Jones (Eds.), *Handbook of emotions* (2nd ed., pp. 417–435). New York: Guilford Press.

Kalin, N. H. (1999). Primate models and aggression. *Journal of Clinical Psychiatry Monograph Series, 17,* 22–24.

Kochanska, G. (1997). Multiple pathways to conscience for children with different temperaments: From toddlerhood to age 5. *Developmental Psychology, 33,* 228–240.

Kochanska, G., Murray, K. T., & Harlan, E. T. (2000). Effortful control in early childhood: Continuity and change, antecedents, and implications for social development. *Developmental Psychology, 36,* 220–232.

Leary, M. R., Tambor, E. S., Terdal, S. K., & Downs, D. L. (1995). Self-esteem as an interpersonal monitor: The sociometer hypothesis. *Journal of Personality and Social Psychology, 68,* 518–530.

Lease, A. M., Musgrove, K. T., & Axelrod, J. L. (2002). Dimensions of social status in preadolescent peer groups: Likability, perceived popularity, and social dominance. *Social Development, 11,* 508–533.

LeDoux, J. E. (1996). *The emotional brain.* New York: Simon & Schuster.

Luu, P., & Tucker, D. M. (2001). Regulating action: Alternating activation of midline frontal and motor cortical networks. *Clinical Neurophysiology, 112,* 1295–1306.

Luu, P., & Tucker, D. M. (2003). Self-regulation and the executive functions: Electrophysiological clues. In A. Zani & A. M. Preverbio (Eds.), *The cognitive electrophysiology of mind and brain* (pp. 199–223). San Diego: Academic Press.

Lynch, M., & Ciccheti, D. (1991). Patterns of relatedness in maltreated and nonmaltreated children: Connections among multiple representational models. *Development and Psychopathology, 3,* 207–226.

MacDonald, K. (1992). Warmth as a developmental construct: An evolutionary analysis. *Child Development, 63,* 753–773.

Maier, S. F., & Watkins, L. R. (1998). Cytokines for psychologists: Implications of bi-directional immune-to-brain communication for understanding behavior, mood, and cognition. *Psychological Review, 105,* 83–107.

Mathews, A., & Macintosh, B. (in press). Take a closer look: Emotion modifies the boundary extension effect. *Emotion.*

Matthews, G. (1997). Extraversion, emotion and performance: A cognitive-adaptive model. In G. Matthews (Ed.), *Cognitive science perspectives on personality and emotion* (pp. 399–442). Amsterdam, The Netherlands: Elsevier.

McCabe, R. E. (1999). Implicit and explicit memory for threat words in high- and low-anxiety-sensitive participants. *Cognitive Therapy and Research, 23,* 21–38.

McGaugh, J. L., & Cahill, L. (2002). Emotion and memory: Central and peripheral contributions. In R. J. Davidson, K. R. Scherer, & H. H. Goldsmith (Eds.), *Handbook of affective science* (pp. 93–116). New York: Oxford University Press.

McNally, R., Lasko, N., Macklin, M., & Pitman, R. (1995). Autobiographical memory disturbance in combat-related posttraumatic stress disorder. *Behaviour Research and Therapy, 33,* 619–630.

Mesulam, M. (1988). Central cholinergic pathways: Neuroanatomy and some behavioral implications. In M. Avoli, T. A. Reader, R. W. Dykes, & P. Gloor (Eds.), *Neurotransmitters and cortical function: From molecules to mind* (pp. 237–260). New York: Plenum Press.

Metcalfe, J., & Mischel, W. (1999). A hot/cool-system analysis of delay of gratification: Dynamics of willpower. *Psychological Review, 106,* 3–19.

Mineka, S., Pury, C. L., & Luten, A. G. (1995). Explanatory style in anxiety and depression. In G. M. Buchanan & M. E. P. Seligman (Eds.), *Explanatory style* (pp. 135–158). Hillsdale, NJ: Erlbaum.

Moll, J., de Oliviera-Souza, R., Eslinger, P., Bramati, I., Mourao-Miranda, J., Andreiuolo, P., et al. (2002). The neural correlates of moral sensitivity: A functional magnetic resonance imaging investigation of basic and moral emotions. *Journal of Neuroscience, 22,* 2730–2736.

Morris, J. S., & Dolan, R. J. (2001). Involvement of human amygdala and orbitofrontal cortex in hunger-enhanced memory for food stimuli. *Journal of Neuroscience, 21,* 5304–5310.

Muraven, M., Tice, D. M., & Baumeister, R. F. (1998). Self-control as limited resource: Regulatory depletion patterns. *Journal of Personality and Social Psychology, 74,* 774–789.

Murray, K. T., & Kochanska, G. (2002). Effortful control: Factor structure and relation to externalizing and internalizing behaviors. *Journal of Abnormal Child Psychology, 30,* 503–514.

Nauta, W. J. H. (1971). The problem of the frontal lobe: A reinterpretation. *Journal of Psychiatric Research, 8,* 167–187.

Ochsner, K. N., Bunge, S. A., Gross, J. J., & Gabrieli, J. D. (2002). Rethinking feelings: An fMRI study of the cognitive regulation of emotion. *Journal of Cognitive Neuroscience, 14,* 1215–1229.

Ochsner, K. N., & Schacter, D. L. (2000). A social cognitive neuroscience approach to emotion and memory. In J. C. Borod (Ed.), *The neuropsychology of emotion* (pp. 163–193). New York: Oxford University Press.

Panksepp, J. (1998). *Affective neuroscience.* New York: Oxford University Press.

Passingham, R. E. (1987). Two cortical systems for directing movement. In C. Foundation (Ed.), *Motor areas of the cerebral cortex* (pp. 151–164). New York: Wiley.

Pearce, J. M. (1987). *An introduction to animal cognition.* Hillsdale, NJ: Erlbaum.

Pickering, A. D., & Gray, J. A. (2001). Dopamine, appetitive reinforcement, and the neuropsychology of human learning: An individual differences approach. In A. Eliasz & A. Angleitner (Eds.), *Advances in research on temperament* (pp. 113–146). Lengerich, Germany: PABST Science.

Pliszka, S. R. (1992). Comorbidity of attention-deficit hyperactivity disorder and overanxious disorder. *Journal of the American Academy of Child and Adolescent Psychiatry, 31,* 197–203.

Porges, S. W., Doussard-Roosevelt, J. A., & Maiti, A. K. (1994). Vagal tone and the physiological regulation of emotion. *Monographs of the Society for Research in Child Development, 59*(2–3, Serial No. 240), 167–186.

Posner, M. I., & DiGirolamo, G. J. (1998). Executive attention: Conflict, target detection and cognitive control. In R. Parasuraman (Ed.), *The attentive brain* (pp. 401–423). Cambridge, MA: MIT Press.

Posner, M. I., & Raichle, M. E. (1994). *Images of mind.* New York: Scientific American Library.

Posner, M. I., & Rothbart, M. K. (1998). Attention, self-regulation and consciousness. *Philosophical Transactions of the Royal Society of London. Series B, Biological Sciences, 353,* 1915–1927.

Quay, H. C. (1993). The psychobiology of undersocialized aggressive conduct disorder: A theoretical perspective. *Development and Psychopathology, 5,* 165–180.

Rapee, R. M., & Heimberg, R. G. (1997). A cognitive-behavioral model of anxiety in social phobia. *Behavior Research and Therapy, 35,* 741–756.

Reidy, J., & Richards, A. (1997). A memory bias for threat in high-trait anxiety. *Personality and Individual Differences, 23,* 653–663.

Rothbart, M. K., Ahadi, S. A., & Hershey, K. L. (1994). Temperament and social behavior in childhood. *Merrill-Palmer Quarterly, 40,* 21–39.

Rothbart, M. K., Derryberry, D., & Posner, M. I. (1994). A psychobiological approach to the development of temperament. In J. E. Bates & T. D. Wachs (Eds.), *Temperament: Individual differences at the interface of biology and behavior* (pp. 83–116). Washington, DC: American Psychological Association.

Scarr, S., & McCartney, K. (1983). How people make their own environments: A theory of genotype-environment effects. *Child Development, 54,* 424–435.

Schoenbaum, G., Chiba, A., & Gallagher, M. (2003). Orbitofrontal cortex and basolateral amygdala encode expected outcomes during learning. *Journal of Neurophysiology, 89,* 2823–2838.

Schoenbaum, G., Setlow, B., Nugent, S. L., Saddoris, M. P., & Gallagher, M. (2003). Lesions of orbito frontal cortex and basolateral amygdala complex disrupt acquisition of odor-guided discriminations and reversals. *Learning and Memory, 10,* 129–140.

Schulkin, J., Gold, P. W., & McEwen, B. S. (1998). Induction of corticotropin-releasing hormone gene expression by glucocorticoids: Implication for understanding the states of fear and anxiety and allostatic load. *Psychoneuroendocrinology, 23,* 219–243.

Schulkin, J., McEwen, B. S., & Gold, P. W. (1994). Allostasis, amygdala, and anticipatory angst. *Neuroscience and Biobehavioral Reviews, 18,* 385–396.

Schultz, W. (1998). Predictive reward signal of dopamine neurons. *Journal of Neurophysiology, 80,* 1–27.

Schultz, W., Tremblay, L., & Hollerman, J. R. (2000). Reward processing in primate orbitofrontal cortex and basal ganglia. *Cerebral Cortex, 10,* 272–283.

Sewards, T. V., & Sewards, M. A. (2000). The awareness of thirst: Proposed neural correlates. *Consciousness and Cognition, 9,* 463–487.

Shallice, T., Marzocchi, G. M., Coser, S., Del Savio, M., Meuter, R. F., & Rumiati, R. I. (2002). Executive function profile of children with attention deficit hyperactivity disorder. *Developmental Neuropsychology, 21,* 43–71.

Shoda, Y., Mischel, W., & Peake, P. K. (1990). Predicting adolescent cognitive and self-regulatory competencies from preschool delay of gratification: Identifying diagnostic conditions. *Developmental Psychology, 26,* 978–986.

Showers, C. J., & Kling, K. C. (1996). The organization of self-knowledge: Implications for mood regulation. In L. L. Martin & A. Tesser (Eds.), *Striving and feeling: Interactions among goals, affect, and self regulation* (pp. 151–174). Mahwah, NJ: Erlbaum.

Singer, W. (1990). Role of acetylcholine in use-dependent plasticity of the visual cortex. In M. Steriade & D. Biesold (Eds.), *Brain cholinergic systems* (pp. 314–336). Oxford: Oxford University Press.

Skinner, E. A., Zimmer-Gembeck, M., & Connell, J. P. (1998). Individual differences and the development of perceived control. *Monographs of the Society for Research in Child Development, 63*(254), pp. 2–3.

Stansbury, K., & Gunnar, M. R. (1994). Adrenocortical activity and emotion regulation. *Monographs of the Society for Research in Child Development, 59*(2–3, Serial No. 240), 108–134.

Stuss, D. T., Shallice, T., Alexander, M. P., & Picton, T. W. (1995). A multidisciplinary approach to anterior attentional functions. In J. Grafman, K. J. Holyoak, & F. Boller (Eds.), *Annals of the New York Academy of Sciences: Vol. 769. Structure and functions of the human prefrontal cortex* (pp. 191–211). New York: New York Academy of Sciences.

Swanson, L. W. (2000). Cerebral hemisphere regulation of motivated behavior. *Brain Research, 886*(1/2), 113–164.

Tanji, J., & Shima, K. (1996). Supplementary motor cortex in organization of movement. *European Neurology, 36*(Suppl. 1), 13–19.

Toth, S. L., Cicchetti, D., Macfie, J., & Emde, R. N. (1997). Representations of self and other in the narratives of neglected, physically abused, and sexually abused preschoolers. *Development and Psychopathology, 9*, 781–796.

Toth, S. L., Cicchetti, D., Macfie, J., Maugan, A., & VanMeenen, K. (2000). Narrative representations of caregivers and self in mal-treated preschoolers. *Journal of Clinical Child Psychology, 29*, 307–318.

Tucker, D. M. (2001). Motivated anatomy: A core-and-shell model of corticolimbic architecture. In G. Gainotti (Ed.), *Handbook of neuropsychology: Vol. 5. Emotional behavior and its disorders* (2nd ed., pp. 125–160). Amsterdam: Elsevier.

Tucker, D. M., & Derryberry, D. (1992). Motivated attention: Anxiety and the frontal executive mechanisms. *Neuropsychiatry, Neuropsychology, and Behavioral Neurology, 5*, 233–252.

Tucker, D. M., Derryberry, D., & Luu, P. (2000). Anatomy and physiology of human emotion: Vertical integration of brain stem, limbic, and cortical systems. In J. C. Borod (Ed.), *The neuropsychology of emotion* (pp. 56–79). New York: Oxford University Press.

Uphouse, L. (1998). Multiple serotonin receptors: Too many, not enough, or just the right number? *Neuroscience and Biobehavioral Reviews, 21*, 679–698.

Vasey, M. W., & Daleiden, E. L. (1996). Information-processing pathways to cognitive interference in childhood. In I. G. Sarason, G. R. Pierce, & B. R. Sarason (Eds.), *Cognitive interference: Theories, methods, and findings* (pp. 117–138). Mahwah, NJ: Erlbaum.

Watson, D., & Clark, L. A. (1992). On traits and temperament: General and specific factors of emotional experience and their relation to the five-factor model. *Journal of Personality, 60*, 441–476.

Wells, A., & Matthews, G. (1994). *Attention and emotion: A clinical perspective.* Hillsdale, NJ: Erlbaum.

Wise, R. A. (1987). Sensorimotor modulation and the variable action pattern (VAP): Toward a noncircular definition of drive and motivation. *Psychobiology, 15*, 7–20.

CHAPTER 13

Stress Neurobiology and Developmental Psychopathology

MEGAN R. GUNNAR and DELIA VAZQUEZ

Maladaptive responses to stress are components of both the etiology and expression of many psychiatric disorders (e.g., Dawes et al., 1999). In addition, individuals differ in their stress vulnerability, with some seeming to thrive despite the odds and others succumbing to even relatively mild adversity (Masten, 1999). Early adverse experiences likely contribute to both individual differences in stress vulnerability and their expression in psychiatric disorder (Heim, Owen, Plotsky, & Nemeroff, 1997). Explicating these individual differences and their role in psychiatric etiology is one of the central issues in developmental psychopathology. The goals of this chapter are to describe the current state of our knowledge regarding the developmental neurobiology of stress, its relation to psychiatric disorders, and the impact of early adverse experiences on stress vulnerability and resilience. We focus on studies of the limbic-hypothalamic-pituitary adrenocortical (LHPA) system, a critical system fostering both resilience and vulnerability to stress in animals and humans. Research on this neuroendocrine system has a long history.

HISTORICAL OVERVIEW

In 1957, Levine (see review, in press) published a landmark *Science* paper demonstrating that removing rat pups from their mother for a few minutes daily during the first weeks of life permanently reduced activity of the LHPA system. This publication followed one from the previous year demonstrating that this *handling* manipulation also reduced fearful, anxious behavior. The half-century since these publications has seen remarkable advances in preclinical (animal) research on stress and early experience (see Levine, in press). This work built on insights into stress physiology that began with Cannon (1914) and Selye (1936) and took on new meaning with Harris's (1948) work showing that the brain controlled endocrine activity, including that of the

This work was supported by the National Institute of Mental Health "Early Experience, Stress, and Prevention Science" research network (MH60766) and a National Institute of Mental Health Research Scientist Award (MH00946) to the first author and National Institute of Mental Health (MH59396, MH01-0328) and National Institute of Child Health and Human Development (HD/DK37431) grants to the second author.

pituitary-adrenocortical system. More recently, McEwen's (e.g., McEwen, Weiss, & Schwartz, 1968) evidence that glucocorticoids (GCs; cortisol in humans and nonhuman primates, corticosterone in rats), the hormonal products of the LHPA system, both sustain normal brain function and paradoxically endanger nerve cells, ushered in heightened awareness of the critical role of this neuroendocrine system in psychiatric health and disease.

Our understanding of the role of GCs in shaping the developing brain has been enriched through evidence that they contribute to the regulation of brain-derived neurotropic factors (Smith et al., 1995), up-regulate activity of the amygdala (Makino, Gold, & Schulkin, 1994), and target prefrontal systems involved in stress and emotion (Sullivan & Gratton, 2002). Meanwhile, research by Meaney (e.g., Weaver, Cervoni, Diorio, Szyf, & Meaney, 2001), among others, has explicated some of the molecular processes through which early experiences may produce their lifelong effects on stress neurobiology. Critically, in rodents it appears that these molecular processes are set into motion by maternal behavior (see Cirulli & Alleva, 2003).

GCs are only part of the picture. A critical link to psychopathology came with awareness that corticotropin-releasing hormone (CRH), the major LHPA activating hormone in the hypothalamus, also has neurostimulatory and neuromodulatory effects in many regions of the brain involved in stress and emotion (e.g., Heim et al., 1997). When produced and acting outside the hypothalamus, CRH has been shown to play a role in a variety of psychiatric conditions, most principally affective disorders (see Nemeroff, 1996). CRH acts through a family of receptors that mediate different components of behavioral and physiological responses to stress. The development of this receptor system may be another key to how experience shapes stress vulnerability and resilience (reviewed in Heim et al., 1997). Thus, as Levine (in press) noted, what began as a story about the role of GCs in stress regulation may eventually extend into many areas of pathophysiology that are not associated with regulation of the LHPA system.

The history of any field rests on both conceptual and methodological advances. Conceptually, evidence that the stress-emotion system is highly plastic during development and that parental care shapes its development forms the basis for translation of the preclinical work into research on developmental psychopathology. Technically, the critical advances are legion, encompassing much of the armamentaria of modern-day neuroscience (e.g., cloning, knock-outs, neuroimaging). All of these advances are essential for understanding the processes that transduce experience into altered stress vulnerability, yet advances in the translation of preclinical and neuroscience research into the field of human developmental psychopathology rests on something much more mundane: spit.

Initial measures of adrenocortical activity were indirect and crude (Levine, in press). The development of competitive binding assays allowed measurement of GCs in urine and blood, thus permitting study of the adrenocortical system in humans. Soon after competitive binding assays were available, the first studies of GCs in children appeared (for review, see Gunnar, 1986). However, the immense challenge of collecting urine reliably and the invasiveness of plasma sampling limited the studies that could be conducted on children (reviewed in Gunnar, 1986). Then, in the early 1980s, assay techniques were refined to allow the measurement of cortisol in small amounts of free-flowing saliva (Riad-Fahmy, Read, Walker, & Griffiths, 1982). Salivary cortisol reflects the unbound or biologically active fraction of the hormone and is highly correlated with plasma cortisol concentrations (see Kirschbaum & Hellhammer, 1989, 1994). With the use of salivary cortisol measures, the number of publications on children has increased from fewer than a dozen in the 1970s to nearly that many each month in the first years of the twenty-first century.

The emergence of a developmental systems perspective in child psychology and developmental psychopathology (e.g., Cicchetti & Tucker, 1994) has also encouraged hormone-behavior studies in children. According to this perspective, development involves complex, bidirectional flows of influence across hierarchically organized systems and subsystems, from the level of the gene to the level of social systems. This approach permits inclusion of biological measures in developmental research without implying that behavioral development can be reduced to biological explanations. Nonetheless, these perspectives are not theories and do not provide theory-driven predictions about how physiological measures should be related to behavioral outcomes. Such focused predictions need to be derived from specific models pertaining to the behavioral and biological systems under study.

Recently, investigators have called for more theory-driven studies of cortisol-behavior relations in human developmental research (e.g., Granger & Kivlighan, 2003). Although laudatory, attempts to predict activity of the LHPA system in human development will be problematic as long as most studies of children are restricted to assessing only one level (the adrenal) of this very dynamic, self-regulating system (Gunnar & Vazquez, 2001). One goal of this chapter is to discuss the complex, multifactorial regulation of the LHPA system and to clarify why testing theory-driven predictions requires probing levels of the axis above the adrenal, up to and including corticolimbic pathways into the LHPA system. Because we are limited in our ability to do this kind of research in children, theory-driven research on the LHPA system requires close integration of human developmental research with preclinical animal studies. Theory-driven work in human development also benefits greatly from studies of clinical populations, including adult populations, in which it is ethical to use pharmacological probes and more invasive sampling techniques.

Another stumbling block to theory-driven developmental psychopathology research on the LHPA system has been the lack of criteria for defining and assessing dysregulation. As we will see, most of the studies of children involve assessment of GC levels and GC change or responsivity scores. In addition, there is a growing body of literature on the daily or circadian pattern of GC production. If children with behavior problems and/or adverse early histories exhibit levels, responses, or circadian patterns in GC production that differ from children with fewer behavior problems or less adverse histories, the temptation has been to describe the differences as a reflection of dysregulation of the LHPA system. However, the system might merely be acting differently along some parameter(s), though not be *dysregulated*. Derived from arguments made by Siever and Davis (1985), dysregulation in many physiological systems can be conceptualized as persistent disturbances *in one or more* of the system's homeostatic regulatory mechanisms. We discuss the specific mechanisms later in the chapter, but the observed phenomena indicative of dysregulation can be listed here: (1) Basal output is more erratic; (2) normal periodicities are disrupted; (3) efficiency of feedback mechanisms is increased or decreased, resulting in overly rapid or overly slow return to set points following perturbation; (4) adjustment to repeated stimulation fails; and (5) clinically efficacious treatments restore efficient regulation. Although few studies of children provide enough information to determine whether the LHPA system is dysregulated in relation to either behavior disorders or adverse experiences, preclinical studies do allow such assessments, as do some of the studies of adults that we consider.

In what follows, we provide an overview of the neurobiology of the mature LHPA system and its role in stress and adaptation. We then describe the developmental neurobiology of the system based on preclinical research, with links to human development when feasible. Next, we examine associations between LHPA activity and psychopathology in children as a prelude to examining the role of experience in shaping the activity of the LHPA system in animals and humans.

THE MATURE LIMBIC-HYPOTHALAMIC-PITUITARY-ADRENOCORTICAL SYSTEM

The LHPA axis is the classical stress system (Selye, 1936). Once labeled the HPA axis, an L for limbic is now commonly added to indicate the critical role of the limbic system in its activity. Two molecules at the opposite ends of the activating pathway regulate LHPA activity: CRH and GCs. CRH activates both hormonal and behavioral stress responses (e.g., Heim et al., 1997). CRH-stimulated behaviors include heightened vigilance, defense-related learning and memory, and context-dependent motor responses: freezing, fighting, or fleeing. Activation of the LHPA axis leads to increases in GCs, extremely potent steroids that function to facilitate adaptation and to restore homeostasis through changing internal dynamics. McEwen (1998) has described this dynamic regulation as *allostasis,* or the maintenance of stability through change. The capacity of organisms to make allostatic adjustments is necessary for survival. However, the biological processes set into motion are meant for short-term adaptations and are potentially damaging to physical and mental health if they persist too long or occur too frequently. The cost of allostasis has been described as *allostatic load.*

GCs orchestrate allostatic adjustments by operating on the DNA to activate, enhance, or inhibit the gene transcription in most organs and tissues of the body (Sapolsky, Romero, & Munck, 2000). In the periphery, among other actions, GCs promote glycolysis, a process that provides glucose from hepatic stores and facilitates increases in oxygen levels. In the brain, GCs help orchestrate motivation, reward, and mood (de Kloet, 1991). Brief and controllable stress with high but controllable GC levels stimulates exhilarated mood and health-promoting actions. In contrast, as first described by Seyle in 1936 (see Table 13.1), prolonged, uncontrollable, or chronic states of distress leading to high or prolonged GC levels can have deleterious mental and

TABLE 13.1   Behavioral and Physiological Adaptations of Acute Stress

Physiological Responses: Redirection of Function	Behavioral Responses: Redirection of Behavior	Physiological Outcome: Redirection of Energy	LHPA Hormone
Increased respiratory function	Increased arousal, vigilance, and attention	Oxygen shunted to CNS and critical body sites	CRH
Increased cardiovascular tone	Increased cognition		GCs
Increased gluconeogenesis; increased lipolysis	Suppression of feeding	Increased body temperature; suppressed appetite	CRH
		Glucose and nutrients shunted to CNS and critical body sites	GCs
Inhibition of growth and reproductive hormones, inflammatory processes, immune system	Suppression of sexual behavior	No reproduction; decreased immune function	CRH and GCs
Limitation of stress (LHPA) activation/ response		Demands to cope with stress predominate	GCs

Source: Modified from "The Concepts of Stress and Stress System Disorders: Overview of Physical and Behavioral Homeostasis," by G. P. Chrousos and P. W. Gold, 1992, *Journal of the American Medical Association, 267*(9), pp. 1244–1252.

physical consequences (Sapolsky et al., 2000). The repercussion of prolonged CRH and GC activity may be especially costly during development. High CRH levels, with or without elevated GCs, inhibit physical and neural development (Avishai-Eliner, Brunson, Sandman, & Baram, 2002). CRH and GCs also shape brain systems involved in perception and response to threat and, in genetically vulnerable individuals, may facilitate the development of psychopathology (Heim et al., 1997).

LHPA studies in humans are still largely confined to measures of cortisol and, more recently, the *anticortisol,* dehydroepiandrosterone (DHEA). Cortisol is a glucocorticoid that has catabolic effects; DHEA is an androgenic steroid that has anabolic effects. Both are produced by the adrenal cortex. Because measurements in humans are focused on these adrenocortical hormones, this has led to the misleading view that the pituitary-adrenal axis is at the center of the stress response. However, animal models and advanced molecular techniques make it clear that CRH and its system of receptors are as central as GCs (cortisol and corticosterone) for stress and adaptation. This can be demonstrated through description of stress-activating and regulatory pathways.

The Hypothalamic-Pituitary-Adrenocortical Axis

The circuits that originate in specific brain areas and activate the LHPA system converge, directly or indirectly, on the medial parvocellular region of the paraventricular nucleus (mpPVN) of the hypothalamus that secretes CRH and arginine vasopressin (AVP; see Figure 13.1). Inputs to the mpPVN include both *activating* and *inhibiting pathways.* These pathways are similar in the rat and human (reviewed in Lopez, Akil, & Watson, 1999). Once released, both CRH and AVP interact with their receptors on corticotropic cells of the anterior pituitary (AP), where the proopiomelanocortin (POMC) molecule is synthesized and processed into adrenocorticotropic hormone (ACTH). Binding of CRH to pituitary CRH receptor 1 (CRH r1) leads to the secretion of ACTH. AVP potentiates CRH-induced ACTH release. ACTH circulates in blood and binds to its own receptors on the adrenal cortex, leading to the synthesis and release of GCs.

Mineralocorticoid and Glucocorticoid Receptors

GCs target many organs and tissues, including the brain. They have their effects through two types of receptors: mineralocorticoid (MR) and glucocorticoid (GR). Receptor binding, particularly to GR, also accomplishes negative feedback whereby GCs inhibit their own production. There are three types of negative feedback: fast, intermediate, and delayed. Fast feedback is rapid (within minutes) and dependent on the rate rather than the absolute magnitude of GC increase. It is achieved, at least in part, through GC binding to receptors in the mpPVN, AP, and hippocampus (reviewed in Dallman et al., 1992). Intermediate and delayed feedback, on the other hand, work over the course of hours to days to suppress CRH and POMC gene expression in the hypothalamus and AP, respectively, thereby decreasing the ACTH secretory drive. Thus, multiple feedback

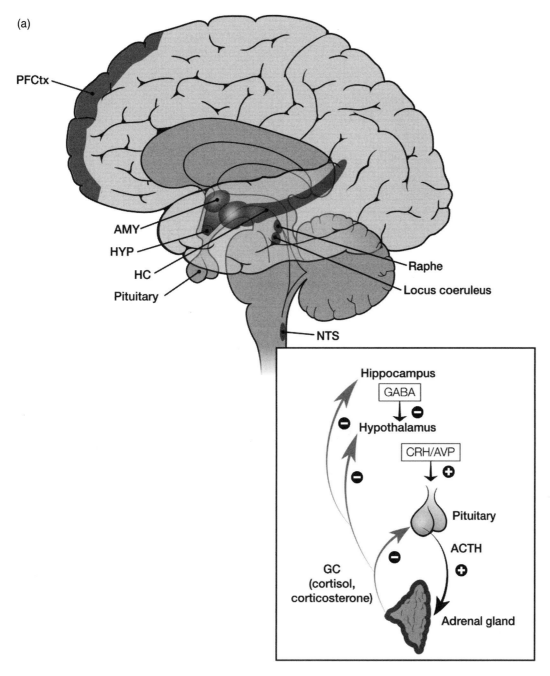

(a)

Figure 13.1   The LHPA System. Panel A depicts the anatomy of the LHPA system and structures important in its regulation. AMY = Amygdala, HC = Hippocampus, HYP = Hypothalamus, NTS = Nucleus of the tractus solitarius, PFCtx = Prefrontal cortex. Panel B depicts the activation (+) and negative feedback inhibition (−) pathways of the HPA system. Increases in GCs are initiated by the release of CRH/AVP from the medial parvocellular region of the paraventricular nucleus (mpPVN) in the hypothalamus. Negative feedback inhibition operates through GCs acting at the level of the pituitary, hypothalamus and hippocampus. ACTH = Adreno-corticotropic hormone, AVP = Arginine vasopressin, CRH = Corticotropin releasing hormone, GABA = Gamma animobutyric acid.

loops operate in different time domains and through different processes (neuronal signaling as well as gene regulation) to maintain GCs within normal basal levels.

The effects of GCs depend on which receptor is bound (MR or GR), the ratio of MR to GR binding, and the receptor's location (de Kloet, 1991). In the rodent brain, MRs are expressed in limbic regions (e.g., septum, hippocampus) and GRs are distributed throughout the brain. However, unlike rodents, humans express MR in cortical regions, suggesting an MR role in processive functions related to stress (see later discussion, and reviewed in Lopez et al., 1999). MRs bind GCs readily (high affinity), and GRs bind GCs less readily (lower affinity); therefore, GCs bind first to MRs and then to GRs as MR sites saturate. MRs are typically about 80% to 90% bound or occupied when GCs are in basal ranges, with GRs being bound only at the peak of the circadian cycle or when stressors stimulate elevations over basal concentrations.

In addition to mediating negative feedback, in the brain both MRs and GRs mediate all GC effects. Outside the brain, MRs regulate water/salt balance through binding by aldosterone, another steroid hormone. In the periphery, GCs do not occupy MRs because of the presence of the enzyme 11 beta hydroxysteroid dehydrogenase (11ß-HSD) that inactivates GCs. In the brain, 11ß-HSD is minimally expressed so that MR exhibits its high affinity for GCs (Reul & de Kloet, 1985). Through brain MRs and GRs, GCs serve at least four critical stress functions (reviewed in Sapolsky et al., 2000). MRs mediate *permissive* GC effects that sustain an organism's ability to make adaptive responses to changing environmental demands. For example, MRs maintain steady and persistent electrical current, allowing neurons to be responsive to their neurotransmitters. In contrast, GRs have *suppressive* effects, inhibiting ongoing behavioral and neurophysiological responses. *MR and GR, thus, tend to have opposing effects.* Several additional examples of these opposing effects help demonstrate this general rule. MRs facilitate cerebral glucose utilization, and GRs inhibit glucose utilization throughout the brain. MRs mediate forms of synaptic plasticity that underlie learning; GRs, operating over hours or days, disrupt the same mechanisms of synaptic plasticity, endanger cell survival, and blunt hippocampal excitability, disrupting memory formation. The opposing effects of MR and GR combined with the differential affinity of GCs for these two receptors is believed to be why the relations between GCs and adaptive functioning often takes an inverted-U function. Thus, very low and very high GC concentrations are associated with deleterious health and behavior consequences, and moderate levels and small or well-constrained elevations tend to support adaptive functioning.

In addition to levels and duration, the timing of the GC response also influences its role in stress and adaptation. Initial effects of increasing levels of GCs tend to be *stimulatory* and permissive as these operate through MR and initial GR effects of liberating hepatic energy stores, resulting in increased glucose levels and permissive GR effects on other stress-stimulated physiological systems. Well-timed anticipatory responses to stressors thus can place the organism in an optimal state to handle challenge and constrain or suppress the operation of other stress-sensitive systems. Therefore, not only too persistent but also too shallow GC responses above resting basal levels can be damaging, particularly when this permits other stress-stimulated physiological responses to continue unchecked (e.g., immune reactions). The final category of GC effects is *preparatory,* denoting GC-induced changes in neurobiology that affect the way organisms responds to subsequent stressors. Thus, for example, operating through GRs, GCs up-regulate the sensitivity of the amygdala to threat stimuli, resulting in heightened sensitivity to subsequent threats (for review, see Rosen & Schulkin, 1998).

The effects of GCs depend not only on their level and timing, but also on the ratio of MRs to GRs that are occupied in different brain regions (de Kloet, 1991). This is demonstrated using transgenic preparations (reviewed in Korte, 2001). Transgenic mice that underexpress GR produce high and prolonged GC responses (impaired feedback), are hyperactive, and have great difficulty with spatial learning, presumably because of secondary hippocampal effects. Transgenic mice that overexpress GR have increased anxiety-related behavior with increased CRH expression in the amygdala, unaltered CRH levels in the PVN, and normal basal GC levels. MR knock-outs have impaired neurogenesis presumably secondary to chronic elevations in basal GC levels.

Systemic versus Processive Stress and Their Neuroanatomical Pathways

A number of seemingly disparate stimuli activate the LHPA axis. Some stimuli activate the axis through *systemic* paths; others require interpretation by the organism and thus are termed *processive or collative* (reviewed in Herman & Cullinan, 1997). Systemic stressors are physical and context-independent. Thus, they stimulate the LHPA axis even in an unconscious animal. Examples are hypotension (decreases in blood pressure), hypoxia (decreases in oxygen levels), and infection. In contrast, processive stressors are context-dependent, requiring the comparison of current information with past experience and the assignment of *emotional meaning.* Systemic and processive stressors operate through diffuse networks of neurons that converge at the level of the mpPVN. For systemic stressors, the information stimulating activation of the LHPA is relayed to the mpPVN via the brain stem through afferents originating in the dorsal roots of the autonomic system and the glossopharyngeal and vagus cranial nerves. For example, the nucleus of the tractus solitarius (NTS, a key parasympathetic relay station) receives afferent fibers that indicate hypotension as a result of hemorrhage. In turn, *efferent fibers travel away* from NTS into the CRH-rich mpPVN area to activate an LHPA response. Some of these autonomic connections are direct into the mpPVN, but most are indirect via other limbic structures.

Limbic centers transmit processive stressor information to the mpPVN via corticolimbic *efferent* pathways involving the BNST (bed nucleus of the stria terminalis), preoptic nucleus, lateral and medial septum, the amygdala, prefrontal cortex, and ventral subiculum (reviewed in Herman et al., 2003). Efferent pathways converge in the fimbria/fornix, a collection of nerve bundles emanating from the hippocampus, subiculum, and cortical regions. Some of these pathways provide activating and others inhibiting input to the mpPVN. The medial amygdala and lateral BNST are centrally involved in *activating pathways*. The various nuclei of the amygdala mediate behavioral and also autonomic cardiovascular responses to stress indirectly using the BNST or NTS as relay stations, with the fibers terminating two or more steps removed from the mpPVN (de Olmos, Alheid, & Beltramino, 1985). Whether or not cardiovascular effects are induced along with LHPA activation depends on the nuclei excited by stress-induced amygdala activation (e.g., basolateral versus basomedial; M. Davis, 1992).

For processive stressors, *inhibitory influences* are also mediated through limbic structures: the ventral subiculum, preoptic area, medial BNST, and cingulate/prefrontal cortex (Herman, Muller, & Figueiredo, 2004). Damage to the subiculum, its major outflow pathway (the fimbria/fornix), or the medial frontal cortex increases CRH mpPVN expression and enhances GC production to processive stressors. However, some overlap in excitatory and inhibitory inputs exists as medial prefrontal cortex damage has been shown to both increase and decrease GC production and autonomic activation (reviewed in Herman et al., 2003; C. D. Walker, Welberg, & Plotsky, 2002).

Neurotransmitters and the Limbic-Hypothalamic-Pituitary-Adrenocortical Axis

Neurotransmitters are the mediators of LHPA activity that operate along the neuroanatomical pathways outlined earlier (see Figure 13.2). Many neurotransmitter systems exist in the brain, but noradrenaline (NA), serotonin (5-HT), glutamate, and gamma-aminobutyric-acid (GABA) are particularly important in modulation of the LHPA system. All of these molecules have excitatory effects on the LHPA

axis through their innervation of limbic structures that, in turn, have direct access to the mpPVN (reviewed in Herman et al., 2003). This excitatory stimulation operates through ascending monoaminergic input from the pons area, where presynaptic neurons containing NA (locus coeruleus) and 5-HT (raphe nuclei) originate. Direct activation of the LHPA system, however, involves short circuits arising from glutamate neurons within the mpPVN that act on glutaminergic receptors (NMDA, kainate, or AMPA) and through inhibition of inhibitory GABA-ergic afferents (because double negative equals positive; see later discussion and Figure 13.2).

Inhibition of the LHPA axis at the level of the mpPVN is mediated through GABA-ergic neurons. The inhibitory structures (e.g., septum, prefrontal cortex, medial BNST, and suprachiasmatic nucleus) are rich in GABA neurons (Herman et al., 2004). GABA modulation is how GRs in the hippocampus mediate negative feedback. GR-activated electrical currents travel through hippocampal efferents to interact with GABA-containing neurons in the BNST, preoptic area, and hypothalamus, achieving a net inhibition on the mpPVN. Activation of the LHPA system also can involve GABA activity. In this case, GABA interacts with adjacent GABA neurons and results in a decrease of the downstream inhibition (first GABA neuron inhibits the release of a second GABA neuron). Amygdala innervation of the mpPVN is a good example of this double negative. Enhanced amygdaloid activity leads to disinhibition of disynaptic GABA-ergic input to the mpPVN and therefore enhances LHPA activity (see Figure 13.2). GABA-ergic tone is also the main factor influencing resting basal state of the LHPA axis, characterized by circadian oscillations of its key hormones (see later discussion).

Critical Features of Processive Stressors in Humans

Although the neuroanatomical pathways of processive stressors are beginning to be worked out in studies of animals, in human research the key features of processive stimuli capable of activating an LHPA response are still uncertain. These features have variously been described as novelty, uncertainty, unpredictability, uncontrollability, and potential for harm or loss (see reviews by Kirschbaum & Hellhammer, 1989, 1994). Distressingly, however, despite arguments that the LHPA axis is highly sensitive to processive stressors, it is often difficult to provoke GC responses in the laboratory (see review by Biondi & Picardi, 1999). Indeed, in many laboratory studies of children and adolescents, rather than an increase in cortisol to the

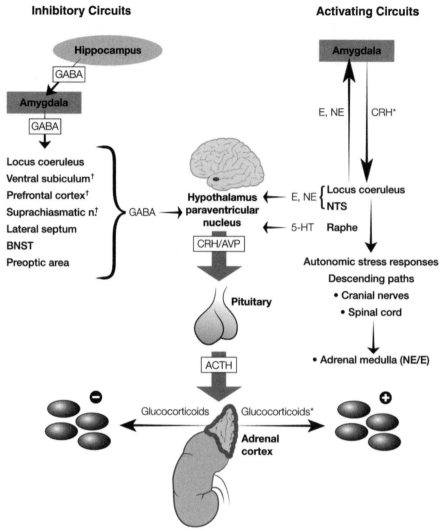

Inhibitory Circuits

Hippocampus

GABA

Amygdala

GABA

Locus coeruleus
Ventral subiculum†
Prefrontal cortex†
Suprachiasmatic n.†   GABA → Hypothalamus
Lateral septum   paraventricular
BNST   nucleus
Preoptic area

CRH/AVP

Pituitary

ACTH

⊖ Glucocorticoids

Activating Circuits

Amygdala

E, NE   CRH*

E, NE { Locus coeruleus
         NTS

5-HT   Raphe

Autonomic stress responses
Descending paths
• Cranial nerves
• Spinal cord

• Adrenal medulla (NE/E)

Glucocorticoids*   ⊕

Adrenal
cortex

* Glucocorticoids provide positive stimulation to the amygdala for the synthesis and release of CRH, but negative to the pituitary, hypothalamus and hippocampus.

† Interaction is through glutamate outflow from these regions that synapse on local GABAergic neurons, producing inhibition of mpPVN.

Figure 13.2   Schematic representation of the activating (right side) and and inhibiting (left side) circuits that contribute to regulation of the LHPA system. Catecholamines, *norepinephrine (NE) and epinephrine (E)* arising from medullary nuclei of the brainstem are the primary neurotransmitters providing activation of CRH synthesis and release from the mpPVN. *Serotonin* originating from dorsal raphe is weakly activating; it act both directly on mpPVN and indirectly through *excitatory glutamate neurons* or *inhibitory gamma animobutyric acid (GABA)* inputs. Paradoxically, the inhibitory GABA neurotransmitter activates the mpPVN to secrete CRH since two GABA neurons activated in series leads to excitation and not inhibition. *Extra-hypothalamic CRH also acts as a neurotransmitter to initiate autonomic and behavioral responses to stress.* The activation of the extra-hypothalamic CRH system is initiated by *rising* glucocorticoids levels that operate on the amygdala to secrete CRH that, in turn, impacts on the locus cerouleus (LC). Through the activation of catecholaminergic brainstem nuclei there is also stimulation of descending pathways leading to NE/E release form the adrenal medulla that facilitates cardiovascular autonomic responses to stress. Inhibition of the LHPA axis seen in the left side is provided by *glucocorticoids* acting on glucocorticoids receptors (GR) in the hypothalamus and pituitary where CRH and ACTH release is halted. The hippocampus serves to inhibit the stress response via multiple circuits, some of which are direct inhibitory GABA inputs; others are indirect through glutamate excitatory inputs to GABA neurons converging in the mpPVN. GABA neurons located in each of the structures further modify the stress reactivity and inhibition from other brain regions such as the thalamus, association cortex, cortical and limbic afferents.

intended stressor, cortisol levels for most subjects fall over the testing period! This may reflect anticipatory increases in GCs and inadequate periods for adaptation to the laboratory, but it may also reflect our lack of understanding of the stimuli capable of activating the LHPA axis in humans.

In a recent meta-analytic review of 208 adult studies, Dickerson and Kemeny (2004) provide an empirical test of the core features of potent GC-stimulating tasks. They argued that for an event to activate the LHPA system, goals that are central to the individual must be threatened. Self-preservation is a central goal of all living organisms. Certainly, physical threats to self-preservation are likely to produce marked increases in cortisol, as evidenced by studies of individuals in emergency rooms assessed shortly after life-threatening events (see Yehuda, 2000). These authors argue, however, that the preservation of the *social self* is also a central goal for humans. The results of their meta-analysis showed that paradigms that threaten the social self (e.g., social evaluation by an audience of judges) are potent stimulators of the LHPA axis. Tasks that require mental effort but where poor performance poses little threat to the social self are not very effective in elevating cortisol. Tasks that produce negative emotions but do not threaten the social self are not effective in elevating GCs. Novelty, unpredictability, and uncontrollability act synergistically with threats to central goals to produce the most marked GC responses.

No one has conducted a similar meta-analysis of stressors in children. However, in early childhood, separation activates the LHPA axis, an event that has an evolutionary history of threatening self-preservation. Later in childhood, Flinn and England (1995) have reported, serious family conflicts and threats of rejection/abandonment are highly potent in elevating cortisol in their study of Caribbean children. In addition, even very early in life, social rejection by peers is associated with high GC levels among preschool children (Gunnar, Tout, Donzella, & van Dulmen, 2003). Thus, it seems likely that the Dickerson and Kemeny (2004) analysis will apply to children. Critically, because it is rare to find a laboratory study beyond the infancy period in which the stressor elevates cortisol in most children, it is challenging to interpret the result of most laboratory-based, GC human developmental stress studies.

A System with a Rhythm

The LHPA axis is not just an alarm system waiting to be activated. It is also a system that exhibits a *circadian* or 24-hour rhythm. GC levels reach their peak approximately 30 minutes after waking, although they begin to rise in the last hours of sleep. From peak levels, GCs fall throughout the day, with transient increases about 45 minutes following protein-rich meals (postprandial surge), until levels reach their lowest point or nadir at the end of the activity phase (e.g., Kwak, Morano, Young, Watson, & Akil, 1993). GCs measured in saliva follow the same pattern, offset by approximately 2 minutes, from GCs measured in plasma. The circadian rhythm not only alters basal levels of the hormones along the LHPA axis, but also changes in its sensitivity to stressful stimuli. At the nadir of the rhythm (roughly 10 to 12 P.M. in humans on a regular day/night schedule), the LHPA system is more responsive to both activating and inhibiting (negative feedback) signals (Dallman et al., 1992). Thus, time of day is a critical factor in interpreting LHPA effects and designing LHPA studies.

The need to control for diurnal rhythm in assessing activity of the LHPA system places critical restrictions on researchers studying this system. However, in human developmental research, time of day often is not controlled. It is not clear how much of a problem this poses. In their review, Dickerson and Kemeny (2004) were not able to detect differences in the magnitude of the adult GC response depending on whether assessments were made in the morning or afternoon. Although this would seem to stand in marked contrast to the animal studies, the human studies deal with a smaller time of day variation. Rather than contrasting LHPA activity at the peak and nadir of the cycle (wake-up and bedtime), testing times in human studies typically vary across the midportion of the day. This is especially true for studies with children, for whom testing schedules are constrained by such factors as when the child typically naps and when other family members get home from work or school. It may be that when testing occurs between 9 A.M. and 5 P.M., variations in testing times introduce little variability in the responsiveness of the system. On the other hand, until the appropriate meta-analysis of the child development literature on cortisol reactivity is conducted, it is probably better to avoid testing times that vary uncontrollably between subjects.

The LHPA circadian rhythm is one of many physiological (e.g., body temperature) and behavioral (e.g., sleep, feeding) rhythms in mammals. The suprachiasmatic nucleus (SCN) is the master pacemaker controlling circadian rhythms (reviewed in van Esseveldt, Lehman, & Boer, 2000). It oscillates with a near 24-hour period under constant light conditions but is entrained to day/night rhythm by periodicity of light exposure and nonphotic modulators, including patterns of locomotor activity, feeding and sleep (Follenius, Brandenberger, Bandesapt, Libert, & Ehrhart, 1992; Follenius, Brandenberger, Hietter, Simeoni, & Reinhardt, 1982). In humans, the SCN is also entrained by our expectations about when we are to wake up in the morning (Born, Hansen, Marshall, Molle, & Fehm, 1999). For example, if we expect to wake up at 6 A.M., activity of the LHPA system will reflect that expectation, regardless of when we actually wake up. Thus, not only the time since waking but also whether the individual is waking at his or her usual time is important to consider in assessing early morning cortisol concentrations. Unfortunately, we do not know what happens to the circadian rhythm when bedtimes and wake-up times are unpredictable, as they may be in more chaotic households. Sleep restriction also modifies LHPA axis activity, leading to elevated resting GC levels (Leproult, Copinschi, Buxton, & Van Cauter, 1997). Thus, sleep-wake rhythms are important to consider in studies of LHPA activity.

The pathways that integrate the perception of light into the SCN are the retinohypothalamic tract (GABA-ergic), the geniculohypothalamic tract (neuropeptide Y or NPY), and raphe (5-HT). The nonphotic input is received from the cortex, basal forebrain, and hypothalamus using NPY, 5-HT, and possibly GCs (Liu & Reppert, 2000). A myriad of neuropeptides are expressed in the SCN; however, it is likely that the GABA-ergic system plays a more important role than these neuropeptides in transmitting the rhythmic function of the SCN to other brain regions (Liu & Reppert, 2000). Once a circadian rhythm is generated in the SCN, it is imposed on the mpPVN primarily via projections into the brain stem autonomic centers (Herman et al., 2003). But there is also an ACTH independent multisynaptic projection to the adrenal that results in a fast decrease of circulating GCs at the beginning of sleep (Buijs et al., 1999). This pathway helps explain why activation of the axis at the nadir of the LHPA rhythm around the onset of nighttime sleep in humans results in greater GC responses than activation at the peak of the circadian rhythm (Kaneko, Hiroshige, Shinsako, & Dallman, 1980).

In the LHPA system, MRs play a critical role in maintaining the LHPA basal rhythm. This relationship has been demonstrated by using antagonists that are specific to MR or GR (reviewed in de Kloet, 1991). Selective MR antagonists produce *elevated* basal GCs near the nadir of the rhythm without affecting levels near the circadian peak or responses to a processive stressor. Conversely, selective GR antagonists have *no effect on resting basal* or restraint stress GC levels at any time of day. Combining MR and GR antagonists, however, produces elevated GCs over the entire day as well as increased elevations to stressors. In humans, pharmacological MR antagonists also increase cortisol levels in the evening, near the nadir of the LHPA rhythm (e.g., Grottoli et al., 2002; but see Michelson, Chrousos, & Gold, 1994). In sum, MR activation is necessary and sufficient to maintain low basal GC levels during the nadir of the circadian rhythm, whereas MR and GR activation is necessary to constrain GC secretion during the circadian peak and during acute stress.

The circadian rhythm of cortisol can be observed in humans as early as 6 to 12 weeks of life (Larson, White, Cochran, Donzella, & Gunnar, 1998). However, throughout infancy and early childhood, cortisol production from midmorning through late afternoon fluctuates markedly with naps and feedings (for review, see Gunnar & Donzella, 2002). As children give up their daytime naps, the typical adult diurnal pattern of cortisol production emerges (Watamura, Donzella, Kertes, & Gunnar, 2004). Ambulatory studies of salivary cortisol have shown that not all individuals reliably produce this diurnal pattern of cortisol production. Even in the absence of frank physical or mental disorders, about 10% to 15% of the adult population appears to have days when early morning levels are not high and/or evening levels are not low (Smyth et al., 1997). The etiology and significance of these atypical patterns is not well understood (see Heim, Ehlert, & Hellhammer, 2000), although they have been associated with emotional and mental exhaustion (e.g., burnout), chronic pain disorders (e.g., fibromyalgia), and, in infants and young children, conditions of chronic neglect (Gunnar & Vazquez, 2001).

In addition to the classic diurnal pattern, recently it has been noted that there is about a 60% increase in salivary cortisol concentration in the 30 to 40 minutes after waking. Termed the *cortisol awakening response* (CAR), this increase is stable within individuals and reflects genetic as well as other factors (Wüst, Federenko, Hellhammer, & Kirschbaum, 2000). Individuals with constant work overload and chronic worries tend to exhibit larger increases in cortisol upon waking (Schlotz, Hellhammer, Schultz, & Stone, 2004).

Stability and Heritability

Studies of the LHPA axis often focus on individual differences, thus making it essential that we understand the reliability of these differences. Regarding *basal cortisol,* using latent state-trait modeling it has been shown that the balance of state and trait components varies over the day, with generally larger trait components obtained soon after morning awakening and larger state components obtained later in the day (Kirschbaum et al., 1990; Shirtcliff, Granger, Booth, & Johnson, in press). In fact, it has been difficult to fit state-trait models to cortisol measures obtained later in the day because state variability is so large that stable trait components are difficult to discern (e.g., Kirschbaum et al., 1990). Assessing the stability of the LHPA *stress* response is more complicated because the same stressor repeated a second time is not as novel and thus would be expected to produce less activation. Furthermore, different stressors operate over different neural pathways and thus produce different responses. However, several researchers have recently reported modest test-retest stability (e.g., *r*s of around .5) in cortisol responses to stressors in infancy (e.g., Goldberg et al., 2003; Lewis & Ramsay, 1995). E. F. Walker, Walder, and Reynolds (2001) also noted rank-order stability of a similar magnitude in their study of adolescents assessed over a 2-year period. As in other psychometric measurement, aggregation tends to produce more reliable indices. For example, in one study using the Trier Social Stress Test (TSST) administered repeatedly over several days, the GC response to the first TSST did not correlate with responses to the later TSSTs, but GC responses to the later TSSTs were correlated (Pruessner et al., 1997). In addition, although the GC response to the first TSST was not correlated with personality traits, responses to the later TSSTs were, particularly when these responses were averaged. Unfortunately, there is little information on how many GC values need to be aggregated before reliable individual difference estimates are obtained. And, given the state-trait modeling results, the number needed likely varies with time of day. Another reliability-reducing factor may be individual differences in the rise time of the response. Ramsay and Lewis (2003) showed that when cortisol measures were taken repeatedly following an inoculation stressor in infants, the average peak response was at approximately 25 minutes poststimulation. However, there was a substantial number of infants who reached their peak cortisol levels at other time points. When only two measures (pre- and post-) are taken, it is very possible that delta cortisol underestimates cortisol reactivity for many individuals.

Stable individual differences in LHPA activity may partly reflect genetic influences. A recent review of human twin studies concluded that these influences were only modest (Bartels, van den Berg, Sluyter, Boomsma, & de Geus, 2003). However, in most of the reviewed studies, only a single, potentially unreliable, cortisol measure was obtained. To address the problem of limited measurement, these authors analyzed salivary cortisol data collected at four points over the day on 2 school days in 209 12-year-old twin pairs. Heritability estimates varied over the daytime cycle. They were weak ($h^2 = .32$) at the moment of waking, highest 30 to 40 minutes postwaking ($h^2 = .71$), modest late in the morning ($h^2 = .43$), and absent or undetectable in the evening before bed. These data fit with the latent state-trait modeling results, suggesting that cortisol levels 30 to 40 minutes after morning awakening exhibit a heritable trait

component, whereas those taken at other points in the day reflect stronger, unique, and possibly transient environmental or internal state effects. Basal levels later in the day are likely to exhibit heritable influences, but it may take many more than 2 days of cortisol assessment to obtain measures that are reliable enough to yield significant heritability estimates.

THE DEVELOPING LIMBIC-HYPOTHALAMIC-PITUITARY-ADRENOCORTICAL SYSTEM

The rules governing activity of the LHPA axis in adults differ from those for the neonate. Most of this evidence comes from studies of rats. We describe preclinical or animal research and then consider how this information applies to human development. In rats, during the first 2 postnatal weeks (postnatal days 4 to 14), ACTH and GC responses to many stressors are markedly diminished. This period has been termed the relative stress-hyporesponsive period (SHRP). Although GC responses are low during the SHRP, marked stressor responses can be observed in the hypothalamus and other brain regions in a species- and developmentally specific manner (Smith, Kim, Van Oers, & Levine, 1997; C. D. Walker, Scribner, Cascio, & Dallman, 1991). Structural and functional brain immaturity and marked developmental changes in the adrenal gland appear to underlie these developmental differences.

Key Features of the Developing Limbic-Hypothalamic-Pituitary-Adrenocortical System

The LHPA system undergoes marked changes during development. Here we briefly review the changes most pertinent to our understanding of developmental psychopathology in relation to LHPA functioning.

The Adrenal and Glucocortical Secretion

In the mature animal, the adrenal glands consist of two divisions: a cortex that produces three types of steroids and a medulla that produces catecholamines. The three steroids produced by the cortex are derived from morphologically and functionally distinct zones (Parker & Schimmer, 2001). The zona glomerulosa (ZG) synthesizes GCs; the zona fasciculata (ZF) produces mineralocorticoids (MCs), and the zona reticulata (ZR) produces sex steroids. Prenatally, the maternal placenta and the fetal adrenal cortex constitute a fetal-placental unit. The fetal adrenal cortex consists primarily of one zone (fetal zone), which is equivalent to the reticulata and is geared to the production of estrogen precursors. These molecules are transferred from the fetus to the placenta, where they are metabolized to estrogen, essential for the maintenance of pregnancy. As gestation progresses, a primitive ZG develops and begins producing GCs. At birth, GC levels are elevated as a consequence of the stress of parturition. In the rat, due to hepatic immaturity, it takes a long time for the pup to clear GCs from circulation. However, by postnatal day (PND) 4, basal GC levels are low in the rat pup and remain low through PND 14, the period of the SHRP (C. D. Walker et al., 1991). Parturition also initiates an ischemic process resulting in involution (developmental removal) of the fetal zone.

For ACTH to stimulate GC production, cell-specific gene expression leading to specific enzyme synthesis is required in the ZG. However, the development of chromaffin cells in the adrenal medulla also plays a role (reviewed in Vazquez & Levine, in press). Isolated adrenal cells lose the capacity to produce GCs unless chromaffin cells from the medulla are added to cell culture preparations. In the rat, the adrenal medulla does not become a well-defined region until the end of the first postnatal week, corresponding to a period of rapid development of the GC- and MC-producing zones of the adrenal cortex. Thus, the adrenal is quite immature in the rat during the first 2 weeks postnatal, a fact consistent with the SHRP.

Yet, there are environmental events that can stimulate marked GC responses in the neonatal rat. Among these is removal of the mother for 24 hours. Maternal absence for this duration raises GC levels and permits the adrenal to respond to both stressors and ACTH (see Vazquez & Levine, in press). Feeding (milk into the gut) and stroking help to block this effect, suggesting that it may be partially mediated by feedback through autonomically mediated pathways from the gut and skin. Recent studies suggest that the nutritive components in milk can also modulate the response of the neuroendocrine system to stress and, possibly, influence some aspects of brain development (see review, C. D. Walker et al., 2004). In particular, fat and leptin, a protein produced in the adipose tissue and present in maternal milk in both humans and rodents, reduces responses to stress in the infant. This is different in the adult, in which high-fat feedings exacerbates the LHPA response to stress. Although the mechanisms involved in this phenomenon are not clear, Walker and colleagues suggest that leptin acts on both central (hypothalamus and hippocampus) and peripheral (pituitary, adrenal gland) systems in the infant to reduce exposure to GCs and enhance hippocampal development during a sensitive period of brain development. Table 13.2 lists genes that are modulated by endogenous and synthetic GCs in developing mammals.

The Anterior Pituitary

Consistent with the immaturity of the adrenal and the relevance of the adrenal fetal zone during gestation, the anterior pituitary (AP) also displays marked morphological and functional changes during fetal and early postnatal development in the rat pup. The development of the AP from epidermal precursor cells is under the control of transcription factors that are expressed early in embryogenesis (reviewed in Swanson, 1992). Hypothalamic hormones help differentiate specific AP cells that produce specific hormones. In the late fetal/early postnatal period, the AP contains more ACTH-producing cells (corticotrophs) than in the mature rat. Corticotrophs are among the first AP cells to mature, being functional by gestational day 16. However, the ability to process POMC into mature ACTH develops only gradually (for review, see Vazquez, 1998; C. D. Walker et al., 2002). During gestation, high molecular ACTH forms predominate that may be important for fostering development of the adrenal and for maintaining the fetal-placental unit but stimulate minimal GC production. During the late fetal and early postnatal period, the ACTH molecules produced by corticotroph cells gradually change to increasingly yield GC-stimulating forms. Corticotroph cells express receptors for CRH (i.e., CRHr1) by late gestation, with numbers declining from PND 5 to adulthood. AVP receptors follow a similar developmental pattern but are not functionally coupled to second messenger systems until PND 10. Thus, consistent with the waning of the SHRP, after PND 10, the AP exhibits increasing capacity to produce mature ACTH and mature responses to both CRH and AVP by the end of the 2nd week.

Hypothalamic Corticotropin-Releasing Hormone

In the rat, by gestational day (GD) 17, neurosecretory neurons appear in the mpPVN along with evidence of CRH mRNA. One day later, AVP mRNA can be observed. Soon after, CRH and AVP levels begin to increase. At approximately this same time, axon terminals containing granular vesicles can be seen in the external layer of the median eminence. However, the mpPVN is not completely mature until PND 28, the time of typical weaning in the wild (Bugnon, Fellmann, Gouget, & Cardot, 1982). CRH receptors herald the emergence of a functional role for CRH in the brain and pituitary. The distribution of these CRH receptors (1 and 2) is very similar in both the developing and mature rodent. However, several brain regions have high expression of both CRHr1 and r2 early in life, followed by a

TABLE 13.2   Partial Listing of Genes Modulated by Endogenous and Synthetic Glucocorticoids in the Developing Mammal

Brain Cell Lineages and Differentiation

Bax induces apoptosis. Low GCs increase bax mRNA levels in adult rats (Cardenas et al., 2002).

Bcl-2 prevents apoptosis and neutralizes effects of bax. Low GCs increase bcl-2 mRNA levels (Cardenas et al., 2002).

Ay controls epidermal cell lineage migration. GCs decrease birthweights and increase rates of cleft palate, as examined using prenatal rats (E18; Teramoto, Hatakenaka, & Shirasu, 1991).

Myelin basic protein functions in the development of myelin. GCs increase mRNA levels of this gene in oligodendrocytes, as detected in the neonatal rat (Kumar, Cole, Chiappelli, & de Vellis, 1989).

GPDH plays a role in oligodendrocyte differentiation and myelinogenesis. GCs increase its tRNA levels in oligodendrocyte nuclei (Kumar et al., 1989).

GFAP is an astrocytic marker. In postnatal (2 wks) rats, GCs increase GFAP expression (O'Callaghan, Brinton, & McEwen, 1991).

NGF is required for the development of sympathetic neurons and some sensory neurons. In postnatal (PND11) rats, GCs increase prefrontal cortex (both sexes) and hippocampal (males) NGF; low GCs cause changes in distribution and expression of NGF receptors in the hippocampus (Scaccianoce, Catalani, Lombardo, Consoli, & Angelucci, 2001).

Glutamine synthetase catalyzes recycling of glutamine in glial cells. In embryonic rats, inhibition of GC receptors suppresses the expression of this gene (Vardimon, Ben-Dror, Avisar, Oren, & Shiftan, 1999).

Glucocorticoid receptor plays a critical role in regulation of the HPA axis. In sheep and rats late in gestation, GCs increase GR mRNA levels (Holloway, Whittle, & Challis, 2001).

Anterior Pituitary

POMC is the pro-hormone that is cleaved to yield ACTH. GCs reduce POMC mRNA levels, as noted in late-gestation sheep (Holloway et al., 2001).

Vasopressin receptor (**V1b**) regulates AP response to vasopressin. GCs decrease V1b receptor expression in the AP, as shown in sheep (E100; Young, Smith, Figueroa, & Rose, 2003).

Prolactin is critical in lactation and delivery. GCs in sheep (E130-E140) increase prolactin mRNA in the AP (Phillips, Fielke, Young, & McMillen, 1996).

FTB controls maturation of glycoprotein galactosylation and fucosylation processes important for hormonal bioactivity. In neonatal rats, GCs increase its transcriptional regulation (Biol-N'gargba, Niepceron, Mathian, & Louisot, 2003).

Peripheral Catecholaminergic System

PNMT is the rate-limiting enzyme in adrenaline synthesis. GCs regulate PNMT activity throughout life, and GR appears to be necessary for the developmental appearance of PNMT expression (Anderson & Michelsohn, 1989).

PENK gene regulates enkephaline-related petide in chromaffin cells. GCs reduce adrenal PENK mRNA levels, as shown in fetal sheep (E124; Fraser, Matthews, Braems, Jeffray, & Challis, 1997).

Inflammation

HLA-G plays a critical role in inflammation. In cells cultured from humans (E7-9), GCs enhance transcription of HLA-G in trophoblasts (Moreau et al., 2001).

Proteolipid protein may trigger the immune system to attack myelin. GCs increase mRNA levels in oligodendrocytes, as shown in neonatal rat brain tissue (Kumar et al., 1989).

Physical Growth

IGF-II regulates cell proliferation and metabolism. Low GCs increase hepatic transcription rate of IGF-II, as shown in late-gestation sheep gene culture (Kumar et al., 1989).

CTGF/IGFBP rP2 plays a role in bone formation. In E22 rats, GCs cause a time- and dose-dependent increase in mRNA levels in bone cells and increase transcription rate (Pereira, Durant, & Canalis, 2000).

GHR-1A, GHR-2, and **GHR-3** regulate this family of growth hormone receptors, which directly stimulate the production of IGF-1 in the liver and other tissues. As shown in fetal sheep, increases in GCs during fetal development stimulate increases in GRH mRNA (Li, Gilmour, Saunders, Dauncey, & Fowden, 1999).

IGF binding protein-1 regulates IGF availability in postnatal life and contributes to somatic growth in utero. In fetal rat livers, GCs increase synthesis of IGFBP-1 (Menuelle, Babajko, & Plas, 1999).

Tryptophan oxygenase is an enzyme required for normal growth and development. In neonatal rat livers, GCs increase trypotophan oxygenase mRNA (Nagao, Nakamura, & Ichihara, 1986).

Alpha 1 (I) procollagen plays a role in proper osteoblast proliferation. In rats (calvaria cultures), GCs decrease alpha I (I) procollagen transcripts (Delany, Gabbitas, & Canalis, 1995).

Respiratory System

TTF-1 regulates thyroid transcription factor-1, which plays a role in lung morphogenesis and is involved in the transcription of surfactant proteins. Synthetic GCs increase mRNA expression of TTF-1 in rats with congenital hypoplasia.

LGL2 is coordinated with key transcription factors that regulate signal transduction pathways in the fetal lung. In rats (E14) and humans (gestational week 16), GCs induce LGL2 (Zhang et al., 2000).

SP-A, SP-B, and **SP-C** (surfactant proteins) are critical for respiration. Three variants of these proteins (A, B, and C) work in coordination to reduce alveolar surface tension at the air-liquid interface in lung tissue. In humans, GCs induce surfactant proteins (Losada, Tovar, Xia, Diez-Pardo, & Santisteban, 2000). In rats with congenital hypoplasia, synthetic GCs increase SP-B mRNA levels (Losada et al., 2000). In human lung tissue, synthetic GCs in coordination with DBcAMP reduce SP-A mRNA levels (McCormick & Mendelson, 1994; though see contradictory results in rabbit fetal lung tissue, Durham, Wohlford-Lenane, & Snyder, 1993). In fetal rabbit lung tissue, synthetic GCs, as well as GCs increased due to maternal stress, increase SP-C mRNA levels (Durham et al., 1993).

decline. For example, in the pyramidal region of the hippocampus and frontal cortex, CRHr1 are two- to fourfold higher during the 1st week of life and then decline to adult levels by postnatal day 12 (Avishai-Eliner, Yi, & Baram, 1996). CRHr2 are detected in the frontal cortex only during fetal and early postnatal life (Eghbal-Ahmadi et al., 1998). These distinct developmental profiles indicate a precise regulation of these receptors during development and the possibility that alteration of these profiles in areas critical to physiological and behavioral responses to stressors may be targets of early experience effects.

Monoamines

During the postnatal period in the rat, monoamine circuitry is being laid down and fine-tuned. The pattern of overproliferation and pruning of the major neurotransmitter systems in the rat (discussed in Vazquez et al., 1998) and human (summarized in Spinelli, 1987) have been described elsewhere. For example, in the rat, 5-HT-containing cell bodies are present at birth, reach maximum density by PND 14, and then decline to the adult innervation pattern by puberty (i.e., PND 35 to 45). The 5-HT receptor system follows a similar developmental course. Notably, development of the serotonin system corresponds to development of the LHPA stress response. Thus, increased levels of brain 5-HT metabolites following stress are observed around PND 12 in the rat pup, which is also when the LHPA response to stress becomes more predictable (Mitchell, Iny, & Meaney, 1990). GCs also influence the development of the 5-HT system, affecting the expression of the rate-limiting enzymes for 5-HT production (Singh, Corley, Phan, & Boadle-Bider, 1990). A similar developmental pattern is observed for the central NA system that again is linked closely to the ability of the NA system to activate the LHPA system (Herrenkohl, Ribary, Schlumpf, & Lichtensteiger, 1988). Here, too, GCs influence activity of the adrenergic system, in part through regulating levels of its rate-limiting enzymes (Markey, Towle, & Sze, 1982). Thus, there are bidirectional interactions between the ability to mount an LHPA response and the development of the brain monoaminergic systems.

Glucocorticoid Receptors

Both MR and GR receptors develop quite early in gestation in the rat and presumably also the human brain. Overall, MR density is greater during the early postnatal period than later in life in the rat (Vazquez et al., 1998; Vazquez, Morano, Lopez, Watson, & Akil, 1993). GRs are observed as early as GD 13 and are evident between GD 15 and 22 in the hippocampus, mpPVN, and locus coeruleus. Different regions of the hippocampus display different developmental progressions. MR and GR are most abundant around PND 10 in the rat, with GR mRNA reaching adult levels after this time. In contrast, MR mRNA in the hippocampal dentate gyrus does not reach adult distributions until around PND 28 (for review, see Vazquez, Morano, et al., 1993). Overall, the hippocampal GR system matures long before the animal is capable of feedback inhibition. This likely reflects continued immaturity of connections of the hippocampus to the mpPVN (Vazquez & Akil, 1993). As noted earlier, emotional reactivity appears to be linked to hippocampal corticoid receptor expression, with an optimal balance of MR to GR argued to be critical to a number of functions (de Kloet, 1991). The MR and GR systems exhibit developmental changes and are highly sensitive to early experiences in the rat.

Circulating Glucocorticoids and Their Role in Development

Low GC levels in young organisms do not necessarily mean low levels of biologically active hormone. Most GCs in mature animals are bound to corticosteroid-binding globulin (CBG) and other proteins. Only the unbound or free GC can bind to receptors and thus have biological effects. In neonatal rats and humans, CBG and other binding globulins are low, and thus most circulating GCs have biological activity (Hadjian, Chedin, Cochet, & Chambaz, 1975; Henning, 1978). Furthermore, the clearance of GCs from the circulation is significantly slower in the pup and in the human newborn than in the adult. Thus, despite low plasma levels of GCs during the SHRP in rats and during the newborn period in humans, the levels of biologically active GCs are more than sufficient to have marked physiological effects.

GCs are steroid hormones, and as such, their receptors do not lie on the surface of cells (as is the case for neurotransmitters) but in the cytosol inside the cell (Lombroso & Sapolsky, 1998). In the cytosol of brain cells, GCs bind with either MR or GR to form GC-receptor complexes that then move into the cell nucleus and bind to the promoter regions of many different genes, initiating or inhibiting synthesis of different cell proteins. Rapid brain growth, accelerated synaptogenesis, myelinization, astrocyte proliferation, and the organization of multiple neurotransmitter systems characteristic of the developing organism definitely require GCs. Thus, changes in GC activity can be significant to the developing brain. However, for GCs to affect brain development, they must get into the brain and the cell must express MR or GR. In addition, having the receptors is not enough; GCs must also be able to engage the necessary intracellular mechanisms following receptor binding (reviewed in C. D. Walker et al., 2002). Finally, the impact of GCs on the developing brain also depends on the maturity of other signaling systems and their capacity to interact with GCs. Given that signaling systems have their own development time courses that vary with brain region, the effects of GCs on the developing brain cannot be simply stated. The effects depend on brain region, maturity and activity of other signaling systems, and developmental timing. The interaction of these factors, in addition, varies with species in ways that are not well understood. This poses a major challenge in translating preclinical studies to predictions about GC effects on human development.

As noted earlier, most circulating GCs in the fetus and neonate are unbound and thus potentially biologically active. Furthermore, circulating levels of maternal GCs increase in late pregnancy. This might seem to place the fetal brain at high risk of GC exposure. However, under normal circumstances, in rats and primates high placental levels of the enzyme 11ß-HSD rapidly convert GCs to biologically inert forms (Seckl, Cleasby, & Nyirenda, 2000). There are two known isoforms of 11ß-HSD. Type 1 is bidirectional, capable of converting GCs to inactive forms and then back again, whereas the Type 2 form converts GCs only to less active forms. The expression of the Type 2 form increases with gestation but varies in efficiency among species. In humans, the Type 2 form is the most important, but does not inactivate dexamethasone (DEX) or betamethasone, two GCs used medically to expedite fetal lung maturation in women at risk for premature delivery (Seckl et al., 2000). Thus, in humans, these two medically prescribed GCs pass readily from mother to fetus.

Studies in which endogenous GC was administered to fetal rats show that high levels preferentially affect maturation of neurons in the cerebral cortex, reticular formation, limbic system, and spinal cord. They also globally inhibit neurogenesis, gliogenesis, cell division, and myelinization throughout the brain by altering patterns of gene expression (see Table 13.1). GC-induced cell death and cell survival mechanisms are also normally involved in remodeling of neurocircuit structure and function (e.g., Duman, Malberg, & Thome, 1999). The effects of GCs on fetal brain development have been examined in many studies using DEX, because, as noted, this synthetic hormone is used medically in premature infants (reviewed in Matthews, 2000) and bypasses the placental 11ß-HSD system. These studies indicate that DEX can have profound effects on brain development. DEX exposure in the last week of gestation results in adult rats with *reduced* NA content in the hippocampus and cortex and *reduced* NA turnover in the forebrain. However, maturation of the adrenergic system is actually advanced in the brain stem and forebrain and there is an overexpression of NA transporter, allowing increased NA recycling. No effect has been detected on adrenergic receptor expression. Interestingly, animals exposed to DEX in utero have increased LHPA function and faulty negative feedback. It is unclear whether DEX-induced modifications of the NA system are involved in producing these changes in LHPA function. Indeed, these changes actually may be due to serotonin. In rats, DEX in the last week of gestation leads to male offspring with increased hypothalamus, hippocampal, and brain stem 5-HT concentrations, probably due to an increase in 5-HT transporter synthesis in the raphe. The combination of increased hypothalamic expression of 5-HT transporter and increased availability of 5-HT are, in part, responsible for the elevated LHPA activity observed in DEX-exposed male offspring. Additionally, impairment in negative feedback in the DEX-exposed fetus may be due to reduced NA levels and 5-HT turnover that may reduce hippocampal GR receptor numbers (reviewed in Matthews, 2000).

Behavioral effects of developmental DEX exposure have also been observed in rodents (reviewed in Matthews, 2000). In mice, a single DEX injection on PND 14 affects fear behavior, memory, and social interactions but not sensory, motor, motivation, and learning performance. In primates, DEX and cortisol administered during fetal development have profound effects on the morphology of the hippocampus. Although behavioral effects have not been reported in rhesus monkeys, in humans DEX exposure beginning before the 10th week of gestation and continued until delivery results in heightened emotionality, unsociability, avoidance, and behavioral problems in children 6 months to 6 years of age (Trautman, Meyer-Bahlburg, Postelnek, & New, 1995). Although many older studies of the effects of antenatal steroids in humans have yielded little evidence of long-term effects, recent studies have demonstrated reduced brain volumes at birth (Modi et al., 2001; Murphy, 2001). Thus, it is clear that GCs have a critical role in brain development.

Development and the Limbic-Hypothalamic-Pituitary-Adrenocortical System in Humans

The developmental neurobiology and physiology of the LHPA system in humans are not well understood. Primates, including humans, do possess a fetal adrenal zone that produces estrogen precursors during gestation (Mesiano & Jaffe, 1997). In humans, this zone involutes over the first 6 postnatal months (Reynolds, 1981). CBG levels are low in the human neonate, increasing over the same age period (Hadjian et al., 1975). Consequently, free or unbound cortisol levels decrease slightly, and plasma or total cortisol production increases over the first 4 to 6 months after birth. There is also evidence that the adrenal becomes less sensitive to ACTH over the 1st year (Lashansky et al., 1991). Thus, as in the rodent, the pituitary-adrenocortical system continues to develop postnatally. Whether there is a human or primate equivalent of the SHRP is highly uncertain; however, numerous studies show developmental changes in GC responses from the prenatal through the adolescent period. By 18 to 20 weeks of gestation, the fetal LHPA system produces increases in cortisol to aversive stimulation (Giannakoulpoulous, Sepulveda, Kourtis, Glover, & Fisk, 1994). With increased gestational age, basal levels of plasma cortisol and ACTH increase. Healthy, term babies are capable of mounting cortisol and ACTH reactions to the types of perturbations routinely encountered in the newborn period (i.e., physical examinations, heel stick blood draws, and for boys, circumcision; reviewed in Gunnar, 1992).

Cortisol stress responses decrease over the infancy period (e.g., Gunnar, Brodersen, Krueger, & Rigatuso, 1996; Lewis & Ramsay, 1995). On average, it becomes difficult to produce elevations in cortisol to both laboratory and mild medical stressors by the end of the 1st year (see Gunnar & Donzella, 2002), although the absolute change (irrespective of increase or decrease) is similar in the 2nd year as compared to that observed around 6 months of age (Lewis & Ramsay, 1995). It is unlikely that this diminution of cortisol responses is equivalent to the rodent SHRP because it is highly dependent on the immediate presence and support of the caregiver. This was clearly demonstrated in a recent study of toddlers entering child care (Ahnert, Gunnar, Lamb, & Barthel, 2004). During an adaptation period of several days with the mother present, infants in secure attachment relationships showed only very small increases in cortisol over home baseline levels. However, on the 1st day at child care without the mother and continuing for at least the first 9 days, large increases in cortisol were noted for these same infants. Over the course of the preschool years, children become more capable of maintaining basal cortisol levels in the absence of their attachment figures (for review, see Gunnar & Donzella, 2002). A number of mechanisms likely account for the developmental changes in GC responsivity over the infancy and preschool years, including the development of the attachment system and the child's developing social and emotional regulatory competence.

Whereas GC responses tend to decrease over the early childhood years, it has been argued that, with the transition to adolescence, children become more hormonally responsive and thus perhaps more vulnerable to stressors (e.g., Spear, 2000). Several studies have shown both between-subject correlations of age with basal cortisol levels and within-subject increases in basal GCs in children 6 to 17 years of age (e.g., Kiess et al., 1995; Legro, Lin, Demers, & Lloyd, 2003; Netherton, Goodyer, Tamplin, & Herbert, 2004; Shirtcliff et al., in press). Three studies suggest that the most marked increase in basal GCs occurs between 10 and 14 years (Elmlinger, Kuhnel, & Ranke, 2002; Lupien, S. King, Meaney, & McEwen, 2001; Tornhage, 2002); others yield evidence of more gradual, linear increases (Jonetz-Mentzel & Wiedemann, 1993; Lashansky et al., 1991; E. F. Walker et al., 2001). Studies using Tanner staging have suggested that increases in basal levels are observed around Tanner stage 3 (Halligan, Herbert, Goodyer, & Murray, 2004; Netherton et al., 2004). Thus, although basal GC levels do seem to increase from childhood through adolescence, the precise timing and certainly the mechanisms underlying this effect are not well understood.

All of these studies examined salivary or plasma cortisol levels, which do not provide an integrated measure of total cortisol production over the day. Studies using integrated urinary cortisol sampling tend to be at odds with the plasma/salivary studies. Specifically, although 24-hour urinary free cortisol concentrations do increase across the adolescent years, this finding is no longer significant if urine volume (creatine) and body mass are taken into account (Dimitriou, Maser-Gluth, & Remer, 2003; Gomez, Malozowski, Winterer, Vamvoakopoulos, & Chrousos, 1991; Honour, Kelnar, & Brooks, 1991; Legro, Lin, Demers, & Lloyd, 2003). Lack of evidence for increases in integrated 24-hour cortisol production raises the possibility that increases in basal cortisol with age and/or pubertal status may reflect changes in diurnal patterning of cortisol production rather than overall increases in basal cortisol levels. In this regard, it is noteworthy that most of the studies showing increases in basal salivary or plasma cortisol have collected samples in the morning hours. Furthermore, when both morning and evening samples were obtained, only the morning values were found to correlate positively with pubertal status (Halligan et al., 2004; Netherton et al., 2004). Thus, it is conceivable that changes in basal cortisol may actually reflect the continued maturation of the adult diurnal rhythm that may not become fully mature until around the midpoint of pubertal development.

The vulnerability hypothesis (e.g., Spear, 2000), of course, depends not on basal levels, but on reactivity of the LHPA system. Basal levels may increase with age and/or pubertal status, but it is not clear whether *reactivity* of the LHPA system also increases. There are simply too few studies that actually have produced elevations in cortisol to address this question. E. F. Walker et al. (2001), however, have interpreted their findings as evidence of increased reactivity to the experience of coming to the lab for testing. Studying children 11 to 18 years of age, they took four salivary cortisol measures during a laboratory stressor paradigm. Cortisol levels *decreased* across the stressor period, suggesting that the initial levels were in fact elevations over baseline. It was these initial levels that were positively correlated with age. Furthermore, several years later, when they brought the children in again for testing, only the initial levels were higher than the child's own initial levels several years before. However, two studies using the TSST modified for children failed to note significant effects of age when children 9 to 16 years were studied (Klimes-Dougan, Hastings, Granger, Usher, & Zahn-Waxler, 2001; Kudielka, Buske-Kirschbaum, Hellhammer, & Kirschbaum, 2004). There is also no evidence that the adrenal becomes more sensitive to ACTH (Dahl et al., 1992; Lashansky et al., 1991) or that CRH infusion elicits overall more cortisol and ACTH with age for children between 6 and 16 years (Stroud, Papandonatos, Williamson, & Dahl, 2004). Thus, if the LHPA axis becomes more reactive during adolescence, the effect is likely to be subtle.

All but one of these studies involved typically developing children. Notably, when risk populations are used, there is no evidence of age changes in cortisol activity, basal or response values, over the transition to adolescence (Dahl et al., 1991; Dorn et al., 2003; Goodyer, Park, Netherton, & Herbert, 2001; Granger, Weisz, & Kauneckis, 1994; McBurnett et al., 1991; McBurnett, Lahey, Rathouz, & Loeber, 2000; Scerbo & Kolko, 1994). It seems possible that if changes in cortisol levels and reactivity with age are generally subtle, these age changes may be readily overwhelmed by the stress of emotional problems or life events in high-risk populations.

Sex Differences and Sex Steroids

Subtle changes in basal levels and/or reactivity of the LHPA system during adolescence, if they exist, may be related to changing sex steroid activity. In rats and in humans, sex differences are apparent at many levels of the LHPA axis. In rats, estrogens have excitatory effects and androgens have inhibitory effects on LHPA function. Thus, in rats, females are the more stress-reactive sex (Critchlow, Liebelt, Bar-Sela, Mountcastle, & Lipscomb, 1963; Le Mevel, Abitbol, Beraud, & Maniey, 1979), and both basal and stress levels of ACTH and GC are high when estrogen levels are elevated (e.g., Bohler et al., 1990). Ovariectomy reduces plasma ACTH and GCs, and replacement of estra-

diol returns ACTH and GCs to normal levels (Burgess & Handa, 1992; Viau & Meaney, 1991). Females also exhibit high levels of CBG (Gala & Westphal, 1965) and CRH (Hiroshige & Wada-Okada, 1973). In addition, gonadal hormones modulate GC metabolism (Grant, Forsham, & DiRaimondo, 1965) and hippocampal MR and GR protein and mRNA levels (e.g., Kerr, Beck, & Handa, 1996; Viau & Meaney, 1996).

In humans, the evidence is fairly consistently the reverse. Men show larger GC and ACTH responses than women to most stressors administered in the laboratory, but are not more reactive than females to systemic or pharmacological stressors (for reviews, see Kirschbaum, Kudielka, Gaab, Schommer, & Hellhammer, 1999; Kirschbaum, Wüst, & Hellhammer, 1992). Men also show larger catecholamine responses than women to stressors such as IQ testing, cognitive-conflict tasks, major examinations, and speech tasks (e.g., Frankenhaeuser, 1983). The greater male vulnerability to processive stressors has been related to their greater vulnerability to cardiovascular disease and stroke, disorders related to hyperstress reactivity. In contrast, the blunted response of women to stressors has been related to their greater vulnerability to hyporesponsivity disorders, most notably autoimmune and chronic pain disorders (McEwen, 1998). Depression stands in marked contrast to these patterns of sex difference, being associated with hypercortisolism (Nemeroff, 1996) and being more prevalent in women, beginning about midadolescence (Piccinelli & Wilkinson, 2000).

The central gender stress question always has been whether these male-female differences in humans are psychological or physiological. Those arguing for psychological differences note that men and women likely process and cope with stress differently (e.g., Taylor et al., 2000). In addition, they note that most of the stressors examined in human studies have been instrumental or achievement-oriented and that these types of stressors likely threaten the social self in ways that are more central to male self-construals (see Stroud, Salovey, & Epel, 2002). Consistent with this argument is evidence that males compared to females excreted more adrenaline during major university entrance exams. But, among the young women, those who were adrenaline increasers were more likely to have adopted male achievement values, whereas adrenaline decreasers were more likely to place a high value on marriage and parenting and to perceive themselves as fulfilling traditional feminine social roles (Rauste-von Wright, von Wright & Frankenhauser, 1981). More pertinent is evidence that stressors that threaten affiliation are more provocative among women than men. Using participants age 17 to 23, Stroud and colleagues recently showed that men elevated cortisol to a speech/math stressor, and women elevated cortisol to a social rejection stressor. If replicable, these data suggest serious limitations in the literature on LHPA responses to processive or psychological stressors in human adults—specifically, that the literature is limited to examination of male-biased stressors. We lack adequate evidence of sensitivity to processive stressors in women because we have failed to identify stressors that are ideally designed to threaten core female self-construals.

In contrast, for those taking a physiological perspective on adult sex differences in LHPA reactivity, there is evidence that the sex differences in response to achievement-type stressors varies with the woman's menstrual cycle. Thus, cortisol responses to the TSST do not differ between men and women in the *follicular* phase of their cycles (when estrogen levels rise to their monthly peak), but men respond more than women in the *luteal* phase of the cycle (when estrogen levels are falling; Kirschbaum et al., 1999). These data suggest that failure to control for stage of menstrual cycle may impede our understanding of sex differences in reactivity of the LHPA system in human adults. According to the physiological argument, we would not expect to observe sex differences in basal cortisol at any point in childhood, but we would expect to observe sex differences in responses to processive stressors beginning around the midpoint in puberty. The child data are relatively consistent with these predictions. Of over 20 studies of basal cortisol that included boys and girls, we found only three that reported significant sex differences, one showing higher levels for girls (Smider et al., 2002) and two for boys (Elmlinger et al., 2002; Jonetz-Mentzel & Wiedemann, 1993). Studies of GC responsivity to stressors similarly report few sex differences in infancy and early childhood. One study of newborns did report larger increases for boys (M. Davis & Emory, 1995), and a study of peer entry stress in preschoolers reported larger increases for girls (Sethre-Hofstand, Stansbury, & Rice, 2002). There is some suggestion, however, that studies involving competitive challenges might produce larger GC responses in prepubertal boys than girls (Donzella, Gunnar, Krueger, & Alwin, 2000; Jansen et al., 1999; Kertes & Gunnar, 2004). Furthermore, one study noted that prepubertal boys showed larger GC responses to CRH than did girls (Dahl et al., 1992). However, overall, prior to adolescence, sex differences in GC activity tend to be infrequently reported.

Sex differences in response to processive stressors appear to emerge in adolescence. Male adolescents taking university entrance exams exhibit cortisol increases, but females typically do not (Frankenhaeuser et al., 1978). Boys

between 14 and 16 years of age produce larger cortisol responses than girls to a psychosocial stressor, but this was not the case among younger, 10- to 13-year-old children in the same study (Klimes-Dougan et al., 2001). Among 13- to 17-year-old adolescents, boys have also been observed to exhibit a larger ACTH response to CRH administration (Dorn et al., 1996; although see Stroud et al., 2004). Thus, in a number of studies of typically developing children, boys begin to exhibit larger LHPA responses than girls around the midpoint in puberty. As noted, however, the types of stressors examined to date may be male-biased, involving threats to instrumental competence. We simply do not know whether girls respond more to threats to affiliative competence (i.e., social rejection) and, if so, whether such sex differences in stress reactivity, if they exist, emerge or change from childhood through adolescence.

PSYCHOPATHOLOGY

Adverse early experiences in human and nonhuman primates increase the variability of LHPA functioning, in some individuals producing hyperreactivity and in others, seemingly, hyporesponsivity. This may partly reflect interactions between genetic dispositions to particular disorders and experience. Prior to reviewing the early experience literature, we provide a brief overview of patterns of LHPA activity in three types of behavior disorders associated with adverse early rearing environments: disruptive behavior disorder, anxiety disorders, and depression.

Disruptive Behavior Disorders

Although there are several models of the processes underlying Oppositional Defiant Disorder (ODD) and Conduct Disorder, referred to collectively as disruptive behavior disorders (DBD), they all revolve around constructs of underarousal and underreactivity (Burke, Loeber, & Birmaher, 2002). The general idea is that children at risk for DBD are underreactive to threat stimuli, resulting in impaired avoidance learning and underarousal, which may encourage sensation seeking as a means of increasing arousal. None of the models is complete, and most assume that they may apply only to subgroups of children with DBD (Burke et al., 2002; McBurnett & Lahey, 1994).

Consistent with models of underarousal, low basal or pretest cortisol has been reported in a number of studies, most using variants of the following protocol. Children arrive for testing in the morning, often around 9 A.M. A saliva sample is taken, after which the child is subjected to a mild stressor task, and a second saliva sample is taken at the end of testing 30 to 40 minutes later. Typically developing children exhibit high cortisol levels at pretest with decreasing levels over the testing period. In contrast, DBD children or those at high risk for DBD have low cortisol levels at pretest that do not change over the testing period (Hardie, Moss, Vanyukov, Yao, & Kirillovac, 2002; King, 1998; Moss, Vanyukov, & Martin, 1995; Moss, Vanyukov, Yao, & Kirillovac, 1999). This pattern has been observed in both boys and girls (Hardie et al., 2002; Pajer, Garner, Rubin, Perel, & Neal, 2001). Even in studies that have failed to obtain group differences in cortisol between DBD and control children, disruptive behavior symptom counts have correlated with lower early morning cortisol levels (Pajer, Gardner, Kirillovac, & Vanyukov, 2001; Scerbo & Kolko, 1994; Vanyukov et al., 1993). Although most cortisol studies of DBD children have sampled cortisol in the early morning, not all have. McBurnett and colleagues (McBurnett, Lahey, Frick, et al., 1991; McBurnett, Lahey, & Rathouz, et al., 2000) have reported lower cortisol levels for DBD children, despite not controlling for time of day.

Perhaps more significant, several studies have demonstrated that low cortisol levels predict later disruptive behavior problems. Granger, Weisz, and McCracken (1996) reported that clinic-referred 9- to 16-year-olds who had low cortisol levels at the beginning of a late-afternoon laboratory test displayed more delinquency at follow-up testing several months later. Similarly, in another study (van de Wiel, van Goozen, Matthys, Snoek, & van Engeland, 2004), 8- to 13-year-old boys with DBD who had cortisol levels below the median had higher externalizing, ODD, and overt aggression scores at a 9-month follow-up assessment than did boys with cortisol levels above the median. Finally, in a study of several hundred adolescent boys, resting cortisol levels assessed when the boys were between 10 and 12 years of age were negatively correlated with self-reported aggression and positively correlated with constraint, control, and harm avoidance 5 years later (Shoal, Giancola, & Kirrilova, 2003). Thus, DBD children and those who develop DBD symptoms appear to have lower cortisol levels than do nondisordered children. Low basal or pretest cortisol would be consistent with an underarousal hypothesis, and through impairment of permissive actions of GCs might reduce responsiveness of other stress-sensitive systems (e.g., brain monoamines).

What is not as well established is whether low reactivity of the LHPA system is associated with DBD. To examine the underreactivity hypothesis requires that experimentally imposed stressors elevate cortisol in the control or comparison group. To date, only two studies have met this criterion (van Goozen, Matthys, Cohen-Kettenis, Buittelaar, & van Engeland, 2000; van Goozen et al., 1998). Van Goozen and colleagues exposed severely disordered DBD children and controls to a task during which a peer (on audiotape) denigrated their performance. When the paradigm was conducted during the morning hours, the task prevented the normal decrease in cortisol among the typically developing and DBD children. When performed in the afternoon hours, typically developing but not DBD children exhibited significant cortisol increases. In addition, in both the morning and afternoon studies, DBD children exhibited lower heart rate and skin conductance than did the typically developing children. Of particular importance, in a recent follow-up study, these researchers (van del Wiel et al., 2004) examined the effectiveness of treatment for DBD children as a function of cortisol reactivity to their paradigm. Treatment included medication and individual and family therapy. Children with DBD who exhibited no cortisol response to their stressor paradigm also failed to show improvement in DBD symptoms 9 months after the onset of treatment, whereas those who did show a cortisol response did show improvement. Thus, there is some evidence from at least this research group that DBD, and perhaps especially DBD that is resistant to treatment, is associated with low GC responsivity.

However, not all DBD children exhibit low cortisol levels. In fact, several researchers have noted that the combination of DBD and anxiety disorders is associated with high rather than low cortisol activity relative to controls. Thus, McBurnett and colleagues (1991) found higher levels of cortisol among comorbid (DBD + anxiety) children than in DBD-only children. In both of their studies, van Goozen and colleagues (1998, 2000) found that DBD children, but not normal controls, who showed a cortisol response to the stressor task were more anxious and depressed than those who did not respond. Finally, Scerbo and Kolko (1994) found that parent reports of internalizing problems were positively correlated with cortisol levels in their DBD children. Thus, across all of the studies that included measures of anxiety, low cortisol levels were typically observed *only* for those disruptive children who were not clinically anxious. McBurnett and Lahey (1994) caution that to clarify the relations between cortisol and disruptive behavior problems, we may need to distinguish between aggressive (undersocialized Conduct Disorder) and nonaggressive forms of the disorder. The 10- to 12-year-old boys studied by McBurnett and colleagues (1991) who had the lowest cortisol levels were also described by peers as the meanest and by adults as having the most aggressive symptoms. Pajer and colleagues (2001) noted a similar, but nonsignificant, difference between the aggressive and nonaggressive DBD girls.

It is unclear why at least some subtypes of DBD children might exhibit low basal cortisol levels and possibly hyporeactivity of the HPA axis. Studies of DBD children's response to serotonergic challenges have shown that these children exhibit blunted cortisol reactions to fenfluramine (Soloff, Lynch, & Moss, 2000) and sumatriptan (Snoek et al., 2002), suggesting that serotonergic regulation of the LHPA system is compromised. Monkeys carrying the short version of the serotonin transporter allele are especially vulnerable to disturbances in the early caregiving environments that elevate cortisol (Bennett et al., 2002). Studying children of substance-abusing fathers, investigators have hypothesized that low cortisol levels in these children may be the product of disturbances in their family environment (Hardie et al., 2002; Pajer, Gardner, et al., 2001). Thus, low cortisol levels may be the result of down-regulation of the axis following periods of elevated cortisol. Unfortunately, none of the studies of DBD children or those at risk for DBD problems has started assessing children's neuroendocrine and autonomic reactivity during the first years of life.

In this regard, it is useful to examine relations between disruptive behavior and cortisol activity in community samples of primarily nondisordered children. For school-age and older children, the evidence fairly consistently points to significant associations between low cortisol and more externalizing-type behaviors (e.g., Flinn & England, 1995; Spangler, 1995; Tennes & Kreye, 1985; Tennes, Kreye, Avitable, & Wells, 1986). Using a very large sample of 6- to 16-year-old children, Shirtcliff and colleagues (in press) applied latent state-trait modeling techniques to identify the trait component of early morning cortisol production. Then they examined whether the trait component was associated with either internalizing or externalizing problem behavior in the nonclinical range. For boys, but not girls, they found a significant negative relation between trait cortisol shortly after waking and externalizing problems.

Studies of typically developing children under the age of 7, when oppositional and aggressive behaviors are more normative, have yielded weaker and more mixed results. Lower cortisol levels for more aggressive children have been noted in two studies (de Haan, Gunnar, Tout, Hart, & Stansbury, 1998; Hart, Gunnar, & Cicchetti, 1995). Larger, rather than smaller, cortisol reactivity among more aggressive children to new peer situations was noted in three studies (de Haan et al., 1998; Dettling, Gunnar, & Donzella, 1999) but not in other similar studies (Bruce, Davis, & Gunnar, 2002; Dettling, Parker, Lane, Sebanc, & Gunnar, 2000; Gunnar, Tout, de Haan, Pierce, & Stansbury, 1997). Thus, during the toddler and preschool years, when aggression and oppositional behavior is observed at relatively high frequencies, the relationship between these behaviors and cortisol is unreliable in typically developing children. However, children who persist in more aggressive, oppositional behavior during the school-age and adolescent years, even though their behavior is within the nondisordered range, do appear to have lower basal and perhaps less reactive LHPA systems.

Anxiety Disorders

Pathological anxiety in animals and humans may reflect an exaggeration of normal anticipatory LHPA responses (Rosen & Schulkin, 1998). This argument builds on related models of the LHPA system's role in the pathophysiology of affective disorders (e.g., Gold, Goodwin, & Chrousos, 1988). Anticipatory anxiety involves phasic immobility or freezing, autonomic changes (e.g., increased sympathetic discharge), increased neuroendocrine activity (e.g., elevated levels of GCs), heightened reflexive responses to sensory stimuli (e.g., fear-potentiated startle), hypoanalgesia, and increased urination and defecation (Rosen & Schulkin, 1998). In the presence of elevated GCs and CRH, a cascade of biomolecular events that include increased expression of immediate-early genes (Makino, Gold, & Schulkin, 1994) increases the sensitivity of central fear circuits, heightens anxiety to distal danger cues, and supports the transition from normal to pathological anxiety.

A number of studies of anxiety-disordered children reveal elevations in basal GC levels (Carrion et al., 2002; DeBellis, Baum, et al., 1999; Klimes-Dougan et al., 2001; however, see Martel et al., 1999 for a counterexample). In addition, there is also growing evidence that clinically anxious children are hyper-GC-responsive to some types of stressors, including air puff startle (Ashman, Dawson, Panagiotides, Yamada, & Wilkinson, 2002) and mother-child conflict discussions (Granger, Weisz, et al., 1994), although such associations have not always been found (Dorn et al., 2003; Martel et al., 1999). Cortisol reactivity has also been shown to predict subsequent anxiety symptoms among clinic-referred adolescents (Granger et al., 1996). Finally, as discussed earlier, anxiety plus DBD is associated with higher cortisol activity than observed among control and nonanxious DBD children.

If hyperresponsivity of the LHPA axis constitutes a diathesis for the development of anxiety disorders, then we should find evidence of heightened LHPA axis activity in extremely temperamentally inhibited and/or socially reticent children who are at risk for the development of these disorders (Rosenbaum et al., 1993). However, because novel situations should elevate cortisol in nonanxious as well as anxious individuals, this may be difficult to demonstrate. Many studies of adults have shown that GC elevations are larger the first time individuals confront a challenging or threatening event and diminish markedly with repetition (as reviewed in Kirschbaum & Hellhammer, 1989). Elevating GCs in anticipation of challenge thus is not pathological but instead is an adaptive function of the LHPA axis (Rosen & Schulkin, 1998; Sapolsky et al., 2000). In studies of adults and animals, individuals who exhibit the largest increases in cortisol under normative conditions of uncertainty are sometimes more dominant and assertive, rather than shy or socially reticent (e.g., Golub, Sassenrath, & Goo, 1979; Hellhammer, Buchtal, Ingmar, & Kirschbaum, 1997). Thus, whereas anxious individuals may exhibit anticipatory cortisol reactions, so may competent, assertive individuals. However, as most individuals should show habituation of the LHPA axis response upon repetition of the same stressor, we might find evidence that failure to habituate is associated with risk for developing anxiety and depression.

Indeed, this conclusion appears to be the thrust of work by Pruessner and colleagues (1997). Personality differences among adult subjects did not predict elevations in cortisol to the first stressor trial. However, although most subjects habituated on subsequent trials, responses on these trials were significantly and highly correlated with two risk factors in the etiology of affective disorders: low self-esteem and external locus of control. In a similar vein, van Eck and colleagues (van Eck, Berkhof, Nicolson, & Sulon, 1996; van Eck, Nicolson, Berkhof, & Sulon, 1996) demonstrated that high trait-anxious individuals were more likely to exhibit cortisol elevations to familiar daily hassles (i.e., being late for the bus, a disagreement with a coworker). This was the case even though high trait anxiety was not associated with larger GC responses the first time individuals were subjected to a laboratory stressor (i.e., the TSST). Taken together, these adult findings suggest that continuing to activate the LHPA axis to familiar stressors, rather than exaggerated activation to a novel stressor, may form part of the diathesis for the development of pathological anxiety. If so, then during development, cortisol activity might correlate less often with inhibited, socially reticent temperament when children are tested responding to novel, unfamiliar stressors than when they are tested reacting to familiar challenges at home or school.

There is some support for this hypothesis. Young children who exhibited more facial expressions of fear to emotion-eliciting laboratory events did not have higher cortisol levels in the laboratory, but did at home (Buss et al., 2003). Likewise, in another study, shy/anxious temperament predicted home but not school levels of cortisol during the initial weeks of preschool (de Haan et al., 1998). Similarly, Schmidt and colleagues (Schmidt & Fox, 1998; Schmidt et al., 1997) did not find that extremely shy, inhibited children produced higher GC responses to a laboratory stressor, but did have higher home early morning GC levels. Kagan, Reznick, and Snidman (1987) reported similar results.

Using new peer group settings, several researchers have noted higher cortisol levels among more anxious, introverted children, but only once the play group setting was familiar (e.g., Granger, Stansbury, & Henker, 1994). In one study of children entering a new playgroup, anxious children did have high cortisol levels, but so did the most socially outgoing children (Legendre & Trudel, 1996). In several studies of children starting new school years, we (Bruce et al., 2002; E. Davis, Donzella, Krueger, & Gunnar, 1999) noted that by the 5th day of school, a time when the situation should still be novel especially for first-grade children, exuberant or extroverted children had higher cortisol levels relative to weekend baseline days earlier in the day prior to and during school. In contrast, shy, inhibited children exhibited elevated bedtime cortisol levels hours after they had returned home. Thus, increasing cortisol levels to novel, uncertain stressors may not be unique to shy, inhibited children, but, shy, inhibited children may be less likely to habituate cortisol responses as the situation becomes more familiar, and they may be less able to turn off the cortisol response once they have left the novel situation.

Studies examining relations between fearful temperament and physiological reactivity typically have used laboratory challenges to elicit wary or fearful behavior (e.g., Kagan et al., 1987). Fussing, crying, seeking proximity with attachment figures, and withdrawing from or avoiding contact with the threat stimuli are then used to measure fear. One reason associations between fearful behavior and cortisol may be low is that these behaviors also reflect active attempts to manage or control threat. As long as the individual possesses responses to cope with threat, we would not expect to see elevations in GCs. This may be why several researchers now report that freezing may be the fear behavior that is the most closely correlated with increases in GCs and in sympathetic reactivity (Buss, Davidson, Kalin, & Goldsmith, 2004; Gunnar & Nelson, 1994). Freezing in situations where the child has many avenues available to exert control over the threat may be particularly noteworthy (Buss et al., 2004).

We cannot tell from these studies whether cortisol activity also predicts the development of anxious, internalizing problems. Some evidence suggests that it may. Essex and colleagues (Essex, Klein, Eunsuk, & Kalin, 2002; Smider et al., 2002) obtained salivary cortisol samples at home when the children were 4.5 years of age, and these measures predicted internalizing problems in kindergarten a year later and both internalizing and externalizing problem behavior in first grade. Somewhat similar findings have been reported in studies of young adolescents (Granger et al., 1996; Susman, Dorn, & Chrousos, 1991; Susman, Dorn, Inoff-Germain, Nottelman, & Chrousos, 1997). Notably, however, when behavior and cortisol are both used to predict later behavior problems, behavior is the better predictor (Granger et al., 1996; Susman et al., 1991). However, because cortisol levels are often based on only one or two assessments, the greater predictive value of behavioral measures may reflect their greater statistical reliability. Finally, when family process variables are included in studies of cortisol and internalizing problems, the family measures predict both cortisol levels and internalizing symptoms (Granger et al., 1998).

Depression

There is typically high comorbidity between anxiety and depression. We consider depression here separately from anxiety, however, because so much of the LHPA research on psychiatric disorders has focused on Major Depressive Disorder (MDD), often using anxiety-disordered individuals as a comparison group. Indeed, disturbance in LHPA regulation in adults with MDD is among the most reliable findings in biological psychiatry (see review, Pariante, 2003). Alterations are observed in both the diurnal rhythm and negative feedback regulation of the axis. In many adult MDD patients, basal levels of cortisol and ACTH remain high throughout the day, resulting in hypercortisolemia and a loss of the normal diurnal rhythm. Fast-feedback regulation of the axis is impaired, resulting in larger and more prolonged elevations to stressors and failure to suppress cortisol to DEX. Chronic CRH drive and high cortisol levels produce down-regulation of pituitary ACTH and thus blunted ACTH responses to CRH challenge. Blunted growth hormone responses to a variety of challenges, in-

cluding stimulation with growth hormone releasing hormone (GHRH), are also frequently observed, perhaps reflecting chronic CRH drive at the level of the pituitary (Ryan, 1998). These results meet several of the criteria for dysregulation outlined earlier in this chapter. Indeed, several prominent theories of the etiology of depression focus on dysregulation of the LHPA axis and/or of CRH (e.g., Holsboer, 2000; Nemeroff, 1996).

There have been a number of excellent reviews of LHPA axis functioning in child and adolescent depression (e.g., Goodyer, Park, & Herbert, 2001; Ryan, 1998). Thus, we only briefly review this area of research. Studies using ambulatory measures of salivary cortisol in depressed adolescents often yield evidence of elevated GC levels, similar to results obtained for adults (Goodyer, Herbert, & Altham, 1998; Goodyer, Herbert, Moor, & Altham, 1991). Higher cortisol levels and higher cortisol: DHEA ratios may also predict longer illness duration (Goodyer et al., 1998). Nonetheless, fewer MDD adolescents than MDD adults exhibit evening distortions of the LHPA rhythm (Dahl et al., 1991; Forbes, Williamson, Ryan, & Dahl, 2004; Goodyer et al., 1998). In addition, evidence for hypersecretion of GC in early-onset depression is sparse when depressed children and adolescents are studied under controlled laboratory conditions. Under highly controlled sleep-laboratory conditions, most MDD school-age and adolescent children exhibit normal diurnal patterns of cortisol and ACTH production relative to carefully screened, supernormal controls (e.g., Dahl et al., 1991).

There are many other indications that MDD in children and adolescents is less associated with endogenous dysregulation of the LHPA axis than it is in adults. Nonsuppression of cortisol to DEX is rare in MDD children and adolescents, and ACTH and cortisol responses to CRH are also typically normal, at least in depressed children who have not also been physically abused (for review, see Ryan, 1998). Perhaps important, however, MDD in children, as in adults, is associated with blunted growth hormone responses to provocative challenges as well as to stimulation by GHRH, and this blunted response appears to continue after recovery from the illness (reviewed in Ryan, 1998). As noted, this may reflect the impact of chronic CRH drive. Failure to observe alterations in the axis at the level of the pituitary and adrenal in depressed children and adolescents may reflect the resilience of the axis to endogenous dysregulation during childhood. Furthermore, this would suggest that such endogenous dysregulation might become more apparent by late adolescence or with more chronic, recurrent illness (see also Kutcher et al., 1991).

Given that abnormalities in LHPA axis functioning are less characteristic of early-onset depression than adult-onset depression, it would be surprising to find that pre-morbid activity of the axis predicts the development of depression in high-risk samples. Nonetheless, there is some evidence to this effect. Luby and colleagues (2003) found that anhedonic preschoolers exhibited increases in cortisol to mild laboratory challenges that were not noted among children with more typical affective dispositions. Among adolescents, highly variable early morning basal cortisol levels across days predicted which adolescents would experience their first bout of clinical depression over the next months (Goodyer, Herbert, Tamplin, & Altham, 2000). Specifically, when 4 days of 8 A.M. and 8 P.M. cortisol were obtained, adolescents who spiked (exhibited at least one value in the upper 10% of the distribution of values) were 7 times as likely to develop depression over the next few months. This effect was specific to the morning cortisol samples (see also Halligan, Herbert, Goodyer, & Murray, 2004). Loneliness has also been shown to be a correlate of higher ambulatory cortisol levels in typically developing, low-risk adolescents, and for adolescents at school, being alone at the time of sampling rather than being with friends has been associated with increasing cortisol levels (Adam, 2002). Thus, although an endogenous dysregulation of the LHPA axis does not appear to be present in most children with depression, heightened cortisol reactivity and higher levels associated with loneliness suggest that activity of the LHPA system may contribute to the etiology of depression in children and adolescents. However, in many of these studies of children at risk for depression, the role of anxiety in potentially disturbing activity of the LHPA system was not clearly ruled out. Thus, in some of these studies of at-risk children, high anxiety and LHPA axis disturbances may be indicating risk for the development of depression.

Summary of Limbic-Hypothalamic-Pituitary-Adrenocortical Activity in Child Clinical Disorders

This brief review of the literature on LHPA associations with clinical disorders and subclinical behavior problems in children yields evidence of association with both hypo- (e.g., DBD without anxiety) and hypercortisol activity (anxiety and, to some extent, depression). Because in humans early adverse experiences tend to increase rates of both disruptive and anxious/depressed symptoms, we might expect the impact of early experiences on LHPA functioning to be filtered through individual vulnerabilities to different patterns of disordered functioning. There

is little evidence for this in the rodent research that spawned much of this field of inquiry. However, because the preclinical studies have been conducted on highly inbred strains, we might expect less evidence of the multifinality (different end points associated with similar experiences) typically observed in human studies of early experiences.

EARLY EXPERIENCES AND STRESS REACTIVITY AND REGULATION

Studies of the impact of early experience on the LHPA system have important implications for developmental psychopathology. Here we first review the detailed work conducted in rodents and then examine the implications of this work for our understanding of primate development, including the development of young children.

Rodent Studies

The long history of early experience stress studies in rats provides the basis for attempts to understand how variations in care early in life may impact individual differences in stress resilience and vulnerability to psychiatric disorders. There have been many recent and excellent reviews of this literature (e.g., Cirulli & Alleva, 2003; Graham, Heim, Goodman, Miller, & Nemeroff, 1999; Sanchez, Ladd, & Plotsky, 2001); thus, we only very briefly outline the general findings. A number of early experience paradigms have been used in the rat. Most involve some form of maternal separation. *Handling* involves very brief (3 to 5 minutes) daily removal of the pup from the mother and nest. *Separation* involves longer periods, ranging from 3 hours daily to 6 to 24 hours one or more times prior to weaning. Over 20 years ago, Levine (1975) argued that these manipulations produce their effects, at least in part, by altering mother-pup interaction (but see also Denenberg, 1999). Current evidence suggests that the critical components of maternal behavior affected by early experience manipulations center on feeding interactions. Specifically, they center on how much the mother licks and grooms her pups (typically occurring in conjunction with nursing bouts) and how well she assumes the nursing posture (arched back). Handling seems to stimulate increased licking/grooming and arched-back nursing (LG-ABN), although in some strains (but not in others), separation reduces these aspects of maternal behavior. In strains where these aspects of maternal behavior are not reduced by separation, hyperresponsivity of the LHPA axis is not observed. Similarly, spontaneous variations in LG-ABN among mother rats have also been associated with long-term effects on offspring similar to those observed in handling (high LG-ABN) and separation (low LG-ABN). The effects of handling are greater in the 1st than in the 2nd postnatal week. In addition, 24 hours of maternal separation has opposite effects when performed at the end of the 1st compared to the 2nd postnatal week. Both of these findings suggest sensitive periods for effects on the LHPA system early in postnatal development in the rat.

Handling and high LG-ABN produce offspring who later in life are less fearful and exhibit lower CRH activity in the hypothalamus and amygdala, increased GR in the hippocampus, and better containment of the GC response. They also evidence enhanced functioning of the noradrenergic, dopamine, and serotonin system and increased synaptogenesis in various regions of the brain (see review articles cited earlier). Maternal separation and low LG-ABN produce the opposite: high fearful offspring with heightened CRH and LHPA reactivity. Of particular importance, the early experience manipulations in rodents appear to affect responses to processive stressors more than systemic stressors, thus implicating corticolimbic components of the stress-emotion system. GCs may not mediate the effects of maternal separation, as suppression of GCs has no ameliorating effects on pups separated for 24 hours. Instead, there is evidence that CRH operating through CRHr1 may contribute to the effects of these early experience manipulations. In addition, although the effects of early experience manipulations on GR may be permanent, exposing juvenile rats to environmental enrichment can reverse many of the other behavioral and neurobiological effects of maternal separation. This suggests that in the rat, postweaning manipulations continue to shape neural components of the stress-emotion system (Francis, Diorio, Plotsky, & Meaney, 2002).

Because so much of the data on early experiences and later stress reactivity and regulation comes from rat models, we face a number of challenges in translating this literature to human or, for that matter, primate development. Critically, gestational time varies such that birth occurs at a different point of neurobiological development: 3 weeks for the rat, 7 months for the monkey, and 9 months for the human. Rats are weaned at 21 to 22 days of age in the laboratory (28 days in the wild), monkeys at 1 year, and 2 to 3 years of nursing is not uncommon for human infants in hunter-gatherer cultures. Based on first signs of reproductive ability, rats are juvenile between 35 and 45 days of age, nonhuman primates around 3 to 4 years of age, and humans until the 2nd decade of life. The central nervous system is much more immature in the rat at birth than in the human and nonhuman primate, although at this time, there is no agreed upon method of identifying corresponding developmental periods of neural plasticity among species. Nonetheless, there is reason to believe that the 1st postnatal week in the rat likely corresponds to prenatal development in humans (Dobbing, 1981; Vazquez, 1998). Postnatal experiences should operate primarily on brain regions that develop after birth. Because at birth the HPA system is more mature in the primate than in the rat, we might expect that postnatal effects on the stress-emotion system in primates would be less apparent in the HPA system than in the corticolimbic pathways influencing stress reactivity and regulation.

Nonhuman Primate Studies

Early experience research in nonhuman primates has largely progressed through the lens of attachment theory. Accordingly, the mother-infant relationship has been conceptualized as a social buffer against stress (Bowlby, 1969; Suomi, 1995). Maternal buffering describes situations in which the infant may be behaviorally distressed but physiological stress responses are attenuated. For example, capture and handling elicits intense behavioral distress, but when mother and infant are immediately reunited, cortisol responses are minimal (Levine & Wiener, 1988). Although there is as yet no clear evidence of an SHRP in the monkey infant, maternal buffering may serve the same function, reducing the likelihood of high GC exposure during periods of rapid brain development. In primates, physical contact is critical for the development of the attachment relationship (Harlow, Harlow, & Suomi, 1971). However, monkey infants can also use distal modes of communication with mother to buffer LHPA and NA responses to separation (e.g., Bayart, Hayashi, Faull, Barchas, & Levine, 1990). The natural ecology of most primate species is social. Mother and infant live in troupes that include other mothers and infants, adult males, and the infant's older siblings. Species differ in how often the infant is parented by other members of the troupe, a phenomenon termed *alloparenting* or *aunting*. Although the availability of alloparents does not prevent elevations in cortisol to maternal separation, it does result in a more rapid termination of the GC response and a reduction in the likelihood of despair reactions (I. C. Kaufman & Rosenblum, 1967; Levine & Wiener, 1988). Thus, in primate infants, maternal buffering is not restricted to physical contact between mother and infant and is a function that can be provided to some extent by other nurturing conspecifics.

Separation confronts the infant with two conflicting challenges: Reestablish contact and avoid attack or predation. Two stages of separation response have been described: *protest,* or the period of active searching, and *despair,* a period of passivity and withdrawal (Bowlby, 1973). Although once described as a necessary biphasic process following maternal loss (Bowlby, 1973), infant behavior during both phases is affected by the context of separation. Protest appears to be related to preseparation factors (e.g., Gunnar, Gonzalez, Goodlin, & Levine, 1981) and cues signifying predation/attack (Kalin, Shelton, Rickman, & Davidson, 1998). Despair appears to be affected by the presence of alloparents and the degree of social threat confronting the infant in the mother's absence (Hinde & Davies, 1972). Separation thus is not a unitary phenomenon (Kraemer, Ebert, Schmidt, & McKinney, 1991). Its complexity may help explain why protest behaviors at times are inversely related to separation-induced LHPA activity and why during prolonged and/or repeated separations protest behaviors are sometimes reduced, while LHPA continues or sometimes increases (e.g., Coe, Glass, Wiener, & Levine, 1983). Levine and Wiener (1988) have argued that protest reflects the active attempts to cope with separation, and LHPA responses reflect failed coping. An alternative, but not mutually exclusive, explanation is that protest reflects operation of the attachment system, and LHPA activity reflects actions of central fear/anxiety systems.

Support for this latter argument comes from studies by Kalin and his colleagues. In rhesus infants, administering exogenous opiates during separation reduces protest behavior but not GCs or defensive behaviors (e.g., freezing and threatening experimenters; Kalin, Shelton, & Barksdale, 1988). In contrast, intraventricular CRH administration during separation increases GCs and defensive behavior but not protest (Kalin, Shelton, & Barksdale, 1989; Kalin, Shelton, & Turner, 1992). In rhesus infants, there is a close correspondence between defensive behaviors (e.g., freezing) and LHPA activity. LHPA activity in rhesus infants is also associated with greater right frontal EEG asymmetry, suggesting corticolimbic organization of defensive, withdrawal behaviors (Kalin et al., 1998). Combined, these data argue that separation can produce fear in infant primates, and that when it does, we see marked elevations in LHPA activity and defensive behaviors, perhaps orchestrated, at least in part, by extrahypothalamic CRH. How much the infant protests, however, is often uncorrelated with activity of the LHPA axis and may be organized along different neurobiological pathways. There is evidence of a similar dissociation between separation-induced crying and cortisol elevations in human infants (e.g., Spangler & Schieche, 1998).

Whereas repeated separation in rats produces hypercortisolism, in monkeys it may reduce LHPA activity. Infant squirrel monkeys do not exhibit habituation of the LHPA response to repeated 6-hour separations, even with as many as 80 trials (Hennessy, 1986). However, several years later, previously separated juveniles demonstrate blunted GC and NA responses to social isolation stress (Levine, Lyons, & Schatzberg, 1997). Repeated, daily separations of several hours in marmosets during the 1st month of life lower basal cortisol near the peak of the circadian cycle while increasing fearful, anxious behaviors (Dettling, Feldon, & Price, 2002). In contrast, in squirrel monkeys, 1 hour of separation weekly for 10 weeks had the opposite effect, reducing clinging and increasing exploration of a novel environment and blunting LHPA responsivity (Lyons et al., 1999; Parker, Buckmaster, Schatzberg, & Lyons, 2004). Lyons and colleagues (e.g., 1999) suggest that brief separations in monkeys may function like handling in rats. However, a recent study of repeated, unpredictable separations in rhesus infants questions this conclusion (Sanchez et al., in press). Monkey infants typically spend less time in close proximity to mother with age; however, infants who experienced the series of unpredictable separations showed the reverse: *increases* in proximity with age. Evidence of heightened stress reactivity was noted, although this was more apparent for females in cortisol reactivity and males in heightened acoustic startle reactions. Of importance for comparison with human studies of early trauma and deprivation, both males and females exhibited disturbances in diurnal cortisol production, although the disturbances varied by sex, with males showing a shallower rhythm over the morning hours and females exhibiting a flatter rhythm from morning to evening. Thus, repeated separation paradigms produce alterations in fear/anxiety and LHPA activity in monkey infants. Nonetheless, these changes do not always suggest heightened stress reactivity. In some cases, they appear to produce blunted responsivity to subsequent stressors. Whether these differences reflect species differences, differences in developmental timing, and/or differences in the supportiveness of the separation environment (e.g., presence of alloparents) is not yet clear. These findings do, however, raise critical questions about how best to translate the rodent findings to primates, including humans.

The challenge of translating the rodent findings is also demonstrated by work on prolonged separations in infant monkeys. Separations of several days or weeks increase fearful, anxious behavior in monkey infants. Tested months and years after the separation experience, juvenile rhesus who were separated once or twice in infancy were found to be more neophobic and behaviorally reactive than never-separated animals (Spencer-Booth & Hinde, 1971). These effects were greater when the infant was left in the social group than when it was removed and the mother remained in her familiar surroundings (Hinde, Leighton-Shapiro, & McGinnis, 1978). Continuing the theme of maternal mediation of separation effects, Hinde argued that removing the mother from the social group was more devastating than removing the infant because, in the former case, the mother had to ignore the infant and reestablish her social position in the troupe upon her return. However, there is also evidence that leaving the infant in the social group, if it is not adopted by another female, also results in prolonged GC increases and other neurobiological disturbances (Laudenslager et al., 1995; Reite, Harbeck, & Hoffman, 1981). In contrast, if infant rhesus monkeys are placed alone in single cages during separation, GC levels return to near baseline within 24 hours (Gunnar et al., 1981). These findings are consistent with Kalin's (Kalin, Shelton, & Barksdale, 1988) argument that LHPA activity during separation reflects the degree of ongoing threat in the separation environment. Despite evidence of continued elevations in GCs during prolonged separations, however, there is little evidence of long-term changes in the LHPA axis (Capitanio, Rasmussen, Snyder, Laudenslager, & Reite, 1986).

In addition to separation, the effects of several aberrant rearing environments have been studied, including total and partial social isolation rearing, surrogate-peer rearing, and peer-only rearing. Sensitive periods have been demonstrated for behavioral abnormalities with deprivation during the first 6 months, resulting in more drastic effects than similar deprivation periods later in life (for review, see Kraemer, 1992). As in the research on separation, despite marked increases in bizarre behavior and anxious, neophobic reactions, long-term effects on the LHPA axis rarely have been observed. Considering social isolation rearing first, although there is evidence of marked aberrations in the coordination of central monoamine systems (Kraemer, Ebert, Schmidt, & McKinney, 1989), isolate-reared monkeys do not show increased LHPA reactivity (Meyer & Bowman, 1972; Sanchez, Young, Mathys, Plotsky, & Insel, 1999). Indeed, normalizing experience in these paradigms tends, if anything, to increase basal GCs and autonomic responsivity to stressors (Hill, McCormack, & Mason, 1972; Wood, Mason, & Kenney, 1979). Structural and neurochemical studies also have failed to reveal effects on the LHPA system (Sanchez et al., 2001). Changes have *not* been detected in BNST, in the number of hypothalamic dopaminergic neurons, the density of CRH neurons in the PVN or in CRH or AVP or their receptors in the hypothalamus, including the mpPVN (Sanchez et al.,

1999). Failure to find effects on the LHPA axis may reflect the greater maturity of this system at birth in the primate as compared to the rodent. Nonetheless, corticolimbic areas important in the regulation of fear/anxiety and LHPA activity are affected by isolation rearing (see Sanchez et al., 2001). Isolate-reared animals exhibit increased intensity of neurofilament protein immunoreactivity in the hippocampus (Siegel et al., 1993), as well as increased density of CRF1 receptors in the prefrontal cortex and downregulation of CRF2 receptors in the amygdala (Sanchez et al., 1999).

Allowing surrogate-reared infants daily peer experience supports reasonably normal social development (Suomi & Harlow, 1972). LHPA effects, however, are variable (Champoux, Coe, Schanberg, Kuhn, & Suomi, 1989; Clarke, 1993; Shannon, Champoux, & Suomi, 1998). Similar to repeatedly separated infants, smaller LHPA responses to brief periods of social isolation have been observed (Shannon et al., 1998), along with atypically low GC levels early in the morning, near the peak of the rhythm (Boyce, Champoux, Suomi, & Gunnar, 1995). Diurnal temperature and rest-activity rhythms have also been found to be dysregulated in surrogate-reared animals (Lubach, Kittrell, & Coe, 1992). Peer-only rearing, in which infants are reared with only other infants as attachment figures, produces more markedly deviant stress responsivity and behavior than surrogate-peer rearing (Suomi, 1997). Studies of these animals indicate larger and more prolonged LHPA responses to separation, increased alcohol consumption as juveniles that correlates with separation-induced cortisol reactions, and a combination of both neophobia and heightened reactive aggression (Higley, Suomi, & Linnoila, 1992). Unfortunately, there have been no published anatomical analyses of surrogate-peer and peer-only reared animals. Consequently, we do not know whether their LHPA axis anomalies reflect changes in the LHPA system proper or in corticolimbic inputs to the LHPA system.

In addition to separations and various deprivation rearing manipulations, researchers have manipulated demands on the mother to disturb maternal behavior. For example, they have altered maternal foraging demands. When foraging demands are unpredictable (i.e., variable foraging demand or VFD paradigm), marked alterations in the social organization of female bonnet macaques have been noted (Rosenblum & Andrews, 1994). Specifically, VFD reduces the maternal responsiveness to infant signals, resulting in insecure patterns of attachment behavior and long-term effects on offspring development (Andrews & Rosenblum, 1994). As juveniles and young adults, VFD-reared animals tend to be fearful of new social situations and low in dominance. They also have elevated CSF levels of CRH and monoamine abnormalities, suggesting that their early experiences sensitized the hypothalamic and/or extrahypothalamic CRH system (Coplan et al., 1996; Rosenblum et al., 1994).

Finally, monkey mothers do spontaneously abuse their infants. In rhesus, approximately 2% of infants are physically abused by mothers who were likely to have been abused themselves as infants (Maestripieri, 1999). Abusive behavior includes violent behaviors such as dragging the infant on the ground, crushing, throwing, or stepping/sitting on it. These abusive behaviors are observed most frequently in the first 3 postnatal months. In recent work, McCormack and colleagues (2003) noted significant alterations in LHPA functioning among abused infants. Specifically, compared to nonabused controls, abused infants exhibited higher basal morning levels of cortisol during the 1st postnatal month when abuse rates were the highest, but beginning in the 2nd postnatal month and continuing at least through the 6th postnatal month, their basal cortisol levels were suppressed, especially in the early morning hours. At 2 months of age, abused infants were unable to use maternal contact to buffer elevations in cortisol when mother and infant were captured together and singly caged for 30 minutes; in contrast, nonabused infants showed no increase in cortisol to these procedures. Of particular importance, disturbances in the LHPA system were also noted using pharmacological challenges. Specifically, the abused relative to the nonabused infants exhibited blunted ACTH responses to CRH, suggesting that some of their alterations in HPA function could be due to CRF receptor down-regulation at the level of the pituitary. Notably, down-regulation of ACTH to CRH was detected at both 6 and 12 months, many months after the infants were no longer highly dependent on maternal care. Similar but less dramatic effects of harsh treatment have also been noted in Goeldi's monkey infants (Dettling, Pryce, Martin, & Döbeli, 1998), where larger cortisol responses and behavioral distress to brief separations were obtained from infants whose parents engaged in more aggressive weaning behavior.

Summary of the Monkey Infant Studies

As in rodents, monkey mothers provide an external regulator of the LHPA and other stress-sensitive systems. In primates, separation protest (crying and searching) does not appear to be associated with LHPA activation, but defensive behaviors do, perhaps coordinated by extrahypothalamic CRH. The separation context influences the magnitude of the LHPA response. When the infant is nurtured by other conspecifics in the mother's absence, small GC responses are obtained that resolve quickly. When the separation environment is more threatening, high GC responses are produced that may not habituate over trials. The long-term impact of the various separation and rearing environment paradigms that have been studied in monkeys are difficult to summarize. *Overall, however, as in the rodent research, the clearest impacts on infant behavior and stress neurobiology appear to arise in those paradigms that produce disturbances in mother-infant interaction or, in the case of peer-only rearing, in the supportiveness of the infant's attachment figures.* Thus, as in the rodent research, the behavior of the infant's caregivers may be the most important factor in determining the long-term impact of early adverse experiences on the development of the LHPA system. Furthermore, unlike in the rodent, more of the effects of postnatal adversity in monkeys appear to be evident on limbic circuits impacting activity of the HPA axis than on the HPA axis proper. This is consistent with the greater maturity of the HPA axis at birth in primates than in rodents.

Human Studies

In this section, we cover studies of caregiving and LHPA activity in human infants and children. These studies have been conducted through two major theoretical lenses. First, as in the nonhuman primate research, concepts and assumptions of attachment theory have guided much of the work. Second, in work on childhood maltreatment, research on adult Posttraumatic Stress Disorder (PTSD) has shaped the questions asked as well as interpretation of the findings. We first examine LHPA associations with variations in caregiving in the normative or nonabusive range and then consider LHPA studies of maltreated children.

Normative Variations in Caregiving

Consistent with attachment theory, in human infants insensitive, intrusive maternal care is associated with heightened GC activity. Insensitive or intrusive caregiving has been associated with GC increases during mother-infant play bouts (Spangler, Schieche, Ilg, Maier, & Ackermann, 1994), higher presession GC levels during well-child health checkups (Gunnar, Brodersen, Nachmias, Buss, & Rigatuso, 1996), and larger GC responses to strange and potentially threatening events (Nachmias, Gunnar, Mangelsdorf, Parritz, & Buss, 1996). In these studies, the sensitivity rather than the amount of maternal behavior seems to be the critical factor. Thus, mothers who engaged in both more and more varied, but not necessarily more sensitive, soothing activities have not been found to have infants who exhibited smaller GC response to an inoculation stressor (Lewis & Ramsay, 1999). Similarly, mothers who engaged in more, but not more sensitive, interactions with fearful toddlers did not reduce their toddlers' GC responses to potentially threatening events (Nachmias et al., 1996).

Maternal sensitivity associated with reduced GC responses has also been shown to predict whether the mother-infant relationship would be classified as secure based on Ainsworth and Wittag's Strange Situation assessment (Gunnar, Brodersen, Nachmias, et al., 1996; Nachmias et al., 1996). When cortisol is not sampled too early following the stressor to detect the effect (e.g., Gunnar, Mangelsdorf, Larson, & Hertsgaard, 1989), the evidence fairly consistently supports the hypothesis that by the end of the 1st year, attachment security provides a powerful stress buffer in humans. There is evidence for this conclusion using stressors ranging from the Strange Situation (Spangler & Grossmann, 1993; Spangler & Schieche, 1998), to novel, arousing stimuli (Nachmias et al., 1996), to inoculations (Gunnar, Brodersen, Krueger, et al., 1996). However, as yet there is no evidence that a history of secure attachment reduces infant or toddler GC reactivity when the attachment figure is not available or when separations last more than a few minutes (see Ahnert et al., 2004). Secure attachment may foster better stress regulation, but this has been observed only in the presence of the attachment figure during the infant and toddler periods.

The hypothesis that sensitive and responsive caregiving is critical in regulating stress hormones in young children is also supported by research on nonparental caregivers. In a study in which 9-month-olds were separated from their mother for 30 minutes, infants who were randomly assigned to a sensitive and supportive babysitter condition did not produce elevations in cortisol, but those who were assigned to an unresponsive and inattentive babysitter condition did (Gunnar, Larson, Hertsgaard, Harris, & Brodersen, 1992). In a study of home-based child care, preschoolers produced increases in cortisol over the child care day if their care providers were less attentive and provided less supportive stimulation (Dettling et al., 2000).

Given evidence that unresponsive, insensitive, and/or intrusive care fails to provide an adequate stress buffer, it is not surprising that maternal depression has been associated with higher GC levels in young children. Depressed mothers are often more insensitive, erratically responsive, and/or intrusive with their children (Dawson & Ashman, 2000). Dawson and Ashman reported that right frontal EEG asymmetry in toddlers of depressed mothers was largely mediated by these aspects of maternal care. Furthermore, they found that at 3 years of age, morning GC levels could be predicted by how clinically depressed the mother had been during the child's 1st year of life. At 7 years, these children's laboratory pretest GC levels were higher if their mother had been clinically depressed during their first 2 years (Ashman et al., 2002). Similarly, adolescents whose mother had been depressed in their 1st postnatal years were more likely to produce one or more days of elevated cortisol in the early morning, a pattern predictive of depression in previous work (Halligan et al., 2004). Furthermore, Halligan and colleagues found this effect of early maternal depression while controlling for the total number of months the mother had been depressed during the child's life and the mother's current depression status. These findings are important for two reasons. First, they suggest that higher GC levels in offspring of depressed mothers are not due merely to shared genetics. Second, they support the possibility that insensitive, unresponsive care in the early years of the child's life may shape LHPA activity.

This latter point is one implication of another study that also examined maternal depression. Essex and colleagues (2002) found that home GC levels in 4.5-year-old children were higher if the mother scored high on depressive symptoms both during the prior year and during the children's infancy. Mothers with high depression symptoms only when their children were 4 or only during infancy did not have children with higher GC levels than mothers who never had high symptom counts. Unfortunately, the researchers did not examine whether the effects of maternal depressive symptoms were mediated by intrusive, unresponsive, or insensitive treatment of the child. Furthermore, these data do not allow us to untangle the impact of chronic maternal depression from organizational effects of early maternal care that then heightens vulnerability to stressors later in the child's life.

Unfortunately, few of the studies of postnatal maternal behavior permit us to rule out prenatal influences on the development of the child's LHPA system. This is a serious shortcoming as there is increasing evidence of fetal programming of the stress neuraxis. Several recent studies suggest that exposure to elevated levels of CRH and/or cortisol prenatally may influence the behavioral and physiological reactivity of the child, at least shortly after birth (see Wadhwa, Sandman, & Garite, 2001). For example, depressed mothers tend to produce higher urinary cortisol levels around midpregnancy than do nondepressed mothers, and these levels predict the newborn's urinary cortisol levels (Diego et al., 2004). Of particular importance, it was prenatal, not concurrent postnatal, maternal cortisol values that were predictive of infant cortisol activity. We do not know how long such effects persist.

Finally, as in so many other areas, we have very little evidence that maternal depression and associated insensitive, intrusive care increase cortisol *reactivity*. In all of the studies described, maternal depression was either associated with home baseline GC or laboratory pretest GC levels. In the one study describing GC responses to a stressor, Ashman and colleagues (2002) did not find effects of depression on the GC stress response, even though associations with pretest GC levels were obtained. They did, however, find an interaction between maternal depression during the child's infancy and the child's current internalizing problems. Children with internalizing problems who had been cared for by a mother who was clinically depressed during their first 2 years had the largest GC responses to the stressor. As we will see, activity of the LHPA axis in a number of studies of maltreated children also is a function of the interaction between the individual's history of care and his or her current mental health status.

Maltreatment

Because most maltreatment occurs at the hands of parents or guardians, childhood maltreatment typically represents a profound failure of the caregiving system (Cicchetti & Rogosch, 2001a). It is also associated with host of pathological outcomes, including both affective (anxiety, depression) and disruptive behavior disorders (for review, see Pine, & Cohen, 2002). Recently, there has been increased interest in identifying the various neurobiological mechanisms through which maltreatment produces its deleterious effects (e.g., Bremner & Vermetten, 2001; Cicchetti & Tucker, 1994; J. Kaufman & Charney, 2001; Teicher, Andersen, Polcarri, Anderson, & Navalta, 2002). Most of this work has started with the assumption that maltreatment is stressful and/or traumatic and that it produces its effects, at least in part, through episodic or chronic stress. No investigator expects the effects of maltreatment to be mediated by any one neurobiological system, but most include GCs and CRH in their models. This means that there have been a relatively large number of studies of the LHPA system in relation to childhood maltreatment (see recent reviews by Bremner & Vermetten, 2001; Glaser, 2000; Heim, Ehlert, Hanker, & Hellhammer, 1998; J. Kaufman & Charney, 2001).

Childhood maltreatment, however, is a multifaceted phenomena (Glaser, 2000). It differs in type (physical, sexual, emotional, neglectful), severity, and duration, and often several types are inflicted on the same child, sometimes at different points in his or her development (Barnett, Manly, & Cicchetti, 1993). Furthermore, it often occurs in the context of family conflict, parental psycho-

pathology, economic adversity, and other factors that may also impact the child's developing stress system. As is the case for other stressors, the impact of child maltreatment on the neurobiology of stress and emotion likely depends on the age of the child, the child's gender, his or her premorbid functioning, and genetic factors. Finally, its effects on the developing stress system will depend on the individual's age when these effects are assessed, current life stressors, social support, mental health status, time since maltreatment, and the measure(s) chosen for assessment. Given all of these factors, it is no surprise that the literature on maltreatment and stress neurobiology includes contradictory findings.

As noted earlier, much of the research on childhood maltreatment has been generated from a trauma framework. As such, many of the questions have been derived from adult work on PTSD. In adults, PTSD in response to traumas experienced in adulthood has been sometimes (Yehuda, 2000), but not always (Bremner et al., 2003), associated with low basal GCs (particularly late in the day), prolonged GC suppression to DEX, increased GR as measured on lymphocytes, and possibly heightened negative feedback regulation of the axis. One central question in this literature is whether these LHPA abnormalities predate rather than follow from the trauma (see Yehuda, 2000). Childhood maltreatment is one of the risk factors for developing PTSD in response to a traumatic event experienced in adulthood. Thus, researchers have been interested in whether adults who were maltreated as children exhibit prolonged suppression of the LHPA axis in response to a low dose of DEX regardless of their current PTSD status. If so, this might indicate that early maltreatment produces LHPA alterations that serve as a risk factor for the development of PTSD to traumas encountered in adulthood. In one small study, adult women who had been sexually abused as children were given a low-dose DEX test (Stein, Yehuda, Koverola, & Hanna, 1987). Compared to controls, the maltreated women did show prolonged cortisol suppression, regardless of their current PTSD status. We do not know whether this would also be true of men or of individuals who experienced other forms of childhood maltreatment.

Other studies of adults maltreated as children provide evidence of hypofunctioning at the adrenal but not necessarily at other levels of the LHPA system. These results were obtained in individuals without current psychiatric diagnoses. Using pharmacological probes, Heim, Newport, Bonsall, Miller, and Nemeroff (2001) found elevated ACTH production in response to CRH in women who had been abused prior to puberty. At the level of the adrenal, however, they obtained evidence of relative adrenal insufficiency. In response to both CRH and ACTH challenge tests, these women showed blunted GC responses relative to control women who had not experienced childhood abuse. Similarly, when a processive stressor rather than a pharmacological probe was used, they obtained evidence of elevated ACTH responses and normal GC reactions (Heim, Newport, et al., 2000). When the data from Heim et al. were subjected to a regression analysis to examine the effects of childhood abuse after controlling for current life events and psychopathology, peak GC and ACTH responses were both found to correlate positively with childhood abuse scores (Heim & Nemeroff, 2001). Finally, several studies of adults (male and female) who experienced physical and emotional abuse as children have reported low 24-hour urinary free cortisol (UFC) production (Roy, 2002; Yehuda, Halligan, & Grossman, 2001), although interestingly, not in women who were sexually maltreated as children (Yehuda et al., 2001).

Current psychiatric diagnosis interacts with childhood abuse in studies of the LHPA axis in adults abused as children. Thus, among depressed women maltreated as children, Heim and colleagues (Heim & Nemeroff, 2001; Heim, Newport, et al., 2000) noted elevated GC as well as ACTH responses to the TSST relative to nonabused, depressed controls. Indeed, the combination of childhood abuse and adult depression accounted for 21% of the variance in LHPA responses to the TSST. However, when a pharmacologic probe of the axis was used (i.e., CRH challenge test), similar to other depressed adults, these women exhibited a blunted ACTH reaction. In contrast, women with borderline personality diagnoses who had been maltreated as children showed augmented ACTH responses to CRH relative to similarly diagnosed women without a history of childhood maltreatment (Rinne et al., 2002). There is also evidence that adults with PTSD pursuant to childhood abuse may exhibit hyper- rather than hypo-LHPA functioning to processive stressors. Bremner and colleagues (2003) recently reported markedly elevated salivary GCs during an hour-long anticipatory period in a small sample of PTSD adults (male and female) maltreated in various ways as children. For women, no GC differences from nonpsychiatric, nonmaltreated controls were obtained in response to a cognitive stressor in this study, although PTSD males abused as children showed significantly higher GC reactions.

In summary, there is some evidence that childhood maltreatment is associated with low 24-hour GC production in adulthood, consistent with other work on adults with PTSD. However, there is little evidence that childhood maltreatment decreases LHPA reactivity at levels of the axis above the adrenal. Furthermore, there is little evidence, so far, that GC and ACTH responses to processive stressors are blunted in adults who were maltreated as children. Indeed, increased ACTH and GC reactivity to such stressors has been obtained. The LHPA effects of childhood maltreatment, however, appear to be influenced by the individual's current mental health status. Maltreated, depressed patients exhibit LHPA activity characteristic of MDD adults. Specifically, they show blunted ACTH responses to CRH challenge. Adults with PTSD who are not also clinically depressed may show exaggerated LHPA responses to psychological or processive stressors, similar to other studies of LHPA reactivity in clinical anxiety-disordered subjects.

Of course, despite the work just described, there is a great deal that is not yet known about the impact of childhood maltreatment on the activity of the mature stress system. Most of the studies have included only women. Few of the studies controlled for current life stressors, social supports, and/or recent trauma experiences. Most have had small samples that did not allow researchers to examine the timing, duration, or combinations of types of abuse to which the individual was exposed in childhood. Nonetheless, even given these limitations, the studies of adults maltreated as children tend to support the hypothesis that childhood maltreatment sensitizes the LHPA system, perhaps rendering individuals more vulnerable to stressors and increasing their risk for stress-related disorders.

This research on adults maltreated in childhood should caution us against assuming that childhood maltreatment will produce evidence of heightened activity at all levels of the axis and for all individuals. Increased pituitary responsivity to ACTH and to psychosocial stressors may exist in concert with low cortisol baselines. Responses to pharmacological probes specific for different levels of the axis may reveal patterns of response that are markedly different from, or even the opposite of, those obtained when processive stressors that involve corticolimbic circuitry are used. Given the complexity of the findings for adults, we should anticipate that the data on children, obtained while the stress system is still maturing, might be even more complex and challenging to interpret.

As in adults, whether maltreatment is associated with increased or suppressed LHPA activity in children appears to depend, at least in part, on the child's current psychiatric diagnoses and/or behavioral disposition. Internalizing problems and/or affective disorders (PTSD or depression) interact with abuse history to produce evidence of heightened reactivity of the LHPA system. In contrast, externalizing problems in the absence of concurrent anxiety disorders appear to reduce evidence of altered LHPA activity, at least when maltreated children are compared to normal controls. As discussed subsequently, ongoing adversity in the home may also stimulate higher LHPA activity in previously maltreated children. As current adversity is often unanalyzed, this makes interpretation of many of the studies difficult.

First we consider studies of maltreated children with PTSD. Here, unlike in adults, there is evidence of elevated rather than suppressed basal cortisol levels. Thus, DeBellis, Baum, and colleagues (1999) reported that, compared to normal controls, 24-hour UFC and urinary catecholamine concentrations were elevated in children (Tanner stage < III) with chronic PTSD pursuant to early, severe, and prolonged maltreatment. UFC and urinary catecholamine levels were also correlated positively with the duration of abuse and the number and severity of PTSD symptoms. These children's UFC concentrations, however, were only marginally higher than nonabused, clinically anxious children. Some of the children from this study were part of a larger neuroimaging study that revealed smaller brain volumes and smaller corpus callosum size but not smaller hippocampal volumes in maltreated children with PTSD relative to normal controls (DeBellis, Keshavan, et al., 1999). In a very similar set of studies, Carrion and colleagues (2001, 2002) found elevated salivary GC levels over the day in maltreated, PTSD children relative to normal controls. Using the subjects from the cortisol study plus others, they also reported reduced brain volumes and corpus callosum size, lack of hippocampal volume differences, and less asymmetry of the prefrontal cortex.

There is also evidence that depression interacts with maltreatment history to produce heightened LHPA activity. Thus, in a study of 7- to 15-year-old sexually abused girls studied within 3 to 4 years of abuse reporting, DeBellis and colleagues (1994) found marginally higher 24-hour GC levels (averaged over 3 days). Consistent with adult depression, they also found blunted ACTH but not GC responses to CRH challenge. Most of the girls in the study were dysthymic, and nearly half had attempted suicide. In contrast, J. Kaufman and colleagues (1997) found that depressed, maltreated 7- to 13-year-old children exhibited larger ACTH responses to CRH than did nondepressed maltreated children. However, this was true only of the girls who were still living under conditions of ongoing economic and social adversity. Similarly, in a study of DEX suppression, adolescent girls with PTSD pursuant to early abuse showed similar suppression of the HPA axis to the low-dose DEX test compared to a trauma/no PTSD and normal control group. Only the traumatized girls who met criteria for clinical de-

pression differed, exhibiting less DEX suppression than the other girls. Finally, there are two studies of depressed, maltreated children that have used Cicchetti's day camp paradigm to collect salivary cortisol measures (Hart, Gunnar, & Cicchetti, 1996; J. Kaufman, 1991). In both of these studies, depressed, maltreated children exhibited increasing GC levels over the camp day, but this was not observed among the nondepressed maltreated children or among the comparison children. As in the J. Kaufman et al. (1997) study, many of these depressed children were living under conditions of ongoing adversity. This was also true of maltreated children with internalizing behavior disorders studied by Cicchetti and Rogosch (2001a, 2001b). These children had higher 9 A.M. and 4 P.M. salivary GC levels averaged over 5 days of summer camp than did nonabused children with clinical levels of internalizing problems.

As noted earlier, children with externalizing problems in the absence of comorbid anxiety disorders and those with aggressive, oppositional dispositions in the nonclinical range tend to exhibit low levels of LHPA activity. If maltreatment increases LHPA activity in these children, their basal cortisol following maltreatment may not appear elevated compared to nondisordered controls, but they may still be elevated relative to nonmaltreated children with externalizing problems. Indeed, Hart and colleagues (1995) found that median cortisol levels at school did not differ among maltreated preschoolers relative to age-, sex-, and economically matched controls. However, maltreated children did exhibit less day-to-day cortisol variability, especially if they were *less* socially competent, or rather, more aggressive and undercontrolled. In addition, among the maltreated children who were so out of control that they had to be gently restrained, cortisol levels on the days requiring restraint were lower than on days when the children's behavior was more appropriate. Cicchetti and Rogosch (2001b) also found that maltreated boys, but not girls, with clinical levels of externalizing problems had higher cortisol levels at summer camp relative to nonmaltreated boys with externalizing problems. For the maltreated, externalizing boys, however, cortisol levels were not elevated over levels exhibited by nondisordered, nonmaltreated controls.

Not all maltreated children exhibit these effects. Children without behavior disorders have not been shown to have elevated basal cortisol levels (see Cicchetti & Rogosch, 2001b). These children, however, may have experienced less prolonged, varied, and/or severe maltreatment (Cicchetti & Rogosch, 2001a) and/or may be less genetically vulnerable (J. Kaufman et al., 1998). And, as noted, the presence of ongoing adversity and family dysfunction may contribute to heightened LHPA activity in maltreated children. Despite all that remains to be understood regarding maltreatment and LHPA activity during childhood, we can at least conclude that there is little evidence of hypofunctioning or lowered basal GC levels in maltreated children, unlike the results described in studies of adults who were maltreated as children.

This difference between hypercortisolism in studies of children and hypocortisolism in studies of adults has led some to argue that hypofunctioning at the level of the adrenal, at least, emerges as a function of living for a prolonged period of time with the sequelae of trauma exposure (Yehuda et al., 2001). A longitudinal study of sexually abused girls by Frank Putnam and colleagues is cited as the best evidence for a transition from hyper- to hypofunctioning. Unfortunately, as yet, most of the results of this study are available only as conference presentations. Putnam and colleagues (Frank Putnam, personal communication, June 10, 2003) collected a group of sexually abused girls (averaging 11 years of age) who were first studied within 6 months of the abuse reporting. At this point, elevated cortisol levels were reported for girls tested in the morning hours; suppressed levels were noted for a small group of girls who self-selected into an early afternoon testing slot. DeBellis and colleagues (1994), in the study described earlier, examined a small subsample of these girls several years after abuse reporting. At that time, measures of cortisol (24-hour UFC, late afternoon baseline, response to CRH) did not differ from nonmaltreated controls. Nonetheless, low baseline ACTH and blunted ACTH responses to CRH were noted. This pattern of hypopituitary ACTH and normal cortisol activity suggests that the adrenal may have been hyperresponsive to ACTH in these girls at this point in their development. That is, the adrenal was able to sustain normal GC levels despite reduced ACTH drive. Finally, at a 7-year follow-up visit, when most of the girls were in their teens, evidence of hypocortisolism was obtained. Specifically, the previously maltreated girls had *lower* plasma GC levels than controls both at the beginning of a laboratory cognitive task and in serial samples obtained over the 30-minute cognitive challenge. Thus, this study suggests a transition from hyper- to hypocortisolism with time or pubertal development. Clearly, more longitudinal work is needed to examine dynamic changes in LHPA activity pursuant to early maltreatment and family adversity.

In this respect, an ongoing study of response to the trauma of a natural disaster may provide some useful insights. Children exposed at around age 8 to the 1988 Armenian earthquake have been examined at 5 and 6.5 years following the disaster (Goenjian et al., 1996, 2003). The children were recruited from two towns, one near the epicenter that experienced incredible destruction and loss of life, and one farther away that was much less devastated. Children living near the epicenter exhibited more evidence of PTSD and depression than did those farther from the epicenter. Using one sample of children studied 5 years posttrauma, the researchers reported prolonged suppression to low-dose DEX of the adrenocortical axis in the more traumatized children, along with lower early morning, but not late afternoon, basal cortisol levels. Drawing another sample from these cities, 6.5 years posttrauma lower basal ACTH, but not cortisol, levels were noted. However, in this study, no differences in ACTH or cortisol responses to a mild exercise stressor were obtained. In both cases, measures of LHPA functioning were negatively correlated with PTSD and depression scores. These children, who were in their early adolescent years when tested, tended to exhibit the suppression of LHPA axis functioning that has been more characteristic of the adult PTSD than child PTSD literature. Although this could be because they were tested many years after the trauma exposure, several of the studies described earlier (e.g., Carrion et al., 2002; DeBellis, Baum, et al., 1999) that examined younger children were also conducted after at least this many years had transpired since the *onset* of maltreatment. This would seem to leave concurrent adversity and age at assessment (childhood versus adolescence) as critical variables needing further exploration. Of course, the neurobiological sequelae of trauma due to maltreatment and trauma due to natural disaster may well be different.

Another factor that confounds our understanding of the impact of abuse on the developing LHPA system is that many maltreated children also experience significant neglect. Neglect, while it may characterize deficient or depriving care, needs to be considered separately from abuse, as it may not, by itself, be traumatic or frightening to children. Furthermore, neglect or deprivation of care is more similar to the primate deprivation rearing paradigms (i.e., isolation, surrogate-peer rearing), which, as noted, tend to be associated with few long-term effects on the LHPA system. In most studies of maltreatment, it is extremely difficult to isolate the effects of neglect from other types of abuse, as children who are physically, sexually, and/or emotionally abused are also likely to be neglected. Indeed, in a study of nearly 400 maltreated children, after careful background checks, Cicchetti and Rogosch (2001a) were able to identify only 8% of their summer camp population as having been subject solely to neglect. Furthermore, neglect-only histories were not associated with altered GC levels among the children studied in the day camp paradigm.

Most of the work on LHPA effects of severe neglect comes from studies of institutionally reared children. Here there is evidence of marked abnormalities in diurnal GC patterns for infants and toddlers living in institutions in Russia and Eastern Europe (as reviewed in Gunnar & Vazquez, 2001). Specifically, low early morning GC levels and a general lack of diurnal variation have been found. These results mimic those reported for rhesus infants in surrogate-peer rearing paradigms (Boyce et al., 1995). It is unlikely that the lack of what has been called the short or daytime rhythm (wake-up to bedtime) is permanent, as several years after adoption, most institutionally reared children exhibit fairly normal decreases in cortisol from wake-up to bedtime (Gunnar, Morison, Chisholm, & Schuder, 2001). There is some evidence that those from the most deprived preadoption environments, however, may exhibit slightly elevated salivary GC levels at least at some times during the day (Gunnar et al., 2001). In a recent study of postinstitutionalized children adopted from around the world, slightly higher early morning GC levels were noted only for those children who also were physically stunted at adoption and/or had parents who reported that the children experienced extreme privation prior to adoption (Kertes, Madsen, & Gunnar, 2005). Given these data, it seems likely that basal GC levels may not be strongly affected by early deprivation in human children. If so, this conclusion would be consistent with much of the animal data we reviewed earlier. What has not been studied yet is whether *reactivity* of the LHPA system is altered in children pursuant to early deprivation.

CONCLUSIONS AND FUTURE DIRECTION

In the nearly 50 years since Levine (1957) published the paper in *Science* that launched this field of inquiry, we have learned a great deal about how regulation of the LHPA system in early development influences the development of stress vulnerability and resilience. In rats, monkeys, and children, it is now well established that caregivers are potent regulators of this neuroendocrine system. In primates, sensitive, responsive care from mothers and other nurturing figures buffers the system from being activated when youngsters confront strange or threatening events. In rats, maternal behaviors surrounding feeding bouts keep this system operating in low ranges characteristic of the stress-hyporesponsive period. In rats, monkeys, and children, separation can provoke large increases in the activity of this system, especially when separation results in a reduction in nurturance from the mother and other nurturing figures and confronts the youngster with conditions that are frightening.

We are still a long way, though, from understanding how disturbances in early care may affect the development of this system. Tremendous advances have been made in understanding these processes at the molecular level in rats. In rats, we also have a fairly detailed understanding of the developmental neurobiology of this system in relation to other neural systems involved in stress reactivity and regulation. However, as we have seen, translating the rodent findings to primates and humans is not trivial. One unanswered problem is how best to map developmental periods across species. There is no agreed upon metric. The 1st week of life in the rat is often mapped to the last trimester of gestation in humans. Each month of development in monkeys is often mapped to 4 months in humans. However, this mapping is largely based on motor maturity. Clearly, a better metric would be based on the development of the specific neural systems, in this case, the components of the LHPA system and its corticolimbic regulatory pathways. However, we lack so much information about the normative developmental neurobiology of the relevant systems in the monkey and the human that any attempt at mapping the timing from rats to monkeys to humans is crude at best. And of course, in making this mapping we cannot consider all monkeys together. The developmental neurobiology of the marmoset, squirrel monkey, and rhesus will be different. Thus, even translating across monkey species is fraught with questions about developmental neurobiology that cannot yet be answered. Yet another consideration is the fact that cortical development and therefore executive function differ among rodents, monkeys, and humans. Thus, we might expect that aspects of early experience, stress, and emotion regulation that depend on the development of corticolimbic circuits will be difficult to map across species.

One solution to this problem might seem to be to abandon preclinical models. If we are interested in human development, concentrate on studies of human development. However, there are good reasons this is not the best solution. In human infants and children, we can measure the production of GCs noninvasively using salivary measures of cortisol. We can also measure DHEA, an androgenic steroid hormone that is believed to have anticortisol effects (see, e.g., Granger & Kivlighan, 2003). However, as this review has repeatedly demonstrated, activity of the LHPA system at the level of the adrenal (cortisol and DHEA) is only part of the story. The impact of early experiences on activity of the LHPA system can be seen at higher levels of the system (e.g., pituitary), even when it is not readily apparent at the adrenal level. Currently, blood sampling is needed to assess ACTH. Unless techniques are developed that allow noninvasive assessment of ACTH in infants and children, those of us conducting developmental studies with children will be limited in what we can understand when only humans are a part of the developmental analysis.

More critical, the long history of research that was reviewed in this chapter demonstrates that many of the important impacts of early experiences are likely operating at levels above the pituitary. Recall that in rats, early experience manipulations during the SHRP appear to produce no responses at the pituitary and adrenal level. However, measures of early genes in the hypothalamus indicate that the mpPVN may be responsive to these manipulations (see review by Cirulli & Alleva, 2003). Thus, CRH may increase in the hypothalamus and likely also in extrahypothalamic regions during the period when it is difficult to elevate ACTH and GCs in the rat. CRH in rats has been shown to have effects on the developing hippocampus and likely on other neural systems involved in stress reactivity and regulation. We do not know whether this is true in human development or, if it is true, when during development these effects might be observed. However, findings such as these should make us very wary of relying only on measures of cortisol and ACTH to understand whether activity of the LHPA system may mediate the effects of early perturbations. Thus, we need the preclinical models because of the opportunity they provide to perform the highly invasive procedures that allow measures of central CRH activity and explication of the molecular processes through which the activity of stress-sensitive systems may affect brain development. However, we must be very cautious in translating these models directly to human development.

The monkey studies provide an important lesson in this regard. These studies, along with some of the recent work with rats, challenge us to understand and integrate the impact of early experiences on corticolimbic stress and emotion regulatory pathways into the neuroendocrine early experience story. They also point to the possibility that activity of the LHPA system may be significant in shaping postnatal brain development in primates, without at the same time affecting the neurobiology of the HPA system proper. It seems very likely that some of the molecular

events that permanently alter activity of the HPA system in rodents during the first 2 postnatal weeks are events, which, if they operate in primates (including humans), typically occur prior to birth. Although this still needs to be determined, it is clear that corticolimbic pathways that are involved in regulating emotional, behavioral, and physiological responses to perturbations are immature at birth in primates and that these systems exhibit very protracted postnatal development. In humans, it is likely that these systems are not fully mature until late adolescence. The molecular evidence obtained in preclinical studies of rats and mice clearly indicates that GCs are involved in regulating genes that affect the development of relevant corticolimbic pathways and their neurotransmitter systems. Thus, it is likely that postnatal experiences that affect concurrent GC activity may affect the development frontal systems underlying stress vulnerability and resilience, without at the same time affecting the neuroanatomy and physiology of the HPA system. As noted, in primates, including humans, the time when GCs might affect developing corticolimbic pathways without altering the neurobiology of the HPA system probably covers much of the postnatal developmental period.

If true, this alters the end points we need to be examining in studies of monkeys and humans. Unlike in the rat, we are probably not looking for evidence of endogenous dysregulation of the HPA system. And, if we find this evidence, as has been shown in studies of adults who were maltreated as children, it probably means that the mechanisms are not the same as those uncovered in preweaning studies of rodents. Instead, we need to be examining measures of the relevant stress- and emotion-regulating corticolimbic systems. And, for those of us interested in whether disturbances in regulation of the LHPA system in early life may have altered development of these later-maturing systems, we need to be assessing activity of the LHPA system during the time when we expect these effects may be occurring.

Here we are in relatively uncharted waters; however, as demonstrated in this review, there are a number of indicators that this approach will be fruitful. First, there are several indications that activity of the LHPA system, as measured using salivary cortisol, predicts the emergence of emotional problems even when those problems are not apparent at the time of cortisol assessment. Thus, in the work by Essex and colleagues (Essex et al., 2002; Smider et al., 2002), higher later afternoon cortisol levels when children were 4.5 years of age were not correlated with behavior problems at that time, but they predicted the emergence of behavior problems 1 and 2 years later. Second, in adolescents at risk for depression, spiking cortisol one or more times over the course of basal assessment predicted the onset of depression within the next few months (Goodyer et al., 2000). This was the case even though studies of early-onset depression under highly controlled conditions indicate that the LHPA system functions normally in children and adolescents with MDD (Ryan, 1998). Third, studies of children reared in orphanages reveal very atypical patterns of basal cortisol production while the children are in these orphanages. However, once adopted into families, most of the children display normal patterns of diurnal cortisol activity (Kertes et al., 2005). This is true despite that fact that many of the postinstitutionalized children with typical patterns of cortisol production exhibit elevated behavioral problems. Certainly, the studies just described do not prove the point. However, they do raise the possibility that longitudinal studies tracing relationships between LHPA regulation and adverse patterns of care during periods of rapid corticolimbic development are needed, rather than focusing our attention so narrowly on dysregulation of the LHPA system as the critical end point.

The primate studies and the presumed maturity of the LHPA system early in infancy in humans should also caution us against interpreting altered patterns of GC activity in children from adverse life conditions as evidence of dysregulation of the LHPA system. Rather, it is possible that differences in GC production under basal or response conditions may reflect ongoing adversity in the child's life. Overall, we have probably paid too little attention to children's current life circumstances in assessing LHPA activity in high-risk populations. As mentioned, sleep disturbances, unpredictable bedtimes and wake-up times, family conflict, and other circumstances of children's daily lives can affect basal GC levels, diurnal patterns of GC production, and reactivity to stressors. Assessing the impact of experiences earlier in life on current activity of the LHPA system should be greatly enhanced by careful attention to such factors in the child's life at the time of assessment. Again, as demonstrated in the work by Essex and colleagues (2002), neither early nor concurrent circumstances may be associated with GC levels in children; however, when combined, the interaction may be highly predictive. Also, as demonstrated by J. Kaufman and colleagues (1997), what appears to be dysregulation of the LHPA system may on closer inspection be evidence that when children are living in highly stressful families, their system is more sensitive to stimulation.

A call to include better assessments of the stressfulness of children's current life circumstances, however, presumes that we have a good understanding of the characteristics of situations that activate the LHPA system in children of different ages. We don't. There is good evidence in infants and young children that the security of the parent-child attachment system predicts the power of the parent's presence to buffer increases in GCs to novel, arousing, or distress-eliciting events (see review by Gunnar & Donzella, 2002). Work by Flinn and England (1995) clearly suggest that significant family conflicts can provoke elevations in GCs in children that may last several days. However, we have no clear theory of the psychosocial processes that impact the activity of the LHPA system in children. The meta-analysis of laboratory stressors used in studies of adults (Dickerson & Kemeny, 2004) may provide some guidelines for developing such a theory in developmental research. Indeed, the time may be ripe for a similar meta-analytic synthesis of the research on children. Certainly, we need clear guidelines so that we can develop laboratory paradigms that actually produce elevations in GCs in children and adolescents if we are to move beyond primarily basing our research on measures of basal and/or pretest GC levels.

In addition, we need to better understand the interaction between early experiences and individual differences in predispositions to different disorders. As demonstrated in this review, there does not seem to be a sharp or qualitative difference in the association of LHPA activity for children with behavior problems and those with temperaments or emotional dispositions that place them at risk for developing these disorders. Children with anxiety disorders tend to be more stress-reactive, but those with shy or inhibited temperament also tend to exhibit higher GC activity, at least under certain conditions. Children with disruptive behavior disorders (in the absence of comorbid anxiety) tend to exhibit low GC activity. However, school-age and older children with externalizing behaviors within the normal or nonclinical range also show negative correlations between cortisol levels and externalizing behaviors. We need a better understanding of the neurobiology of these individual differences. We also need models that will help us predict the impact of adverse experiences on the developing stress system of children with these different dispositions. These models will likely include an understanding of the role of experience in gene expression (e.g., Bennett et al., 2002). With regard to studies of LHPA activity, this will likely mean understanding how GCs and CRH interact with genes regulating the activity of monoamine systems involved in anxiety and disruptive behaviors. However, as research in developmental psychopathology has amply demonstrated, transactional models are needed to understand development, and these models need to include how individuals influence and increasingly select their environments. Thus, research on early experiences, stress neurobiology, and developmental psychopathology will likely benefit from advances in molecular genetics, particularly if studies can be conducted in which gene and environment interactions are investigated and with a focus on how individuals both influence and are influenced by their experiences over time.

As this review demonstrates, research on early experience and stress has been fruitful. Despite this, as we attempt to adequately translate the preclinical research into its appropriate implications for human development, we have our work cut out for us. Based on the human research that has already been conducted, there is ample reason to believe that there are insights to be gained by pursuing such translational research. As the work thus far indicates, however, the translation is not likely to be direct. Nonetheless, animal models are needed to help explicate the mechanisms that transduce experience into altered neurobiological development. Adequate translation and integration of early experience stress research, therefore, will require researchers to be familiar with not only the findings but also the challenges of translating preclinical studies. This forms the basis for our final argument about future directions for this research area: Much more attention is needed in training human and animal researchers in translation and integration. To move this field forward most fruitfully, researchers studying human development need to understand both the promises and pitfalls of using the early experience animal studies as the basis for predictions about human development. Similarly, researchers doing preclinical work need to go beyond suggesting that their findings have implications for human development. Somehow, the bridge between those doing human developmental and those doing animal developmental research on early experiences and stress vulnerability needs to be built so that we can make real progress in understanding how adverse early experiences increase the risk for psychopathology.

REFERENCES

Adam, E. K. (2002, April). *Momentary emotion and cortisol activity in adolescents' everyday lives.* Paper presented at the Society for Research on Adolescence, New Orleans, LA.

Ahnert, L., Gunnar, M., Lamb, M., & Barthel, M. (2004). Transition to child care: Associations with infant-mother attachment, infant negative emotion and cortisol elevations. *Child Development, 75,* 639–650.

Anderson, D. J., & Michelsohn, A. (1989). Role of glucocorticoids in the chromaffin neurondevelopmental decision. *International Journal of Developmental Neuroscience, 7,* 475–487.

Andrews, M. W., & Rosenblum, L. A. (1994). The development of affiliative and agonistic social patterns in differentially reared monkeys. *Child Development, 65,* 1398–1404.

Ashman, S. B., Dawson, G., Panagiotides, H., Yamada, E., & Wilkinson, C. W. (2002). Stress hormone levels of children of depressed mothers. *Development and Psychopathology, 14,* 333–349.

Avishai-Eliner, S., Brunson, K. L., Sandman, C. A., & Baram, T. Z. (2002). Stressed-out, or in utero? *Trends in Neuroscience, 25,* 518–524.

Avishai-Eliner, S., Yi, S. J., & Baram, T. Z. (1996). Developmental profile of messenger RNA for the corticotropin-releasing hormone receptor in the rat limbic system. *Brain Research and Developmental Brain Research, 91,* 159–163.

Barnett, D., Manly, J. T., & Cicchetti, D. (1993). Defining child maltreatment: The interface between policy and research. In D. Cicchetti & S. L. Toth (Eds.), *Child abuse, child development, and social policy* (Vol. 8, pp. 7–73). Rochester, NY: ABLEX.

Bartels, M., van den Berg, M., Sluyter, F., Boomsma, D., & de Geus, E. (2003). Heritability of cortisol levels: Review and simultaneous analysis of twin studies. *Psychoneuroendocrinology, 28,* 121–137.

Bayart, F., Hayashi, K. T., Faull, K. F., Barchas, J. D., & Levine, S. (1990). Influence of maternal proximity on behavioral and physiological responses to separation in infant rhesus monkeys (Macaca mulatta). *Behavioral Neuroscience, 104,* 98–107.

Bennett, A. J., Lesch, K. P., Heils, A., Long, J. C., Lorenz, J. G., Shoal, S. E., et al. (2002). Early experience and serotonin transporter gene variation interact to influence primate CNS function. *Molecular Psychiatry, 7,* 118–122.

Biondi, M., & Picardi, A. (1999). Psychological stress and neuroendocrine function in humans: The last two decades of research. *Psychotherapy and Psychosomatics, 68,* 114–150.

Biol-N'garagba, M. C., Niepceron, E., Mathian, B., & Louisot, P. (2003). Glucocorticoid-induced maturation of glycoprotein galactosylation and fucosylation processes in the rat small intestine. *Journal of Steroid Biochemistry and Molecular Biology, 84,* 411–422.

Bohler, H., Zoeller, R., King, J., Rubin, B., Weber, R., & Merriam, G. (1990). Corticotropin releasing hormone mRNA is elevated on the afternoon of proestrus in the parvocellular paraventricular nuclei of the female rat. *Brain Research and Molecular Brain Research, 8,* 259–262.

Born, J., Hansen, K., Marshall, L., Molle, M., & Fehm, H. L. (1999). Timing the end of nocturnal sleep. *Nature, 397,* 29–30.

Bowlby, J. (1969). *Attachment and loss: Attachment* (Vol. 1). New York: Basic Books.

Bowlby, J. (1973). *Attachment and loss: Separation* (Vol. 2). New York: Basic Books.

Boyce, W. T., Champoux, M., Suomi, S. J., & Gunnar, M. R. (1995). Salivary cortisol in nursery reared rhesus monkeys: Reactivity to peer interactions and altered circadian activity. *Developmental Psychobiology, 28,* 257–267.

Bremner, J. D., & Vermetten, E. (2001). Stress and development: Behavioral and biological consequences. *Development and Psychopathology, 13,* 473–490.

Bremner, J. D., Vythilingam, N., Vermeetn, E., Adil, J., Khan, S., Nazeer, A., et al. (2003). Cortisol response to a cognitive stress challenge in posttraumatic stress disorder (PTSD) related to childhood abuse. *Psychoneuroendocrinology, 28,* 733–750.

Bruce, J., Davis, E. P., & Gunnar, M. (2002). Individual differences in children's cortisol response to the beginning of a new school year. *Psychoneuroendocrinology, 27,* 635–650.

Bugnon, C., Fellmann, D., Gouget, A., & Cardot, J. (1982). Ontogeny of the corticoliberin neuroglandular system in rat brain. *Nature, 298,* 159.

Buijs, R. M., Wortel, J., van Heerikhuize, J. J., Feenstra, M. G., Horst, G. J. T., Romijn, H. J., et al. (1999). Anatomical and functional demonstration of a multisynaptic suprachiasmatic adrenal (cortex) pathway. *European Journal of Neuroscience, 11,* 1535–1544.

Burgess, L. H., & Handa, R. J. (1992). Chronic estrogen-induced alterations in adrenocorticotropin and corticosterone secretion, and glucocorticoid receptor-mediated functions in female rats. *Endocrinology, 131,* 1261–1269.

Burke, J. D., Loeber, R., & Birmaher, B. (2002). Oppositional defiant disorder and conduct disorder: A review of the past 10 years, Part II. *Journal of the American Acadamy of Child and Adolescent Psychiatry, 41,* 1275–1293.

Buss, K. A., Davidson, R. J., Kalin, N., & Goldsmith, H. H. (2004). Context-specific freezing and associated physiological reactivity as a dysregulated fear response. *Developmental Psychology, 40,* 583–594.

Buss, K. A., Schumacher, J. R. M., Dolski, I., Kalin, N. H., Goldsmith, H. H., & Davidson, R. J. (2003). Right frontal brain activity, cortisol, and withdrawal behavior in 6-month-old infants. *Behavioral Neuroscience, 117,* 11–20.

Cannon, W. B. (1914). The emergency function of the adrenal medulla in pain and the major emotions. *American Journal of Physiology, 33,* 356–372.

Capitanio, J. P., Rasmussen, K. L. R., Snyder, D. S., Laudenslager, M. L., & Reite, M. (1986). Long term followup of previously separated pigtail macaques: Group and individual differences in response to novel situations. *Journal of Child Psychology and Psychiatry, 27,* 531–538.

Cardenas, S. P., Parra, C., Bravo, J., Morales, P., Lara, H. E., Herrera-Marschitz, M., et al. (2002). Corticosterone differentially regulates bax, bcl-2 and bcl-x mRNA levels in the rat hippocampus. *Neuroscience Letters, 331,* 9–12.

Carrion, V., Weems, C., Eliez, S., Patwardhan, A., Brown, W., Ray, R., et al. (2001). Attenuation of frontal asymmetry in pediatric posttraumatic stress disorder. *Biological Psychiatry, 50,* 943–951.

Carrion, V., Weems, C., Ray, R., Glaser, B., Hessl, D., & Reiss, A. (2002). Diurnal salivary cortisol in pediatric posttraumatic stress disorder. *Biological Psychiatry, 51,* 575–582.

Champoux, M., Coe, C., Schanberg, S., Kuhn, C., & Suomi, S. (1989). Hormonal effects of early rearing conditions in the infant rhesus monkey. *American Journal of Primatology, 19,* 111–117.

Chrousos, G. P., & Gold, P. W. (1992). The concepts of stress and stress system disorders: Overview of physical and behavioral homeostasis. *Journal of the American Medical Association, 267*(9), 1244–1252.

Cicchetti, D., & Rogosch, F. A. (2001a). Diverse patterns of neuroendocrine activity in maltreated children. *Development and Psychopathology, 13,* 677–720.

Cicchetti, D., & Rogosch, F. (2001b). The impact of child maltreatment and psychopathology on neuroendocrine functioning. *Development and Psychopathology, 13,* 783–804.

Cicchetti, D., & Tucker, D. (1994). Development and self-regulatory structures of the mind. *Development and Psychopathology, 6,* 533–549.

Cirulli, F., & Alleva, B. E. (2003). Early disruption of the mother-infant relationship: Effects on brain plasticity and implications for psychopathology. *Neuroscience and Biobehavioral Reviews, 27,* 73–82.

Clarke, A. S. (1993). Social rearing effects on HPA axis activity over early development and in response to stress in rhesus monkeys. *Developmental Psychobiology, 26,* 433–446.

Coe, C., Glass, J., Wiener, S., & Levine, S. (1983). Behavioral, but not physiological, adaptation to repeated separation in mother and infant primates. *Psychoneuroendocrinology, 8,* 401–409.

Coplan, J., Andrews, M., Rosenblum, L., Owens, M., Friedman, S., Gorman, J., et al. (1996). Persistent elevations of cerebrospinal fluid concentrations of corticotropin-releasing factor in adult nonhuman primates exposed to early-life stressors: Implications for the pathophysiology of mood and anxiety disorders. *Proceedings of the National Academy of Sciences of the United States of America, 93,* 1619–1623.

Critchlow, V., Liebelt, R., Bar-Sela, M., Mountcastle, W., & Lipscomb, H. (1963). Sex difference in resting pituitary-adrenal function in the rat. *American Journal of Physiology, 205,* 807–815.

Dahl, R., Ryan, N., Puig-Antich, J., Nguyen, N., al-Shabbout, M., Meyer, V., et al. (1991). 24-hour cortisol measures in adolescents with major depression: A controlled study. *Biological Psychiatry, 30,* 25–36.

Dahl, R., Siegel, S., Williamson, D., Lee, P., Perel, J., Birmaher, B., et al. (1992). Corticotropin releasing hormone stimulation test and nocturnal cortisol levels in normal children. *Pediatric Research, 32,* 64–68.

Dallman, M., Akana, S., Scribner, K., Bradbury, M., Walker, C., Strack, A., et al. (1992). Stress, feedback and facilitation in the hypothalamo-pituitary-adrenal axis. *Journal of Neuroendocrinology, 4,* 517–526.

Davis, E., Donzella, B., Krueger, W. K., & Gunnar, M. (1999). The start of a new school year: Individual differences in salivary cortisol response in relation to child temperament. *Developmental Psychobiology, 35,* 188 196.

Davis, M. (1992). The role of the amygdala in fear and anxiety. *Annual Review of Neuroscience, 15,* 353–375.

Davis, M., & Emory, E. (1995). Sex differences in neonatal stress reactivity. *Child Development, 66,* 14–27.

Dawes, M., Dorn, L., Moss, H., Yao, J., Kirisci, L., Ammerman, R., et al. (1999). Hormonal and behavioral homeostasis in boys at risk for substance abuse. *Drug and Alcohol Dependence, 55,* 165–176.

Dawson, G., & Ashman, S. (2000). On the origins of a vulnerability to depression: The influence of early social environment on the development of psychobiological systems related to risk for affective disorder. In C. A. Nelson (Ed.), *Minnesota Symposia on Child Psychology: Vol. 31. The effects of adversity on neurobehavioral development* (pp. 245–278). New York: Erlbaum.

DeBellis, M. D., Baum, A., Birmaher, B., Keshavan, M., Eccard, C., Boring, A., et al. (1999). Developmental traumatology: Pt. 1. Biological stress systems. *Biological Psychiatry, 9,* 1259–1270.

DeBellis, M. D., Chrousos, G., Dorn, L., Burke, L., Helmers, K., Kling, M., et al. (1994). Hypothalamic-pituitary-adrenal axis dysregulation in sexually abused girls. *Journal of Clinical Endocrinology and Metabolism, 78,* 249–255.

DeBellis, M. D., Keshavan, M., Clark, D., Casey, B., Giedd, J., Boring, A., et al. (1999). Developmental traumatology: Pt. 2. Brain development. *Biological Psychiatry, 45,* 1271–1284.

de Haan, M., Gunnar, M., Tout, K., Hart, J., & Stansbury, K. (1998). Familiar and novel context yield different associations between cortisol and behavior among 2-year-olds. *Developmental Psychobiology, 31,* 93–101.

de Kloet, E. R. (1991). Brain corticosteroid receptor balance and homeostatic control. *Frontiers in Neuroendocrinology, 12,* 95–164.

Delany, A., Gabbitas, B., & Canalis, E. (1995). Cortisol downregulates osteoblast alpha 1 (I) procollagen mRNA by transcriptional and posttranscriptional mechanisms. *Journal of Cellular Biochemistry, 57,* 488–494.

Denenberg, V. H. (1999). Commentary: Is maternal stimulation the mediator of the handling effects in infancy? *Developmental Psychobiology, 34,* 1–3.

De Olmos, J., Alheid, G., & Beltramino, C. (1985). *The rat nervous system* (Vol. 1). San Diego: Academic Press.

Dettling, A., Feldon, J., & Pryce, C. (2002). Repeated parental deprivation in the infant common marmoset and analysis of its effects on early development. *Biological Psychiatry, 52*, 1037–1046.

Dettling, A., Gunnar, M., & Donzella, B. (1999). Cortisol levels of young children in full-day childcare centers: Relations with age and temperament. *Psychoneuroendocrinology, 24*, 505–518.

Dettling, A., Parker, S. W., Lane, S., Sebanc, A., & Gunnar, M. R. (2000). Quality of care and temperament determine whether cortisol levels rise over the day for children in full-day childcare. *Psychoneuroendocrinology, 25*, 819–836.

Dettling, A., Pryce, C. R., Martin, R. D., & Döbeli, M. (1998). Physiological responses to parental separation and a Strange Situation are related to parental care received in juvenile Goeldi's monkeys (Callimico goeldii). *Developmental Psychobiology, 33*, 21–31.

Dickerson, S. S., & Kemeny, M. E. (2004). Acute stressors and cortisol responses: A theoretical integration and synthesis of laboratory research. *Psychological Bulletin, 130*, 355–391.

Diego, M. A., Field, T., Hernandez-Reif, M., Cullen, C., Schanberg, S. M., & Kuhn, C. M. (2004). Prepartum, postpartum, and chronic depression effects on newborns. *Psychiatry, 67*, 63–80.

Dimitriou, T., Maser-Gluth, C., & Remer, T. (2003). Adrenocortical activity in healthy children is associated with fat mass. *American Journal of Clinical Nutrition, 77*, 731–736.

Dobbing, J. (1981). *The later development of the brain and its vulnerability*. London: Heinemann Medical Books.

Donzella, B., Gunnar, M., Krueger, K., & Alwin, A. (2000). Cortisol and vagal tone responses to competitive challenge in preschoolers: Associations with temperament. *Developmental Psychobiology, 37*, 209–220.

Dorn, L. D., Burgess, E. S., Susman, E. J., von Eye, A., DeBellis, M. D., Gold, P. W., et al. (1996). Response to CRH in depressed and nondepressed adolescents: Does gender make a difference? *Journal of the American Academy of Child and Adolescent Psychiatry, 35*, 764–773.

Dorn, L. D., Campo, J. C., Thato, S., Dahl, R. E., Lewin, D., Chandra, R., et al. (2003). Psychological comorbidity and stress reactivity in children and adolescents with recurrent abdominal pain and anxiety disorders. *Journal of the American Academy of Child and Adolescent Psychiatry, 42*, 66–75.

Duman, R. S., Malberg, J., & Thome, J. (1999). Neural plasticity to stress and antidepressant treatment. *Biological Psychiatry, 46*, 1181–1191.

Durham, P. L., Wohlford-Lenane, C. L., & Snyder, J. M. (1993). Glucocorticoid regulation of surfactant associated proteins in rabbit fetal lung in vivo. *Anatomical Record, 237*, 365–377.

Eghbal-Ahmadi, M., Hatalski, C., Lovenberg, T., Avishai-Eliner, S., Chalmers, D., & Baram, T. (1998). The developmental profile of the corticotropin releasing factor receptor (CRF2) in rat brain predicts distinct age-specific functions. *Developmental Brain Research, 107*, 81–90.

Elmlinger, M. W., Kuhnel, W., & Ranke, M. B. (2002). Reference ranges for serum concentrations of flutropin (LH), follitropin (FSH), estradiol (E2), prolactin, progesterone, sex hormone-binding globulin (SHBG), dehydroepiandrosterone sulfate (DHEA), cortisol and ferritin in neonates, children and young adults. *Clinical Chemistry and Laboratory Medicine, 401*, 1151–1160.

Essex, M. J., Klein, J. H., Eunsuk, C., & Kalin, N. H. (2002). Maternal stress beginning in infancy may sensitize children to later stress exposure: Effects on cortisol and behavior. *Biological Psychiatry, 52*, 776–784.

Flinn, M. V., & England, B. G. (1995). Childhood stress and family environment. *Current Anthropolgy, 36*, 1995.

Follenius, M., Brandenberger, G., Bandesapt, J. J., Libert, J. P., & Ehrhart, J. (1992). Nocturnal cortisol release in relation to sleep structure. *Sleep, 15*, 21–27.

Follenius, M., Brandenberger, G., Hietter, B., Simeoni, M., & Reinhardt, B. (1982). Diurnal cortisol peaks and their relationship to meals. *Journal of Clinical Endocrinology and Metabolism, 55*, 757–761.

Forbes, E., Williamson, D., Ryan, N., & Dahl, R. (2004). Positive and negative affect in depression: Influence of sex and puberty. *Annals of the New York Academy of Sciences, 1021*, 341–347.

Francis, D., Diorio, J., Plotsky, P., & Meaney, M. (2002). Environmental enrichment reverses the effects of maternal separation on stress reactivity. *Journal of Neuroscience, 22*, 7840–7843.

Frankenhaeuser, M. (1983). The sympathetic-adrenal and pituitary-adrenal response to challenge: Comparison between the sexes. In T. M. Dembroski, T. H. Cologne, & G. Blumchen (Eds.), *Biobehavioral bases of coronary heart disease* (Vol. 2, pp. 91–105). Basel, Switzerland: Karger.

Frankenhaeuser, M., Rauste von Wright, M., Collins, A., von Wright, J., Sedvall, G., & Swahn, C. (1978). Sex differences in psychoneuroendocrine reactions to examination stress. *Psychosomatic Medicine, 40*, 334–343.

Fraser, M., Matthews, S., Braems, G., Jeffray, T., & Challis, J. (1997). Developmental regulation of preproenkephalin (PENK) gene expression in the adrenal gland of the ovine fetus and newborn lamb: Effects of hypoxemia and exogenous cortisol infusion. *Journal of Endocrinology, 155*, 143–149.

Gala, R. R., & Westphal, U. (1965). Corticosteroid-binding globulin in the rat: Studies on the sex difference. *Endocrinology, 77*, 841–851.

Giannakoulpoulous, X., Sepulveda, W., Kourtis, P., Glover, V., & Fisk, N. M. (1994). Fetal plasma and beta endorphin response to intrauterine needling. *Lancet, 344*, 77–81.

Glaser, D. (2000). Child abuse and neglect and the brain: A review. *Journal of Child and Adolescent Psychiatry, 41*, 97–116.

Goenjian, A. K., Pynoos, R. S., Steinberg, A. M., Endres, D., Abraham, K., Geffner, M. E., et al. (2003). Hypothalamic-pituitary-adrenal activity among Armenian adolescents with PTSD symptoms. *Journal of Traumatic Stress, 16*, 319–323.

Goenjian, A. K., Yehuda, R., Pynoos, R. S., Steinberg, A. M., Tashjian, M., Yang, R., et al. (1996). Basal cortisol, dexamethasone suppression of cortisol, and MHPG in adolescents after the 1988 earthquake in Armenia. *American Journal of Psychiatry, 153*, 929–934.

Gold, P., Goodwin, F., & Chrousos, G. (1988). Clinical and biochemical manifestations of depression: Relations to the neurobiology of stress. *New England Journal of Medicine, 319*, 348–353.

Goldberg, S., Levitan, R., Leung, E., Masellis, M., Basile, V., Nemeroff, C., et al. (2003). Cortisol concentrations in 12- to 18-month-old infants: Stability over time, location, and stressor. *Biological Psychiatry, 54*, 719–726.

Golub, M. S., Sassenrath, E. N., & Goo, G. P. (1979). Plasma cortisol levels and dominance in peer groups of rhesus monkey weanlings. *Hormones and Behavior, 12*, 50–59.

Gomez, M., Malozowski, S., Winterer, J., Vamvoakopoulos, N., & Chrousos, G. P. (1991). Urinary free cortisol values in normal children and adolescents. *Journal of Pediatrics, 118*, 256–258.

Goodyer, I. M., Herbert, J., & Altham, P. (1998). Adrenal steroid secretion and major depression in 8- to 16-year olds, III. Influence of cortisol/DHEA ratio at presentation on subsequent rates of disappointing life events and persistent major depression. *Psychological Medicine, 28*, 265–273.

Goodyer, I. M., Herbert, J., Moor, S., & Altham, P. (1991). Cortisol hypersecretion in depressed school aged children and adolescents. *Psychiatry Research, 37*, 237–244.

Goodyer, I. M., Herbert, J., Tamplin, A., & Altham, P. (2000). First-episode major depression in adolescents: Affective, cognitive and endocrine characteristics of risk status and predictors of onset. *British Journal of Psychiatry, 176,* 142–149.

Goodyer, I. M., Park, R., & Herbert, J. (2001). Psychosocial and endocrine features of chronic first episode major depression in 8–16 year olds. *Biological Psychiatry, 50,* 351–357.

Goodyer, I. M., Park, R. J., Netherton, C. M., & Herbert, J. (2001). Possible role of cortisol and dehydroepiandrosterone in human development and psychopathology. *British Journal of Psychiatry, 173,* 243–249.

Graham, Y. P., Heim, C., Goodman, S. H., Miller, A. H., & Nemeroff, C. B. (1999). The effects of neonatal stress on brain development: Implications for psychopathology. *Development and Psychopathology, 11,* 545–565.

Granger, D., & Kivlighan, K. T. (2003). Integrating biological, behavioral, and social levels of analysis in early child development: Progress, problems, and prospects. *Child Development, 74,* 1–6.

Granger, D., Serbin, L., Schwartzman, A., Lehoux, P., Cooperman, J., & Ikeda, S. (1998). Children's salivary cortisol, internalizing behaviour problems, and family environment: Results from the Concordia longitudinal risk project. *International Journal of Behavioral Development, 22,* 707–728.

Granger, D., Stansbury, K., & Henker, B. (1994). Preschoolers' behavioral and neuroendocrine responses to social challenge. *Merrill-Palmer Quarterly, 40,* 20–41.

Granger, D., Weisz, J. R., & Kauneckis, D. (1994). Neuroendocrine reactivity, internalizing behavior problems, and control-related cognitions in clinic-referred children and adolescents. *Journal of Abnormal Psychology, 103,* 267–276.

Granger, D., Weisz, J. R., & McCracken, J. T. (1996). Reciprocal influences among adrenocortical activation, psychosocial processes, and the behavioral adjustment of clinic-referred children. *Child Development, 67,* 3250–3262.

Grant, S., Forsham, P., & DiRaimondo, V. (1965). Suppression of 17 hydroxycorticosteroids in plasma and urine by single and divided doses of triamcinolone. *New England Journal of Medicine, 273,* 1115–1118.

Grottoli, S., Giordano, R., Maccagno, B., Pellegrino, M., Ghigo, E., & Arvat, E. (2002). The stimulatory effect of canrenoate, a mineralocorticoid antagonist, on the activity of the hypothalamus-pituitary-adrenal axis is abolished by alprazolam, a benzodiazepine, in humans. *Journal of Clinical Endocrinolology and Metabolism, 87,* 4616–4620.

Gunnar, M. (1986). Human developmental psychoendocrinology: A review of research on neuroendocrine responses to challenge and threat in infancy and childhood. In M. Lamb, A. Brown, & B. Rogoff (Eds.), *Advances in developmental psychology* (Vol. 4, pp. 51–103). Hillsdale, NJ: Erlbaum.

Gunnar, M. (1992). Reactivity of the hypothalamic-pituitary-adrenocortical system to stressors in normal infants and children. *Pediatrics, 80,* 491–497.

Gunnar, M., Brodersen, L., Krueger, K., & Rigatuso, J. (1996). Dampening of adrenocortical responses during infancy: Normative changes and individual differences. *Child Development, 67,* 877–889.

Gunnar, M., Brodersen, L., Nachmias, M., Buss, K., & Rigatuso, R. (1996). Stress reactivity and attachment security. *Developmental Psychobiology, 29,* 10–36.

Gunnar, M., & Donzella, B. (2002). Social regulation of the LHPA axis in early human development. *Psychoneuroendocrinology, 27,* 199–220.

Gunnar, M., Gonzalez, C., Goodlin, B., & Levine, S. (1981). Behavioral and pituitary-adrenal responses during a prolonged separation period in infant rhesus macaques. *Psychoneuroendocrinology, 6,* 65–75.

Gunnar, M., Larson, M., Hertsgaard, L., Harris, M., & Brodersen, L. (1992). The stressfulness of separation among 9-month-old infants: Effects of social context variables and infant temperament. *Child Development, 63,* 290–303.

Gunnar, M., Mangelsdorf, S., Larson, M., & Hertsgaard, L. (1989). Attachment, temperament and adrenocortical activity in infancy: A study of psychoendocrine regulation. *Developmental Psychology, 25,* 355–363.

Gunnar, M., Morison, S. J., Chisholm, K., & Schuder, M. (2001). Salivary cortisol levels in children adopted from Romanian orphanages. *Development and Psychopathology, 13,* 611–628.

Gunnar, M., & Nelson, C. A. (1994). Event-related potentials in year-old infants: Relations with emotionality and cortisol. *Child Development, 65,* 80–94.

Gunnar, M., Tout, K., de Haan, M., Pierce, S., & Stansbury, K. (1997). Temperament, social competence, and adrenocortical activity in preschoolers. *Developmental Psychobiology, 31,* 65–85.

Gunnar, M., Tout, K., Donzella, M. A., & van Dulmen, M. (2003). Temperament, peer relationships, and cortisol activity in preschoolers. *Developmental Psychobiology, 43,* 346–358.

Gunnar, M., & Vazquez, D. M. (2001). Low cortisol and a flattening of the expected daytime rhythm: Potential indices of risk in human development. *Development and Psychopathology, 13,* 516–538.

Hadjian, A. J., Chedin, M., Cochet, C., & Chambaz, E. M. (1975). Cortisol binding to proteins in plasma in the human neonate and infant. *Pediatric Research, 9,* 40–45.

Halligan, S., Herbert, J., Goodyer, I. M., & Murray, L. (2004). Exposure to postnatal depression predicts elevated cortisol in adolescent offspring. *Biological Psychiatry, 55,* 376–381.

Hardie, T., Moss, H., Vanyukov, M., Yao, J., & Kirillovac, G. (2002). Does adverse family environment or sex matter in the salivary cortisol responses to anticipatory stress? *Psychiatry Research, 111,* 121–131.

Harlow, H. F., Harlow, M. K., & Suomi, S. J. (1971). From thought to therapy: Lessons from a primate laboratory. *American Scientist, 59,* 538–549.

Harris, G. W. (1948). Neural control of the pituitary gland. *Physiological Review, 28,* 139–179.

Hart, J., Gunnar, M., & Cicchetti, D. (1995). Salivary cortisol in maltreated children: Evidence of relations between neuroendocrine activity and social competence. *Development and Psychopathology, 7,* 11–26.

Hart, J., Gunnar, M., & Cicchetti, D. (1996). Altered neuroendocrine activity in maltreated children related to symptoms of depression. *Development and Psychopathology, 8,* 201–214.

Heim, C., Ehlert, U., Hanker, J. P., & Hellhammer, D. H. (1998). Abuse-related posttraumatic stress disorder and alterations of the hypothalamic-pituitary-adrenal axis in women with chronic pelvic pain. *Psychosomatic Medicine, 60,* 309–318.

Heim, C., Ehlert, U., & Hellhammer, D. K. (2000). The potential role of hypocortisolism in the pathophysiology of stress-related bodily disorders. *Psychoneuroendocrinology, 25,* 1–35.

Heim, C., & Nemeroff, C. B. (2001). The role of childhood trauma in the neurobiology of mood and anxiety disorders: Preclinical and clinical studies. *Biological Psychiatry, 49,* 1023–1039.

Heim, C., Newport, D., Bonsall, R., Miller, A., & Nemeroff, C. (2001). Altered pituitary adrenal axis responses to provocative challenge tests in adult survivors of childhood abuse. *American Journal of Psychiatry, 158,* 575–581.

Heim, C., Newport, D. J., Heit, S., Graham, Y. P., Wilcox, M. B. R., Miller, A. H., et al. (2000). Pituitary-adrenal and autonomic responses to stress in women after sexual and physical abuse in childhood. *Journal of the American Medical Association, 284,* 592–597.

Heim, C., Owen, M., Plotsky, P., & Nemeroff, C. (1997). The role of early adverse life events in the etiology of depression and posttraumatic stress disorder: Focus on corticotropin releasing factor. *Annals of the New York Academy of Science, 821,* 194–207.

Hellhammer, D. H., Buchtal, J., Ingmar, G., & Kirschbaum, C. (1997). Social hierarchy and adrenocortical stress reactivity in men. *Psychoneuroendocrinology, 22,* 643–665.

Hennessy, M. B. (1986). Multiple, brief maternal separations in the squirrel monkey: Changes in hormonal and behavioral responses. *Physiology and Behavior, 36,* 245–250.

Henning, S. (1978). Plasma concentrations of total and free corticosterone during development in the rat. *American Journal of Physiology, 23,* E451–E456.

Herman, J. P., & Cullinan, W. E. (1997). Neurocircuitry of stress: Central control of the hypothalamo pituitary adrenocortical axis. *Trends in Neuroscience, 20,* 78–84.

Herman, J. P., Figueiredo, H., Muller, N. K., Ulrich-Lai, Y., Ostrander, M. M., Choi, D. C., et al. (2003). Central mechanisms of stress integration: Hierarchical circuits controlling hypothalamic pituitary adrenocortical responses. *Frontiers in Endocrinology, 24,* 151–180.

Herman, J. P., Muller, N. K., & Figueiredo, H. (2004). Role of GABA and glutamate circuitry in hypothalamo-pituitary adrenocortical stress integration. *Annals of the New York Academy of Science, 1018,* 35–45.

Herrenkohl, L. R., Ribary, U., Schlumpf, M., & Lichtensteiger, W. (1988). Maternal stress alters monoamine metabolites in fetal and neonatal rat brain. *Experientia, 44,* 457–459.

Higley, J. D., Suomi, S. J., & Linnoila, M. (1992). A longitudinal study of CSF monoamine metabolite and plasma cortisol concentrations in young rhesus monkeys: Effects of early experience, age, sex, and stress on continuity of individual differences. *Biological Psychiatry, 32,* 127–145.

Hill, S. D., McCormack, S. A., & Mason, W. A. (1972). Effects of artificial mothers and visual experiences on adrenal responsiveness in infant monkeys. *Developmental Psychobiology, 6,* 421–429.

Hinde, R. A., & Davies, L. (1972). Removing infant rhesus from mother for 13 days compared with removing mother from infant. *Journal of Child Psychology and Psychiatry and Allied Disciplines, 13,* 227–237.

Hinde, R. A., Leighton-Shapiro, M. E., & McGinnis, L. (1978). Effects of various types of separation experience on rhesus monkeys 5 months later. *Journal of Child Psychology and Psychiatry, 19,* 199–211.

Hiroshige, T., & Wada-Okada, S. (1973). Diurnal changes of hypothalamic content of corticotropin releasing activity in female rats at various stages of the estrous cycle. *Neuroendocrinology, 12,* 316–319.

Holloway, A. C., Whittle, W. L., & Challis, J. R. (2001). Effects of cortisol and estradiol on pituitary expression of proopiomelanocortin, prohormone convertase-1, prohormone convertase 2, and glucocorticoid receptor mRNA in fetal sheep. *Endocrine Journal, 14,* 343–348.

Holsboer, F. (2000). The corticosteroid receptor hypothesis of depression. *Neuropsychopharmacology, 23,* 477–501.

Honour, J. W., Kelnar, C. J. H., & Brook, C. G. D. (1991). Urine steroid excretion rates in childhood reflect growth and activity of the adrenal cortex. *Acta Endocrinologica, 124,* 219–224.

Jansen, L. M. C., Gispen-deWied, C. C., Jasen, M. A., vander Gaag, R.-J., Matthys, W., & van Engeland, H. (1999). Pituitary-adrenal reactivity in a child psychiatric population: Salivary cortisol response to stressors. *European Neuropsychopharmacology, 9,* 67–75.

Jonetz-Mentzel, L., & Wiedemann, G. (1993). Establishment of reference ranges for cortisol in neonates, infants, children and adolescents. *European Journal of Clinical Chemistry and Clinical Biochemistry, 31,* 525–529.

Kagan, J., Reznick, J. S., & Snidman, N. (1987). The physiology and psychology of behavioral inhibition in children. *Child Development, 58,* 1459–1473.

Kalin, N., Shelton, S., & Barksdale, C. (1988). Opiate modulation of separation-induced distress in non-human primates. *Brain Research, 440,* 856–862.

Kalin, N., Shelton, S., & Barksdale, C. (1989). Behavioral and physiologic effects of CRH administered to infant primates undergoing maternal separation. *Neuropsychopharmacology, 2,* 97–104.

Kalin, N., Shelton, S. E., Rickman, M., & Davidson, R. J. (1998). Individual differences in freezing and cortisol in infant and mother rhesus monkeys. *Behavioral Neuroscience, 112,* 251–254.

Kalin, N., Shelton, S. E., & Turner, J. G. (1992). Effects of ß-carboline on fear-related behavioral and neurohormonal responses of infant rhesus monkeys. *Biological Psychiatry, 31,* 1008–1019.

Kaneko, M., Hiroshige, T., Shinsako, J., & Dallman, M. F. (1980). Diurnal changes in amplification of hormone rhythms in the adrenocortical system. *American Journal of Physiology, 239,* 309–316.

Kaufman, I. C., & Rosenblum, L. A. (1967). The reaction to separation in infant monkeys: Anaclitic depression and conservation-withdrawal. *Psychosomatic Medicine, 29,* 648–675.

Kaufman, J. (1991). Depressive disorders in maltreated children. *Journal of the American Academy of Child and Adolescent Psychiatry, 30,* 257–265.

Kaufman, J., Birmaher, B., Brent, D., Dahl, R., Bridge, J., & Ryan, N. D. (1998). Psychopathology in the relatives of depressed-abused children. *Child Abuse and Neglect, 22,* 171–181.

Kaufman, J., Birmaher, B., Perel, J., Dahl, R. E., Moreci, P., Nelson, B., et al. (1997). The corticotropin-releasing hormone challenge in depressed abused, depressed nonabused, and normal control children. *Biological Psychiatry, 42,* 669–679.

Kaufman, J., & Charney, D. S. (2001). Effects of early stress on brain structure and function: Implications for understanding the relationship between child maltreatment and depression. *Development and Psychopathology, 13,* 451–472.

Kerr, J., Beck, S., & Handa, R. (1996). Androgens modulate glucocorticoid receptor mRNA, not mineralocorticoid receptor mRNA levels, in the rat hippocampus. *Journal of Neuroendocrinology, 8,* 439–447.

Kertes, D., & Gunnar, M. (2004). Evening activities as a potential confound in research on the adrenocortical system in children. *Child Development, 75,* 193–204.

Kertes, D. A., Madsen, N. J., & Gunnar, M. (2005). Early deprivation and home basal cortisol levels: A study of internationally-adopted children. Under revision. *Development and Psychopathology.*

Kiess, W., Meidert, R. A., Dressensorfer, K., Schriever, U., Kessler, A., Konig, A., et al. (1995). Salivary cortisol levels throughout childhood and adolescence: Relation with age, pubertal stage, and weight. *Pediatric Research, 37,* 502–506.

King, J. (1998). Attention-deficit hyperactivity disorder and the stress response. *Biological Psychiatry, 44,* 72–74.

Kirschbaum, C., & Hellhammer, D. H. (1989). Salivary cortisol in psychobiological research: An overview. *Neuropsychobiology, 22,* 150–169.

Kirschbaum, C., & Hellhammer, D. H. (1994). Salivary cortisol in psychoneuroendocrine research: Recent developments and application. *Psychoneuroendocrinology, 19,* 313–333.

Kirschbaum, C., Kudielka, B. M., Gaab, J., Schommer, N. C., & Hellhammer, D. H. (1999). Impact of gender, menstrual cycle phase, and oral contraceptives on the activity of the hypothalamus pituitary adrenal axis. *Psychosomatic Medicine, 61,* 154–162.

Kirschbaum, C., Steyer, R., Eid, M., Patalla, U., Schwenkmezger, P., & Hellhammer, D. (1990). Cortisol and behavior: 2. Application of a latent state-trait model to salivary cortisol. *Psychoneuroendocrinology, 15,* 297–307.

Kirschbaum, C., Wüst, S., & Hellhammer, D. (1992). Consistent sex differences in cortisol responses to psychological stress. *Psychosomatic Medicine, 54,* 648–657.

Klimes-Dougan, B., Hastings, P. D., Granger, D. A., Usher, B. A., & Zahn-Waxler, C. (2001). Adrenocortical activity in at-risk and normally developing adolescents: Individual differences in salivary cortisol basal levels, diurnal variation, and responses to social challenges. *Development and Psychopathology, 13,* 695–719.

Korte, S. M. (2001). Corticosteroids in relation to fear, anxiety and psychopathology. *Neuroscience and Biobehavioral Reviews, 25,* 117–142.

Kraemer, G. W. (1992). Psychobiological attachment theory and psychopathology. *Behavioral and Brain Sciences, 15,* 525–541.

Kraemer, G. W., Ebert, M. H., Schmidt, D. E., & McKinney, W. T. (1989). A longitudinal study of the effect of different social rearing conditions on cerebrospinal fluid, norepinephrine and biogenic amine metabolites in rhesus monkeys. *Neuropsychopharmacology, 2,* 175–189.

Kraemer, G. W., Ebert, M. H., Schmidt, D. E., & McKinney, W. T. (1991). Strangers in a strange land: A psychobiological study of infant monkeys before and after separation from real or inanimate mothers. *Child Development, 62,* 548–566.

Kudielka, B. M., Buske-Kirschbaum, A., Hellhammer, D., & Kirschbaum, C. (2004). HPA responses to laboratory psychosocial stress in healthy elderly adults, young adults, and children: Impact of age and gender. *Psychoneuroendocrinology, 29,* 83–98.

Kumar, S., Cole, R., Chiappelli, F., & de Vellis, J. (1989). Differential regulation of oligodendrocyte markers by glucocorticoids: Post-transcriptional regulation of both proteolipid protein and myelin basic protein and transcriptional regulation of glycerol phosphate dehydrogenase. *Proceedings of the National Academy of Sciences, USA, 87,* 6807–6811.

Kutcher, S., Malkin, D., Silverberg, J., Marton, P., Williamson, P., Malkin, A., et al. (1991). Nocturnal cortisol, thyroid stimulating hormone, and growth hormone secretory profiles in depressed adolescents. *Journal of the American Acadamy of Child and Adolescent Psychiatry, 30,* 407–414.

Kwak, S., Morano, M., Young, E., Watson, S., & Akil, H. (1993). Diurnal CRH mRNA in the hypothalamus: Decreased expression in the evening is not dependent on endogenous glucocorticoids. *Neuroendocrinology, 57,* 96–105.

Larson, M., White, B. P., Cochran, A., Donzella, B., & Gunnar, M. (1998). Dampening of the cortisol response to handling at 3-months in human infants and its relation to sleep, circadian cortisol activity, and behavioral distress. *Developmental Psychobiology, 33,* 327–337.

Lashansky, G., Saenger, P., Kishman, K., Gautier, T., Mayes, D., Berg, G., et al. (1991). Normative data for adrenal steroidogenesis in a healthy pediatric population: Age- and sex-related changes after adrenocorticotropin stimulation. *Journal of Clinical Endocrinology and Metabolism, 76,* 674–686.

Laudenslager, M. L., Boccia, M. L., Berger, C. L., Gennaro-Ruggles, M. M., McFerran, B., & Reite, M. L. (1995). Total cortisol, free cortisol, and growth hormone associated with brief social separation experiences in young macaques. *Developmental Psychobiology, 28,* 199–211.

Legendre, A., & Trudel, M. (1996). Cortisol and behavioral responses of young children coping with a group of unfamiliar peers. *Merrill-Palmer Quarterly, 42,* 554–577.

Legro, R. S., Lin, H. M., Demers, L. M., & Lloyd, T. (2003). Urinary free cortisol increases in adolescent Caucasian females during perimenarche. *Journal of Clinical Endocrinology and Metabolism, 88,* 215–219.

Le Mevel, J. C., Abitbol, S., Beraud, G., & Maniey, J. (1979). Temporal changes in plasma adrenocorticotropin concentration after repeated neurotropic stress in male and female rats. *Endocrinology, 105,* 812–817.

Leproult, R., Copinschi, G., Buxton, O., & Van Cauter, E. (1997). Sleep loss results in an elevation of cortisol levels the next evening. *Sleep, 20,* 865–870.

Levine, S. (1957). Infantile experience and resistance to physiological stress. *Science, 126,* 405–406.

Levine, S. (1975). Psychosocial factors in growth and development. In L. Levi (Ed.), *Society, stress and disease* (pp. 43–50). London: Oxford University Press.

Levine, S. (in press). Stress: An historical perspective. In T. Steckler, N. Kalin, & J. M. Reul (Eds.), *Handbook on stress, immunology and behavior.* New York: Academic Press.

Levine, S., Lyons, D. M., & Schatzberg, A. F. (1997). Psychobiological consequences of social relationships. *Annals of the New York Academy of Science, 807,* 210–218.

Levine, S., & Wiener, S. G. (1988). Psychoendocrine aspects of mother-infant relationships in nonhuman primates. *Psychoneuroendocrinology, 13,* 143–154.

Lewis, M., & Ramsay, D. S. (1995). Developmental change in infants' responses to stress. *Child Development, 66,* 657–670.

Lewis, M., & Ramsay, D. S. (1999). Effect of maternal soothing on infant stress response. *Child Development, 70,* 11–20.

Li, J., Gilmour, R. S., Saunders, J. C., Dauncey, M. J., & Fowden, A. L. (1999). Activation of the adult mode of ovine growth hormone receptor gene expression by cortisol during late fetal development. *FASEB Journal, 13,* 545–552.

Liu, C., & Reppert, S. M. (2000). GABA synchronizes clock cells within the suprachiasmatic circadian clock. *Neuron, 25,* 123–128.

Lombroso, P., & Sapolsky, R. (1998). Development of the cerebral cortex: XIII. Stress and brain development. *Journal of the American Academy of Child and Adolescent Psychiatry, 37,* 1337–1339.

Lopez, J., Akil, H., & Watson, S. (1999). Neural circuits mediating stress. *Biological Psychiatry, 46,* 1461–1471.

Losada, A., Tovar, J. A., Xia, H. M., Diez-Pardo, J. A., & Santisteban, P. (2000). Down-regulation of thyroid transcription factor-1 gene expression in fetal lung hypoplasia is restored by glucocorticoids. *Endocrinology, 141,* 2166–2173.

Lubach, G. R., Kittrell, E. M. W., & Coe, C. L. (1992). Maternal influences on body temperature in the infant primate. *Physiology and Behavior, 51,* 987–994.

Luby, J., Heffelfinger, A., Mrakotsky, C., Brown, K., Hessler, M., & Spitznagel, E. (2003). Alterations in stress cortisol reactivity in depressed preschoolers relative to psychiatric and no-disorder comparison groups. *Archives of General Psychology, 60,* 1248–1255.

Lupien, S., King, S., Meaney, M. J., & McEwen, B. (2001). Can poverty get under your skin? Basal cortisol levels and cognitive function in children from low and high socioeconomic status. *Development and Psychopathology, 13,* 653–676.

Lyons, D. M., Wang, O. J., Lindley, S. E., Levine, S., Kalin, N. H., & Schatzberg, A. F. (1999). Separation induced changes in squirrel monkey hypothalamic-pituitary-adrenal physiology resemble aspects of hypercortisolism in humans. *Psychoendocrinology, 24,* 131–142.

Maestripieri, D. (1999). The biology of human parenting: Insights from nonhuman primates. *Neuroscience and Biobehavioral Reviews, 23,* 411–422.

Makino, S., Gold, P. W., & Schulkin, J. (1994). Corticosterone effects on corticotropin-releasing hormone mRNA in the central nucleus of the amygdala and the parvocellular region of the paraventricular nucleus of the hypothalamus. *Brain Research, 640,* 105–112.

Markey, K. A., Towle, A. C., & Sze, P. Y. (1982). Glucocorticoid influence on tyrosine hydroxylase activity in mouse locus coeruleus during postnatal development. *Endocrinology, 111,* 1519–1523.

Martel, F. L., Hayward, C., Lyon, G. M., Sanborn, K., Varady, S., & Schatzberg, A. F. (1999). Salivary cortisol levels in socially phobic adolescent girls. *Depression and Anxiety, 10,* 25–27.

Masten, A. S. (1999). Resilience comes of age: Reflections on the past and outlook for the next generation of research. In M. D. Glantz, J. Johnson, & L. Huffman (Eds.), *Resilience and development: Positive life adaptations* (pp. 281–296). New York: Plenum Press.

Matthews, S. G. (2000). Antenatal glucocorticoids and programming of the developing CNS. *Pediatric Research, 47,* 291–300.

McBurnett, K., & Lahey, B. B. (1994). Psychophysiological and neuroendocrine correlates of conduct disorder and antisocial behavior in children and adolescents. *Progress in Experimental Personality and Psychopathology,* 199–231.

McBurnett, K., Lahey, B. B., Frick, P. J., Risch, C., Loeber, R., Hart, E. L., et al. (1991). Anxiety, inhibition, and conduct disorder in children: II. Relation to salivary cortisol. *Journal of the American Academy of Child and Adolescent Psychiatry, 30,* 192–196.

McBurnett, K., Lahey, B. B., Rathouz, P. K., & Loeber, R. (2000). Low salivary cortisol and persistent aggression in boys referred for disruptive behavior. *Archives of General Psychiatry, 57,* 38–43.

McCormack, K., Grand, A., LaPrairie, J., Fulks, R., Graff, A., Maestripieri, D., et al. (2003). Behavioral and neuroendocrine outcomes of infant maltreatment in rhesus monkeys: The first four months. *Society for Neuroscience Abstracts, 641,* 14.

McCormick, S., & Mendelson, C. (1994). Human SP-A1 and SP-A2 genes are differentially regulated during development and by cAMP and glucocorticoids. *American Journal of Physiology, 266,* 367–374.

McEwen, B. S. (1998). Stress, adaptation, and disease: Allostasis and allostatic load. *Annals of the New York Academy of Science, 840,* 33–44.

McEwen, B. S., Weiss, J. M., & Schwartz, L. S. (1968). Selective retention of corticosterone by limbic structures in rat brain. *Nature, 220,* 911–912.

Menuelle, P., Babajko, S., & Plas, C. (1999). Insulin-like growth factor (IGF) binding proteins modulate the glucocorticoid-dependent biological effects of IGF-II in cultured fetal rat hepatocytes. *Endocrinology, 140,* 2232–2240.

Mesiano, S., & Jaffe, R. B. (1997). Developmental and functional biology of the primate fetal adrenal cortex. *Endocrine Reviews, 18,* 378–403.

Meyer, J. S., & Bowman, R. E. (1972). Rearing experience, stress, and adrenocortical steroids in the rhesus monkey. *Hormones and Behavior, 8,* 339–343.

Michelson, D., Chrousos, G. P., & Gold, P. W. (1994). Type 1 glucocorticoid receptor blockade does not affect baseline or ovine corticotropin releasing hormone, stimulated adrenocorticotropic hormone and cortisol secretion. *Neuroimmunomodulation, 1,* 274–277.

Mitchell, J. B., Iny, L. J., & Meaney, M. J. (1990). The role of serotonin in the development and environmental regulation of type II corticosteroid receptor binding in rat hippocampus. *Brain Research, 55,* 231–235.

Modi, N., Lewis, H., Al-naqeeb, N., Ajayi-obe, M., Dore, C., & Rutherford, M. (2001). The effects of repeated antenatal glucocorticoid therapy on the developing brain. *Pediatric Research, 50,* 581–585.

Moreau, P., Faure, O., Lefebvre, S., Ibrahim, E. C., O'Brien, M., Gourand, L., et al. (2001). Glucocorticoid hormones upregulate levels of HLA-G transcripts in trophoblasts. *Transplantation Proceedings, 33*(3), 2277–2280.

Moss, H. B., Vanyukov, M. M., & Martin, C. S. (1995). Salivary cortisol responses and the risk for substance abuse in prepubertal boys. *Biological Psychiatry, 38,* 547–555.

Moss, H. B., Vanyukov, M. M., Yao, J. K., & Kirillovac, G. P. (1999). Salivary cortisol responses in prepubertal boys: The effects of parental substance abuse and association with drug use behavior during adolescence. *Biological Psychiatry, 45,* 1293–1299.

Murphy, D. J. (2001). Effects of antenatal corticosteroids on postmortem brain weight of preterm babies. *Early Human Development, 63,* 113–122.

Nachmias, M., Gunnar, M., Mangelsdorf, S., Parritz, R., & Buss, K. (1996). Behavioral inhibition and stress reactivity: Moderating role of attachment security. *Child Development, 67,* 508–522.

Nagao, M., Nakamura, T., & Ichihara, A. (1986). Developmental control of gene expression of tryptophan 2, 3 dioxygenase in neonatal rat liver. *Biochimica et Biophysica Acta, 867,* 179–186.

Nemeroff, C. B. (1996). The corticotropin-releasing factor (CRF) hypothesis of depression: New findings and new directions. *Molecular Psychiatry, 1,* 336–342.

Netherton, C. M., Goodyer, I. M., Tamplin, A., & Hertbert, J. (2004). Salivary cortisol and dehydroepiandrosterone in relation to puberty and gender. *Psychoneuroendocrinology, 29,* 125–140.

O'Callaghan, J. P., Brinton, R. E., & McEwen, B. S. (1991). Glucocorticoids regulate the synthesis of glial fibrillary acidic protein in intact and adrenalectomized rats but do not affect its expression following brain injury. *Journal of Neurochemistry, 57,* 860–869.

Pajer, K., Gardner, W., Kirillovac, G. P., & Vanyukov, M. M. (2001). Sex differences in cortisol level and neurobehavioral disinhibition in children of substance abusers. *Journal of Child and Adolescent Substance Abuse, 10,* 65–76.

Pajer, K., Garner, W., Rubin, R. T., Perel, J., & Neal, S. (2001). Decreased cortisol levels in adolescent girls with conduct disorder. *Archives of General Psychiatry, 58,* 297–302.

Pariante, C. M. (2003). Depression, stress and the adrenal axis. *Journal of Neuroendocrinology, 15,* 811–812.

Parker, K. J., Buckmaster, C. L., Schatzberg, A. F., & Lyons, D. M. (2004). Prospective investigation of stress inoculation in young monkeys. *Archives of General Psychiatry, 61,* 933–941.

Parker, K. L., & Schimmer, B. P. (2001). Genetics of the development and function of the adrenal cortex. *Reviews in Endocrine and Metabolic Disorders, 2,* 245–252.

Pereira, R. C., Durant, D., & Canalis, E. (2000). Transcriptional regulation of connective tissue growth factor by cortisol in osteoblasts. *American Journal of Physiology: Endocrinology and Metabolism, 279,* E570–E576.

Phillips, I. D., Fielke, S. L., Young, I. R., & McMillen, I. C. (1996). The relative roles of the hypothalamus and cortisol in the control of prolactin gene expression in the anterior pituitary of the sheep fetus. *Journal of Neuroendocrinology, 8,* 929–933.

Piccinelli, M., & Wilkinson, G. (2000). Gender differences in depression: Critical review. *British Journal of Psychiatry, 177,* 486–492.

Pine, D., & Cohen, J. A. (2002). Trauma in children and adolescents: Risk and treatment of psychiatric sequelae. *Biological Psychiatry, 51,* 519–531.

Pruessner, J. C., Gaab, J., Hellhammer, D. H., Lintz, D., Schommer, N., & Kirschbaum, C. (1997). Increasing correlations between personality traits and cortisol stress responses obtained by data aggregation. *Psychoneuroendocrinology, 22,* 615–625.

Ramsay, D. S., & Lewis, M. (2003). Reactivity and regulation in cortisol and behavioral responses to stress. *Child Development, 74,* 456–464.

Rauste von Wright, M., von Wright, J., & Frankenhaeuser, M. (1981). Relationships between sex related psychological characteristics during adolescence and catecholamine excretion during achievement stress. *Psychophysiology, 18,* 362–370.

Reite, M., Harbeck, R., & Hoffman, A. (1981). Altered cellular response following peer separation. *Life Sciences, 29,* 1133–1136.

Reul, J. M., & de Kloet, E. R. (1985). Two receptor systems for corticosterone receptors in rat brain: Microdistribution and differential occupation. *Endocrinology, 117,* 2505–2511.

Reynolds, J. W. (1981). Development and function of the human fetal adrenal cortex. In M. J. Novy & J. A. Resko (Eds.), *Fetal endocrinology* (pp. 35–52). New York: Academic Press.

Riad-Fahmy, D., Read, G. F., Walker, R. F., & Griffiths, K. (1982). Steroids in saliva for assessing endocrine function. *Endocrine Review, 3,* 367–395.

Rinne, T., de Kloet, E. R., Wouters, L., Goekoop, J. G., DeRijk, R. H., & van den Brink, W. (2002). Hyperreponsiveness of hypothalamic-pituitary-adrenal axis to combined dexamethasone/corticotropin-releasing hormone challenge in female borderline personality disorder subjects with a history of sustained childhood abuse. *Biological Psychiatry, 52,* 1102–1112.

Rosen, J. B., & Schulkin, J. (1998). From normal fear to pathological anxiety. *Psychological Review, 105,* 325–350.

Rosenbaum, J. F., Biederman, J., Bolduc-Murphy, E. A., Faraone, S. V., Chaloff, J., Hirshfeld, D. R., et al. (1993). Behavioral inhibition in childhood: A risk factor for anxiety disorders. *Harvard Review of Psychiatry, 1,* 2–16.

Rosenblum, L. A., & Andrews, M. W. (1994). Influences of environmental demand on maternal behavior and infant development. *Acta Paediatrica, 397,* 57–63.

Rosenblum, L. A., Coplan, J. D., Friedman, S., Bassoff, T., Gorman, J. M., & Andrews, M. W. (1994). Adverse early experiences affect noradrenergic and serotonergic functioning in adult primates. *Biological Psychiatry, 35,* 221–227.

Roy, A. (2002). Urinary free cortisol and childhood trauma in cocaine dependent adults. *Journal of Psychiatric Research, 36,* 173–177.

Ryan, N. D. (1998). Psychoneuroendocrinology of children and adolescents. *Psychiatric Clinics of North America, 21,* 435–441.

Sanchez, M., Ladd, C., & Plotsky, P. (2001). Early adverse experience as a developmental risk factor for later psychopathology: Evidence from rodent and primate models. *Development and Psychopathology, 13,* 419–450.

Sanchez, M., Noble, P., Lyon, C., Plotsky, P., Davis, M., Nemeroff, C., et al. (in press). Alterations of diurnal cortisol rhythm and the acoustic startle response in non-human primates with adverse rearing experience. *Biological Psychiatry.*

Sanchez, M., Young, L., Mathys, K., Plotsky, P., & Insel, T. (1999). Different rearing conditions affect the development of corticotropin releasing factor (CRF) and vasopressin (AVP) systems in non human primates. *Society for Neuroscience Abstracts, 25,* 443.

Sapolsky, R. M., Romero, L. M., & Munck, A. U. (2000). How do glucocorticoids influence stress responses? Integrating permissive, suppressive, stimulatory, and preparative actions. *Endocrine Reviews, 21,* 55–89.

Scaccianoce, S., Catalani, A., Lombardo, K., Consoli, C., & Angelucci, L. (2001). Maternal glucocorticoids hormone influences nerve growth factor expression in the developing rat brain. *NeuroReport, 12,* 2881–2884.

Scerbo, A. S., & Kolko, D. J. (1994). Salivary testosterone and cortisol in disruptive children: Relation to aggressive, hyperactive, and internalizing behavior. *Journal of the American Academy of Child Psychiatry, 33,* 1174–1184.

Schlotz, W., Hellhammer, D., Schulz, P., & Stone, A. (2004). Perceived work overload and chronic worrying predict weekend-weekday differences in the cortisol awakening response. *Psychosomatic Medicine, 66,* 207–214.

Schmidt, L., & Fox, N. (1998). Fear-potentiated startle responses in temperamentally different human infants. *Developmental Psychobiology, 32,* 113–120.

Schmidt, L., Fox, N., Rubin, K., Sternberg, E., Gold, P., Smith, C., et al. (1997). Behavioral and neuroendocrine responses in shy children. *Developmental Psychobiology, 30,* 127–140.

Seckl, J. R., Cleasby, M., & Nyirenda, M. J. (2000). Glucocorticoids, 11-beta-hydroxysteroid dehydrogenase, and fetal programming. *Kidney International, 57,* 1412–1417.

Selye, H. (1936). A syndrome produced by diverse nocuous agents. *Nature, 38,* 32–36.

Sethre-Hofstand, L., Stansbury, K., & Rice, M. A. (2002). Attunement of maternal and child adrenocortical response to child challenge. *Psychoneuroendocrinology, 27,* 731–747.

Shannon, C., Champoux, M., & Suomi, S. J. (1998). Rearing condition and plasma cortisol in rhesus monkey infants. *American Journal of Primatology, 46,* 311–321.

Shirtcliff, E., Granger, D., Booth, A., & Johnson, D. (in press). Low salivary cortisol levels and externalizing behavior problems: A latent state trait model in normally developing youth. *Development and Psychopathology.*

Shoal, G. D., Giancola, P. R., & Kirillovac, G. P. (2003). Salivary cortisol, personality, and aggressive behavior in adolescent boys: A 5-year longitudinal study. *Journal of the American Academy of Child and Adolescent Psychiatry, 42,* 1101–1107.

Siever, L. J., & Davis, K. L. (1985). Overview: Towards a dysregulation hypothesis of depression. *American Journal of Psychiatry, 142,* 1017–1031.

Siegel, S. J., Ginsberg, S. D., Hof, P. R., Foote, S. L., Young, W. G., Draemer, G. W., et al. (1993). Effects of social deprivation in prepubescent rhesus monkeys: Immunohistochemical analysis of the neurofilament protein triplet in the hippocampal formation. *Brain Research, 619,* 299–305.

Singh, V., Corley, K., Phan, H., & Boadle-Bider, M. (1990). Increases in the activity of tryptophan hydroxylase from rat cortex and midbrain in response to acute or repeated sound stress are blocked by adrenalectomy and restored by dexamethasone treatment. *Brain Research, 516,* 66–76.

Smider, N., Essex, M. J., Kalin, N., Buss, K. A., Klein, M. H., Davidson, R. J., et al. (2002). Salivary cortisol as a predictor of socioemotional adjustment during kindergarten: A prospective study. *Child Development, 73,* 75–92.

Smith, M., Davidson, J., Ritchie, J., Makino, S., Kvetnansky, R., & Post, R. (1995). Stress and glucocorticoids affect the expression of brain derived neurotropic factors and neurotrophin-3 mRNA in the hippocampus. *Journal of Neuroscience, 15,* 1768–1777.

Smith, M., Kim, S., Van Oers, H., & Levine, S. (1997). Maternal deprivation and stress induce immediate early genes in the infant rat brain. *Endocrinology, 138,* 4622–4628.

Smyth, J., Ockenfels, M., Gorin, A., Catley, D., Porter, L., Kirschbaum, C., et al. (1997). Individual differences in the diurnal cycle of cortisol. *Psychoneuroendocrinology, 22,* 89–106.

Snoek, H., van Goozen, S., Matthys, W., Sigling, H., Koppenschaar, H., Westenberg, H., et al. (2002). Serotonergic functioning in children with oppositional defiant disorder: A sumatriptan challenge study. *Biological Psychiatry, 51,* 319–325.

Soloff, P. H., Lynch, K. G., & Moss, H. B. (2000). Serotonin, impulsivity, and alcohol use disorders in the older adolescent: A psychobiological study. *Alcoholism, Clinical and Experimental Research, 24,* 1609–1619.

Spangler, G. (1995). School performance, type A behavior, and adrenocortical activity in primary school children. *Anxiety, Stress, and Coping, 8,* 299–310.

Spangler, G., & Grossmann, K. E. (1993). Biobehavioral organization in securely and insecurely attached infants. *Child Development, 64,* 1439–1450.

Spangler, G., & Schieche, M. (1998). Emotional and adrenocortical responses of infants to the Strange Situation: The differential function of emotional expression. *International Journal of Behavioral Development, 22,* 681–706.

Spangler, G., Schieche, M., Ilg, U., Maier, U., & Ackermann, C. (1994). Maternal sensitivity as an external organizer for biobehavioral regulation in infancy. *Developmental Psychobiology, 27,* 425–437.

Spear, L. P. (2000). The adolescent brain and age-related behavioral manifestations. *Neuroscience and Biobehavioral Reviews, 24,* 417–463.

Spencer-Booth, Y., & Hinde, R. A. (1971). Effects of brief separations from mothers during infancy on behaviour of rhesus monkeys 6–24 months later. *Journal of Child Psychological Psychiatry, 12,* 157–172.

Spinelli, D. N. (1987). Plasticity triggering experiences, nature, and the dual genesis of brain structure and function. In N. Gunzenhauser (Ed.), *Infant stimulation: For whom, what kind, when and how much?* (pp. 21–29). Safe Harbor, CT: Johnson & Johnson.

Stein, M. B., Yehuda, R., Koverola, C., & Hanna, C. (1987). Enhanced dexamethasone suppression of plasma cortisol in adult women traumatized by childhood sexual abuse. *Biological Psychiatry, 42,* 680–686.

Stroud, L. R., Papandonatos, G. D., Williamson, D. E., & Dahl, R. E. (2004). Sex differences in the effects of pubertal development on responses to a corticotropin-releasing hormone challenge: The Pittsburgh psychobiologic studies. *Annals of the New York Academy of Sciences, 1021,* 348–351.

Stroud, L. R., Salovey, P., & Epel, E. S. (2002). Sex differences in stress responses: Rejection versus achievement stress. *Biological Psychiatry, 52,* 318–327.

Sullivan, R. M., & Gratton, A. (2002). Prefontal cortical regulation of hypothalamic-pituitary adrenal function in the rat and implications for psychopathology: Side matters. *Psychoneuroendocrinology, 27,* 99–114.

Suomi, S. J. (1995). Influence of attachment theory on ethological studies of biobehavioral development in nonhuman primates. In S. Goldberg, R. Muir, & J. Kerr (Eds.), *Attachment theory: Social, developmental, and clinical perspectives* (pp. 185–201). Hillsdale, NJ: Analytic Press.

Suomi, S. J. (1997). Early determinants of behavior: Evidence from primate studies. *British Medical Bulletin, 53,* 170–184.

Suomi, S. J., & Harlow, H. F. (1972). Social rehabilitation of isolate-reared monkeys. *Developmental Psychology, 6,* 487–496.

Susman, E., Dorn, L., & Chrousos, G. (1991). Negative affect and hormone levels in young adolescents: Concurrent and predictive perspectives. *Journal of Youth and Adolescence, 20,* 167–190.

Susman, E., Dorn, L., Inoff-Germain, G., Nottelman, E., & Chrousos, G. (1997). Cortisol reactivity, distress behavior, and behavioral and psychological problems in young adolescents: A longitudinal perspective. *Journal of Research on Adolescence, 70,* 81–105.

Swanson, L. W. (1992). Spatiotemporal patterns of transcription factor gene expression accompanying the development and plasticity of cell phenotypes in the neuroendocrine system. *Progress in Brain Research, 92,* 97–113.

Taylor, S., Klein, L., Lewis, B., Gruenewald, T., Gurung, R., & Updegraff, J. (2000). Biobehavioral responses to stress in females: Tend-and-befriend, not fight-or-flight. *Psychological Review, 107,* 411–429.

Teicher, M., Andersen, S., Polcarri, A., Anderson, C., & Navalta, C. (2002). Developmental neurobiology of childhood stress and trauma. *Psychiatric Clinics of North America, 25,* 397–426.

Tennes, K., & Kreye, M. (1985). Children's adrenocortical responses to classroom activities and tests in elementary school. *Psychosomatic Medicine, 47,* 451–460.

Tennes, K., Kreye, M., Avitable, N., & Wells, R. (1986). Behavioral correlates of excreted catecholamines and cortisol in second-grade children. *Journal of the American Academy of Child Psychiatry, 25,* 764–770.

Teramoto, S., Hatakenaka, N., & Shirasu, Y. (1991). Effects of the Ay gene on susceptibility to hydrocortisone fetotoxicity and teratogenicity in mice. *Teratology, 44,* 101–106.

Tornhage, C.-J. (2002). Reference values for morning salivary cortisol concentrations in healthy school aged children. *Journal of Pediatric Endocrinology and Metabolism, 15,* 197–204.

Trautman, P. D., Meyer-Bahlburg, H. F. L., Postelnek, J., & New, M. I. (1995). Effects of early prenatal dexamethasone on the cognitive and behavioural development of young children: Results of a pilot study. *Psychoneuroendocrinology, 20,* 439–449.

van de Wiel, N. M. H., van Goozen, S. H., Matthys, W., Snoek, H., & van Engeland, H. (2004). Cortisol and treatment effect in children with disruptive behavior disorders: A preliminary study. *Journal of the American Academy of Child and Adolescent Psychiatry, 43,* 1011–1018.

van Eck, M., Berkhof, H., Nicolson, N., & Sulon, J. (1996). The effects of perceived stress, traits, mood states, and stressful daily events on salivary cortisol. *Psychosomatic Medicine, 58,* 447–458.

van Eck, M., Nicolson, N. A., Berkhof, H., & Sulon, J. (1996). Individual differences in cortisol responses to a laboratory speech task and their relationships to responses to stressful daily events. *Biological Psychology, 43,* 69–84.

van Esseveldt, L. K. E., Lehman, M. N., & Boer, G. J. (2000). The suprachiasmatic nucleus and the circadian time-keeping system revisited. *Brain Research, 33,* 34–77.

van Goozen, S., Matthys, W., Cohen-Kettenis, P., Buittelaar, J., & van Engeland, H. (2000). Hypothalamic-pituitary-adrenal axis and autonomic nervous system activity in disruptive children and matched controls. *Journal of the American Academy of Child and Adolescent Psychiatry, 39,* 1438–1445.

van Goozen, S., Matthys, W., Cohen-Kettenis, P., Gispen-de Wied, C., Wiegant, V., & van Engeland, H. (1998). Salivary cortisol and cardiovascular activity during stress in oppositional defiant disordered boys and normal controls. *Biological Psychiatry, 43,* 531–539.

Vanyukov, M., Moss, H., Plial, J., Blackson, T., Mezzich, A., & Tarter, R. (1993). Antisocial symptoms in preadolescent boys and in their parents: Associations with cortisol. *Psychiatry Research, 46,* 9–17.

Vardimon, L., Ben-Dror, I., Avisar, N., Oren, A., & Shiftan, L. (1999). Glucocorticoid control of glial gene expression. *Journal of Neurobiology, 40,* 513–527.

Vazquez, D. M. (1998). Stress and the developing limbic-hypothalamic-pituitary-adrenal axis. *Psychoneuroendocrinology, 23,* 663–700.

Vazquez, D. M., & Akil, H. (1993). Pituitary-adrenal response to ether vapor in the weanling animal: Characterization of the inhibitory effect of glucocorticoids on adrenocorticotropin secretion. *Pediatric Research, 34*(5), 646–653.

Vazquez, D. M., & Levine, S. (in press). The hypothalamic-pituitary-adrenal axis in postnatal life. In T. Steckler, N. Kalin, & J. M. Reul (Eds.), *Handbook on stress, immunology and behavior.*

Vazquez, D. M., López, J. F., Morano, M. I., Kwak, S. P., Watson, S. J., & Akil, H. (1998). Alpha, beta and gamma mineralocorticoid receptor mRNA splice variants: Differential expression and rapid regulation in the developing hippocampus. *Endocrinology, 139,* 3165–3177.

Vazquez, D. M., Morano, I. M., Lopez, J. F., Watson, S. J., & Akil, H. (1993). Short term adrenalectomy increases glucocorticoid and mineralocorticoid receptor mRNA in selective areas of the developing hippocampus. *Molecular and Cellular Neuroscience, 4,* 455–471.

Viau, V., & Meaney, M. J. (1991). Variations in the hypothalamic-pituitary-adrenal response to stress during the estrous cycle in the rat. *Endocrinology, 129,* 2503–2511.

Viau, V., & Meaney, M. J. (1996). The inhibitory effect of testosterone on hypothalamic-pituitary adrenal responses to stress is mediated by the medial preoptic area. *Journal of Neuroscience, 16,* 1866–1876.

Wadhwa, P. D., Sandman, C. A., & Garite, T. J. (2001). The neurobiology of stress in human pregnancy: Implications for development of the fetal central nervous system. *Progress in Brain Research, 133,* 131–142.

Walker, C. D., Deschamps, S., Proulx, K., Tu, M., Salzman, C., Woodside, B., et al. (2004). Mother to infant or infant to mother? Reciprocal regulation of responsiveness to stress in rodents and the implications for humans. *Journal of Psychiatry and Neuroscience, 29,* 364–382.

Walker, C. D., Scribner, K. A., Cascio, C. S., & Dallman, M. F. (1991). The pituitary-adrenocortical system in the neonatal rat is responsive to stress throughout development in a time dependent and stressor-specific fashion. *Endocrinology, 128,* 1385–1395.

Walker, C. D., Welberg, L. A. M., & Plotsky, P. M. (2002). Glucocorticoids, stress, and development. In D. W. Pfaff, A. P. Arnold, A. M. Etgen, S. E. Fahrbach, & R. T. Rubin (Eds.), *Hormones, brain and behavior* (pp. 387–534). San Diego: Academic Press.

Walker, E. F., Walder, D. J., & Reynolds, F. (2001). Developmental changes in cortisol secretion in normal and at risk youth. *Development and Psychopathology, 13,* 721–732.

Watamura, S., Donzella, B., Kertes, D., & Gunnar, M. (2004). Developmental changes in baseline cortisol activity in early childhood: Relations with napping and effortful control. *Developmental Psychobiology, 45,* 125–133.

Weaver, I., Cervoni, N., Diorio, J., Szyf, M., & Meaney, M. (2001). Maternal behavior in infancy regulates methylation of the hippocampal glucocorticoid receptor promoter. *Society of Neuroscience Abstracts, 27,* 615–697.

Wood, B. S., Mason, W. A., & Kenney, M. D. (1979). Contrasts in visual responsiveness and emotional arousal between rhesus monkeys raised with living and those raised with inanimate substitute mothers. *Journal of Comparative and Physiological Psychology, 93,* 368–377.

Wüst, S., Federenko, I., Hellhammer, D. H., & Kirschbaum, C. (2000). Genetic factors, perceived chronic stress, and the free cortisol response to awakening. *Psychoneuroendocrinology, 25,* 707–720.

Yehuda, R. (2000). Biology of posttraumatic stress disorder. *Journal of Clinical Psychiatry, 61*(Suppl. 7), 12–21.

Yehuda, R., Halligan, S. L., & Grossman, R. (2001). Childhood trauma and risk for PTSD: Relationship to intergenerational effects of trauma, parental PTSD, and cortisol excretion. *Development and Psychopathology, 13,* 733–753.

Young, S. F., Smith, J. L., Figueroa, J. P., & Rose, J. C. (2003). Ontogeny and effect of cortisol on vasopressin-1b receptor expression in anterior pituitaries of fetal sheep. *American Journal of Physiology: Regulatory Integrative and Comparative Physiology, 284,* R51–R56.

Zhang, C., Sweezey, N. B., Gagnon, S., Muskat, B., Koehler, D., Post, M., et al. (2000). A novel karyopherin-beta homolog is developmentally and hormonally regulated in fetal lung. *American Journal of Respiratory Cell and Molecular Biology, 22,* 451–459.

CHAPTER 14

Beyond the Stress Concept: Allostatic Load—A Developmental Biological and Cognitive Perspective

SONIA J. LUPIEN, ISABELLE OUELLET-MORIN, ALMUT HUPBACH, MAI T. TU, CLAUDIA BUSS, DOMINIQUE WALKER, JENS PRUESSNER, and BRUCE S. MCEWEN

Stress is a popular topic these days. A week seldom passes without hearing or reading about stress and its deleterious effects on health. Given this negative impact of stress on human health, many types of stress management therapies have been put forward to decrease stress and thus promote health. However, there is a great paradox in the field of stress research, and it relates to the fact that the popular definition of stress is very different from the scientific definition of stress. This has left a multitude of people and experts talking about, and working on, very different aspects of the stress response.

In popular terms, stress is mainly defined as time pressure. We feel stressed when we do not have the time to perform the tasks we want to perform. This time pressure usually triggers a set of physiological reactions (see discussion) that give us the indication that we are stressed. Although this definition is certainly accurate in terms of one component of the stress response, it is important to acknowledge that in scientific terms, stress is not equivalent to time pressure. If this were true, every individual would feel stressed when pressured by time. However, we all know peo-ple who are extremely stressed by time pressure and others who actually seek time pressure to perform adequately (so-called procrastinators). This shows that stress is a highly individual experience that does not depend on a particular event such as time pressure; rather, it depends on specific psychological determinants that trigger a stress response.

THE ALLOSTATIC LOAD MODEL

The allostatic load model proposed by McEwen and Stellar (1993) refers to the wear and tear that the body experiences due to the repeated use of adaptive responses to stress, as well as the inefficient turning on or shutting off of these responses. Allostatic load refers to the cost the body pays for this adaptation, when this adaptation needs to be maintained for long periods of time.

Stress: Historical Background

Prior to becoming part of our day-to-day conversations, the term "stress" was used by engineers to explain forces that can put strain on a structure. For example, one could place strain on a piece of metal in such a way that it would break like glass when it reached its stress level. In 1936, Hans Selye (reproduced in Selye, 1998) borrowed the term from the field of engineering and talked about stress as being a nonspecific phenomenon representing the intersection of symptoms produced by a wide variety of noxious agents. For many years, Selye tested various conditions (e.g., fasting, extreme cold, operative injuries, and drug administration) that would produce morphological changes in the body that were representative of a stress response, such as enlargement of the adrenal gland, atrophy of the thymus, and gastric ulceration. Selye's view of the concept of stress was that the determinants of the stress response are nonspecific; that is, many unspecific conditions can put strain on the organism and lead to disease, the same way that many unspecific conditions can put strain on a piece of metal and break it like glass.

Not all researchers agreed with Selye's model, particularly with the notion that the determinants of the stress response are nonspecific. The reason for this was simple. Selye spent his entire career working on physical stressors (e.g., heat, cold, and pain), but we all know that some of the worst stressors we encounter in life are psychological in nature and are induced by our interpretation of events. For this reason, a psychologist named John Mason (1968) spent many years measuring stress hormone levels in humans subjected to various conditions that he thought would be stressful; he intended to describe the psychological characteristics that would make any condition stressful to anyone exposed to it. This work was made possible in the early 1960s due to the development of new technology that allowed scientists to measure levels of hormones that are released during reactivity to stress. The release of stress hormones is made possible through activation of a neuroendocrine axis named the hypothalamic-pituitary-adrenal (HPA) axis.

The Hypothalamic-Pituitary-Adrenal Axis

When a situation is interpreted as being stressful, it triggers the activation of the HPA axis, whereby neurons in the hypothalamus, a brain structure often termed the "master gland," releases corticotropin-releasing hormone (CRH). The release of CRH triggers the subsequent secretion and release of another hormone, adrenocorticotropin (ACTH), from the pituitary gland, also located in the brain. When ACTH is secreted by the pituitary gland, it travels in the blood and reaches the adrenal glands, which are located above the kidneys, and triggers secretion of the so-called

stress hormones. There are two main stress hormones, the glucocorticoids (corticosterone in animals and cortisol in humans) and the catecholamines (epinephrine and norepinephrine). In humans, cortisol secretion shows pronounced circadian rhythmicity, where concentrations are at their highest in the morning (the circadian peak), progressively decline from late afternoon to early nocturnal periods (the circadian trough), and show abrupt elevations after the first few hours of sleep. The acute secretion of glucocorticoids and catecholamines in response to a stressor constitutes the primary mediators in the chain of hormonal events triggered in response to stress. When these two hormones are secreted in response to stress, they act on the body to give rise to the fight-or-flight response, whereby one would, for instance, experience an increase in heart rate and blood pressure.

By summarizing the results of studies measuring the circulating levels of these hormones before and after individuals were exposed to various jobs or situations that were deemed to be stressful (e.g., air-traffic controllers and parachute jumping), Mason (1968) was able to describe three main psychological determinants that would induce a stress response in any individual exposed to them. Using this methodology, he showed that for a situation to induce a stress response, it has to be interpreted as being *novel* and/or *unpredictable,* and/or the individual must have the feeling that he or she *does not have control over the situation.* Although this work led to a general debate between Selye (1975a) and Mason, further studies confirmed that the determinants of the stress response are highly specific and, therefore, potentially predictable and measurable.

Stress, Stressor, Stress Response, Eustress, and Distress

From this short historical background, it is becoming clear that various definitions have been given to stress. In the past few years, a growing number of scientists started to feel the need to clarify these concepts to increase our understanding of the effects of stress on human health. Based on recent reviews, McEwen and Wingfield (2003) proposed a clarification of these different concepts of stress that we use in this review. Thus, we define stress as a threat, *real or implied,* to homeostasis. In this sense, stress can be absolute (a *real* threat induced by an earthquake in a town, leading to a significant stress response in every person facing this threat), or it can be relative (an *implied* threat induced by the interpretation of a situation as being novel and/or unpredictable and/or uncontrollable, for example, a public speaking task).

Absolute versus Relative Stressors

Absolute stressors serve adaptive purposes and are those events or situations that will necessarily lead to a stress response in the majority (if not the totality) of individuals when they are first confronted with it. Being in or witnessing an accident, confronting a dangerous animal, being submitted to extreme cold or heat are all examples of absolute stressors. These extreme and particular situations constitute absolute stressors in that, due to their aversive nature, a stress response *has to* be elicited for one's survival and/or well-being. In Western societies, absolute stressors are rare but are nonetheless those that elicit the greatest physiological response. Conversely, relative stressors are those events or situations that will elicit a stress response only in a certain proportion of individuals. Moreover, this response may be mild or strong. For example, having to unexpectedly deliver a speech that will be videotaped may be very stressful for one individual and not at all for another. Large interindividual variations in the stress response to psychological challenges have been frequently reported (Hellhammer, Buchtal, Gutberlet, & Kirschbaum, 1997; Kirschbaum & Hellhammer, 1989; Kirschbaum, Klauer, Filipp, & Hellhammer, 1995; Kirschbaum, Kudielka, Gaab, Schommer, & Hellhammer, 1999; Kirschbaum, Prussner, et al., 1995; Kudielka, Buske-Kirschbaum, Hellhammer, & Kirschbaum, 2004; Kudielka, Schommer, Hellhammer, & Kirschbaum, 2004; Lupien et al., 1997; M. Pruessner, Hellhammer, Pruessner, & Lupien, 2003; Rohleder, Wolf, & Kirschbaum, 2003; Roy, Steptoe, & Kirschbaum, 1998). As discussed in section II of this chapter, these individual differences in response to relative stressors may be due to differences in past experiences, learning, or genetic or cognitive processes. However, most of the relative stressors that lead to large interindividual variations are those stressors that imply a cognitive and/or psychosocial component (Dickerson & Kemeny, 2002). It may be argued that absolute stressors are closely linked to physiological systems due to their life- or self-threatening nature. On the contrary, relative stressors, because they are milder or because they necessitate a cognitive interpretation to elicit a response, will not necessarily lead to a physiological response, and the presence or absence of a physiological response will depend on the outcome of the cognitive analysis.

Eustress versus Distress

Situations can be interpreted as being positive, leading to eustress (good stress), or as being negative, leading to distress (bad stress). The nature (eustress versus distress) of the stress response elicited by these situations relates more to the cognitive interpretation given to the situation (as being positive or negative to the individual) than to the physical consequence of it. To date, very few studies have been performed to assess the body's different responses to eustress or distress. However, a study performed in 1989 by Berk and collaborators assessed the hormonal response to a mirthful laughter experience in 10 healthy male subjects. In this study, half of the participants viewed a 60-minute humorous video and the other half did not. Measures of cortisol, 3,4-dihydrophenylacetic acid (dopac, the major serum neuronal catabolite of the neurotransmitter dopamine), epinephrine, and norepinephrine were assessed before and after exposure to the experimental or control conditions. The results showed that cortisol and dopac in the experimental group decreased more rapidly from baseline than in the control group, whereas epinephrine levels in the experimental group were significantly lower than in the control group at all time points. Although the authors stated that these biochemical changes have implications for the reversal of the neuroendocrine and classical stress hormone response, it has to be noted that the study was performed with a very small sample of participants (5 in each group), and the cortisol changes in response to the funny movie were not compared to the cortisol changes after exposure to a sad or aggressive movie. Consequently, it is not clear at this time whether feelings of eustress or distress lead to different hormonal responses in humans.

Stressor versus Stress Response

The stressor is the event itself, such as the earthquake in the case of the absolute stress or the public speaking task in the case of the relative stress. The stress response is the body's reaction to the event (Selye, 1975b, 1998) and can be measured by monitoring levels of cortisol and ACTH in blood or cortisol in saliva or urine. Activity within the sympathetic nervous system is measurable as levels of catecholamines in blood, urine, or saliva or by monitoring heart rate and blood pressure. Although the subjective experience of stress does not always correlate with the output of the physiological mediators of stress (Kirschbaum et al., 1999), the measurement of the body's physiological responses to environmental challenges (real or implied) nonetheless constitutes the primary means of connecting experience with resilience or the risk of disease.

Acute versus Chronic Stress

Activation of the stress response in the face of a threat (real or implied) is primordial for the survival of the species. This acute stress response, which has been called the fight-or-flight response, allows the individual to mobilize the energy required to deal with threat. However, chronic exposure to these threats can have detrimental effects on the body. Although a wealth of data has been gathered on the effects of chronic stress on the body, almost no model has been offered to explain, predict, and measure the impact of chronic stress on the body. The main reason for this is the fact that no model has proposed a clear distinction between the positive impact of an acute response to stress and the negative impact of a chronic activation of the stress systems. Moreover, in many cases, a stressor is thought to refer to any situation that challenges the body's homeostasis and consequently is seen as being negative. However, in recent years, a new model has been developed to disentangle these different concepts and allow for a clearer description of the positive and negative effects of acute and chronic stress on the organism. This is the allostatic load model (McEwen & Stellar, 1993), but to understand what allostatic load is, one has to first understand the notion of allostasis and how it differs from the notion of homeostasis.

Allostasis versus Homeostasis

In 1929, Cannon introduced the term "homeostasis" to refer to the operation of coordinated physiological processes that maintain most of the steady states of the organism. Consequently, homeostasis is the stability of physiological systems that maintain life, such as pH, body temperature, glucose levels, and oxygen tension. These physiological systems are truly essential for life and are therefore maintained within an optimal range. The daily routines of animals and humans include nutritional inputs to maintain normal activities and to anticipate additional requirements (such as breeding, acclimating to environmental changes) during the day-night cycle and the seasons. These homeostatic mechanisms allow the individual to maintain physiological and behavioral stability despite fluctuating environmental conditions.

However, life is not always stable, and superimposed on these predictable events are facultative physiological and behavioral responses to unpredictable events that have the potential to be stressors. To respond to these unpredictable events, the system requires extra energy from endogenous stores of fat, glycogen, and protein. Consequently, to survive, an organism must be able to maintain such emergency responses. The capacity to maintain these emergency responses has been called "allostasis" (Sterling & Eyer, 1988), which implies the process of adaptation (McEwen & Stellar, 1993). Allostasis, mean-

ing literally "maintaining stability through change," describes the process of adaptation to challenge. It was introduced by Sterling and Eyer in 1988 to describe how the cardiovascular system adjusts to resting and active states of the body. This notion was generalized to other physiological mediators, such as the secretion of cortisol and catecholamines (McEwen, 1998a, 1998b; McEwen & Seeman, 1999; McEwen & Stellar, 1993).

Allostasis is positive and necessary to life. It is different from homeostasis in that it supports homeostasis; that is, it supports those physiological parameters essential for life, as environments and/or life history stages change. Indeed, homeostasis keeps "set-points" and various boundaries of control (such as pH), whereas allostasis allows for a modification of these set-points in order to face challenges. Consequently, homeostasis involves systems that are essential for life, and allostasis maintains these systems in balance as environment and life history stage change (McEwen & Wingfield, 2003).

For each system of the body, allostasis allows for short-term adaptive actions of the organism in response to environmental change. As presented in Table 14.1, for the cardiovascular system, one good example of allostasis is the role of catecholamines in promoting adaptation by adjusting heart rate and blood pressure to various conditions such as sleeping, waking, and physical exertion (Sterling & Eyer, 1988). For the metabolic system, one example of allostasis is the role of glucocorticoids at enhancing food intake and facilitating the replenishment of energy reserves after an environmental challenge (Beauman, 2000; Kuenzel, Beck, & Teruyama, 1999). For the brain, a good example of allostasis is the involvement of both glucocorticoids and catecholamines in promoting memory for emotionally meaningful events related to the environmental changes (Cahill, Prins, Weber, & McGaugh, 1994; Maheu, Joober, Beaulieu, & Lupien, 2004; Maheu & Lupien, 2003; Roozendaal, 2000, 2003; Roozendaal, Hahn, Nathan, de Quervain, & McGaugh, 2004; van Stegeren, Everaerd, Cahill, McGaugh, & Gooren, 1998). For the immune system, an example of allostasis is the role of glucocorticoids and catecholamines in promoting trafficking of immune cells to organs and tissues where they are needed to fight an infection or other challenges (Dhabhar & McEwen, 1999). All these body responses go above homeostatic functions and serve to maintain the stability of the various systems of the body in response to environmental challenges. It is because allostasis allows for a change in the set-points of these various physiological systems that homeostasis is kept, and the body can respond adequately to environmental changes.

TABLE 14.1   Examples of Allostasis and Allostatic Load Processes, along with the Primary Stress Mediators Involved, for the Cardiovascular, Metabolic, Immune, and Brain Systems

System	Primary Stress Mediator Involved	Allostasis	Allostatic Load
Cardiovascular	Catecholamines	Act by promoting adaptation by adjusting heart rate (HR) and blood pressure (BP) to sleeping, waking, and physical exertion.	Repeated surges of BP accelerates atherosclerosis and synergizes with metabolic hormones to produce Type II diabetes.
Metabolic	Glucocorticoids	Enhance food intake and facilitate replenishment of energy reserves.	Repeated HPA activity leads to insulin resistance, accelerating toward progression of Type II diabetes, including abdominal obesity, atherosclerosis, and hypertension.
Immune	Glucocorticoids and Catecholamines	Promote trafficking (movement) of immune cells to organs and tissues where they are needed to fight infections or other challenges and modulate the expression of the hormones of the immune system, i.e., the cytokines and the chemokines.	Chronic overactivity of these mediators leads to immunosuppressive effects.
Brain	Glucocorticoids and Catecholamines	Promote retention of memories for emotionally charged events, both positive and negative.	Overactivity of these mediators lead to cognitive dysfunction, reduces neuronal excitability, induces neuronal atrophy, and in extreme cases, causes death of brain cells.

Allostatic Load: When Things Turn Bad

In 1993, McEwen and Stellar proposed the term "allostatic load" to refer to the wear and tear that the body experiences due to the repeated use of allostatic responses as well as the inefficient turning on or shutting off of these responses. Allostatic load refers to the cost the body pays for this adaptation, when this adaptation needs to be maintained for long periods of time. From the standpoint of survival and health of the individual, the most important feature of the primary stress mediators associated with allostasis is that they have protective effects in the short run. However, they can have damaging effects at longer time intervals if there are many adverse life events or if the secretion of hormones is dysregulated due to sustained stress responses. When this happens, it leads to allostatic load. As presented in Figure 14.1, McEwen and Stellar's model describes the operating factors and the general sequence of events that occurs under conditions of acute and chronic stress (for reviews of the concept, see McEwen, 1998a, 1998b; McEwen & Seeman, 1999; McEwen & Stellar, 1993; McEwen & Wingfield, 2003; Seeman, McEwen, Rowe, & Singer, 2001). The model comprises a behavioral side, on which the individual interprets and reacts to a challenge, and a biological side, on which the body reacts to the perceived stress. The model thus comprises both a top-down processing side (interpretation of a situation as being stressful, leading to activation of the various stress systems) and a bottom-up side (the effects of the acute and/or prolonged activation of these systems on the body and the brain).

Top-Down Processing and Allostasis

The first factor in McEwen and Stellar's (1993) model is the reaction of the individual to physical and psychological stimuli. As presented in Figure 14.1, this reaction is in part determined by the social context and the social status of the individual. Second, the stimulus will have an effect on the individual's information-processing system (the "processor"). The response of the processor will be determined by genetic makeup, stage of biological development, gender, past learning, and social history. If the stimulus is perceived as a threat and the source of the threat is unknown, the individual will become highly vigilant and try to determine the real nature (threat versus nonthreat) of the stimulus. If the stimulus is perceived as a threat and its source is known, the individual will try to find a coping response to the threat. If no response is available, helplessness or hopelessness may appear, with its altered physiologic responses. If a response is available, the outcome of it will depend on the cost of that response. If a low-cost response is appropriate, no stress response will be initiated. If a high-cost response is needed, it may necessitate the appearance of aggression or sensation-seeking or risk-taking behaviors. However, the available response can also be thwarted, which will eventually lead to displaced frustration or aggression. So, perceptions of threat and choice of response are central aspects of the assessment

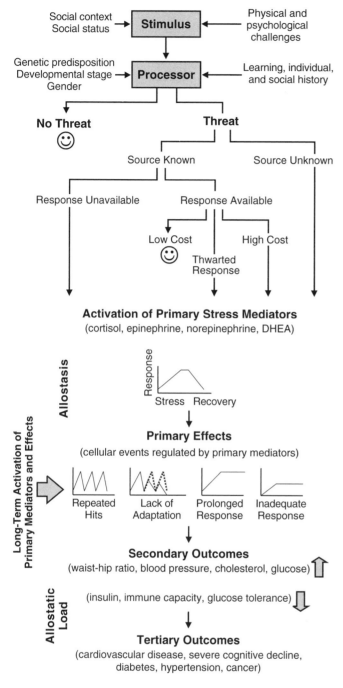

Figure 14.1 Schematic representation of the Allostatic Load model.

which will help trigger a stress response allowing the individual to deal with the threat. What is important to understand here is that the same mediators (glucocorticoids and catecholamines) that are protective and adaptive in the short run can have extremely damaging consequences if they are overproduced and/or are dysregulated for a longer period of time (McEwen, 1998a), leading to biphasic actions of the primary stress mediators.

The long-term cost to the body from allostatic load may be subdivided into at least four subtypes (McEwen, 1998a), as summarized in Figure 14.1. The first type is simply too much stress in the form of repeated, novel events that cause repeated elevations of stress mediators. For example, the amount and frequency of economic hardship predicts decline of physical and mental functioning as well as mortality (Adler et al., 1994). A second type of allostatic load involves a failure to habituate or adapt to the multiple occurrences of the same stressor. This leads to the overexposure to stress mediators because the body fails to dampen or eliminate the hormonal stress response to a repeated event. For example, when confronted with repeated public speaking challenges, most individuals habituated their cortisol response, but a few individuals continued to show cortisol response (Kirschbaum, Prussner, et al., 1995). A third type of allostatic load involves the failure to shut off either the hormonal stress response or the normal trough of the diurnal cortisol pattern. Examples of this include blood pressure elevations in work-related stress (Gerin, Litt, Deich, & Pickering, 1996; Kunz-Ebrecht, Kirschbaum, & Steptoe, 2004; Lundberg, 1996; Ming et al., 2004; Pickering, 1996a, 1996b; Pickering et al., 1996; Schwartz, Pickering, & Landsbergis, 1996; Steptoe, Siegrist, Kirschbaum, & Marmot, 2004; Steptoe & Willemsen, 2004), sleep deprivation leading to elevated evening cortisol and hyperglycemia within 5 days (Leproult, Copinschi, Buxton, & Van Cauter, 1997; Van Cauter, Polonsky, & Scheen, 1997), and depressive illness leading to chronically elevated cortisol and loss of bone mineral mass (Coelho, Silva, Maia, Prata, & Barros, 1999; Michelson et al., 1996; Robbins, Hirsch, Whitmer, Cauley, & Harris, 2001; Wong et al., 2005). The fourth type of allostatic load involves an inadequate hormonal stress response which allows other systems, such as the inflammatory cytokines, to become overactive (Chrousos & Elenkov, 2000; Elenkov, Chrousos, & Wilder, 2000). The Lewis rat is an example of an animal strain in which increased susceptibility to inflammatory and autoimmune disturbances is related to inadequate levels of cortisol (for a review, see Fournie et al., 2001). Next, we give an example of allostasis turning into allostatic load for the primary stress mediator glucocorticoids.

of risk and making choices leading to health-damaging or health-promoting behaviors.

Bottom-Up Effects and Allostatic Load

When a given situation is perceived as stressful or threatening, there will be activation of the primary stress mediators (glucocorticoids, catecholamines, dehydroepiandrosterone [DHEA]; a complete description of these mediators follows),

Glucocorticoids and Allostatic Load: An Example. The traditional role of glucocorticoids is to promote conversion of protein and lipids to usable carbohydrates. In the short run, this is a positive aspect of this stress mediator as glucocorticoids will serve to replenish energy reserves after a period of activity such as running away from a house on fire. The same glucocorticoid will also act on the brain during this period to increase appetite for food (to replenish energy reserves) and to increase locomotor activity and food-seeking behavior (to increase energy expenditures; Leibowitz & Hoebel, 1997; Tang, Akabayashi, Manitiu, & Leibowitz, 1997). These effects of glucocorticoids are very beneficial when we have to run as fast as we can from a house on fire and when we have to replenish our energy after this intense running to maintain our daily activities. However, these effects can be detrimental when the stress response is triggered chronically by an absolute (e.g., always having to run away from a predator) or relative (e.g., a low sense of control at work) stressor.

There is an important point to make with regard to the impact of relative stressors on allostasis and allostatic load. The primary stress mediator (here, glucocorticoids) does not distinguish between a real (a house on fire) and an implied (low sense of control) threat; consequently, its activation will occur at each occurrence of the stressor (real or implied), leading to long-term secretion of glucocorticoids. Moreover, the action of glucocorticoids will be the same, that is, action on the brain to increase appetite for food (replenishment of energy reserves) and increase locomotor activity (energy expenditures). Given that, in the case of a relative stressor, the stress response has been triggered by a psychological situation rather than a real threat to survival (absolute stressor), the energy expenditure is less, but the glucocorticoids have been secreted at the same levels, activating the brain in the same way to increase food intake, with a preference for carbohydrates. Given that in Western societies, food is easily available and does not necessitate a lot of food-seeking behaviors, the energy expenditure resulting from food-seeking behavior is low. In the long run, inactivity and lack of energy expenditure, along with increased secretion of glucocorticoids, creates a situation where chronically elevated glucocorticoids can impede the action of insulin to promote glucose uptake. One of the results of this interaction is that insulin levels increase and, together, high insulin and glucocorticoids concentrations promote the deposition of body fat. This combination of hormones will also promote the formation of atherosclerotic plaques in coronary arteries, increasing the risk for coronary diseases (Brindley & Rolland, 1989).

It is when a dysregulation of other hormones occurs in response to the long-term secretion of the primary stress mediators that allostatic load appears. Other examples of allostatic load are depicted in Table 14.1 for the cardiovascular, metabolic, immune, and brain systems.

When Top-Down Processing Meets Bottom-Up Effects

As we have summarized above, once a situation has been interpreted as being threatening, a stress response will be activated, which might lead to allostatic load. What is interesting to take into account in this context is that some of the hormones secreted during the stress response will access the brain and will modify the way that further upcoming information is processed.

Allostatic Load and the Brain.   As we noted earlier, one of the most important parts of the allostatic load model is the cognitive processor, which acts by deciding whether a situation constitutes a threat or not. Once this processing has been done, there will be activation (threat) or not (nonthreat) of the primary stress mediators.

It is important to note here that these primary mediators (particularly glucocorticoids and catecholamines) have been shown to have important effects on the brain, leading to changes in cognitive processing. Here again, a process of allostasis and allostatic load has been observed with regard to the effects of the primary stress mediators on the brain.

Allostatic Effects on the Brain.   Given the lipophilic properties of glucocorticoids, these adrenal hormones can easily cross the blood-brain barrier and enter the brain, where they can influence brain function and behavior by way of binding to different receptor types. Three of the most important brain areas containing glucocorticoid receptors are the hippocampus, amygdala, and frontal lobes, which are brain structures known to be involved in learning and memory (for reviews, see Lupien & Lepage, 2001; Lupien & McEwen, 1997). Although epinephrine does not readily access the brain due to absence of lipophilic properties, it can still act on the brain through its action on the sensory vagus outside of the blood-brain barrier, with information transmitted into the brain via the nucleus of the solitary tract (for a review, see Roozendaal, 2000). The most important brain area containing adrenergic receptors is the amygdala, which has been shown to play an important role in fear processing (for a recent review, see LeDoux, 2003) and memory for emotionally relevant information (for a recent review, see McGaugh, 2000).

Because of their actions on brain structures known to be involved in fear detection and memory for emotionally relevant information, the stress mediators enhance the formation of the so-called flashbulb memories of events associated with strong emotions, including fear but also positive emotions. This process involves the amygdala, and the pathway for encoding these memories involves the interaction between neurotransmitters in the amygdala and in related brain areas such as the hippocampus along with circulating stress hormones of the adrenal cortex and adrenal medulla (McGaugh, 2000; Roozendaal, Hahn, et al., 2004; Roozendaal, McReynolds, & McGaugh, 2004; van Stegeren et al., 1998). The importance of these stress mediators on memory for emotionally relevant information has been recently confirmed by studies in which blockade of either glucocorticoid (Maheu et al., 2004) or norepinephrine (Cahill et al., 1994) activity impaired the recall of emotionally relevant information. Consequently, secretion of these primary stress mediators is necessary for the adequate encoding of emotionally relevant information. This enhancement of memory for stimuli inducing stressful and/or emotional responses may be essential for a species' survival.

At the same time as the brain encodes information and controls the behavioral responses, it is also changed structurally and chemically by those experiences. Although for a long time it was thought that the brain of adult mammals does not generate new nerve cells, more recent evidence showed that neurons are born in the adult mammalian brain (Altman & Das, 1965). Interestingly, in the adult brain, the generation of new neurons (called neurogenesis) occurs in two regions. The first region is the subventricular zone in the wall of the lateral ventricle, where new interneurons are generated for the olfactory bulb; the second region is the subgranular zone of the dentate gyrus of the hippocampus, which gives rise to the granule cells. Moreover, recent evidence shows that adult neurogenesis in the dentate gyrus of the hippocampus is a feature of all mammalian species, occurring in rats, mice, tree shrews, marmosets, macaques, and humans (H. A. Cameron, Woolley, McEwen, & Gould, 1993; Eriksson et al., 1998; Gould, McEwen, Tanapat, Galea, & Fuchs, 1997; Gould et al., 1999; Gould, Tanapat, McEwen, Flugge, & Fuchs, 1998; Kempermann, Kuhn, & Gage, 1997). Although the functional significance of hippocampal neurogenesis has been questioned in the past, a study published in the March 2001 issue of Nature reported that neurogenesis in the adult is involved in the formation of trace memories, suggesting that the new neurons actually contribute to the function of the adult brain (Shors et al., 2001).

Gould and collaborators (1999) reported that training on a task that requires the hippocampal formation results in an increase in the number of adult-generated granule cells. Of particular importance, these authors showed that in untrained adult laboratory animals, the majority of generated cells degenerate within 2 weeks of production, whereas training on hippocampal-dependent tasks rescued a significant proportion of these cells. In line with experiments showing experience-dependent changes in hippocampal volumes, studies performed in adult neurogenesis show that learning can enhance the number of granule neurons. Also, comparative studies of different species show that hippocampal volume is increased in mammalian and avian species that depend critically on spatial memory for survival. Examples of such critical memory skills involve home-range navigation, migration, brood parasitism, and memory-based cache recovery in birds that hide food (Suzuki & Clayton, 2000). This association between performance of spatial tasks and hippocampal size could be explained in terms of the impact of environmental demands on hippocampal volume, rather than the converse. For example, Clayton and collaborators (Clayton & Krebs, 1994; Gerlai & Clayton, 1999) reported that the hippocampus of titmice and chickadees increases in volume in association with the experience of storing and recovering food caches. This result shows that in animals, there can be an experience-dependent hippocampal growth that occurs at a relatively late stage in development. Similar results of experience-based changes in hippocampal volumes were recently reported by Maguire and collaborators (2000) in humans. These authors tested the hypothesis that the ability of London taxi cab drivers to navigate to a specific destination correlates with hippocampal volume. They showed that compared to age-matched controls, the taxi drivers had larger posterior hippocampi. Although these results surely do not confirm that the experience of driving a taxi in the complex streets of London has a significant effect on hippocampal volumes, they nonetheless raise the intriguing possibility of hippocampal plasticity in response to environmental demands.

Allostatic Load Effects on the Brain. Although short-term responses of the brain to novel and potentially threatening situations may be adaptive and result in new learning and acquired behavioral strategies for coping, as may be the case for certain types of fear-related memories, repeated stress can cause both cognitive impairments and structural changes in the hippocampus. Each of these processes may be occurring somewhat independently of each other and contribute in various degrees to different pathophysiological situations involving traumatic stress, depression, or aging.

The cognitive effects of long-term elevations of glucocorticoids in human populations have been studied in disorders affecting glucocorticoid levels and using exogenous administration of the synthetic compound to healthy subjects (for a review, see Lupien & Lepage, 2001). Mental disturbances mimicking mild dementia (such as decrements in simple and complex attentional tasks, verbal and visual memory, encoding, storage, and retrieval) have been described in depressed patients with hypercortisolism (R. M. Cohen, Weingartner, Smallberg, Pickar, & Murphy, 1982; Rubinow, Post, Savard, & Gold, 1984; Vythilingam et al., 2004; Weingartner, Cohen, Murphy, Martello, & Gerdt, 1981; Wolkowitz et al., 1988; Wolkowitz et al., 1990) and in steroid psychosis following glucocorticoid treatment (Hall, Popkin, Stickney, & Gardner, 1979; Ling, Perry, & Tsuang, 1981; Varney, Alexander, & MacIndoe, 1984; Wolkowitz, Reus, Canick, Levin, & Lupien, 1997). Similar cognitive deficits are also reported in patients suffering from Cushing's disease (O. G. Cameron, Starkman, & Schteingart, 1995; Starkman, Gebarski, Berent, & Schteingart, 1992; Starkman, Giordani, Berent, Schork, & Schteingart, 2001; Starkman et al., 1999; Starkman, Giordani, Gebarski, & Schteingart, 2003). During human aging, a significant proportion of elderly individuals present an endogenous increase of glucocorticoid levels (Lupien et al., 1996), and this increase has been related to impaired memory performance (Lupien et al., 1994).

Although an allostatic process has been shown to lead to positive structural changes of the hippocampus, it is important to note that an allostatic load process has also been shown to have significant detrimental effects on this brain structure. For example, treatment of adult rats with corticosterone decreases the proliferation of granule cell precursors (H. A. Cameron & Gould, 1994), and removal of adrenal steroids stimulated the generation of new granule neurons (H. A. Cameron & McKay, 1999). Given the suppressive actions of glucocorticoids on hippocampal neurogenesis, stressful experiences have been suggested to inhibit cell proliferation in adulthood, a hypothesis that has been demonstrated. Long-term stressful experience decreases the number of adult-generated neurons in the dentate gyrus in various species, including the rat (Heale, Vanderwolf, & Kavaliers, 1994; Sgoifo, de Boer, Haller, & Koolhaas, 1996), tree shrew (Gould et al., 1997), and marmoset (Gould et al., 1998). In a similar vein, repeated stress produces prolonged suppression of cell proliferation

in the dentate gyrus of the adult tree shrew (Fuchs, Uno, & Flugge, 1995). Stress-induced decreases in dentate gyrus cell proliferation could also contribute, in line with atrophy of the pyramidal cells of the hippocampus, to changes in hippocampal volumes observed after chronic exposure to stress.

Smaller hippocampal volumes associated with chronic elevations of glucocorticoids have also been reported in humans. Over the past 2 decades, many studies revealed the presence of smaller hippocampal volumes in various psychiatric disorders, such as depression (Krishnan et al., 1991; Sheline, 1996; Sheline, Gado, & Kraemer, 2003; Sheline, Sanghavi, Mintun, & Gado, 1999; Sheline, Wang, Gado, Csernansky, & Vannier, 1996; Vythilingam et al., 2004), Posttraumatic Stress Disorder (Bremner, 2002, 2003; Vythilingam et al., 2002), and Schizophrenia (Heckers, 2001; Nelson, Saykin, Flashman, & Riordan, 1998), all of which involve glucocorticoid-level dysregulations. Hippocampal atrophy associated with chronic exposure to high levels of glucocorticoids is also reported in patients with Cushing's disease (Starkman et al., 1992; Starkman et al., 1999) and elderly individuals (Lupien et al., 1998). A recent study of Cushing's patients revealed that surgical treatment of hypercortisolism in these patients leads to a reversal of the glucocorticoid-induced hippocampal atrophy reported to occur in this population, with an average volume increase of 3.2% and variations up to 10% in some patients (Starkman et al., 1999). This is a significant finding as it implies the possibility of functional reorganization of the hippocampus once the allostatic load process has been taken away. Reversibility and/or preventability of such atrophy is a major topic for future research, as is the implication of such treatment for cognitive function.

Chronology of the Allostatic Load Process. As we have stated in previous sections, the activation of the primary stress mediators represents an allostatic process whereby an adaptive response to an environmental threat is organized. However, after repeated exposure to various situations that lead to activation of these stress mediators (either through repetitive hits, failure to habituate, prolonged response, or inadequate response), allostatic load will develop. Consequently, there exists a chronology of hormonal and cellular events in the development of allostatic load that can allow for a measure of the level of allostatic load in any given individual. The chain of events in the allostatic load process begins with the allostatic activation of primary mediators, with the resulting primary effects. After prolonged allostatic attempts at adaptation, other hormonal and cellular processes will become dysregulated, leading to secondary and tertiary outcomes. We summarize these next.

Primary Mediators of Allostatic Load.   The primary mediators of allostatic load are those chemical messengers that are released as part of allostasis (see Table 14.2). At present, there are four primary mediators included in the assessment of allostatic load: cortisol, epinephrine, norepinephrine (the catecholamines), and DHEA. These chemical messengers are primary mediators because they have widespread influence throughout the body and are very useful (when measured correctly) at predicting a variety of secondary and tertiary outcomes.

As summarized earlier, cortisol (the most important glucocorticoid in humans) has wide-ranging effects throughout the body. Receptors for glucocorticoids are present in virtually every tissue and organ in the body and mediate effects ranging from the induction of liver enzymes involved in energy metabolism to regulating the trafficking of immune cells and cytokine production to facilitating the formation of fear-related memories.

DHEA is a functional antagonist of cortisol (May, Holmes, Rogers, & Poth, 1990; Wright, Porter, Browne, & Svec, 1992) that may also have effects via other signaling pathways (Araneo & Daynes, 1995); generally, low DHEA is considered deleterious, as is chronically high cortisol (Morales, Nolan, Nelson, & Yen, 1994). Blood level of DHEA, most of which is present in the sulfated form (DHEAS), peaks at approximately 20 years of age and declines rapidly and markedly after age 25 (Orentreich, Brind, Rizer, & Vogelman, 1984). The accumulation of abdominal fat increases with aging, and abdominal obesity increases the risk for development of insulin resistance, diabetes, and atherosclerosis (Cefalu et al., 1995). In rats, DHEA has protective effects against both the insulin resistance induced by a high-fat diet (Hansen, Han, Nolte, Chen, & Holloszy, 1997) and the decrease in insulin responsiveness that occurs with advancing age (Han, Hansen, Chen, & Holloszy, 1998).

The catecholamines epinephrine and norepinephrine are released by the adrenal medulla and sympathetic nervous system, respectively, and produce widespread effects throughout the body, ranging from vasoconstriction and acceleration of heart rate to trafficking of immune cells to targets, as well as enhancement of fear-related memory formation (Cahill et al., 1994). Adrenergic receptors are widespread throughout the body, in blood vessels and target organs such as the liver, pancreas, and brain, which is not

TABLE 14.2   Various Stages of Allostatic Load and the Physiological and Clinical Markers Used to Assess the Degree of Allostatic Load

Stages of Allostatic Load	Physiological and Clinical Markers
Primary mediators	Glucocorticoids
	DHEA
	Adrenaline
	Noradrenaline
	Cytokines
Primary effects	Cellular events (enzymes, receptors, ion channels, structural proteins) that are regulated by the primary mediators as part of allostasis (not well studied).
Secondary outcomes	Reflect the cumulative outcomes of the primary effects and the outcomes of more than one primary mediator.
	Waist-hip ratio
	Blood pressure (systolic and diastolic)
	Heart rate
	Glycosylated hemoglobin
	HDL (High Density Lipoprotein)
	Total cholesterol
	Glucose
	Insulin
	Poor glucose tolerance
	Nitric oxide
	Fibrinogen
	Immune delayed-type hypersensitivity
	Immunization challenge response
	Frequency and severity of common cold
	Mild cognitive decline unrelated to age
Tertiary outcomes	Actual diseases or disorders that are the result of the allostatic load that are predicted from the extreme values of the secondary outcomes and of the primary mediators.
	Cardiovascular disease
	Severe cognitive decline
	Decreased physical capacity
	Cancer

Note: It is important to note that there are other primary mediators that may be included in the allostatic load model, but we have selected a subset of these for clarity. These potential additional mediators are presented in italics and are not discussed in the text. Also, it is important to underline that all these mediators operate as an interacting network and not necessarily in a linear fashion, as the table might suggest.

accessible to circulating catecholamines. However, catecholamines signal the brain through the sensory vagus and the nucleus of the solitary tract, as in learned fear.

Primary Effects of Allostatic Load.   The primary effects of allostatic load have not been measured extensively, but these include cellular events, the actions of enzymes, receptors, ion channels, and/or structural proteins that are induced genomically or phosphorylated via second messenger systems that are regulated as part of allostasis by the primary mediators (see Table 14.2).

For example, glucocorticoids regulate gene expression via several pathways, involving interactions with DNA via the glucocorticoid response elements and also via protein-protein interactions with other transcriptional regulators (Miner, Diamond, & Yamamoto, 1991). As noted earlier, DHEA antagonizes glucocorticoid actions in a number of systems. Catecholamines act via alpha and beta adrenergic receptors, and beta receptors stimulate the formation of the intracellular second messenger, cyclic AMP (cAMP), which, in turn, regulates intracellular events via phosphorylation, including transcription regulators via the CREB family of proteins (Siegel, Agranoff, Albers, Fisher, & Uhler, 1999).

In some cases, the glucocorticoid and cAMP pathways converge at the level of gene expression (e.g., see Yamada, Duong, Scott, Wang, & Granner, 1999). Therefore, it is not surprising that secondary outcomes (see later discussion) are the result of more than one primary mediator. Consequently, primary effects are organ- and tissue-specific, and secondary outcomes reflect the integrated actions of the primary effects.

Secondary Outcomes. The secondary outcomes are the integrated processes that reflect the cumulative outcomes of the primary effects in a tissue/organ-specific manner in response to the primary mediators (see Table 14.2). Consequently, they often reflect the actions of more than one primary mediator. Examples of secondary outcomes are evident in waist-hip ratio (abdominal fat deposition), blood pressure elevation, glycosylated hemoglobin, the ratio of cholesterol to HDL High Density Lipoproteins (HDL), and HDL cholesterol. These are secondary outcomes because they reflect the effects of sustained elevations in glucose and the insulin resistance that develop as a result of elevated cortisol and elevated sympathetic nervous system activity (primary mediators). Blood pressure elevation is part of the pathophysiological pathway of metabolic syndrome but is also a more primary indication of the allostatic load that can lead to accelerated atherosclerosis as well as insulin resistance. Cholesterol and HDL cholesterol are measures of metabolic imbalance in relation to obesity and atherosclerosis and also reflect the operation of the same primary mediators as well as other metabolic hormones.

Another important secondary outcome is mild cognitive decline without dementia; this secondary outcome relates to the detrimental effects of long-term exposure to high levels of glucocorticoids and catecholamines on cognitive processing in humans (Lupien et al., 1998; Lupien et al., 1994). More recently, we have also included specific outcomes related to the damaged pathway in cardiovascular disease and risk for myocardial infarction (e.g., nitric oxide, fibrinogen). Fibrinogen, one of the blood-clotting factors, has already been used as an allostatic load measure in relation to job stress and socioeconomic status (Markowe et al., 1985). Finally, outcomes related to other systems such as the immune system have now been included. Here, integrated measures of the immune response such as delayed-type hypersensitivity (Dhabhar & McEwen, 1999) and immunization challenge (Kiecolt-Glaser, Glaser, Gravenstein, Malarkey, & Sheridan, 1996) should reveal the impact of allostatic load on cellular and humoral immune function and help distinguish between the immunoenhancing effects of acute stress and immunosuppressive effects of chronic stress. Moreover, assessment of the frequency and severity of the common cold (S. Cohen et al., 1997; S. Cohen, Tyrrell, & Smith, 1991) is another indirect way of assessing immune function, and this might be considered a secondary outcome.

Tertiary Outcomes. The tertiary outcomes are the actual diseases or disorders that are the results of the allostatic load that is predicted from the extreme values of the secondary outcomes and of the primary mediators (see Table 14.2). Thus far, the tertiary outcomes that are thought to result from allostatic load are cardiovascular disease, decreased physical capacity, severe cognitive decline, and cancer.

With regard to the chronology of the allostatic load model, it is important to note that in the allostatic load formulation, the impact on health risk is thought to result not only from large and clinically significant deviations from normal operating ranges, but also from more modest dysregulations if they are present in multiple systems. McEwen and Stellar (1993) hypothesized that the cumulative impact on health risk from modest dysregulations in multiple systems can be substantial, even if they individually have minimal and insignificant health effects.

Validation of the Allostatic Load Model

Although the concept of allostatic load offers a great opportunity to explain various stress-related disorders, the model remains static as long as it has not been validated with experimental data. It thus became important to assess the predictive power of the allostatic load model in various populations.

Allostatic Load and Aging. In a first validation study, data were used from the MacArthur Successful Aging Study that pertains to levels of physiologic activity across a range of important regulatory systems, including the HPA and sympathetic nervous systems as well as the cardiovascular system and metabolic processes (Seeman et al., 1994; Seeman & Chen, 2002; Seeman, McEwen et al., 2001; Seeman, Singer, Rowe, Horwitz, & McEwen, 1997). In this study, Seeman and collaborators (Seeman, Crimmins, et al., 2004) evaluated the capacity of an allostatic load score to predict four categories of health outcomes in 1,189 men and women aged 70 to 79 followed over a period of 7 years. The measure of allostatic load used in this first validation study reflected only one of the two aspects of physiologic activity postulated to contribute to allostatic load, namely, higher, chronic, steady state levels of activity related to the diurnal variation as well as any residual activity reflecting chronic stress or failure to shut off responses to acute stressors. The parameters that were available for determining allostatic load scores included urinary cortisol, adrenaline, noradrenaline; serum DHEA; waist-hip ratio, diastolic and systolic blood pressure, glycosylated hemoglobin, serum HDL, and total cholesterol. For each of the 10 indicators of allostatic load, subjects were classified into quartiles based on the distribution of scores in the baseline cohort. Allostatic load was measured by summing the number of parameters for which the subject fell into the highest risk quartile, leading to an allostatic load score for each participant. The results showed that higher baseline allostatic load scores were associated with significantly increased risk for 2.5-year (Seeman et al., 1997) and 7-year (Karlamangla, Singer, McEwen, Rowe, & Seeman, 2002; Seeman, McEwen et al., 2001) mortality, as well as declines in cognitive and physical functioning, and were marginally associated with incident cardiovascular disease events. More important, although none of the 10 components of allostatic load exhibited significant associations on its own with health outcome, the summary measure of allostatic load was found to be significantly associated with these four major health outcomes. These findings were consistent with the idea that although a modest deviation in the level of activity of a single physiologic system may not be predictive of poor future health, the cumulative toll from modest alterations in several physiologic systems is a prognosis of poor health.

Allostatic Load across the Life Span. In a more recent study, Crimmins and collaborators (Crimmins, Johnston, Hayward, & Seeman, 2003) assessed age differences in allostatic load from a large nationally representative sample in the United States. The National Health and Nutrition Examination Suvery involved the collection of data over the period 1988 to 1994 in 18,000 individuals 20 years of age and older. Using the data from this study, an allostatic load index was constructed using 13 indicators of physiological dysregulation and analyzed using the quartile method of Seeman and colleagues (Seeman, McEwen, et al., 2001; Seeman et al., 1997). Results showed that allostatic load score increased with age through the 60s and then leveled off, so that individuals above 60 years of age had fairly similar levels of allostatic load. The ratios of one age group to the preceding showed that the increase in allostatic load score from one age group to the next was .4 or .5 in the first 2 decades of adulthood, and was .2 to .3 in the next decades. The change in allostatic load score after these decades (after 60 years) did not change significantly. Although these results were not linked to subsequent health outcomes, they revealed an interesting pattern of increasing allostatic load score, starting in the early decades of adulthood.

Allostatic Load and Work Conditions. Adverse work characteristics and poor social support have been associated with an increased risk for cardiovascular disease and other adverse health outcomes. To assess whether an allostatic load index could be a good predictor of work characteristics, Schnorpfeil and collaborators (2003) performed a cross-sectional study with 324 industrial workers in Germany. Psychosocial work characteristics were assessed using various validated questionnaires, and an allostatic load index was assessed using 14 physiological components of the allostatic load model; the analysis was performed using the quartile method (Seeman, McEwen et al., 2001; Seeman et al., 1997). The results revealed that older individuals, particularly men, had significantly higher allostatic load scores than younger participants or women. Of the various work characteristics evaluated, only job demands related significantly with the allostatic load score. This association persisted after controlling for smoking status and gender and after excluding participants reporting hypertension, cardiovascular disease, or diabetes. However, the authors also showed that the association between job demands and allostatic load was highly dependent on age, with little or no association in younger participants, and an increasing effect of job demands on allostatic load score in participants over 45. These results go along with the notion that allostatic load results from the cumulative impact of wear and tear that occurs throughout life and that adds up with increasing age.

Allostatic Load and Socioeconomic Status. In a more recent study, the data from the MacArthur Studies of Successful Aging were used to assess whether the socioeconomic status (SES) differences in mortality can be partially explained by differences in allostatic load (Seeman, Crimmins, et al., 2004). Results showed that the score of allostatic load explained 35.4% of the difference in mortality risk between those with higher versus those with lower SES. Of importance, it was shown that the cumulative index provided independent explanatory power over and above a measure of doctor-diagnosed disease. Here again, the summary measure (allostatic load score) accounted for more variance than individual biological parameters in predicting health outcomes, suggesting the high potential value of this multisystem view of biological pathways through which SES ultimately affects morbidity and mortality.

Allostatic Load and Social Support. Allostatic load scores have not only been associated with negative outcomes; new studies now show that the presence of social support in an individual's life is a strong predictor of low allostatic load scores later in life. The first report of a significant association between allostatic load score and social support was published by Singer and Ryff in 1999. These authors used data from the Wisconsin Longitudinal Study and searched for precursors to allostatic load via ordered categories of cumulative adversity relative to advantage over the life course. They operationalized life trajectories via economic circumstances and social relationship experiences (e.g., parent-child interactions, quality of spousal ties). The results of this study revealed a strong association between the extent of adversity early in life and the likelihood of high allostatic load later in life. More important, they showed that resilient individuals with economic disadvantage but compensating positive social relationship histories showed low prevalence of high allostatic load. In 2001, using data from the MacArthur Study of Successful Aging, Seeman and collaborators (Seeman, Lusignolo, Albert, & Berkman, 2001) reported that greater baseline emotional support in the participants of this longitudinal study was a significant predictor of better cognitive function at the 7.5-year follow-up, controlling for baseline cognitive function and known sociodemographic, behavioral, psychological, and health status predictors of cognitive aging. Finally, in a recent study using data from the Social Environment and Biomarkers of Aging Study in Taiwan, Seeman and collaborators (Seeman, Glei, et al., 2004) examined relationships between social environment characteristics and allostatic load in two groups of older Taiwanese individuals split as a function of age (54 to 70, and

71 and older). They used the longitudinal data on levels of social integration and extent of social support as predictors of cumulative allostatic load. The results showed that in the 54 to 70 age group, the presence of a spouse in early years (6 to 8 years prior to the collection of data) was associated with lower allostatic load in men, but not women. In the older group of participants (71 years and above), it was found that ties with close friends and/or neighbors were significantly related to lower allostatic load score for both men and women. Interestingly, although significant, these relationships between social support and allostatic load were more modest than the associations reported to occur in Western societies. The authors suggested that contextual, normative influences on social experience may affect the patterns of association between features of these social worlds and the physiological substrates of health.

Conclusion

Many important points result from our analysis of the allostatic load model. First, cumulative wear and tear have effects on the body through lifelong exposure to various challenges. Second, the data obtained so far show that allostatic load tends to develop in time and increase sharply in the later decades of adult life. These data also show that environmental conditions, such as high job demands and poverty, are associated with higher allostatic load scores. However, the presence of social support, either in early life or later in life, is a strong predictor of low allostatic load. These results suggest that allostatic load is a process that could begin very early in life, and that, depending on the environmental conditions to which children are exposed, they may develop an allostatic load process very early in development.

In the next sections of this chapter, we summarize data and concepts pertaining to the potential pathways by which allostatic load can develop in children facing adversities.

EARLY ADVERSITY AND THE DEVELOPMENT OF ALLOSTATIC LOAD

Following a definition by Sandler (2001), adversity can be characterized as a condition that threatens the satisfaction of basic human needs and goals (including physical safety, self-esteem, efficacy, and social relatedness) and constrains the accomplishment of developmental tasks such as school success and positive role functioning at home. Many conditions have been related to early adversity, the most important of them being low SES, child maltreatment, and war. In the following, we discuss some data related to these different types of early adversities. Although we are aware that each type of adversity may have very different effects on the body's response to stress, it is important to note that there have not been enough studies performed so far on this particular issue to allow us to offer a clear distinction across these different forms of adversity. Consequently, we discuss these adversities generally as conditions very early in life that threaten the satisfaction of a child's basic needs and goals (Sandler, 2001).

Many studies on adversity have looked at the effects of low SES on health and well-being. It has been found that individuals from high SES environments enjoy better health than individuals from low SES environments. Various studies have shown that blood pressure (Breier et al., 1987) increases significantly as employment grade (B. S. Dohrenwend, 1973), occupational status (Adelstein, 1980), income (Folkman, Schaefer, & Lazarus, 1979), or years of education (Adelstein, 1980) decrease. Although most of the literature has concentrated on systemic diseases, other studies have shown a significant relationship between SES and mental health. For instance, inverse associations have been reported between SES and the prevalence of Schizophrenia, Posttraumatic Stress Disorder, Major Depression, alcoholism, substance abuse, Antisocial Personality Disorder, and nonspecific distress (B. P. Dohrenwend, 2000).

With regard to developmental pathways, the exposure to adverse conditions in childhood is closely related to the development of physical and mental health problems in adulthood (Sandler, 2001). The relationship is of a cumulative nature; that is, the greater the number of adverse experiences, the more likely is development of a variety of problems later in life. For instance, Felitti et al. (1998) reported a 4- to 12-fold increased risk for alcoholism, drug abuse, depression, and suicide attempts in adults who had experienced four or more adversities in childhood.

Although the relationship between early adversity and health is well documented, the mechanisms that account for the relationship are not clearly understood (e.g., Sandler, 2001). One possible pathway that links adversity to health problems is stress (e.g., Lupien, King, Meaney, & McEwen, 2001; McLoyd, 1998): As stated earlier, adversity is a condition that threatens the satisfaction of basic human needs. The consequence of perceiving such a threat is a state of stressful arousal (e.g., Sandler, 2001). With respect to SES, it has been shown that low SES individuals are exposed to a greater amount of chronic and acute threats/stressors than high SES individuals (e.g., Bradley & Corwyn, 2002). Environmental as well as social/psychological factors contribute to the increased stress levels. With regard to environmental factors, low SES is associ-

ated with poor living conditions, overcrowding, exposure to environmental hazards, and crime (e.g., Bradley & Corwyn, 2002; Haan, Kaplan, & Syme, 1989). With regard to sociological/psychological factors, it has been shown that lower SES increases the likelihood of exposure to negative events such as social aggression, family conflict, and risk behaviors (B. S. Dohrenwend & Dohrenwend, 1970). Additionally, low SES individuals are exposed to a higher rate of change and instability in their lives such as family dissolution and household moves. This instability has been found to produce a higher level of individual distress in these individuals (Broadhead et al., 1983; B. S. Dohrenwend & Dohrenwend, 1970). Moreover, individuals who have access to psychological and material support from family, spouses, or friends during stressful events appear to be in better health compared to individuals without significant support (Broadhead et al., 1983; S. Cohen, 1988; Schwarzer & Leppin, 1989; Starfield, 1982). Individuals low on the SES hierarchy have fewer of these social and psychological resources to cope with stressful life events than individuals higher in the SES hierarchy (S. Cohen, 1988; House et al., 1994; McLeod & Kessler, 1990).

To assess whether the development of the relationship between SES and mental health is sustained, at least in part, by exposure to high levels of glucocorticoids, Lupien and collaborators (Lupien, King, Meaney, & McEwen, 2000; Lupien et al., 2001) measured morning salivary cortisol levels and cognitive function (memory, attention, language, and emotional processing) in 396 children (from 6 to 16 years of age) from low versus high SES in the Montreal area in Canada (Lupien et al., 2001). Depressive symptomatology and exposure to stressful events were also assessed in each child's mother through a semistructured phone interview. The results revealed that low SES children from 6 to 10 years old presented significantly higher salivary cortisol levels when compared to children from high SES. This difference disappeared at the time of school transition, that is, at 12 years old, and no SES differences were observed at 12, 14, and 16 years of age. The absence of SES differences in cortisol levels during high school could be due to changes in cortisol secretion in relation to social roles (importance of peers over family, youth culture, etc.; see Lupien et al., 2001), or to the fact that those teenagers from low SES who were available to perform this study were the most resilient, that is, were those teenagers who decided not to quit school. Neuropsychological data showed that although children from low and high SES do not differ with regard to memory, attentional, and linguistic functions, children from low SES (at all ages) presented a significantly higher level of negative emotional processing (Lupien et al., 2005). Scores on the depression and stress questionnaires were significantly higher for low SES mothers, when compared to high SES mothers. More important, the authors reported a significant positive correlation between the mother's depressive symptomatology and her child's cortisol level (Lupien et al., 2000). This showed that the higher the score of the mother on the depressive scale, the higher the cortisol level of her child. Altogether, these results showed that low SES in young children is related to increased cortisol secretion and negative emotional processing. Moreover, they showed that depression in the mother is, in conjunction with low SES, a significant factor predicting high cortisol levels in children.

Other studies have reported a significant association between early adversities and/or mother's depression on a child's glucocorticoid levels. For example, numerous retrospective studies of adults and children have shown that increased reactivity of the HPA system is associated with early trauma (Cicchetti & Rogosch, 2001; Heim et al., 2000; Kaufman et al., 1997; Yehuda, Halligan, & Grossman, 2001), as well as severe deprivation (Gunnar, Morison, Chisholm, & Schuder, 2001). Moreover, studies of infants and toddlers suggest that maternal postpartum depression and behaviors, with the insecure mother-child attachments that can result from these conditions, are positively associated with children's cortisol levels (Field, 1994; Spangler & Grossmann, 1993). In a longitudinal study of children of depressed mothers, Hessl and collaborators (1998) found that postpartum depression was positively associated with children's cortisol at 3 years of age, although another study reported no effect of maternal depression on cortisol levels when the children were age 7 (Ashman, Dawson, Panagiotides, Yamada, & Wilkinson, 2002).

However, in another study, Essex and collaborators (Essex, Klein, Cho, & Kalin, 2002) measured salivary cortisol levels in 282 children age 4.5 years and 154 of their siblings. The authors were able to obtain maternal reports of stress when the children were ages 1, 4, and 12 months and again at 4.5 years. Finally, they assessed the child's mental health symptoms in the first grade of school. In the first cross-sectional analysis of the association between actual maternal stress and the actual child's cortisol levels, Essex and collaborators found that at 4.5 years of age, the children exposed to high levels of concurrent maternal stress presented significantly higher cortisol levels than children exposed to moderate or low levels of maternal stress. Very interestingly, they also revealed a similar association of exposure to concurrent maternal stress and cortisol levels in the siblings of these children. The analysis of the longitudinal data revealed that the children who were

exposed to high levels of concurrent actual maternal stress and who were initially exposed to high maternal stress in infancy (thus exposed to high maternal stress both in infancy and at 4.5 years of age) were the only group that had significantly higher cortisol levels. No effects of maternal stress on child's cortisol levels were observed for children exposed to maternal stress in infancy only. These results suggest that exposure to concurrent maternal stress is associated with increased cortisol levels only for children whose exposure began in infancy. The authors then addressed the potential association between child's cortisol levels and behavioral problems. Results showed that the preschoolers with high cortisol levels presented greater internalizing and externalizing symptoms when assessed 2 years later. Finally, the link reported between low SES and higher cortisol levels in children (Lupien et al., 2001) was replicated in this study.

In a more recent study, G. W. Evans and Marcynyszyn (2004) analyzed cross-sectional data from 216 third-through fifth-grade low- and middle-income children in upstate New York. The data of this study included overnight urinary neuroendocrine levels, noise levels, residential crowding (people per room), and housing quality. The authors calculated an index of cumulative environmental risk exposure based on the number of risk factors (i.e., crowding, indoor noise, and housing quality). Risk exposure for each factor was designated as greater than 1 standard deviation above the mean and given a score of 1. The other exposure levels were considered lower risk and coded as 0. The results revealed that cumulative environmental risk exposure was significantly greater for low-income children. More important, the authors showed that cumulative environmental risk was positively correlated with elevated overnight epinephrine, norepinephrine, and cortisol in the low-income sample but not in the middle-income sample. These results remained significant after controlling for income, maternal education, family structure, age, and gender.

Altogether, these results strongly suggest that early exposure to adversity (through low SES, maternal stress/depression, or maltreatment) can have potent and long-lasting effects on the secretion of glucocorticoids in children. Although these studies provide very interesting results with regard to the influence of early adversities on a child's basal cortisol levels, they do not provide an answer to a very important question about the allostatic load model: What determines the initial processing of an information as being threatening (leading to the secretion of the primary stress mediators) or nonthreatening? Indeed, as we have discussed in previous sections, various situations can be real threats (a house on fire) or implied threats (interpretation of a situation as being novel and/or unpredictable and/or uncontrollable), and both types of stressors will lead to the activation of primary stress mediators and potentially to allostatic load. It is thus becoming extremely important to understand the mechanisms by which early adversities might shape a child's cognitive processing and lead to a healthy or biased processing of incoming information and, consequently, to cumulative allostatic load due to repeated activation of the primary stress mediators when situations are interpreted most of the time as being stressful.

The Subjective Nature of Reality: The Human Information-Processing System

Cognitive psychology is concerned with how people perceive, learn, remember, and think about information. Since the 1960s, the human brain has often been conceptualized as an information-processing device. From studies in cognitive psychology, we have learned that what we perceive is not an exact replica of the external world. Instead, perceptual processes transform and interpret information from the external world. Additionally, our mental capacities are limited, and to further process information, we have to allocate our mental resources to certain stimuli, a process called selective attention. Stimuli we attend to enter a short-term or working memory store; from there, some of the information will eventually be transferred into long-term memory, the memory system that stores our experiences (episodic memory) and factual knowledge (semantic memory; for criticism and modifications of this view of memory, see, e.g., Baddeley, 1999, chap. 2). The content of the long-term memory store will also determine how the incoming information is interpreted and what behavioral responses are elicited. In sum, what has become clear is that incoming information is modulated at every stage of the information-processing flow, finally resulting in an individual's very own construction of reality.

The aspects of a situation an individual attends to, the interpretation of these aspects, and the behavioral responses that follow are largely determined by the individual's history and previous experiences. It can be assumed that the cognitive systems are largely "shaped" during childhood (e.g., Cicchetti, 2002), when those neurological systems (frontal lobe, amygdala, and hippocampus) undergo major developmental changes that subserve attention and memory as well as other higher-order cognitive processes such as problem solving and decision making.

In the following, we describe cognitive processes that we think can explain parts of the association that has been found between adversity and allostatic load/health damage. We introduce an information-processing model of adaptation to threatening information that highlights two different adaptation pathways that can lead to allostatic load. We argue that both pathways are likely to be found in individuals who grew up in disadvantaged and/or adverse environments and who lacked protective mechanisms that could counteract the influence of adversity.

An Information-Processing Model of Adaptation to Threatening Information

As described earlier, individuals growing up in disadvantaged environments frequently face threatening situations: instability, financial problems, limited residential choices, crime, conflict, social aggression, and so on. Some of these threats constitute absolute stressors (e.g., maltreatment, crime); others constitute relative stressors (e.g., instability, financial problems). As presented in Figure 14.2, the frequent encounter with threatening information will likely result in a cognitive system that reacts hypersensitively to threatening information. This is accomplished by an attentional system that is highly vigilant, because the individual is expecting threatening information. The expectation of threats and a bias toward interpreting situations as threatening is probably due to a memory system that contains a variety of highly interconnected and easily accessible threat-related information (Pollak & Sinha, 2002). A cognitive system that is biased toward the detection and processing of threatening information can be viewed as adaptive in the short run (allostasis), because an early and

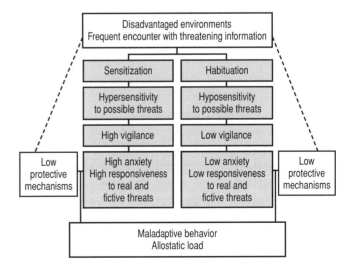

Figure 14.2 Schematic representation of how early adversity can modify the processing of threatening information, leading to habituation or sensitization of detection of threatening information.

facilitated threat detection might give individuals the necessary time to counteract the threat (Pollak & Sinha, 2002). This cognitive system, however, has at least two drawbacks in the long run. First, a hypervigilant system is likely to wear out quickly (allostatic load; McEwen, 1998b). Second, the cost of high vigilance is false alarms to relative stressors; that is, nonthreatening information might be falsely identified as threatening (Pollak & Kistler, 2002). Protective mechanisms, such as well-functioning parent-child relationships and cognitive abilities, are often compromised as a consequence of adversity. If protective mechanisms fail, sensitization to threatening information is likely to result in maladaptive psychological (e.g., stress, anxiety) and behavioral (e.g., aggressive, health-damaging) responses (e.g., Masten, 2001). Prolonged states of anxiety and anticipation of negative events can result in allostatic load (McEwen, 1998b).

One can think of another, and in some sense opposite way of dealing with frequent exposure to threatening information, namely, habituation (see Figure 14.2). Habituation is the tendency to become accustomed to a stimulus, resulting in the stimulus becoming less and less noticed. Individuals from disadvantaged environments might get accustomed to threatening situations and might filter out threatening stimuli. This can be adaptive in the short run, because the individual will be less anxious and less vigilant (allostasis). On the other hand, the late detection of and the general hyporesponsiveness to real threats prevent individuals from proactive planning of adequate responses. The consequence is that no stress response is initiated in situations where such a response would be adequate. The inadequate response of allostatic systems is one pathway that has been linked to allostatic load (Type 4 allostatic load, inadequate response; McEwen, 1998b). Furthermore, the hyporesponsiveness to threatening information might promote risk-taking and thrill-seeking behaviors that can lead to further health damage and greater allostatic load, especially when protective mechanisms fail.

Next, we review some empirical evidence for the adaptive processes described in the model. We describe studies that demonstrate the specific influence that adversity has on the development of several cognitive processes, including attention, perception, memory, language, and theory of mind. The research reviewed here comprises a rather heterogeneous set of studies covering very different aspects of adversity, from low SES to different kinds of child maltreatment. We are aware of the fact that different experiences lead to very specific outcomes. The heterogeneous sample of studies we describe serves the purpose of illustrating how the environment shapes cognitive processes in

such a way that the individual is more susceptible to stress, and is not meant to give a comprehensive overview of the complex literature on adversity and cognitive development. Throughout the chapter, the reader should keep in mind that high adversity alone has only a weak predictive value for poor developmental outcome. Only the combination of high adversity and weak protective resources leads to maladaptive profiles (Masten, 2001).

Before describing the studies, we briefly review the brain structures that are involved in the stress response and that might therefore be modified by early adversities. These brain structures play an important role in interpreting situations and selecting possible responses.

Brain Structures Involved in the Stress Response

Three brain structures are critically involved in the stress response: the prefrontal cortex, the amygdala, and the hippocampal formation. Each of these brain structures is affected by stress hormones and/or involved in the regulation of stress hormone secretion. At the same time, these brain structures play a crucial role in the interpretation of a situation (as being stressful) and in the subsequent selection and inhibition of possible responses.

The prefrontal cortex is sometimes described as the highest part of the brain as it is involved in most higher cognitive functions such as reasoning, planning, attention, working memory, and some aspects of language (e.g., Connolly, Goodale, Menon, & Munoz, 2002; Owen, Doyan, Petrides, & Evans, 1996). For instance, the prefrontal cortex determines which information will be considered and which information will be inhibited during the performance of goal-directed behaviors (e.g., Bunge, Ochsner, Desmond, Glover, & Gabrieli, 2001). It also plays an important role in retrieval processes, especially in recalling the temporal order and source of memories (e.g., Fan, Snodgrass, & Bilder, 2003). Many other specific functions of the prefrontal cortex could be named. Because of its involvement in nearly all higher cognitive processes, some authors regard the prefrontal cortex as the "frontal moral guidance system" that regulates social/moral behaviors (e.g., Bigler, 2001, p. 610).

The amygdala is critically involved in assessing the emotional significance of events (e.g., Anderson & Phelps, 2001). It is especially important for the processing of the emotions of anger, aggression, and fear. Recent studies with rats suggest that the amygdala also plays a crucial role in forming associations between cues and outcomes (Schoenbaum, Setlow, Saddoris, & Gallagher, 2003).

The hippocampal formation is involved in learning and memory. It specifically subserves the formation and retrieval of episodic memories, that is, the human ability to mentally travel back in time and remember where (spatial component) and when (temporal component) a specific event occurred (e.g., Tulving, 2002). During encoding, the hippocampal formation is engaged in relational learning mechanisms that bind the different components of an event into an integrated memory trace (e.g., Davachi & Wagner, 2002). Damage to the hippocampal formation results in profound amnesia, especially an inability to remember new episodes (e.g., Vargha-Khadem et al., 1997).

Roughly speaking, the described brain structures are critically involved in evaluating a situation and selecting an appropriate response (prefrontal cortex) with regard to the emotional content of the situation (amygdala) and in relation to past experiences (hippocampal formation, prefrontal cortex).

Selective Attention to Threatening Information in Maltreated Children

As described earlier, it is impossible to process all information to which an individual is exposed because attentional resources are limited. Therefore, some environmental cues are filtered out or attenuated and other stimuli are selected for further processing (e.g., Treisman, 1964). Which stimuli are attended to is a function of the physical and psychological state of the individual, as is the saliency of these cues. Children's information-processing capacities are much more limited than those of adults (e.g., Case, 1985). Therefore, they are much more selective in their attentional processes. Pollak and Sinha (2002) argue that children selectively attend to those features of the environment that are closely linked with highly positive or highly negative outcomes.

Pollak and colleagues (Pollak, Cicchetti, Hornung, & Reed, 2000; Pollak & Tolley-Schell, 2003) have demonstrated in several studies using a variety of methods that early experiences shape attentional processes and determine which stimuli children select for attention. They found that maltreated and nonmaltreated children differed in their attention allocation to certain emotional stimuli. Specifically, physically abused children were highly sensitive to information that signals threat and possible harm, namely, angry facial expressions. At the same time, these children had problems shifting their attentional focus away from angry faces; that is, they had less control over their attentional processes than nonabused controls.

Physically abused children are not only especially sensitive to anger cues, they also experience more fear than nonabused controls when witnessing angry interactions. For instance, in a study by Hennessy, Rabideau, Cicchetti, and Cummings (1994), physically abused children reported more fear than nonabused controls when watching videotapes of adults in angry interactions. Over time, the frequent experience of fear and the accompanying stress response can result in allostatic load (e.g., McEwen, 1998b).

It is important to note that the studies by Pollak and colleagues (2000) show that abused children do not experience a general attentional deficit. Rather, abused children's attention is biased toward the detection of anger cues. Additionally, abused children have difficulties exerting control over their attentional processes when faced with threatening information. In the next section, we describe how this sensitization to threat affects perceptual and memory processes in abused children.

Effects of Adversity on Perceptual and Representational Systems

As described earlier, the long-term memory store contains an individual's knowledge about the world and past experiences. It can be hypothesized that the long-term memory store differs greatly in its content for children facing adversities when compared to children in less adverse conditions. Whereas children living in adverse conditions may experience a lot of stressful situations and daily hassles and acquire a lot of factual knowledge about how to survive in threatening environments, children living in more favorable conditions may experience a great variety of nonstressful situations. Thus, it can be assumed that the memory content of children facing adversity is biased toward threatening/stressful information. It can be further speculated that children facing adversity are more likely to interpret a situation as threatening and to select threat-oriented coping strategies, whereas children living in more favorable conditions are more likely to interpret a situation as nonthreatening and to select a nonthreat strategy to meet the situational demands.

The assumption that memory processes are shaped or fine-tuned by early experiences is again supported by the work of Pollak and colleagues (Pollak et al., 2000; Pollak & Sinha, 2002), who studied emotion recognition in children. Pollak et al. presented physically abused, neglected, and nonmaltreated children with several emotional stories. After hearing each story, the children were shown photographs depicting facial expressions of different emotions and were asked to select the photograph that would best fit what the story's protagonist felt. Neglected children, who have experienced a lack of care and responsiveness from their parents, had difficulties recognizing different emotional states. In contrast, physically abused children were as sensitive as controls in differentiating emotions, and they performed especially well in recognizing anger-related situations. Both maltreated groups showed a response bias: Neglected children displayed a response bias for sad facial expressions, and physically abused children showed a tendency toward selecting angry facial expressions. This study clearly shows that early experiences shape how individuals interpret emotional signals in a very specific way. For instance, the response bias for anger in physically abused children might be due to their experience of frequent anger outbursts that are often unpredictable and that appear not to be related to the specific situation.

Physically abused children do not only show a response bias for anger. Already at a perceptual level, these children are especially sensitive to anger cues. This was experimentally shown by Pollak and Sinha (2002), who asked physically abused and nonabused children to recognize emotions from degraded pictures of happy, angry, sad, and fearful faces in a priming task. Faces were initially presented in highly degraded formats. Over time, the pictures became more organized and easier to identify. Physically abused children were able to correctly identify angry facial expressions on the basis of more degraded picture versions than were nonmaltreated children. Physically abused children needed more information than controls to recognize sadness. No group differences were found for happiness or fearfulness.

Taken together, these studies show that an abusive environment makes children especially sensitive for the detection of anger. According to Pollak and Sinha (2002), this is accomplished by a memory system that is fine-tuned by early experiences to allow for facilitated access to the representation of anger. Physically abused children grow up in an environment that is characterized by uncontrollable sudden outbursts of violence. The early detection of anger might give children additional time to prepare for hostile interactions. In this sense, abused children's early detection of threatening information can be viewed as adaptive. However, it becomes maladaptive when premature decisions about facial expressions are made (see Pollak & Sinha, 2002, for these arguments). In cases of uncertainty, abused children tend to interpret facial expressions as angry, a bias that restricts them from considering other possible interpretations (Pollak & Kistler, 2002). Later in life, a bias toward interpreting situations as threatening and therefore stressful is likely to result in allostatic load and situational-inadequate responses such as conduct disorders, aggressive behavior, depression, and anxiety.

Effects of Adversity on Language Development

Interpersonal communication is one mechanism that helps individuals to cope with stressful situations. This coping

mechanism is often spontaneously used with family and friends, and it is a basic element of many psychological counseling approaches (e.g., client-centered therapy; Rogers, 1951). For this coping mechanism to work, individuals need to be able to verbally express their problems and feelings; that is, communicative skills play an important role.

Language develops in a very constrained and predictable way in all normally developing children, and many researchers have emphasized the biological-maturational component of language acquisition (e.g., Chomsky, 1972; Pinker, 1994). This component might explain why individuals reared in very different cultural and linguistic environments all acquire their native language. Although almost all individuals become fluent speakers, environmental factors likely influence the grade of linguistic proficiency that is reached. It has been shown that disadvantaged environments can influence the pathways of language acquisition, possibly resulting in language and communicative deficits later in life. For instance, children from lower SES families show slower rates of vocabulary growth than children from higher SES families (Hoff, 2003). This effect is mediated by the speech children hear at home. Hoff showed that the speech of mothers from lower and higher SES differs in quantity, lexical richness, and sentence complexity, and that these differences explained over 20% of the variance in 2-year-olds' size of productive vocabulary.

Cicchetti and colleagues (Beeghly & Cicchetti, 1994; Coster, Gersten, Beeghly, & Cicchetti, 1989) looked at language development in maltreated children and found delays in language structure, expressive vocabulary, and expression of internal states. Eigsti and Cicchetti (2004) extended these findings by showing that not only the content but also the linguistic form is affected by maltreatment and SES: 5-year-old maltreated children and nonmaltreated children from low SES both scored below age-expected levels of syntactic abilities, with maltreatment causing a significantly greater amount of developmental delay.

What are the long-term effects of these developmental delays? Because longitudinal studies are missing, there is no definite answer to that question. However, Eigsti and Cicchetti (2004) suspect that language delays lead to later emotional, social, and cognitive delays and exacerbate existing problems. The observation that the speech of mothers from lower and higher SES differs in many aspects (Hoff, 2003) further supports long-lasting detrimental effects of disadvantaged environments on language skills. The less an individual is able to communicate his or her problems and internal states, the more difficulties he or she might have coping with stressful situations, because interpersonal communication might not lead to the desired stress-releasing effect.

Effects of Adversity on False Belief Understanding

A 3-year-old child's understanding of the mind is very different from that of a 5-year-old child. Whereas 3-year-old children roughly assume that all people share the same knowledge, 5-year-old children have realized that people's beliefs may be true or false and that people's behavior is based on these beliefs rather than on reality. In their now-classic set of experiments on false belief understanding, Gopnik and Astington (1988) showed children of different ages a box with pictures of candy on it and asked the children what they thought was in the box. The children assumed that the box contained candy and were surprised when they opened the box and found crayons. When asked what another child who has not yet looked inside the box would think was in the box, 5-year-old children seemed to understand the concept of deception and said "candy." Three-year-old children, in contrast, answered that the other child would think that the box contained crayons. Moreover, 3-year-old children also denied their own original deception; that is, they said they had always thought that the box contained crayons. Since the original work by Gopnik and Astington several studies have shown that major changes in false belief understanding take place around 4 years of age (Wellman, Cross, & Watson, 2001).

Does false belief understanding follow a different developmental pattern in maltreated children? In a recent study by Cicchetti and colleagues (Cicchetti, Rogosch, Maughan, Toth, & Bruce, 2003), 3- to 8-year-old maltreated and non-maltreated children performed two false belief tasks. Among children with a verbal mental age of 49 months or greater, maltreated children demonstrated less false belief understanding than nonmaltreated children. Performance was worst for children who were physically abused and whose maltreatment started during the toddler years. Cicchetti et al. suggest two possible pathways by which maltreatment can affect false belief understanding. First, deficits in caregiving, especially the lack of parental empathy and sensitivity to the child's internal experiences, and the limited communication of feelings and emotions by the parents may contribute to a delay in the child's understanding of beliefs of self and others. This suggestion is strengthened by studies showing that maternal language to toddlers about internal states mirrors their children's abilities to become increasingly other-oriented (Beeghly, Bretherton, & Mervis, 1986; J. Dunn, Bretherton, Munn, 1987). Dunn and collaborators (J. Dunn, Brown, & Beard-

sall, 1991) found that individual differences in the amount of family discussions about feelings and emotions predicted young children's understanding of other people's feelings and beliefs, even when children's language skills were controlled for analytically. From these results, it is becoming clear that a child does not necessarily need to be exposed to significant adversities (e.g., maltreatment) in order to present weaknesses in the development of verbal abilities and emotional understanding, but that exposure to a family environment lacking the richness of interactions necessary to develop these skills may be sufficient to prevent adequate cognitive and emotional abilities later in life. Also, given the fact that the ability to make judgments about mental states is critical to social interactions, it may be possible that a lack of adequate development of this skill may prevent children from coping efficiently in the face of the various stressors of life.

Second, neurobiological maturation processes might be more directly altered by maltreatment in that "children subjected to pathological care giving may acquire neuropathological connections instead of functional neural connections" (Cicchetti et al., 2003, p. 1087). This pathway could explain why an onset of maltreatment during the toddler years is especially detrimental to the development of false belief understanding, because the toddler period is a time of rapid creation and modification of neuronal connections (see also Cicchetti, 2002), and many of the precursors of false belief understanding develop during that period, for example, language development (especially the verbal expression of internal states), conceptual development, increased individuation, and self-other differentiation (Cicchetti, 1991).

Regarding the influence of SES on theory of mind development, findings are somewhat mixed. For instance, Cutting and Dunn (1999) found differences in false belief understanding in relation to parental occupational class and mother's education (see also Pears & Moses, 2003). Other researchers have found that SES and performance in theory of mind tasks were not (Cicchetti et al., 2003) or only weakly (Murray, Woolgar, Briers, & Hipwell, 1999) related and that parental behaviors (Hughes, Deater-Deckard, & Cutting, 1999) or general and verbal intelligence (Murray et al., 1999) were better predictors of theory of mind performance.

Taken together, studies have shown that adversity can alter false belief understanding and other aspects of theory of mind development in children. For the case of maltreatment, the pathways through which maltreatment contributes to developmental delays have been specified. For low SES, the literature is less clear and the multifaceted factors that may lead to successful or unsuccessful development need further specification.

Positive Outcome in the Context of Adversity: The Concept of Resilience

Not everybody reared in disadvantaged environments will face problems later in life. In the literature, the phenomenon that similar stressful experiences can lead to very different individual outcomes is referred to as multifinality (Curtis & Cicchetti, 2003). At the same time, not everybody who experiences problems later in life has faced adversity, a phenomenon referred to as equifinality (Curtis & Cicchetti, 2003). Both concepts highlight the important fact that early experiences do not ultimately determine further developmental pathways. This brings us to the concept of resilience. Resilience can be defined as successful adaptation or competent developmental outcome in the face of risk and adversity. Curtis and Cicchetti conceptualize resilience as "a dynamic process that is influenced by neural and psychological self-organization, as well as transactions between the ecological context and the developing organism" (p. 776). Thus, many different interdependent factors contribute to resilient functioning, including biological factors such as genetic makeup, brain organization, and neuroendocrine functioning; psychological factors such as emotion regulation, attachment, and locus of control; and environmental factors such as parenting (for overviews, see, e.g., Curtis & Cicchetti, 2003; Luthar, 2003; Masten, 2001). Here, we focus on cognitive processes that contribute to resilience.

An interesting longitudinal study on adversity and resilience was conducted by Masten et al. (1999), who followed children over 10 years from childhood through adolescence and assessed three major domains of competence: academic achievement, conduct, and peer social competence. Adversity was measured as the occurrence of major life events and experiences that are likely to be stressful (e.g., death of a family member). The study focused on two possible resources that are assumed to protect children from the effects of adversity: intellectual functioning (intelligence) and parenting quality. The authors found that both resources protected children from developing competence problems. High-adversity children with high intelligence scores and well-functioning parent-child relationships were as competent as low-adversity children. At the same time, low-adversity children with low resources developed competence similar to high-resource children. This shows that only the combination of high adversity and low resources resulted in competence problems. Specific to intellectual functioning, intelligence was related to academic achievement and to social competence

in childhood. Academic achievement is negatively associated with mental health problems (Sandler, 2001). Most interesting, high intellectual functioning in childhood was a protective factor against developing conduct problems in adolescence, thus pointing to the long-term moderating effect of early cognitive functioning on adversity. This finding also replicates previous studies that have shown that intellectual functioning is an important moderating variable of antisocial behavior in high-risk groups (White, Moffitt, & Silva, 1989). As Masten et al. (1999, p. 163) point out, "Numerous processes could underlie this effect: Good verbal, learning or problem solving aptitude could play a role in assessing threat, accessing resources, effective seeking of healthier environments or relationships for development, appealingness to teachers, etc."

In summary, the data suggest that the capacity to detect threatening and nonthreatening information develops very early in life and is sensitive to environmental conditions. This modification of the selective attention process will lead to more threatening cues and information being stored in long-term memory, with the resulting effect that when the time comes to find a response to a threat (relative or absolute, real or implied), a threat-related type of response (aggression, violence, etc.) may be more readily available for immediate action. Although this response may be adaptive in the short run, the frequent detection of threat and/or threat response may lead to an allostatic load process, affecting the behavior, the body, and the brain. In terms of behavior, this decision process might lead in the long run to the development of externalizing behaviors and/or a diagnosis of a Conduct Disorder. If this is the case, then some bodily markers of allostatic load may be related to externalized behaviors in children.

To assess whether such a process might occur in developing children, we have reviewed the literature on externalized behavior and Conduct Disorders in children, in association with biological processes known to be involved in allostatic load. In our literature search, we found various markers of allostatic load that have been studied in relation to externalized behaviors or Conduct Disorders in children. Some of these biological processes are primary stress mediators (cortisol, DHEAS), and others are secondary outcomes (waist-hip ratio, cholesterol, and heart rate). We summarize these data in the following sections.

Allostatic Load and Externalized Behaviors/Conduct Disorder in Children

Conduct Disorder (CD) refers to a group of symptoms or problematic externalized behaviors. The description of CD in the *Diagnostic and Statistical Manual of Mental Disorders,* fourth edition (*DSM-IV*), includes four types of behavior: (1) aggression toward people or animals, (2) destruction of property, (3) deceitfulness or theft, and (4) serious violations of rules; all of these are referred to as externalizing behaviors. Because it is a very heterogeneous disorder both in its occurrence and in its etiology, Frick (1998) proposed using the plural term Conduct Disorders. Two different types of CD are nowadays distinguished: the childhood-onset (*DSM-IV*) or life-course-persistent type (Caspi & Moffitt, 1995) and the adolescent-onset (*DSM-IV*) or adolescence-limited type (Caspi & Moffitt, 1995), each with a different etiology. The spectrum of CD also includes more extreme forms of behaviors, such as psychopathic behavior. It has been acknowledged that the distinction between these two types of CD is of importance for their causal accounts and treatment decisions (Caspi & Moffitt, 1995; Frick, 1998; Moffitt, Caspi, Harrington, & Milner, 2002). In our review of allostatic load markers, we focus on the childhood-onset or life-course-persistent type, and we intermix by sections the results of studies that have assessed either externalized behaviors in children or children diagnosed with Conduct Disorders. However, for the sake of clarity, we refer to only Conduct Disorders in each section's title.

Commonly, adverse environmental factors are suggested to contribute, at least partially, to the onset, maintenance, and exacerbation of externalizing behaviors among children (Haapasalo & Tremblay, 1994; McLeod & Shanahan, 1993). The adverse environmental conditions studied in relation to externalizing behaviors include SES (Brooks-Gunn & Duncan, 1997; McLoyd, 1998), low parental education attainment (Hanson, McLanahan, & Thomson, 1997), negative parental behaviors (Lempers, Clark-Lempers, & Simons, 1989), single motherhood (Corcoran & Chaudry, 1997), exposure to violence (Miller, Wasserman, Neugebauer, Gorman-Smith, & Kamboukos, 1999), and low quality of schools and neighborhoods (Bradley & Corwyn, 2002).

Here, it is important to note that the importance of these environmental variables in the development of externalized behaviors may stem from their actions on parental behavior. For example, economic hardship may decrease the mother's self-esteem (McLeod & Nonnemaker, 2000) and the parents' investment in the child (Bolger, Patterson, Thompson, & Kupersmidt, 1995; Jackson, Brooks-Gunn, Huang, & Glassman, 2000), may induce frequent use of physical discipline (Conger, Patterson, & Ge, 1995; Deater-Deckard, Dodge, Bates, & Pettit, 1996), and may exacerbate mothers' depressive symptoms (McLeod & Nonnemaker, 2000). So, the response that is induced by exposure to adverse environmental factors may be mediated by the psychological and physiological stress induced by these adversities, which in turn may be responsible for enhanced propensity to manifest externalizing behaviors (G. W. Evans, 2003; G. W. Evans & English, 2002).

A child who manifests externalization problems may react and cope (at physiological, cognitive, or behavioral levels) differently when confronted by threats as a function of his or her age. For example, a 10-year-old child with externalization problems may decide to either fight or lie to escape negative consequences, whereas an adolescent with externalization problems may be prone to select dangerous health-related behaviors (e.g., substance abuse, smoking) or adopt risk behaviors such as antisocial behaviors (e.g., stealing, fighting), drop out of school, or engage in sensation-seeking activities. From society's viewpoint, these behaviors may be unacceptable or at least impede access to better living conditions. Nevertheless, in the short run, some of these behaviors may enhance the child's or adolescent's perceived adaptation to threats by enhancing self-esteem or offering an alternative access to prestige or money, being recognized and respected, or having a thrill. Furthermore, children and adolescents manifesting externalized behaviors may also elicit more negative interactions and coercion from their environment. In attempting to adapt to threats in a cost-effective way according to their initial individual differences, some of them may exacerbate the likelihood of negative reactions from the environment, which could eventually lead to a sustained engagement in externalizing behaviors (Brennan & Raine, 1997). Thus, children with externalization problems may select different coping strategies from children without these problems as a result of both individual characteristics and adverse environmental conditions.

General Cognitive/Brain Dysfunctions in Conduct Disorders

The three brain structures (prefrontal cortex, amygdala, hippocampal formation) that are involved in the stress response (see earlier discussion) have been found to be structurally and/or functionally different in individuals with CD or other forms of antisocial disorders, including criminal psychopaths, when compared to normal controls.

With regard to structural differences, right temporal and prefrontal lobe volumes were reported to be smaller in early-onset CD and in Antisocial Personality Disorder (APD; Kruesi, Casanova, Mannheim, & Johnson-Bilder, 2004; Raine, Lencz, Bihrle, LaCasse, & Colletti, 2000). Bigler (2001) put forward the hypothesis that the prefrontal cortex as the major instance of moral guidance never developed a functional role in individuals with APD, thus explaining the deficiency of moral decision making in these individuals. It might be speculated that smaller prefrontal lobe volumes are also related to the impulsive behavior seen in individuals with CD and APD, because the prefrontal cortex plays a major role in response inhibition.

With regard to functional differences, Kiehl et al. (2001) showed that criminal psychopaths showed less activation of the amygdala and hippocampal formation when processing affective stimuli in comparison to criminal nonpsychopaths and controls. As described earlier, the amygdala is critically involved in fear processing and the formation of associations between cues and outcomes. The lower affect-related amygdala activation in criminal psychopaths therefore goes hand in hand with the finding that psychopaths are insensitive to several types of fear and punishment contingencies (e.g., Hare, 1965; Patrick et al., 1994). At the same time, in the study by Kiehl et al., criminal psychopaths showed an overactivation in the prefrontal cortex when processing affective stimuli. According to Kiehl et al., this overactivation might imply that criminal psychopaths need more cognitive resources to process affective stimuli.

As discussed earlier, allostatic load is intimately linked to brain integration of the environment. The interpretation of events as threatening or not leads to behavioral responses selected to cope with the threat, which in turn contribute to an increase of allostatic load in the long run (McEwen, 2000b). Children experiencing externalizing problems may modify *in their own way* (not necessarily consciously) their information-processing system (e.g., selection of coping behaviors and evaluation of their cost-effectiveness) to minimize the intensity/frequency of their subsequent reactions to further threats at physiological, attentional, and emotional levels. In other words, information processes may act to inhibit relevant events initially processed as threatening (habituation). As a consequence, physiological reactions induced by these initial threatening events may be reduced, leading to an allostatic response (inadequate response). This modification of the perception of threat will likely influence the physiological response of the child to environmental threats, which may then act to enhance externalizing behaviors through higher tolerance to negative events (e.g., punishment, pain, emotional arousal), reducing the child's response to social rules and frequent risky and sensation-seeking behaviors adopted by the child in order to cope with physiological underarousal (Raine, 1993).

We acknowledge that sustained externalizing problems during childhood and adolescence are not exclusively in-duced through modifications of brain chemistry. Yet, a closer examination of the physiological markers related to allostatic load is a challenging and promising way to understand the mechanisms by which markers of allostatic load may relate to externalizing behaviors.

Cortisol and Conduct Disorder

Among all the components of allostatic load, the primary stress mediator cortisol has been the most widely studied in relation to Conduct Disorders in children. To this day, the most consistent finding with regard to the secretion of cortisol levels in children with CD is the presence of lower basal levels of cortisol, although some discrepancies in the results are clearly observable. The first study of children with CD was by Kruesi and collaborators in 1989 (Kruesi, Schmidt, Donnelly, Hibbs, & Hamburger, 1989). They measured 24-hour urinary cortisol excretion in 19 boys with Attention Deficit and/or CD and 19 age-, race-, and IQ-matched normal controls. The results revealed no difference in the 24-hour urinary cortisol secretion between the two groups. However, 2 years later, McBurnett and collaborators (1991) assessed salivary cortisol levels in 67 boys (ages 8 to 13 years) with Anxiety Disorders and/or CD. The results showed that children with both CD and Anxiety Disorder had higher levels of salivary cortisol than children with CD without comorbid Anxiety Disorder. After this first report of significantly lower cortisol levels in children with CD, a wealth of studies reported either a negative correlation between cortisol levels and symptoms of CD (McBurnett & Lahey, 1994; McBurnett, Lahey, Capasso, & Loeber, 1996; McBurnett, Lahey, Rathouz, & Loeber, 2000; Pajer, Gardner, Rubin, Perel, & Neal, 2001) or the presence of significantly lower cortisol levels in children with CD when compared to children without CD (Pajer et al., 2001).

Although a significant number of studies have reported a link between low cortisol levels and Conduct Disorders, it is important to note that, similarly to Kruesi and collaborators' (1989) study, other studies did not report such an association. For example, in 1997, Schulz and collaborators (Schulz, Halperin, Newcorn, Sharma, & Gabriel, 1997) tested plasma salivary cortisol levels in aggressive and nonaggressive boys with Attention Deficit Disorder and reported no differences in cortisol levels between the groups. Other studies performed with adolescent mothers with CD did not report the negative correlation between cortisol levels and symptoms of CD (Susman et al., 1999) or did not report a significant difference between cortisol levels in adolescent mothers with or without CD (Azar et al., 2004). The discrepancy observed in the literature on cortisol and symptoms of CD may stem from a variety of factors, including the diagnosis of CD, the externalizing behavior measured, and the time and method of assessment of cortisol. Indeed, in the various studies that were performed on the link between cortisol levels and Conduct Disorders, important methodological differences are observed, with some authors assessing the 24-hour urinary pattern of cortisol secretion (Kruesi et al., 1989), others assessing plasma cortisol levels measured immediately to 115 minutes after insertion of a catheter (Pajer et al., 2001; Schulz et al., 1997; Susman et al., 1999), and others assessing cortisol in saliva samples taken in the morning period (Azar et al., 2004; Vanyukov et al., 1993) or at any time (not controlled for) over a 2-year period (McBurnett & Lahey, 1994; McBurnett et al., 1991, 1996, 2000).

Here, we remind the reader that basal levels of cortisol follow a circadian cycle, with higher levels in the morning and declining levels throughout the day. It is thus extremely important when assessing cortisol levels in humans to control for the time of day at which the samples are taken. Moreover, any cortisol difference pertaining to samples obtained in the morning cannot be taken as direct evidence that cortisol secretion is lower in children with Conduct Disorders, given that it may be possible that the total excretion of cortisol throughout the day is not different in these children when compared to control children. Also, there is a major difference between plasma and salivary measures of cortisol, as the plasma concentrations of cortisol include both the free (biologically active) and bound (to carrier proteins and thus inactive) portions of cortisol, whereas salivary samples assess the free portion of cortisol. Given that it is the free portion of cortisol that will be active, salivary cortisol may represent a better measure of the biologically active cortisol levels than plasma cortisol levels. Moreover, cortisol levels have been shown to present a significant increase at 30 and 60 minutes after waking (called the cortisol awakening response; J. C. Pruessner et al., 1997), and this pronounced cortisol increase during the first hour after waking in the morning has been found to be associated with higher measures of self-reported stress (J. C. Pruessner, Hellhammer, & Kirschbaum, 1999; M. Pruessner et al., 2003; Schulz, Kirschbaum, Pruessner, & Hellhammer, 1998; Wüst, Federenko, Hellhammer, & Kirschbaum, 2000). Finally, venipuncture has been shown to induce a potent response of the HPA axis (Meeran, Hattersley, Mould, & Bloom, 1993), and it is possible that the cortisol response to venipuncture induces large inter- and intraindividual cortisol responses, explaining some of the discrepant findings. For a complete review of the methodological factors that could account for the discrepancies of data and for more in-

formation on the best method to assess cortisol levels in humans, see the recent review by Goodyer and collaborators (Goodyer, Park, Netherton, & Herbert, 2001).

Be that as it may, some mechanisms have been proposed to explain the link between low cortisol levels and externalizing behaviors. Low cortisol levels noted in aggressive individuals are understood in the light of an underaroused sympathetic autonomous nervous system and HPA axis (Lahey, McBurnett, Loeber, & Hart, 1995). Consequently, a dampened HPA axis secretion pattern would constitute an adaptive response (habituation) to aversive situations such as pain and parental coercive behaviors (Vanyukov et al., 1993). Moreover, lower reactive secretion in individuals manifesting externalizing behaviors may be explained as a higher HPA axis activation threshold (Kruesi et al., 1989). For these individuals, moderate stressful events may be inefficient to induce HPA axis activation. As a result, those individuals may feel understimulated and be prone to searching for sensation-seeking activities.

The low cortisol-CD link could also be interpreted as a physiological marker of a tendency toward (or an absence of) behavioral inhibition (Kagan, Reznick, & Snidman, 1987). Gray (1982, 1987) suggested that two neurophysiological systems are implicated in antisocial behaviors: the behavior inhibition system (BIS) and the behavior activation system (BAS). The BIS has received considerable attention in regard to the low cortisol levels noted in externalizing individuals. One of the main functions of the BIS is to down-regulate (inhibit) nonreinforced behaviors (e.g., aggressive behaviors) while perceiving aversive cues in the environment (e.g., punishment). BIS activation is expressed at the behavioral level through inhibition responses and at the physiological level in cortisol, serotonin, and noradrenalin secretion (King, Barkley, & Barrett, 1998). Convergent with the BIS, higher cortisol levels appear to be a protective feature against manifesting externalizing behavior problems (because facilitating inhibition of these behaviors), and lower cortisol levels may be a marker of a behavioral disinhibition already associated with externalizing behaviors (King et al., 1998; McBurnett et al., 1996).

Interestingly, most studies assessing the association between cortisol levels and the *development* of disruptive behaviors in preschoolers report a *positive* association between cortisol and some psychological correlates of externalizing behaviors (e.g., negative affect, aggression, difficult or instable temperament; E. P. Davis, Donzella, Krueger, & Gunnar, 1999; de Haan, Gunnar, Tout, Hart, & Stansbury, 1998; Gunnar, Tout, de Haan, Pierce, & Stansbury, 1997). For example, Dettling, Gunnar, and Donzella (1999) reported a positive association between cortisol levels secreted during the day and negative affect and aggression in preschoolers. To explain this result, they suggested that immature regulation systems and negative peer relationships might be correlated with higher cortisol secretion. In this sense, the higher cortisol levels associated with aggression in preschoolers may be related to a stress-induced cortisol release rather than to basal levels of cortisol. Higher cortisol levels have also been interpreted as a marker of the effort to adapt to a demanding and unfamiliar social environment (Stansbury & Harris, 2000). Even though moderate cortisol secretion may enhance the child's capacity to cope with an unfamiliar environment, large secretions of cortisol may be a marker of dysfunctional social adaptation (McEwen, 2002). Consequently, an inverted U-shape relationship between cortisol and social functioning may best characterize this association in childhood (E. P. Davis et al., 1999) and adulthood (McEwen, 2003).

In the preschool years, the mechanisms involved in the modified HPA axis resulting from adverse environmental conditions remain to be clarified. The first years of life possibly constitute a sensitive period in which several physiological systems complete their maturation and show greater plasticity to environmental factors (De Kloet, Vreugdenhil, Oitzl, & Joels, 1998; Gunnar & Donzella, 2002). Consequently, adverse environmental conditions experienced during this sensitive period may be particularly determinant in inducing changes in the HPA axis (Heim et al., 2000; Meaney et al., 1996). Essex, Klein, Cho, and Kalin (2002) observed that children who experienced chronic stress during their 1st year of life have higher cortisol levels at 4.5 years of age, suggesting that cumulative rather than acute stressful events are linked to permanent physiological changes (G. W. Evans & English, 2002). Modified HPA axis secretion patterns observed in childhood and adulthood are thought to be one of several physiological outcomes of chronic stress experienced early in life (Gunnar et al., 2001; Gunnar & Vazquez, 2001).

Dehydroepiandrosterone and Conduct Disorder

DHEA and its sulfate (DHEAS) is another primary stress mediator that has been studied in relation to CD. The rationale here is that from around age 6, children exhibit a gradual increase in androgens, but these androgens are of adrenal origin, a period called the adrenarche. It is not until puberty that gonadal androgens (of gonadal origin), such as testosterone, become more important. Researchers (Buydens-Branchey & Branchey, 2004; Dmitrieva, Oades, Hauffa, & Eggers, 2001; Goodyer et al., 2001; van Goozen, Matthys, Cohen-Kettenis, Thijssen, & van Engeland, 1998; van Goozen, van den Ban et al., 2000) have thus concluded that studies of Conduct Disorders in prepubertal children should therefore not focus on testosterone, but on adrenal androgens, such as DHEA and DHEAS. DHEA and DHEAS are also very interesting for the study of Conduct Disorders because, besides being secreted in the adrenal glands, they are also endogenously synthesized by the brain (Robel & Baulieu, 1995). Many studies have shown that DHEA acts by increasing neuronal excitability, enhancing neuronal plasticity and having neuroprotective properties (Wolf & Kirschbaum, 1999). From the effects of DHEA on the body and the brain, many authors have suggested that DHEA/DHEAS should be elevated in individuals who are aggressive. This suggestion has been confirmed.

In a study performed in 1998, van Goozen and collaborators examined the relationship between plasma levels of testosterone and DHEAS in 15 boys with CD and 25 normal controls boys. The intensity of aggression and delinquency of the boys were rated by parents and teachers over a period of 6 months. The results showed that boys with CD had significantly higher levels of DHEAS, although testosterone levels did not differ between groups. Also, the authors reported that levels of DHEAS were significantly and positively correlated with the intensity of aggression and delinquency as rated by both parents and teachers. The authors interpreted these results as suggesting that adrenal androgen functioning plays an important role in the onset and maintenance of aggression in young boys. In a second study, van Goozen and collaborators (van Goozen, van den Ban, et al., 2000) measured DHEAS in children with oppositional and antisocial behavior and normal controls. The results showed that children with oppositional and antisocial behavior had higher DHEAS levels than the control groups. An increase in DHEAS in children and adolescents with CD was also reported by Dmitrieva et al. (2001).

Cholesterol and Conduct Disorder

Cholesterol and, more generally, lipid concentrations and metabolism have received substantial attention in relation to externalizing behaviors and more specifically violence and delinquency. Interestingly, while allostatic load in adults and older individuals is associated with high cholesterol levels, a negative relation is usually noted between cholesterol and violence in both young and adults. Golomb, Stattin, and Mednick (2000) reported that low cholesterol levels in males were most frequently associated with violent crimes committed against others. The participants' age was related to both cholesterol levels and violent crimes, but the association remained significant when age was taken into account. Similar results were noted in relation to physical aggression (Hillbrand & Spitz, 1999; Hillbrand, Waite,

Miller, Spitz, & Lingswiler, 2000), past history of aggression in inpatients of a drug rehabilitation unit (Buydens-Branchey, Branchey, Hudson, & Fergeson, 2000), violent offenders with Antisocial Personality Disorder (Virkkunen, 1979), violent suicidal attempts (Vevera, Zukov, Morcinek, & Papezova, 2003), and cholesterol-lowering interventions in humans (Golomb, 1998; Muldoon, Manuck, & Matthews, 1990) and in nonhuman primates (Kaplan et al., 1994).

In contrast to the overall negative association generally reported between cholesterol and aggression, nonsignificant or positive relationships have been noted between cholesterol and psychological aggression, expressive hostility, and anger attacks (C. C. Chen, Lu, Wu, & Chang, 2001; Hillbrand & Spitz, 1999; Wing, Matthews, Kuller, Meilahn, & Plantinga, 1991). These results suggest that the cholesterol and aggression association is restricted to physical aggression and violence.

However, previous results obtained on the association between cholesterol and CD must be accepted cautiously for several reasons. First, most of these studies were conducted exclusively with male participants, which limits the generalization of results to females. A study conducted by Lindberg, Rastam, Gullberg, and Eklund (1992) reported a similar negative association between cholesterol and aggression in female participants, although the magnitude of the association was much weaker. Young age is related to the cholesterol-aggression association, but the link remains significant once age is taken into account, which suggests that the association between cholesterol and aggression is not essentially explained by the age of the child (Golomb et al., 2000). Note that alcohol use (linked to increased HDL level with no change in cholesterol) and SES levels (inversely correlated to cholesterol) do not explain the overall relation (Golomb, 1998).

The mechanisms connecting cholesterol to physical aggression are still unknown, but modified serotonin function has been proposed to mediate this association (Buydens-Branchey et al., 2000; Mysterud & Poleszynski, 2003). Low cholesterol levels reduce lipid microviscosity in the brain cell membrane, resulting in dampened activity in serotonergic systems (Kaplan et al., 1994; Vevera et al., 2003). Low serotonin levels are commonly related to a reduced capacity to inhibit aggressive behaviors and impulsivity (Coccaro, 1992; Linnoila & Virkkunen, 1992; Virkkunen, De Jong, Bartko, & Linnoila, 1989). Cognitive information and emotional processing are once again thought to be implicated in the serotonin-aggression association (Berman, Tracy, & Coccaro, 1997), namely by reducing sensitivity to external clues referring to punishment or norm violation (Spoont, 1992).

Other mechanisms have been shown to play a role in the aggression-cholesterol association. Negative mood states, low cognitive efficacy, and a reduced interpersonal involvement are also linked to low cholesterol levels in an inpatient sample (Hillbrand et al., 2000). These results suggest that the association between aggression and cholesterol may partially be accounted for by other psychological and behavioral correlates.

Waist-Hip Ratio and Conduct Disorder

Very few studies have assessed the link between waist-hip ratio and Conduct Disorders. In 2001, Ishikawa and collaborators (Ishikawa, Raine, Lencz, Bihrle, & LaCasse, 2001) measured height, weight, body mass index, bulk, and psychosocial adversity in 44 controls and 43 adolescents and adults with antisocial personalities. They reported that adult antisocial individuals, regardless of age of onset, were significantly taller and had greater body bulk than controls. However, they also reported that although groups tended to differ on weight, they did not differ on body mass index. In 2003, Mustillo and collaborators assessed the association between obesity and the development of psychiatric disorders in 991 children ages 9 to 16 who were evaluated annually over an 8-year period for height, weight, psychiatric disorder, and vulnerabilities for psychiatric disorder. The results showed that of the four developmental trajectories of obesity tested—no obesity (73%), chronic obesity (15%), childhood obesity (5%), and adolescent obesity (7%)—only chronic obesity was associated with Oppositional Defiant Disorder in boys and girls and depressive disorders in boys.

Heart Rate and Conduct Disorder

Increased cardiovascular activity is a secondary outcome in the allostatic load model, which is operationalized by higher heart rate and blood pressure (both systolic and diastolic). Cardiovascular parameters (heart rate, blood pressure, etc.) are easy, noninvasive, and inexpensive to collect. Despite this apparent simplicity, it has to be noted that the context in which measures of heart rate are collected (resting rate or activation/anticipation heart rate) may have a major impact on the results obtained in a given study. This makes results harder to interpret and requires at least some caution. Also, very few studies have been conducted with children showing the full spectrum of Conduct Disorder. However, various studies have been performed on some of the externalizing behaviors present in Conduct Disorders. We summarize these two types of studies next.

A relationship between anger, hostility, elevated heart rate, and blood pressure has been noted in several studies (M. C. Davis, Matthews, & McGrath, 2000; Galovski,

Blanchard, Malta, & Freidenberg, 2003). Competition challenge, harassment, and provocative insults are thought to be central in the increased physiological reactivity associated with anger (Garcia-Leon, Reyes del Paso, Robles, & Vila, 2003). In contrast, instrumental and less emotionally aroused antisocial behaviors are associated with *lower* heart rate and have been suggested to reflect both an underarousal state and fearlessness (Scarpa & Raine, 1997). These sensation-seeking behaviors have been shown to enhance the propensity for risk-taking behaviors (e.g., alcohol and drugs, sexual promiscuity, extreme sports), physical aggression, and criminal activities (Raine, Venables, & Williams, 1995; Scarpa & Ollendick, 2003).

A meta-analysis conducted by Ortiz and Raine (2004) of 40 studies indicated that both resting heart rate (n = 5,868 with a mean age of 10.8 years) and reactive heart rate (n = 578 with a mean age of 12.6 years) were negatively related to antisocial behaviors. In their prospective study, Raine, Venables, and Mednick (1997) have reported that a low resting heart rate assessed at age 3 in 1,795 children was associated with higher rates of physical behaviors at age 11. Low resting heart rates have also been linked with fighting behaviors at age 9 to 12 years in children from low SES (Kindlon et al., 1995). This association is still significant when body size and pubertal status are taken into account.

Interestingly, it has been shown that stressful characteristics of inner-city environments, compared to suburban and rural area lifestyles and environments, are generally linked to higher blood pressure (Thomas & Groer, 1986). For some children, these adverse environmental conditions may sensitize them to further threats, contributing to increasing or maintaining higher resting heart rates. However, other children confronted with the same adverse conditions may be desensitized (habituation) to threatening events encountered on a daily basis. Convergent with this hypothesis, Cooley-Quille and Lorion (1999) reported that youths exposed to the highest levels of community violence have the lowest resting heat rate. Such physiological adaptation may be protective in the short run by dampening physiological activation associated with stressful environments, but it can become detrimental in the long run, placing these children at risk to engage in developmental trajectories characterized by externalizing problems such as delinquency and violence.

A second hypothesis for these discrepant results is that lower heart rates in aggressive and violent individuals may partially be explained through inherited differences in cardiovascular activity. Moderate to strong heritability estimates in cardiovascular indices are noted in several studies

in infancy (Dubreuil et al., 2003; Healy, 1992), childhood (Boomsma & Plomin, 1986; Schieken et al., 1989), and adulthood (An et al., 2000; Ditto, 1993; Somes, Harshfield, Alpert, Goble, & Schieken, 1995). Inherited differences in heart rate may enhance the propensity of individuals with lower heart rate to manifest externalizing behaviors while protecting individuals with higher heart rate from personal involvement in contexts where externalizing behaviors are adaptive or required (Kindlon et al., 1995; Raine et al., 1995). These working models appear at first sight hard to reconcile. Yet, although distinct, they are not mutually exclusive. From a developmental perspective, potential factors linked to the onset of externalizing problems are generally thought to be multidimensional and influenced simultaneously by genes and environment throughout one's lifetime.

Immune Function and Conduct Disorder

To this day, only one study has assessed the unique influence of Conduct Disorder on immune function. Birmaher et al. (1994) assessed total white blood cells, lymphocytes subsets, natural killer cell activity, and lymphocyte proliferation in adolescents with either Major Depressive Disorder or Conduct Disorder and normal adolescents. They reported that although there were no significant between-group differences in any of the cellular immune measurements, natural killer cell activity was significantly negatively correlated with past year and lifetime adverse life events across all effector-target cell ratios. This result remained significant after controlling for diagnoses and SES.

Allostatic Load and Conduct Disorder

Although the studies performed on the primary stress mediators and secondary outcomes of allostatic load have shown some associations with Conduct Disorders, it is important to remind the reader that the studies that validated the allostatic load model clearly showed that none of the components of allostatic load exhibited significant associations on their own with health outcome. Indeed, it was shown that it is the summary measure of allostatic load that is significantly associated with major health outcomes. These findings were consistent with the idea that although a modest deviation in the level of activity of a single physiologic system may not be predictive of poor future health, the cumulative toll from modest alterations in several physiologic systems is prognostic for poor health. Consequently, it may be possible that some of the discrepant findings related to primary stress mediators and/or secondary outcomes and CD may be due to the fact that only one component of the allostatic load model has been assessed. Although no study has assessed all components of the allostatic load model in children with Conduct Disorders, recent studies measured two or more markers of allostatic load, and the results reveal a very interesting pattern of developmental allostatic load in childhood Conduct Disorders. We summarize these next.

Low Cortisol and High Sulfated Dehydroepiandrosterone in Conduct Disorder.   As we have summarized, independent studies have reported low cortisol levels and high DHEAS in children with Conduct Disorders. This is an interesting finding because the opposite pattern is observed in depressed children ages 8 to 16 years, namely, high levels of cortisol and low levels of DHEA/DHEAS (Goodyer et al., 1996). A recent study performed in 2004 by Buydens-Branchey and Branchey assessed levels of cortisol and DHEAS in 40 adult cocaine addicts with a retrospective diagnosis of Antisocial Personality Disorder or childhood CD. Given that DHEAS and cortisol were assessed in blood taken with venipuncture, the authors attributed any group differences in DHEAS and/or cortisol to a difference in reactivity to the stress induced by the venipuncture. The results showed that the men who had a retrospective diagnosis of CD had significantly increased DHEAS levels and less cortisol in response to venipuncture. Comparisons between patients who did and did not meet the APD adult criteria did not reveal any significant difference in DHEAS or in cortisol responsivity.

Low Cortisol and Low Heart Rate in Conduct Disorder.   Again, low cortisol levels and lower heart rate have been reported in children with Conduct Disorders, but very few studies measured these two markers at the same time in children with Conduct Disorder. In 2000, van Goozen and collaborators (van Goozen, Matthys, Cohen-Kettenis, Buitelaar, & van Engeland, 2000) investigated whether a pattern of lower autonomic nervous system and HPA axis activity can be found in children with disruptive behavior disorders under nonstressful and stressful conditions. They also assessed whether the pattern of hormonal responses to stress would correspond with the child's feelings of control and negative emotionality. In this study, they assessed cortisol levels, heart rate, skin conductance levels, and subjective feelings of control and negative emotionality in 26 children with disruptive behavior disorder and 26 control children. The results showed that in the baseline, nonstressful condition, heart rate and skin conductance levels were lower in children with CD, although cortisol levels were

similar in all groups. When exposed to a stressful situation, children with disruptive behavior disorders presented a lower increase in heart rate and cortisol, when compared to children without disruptive behavior disorder, but they reported higher levels of emotional arousal.

In a more recent study, Snoek and collaborators (Snoek, Van Goozen, Matthys, Buitelaar, & van Engeland, 2004) assessed heart rate and cortisol levels in children with Oppositional Defiant Disorder (ODD) and children with Attention-Deficit/Hyperactivity Disorder (ADHD) under baseline and stressful conditions. The results showed that under baseline conditions, the groups did not differ for cortisol levels, although the group of children with ODD presented lower heart rates than the ADHD group. The results also showed that in response to stress, children with ODD presented weaker cortisol and heart rate responses to stress when compared to children with ADHD and control children. Altogether, these results suggest the presence of a hyperreactivity of the primary stress mediators (cortisol and catecholamines/heart rate) in response to stress in children with ODD.

Cortisol and Immune Function in Conduct Disorder. In the immune system, white blood cells called lymphocytes are very diverse in their functions. The most abundant lymphocytes are the B lymphocytes (B cells) and the T lymphocytes (T cells). The B cells are designated as such because they are produced and mature in the *B*one marrow, and T cells are designated as such because their precursors leave the bone marrow and mature in the *T*hymus. Chief among the regulatory T cells are helper/inducer T cells. These cells are needed to activate many immune cells, including B cells and other T cells. Another subset of regulatory T cells acts to turn off or suppress immune cells. There are two types of helper T cells. The Th1 type participates in cell-mediated immunity and are essential for controlling intracellular pathogens such as viruses and certain bacteria. The Th2 type provides help for B cells and, in so doing, are essential for antibody-mediated immunity. Antibodies are needed to control extracellular pathogens which, unlike intracellular parasites, are exposed to antibodies in blood and other fluids.

Glucocorticoids have been shown to regulate the expression of Th1 and Th2 (Chrousos & Elenkov, 2000; Elenkov et al., 2000; Elenkov, Papanicolaou, Wilder, & Chrousos, 1996; Milburn, Poulter, Dilmec, Cochrane, & Kemeny, 1997). High levels of glucocorticoids have been shown to suppress Th1 and favor the expression of a Th2 response (a Th2 shift), whereas decreased concentrations of cortisol produce a shift toward Th1 function and suppress Th2 (a Th1 shift; Chrousos & Elenkov, 2000; Elenkov et al., 2000). This is an interesting finding because Th2 shifts are associated with susceptibility to infections from most types of intracellular pathogens and vulnerability to cancer (Rabin, 1999; Shurin, Lu, Kalinski, Stewart-Akers, & Lotze, 1999; Sprietsma, 1999). In contrast, and although a Th1 shift has been shown to confer some protection from these problems, it has been associated with increased susceptibility to "stress-related" disorders such as fibromyalgia and chronic fatigue syndrome (Clauw & Chrousos, 1997; Crofford, Jacobson, & Young, 1999; Griep et al., 1998; Lentjes, Griep, Boersma, Romijn, & de Kloet, 1997; Scott, Medbak, & Dinan, 1998), as well as autoimmune (al-Wabel, al-Janadi, & Raziuddin, 1993; Balomenos, Rumold, & Theofilopoulos, 1998; Gutierrez, Garcia, Rodriguez, Rivero, & Jacobelli, 1998), and inflammatory (Chrousos, 1995; Harbuz, Jessop, & Lightman, 1997) disease.

Given that low cortisol levels have been correlated with a shift toward Th1 (predominance of Th1 with suppression of Th2), Pajer and collaborators (Pajer, Rabin, & Gardner, 2002) recently conducted a study in young girls with antisocial behavior to assess whether the low cortisol profile generally observed in children with Conduct Disorder is associated with a shift toward Th1. In this study, the authors used plasma levels of IgG3 and IgG4 as markers for Th1 and Th2 activity and assessed the IgG 3:4 ratios in 42 teenage girls with CD or controls. Results showed that the mean IgG 3:4 ratio was higher in the girls with CD and that cortisol levels were significantly and negatively correlated with IgG 3:4 ratio. These new findings indicate that immunologic abnormalities are present in relation to low cortisol levels in adolescents with CD.

The various studies that have been performed in relation to hormonal and immune dysfunctions in Conduct Disorders tend to show that lower levels of the primary stress mediators cortisol and catecholoamines (through cardiovascular indices) are associated with Conduct Disorders and that these lower levels of activity are associated with higher levels of DHEAS and immune changes. It is interesting to note that the pattern of changes in the mediators of allostatic load is different from the pattern that has been observed in older adults. Indeed, in older populations, increased levels of the primary stress mediators cortisol and catecholamines and lower levels of DHEAS have been reported to predict functional decline later in life (Seeman, McEwen et al., 2001; Seeman et al., 1997). It is therefore possible that the differences in allostatic stress mediators reported to occur in children and older adults

may be due to differences in psychological characteristics of the populations (Conduct Disorders versus normal populations) or to significant developmental differences in the pattern of allostatic load across the life span (younger versus older adults).

Validation of Allostatic Load in Children

A very interesting study published in 2003 by G. W. Evans gives us very valuable data about normal childhood and allostatic load. Actually, this is the only study published to date that specifically assessed the various components of allostatic load in a population of children. In this study, 339 low-income children with a mean age of 9 were recruited from public schools in New York State. Evans evaluated the cumulative environmental risk factors using the same method previously described for physical environmental risk (crowding, noise, housing quality; see G. W. Evans & Marcynyszyn, 2004). Moreover, psychological risk factors (child separation, turmoil, violence) were also assessed, as well as aspects of the home environment and personal characteristics (poverty, single parenthood, maternal high school dropout). As well, two behavioral protocols were included to examine self-regulatory behavior and learned helplessness. The child's ability to delay gratification was used as an index of self-regulatory behavior, and learned helplessness was evaluated with a standard behavioral protocol. Finally, measures of allostatic load included resting blood pressure (diastolic and systolic), overnight urinary neuroendocrine measures (cortisol, epinephrine, and norepinephrine), an index of fat deposition (body mass index), and a total allostatic load index (0 to 6) reflecting the number of these six singular physiological indicators on which each child scored in the top quartile of risk. The results of this study showed that all three primary stress mediators (cortisol, epinephrine, norepinephrine) were elevated by cumulative risk exposure and that body mass index was significantly and positively related to cumulative risk exposure. More important, the author reported that the total allostatic load index was significantly related to cumulative environmental risk. Interestingly, it was found that children's own perceptions of self-worth were unrelated to any allostatic load indicators but were positively correlated with task persistence on the learned helplessness puzzle. Besides being the first study specifically assessing allostatic load in normally developing children, this study is very important because it shows that in low-income children without Conduct Disorders (although presence or absence of Conduct Disorder was not specifically assessed in this study), *higher* allostatic load scores on primary stress mediators and secondary outcomes are observed. This is a very interesting finding in line with previous data summarized in children with Conduct Disorders, suggesting that when behavioral problems and/or symptoms become apparent in children, most markers of allostatic load are decreased. In his study, Evans tested the presence of a curvilinear function between cumulative environmental risk and allostatic load score, and the quadratic function proved to be significant. This result strongly suggests that a mechanism of early adaptation to allostatic load may exist, whereby the organism tries to adapt to environmental demands. As we have argued in previous sections of this chapter, this mechanism of adaptation may be closely related to the cognitive interpretation given to adverse events in order to adapt to the various challenges of life.

However, another possibility has to be raised with regard to the different results obtained on allostatic load in various populations. Indeed, it is quite possible that these different patterns of allostatic load are due to genetic influences acting on the stress mediators, leading to increased risk for the development of CD during childhood.

McEwen and Stellar (1993) have highlighted the idea that, early in infancy, genetic predispositions and environmental factors contribute to laying down the individual differences in subjective perceptions attributed to a threat (relevant or not) and then physiologically responding to it. As a result of cumulative threats (or less intense experiences) over time, initial differences in the response to stressful events could be altered (either minimized or enhanced), resulting in vulnerability to diseases (Repetti, Taylor, & Seeman, 2002; Rutter, 1994). To date, researchers in developmental psychopathology have devoted great effort to studying the associations and mechanisms linking early proximal (e.g., parental behaviors, parent-child relationships) and distal (e.g., poverty, dangerousness of neighborhood) environmental characteristics and the individual differences of presenting pathology. Results obtained from animal models (Meaney et al., 1991) and studies conducted with humans (G. W. Evans, 2003; Felitti et al., 1998; Gunnar et al., 2001; Hertsgaard, Gunnar, Erickson, & Nachmias, 1995) show promising features in our understanding of the trajectories leading to allostatic load. Less is known about the potent influences that genetic factors may have on allostatic load.

Considering that allostatic load is a complex syndrome involving several physiological mediators, regulatory systems, and stress-related structures (Repetti et al., 2002; Seeman, McEwen et al., 2001; Seeman, Singer, Ryff, Dienberg Love, & Levy-Storms, 2002), the estimation of the overall impact of genes on allostatic load appears premature and questionable for several reasons. First, no empirical evidence allows for the assumption that individuals are similarly characterized across primary mediators: Are individual differences in primary mediators correlated? Second, primary mediators may have distinct trajectories leading to diseases: Does a dysfunction of the HPA axis induce a similar vulnerability for anxiety-related problems compared to an altered catecholamine system? Third, primary mediators may show different etiological patterns: Are primary mediators regulated by common or different genes/environments? Are primary mediators regulated by the same genes/environments across the life span? Current data show that genetic influences on some phenotypes might be enhanced during development, whereas the genetic influence on other phenotypes might be "turned on" or "turned off" later in life (Plomin, DeFries, McClearn, & McGuffin, 2001). Finally, considering that allostasis and allostatic load are probably multifactorial (e.g., influenced by several genes and environments), as are most complex phenotypes, the remaining question in estimating genetic and environmental influences on individual differences in allostatic load should be considered cautiously. Accordingly, the genetic influences on allostatic load could be more efficiently understood through studying their impact on more elementary neurobiological traits, such as primary mediators (de Geus, 2002). That is, primary mediators may be referred as endophenotypes of allostatic load, which allows a more valid examination of the respective roles of etiological factors (environments and genes) to each primary mediator (HPA axis, catecholamine, and DHEA) and consequently to the complex construct of allostatic load.

Genetic Influences on the Hypothalamic-Pituitary-Adrenal Axis: Results from Twin Studies

The HPA axis is one of the most studied primary mediators. Behavioral genetic analyses offer a powerful tool to investigate the etiology of individual variations for a trait in a population (D. M. Evans, Gillespie, & Martin, 2002). In behavioral genetic modeling, genetic and environmental sources of variance of a phenotype (or endophenotype) are disentangled by using measures collected from participants who differ in their degree of genetic relatedness (Plomin et al., 2001). In twin studies, genetic models are based on monozygotic (MZ; identical twins, sharing 100% of their genes) and dizygotic (DZ; fraternal twins, sharing approximately 50% of their genes) twin intraclass correlation comparisons. Typically, four main sources of variance can be assessed and generally symbolized by the following capital letters (parameters): [A] represents the additive genetic effect (the effect of an allele is added to the effect of other alleles); [D] the nonadditive genetic effect (resulting from interaction between alleles at the same locus, *dominance,* or at different loci, *epistasis*); [C] the common environment effect, linked to the experience of similar environments within twin pairs; and [E] the unique environment effect, which also includes the measurement errors (Posthuma et al., 2000). In short, twin design studies allows us to estimate the magnitude of the genetic and environmental effects on a phenotype, and the mode of transmission (i.e., additive or nonadditive) that best reflects genetic covariation between participants (for extended description of genetic modeling in twin design studies, see D. M. Evans et al., 2002; Neale & Cardon, 1992; Posthuma et al., 2000). We highlight some empirical results of heritability reported from twin studies about individual differences in HPA axis (re)activity, underlining the main limitations and interpretations from a heuristic and methodological standpoint, and identifying future areas that will need to be investigated to initiate a comprehensive conceptual framework of modulatory influences of genes to allostatic load and psychopathology.

Large individual variations are noted in HPA axis (re)activity (Wüst et al., 2000). Genetic factors are thought to play an important role in the individual differences in HPA axis (re)activity. Surprisingly few studies have attempted to estimate the heritability of cortisol levels, although twin designs offer a great opportunity to assess genetic and environmental influences. Concerning nonreactive cortisol levels, reported heritability estimates vary considerably from one study to another, ranging from 0 to 74% (for a review, see Bartels, Van den Berg, Sluyter, Boomsma, & de Geus, 2003). Wüst and his colleagues have collected saliva samples after awakening on two consecutive days from 52 MZ and 52 DZ twin pairs ages 8 to 65 years old. They observed moderate genetic effects on saliva cortisol levels for the main increase in awakening cortisol response ($h^2 = .40$) and for the area under the curve ($h^2 = .48$). This finding is consistent with that of Kirschbaum and collaborators (Kirschbaum, Wüst, Faig, & Hellhammer, 1992), who reported a significant influence of genetic factors on the three baseline measures of salivary cortisol levels collected before stimulation procedures (CRH test, ergometry, and public speech). Meikle, Stringham, Woodward, and Bishop (1988) obtained similar heritability estimates with plasma cortisol levels ($h^2 = .45$ for total cortisol and $h^2 = .51$ for unbound cortisol) in 20 MZ and 20 DZ twin male pairs. Bartels, de Geus, Kirschbaum, Sluyter, and Boomsma (2003) recently reported significant heritability estimates on cortisol levels sampled at several times on two consecutive days in 12-year-old twin pairs ($n = 180$). Results showed higher cortisol heritability estimates for samples collected 45 minutes after awakening ($h^2 = .60$), moderate estimates around noon ($h^2 = .30$), and null estimates in the evening. Other results also suggest moderate genetic influences for nonreactive cortisol levels (Inglis et al., 1999; Young, Aggen, Prescott, & Kendler, 2000). In spite of these results, other studies report null heritability estimates for basal cortisol levels (Froehlich, Zink, Li, & Christian, 2000; Meikle et al., 1988; Pritchard et al., 1998). Furthermore, some empirical results showed that the daytime cortisol profile is moderately influenced by shared environments (Wüst et al., 2000), although this finding appears inconsistent (Linkowski et al., 1993).

Heritability estimates of reactive cortisol levels (in response to stress) lead to divergent results, although most of them suggest no or minor genetic effects in cortisol responses to various stressful events or tasks (Nurnberger et al., 1982; Pritchard et al., 1998). For example, Kirschbaum et al. (1992) found no significant intraclass correlation differences between MZ and DZ twin pairs' cortisol levels in response to physical and psychological stress paradigms. In contrast, they obtained significant intraclass correlation differences during the administration of corticotropin-releasing factor (CRF; stimulates the HPA axis), suggesting that HPA axis responses to CRF may be influenced by genes via negative feedback retroaction loops. In these studies, no significant estimate of common environmental factors was reported.

Disparities noted for heritability estimates may be accounted for by various methodological procedures, such as collection methods (plasma, salivary, and urine samples), time of collection (at waking, before bedtime, before or after a stressful activity), and small sample size (Bartels, Van den Berg et al., 2003). Time of sampling and the nature of sampling (reactive or not) are particularly important as we are still unsure whether different genes may influence cortisol levels at different times of the day and what may be the common or different etiological factors related to nonreactive and reactive cortisol levels. Recent results suggest that estimates of genetic and environmental variance components vary sufficiently across the day to induce distinct etiological patterns of cortisol secretion at different times of the day (Bartels, de Geus et al., 2003). Why there are differences in genetic and environmental estimates in cortisol levels sampled at distinct times of the day is still unknown. Small sample size is another issue that could partially explain discrepancies between reported heritability estimates. Most of these studies do not allow sufficient statistical power to distinguish the variance related to genes from the variance associated with common environments (Bartels, Van den Berg et al., 2003). As a result, genetic, common, and unique environment variance components are estimated, more often than not, through MZ and DZ intraclass correlations (except Bartels, de Geus et al., 2003; Bartels, Van den Berg et al., 2003). The main limitation of estimating heritability through rough comparisons of intraclass correlation is that it does not take into account the dispersion indices related to the evaluated phenotype. Moreover, this statistical procedure does not allow us to estimate confidence intervals and does not provide any statistical parameters that specify how well the chosen model (rather than other tested models) best describes the observed data (Posthuma et al., 2000).

To overcome these limitations, Bartels and her colleagues (Bartels, Van den Berg et al., 2003) have performed a simultaneous analysis by using structural equation modeling to fit data collected in five distinct studies selected on the basis of similar methodological characteristics (Froehlich et al., 2000; Inglis et al., 1999; Linkowski et al., 1993; Meikle et al., 1988; Wüst et al., 2000). A heritability estimate of 62% was obtained for nonreactive cortisol levels, suggesting that over half of the individual differences observed in basal cortisol levels can be attributed to additive genetic factors. The most parsimonious model includes no parameter for common environment. The remaining variance (38%) was attributed to uniquely experienced environment (i.e., environmental factors affecting the children within the twin pair differently). This result points to a moderate genetic component of basal cortisol levels across a large age span (i.e., 8 to 67 years old).

Theoretical Implications and Misleading Interpretations of Twin Studies' Results

No influence of the twins' shared environments on the HPA axis? In light of the results emerging from twin studies, one might be tempted to conclude that common environmental factors do not exert a significant influence on individual differences in nonreactive cortisol secretion. These findings are surprising given the fact that other studies have reported that adverse environments, including poverty, low parental education attainment, placement in orphanage, and parental negative behaviors, have a detrimental effect on cortisol levels and circadian rhythms (Flinn & England, 1997; Gunnar et al., 2001; Lupien et al., 2000; Taylor, Repetti, & Seeman, 1997). Can we reconcile these divergent conclusions? One interpretation may reside in distinguishing the characteristics of those studies from the twin

studies' samples. Bear in mind that environmental and genetic estimates can be interpreted only in the population from whom data have been collected (Plomin et al., 2001). No generalization of the results can be drawn to other populations. The majority of the heritability estimates reported in twin studies are issued from normative samples of twins mostly not confronted with intense and chronic stressful environments. Accordingly, the reported heritability estimates should not be extended or compared to clinical samples, which are particularly at risk in light of highly adverse environments, mainly because it is still unknown if there are relevant differences in genetic and environmental estimates that result from normative samples in comparison to clinical samples.

Another interpretation of the nonsignificant shared environmental factors reported by twin studies refers to different processes by which environmental factors may influence the HPA axis (re)activity at different periods of development. Infancy has long been conceived as a sensitive period of development mostly because several physiological systems have not completed their maturational processes and thus show considerable plasticity to environmental conditions (Andersen, 2003; De Kloet et al., 1998). Prenatal and early environments have been suggested to have important organizational and stable effects on primary mediators and, to a greater extent, on several regulatory systems, including the stress-related system (e.g., hippocampus, amygdala, hypothalamus; Repetti et al., 2002; Weinstock, 1997). Increased sensitivity to environmental conditions may allow the organism to achieve short-term or long-term adaptations to this environment (Huether, 1998; Teicher et al., 2003). However, the cost of stable modifications in stress-related systems, as induced by environmental factors experienced during the sensitive period, may not always be optimal, sometimes placing the organism in a long-standing allostatic load (McEwen, 2003).

Although the mechanisms associated with the permanent effects of early environments on individual differences in HPA axis (re)activity have not been fully understood, the role of glucocorticoid receptors is highlighted (Blackhurst et al., 2002; Takahashi, 1998; Welberg & Seckl, 2001). In rodents, postnatal handling during the 1st week of life has been shown to decrease stress reactivity later in life, perhaps through alterations in CRF gene expression in the paraventricular nucleus of the hypothalamus and the amygdala, resulting in increased glucocorticoid negative feedback via the glucocorticoid receptors (Meaney, 2001; Plotsky & Meaney, 1993; Vallee et al., 1997). In contrast, maternal separation occurring early in life induces increased HPA axis responses to stress that are sustained in adulthood (Plotsky & Meaney, 1993). Alterations in CRF gene expression may contribute to this association. The effects in HPA axis regulation through manipulations of the pups' early proximal environments have been closely related to the overall modifications in time and/or quality of maternal care of the offspring (Champagne, Francis, Mar, & Meaney, 2003). Furthermore, mothers' individual differences in maternal care have been reported to have a nongenomic effect on HPA axis regulatory functions of their offspring, rather than inherited common genes related to the phenotype characterizing reactivity to stress (Francis, Champagne, Liu, & Meaney, 1999; Francis, Diorio, Liu, & Meaney, 1999). In other words, pups' individual differences in (re)activity are suggested to be genetically encrypted in their genotype, not through inherited characteristics but through epigenetic programming induced by maternal care (Weaver et al., 2004).

Can the results indicating an important influence of early environments to later HPA axis (re)activity be reconciled with those from twin studies indicating nonsignificant contributions of shared environmental factors? Note that the estimations of shared environmental factors' influence in twin studies are exclusively conducted from late in childhood to old age, thus, after the sensitive period highlighted in the studies that show considerable organizational effects of early environment to HPA axis (re)activity. This could explain, at least in part, some inconsistencies. Furthermore, bear in mind that behavioral genetic modeling estimating the sources of variance related to genetic and environmental factors in individual differences in HPA axis (re)activity are conducted without any specific consideration for the organizational effects of environments experienced during the sensitive period. To what extent those environments increase or decrease similarities within MZ and DZ twin pairs is therefore unknown. Taken together, these considerations underline the importance of adopting a prospective view of genetic and environmental influences in individual differences on HPA axis (re)activity. A closer examination of etiological sources of variance in individual differences in HPA axis (re)activity in infancy is then strongly needed because other mechanisms may be associated with individual differences in HPA axis throughout development.

Gene-Environment Interactions. Early environments have been shown to have organizational and longstanding influences in shaping individual differences in HPA axis (re)activity, particularly during the sensitive period in infancy. After this period, individual differences in HPA axis (re)activity from both inherited and early environmentally settled genetic factors are suggested to interact with incoming environmental factors to determine the larger observed individual differences in HPA axis (re)activity (Anisman, Zaharia, Meaney, & Merali, 1998; McEwen, 2000a; Repetti et al., 2002). Interaction between genes and the environment refers to the idea that genetic factors influence the sensitivity of a given phenotype to distinct environmental settings (Rutter & Silberg, 2002). For example, a child who inherits a phenotype linked to high reactive responses to stress may be more vulnerable when confronted with more adverse stressful environments (e.g., environments exacerbate his or her genotype) relative to environments that do not present any significant stress factors. Bronfenbrenner and Ceci (1994) have gone beyond this assertion to specify that when synergistic effects resulting from genetic-environment interactions are weak, genetic potentials related to the phenotype (e.g., genotype) remain relatively unrealized. However, the potential should be progressively more actualized when gene-environment interactions become more stringent, specifically referring to more adverse stressful environments in association with HPA axis (re)activity. No twin studies have tested models including a parameter for the gene-environment interactions. In the context of significant genetic-environment interactions, the variance associated with the interaction factor is relegated to the genetic component, resulting in spurious inflated estimations of the genetic parameters and misleading interpretations about shared environment contributions. Further studies should address the conceptual and prospective processes related to individual differences in HPA axis (re)activity.

Unique Environments. According to the reported studies, a significant proportion of the total individual variance in the HPA axis (re)activity is consistently attributed to the unique environment parameters (Wüst et al., 2000). Unique environment components include, in addition to all measurement errors (e.g., sampling procedures and collecting time), environmental factors not shared within twin pairs. Nonshared environmental factors involved in the unique environment's estimate are theoretically unlimited, varying from different classes at school and distinct significant friends to more complex factors that constitute the cognitive processing of information. Confronted by similar threatening contexts, individuals may show different physiological responses according to the unique cognitive schemas activated and to the perceived coping response availability and efficiency. Those nonshared environments contribute to increasing the nonshared source of variance estimated. However, these nonshared environmental factors may represent promising areas of interventions (e.g., cognitive therapy).

FUTURE DIRECTIONS

Based on our review of the model of allostatic load and our description of the potential effects of allostatic load on child development as a function of early adversity, we believe that there are two major issues that should be investigated in the next decade. The first relates to the importance of taking into consideration the hormonal milieu of the mother (both pre- and postnatally) when studying stress reactivity and allostatic load in children. The second relates to the importance of considering how early adversities can impact the developing brain and lead to increased reactivity to stress and/or trauma in adulthood.

The Hormonal Milieu of the Mother in the Prenatal and Postnatal Periods

Pregnancy is associated with major changes in hormone levels, and the post-partum period that follows birth is also associated with drastic modifications of hormone levels. Recent studies performed in both animals and humans suggest that the hormonal milieu of the mother in the prenatal and postnatal period might have significant impact on the child's development.

Prenatal Period

A growing body of empirical evidence, based on methodologically rigorous studies of pregnant women of different ethnic, socioeconomic, and cultural backgrounds, supports the premise that mothers experiencing high levels of psychological or social stress during pregnancy are at significantly increased risk for preterm birth or low birthweight (Hedegaard, Henriksen, Sabroe, & Secher, 1993; McLean et al., 1995; Paarlberg, Vingerhoets, Passchier, Dekker, & Van Geijn, 1995; Rini, Dunkel-Schetter, Wadhwa, & Sandman, 1999; Wadhwa, Sandman, Porto, Dunkel-Schetter, & Garite, 1993). Recent epidemiological studies in Europe, North America, and the developing world suggest that babies born at term with low weight (intrauterine growth retardation; IUGR) will develop with high prevalence several pathologies, including insulin resistance, Type 2 diabetes, hypertension, and ischemic heart disease, during adult life

(Barker et al., 1993; Phillips, 1998). It is interesting to note that the physiological disorders observed in low birthweight babies have all been associated with secondary outcomes of allostatic load in adult life (see earlier discussion). Such an association between IUGR and the appearance of diseases in later life has led to the fetal origin hypothesis (Barker et al., 1993), which suggests that adverse environmental factors acting in utero program the development of fetal tissues, producing later dysfunctions and diseases.

The effect sizes of maternal stress on birthweight in well-controlled prospective studies with large sample sizes (more than 1,000 women) have typically ranged between 1.5-fold and 2-fold increase (Hedegaard et al., 1993; Hedegaard, Henriksen, Sabroe, & Secher, 1996; Peacock, Bland, & Anderson, 1995). Most of these studies have shown that within the range of stressors that are related to low birthweight, the time of exposure to the stressor is the important variable. Chronic exposure to stress in the pregnant mother, more than exposure to acute stress per se, is the most important variable related to low birthweight in the child (Hedegaard et al., 1993; McLean et al., 1995; Paarlberg et al., 1995; Rini et al., 1999; Wadhwa et al., 1993). A human study performed by Wadhwa and collaborators found that, independent of biomedical risk, each unit increase of prenatal life event stress (from a possible sample range of 14.7 units) was associated with a 55.03 g decrease in infant birthweight and a significant increase in the likelihood of low birthweight (odds ratio = 1.32).

Programming is related to a specific time window during development and persists during the whole life span (Seckl, Cleasby, & Nyirenda, 2000). One reason the programming effects of prenatal environmental stress are permanent is assumed to be due to enduring effects on the HPA axis (Ader, 1969; De Kloet et al., 1998; Meaney, 2001; Meaney, Aitken, Viau, Sharma, & Sarrieau, 1989; Meaney et al., 1996; Menard, Champagne, & Meaney, 2004; Plotsky & Meaney, 1993; Weaver et al., 2004; Weinstock, 1997) and the resulting high secretion of glucocorticoids. Recently, it has been shown that these changes in programming are linked to alterations in glucocorticoid receptors in the limbic system (Lesage, Blondeau, Grino, Breant, & Dupouy, 2001; Levitt, Lindsay, Holmes, & Seckl, 1996; Lingas, Dean, & Matthews, 1999). Because the hippocampus contains high levels of glucocorticoid receptors and is an important regulator of glucocorticoid negative feedback (De Kloet et al., 1998; Jacobson & Sapolsky, 1991), it has been assumed that changes in receptor expression will potentially alter negative feedback thresholds within the HPA axis, leading to chronically high levels of glucocorticoids in prenatally stressed individuals, which could in turn impact cognitive development in the child.

Indeed, rats exposed in utero to high levels of glucocorticoids have been shown to present significant memory impairments when compared to rats not exposed to stress in utero (Lemaire, Koehl, Le Moal, & Abrous, 2000; Szuran, Pliska, Pokorny, & Welzl, 2000; Welberg & Seckl, 2001). In humans, studies reveal an association between prenatal glucocorticoid overexposure and impaired cognitive development (for a review, see Buitelaar, Huizink, Mulder, de Medina, & Visser, 2003) and between stress during pregnancy and general cognitive development and language functioning in toddlers (Laplante et al., 2004). Both prematurity and IUGR are consistently associated with cognitive impairments (Buitelaar et al., 2003). Other data suggest that cognitive outcomes are more seriously compromised by growth restriction than by prematurity (Lagercrantz, 1997). Earlier studies, using more global measures of cognitive development, such as IQ tests, reported significant impairments among IUGR children (Breslau, Chilcoat, DelDotto, Andreski, & Brown, 1996; Hutton, Pharoah, Cooke, & Stevenson, 1997; Landry, Smith, Miller-Loncar, & Swank, 1997; Martyn, Gale, Sayer, & Fall, 1996; Seidman et al., 1992). As adults, IUGR babies are less likely to hold managerial/professional employment and earn less income (Strauss, 2000), suggesting that growth-related impairments in cognitive development are functionally relevant.

Altogether, these findings provide a strong set of data suggesting that exposure to stress in pregnancy might have a profound influence on birthweight and postnatal cognitive development, and consequently, that one could use an individual's birthweight/gestational age as a good proxy for exposure to prenatal early adversity. Future studies assessing the effects of maternal stress during pregnancy and reactivity to stress and cognitive function in the children should provide very valuable data on the effects of prenatal exposure to stress on allostatic load later in life.

Postnatal Period

Giving birth and caring for a newborn is a highly emotional and stressful experience for a new mother. Across all species, physiological and behavioral changes prepare the mother for the arrival of her offspring. In the past few decades, animal studies have documented considerable plasticity in the maternal brain during pregnancy and lactation (for a review, see Russell, Douglas, & Ingram, 2001). These changes, which span late gestation throughout lactation, ensure optimal infant development through the establishment of maternal behavior (animal's nest building, retrieval, licking and grooming; reviewed by Numan, 1994), metabolic resetting, and neuroendocrine changes. During human pregnancy and the transition to lactation, major hormonal changes occur within a short period of time. Maternal levels of estrogens and progesterone, which increase gradually during pregnancy (about 10- to 20-fold for progesterone and 100-fold for estradiol concentrations), suddenly drop at delivery and return to pregravid levels within a few days. Just as in any other mammalian species, human maternal behavior and changes in mood, emotion, and cognition are then initiated in the preparation for motherhood (Russell et al., 2001).

Feeding Choice

It is interesting to note that earlier studies conducted in rodents have demonstrated that lactation is associated with a period of *hyporesponsiveness* to various stressors in mothers (Carter & Lightman, 1987; Higuchi, Honda, Takano, & Negoro, 1988; I. D. Neumann et al., 1998; Toufexis et al., 1998). More important, it has been shown that this period of stress hyporesponsiveness in mothers is associated with the same stress hyporesponsiveness period in pups (Dent, Smith, & Levine, 2000; Levine, 1994; Schapiro, Geller, & Eiduson, 1962). The main characteristics of this period in pups are very low basal glucocorticoid levels and an inability of many stressors to elicit a glucocorticoid response (Levine, 1994).

The presence of a stress hyporesponsiveness period in the mother is related to lactation (Hard & Hansen, 1985; Hary, Dupouy, & Chatelain, 1981; Lightman & Young, 1989; I. D. Neumann, Toschi, Ohl, Torner, & Kromer, 2001; Shanks et al., 1999; Stern, Goldman, & Levine, 1973; Walker, Lightman, Steele, & Dallman, 1992; Walker, Trottier, Rochford, & Lavallee, 1995; Windle, Brady, et al., 1997; Windle, Wood, et al., 1997; Witek-Janusek, 1988) and to the role of central oxytocin and prolactin release in discrete regions of the hypothalamus throughout lactation (for a review, see Torner & Neumann, 2002; Torner, Toschi, Nava, Clapp, & Neumann, 2002). Oxytocin and prolactin, respectively involved in milk ejection and production, not only have known anxiolytic effects in both male and female virgin rats, but also play an important role in the onset of maternal behavior (Bridges, 1984; Bridges, Numan, Ronsheim, Mann, & Lupini, 1990; Carter & Lightman, 1987; Higuchi et al., 1988; I. D. Neumann, Russell, & Landgraf, 1993; I. D. Neumann et al., 2001; Torner et al., 2002).

Humans differ from animals in their choice to breast-feed or not. In contrast to bottle-feeding, breast-feeding will initiate the hormonal response of oxytocin and prolactin, which have been shown to be involved in the stress hyporesponsive period. Consequently, women who breast-feed may present a hyporesponsive response to stress when compared to women who bottle-feed. Such a result has been obtained in human mothers. For example, Wiesenfeld and collaborators (Wiesenfeld, Malatesta, Whitman, Granrose, & Uili, 1985) first showed that breast-feeding women exposed to infant signals display blunted autonomic skin conductance responses, compared to bottle-feeding mothers. Along with these findings, about a decade later, it was shown that, at 8 to 18 weeks postpartum, breast-feeding mothers have blunted HPA axis responses to a stressful treadmill exercise, compared to bottle-feeding mothers (Altemus, Deuster, Galliven, Carter, & Gold, 1995). These findings seem to suggest that women who breast-feed have blunted physiological responses to potentially stressful events. This could differentially impact reactivity to stress directly relevant to the infant and/or impact the child's hyporesponsivity to stress as well.

Consequently, it could be proposed that by inducing stress hyporesponsivity to environmental stressors, breast-feeding could serve as a protective factor for the mother (and possibly for her child) from repeated and/or excessive secretion of plasma and milk glucocorticoids during the postpartum period (Patacchioli et al., 1992; Yeh, 1984). In contrast, by preventing the emergence of the naturally occurring hyporesponse to neutral stressors, bottle-feeding might enhance the woman's reactivity to stressors and thus lead to repeated and/or excessive secretion of glucocorticoids. As we have summarized in this review, excessive secretion of cortisol levels in humans has been associated with memory impairments (Lupien et al., 1997, 2005; Lupien & Lepage, 2001; Lupien & McEwen, 1997; Maheu et al., 2004) and emotional disturbances (Sachar et al., 1973). Interestingly, a study published in 1992 reported a significant negative correlation between glucocorticoid levels and the mood of mothers who bottle-fed their babies (Bonnin, 1992). Breast-feeding is certainly not the only protective factor during this critical period, but as one that is easily accessible to all mothers, it might be one that could be strongly encouraged in specific populations exposed to high levels of environmental stress (i.e., low SES communities). These populations also choose more frequently not to breast-feed. It is thus possible that some of the effects of early adversities that are shown in children's development are due to the hormonal milieu of mothers at the time of birth of the child, induced by the feeding mode chosen by mothers. Clearly, further studies assessing the impact of infant feeding choice on the child's behavior are needed to elucidate this intriguing association between in-

fant feeding mode and stress reactivity in both the mother and her child.

Parity

Studies investigating stress responses have concentrated mostly on primiparous mothers, as the most dramatic changes in lifestyle occur after the first childbirth. Being a mother for the first time can at times be an emotionally intense and stressful experience in a woman's life. Even though fatigue and sleep disruption in maternal role "acquisition" in primiparous mothers is comparable to those experiences associated with the role of "expansion" in multiparous mothers (Waters & Lee, 1996), women with prior childbirth experience are less anxious and depressed (Fleming, Ruble, Krieger, & Wong, 1997; Fleming, Steiner, & Corter, 1997), undergo shorter and less painful labor (Mahon, Chazotte, & Cohen, 1994), and are less likely to experience gestational complications (Da Costa, Larouche, Dritsa, & Brender, 2000) and delayed lactogenesis in the days following delivery (D. C. Chen, Nommsen-Rivers, Dewey, & Lonnerdal, 1998), compared to primiparous mothers. In fact, parity is inversely correlated with the amount of life change (Grace, 1993). Thus, it is not surprising that multiparous mothers also display lower glucocorticoid levels during the days following delivery (Grajeda & Perez-Escamilla, 2002) and have more positive maternal attitudes and attractiveness to infant odors (Fleming, Steiner, et al., 1997). However, currently no study has investigated the changes in stress responsiveness as a function of parity. Future studies assessing stress reactivity in both mothers and children as a function of parity could lead to very interesting results.

Indeed, a few studies in the animal literature have investigated "habituation" of neuronal functions with respect to parity. This habituation process might also be present in the human population. Boukydis and Burgess (1982) observed higher arousal to infant cries in first-time mothers compared to mothers with several children and nonparents. This parity-induced attenuation in responsiveness is not surprising considering the fact that with repetitive exposure, the novelty characteristic of a stressful or emotional event is lost as the subject gains experience. This, in turn, can alter stress appraisal to the benefit of the mother, so that responsiveness to stress should be high only in situations of actual child endangerment. On the other hand, multiple demands placed on multiparous mothers increase fatigue (Sammons, 1990), which could enhance vulnerability to external stressors and lead to increased risk for postpartum depression (Righetti-Veltema, Conne-Perreard, Bousquet, & Manzano, 1998). Even though parity does not play a significant role in occupational fatigue in working women (Newman et al., 2001), increased household demands, particularly linked to child care, can induce more daily stressful challenges and are linked to lower morning glucocorticoid levels (Adam & Gunnar, 2001). Interestingly, parity is also associated with elevations in the diastolic blood pressure observed during the daytime (James, Cates, Pickering, & Laragh, 1989), suggesting that multiple physiological systems, in multiple states (i.e., basal or stimulated), can be modified by parity. This result suggests that parity could have a significant impact on allostatic load in mothers and/or children.

Influences of Early Adversities on Brain Development

Every day, parents observe the growing behavioral repertoire of infants and young children, as well as the corresponding changes in cognitive and emotional functions. These changes are thought to be related to normal brain development, particularly to the growth of the hippocampus and frontal lobe regions from infancy to childhood. Results of various studies assessing developmental changes in brain structures showed that the volumes of whole brain and frontal and temporal lobes increase rapidly during the first 2 years after birth, followed by a more gradual expansion restricted to white matter (Matsuzawa et al., 2001; Pfefferbaum et al., 1994). Examination of the spatial and temporal patterns of brain growth, brain shrinkage, and cortical thinning over time may help to explain the cognitive and behavioral changes that occur from infancy to childhood. The volume of the hippocampal formation increases sharply until the age of 2 years (Utsunomiya, Takano, Okazaki, & Mitsudome, 1999), and the prefrontal volume increases rapidly between 8 and 14 years of age (Kanemura et al., 1999). Late growth in prefrontal volumes is consistent with data showing that this region is known to develop latest in terms of myelination and synaptic density (Yakovlev, 1967). In summary, by the age of 2 years, the hippocampal formation has stabilized, and the prefrontal cortex volume presents a sharp increase in volume by the age of 8. The observed maturation in the frontal lobes has been shown to correlate with measures of cognitive functioning during childhood and adolescence (Reiss, Abrams, Singer, Ross, & Denckla, 1996; Sowell, Thompson, Tessner, & Toga, 2001).

Although the changes in brain structures observed during childhood and adolescence are likely maturational in nature and may be related to pubertal and hormonal changes that occur during the adolescent years, it is important to underline that, as summarized earlier, various animal studies have shown differential changes in dendritic arborization and cortical thickening of the hippocampus as a function of enriched, stressful, or demanding environmental experiences. It is thus conceivable that exposure to early adversities (prenatally and/or postnatally) in developing children might impact the development of the brain structures involved in the response to stress (hippocampus, amygdala, and frontal lobes; see earlier discussion) and lead them to become more reactive to stress in adulthood.

A recent study by Gilbertson and collaborators (2002) goes along with this suggestion. Earlier studies assessing the volume of the hippocampus in adult individuals who were exposed to traumatic events and who developed Posttraumatic Stress Disorder (PTSD) revealed that these individuals present smaller hippocampal volumes when compared to individuals exposed to the same trauma, but who did not develop PTSD (Bremner, 2002, 2003; Vythilingam et al., 2002). These results led to the suggestion that exposure to a traumatic event induces an atrophy of the adult hippocampus due to the neurotoxic effects of glucocorticoids on the hippocampus (the "neurotoxicity hypothesis" or "glucocorticoid-cascade hypothesis"; Jacobson & Sapolsky, 1991; Sapolsky, Krey, & McEwen, 1986). However, in 2002, Gilbertson et al. tested another possible hypothesis (called the "vulnerability hypothesis"), whereby *predetermined* smaller hippocampal volumes could explain increased reactivity to traumatic events in adults exposed to trauma, leading them to develop PTSD when exposed to a traumatic experience. To test this hypothesis, these authors measured hippocampal volumes in Vietnam War veterans who developed PTSD (PTSD+ group) and in others who did not develop PTSD (the PTSD− group) in response to the trauma of war. By comparing the hippocampal volumes of these two groups, they replicated earlier findings showing that the PTSD+ group had smaller hippocampal volumes then the PTSD− group (the neurotoxicity hypothesis). However, in the same study, they also measured the hippocampal volumes of the homozygotic twin brother of each of the Vietnam War veterans (PTSD+ and PTSD−), *who never went to war.* Here, they showed that the homozygotic twin brothers of the PTSD+ group *also* had small hippocampal volumes when compared to the homozygotic twin brothers of the PTSD− group. These results strongly suggest that the men who went to war and developed PTSD entered the war zone with a smaller hippocampal volume to begin with, relative to the men who went to war and did not develop PTSD (the vulnerability hypothesis). Consequently, hippocampal volume may actually be a preexisting condition that increases vulnerability to PTSD upon exposure to a traumatic experience, rather than (or along with) being a consequence of the trauma.

Still, the smaller hippocampal volumes in the men who developed PTSD on exposure to war could have been determined by early exposure to stress, which could then have delayed the development of this structure and rendered these individuals more vulnerable to the effects of stress and trauma later in life. Indeed, it is important to remind the reader that stress, environmental enrichment, and environmental demands are among the most potent inducers of changes in neurogenesis and/or dendritic arborization in the hippocampus, documented to lead to changes in hippocampal volumes.

Based on these data, we believe that there is an urgent need to test the influence of early adversity on the developing hippocampus (and other brain structures). Here, two contradictory hypotheses emerge with regard to the influence that early adversity might have on the development of the hippocampus. First, it could be postulated that children facing adversity due to lower levels of environmental enrichment and/or higher levels of stress could eventually present a delay in the development of the hippocampus (either due to a decrease in neurogenesis or a stress-induced decrease in dendritic arborization), which could eventually result in smaller hippocampal volumes in children facing early adversity when compared to children who do not. If this is the case, one could predict that smaller hippocampal volumes in children facing adversities could render these children more vulnerable to the effects of stress on both cognition and mental health. However, another hypothesis can also be proposed with regard to the development of the hippocampus in the face of adversity. Indeed, a wealth of animal data has now shown that hippocampal volume increases in relation to environmental *demands* due to the presence of stressful situations (see earlier discussion). It may thus be possible that growing up in adversity could lead to significant changes in hippocampal neurogenesis and/or growth and contribute to larger hippocampal volumes. If this is the case, one would have to predict that the larger hippocampal volumes in children facing adversity could render these children less vulnerable to the effects of stress on both cognition and mental health.

However, both hypotheses could coexist. Developmental pathways leading to small versus large hippocampi in children facing adversities could be determined by the child's perception of what the adverse environment can offer. If nothing is perceived as coming out of the adverse environment, stress could impact negatively on the developing hippocampus and lead to smaller volumes and to an increased vulnerability to stress in future years. However, if exposure to adverse events pushes the child to search for more appropriate environments (increased demands), this could impact positively on the developing hippocampus, lead to larger volumes and, consequently, to a decreased vulnerability to stress in future years. If this is the case, then for the first time, a structural and biological basis of resilience would be described. However, the process that leads a child to believe that a neglectful environment has nothing to offer (learned helplessness) or that pushes him or her to search for a better environment (meeting demands) is one of the most intriguing processes that the field of developmental psychopathology might have to face in the next decade.

GENERAL CONCLUSION

The concepts of allostasis and allostatic load are inclusive of what we mean by stress, but they are much broader because they include aspects of lifestyle as well as genetic influences and developmental effects, including early life experiences and adversities. In this way, allostasis and allostatic load provide a general conceptual framework that allows us to evaluate the overall impact of the physical and social environment on individuals and groups of individuals. It should be emphasized that, although most of the work done so far has focused on the role of HPA activity and autonomic nervous system reactivity in these nature-nurture interactions, the allostasis/allostatic load model can be generalized to other physiological systems that respond to environmental stimuli. In other words, allostasis and allostatic load attempt to embody a general biological principle: that the systems that help protect the body and promote adaptation in the short term can also participate in pathophysiological processes when they are overused or inefficiently managed.

The most important feature of allostatic load is that it operates gradually over long periods of time in the life of an individual. In fact, as summarized in this chapter, influences of genetic factors and early experiences, when coupled with the subsequent life experiences of each individual, exert a lifelong effect on the physiology of an individual and alter the risk for developing a variety of pathophysiological conditions and diseases later in life as well as the rate of certain aspects of the aging process. More important, given that the primary stress mediators of allostatic load can access the brain, they can alter the way incoming information is processed, leading to important differences in the interpretation of events as being stressful (threatening) or nonstressful (nonthreatening).

This multidisciplinary view of stress as a form of allostatic load should eventually allow us to identify very early in the life of an individual what are the potential risk factors for the negative effects of stress on physical and mental health. For example, personality traits such as anger, negative affect, low self-esteem, and emotional inhibition modify HPA and autonomic nervous system reactivity on an acute and/or chronic basis (for an example, see Kirschbaum, Prussner, et al., 1995). These changes, in turn, contribute to allostatic load when they represent a lifelong pattern of response to challenges. We have seen that these personality traits might themselves be the result of early life experiences as well as reflections of genetic factors. Fortunately, none of these traits, or the genetic and/or environmental factors that produce them, reflects an irreversible change in either behavior or allostatic load, and there are many intervention strategies that are likely to be very helpful early in development as well as later in life. However, before intervening in the early and/or later life period, one has to detect the presence of a chronic stress state. This is what allostatic load is about: detecting, in order to prevent.

REFERENCES

Adam, E. K., & Gunnar, M. R. (2001). Relationship functioning and home and work demands predict individual differences in diurnal cortisol patterns in women. *Psychoneuroendocrinology, 26*(2), 189–208.

Adelstein, A. M. (1980). Life-style in occupational cancer. *Journal of Toxicology and Environmental Health, 6*(5/6), 953–962.

Ader, R. (1969). Early experiences accelerate maturation of the 24-hour adrenocortical rhythm. *Science, 163*(872), 1225–1226.

Adler, N. E., Boyce, W. T., Chesney, M. A., Cohen, S., Folkman, S., Kahn, R. L., et al. (1994). Socioeconomic status and health: The challenge of the gradient. *American Psychologist, 49*(1), 15–24.

Altemus, M., Deuster, P. A., Galliven, E., Carter, C. S., & Gold, P. W. (1995). Suppression of hypothalmic-pituitary-adrenal axis responses to stress in lactating women. *Journal of Clinical Endocrinology and Metabolism, 80*(10), 2954–2959.

Altman, J., & Das, G. D. (1965). Autoradiographic and histological evidence of postnatal hippocampal neurogenesis in rats. *Journal of Comparative Neurology, 124*(3), 319–335.

al-Wabel, A., al-Janadi, M., & Raziuddin, S. (1993). Cytokine profile of viral and autoimmune chronic active hepatitis. *Journal of Allergy and Clinical Immunology, 92*(6), 902–908.

An, P., Rice, T., Perusse, L., Borecki, I. B., Gagnon, J., Leon, A. S., et al. (2000). Complex segregation analysis of blood pressure and heart rate measured before and after a 20-week endurance exercise training program: The HERITAGE Family Study. *American Journal of Hypertension, 13*(5, Pt. 1), 488–497.

Andersen, S. L. (2003). Trajectories of brain development: Point of vulnerability or window of opportunity? *Neuroscience and Biobehavioral Reviews, 27*(1/2), 3–18.

Anderson, A. K., Phelps, E. A. (2001). Lesions of the human amygdala impair enhanced perception of emotionally salient events. *Nature, 411,* 305–309.

Anisman, H., Zaharia, M. D., Meaney, M. J., & Merali, Z. (1998). Do early-life events permanently alter behavioral and hormonal responses to stressors? *International Journal of Developmental Neuroscience, 16*(3/4), 149–164.

Araneo, B., & Daynes, R. (1995). Dehydroepiandrosterone functions as more than an antiglucocorticoid in preserving immunocompetence after thermal injury. *Endocrinology, 136*(2), 393–401.

Ashman, S. B., Dawson, G., Panagiotides, H., Yamada, E., & Wilkinson, C. W. (2002). Stress hormone levels of children of depressed mothers. *Development and Psychopathology, 14*(2), 333–349.

Azar, R., Zoccolillo, M., Paquette, D., Quiros, E., Baltzer, F., & Tremblay, R. E. (2004). Cortisol levels and conduct disorder in adolescent mothers. *Journal of the American Academy of Child and Adolescent Psychiatry, 43*(4), 461–472.

Baddeley, A. D. (1999). *Essentials of human memory.* London: Taylor & Francis.

Balomenos, D., Rumold, R., & Theofilopoulos, A. N. (1998). Interferongamma is required for lupus-like disease and lymphoaccumulation in MRL-lpr mice. *Journal of Clinical Investigation, 101*(2), 364–371.

Barker, D. J., Hales, C. N., Fall, C. H., Osmond, C., Phipps, K., & Clark, P. M. (1993). Type 2 (non-insulin-dependent) diabetes mellitus, hypertension and hyperlipidaemia (syndrome X): Relation to reduced fetal growth. *Diabetologia, 36*(1), 62–67.

Bartels, M., de Geus, E. J., Kirschbaum, C., Sluyter, F., & Boomsma, D. I. (2003). Heritability of daytime cortisol levels in children. *Behavior Genetics, 33*(4), 421–433.

Bartels, M., Van den Berg, M., Sluyter, F., Boomsma, D. I., & de Geus, E. J. (2003). Heritability of cortisol levels: Review and simultaneous analysis of twin studies. *Psychoneuroendocrinology, 28*(2), 121–137.

Beauman, D. E. (2000). Regulation of nutrient partitioning during lactation: Homeostasis and homeorhesis revisited. In P. J. Cronje (Ed.), *Ruminant physiology: Digestion, metabolism, and growth and reproduction* (pp. 311–327). New York: CAB Publishing.

Beeghly, M., Bretherton, I., & Mervis, C. (1986). Mother's internal state language to toddlers. *British Journal of Developmental Psychology, 4,* 247–260.

Beeghly, M., & Cicchetti, D. (1994). Child maltreatment, attachment and the self system: Emergence of an internal state lexicon in toddlers at high social risk. *Development and Psychopathology, 6,* 5–30.

Berk, L. S., Tan, S. A., Fry, W. F., Napier, B. J., Lee, J. W., Hubbard, R. W., et al. (1989). Neuroendocrine and stress hormone changes during mirthful laughter. *American Journal of the Medical Sciences, 298*(6), 390–396.

Berman, M. E., Tracy, J. I., & Coccaro, E. F. (1997). The serotonin hypothesis of aggression revisited. *Clinical Psychology Review, 17*(6), 651–665.

Bigler, E. D. (2001). Frontal lobe pathology and antisocial personality disorder. *Archives of General Psychiatry, 58,* 609–611.

Birmaher, B., Rabin, B. S., Garcia, M. R., Jain, U., Whiteside, T. L., Williamson, D. E., et al. (1994). Cellular immunity in depressed, conduct disorder, and normal adolescents: Role of adverse life events. *Journal of the American Academy of Child and Adolescent Psychiatry, 33*(5), 671–678.

Blackhurst, G., McElroy, K. P., Kenyon, C. J., Fraser, R., Swan, L., Anderson, N., et al. (2002). Glucocorticoid receptor binding in twin pairs is affected by shared environment but not by shared genes. *Journal of Steroid Biochemistry and Molecular Biology, 80*(4/5), 395–400.

Bolger, K. E., Patterson, C. J., Thompson, W. W., & Kupersmidt, J. B. (1995). Psychosocial adjustment among children experiencing persistent and intermittent family economic hardship. *Child Development, 66*(4), 1107–1129.

Bonnin, F. (1992). Cortisol levels in saliva and mood changes in early puerperium. *Journal of Affective Disorders, 26*(4), 231–239.

Boomsma, D. I., & Plomin, R. (1986). Heart rate and behavior of twins. *Merrill-Palmer Quarterly, 32*(2), 141–151.

Boukydis, C. F., & Burgess, R. L. (1982). Adult physiological response to infant cries: Effects of temperament of infant, parental status, and gender. *Child Development, 53*(5), 1291–1298.

Bradley, R. H., & Corwyn, R. F. (2002). Socioeconomic status and child development. *Annual Review of Psychology, 53,* 371–399.

Breier, A., Albus, M., Pickar, D., Zahn, T. P., Wolkowitz, O. M., & Paul, S. M. (1987). Controllable and uncontrollable stress in humans: Alterations in mood and neuroendocrine and psychophysiological function. *American Journal of Psychiatry, 144*(11), 1419–1425.

Bremner, J. D. (2002). Neuroimaging studies in post-traumatic stress disorder. *Current Psychiatry Reports, 4*(4), 254–263.

Bremner, J. D. (2003). Functional neuroanatomical correlates of traumatic stress revisited 7 years later, this time with data. *Psychopharmacology Bulletin, 37*(2), 6–25.

Brennan, P. A., & Raine, A. (1997). Biosocial bases of antisocial behavior: Psychophysiological, neurological, and cognitive factors. *Clinical Psychology Review, 17*(6), 589–604.

Breslau, N., Chilcoat, H., DelDotto, J., Andreski, P., & Brown, G. (1996). Low birth weight and neurocognitive status at six years of age. *Biological Psychiatry, 40*(5), 389–397.

Bridges, R. S. (1984). A quantitative analysis of the roles of dosage, sequence, and duration of estradiol and progesterone exposure in the regulation of maternal behavior in the rat. *Endocrinology, 114*(3), 930–940.

Bridges, R. S., Numan, M., Ronsheim, P. M., Mann, P. E., & Lupini, C. E. (1990). Central prolactin infusions stimulate maternal behavior in steroid-treated, nulliparous female rats. *Proceedings of the National Academy of Sciences of the United States of America, 87*(20), 8003–8007.

Brindley, D. N., & Rolland, Y. (1989). Possible connections between stress, diabetes, obesity, hypertension and altered lipoprotein metabolism that may result in atherosclerosis. *Clinical Science, 77*(5), 453–461.

Broadhead, W. E., Kaplan, B. H., James, S. A., Wagner, E. H., Schoenbach, V. J., Grimson, R., et al. (1983). The epidemiologic evidence for a relationship between social support and health. *American Journal of Epidemiology, 117*(5), 521–537.

Bronfenbrenner, U., & Ceci, S. J. (1994). Nature-nurture reconceptualized in developmental perspective: A bioecological model. *Psychological Review, 101*(4), 568–586.

Brooks-Gunn, J., & Duncan, G. J. (1997). The effects of poverty on children. *Future of Children, 7*(2), 55–71.

Buitelaar, J. K., Huizink, A. C., Mulder, E. J., de Medina, P. G., & Visser, G. H. (2003). Prenatal stress and cognitive development and temperament in infants. *Neurobiology of Aging, 24*(Suppl. 1), S53–S60.

Bunge, S. A., Ochsner, K. N., Desmond, J. E., Glover, G. H., & Gabrieli, J. D. (2001). Prefrontal regions involved in keeping information in and out of mind. *Brain, 124,* 2074–2086.

Buydens-Branchey, L., & Branchey, M. (2004). Cocaine addicts with conduct disorder are typified by decreased cortisol responsivity and high plasma levels of DHEA-S. *Neuropsychobiology, 50*(2), 161–166.

Buydens-Branchey, L., Branchey, M., Hudson, J., & Fergeson, P. (2000). Low HDL cholesterol, aggression and altered central serotonergic activity. *Psychiatry Research, 93*(2), 93–102.

Cahill, L., Prins, B., Weber, M., & McGaugh, J. L. (1994). Beta-adrenergic activation and memory for emotional events. *Nature, 371*(6499), 702–704.

Cameron, H. A., & Gould, E. (1994). Adult neurogenesis is regulated by adrenal steroids in the dentate gyrus. *Neuroscience, 61*(2), 203–209.

Cameron, H. A., & McKay, R. D. (1999). Restoring production of hippocampal neurons in old age. *Nature Neuroscience, 2*(10), 894–897.

Cameron, H. A., Woolley, C. S., McEwen, B. S., & Gould, E. (1993). Differentiation of newly born neurons and glia in the dentate gyrus of the adult rat. *Neuroscience, 56*(2), 337–344.

Cameron, O. G., Starkman, M. N., & Schteingart, D. E. (1995). The effect of elevated systemic cortisol levels on plasma catecholamines in Cushing's syndrome patients with and without depressed mood. *Journal of Psychiatric Research, 29*(5), 347–360.

Cannon, W. (1929). The wisdom of the body. *Physiological Review, 9,* 399–431.

Carter, D. A., & Lightman, S. L. (1987). Oxytocin responses to stress in lactating and hyperprolactinaemic rats. *Neuroendocrinology, 46*(6), 532–537.

Case, R. (1985). *Intellectual development: Birth to adulthood.* New York: Academic Press.

Caspi, A., & Moffitt, T. E. (1995). The continuity of maladaptive behavior: From description to understanding in the study of antisocial behavior. In D. Cicchetti & D. J. Cohen (Eds.), *Developmental psychopathology: Vol. 2. Risk, disorder and adaptation* (pp. 472–511). New York: Wiley.

Cefalu, W. T., Wang, Z. Q., Werbel, S., Bell-Farrow, A., Crouse, J. R., III, Hinson, W. H., et al. (1995). Contribution of visceral fat mass to the insulin resistance of aging. *Metabolism, 44*(7), 954–959.

Champagne, F. A., Francis, D. D., Mar, A., & Meaney, M. J. (2003). Variations in maternal care in the rat as a mediating influence for the effects of environment on development. *Physiology and Behavior, 79*(3), 359–371.

Chen, C. C., Lu, F. H., Wu, J. S., & Chang, C. J. (2001). Correlation between serum lipid concentrations and psychological distress. *Psychiatry Research, 102*(2), 153–162.

Chen, D. C., Nommsen-Rivers, L., Dewey, K. G., & Lonnerdal, B. (1998). Stress during labor and delivery and early lactation performance. *American Journal of Clinical Nutrition, 68*(2), 335–344.

Chomsky, N. (1972). *Language and mind.* San Diego: Harcourt Brace Jovanovich.

Chrousos, G. P. (1995). The hypothalamic-pituitary-adrenal axis and immune-mediated inflammation. *New England Journal of Medicine, 332*(20), 1351–1362.

Chrousos, G. P., & Elenkov, I. (2000). Interactions of the endocrine and immune systems. In L. DeGroot (Ed.), *Endocrinology* (4th ed., pp. 571–586). Philadelphia: Saunders.

Cicchetti, D. (1991). Fractures in the crystal: Developmental psychopathology and the emergence of self. *Developmental Review, 11*(3), 271–287.

Cicchetti, D. (2002). The impact of social experience on neurobiological systems: Illustration from a constructivist view of child maltreatment. *Cognitive Development, 17*(3), 1407–1428.

Cicchetti, D., & Rogosch, F. A. (2001). Diverse patterns of neuroendocrine activity in maltreated children. *Development and Psychopathology, 13*(3), 677–693.

Cicchetti, D., Rogosch, F. A., Maughan, A., Toth, S. L., & Bruce, J. (2003). False belief understanding in maltreated children. *Development and Psychopathology, 15*(4), 1067–1091.

Clauw, D. J., & Chrousos, G. P. (1997). Chronic pain and fatigue syndromes: Overlapping clinical and neuroendocrine features and potential pathogenic mechanisms. *Neuroimmunomodulation, 4*(3), 134–153.

Clayton, N. S., & Krebs, J. R. (1994). Hippocampal growth and attrition in birds affected by experience. *Proceedings of the National Academy of Sciences of the United States of America, 91*(16), 7410–7414.

Coccaro, E. F. (1992). Impulsive aggression and central serotonergic system function in humans: An example of a dimensional brain behavior relationship. *International Clinical Psychopharmacology, 7*(1), 3–12.

Coelho, R., Silva, C., Maia, A., Prata, J., & Barros, H. (1999). Bone mineral density and depression: A community study in women. *Journal of Psychosomatic Research, 46*(1), 29–35.

Cohen, R. M., Weingartner, H., Smallberg, S. A., Pickar, D., & Murphy, D. L. (1982). Effort and cognition in depression. *Archives of General Psychiatry, 39*(5), 593–597.

Cohen, S. (1988). Psychosocial models of the role of social support in the etiology of physical disease. *Health Psychology, 7*(3), 269–297.

Cohen, S., Line, S., Manuck, S. B., Rabin, B. S., Heise, E. R., & Kaplan, J. R. (1997). Chronic social stress, social status, and susceptibility to upper respiratory infections in nonhuman primates. *Psychosomatic Medicine, 59*(3), 213–221.

Cohen, S., Tyrrell, D. A., & Smith, A. P. (1991). Psychological stress and susceptibility to the common cold. *New England Journal of Medicine, 325*(9), 606–612.

Conger, R. D., Patterson, G. R., & Ge, X. (1995). It takes two to replicate: A mediational model for the impact of parents' stress on adolescent adjustment. *Child Development, 66*(1), 80–97.

Connolly, J. D., Goodale, M. A., Menon, R. S., & Munoz, D. P. (2002). Human fMRI evidence for the neural correlates of preparatory set. *Nature Neuroscience, 5,* 1345–1352.

Cooley-Quille, M., & Lorion, R. (1999). Adolescents' exposure to community violence: Sleep and psychophysiological functioning. *Journal of Community Psychology, 27*(4), 367–375.

Corcoran, M. E., & Chaudry, A. (1997). The dynamics of childhood poverty. *Future Child, 7*(2), 40–54.

Coster, W. J., Gersten, M. S., Beeghly, M., & Cicchetti, D. (1989). Communicative functioning in maltreated toddlers. *Developmental Psychology, 25*(6), 1020–1029.

Crimmins, E. M., Johnston, M., Hayward, M., & Seeman, T. (2003). Age differences in allostatic load: An index of physiological dysregulation. *Experimental Gerontology, 38*(7), 731–734.

Crofford, L. J., Jacobson, J., & Young, E. (1999). Modeling the involvement of the hypothalamic-pituitary-adrenal and hypothalamic-pituitary-gonadal axes in autoimmune and stress-related rheumatic syndromes in women. *Journal of Women's Health, 8*(2), 203–215.

Curtis, W. J., & Cicchetti, D. (2003). Moving research on resilience into the 21st century: Theoretical and methodological considerations in examining the biological contributors to resilience. *Development and Psychopathology, 15*(3), 773–810.

Cutting, A. L., & Dunn, J. (1999). Theory of mind, emotion understanding, language, and family background: Individual differences and interrelations. *Child Development, 70*(4), 853–865.

Da Costa, D., Larouche, J., Dritsa, M., & Brender, W. (2000). Psychosocial correlates of prepartum and postpartum depressed mood. *Journal of Affective Disorders, 59*(1), 31–40.

Davachi, L., & Wagner, A. D. (2002). Hippocampal contributions to episodic encoding: Insights from relational and item-based learning. *Journal of Neurophysiology, 88,* 982—990.

Davis, E. P., Donzella, B., Krueger, W. K., & Gunnar, M. R. (1999). The start of a new school year: Individual differences in salivary cortisol response in relation to child temperament. *Developmental Psychobiology, 35*(3), 188–196.

Davis, M. C., Matthews, K. A., & McGrath, C. E. (2000). Hostile attitudes predict elevated vascular resistance during interpersonal stress in men and women. *Psychosomatic Medicine, 62*(1), 17–25.

Deater-Deckard, K., Dodge, K. A., Bates, J. E., & Pettit, G. S. (1996). Physical discipline among African American and European American mothers: Links to children's externalizing behaviors. *Developmental Psychology, 32*(6), 1065–1072.

de Geus, E. J. (2002). Introducing genetic psychophysiology. *Biological Psychology, 61*(1/2), 1–10.

de Haan, M., Gunnar, M. R., Tout, K., Hart, J., & Stansbury, K. (1998). Familiar and novel contexts yield different associations between cortisol and behavior among 2-year-old children. *Developmental Psychobiology, 33*(1), 93–101.

De Kloet, E. R., Vreugdenhil, E., Oitzl, M. S., & Joels, M. (1998). Brain corticosteroid receptor balance in health and disease. *Endocrine Reviews, 19*(3), 269–301.

Dent, G. W., Smith, M. A., & Levine, S. (2000). Rapid induction of corticotropin-releasing hormone gene transcription in the paraventricular nucleus of the developing rat. *Endocrinology, 141*(5), 1593–1598.

Dettling, A. C., Gunnar, M. R., & Donzella, B. (1999). Cortisol levels of young children in full-day childcare centers: Relations with age and temperament. *Psychoneuroendocrinology, 24*(5), 519–536.

Dhabhar, F. S., & McEwen, B. S. (1999). Enhancing versus suppressive effects of stress hormones on skin immune function. *Proceedings of the National Academy of Sciences of the United States of America, 96*(3), 1059–1064.

Dickerson, S. S., & Kemeny, M. E. (2002). Acute stressors and cortisol reactivity: A meta-analytic review. *Psychosomatic Medicine, 54,* 105–123.

Ditto, B. (1993). Familial influences on heart rate, blood pressure, and self-report anxiety responses to stress: Results from 100 twin pairs. *Psychophysiology, 30*(6), 635–645.

Dmitrieva, T. N., Oades, R. D., Hauffa, B. P., & Eggers, C. (2001). Dehydroepiandrosterone sulphate and corticotropin levels are high in young male patients with conduct disorder: Comparisons for growth factors, thyroid and gonadal hormones. *Neuropsychobiology, 43*(3), 134–140.

Dohrenwend, B. P. (2000). The role of adversity and stress in psychopathology: Some evidence and its implications for theory and research. *Journal of Health and Social Behavior, 41*(1), 1–19.

Dohrenwend, B. S. (1973). Social status and stressful life events. *Journal of Personality and Social Psychology, 28*(2), 225–235.

Dohrenwend, B. S., & Dohrenwend, B. P. (1970). Class and race as status-related sources of stress. In S. Levine & N. A. Scotch (Eds.), *Social stress* (pp. 111–140). Chicago: Aldine.

Dubreuil, E., Ditto, B., Dionne, G., Pihl, R. O., Tremblay, R. E., Boivin, M., et al. (2003). Familiality of heart rate and cardiac-related autonomic activity in five-month-old twins: The Quebec newborn twins study. *Psychophysiology, 40*(6), 849–862.

Dunn, J., Bretherton, I., & Munn, P. (1987). Conversations about feeling states between mothers and their young children. *Developmental Psychology, 23,* 132–139.

Dunn, J., Brown, J., & Beardsall, L. (1991). Family talk about feeling states and children's later understanding of other's emotions. *Developmental Psychology, 27,* 448–455.

Eigsti, I. M., & Cicchetti, D. (2004). The impact of child maltreatment on expressive syntax at 60 months. *Developmental Science, 7*(1), 88–102.

Elenkov, I. J., Chrousos, G. P., & Wilder, R. L. (2000). Neuroendocrine regulation of IL-12 and TNF-alpha/IL-10 balance: Clinical implications. *Annals of the New York Academy of Sciences, 917,* 94–105.

Elenkov, I. J., Papanicolaou, D. A., Wilder, R. L., & Chrousos, G. P. (1996). Modulatory effects of glucocorticoids and catecholamines on human interleukin-12 and interleukin-10 production: Clinical implications. *Proceedings of the Association of American Physicians, 108*(5), 374–381.

Eriksson, P. S., Perfilieva, E., Bjork-Eriksson, T., Alborn, A. M., Nordborg, C., Peterson, D. A., et al. (1998). Neurogenesis in the adult human hippocampus. *Nature Medicine, 4*(11), 1313–1317.

Essex, M. J., Klein, M. H., Cho, E., & Kalin, N. H. (2002). Maternal stress beginning in infancy may sensitize children to later stress exposure: Effects on cortisol and behavior. *Biological Psychiatry, 52*(8), 776–784.

Evans, D. M., Gillespie, N. A., & Martin, N. G. (2002). Biometrical genetics. *Biological Psychology, 61*(1), 33–51.

Evans, G. W. (2003). A multimethodological analysis of cumulative risk and allostatic load among rural children. *Developmental Psychology, 39*(5), 924–933.

Evans, G. W., & English, K. (2002). The environment of poverty: Multiple stressor exposure, psychophysiological stress, and socioemotional adjustment. *Child Development, 73*(4), 1238–1248.

Evans, G. W., & Marcynyszyn, L. A. (2004). Environmental justice, cumulative environmental risk, and health among low- and middle-income children in upstate New York. *American Journal of Public Health, 94*(11), 1942–1944.

Fan, J., Snodgrass, J., & Bilder, R. M. (2003). Functional magnetic resonance imaging of source versus item memory. *Neuroreport, 2,* 2275–2281.

Felitti, V. J., Anda, R. F., Nordenberg, D., Williamson, D. F., Spitz, A. M., Edwards, V., et al. (1998). Relationship of childhood abuse and household dysfunction to many of the leading causes of death in adults: The Adverse Childhood Experiences (ACE) Study. *American Journal of Preventive Medicine, 14*(4), 245–258.

Field, T. (1994). The effects of mother's physical and emotional unavailability on emotion regulation. In N. A. Fox (Ed.), *The development of emotion regulation* (pp. 208–227). Chicago: University of Chicago Press.

Fleming, A. S., Ruble, D., Krieger, H., & Wong, P. Y. (1997). Hormonal and experiential correlates of maternal responsiveness during pregnancy and the puerperium in human mothers. *Hormones and Behavior, 31*(2), 145–158.

Fleming, A. S., Steiner, M., & Corter, C. (1997). Cortisol, hedonics, and maternal responsiveness in human mothers. *Hormones and Behavior, 32*(2), 85–98.

Flinn, M. V., & England, B. G. (1997). Social economics of childhood glucocorticoid stress response and health. *American Journal of Physical Anthropology, 102*(1), 33–53.

Folkman, S., Schaefer, C., & Lazarus, R. S. (1979). Cognitive processes as mediators of stress and coping. In V. Hamilton & D. W. Warburton (Eds.), *Human stress and cognition: An information processing approach* (pp. 265–298). New York: Wiley.

Fournie, G. J., Cautain, B., Xystrakis, E., Damoiseaux, J., Mas, M., Lagrange, D., et al. (2001). Cellular and genetic factors involved in the difference between Brown Norway and Lewis rats to develop respectively type-2 and type-1 immune-mediated diseases. *Immunological Reviews, 184,* 145–160.

Francis, D. D., Champagne, F. A., Liu, D., & Meaney, M. J. (1999). Maternal care, gene expression, and the development of individual differences in stress reactivity. *Annals of the New York Academy of Sciences, 896,* 66–84.

Francis, D. D., Diorio, J., Liu, D., & Meaney, M. J. (1999). Nongenomic transmission across generations of maternal behavior and stress responses in the rat. *Science, 286*(5442), 1155–1158.

Frick, P. J. (1998). *Conduct disorders and severe antisocial behavior.* New York: Plenum Press.

Froehlich, J. C., Zink, R. W., Li, T. K., & Christian, J. C. (2000). Analysis of heritability of hormonal responses to alcohol in twins: Beta-endorphin as a potential biomarker of genetic risk for alcoholism. *Alcoholism, Clinical and Experimental Research, 24*(3), 265–277.

Fuchs, E., Uno, H., & Flugge, G. (1995). Chronic psychosocial stress induces morphological alterations in hippocampal pyramidal neurons of the tree shrew. *Brain Research, 673*(2), 275–282.

Galovski, T. E., Blanchard, E. B., Malta, L. S., & Freidenberg, B. M. (2003). The psychophsiology of aggressive drivers: Comparison to non-aggressive drivers and pre- to post-treatment change following a cognitive-behavioural treatment. *Behaviour Research and Therapy, 41*(9), 1055–1067.

Garcia-Leon, A., Reyes del Paso, G. A., Robles, H., & Vila, J. (2003). Relative effects of harassment, frustration, and task characteristics on cardiovascular reactivity. *International Journal of Psychophysiology, 47*(2), 159–173.

Gerin, W., Litt, M. D., Deich, J., & Pickering, T. G. (1996). Self-efficacy as a component of active coping: Effects on cardiovascular reactivity. *Journal of Psychosomatic Research, 40*(5), 485–493.

Gerlai, R., & Clayton, N. S. (1999). Analysing hippocampal function in transgenic mice: An ethological perspective. *Trends in Neuroscience, 22*(2), 47–51.

Gilbertson, M. W., Shenton, M. E., Ciszewski, A., Kasai, K., Lasko, N. B., Orr, S. P., et al. (2002). Smaller hippocampal volume predicts pathologic vulnerability to psychological trauma. *Nature Neuroscience, 5*(11), 1242–1247.

Golomb, B. A. (1998). Cholesterol and violence: Is there a connection? *Annals of Internal Medicine, 128*(6), 478–487.

Golomb, B. A., Stattin, H., & Mednick, S. (2000). Low cholesterol and violent crime. *Journal of Psychiatric Research, 34*(4/5), 301–309.

Goodyer, I. M., Herbert, J., Altham, P. M., Pearson, J., Secher, S. M., & Shiers, H. M. (1996). Adrenal secretion during major depression in 8- to 16-year-olds: I. Altered diurnal rhythms in salivary cortisol and dehydroepiandrosterone (DHEA) at presentation. *Psychological Medicine, 26*(2), 245–256.

Goodyer, I. M., Park, R. J., Netherton, C. M., & Herbert, J. (2001). Possible role of cortisol and dehydroepiandrosterone in human development and psychopathology. *British Journal of Psychiatry, 179,* 243–249.

Gopnik, A., & Astington, J. W. (1988). Children's understanding of representational change and its relation to the understanding of false belief and the appearance-reality distinction. *Child Development, 59*(1), 26–37.

Gould, E., McEwen, B. S., Tanapat, P., Galea, L. A., & Fuchs, E. (1997). Neurogenesis in the dentate gyrus of the adult tree shrew is regulated by psychosocial stress and NMDA receptor activation. *Journal of Neuroscience, 17*(7), 2492–2498.

Gould, E., Reeves, A. J., Fallah, M., Tanapat, P., Gross, C. G., & Fuchs, E. (1999). Hippocampal neurogenesis in adult Old World primates. *Proceedings of the National Academy of Sciences of the United States of America, 96*(9), 5263–5267.

Gould, E., Tanapat, P., McEwen, B. S., Flugge, G., & Fuchs, E. (1998). Proliferation of granule cell precursors in the dentate gyrus of adult monkeys is diminished by stress. *Proceedings of the National Academy of Sciences of the United States of America, 95*(6), 3168–3171.

Grace, J. T. (1993). Mothers' self-reports of parenthood across the first 6 months postpartum. *Research in Nursing and Health, 16*(6), 431–439.

Grajeda, R., & Perez-Escamilla, R. (2002). Stress during labor and delivery is associated with delayed onset of lactation among urban Guatemalan women. *Journal of Nutrition, 132*(10), 3055–3060.

Gray, J. A. (1982). *The neurophysiology of anxiety: An enquiry into the functions of the septo-hippocampal system.* Oxford: Oxford University Press.

Gray, J. A. (1987). *The psychology of fear and stress* (2nd ed.). Cambridge, MA: Cambridge University Press.

Griep, E. N., Boersma, J. W., Lentjes, E. G., Prins, A. P., van der Korst, J. K., & de Kloet, E. R. (1998). Function of the hypothalamic-pituitary-adrenal axis in patients with fibromyalgia and low back pain. *Journal of Rheumatology, 25*(7), 1374–1381.

Gunnar, M. R., & Donzella, B. (2002). Social regulation of the cortisol levels in early human development. *Psychoneuroendocrinology, 27*(1/2), 199–220.

Gunnar, M. R., Morison, S. J., Chisholm, K., & Schuder, M. (2001). Salivary cortisol levels in children adopted from Romanian orphanages. *Development and Psychopathology, 13*(3), 611–628.

Gunnar, M. R., Tout, K., de Haan, M., Pierce, S., & Stansbury, K. (1997). Temperament, social competence, and adrenocortical activity in preschoolers. *Developmental Psychobiology, 31*(1), 65–85.

Gunnar, M. R., & Vazquez, D. M. (2001). Low cortisol and a flattening of expected daytime rhythm: Potential indices of risk in human development. *Development and Psychopathology, 13*(3), 515–538.

Gutierrez, M. A., Garcia, M. E., Rodriguez, J. A., Rivero, S., & Jacobelli, S. (1998). Hypothalamic-pituitary-adrenal axis function and prolactin secretion in systemic lupus erythematosus. *Lupus, 7*(6), 404–408.

Haan, M. N., Kaplan, G. A., & Syme, S. L. (1989). Socioeconomic status and health: Old observations and new thoughts. In J. Bunker, D. Gomby, & B. Kehrer (Eds.), *Pathways to health: The role of social factors* (pp. 31–43). Menlo Park, CA: Henry H. Kaiser Family Foundation.

Haapasalo, J., & Tremblay, R. E. (1994). Physically aggressive boys from ages 6 to 12: Family background, parenting behavior, and prediction of delinquency. *Journal of Consulting and Clinical Psychology, 62*(5), 1044–1052.

Hall, R. C., Popkin, M. K., Stickney, S. K., & Gardner, E. R. (1979). Presentation of the steroid psychoses. *Journal of Nervous and Mental Diseases, 167*(4), 229–236.

Han, D. H., Hansen, P. A., Chen, M. M., & Holloszy, J. O. (1998). DHEA treatment reduces fat accumulation and protects against insulin resistance in male rats. *Journals of Gerontology. Series A, Biological Sciences and Medical Sciences, 53*(1), B19–B24.

Hansen, P. A., Han, D. H., Nolte, L. A., Chen, M., & Holloszy, J. O. (1997). DHEA protects against visceral obesity and muscle insulin resistance in rats fed a high-fat diet. *American Journal of Physiology, 273*(5, Pt. 2), R1704–R1708.

Hanson, T. L., McLanahan, S., & Thomson, E. (1997). Economic resources, parental practices, and children's well-being. In G. J. Duncan & J. Brooks-Gunn (Eds.), *Consequences of growing up poor* (pp. 190–238). New York: Russell Sage Foundation.

Harbuz, M. S., Jessop, D. S., & Lightman, S. L. (1997). Hypothalamo-pituitary-adrenal activity in experimental models of autoimmune-inflammatory disease. In J. C. Buckingham, G. E. Gillies, & A. M. Cowell (Eds.), *Stress, stress hormones and the immune system* (pp. 95–123). New York: Wiley.

Hard, E., & Hansen, S. (1985). Reduced fearfulness in the lactating rat. *Physiology and Behavior, 35*(4), 641–643.

Hare, R. D. (1965). Psychopathy, fear arousal and anticipated pain. *Psychological Reports, 16*, 499–502.

Hary, L., Dupouy, J. P., & Chatelain, A. (1981). Pituitary response to bilateral adrenalectomy, metyrapone treatment and ether stress in the newborn rat. *Biology of the Neonate, 39*(1/2), 28–36.

Heale, V. R., Vanderwolf, C. H., & Kavaliers, M. (1994). Components of weasel and fox odors elicit fast wave bursts in the dentate gyrus of rats. *Behavioral Brain Research, 63*(2), 159–165.

Healy, B. T. (1992). The heritability of autonomic nervous system processes. In T. M. Field & P. M. McCabe (Eds.), *Stress and coping in infancy and childhood* (pp. 69–82). New York: Erlbaum.

Heckers, S. (2001). Neuroimaging studies of the hippocampus in Schizophrenia. *Hippocampus, 11*(5), 520–528.

Hedegaard, M., Henriksen, T. B., Sabroe, S., & Secher, N. J. (1993). Psychological distress in pregnancy and preterm delivery. *British Medical Journal, 307*(6898), 234–239.

Hedegaard, M., Henriksen, T. B., Sabroe, S., & Secher, N. J. (1996). The relationship between psychological distress during pregnancy and birth weight for gestational age. *Acta Obstetricia et Gynecologica Scandinavica, 75*(1), 32–39.

Heim, C., Newport, D. J., Heit, S., Graham, Y. P., Wilcox, M., Bonsall, R., et al. (2000). Pituitary-adrenal and autonomic responses to stress in women after sexual and physical abuse in childhood. *Journal of the American Medical Association, 284*(5), 592–597.

Hellhammer, D. H., Buchtal, J., Gutberlet, I., & Kirschbaum, C. (1997). Social hierarchy and adrenocortical stress reactivity in men. *Psychoneuroendocrinology, 22*(8), 643–650.

Hennessy, K. D., Rabideau, G. J., Cicchetti, D., & Cummings, E. M. (1994). Responses of physically abused and nonabused children to different forms of interadult anger. *Child Development, 65*(3), 815–828.

Hertsgaard, L., Gunnar, M., Erickson, M. F., & Nachmias, M. (1995). Adrenocortical responses to the Strange Situation in infants with disorganized/disoriented attachment relationships. *Child Development, 66*(4), 1100–1106.

Hessl, D., Dawson, G., Frey, K., Panagiotides, H., Self, H., Yamada, E., et al. (1998). A longitudinal study of children of depressed mothers: Psychobiological findings related to stress. In D. M. Hann, L. C. Huffman, K. K. Lederhendler, & D. Minecke (Eds.), *Advancing research on developmental plasticity: Integrating the behavioral sciences and the neurosciences of mental health* (pp. 256). Bethesda, MD: National Institutes of Mental Health.

Higuchi, T., Honda, K., Takano, S., & Negoro, H. (1988). Reduced oxytocin response to osmotic stimulus and immobilization stress in lactating rats. *Journal of Endocrinology, 116*(2), 225–230.

Hillbrand, M., & Spitz, R. T. (1999). Cholesterol and aggression. *Aggression and Violent Behavior, 4*(3), 359–370.

Hillbrand, M., Waite, B. M., Miller, D. S., Spitz, R. T., & Lingswiler, V. M. (2000). Serum cholesterol concentrations and mood states in violent psychiatric patients: An experience sampling study. *Journal of Behavioral Medicine, 23*(6), 519–529.

Hoff, E. (2003). The specificity of environmental influence: Socioeconomic status affects early vocabulary development via maternal speech. *Child Development, 74*(5), 1368–1378.

House, J. S., Lepkowski, J. M., Kinney, A. M., Mero, R. P., Kessler, R. C., & Herzog, A. R. (1994). The social stratification of aging and health. *Journal of Health and Social Behavior, 35*(3), 213–234.

Huether, G. (1998). Stress and the adaptive self-organization of neuronal connectivity during early childhood. *International Journal of Developmental Neuroscience, 16*(3/4), 297–306.

Hughes, C., Deater-Deckard, K., & Cutting, A. L. (1999). Speak roughly to your little boy? Sex differences in the relations between parenting and preschoolers' understanding of mind. *Social Development, 8*(2), 143–160.

Hutton, J. L., Pharoah, P. O., Cooke, R. W., & Stevenson, R. C. (1997). Differential effects of preterm birth and small gestational age on cognitive and motor development. *Archives of Disease in Childhood: Fetal and Neonatal Edition, 76*(2), F75–F81.

Inglis, G. C., Ingram, M. C., Holloway, C. D., Swan, L., Birnie, D., Hillis, W. S., et al. (1999). Familial pattern of corticosteroids and their metabolism in adult human subjects: The Scottish Adult Twin Study. *Journal of Clinical Endocrinology and Metabolism, 84*(11), 4132–4137.

Ishikawa, S. S., Raine, A., Lencz, T., Bihrle, S., & LaCasse, L. (2001). Increased height and bulk in antisocial personality disorder and its subtypes. *Psychiatry Research, 105*(3), 211–219.

Jackson, A. P., Brooks-Gunn, J., Huang, C. C., & Glassman, M. (2000). Single mothers in low-wage jobs: Financial strain, parenting, and preschoolers' outcomes. *Child Development, 71*(5), 1409–1423.

Jacobson, L., & Sapolsky, R. (1991). The role of the hippocampus in feedback regulation of the hypothalamic-pituitary-adrenocortical axis. *Endocrine Reviews, 12*(2), 118–134.

James, G. D., Cates, E. M., Pickering, T. G., & Laragh, J. H. (1989). Parity and perceived job stress elevate blood pressure in young normotensive working women. *American Journal of Hypertension, 2*(8), 637–639.

Kagan, J., Reznick, J. S., & Snidman, N. (1987). The physiology and psychology of behavioral inhibition in children. *Child Development, 58*(6), 1459–1473.

Kanemura, H., Aihara, M., Aoki, S., Hatakeyama, K., Kamiya, Y., Ono, C., et al. (1999). Quantitative measurement of prefrontal lobe volume on three-dimensional magnetic resonance imaging scan. *Brain and Development, 31*(6), 519–524.

Kaplan, J. R., Shively, C. A., Fontenot, M. B., Morgan, T. M., Howell, S. M., Manuck, S. B., et al. (1994). Demonstration of an association among dietary cholesterol, central serotonergic activity, and social behavior in monkeys. *Psychosomatic Medicine, 56*(6), 479–484.

Karlamangla, A. S., Singer, B. H., McEwen, B. S., Rowe, J. W., & Seeman, T. E. (2002). Allostatic load as a predictor of functional decline: MacArthur studies of successful aging. *Journal of Clinical Epidemiology, 55*(7), 696–710.

Kaufman, J., Birmaher, B., Perel, J., Dahl, R. E., Moreci, P., Nelson, B., et al. (1997). The corticotropin-releasing hormone challenge in depressed abused, depressed nonabused, and normal control children. *Biological Psychiatry, 42*(8), 669–679.

Kempermann, G., Kuhn, H. G., & Gage, F. H. (1997). More hippocampal neurons in adult mice living in an enriched environment. *Nature, 386*(6624), 493–495.

Kiecolt-Glaser, J. K., Glaser, R., Gravenstein, S., Malarkey, W. B., & Sheridan, J. (1996). Chronic stress alters the immune response to influenza virus vaccine in older adults. *Proceedings of the National Academy of Sciences of the United States of America, 93*(7), 3043–3047.

Kiehl, K. A., Smith, A. M., Hare, R. D., Mendrek, A., Forster, B. B., Brink, J., et al. (2001). Limbic abnormalities in affective processing by criminal psychopaths as revealed by functional magnetic resonance imaging. *Biological Psychiatry, 50*, 677–684.

Kindlon, D. J., Tremblay, R. E., Mezzacappa, E., Earls, F., Laurent, D., & Schaal, B. (1995). Longitudinal patterns of heart rate and fighting behavior in 9- through 12-year-old boys. *Journal of the American Academy of Child and Adolescent Psychiatry, 34*(3), 371–377.

King, J. A., Barkley, R. A., & Barrett, S. (1998). Attention-deficit hyperactivity disorder and the stress response. *Biological Psychiatry, 44*(1), 72–74.

Kirschbaum, C., & Hellhammer, D. (1989). Response variability of salivary cortisol under psychological stimulation. *Journal of Clinical Chemistry and Clinical Biochemistry, 27*(4), 237.

Kirschbaum, C., Klauer, T., Filipp, S. H., & Hellhammer, D. H. (1995). Sex-specific effects of social support on cortisol and subjective responses to acute psychological stress. *Psychosomatic Medicine, 57*(1), 23–31.

Kirschbaum, C., Kudielka, B. M., Gaab, J., Schommer, N. C., & Hellhammer, D. H. (1999). Impact of gender, menstrual cycle phase, and oral contraceptives on the activity of the hypothalamus-pituitary-adrenal axis. *Psychosomatic Medicine, 61*(2), 154–162.

Kirschbaum, C., Prussner, J. C., Stone, A. A., Federenko, I., Gaab, J., Lintz, D., et al. (1995). Persistent high cortisol responses to repeated psychological stress in a subpopulation of healthy men. *Psychosomatic Medicine, 57*(5), 468–474.

Kirschbaum, C., Wüst, S., Faig, H. G., & Hellhammer, D. H. (1992). Heritability of cortisol responses to human corticotropin-releasing hormone, ergometry, and psychological stress in humans. *Journal of Clinical Endocrinology and Metabolism, 75*(6), 1526–1530.

Krishnan, K. R., Doraiswamy, P. M., Figiel, G. S., Husain, M. M., Shah, S. A., Na, C., et al. (1991). Hippocampal abnormalities in depression. *Journal of Neuropsychiatry and Clinical Neurosciences, 3*(4), 387–391.

Kruesi, M. J., Casanova, M. F., Mannheim, G., & Johnson-Bilder, A. (2004). Reduced temporal lobe volume in early onset conduct disorder. *Psychiatry Research, 132*, 1–11.

Kruesi, M. J., Schmidt, M. E., Donnelly, M., Hibbs, E. D., & Hamburger, S. D. (1989). Urinary free cortisol output and disruptive behavior in children. *Journal of the American Academy of Child and Adolescent Psychiatry, 28*(3), 441–443.

Kudielka, B. M., Buske-Kirschbaum, A., Hellhammer, D. H., & Kirschbaum, C. (2004). HPA axis responses to laboratory psychosocial stress in healthy elderly adults, younger adults, and children: Impact of age and gender. *Psychoneuroendocrinology, 29*(1), 83–98.

Kudielka, B. M., Schommer, N. C., Hellhammer, D. H., & Kirschbaum, C. (2004). Acute HPA axis responses, heart rate, and mood changes to psychosocial stress (TSST) in humans at different times of day. *Psychoneuroendocrinology, 29*(8), 983–992.

Kuenzel, W. J., Beck, M. M., & Teruyama, R. (1999). Neural sites and pathways regulating food intake in birds: A comparative analysis to mammalian systems. *Journal of Experimental Zoology, 283*(4/5), 348–364.

Kunz-Ebrecht, S. R., Kirschbaum, C., & Steptoe, A. (2004). Work stress, socioeconomic status and neuroendocrine activation over the working day. *Social Science and Medicine, 58*(8), 1523–1530.

Lagercrantz, H. (1997). Better born too soon than too small. *Lancet, 350*(9084), 1044–1045.

Lahey, B. B., McBurnett, K., Loeber, R., & Hart, E. L. (1995). Psychobiology. In G. Sholevar (Ed.), *Conduct disorders in children and adolescents* (pp. 27–44). Washington, DC: American Psychiatric Press.

Landry, S. H., Smith, K. E., Miller-Loncar, C. L., & Swank, P. R. (1997). Predicting cognitive-language and social growth curves from early maternal behaviors in children at varying degrees of biological risk. *Developmental Psychology, 33*(6), 1040–1053.

Laplante, D. P., Barr, R. G., Brunet, A., Galbaud du Fort, G., Meaney, M. L., Saucier, J. F., et al. (2004). Stress during pregnancy affects general intellectual and language functioning in human toddlers. *Pediatric Research, 56*(3), 400–410.

LeDoux, J. E. (2003). The emotional brain, fear, and the amygdala. *Cellular and Molecular Neurobiology, 23*(4/5), 727–738.

Leibowitz, S. F., & Hoebel, B. G. (1997). Behavioral neuroscience of obesity. In G. A. Bray, C. Bouchard, & W. P. T. James (Eds.), *Handbook of obesity* (pp. 313–358). New York: Marcel Dekker.

Lemaire, V., Koehl, M., Le Moal, M., & Abrous, D. N. (2000). Prenatal stress produces learning deficits associated with an inhibition of neurogenesis in the hippocampus. *Proceedings of the National Academy of Sciences of the United States of America, 97*(20), 11032–11037.

Lempers, J. D., Clark-Lempers, D., & Simons, R. L. (1989). Economic hardship, parenting, and distress in adolescence. *Child Development, 60*(1), 25–39.

Lentjes, E. G., Griep, E. N., Boersma, J. W., Romijn, F. P., & de Kloet, E. R. (1997). Glucocorticoid receptors, fibromyalgia and low back pain. *Psychoneuroendocrinology, 22*(8), 603–614.

Leproult, R., Copinschi, G., Buxton, O., & Van Cauter, E. (1997). Sleep loss results in an elevation of cortisol levels the next evening. *Sleep, 20*(10), 865–870.

Lesage, J., Blondeau, B., Grino, M., Breant, B., & Dupouy, J. P. (2001). Maternal undernutrition during late gestation induces fetal overexposure to glucocorticoids and intrauterine growth retardation, and disturbs the hypothalamo-pituitary-adrenal axis in the newborn rat. *Endocrinology, 142*(5), 1692–1702.

Levine, S. (1994). The ontogeny of the hypothalamic-pituitary-adrenal axis: The influence of maternal factors. *Annals of the New York Academy of Sciences, 746,* 275–293.

Levitt, N. S., Lindsay, R. S., Holmes, M. C., & Seckl, J. R. (1996). Dexamethasone in the last week of pregnancy attenuates hippocampal glucocorticoid receptor gene expression and elevates blood pressure in the adult offspring in the rat. *Neuroendocrinology, 64*(6), 412–418.

Lightman, S. L., & Young, W. S., III. (1989). Lactation inhibits stress-mediated secretion of corticosterone and oxytocin and hypothalamic accumulation of corticotropin-releasing factor and enkephalin messenger ribonucleic acids. *Endocrinology, 124*(5), 2358–2364.

Lindberg, G., Rastam, L., Gullberg, B., & Eklund, G. A. (1992). Low serum cholesterol concentration and short term mortality from injuries in men and women. *British Medical Journal, 305*(6848), 277–279.

Ling, M. H., Perry, P. J., & Tsuang, M. T. (1981). Side effects of corticosteroid therapy: Psychiatric aspects. *Archives of General Psychiatry, 38*(4), 471–477.

Lingas, R., Dean, F., & Matthews, S. G. (1999). Maternal nutrient restriction (48 h) modifies brain corticosteroid receptor expression and endocrine function in the fetal guinea pig. *Brain Research, 846*(2), 236–242.

Linkowski, P., Van Onderbergen, A., Kerkhofs, M., Bosson, D., Mendlewicz, J., & Van Cauter, E. (1993). Twin study of the 24-h cortisol profile: Evidence for genetic control of the human circadian clock. *American Journal of Physiology, 264*(2, Pt. 1), E173–E181.

Linnoila, V. M., & Virkkunen, M. (1992). Aggression, suicidality, and serotonin. *Journal of Clinical Psychiatry, 53*(Suppl.), 46–51.

Lundberg, U. (1996). Influence of paid and unpaid work on psychophysiological stress responses of men and women. *Journal of Occupational Health Psychology, 1*(2), 117–130.

Lupien, S. J., de Leon, M., de Santi, S., Convit, A., Tarshish, C., Nair, N. P., et al. (1998). Cortisol levels during human aging predict hippocampal atrophy and memory deficits. *Nature Neuroscience, 1*(1), 69–73.

Lupien, S. J., Fiocco, A., Wan, N., Maheu, F., Lord, C., Schramek, T., et al. (2005). Stress hormones and human memory function across the lifespan. *Psychoneuroendocrinology, 30*(3), 225–242.

Lupien, S. J., Gaudreau, S., Tchiteya, B. M., Maheu, F., Sharma, S., Nair, N. P., et al. (1997). Stress-induced declarative memory impairment in healthy elderly subjects: Relationship to cortisol reactivity. *Journal of Clinical Endocrinology and Metabolism, 82*(7), 2070–2075.

Lupien, S. J., King, S., Meaney, M. J., & McEwen, B. S. (2000). Child's stress hormone levels correlate with mother's socioeconomic status and depressive state. *Biological Psychiatry, 48*(10), 976–980.

Lupien, S. J., King, S., Meaney, M. J., & McEwen, B. S. (2001). Can poverty get under your skin? Basal cortisol levels and cognitive function in children from low and high socioeconomic status. *Development and Psychopathology, 13,* 651–674.

Lupien, S. J., Lecours, A. R., Lussier, I., Schwartz, G., Nair, N. P., & Meaney, M. J. (1994). Basal cortisol levels and cognitive deficits in human aging. *Journal of Neuroscience, 14*(5, Pt. 1), 2893–2903.

Lupien, S. J., Lecours, A. R., Schwartz, G., Sharma, S., Hauger, R. L., Meaney, M. J., et al. (1996). Longitudinal study of basal cortisol levels in healthy elderly subjects: Evidence for subgroups. *Neurobiology of Aging, 17*(1), 95–105.

Lupien, S. J., & Lepage, M. (2001). Stress, memory, and the hippocampus: Can't live with it, can't live without it. *Behavioral Brain Research, 127*(1/2), 137–158.

Lupien, S. J., & McEwen, B. S. (1997). The acute effects of corticosteroids on cognition: Integration of animal and human model studies. *Brain Research Reviews, 24*(1), 1–27.

Luthar, S. S. (2003). *Resilience and vulnerability: Adaptation in the context of childhood adversities.* Cambridge, England: Cambridge University Press.

Maguire, E. A., Gadian, D. G., Johnsrude, I. S., Good, C. D., Ashburner, J., Frackowiak, R. S., et al. (2000). Navigation-related structural change in the hippocampi of taxi drivers. *Proceedings of the National Academy of Sciences of the United States of America, 97*(8), 4398–4403.

Maheu, F. S., Joober, R., Beaulieu, S., & Lupien, S. J. (2004). Differential effects of adrenergic and corticosteroid hormonal systems on human short- and long-term declarative memory for emotionally arousing material. *Behavioral Neuroscience, 118*(2), 420–428.

Maheu, F. S., & Lupien, S. J. (2003). Memory in the grip of emotions and stress: A necessarily harmful impact. *Medicine Sciences, 19*(1), 118–124.

Mahon, T. R., Chazotte, C., & Cohen, W. R. (1994). Short labor: Characteristics and outcome. *Obstetrics and Gynecology, 84*(1), 47–51.

Markowe, H. L., Marmot, M. G., Shipley, M. J., Bulpitt, C. J., Meade, T. W., Stirling, Y., et al. (1985). Fibrinogen: A possible link between social class and coronary heart disease. *British Medical Journal, 291*(6505), 1312–1314.

Martyn, C. N., Gale, C. R., Sayer, A. A., & Fall, C. (1996). Growth in utero and cognitive function in adult life: Follow up study of people born between 1920 and 1943. *British Medical Journal, 312*(7043), 1393–1396.

Mason, J. W. (1968). A review of psychoendocrine research on the sympathetic-adrenal medullary system. *Psychosomatic Medicine, 30*(5, Suppl.), 631–653.

Masten, A. S. (2001). Ordinary magic: Resilience processes in development. *American Psychologist, 56*(3), 227–238.

Masten, A. S., Hubbard, J. J., Gest, S. D., Tellegen, A., Garmezy, N., & Ramirez, M. (1999). Competence in the context of adversity: Pathways to resilience and maladaptation from childhood to late adolescence. *Development and Psychopathology, 11*(1), 143–169.

Matsuzawa, J., Matsui, M., Konishi, T., Noguchi, K., Gur, R. C., Bilker, W., et al. (2001). Age-related volumetric changes of brain gray and white matter in healthy infants and children. *Cerebral Cortex, 11*(4), 335–342.

May, M., Holmes, E., Rogers, W., & Poth, M. (1990). Protection from glucocorticoid induced thymic involution by dehydroepiandrosterone. *Life Sciences, 46*(22), 1627–1631.

McBurnett, K., & Lahey, B. B. (1994). Psychophysiological and neuroendocrine correlates of conduct disorder and antisocial behavior in children and adolescents. *Progress in Experimental Personality and Psychopathology Research,* 199–231.

McBurnett, K., Lahey, B. B., Capasso, L., & Loeber, R. (1996). Aggressive symptoms and salivary cortisol in clinic-referred boys with conduct disorder. *Annals of the New York Academy of Sciences, 794,* 169–178.

McBurnett, K., Lahey, B. B., Frick, P. J., Risch, C., Loeber, R., Hart, E. L., et al. (1991). Anxiety, inhibition, and conduct disorder in children: II. Relation to salivary cortisol. *Journal of the American Academy of Child and Adolescent Psychiatry, 30*(2), 192–196.

McBurnett, K., Lahey, B. B., Rathouz, P. J., & Loeber, R. (2000). Low salivary cortisol and persistent aggression in boys referred for disruptive behavior. *Archives of General Psychiatry, 57*(1), 38–43.

McEwen, B. S. (1998a). Protective and damaging effects of stress mediators. *New England Journal of Medicine, 338*(3), 171–179.

McEwen, B. S. (1998b). Stress, adaptation, and disease: Allostasis and allostatic load. *Annals of the New York Academy of Sciences, 840,* 33–44.

McEwen, B. S. (2000a). Allostasis and allostatic load: Implications for neuropsychopharmacology. *Neuropsychopharmacology, 22*(2), 108–124.

McEwen, B. S. (2000b). The neurobiology of stress: From serendipity to clinical relevance. *Brain Research, 886*(1/2), 172–189.

McEwen, B. S. (2002). Protective and damaging effects of stress mediators: The good and bad sides of the response to stress. *Metabolism, 51*(6, Suppl. 1), 2–4.

McEwen, B. S. (2003). Mood disorders and allostatic load. *Biological Psychiatry, 54*(3), 200–207.

McEwen, B. S., & Seeman, T. (1999). Protective and damaging effects of mediators of stress: Elaborating and testing the concepts of allostasis and allostatic load. *Annals of the New York Academy of Sciences, 896,* 30–47.

McEwen, B. S., & Stellar, E. (1993). Stress and the individual: Mechanisms leading to disease. *Archives of Internal Medicine, 153*(18), 2093–2101.

McEwen, B. S., & Wingfield, J. C. (2003). The concept of allostasis in biology and biomedicine. *Hormones and Behavior, 43*(1), 2–15.

McGaugh, J. L. (2000). Memory: A century of consolidation. *Science, 287*(5451), 248–251.

McLean, M., Bisits, A., Davies, J., Woods, R., Lowry, P., & Smith, R. (1995). A placental clock controlling the length of human pregnancy. *Nature Medicine, 1*(5), 460–463.

McLeod, J. D., & Kessler, R. C. (1990). Socioeconomic status differences in vulnerability to undesirable life events. *Journal of Health and Social Behavior, 31*(2), 162–172.

McLeod, J. D., & Nonnemaker, J. M. (2000). Poverty and child emotional and behavioral problems: Racial/ethnic differences in processes and effects. *Journal of Health and Social Behavior, 41,* 137–161.

McLeod, J. D., & Shanahan, M. J. (1993). Poverty, parenting, and children's mental health. *American Sociological Review, 58*(3), 351–366.

McLoyd, V. C. (1998). Socioeconomic disadvantage and child development. *American Psychologist, 53*(2), 185–204.

Meaney, M. J. (2001). Maternal care, gene expression, and the transmission of individual differences in stress reactivity across generations. *Annual Review of Neuroscience, 24,* 1161–1192.

Meaney, M. J., Aitken, D. H., Viau, V., Sharma, S., & Sarrieau, A. (1989). Neonatal handling alters adrenocortical negative feedback sensitivity and hippocampal type II glucocorticoid receptor binding in the rat. *Neuroendocrinology, 50*(5), 597–604.

Meaney, M. J., Diorio, J., Francis, D., Widdowson, J., LaPlante, P., Caldji, C., et al. (1996). Early environmental regulation of forebrain glucocorticoid receptor gene expression: Implications for adrenocortical responses to stress. *Developmental Neuroscience, 18*(1/2), 49–72.

Meaney, M. J., Mitchell, J. B., Aitken, D. H., Bhatnager, J., Bodnoff, S. R., Iny, L. J., et al. (1991). The effects of neonatal handling on the development of the adrenocortical response to stress: Implications for neuropathology and cognitive deficits in later life. *Psychoneuroendocrinology, 16,* 85–103.

Meeran, K., Hattersley, A., Mould, G., & Bloom, S. R. (1993). Venepuncture causes rapid rise in plasma ACTH. *British Journal of Clinical Practice, 47*(5), 246–247.

Meikle, A. W., Stringham, J. D., Woodward, M. G., & Bishop, D. T. (1988). Heritability of variation of plasma cortisol levels. *Metabolism, 37*(6), 514–517.

Menard, J. L., Champagne, D. L., & Meaney, M. J. (2004). Variations of maternal care differentially influence "fear" reactivity and regional patterns of cFos immunoreactivity in response to the shock-probe burying test. *Neuroscience, 129*(2), 297–308.

Michelson, D., Stratakis, C., Hill, L., Reynolds, J., Galliven, E., Chrousos, G., et al. (1996). Bone mineral density in women with depression. *New England Journal of Medicine, 335*(16), 1176–1181.

Milburn, H. J., Poulter, L. W., Dilmec, A., Cochrane, G. M., & Kemeny, D. M. (1997). Corticosteroids restore the balance between locally produced Th1 and Th2 cytokines and immunoglobulin isotypes to normal in sarcoid lung. *Clinical and Experimental Immunology, 108*(1), 105–113.

Miller, L. S., Wasserman, G. A., Neugebauer, R., Gorman-Smith, D., & Kamboukos, D. (1999). Witnessed community violence and antisocial behavior in high-risk, urban boys. *Journal of Clinical Child Psychology, 28*(1), 2–11.

Miner, J. N., Diamond, M. I., & Yamamoto, K. R. (1991). Joints in the regulatory lattice: Composite regulation by steroid receptor-AP1 complexes. *Cell Growth and Differentiation, 2*(10), 525–530.

Ming, E. E., Adler, G. K., Kessler, R. C., Fogg, L. F., Matthews, K. A., Herd, J. A., et al. (2004). Cardiovascular reactivity to work stress predicts subsequent onset of hypertension: The Air Traffic Controller Health Change Study. *Psychosomatic Medicine, 66*(4), 459–465.

Moffitt, T. E., Caspi, A., Harrington, H., & Milner, B. J. (2002). Males on the life-course-persistent and adolescence-limited antisocial pathways: Follow-up at age 26 years. *Development and Psychopathology, 14,* 179–207.

Morales, A. J., Nolan, J. J., Nelson, J. C., & Yen, S. S. (1994). Effects of replacement dose of dehydroepiandrosterone in men and women of advancing age. *Journal of Clinical Endocrinology and Metabolism, 78*(6), 1360–1367.

Muldoon, M. F., Manuck, S. B., & Matthews, K. A. (1990). Lowering cholesterol concentrations and mortality: A quantitative review of primary prevention trials. *British Medical Journal, 301*(6747), 309–314.

Murray, L., Woolgar, M., Briers, S., & Hipwell, A. (1999). Children's social representations in dolls' house play and theory of mind tasks, and their relation to family adversity and child disturbance. *Social Development, 8*(2), 179–200.

Mustillo, S., Worthman, C., Erkanli, A., Keeler, G., Angold, A., & Costello, E. J. (2003). Obesity and psychiatric disorder: Developmental trajectories. *Pediatrics, 111*(4, Pt. 1), 851–859.

Mysterud, I., & Poleszynski, D. V. (2003). Expanding evolutionary psychology: Toward a better understanding of violence and aggression. *Social Science Information, 23,* 5–50.

Neale, M. C., & Cardon, L. R. (1992). *Methodology for genetic studies of twins and families.* Dordrecht, The Netherlands: Kluwer Academic.

Nelson, M. D., Saykin, A. J., Flashman, L. A., & Riordan, H. J. (1998). Hippocampal volume reduction in Schizophrenia as assessed by magnetic resonance imaging: A meta-analytic study. *Archives of General Psychiatry, 55*(5), 433–440.

Neumann, I. D., Johnstone, H. A., Hatzinger, M., Liebsch, G., Shipston, M., Russell, J. A., et al. (1998). Attenuated neuroendocrine responses to emotional and physical stressors in pregnant rats involve adenohypophysial changes. *Journal of Physiology, 508*(Pt. 1), 289–300.

Neumann, I. D., Russell, J. A., & Landgraf, R. (1993). Oxytocin and vasopressin release within the supraoptic and paraventricular nuclei of pregnant, parturient and lactating rats: A microdialysis study. *Neuroscience, 53*(1), 65–75.

Neumann, I. D., Toschi, N., Ohl, F., Torner, L., & Kromer, S. A. (2001). Maternal defense as an emotional stressor in female rats: Correlation of neuroendocrine and behavioural parameters and involvement of brain oxytocin. *European Journal of Neuroscience, 13*(5), 1016–1024.

Newman, R. B., Goldenberg, R. L., Moawad, A. H., Iams, J. D., Meis, P. J., Das, A., et al. (2001). Occupational fatigue and preterm premature rupture of membranes: National Institute of Child Health and Human Development Maternal-Fetal Medicine Units Network. *American Journal of Obstetrics and Gynecology, 184*(3), 438–446.

Nurnberger, J. I., Jr., Gershon, E. S., Simmons, S., Ebert, M., Kessler, L. R., Dibble, E. D., et al. (1982). Behavioral, biochemical and neuroendocrine responses to amphetamine in normal twins and "wellstate" bipolar patients. *Psychoneuroendocrinology, 7*(2/3), 163–176.

Orentreich, N., Brind, J. L., Rizer, R. L., & Vogelman, J. H. (1984). Age changes and sex differences in serum dehydroepiandrosterone sulfate concentrations throughout adulthood. *Journal of Clinical Endocrinology and Metabolism, 59*(3), 551–555.

Ortiz, J., & Raine, A. (2004). Heart rate level and antisocial behavior in children and adolescents: A meta-analysis. *Journal of the American Academy of Child and Adolescent Psychiatry, 43*(2), 154–162.

Owen, A. M., Doyon, J., Petrides, M., & Evans, A. C. (1996). Planning and spatial working memory: A positron emission tomography study in humans. *European Journal of Neuroscience, 8,* 353–364.

Paarlberg, K. M., Vingerhoets, A. J., Passchier, J., Dekker, G. A., & Van Geijn, H. P. (1995). Psychosocial factors and pregnancy outcome: A review with emphasis on methodological issues. *Journal of Psychosomatic Research, 39*(5), 563–595.

Pajer, K., Gardner, W., Rubin, R. T., Perel, J., & Neal, S. (2001). Decreased cortisol levels in adolescent girls with conduct disorder. *Archives of General Psychiatry, 58*(3), 297–302.

Pajer, K., Rabin, B., & Gardner, W. (2002). Increased IgG 3, 4 ratios in adolescent antisocial females: Evidence of Th1/Th2 imbalance? *Brain, Behavior, and Immunity, 16*(6), 747–756.

Patacchioli, F. R., Cigliana, G., Cilumbriello, A., Perrone, G., Capri, O., Alema, G. S., et al. (1992). Maternal plasma and milk free cortisol during the first 3 days of breast-feeding following spontaneous delivery or elective cesarean section. *Gynecologic and Obstetric Investigation, 34*(3), 159–163.

Patrick, C. J., Cuthbert, B. N., & Lang, P. J. (1994). Emotion in the criminal psychopath: Fear image processing. *Journal of Abnormal Psychology, 103,* 523–534.

Peacock, J. L., Bland, J. M., & Anderson, H. R. (1995). Preterm delivery: Effects of socioeconomic factors, psychological stress, smoking, alcohol, and caffeine. *British Medical Journal, 311*(7004), 531–535.

Pears, K. C., & Moses, L. J. (2003). Demographics, parenting, and theory of mind in preschool children. *Social Development, 12*(1), 1–19.

Pfefferbaum, A., Mathalon, D. H., Sullivan, E. V., Rawles, J. M., Zipursky, R. B., & Lim, K. O. (1994). A quantitative magnetic resonance imaging study of changes in brain morphology from infancy to late adulthood. *Archives of Neurology, 51*(9), 874–887.

Phillips, D. I. (1998). Birth weight and the future development of diabetes: A review of the evidence. *Diabetes Care, 21*(Suppl. 2), B150–B155.

Pickering, T. G. (1996a). Job strain and the prevalence and outcome of coronary artery disease. *Circulation, 94*(5), 1138–1139.

Pickering, T. G. (1996b). White coat hypertension. *Current Opinion in Nephrology and Hypertension, 5*(2), 192–198.

Pickering, T. G., Devereux, R. B., James, G. D., Gerin, W., Landsbergis, P., Schnall, P. L., et al. (1996). Environmental influences on blood pressure and the role of job strain. *Journal of Hypertension, 14*(5, Suppl.), S179–S185.

Pinker, S. (1994). *The language instinct.* New York: Morrow.

Plomin, R., DeFries, J. C., McClearn, G. E., & McGuffin, P. (2001). *Behavioral genetics* (4th ed.). New York: Worth.

Plotsky, P. M., & Meaney, M. J. (1993). Early, postnatal experience alters hypothalamic corticotropin-releasing factor (CRF) mRNA, median eminence CRF content and stress-induced release in adult rats. *Brain Research. Molecular Brain Research, 18*(3), 195–200.

Pollak, S. D., Cicchetti, D., Hornung, K., & Reed, A. (2000). Recognizing emotion in faces: Developmental effects of child abuse and neglect. *Developmental Psychology, 36*(5), 679–688.

Pollak, S. D., & Kistler, D. J. (2002). Early experience is associated with the development of categorical representations for facial expressions of emotion. *Proceedings of the National Academy of Sciences of the United States of America, 99*(13), 9072–9076.

Pollak, S. D., & Sinha, P. (2002). Effects of early experience on children's recognition of facial displays of emotion. *Developmental Psychology, 38*(5), 784–791.

Pollak, S. D., & Tolley-Schell, S. A. (2003). Selective attention to facial emotion in physically abused children. *Journal of Abnormal Psychology, 112*(3), 323–338.

Posthuma, D., de Geus, E. J. C., Neale, M. C., Hulshoff Pol, H. E., Baaré, W. F. C., Kahn, R. S., et al. (2000). Multivariate genetic analysis of brain structure in an extended twin design. *Behavior Genetics, 30,* 311–319.

Pritchard, J., Despres, J. P., Gagnon, J., Tchernof, A., Nadeau, A., Tremblay, A., et al. (1998). Plasma adrenal, gonadal, and conjugated steroids before and after long-term overfeeding in identical twins. *Journal of Clinical Endocrinology and Metabolism, 83*(9), 3277–3284.

Pruessner, J. C., Hellhammer, D. H., & Kirschbaum, C. (1999). Burnout, perceived stress, and cortisol responses to awakening. *Psychosomatic Medicine, 61*(2), 197–204.

Pruessner, J. C., Wolf, O. T., Hellhammer, D. H., Buske-Kirschbaum, A., von Auer, K., Jobst, S., et al. (1997). Free cortisol levels after awakening: A reliable biological marker for the assessment of adrenocortical activity. *Life Sciences, 61*(26), 2539–2549.

Pruessner, M., Hellhammer, D. H., Pruessner, J. C., & Lupien, S. J. (2003). Self-reported depressive symptoms and stress levels in healthy young men: Associations with the cortisol response to awakening. *Psychosomatic Medicine, 65*(1), 92–99.

Rabin, B. S. (1999). *Stress, immune function, and health: The connection.* New York: Wiley-Liss & Sons.

Raine, A. (1993). *The psychopathology of crime: Criminal behavior as a clinical disorder.* Academic Press.

Raine, A., Lencz, T., Bihrle, S., LaCasse, L., & Colletti, P. (2000). Reduced prefrontal gray matter volume and reduced autonomic activity in antisocial personality disorder. *Archives of General Psychiatry, 57,* 119–127.

Raine, A., Venables, P. H., & Mednick, S. A. (1997). Low resting heart rate at age 3 years predisposes to aggression at age 11 years: Evidence from the Mauritius Child Health Project. *Journal of the American Academy of Child and Adolescent Psychiatry, 36*(10), 1457–1464.

Raine, A., Venables, P. H., & Williams, M. (1995). High autonomic arousal and electrodermal orienting at age 15 years as protective factors against criminal behavior at age 29 years. *American Journal of Psychiatry, 152*(11), 1595–1600.

Reiss, A. L., Abrams, M. T., Singer, H. S., Ross, J. L., & Denckla, M. B. (1996). Brain development, gender and IQ in children: A volumetric imaging study. *Brain, 119*(Pt. 5), 1763–1774.

Repetti, R. L., Taylor, S. E., & Seeman, T. E. (2002). Risky families: Family social environments and the mental and physical health of offspring. *Psychological Bulletin, 128*(2), 330–366.

Righetti-Veltema, M., Conne-Perreard, E., Bousquet, A., & Manzano, J. (1998). Risk factors and predictive signs of postpartum depression. *Journal of Affective Disorders, 49*(3), 167–180.

Rini, C. K., Dunkel-Schetter, C., Wadhwa, P. D., & Sandman, C. A. (1999). Psychological adaptation and birth outcomes: The role of personal resources, stress, and sociocultural context in pregnancy. *Health Psychology, 18*(4), 333–345.

Robbins, J., Hirsch, C., Whitmer, R., Cauley, J., & Harris, T. (2001). The association of bone mineral density and depression in an older population. *Journal of the American Geriatrics Society, 49*(6), 732–736.

Robel, P., & Baulieu, E. E. (1995). Dehydroepiandrosterone (DHEA) is a neuroactive neurosteroid. *Annals of the New York Academy of Sciences, 774,* 82–110.

Rogers, C. R. (1951). *Client-centered therapy*. Boston: Houghton Mifflin.

Rohleder, N., Wolf, J. M., & Kirschbaum, C. (2003). Glucocorticoid sensitivity in humans: Interindividual differences and acute stress effects. *Stress, 6*(3), 207–222.

Roozendaal, B. (2000). 1999 Curt P. Richter Award: Glucocorticoids and the regulation of memory consolidation. *Psychoneuroendocrinology, 25*(3), 213–238.

Roozendaal, B. (2003). Systems mediating acute glucocorticoid effects on memory consolidation and retrieval. *Progress in Neuropsychopharmacology and Biological Psychiatry, 27*(8), 1213–1223.

Roozendaal, B., Hahn, E. L., Nathan, S. V., de Quervain, D. J., & McGaugh, J. L. (2004). Glucocorticoid effects on memory retrieval require concurrent noradrenergic activity in the hippocampus and basolateral amygdala. *Journal of Neuroscience, 24*(37), 8161–8169.

Roozendaal, B., McReynolds, J. R., & McGaugh, J. L. (2004). The basolateral amygdala interacts with the medial prefrontal cortex in regulating glucocorticoid effects on working memory impairment. *Journal of Neuroscience, 24*(6), 1385–1392.

Roy, M. P., Steptoe, A., & Kirschbaum, C. (1998). Life events and social support as moderators of individual differences in cardiovascular and cortisol reactivity. *Journal of Personality and Social Psychology, 75*(5), 1273–1281.

Rubinow, D. R., Post, R. M., Savard, R., & Gold, P. W. (1984). Cortisol hypersecretion and cognitive impairment in depression. *Archives of General Psychiatry, 41*(3), 279–283.

Russell, J. A., Douglas, A. J., & Ingram, C. D. (2001). Brain preparations for maternity: Adaptive changes in behavioral and neuroendocrine systems during pregnancy and lactation. An overview. *Progress in Brain Research, 133,* 1–38.

Rutter, M. (1994). Stress research: Accomplishments and tasks ahead. In R. J. Haggerty, L. R. Sherrod, N. Garmezy, & M. Rutter (Eds.), *Stress, risk, and resilience in children and adolescents: Processes, mechanisms, and interventions* (pp. 304–329). Cambridge, England: Cambridge University Press.

Rutter, M., & Silberg, J. (2002). Gene-environment interplay in relation to emotional and behavioral disturbance. *Annual Review of Psychology, 53,* 463–490.

Sachar, E. J., Hellman, L., Roffwarg, H. P., Halpern, F. S., Fukushima, D. K., & Gallagher, T. F. (1973). Disrupted 24-hour patterns of cortisol secretion in psychotic depression. *Archives of General Psychiatry, 28*(1), 19–24.

Sammons, L. N. (1990). Psychological aspects of second pregnancy. *NAACOG's Clinical Issues in Perinatal and Women's Health Nursing, 1*(3), 317–324.

Sandler, I. (2001). Quality and ecology of adversity as common mechanisms of risk and resilience. *American Journal of Community Psychology, 29*(1), 19–61.

Sapolsky, R. M., Krey, L. C., & McEwen, B. S. (1986). The neuroendocrinology of stress and aging: The glucocorticoid cascade hypothesis. *Endocrine Reviews, 7*(3), 284–301.

Scarpa, A., & Ollendick, T. H. (2003). Community violence exposure in a young adult sample: III. Psychophysiology and victimization interact to affect risk for aggression. *Journal of Community Psychology, 31*(4), 321–338.

Scarpa, A., & Raine, A. (1997). Psychophysiology of anger and violent behavior. *Psychiatric Clinics of North America, 20*(2), 375–394.

Schapiro, S., Geller, E., & Eiduson, S. (1962). Neonatal adrenal cortical response to stress and vasopressin. *Proceedings of the Society for Experimental Biology and Medicine, 109,* 937–941.

Schieken, R. M., Eaves, L. J., Hewitt, J. K., Mosteller, M., Bodurtha, J. N., Moskowitz, W. B., et al. (1989). Univariate genetic analysis of blood pressure in children (the Medical College of Virginia Twin Study). *American Journal of Cardiology, 64*(19), 1333–1337.

Schnorpfeil, P., Noll, A., Schulze, R., Ehlert, U., Frey, K., & Fischer, J. E. (2003). Allostatic load and work conditions. *Social Science and Medicine, 57*(4), 647–656.

Schoenbaum, G., Setlow, B., Saddoris, M. P., & Gallagher, M. (2003). Encoding predicted outcome and acquired value in orbitofrontal cortex during cue sampling depends upon input from basolateral amygdala. *Neuron, 39,* 855–867.

Schulz, K. P., Halperin, J. M., Newcorn, J. H., Sharma, V., & Gabriel, S. (1997). Plasma cortisol and aggression in boys with ADHD. *Journal of the American Academy of Child and Adolescent Psychiatry, 36*(5), 605–609.

Schulz, K. P., Kirschbaum, C., Pruessner, J. C., & Hellhammer, D. (1998). Increased free cortisol secretion after awakening in chronically stressed individuals due to work overload. *Stress Medicine, 14*(2), 91–97.

Schwartz, J. E., Pickering, T. G., & Landsbergis, P. A. (1996). Work-related stress and blood pressure: Current theoretical models and considerations from a behavioral medicine perspective. *Journal of Occupational Health Psychology, 1*(3), 287–310.

Schwarzer, R., & Leppin, A. (1989). Social support and health: A meta-analysis. *Psychology and Health, 3*(1), 1–15.

Scott, L. V., Medbak, S., & Dinan, T. G. (1998). Blunted adrenocorticotropin and cortisol responses to corticotropin-releasing hormone stimulation in chronic fatigue syndrome. *Acta Psychiatrica Scandinavica, 97*(6), 450–457.

Seckl, J. R., Cleasby, M., & Nyirenda, M. J. (2000). Glucocorticoids, 11beta-hydroxysteroid dehydrogenase, and fetal programming. *Kidney International, 57*(4), 1412–1417.

Seeman, T. E., Charpentier, P. A., Berkman, L. F., Tinetti, M. E., Guralnik, J. M., Albert, M., et al. (1994). Predicting changes in physical performance in a high-functioning elderly cohort: MacArthur studies of successful aging. *Journal of Gerontology, 49*(3), M97–M108.

Seeman, T. E., & Chen, X. (2002). Risk and protective factors for physical functioning in older adults with and without chronic conditions: MacArthur Studies of Successful Aging. *Journals of Gerontology. Series B, Psychological Sciences and Social Sciences, 57*(3), S135–S144.

Seeman, T. E., Crimmins, E., Huang, M. H., Singer, B., Bucur, A., Gruenewald, T., et al. (2004). Cumulative biological risk and socio-economic differences in mortality: MacArthur studies of successful aging. *Social Science and Medicine, 58*(10), 1985–1997.

Seeman, T. E., Glei, D., Goldman, N., Weinstein, M., Singer, B., & Lin, Y. H. (2004). Social relationships and allostatic load in Taiwanese elderly and near elderly. *Social Science and Medicine, 59*(11), 2245–2257.

Seeman, T. E., Lusignolo, T. M., Albert, M., & Berkman, L. (2001). Social relationships, social support, and patterns of cognitive aging in healthy, high-functioning older adults: MacArthur studies of successful aging. *Health Psychology, 20*(4), 243–255.

Seeman, T. E., McEwen, B. S., Rowe, J. W., & Singer, B. H. (2001). Allostatic load as a marker of cumulative biological risk: MacArthur studies of successful aging. *Proceedings of the National Academy of Sciences of the United States of America, 98*(8), 4770–4775.

Seeman, T. E., Singer, B. H., Rowe, J. W., Horwitz, R. I., & McEwen, B. S. (1997). Price of adaptation: Allostatic load and its health consequences: MacArthur studies of successful aging. *Archives of Internal Medicine, 157*(19), 2259–2268.

Seeman, T. E., Singer, B. H., Ryff, C. D., Dienberg Love, G., & Levy-Storms, L. (2002). Social relationships, gender, and allostatic load across two age cohorts. *Psychosomatic Medicine, 64*(3), 395–406.

Seidman, D. S., Laor, A., Gale, R., Stevenson, D. K., Mashiach, S., & Danon, Y. L. (1992). Birth weight and intellectual performance in late adolescence. *Obstetrics and Gynecology, 79*(4), 543–546.

Selye, H. (1975a). Confusion and controversy in the stress field. *Journal of Human Stress, 1*(2), 37–44.

Selye, H. (1975b). Stress and distress. *Comprehensive Therapy, 1*(8), 9–13.

Selye, H. (1998). A syndrome produced by diverse nocuous agents: 1936. *Journal of Neuropsychiatry and Clinical Neurosciences, 10*(2), 230–231.

Sgoifo, A., de Boer, S. F., Haller, J., & Koolhaas, J. M. (1996). Individual differences in plasma catecholamine and corticosterone stress responses of wild-type rats: Relationship with aggression. *Physiology and Behavior, 60*(6), 1403–1407.

Shanks, N., Windle, R. J., Perks, P., Wood, S., Ingram, C. D., & Lightman, S. L. (1999). The hypothalamic-pituitary-adrenal axis response to endotoxin is attenuated during lactation. *Journal of Neuroendocrinology, 11*(11), 857–865.

Sheline, Y. I. (1996). Hippocampal atrophy in major depression: A result of depression-induced neurotoxicity? *Molecular Psychiatry, 1*(4), 298–299.

Sheline, Y. I., Gado, M. H., & Kraemer, H. C. (2003). Untreated depression and hippocampal volume loss. *American Journal of Psychiatry, 160*(8), 1516–1518.

Sheline, Y. I., Sanghavi, M., Mintun, M. A., & Gado, M. H. (1999). Depression duration but not age predicts hippocampal volume loss in medically healthy women with recurrent major depression. *Journal of Neuroscience, 19*(12), 5034–5043.

Sheline, Y. I., Wang, P. W., Gado, M. H., Csernansky, J. G., & Vannier, M. W. (1996). Hippocampal atrophy in recurrent major depression. *Proceedings of the National Academy of Sciences of the United States of America, 93*(9), 3908–3913.

Shors, T. J., Miesegaes, G., Beylin, A., Zhao, M., Rydel, T., & Gould, E. (2001). Neurogenesis in the adult is involved in the formation of trace memories. *Nature, 410*(6826), 372–376.

Shurin, M. R., Lu, L., Kalinski, P., Stewart-Akers, A. M., & Lotze, M. T. (1999). Th1/Th2 balance in cancer, transplantation and pregnancy. *Springer Seminars in Immunopathology, 21*(3), 339–359.

Siegel, G. J., Agranoff, B. W., Albers, R. W., Fisher, S. K., & Uhler, M. D. (1999). *Basic neurochemistry.* New York: Lippincott-Raven.

Singer, B., & Ryff, C. D. (1999). Hierarchies of life histories and associated health risks. *Annals of the New York Academy of Sciences, 896,* 96–115.

Snoek, H., Van Goozen, S. H., Matthys, W., Buitelaar, J. K., & van Engeland, H. (2004). Stress responsivity in children with externalizing behavior disorders. *Development and Psychopathology, 16*(2), 389–406.

Somes, G. W., Harshfield, G. A., Alpert, B. S., Goble, M. M., & Schieken, R. M. (1995). Genetic influences on ambulatory blood pressure patterns: The Medical College of Virginia Twin Study. *American Journal of Hypertension, 8*(5, Pt. 1), 474–478.

Sowell, E. R., Thompson, P. M., Tessner, K. D., & Toga, A. W. (2001). Mapping continued brain growth and gray matter density reduction in dorsal frontal cortex: Inverse relationships during postadolescent brain maturation. *Journal of Neuroscience, 21*(22), 8819–8829.

Spangler, G., & Grossmann, K. E. (1993). Biobehavioral organization in securely and insecurely attached infants. *Child Development, 64*(5), 1439–1450.

Spoont, M. R. (1992). Modulatory role of serotonin in neural information processing: Implications for human psychopathology. *Psychological Bulletin, 112*(2), 330–350.

Sprietsma, J. E. (1999). Modern diets and diseases: NO-zinc balance—Under Th1, zinc and nitrogen monoxide (NO) collectively protect against viruses, AIDS, autoimmunity, diabetes, allergies, asthma, infectious diseases, atherosclerosis and cancer. *Medical Hypotheses, 53*(1), 6–16.

Stansbury, K., & Harris, M. L. (2000). Individual differences in stress reactions during a peer entry episode: Effects of age, temperament, approach behavior, and self-perceived peer competence. *Journal of Experimental Child Psychology, 76*(1), 50–63.

Starfield, E. L. (1982). Child health and social status. *Pediatrics, 69,* 550–557.

Starkman, M. N., Gebarski, S. S., Berent, S., & Schteingart, D. E. (1992). Hippocampal formation volume, memory dysfunction, and cortisol levels in patients with Cushing's syndrome. *Biological Psychiatry, 32*(9), 756–765.

Starkman, M. N., Giordani, B., Berent, S., Schork, M. A., & Schteingart, D. E. (2001). Elevated cortisol levels in Cushing's disease are associated with cognitive decrements. *Psychosomatic Medicine, 63*(6), 985–993.

Starkman, M. N., Giordani, B., Gebarski, S. S., Berent, S., Schork, M. A., & Schteingart, D. E. (1999). Decrease in cortisol reverses human hippocampal atrophy following treatment of Cushing's disease. *Biological Psychiatry, 46*(12), 1595–1602.

Starkman, M. N., Giordani, B., Gebarski, S. S., & Schteingart, D. E. (2003). Improvement in learning associated with increase in hippocampal formation volume. *Biological Psychiatry, 53*(3), 233–238.

Steptoe, A., Siegrist, J., Kirschbaum, C., & Marmot, M. (2004). Effort-reward imbalance, overcommitment, and measures of cortisol and blood pressure over the working day. *Psychosomatic Medicine, 66*(3), 323–329.

Steptoe, A., & Willemsen, G. (2004). The influence of low job control on ambulatory blood pressure and perceived stress over the working day in men and women from the Whitehall II cohort. *Journal of Hypertension, 22*(5), 915–920.

Sterling, P., & Eyer, J. (1988). Allostatis: A new paradigm to explain arousal pathology. In S. Fisher & J. Reason (Eds.), *Handbook of life stress, cognition and health* (pp. 629–649). New York: Wiley.

Stern, J. M., Goldman, L., & Levine, S. (1973). Pituitary-adrenal responsiveness during lactation in rats. *Neuroendocrinology, 12*(3), 179–191.

Strauss, R. S. (2000). Adult functional outcome of those born small for gestational age: Twenty-six-year follow-up of the 1970 British Birth Cohort. *Journal of the American Medical Association, 283*(5), 625–632.

Susman, E. J., Schmeelk, K. H., Worrall, B. K., Granger, D. A., Ponirakis, A., & Chrousos, G. P. (1999). Corticotropin-releasing hormone and cortisol: Longitudinal associations with depression and antisocial behavior in pregnant adolescents. *Journal of the American Academy of Child and Adolescent Psychiatry, 38*(4), 460–467.

Suzuki, W. A., & Clayton, N. S. (2000). The hippocampus and memory: A comparative and ethological perspective. *Current Opinion in Neurobiology, 10*(6), 768–773.

Szuran, T. F., Pliska, V., Pokorny, J., & Welzl, H. (2000). Prenatal stress in rats: Effects on plasma corticosterone, hippocampal glucocorticoid receptors, and maze performance. *Physiology and Behavior, 71*(3/4), 353–362.

Takahashi, L. K. (1998). Prenatal stress: Consequences of glucocorticoids on hippocampal development and function. *International Journal of Developmental Neuroscience, 16*(3/4), 199–207.

Tang, C., Akabayashi, A., Manitiu, A., & Leibowitz, S. F. (1997). Hypothalamic galanin gene expression and peptide levels in relation to circulating insulin: Possible role in energy balance. *Neuroendocrinology, 65*(4), 265–275.

Taylor, S. E., Repetti, R. L., & Seeman, T. (1997). Health psychology: What is an unhealthy environment and how does it get under the skin? *Annual Review of Psychology, 48,* 411–447.

Teicher, M. H., Andersen, S. L., Polcari, A., Anderson, C. M., Navalta, C. P., & Kim, D. M. (2003). The neurobiological consequences of early stress and childhood maltreatment. *Neuroscience Biobehavioral Review, 27*(1/2), 33–44.

Thomas, S. P., & Groer, M. W. (1986). Relationship of demographic, life-style, and stress variables to blood pressure in adolescents. *Nursing Research, 35*(3), 169–172.

Torner, L., & Neumann, I. D. (2002). The brain prolactin system: Involvement in stress response adaptations in lactation. *Stress, 5*(4), 249–257.

Torner, L., Toschi, N., Nava, G., Clapp, C., & Neumann, I. D. (2002). Increased hypothalamic expression of prolactin in lactation: Involvement in behavioural and neuroendocrine stress responses. *European Journal of Neuroscience, 15*(8), 1381–1389.

Toufexis, D. J., Thrivikraman, K. V., Plotsky, P. M., Morilak, D. A., Huang, N., & Walker, C. D. (1998). Reduced noradrenergic tone to the hypothalamic paraventricular nucleus contributes to the stress hyporesponsiveness of lactation. *Journal of Neuroendocrinology, 10*(6), 417–427.

Treisman, A. (1964). Monitoring and storage of irrelevant messages in selective attention. *Journal of Verbal Learning and Verbal Behavior, 3*(6), 449–459.

Tulving, E. (2002). Episodic memory: from mind to brain. *Annual Review of Psychology, 53,* 1–25.

Utsunomiya, H., Takano, K., Okazaki, M., & Mitsudome, A. (1999). Development of the temporal lobe in infants and children: Analysis by MR-based volumetry. *American Journal of Neuroradiology, 20*(4), 717–723.

Vallee, M., Mayo, W., Dellu, F., Le Moal, M., Simon, H., & Maccari, S. (1997). Prenatal stress induces high anxiety and postnatal handling induces low anxiety in adult offspring: Correlation with stress-induced corticosterone secretion. *Journal of Neuroscience, 17*(7), 2626–2636.

Van Cauter, E., Polonsky, K. S., & Scheen, A. J. (1997). Roles of circadian rhythmicity and sleep in human glucose regulation. *Endocrine Reviews, 18*(5), 716–738.

van Goozen, S. H., Matthys, W., Cohen-Kettenis, P. T., Buitelaar, J. K., & van Engeland, H. (2000). Hypothalamic-pituitary-adrenal axis and autonomic nervous system activity in disruptive children and matched controls. *Journal of the American Academy of Child and Adolescent Psychiatry, 39*(11), 1438–1445.

van Goozen, S. H., Matthys, W., Cohen-Kettenis, P. T., Thijssen, J. H., & van Engeland, H. (1998). Adrenal androgens and aggression in conduct disorder prepubertal boys and normal controls. *Biological Psychiatry, 43*(2), 156–158.

van Goozen, S. H., van den Ban, E., Matthys, W., Cohen-Kettenis, P. T., Thijssen, J. H., & van Engeland, H. (2000). Increased adrenal androgen functioning in children with oppositional defiant disorder: A comparison with psychiatric and normal controls. *Journal of the American Academy of Child and Adolescent Psychiatry, 39*(11), 1446–1451.

van Stegeren, A. H., Everaerd, W., Cahill, L., McGaugh, J. L., & Gooren, L. J. (1998). Memory for emotional events: Differential effects of centrally versus peripherally acting beta-blocking agents. *Psychopharmacology, 138*(3/4), 305–310.

Vanyukov, M. M., Moss, H. B., Plail, J. A., Blackson, T., Mezzich, A. C., & Tarter, R. E. (1993). Antisocial symptoms in preadolescent boys and in their parents: Associations with cortisol. *Psychiatry Research, 46*(1), 9–17.

Vargha-Khadem, F., Gadian, D. G., Watkins, K. E., Connelly, A., Van Paesschen, W., & Mishkin, M. (1997). Differential effects of early hippocampal pathology on episodic and semantic memory. *Science, 277,* 376–380.

Varney, N. R., Alexander, B., & MacIndoe, J. H. (1984). Reversible steroid dementia in patients without steroid psychosis. *American Journal of Psychiatry, 141*(3), 369–372.

Vevera, J., Zukov, I., Morcinek, T., & Papezova, H. (2003). Cholesterol concentrations in violent and non-violent women suicide attempters. *European Psychiatry, 18*(1), 23–27.

Virkkunen, M. (1979). Serum cholesterol in antisocial personality. *Neuropsychobiology, 5*(1), 27–30.

Virkkunen, M., De Jong, J., Bartko, J., & Linnoila, M. (1989). Psychobiological concomitants of history of suicide attempts among violent offenders and impulsive fire setters. *Archives of General Psychiatry, 46*(7), 604–606.

Vythilingam, M., Heim, C., Newport, J., Miller, A. H., Anderson, E., Bronen, R., et al. (2002). Childhood trauma associated with smaller hippocampal volume in women with major depression. *American Journal of Psychiatry, 159*(12), 2072–2080.

Vythilingam, M., Vermetten, E., Anderson, G. M., Luckenbaugh, D., Anderson, E. R., Snow, J., et al. (2004). Hippocampal volume, memory, and cortisol status in major depressive disorder: Effects of treatment. *Biological Psychiatry, 56*(2), 101–112.

Wadhwa, P. D., Sandman, C. A., Porto, M., Dunkel-Schetter, C., & Garite, T. J. (1993). The association between prenatal stress and infant birth weight and gestational age at birth: A prospective investigation. *American Journal of Obstetrics and Gynecology, 169*(4), 858–865.

Walker, C. D., Lightman, S. L., Steele, M. K., & Dallman, M. F. (1992). Suckling is a persistent stimulus to the adrenocortical system of the rat. *Endocrinology, 130*(1), 115–125.

Walker, C. D., Trottier, G., Rochford, J., & Lavallee, D. (1995). Dissociation between behavioral and hormonal responses to the forced swim stress in lactating rats. *Journal of Neuroendocrinology, 7*(8), 615–622.

Waters, M. A., & Lee, K. A. (1996). Differences between primigravidae and multigravidae mothers in sleep disturbances, fatigue, and functional status. *Journal of Nurse-midwifery, 41*(5), 364–367.

Weaver, I. C., Cervoni, N., Champagne, F. A., D'Alessio, A. C., Sharma, S., Seckl, J. R., et al. (2004). Epigenetic programming by maternal behavior. *Nature Neuroscience, 7*(8), 847–854.

Weingartner, H., Cohen, R. M., Murphy, D. L., Martello, J., & Gerdt, C. (1981). Cognitive processes in depression. *Archives of General Psychiatry, 38*(1), 42–47.

Weinstock, M. (1997). Does prenatal stress impair coping and regulation of hypothalamic-pituitary-adrenal axis? *Neuroscience and Biobehavioral Reviews, 21*(1), 1–10.

Welberg, L. A., & Seckl, J. R. (2001). Prenatal stress, glucocorticoids and the programming of the brain. *Journal of Neuroendocrinology, 13*(2), 113–128.

Wellman, H. M., Cross, D., & Watson, J. (2001). Meta-analysis of theory-of-mind development: The truth about false belief. *Child Development, 72*(3), 655–684.

White, J. L., Moffitt, T. E., & Silva, P. A. (1989). A prospective replication of the protective effects of IQ in subjects at high risk for juvenile delinquency. *Journal of Consulting and Clinical Psychology, 57*(6), 719–724.

Wiesenfeld, A. R., Malatesta, C. Z., Whitman, P. B., Granrose, C., & Uili, R. (1985). Psychophysiological response of breast- and bottle-feeding mothers to their infants' signals. *Psychophysiology, 22*(1), 79–86.

Windle, R. J., Brady, M. M., Kunanandam, T., Da Costa, A. P., Wilson, B. C., Harbuz, M., et al. (1997). Reduced response of the hypothalamo-pituitary-adrenal axis to alpha1-agonist stimulation during lactation. *Endocrinology, 138*(9), 3741–3748.

Windle, R. J., Wood, S., Shanks, N., Perks, P., Conde, G. L., Da Costa, A. P., et al. (1997). Endocrine and behavioural responses to noise stress: Comparison of virgin and lactating female rats during non-disrupted maternal activity. *Journal of Neuroendocrinology, 9*(6), 407–414.

Wing, R. R., Matthews, K. A., Kuller, L. H., Meilahn, E. N., & Plantinga, P. (1991). Waist to hip ratio in middle-aged women: Associations with behavioral and psychosocial factors and with changes in cardiovascular risk factors. *Arteriosclerosis and Thrombosis, 11*(5), 1250–1257.

Witek-Janusek, L. (1988). Pituitary-adrenal response to bacterial endotoxin in developing rats. *American Journal of Physiology, 255*(4, Pt. 1), E525–E530.

Wolf, O. T., & Kirschbaum, C. (1999). Actions of dehydroepiandrosterone and its sulfate in the central nervous system: Effects on cognition and emotion in animals and humans. *Brain Research Reviews, 30*(3), 264–288.

Wolkowitz, O. M., Breier, A., Doran, A., Rubinow, D., Berrettini, W., Coppola, R., et al. (1988). Prednisone-induced behavioral and biological changes in medically healthy volunteers. *Psychopharmacology Bulletin, 24*(3), 492–494.

Wolkowitz, O. M., Reus, V. I., Canick, J., Levin, B., & Lupien, S. J. (1997). Glucocorticoid medication, memory and steroid psychosis in medical illness. *Annals of the New York Academy of Sciences, 823*, 81–96.

Wolkowitz, O. M., Reus, V. I., Weingartner, H., Thompson, K., Breier, A., Doran, A., et al. (1990). Cognitive effects of corticosteroids. *American Journal of Psychiatry, 147*(10), 1297–1303.

Wong, S. Y., Lau, E. M., Lynn, H., Leung, P. C., Woo, J., Cummings, S. R., et al. (2005). Depression and bone mineral density: Is there a relationship in elderly Asian men? Results from Mr. Os (Hong Kong). *Osteoporosis International, 16*, 610–615.

Wright, B. E., Porter, J. R., Browne, E. S., & Svec, F. (1992). Antiglucocorticoid action of dehydroepiandrosterone in young obese Zucker rats. *International Journal of Obesity and Related Metabolic Disorders, 16*(8), 579–583.

Wüst, S., Federenko, I., Hellhammer, D. H., & Kirschbaum, C. (2000). Genetic factors, perceived chronic stress, and the free cortisol response to awakening. *Psychoneuroendocrinology, 25*(7), 707–720.

Yakovlev, P. L., & Lecours, A. R. (1967). The myelogenetic cycles of regional maturation of the brain. In A. Minkowski (Ed.), *Regional development of the brain in early life* (pp. 3–70). Oxfort: Blackwell.

Yamada, K., Duong, D. T., Scott, D. K., Wang, J. C., & Granner, D. K. (1999). CCAAT/enhancer-binding protein beta is an accessory factor for the glucocorticoid response from the cAMP response element in the rat phosphoenolpyruvate carboxykinase gene promoter. *Journal of Biological Chemistry, 274*(9), 5880–5887.

Yeh, K. Y. (1984). Corticosterone concentrations in the serum and milk of lactating rats: Parallel changes after induced stress. *Endocrinology, 115*(4), 1364–1370.

Yehuda, R., Halligan, S. L., & Grossman, R. (2001). Childhood trauma and risk for PTSD: Relationship to intergenerational effects of trauma, parental PTSD, and cortisol secretion. *Development and Psychopathology, 13*, 733–753.

Young, E. A., Aggen, S. H., Prescott, C. A., & Kendler, K. S. (2000). Similarity in saliva cortisol measures in monozygotic twins and the influence of past major depression. *Biological Psychiatry, 48*(1), 70–74.

CHAPTER 15

Memory and Developmental Psychopathology

MARK L. HOWE, SHEREE L. TOTH, and DANTE CICCHETTI

How does children's memory operate and what are the critical developmental shifts during childhood that change memory from a less mature to a more mature system? How are these processes altered, if at all, in children experiencing trauma or psychopathology? In this chapter, we address these questions in the context of child maltreatment and the chronic stress and psychiatric sequelae associated with child abuse and neglect. Very solid theoretical grounds encourage us to anticipate that stress, particularly the stress associated with early aversive childhood experiences such as maltreatment, produces alterations in basic memory processes. Throughout this review, however, we show that the evidence does not substantiate such a claim.

Drawing on a developmental psychopathology perspective, we begin by discussing how childhood trauma might affect the normal course of memory development. Although there are scant data to date, there are a number of theories that lead us to believe that fundamental processes may be altered as a function of childhood trauma. In what follows,

we outline these theories and then evaluate them in the context of specific memory data related to children's basic memory processes and autobiographical memory. We conclude with a discussion of future research directions that should be undertaken to affirm or challenge our contention that, based on extant empirical findings, memory operates similarly in traumatized and nontraumatized individuals.

HOW DOES TRAUMA AFFECT MEMORY AND MEMORY DEVELOPMENT?

Trauma and the stress associated with it are thought to have a variety of effects on basic memory processes as well as on memory for traumatic events themselves. In an early description of the field of developmental psychopathology, Sroufe and Rutter (1984) stated ". . . the focus is on the ontogenetic process whereby early patterns of individual adaptation evolve to later patterns of adaptation. . . . At times, studying the course of adaptation in selected nondisordered individuals also is of great interest . . ." (p. 25). In a further elaboration of the parameters of the field, Cicchetti and Cohen (1995a, 1995b) highlighted the interplay between normal and atypical development and argued that investigations with both populations are

The writing of this chapter was supported by grants from the Natural Sciences and Engineering Research Council of Canada (to MLH), National Institute of Mental Health (to DC, MLH, and SLT), and the Spunk Fund, Inc. (to DC and SLT).

necessary to truly understand developmental mechanisms and processes. Therefore, in this chapter, we build on one of the central tenets of developmental psychopathology, namely, that investigations with normal populations can serve to inform approaches to atypical populations. Knowledge of the development of memory in normal populations of children provides a baseline with which similar or divergent memory processes in children who have been traumatized can be compared.

Because a number of reviews of the scientific and theoretical literature on the overall impact of stress on biological functioning (including the consequences of chronic Posttraumatic Stress Disorder [PTSD]) have recently appeared, we do not reiterate them here (see Bremner & Narayan, 1998; Bremner & Vermetten, 2001; Brewin, 2003; Dalgleish, 2004; Dickerson & Kemeny, 2004; Engleberg & Christianson, 2002; Kemeny, 2003; McEwen & Schmeck, 1994; Sapolsky, Romero, & Munck, 2000). Instead, we focus on specific aspects of stress responses that affect basic memory processes as well as those that are purported to affect memory for traumatic experiences themselves. We begin by providing an overview of physiological reactivity and stress, including a description of the measures most commonly used to index stress reactivity. This is followed by a synthesis of what is known about the effects of stress on the neural substrates of memory. In the penultimate section, we discuss theories and research concerned with acute versus chronic stress and memory development in childhood. We conclude by discussing clinical implications of this work and proposing directions for future research.

Physiological Reactivity and Stress

Stressful events frequently lead to the release of adrenal stress hormones, including catecholamines and glucocorticoids (McGaugh, 2000; Sapolsky et al., 2000). Studies with animals and humans have shown that the release of these hormones is correlated with dramatic changes in memory and cognition (Cahill & McGaugh, 1998; Lupien & McEwen, 1997; McEwen & Sapolsky, 1995; McGaugh, Cahill, & Roozendaal, 1996). Although exposure to acute stressors can enhance memory storage and consolidation (for a review, see Howe, 1998), impairment of memory and cognitive processes has been associated with chronic exposure to stressors (McEwen & Sapolsky, 1995). Clearly, however, the presence of either acute or chronic stressors can both enhance and impair memory and cognition depending on a number of factors, including the intensity of

the stressor (see Howe, 1998) as well as individual differences in stress reactivity (see Quas, Bauer, & Boyce, 2004). In what follows, we provide a brief overview of the basic mechanisms involved in biopsychological reactivity to stressors and show how these reactions enhance or compromise memory and cognition. We consider research with animals and humans and, in the latter case, with both adults and children.

Catecholamines and Glucocorticoids

It has been known for some time that physiological and psychological stress provoke an integrated response involving neural (including sympathetic and parasympathetic responses) and neuroendocrine (including the hypothalamic-pituitary-adrenocorticol [HPA] axis) systems. The neural (sympathetic) contribution includes the secretion of the catecholamines epinephrine and norepinephrine, and the neuroendocrine contribution includes the secretion of glucocorticoids by the adrenal gland. A key similarity between these systems is that both catecholamines and glucocorticoids exhibit an inverted U-shaped relationship between the amount secreted and memory: Small amounts have little effect on memory, moderate amounts can enhance memory, and extreme amounts can impair memory (Gold & McCarty, 1995; Izquierdo & Medina, 1997; Korneyev, 1997; McGaugh, 1995). Although there is considerable debate as to whether such extreme levels exist in children's real-world experiences (see Chen, Zeltzer, Craske, & Katz, 2000), there are experimental studies that clearly show high levels to be deleterious to memory (see Sapolsky et al., 2000). Thus, stress can have seemingly opposite effects on memory depending on its intensity and chronicity. Further, these different effects can be either specific and experience-dependent (e.g., affecting only the specific event memory) or general and more globally relevant to basic memory processes (e.g., exhibiting long-lasting structural and functional consequences such as hippocampal cell loss or elevated levels of circulating catecholamines). In this chapter, we are concerned with both of these effects—the former because it addresses the issue of what can be remembered about traumatic experiences and the latter because it goes directly to the issue of how basic memory processes may be affected more generally by trauma and stress.

We should note that there are also differences in how catecholamines and glucocorticoids function. Catecholamines do not enter the brain directly but exert their effects indirectly (i.e., through secondary-messenger cascades at postsynaptic sites). Glucocorticoids directly affect receptors especially in the hippocampus, a structure well-known to play an important role in learning and memory (particularly in the consolidation of memories). If this latter structure is permanently altered by glucocorticoid activity in response to stress and trauma, then questions arise concerning the longevity of memories from the traumatic experiences.

Two other distinctions between catecholamines and glucocorticoids are important. The first of these concerns the time course: The indirect effects of catecholamines develop over a relatively short interval (within seconds), whereas the glucocorticoids are secreted over a matter of minutes and their effects can take hours to emerge. Because memories are not formed instantaneously, taking a rather protracted time course to emerge (from hours to days depending on which model of consolidation one adheres to), both of these effects will be important but at different points in the time course of memory formation. The second difference concerns the site of their effects: Stress-induced catecholamine effects are localized primarily in the amygdaloid complex, whereas stress-induced glucocorticoid effects are localized primarily in the hippocampal complex (McEwen & Sapolsky, 1995).

Although different sites are affected, there is good reason to believe that both catecholamines and glucocorticoids can enhance or inhibit memory formation. That is, considerable evidence exists showing that the amygdaloid complex plays a central role in modulating (either enhancing or impairing) memories for stressful experiences (Cahill, 2000; Cahill & McGaugh, 1996; McGaugh, 1995, 2000, 2003; Pelletier & Pare, 2004). Similar memory-enhancing and memory-impairing effects have been observed with the stress-induced release of the endogenous glucocorticoids corticosterone (in rats) and cortisol (in humans), and these effects are believed to influence the neural processes linked to consolidation of memories (Diamond, Fleshner, Ingersoll, & Rose, 1996; Newcomer, Craft, Hershey, Askins, & Bardgett, 1994; Oades, 1979; Pugh, Tremblay, Fleshner, & Rudy, 1997).

Regardless of the locus of these effects, both catecholamines and glucocorticoids modulate what gets stored in memory and may do so by altering processes involved in consolidation (Abel et al., 1995; Cahill & McGaugh, 1996; Izquierdo & Medina, 1997). Consolidation is that process through which initially encoded information is transformed from its initial labile, transient form to a more stable, less volatile form (for a recent overview, see Dash, Hebert, & Runyan, 2004). More formally, consolidation refers to a phase of memory formation in which, among other things,

synaptic connections are strengthened, a process that is similar in duration at both the cellular and behavioral levels (for a more complete description, see Abel et al., 1995; Dash et al., 2004; McGaugh, 2003). Because it is during this consolidation interval that memories are most susceptible to interference and distortion, it is important to determine the length of this interval. Originally, consolidation referred to the stabilization of memory within the first few hours following encoding. Subsequently, it has been used to refer to a more protracted interval (months to years) that involves greater transformations, ones that may involve transfer of memory traces from one region of the brain (e.g., the hippocampus) to another (e.g., neocortex; Squire, Cohen, & Nadel, 1984). The modulatory effects of stress are thought to be relevant to the original sense of consolidation as most of the biochemical cascade effects occur over a briefer time course involving hours, not weeks, months, or years (Abel et al., 1995; Izquierdo & Medina, 1997). Thus, stress-induced release of catecholamines and glucocorticoids most likely modulate memories for traumatic events by altering (enhancing or inhibiting) the course of consolidation (also see Richter-Levin & Akirav, 2003).

However, there is some evidence that although glucocorticoids may act to enhance consolidation of memories, the same dose levels can act to inhibit subsequent retrieval of those memories. That is, stress-induced or exogenously administered glucocorticoids can have contradictory effects on memory, enhancing storage (consolidation) but inhibiting later retrieval. This is true even with acute doses of glucocorticoids. For example, de Quervain, Roozendaal, and McGaugh (1998) found that glucocorticoid doses sufficient to enhance consolidation profoundly impaired later retrieval. It should be noted that these effects have been obtained in spatial memory tasks with rats and may not generalize to humans.

Glucose and Oxygenation

Additional biological mechanisms can mediate the effects of stress on memory. In particular, catecholamine effects due to stress may arise because of changes in the delivery of oxygen and glucose to the brain. The catecholamine epinephrine, for example, may affect memory through its well-established effects on blood glucose. The modulatory effects of glucose on memory are, of course, dependent on a central cholinergic mechanism (Kopf & Baratti, 1995) and may be specific to the learning situation itself (Cahill & McGaugh, 1996). Specifically, when epinephrine release is experimentally blocked during an emotional episode (and glucose levels do not change), it is likely that ß-adrenergic receptor activation (by norepinephrine) may produce memory enhancement. In fact, the neurotransmitter norepinephrine, also important to memory, has been thought to enhance firing in neurons that participate in the encoding of environmentally significant information (Kety, 1970). Of particular importance, novelty is directly linked to norepinephrine release and subsequently enhanced retention in some animals (Kitchigina, Vankov, Harley, & Sara, 1997). In humans, blocking norepinephrine reduces the normal memory-enhancing effects of surprise (Cahill, Prins, Weber, & McGaugh, 1994; Nielson & Jensen, 1994). Relevant to this chapter, Cahill et al. found that the ß-adrenergic blocking drug propanolol selectively impaired memory for an emotionally arousing story in healthy adults, supporting the claim that memory modulation due to emotional arousal is contingent on the activation of these ß-adrenergic receptors even though they are not required for the formation of nonemotional (neutral) memories.

Effects of Prolonged Stress

Chronic stress (specifically, the release of glucocorticoids) in animals can lead to the atrophy of dendritic branches in the pyramidal neurons of the CA3 region of the hippocampus (Watanabe, Gould, & McEwen, 1992; Woolley, Gould, & McEwen, 1990). Although some of this loss is reversible, irreversible neuronal loss in the hippocampus does occur with prolonged exposure to glucocorticoids (Kerr, Campbell, Applegate, Brodish, & Landfield, 1991; Mizoguchi, Kunishita, Chui, & Tabira, 1992; Sapolsky, Krey, & McEwen, 1985; Uno, Ross, Else, Suleman, & Sapolsky, 1989). The fact that chronic exposure to stress-induced glucocorticoids affects dendritic branching first followed by neuron loss does not appear to be species-specific because such findings have been obtained in rats, monkeys, and tree shrews (McEwen & Sapolsky, 1995). Although studies with humans are less well controlled, they, too, suggest that hippocampal atrophy is associated with prolonged glucocorticoid exposure (Axelson et al., 1993; Starkman, Gebarski, Berent, & Schteingart, 1992). Indeed, it has been known for some time that prolonged exposure to elevated levels of glucocorticoids is accompanied by cognitive impairment, including impairment of declarative memory and visual episodic memory (Nasrallah, Coffman, & Olson, 1989). Although some of these findings with human participants are compromised because of coincident disease, studies with healthy adults have also shown that a decline in declarative (explicit) measures of memory, but not in implicit measures, can be associated with sustained increases in glucocorticoids (Lupien et al., 1994; Newcomer et al.,

1994; Wolkowitz et al., 1990). Functional magnetic resonance imaging (fMRI) studies with adults who have been exposed to prolonged stress, for example, abused women (Schacter, Koustaal, & Norman, 1996) and individuals who have been diagnosed with combat-related PTSD (Bremner, Krystal, Southwick, & Charney, 1995), as well as primates (Sapolsky, Uno, Rebert, & Finch, 1990) and humans (Keenan, Jacobson, Soleymani, & Newcomer, 1995) who have been exposed to elevated glucocorticoids over prolonged treatment intervals, show decreased hippocampal volume. Although this decrease may be subject to a variety of interpretations, it is possible that toxic levels of glucocorticoids were reached given the prolonged exposure to stress or to steroid (e.g., prednisone) therapy.

Although few studies have been conducted with children, it is known that high-dose prednisone treatment of asthmatic children leads to poorer verbal memory than low-dose treatment (Bender, Lerner, & Poland, 1991). In addition, maltreated children whose abuse is tantamount to chronic stress tend to exhibit altered patterns of diurnal cortisol activity. Specifically, depressed maltreated children, relative to nonmaltreated depressed children, exhibit lower concentrations of cortisol in the morning and show an increase rather than the normal decrease in cortisol from the morning to the afternoon (Cicchetti & Rogosch, 2001; Hart, Gunnar, & Cicchetti, 1996). There is additional evidence that children exposed to prolonged stress, including sexually abused girls (DeBellis et al., 1994), experience some deficits on explicit (declarative) memory tasks, although it is not clear that these problems are directly attributable to prolonged stress (Schacter et al., 1996). Although it is apparent that such individuals can have problems remembering (e.g., transient amnesia) aspects of the precipitating event (e.g., sexual abuse), it is also clear that they can have related deficits associated with the recall of autobiographical events (Kuyken & Brewin, 1995; Parks & Balon, 1995).

Individual and Developmental Differences in Stress Reactivity

As we have seen, traumatic events usually elicit high levels of stress hormones that are often maintained for a long period of time following the event (Sapolsky et al., 2000). This means that recently traumatized individuals should exhibit an exaggerated tonic level of arousal (e.g., elevated heart rate, hypersensitive startle response), something that leads to changes in information processing (e.g., attention may become narrowed and focused on a critical aspect of the traumatic event—so-called weapon focus; Loftus, Loftus, & Messo, 1987). Information that gets encoded will be determined to some degree by this narrowing of attention, and what can be retrieved later is constrained by what was initially encoded (see Howe, 1997, 1998).

Thus, in general, there is a negative relationship between physiological arousal and attention, particularly in children (Richards & Casey, 1991; Suess, Porges, & Plude, 1994). In terms of children's memory and stress reactivity, reactive children have difficulty attending to external information when they are experiencing stress. This, in turn, limits information that gets encoded and stored; hence, memory traces may be more impoverished and less durable. Moreover, reactive children's arousal level can impact not only encoding, but also retrieval processes. That is, arousal levels may be too high for children to adequately search memory or utilize cues effectively (e.g., interviewer's questions or other available prompts). This is especially true when reactive children are being queried about stressful events or when the retrieval situation itself is stressful (see Quas et al., 2004).

But exactly how are these variations in stress and stress reactivity measured? Physiological reactivity has been measured in a variety of ways that reflect activation of the (1) autonomic nervous system (e.g., heart rate; respiratory sinus arrhythmia, an index of parasympathetic activity on the cardiac cycle; preejection period, an index of sympathetic activity on the cardiac cycle) or (2) HPA axis, most frequently operationalized in terms of salivary cortisol. As it turns out, measures of increased heart rate during the to-be-encoded event are negatively related to children's subsequent memory for those events (Bugental, Blue, Cortez, Fleck, & Rodriguez, 1992; N. Stein & Boyce, 1995). It appears that increased heart rate interferes with encoding, leading to impoverished representations of the event in memory. Although there are a number of limitations to studies such as these with children (see Quas et al., 2004), additional work using autonomic measures is clearly warranted, particularly investigations that also measure changes in heart rate during retrieval.

Considerably more research has used cortisol rather than variation in autonomic reactivity as an index of stress. For example, Merritt, Ornstein, and Spicker (1994) examined the relationship between salivary cortisol and a stressful medical procedure and found no relationship between cortisol levels and children's memory for the stressful event. Similarly, Chen et al. (2000) found no relationship between cortisol levels and children's memory for lumbar punctures. Unfortunately, the results of both of these stud-

ies are difficult to interpret given the relatively small sample sizes and the manner in which cortisol levels were calculated (Merritt et al., 1994) and because additional, potentially memory-relevant medications were present prior to the stressful procedure (Chen et al., 2000).

More recently, Quas et al. (2004) examined the interaction between physiological reactivity (autonomic responses and salivary cortisol) and social support (supportive versus nonsupportive interviewer style) on children's initial and long-term recollection of a stressful event (memory for an event involving a fire alarm). Although few significant relationships emerged at initial recollection, cortisol reactivity was associated with poorer long-term retention of the event. Moreover, autonomic reactivity was related to higher accuracy during a supportive interview and lower accuracy during a nonsupportive interview. It would seem that, at least in this study, autonomic and cortisol measures tap different aspects of memory processing for stressful materials (overall retention versus interview style), although both appear to be related to retrieval components of long-term retention.

Overall, the research on stress and memory with human and nonhuman participants suggests that both storage and retrieval processes are affected by stress. Although the results are often clearer in nonhuman animal studies, the results of the study by Quas et al. (2004) does suggest that retrieval of stressful memories is influenced by the type of interview being conducted and that overall retention levels may be influenced by children's stress reactivity. In terms of storage, although often difficult to demonstrate empirically with human child samples, "it seems reasonable that the storage of memories should be moderated in some way to enhance the contrast between memories of important events from those of less relevant memories—to enhance the distinction between signal and noise" (Nielson & Jensen, 1994, p. 190).

But why should it be so hard to demonstrate this connection between stress and enhanced storage or consolidation of information in children? As we have already pointed out, one reason is that a number of measurement issues exist when children are the sample of choice. In fact, with children, there is no consensus on the best index of stress. As previously discussed, a variety of techniques have been used to measure stress in children, including subjective self-ratings (where children rate their own level of stress), behavioral and objective rating scales (where parents or objective observers adduce the child's level of stress), physiological indices (heart rate, blood pressure, and the other indices listed earlier), and neuroendocrine measures (salivary cortisol). Unfortunately, all of these measures have their weaknesses and have faired poorly with respect to predicting children's event memory. In addition to those studies already mentioned, Howe, Courage, and Peterson (1994, 1995) failed to find a relationship between self- or parent ratings of a child's stress and children's memory for emergency room treatment, even up to a year after the experience. Goodman and Quas (1997) also failed to find a relationship between subjective and behavioral measures of stress and memory for a stressful medical procedure, the voiding cystourethrogram (VCUG). Of course, the inability to find relationships between memory and stress as measured by subjective and behavioral scales may not be a surprise as such indices may be insensitive to the underlying physiological changes that are associated with stress (also see Howe, 1997, 1998). Thus, similar to the autonomic and neuroendocrine measures of stress reactivity, studies using subjective, objective, and behavioral scales have been unable to unambiguously link changes in children's stress with subsequent memory for those stressful events.

Another reason these measures, salivary cortisol in particular, may not predict event memory in studies with children is that the extent of these reactions can vary both developmentally and across individuals. For example, there are marked developmental and individual differences in cortisol responses to stress (for a review, see Gunnar, Tout, de Haan, Pierce, & Standbury, 1997). That is, neuroendocrine reactivity can fluctuate with other variables, including age, attachment styles (Nachmias, Gunnar, Manglesdorf, Parritz, & Buss, 1996), temperament (Boyce, Barr, & Zeltzer, 1992; Kagan, 1994), stress reactivity (Gunnar et al., 1997), and knowledge (N. Stein & Liwag, 1997; for a review, see Howe, 1998). Salivary cortisol is a marker worth studying, especially because of its sensitivity to cognitive and social factors, as long as when it is examined, these other covariates are considered simultaneously. To do so, and to link cortisol and memory, Goodman and Quas (1997) pointed out that it is important to consider not only these individual differences, but also individual differences in the quality and quantity of memories for traumatic events. Frequently, such differences can be related to individual differences in the rememberer's reactions to and consequences from traumatic experiences (Brewin, Andrews, & Gotlib, 1993; Malinowsky-Rummell & Hansen, 1993). Thus, although a number of promising measures that may lead to a better understanding of the link between stress and memory in children exist, few studies have incorporated these measures into a single design. It is only when all of these individual differences factors are considered in concert that

relationships between neuroendocrine measures of stress reactivity and memory for stressful experiences will be discovered.

Effects of Stress and Trauma on Neural Development

Now that we have examined the extant research on physiological reactivity and stress in memory, we direct our attention to neural development. Specifically, what are the long-term consequences of prolonged stress, especially that associated with maltreatment, on neurological development? Although research on this question has really flourished only in the past decade or so, there is evidence that childhood physical and sexual abuse is associated with decreased cortical integration (Schiffer, Teicher, & Papanicolaou, 1995; Teicher, 1994), increased electroencephalogram abnormalities (Ito et al., 1993), and diminished size of the corpus callosum (DeBellis et al., 1999; Teicher et al., 1997). There is also evidence of similar, attenuated maturation of the corpus callosum in neglected children (Teicher et al., 2004). Moreover, studies have found that early maltreatment (neglect, physical and sexual abuse) exerts a larger negative impact on the developing corpus callosum in boys than in girls (DeBellis & Keshaven, 2003; Teicher et al., 2004). This gender difference was more important (accounting for more of the variance) than whether children developed PTSD as a function of the occurrence maltreatment. Thomas and DeBellis (2004) also found that the prolonged exposure to stress in traumatized children who develop PTSD is related to those children having greater differences in pituitary volume with age than that of control children.

Although it is not clear what these differences in neurological development might mean for the functioning of basic memory processes in neglected and abused children, some of the results concerning changes in hippocampal development are suggestive. For example, a number of researchers have found that maltreatment during childhood (physical and sexual abuse) is associated with diminished left hippocampal development in adulthood (Bremner et al., 1997; Ito, Teicher, Glod, & Ackerman, 1998; M. B. Stein, 1997) especially when it is comorbid with PTSD (Bremner, Vythilingam, Vermetten, Southwick, McGlashan, Nazeer, et al., 2003; Bremner, Vythilingam, Vermetten, Southwick, McGlashan, Staib, et al., 2003). Other investigators have not found changes in hippocampal volume as a function of trauma, even in those who develop PTSD (Bonne et al., 2001), and still other researchers have not found any support for the premise that hippocampal development differs in maltreated and nonmaltreated populations (DeBellis, Hall, Boring, Frustaci, & Moritz, 2001; Pederson et al., 2004). Part of the reason for this discrepancy in outcome may have to do with the age of the maltreated subjects when examined; for example, in the Bremner et al. (1997) study, the participants were adults who retrospectively reported childhood abuse, whereas in the DeBellis et al. study, the participants were children whose abuse was documented. Caution is also needed when interpreting these outcomes because the sample sizes are often somewhat small (e.g., $ns = 9$ maltreated and 9 control in DeBellis et al., 2001, and $ns = 17$ maltreated and 17 control in Bremner et al., 1997).

Finally, some reports suggest an abnormal connectivity among brain regions involved in the recall of traumatic events in individuals who develop PTSD, but not in those who do not develop PTSD (Lanius et al., 2001, 2003, 2004). It may be that such dysregulation results in changes in how traumatic experiences are retrieved for people who develop PTSD, not in how or that such experiences are represented (encoded, stored, retained) in memory. Overall, then, although there is good reason to believe that the neurological substrates that subserve basic memory functioning should be altered as a consequence of early stressful experiences (e.g., child maltreatment), the empirical evidence is at best mixed.

EXTANT THEORIES OF MEMORY AND TRAUMA

This review of the cognitive neuroscience literature has shown that there are any number of reasons we should suspect that memories of trauma are somehow different from memories of ordinary events. As we have also seen in this review, although there is some evidence that individuals who develop PTSD may retrieve traumatic memories somewhat differently from those who do not, there is little evidence to suggest that the basic memory processes of traumatized individuals are somehow fundamentally different from that of other individuals. These facts notwithstanding, there exists theoretical speculation that victims of trauma may have fundamentally altered basic memory processes. In this section, we consider a number of these theories.

Terr's Theory

Contrary to what is known from the vast literature on memory, where amount remembered is directly related to the number of times one has experienced an event, Terr (1988, 1994) has suggested that memory for trauma is inversely related to the number of traumatic experiences a person has encountered. That is, Terr believes that children often forget repeated traumas (what she calls Type II syndromes) but remember single traumatic experiences (what she calls Type I syndromes). Type I events revolve around a single incident, such as a kidnapping or schoolyard sniper attack, and tend to be memorable because they are distinctive inasmuch as they are unexpected and potentially life threatening. Type II events involve multiple repeated incidents of physical or sexual abuse and are not as memorable as Type I events because they are predictable and repetitive and become anticipated. Because such events become expected, children will employ defensive techniques such as denial and psychic numbing to reduce the emotional impact of these events, practices that in turn alter the encoding of these experiences such that later retention is difficult and such experiences become easily forgotten.

As has been shown in this chapter, the sorts of experiences Terr labels as Type I are, in fact, well remembered (for a review, see Howe, 2000). However, there is very little (if any) evidence that Terr's Type II events are forgotten or more poorly remembered. In fact, the only evidence that Type II experiences are not well remembered comes from Terr's (1988) own examination of 20 children's recollection of trauma they experienced prior to the age of 5 years. Of the seven who had Type II, repeated experiences, three were unable to verbally recall the events 5 months to 12 years later and four retained what were called "spotty" memories.

As others have pointed out, there are any number of reasons these conclusions about Type I and II event memories are flawed. First, Type I and II events were confounded with the child's age at the time of the trauma (also see McNally, 2003). That is, the children who could not produce verbal recall of Type II traumas were on average younger when their traumas ended than children who had single-incident Type I traumas. In fact, they were so young (6 months, 24 months, and 28 months of age) that many of these findings can be accounted for more parsimoniously by noting that this is exactly the time frame that is coincident with childhood amnesia (see Howe, 2000; Howe & Courage, 1993, 1997). Second, as Roediger and Bergman (1998) noted, the memory literature is replete with studies showing that repeated events are better remembered than one-time events. Although event repetition may lead to schematization of the memory, making some of the details concerning individual episodes difficult to discriminate, that such events are remembered and are remembered better than events that occurred only once is not in question. The extant literature on memory and repetition shows that the greater the repetition, the better the memory. Although some might argue that such findings pertain only to non-traumatic event memories and that somehow the nature of traumatic events violates the general laws of memory, even in the context of traumatic experiences, most clinicians and researchers have found excellent recollection of repeated abuse (Goleman, 1992; Yapko, 1994), including physical (Pelcovitz et al., 1994) and sexual abuse (Archdiocesan Commission, 1990), community violence (Fitzpatrick & Boldizar, 1993), and horrific events such as the Cambodian holocaust (Kinzie, Sack, Angell, Manson, & Rath, 1986). Thus, contrary to Terr's notion that Type II repeated traumas are more poorly remembered than one-time events, there is abundant evidence that repeated abusive experiences are well remembered. Moreover, studies of intrusive memories of victims of abuse have clearly shown that people remember their abuse all too well (Ehlers et al., 2002; Hackmann, Ehlers, Speckens, & Clark, 2004; Holmes, Grey, & Young, 2005). In fact, it has been proposed that these involuntary memories occur in response to stimuli that bear a resemblance to stimuli experienced immediately prior to the traumatic event(s) and may serve as a "warning signal" (Charney, Deutch, Krystal, Southwick, & Davis, 1993; Ehlers et al., 2002; Foa & Rothbaum, 1998). Thus, Terr's idea contradicts what is known empirically. Indeed, all of the scientific evidence runs counter to Terr's assertions that the more children are abused, the more likely it is that they will forget having been abused.

Freyd's Betrayal Trauma Theory

Freyd (1996; Freyd, DePrince, & Zurbriggen, 2001) proposed that children are more likely to experience amnesia for abuse inflicted by parents or caretakers than by strangers because of evolutionary pressures to maintain attachments to those who are vital to one's survival. That is, it is adaptive to forget abuse that involves such betrayals of trust to ensure one's own survival. Although she agrees with Terr that repeated traumas are more likely to be forgotten, she does so because she believes that such abuse is more likely to have occurred at the hands of a caretaker. Thus, it is the status of the abuser (caretaker or stranger) that determines forgetting, not the number of abuse incidents.

As we have already seen and will see again later when all of the evidence is discussed, abuse tends not to be forgotten but rather to be remembered (Herman, 1981). In fact, Russell's (1999) epidemiologic study found that not one incest survivor had ever forgotten his or her molestation experience. Goodman et al. (2003) found no relationship between abuser status (parent/caregiver versus

stranger) and failure to report abuse years after the abuse. Thus, as for most, if not all, survivors of trauma, there is little or no support for the idea that incest survivors experience amnesia for their abuse.

Van der Kolk's Theory

According to van der Kolk (1994; van der Kolk & Fisler, 1995), trauma interferes with explicit (declarative), but not implicit, memory. This is because trauma leads to the release of stress hormones, hormones that create a sort of state-dependent memory for the traumatic experience. Further, van der Kolk argues that state-dependent memories are inaccessible to conscious recollection until the same state is induced again, and that until that time such memories remain intact and unchanged. That is, unlike other memories, van der Kolk maintains that traumatic memories are not subject to the normal deterioration processes that other memories are subject to; rather, they remain indelible. However, unlike explicit memories, implicit memories are said to appear spontaneously in the guise of flashbacks, dreams, body memories, avoidant behaviors, and so forth (Brown, Scheflin, & Hammond, 1998). Moreover, it is through these implicit memories that those who have been traumatized can "recover" an explicit memory of the traumatic experience.

This theory, too, is plagued by empirical and conceptual problems. First, as we have already discussed and will explicate more completely later, trauma does not prevent the formation of explicit, declarative memories. In fact, more often than not, stress aids the consolidation of memories for traumatic events. Although extreme levels of stress can impair consolidation, this does not result in memories that last forever, unchanged. Rather, it means that these memories do not get stored, so they cannot be recovered later. However, there is little evidence that such extreme levels of stress occur naturally. It is more likely, therefore, that such memories do get stored and that stress experiences enhance and promote the formation of explicit, declarative memory for traumatic events.

Second, even if trauma resulted in state-dependent memories that could not be accessed consciously, the evidence concerning state-dependent memories does not support the idea that such memories would be dissociated from consciousness. Specifically, research on state-dependent memories shows that although people tend to have less extensive access to those memories, they are not amnesic for the experience (Eich, 1995; Eich, Macaulay, Loewenstein, & Dihle, 1997). Of course, state dependency cannot explain why memories of trauma would be recovered in a therapeutic environment that was presumably devoid of such trauma. Even individuals who report dissociative alterations in consciousness (e.g., slowing of time, out of body experiences) during traumatic events such as near-death experiences (for a review, see Greyson, 2000) or first-time skydiving (Sterlini & Bryant, 2002) do not become amnesic for these experiences, but are capable of providing detailed declarative recollections of such experiences.

Third, implicit memory does not contain an unchanging, veridical record of experience, traumatic or otherwise (see Howe, 2000). In fact, implicit memory is as subject to change and distortion as is explicit memory (Howe, 2000; Lustig & Hasher, 2001). Even if implicit memories did return as bodily sensations, unexplained feelings, and flashbacks, there is nothing in implicit memory traces that reveal their source. That is, such traces do not contain information that indexes their origin, and hence it is impossible to use them to accurately re-create the original experience. As Roediger and Bergman (1998) point out, sparsely encoded traces do not become more accurate with time. Instead, such traces undergo greater reconstruction, and hence are potentially more inaccurate, than more completely encoded traces. Moreover, such memories are not stored in muscle tissue—the idea of "body memories" is inconsistent with the cognitive neuroscience of memory, even the neuroscience of traumatic memories (see earlier section). In fact, animal research has shown that there is no such thing as indelibly etched emotional memories. Even well-established memories based on fear conditioning are labile and subject to alteration (Morrison, Allardyce, & McKane, 2002; Nader, Schafe, & LeDoux, 2000; Zola, 1997).

Foa's Fear Networks

It is well-known that many traumatized individuals develop a heightened sensitivity to trauma-related information (Field et al., 2001; J. M. G. Williams, Mathews, & MacLeod, 1996) as well as heightened memory for, and less forgetting of, trauma-related information (Amir, McNally, & Wiegartz, 1996; Cloitre, Cancienne, Brodsky, Dulit, & Perry, 1996; McNally, Metzger, Lasko, Clancy, & Pitman, 1998; Paunovic, Lundh, & Oest, 2002). Foa (Foa & Kozak, 1991; Foa & Rothbaum, 1998) has attempted to explain these phenomena by arguing that traumatized individuals, especially those who develop PTSD, develop semantic "fear" networks that serve to organize trauma-relevant information. These networks, like other semantic networks, are developed to integrate information about a specific theme, in this case trauma, and may be used to alert their users to the warning signs of impending threat of trauma. Not only do these networks create states of hypervigilance, but they can also serve to preserve information about trauma (e.g., through rehearsal of information) and link similar experiences together in memory (making for stronger traces). Repeated traumatic experiences should, contrary to Terr, increase the likelihood of creating these networks, hence increasing memory for traumatic experiences. These networks are also said to be linked to intrusive memories for the traumatic experience(s).

There is some evidence supporting this idea. For example, it might be predicted that individuals who have been abused (e.g., childhood sexual abuse, or CSA) might have particularly robust CSA memories as PTSD symptomatology increases, with more severe abuse resulting in better CSA memory. This is exactly what Alexander et al. (2005) found: Individuals with documented CSA and individuals with more PTSD symptomatology had particularly accurate CSA memories. Thus, emotional events such as CSA may be better preserved in trauma-related semantic networks resulting in better, not worse, recollection later in adulthood.

Conversely, traumatized individuals who have subsequently developed PTSD should exhibit anxiety responses that are specific to trauma-relevant materials. Alternatively, PTSD may be the result of pathological memory formation (Keane, Fairbank, & Caddell, 1985) in which associative learning coalesces trauma-specific cues with neuroendocrine responses in what has been called a "fear network" (Foa & Kozak, 1991; Foa & Rothbaum, 1998; Foa, Steketee, & Rothbaum, 1989). The more an individual reexperiences the traumatic event, the greater the potential increase in tonic levels of sympathetic activation. This means that victims of recent trauma should exhibit fear responses to specific trauma-related cues (as the fear network continues to emerge) and that only individuals with chronic PTSD will exhibit generally increased levels of reactivity to all stimuli.

Recent reviews of physiological research with chronic PTSD patients have routinely concluded that these individuals have heightened responses to stimuli that are related to the traumatic event (Orr, Metzger, & Pittman, 2002). In fact, this pattern seems to hold for recently traumatized individuals as well (Elsesser, Sartory, & Tackenberg, 2004). That is, both recently traumatized individuals and those with chronic PTSD exhibited similar elevated levels of activation to trauma-related materials, but the groups did not differ with respect to levels of generalized activation.

In summary, although the theories that exist regarding the effects of trauma on memory have proffered some intriguing ideas and speculations, extant empirical studies do not substantiate the theoretical claims that traumatized individuals utilize fundamentally different memory processes than nontraumatized persons. These investigations are reviewed in a subsequent section of this chapter.

CHILDREN'S MEMORY DEVELOPMENT AND TRAUMA

Given all of the neurophysiological evidence and theoretical speculation we have just reviewed, there is good reason to expect that early trauma may result in changes so fundamental to the neural machinery necessary to encode, store, retain, and retrieve memories that the development of these basic processes will be compromised sufficiently to effect performance on everyday memory tasks. Indeed, a number of researchers have suggested that prolonged physiological reactivity to the effects of stress results in significant global changes in functioning during childhood, including increased risk of physical and mental disorders, emotional dysregulation, and cognitive dysfunction (Johnston-Brooks, Lewis, Evans, & Whalen, 1998; Porges, 1997; Raine, Venables, & Mednick, 1997; Rieder & Cicchetti, 1989; Scarpa, 1997). Despite the seeming obviousness of this linkage, there have been a number of failures to provide direct evidence of such a one-to-one mapping. Indeed, it seems more prudent to conclude that the mapping is one-to-many at best and, more realistically, many-to-many and that, rather than seeing reactivity as always being a risk factor, it is more appropriately conceived of as a form of biological sensitivity to environmental and contextual influences (also see Quas et al., 2004).

Despite these complexities, theoretical accounts of how basic memory processes might be compromised by early trauma do exist. Of the theories of memory and trauma we have just reviewed, only Foa's has received empirical support, but even here, this support has been limited. Although this theory, like the others just reviewed, is applicable to children as well as adults, none of the theories have explicitly addressed questions related to the potential changes to memory development that trauma and stress might produce. To address this question, we must first know something about the normal course of memory development. Because a complete exegesis would require numerous tomes, some of which have appeared recently (e.g., Brainerd & Reyna, 2005; Howe, 2000; Rovee-Collier, Hayne, & Columbo, 2001; Schneider & Pressley, 1997), we restrict our presentation to those aspects of children's memory development most likely to be affected by stress, the sequelae of child maltreatment, and psychiatric disorder.

Development of Basic Memory Processes

To begin, a number of investigators have theorized that there is considerable continuity in basic memory processes across childhood and into adulthood (Bauer, 1996; Howe, 2000). That is, infants', toddlers', and children's memory, like that of adults, is subject to misleading information and false memories (Brainerd & Reyna, 2005; Rovee-Collier et al., 2001) and interfering information (Howe, 1995; Rovee-Collier et al., 2001), can be recoded once in storage (Howe, 2004b; Rovee-Collier et al., 2001), can be selectively "forgotten" when directed to do so (Howe, 2002), benefits from distinctiveness (Howe, in press; Howe, Courage, Vernescu, & Hunt, 2000; Rovee-Collier et al., 2001), and is subject to spacing effects (Dempster, 1988; Rovee-Collier et al., 2001) and to many other factors that are well-known in the adult memory literature. Although there is continuity in basic memory processes across development, there is also considerable growth. For example, memory improves as children's knowledge base increases (Bjorklund, 1987), as their ability to encode source information (the context in which information was acquired) improves (Drummey & Newcombe, 2002), as effective strategies (e.g., rehearsal, organization) improve (Schneider & Pressley, 1997), and as metamemory improves (Howe & O'Sullivan, 1990). This growth results in increases in the *complexity* of the information that can be retained, the *duration* of the interval over which information can be retained, and the *representational flexibility* of information in memory, as well as a reduction in the *context-specificity* of what is retained, to name a few outcomes (see Howe, 2000; Rovee-Collier et al., 2001).

Despite our ability to scientifically document these and other remarkable achievements in children's memory, the question remains: What is it that develops? That is, given the striking processing continuity that exists in the face of such prodigious growth, does there exist a common set of basic processes that underlie this dramatic growth in memory functioning and capacity? There is a singular dearth of theories concerning memory development, but those that do exist either emphasize neuroscience (i.e., advances in brain maturation) or cognitive science (i.e., advances in organizational efficiency) in their explanation of growth in memory throughout childhood, although these two approaches are not mutually exclusive. We next consider the neuroscience explanations, followed by the cognitive science explanations.

The Neuroscience of Memory Development

According to C. A. Nelson (1995, 1997, 2000), improvements in memory during childhood are mediated by the extensive and rapid growth of structures in the brain. Specifically, Nelson argues that there are multiple memory systems (e.g., procedural versus declarative) that have different developmental trajectories. Some early developing neurological structures (e.g., the hippocampus, striatum, cerebellum, and olivary-cerebellar complex) are sufficiently well developed early in life to subserve a procedural, or what he calls a "preexplicit," memory system. This is the system that makes recognition memory possible, and it is the system that he argues is necessary for the types of memory performance seen in early infancy (e.g., novelty preference, habituation, operant and classical conditioning, visual expectancy). By contrast, performance on explicit, declarative memory tasks depends on the addition of later developing structures of the medial temporal lobe (e.g., the amygdala), inferior temporal cortical regions, and some aspects of the prefrontal cortex. These memory-relevant structures are not available until some time in the second half of the 1st postnatal year.

In addition, early life brings with it a number of ongoing neural developments, including proliferation of synapses, dendrites, fiber bundles, neurotransmitters, and myelin (see Johnson, 1997, 2000). In fact, the process of synaptogenesis peaks in infancy and toddlerhood and, following a period of overproduction, connections are pruned back and decline thereafter in early childhood (Huttenlocher, 1999). A key point for the purposes of this chapter is that experience is critical to this neural development. Specifically, the selective survival or loss of certain synaptic connections as well as the growth of new ones hinges on experience and interaction with the environment (Greenough & Black, 1999; Greenough, Black, & Wallace, 1987). Experience-based synaptogenesis and related changes in connectivity contribute to some of the neural infrastructure or hardware that supports advances in memory software (e.g., encoding, storage, retrieval). The extent to which and the manner in which different types of early experience affect neural development and hence the development of basic memory hardware and software is not well documented. Although this important area of investigation remains young, it is clear that a complete understanding of the development and malleability of basic memory processes early in life is contingent on

mapping the interaction of experience with the structural and functional plasticity of early neural development.

Cognitive Science of Memory Development

The ideas discussed in the previous section are not without their detractors due to some rather contentious assumptions. For example, some of the work has been conducted in brain-damaged adult populations or with lesioned animals. It is not clear that such findings generalize to intact, human children. Moreover, it is not at all clear that multiple memory systems exist. Indeed, there is evidence against this hypothesis (for a review, see Howe, 2000; Rovee-Collier et al., 2001). Even if there are multiple memory systems, it is not clear whether they develop sequentially or in parallel.

A good example of this debate concerns the idea that there exist separate implicit (i.e., nondeclarative memories that are said to be outside of conscious awareness) and explicit (i.e., declarative memories that are available to consciousness) memory systems. It has been argued that even though we may not have a conscious recollection of a traumatic experience, its residue nonetheless persists in our implicit, nondeclarative system and can still influence our behaviors, unbeknownst to us (for a brief overview, see Howe & Courage, 2004). The problem here is that extreme caution must be exercised when interpreting nonverbal behaviors (the quintessential index of implicit memory) as indices of memories of past traumatic events. This is because there is no direct mapping of specific traumatic experiences onto specific behaviors (e.g., a child's fear of loud noises cannot be inextricably linked to an earlier experience of hearing gunshots while witnessing the murder of his or her parents). Although it is important to remain open to the possible nonverbal behaviors that may signal memories for traumatic events, it is nonetheless prudent to be wary of the circularity of such observations (Howe & Courage, 2004). In any event, the available evidence suggests that even if there exist separate declarative and nondeclarative memory systems, they are both available and functioning very early in life and most likely develop in parallel (Howe, 2000; Rovee-Collier et al., 2001).

Because of these and other concerns about a pure neuroscience approach to memory development, cognitive science models of memory development (e.g., Brainerd & Reyna's, 2005, fuzzy-trace theory; Howe's, 2000, trace-integrity theory) have been constructed. Although these models were constructed independent of the ones just reviewed, they are consistent with findings in the neuroscience literature. For example, in fuzzy-trace theory, memory consists of two traces: a verbatim trace (one that contains surface features of the experience as well as item-specific information) and a gist trace (one that contains the meaning of the experience as well as other relational, elaborative information). Although both types of traces develop early and in parallel, verbatim processing tends to dominate early in memory development, with gist processing becoming more dominant (depending on the task at hand) as development proceeds.

In contrast, trace-integrity theory views memory as consisting of unitary traces and memory development as a continuous process (Howe, 2000). This means that both verbatim and gist, implicit and explicit, procedural and declarative aspects of memory are contained within the same unified trace in memory. Differences in the retrievability of these different components of memory traces are controlled by trace integration and access features of the retrieval task and not by differences in the availability of different memory traces.

Regardless of which theory one adopts, the key to memory development is corresponding changes in organizational capacity. In fuzzy-trace theory, this may seem obvious inasmuch as gist processing begins to take on more and more importance as memory development unfolds. Perhaps the role of organization is equally obvious in the trace-integrity theory. Here, memory traces are viewed as collections of basic elements (e.g., features, nodes) that come to be integrated through processes linking the current functional information (that subset of features extracted and encoded from the current environment) with knowledge already stored in memory. Traces lie on a continuum from little or no integration to high integration, in which the elements within the trace have great cohesion and the trace itself is distinct from other traces in memory, making it highly discriminable for retrieval. The relationships among items or elements within the trace provides the "glue" for these traces. As children's ability to organize and extract features from the environment grows, their ability to store and retrieve more durable traces increases. Because children's ability to extract more and more abstract information from displays increases with conceptual development, as does their knowledge base, their ability to store and retrieve more conceptually sophisticated information also burgeons.

As an example, consider the onset of autobiographical memory or personal memories for events that happened to "me" (a more complete account is provided in the later section on autobiographical memory). It is well-known that before 18 to 24 months of age, children can remember events, but those events are not organized as events that happened to "me," nor are they remembered in later childhood or adulthood (so-called infantile amnesia). Event memory can become autobiographical only when there is a cognitive self (a me with recognizable features) that provides an organizational framework for storing and retrieving event information (Howe, 2004a).

Most theories of memory development concur that traumatic experiences should be well remembered due to their distinctive (e.g., emotional, unique) character (better discrimination of traces). The effects of chronic stress may be outweighed by effects due to differences in the semantic organization of experiences. That is, because maltreated children are often those who come from the lowest socioeconomic strata of our society, and because it is well-known that socioeconomic status (SES) is linked to differences in memory performance due to variation in knowledge base, it may well be that maltreated children's basic memory processes are the same as those of nonmaltreated children (unless there is demonstrable brain injury) and differ only in the manner in which information is organized semantically (see Howe, Cicchetti, Toth, & Cerrito, 2004, for further discussion).

MEMORY DEVELOPMENT AND CHILDHOOD TRAUMA

The question as to whether childhood trauma alters the course of normal memory development is a difficult one to answer and is the subject of a number of ongoing research programs. In this section, we review what is known about this topic by addressing questions concerning the nature of children's memory for stressful and traumatic experiences and whether there is any evidence that traumatized children's basic memory processes have been altered by their trauma experience(s).

Children's Memory for Stressful and Traumatic Experiences

A number of recent reviews have appeared on the topic of children's recollection of stressful and traumatic experiences (e.g., Cordon, Pipe, Sayfan, Melinder, & Goodman, 2004; Howe, 1997, 1998, 2000), and all of them have concluded that, barring accompanying cerebral assault, children can and do remember many of the central elements of a traumatic event. For example, Howe and colleagues (1994, 1995) reported a series of studies in which young (18 months to 5 years) children's memory for an accident and subsequent emergency room treatment was examined immediately (within 2 to 3 days of treatment), after 6 months, and following a 1-year delay. Using free recall as well as open-ended cued recall, Howe et al. found that although details peripheral to the event were forgotten over time, the gist of the event was well remembered even after a 1-year interval. Interestingly, a subset of children who experienced additional emergency room experiences during the retention interval often blended these experiences into a single report (Howe et al., 1995). Although these intrusions did not retroactively interfere with recall of the original experience, an interviewer naïve to the original experience would not have been able to separate the information from the different experiences. Similar findings have been obtained in studies examining children's recall of medical examinations (Bruck, Ceci, Francoeur, & Barr, 1995; Ornstein, Shapiro, Clubb, Follmer, & Baker-Ward, 1997) and memories for anticipated painful medical procedures such as bone marrow transplants (Stuber, Nader, Yasuda, Pynoos, & Cohen, 1991), lumbar punctures (Chen et al., 2000), and the VCUG (Goodman, Quas, Batterman-Faunce, Riddlesberger, & Kuhn, 1994; Merritt et al., 1994). Overall, the findings from studies such as these converge on the conclusion that even recall of traumatic experiences is reconstructive and prone to the same type of errors commonly found in the recall of more mundane events.

Similar conclusions have been reached concerning children's memory for other, naturally occurring traumatic events. For example, children's memory for sniper attacks (Pynoos & Nader, 1989; Schwartz & Kowalski, 1991), hurricanes (Ackil, van Abbema, & Bauer, 2003; Bahrick, Parker, Fivush, & Levitt, 1998; Shaw, Applegate, & Schorr, 1996), earthquakes (Najarian, Goenjian, Pelcovitz, Mandel, & Najarian, 1996), a fatal bus-train collision in Israel (Tyano et al., 1996), attacks during the Gulf War (Dyregov, Gjestad, & Raundalen, 2002; Laor et al., 1997), and imprisonment in Cambodia (Kinzie et al., 1986), although accurate concerning the gist of the traumatic experience, is also subject to significant reconstruction. Not only do children tend to remember traumatic experiences reconstructively, but, like adults, they also experience involuntary, intrusive memories of these events (Malmquist, 1986; Pynoos & Eth, 1984). Such intrusive memories may serve as a warning signal that similar traumatic experiences are about to occur (see Ehlers et al., 2002; Hackmann et al., 2004).

Finally, children's and adults' recollections of childhood abuse (sexual and physical) are not only well remembered, but, as already noted, the probability of remembering tends to increase with the number of abusive incidents (Archdiocesan Commission, 1990; Goleman, 1992; Yapko, 1994). Like memories of natural disasters (Green et al., 1994), recollections of abusive experiences tend to be fairly durable,

being recallable many years later (see Alexander et al., 2005; Femina, Yeager, & Lewis, 1990; Loftus, Polonsky, & Fullilove, 1994; L. M. Williams, 1994). However, such recollections, like all recollections, are subject to reconstructive memorial processes.

Thus, the evidence indicates that, similar to memory for more mundane events, children's memory for traumatic experiences is good for central or gist information even though it is reconstructive in nature. One important difference may be that traumatic experiences are more durable than nontraumatic ones. The reason for this might be that traumatic or stressful memories carry with them some adaptive significance. That is, they can signal impending threat when the appropriate warning stimuli are present in the environment (e.g., Ehlers et al., 2002; Foa & Rothbaum, 1998). The preservation of such memories then helps to assure the organism's survival by assisting in the avoidance of similar threatening events (also see Wiedenmayer, 2004). In addition, such experiences are distinctive and personally significant, qualities that are well-known in autobiographical memory research (Brewer, 1986; Conway, 1996; Howe, 1997) for promoting longevity. More generally, naturally occurring distinctive experiences, as well as those created in the lab, are well-known to be better remembered than less distinct experiences (Howe, in press; Howe et al., 2000). Thus, there is considerable continuity in the memory processes governing recollection of traumatic experiences and those governing more traditionally studied memory experiences. The question that remains, however, is whether these general processes that govern memory and memory development are somehow altered by stressful and traumatic experiences, causing them to differ over time, particularly in children who have experienced chronic stress.

Traumatized Children's Basic Memory Processes

As previously discussed, autobiographical memory can begin as early as 2 years of age, the time at which the cognitive self emerges (Howe, 2004a). Although we will defer discussion of autobiographical memory until the next section, it is of interest to note that the clinical literature is replete with examples of nonverbal indices of traumatic memories from before the age of 2 years in traumatized infants (Gaensbauer, 1995, 2002; Paley & Alpert, 2003; Terr, 1988). Most of these infant memories are revealed during play therapy and, as cautioned earlier, need to be interpreted carefully. In fact, it is not clear that these nonverbal play behaviors represent actual memories as they require considerable prompting to be elicited, are heavily dependent on context (events, places, people, etc.), and may be elicited because of the demand characteristics of the props and context (Cordon et al., 2004; see Howe et al., 1994, for a case study). Generally speaking, then, there is little evidence to substantiate the claim that traumatic experiences are retained, implicitly or explicitly, before the age of 18 to 24 months, and it is very clear that they do not become part of our adult memories for events (L. M. Williams, 1994).

By approximately 2 years of age, children are capable of remembering distinctive and traumatic events. Traumatized children are also capable of remembering events at this age (see the section on autobiographical memory), but the relevant question here is whether these experiences subvert the normal course of memory development. That is, do traumatized and maltreated children's basic memory processes begin to work in ways that are fundamentally different from those of nonmaltreated children?

This question has been addressed in only a handful of studies, most of which have been published only recently. For example, Eisen, Qin, Goodman, and Davis (2002) examined maltreated children's memory and suggestibility about an anogenital examination and clinical assessment. The children, ages 3 to 17 years, had all been referred to an inpatient hospital unit specializing in the assessment of child abuse and neglect. Children were partitioned into three groups: (1) the abuse group that included children who were physically abused, sexually abused, or both; (2) the neglect group that included neglected children and children whose parent had a documented addiction but where there was no indication of abuse; and (3) a nonabused group consisting of children who had been referred to the clinic but where claims of abuse or neglect were not substantiated. Children were administered a series of standard tests (including scales measuring dissociation, memory, and general psychological functioning), measures of stress, and a questionnaire concerning memory for the psychological consultation, including a photo identification task concerning the clinician who conducted the interview. Of particular interest were the children's responses to a questionnaire designed specifically to examine suggestibility in the context of the child's anogenital examination. This contained questions about events that happened (e.g., "Was there a nurse in the doctor's room with you?") as well as misleading questions (e.g., "The nurse took her clothes off, didn't she?").

The results showed the typical age effects in memory, where older children remembered more than younger children and younger children were more susceptible to misleading suggestions than were older children. Of particular importance, maltreated children were no more likely than nonmaltreated children to confuse details about the medical examination. In other words, maltreated children were no more susceptible to suggestion than nonmaltreated control children.

Although maltreatment may not affect children's ability to correctly remember a medical examination or their ability to resist suggestions about the examination, they may be more susceptible to false memories, particularly those that are relatively automatically generated. In particular, if stress and maltreatment result in lowered cognitive inhibition (e.g., it is more difficult to "screen" intrusive memories or selectively attend to only certain aspects of a stimulus display), then maltreated children may be more susceptible to falsely remembering strong semantic associations when memorizing lists of interrelated concepts. Previous research with nonmaltreated children has shown that, unlike suggestibility effects, false memories such as the ones just described (i.e., those obtained using the Deese-Roediger-McDermott or DRM procedure) increase rather than decrease with age in childhood (for a review, see Brainerd & Reyna, 2005). This is because, although such false memories occur relatively automatically, they do depend on children's being able to extract the meaning of not only each individual concept, but also the common meaning across all of the list members. For example, upon hearing (and trying to remember) the list *bed, rest, awake, tired, dream, wake, snooze, blanket, doze, slumber, snore, nap*, older children are more likely to falsely remember *sleep* than younger children.

To see whether maltreated children were more (or less) susceptible to these types of false memories, Howe et al. (2004) examined three groups of children's performance on the DRM task. Specifically, 60 middle-SES children (the children most frequently sampled when studying memory development and false memories in particular), 48 maltreated low-SES children (all of whom had documented physical, sexual, or emotional abuse or were neglected), and 51 nonmaltreated low-SES comparison children (none of whom were abused or neglected) ages 5 to 12 years studied a series of DRM lists. Recall measures were taken following the presentation of each list and a final recognition test was administered after all of the lists had been presented.

The results showed that all of the children exhibited age increases in both true and false memories, consistent with previous research, and that these patterns were the same regardless of maltreatment status. That is, both maltreated and nonmaltreated children exhibited false memories, and the number of false memories increased with age at the same rate. The only differences that emerged were associated with SES. That is, consistent with prior studies, low-SES children exhibited poorer overall performance (lower true and false memories) than did middle-SES children.

To summarize, there is considerable reason to believe that maltreated (abused and neglected) children's basic memory processes should be adversely affected if for no other reason than the chronic stress such children have experienced. However, like the conclusion concerning similar subversive effects on neural development, particularly neural developments relevant to memory performance, empirical findings to date do not substantiate such claims. Although admittedly few studies have been published and there are clearly other basic memory processes that need to be examined, those that have been conducted do not reveal differences in basic memory performance between maltreated children and demographically similar nonmaltreated control children.

Perhaps these differences are more apt to show up in maltreated children's recollections of traumatic experiences themselves. Although we have already seen that children tend to be reasonably accurate at remembering traumatic experiences, due perhaps to their distinctiveness (Howe, in press), there exists a strong theoretical rationale for the belief that these memories, indeed all of autobiographical memory, may be fundamentally different in children who have been maltreated compared to those who have not (Foa & Rothbaum, 1998; Terr, 1988). We examine this belief next in the context of research on children's (maltreated and nonmaltreated) autobiographical memory.

AUTOBIOGRAPHICAL MEMORY

The stress and trauma of child maltreatment (acute or chronic) can be associated with subsequent psychiatric impairment (MacMillan et al., 2001). In particular, child maltreatment is a risk factor for Major Depressive Disorders (Heim & Nemeroff, 2001) and PTSD (Kessler, Sonnega, Bromet, Hughes, & Nelson, 1995). The interaction of individual differences characteristics in stress reactivity, cognitive as well as psychobiological, and child maltreatment are complex and lead to considerable variation in predicting which children will come to have psychopathologies (Delahanty, Nugent, Christopher, & Walsh, 2005; Shea, Walsh, MacMillan, & Steiner, 2005). In fact, diversity in process and outcome is a hallmark of a developmental psychopathology perspective (Cicchetti & Rogosch, 1996). These concepts are important to consider when examining memory in victims of trauma. Rather than focusing on main effect models that look broadly at the effects of

trauma on memory, it is necessary to recognize that not all trauma victims are affected similarly (Cicchetti, 2002; Cicchetti & Toth, 1995). The principle of multifinality suggests that similar experiences of trauma may not affect memory in the same way in different individuals. Thus, for example, it is unlikely that all physically or sexually abused children will evidence similar memory changes. This principle is also useful in addressing seemingly discrepant findings in the literature regarding enhanced versus impaired memory in traumatized populations. Conversely, equifinality suggests that there are multiple pathways to the same outcome. Accordingly, various types of traumatic experiences may eventuate in similar effects on memory.

Despite diversity in process and outcome with respect to the emergence of psychopathology, there are some important implications for memory functioning when these pathologies are a consequence of child maltreatment. In this section, we concentrate on those consequences that are associated with autobiographical memory.

Autobiographical memory begins as early as 18 to 24 months of age (see Howe, 2000, 2004a; Howe & Courage, 1993, 1997; Howe, Courage, & Edison, 2003). As noted in trace-integrity theory, this time corresponds to the point at which children acquire a cognitive sense of self, an important ingredient to organizing memories as autobiographical. That is, although as we have already noted that children have both implicit and explicit memory from very early in life, such memories are fragmentary and somewhat disorganized and are not well retained over time. With the advent of the cognitive self, such memories become organized not just as events but as events that happened to "me." Like all other advances in early memory development, information is better retained, becoming more durable, as it becomes better organized. Once children can use the cognitive self to organize events, autobiographical memory emerges and children's memories of events that happened to them become more stable and durable.

This theory not only is logically appealing but also has received empirical support (see Howe, 2004a; Howe et al., 2003). An interesting feature of this theory is that the onset of the cognitive self, and hence autobiographical memory, appears to be controlled more by maturational factors than by environmental factors. For example, infants who have delayed maturation (e.g., due to Down syndrome, familial mental retardation, Autism) show marked delays in the onset of the cognitive self (Cicchetti, 1991; Hill & Tomlin, 1981; Loveland, 1987, 1993; Mans, Cicchetti, & Sroufe, 1978; Schneider-Rosen & Cicchetti, 1984, 1991; Spiker & Ricks, 1984). These children do acquire a cognitive self if and when they achieve a mental age comparable to that of nondelayed infants who do have a cognitive sense of self. Other recent data have shown a link between the onset of the cognitive self and constitutional factors, such as stress reactivity and temperament (DiBiase & Lewis, 1997; Lewis & Ramsay, 1997). DiBiase and Lewis found that infants with a difficult temperament at 5 months of age were more likely to show earlier acquisition of the cognitive self than were infants with an easy temperament. Lewis and Ramsay found that children with higher stress reactivity (measured in terms of cortisol levels and behavioral responses to inoculations at 2, 4, 6, and 18 months) also had earlier onset of the cognitive self than did those with lower stress reactivity. In contrast, Lewis and Brooks-Gunn (1979) have shown that the onset of the cognitive self is not related to a child's sex, maternal education, family SES, birth order, or number of siblings. Likewise, maltreated infants whose aberrant caretaking environments are associated with delays or deviations in emotional development as it relates to the self are not delayed in the onset of the cognitive self (Cicchetti, 1991; Cicchetti & Beeghly, 1987; Schneider-Rosen & Cicchetti, 1984, 1991), although they do exhibit a more negative reaction to their mirror image (Cicchetti, Beeghly, Carlson, & Toth, 1990; Schneider-Rosen & Cicchetti, 1984, 1991). Thus, the onset of the cognitive self, the critical achievement necessary to kick-start autobiographical memory, is linked more to maturation-constitutional factors than to social-experiential factors. That is, the emergence of the cognitive self and autobiographical memory is associated with maturational achievements and does not appear to be influenced by variations in social or child-care experiences in any obvious way.

Autobiographical memory is, of course, memory for our personal history. When asked to generate detailed personal memories for events, most people can generate fairly specific responses. For example, when a child (or an adult) is presented with the cue word *holiday,* he or she might respond with a fairly specific accounting of a trip to Disney World in Florida (e.g., Hammond & Fivush, 1991). The same cannot be said for people suffering from depression. Such individuals tend to provide an overly general response, such as "I remember enjoying holidays as a child," to autobiographical memory cues. This effect was first discovered in suicidal individuals (J. M. G. Williams & Broadbent, 1986; J. M. G. Williams & Dritschel, 1988) and has subsequently been replicated in other populations of depressed individuals (Brittlebank, Scott, Williams, & Ferrier, 1993; Croll & Bryant, 2000; Dalgleish, Spinks, Yiend, & Kuyken, 2001; Goddard, Dritschel, & Burton, 1996; Henderson, Hargreaves, Gregory, & Williams, 2002;

Kuyken & Dalgleish, 1995; Moore, Watts, & Williams, 1988; Puffet, Jehin-Marchot, Timsit-Berthier, & Timsit, 1991; Wessel, Meeren, Peeters, Arntz, & Merckelbach, 2001; J. M. G. Williams & Scott, 1988), those suffering from Bipolar Disorder (Scott, Stanton, Garland, & Ferrier, 2000), postpsychotic depression (Iqbal, Birchwood, Hemsley, Jackson, & Morris, 2004), adolescent mood disturbances (Swales, Williams, & Wood, 2001), and individuals remitted from Major Depression (Mackinger, Pachinger, Leibetseder, & Fartacek, 2000). Overgenerality of autobiographical memory responses has been found in other clinical populations, including persons suffering from PTSD (McNally, Lasko, Maclin, & Pitman, 1995; McNally, Litz, Prassas, Shin, & Weathers, 1994), Acute Stress Disorder (Harvey, Bryant, & Dang, 1998), Borderline Personality Disorder (Jones et al., 1999; Startup et al., 2001), Obsessive-Compulsive Disorder with comorbid depression (Wilhelm, McNally, Baer, & Florin, 1997), and persecutory delusional patients (Kaney, Bowen-Jones, & Bentall, 1999). These populations all exhibit (or exhibited) significant levels of depression, a history of trauma (particularly childhood trauma), or both. Interestingly, populations that do not have these characteristics do not tend to recall overgeneral autobiographical memories. This latter group includes populations suffering from Seasonal Affective Disorder (Dalgleish et al., 2001), Obsessive-Compulsive Disorder without comorbid depression (Wilhelm et al., 1997), and Generalized Anxiety Disorder (Burke & Mathews, 1992; Wessel et al., 2001), except for those associated with trauma giving rise to PTSD or Acute Stress Disorder.

A variety of explanations have been proposed for why overgeneral retrieval of autobiographical memories occurs in depressed or traumatized populations but not other clinical groups. Although some theories focus on the neurobiological effects of stress, the majority have to do more with cognitive explanations of changes in retrieval patterns than with neurobiologically based problems that necessarily affect the encoding and storage of information. Specifically, J. M. G. Williams (1996) has suggested that autobiographical memory is organized hierarchically (as in Conway & Pleydell-Pearce, 2000). In this model, there are two types of hierarchies in which events are stored and organized: *general categories,* in which information relating to events, people, activities, and places are stored, and *extended time periods,* in which information relating to different life periods, or periods lasting longer than a day, are stored. Within each hierarchy, more specific details are nested. Because information is organized in this top-down fashion, and because retrieval proceeds in a top-down manner, retrieval can be aborted at the highest level before specific information is accessed, leading to overgeneral or generic autobiographical recall. Ending a search prematurely in the general categories hierarchy leads to categoric overgeneral memory, in which participants report a summary of several episodes sharing common features (e.g., "I like theme parks"), whereas ending a search prematurely in the extended time period category leads to an extended overgeneral memory that summarizes several episodes from a common time period (e.g., "I enjoyed holidays as a child"). As it turns out, not only are depressed individuals more likely than nondepressed to produce generic memories than specific ones, but they are also more likely to produce categoric overgeneral recall than extended overgeneral memory, whereas the different generic responses when given by nondepressed individuals are equally common (J. M. G. Williams & Dritschel, 1992).

J. M. G. Williams (1996) attempted to link this model to an early sociolinguistic approach to autobiographical memory in childhood (K. Nelson & Gruendel, 1981) in which children were said to first represent and retrieve events generically.[1] Williams hypothesized that stressful experiences during childhood might have led depressed patients to become "arrested" in their generic retrieval of experiences. That is, they adopt a generic retrieval strategy to avoid specifics of past events and hence reduce the negative affect associated with them.

What aspects of a person's history cause him or her to adopt a retrieval style that stops searching for specific memories and reports only generic information? Studies that have compared prior trauma and depression provide mixed results. First, as we have already indicated, numerous studies (listed earlier) have found that overgeneral autobiographical memories are correlated with depression.

However, what is not clear is whether these effects represent true retrieval effects or simply a more general reluctance to report retrieved memories. That is, specific memories may have been retrieved, but depressed patients are simply less likely to report them to an interviewer than are nondepressed individuals. This is consistent with the finding that depressed individuals exhibit global cognitive and memory deficits due to lapses in attention and motivation (Burt, Zembar, & Niederehe, 1995). Although a promising idea, Wessel, Merckelbach, and Dekkers (2002) reported no such association between standardized measures of memory performance and overgeneral autobiographical memory. A further complication, and one that may suggest that overgeneral memory is not simply a reporting issue, are the findings that depressed individuals do produce specific memories as well as overgeneral ones and sometimes produce more specific memories to negatively valenced cues, sometimes produce more specific memories to positively valenced cues, and sometimes there is no difference between positive and negative cues (see Dalgleish et al., 2003).

The view that overgeneral memory may be the result of trauma, particularly trauma in childhood, is supported by Kuyken and Brewin's (1995) reanalysis of their data set (reported in Dalgleish et al., 2003), in which more overgeneral memories were produced by a clinical sample of individuals who reported having been abused than by those not reporting abuse, even when depressed mood was controlled. The finding that self-reported abuse is linked to overgeneral memory has been replicated in a nonclinical community sample of abuse victims (Henderson et al., 2002). Taken together, these results suggest that self-reported abuse, not depression, may be responsible for overgeneral autobiographical memories. This is consistent with J. M. G. Williams's (1996) suggestion that exposure to psychological trauma in childhood perturbs the normal development of autobiographical memory (for negative experiences primarily, but may also affect recall of positive experiences) and that children learn a specific retrieval style that minimizes recall of specific experiences. Unfortunately, other researchers have not found a similar link between childhood trauma (self-reported or verified) and overgeneral memory. For example, Wessel et al. (2001) found no relationship between early abuse and overgeneral memory but did find one between depression and overgenerality. Similarly, Wessel et al. (2002) found no relationship between overgeneral memory and childhood trauma but did find an association between depression and overgenerality.

---

[1] It is now known that children's event representations, like that of other domains of cognitive functioning, are represented quite specifically in memory and that memory development proceeds from specific, verbatim, contextually driven representations to more general, generic, gist-like representations (Brainerd & Reyna, 2005; Howe, 2000; Mandler, 2004). As well, as we have already described in this chapter, it is also known that even young children's autobiographical memories contain very specific, verbatim details of their experience and are not represented generically (also see Howe, 2000). Of course, although the developmental arrest component of this model is not supported in theory or data, Williams's point that people in some clinical populations report only generic rather than specific autobiographical information is still seen as feasible by some in the clinical literature today.

One reason for these discrepant findings concerning the role of abuse may be that the participants in the different studies suffered from varying severities of abuse. That is, studies that have shown a link between abuse and overgeneral memory (Henderson et al., 2002; Kuyken & Brewin, 1995) have differed from those that have not found this link (Wessel et al., 2001) on a number of dimensions, including severity of abuse and/or the presence/absence of abuse. Although the clinical group in the Wessel et al. (2002) study had been interned in Japanese concentration camps during World War II as children and were no doubt exposed to traumatic events at that time, it is not clear what the overall level of trauma exposure was during the internment. It may be, then, that the latter studies did not evince sufficient levels of abuse to detect a relationship with overgeneral memory. Indeed, when a clinical sample is selected such that levels of reported abuse are likely elevated relative to healthy controls, and who do not suffer from mood disorders, there exists a clear association between abuse and overgeneral memory (Dalgleish et al., 2003). Of course, the limitation with these studies is that the association is between overgeneral autobiographical memory and self-reported abuse and not abuse that has been independently corroborated.

It may be that individuals who have been abused in childhood or those who are depressed exhibit overgeneral memory because they may have something in common; that is, traumatic experiences such as physical and sexual abuse in childhood are often associated with depression in both children and adults (Allen & Tarnowski, 1989; Andrews, Valentine, & Valentine, 1995; Bemporad & Romano, 1992; Bifulco, Brown, & Harris, 1994; Carlin et al., 1994; Cicchetti & Rogosch, 2001; Downey, Feldman, Khuri, & Friedman, 1994; Fox & Gilbert, 1994; Kazdin, Moser, Colbus, & Bell, 1985; Kessler & Magee, 1994; Kuyken & Brewin, 1994, 1995; Sternberg et al., 1993; Stone, 1993; Straus & Kantor, 1994; Toth, Manly, & Cicchetti, 1992). This is consistent with J. M. G. Williams's (1996) idea that early traumatic experience leads to a failure to reduce retrieval inhibition in autobiographical memory. That is, because specific emotional information associated with traumatic events is too painful to reexperience, it is defended against by stopping the retrieval process at the overgeneral level. In the only study to examine these effects in traumatized children, Orbach, Lamb, Sternberg, Williams, and Dawud-Noursi (2001) found that children who had been exposed to family violence produced overgeneral autobiographical memories but only for that subsample who was comorbid for depression. Thus, for children, traumatic experiences alone may not be sufficient for the develop-

ment of overgeneral autobiographical recall. Rather, these traumatic experiences must be accompanied by depression.

Somewhat problematic for J. M. G. Williams's (1996) approach is that the developmental sequence for memory is incorrect. As reviewed earlier, memory development from infancy onward (including autobiographical memory) proceeds from remembering highly specific, contextually bound, verbatim information to learning about more general, categorizable gist-like meanings (Brainerd & Reyna, 2005; Howe, 2000; Rovee-Collier et al., 2001). Thus, we do not proceed from the general to the more specific but go from the specific to the more general (also see note 1). Three additional facts are at odds with Williams's account: (1) Depressed and traumatized individuals do remember specific episodes, not just generic information; in fact, the percentage of memories recalled that are specific always exceeds 50% and often exceeds 75% across studies (see Dalgleish et al., 2003), suggesting that lapses into overgeneral retrieval are the exception rather than the rule; (2) when depressed individuals recall specific information, it is more likely when they are given negative cues than positive cues; and (3) individuals with PTSD tend to have intrusive, specific, and very detailed autobiographical recollections of the event related to PTSD (although there may be a difference between involuntary and voluntary autobiographical recall). In fact, concerning this last point, the rate of memory intrusions tends to be highly correlated with overgenerality in autobiographical recall (Brewin, Reynolds, & Tata, 1999; Wessel et al., 2002). Perhaps this association emerges because some individuals use a repressive coping style to avoid consciously ruminating about traumatic memories, increasing the likelihood that they appear as intrusive recollections. Whatever the case may be, it is clear that an alternative theoretical framework is necessary to accommodate the empirical findings.

In summary, what this review has shown is that similar to more basic neurological and memory processes discussed earlier, although there is good reason to suspect that autobiographical memory processes may be perturbed in the presence of childhood maltreatment and the ensuing psychopathology, the empirical evidence is not consistent with that viewpoint. First, there appear to be no differences in the age of onset of autobiographical memory unless a maturational delay exists (e.g., due to Down syndrome, Autism). Second, although childhood trauma and maltreatment have been linked to an overgeneral reporting bias of autobiographical memories, it is not clear that these effects are related to maltreatment per se or to the comorbidity factors such as depression. Indeed, it is not clear that these effects are memory effects at all and are not simply a more general and global characteristic of depression in which there is frequently a cognitive bias affecting the motivation to participate in tasks or to report memories of experiences. Before we can be certain, considerable research will be needed to sort through these different issues and determine whether changes in autobiographical memory occur as a result of maltreatment or comorbidity factors, and if so, whether such overgeneral reporting is simply a motivational issue consistent with other biases associated with depression or is really a memory retrieval phenomenon.

CONCLUSION AND FUTURE DIRECTIONS

We began this chapter by asking how stress, particularly the chronic stress associated with child maltreatment, affects the development of children's basic memory processes as well as how it affects children's recollection of the stressful and traumatic experiences themselves. Although there are sound theoretical reasons to believe that stress may affect basic memory processes and memory for traumatic experiences (e.g., enhanced consolidation and storage, inhibition of retrieval), the data in hand suggest otherwise. What this review has shown is that the experience of trauma, acute or chronic, does not exert any special effects on memory that fundamentally change the operation of memory from that observed in nontraumatized populations. With that said, however, we want to underscore the fact that research in this area is still in its infancy. Because of the paucity of work in this area, we use the remainder of this chapter to highlight future directions that need to be pursued in order to have confidence that memory operates similarly in traumatized and nontraumatized individuals.

First, and perhaps foremost, we want to emphasize the importance of conducting investigations with individuals who have experienced trauma rather than trying to extrapolate from studies conducted with normal populations or from analogue studies. This recommendation is consistent with developmental psychopathology's commitment to examining atypical as well as normal populations. Unfortunately, historically much of the work on trauma and memory has been conducted with normal populations involved in simulated analogue studies. For example, in investigations of eyewitness testimony, Yuille and Cutshall (1986) reported that between 1974 and 1982, 92% of investigations purporting to examine eyewitness testimony involved college students participating in simulation studies. Much of the early work on false and suggested memories in

children similarly involved simulated studies with normative groups of children (Ceci & Bruck, 1995). Although these studies provide a valuable starting point for examining complex issues, they cannot be viewed as definitive or as the end point. Rather, such studies provide building blocks on which investigations with actual victims of trauma can be initiated. Only when a sufficient body of studies cohere can we truly have confidence about how trauma does, or does not, affect memory.

Related to this, the nature of materials utilized to investigate memory needs to be carefully considered. The normative literature on basic memory provides an excellent point for beginning to determine how memory may operate similarly or differently in traumatized children. However, the fact that memory for standard lists of words utilized with normative populations is not affected by trauma does not mean that memory for emotionally laden words will operate similarly (Rieder & Cicchetti, 1989). Therefore, although beginning with standard memory paradigms allows comparisons with a large normative literature to be made, memory for traumatic material also must be investigated. In this regard, investigations of autobiographical memory may be particularly germane. However, to conduct such investigations, accurate information must be available on the actual event that occurred and on what information an individual recalled immediately following the event. The conduct of such investigations is likely to be particularly challenging and to pose logistic as well as ethical challenges. Immediately following an event, an individual may be involved in investigative and/or court proceedings, and interviews could potentially contaminate the accuracy of the recall of the event. Moreover, over time it might prove to be troubling to an individual to be queried about past trauma. Although utilization of court testimony from the victim and witnesses might provide a window into immediate recall, sensitivity in assessing memory over time is needed. Because it is critically important to enhance our knowledge of autobiographical memory in victims of trauma, the design and conduct of investigations in this arena hold much promise for informing our understanding of trauma and memory.

A number of issues exist in the memory and trauma literature that must be addressed if the field is to move forward in attaining a comprehensive understanding of this important area. A major omission in the extant literature on trauma and memory involves the absence of studies of extreme and chronic stress. It may be that in cases of extreme stress, an event is not stored. However, such a conclusion cannot be drawn in the absence of studies with highly stressed individuals.

The presence of co-occurring risk factors in samples of traumatized individuals has also contributed to difficulty in ascertaining exactly what may be operating to affect memory. For example, in populations who have experienced PTSD, the effects of the trauma on memory per se are confounded with issues such as hospitalization, utilization of medication, the provision of psychotherapy, substance use and abuse, and comorbid mental illness (e.g., depression). Sufficiently large samples with improved control over potentially confounding factors must be conducted to better parse the effects of trauma from other factors.

With the advent of neuroimaging technology, new avenues for examining brain structure and functioning in victims of trauma have emerged. Although such technologies are appealing and may help to elucidate how trauma affects the brain, caution also is in order. Technological advances cannot compensate for the absence of sound theory, careful experimental design, meticulous execution of empirical investigations, and rigorous scientific methodology. It is crucial that these conceptual and methodological issues be placed at the forefront of research on neuroimaging and memory in traumatized populations. Otherwise, it will be unclear whether neuroimaging findings reflect genuine differential physiological processes between traumatized and nontraumatized individuals, whether these processes are merely epiphenomena, or whether these physiological differences represent compensatory or adaptive neurobiological changes (Cicchetti, 2002; Curtis & Cicchetti, 2003; Peterson, 2003). As our understanding of basic memory processes increases, the incorporation of studies involving MRI and fMRI is more likely to yield fruitful results. To date, investigations of brain structure and memory processes have rarely been conducted in the same individuals who have experienced trauma. In the future, it is essential that increasing multiple-levels-of-analysis research on memory and brain structure and function be conducted with traumatized populations.

Although we are increasingly accruing knowledge about trauma and memory, clinical, social policy, and legal implications are inherent in how the questions posed in this chapter are answered. Therefore, a significant responsibility exists to build on current knowledge with normative populations and to design increasingly methodologically rigorous and theoretically sophisticated investigations of trauma and memory. For example, understanding how various types of trauma interact with developmental status to affect memory will be critical for suggesting what type of therapeutic intervention to utilize. Because scientific evidence does not support views that memories can be stored in the body preverbally, efforts to help young trauma victims recall an event that they, in truth, have no knowledge of could prove to be countertherapeutic. Because trauma may actually alter neuronal connections in the brain (Cicchetti, 2002; DeBellis, 2001), therapies that require victims to relive traumatic events might actually consolidate the maladaptive negative neuronal pathways that may be associated with the experience of trauma. The area of "repressed" memory is particularly salient, and much has been written about the perils inherent in therapists' suggestion of trauma to patients who may not consciously recall (or who may not have experienced) such trauma (Loftus & Ketcham, 1994). Given our current state of knowledge regarding trauma and memory, unless children or adults seek help specifically to address their reactions to trauma, caution in exploring such events is indicated.

In the policy and legal arenas, we are beginning to attain evidence that memory in victims of trauma is certainly no worse than in the general population. Conversely, we also do not have reason to believe that memories of trauma are indelible or somehow enhanced, nor are they protected from reconstructive processes common to most, if not all, memories. Again, however, we urge caution, as the seminal studies that can shed light on these issues remain to be conducted.

In closing, we are embarking on a new era of investigations of trauma and memory that will involve actual victims of trauma and that will utilize both basic memory paradigms and those that are likely to be more emotionally arousing. We are guardedly optimistic that such investigations not only will enhance our understanding of the operation of memory in victims of trauma, but also will assist in refining and enhancing developmental theories of memory.

REFERENCES

Abel, T., Alberini, C., Ghirardi, M., Huang, Y.-Y., Nguyen, P., & Kandel, E. R. (1995). Steps toward a molecular definition of memory consolidation. In D. L. Schacter, J. T. Coyle, G. D. Fischbach, M. M. Mesulam, & L. E. Sullivan (Eds.), *Memory distortion* (pp. 298–325). Cambridge, MA: Harvard University Press.

Ackil, J. K., van Abbema, D. L., & Bauer, P. J. (2003). After the storm: Enduring differences in mother-child recollections of traumatic and nontraumatic events. *Journal of Experimental Child Psychology, 84,* 286–309.

Alexander, K. W., Quas, J. A., Goodman, G. S., Ghetti, S., Edelstein, R. S., Redlich, A. D., et al. (2005). Traumatic impact predicts long-term memory for documented child sexual abuse. *Psychological Science, 16,* 33–40.

Allen, D. M., & Tarnowski, K. J. (1989). Depressive characteristics of physically abused children. *Journal of Abnormal Child Psychology, 17,* 1–11.

Amir, N., McNally, R., & Wiegartz, P. S. (1996). Implicit memory bias for threat in posttraumatic stress disorder. *Cognitive Therapy and Research, 20,* 625–635.

Andrews, B., Valentine, E. R., & Valentine, J. D. (1995). Depression and eating disorders following abuse in childhood in two generations of women. *British Journal of Clinical Psychology, 34,* 37–52.

Archdiocesan Commission. (1990). *The report of the Archdiocesan Commission of the inquiry into the sexual abuse of children by members of the clergy* (St. John's Winter Report). Newfoundland, Canada: Archdiocese of St. John's.

Axelson, D., Dorsaiswamy, P., McDonald, W., Boyko, O., Typler, L., Patterson, L., et al. (1993). Hypercortisolemia and hippocampal changes in depression. *Psychiatry Research, 47,* 163–173.

Bahrick, L. E., Parker, J. F., Fivush, R., & Levitt, M. (1998). The effects of stress on young children's memory for a natural disaster. *Journal of Experimental Psychology: Applied, 4,* 308—331.

Bauer, P. J. (1996). What do infants recall of their lives? Memory for specific events by one- and two-year-olds. *American Psychologist, 51,* 29–41.

Bemporad, J. R., & Romano, S. J. (1992). Childhood maltreatment and adult depression: A review of research. In D. Cicchetti & S. L. Toth (Eds.), *Rochester Symposium on Developmental Psychopathology: Vol. 4. Developmental perspectives on depression* (pp. 351–376). Rochester, NY: University of Rochester Press.

Bender, B. G., Lerner, J. A., & Poland, J. E. (1991). Association between corticosteroids and psychologic change in hospitalized asthmatic children. *Annals of Allergy, 66,* 414–419.

Bifulco, A., Brown, G. W., & Harris, T. O. (1994). Childhood Experience of Care and Abuse (CECA): A retrospective interview measure. *Journal of Child Psychology, Psychiatry, and Allied Disciplines, 35,* 1419–1435.

Bjorklund, D. F. (1987). How changes in knowledge base contribute to the development of organization in children's memory: An interpretative review. *Developmental Review, 7,* 93–130.

Bonne, O., Brandes, D., Gilboa, A., Gomori, J. M., Shenton, M. E., Pitman, R. K., et al. (2001). Longitudinal MRI study of hippocampal volume in trauma survivors with PTSD. *American Journal of Psychiatry, 158,* 1248–1251.

Boyce, W. T., Barr, R. G., & Zeltzer, L. K. (1992). Temperament and the psychobiology of childhood stress. *Pediatrics, 90,* 483–486.

Brainerd, C. J., & Reyna, V. F. (2005). *The science of false memory.* New York: Oxford University Press.

Bremner, J. D., Krystal, J. H., Southwick, S. M., & Charney, D. S. (1995). Functional neuroanatomical correlates of the effects of stress on memory. *Journal of Traumatic Stress, 8,* 527–553.

Bremner, J. D., & Narayan, M. (1998). The effects of stress on memory and the hippocampus throughout the life cycle: Implications for child development and aging. *Development and Psychopathology, 10,* 871–885.

Bremner, J. D., Randall, P., Vermetten, E., Staib, L., Bronen, R. A., Mazure, C., et al. (1997). Magnetic resonance imaging-based measurement of hippocampal volume in posttraumatic stress disorder related to childhood physical and sexual abuse: A preliminary report. *Biological Psychiatry, 41,* 23–32.

Bremner, J. D., & Vermetten, E. (2001). Stress and development: Behavioral and biological consequences. *Development and Psychopathology, 13,* 473–489.

Bremner, J. D., Vythilingam, M., Vermetten, E., Southwick, S. M., McGlashan, T., Nazeer, A., et al. (2003). MRI and PET study of deficits in hippocampal structure and function in women with childhood sexual abuse and posttraumatic stress disorder. *American Journal of Psychiatry, 160,* 924–932.

Bremner, J. D., Vythilingam, M., Vermetten, E., Southwick, S. M., McGlashan, T., Staib, L. H., et al. (2003). Neural correlates of declarative memory for emotionally valenced words in women with posttraumatic stress disorder related to early childhood sexual abuse. *Biological Psychiatry, 53,* 879–889.

Brewer, W. F. (1986). What is autobiographical memory? In D. C. Rubin (Ed.), *Autobiographical memory* (pp. 25–49). Cambridge, England: Cambridge University Press.

Brewin, C. R. (2003). *Posttraumatic stress disorder: Malady or myth?* New Haven, CT: Yale University Press.

Brewin, C. R., Andrews, B., & Gotlib, I. (1993). Psychopathology and early experience: A reappraisal of retrospective reports. *Psychological Bulletin, 113,* 82–98.

Brewin, C. R., Reynolds, M., & Tata, P. (1999). Autobiographical memory processes and the course of depression. *Journal of Abnormal Psychology, 108,* 511–517.

Brittlebank, A. D., Scott, J., Williams, J. M. G., & Ferrier, I. N. (1993). Autobiographical memory in depression: State or trait marker? *British Journal of Psychiatry, 162,* 118–121.

Brown, D., Scheflin, A. W., & Hammond, D. C. (1998). *Memory, trauma treatment, and the law.* New York: Norton.

Bruck, M., Ceci, S. J., Francoeur, E., & Barr, R. (1995). I hardly cried when I got my shot! Influencing children's reports about a visit to the pediatrician. *Child Development, 66,* 193–208.

Bugental, D. B., Blue, J., Cortez, V., Fleck, K., & Rodriguez, A. (1992). The influence of witnessed affect on information processing in children. *Child Development, 63,* 774–786.

Burke, M., & Mathews, A. (1992). Autobiographical memory and clinical anxiety. *Cognition and Emotion, 6,* 23–35.

Burt, D. B., Zembar, M. J., & Niederehe, G. (1995). Depression and memory impairment: A meta-analysis of the association, its pattern, and specificity. *Psychological Bulletin, 117,* 285–305.

Cahill, L. (2000). Modulation of long-term memory storage in humans by emotional arousal: Adrenergic activation and the amygdala. In J. P. Aggleton (Ed.), *The amygdala: A functional analysis* (pp. 425–445). Oxford: Oxford University Press.

Cahill, L., & McGaugh, J. L. (1996). Modulation of memory storage. *Current Opinion in Neurobiology, 6,* 237–242.

Cahill, L., & McGaugh, J. L. (1998). Mechanisms of emotional arousal and lasting declarative memory. *Trends in Neuroscience, 21,* 294–299.

Cahill, L., Prins, B., Weber, M., & McGaugh, J. L. (1994). ß-adrenergic activation and memory for emotional events. *Nature, 371,* 702–704.

Carlin, A. S., Kemper, K. J., Ward, N. G., Sowell, H., Gustafson, B., & Stevens, N. (1994). The effect of differences in objective and subjective definitions of childhood physical abuse on estimates of its incidence and relationship to psychopathology. *Child Abuse and Neglect, 18,* 393–399.

Ceci, S. J., & Bruck, M. (1995). *Jeopardy in the courtroom: A scientific analysis of children's testimony.* Washington, DC: American Psychological Association.

Charney, D. S., Deutch, A. Y., Krystal, J. H., Southwick, S. M., & Davis, M. (1993). Psychobiologic mechanisms of posttraumatic stress disorder. *Archives of General Psychology, 50,* 294–305.

Chen, E., Zeltzer, L. K., Craske, M. G., & Katz, E. R. (2000). Children's memories for painful cancer treatment procedures: Implications for distress. *Child Development, 71,* 933–947.

Cicchetti, D. (1991). Fractures in the crystal: Developmental psychopathology and the emergence of the self. *Developmental Review, 11,* 271–287.

Cicchetti, D. (2002). The impact of social experience on neurobiological systems: Illustration from a constructivist view of child maltreatment. *Cognitive Development, 17,* 1407–1428.

Cicchetti, D., & Beeghly, M. (1987). Symbolic development in maltreated youngsters: An organizational perspective. *New Directions for Child Development, 36,* 47–68.

Cicchetti, D., Beeghly, M., Carlson, V., & Toth, S. (1990). The emergence of the self in atypical populations. In D. Cicchetti & M.

Beeghly (Eds.), *The self in transition: Infancy to childhood* (pp. 309–344). Chicago: University of Chicago Press.

Cicchetti, D., & Cohen, D. J. (Eds.). (1995a). *Developmental psychopathology: Vol. 1. Theory and method.* New York: Wiley.

Cicchetti, D., & Cohen, D. J. (Eds.). (1995b). *Developmental psychopathology: Vol. 2. Risk, disorder, and adaptation.* New York: Wiley.

Cicchetti, D., & Rogosch, F. A. (1996). Equifinality and multifinality in developmental psychopathology. *Development and Psychopathology, 8,* 597–600.

Cicchetti, D., & Rogosch, F. A. (2001). The impact of child maltreatment and psychopathology upon neuroendocrine functioning. *Development and Psychopathology, 13,* 783–804.

Cicchetti, D., & Toth, S. L. (1995). A developmental psychopathology perspective on child abuse and neglect. *Journal of the American Academy of Child and Adolescent Psychiatry, 34,* 541–565.

Cloitre, M., Cancienne, J., Brodsky, B., Dulit, R., & Perry, S. W. (1996). Memory performance among women with parental abuse histories: Enhanced directed forgetting or directed remembering? *Journal of Abnormal Psychology, 105,* 204–211.

Conway, M. A. (1996). Autobiographical knowledge and autobiographical memories. In D. C. Rubin (Ed.), *Remembering our past: Studies in autobiographical memory* (pp. 67–93). New York: Cambridge University Press.

Conway, M. A., & Pleydell-Pearce, C. (2000). The construction of autobiographical memories in the self-memory system. *Psychological Review, 107,* 261–268.

Cordon, I. M., Pipe, M.-E., Sayfan, L., Melinder, A., & Goodman, G. S. (2004). Memory for traumatic experiences in early childhood. *Developmental Review, 24,* 101–132.

Croll, S., & Bryant, R. A. (2000). Autobiographical memory in postnatal depression. *Cognitive Therapy and Research, 24,* 419–426.

Curtis, W. J., & Cicchetti, D. (2003). Moving research on resilience into the 21st century: Theoretical and methodological considerations in examining the biological contributors to resilience. *Development and Psychopathology, 15,* 773–810.

Dalgleish, T. (2004). Cognitive approaches to posttraumatic stress disorder: The evolution of multirepresentational theorizing. *Psychological Bulletin, 130,* 228–260.

Dalgleish, T., Spinks, H., Yiend, J., & Kuyken, W. (2001). Autobiographical memory style in seasonal affective disorder and its relationship to future symptom remission. *Journal of Abnormal Psychology, 110,* 335–340.

Dalgleish, T., Tchanturia, K., Serpell, L., Hems, S., Yiend, J., de Silva, P., et al. (2003). Self-reported parental abuse relates to autobiographical memory style in patients with eating disorders. *Emotion, 3,* 211–222.

Dash, P. K., Hebert, A. E., & Runyan, J. D. (2004). A unified theory for systems and cellular memory consolidation. *Brain Research Reviews, 45,* 30–37.

DeBellis, M. D. (2001). Developmental traumatology: The psychological development of maltreated children and its implications for research, treatment, and policy. *Development and Psychopathology, 13,* 539–564.

DeBellis, M. D., Chrousos, G. P., Dorn, L. D., Burke, L., Helmers, K., Kling, M. A., et al. (1994). Hypothalamic-pituitary-adrenal axis dysregulation in sexually abused girls. *Journal of Clinical Endocrinology and Metabolism, 78,* 249–255.

DeBellis, M. D., Hall, J., Boring, A., Frustaci, K., & Moritz, G. (2001). A pilot longitudinal study of hippocampal volumes in pediatric maltreatment-related posttraumatic stress disorder. *Biological Psychiatry, 50,* 305–309.

DeBellis, M. D., & Keshaven, M. S. (2003). Sex differences in brain maturation in maltreatment-related pediatric posttraumatic stress disorder. *Neuroscience and Biobehavioral Reviews, 27,* 103–117.

DeBellis, M. D., Keshaven, M. S., Clark, D. B., Casey, B. J., Giedd, J. N., Boring, A. M., et al. (1999). Developmental traumatology: Part II. Brain development. *Biological Psychiatry, 45,* 1271–1284.

Delahanty, D. L., Nugent, N. R., Christopher, N. C., & Walsh, M. (2005). Initial urinary epinephrine and cortisol levels predict acute PTSD symptoms in child trauma victims. *Psychoneuroendocrinology, 30,* 121–128.

Dempster, F. N. (1988). The spacing effect: A case study in the failure to apply the results of psychological research. *American Psychologist, 43,* 627–634.

de Quervain, D. J.-F., Roozendaal, B., & McGaugh, J. L. (1998). Stress and glucocorticoids impair retrieval of long-term spatial memory. *Nature, 394,* 780–787.

Diamond, D. M., Fleshner, M., Ingersoll, N., & Rose, G. M. (1996). Psychological stress impairs spatial working memory: Relevance to electrophysiological studies of hippocampal function. *Behavioral Neuroscience, 110,* 661–672.

DiBiase, R., & Lewis, M. (1997). The relation between temperament and embarrassment. *Cognition and Emotion, 11,* 259–271.

Dickerson, S. S., & Kemeny, M. E. (2004). Acute stressors and cortisol responses: A theoretical integration and synthesis of laboratory research. *Psychological Bulletin, 130,* 355–391.

Downey, G., Feldman, S., Khuri, J., & Friedman, S. (1994). Maltreatment and childhood depression. In W. M. Reynolds & H. F. Johnson (Eds.), *Handbook of depression in children and adolescents: Issues in clinical child psychology* (pp. 481–508). New York: Plenum Press.

Drummey, A. B., & Newcombe, N. S. (2002). Developmental changes in source memory. *Developmental Science, 5,* 502–513.

Dyregov, A., Gjestad, R., & Raundalen, M. (2002). Children exposed to warfare: A longitudinal study. *Journal of Traumatic Stress, 15,* 59–68.

Ehlers, A., Hackmann, A., Steil, R., Clohessy, S., Wenninger, K., & Winter, H. (2002). The nature of intrusive memories after trauma: The warning signal hypothesis. *Behavior Research and Therapy, 40,* 995–1002.

Eich, E. (1995). Searching for mood dependent memory. *Psychological Science, 6,* 67–75.

Eich, E., Macaulay, D., Loewenstein, R. J., & Dihle, P. H. (1997). Memory, amnesia, and dissociative identity disorder. *Psychological Science, 8,* 417–422.

Eisen, M. L., Qin, J., Goodman, G. S., & Davis, S. L. (2002). Memory and suggestibility in maltreated children: Age, stress, arousal, dissociation, and psychopathology. *Journal of Experimental Child Psychology, 83,* 167–212.

Elsesser, K., Sartory, G., & Tackenberg, A. (2004). Attention, heart rate, and startle response during exposure to trauma-relevant pictures: A comparison of recent trauma victims and patients with posttraumatic stress disorder. *Journal of Abnormal Psychology, 113,* 289–301.

Engleberg, E., & Christianson, S.-A. (2002). Stress, trauma, and memory. In M. L. Eisen, J. A. Quas, & G. S. Goodman (Eds.), *Memory and suggestibility in the forensic interview* (pp. 143–164). Mahwah, NJ: Erlbaum.

Femina, D. D., Yeager, C. A., & Lewis, D. O. (1990). Child abuse: Adolescent records vs. adult recall. *Child Abuse and Neglect, 14,* 227–231.

Field, N. P., Classen, C., Butler, L. D., Koopman, C., Zarcone, J., & Spiegel, D. (2001). Revictimization and information processing in women survivors of childhood sexual abuse. *Journal of Anxiety Disorders, 15,* 459–469.

Fitzpatrick, K. M., & Boldizar, J. P. (1993). The prevalence and consequences of exposure to violence among African-American youth.

Journal of the American Academy of Child and Adolescent Psychiatry, 32, 424–430.

Foa, E. B., & Kozak, M. J. (1991). Emotional processing: Theory, research, and clinical implications of anxiety disorders. In J. D. Safran & L. S. Greenberg (Eds.), *Emotion, psychotherapy, and change* (pp. 21–49). New York: Guilford Press.

Foa, E. B., & Rothbaum, B. O. (1998). *Treating the trauma of rape.* New York: Guilford Press.

Foa, E. B., Steketee, G., & Rothbaum, B. O. (1989). Behavioral/cognitive conceptualizations of post-traumatic stress disorder. *Behavior Research and Therapy, 20,* 155–176.

Fox, K. M., & Gilbert, B. O. (1994). The interpersonal and psychological functioning of women who experienced childhood physical abuse, incest, and parental alcoholism. *Child Abuse and Neglect, 18,* 849–858.

Freyd, J. (1996). *Betrayal trauma.* Cambridge, MA: Harvard University Press.

Freyd, J., DePrince, A. P., & Zurbriggen, E. L. (2001). Self-reported memory for abuse depends upon victim-perpetrator relationship. *Journal of Trauma and Dissociation, 2,* 5–16.

Gaensbauer, T. J. (1995). Trauma in the preverbal period: Symptoms, memories, and developmental impact. *Psychoanalytic Study of the Child, 49,* 412–433.

Gaensbauer, T. J. (2002). Representations of trauma in infancy: Clinical and theoretical implications for the understanding of early memory. *Infant Mental Health Journal, 23,* 259–277.

Goddard, L., Dritschel, B., & Burton, A. (1996). Role of autobiographical memory in social problem solving and depression. *Journal of Abnormal Psychology, 105,* 609–616.

Gold, P. E., & McCarty, R. C. (1995). Stress regulation of memory processes: Role of peripheral catecholamines and glucose. In M. J. Friedman, D. S. Charney, & A. Y. Deutch (Eds.), *Neurobiological and clinical consequences of stress* (pp. 151–162). Philadelphia: Lippincott-Raven.

Goleman, D. (1992, July 21). Childhood trauma: Memory or invention? *New York Times,* p. B5.

Goodman, G. S., Ghetti, S., Quas, J. A., Edelstein, R. S., Alexander, K. W., Redlich, A. D., et al. (2003). A prospective study of memory for child sexual abuse: New findings relevant to the repressed-memory controversy. *Psychological Science, 14,* 113–118.

Goodman, G. S., & Quas, J. A. (1997). Trauma and memory: Individual differences in children's recounting of a stressful experience. In N. L. Stein, P. A. Ornstein, B. Tversky, & C. J. Brainerd (Eds.), *Memory for everyday and emotional events* (pp. 267–294). Mahwah, NJ: Erlbaum.

Goodman, G. S., Quas, J. A., Batterman-Faunce, J. M., Riddlesberger, M. M., & Kuhn, J. (1994). Predictors of accurate and inaccurate memories of traumatic events experienced in childhood. *Consciousness and Cognition, 3,* 269–294.

Green, B. L., Grace, M. C., Vary, M. G., Kramer, T. L., Cleser, G. C., & Leonard, A. C. (1994). Children of disaster in the second decade: A 17-year follow-up study of Buffalo Creek survivors. *Journal of the American Academy of Child and Adolescent Psychiatry, 33,* 71–79.

Greenough, W. T., & Black, J. E. (1999). Experience, neural plasticity, and psychological development. In N. A. Fox, L. A. Leavitt, & J. G. Warhol (Eds.), *The role of early experience in infant development* (pp. 29–40). Pompton Plains, NJ: Johnson & Johnson Pediatric Institute.

Greenough, W. T., Black, J. E., & Wallace, C. S. (1987). Experience and brain development. *Child Development, 58,* 539–559.

Greyson, B. (2000). Near-death experiences. In E. Cardena, S. J. Lynn, & S. Krippner (Eds.), *Varieties of anomolous experience: Examining the scientific evidence* (pp. 315–352). Washington, DC: American Psychological Association.

Gunnar, M. R., Tout, K., de Haan, M., Pierce, S., & Stansbury, K. (1997). Temperament, social competence, and adrenocortical activity in preschoolers. *Developmental Psychobiology, 31,* 65–85.

Hackmann, A., Ehlers, A., Speckens, A., & Clark, D. M. (2004). Characteristics and content of intrusive memories in PTSD and their changes with treatment. *Journal of Traumatic Stress, 17,* 231–240.

Hammond, N. R., & Fivush, R. (1991). Memories of Mickey Mouse: Young children recount their trip to Disneyworld. *Cognitive Development, 6,* 433–448.

Hart, J., Gunnar, M., & Cicchetti, D. (1996). Altered neuroendocrine activity in maltreated children related to symptoms of depression. *Development and Psychopathology, 8,* 201–214.

Harvey, A. G., Bryant, R. A., & Dang, S. T. (1998). Autobiographical memory in acute stress disorder. *Journal of Consulting and Clinical Psychology, 66,* 500–506.

Heim, C., & Nemeroff, C. B. (2001). The role of childhood trauma in the neurobiology of mood and anxiety disorders: Preclinical and clinical studies. *Biological Psychiatry, 49,* 1023–1039.

Henderson, D., Hargreaves, I., Gregory, S., & Williams, J. M. G. (2002). Autobiographical memory and emotion in a nonclinical sample of women with and without a reported history of childhood sexual abuse. *British Journal of Clinical Psychology, 41,* 129–141.

Herman, J. L. (1981). *Father-daughter incest.* Cambridge, MA: Harvard University Press.

Hill, S., & Tomlin, C. (1981). Self-recognition in retarded children. *Child Development, 52,* 145–150.

Holmes, E. A., Grey, N., & Young, K. A. D. (2005). Intrusive images and "hotspots" of trauma memories in posttraumatic stress disorder: An exploratory investigation of emotions and cognitive themes. *Journal of Behavior Therapy and Experimental Psychiatry, 36,* 3–17.

Howe, M. L. (1995). Interference effects in young children's long-term retention. *Developmental Psychology, 31,* 579–596.

Howe, M. L. (1997). Children's memory for traumatic experiences. *Learning and Individual Differences, 9,* 153–174.

Howe, M. L. (1998). Individual differences in factors that modulate storage and retrieval of traumatic memories. *Development and Psychopathology, 10,* 681–698.

Howe, M. L. (2000). *The fate of early memories: Developmental science and the retention of childhood experiences.* Washington, DC: American Psychological Association.

Howe, M. L. (2002). The role of intentional forgetting in reducing children's retroactive interference. *Developmental Psychology, 38,* 3–14.

Howe, M. L. (2004a). Early memory, early self, and the emergence of autobiographical memory. In D. Beike, J. M. Lampinen, & D. A. Behrend (Eds.), *The self and memory* (pp. 45–72). New York: Psychology Press.

Howe, M. L. (2004b). The role of conceptual recoding in reducing children's retroactive interference. *Developmental Psychology, 40,* 131–139.

Howe, M. L. (in press). The role of distinctiveness in children's memory. In R. R. Hunt & J. Worthen (Eds.), *Distinctiveness and human memory.* New York: Oxford University Press.

Howe, M. L., Cicchetti, D., Toth, S. L., & Cerrito, B. (2004). True and false memories in maltreated children. *Child Development, 75,* 1402–1417.

Howe, M. L., & Courage, M. L. (1993). On resolving the enigma of infantile amnesia. *Psychological Bulletin, 113,* 305–326.

Howe, M. L., & Courage, M. L. (1997). The emergence and early development of autobiographical memory. *Psychological Review, 104,* 499–523.

Howe, M. L., & Courage, M. L. (2004). Demystifying the beginnings of memory. *Developmental Review, 24,* 1–5.

Howe, M. L., Courage, M. L., & Edison, S. (2003). When autobiographical memory begins. *Developmental Review, 23,* 471–494.

Howe, M. L., Courage, M. L., & Peterson, C. (1994). How can I remember when "I" wasn't there: Long-term retention of traumatic experiences and emergence of the cognitive self. *Consciousness and Cognition, 3,* 327–355.

Howe, M. L., Courage, M. L., & Peterson, C. (1995). Intrusions in preschoolers' recall of traumatic childhood events. *Psychonomic Bulletin and Review, 2,* 130–134.

Howe, M. L., Courage, M. L., Vernescu, R., & Hunt, M. (2000). Distinctiveness effects in children's long-term retention. *Developmental Psychology, 36,* 778–792.

Howe, M. L., & O'Sullivan, J. T. (1990). The development of strategic memory: Coordinating knowledge, metamemory, and resources. In D. F. Bjorklund (Ed.), *Children's strategies: Contemporary views of cognitive development* (pp. 129–155). Hillsdale, NJ: Erlbaum.

Huttenlocher, P. R. (1999). Synaptogenesis in human cerebral cortex and the concept of critical periods. In N. A. Fox, L. A. Leavitt, & J. G. Warhol (Eds.), *The role of early experience in infant development* (pp. 15–28). Pompton Plains, NJ: Johnson & Johnson Pediatric Institute.

Iqbal, Z., Birchwood, M., Hemsley, D., Jackson, C., & Morris, E. (2004). Autobiographical memory and post-psychotic depression in first episode psychosis. *British Journal of Clinical Psychology, 43,* 97–104.

Ito, Y., Teicher, M. H., Glod, C. A., & Ackerman, E. (1998). Preliminary evidence for aberrant cortical development in abused children: A quantitative EEG study. *Journal of Neuropsychiatry and Clinical Neuroscience, 10,* 298–307.

Ito, Y., Teicher, M. H., Glod, C. A., Harper, D., Magnus, E., & Gelbard, H. A. (1993). Increased prevalence of electrophysiological abnormalities in children with psychological, physical, and sexual abuse. *Journal of Neuropsychiatry and Clinical Neuroscience, 5,* 401–408.

Izquierdo, I., & Medina, J. H. (1997). The biochemistry of memory formation and its regulation by hormones and neuromodulators. *Psychobiology, 25,* 1–9.

Johnson, M. H. (1997). *Developmental cognitive neuroscience.* Cambridge, MA: Blackwell.

Johnson, M. H. (2000). Functional brain development in infants. *Child Development, 71,* 75–81.

Johnston-Brooks, C. H., Lewis, M. A., Evans, G. W., & Whalen, C. K. (1998). Chronic stress and illness in children: The role of allostatic load. *Psychosomatic Medicine, 60,* 597–603.

Jones, B., Heard, H. L., Startup, M., Swales, M. A., Williams, J. M. G., & Jones, R. (1999). Autobiographical memory, dissociation, and parasuicide in borderline personality disorder. *Psychological Medicine, 29,* 1397–1404.

Kagan, J. (1994). *Galen's prophecy: Temperament in human nature.* New York: Basic Books.

Kaney, S., Bowen-Jones, K., & Bentall, R. P. (1999). Persecutory delusions and autobiographical memory. *British Journal of Clinical Psychology, 38,* 97–102.

Kazdin, A. E., Moser, J., Colbus, D., & Bell, R. (1985). Depressive symptoms among physically abused and psychiatrically disturbed children. *Journal of Abnormal Psychology, 94,* 298–307.

Keane, T. M., Fairbank, J. P., & Caddell, J. M. (1985). A behavioral approach to assessing and treating posttraumatic stress disorder in Vietnam veterans. In C. R. Figley (Ed.), *Trauma and its wake: The study and treatment of posttraumatic stress disorder* (pp. 257–294). New York: Brunner/Mazel.

Keenan, P. A., Jacobson, M. W., Soleymani, R. M., & Newcomer, J. W. (1995). Commonly used therapeutic doses of glucocorticoids impair explicit memory. *Annals of the New York Academy of Sciences, 761,* 400–402.

Kemeny, M. E. (2003). The psychobiology of stress. *Current Directions in Psychological Science, 12,* 124–129.

Kerr, D., Campbell, L., Applegate, M., Brodish, A., & Landfield, P. (1991). Chronic stress-induced acceleration of electrophysiologic and morphometric biomarkers of hippocampal aging. *Journal of Neuroscience, 11,* 1316–1322.

Kessler, R. C., & Magee, W. J. (1994). Childhood family violence and adult recurrent depression. *Journal of Health and Social Behavior, 35,* 13–27.

Kessler, R. C., Sonnega, A., Bromet, E., Hughes, M., & Nelson, C. B. (1995). Posttraumatic stress disorder in the National Comorbidity Survey. *Archives of General Psychiatry, 52,* 1048–1060.

Kety, S. S. (1970). The biogenic amines in the central nervous system: Their possible role in arousal, emotion, and learning. In F. O. Schmitt (Ed.), *The neurosciences: Second study program* (324–335). New York: Rockefeller University Press.

Kinzie, J. D., Sack, W. H., Angell, R. H., Manson, S., & Rath, B. (1986). The psychiatric effects of massive trauma on Cambodian children: I. The children. *Journal of the American Academy of Child and Adolescent Psychiatry, 25,* 370–376.

Kitchigina, V., Vankov, A., Harley, C., & Sara, S. J. (1997). Novelty-elicited, noradrenaline-dependent enhancement of excitability in the dentate gyrus. *European Journal of Neuroscience, 9,* 41–47.

Kopf, S. R., & Baratti, C. M. (1995). Memory-improving actions of glucose: Improvement of a central cholinergic mechanism. *Behavioral and Neural Biology, 62,* 237–243.

Korneyev, A. Y. (1997). The role of hypothalamic-pituitary-adrenocortical axis in memory-related effects of anxiolytics. *Neurobiology of Learning and Memory, 67,* 1–13.

Kuyken, W., & Brewin, C. R. (1994). Intrusive memories of childhood abuse during depressive episodes. *Behavior Research and Therapy, 32,* 525–528.

Kuyken, W., & Brewin, C. R. (1995). Autobiographical memory functioning in depression and reports of early abuse. *Journal of Abnormal Psychology, 104,* 585–591.

Kuyken, W., & Dalgleish, T. (1995). Autobiographical memory and depression. *British Journal of Clinical Psychology, 33,* 89–92.

Lanius, R. A., Williamson, P. C., Densmore, M., Boksman, K., Gupta, M. A., Neufeld, R. W., et al. (2001). Neural correlates of traumatic memories in posttraumatic stress disorder: A functional MRI investigation. *American Journal of Psychiatry, 158,* 1920–1922.

Lanius, R. A., Williamson, P. C., Densmore, M., Boksman, K., Neufeld, R. W., Gati, J. S., et al. (2004). The nature of traumatic memories: A 4-T fMRI functional connectivity analysis. *American Journal of Psychiatry, 161,* 36–44.

Lanius, R. A., Williamson, P. C., Hopper, J., Densmore, M., Boksman, K., Gupta, M. A., et al. (2003). Recall of emotional states in posttraumatic stress disorder: An fMRI investigation. *Biological Psychiatry, 53,* 204–210.

Laor, N., Wolmer, L., Mayes, L. C., Gershon, A., Weizman, R., & Cohen, D. J. (1997). Israeli preschool children under Scuds: A 30-month follow-up. *Journal of the American Academy of Child and Adolescent Psychiatry, 36,* 349–356.

Lewis, M., & Brooks-Gunn, J. (1979). *Social cognition and the acquisition of self.* New York: Plenum Press.

Lewis, M., & Ramsay, D. (1997). Stress reactivity and self-recognition. *Child Development, 68,* 621–629.

Loftus, E. F., & Ketcham, K. (1994). *The myth of repressed memory.* New York: St. Martin's Press.

Loftus, E. F., Loftus, G. R., & Messo, J. (1987). Some facts about "weapon focus." *Law and Human Behavior, 11,* 55–62.

Loftus, E. F., Polonsky, S., & Fullilove, M. T. (1994). Memories of childhood sexual abuse: Remembering and repressing. *Psychology of Women Quarterly, 18,* 67–84.

Loveland, K. (1987). Behavior of young children with Down syndrome before the mirror: Finding things reflected. *Child Development, 58,* 928–936.

Loveland, K. (1993). Autism, affordances, and the self. In U. Neisser (Ed.), *The perceived self* (pp. 237–253). New York: Cambridge University Press.

Lupien, S. J., Lecours, A., Lussier, I., Schwartz, G., Nair, N., & Meany, M. (1994). Basalcortisol levels and cognitive deficits in human aging. *Journal of Neuroscience, 14,* 2893–2903.

Lupien, S. J., & McEwen, B. S. (1997). The acute effects of glucocorticoids on cognition: Integration of animal and human model studies. *Brain Research Reviews, 24,* 1–27.

Lustig, C., & Hasher, L. (2001). Implicit memory is not immune to interference. *Psychological Bulletin, 127,* 618–628.

Mackinger, H. F., Pachinger, M. M., Leibetseder, M. M., & Fartacek, R. R. (2000). Autobiographical memories in women remitted from major depression. *Journal of Abnormal Psychology, 109,* 331–334.

MacMillan, H., Fleming, J. E., Streiner, D. L., Lin, E., Boyle, M. H., Jamieson, E., et al. (2001). Childhood abuse and lifetime psychopathology in a community sample. *American Journal of Psychiatry, 158,* 1878–1883.

Malinowsky-Rummell, R., & Hansen, D. J. (1993). Long-term consequences of childhood physical abuse. *Psychological Bulletin, 114,* 68–79.

Malmquist, C. P. (1986). Children who witness parental murder: Posttraumatic aspects. *Journal of the American Academy of Child and Adolescent Psychiatry, 25,* 320–325.

Mandler, J. M. (2004). *The foundations of mind.* New York: Oxford University Press.

Mans, L., Cicchetti, D., & Sroufe, L. A. (1978). Mirror reaction of Down syndrome toddlers: Cognitive underpinnings of self recognition. *Child Development, 49,* 1247–1250.

McEwen, B. S., & Sapolsky, R. M. (1995). Stress and cognitive function. *Current Opinion in Neurobiology, 5,* 205–216.

McEwen, B. S., & Schmeck, H. M. (1994). *The hostage brain.* New York: Rockefeller University Press.

McGaugh, J. L. (1995). Emotional activation, neuromodulatory systems, and memory. In D. Schacter, J. T. Coyne, G. D. Fischbach, M.-M. Mesulam, & L. E. Sullivan (Eds.), *Memory distortion* (pp. 255–273). Cambridge, MA: Harvard University Press.

McGaugh, J. L. (2000). Memory: A century of consolidation. *Science, 287,* 248–251.

McGaugh, J. L. (2003). *Memory and emotion.* London: Weidenfeld & Nicholson.

McGaugh, J. L., Cahill, L., & Roozendaal, B. (1996). Involvement of the amygdala in memory storage: Interaction with other brain systems. *Proceedings of the National Academy of Science, USA, 93,* 13508–13514.

McNally, R. J. (2003). *Remembering trauma.* Cambridge, MA: Harvard University Press.

McNally, R. J., Lasko, N. B., Maclin, M. L., & Pitman, R. K. (1995). Autobiographical memory disturbance in combat-related posttraumatic stress disorder. *Behavior Research and Therapy, 33,* 619–630.

McNally, R. J., Litz, B. T., Prassas, A., Shin, L. M., & Weathers, F. W. (1994). Emotional priming and autobiographical memory in posttraumatic stress disorder. *Cognition and Emotion, 8,* 351–368.

McNally, R. J., Metzger, L. J., Lasko, N. B., Clancy, S. A., & Pitman, R. K. (1998). Directed forgetting of trauma cues in adult survivors of childhood sexual abuse with and without posttraumatic stress disorder. *Journal of Abnormal Psychology, 107,* 596–601.

Merritt, K. A., Ornstein, P. A., & Spicker, B. (1994). Children's memory for a salient medical procedure: Implications for testimony. *Pediatrics, 94,* 17–23.

Mizoguchi, K., Kunishita, T., Chui, D., & Tabira, T. (1992). Stress induces neuronal death in the hippocampus of castrated rats. *Neuroscience Letters, 138,* 157–164.

Moore, R. G., Watts, F. N., & Williams, J. M. G. (1988). The specificity of personal memories in depression. *British Journal of Clinical Psychology, 27,* 275–276.

Morrison, P. D., Allardyce, J., & McKane, J. P. (2002). Fear knot: Neurobiological disruption of long-term memory. *British Journal of Psychiatry, 180,* 195–197.

Nachmias, M., Gunnar, M., Manglesdorf, S., Parritz, R. H., & Buss, K. (1996). Behavioral inhibition and stress reactivity: The moderating role of attachment security. *Child Development, 67,* 508–522.

Nader, K., Schafe, G. E., & LeDoux, J. E. (2000). Fear memories require protein synthesis in the amygdala for reconsolidation after retrieval. *Nature, 406,* 722–726.

Najarian, L. M., Goenjian, A. K., Pelcovitz, D., Mandel, E., & Najarian, B. (1996). Relocation after a disaster: Posttraumatic stress disorder in Armenia after the earthquake. *Journal of the American Academy of Child and Adolescent Psychiatry, 35,* 374–383.

Nasrallah, H., Coffman, J., & Olson, S. (1989). Structural brain-imaging findings in affective disorders: An overview. *Journal of Neuropsychiatry and Clinical Neuroscience, 1,* 21–32.

Nelson, C. A. (1995). The ontogeny of human memory: A cognitive neuroscience perspective. *Developmental Psychology, 31,* 723–738.

Nelson, C. A. (1997). The neurobiological basis of early memory development. In N. Cowan (Ed.), *The development of memory in early childhood* (pp. 41–82). Hove, East Sussex, England: Psychology Press.

Nelson, C. A. (2000). Neural plasticity in human development: The role of early experience in sculpting memory systems. *Developmental Science, 3,* 115–130.

Nelson, K., & Gruendel, J. (1981). Generalized event representation: Basic building blocks of cognitive development. In M. Lamb & A. Brown (Eds.), *Advances in developmental psychology* (Vol. 1, pp. 131–158). Hillsdale, NJ: Erlbaum.

Newcomer, J. W., Craft, S., Hershey, T., Askins, K., & Bardgett, M. E. (1994). Glucocorticoid-induced impairment in declarative memory performance in adult humans. *Journal of Neuroscience, 14,* 2047–2053.

Nielson, K. A., & Jensen, R. A. (1994). Beta-adrenergic receptor antagonist antihypertensive medications impair arousal-induced modulation of working memory in elderly humans. *Behavioral and Neural Biology, 62,* 190–200.

Oades, R. D. (1979). Search and attention: Interactions of the hippocampal-septal axis, adrenalcortical, and gonadal hormones. *Neuroscience and Biobehavioral Reviews, 3,* 31–48.

Orbach, Y., Lamb, M. E., Sternberg, K. J., Williams, J. M. G., & Dawud-Noursi, S. (2001). The effect of being a victim or witness of family violence on the retrieval of autobiographical memories. *Child Abuse and Neglect, 25,* 1427–1437.

Ornstein, P. A., Shapiro, L. R., Clubb, P. A., Follmer, A., & Baker-Ward, L. (1997). The influence of prior knowledge on children's memory for salient medical experiences. In N. L. Stein, P. A. Ornstein, B. Tversky & C. J. Brainerd (Eds.), *Memory for everyday and emotional events* (pp. 83–112). Mahwah, NJ: Erlbaum.

Orr, S. P., Metzger, L. J., & Pitman, R. K. (2002). Psychophysiology of posttraumatic stress disorder. *Psychiatric Clinics of North America, 25,* 271–293.

Paley, J., & Alpert, J. (2003). Memory of infant trauma. *Psychoanalytic Psychology, 20,* 329–347.

Parks, E. D., & Balon, R. (1995). Autobiographical memory for childhood events: Patterns of recall in psychiatric patients with a history of alleged trauma. *Psychiatry, 58,* 199–208.

Paunovic, N., Lundh, L.-G., & Oest, L.-G. (2002). Attentional and memory bias for emotional information in crime victims with acute posttraumatic stress disorder. *Journal of Anxiety Disorders, 16,* 675–692.

Pederson, C. L., Maurer, S. H., Kaminski, P. L., Zander, K. A., Peters, C. M., Stokes-Crowe, L. A., et al. (2004). Hippocampal volume and memory performance in a community-based sample of women with posttraumatic stress disorder secondary to child abuse. *Journal of Traumatic Stress, 17,* 37–40.

Pelcovitz, D., Kaplan, S., Goldenberg, B., Mandel, F., Lehane, J., & Guarrera, J. (1994). Post-traumatic stress disorder in physically abused adolescents. *Journal of the American Academy of Child and Adolescent Psychiatry, 33,* 305–312.

Pelletier, J. G., & Pare, D. (2004). Role of amygdala oscillations in the consolidation of emotional memories. *Biological Psychiatry, 55,* 559–562.

Peterson, B. S. (2003). Conceptual, methodological, and statistical challenges in brain imaging studies of developmentally based psychopathologies. *Development and Psychopathology, 15,* 811–832.

Porges, S. W. (1997). Emotion: An evolutionary by-product of the neural regulation of the autonomic nervous system. In C. S. Carter, I. Lederhendler, & B. Kirkpatrick (Eds.), *The integrative neurobiology of affiliation* (pp. 62–77). New York: New York Academy of Sciences.

Puffet, A., Jehin-Marchot, D., Timsit-Berthier, M., & Timsit, M. (1991). Autobiographical memory and major depressive states. *European Psychiatry, 6,* 141–145.

Pugh, C. R., Tremblay, D., Fleshner, M., & Rudy, J. W. (1997). A selective role for corticosterone in contextual-fear conditioning. *Behavioral Neuroscience, 111,* 503–511.

Pynoos, R. S., & Eth, S. (1984). The child as witness to homicide. *Journal of Social Issues, 2,* 87–104.

Pynoos, R. S., & Nader, K. (1989). Children's memory and proximity to violence. *Journal of the American Academy of Child and Adolescent Psychiatry, 28,* 236–241.

Quas, J. A., Bauer, A., & Boyce, W. T. (2004). Physiological reactivity, social support, and memory in early childhood. *Child Development, 75,* 797–814.

Raine, A., Venables, P. H., & Mednick, S. A. (1997). Low resting heart rate at age 3 years predisposes to aggression at age 11 years: Evidence from the Mauritius Child Health Project. *Journal of the American Academy of Child and Adolescent Psychiatry, 36,* 1457–1464.

Richards, J. E., & Casey, B. J. (1991). Heart rate variability during attention phases in young infants. *Psychophysiology, 28,* 43–53.

Richter-Levin, G., & Akirav, I. (2003). Emotional tagging of memory formation: In the search for neural mechanisms. *Brain Research Reviews, 43,* 247–256.

Rieder, C., & Cicchetti, D. (1989). An organizational perspective on cognitive control functioning and cognitive affective balance in maltreated children. *Developmental Psychology, 25,* 382–393.

Roediger, H. L., III, & Bergman, E. T. (1998). The controversy over recovered memories. *Psychology, Public Policy, and Law, 4,* 1091–1109.

Rovee-Collier, C., Hayne, H., & Columbo, M. (2001). *The development of implicit and explicit memory.* Amsterdam, The Netherlands: John Benjamins.

Russell, D. E. H. (1999). *The secret trauma: Incest in the lives of girls and women* (Rev. ed.). New York: Basic Books.

Sapolsky, R. M., Krey, L., & McEwen, B. S. (1985). Prolonged glucocorticoid exposure reduces hippocampal neuron number: Implications for aging. *Journal of Neuroscience, 5,* 1121–1127.

Sapolsky, R. M., Romero, M., & Munck, A. U. (2000). How do glucocorticoids influence stress responses? Integrating permissive, suppressive, stimulatory, and preparative actions. *Endocrine Reviews, 21,* 55–89.

Sapolsky, R. M., Uno, H., Rebert, C. S., & Finch, C. E. (1990). Hippocampal damage associated with prolonged glucocorticoid exposure in primates. *Journal of Neuroscience, 10,* 2897–2902.

Scarpa, A. (1997). Aggression in physically abused children: The interactive role of emotion regulation. In A. Raine, P. A. Brennan, D. Farrington, & S. A. Mednick (Eds.), *Biosocial bases of violence* (pp. 341–343). New York: Plenum Press.

Schacter, D., Koustaal, W., & Norman, K. A. (1996). Can cognitive neuroscience illuminate the nature of traumatic childhood memories? *Current Opinion in Neurobiology, 6,* 207–214.

Schiffer, F., Teicher, M. H., & Papanicolaou, A. C. (1995). Evoked potential evidence for right brain activity during the recall of traumatic memories. *Journal of Neuropsychiatry and Clinical Neuroscience, 7,* 169–175.

Schneider, W., & Pressley, M. P. (1997). *Memory development between two and twenty* (2nd ed.). Mahwah, NJ: Erlbaum.

Schneider-Rosen, K., & Cicchetti, D. (1984). The relationship between affect and cognition in maltreated infants: Quality of attachment and the development of visual self-recognition. *Child Development, 55,* 648–658.

Schneider-Rosen, K., & Cicchetti, D. (1991). Early self-knowledge and emotional development: Visual self-recognition and affective reactions to mirror self-images in maltreated and non-maltreated infants. *Developmental Psychology, 27,* 471–478.

Schwartz, E. D., & Kowalski, J. M. (1991). Malignant memories: PTSD in children and adults after a school shooting. *Journal of the American Academy of Child and Adolescent Psychiatry, 30,* 936–944.

Scott, J., Stanton, B., Garland, A., & Ferrier, I. N. (2000). Cognitive vulnerability in patients with bipolar disorder. *Psychological Medicine, 30,* 467–472.

Shaw, J. A., Applegate, B., & Schorr, C. (1996). Twenty-one month follow-up study of school-age children exposed to Hurricane Andrew. *Journal of the American Academy of Child and Adolescent Psychiatry, 35,* 359–364.

Shea, A., Walsh, C., MacMillan, H., & Steiner, M. (2005). Child maltreatment and HPA axis dysregulation: Relationship to major depressive disorder and post traumatic stress disorder in females. *Psychoneuroendocrinology, 30,* 162–178.

Spiker, D., & Ricks, M. (1984). Visual self-recognition in autistic children: Developmental relationships. *Child Development, 55,* 214–225.

Squire, L. R., Cohen, N., & Nadel, L. (1984). The medial temporal region and memory consolidation: A new hypothesis. In H. Weingartner & E. Parker (Eds.), *Memory consolidation* (pp. 87–105). Hillsdale, NJ: Erlbaum.

Sroufe, L. A., & Rutter, M. (1984). The domain of developmental psychopathology. *Child Development, 55,* 17–29.

Starkman, M. N., Gebarski, S., Berent, S., & Schteingart, D. (1992). Hippocampal formation volume, memory dysfunction, and cortisol levels in patients with Cushing's syndrome. *Biological Psychiatry, 32,* 756–765.

Startup, M., Heard, H., Swales, M., Jones, B., Williams, J. M. G., & Jones, R. S. P. (2001). Autobiographical memory and parasuicide in borderline personality disorder. *British Journal of Clinical Psychology, 40,* 113–120.

Stein, M. B. (1997). Hippocampal volume in women victimized by childhood sexual abuse. *Psychological Medicine, 27,* 951–959.

Stein, N., & Boyce, W. T. (1995, April). The role of physiological reactivity in attending to, remembering, and responding to an emotional event. In G. Goodman & L. Baker-Ward (Chairs), *Children's memory for emotional and traumatic events.* Symposium conducted at the Society for Research in Child Development Meetings, Indianapolis, IN.

Stein, N., & Liwag, M. D. (1997). Children's understanding, evaluation, and memory for emotional events. In P. van den Broek, P. Bauer, & T. Bourg (Eds.), *Developmental spans in event comprehension and representation: Bridging fictional and actual events* (pp. 199–235). Mahwah, NJ: Erlbaum.

Sterlini, G. L., & Bryant, R. A. (2002). Hyperarousal and dissociation: A study of novice skydivers. *Behavior Research Therapy, 40,* 431–437.

Sternberg, K. J., Lamb, M. E., Greenbaum, C., Cicchetti, D., Dawud, S., Cortes, R. M., et al. (1993). Effects of family violence on children's behavior problems and depression. *Developmental Psychology, 29,* 44–52.

Stone, N. M. (1993). Parental abuse as a precursor to childhood onset depression and suicidality. *Child Psychiatry and Human Development, 24,* 13–24.

Straus, M. A., & Kantor, G. K. (1994). Corporal punishment of adolescents by parents: A risk factor in the epidemiology of depression, suicide, alcohol abuse, child abuse, and wife beating. *Adolescence, 29,* 543–561.

Stuber, M. L., Nader, K., Yasuda, P., Pynoos, R. S., & Cohen, S. (1991). Stress responses after pediatric bone marrow transplantation: Preliminary results of a prospective longitudinal study. *Journal of the American Academy of Child and Adolescent Psychiatry, 30,* 952–957.

Suess, P. E., Porges, S. W., & Plude, D. J. (1994). Cardiac vagal tone and sustained attention in school-age children. *Psychophysiology, 31,* 17–22.

Swales, M. A., Williams, J. M. G., & Wood, P. (2001). Specificity of autobiographical memory and mood disturbance in adolescents. *Cognition and Emotion, 15,* 321–331.

Teicher, M. H. (1994). Early abuse, limbic system dysfunction, and borderline personality disorder. In K. Silk (Ed.), *Biological and neurobehavioral studies of borderline personality disorder* (pp. 177–207). Washington, DC: American Psychiatric Press.

Teicher, M. H., Dumont, N. L., Ito, Y., Vaituzis, C., Giedd, J. N., & Andersen, S. L. (2004). Childhood neglect is associated with reduced corpus callosum area. *Biological Psychiatry, 56,* 8085.

Teicher, M. H., Ito, Y., Glod, C. A., Andersen, S. L., Dumont, N., & Ackerman, E. (1997). Preliminary evidence for abnormal cortical development in physically and sexually abused children using EEG coherence and MRI. *Annals of the New York Academy of Science, 821,* 160–175.

Terr, L. (1988). What happens to early memories of trauma? A study of twenty children under age five at the time of documented events. *Journal of the American Academy of Child and Adolescent Psychiatry, 27,* 96–104.

Terr, L. (1994). *Unchained memories: True stories of traumatic memories, lost and found.* New York: Basic Books.

Thomas, L. A., & De Bellis, M. D. (2004). Pituitary volumes in pediatric maltreatment-related posttraumatic stress disorder. *Biological Psychiatry, 55,* 752–758.

Toth, S. L., Manly, J. T., & Cicchetti, D. (1992). Child maltreatment and vulnerability to depression. *Development and Psychopathology, 4,* 97–112.

Tyano, S., Iancu, I., Solomon, Z., Sever, J., Goldstein, I., Touveiana, Y., et al. (1996). Seven-year follow-up of child survivors of a bus-train collision. *Journal of the American Academy of Child and Adolescent Psychiatry, 35,* 365–373.

Uno, H., Ross, T., Else, J., Suleman, M., & Sapolsky, R. M. (1989). Hippocampal damage associated with prolonged and fatal stress in primates. *Journal of Neuroscience, 9,* 1705–1711.

Van der Kolk, B. (1994). The body keeps the score: Memory and the evolving psychobiology of posttraumatic stress. *Harvard Review of Psychiatry, 1,* 253–265.

Van der Kolk, B., & Fisler, R. (1995). Dissociation and the fragmentary nature of traumatic memories: Overview and exploratory study. *Journal of Traumatic Stress, 8,* 505–525.

Watanabe, Y., Gould, E., & McEwen, B. S. (1992). Stress induces atrophy of apical dendrites of hippocampus CA3 pyramidal neurons. *Brain Research, 588,* 341–344.

Wessel, I., Meeren, M., Peeters, F., Arntz, A., & Merckelbach, H. (2001). Correlates of autobiographical memory specificity: The role of depression, anxiety, and childhood trauma. *Behavior Research and Therapy, 39,* 409–421.

Wessel, I., Merckelbach, H., & Dekkers, T. (2002). Autobiographical memory specificity, intrusive memory, and general memory skills in Dutch-Indonesian survivors of the World War II era. *Journal of Traumatic Stress, 15,* 227–234.

Wiedenmayer, C. P. (2004). Adaptations or pathologies? Long-term changes in brain and behavior after a single exposure to severe threat. *Neuroscience and Biobehavioral Reviews, 28,* 1–12.

Wilhelm, S., McNally, R. J., Baer, L., & Florin, I. (1997). Autobiographical memory in obsessive-compulsive disorder. *British Journal of Clinical Psychology, 36,* 21–32.

Williams, J. M. G. (1996). Depression and the specificity of autobiographical memory. In D. C. Rubin (Ed.), *Remembering our past: Studies in autobiographical memory* (pp. 244–267). New York: Cambridge University Press.

Williams, J. M. G., & Broadbent, K. (1986). Autobiographical memory in suicide attempters. *Journal of Abnormal Psychology, 95,* 144–149.

Williams, J. M. G., & Dritschel, B. H. (1988). Emotional disturbance and the specificity of autobiographical memory. *Cognition and Emotion, 2,* 221–234.

Williams, J. M. G., Mathews, A., & MacLeod, C. (1996). The emotional Stroop task and psychopathology. *Psychological Bulletin, 120,* 3–24.

Williams, J. M. G., & Scott, J. (1988). Autobiographical memory in depression. *Psychological Medicine, 18,* 689–695.

Williams, L. M. (1994). Recall of childhood trauma: A prospective study of women's memories of child sexual abuse. *Journal of Consulting and Clinical Psychology, 62,* 1167–1176.

Wolkowitz, O. M., Reus, V. I., Weingartner, H., Thompson, K., Breier, A., Doran, A., et al. (1990). Cognitive effects of corticosteroids. *American Journal of Psychiatry, 147,* 1297–1303.

Woolley, C. S., Gould, E., & McEwen, B. S. (1990). Exposure to excess glucocorticoids alters dendritic morphology of adult hippocampal pyramidal neurons. *Brain Research, 531,* 225–231.

Yapko, M. (1994). *Suggestions of abuse: Real and imagined memories.* New York: Simon & Schuster.

Yuille, J. C., & Cutshall, J. (1986). Analysis of statements of victims, witnesses, and suspects. In J. C. Yuille (Ed.), *Credibility assessment: NATO Advanced Institutes Series [Series D: Behavioral and social sciences]* (Vol. 47, pp. 175–191). New York: Kluwer Academic/ Plenum Press.

Zola, S. M. (1997). The neurobiology of recovered memory. *The Journal of Neuropsychiatry and Clinical Neuroscience, 9,* 449–459.

CHAPTER 16

Traumatic Stress from a Multiple-Levels-of-Analysis Perspective

J. DOUGLAS BREMNER

Traumatic stress is ubiquitous in our society and represents an enormous public health burden (Kessler & Magee, 1993). Psychological traumas are unique in standing at the crossroads of mind, body, psyche, the individual, and society. As such, trauma can be approached from a variety of perspectives, including biological, genetic, psychological, social, philosophical, literary, and artistic. To fully understand the effects of trauma on the individual, one must consider biological consequences of stress, effects on the individual's psychology, spirit, and character, and the impact on the family, community, and culture. Thus, it is necessary to look at traumatic stress from multiple perspectives at the same time.

Some aspects of the trauma response act as mediators or moderators of other outcomes. For example, spirituality or culture may affect Posttraumatic Stress Disorder (PTSD) outcome, and amygdala sensitivity may (theoretically) influence acute anxiety and chronic stress-related disorders like PTSD. Traumatic stress can also lead to a range of mental health outcomes that have been termed

The work presented in this review was supported by grants from the National Institute of Mental Health (MH56120), the Emory Conte Center for Early Life Stress, and the Department of Veterans Affairs Traumatic Stress from Multiple Levels of Analysis.

trauma-spectrum disorders (Bremner, 1999, 2002a), including PTSD, depression, dissociation, anxiety, substance abuse, and eating disorders. This multitude of outcomes is an illustration of the principle of multifinality: one cause leading to multiple outcomes (Cicchetti & Rogosch, 1996).

The multiple-layers approach to trauma requires a focus on development. Trauma can lead to a succession of diverse outcomes as the individual moves through childhood and adolescence to adulthood (Feiring & Lewis, 1996). It is also possible that individuals can end up at the same place but travel different paths. As an example, studies of women with depression show that some were abused in childhood and others were not, suggesting that depression may be related to abuse in some individuals, and other factors (e.g., genetics) may contribute to depression in other individuals. Furthermore, in these studies there were important biological differences in the different groups; for example, the abused depressed women had smaller hippocampal volume (Vythilingam et al., 2002) and potentiated cortisol reactions to stress (Heim et al., 2000). This suggests that one can arrive at the final depression end point by two different paths, for example, early abuse or inherent disposition. Emerging evidence shows that these subtypes have different treatment responses; for example, depression due to early abuse responds more to therapy and less to medication. Thus, looking at a problem such as traumatic stress from multiple levels has clinical relevance.

Richters and Hinshaw (1999) have argued that the development of the American Psychiatric Association's (APA, 2000) *Diagnostic and Statistical Manual of Mental Disorders* (*DSM-IV-TR*) represented an abduction of psychological distress into the realm of disorder. Psychological symptoms and mental distress were described as manifestations of primary diseases that, by definition, represented underlying dysfunction in the individual (Wakefield, 1999). This viewpoint made sense and explained much of what clinicians were seeing, but like all easy fixes, it had a downside. Although it fit the medical model, where a specific disease is associated with a specific pathogen, and allowed psychiatrists and psychologists to share a common language with medical doctors and claim common cause, there was never an easy fit. First of all, the model never fully described the phenomena. Not everything about patients with psychological complaints can be defined by the single disease model. Because of this, practitioners had to abandon the model in the real world even though they pretended to follow the model to retain the approval of the experts in their own field. Although taught to diagnose a single condition and apply a single remedy, many clinicians treat clusters of symptoms, or respond to patients on a one-to-one basis. Second, psychiatry has never been fully incorporated into the medical fold, perhaps because of the suspicion that the disorders treated by psychiatrists were fundamentally different from physical conditions, or because of qualms about the scientific foundation for the disorders. In fact, whenever the pathophysiological basis of a disorder in the psychiatry realm is nailed down, it is spirited away to the physical side of medicine. Take the case of Parkinson's disease, which only belatedly was discovered to be due to a degeneration of dopamine neurons in the striatum, or epilepsy, found to be due typically to lesions in the hippocampus rather than possession by evil spirits.

The so-called abduction of disorder has had several consequences. First, it does not fully describe all of the phenomena. Rather than reconsider the paradigm, the response to this has been to add more diagnoses, leading to exponential growth in the size of successive editions of the *DSM*. Second, the disease model implies that each disease is unique and does not overlap with other diseases; however, this has never been the case in psychiatry. Third, inherent in the disease model is the idea that every specific disease has a specific treatment, and the education of clinicians in the proper identification of disease would lead to the proper application of medication treatment. Never mind the fact that the treatment is always the same (i.e., selective serotonin reuptake inhibitors [SSRIs] for all mood and anxiety disorders). Although the *DSM* was developed by psychiatrists, it was marketed by the pharmaceutical industry, for whom the expansion of diagnosis (and therefore treatment) was in their best interest; therefore, if we are to follow the trail of clues to discover who is the source of abduction of disorder in psychiatry, it would have to lead back to that source.

Traumatic stress can also be viewed from the larger philosophical perspective. All behaviors have to have some evolutionary advantage in order to be preserved. The withdrawal and decreased interest in things that occurs after trauma may have had an evolutionary advantage. For example, individuals under constant threat may have withdrawn more, which may have had survival value. Remember, survival was based on ability to live long enough to reproduce the species, not to have a long life span.

The abduction of disorder by psychiatry has led to the current, somewhat silly situation in which clinicians pay lip service to psychiatric diagnosis because they think it is what the experts expect of them, but in reality do whatever they want. In the academic arena, there is an equally absurd situation, where diagnoses are expected to be "pure" and without comorbidity, leading investigators on a silly goose chase to mollify their readership and get their papers published and grants funded. What is worse, some misguided investigators, in the search for a pure disorder, perform studies on patient groups that are so unusual that they have no applicability to the patients who actually present to clinical practice. However, increasingly findings from the biological arena are not supporting the specificity of disorders; this has led some to think about the comorbidity issue as something other than their "problem." In fact, fields such as genetics and brain imaging, which are empirically based, rather than validating the single, discrete disease model, as they are expected to do, may actually open things up to a more rich appreciation of our patients. That is, they may facilitate the multiple-levels-of-analysis approach.

One area of investigation that may turn the whole issue on its head is the emerging field of the relationship between physical health and mental disorders. Studies have shown that stress, PTSD, and depression can increase the risk of several physical disorders, including heart disease, cancer, infection, diabetes, and asthma. In fact, it is increasingly clear that for many patients presenting to their doctors with a range of mental conditions, there are profound lifestyle, spiritual, and traumatic factors that lie behind their diseases. In many cases, those factors are simply ignored. Rather than asking for psychiatry to be medicalized, maybe we should be asking medicine to be psychiatrized. That may be better in the long run for patients.

In trying to move beyond the gridlock created by the abduction of disorder, it helps to have a perspective on mental disorders that goes beyond the current *DSM* era. This chapter reviews the long history of research in the traumatic stress area of psychiatry and an even longer history of recognition of the effects of traumatic stress in popular culture that predates the *DSM* era. This chapter argues that, to understand the complete effects of traumatic stress, it is necessary to understand the effects of trauma on the individual psyche, in the context of the individual within society, on the brain, individual physiology, and physical health, predisposition, risk factors, and resiliency—in other words, a multiple-levels-of-analysis perspective.

10,000 YEARS OF TRAUMA

Most research in the area of traumatic stress has taken place in the past 20 years, since the establishment of PTSD as a diagnosis in the *DSM* in 1980 (APA, 1980). However, there is a long history of work in the field of traumatic stress, going back to 1830, with the first description of what was called "railway spine" or railway injuries in England. This was a disorder that occurred after train accidents and was described as involving problems with memory, pain in the back, confusion, amnesia, and increased anxiety—many of the symptoms that today we would call PTSD. The etiology of railway spine was felt to be related to contusions of the spine, which were below the ability of pathological diagnosis to detect. A paper in *Lancet* appeared describing railway spine as a disorder of railway injury without physical trauma. This was the first description of an effect on the individual of a psychological trauma in which there was not actually a physical injury. Subsequently, Erichsen (1866/2001) wrote a book on *Railway and Other Injuries of the Spine* describing in detail the effects of railway injuries.

In parallel with developments in England, the first patients with trauma-related disorders were being recognized in Germany. The German psychiatrist Oppenheim (2001) first described traumatic neurosis, in which a traumatic event leads to long-term symptoms. Oppenheim said that psychological stress or extreme shock could lead to long-term changes in physiology that were unrelated to an actual physical injury, but actually caused changes in physiology in the brain.

With the advent of the First World War in Germany, Italy, and England, shell shock was first described, in which people would forget their name or who they were or where they were on the battlefield. Shell shock was felt to be caused by the shock of exploding shells. However, psychiatrists soon realized that shell shock could occur even when soldiers were far from an exploding shell. This led to the idea that shell shock might be related to psychological trauma.

Things changed in psychiatry at that time as Freud's (1995) view of the psychoneuroses gained predominance. With Freud, there was more of an emphasis on the unconscious and fantasy, and the idea of traumatic neurosis lost favor. In addition, there was an emphasis on keeping soldiers on the battlefield, and psychiatrists were discouraged from providing diagnoses that explained soldiers' inability to perform on the battlefield. This added to the demise of traumatic neurosis. In the middle part of the twentieth century, psychoanalysis dominated in the United States and there was no trauma-specific diagnosis such as PTSD.

The rise of biological psychiatry in the United States laid the foundations for examining the physical role in the development of symptoms whose etiology is emotional trauma. Initially, the biological psychiatrists focused on Schizophrenia as being a "real" disorder and left the neuroses to the psychoanalysts. However, with *DSM-III* (1980) the neuroses were written out of the psychiatric nomenclature and replaced with a plethora of specific mood and anxiety disorders. The veterans returning from the Vietnam War in the 1970s became a potent political group that lobbied for recognition. This led to the description of a Vietnam War syndrome that captured the suffering of many veterans related to their war-time experiences. Debate went back and forth about whether war-time experiences caused the veterans' symptoms or preexisting personality problems were responsible. At the core of the debate was whether war caused mental disorders, with the implications for whether the government should be responsible for the disabilities of veterans. The development of rating scales allowed researchers to show a correlation between trauma severity and symptom outcomes (Keane, Caddell, & Taylor, 1988; Keane, Wolfe, & Taylor, 1987), leading to a total triumph of the war etiology group. This led to the inclusion of PTSD in the *DSM-III* in 1980, emphasizing for the first time in the twentieth century the central role of trauma.

PTSD has always been unique in requiring a trauma exposure for the diagnosis, even though other disorders, such as the dissociative disorders, are just as strongly linked to trauma exposure. This requirement for trauma exposure, called Criteria A in *DSM-III,* involved exposure to an event beyond the range of normal human experience. However it quickly became apparent that many traumas are fairly common, so in *DSM-IV,* there is the requirement of exposure to a threat to life, to self, or significant other accompanied by intense fear, horror, or helplessness (Saigh & Bremner, 1999). Traumatic stress so defined affects more than half of the U.S. population.

The creation of the diagnosis allowed biological research on PTSD and also controlled trials of treatment with medication or psychotherapy. The acknowledgment of PTSD in veterans led to research on child sexual trauma in the United States.

Throughout all of this history there is a pattern of multiple threads moving parallel to one another but never really connecting and informing one another. For instance, the false memory thread developed oblivious to the biological correlates of the PTSD thread, even though they had information that was mutually informative. Sometimes this is driven by institutional or disciplinary chauvinism (e.g., who are the "real scientists" or the "real researchers," or alternatively, who is doing "relevant" research). Like all forms of prejudice, this type of thinking helps to keep things orderly and risk-free but limits the capacity to think outside the box. An analysis from multiple levels implicitly crosses these boundaries and offers a different perspective, moving toward the goalposts that the National Institutes of Health "road map" has been nudging us toward.

THE FAUSTIAN BARGAIN OF THE *DIAGNOSTIC AND STATISTICAL MANUAL III*

Although the development of the *DSM-III* resulted in greater research and recognition in the field of traumatic stress, in some sense it has been a Faustian bargain. To throw out the old psychoanalytic system, the Faustian bargain of *DSM-III* was to allow no theoretical or etiological constructs to come into play in the development of the individual psychiatric syndromes. Although *DSM-III* provided crisper definitions of mental disorders, it also sold the concept of multiple stand-alone mental disorders, defined only by the face value of their presenting symptoms. In cases where the same symptoms were identical between disorders, they were simply reworded to appear unique to the disorder. For example, rather than state that veterans could reexperience a traumatic event in a dissociated state with elements of derealization, depersonalization, and amnesia, much as a childhood abuse victim does, it was stated that

veterans experienced "flashbacks," which were felt to be unique to the veteran experience. Implicit in this was a desire to fight for the diagnosis of the veteran with PTSD as being distinct from other disorders, such as dissociative disorders, that could drag the whole enterprise down with it. The result was a poor understanding by clinicians of the symptoms, their etiology, and phenomenology. Needless to say, the drug companies had a field day with this plethora of diagnoses, as it boosted sales of their antidepressants, and hurried to train clinicians in the new diagnoses as well as, of course, the new treatments to be applied.

In an editorial (Bremner, 1999) and later in *Does Stress Damage the Brain?* (Bremner, 2002a), I argued for the concept of trauma-spectrum psychiatric disorders, or a grouping of disorders with a common link to trauma. In this model, stress acting against a background of genetic predisposition and a history of prior stressors (which we know increases the risk for psychopathology with retraumatization) leads to a number of psychiatric disorders, including PTSD. There is overlap between symptoms of PTSD, depression, dissociation, Borderline Personality Disorder, and other stress-related disorders. Symptoms of flashbacks seen in PTSD are really dissociative phenomena. Amnesia and identity disturbance are seen in personality disorders, PTSD, and dissociative disorders. I advocated for disorders related to trauma being included in a separate diagnostic category. PTSD is an anxiety disorder, in a separate category from dissociative disorders, although it shares in common with dissociative disorders the trauma ideology and has less in common with such disorders as Obsessive-Compulsive Disorder. According to this argument, there are not separate distinct disorders, but instead a single spectrum of disorders that have been improperly categorized as distinct by our current diagnostic schema.

TRAUMA AND THE SELF

The development of the *DSM* represented an embrace of the one disease, and by implication, one etiology model. In the case of psychological trauma, the one disease was PTSD and the etiology was the trauma. Trauma was construed as something like a bacterium that caused an infection and could be treated by a single drug. This represented a medicalization of trauma. However, it ignored the profound effect that traumatic experiences have on the self, character, psyche, and the individual in society and culture.

Psychological trauma can lead to more than the development of specific psychiatric disorders: It can have a major impact on our total way of viewing the world and ourselves that transcends a specific disorder. We all have an illusion that the world is a safe and just place. That's because we need such an illusion to survive. The world would be a terrible place if we could foresee the future, if we knew everything that was going to happen to us. It is our ignorance of the true nature of the world that keeps us sane. Traumatized patients with the diagnosis of PTSD often do not see the world as a safe place. A woman who has a child snatched from her arms by a kidnapper will forever after live with the knowledge that anyone at any time could suddenly take another of her children from her. Someone who was taken hostage will never feel safe walking down a city street.

Not only individuals but entire nations and cultures can be traumatized as well. We saw that play out on a national scale with 9/11. Studies in the aftermath of 9/11 demonstrated that the amount of time spent watching TV was correlated with poor mental outcomes. In other words, the media of this country had become the agent of traumatization. The media also extended the reach of the trauma far beyond the immediate vicinity of Manhattan. More recently, we have had the worldwide traumatization of the tsunami in the Indian Ocean.

By its very nature, trauma extends beyond the individual and takes political and societal dimensions. Terrorists recognize the political potential of psychological trauma and use it well. Terrorists target aspects of life that we take for granted, such as the public mail system and public transportation, in an effort to jolt us out of a sense of safety and security. By doing things like sending anthrax in the mail, terrorists create a sense of national fear, where everyone is hanging on every piece of news, trying to understand what is happening and to protect themselves. The anthrax scare effectively created a traumatic event for the entire nation, as every one, to varying degrees, feels the potential threat of receiving infected mail.

GENETIC CONTRIBUTIONS TO TRAUMA-INDUCED PSYCHOPATHOLOGY

When considering the trauma response from multiple levels it is important to assess the role of genetics. Twin pair studies offer an ideal method for examining the contribution of genetic and environmental factors to variables such as the trauma response. By definition, monozygotic (identical) twins share the same genetic material, and dizygotic (fraternal) twins share 50% of the same genetic material. In addition, because these twins share the same household, they have shared environmental experiences. Therefore, twins

are similar for all variables except the variable of interest. The Vietnam Era Twin Registry has been used for studies of the relative contribution of genetics and environment to trauma-related psychopathology (Eisen, Neuman, Goldberg, Rice, & True, 1989; Goldberg, True, Eisen, Henderson, & Robinette, 1987; Henderson et al., 1990). The Registry consists of 7,375 male-male twin pairs born between 1939 and 1957 with both brothers having served in the U.S. military during the Vietnam era (Henderson et al., 1990). The Twin Registry categorizes pairings where only one brother was in combat in Vietnam, neither went to Vietnam, and both went to Vietnam (Goldberg et al., 1987). By examining all possible combinations of twins, it is possible to determine the relative role of genetics and environment in the development of trauma-related outcomes such as PTSD. Using these methods, a telephone survey was conducted with 2,090 monozygotic twin pairs with Vietnam era military service; 715 monozygotic twins served in Southeast Asia (SEA) and had a twin who did not serve in SEA. PTSD was found to be strongly associated with military service in SEA, with a nine-fold increase in PTSD in the SEA twins who experienced high levels of combat compared to the non-SEA twin (95% confidence interval, 4.8 to 17.6; Goldberg, True, Eisen, & Henderson, 1990). Other studies found a substantial contribution of genetic factors to PTSD symptomatology, with 13% to 34% of the variance in liability for symptoms in the different PTSD symptom clusters accounted for by genetic factors (Goldberg et al., 1990; True et al., 1993). These findings show that there is a combined genetic and environmental (i.e., stress) contribution to PTSD. The exact mechanism by which genetics confers an increased risk for PTSD is not known.

Genetic factors can confer risk for trauma-related psychopathology in several ways. One study found that individuals with a genetic polymorphism for the short form of the serotonin transporter were at risk for depression if they were exposed to a major stressor (Caspi et al., 2003). Thus, in two individuals exposed to the same stress, those with the short form of the serotonin transporter will be at increased risk. Studies have shown that traumatic stress is associated with an increased risk of depression. In addition, some individuals may actually be at increased risk for being exposed to traumatic stressors, which underlies their increased risk of depression (Kendler, Thornton, & Gardner, 2000), rather than some genetic alteration.

Looking at the problem of PTSD from multiple levels of analysis can involve assessing how genetic factors act in the brain to confer risk for PTSD. Some studies have found evidence for lower IQ before trauma exposure predicting risk for PTSD (Macklin et al., 1998; McNally & Shin, 1995);

other studies found smaller hippocampal volume in twins whose brothers developed PTSD secondary to combat exposure (Gilbertson et al., 2002). Genetic contributions to smaller hippocampal volume in PTSD could be mediated either by smaller hippocampal volume at birth (Pitman, 2001) and/or increasing vulnerability for stress exposure or increased responsiveness to stressors (Kendler et al., 2000). Our own preliminary data in twins show a 9% reduction in hippocampal volume in twins with combat-related PTSD relative to their non-combat-exposed twin brothers; these results are consistent with a combined genetic and environmental contribution to smaller hippocampal volume.

NEUROPHYSIOLOGICAL RESPONSES TO TRAUMA

Trauma also has lasting effects on the body and physiological systems (Figure 16.1). Stress circuits, such as the cortisol and norepinephrine systems, and brain regions involved in memory, including the hippocampus, amygdala, and prefrontal cortex, are sensitive to stress (Bremner, 2002b; Bremner & Vermetten, 2001). Changes in these circuits and systems lead to symptoms of PTSD and other stress-re-

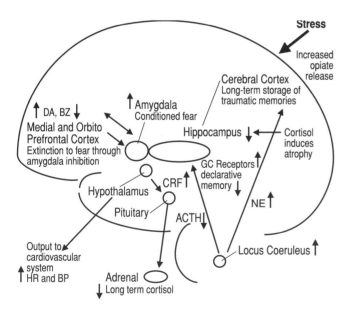

Figure 16.1 Model of how traumatic stress affects the brain. Stress is associated with acute increases in cortisol and norepinephrine. With chronic stress there is dysregulation of these systems, with increased amygdala function and decreased hippocampal and medial prefrontal function. Outputs through the hypothalamus and medial prefrontal cortex increase peripheral sympathetic and cortisol function, increasing the risk of heart disease.

lated psychiatric disorders such as depression and dissociative disorders (Bremner, 2002a).

Stress is associated with activation of the hypothalamic-pituitary-adrenal (HPA) axis. Corticotropin-releasing factor (CRF) is released from the hypothalamus, with stimulation of adrenocorticotropin hormone (ACTH) release from the pituitary, resulting in cortisol release from the adrenal gland. This process, in turn, has a negative feedback effect on the HPA axis at the level of the pituitary as well as central brain sites, including the hypothalamus and hippocampus. In addition to its role in activating the HPA axis, CRF acts centrally to mediate fear-related behaviors (Arborelius, Owens, Plotsky, & Nemeroff, 1999) and triggers other neurochemical responses to stress such as the noradrenergic neurotransmitter system via the brain stem's locus coeruleus (Melia & Duman, 1991). Early life stress leads to long-term sensitization of the HPA axis and increases in CRF (Levine, Weiner, & Coe, 1993; Stanton, Gutierrez, & Levine, 1988). Rats deprived of their mother had decreased numbers of glucocorticoid receptors, as measured by binding of the drug dexamethasone, in the hippocampus, hypothalamus, and frontal cortex (Ladd, Owens, & Nemeroff, 1996), increased CRF stress (Coplan et al., 1996; Makino, Smith, & Gold, 1995), and stress-induced glucocorticoid (Plotsky & Meaney, 1993) and ACTH release (Ladd et al., 1996). Stress also results in chronic overactivation of the norepinephrine system, which plays a critical role in the fight-or-flight response (Bremner, Krystal, Southwick, & Charney, 1996a, 1996b).

The hippocampus, a brain area involved in learning and memory, is particularly sensitive to the effects of stress (McEwen et al., 1997; Sapolsky, 1996). Psychosocial stress with associated elevated levels of glucocorticoids results in decreased branching of dendrites, which carry electrical signals to cells, and/or neuronal loss in a region of the hippocampus (Uno, Tarara, Else, Suleman, & Sapolsky, 1989) and a decrease in the regeneration of neurons (Gould, Tanapat, McEwen, Flugge, & Fuchs, 1998) in the hippocampus. High levels of glucocorticoids seen with stress have also been associated with deficits in new learning, in addition to damage to the hippocampus (Diamond, Fleshner, Ingersoll, & Rose, 1996; Lemaire, Koehl, Le Moal, & Abrous, 2000; Luine, Villages, Martinex, & McEwen, 1994). Brain-derived neurotrophic factor (BDNF) is a recently isolated neuropeptide that has important nutritional effects on the hippocampus and other brain regions. Stress results in a reduction in BDNF messenger RNA in the hippocampus, suggesting that stress reduces the brain's ability to grow and thrive. CRF also has a direct effect on the hippocampus in early development (Brunson, Eghbal-Ahmadi,

Bender, Chen, & Baram, 2001). In one study, antidepressant drugs and electroconvulsive therapy increased BDNF levels in two regions (CA3 and CA1) of the hippocampus, reversing the effects seen in stress (Nibuya, Morinobu, & Duman, 1995). Serotonin reuptake inhibitors also increase dendritic branching and neurogenesis within the hippocampus (Malberg, Eisch, Nestler, & Duman, 2000). Phenytoin (Dilantin), a medication used to treat epilepsy, inhibits excitatory amino acid transmission and blocks the effects of stress on the hippocampus (Watanabe, Gould, Cameron, Daniels, & McEwen, 1992). These findings have implications for treatment of PTSD and depression and have stimulated clinical trials of these agents to look at their effects on memory and hippocampal volume in PTSD and depression. Thus, there may be potential to treat or perhaps even reverse some of the detrimental effects of child abuse.

The hippocampus demonstrates an unusual capacity for plasticity, the ability of neurons to change and regenerate in response to environmental inputs. In addition to findings noted earlier related to the negative effects of stress on neurogenesis, it has recently been demonstrated that changes in the environment, for example, social enrichment, can modulate generation of neurons in the dentate gyrus of the hippocampus and slow the normal age-related decline in neurogenesis (Kempermann, Kuhn, & Gage, 1998). These findings may have implications for victims of abuse as well as emotional neglect.

An animal model that has been applied to study beneficial early interventions is postnatal handling—the quality of physical contact between a caregiver and an infant. Postnatal handling has important effects on the development of behavioral and endocrine responses to stress. For example, daily handling within the first few weeks of life (picking up rat pups and then returning them to their mother) resulted in increased Type II glucocorticoid receptor binding, which persisted throughout life. This was associated with increased feedback sensitivity to glucocorticoids and reduced glucocorticoid-mediated hippocampal damage in later life (Meaney, Aitken, van Berkel, Bhatnager, & Sapolsky, 1988). These effects appear to be due to a type of "stress inoculation" from the mother's repeated licking of the handled pups (Liu, Diorio, Day, Francis, & Meaney, 2000). Considered together, these findings suggest that early in the postnatal period there is a naturally occurring brain plasticity in key neural systems that may "program" an organism's biological response to stressful stimuli.

The medial prefrontal cortex includes the anterior cingulate, orbitofrontal cortex, and ventral prefrontal cortex and is a major target area of the neurotransmitters dopamine and norepinephrine. The prefrontal cortex has been suggested to play a role in working memory in conjunction with other brain areas, such as the hippocampus. A critical range of dopamine and norepinephrine turnover is necessary for keeping this working memory system active and ready for optimal cognitive functioning (Horger & Roth, 1996), a situation that is impaired in situations of extreme or chronic stress (Arnsten, 2000). The mesofrontal dopaminergic system also plays a role in emotional responses, selective information processing, and coping with the external world (Devinsky, Morrell, & Vogt, 1995; Pani, Porcella, & Gessa, 2000). The medial prefrontal cortex has inhibitory inputs to the amygdala that have been hypothesized to play a role in the extinction of fear responses (Milad & Quirk, 2002; Morgan & LeDoux, 1995). The area of the effects of early stress on mesofrontal dopamine function is not well developed; however, imaging findings from patients with childhood abuse implicate dysfunction of the medial prefrontal cortex.

The medial prefrontal cortex plays a critical role in regulation of peripheral neurohormonal responses to stress (Feldman, Conforti, & Weidenfeld, 1995). In addition to the amygdala and the hypothalamus, portions of the medial prefrontal cortex (infralimbic, ventral prelimbic) project to the nucleus solitarius and nucleus ambiguous in the brain stem, where they regulate heart rate and blood pressure responses to stress. Lesions of the dorsal part of this region (anterior cingulate) resulted in increased heart responses to conditioned stimuli, suggesting that this region decreases heart rate response to stress; lesions in the ventral portion decreased heart response, suggesting that this region increases heart rate response to stress (Frysztak & Neafsey, 1994). Lesions of the medial prefrontal cortex are associated with a blunted cortisol and ACTH response to stress, with no effect on resting cortisol (Diorio, Viau, & Meaney, 1993).

THE NEUROBIOLOGY OF EARLY STRESS IN CHILDREN

The few studies of the effects of early stress on neurobiology conducted in clinical populations of traumatized children have generally been consistent with findings from animal studies. Research with traumatized children has been complicated by issues related to psychiatric diagnosis and assessment of trauma (Cicchetti & Walker, 2001). Some studies have not specifically examined psychiatric diagnosis, whereas others have focused on children with trauma and depression and still others on children with trauma and PTSD. In our view, the issues of diagnosis are important in this area. Not all children will develop psychopathology following exposure to abuse, and we hypothesize that stress-induced changes in neurobiology that individuals are uniquely susceptible to underlie the development of psychiatric symptoms (Bremner, 2002a; Bremner & Vermetten, 2001).

Studies in adults with a history of early childhood abuse and the diagnosis of PTSD have been consistent with long-term changes in the HPA axis, hippocampal morphology, and hippocampal-based memory function (Bremner & Vermetten, 2001). An increase in cerebrospinal fluid concentrations of CRF was shown in adult patients with combat-related PTSD compared to healthy controls (Baker et al., 1999; Bremner, Licinio, et al., 1997). Consistent with increased levels of CRF, combat-related PTSD patients had a blunted ACTH response to CRF challenge (Smith et al., 1989), although adult women with PTSD showed the opposite response (Rasmusson, Lipschitz, Bremner, Southwick, & Charney, 2001). Some studies (Yehuda, Southwick, Nussbaum, Giller, & Mason, 1991) but not others (Pitman & Orr, 1990) of adults with chronic PTSD found decreased levels of cortisol in 24-hour urines. Other findings in combat-related PTSD include increased suppression of cortisol with low-dose (0.5 mg) dexamethasone (Yehuda et al., 1993) and increased number of glucocorticoid receptors on peripheral lymphocytes (Yehuda, Lowry, Southwick, Mason, & Giller, 1991). Sexually abused girls (in which effects of specific psychiatric diagnosis was not examined) had blunted ACTH response to CRF (DeBellis, Chrousos, et al., 1994), and women with childhood abuse-related PTSD had hypercortisolemia (Lemieux & Coe, 1995). Another study of traumatized children in which the diagnosis of PTSD was established showed increased levels of cortisol measured in 24-hour urines (DeBellis, Baum, et al., 1999). Emotionally neglected children from a Romanian orphanage had elevated cortisol levels over a diurnal period compared to controls (Gunnar, Morison, Chisolm, & Schuder, 2001). Maltreated school-age children with clinical-level internalizing problems such as depression and anxiety had elevated cortisol compared to controls (Cicchetti & Rogosch, 2001). Adult women with a history of childhood abuse showed increased suppression of cortisol with low-dose (0.5 mg) dexamethasone (Stein, Yehuda, Koverola, & Hanna, 1997). In a study of women with PTSD related to early childhood sexual abuse, Bremner and colleagues showed decreased baseline cortisol in the afternoon (12 to 8 P.M.) based on 24-hour diurnal assessments of plasma cortisol and exaggerated cortisol response to stressors (traumatic stressors; Elzinga, Schmahl, Vermetten, van Dyck, & Bremner, 2002) more than neutral cognitive stressors (Bremner, Vythilingam, Vermetten, Adil, et al., 2002) relative to controls.

Few studies have examined noradrenergic function related to childhood abuse. Studies have found increased noradrenergic function in adults with PTSD (Bremner, Krystal, et al., 1996b). Studies in children with abuse in which diagnosis of PTSD was not established found increased catecholamines in 24-hour urine (including norepinephrine, epinephrine, and dopamine; DeBellis, Lefter, Trickett, & Putnam, 1994). Studies in children with the diagnosis of PTSD are also consistent with elevations in catecholamine (DeBellis, Baum, et al., 1999). These findings are consistent with animal studies showing increased noradrenergic activity following early stress.

Another important outcome of childhood abuse is depression. Hypercortisolemia is a well-replicated finding in a subgroup of patients with depression. Depressed patients also showed increased rates of nonsuppression on the dexamethasone suppression test (consistent with excessive levels of cortisol in the periphery), elevated CRF levels in cerebrospinal fluid (Nemeroff et al., 1984), and blunted ACTH response to CRF challenge (consistent with excessive CRF release; Gold et al., 1986). Findings in adolescents with depression are less clear, with a smaller number of patients exhibiting hypercortisolemia, which may be specific to nighttime cortisol levels (Birmaher et al., 1992; Dahl et al., 1991; Dorn et al., 1996; Kutcher et al., 1991). These discrepant findings may be related to the fact that hypercortisolemia is more common in patients with trauma histories (Hart, Gunnar, & Cicchetti, 1996). Adult women with depression and a history of early childhood abuse had an increased cortisol response to a stressful cognitive challenge relative to controls (Heim et al., 2000) and a blunted ACTH response to CRF challenge (Heim, Newport, Bonsall, Miller, & Nemeroff, 2001).

Childhood abuse has also been associated with changes in central brain function. Several studies have shown alterations in electroencephalogram (EEG) measures of brain activity in children with a variety of traumas who were not selected for diagnosis compared to healthy children. About half of the children in these studies had a psychiatric diagnosis. Abnormalities were located in the anterior frontal cortex and temporal lobe and were localized to the left hemisphere (Ito et al., 1993; Schiffer, Teicher, & Papanicolaou, 1995).

Studies in adult survivors of childhood abuse have found abnormalities in the hippocampus. Neuropsychological tests of long-term memory function, such as the verbal Selective Reminding Test (vSRT), and percentage of retention during paragraph recall on the Wechsler Memory Scale (WMS) can be used as probes of hippocampal function. Bremner, Randall, Capelli, et al. (1995) found deficits in verbal declarative memory as measured by the WMS and vSRT in patients with childhood physical and sexual abuse in comparison to controls. Deficits in verbal memory in the childhood abuse patients were significantly correlated with severity of childhood sexual abuse.

Based on the animal studies reviewed earlier, there was a rationale to measure hippocampal volume in patients with PTSD and depression. An initial study used magnetic resonance imaging (MRI) volumetric (i.e., size measurement) techniques to show an 8% reduction in hippocampal volume in patients with combat-related PTSD compared to controls (Bremner, Randall, Scott, et al., 1995; Figure 16.2). In a second study comparing 17 patients with PTSD related to early childhood abuse to 17 case-matched controls, there was a 12% reduction in left hippocampal volume ($p < .05$; Bremner, Randall, et al., 1997). Other published studies showed hippocampal volume reduction, for example, in combat-related PTSD (Gurvits et al., 1996) and in women with early sexual abuse, most of whom met criteria for PTSD (Stein, Koverola, Hanna, Torchia, & McClarty, 1997). We recently found a reduction in bilateral hippocampal volume in women with early childhood sexual abuse and PTSD, relative to abused women without PTSD and nonabused non-PTSD women (Bremner, Vythilingam,

Vermetten, Southwick, McGlasha, Nazeer, et al., 2003). In studies of children with abuse-related PTSD, there was a smaller intracranial and cerebral volume, with no reduction in hippocampal volume (Carrion et al., 2001; DeBellis, Keshavan, et al., 1999) and no change in hippocampal volume over a 2-year period (DeBellis, Hall, Boring, Frustaci, & Moritz, 2001). Adults with new-onset PTSD showed no difference in hippocampal volume relative to controls (Bonne et al., 2001). MRI studies in adult depression showed smaller hippocampal volume in adults with depression (Bremner, 2002c). Recently, we found that smaller left hippocampal volume was seen only in women with depression and a history of childhood abuse, but not in depressed women without childhood abuse (Vythilingam et al., 2002). These studies suggest that chronicity of PTSD illness may be a factor determining hippocampal volume reduction. Similarly, chronicity of depression has been associated with degree of hippocampal atrophy.

NEUROIMAGING OF BRAIN FUNCTION IN EARLY TRAUMA

Neuroimaging studies have provided a map for the neural circuitry of early childhood abuse (Bremner, 2002b). The medial prefrontal cortex has been implicated in the stress response. The medial prefrontal cortex in the human consists of several related areas, including the orbitofrontal cortex, anterior cingulate (area 25-subcallosal gyrus, and Area 32), and anterior prefrontal cortex (area 9). This area plays a critical role in extinction of fear (Milad & Quirk, 2002; Morgan & LeDoux, 1995). Human subjects with lesions of the prefrontal cortex showed dysfunction of normal emotions and an inability to relate in social situations that require correct interpretation of the emotional expressions of others (Damasio, Grabowski, Frank, Galaburda, & Damasio, 1994). These findings suggest that dysfunction of the medial prefrontal cortex may play a role in pathological emotions that sometimes follow exposure to extreme stressors such as childhood sexual abuse. Other regions, including the posterior cingulate, parietal and motor cortex, and cerebellum, are functionally related to the anterolateral prefrontal cortex (superior and middle frontal gyri), mediating visuospatial processing that is critical to survival in life-threatening situations. We have hypothesized that the excessive vigilance seen in PTSD is associated with increased demands on brain areas involved in visuospatial aspects of memory function and planning of response to potentially threatening stimuli.

Hippocampal Volume Reduction in PTSD

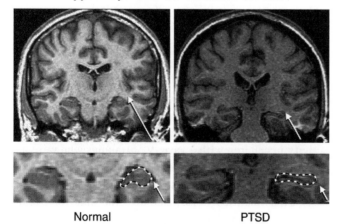

Normal   PTSD

Figure 16.2 Hippocampal volume in PTSD on a coronal MRI. The hippocampus is visibly smaller in the PTSD patient compared to a normal control.

In a study that followed up on findings of reduced hippocampal volume in abuse-related PTSD, we measured hippocampal function and structure in childhood abuse-related PTSD. Hippocampal function during the performance of hippocampal-based verbal declarative memory tasks was measured using positron emission tomography (PET) and [^{15}O]H$_2$O (radioactive water that binds in the brain to show change in blood flow) in women with a history of early childhood sexual abuse with and without PTSD. Hippocampal volume was measured with MRI in three subject groups: women with early childhood sexual abuse and PTSD, women with early abuse without PTSD, and women without early abuse or PTSD. A failure of hippocampal activation ($F = 14.94$; $df = 1,20$; $p < .001$) and 16% smaller volume of the hippocampus was seen in women with abuse and PTSD compared to women with abuse without PTSD. Abused PTSD women also had a 19% smaller hippocampal volume relative to women without abuse or PTSD (Bremner, Vythilingam, Vermetten, Southwick, et al., 2002). These results are consistent with the hypothesis that early abuse with associated PTSD results in deficits in hippocampal function and structure, possibly through damage to hippocampal neurons.

Functional neuroimaging studies have been performed in childhood abuse-related PTSD to map out the neural circuitry of abuse-related PTSD (Figure 16.3). These studies are consistent with dysfunction in a network of related brain areas, including the medial prefrontal cortex, hippocampus, and amygdala (Figure 16.4). We measured brain blood flow with PET and [^{15}O]H$_2$O during exposure to personalized scripts of childhood sexual abuse. Twenty-two women with a history of childhood sexual abuse underwent injection of [^{15}O]H$_2$O followed by PET imaging of the brain while listening to neutral and traumatic (personalized childhood sexual abuse events) scripts. Brain blood flow during exposure to traumatic versus neutral scripts was compared between sexually abused women with and without PTSD. Memories of childhood sexual abuse were associated with greater increases in blood flow in portions of the anterior prefrontal cortex (superior and middle frontal gyri-areas 6 and 9), posterior cingulate (area 31), and motor cortex in sexually abused women with PTSD compared to sexually abused women without PTSD. Abuse memories were associated with alterations in blood flow in the medial prefrontal cortex, with decreased blood flow in subcallosal gyrus-area 25 and a failure of activation in anterior cingulate-area 32. There was also decreased blood flow in the right hippocampus, fusiform/inferior temporal gyrus, supramarginal gyrus, and visual association cortex in PTSD relative to non-PTSD women (Bremner, Narayan, et al., 1999). This study replicated findings of decreased function in the medial prefrontal cortex and increased function in the posterior cingulate in combat-related PTSD during exposure to combat-related slides and sounds (Bremner, Staib, et al., 1999; Figure 16.5). Shin et al. (1999) studied 8 women with childhood sexual abuse and PTSD and 8 women with abuse without PTSD using PET during exposure to script-driven imagery of childhood abuse. The authors found blood-flow increases in the orbitofrontal cortex and anterior temporal pole in both groups of subjects, with greater increases in these areas in the PTSD group. PTSD patients showed a relative failure of the anterior cingulate activation compared to controls. The PTSD patients (but not controls) showed decreased blood flow in anteromedial portions of the prefrontal cortex and left inferior frontal gyrus.

These studies have relied on specific traumatic cues to activate personalized traumatic memories of childhood abuse and PTSD symptoms in patients with PTSD. Another method to probe neural circuits in PTSD is to assess neural correlates of retrieval of emotionally valenced declarative memory. In this type of paradigm, instead of using a traditional declarative memory task, such as retrieval of word pairs like "gold-west," which has been the standard of memory research for several decades, words with emotional valence, such as "stench-fear" are utilized (Bremner et al., 2001). Although there has been relatively little research on retrieval of emotionally valenced words, it is of interest from the standpoint of PTSD as a method for activating neural pathways relevant to trauma and memory. If PTSD patients demonstrate a pattern of brain

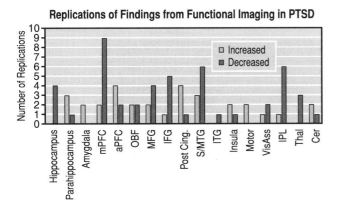

Figure 16.3 Replicated findings in PTSD. The most replicated findings related to symptom provocation are decreased medial prefrontal function. Other findings include decreased hippocampal and dorsolateral prefrontal function and increased amygdala function.

**Increased Blood Flow with Fear Acquisition
versus Control in Abuse-Related PTSD**

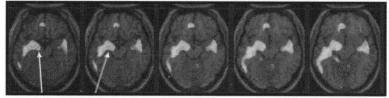

Left Amygdala

Figure 16.4   Amygdala function in PTSD. With classical fear conditioning (pairing of an unconditioned stimulus [shock] with a conditioned stimulus [seeing a blue square on a screen]), there was increased amygdala activation in PTSD relative to controls, suggesting increased sensitivity of the amygdala in the learning of fear.

activation during retrieval of emotionally valenced declarative memory that is similar to that seen during exposure to other tasks that stimulate brain networks mediating PTSD symptoms, such as exposure to personalized scripts of childhood trauma or exposure to trauma-related pictures and sounds, then that would provide convergent evidence for dysfunction of a specific neural circuit in the processing of emotional memory in PTSD. We recently used PET in the examination of neural correlates of retrieval of emotionally valenced declarative memory in 10 women with a history of childhood sexual abuse and the diagnosis of PTSD and 11 women without abuse or PTSD. We hypothesized that retrieval of emotionally valenced words would result in an altered pattern of brain activation in patients with PTSD similar to that seen in prior studies of exposure to cues of personalized traumatic memories. Specifically, we hypothesized that retrieval of emotionally valenced

words in PTSD relative to non-PTSD subjects would result in decreased blood flow in the medial prefrontal cortex (subcallosal gyrus and other parts of the anterior cingulate), hippocampus, and fusiform gyrus/inferior temporal cortex, with increased blood flow in the posterior cingulate, motor and parietal cortex, and dorsolateral prefrontal cortex. PTSD patients during retrieval of emotionally valenced word pairs showed greater decreases in blood flow in an extensive area that included the orbitofrontal cortex, anterior cingulate, and medial prefrontal cortex (Brodmann's areas 25, 32, 9), left hippocampus, and fusiform gyrus/inferior temporal gyrus, with increased activation in the posterior cingulate, left inferior parietal cortex, left middle frontal gyrus, and visual association and motor cortex. There were no differences in patterns of brain activation during retrieval of neutral word pairs between patients and controls (Bremner, Vythilingam, Vermetten, South-

Medial PFC
(BA 25)

**Medial Prefrontal Cortical Dysfunction
with Traumatic Memories in PTSD**

AC
(BA 32)

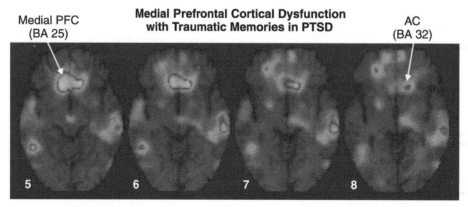

Decreased function in medial prefrontal cortical areas. Anterior Cingulate BA 25, BA 32 in veterans with PTSD compared to veterans without PTSD during viewing of combat-related slides and sounds. Z score > 3.00; p < .001

Figure 16.5   Effects of combat-related slides and sounds on brain function. Identified area shows decreased blood flow with combat slides and sounds in combat veterans with PTSD. This area normally inhibits the amygdala (involved in fear responses).

wick, McGlashan, Staib, et al., 2003). A similar failure of activation in the anterior cingulate/medial prefrontal cortex was seen in women with abuse and PTSD while performing an emotional Stroop involving naming the color of a word like "rape" (Bremner et al., 2004). These findings were similar to prior imaging studies in PTSD from our group using trauma-specific stimuli for symptom provocation, adding further supportive evidence for a dysfunctional network of brain areas involved in memory, including the hippocampus, medial prefrontal cortex, and cingulate, in PTSD.

Other studies have used MRI to look at structural changes in other brain areas besides the hippocampus in childhood abuse. One study used single voxel proton magnetic resonance spectroscopy (proton MRS) to measure relative concentration of N-acetylaspartate and creatinine (a marker of neuronal viability) in the anterior cingulate of 11 children with maltreatment-related PTSD and 11 controls. The authors found a reduction in the ratio of N-acetylaspartate to creatinine in PTSD relative to controls (DeBellis, Keshavan, Spencer, & Hall, 2000). Studies have also found smaller brain size and smaller size of the corpus callosum in children with abuse and PTSD relative to controls (DeBellis, Keshavan, et al., 1999). In a study of abused children in whom diagnosis was not specified, there was an increase in T2 relaxation time in the cerebellar vermis, suggesting dysfunction in this brain region (Anderson, Teicher, Polcari, & Renshaw, 2002).

We developed a method for assessing neural correlates of fear conditioning in abuse-related PTSD. In the fear conditioning paradigm, pairing of a light with a shock leads to a fear reaction to the light alone, an effect mediated by the amygdala. Women with early childhood sexual abuse-related PTSD (n = 8) and women without abuse or PTSD (n = 11) underwent measurement of psychophysiological responding as well as PET measurement of cerebral blood flow during habituation, acquisition, and extinction of conditioned fear conditions. During habituation, subjects were exposed to a blue square on a screen, 4 seconds in duration, eight times at regular intervals over 90 seconds. During acquisition, exposure to the blue square was paired with an electric shock to the forearm. With extinction, subjects were again exposed to the blue square but without shock. On the 2nd day, subjects went through the same procedure but with random electric shocks (an equal number as on day 1) during the acquisition phase. The control paradigm was identical to the acquisition of conditioned fear paradigm, with the exception that subjects underwent scanning during sensitization trials instead of acquisition of conditioned fear trials for scans 3 and 4. Subjects underwent

sensitization trials, which involved exposure to the conditioned stimulus (blue square) and random electric shocks not paired with the conditioned stimulus. Both PTSD patients and control subjects showed activation of the amygdala with acquisition of conditioned fear (pairing of unconditioned stimulus and conditioned stimulus) relative to the control condition ($p < .005$). Greater left amygdala activation during fear conditioning was seen in PTSD patients relative to comparison subjects (Figure 16.4). Extinction of fear responses was associated with decreased function in the orbitofrontal and medial prefrontal cortex (including the subcallosal gyrus, BA 25, and anterior cingulate BA 32) in the PTSD patients, but not in the controls (Bremner et al., in press). Extinction of fear responding was associated with a greater decrease in medial prefrontal function (anterior cingulate, BA 25, 32, 24) in PTSD compared to controls. These findings are consistent with increased amygdala function in PTSD.

TRAUMA AND PHYSICAL HEALTH

The multiple levels of analysis approach also requires an examination of the relationship between traumatic stress and physical disorders, which may act directly or through trauma-related disorders like depression and PTSD. Traumatic stress has a wide range of effects on behavior and health (Proctor, Harley, Wolfe, Heeren, & White, 2001; Proctor et al., 1998; Wagner, Wolfe, Rotnitsky, Proctor, & Erickson, 2000; Zatzick et al., 1997). Work from the Centers for Disease Control showed that early adverse events are associated with dramatic increases in anxiety, substance abuse, obesity, and variables such as smoking that represent a risk factor for heart disease (Dube, Felitti, Dong, Giles, & Anda, 2003; Williamson, Thompson, Anda, Dietz, & Felitti, 2002). The cardiovascular system is particularly sensitive to stress and emotion (Berkman, Vaccarino, & Seeman, 1993; Krumholz et al., 1998; Rozanski, Blumenthal, & Kaplan, 1999). Increased risk of heart disease was associated with depression (Anda, Williamson, & Jones, 1993), anxiety, and personality (Mendes de Leon et al., 1998; Musselman, Evans, & Nemeroff, 1998; Rozanski et al., 1999). Laboratory studies showed an increase in ischemia with mental stressors like mental arithmetic in certain vulnerable individuals (Arrighi et al., 2000; Arrighi, Burg, Cohen, & Soufer, 2003; Burg, Jain, Soufer, Kerns, & Zaret, 1993; Soufer et al., 1998). Mental stress was also associated with a decrease in heart rate variability (Lampert, Ickovics, Viscoli, Horwitz, & Lee, 1998), which increases the risk of sudden death from arrhythmia. Patients with acute stressors were found to have a reversible left ventricular dysfunction with myocardial inflammation on biopsy; markedly elevated levels of plasma epinephrine and norepinephrine showed that the patients were under severe stress (Wittstein et al., 2005). One study found an increased risk of cerebrovascular disease in veterans who had undergone captivity stress during WWII; the risk was compounded by a diagnosis of PTSD (Brass & Page, 1996). Other studies have shown a relationship between stress, PTSD, and heart disease (Boscarino, 1997; Engel, Liu, McCarthy, Miller, & Ursano, 2000).

Epidemiological studies have established a relationship between episodes of Major Depression, which is often linked to stress, and cardiovascular events in patients with (Barefoot, Helms, & Mark, 1996; Carney, Rich, & Freedland, 1988; Frasure-Smith, Lesperance, Juneau, Talajic, & Bourassa, 1999; Frasure-Smith, Lesperance, & Talajic, 1993) and without (Anda et al., 1993; Barefoot & Schroll, 1996; Ford et al., 1998; Fredman, Magaziner, Hebel, Hawkes, & Zimmerman, 1999; Hippisley-Cox, Fielding, & Pringle, 1998; Pratt et al., 1996) a prior history of coronary heart disease (CHD). Episodes of depressed mood were associated with a triggering of myocardial ischemia (Gullette, Blumenthal, & Babyak, 1997). Depression is associated with an increased risk of mortality, which is primarily related to increased cardiovascular death, particularly in men (Wulsin, Vaillant, & Wells, 1999).

The mechanisms through which depression increases CHD risk are unclear. Depression could increase CHD risk through its known association with unhealthy behaviors, such as lack of exercise, smoking, and poor diet, or through direct effects on the cardiovascular system (Hemingway & Marmot, 1999; Musselman et al., 1998; Wulsin et al., 1999). Stressful life events have been linked to the onset of episodes of Major Depression (Kendler et al., 2000), but it is not known whether stress leads to both heart disease and depression independently, or whether stress mediates an effect on heart disease through the development of depression.

Elevations in cortisol and sympathetic function in depressed individuals could lead to cardiac events through several possible pathways. Increased sympathetic function leads to increases in heart rate and blood pressure, which is associated with endothelial injury, platelet aggregation, and increased vascular reactivity (Musselman et al., 1998). These factors are all associated with increased risk of myocardial infarction. Some studies have directly linked changes in platelet aggregation and vascular reactivity with depression (Musselman et al., 1998). Stress (which increases the risk of depressive episodes) results in increased cortisol and norepinephrine release, as well as increased heart rate and blood pressure (Bremner, Krystal, et al., 1996a, 1996b), which can impact negatively on cardiovascular function. Studies in monkeys using social stress (in which dominance hierarchies are changed over time) have demonstrated a relationship between stress and accelerated cardiovascular disease (Kaplan, Manuck, Clarkson, Lusso, & Taub, 1982). Monkeys undergoing stressors had increased activation of the cortisol and norepinephrine systems, which was associated with acceleration of the development of atherosclerosis. Stressed monkeys also developed increased endothelial injury, which led to increased platelet aggregation and plaque formation at the site of the injury. These effects were shown to be blocked with propanolol, the beta-adrenergic receptor antagonist, indicating that the effects were mediated through norepinephrine (Kaplan, Manuck, Adams, Weingand, & Clarkson, 1987). Stress also resulted in impairment in endothelial responsivity to acetylcholine. Elevated morning plasma cortisol levels have been related to coronary atherosclerosis in young and middle-aged men (Troxler, Sprague, Albanese, Fuchs, & Thompson, 1977). An excess in cortisol level may increase the risk for cardiovascular disease by injuring the intima (Kemper, Baggenstoss, & Slocumb, 1957; Nahas, Brunson, King, & Cavert, 1958) or by inducing inflammation in the artery wall (Gabay & Kushner, 1999; Musselman et al., 1998).

The effects of traumatic stress on heart disease might be mediated through brain areas sensitive to stress that are affected by PTSD, including the amygdala, medial prefrontal cortex, hippocampus, posterior cingulate, and anterior cingulate. These brain circuits have direct or indirect outputs through the hypothalamus and medial prefrontal cortex to neurohormonal systems (cortisol, norepinephrine) that influence myocardial function. For instance, the hippocampus and medial prefrontal cortex (which includes the anterior cingulate) have inhibitory pathways to the amygdala (Milad & Quirk, 2002; Morgan & LeDoux, 1995; Morgan, Romanski, & LeDoux, 1993; Phillips & LeDoux, 1992), which plays a critical role in the stress response (Davis, 1992; Hitchcock & Davis, 1986; Hitchcock, Sananes, & Davis, 1989; J. L. LeDoux, 1993; Miserendino, Sananes, Melia, & Davis, 1990; Rosen & Davis, 1988). In addition to activating increased arousal and fear behaviors, the amygdala has pathways through the lateral hypothalamus that activate cortisol and sympathetic pathways in the periphery (Hitchcock & Davis, 1991). Other brain areas implicated in a study of CHD patients (who were hostile but without psychiatric disorder) who experienced mental stress-induced ischemia included the parietal, temporal, and visual cortex and dorsolateral prefrontal cortex. Also, activations and deactivations were seen in different parts of the prefrontal cortex, including the medial prefrontal cortex and anterior cingulate. Some of these regions were involved in the cognitive and visual appraisal of the stress or in the mathematics (visual, parietal, temporal cortex; Soufer et al., 1998). The medial prefrontal cortex and anterior cingulate are unique in also mediating directly cortisol and sympathetic responses through direct connections to the brain stem (Diorio et al., 1993). The amygdala has a direct pathway to the lateral nucleus of the hypothalamus that stimulates the peripheral stress response system. The hippocampus has direct inputs to the amygdala. The posterior cingulate also has connections with these regions and is involved in visuospatial processing of threat. These brain regions are included in the list of limbic regions (J. E. LeDoux, 1996). Cats with a loss of the cerebral cortex have increased sympathetic responses (MacLean, 1949; Papez, 1937); this neurohormonal activation is critical for survival. However, with chronic stress and chronic activation, these neurohormonal systems lead to changes in the endothelium, acceleration of atherosclerosis, alterations in heart rate variability, increased risk for arrhythmias, increased platelet aggregation, and other factors that increase the risk for cardiovascular mortality after stress. In our ongoing studies, we are finding that patients with a history of traumatic stress and depression have increased stress-induced myocardial ischemia measured with cardiac single photon emission computed tomography. These patients experienced ischemia in the absence of chest pain. Our ongoing twin study shows very high rates of undetected heart disease in depression, measured with cardiac PET. It could be that exposure to traumatic stress with the negative outcome of depression is necessary for the development of stress-induced ischemia. There could be a large number of patients with depression and traumatic stress who are at risk for heart disease. The increased mortality after heart attack could be due to stress-induced episodes of ischemia that put vulnerable myocardium at risk.

MULTIPLE LEVELS OF ANALYSIS

Traditionally, researchers have approached problems from a single dimension. For instance, epidemiologists focus on prevalence of disease and risk factors in the population at large. Psychologists and psychiatrists focus on groups of patients, often funneled to the same clinic because they have similar complaints. Or there may be a group of investigators in an engineering department who have a nifty technology that could provide vital clues about a group of patients with a mental disorder, but they don't want to be bothered with driving across town to meet with a group of behavioral researchers or mental health clinicians. You may have a situation where two different groups, say, psychosocial epidemiologists and behavioral psychologists, are studying essentially the same phenomena but conversing in a different jargon, publishing in different journals that the other group never reads, attending different meetings, sending grants to different study sections, and basically knowing nothing of the parallel culture. You can point to a similar disjunct between biological psychiatrists and developmental psychologists. Cardiologists treat heart disorders caused by sadness or stress and have no idea what the true etiology is of their patients' disorders.

The language of the new National Institutes of Health "road map" is aimed at batting down such barriers between research groups and disciplines. It talks about the need to eliminate "silos" and promote interdisciplinary research. Although we all can agree that more cross-fertilization will help everyone, the fact is that sometimes people in silos are actually battened down in bunkers, fighting a war to keep the money flowing in so that they can continue an independent line of research.

However, because researchers have always gone and will continue to go where the money is, it seems that the new road map ushers in a new way to look at the old problems. And what way is that? It seems to mean getting out of the straitjacket of looking at a single dimension of a problem such as traumatic stress and looking at the problem from multiple levels at the same time (Cicchetti & Dawson, 2002). This means thinking about the impact of trauma from the standpoint of biology, psychology, individual meaning, spirituality, and other dimensions. Most psychological research is based on self-report data provided by subjects about the symptoms they are experiencing. However, they may have arrived at this point from multiple pathways; therefore, self-report data may not be helpful, and in fact may even be misleading. Adding biological or genetic data to the self-report data may better inform the phenotype, leading to a view of the endophenotype (Kagan, Snidman, McManis, Woodward, & Hardway, 2002).

Biological mediators may also have an impact on psychological outcomes (Kopnisky, Cowan, & Hyman, 2002). For instance, in the aftermath of traumatic stress, there can be preoccupation and rumination that lead to memory rehearsing. This memory rehearsing can lead to feelings of upset, with enhanced cortisol and norepinephrine outflow, which modulate memory and actually change how memory is stored. Activation of the amygdala and decreased function in the prefrontal cortex further enforce the circuitry that maintains the memory. However, teaching individuals how to let these thoughts go and to prevent endless cycles of rumination about the trauma through meditation and self-healing may prevent the consolidation of the memory circuits that maintain indelible memories and reduce long-term anxiety (Bishop et al., 2004; Bishop & Sativihari, in press).

There are other ways a multiple-levels-of-analysis approach can better inform our models of mental illness. One can look specifically at the domain of clinical neuroscience and see that a multilayered approach is necessary, even discounting other disciplines. Specifically, the initial assumption was that the advent of brain imaging (and genetics) would help us find "the lesion" that was responsible for the disorder. However, years of research have shown that this is not the case, forcing us to fall back on models of circuits of multiple regions functioning (or dysfunctioning) in tandem to lead to symptoms of the disorder (Johnson, Halit, Grice, & Karmiloff-Smith, 2002).

Looking at the issue of development represents another face of the multidimensional cube. Psychiatric disorders in adults have a fairly uniform and continuous face, at least on the surface. However, to follow psychopathology in children, throughout the developmental periods of infancy, childhood, adolescence, and finally into adulthood, can be like following Alice through the looking glass. Symptoms that appear as one disorder in one stage of development can look very different in another stage of development (Harrington, Rutter, & Fombonne, 1996). Adding the element of trauma makes things even more confusing. We know very little about how risk and resilience influence children's responses to trauma. Children seem to flip from one diagnosis to another throughout childhood, and there is little consensus about what is going on here (Harrington et al., 1996; Saigh et al., 2000). On top of that, assessment of PTSD in children has been notoriously difficult (Saigh et al., 2000).

Because a variety of mediators and modulators can influence the eventual outcomes of the trauma response, a multilevel analysis would be beneficial. Individuals could be born with an inherent resilient constitution that makes them resistant to the effects of the trauma (Bonanno, 2004). An inherently strong social support network (Keane et al., 1987) or lack of previous traumas (Bremner, South-

wick, Johnson, Yehuda, & Charney, 1993) may positively affect long-term outcome. Our understanding of these variables is limited by the fact that most research on trauma was conducted with Vietnam veterans 20 years after their trauma exposure. Before 1990, the diagnosis of PTSD was never made by VA clinicians (Bremner, Southwick, Darnell, & Charney, 1996), even though the diagnosis was established in 1980. To understand why some individuals develop chronic PTSD from early abuse and others don't, we can't wait until 20 years after the fact. Research is needed longitudinally to follow traumatized individuals through the different stages of development to assess the effects of trauma using multiple layers of analysis.

CONCLUSIONS AND FUTURE DIRECTIONS

Trauma has effects on multiple levels, including psychological, biological, physical, social, and political. At times, biological correlates of traumatic stress can become metaphors for individual, political, and social responses to trauma. Understanding all of these facets is important because they often cannot be separated. For instance, a person's sense of meaning may be altered after trauma, but that may be driven by the physiological changes associated with the trauma. And recovery may involve a spiritual process that in fact changes brain function. The public health implications of biological changes with childhood abuse are also relevant. If childhood stress and maltreatment leads to an inhibition of neuronal growth and/or damage in brain areas such as the hippocampus that are critical for new learning and memory, this could have detrimental effects on the ability of children to succeed in school. Also, if stress results in dysfunction of brain areas such as the medial portion of the prefrontal cortex that are involved in the regulation of social behavior, early stress could lead to a biological vulnerability to future acts of antisocial behavior, leading to a vicious cycle of repeated violence and abuse.

Looking at traumatized patients from a multiple-levels-of-analysis approach has implications for treatment and future directions of research. By throwing out the one disease/one etiology model, the limitations of a single treatment are highlighted. In the future, we need to go beyond thinking of a single medication or psychotherapy treatment being applicable to all traumatized patients. Medications like the SSRIs do have a role to play, but other aspects of the traumatized patient need to be addressed as well. Tools that can be given to patients to help themselves can be very powerful. For instance, meditation has been shown to increase overall sense of control (Weissbecker et al., 2002) through a positive accepting mode of control (Astin, 1997). Meditation may provide a way for trauma victims who are vulnerable to PTSD to experience a greater sense of control in relation to their thoughts and memories and to be less emotionally reactive to their presence in the midst of other activities. For example, if a distressing memory/thought is noticed, no attempt is necessarily made to change it. Thus, the focused attention required to sustain the thought (with its attendant distress) is diverted, preventing the escalation of negative thoughts into ruminative patterns (Teasdale, Segal, & Williams, 1995), which in turn can lead to increases in negative psychological states such as mental distress and depression (Teasdale et al., 2000). This process may also prevent the rehearsing and replay of traumatic memories that may modify the way they are stored and make them indelible or resistant to further modification. Reduction of negative thoughts and behaviors may also promote self-healing through the promotion of positive rather than negative behaviors and coping styles.

More attention needs to be paid to the ability of trauma victims to heal themselves in other ways. Our focus on the disease model in PTSD carries the assumption that trauma is always a bad thing that inevitably leads to psychopathology. However, many individuals are extremely resilient in the face of trauma and report their reaction in the aftermath of trauma as a growth experience (Bonanno, 2004). Some patients are better left alone, or can help themselves through programs of self-healing.

Future research needs to examine the role of such alternative approaches in helping trauma victims in their recovery. Studies also need to go beyond the false dichotomies of mind/brain/body and address the important effects that stress has on physical health, perhaps mediated through the brain. Then treatments of physical disorders can incorporate elements of behavior, emotion, spirituality, and cognition that are closer to the root of the distress. Studies also need to incorporate in their designs multiple outcomes of behavior, spirituality, physical indicators, brain measures, cognitive assessments, and the multitude of factors that go into the development of distress. These studies should be performed longitudinally, so that the interaction between physical, neural, emotional, and psychological development and trauma can be fully assessed. More attention is needed to research that goes beyond the boundaries of discipline or expertise, including studies on the relationship between stress and physical disorders like heart disease, and the play between genetics and mental symptoms. In promoting a multiple-levels-of-analysis approach, we may be getting closer to what is really bothering our patients and have a better chance at giving them the best treatments.

REFERENCES

American Psychiatric Association. (1980). *Diagnostic and statistical manual of mental disorders* (3rd ed.). Washington, DC: Author.

American Psychiatric Association. (2000). *Diagnostic and statistical manual of mental disorders* (4th ed., text rev.). Washington, DC: Author.

Anda, R., Williamson, D., & Jones, D. (1993). Depressed affect, hopelessness, and the risk of ischemic heart disease in a cohort of U.S. adults. *Epidemiology, 4,* 285–294.

Anderson, C. M., Teicher, M. H., Polcari, A., & Renshaw, P. F. (2002). Abnormal T2 relaxation time in the cerebellar vermis of adults sexually abused in childhood: Potential role of the vermis in stress-enhanced risk for drug abuse. *Psychoneuroendocrinology, 27,* 231–244.

Arborelius, L., Owens, M. J., Plotsky, P. M., & Nemeroff, C. B. (1999). The role of corticotropin-releasing factor in depression and anxiety disorders. *Journal of Endocrinology, 160,* 1–12.

Arnsten, A. F. (2000). Stress impairs prefrontal cortical function in rats and monkeys: Role of dopamine D1 and norepinephrine alpha-1 receptor mechanisms. *Progress in Brain Research, 126,* 183–192.

Arrighi, J. A., Burg, M., Cohen, I. S., Kao, A. H., Pfau, S., Caulin-Glaser, T., et al. (2000). Myocardial blood-flow response during mental stress in patients with coronary artery disease. *Lancet, 356*(9226), 310–311.

Arrighi, J. A., Burg, M., Cohen, I. S., & Soufer, R. (2003). Simultaneous assessment of myocardial perfusion and function during mental stress in patients with chronic coronary artery disease. *Journal of Nuclear Cardiology, 10*(3), 267–274.

Astin, J. (1997). Stress reduction through mindfulness meditation: Effects on psychological symptomatology, sense of control, and spiritual experiences. *Psychotherapy and Psychosomatics, 66,* 97–106.

Baker, D. B., West, S. A., Nicholson, W. E., Ekhator, N. N., Kasckow, J. W., Hill, K. K., et al. (1999). Serial CSF corticotropin-releasing hormone levels and adrenocortical activity in combat veterans with posttraumatic stress disorder. *American Journal of Psychiatry, 156,* 585–588.

Barefoot, J. C., Helms, M. J., & Mark, D. B. (1996). Depression and long-term mortality risk in patients with coronary artery disease. *American Journal of Cardiology, 78,* 613–617.

Barefoot, J. C., & Schroll, M. (1996). Symptoms of depression, acute myocardial infarction, and total mortality in a community sample. *Circulation, 93,* 1976–1980.

Berkman, L. F., Vaccarino, V., & Seeman, T. (1993). Gender differences in cardiovascular morbidity and mortality: The contribution of social networks and support. *Annals of Behavioral Medicine, 15,* 112–118.

Birmaher, B., Dahl, R. E., Ryan, N. D., Rabinovich, H., Ambrosini, P., al-Shabbout, M., et al. (1992). The dexamethasone suppression test in adolescent outpatients with major depressive disorder. *American Journal of Psychiatry, 149,* 1040–1045.

Bishop, S. R., Lau, M., Shapiro, S., Carlson, L., Anderson, N. D., Carmody, J., et al. (2004). Mindfulness: A proposed operational definition. *Clinical Psychology, 11,* 230–241.

Bishop, S. R., & Sativihari, R. (in press). Effect of mindfulness meditation on anxiety sensitivity: Preliminary findings. *Cognitive Therapy and Research.*

Bonanno, G. A. (2004). Loss, trauma, and human resilience: Have we underestimated the human capacity to thrive after extremely aversive events? *American Psychologist, 59*(1), 20–28.

Bonne, O., Brandes, D., Gilboa, A., Gomori, J. M., Shenton, M. E., Pitman, R. K., et al. (2001). Longitudinal MRI study of hippocampal volume in trauma survivors with PTSD. *American Journal of Psychiatry, 158,* 1248–1251.

Boscarino, J. A. (1997). Diseases among men 20 years after exposure to severe stress: Implications for clinical research and medical care. *Psychosomatic Medicine, 59,* 605–615.

Brass, L., & Page, W. (1996). Stroke in former prisoners of war (POW). *Journal of Stroke and Cerebrovascular Disease, 6,* 72–78.

Bremner, J. D. (1999). Acute and chronic responses to stress: Where do we go from here? [Editorial]. *American Journal of Psychiatry, 156,* 349–351.

Bremner, J. D. (2002a). *Does stress damage the brain? Understanding trauma-related disorders from a mind-body perspective.* New York: Norton.

Bremner, J. D. (2002b). Neuroimaging of childhood trauma. *Seminars in Clinical Neuropsychiatry, 7,* 104–112.

Bremner, J. D. (2002c). Structural changes in the brain in depression and relationship to symptom recurrence. *CNS Spectrums, 7,* 129–139.

Bremner, J. D., Krystal, J. H., Southwick, S. M., & Charney, D. S. (1996a). Noradrenergic mechanisms in stress and anxiety: I. Preclinical studies. *Synapse, 23,* 28–38.

Bremner, J. D., Krystal, J. H., Southwick, S. M., & Charney, D. S. (1996b). Noradrenergic mechanisms in stress and anxiety: II. Clinical studies. *Synapse, 23,* 39–51.

Bremner, J. D., Licinio, J., Darnell, A., Krystal, J. H., Owens, M., Southwick, S. M., et al. (1997). Elevated CSF corticotropin-releasing factor concentrations in posttraumatic stress disorder. *American Journal of Psychiatry, 154,* 624–629.

Bremner, J. D., Narayan, M., Staib, L. H., Southwick, S. M., McGlashan, T., & Charney, D. S. (1999). Neural correlates of memories of childhood sexual abuse in women with and without posttraumatic stress disorder. *American Journal of Psychiatry, 156,* 1787–1795.

Bremner, J. D., Randall, P. R., Capelli, S., Scott, T. M., McCarthy, G., & Charney, D. S. (1995). Deficits in short-term memory in adult survivors of childhood abuse. *Psychiatry Research, 59,* 97–107.

Bremner, J. D., Randall, P. R., Scott, T. M., Bronen, R. A., Delaney, R. C., Seibyl, J. P., et al. (1995). MRI-based measurement of hippocampal volume in patients with combat-related posttraumatic stress disorder. *American Journal of Psychiatry, 152,* 973–981.

Bremner, J. D., Randall, P. R., Vermetten, E., Staib, L., Bronen, R. A., Mazure, C. M., et al. (1997). MRI-based measurement of hippocampal volume in posttraumatic stress disorder related to childhood physical and sexual abuse: A preliminary report. *Biological Psychiatry, 41,* 23–32.

Bremner, J. D., Soufer, R., McCarthy, G., Delaney, R. C., Staib, L. H., Duncan, J. S., et al. (2001). Gender differences in cognitive and neural correlates of remembrance of emotional words. *Psychopharmacology Bulletin, 35,* 55–87.

Bremner, J. D., Southwick, S. M., Darnell, A., & Charney, D. S. (1996). Chronic PTSD in Vietnam combat veterans: Course of illness and substance abuse. *American Journal of Psychiatry, 153,* 369–375.

Bremner, J. D., Southwick, S. M., Johnson, D. R., Yehuda, R., & Charney, D. S. (1993). Childhood physical abuse and combat-related posttraumatic stress disorder in Vietnam veterans. *American Journal of Psychiatry, 150,* 235–239.

Bremner, J. D., Staib, L., Kaloupek, D., Southwick, S. M., Soufer, R., & Charney, D. S. (1999). Neural correlates of exposure to traumatic pictures and sound in Vietnam combat veterans with and without posttraumatic stress disorder: A positron emission tomography study. *Biological Psychiatry, 45,* 806–816.

Bremner, J. D., & Vermetten, E. (2001). Stress and development: Behavioral and biological consequences. *Development and Psychopathology, 13,* 473–489.

Bremner, J. D., Vermetten, E., Schmahl, C., Vaccarino, V., Vythilingam, M., Afzal, N., et al. (in press). Positron emission tomographic imaging of neural correlates of a fear acquisition and extinction paradigm in women with childhood sexual abuse–related posttraumatic stress disorder. *Psychological Medicine.*

Bremner, J. D., Vermetten, E., Vythilingam, M., Afzal, N., Schmahl, C., Elzinga, B. E., et al. (2004). Neural correlates of the classical color and emotional Stroop in women with abuse-related posttraumatic stress disorder. *Biological Psychiatry, 55*(6), 612–620.

Bremner, J. D., Vythilingam, M., Vermetten, E., Adil, J., Khan, S., Nazeer, A., et al. (2002). Cortisol response to a cognitive stress challenge in posttraumatic stress disorder (PTSD) related to childhood abuse. *Psychoneuroendocrinology, 28,* 733–750.

Bremner, J. D., Vythilingam, M., Vermetten, E., Southwick, S. M., McGlashan, T., Nazeer, A., et al. (2002). Deficits in hippocampal structure and function in women with childhood sexual abuse–related posttraumatic stress disorder (PTSD) measured with magnetic resonance imaging and positron emission tomography. *American Journal of Psychiatry, 160*(5), 924–932.

Bremner, J. D., Vythilingam, M., Vermetten, E., Southwick, S. M., McGlashan, T., Nazeer, A., et al. (2003). MRI and PET study of deficits in hippocampal structure and function in women with childhood sexual abuse and posttraumatic stress disorder (PTSD). *American Journal of Psychiatry, 160,* 924–932.

Bremner, J. D., Vythilingam, M., Vermetten, E., Southwick, S. M., McGlashan, T., Staib, L., et al. (2003). Neural correlates of declarative memory for emotionally valenced words in women with posttraumatic stress disorder (PTSD) related to early childhood sexual abuse. *Biological Psychiatry, 53,* 289–299.

Brunson, K. L., Eghbal-Ahmadi, M., Bender, R., Chen, Y., & Baram, T. Z. (2001). Long-term, progressive hippocampal cell loss and dysfunction induced by early-life administration of corticotropin-releasing hormone reproduce the effects of early-life stress. *Proceedings of the National Academy of Sciences, USA, 98*(15), 8856–8861.

Burg, M. M., Jain, D., Soufer, R., Kerns, R. D., & Zaret, B. L. (1993). Role of behavioral and psychological factors in mental stress-induced silent left ventricular dysfunction in coronary artery disease. *Journal of the American College of Cardiology, 22*(2), 440–448.

Carney, R. M., Rich, M. W., & Freedland, K. E. (1988). Major depressive disorder predicts cardiac events in patients with coronary artery disease. *Psychosomatic Medicine, 50,* 627–633.

Carrion, V. G., Weems, C. F., Eliez, S., Patwardhan, A., Brown, W., Ray, R. D., et al. (2001). Attenuation of frontal asymmetry in pediatric posttraumatic stress disorder. *Biological Psychiatry, 50,* 943–951.

Caspi, A., Sugden, K., Moffitt, T. E., Taylor, A., Craig, I. W., Harrington, H., et al. (2003). Influence of life stress on depression: Moderation by a polymorphism in the 5-HTT gene. *Science, 301*(5631), 386.

Cicchetti, D., & Dawson, G. (2002). Editorial: Multiple levels of analysis. *Development and Psychopathology, 14,* 417–420.

Cicchetti, D., & Rogosch, F. A. (1996). Equifinality and multifinality in developmental psychopathology. *Development and Psychopathology, 8,* 597–600.

Cicchetti, D., & Rogosch, F. A. (2001). The impact of child maltreatment and psychopathology on neuroendocrine functioning. *Development and Psychopathology, 13,* 783–804.

Cicchetti, D., & Walker, E. F. (2001). Stress and development: Biological and psychological consequences. *Development and Psychopathology, 13,* 413–418.

Coplan, J. D., Andrews, M. W., Rosenblum, L. A., Owens, M. J., Friedman, S., Gorman, J. M., et al. (1996). Persistent elevations of cerebrospinal fluid concentrations of corticotropin-releasing factor in adult nonhuman primates exposed to early-life stressors: Implications for the pathophysiology of mood and anxiety disorders. *Proceedings of the National Academy of Sciences, USA, 93,* 1619–1623.

Dahl, R. E., Ryan, N. D., Puig-Antich, J., Nguyen, N. A., al-Shabbout, M., Meyer, V. A., et al. (1991). 24-hour cortisol measures in adolescents with major depression: A controlled study. *Biological Psychiatry, 30,* 25–36.

Damasio, H., Grabowski, T., Frank, R., Galaburda, A. M., & Damasio, A. R. (1994). The return of Phineas Gage: Clues about the brain from the skull of a famous patient. *Science, 264,* 1102–1105.

Davis, M. (1992). The role of the amygdala in fear and anxiety. *Annual Review of Neuroscience, 15,* 353–375.

DeBellis, M. D., Baum, A. S., Keshavan, M. S., Eccard, C. H., Boring, A. M., Jenkins, F. J., et al. (1999). A. E. Bennett Research Award: Developmental traumatology: Pt. I. Biological stress systems. *Biological Psychiatry, 45,* 1259–1270.

DeBellis, M. D., Chrousos, G. P., Dorn, L. D., Burke, L., Helmers, K., Kling, M. A., et al. (1994). Hypothalamic pituitary adrenal dysregulation in sexually abused girls. *Journal of Clinical Endocrinology and Metabolism, 78,* 249–255.

DeBellis, M. D., Hall, J., Boring, A. M., Frustaci, K., & Moritz, G. (2001). A pilot longitudinal study of hippocampal volumes in pediatric maltreatment-related posttraumatic stress disorder. *Biological Psychiatry, 50,* 305–309.

DeBellis, M. D., Keshavan, M. S., Clark, D. B., Casey, B. J., Giedd, J. N., Boring, A. M., et al. (1999). A. E. Bennett Research Award: Developmental traumatology: Pt. II. Brain development. *Biological Psychiatry, 45,* 1271–1284.

DeBellis, M. D., Keshavan, M. S., Spencer, S., & Hall, J. (2000). N-acetylaspartate concentration in the anterior cingulate of maltreated children and adolescents with PTSD. *American Journal of Psychiatry, 157,* 1175–1177.

DeBellis, M. D., Lefter, L., Trickett, P. K., & Putnam, F. W. (1994). Urinary catecholamine excretion in sexually abused girls. *Journal of the American Academy of Child and Adolescent Psychiatry, 33,* 320–327.

Devinsky, O., Morrell, M. J., & Vogt, B. A. (1995). Contributions of anterior cingulate to behavior. *Brain, 118,* 279–306.

Diamond, D. M., Fleshner, M., Ingersoll, N., & Rose, G. M. (1996). Psychological stress impairs spatial working memory: Relevance to electrophysiological studies of hippocampal function. *Behavioral Neuroscience, 110,* 661–672.

Diorio, D., Viau, V., & Meaney, M. J. (1993). The role of the medial prefrontal cortex (cingulate gyrus) in the regulation of hypothalamic-pituitary-adrenal responses to stress. *Journal of Neuroscience, 13*(9), 3839–3847.

Dorn, L. D., Burgess, E. S., Susman, E. J., von Eye, A., DeBellis, M. D., Gold, P. W., et al. (1996). Response to CRH in depressed and nondepressed adolescents: Does gender make a difference? *Journal of the American Academy of Child and Adolescent Psychiatry, 35,* 764–773.

Dube, S. R., Felitti, V. J., Dong, M., Giles, W. H., & Anda, R. F. (2003). The impact of adverse childhood experiences on health problems: Evidence from four birth cohorts dating back to 1900. *Preventive Medicine, 37,* 268–277.

Eisen, S., Neuman, R., Goldberg, J., Rice, J., & True, W. (1989). Determining zygosity in the Vietnam Era Twin Registry: An approach using questionnaires. *Clinical Genetics, 35,* 423–432.

Elzinga, B. M., Schmahl, C. S., Vermetten, E., van Dyck, R., & Bremner, J. D. (2002). Increased cortisol responses to the stress of traumatic reminders in abuse-related PTSD. *Neuropsychopharmacology, 28* 1656–1665.

Engel, C. C., Liu, X., McCarthy, B. D., Miller, R. F., & Ursano, R. (2000). Relationship of physical symptoms to posttraumatic stress disorder among veterans seeking care for Gulf War related health conditions. *Psychosomatic Medicine, 62*(6), 739–745.

Feiring, C., & Lewis, M. (1996). Finality in the eye of the beholder: Multiple sources, multiple time points, multiple paths. *Development and Psychopathology, 8,* 721–733.

Feldman, S., Conforti, N., & Weidenfeld, J. (1995). Limbic pathways and hypothalamic neurotransmitters mediating adrenocortical responses to neural stimuli. *Neuroscience and Biobehavioral Reviews, 19*(2), 235–240.

Ford, D. E., Mead, L. A., Chang, P. P., Cooper-Patrick, L., Wang, N., & Klag, M. J. (1998). Depression is a risk factor for coronary artery disease in men. *Archives of Internal Medicine, 158*(10), 54–59.

Frasure-Smith, N., Lesperance, F., Juneau, M., Talajic, M., & Bourassa, M. G. (1999). Gender, depression and one-year prognosis after myocardial infarction. *Psychosomatic Medicine, 61,* 26–37.

Frasure-Smith, N., Lesperance, F., & Talajic, M. (1993). Depression following myocardial infarction. *Journal of the American Medical Association, 270,* 1819–1825.

Fredman, L., Magaziner, J., Hebel, J. R., Hawkes, W., & Zimmerman, S. I. (1999). Depressive symptoms and 6-year mortality among elderly community-dwelling women. *Epidemiology, 10,* 54–59.

Freud, S. (1995). *The basic writings of Sigmund Freud.* New York: Modern Library.

Frysztak, R. J., & Neafsey, E. J. (1994). The effect of medial frontal cortex lesions on cardiovascular conditioned emotional responses in the rat. *Brain Research, 643,* 181–193.

Gabay, C., & Kushner, I. (1999). Acute-phase proteins and other systemic responses to inflammation. *New England Journal of Medicine, 340,* 448–454.

Gilbertson, M. W., Shenton, M. E., Ciszewski, A., Kasai, K., Lasko, N. B., Orr, S. P., et al. (2002). Smaller hippocampal volume predicts pathologic vulnerability to psychological trauma. *Nature Neuroscience, 5*(11), 1242–1247.

Gold, P. W., Loriaux, D. L., Roy, A., Kling, M. A., Calabrese, J. R., Kellner, C. H., et al. (1986). Response to corticotropin-releasing hormone in the hypercortisolism of depression and Cushing's disease. *New England Journal of Medicine, 314,* 1329–1335.

Goldberg, J., True, W. R., Eisen, S. A., & Henderson, W. G. (1990). A twin study of the effects of the Vietnam War on posttraumatic stress disorder. *Journal of the American Medical Association, 263,* 1227–1232.

Goldberg, J., True, W. R., Eisen, S. A., Henderson, W., & Robinette, C. D. (1987). The Vietnam Era Twin (VET) Registry: Ascertainment bias. *Acta Genetica and Medical Gemellology, 36,* 67–78.

Gould, E., Tanapat, P., McEwen, B. S., Flugge, G., & Fuchs, E. (1998). Proliferation of granule cell precursors in the dentate gyrus of adult monkeys is diminished by stress. *Proceedings of the National Academy of Sciences, USA, 95,* 3168–3171.

Gullette, E. C. D., Blumenthal, J. A., & Babyak, M. (1997). Effect of mental stress on myocardial ischemia during daily life. *Journal of the American Medical Association, 277,* 1521–1526.

Gunnar, M. R., Morison, S. J., Chisolm, K., & Schuder, M. (2001). Salivary cortisol levels in children adopted from Romanian orphanages. *Development and Psychopathology, 13,* 611–628.

Gurvits, T. G., Shenton, M. R., Hokama, H., Ohta, H., Lasko, N. B., Gilbertson, M. B., et al. (1996). Magnetic resonance imaging study of hippocampal volume in chronic combat-related posttraumatic stress disorder. *Biological Psychiatry, 40,* 192–199.

Harrington, R., Rutter, M., & Fombonne, E. (1996). Developmental pathways in depression: Multiple meanings, antecedents, and endpoints. *Development and Psychopathology, 8,* 601–616.

Hart, J., Gunnar, M., & Cicchetti, D. (1996). Altered neuroendocrine activity in maltreated children related to symptoms of depression. *Development and Psychopathology, 8,* 201–214.

Heim, C., Newport, D. J., Bonsall, R., Miller, A. H., & Nemeroff, C. B. (2001). Altered pituitary-adrenal axis responses to provocative challenge tests in adult survivors of childhood abuse. *American Journal of Psychiatry, 158,* 575–581.

Heim, C., Newport, D. J., Heit, S., Graham, Y. P., Wilcox, M., Bonsall, R., et al. (2000). Pituitary-adrenal and autonomic responses to stress in women after sexual and physical abuse in childhood. *Journal of the American Medical Association, 284,* 592–597.

Hemingway, H., & Marmot, M. (1999). Psychosocial factors in the aetiology and prognosis of coronary heart disease: Systematic review of prospective cohort studies. *British Medical Journal, 318,* 1460–1467.

Henderson, W. G., Eisen, S., Goldberg, J., True, W. R., Barnes, J. E., & Vitek, M. E. (1990). The Vietnam Era Twin Registry: A resource for medical research. *Public Health Reports, 105,* 368–373.

Hippisley-Cox, J., Fielding, K., & Pringle, M. (1998). Depression as a risk factor for ischemic heart disease in men: Population based case-control study. *British Medical Journal, 316,* 1714–1719.

Hitchcock, J. M., & Davis, M. (1986). Lesions of the amygdala, but not of the cerebellum or red nucleus, block conditioned fear as measured with the potentiated startle paradigm. *Behavioral Neuroscience, 100,* 11–22.

Hitchcock, J. M., & Davis, M. (1991). Efferent pathway of the amygdala involved in conditioned fear as measured with the fear-potentiated startle paradigm. *Behavioral Neuroscience, 105,* 826–842.

Hitchcock, J. M., Sananes, C. B., & Davis, M. (1989). Sensitization of the startle reflex by footshock: Blockade by lesions of the central nucleus of the amygdala or its efferent pathway to the brainstem. *Behavioral Neuroscience, 103,* 509–518.

Horger, B. A., & Roth, R. H. (1996). The role of mesoprefrontal dopamine neurons in stress. *Critical Reviews in Neurobiology, 10,* 395–418.

Ito, Y., Teicher, M. H., Glod, C. A., Harper, D., Magnus, E., & Gelbard, H. A. (1993). Increased prevalence of electrophysiological abnormalities in children with psychological, physical and sexual abuse. *Journal of Neuropsychiatry and Clinical Neuroscience, 5,* 401–408.

Johnson, M. H., Halit, H., Grice, S. J., & Karmiloff-Smith, A. (2002). Neuroimaging of typical and atypical development: A perspective from multiple levels of analysis. *Development and Psychopathology, 14,* 521–536.

Kagan, J., Snidman, N., McManis, M., Woodward, S., & Hardway, C. (2002). One measure, one meaning: Multiple measures, clearer meaning. *Development and Psychopathology, 14,* 463–475.

Kaplan, J. R., Manuck, S. B., Adams, M. R., Weingand, K. W., & Clarkson, T. B. (1987). Inhibition of coronary atherosclerosis by propanolol in behaviorally predisposed monkeys fed an atherogenic diet. *Circulation, 76,* 1365–1372.

Kaplan, J. R., Manuck, S. B., Clarkson, T. B., Lusso, F. M., & Taub, D. B. (1982). Social status, environment, and atherosclerosis in cynomolgus monkeys. *Arteriosclerosis, 2,* 359–368.

Keane, T. M., Caddell, J. M., & Taylor, K. L. (1988). Mississippi Scale for Combat-Related Post-Traumatic Stress Disorder: Three studies in reliability and validity. *Journal of Consulting and Clinical Psychology, 56,* 85–90.

Keane, T. M., Wolfe, J., & Taylor, K. L. (1987). Post-traumatic stress disorder: Evidence for diagnostic validity and method for psychological assessment. *Journal of Clinical Psychology, 43,* 32–43.

Kemper, J. W., Baggenstoss, A. H., & Slocumb, C. H. (1957). The relationship of therapy with cortisone to the incidence of vascular lesions in rheumatoid arthritis. *Annals of Internal Medicine, 46,* 831–851.

Kempermann, G., Kuhn, H. G., & Gage, F. H. (1998). Experience-induced neurogenesis in the senescent dentate gyrus. *Journal of Neuroscience, 18,* 3206–3212.

Kendler, K. S., Thornton, L. M., & Gardner, C. O. (2000). Stressful life events and previous episodes in the etiology of major depression in women: An evaluation of the "kindling" hypothesis. *American Journal of Psychiatry, 157,* 1243–1251.

Kessler, R. C., & Magee, W. J. (1993). Childhood adversities and adult depression: Basic patterns of association in a U.S. national survey. *Psychological Medicine, 23,* 679–690.

Kopnisky, K. L., Cowan, W. M., & Hyman, S. E. (2002). Levels of analysis in psychiatric research. *Development and Psychopathology, 14,* 437–461.

Krumholz, H. M., Butler, J., Miller, J., Vaccarino, V., Williams, C. S., Mendes de Leon, C. F., et al. (1998). Prognostic importance of emotional support for elderly patients hospitalized with heart failure. *Circulation, 97,* 958–964.

Kutcher, S., Malkin, D., Silverberg, J., Marton, P., Williamson, P. C., Malkin, A., et al. (1991). Nocturnal cortisol, thyroid stimulating hormone, and growth hormone secretory profiles in depressed adolescents. *Journal of the American Academy of Child and Adolescent Psychiatry, 30,* 407–414.

Ladd, C. O., Owens, M. J., & Nemeroff, C. B. (1996). Persistent changes in CRF neuronal systems produced by maternal separation. *Endocrinology, 137,* 1212–1218.

Lampert, R., Ickovics, J., Viscoli, C., Horwitz, R., & Lee, W. (1998). Inter-relationship between effect on heart rate variability and effect on outcome by beta-blockers in the Beta Blocker Heart Attack Trial (BHAT). *Circulation, 98,* 1–80.

LeDoux, J. E. (1996). *The emotional brain: The mysterious underpinnings of emotional life.* New York: Simon & Schuster.

LeDoux, J. L. (1993). In search of systems and synapses. *Annals of the New York Academy of Sciences, 702,* 149–157.

Lemaire, V., Koehl, M., Le Moal, M., & Abrous, D. N. (2000). Prenatal stress produces learning deficits associated with an inhibition of neurogenesis in the hippocampus. *Proceedings of the National Academy of Sciences, USA, 97*(20), 11032–11037.

Lemieux, A. M., & Coe, C. L. (1995). Abuse-related posttraumatic stress disorder: Evidence for chronic neuroendocrine activation in women. *Psychosomatic Medicine, 57,* 105–115.

Levine, S., Weiner, S. G., & Coe, C. L. (1993). Temporal and social factors influencing behavioral and hormonal responses to separation in mother and infant squirrel monkeys. *Psychoneuroendocrinology, 4,* 297–306.

Liu, D., Diorio, J., Day, J. C., Francis, D. D., & Meaney, M. J. (2000). Maternal care, hippocampal synaptogenesis and cognitive development in rats. *Nature Neuroscience, 8,* 799–806.

Luine, V., Villages, M., Martinex, C., & McEwen, B. S. (1994). Repeated stress causes reversible impairments of spatial memory performance. *Brain Research, 639,* 167–170.

Macklin, M. L., Metzger, L. J., Litz, B. T., McNally, R. J., Lasko, N. B., Orr, S. P., et al. (1998). Lower precombat intelligence is a risk factor for posttraumatic stress disorder. *Journal of Consulting and Clinical Psychology, 66,* 323–326.

MacLean, P. D. (1949). Psychosomatic disease and the visceral brain: Recent developments bearing on the Papez theory of emotion. *Psychosomatic Medicine, 11,* 338–353.

Makino, S., Smith, M. A., & Gold, P. W. (1995). Increased expression of corticotropin-releasing hormone and vasopressin messenger-ribonucleic acid (messenger RNA) in the hypothalamic paraventricular nucleus during repeated stress: Association with reduction in glucocorticoid messenger-RNA levels. *Endocrinology, 136,* 3299–3309.

Malberg, J. E., Eisch, A. J., Nestler, E. J., & Duman, R. S. (2000). Chronic antidepressant treatment increases neurogenesis in adult rat hippocampus. *Journal of Neuroscience, 20,* 9104–9110.

McEwen, B. S., Conrad, C. D., Kuroda, Y., Frankfurt, M., Magarinos, A. M., & McKittrick, C. (1997). Prevention of stress-induced morphological and cognitive consequences. *European Neuropsychopharmacology, 7,* S322–E328.

McNally, R. J., & Shin, L. H. (1995). Association of intelligence with severity of posttraumatic stress disorder symptoms in Vietnam combat veterans. *American Journal of Psychiatry, 152,* 936–938.

Meaney, M. J., Aitken, D., van Berkel, C., Bhatnager, S., & Sapolsky, R. M. (1988). Effect of neonatal handling on age-related impairments associated with the hippocampus. *Science, 239,* 766–769.

Melia, K. R., & Duman, R. S. (1991). Involvement of corticotropin-releasing factor in chronic stress regulation of the brain noradrenergic system. *Proceedings of the National Academy of Sciences, USA, 88,* 8382–8386.

Mendes de Leon, C. F., Krumholz, H. M., Seeman, T. S., Vaccarino, V., Williams, C. S., Kasl, S. V., et al. (1998). Depression and risk of coronary heart disease in elderly men and women: Prospective evidence from the New Haven EPESE. *Archives of Internal Medicine, 158,* 2341–2348.

Milad, M. R., & Quirk, G. J. (2002). Neurons in medial prefrontal cortex signal memory for fear extinction. *Nature, 420,* 70–73.

Miserendino, M. J. D., Sananes, C. B., Melia, K. R., & Davis, M. (1990). Blocking of acquisition but not expression of conditioned fear-potentiated startle by NMDA antagonists in the amygdala. *Nature, 345,* 716–718.

Morgan, C. A., & LeDoux, J. E. (1995). Differential contribution of dorsal and ventral medial prefrontal cortex to the acquisition and extinction of conditioned fear in rats. *Behavioral Neuroscience, 109,* 681–688.

Morgan, C. A., Romanski, L. M., & LeDoux, J. E. (1993). Extinction of emotional learning: Contribution of medial prefrontal cortex. *Neuroscience Letters, 163,* 109–113.

Musselman, D. L., Evans, D. L., & Nemeroff, C. B. (1998). The relationship of depression to cardiovascular disease. *Archives of General Psychiatry, 55,* 580–592.

Nahas, G. G., Brunson, J. G., King, W. M., & Cavert, H. M. (1958). Functional and morphologic changes in heart lung preparations following administration of adrenal hormones. *American Journal of Clinical Pathology, 34,* 717–729.

Nemeroff, C. B., Widerlov, E., Bissette, G., Walleus, H., Karlsson, I., Eklund, K., et al. (1984). Elevated concentrations of CSF corticotropin-releasing factor-like immunoreactivity in depressed patients. *Science, 226,* 1342–1344.

Nibuya, M., Morinobu, S., & Duman, R. S. (1995). Regulation of BDNF and trkB mRNA in rat brain by chronic electroconvulsive seizure and antidepressant drug treatments. *Journal of Neuroscience, 15,* 7539–7547.

Oppenheim, H. (2001). Traumatic pasts: History, psychiatry, and trauma in the modern age, 1870–1930 (M. S. Micale & P. Lerner, Eds.). Cambridge, London: Cambridge University Press.

Pani, L., Porcella, A., & Gessa, G. L. (2000). The role of stress in the pathophysiology of the dopaminergic system. *Molecular Psychiatry, 5,* 14–21.

Papez, J. W. (1937). A proposed mechanism of emotion. *American Medical Association Archives of Neurology and Psychiatry, 38,* 725–743.

Phillips, R. G., & LeDoux, J. E. (1992). Differential contribution of amygdala and hippocampus to cued and contextual fear conditioning. *Behavioral Neuroscience, 106,* 274–285.

Pitman, R. K. (2001). Hippocampal diminution in PTSD: More (or less?) than meets the eye. *Hippocampus, 11*(2), 73–74.

Pitman, R. K., & Orr, S. P. (1990). Twenty-four hour urinary cortisol and catecholamine excretion in combat-related posttraumatic stress disorder. *Biological Psychiatry, 27,* 245–247.

Plotsky, P. M., & Meaney, M. J. (1993). Early, postnatal experience alters hypothalamic corticotropin-releasing factor (CRF) mRNA, median eminence CRF content and stress-induced release in adult rats. *Molecular Brain Research, 18*(3), 195–200.

Pratt, L. A., Ford, D. E., Crum, R. M., Armenian, H. K., Gallo, J. J., & Eaton, W. W. (1996). Depression, psychotropic medication, and risk of myocardial infarction: Prospective data from the Baltimore ECA follow-up. *Circulation, 94,* 3123–3129.

Proctor, S. P., Harley, R., Wolfe, J., Heeren, T., & White, R. F. (2001). Health-related quality of life in Persian Gulf War veterans. *Military Medicine, 166*(6), 510–519.

Proctor, S. P., Heeren, T., White, R. F., Wolfe, J., Borgos, M. S., Davis, J. D., et al. (1998). Health status of Persian Gulf War veterans: Self-reported symptoms, environmental exposures, and the effect of stress. *International Journal of Epidemiology, 27*(6), 1000–1010.

Rasmusson, A. M., Lipschitz, D. S., Bremner, J. D., Southwick, S. M., & Charney, D. S. (2001). Increased pituitary and adrenal reactivity in premenopausal women with posttraumatic stress disorder. *Biological Psychiatry, 50,* 965–977.

Richters, J. E., & Hinshaw, S. P. (1999). The abduction of disorder in psychiatry. *Journal of Abnormal Psychology, 108*(3), 438–445.

Rosen, J. B., & Davis, M. (1988). Enhancement of acoustic startle by electrical stimulation of the amygdala. *Behavioral Neuroscience, 102,* 195–202.

Rozanski, A., Blumenthal, J. A., & Kaplan, J. (1999). Impact of psychological factors on the pathogenesis of cardiovascular disease and implications for therapy. *Circulation, 99,* 2192–2217.

Saigh, P. A., & Bremner, J. D. (1999). The history of posttraumatic stress disorder. In P. A. Saigh & J. D. Bremner (Eds.), *Posttraumatic stress disorder: A comprehensive text* (pp. 1–17). Needham Heights, MA: Allyn & Bacon.

Saigh, P. A., Yasik, A. E., Oberfield, R. A., Green, B. L., Halamandaris, P. V., Rubenstein, H., et al. (2000). The Children's PTSD Inventory: Development and reliability. *Journal of Traumatic Stress, 13,* 369–380.

Sapolsky, R. M. (1996). Why stress is bad for your brain. *Science, 273,* 749–750.

Schiffer, F., Teicher, M. H., & Papanicolaou, A. C. (1995). Evoked potential evidence for right brain activity during the recall of traumatic memories. *Journal of Neuropsychiatry and Clinical Neuroscience, 7,* 169–175.

Shin, L. H., McNally, R. J., Kosslyn, S. M., Thompson, W. L., Rauch, S. L., Alpert, N. M., et al. (1999). Regional cerebral blood flow during script-driven imagery in childhood sexual abuse–related PTSD: A PET investigation. *American Journal of Psychiatry, 156,* 575–584.

Smith, M. A., Davidson, R., Ritchie, J. C., Kudler, H., Lipper, S., Chappell, P., et al. (1989). The corticotropin-releasing hormone test in patients with posttraumatic stress disorder. *Biological Psychiatry, 26,* 349–355.

Soufer, R., Bremner, J. D., Arrighi, J. A., Cohen, I., Zaret, B. L., Burg, M. M., et al. (1998). Cerebral cortical hyperactivation in response to mental stress in patients with coronary artery disease. *Proceedings of the National Academy of Sciences, USA, 95,* 6454–6459.

Stanton, M. E., Gutierrez, Y. R., & Levine, S. (1988). Maternal deprivation potentiates pituitary-adrenal stress responses in infant rats. *Behavioral Neuroscience, 102,* 692–700.

Stein, M. B., Koverola, C., Hanna, C., Torchia, M. G., & McClarty, B. (1997). Hippocampal volume in women victimized by childhood sexual abuse. *Psychological Medicine, 27,* 951–959.

Stein, M. B., Yehuda, R., Koverola, C., & Hanna, C. (1997). Enhanced dexamethasone suppression of plasma cortisol in adult women traumatized by childhood sexual abuse. *Biological Psychiatry, 42,* 680–686.

Teasdale, J. D., Segal, A., & Williams, J. M. G. (1995). How does cognitive therapy prevent depressive relapse and why should attentional control (mindfulness) training help? *Behavior Research and Therapy, 33*(1), 25–39.

Teasdale, J. D., Segal, Z. V., Williams, J. M. G., Ridgeway, V. A., Soulsby, J. M., & Lau, M. A. (2000). Prevention of relapse/recurrence in major depression by mindfulness-based cognitive therapy. *Journal of Consulting and Clinical Psychology, 68,* 615–623.

Troxler, R. G., Sprague, E. A., Albanese, R. A., Fuchs, R., & Thompson, A. J. (1977). The association of elevated plasma cortisol and early atherosclerosis as demonstrated by coronary angiography. *Atherosclerosis, 26,* 151–162.

True, W. R., Rice, J., Eisen, S. A., Heath, A. C., Goldberg, J., Lyons, M. J., et al. (1993). A twin study of genetic and environmental contributions to liability for posttraumatic stress disorder symptoms. *Archives of General Psychiatry, 50,* 257–264.

Uno, H., Tarara, R., Else, J. G., Suleman, M. A., & Sapolsky, R. M. (1989). Hippocampal damage associated with prolonged and fatal stress in primates. *Journal of Neuroscience, 9,* 1705–1711.

Vythilingam, M., Heim, C., Newport, C. D., Miller, A. H., Vermetten, E., Anderson, E., et al. (2002). Childhood trauma associated with smaller hippocampal volume in women with major depression. *American Journal of Psychiatry, 159,* 2072–2080.

Wagner, A. W., Wolfe, J., Rotnitsky, A., Proctor, S. P., & Erickson, D. J. (2000). An investigation of the impact of posttraumatic stress disorder on physical health. *Journal of Traumatic Stress, 13*(1), 41–55.

Wakefield, J. C. (1999). Evolutionary versus prototype analyses of the concept of disorder. *Journal of Abnormal Psychology, 108,* 374–399.

Watanabe, Y. E., Gould, H., Cameron, D., Daniels, D., & McEwen, B. S. (1992). Phenytoin prevents stress and corticosterone induced atrophy of CA3 pyramidal neurons. *Hippocampus, 2,* 431–436.

Weissbecker, I., Salmon, P., Studts, J. L., Floyd, A. R., Dedert, E. A., & Sephton, S. E. (2002). Mindfulness-based stress reduction and sense of coherence among women with fibromyalgia. *Journal of Clinical Psychology in Medical Settings, 9,* 297–307.

Williamson, D. F., Thompson, T. J., Anda, R. F., Dietz, W. H., & Felitti, V. J. (2002). Body weight, obesity, and self-reported abuse in childhood. *International Journal of Obesity, 26,* 1075–1082.

Wittstein, I. S., Thiemann, D. R., Lima, J. A. C., Baughman, K. L., Schulman, S. P., Gerstenblith, G., et al. (2005). Neurohormonal features of myocardial stunning due to sudden emotional stress. *New England Journal of Medicine, 352,* 539–548.

Wulsin, L. R., Vaillant, G. E., & Wells, V. E. (1999). A systematic review of the mortality of depression. *Psychosomatic Medicine, 61,* 6–17.

Yehuda, R., Lowry, M. T., Southwick, S. M., Mason, J. W., & Giller, E. L. (1991). Increased number of glucocorticoid receptors in posttraumatic stress disorder. *American Journal of Psychiatry, 148,* 499–504.

Yehuda, R., Southwick, S. M., Krystal, J. H., Bremner, J. D., Charney, D. S., & Mason, J. (1993). Enhanced suppression of cortisol with low dose dexamethasone in posttraumatic stress disorder. *American Journal of Psychiatry, 150,* 83–86.

Yehuda, R., Southwick, S. M., Nussbaum, E. L., Giller, E. L., & Mason, J. W. (1991). Low urinary cortisol in PTSD. *Journal of Nervous and Mental Diseases, 178,* 366–369.

Zatzick, D. F., Marmar, C. R., Weiss, D. S., Browner, W. S., Metzler, T. J., Golding, J. M., et al. (1997). Posttraumatic stress disorder and functioning and quality of life outcomes in a nationally representative sample of male Vietnam veterans. *American Journal of Psychiatry, 154*(12), 1690–1695.

CHAPTER 17

Immunology and Developmental Psychopathology

DOUGLAS A. GRANGER, GALE A. GRANGER, and STEVE W. GRANGER

Exponential growth in knowledge of the interactions among the central and peripheral nervous systems and the immune system has been achieved in the past 3 decades (Ader, 1981, 2000; Ader, Felten, & Cohen, 1991; Ader, Cohen, & Felten, 1995). The signals and routes via which psychological and physical stressors lead to endocrine and immune responses have been studied extensively. Theorists, applied researchers, and professionals are extrapolating these basic findings to consider how individual differences in psychological states might be associated with immunity, illness susceptibility, and negative health outcomes (see Cohen & Herbert, 1996; Herbert & Cohen, 1993b; Kemeny & Gruenewald, 1999; Kemeny & Laudenslager, 1999; Kiecolt-Glaser & Glaser, 1995). By contrast, how such processes affect children's immunity has received only scant empirical attention (e.g., Adamson-Macedo, 2000; Boyce et al., 1995; C. K. Coe, 1999; C. L.

Coe, 1996). Although developmental science should be concerned with the ultimate impact of these phenomena on children's health and well-being, and additional research with this particular emphasis seems to be a high priority, the focus of this chapter is on another leading edge of psychoneuroimmunologic research (e.g., Maier & Watkins, 1998a, 1998b; Maier, Watkins, & Fleshner, 1994) that has substantially altered assumptions regarding the direction and nature of effects among the brain, behavior, and immunity (e.g., Blalock, 1994; Dantzer, 2001).

Our overarching objective is to introduce a new world of ideas to developmental scientists and to reveal how the implications of this new knowledge extends into their realm of inquiry and influences theories about the origins of individual differences in and extremes of behavior (Cicchetti & Lynch, 1995; Gottlieb, 1992). To place these ideas into a meaningful context, a historical overview of our understanding regarding the neuroendocrine immune (NEI) network is provided. Whenever possible, road maps to seminal papers for interested readers are offered. We assume that developmental psychopathology has only rarely cross-trained its students in immunology, and therefore we digress to introduce the basic features of the immune system with an emphasis on its proposed function as our "sixth sense." Then the concomitants and consequences of the intracellular regulatory molecules of the NEI network (e.g., cytokines) for the brain and ultimately behavior are described with direct reference to their association with developmental psychopathology. Next, we review the available evidence that supports immune system-stimulated changes in central nervous and endocrine systems during early development as they effect permanent changes in these processes as well as in social behavior that persists into adulthood. Genetic-developmental and social environmental forces are also explored as examples of potential moderators of the developmental effects of early illness on later life outcomes. Collectively, the findings support the biological plausibility that the search for environmental forces that shape microevolution and individual development has largely overlooked a large class of ubiquitous and omnipresent stimuli: physical antigens such as viruses, bacteria, and toxins. We conclude by presenting a theoretical model of how psychoneuroimmunologic processes affect developmental plasticity, and we make recommendations for research to integrate such ideas into developmental science in the next generation of studies.

THE NEUROENDOCRINE IMMUNE NETWORK: ABBREVIATED HISTORY OF THE SCIENCE

Robert Ader (1996, 2000) has thoughtfully documented the history of science linking behavior and psychological states to changes in immune function. He describes a modern set of assumptions that has evolved from a series of major discoveries that punctuate three major eras of inquiry. The first era spans the turn of the prior century through the early 1950s. During this period, the field of immunology made substantial strides and expanded our understanding of lymphoid cell and tissue function, antibody specificity and activity, and most other basic features of the immune system. These advances had profound implications for research and treatment of infectious disease, allergy, cancer, and tissue rejection/transplantation. But classically trained immunologists of this time were in some respects myopic. It was determined that the central nervous system (CNS) lacked a lymphatic system to drain its tissues and capture

potential antigens and was protected from infiltration of many soluble substances (i.e., cytokines) and the inward migration of lymphoid cells by the blood-brain barrier (Benveniste, 1992a, 1992b). Correspondingly, the dominant assumption was that the CNS operated relatively isolated from, and independent of, the immune system. The CNS was considered an immunologically privileged site. There was no available evidence to support the biological plausibility that the immune system might be influenced by psychological, cognitive, affective, or behavioral states. With only a few exceptions, this set of ideas attracted little or no empirical attention. There were some Russian scientists (Kopeloff, Kopeloff, & Raney, 1933) who published findings in the 1930s suggesting that components of the immune response could be classically conditioned (see Ader, 1996), but this potentially groundbreaking work was largely overlooked by the scientific establishment. Needless to say, the possibility that the immune system may affect the brain and behavior was never addressed in the scientific literature of this time.

Observations made by George Solomon (1969; Solomon, Amkraut, & Kasper, 1974; Solomon & Moos, 1965), then working at Stanford University, are considered by many to have initiated a paradigm shift in the 1960s. Solomon and his colleagues reported clinical evidence of associative relationships between socioemotional events and immune activity. He claimed that individual differences in symptoms of autoimmune arthritis varied as a function of social and psychological features (conflict, cohesion, emotional climate) of the family environment (Solomon & Moos, 1965). Unfortunately, as with the observations of the Russian scientists 30 years earlier, Solomon's reports were not well received by the scientific establishment. They did attract attention, but they were largely dismissed as being "biologically implausible." Journal editors and study sections serially rejected his manuscripts and proposals, and in the face of strong resistance to his ideas, he temporarily closed his laboratory due to lack of support.

The evidence of "biological plausibility" that Solomon needed to support the veridicality of his clinical observations was not obtained until the late 1970s and early 1980s. Anatomical pathways were discovered that physiochemically linked the central nervous and lymphoid systems (see Figure 17.1). Most notably, a team led by David and Susan Felten at the University of Rochester identified specific efferent nerve tracts that terminated in lymphoid tissues and organs, including the spleen (D. L. Felten, Ackerman, Wiegand, & Felten, 1987), lymph nodes (D. L. Felten et al., 1984), thymus (Williams et al., 1981), and appendix (D. L. Felten, Overhage, Felten, & Schmedtje, 1981). Receptors

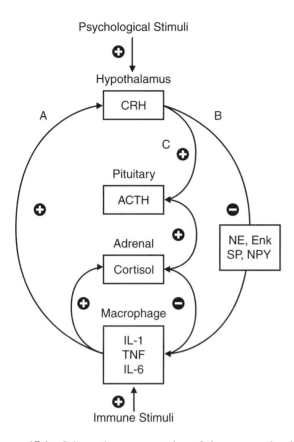

Psychological Stimuli

Hypothalamus

CRH

A   B

C

Pituitary

ACTH

NE, Enk
SP, NPY

Adrenal

Cortisol

Macrophage

IL-1
TNF
IL-6

Immune Stimuli

Figure 17.1 Schematic representation of the neuroendocrine-immune system and its signaling routes and molecules. Pathway A indicates the immune-to-brain communication link via the activity of cytokines (IL-1 = Interleukin-1; IL-6 = Interleukin-6; TNF = Tumor necrosis factor). Pathway B indicates the communication route between the autonomic nervous system (ANS) and the immune system (ENK = Enkephalin; NE = Norepinephrine; NPY = Neuropeptide YSP = Substance P). Pathway C indicates the communication link between the Hypothalamic-pituitary-adrenal axis and the immune system (ACTH = Adrenocorticotropic hormone; CORT = Cortisol or corticosterone; CRF = Corticotropin-releasing hormone). Plus (+) and minus (−) identify pathways with primarily excitatory or inhibitory effects. *Source:* From "Developmental Psychoneuroimmunology: The Role of Cytokine Network Activation in the Epigenesis of Developmental Psychopathology" (pp. 293–323), by D. A. Granger, N. A. Dreschel, and E. A. Shirtcliff, in *Neurodevelopmental Mechanisms in Psychopathology* by D. Cicchetti and E. Walker (Eds.), 2003, New York: Cambridge University Press.

were identified on lymphoid cells for a variety of the products (e.g., epinephrine, norepinephrine) secreted by these nerve terminals (S. Y. Felten, Felten, Bellinger, & Olschowka, 1992). Lymphoid cell function was altered in the presence of these substances. Then it was established that the hypothalamic-pituitary-adrenal (HPA) axis (i.e., adrenocorticotropic hormone, glucocorticoids) and autonomic nervous systems (i.e., substance P, neuropeptide Y,

norepinephrine) were able to communicate with lymphoid cells via releasing factors and hormones secreted into the general circulation (see Carr, Radulescu, DeCosta, Rice, & Blalock, 1992). These discoveries of both hard-wired and soluble chemical messenger routes of communication served to establish the scientific legitimacy of studying interrelationships among the brain, behavior, and immunity (Ader, 1981; Ader et al., 1991; Kiecolt-Glaser & Glaser, 1989). Subsequently, research focused on explaining individual differences in links between stress, behavior, and health risk as mediated or moderated by the effects of psychological states on immune function. Research reports from this effort now fill many of the pages of health-oriented scientific journals, such as *Health Psychology, Annals of Behavioral Medicine, Brain, Behavior and Immunity,* and *Psychosomatic Medicine.*

The interested reader is referred to a meta-analytic review on stress and immunity by Herbert and Cohen (1993b). Briefly, the review reveals that subjective experiences related to stress are capable of suppressing immune activity. However, there are several important caveats. The effects are not necessarily consistent within any or across the many different compartments of the immune system (see later discussion). The magnitude of the suppressive effect, averaging across all available studies, is approximately 10%. The duration of effects is best characterized as a temporary "delay" rather than an absolute shutdown in any particular immune process.

Although the basic immunosuppressive effect of stress on immunity is consistently observed across studies, there remain questions regarding the clinical significance and ultimate impact on health of such effects. That is, only a handful of studies (e.g., Cohen, Tyrell, & Smith, 1991) have come close to *causally* linking stress-induced suppression of immune activity in humans to increased risk for negative health outcomes. The small magnitude and short duration of these effects, when considered in light of the complexity of the immune system (adaptability, broad range of normative activity, extensive redundancy between subsystems), suggest that a causal link is unlikely. Indeed, it takes a substantial stretch of the imagination to consider why a causal link would have adaptive significance. This realization has influenced the drift in National Institutes of Health funding priorities away from basic research questions on the links between stress and immunity.

During the late 1960s and 1970s, basic research on the immune system progressed at a very rapid pace. One discovery was paramount. Until this time, it was assumed that cellular communication within the immune system depended largely on physical cell-to-cell contact. This set of assumptions was challenged by Gale Granger and colleagues (e.g., G. A. Granger & Williams, 1968; Hessinger, Daynes, & Granger, 1973) at the University of California, Irvine. In a series of landmark studies, they revealed that cells of the immune system secreted soluble chemical messengers of their own to initiate, maintain, and regulate cellular immune responses. These messengers were originally defined as "lymphokines," and for years their effects were considered to be limited to the immune system. More important, for present purposes, it was discovered that these lymphokines (see Maier & Watkins, 1998b; E. Smith, 1992; Vilcek, 1998) also had "hormonal" effects on nonlymphoid cells at considerable distances from the cells that secreted them. Receptors for these molecules were also identified on cells of the central nervous and endocrine systems (e.g., Besedovsky et al., 1983; Besedovsky & Del Rey, 1989). In recognition of their functional diversity, this group of molecules was relabeled cytokines in the early 1980s. Since that time an explosion of information has accumulated about these molecules and their effects. For instance, a computerized search of Medline using cytokine as the keyword yields more than 299,255 publications on the topic.

For the budding field of psychoneuroimmunology, this wave of new information completed a critically important communication loop. It was biologically plausible that the immune system could both receive *and* send biochemical signals to the central nervous system (see Figure 17.1). These advances stimulated a shift in our assumptions regarding how the brain, behavior, and immune system influenced one another (see Maier & Watkins, 1998a, 1998b). Today, a third era of understanding and research on psychoneuroimmunology has evolved that has been heavily influenced by technical and theoretical advances made during the 1990s (declared by the U.S. Congress as "the decade of the brain"). Psychoneuroimmunology research has attracted considerable attention from molecular biologists and neuroscientists (Ader, 2000; Altman, 1997). The findings from their efforts are unequivocal: Cells of the lymphoid, central nervous, and endocrine systems use the same hormones, neurotransmitters, and other critical effector molecules to send and receive signals among one another. These once considered independent systems are now viewed as sharing a common set of signaling molecules and receptors and "speak" a similar chemical language (Ader et al., 1991; Blalock, 1994, 1997; Maier & Watkins, 1998a).

Our contemporary assumptions are that the brain, endocrine system, and immune system constitute an interactive information network, with each node capable of affecting and being affected by the activity of the others

(Ader, 2000; Black, 1995; Cotman, Brinton, Glaburda, McEwen, & Schneider, 1987). A schematic diagram of these interactive systems with representative signaling molecules and communication routes is depicted in Figure 17.1. Pathway A indicates the immune-to-brain communication link triggered by immune activation and carried forward via the activity of cytokines, such as interleukin-1 (IL-1) tumor necrosis factor (TNF) and interleukin-6 (IL-6). Consequences involve activation of the HPA axis at the level of the hypothalamus, pituitary, and adrenal. Pathway B indicates the communication route between the autonomic nervous system (ANS) and the immune system involving signals such as norepinephrine (NE), enkephalin (ENK), substance P (SP), and neuropeptide Y (NPY). Pathway C indicates the communication link between the HPA axis and the immune system (CRF = corticotropin-releasing hormone; ACTH = adrenocorticotropic hormone; CORT = cortisol or corticosterone). Consequences of the activation of pathways B and C involve suppression of the immune response. The interconnection of these pathways (A to BC and back to A) is considered highly adaptive. This negative feedback loop from the ANS and HPA axis prevents the inflammatory response from proceeding unchecked and damaging the host.

OVERVIEW OF THE IMMUNE SYSTEM

A basic understanding of the immune system is fundamental to thinking about its potential interactions with behavior and developmental psychopathology. Here we provide an introductory (101-level) overview to highlight its key properties and functional divisions. Some of the key immune component processes are described in sufficient detail so the naïve reader can appreciate the immune system's complexity. Interested readers are referred to introductory texts by Janeway (2005) and Goldsby (2003) for additional basic background information and are also encouraged to audit a basic immunology course.

Basic Properties and Divisions

The immune system functions to protect individuals from infectious organisms, microbes, transformed cells (virally infected or malignant), and toxins. To do this, it has the capacity to (1) distinguish between cells and molecules that belong (self antigens) and those that do not belong (nonself antigens); (2) destroy foreign antigens without doing damage to the host; and (3) record antigenic experience so the immune response is more efficient and effective later, if re-exposure occurs (Clough & Roth, 1998). The immune system is divided into two functional branches: innate or natural immunity and specific or acquired immunity.

Innate or Natural Immunity

These mechanisms are termed natural because they do not require exposure to a foreign agent to be acquired. They are present at birth or develop over the course of maturation without environmental input. This is the first line of defense against invading microorganisms. Natural immunity is composed of physical, mechanical, and chemical barriers found on all body surfaces. For example, skin is acidic and its surface is composed of a cornified, nonviable, impervious layer of cells. Internal body surfaces (mucus membranes) are washed by a continuous flow of mucus, which can contain antibacterial enzymes and peptides, termed defensins. If a surface barrier is breached, the invading organism is immediately confronted by various types of lymphoid cells (e.g., macrophages, neutrophils). Mobilized from the blood stream or found in the local tissue, phagocytic cells (e.g., macrophage) ingest and digest nonself antigens. If the organism gains entrance into the blood stream, it will be confronted by large numbers of phagocytic cells located in the spleen and liver. These cells also include a specialized subpopulation of lymphocytes, termed natural killer (NK) cells. NK cells identify and destroy cells that are virally infected or transformed (malignant). The majority of nonself antigens and invading organisms are stopped from infecting the host by the innate immune system's first line of defense.

Specific or Acquired Immunity

As opposed to natural or innate defenses, the adaptive immune response only becomes operative when the nonspecific natural barriers are breached. At this point, the host is infected. Organisms and materials that activate the immune response are called antigens (Ags) and must be foreign to the host immune system. The immune system distinguishes foreign from self by differences in the shape of the Ag when compared to self molecules. The most effective Ags are usually large, complex molecules; for example, proteins and carbohydrates are the best, whereas lipids and nucleic acids, though large, are not complex and therefore are least effective. But small molecules can become immunogenic if they can covalently link to a larger carrier molecule. When this occurs, the complex is termed a hapten.

Cells and Tissues

The lymphoid system comprises interconnected vessels and organs disseminated throughout the body but missing in the central nervous system. Lymphatics are an interconnected system of vessels and associated lymph nodes located in most body tissues. Lymphatic vessels have multiple functions: (1) facilitate lymphoid cell movement, (2) return fluids from tissues back to the blood stream, and (3) collect foreign materials that have entered our tissues. Lymph nodes capture and localize foreign materials in the lymph fluid and are primary sites of the specific immune response. Gut-associated lymphoid tissue collects and responds against materials that gain entrance into tissues via the gastrointestinal tract. The spleen and bone marrow are lymphoid tissues that capture foreign materials that gain entrance into the blood stream. Bone marrow is the source of stem cells, which can reconstitute the lymphoid system.

During development in utero, one population of lymphocytes leaves the bone marrow and enters the thymus, where they acquire the capacity of self-recognition and migrate into the lymphoid tissue; they are termed T lymphocytes. A second population of lymphocytes leaves the bone marrow and migrates directly into the lymphoid tissues; these are termed B lymphocytes. Mononuclear phagocytes are derived from the bone marrow. T and B lymphocytes and monocytes can be found circulating in blood and lymph, but the majority are localized in lymphatic tissues. As will be shown in a subsequent section, lymphocytes collaborate to recognize, destroy, and eliminate foreign Ags.

Ontogeny

The immune system in humans becomes functional 2 to 4 months after birth but does not completely mature until puberty (see Figure 17.2). The newborn human is protected during the first few months after birth by maternal antibodies (Ab)/immunoglobulins (Ig). Antibodies are proteins

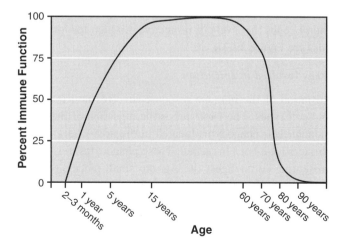

Figure 17.2 Curvilinear trajectory of immune system ontogeny.

secreted from lymphocytes (B cells) and will be fully explained in a subsequent section. Maternal antibodies are passed to the fetus via the placenta and passed to the newborn via colostrum during early breast-feeding. Maternal Ab gradually decay, and the immune system of the newborn gradually becomes functional. There are also cases of genetic and acquired complete or partial immunodeficiency in both adults and children. The functional capacity of the immune system declines as we reach old age. The rate and timing of this decline vary from individual to individual but generally starts during the 6th decade of life and continues until death. This decline is not due to a loss of lymphoid cells but to their ability to respond to new Ags.

Primary and Secondary Response

The immune response generated to the first exposure of an individual to an Ag is termed the *primary response*. The timing and level of response depend on the route of entry, how distinct the Ag is from self, and the amount of Ag involved. There are two components to the immune response: formation of soluble proteins by B lymphocytes (Abs) and cell-mediated immunity (CMI) residing in populations of T lymphocytes. One or both types of response may occur to a single Ag. Antibodies appear within 3 to 5 days in the serum of an individual during the primary response. The levels continue to rise for 15 to 20 days, and then, as they induce destruction of the Ag, level off and decline to a low baseline level, which is maintained for long periods. If the Ag is an infectious agent, the host may show clinical symptoms and recover if the agent can be destroyed. Upon reexposure to the same Ag, Abs appear in a few hours and the levels rise much higher than those reached in the primary response. The host may not show signs of infection, and Ab levels can remain high for long periods. This *secondary response* phenomenon is the scientific basis for the concept of booster shots. Subsequent exposure to Ag (such as booster shots) keeps the levels of protective Ab high for long periods (see Figure 17.3).

Steps Involved in Initiation

Initiation of the immune response involves multiple steps and cell types. The first step is the ingestion of the Ag by mononuclear phagocytes located in the area where natural barriers have been breached. These phagocytes, termed Ag presenting cells, digest the Ag into small pieces, then express the pieces in combination with special receptors on the exterior of the plasma membrane. The Ag presenting cells then migrate into a lymphoid tissue, and the membrane complex is presented to helper CD4+ T lymphocytes. The helper cells then activate small populations of Ag-

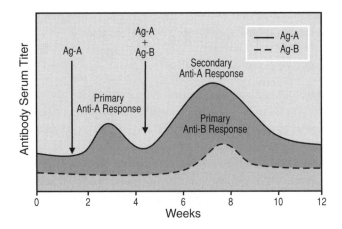

Figure 17.3 Specificity, memory, and regulation of immune response. Antigens A and B induce the production of different antibodies (specificity). The secondary response to antigen A is more rapid and larger than the primary response (memory). Antibody levels (titers) decline with time after each immunization (regulation).

specific T and/or B lymphocytes. Once activated, the Ag-specific T and B cells rapidly expand their numbers. The effector T lymphocytes are responsible for cell-mediated immunity and the B lymphocytes differentiate into Ab-forming plasma cells. Cytokines secreted by activated cells at each step are the stimulus that promotes both cellular differentiation and proliferation. The end result of this process is the generation of large numbers of Ag-specific T cells and specific Abs whose job it is to leave the lymphoid tissues and inactivate and destroy the Ag. The humoral Ab response is referred to as TH1 type reaction, and cellular immunity is referred to a TH2 type response. After the destruction and removal of the Ag, memory T and B cells can remain in lymphoid tissues for years. These long-lived memory cells can rapidly respond upon a second contact with the specific Ag.

Antibodies/Immunoglobulins

There are five classes of antibodies/immunoglobulins in humans that are an interrelated family of proteins. The most predominant classes are IgG, IgM, IgA, IgD, and IgE. IgM is the first Ab formed, followed by IgG, which becomes the major class in serum. IgA is found in serum and is also the major class in body secretions. Only a minor-class IgE is often the culprit responsible for most allergies. All classes of Ab can be formed with the same specificity against a single Ag. Each class can have a different functional capability. Each class of Abs is formed by assembly of distinct heavy (2) and light (2) peptide chains folded together to form a Y-shaped molecule. Each complete molecule has two identical

Ag binding sites at the ends of the Y. Serum IgG, IgE, IgD, and IgA are single units, and IgM and secreted IgA are polymers of 5 and 2 monomer units, respectively. Various portions of the molecule are referred to as either "fragment with Ab activity" (FaB) or "fragment crystalizable" (Fc), based on digestion of the molecule with proteases.

Cell-Mediated Immunity

The mediators of cellular immunity are antigen specific T lymphocytes. They possess a specific Ag-recognizing receptor expressed on their external plasma membrane. The T cell receptor is able to recognize Ag only when it is has been processed and is complexed to special receptors expressed on the external membrane on most body cells. These Ag-reactive T cells are referred to as cytotoxic T cells (CTL) and cytokine-releasing cells.

Adaptive Immunity: Effector Phase

Once initiated, the purpose of the immune response is to inactivate and destroy the foreign antigen(s). There are two broad classes of immunity: *humoral*, mediated by immunoglobulins, and *cellular*, mediated by immune T cells.

Effects of IgM, IgG, and IgA

Abs molecules have multiple specific binding sites for the Ag. Once bound to an Ag, they can cause neutralization of enzymes, toxins, and viral particles. They also localize the Ag by forming Ag-Ab complexes with both soluble and particulate Ags. These Ag-Ab complexes can activate secondary mechanisms, which help in the destruction of the Ag. The complement system is a family of 9 proteins, found in both serum and tissue fluids, which are activated in a cascade fashion to result in formation of the "attack complex" and in release of several chemo-attractant peptides. The attack complex causes cell lyses and the peptides induce immigration of phagocytic cells from the blood stream. Phagocytes can recognize Ag-Ab-complement complexes and will phagocytose and digest the entire complex. The NK cell can also recognize an Ab-coated cell and cause its destruction. The NK cell must make physical contact with the Ab-coated cell. This class of cytotoxic reactions is termed antibody-dependent cellular cytotoxicity (ADCC).

IgE Allergies

IgE is the main but not the only cause of most allergic reactions. Allergies occur in families and affect a large percentage of the human population. The IgE molecule has the unique ability to bind via the tail or Fc portion of the molecule to mediator-containing basophils and mast cells. These mediator-containing cells are widely distributed in body tissues and in the blood stream. An individual can become allergic by exposure to Ag, formation of IgE, and coating of mast and basophil cells with IgE. Subsequent exposure to Ag results in specific release of histamine, chemokines, and lipid mediators, which induce the tissue changes associated with allergies. The severity of these reactions is affected by a variety of factors, including IgE levels, mast cell reactivity, and amount of Ag reaching the mast cells.

Cell-Mediated Immunity

Cell-mediated immunity is those classes of reactions mediated by immune cytotoxic and cytokine-releasing T lymphocytes. Cytotoxic T lymphocytes (CTL) recognize processed Ag peptides complexed with receptors on a target cell surface. They identify these peptides via a specific T cell receptor on the surface of the CTL. Subsequent interaction of membrane proteins on both cells induces the CTL to destroy the target cell via two mechanisms: deposition of cytolysines on the target cell surface, which induces membrane disruption, and secretion of chemokines and cytokines, which can induce inflammation and a slower form of cell death (apoptosis). This type of immunity is important in destruction of allografts, virus-infected cells, tumor cells, and self cells in various forms of autoimmune disease.

Although CTL and cytokines secreting T cells do not have a direct effect on microorganisms, they are important in microbial immunity. They exert their effects by recruiting and activating blood monocytes to become highly phagocytic macrophages, which can ingest and destroy the microorganism. The T cells are stimulated to release chemokines and cytokines by interaction with processed microbial Ags on the surface of tissue-fixed mononuclear phagocytes at the site of infection. These mediators induce emigration of monocytes from the blood stream into the affected tissue, and they are further induced to differentiate into macrophages. The activated macrophage has the ability to destroy the microorganism via its increased phagocytic and digestive capacity. This type of reactivity is very important in resistance to different types of bacterial, fungal, and viral infections. These reactions also have a role in tumor immunity and various types of autoimmune syndromes and have been termed delayed hypersensitivity (DTH).

Summary

Natural resistance mechanisms serve to slow the initial progress of a pathogen while the adaptive immune system becomes engaged. Once initiated, soluble antibodies, secreted by plasma cells in lymphoid tissue, reach the site of infection via the blood stream and neutralize and localize the pathogen and soluble toxins and enzymes. The Ag-Ab complex is formed and the complement system is activated, which can kill certain pathogens and will induce emigration of phagocytes from the blood stream into the site of infection. Phagocytes recognize the Ag-Ab complement complexes and ingest and digest them. Later, Ag-specific T cells enter the site, become activated to secrete cytokines, induce monocytes from the blood to enter the tissue, and activate to become macrophages. The activated macrophages also ingest and destroy the Ag-Ab complexes. Once the Ag is removed, the normal healing process can begin and the tissue is repaired and returned to normal.

THE IMMUNE SYSTEM AS OUR "SIXTH SENSE"

Decoding the syntax of the NEI axis has enabled theorists to attribute new features to the immune system's already extensive functional repertoire. Blalock (e.g., 1994, 1997) was among the first to propose that the immune system recognizes unique environmental stimuli (i.e., viruses, bacteria, microbes, toxins) that are essentially undetectable by our classic visual, auditory, olfactory, and gustatory sensory systems. More specifically, one cannot see, hear, smell, taste, or feel an individual microbe. However, the immune system is designed to recognize and respond to 10^9 different specific antigens. Just as is true with our other sensory inputs, when the immune system recognizes such stimuli, the encounter is converted into a cascade of biochemical messages. We now know that those messages are responsible for inducing changes in the host's metabolic, thermogenic, and behavioral states in response to infection.

The adaptive significance of the biobehavioral (metabolic, thermogenic) reaction to systemic infection provides a supportive physiologic environment for the immune system to fight pathogens most effectively. For example, increased sleepiness combined with reduced activity, motivation, and arousal may conserve energy stores needed by the immune system. It might seem paradoxical to have a decreased appetite when sick (one is sacrificing calorie and protein intake by not eating), but it is adaptive for a sick animal in the wild not to forage for food, but to stay in one place, conserving energy and avoiding predators (Hart, 1988). Fever is stimulated by action of proinflammatory molecules (cytokines and acute phase proteins) on the hypothalamus. These signals produce an unfavorable environment for the growth of many microbial pathogens (see Kluger, 1979). For instance, the rate of bacterial growth is consistently slower in environments with temperatures greater than 98°F. The afflicted individual's expression of sickness behaviors (see subsequent discussion) also serves an adaptive purpose. The sick are more socially inhibited and withdrawn, a behavior change that conveys benefits to the individual, as noted, but also to the population and immediate social group. In the cases of communicable infectious pathogens, social withdrawal of those infected limits the exposure of others to the agent of disease.

The advances in our understanding of the interactions among the immune, central nervous, and endocrine systems reveal that individual differences in biobehavioral responses to infection may be relevant to developmental science in ways previously unrealized. Characterizing the immune system as a sixth sense highlights the biological plausibility that immune system-to-brain communications represent a largely unexplored pathway through which individual differences in experience with environmental factors (nonself antigens) shape and reshape the structure and function of biological systems underlying behavior. With few exceptions (e.g., Adamson-Macedo, 2000; C. L. Coe, 1996; Crnic, 1991; Shanks, Larocque, & Meaney, 1995), this set of ideas has attracted only minimal attention from mainstream psychoneuroimmunology or developmentally oriented researchers. Figure 17.4 presents a summary of the major shifts in the evolution of our knowledge regarding the central nervous system and the immune system, as well as the corresponding assumptions regarding the links between the immune system and behavior.

A PRIMER ON CYTOKINES FOR DEVELOPMENTAL SCIENTISTS

In this section, we describe the general properties of cytokine (the critical effector molecules thought to mediate the aforementioned sensory functions) and how peripherally activated cytokines communicate with and affect the brain, endocrine system, and behavior. Readers interested in additional detail are referred to Maier and Watkins (1998b), who present an overview of cytokines for psychologists, or S. W. Granger and Ware (2003). *The Cytokine Handbook,* fourth edition (Thomson & Lotze, 2003), provides basic detail on individual cytokines as well as their interactions and therapeutic uses. As this is a rapidly expanding area of knowledge, interested readers may also find cutting-edge information in scientific journals such as *Science, Nature, Cell, Journal of Experimental Medicine,*

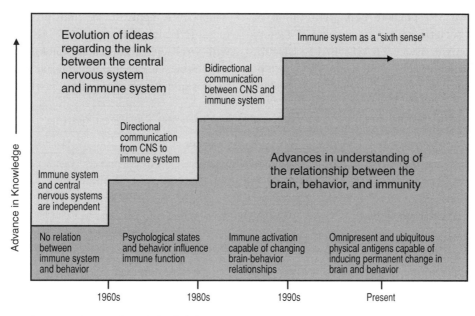

Figure 17.4   Advances in our understanding of the link between the central nervous system and the immune system has progressed in a stepwise function over the past 50 years. The basic developments have profoundly changed our assumptions about how the immune system effects and is influenced by behavioral and psychological states.

Journal of Clinical Investigation, Lancet, Journal of the American Medical Association, Cytokine, Lymphokine Research, Proceedings of the National Academy of Sciences, and various immunology-related journals such as *Immunity, Nature Immunology, Journal of Immunology,* and *Journal of Neuroimmunomodulation.*

Basic Properties and Functions

Although work on lymphokines and interferons (two types of molecules now recognized to have cytokine actions) began in the 1960s, it wasn't until 1974 that the term cytokine was proposed to describe the entire class of molecules with these properties (Vilcek, 1998). Since then, the number of molecules that have cytokine-like properties has been expanding at a very rapid pace. This can be attributed to technological advances in molecular biology and genome sequencing, which have led to the discovery of more than 200 members. In fact, a relatively new family of molecules called chemokines has experienced its own wave of discovery, leading to the identification of four subfamilies of these molecules, totaling 47 members in all. Hence, the complexity of this network continues to grow as the intertwining biologic functions of these molecules are elucidated.

Cytokines are small protein molecules that act as intercellular messengers (see Goldsby, 2003; Thomson & Lotze, 2003). They range in size from 8 to 30 kiloDaltons

(kDa) and induce their effects as soluble or membrane-bound proteins by binding to high-affinity receptors on target cell membranes. Unlike hormones, cytokines usually act over short distances in an autocrine or paracrine fashion. Virtually all nucleated cells can produce cytokines, but white blood cells are the major source. Monocytes and macrophages are especially efficient cytokine producers. Some cytokines are stored preformed in the intracellular granules for instantaneous release. However, most cytokine secretion involves de novo protein synthesis, a process that takes hours.

Cytokines are pleiotropic, meaning they have multiple target cells and multiple actions, and their effects are often redundant, sometimes synergistic; they often induce the production of other cytokines and are less frequently antagonistic. They play important roles in maintaining health and are the causative agents in disease. In addition to regulating immune and inflammatory responses, the biologic consequences of cytokine signaling are critical for development, growth, healing, and maintenance of just about every tissue and organ of the body. Cytokines can be grouped into families according to their structure, common receptor usage, and whether they have predominantly anti-inflammatory, proinflammatory, chemotactic, or growth-promoting functions. Within the immune system, in general, interleukins (e.g., IL-1 through IL-28) are molecules that have a functional activity involving leukocytes; colony-stimulating and growth factors (e.g., IL-3,

G-CSF, m-CSF, GMCSF) promote cell proliferation of hematopoeitic and somatic cells; tumor necrosis factors (e.g., TNF, lymphotoxin, FasL, TRAIL, BAFF, CD40L, OX40L) initiate inflammation, orchestrate the development and maintenance of lymphoid organs, and regulate lymphocyte homeostasis and proliferation; interferons (e.g., INF-alpha/beta and INF-gamma) act to interfere with viral replication; and chemokines (e.g., CC and CXC chemokines) are chemotactic agents that recruit leukocytes to sites of inflammation and orchestrate lymphoid architec-

TABLE 17.1 Representative Members of the Cytokine Family and Some of Their Major Biological Activities

Family	Representative Members	Secreted By	Major Biological Activity
Interleukins (IL1–IL29)	Interleukin-1 (IL-1α, IL-1ß)	Monocytes/macrophages	Induces synthesis of acute-phase proteins Induces fever Stimulates lymphocyte activation
	Interleukin-2 (IL-2)	T Lymphocytes	Induces T lymphocyte proliferation Enhances activity of NK cells
	Interleukin-4 (IL-4)	T Lymphocytes	Stimulates T and B lymphocyte proliferation, Th2 polarization Increases phagocytic (ingestive) activity of macrophage
	Interleukin-6 (IL-6)	Monocytes/macrophages	Induces synthesis of acute-phase proteins Stimulates antibody production
	Interleukin-10 (IL-10)	T Lymphocytes	Suppresses macrophage cytokine secretion Down-regulates antigen presentation
	Interleukin-12 (IL-12)		Stimulates cellular immune responses, Th1 polarization
Interferons	Interferon gamma (IFN-γ)	NK cells/T lymphocytes	Enhances activity of macrophages Induces proliferation of B lymphocytes Inhibits viral replication
	Type I Interferon (IFN) IFNα and IFNß	IFNα- Neutrophils, dendritic cells IFNß- fibroblasts	MHC class I induction, antiviral, anti-proliferative
Colony-stimulating and growth factors	Transforming Growth Factor ß (TGF-ß)	Macrophages/lymphocytes	Induces macrophage IL-1 production Limits inflammatory response and promotes wound healing
	Granulocyte Macrophage Colony Stimulating Factor (GMCSF)	T lymphocytes/activated macrophages	Stimulate the formation of macrophages, neutrophils, eosinophiles, and basophiles
	Granulocyte Colony Stimulating Factor (GCSF)		
	Macrophage Colony Stimulating Factor (MCSF)		
Tumor necrosis factor superfamily (TNFSF1–TNFSF18)	Tumor Necrosis Factor (TNF)	Macrophages	Has cytotoxic (cell-killing) effects Induces cytokine secretion Associated with chronic inflammation
	Lymphotoxin (LT/TNFß)	Lymphocytes	Development and maintenance of lymphoid organs, chemokine induction
	CD40L	Lymphocytes	T cell proliferation
	FasL	Lymphocytes	Apoptosis, lymphocyte homeostasis
	BAFF	Myeloid cells	B cell survival
	TRAIL	Most normal tissues	Apoptosis
	OX40, CD27L, 4-1BBL	Antigen-presenting cells	T cell costimulation
Chemokines CC chemokines (CCL1–CCL28), CXC chemokines (CXCL1–CXCL16), C chemokines, and CX3CL1	IP-10 (CXCL10) IL-8 (CXCL8) Rantes (CCL5)	Monocytes Epithelial cells T cells	Chemotaxis, adhesion, histamine release Neutrophil recruitment Chemoattraction of leukocytes

ture and leukocyte trafficking. The nomenclature hints at their major functions, but most cytokines have extremely diverse effects (Clough & Roth, 1998). Some specific examples of cytokines and their main biological functions in the immune system are listed in Table 17.1.

Cytokine Regulation

Cytokines are extremely potent signaling molecules, and their presence even in very low pg/ml (picogram per milliliter) levels can induce substantial cellular consequences. A complex set of mechanisms exists to prevent cytokines from doing damage to the host. At least three types of endogenous cytokine inhibitors have been identified: cytokine antagonists (e.g., IL-1ra), molecules homologous to cytokines and able to bind cytokine receptors without leading to signal transduction; shed cytokine receptors (e.g., s-TNF-R type I and II), which bind cytokines in the intercellular fluid space and stop it from reaching its target cell or tissue (Gatanaga, Hwang, et al., 1990; Gatanaga, Lentz, et al., 1990); and other molecules that act through independent receptors that exert opposite effects on the cell (Thomson & Lotze, 2003). Some cytokines also inhibit each other (e.g., IL-10 inhibits synthesis of TNF, IL-1, IL-6, and others).

The regulation of cytokines is complex and has profound consequences for the host. Inadequate production of cytokines will result in an insufficient cellular immune response and a potentially negative outcome related to pathogenesis of the microbe or virus (see Figure 17.5). Without medical intervention, individuals expressing consistent hypoarousal of the cytokine network would be unlikely to survive. It is highly likely that in nature, this phenotype would be removed from the gene pool within one generation, as these individuals would succumb to pathogenesis (or predation). On the other hand, excessive cytokine secretion has been linked to "sickness behaviors" (see subsequent discussion), autoimmune disorders (i.e., arthritis), neurological disease (e.g., multiple sclerosis), toxic shock, and death (i.e., sepsis; see Figure 17.5). It is plausible that in populations under selective pressure, individuals expressing hyperarousal of the cytokine network would also be removed from the gene pool. That is, when challenged by immune stimuli, these individuals would experience severe fatigue, fever, loss of appetite, inactivity, social withdrawal, weight loss, and cognitive slowing, which together significantly increase risk of predation. Thus, in the wild, selective pressure from microorganisms and predators may serve to regulate the gene pool such that reproductively fit individuals have cytokine networks that operate within an optimal range of function (see Figure 17.5).

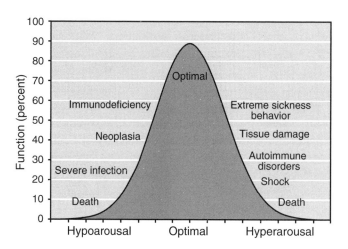

Figure 17.5 Individual differences in the activity of the cytokine network have an inverse parabolic relationship with physical and mental health. Regulation of cytokine activity within an optimal range is essential to avoid the negative biobehavioral consequences linked with either hypoarousal or hyperarousal of the immune system. *Source:* From "Developmental Psychoneuroimmunology: The Role of Cytokine Network Activation in the Epigenesis of Developmental Psychopathology" (pp. 293–323), by D. A. Granger, N. A. Dreschel, and E. A. Shirtcliff, in *Neurodevelopmental Mechanisms in Psychopathology* by D. Cicchetti and E. Walker (Eds.), 2003, New York: Cambridge University Press.

How Peripherally Activated Cytokines Talk to the Brain

The most well-characterized pathway through which peripheral immunological stimuli signal changes in the brain begins with the macrophage. When activated, macrophages secrete a cascade of cytokines and other chemical messengers (see Table 17.1). Of particular importance, it is the cytokine products released in response to immune stimulation, not the direct effect of the immunological stimulus (e.g., bacterial or viral pathogenesis), that are thought to mediate many of the resulting changes in the brain (Dantzer, Bluthe, & Goodall, 1993; Dinarello, 1984a, 1984b).

Molecular, cellular, and in vivo evidence suggests that macrophage-derived interleukin-1 (IL-1) has the most systemic and hormonal-type effects of all the cytokines (E. Smith, 1992), with widespread consequences for the brain (Weiss, Quan, & Sundar, 1994). Two forms of IL-1 exist, α and ß (Dinarello, 1988, 1992). IL-1ß is the dominant soluble, biologically active form in the circulation and brain (Benveniste, 1992b; Chensue, Shmyre-Forsch, Otterness, & Kunkel, 1989; E. Smith, 1992). Peripheral administration of nanogram amounts of IL-1ß stimulate corticotropin-releasing factor (CRF) from hypothalamic neurons (Harbuz & Lightman, 1992; Sapolsky, Rivier, Yamamoto, Plotsky, & Vale, 1987; Woloski, Smith, Meyer,

Fuller, & Blalock, 1985), resulting in increased circulating levels of ACTH and corticosterone (Dunn, 1988, 1990). Interestingly, reports by Berkenbosch (Berkenbosch, de Goeij, Del Rey, & Besedovsky, 1989; Berkenbosch, De Rijk, Del Rey, & Besedovsky, 1990; Berkenbosch, Van Dam, De Rijk, & Schotanus, 1992) and Dunn (e.g., Chuluyan, Saphier, Rohn, & Dunn, 1992; Dunn, 1992a, 1992b) demonstrate that peripheral administration of IL-1ß may also potentiate the HPA axis response to environmental challenge. IL-6 and TNF are functioning similar to IL-1ß in that they also stimulate the HPA axis during inflammatory stress (E. Smith, 1992).

Cytokines have a variety of effects on cerebral neurotransmission (see Dunn & Wang, 1995; Dunn, Wang, & Ando, 1999). IL-1ß acts to stimulate cerebral norepinephrine (NE) metabolism, probably reflecting increased synaptic release. IL-1, IL-6, and TNF also stimulate indolamine metabolism of tryptophan and decrease the concentration of serotonin (5-HT). Through their action on indolamines, cytokines also affect the synthesis of quinolinic (QUIN) and kynurenic acid (see Figure 17.6). QUIN is an agonist of the N-methyl-d-aspartate (NMDA) receptor and other excitatory amino acid receptors. These receptors mediate excitatory amino acid neurotransmission in the hippocampus, basal ganglia, and cerebral cortex and, when activated for sufficient periods, have been implicated in nerve cell death and dysfunction (Heyes, 1992; Heyes, Brew, et al., 1992; Heyes, Quearry, & Markey, 1989; Heyes, Saito, et al., 1992; Saito, Markey, & Heyes, 1992). On the other hand, kynurenic acid is an antagonist of NMDA receptors and could modulate the neurotoxic effects of QUIN as well as disrupt excitatory amino acid transmission. Heyes and colleagues report that QUIN and kynurenic acid are mediators of neuronal dysfunction and nerve cell death in inflammatory diseases. A schematic diagram of the cerebral effects of cytokines is depicted in Figure 17.6.

It is apparent that many of the peripherally stimulated effects on the central nervous system result from activation of IL-1ß in the brain (Quan, Sundar, & Weiss, 1994). That is, within hours after peripheral immune activation, expression of IL-1ß transcripts is induced in the hippocampus, hypothalamus, and pituitary (Ban, Haour, & Lenstra, 1992; Laye, Parnet, Goujon, & Dantzer, 1994). Studies also show that IL-1 receptors are widely distributed throughout the brain and endocrine tissues (Cunningham & De Souza, 1993), with high densities observed in the hippocampal area and the choroid plexus (Takao, Tracy, Mitchell, & De Souza, 1990). Thus, it is not surprising that the behavioral and physiological effects can be mimicked by administration of IL-1ß directly into the brain (Weiss et al., 1994) and that they can be attenuated by intracerebraventricular in-

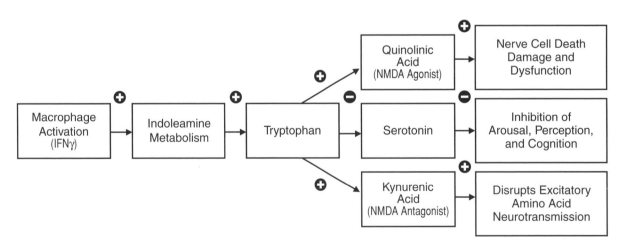

Figure 17.6   Immune activation has a variety of effects on cerebral neurotransmission. Bacterial, viral, fungal, and parasitic infections result in macrophage release of cytokines, including those that activate indoleamine-2,3-dioxygenase (IDO). Increases in IDO activity accelerate the degradation of L-tryptophan to neuroreactive kynurenines, including the excitotoxin quinolinic acid (QUIN) and the antagonist of excitatory amino acid receptors, kynurenic acid (KYNA). QUIN and KYNA influence the activity of N-methyl-D-aspartate (NMDA) receptors. Degradation of L-tryptophan via this kynurenic pathway results in reduced serotonin levels. Consequences of this immune-to-brain pathway include neural damage and dysfunction, neurologic deficits and neurodegeneration, and inhibition of arousal, perception, and cognition. *Source:* From "Developmental Psychoneuroimmunology: The Role of Cytokine Network Activation in the Epigenesis of Developmental Psychopathology" (pp. 293–323), by D. A. Granger, N. A. Dreschel, and E. A. Shirtcliff, in *Neurodevelopmental Mechanisms in Psychopathology,* by D. Cicchetti and E. Walker (Eds.), 2003, New York: Cambridge University Press.

jection of the IL-1 receptor antagonist, IL-1ra (Bluthe, Dantzer, & Kelley, 1992).

Interestingly, IL-1ß in the general circulation does not cross the blood-brain barrier in humans. Rather, peripheral release of IL-1ß somehow signals cytokine synthesis within the CNS. Studies suggest that this process proceeds by both humoral and neural pathways (see Dantzer, Konsman, Bluthe, & Kelley, 2000). The first studies carried out on the mechanisms by which peripheral immune stimuli signal the brain to induce fever, activation of the HPA axis, and sickness behavior emphasized parts of the blood-brain barrier (the circumventricular organs) that allow proinflammatory cytokines to act on the brain. Rodents have circumventricular organs but humans do not, raising an important question regarding the communication route in humans. In the mid-1990s, it was discovered that the subdiaphragmatic section of the vagus nerve attenuates the brain effects of systemic cytokines, suggesting that the mechanism in humans involves cytokine induction in the brain. Since then, neuroanatomical pathways have been confirmed that reveal a fast route of communication from the immune system to the brain via the vagus nerves. In rodents, this neural afferent pathway complements a humoral pathway that involves cytokines produced locally at the circumventricular organs and in the brain parenchyma (see reviews by Dantzer, Bluthe, Gheusi, et al., 1998; Dantzer, Bluthe, Laye, et al., 1998; Dantzer et al., 2000).

In summary, the biological pathways via which cytokines affect the central nervous system have been well characterized. The effects of cytokines in the brain involve changes in neurotransmission in brain regions (i.e., limbic system, hypothalamus), with well-established links to learning and memory, emotion regulation, and the psychobiology of the stress response.

It is tempting to speculate that humans' sweeping elimination of natural predators and widespread application of medical interventions to eradicate infectious diseases (i.e., antibiotics, immunizations) may have created an opportunity for the expression of a wide range of individual differences in the activity of the cytokine network in the modern human population. The next sections detail our understanding of the links between immune activation and behavior and cytokines and psychopathology.

CYTOKINES AND THE BEHAVIORAL SURFACE

The pioneering work of Robert Dantzer at the Neurobiologie Integrative, INSERUM, Bordeaux, has defined the cutting edge of our knowledge regarding the behavioral effects of cytokines. Numerous animal model studies show

that IL-1ß administration elicited anorexia (Hart, 1988; Moldawer, Andersson, Gelin, & Lundholm, 1988), increased sleep time (Opp, Orbal, & Kreuger, 1991), decreased social and nonsocial exploration (Sparado & Dunn, 1990), decreased sexual activity (Avitsur & Yirmiya, 1999), increased defensive withdrawal, and affected other behaviors characteristic of the nonspecific symptoms of sickness (Dantzer, 2001; Dantzer et al., 1993; Dunn, Antoon, & Chapman, 1991; Kent, Rodriguez, Kelley, & Dantzer, 1994; Kreuger, Walter, Dinarello, Wolff, & Chedid, 1984). At the behavioral level, some suggest that "sickness behavior" is the expression of a disruption in motivation and arousal that reorganizes the organism's priorities to cope with infectious pathogens (Aubert, 1999; Dantzer, 2001; Gahtan & Overmier, 2001).

Mild to moderate levels of cognitive and behavioral effects of peripherally released cytokines, such as IL-1ß, can be recognized in any person with an active systemic influenza infection. That these effects are commonplace and are experienced to some degree by all of us is illustrated by the sea of hands raised in unanimity when introduction to health psychology students are asked, "Do you agree that your behavior, appetite, and interest in sleep and sex are different when you are sick?" By contrast, only about one-third of the hands are raised when the complementary question, "How many have had the experience of getting sick soon after experiencing a major life event (e.g., loss of a loved one or pet, breakup with a significant other, major challenge in your job or school)?" is asked. Our common experience is consistent with a robust pattern emerging in the literature. That is, the magnitude and breadth of the effects of immune activation at the behavioral surface is considerably more substantial than the effects of our behavior and subjective experience on our immune function.

Tyrell and colleagues (A. P. Smith et al., 1987; A. P. Smith, Tyrell, Coyle, & Higgins, 1988; R. W. Smith, Tyrell, Coyle, & Willman, 1987) rigorously documented adverse effects of experimentally induced respiratory virus infection and cytokine administration on human psychomotor performance, mood, and memory. But the vast majority of information comes from studies of cytokines as biological response modifiers or immunotherapeutics. The discovery of cytokines was considered a major advance in decoding the communication signals used by lymphoid cells, and high expectations were set for their use in treatment of immune-related disease. Clinical trials proved these assumptions to be correct, but there were behavioral and psychological iatrogenic effects that caused many involved as participants in the early trials to withdraw. Many oncology patients treated with cytokines complained of headache, fever, anorexia, fatigue, and social withdrawal

(Gutterman et al., 1982; Mannering & Deloria, 1986). Studies showed that oncology patients treated with cytokines (in this case, interleukin-2 or interferon-alpha) for only 3 to 5 days had significantly higher depression and anxiety symptoms (Capuron, Bluthe, & Dantzer, 2001; Capuron, Ravaud, & Dantzer, 2000, 2001; Capuron, Ravaud, Gualde, et al., 2001). Repeated prolonged exposure to cytokines resulted in increased irritability, short temper, agitation, and aggressiveness; extreme emotional liability, depression, and fearfulness; and more severe symptoms, such as disorientation, paranoia, and suicidal ideation (e.g., Renault et al., 1987). Although these adverse effects were generally attenuated with the termination of the protocol, some participants remained emotionally vulnerable for weeks after the cessation.

In summary, the experimental studies provide strong support for the conclusion that cytokine production (or administration) is causally linked to the expression of change in psychological, emotional, behavioral, and cognitive function. The severity of the symptoms clearly extends into the clinical range. The symptoms linked to cytokines include primarily those related to internalizing (such as cognitive processes, psychosis, anxiety, fearfulness, depression, thoughts about suicide) disorders. Generally, the effects of cytokines at the behavioral surface are consistent with our knowledge about the effects cytokines have on the central nervous and neuroendocrine systems.

INTERNALIZING PROBLEM BEHAVIOR AND CYTOKINES

There have been very few published studies devoted to a comprehensive evaluation of the relationship between psychiatric disorder and cytokine regulation. Some studies report adult patients with severe depression, anxiety, and symptoms of stress-related psychiatric disorders have associated immune abnormalities (e.g., Kelly, Ganguli, & Rabin, 1987; Kronfol, 1999; Kronfol & Remick, 2000). The findings are not always consistent across studies, but the pattern largely supports the hypothesis of an association between internalizing behavior problems and activation of the cytokine network (Connor & Leonard, 1998; Dantzer, Wollman, Vitkovic, & Yirmiya, 1999).

Depression

The rationale that cytokines play a role in the pathophysiology of Major Depression is based on assumptions that (1) depression is closely associated with stress and is often portrayed as an exaggerated response to stress, (2) depression is accompanied by atypical HPA axis activity, and (3) the cardinal manifestations of depression include changes in sleep, appetite, sex drive, social withdrawal, and cognitive slowing (Kronfol, 1999). There is evidence that cytokines are associated with, or influence, many of these individual symptoms (see Anderson et al., 1996; Herbert & Cohen, 1993a). For instance, in early studies, Maes (Maes, Bosmans, Meltzer, Scharpe, & Suy, 1993; Maes et al., 1995) reported significant elevations of IL-1ß and IL-6 in the plasma of depressed patients. Owen, Eccleston, Ferrier, and Young (2001) report elevated levels of IL-1ß in Major Depression and postviral depression. Musselman et al. (2001) report that cancer patients with depression had markedly higher plasma concentrations of IL-6 than healthy comparison subjects and cancer patients without depression. Berk, Wadee, Kuschke, and O'Neill-Kerr (1997) report that levels of c-reactive protein and IL-6 were significantly raised in a group with Major Depression. Suarez et al. (2003) showed that men with Beck Depression Inventory scores of 10 or above (mild- to moderate-level symptoms) exhibited an overexpression of IL-1ß, TNF-alpha, and IL-8. Capuron et al. (2003) recently showed that tryptophan degradation into kynurenine by the enzyme indoleamine-2,3-dioxygenase during immune activation may contribute to the development of depressive symptoms during interferon α therapy.

But Haack and colleagues (1999) caution that the association between depressive symptoms and cytokines may be in part due to incomplete control of numerous potential confounding influences. In one of the largest studies to date (361 psychiatric patients, 64 health controls), they report that once age, body mass, gender, smoking habits, ongoing or recent infectious diseases, and medications are carefully taken into account, plasma levels of cytokines and cytokine receptors yield little, if any, evidence for immunopathology in Major Depression.

Very few studies have explored relationships between psychiatric symptoms or problem behavior and cytokine levels in youth. Birmaher et al. (1994) studied 20 adolescents with Major Depressive Disorder, 17 nondepressed subjects with Conduct Disorder, and 17 healthy controls. Blood samples were drawn for total white blood cells, lymphocyte subsets, NK cell activity, and lymphocyte proliferation assays. Overall, there were no significant between-group differences, but the project did not measure cytokines. A preliminary study in our lab revealed that serum levels of cytokines were significantly correlated with behavior problems in clinic-referred youth but not in nonreferred age-matched comparisons. In the study (M age = 11.3 years, range 8 to 17), it was observed that individual differences in serum levels of IL-1 were positively correlated (rs (17) = .59 and .55, $ps < .05$) with self-reported anxiety/depression on the Youth Self-Report version of the Child Behavior Checklist (Achenbach, 1991a, 1991b) and Children's Depression Inventory (Kovacs, 1983) in a clinic-referred group ($n = 20$) but not in a normally developing comparison ($n = 19$) group (D. A. Granger, Ikeda, & Block, 1997). Most recently, Brambilla, Monteleone, and Maj (2004) studied 11 children and adolescents with Dysthymia (DYS), 11 with recurrent Major Depressive Disorder (MDD), and 11 healthy age-sex matched controls. IL-1ß levels were significantly higher in the DYS group compared to controls and were correlated with anxious and depressive symptomatology in the MDD but not DYS patients (Brambilla et al., 2004). No studies to our knowledge have yet followed the relationship between depression and immune activation prospectively in youth. Although few in number, the consistency of the findings suggests that this would be a worthwhile next step.

Anxiety Disorders

Depression is often comorbid with anxiety symptoms and other anxiety-related disorders, but data linking cytokines to anxiety disorders are scant. There is a growing body of evidence suggesting a role for autoimmune mechanisms in some specific cases of Obsessive-Compulsive Disorder (OCD; Garvey, Giedd, & Swedo, 1998; Leonard et al., 1999; Swedo et al., 1998). Maes, Meltzer, and Bosmans (1994b) noted a positive association between IL-6 and the severity of compulsive symptoms. Mittleman et al. (1997) reported atypical cytokine levels in the cerebral spinal fluid of patients with childhood-onset OCD. Studies do not consistently support a link between immune abnormalities and Panic Disorders (PD). Brambilla et al. (1992, 1994) reported plasma IL-1ß was significantly higher in patients with PD than controls, before and after treatment with benzodiazepine. Studies by Rapaport and Stein (1994) and Weizman, Laor, Wiener, Wolmer, and Bessler (1999) failed to find that immune measures differentiated patients with PD from normal controls. Spivak et al. (1997) found circulating levels of IL-1ß were significantly higher in patients with combat-related Posttraumatic Stress Disorder (PTSD), with IL-1ß levels correlating with duration of PTSD and severity of anxiety and depression. To our knowledge, no studies have explored relationships between cytokines and anxiety disorders in youth.

The findings to date suggest that cytokines are capable of causing rapid reorganization in behavioral, affective, and cognitive domains; the intensity of such effects ranges from mild to extreme, and the duration of the effects can outlast the events that precipitated their release. The breadth, magnitude, and duration of the biobehavioral effects of cytokines underscore the plausibility that their dysregulation might alter the organization of human physiology and behavior in ways that affect microevolution and individual development. In particular, accumulating literature highlights the possibility that variation in the expression of socioemotional, cognitive, and behavioral symptoms associated with depression and/or socially inhibited behaviors may be partially explained by differential sensitivities to the effects of exposure to naturally occurring ubiquitous immune stimuli (e.g., see Dantzer, 2001; Kronfol & Remick, 2000; Watson, Mednick, Huttunen, & Wang, 1999). However, although cytokines are sufficient to cause psychiatric symptoms, it is clear that they are *not both necessary and sufficient;* many internalizing psychiatric symptoms and patterns of disorder clearly occur in the absence of cytokine aberrations.

METHODS TO STUDY BEHAVIORAL EFFECTS OF CYTOKINES

Cytokines and their inhibitors can be measured in most biological fluids in the pg/ml (e.g., serum, plasma, urine, cerebrospinal fluid, and possibly saliva) range. There are several approaches, and each has specific advantages and disadvantages. We describe some of the key challenges here and refer the interested reader to more detailed discussions elsewhere.

Traditional in Vitro Methods

There are several challenges to researchers studying cytokine-behavior relationships. Under normal conditions, unless the immune system has been stimulated, the level of most cytokines is in the very low to undetectable range (Wadhwa & Thorpe, 1998). During periods of systemic immune activation, cytokine levels in serum can rise substantially within hours, but there are wide-ranging individual differences. This creates considerable obstacles to evaluating correlates of individual differences as the range of scores is often restricted to present or absent. Also, the variation in levels for the detectable scores can be considerable and is, in our experience, rarely normally distributed. To reveal the full range of individual differences, investigators are often forced to study cytokine responses or production in reaction to an immune challenge. This is most often accomplished in vitro. Blood is collected and lymphoid cells are isolated in single-cell suspension, cultured in media containing bovine serum products and antibiotics, and challenged with a stimulus. After a specified period, the media (supernatant) and/or cells are collected and assayed.

Assay reagents and materials are now widely commercially available, and assays for these biomarkers are routine in most clinical and biomedical research laboratories. *Immunoreactive* cytokine levels would be subsequently assessed using a detection system designed around a highly specific antibody. These methods include competitive radio or enzyme immunoassays (Chard, 1990; Brambilla et al., 2004). These protocols are efficient, economical, and relatively high through-put. They require basic laboratory skills and equipment. The *functional* activity of cytokines is measured using a different approach, called generally bioassays. Here, supernatant from stimulated cultures is applied to a different set of cells (specialized cell-line), and the amount of cytokine bioactivity is extrapolated from the degree of their response (number that grow or die). These tests provide qualitatively different information than immunoassays. They are complex and time-consuming and require advanced laboratory skill and equipment. In addition, many researchers measure cytokine messenger RNA (mRNA) transcripts extracted from stimulated lymphoid cells. These assays require knowledge of polymerase chain reaction techniques. Kiecolt-Glaser and Glaser (1988), Vedhara, Fox, and Wang (1999), and Wadhwa and Thorpe (1998) present overviews of the measurement of the immune response with specific attention to cytokines.

Experimental in Vivo Methods

The ecological validity of in vitro data on cytokine levels, bioactivity, and mRNA has been questioned (Kiecolt-Glaser & Glaser, 1988), based on the fact that the cells have been handled, maintained, and manipulated in ways that would not occur in the body. As an alternative to in vitro methods, investigators study individual differences or intraindividual change in cytokine production and behavior in whole organisms during acute or chronic illnesses that have inflammatory components. This approach has its own limitations. Are the behavioral consequences of illness in whole organisms (especially in humans) the consequence of the infectious agent itself or of the immune response to that agent? Our overarching assumption is that some individuals generate more proinflammatory cytokines in response to immune challenge and/or that some individuals'

nervous and/or endocrine system components are more sensitive to the effects of cytokines than others'. Correspondingly, we are not particularly invested in the specifics of any particular pathogen or pathogenic process. Rather, we treat the pathogen as a stimulus and are most interested in the characteristics of individuals that create exaggerated cytokine responses or sensitivities when exposed to any number of immune stimuli.

To resolve these issues, in experimental paradigms it is common to employ a standard nonreplicating immune stimulus (e.g., lipopolysaccharide, LPS) as a proxy for systemic viral or bacterial infection (Tilders et al., 1994). LPS (also referred to as endotoxin) is the immunologically active component of gram-negative bacteria cell walls. LPS is derived from bacteria that are endemic to most mammalian species (*E. coli, Salmonella*), and vertebrates have specific LPS receptors on the surface of macrophages. Numerous animal studies show that LPS administration mimics the behavioral, neurochemical, and neuroendocrine response to cytokines (i.e., IL-1ß) very closely (see Dunn, 1996). Use of substances like LPS also enables investigators to standardize exposure (e.g., dose by weight, duration of exposure, and strain of virus) to the immune stimulus, a control that is not easy to implement in more ecologically valid contexts. In one of the few studies conducted with humans, Reichenberg et al. (2001) employed a double-blind crossover design with 20 healthy male volunteers. Participants completed psychological questionnaires and neuropsychological tests 1, 3, and 9 hours after intravenous injection of endotoxin (0.8 ng/kg, *Salmonella*). Reichenberg et al. observed that after endotoxin administration, the subjects showed a transient increase in anxiety and depressed mood, with decreased verbal and nonverbal memory. These changes were associated with increased levels of cytokine secretion (i.e., IL-1ß, TNF-a, IL-6) released in response to endotoxin.

Natural Experiments

Interestingly, substances like endotoxin have been used as adjuvants in vaccine preparations (e.g., whole-cell DTP vaccine). Adjuvants are added to stimulate the immune response sufficiently so that adequate antibody is produced to the particular antigen species included in the vaccine preparation. Investigators studying the effects of stress on immunity in adults have often taken advantage of immunizations as natural experiments (Bonneau, Sheridan, Feng, & Glaser, 1993; Kiecolt-Glaser, Glaser, Gravenstein, Malarkey, & Sheridan, 1996). Child immunizations offer a similar opportunity. In the United States, for instance, parents are encouraged to have their children immunized starting at 3 months of age and continuing on a regular basis through the preschool years. Studies of immunizations represent a natural experiment in which to explore individual differences in cytokine-behavior relationships (Morag, Yirmiya, Lerer, & Morag, 1998). Several studies predate the current rationale but do show mild to moderate short-term behavioral effects of childhood immunizations (Cody, Baraff, Cherry, Marcy, & Manclark, 1981). The side effects include fever, irritability, lack of appetite, and increased sleep and parallel the nonspecific symptoms of sickness induced by cytokines.

On a side note, in general, we know very little about the determinants of individual, developmental, or gender differences in the expression of sickness behaviors in children. Research on the efficacy of most childhood vaccines was conducted largely before cytokines were known as regulators of the NEI network. For instance, the whole-cell version of the DPT vaccine contained endotoxin as an adjuvant. The vaccine was causally linked to adverse reactions and behavior disorders (e.g., Blumberg et al., 1993; Borg, 1958; Cody et al., 1981; Long, DeForest, Smith, Lazaro, & Wassilak, 1990). A government-mandated scientific panel called for studies of biobehavioral predictors of individual differences in the severity of adverse responses to vaccines, as well as the specific biological mechanisms responsible for vaccine-induced behavioral effects (Howson, Howe, & Fineberg, 1991). The use of the whole-cell DTP vaccine was discontinued in the late 1990s. Thus far, immunizations have been used to study the effects of stress on immunity and health; we highlight the potential of this natural experiment as a model in which to study sickness behaviors and immune-endocrine relationships across the life span.

Noninvasive Measurement in Saliva

The ability to measure biological variables noninvasively in saliva has created many opportunities for behavioral scientists to test biosocial models of individual differences and intraindividual change in mood, cognition, behavior, and psychopathology (Kirschbaum, Read, & Hellhammer, 1992; Malamud & Tabak, 1993). For instance, the integration of salivary measures of steroid hormones such as cortisol (Schwartz et al., 1998), testosterone (D. A. Granger et al., 2004), and dehydroepiandrosterone (D. A. Granger, Schwartz, Booth, Curran, & Zakaria 1999) has become routine in developmental science. Yet, as the number of studies doing so has increased, special circumstances capable of compromising the value of the information generated have been documented. In a series of studies, we show that the measurement of salivary biomarkers can be substantially influenced during the process of sample collection (Schwartz, Granger, Susman, Gunnar, & Laird, 1998; Shirtcliff, Granger, Schwartz, & Curran, 2001), are susceptible to interference effects caused by the leakage of blood (plasma) into saliva (Kivlighan, Granger, Schwartz, Nelson, & Curran, 2004), and are sensitive to storage conditions when samples are archived (D. A. Granger et al., 2004). Although we show workable solutions to each of these problems, they are raised here because these issues are relevant to the measurement of immune markers in saliva but have yet to be addressed in the literature.

There are other caveats. The immune system is highly compartmentalized, and immune activity in the oral mucosa may reflect a localized response that is relatively independent of the more general systemic level of activation. Indeed, there is a highly specialized literature on oral biology and disease. Consistent with this explanation, and in contrast to the near-perfect linear serum-saliva associations for some endocrine markers (i.e., cortisol), the serum-saliva correlations for immune markers has been shown to be small to modest (Nishanian, Aziz, Chung, Detels, & Fahey, 1998). In our preliminary studies, we have documented the internal validity (i.e., linearity, spike recovery) of experimental immunoassay protocols for sIgA, c-reactive protein, interleukin-6, and surrogate markers of immune activation such as ß-2-microglobulin and neopterin. However, important questions remain unanswered: To what degree, and under which circumstances, do the levels of salivary immune markers reflect systemic immune activation? Do individual differences in these parameters provide information beyond the status of the immune system in the oral mucosa? Studies to establish external validity of these markers are now under way.

DO CYTOKINES AFFECT DEVELOPMENTAL PLASTICITY OF THE BIOLOGICAL BASIS OF BEHAVIOR?

It is clear that cytokines cause short-term behavioral changes, but is it possible that activation of the cytokine network could affect the long-term plasticity of biological systems underlying important behavioral, emotional, or cognitive capacities? Can cytokines change enduring aspects of our temperament or personality? The overwhelming evidence of cytokine effects on cerebral and neuroendocrine systems underscores that this may be biologically plausible. Yet, at first glance, this possibility seems to contradict our everyday experience. When adults have systemic viral or bacterial infections (e.g., influenza, *E. Coli*), the majority clearly express sickness behaviors, albeit to different degrees. But even those of us who become the most agitated, withdrawn, sleepy, and irritable when we are sick return to our regular selves within days after the obvious signs of infection (fever, swollen glands) subside.

Theoretical Background and Biological Plausibility

Are there developmental periods when humans are more susceptible to longer-term or permanent effects? Several facts suggest that humans may be more susceptible earlier than later in life. Each of the main components of the NEI axis develops rapidly during the 1st year of life. As noted earlier, the immune system starts to function 2 to 4 months after birth and does not reach full maturity until puberty. The HPA axis is functional and stress-responsive at birth, but not yet synchronized with a diurnal rhythm. The threshold or set point of cortisol reactivity is substantially influenced by environmental input (i.e., the caregiving environment) during early childhood. The adrenal gland, however, doesn't fully mature until middle childhood—a period of development termed adrenarche that begins for most around age 6 to 8. By contrast, in the last decades of life, the lymphoid system's ability to recognize and respond to antigens declines dramatically, as do levels of most endocrine system products.

Shanks et al. (1995) suggest the possibility that experience with the antigenic environment early is critical with respect to setting the tone of neuroendocrine reactivity throughout life. This logic closely parallels Michael Meaney's (Liu et al., 1997; Meaney, Aitken, Bhatnagar, Van Berkel, & Sapolsky, 1988) behavioral studies showing that characteristics of the early caregiving environment are determinants of individual differences in HPA reactivity in later life. Shanks speculates that the antigenic environment mammals are born into remains remarkably stable throughout life. Thus, she considers the influence of early illness on the developing HPA axis to be adaptive. HPA responsiveness to the secretion of proinflammatory cytokines is essential to regulating the magnitude and duration of the systemic immune response. It follows, then, that the NEI system would not be one size fits all but would have the potential to assimilate and accommodate the antigenic topography early in development. This logic is consistent with the notion that the immune system plays a highly specialized sensory role in this process of fine-tuning the threshold of reactivity for the developing NEI.

To adequately investigate this possibility, studies are needed that employ longitudinal designs and focus on the link between the activity of cytokines (and processes that influence their regulation) and the onset, changes, and continuities of atypical behavioral and biological function. To our knowledge, such studies have yet to be conducted with humans. The evidence from animal studies, however, is revealing.

Effects of Early Illness on Physiology Later in Life

Studies with rodents show conclusively that exposure to immune system products (i.e., cytokines) during early development permanently changes biological systems with well-known organizational influences on the brain and behavior. O'Grady and colleagues (O'Grady & Hall, 1990, 1991; O'Grady, Hall, & Goldstein, 1987) reported that immune activation during pre- and neonatal periods affects changes in the size of the adrenal glands, ovaries, and testes that persist into adulthood. Shanks et al. (1995) showed that immune activation during a critical neonatal period of HPA axis development had profound effects on neuroendocrine (i.e., ACTH, corticosterone) responsiveness to environmental challenge during adulthood. Specifically, administration of endotoxin (0.05 mg/kg) on days 3 and 5 of life resulted in decreased glucocorticoid negative-feedback inhibition of ACTH synthesis, thereby potentiating HPA responsiveness to restraint stress. These studies are perhaps the first to reveal that exposure to immune products early in life can permanently alter neural systems, that is, HPA and hypothalamic-pituitary-gonadal axes, governing the impact of maturational processes and environmental events on development. They suggest indirect effects on behavioral, emotional, and social processes via permanent changes induced in these biological systems.

Effects of Early Illness on Later Behavior

This developmental phenomenon was first extended into the behavioral domain by Crnic and colleagues (Crnic, 1991; Segall & Crnic, 1990). Their studies reveal striking evidence that immune activation in neonates induced behavioral changes that persisted into adulthood. Neonatal mice administered herpes simplex virus or interferon became spontaneously hyperactive for life (Crnic & Pizer, 1988). Of particular importance, this radical reorganization of behavior was mediated by the impact of products of cellular immune activation, not necessarily viral pathogenesis, on the migration of granule cells from the cerebellum.

Crnic's findings are groundbreaking in that they provide solid evidence of neuroanatomical changes induced by immune activation early in life that underlie permanent behavioral change expressed later in life. Crnic (1991) postulated that individual differences in the development of atypical behavior may be caused by common immunological stimuli that have uncommon effects on the biological basis of behavior.

UNCOMMON BIOBEHAVIORAL EFFECTS OF IMMUNE STIMULI: IMPLICATIONS FOR DEVELOPMENTAL PSYCHOPATHOLOGY?

In a series of studies, we attempted to extend the basic ideas forwarded by Crnic (1991) by exploring sources of individual differences in the uncommon biobehavioral effects of common immune stimuli. It was anticipated that by doing so, important clues would be revealed that would contribute to a more general understanding of individual development, microevolution, and the development of psychopathology. The studies employed a well-established animal model that represents the major dimensions of atypical social development: internalizing and externalizing behavior problems. The model system, developed by Robert Cairns at the University of North Carolina at Chapel Hill, involves two lines of mice (ICR) that have been selectively bred for differences in social interaction patterns and a control line of mice bred without selection for behavior (for details, see R. B. Cairns, MacCombie, & Hood, 1983). Selection for breeding was based on the social isolation-induced aggressive behavior of adult males assessed in a 10-minute observation of dyadic social interaction. Within a few generations, the program resulted in a high-aggressive and low-aggressive line. Selective breeding was continued for 30 generations. Presently, the lines are maintained by Kathryn Hood at the Pennsylvania State University without further selective pressure.

The model has several advantages that make it valuable for testing hypotheses about the uncommon effects of common immune stimuli on biobehavioral outcomes. There are demonstrated sensitive periods for early experiences that influence later social behavior (B. D. Cairns, Hood, & Midlam, 1985; Hood & Cairns, 1989) and established procedures for assessing adult levels of social behavior (R. B. Cairns, Gariepy, & Hood, 1990; Hood & Cairns, 1988). At 44 to 46 days of age, animals are observed in a dyadic test during the dark period of the diurnal cycle. Subjects are placed into a rectangular Plexiglas chamber (20 × 21 × 31 cm), with a metal barrier dividing the chamber in half. An unfamiliar same-age male is placed in the other half. After a 5-minute habituation period, the barrier is removed and the mice are allowed to interact for 10 minutes. Dyadic behaviors are videotaped under dim red light. Social behaviors are coded from videotapes in 120 5-second sequential blocks of the 10-minute test period. Within each 5-second period, an observer scores the presence of the following behaviors: attacks (a vigorous lunge accompanied by biting and wrestling); attack latency (the number of seconds until the first attack by the subject); behavioral immobility/freeze (subject does not move for at least 2 seconds); social reactivity/startle (a startle response, jumped or kicked with the hind leg in response to mild social stimulation, such as a sniff or groom from the partner); and social exploration (sniffing, climbing on, or grooming the social partner). Dependent measures are compiled as the number of 5-second periods in which a behavior occurred, with a maximum score of 1 for each behavior in each 5-second period.

A series of studies by John Pettito and colleagues show line differences in immune responsiveness at the cellular level. When challenged with 3-methylcholanthrene, 100% of the mice from the socially inhibited/low-aggressive line developed tumors, compared to only 44% of the high-aggressive line animals. The line differences were extended to include NK cell and T and B cell responsiveness in vitro. Compared to aggressive mice, low-aggressive mice had significantly lower T cells, lower proliferative responses to concanavalin A, lower IL-2 and interferon gamma production, and lower NK cell activity (Pettito, Lysle, Gariepy, Clubb, et al., 1994; Pettito, Lysle, Gariepy, & Lewis, 1992, 1994). Pettito speculates that this association may be due to a genetic linkage between subsets of genes involved in determining these complex behavioral and immunological traits (Pettito et al., 1999).

Individual Differences

In an attempt to complement Pettito et al.'s work, D. A. Granger, Hood, et al. (1997) explored the possibility that genetic-developmental differences in social behavior are associated with differences in the biobehavioral effects of induced illness in adult animals. The expectation was that animals from the high-aggressive line would show a more robust proinflammatory response than the low-aggressive line mice. Adult males from high- and low-aggressive behavior lines were injected with endotoxin (LPS: 0.25 mg/kg, 1.25 mg/kg, or 2.5 mg/kg) or saline. Body temperature, weight, and locomotor activity were monitored before and 8 and 24 hours after injection. Twenty-four hours after injection, social behaviors were assessed in a 10-minute dyadic test, and tissue (spleens and hypothalami) were collected. As hypothesized, high-aggressive line males had a lower threshold to endotoxin-induced effects on body temperature, weight loss, spleen weight, hypothalamic norepinephrine, and corticosterone than did males from the low-aggressive line. In the high-aggressive line only, social reactivity (startle response to mild social investigation) increased, and attack frequency and latency to attack decreased for endotoxin-treated compared to saline-treated mice. Table 17.2 presents bivariate correlations among the biobehavioral effects of endotoxin by selected line. Noteworthy is the fact that endotoxin-induced differences in activation of the immune response (crudely estimated here by spleen weight) and HPA axis (i.e., corticosterone) were significantly associated with activity levels, weight, and body temperature 8 and 24 hours postinjection in the high-aggressive but not low-aggressive line mice. The selected line (genotype) × endotoxin treatment (environment) interactions demonstrate that genetic-developmental differences in social and aggressive behavior may indicate the extent to which immune stimuli function as biobehavioral stressors.

In a companion set of studies, we attempted to link the time course of the biobehavioral effects of endotoxin to proinflammatory cytokine (IL-1ß) production (D. A. Granger, Hood, & Banta, 2000). In a between-subjects design ($N = 120$; 5 per design cell), adult male mice from the high- and low-aggressive lines were administered endotoxin (1.25 mg/kg) and social behavior was assessed (as described earlier) and serum harvested (immediately following cervical dislocation via cardiac puncture) at 12 time points (0.5 to 6, 18, and 24 hours) postinjection. As in the earlier study, in contrast to low-aggressive line mice, high-aggressive line mice showed endotoxin-induced reduction in attack frequency, an increase in attack latency, more pronounced increases in behavioral immobility, and more socially reactive behaviors. As can be seen in Figure 17.7, high-aggressive mice produced IL-1ß more quickly and at higher levels than did low-aggressive mice. Although there was not a significant line difference in the production of corticosterone, endotoxin-related differences in levels of IL-1ß, corticosterone, and behavior change were positively associated in the high-aggressive line only. For example, Figure 17.7 illustrates that the increases in IL-1ß, corticosterone, and socially reactive behavior postinjection were closely coordinated in time in the high-aggressive but not the low-aggressive line. Because an endotoxin dose of 1.25 mg/kg is on the high end of the scale, a follow-up experiment confirmed that the basic finding—the line difference

TABLE 17.2   Bivariate Correlations among the Biobehavioral Effects of Endotoxin in Adult Male Mice Selectively Bred for Differences in Social Behavior

	CORT	Spleen Weight	Attack Frequency	Behavioral Immobility	Social Exploration	Reactivity
High-Aggressive						
8 hours postinjection						
Activity	−.68[a]	−.50[c]	.23	−.22	.05	−.36
Weight	.59[b]	.49[c]	−.50[c]	.69[a]	−.57[b]	.68[b]
Temperature	−.62[b]	−.58[b]	.51[c]	−.62	.39	−.63[b]
24 hours postinjection						
Activity	−.64[b]	−.47[c]	.23	−.19	.03	−.28
Weight	−.70[a]	−.56[c]	.36	−.47[c]	.25	−.47[c]
Temperature	−.55[b]	.25	.30	−.79[a]	.51[c]	−.47[c]
Corticosterone	—	.28	−.08	.41[d]	−.37	.43[c]
Low-Aggressive						
8 hours postinjection						
Activity	.04	.10	—	−.32	.00	.56[b]
Weight	.16	.05	—	.21	−.35	−.39
Temperature	−.08	.02	—	−.34	.38	.16
24 hours postinjection						
Activity	−.11	−.23	—	−.44[c]	.15	.63[b]
Weight	−.19	.00	—	−.29	.42[d]	.27
Temperature	.16	.19	—	−.25	.03	.37
Corticosterone	—	.53[c]	—	.05	−.45[c]	.48[c]

Notes: Data were averaged across endotoxin dose. Activity, weight, and temperature scores represent percent change from baseline (preinjection) levels at 8- and 24-hours postinjection. Serum corticosterone (CORT) levels and social behaviors were assessed 24 hours postinjection. [a]$p < .001$ (all dfs = 19, two-tailed tests); [b]$p < .01$; [c]$p < .05$; [d]$p < .06$. *Source:* From "Effects of Peripheral Immune Activation on Social Behavior and Adrenocortical Activity in Aggressive Mice: Genotype-Environment Interactions," by D. A. Granger et al., 1997, *Aggressive Behavior, 23,* pp. 93–105.

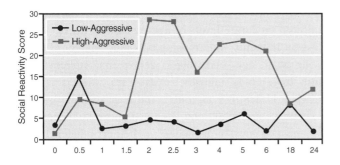

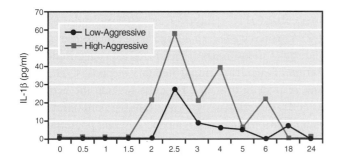

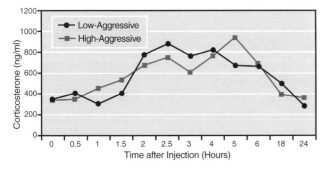

Figure 17.7 Time course effects of endotoxin (1.25 mg/kg) for Interluekin-1β and socially reactive (startle) behaviors are correlated, but distinctly differ in mice selectively bred for high versus low levels of aggressive behavior. *Source: From Individual Differences in Endotoxin Effects on Social Behavior and Interleukin-1β, by D. A. Granger, K. E. Hood, and M. B. Banta, 2000, unpublished manuscript, University Park, Pennsylvania State University.*

in IL-1ß production—was evident even at a fivefold lower endotoxin dose (0.25 mg/kg).

Taken together with the findings with parallel lines of mice (e.g., Pettito et al., 1999; Pettito, Lysle, Gariepy, Clubb, et al., 1994; Pettito, Lysle, Gariepy, & Lewis, 1992, 1994), these data suggest that the observed pattern may in part be due to line differences in peripheral proinflammatory cytokine production. Clearly, the possibility cannot be ruled out that there may be line-differential CNS or HPA axis sensitivity to the afferent signals of cytokines, to other acute phase proteins, or to endotoxin itself. However, the lack of a corticosterone difference

between lines in response to endotoxin suggests the last possibility is unlikely.

In the next experiment, the possibility of a line difference in sensitivity to proinflammatory cytokines was examined. Endotoxin was removed from the equation, and the direct effect of IL-1ß on biobehavioral outcomes was tested. Adult males from the high- and low-aggressive lines were administered a standard dose of IL-1ß IP (0.25 to 1.0 ug/ml) or saline. Consistent with Pettito's findings, high-aggressive line mice showed higher circulating levels of IL-6 than did low-aggressive mice (see Figure 17.8), but the difference was most pronounced at the highest (1.0 ug/mL) IL-1ß dose. As can be seen in Table 17.3, in the high-aggressive line, individual differences in IL-6 levels in response to IL-1ß injection were associated with higher levels of corticosterone, temperature loss, and behavioral immobility and reduced social exploration in observed social interactions.

The mechanisms responsible for the apparent linkage between these behavioral traits and immune function are unclear. Pettito and colleagues (1999) raise two possibilities: that the association between selective line and immune

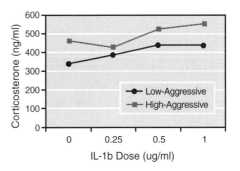

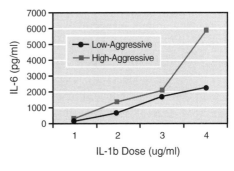

Figure 17.8 Exogenous administration of Interluekin-1β (ug/mL) induces Interleukin-6 and corticosterone differently in adult male mice selectively bred for high versus low levels of aggressive behavior. *Source: From Individual Differences in Endotoxin Effects on Social Behavior and Interleukin-1β, by D. A. Granger, K. E. Hood, and M. B. Banta, 2000, unpublished manuscript, University Park, Pennsylvania State University.*

TABLE 17.3   IL-1ß-Induced Circulating Levels of Interleukin-6 Are Correlated with Measures of HPA Axis Activation and Social Behavior

Selected Line	Low-Aggressive			High-Aggressive		
	IL-1ß	IL-6	CORT	IL-1ß	IL-6	CORT
Temperature loss						
30 minute postinjection	−.20	−.27	−.21	−.30	−.20	−.20
60 minute postinjection	−.13	−.20	−.27	−.50[a]	−.44[a]	−.56[a]
120 minute postinjection	−.44[a]	−.43+	−.38	−.52[a]	−.45[a]	−.37
Social reactivity	.17	.41+	−.09	−.24	−.11	.09
Behavioral immobility	.51[a]	.39	.30	.45[a]	.68[c]	.52[a]
Social exploration	−.15	−.30	.08	−.23	−.43+	−.22
IL-6	.81[c]	—	—	.91[c]	—	—
Corticosterone	.33	.56[b]	—	.59[b]	.64[b]	—

Note: $+ p < .07$, [a] $p < .05$, [b] $p < .01$, [c] $p < .001$. IL-1ß indicates dose condition (vehicle, 0.25 µ/mL, 0.50 µ/mL, 1.0 µ/mL). Corticosterone measured in ng/mL and IL-6 in pg/mL units. Social behavior data are frequency scores during a 10-minute dyadic test. *Source:* From *Individual Differences in Endotoxin Effects on Social Behavior and Interleukin-ß,* by D. A. Granger, K. E. Hood, and M. B. Banta, 2000, unpublished manuscript, University Park, Pennsylvania State University.

function may be due to a genetic linkage between subsets of genes involved in determining these complex traits, or that these results may represent a fortuitous association that occurred during selective breeding. There is some independent evidence that the aggression-immunity link may not be random. Experimental nonhuman primate studies (Macaca Fascicularis) reveal that changes in cellular immunity in response to the stress of repeated social reorganization are associated with individual differences in aggressive behavior (Cohen et al., 1997), and high-aggressive monkeys have higher lymphocyte counts than low-aggressive monkeys (Line et al., 1996).

In the largest study to date of the relationship between aggression and immunologic processes in humans, D. A. Granger, Booth, and Johnson (2000) evaluated two conflicting models: a positive association stemming from an adaptive mechanism protecting aggressive individuals from increased exposure to immune stimuli and a negative association due to potential immunosuppressive effects of high testosterone levels. The models were tested using enumerative measures of cellular and humoral immunity in a sample of 4,415 men ages 30 to 48 who were interviewed and underwent a medical exam. The findings provided clear evidence in support of the first model and failed to support the second. Analyses revealed positive (and curvilinear) associations between aggressive behavior and enumerative measures of helper/inducer and suppressor/cytolytic T lymphocytes and B lymphocytes. More specifically, men with very high levels of aggressive behavior did not show correspondingly higher numbers of circulating lymphoid

cells. In contrast, the relationship was robust for men who exhibited moderate levels of aggressive behaviors. The aggression-immunity relationship was independent of testosterone level, age, body mass, depression, current health status (e.g., colds, injuries, sexually transmitted diseases, and general health symptoms), and negative health behaviors (tobacco, alcohol, and drug use and sexual promiscuity) and was most pronounced for helper/inducer T cells. There was no association between testosterone and any immune measure. It may be noteworthy that the aggression-immunity association was strongest for the numbers of T helper cells (CD4), cytolytic T cells (CD8), and B lymphocytes. As noted earlier, to a large extent this subset of lymphoid cells determines the initiation, magnitude, and duration of specific cellular immune responses. The functional responsibilities of CD4 cells include the activation of B cells, secretion of cytokines that regulate intercellular communications among T lymphocytes, and potentiation of the cytolytic activity of natural killer cells. CD4 cells facilitate both humoral and cellular branches of specific immunity and thus affect the immune response to both extracellular (bacteria) and intracellular (e.g., malignant or virally infected cells) antigens. The functional significance of B cells includes specific antigen recognition, antigen presentation, antibody production, and maintenance of immunologic memory.

Although these findings focus attention on aspects of specific cell-mediated immunity, there is scant empirical evidence to suggest which of the many physiological pathways possibly responsible for the association should receive priority research attention. As noted earlier, even among the best-developed animal models, the source of the link between aggression and immunity remains unknown. Research focused on elaborating the nature and sources of the apparent aggression-lymphoctye link would seem to be the next logical step to begin the process of ruling out the many alternative hypotheses. However, in our opinion, it would be shortsighted to focus this effort on aggression exclusively. No research to date has ruled out the possibility that other behavior profiles may be associated with the uncommon effects of common immune stimuli.

Developmental Effects

Among the enduring issues in developmental psychobiology are the origins of individual adaptations to changing environments and how these influences are integrated with maturational processes to produce differences in social behavior (Cicchetti & Dawson, 2002). In general, it has been proposed that developmental integration occurs in response to environmental forces that are predictable and omnipresent but often nonobvious. In this developmental integration, very early stimulation may lead to differences in later life in the threshold or sensitivity of behavioral and physiological responsiveness to challenge (Hood, Dreschel, & Granger, 2003).

To explore individual differences in the developmental consequences of early immune stress, D. A. Granger, Hood, Ikeda, Reed, and Block (1996) evaluated neonatal immune stress and differences in social expression at adulthood. Neonatal male mice from the high- and low-aggressive lines were administered saline or 0.05 mg/kg endotoxin at age 5 or 6 days. There was a transient endotoxin-induced reduction in the growth rate (72 hours after injection) of the neonates from the high-aggressive line only. At adulthood, social behaviors were observed in the dyadic test (as in the earlier studies). As young adults, endotoxin-treated males show more socially reactive behavior (startle responses) to a novel social partner's contact compared to saline controls. For the high-aggressive line only, endotoxin treatment increased behavioral immobility, decreased attack frequency, and increased attack latency compared to same-line saline-treated controls. Within 20 minutes of the conclusion of the dyadic test, sera and hypothalmi were harvested. Neonatal endotoxin-treated males from the high-aggressive line as adults show decreased levels of hypothalamic CRF. The effects of endotoxin exposure in early life on socially reactive behavior in later life were associated with endotoxin-induced individual differences in CRF levels in the high-aggressive but not low-aggressive line mice. These findings suggest that variation in the expression of socially inhibited behaviors in later life may be partially explained by differential sensitivities to the effects of exposure to immune stimuli in early life.

These developmental findings are consistent with the multiple studies described earlier that show adult males from the high-aggressive line are intrinsically more immunologically reactive to endotoxin compared to males from the low-aggressive line. In a follow-up experiment, it was confirmed that early in development (age 6 to 8 days), males from the selected lines were capable of producing IL-1ß in response to endotoxin. Neonates ($N = 100$) were injected IP with saline or 0.5, 0.25, or 1.25 mg/kg endotoxin. Two hours postinjection, trunk blood was collected and frozen for later assay. To ensure sufficient test volume, whole blood samples were pooled across two male siblings. There was a highly significant main effect of endotoxin dose on IL-1ß, with means (and standard deviations) of 2.62 pg/ml (4.73), 16.71 pg/ml (21.74), and 87.49 pg/ml (61.03), for the saline, 0.25 mg/kg, and 1.25 mg/kg conditions, respectively. The variation within dose conditions was sufficiently large that line differences in IL-1ß were not evident.

Hood et al. (2003) note that these convergent findings impel a consideration of the biobehavioral pathways through which these effects are realized. Are alterations in social development a direct result of immune stimulation, perhaps mediated by the HPA axis? A complementary hypothesis is that concurrent changes in dam-pup interactions produced by pup immune stimulation and related changes in pup behaviors might be reflected by changes in dam's behavior, which then may impact pup's behavior in a circular reaction over the course of early development to bring about long-term changes in social expression.

The Role of the Social Environment: Early Maternal Caregiving

In mammalian species, early development is embedded in the social context of maternal caregiving (Hofer, 1994; Krasnegor & Bridges, 1990). Differences in maternal responsiveness during interactions with neonates are sufficient to alter adult offspring behaviors in important ways. A major hypothesis is that the developing HPA axis in young animals is regulated by maternal behavior (Hofer, 1987; Levine, 1994). Much of the research on this question employs a handling manipulation—a brief daily removal of young from the maternal cage sufficient to activate maternal behaviors, especially licking and grooming of pups when they are returned to the dam. The general finding is that increased maternal licking and grooming promotes in later life a more efficient HPA response to severe stress and decreased HPA response to moderate stress, such as a novel environment. In rats, handled offspring develop faster and show earlier maturation of the HPA system. As adults, handled offspring show increased resistance to stress and disease and reduced fear-related behaviors. These favorable response patterns persist throughout the life span (Meaney, Aitken, Bhatnagar, Van Berkel & Sapolsky, 1988).

Immune stimulation, by contrast, may produce a different pattern of developmental effects. After early handling, the adult HPA axis is less responsive to stress; however, after endotoxin exposure, the HPA axis is more responsive (Shanks et al., 1995). This pattern is similar to the effects of prolonged maternal separation (deprivation) in rats, which produces lifelong HPA hyperresponsiveness to stress and associated vulnerabilities (Plotsky & Meaney, 1993).

Experimental manipulation of pups may change the stimulus value of pups for dams and thus may constitute another route of developmental effects (Hood et al., 2003).

Two lines of evidence suggest that line-specific maternal responsiveness to endotoxin-treated pups may contribute to differences in early endotoxin exposure effects later in life. Shanks and colleagues (1995, p. 382) reported anecdotal evidence of changes in dam-pup interactions following endotoxin administration to neonates: "At 3–4 hours postinjection, the dam was consistently off the nest, and this persisted until about 8 hr following treatment." Another source of variation in dam-pup interactions derives from systematic individual differences in dam or pup characteristics. Two studies using lines of mice that are related to those in the present report show line differences in maternal behaviors in a daily handling paradigm (Gariepy, Nehrenberg, & Mills-Koonce, 2001) and in observations of undisturbed litters (Rodriguiz, Gariepy, & Jones, 1998), with different patterns of line differences in the two observation protocols. Gariepy et al. showed, for example, that dams from the high-aggressive line are naturally more active (more licking, handling of pups, social contacts) in maternal caregiving than are dams from the low-aggressive line.

The evidence suggests several developmental pathways for the effects of early immune stimulation on later social expression. The first model specifies a physiological pathway of endotoxin-immune-HPA effects that directly alter behavior by intrinsic line differences in susceptibility to endotoxin. A second model proposes a possible pathway through the social-behavioral milieu of early development. Differences in maternal responsiveness to endotoxin-treated pups many contribute to or may completely constitute the pathway of early endotoxin effects on social development. Alternatively, differential susceptibility of pups to endotoxin effects may alter pups' contributions to dam-pup interactions, with consequent changes in the early social milieu (Hood et al., 2003). Finally, a third model proposes there may be combinations of these factors that produce development change. An example would be easily disrupted dams paired with more susceptible pups resulting in ineffective maternal care and associated effects.

In a recent report, D. A. Granger, Hood, Dreschel, Sergeant, and Likos (2001) directly addressed one of these models. The origins of individual differences in social behavior were examined in relation to early stress (immune challenge) and the social milieu (maternal behavior) using the genetic-developmental model. The study examined the persistence of line differences in the developmental effects of induced illness early in life under two conditions of maternal care (see Table 17.4). Neonatal mice from the high- and low-aggressive selectively bred lines received saline or 0.05 mg/kg LPS on day 5 or 6, as before. Litters were reared either by their line-specific biological dam or by a foster dam from a line bred without selection. As before, adult social behaviors were assessed in a dyadic test. If the first model is correct, then regardless of the maternal caregiving environment, high-aggressive line mice will show more pronounced developmental effects of immune challenge early in life than low-aggressive line mice. If the second model is correct, then effects of the early social milieu (being reared with the biological dam or being fostered to a control-line dam) will appear. A third possibility is that both sources of individual (selective breeding) and environmental (maternal caregiving) differences will contribute to patterns of adult social expression after early immune stress.

As in previous studies, mice from the high-aggressive line showed more developmental sensitivity to immune challenge than mice from the low-aggressive line. As adults, endotoxin-treated mice from the high-aggressive line have lower levels of aggressive behavior, longer latency to attack, and higher rates of socially reactive and inhibited behaviors compared to saline controls (see Table 17.5).

TABLE 17.4   Predictions on Developmental Integration of Early Immune Exposure: Effects on Adult Social Behaviors

Family of Origin	Maternal Caregiving	Intrinsic Sensitivity to Immune Challenge	Adult Social Behavioral Outcome
High-aggressive Low-inhibition	Low caregiving	More sensitive	Lower externalizing Higher internalizing
Low-aggressive High inhibition	High caregiving	Less sensitive	Higher internalizing

Note: Externalizing behaviors in the model include attack frequency and latency. Internalizing behaviors include social inhibition and social reactivity. Reprinted from "Developmental Effects of Early Immune Stress on Aggressive, Socially Reactive, and Inhibited Behaviors," by D. A. Granger, K. E. Hood, N. A. Dreschel, E. Sergeant, and A. Likos, 2001, *Development and Psychopathology, 13,* pp. 599–610.

TABLE 17.5   Differential Effects of Endotoxin Exposure by Selectively Bred Line: Mean (and Standard Deviations) for Social Behaviors

Selected Line Neonatal Exposure	Low-Aggressive		High-Aggressive	
	Saline ($n = 18$)	Endotoxin ($n = 21$)	Saline ($n = 22$)	Endotoxin ($n = 19$)
Attack frequency	00.00 (00.00)	00.00 (00.00)	48.86 (17.87)	32.68[a] (22.32)
Attack latency	—	—	28.41 (28.09)	137.37[a] (197.46)
Behavioral immobility	21.17 (12.97)	25.81 (16.70)	0.68 (1.78)	4.95[a] (6.68)
Social reactivity	0.72 (0.89)	2.71[b] (3.20)	1.54 (2.72)	6.26[b] (8.32)
Social exploration	71.00 (18.69)	67.05 (18.74)	16.68 (14.11)	26.74 (24.45)

Note: [a] $p < .01$; [b] $p < .05$; T-tests (two-tailed) comparing neonatal endotoxin versus saline exposure conditions within selected line. The unit of measurement for attack latency is the number of 5-s observation periods to first attack. All other behaviors are scored as the number of 5-s periods in which the specific behavior was observed. Reprinted from "Developmental Effects of Early Immune Stress on Aggressive, Socially Reactive, and Inhibited Behaviors," by D. A. Granger, K. E. Hood, N. A. Dreschel, E. Sergeant, and A. Likos, 2001, *Development and Psychopathology, 13,* pp. 599–610.

The data support a robust pattern of individual differences, with variation in the developmental effect of early immune challenge that is systematically related to preexisting individual differences in aggressive behavior. Beyond these confirmatory observations, several new findings are noteworthy. The systematic developmental effects within the high-aggressive line are relatively unaffected when the social environment of early rearing is held constant by fostering animals to mothers from a control line of mice. By contrast, within the low-aggressive line there is only one behavior that is sensitive to early immune challenge (social reactivity), and that effect is strongly dependent on pup-dam interactions with the biological mother. Moreover, the effects of rearing environment are markedly different between the lines. In the high-aggressive line, there are multiple effects of endotoxin and only a single effect of rearing environment. In the low-aggressive line, there are multiple behaviors affected by fostering and only a single behavior influenced by endotoxin, in interaction with the fostering conditions. That the effects of endotoxin are robust in the high-aggressive line regardless of rearing condition rules out line differences in maternal behavior as the primary source of the development effect. However, there remains the possibility that high-aggressive pups treated with endotoxin are eliciting different behaviors from their own dams and from foster dams, compared to pups treated with saline.

In a design that complements this study, Hood et al. (2003) rigorously examined whether differences in mater-

nal responsiveness during interactions with endotoxin-treated pups might contribute to endotoxin effects on social development. Based on the findings reported earlier (see Table 17.5), it was hypothesized that when intrinsic differences in immune responsiveness are extreme (as with individuals from the high- versus low-aggressive lines), maternal responsiveness to endotoxin-treated ("sick") pups may have little or no influence on social behavior outcomes later in life. The social environment's capacity to influence the developmental outcome under these conditions may be orders of magnitude less than the contribution made to the outcome by the intrinsic differences in immunologic reactivity (D. A. Granger et al., 2001). Alternatively, when intrinsic differences in immunologic reactivity are not as extreme (or within the normal range as depicted in Figure 17.5), the ontogenic process should be more open to the influence of differential experience with social environmental processes. Hood et al. examined the latter possibility. Figure 17.9 presents an overview of this complex design. Neonatal mice bred without selection for behavior or differences in immune reactivity were fostered to dams from either the high- or low-aggressive lines of mice (because they show distinct differences in maternal caregiving behaviors; Gariepy et al., 2001; Rodriguiz et al., 1998) or dams from a control line bred without selection. Repeated naturalistic observations of maternal behavior on postnatal days 2, 4, 5, 6, and 8 were conducted. Scan-sampling procedures were implemented by observers blind to dam line and endotoxin treatment conditions to record the following

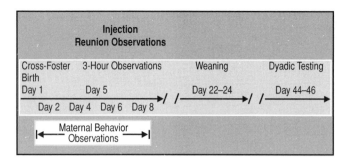

Figure 17.9 Developmental research design: time line of fostering, injections, and assessments. *Source:* From "Maternal Behavior Changes after Immune Challenge of Neonates with Developmental Effects on Adult Social Behavior," by K. E. Hood, N. Dreschel, and D. A. Granger, 2003, *Developmental Psychobiology, 42,* pp. 17–34.

maternal behaviors: off-nest (dam off nest and not in contact with pups), nursing (dam in a nursing posture), lick (dam licking pups with mouth or tongue movements), and handle (dam nosing, touching with paws or moving pups). To provide a special focus on licking of pups by dams (this behavior is low-frequency), an additional event sampling procedure was implemented on each observation day (see Hood et al., 2003, for detail). As in the earlier studies, on postnatal day 5, neonates were administered saline or 0.05 mg/kg endotoxin. However, this time two observation periods on postnatal day 5 were of interest. Reunion episodes were observed to capture the immediate reactions of dams to pups that had been removed from the nest after handling and treatment with endotoxin. For 5 minutes after the pups' return, observers recorded maternal behavior (i.e., latency to first retrieve of a pup, latency to last retrieve, off-nest, touching or handling a pup, licking, and nursing). Simultaneously, ultrasonic vocalizations (USV) from the pups as an index of individual differences in their solicitation/response to the social environment during the reunion episode. Additional scan and event sample observations of maternal behavior were recorded 3 hours postinjection, when the illness response of pups to endotoxin was expected to be at peak intensity.

Result showed for the first time (to our knowledge) that the early maternal caregiving environment may influence the effects of early illness on social development. Consistent with the time course of endotoxin-induced illness, we observed dramatic but temporary effects on maternal caregiving. Dam responsiveness to induced pup illness was related to later social development, with changes in prosocial behaviors (social exploration) and antisocial behaviors (attack frequency and latency) that occur in different patterns in pups reared in the three dam lines. The immediate im-

pact of endotoxin treatment on dam-neonate interactions is evidenced by slower retrieval of pups, more time off-nest, less contact with pups, and fewer USVs from pups. At the peak of pups' induced illness, 3 or 4 hours after endotoxin treatment, maternal care is restored and enhanced, with more licking and less time off-nest for endotoxin-treated than saline-treated pups. By days 6 and 8 (24 and 72 hours postinjection), endotoxin effects on maternal behavior are not evident. Similarly, weights at weaning (day 22 to 24) show no effect of endotoxin treatment. As expected, line differences in maternal responsiveness were pronounced. More important, males exposed to endotoxin early in life showed changes in adult social behaviors that depended on foster dam line as well as individual differences in maternal responsiveness.

This study highlighted the potential usefulness of a social-contextual analysis for understanding early experience effects (e.g., Cicchetti & Richters, 1997). Specifically, it showed that when intrinsic individual differences in immune reactivity are within the normative range, maternal responsiveness to stressed neonates can ameliorate the social-developmental effects of early illness (Hood et al., 2003). Collectively, this series of studies (D. A. Granger et al., 1996, 2001; Hood et al., 2003) demonstrate that nonobvious but omnipresent features of the physical environment early in life, such as antigenic load, may interact with intrinsic differences in immunologic reactivity and the social environment to determine individual social developmental outcomes. The findings support Crnic's (1991) proposal that individual differences in development may be caused by common immune stimuli that have "uncommon effects" on the psychobiological basis of behavior. They extend Crnic's observations by specifying factors that influence susceptibility, including intrinsic differences in social behavior, immunologic reactivity, risk of exposure, and the capacity of the early caregiving environment to facilitate recovery.

CONCLUDING COMMENTS AND FUTURE RESEARCH DIRECTIONS

Contemporary developmental theorists place behavioral adaptation in a pivotal position with respect to the bidirectional nature of environmental and biological influences on individual development. Cognitive-behavioral responsiveness to environmental events is thought to mediate or moderate the impact of such events on rapid (e.g., hormones, neurotransmitters) and slower acting (e.g., genetic activity) biological systems (Gottlieb, 1992). Subsequently, the effects of these biological systems manifest as adjustments in behavioral organization or responsiveness, or both. The functional and integrative integrity of the reciprocal influences among these systems is considered essential for optimal development (Cicchetti & Dawson, 2002). For instance, these processes enable individuals to continuously adapt to the ever-changing topography of social ecological landscapes, as well as appropriately engage the social context during life periods characterized by rapid acquisition of new skills and abilities (e.g., infancy, toddlerhood, adolescence).

It seems reasonable that cytokines may affect developmental plasticity via their impact on biobehavioral processes that set the stage for successful behavioral, emo-tional, social, and cognitive adaptation. As noted, there is unequivocal evidence that cytokines restrict the range of adaptive behaviors in several domains and may induce some maladaptive behavioral and psychological states. These cytokine-induced changes may potentiate the impact of environmental events on stress-responsive biological systems. For instance, cytokine effects may limit the behavioral surface's ability to effectively moderate the impact of environment challenge on HPA axis and sympathetic nervous system activation. Alternatively, cytokine-induced psychological states (maladaptive coping strategies, emotion regulation, cognitive slowing) may potentiate the responsiveness of environmentally sensitive

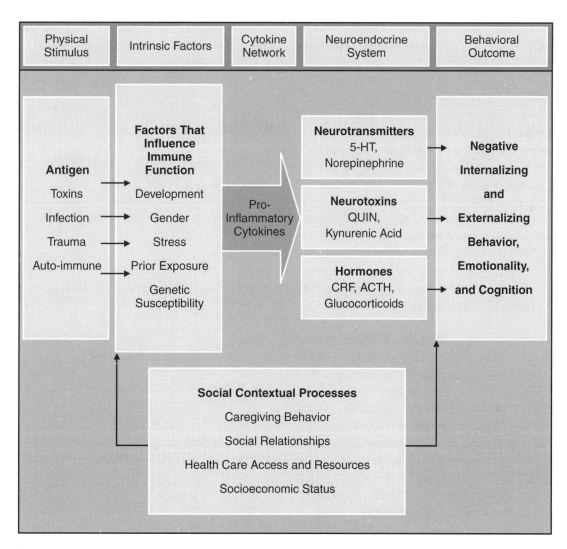

Figure 17.10.   Theoretical model of interacting processes contributing to individual differences in the developmental effects of the activation of the cytokine network. *Source:* From "Developmental Psychoneuroimmunology: The Role of Cytokine Network Activation in the Epigenesis of Developmental Psychopathology" (pp. 293–323), by D. A. Granger, N. A. Dreschel, and E. A. Shirtcliff, in *Neurodevelopmental Mechanisms in Psychopathology* by D. Cicchetti and E. Walker (Eds.), 2003, New York: Cambridge University Press.

biological systems. Still another possibility is that cytokine effects at the behavioral surface level restrict individual opportunities to engage contexts that nurture social, cognitive, or behavioral development. For instance, cytokine-induced social and defensive withdrawal or cognitive slowing would limit experiences in ways that would preclude vicarious or trial-and-error learning, parent-child interactions, or peer relationships.

In the field of child development, etiologic factors determining vulnerability to specific atypical developmental outcomes have for the most part consistently eluded detection. Even when the range of potential causal factors has been narrowed, it is clear that individual differences in the expression of their effects are the rule rather than the exception. Given this somewhat discouraging state of our knowledge, it is not surprising that theorists commonly assume that atypical developmental outcomes represent the final common pathway of multiple independent and interacting factors. This perspective has proven useful for some purposes (i.e., identifying the range of prospective causal factors) but has not necessarily resulted in progress toward defining the nature of cause and effect.

We forward an alternative perspective: that a common set of biobehavioral processes may be responsible for causing subtle deviations in biological and behavioral plasticity. The effects of this common initial pathway may modify developmental processes impacting a range of atypical developmental outcomes. It follows that individual differences in the nature of these effects would be shaped by person factors (i.e., polygenic control of the immune response, central nervous system sensitivity to cytokines, critical periods of the development of the neuroendocrine-immune network), environmental factors (i.e., frequency, duration, or timing of exposure to immunologic stimuli), as well as social processes.

A theoretical model representing the possible direct and indirect pathways between dysregulation of the cytokine network and developmental psychopathology is presented in Figure 17.10. At least five levels of analysis are relevant to understanding individual differences in the uncommon effects of common immune stimuli: (1) features of the physical environment or socioeconomic factors that increase risk or exposure to immune stimuli (e.g., population density, hygiene, water and food quality, heath care access or quality); (2) psychological factors that limit individuals' understanding or perceptions of susceptibility, severity of consequences, and risk or threat of exposure to antigens; (3) physiological predispositions or states that affect the synthesis of immune-derived molecules or that influence the sensitivity of target organs and tissues; (4) the capacity

of the social environment to facilitate or disrupt recovery once a susceptible individual has been exposed; or (5) the competence of the individual at risk to elicit assistance and support from the social environment. Adopting this biosocial model leads to testable hypotheses at several levels of analysis.

It is our expectation that the findings of studies that integrate this perspective and these psychoneuroimmunologic concepts into developmental science may engender strong inferences focused on explaining the nature of causation rather than simply describing phenomena and their correlates. To adequately investigate this model, studies are needed that employ prospective longitudinal designs and focus on the link between the activity of cytokines and the onset, changes, and continuities of atypical behavioral and biological function. Studies to elaborate these uncommon developmental effects in the context of experiments of nature (Cicchetti, 2003), such as childhood immunizations, early childhood infections or inflammatory diseases, and in special populations at high risk of exposure to immune stimuli early in life would seem an appropriate next step.

REFERENCES

Achenbach, T. M. (1991a). *Manual for the Child Behavior Checklist/4–18 and 1991 profile*. Burlington: University of Vermont.

Achenbach, T. M. (1991b). *Manual for the Youth Self-Report and 1991 profile*. Burlington: University of Vermont, Department of Psychiatry.

Adamson-Macedo, E. N. (2000). Neonatal psychoneuroimmunology: Emergence, scope and perspectives. *Neuroendocrinology Letters, 21,* 175–186.

Ader, R. (1981). *Psychoneuroimmunology.* San Diego: Academic Press.

Ader, R. (1996). Historical perspectives on psychoneuroimmunology. In H. Friedman, T. W. Klein, & A. L. Friedman (Eds.), *Psychoneuroimmunology, stress, and infection* (pp. 1–24). New York: CRC Press.

Ader, R. (2000). On the development of psychoneuroimmunology. *European Journal of Pharmacology, 405* 167–176.

Ader, R., Cohen, N., & Felten, D. (1995). Psychoneuroimmunology: Interactions between the nervous system and the immune system. *Lancet, 345,* 99–103.

Ader, R., Felten, D. L., & Cohen, D. J. (1991). *Psychoneuroimmunology.* San Diego: Academic Press.

Altman, F. (1997). Where is the "neuro" in psychoneuroimmunology? A commentary on increasing research on the "neuro" component of psychoneuroimmunology. *Brain Behavior and Immunity, 11,* 1–8.

Anderson, J. A., Lentsch, A. B., Hadjiminas, D. J., Miller, F. N., Martin, A. W., Nakagawa, K., et al. (1996). The role of cytokines, adhesion molecules, and chemokines in interleukin-2-induced lymphocytic infiltration in C57BL/6 mice. *Journal of Clinical Investigation, 97,* 1952–1959.

Aubert, A. (1999). Sickness and behaviour in animals: A motivational perspective. *Neuroscience and Biobehavioral Reviews, 23,* 1029–1036.

Avitsur, R., & Yirmiya, R. (1999). The immunobiology of sexual behavior: Gender differences in the supression of sexual activity during illness. *Pharmacology Biochemistry and Behavior, 64,* 787–796.

Ban, E. M., Haour, F. G., & Lenstra, R. (1992). Brain interleukin-1 gene expression induced by peripheral lipopolysaccharide administration. *Cytokine, 4,* 48–54.

Benveniste, E. N. (1992a). Cytokines: Influence on glial cell gene expression and function. In J. E. Blalock (Ed.), *Neuroimmunoendocrinology* (2nd ed., pp. 106–153). New York: Karger.

Benveniste, E. N. (1992b). Inflammatory cytokines within the central nervous system: Sources, function and mechanism of action. *Cell Physiology, 32,* 1–16.

Berk, M., Wadee, A. A., Kuschke, R. H., & O'Neill-Kerr, A. (1997). Acute phase proteins in major depression. *Journal of Psychosomatic Research, 43,* 529–534.

Berkenbosch, F., de Goeij, D. E., Del Rey, A. D., & Besedovsky, H. O. (1989). Neuroendocrine, sympathetic and metabolic responses induced by interleukin-1. *Neuroendocrinology, 50,* 570–576.

Berkenbosch, F., De Rijk, R., Del Rey, A., & Besedovsky, H. (1990). Neuroendocrinology of interleukin-1. *Advances in Experimental Medicine and Biology, 274,* 303–314.

Berkenbosch, F., Van Dam, A.-M., De Rijk, R., & Schotanus, K. (1992). Role of the immune hormone interleukin-1 in brain adaptive responses to infection. In R. Kvetnansky, R. McCarty, & J. Axelrod (Eds.), *Stress: Neuroendocrine and molecular approaches* (pp. 623–640). New York: Gordon and Breach Science.

Besedovsky, H. O., & Del Rey, A. (1989). Mechanism of virus-induced stimulation of the hypothalamus-pituitary-adrenal axis. *Journal of Steroid Biochemistry, 34,* 235–239.

Besedovsky, H. O., Del Rey, A., Sorkin, E., Da Prada, M., Burri, R., & Honegger, C. (1983). The immune response evokes changes in brain noradrenergic neurons. *Science, 221,* 564–566.

Birmaher, B., Rabin, B. S., Garcia, M. R., Jain, U., Whiteside, T. L., Williamson, D. E., et al. (1994). Cellular immunity in depressed, conduct disorder, and normal adolescents: Role of adverse life events. *Journal of the American Academy of Child and Adolescent Psychiatry, 33,* 671–678.

Black, P. H. (1995). Psychoneuroimmunology: Brain and immunity. *Scientific American Science and Medicine, 1,* 16–25.

Blalock, J. E. (1994). The immune system: Our sixth sense. *Immunologist, 2,* 8–15.

Blalock, J. E. (1997). The syntax of immune-neuroendocrine communication. *Immunology Today, 15,* 504–511.

Blumberg, D. A., Lewis, K., Mink, C. M., Christenson, P. D., Chatfield, P., & Cherry, J. D. (1993). Severe reactions associated with diphtheria-tetanus-pertussis vaccine: Detailed study of children with seizures, hypotonic-hyporesponsive episodes, high fevers, and persistent crying. *Pediatrics, 91,* 1158–1165.

Bluthe, R. M., Dantzer, R., & Kelley, K. W. (1992). Effects of interleukin-1 receptor antagonist on the behavioral effects of lipopolysaccharide in rat. *Brain Research, 573,* 318–320.

Bonneau, R. H., Sheridan, J. F., Feng, N., & Glaser, R. (1993). Stress-induced modulation of the primary cellular immune response to herpes simplex virus infection is mediated by both adrenal-dependent and independent mechanisms. *Journal of Neuroimmunology, 42,* 167–176.

Borg, J. M. (1958). Neurological complications of pertussis immunization. *British Medical Journal, 2,* 24.

Boyce, W. T., Chesney, M., Alkon, A., Tschann, J. M., Adams, S., Chesterman, B., et al. (1995). Psychobiologic reactivity to stress and childhood respiratory illness: Results of two prospective studies. *Psychosomatic Medicine, 57,* 411–426.

Brambilla, F., Bellodi, L., Perna, G., Battaglia, M., Sciuto, G., Diaferia, G., et al. (1992). Psychoimmunoendocrine aspects of panic disorder. *Neuropsychobiology, 26,* 12–22.

Brambilla, F., Bellodi, L., Perna, G., Bertani, A., Panerai, A., & Sacerdote, P. (1994). Plasma interleukin-1 beta concentrations in panic disorder. *Psychiatry Research, 54,* 135–142.

Brambilla, F., Monteleone, P., & Maj, M. (2004). Interleukin-1 beta and tumor necrosis factor-alpha in children with major depressive disorder or dysthymia. *Journal of Affective Disorders, 78,* 273–277.

Cairns, B. D., Hood, K., & Midlam, J. (1985). On fighting mice: Is there a sensitive period for isolation effects? *Animal Behavior, 33,* 166–180.

Cairns, R. B., Gariepy, J. L., & Hood, K. E. (1990). Development, microevolution, and social behavior. *Psychological Review, 97,* 49–65.

Cairns, R. B., MaCombie, D. J., & Hood, K. E. (1983). A developmental-genetic analysis of aggressive behavior in mice. *Journal of Comparative Psychology, 97,* 69–89.

Capuron, L., Bluthe, R. M., & Dantzer, R. (2001). Cytokines in clinical psychiatry. *American Journal of Psychiatry, 158,* 1163–1164.

Capuron, L., Neurauter, G., Musselman, D. L., Lawson, D. H., Nemeroff, C. B., Fuchs, D., et al. (2003). Interferon-alpha-induced changes in tryptophan metabolism: Relationship to depression and paroxetine treatment. *Biological Psychiatry, 54,* 906–914.

Capuron, L., Ravaud, A., & Dantzer, R. (2000). Early depressive symptoms in cancer patients receiving interleukin 2 and/or interferon alpha-2b therapy. *Journal of Clinical Oncology, 18,* 2143–2151.

Capuron, L., Ravaud, A., & Dantzer, R. (2001). Timing and specificity of the cognitive changes induced by interleukin-2 and interferon-alpha treatments in cancer patients. *Psychosomatic Medicine, 63,* 376–386.

Capuron, L., Ravaud, A., Gualde, N., Bosmans, E., Dantzer, R., Maes, M., et al. (2001). Association between immune activation and early depressive symptoms in cancer patients treated with interleukin-2-based therapy. *Psychoneuroendocrinology, 26,* 797–808.

Carr, D. J., Radulescu, R. T., DeCosta, B. R., Rice, K. C., & Blalock, J. E. (1992). Opioid modulation of immunoglobulin production by lymphocytes isolated from Peyer's patches and spleen. *Annals of the New York Academy of Science, 650,* 125–127.

Chard, T. (1990). *An introduction to radioimmunoassay and related techniques, 4th ed.* Amsterdam, The Netherlands: Elsevier.

Chensue, S. W., Shmyre-Forsch, C., Otterness, I. G., & Kunkel, S. L. (1989). The beta form is the dominant interleukin-1 released by peritoneal macrophages. *Biochemical Biophysical Research Communications, 160,* 404–408.

Chuluyan, H. E., Saphier, D., Rohn, W. M., & Dunn, A. J. (1992). Noradrenergic innervation of the hypothalamus participates in adrenocortical responses to interleukin-1. *Neuroendocrinology, 56,* 106–111.

Cicchetti, D. (2003). Experiments of nature: Contributions to developmental theory. *Development and Psychopathology, 15,* 833–835.

Cicchetti, D., & Dawson, G. (2002). Multiple levels of analysis. *Development and Psychopathology, 14,* 417–420.

Cicchetti, D., & Lynch, M. (1995). Failures in the expectable environment and their impact on individual development: The case of child maltreatment. In D. Cicchetti & D. J. Cohen (Eds.), *Developmental psychopathology: Vol. 2. Risk, disorder and adaptation* (pp. 32–71). New York: Wiley.

Cicchetti, D., & Richters, J. E. (1997). Examining the conceptual and scientific underpinnings of research in developmental psychopathology. *Developmental Psychopathology, 9,* 182–192.

Clough, N. C., & Roth, J. A. (1998). *Understanding immunology.* St. Louis: Mosby-Year Book.

Cody, C. L., Baraff, L. J., Cherry, J. D., Marcy, S. M., & Manclark, C. R. (1981). Nature and rates of adverse reactions associated with DTP and DT immunizations in infants and children. *Pediatrics, 68,* 650–659.

Coe, C. K. (1999). Psychosocial factors and psychoneuroimmunology within a lifespan perspective. In D. P. Keating & C. Hertzman (Eds.),

Developmental health and the wealth of nations (pp. 201–219). New York: Guilford Press.

Coe, C. L. (1996). Developmental psychoneuroimmunology revisited. *Brain Behavior and Immunity, 10,* 185–187.

Cohen, S., & Herbert, T. B. (1996). Health psychology: Psychological factors and physical disease from the perspective of human psychoneuroimmunology. *Annual Review of Psychology, 47,* 113–142.

Cohen, S., Line, S., Manuck, S. B., Rabin, B. S., Heise, E., & Kaplan, J. R. (1997). Chronic stress, social status, and susceptibility to upper respiratory infections in nonhuman primates. *Psychosomatic Medicine, 59,* 213–221.

Cohen, S., Tyrell, D., & Smith, A. (1991). Psychological stress and susceptibility to the common cold. *New England Journal of Medicine, 325,* 606.

Connor, T. J., & Leonard, B. E. (1998). Depression, stress and immunological activation: The role of cytokines in depressive disorders. *Life Sciences, 62,* 583–606.

Cotman, C. W., Brinton, R. E., Glaburda, A., McEwen, B. S., & Schneider, D. M. (1987). *The neuro-immune-endocrine connection.* New York: Raven Press.

Crnic, L. S. (1991). Behavioral consequences of viral infection. In R. Ader, D. L. Felten, & N. Cohen (Eds.), *Psychoneuroimmunology* (2nd ed., pp. 749–770). New York: Academic Press.

Crnic, L. S., & Pizer, L. I. (1988). Behavioral effects of neonatal herpes simplex type 1 infection of mice. *Neurotoxicology and Teratology, 10,* 381–386.

Cunningham, E. T., & De Souza, E. B. (1993). Interleukin-1 receptors in the brain and endocrine tissues. *Immunology Today, 14,* 171–176.

Dantzer, R. (2001). Cytokine-induced sickness behavior: Where do we stand? *Brain Behavior and Immunity, 15,* 7–24.

Dantzer, R., Bluth, R.-M., & Goodall, G. (1993). Behavioral effects of cytokines: An insight into mechanisms of sickness behavior. *Methods in Neuroscience, 16,* 130–150.

Dantzer, R., Bluthe, R. M., Gheusi, G., Cremona, S., Laye, S., Parnet, P., et al. (1998). Molecular basis of sickness behavior. *Annals of the New York Academy of Science, 856,* 132–138.

Dantzer, R., Bluthe, R. M., Laye, S., Bret-Dibat, J. L., Parnet, P., & Kelley, K. W. (1998). Cytokines and sickness behavior. *Annals of the New York Academy of Science, 840,* 586–590.

Dantzer, R., Konsman, J. P., Bluthe, R. M., & Kelley, K. W. (2000). Neural and humoral pathways of communication from the immune system to the brain: Parallel or convergent? *Autonomic Neuroscience, 85,* 60–65.

Dantzer, R., Wollman, E., Vitkovic, L., & Yirmiya, R. (1999). Cytokines and depression: Fortuitous or causative association? *Molecular Psychiatry, 4,* 328–332.

Dinarello, C. A. (1984a). Interleukin-1. *Review of Infectious Disease, 6*(1), 51–95.

Dinarello, C. A. (1984b). Interleukin 1 as mediator of the acute-phase response. *Survey of Immunology Research, 3,* 29–33.

Dinarello, C. A. (1988). Biology of interleukin 1. *Journal of the Federation for the Advancement of Science and Experimental Biology, 2,* 108–115.

Dinarello, C. A. (1992). The biology of interleukin-1. *Chemical Immunology, 51,* 1–32.

Dunn, A. J. (1988). Systemic interleukin-1 administration stimulates hypothalamic norepinephrine metabolism paralleling the increased plasma corticosterone. *Life Science, 43,* 429–435.

Dunn, A. J. (1990). Interleukin-1 as a stimulator of hormone secretion. *Progress in Neuroimmunology, 3,* 26–34.

Dunn, A. J. (1992a). Endotoxin-induced activation of cerebral catecholamine and serotonin metabolism: Comparison with interleukin-1. *Journal of Pharmacology and Experimental Therapy, 261,* 964–969.

Dunn, A. J. (1992b). The role of interleukin-1 and tumor necrosis factor alpha in the neurochemical and neuroendocrine responses to endotoxin. *Brain Research Bulletin, 29,* 807–812.

Dunn, A. J. (1996). Psychoneuroimmunology, stress and infection. In H. Friedman, T. W. Klein, & A. Friedman (Eds.), *Psychoneuroimmunology, stress and infection* (pp. 25–46). New York: CRC Press.

Dunn, A. J., Antoon, M., & Chapman, Y. (1991). Reduction of exploratory behavior by intraperitoneal injection of interleukin-1 involves brain corticotropin-releasing factor. *Brain Research Bulletin, 26,* 539–542.

Dunn, A. J., & Wang, J. (1995). Cytokine effects on CNS biogenic amines. *Neuroimmunomodulation, 2,* 319–328.

Dunn, A. J., Wang, J., & Ando, T. (1999). Effects of cytokines on cerebral neurotransmission: Comparison with the effects of stress. *Advances in Experimental Medicine and Biology, 461,* 117–127.

Felten, D. L., Ackerman, K. D., Wiegand, S. J., & Felten, S. Y. (1987). Noradrenergic sympathetic innervation of the spleen: I. Nerve fibers associate with lymphocytes and macrophages in specific compartments of the splenic white pulp. *Journal of Neuroscience Research, 18,* 28–36.

Felten, D. L., Livnat, S., Felten, S. Y., Carlson, S. L., Bellinger, D. L., & Yeh, P. (1984). Sympathetic innervation of lymph nodes in mice. *Brain Research Bulletin, 13,* 693–699.

Felten, D. L., Overhage, J. M., Felten, S. Y., & Schmedtje, J. F. (1981). Noradrenergic sympathetic innervation of lymphoid tissue in the rabbit appendix: Further evidence for a link between the nervous and immune systems. *Brain Research Bulletin, 7,* 595–612.

Felten, S. Y., Felten, D. L., Bellinger, D. L., & Olschowka, J. A. (1992). Noradrenergic and peptidergic innervation of lymphoid organs. *Chemical Immunology, 52,* 25–48.

Gahtan, E., & Overmier, J. B. (2001). Performance more than working memory disrupted by acute systemic inflammation in rats in appetitive tasks. *Physiology and Behavior, 73,* 201–210.

Gariepy, J.-L., Nehrenberg, D., & Mills-Koonce, R. (2001). Maternal care and separation stress in high- and low-aggressive mice [Abstract]. *Developmental Psychobiology, 38,* 203.

Garvey, M., Giedd, J., & Swedo, S. E. (1998). PANDAS: The search for environmental triggers of pediatric neuropsychiatric disorders: Lessons from rheumatic fever. *Journal of Child Neurology, 13,* 413–423.

Gatanaga, T., Hwang, C. D., Kohr, W., Cappuccini, F., Lucci, J. A., III, Jeffes, E. W., et al. (1990). Purification and characterization of an inhibitor (soluble tumor necrosis factor receptor) for tumor necrosis factor and lymphotoxin obtained from the serum ultrafiltrates of human cancer patients. *Proceedings of the National Academy of Sciences, USA, 87,* 8781–8784.

Gatanaga, T., Lentz, R., Masunaka, I., Tomich, J., Jeffes, E. W., III, Baird, M., et al. (1990). Identification of TNF-LT blocking factor(s) in the serum and ultrafiltrates of human cancer patients. *Lymphokine Research, 9,* 225–229.

Goldsby, R. A. (2003). *Immunology* (5th ed.). New York: Freeman.

Gottlieb, G. (1992). *Individual development and evolution: The genesis of novel behavior.* New York: Oxford University Press.

Granger, D. A., Booth, A., & Johnson, D. (2000). Human aggression and enumerative measures of immunity. *Psychosomatic Medicine, 62,* 583–590.

Granger, D. A., Dreschel, N. A., & Shirtcliff, E. A. (2003). Developmental psychoneuroimmunology: The role of cytokine network activation in the epigenesis of developmental psychopathology. In D. Cicchetti & E. Walker (Eds.), *Neurodevelopmental mechanisms in psychopathology* (pp. 293–323). New York: Cambridge University Press.

Granger, D. A., Hood, K. E., & Banta, M. B. (2000). *Individual differences in endotoxin effects on social behavior and interleukin-1β.* Unpublished manuscript, University Park, Pennsylvania State University.

Granger, D. A., Hood, K. E., Dreschel, N. A., Sergeant, E., & Likos, A. (2001). Developmental effects of early immune stress on aggressive, socially reactive, and inhibited behaviors. *Development and Psychopathology, 13,* 599–610.

Granger, D. A., Hood, K. E., Ikeda, S. C., Reed, C. L., & Block, M. L. (1996). Neonatal endotoxin exposure alters the development of social behavior and the hypothalamic-pituitary-adrenal axis in selectively bred mice. *Brain Behavior and Immunity, 10,* 249–259.

Granger, D. A., Hood, K. E., Ikeda, S. C., Reed, C. L., Jones, B. C., & Block, M. L. (1997). Effects of peripheral immune activation on social behavior and adrenocortical activity in aggressive mice. *Aggressive Behavior, 23,* 93–105.

Granger, D. A., Ikeda, S., & Block, M. B. (1997, April). *Developmental psychoneuroimmunology: Integrating effects of environmental, biological, and behavioral processes on child development.* Paper presented at the annual meeting of the Society for Research in Child Development, Washington, DC.

Granger, D. A., Schwartz, E. B., Booth, A., Curran, M., & Zakaria, D. (1999). Assessing dehydroepiandrosterone in saliva: A simple radioimmunoassay for use in studies of children, adolescents, and adults. *Psychoneuroendocrinology, 24,* 567–579.

Granger, D. A., Shirtcliff, E. A., Booth, A., Kivlighan, K. T., & Schwartz, E. B. (2004). The "trouble" with salivary testosterone. *Psychoneuroendocrinology, 29,* 1229–1240.

Granger, G. A., & Williams, T. W. (1968). Lymphocyte cytotoxicity in vitro: Activation and release of a cytotoxic factor. *Nature, 218,* 1253–1254.

Granger, S. W., & Ware, C. F. (2003). Lymphotoxins. In A. W. Thomson & M. T. Lotze (Eds.), *The cytokine handbook* (4th ed., pp. 825–836). San Diego: Academic Press.

Gutterman, J. U., Fein, S., Quesacia, J., Hornings, S. J., Levine, J. F., Alexanian, R., et al. (1982). Recombinant leukocyte A interferon: Pharmacokinetics, single dose tolerance, and biological effects in cancer patients. *Annals of Internal Medicine, 96,* 549–556.

Haack, M., Hinze-Selch, D., Fenzel, T., Kraus, T., Kuhn, M., Schuld, A., et al. (1999). Plasma levels of cytokines and soluble cytokine receptors in psychiatric patients upon hospital admission: Effects of confounding factors and diagnosis. *Journal of Psychiatry Research, 33,* 407–418.

Harbuz, M. S., & Lightman, S. L. (1992). Stress and the hypothalamic-pituitary-adrenal axis: Acute, chronic and immunological activation. *Journal of Endocrinology, 134,* 327–339.

Hart, B. L. (1988). Biological basis of the behavior of sick animals. *Neuroscience and Biobehavioral Review, 12,* 123–137.

Herbert, T. B., & Cohen, S. (1993a). Depression and immunity: A meta-analytic review. *Psychological Bulletin, 113,* 472–486.

Herbert, T. B., & Cohen, S. (1993b). Stress and immunity in humans: A meta-analytic review. *Psychosomatic Medicine, 55,* 364–379.

Hessinger, D. A., Daynes, R. A., & Granger, G. A. (1973). Binding of human lymphotoxin to target-cell membranes and its relation to cell-mediated cytodestruction. *Proceedings of the National Academy of Sciences, USA, 70,* 3082–3086.

Heyes, M. P. (1992). Quinolinic acid in culture media used for in vitro neurotoxicology studies. *Neuroscience Letters, 145,* 234–235.

Heyes, M. P., Brew, B. J., Saito, K., Quearry, B. J., Price, R. W., Lee, K., et al. (1992). Inter-relationships between quinolinic acid, neuroactive kynurenines, neopterin and beta 2-microglobulin in cerebrospinal fluid and serum of HIV-1-infected patients. *Journal of Neuroimmunology, 40,* 71–80.

Heyes, M. P., Quearry, B. J., & Markey, S. P. (1989). Systemic endotoxin increases L-tryptophan, 5-hydroxyindoleacetic acid, 3-hydroxykynurenine and quinolinic acid content of mouse cerebral cortex. *Brain Research, 491,* 173–179.

Heyes, M. P., Saito, K., Crowley, J. S., Davis, L. E., Demitrack, M. A., Der, M., et al. (1992). Quinolinic acid and kynurenine pathway metabolism in inflammatory and non-inflammatory neurological disease. *Brain, 115,* 1249–1273.

Hofer, M. A. (1987). Early social relationships: A psychobiologist's view. *Child Development, 58,* 633–647.

Hofer, M. A. (1994). Early relationships as regulators of infant physiology and behavior. *Acta Paediatrica, 397,* 9–18.

Hood, K. E., & Cairns, R. B. (1988). A developmental-genetic analysis of aggressive behavior in mice: II. Cross-sex inheritance. *Behavioral Genetics, 18,* 605–619.

Hood, K. E., & Cairns, R. B. (1989). A developmental-genetic analysis of aggressive behavior in mice: IV. Genotype-environment interaction. *Aggressive Behavior, 15,* 361–380.

Hood, K. E., Dreschel, N., & Granger, D. A. (2003). Maternal behavior changes after immune challenge of neonates with developmental effects on adult social behavior. *Developmental Psychobiology, 42,* 17–34.

Howson, C. P., Howe, C. J., & Fineberg, H. V. (1991). *Adverse effects of pertussis and rubella vaccines: A report of the committee to review the adverse consequences of pertussis and rubella vaccines.* Unpublished manuscript.

Janeway, C. A., Jr. (2005). *Immunobiology: The immune system in health and disease.* New York: Garland Science.

Kelly, R. H., Ganguli, R., & Rabin, B. S. (1987). Antibody to discrete areas of the brain in normal individuals and patients with Schizophrenia. *Biological Psychiatry, 22,* 1488–1491.

Kemeny, M. E., & Gruenewald, T. L. (1999). Psychoneuroimmunology update. *Seminars in Gastrointestinal Disease, 10,* 20–29.

Kemeny, M. E., & Laudenslager, M. L. (1999). Introduction beyond stress: The role of individual difference factors in psychoneuroimmunology. *Brain Behavior and Immunity, 13,* 73–75.

Kent, S., Rodriguez, F., Kelley, K. W., & Dantzer, R. (1994). Reduction in food and water intake induced by microinjection of interleukin-1 beta in the ventromedial hypothalamus of the rat. *Physiology and Behavior, 56,* 1031–1036.

Kiecolt-Glaser, J. K., & Glaser, R. (1988). Methodological issues in behavioral immunology research with humans. *Brain Behavior and Immunity, 2,* 67–78.

Kiecolt-Glaser, J. K., & Glaser, R. (1989). Psychoneuroimmunology: Past, present, and future. *Health Psychology, 8,* 677–682.

Kiecolt-Glaser, J. K., & Glaser, R. (1995). Psychoneuroimmunology and health consequences: Data and shared mechanisms. *Psychosomatic Medicine, 57,* 269–274.

Kiecolt-Glaser, J. K., Glaser, R., Gravenstein, S., Malarkey, W. B., & Sheridan, J. (1996). Chronic stress alters the immune response to influenza virus vaccine in older adults. *Proceedings of the National Academy of Science, USA, 93,* 3043–3047.

Kirschbaum, C., Read, G. F., & Hellhammer, D. H. (1992). *Assessment of hormones and drugs in saliva in biobehavioral research.* Kirkland, WA; Hogrefe & Huber Publishers.

Kivlighan, K. T., Granger, D. A., Schwartz, E. B., Nelson, V., & Curran, M. (2004). Quantifying blood leakage into the oral mucosa and its effects on the measurement of cortisol, dehydroepiandrosterone, and testosterone in saliva. *Hormones and Behavior, 46,* 3–46.

Kluger, M. J. (1979). *Fever: Its biology, evolution, and function.* Princeton, NJ: Princeton University Press.

Kopeloff, N., Kopeloff, L. M., & Raney, M. E. (1933). The nervous system and antibody production. *Psychiatry Quarterly, 7,* 84.

Kovacs, M. (1983). *The Children's Depression Inventory: A self-rated depression scale for school-aged youngsters.* Unpublished manuscript, University of Pittsburgh, School of Medicine.

Krasnegor, N. A., & Bridges, R. S. (1990). *Mammalian parenting: Biochemical, neurological, and behavioral determinants.* New York: Oxford University Press.

Kreuger, J. M., Walter, J., Dinarello, C. A., Wolff, S. M., & Chedid, L. (1984). Sleep promoting effects of endogenous pyrogen (IL-1). *American Journal of Physiology, 246,* 9994–9999.

Kronfol, Z. (1999). Depression and immunity: The role of cytokines. In N. P. Plotnikoff, R. E. Faith, A. J. Murgo, & R. A. Good (Eds.), *Cytokines: Stress and immunity* (pp. 51–60). New York: CRC Press.

Kronfol, Z., & Remick, D. G. (2000). Cytokines and the brain: Implications for clinical psychiatry. *American Journal of Psychiatry, 157,* 683–694.

Laye, S., Parnet, P., Goujon, E., & Dantzer, R. (1994). Peripheral administration of lipopolysaccharide induces the expression of cytokine transcripts in the brain and pituitary of mice. *Brain Research and Molecular Brain Research, 27,* 157–162.

Leonard, H. L., Swedo, S. E., Garvey, M., Beer, D., Perlmutter, S., Lougee, L., et al. (1999). Postinfectious and other forms of obsessive-compulsive disorder. *Child and Adolescent Psychiatric Clinics of North America, 8,* 497–511.

Levine, S. (1994). The ontogeny of the hypothalamic-pituitary-adrenal axis: The influence of maternal factors. *Annuals of the New York Academy of Sciences, 746,* 275–288.

Line, S., Kaplan, J. R., Heise, E., Hilliard, J. K., Cohen, S., & Rabin, B. S. (1996). Effects of social reorganization on cellular immunity in male cynomolgus monkeys. *American Journal of Primatology, 39,* 235–249.

Liu, D., Dioria, J., Tannenbaum, B., Caldji, C., Francis, D., Freedom, A., et al. (1997). Maternal care, hippocampal, glucocorticoid receptors, and hypothalamic-pituitary-adrenal responses to stress. *Science, 277,* 1659–1662.

Long, S. A., DeForest, A., Smith, D. G., Lazaro, C., & Wassilak, S. G. F. (1990). Longitudinal study of adverse reactions following diphtheria-tetanus-pertussis vaccine in infancy. *Pediatrics, 85,* 294–302.

Maes, M., Bosmans, E., Meltzer, H. Y., Scharpe, S., & Suy, E. (1993). Interluekin-1 beta: A putative mediator of HPA axis hyperactivity in major depression. *American Journal of Psychiatry, 150,* 1189–1193.

Maes, M., Meltzer, H. Y., & Bosmans, E. (1994a). Immune-inflammatory markers in Schizophrenia: Comparison to normal controls and effects of clozapine. *Acta Psychiatrica Scandinavica, 89,* 346–351.

Maes, M., Meltzer, H. Y., & Bosmans, E. (1994b). Psychoimmune investigation in obsessive-compulsive disorder: Assays of plasma transferrin, IL-2 and IL-6 receptor, and IL-1b and IL-6 concentrations. *Neuropsychobiology, 30,* 57.

Maes, M., Meltzer, H. Y., Bosmans, E., Bergmans, R., Vandoolaeghe, E., Ranjan, R., et al. (1995). Increased plasma concentrations of interleukin-6, soluble interleukin-6, soluble interleukin-2 and transferrin receptor in major depression. *Journal of Affective Disorders, 34,* 301–309.

Maier, S. F., & Watkins, L. R. (1998a). Bidirectional communication between the brain and the immune system: Implications for behavior. *Animal Behaviour, 57,* 741–751.

Maier, S. F., & Watkins, L. R. (1998b). Cytokines for psychologists: Implications of bidirectional immune-to-brain communication for understanding behavior, mood, and cognition. *Psychological Review, 105,* 83–107.

Maier, S. F., Watkins, L. R., & Fleshner, M. (1994). Psychoneuroimmunology: The interface between behavior, brain, and immunity. *American Psychologist, 49,* 1004–1017.

Malamud, D., & Tabak, L. (Eds.). (1993). Saliva as a diagnostic fluid. *Annals of the New York Academy of Sciences, 694.*

Mannering, G. J., & Deloria, L. B. (1986). The pharmacology and toxicity of the interferons: An overview. *Annual Review of Pharmacology and Toxicology, 26,* 455–515.

Meaney, M. J., Aitken, D. H., Bhatnagar, S., Van Berkel, C., & Sapolsky, R. M. (1988). Postnatal handling attenuates neuroendocrine, anatomical, and cognitive impairments related to the aged hippocampus. *Science, 238,* 766–768.

Mittleman, B. B., Castellanos, F. S., Jacobsen, L. K., Rapoport, J. L., Swedo, S. E., & Shearer, G. M. (1997). Cerebrospinal fluid cytokines in pediatric neuropsychiatric disease. *Journal of Immunology, 159,* 2994–2999.

Moldawer, L. L., Andersson, C., Gelin, J., & Lundholm, K. G. (1988). Regulation of food intake and hepatic protein synthesis by recombinant-derived cytokines. *American Journal of Physiology, 254,* 450–456.

Morag, M., Yirmiya, R., Lerer, B., & Morag, A. (1998). Influence of socioeconomic status on behavioral, emotional and cognitive effects of rubella vaccination: A prospective, double blind study. *Psychoneuroendocrinology, 23,* 337–351.

Musselman, D. L., Miller, A. H., Porter, M. R., Manatunga, A., Gao, F., Penna, S., et al. (2001). Higher than normal plasma interleukin-6 concentrations in cancer patients with depression: Preliminary findings. *American Journal of Psychiatry, 158,* 1252–1257.

Nishanian, P., Aziz, N., Chung, J., Detels, R., & Fahey, J. L. (1998). Oral fluids as an alternative to serum for measurement of immune activation. *Clinical and Diagnostic Laboratory Immunology, 5,* 507–512.

O'Grady, M. P., & Hall, N. R. S. (1990). Postnatal exposure to Newcastle's disease virus alters endocrine development. *Teratology, 41,* 623–624.

O'Grady, M. P., & Hall, N. R. S. (1991). Long-term effects of neuroendocrine-immune interactions during early development. In R. Ader, D. L. Felten, & N. Cohen (Eds.), *Psychoneuroimmunology* (2nd ed., pp. 561–572). New York: Academic Press.

O'Grady, M. P., Hall, N. R. S., & Goldstein, A. L. (1987). Developmental consequences of prenatal exposure to thymosin: Long term changes in immune and endocrine parameters. *Society for Neuroscience, 13,* 1380.

Opp, M. R., Orbal, F., & Kreuger, J. M. (1991). Interleukin-1 alters rat sleep: Temporal and dose-related effects. *American Journal of Physiology, 260,* 52–58.

Owen, B. M., Eccleston, D., Ferrier, I. N., & Young, A. H. (2001). Raised levels of plasma interleukin-1beta in major and postviral depression. *Acta Psychiatrica Scandinavica, 103,* 226–228.

Pettito, J. M., Gariepy, J., Gendreau, P. L., Rodriguiz, R., Lewis, M., & Lysle, D. T. (1999). Differences in NK cell function in mice bred for high and low aggression: Genetic linkage between complex behavior and immunological traits? *Brain, Behavior, and Immunity, 13,* 175–186.

Pettito, J. M., Lysle, D. T., Gariepy, J., Clubb, P. H., Cairns, B. D., & Lewis, M. (1994). Genetic differences in social behavior and cellular immune responsiveness: Effects of social experience. *Brain, Behavior, and Immunity, 8,* 111–112.

Pettito, J. M., Lysle, D. T., Gariepy, J., & Lewis, M. (1992). The expression of genetic differences in social behavior in ICR mice correlates with differences in cellular immune responsiveness. *Clinical Neuropharmacology, 15,* 658–659.

Pettito, J. M., Lysle, D. T., Gariepy, J., & Lewis, M. (1994). Association of genetic differences in social behavior and cellular immune responsiveness. *Brain, Behavior, and Immunity, 8,* 111–112.

Plotsky, P. M., & Meaney, M. J. (1993). Early postnatal experience alters hypothalamic corticotrophin-releasing factor (CRF) mRNA, median eminence CRF content, and stress-induced release in adult rats. *Molecular Brain Research, 18,* 195–200.

Quan, N., Sundar, S. K., & Weiss, J. M. (1994). Induction of interleukin-1 in various brain regions after peripheral and central injections of lipopolysaccharide. *Journal of Neuroimmunology, 49,* 125–134.

Rapaport, M. H., & Stein, M. B. (1994). Serum cytokine and soluble interleukin-2 receptors in patients with panic disorder. *Anxiety, 1,* 22–25.

Reichenberg, A., Yirmiya, R., Schuld, A., Kraus, T., Haack, M., Morag, A., et al. (2001). Cytokine-associated emotional and cognitive disturbances in humans. *Archives of General Psychiatry, 58,* 445–452.

Renault, P. F., Hoofnagle, J. H., Parky, Y., Mullen, K. D., Peters, M., Jones, D., et al. (1987). Psychiatric complications of long-term interferon-alpha therapy. *Archives of Internal Medicine, 147,* 1577–1580.

Rodriguiz, R. M., Gariepy, J.-L., & Jones, B. C. (1998). Genetic contraints and the developmental plasticity of behavioral and neuroendocrine systems and their coupling in a stressful situation. In D. M. Hann, L. C. Huffman, I. I. Lederhendler, & D. Meinecke (Eds.), *Advancing research on developmental plasticity: Integrating the behavioral science and neuroscience of mental health* (pp. 417–418). Bethesda, MD: National Institutes of Mental Health.

Saito, K., Markey, S. P., & Heyes, M. P. (1992). Effects of immune activation on quinolinic acid and neuroactive kynurenines in the mouse. *Neuroscience, 51,* 25–39.

Sapolsky, R., Rivier, C., Yamamoto, G., Plotsky, P., & Vale, W. (1987). Interleukin-1 stimulates the secretion of hypothalamic corticotropin-releasing factor. *Science, 238,* 522–524.

Schwartz, E., Granger, D. A., Susman, E. J., Gunnar, M., & Laird, B. (1998). Assessing salivary cortisol in studies of child development. *Child Development, 69,* 1503–1513.

Segall, M. A., & Crnic, L. S. (1990). An animal model for the behavioral effects of interferon. *Behavioral Neuroscience, 104,* 612–618.

Shanks, N., Larocque, S., & Meaney, M. J. (1995). Neonatal endotoxin exposure alters the development of the hypothalamic-pituitary-adrenal axis: Early illness and later responsivity to stress. *Journal of Neuroscience, 15,* 376–384.

Shirtcliff, E. A., Granger, D. A., Schwartz, E., & Curran, M. J. (2001). Use of salivary biomarkers in biobehavioral research: Cotton based sample collection methods can interfere with salivary immunoassay results. *Psychoneuroendocrinology, 26,* 165–173.

Smith, A. P., Tyrell, D. A., Al-Nakib, W., Coyle, K. B., Donovan, C. B., Higgins, P. G., et al. (1987). Effects of experimentally induced respiratory virus infection and illness on psychomotor performance. *Neuropsychobiology, 18,* 144–148.

Smith, A. P., Tyrell, D. A., Coyle, K., & Higgins, P. (1988). Effects of interferon alpha on performance in man: A preliminary report. *Psychopharmacology, 96,* 414–416.

Smith, E. (1992). Hormonal effects of cytokines. In J. E. Blalock (Ed.), *Neuroimmunoendocrinology* (pp. 154–169). New York: Krager.

Smith, R. W., Tyrell, D., Coyle, K., & Willman, J. S. (1987). Selective effects of minor illnesses on human performance. *British Journal of Psychology, 78,* 183–188.

Solomon, G. F. (1969). Emotions, stress, the central nervous system, and immunity. *Annals of the New York Academy of Science, 164,* 335–343.

Solomon, G. F., Amkraut, A. A., & Kasper, P. (1974). Immunity, emotions and stress: With special reference to the mechanisms of stress effects on the immune system. *Annals of Clinical Research, 6,* 313–322.

Solomon, G. F., & Moos, R. H. (1965). The relationship of personality to the presence of rheumatiod factor in asymptomatic relatives of patients with rheumatoid arthritis. *Psychosomatic Medicine, 27,* 350.

Sparado, F., & Dunn, A. J. (1990). Intracerebrovascular administration of interleukin-1 to mice alters investigation of stimulus in a novel environment. *Brain, Behavior, and Immunity, 4,* 308–322.

Spivak, B., Shohat, B., Mester, R., Avraham, S., Gil-Ad, I., Bleich, A., et al. (1997). Elevated levels of serum interleukin-1 beta in combat-related posttraumatic stress disorder. *Biological Psychiatry, 42,* 345–348.

Suarez, E. C., Krishnan, R. R., & Lewis, J. G. (2003). The relation of severity of depressive symptoms to monocyte-induced proinflammatory cytokines and chemokines in apparently healthy men. *Psychosomatic Medicine, 65,* 362–368.

Swedo, S. E., Leonard, H. L., Garvey, M., Mittleman, B. B., Allen, A. J., Perlmutter, S., et al. (1998). Pediatric autoimmune neuropsychiatric disorders associated with streptococcal infections: Clinical description of the first 50 cases. *American Journal of Psychiatry, 155,* 264–271.

Takao, T., Tracy, D. E., Mitchell, W. M., & De Souza, E. B. (1990). Interleukin-1 receptors in the mouse brain: Characterization and neuronal localization. *Endocrinology, 127,* 3070–3078.

Thomson, A., & Lotze, M. T. (2003). *The cytokine handbook* (4th ed.). San Diego: Academic Press.

Tilders, F. J. H., DeRuk, R. H., VanDam, A.-M., Vincent, V. A. M., Schotanus, K., & Persoons, J. H. A. (1994). Activation of the hypothalamus-pituitary-adrenal axis by bacterial endotoxins: Routes and intermediate signals. *Psychoneuroendocrinology, 19,* 209–232.

Vedhara, K., Fox, J. D., & Wang, E. C. (1999). The measurement of stress-related immune dysfunction in psychoneuroimmunology. *Neuroscience Biobehavioral Reviews, 23,* 699–715.

Vilcek, J. (1998). The cytokines: An overview. In A. W. Thomson (Ed.), *The cytokine handbook* (pp. 1–20). San Diego: Academic Press.

Wadhwa, M., & Thorpe, R. (1998). Assays for cytokines. In A. W. Thomson (Ed.), *The cytokine handbook* (pp. 856–884). San Diego: Academic Press.

Watson, J. B., Mednick, S. A., Huttunen, M., & Wang, X. (1999). Prenatal teratogens and the development of adult mental illness. *Development and Psychopathology, 11,* 457–466.

Weiss, J. M., Quan, N., & Sundar, S. K. (1994). Widespread activation and consequences of interleukin-1 in the brain. *Annals of the New York Academy of Sciences, 741,* 338–357.

Weizman, R., Laor, N., Wiener, Z., Wolmer, L., & Bessler, H. (1999). Cytokine production in panic disorder patients. *Clinical Neuropharmacology, 22,* 107–109.

Williams, J. M., Peterson, R. G., Shea, P. A., Schmedtje, J. F., Bauer, D. C., & Felten, D. L. (1981). Sympathetic innervation of murine thymus and spleen: Evidence for a functional link between the nervous and immune systems. *Brain Research Bulletin, 6,* 83–94.

Woloski, B. M. R. N. J., Smith, E., Meyer, W. J., Fuller, G. M., & Blalock, J. E. (1985). Corticotropin-releasing activity of monokines. *Science, 230,* 1035–1037.

CHAPTER 18

The Study of Developmental Psychopathology in Adolescence: Integrating Affective Neuroscience with the Study of Context

LAURENCE STEINBERG, RONALD DAHL, DANIEL KEATING, DAVID J. KUPFER, ANN S. MASTEN, and DANIEL S. PINE

The transitional, formative, and malleable nature of adolescence makes it arguably the most important period of development for the study of developmental psychopathology. As a transitional period, adolescence is marked by rapid and dramatic intraindividual change in the realms of biology, cognition, emotion, and interpersonal relationships and by equally impressive transformations in the major contexts in which children spend time: the family, the peer group, and school. These transformations alter individual strengths and vulnerabilities and present both opportunities and challenges that require adaptation on the part of the developing adolescent. For a significant proportion of adolescents, the interaction between these changes in intraindividual functioning and changes in context result in the emergence of some emotional and behavioral problems. Notably, many behavioral and affective problems, such as substance abuse and disordered eating, are seldom or rarely seen before adolescence, and others, such as Major depression and bipolar illness, show a dramatic increase in prevalence during this period. For many more adolescents, the period is one of experimentation with risky activity, behavior that, though not formally considered psychopathology, nonetheless increases morbidity and mortality considerably.

As a formative period, adolescence is important to the study of developmental psychopathology because after this

The development of the framework described in this chapter was supported by the John D. and Catherine T. MacArthur Foundation Research Network on Psychopathology and Development under the leadership of David Kupfer. The authors express their deep appreciation to the MacArthur Foundation and to all the members of this network for their contributions to our thinking about development and psychopathology in the transition to adolescence. The ideas expressed in this chapter are collaborative, with all authors contributing to writing the chapter. The first author coordinated the preparation of this chapter; all other authors are listed alphabetically.

maturational interval, some patterns of emotional and be-havioral difficulty may become more difficult to alter. For reasons not yet understood, there appears to be relatively more consolidation of psychopathology in adolescence than in earlier periods. Prospective longitudinal studies suggest that the majority of chronic and recurrent psychiatric problems that afflict adults have begun by the end of adoles-cence. Indeed, the initial manifestations of affective distur-bance, antisocial behavior, and substance abuse emerge much less frequently in adulthood than in previous develop-mental periods and are generally preceded by problems in these or other domains during adolescence. This applies both to problems with behavior, as in the disruptive behavior disorders, and to problems with emotion regulation, as in the mood and anxiety disorders (Moffitt & Caspi, 2001; Pine, Cohen, Gurley, Brook, & Ma, 1998). Adolescence is also critical in setting lifestyle trajectories with enormous long-term implications for adult health. These trajectories in-clude early patterns of behavior in the realms of exercise; nutrition; the use of tobacco, caffeine, alcohol, and other mood-altering substances; and sleep and other health habits. Adolescence is the period for establishing the foundation for advanced education, major life roles, relationships, and working toward long-term productive goals. Accordingly, adolescence is an *important period for the development of preventive interventions designed to head off the develop-ment of more serious psychopathology in adulthood.*

Finally, despite its formative nature, adolescence is a period of malleability, or developmental plasticity. Pat-terns of neural connection among and between systems of emotion, motivation, and cognitive processes related to the pursuit of long-term goals undergo a natural reorganization during adolescence. For example, the onset of puberty is associated with biologically based changes in motivational and emotional systems linked to reproductive behavior in ways that contribute to the development of sexual and ro-mantic interests. A second example is how the developing concept of *self* along with the cognitive abilities to imagine future versions of this self—and affective experiences of fears or excitement linked to tragic or heroic versions of the future self—emerge during adolescence. Early experi-ences in these domains not only influence youth in psycho-logical and emotional domains, but also have an impact through brain-behavior interactions on the patterns of con-nections among neural systems.

As reviewed in a subsequent section of this chapter, there is also increasing evidence that maturational brain processes are continuing throughout adolescence (Dahl & Spear, 2004; Spear, 2000). For example, even relatively simple structural measures, such as the ratio of white to gray matter in the brain, demonstrate large-scale changes into the late teenage years (Giedd et al., 1999; Sowell, Delis, Stiles, & Jernigan, 2001; Sowell, Trauner, Gamst, & Jernigan, 2002). The impact of this continued maturation on emotional, intellectual, and behavioral development has yet to be thoroughly studied, but the evidence for ongoing developmental processes and apparent plasticity of brain development in adolescence suggests that this period may present some unique opportunities for intervention (includ-ing cognitive-behavioral, psychopharmacological, and/or other psychotherapeutic treatments).

Furthermore, any discussion of developmental psycho-pathology in adolescence must also consider the broader historical context that suggests that adolescence in modern society may reflect a convergence of recent biological and social changes that together have greatly expanded this maturational interval. Most contemporary writers, includ-ing the present authors, define adolescence as the interval between the onset of puberty (ordinarily seen as the most important marker of the onset of the period) and the transi-tion into adult roles (ordinarily seen as the most important marker of the period's conclusion). Both historical data and anthropological studies indicate that the mean age of sexual maturation in premodern societies was around 16 or 17 years—very close to the age at which young people began assuming the adult responsibilities of work and fam-ily formation. Thus, throughout most of human history, adolescence—the interval between the onset of sexual ma-turity and the assumption of adult responsibilities—was often only a few years in length.

More recently, however, the physical manifestations of puberty have been occurring at earlier ages, particularly among girls. At the same time, and especially in the most recent decades, the end of adolescence (taking on full adult roles and responsibilities) has been occurring at a relatively later time, with the prolongation of formal schooling and the extension of the adolescent's economic dependency on his or her family of origin. In the United States, for example, the *average* age of menarche (one of the final steps in pubertal maturation in girls) occurs at 12.5 years (Steinberg, 2005), but full entry into adult roles is delayed for the majority of the population until at least 20 years of age and often well beyond (Arnett & Tanner, in press). Thus, in most contemporary industrialized soci-eties, many youth spend close to a decade with sexually mature bodies and reproductively activated brains prior to taking on adult roles or status.

This general expansion of the adolescent interval makes early adolescence in contemporary industrialized society a period of particular vulnerability for maturational disjunctions among biologic, behavioral, and social processes. More specifically, this confluence of historical and individual changes in patterns of biological maturity, contextual demands, and contextual supports appears to have opened a window of risk for behavioral and emotional health problems for many young members of modern societies as they negotiate the transition from childhood to adolescence and from adolescence to adulthood.

Adolescence is therefore a period of heightened risk in general. However, some individuals are at greater risk than others. Children at greatest risk include those who enter this demanding transition already vulnerable, as well as those who become vulnerable during this challenging time (due to genetic predispositions and/or earlier adverse experiences), those for whom the disjunctions between developmental domains are greatest, those facing the greatest challenges during the transition, those with the least contextual support, and those with bad combinations of low resources and heightened genetic and/or developmentally acquired vulnerability. One of the most important goals of research on psychopathology in adolescence is to achieve a better understanding of the processes—and mechanisms—by which neurobiology, behavior, and context interact during this transition to create vulnerability and risk that for some individuals can spiral into significant long-term impairments and psychopathology.

On the other hand, risk does not inevitably lead to bad outcomes. Risk is a probability relating to a specific outcome of interest in a group or population; individual adolescents can manifest considerable resilience despite their status as members of a group at risk for negative outcomes. It is equally important to understand why other individuals navigate this interval of development quite successfully, to better understand patterns and processes of protection and resilience. An informative research agenda will thus need to focus both on mechanisms and on the trajectories of development during the adolescent transition, as well as preceding transitions. The adolescent transition may activate preexisting risk conditions—conditions that may reflect a cumulative "chain of risk," divergence into a pathway of vulnerability, or the expression of a latent problem from an earlier critical period (Boyce & Keating, 2004)—or introduce new risks that are specific to this developmental period. Increasing our knowledge of these developmental processes is crucial to inform policies and programs aimed at improving the health and well-being of adolescents and the adults they will become. The very fact that multiple transformations are occurring in adolescence may provide windows of opportunity for

positive influence as well as windows of risk (see also Cicchetti & Rogosch, 2002).

Our goal in this chapter is to stimulate the development of a research agenda that will lead to identifying specific developmental processes for specific types of psychopathology in ways that can be used to leverage interventions. For example, a better understanding of the processes underlying changes in affect regulation during pubertal maturation may ultimately inform interventions targeted at children at high risk for developing a depressive disorder (such as those with a strong family history of depression, or individuals with symptoms of anxiety) *before* the development of a more serious disorder. In a similar way, a deeper understanding of the developmental processes and unique opportunities in this maturational interval can eventually inform a broad range of policies and programs designed to decrease vulnerability and risk and promote healthier adolescent development and increase resilience.

This chapter is organized as follows. In the first section, we offer several general observations about psychopathology in adolescence that have emerged from research over the past several decades and that motivated the development of the present heuristic approach. Rather than review research on the nature, antecedents, and developmental course of specific disorders, we emphasize overarching principles that apply across different types of psychopathology and serve as a basis for understanding what is unique about developmental psychopathology in adolescence. This discussion of broad principles is followed by a section in which we introduce a new framework for research on psychopathology in adolescence. Within this framework, the development of psychopathology in adolescence is linked to the convergence of specific biological, cognitive, and contextual factors characteristic of the adolescent decade. Following our overview of the framework, we examine several aspects of developmental and contextual change that occur in adolescence, with detailed sections on changes in brain structure and function; in arousal, motivation, and affect regulation; in the development of regulatory competence; and in the major contexts in which adolescents spend time. The chapter concludes with a call for new, interdisciplinary research that examines the interplay among neurobiological, psychological, and contextual influences on psychopathology in adolescence.

PSYCHOPATHOLOGY IN ADOLESCENCE: SOME GENERAL OBSERVATIONS

For centuries, the study of psychological maladjustment and the study of adolescent development have been inextricably linked, both conceptually and empirically. Philosophers, clinicians, scientists, and virtually all observers of human behavior have long noted that adolescence is a period of special significance for the emergence or intensification of various forms of emotional and behavioral disorder, including many internalizing problems (e.g., depression, bipolar illness, eating disorders), externalizing problems (e.g., delinquency, violence), and addictive disorders (e.g., alcohol abuse and dependency, drug abuse and dependency). Although scholars may disagree about *why* adolescence is so important to the study of clinical phenomena, there is little dispute over whether it *is* important. Indeed, the list of clinical phenomena that are *not* in some way centrally associated with adolescence is probably shorter than the list of clinical phenomena that are. Nevertheless, controversy remains concerning the scope of these developmental trends. On the one hand, marked changes in the prevalence of clinically meaningful emotional and behavioral problems clearly occur during adolescence. On the other hand, the majority of adolescents pass through this developmental period with no more than transient or mild signs of impairment stemming from psychopathology.

Four observations surface repeatedly in discussions of the development of psychopathology in adolescence (Masten, 1988). First, there is a notable increase in the prevalence of certain types of psychopathology during adolescence, including depression, social anxiety, eating disorders, psychosis, and substance abuse and dependence. Many, if not most, disorders have their initial onset during adolescence (Kessler et al., 2005). Such data support the notion that early adolescence is a period of heightened vulnerability for affective and behavioral disorders. In each case, these changes in prevalence appear relatively dramatic. For example, Major Depressive Disorder (MDD) is relatively rare before puberty. However, adolescents face a particularly high risk for MDD upon entering puberty. Even by conservative estimates, point prevalence of MDD changes during this developmental period from less than 5% to more than 10% (Angold, Costello, & Worthman, 1998; Costello et al., 2002).

Second, there are important changes in the manifestations of many forms of psychopathology during adolescence. For example, the cognitive symptoms of depression, such as hopelessness, become a more salient feature of affective disturbance as individuals become more capable of hypothetical and abstract thinking. In fact, maturation in cognitive processes early in adolescence are thought to create a new state of vulnerability in some individuals. The combination of adverse life experiences with this underlying cognitive diathesis that becomes manifest during adolescence is thought to account for adolescent increases in rates of MDD (Hankin & Abramson, 2001). Similarly, the outward manifestations of conduct problems become more serious, as antisocial behavior becomes connected more with criminal activity. Notably, relatively few studies examine the way symptom profiles are transformed between childhood and adolescence and between adolescence and adulthood (but see, e.g., Avenevoli & Steinberg, 2001).

Third, new patterns of gender differences in psychopathology emerge during adolescence. Most notably, whereas rates of depression are similar among boys and girls prior to puberty, by middle adolescence depression is twice as common among females as males, a ratio that is maintained into and through adulthood. Interestingly, some evidence suggests that opposite trends emerge for behavioral disorders, with decreasing gender divergence for various markers of behavior problems (Moffitt & Caspi, 2001). The emergence or intensification of gender differences in affective psychopathology in adolescence is consistent with the more general intensification of gender differences in personality and behavior that occurs during the 2nd decade of life (J. P. Hill & Lynch, 1983). Any comprehensive theory about why psychopathology increases in adolescence must be able to account for impressive gender differences in relative rates of certain disorders.

Finally, some, but not all, forms of psychopathology in adolescence have shown important changes in prevalence over historical time, generally, with prevalence increasing with successive generations. Thus, although the process of transition from childhood to adulthood has probably always held hazards for human development, current conditions of adolescent development may have elevated the risk for specific problems that can be observed in patterns of risk-taking behaviors, affective disturbance, eating disorders, and substance abuse. We recognize that considerable complications arise in efforts to examine changes in prevalence of adolescent mental disorders over time. Given changes in perceptions of various sorts of mental illness and advances in methods for assessing rates of psychiatric disorders over time, the sensitivity for detecting disorders may change across successive cohorts of adolescence. However, data on completed suicide appear to be less susceptible to these influences than data on specific conditions such as MDD. Data documenting increased during adolescence in rates both of completed suicide and Major depression during the second half of the twentieth century suggest that rates of psychopathology among adolescents have genuinely increased (Costello et al., 2002). These historical changes suggest that, despite the obvious importance of biological change as a defining feature of adolescence and a potential contributor to psychopathology, contextual factors must play a very important role in the development of affective and behavioral problems during this period.

ADOLESCENT DEVELOPMENT, SELF-REGULATION, AND PSYCHOPATHOLOGY

There has been a recent paradigm shift in the study of adolescent psychopathology away from seeing psychological disturbance during adolescence as either the grown-up version of childhood disorder or the immature or prodromal counterpart of adult pathology. In our view, the study of psychopathology in adolescence necessitates the study of clinical phenomena in the context of adolescence as a developmental period, rather than the study of clinical phenomena among individuals who merely happen to be older than children and younger than adults. For example, adolescence represents a time of unusual passion, manifest in extreme levels of reported feeling states. These normal developmental changes appear to be reflected in the manifestations of adolescent episodes of MDD.

A more comprehensive approach to research in this area requires linking developmental changes in the prevalence, nature, and manifestation of psychopathology in adolescence to specific aspects of biological, cognitive, emotional, social, and contextual transformation that define the period. Thus, for example, one might study the specific links between changes in depressive symptomatology and the development of abstract thinking, hormonal changes related to pubertal processes, and school transitions in early adolescence, or the connections between changes in peer relations, body shape, school contexts, and media utilization and the development of eating disturbances. Unfortunately, however, most studies of the development of psychopathology in adolescence chart symptoms of disturbance as a function of chronological age (a poor proxy for development) and do not examine how these same symptoms vary as a function of various aspects of intraindividual and contextual transformation.

We share with numerous other writers the belief that many aspects of psychopathology can be usefully cast as problems of self-regulation (see Steinberg & Avenevoli, 2000). With reference to adolescence in particular, we begin from the premise that adolescence is characterized by an increased need to regulate affect and behavior in accordance with long-term goals and consequences, often at a distance from the adults who provided regulatory structure and guidance during childhood. In fact, this characterizes the central psychological task of adolescence in contemporary society. (Data on the development of a sense of identity, long portrayed as the fundamental developmental task of the period, e.g., Erikson, 1959, shows that most of the psychological work surrounding this issue takes place in late adolescence and early adulthood; Waterman, 1982.) As they mature toward adulthood, adolescents must increasingly control their *own* feelings and actions on the basis of learned principles, rules, and future risks and rewards that may not seem emotionally salient in the moment. This process is not simply a matter of cognitive understanding of consequences (e.g., knowing the risks of HIV, pregnancy, or driving drunk or the long-term rewards of hard work, discipline, or academic accomplishments). Rather, adolescents must develop the ability to use such knowledge to reliably guide behavior in the absence of adult supervision.

Further, this new level of self-regulation must be achieved at the same time that maturational changes may alter the nature and strength of emotions evoked by contexts that are also undergoing change. Successful navigation of *behavior* through complex social challenges and ambiguous conflicts in adolescence requires a complex balancing of many strong competing feelings related to goals, fears, and desires. Mature judgment and behavioral control in the face of strong feelings and desires are only partially in place at the end of childhood and are skills that continue to show maturational improvements well beyond early adolescent years and into the mid-20s. It is precisely this increased ability and necessity of integrating maturing cognitive elements and emerging emotional and motivational factors in a complex system of conscious control that is in many ways the hallmark of adolescence (Keating, 2004). As noted earlier, contemporary neuroscience evidence supports the view that systematic integration of an "executive suite" lies at the core of the adolescent transition (Keating, 2004), shown particularly in the enhanced development of the prefrontal cortex, in expanded corticocortical communication (prefrontal and whole brain increases in white matter density), and in apparent synaptic pruning (proliferation and then decrease in gray matter density).

Puberty and adrenarche (the maturation of the adrenal system that occurs in preadolescence), however, begin to exert large changes in young bodies and brain systems more than a decade before mature judgment and self-control are achieved. The temporal gap between the heightened arousal set in motion by puberty and the onset of adult like regulatory competence, which does not fully mature until early adulthood, creates the special vulnerability and challenge of adolescence. One explanation for the historical rise in the prevalence of many forms of psychopathology is that this gap has become more pronounced over the course of the past century, especially among girls. Specifically, there has been a dramatic historical change toward the earlier onset of puberty among girls such that menarche (one of the *final* events in female pubertal maturation) typically occurs *before* age 13 in most industrialized societies. Further, the early rise in adrenarcheal hormones (an early maturational process associated with puberty) is well under way by 8 to 9 years of age in both boys and girls. (We do not have historical data on whether adrenarche occurs earlier today than in previous eras, but there is reason to suspect that this is the case given the secular trend in menarche and other external manifestations of puberty.) The onset of puberty in children not only impacts physical growth and sexual maturation, but also activates new drives, impulses, emotions, motivations, changes in arousal, and new behaviors and experiences that challenge self-regulatory abilities. Therefore, early adolescence in contemporary society is a time of potential mismatch between rapidly changing emotional and motivational systems and the slowly maturing systems of self-control.

These interrelated emotional, motivational, physical, and cognitive developments must also be considered in light of the context of early adolescence in modern life. Three aspects of the context of contemporary adolescence are especially important. First, the dramatic historical change to earlier onset of puberty impacts not only the physical aspects of development but also the social experiences of young adolescents. The appearance of secondary sex characteristics at an earlier age likely leads to the earlier onset of dating, romantic involvement, and sexual experimentation. In addition, in light of research suggesting that changes in the physical appearance of individuals at puberty provoke changes in parent-child relations, especially with respect to increases in adolescent assertiveness and autonomy seeking (e.g., Steinberg, 1988), the earlier onset of puberty may set in motion changes in family dynamics before parents expect these shifts to occur. As Collins (1990) has noted, difficulties in parent-child relationships often increase when family members' expectations of each other are "violated." Previous generations of parents may have expected, and perhaps tolerated, increased autonomy seeking in their child when it occurred in conjunction with the adolescent's entrance into the labor force, for example, but today's parents may react very dif-

ferently to the same sort of assertiveness now that it comes at a much earlier age.

Second, young adolescents are typically dealing with increasingly more difficult decision making and challenges to self-control in complex environments that activate many arousing but conflicting feelings and desires, as well as the need to navigate complex choices and ambiguities. The range of options available to adolescents, from choosing among alternative sources of entertainment to choosing among alternative educational or vocational pathways, has increased dramatically in contemporary industrialized society. Thus, today's adolescents face more decisions, and more complicated decisions, than their counterparts did in previous eras. These changes are reflected in higher rates of adverse experiences that are thought to interact with maturation in cognitive capacities to precipitate episodes of depression in vulnerable individuals.

Third, there has been a historical shift toward increased behavioral autonomy among teenagers, such that external constraints on their behavior (in the form of parental and adult supervision) are diminishing and are often absent. Changes in patterns of parental employment, in rates of divorce and separation, and in patterns of residential mobility, which have led to disruptions in community ties, have decreased the amount of time that young people spend in the company of parents, adult neighbors, and members of their extended family. As a consequence, today's adolescents have fewer resources on which to draw in the task of regulating new emotions and drives. These contextual changes may exacerbate special vulnerability of adolescents to emotional and behavioral problems.

In this chapter, we argue that disjunctions in biology, cognitive capability, and contextual demands in adolescence create vulnerabilities for certain types of emotional and behavioral difficulties, in particular, those that involve the regulation of affect (e.g., depression, social anxiety), appetite (e.g., substance abuse and dependence, eating disorders), and impulsivity (e.g., antisocial behavior, excessive risk taking). The framework we propose is relevant to the study of a wide range of psychopathologies, including internalizing, externalizing, and addictive disorders. To understand the development of psychopathology in adolescence, therefore, we need to understand changes in patterns of arousal and motivation, the development of regulatory competence, and the ways this competence may be compromised or strengthened by the interplay among biology, cognition, and context.

In each of these areas of study, there have been major scientific advances in recent years. A conceptual framework to productively advance our understanding must therefore confront two competing demands. The first is to capture the complexities of development within and between multiple domains. The second is to draw a picture of the interplay among multiple systems that is sufficiently coherent to organize a research agenda and to inform policy and practice.

Three propositions guide the framework we offer in this chapter. First, we hypothesize that various forms of psychopathology in adolescence are related to the neurobehavioral changes of puberty, which include changes in brain systems regulating arousal and appetite that subsequently influence the intensity and duration of emotion and motivation. Adolescents, we hypothesize, experience emotions and motivations that are qualitatively and subjectively stronger than those experienced by prepubertal children. Thus, for example, whereas children experience sadness, euphoria, anxiety, and anger, the biological changes of puberty result in the capacity of individuals to feel sadder, more euphoric, more anxious, and angrier and, furthermore, to experience these more intense affective states for longer periods of time. Similarly, the biological changes of puberty stimulate changes in the intensity and duration of various drives, not only the sex drive, which is presumed to intensify at puberty, but all drives relevant to reward, novelty, and stimulation seeking. In addition, motivational drives related to social status appear to increase during adolescence.

Second, we hypothesize that the increased intensity and duration of emotion and the increased strength of at least some appetitive drives create new regulatory challenges, particularly with respect to self-regulation in the face of high-intensity emotions and motivation and in the midst of emotional conflicts. During adolescence, there is a shift in regulatory capability away from regulation that is assisted by external agents, such as parents, toward regulation that is primarily internal, cognitive in nature, and involving higher-order executive functioning. The type of executive function that is assembled during the adolescent transition is in fact an integration of a number of specific cognitive achievements, particularly in planning, monitoring, evaluating, and reflecting. Together, these can be thought of as an executive suite that comes increasingly, but gradually, under conscious control during adolescence (Keating, 2004). Because the maturation of regulatory systems relevant to the modulation of emotion and motivation is not driven by pubertal development and is still taking place during late adolescence, however, adolescents are relatively more vulnerable than children (whose levels of arousal and motivation are lower) or adults (whose regula-

tory capabilities are stronger) to extremes in affective and drive states, which may leave adolescents more susceptible to psychopathology. Regulatory problems may result either from inadequate or incompletely developed regulatory capacities or both. Bringing the potent and novel affective and motivational systems into an integrated, functioning system is a lengthy and effortful process. Thus, emotional and behavioral disorders may result from underregulation (e.g., where the underregulation of anger may lead to conduct problems) or inappropriate regulation (e.g., where the overregulation of sadness by rumination may lead to the development of depressive disorder). As regulatory capacities mature, individuals become less susceptible to the development of psychopathology.

Third, we hypothesize that during the period of greatest disjunction between affect and appetitive motivations on the one hand, and regulatory competence on the other, individuals may be protected from extremes in emotion or drive by a context that provides adequate external regulation in the form of support, control, and predictability. Thus, although many individuals may experience emotions and drives whose intensity and duration exceeds their regulatory competence, those adolescents who enjoy supportive home, peer, school, and neighborhood contexts are buffered from the ill effects of the emotion-cognition disjunction. In addition, their transition to an internal, consciously controlled regulatory system is more effectively scaffolded compared with individuals lacking in such support. Conversely, individuals whose environments do not provide sufficient support, control, and predictability are relatively more vulnerable to the development of psychopathology. In our view, the adolescent is not merely the passive recipient of contextual support, however. We view context as a resource that is both provided by outside agents (such as parents or teachers) and also actively recruited by adolescents. An important, yet remarkably understudied question, is how individuals develop the capacity to identify, enlist, and employ sources of contextual support during times of stress as a means of protection against the development of emotional and behavioral difficulty. In this regard, *resilience* in the face of adversity may reflect in part the ability to engage contextual resources in the service of self-protection.

BRAIN DEVELOPMENT IN ADOLESCENCE

Despite the widely held notion that the brain "changes" at puberty, there is a surprising dearth of neuroscience data that specifically refer to the links between brain development and pubertal maturation. As a consequence, in this section, we draw on other areas of neuroscience that frame our understanding of maturational changes more specific to the interval surrounding pubertal development. This includes general aspects of brain development, contextual effects on brain development, and a discussion of what is known about changes in brain function in specific brain regions during adolescence.

It is important to note at the outset that not all brain development in adolescence is closely linked to processes of pubertal maturation. One limitation of extant views of adolescent development, and of psychopathology in adolescence in particular, is that "biology" has been used as an explanatory construct without sufficient attention paid to the fact that biological change in adolescence is multisystemic, and that even pubertal change itself is not a unitary phenomenon. Thus, it is important to distinguish between aspects of brain development and function that are closely tied to puberty and those that appear to take place relatively independent of pubertal maturation (i.e., that follow a different timetable and are influenced by other aspects of aging and/or experience). Moreover, even within puberty, some aspects of brain development may be particularly heavily influenced by specific facets of puberty but unrelated to others (e.g., those that are closely linked to changes along the hypothalamic-pituitary-adrenal axis versus those that are closely linked to changes along the hypothalamic-pituitary-gonadal axis).

Research on the impact of biology cn psychopathology in adolescence is further complicated by the fact that some links between biology and behavior are best understood with reference to neurobiological processes unfolding in brain systems, others with respect to endocrinological processes occurring at a more holistic level, and still others with regard to changes in the physical appearance and competencies of the adolescent. Thus, to say that the onset, intensification, or transformation of any form of psychopathology in adolescence is linked to the biological changes of the period is no longer adequate, given our understanding of the complexity of biological change during the years between childhood and adulthood. As we move forward into the twenty-first century, questions about biological change and psychological functioning in adolescence will need to be framed with much greater specificity. Some aspects of functioning are linked to puberty, others are linked to biological change that takes place in adolescence but that is not pubertal in nature, and still others are linked only secondarily to processes of normative biological maturation. And among those changes linked to puberty, there is considerable heterogeneity with respect to the aspects of pubertal maturation that are most important.

Brain Development in Mammalian Species

Brain development in mammalian species follows an orderly progression that begins with differentiation of the brain and spinal cord in the longitudinal, circumferential, and radial dimensions. This process is followed by increases in cell numbers, repositioning of cell locations, and maturation of connections among brain cells and supporting constituents (Nowakowski & Hayes, 1999; Rakic & Nowakowski, 1981). Three aspects of brain development appear relevant for theories of developmental psychopathology in adolescence. First, perhaps the most extensive data relate to evidence of active changes within cells after they have already ceased to divide (Kolb, Forgie, Gibb, Gorny, & Bowntree, 1998; Lewis, 1997). There is robust evidence of prolonged refinements in synapses, the connections among nerve cells, well into adolescence, as reflected by changes in the morphology and functional integrity of dendrites, the part of the neuron or nerve cell that receives information from other parts of the nervous system. Synapses exhibit marked changes during adolescence in absolute number, precise localization on dendrites, and functional integrity (Kolb, 1999). In general, there is some evidence that such changes occur more profoundly in parts of the brain devoted to multimodal sensory processes or abstract motor plans, as opposed to primary sensory areas involved in perception of low-level stimulus features or primary motor areas involved in control of isolated muscle groups. On the other hand, only broad, tentative conclusions can be made about the nature of these changes in adolescence, given the relatively limited developmental research on region-specific patterns of cellular differentiation in humans or among nonhuman primates (Fuster, 1997; Huttenlocher, 2002; Lewis, 1997). Developmental changes of ascending brain stem monoamine systems effects on cortical-cortical synapses may be particularly important as regulators of behavior. For example, studies in nonhuman primates demonstrate adolescent maturation in dopaminergic innervation of neurons in the prefrontal cortex (Goldman-Rakic, 1987; Kolb, 1999; Lewis, 1997). Advances in neuroimaging methodology provide the means for generating comparable data in human adolescents (Gogtay et al., 2004; McClure et al., 2004; Monk et al., 2003; Thompson, Cannon, & Toga, 2002).

Second, conduction along neurons is facilitated by the maturation of myelin sheaths. There is evidence of extensive myelination during adolescence, though this evidence carries less direct implications for current theories of normative and psychopathological functioning, given the incomplete understanding of relations between myelination and cognitive function (Evans et al., 1999; Fuster et al., 1997; Gabrielli et al., 1999; Kolb, 1999). On the other hand, to the extent that cortical-cortical interactions represent a key aspect of complex thought, maturation in myelination, by increasing the speed of nerve cell conduction, is likely to facilitate maturation in complex thought processes.

Finally, recent studies provide emerging evidence that new neurons may actually arise in at least some brain regions, particularly the hippocampus and olfactory cortex (Gould & Tanapat, 1999). This represents a relatively marked departure from initial thinking on aspects of primate neural development, which did not allow for the genesis of new neurons after early development. In the hippocampus, where adult neurogenesis has been most convincingly documented, newly synthesized neurons are integrated into extant neural circuits to refine acquired abilities (Gould & Tanapat, 1999). Taken together, data on synaptic plasticity, myelination, and neurogenesis suggest that refinements in neural connectivity represent key neural processes that are relevant for understanding normative and atypical adolescent development.

An emerging irony in the expanding horizon of neuroscience research relates to the growing shortage of developmentally oriented studies necessary for informing integrative perspectives on human adolescence. Whereas working knowledge of brain circuitry is growing in an exponential fashion, knowledge is growing relatively slowly in areas related to developmental or pubertal influences on brain circuitry. Work in developmental psychology, clinical neuroscience, and psychiatry raises key questions pertaining to changes in brain function during puberty related to the regulation of affective states. These questions reflect the fact that puberty signals relatively abrupt changes in behavior, particularly emotionally modulated behaviors, in humans and other mammals. Neuroscience research encounters considerable hurdles in attempting to address developmental questions related to emotion and pubertal development among humans, however. Much of the neuroscience database derives from studies of rodents (LeDoux, 1998). Such work carries unclear implications for humans, however, given the large cortical contribution to the regulation of emotion in primates (Rolls, 1999). Conversely, much of the clinical database derives from observations of symptom patterns, which are not easily modeled in animals. In the current chapter, emphasis is placed on clinical data from neuropsychology, electrophysiology, and brain imaging methods. These methods generate data in humans that can be more readily compared to data in nonhuman primates and rodents. Finally, independent of any changes related to puberty, other aspects of brain development are likely to impact adolescent changes in behavior over relatively prolonged periods. Here, too, considerable research is needed that delineates changes across the full adolescent period as they impact aspects of abstract thinking and other cognitive abilities that continue to emerge long after pubertal transitions have ceased.

Contextual Effects on Brain Development

Discussions of brain development in adolescence and its implications for psychopathology must acknowledge not only the importance of normative maturational processes during this time but also the role of the environment in shaping patterns of growth and maturation. Brain development appears to be more plastic and susceptible to environmental influence in adolescence than had been previously thought. Indeed, current neuroscience research on contextual influences suggests that environmental factors might conceivably profoundly affect brain development in adolescence and that neurodevelopmental processes are affected on varying time scales. Thus, one of the reasons for the heightened vulnerability of adolescents to various forms of psychopathology could inhere in the vulnerability of the adolescent brain to contextual influence. To most clearly summarize available data, this section separately discusses long-term, intermediate, and acute effects of context on brain function, while acknowledging the somewhat artificial nature of these temporal distinctions.

In terms of effects that persist across the life span, some contextual factors produce permanent change in neural circuitry by affecting developmental processes. One of the best-understood effects in this area derives from the work by Meaney and colleagues (Liu et al., 1997; Meaney, 2001b), revealing an effect of handling manipulations on rodent pups prior to adolescence. Contextual manipulations early in development permanently alter the rat's physiological response to various stressors by affecting the sensitivity of feedback regulation in limbic brain regions, including the hippocampus and ventral prefrontal region. The precise developmental period during which these effects can occur has not been established. Interestingly, however, it appears that an enriched social and learning environment during the peripubertal period in rats is capable of reversing many of the adverse effects of early maternal separation (Francis, Diorio, Plotsky, & Meaney, 2002) and that these experiences later in development influence some, but not all, of the brain systems impacted by the early handling and separation paradigms. Variations in maternal care alter the expression of genes that regulate responses to stress, synaptic development in the hippocampus, and later maternal behavior among female offspring (Meaney, 2001a).

Other work, examining contextual effects on synaptic plasticity in the rodent cerebral cortex, emphasizes the need for research on contextual effects on prefrontal and limbic regions in adolescence. In work on plasticity in the cortex, contextual manipulations exert effects on dendrite patterns in adult animals, and these effects vary as a function of developmental stage (Greenough, Black, & Wallace, 1987; Kolb, 1999). Contextual factors appear to produce, particularly robust long-term changes in dendrites when they operate during periods of intense synapse formation. This is important, because some regions of the brain may undergo particularly marked synapse formation in adolescence (Lewis, 1997), and as a result, the development of these brain regions may be particularly susceptible to the effects of context. This emphasizes the need to extend work exemplified in the studies from Meaney and colleagues through the adolescent period.

Beyond such long-term neurodevelopmental effects, other studies demonstrate contextual effects on neural function that operate over days to weeks. Such intermediate effects are elucidated in a particularly compelling fashion through studies examining the response, following contextual manipulations, in the hippocampus, a part of the brain in the temporal lobe involved in memory. Specifically, relatively brief periods of stress alter dendrite patterns in one group of neurons as well as survival rates for another group of newly generated neurons. Interestingly, less extreme contextual manipulations, such as learning experiences, can exert comparable effects. Both monoamines and neurohormones are central regulators of these processes. As a result, changes in the functioning of monoamine and neurohormonal systems during puberty may alter the response of neural systems, including the hippocampus, to contextual effects operating on an intermediate time scale.

Finally, contextual factors exert acute effects on functioning in neural circuits. Because these effects are at least partially mediated by systems that undergo robust developmental changes during adolescence, acute contextual effects on neural function may change with the initiation of puberty. For example, hormonal systems that signal the onset of puberty have robust effects on functional aspects of neural sys-

tems in animals that appear relevant for human cognitive functioning. A series of neuroimaging studies among adults demonstrates a robust effect of sex hormones on executive tasks that engage prefrontal regions (Berman et al., 1997; Shaywitz et al., 1999). Given the particularly high levels of steroid hormone receptors in medial temporal regions, changes in the hormonal milieu during adolescence may also affect performance on tasks that engage these regions. Similarly, autonomic systems that mature during puberty affect functional aspects of neural systems in animals. For example, emotional modulation of mnemonic functions results from the acute peripherally mediated effects of stress on the noradrenergic system that, in turn, affects a neural circuit involving the basolateral amygdala and hippocampus (Roozendaal, 2002). Sensitivity of the noradrenergic system to stress, as reflected in peripheral measures, appears to increase during the pubertal years (Galanter, Wasserman, Sloan, & Pine, 1999). Finally, contextual factors may exert unique acute effects on brain function during adolescence due to interactions between changes in hormonal or autonomic systems and the underlying brain regions on which they act. For example, executive functions mediated by dorsal prefrontal regions are modulated by dopamine input to this region (Arnsten, 1999). Stress effects on prefrontal function may change during adolescence due to developmental changes in the dopamine system as well as in prefrontal targets (Lewis, 1997). These changes may be particularly observable during adolescence, in light of the key modulatory role for the dopamine system in prefrontal functions (Cohen, Aston-Jones, & Gilzenrat, 2004). Hence, changes in the hormonal, autonomic, and monoamine milieus during adolescence may alter the brain's response to acute stress.

Adolescent Development in Specific Brain Regions

As elucidated in the preceding section, adolescence may represent a time of marked cellular differentiation in brain regions known to play a role in emotional regulation. The nature of ongoing neural processes in these regions at adolescence may create a window for particularly marked effects of context on emotional processing (Kolb, 1999). This section summarizes available data on adolescent brain development that support this possibility. Because data for the prefrontal and the inferior temporoparietal cortices most clearly support this premise, only data for these specific brain regions are reviewed. Nevertheless, given changes during adolescence in monoamine and hormonal systems with widespread modulatory influences, changes during this period in other brain regions may exert equally compelling effects on behavior.

Changes in the prefrontal cortex represent one of the most consistently studied aspects of adolescent brain development. Data from neuropsychology, brain imaging, and postmortem studies in primates all point to considerable changes in prefrontal structure and function in adolescence. Given the complexity of this brain region and the wealth of available data, considerable disagreement remains on the most appropriate model of prefrontal function. Nevertheless, most investigators view one set of functions as particularly dependent on dorsal aspects of this brain region. These include functions usually subsumed under the concepts of "working memory" and "preparatory set." Another set of functions is typically viewed as particularly dependent on ventral or orbitofrontal aspects of the prefrontal cortex. These include functions often subsumed under the concept of "inhibitory functions." Ventral frontal regions in particular also may be more intimately tied to the calibration and regulation of emotions or behaviors associated with rewards and punishments. Finally, a third set of functions related to motivation and performance monitoring typically is viewed as dependent on medial frontal regions, including the cingulate gyrus.

There is some evidence that dorsal aspects of the prefrontal cortex reach functional maturity later in adolescence, as compared to ventral and medial aspects of the prefrontal cortex. This evidence derives from neuropsychological studies in humans (Luciana & Nelson, 1998), brain imaging studies in humans (Chugani, 1999; Giedd et al., 1999; Thompson et al., 2000), and postmortem studies in nonhuman primates (Lewis, 1997). Interestingly, this may require that certain functions ordinarily subserved by the dorsal region in adulthood be mediated by ventral regions prior to late adolescence. For example, at adolescence, transient deactivation of dorsal prefrontal regions has an increasingly profound effect on certain functions, such as delayed response, usually attributed to this region (Alexander, 1982). As such, these developmental data raise the possibility of an asynchrony between developments in prefrontal regions most intimately tied to emotion (which appear to come online relatively earlier in adolescence) as opposed to those most closely linked to executive functions (which appear to come online relatively later). Surprisingly little is known about the functional development of the ventral, medial, and orbitofrontal regions of the cortex, however, or about the interrelations between functions that are mediated in the ventral and dorsal regions—and this represents a critical area of focus for current and future research aimed at understanding the development of affect regulation and the emergence of self-regulatory capacities in adolescence (as discussed in more detail in the following section on affect regulation).

Changes in the temporoparietal cortex represent a second aspect of brain development where there is evidence of adolescent changes. This brain region plays a key role in forming representations of objects through the integration of more specific perceptual aspects of objects. In terms of emotional salience, studies in nonhuman primates document interactions between inferior temporal regions and medial temporal structures, including the amygdala and hippocampus. As reviewed elsewhere (Pine, 2003), maturation in linguistic capacity may signal maturation of the ventral temporal region. This maturation may reflect a stronger role for linguistic and other cognitive processes related to categorization skill in the regulation of emotion.

In summary, then, although research on adolescent brain development is still in its infancy, there is considerable evidence that the 2nd decade of life is a period of great activity with respect to changes in brain structure and function, especially in regions and systems associated with response inhibition, the calibration of risk and reward, and emotion regulation (see Dahl & Spear, 2004). Contrary to earlier beliefs about brain maturation in adolescence, this activity is not limited to the early adolescent period, or is it invariably linked to processes of pubertal maturation. Two particular observations about brain development in adolescence are especially pertinent to our understanding of the development of psychopathology during this period. First, the fact that much brain development during adolescence is in the particular brain regions and systems that are key to the regulation of behavior and emotion and to the perception and evaluation of risk and reward is important, as many forms of psychological disorder in adolescence are linked conceptually and empirically to problems in impulse control, sensation seeking, and affect regulation. Second, growing evidence that patterns of brain change in adolescence are susceptible to environmental influence suggests that contextual factors undoubtedly play an important role in accounting for individual differences in patterns of normative and atypical development. The integration of neuroscience-based research efforts with those that are more contextually oriented will permit a vast improvement in our understanding of how context gets "into" the brain during the adolescent years and how this process may help inform future study of the onset and developmental course of psychopathology.

AROUSAL, MOTIVATION, AND AFFECT REGULATION DURING PUBERTY AND ADOLESCENCE

As noted earlier, the framework we have proposed emphasizes the links between psychopathology and self-regulation in adolescence. Central to our argument is the notion that changes in arousal and motivation brought on by pubertal maturation precede the development of regulatory competence in a manner that creates a disjunction between the adolescent's affective experience and his or her ability to regulate arousal, motivation, and emotion, all of which have implications for the regulation of behavior. As we have noted elsewhere (e.g., Dahl, 2001), the developments of early adolescence create a situation in which one is starting an engine without yet having a skilled driver.

In this section, we outline some of the emerging understanding regarding maturational changes in arousal, motivation, and emotion during adolescence. This includes some discussion of the neurobiology of affect regulation and the regulation of sleep and arousal. Affect regulation is considered within a framework of the developing neurobehavioral systems that underpin emotion and its regulation, systems that are hypothesized to be of clinical relevance to understanding affect dysregulation and the emergence of affective and behavioral disorders in adolescence.

The Neurobiology of Affect Regulation

From a neuroscience perspective, emotions have been conceptualized as brain states associated with rewards and punishments (Rolls, 1999). Affect regulation involves major contributions from a group of interconnected brain structures, including the amygdala, extended amygdala/ventral striatum, and several cortical areas, particularly areas of the medial and orbitofrontal cortex (Davidson, 2000; Davidson, Jackson, & Kalin, 2000; Davidson, Pizzagalli, Nitschke, & Putnam, 2002; Drevets, 2003; Rolls, 1999). Medial frontal areas, encompassing the anterior and posterior cingulate cortex, appear to be involved, especially in situations of performance monitoring, response conflict, and/or error detection in relation to an emotional state (Carter et al., 1998). The amygdala is typically recognized as a key structure for integrating the perception of rewarding/punishing stimuli and orchestrating some aspects of an organism's response to these stimuli. In terms of acute regulation of these responses, neurons in some amygdala nuclei exhibit long-term potentiation as well as habituation following the pairing of a rewarding or punishing stimulus with a neutral stimulus (Rogan, Staubli, & LeDoux, 1997). Neurons in other amygdala nuclei may undergo sensitization under different stimulus-pairing conditions (Davis, 1992). The degree to which intrinsic aspects of amygdala functions change during adolescence remains unclear. The underlying circuitry of the primate amygdala, as well as its connections with key afferents and efferents, appears to develop relatively early in life.

Nevertheless, Kellogg and colleagues (Kellogg, Awatramani, & Piekut, 1998) have documented increases during adolescence in stress-induced gene expression in the rodent amygdala. Such adolescent changes could partially reflect changes in other structures or hormonal systems that interact with amygdala nuclei as part of circuits mediating responses to reward and punishment.

Left unclear in extant attempts to apply affective neuroscience methods to the investigation of affective disorders in adolescence is specificity regarding the particular components of affect that are dysregulated. Even a cursory analysis of the complexity of most forms of psychopathology indicates how complex a problem this is. For example, the development of Major depression in adolescents could be associated with altered perception of emotional cues, a lower threshold to activate negative emotions such as sadness, a tendency to activate a greater intensity of negative affective states, difficulties terminating negative affective states once they are activated, difficulties activating *positive* emotional states, altered interpretation or monitoring of internal affective states, or patterns of behavior resulting in fewer emotionally rewarding experiences—or, most likely, some combination of these and other factors. Similarly, the development of conduct problems could be due to deficient capacity in using emotion or emotion-related attentional processes in the regulation of behavior, difficulties in the regulation of appetitive drives, problems in the regulation of affective states such as anger, deficiencies in inhibitory control, or some amalgamation of these.

Pubertal Maturation and Affective Development

In contrast to most measures of cognitive development, which seem to correlate more closely with age and experience rather than the timing of pubertal maturation, there is evidence for a specific link between pubertal maturation and developmental changes in various aspects of arousal, motivation, and emotion. For example, there is evidence that pubertal development directly influences the development of romantic interest and sexual motivation (Udry, 1987). There is also evidence that some changes in emotional intensity and reactivity are more closely linked to pubertal maturation than to age, such as measures of parent-adolescent conflict (Steinberg, 1987). Some cognitive skills related to human face-processing have also shown intriguing alterations in midadolescent development: an apparent *decrement* in face-processing skills that is associated with sexual maturation (measured by Tanner staging by physical examinations) rather than with age or grade level (Diamond, Carey, & Back, 1983). A parallel finding has been reported for voice recognition (Mann, Diamond, & Carey, 1979).

There is also evidence that the increase in sensation seeking and risk taking and some proclivity toward reckless behavior is influenced by puberty. For example, in a recent study by Martin et al. (2002), where sensation-seeking and risk-taking behaviors were examined in a large group of young adolescents ages 11 to 14, there was no significant correlation between age and sensation seeking, but a significant correlation between sensation seeking and pubertal stage among both boys and girls. There is also evidence in animal and human studies supporting a link between increasing levels of reproductive hormones and sensitivity to social status (Book, Starzyk, & Qunisey, 2001; Josephs, Newman, Brown, & Beer, 2003), which is consistent with the link between puberty and risk taking, as several influential theories of adolescent risk taking (e.g., Moffitt, 1993) suggest that at least some of this behavior is done in the service of enhancing one's standing with peers. There is evidence, as well, that adolescent girls prefer and find more attractive dominant and aggressive boys, although this preference appears to wane as girls mature out of adolescence (Pellegrini & Long, 2003).

Sleep and Arousal at Puberty

Another area of investigation where puberty-specific maturational processes have been well documented concerns changes in the regulation of sleep and arousal. Dahl, Trubnick, al-Shabbout, and Ryan's (1997) longitudinal study of normal sleep found that changes in REM sleep measures showed a strong link to pubertal increases in reproductive hormones, whereas changes in stages 3 and 4 non-REM sleep appeared to be more strongly linked to the rapid physical growth at puberty (as measured by body mass index). There is also a circadian shift (delay) resulting in a biologically based tendency to stay up later (and sleep in later) that occurs in early to midpuberty and an increase in objectively measured daytime sleepiness (which may represent an increased biologic need for sleep during pubertal maturation; Carskadon, 1990, 1999; Carskadon et al., 1980). There are also maturational changes in the effects of sleep loss in adolescence. By midpuberty, adolescents show much greater objectively measured sleepiness, as well as complex changes in mood and affect regulation, in response to sleep loss (Dahl, 1996, 1999; Dahl, Bernhisel-Broadbent, Scanlon-Holdford, Sampson, & Lupo, 1995; Dahl, Pelham, & Wierson, M., 1991; Maayan et al., 1998).

The impact of pubertal change on sleep and arousal may have important implications for the development of psycho-

pathology. In addition to the direct effects of sleep loss on mood and motivation, sleep loss in adolescents can also increase stimulant use during the day (including caffeine, nicotine, and methylphenidate, as well as illicit stimulants). Some of the behavioral adaptations to accumulated sleep loss (such as extensive catch-up sleep on the weekends by sleeping in very late) can also have negative effects on the slowly adapting circadian systems. In these ways, it appears that insufficient sleep can sometimes contribute to a spiral of problems with emotional dysregulation. Further, adolescent depression is associated with disturbed sleep, particularly difficulties falling asleep.

Puberty and Psychopathology

Although the specific mechanisms connecting pubertal maturation and many types of psychopathology in adolescence have yet to be established, increases in certain types of affective disturbance have been convincingly linked to pubertal maturation, especially among girls. As noted earlier, the prevalence of Major depression exhibits a two- to fivefold increase during adolescence, particularly among adolescent girls, and this increase is associated with pubertal stage (Angold et al., 1998). Similarly, panic attacks are extremely rare prior to puberty but exhibit a marked increase, particularly among girls, with pubertal onset (Hayward et al., 1992; Pine et al., 1998). Angold et al. (1998) reported data from a longitudinal epidemiological sample indicating that the *rise* in pubertal hormones was the best predictor of increased risk for depression among girls.

Numerous studies have shown that individuals who go through puberty earlier than their same-age peers are especially vulnerable to a wide range of affective and behavioral disorders. Indeed, one of the most robust findings in the literature on pubertal development and adolescent adjustment is that early maturing females and, to a lesser extent, early maturing males evince relatively higher rates of virtually all sorts of adjustment difficulties, including depression and suicide, delinquency, risk taking, emotional disorders, and other psychological difficulties (Alsaker & Olweus, 1993; Caspi, Lynam, Moffitt, & Silva, 1993; Ge, Conger, & Elder, 1996; Graber, Lewinsohn, Seeley, & Brooks-Gunn, 1997; Orr & Ingersoll, 1995). As with the case of pubertal status and psychopathology, the underlying links between pubertal timing and psychopathology have remained largely unexplained. Some investigators have emphasized the effects of off-time development (i.e., different from peers) as the key factor in risk for depression (Graber et al.,1997); others have attributed the increased vulnerability of early maturers to a wider array of problems to social factors (e.g., among girls, heightened expectations for involvement in sexual activity, especially with older boys, and among both males and females, association with older peers who may lead them into early experimentation with drugs and delinquency; Magnusson, Stattin, & Allen, 1986). Another strong possibility, suggested by our earlier analysis, is that the disjunction between changes in affective arousal (which are linked to puberty) and the development of self-regulatory competence (which is not) is wider among early maturers than their peers.

It is important to emphasize the limitations of these studies of puberty and psychopathology: Many have relied on self-report measures of pubertal development, and few have obtained objective measures of pubertal maturation or hormone levels. As a consequence, information on underlying mechanisms is sparse. Current theories adopt an integrative perspective (Angold et al., 1998; Dahl, 2001) consistent with the idea that biological changes associated with puberty increase adolescents' vulnerability to social stress, but these models are not inconsistent with those that focus more on the direct links between pubertal maturation and the development of various brain systems. Given the magnitude, significance, and complexity of these problems, there is a need for studies examining changes in affect regulation within a framework of affective neuroscience. In addition to methodological advances, there is also a need for conceptual and modeling work focused on pubertal effects on brain maturation, emotion, and emotion regulation.

In some models of the development of affect regulation, there is an explicit emphasis on cognitive systems exerting control over emotions and emotion-related behavior (see Thompson, 1994). Many aspects of affect regulation involve the ability to inhibit, delay, or modify an emotion or its expression in accordance with some rules, goals, or strategies or to avoid learned negative consequences. However, there is increasing understanding that cognitive-emotional interactions also unfold in the other direction in important ways. Thus, just as cognition has an important impact on emotion, emotion has an important impact on basic cognitive processes, including decision making and behavioral choice. These issues are not traditionally considered within the scope of affect regulation, but they are important within the larger framework of affective changes during adolescence, especially with respect to the study of psychopathology. Similarly, maturation in other aspects of cognition is thought to contribute to vulnerability for affective disturbances. For example, as individuals enter early adolescence, they demonstrate the capacity to manifest specific cognitive profiles associated with risk for affective disturbances (Hankin & Abramson, 2001). When confronted with certain types of adverse contextual circumstances, adolescents who have developed to manifest this cognitive profile face a particularly high risk for affective disorders, particularly major depression.

Behavioral data have often made it appear that adolescents are poor decision makers (i.e., high rates of participation in dangerous activities, automobile accidents, drug use, and unprotected sex). This led initially to hypotheses that adolescents had poor cognitive skills in decision making or that information about consequences of risky behavior may have been unclear (Botvin, 1991; Tobler, 1986). In contrast to those hypotheses, however, there is substantial evidence that adolescents engage in dangerous activities *despite* understanding (cognitively) the risks involved (Benthin et al., 1995; Cauffman & Steinberg, 1995; Dahl, 2001; Slovic, 1987, 1998, 2000a, 2000b). In real-life situations, adolescents do not simply rationally weigh (in conscious thought) the relative risks and consequences of their behavior: Their actions are largely influenced by feelings (Steinberg, 2003). Likes and dislikes, as well as emotional expectancies (including fears and desires), impact strongly on behavioral choices.

In contrast to much previous work on adolescent decision making that emphasized cognitive processes and mainly ignored affective ones, there is now increasing recognition of the importance of emotion in decision making (Loewenstein & Lerner, in press). The decision to engage in a specific behavior with long-term health consequences—such as smoking a cigarette, drinking alcohol, or engaging in unprotected sex—cannot be completely understood within the framework of cold cognitive processes. (*Cold* cognition refers to thinking processes under conditions of low emotion and/or arousal; *hot* cognition refers to thinking under conditions of strong feelings or high arousal and therefore may be much more important to understanding risky choices in real-life situations.) These affective influences are relevant in many day-to-day decisions that are made at the level of gut feelings regarding what to do in a particular situation (rather than deliberate thoughts about outcome probabilities or risk value). These gut feelings appear to be the products of affective systems in the brain that are performing computations that are largely outside conscious awareness (except for the feelings they evoke; Bechara, Damasio, & Damasio, 2000; Bechara, Damasio, Damasio, & Lee, 1999). How these feelings develop and become calibrated during maturation and how the strengths of fears versus desires are influenced by particular types of experiences at particular points in development are only beginning to be studied within the framework of affective neuroscience (Dahl, 2001). It does appear, however, that puberty and sexual maturation have important influences on at least some aspects of behavior through new drives, motivations, and intensity of feelings, as well as new experiences that evoke strong feelings (such as developing romantic involvement; Keating & Sasse, 1996; Keating & Shapka, 1999; Richards, Crowe, Larson, & Swarr, 1998). In the next section, we examine the development of the cognitive tools that permit the adolescent to regulate emotion and behavior in the face of these new and intense emotions.

THE DEVELOPMENT OF REGULATORY COMPETENCE IN ADOLESCENCE

A central feature of the emerging framework on adolescent psychopathology we propose is the role of regulatory systems. During the adolescent transition, we argue, regulatory systems are gradually brought under the control of central executive functions, with a special focus on the interface of cognition and emotion. In this section, we provide a new look at cognitive development in adolescence that is grounded in recent discoveries in neuroscience and examine the significance of cognitive change in adolescence for the development of regulatory competence.

Two important observations about cognitive development in adolescence are especially relevant to our assertion that psychopathology in adolescence is related to the disjunction between affective arousal and regulatory competence. The first is that the development of an integrated and consciously controlled executive suite of regulatory capacities is a lengthy process. Yet, adolescents confront major, emotionally laden life dilemmas from a relatively early age—perhaps, as we have suggested, getting earlier over historic time, with a decline in the age of pubertal onset and in the age at which a wide range of choices are thrust on them.

The second observation is that the acquisition of a fully coordinated and controlled set of executive functions occurs relatively later in development, both ontogenetically and phylogenetically (Keating, 2004). As such, it is less likely to be canalized (to the same degree as, say, early language acquisition), leaving greater opportunities for suboptimal trajectories. As noted, these suboptimal patterns of development take many different forms, clusters of which are associated with broad categories of psychopathology,

such as the excessive down-regulation of mood and motivation that characterizes many internalizing difficulties or the inadequate control of arousal that is associated with a wide range of risky behaviors typically seen as externalizing. Understanding the normative course of cognitive and brain development as it relates to the development of executive functions will be important elements of a framework that can address issues of disjunction in developmental timing as well as developmental difficulties in regulatory systems per se (Steingard et al., 2002).

A Neuroscience Perspective on Cognitive Development in Adolescence

Until recently, much of the work on adolescent cognitive development was devoted to a search for a core mechanism that could account parsimoniously for the broad changes in adolescent thinking that are observed at a more general level (Keating, 2004). After nearly 50 years of searching, what has emerged instead is the necessity of an integrated account. What lies at the core of adolescent cognitive development is not likely to be any single device that drives it. Rather, it is the attainment of a more fully conscious, self-directed, and self-regulating mind that characterizes the adolescent transition. This is achieved principally through the assembly of an advanced executive suite of capabilities (Donald, 2001) rather than through specific advancement in any one of the constituent elements. This represents a major shift in prevailing views of cognition, going beyond the search for underlying elements (or hidden "demons"; Dennett, 1996) that are formed and operate largely outside of awareness.

The plausibility of such an integrative account has been substantially enhanced by recent major advances in the neurosciences (e.g., Casey, Giedd, & Thomas, 2000; Giedd et al., 1999; Johnson, 2001; Luna et al., 2001; Nelson, 1999; Paus et al., 1999; Sowell et al., 2001; Sowell et al., 2002; Steingard et al., 2002), in comparative neuroanatomy across closely related primate species that illuminate core issues of human cognitive evolution (Donald, 2001; Rilling & Insel, 1999), and in a deepened understanding of the critical role of culture and context in the shaping of cognitive and brain development (Donald, 2001; Francis et al., 2002). Much of the underlying action is focused on specific developments in the prefrontal cortex, but with an equally significant role for rapidly expanding linkages to the whole brain (Donald, 2001; Luna et al., 2001; Newman & Grace, 1999). This complex process of assembly is supported by increasingly rapid connectivity (through continued myelination of nerve fibers), particularly in communication among different brain regions, and by significant and localized synaptic pruning especially in frontal areas that are crucial to executive functioning (Giedd et al., 1999; Sowell et al., 2001, 2002; Steingard et al., 2002). In the same way that new research on pubertal processes has made it eminently clear that our understanding of psychopathology in adolescence is not likely to hinge on models that are based on the identification of single-bullet accounts of pubertal maturation, new research on cognitive development in adolescence makes it clear that the search for a unitary aspect of cognitive development in adolescence that explains the onset or course of psychopathology in adolescence is unlikely to bear fruit.

The Role of the Prefrontal Cortex in the Development of Regulatory Competence

It is noteworthy that the most marked differences between adult humans and nonhuman primates (Rilling & Insel, 1999) occur precisely in those features of brain development that emerge most strikingly during adolescence: differentially greater increases in neocortical volume (beyond the expected increase owing to larger brain volume overall); differentially greater gyrification of the prefrontal cortex, indicating a more convoluted design that affords both more capacity for central coordination and more rapid communication; and a greater relative increase in cerebral white matter relative to neocortical gray matter, "suggesting that axonal connections between neocortical neurons may increase faster than the number of neurons as brain size increases" (p. 222). The prefrontal cortex is thus among the latest brain systems to develop, both phylogenetically and ontogenetically, especially the dorsolateral prefrontal cortex (Fuster, 2000). Its importance for adolescent cognitive development can be inferred from this convergence but is more directly evident from its integrative functions. The importance of the relatively late development of systems mediated by the dorsolateral prefrontal cortex is especially important for understanding aspects of psychopathology in adolescence that are somehow related to deficiencies in the coordination of cognitive and affective systems.

The prefrontal lobes have long been seen as central to the coordination of cognitive activity (Case, 1992; Stuss, 1992), whose function is to sustain "many high-level metacognitive operations, such as self-evaluation, long-term planning, prioritizing values, maintaining fluency, and the production of appropriate social behavior" (Donald, 2001, p. 198). The reach and complexity of the prefrontal cortex have been further emphasized in recent work identifying important details of its structure and function

(Barbas & Hilgetag, 2002; Fuster, 2000; Fuster, Van Hoesen, Morecraft, & Semendeferi, 2000; Watanabe, 2002). In particular, the temporal integration of retrospective memory and preparatory set in the dorsolateral prefrontal cortex (Fuster, 2000) creates the conditions for a broader, more fully conscious control of cognition and behavior.

In other words, the narrow window of active awareness that is the focus of much of experimental cognitive science, which seems to undermine assertions of a broader consciousness with significant agency in decision making and planning, captures too little of the important cognitive action (Donald, 2001). In addition, the close connection and communication among regions of the prefrontal cortex that are more cognitive with those that have important linkages with emotional processing, especially the orbitofrontal cortex (Barbas & Hilgetag, 2002), support the view of the prefrontal cortex as a more general synthesizer of experience and governor of action. Thus, the role of the prefrontal cortex as not only an integrator of cognitive functions but also a governing regulator of emotion, attention, and behavior takes on special importance during adolescence in three ways.

First, patterns of individual differences in how cognition, emotion, and behavior become integrated during adolescence may well have a long reach with respect not only to the development of psychopathology but also to normative habits of mind (Keating, 1996a, 1996b, 1996c) that influence trajectories of competence and coping. Second, as already noted, the pubertal influences on many hormonal and neuroendocrine systems are dramatic (Angold et al., 1998), entailing the cascading reorganization of body and brain systems. Third, recent evidence from animal models has demonstrated the partial reversibility of damage acquired during early development, at both the behavioral and the physiological levels, as a function of enriched environments during puberty (Francis et al., 2002). In combination, this evidence points strongly toward both enduring (but not limitless) neural plasticity and the critical role of developmental experience in shaping future developmental trajectories in cognition and behavior (Nelson, 1999; Nelson et al., 2002).

Like early childhood, adolescence may well be a sensitive or critical developmental period for both normative and maladaptive patterns of development through the shaping of future trajectories and in the biological embedding of developmental experiences as the principal method through which this occurs (Boyce & Keating, 2004; Keating & Hertzman, 1999; Meaney, 2001a). Several aspects of development during this period are especially significant in this regard: the interdependence and developmental coordination of numerous cognitive elements, and of cognition with emotion and behavior; the role of puberty in a fundamental restructuring of many body systems; the apparent concentration of changes in the adolescent brain in the prefrontal cortex (which serves as a governor of cognition and action), together with the enhanced interregional communication between the prefrontal cortex and other brain regions; and the evidence for substantial synaptic pruning and nontrivial physiological reversibility of behavioral and neuroendocrine patterns arising from early developmental experiences.

Taken together, these developments reinforce the emerging understanding of adolescence as a critical or sensitive period for a reorganization of regulatory systems, a reorganization that is fraught with both risks and opportunities for trajectories of psychopathology. A key difference between the early development of regulatory systems that control patterns of arousal and soothing without necessarily invoking cognitive mechanisms and the maturing of regulatory systems in the adolescent transition is the potential for bringing such systems under conscious, self-aware, cognitive control. Recent work from both neuroscience and human evolution supports the view that adolescence is a focal period for this integration of regulatory systems and conscious control. It also supports the view that this developmental integration occurs under the direct influence of the social context, both phylogenetically and ontogenetically.

In a summary of recent work from cognitive neuroscience and evolutionary studies, Donald (2001) proposed three major transitions as levels of consciousness beyond the episodic awareness that we share with our nonhuman primate cousins. Each rests on continuing development and refinement of the executive suite that is concentrated in the prefrontal cortex (including its interregional connectivity): "(1) more precise and self-conscious control of action in mimesis; (2) richer and faster accumulation of cultural knowledge, in speech; and (3) much more powerful and reflective cultures, driven by symbolic technology" (p. 262). Note that each of these proceeds as a coevolution of brain and culture; indeed, the signal species characteristic of *Homo sapiens* can be thought of as cultural mind-sharing that activates individual minds (whose brains have been "designed" by evolution to participate in just such activity). The implication of these convergences is that there exist potentially homologous qualitative transitions in the evolution of the human brain, the nature of primate group interaction, and adolescent cognitive and brain development. The essence of the homology lies in the nature of human consciousness, including its phylogeny, ontogeny, and inseparability from culture and context.

Fully attained human consciousness is thus potentiated by key developments in the brain that are late arrivals in evolutionary history and become fully available for assembly in individual ontogeny only during the adolescent transition. But this potential assembly becomes actual only in close interplay with the surrounding cultural and cognitive web, in which the individual adolescent experiences culture not passively as an external entity, but as an active force (Swidler, 1986) that can be used to both define and achieve goals and serves simultaneously as a fundamental coconstructor of cognition and consciousness.

This coordination of cognitive and cognition-emotion subsystems into a more centrally governed metasystem is thus unlikely to be smooth developmentally or uniform in execution. As we have argued, understanding deviations from optimal developmental pathways will thus require attention to developmental trajectories preceding and subsequent to the adolescent transition, to the fundamental mechanisms of cognitive, emotional, and regulatory systems that are increasingly governed by a centrally coordinated executive system, and to the multiple contexts that coconstitute the integrated control systems. At the same time that we probe more deeply into neural and neuroendocrine circuitry, to get a full picture, we will need to gain a more precise understanding of the contexts that shape those central developments. It is to the role of context that we now turn.

THE ROLE OF CONTEXT IN THE DEVELOPMENT OF PSYCHOPATHOLOGY IN ADOLESCENCE

Contemporary adolescence is characterized not only by changes within the individual adolescent but also by changes in the contexts in which adolescents live and in their interactions with those contexts. As articulated in ecological models and developmental systems theory (Bronfenbrenner, 1979; Ford & Lerner, 1992; Gottlieb & Halpern, 2002; Thelen & Smith, 1998), individual development is embedded in processes of interaction with family, peers, school, neighborhood, and society. Adolescents in many modern societies spend increasing amounts of time outside the supervision of their parents and in the company of peers, make transitions to secondary schooling, begin to try out the worlds of work and romantic relationships, and engage with media in many forms, often for many hours a week (B. B. Brown & Theobald, 1999; J. Brown & Witherspoon, 2002; Hernandez, 1994; Steinberg & Morris, 2001). The nature of these contexts and the interactions of adolescents with them have been widely implicated in the development, maintenance, and prevention of psychopathology, although the conceptual models of how and why context and psychopathology may be linked continue to undergo transformation.

Central to the framework advanced in this chapter is the thesis that, during the transition from childhood into adolescence, and over the course of early adolescence in particular, contextual interactions may play a key role in protecting or exacerbating the adaptation of individuals who enter the transition with regulatory vulnerabilities. That is, during early adolescence, a developmental period characterized by a disjunction between arousal activation (which is high) and regulatory competence (which is not yet fully developed), individuals need the assistance and protection provided by a structured and supportive context. In concrete terms, adolescents need the presence of other individuals and institutions that will enable them to develop in healthy ways through a potentially challenging developmental transition by facilitating the development of regulatory competence and protecting from the harmful effects of deficiencies in regulatory skills until these capabilities have matured sufficiently. Concomitantly, this time is particularly risky for young people with little or no contextual support and those with high vulnerability due to regulatory deficiencies.

Context and adolescent psychopathology connections were studied initially in terms of risk factors for psychopathology and problems, such as delinquency, substance abuse, school dropout, depression, eating disorders, and suicidal behavior, all of which were linked in some way to "bad" environments (Dryfoos, 1990; Garmezy, 1983; Lerner & Galambos, 1998; Masten, 1988; Masten & Garmezy, 1985; Repetti, Taylor, & Seeman, 2002). Poor parenting, poverty, divorce, and many other stressful life events, as well as bad neighborhoods and deviant peers were each studied as risk factors for psychopathology. Extensive evidence pointed to unsupportive or dangerous environments and relationships as predictors of psychopathology, although the processes accounting for these outcomes were not well understood. It also became clear that risky conditions often co-occurred, such that some youth faced very hazardous transitions to adolescence, fraught with stressful experiences and little in the way of positive resources; psychopathology was often associated with high net or cumulative risk (Masten, 1988; Masten, Best, & Garmezy, 1990; Masten & Coatsworth, 1998; Rutter, 1979; Sameroff, 2000; Sameroff, Gutman, & Peck, 2003; Yoshikawa, 1994).

With the emergence of developmental approaches to psychopathology, thinking about the connections of context

and adolescent behavior problems has changed in several respects. First, the role of context in normative developmental transitions has received closer examination in efforts to use findings from research on typical development to inform our understanding of maladaptive developmental pathways. Second, more dynamic models of person-environment interaction have gained ground, emphasizing the role of adolescents as agents in the shaping of their own experiences and the importance of relationships in the development and course of problematic and positive behavior during adolescence. Attention is increasingly focused on how contexts and adolescents interact or coact to shape development leading toward or away from psychopathology, with more focus on regulatory processes and concepts such as self-regulation, coregulation, and scaffolding. Finally, there has been a movement away from research on single contexts considered in isolation toward the study of the ways in which multiple, interdependent, and sometimes nested contexts may interact to influence patterns of individual development. These changes reflect the influence of systems theory on conceptualizations of normative and deviant development and also herald an evolving framework for a developmental psychopathology of adolescence.

Over the past 20 years, since Hill (J. P. Hill, 1980, 1983) first published his framework for research in adolescence, there have been marked changes in the study of context in relation to adolescent development, and it is clear that more changes are on the way (Masten, 2001, 2004, 2005, in press; Roberts & Masten, 2005). Studies of traditional contexts, such as peers, families, and schools, continue, but the focus of work has shifted to more complex and dynamic questions. Contexts that had received little study before, including romantic relationships, work, extracurricular activities, and media, are now undergoing more intensive investigation. Emerging technologies have created virtual contexts for adolescent interaction, including electronic friendships, neighborhoods, fantasy worlds, and many other kinds of contexts and contextual interactions. These same technologies have altered the study of context-adolescent interaction as investigators capitalize on computers, cell phones, and pagers to assess the ongoing interactions of adolescents with their environments. This section highlights some of these changes, as investigators try to understand the nature of adolescent interactions with their environments—particularly the interplay of affective systems and context—and how these interactions may contribute to the etiology, maintenance, or prevention of or recovery from psychopathology and other problems in adolescent development.

Several overarching themes in the study of psychopathology and context in adolescence have emerged in the past decade. First, there is growing evidence that the role of context in the development of psychopathology is typically nonspecific. That is, it is difficult to find links between specific contextual stressors (either chronic or acute) and specific manifestations of dysfunction; divorce, poverty, maltreatment, exposure to neighborhood violence, and peer rejection, for example, are risk factors for many types of problems in adolescence (Steinberg & Avenevoli, 2000). Thus, it appears likely that specificity in the manifestations of emotional and behavioral disorder (i.e., why one individual develops depression but another develops alcohol dependence) likely reflects individual differences (genetic or acquired) in biological diatheses rather than differences in contextual experience.

Second, the impact of contextual stress on psychopathology is cumulative. Individuals whose lives are characterized by a greater number of contextual risks are more likely to show manifestations of internalizing, externalizing, or addictive problems than are those whose lives are characterized by fewer risk factors.

Third, there are significant links among contextual risk factors that make it difficult to study them as independent influences. Adolescents who grow up in dysfunctional family environments, for example, are more likely to experience poverty, attend inadequate schools, encounter antisocial peers, and witness neighborhood violence. By the same token, adolescents who enjoy one form of contextual benefit (e.g., supportive teachers) are also more likely to have lives that are characterized by multiple advantages.

Fourth, contextual risk exerts its impact on psychopathology through both objective and subjective means (Boyce et al., 1998). Thus, in research on context and psychopathology, it is important to document both the objective level of stress and the adolescent's subjective appraisal of it. This is especially important in research involving adolescents from different demographic groups, because the same stressor may be appraised differently by individuals with different backgrounds. What might be considered harsh parenting among middle-class suburban adolescents, for example, may be considered protective among impoverished inner-city youth. To the extent that the impact of parenting is mediated by the way it is interpreted by the adolescent, we would expect that parental strictness would have different effects in these different settings.

Fifth, a complete understanding of the role of context in the development of psychopathology necessitates that attention be paid to the interactive and nested relations among contexts. Until quite recently, investigators focused on one context at a time, such as the family in isolation from the school or neighborhood, or on the peer group as a context separate from the home or workplace. We know, however, that contexts interact in ways that may exacerbate, compensate for, or cancel out each other's influence on normative and atypical development. Additionally, contemporary research on contextual influence, reflecting the work of Bronfenbrenner (1979) and others, has documented the importance of examining the ways the influence of proximal settings, such as the family, are moderated by factors within the broader contexts that contain them, such as neighborhoods (e.g., Furstenberg, Cook, Eccles, Elder, & Sameroff, 1999; Leventhal & Brooks-Gunn, 2000).

Finally, adolescents are not the passive recipients of contextual influence, but are active agents who choose, transform, and recruit contextual resources. Unlike younger children, who have little control over where and with whom they spend time, adolescents are more active in selecting the contexts to which they are exposed; although adolescents have little say over their family or school environments, they choose their friends, decide whether to work or engage in extracurricular activities, and pick the media to which they are exposed. This fact poses a challenge to researchers interested in demonstrating causal influences of context on psychopathology, because often it is not clear whether it is the context that is driving the psychopathology or the reverse. Thus, for example, the links between externalizing problems and affiliation with antisocial peers may result from the self-selection of antisocial adolescents into deviant peer groups as well as the recruitment of alienated youth into deviant groups. Deviant peer association may then function to exacerbate antisocial behavior through reinforcement, modeling, opportunities, or combined influences of this kind. It is not easy to sort out causality when there is so much reciprocal influence. In addition, and operating above and beyond any selection process, is the fact that adolescents actually influence their parents, friends, teachers, and neighbors in ways that affect the home, peer, school, and community contexts, which then, in turn, influence the adolescent's development. An important but understudied issue is how, under what circumstances, and through what processes adolescents actively employ contextual resources (from relationships with parents, friends, and teachers to video games and Internet chat rooms) as a means of protection against the adverse effects of environmental stress and for the amelioration of psychological distress.

A detailed review of the vast literature on specific aspects of context that have been associated with various forms of psychopathology in adolescence is beyond the scope of this chapter. In the sections that follow, we highlight points of consensus and areas of converging evidence in different contexts.

The Role of the Family

Of the many contexts that have been studied in relation to adolescent psychopathology, none has received as much attention as the family. Parent-adolescent relationships characterized by warmth, support, age- and context-appropriate monitoring, and clear expectations for positive behavior—the kind of parenting known as "authoritative" in style (Baumrind, 1973, 1991)—continues to be widely associated with positive adaptation in adolescence (Steinberg, 2001). Conversely, families that provide little warmth, structure, or resources or that expose the adolescent to high levels of hostility may not only exacerbate risk for psychopathology, but also fail to scaffold successful transitions in adolescence, leaving their adolescent children unprotected during a challenging time of change (Ge, Lorenz, Conger, Elder, & Simons, 1994; Masten, 1988; Repetti et al., 2002). If is, of course, quite possible that parents who do not function well transmit genetic vulnerability to psychopathology along with providing a risk-laden or neglectful environment. This is a classic confound in diathesis-stressor models of psychopathology, and the issue has reemerged in contemporary debates about the importance of parenting in development (Collins, Maccoby, Steinberg, & Hetherington, 2000; Masten & Shaffer, in press; Repetti et al., 2002; Scarr & McCartney, 1983).

Nonetheless, research implicates parenting as a key mediator of adverse life experiences and psychosocial disadvantage on adolescent behavior (Bradley & Corwyn, 2002; Elder & Conger, 2000; McLoyd, 1998; Sampson & Laub, 1994; Yoshikawa, 1994). In these models, with compelling supportive data, adversity undermines parental functioning, which in turn affects adolescent functioning. Not surprisingly, adolescents who achieve more positive adaptation in the presence of adversity or psychosocial risk often have better-functioning parents or other adults who provide effective parent resources for them in spite of high-adversity exposure (Masten, 2001; Masten et al., 1999). Recent studies also hint at the potential role of parenting in scaffolding self-regulation skills in the transition to adolescence; in a recent study of competence development among rural African American adolescents living in poverty, the effects of effective parenting on competence in young adolescents was mediated by self-regulation in the adolescents (Brody, Murry, Kim, & Brown, 2002). Moreover, interventions to facilitate or protect the quality of parent functioning under adverse conditions appear to be effective in altering the risk for prob-

lems developing in children and adolescents (Forgatch & DeGarmo, 1999; Hawkins et al., 2003; Tremblay, Vitaro, Nagin, Pagani, & Séguin, 2003; Wolchik et al., 2002).

Recent studies of families also focus on indirect and possible long-term effects that families may have in protecting or harming development in adolescence indirectly, through their influence on the opportunities, peers, schools, and neighborhood resources available to their children. Long before the challenges of adolescence arrive, effective parents may facilitate the successes of their children in peer relations and schools, indirectly increasing the likelihood of bonding to prosocial peers and school engagement that may be a key to avoiding increases in antisocial and other risk-taking behaviors that tend to accompany transitions to adolescence (B. B. Brown, Mounts, Lamborn, & Steinberg, 1993; Collins et al., 2000; Galambos, Barker, & Almeida, 2003; Pettit, Bates, Dodge, & Meece, 1999; Wagner & Reiss, 1995).

It is also interesting to note that normative data on changes in adolescent-parent interactions through the transitions of early adolescence suggest some kind of transformation in coregulation within these relationships. A meta-analysis of studies of parent-adolescent conflict indicates that although conflict generally declines across adolescence, the intensity of affect characterizing these conflicts rises in early adolescence (Laursen, Coy, & Collins, 1998). Sufficient data are not yet available to discern subtle patterns or differentiate age, context, and pubertal effects in these parent-adolescent interactions. However, studies do corroborate the general idea prominent in many theories of adolescent maturation that reorganizations occur in parent-adolescent interactions around adolescence and that these transformations involve affect regulation. It is therefore important to understand how variations in parenting practices may contribute to the development of regulatory competence.

Peers as Positive and Negative Influences on Adolescent Development

In most modern societies, adolescents spend more unsupervised time in the company of their peers than do younger children, and it is widely accepted that peers play an increasing role in the lives of adolescents as compared to younger children (B. B. Brown & Theobold, 1999; Bukowski, Newcomb, & Hartup, 1998; Collins & Laursen, 1999; Hartup, 1996; Hartup & van Lieshout, 1995; Parker, Rubin, Price, & DeRosier, 1995; Steinberg & Morris, 2001). As children grow older, they typically have more freedom of choice about whom they associate with. Adolescents may choose peers who reinforce their own beliefs, enable them to explore new roles, or engage in exciting activities. They also may be recruited by peers for similar reasons. Thus, peers have increasing potential as part of the regulatory systems available to adolescents. Adolescents may self-regulate by actively seeking peer interactions; peers also may deliberately act to cheer up, calm down, or recruit a friend for illicit activities. Evidence suggests that adolescents actively select peer contexts that reflect their personalities or preferences and that peer groups in turn influence adolescents' mood states and behavior (B. B. Brown & Theobald, 1999; Cairns & Cairns, 1994; Collins et al., 2000; Dishion & Patterson, this *Handbook,* Volume 3; Tremblay et al., 2003). Teens in the popular groups at some high schools appear to have increased risk for substance abuse problems (B. B. Brown et al., 1993). In the Michigan Study of Adolescent Life Transitions (see Eccles, Barber, Stone, & Hunt, 2003), male and female seniors involved in team sports (often among the most popular youth in high school) reported more alcohol use and drinking problems than nonathletes, despite better academic achievement, enjoyment of school, and subsequent educational and occupational success. With respect to psychopathology, antisocial behavior can lead to rejection by normative peers in middle childhood and also to affiliation with deviant peers, who subsequently encourage negative behaviors ranging from delinquent activities to health-risk behaviors (Catalano & Hawkins, 1996; Deater-Deckard, 2001; Dishion, Andrews, & Crosby, 1995; Dodge & Pettit, 2003; J. P. Hill, 2002; Parker et al., 1995; Patterson, Reid, & Dishion, 1992; Tremblay et al., 2003). Other children may withdraw from social interaction with peers due to shyness or anxiety and become more lonely and sad as a result (Deater-Deckard, 2001; Rubin & Bukowski, 1998). It is interesting to note that anxious solitude may contain the growth of antisocial behavior in adolescence, suggesting that this variable (likely reflecting high inhibition or social anxiety) may function as a risk factor for internalizing problems and a protective factor for externalizing problems (Masten et al., in press; Mesman, Bongers, & Koot, 2001; Moffitt, Caspi, Harrington, & Miline, 2002; Pine, Cohen, & Cohen, 2000).

Peer-Family Joint Effects

One of the advances in the study of peer and family contexts in recent years has come in the form of considering how each of these systems may influence the effects of the other. Poor parenting may elevate the risk for association with deviant peers; concomitantly, lack of monitoring may increase unstructured time with antisocial peers, facilitating "deviancy training" (Bogenschneider, Wu, Raffaelli, & Tsay, 1998; Deater-Deckard, 2001; Dishion, McCord, & Poulin, 1999;

Parker et al., 1995). Peer relations have been found to increase the influence of negative parenting on externalizing behavior (Lansford, Criss, Pettit, Dodge, & Bates, 2003). On the positive side, close parent-adolescent relationships may enhance the likelihood of exposure to positive peer networks as well as the socioemotional skills to engage effectively with peers (B. B. Brown & Theobald, 1999; Collins et al., 2000; Sroufe, Egeland, & Carlson, 1999). Evidence also suggests that good-quality relationships with parents may moderate the influence of deviant friends (Galambos et al., 2003; Vitaro, Brendgen, & Tremblay, 2000).

Romantic Relationships

Another change evident over the past 20 years is the increasing attention to romantic relationships as contexts for adolescent development (Collins & Laursen, 1999; Furman, Brown, & Feiring, 1999; Steinberg & Morris, 2001). Romantic relationships emerge in adolescence, though they may remain exploratory until early adulthood; this domain can be conceptualized as an emerging developmental task in adolescence and a salient developmental task of early adulthood (Roisman, Masten, Coatsworth, & Tellegen, 2004). These special peer relationships, spurred by new motivational systems, pubertal processes, and a culture promoting adolescent sexuality and romance, offer a new realm of possibilities for adolescents to experience emotional extremes of happiness, excitement, disappointment, and despair. Romantic feelings appear to be powerful activators of behavior; concomitantly, romantic relationships appear to be powerful regulators of arousal and affect (Furman et al., 1999; Larson, Clore, & Wood, 1999; Maccoby, 1998; Richards et al., 1998). We noted previously that early maturing is a risk factor for a variety of problems; for some girls, this risk appears to be mediated by romantic relationships with older boys (Steinberg & Morris, 2001). Breakups of romantic relationships also may trigger great distress in adolescents (Larson et al., 1999). Recent work based on sexual selection theory suggests that peer group dominance among males and relational aggression among females are related over time to dating popularity in young adolescents (Pellegrini & Long, 2003). Though still limited, the growing literature on romantic relationships in adolescence suggests that these relationships may play complex roles in social development and the regulation of affect, with positive and negative ramifications.

Schools and Psychopathology in Adolescence

School contexts play a salient role in the lives of modern youth for many years and in multiple ways. The transition to secondary schooling in adolescence presents new challenges and opportunities for learning, peer relationships, extracurricular activities, and having fun, with all the attendant complexities of cognitive, emotional, social, and cultural processes (Entwisle, 1990; Roeser, Eccles, & Freedman-Doan, 1999; Roeser, Eccles, & Sameroff, 1998, 2000). Substantial progress has been made in documenting the significance of schools in the lives of adolescents (Blum, McNeely, & Rinehart, 2002; Eccles & Roeser, 1999; Hawkins, Catalano, Kosterman, Abbott, & Hill, 1999; Roeser, Eccles, & Sameroff, 1998, 2000; Stipek, 1997). Transitions into junior high school and high school often are accompanied by normative changes in motivation, attendance, involvement, and achievement.

Psychopathology has been linked to school failure and disengagement in various ways. For example, adolescents who are antisocial, anxious, or depressed may not go to school or perform well when they get there; academic failure may increase the likelihood of dropping out, affiliation with deviant peers, or internalizing symptoms; or youth may be victimized at school (Masten et al., in press; Roeser et al., 2000; Stipek, 1997). Perhaps the most striking conclusion to be drawn from recent studies of competence in the school context and either externalizing or internalizing symptoms in adolescence is the *salience* of academic success or failure as a mediator, outcome, and predictor of adolescent symptoms and disorders (Elder & Conger, 2000; Hawkins et al., 1999, 2003; Hinshaw, 2002; Maguin & Loeber, 1996; Masten, 2003, in press; Masten et al., 1995, in press; Roeser et al., 1999; Roeser, Eccles, & Strobel, 1998; Stipek, 1997).

Interventions to promote positive bonding to school and academic achievement have shown success, increasing academic attainment and reducing dropout and delinquency. The mediating processes by which these interventions work are not well understood, though increasingly, interventions are designed strategically to shed some light on the mediating processes. Hawkins et al. (2003), in the Seattle Social Development Project, have shown that multifaceted elementary school interventions increase positive bonding to school in the high school years, which is associated with school success and lower risk for multiple problems. A study of mentoring as an intervention by Rhodes, Grossman, and Resch (2000) suggested that the Big Brother Big Sister program improves relationships with parents along with school involvement and achievement. Mentoring may have some direct influences on school values and behavior, but these interventions also may provide indirect benefits in the lives of adolescents that are mediated by parent-adolescent relationships.

Recent attention also has focused on the role of extracurricular activities in adolescent development (Mahoney, 2000). Such activities may provide opportunities for triumphs and risk for tragedies, but also may serve the more mundane but important function of bonding youth to the normative school context and normative peers, with important socialization sequelae. Little is known about the general regulatory role sports and other activities may play in the healthy development of adolescents, though studies of the joys and stresses of sport involvement suggest intense possibilities for affect regulation, for good or ill (Gatz, M., Messner, & Ball-Rokeach, 2002; President's Council on Physical Fitness and Sports, 1997; Smoll & Smith, 2002). Structured activities of diverse kinds could play a powerful regulatory role in stress management and arousal regulation, may help adolescents acquire self-control and related regulatory competencies, and may serve to facilitate relationships with peers and coaches who can also play such regulatory roles.

Work as a Context for Adolescent Development

The role of the work context in adolescent development and psychopathology has also seen increased research over the past 20 years (Mortimer, 2003; Mortimer & Staff, in press; Roisman et al., 2004; Steinberg & Morris, 2001). Considerable attention has been given to the question of relative risks and benefits of work. In terms of psychopathology or positive adaptation, work may exacerbate stress and distress, increase self-efficacy, take time from schoolwork, or motivate youth to success in school. Generally, moderate work hours in the lives of ordinary adolescents who are succeeding in other aspects of their lives appears to have at least short-term benefits (e.g., extra money and self-confidence) and few costs. For some youth, steady low-intensity work during adolescence may also have long-term benefits in vocational development (Mortimer, 2003). However, working long hours at unskilled jobs may contribute to symptoms, either directly (stress) or indirectly, by contributing to school problems.

The extent to which work may contribute to regulatory competence likely depends on the nature of the work environment, the number of hours per week the adolescent works, and the extent to which working facilitates or interferes with the successful negotiation of other tasks, such as those affecting achievement in school (Roisman et al., 2004). In an appropriately challenging job with adequate supervision, where the adolescent is acquiring skills and not unduly stressed by demanding work hours, employment may contribute to the development of responsibility, time management skills, and self-confidence. In a menial job with inadequate supervision, where work is stressful and hours long, however, employment may contribute to mental health problems, alcohol and drug use, and diminished attachment to school (Staff, Mortimer, & Ugen, in press).

Community, Society, and Culture

One of the marked changes characteristic of adolescence in many modern societies is the increased level of mobility in society and the potential for engaging and being engaged by more aspects of community, culture, and society outside the family and school contexts. Recent studies have begun to address the potency of neighborhoods as sources of risks, assets, and moderators of adolescent development (Duncan & Raudenbush, 2001; Leventhal & Brooks-Gunn, 2000; Lynam et al., 2000; Sampson, Morenoff, & Gannon-Rowley, 2002; Sampson, Raudenbush, & Earls, 1997; Sampson, Squires, & Zhou, 2001). There are hints in this literature that social structures in neighborhoods may function as regulatory systems for the behavior of youth, although it is difficult methodologically to sort out the role of larger social systems from the influence of the individuals and families that compose them (Duncan & Raudenbush, 2001). Studies of resilience in youth at risk due to family adversity or poverty suggest that external regulatory systems in communities (provided by churches, boys' and girls' clubs, recreational centers and teams, etc.) may play a protective role for the development of competence (Masten & Coatsworth, 1998). Who chooses to engage such systems and why remains an intriguing mystery. Coaches and youth ministers may seek out youth, youth may seek out competent and trustworthy adults, or juvenile systems may assign youth to some of these connections. Yet, for these external systems to work, adolescents must participate, and it seems likely that the bonding of youth to positive community systems is scaffolded through the relationships they form with mentors and other program participants.

Macrosystem influences on the regulation of adolescent risk behavior and, accordingly, vulnerability to certain forms of psychopathology also are beginning to be studied. Examples include studies of cigarette tax policy on adolescent tobacco use (Flay & Petraitis, 1994), the impact of gun-control policies on access to weapons (Elliott, Hamburg, & Williams, 1998), the effects of condom distribution in school-based health clinics, and the impact of graduated driver's licensing policies on automobile accidents. Although these policies are rarely thought of as interventions designed to prevent or reduce psychopathology, they can be viewed as attempts to impose external regulation on individuals whose judgment and regulatory compe-

tence is not yet fully mature. One interesting but unstudied question is the relative effectiveness of policies designed to impose regulatory control on adolescents as a means of limiting risk behavior versus those designed to limit risk behavior by increasing adolescents' regulatory competence (e.g., through educational intervention).

Media and Virtual Contexts

Whereas many of the traditional contexts of adolescence development—involving family, peers, school, neighborhoods, and work—readily fit an embedded systems model of development, as proposed by Bronfenbrenner (1979) and others, other elements of context in adolescents' lives do not fit so neatly. Yet, these experiences may play an enormous and growing role in adolescent development. In particular, music, movies, and television, as well as the new virtual worlds of electronic games, web sites, and Internet chat rooms, saturate the lives of many adolescents many hours a day, penetrating most other contexts of interaction. The "media diet" (J. D. Brown, 2000; J. D. Brown & Witherspoon, 2002) of American teenagers reflects a rapidly changing and increasingly individualized context for learning, self-regulation, victimization, friendship formation, sex, violence, illegal activity, and self-discovery, among other processes. Teenagers clearly utilize music, phones, movies, games, chat rooms, instant messaging, e-mail, and other electronic media to meet all kinds of needs. Increasingly, these media can be tailored to individual desires, so that adolescents can fine-tune their own experiences. Concomitantly, the same strategies can be utilized by marketers to recruit teenagers as consumers, often with the promise of happiness or sex appeal through consumption of food or drugs or the purchase of goods and services. The role of these transactions in the development or avoidance of psychopathology, misery, antisocial behavior, or risk-taking behavior is only beginning to be considered, as concern grows about the unmonitored interactions of adolescents through these media on violence, depression, self-injury behavior, substance use, and many other problems or risky behaviors.

New Approaches to Context in Relation to Adolescent Psychopathology: A Summary

Over the past 20 years, there has been a rapid expansion of research and theory on the significance of context-adolescent interactions for adolescent development and psychopathology. Work and romantic relationships have gained more attention, as have the moderating and mediating roles of one context in regard to another. A profound change has occurred in the conceptualization of context in relation to adolescent development. Relationships, media, drugs, food, and activities, for example, are viewed as ways for adolescents to develop and exercise regulatory competence and to modulate levels of negative affect.

Our point is that adolescents recruit context to regulate their emotion, arousal, motivation, and behavior, sometimes deliberately and sometimes without any awareness of the process. To manage their affect, thoughts, and actions, adolescents listen to music, phone their friends, pick fights with their parents, ask romantic partners for advice, meet their classmates at coffee shops, drink alcohol at parties, play basketball, or go dancing. Conversely, contexts actively recruit adolescents. As adolescents in modern societies gain economic influence, more and more films, television program, games, clothes, drugs, food, and consumer products are marketed to them, often blatantly advertised for the purpose of regulating mood or arousal. In relationships and in virtual worlds of interactions, friends, romantic partners, and strangers may have ample opportunity to engage in coregulation of each other's affect and behavior.

Concerns about deviant outcomes from adolescent-context interactions have increased, perhaps in part as a function of the decreasing control of adults over these transactions. Major concerns include social contagion of maladaptive behaviors, such as violence, self-injury, depression, or suicide. On the other hand, emerging contexts for adolescent development, such as virtual friends and support networks, could conceivably offer just as many positive as negative opportunities (J. D. Brown & Witherspoon, 2002). The extensive and expanding contexts available to adolescents may be challenging and overwhelming or supportive and protective.

As adolescents, who might be viewed as novice adults, negotiate the many changes of adolescence and the transition to self-regulated behavior, they may call on people in the various contexts of their lives for help. At the same time, adults, especially parents, may deliberately scaffold this long-term transition to adulthood through provision of adequate structure, support, and opportunities to facilitate success. If developmental decalage occurs, with major differences in the functional maturity of affective, sexual, cognitive, and social systems utilized by adolescents to adapt, resources in the external context, in relationships, and in formal and informal institutions may provide compensatory or protective effects that temporarily close the functional gaps in emotional and cognitive maturity with and across individuals. Conceptualizing the role of context

in this way may offer important perspectives for interventions to prevent and ameliorate behavioral and emotional problems in adolescence.

CONCLUDING COMMENTS AND FUTURE DIRECTIONS

The framework we have advanced in this chapter articulates a new view of psychopathology in adolescence that is grounded in an emerging understanding of the ways neurobiology and context interact during the transition from childhood to adulthood. This framework begins from the premise that adolescence is characterized by an increased need to regulate affect and behavior in accordance with long-term goals and consequences, often at a distance from the adults who provided regulatory structure and guidance during childhood. From this vantage point, adolescence is a time of especially heightened vulnerability to psychopathology specifically as a result of disjunctions between and among developing brain, behavioral, and cognitive systems that mature along different timetables and under the control of both common and independent biological processes. These disjunctions, in turn, create gaps between affect, thinking, and action. Viewed from this perspective, symptoms of various types of psychopathology in adolescence can be profitably understood as reflecting difficulties in the coordination of emotional, intellectual, and behavioral proclivities, capacities, and capabilities. By all indications, adolescence may well be a sensitive or critical developmental period for both normative and maladaptive patterns of development through the shaping of future trajectories and in the biological embedding of developmental experiences as the principal method through which this occurs.

Although adolescence is a time of increased vulnerability to psychological dysfunction, the fact remains that only a minority of adolescents develop psychopathology. To be useful, then, any framework that purports to aid in our understanding of psychopathology in adolescence must account not only for the heightened vulnerability that is characteristic of the period in general, but also for the wide variability between individuals in whether and to what extent this vulnerability is ever actualized. Virtually all adolescents will experience the sorts of disjunctions between affect, cognition, and behavior to which we have alluded, but most individuals will weather these difficulties and move into adulthood having experienced no or few serious difficulties.

In our view, individual differences in emotional and behavioral dysfunction during this period inhere in differences among adolescents in the nature and extent of these disjunctions and in the availability of contextual support and the presence of contextual risk during times of heightened neurobiological vulnerability. Research on early maturing girls is a case in point. As we have noted, for example, early maturing girls are, on average, at greater risk for the development of emotional and behavioral problems than their on-time or late-maturing peers. This is likely because earlier pubertal maturation brings with it changes in arousal that precede, by a fairly long stretch of time, the development of the regulatory competence necessary to modulate these drives; this is the sort of disjunction between arousal and regulatory competence that heightens vulnerability to problems. Moreover, the physical changes that accompany puberty also elicit new interactions with context (e.g., attracting attention from older peers and unwelcome advances from adult strangers) that may be difficult for a young girl to handle. Yet, most early maturing girls do not develop psychopathology. This is because early puberty is a risk factor for psychopathology among adolescent girls only under conditions of specific contextual risk: in families that expose the adolescent to stressful life events, in schools in which older boys are present, in communities in which students are especially body conscious, and in cultures that place a premium on thinness (Steinberg, 2005).

The past 2 decades have seen considerable progress in our understanding of the most important sources of contextual risk and support. We now have a very good sense of what adolescents need in the family, school, peer, and neighborhood contexts to maximize positive youth development and minimize emotional and behavioral problems. There is an especially rich literature on familial risk and protective factors and, to a lesser extent, on the influence of peer, school, and work settings. Overall, the study of environmental influence on psychopathology in adolescence has yielded a solid basis for the development of preventive interventions and treatments, but research has focused largely on the influence of family and friends, and much work remains to be done on understudied contextual influences, such as those of romantic partners, neighborhoods, and electronic media.

In contrast to our understanding of the role of context in the development of psychopathology, considerably less is known about the neurobiological factors—both genetic and acquired, individual-specific and developmentally universal—that place individuals at risk for psychopathology as they move into and through adolescence. Scholars have long recognized that the biological changes of adolescence must play some role in the development of disorder, but until recently, this recognition has been largely nonspe-

cific. There is no doubt that today we are on the cusp of a biological revolution in the study of normative and atypical adolescent development—a revolution made possible by tremendous advances in the study of molecular genetics, endocrinology, neurotransmission, and structural and functional brain anatomy. These advances will enable the field to move beyond sweeping generalizations about the significance of puberty or of changes in certain brain regions in the development of psychopathology in adolescence and to begin to identify the specific aspects of pubertal maturation and brain development that are linked to specific forms of psychological malady. This will require a careful unpacking of puberty as a multifaceted phenomenon that involves endocrinological, neuroendocrinological, somatic, and social processes and an equally careful unpacking of brain development in adolescence that links maturational change within and across specific systems (note: *systems, not regions*) to changes in behavior, cognition, and affect.

Recent breakthroughs in neuroscience generate considerable enthusiasm for expanding knowledge on the mechanisms behind adolescent changes in behavior associated with successful or unsuccessful transitions in development. Although this process is widely known to be regulated by multiple factors acting across various levels, recent studies have begun to delineate the nature of such interactions. For example, specific genetic factors have been shown to moderate developmental trajectories following exposure to trauma (Caspi et al., 2002, 2003). Such concrete demonstrations of interactions between genetic and environmental factors provide insights for future work. Further studies are needed that delineate other examples of interactions between genetic or other person-specific factors and environmental factors as mediators of the adolescent transition. Moreover, following successful demonstration of such interactions, experimental studies are now needed that examine the effects of targeted manipulations on long-term outcome. For example, given evidence of gene-environment interactions, interventions designed to remove potentially noxious environmental effects might be expected to have more potent effects on one or another subgroup of adolescents. Finally, documenting interactions between genes and environments should increase efforts to delineate the path that extends from genetics to behavior, a path that must ultimately involve changes in specific neural circuits. Advances in neuroimaging techniques provide the tools for delineating relevant functional, developmental changes in underlying neural circuits that occur during adolescence (McClure et al., 2004; Monk et al., 2003; Pine et al., 2002, 2004). For such techniques to be used most effectively, further work is needed developing experimental paradigms sensitive to relevant behavioral dimensions manifest in the laboratory.

It is a well-worn cliché to note that progress in the study of psychological development, whether normative or atypical, will require interdisciplinary collaboration among scholars trained in different disciplines. But like all clichés, this one has many elements of truth to it. Despite its obvious importance, the biological revolution that is currently unfolding in the study of adolescence will not suffice in the search for a complete understanding of the development, prevention, and treatment of psychopathology during this stage of life. Biological vulnerabilities may set the stage for psychopathology, but they by no means determine its course. Biological vulnerabilities expressed in different contexts often lead to vastly different outcomes.

Nor will the answer to questions about the onset, nature, and course of psychopathology be found in the study of context alone. We have noted numerous times in this chapter that the sources of contextual risk and protection in adolescence are nonspecific and cumulative. A wide variety of risk and protective factors are associated with the presence or absence of a wide range of difficulties, and the likelihood of psychopathology increases as a function of the sheer number of risk factors in the individual's environment and decreases as a function of the sheer number of protective factors.

Future progress in the developmental psychopathology of adolescence demands an integration of research on brain, behavior, and context. This will require cross-training and collaboration of scientists who specialize in neuroscience, behavioral development, and influential contextual systems, including families, peers, communities, media, policy, and multiple aspects of culture. In this chapter, we offer a framework that we hope will launch many such efforts.

REFERENCES

Alexander, G. (1982). Functional development of front association cortex in monkeys: Behavioral and eletrophysiological studies. *Neuroscience Research Program Bulletin, 20,* 471–479.

Alsaker, F., & Olweus, D. (1993). Global self-evaluations and perceived instability of self in early adolescence: A cohort longitudinal study. *Scandinavian Journal of Psychology, 34,* 47–63.

Angold, A., Costello, E., & Worthman, C. (1998). Puberty and depression: The roles of age, pubertal status and pubertal timing. *Psychological Medicine, 28,* 51–61.

Arnett, J. J., & Tanner, J. (in press). *Growing into adulthood: The lives and contexts of emerging adults.* Washington, DC: American Psychological Association.

Arnsten, A. (1999). Development of the cerebral cortex: Stress impairs prefrontal cortical function. *Journal of the American Academy of Child and Adolescent Psychiatry, 38,* 220–222.

Avenevoli, S., & Steinberg, L. (2001). The continuity of depression across the adolescent transition. In H. Reese & R. Kail (Eds.), *Advances in child development and behavior* (Vol. 28, pp. 139–173). New York: Academic Press.

Barbas, H., & Hilgetag, C. C. (2002). Rules relating connections to cortical structure in primate prefrontal cortex. *Neurocomputing, 44–46,* 301–308.

Baumrind, D. (1973). The development of instrumental competence through socialization. In A. D. Pick (Ed.), *Minnesota Symposia on Child Psychology* (Vol. 7, pp. 3–46). Minneapolis: University of Minnesota Press.

Baumrind, D. (1991). The influence of parenting style on adolescent competence and substance use. *Journal of Early Adolescence, 11,* 56–95.

Bechara, A., Damasio, H., & Damasio, A. R. (2000). Emotion, decision making and the orbitofrontal cortex. *Cerebral Cortex, 10,* 295–307.

Bechara, A., Damasio, H., Damasio, A. R., & Lee, G. P. (1999). Different contributions of the human amygdala and ventromedial prefrontal cortex to decision-making. *Journal of Neuroscience, 19,* 5473–5481.

Benthin, A., Slovic, P., Moran, P., Severson, H., Mertz, C. K., & Gerrard, M. (1995). Adolescent health-threatening and health-enhancing behaviors: A study of word association and imagery. *Journal of Adolescent Health, 17,* 143–152.

Berman, K., Schmidt, P., Rubinow, D., Danaceau, M., Van Horn, J., Esposito, G., et al. (1997). Modulation of cognition-specific cortical activity by gonadal steroids: A positron-emission tomography study in women. *Proceedings of the National Academy of Sciences, 94,* 8836–8841.

Blum, R. W., McNeely, C. A., & Rinehart, P. M. (2002). *Improving the odds: The untapped power of schools to improve the health of teens.* Minneapolis: Center for Adolescent Health and Development, University of Minnesota.

Bogenschneider, K., Wu, M., Raffaelli, M., & Tsay, J. C. (1998). Parent influences on adolescent peer orientation and substance use: The interface of parenting practices and values. *Child Development, 69,* 1672–1688.

Book, A., Starzyk, K., & Qunisey, V. (2001). The relationship between testosterone and aggression: A meta-analysis. *Aggression and Violent Behavior, 6,* 579–599.

Botvin, G. (1991). Substance abuse prevention: Theory, practice, and effectiveness. In M. Tonry (Ed.), *Crime and justice* (pp. 461–519). Chicago: University of Chicago Press.

Boyce, W. T., Frank, E., Jensen, P., Kessler, R., Nelson, C., & Steinberg, L. (1998). The role of context in the development of psychopathology. *Development and Psychopathology, 10,* 143–164.

Boyce, W. T., & Keating, D. P. (2004). Should we intervene to improve childhood circumstances? In D. Kuh & Y. Ben-Shlomo (Eds.), *A life course approach to chronic disease epidemiology* (2nd ed., pp. 415–445). Oxford: Oxford University Press.

Bradley, R. H., & Corwyn, R. F. (2002). Socioeconomic status and child development. *Annual Review of Psychology, 53,* 371–399.

Brody, G. H., Murry, V. M., Kim, S., & Brown, A. C. (2002). Longitudinal pathways to competence and psychological adjustment among African American children living in rural single-parent households. *Child Development, 73,* 1505–1516.

Bronfenbrenner, U. (1979). *The ecology of human development: Experiments by nature and design.* Cambridge, MA: Harvard University Press.

Brown, B. B., Mounts, N., Lamborn, S. D., & Steinberg, L. (1993). Parenting practices and peer group affiliation in adolescence. *Child Development, 64,* 467–482.

Brown, B. B., & Theobald, W. (1999). How peers matter: A research synthesis of peer influences on adolescent pregnancy. In P. Bearman, H. Brückner, B. Brown, W. Theobald, & S. Philliber (Eds.), *Peer potential: Making the most of how teens influence each other: A report from the National Campaign to Prevent Teen Pregnancy* (pp. 27–80). Washington, DC: National Campaign to Prevent Teen Pregnancy.

Brown, J. D. (2000). Adolescents' sexual media diets. *Journal of Adolescent Health, 27S,* 35–40.

Brown, J. D., & Witherspoon, E. M. (2002). The mass media and American adolescents' health. *Journal of Adolescent Health, 31,* 153–170.

Bukowski, W. M., Newcomb, A. F., & Hartup, W. W. (1998). *The company they keep: Friendships in childhood and adolescence.* New York: Cambridge University Press.

Cairns, R. B., & Cairns, B. D. (1994). *Lifelines and risks: Pathways of youth in our time.* New York: Cambridge University Press.

Carskadon, M. A. (1990). Adolescent sleepiness: Increased risk in a high-risk population. *Alcohol, Drugs, and Driving, 6,* 317–328.

Carskadon, M. A. (1999). *Adolescent sleep patterns: Biological, social, and psychological influences.* New York: Cambridge University Press.

Carskadon, M. A., Harvey, K., Duke, P., Anders, T. F., Litt, I. F., & Dement, W. C. (1980). Pubertal changes in daytime sleepiness. *Sleep, 2,* 453–460.

Carter, C. S., Braver, T. S., Barch, D. M., Botvinick, M. M., Noll, D., & Cohen, J. D. (1998). Anterior cingulate cortex, error detection, and the online monitoring of performance. *Science, 280,* 747–749.

Case, R. (1992). The role of the frontal lobes in the regulation of cognitive development. *Brain and Cognition, 20,* 51–73.

Casey, B. J., Giedd, J. N., & Thomas, K. M. (2000). Structural and functional brain development and its relation to cognitive development. *Biological Psychology, 54,* 241–257.

Caspi, A., Lynam, D., Moffitt, T. E., & Silva, P. A. (1993). Unraveling girls' delinquency: Biological, dispositional, and contextual contributions to adolescent misbehavior. *Developmental Psychology, 29,* 19–30.

Caspi, A., McClay, J., Moffitt, T., Mill, J., Martin, J., Craig, I., et al. (2002). Evidence that the cycle of violence in maltreated children depends on genotype. *Science, 297,* 851–854.

Caspi, A., Sugden, K., Moffitt, T., Taylor, A., Craig, I., Harrington, H., et al. (2003). Influence of life stress on depression: Moderation by a polymorphism in the 5-HTT gene. *Science, 301,* 386–389.

Catalano, R. F., & Hawkins, J. D. (1996). The social development model: A theory of antisocial behavior. In J. D. Hawkins (Ed.), *Delinquency and crime: Current theories* (pp. 149–197). New York: Cambridge University Press.

Cauffman, E., & Steinberg, L. (1995). The cognitive and affective influences on adolescent decision-making. *Temple Law Review, 68,* 1763–1789.

Chugani, H. T. (1999). Metabolic imaging: A window on brain development and plasticity. *Neuroscientist, 5,* 29–40.

Cicchetti, D., & Rogosch, F. (2002). A developmental psychopathology perspective on adolescence. *Journal of Consulting and Clinical Psychology, 70,* 6–20.

Cohen J., Aston-Jones, G., & Gilzenrat, M. (2004). A systems level perspective on attention and cognitive control: Guided activation, adaptive gating, conflict monitoring, and exploitation vs. exploration, In M. Posner (Ed.), *Cognitive neuroscience of attention* (pp. 71–90). New York: Guilford Press.

Collins, W. A. (1990). Parent-child relationships in the transition to adolescence: Continuity and change in interaction, affect, and cognition. In R. Montemayor, G. Adams, & T. Gullotta (Eds.), *Advances in adolescent development: Vol. 2.The transition from childhood to adolescence* (pp. 85–106). Beverly Hills, CA: Sage.

Collins, W. A., & Laursen, B. (Eds.). (1999). *Minnesota Symposia on Child Psychology: Vol. 30. Relationships as developmental contexts.* Mahwah, NJ: Erlbaum.

Collins, W. A., Maccoby, E. E., Steinberg, L., & Hetherington, E. M. (2000). Contemporary research on parenting: The case for nature and nurture. *American Psychologist, 55,* 218–232.

Costello, E. J., Pine, D. S., Hammen, C., March, J. S., Plotsky, P. M., Weissman, M. M., et al. (2002). Development and natural history of mood disorders. *Biological Psychiatry, 52,* 529–542.

Dahl, R. E. (1996). The impact of inadequate sleep on children's daytime cognitive function. *Seminars in Pediatric Neurology, 3,* 44–50.

Dahl, R. E. (1999, January). The consequences of insufficient sleep for adolescents: Links between sleep and emotional regulation. *Phi Delta Kappan,* 354–359.

Dahl, R. E. (2001). Affect regulation, brain development, and behavioral/emotional health in adolescence. *CNS Spectrums, 6*(1), 1–12.

Dahl, R. E., Bernhisel-Broadbent, J., Scanlon-Holdford, S., Sampson, H. A., & Lupo, M. (1995). Sleep disturbances in children with atopic dermatitis. *Archives of Pediatric and Adolescent Medicine, 149,* 856–860.

Dahl, R. E., Pelham, W. E., & Wierson, M. (1991). The role of sleep disturbances in attention deficit disorder symptoms: A case study. *Journal of Pediatric Psychology, 16,* 229–239.

Dahl, R. E., & Spear, L. (Eds.). (2004). Adolescent brain development: Vulnerabilities and opportunities. *Annals of the New York Academy of Sciences, 1021.*

Dahl, R. E., Trubnick, L., al-Shabbout, M., & Ryan, N. (1997). Normal maturation of sleep: A longitudinal EEG study in children. *Sleep Research, 26,* 155.

Davidson, R. J. (2000). Affective style, psychopathology, and resilience: Brain mechanisms and plasticity. *American Psychologist, 55,* 1196–1214.

Davidson, R. J., Jackson, D., & Kalin, N. (2000). Emotion, plasticity, context, and regulation: Perspectives from affective neuroscience. *Psychological Bulletin, 126,* 890–909.

Davidson, R. J., Pizzagalli, D., Nitschke, J. B., & Putnam, K. M. (2002). Depression: Perspectives from affective neuroscience. *Annual Review of Psychology, 53,* 545–574.

Davis, M. (1992). The role of the amygdala in fear and anxiety. *Annual Review of Neuroscience, 15,* 353–375.

Deater-Deckard, K. (2001). Annotation: Recent research examining the role of peer relationships in the development of psychopathology. *Journal of Child Psychology and Psychiatry, 42,* 565–579.

Dennett, D. C. (1996). *Kinds of minds: Toward an understanding of consciousness.* New York: Basic Books.

Diamond, R., Carey, S., & Back, K. (1983). Genetic influences on the development of spatial skills during early adolescence. *Cognition, 13,* 167–185.

Dishion, T. J., Andrews, D. W., & Crosby, L. (1995). Antisocial boys and their friends in early adolescence: Relationship characteristics, quality, and interactional process. *Child Development, 66,* 139–151.

Dishion, T. J., McCord, J., & Poulin, F. (1999). When interventions harm: Peer groups and problem behavior. *American Psychologist, 54,* 755–764.

Dodge, K. A., & Pettit, G. S. (2003). A biopsychosocial model of the development of chronic conduct problems in adolescence. *Developmental Psychology, 39,* 349–371.

Donald, M. (2001). *A mind so rare: The evolution of human consciousness.* New York: Norton.

Drevets, W. C. (2003). Neuroimaging abnormalities in the amygdala in mood disorders. *Annals of the New York Academy of Sciences, 985,* 420–444.

Dryfoos, J. G. (1990). *Adolescents at risk: Prevalence and prevention.* New York: Oxford University Press.

Duncan, G. J., & Raudenbush, S. W. (2001). Neighborhoods and adolescent development: How can we determine the links? In A. Booth & N. Crouter (Eds.), *Does it take a village? Community effects on children, adolescents, and families* (pp. 105–136). State College: Pennsylvania State University Press.

Eccles, J. S., Barber, B. L., Stone, M., & Hunt, J. (2003). Extracurricular activities and adolescent development. *Journal of Social Issues, 59,* 865–889.

Eccles, J. S., & Roeser, R. W. (1999). School and community influences on human development. In M. H. Bornstein & M. E. Lamb (Eds.), *Developmental psychology: An advanced textbook* (4th ed., pp. 503–554). Mahwah, NJ: Erlbaum.

Elder, G. H., Jr., & Conger, R. D. (2000). *Children of the land: Adversity and success in rural America.* Chicago: University of Chicago Press.

Elliot, D. S., Hamburg, B. A., & Williams, K. R. (Eds.). (1998). *Violence in American schools: A new perspective.* New York: Cambridge University Press.

Entwisle, D. R. (1990). Success in school. In S. S. Feldman & G. R. Elliott (Eds.), *At the threshold: The developing adolescent* (pp. 197–224). Cambridge, MA: Harvard University Press.

Erikson, E. H. (1959). *Identity and the life cycle.* New York: W. W. Norton.

Flay, B. R., & Petraitis, J. (1994). The theory of triadic influence: A new theory of health behavior with implications for preventive interventions. In G. S. Albrecht (Ed.), *Advances in medical sociology: Vol. 4. Reconsiderations of Models of Health Behavior Change* (pp. 19–44). Greenwich, CT: JAI.

Ford, D. H., & Lerner, R. M. (1992). *Developmental systems theory: An integrative approach.* Newbury Park, CA: Sage.

Forgatch, M. S., & DeGarmo, D. S. (1999). Parenting through change: An effective prevention program for single mothers. *Journal of Consulting and Clinical Psychology.*

Francis, D. D., Diorio, J., Plotsky, P. M., & Meaney, M. J. (2002). Environmental enrichment reverses the effects of maternal separation on stress reactivity. *Journal of Neuroscience, 22,* 7840–7843.

Furman, W., Brown, B. B., & Feiring, C. (Eds.). (1999). *The development of romantic relationships in adolescence.* New York: Cambridge University Press.

Furstenberg, F., Jr., Cook, T., Eccles, J., Elder, G. H., Jr., & Sameroff, A. (1999). *Managing to make it: Urban families and adolescent success.* Chicago: University of Chicago Press.

Fuster, J. M. (1997). *The prefrontal cortex: Anatomy, physiology, and neuropsychology of the frontal lobe* (3rd ed.). Philadelphia: Lippincott-Raven Press.

Fuster, J. M. (2000). The prefrontal cortex of the primate: A synopsis. *Psychobiology, 28,* 125–131.

Fuster, J. M., Van Hoesen, G. W., Morecraft, R. J., & Semendeferi, K. (2000). Executive systems. In B. S. Fogel, R. B. Schiffer, & S. M. Rao (Eds.), *Synopsis of neuropsychiatry* (pp. 229–242). Philadelphia: Lippincott, Williams, & Wilkins.

Galambos, N. L., Barker, E. T., & Almeida, D. M. (2003). Parents *do* matter: Trajectories of change in externalizing and internalizing problems in early adolescence. *Child Development, 74,* 578–594.

Galanter, C. A., Wasserman, G., Sloan, R. P., & Pine, D. S. (1999). Changes in autonomic regulation with age: Implications for psychopharmacologic treatments in children and adolescents. *Journal of Child and Adolescent Psychopharmacology, 9,* 257–265.

Garmezy, N. (1983). Stressors of childhood. In N. Garmezy & M. Rutter (Eds.), *Stress, coping, and development in children* (pp. 43–84). New York: McGraw-Hill.

Gatz, M., Messner, M. A., & Ball-Rokeach, S. J. (Eds.). (2002). *Paradoxes of youth and sport.* Albany, NY: State University of New York Press.

Ge, X., Conger, R. D., & Elder, G. H., Jr. (1996). Coming of age too early: Pubertal influence on girls' vulnerability to psychological distress. *Child Development, 67,* 3386–3400.

Ge, X., Lorenz, F. O., Conger, R. D., Elder, G. H., Jr., & Simons, R. L. (1994). Trajectories of stressful life events and depressive symptoms during adolescence. *Developmental Psychology, 30,* 467–483.

Giedd, J., Blumenthal, J., Jeffries, N., Castllanos, F., Liu, H., Zijdenbos, A., et al. (1999). Brain development during childhood and adolescence: A longitudinal MRI study. *Nature Neuroscience, 2,* 861–863.

Gogtay, N., Giedd, J., Lusk, L., Hayashi, K., Greenstein, D., Vaituzis, A., et al. (2004). Dynamic mapping of human cortical development during childhood through early adulthood. *Proceedings of the National Academy of Sciences, 101,* 8174–8179.

Goldman-Rakic, P. S. (1987). Development of cortical circuitry and cognitive function. *Child Development, 58,* 601–622.

Gottlieb, G., & Halpern, C. T. (2002). A relational view of causality in normal and abnormal development. *Development and Psychopathology, 14,* 421–435.

Gould, E., & Tanapat, P. (1999). Stress and hippocampal neurogenesis. *Biological Psychiatry, 46,* 1472–1479.

Graber, J. A., Lewinsohn, P. M., Seeley, J. R., & Brooks-Gunn, J. (1997). Is psychopathology associated with the timing of pubertal development? *Journal of the American Academy of Child and Adolescent Psychiatry, 36,* 1768–1776.

Greenough, W. T., Black, J. E., & Wallace, C. S. (1987). Experience and brain development. *Child Development, 58,* 539–559.

Hankin, B. L., & Abramson, L. Y. (2001). Development of gender differences in depression: An elaborated cognitive vulnerability-transactional stress theory. *Psychological Bulletin, 127,* 773–776.

Hartup, W. (1996). The company they keep: Friendships and their developmental significance. *Child Development, 67,* 1–13.

Hartup, W. W., & van Lieshout, C. F. M. (1995). Personality development in social context. *Annual Review of Psychology, 46,* 655–687.

Hawkins, J. D., Catalano, R. F., Kosterman, R., Abbott, R., & Hill, K. G. (1999). Preventing adolescent health-risk behaviors by strengthening protection during childhood. *Archives of Pediatrics and Adolescent Medicine, 153,* 226–234.

Hawkins, J. D., Smith, B. H., Hill, K. G., Kosterman, R. F. C., & Abbott, R. D. (2003). Understanding and preventing crime and violence: Findings from the Seattle Social Development Project. In T. P. Thornberry & M. D. Krohn (Eds.), *Taking stock of delinquency: An overview of findings from contemporary longitudinal studies* (pp. 255–312). New York: Kluwer Academic/Plenum Publishers.

Hayward, C., Killen, J. D., Hammer, L. D., Litt, I. F., Wilson, D. M., Simmonds, B., et al. (1992). Pubertal stage and panic attack history in sixth- and seventh-grade girls. *American Journal of Psychiatry, 149,* 1239–1243.

Hernandez, D. J. (1994). Children's changing access to resources: A historical perspective. *Social Policy Report: Society for Research in Child Development, 8.*

Hill, J. P. (1980). *Understanding early adolescence: A framework.* Carrboro, NC: Center for Early Adolescence.

Hill, J. P. (1983). Early adolescence: A research agenda. *Journal of Early Adolescence, 3,* 1–21.

Hill, J. P. (2002). Biological, psychological and social processes in the conduct disorders. *Journal of Child Psychology and Psychiatry, 43,* 133–164.

Hill, J. P., & Lynch, M. (1983). The intensification of gender-related role expectations during adolescence. In J. Brooks-Gunn & A. Peterson (Eds.), *Female puberty* (pp. 201–228). New York: Plenum Press.

Hinshaw, S. P. (2002). Process, mechanism, and explanation related to externalizing behavior in developmental psychopathology. *Journal of Abnormal Child Psychology, 30,* 431–446.

Huttenlocher, P. (2002). *Neural plasticity: The effects of the environment on the development of the cerebral cortex.* Cambridge, MA: Harvard University Press.

Johnson, M. H. (2001). Functional brain development in humans. *Nature Reviews Neuroscience, 2*, 475–483.

Josephs, R. A., Newman, M.L., Brown, R. P., & Beer, J. M. (2003). Status, testosterone, and human intellectual performance: Stereotype threat as status concern. *Psychological Science, 14*, 158–163.

Keating, D. P. (1996a). Habits of mind: Developmental diversity in competence and coping. In D. K. Detterman (Ed.), *Current topics in human intelligence: Vol. 5. The environment* (pp. 31–44). Norwood, NJ: Ablex.

Keating, D. P. (1996b). Habits of mind for a learning society: Educating for human development. In D. R. Olson & N. Torrance (Eds.), *Handbook of education and human development: New models of learning, teaching and schooling* (pp. 461–481). Oxford: Blackwell.

Keating, D. P. (1996c). Human developmental diversity: A learning society perspective. In D. K. Detterman (Ed.), *Current topics in human intelligence: Vol. 5. The evnironment* (pp. 211–215). Norwood, NJ: Ablex.

Keating, D. P. (2004). Cognitive and brain development. In R. J. Lerner & L. D. Steinberg (Eds.), *Handbook of adolescent psychology* (2nd ed., pp. 45–84). Hoboken, NJ: Wiley.

Keating, D. P., & Hertzman, C. (Eds.). (1999). *Developmental health and the wealth of nations: Social, biological, and educational dynamics.* New York: Guilford Press.

Keating, D. P., & Sasse, D. K. (1996). Cognitive socialization in adolescence: Critical period for a critical habit of mind. In T. P. Gullota (Ed.), *Psychosocial development during adolescence: Progress in developmental contextualism* (pp. 232–258). Thousand Oaks, CA: Sage.

Keating, D., & Shapka, J. (1999). *Pubertal change, cognitive change, and the development of psychopathology in adolescence: Summary of current work: Vol. 1.* Prepared for the MacArthur Foundation Research Network on Psychopathology and Development. (Available from the first author, University of Michigan, Ann Arbor)

Kellogg, C. K., Awatramani, G. B., & Piekut, D. T. (1998). Adolescent development alters stressor-induced Fos immunoreactivity in rat brain. *Neuroscience, 83*, 681–689.

Kessler, R. C., Berglund, P., Demler, O., Jin, R., Merikangas, K. R., & Walters, E. E. (2005). Lifetime prevalence and age-of-onset distributions of DSM-IV disorders in the national comorbidity survey replication. *Archives of General Psychiatry, 62*, 593–602.

Kolb, B. (1999). Synaptic plasticity and the organization of behavior after early and late brain injury. *Journal of Experimental Psychology, 53*, 62–75.

Kolb, B., Forgie, M., Gibb, R., Gorny, G., & Bowntree, S. (1998). Age, experience, and the changing brain. *Neuroscience Biobehavior Review, 22*, 143–159.

Lansford, J. E., Criss, M. M., Pettit, G. S., Dodge, K. A., & Bates, J. E. (2003). Friendship quality, peer group affiliation, and peer antisocial behavior as moderators of the link between negative parenting and adolescent externalizing behavior. *Journal of Research on Adolescence, 13*, 161–184.

Larson, R. W., Clore, G. L., & Wood, G. A. (1999). The emotions of romantic relationships: Do they wreak havoc on adolescents? In W. Furman, B. B. Brown, & C. Feiring (Eds.), *The development of romantic relationships in adolescence* (pp. 19–49). New York: Cambridge University Press.

Laursen, B., Coy, K. C., & Collins, W. A. (1998). Reconsidering changes in parent-child conflict across adolescence: A meta-analysis. *Child Development, 69*, 817–832.

LeDoux, J. E. (1998). Fear and the brain: Where have we been, and where are we going? *Biological Psychiatry, 44*, 1229–1238.

Lerner, R. M., & Galambos, N. L. (1998). Adolescent development: Challenges and opportunities for research, programs, and policies. *Annual Review of Psychology, 49*, 413–446.

Leventhal, T., & Brooks-Gunn, J. (2000). The neighborhoods they live in: The effects of neighborhood residence on child and adolescent outcomes. *Psychological Bulletin, 126*(2), 309–337.

Lewis, D. A. (1997). Development of the prefrontal cortex during adolescence: Insights into vulnerable neural circuits in Schizophrenia. *Neuropsychopharmacology, 16*, 385–398.

Liu, D., Diorio, J., Tannenbaum, B., Caldji, C., Francis, D., Freedman, A., et al. (1997). Maternal care, hippocampal glucocorticoid receptors, and hypothalamic-pituitary-adrenal responses to stress. *Sciene, 277*, 1659-1662.

Loewenstein, G., & Lerner, J. S. (in press). The role of affect in decision-making. In H. Goldsmith (Ed.), *Handbook of affective science.* New York: Oxford University Press.

Luciana, M., & Nelson, C. A. (1998). The functional emergence of prefrontally-guided working memory systems in four- to eight-year-old children. *Neuropsychologia, 36*, 273–293.

Luna, B., Thulborn, K. R., Munoz, D. P., Merriam, E. P., Garver, K. E., Minshew, N. J., et al. (2001). Maturation of widely distributed brain function subserves cognitive development. *Neuroimage, 13*, 786–793.

Lynam, D. R., Caspi, A., Moffitt, T. E., Wikström, P., Wikström, P.-O. H., Loeber, R., et al. (2000). The interaction between impulsivity and neighborhood context of offending: The effects of impulsivity are stronger in poorer neighborhoods. *Journal of Abnormal Psychology, 109*, 563–574.

Maayan, L. A., Roby, G., Casey, B. J., Livnat, R., Kydland, E. T., Williamson, D. E., et al. (1998). Sleep deprivation in adolescents: Effects on emotional and cognitive processing. *Journal of Sleep and Sleep Disorders Research, 21*, 250.

Maccoby, E. E. (1998). *The two sexes: Growing up apart, coming together.* Cambridge, MA: Harvard University Press.

Magnusson, D., Stattin, H., & Allen, V. (1986). Differential maturation among girls and its relation to social adjustment in a longitudinal perspective. In P. Baltes, D. Featherman, & R. Lerner (Eds.), *Life span development and behavior* (Vol. 7, pp. 135–172). Hillsdale, NJ: Erlbaum.

Maguin, E., & Loeber, R. (1996). Academic performance and delinquency. *Crime and Justice: A Review of Research, 20*, 145–264.

Mahoney, J. L. (2000). School extracurricular activity participation as a moderator in the development of antisocial patterns. *Child Development, 71*, 502–516.

Mann V., Diamond, R., & Carey, S. (1979). Development of voice recognition: Parallels with face recognition. *Journal of Experimental Child Psychology, 27*, 153–165.

Martin, C. A., Kelly, T. H., Rayens, M., Brogli, B. R., Brenzel, A., Smith, W. J., et al. (2002). Sensation seeking, puberty and nicotine, alcohol and marijuana use in adolescence. *Journal of the American Academy of Child and Adolescent Psychiatry, 41*(12), 1495–1502.

Masten, A. S. (1988). Toward a developmental psychopathology of early adolescence. In M. D. Levine & E. R. McAnarney (Eds.), *Early adolescent transitions* (pp. 261–278). Lexington, MA: Heath.

Masten, A. S. (2001). Ordinary magic: Resilience processes in development. *American Psychologist, 56*, 227–238.

Masten, A. S. (2003). Commentary: Developmental psychopathology as a unifying context for mental health and education models, research, and practice in schools. *School Psychology Review, 32*, 169–173.

Masten, A. S. (2004). Regulatory processes, risk and resilience in adolescent development. *Annals of the New York Academy of Sciences, 1021*, 310–319.

Masten, A. S. (2005). Peer relations and psychopathology in developmental perspective: Reflections on progress and promise. *Journal of Clinical Child and Adolescent Psychology, 34,* 87–92.

Masten, A. S. (Ed.). (in press). Multilevel dynamics in developmental psychopathology: Pathways to the future. *Minnesota Symposia on Child Psychology* (Vol. 34). Mahwah, NJ: Erlbaum.

Masten, A. S., Best, K. M., & Garmezy, N. (1990). Resilience and development: Contributions from the study of children who overcome adversity. *Development and Psychopathology, 2,* 425–444.

Masten, A. S., & Coatsworth, J. D. (1998). The development of competence in favorable and unfavorable environments: Lessons from research on successful children. *American Psychologist, 53,* 205–220.

Masten, A. S., Coatsworth, J. D., Neemann, J., Gest, S. D., Tellegen, A., & Garmezy, N. (1995). The structure and coherence of competence from childhood through adolescence. *Child Development, 66*(6), 1635–1659.

Masten, A. S., & Garmezy, N. (1985). Risk, vulnerability, and protective factors in developmental psychopathology. In B. B. Lahey & A. E. Kazdin (Eds.), *Advances in clinical child psychology* (Vol. 8, pp. 1–52). New York: Plenum Press.

Masten, A. S., Hubbard, J., Gest, S. D., Tellegen, A., Garmezy, N., & Ramirez, M. (1999). Adversity, resources and resilience: Pathways to competence from childhood to late adolescence. *Development and Psychopathology, 11,* 143–169.

Masten, A. S., Roisman, G. I., Long, J. D., Burt, K. B., Obradovic, J., Riley, J. R., et al. (in press). Developmental cascades: Linking academic achievement, externalizing and internalizing symptoms over 20 years. *Developmental Psychology.*

Masten, A. S., & Shaffer, A. (in press). How families matter in child development: Reflections from research on risk and resilience. In A. Clarke-Stewart & J. Dunn (Eds.), *Families count: Effects on child and adolescent development.* Cambridge: University Press.

McClure E., Nelson, E., Zarahn, E., Leibenluft, E., Bilder, R., Charney, D., et al. (2004). A developmental examination of gender differences in brain engagement during evaluation of threat. *Biological Psychiatry, 55,* 1047–1055.

McLoyd, V. C. (1998). Socioeconomic disadvantage and child development. *American Psychologist, 53,* 185–204.

Meaney, M. J. (2001a). Maternal care, gene expression, and the transmission of individual differences in stress reactivity across generations. *Annual Review of Neuroscience, 24,* 1161–1192.

Meaney, M. J. (2001b). Nature, nurture, and the disunity of knowledge. *Annals of the New York Academy of Sciences, 935,* 50–61.

Mesman, J., Bongers, I. L., & Koot, H. M. (2001). Preschool developmental pathways to preadolescent internalizing and externalizing problems. *Journal of Child Psychology and Psychiatry, 42,* 679–689.

Moffitt, T. E. (1993). Adolescence-limited and life-course-persistent antisocial behavior: A developmental taxonomy. *Psychological Review, 100,* 674–701.

Moffitt, T. E., & Caspi, A. (2001). Childhood predictors differentiate life-course persistent and adolescence-limited antisocial pathways among males and females. *Developmental Psychopathology, 13,* 355–375.

Moffitt, T. E., Caspi, A., Harrington, H., & Milne, B. J. (2002). Males on the life-course-persistent and adolescence-limited antisocial pathways: Follow-up at age 26 years. *Development and Psychopathology, 14,* 179–207.

Monk, C., McClure E., Nelson, E., Zarahn E., Bilder, R., Leibenluft, E., et al. (2003). Adolescent immaturity in attention-related brain engagement to emotional facial expressions. *NeuroImage, 20,* 420–428.

Mortimer, J. T. (2003). *Working and growing up in America.* Cambridge, MA: Harvard University Press.

Mortimer, J. T., & Staff, J. (in press). Adolescent work and the early socioeconomic career. In J. T. Mortimer & M. Shanahan (Eds.), *Handbook of the life course.* New York: Plenum Press.

Nelson, C. A. (1999). Neural plasticity and human development. *Current Directions in Psychological Science, 8,* 42–45.

Nelson, C. A., Bloom, F. E., Cameron, J. L., Amaral, D., Dahl, R. E., & Pine, D. (2002). An integrative, multidisciplinary approach to the study of brain-behavior relations in the context of typical and atypical development. *Development and Psychopathology, 14,* 499–520.

Newman, J., & Grace, A. A. (1999). Binding across time: The selective gating of frontal and hippocampal systems modulating working memory and attentional states. *Consciousness and Cognition, 8,* 196–212.

Nowakowski, R. S., & Hayes, N. L. (1999). CNS development: An overview. *Development and Psychopathology, 11,* 395–417.

Orr, D. P., & Ingersoll, G. M. (1995). The contribution of level of cognitive complexity and pubertal timing to behavioral risk in young adolescents. *Pediatrics, 95,* 528–533.

Parker, J. G., Rubin, K. H., Price, J. M., & DeRosier, M. E. (1995). Peer relationships, child development and adjustment: A developmental psychopathology perspective. In D. Cicchetti & D. Cohen (Eds.), *Developmental psychopathology: Vol. 2. Risk, disorder, and adaptation* (pp. 96–161). New York: Wiley.

Patterson, G. R., Reid, J. B., & Dishion, T. J. (1992). *A social interactional approach: Vol. 4. Antisocial boys.* Eugene, OR: Castalia.

Paus, T., Zijdenbos, A., Worsley, K., Collins, D. L., Blumenthal, J., Geidd, J., et al. (1999). Structural maturation of neural pathways in children and adolescents: In vivo study. *Science, 283,* 1908–1911.

Pellegrini, A. D., & Long, J. D. (2003). A sexual selection theory longitudinal analysis of sexual segregation and integration in early adolescence. *Journal of Experimental Child Psychology, 85,* 257–278.

Pettit, G. S., Bates, J. E., Dodge, K. A., & Meece, D. W. (1999). The impact of after-school peer contact on early adolescent externalizing problems is moderated by parental monitoring, perceived neighborhood safely, and prior adjustment. *Child Development, 70,* 768–778.

Pine, D. S. (2003). Developmental psychobiology and response to threats: Relevance to trauma in children and adolescents. *Biological Psychiatry, 53,* 796–808.

Pine, D. S., Cohen, E., & Cohen, P. (2000). Social phobia and the persistence of conduct problems. *Journal of Child Psychology and Psychiatry, 41,* 657–665.

Pine, D. S., Cohen, P., Gurley, D., Brook, J., & Ma, Y. (1998). The risk for early-adulthood anxiety and depressive disorders in adolescents with anxiety and depressive disorders. *Archives of General Psychiatry, 55,* 56–64.

Pine, D. S., Grun, J., Maguire, E., Burgess, N., Zarahn, E., Koda, V., et al. (2002). Neurodevelopmental aspects of spatial navigation: A virtual reality fMRI study. *Neuroimage, 15,* 396–406.

Pine, D. S., Lissek, S., Klein, R. G., Mannuzza, S., Moulton, J. L., III, Guardino, M., et al. (2004). Face-memory and emotion: Associations with major depression in children and adolescents. *Journal of Child Psychology and Psychiatry, 45,* 1199–1208.

President's Council on Physical Fitness and Sport. (1997, May). *Physical activity and sport in the lives of girls: Physical and mental health dimensions from an interdisciplinary approach.* Washington, DC: Author.

Rakic, P., & Nowakowski, R. S. (1981). The time of origin of neurons in the hippocampal region of the rhesus monkey. *Journal of Comparative Neurology, 196,* 99–128.

Repetti, R. L., Taylor, S. E., & Seeman, T. E. (2002). Risky families: Family social environments and the mental and physical health of offspring. *Psychological Bulletin, 128,* 330–366.

Rhodes, J. E., Grossman, J. B., & Resch, N. L. (2000). Agents of change: Pathways through which mentoring relationships influence adolescents' academic adjustment. *Child Development, 71,* 1662–1671.

Richards, M. H., Crowe, P. A., Larson, R., & Swarr, A. (1998). Developmental patterns and gender differences in the experience of peer companionship during adolescence. *Child Development, 69,* 154–163.

Rilling, J. K., & Insel, T. R. (1999). The primate neocortex in comparative perspective using magnetic resonance imaging. *Journal of Human Evolution, 37,* 191–223.

Roberts, J. M., & Masten, A. S. (2005). Resilience in context. In R. DeV. Peters, B. Leadbeater, & R. J. McMahon (Eds.), *Resilience in children, families, and communities: Linking context to practice and policy* (pp. 13–25). New York: Kluwer Academic/Plenum Press.

Roeser, R. W., Eccles, J. S., & Freedman-Doan, C. (1999). Academic functioning and mental health in adolescence: Patterns, progressions, and routes from childhood. *Journal of Adolescent Research, 14,* 135–174.

Roeser, R. W., Eccles, J. S., & Sameroff, A. J. (1998). Academic and emotional functioning in early adolescence: Longitudinal relations, patterns, and prediction by experience in middle school. *Development and Psychopathology, 10,* 321–352.

Roeser, R. W., Eccles, J. S., & Sameroff, A. J. (2000). School as a context of early adolescents' academic and social-emotional development: A summary of research findings. *Elementary School Journal, 100,* 443–471.

Roeser, R. W., Eccles, J. S., & Strobel, K. R. (1998). Linking the study of schooling and mental health: Selected issues and empirical illustrations at the level of the individual. *Educational Psychologist, 33,* 153–176.

Rogan, M. T., Staubli, U. V., & LeDoux, J. E. (1997). Fear conditioning induces associative long-term potentiation in the amygdala. *Nature, 390,* 604–607.

Roisman, G. I., Masten, A. S., Coatsworth, J. D., & Tellegen, A. (2004). Salient and emerging developmental tasks in the transition to adulthood. *Child Development, 75,* 123–133.

Rolls, E. T. (1999). *The brain and emotion.* New York: Oxford University Press.

Roozendaal, B. (2002). Stress and memory: Opposing effects of glucocorticoids on memory consolidation and memory retrieval. *Neurobiology of Learning and Memory, 78,* 578–595.

Rubin, K. H., & Bukowski, W. (1998). Peer interactions, relationships, and groups. In W. Damon (Series Ed.) & N. Eisenberg (Vol. Ed.), *Handbook of child psychology: Vol. 3. Social, emotional, and personality development* (5th ed., pp. 619–700). New York: Wiley.

Rutter, M. (1979). Protective factors in children's responses to stress and disadvantage. *Annals of the Academy of Medicine, Singapore, 8,* 324–338.

Sameroff, A. J. (2000). Developmental systems and psychopathology. *Development and Psychopathology, 12,* 297–312.

Sameroff, A. J., Gutman, L. M., & Peck, S. C. (2003). Adaptation among youth facing multiple risks. In S. S. Luthar (Ed.), *Resilience and vulnerability: Adaptation in the context of childhood adversities* (pp. 364–391). New York: Cambridge University Press.

Sampson, R. J., & Laub, J. H. (1994). Urban poverty and the family context of delinquency: A new look at structure and process in a classic study. *Child Development, 65,* 523–540.

Sampson, R. J., Morenoff, J. D., & Gannon-Rowley, T. (2002). Assessing "Neighborhood Effects": Social processes and new directions in research. *Annual Review of Sociology, 28,* 443–478.

Sampson, R. J., Raudenbush, S. W., & Earls, F. (1997). Neighborhoods and violent crime: A multilevel study of collective efficacy. *Science, 277,* 918–924.

Sampson, R. J., Squires, G. D., & Zhou, M. (2000). *How neighborhoods matter: The value of investing at the local level.* Washington, DC: American Psychological Association.

Scarr, R. J., & McCartney, K. (1983). How people make their own environments: A theory of genotype: Environment effects. *Child Development, 54,* 424–435.

Shaywitz, S., Shaywitz, B., Pugh, K., Fulbright, R., Skudlarski, P., Mencl, W., et al. (1999). Effect of estrogen on brain activation patterns in postmenopausal women during working memory tasks. *Journal of the American Medical Association, 281,* 1197–1202.

Slovic, P. (1987). Perception of risk. *Science, 236,* 280–285.

Slovic, P. (1998). Do adolescent smokers know the risks? *Duke Law Journal, 47,* 1133–1141.

Slovic, P. (2000a). Rejoinder: The perils of Viscusi's analyses of smoking risk perceptions. *Journal of Behavioral Decision Making, 13,* 273–276.

Slovic, P. (2000b). What does it mean to know a cumulative risk? Adolescent's perceptions of short-term and long-term consequences of smoking. *Journal of Behavioral Decision Making, 13,* 259–266.

Smoll, F. L., & Smith, R. E. (Eds.). (2002). *Children and youth in sport: A biopsychosocial perspective.* Dubuque, IA: Kendall/Hunt Publishing.

Sowell, E. R., Delis, D., Stiles, J., & Jernigan, T. L. (2001). Improved memory functioning and frontal lobe maturation between childhood and adolescence: A structural MRI study. *Journal of the International Neuropsychological Society, 7,* 312–322.

Sowell, E. R., Trauner, D. A., Gamst, A., & Jernigan, T. L. (2002). Development of cortical and subcortical brain structures in childhood and adolescence: A structural MRI study. *Developmental Medicine and Child Neurology, 44,* 4–16.

Spear, P. (2000). The adolescent brain and age-related behavioral manifestations. *Neuroscience and Biobehavioral Reviews, 24,* 417–463.

Sroufe, L. A., Egeland, B., & Carlson, E. A. (1999). One social world: The integrated development of parent-child and peer relationships. In W. A. Collins & B. Laursen (Eds.), *Minnesota Symposium on Child Psychology: Vol. 30. Relationships as developmental contexts* (pp. 241–261). Mahwah, NJ: Erlbaum.

Staff, J., Mortimer, J., & Ugen, C. (in press). Work and leisure in adolescence. In R. Lerner & L. Steinberg (Eds.), *Handbook of adolescent psychology.* Hoboken, NJ: Wiley.

Steinberg, L. (1987). The impact of puberty on family relations: Effects of pubertal status and pubertal timing. *Developmental Psychology, 23,* 451–460.

Steinberg, L. (1988). Reciprocal relation between parent-child distance and pubertal maturation. *Developmental Psychology, 24,* 122–128.

Steinberg, L. (2001). We know some things: Adolescent-parent relationships in retrospect and prospect. *Journal of Research on Adolescence, 11,* 1–20.

Steinberg, L. (2003). Is decision-making the right framework for the study of adolescent risk-taking? In D. Romer (Ed.), *Reducing adolescent risk: Toward an integrated approach* (pp. 18–24). Thousand Oaks, CA: Sage.

Steinberg, L. (2005). *Adolescence* (7th ed.). New York: McGraw-Hill.

Steinberg, L., & Avenevoli, S. (2000). The role of context in the development of psychopathology: A conceptual framework and some speculative propositions. *Child Development, 71,* 66–74.

Steinberg, L., & Morris, A. S. (2001). Adolescent development. *Annual Review of Psychology, 52,* 83–110.

Steingard, R. J., Renshaw, P. F., Hennen, J., Lenox, M., Cintron, C. B., Young, A. D., et al. (2002). Smaller frontal lobe white matter volumes in depressed adolescents. *Journal of Biological Psychiatry, 52,* 413–417.

Stipek, D. (1997). Success in school: For a head start in life. In S. S. Luthar, J. A. Burack, D. Cicchetti, & J. R. Weisz (Eds.), *Developmen-*

tal psychopathology: Perspectives on adjustment, risk, and disorder (pp. 75–92). New York: Cambridge University Press.

Stuss, D. T. (1992). Biological and psychological development of executive functions. *Brain and Cognition, 20,* 8–23.

Swidler, A. (1986). Culture in action: Symbols and strategies. *American Sociological Review, 51,* 273–286.

Thelen, E., & Smith, L. (1998). Dynamic systems theories. In W. Damon (Series Ed.) & R. M. Lerner (Vol. Ed.), *Handbook of child psychology: Vol. 1. Theoretical models of human development* (5th ed., pp. 563–634). New York: Wiley.

Thompson, P. M., Cannon, T., & Toga, A. (2002). Mapping genetic influences on human brain structure. *Annals of Medicine, 34,* 523–536.

Thompson, P. M., Giedd, J. N., Woods, R. P., MacDonald, D., Evans, A. C., & Toga, A. W. (2000). Growth patterns in the developing brain detected by using continuum mechanical tensor maps. *Nature, 404,* 190–193.

Thompson, R. A., & Fox, N. A. (Eds.). (1994). Emotion regulation: A theme in search of definition. *Monographs of the Society for Research in Child Development, 59*(Serial No. 240).

Tobler, N. (1986). Meta-analysis of 143 adolescent prevention programs: Quantitative outcome results of program participants compared to a control or comparison group. *Journal of Drug Issues, 16,* 537–567.

Tremblay, R. E., Vitaro, F., Nagin, D., Pagani, L., & Séguin, J. R. (2003). The Montreal Longitudinal and Experimental Study: Rediscovering the power of descriptions. In T. P. Thornberry & M. D. Krohn (Eds.), *Taking stock of delinquency: An overview of findings from contemporary longitudinal studies* (pp. 205–254). New York: Kluwer Academic/Plenum Publishers.

Udry, J. (1987). Hormonal and social determinants of adolescent sexual initiation. In J. Bancroft (Ed.), *Adolescence and puberty* (pp. 70–87). New York: Oxford University Press.

Vitaro, F., Brendgen, M., & Tremblay, R. E. (2000). Influence of deviant friends on delinquency: Searching for moderator variables. *Journal of Abnormal Child Psychology, 28,* 313–326.

Wagner, B., & Reiss, D. (1995). Family systems and developmental psychopathology: Courtship, marriage, or divorce. In D. Cicchetti & D. J. Cohen (Eds.), *Developmental psychopathology: Vol. 1. Theory and methods* (pp. 696–730). New York: Wiley.

Watanabe, M. (2002). Integration across multiple cognitive and motivational domains in monkey prefrontal cortex. In D. T. Stuss & R. T. Knight (Eds.), *Principles of frontal lobe function* (pp. 326–337). New York: Oxford University Press.

Waterman, A. (1982). Identity development from adolescence to adulthood: An extension of theory and a review of research. *Developmental Psychology, 18,* 341–358.

Wolchik, S. A., Sandler, I. N., Milsap, R. E., Plummer, B. A., Greene, S. M., Anderson, E. R., et al. (2002). Six-year follow-up of preventive interventions for children of divorce: A randomized control trial. *Journal of the American Medical Association, 288,* 1874–1881.

Yoshikawa, H. (1994). Prevention as cumulative protection: Effects of early family support and education on chronic delinquency and its risks. *Psychological Bulletin, 115,* 28–54.

CHAPTER 19

White Matter Pathology, Brain Development, and Psychiatric Disorders: Lessons from Corpus Callosum Studies

VAIBHAV A. DIWADKAR and MATCHERI S. KESHAVAN

Brain development occurs along a complex yet systematic schedule dictated by a combination of genetic and epigenetic influences (Rubenstein & Rakic, 1999). Prenatal gray matter development is marked by rapid neurogenesis resulting in a proliferation of redundant synaptic matter during early postnatal development (Huttenlocher & Dabholkar, 1997). Redundant synaptic matter is subsequently pruned during the course of childhood and adolescence, reflecting a functional coupling between interactions with the environment and neurodevelopment (Lund, 1997). White matter development follows a complementary course with early postnatal myelination observed in the pons and the cerebellum, followed by myelination in the corpus callosum and its subregions and finally in white matter in the heteromodal association regions (van der Knaap & Valk, 1990). Neurodevelopment is a continuous process; in the absence of derailments due to deep or subtle pathology, the resultant output of these vastly complicated and interdependent processes of genetically driven development and sensory innervation is a brain that is balanced both in terms of its structural organization and in its functional specification

(Laughlin & Sejnowski, 2003; Rakic, 1999). However, this delicate balance is vulnerable to pathological insults that may have diverse origins.

BACKGROUND: NEURODEVELOPMENT

Neuropsychiatric illnesses are increasingly thought to result from processes of abnormal neurodevelopment at critical stages of the individual's growth (Lewis & Levitt, 2002; Marenco & Weinberger, 2001; Nasrallah, 1997). Several lines of evidence suggest this. Psychopathological signs of abnormal behavior are evident before the onset of frank psychosis, particularly during adolescence, and may be predictive of the onset of illness (Aarkrog & Mortensen, 1985; Keshavan, 1999; Keshavan, Dick, et al., 2002; Keshavan, Stanley, Montrose, Minshew, & Pettegrew, 2003; Montrose et al., 1997; Winters, Cornblatt, & Erlenmeyer-Kimling, 1991). A handful of cross-sectional and longitudinal studies have documented progressive changes in brain structure during adolescence in illnesses such as early-onset Schizophrenia, including accelerated ventricular expansion and cortical gray matter loss (Gogtay et al., 2003; Rapoport et al., 1997, 1999). Studies of young populations at genetic risk for illnesses such as

This work was supported in part by NIMH grants 68680 (VAD), 64023, 01180 (MSK), a NARSAD Young Investigator award (VAD), and a NARSAD Independent Investigator award (MSK).

742

Schizophrenia point to abnormal brain morphology and function of crucial cortical structures such as the prefrontal cortex and the superior temporal cortex that are qualitatively similar to those observed in first-episode patients (Job et al., 2003; Keshavan, Dick, et al., 2002; Keshavan et al., 2003). These and other lines of evidence motivate the search for developmental correlates of neuropsychiatric illnesses that may result from complex interactions among genetic predispositions, the environment, and alterations in programmed neurodevelopment (Lewis & Levitt, 2002; Tsuang, 2000).

Clearly, any number of facets of neurodevelopment may be studied to examine their impact on neuropsychiatric illness. The majority of studies have focused on changes in the trajectory of gray matter development measured using high-resolution magnetic resonance imaging (MRI), probably because synaptic (i.e., gray matter) activity is associated most closely with cognition and behavior. Furthermore, as mentioned earlier, the profile of gray matter change starting with synapse production and continuing on through neuronal and synaptic pruning during adolescence has been well established by experimental methods ranging from tissue analysis to analyses of in vivo MRI (Gogtay et al., 2004; Sowell, Thompson, Tessner, & Toga, 2001; Webb, Monk, & Nelson, 2001). Finally, accelerated synaptic pruning during adolescence (Feinberg, 1990; Keshavan, Anderson, & Pettegrew, 1994) is an important explanation for widespread reductions in cortical gray matter volume that have been reported in neuropsychiatric illnesses such as Schizophrenia and Bipolar Disorder (Lim, Rosenbloom, Faustman, Sullivan, & Pfefferbaum, 1999; Lyoo et al., 2004; Shenton, Dickey, Frumin, & McCarley, 2001). However, recent paradigm shifts have led to a departure from a focal lesion(s) model of neuropsychiatric illness to a view of these illnesses as being disorders of connections between brain regions. Therefore, there has been an increasing interest in the development of white matter and the role that altered white matter expansion or connectivity may play in psychiatric illnesses and disorders.

The maturation of white matter in the brain follows an orderly pattern that has been elucidated in both the early postnatal phase and through adolescence using MRI (Barkovich, 2000). Qualitative analyses have indicated early myelination in subcortical structures such as the pons and the cerebellar peduncles, followed by the internal capsule, the corpus callosum, and finally in corticocortical white matter tracks (Barkovich, Kjos, Jackson, & Norman, 1988; Barkovich & Maroldo, 1993; Girard, Raybaud, & du Lac, 1991; McCardle et al., 1987; van der Knaap & Valk,

1990). A significant increase in the absolute volume of cortical white matter has been reported through adolescence and young adulthood (Giedd, Blumenthal, Jeffries, Castellanos, et al., 1999), with an increase in white matter density particularly prominent in structures such as the internal capsule that may be associated with an expansion in motor and linguistic capacity in this period (Paus et al., 1999). White matter expansion in conjunction with programmed gray matter loss continues into young adulthood, by which time the ratio of cortical gray to white matter asymptotes, signaling a large degree of stability in the structural organization of the brain (Pfefferbaum et al., 1994). It is the simultaneous decrease of metabolically expensive gray matter along with the increase of metabolically inexpensive white matter that results in an "optimized" ratio of gray to white matter (Zhang & Sejnowski, 2000). As with cortical folding, the corticocortical connectivity provided by white matter connections enables the efficient computation and transfer of information in spite of the brain's limitations of finite volume (Karbowski, 2003). MRI investigations in the primate brain have revealed that the rate of increase of cerebral white matter expansion outpaces that in neocortical gray matter (Rilling & Insel, 1999), indicating the fundamental role of developmentally driven white matter expansion in cortical organization. Through this connective network, neuronal impulses are efficiently conveyed between cortical and subcortical regions that have been endowed with relative specialization for particular tasks through evolution. It is largely this interregional and interhemispheric communication that makes higher-order cognitive activity possible (Gazzaniga, 1989; Goldman-Rakic, 1988). Disturbances in communication are most likely to give rise to disturbances in higher-order cognitive processes that are the hallmark of many neuropsychiatric disorders (Lee, Williams, Breakspear, & Gordon, 2003).

Many neuropsychiatric illnesses such as Schizophrenia and Bipolar Disorder are marked by disordered thought and persistent cognitive impairment. These impairments in higher-order functions are among the core symptoms of these disorders and are thought to be predictive of outcome (Kuperberg & Heckers, 2000). Cognitive symptoms include impairments in social cognition (Insel & Fernald, 2004), lowering of working memory capacity (Goldman-Rakic, 1994), loss of executive control and planning, and impairments in attention (Elvevag & Goldberg, 2000; Quraishi & Frangou, 2002). The widespread pattern of these cognitive symptoms (particularly in Schizophrenia) suggests more than simply focal impairments to a few cortical structures. Rather, they suggest a fundamental dysfunction in the integrity of neuronal networks in the brain. This pattern of observed cognitive impairment has in part given rise to "disconnection hypotheses" (Friston, 1998; McGlashan & Hoffman, 2000), which suggest that neuropsychiatric illnesses arise not from focal insults to specific regions of interest in the brain, but imbalances in neural circuitry (Grossberg, 2000). This implies that it is not gray matter alone but also abnormal white matter that may be a core correlate of neuropsychiatric illnesses (Lim & Helpern, 2002), motivating the need to identify structural and functional impairments in cortical and subcortical white matter. Of the white matter structures in the brain, the corpus callosum is perhaps the most important from the perspective of its function, structure, and development.

THE CORPUS CALLOSUM: DEVELOPMENT AND INFORMATION PROCESSING

The corpus callosum is the principal commissure connecting the right and left hemispheres of the brain. The structure (most clearly visible in a midsagittal MRI section; see Figure 19.1a) consists of packed bundles of white matter fibers arranged along the midbrain and connecting the hemispheres. Developmental increases in callosal size are largely related to increases in axonal size and myelination (S. Clarke, Kraftsik, Van der Loos, & Innocenti, 1989); therefore, illnesses that may be associated with abnormal axonal size, number, or myelination, such as Schizophrenia, may be particularly vulnerable to callosal pathology.

The corpus callosum remains largely responsible for the interhemispheric integration of sensory, motor, and cognitive experiences (Seymour, Reuter-Lorenz, & Gazzaniga, 1994), and its developed nature is thought to largely enable conscious experience and performance (Dimond, 1976; Gazzaniga, 2000). In addition, fibers in the corpus callosum are topographically organized along an anterior to posterior scheme (Figure 19.1b). As shown, the callosum can be divided into subdivisions: the genu, the body, the isthmus, and the splenium. Postmortem tissue analyses have revealed systematic associations between callosal subregions and interconnectivity between hemispheric regions as Wallerian degeneration in callosal subregions are associated with specific cortical lesions due to infarctions or contusions. Degeneration of the genu was associated with prefrontal cortical infarctions, the body with temporoparietal infarctions, and the splenium with temporo-occipital infarctions (deLacoste, Kirkpatrick, & Ross, 1985). These and other investigations in humans and other primates have established that the interhemispheric

transfer of white matter bundles is spatially organized in the corpus callosum to broadly reflect cortical neuroanatomy (Aboitz, Scheibel, Fisher, & Zaidel, 1992; LaMantia & Rakic, 1990; Pandya & Seltzer, 1986). The macro organization of callosal connections promotes broad flexibility and efficiency of interhemispheric connections (Innocenti, Aggoun-Zouaoui, & Lehmann, 1995), and it has been proposed that the development of the corpus callosum in humans has enabled a more detailed pattern of hemispheric specialization and a more efficient use of intrahemispheric resources (Gazzaniga, 2000). An analysis of the callosum and its subregions may provide useful models of cortical development generally (Innocenti, 1994; Keshavan, Diwadkar, DeBellis, et al., 2002). By corollary, abnormalities in callosal connections may indicate more general impairments in corticocortical connections that may arise from altered neurodevelopment (Innocenti, Ansermet, & Parnas, 2003).

The corpus callosum has a rich developmental profile, maturing from early neonatal development well into the 3rd

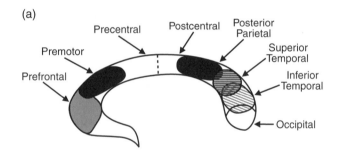

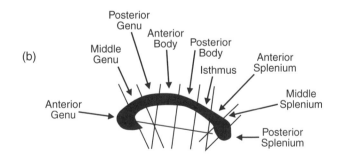

Figure 19.1 Histological based topographic relationships between the corpus callosum sub-regions (shaded and hashed regions) and labeled regions of the neocortex (Witelson, 1989) are shown (a). Morphometric schemes that have been used by our group and others to sub-divided the corpus callosum in its midsagittal section show good correspondence with the known topographic mapping (b). Adapted from "Abnormalities of the Corpus Callosum in First Episode, Treatment Naive Schizophrenia," by M. S. Keshavan, V. A. Diwadkar, K. Harenski, Rosenberg, et al., 2002, *Journal of Neurology, Neurosurgery, and Psychiatry, 72*(6), pp. 757–760.

decade of life. At birth, the corpus callosum is relatively iso-intense compared to other white matter, with its intensity in T_1-weighted structural MRI images increasing rapidly within the first 8 months of postnatal development (Ballesteros, Hansen, & Soila, 1993; Georgy, Hesselink, & Jernigan, 1993). This increase in intensity is most likely related to profound changes in myelination and axonal development (Barkovich, 2000; Holland, Haas, Norman, Brant-Zawadzki, & Newton, 1986) and may relate to increased corticocortical and interhemispheric functional organization, particularly during childhood and adolescence (Giedd, 1999). Both cross-sectional and longitudinal studies have documented systematic structural growth during childhood and adolescence (DeBellis et al., 2001). Age-related correlations in cross-sectional samples (ages 4 to 18) are particularly notable in the splenium and isthmus (Rajapakse et al., 1996), and longitudinal studies in the same age range have confirmed systematic expansion of mid- and posterior callosal regions (Giedd, Blumenthal, Jeffries, Rajapakse, et al., 1999). Recent studies of callosal expansion have modified our understanding of the extent of the neurodevelopmental period as increases in callosal size have been reported up to the 4th decade of life (Pujol, Vendrell, Junque, Marti-Vilalta, & Capdevila, 1993), though the estimated rate of change, which is highest in childhood, decreases through adolescence and adulthood (Keshavan, Diwadkar, DeBellis, et al., 2002).

The known developmental profile of the corpus callosum in normative development has implications for neuropsychiatric illnesses and disorders. As alluded to earlier, many of these conditions are thought to be mediated by abnormal neurodevelopment at critical periods. In particular, vulnerability to Schizophrenia increases through adolescence, with the highest incidence coming in young adulthood. Abnormal callosal development may contribute to cortical disconnection, which is increasingly being seen as a core feature of the neurobiology of the illness (McGlashan & Hoffman, 2000). Furthermore, the critical neurodevelopmental period in psychiatric illness may extend beyond late adolescence and young adulthood, as initially thought. Recent neurobiological investigations have revealed developmental effects beyond adolescence (Bartzokis, 2002), findings that are relevant given that callosal development extends at least into the 4th decade of life (Pujol et al., 1993). Callosal development is also related to obstetric complications and environmental and cognitive influences, which are all associated with psychiatric disorders. For example, preterm children show marked abnormalities in callosal development (Stewart et al., 1999). Callosal width has been shown to be a function of literacy; illiterate subjects have thinner callosa

(Castro-Caldas et al., 1999). Callosal size has also been related to environmental and social effects. Monkeys reared in artificial and impoverished social environments show immature development of the corpus callosum compared to monkeys reared in more naturalistic and socially rich environments (Sanchez, Hearn, Do, Rilling, & Herndon, 1998). Such studies assume particular relevance in the context of illnesses such as Schizophrenia, mood disorders, and Autism, which may be associated with an aberrant pattern of neuroregulatory development as a result of abnormal social interaction during the critical stages of development. However, the modulatory role of development in the corpus callosum in psychiatric illness remains understudied.

Several assumptions regarding the corpus callosum and its role in information processing in mental illness have been made. Principal among them is the idea that interhemispheric connectivity in psychoses may be altered, either too much or, more likely, too little (David, 1994; Schrift, Bandla, Shah, & Taylor, 1986). Numerous psychological experiments and biological studies have been applied to answering these questions (Coger & Serafetinides, 1990). However, the evidence remains unclear, and it is not obvious how to reconcile findings from psychological experiments (in illnesses such as Schizophrenia) with the findings from MRI-based anatomical studies. Psychological studies on the integrity of the corpus callosum have used tasks that study patterns of the interhemispheric transfer of information.

The interhemispheric transfer of information has typically been studied using dichotic listening or split visual field paradigms. In these studies, information required for making judgments about stimuli is divided, with partial information being presented to each hemisphere of the brain; the information must then be integrated across hemispheres to facilitate a response (Baynes, Eliassen, Lutsep, & Gazzaniga, 1998). Alternatively, competing information is presented to each hemisphere, and it is presumed that interhemispheric integration results in response interference (David, 1993). Studies on facilitation have revealed decreased performance in Schizophrenia patients when information was presented to opposite visual hemifields or different hands (Carr, 1980; Craft, Willerman, & Bigler, 1987; Dimond, Scammell, Pryce, Huws, & Gray, 1979; Green, 1978). These results suggest that patients are impaired when required to make judgments based on the interhemispheric integration of information, therefore implying reduced callosal integrity. Studies on response inhibition using Stroop interference tasks have suggested an opposite pattern of interhemispheric transfer. In conditions in which the interhemispheric transfer of information would impede performance, Schizophrenia patients performed worse than controls (David, 1993). The decrease in performance is attributed to increased response interference resulting from increased callosal information transfer. These results appear difficult to reconcile. However, recent experiments suggest a possible dichotomy in callosal transfer during conscious or automatic tasks. Patients may be particularly deficient when interhemispheric transfer must be done consciously, as in integration tasks, but may evince an opposite pattern during unconscious processing, such as during the interference tasks (Narr, Green, Capetillo-Cunliffe, Toga, & Zaidel, 2003).

Abnormal interhemispheric integration has also been associated with some of the core symptoms in Schizophrenia, specifically Schneiderian delusions (Nasrallah, 1985). The hypothesized mechanism for this is that a lack of appropriate integration may lead to a disinhibition of "awareness" between the two hemispheres, leading to a lack of unity of conscious experience. The result of this disinhibition may be an increase in positive symptoms such as delusions and thought insertions, which arise from the impaired brain's inability to appropriately unify interhemispheric information into an undifferentiated percept. This theory is highly exploratory but is logically consistent with both the neuropsychological evidence and the phenotypic expressions of Schizophrenia.

CORPUS CALLOSUM AND NEUROPSYCHIATRIC ILLNESS

Perhaps the most informative studies on the callosum are those that use MRI to assess structure in vivo. We present a selective review of studies of callosal structure in three major areas of neuropsychiatric illness: Schizophrenia, mood disorders, and developmental disorders (with a focus on Autism). The neurodevelopmental bases of these disorders has either been widely established (e.g., Autism) or largely accepted as likely (e.g., Schizophrenia and mood disorders; Harrison, 2002; Lewis & Levitt, 2002). Further, all three may be associated with disturbances in the integrity of key neural networks within the cortex and between cortical and subcortical regions (Andreasen et al., 1999; Drevets et al., 1992; C. Frith, 2004). Impaired communication is suggestive of white matter pathology or impairment, making the corpus callosum an important candidate region for inquiry.

Schizophrenia

Schizophrenia is a particularly devastating mental illness marked by severe deficits in cognition and thought, disor-

dered thinking, and generally poor mental function. The illness is thought to be of polygenic origin and in part epigenetically expressed in abnormal neurodevelopment (Lewis & Levitt, 2002; Petronis, 2004). The widespread cognitive and thought impairments that are observed have led to the idea of Schizophrenia as an illness of disordered neurocircuitry or connectivity (Friston, 1999; Harrison, 1999; McGlashan & Hoffman, 2000; Selemon & Goldman-Rakic, 1999). Several abnormal pathways have been proposed, including the corticothalamic (Glantz & Lewis, 2000), corticothalamic-cerebellar (Andreasen, 1999), and corticocortical (Selemon & Goldman-Rakic, 1999). Recent studies have gone beyond looking at the loss of neuropil or decreases in the dendritic spine density of pyramidal neurons, and have shown extensive abnormalities in MRI-measured white matter integrity. The corpus callosum is a natural candidate for analyses of possible pathology.

The role of callosal abnormalities in Schizophrenia in particular and mental illness in general has been long suspected (B. Clarke, 1987), and several lines of work have provided experimental evidence of the relevance of its pathology in Schizophrenia. Whereas healthy brains are characterized by systematic asymmetric cortical organization in specific structures (Galuske, Schlote, Bratzke, & Singer, 2000), Schizophrenia is characterized by alterations in the normal patterns of structural and functional cerebral asymmetry (Crow, Colter, Frith, Johnstone, & Owens, 1989; Sommer, Ramsey, & Kahn, 2001). Patients show altered cerebral volumes and patterns of fMRI-measured activation during language tasks and decreases in right-handed preference (Delisi et al., 2002). The altered pattern of cerebral asymmetry is suggestive of altered interhemispheric pathways. More selective white matter imaging techniques have implicated disordered white matter connectivity in Schizophrenia, supporting the hypothesis of dysfunctional connectivity in the illness (Friston, 1999; Lim, Hedehus, et al., 1999; Lim & Helpern, 2002) and suggesting a role of callosal dysfunction in the illness. Investigations of callosal dysfunction in Schizophrenia have been based on neurobiological and behavioral approaches.

Studies on Callosal Tissue Integrity

Until recently, probing the integrity of neural tissue in psychiatric illness was restricted to the use of postmortem analyses of patient brains. The earliest study of postmortem chronic Schizophrenia patient brains suggested a thickening of the corpus callosum (Rosenthal & Bigelow, 1972), with subsequent reanalysis and remeasurement of the data indicating an increased effect in the anterior section of the structure, presumably encompassing the genu and the body (Bigelow, Nasrallah, & Rauscher, 1983).

However, negative studies have shown an absence of differences in axonal counts between patients and controls (Casanova et al., 1989). Generally consistent with these findings, it has been argued that Schizophrenia is characterized by unique myelinated interhemispheric pathways not observed in healthy control subjects, resulting in hyperconnective interhemispheric interaction (Randall, 1980) or by misconnections between late-evolving brain regions such as the prefrontal and temporal cortices (Crow, 1998). More recent postmortem studies have identified selective reductions in axonal density across the subregions of the structure in the brains of female patients, suggesting subtle gender-related pathologies, with a decrease in the number of axons (Highley et al., 1999). These findings (although limited to female patients) are inconsistent with the hyperconnective idea, particularly in the genu (connecting the prefrontal cortex). Postmortem studies have suffered from the confounding of possible prolonged illness-related effects or medication effects on brain pathology; these problems are alleviated by in vivo MRI techniques.

MRI techniques are as yet imperfectly suited to assess in vivo tissue morphology; however, the selective application of structural and diffusion tensor imaging has proven informative. Signal intensities in T_1-weighted images are general and nonspecific measures of tissue integrity and are sensitive to quantities of MR-visible water, which may in turn be revealing markers of tissue pathology (Diwadkar & Keshavan, 2002).

MRI signal intensity analyses have provided evidence of systematic changes in signal intensity with age across callosal substructures (Keshavan, Diwadkar, DeBellis, et al., 2002), plausibly associated with demonstrated changes in age-related myelination in the structure (S. Clarke et al., 1989). Analysis of callosal substructures in Schizophrenia showed significant decreases in signal intensity across most of the subregions—the genu, body, and isthmus (excluding the splenium)—suggesting an alteration in the integrity of white matter, possibly resulting from decreased myelination or microtubular density of callosal white matter (Diwadkar, DeBellis, Sweeney, Pettegrew, & Keshavan, 2004). These changes appear to be in part developmentally mediated. Age-related changes observed in controls are absent in patients, indicating that the continually developing profile of the structure may be arrested in individuals with the illness. Voxel-based analyses have provided evidence of statistical relationships between clinical symptoms and callosal white matter density. Reductions in white matter density have been documented in the genu of the corpus callosum (Hulshoff Pol et al., 2004), indicating possibly aberrant interhemispheric transfer between the frontal lobes. Significant negative correlations between reality distortion scores

measured from the Scale for the Assessment of Positive Symptoms (SAPS) subscales for hallucinations and delusions (Andreasen, 1984) and white matter density across the inferior surface of the corpus callosum have been reported, suggesting that increases in the magnitude of reality distortion are related to possible decreases in callosal integrity (Wright et al., 1995).

The nonspecificity of T_1-weighted images can be overcome by the use of more specific techniques, such as diffusion tensor imaging (DTI; Rowley, Grant, & Roberts, 1999) or magnetization transfer imaging (MTI; van Buchem & Tofts, 2000). DTI is sensitive to the diffusion of water in the region of myelin sheaths, membranes, and white matter tracts. Neuropathology of white matter can result in changes in the patterns of anisotropic diffusion of water, leading to altered measurements of diffusion in DTI. Similarly, MTI depends on the transfer of magnetization between relatively mobile protons present in water, for example, and protons bound to macromolecules, fiber tracts, and myelin, and the transfer of magnetization is sensitive to changes in tissue integrity.

Both DTI and MTI are sensitive to age-related changes in white matter development, particularly in the corpus callosum (Sullivan & Pfefferbaum, 2003). Recent studies have documented age-related increases in fractional anisotropy (signifying better organization of white matter) in the genu and the splenium of the corpus callosum in neonates (Gilmore et al., 2004). Both techniques have been applied to the study of callosal integrity in Schizophrenia. A recent study examined changes in mean diffusivity (a general index of diffusion) and fractional anisotropy (an index of regional compared to global diffusion) in the genu and splenium of the corpus callosum. In the splenium, mean diffusivity was increased and fractional anisotropy decreased, suggesting impairments in the integrity of callosal tissue in those subregions (Foong et al., 2000). Subsequent support for these findings has been mixed. Adult studies have provided support for these findings in the splenium (Agartz, Andersson, & Skare, 2001), though few studies have attempted to examine diffusivity or anisotropy in callosal subregions (Ardekani, Nierenberg, Hoptman, Javitt, & Lim, 2003). At least one study in childhood-onset patients has been negative in both the genu and the splenium (Kumra et al., 2004).

Studies assessing altered patterns of symmetry provide another approach to study callosal dysfunction. For example, a normal pattern of greater leftward asymmetry in anisotropy values observed in the region of the genu in control subjects is reduced in Schizophrenia patients, suggesting possible reorganization of callosal fibers connecting the frontal hemispheres (Park et al., 2004). Recent work has speculated that relative hyperconnectivity of callosal fibers in the anterior portion of the corpus callosum may be associated with the experience of auditory hallucinations. Fractional anisotropy values in the anterior aspects of the corpus callosum in patients experiencing frequent auditory hallucinations have been shown to be *greater* than in those experiencing infrequent hallucinators and even healthy controls (but see Rossell et al., 2001, for negative results in a similar study). This result is suggestive of greater white matter connectivity, which may result in spurious communications between brain regions, leading to the experience of auditory hallucinations (Gunther et al., 1991; Hubl et al., 2004). Similar positive relationships between positive symptoms (hallucinations and delusions) and callosal size have been demonstrated (Gunther et al., 1991).

Studies in Callosal Area and Shape

Studies in callosal shape follow a long tradition of morphometric investigations of neural structures in clinical neuroscience, and in particular Schizophrenia (Shenton et al., 2001). The assumption behind morphometry in clinical neuroscience is that microstructural abnormalities will express themselves as volumetric abnormalities in the structures of interest. With respect to the corpus callosum, most morphometric studies have been area-based rather than volumetric, partly as a result of difficulties in visualizing the lateral boundaries of this structure in midsagittal images of the brain (Bishop & Wahlsten, 1997).

Changes in callosal size in Schizophrenia have been investigated since the inception of high-resolution MRI in research. In a meta-analysis conducted approximately 10 years since the onset of the earliest work in this area, Woodruff and colleagues (Woodruff, McManus, & David, 1995) demonstrated that there was a decrease in callosal size in Schizophrenia of about 0.5 cm^2. Subsequent reviews have reiterated the findings of the earlier meta-analysis, demonstrating that a majority of studies document decreases in callosal area in Schizophrenia (Shenton et al., 2001). Problems of interpretation abound, though, as patient samples continue to differ in terms of age and primary diagnoses, and techniques for callosal measurement lack standardized validation. Statistical analyses of the data may or may not always correct for intracranial or total brain volume (Bishop & Wahlsten, 1997).

Some of our own recent work has indicated developmentally associated reductions in callosal area across the entire structure. Using a parcellation scheme from deLacoste and colleagues (1985), we conducted size and other image analyses of the genu, body, isthmus, and splenium in a sample of first-episode Schizophrenia patients ($n = 31$),

non-Schizophrenia psychotic controls, and healthy comparison subjects (Diwadkar et al., 2004; Keshavan, Diwadkar, Harenski, et al., 2002). Several striking results were observed. Area reductions specific to Schizophrenia patients were seen across all the subregions of the structure, confirmed by planned statistical contrasts. Further, these reductions appeared to be developmentally mediated: Significant age-related increases were observed in the size of substructures in healthy control subjects, but there was an absence of significant correlations in first-episode Schizophrenia patients. These results conform to the analyses of MRI signal intensity (see earlier discussion). In the sample of young first-episode patients in our studies (mean age = 24 years), reductions in callosal size were observed across all the principal subregions, suggesting a plausible decrease in the number or size of axonal fibers connecting the cortical hemispheres in Schizophrenia. Further, these reductions corroborated shape-based alterations of the callosum that had been previously documented in the same group of subjects (DeQuardo et al., 1999).

Our findings are broadly consistent with other MRI-based investigations of callosal size (Tibbo, Nopoulos, Arndt, & Andreasen, 1998), though negative results also exist (Meisenzahl et al., 1999). Investigations in first-episode patients with mild neuroleptic exposure have yielded similar results (Bachmann et al., 2003), with the additional finding of decreases being greater in men than in women. Studies have also demonstrated a positive relationship between callosal length and age of illness onset (Colombo, Bonfanti, & Scarone, 1994).

Investigations of callosal size abnormalities in the premorbid phase of Schizophrenia are lacking, and only limited studies exist in very early-onset patients. At least one study has documented callosal abnormalities in very young subjects showing symptoms of Schizophrenia or Schizotypal Personality Disorder. Compared to a group of age-matched controls, these patients showed a reduction in undifferentiated callosal area (Hendren et al., 1995). These findings are of importance because of the young age of the subject sampled (<12 years), which indicates a plausible callosal abnormality at very early stages of neurodevelopment. Other studies of young at-risk populations have been negative. Chua and colleagues (Chua, Sharma, Takei, Murray, & Woodruff, 2000) examined total and differentiated callosal size in a cohort of patients, their first-degree relatives, and healthy controls and were unable to replicate differences between patients and controls and correspondingly failed to document reductions in first-degree relatives. This negative result is perhaps important given the reasonable size of the sample ($n > 25$ in all groups), though the average age of the samples exceeded 30, which may extend beyond the known developmental profile of the structure (Pujol et al., 1993). Some developmentally related analyses of callosal size have suggested altered profiles of maturation in childhood-onset Schizophrenia. In analyses of large samples (ages 8 to 24) of very young-onset patients, it appears that splenial size in this population appears to decline in late adolescence and young adulthood (compared to continuing increases in healthy controls; Keller et al., 2003; but see Jacobsen et al., 1997).

Collectively, the reviewed studies suggest a complex relationship between callosal integrity and Schizophrenia. The clarity of results has been confounded by differences in patient sample characteristics, in particular a dependence on study patients in the chronic phase and a relative absence of studies using neuroleptic-naïve first-episode subjects. The use of first-episode patients is particularly important as it avoids confounds of illness chronicity and effects of neuroleptic exposure and prolonged illness duration (Keshavan & Schooler, 1992). These are concerns given the demonstrated effect of antipsychotics on gray matter volume and the neurodegeneration observed following illness onset (Lieberman, 1999) and is an insurmountable limitation of most histopathological investigations. This may explain why the histopathological data have not been clearly confirmed by subsequent in vivo MRI investigations, and why studies on callosal morphometry have proven variable (Woodruff, Pearlson, Geer, Barta, & Chilcoat, 1993). Many important subgroups also remain understudied. For example, no in vivo studies of tissue integrity exist in young individuals at risk for Schizophrenia; therefore, knowledge of the development of the structure in the premorbid course of the illness is absent. It will be important to fill in these lacunae in knowledge to ascertain the relationship between abnormal neurodevelopment, callosal morphology, and Schizophrenia.

Other Psychiatric Disorders

It has been proposed that right hemisphere dysfunction is characteristic of depressive illness, and that interhemispheric communication may be disrupted. Studies using sleep electroencephalogram (EEG) have also shown low interhemispheric coherence in depressive patients (Armitage, 1995), suggesting callosal disconnectivity. Only one available study has examined the corpus callosum in unipolar depression and has found an increase in size (Wu et al., 1993). The corpus callosum appears to be larger in Bipolar Disorder as well (Hauser, Dauphinais, & Berrettini, 1989; Hauser et al., 1989).

Impaired interhemispheric connectivity has also been suggested in Obsessive-Compulsive Disorder (OCD; Mal-

let, Mazoyer, & Martinot, 1998). The corpus callosum appears to be bigger in OCD patients compared to controls (Farchione, Lorch, & Rosenberg, 2002; Rosenberg et al., 1997), contrasting with the reductions in this structure seen in Schizophrenia and Attention-Deficit/Hyperactivity Disorder (ADHD). The mean signal intensity is also altered in OCD patients, suggesting a possible increase in myelination. However, not all studies show corpus callosum changes in OCD (Kellner et al., 1991).

Severe early stress and maltreatment may produce a cascade of events that have the potential to alter brain development. Reduced area of the corpus callosum has been reported in both childhood Posttraumatic Stress Disorder (PTSD; DeBellis, Keshavan, et al., 1999) and in adults with this disorder (Villarreal et al., 2004). In the DeBellis study, subjects with PTSD did not show the normal age-related increases in the area of the total corpus callosum and its posterior region (splenium) compared to nonmaltreated subjects; however, this finding was more prominent in males with PTSD. Overall, callosal changes have been observed in a variety of psychiatric disorders, but the findings are not as consistent as in Schizophrenia. The small number of studies available and the variations in study populations limit conclusions that can be drawn.

Autism

Autism is a neurodevelopmental disorder characterized by abnormalities in social interaction and communication and by behavioral repetition or obsessive interest (Baron-Cohen, 2004). The syndrome is also typically accompanied by developmental delays in the onset of language. The phenotype of the syndrome is complex, and diagnosis is based on the presence of a subset of symptoms related to these impairments that by the age of 3 (Rapin, 1999). Autism is not a monolithic diagnosis; a complex subgroup Asperger's syndrome shares many of the core features but is characterized by an absence of delays in language, by an IQ in or above the average range, and by above-average abilities narrowly focused in limited domain(s). A specific characterization of the social deficits in cognition in Autism is the absence of a "theory of mind," or an inability to interpret correctly or attribute mental states to others (U. Frith, 1996), though this theory is narrow and excludes many of the secondary cognitive deficits, such as attentional and executive function impairments, that are also observed in the syndrome (U. Frith & Happé, 1994).

Because Autism presents itself early in development, it is thought of as fundamentally a developmental disorder, though its etiology remains generally obscure (Rapin &

Katzman, 1998). Heritability studies provide strong evidence of very high concordance rates in monozygotic twins (Bailey et al., 1995), suggesting a significant genetic component, and linkage studies are beginning to identify susceptibility genes (Lamb, Parr, Bailey, & Monaco, 2002). Like Schizophrenia, this syndrome may best be characterized as resulting from a complex interaction between genetic susceptibility and early environmental insults, leading to alterations in programmed neurodevelopment (Courchesne, Redcay, & Kennedy, 2004; Muhle, Trentacoste, & Rapin, 2004; Nicolson & Szatmari, 2003). The broad nature of cognitive deficits is suggestive of disconnectivity in the cortex or between cortical and subcortical circuits (Skoyles, 2002). Morphometric studies have also mapped out a diverse range of volumetric alterations in autistic individuals, including abnormal volumes of the cerebellum, subcortical structures (midbrain and brain stem), and total brain as well as parietal, temporal and frontal volumes (Brambilla et al., 2003). More focused structural MRI studies have provided plausible evidence of disordered connectivity between corticolimbic circuits in the form of reduced correlations in gray matter volume between key cortical and limbic regions (McAlonan et al., 2005). Functional MRI studies have hinted at disordered uni- and bilateral functional connectivity during language comprehension in Autism (Just, Cherkassky, Keller, & Minshew, 2004). Finally, recent evidence suggests an alteration in the pattern of cerebral asymmetry in Autism, with autistic subjects showing greater rightward structural asymmetry in an analysis of several cortical regions (Herbert et al., 2005). The combination of dysregulated early development and disconnections are suggestive of plausible corpus callosum pathology in Autism (Piven, 1997).

Studies on Callosal Tissue Integrity

The earliest study of in vivo tissue integrity in Autism using MRI signal intensity analysis suggested an absence of differences in MRI between controls and autistic subjects and a similar profile of intensity change as a function of age in both groups (Belmonte, Egaas, Townsend, & Courchesne, 1995). The authors suggested that these results indicated normal patterns of developmental myelination of the corpus callosum in Autism. On the other hand, recent voxel-based and DTI-based studies have provided evidence of positive findings, specifically reductions in white matter concentration and decreases in anisotropic diffusion.

In a sample of adolescent male autistics, significant reductions in white matter density were observed in the splenium of the corpus callosum (Waiter et al., 2005). More general reductions in the genu were observed in a sample of 16 high-functioning autistics (Chung, Dalton, Alexander, & Davidson, 2004). Few studies have applied DTI to the study of tissue integrity in Autism. Recent evidence indicates reduced anisotropy in the genu of the callosum (Barnea-Goraly et al., 2004). These studies (as in Schizophrenia) provide generally consistent evidence of abnormal tissue integrity in the corpus callosum in the Autism spectrum. The evidence from morphometric investigations of callosal size is similarly consistent.

Studies on Callosal Area

Discounting a few negative results showing an absence of changes in callosal area (Herbert et al., 2004), several studies of independent samples have documented robust changes in callosal size (Egaas, Courchesne, & Saitoh, 1995). Reductions in callosal area in both high-functioning and mentally retarded autistic patients have been reported (Manes et al., 1999), suggesting that deficits are not restricted to a particular IQ-based subgroup. Regional analyses have documented reductions in the area of the genu and the body of the structure as well (Hardan, Minshew, Harenski, & Keshavan, 2001; Piven, Bailey, Ranson, & Arndt, 1997).

Too few studies exist to discern a systematic regional pattern of callosal alteration in Autism. The pattern of evidence indicates both microstructural and morphometric changes, suggestive of a reduced integrity of the structure in the disorder.

Attention-Deficit/Hyperactivity Disorder

Interest in studying callosal impairment in ADHD stems from several observations. The corpus callosum contributes to attention by modulating resource allocation between the hemispheres and filtering interhemispheric signal transmission (Mikels & Reuter-Lorenz, 2004). ADHD has been thought to be associated with defects in interhemispheric communication (Magara, Ricceri, Wolfer, & Lipp, 2000). Furthermore, ADHD-like features are often seen in individuals with hypoplasia of the corpus callosum. Studies examining the corpus callosum in ADHD have generally shown reductions in the size of this structure (Giedd, Blumenthal, Molloy, & Castellanos, 2001; D. E. Hill et al., 2003), similar to reductions observed in Schizophrenia. Increased attentional problems have been associated with more prominent reductions in corpus callosal size (Kayl, Moore, Slopis, Jackson, & Leeds, 2000). ADHD patients also show a higher signal intensity ratio in the posterior regions in T_2-weighted MRI, probably reflecting alterations in myelination (Pueyo et al., 2003).

Other Developmental Disorders

Callosal abnormalities have also been implicated in other developmental disorders, particularly those associated with risk for psychoses. For example, DiGeorge syndrome (also known as velocardial facial syndrome, or VCFS), caused by a specific deletion of chromosome 22q11, is associated with increased risk and rates of Schizophrenia and mood disorders, with studies showing an increased incidence rate of this deletion in Schizophrenia patients compared to healthy subjects (Usiskin et al., 1999). Investigations of callosal size in nonpsychotic children afflicted by the 22q11 deletion syndrome have shown abnormal increases compared to healthy controls (Shashi et al., 2004; Usiskin et al., 1999) in the body and the isthmus of the structure. Further, a relative lack of age-related changes in 22q11 samples has been observed. Reductions in total and regional callosal size have been reported in young individuals with Tourette's syndrome (Peterson et al., 1994), and Williams's syndrome (Schmitt, Eliez, Warsofsky, Bellugi, & Reiss, 2001; Tomaiuolo et al., 2002).

SUBSTANCE ABUSE AND CALLOSAL MORPHOLOGY

Substance abuse is widely associated with widespread teratogenic effects. Because the prenatal genesis and development of the corpus callosum begins to take place at around the same time as the greatest embryonic vulnerability to alcohol damage (Loeser & Alvord, 1968), it has been argued that the structure may embody the prenatal teratogenic defects due to maternal substance abuse and therefore a particularly crucial target for study (Bookstein, Sampson, Connor, & Streissguth, 2002; Johnson, Swayze, Sato, & Andreasen, 1996).

MRI-based investigations of brain morphology in chronic substance abusers and individuals prenatally exposed to high levels of cocaine and alcohol have documented widespread impairments in brain structure (Archibald et al., 2001; Roebuck, Mattson, & Riley, 1998; Sowell, Thompson, Mattson, et al., 2001) and cognitive function (Riley, McGee, & Sowell, 2004). Increases in impulsivity, suggesting a lack of prefrontal cortical-directed cognitive control (Moeller et al., 2005), and deficits in attention and visuospatial function have been documented (Sowell, Mattson, et al., 2001), along with reductions in prefrontal gray and white matter (Fein, Di Sclafani, Cardenas, et al., 2002; Fein, Di Sclafani, & Meyerhoff, 2002; O'Neill, Cardenas, & Meyerhoff, 2001). Midtemporal lobe structures such as the hippocampus may also be particularly affected by adolescent alcohol abuse (DeBellis et al., 2000).

Significantly, substance abuse may have a critical developmental basis. Studies indicate a reduction in key electrophysiological components such as the P300 amplitude during visual and auditory processing (S. Y. Hill, Shen, Lowers, & Locke, 2000; S. Y. Hill & Steinhauer, 1993) in children at high risk for developing alcoholism. Further, studies of cocaine-dependent individuals have documented an absence of age-related expansion of frontal white matter, indicating plausibly reduced myelin expansion and, by inference, reduced functional connectivity of the neocortex (Bartzokis et al., 2002). The idea of reduced connectivity is supported by studies indicating an impairment in the interhemispheric transfer of information in children with heavy prenatal alcohol exposure (Roebuck, Mattson, & Riley, 2002) and in adults with chronic alcohol abuse (Schulte, Pfefferbaum, & Sullivan, 2004). Electrophysiological studies indicate reduced coherence of brain wave activity (reduced theta and gamma band coherence) among heavy drinkers compared to light drinkers (de Bruin et al., 2004), and resting state fMRI studies in cocaine abusers show reduced functional connectivity in the early visual system (Li et al., 2000). The widespread pattern of brain abnormalities, evidence of reduced cognitive function and connectivity, and patterns of developmental alterations in neurobiology suggest the corpus callosum as a target for impairment in substance abuse.

Midsagittal analyses of MRI images have helped elucidate many of the abnormalities associated with callosal morphology in children and adolescents suffering from neurotoxic effects of fetal alcohol exposure. These studies have suggested a higher rate of agenesis of the corpus callosum in children prenatally exposed to alcohol (Mattson, Schoenfeld, & Riley, 2001). Quantitative morphometric analyses have provided more evidence of callosal abnormalities: Reductions in callosal area of the genu and splenium in children with Fetal Alcohol Syndrome compared to controls have been reported (Riley et al., 1995). These more conventional morphometric analyses were extended using novel methods to detect changes in callosal shape, using landmark analyses (Bookstein, 1997) to assess changes in the shape of the structure as opposed to area. These studies have documented patterns of systematic displacement and increased variability of callosal shape in fetal alcohol-exposed subjects. In a study of adult males and females, Bookstein and colleagues (Bookstein, Sampson, Streissguth, & Connor, 2001) demonstrated that exposed individuals had increased variability in the shape of the callosum compared to controls. This pattern of variability led to different patterns of differences between males and females. More significant variance for exposed males was observed under the isthmus (and, to some extent, the genu). For exposed females, the variance was primarily increased in the height of the callosal arch (i.e., the anterior and posterior divisions of the body), with some increases also observed in the ventral aspects of the isthmus and splenium. Similar shape analyses of callosal contouring have provided evidence of hyperdisplacement of the posterior aspects of the structure in exposed adolescents and young adults. In general, these studies suggest that the callosum is more inferiorly and anteriorly placed in exposed patients compared to controls (Sowell, Mattson, et al., 2001). These patterns were also related to the degree of alcohol exposure, providing evidence of a dose-related effect. Furthermore, studies have shown an increase in callosal white matter in patients with longer periods of sobriety, suggesting that the neurotoxic impact of substance abuse may not be irreversible (Pfefferbaum, Rosenbloom, Serventi, & Sullivan, 2002).

Recent examinations of callosal microstructure in substance abuse disorders also provide evidence of significant alterations. Chronic alcoholism is associated with reduced integrity of white matter in the genu of the corpus callosum (Pfefferbaum & Sullivan, 2002), and similar reductions have been documented in cocaine abusers (Moeller et al., 2005). These reductions have been related to impaired neurocognitive function, including increases in impulsivity and a reduction in the speed of interhemispheric processing, suggesting a neurobehavioral expression of such microstructural changes (Schulte, Sullivan, Muller-Oehring, Adalsteinsson, & Pfefferbaum, 2005). Recent studies suggest that these decreases may be associated with significant increase in intra- and extracellular fluid in callosal regions (Pfefferbaum & Sullivan, 2005), providing some evidence of the microstructural pathway for impairment in alcoholism.

The dramatic effects of substance abuse on callosal integrity indicate a pattern of structural vulnerability that includes both intrinsic factors (more likely to be associated with psychiatric conditions) and extrinsic factors, indicating reactivity to neurotoxic substances. The striking impairments that are observed in Fetal Alcohol Syndrome are of particular relevance in considering the role of experience-independent development on callosal development. As noted earlier, callosal development begins around approximately the 39th day postconception. This period is marked by the formation and differentiation of the commissural plate. Callosal fibers differentiate from the commissural

plate around the 75th postconception day, and adult-like morphology is achieved at around the 115th day (Loeser & Alvord, 1968). This pattern of prenatal development in the first trimester renders the corpus callosum particularly vulnerable to the toxic effects of ethanol, which are known to disrupt cell division, proliferation and migration, and the development of glia (Guerri, 1998). The relatively well-understood mechanisms of induced neurotoxicity in vitro in Fetal Alcohol Syndrome provide clear evidence of a neurodevelopmental lesion at a critical stage of callosal formation and development. The impact of this early lesion to the callosum on behavioral performance is profound, leading to severe mental and motor retardation in children exposed prenatally to alcohol or cocaine (Riley et al., 2004; Singer et al., 1997).

CONCLUSION AND FUTURE DIRECTIONS

As the major intercommissural pathway, the corpus callosum is an important white matter structure that is a natural target for investigation in neuropsychiatric illness. The developmental and topographic relationship with the neocortex further advances its importance as a region of interest. As reviewed here, the hyper- or hypoplasia of the corpus callosum is associated with a diverse variety of psychiatric illnesses and disorders. The findings are summarized in Table 19.1.

The precise mapping between in vivo MRI measurements of white matter volume or area and cellular processes such as

TABLE 19.1 Summary of Callosal Findings across Illnesses/Disorders

	Direction of Impairment	Regional Specifics	Developmental Effects
Schizophrenia	↓	Genu Body Splenium	Altered
Mood disorders	↑	N/A	N/A
Autism	↓	Genu Body Splenium	Altered
ADHD	↓	N/A	N/A
PTSD	↓	N/A	Altered
VCFS (22q11 deletion)	↑	Body Isthmus	Altered
OCD	↑	N/A	N/A

gliosis, myelination, or axonal integrity is not yet well understood. However, there are plausible justifications to correlate the observed in vivo findings to ex vivo or postmortem work in these illnesses.

In Schizophrenia, studies have suggested excessive gliosis in the corpus callosum in later-onset patients (Nasrallah, McCalley-Whitters, Bigelow, & Rauscher, 1983). In mood disorders, there is a suggestion of relative lack of subgenual prefrontal glia (potentially related to callosal morphology; Drevets, Ongur, & Price, 1998). None of the published work is specific to the corpus callosum, however, and to our knowledge, no histopathological data exist in developmental disorders such as Autism or in ADHD.

Accumulating studies have implicated myelin dysfunction as a principal neurobiological correlate of Schizophrenia (Davis et al., 2003), Bipolar Disorder (Tkachev et al., 2003), and developmental disorders such as Autism (Reiss, Feinstein, & Rosenbaum, 1986). In Schizophrenia, studies using MRI relaxometry have demonstrated plausibly lower myelin fraction, particularly in the genu of the structure (Flynn et al., 2003). Reduced myelination (expressed as reductions in myelin basic protein) in the limbic system of female bipolar patients has been reported, though no reports from the corpus callosum exist (Chambers & Perrone-Bizzozero, 2004). With recent explorations implicating myelin- and oligodendrocyte-related genes in the pathophysiology of both Bipolar Disorder and Schizophrenia (Tkachev et al., 2003), it is likely that reduced myelin in the corpus callosum may be associated with the reductions in callosal volume (Ogden et al., 2004). In Autism, evidence suggests that white matter abnormalities may stem from changes in oligodendrocytes and/or myelination; autistic children show a higher incidence of myelin basic protein antibodies, suggestive of altered myelination, and abnormalities in the expression of oligodendrocyte myelin glycoprotein, which may lead to impaired proliferation of oligodendrocytes or myelin (Dong & Greenough, 2004). Again, however, direct evidence linking such processes locally to the corpus callosum is lacking.

Axonal differences may also contribute to in vivo estimates of callosal abnormalities. In Schizophrenia, subtle differences in axonal density have been observed between patients and controls (Highley et al., 1999). Similar data in other disorders or syndromes are lacking, however.

An intriguing yet unresolved question is the potential relationship between impaired white matter and associated gray matter in psychiatric illness. Gray : white matter ratios are of importance in in vivo imaging for several reasons.

Segmentation procedures used to separate T_1-weighted MRI images into gray, white, and cerebrospinal fluid components are subject to error from partial volume effects that limit the effectiveness of such techniques to absolutely quantitate either gray or white volume (Hohne & Pommert, 1996). Further, the balance of cortical gray and white matter is thought to be a metric of brain organization generally (Zhang & Sejnowski, 2000). Limited evidence in Schizophrenia suggests complementary reductions in gray and white matter in the heteromodal association cortices and the limbic lobe, suggesting convergent deficits in regional synaptic and axonal integrity, particularly in patients with negative symptoms (Sanfilipo et al., 2000; Sigmundsson et al., 2001). Alterations in gray : white brain ratio have been documented in adult and late-onset Schizophrenia patients as well (Bartzokis et al., 2003; Casanova & Lindzen, 2003). In general, given the high degree of interrelatedness in the developmental processes associated with synaptic proliferation and pruning and myelin and white matter development, it is reasonable to assume that callosal abnormalities are related to complementary gray matter impairments. Indeed (at least in Schizophrenia), gray matter reductions have been documented in the regions that impaired callosal areas connect (Shenton et al., 2001).

Direct evidence that speaks to developmental trajectories in callosal change in illnesses and disorders is relatively sparse. As noted earlier, a few studies have demonstrated alternative pathways of callosal change in cross-sectional Schizophrenia samples compared to healthy controls (Keshavan, Diwadkar, Harenski, et al., 2002), though similar data in other illnesses and disorders are lacking. More thorough analyses of age-related callosal changes in different disorders may be compelling for several reasons. Illnesses such as Schizophrenia and Bipolar Disorder and disorders such as Autism are illnesses of neurodevelopment. In fact, several genes implicated in their pathophysiology are the genes that are thought to be involved in neurodevelopment as well (Jones & Murray, 1991; Muhle et al., 2004). Furthermore, changes in expression of myelin-encoding genes have been documented in Schizophrenia and Bipolar Disorder (Aston, Jiang, & Sokolov, 2005; Tkachev et al., 2003). From such studies we can extrapolate that the relative phenotypic distinctions between Schizophrenia and Bipolar Disorder emerge as a result of different neurodevelopmental expressions at different time points (J. Walker, Curtis, Shaw, & Murray, 2002). As our own work has recently established, different patterns of change in MRI-measured callosal morphology are observed in childhood, adolescence, and young adulthood (Keshavan, Diwadkar, DeBellis, et al., 2002).

Given the emerging consensus that derailed neurodevelopment is a mechanism that may underlie psychiatric illness in general (Kreipke, Rosenberg, & Keshavan, 2004), comparative studies in at-risk psychiatric populations may provide information on specific time points at which derailment of callosal development occurs. The timing and the extent of such derailment may provide important insights on the future emergence of phenotypically nonoverlapping psychiatric diagnoses such as Schizophrenia and Bipolar Disorder (J. Walker, Curtis, & Murray, 2002) and may elucidate the developmental course of syndromes such as Autism (McAlonan et al., 2005) and ADHD (Giedd et al., 2001).

The corpus callosum's unique spatial relationship with cortical regions provides opportunities to estimate the patterns of derailed neurocircuitry in development. Different patterns of change in callosum regions may be associated with different clinical phenotypes and may implicate overlapping or nonoverlapping circuits in the brain. As an example, although the effect of alterations in callosal morphology in an illness such as Schizophrenia is largest in the genu (which connects the prefrontal cortices), alterations are observed across all subregions, consistent with the idea of the illness being a more generalized disconnection syndrome of the brain. Detailed analyses of this nature in other disorders may help clarify the nature and the degree of estimated disconnection.

A general framework with which to understand the nature and the directionality of callosal alterations in diverse syndromes remains elusive. The understanding of abnormal neurobiology in many of these syndromes is continually evolving, but at present, there is no plausible single unitary mechanism or set of mechanisms that may explain callosal abnormalities. One candidate mechanism may be stress or trauma to the brain that impacts at critical stages of development (DeBellis, Baum, et al., 1999; Teicher, Andersen, Polcari, Anderson, & Navalta, 2002; Teicher et al., 2003), leading to axonal damage in critical cortical and callosal regions.

Increasingly, childhood stress and abuse have been associated with abnormal development of the brain in general and the corpus callosum in particular. In an early study, Teicher and colleagues (1997) demonstrated significant reductions in the size of the body of the corpus callosum in young patients with a history of childhood abuse. These patients also demonstrated an abnormal pattern of EEG-measured inter- and intrahemispheric coherence of brain activation, suggesting that abuse may have altered the normative pattern of brain development (Ito, Teicher, Glod, & Ackerman, 1998). Recent studies have extended this work to indicate callosal abnormalities not only in abused but in neglected children as well (Teicher et al., 2004). These

MRI-measured reductions in humans are consistent with experimental studies documenting profound effects of rearing and isolation on the corpus callosum in the rhesus monkey (Sanchez et al., 1998) and suggest that early stress through trauma or neglect to compacted white matter structures like the corpus callosum may derail or reverse the known patterns of myelination in that structure (McGraw, Liang, & Provenzale, 2002). The cascading effects of alterations in the stress-response system may lead to reverberating effects throughout development. For example, prolonged stress is known to impair the development of the glucocorticoid receptors, eventually leading to enhanced noradrenergic, corticosteroid, and vasopressin responses to stress (Teicher et al., 2002). Consistent with this, experimental studies have demonstrated that early glucocorticoid administration interferes with glial cell division and myelination (Lauder, 1983).

Psychosocial stress is implicated as a precipitating factor in several mental illnesses, including Schizophrenia. In particular, the biological effects of stress are modulated by the hypothalamic-pituitary-adrenal axis, which is known to function abnormally in the illness (Corcoran et al., 2003), and may impact normal development in Schizophrenia (E. F. Walker, Diforio, & Baum, 1999). It is likely that certain stressors may severely compromise the stress hormone response and may lead to unpredictable and myriad effects on neural differentiation and myelination, leading to hypodevelopment of the corpus callosum (and other structures) in a number of psychiatric disorders, such as Schizophrenia and Bipolar Disorder, and environmental insults, including drug abuse and Fetal Alcohol Syndrome. Thus, the pathways to callosal impairment may be diverse in origin but may converge on a similar end point.

The effects of stress and neurotoxicity are not specific to the corpus callosum. For example, malfunctions of the glutamate system leading to neurotoxic-related neuronal loss and abnormal neuron development have been generally implicated in Schizophrenia (Konradi & Heckers, 2003) and may impact several regions of the brain. Genetic factors may also play a critical role in abnormal callosal morphology. Recent studies have identified displacements of the corpus callosum in unaffected monozygotic twins of Schizophrenia patients, suggesting a heritable component to callosal morphology (Narr et al., 2002). Studies in healthy monozygotic and dizygotic twin populations and elderly populations have also confirmed a heritable basis to callosal morphology, with a large proportion of variance in structure size accounted for by genetic factors (Pfefferbaum, Sullivan, & Carmelli, 2004; Scamvougeras, Kigar, Jones, Weinberger, & Witelson, 2003).

Emerging MRI techniques may contribute to increased understanding of the specific abnormalities of in vivo microstructure of the corpus callosum. For instance, fiber pathway abnormalities may be the endophenotype of interest, but conventional MRI is not informative of such deficits. White matter imaging techniques such as DTI and MTI may provide more focused answers, though they are also limited by the underlying topography of fiber pathways. Magnetic resonance spectroscopy techniques, especially with the use of high-field magnets (3 Tesla or higher), can quantify changes in in vivo neurochemical markers such as glutamine and glutamate that are integral to glial and neuronal interactions.

Psychiatric illness and disorder may render some brain regions more generally vulnerable than others. The corpus callosum occupies a unique place in the taxonomy of regions, and it is not surprising that it is weakly or strongly implicated in a variety of disorders. Key directions for the future are to understand the specific timing (in terms of developmental stage) when callosal impairments begin to be manifest and the relationship between such impairments and neuropsychological function. Longitudinal studies that employ multimodal imaging techniques (fMRI, DTI, etc.) in conjunction with focused tasks (e.g., split-hemispheric integration tasks) may provide answers about the progression and the nature of callosal impairments. The role of white matter in psychiatric illnesses and conditions is becoming better elucidated (Kumar & Cook, 2002). Therefore, studies of the corpus callosum may play a key role in revealing important aspects of the developmental pathophysiology of psychiatric illnesses and disorders.

REFERENCES

Aarkrog, T., & Mortensen, K. V. (1985). Schizophrenia in early adolescence: A study illustrated by long-term cases. *Acta Psychiatrica Scandinavica, 72*(5), 422–429.

Aboitz, F., Scheibel, A. B., Fisher, R. S., & Zaidel, E. (1992). Fiber composition of the human corpus callosum. *Brain Research, 598,* 143–153.

Agartz, I., Andersson, J. L., & Skare, S. (2001). Abnormal brain white matter in Schizophrenia: A diffusion tensor imaging study. *NeuroReport, 12*(10), 2251–2254.

Andreasen, N. C. (1984). *Scale for the Assessment of Positive Symptoms (SAPS).* Iowa City: University of Iowa.

Andreasen, N. C. (1999). A unitary model of Schizophrenia: Bleuler's "fragmented phrene" as schizencephaly. *Archives of General Psychiatry, 56*(9), 781–787.

Andreasen, N. C., Nopoulos, P., O'Leary, D. S., Miller, D. D., Wassink, T., & Flaum, M. (1999). Defining the phenotype of Schizophrenia: Cognitive dysmetria and its neural mechanisms. *Biological Psychiatry, 46*(7), 908–920.

Archibald, S. L., Fennema-Notestine, C., Gamst, A., Riley, E. P., Mattson, S. N., & Jernigan, T. L. (2001). Brain dysmorphology in individuals with severe prenatal alcohol exposure. *Developmental Medicine and Child Neurology, 43*(3), 148–154.

Ardekani, B. A., Nierenberg, J., Hoptman, M. J., Javitt, D. C., & Lim, K. O. (2003). MRI study of white matter diffusion anisotropy in Schizophrenia. *NeuroReport, 14*(16), 2025–2029.

Armitage, R. (1995). Microarchitectural findings in sleep EEG in depression: Diagnostic implications. *Biological Psychiatry, 37*(2), 72–84.

Aston, C., Jiang, L., & Sokolov, B. P. (2005). Transcriptional profiling reveals evidence for signaling and oligodendroglial abnormalities in the temporal cortex from patients with major depressive disorder. *Molecular Psychiatry, 10*(3), 309–322.

Bachmann, S., Pantel, J., Flender, A., Bottmer, C., Essig, M., & Schroder, J. (2003). Corpus callosum in first-episode patients with Schizophrenia: A magnetic resonance imaging study. *Psychological Medicine, 33*(6), 1019–1027.

Bailey, A., Le Couteur, A., Gottesman, I., Bolton, P., Simonoff, E., Yuzda, E., et al. (1995). Autism as a strongly genetic disorder: Evidence from a British twin study. *Psychological Medicine, 25*(1), 63–77.

Ballesteros, M. C., Hansen, P. E., & Soila, K. (1993). MR imaging of the developing human brain: Pt. 2. Postnatal development. *Radiographics, 13*(3), 611–622.

Barkovich, A. J. (2000). Concepts of myelin and myelination in neuroradiology. *American Journal of Neuroradiology, 21*(6), 1099–1109.

Barkovich, A. J., Kjos, B. O., Jackson, D. E., Jr., & Norman, D. (1988). Normal maturation of the neonatal and infant brain: MR imaging at 1.5 T. *Radiology, 166*(1, Pt. 1), 173–180.

Barkovich, A. J., & Maroldo, T. V. (1993). Magnetic resonance imaging of normal and abnormal brain development. *Topics in Magnetic Resonance Imaging, 5*(2), 96–122.

Barnea-Goraly, N., Kwon, H., Menon, V., Eliez, S., Lotspeich, L., & Reiss, A. L. (2004). White matter structure in Autism: Preliminary evidence from diffusion tensor imaging. *Biological Psychiatry, 55*(3), 323–326.

Baron-Cohen, S. (2004). The cognitive neuroscience of Autism. *Journal of Neurology, Neurosurgery, and Psychiatry, 75*(7), 945–948.

Bartzokis, G. (2002). Schizophrenia: Breakdown in the well-regulated lifelong process of brain development and maturation. *Neuropsychopharmacology, 27*(4), 672–683.

Bartzokis, G., Beckson, M., Lu, P. H., Edwards, N., Bridge, P., & Mintz, J. (2002). Brain maturation may be arrested in chronic cocaine addicts. *Biological Psychiatry, 51*(8), 605–611.

Bartzokis, G., Nuechterlein, K. H., Lu, P. H., Gitlin, M., Rogers, S., & Mintz, J. (2003). Dysregulated brain development in adult men with Schizophrenia: A magnetic resonance imaging study. *Biological Psychiatry, 53*(5), 412–421.

Baynes, K., Eliassen, J. C., Lutsep, H. L., & Gazzaniga, M. S. (1998). Modular organization of cognitive systems masked by interhemispheric integration. *Science, 280*(5365), 902–905.

Belmonte, M., Egaas, B., Townsend, J., & Courchesne, E. (1995). NMR intensity of corpus callosum differs with age but not with diagnosis of Autism. *NeuroReport, 6*(9), 1253–1256.

Bigelow, L. B., Nasrallah, H. A., & Rauscher, F. P. (1983). Corpus callosum thickness in chronic Schizophrenia. *British Journal of Psychiatry, 142,* 284–287.

Bishop, K., & Wahlsten, D. (1997). Sex differences in the human corpus callosum: Myth or reality? *Neuroscience and Biobehavioral Reviews, 21,* 581–601.

Bookstein, F. L. (1997). Landmark methods for forms without landmarks: Morphometrics of group differences in outline shape. *Medical Image Analysis, 1,* 225–243.

Bookstein, F. L., Sampson, P. D., Connor, P. D., & Streissguth, A. P. (2002). Midline corpus callosum is a neuroanatomical focus of fetal alcohol damage. *Anatomical Record, 269*(3), 162–174.

Bookstein, F. L., Sampson, P. D., Streissguth, A. P., & Connor, P. D. (2001). Geometric morphometrics of corpus callosum and subcortical structures in the fetal-alcohol-affected brain. *Teratology, 64*(1), 4–32.

Brambilla, P., Hardan, A., di Nemi, S. U., Perez, J., Soares, J. C., & Barale, F. (2003). Brain anatomy and development in Autism: Review of structural MRI studies. *Brain Research Bulletin, 61*(6), 557–569.

Carr, S. A. (1980). Interhemispheric transfer of stereognostic information in chronic schizophrenics. *British Journal of Psychiatry, 136,* 53–58.

Casanova, M. F., & Lindzen, E. C. (2003). Changes in gray-/white-matter ratios in the parahippocampal gyri of late-onset Schizophrenia patients. *American Journal of Geriatric Psychiatry, 11*(6), 605–609.

Casanova, M. F., Zito, M., Bigelow, L. B., Berthot, B., Sanders, R. D., & Kleinman, J. E. (1989). Axonal counts of the corpus callosum of schizophrenic patients. *Journal of Neuropsychiatry and Clinical Neurosciences, 1*(4), 391–393.

Castro-Caldas, A., Miranda, P. C., Carmo, I., Reis, A., Leote, F., Ribeiro, C., et al. (1999). Influence of learning to read and write on the morphology of the corpus callosum. *European Journal of Neurology, 6*(1), 23–28.

Chambers, J. S., & Perrone-Bizzozero, N. I. (2004). Altered myelination of the hippocampal formation in subjects with Schizophrenia and bipolar disorder. *Neurochemical Research, 29*(12), 2293–2302.

Chua, S. E., Sharma, T., Takei, N., Murray, R. M., & Woodruff, P. W. (2000). A magnetic resonance imaging study of corpus callosum size in familial schizophrenic subjects, their relatives, and normal controls. *Schizophrenia Research, 41*(3), 397–403.

Chung, M. K., Dalton, K. M., Alexander, A. L., & Davidson, R. J. (2004). Less white matter concentration in Autism: 2D voxel-based morphometry. *Neuroimage, 23*(1), 242–251.

Clarke, B. (1987). Arthur Wigan and the duality of the mind. *Psychological Medicine Monograph, 11*(Suppl.), 1–52.

Clarke, S., Kraftsik, R., Van der Loos, H., & Innocenti, G. M. (1989). Forms and measures of adult and developing human corpus callosum: Is there sexual dimorphism? *Journal of Comparative Neurology, 280*(2), 213–230.

Coger, R. W., & Serafetinides, E. A. (1990). Schizophrenia, corpus callosum and interhemispheric communication: A review. *Psychiatry Research, 34,* 163–184.

Colombo, C., Bonfanti, A., & Scarone, S. (1994). Anatomical characteristics of the corpus callosum and clinical correlates in Schizophrenia. *European Archives of Psychiatry and Clinical Neuroscience, 243*(5), 244–248.

Corcoran, C., Walker, E., Huot, R., Mittal, V., Tessner, K., Kestler, L., et al. (2003). The stress cascade and Schizophrenia: Etiology and onset. *Schizophrenia Bulletin, 29*(4), 671–692.

Courchesne, E., Redcay, E., & Kennedy, D. P. (2004). The autistic brain: Birth through adulthood. *Current Opinion in Neurology and Neurosurgery, 17*(4), 489–496.

Craft, S., Willerman, L., & Bigler, E. D. (1987). Callosal dysfunction in Schizophrenia and schizo-affective disorder. *Journal of Abnormal Psychology, 96*(3), 205–213.

Crow, T. J. (1998). Schizophrenia as a transcallosal misconnection syndrome. *Schizophrenia Research, 30*(2), 111–114.

Crow, T. J., Colter, N., Frith, C. D., Johnstone, E. C., & Owens, D. G. (1989). Developmental arrest of cerebral asymmetries in early onset Schizophrenia. *Psychiatry Research, 29*(3), 247–253.

David, A. S. (1993). Callosal transfer in Schizophrenia: Too much or too little? *Journal of Abnormal Psychology, 102*(4), 573–579.

David, A. S. (1994). Schizophrenia and the corpus callosum: Developmental, structural, and functional relationships. *Behavioral Brain Research, 64,* 203–211.

Davis, K. L., Stewart, D. G., Friedman, J. I., Buchsbaum, M., Harvey, P. D., Hof, P. R., et al. (2003). White matter changes in Schizophrenia: Evidence for myelin-related dysfunction. *Archives of General Psychiatry, 60*(5), 443–456.

DeBellis, M. D., Baum, A., Birmaher, B., Keshavan, M. S., Eccard, C. H., Boring, A. M., et al. (1999). Developmental traumatology: Biological stress systems and brain development in maltreated children with PTSD, Part I: The association of increased urinary cortisol and catecholamine excretion with characteristics of trauma and psychiatric symptoms in prepubertal maltreated children with PTSD [A. E. Bennett Award paper]. *Biological Psychiatry, 45,* 1259–1270.

DeBellis, M. D., Clark, D. B., Beers, S. R., Soloff, P. H., Boring, A. M., Hall, J., et al. (2000). Hippocampal volume in adolescent-onset alcohol use disorders. *American Journal of Psychiatry, 157,* 737–744.

DeBellis, M. D., Keshavan, M. S., Beers, S. R., Hall, J., Frustaci, K., Masalehdan, A., et al. (2001). Sex differences in brain maturation during childhood and adolescence. *Cerebral Cortex, 11*(6), 552–557.

DeBellis, M. D., Keshavan, M. S., Clark, D. B., Casey, B. J., Giedd, J. N., Boring, A. M., et al. (1999). A. E. Bennett Research Award: Developmental traumatology: Pt. II. Brain development. *Biological Psychiatry, 45*(10), 1271–1284.

de Bruin, E. A., Bijl, S., Stam, C. J., Bocker, K. B., Kenemans, J. L., & Verbaten, M. N. (2004). Abnormal EEG synchronisation in heavily drinking students. *Clinical Neurophysiology, 115*(9), 2048–2055.

deLacoste, M. C., Kirkpatrick, J. B., & Ross, E. D. (1985). Topography of the human corpus callosum. *Journal of Neuropathology and Experimental Neurology, 44,* 578–591.

Delisi, L. E., Svetina, C., Razi, K., Shields, G., Wellman, N., & Crow, T. J. (2002). Hand preference and hand skill in families with Schizophrenia. *Laterality, 7*(4), 321–332.

DeQuardo, J. R., Keshavan, M. S., Bookstein, F. L., Bagwell, W. W., Green, W. D., Sweeney, J. A., et al. (1999). Landmark-based morphometric analysis of first-episode Schizophrenia. *Biological Psychiatry, 45*(10), 1321–1328.

Dimond, S. J. (1976). Brain circuits for consciousness. *Brain Behaviour and Evolution, 13*(5), 376–395.

Dimond, S. J., Scammell, R. E., Pryce, I. G., Huws, D., & Gray, C. (1979). Callosal transfer and left-hand anomia in Schizophrenia. *Biological Psychiatry, 14*(5), 735–739.

Diwadkar, V. A., DeBellis, M. D., Sweeney, J. A., Pettegrew, J. W., & Keshavan, M. S. (2004). Abnormalities in MRI-measured signal intensity in the corpus callosum in Schizophrenia. *Schizophrenia Research, 67*(2/3), 277–282.

Diwadkar, V. A., & Keshavan, M. S. (2002). Newer techniques in magnetic resonance imaging and their potential for neuropsychiatric research. *Journal of Psychosomatic Research, 53,* 677–685.

Dong, W. K., & Greenough, W. T. (2004). Plasticity of nonneuronal brain tissue: Roles in developmental disorders. *Mental Retardation and Developmental Disabilities Research Review, 10*(2), 85–90.

Drevets, W. C., Ongur, D., & Price, J. L. (1998). Neuroimaging abnormalities in the subgenual prefrontal cortex: Implications for the pathophysiology of familial mood disorders. *Molecular Psychiatry, 3*(3), 220–226, 190–221.

Drevets, W. C., Videen, T. O., Price, J. L., Preskorn, S. H., Carmichael, S. T., & Raichle, M. E. (1992). A functional anatomical study of unipolar depression. *Journal of Neuroscience, 12*(9), 3628–3641.

Egaas, B., Courchesne, E., & Saitoh, O. (1995). Reduced size of corpus callosum in Autism. *Archives of Neurology, 52*(8), 794–801.

Elvevag, B., & Goldberg, T. E. (2000). Cognitive impairment in Schizophrenia is the core of the disorder. *Critical Reviews in Neurobiology, 14*(1), 1–21.

Farchione, T. R., Lorch, E., & Rosenberg, D. R. (2002). Hypoplasia of the corpus callosum and obsessive-compulsive symptoms. *Journal of Child Neurology, 17*(7), 535–537.

Fein, G., Di Sclafani, V., Cardenas, V. A., Goldmann, H., Tolou-Shams, M., & Meyerhoff, D. J. (2002). Cortical gray matter loss in treatment-naive alcohol dependent individuals. *Alcoholism: Clinical and Experimental Research, 26*(4), 558–564.

Fein, G., Di Sclafani, V., & Meyerhoff, D. J. (2002). Prefrontal cortical volume reduction associated with frontal cortex function deficit in 6-week abstinent crack-cocaine dependent men. *Drug and Alcohol Dependence, 68*(1), 87–93.

Feinberg, I. (1990). Cortical pruning and the development of Schizophrenia. *Schizophrenia Bulletin, 16*(4), 567–570.

Flynn, S. W., Lang, D. J., Mackay, A. L., Goghari, V., Vavasour, I. M., Whittall, K. P., et al. (2003). Abnormalities of myelination in Schizophrenia detected in vivo with MRI and post-mortem with analysis of oligodendrocyte proteins. *Molecular Psychiatry, 8*(9), 811–820.

Foong, J., Maier, M., Clark, C. A., Barker, G. J., Miller, D. H., & Ron, M. A. (2000). Neuropathological abnormalities of the corpus callosum in Schizophrenia: A diffusion tensor imaging study. *Journal of Neurology, Neurosurgery, and Psychiatry, 68*(2), 242–244.

Friston, K. J. (1998). The disconnection hypothesis. *Schizophrenia Research, 10*, 115–125.

Friston, K. J. (1999). Schizophrenia and the disconnection hypothesis. *Acta Psychiatrica Scandinavica, 395*(Suppl.), 68–79.

Frith, C. (2004). Is Autism a disconnection disorder? *Lancet Neurol, 3*(10), 577.

Frith, U. (1996). Cognitive explanations of Autism. *Acta Paediatrica, 416*(Suppl.), 63–68.

Frith, U., & Happé, F. (1994). Autism: Beyond "theory of mind." *Cognition, 50*(1/3), 115–132.

Galuske, R. A., Schlote, W., Bratzke, H., & Singer, W. (2000). Interhemispheric asymmetries of the modular structure in human temporal cortex. *Science, 289*(5486), 1946–1949.

Gazzaniga, M. S. (1989). Organization of the human brain. *Science, 245*(4921), 947–952.

Gazzaniga, M. S. (2000). Cerebral specialization and interhemispheric communication: Does the corpus callosum enable the human condition? *Brain, 123*(Pt. 7), 1293–1326.

Georgy, B. A., Hesselink, J. R., & Jernigan, T. L. (1993). MR imaging of the corpus callosum. *American Journal of Roentgenology, 160*(5), 949–955.

Giedd, J. N. (1999). Brain development: IX. Human brain growth. *American Journal of Psychiatry, 156*(1), 4.

Giedd, J. N., Blumenthal, J., Jeffries, N. O., Castellanos, F. X., Liu, H., Zijdenbos, A., et al. (1999). Brain development during childhood and adolescence: A longitudinal MRI study. *Nature Neuroscience, 2*(10), 861–863.

Giedd, J. N., Blumenthal, J., Jeffries, N. O., Rajapakse, J. C., Vaituzis, A. C., Liu, H., et al. (1999). Development of the human corpus callosum during childhood and adolescence: A longitudinal MRI study. *Progress in Neuro-Psychopharmacology and Biological Psychiatry, 23*(4), 571–588.

Giedd, J. N., Blumenthal, J., Molloy, E., & Castellanos, F. X. (2001). Brain imaging of attention deficit/hyperactivity disorder. *Annals of the New York Academy of Science, 931*, 33–49.

Gilmore, J. H., Zhai, G., Wilber, K., Smith, J. K., Lin, W., & Gerig, G. (2004). 3 Tesla magnetic resonance imaging of the brain in newborns. *Psychiatry Research, 132*(1), 81–85.

Girard, N., Raybaud, C., & du Lac, P. (1991). MRI study of brain myelination. *Journal of Neuroradiology, 18*(4), 291–307.

Glantz, L. A., & Lewis, D. A. (2000). Decreased dendritic spine density on prefrontal cortical pyramidal neurons in Schizophrenia. *Archives of General Psychiatry, 57*(1), 65–73.

Gogtay, N., Giedd, J. N., Lusk, L., Hayashi, K. M., Greenstein, D., Vaituzis, A. C., et al. (2004). Dynamic mapping of human cortical development during childhood through early adulthood. *Proceedings of the National Academy of Sciences, USA, 101*(21), 8174–8179.

Gogtay, N., Sporn, A., Clasen, L. S., Greenstein, D., Giedd, J. N., Lenane, M., et al. (2003). Structural brain MRI abnormalities in healthy siblings of patients with childhood-onset Schizophrenia. *American Journal of Psychiatry, 160*(3), 569–571.

Goldman-Rakic, P. S. (1988). Topography of cognition: Parallel distributed networks in primate association cortex. *Annual Review of Neuroscience, 11*, 137–156.

Goldman-Rakic, P. S. (1994). Working memory dysfunction in Schizophrenia. *Journal of Neuropsychiatry and Clinical Neuroscience, 6*, 348–357.

Green, P. (1978). Defective interhemispheric transfer in Schizophrenia. *Journal of Abnormal Psychology, 87*(5), 472–480.

Grossberg, S. (2000). The imbalanced brain: From normal behavior to Schizophrenia. *Biological Psychiatry, 48*(2), 81–98.

Guerri, C. (1998). Neuroanatomical and neurophysiological mechanisms involved in central nervous system dysfunctions induced by prenatal alcohol exposure. *Alcoholism: Clinical and Experimental Research, 22*(2), 304–312.

Gunther, W., Petsch, R., Steinberg, R., Moser, E., Streck, P., Heller, H., et al. (1991). Brain dysfunction during motor activation and corpus callosum alterations in Schizophrenia measured by cerebral blood flow and magnetic resonance imaging. *Biological Psychiatry, 29*(6), 535–555.

Hardan, A. Y., Minshew, N. J., Harenski, K., & Keshavan, M. S. (2001). Posterior fossa magnetic resonance imaging in Autism. *Journal of the American Academy of Child and Adolescent Psychiatry, 40*, 666–672.

Harrison, P. J. (1999). The neuropathology of Schizophrenia. A critical review of the data and their interpretation. *Brain, 122*(Pt. 4), 593–624.

Harrison, P. J. (2002). The neuropathology of primary mood disorder. *Brain, 125*(Pt. 7), 1428–1449.

Hauser, P., Dauphinais, I. D., & Berrettini, W. (1989). Corpus callosum dimensions measured by magnetic resonance imaging in bipolar affective disorder and Schizophrenia. *Biological Psychiatry, 26*, 659–668.

Hauser, P., Dauphinais, I. D., Berrettini, W., DeLisi, L. E., Gelernter, J., & Post, R. M. (1989). Corpus callosum dimensions measured by magnetic resonance imaging in bipolar affective disorder and Schizophrenia. *Biological Psychiatry, 26*(7), 659–668.

Hendren, R. L., Hodde-Vargas, J., Yeo, R. A., Vargas, L. A., Brooks, W. M., & Ford, C. (1995). Neuropsychophysiological study of children at risk for Schizophrenia: A preliminary report. *Journal of the American Academy of Child and Adolescent Psychiatry, 34*(10), 1284–1291.

Herbert, M. R., Ziegler, D. A., Deutsch, C. K., O'Brien, L. M., Kennedy, D. N., Filipek, P. A., et al. (2005). Brain asymmetries in Autism and developmental language disorder: A nested whole-brain analysis. *Brain, 128*(Pt. 1), 213–226.

Herbert, M. R., Ziegler, D. A., Makris, N., Filipek, P. A., Kemper, T. L., Normandin, J. J., et al. (2004). Localization of white matter volume increase in Autism and developmental language disorder. *Annals of Neurology, 55*(4), 530–540.

Highley, J. R., Esiri, M. M., McDonald, B., Cortina-Borja, M., Herron, B. M., & Crow, T. J. (1999). The size and fibre composition of the corpus callosum with respect to gender and Schizophrenia: A post-mortem study. *Brain, 122*(Pt. 1), 99–110.

Hill, D. E., Yeo, R. A., Campbell, R. A., Hart, B., Vigil, J., & Brooks, W. (2003). Magnetic resonance imaging correlates of attention-deficit/hyperactivity disorder in children. *Neuropsychology, 17*(3), 496–506.

Hill, S. Y., Shen, S., Lowers, L., & Locke, J. (2000). Factors predicting the onset of adolescent drinking in families at high risk for developing alcoholism. *Biological Psychiatry, 48*(4), 265–275.

Hill, S. Y., & Steinhauer, S. R. (1993). Assessment of prepubertal and postpubertal boys and girls at risk for developing alcoholism with P300 from a visual discrimination task. *Journal of Studies of Alcohol, 54,* 350–358.

Hohne, K. H., & Pommert, A. (1996). Volume visualization. In A. W. Toga & J. C. Mazziotta (Eds.), *Brain mapping: The methods* (pp. 423–444). San Diego: Academic Press.

Holland, B. A., Haas, D. K., Norman, D., Brant-Zawadzki, M., & Newton, T. H. (1986). MRI of normal brain maturation. *American Journal of Neuroradiology, 7*(2), 201–208.

Hubl, D., Koenig, T., Strik, W., Federspiel, A., Kreis, R., Boesch, C., et al. (2004). Pathways that make voices: White matter changes in auditory hallucinations. *Archives of General Psychiatry, 61*(7), 658–668.

Hulshoff Pol, H. E., Schnack, H. G., Mandl, R. C., Cahn, W., Collins, D. L., Evans, A. C., et al. (2004). Focal white matter density changes in Schizophrenia: Reduced inter-hemispheric connectivity. *Neuroimage, 21*(1), 27–35.

Huttenlocher, P. R., & Dabholkar, A. S. (1997). Regional differences in synaptogenesis in human cerebral cortex. *Journal of Comparative Neurology, 387*(2), 167–178.

Innocenti, G. M. (1994). Aspects of dendritic maturation of callosally projecting neurons. In M. Lassonde & M. A. Jeeves (Eds.), *Callosal agenesis: A natural split brain?* (pp. 119–123). New York: Plenum Press.

Innocenti, G. M., Aggoun-Zouaoui, D., & Lehmann, P. (1995). Cellular aspects of callosal connections and their development. *Neuropsychologia, 33*(8), 961–987.

Innocenti, G. M., Ansermet, F., & Parnas, J. (2003). Schizophrenia, neurodevelopment and corpus callosum. *Molecular Psychiatry, 8*(3), 261–274.

Insel, T. R., & Fernald, R. D. (2004). How the brain processes social information: Searching for the social brain. *Annual Review of Neuroscience, 27,* 697–722.

Ito, Y., Teicher, M. H., Glod, C. A., & Ackerman, E. (1998). Preliminary evidence for aberrant cortical development in abused children: A quantitative EEG study. *Journal of Neuropsychiatry and Clinical Neurosciences, 10*(3), 298–307.

Jacobsen, L. K., Giedd, J. N., Rajapakse, J. C., Hamburger, S. D., Vaituzis, A. C., Frazier, J. A., et al. (1997). Quantitative magnetic resonance imaging of the corpus callosum in childhood onset Schizophrenia. *Psychiatry Research, 68*(2/3), 77–86.

Job, D. E., Whalley, H. C., McConnell, S., Glabus, M., Johnstone, E. C., & Lawrie, S. M. (2003). Voxel-based morphometry of grey matter densities in subjects at high risk of Schizophrenia. *Schizophrenia Research, 64,* 1–13.

Johnson, V. P., Swayze, V. W., II, Sato, Y., & Andreasen, N. C. (1996). Fetal alcohol syndrome: Craniofacial and central nervous system manifestations. *American Journal of Medical Genetics, 61*(4), 329–339.

Jones, P., & Murray, R. M. (1991). The genetics of Schizophrenia is the genetics of neurodevelopment. *British Journal of Psychiatry, 158,* 615–623.

Just, M. A., Cherkassky, V. L., Keller, T. A., & Minshew, N. J. (2004). Cortical activation and synchronization during sentence comprehension in high-functioning Autism: Evidence of underconnectivity. *Brain, 127*(Pt. 8), 1811–1821.

Karbowski, J. (2003). How does connectivity between cortical areas depend on brain size? Implications for efficient computation. *Journal of Computational Neuroscience, 15*(3), 347–356.

Kayl, A. E., Moore, B. D., III, Slopis, J. M., Jackson, E. F., & Leeds, N. E. (2000). Quantitative morphology of the corpus callosum in children with neurofibromatosis and attention-deficit hyperactivity disorder. *Journal of Child Neurology, 15*(2), 90–96.

Keller, A., Jeffries, N. O., Blumenthal, J., Clasen, L. S., Liu, H., Giedd, J. N., et al. (2003). Corpus callosum development in childhood-onset Schizophrenia. *Schizophrenia Research, 62*(1/2), 105–114.

Kellner, C. H., Jolley, R. R., Holgate, R. C., Austin, L., Lydiard, R. B., Laraia, M., et al. (1991). Brain MRI in obsessive-compulsive disorder. *Psychiatry Research, 36*(1), 45–49.

Keshavan, M. S. (1999). Development, disease and degeneration in Schizophrenia: A unitary pathophysiological model. *Journal of Psychiatry Research, 33*(6), 513–521.

Keshavan, M. S., Anderson, S., & Pettegrew, J. W. (1994). Is Schizophrenia due to excessive synaptic pruning in the prefrontal cortex? *Journal of Psychiatric Research, 28,* 239–265.

Keshavan, M. S., Dick, E., Mankowski, I., Harenski, K., Montrose, D. M., Diwadkar, V., et al. (2002). Decreased left amygdala and hippocampal volumes in young offspring at risk for Schizophrenia. *Schizophrenia Research, 58,* 173–183.

Keshavan, M. S., Diwadkar, V. A., DeBellis, M. D., Dick, E., Kotwal, R., Rosenberg, D. R., et al. (2002). Development of the corpus callosum in childhood, adolescence and early adulthood. *Life Sciences, 70*(16), 1909–1922.

Keshavan, M. S., Diwadkar, V. A., Harenski, K., Rosenberg, D. R., Sweeney, J. A., & Pettegrew, J. W. (2002). Abnormalities of the corpus callosum in first episode, treatment naive Schizophrenia. *Journal of Neurology, Neurosurgery, and Psychiatry, 72*(6), 757–760.

Keshavan, M. S., & Schooler, N. R. (1992). First-episode studies in Schizophrenia: Criteria and characterization. *Schizophrenia Bulletin, 18,* 491–513.

Keshavan, M. S., Stanley, J. A., Montrose, D. M., Minshew, N. J., & Pettegrew, J. W. (2003). Prefrontal membrane phospholipid metabolism of child and adolescent offspring at risk for Schizophrenia or schizoaffective disorder: An in vivo 31P MRS study. *Molecular Psychiatry, 8*(3), 316–323.

Konradi, C., & Heckers, S. (2003). Molecular aspects of glutamate dysregulation: Implications for Schizophrenia and its treatment. *Pharmacology and Therapeutics, 97*(2), 153–179.

Kreipke, C. W., Rosenberg, D. R., & Keshavan, M. S. (2004). Does disordered brain development occur across diagnostic boundaries? In M. S. Keshavan, J. Kennedy, & R. M. Murray (Eds.), *Neurodevelopment and Schizophrenia* (pp. 390–411). New York: Cambridge University Press.

Kumar, A., & Cook, I. A. (2002). White matter injury, neural connectivity and the pathophysiology of psychiatric disorders. *Developmental Neuroscience, 24*(4), 255–261.

Kumra, S., Ashtari, M., McMeniman, M., Vogel, J., Augustin, R., Becker, D. E., et al. (2004). Reduced frontal white matter integrity in early-onset Schizophrenia: A preliminary study. *Biological Psychiatry, 55*(12), 1138–1145.

Kuperberg, G., & Heckers, S. (2000). Schizophrenia and cognitive function. *Current Opinion on Neurobiology, 10*(2), 205–210.

LaMantia, A. S., & Rakic, P. (1990). Cytological and quantitative characteristics of four cerebral commissures in the rhesus monkey. *Journal of Comparative Neurology, 291,* 520–537.

Lamb, J. A., Parr, J. R., Bailey, A. J., & Monaco, A. P. (2002). Autism: In search of susceptibility genes. *Neuromolecular Medicine, 2*(1), 11–28.

Lauder, J. M. (1983). Hormonal and humoral influences on brain development. *Psychoneuroendocrinology, 8*(2), 121–155.

Laughlin, S. B., & Sejnowski, T. J. (2003). Communication in neuronal networks. *Science, 301*(5641), 1870–1874.

Lee, K. H., Williams, L. M., Breakspear, M., & Gordon, E. (2003). Synchronous gamma activity: A review and contribution to an integrative neuroscience model of Schizophrenia. *Brain Research. Brain Research Reviews, 41*(1), 57–78.

Lewis, D. A., & Levitt, P. (2002). Schizophrenia as a disorder of neurodevelopment. *Annual Review of Neuroscience, 25,* 409–432.

Li, S. J., Biswal, B., Li, Z., Risinger, R., Rainey, C., Cho, J. K., et al. (2000). Cocaine administration decreases functional connectivity in human primary visual and motor cortex as detected by functional MRI. *Magnetic Resonance in Medicine, 43,* 45–51.

Lieberman, J. A. (1999). Is Schizophrenia a neurodegenerative disorder? A clinical and neurobiological perspective. *Biological Psychiatry, 46,* 729–739.

Lim, K. O., Hedehus, M., Moseley, M., de Crespigny, A., Sullivan, E. V., & Pfefferbaum, A. (1999). Compromised white matter tract integrity in Schizophrenia inferred from diffusion tensor imaging. *Archives of General Psychiatry, 56*(4), 367–374.

Lim, K. O., & Helpern, J. A. (2002). Neuropsychiatric applications of DTI: A review. *NMR in Biomedicine, 15,* 587–593.

Lim, K. O., Rosenbloom, M. J., Faustman, W. O., Sullivan, E. V., & Pfefferbaum, A. (1999). Cortical gray matter deficit in patients with bipolar disorder. *Schizophrenia Research, 40*(3), 219–227.

Loeser, J. D., & Alvord, E. C. (1968). Agenesis of the corpus callosum. *Brain, 91,* 553–570.

Lund, J. S. (1997). Development of the cerebral cortex: An overview. In M. S. Keshavan & R. M. Murray (Eds.), *Neurodevelopment and adult psychopathology* (pp. 3–11). Cambridge, England: Cambridge University Press.

Lyoo, I. K., Kim, M. J., Stoll, A. L., Demopulos, C. M., Parow, A. M., Dager, S. R., et al. (2004). Frontal lobe gray matter density decreases in bipolar I disorder. *Biological Psychiatry, 55*(6), 648–651.

Magara, F., Ricceri, L., Wolfer, D. P., & Lipp, H. P. (2000). The acallosal mouse strain I/LnJ: A putative model of ADHD? *Neuroscience and Biobehavioral Reviews, 24*(1), 45–50.

Mallet, L., Mazoyer, B., & Martinot, J. L. (1998). Functional connectivity in depressive, obsessive-compulsive, and schizophrenic disorders: An explorative correlational analysis of regional cerebral metabolism. *Psychiatry Research, 82*(2), 83–93.

Manes, F., Piven, J., Vrancic, D., Nanclares, V., Plebst, C., & Starkstein, S. E. (1999). An MRI study of the corpus callosum and cerebellum in mentally retarded autistic individuals. *Journal of Neuropsychiatry and Clinical Neurosciences, 11*(4), 470–474.

Marenco, S., & Weinberger, D. R. (2001). The neurodevelopmental hypothesis of Schizophrenia: Following a trail of evidence from cradle to grave. *Developmental Psychopathology, 12,* 501–527.

Mattson, S. N., Schoenfeld, A. M., & Riley, E. P. (2001). Teratogenic effects of alcohol on brain and behavior. *Alcohol Research and Health, 25*(3), 185–191.

McAlonan, G. M., Cheung, V., Cheung, C., Suckling, J., Lam, G. Y., Tai, K. S., et al. (2005). Mapping the brain in Autism. A voxel-based MRI study of volumetric differences and intercorrelations in Autism. *Brain, 128*(2), 268–276.

McCardle, C. B., Richardson, C. J., Nicholas, D. A., Mirfakhraee, M., Hayden, C. K., & Amparo, E. G. (1987). Developmental features of the neonatal brain: MR imaging: Pt. I. Gray-white matter differentiation and myelination. *Pediatric Radiology, 162,* 223–229.

McGlashan, T. H., & Hoffman, R. E. (2000). Schizophrenia as a disorder of developmentally reduced synaptic connectivity. *Archives of General Psychiatry, 57*(7), 637–648.

McGraw, P., Liang, L., & Provenzale, J. M. (2002). Evaluation of normal age-related changes in anisotropy during infancy and childhood as shown by diffusion tensor imaging. *American Journal of Roentgenology, 179*(6), 1515–1522.

Meisenzahl, E. M., Frodl, T., Greiner, J., Leinsinger, G., Maag, K. P., Heiss, D., et al. (1999). Corpus callosum size in Schizophrenia: A magnetic resonance imaging analysis. *European Archives of Psychiatry and Clinical Neuroscience, 249*(6), 305–312.

Mikels, J. A., & Reuter-Lorenz, P. A. (2004). Neural gate keeping: The role of interhemispheric interactions in resource allocation and selective filtering. *Neuropsychology, 18*(2), 328–339.

Moeller, F. G., Hasan, K. M., Steinberg, J. L., Kramer, L. A., Dougherty, D. M., Santos, R. M., et al. (2005). Reduced anterior corpus callosum white matter integrity is related to increased impulsivity and reduced discriminability in cocaine-dependent subjects: Diffusion tensor imaging. *Neuropsychopharmacology, 30*(3), 610–617.

Montrose, D. M., Dick, E., Pierri, J. N., Chris, K., Sweeney, J. A., & Keshavan, M. S. (1997). Intellectual function and psychopathology in offspring at risk for Schizophrenia. *Schizophrenia Research, 24,* 117.

Muhle, R., Trentacoste, S. V., & Rapin, I. (2004). The genetics of Autism. *Pediatrics, 113*(5), E472–E486.

Narr, K. L., Cannon, T. D., Woods, R. P., Thompson, P. M., Kim, S., Asunction, D., et al. (2002). Genetic contributions to altered callosal morphology in Schizophrenia. *Journal of Neuroscience, 22*(9), 3720–3729.

Narr, K. L., Green, M. F., Capetillo-Cunliffe, L., Toga, A. W., & Zaidel, E. (2003). Lateralized lexical decision in Schizophrenia: Hemispheric specialization and interhemispheric lexicality priming. *Journal of Abnormal Psychology, 112*(4), 623–632.

Nasrallah, H. A. (1985). The unintegrated right cerebral hemispheric consciousness as alien intruder: A possible mechanism for Schneiderian delusions in Schizophrenia. *Comprehensive Psychiatry, 26*(3), 273–282.

Nasrallah, H. A. (1997). Neurodevelopmental models of affective disorders. In M. S. Keshavan & R. M. Murray (Eds.), *Neurodevelopment and adult psychopathology* (pp. 99–105). New York: Cambridge University Press.

Nasrallah, H. A., McCalley-Whitters, M., Bigelow, L. B., & Rauscher, F. P. (1983). A histological study of the corpus callosum in chronic Schizophrenia. *Psychiatry Research, 8,* 251–260.

Nicolson, R., & Szatmari, P. (2003). Genetic and neurodevelopmental influences in autistic disorder. *Canadian Journal of Psychiatry, 48*(8), 526–537.

Ogden, C. A., Rich, M. E., Schork, N. J., Paulus, M. P., Geyer, M. A., Lohr, J. B., et al. (2004). Candidate genes, pathways and mechanisms for bipolar (manic-depressive) and related disorders: An expanded convergent functional genomics approach. *Molecular Psychiatry, 9*(11), 1007–1029.

O'Neill, J., Cardenas, V. A., & Meyerhoff, D. J. (2001). Separate and interactive effects of cocaine and alcohol dependence on brain structures and metabolites: Quantitative, MRI and proton MR spectroscopic imaging. *Addiction Biology, 6*(4), 347–361.

Pandya, D. N., & Seltzer, B. (1986). The topography of commissural fibers. In F. Lepore, M. Ptito, & H. H. Jasper (Eds.), *Two hemispheres, one brain: Functions of the corpus callosum* (pp. 47–73). New York: Alan R. Liss.

Park, H. J., Westin, C. F., Kubicki, M., Maier, S. E., Niznikiewicz, M., Baer, A., et al. (2004). White matter hemisphere asymmetries in healthy subjects and in Schizophrenia: A diffusion tensor MRI study. *Neuroimage, 23*(1), 213–223.

Paus, T., Zijdenbos, A., Worsley, K., Collins, D. L., Blumenthal, J., Giedd, J. N., et al. (1999). Structural maturation of neural pathways in children and adolescents: In vivo study. *Science, 283*(5409), 1908–1911.

Peterson, B. S., Leckman, J. F., Duncan, J. S., Wetzles, R., Riddle, M. A., Hardin, M. T., et al. (1994). Corpus callosum morphology from magnetic resonance images in Tourette's syndrome. *Psychiatry Research, 55*(2), 85–99.

Petronis, A. (2004). Schizophrenia, neurodevelopment and epigenetics. In M. S. Keshavan, J. Kennedy, & R. M. Murray (Eds.), *Neurodevelopment and Schizophrenia* (pp. 174–190). New York: Cambridge University Press.

Pfefferbaum, A., Mathalon, D. H., Sullivan, E. V., Rawles, J. M., Zipursky, R. B., & Lim, K. O. (1994). A quantitative magnetic resonance imaging study of changes in brain morphology from infancy to late adulthood. *Archives of Neurology, 51*(9), 874–887.

Pfefferbaum, A., Rosenbloom, M., Serventi, K. L., & Sullivan, E. V. (2002). Corpus callosum, pons, and cortical white matter in alcoholic women. *Alcoholism: Clinical and Experimental Research, 26*(3), 400–406.

Pfefferbaum, A., & Sullivan, E. V. (2002). Microstructural but not macrostructural disruption of white matter in women with chronic alcoholism. *Neuroimage, 15*(3), 708–718.

Pfefferbaum, A., & Sullivan, E. V. (2005). Disruption of brain white matter microstructure by excessive intracellular and extracellular fluid in alcoholism: Evidence from diffusion tensor imaging. *Neuropsychopharmacology, 30*(2), 423–432.

Pfefferbaum, A., Sullivan, E. V., & Carmelli, D. (2004). Morphological changes in aging brain structures are differentially affected by time-linked environmental influences despite strong genetic stability. *Neurobiology and Aging, 25*(2), 175–183.

Piven, J. (1997). The biological basis of Autism. *Current Opinion on Neurobiology, 7*(5), 708–712.

Piven, J., Bailey, J., Ranson, B. J., & Arndt, S. (1997). An MRI study of the corpus callosum in Autism. *American Journal of Psychiatry, 154*(8), 1051–1056.

Pueyo, R., Maneru, C., Junque, C., Vendrell, P., Pujol, J., Mataro, M., et al. (2003). Quantitative signal intensity measures on magnetic resonance imaging in attention-deficit hyperactivity disorder. *Cognitive and Behavioral Neurology, 16*(1), 75–81.

Pujol, J., Vendrell, P., Junque, C., Marti-Vilalta, J. L., & Capdevila, A. (1993). When does human brain development end? Evidence of corpus callosum growth up to adulthood. *Annals of Neurology, 34*, 71–75.

Quraishi, S., & Frangou, S. (2002). Neuropsychology of bipolar disorder: A review. *Journal of Affective Disorders, 72*(3), 209–226.

Rajapakse, J. C., Giedd, J. N., Rumsey, J. M., Vaituzis, A. C., Hamburger, S. D., & Rapoport, J. L. (1996). Regional MRI measurements of the corpus callosum: A methodological and developmental study. *Brain Development, 18*(5), 379–388.

Rakic, P. T. (1999). The importance of being well placed and having the right connections. *Annals of the New York Academy of Science, 882*, 90–106.

Randall, P. L. (1980). A neuroanatomical theory on the aetiology of Schizophrenia. *Medical Hypotheses, 6*(6), 645–658.

Rapin, I. (1999). Autism in search of a home in the brain. *Neurology, 52*(5), 902–904.

Rapin, I., & Katzman, R. (1998). Neurobiology of Autism. *Annals of Neurology, 43*(1), 7–14.

Rapoport, J. L., Giedd, J. N., Blumenthal, J., Hamburger, S., Jeffries, N., Fernandez, T., et al. (1999). Progressive cortical change during adolescence in childhood-onset Schizophrenia: A longitudinal magnetic resonance imaging study. *Archives of General Psychiatry, 56*(7), 649–654.

Rapoport, J. L., Kumra, S., Jacobsen, L., Smith, A., Lee, P., Nelson, J., et al. (1997). Childhood onset Schizophrenia: Progressive ventricular change during adolescence. *Archives of General Psychiatry, 54*, 897–903.

Reiss, A. L., Feinstein, C., & Rosenbaum, K. N. (1986). Autism and genetic disorders. *Schizophrenia Bulletin, 12*(4), 724–738.

Riley, E. P., Mattson, S. N., Sowell, E. R., Jernigan, T. L., Sobel, D. F., & Jones, K. L. (1995). Abnormalities of the corpus callosum in children prenatally exposed to alcohol. *Alcoholism: Clinical and Experimental Research, 19*(5), 1198–1202.

Riley, E. P., McGee, C. L., & Sowell, E. R. (2004). Teratogenic effects of alcohol: A decade of brain imaging. *American Journal of Medical Genetics Part C (Seminars in Medical Genetics), 127*(1), 35–41.

Rilling, J. K., & Insel, T. R. (1999). The primate neocortex in comparative perspective using magnetic resonance imaging. *Journal of Human Evolution, 37*(2), 191–223.

Roebuck, T. M., Mattson, S. N., & Riley, E. P. (1998). A review of the neuroanatomical findings in children with fetal alcohol syndrome or prenatal exposure to alcohol. *Alcoholism: Clinical and Experimental Research, 22*(2), 339–344.

Roebuck, T. M., Mattson, S. N., & Riley, E. P. (2002). Interhemispheric transfer in children with heavy prenatal alcohol exposure. *Alcoholism: Clinical and Experimental Research, 26*(12), 1863–1871.

Rosenberg, D. R., Keshavan, M. S., Dick, E. L., Bagwell, W. W., MacMaster, F. P., & Birmaher, B. (1997). Corpus callosal morphology in treatment-naive pediatric obsessive compulsive disorder. *Progress in Neuro-Psychopharmacology and Biological Psychiatry, 21*(8), 1269–1283.

Rosenthal, R., & Bigelow, L. B. (1972). Quantitative brain measurements in chronic Schizophrenia. *British Journal of Psychiatry, 121*, 259–264.

Rossell, S. L., Shapleske, J., Fukuda, R., Woodruff, P. W., Simmons, A., & David, A. S. (2001). Corpus callosum area and functioning in schizophrenic patients with auditory-verbal hallucinations. *Schizophrenia Research, 50*(1/2), 9–17.

Rowley, H. A., Grant, P. E., & Roberts, T. P. (1999). Diffusion MR imaging: Theory and applications. *Neuroimaging Clinics of North America, 9*, 343–361.

Rubenstein, J. L., & Rakic, P. (1999). Genetic control of cortical development. *Cerebral Cortex, 9*(6), 521–523.

Sanchez, M. M., Hearn, E. F., Do, D., Rilling, J. K., & Herndon, J. G. (1998). Differential rearing affects corpus callosum size and cognitive function of rhesus monkeys. *Brain Research, 812*(1/2), 38–49.

Sanfilipo, M., Lafargue, T., Rusinek, H., Arena, L., Loneragan, C., Lautin, A., et al. (2000). Volumetric measure of the frontal and temporal lobe regions in Schizophrenia: Relationship to negative symptoms. *Archives of General Psychiatry, 57*(5), 471–480.

Scamvougeras, A., Kigar, D. L., Jones, D., Weinberger, D. R., & Witelson, S. F. (2003). Size of the human corpus callosum is genetically determined: An MRI study in mono and dizygotic twins. *Neuroscience Letters, 338*(2), 91–94.

Schmitt, J. E., Eliez, S., Warsofsky, I. S., Bellugi, U., & Reiss, A. L. (2001). Corpus callosum morphology of Williams syndrome: Relation to genetics and behavior. *Developmental Medicine and Child Neurology, 43*(3), 155–159.

Schrift, M. J., Bandla, H., Shah, P., & Taylor, M. A. (1986). Interhemispheric transfer in major psychoses. *Journal of Nervous and Mental Diseases, 174*(4), 203–207.

Schulte, T., Pfefferbaum, A., & Sullivan, E. V. (2004). Parallel interhemispheric processing in aging and alcoholism: Relation to corpus callosum size. *Neuropsychologia, 42*(2), 257–271.

Schulte, T., Sullivan, E. V., Muller-Oehring, E. M., Adalsteinsson, E., & Pfefferbaum, A. (2005). Corpus callosal microstructural integrity influences interhemispheric processing: A diffusion tensor imaging study. *Cerebral Cortex.*

Selemon, L. D., & Goldman-Rakic, P. S. (1999). The reduced neuropil hypothesis: A circuit based model of Schizophrenia. *Biological Psychiatry, 45*(1), 17–25.

Seymour, S. E., Reuter-Lorenz, P. A., & Gazzaniga, M. S. (1994). The disconnection syndrome: Basic findings reaffirmed. *Brain, 117*(Pt. 1), 105–115.

Shashi, V., Muddasani, S., Santos, C. C., Berry, M. N., Kwapil, T. R., Lewandowski, E., et al. (2004). Abnormalities of the corpus callosum in nonpsychotic children with chromosome 22q11 deletion syndrome. *Neuroimage, 21*(4), 1399–1406.

Shenton, M. E., Dickey, C. C., Frumin, M., & McCarley, R. W. (2001). A review of MRI findings in Schizophrenia. *Schizophrenia Research, 49,* 1–52.

Sigmundsson, T., Suckling, J., Maier, M., Williams, S., Bullmore, E., Greenwood, K., et al. (2001). Structural abnormalities in frontal, temporal, and limbic regions and interconnecting white matter tracts in schizophrenic patients with prominent negative symptoms. *American Journal of Psychiatry, 158*(2), 234–243.

Singer, L., Arendt, R., Farkas, K., Minnes, S., Huang, J., & Yamashita, T. (1997). Relationship of prenatal cocaine exposure and maternal postpartum psychological distress to child developmental outcome. *Developmental Psychopathology, 9*(3), 473–489.

Skoyles, J. R. (2002). Is Autism due to cerebral-cerebellum disconnection? *Medical Hypotheses, 58*(4), 332–336.

Sommer, I. E., Ramsey, N. F., & Kahn, R. S. (2001). Language lateralization in Schizophrenia: An fMRI study. *Schizophrenia Research, 52,* 57–67.

Sowell, E. R., Mattson, S. N., Thompson, P. M., Jernigan, T. L., Riley, E. P., & Toga, A. W. (2001). Mapping callosal morphology and cognitive correlates: Effects of heavy prenatal alcohol exposure. *Neurology, 57*(2), 235–244.

Sowell, E. R., Thompson, P. M., Mattson, S. N., Tessner, K. D., Jernigan, T. L., Riley, E. P., et al. (2001). Voxel-based morphometric analyses of the brain in children and adolescents prenatally exposed to alcohol. *NeuroReport, 12*(3), 515–523.

Sowell, E. R., Thompson, P. M., Tessner, K. D., & Toga, A. W. (2001). Mapping continued brain growth and gray matter density reduction in dorsal frontal cortex: Inverse relationships during postadolescent brain maturation. *Journal of Neuroscience, 21*(22), 8819–8829.

Stewart, A. L., Rifkin, L., Amess, P. N., Kirkbride, V., Townsend, J. P., Miller, D. H., et al. (1999). Brain structure and neurocognitive and behavioural function in adolescents who were born very preterm. *Lancet, 353*(9165), 1653–1657.

Sullivan, E. V., & Pfefferbaum, A. (2003). Diffusion tensor imaging in normal aging and neuropsychiatric disorders. *European Journal of Radiology, 45*(3), 244–255.

Teicher, M. H., Andersen, S. L., Polcari, A., Anderson, C. M., & Navalta, C. P. (2002). Developmental neurobiology of childhood stress and trauma. *Psychiatric Clinics of North America, 25*(2), 397–426.

Teicher, M. H., Andersen, S. L., Polcari, A., Anderson, C. M., Navalta, C. P., & Kim, D. M. (2003). The neurobiological consequences of early stress and childhood maltreatment. *Neuroscience and Biobehavioral Reviews, 27*(1/2), 33–44.

Teicher, M. H., Dumont, N. L., Ito, Y., Vaituzis, C., Giedd, J. N., & Andersen, S. L. (2004). Childhood neglect is associated with reduced corpus callosum area. *Biological Psychiatry, 56*(2), 80–85.

Teicher, M. H., Ito, Y., Glod, C. A., Andersen, S. L., Dumont, N., & Ackerman, E. (1997). Preliminary evidence for abnormal cortical development in physically and sexually abused children using EEG coherence and MRI. *Annals of the New York Academy of Science, 821,* 160–175.

Tibbo, P., Nopoulos, P., Arndt, S., & Andreasen, N. C. (1998). Corpus callosum shape and size in male patients with Schizophrenia. *Biological Psychiatry, 44*(6), 405–412.

Tkachev, D., Mimmack, M. L., Ryan, M. M., Wayland, M., Freeman, T., Jones, P. B., et al. (2003). Oligodendrocyte dysfunction in Schizophrenia and bipolar disorder. *Lancet, 362*(9386), 798–805.

Tomaiuolo, F., Di Paola, M., Caravale, B., Vicari, S., Petrides, M., & Caltagirone, C. (2002). Morphology and morphometry of the corpus callosum in Williams syndrome: A T1-weighted MRI study. *NeuroReport, 13*(17), 2281–2284.

Tsuang, M. (2000). Schizophrenia: Genes and environment. *Biological Psychiatry, 47*(3), 210–220.

Usiskin, S. I., Nicolson, R., Krasnewich, D. M., Yan, W., Lenane, M., Wudarsky, M., et al. (1999). Velocardiofacial syndrome in childhood-onset Schizophrenia. *Journal of the American Academy of Child and Adolescent Psychiatry, 38*(12), 1536–1543.

van Buchem, M. A., & Tofts, P. S. (2000). Magnetization transfer imaging. *Neuroimaging Clinics of North America, 10,* 771–788.

van der Knaap, M. S., & Valk, J. (1990). MR imaging of the various stages of normal myelination during the first year of life. *Neuroradiology, 31*(6), 459–470.

Villarreal, G., Hamilton, D. A., Graham, D. P., Driscoll, I., Qualls, C., Petropoulos, H., et al. (2004). Reduced area of the corpus callosum in posttraumatic stress disorder. *Psychiatry Research, 131*(3), 227–235.

Waiter, G. D., Williams, J. H., Murray, A. D., Gilchrist, A., Perrett, D. I., & Whiten, A. (2005). Structural white matter deficits in high-functioning individuals with autistic spectrum disorder: A voxel-based investigation. *Neuroimage, 24*(2), 455–461.

Walker, E. F., Diforio, D., & Baum, K. (1999). Developmental neuropathology and the precursors of Schizophrenia. *Acta Psychiatrica Scandinavica, 395*(Suppl.), 12–19.

Walker, J., Curtis, V., & Murray, R. M. (2002). Schizophrenia and bipolar disorder: Similarities in pathogenic mechanisms but differences in neurodevelopment. *International Clinical Psychopharmacology, 17* (Suppl., 3), S11–S19.

Walker, J., Curtis, V., Shaw, P., & Murray, R. M. (2002). Schizophrenia and bipolar disorder are distinguished mainly by differences in neurodevelopment. *Neurotoxicity Research, 4*(5/6), 427–436.

Webb, S. J., Monk, C. S., & Nelson, C. A. (2001). Mechanisms of postnatal neurobiological development: Implications for human development. *Developmental Neuropsychology, 19*(2), 147–171.

Winters, L., Cornblatt, B. A., & Erlenmeyer-Kimling, L. (1991). The prediction of psychiatric disorders in late adolescence. In E. F. Walker (Ed.), *Schizophrenia: A life-course developmental perspective* (pp. 123–137). San Diego: Academic Press.

Woodruff, P. W., McManus, I. C., & David, A. S. (1995). Meta-analysis of corpus callosum size in Schizophrenia. *Journal of Neurology, Neurosurgery, and Psychiatry, 58*(4), 457–461.

Woodruff, P. W., Pearlson, G. D., Geer, M. J., Barta, P. E., & Chilcoat, H. D. (1993). A computerized magnetic resonance imaging study of corpus callosum morphology in Schizophrenia. *Psychological Medicine, 23*(1), 45–56.

Wright, I. C., McGuire, P. K., Poline, J. B., Travere, J. M., Murray, R. M., Frith, C. D., et al. (1995). A voxel-based method for the statistical analysis of gray and white matter density applied to Schizophrenia. *Neuroimage, 2,* 244–252.

Wu, J. C., Buchsbaum, M. S., Johnson, J. C., Hershey, T. G., Wagner, E. A., Teng, C., et al. (1993). Magnetic resonance and positron emission tomography imaging of the corpus callosum: Size, shape and metabolic rate in unipolar depression. *Journal of Affective Disorders, 28*(1), 15–25.

Zhang, K., & Sejnowski, T. J. (2000). A universal scaling law between gray matter and white matter of cerebral cortex. *Proceedings of the National Academy of Sciences, USA, 97*(10), 5621–5626.

CHAPTER 20

Toward a Developmental Psychopathology of Personality Disturbance: A Neurobehavioral Dimensional Model

RICHARD A. DEPUE and MARK F. LENZENWEGER

The personality disorders, as defined by the *Diagnostic and Statistical Manual of Mental Disorders,* fourth edition (*DSM-IV;* American Psychiatric Association [APA], 1994), are thought to represent stable, enduring, and consistent maladaptive personality configurations that result in considerable occupational and social impairment as well as subjective distress for many who suffer from them. However, relatively little is known about what causes personality disorders to develop or how they are maintained to varying degrees over time. Although the 1980s saw an upsurge in interest in the definition and assessment of personality pathology, it is fair to say that even 20 years later, many questions remain as to the proper classification architecture for personality pathology, the nature of the relationship between normal personality and temperament processes and personality pathology, and the life span trajectories for those who are afflicted with personality pathology (Lenzenweger & Clarkin, 2005). In short, the cause of personality pathology remains essentially unknown.

This work was supported by National Institute of Mental Health research grants MH-55347 awarded to R. A. Depue and MH-45448 awarded to M. F. Lenzenweger.

Before tackling the substantive focus of this chapter, which is to provide a provisional sketch for aspects of a developmental psychopathology for personality disorders, we would like to mention two "big facts" regarding personality disorders as presently conceived. These big facts, as it were, have impacted our thinking and provided the impetus, in part, for many of the ideas developed here, and they have implications for the developmental psychopathology approach. Although long thought to be relatively prevalent based on impressions from practitioners in office and clinic settings, only recently have quality prevalence estimates emerged for personality pathology in the nonclinical and general population. Lenzenweger, Loranger, Korfine, and Neff (1997) provided the first empirical prevalence estimate for personality pathology derived from a nonclinical sample and employing experienced diagnosticians. These investigators reported a prevalence of 11% for "any personality disorder" (Lenzenweger et al., 1997), a rate that was replicated in subsequent studies by Torgersen, Kringlen, and Cramer (2001; 13%), Samuels et al. (2002; 9%), and Grant et al. (2004; 14.8%). Thus, although there is considerable debate about the proper way to define personality pathology, it is safe to say that there is a rate of impairing psychopathology in the general population that is nontrivial. In fact, it appears that somewhere between 1 in 7 and 1 in 10 adults in the population is likely to suffer from a diagnosable personality disorder. This is clearly a problem of considerable proportion, worthy of both clinical and scientific interest. This rate of psychopathology suggests that the developmental determinants of personality pathology are not likely to be rare. Moreover, as with any complex phenotype, we anticipate that multiple lines of influence will interact to create what is known as a personality disorder; thus, one should not expect to find simple, causal explanations for the development of these forms of psychopathology (e.g., personality disorder develops solely from severe childhood sexual abuse).

A second big fact concerns the manner in which personality disorders are actually defined in terms of their basic nature, specifically their putative stability over time. The current diagnostic nomenclature (*DSM-IV*, APA, 1994) and its immediate predecessors (*DSM-III*, APA, 1980; *DSM-III-R*, APA, 1987) all defined personality disorders as "enduring patterns" of behavior that are "inflexible" and "stable over time." Clearly, the picture that the *DSM* model has painted is one of considerable temporal stability for personality pathology; however, it is noteworthy that these descriptions of stability in the APA nomenclature were *never* based on empirical data. At the time the *DSM-III* was published, there were no empirical data available from prospective, multiwave longitudinal studies on which such assertions could be based. The basis for the *DSM* position on the temporal stability of the personality disorders came largely from the impressions of practitioners, long held beliefs about the basic nature of personality pathology, and a small number of test-retest studies. The test-retest studies, though useful for the establishment of psychometric characteristics for assessment instruments, provided little to no insight into the question of long-term stability of the personality disorders owing to the well-known limitations and artifacts inherent in the test-retest study design. The first major longitudinal study in this area that met contemporary design criteria, known as the Longitudinal Study of Personality Disorders (LSPD; Lenzenweger, 1999; Lenzenweger et al., 1997; Lenzenweger, Johnson, & Willett, 2004), was only begun in 1990. Other longitudinal studies of the personality disorders were begun later (e.g., Gunderson et al., 2000; J. G. Johnson et al., 2000; Shea et al., 2002; Zanarini, Frankenburg, Hennen, & Silk, 2003). With the passage of nearly 10 years, during which the various longitudinal studies have been under way, a clear pattern has begun to emerge re-

garding the stability of personality pathology over time. Despite one or another methodological artifacts, all of the existing longitudinal studies show consistent and compelling evidence of mean level decreases in personality disorder features over time (J. G. Johnson et al., 2000; Lenzenweger, 1999; Lenzenweger, Johnson, et al., 2004; Shea et al., 2002; Zanarini et al., 2003). Data from the LSPD revealed mean level change in personality disorder features over time (Lenzenweger, 1999), and more recent analyses of the LSPD data, using the more sensitive approach of individual growth curve analysis, revealed a decline of 1.4 personality disorder features per year (Lenzenweger, Johnson, et al., 2004). Such change represented a "medium" effect size (Rosenthal & Rosnow, 1991). It is important to note that the change observed in the LSPD subjects was not accounted for by other comorbid mental disorders (e.g., unipolar depression, anxiety disorders, substance abuse) or exposure to conventional psychiatric treatments. With respect to the other longitudinal efforts, in a study limited to Borderline Personality Disorder (BPD), Zanarini et al. found massive declines in symptoms, such that 73.5% of previously diagnosed BPD subjects were remitted at 6-year follow-up, suggesting nontrivial mean level changes in BPD symptoms. J. G. Johnson et al. found 28% to 48% reductions in personality disorder features with time in a study based on careful chart reviews of the same people over time. Shea et al. found 66% of the participants in a longitudinal study of diagnosed personality disorder patients dropped below diagnostic thresholds in 1 year, with highly significant (revealing substantial effects) declines for continuously measured personality disorder symptoms. The Shea et al. data are somewhat difficult to interpret, as the assessors of the patients were not blind to previous assessments and all of the patients in the study were also in treatment during the course of the study. Nonetheless, the assumption of stability of the personality disorders over time, despite being widely espoused as well as included in the formal diagnostic nomenclature, is eroding in the face of empirical data.

Thus, from the standpoint of developmental psychopathology, the personality disorders represent a domain of psychopathology that actually shows clear evidence of change over time, although the precise determinants of such change remain to be specified. Moreover, such change also suggests that the phenomena known as personality disorders are best thought of as plastic or dynamic constructs that can show flexibility with the passage of time. Any developmental psychopathology account of the emergence and development of such disorders must take into account this plastic and dynamic nature. Finally, regarding the long-term developmental picture of the personality disorders, it is fair to say that, as a field, we still have no idea, from properly designed multiwave studies, what the exact nature of personality disorder stability and change is over the life span.

The developmental psychopathology perspective (Cicchetti & Cohen, 1995; Rutter, 1997, 2000; see also Lenzenweger & Haugaard, 1996) seeks to illuminate the interaction between normative and abnormal development. The study of personality disorders from a developmental psychopathology perspective strikes us as having considerable potential. In our theoretical work on the neurobehavioral underpinnings of personality disorders, we have sought to integrate what is known about normal personality and temperament systems with what is known about the most common personality disorder phenotypes. Moreover, personality pathology, by its very definition, calls out to be studied from a longitudinal perspective and thus should be properly studied using methods, measures, and time frames that will help to illuminate change and development across the life span. Within this life span developmental perspective, which can be developed only in preliminary form here, we can well imagine that there are not only risk factors that can facilitate the emergence of personality disorders (both within the person and in the environment), but that there are also protective factors that mitigate against the emergence of a personality disorder. Clearly, whether or not one develops a personality disorder depends on a number of contingencies, and the pathway that runs from such risks and underlying liabilities to a disordered personality organization is not one that is fixed in granite. Rather, we envision a relatively complex, interactive dance taking place between neurobehavioral systems, brain development, and environmental inputs that can result, but may not necessarily result, in recognizable personality pathology. In this context, we note the importance of *multiple levels of analysis* (Cicchetti & Dawson, 2002; Kosslyn & Rosenberg, 2001) in the conceptualization of personality pathology. A multiple-levels-of-analysis approach represents a research and theoretical vantage point that seeks to understand and model complex psychological processes and constructs at levels ranging from the cellular to the interpersonal and social. Ideally, models of complex phenomena, such as personality pathology, should seek to simultaneously consider factors within the person (e.g., neurobiology, neural circuitry), at the level of the person (e.g., individual differences), and between persons (e.g., interpersonal, social functioning). We endorse this valuable research perspec-

tive, and the model we present seeks to understand personality pathology across multiple levels of analysis.

In our chapter, we sketch out what we believe to be the foundational elements of personality pathology; however, we emphasize that the interaction of these elements likely continues across time and that even in the case of personality disordered individuals, it is likely that their disorder, as it were, continues to exert some influence on psychological development and functioning over time. In summary, in our view of the development of what we term "personality disturbance," such disturbance is the product of a matrix of highly interactive systems of neurobehavioral processes. This matrix, of course, interacts with the environment through time and across contexts, including developmental transitions, to allow for the emergence of personality pathology.

THE PROBLEM OF MODELING NONENTITIES

From a scientific perspective, it is really no longer possible to accept the notion that personality disorders (PDs) represent distinct, categorical diagnostic entities. The behavioral features of PDs are not organized into discrete diagnostic entities, and multivariate studies of behavioral criteria fail to identify factors that resemble existing diagnostic constructs (Block, 2001; Ekselius, Lindstrom, von Knorring, Bodlund, & Kullgren, 1994; Livesley, 2001; Livesley, Schroeder, Jackson, & Jang, 1994). Indeed, just the opposite is observed: The behavioral features of PDs merge imperceptibly in a continuous fashion across diagnostic categories, resulting in (1) significant overlap of behavioral features across categories and hence diagnostic comorbidity within individuals and (2) symptom heterogeneity within categories and hence frequent (and most common in some studies) application of the ambiguous diagnosis of Personality Disorder Not Otherwise Specified (Livesley, 2001; Saulsman & Page, 2004). Moreover, aside from schizotypy/schizotypic disorders, the existing latent class and taxometric analysis literature on PDs generally does *not* provide support for distinct entities in the PD realm in any compelling fashion, and some provisional taxonic findings for Borderline and Antisocial PDs are open to doubt. It is, accordingly, not surprising that diagnostic membership is not significantly associated with predictive validity as to prognosis or psychological or pharmacological treatments (Livesley, 2001). Such a state of affair recently led Livesley to declare that "evidence on these points has accumulated to the point that it can no longer be ignored" (p. 278).

Such a state of affairs supports proponents of a dimensional approach to PDs, who note that (1) the behavioral features of PDs not only overlap diagnostic categories, but also merge imperceptibly with normality (Livesley, 2001; Saulsman & Page, 2004); and (2) the factorial structure of behavioral traits associated with PDs is similar in clinical and nonclinical samples (Livesley, Jackson, & Schroeder, 1992; Reynolds & Clark, 2001). Furthermore, the higher-order structure of PD traits resembles four of the five major traits identified in the higher-order structure of normal personality (Clark & Livesley, 1994; Clark, Livesley, Schroeder, & Irish, 1996; Reynolds & Clark, 2001). These findings suggest that PDs may be better understood as emerging at the extremes of personality dimensions that define the structure of behavior in the normal population (for reviews of this position, see P. T. Costa & Widiger, 1994; Depue & Lenzenweger, 2001; Lenzenweger & Clarkin, 1996; Livesley, 2001; Reynolds & Clark, 2001; Saulsman & Page, 2004; Widiger, Trull, Clarkin, Sanderson, & Costa, 1994).

This realization has led to innumerable attempts to illustrate the association of personality traits to PD diagnostic categories. Most of these studies have relied on the so-called five-factor model of personality, which defines a structure characterized by the five higher-order traits of extraversion, neuroticism, agreeableness, conscientiousness, and openness to experience. Although Reynolds and Clark (2001) demonstrated that four of these traits (openness shows no consistent relation to PDs; Saulsman & Page, 2004) account for a substantial proportion of the variance in interview-based ratings of *DSM-IV* PD diagnoses, a recent meta-analysis of similar studies demonstrated the limitation of the approach of correlating four traits with PDs (Saulsman & Page, 2004). The meta-analysis showed that most such studies illustrate the following problems: (1) The correlation of these four traits with PD categories is moderate to weak; (2) the complex "entity" of a PD category is defined by as little as one trait but never by four traits in a significant way; and (3) single traits (e.g., neuroticism) characterize more than one, and sometimes several, putatively distinct PDs. For example, how helpful is it to know that Histrionic PD is characterized by moderately high extraversion but by no other trait; or, similarly, that Dependent PD is associated with moderately high neuroticism but by no other trait? To what line of research or clinical intervention does that knowledge lead? Moreover, the traits relate more highly to PD categories that are studied in nonclinical samples, indicating that the traits may be less valuable in defining clinical entities. What the meta-analysis did reveal is that most PDs manifest, in common, higher trait levels of neuroticism and lower trait levels of agreeableness, meaning that most individuals with PDs are subject to negative emotionality and impaired affiliative or interpersonal behavior. Thus, again, when PD categories serve as the outcome variable, personality traits provide little in the way of power to discriminate between such categories. Overall, then, it is probably not unfair to conclude that such correlational studies have done little to inform the issue of continuity from personality systems to states of disorder, most of them having merely specified correlates of PDs and nothing more, and most of these studies lacked an underlying framework for understanding both personality and PDs.

The paradox in all of this is that, despite knowing that the PD diagnostic categories are unreliable and lack compelling construct and predictive validity, researchers cling to the approach of relating major personality traits, typically considered at the conceptual level of analysis one trait at a time, to *nonentities* of PDs. How can one learn something substantive by relating four higher-order traits to heterogeneous behavioral phenomena that are clustered conceptually (not statistically or theoretically) into diagnostic entities? As Livesley (2001) aptly notes, because PD diagnoses are so fundamentally flawed, it is not important to know whether each PD diagnosis can be accommodated by a dimensional model. Furthermore, the problem in this approach does not appear to be explained simply by use of a small number of broad traits. When the 30 facet scales of the NEO-PI (Personality Inventory) were correlated with PD categories, only modest gains were achieved relative to the use of the four major traits (mean difference in $R^2 \sim 0.04$; Dyce & O'Connor, 1998; Millon, 1997).

Perhaps one of the most crucial issues associated with a dimensional personality approach to PDs is that the substantive meaning of the four major traits is not clear and generally has been a neglected topic (Block, 2001). Put differently, there is not a clear understanding as to which underlying neurobehavioral systems these traits reflect, which the behavioral genetic literature implies they must (Tellegen et al., 1988). Accordingly, in this chapter, we promote an alternative empirical and theoretical approach to PDs. First, we embrace the fact that PDs do not exist as *distinct entities;* therefore, we refer to the behavioral manifestations that emerge at the extremes of personality dimensions as *personality disturbance* rather than disorder. We exclude Schizotypal and Paranoid Personality Disorders from our model, because there is evidence that they may be genetically related to Schizophrenia (e.g., Kendler et al., 1993; Lenzenweger & Loranger, 1989), representing an alternative manifestation of Schizophrenia liability (Lenzenweger, 1998), and studies of the latent class structure of schizotypy show evidence that its underlying nature is more likely of a taxonic or qualitative nature (Korfine & Lenzenweger, 1995; Lenzenweger & Korfine, 1992). The term *disorder,* though less formal and regimented than the term *disease,* nevertheless connotes a relatively coherent symptomatic entity that, with more empirical attention, will be characterized by distinct boundaries and underlying dysfunction. We do not believe that, as PDs are currently conceived, such a state of scientific credibility will be achieved and hence warrant the use of the terms syndrome, disorder, or disease. Second, we attempt to delineate the nature of the neurobehavioral systems that we postulate underlie the four major traits of personality. In so doing, we hope to provide a substantive meaning to the four major personality traits that supersedes the extant variation in trait labels and psychological concepts.

The implications of defining personality traits in terms of neurobehavioral systems leads to a third part of the chapter, where we derive a model of personality disturbance based on the *interaction* of these neurobehavioral systems. Though genetically speaking, it may be possible to conceive of the neurobiological variables associated with neurobehavioral systems as subject to independent influences, it is impossible to imagine that neurobehavioral systems are independent at a functional level. Similarly, it is impossible to imagine that personality traits can be associated in an independent manner to PDs. Neurobehavioral systems, and the personality traits that reflect their influence, interact to produce complex behavior patterns—personality as a whole—in a multivariate fashion. Therefore, our model of personality disturbance rests on a foundation of multivariate interaction of neurobehavioral systems. Such an interaction may yield a phenotypic clustering of behavioral signs or symptoms that could be taken to suggest a demarcation, perhaps indicative of latent threshold effects in the neurobehavioral systems, but the observed clustering represents the end product of underlying continuous dimensional neurobehavioral systems. Furthermore, although it is true that our model is dimensional in nature, where personality disturbance lies at the extreme of normal, interacting personality dimensions, it is worth noting that no assumption is made herein that phenotypic dimensions of personality are genetically continuous. The phenotypic continuity could well represent several underlying, *distinct* genotypic distributions (Gottesman, 1997), as may be the case even within the

normal range of variation of some personality traits (Benjamin et al., 1996; Ebstein et al., 1996).

NEUROBEHAVIORAL SYSTEMS UNDERLYING HIGHER-ORDER PERSONALITY TRAITS

The higher-order structure of personality converges on three to seven factors that account for the phenotypic variation in behavior (Digman, 1997; Tellegen & Waller, in press). Although there is considerable agreement on the robustness of at least four higher-order traits, there is nevertheless substantial variation in the definition of these traits because researchers emphasize different characteristics depending on their trait concepts. Our model focuses on four higher-order traits that are robustly identified in the psychometric literature and that we define with reference to coherent neurobehavioral systems. Higher-order traits resembling *extraversion* and *neuroticism* (anxiety) are identified in virtually every taxonomy of personality. Affiliation, termed *agreeableness* (P. Costa & McCrae, 1992; Goldberg & Rosolack, 1994) or *social closeness* (Tellegen & Waller, in press), has emerged more recently as a robust trait and comprises affiliative tendencies, cooperativeness, and feelings of warmth and affection (Depue & Morrone-Strupinksy, in press). Finally, some form of impulsivity, more recently termed *constraint* (Tellegen & Waller, in press) or *conscientiousness* (due to an emphasis on the unreliability, unorderliness, and disorganization accompanying an impulsive disposition; P. Costa & McCrae, 1992; Goldberg & Rosolack, 1994), frequently emerges in factor studies.

Agentic Extraversion and Affiliation

Agentic extraversion and affiliation represent well established neurobehavioral systems. Modeling these systems entails consideration of both the complexities of interpersonal behavior as well as the relations between the two systems.

Trait Complexities Related to Interpersonal Behavior

Interpersonal behavior is not a unitary characteristic, but has two major components. One component, *affiliation,* reflects enjoying and valuing close interpersonal bonds and being warm and affectionate; the other component, *agency,* reflects social dominance, assertiveness, exhibitionism, and a subjective sense of potency in accomplishing goals. These two components are consistent with the two independent major traits identified in the theory of interpersonal behavior: warm-agreeable versus assured-dominant (Wiggins, 1991). Recent studies have consistently supported a two-component structure of interpersonal behavior in joint factor analyses of multidimensional personality questionnaires (Church, 1994; Church & Burke, 1994; Digman, 1997; Morrone-Strupinsky, Depue, Scherer, & White, 2000; Morrone-Strupinsky & Depue, 2004; Tellegen & Waller, in press), where two general traits were identified in each case as affiliation and agency (Depue & Collins, 1999). Lower-order traits of social dominance, achievement, endurance, persistence, efficacy, activity, and energy all loaded much more strongly on agency than on affiliation, whereas traits of sociability, warmth, and agreeableness showed a reverse pattern. Such findings have led trait psychologists to propose that affiliation and agency represent distinct dispositions (Depue & Collins, 1999; Depue & Morrone-Strupinsky, in press; Tellegen & Waller, in press): Whereas affiliation is clearly interpersonal in nature, agency represents a more general disposition that is manifest in a range of achievement-related, as well as interpersonal, contexts (P. Costa & McCrae, 1992; Goldberg & Rosolack, 1994; Tellegen & Waller, in press; Watson & Clark, 1997; Wiggins, 1991).

Association of Agentic Extraversion and Affiliation with Two Neurobehavioral Systems

Behavioral systems may be understood as behavior patterns that evolved to adapt to stimuli critical for survival and species preservation (Gray, 1973, 1992; MacLean, 1986; Schneirla, 1959). As opposed to specific behavioral systems that guide interaction with very specific stimulus contexts, *general* behavioral systems are more flexible and have less immediate objectives and more variable topographies (Blackburn et al., 1989; MacLean, 1986). General systems are activated by broad *classes* of stimulus (Depue & Collins, 1999; Gray, 1973, 1992) and regulate general emotional-behavioral dispositions, such as desire-approach, fear-inhibition, and affiliative tendencies, that modulate goal-directed activity. It is the general systems that directly influence the structure of mammalian behavior at higher-order levels of organization, because, like higher-order personality traits, their pervasive modulatory effects on behavior derive from frequent activation by broad stimulus classes. *Thus, the higher-order traits of personality, which are general and few, most likely reflect the activity of the few, general neurobehavioral systems.*

We have suggested that the two traits of agentic extraversion and affiliation reflect the activity of two neurobe-havioral systems involved in guiding behavior to *rewarding* goals (Depue & Collins, 1999; Depue & Morrone-Strupinsky, in press). Reward involves several dynamically interacting neurobehavioral processes occurring across two phases of goal acquisition: appetitive and consummatory. Although both phases are elicited by unconditioned incentive (reward-connoting) stimuli, their temporal onset, behavioral manifestations, and putative neural systems differ (Berridge, 1999; Blackburn et al., 1989; Depue & Collins, 1999; Di Chiara & North, 1992; Wyvell & Berridge, 2000) and are dissociated in factor-analytic studies based on behavioral characteristics of animals (Pfaus, Smith, & Coopersmith, 1999).

An appetitive, preparatory phase of goal acquisition represents the first step toward attaining biologically important goals (Blackburn et al., 1989; Hilliard, Domjan, Nguyen, & Cusato, 1998). It is based on a mammalian behavioral system that is activated by, and serves to bring an animal in contact with, unconditioned and conditioned rewarding incentive stimuli (Depue & Collins, 1999; Gray, 1973; Schneirla, 1959). This system is consistently described in all animals across phylogeny (Schneirla, 1959). We define this system as *behavioral approach based on incentive motivation* (Depue & Collins, 1999).

The nature of this behavioral system, as well as the system associated with a consummatory phase of reward (discussed next), can be most efficiently described by using an affiliative object (e.g., a potential mate) as the rewarding goal object. Thus, an affiliative goal is referred to throughout this and the next sections. In the appetitive phase of affiliation (see Figure 20.1), specific, *distal* affiliative stimuli of potential bonding partners—for example, facial features and smiles, friendly vocalizations and gestures, and bodily features (Porges, 1998)—serve as unconditioned incentive stimuli based on their distinct patterns of sensory properties, such as smell, color, shape, and temperature (Di Chiara & North, 1992; Hilliard et al., 1998). For instance, Breiter, Aharon, Kahneman, Dale, and Shizgal (2001) and Aharon et al. (2001) have shown that even passive viewing of attractive female faces unconditionally activates the anatomical areas that integrate reward, incentive motivation, and approach behavior in heterosexual males. These incentives are inherently evaluated as positive in valence and activate incentive motivation, increased energy through sympathetic nervous system activity, and forward locomotion as a means of bringing individuals into close proximity (Di Chiara & North, 1992). Moreover, the incentive state is inherently rewarding but in a highly activated manner,

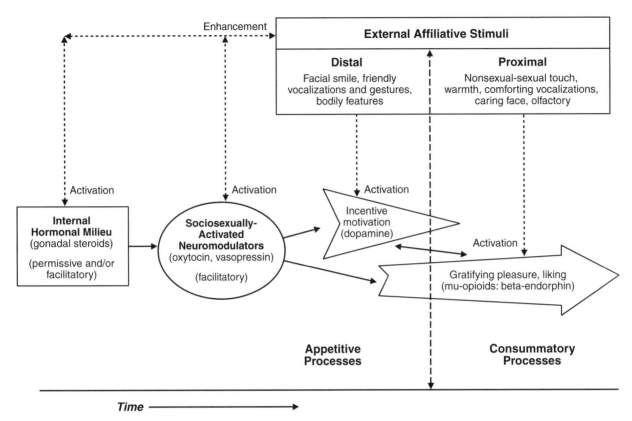

Figure 20.1   The development and maintenance of affiliative bonds across two phases of reward. Distal affiliative stimuli elicit an incentive-motivated approach to an affiliative goal, accompanied by strong emotional-motivational feelings of wanting, desire, and positive activation. The approach phase ensures not only sociosexual interaction with an affiliative object, but also acquisition of a memory ensemble or network of the context in which approach, reward, and goal acquisition occur. Next, proximal affiliative stimuli emanating from interaction with the affiliative object elicit strong feelings of consummatory reward, liking, and physiological quiescence, all of which become associated with these stimuli as well as the context predictive of reward. As discussed in the text, dopamine encodes the incentive salience of contextual stimuli predictive of reward during the approach phase and, in collaboration with consummatory reward mediated by μ-opiate, encodes the incentive salience of proximal stimuli directly linked to the affiliative object. The end result of this sequence of processes is an incentive-encoded affiliative memory network that continues to motivate approach toward and interaction with the affiliative object. Specialized processes ensure that affiliative stimuli are weighted as significant elements in the contextual ensembles representing affiliative memory networks. These specialized processes include the construction of a contextual ensemble via affiliative stimulus-induced opiate potentiation of dopamine processes and the influence of permissive and/or facilitatory factors such as gonadal steroids, oxytocin, and vasopressin on (1) sensory, perceptual, and attentional processing of affiliative stimuli and (2) formation of social memories. See Depue and Morrone-Strupinsky (in press) for details.

and animals will work intensively to obtain that reward without evidence of satiety (Depue & Collins, 1999).

In humans, the incentive state is associated with subjective feelings of desire, wanting, excitement, elation, enthusiasm, energy, potency, and self-efficacy that are distinct from, but typically co-occur with, feelings of pleasure and liking (Berridge, 1999; Watson & Tellegen, 1985). This subjective experience is concordant with the nature of the lower-order traits of social dominance, achievement, endurance, persistence, efficacy, activity, and energy that all load strongly on the *agency* personality factor (see earlier discussion) and with the adjectives that define the subjective *state* of positive affect that is so

closely associated with agentic extraversion (activated, peppy, strong, enthused, energetic; Watson & Tellegen, 1985). Therefore, we have proposed that agentic extraversion reflects the activity of a behavioral approach system based on *positive incentive motivation*.

When close proximity to a rewarding goal is achieved, incentive-motivational approach gives way to a consummatory phase of goal acquisition (Herbert, 1993). In this phase, specific *interoceptive* and *proximal exteroceptive* stimuli related to critical primary biological aims elicit behavioral patterns that are relatively specific to those conditions (e.g., sexual, social, or food-related; Blackburn et al., 1989; Hilliard et al., 1998; MacLean, 1986; Timberlake &

Silva, 1995). Performance of these behavioral patterns is inherently rewarding (Berridge, 1999). In the case of potential mate acquisition, examples of affiliative behavioral patterns are courtship, gentle stroking and grooming, mating, and certain maternal patterns such as breast-feeding, all of which may include facial, caressive tactile, gestural, and certain vocal behaviors (Polan & Hofer, 1998). Tactile stimulation may be particularly effective in activating affiliative reward processes in animals and humans (Fleming, Korsmit, & Deller, 1994). Significantly, light, pleasant touch that occurs to caress-like, skin-to-skin contact between individuals is transmitted by different afferents from hard or unpleasant touch (Olausson et al., 2002); light, pleasant touch is transmitted by slow-conducting, unmyelinated afferents that project to the insular cortex but not to somatosensory areas S1 and S2, whereas hard, unpleasant touch is transmitted by fast-conducting myelinated afferents to S1 and S2 (anterior parietal). The insular cortex is a paralimbic region known to integrate several sensory modalities, including autonomic, gustatory, visual, auditory, and somatosensory, to characterize the emotional nature of sensory input (Damasio, 2003; Mesulam, 1990).

As opposed to an incentive motivational state of activation, desire, and wanting, the expression of *consummatory* behavioral patterns elicits intense feelings of pleasure, gratification, and liking, plus physiological quiescence characterized by rest, sedation, anabolism, and parasympathetic nervous system activity, thereby reinforcing the production and repetition of those behaviors (Berridge, 1999; Di Chiara & North, 1992; Porges, 1998, 2001). Thus, whereas appetitive approach processes bring an individual into contact with unconditioned incentive stimuli, consummatory processes bring behavior to a gratifying conclusion (Hilliard et al., 1998). Whether the pleasurable state generated in affiliative interactions shares a common neurobiology with the pleasure generated by other consummatory behaviors (e.g., feeding) is not certain but is assumed by some to be so (Di Chiara & North, 1992; Panksepp, 1998).

The core content of affiliation scales seems to reflect the operation of neurobehavioral processes that (1) create a warm, affectionate, gratifying subjective emotional state elicited by others, which (2) motivate close interpersonal behavior. Our hypothesis is that the subjective experience of warmth and affection reflects the *capacity to experience consummatory reward that is elicited by a broad array of affiliative stimuli* (Depue & Morrone-Strupinsky, in press). This capacity is viewed as providing the key element utilized in additional psychobiological processes that permit the development and maintenance of longer-term affective bonds, defined as long-term selective social attachments

observed most intensely between infants and parents and between adult mates, and that are characteristic of social organization in human and other primate societies (Gingrich, Liu, Cascio, Wang, & Insel, 2000; Wang et al., 1999). It is important to emphasize that a core capacity for affiliative reward and bonding is not viewed as a sufficient determinant of close social relationships, only as a necessary one, a sine qua non. Such affiliative reward is hypothesized to underlie all human social relationships having a positive affective component. Other interpersonal constructs of sociability, attachment, and separation anxiety are accordingly viewed as either broader than affiliation, as defined here, and/or as based on different neurobehavioral systems (see Depue & Morrone-Strupinsky, in press, for a full discussion).

Through Pavlovian associative learning, the experience of reward generated throughout appetitive and consummatory phases is associated with previously affectively neutral stimulus contexts (objects, acts, events, places) in which pleasure occurred, thereby forming conditioned incentive stimuli that are predictive of reward and that have gained the capacity to elicit anticipatory pleasure and incentive motivation (Berridge, 1999; Ostrowski, 1998; Timberlake & Silva, 1995). Because of the predominance of symbolic (conditioned) processes in guiding human behavior in the absence of unconditioned stimuli, conditioned incentives are likely to be particularly important elicitors of *enduring* reward processes (Fowles, 1987). Thus, the acquisition and maintenance of a mate relationship, for example, depends closely on Pavlovian associative learning that links the experience of reward with (1) the salient contextual cues that predict reward during the appetitive phase (e.g., features of a laboratory cage) and (2) a mate's individualistic cues associated directly with consummatory reward (e.g., individual characteristics of a sexually receptive female mate; Domjan, Cusato, & Villarreal, 2000). Taken together, these processes support acquisition of affiliative memories, where contextual ensembles are formed and weighted in association with the reward provided by interaction with the potential mate.

Neurobiology of Incentive Motivation and Affiliative Reward

By drawing an association between traits and behavioral systems, that is, agentic extraversion and incentive motivation, affiliation and affiliative reward, we are able to utilize the behavioral neurobiology animal literature to discern the neurobiology associated with these behavioral systems and, by analogy, with the personality traits of agentic extraversion and affiliation. As reviewed recently (Depue & Collins, 1999), animal research demonstrates that the positive incentive motivation and experience of reward that underlies a behavioral system of approach is dependent on the functional properties of the midbrain ventral tegmental area (VTA) dopamine (DA) projection system. DA agonists or antagonists in the VTA or nucleus accumbens (NAS), which is a major terminal area of VTA DA projections, in rats and monkeys facilitate or markedly impair, respectively, a broad array of incentive motivated behaviors. Furthermore, dose-dependent DA receptor activation in the VTA-NAS pathway facilitates the acute rewarding effects of stimulants, and the NAS is a particularly strong site for intracranial self-administration of DA agonists (Le Moal & Simon, 1991; Pich et al., 1997). DA agonists injected in the NAS also modulate behavioral responses to *conditioned* incentive stimuli in a dose-dependent fashion (Cador, Taylor, & Robbins, 1991; Robbins, Cador, Taylor, & Everitt, 1989; Wolterink, Cador, Wolterink, Robbins, & Everitt, 1989). In single-unit recording studies, VTA DA neurons are activated preferentially by appetitive incentive stimuli (Schultz, Dayan, & Montague, 1997). DA cells, most numerously in the VTA, respond vigorously to and in proportion to the magnitude of both conditioned and unconditioned incentive stimuli and in anticipation of reward (Schultz et al., 1997).

Incentive motivation is associated in humans with both positive *emotional* feelings, such as elation and euphoria, and *motivational* feelings of desire, wanting, craving, potency, and self-efficacy. In humans, DA-activating psychostimulant drugs induce both sets of feelings (Drevets et al., 2001). Neuroimaging studies of cocaine addicts found that during acute administration, the intensity of a subject's subjective euphoria increased in a dose-dependent manner in proportion to cocaine binding to the DA uptake transporter (and hence to DA levels) in the striatum (Volkow et al., 1997). Moreover, cocaine-induced activity in the NAS was linked equally strongly (if not more strongly) to motivational feelings of desire, wanting, and craving as to the emotional experience of euphoric rush (Breiter et al., 1997). The degree of amphetamine-induced DA release in the healthy human ventral striatum assessed by PET was correlated strongly with feelings of euphoria (Drevets et al., 2001). Hence, taken together, the animal and human evidence demonstrates that the VTA DA-NAS pathway is a primary neural circuit for incentive motivation and its accompanying subjective state of reward.

With respect to consummatory reward and affiliative behavior, a broad range of evidence suggests a role for endogenous opiates. Endogenous opiate release or receptor binding is increased in rats, monkeys, and humans by lacta-tion and nursing, sexual activity, vaginocervical stimulation, maternal social interaction, brief social isolation, and grooming and other nonsexual tactile stimulation (Depue & Morrone-Strupinsky, in press; Keverne, 1996; Silk, Alberts, & Altmann, 2003). Opiate receptor (OR) antagonists naltrexone or naloxone in small doses apparently reduce the reward derived from social interactions because they increase attempts to obtain such reward, manifested as increases in the amount of maternal contact by young monkeys and solicitations for grooming and frequency of being groomed in mature female monkeys, which has been associated with increased cerebrospinal fluid levels of ß-endorphin (Graves, Wallen, & Maestripieri, 2002; Martel, Nevison, Simpson, Keverne, 1995). In addition, the endogenous opiate ß-endorphin stimulates play behavior and grooming in juvenile rats, whereas naltrexone leads to reduced grooming of infants and other group members in monkeys and rats, and to maternal neglect in monkeys and sheep that is similar to the neglect shown by human mothers who abuse opiates (Keverne, 1996; Martel et al., 1995). Similarly, human females administered the opiate antagonist naltrexone showed an increased amount of time spent alone, a reduced amount of time spent with friends, and a reduced frequency and pleasantness of their social interactions relative to placebo. Such findings suggest that opiates provide a critical part of the neural basis on which primate sociality has evolved (Nelson & Panksepp, 1998). Particularly important is the relation between μ-opiates and grooming, because the primary function of primate grooming may well be to establish and maintain social bonds (Matheson & Bernstein, 2000).

Perhaps most relevant to affiliative reward is the mu (μ) OR family, which is the main site of exogenously administered opiate drugs (e.g., morphine) and of endogenous endorphins (particularly, ß-endorphin; LaBuda, Sora, Uhl, Fuchs, 2000; Schlaepfer et al., 1998; Shippenberg & Elmer, 1998; Stefano et al., 2000; Wiedenmayer & Barr, 2000). μORs also appear to be the main site for the effects of endogenous ß-endorphins and endogenous morphine on the subjective feelings in humans of *increased* interpersonal warmth, euphoria, well-being, and peaceful calmness, as well as of *decreased* elation, energy, and incentive motivation (Schlaepfer et al., 1998; Shippenberg & Elmer, 1998; Stefano et al., 2000; Uhl, Sora, & Wang, 1999).

The facilitatory effects of opiates on affiliative behavior are thought to be exerted by fibers that arise mainly from the hypothalamic arcuate nucleus and terminate in brain regions that typically express μORs. μORs may facilitate the rewarding effects associated with many motivated behaviors (Nelson & Panksepp, 1998; Niesink, Vanderschuren, & van Ree, 1996; Olive, Koenig, Nannini, & Hodge, 2001; Olson, Olson, & Kastin, 1997; Stefano et al., 2000; Strand, 1999). For instance, whereas DA antagonists block appetitive behaviors in pursuit of reward but not the actual consumption of reward (e.g., sucrose; Ikemoto & Panksepp, 1996), μOR-antagonists block rewarding effects of sucrose and sexual behavior, and in neonatal rats persistently impair the response to the inherently rewarding properties of novel stimulation (Herz, 1998). Rewarding properties of μOR agonists are directly indicated by the facts that animals will work for the prototypical μ-agonists morphine and heroin and that they are dose-dependently self-administered in animals and humans (Di Chiara, 1995; Nelson & Panksepp, 1998; Olson et al., 1997; Shippenberg & Elmer, 1998). There is a significant correlation between an agonist's affinity at the μOR and the dose that maintains maximal rates of drug self-administration behavior (Shippenberg & Elmer, 1998).

The rewarding effect of opiates may be especially mediated by μORs located in the NAS and VTA, both of which support self-administration of μOR agonists that is attenuated by intracranially administered μOR antagonists (David & Cazala, 2000; Herz, 1998; Schlaepfer et al., 1998; Shippenberg & Elmer, 1998). When opiate- and DA-specific antagonists were given prior to cocaine or heroin self-administration, the opiate antagonist selectively altered opiate self-administration, and DA antagonists selectively altered the response to the DA agonist cocaine (Shippenberg & Elmer, 1998). Destruction of DA terminals in the NAS also showed that opiate self-administration is independent of DA function, at least at the level of the NAS (Dworkin, Guerin, Goeders, & Smith, 1988). Furthermore, NAS DA functioning was specifically related to the incentive salience of reward cues but was unrelated to the hedonic state generated by consuming the rewards (Wyvell & Berridge, 2000). *Thus, DA and opiates appear to functionally interact in the NAS, but they apparently provide independent contributions to rewarding effects.* This appears to be particularly the case for the *acute* rewarding effects of opiates, which are thought to occur through a DA-independent system that is mediated through brain stem reward circuits, including the tegmental pedunculopontine nucleus (Laviolette, Gallegos, Henriksen, & van der Kooy, 2004).

Rewarding effects of opiates are also directly indicated by the fact that a range of μOR agonists, when injected intracerebroventricularly or directly into the NAS, serve as unconditioned rewarding stimuli in a dose-dependent

manner in producing a conditioned place preference, a behavioral measure of reward (Narita, Aoki, & Suzuki, 2000; Nelson & Panksepp, 1998; Shippenberg & Elmer, 1998). VTA-localized μORs, particularly in the rostral zone of the VTA (Carlezon et al., 2000), mediate (1) rewarding effects such as self-administration behavior and conditioned place preference (Carlezon et al., 2000; Shippenberg & Elmer, 1998; Wise, 1998), (2) increased sexual activity and maternal behaviors (Callahan et al., 1996; Leyton & Stewart, 1992; van Furth & van Ree, 1996), and (3) the persistently increased play behavior, social grooming, and social approach of rats subjected to morphine in utero (Hol, Niesink, van Ree, & Spruijt, 1996). Indeed, microinjections of morphine or a selective μOR agonist into the VTA produced marked place preferences, whereas selective antagonism of μORs prevented morphine-induced conditioned place preference (Olmstead & Franklin, 1997). Indeed, transgenic mice lacking the μOR gene show no morphine-induced place preferences or physical dependence from morphine consumption, whereas morphine induces both of these behaviors in wild-type mice (Matthes et al., 1996; Simonin et al., 1998). Significantly, opiate but not oxytocin antagonists block the development of partner preference that is induced specifically by *repeated* exposure and *repeated* sexual activity in rodents (Carter, Lederhendler, & Kirkpatrick, 1997).

An *interaction* of DA and μ-opiates in the experience of reward throughout appetitive and consummatory phases of *affiliative* engagement appears to involve two processes. During the anticipatory phase of goal acquisition, μOR activation in the VTA can increase DA release in the NAS and hence the experience of reward (Marinelli & White, 2000). Subsequently, the firing rate of VTA neurons decreases following delivery and consumption of appetitive reinforcers (e.g., food, sex, liquid; Schultz et al., 1997). At the same time, μOR activation in the NAS (perhaps by opiate release from higher-threshold NAS terminals that colocalize DA and opiates; Le Moal & Simon, 1991) decreases NAS DA release, creating an opiate-mediated experience of reward associated with consummation that is independent of DA (Churchill, Rogues, & Kalivas, 1995). Thus, in contrast to the incentive motivational effects of DA during the anticipation of reward, opiates may subsequently induce calm pleasure and bring consummatory behavior to a gratifying conclusion. This may explain the fact that higher doses of μOR agonists administered into the NAS can block the self-administration of certain psychostimulant drugs of abuse in animals and reduce appetitive behaviors

(Hyztia & Kiiannaa, 2001; B. Johnson & Ait-Daoud, 2000; Kranzler, 2000).

In sum, as illustrated in Figure 20.1, distal affiliative cues (e.g., friendly smiles and gestures, sexual features) serve as incentive stimuli that activate DA-facilitated incentive-reward motivation, desire, wanting, and approach to affiliative objects. As these objects are reached, more proximal affiliative stimuli (e.g., pleasant touch) strongly activate μ-opiate release, which promotes an intense state of pleasant reward, warmth, affection, and physiological quiescence and brings approach behavior to a gratifying conclusion. Throughout this entire sequence of goal acquisition, the contextual cues associated with approach to the goal, and the cues specifically related to the goal, are all associated with the experience of reward. It is beyond the scope of this chapter, but it is worth noting that DA and μ-opiates play a critical role in strengthening the association between these contextual cues and reward (Depue & Morrone-Strupinsky, in press). Thus, these two neuromodulators are critical to establishing our preferences and memories for particular contexts and affiliative cues predictive of reward.

Individual Differences in Dopamine Incentive and μOpiate Receptor Reward Processes

Individual differences in agentic extraversion and affiliation are subject to strong genetic influence (Tellegen et al., 1988). If personality disturbance occurs in the region located at the extreme tails of individual difference distributions in the traits of agentic extraversion and affiliation, it is important to show that the neuromodulators associated with incentive motivation and affiliative reward are sources of individual differences in these behavioral systems. Animal research demonstrates that individual differences in DA functioning contribute significantly to variation in incentive-motivated behavior, as does much human work (Depue & Collins, 1999; Depue, Luciana, Arbisi, Collins, & Leon, 1994). Inbred mouse and rat strains with variation in the number of neurons in the VTA DA cell group or in several indicators of enhanced DA transmission show marked differences in behaviors dependent on DA transmission in the VTA-NAS pathway, including levels of spontaneous exploratory activity and DA agonist-induced locomotor activity and increased acquisition of self-administration of psychostimulants (Depue & Collins, 1999).

Similar findings for μ-opiates exist (Depue & Morrone-Strupinsky, in press). Individual differences in humans and rodents have been demonstrated in levels of μOR expression and binding that are associated with a preference for μOR-agonists such as morphine (Uhl et al., 1999; Zubieta et al., 2001). In humans, individual differences in central nervous system (CNS) μOR densities show a range of up to 75% between lower and upper thirds of the distribution (Uhl et al., 1999), differences that appear to be related to variation in the rewarding effects of alcohol in humans and rodents (Berrettini et al., 1997; De Waele et al., 1995; Gianoulakis et al., 1996; McCall et al., 2000a, 2000b; Olson et al., 1997).

Differences of this magnitude in the *expressive* properties of the μOR gene could contribute substantially to individual variation in μOR-induced *behavioral* expression via an effect on ß-endorphin functional potency. For instance, one source of this individual variation is different single-nucleotide polymorphisms (SNPs) in the μOR gene OPRM1 (Berrettini, Hoehe, Ferraro, DeMaria, & Gottheil, 1997; Bond et al., 1998; Gelernter, Kranzler, & Cubells, 1999). The most prevalent of these is A118G, which is characterized by a substitution of the amino acid Asn by Asp at codon 40, with an allelic frequency of 10% in a mixed sample of former heroin abusers and normal controls (Bond et al., 1998). Although this SNP did not bind all opiate peptides more strongly than other SNPs or the normal nucleotide sequence, it did bind ß-endorphin 3 times more tightly than the most common allelic form of the receptor (Bond et al., 1998). Furthermore, ß-endorphin is 3 times more effective in agonist-induced activation of G-protein-coupled potassium channels at the A118G variant receptor compared to the most common allelic form (Bond et al., 1998).

Genetic variation in μOR properties is related to response to rewarding drugs, such as morphine, alcohol, and cocaine, and to opiate self-administration behavior in animals (Berrettini et al., 1997). For instance, when transgenic insertion was used to increase μOR density specifically in mesolimbic areas thought to mediate substance abuse via VTA DA neurons, transgenic mice showed increased self-administration of morphine compared to wild-type mice, even when the amount of behavior required to maintain drug intake increased 10-fold (Elmer, Pieper, Goldberg, & George, 1995). Thus, the efficacy of morphine as a reinforcer was substantially enhanced in transgenic mice. Conversely, μOR knock-out mice do not develop conditioned place preference and physical dependence on morphine, whereas morphine induces both of these behaviors in wild-type mice (Matthes et al., 1996).

Taken together, these studies suggest that genetic variation in DA and μOR properties in humans and rodents is (1) substantial, (2) an essential element in the variation in the rewarding value of DA and opiate agonists, and (3) critical in accounting for variation in the Pavlovian learning that underlies the association between contextual cues and reward, as occurs in partner and place preferences (Elmer et al., 1995; Matthes et al., 1996).

Anxiety or Neuroticism

Here we consider the nature and independence of anxiety and fear as behavioral systems as well as consider their neurobiological foundations.

Anxiety and Fear as Two Distinct Behavioral Systems

Adaptation to aversive environmental conditions is crucial for species survival, and at least two distinct behavioral systems have evolved to promote such adaptation. One system is fear (often labeled "harm avoidance" in the trait literature, but this is different from Cloninger, Svrakic, and Przybeck's, 1993, harm avoidance, which actually assesses anxiety), which is a very specific behavioral system that evolved as a means of escaping unconditioned aversive stimuli that are inherently dangerous to survival, such as tactile pain, injury contexts, snakes, spiders, heights, approaching strangers, and sudden sounds. These stimuli are specific, discrete, and explicit and in turn elicit specific, short-latency, high-magnitude phasic responses of autonomic arousal, subjective feelings of panic, and behavioral escape. Specific, discrete, neutral stimuli associated with these unconditioned events elicit conditioned fear. Such conditioned stimuli elicit a different behavioral profile from that of unconditioned stimuli, in that freezing and suppression of operant behavior (i.e., behavioral inhibition), as opposed to active escape, characterize the former, though both response systems involve autonomic arousal, pain inhibition, and reflex potentiation.

There are, however, many aversive circumstances that do not involve specific, discrete, explicit stimuli that evolutionarily have been neurobiologically linked to subjective fear and escape. That is, there are many situations in which specific aversive cues do not exist; rather, the stimulus conditions are associated with an elevated *potential* risk of danger or aversive consequences. In such cases, no explicit aversive stimuli are present to inherently activate escape circuitries. Nevertheless, the stimuli can be unconditioned in nature, as in darkness, open spaces, unfamiliarity, and predator odors, or they can be conditioned contextual cues (general textures, colors, relative spatial locations, sounds) that have been associated with previous exposure to specific aversive stimuli (Davis & Shi, 1999; Davis, Walker, & Lee, 1997; Fendt, Endres, & Apfelbach, 2003). Conceptually, these stimuli are characterized in common by unpredictability and uncontrollability—or, more simply, uncertainty.

To reduce the risk of danger in such circumstances, a second behavioral system evolved: *anxiety.* Anxiety is characterized by negative emotion or affect (anxiety, depression, hostility, suspiciousness, distress) that serves the purpose of informing the individual that, though no explicit, specific aversive stimuli are present, conditions are potentially threatening (White & Depue, 1999). This affective state, and the physiological arousal that accompanies it, continues or reverberates until the uncertainty is resolved. Associated responses that may functionally help to resolve the uncertainty are heightened attentional scanning of the uncertain environment and cognitive worrying and rumination over possible response-outcome scenarios. An important point is that no specific motor response is linked to anxiety, because no motor response is specified under stimulus conditions of uncertainty. Caution and locomotor modulation are necessary, but behavioral inhibition will not allow the individual to explore the environment to discover if danger is indeed lurking. An example is a deer entering an open meadow: Caution, slow approach, heightened attentional scanning, and enhanced cognitive activity are optimal, not freezing. This is in direct contradiction to Gray's (1973) theory that the best marker for anxiety is behavioral inhibition; rather, conditioned stimulus fear is associated with such inhibition. Thus, Davis et al. (1997) and Barlow (2002) suggest that the stimulus conditions and behavioral characteristics of fear and anxiety are different, although a similar state of intense autonomic arousal is associated with both emotional states, rendering them similar at the subjective level. The prolonged negative subjective state of anxiety, however, distinguishes its subjective state from the rapid, brief state of panic associated with the presence of a specific fear stimulus.

There is another important difference between fear and anxiety at the trait level of analysis. In personality inventories, fear typically is represented as a primary or facet-level scale, not a higher-order factor (Tellegen & Waller, in press). Fear usually also is associated with a higher-order trait of constraint. In contrast, anxiety, which is typically referred to as neuroticism, is one of the most reliably identified higher-order traits and does not load highly on a constraint higher-order factor. This higher-order nature of anxiety but not fear is related to the fact that, just like

TABLE 20.1 Correlation between Trait Measures of Fear and Anxiety

Fear	Anxiety		
	Tellegen NEM	Eysenck N	STAI
Tellegen Harm Avoidance	−.03	−.02	
Jackson Harm Avoidance			.05
Lykken Physical Activity		−.01	.05
Hodges Physical Danger			.02
Zuckerman SSS (reversed)	.08	.04	

Notes: Eysenck N = Eysenck neuroticism; NEM = Negative emotionality; and STAI = State Trait Anxiety Inventory.

agentic extraversion, the eliciting stimuli for anxiety occur frequently in a civilized society, whereas the specific stimuli that elicit fear do not. This means that anxiety represents a general behavioral system that is activated by a broad *class* of stimuli, whereas fear represents a more specific behavioral system that evolved to respond to specific stimuli critical for survival.

The trait literature supports the *independence* of anxiety and fear, which as personality traits are subject to distinct sources of genetic variation (Tellegen et al., 1988). As the averaged correlations derived from numerous studies in Tables 20.1, 20.2, and 20.3 show, the relation between neuroticism (anxiety) and harm avoidance (fear) is essentially zero (White & Depue, 1999). As shown in Tables 20.2 and 20.3, the magnitude of emotional distress and autonomic arousal elicited by discrete stimuli associated with physical harm (Table 20.2) is significantly related to harm avoidance but not neuroticism, whereas conditions of uncertainty associated with external evaluations of the self (Table 20.3) are significantly related to neuroticism but not harm avoidance (White & Depue, 1999). Furthermore, Table 20.2 shows that, in contrast to Gray's (1973, 1992) and Cloninger's (Cloninger et al., 1993) theoretical position that anxiety is associated with behavioral inhibition, it is harm avoidance rather than neuroticism that correlates significantly with indices of behavioral inhibition in contexts of physical danger. Indeed, one of the most reliable indices of conditioned fear in animals is behavioral inhibition (Davis

TABLE 20.3 Correlation of Emotional Distress to Contexts Associated with Threats to the Self with Trait Measures of Fear and Anxiety

Trait	Emotional Distress			
	Exam	Intelligence Test	Public Speaking	Failure Feedback
Fear	.11	.09	.05	.08
Anxiety	.48	.47	.57	.52

et al., 1997; LeDoux, 1998; Panksepp, 1998), which is not the case for stimulus-induced anxiety (Davis et al., 1997). These various findings suggest that anxiety and fear are distinctly different traits, and analysis of clinical anxiety disorders reached equivalent conclusions (Barlow, 2002).

Neurobiology of Anxiety

The psychometric independence of fear and anxiety is mirrored in their dissociable neuroanatomy. Species-specific unconditioned stimuli having an evolutionary history of danger eliciting fear and defensive motor escape, facial and vocal signs, autonomic activation, and antinociception, specifically from the lateral longitudinal cell column in the midbrain periaquiductal gray (PAG; see Figure 20.2; Bandler & Keay, 1996). In turn, PAG efferents converge on the ventromedial and rostral ventrolateral regions of the medulla, where somatic-motor and autonomic information, respectively, are integrated and transmitted to the spinal cord (Guyenet et al., 1996; Holstege, 1996). Although these processes can occur without a cortex (Panksepp, 1998), association of discrete, explicit neutral stimuli (fear conditioned stimulus) with an unconditioned stimulus and primary negative reinforcement occurs via cortical uni- and polymodal sensory efferents that converge on the basolateral complex of the amygdala (although crude representations of external stimuli can rapidly reach the basolateral amygdala subcortically from the thalamus; Aggleton, 1992; Davis et al., 1997; LeDoux, 1998). Fear conditioned stimuli elicit a host of behavioral, neuropeptide, and autonomic responses via output from the basolateral amygdala to the central

TABLE 20.2 Correlation of Emotional Distress, Behavioral Inhibition, and Heart Rate and Electrodermal Responses to Aversive Stimuli with Trait Measures of Fear and Anxiety

Trait	Emotional Distress				Behavioral Inhibition				Threatened Shock Electrodermal		
	Hts	Rat	Snake	Shock	Hts	Rat	Snake	Cockroach	HR	Specific	Nonspecific
Fear	.43	.54	.62	.64	.44	.35	.51	.46	.48	.43	.53
Anxiety	.17	.20	.14	.04	.15		.07		.09	.14	.17

Note: HR = Heart rate, Hts = Heights.

amygdala, which in turn sends functionally *separable* efferents to many hypothalamic and brain stem targets (Aggleton, 1992; LeDoux, Cicchetti, Xagoraris, & Romanski, 1990). In the case of fear conditioned stimulus, as noted earlier, the motor response is not escape but rather freezing or *behavioral inhibition,* which involves activation of the caudal ventrolateral cell column of the PAG, shown in Figure 20.2 (LeDoux, 1998).

The neuroanatomic distinction between fear and anxiety has been delineated by use of the fear-potentiated auditory-induced startle paradigm. In this paradigm, an established, explicit light conditioned stimulus activates a cell assembly representing the association among conditioned stimulus, unconditioned stimulus (e.g., shock), and tactile pain located in the basolateral amygdala. Excitation of this assembly by the conditioned stimulus activates efferents to the central amygdala, which in turn monosynaptically potentiates startle reflex circuitry in the reticular nucleus of the caudal pons that is activated simultaneously by, for example, a loud, sudden noise. This potentiation of the startle reflex by a fear conditioned stimulus is *phasic* in nature, occurring almost immediately after light onset, but returning to baseline amplitude shortly after light offset (Davis et al., 1997). Lesions of the central amygdala reliably block explicit fear conditioned stimulus-potentiated startle and behavioral inhibition. In contrast, nondiscrete, contextually related aversive stimulation—for example, prolonged bright light in an unfamiliar environment, which are aversive unconditioned stimuli for nocturnal rats—elicits robust startle potentiation that endures *tonically* as long as the aversive conditions are present, even when the central amygdala is lesioned. These findings suggest that these types of stimulus conditions,

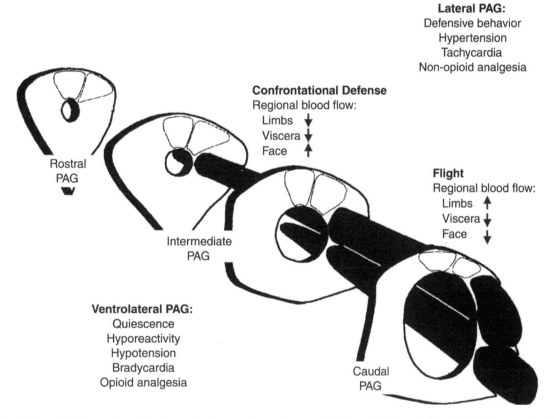

Figure 20.2 Schematic illustration of the lateral and ventrolateral neuronal columns in (from left to right) the rostral midbrain periaqueductal gray (PAG), the intermediate PAG (2 sections), and the caudal PAG. Injections of excitatory amino acids (EAA) in the lateral and ventrolateral PAG column evoke fundamentally opposite alterations in sensory responsiveness and somatic and autonomic adjustments. EAA injections made in the intermediate, lateral PAG evoke a confrontational defensive reaction, tachycardia, and hypertension associated with decreased blood flow to limbs and viscera and increased blood flow to extracranial vascular beds. EAA injections into the caudal, lateral PAG evoke flight, tachycardia, and hypertension associated with decreased blood flow to visceral and extracranial vascular beds and increased blood flow to limbs. In contrast, EAA injections into the ventrolateral PAG evoke cessation of all spontaneous activity (i.e., quiescence), a decreased responsiveness to the environment, hypotension, and bradycardia. The lateral and ventrolateral PAG also mediate different types of analgesia. *Source:* From Bandler & Keay, (1996).

which are typically associated with the elicitation of anxiety, rely on a different neuroanatomical foundation in generating an enduring potentiation of the startle reflex (Davis et al., 1997).

The enduring potentiating effects of nondiscrete, contextually related aversive stimuli on the startle reflex is dependent on a group of structures collectively referred to as the *extended amygdala,* which receives massive projections from basolateral and olfactory amygdala complexes, and which represents a macrostructure that is characterized by two divisions, central and medial (Heimer, 2003; McGinty, 1999). As shown in Figure 20.3, these two divisions originate from the central and medial nuclei of the amygdala and consist of cell groups that are distributed throughout the sublenticular area, bed nucleus of the stria terminalis (BNST), around striatal and pallidal structures, and back to merge specifically with the caudomedial region of the

NAS. Contextual stimuli are conveyed to the BNST and other central extended amygdala regions via perirhinal plus basolateral amygdala (e.g., bright light) and parahippocampal + entorhinal + hippocampal (contextual stimuli) glutamatergic efferents (Annett, McGregor, & Robins, 1989; Bechara et al., 1995; Everitt & Robbins, 1992; Gaffan, 1992; Heimer, 2003; LeDoux, 1998; Selden, Everitt, Jarrard, & Robbins, 1991; Sutherland & McDonald, 1990). Viewing the sublenticular area and lateral BNST as a foundation for anxiety processes is supported in part by the fact that, in contrast to the central amygdala, (1) neurons in the sublenticular area show maximal prolonged responsiveness specifically to unfamiliar stimuli (Rolls, 1999) and (2) electrical stimulation or lesions of the BNST did not initiate or block, respectively, the behavioral inhibition elicited by an explicit fear conditioned stimulus (LeDoux et al., 1990), which mirrors the lack of association of behavioral inhibition with trait anxiety, discussed earlier.

Similar to the outputs from the central nucleus of the amygdala, most structures of the central division of the extended amygdala can transmit this motivationally relevant information to some or all hypothalamic and brain stem structures related to emotional expression (Heimer, 2003; Holstege, 1996). Whereas the basolateral complex of the amygdala is involved in pairing positive and negative reinforcement with stimuli that are discrete and explicit and that have been analyzed for their specific characteristics, at least the central division of the extended amygdala appears to associate *general contextual features and nonexplicit, nondiscrete* conditioned and unconditioned stimuli with reinforcement (e.g., light conditions, physical features, spatial relations; Davis & Shi, 1999; Davis et al., 1997; McDonald, Shammah-lagnado, Shi, & Davis, 1999). Thus, two emotional learning systems may have evolved: the basolateral amygdala to associate reinforcement with explicit, specific characteristics of objects (i.e., for fear), and the BNST to associate reinforcement with nonexplicit spatial and contextual stimulus aspects (i.e., for anxiety).

A major finding of importance in understanding the association between anxiety and the central extended amygdala is that injection of corticotropin-releasing hormone (CRH) into the BNST potentiates startle in a dose-dependent manner for up to 2 hours duration (Davis et al., 1997). It is not surprising, then, that lesions of the BNST or injection of a CRH antagonist in the BNST significantly attenuates both bright light- or CRH-enhanced startle without having any effect on discrete fear conditioned stimulus-potentiated startle (Davis et al., 1997). In contrast, lesions of the central amygdala eliminate the discrete fear conditioned stimulus-potentiated startle, but have no effect on CRH-enhanced startle.

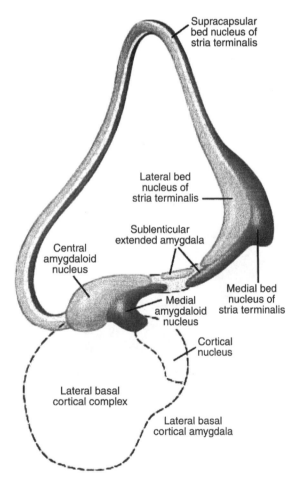

Figure 20.3 The central (dark gray) and medial (light gray) divisions of the extended amygdala, shown in isolation from the rest of the brain. *Source:* From "A New Anatomical Framework for Neuropsychiatric Disorders and Drug Abuse," by L. Heimer, 2003, *American Journal of Psychiatry, 160,* pp. 1726–1739.

Prolonged bright light-induced startle potentiation is also blocked by (1) lesions of the fornix, which carries hippocampal efferents conveying salient context to the BNST (Amaral & Witter, 1995); (2) glutamatergic antagonists injected into the BNST that block hippocampal efferent input; and (3) buspirone, a potent anxiolytic (Davis et al., 1997). Conversely, lesions of or glutamate antagonists injected in the central amygdala blocked fear conditioned stimulus-potentiated startle but had no effect on startle elicited by bright light conditions or on anxiolytic effects in the elevated + maze, where benzodiazepines have a robust anxiolytic effect (Davis et al., 1997; Treit, Pesold, & Rotzinger, 1993). The basolateral amygdala is involved in both bright light- and conditioned stimulus-potentiated startle due to processing of visual information, but not in CRH-enhanced startle.

Thus, with respect to potentiation of the startle reflex, there is a multivariate double dissociation of the central amygdala and the BNST. As summarized in Figure 20.4

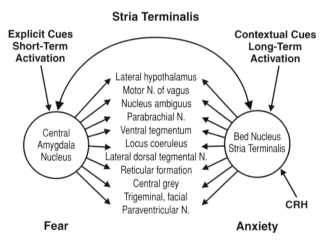

Figure 20.4 Hypothetical schematic suggesting that the central nucleus of the amygdala and the bed nucleus of the stria terminalis may be differentially involved in fear and anxiety, respectively. Both brain areas have highly similar hypothalamic and brain stem targets known to be involved in specific signs and symptoms of fear and anxiety. However, the stress peptide corticotropin-releasing hormone (CRH) appears to act on receptors in the bed nucleus of the stria terminalis rather than the amygdala, at least in terms of an increase in the startle reflex. Furthermore, the bed nucleus of the stria terminalis seems to be involved in the anxiogenic effects of a very bright light presented for a long time but not when that very same light was previously paired with a shock. Just the opposite is the case for the central nucleus of the amygdala, which is critical for fear conditioning using explicit cues such as a light or tone paired with aversive stimulation (i.e., conditioned fear). *Source:* From "Roles of the Amygdala and Bed Nucleus of the Stria Terminalis in Fear and Anxiety Measured with the Acoustic Startle Reflex," by M. Davis, D. Walker, and Y. Lee, 1997, *Annals of the New York Academy of Sciences, 821,* pp. 305–331.

(Davis et al., 1997), the nature of the different stimulus conditions that activate these two structures suggests that the amygdala connects explicit phasic stimuli that predict aversive unconditioned stimuli with rapidly activated evasive responses and subjective fear. In contrast, prolonged contextual and/or unfamiliar stimuli that connote uncertainty about expected outcome are associated with a neurobehavioral response system that coordinates activation of (1) the negative affective state of anxiety to inform the individual that the current context is uncertain and potentially dangerous, (2) autonomic arousal to mobilize energy for potential action, (3) selective attention to maximize sensory input at specified locations in the visual field, and (4) cognition to derive a response strategy. Nevertheless, as shown in Figure 20.4, efferents from the BNST and sublenticular area innervate many of the same hypothalamic and brain stem regions as the central amygdala (Heimer, 2003), suggesting that fear and anxiety derive their somewhat similar subjective nature from common neuroendocrine and autonomic response systems (Davis et al., 1997; LeDoux, 1998; Rolls, 1999).

The significance of the prolonged startle-potentiation effects of CRH in the BNST is that CRH and the BNST appear to be integrators of behavioral, neuroendocrine, and autonomic responses to stressful circumstances (Leri, Flores, Rodaros, & Stewart, 2002; Pacak, McCarty, Palkovits, Kopin, & Goldsteing, 1995; Shaham, Erb, & Stewart, 2000). This integration is accomplished by the activity of both the peripheral and central CRH systems. The peripheral system involves CRH neurons located in the paraventricular nucleus of the hypothalamus, which, when activated, initiate the series of events that ends in the release of cortisol from the adrenal cortex (Strand, 1999). Cortisol then circulates in the bloodstream and increases energy reserves (gluconeogenesis) and, if not excessive in quantity, can enhance neurotransmitters involved in modulating emotion and memory (Kim & Diamond, 2002).

In contrast, the central CRH system is composed of CRH neurons located in many different subcortical brain regions that modulate emotion, memory, and CNS arousal (Strand, 1999). Whereas the majority of CRH neurons in the CNS do not mediate the effects of stress, some of the CRH-containing regions that are important in mediating stress effects are illustrated in Figure 20.5. For instance, the basolateral amygdala detects discrete aversive stimuli associated with the stressful circumstances and activates the extensive array of CRH neurons located in the central amygdala. These CRH neurons project to many brain regions that modulate emotion, memory, and arousal, including the peripheral CRH neurons in the paraventricular nucleus in the hypothalamus

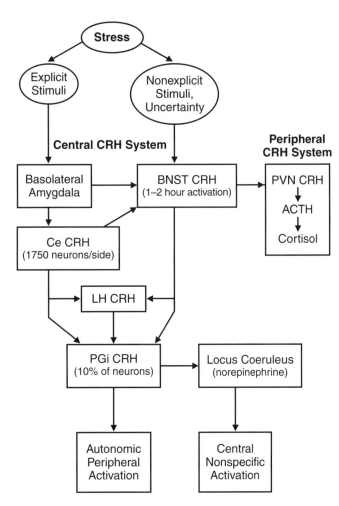

Figure 20.5 Components of the central and peripheral CRH systems. ACTH = Corticotropic hormone from the anterior pituitary; BNST = Bed nucleus of the stria terminalis; Ce = Central amygdala nucleus; LH = Lateral hypothalamus; PGi = Paragiganticocellularis; PVN = Paraventricular nucleus of the hypothalamus.

(Strand, 1999). Stress variables associated with context and uncertainty activate CRH neurons in the BNST, which have similar projection targets as the central amygdala (Erb, Salmaso, Rodaros, & Stewart, 2001; Macey, Smith, Nader, & Porrino, 2003; Shaham et al., 2000). Both the central amygdala and the BNST can activate CRH neurons in the lateral hypothalamus, a region that integrates CNS arousal. In turn, the lateral hypothalamic CRH projections modulate autonomic nervous system activity. Of particular importance, as illustrated in Figure 20.5, all three sources of CRH projections—the central amygdala, BNST, and lateral hypothalamus—innervate CRH neurons in the paragiganticocellularis (PGi; Aston-Jones, Rajkowski, Kubiak, Valentino, & Shiptley, 1996), which is located in the rostral ventrolateral area of the medulla in the brain stem. The PGi is a massive nu-

cleus that provides major integration of central and autonomic arousal and, in turn, coordinates and triggers arousal responses to urgent stimuli via two main pathways emanating from its own population of CRH neurons, which make up 10% of PGi neurons (Aston-Jones et al., 1996). One CRH pathway modulates the autonomic nervous system and hence peripheral arousal effects via projections to the intermediolateral cell column of the spinal cord, activating sympathetic preganglionic autonomic neurons.

The other CRH pathway modulates central arousal effects via activation of the locus coeruleus (LC), where PGi CRH innervation of the LC in humans and monkeys is dense (Aston-Jones et al., 1996). The LC, which is composed of ~20,000 neurons that provide the major source of norepinephrine (NE) in the brain, innervates the entire brain (Oades, 1985). LC neurons that release NE onto ß-adrenergic receptors are responsible for producing a nonspecific emotional activation via broadly collateralizing axons to the central nervous system (Aston-Jones et al., 1996), and this NE release to chronic stress is increased in inbred rat strains with high anxiety (Blizzard, 1988) and in Posttraumatic Stress Disorder patients (Charney, Grillon, & Bremner, 1998). This nonspecific emotional activation pattern constitutes a global urgent response system that responds to unpredicted events and hence facilitates behavioral readiness alerting (enhanced sensory processing) and attention (enhanced selection of stimuli; Aston-Jones et al., 1996), which are characteristic of states of anxiety in highly stress-reactive rodents and monkeys (Blizzard, 1988; Redmond, 1987). This central arousal can be enduring: PGi CRH activation of LC neurons endures and peaks 40 minutes after stimulation of the PGi (Aston-Jones et al., 1996). This persistent activation of spontaneous activity in the LC renders the short-lived, nonsalient stimuli of little effect on the LC, such that salient stimuli have an inordinate effect on LC activity and hence, in turn, on central activation. Thus, taken together, the central CRH neuron system is capable of activating a vast array of behaviorally relevant processes during stressful conditions, including activation of the peripheral CRH system.

CRH administration in rodents, as well as in transgenic mice that have an overproduction of CRH centrally (but not peripherally), generates specifically via CRH2 receptors anxiogenic effects, including reduced exploration of unfamiliarity and of the elevated T-maze, reduced sleep, reduced food intake and sexual activity, and increased sympathetic and behavioral signs of anxiety (Nie et al., 2004; Strand, 1999).

These findings, taken together, suggest that anxiety is essentially a stress-response system that relies on a network of

CRH neuron populations to modulate behaviorally relevant responses to the stressor. The most potent factors in determining the magnitude of a stressor are the very psychological factors that are eliciting stimuli of the anxiety system: uncontrollability, unpredictability, unfamiliarity, unavoidability, and uncertainty. For example, an animal that can control shock shows little evidence of stress, but the animal that is yoked to the first animal and receives shock without control shows severe behavioral and physiological effects of stress. Thus, it is not the physical nature of the shock that is stressful, but the psychological factor of uncontrollability and unpredictability. Furthermore, from the standpoint of trait anxiety or neuroticism, the strongest primary or facet scale in the higher-order factor of anxiety in Tellegen's personality questionnaire is termed *Stress Reactivity* due to the stress-related content of items loading on the scale (Tellegen & Waller, in press).

Nonaffective Constraint or Impulsivity

Here we consider the nature of impulsivity and place this construct within a perspective that emphasizes nonaffective constraint as a major underlying neurobehavioral system. We also explore the neurobiology of nonaffective constraint as a modulatory system.

Delimiting the Heterogeneity of Impulsivity/Constraint

Impulsivity comprises a heterogeneous cluster of lower-order traits that includes sensation seeking, risk taking, novelty seeking, boldness, adventuresomeness, boredom susceptibility, unreliability, and unorderliness. This lack of specificity is reflected in the fact that the content of the measures of impulsivity is heterogeneous, and that not all of these measures are highly interrelated. We (Depue & Collins, 1999) demonstrated elsewhere that at least three different neurobehavioral systems may underlie this trait complex:

1. *Positive incentive motivation,* associated with exploration of novel stimulus conditions.

2. *Low fear,* as indicated in risk taking, attraction to physically dangerous activities, and lack of fear of physical harm.

3. *Low levels of a nonaffective form of impulsivity,* which results in disinhibition of the earlier neurobehavioral systems, as suggested by several researchers (Depue, 1995, 1996; Depue & Spoont, 1986; Panksepp, 1998; Spoont, 1992; Zuckerman, 1994).

As a means of disentangling and clarifying this complexity (see Figure 20.6), we plotted the trait loadings derived in 11 studies (see Appendix) in which two or more multidimensional personality questionnaires were jointly factor-analyzed to derive general, higher-order traits of personality. All studies identified a higher-order trait of impulsivity that *lacks affective content,* which in Figure 20.6 was labeled *constraint* following Tellegen (Tellegen & Waller, in press), who introduced the term to emphasize its independence from emotional traits such as extraversion and neuroticism. All studies also found constraint to be orthogonal to a general, higher-order extraversion trait. Figure 20.6 shows a continuous distribution of traits within the two intersecting orthogonal dimensions of extraversion and constraint. Nevertheless, three relatively homogeneous clusterings of traits can be delineated on the basis of the position and content of traits, relative to extraversion and constraint. First, lower-order traits associated with agentic extraversion (sociability, dominance, achievement, positive emotions, activity, energy) cluster at the high end of the extraversion dimension without substantial association with constraint. A tight clustering of most of these traits to extraversion is evident. Second, various traits of impulsivity that *do not incorporate strong positive affect* (e.g., conscientiousness) cluster tightly around the high end of the constraint dimension without substantial association with extraversion; Eysenck's psychoticism trait and various aggression measures are located at the low end of constraint and show little association with extraversion. Third, all but one trait measure of impulsivity *that incorporate positive affect* (sensation seeking, novelty seeking, risk taking) are located within the dashed lines in Figure 20.6 and are moderately associated with both extraversion and constraint. Thus, currently, most trait models of personality separate a nonaffective form of impulsivity and extraversion into distinct traits, although the terms used for the former vary from conscientiousness (P. Costa & McCrae, 1992; Goldberg & Rosolack, 1994) to constraint (Tellegen & Waller, in press) and impulsivity-unsocialized sensation seeking (Zuckerman, 1994).

Conceptually, the complexity of impulsivity can be clarified by hypothesizing that *nonaffective* constraint lacks ties to a specific motivational-emotional system (Depue & Collins, 1999). As discussed later, a vast body of animal and human literature demonstrates that constraint so conceived functions as a central nervous system variable that modulates the threshold of stimulus elicitation of motor behavior, both positive and negative emotions, and cognition (Coccaro & Siever, 1991; Depue, 1995, 1996; Depue & Spoont, 1986; Panksepp, 1998; Spoont, 1992; Zald & Depue, 2001; Zuck-

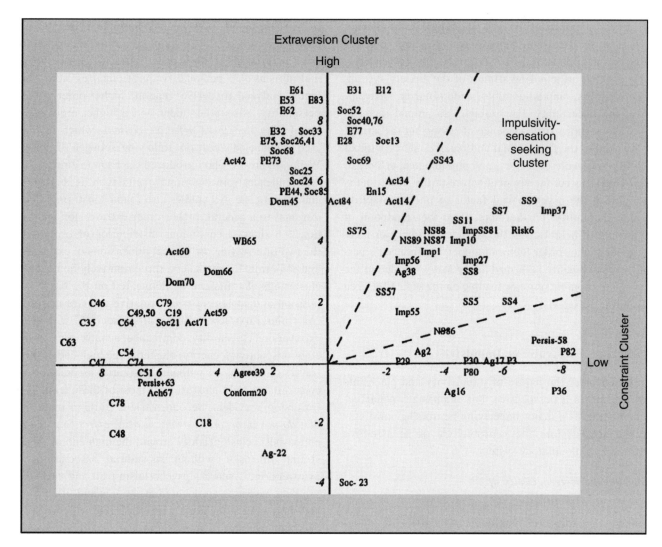

Figure 20.6.   A plotting of loadings of personality traits derived in 11 studies in which more than one multidimensional personality questionnaire was jointly factor-analyzed as a means of deriving general traits of personality. All of these studies defined a general nonaffective impulsivity trait, referred to as constraint (horizontal dimension in the figure), that was separate from the general extraversion trait (vertical dimension in the figure). The figure illustrates three clusterings of traits: an extraversion cluster at the high end of the extraversion dimension; conscientiousness and psychoticism-aggression cluster at the high and low end of the constraint dimension, respectively; and an impulsivity/sensation seeking cluster within the dashed lines. The figure illustrates that extraversion and *non*affective constraint dimensions are generally identified and found to be orthogonal, and that impulsivity/sensation seeking traits associated with strong positive affect arise as a joint function of the interaction of extraversion and constraint. See Appendix A for the identity of the trait measure abbreviations with numbers, the questionnaires to which the abbreviations correspond, and the studies providing the trait loadings. *Source:*   From "Neurobiology of the Structure of Personality: Dopamine, Facilitation of Incentive Motivation, and Extraversion," by R. Depue and P. F. Collins, 1999, *Behavioral and Brain Sciences, 22,* pp. 491–569.

erman, 1994). This formulation is consistent with findings that low constraint is associated in both animals and humans with a generalized motor-cognitive-affective impulsivity but is not preferentially associated with any specific motivational system (Depue & Spoont, 1986; Spoont, 1992; Zald & Depue, 2001). Alternatively, *affective* impulsivity emerges from the interaction of nonaffective constraint with other

distinct affective-motivational systems, such as positive incentive motivation-agentic extraversion (as in Figure 20.6) and anxiety-neuroticism.

Elicitation of behavior can be modeled neurobiologically by use of a minimum threshold construct, which represents a central nervous system weighting of the external and internal factors that contribute to the probability of response expression (Depue & Collins, 1999). External factors are characteristics of environmental stimulation, including magnitude, duration, and psychological salience. Internal factors consist of both state (e.g., stress-induced endocrine levels) and trait biological variation. We propose that nonaffective constraint is the personality trait that reflects the greatest CNS weight on the construct of a minimum response threshold. As such, constraint exerts a general influence over the elicitation of any emotional behavior, and hence constraint is not preferentially associated with any specific neurobehavioral-motivational system. In this model, other higher-order personality traits would thus reflect the influence of neurobiological variables that strongly contribute to the threshold for responding, such as DA in the facilitation of incentive-motivated behavior, μ-opiates in the experience of affiliative reward, and CRH in the potentiation of anxiety.

Neurobiology of Nonaffective Constraint

The important question is what type of CNS variables could provide a major weighting of behavioral elicitation thresholds. Functional levels of neurotransmitters that provide a strong, relatively generalized *tonic inhibitory* influence on behavioral responding would be good candidates as significant modulators of a response elicitation threshold, and hence would likely account for a large proportion of the variance in the trait of nonaffective constraint. We and others previously (Coccaro & Siever, 1991; Depue, 1995, 1996; Depue & Spoont, 1986; Panksepp, 1998; Spoont, 1992; Zald & Depue, 2001; Zuckerman, 1994) and Lesch (1998) most recently suggested that serotonin (5HT), acting at multiple receptor sites in most brain regions, is such a modulator (Azmitia & Whitaker-Azmitia, 1997; Tork, 1990). As reviewed many times in animal and human literatures (Coccaro & Siever, 1991; Coccaro et al., 1989; Depue, 1995, 1996; Depue & Spoont, 1986; Lesch, 1998; Spoont, 1992; Zald & Depue, 2001; Zuckerman, 1994), 5HT modulates a diverse set of functions (including emotion, motivation, motor, affiliation, cognition, food intake, sleep, and sexual activity) and sensory reactivity (such as nociception, sensitization to auditory and tactile startle stimuli, and escape latencies following PAG stimulation) and is associated with many clinical conditions, including violent suicide across several types of disorder, Obsessive-Compulsive Disorder, disorders of impulse control, aggression, depression, anxiety, arson, and substance abuse (Coccaro & Siever, 1991; Depue & Spoont, 1986; Lesch, 1998; Spoont, 1992). Furthermore, *reduced* 5HT functioning in

animals (Depue & Spoont, 1986; Spoont, 1992) and humans (Coccaro et al., 1989) is accompanied by *irritability* and *hypersensitivity* to stimulation in most sensory modalities (Spoont, 1992), which may be due to the important role played by 5HT in the inhibitory modulation of sensory input at several levels of the brain (Azmitia & Whitaker-Azmitia, 1997; Tork, 1990), as well as to significant 5HT modulation of the lateral hypothalamic region that activates autonomic reactivity under stressful conditions (Azmitia & Whitaker-Azmitia, 1997). Thus, 5HT plays a substantial modulatory role in general neurobiological functioning that affects many forms of motivated behavior. In this sense, nonaffective constraint might be viewed as reflecting the influence of the CNS variable of 5HT, which we refer to later as *neural constraint*.

An important but difficult area of research is to determine which personality traits best assess the general modulatory role of 5HT. As a beginning, we found that 5HT agonist-induced increases in serum prolactin secretion were correlated significantly and specifically only with the Constraint/Impulsivity scale (-0.44, $p < .01$) from Tellegen's personality questionnaire of 13 primary scales (Depue, 1995, 1996).

Conceptualizing Individual Differences Underlying Personality Traits

As discussed earlier, models of elicitation of behavioral processes often employ a minimum threshold that represents a central nervous system weighting of the external and internal factors that contribute to initiation of those processes (Depue & Collins, 1999). In addition to the effects of neural constraint (5HT; or nonaffective constraint at the behavioral level), the threshold is weighted most strongly by the joint function of two main variables: magnitude of eliciting stimulation and level of postsynaptic receptor activation of the neurobiological variable thought to contribute most variance to the behavioral process in question, such as DA to incentive motivation, μ-opiates to affiliative reward, and CRH to anxiety. The relation between these two variables is represented in Figure 20.7 as a trade-off function (White, 1986), where pairs of values (of stimulus magnitude and receptor activation) specify a diagonal representing the minimum threshold value for elicitation of a behavioral process. Findings reviewed earlier show that agonist-induced *state* changes in DA, μOR, and CRH activation influence the threshold of incentive motivated behavior, affiliative reward, and anxiety, respectively. Because the two input variables (stimulus magnitude and receptor activation) are interactive, independent variation in

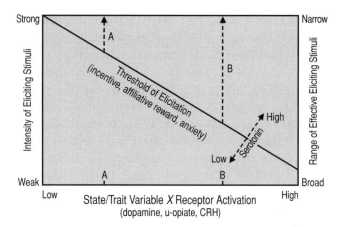

Figure 20.7   A minimum threshold for elicitation of a behavioral process (e.g., incentive motivation-positive affect, affiliative reward-affection, anxiety-negative affect) is illustrated as a trade-off function between eliciting stimulus magnitude (left vertical axis) and *variable X* (e.g., dopamine, μ-opiate, CRH) postsynaptic receptor activation (horizontal axis). Range of effective (eliciting) stimuli is illustrated on the right vertical axis as a function of level of receptor activation. Two hypothetical individuals with low and high *trait* postsynaptic receptor activation (demarcated on the horizontal axis as A and B, respectively) are shown to have narrow (A) and broad (B) ranges of effective stimuli. Threshold effects due to serotonin modulation are illustrated as well.

either one not only modifies the probability of eliciting the behavioral process, but it also simultaneously modifies the value of the other variable that is required to reach a minimum threshold of elicitation. Finally, individual variation in variables that significantly modulate the threshold, especially 5HT-related neural constraint (or nonaffective constraint), would serve as a source of modulation of the threshold of elicitation of *all* behavioral processes. This is shown for 5HT in Figure 20.7.

A threshold model allows behavioral predictions that help to conceptualize the effects of individual differences in neurobiological functioning on personality traits. A trait dimension of postsynaptic receptor activation of variable X (e.g., DA, μ-opiate, or CRH) is represented on the horizontal axis of Figure 20.7, where two individuals with divergent trait levels are demarcated: A (low trait level) and B (high trait level). These two divergent individuals may be used to illustrate the effects of trait differences in variable X receptor activation on elicitation of behavioral processes (e.g., incentive-motivated behavior, affiliative reward, or anxiety).

As Figure 20.7 indicates, for any given eliciting stimulus, the degree of variable X reactivity will, on average, be larger in individual B versus A. Hence, the subjective

emotional and motivational experiences that are facilitated by variable X (e.g., incentive, affection, anxiety) will also be more enhanced in B versus A (Depue & Collins, 1999; Depue & Morrone-Strupinsky, in press). In addition, the difference between individuals A and B in magnitude of subjective experience may contribute to variation in the contemporaneous encoding of a stimulus's intensity or salience (a form of state-dependent learning) and, hence, in the stimulus's encoded salience in subsequent memory consolidation. Accordingly, individuals A and B may develop differences in the capacity of mental representations of (incentive, affiliative, anxiety) contexts to activate the relevant motivational (incentive, affiliative, anxiety) processes, which is significant due to the predominant motivation of behavior in humans by symbolic representations of goals.

If individual differences in encoding apply across the full range of stimulus magnitudes, trait differences in the reactivity of variable X may have marked effects on the *range* of effective (i.e., eliciting) stimuli. This is illustrated in Figure 20.7, where the right vertical axis represents the range of effective (eliciting) stimuli. Increasing trait levels of variable X (horizontal axis) are associated with an increasing efficacy of weaker stimuli (left vertical axis) and, thus, with an increasing range of effective stimuli (right vertical axis). In Figure 20.7, individuals A and B are shown to have a narrow versus broad range, respectively. Significantly, the broader range for individual B suggests that, on average, B will experience more frequent elicitation of subjective emotional experiences associated with variable X activity (incentive, affection, anxiety). This means that the probability at any point in time of being in a variable X-facilitated state for individual B is higher than for A. Therefore, when subsequent relevant stimuli are encountered, their subjectively evaluated magnitude will show a stronger positive bias for B than for A. Thus, trait differences in variable X may *proactively* influence the evaluation and encoding of relevant stimuli and may not be restricted to *reactive* emotional processes. This raises the possibility of variation in the *dynamics* of behavioral engagement with the environment. A positive relation between state variable X activation and stimulus efficacy in the threshold model suggests that, as an initial stimulus enhances variable X activation, the efficacy of subsequently encountered stimuli may be increased proportionally to the degree of the initial variable X activation. Under conditions of strong variable X activation, perhaps even previously subthreshold stimuli may come to elicit behavioral processes (incentive, affiliative reward, anxiety).

THE INTERACTIVE NATURE OF EMOTIONAL TRAITS AND CONSTRAINT

Three of the higher-order personality traits discussed (agentic extraversion, affiliation, anxiety) provide the qualitative emotional content of contemporaneous behavior, depending on which neurobehavioral-motivational system is being elicited at any point in time. The fourth trait, nonaffective constraint, modulates the probability of elicitation of all of those systems. As the very construct of personality connotes, however, the affective or emotional *style* of an individual is determined by the interaction of all four higher-order traits. This means that differential strength between these personality traits, or differential reactivity of their underlying neurobehavioral systems, will determine the relative predominance of particular affective or emotional behavior in individuals. We now consider some of these relevant trait interactions as preparatory discussion for the model of personality disturbance that follows.

Agentic Extraversion × Anxiety

Differential relative strength of the traits of agentic extraversion and anxiety has a substantial influence on the predominant affective or emotional style of an individual. Agentic extraversion is associated with a highly positive affective state, whereas anxiety is associated with a negative affective state. Moreover, both traits are associated with *general* neurobehavioral systems, meaning that they both are subject to frequent elicitation by a broad class of stimuli (incentives and uncertainty, respectively). As illustrated in Figure 20.8, the interaction of these two traits leads to various types of affective style depending on the values of the two traits. The upper right (positive) and lower left (negative) quadrants manifest the greatest contrast and consistency in affective styles, whereas the affective style of individuals in the upper left quadrant is mixed, depending on the relative salience of the most recent incentive versus uncertainty context. The lower right quadrant is characterized by both low positive and negative affective activation and therefore manifests as impoverished affective-emotional behavior reminiscent of clinical descriptions of schizoid behavior.

Agentic Extraversion × Affiliation

The nature of an individual's interpersonal behavior is dependent on the relative strength of agentic extraversion and affiliation. Agentic extraversion is associated with social

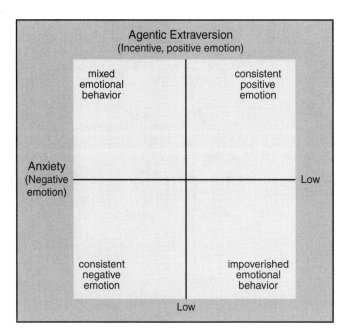

Figure 20.8   Interaction of the higher-order personality traits of agentic extraversion and anxiety. See text for details.

engagement and dominance, whereas affiliation reflects the capacity to experience reward from affiliative interactions. As discussed in the chapter's introduction, theories and research on interpersonal behavior have demonstrated that these two traits are independent and characterize most of the variance in interpersonal behavior. As illustrated in Figure 20.9, their interaction produces substantive differences in interpersonal style. Affiliation at the high end modulates the dominance and competitive aggression of agentic extraversion, creating an *amiable* interpersonal style, ranging from follower to leader depending on the level of agentic extraversion. Perhaps more relevant to personality disturbance, the low end of affiliation manifests as aloof, cold, and uncaring, which ranges from isolated and submissive to manipulative and domineering with increasing levels of agentic extraversion. The lower left quadrant is reminiscent of clinical descriptions of schizoid behavior, whereas the lower right is more in keeping with antisocial behavior.

Affiliation × Separation Anxiety

An additional trait interaction would seem particularly relevant to characterizing interpersonal behavior in personality disturbance: an interaction between affiliation and separation anxiety or distress. The latter trait is rarely assessed in personality inventories, but it is a significant influence in most interpersonal relations at one

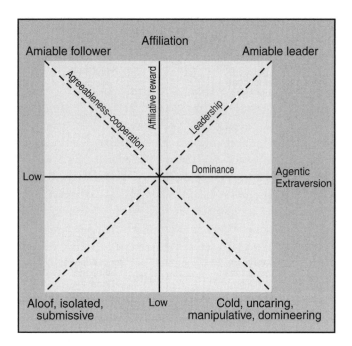

Figure 20.9 Interaction of the higher-order personality traits of agentic extraversion and affiliation. See text for details.

time or another and becomes impairing at extreme levels. Although manifestation of separation anxiety or distress is correlated with the existence of an affiliative bond, we take the position with others (Insel, 1997; Nelson & Panksepp, 1998; Panksepp, 1998; Young, Wang, & Insel, 1998) that processes underlying affiliative bonding are not the same as those involved in social separation distress. Affectively, affiliation and separation are distinctly different and not two sides of a coin. Separation is characterized by the presence of frustration, protest, and anxiety, and not just the absence of warmth and pleasure (and vice versa). In fact, there are data that support a bidimensional organization of affiliation and separation distress, because the neural pathways underlying affiliative engagement (e.g., maternal behavior) are different from those that allow for inhibition of separation distress (Eisenberger, Lieberman, & Williams, 2003; Insel, 1997; Nelson & Panksepp, 1998).

In behavioral terms, separation anxiety or distress may reflect the anxiety of *uncertainty* generated by removal of protective, supportive, safety cues. From a broader evolutionary perspective, separation leading to social isolation can be characterized as unconditionally aversive, having *no discrete, explicit stimulus source*—similar to the human experience of being in the dark (Davis & Shi, 1999; Davis et al., 1997; White & Depue, 1999). In humans, social isolation, rejection, and/or ostracism generates a sense of anxiety, guilt, and apprehension. Put differently, separa-

tion anxiety or distress may in part reflect a very basic neurobehavioral anxiety system that serves to motivate attempts to reverse social isolation via reintegration into a social group (Barlow, 2002; White & Depue, 1999). It may be that separation anxiety or distress is associated to other related traits such as rejection sensitivity and dependency, both of which reflect anxiety over social isolation. This system would be associated with neural networks involved in recognition of social uncertainty and rejection, experience of psychic pain (Eisenberger et al., 2003), and expression of anxiety.

Future research needs to establish the extent to which separation anxiety and the higher-order trait of anxiety are related: Do they reflect the same underlying neurobehavioral system elicited by uncertainty, or do they reflect distinct systems? The answer to this question may help to clarify the fundamental distinctions, if they exist, between negative affect, rejection sensitivity, and separation anxiety that characterizes borderline-, dependent-, and avoidant-like personality disturbance.

As illustrated in Figure 20.10, the dimension of separation distress is portrayed as one of dependency. In interaction with affiliation, the four quadrants can be seen to represent four different social attachment styles frequently described in the literature: (1) *secure* (upper left, where the individual is affectively bonded and not overly distraught with anxiety about losing that bond, and is therefore socially gratified); (2) *ambivalent* (upper right), where the individual is adequately bonded but has intense anxiety about sepa-

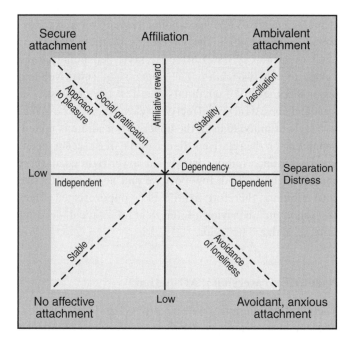

Figure 20.10 Interaction of the higher-order personality traits of affiliation and separation distress. See text for details.

ration from the bond, thereby vacillating between the desire for closeness and protective interpersonal distance. It is in this quadrant that one might expect borderline-, avoidant-, and dependent-like interpersonal disturbance. Moreover, when this quadrant is accompanied by elevation on the higher-order trait of anxiety, the interpersonal disturbance will also be associated with alienation and suspicion of the motives of others, because interpersonal alienation is a strong marker of this trait; Tellegen & Waller, in press; (3) *avoidant-anxious* (lower right, where the individual is not affectively bonded but is anxious about being isolated and alone and thereby avoids loneliness through nonbonded interpersonal relations); and (4) *no affective attachment* (lower left, where there is an absence of affiliative bonding and little anxiety in being separated from social contact, resulting in a stable absence of social attachment that characterizes schizoid-like interpersonal disturbance).

Agentic Extraversion, Anxiety, Aggression, Affiliation × Nonaffective Constraint

A vast body of animal and human evidence consistently associates reduced functioning of 5HT neurotransmission with *behavioral instability.* This instability is manifested as lability, that is, a heightened probability of competing behavioral responses due to a reduced threshold of response elicitation (Spoont, 1992). Therefore, instability or lability will increase as a function of increasing stimulus influences on response elicitation of other behavioral systems (Depue & Spoont, 1986). This means that the effects of constraint depend on interactions with other personality traits that reflect activity in those behavioral systems. That is, the *qualitative content* of unstable behavior will depend on which neurobehavioral-motivational system, or *affective* personality trait, is being elicited at any point in time (Zald & Depue, 2001), although differential strength of various personality traits will obviously produce relative predominance of particular affective behaviors *within individuals.*

An example of the interaction of neurobiological variables associated with constraint (5HT) and agentic extraversion (DA) helps to illustrate the behavioral instability resulting from low constraint. 5HT is an inhibitory modulator of a host of DA-facilitated behaviors, including the reinforcing properties of psychostimulants, novelty-induced locomotor activity, the acquisition of self-administration of cocaine, and DA utilization in the NAS (Ashby, 1996; Depue & Spoont, 1986; Spoont, 1992). This modulatory influence arises in large part from the dense dorsal raphe efferents to the VTA and NAS, connections that are known to modulate DA activity (Ashby, 1966; Azmitia & Whitaker-Azmitia, 1997; Spoont, 1992). A 5HT-related reduction in the threshold of DA facilitation of

behavior results in an exaggerated response to incentive stimuli, which is most apparent in reward-punishment conflict situations. In such situations, exaggerated responding to incentives results in (1) a greater weighting of immediate versus delayed future rewards; (2) increased reactivity to the reward of safety or relief associated with active avoidance (e.g., suicidal behavior); (3) impulsive behavior, that is, a propensity to respond to reward when withholding or delaying a response may produce a more favorable long-term outcome; and (4) various attempts to experience the increased magnitude and frequency of incentive reward, for example, self-administration of DA-active substances (Babor, Hofmann, & Delboca, 1992; Coccaro & Siever, 1991; Depue & Iacono, 1989; Lesch, 1998). All of these effects impair the ability to sustain long-term goal-directed behavior programs (such as obtaining a college degree) by mental representations of expected rewards that can be repeatedly accessed, held online in the prefrontal cortex, and thereby symbolically motivate behavior (Depue & Collins, 1999; Goldman-Rakic, 1987).

A 5HT-DA interaction is more formally illustrated in the threshold model of behavioral facilitation in Figure 20.7, where 5HT values modulate the probability of DA facilitation (variable X) of incentive behavior across the entire range of incentive stimulus magnitude (Depue & Collins, 1999). This interaction is also modeled in Figure 20.11 within a personality framework, where the affectively unipolar dimension of agentic extraversion (DA facilitation) is seen in interaction with nonaffective

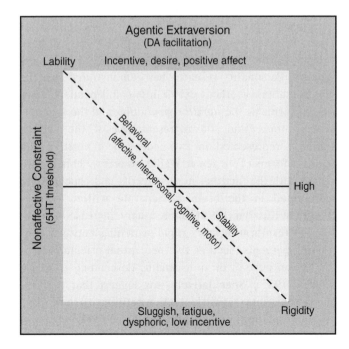

Figure 20.11 Interaction of the higher-order personality traits of agentic extraversion and nonaffective constraint.

constraint (5HT inhibition; Depue, 1996). The interaction of these two traits creates a diagonal dimension of *behavioral stability* that applies equally to affective, cognitive, interpersonal, motor, and incentive processes (Depue & Spoont, 1986; Spoont, 1992; Zald & Depue, 2001). The diagonal represents the line of greatest variance in stability, ranging from lability in the upper left quadrant of the two-space (low 5HT, high DA) to rigidity in the lower right (high 5HT, low DA).

It is important to note that the extent of lability is affected not only by a 5HT influence, but also by DA's more general facilitatory effects on the flow of neural information, where increased DA activity promotes *switching* between response alternatives (i.e., behavioral flexibility; Depue & Iacono, 1989; Oades, 1985; Spoont, 1992). Indeed, when DA transmission is very low, a problem in exceeding the response facilitation threshold occurs, whereas at very high DA transmission levels, a high rate of switching between response alternatives is seen, which can evolve into a low *variety* of responses when abnormally high (e.g., stereotypy; Oades, 1985). Thus, DA's role in switching between response alternatives may explain several of the *non*affective manifestations of extraverted behavior, such as rapidity of attentional shifts and cognitive switching between ideas.

This conceptualization of the interaction of 5HT and DA may be relevant to interpersonal behavior. Brothers and Ring (1992) and others (Adolphs, 2003) have argued that humans have an innate cognitive *alphabet* of ethologically significant behavioral signs that signal the emotional intention of others. This alphabet is integrated into its highest representation in human social cognition as a *person* with propensities and dispositions that have valence for the observer, a social construct akin to personality. Personality research has demonstrated that the representation of others exists in two independent, contrasted forms as the *familiar-good other* and the *unfamiliar-evil other,* and the representation of the self is similarly represented in two independent positive and negative forms (Tellegen & Waller, in press). This is consistent with the fact that most percepts and concepts are represented in the brain as separate unified entities (Squire & Kosslyn, 1998). Interestingly, increased DA activation results in a more rapid switching between contrasting percepts, such as two perceptual orientations of the Necker cube or of an ascending-descending staircase (Oades, 1985). Speculatively, we suggest that the frequent, sometimes rapid fluctuation between extreme mental representations of others and/or the self as *good* or *bad* that characterize several forms of personality disorders is related primarily to reduced 5HT functioning (e.g., bor-

derline-like interpersonal disturbance). Furthermore, this condition would be exaggerated when in interaction with increasing DA functioning (e.g., histrionic-like interpersonal disturbance).

As illustrated in Figure 20.12, interaction between constraint-5HT and trait anxiety-CRH dimensions may create a range of anxious phenotypes that vary in their stability, ranging from most highly labile, episodic, and stress-reactive in the upper left quadrant, to chronically anxious with persistent reverberating negative affect that creates an attitudinal hostility in the upper right quadrant (Zald & Depue, 2001). In support of this interaction, Goddard, Charney, and Germine (1995) recently demonstrated in normal subjects that, when combined with a 5HT antagonist, activation by an NE agonist of LC norepinephrine projections (which is activated by stress-induced PGi CRH neurons) resulted in significantly *greater* NE release in the brain and subjective feelings of anxiety, nervousness, and restlessness than when the NE agonist was administered without a 5HT antagonist. Moreover, together with these findings, our model would account for the weak relation (accounting for 3% to 4% of the variance in behavior) between trait anxiety and a genotypic variant of the 5HT uptake transporter, which may lead to reduced 5HT functioning via negative feedback effects on 5HT cells (Lesch, 1998). In this case, reduced 5HT functioning may disinhibit the LC NE activity-induced autonomic arousal thought to contribute to subjective anxiety (Azmitia & Whitaker-Azmitia, 1997).

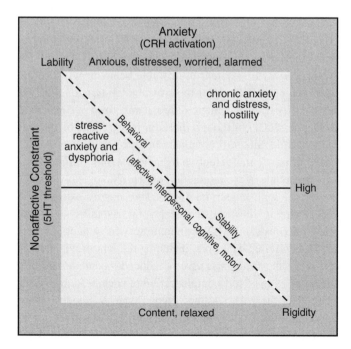

Figure 20.12 Interaction of the higher-order personality traits of anxiety and nonaffective constraint.

Affective aggression is a goal-oriented pattern of attack behavior that is strongly modulated by incentive motivational processes and is markedly disinhibited by conditions of reduced 5HT functioning (Coccaro & Siever, 1991; Depue & Spoont, 1986; Lesch, 1998; Panksepp, 1998; Spoont, 1992). This interaction is likely more complex in that behavioral expression of affective aggression is relative to the strength of the separate but tightly linked neurobehavioral system of fear (Panksepp, 1998). Thus, in Figure 20.13, the vertical axis is represented as a ratio of the strength of affective aggression to fear, and this ratio is modulated by constraint-5HT to produce heightened episodic, impulsive aggression in the upper left quadrant and more chronic aggression and attitudinal hostility in the upper right quadrant. The common finding that reduced 5HT functioning is associated with increased affective aggression is thus expressed in Figure 20.13 but is seen as a function of fear as well.

An interaction of 5HT variation with affiliation was discussed earlier, where reduced 5HT functioning creates frequent, rapid fluctuations between extreme mental representations of others as *good* or *bad*. Such unstable evaluations of others greatly impairs interpersonal relations and may be aggravated in individuals with elevated trait anxiety levels (e.g., borderline-like interpersonal impairment). Another effect of reduced 5HT on affiliation was observed by Higley, Mehlman, Taub, and Higley (1992), who demon-strated that monkeys with low 5HT functioning are overly aggressive and socially rejected by peers. Such monkeys manifest appropriate sociosexual behavior, but its expressive features, in terms of timing and magnitude, appear to be poorly modulated, thereby negatively arousing peers (Higley et al., 1992). It may be that this effect is enhanced in individuals with elevated trait aggression levels.

Conclusions, Implications, and Future Directions

Models of personality traits based on only one neurotransmitter are clearly simplistic and require other modifying factors (Ashby, 1996). In addition, individual differences of psychobiological origin in lower-order traits will represent error variance in predicting higher-order traits from any one variable alone (Livesley, Jang, & Vernon, 1998). Using agentic extraversion as an example, 5HT will certainly not be the only tonic inhibitory modulator of an elicitation threshold. For instance, functional levels of gamma-aminobutyric acid (GABA) tonic inhibitory activity may also influence the threshold of behavioral facilitation as an inhibitor of substance P, a neuromodulator having excitatory effects on VTA DA neurons (Kalivas, Churchill, & Klitenick, 1993; Le Moal & Simon, 1991). Moreover, receptors for GABA, CCK (cholecystokinin), opiates, substance P, and neurotensin are found in the VTA, and their activation can markedly affect DA activity (Kalivas et al., 1993; Le Moal & Simon, 1991). Also, because monoamine oxidase (MAO) is responsible for presynaptic degradation of biogenic amines (DA, 5HT, NE), it may be an important variable in interaction with DA functioning, particularly MAO-B, which predominates in primates and has DA as a specific substrate (Mitra, Mohanakumar, & Ganguly, 1994).

Despite the complexity inherent in the interaction of neurotransmitters in emotional traits, there is good reason to start with one neurotransmitter of substantial effect within the neurobehavioral system underlying a trait, explore the details of its relation to that trait first, and then gradually build complexity by adding additional factors one at a time. This is particularly true of biogenic amines and neuropeptides, because they are phylogenetically old and modulate brain structures associated with behavioral processes relevant to personality, including emotions, motivation, motor propensity, and cognition (Depue & Collins, 1999; Lesch, 1998; Luciana, Collins, & Depue, 1998; Luciana, Depue, Arbisi, & Leon,1992; Oades, 1985). Furthermore, considering their nonspecific modulatory influence and broad distribution patterns in the brain (Ashby, 1996; Aston-Jones et al., 1996; Oades & Halliday, 1987; Tork, 1990), variation in a single neuromodulator

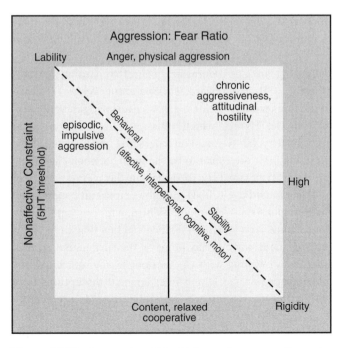

Figure 20.13   Interaction of the higher-order personality traits of anxiety and nonaffective constraint.

can have widespread effects on behavior and on the functioning of multifocal neural networks (Mesulam, 1990), as animal research on the behavioral effects of DA, CRH, μ-opiates, and 5HT has clearly demonstrated. Therefore, variation in biogenic amines and neuropeptides may provide powerful predictors of human behavioral variation. Such neuromodulators may serve as important building blocks for more complex models of personality traits.

Illustration of the interactions of two traits taken at a time, as in this chapter, is informative, but of course underestimates the complexity of reality. The neurobehavioral systems underlying all of the higher-order traits interact. Therefore, we conceive of personality disturbance as *emergent* phenotypes arising from the interaction of the neurobehavioral systems underlying major personality traits.

Our multidimensional model is illustrated in Figure 20.14. In the model, the axes are defined by neurobehavioral systems rather than by traits, because traits are only approximate, fallible estimates of these systems, and trait measures vary in content and underlying constructs. In Figure 20.14, behavioral approach based on positive incentive motivation (underlying agentic extraversion) and anxiety (underlying neuroticism or trait anxiety) are modeled as a ratio of their relative strength, because the opposing nature of their eliciting stimuli affects behavior in a reciprocal manner, such that the *elicitation* or *expression* of one system is influenced by the strength of the other (Gray, 1973). As we discussed, the interaction of these two systems strongly influences the style of an individual's emotional behavior. The affiliative reward dimension (underlying trait affiliation) in the model largely influences the interpersonal domain, whereas the neural constraint dimension (underlying the trait of nonaf-

fective constraint) modulates the expressive features of the other systems. Due to the limitation of graphing more than three dimensions, it should be noted that the model includes two other systems/traits that we suggest influence the manifestation of personality disturbance. As suggested in the section on trait interactions, we believe that a dimension of affective aggression/fear is necessary to account for the full range of antisocial (high aggression/low fear) behavior, and that a dimension of separation anxiety/rejection sensitivity strongly contributes to dependent-, avoidant-, and borderline-like disturbance (all high on this dimension). Taken together, then, the model proposes that the interaction of at least six neurobehavioral systems underlying dimensional personality traits is necessary to account for the emergent phenotypes observed in personality disturbance.

Three significant features of the model are worth emphasizing. First, the phenotypic expression of personality disturbance, represented by the gray-shaded *reaction* surface in the figure (accounting for ~10% of the population; Grant et al., 2004; Lenzenweger et al., 1997; Samuels et al., 2002; Torgersen et al., 2001), is continuous in nature, changing in character gradually but seamlessly across the surface in a manner that reflects the changing product of the multidimensional interactions. It may be that certain areas of the surface are associated with increased probability (risk) of certain features of personality disturbance, and this is represented in the right-back area of the figure as an elevation in the surface that is continuous rather than distinct in contour. Thus, this representation is not meant to imply that a distinct disorder or category exists in that particular area of the surface. Second, the extent and positioning of the reaction surface is weighted most heavily by increasing anxiety, decreasing neural constraint, and decreasing affiliative reward. This weighting is also reflected in the lines with directional arrows overlaying the gray surface in the figure, which illustrate increasing negative emotionality, lability, and interpersonal impairment. These three factors were found to be the most common characteristics of all personality disorders in the meta-analysis of Saulsman and Page (2004), thereby empirically supporting their emphasis in our model. Third, viewing personality disturbance as a *reaction* surface implies that the magnitude of disturbance at any point on the surface is variable, waxing and waning with fluctuations in environmental circumstances, stressors, and interpersonal disruptions both within and across persons over time. Indeed, we recently demonstrated in a longitudinal assessment of the stability of formally defined personality disorders that phenotypic intensity varied markedly over time, thereby affecting the presence/absence of diagnostic status as well as level of symptomatology (Lenzenweger, Johnson, et al., 2004).

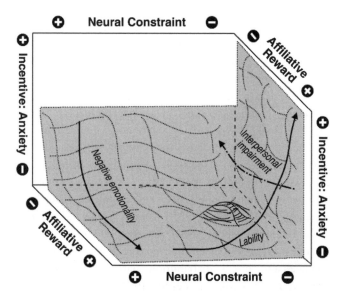

Figure 20.14   A multidimensional model of personality disturbance. See text for details.

Implications of the Model

Several implications of the model can be outlined. First, the model may help to explain sex differences in some forms of personality disturbance. The increased prevalence of males with antisocial behavior may reflect the higher mean of males in the population on the trait of aggression/fear and a lower mean on nonaffective constraint (including 5HT functioning; Spoont, 1992). Additionally, the increased prevalence of females in clinical populations with borderline- and dependent-like personality disturbance may reflect a combination of (1) their higher mean on both trait anxiety (borderline) and separation distress (dependent); (2) their higher mean on affiliation, thereby increasing the need for social relationships whose loss is feared; (3) their lower mean on agentic extraversion, particularly social dominance, hence enhancing the predominance of high levels of trait anxiety; and (4) their lower mean on aggression/fear, hence decreasing the prevalence of antisocial behavior (Depue & Collins, 1999; Kohnstamm, 1989; Tellegen & Waller, in press).

Second, the model suggests that research on the lines of causal neurobiological influence within the structure of *normal* personality will need to be a primary focus if the neurobiological nature of personality disturbance is to be fully understood. At present, there is a paucity of systematic research in this domain (Depue & Collins, 1999; Depue & Morrone-Strupinsky, in press). Third, the multidimensional nature of the model indicates that univariate biological research in personality disturbance will inadequately discover the neurobiological nature of personality disturbance. Thus, not only is multivariate assessment suggested, but methods of *combinatorial* representation of those multiple variables—as in profile, finite mixture modeling, latent class, discriminant function, and multivariate taxonomic analyses—will need to be more fully integrated in this area of research. Fourth, we propose that this neurobehavioral approach should be found in a multitude of venues, not merely in basic wet-lab investigations, if one wants to fully understand other aspects of personality disturbance at other levels of analysis. For example, in a recent study of the executive neurocognitive processing of individuals with Borderline Personality Disorder (Lenzenweger, Clarkin, Fertuck, & Kernberg, 2004), it was found that the constraint system was strongly associated with executive functioning deficits, whereas positive emotion and negative emotion (anxiety) were not. Moreover, constraint remained predictive of executive functioning deficits even when depression and anxiety, well-known features of Borderline Personality Disorder, were taken into account. These findings were particularly interesting as the number of borderline features was unrelated to the executive functioning deficits, which highlights the utility of making use of neurobehavioral systems and their indicators as a way of parsing cognitive performance data. Finally, the trend in development of neurotransmitter-specific drugs may not fully complement the pharmacotherapy requirements of personality disturbance. If personality disturbance represents emergent phenotypes of multiple, interacting neurobehavioral systems, then basic research on the pharmacological modulation of neurobehavioral systems and clinical research on multiregiment pharmacotherapy are greatly needed.

APPENDIX: PERSONALITY QUESTIONNAIRE TRAITS USED IN 11 STUDIES THAT CORRESPOND TO THE NUMBERED TRAIT ABBREVIATIONS ILLUSTRATED IN FIGURE 20.5

See table on pages 795–796.

REFERENCES

Adolphs, R. (2003). Cognitive neuroscience of human social behavior. *Nature Reviews Neuroscience, 4,* 165–178.

Aggleton, J. (1992). *The amygdala: Neurobiological aspects of emotion, memory, and mental dysfunction.* New York: Wiley-Liss.

Aharon, I., Etcoff, N., Ariety, D., Chabris, C., O'Connor, E., & Breiter, H. (2001). Beautiful faces have variable reward value. *Neuron, 32,* 537–551.

Amaral, D., & Witter, M. (1995). Hippocampal formation. In G. Paxinos (Ed.), *The rat nervous system* (pp. 443–494). New York: Academic Press.

Angleitner, A., & Ostendorf, F. (1994). Temperament and the big five factors of personality. In C. F. Halverson, G. A. Kohnstamm, & R. P. Martin (Eds.), *The developing structure of temperament and personality from infancy to adulthood.* Hillsdale, NJ: Erlbaum.

Annett, L., McGregor, A., & Robbins, T. (1989). The effects of ibotenic acid lesions of the nucleus accumbens on spatial learning and extinction in the rat. *Behavioral and Brain Research, 31,* 231–242.

Ashby, C. (1996). *The modulation of dopaminergic neurotransmission by other neurotransmitters.* Boca Raton, FL: CRC Press.

Aston-Jones, G., Rajkowski, J., Kubiak, P., Valentino, R., & Shiptley, M. (1996). Role of the locus coeruleus in emotional activation. In G. Holstege, R. Bandler, & C. Saper (Eds.), *The emotional motor system* (pp. 254–279). New York: Elsevier.

Azmitia, E., & Whitaker-Azmitia, P. (1997). Development and adult plasticity of serotonergic neurons and their target cells. In H. Baumgarten & M. Gothert (Eds.), *Serotonergic neurons and 5HT receptors in the CNS* (Vol. 129, pp. 1–39). New York: Springer.

Babor, T., Hofmann, M., & Delboca, F. (1992). Types of alcoholics: 1. Evidence for an empirically derived typology based on indicators of vulnerability and severity. *Archives of General Psychiatry, 49,* 599–608.

Bandler, R., & Keay, K. (1996). Columnar organization in the midbrain periaqueductal gray and the integration of emotional expression. In G. Holstege, R. Bandler, & C. Saper (Eds.), *The emotional motor system* (pp. 571–605). New York: Elsevier.

Barlow, D. H. (2002). *Anxiety and its disorders* (2nd ed.). New York: Guilford Press.

Bechara, A., Tranel, D., Damasio, H., Adolphs, R., Rockland, C., & Damasio, A. (1995). Double dissociation of conditioning and declarative knowledge relative to the amygdala and hippocampus in humans. *Science, 269,* 1115–1118.

Benjamin, J., Li, L., Patterson, C., Geenberg, B., Murphy, D., & Hamer, D. (1996). Population and familial association between the D4 dopamine receptor gene and measures of novelty seeking. *Nature Genetics, 12,* 81–84.

Berrettini, W. H., Hoehe, M., Ferraro, T. N., DeMaria, P., & Gottheil, E. (1997). Human mu opioid receptor gene polymorphisms and vulnerability to substance abuse. *Addiction and Biology, 2,* 303–308.

Berridge, K. C. (1999). Pleasure, pain, desire, and dread: Hidden core processes of emotion. In D. Kahneman, E. Diener, & N. Schwarz (Eds.), *Well-being: The foundations of hedonic psychology* (pp. 525–557). New York: Russell Sage Foundation.

Blackburn, J. R., Phillips, A. G., Jakubovic, A., & Fibiger, H. C. (1989). Dopamine and preparatory behavior: II. A neurochemical analysis. *Behavioral Neuroscience, 103,* 15–23.

Blizzard, D. A. (1988). The locus coeruleus: A possible neural focus for genetic differences in emotionality. *Experientia, 44,* 491–495.

Block, J. (2001). Millennial contrarianism: The five-factor approach to personality description 5 years later. *Journal of Personality, 69,* 98–107.

Bond, C., LaForge, K. S., Tian, M., Melia, D., Zhang, S., Borg, L., et al. (1998). Single-nucleotide polymorphism in the human mu opioid receptor gene alters ß-endorphin binding and activity: Possible implications for opiate addiction. *Proceedings of the National Academy of Sciences, 95,* 9608–9613.

Breiter, H. C., Aharon, I., Kahneman, D., Dale, A., & Shizgal, P. (2001). Functional imaging of neural responses to expectancy and experience of monetary gains and losses. *Neuron, 30,* 619–639.

Breiter, H. C., Gollub, R. L., Weisskoff, R. M., Kennedy, D. N., Makris, N., Berke, J. D., et al. (1997). Acute effects of cocaine on human brain activity and emotion. *Neuron, 19,* 591–611.

Brothers, L., & Ring, B. (1992). A neuroethological framework for the representation of minds. *Journal of Cognitive Neuroscience, 4,* 107–118.

Cador, M., Taylor, J., & Robbins, T. (1991). Potentiation of the effects of reward-related stimuli by dopaminergic-dependent mechanisms in the nucleus accumbens. *Psychopharmacology, 104,* 377–385.

Callahan, P., Baumann, M., & Rabil, J. (1996). Inhibition of tuberoinfundibular dopaminergic neural activity during suckling: Involvement of mu and kappa opiate receptor subtypes. *Journal of Neuroendocrinology, 8,* 771–776.

Carlezon, W., Haile, C., Coopersmith, R., Hayashi, Y., Malinow, R., Nevem, R., et al. (2000). Distinct sites of opiate reward and aversion within the midbrain identified using a herpes simplex virus vector expressing GluR1. *Journal of Neuroscience, 20,* 1–5.

Carter, S., Lederhendler, I., & Kirkpatrick, B. (1997). *The integrative neurobiology of affiliation* (Vol. 187), New York: New York Academy of Sciences.

Charney, D. S., Grillon, C., & Bremner, J. D. (1998). The neurobiological basis of anxiety and fear: Circuits, mechanisms, and neurochemical interactions (Part I). *Neuroscientist, 4,* 35–44.

Church, A. T. (1994). Relating the Tellegen and five-factor models of personality structure. *Journal of Personality and Social Psychology, 67,* 898–909.

Church, A. T., & Burke, P. (1994). Exploratory and confirmatory tests of the Big Five and Tellegen's three- and four-dimensional models. *Journal of Personality and Social Psychology, 66,* 93–114.

Churchill, L., Roques, B. P., & Kalivas, P. W. (1995). Dopamine depletion augments endogenous opioid-induced locomotion in the nucleus accumbens using both mu 1 and delta opioid receptors. *Psychopharmacology, 120,* 347–355.

Cicchetti, D., & Cohen, D. J. (1995). Perspectives on developmental psychopathology. In D. Cicchetti & D. J. Cohen (Eds.), *Developmental psychopathology: Vol. I. Theory and methods* (pp. 3–22). New York: Wiley.

Cicchetti, D., & Dawson, G. (2002). Editorial: Multiple levels of analysis. *Development and Psychopathology, 14,* 417–420.

Clark, L. A., & Livesley, W. J. (1994). Two approaches to identifying the dimensions of personality disorder. In P. T. Costa Jr. & T. A.

Widiger (Eds.), *Personality disorders and the five factor model of personality* (pp. 261–278). Washington, DC: American Psychological Association.

Clark, L. A., Livesley, W. J., Schroeder, M. L., & Irish, S. L. (1996). Convergence of two systems for assessing personality disorder. *Psychological Assessment, 8,* 294–303.

Cloninger, C. R., Svrakic, D., & Przybeck, T. (1993). A psychobiological model of temperament and character. *Archives of General Psychiatry, 50,* 975–990.

Coccaro, E., & Siever, L. (1991). *Serotonin and psychiatric disorders.* Washington, DC: American Psychiatric Press.

Coccaro, E., Siever, L., Klar, H., Maurer, G., Cochrane, K., Cooper, T., et al. (1989). Serotonergic studies in patients with affective and personality disorders. *Archives of General Psychiatry, 46,* 587–599.

Costa, P., & McCrae, R. (1992). *Revised NEO Personality Inventory (NEO-PI-R) and NEO Five-Factor Inventory (NEO-FFI) professional manual.* Odessa, FL: Psychological Assessment Resources.

Costa, P. T., Jr., & Widiger, T. A. (1994). *Personality disorders and the five factor model of personality.* Washington, DC: American Psychological Association.

Damasio, D. (2003). *Looking for Spinoza.* New York: Harcourt.

David, V., & Cazala, P. (2000). Anatomical and pharmacological specificity of the rewarding effect elicited by microinjections of morphine into the nucleus accumbens of mice. *Psychopharmacology, 150,* 24–34.

Davis, M., & Shi, C. (1999). The extended amydala: Are the central nucleus of the amygdala and the bed nucleus of the stria terminalis differentially involved in fear versus anxiety? *Annals of New York Academy of Sciences, 877,* 281–291.

Davis, M., Walker, D., & Lee, Y. (1997). Roles of the amygdala and bed nucleus of the stria terminalis in fear and anxiety measured with the acoustic startle reflex. *Annals of the New York Academy of Sciences, 821,* 305–331.

Depue, R. (1995). Neurobiological factors in personality and depression. *European Journal of Personality, 9,* 413–439.

Depue, R. (1996). Neurobiology and the structure of personality: Implications for the personality disorders. In J. Clarkin & M. Lenzenweger (Eds.), *Major theories of personality disorders* (pp. 149–163). New York: Guilford Press.

Depue, R., & Collins, P. F. (1999). Neurobiology of the structure of personality: Dopamine, facilitation of incentive motivation, and extraversion. *Behavioral and Brain Sciences, 22,* 491–569.

Depue, R., & Iacono, W. (1989). Neurobehavioral aspects of affective disorders. *Annual Review of Psychology, 40,* 457–492.

Depue, R., & Lenzenweger, M. F. (2001). A neurobehavioral dimensional model of personality disorders. In W. J. Livesley (Ed.), *Handbook of personality disorders* (pp. 136–176). New York: Guilford Press.

Depue, R., Luciana, M., Arbisi, P., Collins, P., & Leon, A. (1994). Dopamine and the structure of personality: Relation of agonist-induced dopamine activity to positive emotionality. *Journal of Personality and Social Psychology, 67,* 485–498.

Depue, R., & Morrone-Strupinsky, J. (in press). A neurobehavioral model of affiliative bonding: Implications for conceptualizing a human trait of affiliation. *Behavioral and Brain Sciences.*

Depue, R., & Spoont, M. (1986). Conceptualizing a serotonin trait: A behavioral dimension of constraint. *Annals of the New York Academy of Sciences, 487,* 47–62.

de Waele, J. P., Kiianmaa, K., & Gianoulakis, C. (1995). Distribution of the mu and delta opioid binding sites in the brain of the alcohol-preferring AA and alcohol-avoiding ANA lines of rats. *Journal of Pharmacology and Experimental Therapeutics, 275*(1), 518–527.

Di Chiara, G. (1995). The role of dopamine in drug abuse viewed from the perspective of its role in motivation. *Drug and Alcohol Dependence, 38,* 95–137.

Di Chiara, G., & North, R. A. (1992). Neurobiology of opiate abuse. *Trends in the Physiological Sciences, 13,* 185–193.

Digman, J. M. (1997). Higher-order factors of the Big Five. *Journal of Personality and Social Psychology, 73,* 1246–1256.

Domjan, M., Cusato, B., & Villarreal, R. (2000). Pavlovian feed-forward mechanisms in the control of social behavior. *Behavioral and Brain Sciences, 23,* 1–29.

Drevets, W. C., Gautier, C., Price, J. C., Kupfer, D. J., Kinahan, P. E., Grace, A. A., et al. (2001). Amphetamine-induced dopamine release in human ventral striatum correlates with euphoria. *Biological Psychiatry, 49,* 81–96.

Dworkin, S., Guerin, G., Goeders, N., & Smith, J. (1988). Kainic acid lesions of the nucleus accumbens selectively attenuate morphine self-administration. *Pharmacology, Biochemistry and Behavior, 29,* 175–181.

Dyce, J. A., & Connor, B. P. (1998). Personality disorders and the five-factor model: A test of facet-level predictions. *Journal of Personality Disorders, 12,* 31–45.

Ebstein, R., Novick, O., Umansky, R., Priel, B., Osher, Y., Blaine, D., et al. (1996). Dopamine D4 receptor (DRD4) exon III polymorphism associated with the human personality trait of novelty seeking. *Nature Genetics, 12,* 78–80.

Eisenberger, N., Lieberman, M., & Williams, K. (2003). Does rejection hurt? An fMRI study of social exclusion. *Science, 302,* 290–292.

Ekselius, L., Lindstrom, E., von Knorring, L., Bodlund, O., & Kullgren, G. (1994). A principal component analysis of the DSM-III-R Axis II personality disorders. *Journal of Personality Disorders, 8,* 140–148.

Elmer, G. I., Pieper, J. O., Goldberg, S. R., & George, F. R. (1995). Opioid operant self-administration, analgesia, stimulation and respiratory depression in μ-deficient mice. *Psychopharmacology, 117,* 23–31.

Erb, S., Salmaso, N., Rodaros, D., & Stewart, J. (2001). A role for the CF-containing pathway from central nucleus of the amygdala to the bed nucleus of the stria terminalis in the stress-induced reinstatement of cocaine seeking in rats. *Psychopharmacology, 158,* 360–365.

Everitt, B., & Robbins, T. (1992). Amygdala-ventral striatal interactions and reward-related processes. In J. Aggleton (Ed.), *The amygdala: Neurobiological aspects of emotion, memory, and mental dysfunction* (pp. 145–159). New York: Wiley-Liss.

Fendt, M., Endres, T., & Apfelbach, R. (2003). Temporary inactivation of the bed nucleus of the stria terminalis but not of the amygdala blocks freezing induced by trimethylthiazoline, a component of fox feces. *Journal of Neuroscience, 23,* 23–28.

Fleming, A. S., Korsmit, M., & Deller, M. (1994). Rat pups are potent reinforcers to the maternal animal: Effects of experience, parity, hormones, and dopamine function. *Psychobiology, 22*(1), 44–53.

Fowles, D. C. (1987). Application of a behavioral theory of motivation to the concepts of anxiety and impulsivity. *Journal of Research in Personality, 21,* 417–435.

Gaffan, D. (1992). Amygdala and the memory of reward. In J. Aggleton (Ed.), *The amygdala: Neurobiological aspects of emotion, memory, and mental dysfunction* (pp. 431–458). New York: Wiley-Liss.

Gelernter, J., Kranzler, H., & Cubells, J. (1999). Genetics of two μ opioid receptor gene (OPRM1) exon I polymorphisms: Population studies, and allele frequencies in alcohol- and drug-dependent subjects. *Molecular Psychiatry, 4,* 476–483.

Gianoulakis, C., Krishnan, B., & Thavundayil, J. (1996). Enhanced sensitivity of pituitary beta-endorphin to ethanol in subjects at high risk of alcoholism. *Archives of General Psychiatry, 52*(3), 250–257.

Gingrich, B., Liu, Y., Cascio, C., Wang, Z., & Insel, T. R. (2000). Dopamine D2 receptors in the nucleus accumbens are important for social attachment in female prairie voles (*Microtus ochrogaster*). *Behavioral Neuroscience, 114*(1), 173–183.

Goddard, A., Charney, D., & Germine, M. (1995). Effects of tryptophan depletion on responses to yohimbine in healthy human subjects. *Biological Psychiatry, 38,* 74–85.

Goldberg, L., & Rosolack, T. (1994). The Big Five factor structure as an integrative framework. In C. Halverson, G. Kohnstamm, & R. Marten (Eds.), *The developing structure of temperament and personality from infancy to adulthood* (pp. 275–314). Hillside, NJ: Erlbaum.

Goldman-Rakic, P. S. (1987). Circuitry of the prefrontal cortex and the regulation of behavior by representational memory. In V. Mountcastle (Ed.), *Handbook of physiology* (pp. 373–417). Bethesda, MD: American Physiological Society.

Gottesman, I. I. (1997). Twins: En route to QTLs for cognition. *Science, 276,* 1522–1523.

Grant, B. F., Hasin, D. S., Stinson, F. S., Dawson, D. A., Chou, S. P., Ruan, W. J., et al. (2004). Prevalence, correlates, and disability of personality disorders in the United States: results from the national epidemiologic survey on alcohol and related conditions. *Journal of Clinical Psychiatry, 65,* 948–958.

Graves, F. C., Wallen, K., & Maestripieri, D. (2002). Opioids and attachment in rhesus macaque abusive mothers. *Behavioral Neuroscience, 116,* 489–493.

Gray, J. A. (1973). Causal theories of personality and how to test them. In J. R. Royce (Ed.), *Multivariate analysis and psychological theory* (pp. 302–354). New York: Academic Press.

Gray, J. A. (1992). Neural systems, emotion and personality. In J. Madden, S. Matthysee, & J. Barchas (Eds.), *Adaptation, learning and affect* (pp. 95–121). New York: Raven Press.

Gunderson, J. G., Shea, M. T., Skodol, A. E., McGlashan, T. H., Morey, L. C., Stout, R. L., et al. (2000). The Collaborative Longitudinal Personality Disorders Study: Development, aims, design, and sample characteristics. *Journal of Personality Disorders, 14,* 300–315.

Guyenet, P., Koshiqa, N., Huangfu, D., Baraban, S., Stornetta, R., & Li, Y.-W. (1996). Role of medulla oblongata in generation of sympathetic and vagal outflows. In G. Holstege, R. Bandler, & C. Saper (Eds.), *The emotional motor system* (pp. 510–552). New York: Elsevier.

Heimer, L. (2003). A new anatomical framework for neuropsychiatric disorders and drug abuse. *American Journal of Psychiatry, 160,* 1726–1739.

Herbert, J. (1993). Peptides in the limbic system: Neurochemical codes for co-ordinated adaptive responses to behavioural and physiological demand. *Progress in Neurobiology, 41,* 723–791.

Herz, A. (1998). Opioid reward mechanisms: A key role in drug abuse? *Canadian Journal of Physiology and Pharmacology, 76,* 252–258.

Higley, J., Mehlman, P., Taub, D., & Higley, S. (1992). Cerebrospinal fluid monoamine and adrenal correlates of aggression in free-ranging rhesus monkeys. *Archives of General Psychiatry, 49,* 436–441.

Hilliard, S., Domjan, M., Nguyen, M., & Cusato, B. (1998). Dissociation of conditioned appetitive and consummatory sexual behavior: Satiation and extinction tests. *Animal Learning and Behavior, 26*(1), 20–33.

Hol, T., Niesink, M., van Ree, J., & Spruijt, B. (1996). Prenatal exposure to morphine affects juvenile play behavior and adult social behavior in rats. *Pharmacology, Biochemistry, and Behavior, 55,* 615–618.

Holstege, G. (1996). The somatic motor system. In G. Holstege, R. Bandler, & C. Saper (Eds.), *The emotional motor system* (pp.lnb56–78). New York: Elsevier.

Hyztia, P., & Kiianmaa, K. (2001). Suppression of ethanol responding by centrally administered CTOP and naltrindole in AA and Wistar rats. *Alcohol Clinical and Experimental Research, 25,* 25–33.

Ikemoto, I., & Panksepp, J. (1996). Dissociations between appetitive and consummatory responses by pharmacological manipulations of reward-relevant brain regions. *Behavioral Neuroscience, 110,* 331–345.

Insel, T. R. (1997). A neurobiological basis of social attachment. *American Journal of Psychiatry, 154*(6), 726–733.

Johnson, B., & Ait-Daoud, N. (2000). Neuropharmacological treatments for alcoholism: Scientific basis and clinical findings. *Psychopharmacology, 149,* 327–344.

Johnson, J. G., Cohen, P., Kasen, S., Skodol, A. E., Hamagami, F., & Brook, J. S. (2000). Age-related change in personality disorder trait levels between early adolescence and adulthood: A community-based longitudinal investigation. *Acta Psychiatrica Scandinavica, 102,* 265–275.

Kalivas, P., Churchill, L., & Klitenick, M. (1993). The circuitry mediating the translation of motivational stimuli into adaptive motor responses. In P. Kalivas & C. Barnes (Eds.), *Limbic motor circuits and neuropsychiatry* (pp. 216–252). Boca Raton, FL: CRC Press.

Kendler, K. S., McGuire, M., Gruenberg, A. M., O'Hare, A., Spellman, M., & Walsh, D. (1993). The Roscommon Family Study: III. Schizophrenia-related personality disorders in relatives. *Archives of General Psychiatry, 50,* 781–788.

Keverne, E. B. (1996). Psychopharmacology of maternal behaviour. *Journal of Psychopharmacology, 10*(1), 16–22.

Kim, J., & Diamond, D. (2002). The stressed hippocampus, synaptic plasticity and lost memories. *Nature Reviews Neuroscience, 3,* 453–462.

Kohnstamm, G. (1989). Temperament in childhood: Cross-cultural and sex differences. In G. Kohnstamm, J. Bates, & M. Rothbart (Eds.), *Temperament in childhood* (pp. 317–365). New York: Wiley.

Korfine, L., & Lenzenweger, M. F. (1995). The taxonicity of schizotypy: A replication. *Journal of Abnormal Psychology, 104,* 26–31.

Kosslyn, S. M., & Rosenberg, R. S. (2001). *Psychology: The brain, the person, the world.* Boston: Allyn & Bacon.

Kranzler, H. R. (2000). Pharmacotherapy of alcoholism: Gaps in knowledge and opportunities for research. *Acohol and Alcoholism, 35,* 537–547.

LaBuda, C. J., Sora, I., Uhl, G. R., & Fuchs, P. N. (2000). Stress-induced analgesia in mu-opioid receptor knockout mice reveals normal function of the delta-opioid receptor system. *Brain Research, 869,* 1–10.

Laviolette, S. R., Gallegos, R. A., Henriksen, S. J., & van der Kooy, D. (2004). Opiate state controls bi-directional reward signaling via GABA-A receptors in the ventral tegmental area. *Nature Neuroscience, 10,* 160–169.

LeDoux, J. E. (1998). *The emotional brain.* New York: Simon & Schuster.

LeDoux, J. E., Cicchetti, P., Xagoraris, A., & Romanski, L. (1990). The lateral amygdaloid nucleus: Sensory interface of the amygdala in fear conditioning. *Journal of Neuroscience, 10,* 1062–1069.

Le Moal, M., & Simon, H. (1991). Mesocorticolimbic dopaminergic network: Functional and regulatory roles. *Physiological Reviews, 71,* 155–234.

Lenzenweger, M. F. (1998). Schizotypy and schizotypic psychopathology: Mapping an alternative expression of Schizophrenia liability. In M. F. Lenzenweger & R. H. Dworkin (Eds.), *Origins and development of Schizophrenia: Advances in experimental psychopathology* (pp. 93–121). Washington, DC: American Psychological Association.

Lenzenweger, M. F. (1999). Stability and change in personality disorder features: The Longitudinal Study of Personality Disorders. *Archives of General Psychiatry, 56,* 1009–1015.

Lenzenweger, M. F., & Clarkin, J. F. (1996). The personality disorders: History, development, and research issues. In J. F. Clarkin & M. F. Lenzenweger (Eds.), *Major theories of personality disorder* (pp. 1–35). New York: Guilford Press.

Lenzenweger, M. F., & Clarkin, J. F. (2005). The personality disorders: History, development, and research issues. In J. F. Clarkin & M. F. Lenzenweger (Eds.), *Major theories of personality disorder* (2nd ed., pp. 1–42). New York: Guilford Press.

Lenzenweger, M. F., Clarkin, J. F., Fertuck, E. A., & Kernberg, O. F. (2004). Executive neurocognitive functioning and neurobehavioral systems indicators in borderline personality disorder: A preliminary study. *Journal of Personality Disorders, 18,* 421–438.

Lenzenweger, M. F., & Haugaard, J. (Eds.). (1996). *Frontiers of developmental psychopathology.* New York: Oxford University Press.

Lenzenweger, M. F., Johnson, M. D., & Willett, J. B. (2004). Individual growth curve analysis illuminates stability and change in personality disorder features: The Longitudinal Study of Personality Disorders. *Archives of General Psychiatry, 61,* 1015–1024.

Lenzenweger, M. F., & Korfine, L. (1992). Confirming the latent structure and base rate of schizotypy: A taxometric analysis. *Journal of Abnormal Psychology, 101,* 567–571.

Lenzenweger, M. F., & Loranger, A. W. (1989). Detection of familial Schizophrenia using a psychometric measure of schizotypy. *Archives of General Psychiatry, 46,* 902–907.

Lenzenweger, M. F., Loranger, A. W., Korfine, L., & Neff, C. (1997). Detecting personality disorders in a nonclinical population: Application of a two-stage procedure for case identification. *Archives of General Psychiatry, 54,* 345–351.

Leri, F., Flores, J., Rodaros, D., & Stewart, J. (2002). Blockade of stress-induced but not cocaine-induced reinstatement by infusion of noradrenergic antagonists into the bed nucleus of the stria terminalis or the central nucleus of the amygdala. *Journal of Neuroscience, 22,* 5713–5718.

Lesch, K.-P. (1998). Serotonin transporter and psychiatric disorders. *Neuroscientist, 4,* 25–34.

Leyton, M., & Stewart, J. (1992). The stimulation of central kappa opioid receptors decreases male sexual behavior and locomotor activity. *Brain Research, 594,* 56–74.

Livesley, W. J. (2001). Commentary on reconceptualizing personality disorder categories using trait dimensions. *Journal of Personality, 69,* 277–286.

Livesley, W. J., Jackson, D. N., & Schroeder, M. L. (1992). Factorial structure of traits delineating personality disorders in clinical and general population samples. *Journal of Abnormal Psychology, 101,* 432–440.

Livesley, W. J., Jang, K., & Vernon, P. (1998). Phenotypic and genetic structure of traits delineating personality disorder. *Archives of General Psychiatry, 55,* 941–948.

Livesley, W. J., Schroeder, M. L., Jackson, D. N., & Jang, K. L. (1994). Categorical distinctions in the study of personality disorder: Implication for classification. *Journal of Abnormal Psychology, 103,* 6–17.

Luciana, M., Collins, P., & Depue, R. (1998). Opposing roles for dopamine and serotonin in the modulation of human spatial working memory functions. *Cerebral Cortex, 8,* 218–226.

Luciana, M., Depue, R. A., Arbisi, P., & Leon, A. (1992). Facilitation of working memory in humans by a D2 dopamine receptor agonist. *Journal of Cognitive Neurosciences, 4,* 58–68.

Macey, D., Smith, H., Nader, M., & Porrino, L. (2003). Chronic cocaine self-administration upregulates the norepinephrine transporter and alters functional activity in the bed nucleus of the stria terminalis of the rhesus monkey. *Journal of Neuroscience, 23,* 12–16.

MacLean, P. (1986). Ictal symptoms relating to the nature of affects and their cerebral substrate. In E. Plutchik & H. Kellerman (Eds.), *Emotion: Theory, research, and experience: Vol. 3. Biological foundations of emotion* (pp. 283–328). New York: Academic Press.

Marinelli, M., & White, F. (2000). Enhanced vulnerability to cocaine self-administration is associated with elevated impulse activity of midbrain dopamine neurons. *Journal of Neuroscience, 20,* 8876–8885.

Martel, F., Nevison, C., Simpson, M., & Keverne, E. (1995). Effects of opioid receptor blockade on the social behavior of rhesus monkeys living in large family groups. *Developmental Psychobiology, 28,* 71–84.

Matheson, M. D., & Bernstein, I. S. (2000). Grooming, social bonding, and agonistic aiding in rhesus monkeys. *American Journal of Primatology, 51,* 177–186.

Matthes, H. W., Maldonado, R., Simonin, F., Valverde, O., Slowe, S., Kitchen, I., et al. (1996). Loss of morphine-induced analgesia, reward effect and withdrawal symptoms in mice lacking the μ-opioid-receptor gene. *Nature, 383,* 819–823.

McDonald, A., Shammah-lagnado, S., Shi, C., & Davis, M. (1999). Cortical afferents to the extended amygdala. *Annals of New York Academy of Sciences, 877,* 309–338.

McGinty, J. F. (1999). Regulation of neurotransmitter interactions in the ventral striatum. *Annals of New York Academy of Sciences, 877,* 129–139.

Mesulam, M. (1990). Large-scale neurocognitive networks and distributed processing for attention, language, and memory. *Annals of Neurology, 28,* 597–613.

Millon, T. (1997). *The Millon inventories: Clinical and personality assessment.* New York: Guilford Press.

Mitra, N., Mohanakumar, K., & Ganguly, D. (1994). Resistance of golden hamster: Relationship to MAO-B. *Journal of Neurochemistry, 62,* 1906–1912.

Morrone-Strupinsky, J. V., & Depue, R. A. (2004). Differential relation of two distinct, film-induced positive emotional states to affiliative and agentic extraversion. *Personality and Individual Differences, 36,* 1109–1126.

Morrone-Strupinsky, J. V., Depue, R. A., Sherer, N., & White, T. (2000). Film-induced incentive motivation and positive affect in relation to agentic and affiliative components of extraversion. *Personality and Individual Differences, 36*, 1109–1126.

Narita, M., Aoki, T., & Suzuki, T. (2000). Molecular evidence for the involvement of NR2B subunit containing N-methyl-D-aspartate receptors in the development of morphine-induced place preference. *Neuroscience, 101*, 601–606.

Nelson, E. E., & Panksepp, J. (1998). Brain substrates of infant-mother attachment: Contributions of opioids, oxytocin, and norepinephrine. *Neuroscience and Biobehavioral Reviews, 22*(3), 437–452.

Nie, Z., Schweitzer, P., Roberts, A., Madamba, S., Moore, S., & Siggins, G. (2004). Ethanol augments GABAergic transmission in the central amygdala via CRF1 receptors. *Science, 303*, 1512–1514.

Niesink, R. J., Vanderschuren, L. J., & van Ree, J. M. (1996). Social play in juvenile rats in utero exposure to morphine. *NeuroToxicology, 17*(3–4), 905–912.

Oades, R. (1985). The role of noradrenaline in tuning and dopamine in switching between signals in the CNS. *Neuroscience and Biobehavioral Reviews, 9*, 261–282.

Oades, R., & Halliday, G. (1987). Ventral tegmental (A10) system: Neurobiology: 1. Anatomy and connectivity. *Brain Research Review, 12*, 117–165.

Olausson, H., Lamarre, Y., Backlund, H., Morin, C., Wallin, B. G., Starck, G., et al. (2002). Unmyelinated tactile afferents signal touch and project to insular cortex. *Nature Neuroscience, 5*, 900–904.

Olive, M., Koenig, H., Nannini, M., & Hodge, C. (2001). Stimulation of endorphin neurotransmission in the nucleus accumbens by ethanol, cocaine, and amphetamine. *Journal of Neuroscience, 21*(184), 1–5.

Olmstead, M., & Franklin, K. B. (1997). The development of a conditioned place preference to morphine. *Journal of Neuroscience, 21*(RC184), 1–5.

Olson, G., Olson, R., & Kastin, A. (1997). Endogenous opiates: 1996. *Peptides, 18*, 1651–1688.

Ostrowski, N. L. (1998). Oxytocin receptor mRNA expression in rat brain: Implications for behavioral integration and reproductive success. *Psychoneuroendocrinology, 23*(8), 989–1004.

Pacak, K., McCarty, R., Palkovits, M., Kopin, I., & Goldsteing, D. (1995). Effects of immobilization on in vivo release of norepinephrine in the bed nucleus of the stria terminalis in conscious rats. *Brain Research, 688*, 242–246.

Panksepp, J. (1998). *Affective neuroscience: The foundations of human and animal emotions.* New York: Oxford University Press.

Panter, A. T., Tanaka, J. S., & Hoyle, R. H. (1994). Structural models for multimode designs in personality and temperament research. In C. F. Halverson, G. A. Kohnstamm, & R. P. Martin (Eds.), *The developing structure of temperament and personality from infancy to adulthood.* Hillsdale, NJ: Erlbaum.

Pfaus, J. G., Smith, W. J., & Coopersmith, C. B. (1999). Appetitive and consummatory sexual behaviors of female rats in bilevel chambers: I. A correlational and factor analysis and the effects of ovarian hormones. *Hormones and Behavior, 35*, 224–240.

Pich, E., Pagliusi, S., Tessari, M., Talabot-Ayer, D., van Huijsduijnen, R., & Chiamulera, C. (1997). Common neural substrates for the addictive properties of nicotine and cocaine. *Science, 275*, 83–86.

Polan, H. J., & Hofer, M. A. (1998). Olfactory preference for mother over home nest shavings by newborn rats. *Developmental Psychobiology, 33*, 5–20.

Porges, S. (1998). Love: An emergent property of the mammalian autonomic nervous system. *Psychoneuroendocrinology, 23*, 837–861.

Porges, S. (2001). The polyvagal theory: Phylogenetic substrates of a social nervous system. *International Journal of Psychophysiology, 42*, 123–146.

Redmond, D. E. (1987). Studies of the nucleus locus coeruleus in monkeys and hypotheses for neuropsychopharmacology. In J. Y. Meltzer (Ed.), *Psychopharmacology: The third generation of progress* (pp. 967–975). New York: Raven Press.

Reynolds, S. K., & Clark, L. A. (2001). Predicting dimensions of personality disorder from domains and facets of the five-factor model. *Journal of Personality, 69*, 199–222.

Robbins, T., Cador, M., Taylor, J., & Everitt, B. (1989). Limbic-striatal interactions in reward-related processes. *Neuroscience and Biobehavioral Reviews, 13*, 155–162.

Rolls, E. T. (1999). *The brain and emotion.* New York: Oxford University Press.

Rosenthal, R., & Rosnow, R. L. (1991). *Essentials of behavioral research: Methods and data analysis* (2nd ed.). New York: McGraw-Hill.

Rutter, M. (1997). Developmental psychopathology as an organizing research construct. In D. Magnusson (Ed.), *The lifespan development of individuals: Behavioral, neurobiological, and psychosocial perspectives: A synthesis* (pp. 394–413). New York: Cambridge University Press.

Rutter, M. (2000). Developmental psychopathology: Concepts and challenges. *Developmental and Psychopathology, 12*, 265–296.

Samuels, J. E., Eaton, W. W., Bienvenu, O. J., Brown, C., Costa, P. T., & Nestadt, G. (2002). Prevalence and correlates of personality disorders in a community sample. *British Journal of Psychiatry, 180*, 536–542.

Saulsman, L. M., & Page, A. C. (2004). The five-factor model and personality disorder empirical literature: A meta-analytic review. *Clinical Psychology Review, 23*, 1055–1085.

Schlaepfer, T. E., Strain, E. C., Greenberg, B. D., Preston, K. L., Lancaster, E., Bigelow, G. E., et al. (1998). Site of opioid action in the human brain: Mu and kappa agonists' subjective and cerebral blood flow effects. *American Journal of Psychiatry, 155*(4), 470–473.

Schneirla, T. (1959). An evolutionary and developmental theory of biphasic processes underlying approach and withdrawal. In M. Jones (Ed.), *Nebraska Symposium on Motivation* (pp. 144–171). Lincoln: University of Nebraska Press.

Schultz, W., Dayan, P., & Montague, P. (1997). A neural substrate of prediction and reward. *Science, 275*, 1593–1595.

Selden, N., Everitt, B., Jarrard, L., & Robbins, T. (1991). Complementary roles of the amygdala and hippocampus in aversive conditioning to explicit and contextual cues. *Neuroscience, 42*, 335–350.

Shaham, Y., Erb, S., & Stewart, J. (2000). Stress-induced relapse to heroin and cocaine seeking in rats: A review. *Brain Research Reviews, 33*, 13–33.

Shea, M. T., Stout, R., Gunderson, J. G., Morey, L. C., Grilo, C. M., McGlashan, T. H., et al. (2002). Short-term diagnositc stability of schizotypal, borderline, avoidant, and obsessive-compulsive personality disorders. *American Journal of Psychiatry, 159*, 2036–2041.

Shippenberg, T. S., & Elmer, G. I. (1998). The neurobiology of opiate reinforcement. *Critical Reviews in Neurobiology, 12*(4), 267–303.

Silk, J. B., Alberts, S. C., & Altmann, J. (2003). Social bonds of female baboons enhance infant survival. *Science, 302*, 1231–1234.

Simonin, F., Valverde, O., Smadja, C., Slowe, S., Kitchen, I., Diierich, A., Le Meur, M., et al. (1998). Disruption of the kappa-opioid receptor gene in mice enhances sensitivity to chemical visceral pain, impairs pharmacological actions of the selective kappa-agonist U-50, 488H and attenuates morphine withdrawal. *EMBO Journal, 17*, 886–897.

Spoont, M. (1992). Modulatory role of serotonin in neural information processing: Implications for human psychopathology. *Psychological Bulletin, 112*, 330–350.

Squire, L., & Kosslyn, S. (1998). *Findings and current opinion in cognitive neuroscience.* Cambridge, MA: MIT Press.

Stallings, M., Hewitt, J., Cloninger, C. R., Heath, A., & Eaves, L. (1996). Genetic and environmental structure of the Tridimesional Personality Questionnaire: Three or four temperament dimensions. *Journal of Personality and Social Psychology, 70*, 127–140.

Stefano, G., Goumon, Y., Casares, F., Cadet, P., Fricchione, G., Rialas, C., et al. (2000). Endogenous morphine. *Trends in Neuroscience, 23*, 436–442.

Strand, F. L. (1999). *Neuropeptides: Regulators of physiological processes.* Cambridge, MA: MIT Press.

Sutherland, R., & McDonald, R. (1990). Hippocampus, amygdala and memory deficits in rats. *Behavioral and Brain Research, 37*, 57–79.

Tellegen, A., Lykken, D. T., Bouchard, T. J., Wilcox, K. J., Segal, N. L., & Rich, S. (1988). Personality similarity in twins reared apart and together. *Journal of Personality and Social Psychology, 54,* 1031–1039.

Tellegen, A., & Waller, N. G. (1996). Exploring personality through test construction: Development of the multidimensional personality questionnaire. In S. Briggs & J. Cheek (Eds.), *Personality measures: Development and evaluation* (pp. 133–161). Greenwich: JAI Press.

Tellegen, A., & Waller, N. G. (in press). Exploring personality through test construction: Development of the multidimensional personality questionnaire. In S. Briggs & J. Cheek (Eds.), *Personality measures: Development and evaluation* (Vol. 1). New York: JAI Press.

Timberlake, W., & Silva, K. (1995). Appetitive behavior in ethology, psychology, and behavior systems. In N. Thompson (Ed.), *Perspectives in ethology: Vol. 11. Behavioral design* (pp. 211–253). New York: Plenum Press.

Torgersen, S., Kringlen, E., & Cramer, V. (2001). The prevalence of personality disorders in a community sample. *Archives of General Psychiatry, 58,* 590–596.

Tork, I. (1990). Anatomy of the serotonergic system. *Annals of the New York Academy of Sciences, 600,* 9–32.

Treit, D., Pesold, C., & Rotzinger, S. (1993). Dissociating the anti-fear effects of septal and amygdaloid lesions using two pharmacologically validated models of rat anxiety. *Behavioral Neuroscience, 107,* 770–785.

Uhl, G. R., Sora, I., & Wang, Z. (1999). The μ opiate receptor as a candidate gene for pain: Polymorphisms, variations in expression, nociception, and opiate responses. *Proceedings of the National Academy of Sciences, 96,* 7752–7755.

van Furth, W., & van Ree, J. (1996). Sexual motivation: Involvement of endogenous opioids in the ventral tegmental area. *Brain Research, 729,* 20–28.

Volkow, N., Wang, G., Fischman, M., Foltin, R., Fowler, J., Abumrad, N., et al. (1997). Relationship between subjective effects of cocaine and dopamine transporter occupancy. *Nature, 386,* 827–829.

Waller, N., Lilienfeld, S., Tellegen, A., & Lykken, D. (1991). The Tridimensional Personality Questionnaire: Structural validity and comparison with the Multidimensional Personality Questionnaire. *Multivariate Behavioral Research, 26,* 1–23.

Wang, Z., Yu, G., Cascio, C., Liu, Y., Gingrich, B., & Insel, T. R. (1999). Dopamine D2 receptor-mediated regulation of partner preferences in female prairie voles (*Microtus ochrogaster*): A mechanism for pair bonding? *Behavioral Neuroscience, 113*(3), 602–611.

Watson, C., & Clark, L. (1997). Extraversion and its positive emotional core. In S. Briggs, W. Jones, & R. Hogan (Eds.), *Handbook of personality psychology* (pp.lnb72–96). New York: Academic Press.

Watson, D., & Tellegen, A. (1985). Towards a consensual structure of mood. *Psychological Bulletin, 98,* 219–235.

White, N. (1986). Control of sensorimotor function by dopaminergic nigrostriatal neurons: Influence on eating and drinking. *Neuroscience and Biobehavioral Reviews, 10,* 15–36.

White, T. L., & Depue, R. A. (1999). Differential association of traits of fear and anxiety with norepinephrine- and dark-induced pupil reactivity. *Journal of Personality and Social Psychology, 77*(4), 863–877.

Widiger, T. A., Trull, T. J., Clarkin, J. F., Sanderson, C., & Costa, P. T., Jr. (1994). A description of the DSM-III-R and DSM-IV personality disorders with the five factor model of personality. In P. T. Costa Jr. & T. A. Widiger (Eds.), *Personality disorders and the five factor model of personality* (pp. 41–56). Washington, DC: American Psychological Association.

Wiedenmayer, C., & Barr, G. (2000). M opioid receptors in the ventrolateral periaqueductal gray mediate stress-induced analgesia but not immobility in rat pups. *Behavioral Neuroscience, 114,* 125–138.

Wiggins, J. (1991). Agency and communion as conceptual coordinates for the understanding and measurement of interpersonal behavior. In D. Cicchetti & W. Grove (Ed.), *Thinking clearly about psychology: Essays in honor of Paul Everett Meehl* (pp. 89–113). Minneapolis: University of Minnesota Press.

Wise, R. (1998). Drug-activation of brain reward pathways. *Drug and Alcohol Dependence, 51,* 13–22.

Wolterink, G., Cador, M., Wolterink, I., Robbins, T., & Everitt, B. (1989). Involvement of D1 and D2 receptor mechanisms in the processing of reward-related stimuli in the ventral striatum. *Society of Neuroscience, 15,* 490.

Wyvell, C. L., & Berridge, K. C. (2000). Intra-accumbens amphetamine increases the conditioned incentive salience of sucrose reward: Enhancement of reward "wanting" without enhanced "liking" on response reinforcement. *Journal of Neuroscience, 20,* 8122–8130.

Young, L. J., Wang, Z., & Insel, T. R. (1998). Neuroendocrine bases of monogamy. *Trends in the Neurosciences, 21,* 71–75.

Zald, D., & Depue, R. (2001). Serotonergic modulation of positive and negative affect in psychiatrically healthy males. *Personality and Individual Differences, 30,* 71–86.

Zanarini, M., Frankenburg, F. R., Hennen, J., & Silk, K. R. (2003). The longitudinal course of borderline psychopathology: 6-year prospective follow-up study of the phenomenology of borderline personality disorder. *American Journal of Psychiatry, 160,* 274–283.

Zubieta, J.-K., Smith, Y., Bueller, J., Xu, Y., Kilbourn, M., Jewett, D., et al. (2001). Regional μ opioid receptor regulation of sensory and affective dimensions of pain. *Science, 293,* 311–315.

Zuckerman, M. (1989). Personality in the third dimension: A psychobiological approach. *Personality and Individual Differences, 10,* 391–418.

Zuckerman, M. (1994). An alternative five-factor model for personality. In C. Halverson, G. Kohnstamm, & R. Marten (Eds.), *The developing structure of temperament and personality from infancy to adulthood* (pp. 114–137). Mahwah, NJ: Erlbaum.

Zuckerman, M. (1996, March). A structural test of personality models based on punishment and reward expectancies and sensitivities, and mood traits. Paper presented at the annual meeting of the Eastern Psychological Association, Philadelphia, PA.

Zuckerman, M., Kuhlman, D., Joireman, J., Teta, P., & Kraft, M. (1993). A comparison of three structural models for personality: The big three, the big five, and the alternative five. *Journal of Personality and Social Psychology, 65,* 757-768.

Study	Numbered Trait Abbreviation[b] (in Numerical Order)	Corresponding Personality Questionnaire Trait[c]
Zuckerman, 1989	Imp1	Buss-Plomin EASI, Inhibitory Control
	Ag2	Buss-Plomin EASI Anger
	P3	Eysenck Personality Questionnaire, Psychoticism
	SS4	Sensation Seeking Scales, Boredom Susceptibility
	SS5	Sensation Seeking Scales, Experience Seeking
	Risk6	Jackson Personality Inventory, Risk Taking
	SS7	Buss-Plomin, EASI Sensation Seeking
	SS8	Sensation Seeking Scales, Disinhibition
	SS9	Karolinska Scale of Personality, Monotony Avoidance
	Imp10	Karolinska Scale of Personality, Impulsivity
	SS11	Sensation Seeking Scales, Thrill-Adventure Seeking
	E12	Eysenck Personality Questionnaire, Extraversion
	Soc13	California Personality Inventory, Sociability
	Act14	Buss-Plomin EASI Activity
	En15	Jackson Personality Inventory, Energy Level
	Ag16	Buss-Durkee Hostility Inventory
	Ag17	Personality Research Form, Aggression
	C18	Strelau Temperament Inventory, Restraint
	C19	Jackson Personality Inventory, Responsibility
	Conform20	Jackson Personality Inventory, Conformity
	Soc21	California Personality Inventory, Socialization
	Ag22	Karolinska Scale Personaltiy, Inhibition of Aggression
	Soc23	Karolinska Scale of Personality, Detachment
	Sco24	Buss-Plomin EASI, Sociability
	Soc25	Jackson Personality Inventory, Social Participation
	Soc26	Personality Research Form, Affiliation
	Imp27	Buss-Plomin EASI, Decision Time
Goldberg & Rosolack, 1994	E28	Eysenck Personality Questionnaire, Extraversion (with factors I and III)
	P29	Eysenck Personality Questionnaire, Psychoticism (with factors I and III)
	P30	Eysenck Personality Questionnaire, Psychoticism (with factors I and II)
Zuckerman et al., 1993 (four factor solution with entire scales)	E31	Costa & McCrae NEO Extraversion
	E32	Eysenck Personality Questionnaire, Extraversion
	Soc33	Zuckerman-Kuhlman Personality Questionnaire, Sociability
	Act34	Zuckerman-Kuhlman Personality Questionnaire, Activity
	C35	Costa & McCrae NEO, Conscientiousness
	P36	Eysenck Personality Questionnaire, Psychoticism
	Imp37	Zuckerman-Kuhlman Personality Questionnaire, Impulsive Sensation Seeking
	Ag38	Zuckerman-Kuhlman Personality Questionnaire, Aggression
	Agree39	Costa & McCrae NEO, Agreeableness
Zuckerman et al., 1993 (five factor solution with primary scales included)	Soc40	Costa & McCrae NEO, E2: Gregariousness
	Soc41	Costa & McCrae NEO, E1: Warmth
	Act42	Costa & McCrae NEO, E4: Activity
	SS43	Costa & McCrae NEO, E5: Excitement Seeking
	PE44	Costa & McCrae NEO, E6: Positive Emotions
	Dom45	Costa & McCrae NEO, E3: Assertiveness
	C46	Costa & McCrae NEO, C4: Achievement
	C47	Costa & McCrae NEO, C5: Self-Discipline
	C48	Costa & McCrae NEO, C6: Deliberation
	C49	Costa & McCrae NEO, C3: Dutiful
	C50	Costa & McCrae NEO, C1: Competence
	C51	Costa & McCrae NEO, C2: Order

(continued)

Study	Numbered Trait Abbreviation[b] (in Numerical Order)	Corresponding Personality Questionnaire Trait[c]
Angleitner & Ostendorf, 1994[d]	Soc52	Buss-Plomin EASI III, Sociability I
	E53	Costa & McCrae NEO, Extraversion
	C54	Costa & McCrae NEO, Conscientiousness
	Imp55	Buss-Plomin EASI III, Noninhibition Control
	Imp56	Buss-Plomin EASI III, Short Decision Time
	SS57	Buss-Plomin EASI III, Sensation Seeking
	Persis-58	Buss-Plomin EASI III, Nonpersistence
	Act 59	Buss-Plomin EASI III, Activity: Tempo
	Act60	Buss-Plomin EASI III, Activity: Vigor
Panter, Tanaka & Hoyle, 1994	E61	Goldberg Surgency
	E62	Costa & McCrae NEO, Extraversion
	C63	Goldberg Conscientiousness
	C64	Costa & McCrae NEO, Conscientiousness
Church, 1994	WB65	Tellegen Multidimensional Personality Questionnaire, Well-Being
	Dom66	Tellegen Multidimensional Personality Questionnaire, Social Potency
	Soc68	Costa & McCrae NEO, E1: Warmth
	Soc69	Costa & McCrae NEO, E2: Gregariousness
	Dom70	Costa & McCrae NEO, E3: Assertiveness
	Act71	Costa & McCrae NEO, E4: Activity
	SS72	Costa & McCrae NEO, E5: Excitement Seeking
	PE73	Costa & McCrae NEO, E6: Positive Emotions
	C74	Costa & McCrae NEO, Conscientiousness
Tellegen & Waller, 1996	E75	Tellegen Multidimensional Personality Questionnaire, Positive Emotionality
	Soc76	California Personality Inventory, Personal Orientation
	E77	Eysenck Personality Questionnaire, Extraversion
	C78	Tellegen Multidimensional Personality Questionnaire, Constraint
	C79	California Personality Inventory, Rigidity
	P80	Eysenck Personality Questionnaire, Psychoticism
Zuckerman, 1996	ImpSS81	Zuckerman-Kuhlman Personality Questionnaire, ImpSS
	P82	Eysenck Personality Questionnaire, Psychoticism
	E83	Eysenck Personality Questionnaire, Extraversion
	Act84	Zuckerman-Kuhlman Personality Questionnaire, Activity
	Soc85	Zuckerman-Kuhlman Personality Questionnaire, Sociability
Waller et al., 1991 (interscale correlations, not factor loadings)	NS86	Cloninger Tridimensional Personality Questionnaire, Novelty Seeking (average of NS subscale correlations × Tellegen MPQ Well-Being [best E estimate] and Control [best Constraint estimate])
Stallings et al., 1996 (interscale correlations, not factor loadings)	NS87	Cloninger Tridimensional Personality Questionnaire, Novelty Seeking (NS correlated × EPQ E & P)
	NS88	Cloninger Tridimensional Personality Questionnaire, Novelty Seeking (NS correlated × EPQ E & KSP Impulsivity)
	NS89	Cloninger Tridimensional Personality Questionnaire, Novelty Seeking (NS correlated × EPQ E & KSP Monotony Avoidance)

[a] References for the trait measures may be found in the study which used them.

[b] A "minus" sign appearing after letters but before the number indicates the inverse of the abbreviated descriptor (e.g., Soc23 is Detachment, the inverse of Sociability).

[c] EASI = Energy-Activity-Sociability-Impulsivity; KSP = Karolinska Scale of Personality; MPQ = Multidimensional Personality Questionnaire; NEO = Neuroticism-Extraversion-Openness; Sensation Seeking Scales = of Zuckerman.

[d] Only established questionnaires used.

CHAPTER 21

Symphonic Causation and the Origins of Childhood Psychopathology

W. THOMAS BOYCE

[Science is] the systematic decoding of observed regularities and the reduction of the regularities to more parsimonious and general principles that account for wide ranges of phenotypic detail.

—P. E. CONVERSE, 1986

THE NATURE-NURTURE CULTURE WARS

By and large, investigators and scholars contributing to this second edition of Cicchetti and Cohen's *Developmental Psychopathology,* including the author of this chapter, were academically reared in a scientific generation marked by a confluence of two irreconcilable views of the origins of human disorders. Within a single generation, physicians,

The research and thought on which this chapter is based were supported and funded by the John D. and Catherine T. MacArthur Foundation Research Network on Psychopathology and Development. An earlier version of the chapter was presented at the Millennium Dialogue on Early Child Development sponsored by the Ontario Institute for Studies in Education of the University of Toronto.

clinical and developmental psychologists, social workers, and laboratory investigators were steeped in the twin agendas of environmental and biological determinism. In the former of these views, prominent in the scientific world of the 1960s and 1970s, disease and disorder were held to be products of contextual exposures and adversities. Human afflictions, it was believed, were due almost exclusively to the acute and chronic, cumulative influences of environmental agents of disease. Such agents included psychological stressors, impoverished living conditions, physical toxins, infectious pathogens, and inadequate or malevolent parenting. Prevention and treatment were taken to require alterations in these causative environmental exposures. Thus, Schizophrenia was viewed as the product of psychological "double binds" in dysfunctional family units, Autism was regarded as the legacy of cold, distant mothers, and maternal overprotectiveness figured prominently in the presumed etiology of childhood anxiety disorders.

In a second canonical view, emerging at the pinnacle of the first by virtue of a revolution in molecular biology, human disorder was thought to be principally the result of biological frailties built into the structure of the heritable genome. Individual genetic differences, occurring on average in 1 of every 1,000 nucleotide base pairs, were seen as likely biological substrates for many human disorders, and quantitative trait loci were thought to constitute the multiple gene systems that, in isolation, code for variation in complex behavioral traits (Plomin & Crabbe, 2000). Most, if not all, disease, it was posited by some, would one day become explicable within the frameworks of evolutionary biology and human genetics, and eagerly anticipated "gene therapies" would transform the treatment and prevention of disordered biology. Thus, Alzheimer's disease would one day be accounted for by mutations in the gene coding for apolipoprotein E4; a polymorphism in the promoter region of the serotonin transporter gene would eventually elucidate anxiety disorders and phobias; and the long repeat allele of the DRD4 dopamine receptor gene would explain the etiology of Attention-Deficit/Hyperactivity Disorder and other externalizing behavior problems. Within 3 decades' time, two opposing and mutually exclusive causal orthodoxies captured and held the high ground of scientific discourse on the genesis of human disease.

NEW EVIDENCE FOR BIOLOGY-CONTEXT INTERACTIONS

Vulnerabilities in both positions first became evident as three sets of research findings emerged in the final years of the twentieth century. First, the nascent field of behavioral genetics increasingly documented shared genetic and environmental accounts for variance in the incidence and severity of a broad array of behavioral and psychopathological disorders (Plomin, DeFries, McClearn, & McGuffin, 2001). Using heritability statistics derived from genetically informative research designs, behavioral geneticists became able to decompose phenotypic variance into genetic and environmental components. The genetic component was further subdivided into additive and nonadditive effects, and the environmental component was parsed into shared and nonshared influences (Goldsmith, Gottesman, & Lemery, 1997). While the neuroscience of Schizophrenia provided compelling evidence for a heritable disorder of the brain, epidemiological studies revealed that, even among monozygotic twins, the concordance rate for a diagnosis of Schizophrenia never exceeded 50%. Schizophrenia

was demonstrably a biological disorder with heritable components, but as much as half of the variance in its rate of occurrence was attributable to environmental exposures. The science of behavior and development thus faced a Kierkegaardian dilemma (Kierkegaard, 1843/1986), in which an uncompromising either/or became a more illuminating both/and. Schizophrenia, like virtually all forms of human behavior (Rutter et al., 1997), became understood as a product of *both* biological *and* contextual etiologies.

A second set of findings revealed the previously unsuspected bidirectional influences of biology and context, each on the other. It had become apparent that genes affected both normative and disordered human behavior; now, new evidence indicated the heritability of environmental experience and the potentially profound regulatory effects of social environmental exposures on the transcription of DNA. Discoveries of such bidirectional effects led to a recognition of genotype-environment correlations and to the categorization of such correlations into passive, reactive, and active forms (Plomin, DeFries, & Loehlin, 1977). Studies by Plomin and colleagues demonstrated heritable influences on parental behavior and the home environment (Braungart, Fulker, & Plomin, 1992; O'Connor, Hetherington, Reiss, & Plomin, 1995), and other work showed that even random misfortune, such as stressful events (Kendler, Neale, Kessler, Heath, & Eaves, 1993) and the loss of friends (Bergeman, Plomin, Pederson, McClearn, & Nesselroade, 1990), were partly attributable to genetic variation. Animal research by Meaney and colleagues demonstrated that brief maternal separations among rat pups alter maternal behavior, leading to down-regulation of the corticotropin-releasing hormone (CRH) system and diminished adrenocortical reactivity extending even into adult life (Anisman, Zaharia, Meaney, & Merali, 1998). Other studies in mice found that disruption of social hierarchies led to viral infection-related mortality, which was attributable to an overexpression of genes for cytokine proteins (Sheridan, Stark, Avitsur, & Padgett, 2000), and that caloric restriction prevented aging-related alterations in the expression of genes governing protein metabolism (C.-K. Lee, Klopp, Weindruch, & Prolla, 1999). Although both environmental and biological determinism assumed impenetrable divisions between contexts and genes, new evidence revealed a capacity for the genome to influence environmental experience and for social and physical environments to switch on and off the decoding of genetic material (Cacioppo, Berntson, Sheridan, & McClintock, 2000). Social experience became a heritable predisposition, and the transcription of genes became a process governable by the character of social experience.

The third source of vulnerability in the twin dogmas of biological and environmental determinism was the more recent and accelerating emergence of biology-context interactions in studies of disease etiology. Much of the work examining biological and contextual contributions to pathogenesis was initially preoccupied with partitioning variance into the two distinctive categories of causal factors. Other studies began to illuminate how interplay between biology and context serves a central etiologic role. Mednick, Gabrielli, and Hutchings (1987), for example, found that a child's rearing by an adoptive parent with a criminal conviction did not increase the likelihood of criminality in the child, unless one of the child's biological parents had also been convicted of a crime. Similarly, a polymorphism in the promoter region of the gene encoding CRH has recently been shown to moderate the association between maternal stress and preterm birth (X. Wang et al., 2001). Self-perceived maternal stress was associated overall with pregnancies that were an average of 1.3 weeks shorter, but when a mother possessed a variant allele of the CRH gene, perceived stress was associated with a 2.9-week shortening. A third example is the finding by vanHerwerden et al. (1995) that a polymorphism in the $Fc_\epsilon R1$-ß gene on chromosome 11q13 alters bronchiolar reactivity to house dust mites and environmental tobacco smoke. While dust mites and smoke are known causes of airway inflammation and allergic symptoms (Palmer & Cookson, 2000), polymorphic markers in this gene are associated with the serum IgE production that is thought to mediate airway reactivity. Explorations of gene-environment interactions are perhaps most robustly developed in the field of environmental toxicology, where as many as 100 candidate genes have been identified with potential for metabolically disposing of carcinogens with known links to lung, brain, and bladder cancers (Albers, 1997). Even in so-called monogenic diseases, such as phenylketonuria, phenotypic expression of the disease is highly variable, suggesting that modifier genes and environmental factors may influence disease severity and course (Scriver & Waters, 1999). Common to each of these examples is a biogenetic vulnerability that amplifies the pathological effects of a social or physical environmental exposure.

Taken together, these three lines of evidence constitute a convincing empirical threat to a monodeterministic view of pathogenesis. Although human morbidities will undoubtedly be identified that have their origins in solely genetic or environmental causes, it appears highly plausible at present to anticipate that variation in the onset and course of *most* human disorders will ultimately be explained by interactions among biological and environmental forces

(Weatherall, 2001). It is now time to move past questions of how much of the variation in outcomes is attributable to genes versus environment and into the more complex and potentially rewarding questions of genetic change and continuity, relations among dimensional symptoms and diagnosable psychopathology, and the interplay between biology and context (Plomin & Crabbe, 2000). As noted by Goldsmith et al. (1997) and Rutter et al. (1997), there is pressing need for broader metaphors of gene-environment interaction, which extend beyond "black box analyses" to hypotheses regarding specific interactive processes.

IMPEDIMENTS TO DISCOVERY

Given the difficulties of discovering biology-context interactions (Wachs & Plomin, 1991), it is all the more remarkable that such interactions are being increasingly identified and characterized in studies of human disease. Gene-environment interactions are assessed as the differential risk effects of an exposure among individuals with different genotypes, or as the differing effects of a genotype among those who are heterogeneous with respect to exposure (Kraemer, Stice, Kazdin, Offord, & Kupfer, 2001). As noted by McClelland and Judd (1993), field studies tend to underestimate the magnitude of interaction effects due to the nonoptimal distributions of the component variables. Interactions accounting for as little as 1% of outcome variance in field research may conceal a true R^2 many times that size that would be found using an optimal, experimental design. When demonstrated, biology-context interactions in human populations may disproportionately exist at the extremes of genetic and environmental variation (McGue & Bouchard, 1998). Animal studies are far more likely to reveal etiologic interactions because of their capacity both for true experimentation and for creating genotypes and exposures that are dimensionally more extreme. Indeed, recent animal work in three different laboratories demonstrated that environments may modify the expression of genotypically derived behavioral differences, even when aspects of context are rigorously controlled (Crabbe, Wahlsten, & Dudek, 1999). Mathematically, analyses of variance and related statistical tests often fail to identify nonadditive effects because they have much less power in tests of interactions than in tests of main effects (Wahlsten, 1990). Newer genetic research designs (Andrieu & Goldstein, 1998), along with statistical approaches that are more sensitive to interaction effects (Kraemer et al., 2001), are now abetting the discovery of complex interactions between and among biologically and environmentally based factors.

SYMPHONIC CAUSATION AND THE INTERACTION OF BIOLOGY AND CONTEXT

What such methods are poised to uncover, it is argued here most centrally, is a kind of *symphonic causation,* a set of lawful regularities in the character and effects of biology-context interplay, which might together compose a foundational principle for understanding the origins of human disease. Our early forays into the territories of etiologic complexity seem to suggest that both necessity and insufficiency are the twin hallmarks of the biological and experiential factors that contribute to disease causation. It may plausibly be the case that few if any human disorders are the products of unilateral pathogenesis and that one of the core features of disease is its essential dependence on a confluence of biologically grounded vulnerabilities and contextually based pathogenic influences. If so, then the causation of human morbidities must be viewed as symphonic, in the sense that their etiologies necessitate a coming together, a conjoining, of diverse, categorically distinctive etiologic elements. Symphonic means "sounding together," a chordal synthesis by which two or more elemental sounds create, in their confluence, a new presence not derivable from the attributes of its parts. Disease may thus imply a lawful but unanticipated convergence of the interior self, in the form of heritable or acquired biological susceptibilities, with the exterior environment, in the form of pathogenic agents of disease.

It is essential to note that this argument is focused neither on the statistical evaluation of cross-product interaction terms nor on the benefits of multilevel analysis. As noted earlier, there are important mathematical impediments to the detection and characterization of interaction effects, and there is ground to be gained both in statistical approaches to evaluating potential interactions and in research designs that maximize their detection. Nonetheless, more is needed than simply better, more pliable statistical tools. Rather, there is a deeper, more fundamental need for a theory of disease that incorporates observed invariances in the character of biology-context interactions. Similarly, although multilevel analysis (i.e., concurrent measurement at multiple levels of organizational complexity) is a heuristic and often revelatory tool, a different, though complementary strategy is being advanced here. A search for invariances in biology-context interplay may indeed involve scientific analysis at very different levels of organization (e.g., the levels of gene and family environment), but the promise of such a search lies not in its implicit penetration of multiple organizational strata, but in its *binocularity,* that is, the conjoining of individual biol-

ogy and shared context into a unitary image of disease and health.

There are at least two corollaries of such a vision of health and disease. The first is that the preservation of health and the genesis of disease are seen, in such a framework, as two facets of the same phenomenon rather than as distinctive and oppositional biological processes. Historically, for example, medicine and public health have been mutually self-regarded as separable and discontinuous fields, medicine addressing pathogenesis and the curative treatment of diseased individuals and public health expounding prevention and the safeguarding of population health. Adoption of a symphonic causation model, on the other hand, implies a reconciliation of medical and public health perspectives and invokes an explicit recapitulation of the ancient Greek conception of harmonious and disharmonious relations. Disease is the morbid conjunction of individual susceptibility and external threat, and health is a state of harmony that exists between individual and context. Thus, the prevention of disease occurrence is a stewardship of harmony, a preservation of the *symphonic* congruity between the needs and vulnerabilities of the individual and the provisions and perils of the environment.

A second corollary is the potentially nonstochastic character of such confluences of biology and context. If biology is capable of invoking and changing context, and if context is capable of altering the expression of individual biology, then the possibility arises for the production of autocatalytic, self-promoting feedback loops involving biology-context-biology chains of influence. Examples are the findings that adolescents with Conduct Disorder affiliate actively with other conduct-disordered peers (Dishion, Patterson, Stoolmiller, & Skinner, 1991) and that young people with internalizing symptoms show a predisposition to form relationships with others who are similarly affected (Hogue & Steinberg, 1995). An array of multiple alleles predisposing to social anxiety, as another example, may lead to a child's marginalization in early social groups, which may turn on or off the transcription of genes responsible for the regulation of affect, leading to the development of Major Depression. Such chains of influence could arguably account for the highly nonrandom distribution of disease and for the persistence and acceleration of morbidities within a subset of human populations. The most well-replicated finding in all of child and adult health services research is that a small minority of any given population, usually about 15% to 20%, sustains well over half the morbidity in the population and is responsible for the majority of health services utilization (Boyce, 1992;

Starfield et al., 1984). This disproportionate disease burden, borne by a small subpopulation, has been found repeatedly, among the wealthy and the impoverished, for both industrialized and developing societies, in Western as well as Eastern cultures. It appears to be a universal reality that ill health accumulates and multiplies over time in a relatively small group of disproportionately affected individuals. One plausible account for such misfortune is the existence of positive feedback systems in the interplay of biology and context, in which biological susceptibilities invoke new environmental risks, which in turn induce new biological proclivities to disease, and so on.[1] Such failures of homeostatic control might credibly account for a majority of morbidity, disability, and premature mortality in the human populations of the world. If so, a search for invariances in symphonic causation might reasonably lead to new insights into the sources and solutions for the afflictions of twenty-first-century societies.

SENSITIVITY TO CONTEXT: AN EMERGING EXEMPLAR OF BIOLOGY-CONTEXT INTERACTIONS

In the developmental psychobiology laboratory that I lead with my colleague Abbey Alkon at the University of California, Berkeley, a particular form of invariance in the symphonic interaction between biology and context has emerged from our work over the past 10 years. In an effort to illuminate and understand the unevenness in childhood morbidities, we have studied the joint influences of naturally occurring adversities and psychobiological reactivity on biomedical and psychiatric endpoints in 3- to 8-year-old children. Stressors occurring in family, school, and community settings have been used to operationalize contextual adversities, and adrenocortical, autonomic, and immunologic responses to highly standardized laboratory challenges have been assessed to index psychobiological reactivity. A remarkably consistent set of findings, from prospective, quasi-experimental, and experimental research designs, has been revealed, in which highly reactive children evince either unusually high or distinctly low rates of morbidity, depending on the character of the surrounding social environment. This particular lawful regularity in the patterns of biology-context

interactions suggests that biological factors may regulate individual, organismic sensitivity to environmental influence.

Stress and Child Health

The social epidemiological research on which our program of investigation has been built is a broad expanse of findings, reported over 40 years, indicating reliable associations between stressors and health in both children and adults. With stress alternately conceptualized as stressful life events (e.g., T. W. Miller, 1998), chronic adversities (e.g., Kelly, 2000), or the occurrence of a major natural or man-made disaster (e.g., Pynoos, Goenjian, & Steinberg, 1998), cohort studies with strong prospective designs have repeatedly documented unconfounded associations between stressors and health end points, including acute infections (Cohen, 1999), injuries (Boyce, 1996), chronic medical conditions (Boekaerts & Röder, 1999), psychopathological morbidities (Jensen, Richters, Ussery, Bloedau, & Davis, 1991), and health care utilization (Ward & Pratt, 1996). Such evidence has been extended to experimental designs in which exposures to pathogenic agents of disease have been randomly allocated and prior psychological stressors are predictive of disease onset and severity (Cohen, Miller, & Rabin, 2001). Despite the increasing rigor of such studies and the elegance of the more recent research designs, epidemiological findings have consistently indicated that stress-illness associations, though reliable and significant, are universally modest in magnitude, never accounting for more than about 10% of the variance in health outcomes. Such significant but modest associations suggest that contextual stressors may play a predisposing but not sufficient or directly etiologic role in pathogenesis. The findings further suggest that individual susceptibility to stressors may operate as an additional, perhaps interactive, factor in the pathways leading to disease or disorder.

Psychobiologic Reactivity to Environmental Adversity

Originating in studies of risk factors for the development of coronary heart disease in adults, systematic investigation of individual differences in stress reactivity began with protocols examining heart rate and blood pressure changes during the completion of stressful laboratory-based tasks (Matthews, 1986). Broad variability in such reactivity was documented in early studies of adult subjects, and predictive relations were described with incident hypertension and coronary disease (Cacioppo et al.,

---

[1] Conversations with my colleague David Ragland led to a consideration of positive feedback loops in the uneven production of human morbidities.

1998). The work of Matthews and colleagues (Matthews, Woodall, & Allen, 1993; Matthews, Woodall, & Stoney, 1990) extended such research into studies of adolescents and young adults, and Cacioppo, Berntson, and coworkers (Berntson, Cacioppo, Quigley, & Fabro, 1994; Cacioppo et al., 2000) developed new methods for ascertaining not just integrative, downstream physiologic measures such as heart rate and blood pressure, but direct assessments of sympathetic and parasympathetic activation. Adrenocortical responses to laboratory challenges were pursued by Gunnar (1987) and her colleagues using measures of salivary cortisol, and given the known regulatory effects of catecholamines and cortisol on immune targets, other researchers began examining cellular (Manuck, Cohen, Rabin, Muldoon, & Bachen, 1991) and humoral (Cohen et al., 2001) immunologic responses in standardized reactivity paradigms.

In our Berkeley laboratory, a series of studies have been conducted employing adrenocortical, autonomic, and immunologic reactivity to a set of standardized social, cognitive, physical, and emotional challenges completed over a 20- to 30-minute protocol. As reported in detail elsewhere (Alkon et al., 2003; Boyce, Barr, & Zeltzer, 1992), individual differences commensurate with those found in adults have been identified in children's reactivity to stressors. In addition, developmental trends in the magnitude of such reactivity have been noted, and direct associations have been found with behavior problems indicating risk for internalizing and externalizing forms of developmental psychopathology. Children showing high-magnitude reactivity to laboratory stressors appear to be characterized by predispositions to a shy, inhibited behavioral phenotype (Boyce et al., 1992; Kagan, 1994); precocious capacities for delay of gratification (O'Hara & Boyce, 2001); poorer recall of acutely stressful events (Stein & Boyce, 1997); subordinate positions in early social groups (Boyce, 2004); and high risk for affective and anxiety-related behavioral symptoms and low risk for externalizing behaviors (Boyce et al., 2001).

Stress × Reactivity Interactions

Most pertinent to the interplay of biology and context, however, our studies have nearly invariably found significant interaction effects between indicators of psychobiological reactivity and measures of social environmental adversity (Boyce, 1996; Boyce et al., 1995). As revealed in Figure 21.1, such interactions display a cross-over configuration in which rates of morbidity among low-reactive children are essentially indifferent to the surrounding social context, while rates among high-reactive children are

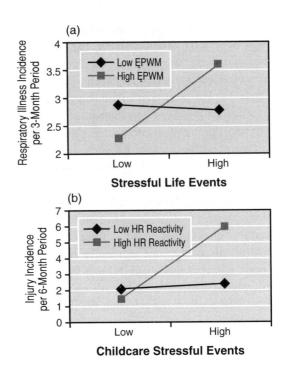

Figure 21.1   Incidences of respiratory illnesses and injuries by level of contextual stress and immunologic (a) pokewee mitogen response) or (b) heart rate reactivity.

highly dependent on contextual effects. Children with low laboratory reactivity have approximately the same incidence of infectious illnesses and injuries in both low- and high-stress settings. By contrast, children with high laboratory reactivity sustain inordinately high rates of illness and injury in stressful settings but inordinately *low* rates in minimally stressful, more nurturant settings.

Although there are several credible accounts for the character of such reactivity × context interactions, the interpretation we have deemed most plausible is that high reactivity is an index of psychobiological sensitivity to social environmental influence. If autonomic and adrenocortical reactivity reflect heightened susceptibility to the nature of the social environment, then highly reactive children could be expected to sustain more of both the pathogenic effects of stressful, unsupportive social circumstances and the protective, salutary effects of highly supportive and predictable social settings. Highly reactive children would thus be expected to reveal, as they have in each of our studies, the best or the worst of observed health outcomes, depending on the character of the ambient social environment.

Replication and Extension

Of particular importance, neither of the prospective studies whose results were summarized earlier was experimental in design. Thus, reactive children in low-stress settings were different from the reactive children in high-stress settings; in neither study were the same high- and low-reactivity children exposed to both low- and high-stress contexts. Because of this inherent deficiency in research design, two subsequent studies employed quasi-experimental and experimental designs, in which low- and high-reactive individuals were observed under both stressful and supportive conditions. The first study examined injury rates before, during, and after a crowding stressor in a troop of semi-free-ranging rhesus macaques; the second was a randomized controlled trial of memory for an acute stressful event under supportive and unsupportive conditions.

The first replication was conducted in a troop of 36 macaques living in a 5-acre natural habitat on the grounds of the National Institutes of Health Primate Center in rural Maryland (Boyce, O'Neill-Wagner, Price, Haines, & Suomi, 1998). One year prior to the study, construction on the grounds of the habitat had imposed, for reasons of animal safety, a 6-month period of troop confinement in a small, 1,000-square-foot building. The crowded conditions of the confinement produced severe stress in the troop, and the incidence of violent attacks and injuries escalated fivefold relative to pre- and postconfinement levels. The animals had been previously assessed, in many hours of individual and group observation, for individual differences in levels of biobehavioral reactivity. As has been observed more generally in rhesus monkeys (Suomi, 1997), approximately 15% to 20% of the animals showed a biobehavioral phenotype marked by predispositions to behavioral inhibition and exaggerated psychobiological reactivity to challenge and novelty. Blinded examination of veterinary records revealed the same form of interaction effect noted in the earlier human studies. Low-reactive monkeys showed little if any escalation in injury rates during confinement, whereas highly reactive, inhibited monkeys sustained dramatic increases in injury rates but strikingly lower rates before and after the stressor. Three of the monkeys died in the period during or immediately following the confinement; all three were high in biobehavioral reactivity. Thus, commensurate with observational results from human studies, the high-reactivity individuals sustained unusually low rates of injuries in normative, low-stress conditions but inordinately high rates under conditions of stress.

A remarkably similar result was obtained in a more recent, formally experimental study conducted in our laboratory by postdoctoral fellow Jodi Quas (Quas, Bauer, & Boyce, 2004). In this experiment, a sample of 56 4- to 6-year-old children completed a standardized reactivity pro-

tocol in a laboratory setting, following which a fire alarm was putatively activated by steam during the preparation of hot chocolate with the child (see Stein & Boyce, 1997, for details of the fire alarm paradigm). The fire alarm episode was highly scripted, ensuring that each child experienced the same verbalizations, events, and sequence. During an interim 2-week period following the first laboratory session, the child's psychobiological data were scored and allocated into categories of high and low reactivity; children were then randomized, for the second session, into high and low support conditions, with stratification by reactivity status. High support consisted of a warm, engaging examiner who requested from the child both spontaneous and probed recall of the events surrounding the reactivity testing and the fire alarm episode; in the low support condition, the same examiner was cold and distant in manner. As shown in Figure 21.2, a significant interaction between reactivity and social condition was again detected. Low-reactivity children showed approximately the same level of memory performance under both conditions. High-reactivity subjects, on the other hand, revealed the highest memory performance of the sample under supportive conditions but the lowest recall accuracy in unsupportive conditions. Results of the quasi-experimental study of injuries in rhesus monkeys and the randomized experiment examining memory effects in young children both confirm significant interactions between biology and context and suggest that reactivity to stressors indexes an openness or "permeability" to social environmental effects. Such findings further suggest a form of constancy in the character of biology-context interactions; that is, one recurring pattern in the interplay between individual biology and social context is that *biology controls sensitivity to environmental influence.*

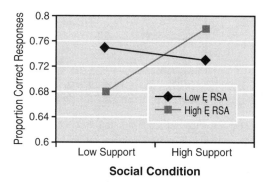

Figure 21.2 Proportion of correct responses on children's memory for stressful event by level of support and autonomic (respiratory sinus arrhythmia) reactivity.

Homologous Findings

Recent reports of gene-environment interactions emanating from the Dunedin Multidisciplinary Health and Development Study (Caspi et al., 2002, 2003), as well as findings on gene × rearing condition effects in rodents (Meaney, 2001) and macaques (Barr et al., 2003), are suggestive of the same biological sensitivity to environmental influence. As shown in Figure 21.3, for example, taken from the reports of Caspi et al., children with polymorphisms conveying enhanced susceptibility (i.e., low monoamine oxidase A activity and the s/s allele in the promoter region of the serotonin transporter gene) had strikingly higher rates of maladaptive outcomes under

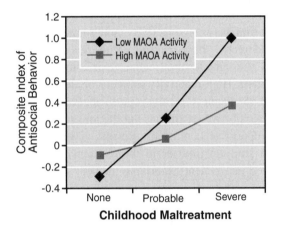

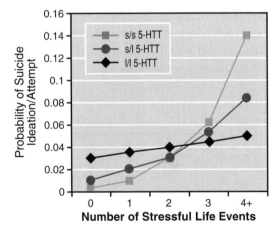

Figure 21.3 Antisocial and suicidal behavior by childhood adversities and genetic polymorphisms. Reprinted with permission from "Role of Genotype in the Cycle of Violence in Maltreated Children," by A. Caspi et al., *Science, 297*(5582), pp. 851–854. Copyright 2002 AAAS; and "Influence of Life Stress on Depression: Moderation by a Polymorphism in the 5-HTT Gene," by A. Caspi et al., *Science, 301*(5631), pp. 386–389. Copyright 2003 AAAS.

conditions of early adversity (child maltreatment in the case of one analysis, and stressful events in the other). The neurobiological plausibility of these epidemiologic findings has been strengthened by recent evidence linking the short allele of the serotonin transporter gene to hyper-reactivity in the human amygdala (Hariri et al., 2005). Although the augmentation of disordered behavior was the principal, widely heralded findings of the Caspi studies, it is also of note that, in both cases, children with the "risk-augmenting" gene actually had *lower* rates of untoward outcomes when growing up in minimally stressful circumstances. Similarly, the work of Meaney and colleagues demonstrated a diminution in adrenocortical activation to stress among rat pups reared by mothers with more attentive, stimulatory maternal behaviors. However, the *lowest* levels of cortisol reactivity were seen among pups with a genetic, strain-specific predisposition to *high* reactivity cross-fostered to constitutionally attentive mothers (Michael Meaney and Moshe Szyf, personal communication, 24 February, 2005). Finally, the recent studies of Barr (Barr et al., 2003), Suomi, and colleagues at the NIH Laboratory of Comparative Ethology have illuminated interactions between the serotonin transporter polymorphism and rearing conditions, such that infant macaques with the s/s or l/s allele who are peer- rather than mother-reared showed significantly higher levels of violent aggression. What has not been as broadly appreciated is the observation that infants with the same allelic genotype raised by their mother were *lower* in aggression than their mother-reared counterparts with the low-risk l/l allele. This observation provides a possible genetic substrate for Suomi's (1991) earlier observation that infant macaques with a "vulnerable" biobehavioral phenotype flourish developmentally when cross-fostered to the care of the troop's most nurturing adult pair.

Taken together, these findings suggest, as indicated earlier in the work of Boyce and colleagues, that the same genotypic variation conferring developmental risk in settings of maltreatment and stress may actually serve protective functions in rearing environments characterized by support, predictability, and care. Such bivalent, context-dependent influences of specific polymorphisms suggest that they operate not as risk factors, but as regulators of environmental *sensitivity*, enhancing susceptibility to both pathogenic and protective aspects of environmental conditions (Boyce & Ellis, 2005; Ellis, Essex, & Boyce, 2005). This bidirectionality in the effects of genotypic variation may also offer a partial account for the paradoxical observation that "risky genes" have been substantially conserved over the evolutionary history of the species involved.

SYMPHONIC CAUSATION: A PROVISIONAL NOSOLOGY OF BIOCONTEXTUAL INTERPLAY

What then are the implications of adopting a symphonic or interactive frame of reference in the study of developmental psychopathology and its origins? Such a view demands, first, a new exploration of *how* biology and context work together to initiate and sustain pathogenesis or to preserve health and well-being. A starting point is a consideration of the nosological or taxonomic regularities in biology-context interactions.

The Need for a Nosological Framework

The existence and importance of biology-context interactions in the genesis of human morbidities have become—finally and rightfully—an article of faith. A recent report from the National Academy of Science's Institute of Human Development said it especially well: "It is time for a new appreciation of the coactivity of nature and nurture in development. Beginning at the moment of conception, hereditary potential unfolds in concert with the environment. The dynamic interplay between gene action and environmental processes continues throughout life" (Shonkoff & Phillips, 2000, p. 39).

Beyond this new canon of interactionism, however, there is a need for more systematic research and reflection on *regularities* in the character of biology-context interactions. It is the observation of such regularities that will begin to reveal deeper truths about *how* genes and environments codetermine human outcomes and *how* individual susceptibility and resilience are conjoined with contextual threat and protection to traverse the severe discontinuity between health and disease. A symphonic view of disease causation would not only acknowledge the bipartite contributions of biology and context, but would begin to codify the systematic congruities in their interactions.

The concept of a symphonic causation of disease, within a nascent philosophy of medicine, bears much in common with Percy's (1989) view of the triadic character of human language. In the same manner in which a conjunction of self and environment produces the experienced *Welt* or world, the confluence of individual biology and environmental peril produces affliction and disease. Pathogenesis and prevention are thus intrinsically triadic; it is out of a symphonic fusion of individual biology and contextual influence that the possibilities for health and disease arise. Among the implications of such a view is a realliance with ancient Platonic and Hippocratic conceptions of health as a harmonious balance between self and society. Thus, the Hippocratic Cor-

pus summarized a view of health as "the expression of a harmonious balance between the various components of man's nature (the four humors that control all of human activities) and the environment and ways of life" (cited in Dubos, 1965, p. 322). Even the pre-Socratic philosopher Alcmaeon of Croton noted the interactive nature of "internal" and "external" causes:

> Disease occurs sometimes from an internal cause such as excess of heat or cold, sometimes from an external cause such as excess or deficiency of food. It may occur in a certain part, such as blood, marrow, or brain; but these parts also are sometimes affected by external causes, such as certain waters, or a particular site, or fatigue, or constraint, or similar reasons. Health is the harmonious mixture of the qualities. (translated by G. Miller, 1962)

Within such a rubric, health and disease are seen as the integrative product of the fit or concordance between individual biological proclivities and dimensions of environmental threat and support. What is now needed is a nosological framework that assembles and classifies observable invariances in the operation of symphonic causation.

A Provisional Nosology

Such a provisional nosology of biology-context interactions is presented in Table 21.1, along with exemplars of each category of interactive association. This five-part nosology makes no claim to comprehensiveness in its description of such interactions, and indeed, emerging research blending assessments of both genetic and environmental risk will almost certainly reveal new varieties of interaction. There is also no implication, in the ordering of categories, that one form predominates over another. Rather, this provisional nosological framework is offered as a first effort to aggregate and order emerging observations of biology-context interactions. As such, the nosology is an attempt to advance the same project begun by Lewontin in a 1974 paper on the analysis of causes, by Meehl in a 1977 exposition on specific etiology and strong influence, and by Kendler and Eaves in their 1986 paper on models for joint effects of genotype and environment. Particular but not exclusive attention has been paid here to interactions predicting developmental psychopathology.

Five forms of biology-context interaction are proposed. First, *potentiation* describes individual biology's amplification of the pathogenicity of contextual forces. Because each category describes a form of interaction, such potentiation implies statistical nonadditivity of effects and a situ-

TABLE 21.1   Observed Regularities and Examples

Observed Regularities	Examples
1. *Potentiation:* Biology amplifies the pathogenicity of context.[a]	Polymorphisms in the genes coding for monoamine oxidase A and the serotonin transporter magnify the pathogenic effects of early maltreatment and stressful events on psychiatric end points (Caspi et al., 2002, 2003).
	A child's rearing by an adoptive parent with a criminal conviction does not increase the likelihood of criminality in the child, unless one of the child's biological parents has also been convicted of a crime (Bohman, 1996; Mednick et al., 1987).
	Type I alcoholism (relatively mild abuse, minimal criminality) requires both genetic risk and a risk-promoting childhood environment for expression (Cloninger et al., 1981).
	Negative environments in adoptive homes have especially harmful effects on adolescent adoptees with antisocial biological parents (Cadoret et al., 1995).
	Positive family history exaggerates adverse effects of smoking on coronary heart disease incidences (R. R. Williams et al., 2000).
	Only children with the A1+ allele of the D2 dopamine receptor gene (DRD2) show declines in cognitive abilities related to family stress (Berman & Noble, 1997).
	Stressful life events are associated with a nearly eightfold increase in risk of autoimmune hyperthyroidism, but only in women (Yoshiuchi et al., 1998).
	Amphetamines increase dominant behavior in high-ranking male rhesus macaques but increase subordinate behavior in low-ranking monkeys (Haber & Barchas, 1983).
2. *Protection:* Biology amplifies the protectiveness of context.	High alcohol consumption protects against coronary heart disease by increasing HDL cholesterol, but only in those with a polymorphism on a lipid metabolism (CETP) gene (Corbex et al., 2000).
	Supportive female audiences lowered blood pressure reactivity to a speech-making task among both males and females, but supportive male audiences diminished reactivity in neither (Glynn et al., 1999).
	Handling induces enhancements of maternal licking and grooming diminishes adrenocortical and behavioral responses to stress in infant mice, especially among animals in the BALB/c strain (Meaney, 2001).
3. *Sensitization:* Biology controls sensitivity to context.	Autonomic reactivity to stress is associated with higher incidence of illness and injury in high-stress contexts but lower incidence in low-stress, supportive contexts (Boyce, 1996; Boyce et al., 1995, 1998; J. A. Quas, Murowchick, Bensadoun, & Boyce, 2002).
	Adoptees with schizophrenic mothers show high rates of disordered thought when placed in communication-deviant families but unusually low rates when placed in effectively communicating families (Wahlberg et al., 1997).
	Highly reactive infant macaques are marginalized and developmentally slow when raised in normative conditions, but when cross-fostered to caring adult pairs, become developmentally precocious, emigrate early from the natal troop, and assume dominant positions in the adult hierarchy (Suomi, 1997).
	Adult female adoptees of alcoholic biological parents have an increased risk of Major Depression when placed in homes with a psychiatrically disturbed adoptive parent, but a lower risk of depression than even subjects with no alcoholic biological parents when placed with psychiatrically healthy adoptive parents (Cadoret et al., 1996).
4. *Specification:* Biology selects the symptomatic expression of contextual pathogenesis.	Relatives of patients with early-onset depression are more likely to be depressed if they are female and more likely to be antisocial if they are male (Winokur et al., 1971).
	Expressed emotion in the family environment is demonstrably related to the relapse of affective disorders, eating disorders, and Schizophrenia, each of which appears to have its own specific biological substrate (Butzlaff & Hooley, 1998).
	Benzene exposure is associated with both hemotoxicity and shortened gestation, but each outcome is moderated by distinctive genetic polymorphisms (Lan et al., 2004; X. Wang et al., 2000).
	(Reverse specification) The short-repeat allele of the serotonin transporter polymorphism confers increased risk of depression on exposure to stressful life events (Caspi et al., 2003) but appears protective against the environmental exposures associated with sudden infant death syndrome (Hunt, 2005).
5. *Facilitation:* Biology controls exposures to contextual pathogenicity.	Genes controlling the melanization of skin determine predispositions to experiences of adversity and racism in North America and other regions of the world (D. R. Williams, 1997).
	Serotonin transporter gene polymorphisms, which systematically differ among Indian and Chinese hybrid rhesus macaque lineages, are associated with aggressive and risk-taking behavior and may account for selective emigration over the Himalyan Mountains in the early history of the species (Champoux et al., 1997; Heinz et al., 1998; S. J. Suomi, personal communication, November 22, 2003).
	Carriers of the gene for excessive iron absorption (HFE) are at risk for hemochromatosis (Cogswell et al., 1998).

[a] It is important to note that the linguistic construction of the five interaction categories is not meant to imply that biological factors are the active component of the interaction, exerting various forms of influence on a set of more passive contextual features. Rather, category descriptions simply adopt the convention of naming biology first and context second, with the understanding that they could be stated In reverse and that examples of opposite effects are abundant.

ation in which individual biology affects the direction or strength of the relation between environmental factors and child outcomes (Baron & Kenny, 1986; Kraemer et al., 2001). A second form of interaction is *protection,* that is, that in which biology amplifies the protectiveness or salutogenic aspects of context. Again, nonadditivity is implied, but the effect of biology is to augment the essentially preventive character of the environmental factor. Third, *sensitization* is the capacity of biological factors to control susceptibility or permeability to environmental influence. This is the form most closely defining the character of psychobiological reactivity × social environmental adversity interactions, which were summarized in the prior section. Fourth, *specification* suggests that biology is capable of selecting the particular symptomatic expression of contextual pathogenesis. This is the interpretation of interaction promulgated by Steinberg and Avenevoli (2000) in their paper noting the tendency for environmental risk to exert generic effects and biological susceptibility to narrow the range of possible disordered outcomes. Finally, a fifth form of interaction, *facilitation,* is that in which biology controls exposures to contextual pathogenicity. Here, the role of individual biology is not one of altering the amplitude of environmental effects, but rather one of determining the presence or degree of exposure to pathogenic or protective contextual elements.

Ottman (1996) has also proposed a five-model nosology of gene-environment interactions, which bears little commonality with the categories presented here. Rather, her models constitute four possible combinations of genotype and exposure in terms of their individual effects on disease risk, along with a noninteractive model in which the genotype increases the production of a nongenetic risk factor (e.g., phenylketonuria). The impetus for the formulation of Ottman's system, however, was entirely commensurate with that motivating the present discussion, that is, the evident need for an interim taxonomy under which categories of interaction could be usefully and perhaps heuristically organized.

Ottman's (1996) nosology also lucidly emphasizes a point important to both categorical systems, that is, the reciprocity between biological and contextual perspectives in describing a given interaction. In defining the character of interaction categories, each has been described in terms of biology's influence on the magnitude, direction, or expression of contextual effects. This convention serves to standardize the format of the nosological categories, but it implies no precedence of biology over context, or the reverse, and each class of interaction can be interchangeably characterized in terms of contextual modification of biolog-

ical effects. Thus, it is in the nature of biology-context interactions that "Biology amplifies the pathogenicity of context" can be reciprocally interpreted as "Context amplifies the pathogenicity of biology." In Wallen's (1996) description of sex differences in rhesus monkey behavior, for example, the interaction of prenatal hormones and social contexts could alternatively, and with equal accuracy, be described either in terms of hormonal influences on sex-specific social rearing effects or as social environmental shaping of prenatal hormonal effects. In the section that follows, specific exemplars of biology-context interplay are explored and examples in each interaction category are presented.

Examples of Biology-Context Interplay

A 1996 lecture by Robert Hinde (1998) offered an elegant model of the complexity inherent in interactions among environment, behavior, and biological state in a vertebrate animal species. For the timing of nest completion to coincide precisely with the laying of eggs, the female canary engages in an elaborately unfolding dialogue among multiple interactive factors, including the physical environment of the nest, reproductive endocrine activity, and maternal behavior. Contextual factors acting on the hypothalamic-pituitary-adrenal system result in gonad development and estrogen release, leading to a heightened responsiveness to the male's courtship behaviors. Changes in hormonal state, in interaction with day length and exposures to the male's song, also induce the construction of a nest and the development of a brood patch, a tactilely sensitive area on the female's ventral surface that loses its feathers and develops increasing vascularity. Stimulation of the brood patch by the physical components of the nest successively initiate alterations in nest-building material from grasses to feathers, a diminution in nest-building behaviors, and, finally, further reproductive development of the mother bird. In an exquisite, sequentially rendered interaction among biology, context, and behavior, the nest's construction is completed just as the eggs are ready to be laid.

Biology-context interactions in human and nonhuman primate species are, at present, in a far more primitive state of elucidation than that portrayed by Hinde, but not surprisingly, early glimpses into the character of such interactions are revealing a picture of equally elegant and exacting complexity. For each of the five categories of interaction—potentiation, protection, sensitization, specification, and facilitation—examples are rapidly accruing in both experimental studies of laboratory animals and observational studies of human subjects. Table 21.1 provides a sampler of such interactions.

The first nosological category, potentiation, is a more general version of the diathesis-stress model of developmental psychopathology (Rosenthal, 1970). In this interactive model, biologically grounded susceptibilities accentuate or amplify the inherent pathogenicity of a given contextual exposure. In addition to the previously noted amplifications of risk for psychopathology by neurotransmitter polymorphisms and criminality among biological parents, studies by Cloninger (Cloninger, Bohman, & Sigvardsson, 1981) and Cadoret (Cadoret, Yates, Troughton, Woodworth, & Stewart, 1995) have documented the interactive roles of genetics and developmental environments in accelerating children's risk for alcoholism and drug dependency. Similarly, a positive family history of coronary heart disease has been shown to augment cardiovascular risk associated with smoking (R. R. Williams, Hopkins, Wu, & Hunt, 2000), and a particular allele of the dopamine receptor gene is known to potentiate cognitive decline in children experiencing severe family stress and adversity (Berman & Noble, 1997). Other examples include the effect of female sex on the link between psychological stressors and autoimmune thyroiditis (Yoshiuchi et al., 1998) and the amplification of dominance/subordination behaviors in specific social settings by the administration of amphetamines to rhesus macaques (Haber & Barchas, 1983).

The second form of interaction, protection, involves a biological amplification of a protective environmental factor. For example, the gene encoding cholesteryl ester transfer protein (CETP) plays a key role in lipid metabolism. CETP decreases the concentration of protective HDL cholesterol, and patients with a deleterious mutation in the CETP gene have abnormally high HDL cholesterol. HDL cholesterol has also been shown to increase with alcohol consumption due to reduced activity of CETP, but this is only the case among individuals with certain CETP polymorphisms (Corbex et al., 2000). Another example is the differential influences of gender on both the protective effects of social support (House, Landis, & Umberson, 1988) and the capacity for provision of such support. In one recent study by Glynn, Christenfeld, and Gerin (1999), blood pressure reactivity to a stress-inducing speech-making task was significantly down-regulated, in both men and women, by the presence of a supportive female audience, but no such effects were found for supportive male audiences. The authors conclude that the sex of supportive companions plays a key role in determining the utility and efficacy of the support provided. Finally, as previously noted, the work of Meaney (2001) and colleagues revealed that handling-induced enhancements of maternal licking and grooming reduced lifelong adrenocortical and behavioral responses to

stress in infant mice. This protective effect was particularly evident in the BALB/c strain.

Sensitization, the third category of biology-context interaction, represents an amalgam of potentiation and protection, except that the same biological factor is capable, through an increased sensitivity or permeability to the environment, of alternately raising or lowering risk. Such interactions are evident in the studies of Boyce and colleagues, reviewed earlier, on autonomic reactivity as an indicator of susceptibility to positive and negative environmental conditions of early childhood. Strikingly similar findings have been published by Wahlberg et al. (1997), who demonstrated inordinately high or low rates of schizophreniform thought among the adopted children of schizophrenic mothers, depending on the level of disordered family communication, and Cadoret et al. (1996), who found exceptionally high or exceptionally low rates of depression in adoptees of alcoholic biological parents, depending on the psychiatric health of the adoptive parents. Finally, Stephen Suomi (1987) presented cross-fostering studies among rhesus monkey infants showing that highly reactive infant macaques, when placed in the care of maximally nurturant adult monkeys, evince a dramatic reversal of developmental course, rising to the top of the dominance hierarchy in the adult troop, becoming developmentally precocious, and, if male, being among the first to emigrate out of the natal troop. Evidence for sensitization interactions suggest that biological, perhaps genetic, factors can calibrate the organism's susceptibility not only to health-diminishing adversities, but also to aspects of health-preserving social supports.

Specification is the fourth form of biology-context interaction. In this form, environmental exposures raise generic, global risk for disorder, and biological or genetic factors focus that risk on specific forms of morbidity. Context thus produces undifferentiated liability, and biology narrows the liability to particular somatic, emotional, or behavioral categories. An example is the study of Winokur and colleagues (Winokur, Cadoret, Dorzab, & Baker, 1971) showing that the relatives of individuals with early-onset major depression were more likely to develop psychopathology and that the form of disorder was more likely to be depression among females and antisocial behavior among males. Thus, common family environments produced an elevated risk for mental disorder, but the form of disorder was determined by the sex of the individual. In a second example, Butzlaff and Hooley (1998) showed, in a meta-analysis, that expressed emotion in the family environment is associated with relapse in affective disorders, eating disorders, and Schizophrenia, but that each form of disorder had its particular biological substrate. Finally, benzene exposure is associated with both hemotoxicity and shortened gestation in humans, but the exposure effects are moderated by two distinctive sets of genetic polymorphisms: genetic variants in metabolizing enzymes in the case of hematological effects and by susceptibility genes CYP1A1 and GSTT1 in reproductive outcomes (Lan et al., 2004; X. Wang et al., 2000).

An example of *reverse* specification is found in the short repeat allele of the serotonin transporter gene. As noted earlier, work by Caspi and colleagues (2003) has demonstrated an elevated risk of depressive symptoms among individuals with one or two copies of the short allele and who also sustain numerous stressful life events. On the other hand, the short repeat allele appears to be protective for sudden infant death syndrome (SIDS), with the long repeat polymorphism overrepresented and the short repeat underrepresented among SIDS victims (Hunt, 2005). The serotonin transporter polymorphism likely interacts with one or more environmental SIDS risk factors, such as smoking, low socioeconomic status, or prone sleeping. Here, a single genetic polymorphism produces up- or down-regulation of risk for two different disorders depending on exposures to environmental and perhaps other contributing factors.

The fifth and final pattern of interaction in this provisional nosology is facilitation, in which biology implements or controls exposures to contextual exposures. Perhaps the most persistent and tragic example of this interactive regularity is the manner in which genes regulating the melanization of skin determine the likelihood of an individual's chronic exposure to social adversities in North American society (D. R. Williams, 1997). Another example is the possible role of serotonin transporter gene polymorphisms in the presumed selective emigration of rhesus macaques across the Himalayas into China (Champoux, Higley, & Suomi, 1997; Heinz et al., 1998; S. J. Suomi, personal communication, 22 November, 2003). Relative to Indian-derived monkeys, Chinese-hybrid macaques show behavioral predispositions to aggression and novelty, lower cerebrospinal fluid levels of 5-HIAA (a metabolite of serotonin), and a higher prevalence of the long repeat allele of the serotonin transporter gene, an example of genotypic variation biasing physical and social environment-based exposures. Finally, a mutation in the iron absorption gene HFE facilitates the development of the disease hemochromatosis by increasing iron absorption in the gut, leading to iron overload and multiorgan dysfunction (Cogswell et al., 1998). Genes and biology may thus interact with environmental agents and pathogens by fostering or facilitating an individual's exposure to such agents.

Molecular Epigenomic Substrates of Symphonic Causation

To whatever extent these nosologic categories of biology × context interactions are validated by future scientific observations, such interactions will be linked in specific and definable ways to underlying molecular processes involving DNA transcription, replication, recombination, and repair, as well as RNA translation and the actions of its protein products. It is also not unreasonable to predict that the character of the interactions described epidemiologically (i.e., their instantiation of potentiating, protecting, sensitizing, specifying, and facilitating interactive processes) will be partially mirrored by cellular events describing the interplay between genomic elements and environmentally activated molecular signals.[2] Although research to date has focused principally on structural variation in DNA sequences, complexities in the regulation of gene *expression* are dramatically expanding the known repertoire of means by which biological and contextual information can interactively operate. Although the control of gene expression can occur via multiple processes affecting DNA transcription/RNA translation (Villard, 2004), three such processes are highlighted here.

First, the initiation of DNA transcription requires the recruitment of RNA polymerase to the promoter region of the gene in question, in close collaboration with a battery of protein *transcription factors*. Internal and external signals—such as developmental events, stressors, or social interactions—are capable of altering the binding of transcription factors to the gene's promoter region, thereby changing the rate of gene expression (Lemon & Tjian, 2000). Each gene has both template and regulatory functions—corresponding to the exon and promoter regions of a given gene sequence—and exposures in social and physical contexts can up- or down-regulate the production of messenger RNA products by changing the availability of transcription factors. An example is the production of c-Fos, an immediate early gene transcription factor, following exposure to an anxiogenic stressor; examining c-Fos expression in high- and low-novelty-seeking rats, significantly lower levels in the CA1 region of the hippocampus have been found among novelty-seeking animals (Kabbaj & Akil,

---

[2] It is acknowledged here that, although molecular genetics form the boundary conditions by which gene × environment interactions take place (Polanyi, 1968), full accounts of such interactions will involve dynamic, irreducible complexities not subsumed by molecular processes, however elegantly defined (Strohman, 2002).

2001). Large-scale, high-throughput DNA microarray technology now allows the identification of patterns of multiple gene expression, changes in such patterns over time or following an exposure, and differences in gene expression profiles among different tissues and individuals. Of greatest relevance to the argument presented here, however, transcription factors can function as either activators or repressors, which accelerate or diminish gene transcription. Transcription factors could thus serve as one molecular genetic substrate for the potentiating or protecting categories of biology × context interactions.

A second set of gene regulatory processes involves the *epigenome,* that is, the chromatin polymer of histone and nonhistone proteins into which genomic DNA is folded and bundled as nucleosomes, which in turn are packaged within chromosomes. Inside this chromatin matrix there exist variable degrees of physical exposure of the DNA to the molecular machinery of transcription (i.e., RNA polymerase, transcription factors). DNA exposure is modified by methylation of cytosine in CG dinucleotide sequences and by acetylation of histone proteins. Methylation and acetylation patterns can thus govern chromatin structure, thereby influencing gene expression. Complex maternal behavior among mother rats, for example, has been shown to calibrate infant stress reactivity by altering histone acetylation and transcription factor binding to the promoter region of a gene coding for the glucocorticoid receptor (Weaver et al., 2004).

A third source of gene regulation is the existence of polygenic networks in which synthetic interactions occur among complex arrays of the genes implicated in a given disorder. A primary mutation involved in cystic fibrosis, for example, produces defective regulation of the transmembrane chloride channel, but the altered gene's expression is also modified by several other polymorphic sites or gene products (Badano & Katsanis, 2002). In another example, digenic mutations in the ROM1 and RDS genes are silent in isolation, but together produce retinitis pigmentosa (Kajiwara, Berson, & Dryja, 1994). In recent work systematically examining the synthetic lethality of mutant gene pairs in yeast, Tong et al. (2004) found an average of 34 digenic interactions among the 143 mutant genes tested, an extraordinary scope of interactive genetic complexity. Gene networks of equal or greater complexity are anticipated in the developmental programs of mammalian organ systems (Sampogna & Nigam, 2004).

Taken together, these categories of symphonic interaction at the molecular genetic level trace a perimeter of means by which biology and context act together in disease pathogenesis and the preservation of health. Although there are both experimental and statistical obstacles to the discovery of such interactions, researchers are progressively assembling a repository of examples, which collectively present an early but informative picture of how genes and environments might work together in etiologic processes. That picture, coming gradually into view, tells a story with vast and immediate implications for the future of health care, biomedical research, and public health policy.

CONCLUSIONS AND FUTURE DIRECTIONS

What conclusions can be reasonably drawn from these observations and what implications for psychiatric care, new research, and mental health policy might be derived from a symphonic interpretation of causal processes?

Implications: Care, Research, and Policy

The implications of biology-context interactions for the future of human health are legion. Advances in our capacity for sampling, analyzing, and employing genetic material in research and practice will arguably revolutionize not only the science of human biology, but also the science of human behavior and development. The capacity for assessing multiple genes using microarray patterns of DNA or RNA sequences will alter fundamentally the ease and practicality of ascertaining human genotypes (P. S. Lee & Lee, 2000). DNA sequence variations comprising single-nucleotide polymorphisms (SNPs), which occur once every 1,000 base pairs between two individuals picked at random, will offer the genetic means of fingerprinting genotypic variation that forms the most basic biological substrate of disease (Evans, Muir, Blackwood, & Porteous, 2001). The dbSNP database, for example, now comprises nearly 9 million SNPs; the HapMap project plans to coalesce information on approximately 300 million human genotypes; and the National Institutes of Health has requested proposals to extend such genotyping to an additional 600 million genomes (Hirschhorn & Daly, 2005). These advances in ascertaining and cataloguing human genetic variation offer the means of fulfilling what Bronfenbrenner and Ceci (1994) have proposed as the need to study proximal processes of organism-environment interaction in order to understand the development of phenotypes. As noted by Reiss (Reiss, Plomin, & Hetherington, 1991), this new genomic knowledge will advance understanding not only of biogenetic pathogenesis, but of human contexts and social environments as well. As researchers become increasingly capable of taking genetic variation into account, the roles of social and physical contextual factors in disease will be discernible with unprecedented clarity. Although much has been achieved by studying social processes in their own right, eliminating the noise of biological variation will produce a level of resolution and focus in studying social contexts never previously attained or even imagined. In our collective scientific pursuit of such precision, however, important methodological, bioethical, and strategic dilemmas arise.

Dilemmas in Computational Biology

First, technological breakthroughs in the ascertainment of genetic variation will facilitate (and are already facilitating) new understandings of biology-context interactions. Much of the difficulty in discovering and analyzing such interactions has been related to the imprecision inherent in using multiple determined, downstream biological measures that are only distantly reflective of the genes and gene expression that are their sources. The ability to assess directly DNA polymorphisms and variable patterns of gene expression not only will allow greater accuracy in the characterization of genetic and epigenetic variation, but will also expedite the choice of more extreme genotypic representation in research designs such as case-control studies.

Along with greater accuracy and efficiency in the measurement of such variation, however, the development of high-throughput data acquisition in the genetic sciences has been accompanied by formidable statistical challenges involving full genome surveys of thousands of SNPs. As reviewed by Hirschhorn and Daly (2005), the sequencing of the human genome, the development of public "libraries" of SNPs, and the dramatic advances in genotyping technology have all contributed to an emerging capacity for detecting disease-linked genetic variation in human populations.

One of the challenges implicit in this capacity for generating unprecedented volumes of genetic information, however, is the choice of *research designs* for ascertaining associations between genetic variation and human disorders. Broadly considered, research approaches for identifying polymorphisms contributing to the prevalent human diseases can be grouped into two broad categories. Candidate gene studies—the approach that has provided most of the knowledge available to date—are those in which genes are selected for assessment based either on their chromosomal location in a region of known linkage to the index disorder or on knowledge of functional characteristics that could influence disease risk. The previously cited work

linking the short repeat allele of the serotonin transporter gene promoter to affective mental disorders, alcohol abuse, and other dependencies are examples of candidate gene studies, in which the 5-HTT promoter was targeted because of known functional linkages between serotonin circuitry and mental health (Barr et al., 2004; Caspi et al., 2003; Kremer et al., 2005). The second, theoretically plausible form of research linking genetic variation to disease is genome-wide association studies, which would survey polymorphic variation across the genome in very large, multiple samples of affected and unaffected individuals. As summarized by W. Y. Wang et al. (W. Y. Wang, Barratt, Clayton, & Todd, 2005), genome-wide study designs remain technically unfeasible at present, though partial surveys of the genome have become possible through the genotyping of many common SNPs in genome-wide association studies. The past 3 decades of genetic research have identified approximately 50 genes and their allelic variants that appear reliably associated with multifactorial human diseases, but it is estimated that as many as 30% of the common disease-associated variants remain undetected, and there are likely hundreds of genetic loci that alter susceptibility to a specific disorder (W. Y. Wang et al., 2005).

The *biometric and computational challenges* of genome-wide studies are also formidable indeed. The statistical power of a study to discover SNPs conferring risk or protection in a given human disorder depends on an array of factors, including the allelic spectrum or architecture of a disease, that is, the number of relevant variants that exist, their allele frequencies, and the potency of their effects on incidence. A review of quantitative trait loci (genetic loci that contribute to variation in continuous phenotypes, such as height), for example, revealed that about half of the candidate causal variants had allele frequencies greater than 5%, whereas the other half had lower prevalences. Further, it is unknown whether the effect sizes of established disease-susceptibility polymorphisms are representative of those yet to be discovered, but the current list bears allelic odds ratios for incident disease in the range of 1.1 to 1.5, that is, relatively small effect sizes that contribute negligibly to familial risks (Risch & Merikangas, 1996).

Partly as a result of these multiple, small contributions of individual SNPs to overall disease risk, genetic investigators and their biostatistical colleagues have increasingly had to contend with the informational tsunamis that result from thousands of genes being screened in samples of thousands of individuals. Extensible, open-source biometric software for use in computational biology and genetics has begun to be made available to the scientific community as an aid to data acquisition, management, and transformation within genetic and bioinformatic applications (Gentleman et al., 2004). Other sophisticated statistical approaches are in development for in vitro studies of dynamic, regulatory networks, such as those involving transcription factor regulation of gene expression and other epigenomic processes (Xing & van der Laan, 2005). Considered together, these technical and computational problems are scientific impediments of remarkable complexity and difficulty, yet molecular biologists and biostatisticians are making steady progress toward tractable solutions to these previously unencountered complexities.

Dilemmas in Bioethics and Health Policy

The bioethical and social policy implications of more rigorous studies of gene-environment interactions are also vast. Wilmoth and colleagues (Wilmoth, Deegan, Lundström, & Horiuchi, 2000) have demonstrated, for example, that contrary to prevailing assumptions, the human life span is not fixed but, in fact, has been slowly advancing for more than a century. Wildner (2000) noted a similar phenomenon in drosophila and suggested that the slowing of mortality among the older age groups of both species may be related to a favorable gene-environment interaction. Maximizing the fit between individual genotypes and the environments that most favor health and well-being could thus have immense consequences not only for the emerging psychopathologies of childhood but for the public health of the world.

Furthermore, a deeper understanding of the genetic sources of vulnerability and of the ways social context can ameliorate or provoke susceptibility may eventually require ethical, democratic societies to move beyond claims of distributive justice as the sole basis for societal obligations to intervene and assist vulnerable children (Halpern & Boyce, in press). If current social institutions and settings are shown to play causal roles in harming such children, increasing their risks of mental and physical illness, society may have the strongest kind of ethical obligation: the obligation to change institutions to desist from harm. At a more fundamental level, there are classical as well as emerging ethical perspectives that give special attention to individuals in vulnerable periods of development, in part due to the inability of not yet mature individuals to argue on their own behalf. These developmental vulnerabilities seem to interact with social contextual adversities, increasing serious risks of disorder during periods of especially high social stress (Boyce & Keating, 2004; Keating & Mustard, 1993). I suggest that these ethical considerations serve as a salient underpinning for the scientific and policy debates that are implied by the scientific observations on vulnerability and resilience that animate this chapter.

Dilemmas Regarding Individual- and Population-Level Interventions

Finally, among the implications of greater knowledge of biology-context interactions is a set of questions surrounding the interventions that would logically follow from such knowledge. On the one hand, one might argue that the genetically grounded, exaggerated sensitivity of certain individuals to ambient environmental adversities should mandate a population-wide reduction in stress exposure and the provision of enhancements to general societal supports. The progressive, federally defined decreases in acceptable environmental lead exposures and blood lead levels in children, for example, were due in part to the discovery of a subset of children with genetically derived special sensitivities to lead effects on heme synthesis pathways (Wetmur, Lehnert, & Desnick, 1991). It was thus the elucidation of a vulnerable subpopulation that prompted a population-wide mandate for decreased exposure.

On the other hand, the identification of genetically vulnerable individuals offers the opportunity to construct surveillance processes and interventions that are specifically targeted to individuals at greatest biological risk for a given category of disease (Khoury, Burke, & Thomson, 2000b). In the field of developmental psychopathology, for example, knowledge of the gene polymorphisms associated with risk for anxiety and affective disorders could potentially lead to school-based interventions capable of preventing entry onto trajectories toward such disorders. In another example, Omenn (2000) pointed out that persons with a genetic trait that decreases the catabolism of nicotine were less likely to be tobacco-dependent, suggesting the possibility of preventive interventions targeting the metabolically at-risk individuals. It is important to note that, as argued by Turkheimer (1998), the establishment of genetic contributions to disease etiology does not necessitate genetic, or even biological, interventions. In Suomi's studies, cited earlier, the provision of expert, highly nurturant foster care for vulnerable young monkeys created dramatically beneficial effects, even though the means of identifying such monkeys involved sophisticated biological assays of stress response. Although adjustments in the environmental component of biology-context interactions may be currently more technically feasible and acceptable, the most recent work of Sapolsky and colleagues (Kaufer et al.,

2004) serves as a harbinger of genetic interventions that could plausibly alter even the most fundamental, molecular aspects of human emotional and behavioral regulation. Whatever the future of gene therapies, the potential for psychosocial and societal intercessions into human adversities could paradoxically be served in unparalleled ways by the study of interactions between biology and context.

Far from a yellow brick road into ascendant knowledge, the path we are now following is rife with new perils and ethical conundrums. Khoury et al. (Khoury, Burke, & Thomson, 2000a) have reviewed comprehensively the scope of such issues that science and human societies must now face, highlighting the dilemmas surrounding privacy and confidentiality, fair use of genetic information, and the prospects for individual and group stigmatization. An outstanding precedent for attending to and addressing such dilemmas is the Ethical, Legal, and Social Implications Program that was established as an integral component of the Human Genome Project (National Human Genome Research Institute, 2005). As new research on gene-environment interactions proceeds, it will be critical for universities and agencies at both national and local levels to follow the Human Genome Project's responsible lead by addressing forthrightly the human and ethical problems that necessarily accompany such research.

CONCLUSION

Despite the difficulties, both philosophical and technical, that will surely attend the continuing and now compelling study of biology-context interaction, it is increasingly clear that such interactions will be among the keys that unlock one of the most ancient and compelling of human mysteries: the etiologies of disease and disorder. Having begun the process of documenting and cataloguing the range of biology-context interactions, it is now time to explore symphonic causation: the patterned, intrinsic regularities in *how* biology and context work together, and what genes and environments *do* in their conjoint elicitation of disease. In seeking to understand the complexity of developmental psychopathology, no problem is more salient and no solution more suffused with potential and hidden rewards.

REFERENCES

Albers, J. W. (1997). Understanding gene-environment interactions [news]. *Environmental Health Perspectives, 105*(6), 578–580.

Alkon, A., Goldstein, L. H., Smider, N., Essex, M., Kupfer, D., & Boyce, W. T. (2003). Developmental and contextual influences on autonomic reactivity in young children. *Developmental Psychobiology, 42*(1), 64–78.

Andrieu, N., & Goldstein, A. M. (1998). Epidemiologic and genetic approaches in the study of gene-environment interaction: An overview of available methods. *Epidemiologic Reviews, 20*(2), 137–147.

Anisman, H., Zaharia, M. D., Meaney, M. J., & Merali, Z. (1998). Do early-life events permanently alter behavioral and hormonal responses to stressors? *International Journal of Developmental Neuroscience, 16*(3/4), 149–164.

Badano, J. L., & Katsanis, N. (2002). Beyond Mendel: An evolving view of human genetic disease transmission. *Nature Reviews: Genetics, 3*(10), 779–789.

Baron, R., & Kenny, D. (1986). The moderator-mediator variable distinction in social psychological research: Conceptual, strategic, and statistical considerations. *Journal of Personality and Social Psychology, 51*(6), 1173–1182.

Barr, C. S., Newman, T. K., Becker, M. L., Parker, C. C., Champoux, M., Lesch, K. P., et al. (2003). The utility of the non-human primate: Model for studying gene by environment interactions in behavioral research. *Genes, Brain, and Behavior, 2*(6), 336–340.

Barr, C. S., Newman, T. K., Lindell, S., Shannon, C., Champoux, M., Lesch, K. P., et al. (2004). Interaction between serotonin transporter gene variation and rearing condition in alcohol preference and consumption in female primates. *Archives of General Psychiatry, 61*(11), 1146–1152.

Bergeman, C. S., Plomin, R., Pederson, N. L., McClearn, G. E., & Nesselroade, J. R. (1990). Genetic and environmental influences on social support: The Swedish Adoption/Twin Study of Aging (SATSA). *Journals of Gerontology, 45,* 101–106.

Berman, S. M., & Noble, E. P. (1997). The D2 dopamine receptor (DRD2) gene and family stress: Interactive effects on cognitive functions in children. *Behavior Genetics, 27,* 33–43.

Berntson, G. G., Cacioppo, J. T., Quigley, K. S., & Fabro, V. T. (1994). Autonomic space and psychophysiological response. *Psychophysiology, 31*(1), 44–61.

Boekaerts, M., & Röder, I. (1999). Stress, coping, and adjustment in children with a chronic disease: A review of the literature. *Disability and Rehabilitation, 21*(7), 311–337.

Bohman, M. (1996). *Predisposition to criminality: Swedish adoption studies in retrospect.* Paper presented at the Genetics of Criminal and Antisocial Behaviour conference, Chichester, England.

Boyce, W. T. (1992). The vulnerable child: New evidence, new approaches. *Advances in Pediatrics, 39,* 1–33.

Boyce, W. T. (1996). Biobehavioral reactivity and injuries in children and adolescents. In M. H. Bornstein & J. Genevro (Eds.), *Child development and behavioral pediatrics: Toward understanding children and health* (pp. 35–58). Mahwah, NJ: Erlbaum.

Boyce, W. T. (2004). Social stratification, health and violence in the very young. *Annals of the New York Academy of Sciences, 1036,* 47–68.

Boyce, W. T., Barr, R. G., & Zeltzer, L. K. (1992). Temperament and the psychobiology of childhood stress. *Pediatrics, 90*(3), 483–490.

Boyce, W. T., Chesney, M., Alkon-Leonard, A., Tschann, J., Adams, S., Chesterman, B., et al. (1995). Psychobiologic reactivity to stress and childhood respiratory illnesses: Results of two prospective studies. *Psychosomatic Medicine, 57,* 411–422.

Boyce, W. T., & Ellis, B. J. (2005). Biological sensitivity to context: Pt. I. An evolutionary-developmental theory of the origins and functions of stress reactivity. *Development and Psychopathology, 17*(2), 271–301.

Boyce, W. T., & Keating, D. P. (2004). Should we intervene to improve childhood circumstances? In D. Kuh & Y. Ben-Shlomo (Eds.), *A life course approach to chronic disease epidemiology* (2nd ed., pp. 415–445). Oxford: Oxford University Press.

Boyce, W. T., O'Neill-Wagner, P., Price, C. S., Haines, M., & Suomi, S. J. (1998). Crowding stress and violent injuries among behaviorally inhibited rhesus macaques. *Health Psychology, 17*(3), 285–289.

Boyce, W. T., Quas, J., Alkon, A., Smider, N., Essex, M., & Kupfer, D. J. (2001). Autonomic reactivity and psychopathology in middle childhood. *British Journal of Psychiatry, 179,* 144–150.

Braungart, J. M., Fulker, D. W., & Plomin, R. (1992). Genetic mediation of the home environment during infancy: A sibling adoption study of the home. *Developmental Psychology, 28,* 1048–1055.

Bronfenbrenner, U., & Ceci, S. J. (1994). Nature-nurture reconceptualization in developmental perspective: A bioecological model. *Psychological Review, 101,* 568–586.

Butzlaff, R. L., & Hooley, J. M. (1998). Expressed emotion and psychiatric relapse: A meta-analysis. *Archives of General Psychiatry, 55,* 547–552.

Cacioppo, J. T., Berntson, G. G., Malarkey, W. B., Kiecolt-Glaser, J. K., Sheridan, J. F., Poehlmann, K. M., et al. (1998). Autonomic, neuroendocrine, and immune responses to psychological stress: The reactivity hypothesis. *Annals of the New York Academy of Sciences, 840,* 664–673.

Cacioppo, J. T., Berntson, G. G., Sheridan, J. F., & McClintock, M. K. (2000). Multilevel integrative analyses of human behavior: Social neuroscience and the complementing nature of social and biological approaches. *Psychological Bulletin, 126*(6), 829–843.

Cadoret, R. J., Winokur, G., Langbehn, D., Troughton, E., Yates, W. R., & Stewart, M. A. (1996). Depression spectrum disease: I. The role of gene-environment interaction. *American Journal of Psychiatry, 153*(7), 892–899.

Cadoret, R. J., Yates, W. R., Troughton, E., Woodworth, G., & Stewart, M. A. (1995). Adoption study demonstrating two genetic pathways to drug abuse. *Archives of General Psychiatry, 52*(1), 42–52.

Caspi, A., McClay, J., Moffitt, T. E., Mill, J., Martin, J., Craig, I. W., et al. (2002). Role of genotype in the cycle of violence in maltreated children. *Science, 297*(5582), 851–854.

Caspi, A., Sugden, K., Moffitt, T. E., Taylor, A., Craig, I. W., Harrington, H., et al. (2003). Influence of life stress on depression: Moderation by a polymorphism in the 5-HTT gene. *Science, 301*(5631), 386–389.

Champoux, M., Higley, J. D., & Suomi, S. J. (1997). Behavioral and physiological characteristics of Indian and Chinese-Indian hybrid rhesus macaque infants. *Developmental Psychobiology, 31*(1), 49–63.

Cloninger, C. R., Bohman, M., & Sigvardsson, S. (1981). Inheritance of alcohol abuse: Cross-fostering analysis of adopted men. *Archives of General Psychiatry, 38*(8), 861–868.

Cogswell, M. E., McDonnell, S. M., Khoury, M. J., Franks, A. L., Burke, W., & Brittenham, G. (1998). Iron overload, public health, and genetics: Evaluating the evidence for hemochromatosis screening. *Annals of Internal Medicine, 129*(11), 971–979.

Cohen, S. (1999). Social status and susceptibility to respiratory infections. *Annals of the New York Academy of Sciences, 896,* 246–253.

Cohen, S., Miller, G. E., & Rabin, B. S. (2001). Psychological stress and antibody response to immunization: A critical review of the human literature. *Psychosomatic Medicine, 63*(1), 7–18.

Converse, P. E. (1986). Generalization and the social psychology of "other worlds." In D. W. Fiske & R. A. Shweder (Eds.), *Metatheory in social science: Pluralisms and subjectivities.* Chicago: University of Chicago Press.

Corbex, M., Poirier, O., Fumeron, F., Betoulle, D., Evans, A., Ruidavets, J. B., et al. (2000). Extensive association analysis between the CETP gene and coronary heart disease phenotypes reveals several putative functional polymorphisms and gene-environment interaction. *Genetic Epidemiology, 19*(1), 64–80.

Crabbe, J. C., Wahlsten, D., & Dudek, B. C. (1999). Genetics of mouse behavior: Interactions with laboratory environment. *Science, 284*(5420), 1670–1672.

Dishion, T., Patterson, G., Stoolmiller, M., & Skinner, M. (1991). Family, school, and behavioral antecedents to early adolescent involvement with antisocial peers. *Developmental Psychology, 27,* 172–180.

Dubos, R. J. (1965). *Man adapting.* New Haven, CT: Yale University Press.

Ellis, B. J., Essex, M. J., & Boyce, W. T. (2005). Biological sensitivity to context: II. Empirical explorations of an evolutionary-developmental hypothesis. *Development and Psychopathology, 17*(2), 303–328.

Evans, K. L., Muir, W. J., Blackwood, D. H., & Porteous, D. J. (2001). Nuts and bolts of psychiatric genetics: Building on the human genome project. *Trends in Genetics, 17*(1), 35–40.

Gentleman, R. C., Carey, V. J., Bates, D. M., Bolstad, B., Dettling, M., Dudoit, S., et al. (2004). Bioconductor: Open software development for computational biology and bioinformatics. *Genome Biology, 5*(10), R80.

Glynn, L. M., Christenfeld, N., & Gerin, W. (1999). Gender, social support, and cardiovascular responses to stress. *Psychosomatic Medicine, 61*(2), 234–242.

Goldsmith, H. H., Gottesman, I. I., & Lemery, K. S. (1997). Epigenetic approaches to developmental psychopathology. *Development and Psychopathology, 9*(2), 365–387.

Gunnar, M. R. (1987). Psychobiological studies of stress and coping: An introduction. *Child Development, 58,* 1403–1407.

Haber, S. N., & Barchas, P. R. (1983). The regulatory effect of social rank on behavior after amphetamine administration. In P. R. Barchas (Ed.), *Social hierarchies: Essays toward a sociophysiological perspective* (pp. 119–132). Westport, CT: Greenwood Press.

Halpern, J., & Boyce, W. T. (in press). Early social dominance and mental health: Ethical obligations to the very young. *International Journal of Law & Psychiatry.*

Hariri, A. R., Drabant, E. M., Munoz, K. E., Kolachana, B. S., Mattay, V. S., Egan, M. F., et al. (2005). A susceptibility gene for affective disorders and the response of the human amygdala. *Archives of General Psychiatry, 62*(2), 146–152.

Heinz, A., Higley, J. D., Gorey, J. G., Saunders, R. C., Jones, D. W., Hommer, D., et al. (1998). In vivo association between alcohol intoxication, aggression, and serotonin transporter availability in nonhuman primates. *American Journal of Psychiatry, 155*(8), 1023–1028.

Hinde, R. A. (1998). Integrating across levels of complexity. In D. M. Hann, L. C. Huffman, I. I. Lederhendler, & D. Meinecke (Eds.), *Advancing research on developmental plasticity: Integrating the behavioral science and neuroscience of mental health* (pp. 165–173). Washington, DC: National Institute of Mental Health.

Hirschhorn, J. N., & Daly, M. J. (2005). Genome-wide association studies for common diseases and complex traits. *Nature Reviews: Genetics, 6*(2), 95–108.

Hogue, A., & Steinberg, L. (1995). Homophily of internalized distress in adolescent peer groups. *Developmental Psychology, 31,* 897–906.

House, J. S., Landis, K. R., & Umberson, D. (1988). Social relationships and health. *Science, 241,* 540–545.

Hunt, C. E. (2005). Gene-environment interactions: Implications for sudden unexpected deaths in infancy. *Archives of Disease in Childhood, 90*(1), 48–53.

Jensen, P. S., Richters, J., Ussery, T., Bloedau, L., & Davis, H. (1991). Child psychopathology and environmental influences: Discrete life events versus ongoing adversity. *Journal of the American Academy of Child and Adolescent Psychiatry, 30,* 303–309.

Kabbaj, M., & Akil, H. (2001). Individual differences in novelty-seeking behavior in rats: A c-Fos study. *Neuroscience, 106*(3), 535–545.

Kagan, J. (1994). *Galen's prophecy.* New York: Basic Books.

Kajiwara, K., Berson, E. L., & Dryja, T. P. (1994). Digenic retinitis pigmentosa due to mutations at the unlinked peripherin/RDS and ROM1 loci. *Science, 264*(5165), 1604–1608.

Kaufer, D., Ogle, W. O., Pincus, Z. S., Clark, K. L., Nicholas, A. C., Dinkel, K. M., et al. (2004). Restructuring the neuronal stress response with anti-glucocorticoid gene delivery. *Nature Neuroscience, 7*(9), 947–953.

Keating, D. P., & Mustard, J. F. (1993). Social economic factors and human development. In D. Ross (Ed.), *Family security in insecure times: National forum on family security* (pp. 87–105). Ottawa, Canada: Canadian Council on Social Development.

Kelly, J. B. (2000). Children's adjustment in conflicted marriage and divorce: A decade review of research. *Journal of the American Academy of Child and Adolescent Psychiatry, 39*(8), 963–973.

Kendler, K. S., & Eaves, L. J. (1986). Models for the joint effect of genotype and environment on liability to psychiatric illness. *American Journal of Psychiatry, 143*(3), 279–289.

Kendler, K. S., Neale, M., Kessler, R., Heath, A., & Eaves, L. (1993). A twin study of recent life events and difficulties. *Archives of General Psychiatry, 50,* 789–796.

Khoury, M. J., Burke, W., & Thomson, E. J. (2000a). Genetics and public health: A framework for the integration of human genetics into public health practice. In M. J. Khoury, W. Burke, & E. J. Thomson (Eds.), *Genetics and public health in the 21st century: Using genetic information to improve health and prevent disease* (Vol. 40, pp. 3–23). Oxford: Oxford University Press.

Khoury, M. J., Burke, W., & Thomson, E. J. (Eds.). (2000b). *Genetics and public health in the 21st century: Using genetic information to improve health and prevent disease* (Vol. 40). Oxford: Oxford University Press.

Kierkegaard, S. (1986). *Either/or* (S. L. Ross & G. L. Stengren, Eds. & Trans.). New York: Harper & Row. (Original work published 1843)

Kraemer, H. C., Stice, E., Kazdin, A., Offord, D., & Kupfer, D. (2001). How do risk factors work together? Mediators, moderators, independent, overlapping and proxy-risk factors. *American Journal of Psychiatry, 158,* 848–856.

Kremer, I., Bachner-Melman, R., Reshef, A., Broude, L., Nemanov, L., Gritsenko, I., et al. (2005). Association of the serotonin transporter gene with smoking behavior. *American Journal of Psychiatry, 162*(5), 924–930.

Lan, Q., Zhang, L., Li, G., Vermeulen, R., Weinberg, R. S., Dosemeci, M., et al. (2004). Hematotoxicity in workers exposed to low levels of benzene. *Science, 306*(5702), 1774–1776.

Lee, C.-K., Klopp, R. G., Weindruch, R., & Prolla, T. A. (1999). Gene expression profile of aging and its retardation by caloric restriction. *Science, 285,* 1390–1393.

Lee, P. S., & Lee, K. H. (2000). Genomic analysis. *Current Opinion in Biotechnology, 11*(2), 171–175.

Lemon, B., & Tjian, R. (2000). Orchestrated response: A symphony of transcription factors for gene control. *Genes & Development, 14*(20), 2551–2569.

Lewontin, R. C. (1974). The analysis of variance and the analysis of causes. *American Journal of Human Genetics, 26,* 400–411.

Manuck, S. B., Cohen, S., Rabin, B. S., Muldoon, M. F., & Bachen, E. A. (1991). Individual differences in cellular immune response to stress. *Psychological Science, 2*(2), 111–115.

Matthews, K. A. (1986). Summary, conclusions and implications. In K. A. Matthews, S. M. Weiss, & T. Detre (Eds.), *Handbook of stress, reactivity and cardiovascular disease.* New York: Wiley-Interscience.

Matthews, K. A., Woodall, K. L., & Allen, M. T. (1993). Cardiovascular reactivity to stress predicts future blood pressure status. *Hypertension, 22,* 479–485.

Matthews, K. A., Woodall, K. L., & Stoney, C. M. (1990). Changes in and stability of cardiovascular responses to behavioral stress: Results from a four-year longitudinal study of children. *Child Development, 61,* 1134–1144.

McClelland, G. H., & Judd, C. M. (1993). Statistical difficulties in detecting interactions and moderator effects. *Psychological Bulletin, 114*(2), 376–390.

McGue, M., & Bouchard, T. J., Jr. (1998). Genetic and environmental influences on human behavioral differences. *Annual Review of Neuroscience, 21*(5), 1–24.

Meaney, M. J. (2001). Maternal care, gene expression, and the transmission of individual differences in stress reactivity across generations. *Annual Review of Neuroscience, 24,* 1161–1192.

Mednick, S. A., Gabrielli, W. F., & Hutchings, B. (1987). Genetic factors in the etiology of criminal behavior. In S. A. Mednick, W. F. Gabrielli, & B. Hutchings (Eds.), *The causes of crime: New biological approaches* (pp. 74–91). Cambridge, England: Cambridge University Press.

Meehl, P. E. (1977). Specific etiology and other forms of strong influence: Some quantitative meanings. *Journal of Medicine & Philosophy, 2*(1), 33–53.

Miller, G. (1962). Airs, waters, and places. *Journal of the History of Medicine, 17,* 129–140.

Miller, T. W. (Ed.). (1998). *Children of trauma: Stressful life events and their effects on children and adolescents.* Madison, CT: International Universities Press.

National Human Genome Research Institute. (2005). *Ethical, legal and social implications of human genetics research.* Available from http://www.genome.gov/10001618.

O'Connor, T. G., Hetherington, E. M., Reiss, D., & Plomin, R. (1995). A twin-sibling study of observed parent-adolescent interactions. *Child Development, 66,* 812–829.

O'Hara, K., & Boyce, W. T. (2001, April). *Behavioral and psychobiological predictors of preschoolers' delayed approach during resistance to temptation.* Paper presented at the Society for Research in Child Development biannual meeting, Minneapolis, MN.

Omenn, G. S. (2000). Genetics and public health: Historical perspectives and current challenges and opportunities. In M. J. Khoury, W. Burke, & E. J. Thomson (Eds.), *Genetics and public health in the 21st century: Using genetic information to improve health and prevent disease* (Vol. 40, pp. 25–44). Oxford: Oxford University Press.

Ottman, R. (1996). Gene-environment interaction: Definitions and study designs. *Preventive Medicine, 25,* 764–770.

Palmer, L. J., & Cookson, W. O. C. M. (2000). Genomic approaches to understanding asthma. *Genome Research, 10,* 1280–1287.

Percy, W. (1989, Summer). The divided creature. *Wilson Quarterly, 13,* 77.

Plomin, R., & Crabbe, J. (2000). DNA. *Psychological Bulletin, 126*(6), 806–828.

Plomin, R., DeFries, J. C., & Loehlin, J. C. (1977). Genotype-environment interaction and correlation in the analysis of human behavior. *Psychological Bulletin, 84,* 309–322.

Plomin, R., DeFries, J. C., McClearn, G. E., & McGuffin, P. (2001). *Behavioral genetics* (4th ed.). New York: Worth.

Polanyi, M. (1968). Life's irreducible structure: Live mechanisms and information in DNA are boundary conditions with a sequence of boundaries above them. *Science, 160*(834), 1308–1312.

Pynoos, R. S., Goenjian, A. K., & Steinberg, A. M. (1998). A public mental health approach to the postdisaster treatment of children and adolescents. *Child and Adolescent Psychiatric Clinics of North America, 7*(1), 195–210.

Quas, J. A., Bauer, A., & Boyce, W. T. (2004). Physiological reactivity, social support, and memory in early childhood. *Child Development, 75*(3), 797–814.

Quas, J. A., Murowchick, E., Bensadoun, J., & Boyce, W. T. (2002). Predictors of children's cortisol activation during the transition to kindergarten. *Journal of Developmental and Behavioral Pediatrics, 23*(5), 304–313.

Reiss, D., Plomin, R., & Hetherington, E. M. (1991). Genetics and psychiatry: An unheralded window on the environment. *American Journal of Psychiatry, 148,* 283–291.

Risch, N., & Merikangas, K. (1996). The future of genetic studies of complex diseases. *Science, 273,* 1516–1517.

Rosenthal, D. (1970). *Genetic theory and abnormal behavior.* New York: McGraw-Hill.

Rutter, M., Dunn, J., Plomin, R., Simonoff, E., Pickles, A., Maughan, B., et al. (1997). Integrating nature and nurture: Implications of person-environment correlations and interactions for developmental psychopathology. *Development and Psychopathology, 9*(2), 335–364.

Sampogna, R. V., & Nigam, S. K. (2004). Implications of gene networks for understanding resilience and vulnerability in the kidney branching program. *Physiology (Bethesda), 19,* 339–347.

Scriver, C. R., & Waters, P. J. (1999). Monogenic traits are not simple: Lessons from phenylketonuria. *Trends in Genetics, 15*(7), 267–272.

Sheridan, J. F., Stark, J. L., Avitsur, R., & Padgett, D. A. (2000). Social disruption, immunity, and susceptibility to viral infection: Role of glucocorticoid insensitivity and NGF. *Annals of the New York Academy of Sciences, 917,* 894–905.

Shonkoff, J. P., & Phillips, D. A. (Eds.). (2000). *From neurons to neighborhoods: The science of early child development.* Washington, DC: National Academy Press.

Starfield, B., Katz, H., Gabriel, A., Livingston, G., Benson, P., Hankin, J., et al. (1984). Morbidity in childhood: A longitudinal view. *New England Journal of Medicine, 310,* 824–829.

Stein, N. L., & Boyce, W. T. (1997, April). *The role of individual differences in reactivity and attention in accounting for memory of a fire-alarm experience.* Paper presented at the Society for Research in Child Development biannual meeting, Washington, DC.

Steinberg, L., & Avenevoli, S. (2000). The role of context in the development of psychopathology: A conceptual framework and some speculative propositions. *Child Development, 71,* 66–74.

Strohman, R. (2002). Maneuvering in the complex path from genotype to phenotype. *Science, 296*(5568), 701–703.

Suomi, S. J. (1987). Genetic and maternal contributions to individual differences in rhesus monkey biobehavioral development. In N. Krasnagor (Ed.), *Psychobiological aspects of behavioral development* (pp. 397–419). New York: Academic Press.

Suomi, S. J. (1991). Early stress and adult emotional reactivity in rhesus monkeys. In G. R. Bock & J. Whelan (Eds.), *The childhood environment and adult disease* (pp. 171–188). Chichester, England: Wiley.

Suomi, S. J. (1997). Early determinants of behaviour: Evidence from primate studies. *British Medical Bulletin, 53*(1), 170–184.

Tong, A. H., Lesage, G., Bader, G. D., Ding, H., Xu, H., Xin, X., et al. (2004). Global mapping of the yeast genetic interaction network. *Science, 303*(5659), 808–813.

Turkheimer, E. (1998). Heritability and biological explanation. *Psychological Review, 105*(4), 782–791.

vanHerwerden, L., Harrap, S., Wong, Z., Abramson, M., Kutin, J., Forbes, A., et al. (1995). Linkage of high-affinity IgE receptor gene with bronchial hyperreactivity, even in the absence of atopy. *Lancet, 346,* 1262–1265.

Villard, J. (2004). Transcription regulation and human diseases. *Swiss Medical Weekly, 134*(39/40), 571–579.

Wachs, T. D., & Plomin, R. (Eds.). (1991). *Conceptualization and measurement of organism-environment interaction.* Washington, DC: American Psychological Association.

Wahlberg, K. E., Wynne, L. C., Oja, H., Keskitalo, P., Pykäläinen, L., Lahti, I., et al. (1997). Gene-environment interaction in vulnerability to Schizophrenia: Findings from the Finnish adoptive family study of Schizophrenia. *American Journal of Psychiatry, 154*(3), 355–362.

Wahlsten, D. (1990). Insensitivity of the analysis of variance to heredity environment interaction. *Behavioral and Brain Sciences, 13*(1), 109–161.

Wallen, K. (1996). Nature needs nurture: The interaction of hormonal and social influences on the development of behavioral sex differences in rhesus monkeys. *Hormones and Behavior, 30,* 364–378.

Wang, W. Y., Barratt, B. J., Clayton, D. G., & Todd, J. A. (2005). Genome-wide association studies: Theoretical and practical concerns. *Nature Reviews: Genetics, 6*(2), 109–118.

Wang, X., Chen, D., Niu, T., Wang, Z., Wang, L., Ryan, L., et al. (2000). Genetic susceptibility to benzene and shortened gestation: Evidence of gene-environment interaction. *American Journal of Epidemiology, 152*(8), 693–700.

Wang, X., Zuckerman, B., Pearson, C., Kaufman, G., Chen, C., Wang, G., et al. (2001, April). *Maternal stress, CRH genotype, and preterm birth.* Paper presented at the Pediatric Academic Societies annual meeting, Baltimore.

Ward, A., & Pratt, C. (1996). Psychosocial influences on the use of health care by children. *Australian and New Zealand Journal of Public Health, 20*(3), 309–316.

Weatherall, D. J. (2001). Phenotype-genotype relationships in monogenic disease: Lessons from the thalassaemias. *Nature Reviews: Genetics, 2*(4), 245–255.

Weaver, I. C., Cervoni, N., Champagne, F. A., D'Alessio, A. C., Sharma, S., Seckl, J. R., et al. (2004). Epigenetic programming by maternal behavior. *Nature Neuroscience, 7*(8), 847–854.

Wetmur, J. G., Lehnert, G., & Desnick, R. J. (1991). The delta-aminolevulinate dehydratase polymorphism: Higher blood lead levels in lead workers and environmentally exposed children with the 1–2 and 2–2 isozymes. *Environmental Research, 56*(2), 109–119.

Wildner, M. (2000). Gene-environment interaction and human lifespan. *Lancet, 356*(9247), 2103.

Williams, D. R. (1997). Race and health: Basic questions, emerging directions. *Annals of Epidemiology, 7,* 322–333.

Williams, R. R., Hopkins, P. N., Wu, L. L., & Hunt, S. C. (2000). Applying genetic strategies to prevent atherosclerosis. In M. J. Khoury, W. Burke, & E. J. Thomson (Eds.), *Genetics and public health in the 21st century: Using genetic information to improve health and prevent disease* (pp. 463–485). Oxford: Oxford University Press.

Wilmoth, J. R., Deegan, L. J., Lundström, H., & Horiuchi, S. (2000). Increase of maximum life-span in Sweden, 1861–1999. *Science, 289*(5488), 2366–2368.

Winokur, G., Cadoret, R., Dorzab, J., & Baker, M. (1971). Depressive disease: A genetic study. *Archives of General Psychiatry, 24*(2), 135–144.

Xing, B., & van der Laan, M. J. (2005). A statistical method for constructing transcriptional regulatory networks using gene expression and sequence data. *Journal of Computational Biology, 12*(2), 229–246.

Yoshiuchi, K., Kumano, H., Nomura, S., Yoshimura, H., Ito, K., Kanaji, Y., et al. (1998). Stressful life events and smoking were associated with Graves' disease in women, but not in men. *Psychosomatic Medicine, 60*(2), 182–185.

Author Index

Subject Index